HARRAP'S

BUSINESS

Italian

DICTIONARY

HARRAP'S BUSINESS
Italian
DICTIONARY

G. Ragazzini and G. Gagliardelli

HARRAP
London

MURSIA
Milan

First published as
Dizionario Commerciale Inglese-Italiano, Italiano-Inglese, edizione concise
by U. Mursia editore,
via Tadino, 29 Milano.

First published in
Great Britain 1990
by HARRAP BOOKS Ltd
26 Market Square, Bromley,
Kent BR1 1NA

ISBN 0 245-60134-1

Printed and bound in Great Britain by
Richard Clay, St Ives Plc, Bungay, Suffolk

PREFACE

This is a concise edition of the well-known Commercial Dictionary *by the same authors, first published by Mursia in 1976. Although smaller in size (both format and type have been reduced), this book contains much the same material as the bigger work, at least as far as entries, equivalents, compounds and phrases are concerned. All sentences, however, have had to be cut out, in order to enable the Publishers to cut down the price of the volume. Moreover, a considerable amount of revising, correcting and updating has been carried out: therefore, it is hoped that this work will prove a useful tool, especially in the hands of students of commerce and economics.*

As can be seen from a glance at the list of abbreviations of subjects dealt with, the lexical register runs from insurance to transport, covering a range of thirty microlanguages (banking, stock market, finance, law, customs, etc.). Apart from legal definitions and standard locutions (contract clauses, commercial usages, etc.), the illustrative phrases, together with the special and idiomatic locutions, comprise a phraseology that is quite new and up to date. The authors are confident that in a world that is growing smaller day after day with the increase of trade and the extension of economic relations between the various countries, the material they have collected, elaborated and arranged in the two sections of this dictionary will be of service both to companies and factories and in schools and universities.

In addition, either section of the work is a faithful mirror of the other, as regards both entries and glosses, as far as the differences in institutions and procedures of the two countries allow. For correct use of the dictionary users are referred to the «Guide».

To conclude, the authors would like to thank Miss Francesca Carabelli, who performed the task of editing, and Miss Giovanna Mascellani, secretary to the authors.

G. R. & G. G.

PREFAZIONE

Questa è l'edizione concise *del noto* Dizionario Commerciale *degli stessi autori, pubblicato per la prima volta da Mursia nel 1976. Benché di mole minore (sono stati ridotti formato e caratteri), questo libro contiene pressoché lo stesso materiale dell'opera maggiore, quanto meno per ciò che riguarda lemmi, traducenti, composti e locuzioni idiomatiche. Tuttavia, è stato necessario eliminare le frasi a senso compiuto, allo scopo di consentire all'Editore di ridurre drasticamente il prezzo del volume. Inoltre, sono state fatte revisioni, correzioni e aggiornamenti vari: si nutre pertanto la speranza che l'opera si rivelerà un utile strumento, specialmente in mano a studenti di commercio e di materie economiche.*

*Come si può vedere scorrendo la lista delle abbreviazioni delle materie trattate, il lessico registrato spazia dalle assicurazioni ai trasporti, coprendo l'intera gamma di trenta microlingue (bancaria, borsistica, finanziaria, giuridica, doganale, ecc.). A parte le definizioni giuridiche e le locuzioni standardizzate (clausole contrattuali, costumanze commerciali, ecc.), la fraseologia presentata, sotto l'aspetto di locuzioni speciali e idiomatiche (*phrases*), è aggiornata, nuova e di prima mano. Gli autori confidano che, in un mondo che si va facendo sempre più piccolo con l'infittirsi degli scambi commerciali e l'intensificarsi dei rapporti economici fra le varie nazioni, il materiale da essi raccolto, elaborato e ordinato nelle due sezioni del dizionario possa rivelarsi utile tanto nelle aziende e nelle fabbriche quanto nelle scuole e nelle università italiane.*

Inoltre, le due sezioni dell'opera si rispecchiano fedelmente l'una nell'altra, sia nei lemmi sia nei traducenti, per quanto è consentito dalla diversità d'istituti e procedure nei due Paesi. Per un corretto uso del dizionario, si rimandano i fruitori alla «guida alla consultazione».

Da ultimo, gli autori desiderano ringraziare calorosamente la dott. Francesca Carabelli, che ha svolto il lavoro di «editing», e la prof. Giovanna Mascellani, segretaria della redazione bolognese.

G. R. e G. G.

LISTA DELLE ABBREVIAZIONI DELLE CATEGORIE GRAMMATICALI E VARIE

LIST OF ABBREVIATIONS REFERRING TO GRAMMATICAL AND OTHER TERMS

a. = aggettivo, aggettivale - *adjective, adjectival*
abbr. = abbreviazione, abbreviato - *abbreviation, abbreviated*
art. = articolo, articolato - *article*
attr. = attributo, attributivo - *attribute, attributive*
avv. = avverbio, avverbiale - *adverb, adverbial*
card. = cardinale - *cardinal*
cfr. = confronta - *compare*
collett. = collettivo - *collective*
cong. = congiunzione - *conjunction*
contraz. = contrazione - *contraction*
def. = definizione, definito - *definition, definite*
deriv. = derivato, derivati - *derived*
determ. = determinativo - *determinative*
difett. = difettivo - *defective*
ecc. = eccetera
es. = esempio - *example*
escl. = esclamazione, esclamativo - *exclamation, exclamatory*
espress. = espressione - *expression*
etc. = *etcetera*
f. = femminile - *feminine*
fam. = familiare - *familiar*
fig. = figurato - *figurative*
G.B. = Gran Bretagna - *Great Britain*
generalm. = generalmente - *generally*
impers. = impersonale - *impersonal*
indef. = indefinito - *indefinite*
ingl. = inglese, anglismo - *English, Anglicism*
inter. = interiezione - *interjection*
inv. = invariabile - *invariable*
irr. = irregolare - *irregular*
ital. = italiano - *Italian*
locuz. = locuzione, locuzioni - *locution*
m. = maschile - *masculine*
n. = nome, nominale - *noun, substantival*
neg. = negazione, negativo - *negation, negative*
neol. = neologismo - *neologism*
n. f. = nome femminile - *noun feminine*
n. m. = nome maschile - *noun masculine*
n. pl. = nome plurale - *noun plural*
n. pr. = nome proprio - *proper name*
num. = numero - *number*
ord. = ordinale - *ordinal*
part. = participio - *participle*
pass. = passato - *past*
pers. = persona, personale - *person, personal*
p. es. = per esempio - *for example*
pl. = plurale - *plural*
poss. = possessivo - *possessive*
pred. = predicato, predicativo - *predicate, predicative*
pref. = prefisso - *prefix*
prep. = preposizione - *preposition*
pres. = presente - *present*
pron. = pronome, pronominale - *pronoun, pronominal*
q. = qualcuno - *someone, somebody*
qc. = qualcosa - *something*
q. V. = quod Vide - *quod vide (which see)*
recipr. = reciproco - *reciprocal*
reg. = regolare - *regular*
relat. = relativo - *relative*
rif. = riferito - *refers to*
rifl. = riflessivo - *reflexive*
scozz. = scozzese - *Scottish*
sim. = simile, simili - *similar*
sing. = singolare - *singular*
sost. = sostantivo, sostantivato - *substantive, used as substantive*
specialm. = specialmente - *specially*
suff. = suffisso - *suffix*
USA = americano, americanismo - *American, Americanism*
U.S.A. = Stati Uniti d'America - *United States of America*
v. = verbo - *verb*
V. = Vedi - *see*
verb. = verbale - *verbal*
v. i. = verbo intransitivo - *verb intransitive*
v. recipr. = verbo reciproco - *reciprocal verb*
v. rifl. = verbo riflessivo - *reflexive verb*
v. t. = verbo transitivo - *verb transitive*

SIMBOLI - SYMBOLS

// = inizio dei composti e delle locuzioni - *beginning of compounds and locutions*
~ = simbolo sostitutivo del lemma - *replaces entry word*
* = rimando alla parte inglese-italiano - *refers reader to the English-Italian section*

N.B. L'asterisco (*) è stato usato, quando necessario, soltanto per i traducenti dei lemmi inglesi. Esso, inoltre, non è stato apposto ai verbi **be** e **have**, le cui forme sono ben note. - *The asterisk (*) has been used, where necessary, only for the glosses of the English entries. It has not been used for the verbs* **be** *and* **have**, *whose forms are well known.*

LISTA DELLE ABBREVIAZIONI DEI LINGUAGGI SETTORIALI

LIST OF ABBREVIATIONS IN LANGUAGES OF SPECIAL FIELDS

amm. = amministrazione, amministrativo - *administration*
ass. = assicurazione, assicurativo - *insurance*
ass. mar. = assicurazioni marittime - *marine insurance*
attr. uff. = attrezzature per ufficio - *office equipment*
banca = attività bancaria - *banking practice*
Borsa = Borsa Valori - *Stock Market*
comm. est. = commercio estero - *foreign trade*
comun. = comunicazioni - *communications*
cred. = credito, creditizio - *credit*
dog. = dogana - *customs*
econ. = economia - *economics, economy*
elab. elettr. = elaboratori elettronici - *computers*
fin. = finanza, finanziario; fisco, fiscale - *finance, financial; fiscal*
giorn. = giornalismo - *journalism*
leg. = legale - *legal*
macch. uff. = macchine per ufficio - *office machines*
market. = marketing - *marketing*
mat. = matematica - *mathematics*
org. az. = organizzazione aziendale - *business organization*
pers. = personale - *personnel*
pubbl. = pubblicità - *advertising*
rag. = ragioneria - *accounting*
sind. = sindacalismo, rapporti di lavoro - *trades unionism, labour relations*
stat. = statistica - *statistics*
trasp. = trasporti - *transport*
trasp. aer. = trasporti aerei - *air transport*
trasp. aut. = trasporti automobilistici - *road transport*
trasp. ferr. = trasporti ferroviari - *rail transport*
trasp. mar. = trasporti marittimi - *sea transport*
tur. = turismo - *tourism*

lemma: (nome)
entry: (noun)

sigla grammaticale: nome
grammatical sign: noun

numeri progressivi per i traducenti delle varie accezioni (8): **1** e **2** significati dell'uso comune o generale; **3** termine della Borsa Valori; **4** termine dell'economia; **5**, **6**, **7**, **8** termini della ragioneria
*progressive numbers referring to glosses of the various meanings (8): **1** and **2** meanings in common general use; **3** a Stock Market term; **4** economic terminology; **5**, **6**, **7**, **8** accounting terminology*

tilde: simbolo sostitutivo del lemma
swing dash: replaces entry word

sbarrette: simbolo d'inizio dei composti e delle locuzioni, ordinati alfabeticamente da ~ **book** ad **accounts variance** (lemma + ×); e poi da **by way of** ~ a **on** ~ (× + lemma)
*double stroke: denotes beginning of compounds and locutions in alphabetical order from ~ **book** to **accounts variance** (entry + ×); then from **by way of** ~ to **on** ~ (× + entry)*

abbreviazioni per i vari linguaggi settoriali
abbreviations for various special languages

breve chiarimento esplicativo, fra parentesi, in corsivo
short explanation, in brackets, in italics

account, *n.* **1** resoconto, relazione, descrizione, esposto. **2** vantaggio. **3** (*Borsa*) liquidazione, termine (*alla Borsa Valori di Londra*). **4** (*econ.*) bilancia. **5** (*rag.*) conto. **6** (*rag.*) esercizio. **7** **accounts**, *pl.* (*rag.*) scritture contabili, contabilità. **8** **accounts**, *pl.* (*rag.*) rendiconto. // ~ **book** (*rag.*) libro contabile, registro contabile; ~ **books** (*rag.*) libri contabili; ~ **current** (*banca*) conto corrente; ~ **current with interest** (*banca*) conto corrente fruttifero; ~ **day** (*Borsa*) giorno di liquidazione; ~ **days** (*Borsa*) giorni di liquidazione, ultimi giorni prima del giorno di liquidazione; **accounts department** (*org. az.*) reparto contabilità; ~ **executive** (*pubbl.*) funzionario d'un'agenzia pubblicitaria il quale mantiene i contatti con i clienti; ~ **holder** (*banca*) titolare d'un conto; **accounts of the business** (*rag.*) conti aziendali; ~ **of expenses** (*rag.*) nota delle spese; ~ **of goods purchased** (*rag.*) conto d'acquisto; ~ **of proceedings** (*rag.*) resoconto; **accounts payable** (*banca*) cambiali in pagamento; (*rag.*) debiti a breve scadenza, effetti passivi; «~ **payee only**» (*banca*) «non trasferibile»; **accounts receivable** (*banca*) cambiali all'incasso; (*rag.*) crediti a breve scadenza, effetti attivi; **accounts receivable department** ufficio esazioni, ufficio incassi; **accounts receivable insurance** (*ass.*) assicurazione sull'incasso dei crediti; ~ **rendered** conto presentato (*al debitore*) per l'approvazione; «~ **rendered**» (*rag.*) «saldo a nuovo»; ~ **settled** conto saldato; ~ **stated** conto approvato (*dal debitore*); «~ **stated**» (*rag.*) «conto liquidato»; **accounts variance** (*rag.*) discrepanza contabile; **by way of** ~ (*cred.*, *rag.*) come acconto; **for one's own** ~ per proprio conto; **Italy's «accounts» with the rest of the world** la situazione «contabile» dell'Italia nei confronti del resto del mondo; **on** ~ (*cred.*, *rag.*) in conto, in acconto.

sigla grammaticale: aggettivo
grammatical sign: adjective

accountable, *a.* **1** (*leg.*) responsabile. **2** (*rag.*) contabile. // ~ **document** lettera contabile; ~ **receipt** ricevuta ufficiale.

due composti del lemma
two compounds of entry word

accountancy, *n.* (*rag.*) ragioneria.

accountant, *n.* ragioniere. // ~ **and Comptroller General** Ragioniere Generale dello Stato.

sbarrette: simbolo d'inizio dei composti e delle locuzioni
double stroke: denotes beginning of compounds and locutions

accounting, *n.* (*rag.*) contabilità. // ~ **data** dati contabili; ~ **date** data di registrazione; ~ **department** (*org. az.*, *rag.*) amministrazione (*d'ufficio*); ~ **machine** (*macch. uff.*) macchina contabile; ~ **offices** (*org. az.*) uffici contabili; ~ **period** (*rag.*) periodo contabile, esercizio; ~ **position** (*rag.*) posizione contabile; ~ **process** (*rag.*) processo contabile; ~ **system** (*rag.*) sistema di contabilità; **from an** ~ **standpoint** (*rag.*) da un punto di vista contabile.

accredit, *v. t.* (*cred.*) accreditare.

baggage, *n.* (*trasp., USA*) bagaglio. // ~ **-check** (*trasp.*) scontrino del bagaglio.

bagman, *n.* (*pl.* **bagmen**) (*pers.*) commesso viaggiatore.

bail[1], *n.* **1** (*leg.*) cauzione. **2** (*leg.*) garanzia, fideiussione. **3** (*leg.*) garante. // ~ **-bond** (*leg.*) cauzione; to **be out on** ~ (*leg.*) essere in libertà provvisoria (*dopo aver pagato la cauzione*); **release on** ~ (*leg.*) rilascio sotto cauzione.

bail[2], *v. t.* **1** (*leg.*) cauzionare. **2** (*leg.*) depositare (*merci: a garanzia*). // to ~ **sb. out** (*slang USA*) aiutare finanziariamente q. (*che si trova nei guai*).

bailee, *n.* **1** (*leg.*) depositario (*di merci: a garanzia*). **2** (*leg.*) comodatario.

bailer, *n.* **1** (*leg.*) depositante (*di merci: a garanzia*). **2** (*leg.*) comodante.

bailiff, *n.* **1** fattore (*d'una grande tenuta*). **2** (*leg.*) ufficiale giudiziario. **3** (*pers.*) usciere di tribunale.

bailment, *n.* **1** (*leg.*) cauzione, garanzia. **2** (*leg.*) deposito a garanzia (*in genere*). **3** (*leg.*) pegno di merci, denaro o altri valori. **4** (*leg.*) comodato.

bailor, *n.* **1** (*leg.*) depositante (*di merci: a garanzia*). **2** (*leg.*) comodante.

bailsman, *n.* (*pl.* **bailsmen**) (*leg.*) garante (*chi offre cauzione per q.*).

balance[1], *n.* **1** equilibrio. **2** (*econ., fin.*) bilancia. **3** (*fin., rag.*) bilancio, ragguaglio. **4** (*fin., rag.*) pareggio. **5** (*fin., rag.*) conguaglio, saldo, differenza a saldo. **6** (*fin., rag.*) rimanenza, resto. **7** (*fin., rag.*) sbilancio (*somma iscritta in bilancio per pareggiare il dare e l'avere*). // ~ **account** conto collettivo; ~ **at** (*o* **in**) **bank** saldo in banca; ~ **book** (*rag.*) libro dei saldi, libro dei bilanci di verifica; ~ **brought forward** (*o* **down**) (*rag.*) saldo riportato, riporto; ~ **brought forward from last account** (*rag.*) saldo riportato dall'esercizio precedente, saldo dell'esercizio precedente; « ~ **can remain** » «saldo (da effettuare) in seguito»; ~ **carried forward** (*o* **down**) (*rag.*) saldo da riportare, saldo a conto nuovo, riporto; ~ **(carried forward) to next account** (*rag.*) saldo a nuovo; ~ **due** (*rag.*) saldo debitore; ~ **from last account** (*rag.*) saldo dell'esercizio precedente; ~ **in cash** (*rag.*) saldo in contanti; ~ **in** (*o* **on**) **hand** (*rag.*) saldo (*o* rimanenza) in cassa; ~ **medium-term loans** (*fin.*) saldo prestiti a medio termine; ~ **method** (*rag.*) metodo amburghese (*per il calcolo degli interessi dei conti correnti fruttiferi*); **the** ~ **of an account** (*rag.*) il saldo d'un conto; ~ **of indebtedness** (*fin., rag.*) bilancio economico, bilancia dei conti; **the** ~ **of international payments** (*fin.*) la

Annotations (left margin):

tre accezioni con traducenti
three meanings with glosses

nomi composti e locuzioni verbali e nominali
compound nouns and verbal and substantival locutions

lemma (verbo munito di esponente² perché omografo del precedente)
entry (verb with exponent², because spelling is the same as in the preceding entry)

lemma (nome, con 7 gruppi di traducenti)
entry (noun, with 7 groups of glosses)

nomi composti e locuzioni idiomatiche
compound nouns and idiomatic locutions

Annotations (right margin):

segnalazione della forma irregolare del plurale
indicates irregular plural form

sigla grammaticale: verbo transitivo
grammatical sign: verb transitive

segnalazione del livello d'uso
indicates level of use

segnalazione della forma irregolare del plurale
indicates irregular plural form

varianti opzionali
optional variants

chiarimento aggiuntivo, fra parentesi, in corsivo
additional explanation, in brackets, in italics

bilancia dei pagamenti internazionali; ~ **of payments** (*fin.*) bilancia dei pagamenti, conti con l'estero; **the ~ of powers** l'equilibrio delle forze (politiche); ~ **of profits carried forward to next account** (*rag.*) saldo degli utili riportato a nuovo sull'esercizio seguente; ~ **of trade** (*econ., fin.*) bilancia commerciale; saldo degli scambi; **the ~ on current account** (*fin., rag.*) la bilancia delle operazioni correnti; ~ **on purchase or sale of securities at settlement date** (*banca*) saldo liquidazione titoli; ~ **-sheet** (*rag.*) bilancio (*prospetto del dare e dell'avere*), stato patrimoniale, bilancio annuale, bilancio commerciale; ~ **-sheet and schedules** (*rag.*) inventario (*bilancio, conto profitti e perdite, conto d'esercizio, ecc.*); ~ **-sheet as at 31st December 1982** bilancio chiuso al 31 dicembre 1982; ~ **-sheet book** (*rag.*) libro dell'inventario; ~ **-sheet items** (*rag.*) capitoli di bilancio; ~ **-sheet made up to (*o* as at) December 31st 1983** bilancio (chiuso) al 31 dicembre 1983; ~ **-sheet value** (*fin., rag.*) valore di bilancio; ~ **-sheets** (*fin., rag.*) bilanci finanziari; **in ~** (*rag.*) in pareggio; **on ~** (*fig.*) tutto considerato, tutto sommato.

nomi composti e locuzioni idiomatiche
compound nouns and idiomatic locutions

note di differenziazione
notes on differentiation

balance², *v. t.* 1 (*rag.*) chiudere, pareggiare, saldare. 2 (*rag.*) bilanciare, equilibrare, conguagliare, ragguagliare. *v. i.* 1 (*fin., rag.*) conguagliarsi, equilibrarsi, chiudere in pareggio. 2 (*rag.*) quadrare. // to ~ **an account** (*rag.*) chiudere un conto, saldare un conto, bilanciare un conto; to ~ **accounts** (*rag.*) ragguagliare le partite, pareggiare il bilancio; to ~ **the books for the year** (*rag.*) fare il bilancio dei libri contabili per l'anno d'esercizio; to ~ **the budget** (*fin., rag.*) pareggiare il bilancio pubblico; to ~ **each other** bilanciarsi, compensarsi; to ~ **the ordinary budget** (*fin., rag.*) equilibrare il bilancio ordinario; to ~ **up** bilanciare.

sigla grammaticale: verbo transitivo
grammatical sign: verb transitive

lemma: verbo, con 4 gruppi di traducenti
entry: verb with 4 groups of glosses

sigla grammaticale: verbo intransitivo
grammatical sign: verb intransitive

locuzioni verbali e verbi composti
verbal locutions and compound verbs

balanced, *a.* 1 equilibrato. 2 (*rag.*) chiuso, saldato. // ~ **development** sviluppo equilibrato; ~ **expansion** espansione equilibrata; **a ~ growth** uno sviluppo equilibrato, uno sviluppo coordinato.

aggettivo seguito da vari sostantivi
adjective followed by various nouns

bale¹, *n.* balla, collo.

bale², *v. t.* (*trasp.*) imballare.

baler, *n.* 1 (*org. az.*) imballatrice (*la macchina*). 2 (*pers.*) imballatore.

baling, *n.* imballaggio, imballatura.

ball, *n.* 1 palla. 2 sfera. // ~ **-pen** penna a sfera; ~ **-point pen** penna a sfera.

lemma (nome, con 2 accezioni e 2 composti)
entry (noun with 2 meanings and 2 compounds)

ballast¹, *n.* (*trasp. mar.*) zavorra. // ~ **passage** (*trasp. mar.*) viaggio in zavorra; **in ~** (*trasp. mar.*) scarico.

lemma (nome)
entry (noun)

ballast², *v. t.* (*trasp. mar.*) zavorrare.

ballasting, *n.* (*trasp. mar.*) zavorramento.

ballooning, *n.* (*Borsa, slang USA*) aumento dei prezzi.

sigla grammaticale: aggettivo
grammatical sign: adjective

sigla grammaticale: verbo transitivo
grammatical sign: verb transitive

assegnabile, *a.* 1 assignable. 2 allottable. 3 awardable (*V.* **assegnare**).

sigla grammaticale: nome maschile
grammatical sign: noun masculine

assegnamento, *n. m.* 1 assignment. 2 (*attribuzione*) allotment, allowance. 3 (*aggiudicazione*) award. 4 (*affidamento, fiducia*) reliance (*V. anche* **assegnare**).

nucleo della voce: 10 gruppi di accezioni, con i traducenti inglesi
nucleus of the entry: 10 groups of meanings with English glosses

asterisco: simbolo di rinvio alla parte inglese-italiano, per reperire le forme irregolari dei verbi
asterisk: refers the reader to the English-Italian section for irregular verb formations

sbarrette: simbolo d'inizio delle locuzioni verbali (10), ordinate alfabeticamente
double stroke: indicates beginning of the verbal locutions (10), in alphabetical order

assegnare, *v. t.* 1 to assign. 2 (*attribuire*) to allot, to allow. 3 (*aggiudicare*) to award. 4 (*dare*) to give★. 5 (*dotare*) to endow. 6 (*ripartire*) to apportion, to portion out. 7 (*fin.*) (*destinare fondi, ecc.*) to direct. 8 (*fin., rag.*) to allocate, to appropriate. 9 (*leg.*) (*beni, diritti, proprietà*) to grant, to vest. 10 (*leg.*) (*un contratto*) to let★. // ~ **a una classe** to class; ~ **compiti a un impiegato** (*anche*) to allocate duties to a clerk; ~ **un compito a q.** to task sb.; ~ **una pensione** to assign a pension; ~ **una pensione a q.** to pension sb.; ~ **tutte le azioni sottoscritte** to allot the shares in full; **non assegnato** (*fin.*) (*di fondo*) unappropriated.

assegnatario, *n. m.* (*leg.*) assignee, allottee, grantee.

le accezioni da **1** a **5** sono proprie dell'uso generale; le accezioni **6, 7** e **8** sono di linguaggi settoriali
*meanings from **1** to **5** belong in general usage; meanings **6, 7, 8** belong to special fields*

tilde: simbolo sostitutivo del lemma
swing dash: stands for entry word

assegnazione, *n. f.* 1 (*di persone, a un lavoro, ecc.*) assignment. 2 (*attribuzione*) allotment, allowance. 3 (*aggiudicazione*) award. 4 (*dotazione*) endowment. 5 (*ripartizione*) apportionment. 6 (*fin., rag.*) allocation, appropriation. 7 (*leg.*) (*di beni, diritti, proprietà*) grant. 8 (*org. az., pers.*) (*del lavoro*) allocation. // ~ **degli incarichi** (*org. az.*) task setting; ~ **di fondi** (*banca, fin.*) funding; ~ **di quote** (*econ., fin.*) allocation of quotas; ~ **di tutte le azioni sottoscritte** (*fin.*) allotment in full; ~ **testamentaria** (*leg.*) devise.

grafie americane
American spelling

sbarrette: simbolo d'inizio dell'apparato locutivo
double stroke: indicates beginning of locutions

notazione sul livello d'uso
indicates level of use

concisa notazione sulla mancanza di corrispondenza fra i due documenti
brief note on the difference between two documents having the same name

assegno, *n. m.* 1 (*banca, cred.*) cheque; check (*USA*). 2 (*pers.*) allowance. // ~ **a vuoto** (*banca, cred.*) dishonoured check, bad cheque, bouncing cheque; dud cheque (*fam.*); ~ **al portatore** (*banca, cred.*) cheque to bearer, bearer cheque; bearer check (*USA*); ~ **all'ordine** (*banca, cred.*) cheque to order; ~ **annuale** annuity; ~ **bancario** (*banca, cred.*) cheque, bank cheque; check, bank check (*USA*); ~ **bancario all'ordine** (*banca, cred.*) order cheque; **un ~ bancario non sbarrato e senza girate** (*banca, cred.*) an open cheque; ~ «**cabriolet**» (*fam.*) kite; flash check (*USA*); ~ **circolare** (*banca, cred.*) «assegno circolare» (*nell'uso, ma non nella forma, corrisponde all'ingl. «bank draft» o «banker's draft»*); circular note; cashier's check (*USA*); ~ **con annesso talloncino di versamento** (*banca, cred.*) cheque with receipt form attached; ~ **con annotazione degli estremi della fattura** (*banca, cred.*) voucher cheque; ~ **con sbarratura generale** (*banca, cred.*) cheque crossed generally; ~ **con sbarratura qualificata** (*banca, cred.*) cheque crossed specially; **assegni d'invalidità** (*pers.*) disability benefits; ~ **d'invalidità** (*o* **di malattia**) (*pers.*) injury benefit; ~ **dono in tagli fissi** (*venduto dagli uffici postali*) (*fin., ingl.*) gift token; ~ **falso** stumer (*fam., ingl.*); stiff (*slang USA*); **assegni familiari** (*pers.*) family allotment cheques; family allowance (*sing.*); child bounty (*fam.*); ~ **in bianco** (*banca, cred.*) blank cheque; **assegni in circolazione** (*cred.*) outstanding cheques; **un ~ non girato** (*banca, cred.*) an unendorsed cheque, an unindorsed cheque; ~ **paga** (*pers.*) paycheck (*USA*); ~ **per accreditamento** (*banca, cred.*) cheque to be credited (to sb.'s account); ~ **per morte** (*di un lavoratore assistito*) (*pers.*) death grant; ~ **sbarrato** (*banca, cred.*) crossed cheque, «for deposit only» cheque; ~ **sbarrato con la dicitura «non negoziabile»** (*banca, cred.*) cheque crossed «not negotiable»; ~ **scoperto** (*banca, cred.*) *V.* ~ **senza copertura;** ~ **senza copertura** (*banca, cred.*) uncovered cheque; non-sufficient funds cheque; kite (*fam.*); flash check (*fam., USA*); ~ **senza valore** stumer, stumour (*fam., ingl.*); ~ **turistico** (*cred.*) traveller's cheque; **un ~ vecchio** (*emesso da più di sei mesi e non ancora incassato*) (*banca, cred.*) a stale cheque; **assegni vistati** (*banca*) marked cheques; ~ **vitalizio** (*ass.*) straight life annuity; **contro ~** cash on delivery, collection on delivery.

assemblaggio, *n. m.* assembly. // ~ **selettivo** (*org. az.*) selective assembly.

assemblea, *n. f.* assembly, meeting; convention(*USA*). // **l'~ degli azionisti** (*fin.*) the meeting of shareholders, the shareholders' meeting; **l'~ dei creditori** (*leg.*) the meeting of creditors, the creditors' meeting; ~ **dei soci** (*d'una società per azioni*) (*fin.*) shareholders' meeting; **un'~ elettiva** an elective assembly; ~ **generale** (*degli azionisti*) (*fin.*) general meeting; ~ **generale annuale** (*fin.*) annual general meeting; ~ **generale per l'approvazione dello statuto** (*d'una società anonima*) (*fin.*) statutory meeting; ~ **legislativa** (*leg.*) legislature; **un'~ ordinaria** (*fin.*) an ordinary meeting; ~ **plenaria** (*leg.*) plenum; **un'~ quindicinale** (*org. az.*) a fortnightly meeting; ~ **straordinaria** (*fin.*) extraordinary meeting; **un'~ trimestrale** a quarterly meeting.

assenteismo, *n. m.* (*econ., sind.*) absenteeism.

assenza, *n. f.* **1** absence. **2** (*leg.*) (*d'una delle due parti*) default. **3** (*leg.*) (*d'imputato o di teste*) non-appearance, non-attendance. // **assenze ingiustificate** (*pers.*) unexcused absences.

asserire, *v. t.* **1** to assert, to affirm, to claim,

spiegazione in corsivo
explanation in italics

notazioni sul livello d'uso dei traducenti
indicates level of use of glosses

rinvio al sublemma successivo (~ **senza copertura**)
refers the reader to sub-entry following (~ ***senza copertura****)*

notazioni sul livello d'uso
indicates level of use

locuzioni nominali (36), ordinate alfabeticamente da ~ **a vuoto** ad ~ **vitalizio** (lemma + ×); e poi la locuzione **contro** ~ (× + lemma)
substantival locutions (36) in alphabetical order from ~ ***a vuoto*** *to ~* ***vitalizio*** *(entry + ×); then the locution* ***contro*** *~ (× + entry)*

sbarrette: inizio di 13 nomi composti e locuzioni
double stroke: beginning of 13 compound nouns and locutions

sigla grammaticale: nome femminile
grammatical sign: noun feminine

lemma (nome), con due accezioni e relativi traducenti
entry (noun) with 2 meanings and respective glosses

sbarrette: simbolo d'inizio dell'apparato locutivo
double stroke: indicates beginning of locutions

biglietto, *n. m.* 1 card, note, ticket. 2 (*trasp.*) ticket. // ~ **a metà prezzo** (*per bambini e cani*) (*trasp.*) half; ~ **a riduzione per bambini** (*trasp.*) child's half-fare ticket; ~ **a tariffa ridotta** (*trasp.*) reduced-rate ticket; ~ **a tariffa ridotta del 50%** (*trasp.*) half-fare ticket; ~ **circolare** (*banca*) circular note; (*trasp.*) circular ticket; ~ **collettivo** (*trasp. ferr.*) party ticket; ~ **combinato** (*trasp.*) combined ticket; ~ **cumulativo** (*trasp. ferr.*) party ticket, through ticket, transfer ticket, transfer; ~ **da cento dollari** hundred-dollar bill; bill (*slang USA*); ~ **da cinque dollari** five-dollar bill; Abe's cabe (*slang USA*); ~ **da dieci dollari** ten-dollar bill; ten (*fam., USA*); ~ **da dieci sterline** ten-pound note; ten (*fam.*); ~ **da mille dollari** thousand-dollar bill; big one (*slang USA*); ~ **da visita** *V.* ~ **di visita**; ~ **d'abbonamento** (*trasp.*) commutation ticket; ~ **d'aereo** aeroplane ticket, air ticket; ~ **d'andata** (*trasp.*) single ticket, single; ~ **d'andata e ritorno** (*trasp., ingl.*) return ticket, return; round-trip ticket (*USA*); ~ **di banca** bank-note, treasury note, note; bank bill, bill (*USA*); **biglietti di banca** (*fin.*) paper currency, paper money, paper (*sing.*); ~ **d'entrata** entrance ticket, admission ticket, card of admission; ~ **di favore** complimentary ticket; ~ **d'ingresso** admission ticket, entrance ticket; ~ **d'invito** invitation card; ~ **di libera circolazione** (*trasp. ferr.*) free pass; **un** ~ **di prima classe** (*trasp.*) a first-class ticket; **un** ~ **di ringraziamento** a note of thanks; **un** ~ **di seconda classe** (*trasp.*) a second-class ticket; **biglietti di Stato a corso forzoso** (*fin.*) currency notes; **biglietti di viaggio** (*tur.*) travel tickets; ~ **di visita** visiting card, business card, ticket; calling-card (*USA*); ~ **ferroviario** (*trasp. ferr.*) railway ticket; ~ **ferroviario valido un solo giorno** (*trasp. ferr.*) day ticket (*ingl.*); ~ **gratuito** (*trasp.*) pass; ~ **natalizio** Christmas card; ~ **per posta aerea** (*comun.*) air letter; ~ **postale** (*pieghevole, e che non abbisogna di busta*) letter sheet; **un** ~ **turistico** (*trasp., tur.*) a tourist ticket.

notazioni sul livello d'uso dei traducenti
indicates level of use of glosses

38 locuzioni nominali, ordinate alfabeticamente da ~ **a metà prezzo** a ~ **turistico**
38 substantival locutions in alphabetical order from ~ **a metà prezzo** *to* ~ **turistico**

notazione grammaticale
grammatical notation

chiarimento esplicativo
explanatory remark

bilancia, *n. f.* 1 (*lo strumento*) weighing machine; scales (*pl.*); pair of scales. 2 (*econ., fin.*) balance, account. // ~ **commerciale** (*econ., fin.*) balance of trade, trade balance, trading balance, current account; **una** ~ **commerciale attiva** (*econ., fin.*) an active balance of trade, a favourable balance of trade; **una** ~ **commerciale deficitaria** (*econ., fin.*) an adverse trade balance, an unfavourable balance of trade; **una** ~ **commerciale passiva** (*econ., fin.*) a passive balance of trade, an adverse trade balance; ~ **dei conti** (*econ., fin.*) balance of indebtedness; ~ **dei**

notazione grammaticale
grammatical notation

accezione economico-finanziaria
economic-financial meaning

ENGLISH - ITALIAN

A

abandon, *v. t.* **1** abbandonare, lasciare per sempre, rinunziare a. **2** (*ass. mar., trasp. mar.*) abbandonare. **3** (*leg.*) abbandonare, desistere da. // to ~ **an option** rinunziare a un'opzione; to ~ **prosecution** (*leg.*) abbandonare un'azione, desistere da un'azione; to ~ **an undertaking (a ship, etc.)** abbandonare un'impresa (una nave, ecc.).

abandonee, *n.* (*ass. mar.*) cessionario dei diritti di proprietà (*assicuratore marittimo cui è ceduta la nave, il relitto, o il carico ricuperato in un naufragio*).

abandonment, *n.* **1** abbandono, rinunzia. **2** (*ass. mar., trasp. mar.*) abbandono. **3** (*leg.*) abbandono, desistenza. // ~ **of action** (*leg.*) abbandono d'un'azione, desistenza da un'azione; ~ **of goods in customs** (*dog.*) abbandono della merce in dogana; ~ **of insured property** (*ass.*) abbandono di cosa assicurata; **the** ~ **of an option** la rinunzia a un'opzione; **the** ~ **of a ship** (*ass. mar.*) l'abbandono d'una nave.

abate, *v. t.* **1** annullare. **2** ribassare, ridurre. // to ~ **prices** ribassare i prezzi.

abated suit, *n.* (*leg.*) causa annullata.

abatement, *n.* **1** annullamento. **2** riduzione, ribasso. **3** abbattimento (*di prezzi*). **4** (*leg.*) sospensione. // ~ **and revival** (*leg.*) sospensione d'una causa (*che può essere ripresa con un atto di riassunzione*); ~ **at law** (*leg.*) annullamento di causa; ~ **of gift (of legacy, etc.)** (*leg.*) riduzione di donazione (di legato, ecc.); **an** ~ **of prices** un ribasso dei prezzi; **an** ~ **of taxes** (*fin.*) una riduzione delle imposte.

abbreviated address, *n.* indirizzo telegrafico.

abdicate, *v. t.* **1** rinunziare a. **2** (*leg.*) diseredare. // to ~ **a right** (*leg.*) rinunziare a un diritto.

Abe's cabe, *n.* (*slang USA*) biglietto da cinque dollari.

abeyance, *n.* **1** (*leg.*) sospensiva. **2** (*leg.*) vacanza (*d'eredità*). // **in** ~ in sospeso; (*leg.*) in sospensiva.

abide, *v. i.* (*pass.* e *part. pass.* **abode** o *reg.*) dimorare. // to ~ **by** attenersi a: to ~ **by the award of the arbitrators** attenersi alla sentenza degli arbitri (al lodo arbitrale).

abiding, *n.* dimora. // ~ **place** luogo di dimora.

ability, *n.* abilità, capacità. // ~ **test** test di capacità, test attitudinale; ~ **theory** (*econ.*) teoria della capacità contributiva (*teoria secondo la quale i tributi dovrebbero essere riscossi dai cittadini a seconda della capacità di questi di pagarli*); ~ **to change domicile** mobilità geografica; ~ **to change occupation** mobilità professionale.

aboard, *avv.* (*trasp.*) a bordo. *prep.* (*trasp.*) a bordo di.

abode, *n.* abitazione.

abolish, *v. t.* abolire, sopprimere. // to ~ **a customs duty** abolire un dazio doganale, sopprimere un dazio doganale; to ~ **distortions of competition** sopprimere le distorsioni di concorrenza.

abolition, *n.* abolizione, soppressione. // ~ **of customs duties** (*dog.*) soppressione dei dazi doganali.

abortion, *n.* (*slang USA*) articolo di qualità scadente.

about, *avv.* in circolazione. *a. attr.* approssimativo. // ~ **ten** una decina.

above, *avv.* e *prep.* sopra. *a. attr.* e *pron.* suddetto. // **the** ~ **clause** la suddetta clausola; ~ **-line** (*fin.*) *V.* ~ **-the-line**; ~ **-the-line** (*fin.*) (*di capitolo d'entrata o spesa di bilancio*) corrente, ordinario; ~ **-the-line payments and receipts** (*fin.*) entrate e spese ordinarie (*voci del bilancio del Governo britannico*); ~ **-the-line surplus** (*fin.*) residuo attivo delle partite correnti; ~ **-mentioned** summenzionato, sopraccennato, sopraindicato, precitato, sopraddetto, surriferito; ~ **-named** sunnominato; ~ **par** (*Borsa*) sopra la pari; ~ **-said** suddetto; ~ **-stated** surriferito; to **be** ~ **par** (*Borsa*) fare aggio.

abridge, *v. t.* limitare, ridurre. // to ~ **sb.'s rights** (*leg.*) limitare i diritti di q.

abridg(e)ment, *n.* **1** riduzione. **2** (*leg.*) restrizione. // ~ **of rights** (*leg.*) restrizione di diritti.

abroad, *avv.* 1 all'estero. 2 sui mercati stranieri.

abrogate, *v. t.* (*leg.*) abrogare.

abrogation, *n.* (*leg.*) abrogazione. // ~ **of the law** abrogazione della legge.

abscond, *v. i.* (*leg.*) darsi alla latitanza. *v. t.* (*leg.*) rendere irreperibile. // to ~ **from justice** (*leg.*) darsi alla latitanza.

absconder, *n.* (*leg.*) latitante.

absconding, *a.* (*leg.*) latitante.

absence, *n.* 1 assenza, mancanza. 2 (*leg.*) contumacia. // ~ **of consideration** (*cred.*) mancanza di copertura; ~ **of consideration for a bill** mancanza di fondi per una cambiale; ~ **of news of a ship** (*trasp. mar.*) mancanza di notizie d'una nave; ~ **to appear** (*leg.*) mancata comparizione in giudizio, contumacia; ~ **to avoid arrest** (*leg.*) latitanza; **in the** ~ **of contrary evidence** (*leg.*) in mancanza di prova contraria; **in the** ~ **of further instructions** in mancanza d'ulteriori istruzioni.

absent, *a.* assente. // ~ **heir** (*leg.*) erede assente; ~ **-mindedness** distrazione.

absenteeism, *n.* (*econ., sind.*) assenteismo.

absolute, *a.* assoluto. // ~ **liability** (*leg.*) responsabilità incondizionata; ~ **majority** (*leg.*) maggioranza assoluta; ~ **monopoly** (*econ.*) monopolio perfetto; ~ **right** (*leg.*) diritto incontestabile; ~ **title** (*leg.*) diritto di proprietà assoluto; ~ **value** valore assoluto.

absolution, *n.* (*leg.*) assoluzione.

absolve, *v. t.* assolvere, liberare.

absolve oneself, *v. rifl.* liberarsi. // to ~ **from further liability** liberarsi da ogni ulteriore responsabilità.

absorb, *v. t.* assorbire.

absorption, *n.* assorbimento. // ~ **potential of a market** (*econ.*) possibilità di assorbimento d'un mercato.

abstinence, *n.* (*econ.*) astinenza.

abstract[1], *n.* 1 estratto, sommario. 2 (*leg.*) estratto di documento. // ~ **of account** (*banca*) estratto (di) conto; ~ **of record** estratto di verbale; ~ **of title** (*leg.*) estratto di certificato di proprietà.

abstract[2], *v. t.* 1 riassumere. 2 (*leg.*) sottrarre. 3 (*rag.*) rilevare. // to ~ **the results of an account** rilevare i risultati di un conto.

abstraction, *n.* (*leg.*) sottrazione. // ~ **of books** (*leg.*) sottrazione dei libri contabili; ~ **of documents** (*o* **of papers**) (*leg.*) sottrazione di documenti.

abundance, *n.* abbondanza.

abundant, *a.* abbondante.

abuse[1], *n.* 1 abuso. 2 (*leg.*) abuso. // ~ **of blank cheque** (*leg.*) abuso di assegno in bianco; ~ **of blank signature** (*leg.*) abuso di bianco segno; ~ **of confidence** (*leg.*) abuso di fiducia; ~ **of power** (*leg.*) abuso d'autorità; ~ **of right** (*leg.*) abuso d'un diritto.

abuse[2], *v. t.* abusare di. // to ~ **one's office** (*leg.*) prevaricare; to ~ **one's power** abusare della propria autorità.

abusive, *a.* (*leg.*) abusivo.

accede, *v. i.* acconsentire, aderire. // to ~ **to an estate** (*leg.*) entrare in possesso d'un bene immobile; to ~ **to a proposal** aderire a una proposta.

acceding, *a.* aspirante, candidato.

accelerate, *v. t.* e *i.* accelerare.

accelerated, *a.* celere. // ~ **service** (*trasp.*) servizio-celere.

accelerating premium, *n.* (*sind.*) premio d'accelerazione.

acceleration, *n.* accelerazione. // ~ **premium** (*sind.*) premio di produttività; ~ **principle** (*econ.*) principio d'accelerazione.

accelerator, *n.* (*econ.*) acceleratore.

accept, *v. t.* accettare, accogliere, gradire. // to ~ **sb.'s apologies** accettare le scuse di q.; to ~ **a bill of exchange** (*cred.*) accettare una cambiale; to ~ **a composition** accettare un concordato; to ~ **firm commitments** accettare impegni precisi; to ~ **in custody** ricevere in custodia; to ~ **a part of the risk to be covered** (*ass.*) accettare una parte del rischio da coprire; to ~ **a suggestion** accettare un suggerimento; to ~ **sb.' terms** accettare le condizioni di q.

acceptability, *n.* accettabilità.

acceptable, *a.* accettabile.

acceptableness, *n.* accettabilità.

acceptance, *n.* 1 accettazione. 2 (*banca, cred.*) accettazione (*nel senso di cambiale recante la dicitura «accettato»*); cambiale accettata. // ~ **against documents** accettazione contro documenti; ~ **bill** tratta documentaria contro accettazione, tratta documentaria; ~ **credit** credito d'accettazione; ~ **for honour** accettazione per intervento; ~ **house** (*fin.*) istituto di accettazione bancaria (*caratteristico del mercato monetario londinese*); ~ **of a bid** (*comm.*) accettazione di un'offerta d'appalto; ~ **of a bill** (*cred.*) accettazione cambiaria; ~ **of a bill by a bank** (*banca, cred.*) accettazione bancaria; ~ **of a judgement** (*leg.*) accettazione di una sentenza; ~ **on account of a customer** accettazione per conto di un cliente (*da parte di una banca*); ~ **qualified as to time** (*banca, cred.*) accettazione condizionata quanto al tempo; ~ **supra protest** (*cred.*) accettazione per intervento; ~ **under**

protest (*cred.*) accettazione per intervento; **non-~** (*banca, cred.*) mancata accettazione.

acceptation, *n.* accettazione, accoglimento.

accepted, *a.* **1** accettato. **2** «**accepted**» «accettato» (*formula di accettazione d'una cambiale*).

accepting, *a.* accettante. // **~ house** (*fin.*) istituto di accettazione bancaria (*caratteristico del mercato monetario londinese*); **~ officer** (*comun.*) addetto all'accettazione (*di raccomandate, telegrammi, ecc.*).

acceptor, *n.* (*banca, cred.*) accettante. // **~ for honour** accettante per intervento; **~ supra protest** accettante per intervento.

access, *n.* accesso. // **~ to the market** (*econ.*) accesso al mercato.

accessary, *a.* e *n.* *V.* **accessory.**

accessible, *a.* (*trasp. aut.*) accessibile.

accession, *n.* accessione. // **~ to an estate** (*leg.*) entrata in possesso d'un bene immobile; **~ to office** entrata in carica.

accessorial, *a.* **1** accessorio. **2** (*leg.*) di complice. // **~ crime** (*leg.*) reato di complicità; **~ guilt** (*leg.*) colpevolezza di complice.

accessory, *a.* e *n.* accessorio. *n.* (*leg.*) complice. // **~ action** (*leg.*) causa accessoria; **the accessories of a motor-car** gli accessori d'un'automobile; **~ to a crime** (*leg.*) complice in un delitto.

accident, *n.* (*ass.*) incidente, infortunio, sinistro. *a. attr.* infortunistico. // **an ~ at sea** (*o* **of the sea**) (*trasp. mar.*) un incidente marittimo; **~ insurance** assicurazione infortuni; **an ~ of navigation** (*trasp. mar.*) un incidente di navigazione; **~ prevention** (*pers.*) antinfortunistica.

accidental, *a.* accidentale, casuale. // **~ collision** (*trasp.*) collisione accidentale; **~ damage** (*leg.*) danno accidentale; **~ loss** (*ass. mar., trasp. mar.*) perdita accidentale; **~ stranding** (*ass. mar., trasp. mar.*) arenamento accidentale.

acclamation, *n.* acclamazione.

accommodate, *v. t.* **1** adattare. **2** agevolare. **3** (*tur.*) accogliere, sistemare. // to **~ a cargo ship for the carriage of emigrants** (*trasp. mar.*) adattare una nave da carico per il trasporto di emigranti; to **~ a quarrel** (*leg.*) comporre una lite.

accommodating movements, *n. pl.* (*fin.*) trasferimenti d'oro e di valuta all'estero (*per sanare il deficit della bilancia dei pagamenti*).

accommodation, *n.* **1** accomodamento, adattamento. **2** agevolazione, facilitazione. **3** (*tur.*) ricettività. **4 accommodations,** *pl.* attrezzature. // **~ acceptance** (*banca, cred.*) accettazione di comodo; **~ bill** (*banca, cred.*) cambiale di comodo, effetto di comodo, cambiale di favore; **~ endorsement** (*banca, cred.*) girata di comodo (*o* di favore); **~ endorser** (*banca, cred.*) girante di comodo; **~ facilities** (*tur.*) esercizi (*alberghieri ed extra-alberghieri*); **~ for payment** facilitazioni di pagamento; **~ ladder** (*trasp. mar.*) barcarizzo; **~ note** (*banca, cred.*) cambiale di comodo; **~ paper** (*banca, cred.*) cambiale di comodo; **~ train** (*trasp. ferr., USA*) treno accelerato, treno locale.

accompanied luggage, *n.* (*trasp.*) bagaglio appresso.

accompany, *v. t.* accompagnare.

accomplice, *n.* (*leg.*) complice, connivente.

accomplish, *v. t.* **1** perfezionare. **2** esaurire (*nel senso di «utilizzare»*).

accomplished, *a.* **1** perfetto, perfezionato. **2** esaurito (*nel senso di «utilizzato»*). **3** (*pers.*) esperto, «finito». // **an ~ fact** un fatto compiuto; **an ~ typist** una dattilografa perfetta; «**five original bills of lading, each of this tenor and date, one of which being ~, the others to stand null and void**» (*trasp. mar.*) «cinque polizze di carico originali, tutte dello stesso tenore e data, una delle quali esaurita, le altre resteranno nulle o di nessun valore».

accord[1], *n.* accordo. // **~ and satisfaction** (*leg.*) mutuo consenso.

accord[2], *v. t.* accordare, concedere.

accordance, *n.* conformità, concordanza. // **in ~ with** (*o* **under**) **the Articles** a norma dello statuto societario.

accordingly, *avv.* conformemente, in conformità, di conseguenza, perciò.

according to, *prep.* secondo, a seconda di. // **~ circumstances** secondo il caso; **~ the law** in base alla legge, a norma di legge, ai sensi (*o* a termini) di legge; **~ usage** secondo le consuetudini; **~ your instructions** come da vostre istruzioni.

account, *n.* **1** resoconto, relazione, descrizione, esposto. **2** vantaggio. **3** (*Borsa*) liquidazione, termine (*alla Borsa Valori di Londra*). **4** (*econ.*) bilancia. **5** (*rag.*) conto. **6** (*rag.*) esercizio. **7 accounts,** *pl.* (*rag.*) scritture contabili, contabilità. **8 accounts,** *pl.* (*rag.*) rendiconto. // **~ book** (*rag.*) libro contabile, registro contabile; **~ books** (*rag.*) libri contabili; **~ current** (*banca*) conto corrente; **~ current with interest** (*banca*) conto corrente fruttifero; **~ day** (*Borsa*) giorno di liquidazione; **~ days** (*Borsa*) giorni di liquidazione, ultimi giorni prima del giorno di liquidazione; **accounts department** (*org. az.*) reparto contabilità; **~ executive** (*pubbl.*) funzionario d'un'agenzia pubblicitaria il quale mantiene i contatti con i clienti; ~ **holder** (*banca*) titolare d'un conto; **accounts of the business** (*rag.*) conti aziendali; ~ **of expenses** (*rag.*) nota delle spese; ~ **of goods purchased** (*rag.*) conto d'acquisto; ~ **of proceedings** (*rag.*) resoconto; **accounts payable** (*banca*) cambiali in pagamento; (*rag.*) debiti a breve scadenza, effetti passivi; «~ **payee only**» (*banca*) «non trasferibile»; **accounts receivable** (*banca*) cambiali all'incasso; (*rag.*) crediti a breve scadenza, effetti attivi; **accounts receivable department** ufficio esazioni, ufficio incassi; **accounts receivable insurance** (*ass.*) assicurazione sull'incasso dei crediti; ~ **rendered** conto presentato (*al debitore*) per l'approvazione; «~ **rendered**» (*rag.*) «saldo a nuovo»; ~ **settled** conto saldato; ~ **stated** conto approvato (*dal debitore*); «~ **stated**» (*rag.*) «conto liquidato»; **accounts variance** (*rag.*) discrepanza contabile; **by way of** ~ (*cred., rag.*) come acconto; **for one's own** ~ per proprio conto; **Italy's «accounts» with the rest of the world** la situazione «contabile» dell'Italia nei confronti del resto del mondo; **on** ~ (*cred., rag.*) in conto, in acconto.

accountable, *a.* 1 (*leg.*) responsabile. 2 (*rag.*) contabile. // ~ **document** lettera contabile; ~ **receipt** ricevuta ufficiale.

accountancy, *n.* (*rag.*) ragioneria.

accountant, *n.* ragioniere. // ~ **and Comptroller General** Ragioniere Generale dello Stato.

accounting, *n.* (*rag.*) contabilità. // ~ **data** dati contabili; ~ **date** data di registrazione; ~ **department** (*org. az., rag.*) amministrazione (*d'ufficio*); ~ **machine** (*macch. uff.*) macchina contabile; ~ **offices** (*org. az.*) uffici contabili; ~ **period** (*rag.*) periodo contabile, esercizio; ~ **position** (*rag.*) posizione contabile; ~ **process** (*rag.*) processo contabile; ~ **system** (*rag.*) sistema di contabilità; **from an** ~ **standpoint** (*rag.*) da un punto di vista contabile.

accredit, *v. t.* (*cred.*) accreditare.

accredited, *a.* accreditato. // ~ **banker** (*fin.*) banchiere accreditato; **the** ~ **party** (*leg.*) l'accreditato.

accreditee, *n.* accreditato, persona accreditata.

accretion, *n.* accrescimento. // ~ **among co-heirs** (*leg.*) accrescimento fra coeredi; ~ **by alluvion** (*leg.*) accrescimento per alluvione.

accrual, *n.* accumulazione. // ~ **basis method** (*rag.*) metodo di rilevazioni contabili secondo il quale la registrazione è effettuata al momento della previsione o dell'impegno; **on an** ~ **basis** (*rag.*) col criterio della competenza economica.

accrue, *v. i.* 1 accumularsi, cumularsi, maturare. 2 decorrere.

accrued, *a.* accumulato, maturato. // ~ **dividends** (*fin.*) dividendi accumulati; ~ **expenses** (*rag.*) ratei passivi; ~ **incomes** (*rag.*) ratei attivi; ~ **interest** (*fin.*) interessi maturati; ~ **items** (*rag.*) ratei; ~ **liability** (*rag.*) rateo passivo; «~ **taxes**» (*rag.*) «fondo tasse».

accruing interest, *n.* interessi da maturare.

accumulate, *v. t.* accumulare. *v. i.* accumularsi. // to ~ **losses** accumulare perdite (su perdite); to ~ **wealth** accumulare ricchezze.

accumulated, *a.* accumulato. // ~ **profit** (*fin.*) utile reinvestito; ~ **surplus value** (*econ.*) plusvalore accumulato.

accumulating society, *n.* società mutualistica con organizzazione centralizzata.

accumulation, *n.* 1 accumulazione. 2 (*fin.*) aumento.

accumulative, *a.* 1 cumulativo. 2 (*fin.*) reinvestito. // ~ **dividends** (*fin.*) dividendi reinvestiti; ~ **judgment** (*o* **sentence**) (*leg.*) cumulo di pene.

accuracy, *n.* esattezza.

accurate, *a.* esatto. // **an** ~ **calculation** un calcolo esatto.

accurately, *avv.* esattamente.

accusable, *a.* (*leg.*) accusabile, incriminabile.

accusation, *n.* (*leg.*) accusa, incriminazione.

accusatorial, *a.* (*leg.*) accusatorio.

accuse, *v. t.* (*leg.*) accusare, incriminare.

accused person, *n.* (*leg.*) imputato, querelato.

ace, *n.* (*slang USA*) banconota da un dollaro. // ~ **in the hole** (*slang USA*) risparmi, malloppo.

achievement test, *n.* (*pers.*) test di profitto.

acid test, *n.* prova con la cartina al tornasole, prova dell'acidità; prova del fuoco (*fig.*). // ~ **ratio** (*rag.*) rapporto fra l'ammontare di cassa, conti e valore di mercato dei titoli e l'ammontare delle passività correnti in bilancio.

acknowledge, *v. t.* riconoscere, ammettere. // to ~ **a claim** riconoscere la validità d'un reclamo; to ~ **receipt** accusare ricevuta.

acknowledgement, *n.* *V.* **acknowledgment.**

acknowledgment, *n.* riconoscimento. // **the** ~ **of a debt** il riconoscimento di un debito; ~ **of delivery** ricevuta (*d'una raccomandata, ecc.*); ~ **of receipt** «accusa» di ricevuta.

acquaint, *v. t.* informare, mettere al corrente, rendere edotto. // to **be acquainted with** essere a conoscenza di, conoscere.

acquaintance, *n.* 1 conoscenza. 2 conoscente.

acquaint oneself with, *v. rifl.* familiarizzarsi con (*qc.*).

acquire, *v. t.* acquisire, acquistare. // to ~ **(st.) by prescription** (*leg.*) usucapire.

acquisition, *n.* acquisto, acquisizione. // **public ~ offer** (*Borsa*) offerta pubblica d'acquisto.

acquit, *v. t.* (*leg.*) assolvere, liberare, sciogliere. // to ~ **sb. from an obligation** sciogliere q. da un obbligo; to ~ **sb. of a charge** assolvere q. da un'accusa; to ~ **under amnesty** assolvere per amnistia.

acquit oneself well, *v. rifl.* assolvere bene un compito.

acquittal, *n.* 1 (*leg.*) assoluzione (*da un capo d'accusa*). 2 (*leg.*) scioglimento (*da un obbligo*).

acquittance, *n.* quietanza.

acquitted, *a.* 1 (*leg.*) assolto (*da una accusa*). 2 (*leg.*) sciolto (*da un obbligo*).

acre, *n.* acro.

across, *prep.* attraverso. // **~ -the-board tariff cuts** (*dog.*) riduzioni generali delle tariffe doganali (*applicate ai dazi su un insieme di molti prodotti*).

act[1], *n.* 1 atto. 2 (*leg.*) legge (*del Parlamento*). // **acts and judicial proceedings** (*leg.*) atti processuali; **~ of bankruptcy** (*leg.*) «atto di fallimento» (*ogni cessazione dei pagamenti da parte del debitore, sia egli un commerciante o no*); **acts of God** casi di forza maggiore; **~ of oblivion** (*leg.*) indulto; **~ of Parliament** legge parlamentare; **~ of a prince** atto di un sovrano; **acts of war** atti di guerra; **in the ~** (*leg.*) sul fatto, in flagrante.

act[2], *v. t.* e *i.* agire, fungere, fare funzione di, fare le veci di. // to ~ **as an agent for sb.** rappresentare q.; to ~ **as chairman** presiedere; to ~ **from base motives** agire per bassi motivi; to ~ **in bad faith** agire in malafede; to ~ **on behalf of sb.** agire per conto di q.

acting, *a.* facente funzione di. // **~ manager** (*pers.*) facente funzione di direttore; **~ partner** socio accomandatario.

action, *n.* 1 azione. 2 (*leg.*) causa. 3 (*leg.*) querela. // **~ at law** (*leg.*) azione legale, querela; **~ barred by lapse of time** (*leg.*) azione intempestiva per decorrenza del termine; **~ for avoidance of contract** (*leg.*) azione per annullamento di contratto; **~ for breach of contract** (*leg.*) causa per violazione di contratto; **~ for damages** (*leg.*) causa per danni; **~ for ejectment** (*leg.*) causa di esproprio; **~ for enforcement of contract** (*leg.*) causa per esecuzione di contratto; **~ for fraud** (*leg.*) causa per truffa; **~ for libel** (*leg.*) querela per diffamazione; **~ for recovery** (*leg.*) azione di regresso (*o* di rivendica); **~ of covenant** (*leg.*) azione d'indennizzo per inadempienza contrattuale; **~ ultra vires** (*leg.*) eccesso di potere; **~ upon a bill** (*leg.*) azione cambiaria; **to bring an ~ against** (*leg.*) sporgere querela contro.

actionable, *a.* (*leg.*) perseguibile (*a termini di legge*).

activate, *v. t.* attivare, animare.

activation research, *n.* (*market.*) ricerca di marketing tendente a stabilire gli effetti d'un'azione pubblicitaria sulle vendite, in un dato periodo.

active, *a.* 1 attivo, vivace. 2 effettivo. // **an ~ balance of trade** (*econ.*) una bilancia commerciale attiva; **an ~ bank account** (*banca*) un conto bancario con un andamento (*o* movimento) regolare; **~ change** (*rag.*) variazione attiva; **~ circulation** (*econ., fin.*) circolazione effettiva; **the ~ farming population** il numero degli addetti all'agricoltura; **an ~ market** (*econ.*) un mercato attivo; **~ partner** socio effettivo, gerente; socio d'opera; socio d'industria; to **be on ~ service** (*pers.*) essere in attività di servizio.

actively, *avv.* attivamente, vivacemente.

activism, *n.* attivismo.

activist, *n.* attivista.

activity, *n.* attività. // **~ variance** (*rag.*) scostamento dovuto a incapacità organizzativa.

actual, *a.* effettivo, reale. // **~ coercion** (*leg.*) coercizione fisica; **~ inflation** (*econ.*) inflazione effettiva; **~ loss** (*ass.*) perdita effettivamente subita; **~ possession** (*leg.*) possesso effettivo; **~ prices** (*econ.*) prezzi reali; **~ tare** tara reale; **~ total loss** (*ass. mar.*) perdita totale effettiva; **~ value** (*mat.*) valore attuale.

actually, *avv.* effettivamente, realmente.

actuarial, *a.* (*mat.*) attuariale. // **~ reserve** (*ass.*) riserva tecnica.

ad, *n.* (*abbr. di* **advertisement**) (*pubbl.*) annuncio pubblicitario, inserzione. // **~ writer** (*pubbl., slang USA*) (agente) pubblicitario, scrittore di testi pubblicitari.

adapt, *v. t.* adattare, adeguare.

adaptability, *n.* adattabilità.

adaptable, *a.* adattabile.

add, *v. t.* (*mat.*) sommare. // to ~ **back** aggiungere; to ~ **freight to the value of the goods** aggiungere il nolo al valore della merce; to ~ **a postscript to a letter** aggiungere un poscritto a una lettera; to ~ **st. to the purchase price to cover one's expenses** maggiorare il prezzo d'acquisto per coprire le spese.

added value, *n.* (*econ., fin.*) valore aggiunto.

adder, *n.* (*macch. uff.*) addizionatrice.

adding, *n.* addizione. // ~ **machine** (*macch. uff.*) addizionatrice; ~ **-subtracting machine** (*macch. uff.*) addizionatrice-sottrattrice.

addition, *n.* 1 aggiunta. 2 (*fin.*) addizionale. 3 (*mat.*) somma.

additional, *a.* addizionale, supplementare. // ~ **assessment** (*fin.*) imposizione addizionale; ~ **charge** spesa supplementare; addizionale (*spesa addizionale*); supplemento di prezzo; (*fin.*) soprattassa; ~ **clause** (*leg.*) clausola addizionale, aggiuntiva (*a un atto*); ~ **freight** (*trasp. mar.*) supplemento di nolo; ~ **information** ulteriori informazioni; ~ **premium** (*ass.*) supplemento di premio; ~ **proof** (*leg.*) prova accessoria; ~ **tax** (*fin.*) addizionale (*imposta addizionale*); sovraimposta, sovrimposta, soprattassa; ~ **taxation** (*fin.*) imposizione addizionale; ~ **worker** (*pers.*) operaio in aggiunta, «extra».

additionally, *avv.* in aggiunta.

add-lister, *n.* (*macch. uff.*) registratore di cassa.

address[1], *n.* 1 indirizzo, recapito. 2 discorso ufficiale, allocuzione. 3 (*trasp. mar.*) raccomandazione (*in un contratto di noleggio*). // ~ **book** indirizzario; ~ **card** scheda con indirizzo; ~ **clause** (*trasp. mar.*) clausola di raccomandazione (*in un contratto di noleggio*); ~ **code** numero codice; ~ **commission** (*trasp. mar.*) commissione di raccomandazione (*in un contratto di noleggio*); ~ **label** etichetta con indirizzo; ~ **side** lato dell'indirizzo (*in una busta*).

address[2], *v. t.* 1 indirizzare. 2 rivolgersi a, rivolgere la parola a, parlare a (*q.*). 3 (*trasp. mar.*) affidare, raccomandare (*una nave*).

addressee, *n.* destinatario (*d'una lettera e sim.*).

addresser, *n.* (*attr. uff.*) targhettatrice, «adrema» (*macchina per stampare indirizzi*).

addressing machine, *n.* (*attr. uff.*) targhettatrice, «adrema» (*macchina per stampare indirizzi*).

addressograph, *n.* (*attr. uff.*) targhettatrice (*macchina per stampare indirizzi*).

address oneself, *v. rifl.* indirizzarsi, rivolgere la parola (*a q.*).

adequacy, *n.* adeguatezza.

adequate, *a.* adeguato, congruo.

adequately, *avv.* adeguatamente.

adhesive, *a.* adesivo. // ~ **stamp** francobollo adesivo; ~ **tape** nastro adesivo.

adjacent, *a.* confinante. // ~ **owner** (*leg.*) proprietario confinante.

adjourn, *v. t.* rimandare, rinviare, differire, aggiornare, posporre. *v. i.* 1 togliere la seduta, sospendere i lavori, aggiornarsi. 2 essere tolto. 3 (*leg.*) (*della Corte*) ritirarsi. // to ~ **a case** (*leg.*) rinviare una causa; to ~ **the hearing** (*o* **the sitting**) (*leg.*) rinviare (*o* sospendere) l'udienza; **adjourned meeting** riunione rinviata.

adjournable, *a.* differibile, rinviabile.

adjournment, *n.* rinvio, aggiornamento. // ~ **by the Court** (*leg.*) rinvio d'ufficio; **the** ~ **of a suit** (*leg.*) il rinvio d'una causa.

adjudge, *v. t.* aggiudicare, accordare. // to ~ **legal damages to sb.** accordare un indennizzo a q.

adjudicate, *v. t.* aggiudicare, dichiarare. // to ~ **sb. bankrupt** (*leg.*) dichiarare q. fallito.

adjudication, *n.* 1 aggiudicazione. 2 (*leg.*) dichiarazione di fallimento. // ~ **of** (*o* **in**) **bankruptcy** (*leg.*) dichiarazione (*o* sentenza dichiarativa) di fallimento; ~ **order** (*leg.*) sentenza dichiarativa di fallimento.

adjust, *v. t.* 1 correggere, adattare, adeguare, rettificare. 2 (*ass. mar.*) liquidare. 3 (*fin., rag.*) conguagliare. // to ~ **accounts at the end of the accounting period** (*rag.*) rettificare i conti alla fine dell'esercizio; to ~ **fundamental imbalances** (*econ., fin.*) correggere squilibri fondamentali; **adjusted balance** (*rag.*) saldo rettificato; **adjusted price** (*Borsa*) prezzo corretto; **adjusted selling price** (*market.*) prezzo di vendita rettificato; **adjusting entry** (*rag.*) scrittura di verifica; **adjusting procedures** (*rag.*) procedimenti di verifica.

adjustable, *a.* (*ass. mar.*) liquidabile. // **an** ~ **peg system** (*fin.*) un sistema a parità adeguabili; **general average** ~ **according to York-Antwerp rules** avaria generale da liquidarsi in base ai regolamenti di York e Anversa.

adjuster, *n.* (*ass. mar.*) liquidatore.

adjustment, *n.* 1 adattamento, adeguamento, rettifica; taratura (*di strumenti, ecc.*). 2 (*ass. mar.*) liquidazione. 3 (*econ.*) allineamento. 4 (*fin., rag.*) conguaglio. 5 **adjustments,** *pl.* (*rag.*) scritture di verifica. // ~ **account** (*rag.*) conto generale; ~ **of average** (*ass. mar.*) liquidazione d'avaria; ~ **of balance statements** (*rag.*) rettifica dei valori iscritti a bilancio; ~ **of creditors' claims** (*leg.*) concordato con i creditori; ~ **of prices** (*econ.*) allineamento dei prezzi; ~ **tax on imports** (*fin.*) imposta di conguaglio per le importazioni; « ~ **value date**» (*banca*) «rettifica di valuta».

adman, *n.* (*pl.* **admen**) 1 (*pubbl.*) agente pubblicitario. 2 (*pubbl., slang USA*) inserzionista.

administer, *v. t.* amministrare. // to ~

justice (*leg.*) amministrare la giustizia; to ~ **an oath** (*leg.*) deferire un giuramento.

administered, *a.* amministrato. // ~ **price** (*econ.*) prezzo amministrato; prezzo praticato in condizioni di oligopolio (*secondo Keynes*); ~ **prices** (*econ.*) prezzi di monopolio (*secondo Keynes*).

administration, *n.* 1 amministrazione, gestione. 2 direzione operativa. // ~ **expenses** (*rag.*) spese d'amministrazione; ~ **of a bankrupt's estate** (*leg.*) curatela d'un fallimento; **the** ~ **of justice** l'amministrazione della giustizia; ~ **procedure** procedura di gestione.

administrative, *a.* amministrativo. // ~ **cost** (*rag.*) costi d'amministrazione; ~ **director** (*pers.*) direttore amministrativo; ~ **expenses** (*fin., rag.*) spese amministrative, spese d'amministrazione; ~ **law** (*leg.*) diritto amministrativo.

administratively, *avv.* amministrativamente.

administrator, *n.* 1 amministratore. 2 (*leg.*) curatore. 3 (*leg.*) esecutore testamentario. // ~ **for a disabled person** (*leg.*) curatore d'un interdetto; ~ **for an insane person** (*leg.*) curatore d'un alienato; ~ **for vacant succession** (*leg.*) curatore d'eredità giacente.

Admiralty, *n.* Ammiragliato (*Ministero della Marina*). // ~ **law** (*leg.*) diritto della navigazione.

admissibility, *n.* ammissibilità.

admissible, *a.* ammissibile.

admission, *n.* 1 ammissione. 2 entrata, ingresso. 3 (*leg.*) confessione (*in cause civili, salvo quelle di divorzio*). // ~ **of evidence** (*leg.*) ammissione di prova; ~ **of proofs** (*leg.*) ammissione di credito insinuato al fallimento; ~ **tax** diritto d'autore, tassa sul biglietto d'ingresso (*a uno spettacolo: computata in percentuale del prezzo*); ~ **temporaire** (*dog.*) ammissione temporanea (*di merci da riesportare dopo lavorazione parziale*); ~ **ticket** biglietto d'ingresso; ~ **to quotation (of stocks and shares)** (*Borsa*) ammissione alla quotazione (di titoli).

admit, *v. t.* e *i.* ammettere, riconoscere. // to ~ **a claim** accogliere un reclamo; (*leg.*) accogliere un ricorso; to ~ **of** ammettere; to ~ **proof of debt in a bankruptcy** (*leg.*) ammettere un credito al passivo d'un fallimento.

admittance, *n.* ammissione, ingresso.

admitted, *a.* ammesso.

admittedly, *avv.* per riconoscimento generale.

adopt, *v. t.* adottare, prendere. // to ~ **a balance** approvare un bilancio; to ~ **a resolution** prendere una decisione; to ~ **strict measures** adottare severi provvedimenti.

adoptee, *n.* (*leg.*) adottato.

adopter, *n.* (*leg.*) adottante.

adoption, *n.* (*leg.*) adozione. // ~ **of a child (of an orphan boy)** adozione d'un bambino (d'un orfano).

adoptive, *a.* (*leg.*) adottivo.

ad referendum, *n.* compromesso.

adulterate, *v. t.* contraffare, falsificare, sofisticare, manipolare. // to ~ **the coinage** (*leg.*) falsificare la moneta.

adulterated, *a.* falsificato.

adulteration, *n.* contraffazione, falsificazione, sofisticazione, manipolazione. // ~ **of the coinage** (*leg.*) falsificazione della moneta.

adulterator, *n.* (*leg.*) sofisticatore.

adulterer, *n.* adulteratore, contraffattore, falsificatore.

ad valorem duty, *locuz. n.* (*dog.*) dazio ad valorem.

ad valorem element, *locuz. n.* elemento ad valorem.

ad valorem stamp, *n.* bollo ad valorem.

advance¹, *n.* 1 acconto. 2 aumento, rialzo. 3 (*banca, cred.*) anticipazione, anticipo, prestito. // ~ **against security** (*banca*) anticipazione su garanzia; ~ **-decline line** (*Borsa*) linea dei rialzi e dei ribassi; ~ **freight** *trasp. mar.*) nolo anticipato; ~ **in price** aumento di prezzo, rincaro; ~ **note** (*banca, cred.*) buono d'anticipazione; **advances on consignment of goods** acconti sulla consegna delle merci; ~ **on current account** (*banca*) anticipo in conto corrente; ~ **on loan account** (*banca*) anticipo in conto prestito; **advances on securities** (*banca*) prestiti su titoli; ~ **refunding** (*fin.*) rimborso anticipato; ~ **repayments of public debts** (*fin.*) rimborsi anticipati di debiti pubblici.

advance², *v. t.* e *i.* 1 aumentare, avanzare, crescere. 2 favorire, far progredire. 3 far avanzare, promuovere. 4 (*banca, cred.*) anticipare. 5 (*leg.*) accampare (*diritti, ecc.*). // to ~ **a claim** avanzare una pretesa; (*leg.*) accampare un diritto; to ~ **in price** aumentare di prezzo; to ~ **money to sb.** anticipare denaro a q.; to ~ **the price of petrol** aumentare il prezzo della benzina; to ~ **rents unfairly** aumentare gli affitti in modo iniquo.

advanced freight, *n.* (*trasp. mar.*) nolo anticipato.

advancement, *n.* (*pers.*) avanzamento, promozione.

advantage¹, *n.* vantaggio, beneficio, profitto, utile.

advantage², *v. t.* avvantaggiare. // to **be ad-**

vantaged by st. essere avvantaggiato da qc.

advantageous, *a.* vantaggioso.

adventure, *n.* 1 avventura. 2 speculazione. 3 (*ass. mar., trasp. mar.*) rischio marittimo. 4 (*trasp. mar.*) viaggio.

adverse, *a.* sfavorevole, ostile. // ~ **economic trend** (*econ.*) congiuntura sfavorevole; **an ~ trade balance** (*econ.*) una bilancia commerciale deficitaria, una bilancia commerciale passiva.

advert, *n.* (*pubbl., slang USA*) annuncio pubblicitario.

advertisable, *a.* (*pubbl.*) propagandabile.

advertise, *v. t.* e *i.* (*pubbl.*) fare pubblicità, fare inserzioni (*su un giornale*), propagandare, pubblicizzare, reclamizzare, annunziare (*un prodotto nuovo*). // to ~ **for a clerk** fare inserzioni per un posto d'impiegato, cercare un impiegato mediante inserzioni; to ~ **in the lost-and-found column** mettere un annunzio nella rubrica degli oggetti smarriti; to ~ **in a newspaper** fare la pubblicità su un giornale; to ~ **on the radio** fare pubblicità alla radio; to ~ **on television** fare pubblicità alla televisione.

advertisement, *n.* (*pubbl.*) annunzio pubblicitario, avviso pubblicitario, inserzione (*su un giornale*). // ~ **canvasser** (*comm.*) produttore di pubblicità; ~ **curtain** sipario ricoperto di avvisi pubblicitari (*a teatro, al cinema, ecc.*); ~ **for bids** (*comm.*) avviso d'appalto; ~ **hoarding** tabellone pubblicitario; **the ~ of a sale** l'annunzio d'una vendita; ~ **rates** tariffe pubblicitarie; ~ **required by law** (*leg.*) annunzio giudiziario.

advertiser, *n.* (*pubbl.*) utente della pubblicità, inserzionista.

advertising, *a.* (*pubbl.*) pubblicitario. *n.* (*pubbl.*) pubblicità, propaganda, réclame. // ~ **agency** (*pubbl.*) agenzia di pubblicità; ~ **agent** (*pubbl.*) agente di pubblicità, agente pubblicitario; ~ **budget** (*org. az.*) stanziamento pubblicitario; ~ **bureau** (*pubbl.*) agenzia di pubblicità; ~ **campaign** (*pubbl.*) campagna pubblicitaria; ~ **contractor** (*pubbl.*) appaltatore di pubblicità, impresario di pubblicità; ~ **expenses** (*org. az., rag.*) spese di pubblicità; ~ **man** (*pubbl.*) agente pubblicitario; ~ **manager** (*pers.*) direttore della pubblicità; ~ **media** (*pubbl.*) mezzi pubblicitari; ~ **office** (*pubbl.*) studio di pubblicità; **the ~ pages** (*giorn.*) le pagine della pubblicità; ~ **research** (*pubbl.*) ricerche pubblicitarie; ~ **standard authority** (*pubbl.*) organismo che fissa livelli qualitativi per la pubblicità.

advertize, *v. t.* e *i.* e *derivati V.* **advertise** e *derivati.*

advice, *n. collett.* 1 consiglio, consigli; parere. 2 avviso. // ~ **boat** (*trasp. mar.*) nave avviso; ~ **note** (*trasp. ferr.*) avviso, lettera d'avviso; **the ~ of the counsel** (*leg.*) il parere dell'avvocato; ~ **of deal** (*Borsa*) avviso d'operazione compiuta; ~ **of delivery** (*trasp.*) avviso di consegna; ~ **of payment** avviso di pagamento; ~ **of receipt** avviso di ricevuta; ~ **of shipment** (*trasp.*) avviso di spedizione; **as per ~** come da avviso.

advisable, *a.* consigliabile.

advise, *v. t.* 1 consigliare. 2 avvisare. // to ~ **with sb.** consultare q.

adviser, *n.* (*amm., org. az.*) consigliere, consulente.

advisor, *n.* (*amm., org. az.*) consulente, consigliere.

advisory, *a.* consultivo. // ~ **body** organismo consultivo; **an ~ bulletin** un bollettino d'informazioni; ~ **committee** (*org. az.*) comitato consultivo; ~ **opinion** parere consultivo.

advocacy, *n.* (*leg.*) avvocatura (*in Scozia*).

advocate[1], *n.* 1 sostenitore, fautore. 2 (*leg.*) avvocato (*in Scozia; cfr.* **barrister** *e* **solicitor**). // **an ~ of dirigisme** (*econ.*) un dirigista; **an ~ of Free Trade** un fautore del liberismo.

advocate[2], *v. t.* perorare la causa di. // to ~ **a fiscal reform** perorare la causa d'una riforma tributaria.

aerial, *a.* aereo. // ~ **navigation** (*trasp. aer.*) navigazione aerea.

aerogram, *n.* (*comun.*) aerogramma.

aeronautic, *a.* aeronautico.

aeronautical, *a.* aeronautico.

aeronautics, *n. pl.* (*col verbo al sing.*) aeronautica.

aeroplane, *n.* (*trasp. aer.*) aeroplano. // ~ **ticket** biglietto d'aereo.

aerospace, *a. attr.* aerospaziale. // ~ **industry** (*econ.*) industria aerospaziale.

affair, *n.* (*di solito al pl.*) affare.

affect, *v. t.* 1 incidere su, influire su, riflettersi su, avere effetto su. 2 avere un effetto deleterio su, nuocere a, colpire, danneggiare, pregiudicare. // to ~ **an account** (*rag.*) incidere su un conto.

affidavit, *n.* (*leg.*) «affidavit»; attestazione ufficiale, asseverazione con giuramento, deposizione giurata, dichiarazione giurata.

affiliate[1], *n.* 1 socio. 2 società affiliata.

affiliate[2], *v. t.* affiliare. // to ~ **with sb.** associarsi con q.

affiliated, *a.* 1 affiliato. 2 affine. // ~ **company** società affiliata; ~ **firm** società affiliata; ~ **member** socio.

affiliation, *n.* affiliazione.

affirm, *v. t.* **1** affermare, asserire. **2** confermare, ratificare.

affirmation, *n.* **1** affermazione, asserzione. **2** conferma, ratifica. // **~ of contract** (*leg.*) accettazione (*espressa o tacita*) d'un contratto; **the ~ of a decision** (*leg.*) la conferma d'un giudizio.

affix, *v. t.* **1** attaccare. **2** apporre. // to **~ one's signature to a document** apporre la firma a un documento; to **~ a stamp** attaccare un francobollo.

affixing, *n.* apposizione. // **the ~ of seals to a legal document** l'apposizione dei sigilli a un documento legale.

affluence, *n.* (*econ.*) benessere economico, opulenza.

affluent, *a.* (*econ.*) benestante, opulento, ricco. // **the ~ society** la società del benessere.

affreight, *v. t.* (*trasp. mar.*) noleggiare (*una nave intera o parte di essa; cfr.* to **charter** *e* to **hire**).

affreighter, *n.* (*trasp. mar.*) trasportatore marittimo (*di merci*); noleggiatore, noleggiante (*di nave*).

affreightment, *n.* (*trasp. mar.*) trasporto marittimo (*delle merci*); noleggio (*d'una nave o di parte di essa; cfr.* **charter party** *e* **bill of lading**). // **~ by bill of lading** (*trasp. mar.*) trasporto marittimo con polizza di carico; **~ by charter** (*trasp. mar.*) noleggio dell'intera nave; **~ by charter party** (*trasp. mar.*) trasporto marittimo con nave noleggiata totalmente (*o* per gran parte di essa).

affront, *n.* ingiuria.

afloat, *avv.* **1** a galla. **2** in mare. **3** (*banca*) (*di effetti*) in circolazione, in sofferenza.

aforementioned, *a.* summenzionato.

aforenamed, *a.* sunnominato.

aforesaid, *a.* suddetto.

aft, *avv.* (*trasp. mar.*) dietro. // **~ draught** pescaggio a poppa.

after, *prep.* dietro. // **~ date** (*banca*) (*di cambiali*) a certo tempo data; **~ hold** (*trasp. mar.*) stiva di poppa; **~ hours** (*Borsa*) dopoborsa; **price ~ hours** prezzo del dopoborsa; **~-sales service** (*market.*) assistenza alla clientela; **~ sight** (*banca*) (*di cambiali*) a certo tempo vista; **at thirty days ~ date** (*banca*) (*di cambiali*) a trenta giorni dalla data.

aftermath, *n.* conseguenza.

afternoon, *n.* pomeriggio. // **~ shift** (*org. az., pers.*) turno pomeridiano.

against, *prep.* contro. // «**~ all risks**» **(a.a.r.)** (*ass.*) «contro tutti i rischi»; **~ delivery** (*Borsa*) salvo consegna.

age[1], *n.* **1** età. **2** epoca. // to **be of ~** (*leg.*) essere maggiorenne; to **be under ~** (*leg.*) essere minorenne; to **come of ~** (*leg.*) diventare maggiorenne.

age[2], *v. i.* invecchiare.

ag(e)ing, *n.* invecchiamento.

agency, *n.* **1** agenzia, rappresentanza, mandato di rappresentanza. **2** (*USA*) ente governativo, organismo. // **~ account** (*rag.*) conto d'un'agenzia; **~ agreement** (*leg.*) contratto di rappresentanza; **~ branch** succursale d'agenzia; **~ commission** compenso d'agenzia; **~ contract** (*leg.*) contratto di rappresentanza; **~ trade** commercio di rappresentanza; **by the ~ of** per opera di; **through the ~ of** per il tramite di.

agenda, *n.* ordine del giorno.

agent, *n.* agente, rappresentante, mandatario. // **~ 's lien** (*leg.*) privilegio generale o speciale per gli agenti e i rappresentanti con deposito (*in forza del quale essi possono far valere i loro crediti, per spese e provvigioni, sulle merci che hanno in deposito*); **the agents of production** (*econ.*) i fattori della produzione; **~ 's tort** (*leg.*) illecito d'agenzia.

aggravating circumstance, *n.* (*leg.*) circostanza aggravante.

aggravation, *n.* aggravamento. // **the ~ of the risk** (*ass.*) l'aggravamento del rischio.

aggregate, *a.* complessivo, globale, totale. *n.* **1** insieme, complesso. **2** (*rag.*) consuntivo. // **~ amount** totale complessivo; **~ deficit** (*rag.*) disavanzo complessivo; **~ demand** (*econ.*) domanda complessiva; **~ rebate** (*market.*) abbuono globale; **~ supply** (*econ.*) offerta complessiva; **~ supply function** (*econ.*) funzione d'offerta complessiva; **in the ~** in totale.

agio, *n.* (*fin.*) aggio.

agiotage, *n.* (*Borsa*) aggiotaggio, speculazione.

agrarian, *a.* agricolo, agrario. // **~ reform programme** (*econ.*) programma di riforma agraria.

agree, *v. i.* **1** essere d'accordo, concordare. **2** mettersi d'accordo, accordarsi. **3** convenire, stabilire. **4** corrispondere. **5** (*rag.*) (*detto di conti*) quadrare. *v. t.* (*fin., rag.*) accettare (*una dichiarazione, un conto, ecc.*). // to **~ on** accordarsi su: to **~ on a price** accordarsi su un prezzo; to **~ to** accedere a, accettare: to **~ to an arbitration** (*leg.*) accettare un arbitrato; to **~ to an arrangement** (*leg.*) accettare un concordato; sottoscrivere un accordo; to **~ to a concession** accordarsi su una concessione; to **~ to a loan** concedere un prestito; to **~ to a sale** acconsentire a vendere; to **~ upon** accordarsi su, stipulare; **as**

agreed upon secondo quanto convenuto, secondo gli accordi presi.

agreeable, *a.* 1 che è d'accordo, consenziente. 2 conforme. // ~ **to** in conformità con; ~ **to the laws of the Country** in conformità con le leggi del paese.

agreeably, *avv.* in modo confacente o conforme, conformemente. // ~ **to repeated instructions** in conformità con le istruzioni ripetutamente impartite.

agreed, *a.* convenuto, pattuito, stabilito. // ~ **consideration** compenso forfettario; **the** ~ **price** il prezzo pattuito; ~ **rate** tariffa concordata; **the** ~ **sum** la somma convenuta; ~ **upon** (*leg.*) stabilito per accordo, stipulato, convenzionale; ~ **valuation clause** (*ass. mar.*) clausola del valore stabilito; **at an** ~ **price** (*o* **sum**) per un prezzo forfettario.

agreeing, *n.* accertamento.

agreement, *n.* **1** accordo, convenzione, stipula, stipulazione, contratto, intesa, patto, trattato. **2** concordanza. **3** (*leg.*) composizione (*d'una vertenza*); compromesso arbitrale. // ~ **clause** (*leg.*) clausola contrattuale; ~ **for sale** (*leg.*) contratto di vendita; ~ **in writing** (*leg.*) contratto scritto; ~ **to sell** (*leg.*) patto di futura vendita, promessa di vendita; «compromesso» (*fam.*).

agricultural, *a.* agricolo, agrario, fondiario. // ~ **bank** banca dell'agricoltura; ~ **credit** credito agrario; ~ **credit bank** banca di credito agricolo; ~ **implements** attrezzi agricoli; ~ **industry** attività agricola; ~ **Mortgage Corporation** (*fin.*) Istituto di Credito Ipotecario per l'Agricoltura; ~ **paper** (*fin.*) titolo di credito agrario; ~ **policy** (*econ.*) politica agraria; ~ **prices** prezzi agricoli; ~ **produce** (*econ.*) prodotti agricoli; ~ **producers' groups** associazioni di produttori agricoli; ~ **products** (*econ.*) prodotti agricoli; ~ **research** ricerca agronomica; ~ **show** esposizione agricola, mostra dell'agricoltura; ~ **support subsidies** (*econ.*) sussidi all'agricoltura; ~ **trade** commercio dei prodotti agricoli; **in the** ~ **sector** in campo agricolo.

agriculture, *n.* agricoltura.

agrimotor, *n.* trattore agricolo.

aid[1]**,** *n.* aiuto, assistenza, contributo, concorso, sussidio. // ~ **disbursement** (*fin.*) aiuto finanziario; **aids for exports** (*comm. est.*) aiuti alle esportazioni; «~ **granted**» (*fin.*) «contributo concesso»; ~ **package** (*econ.*) «pacchetto» di aiuti; ~ **policy** (*econ.*) politica degli aiuti; ~ **system** (*econ.*) regime di aiuti; ~ **to agriculture** (*econ.*) sovvenzioni all'agricoltura; ~ **to developing Countries** (*econ.*) aiuti ai Paesi in via di sviluppo; **aids to individual industries** (*econ.*) aiuti settoriali.

aid[2]**,** *v. t.* aiutare, assistere.

aide-de-press, *n.* (*pubbl., slang USA*) pubblicista.

aim, *n.* fine, scopo.

air, *n.* aria. // ~ **bill** (*abbr. di* ~ **waybill**) (*trasp. aer.*) bolletta di trasporto aereo; ~ **cargo** (*trasp. aer.*) carico trasportato su di un aereo; ~ **carrier** (*trasp. aer.*) vettore aereo; ~ **-conditioned** provvisto d'aria condizionata; ~ **-conditioning** (sistema) d'aria condizionata; ~ **consignment note** (*trasp. aer.*) bolletta di trasporto aereo; ~ **fee** (*comun.*) soprattassa per posta aerea; ~ **freighter** (*trasp. aer.*) aereo da trasporto; ~ **-hostess** hostess, assistente di volo; ~ **journey** viaggio aereo; ~ **letter** (*comun.*) biglietto per posta aerea; ~ **navigation** (*trasp. aer.*) navigazione aerea; ~ **route** via aerea; ~ **service** servizio aereo; ~ **station** (*trasp. aer.*) stazione aeroportuale; ~ **ticket** biglietto d'aereo; ~ **traffic** (*trasp. aer.*) traffico aereo; ~ **transport** trasporto aereo; ~ **transportation** trasporti aerei; ~ **waybill** (*trasp. aer.*) bolletta di trasporto aereo; **by** ~ **dispatch** (*comun.*) per posta pneumatica.

airborne, *a.* (*trasp. aer.*) aerotrasportato.

airbrush, *n.* (*pubbl.*) aerografo.

aircraft, *n.* **1** (*trasp. aer.*) aeroplano, aereo, velivolo. **2** (*trasp. aer.*) aeroplani (*collett.*). // ~ **cargo insurance** (*ass.*) assicurazione del vettore aereo per merci; ~ **carrier** portaerei; ~ **passenger insurance** (*ass.*) assicurazione del vettore aereo per passeggeri.

airdrome, *n.* (*trasp. aer., USA*) aerodromo.

airfield, *n.* (*trasp. aer.*) campo d'aviazione.

airgraph, *n.* (*comun.*) lettera microfilmata spedita per aereo.

airline, *n.* (*trasp. aer.*) linea aerea.

airliner, *n.* (*trasp. aer.*) aereo di linea.

airmail[1]**,** *n.* (*comun.*) posta aerea. // ~ **correspondence** (*comun.*) corrispondenza per via aerea; ~ **fee** soprattassa per posta aerea; ~ **letter** lettera per posta aerea; ~ **parcel** (*trasp. aer.*) pacco spedito per via aerea; ~ **parcel service** servizio di pacchi per via aerea; ~ **remittance** (*cred.*) rimessa per via aerea; **by** ~ per posta aerea, per via aerea.

airmail[2]**,** *v. t.* (*comun.*) spedire (*lettere e sim.*) per posta aerea.

airplane, *n.* (*trasp. aer., USA*) aeroplano.

airport, *n.* (*trasp. aer.*) aeroporto. // ~ **of delivery** aeroporto d'arrivo (*per merci*); ~ **of lading** aeroporto di partenza (*per merci*).

airship, *n.* (*trasp. aer.*) dirigibile.

airstrip, *n.* (*trasp. aer.*) campo d'atterraggio.

airway, *n.* 1 (*trasp. aer.*) via aerea. 2 (*trasp. aer.*) linea aerea.

airworthiness, *n.* (*trasp. aer.*) attitudine alla navigazione aerea, navigabilità.

airworthy, *a.* (*trasp. aer.*) atto alla navigazione aerea, navigabile.

alfalfa, *n.* (*slang USA*) piccola quantità di denaro.

algebraic, *a.* (*mat.*) algebrico. // **an ~ equation** un'equazione algebrica.

alibi, *n.* (*leg.*) alibi.

alien, *a.* estraneo. // **~ corporation** (*fin., USA*) società straniera (*che opera in un dato Paese*).

alienability, *n.* (*leg.*) alienabilità.

alienable, *a.* (*leg.*) alienabile.

alienate, *v. t.* (*leg.*) alienare.

alienation, *n.* 1 (*leg.*) alienazione. 2 (*pers.*) «disaffezione». // **cases of entrepreneurial** fenomeni di «disaffezione» nel mondo imprenditoriale.

alienee, *n.* (*leg.*) cessionario.

alienor, *n.* (*leg.*) cedente.

align, *v. t.* allineare.

alignment, *n.* allineamento.

align oneself, *v. rifl.* allinearsi. // to **~ on the common customs tariff** (*dog.*) allinearsi sulla tariffa doganale comune.

alimony, *n.* (*leg.*) alimenti (*in una causa di separazione o divorzio*).

all, *a.* e *pron.* tutto. // **~ -around** (*USA*) globale; «**~ communications are to be addressed to the secretary**» «ogni comunicazione va rivolta alla segreteria»; **~ in** tutto compreso; **~ -in cost** (*econ., market.*) costo complessivo; **~ -in price** (*market.*) prezzo tutto incluso; **~ -inclusive** tutto compreso; «**~ rights reserved**» (*leg.*) «tutti i diritti riservati», «con riserva di tutti i diritti»; **~ risks policy** (*ass.*) polizza comprensiva di tutti i rischi; **~ -round** globale; **~ -round price** (*econ., market.*) prezzo globale, prezzo tutto incluso; «**~ sailing subject to change with or without notice**» (*trasp. mar.*) «tutte le partenze sono soggette a variazioni con o senza preavviso»; «**~ sailing subject to change without notice**» (*trasp. mar.*) «tutte le partenze sono soggette a variazioni senza preavviso»; **~ the same** ciononostante, lo stesso; **~ -time high** (*econ., fin.*) rialzo massimo; **~ -up service** (*comun., USA*) servizio di spedizione della posta ordinaria per via aerea; **~ -up weight** (*trasp. aer.*) peso a pieno carico (*di un aereo*).

allegation, *n.* 1 asserzione, dichiarazione. 2 allegazione.

allege, *v. t.* 1 asserire, dichiarare. 2 addurre, allegare. // to **~ a decision of the Court** (*leg.*) allegare una sentenza del tribunale; to **~ one's good faith** dichiarare la propria buona fede; to **~ illness as a reason for not going to work** addurre motivi di salute per non andare a lavorare.

alleged, *a.* presunto.

alleviate, *v. t.* alleviare.

alleviation, *n.* alleviamento.

alliance, *n.* alleanza.

allocate, *v. t.* 1 (*fin., rag.*) stanziare, assegnare. 2 (*fin., rag.*) accantonare. 3 (*mat.*) ripartire. // to **~ duties to a clerk** assegnare compiti a un impiegato; to **~ materials for a project** accantonare materiali per un progetto; to **~ a sum of money among several persons** ripartire una somma fra varie persone; to **~ sums** destinare stanziamenti.

allocation, *n.* 1 (*fin., rag.*) stanziamento, assegnazione, ripartizione, somma stanziata. 2 (*fin., rag.*) accantonamento, somma accantonata. 3 (*fin., rag.*) riporto, quota. 4 (*org. az., pers.*) assegnazione (*del lavoro*). // **~ card** (*pers.*) scheda di posizione; **~ of assets and liabilities** (*fin., rag.*) valutazione dell'attivo e del passivo; **~ of profits** (*fin., rag.*) ripartizione degli utili; **~ of quotas** (*econ., fin.*) assegnazione di quote; **~ of resources** (*fin.*) stanziamento di risorse.

allonge, *n.* 1 foglio di prolungamento (*d'un documento*). 2 (*banca, cred.*) allunga, coda (*di cambiale*).

allot, *v. t.* 1 assegnare, aggiudicare. 2 (*fin.*) ripartire (*azioni o obbligazioni*). // to **~ the shares in full** assegnare tutte le azioni sottoscritte.

allotment, *n.* 1 assegnazione, aggiudicazione. 2 (*fin.*) ripartizione (*d'una sottoscrizione azionaria o obbligazionaria*). // **~ in full** (*fin.*) assegnazione di tutte le azioni sottoscritte; **~ letter** (*fin.*) avviso di ripartizione (*di una sottoscrizione azionaria o obbligazionaria*); **~ money** (*fin.*) versamento di ripartizione (*di azioni o obbligazioni*).

allottable, *a.* 1 aggiudicabile, assegnabile. 2 (*fin.*) ripartibile.

allottee, *n.* (*leg.*) assegnatario, aggiudicatario.

allow, *v. t.* 1 permettere, consentire, lasciare. 2 accordare, concedere, dare. 3 accogliere. 4 ammettere. 5 abbonare, bonificare, dedurre. // to **~ a claim** accogliere un reclamo; to **~ closer co-ordination** consentire un maggior coordinamento; to **~ a discount of 3% on the amount of an invoice** concedere uno sconto del 3% sull'importo di una fattura; to **~ for** tener conto di; to ~ **of** ammettere; to ~ **a short delay** concedere una breve dilazione; to ~ **6% interest on deposits** accordare l'interesse del 6% sui depositi.

allowable, *a.* **1** che si può accordare, che può essere concesso. **2** detraibile, deducibile. // **an ~ claim** una richiesta che si può accogliere; **~ income tax deductions** detrazioni ammesse nella denuncia dei redditi.

allowance, *n.* **1** permesso, autorizzazione. **2** assegnazione, concessione, somma di denaro (*per un certo scopo*). **3** abbuono, bonifico, deduzione, detrazione, sconto. **4** tolleranza. **5** indennizzo. **6** (*fin.*) sgravio. **7** (*leg.*) alimenti. **8** (*pers.*) gratifica, assegno, indennità, sussidio. **9** (*pers.*) razione alimentare. **10** (*pers.*) pensione. // **~ for bad debts** (*rag.*) fondo svalutazione crediti; **~ for depreciation** (*rag.*) fondo d'ammortamento; **~ for difference of quality** abbuono per scarto di qualità; **~ for dubious accounts** (*rag.*) fondo svalutazione crediti; **~ for expenses** detrazione per spese; **~ for incollectible accounts** (*rag.*) fondo svalutazione crediti; **~ for necessaries** pensione alimentare; **~ for separate maintenance** (*leg.*) alimenti a seguito di separazione legale; **~ for tare** abbuono per tara; **cost-of-living ~** (*pers.*) (indennità di) carovita.

allowed, *a.* **1** permesso, consentito. **2** ammesso. **3** concesso, accordato.

allow oneself, *v. rifl.* permettersi.

alluvion, *n.* (*leg.*) alluvione.

almost, *avv.* quasi.

along, *prep.* lungo.

alongside, *prep.* **1** a fianco di, a lato di, vicino a. **2** (*trasp. mar.*) sotto bordo.

alongside-date, *n.* (*trasp. mar.*) data di attracco.

already, *avv.* già, di già.

also, *avv.* anche, pure.

alter, *v. t.* **1** alterare, cambiare, modificare, mutare. **2** correggere. // to ~ **an entry** (*rag.*) alterare una scrittura contabile; to ~ **one's plans** modificare i propri progetti.

alteration, *n.* **1** alterazione, cambiamento, modifica, mutamento. **2** correzione. **3** (*fin.*) aggiustamento. // **an ~ in the articles of association** (*leg.*) una modifica allo statuto (*d'una società commerciale*); **the ~ of a deed** (*leg.*) l'alterazione d'un atto ufficiale; **the ~ of an entry** (*rag.*) l'alterazione d'una scrittura contabile.

alternate[1], *a.* (*USA*) sostituto. // **~ manager** (*pers.*) facente funzione di direttore; **~ shift** (*pers.*) turno alternato; **on ~ days** a giorni alterni.

alternate[2], *v. t.* avvicendare. *v. i.* avvicendarsi.

alternating, *a.* che s'alterna, s'avvicenda, ecc. (*V.* **alternate**[2]). // **~ current** corrente alternata.

alternation, *n.* avvicendamento.

alternative, *a.* alternativo, surrogabile. // **~ choice** scelta alternativa; **~ commodity** (*econ.*) bene surrogabile; **~ cost** (*rag.*) costo alternativo; **an ~ offer** un'offerta alternativa.

amalgamate, *v. t.* (*econ.*) fondere, concentrare, incorporare. *v. i.* (*econ.*) fondersi, concentrarsi, incorporarsi.

amalgamated union, *n.* (*sind.*) sindacato che deriva dalla fusione di vari sindacati minori.

amalgamating, *n.* (*econ.*) processo di concentrazione (di fusione, d'incorporazione).

amalgamation, *n.* (*econ.*) fusione, concentrazione, incorporazione. // **~ agreement** (*econ., fin.*) accordo di fusione; **the ~ of companies** la fusione di società commerciali.

amass, *v. t.* accumulare. // to ~ **riches** accumulare ricchezze.

ambiguous, *a.* ambiguo.

amenable, *a.* **1** (*di persona*) trattabile. **2** (*leg.*) passibile.

amend, *v. t.* **1** rettificare. **2** (*leg.*) riformare (*una sentenza*). // to ~ **an account** (*rag.*) rettificare un conto; to ~ **a law** (*leg.*) modificare una legge; **amended budget** (*rag.*) bilancio rettificativo; **an amended invoice** una fattura rettificata.

amendable, *a.* rettificabile.

amendment, *n.* rettifica, riforma. // **the ~ of a judgment** (*leg.*) la riforma d'una sentenza; **~ sheets** fogli mobili d'aggiornamento; **amendments to entries** (*rag.*) rettifiche di scritture contabili.

amends, *n. pl.* (*col v. al sing.*) ammenda. // to **make ~ for st.** fare ammenda di qc.

amicable, *a.* amichevole. // **an ~ discussion** una discussione amichevole; **an ~ settlement** un accordo amichevole.

amortise, *v. t. V.* **amortize.**

amortizable, *a.* (*rag.*) ammortabile, ammortizzabile.

amortization, *n.* (*rag.*) ammortizzamento, ammortamento. // **the ~ of a debt** l'ammortamento di un debito; **~ of workers' housing** (*fin., rag.*) ammortamento case operaie.

amortize, *v. t.* (*rag.*) ammortare, ammortizzare. // to ~ **a debt** ammortare un debito.

amortizement, *n.* (*rag.*) ammortamento, ammortizzamento.

amount[1], *n.* **1** ammontare, somma, cifra, importo. **2** quantità, quantitativo. **3** quota. // **~ brought forward (*o* down)** (*rag.*) somma riportata, riporto; **~ carried forward (*o* down)** (*rag.*)

somma riportata, riporto; **the ~ column** la colonna delle cifre; **«amounts differ»** (*banca*) «le cifre non coincidono con le lettere» (*motivazione del mancato pagamento d'un assegno in cui l'importo in cifre non coincide con quello in lettere*); **~ entered twice** (*rag.*) partita registrata due volte, doppia registrazione; **the ~ invoiced** l'importo fatturato; **the ~ of an invoice** l'importo d'una fattura; **an ~ of money** una somma di denaro; **the ~ of money invested** il capitale investito; **~ paid in advance** importo pagato in anticipo; **~ paid on account** (*banca*) somma versata in conto; **amounts to be made good** (*rag.*) valori creditizi, valori attivi; **~ written off** (*rag.*) cifra di deprezzamento, ammortamento per deprezzamento; **in one ~** in un'unica somma, in una sola volta, in soluzione unica; **to the ~ of** fino all'ammontare di, per un ammontare di, fino alla concorrenza di; **up to the ~ of** fino alla concorrenza di.

amount², *v. i.* ammontare, ascendere, sommare. // to **~ to a crime** (*o* **to an offence**) (*leg.*) costituire reato.

amounting to, *a.* per un ammontare di.

analise, *v. t. V.* **analyse.**

analizable, *a. V.* **analysable.**

analize, *v. t. V.* **analyse.**

analog, *n.* (*USA*) *V.* **analogue.**

analogue, *a.* analogico.

analysable, *a.* analizzabile.

analyse, *v. t.* analizzare. // to **~ an account (a transaction, etc.)** analizzare un conto (un'operazione commerciale, ecc.); to **~ the causes of one's failure** analizzare le cause del proprio insuccesso; to **~ the economic trend** analizzare l'evoluzione economica; **by analysing a sample** (*market.*) sulla base d'un'analisi per campionamento.

analysis, *n.* (*pl.* **analyses**) analisi. // **~ of circulation** (*giorn., pubbl.*) analisi della diffusione; **~ of the cost price into its chief components** (*market.*) scomposizione del prezzo di costo nei suoi principali elementi; **~ of customer acceptance of a new product** (*market.*) analisi dell'accettazione d'un prodotto nuovo; **the ~ of economic policy problems** l'analisi dei problemi di politica economica; **the ~ of expense items** l'analisi dei capitoli di spesa; **~ of market size** (*market.*) analisi delle dimensioni di mercato.

analyst, *n.* analista, analizzatore.

analytic, *a.* analitico.

analytical, *a.* analitico.

analytically, *avv.* analiticamente.

analyzable, *a.* analizzabile.

analyze, *v. t. V.* **analyse.**

analyzer, *n.* analizzatore.

anchor¹, *n.* (*trasp. mar.*) àncora. // to **be** (*o* to **lie**, *o* to **ride**) **at ~** (*trasp. mar.*) essere alla fonda.

anchor², *v. t.* (*trasp. mar.*) ancorare. *v. i.* (*trasp. mar.*) ancorarsi.

anchorage, *n.* 1 (*trasp. mar.*) ancoraggio, fonda. 2 (*trasp. mar.*) diritti di ancoraggio.

anchoring, *n.* (*trasp. mar.*) ancoraggio.

ancillary, *a.* accessorio, sussidiario. // **~ occupations** professioni ausiliarie; **ancillaries to trade** attività ausiliari del commercio (*assicurazioni, banche, trasporti, ecc.*).

«and reduced», *n.* (*leg.*) formula apposta al nome d'una società nella quale, in seguito a riorganizzazione, il capitale è stato ridotto.

angle, *n.* (*mat.*) angolo.

animated, *a.* animato. // **~ cartoons** (*pubbl.*) disegni animati, cartoni animati; **~ display** (*pubbl.*) elemento mobile di richiamo (*per la vetrina d'un negozio*).

animation, *n.* 1 animazione. 2 (*pubbl.*) animazione.

announce, *v. t.* 1 annunciare, annunziare, comunicare, notificare, proclamare, bandire, indire. 2 (*pubbl.*) presentare (*un programma radio-TV*). // to **~ an auction sale** notificare una vendita all'asta; to **~ the payment of a coupon** annunziare il pagamento d'un tagliando.

announcement, *n.* annuncio, annunzio, comunicazione, notifica. // an **~ of marriage** un annunzio di matrimonio; **the ~ of a sale** la notifica d'una vendita.

announcer, *n.* annunciatore, presentatore.

annual, *a.* annuo, annuale. *n.* annuario. // **an ~ boost in income** un aumento annuale dei redditi; **~ convention** raduno annuale; **~ general meeting** assemblea generale annuale; **~ income** (*econ.*) reddito annuo; **~ premium** (*ass.*) premio annuale; **~ report** (*fin., rag.*) resoconto annuale; **~ wage** salario annuo.

annually, *avv.* annualmente.

annuitant, *n.* beneficiario d'un vitalizio, redditiere.

annuity, *n.* 1 annualità. 2 assegno annuale. 3 rendita. 4 pensione. // **~ in redemption of a debt** annualità a rimborso d'un debito; **~ premium** (*ass.*) premio di vitalizio.

annul, *v. t.* 1 annullare, revocare. 2 (*leg.*) rescindere, risolvere (*un contratto*). // to **~ an appointment** revocare una nomina; to **~ a contract** (*leg.*) risolvere un contratto; to **~ a marriage** annullare un matrimonio.

annullable, *a.* 1 annullabile, revocabile. 2

(*leg.*) rescindibile, risolvibile.

annulled, *a.* (*leg.*) annullato, estinto.

annulment, *n.* 1 annullamento, revoca. 2 (*leg.*) rescissione, risoluzione (*d'un contratto*). // ~ **of contract** rescissione di contratto; ~ **of marriage** annullamento di matrimonio.

annum, *n.* anno. // **per** ~ **(p.a.)** all'anno.

answer[1], *n.* risposta; (*comun.*) riscontro. // «~ **prepaid**» (*comun.*) con risposta pagata; **in** ~ **to your letter of June 10th** in risposta alla vostra lettera del 10 giugno.

answer[2], *v. t.* e *i.* rispondere a. // to ~ **for st.** rispondere di qc., farsi garante di qc.; to ~ **in the affirmative** rispondere affermativamente; to ~ **a letter (a question, etc.)** rispondere a una lettera (a una domanda, ecc.); to ~ **a telephone call** (*comun.*) rispondere a una chiamata telefonica; to ~ **to sb. for st.** rispondere di qc. a q.

answerable, *a.* 1 responsabile. 2 cui si può rispondere. // to **be** ~ **to sb. for st.** rispondere di qc. a q., essere responsabile di qc. verso q.

antagonism, *n.* antagonismo.

antagonist, *n.* antagonista.

antagonistic, *a.* antagonistico.

ante, *v. t.* (*slang USA*) finanziare (*un'impresa*).

antedate[1], *n.* antidata.

antedate[2], *v. t.* antidatare, retrodatare. // to ~ **a contract** (*leg.*) antidatare un contratto; **an antedated deed** (*leg.*) un atto retrodatato.

antedating, *n.* retrodatazione, l'antidatare.

anti, *pref.* anti. // ~ **-accident campaign** campagna per la prevenzione degli infortuni; ~ **-competitive** (*econ.*) anticoncorrenziale; ~ **-dumping** (*econ.*) «anti-dumping», «antidumping»; ~ **-dumping duty** (*dog.*) dazio doganale «anti-dumping» (*V.* **dumping**); ~ **-inflationary** (*econ.*) antinflazionistico; ~ **-inflationary measures** (*econ.*) provvedimenti antinflazionistici; ~ **-inflationary policy** (*econ.*) politica antinflazionistica; ~ **-recession measures** (*econ.*) misure anticongiunturali; ~ **-slump** (*econ.*) anticongiunturale; ~ **-trust** (*econ.*) «anti-trust», contro i monopoli, antimonopolistico; ~ **-trust act** (*econ., leg.*) legge contro i monopoli; ~ **-trust laws** (*econ., leg.*) leggi antimonopolistiche, legislazione antimonopolistica; ~ **-trust legislation** (*econ., leg.*) legislazione antimonopolistica.

anticipate, *v. t.* 1 anticipare. 2 prevedere. 3 pregustare. // to ~ **an obligation** pagare un debito in anticipo.

anticipated, *a.* 1 previsto. 2 presunto. // ~ **liabilities** (*rag.*) ratei passivi; ~ **profit** (*fin., rag.*) utile presunto.

anticipation, *n.* 1 anticipo. 2 lo spendere in anticipo. 3 aspettativa, previsione. // **the** ~ **of a payment** l'anticipo d'un pagamento; ~ **rate** (*market.*) sconto supplementare per pagamento anticipato; ~ **survey** (*market.*) indagine previsionale.

anticipatory account, *n.* (*rag.*) bilancio di previsione.

antidumping, *a. V.* **anti-dumping.**

antitrust, *a. V.* **anti-trust.**

any, *a.* e *pron. indef.* qualunque, qualsiasi. // «~ **other business**» (*rag.*) eventuali e varie.

apologize, *v. i.* scusarsi. // to ~ **for doing st.** scusarsi d'aver fatto qc.

apparatus, *n.* apparato.

apparel, *n.* (*trasp. mar.*) attrezzature della nave (*alberi, vele, ancore, ecc.*).

apparent, *a.* 1 apparente. 2 (*leg.*) apparente. // **an** ~ **damage (defect, etc.)** un danno (un difetto, ecc.) evidente.

apparently, *avv.* apparentemente.

appeal[1], *n.* 1 richiamo. 2 (*leg.*) appello, ricorso. // **an** ~ **against a decision** (*leg.*) l'appello contro una sentenza; **Court of** ~ (*leg.*) Corte d'Appello.

appeal[2], *v. i.* 1 fare appello (*a*), essere un richiamo (*per*). 2 (*leg.*) appellarsi, presentare appello, interporre appello, ricorrere. // to ~ **against a judgement** (*leg.*) appellarsi contro una sentenza; to ~ **to** rivolgersi a; (*leg.*) fare appello a; to ~ **to one's customers' tastes** (*market.*) incontrare i gusti della clientela; to ~ **to a higher Court** appellarsi all'autorità giudiziaria superiore.

appealability, *n.* (*leg.*) appellabilità.

appealable, *a.* (*leg.*) appellabile.

appear, *v. i.* 1 apparire, parere. 2 (*leg.*) comparire, presentarsi. 3 (*rag.*) figurare, risultare. // to ~ **at the Bar** (*leg.*) comparire in giudizio; to ~ **before the Court** (*leg.*) comparire in giudizio, costituirsi in giudizio, presentarsi alla sbarra; to ~ **for sb.** (*leg.*) rappresentare q. in giudizio.

appearance, *n.* 1 apparenza. 2 apparizione, comparizione, comparsa. 3 presenza (*aspetto fisico*). // ~ **before the Court** (*leg.*) comparizione in giudizio, costituzione in giudizio; **non** ~ (*leg.*) mancata comparizione in giudizio.

appearer, *n.* (*leg.*) comparente.

appearing party, *n.* (*leg.*) comparente.

appellant, *n.* (*leg.*) appellante.

appellate, *a. attr.* (*leg.*) di appello. // ~ **Court** (*leg.*) Corte d'Appello; ~ **jurisdiction** (*leg.*) giurisdizione d'appello.

appellee, *n.* (*leg.*) appellato.

append, *v. t.* 1 apporre, aggiungere (*per iscritto*). 2 allegare. // to ~ **a clause to a treaty**

aggiungere una clausola a un trattato; to ~ **one's signature** apporre la firma; **with all documents appended** con tutti i documenti allegati.

appending, *n.* apposizione (*della firma, ecc.*).

applicability, *n.* applicabilità.

applicable, *a.* applicabile.

applicant, *n.* 1 aspirante, candidato, concorrente, postulante, richiedente. 2 (*fin.*) sottoscrittore (*di azioni*).

application, *n.* 1 applicazione. 2 domanda (*scritta*), richiesta. 3 (*fin.*) sottoscrizione (*d'azioni*). 4 (*leg.*) istanza. 5 (*rag.*) imputazione (*d'una spesa, ecc.*). // ~ **and allotment sheet** (*fin.*) foglio di sottoscrizione e di ripartizione (*di azioni*); ~ **blank** (*pers.*) modulo d'assunzione; **applications for aid** (*fin.*) domande di concorso (*di contributo*); **an ~ for employment** (*pers.*) una domanda d'impiego; ~ **for quotation** richiesta di quotazione (*d'un prezzo di listino oppure in Borsa*); **applications for reimbursement** domande di rimborso; **an ~ for a situation** (*pers.*) una domanda d'impiego, una domanda d'assunzione; **an ~ for tax discharge** (*fin.*) una domanda di sgravio fiscale; ~ **form** (*fin.*) modulo di sottoscrizione (*di azioni*); (*pers.*) modulo di domanda, modulo d'assunzione; (*fin.*) versamento all'atto della sottoscrizione; **the ~ of a treaty** (*leg.*) l'applicazione d'un trattato; ~ **receipt** (*fin.*) ricevuta d'una sottoscrizione (*di azioni*); ~ **rights** (*fin.*) diritto di sottoscrizione (*di azioni*); ~ **to a bid** (*comm.*) domanda di partecipazione a una gara d'appalto; **on ~** (*market.*) a domanda, su richiesta.

applied, *a.* applicato. // ~ **economics** economia applicata; ~ **research** ricerca applicata.

apply, *v. t.* 1 applicare. 2 (*rag.*) imputare (*una spesa, ecc.*). *v. i.* rivolgersi, indirizzarsi, ricorrere (*a q.*). // to ~ **a brake on the economy** (*fin.*) applicare un freno all'economia; to ~ **for an agency** fare domanda di rappresentanza; to ~ **for a certificate** richiedere un certificato; to ~ **for a job (for a scholarship, etc.)** fare domanda per un impiego (per una borsa di studio, ecc.); to ~ **for shares** (*fin.*) sottoscrivere azioni; to ~ **for so many shares in a company** sottoscrivere un certo numero di azioni di una società; to ~ **the rules to a new case** applicare il regolamento a un caso nuovo; to ~ **to the Court** (*leg.*) fare istanza al tribunale; to ~ **to sb.** (*leg.*) fare istanza a q.; to ~ **to sb. for st.** rivolgersi a q. per ottenere qc.

applying, *a.* richiedente.

apply oneself, *v. rifl.* applicarsi.

appoint, *v. t.* 1 nominare. 2 fissare. 3 ordinare, stabilire. // to ~ **an arbitrator (a liquidator, etc.)** (*leg.*) nominare un arbitro (un liquidatore, ecc.); to ~ **as proxy** (*leg.*) nominare procuratore; to ~ **a committee (the directors of a company, etc.)** nominare un comitato (il consiglio d'amministrazione d'una società, ecc.); to ~ **a day for a meeting** stabilire una data per una riunione; to ~ **sb. heir** (*leg.*) nominare, istituire q. erede; **a newly appointed official** un funzionario di nuova nomina; **a well appointed office** un ufficio ben attrezzato, un ufficio arredato bene.

appointee, *n.* incaricato.

appointing, *n.* nomina.

appointment, *n.* 1 nomina. 2 appuntamento. 3 impiego, posto, ufficio. 4 **appointments,** *pl.* attrezzature, mobilia. // **an ~ as manager** la nomina a direttore; ~ **book** agenda; «**by ~ to H.M. the Queen (*o* H.M. the King)**» «fornitore (*o* fornitori) della Casa Reale».

apportion, *v. t.* 1 assegnare, distribuire, ripartire. 2 lottizzare (*terreni*). // to ~ **a sum of money among several persons** distribuire una somma di denaro a varie persone.

apportionable, *a.* distribuibile, ripartibile.

apportionment, *n.* 1 distribuzione, ripartizione. 2 lottizzazione (*di terreni*). // **the ~ of dividends** (*fin.*) la distribuzione dei dividendi; **the ~ of landed property** la lottizzazione di terreni.

appraisable, *a.* periziabile, stimabile, valutabile.

appraisal, *n.* perizia, stima, valutazione. // ~ **interview** (*pers.*) intervista di valutazione.

appraise, *v. t.* periziare, stimare, valutare, accertare il valore di (*qc.*). // to ~ **again** (*rag.*) rivalutare; to ~ **damages** (*ass.*) fare la stima dei danni; to ~ **property for taxation** (*fin.*) accertare il valore d'una proprietà agli effetti fiscali.

appraisement, *n.* perizia, stima, valutazione.

appraiser, *n.* stimatore, valutatore. // **a group of appraisers** un collegio di periti.

appreciable, *a.* apprezzabile, stimabile, valutabile.

appreciably, *avv.* notevolmente, sensibilmente.

appreciate, *v. t.* 1 apprezzare, stimare, valutare, riconoscere il valore di (*qc.*). 2 (*rag.*) rivalutare. *v. i.* 1 aumentare di prezzo. 2 (*fin., rag.*) aumentare di valore.

appreciated, *a.* apprezzato, gradito.

appreciated surplus, *n.* (*econ., rag.*) plusvalore.

appreciation, *n.* 1 apprezzamento, stima,

valutazione, riconoscimento (*del valore di qc.*). 2 (*fin., rag.*) aumento di valore. 3 (*rag.*) rivalutazione. // ~ **of assets** (*econ., rag.*) plusvalore dell'attivo.

apprentice[1], *n.* (*pers.*) apprendista, praticante, tirocinante.

apprentice[2], *v. t.* (*sind.*) collocare (*q.*) come apprendista.

apprenticeship, *n.* (*pers.*) apprendistato, noviziato, tirocinio.

appro, *n.* (*abbr. di* **approval**) approvazione. // **on** ~ (*market.*) salvo vista e verifica.

approach[1], *n.* 1 approccio. 2 impostazione (*d'un problema*). // **a new** ~ **to foreign trade** una nuova filosofia degli scambi; **a new industrial** ~ un nuovo indirizzo di politica industriale.

approach[2], *v. t.* avvicinare, avvicinarsi a.

approachable, *a.* accessibile.

approbation, *n.* 1 approvazione. 2 (*leg.*) omologazione.

appropriate[1], *a.* 1 adatto, adeguato. 2 competente.

appropriate[2], *v. t.* 1 assegnare, destinare. 2 (*fin., rag.*) stanziare. 3 (*fin., rag.*) accantonare. 4 (*fin., rag.*) prelevare. 5 (*leg.*) appropriarsi di, impadronirsi di; incamerare (*beni*). // to ~ **a certain amount to a special fund for depreciation** stanziare una certa somma per un fondo speciale d'ammortamento; to ~ **funds for the redemption of an annuity** destinare fondi al riscatto d'un'annualità; to ~ **money for the navy** stanziare somme di denaro per la marina da guerra; to ~ **so much out of one's savings** prelevare un tanto dai propri risparmi; to ~ **a sum of money (to oneself)** (*leg.*) appropriarsi d'una somma di denaro.

appropriated, *a.* (*fin., rag.*) (*di fondo*) stanziato.

appropriation, *n.* 1 assegnazione, destinazione. 2 (*fin., rag.*) stanziamento. 3 (*fin., rag.*) accantonamento. 4 (*fin., rag.*) prelievo. 5 (*leg.*) appropriazione; incameramento (*di beni*). 6 (*rag.*) impegno di spesa. 7 (*rag.*) ripartizione. // ~ **account** (*rag.*) bilancio consuntivo; ~ **bills** (*amm., fin.*) disegni di legge per stanziamenti in bilancio; ~ **-in-aid** (*fin., rag.*) stralcio del budget (*riferito a un particolare settore o ufficio della pubblica amministrazione, e che contempli previsioni di entrate per la vendita di beni o servizi*); **the** ~ **of lost property** (*leg.*) l'appropriazione di oggetti smarriti; **the** ~ **of the net profit** (*fin.*) la ripartizione dell'utile netto.

approval, *n.* 1 approvazione, benestare. 2 (*leg.*) omologazione, ratifica (*d'una sentenza*). // ~ **of the Court** (*leg.*) omologazione del tribunale; **on** ~ (*market.*) salvo vista e verifica, salvo prova; in esame, in visione.

approve, *v. t.* e *i.* 1 approvare. 2 (*leg.*) omologare, ratificare. // to ~ **of** approvare; to ~ **a proposal** approvare una proposta.

approximate, *a.* approssimato, approssimativo. // ~ **value** valore approssimativo.

approximately, *avv.* approssimativamente.

approximation, *n.* approssimazione.

appurtenances, *n. pl.* (gli) annessi.

appurtenant, *a.* annesso.

aptitude, *n.* attitudine.

Arabic figures (*o* numerals), *n. pl.* (*mat.*) numeri arabi.

arable, *a.* arabile, lavorativo.

arbiter, *n.* arbitro.

arbitrage, *n.* (*Borsa*) arbitraggio. // ~ **dealer** (*Borsa*) *V.* **arbitrager;** ~ **share** titolo d'arbitraggio; ~ **syndicate** sindacato d'arbitraggio.

arbitrager, *n.* (*Borsa*) operatore in arbitraggi.

arbitrageur, *n.* (*Borsa*) operatore in arbitraggi.

arbitraging, *n.* (*Borsa*) arbitraggio.

arbitragist, *n.* (*Borsa*) operatore in arbitraggi.

arbitral, *a.* arbitrale.

arbitrarily, *avv.* arbitrariamente.

arbitrary, *a.* arbitrario. // **an** ~ **action** (*leg.*) un atto arbitrario; ~ **assessment** (*fin.*) accertamento d'ufficio.

arbitrate, *v. t.* e *i.* arbitrare, fare da arbitro, sottoporre ad arbitrato. // to ~ **between the parties to a suit** (*leg.*) fare da arbitro fra le parti in causa; to ~ **a labour dispute** (*sind.*) sottoporre ad arbitrato una vertenza sindacale; to ~ **a quarrel** (*leg.*) decidere una lite mediante arbitrato; to ~ **upon** sottoporre ad arbitrato; **arbitrated par of exchange** (*fin.*) pari di cambio proporzionale, pari di cambio politico.

arbitration, *n.* (*leg., sind.*) arbitrato, arbitramento, arbitraggio; compromesso arbitrale. // ~ **agreement** (*leg.*) patto arbitrale; clausola compromissoria; ~ **award** (*leg.*) lodo arbitrale; ~ **board** (*leg.*) collegio arbitrale; ~ **bond** (*leg.*) patto arbitrale; ~ **clause** (*leg.*) clausola arbitrale, clausola compromissoria; ~ **Court** (*leg.*) tribunale arbitrale; ~ **fees** (*leg.*) diritti d'arbitrato; ~ **of exchange** (*fin.*) arbitraggio; ~ **proceedings** (*leg.*) procedura arbitrale.

arbitrator, *n.* (*leg., sind.*) arbitro.

arbitrators, *n. pl.* (*leg.*) collegio arbitrale.

archives, *n. pl.* archivio di Stato.

archivist, *n.* archivista.

arch-opponent, *n.* concorrente temibile.

are, *n.* ara (*misura di superficie*).

area, *n.* **1** area, superficie. **2** zona. // ~ **manager** (*market.*) direttore di zona; ~ **of control** area di controllo; ~ **of jurisdiction** (*leg.*) circoscrizione giudiziaria; ~ **sales manager** (*pers.*) direttore alle vendite di zona; ~ **sampling** (*market.*) campionamento su un'area; ~ **test** (*market.*) prova di mercato (*eseguita su un'area ristretta ma rappresentativa*).

argue, *v. i.* discutere, ragionare. // to ~ **sb. into doing st.** persuadere q. a fare qc.

argument, *n.* **1** argomento, ragionamento. **2** discussione.

arise, *v. i.* (*pass.* **arose,** *part. pass.* **arisen**) sorgere, presentarsi.

arithmetical, *a.* aritmetico. // ~ **discount** (*mat.*) sconto razionale.

around, *avv.* e *prep.* intorno, attorno.

arrange, *v. t.* **1** accomodare, disporre. **2** fissare, stabilire. **3** provvedere. // to ~ **a treaty** preparare un trattato; **at an arranged price** a un prezzo stabilito.

arrangement, *n.* **1** accordo, accomodamento. **2 arrangements,** *pl.* disposizioni, preparativi. // **arrangements for implementing regulations** modalità d'applicazione delle norme d'un regolamento; ~ **for importing** (*comm. est.*) regime d'importazione; **the ~ for importing petroleum into France** il regime d'importazione del petrolio in Francia; ~ **with creditors** (*leg.*) concordato con i creditori; ~ **with the Revenue Office** (*fin.*) concordato fiscale.

arrearage, *n.* **1** morosità. **2 arrearages,** *pl.* arretrati.

arrears, *n. pl.* **1** arretrati. **2** (*fin.*) decimi. // ~ **in payments** arretrati dei pagamenti; ~ **of correspondence** corrispondenza in arretrato; ~ **of rent** affitto in arretrato; ~ **of wages** (*pers.*) salario in arretrato; to **be in** ~ (*cred., leg.*) essere moroso; to **be in** ~ **with the rent** essere in arretrato con l'affitto.

arrest[1], *n.* (*anche leg.*) arresto. // to **be** (*o* to **be held) under** ~ essere in stato d'arresto; to **be put** (*o* **placed) under** ~ essere messo in stato d'arresto.

arrest[2], *v. t.* (*anche leg.*) arrestare, fermare.

arrestment, *n.* (*scozz.*) *V.* **attachment,** *def.* 3.

arrival, *n.* **1** arrivo. **2 arrivals,** *pl.* (*tur.*) arrivi. // ~ **station** (*trasp. ferr.*) stazione d'arrivo.

arrive, *v. i.* (*anche fig.*) arrivare. // «to ~» (*market., trasp. mar.*) «salvo arrivo»; to ~ **at a conclusion** giungere a una conclusione; to ~ **at a decision** raggiungere una decisione; to ~ **at a port** (*o* **in harbour)** arrivare in un porto (*o* in porto); to ~ **safely** (*di persona*) arrivare sano e salvo; (*di merce*) arrivare in buone condizioni.

arson, *n.* (*ass., leg.*) incendio doloso.

art, *n.* arte. // ~ **director** (*pers.*) direttore artistico (*d'un'agenzia pubblicitaria*); direttore artistico (*di teatro*); ~ **editor** (*pers.*) direttore artistico (*di giornale*); ~ **of navigation** (*trasp. mar.*) nautica.

article[1], *n.* **1** articolo, clausola. **2** (*giorn.*) articolo «pezzo», servizio. **3 articles,** *pl.* apprendistato, tirocinio, pratica. **4 articles,** *pl.* contratto d'arrolamento. // ~ **of accusation** (*leg.*) capo d'accusa; **articles of apprenticeship** accordo d'apprendistato; **articles of association** (*leg.*) statuto (*d'una società di capitali*); **articles of clothing** articoli di vestiario; **an ~ of the Constitution** (*leg.*) un articolo della Costituzione; **articles of everyday consumption** (*market.*) articoli di consumo corrente; **articles of incorporation** (*leg., USA*) statuto (*d'una società di capitali*); **articles of partnership** (*leg.*) statuto (*d'una società di persone*); ~ **of (the ship's) gear** (*trasp. mar.*) attrezzo.

article[2], *v. t.* impegnare con contratto (*specialm. come apprendista*).

articled clerk, *n.* praticante.

artificial, *a.* artificiale.

artisan, *n.* artigiano. // ~ **production** (*econ.*) produzione artigianale.

artist, *n.* artista.

as, *avv.* come. // ~ **agreed upon** secondo gli accordi; «~ **at**» (*Banca*) «valuta» (*scadenza*); (*rag.*) «chiuso» (*di bilancio*); ~ **customary** come di consueto; ~ **far** ~ fino a (*di luogo*); ~ **fast ~ steamer can deliver according to the custom of the port** (*trasp. mar.*) con la maggior celerità con cui il piroscafo può scaricare secondo le consuetudini del porto; ~ **follows** come segue; ~ **for** quanto a; ~ **instructed** secondo le istruzioni; ~ **long** ~ finché, per tutto il tempo che; ~ **per** come da; ~ **per advice** come da avviso; ~ **per sample** come da campione; ~ **per your invoice** come da vostra fattura; ~ **regards** per quanto riguarda; ~ **requested** come da richiesta; ~ **required** quando sarà necessario; ~ **a rule** di regola; ~ **soon** ~ appena, tosto che; ~ **soon ~ possible** il più presto possibile; ~ **suggested by you** secondo la vostra proposta; ~ **to** quanto a; ~ **well** anche, pure.

ascend, *v. t.* e *i.* ascendere, salire.

ascending, *a.* ascendente.

ascent, *n.* ascesa.

ascertain, *v. t.* accertare, accertarsi di, constatare. // to ~ **the extent of the damage** (*ass.*) accertare l'entità del danno; to ~ **the facts** accertare i fatti; to ~ **what really happened** accertarsi di come sono andate le cose.

ascertainable, *a.* accertabile.

ascertainment, *n.* accertamento, constatazione.

ascribable, *a.* ascrivibile.

ascribe, *v. t.* ascrivere.

ask[1], *n.* (*Borsa, fin.*) prezzo di vendita. // ~ **for bids** (*comm.*) bando (*o* concorso) di gara d'appalto.

ask[2], *v. t.* e *i.* **1** chiedere, domandare. **2** invitare. // to ~ **sb. about st.** chiedere a q. informazioni su qc.; to ~ **after sb.** chiedere notizie di q.; to ~ **a favour of sb.** chiedere un favore a q.; to ~ **for** chiedere: to ~ **(for) advice** chiedere consiglio; to ~ **for references** chiedere referenze; to ~ **for sick-leave** (*pers.*) mettersi in mutua; to ~ **for treatment by one's panel doctor** (*pers.*) mettersi in mutua; to ~ **for trouble** andare in cerca di guai; to ~ **sb. in** invitare q. a entrare; to ~ **a question** fare una domanda (*orale*); to ~ **sb. to lunch** invitare q. a colazione; to ~ **too high a price** (*market.*) chiedere un prezzo troppo alto, esagerare nel prezzo.

aspect, *n.* aspetto.

aspiring, *a.* aspirante.

assault[1], *n.* aggressione, assalto. // ~ **and battery** (*leg.*) vie di fatto.

assault[2], *v. t.* assaltare.

assay[1], *n.* saggio. // ~ **office** banco di saggio.

assay[2], *v. t.* saggiare (*metalli preziosi, ecc.*).

assemblage, *n.* (*org. az.*) montaggio.

assemble, *v. t.* **1** adunare. **2** montare (*i pezzi d'una macchina, ecc.*). *v.i.* adunarsi.

assembly, *n.* **1** assemblea, adunanza, riunione. **2** montaggio, assemblaggio. // ~ **hall** sala di montaggio; ~ **line** catena di montaggio; ~ **-line technique** tecnica della catena di montaggio; ~ **program** programma d'assemblaggio; ~ **room** sala di riunione; ~ **shop** officina di montaggio.

assent[1], *n.* approvazione, consenso.

assent[2], *v. i.* approvare, acconsentire. // to ~ **to a proposal** approvare una proposta.

assert, *v. t.* asserire, affermare. // to ~ **a claim** sostenere un diritto; to ~ **one's innocence** (*leg.*) affermare la propria innocenza.

assertion, *n.* asserzione, affermazione.

assert oneself, *v. rifl.* farsi valere, affermarsi.

assess, *v. t.* **1** determinare, stimare, valutare. **2** (*ass. mar.*) ripartire (*perdite*). **3** (*fin.*) stabilire il valore imponibile di (*beni mobili o immobili*); censire (*a scopo fiscale*). **4** (*fin.*) accertare (*un reddito*). **5** (*fin.*) applicare, fissare (*un'imposta, una multa, ecc.*); tassare. // to ~ **the amount of damages** (*ass.*) determinare l'ammontare dei danni; to ~ **damages after an accident** (*ass.*) accertare i danni dopo un incidente; censire una proprietà; **assessed taxes** (*fin.*) imponibile accertato; **assessed value** (*fin.*) valore imponibile.

assessable, *a.* (*fin.*) accertabile, applicabile, determinabile, imponibile, tassabile. // ~ **income** (*fin.*) imponibile.

assessment, *n.* **1** determinazione, stima, valutazione. **2** giudizio. **3** (*ass. mar.*) ripartizione (*di perdite*). **4** (*fin.*) accertamento, estimo. **5** (*fin.*) imponibile (*fiscale*). **6** (*fin.*) imposta. **7** (*fin., USA*) richiamo dei decimi (*sulle azioni sottoscritte*). // ~ **book** (*fin.*) ruolo delle imposte; **an ~ of damages** (*ass.*) una stima dei danni; **the ~ of a loss** (*ass.*) il regolamento d'un sinistro; (*ass. mar.*) la ripartizione d'una perdita; ~ **on income** (*fin.*) accertamento dei redditi; imposta sul reddito; ~ **on landed property** (*fin.*) imposta fondiaria; **provisional ~ of harvests and stocks** bilancio previsivo dei raccolti e delle scorte.

assessor, *n.* **1** perito, stimatore, valutatore. **2** funzionario del fisco, agente delle imposte.

asset, *n.* **1** bene, dono (*fig.*). **2** qualità, dote (*fig.*). **3 assets,** *pl.* (*leg.*) beni. **4 assets,** *pl.* (*rag.*) attivo, attività, «avere». // **assets and liabilities** (*rag.*) attivo e passivo; **assets brought in** (*fin.*) apporto (*dato a un'azienda*); **assets brought into a business** (*fin.*) apporto a un'azienda; **the assets side** (*rag.*) la colonna delle attività; la parte dell'«avere»; ~ **-stripper** (*econ.*) «asset-stripper» (*acquirente di case, beni industriali, ecc., che li cannibalizza rivendendone poi le parti utilizzabili*); **assets transferred to a company** (*fin.*) apporto a un'azienda; ~ **value** (*Borsa, fin.*) contenuto patrimoniale d'una società (*riferito a un titolo*).

assign[1], *n.* **1** (*leg.*) avente causa, avente diritto. **2** (*leg.*) cessionario.

assign[2], *v. t.* **1** assegnare, attribuire, devolvere. **2** fissare, stabilire. **3** incaricare, nominare. **4** (*leg.*) cedere, trasferire, trasmettere. // to ~ **a bond by endorsement** (*cred., fin.*) trasferire un titolo mediante girata; to ~ **counsel to a defendant** (*leg.*) nominare il difensore d'ufficio per un imputato; to ~ **a day for trial** (*leg.*) fissare il giorno del processo; to ~ **a limit** stabilire un limite; to ~ **a pension** assegnare una pensione.

assignable, *a.* **1** assegnabile, attribuibile. **2** (*leg.*) cedibile, trasferibile, trasmissibile.

assignee, *n.* 1 (*leg.*) avente diritto, avente causa. 2 (*leg.*) assegnatario, cessionario, mandatario. // ~ **in bankruptcy** (*leg.*) amministratore dei beni d'un fallito, curatore d'un fallimento.

assignment, *n.* 1 assegnazione, assegnamento, attribuzione. 2 compito, incarico, nomina. 3 (*leg.*) cessione, trasmissione, trasferimento. 4 (*org. az.*) destinazione (*d'un impiegato a un compito*). // ~ **clause** (*ass.*) clausola di cessione (*per la quale l'assicurato può cedere ad altri i propri diritti verso l'assicuratore*); ~ **of counsel to a defendant** (*leg.*) nomina del difensore d'ufficio per un imputato; ~ **of credit** cessione di credito; ~ **of interest** (*leg.*) cessione d'usufrutto; ~ **of a patent** cessione d'un brevetto; ~ **of property to creditors** (*leg.*) cessione di beni ai creditori; ~ **of share** cessione di quota; ~ **of shares** (*fin.*) trasferimento di azioni.

assignor, *n.* (*leg.*) cedente, mandante.

assist, *v. t.* assistere, aiutare. // to ~ **sb. in doing st.** aiutare q. a fare qc.; to ~ **sb. with a task** assistere q. in un lavoro.

assistance, *n.* assistenza, aiuto, contributo, concorso.

assistant, *n.* (*pers.*) assistente, collaboratore. // ~ **accountant** (*pers.*) aiuto contabile; ~ **cashier** (*pers.*) cassiere in sott'ordine; ~ **editor** (*giorn., pers.*) vicedirettore; ~ **executive editor** (*giorn., pers.*) vice redattore capo; ~ **manager** (*pers.*) vicedirettore; ~ **manageress** (*pers.*) vicedirettrice; ~ **member of a committee** membro aggiunto di un comitato; ~ **secretary** (*pers.*) vicesegretario, vicesegretaria; ~ **station master** (*pers., trasp. ferr.*) vicecapostazione; ~ **to the managing director** (*pers.*) assistente del consigliere delegato.

assizes, *n. pl.* (*leg.*) assise. // **the Assize Court of London** l'Assise di Londra.

associate[1], *a.* associato. // ~ **editor** (*giorn., pers.*) condirettore; ~ **in business** collaboratore in affari; ~ **judge** (*leg.*) giudice «a latere»; ~ **professor** professore associato.

associate[2], *v. t.* associare. *v. i.* associarsi. // to ~ **oneself with sb. in a business undertaking** associarsi con q. in un'impresa commerciale.

associated, *a.* e *n.* collegato. // ~ **company** (*fin.*) società collegata (*società che ha in comune con un'altra tutti i membri del consiglio d'amministrazione o parte di essi*); ~ **in business** che collabora in affari.

association, *n.* 1 associazione. 2 collegamento. // ~ **agreements** accordi d'associazione; **the ~ of fashion with industrial reality** (*market.*) il collegamento della moda con la realtà industriale.

assorted, *a.* assortito.

assortment, *n.* (*market.*) assortimento.

assume, *v. t.* 1 assumere, presumere, accettare. 2 fingere, pretendere. // to ~ **a debt** assumersi un debito; to ~ **the direction of a business** assumere la direzione d'un'azienda; to ~ **a new name** assumere un nome nuovo; to ~ **office** assumere una carica.

assuming, *a.* presuntuoso.

assumption, *n.* 1 assunzione, presunzione, accettazione. 2 finzione, pretesa. // **the ~ of an obligation** l'accettazione di un obbligo; ~ **of ownership** (*leg.*) entrata in possesso (*d'un bene*); **the ~ of power** l'assunzione del potere; ~ **of risks** (*ass.*) assunzione di rischi.

assurable, *a.* (*USA, o, per lo più, sulla vita*) assicurabile.

assurance, *n.* 1 assicurazione. 2 (= **self-assurance**) sicumera. 3 (*ass.*) assicurazione (*USA o, per lo più, sulla vita*). // ~ **company** (*ass.*) compagnia d'assicurazioni; ~ **policy** (*ass.*) polizza d'assicurazione.

assure, *v. t.* 1 assicurare. 2 (*ass.*) assicurare (*USA o, per lo più, sulla vita*). // to ~ **one's life** fare un'assicurazione sulla vita.

assured, *a.* 1 assicurato. 2 (*ass.*) assicurato. **the ~,** *n.* l'assicurato (*USA o, per lo più, sulla vita*).

assure oneself, *v. rifl.* assicurarsi.

assurer, *n.* (*ass.*) assicuratore (*specialm. USA*).

astern, *avv.* (*trasp. mar.*) indietro.

at, *prep.* 1 (*stato in luogo e tempo*) a. 2 (*prezzo*) a. // ~ **large** (*leg.*) latitante.

Atlantic liner, (*trasp. mar.*) transatlantico.

attach, *v. t.* e *i.* 1 attaccare. 2 allegare, accludere. 3 annettere, attribuire. 4 decorrere, aver effetto. 5 (*leg.*) sequestrare, pignorare. // to ~ **demurrage** (*trasp. mar.*) far decorrere le controstallie; to ~ **a document to a letter** allegare un documento a una lettera; to ~ **much importance to st.** attribuire grande importanza a qc.; to ~ **the price tags on each article** attaccare a ogni articolo il cartellino del prezzo; to ~ **to** riferirsi a.

attachable, *a.* (*leg.*) sequestrabile, pignorabile.

attaché, *n.* addetto (*nella carriera diplomatica*).

attached, *a.* (*comm.*) accluso, annesso.

attachment, *n.* 1 legame. 2 attacco (*di un apparecchio*). 3 (*leg.*) decorrenza. 4 (*leg.*) pignoramento, sequestro conservativo. 5 (*trasp. mar.*) talloncino (*allegato a una polizza di carico*). //

~ **of real property** (*leg.*) sequestro immobiliare; ~ **of the risk** (*ass.*) decorrenza della copertura del rischio.

attack[1], *n.* attacco. // **a strong** ~ **on the board's policy** un poderoso attacco alla politica del consiglio d'amministrazione.

attack[2], *v. t.* attaccare. // to ~ **the chairman's proposals** attaccare le proposte del presidente.

attain, *v. t.* conseguire, raggiungere. // to ~ **objectives** raggiungere gli obiettivi.

attainable, *a.* conseguibile.

attainment, *n.* **1** conseguimento, cognizioni. **2 attainments,** *pl.* preparazione.

attempt, *n.* sforzo.

attend, *v. t.* e *i.* **1** frequentare, presenziare, intervenire a (*una riunione, ecc.*). **2** curare, provvedere, occuparsi di. // to ~ **a board meeting** presenziare a una riunione del consiglio d'amministrazione; to ~ **secondary school** frequentare la scuola secondaria; to ~ **to a case** (*leg.*) occuparsi d'una causa; to ~ **to the collection of a bill** (*cred.*) curare l'incasso d'una cambiale; to ~ **to the correspondence** occuparsi della corrispondenza; to ~ **to sb.'s orders with the utmost care** curare le ordinazioni di q. con la massima attenzione; to ~ **to one's work** badare al proprio lavoro; to ~ **a trial** assistere a un processo.

attendance, *n.* frequenza, presenza (*sul posto di lavoro, ecc.*). // ~ **at school** frequenza scolastica; ~ **book** registro delle presenze; ~ **-check** (*pers.*) gettone di presenza; ~ **fee** (*pers.*) gettone di presenza (*il compenso*); ~ **in Court** (*leg.*) comparizione in giudizio; ~ **sheet** (*pers.*) foglio delle presenze.

attendant, *n.* **1** addetto, inserviente. **2** accompagnatore. **3 attendants,** *pl.* personale (*d'un negozio, ecc.*). *a.* inerente (*a*). // ~ **of call office** (*comun., pers.*) telefonista.

attention, *n.* attenzione. // « ~ **of Mr X.Y.** » «all'attenzione di Mr X.Y.».

attenuate, *v. t.* attenuare.

attenuation, *n.* attenuazione.

attest, *v. t.* **1** attestare. **2** (*leg.*) autenticare, vidimare. // to ~ **a fact** attestare un fatto; to ~ **a signature** (*leg.*) autenticare una firma; **attested copy** copia vidimata, copia autentica (*d'un documento*).

attestable, *a.* attestabile.

attestation, *n.* attestazione.

attested, *a.* (*leg.*) autentico. // ~ **affidavit** (*leg.*) atto notorio (*o* di notorietà).

attitude, *n.* atteggiamento. // ~ **survey** (*pers.*) sondaggio di morale aziendale.

attorney, *n.* **1** (*leg.*) procuratore, mandatario. **2** (*leg., USA*) avvocato (*cfr. ingl.* **solicitor**). // ~ **-at-law** (*leg.*) procuratore legale, avvocato; ~ **General** Procuratore Generale; (*USA*) Procuratore Generale (*Ministro della Giustizia*); ~ **'s office** (*leg.*) procura (*ufficio di procuratore*).

attract, *v. t.* attrarre.

attributable, *a.* attribuibile.

attribute, *v. t.* attribuire.

attribution, *n.* attribuzione.

auction[1], *n.* asta pubblica, incanto, licitazione. // ~ **room** sala delle vendite all'asta; ~ **-sale** vendita all'asta, licitazione, incanto.

auction[2], *v. t.* vendere all'asta. // to ~ **st. off** vendere all'asta qc.; (*leg., USA*) appaltare qc.

auctioneer, *n.* banditore (*di vendita all'asta*).

audience, *n.* **1** uditorio, pubblico. **2** udienza.

audimeter, *n.* (*pubbl.*) audimetro.

audio-visual means, *n. pl.* (*pubbl.*) mezzi audiovisivi.

audit[1], *n.* (*amm., org. az., rag.*) controllo, revisione, verifica dei conti, revisione contabile. // ~ **board** commissione di controllo dei conti; ~ **committee** comitato di controllo dei conti.

audit[2], *v. t.* (*amm., org. az., rag.*) controllare, verificare (*i conti*). // to ~ **an account** (*fin., leg.*) verificare un conto e certificarne l'esattezza; to ~ **the cash in hand** (*rag.*) fare un controllo di cassa.

auditing, *n.* **1** (*amm., rag.*) revisione contabile (*dei conti d'un ente pubblico, d'un ministero, ecc.*). **2** (*org. az., rag.*) revisione contabile (*dei conti d'un'azienda: eseguita da professionisti specializzati che svolgono le funzioni attribuite in Italia al collegio dei sindaci*).

auditor, *n.* **1** uditore. **2** (*amm., org. az., rag.*) controllore dei conti, revisore contabile, verificatore, sindaco. // **auditors' committee** collegio dei revisori contabili; ~ **-General** (*amm., rag.*) «Revisore Generale dei Conti» (*in G.B.*); ~ **opinion on fairness of balance-sheet presentation** (*org. az., rag.*) certificazione di bilancio; **auditors' report** relazione dei revisori contabili.

auditorial, *a.* (*fin.*) (*di sindaco di società*) sindacale.

auditorship, *n.* (*amm., org. az., rag.*) ufficio di revisore dei conti.

augment, *v. t.* e *i.* aumentare, accrescere, crescere. // to ~ **one's income by working overtime** aumentare le proprie entrate facendo del lavoro straordinario.

augmentation, *n.* aumento.

austerity, *n.* (*econ.*) austerità. // ~ **programme** programma d'austerità.

autarchic, *a.* (*econ.*) autarchico.

autarchical, *a.* (*econ.*) autarchico.

autarchy, *n.* (*econ.*) autarchia.

autarky, *n.* (*econ.*) autarchia.

authentic, *a.* autentico. // **an** ~ **signature** una firma autentica.

authenticate, *v. t.* (*leg.*) autenticare, legalizzare, vidimare. // to ~ **a certificate** (*leg.*) autenticare un certificato; to ~ **a signature** legalizzare una firma; **authenticated copy of a document** copia autentica d'un documento.

authentication, *n.* (*leg.*) autenticazione, legalizzazione, vidimazione.

authenticity, *n.* autenticità.

authoritative, *a.* autorevole. // **from an** ~ **source** da fonte autorevole.

authority, *n.* **1** autorità, potere, facoltà. **2** autorizzazione. **3** ente (*pubblico o parastatale*). // **by** ~ d'autorità; **the health authorities** il servizio d'igiene; to **be in** ~ comandare; **the Tennessee Valley** ~ l'Ente per la Vallata del Tennessee.

authorization, *n.* autorizzazione. // ~ **for the duty-free reimport of returned goods** (*dog.*) autorizzazione delle reimportazioni in franchigia di merci in precedenza esportate; ~ **to proceed** (*leg.*) autorizzazione a procedere.

authorize, *v. t.* autorizzare. // to ~ **the payment of travelling expenses** autorizzare il pagamento delle spese di viaggio; to ~ **the spending of £ 100,000 on new premises** autorizzare la spesa di 100.000 sterline per una nuova sede.

authorized, *a.* autorizzato. // ~ **act** atto autorizzato; atto d'ordinaria amministrazione; ~ **capital** (*fin.*) capitale nominale.

auto-, *pref.* auto-. // ~ **-rally** autoraduno.

autograph, *n.* autografo. // ~ **book** (*banca*) libro delle firme (*dei clienti*).

automat, *n.* ristorante «automatico».

automatic, *a.* automatico. // ~ **bookkeeping machine** (*macch. uff.*) macchina contabile automatica; ~ **check-off** (*sind.*) trattenuta automatica (*dei contributi sindacali: sulla paga*); ~ **data processing** (*elab. elettr.*) elaborazione automatica dei dati; ~ **exchange** (*comun.*) centralino automatico; ~ **pay increase** (*pers.*) aumento automatico del salario, scatto di stipendio; ~ **stabilizer** (*econ.*) stabilizzatore automatico; ~ **vendor** distributore automatico; ~ **wage adjustment** (*econ., org. az.*) aggiustamento automatico dei salari.

automobile, *n.* (*USA*) automobile.

autonomous, *a.* autonomo. // ~ **investment** (*fin., rag.*) investimento autonomo; ~ **variable** (*mat.*) variabile autonoma.

autonomy, *n.* autonomia.

auxiliary, *a.* ausiliare, strumentale. // ~ **capital** (*econ., fin.*) capitale strumentale; ~ **goods** (*econ., fin.*) beni strumentali.

avail¹, *n.* utile netto.

avail², *v. i.* essere utile, servire (*a qc.*).

availability, *n.* **1** disponibilità. **2** validità. // ~ **of capital** (*fin.*) disponibilità di capitali; ~ **of finance** (*fin.*) possibilità finanziarie.

available, *a.* **1** disponibile. **2** valevole, valido. **3** (*trasp.*) (*di posto a sedere*) libero. // **the** ~ **assets** (*rag.*) le disponibilità; ~ **audience** (*pubbl.*) ascoltatori potenziali; ~ **funds** fondi disponibili, fondi liquidi; **the** ~ **funds** (*rag.*) le disponibilità; ~ **stocks** (*market.*) giacenze disponibili.

availment, *n.* utilizzazione.

avail oneself of, *v. rifl.* valersi di, approfittare di (*qc.*). // to ~ **every opportunity to advertise one's goods** approfittare d'ogni occasione per fare pubblicità alla propria merce; to ~ **a right** (*leg.*) valersi di un diritto.

average¹, *a.* medio. *n.* **1** (*ass. mar.*) avaria. **2** (*mat.*) media. // ~ **adjuster** (*ass. mar.*) liquidatore d'avaria; ~ **adjustment** (*ass. mar.*) liquidazione d'avaria; ~ **adjustor** (*ass. mar.*) liquidatore d'avaria; ~ **bill** (*ass. mar.*) conteggio d'avaria; ~ **bond** (*ass. mar.*) buono (*o* obbligazione) d'avaria; ~ **clause** (*ass. mar.*) clausola d'avaria; ~ **cost** (*econ.*) costo medio; ~ **damage** (*ass. mar.*) danni d'avaria; ~ **expenses** (*ass. mar., trasp. mar.*) spese d'avaria; ~ **income** (*econ.*) reddito medio; **the** ~ **life** la vita media; ~ **payment** (*ass. mar., trasp. mar.*) dividendo d'avaria; ~ **price** (*econ.*) prezzo medio; ~ **statement** (*ass. mar.*) certificato (di liquidazione) d'avaria; liquidazione d'avaria; ~ **stater** (*ass. mar.*) liquidatore d'avaria; ~ **stock** (*market.*) giacenza media; ~ **surveyor** (*ass. mar.*) perito d'avaria; ~ **taker** (*ass. mar.*) liquidatore d'avaria; ~ **tare** tara media; **above the** ~ sopra la media; **below the** ~ sotto la media; **on an** ~ in media; **up to the** ~ pari alla media.

average², *v. t.* e *i.* **1** (*mat.*) fare la media di. **2** (*rag.*) ripartire in modo proporzionale. // to ~ **eight hours a day** fare in media otto ore al giorno (*di lavoro, di studio, ecc.*); to ~ **a loss** (*ass. mar.*) ripartire una perdita in modo proporzionale; to ~ **out** essere in media; to ~ **purchases** fare una media del prezzo degli acquisti; to ~ **sales** fare una media del prezzo delle vendite; to ~ **300 miles a day** fare in media 300 miglia al giorno.

averaging, *a.* che fa una media di. *n.* (*rag.*) ripartizione proporzionale. // ~ **account** (*rag.*) conto di ripartizione.

avoid, *v. t.* **1** evitare. **2** (*fin.*) sottrarsi a (*il fisco*). **3** (*leg.*) rescindere, annullare. // to ~ **a contract** (*leg.*) rescindere un contratto.

avoidable, *a.* (*leg.*) annullabile, rescindibile. // ~ **delay** ritardo evitabile.

avoidance, *n.* (*leg.*) annullamento, rescissione. // ~ **clause** (*leg.*) clausola risolutiva; ~ **of taxation** (*fin.*) l'evitare di pagare le tasse.

avoirdupois, *n.* «avoirdupois» (*sistema di pesi inglesi, la cui unità è la libbra*).

await, *v. t.* attendere. // «to ~ **arrival**» (*comun.*) «fermo posta».

awaited, *a.* atteso.

award[1], *n.* **1** aggiudicazione, assegnazione. **2** (*leg.*) sentenza d'un arbitro, giudizio arbitrale, lodo arbitrale. **3** (*leg.*) sentenza d'un giudice. // **the ~ of a contract** l'aggiudicazione d'un contratto.

award[2], *v. t.* **1** assegnare, aggiudicare. **2** (*leg.*) affidare (*figli minorenni, in caso di divorzio*). // to **be awarded a prize** (*pers.*) ricevere un premio.

awardable, *a.* assegnabile, aggiudicabile.

awarding, *n.* **1** assegnazione, aggiudicazione. **2** (*leg.*) affidamento (*di figli minorenni*).

away, *avv.* via.

ax, *n.* (*slang USA*) licenziamento.

axis, *n.* (*pl.* **axes**) (*mat.*) asse.

B

babbitt, *n.* (*slang USA*) tipico uomo d'affari americano.

baby, *n.* bambino. // ~ **bond** (*fin., USA*) obbligazione del valore nominale di 10, 25 o 50 dollari; ~ **boom** (*stat.*) boom delle nascite; ~ **car** automobile utilitaria.

back[1], *n.* dorso, schiena, retro, tergo, spalle (*fig.*). *a. attr.* **1** posteriore. **2** arretrato. **3** scaduto. *avv.* indietro. // ~ **-bond** (*leg.*) ipoteca; ~ **copy of a newspaper** (*giorn.*) copia arretrata d'un giornale; ~ **-door trade** (*leg.*) commercio illegale; ~ **file** (*attr. uff.*) archivio degli arretrati; ~ **freight** (*trasp. mar.*) spese di nolo impreviste, soprannolo; ~ **office** (*org. az.*) ufficio privato; ~ **order** ordinazione inevasa; ~ **pay** (*org. az., pers.*) arretrati (*del salario*); ~ **rent** affitto arretrato; ~ **-shunt** (*trasp. ferr.*) regresso; ~ **spread** (*fin.*) (*nelle operazioni d'arbitraggio*) condizione che si verifica quando la differenza di prezzo per la stessa merce o per lo stesso titolo in due mercati è minore del normale; ~ **-to-work injunction** (*sind.*) ingiunzione di riprendere il lavoro.

back[2], *v. t.* **1** appoggiare. **2** (*cred.*) sostenere. **3** (*leg.*) patrocinare. **4** (*leg.*) avallare, garantire. // to ~ **a bill** avallare una cambiale, garantire una cambiale; to ~ **down** (*leg.*) recedere, rinunziare a un diritto; to ~ **out of a bargain** ritirarsi da un affare; to ~ **a plan** sostenere un progetto; to ~ **sb. up** appoggiare q.

backdate, *v. t.* retrodatare.

backed, *a.* (*cred.*) avallato, garantito. // ~ **bills** (*cred.*) cambiali avallate; ~ **-note** (*trasp. mar.*) permesso d'imbarco.

backer, *n.* **1** sostenitore. **2** (*cred.*) avallante. // **the** ~ **of a bill of exchange** l'avallante d'una cambiale.

background, *n.* **1** ambiente. **2** (= **economic background**) congiuntura. // **the** ~ **in a business report** i precedenti in una relazione d'affari.

backing, *n.* **1** appoggio, seguito. **2** (*fin.*) copertura (*d'un'emissione di banconote*).

backlog, *n.* **1** arretrato (*di lavoro o affari*). **2** ordinazioni inevase. **3** (*slang USA*) fondo di riserva. // ~ **of demand** (*econ.*) riserva di domanda; ~ **of unfilled orders** elenco delle ordinazioni inevase.

backsliding, *n.* (*Borsa*) scivolata.

backward, *a.* arretrato. // ~ **call** (*trasp. mar.*) scalo (fatto da una nave durante il viaggio) di ritorno; **a** ~ **Country** un Paese arretrato; ~ **economies** economie arretrate; ~ **industries** (*econ.*) industrie arretrate; ~ **method** (*rag.*) metodo retrogrado o indiretto (*usato per il calcolo degli interessi dei conti correnti fruttiferi*); ~ **shifting of tax** (*fin.*) traslazione dell'imposta a un fornitore o a un dipendente, traslazione all'indietro.

backwardation, *n.* (*Borsa, fin.*) deporto, premio del deporto. // ~ **fee** tasso del deporto; ~ **rate** tasso del deporto.

backwardization, *n.* (*Borsa, fin.*) deporto.

backwardized, *a.* (*Borsa, fin.*) a deporto. // ~ **stock (o shares)** titoli a deporto.

backwards, *avv.* all'indietro. // «~ **and/or forwards**» (*trasp. mar.*) «indietro e/o avanti» (*clausola che consente alla nave di fare scalo in qualsiasi porto intermedio*).

bad, *a.* brutto, cattivo, grave. *avv.* male. // **a** ~ **accident** un incidente grave; **a** ~ **blunder** un grosso errore; **a** ~ **business** (*fam.*) un brutto affare; **a** ~ **cheque** un assegno a vuoto; **a** ~ **coin** una moneta falsa; **a** ~ **debt** (*cred.*) un credito inesigibile, un credito di dubbia esigibilità; ~ **debts reserve** (*rag.*) ammortamento dei crediti inesigibili; ~ **delivery of the goods** consegna della merce in cattivo stato; **a** ~ **job** (*fam.*) un brutto affare; **a** ~ **mistake** un grave errore; ~ **news** cattive notizie; **a** ~ **speculation** (*fin.*) una cattiva speculazione; ~ **standing** basso tenore di vita; ~ **stowage** (*trasp. mar.*) stivaggio difettoso; **a** ~ **title** (*leg.*) un titolo di proprietà non valido; ~ **weather** brutto tempo, tempo cattivo; to **be in a** ~ **way** essere a mal partito; **to the** ~ in perdita; (*rag.*) in passivo.

bag, *n.* sacco. // ~ **and baggage** (*fig.*) armi e bagagli; **bags of money** (*fig.*) soldi a palate; **in the** ~ (*fam.*) nel sacco.

baggage, *n.* (*trasp., USA*) bagaglio. // ~ **-check** (*trasp.*) scontrino del bagaglio.

bagman, *n.* (*pl.* **bagmen**) (*pers.*) commesso viaggiatore.

bail[1], *n.* 1 (*leg.*) cauzione. 2 (*leg.*) garanzia, fideiussione. 3 (*leg.*) garante. // ~ **-bond** (*leg.*) cauzione; to **be out on** ~ (*leg.*) essere in libertà provvisoria (*dopo aver pagato la cauzione*); **release on** ~ (*leg.*) rilascio sotto cauzione.

bail[2], *v. t.* 1 (*leg.*) cauzionare. 2 (*leg.*) depositare (*merci: a garanzia*). // to ~ **sb. out** (*slang USA*) aiutare finanziariamente q. (*che si trova nei guai*).

bailee, *n.* 1 (*leg.*) depositario (*di merci: a garanzia*). 2 (*leg.*) comodatario.

bailer, *n.* 1 (*leg.*) depositante (*di merci: a garanzia*). 2 (*leg.*) comodante.

bailiff, *n.* 1 fattore (*d'una grande tenuta*). 2 (*leg.*) ufficiale giudiziario. 3 (*pers.*) usciere di tribunale.

bailment, *n.* 1 (*leg.*) cauzione, garanzia. 2 (*leg.*) deposito a garanzia (*in genere*). 3 (*leg.*) pegno di merci, denaro o altri valori. 4 (*leg.*) comodato.

bailor, *n.* 1 (*leg.*) depositante (*di merci: a garanzia*). 2 (*leg.*) comodante.

bailsman, *n.* (*pl.* **bailsmen**) (*leg.*) garante (*chi offre cauzione per q.*).

balance[1], *n.* 1 equilibrio. 2 (*econ., fin.*) bilancia. 3 (*fin., rag.*) bilancio, ragguaglio. 4 (*fin., rag.*) pareggio. 5 (*fin., rag.*) conguaglio, saldo, differenza a saldo. 6 (*fin., rag.*) rimanenza, resto. 7 (*fin., rag.*) sbilancio (*somma iscritta in bilancio per pareggiare il dare e l'avere*). // ~ **account** conto collettivo; ~ **at** (*o* **in**) **bank** saldo in banca; ~ **book** (*rag.*) libro dei saldi, libro dei bilanci di verifica; ~ **brought forward** (*o* **down**) (*rag.*) saldo riportato, riporto; ~ **brought forward from last account** (*rag.*) saldo riportato dall'esercizio precedente, saldo dell'esercizio precedente; ~ **«can remain»** «saldo (da effettuare) in seguito»; ~ **carried forward** (*o* **down**) (*rag.*) saldo da riportare, saldo a conto nuovo, riporto; ~ **(carried forward) to next account** (*rag.*) saldo a nuovo; ~ **due** (*rag.*) saldo debitore; ~ **from last account** (*rag.*) saldo dell'esercizio precedente; ~ **in cash** (*rag.*) saldo in contanti; ~ **in** (*o* **on**) **hand** (*rag.*) saldo (*o* rimanenza) in cassa; ~ **medium-term loans** (*fin.*) saldo prestiti a medio termine; ~ **method** (*rag.*) metodo amburghese (*per il calcolo degli interessi dei conti correnti fruttiferi*); **the** ~ **of an account** (*rag.*) il saldo d'un conto; ~ **of indebtedness** (*fin., rag.*) bilancio economico, bilancia dei conti; **the** ~ **of international payments** (*fin.*) la bilancia dei pagamenti internazionali; ~ **of payments** (*fin.*) bilancia dei pagamenti, conti con l'estero; **the** ~ **of powers** l'equilibrio delle forze (politiche); ~ **of profits carried forward to next account** (*rag.*) saldo degli utili riportato a nuovo sull'esercizio seguente; ~ **of trade** (*econ., fin.*) bilancia commerciale; saldo degli scambi; **the** ~ **on current account** (*fin., rag.*) la bilancia delle operazioni correnti; ~ **on purchase or sale of securities at settlement date** (*banca*) saldo liquidazione titoli; ~ **-sheet** (*rag.*) bilancio (*prospetto del dare e dell'avere*), stato patrimoniale, bilancio annuale, bilancio commerciale; ~ **-sheet and schedules** (*rag.*) inventario (*bilancio, conto profitti e perdite, conto d'esercizio, ecc.*); ~ **-sheet as at 31st December 1982** bilancio chiuso al 31 dicembre 1982; ~ **-sheet book** (*rag.*) libro dell'inventario; ~ **-sheet items** (*rag.*) capitoli di bilancio; ~ **-sheet made up to** (*o* **as at**) **December 31st 1983** bilancio (chiuso) al 31 dicembre 1983; ~ **-sheet value** (*fin., rag.*) valore di bilancio; ~ **-sheets** (*fin., rag.*) bilanci finanziari; **in** ~ (*rag.*) in pareggio; **on** ~ (*fig.*) tutto considerato, tutto sommato.

balance[2], *v. t.* 1 (*rag.*) chiudere, pareggiare, saldare. 2 (*rag.*) bilanciare, equilibrare, conguagliare, ragguagliare. *v. i.* 1 (*fin., rag.*) conguagliarsi, equilibrarsi, chiudere in pareggio. 2 (*rag.*) quadrare. // to ~ **an account** (*rag.*) chiudere un conto, saldare un conto, bilanciare un conto; to ~ **accounts** (*rag.*) ragguagliare le partite, pareggiare il bilancio; to ~ **the books for the year** (*rag.*) fare il bilancio dei libri contabili per l'anno d'esercizio; to ~ **the budget** (*fin., rag.*) pareggiare il bilancio pubblico; to ~ **each other** bilanciarsi, compensarsi; to ~ **the ordinary budget** (*fin., rag.*) equilibrare il bilancio ordinario; to ~ **up** bilanciare.

balanced, *a.* 1 equilibrato. 2 (*rag.*) chiuso, saldato. // ~ **development** sviluppo equilibrato; ~ **expansion** espansione equilibrata; **a** ~ **growth** uno sviluppo equilibrato, uno sviluppo coordinato.

bale[1], *n.* balla, collo.

bale[2], *v. t.* (*trasp.*) imballare.

baler, *n.* 1 (*org. az.*) imballatrice (*la macchina*). 2 (*pers.*) imballatore.

baling, *n.* imballaggio, imballatura.

ball, *n.* 1 palla. 2 sfera. // ~ **-pen** penna a sfera; ~ **-point pen** penna a sfera.

ballast[1], *n.* (*trasp. mar.*) zavorra. // ~ **passage** (*trasp. mar.*) viaggio in zavorra; **in** ~ (*trasp. mar.*) scarico.

ballast[2], *v. t.* (*trasp. mar.*) zavorrare.

ballasting, *n.* (*trasp. mar.*) zavorramento.

ballooning, *n.* (*Borsa, slang USA*) aumento dei prezzi.

ballot, *n.* 1 pallina (*per votazioni*). 2 scheda (*per votazioni*). // ~ **-paper** scheda (*per votazioni*).

bally, *n.* (*slang USA*) pubblicità.

ballyhoo, *n.* (*slang USA*) pubblicità.

Baltic, *a.* Baltico. **the Baltic,** *n.* 1 il (Mar) Baltico. 2 *V.* ~ **Mercantile and Shipping Exchange.** // **the** ~ **Exchange** (*trasp. mar.*) *V.* ~ **Mercantile and Shipping Exchange;** ~ **Mercantile and Shipping Exchange** (*trasp. mar.*) Borsa dei Noli Marittimi e dei Cereali (*a Londra*); **a** ~ **port** un porto del Baltico; **the** ~ **Sea** il Mar Baltico.

ban[1], *n.* (*leg.*) divieto. // ~ **on prospecting for customers** divieto di pubblicità.

ban[2], *v. t.* (*leg.*) bandire, proscrivere, interdire. // to ~ **from holding public offices** (*leg.*) interdire dai pubblici uffici.

banco, *a.* (*storico*) banco. // **a XIX century Swedish shilling** ~ uno scellino «banco» svedese dell'Ottocento.

band, *n.* banda, fascia. // **bands of fluctuation** (*fin.*) fasce di oscillazione; ~ **within** ~ (*fin.*) fascia entro fascia.

bang, *v. t.* e *i.* battere violentemente, sbattere. // to ~ **the market** (*fin.*) buttar giù il mercato (*provocando un forte ribasso dei prezzi*).

banish, *v. t.* (*leg.*) bandire (*mettere al bando*).

bank[1], *n.* 1 (*cred.*) banca, istituto di credito. 2 **the Bank** (*fin.*) la Banca d'Inghilterra. 3 (*trasp. mar.*) banco (*di sabbia, ecc.*). // ~ **acceptance** accettazione bancaria, tratta spiccata su un banchiere e da lui accettata; ~ **account** conto di (*o* in) banca; ~ **annuities** (*fin.*) titoli del debito consolidato; ~ **balance** saldo in banca; ~ **bill** (*USA*) biglietto di banca, banconota; **Bank bill** cambiale scontabile presso la Banca d'Inghilterra (*e che reca la firma di due «accepting houses»*); ~ **bills** effetti bancari; ~ **book** libretto di banca; (*USA*) libretto per i versamenti; ~ **branch** filiale di banca; ~ **call** (*fin., USA*) richiesta a una banca (*da parte d'un funzionario governativo*) di consegnare le scritture di bilancio; ~ **charges** spese bancarie, commissioni bancarie; ~ **check** (*USA*) assegno bancario; ~ **cheque** assegno bancario; ~ **clearance** benestare bancario; ~ **clerk** (*pers.*) impiegato di banca, bancario; ~ **commission** commissione bancaria, provvigione bancaria; ~ **credit** credito bancario; ~ **credit inflation** (*econ., fin.*) inflazione del credito bancario; ~ **deposit** deposito bancario; ~ **discount** sconto bancario; ~ **draft** «bank draft» (*nell'uso, ma non nella forma, corrisponde al nostro assegno circolare; V. fraseologia sotto* **banker's draft**); ~ **examiner** (*fin., USA*) pubblico ufficiale che controlla periodicamente i conti delle banche soggette alla sua giurisdizione; ~ **guarantee** garanzia bancaria (*rilasciata, dalla banca d'un importatore, sulla solvibilità di quest'ultimo*); ~ **guaranty** assicurazione sui depositi bancari (*contro perdite derivanti da fallimento, ecc.*); ~ **holiday** giorno festivo legale; ~ **loans** (*fin.*) prestiti bancari; ~ **manager** direttore di banca; ~ **money** (*fin.*) titoli di credito; ~ **-note** biglietto di banca, banconota; **the Bank of America** la Banca d'America (*una delle poche banche americane che operi col sistema delle filiali*); ~ **of circulation** banca d'emissione; ~ **of commerce** banca del commercio; ~ **of deposit** banca di deposito; ~ **of discount** (*fin.*) banca di sconto; **the Bank of England** la Banca d'Inghilterra; **the Bank of International Settlements (B.I.S.)** la Banca dei Regolamenti Internazionali (*B.R.I.*); ~ **of issue** banca d'emissione; **the** ~ **of State** la banca dello Stato; ~ **overdraft** emissione allo scoperto (*d'assegni*); (*cred.*) «scoperto» di conto corrente con fido bancario; ~ **paper** (*cred.*) effetto bancario; (*fin.*) moneta cartacea; ~ **pass-book** libretto di deposito vincolato, libretto di risparmio; ~ **rate** (*fin.*) tasso ufficiale di sconto; ~ **rate of discount** (*fin.*) tasso ufficiale di sconto; ~ **reconciliation** (*banca*) riscontro bancario; ~ **reserve** riserva bancaria; ~ **return** rendiconto della situazione d'una banca; ~ **shares** (*fin.*) azioni bancarie; ~ **statement** estratto conto (*mandato dalla banca a un cliente*), rendiconto della situazione d'una banca; ~ **stocks** (*fin.*) bancari; ~ **transfer** trasferimento bancario.

bank[2], *v. i.* 1 essere cliente d'una banca. 2 tenere denaro alla banca. *v. t.* 1 mettere in banca; depositare, versare (*denaro*) in banca. 2 presentare (*titoli*) all'incasso. // to ~ **one's money** versare il proprio denaro in banca.

bankable, *a.* bancabile. // ~ **bills** (*cred.*) effetti bancabili.

banker, *n.* banchiere. // ~**'s acceptance** (*cred.*) accettazione bancaria; **the bankers' bank** la «banca delle banche» (*la banca centrale*); **bankers' clearing house** (*banca, cred.*) stanza di compensazione; **bankers' discount** (*cred.*) sconto bancario; ~ **'s draft** (*cred.*) «banker's draft», credenziale (*nell'uso, ma non nella forma, corrisponde al nostro assegno circolare*); ~ **'s references** referenze bancarie; ~ **'s ticket** conto delle spese bancarie (*su di una cambiale protestata*).

banking, *a.* bancario. *n.* attività bancaria. //

~ **account** conto di (*o* in) banca; ~ **business** attività bancaria; ~ **company** istituto bancario; ~ **concern** azienda bancaria; ~ **customs** prassi bancaria; ~ **establishment** istituto bancario; ~ **firm** istituto bancario; ~ **hours** orario di banca; ~ **house** istituto bancario; ~ **operations** operazioni bancarie; ~ **principle** (*econ., fin.*) principio bancario; **the** ~ **profession** la professione bancaria; ~ **services** servizi bancari; ~ **system** sistema bancario; ~ **technique** tecnica bancaria; ~ **transactions** operazioni bancarie.

bankroll, *v. t.* (*slang USA*) finanziare.

bankrupt[1], *a.* e *n.* (*leg.*) fallito. // **the** ~ **'s estate** la massa fallimentare; ~ **'s indebtedness** debito complessivo del fallito.

bankrupt[2], *v. t.* (*leg.*) far fallire.

bankruptcy, *n.* (*leg.*) fallimento (*in senso proprio*). // ~ **act** (*leg.*) atto fallimentare; ~ **adjudication** (*leg.*) sentenza dichiarativa di fallimento; ~ **assets** (*leg.*) attivo del fallimento; ~ **Court** (*leg.*) tribunale fallimentare; ~ **estates account** conto speciale (*presso la Banca d'Inghilterra*) dove il curatore del fallimento deposita i realizzi in denaro del fallimento stesso; ~ **judge** giudice fallimentare; ~ **law** (*leg.*) legge sul fallimento; diritto fallimentare; ~ **liabilities** (*leg.*) passivo fallimentare; ~ **notice** (*leg.*) preavviso di fallimento; ~ **petition** (*leg.*) istanza fallimentare; ~ **proceedings** (*leg.*) procedura fallimentare.

bankster, *n.* (*slang USA*) banchiere.

banner headline, *n.* (*giorn.*) titolo a tutta pagina.

«banque d'affaires», *n.* (*francese*) banca d'affari.

bar[1], *n.* **1** barra (*alla foce d'un fiume*). **2** verga, lingotto. **3** impedimento, ostacolo. **4** (*leg.*) preclusione. **5 the Bar** (*leg.*) l'avvocatura, la professione forense; l'ordine degli avvocati. **6** (*leg.*) sbarra. **7** (*leg.*) sospensione (*d'un'azione giudiziaria*). *avv.* eccetto. // **the** ~ **Association** (*leg.*) l'Ordine degli Avvocati; ~ **depot** (*fin.*) deposito in contanti; ~ **of the statute of limitations** (*leg.*) prescrizione (*V. anche* **statute**); ~ **to action** (*leg.*) impedimento procedurale; **the Bench and the Bar** la Magistratura e il Foro.

bar[2], *v. t.* **1** sbarrare. **2** ostacolare. **3** impedire, vietare. **4** eccettuare, escludere. **5** (*leg.*) sospendere. // to ~ **sb. from a competitive exam** escludere q. da un esame di concorso; to **be barred by limitation** (*leg.*) essere prescritto; to **be barred by statute of limitations** (*leg.*) essere prescritto, prescriversi.

bare, *a.* **1** nudo. **2** mero. **3** privo, vuoto. // ~ **contract** (*leg.*) contratto di comodato, contratto a titolo gratuito; **the** ~ **minimum of subsistence** il livello minimo di sussistenza; ~ **office premises** una sede spoglia; **the** ~ **subsistence level** il minimo vitale; **a house** ~ **of all comforts** una casa priva d'ogni comodità.

bareboat charter, *n.* (*trasp. mar.*) contratto di noleggio della sola nave.

barely, *avv.* appena, a mala pena, a stento. // **a** ~ **furnished room** una stanza con pochi mobili.

bargain[1], *n.* **1** affare, negozio. **2** buon affare, affare favorevole. **3** (*market.*) «offerta speciale», «occasione». **4 bargains,** *pl.* (*Borsa*) affari conclusi alla Borsa Valori di Londra. // ~ **basement** (*market.*) reparto al piano interrato (*di grande magazzino, ecc.*) per le «offerte speciali»; ~ **-book** (*Borsa*) libro dei contratti; ~ **campaign** (*market.*) campagna di vendita speciale; **bargains done** (*alla Borsa Valori*) corsi praticati; **a** ~ **for the account** (*Borsa*) un affare (*o* un contratto) a termine; **a** ~ **for cash** un affare per contanti; ~ **lot** (*market.*) merce d'occasione; **bargains market** (*Borsa*) lista giornaliera degli affari conclusi alla Borsa Valori di Londra, pubblicata dal «Times»; ~ **price** prezzo di liquidazione, prezzo d'occasione; **a** ~ **sale** una vendita delle rimanenze, una vendita speciale; **into the** ~ per giunta, per sovrammercato.

bargain[2], *v. i.* contrattare, mercanteggiare, tirare sul prezzo.

bargaining, *n.* **1** contrattazione, mercanteggiamento. **2** (*sind.*) trattativa sindacale. // ~ **agent** (*sind.*) rappresentante sindacale; ~ **leverage** (*sind.*) potere contrattuale; ~ **power** (*sind.*) potere contrattuale; ~ **procedure** (*sind.*) procedura delle trattative.

barge, *n.* (*trasp. mar.*) chiatta, barcone. // ~ **hire** (*trasp. mar.*) noleggio di chiatte.

bargee, *n.* (*trasp. mar.*) chiattaiolo.

bargeman, *n.* (*pl.* **bargemen**) (*trasp. mar.*) chiattaiolo.

bark, *n.* (*slang USA*) denaro.

barley, *n.* orzo.

barometer, *n.* barometro. // ~ **stock** (*Borsa, fin.*) «titolo-barometro» (*titolo il cui prezzo di mercato indica l'andamento generale del mercato*).

baron, *n.* magnate.

barratry, *n.* **1** (*leg.*) baratteria (*atto o comportamento doloso di chi ha la responsabilità di un trasporto marittimo*). **2** (*leg.*) dolo. **3** (*leg.*) litigiosità. // ~ **risk** (*ass. mar.*) rischio di baratteria.

barred credit, *n.* (*cred.*) credito prescritto.

barrel, *n.* 1 barile. 2 «barrel» (*misura inglese di capacità per liquidi, pari a litri 163,45*). 3 canna (*d'arma da fuoco*). // ~ **bulk** (*trasp. mar.*) misura di capacità per noli, pari a 5 piedi cubici o 1/8 di tonnellata.

barren, *a.* sterile.

barrier, *n.* barriera.

barring, *avv.* a meno di, salvo. // ~ **by limitation** (*leg.*) prescrizione (*V. anche* **statute**).

barrister, *n.* (*leg.*) avvocato patrocinante. // ~ **-at-law** (*leg.*) avvocato patrocinante.

barter[1], *n.* baratto, scambio, permuta.

barter[2], *v. t.* barattare, scambiare, cedere (*qc.*) in cambio. // to ~ **wheat for machinery** cedere grano in cambio di macchinari.

bascule, *n.* bilico. // ~ **barrier** (*trasp. ferr.*) sbarra a bilico (*di passaggio a livello*).

base, *n.* 1 (*anche mat.*) base. 2 (*Borsa*) punto d'arresto (*nella diminuzione di valore d'un titolo*). *a.* basso, vile. // **a** ~ **coin** una moneta vile; **the** ~ **metals** i metalli vili; ~ **pay** (*pers.*) «paga-base» (*stipendio o salario non comprensivo di straordinari, gratifiche o premi*); ~ **period** (*econ.*) periodo base; ~ **price** (*market.*) prezzo base; ~ **rate** (*pers.*) paga base; ~ **salary** (*pers.*) stipendio base.

base oneself, *v. rifl.* (*detto di persona*) basarsi, fondarsi.

basic, *a.* basilare, di base. // ~ **abatement** (*fin.*) abbattimento alla base (*d'un reddito imponibile*); ~ **capital goods** (*econ.*) beni strumentali essenziali; ~ **crop** (*econ.*) raccolto fondamentale; ~ **duty** dazio di base; ~ **income** (*econ., sind.*) reddito minimo; ~ **industry** industria di base; ~ **intervention price** (*econ.*) prezzo d'intervento di base; ~ **materials** prodotti di base; ~ **quota** quota di base; ~ **rate** (*pers.*) salario base; ~ **research** ricerca di base.

basin, *n.* (*trasp. mar.*) bacino.

basis, *n.* (*pl.* **bases**) base, fondamento. // **the** ~ **of assessment** (*fin.*) la base dell'accertamento (*dell'imponibile*); **the** ~ **of a contract** (*leg.*) la base d'un contratto; ~ **price** (*market.*) prezzo base; ~ **rate** (*market.*) tariffa base.

basket, *n.* 1 (*anche econ.*) paniere. 2 (*fin.*) paniere (*monetario*). // **the** ~ **of goods from which price increases are calculated for indexation purposes** il paniere del carovita.

batch, *n.* 1 complesso (*di cose*). 2 lotto, partita (*di merce*). 3 gruppo (*fig.*). // ~ **production** (*econ.*) produzione in lotti.

battery, *n.* 1 batteria. 2 (*leg.*) percosse. // ~ **-chicken** pollo d'allevamento.

be, *v. i.* (*pass.* **was,** *part. pass.* **been**) 1 essere, esistere. 2 stare. 3 toccare. 4 costare. // to ~ **behind schedule** essere in ritardo (*con le consegne, ecc.*); to ~ **a certain percent off** (*market.*) essere in regresso d'un tanto per cento; to ~ **ill** star male (*di salute*); to ~ **in** essere «in», essere di moda; to ~ **in business** essere in affari; to ~ **in conference** essere in riunione; to ~ **in the employee roll** (*pers.*) essere di ruolo; to ~ **in funds** essere provvisto di denaro; to ~ **in the red** (*banca, cred.*) essere «in rosso» (*fig.*), essere in passivo, essere in deficit; to ~ **late** essere in ritardo; to ~ **off** partire; to ~ **on the market** (*market.*) essere in commercio (*d'un articolo*); to ~ **on the regular staff** (*pers.*) essere di ruolo; to ~ **on the road to completion** essere in via di realizzazione; to ~ **on sale** (*market.*) essere in commercio (*d'un articolo*); to ~ **out** essere fuori; essere fuori moda; to ~ **out of work** (*sind.*) essere disoccupato; to ~ **to** dovere, potere; to ~ **well** stare bene (*di salute*); to ~ **well off** stare bene (*a quattrini*); **for the time being** per il momento; **a would-be banker** uno che pretende d'essere un banchiere.

beach, *v. t.* (*trasp. mar.*) arenare, far arenare. *v. i.* (*trasp. mar.*) arenarsi.

beaching, *n.* (*trasp. mar.*) arenamento.

beacon, *n.* 1 (*trasp. mar.*) faro. 2 (*trasp. mar.*) boa luminosa, gavitello luminoso.

beaconage, *n.* (*trasp. mar.*) diritto di faro.

beak, *n.* (*slang USA*) avvocato.

bear[1], *n.* 1 (*Borsa*) ribassista, giocatore al ribasso, speculatore al ribasso. 2 **bears,** *pl.* (*Borsa*) scoperto. *a. attr.* (*Borsa*) ribassista. // ~ **account** (*Borsa*) scoperto, posizione di ribasso; ~ **campaign** (*Borsa*) campagna al ribasso, campagna ribassista; ~ **position** (*Borsa*) posizione di ribasso; ~ **raid** (*Borsa*) corsa al ribasso, attacco dei ribassisti, manovra al ribasso; ~ **run** (*Borsa*) (tendenza al) ribasso; ~ **sale** (*Borsa*) vendita allo scoperto; ~ **seller** (*Borsa*) venditore allo scoperto; ~ **squeeze** (*Borsa*) stretta ribassista; ~ **stampede** (*Borsa*) corsa alle vendite; ~ **transaction** (*Borsa*) operazione allo scoperto, operazione al ribasso.

bear[2], *v. t.* (*pass.* **bore,** *part. pass.* **born** e **borne**) 1 portare, reggere, sostenere. 2 serbare, tenere. 3 dare, produrre. // to ~ **enquiry** uscire indenne da un'indagine; to ~ **false witness** (*leg.*) deporre il falso; to ~ **heavily on st.** incidere su qc.; to ~ **a loss** sopportare una perdita; to ~ **out** confermare; to ~ **witness** (*leg.*) testimoniare, deporre; to **be borne by** essere sostenuto da.

bear[3], *v. i.* (*Borsa*) giocare, speculare al ribasso. // to ~ **the market** (*Borsa*) vendere allo scoperto.

bearer, *n.* portatore; latore (*d'una lettera, d'una missiva, e sim.*). // ~ **bond** (*fin.*) obbligazione al portatore, titolo al portatore; ~ **certificate** (*fin.*) titolo al portatore; ~ **check** (*banca, USA*) assegno al portatore; ~ **cheque** (*banca*) assegno al portatore; ~ **debenture** (*fin.*) obbligazione al portatore; **the** ~ **of a draft** (*cred.*) il presentatore d'una tratta; **the** ~ **of a letter** il latore di una lettera; ~ **scrip** (*fin.*) titolo al portatore; ~ **security** (*fin.*) titolo al portatore; ~ **shares** (*fin.*) azioni al portatore; ~ **stock** (*fin.*) titolo al portatore; ~ **warrant** (*fin.*) titolo al portatore.

bearing, *n.* **1** portata, influenza. **2** rapporto, relazione. **3** aspetto. **4** (*trasp. mar.*) rilevamento. *a. attr.* producente, produttivo.

bearish, *a.* (*Borsa*) di (*o* da) ribassista; orientato al ribasso, tendente al ribasso. // ~ **tendency** (*Borsa*) tendenza al ribasso; ~ **transaction** (*Borsa*) operazione al ribasso.

bearishness, *n.* (*Borsa*) (tendenza al) ribasso.

beat[1], *n.* battuta.

beat[2], *v. t.* (*pass.* **beat,** *part. pass.* **beat** e **beaten**) battere, sconfiggere, vincere. // to ~ **the competition** vincere la concorrenza; to ~ **down** schiacciare, abbattere; to ~ **down a price** ottenere il ribasso d'un prezzo; to ~ **down a seller** ridurre un venditore a più miti pretese; to ~ **a record** battere un primato.

beating, *n.* battuta.

become, *v. i.* (*pass.* **became,** *part. pass.* **become**) diventare, divenire, farsi. *v. t.* addirsi a, convenire a. // to ~ **applicable** (*leg.*) entrare in applicazione; to ~ **bankrupt** (*leg.*) fallire, far fallimento; to ~ **due** (*cred.*) scadere; to ~ **familiar with sb.** familiarizzarsi con q.; to ~ **final** (*leg.*) passare in giudicato; to ~ **res judicata** (*leg.*) passare in giudicato; to ~ **sanded up** insabbiarsi; to ~ **vacant** (*pers.: d'un posto, d'un impiego*) liberarsi.

bed, *n.* letto.

beeswax, *n.* (*slang USA*) affari.

beewy, *n.* (*slang USA*) denaro.

before, *avv.* e *prep.* davanti (a). // ~ **hours** (*Borsa, fin.*) avamborsa.

beforehand, *avv.* anticipatamente, in anticipo. // ~ **retirement** (*pers.*) pensionamento anticipato.

beg, *v. t.* chiedere, domandare.

begin, *v. i.* (*pass.* **began,** *part. pass.* **begun**) cominciare, incominciare, iniziare.

beginning, *n.* inizio, principio. // ~ **balance** (*rag.*) saldo d'apertura, saldo iniziale; ~ **inventory** (*rag.*) rimanenze iniziali; **the** ~ **of the new fiscal year** l'inizio del nuovo esercizio sociale.

behalf (*soltanto nelle locuz.* **on, in behalf of**) **1** a nome di, per conto di. **2** a favore di, nell'interesse di. // **on** ~ **of a third party** (*leg.*) per conto terzi.

behaviour, *n.* (*market.*) comportamento.

behind, *avv.* e *prep.* **1** dietro. **2** in arretrato. // to **be** ~ **time** essere in ritardo.

behindhand, *avv.* **1** in ritardo. **2** in arretrato.

belga, *n.* (*fin.*) belga (*unità monetaria belga nelle operazioni di cambio*).

believable, *a.* credibile.

believableness, *n.* credibilità.

believe, *v. i.* credere.

bell-ringer, *n.* (*slang USA*) rappresentante, commesso viaggiatore, piazzista.

belong, *v. i.* appartenere.

belongings, *n. pl.* oggetti, cose (*di proprietà personale*); beni. // **personal** ~ effetti personali.

below, *avv.* e *prep.* **1** sotto, sotto a. **2** al disotto di, meno di. **3** in calce, a piè di pagina. **4** oltre. // ~ **the average** al disotto della media; ~ **cost** (*market.*) sotto costo; ~ **-the-line** (*econ.*) (*di capitolo d'entrata o spesa di bilancio*) straordinario; ~ **-the-line payments and receipts** (*fin.*) entrate e spese straordinarie (*voci del bilancio del Governo britannico*); ~ **par** (*fin.*) sotto la pari; ~ **price** (*market.*) sottoprezzo; to **be** ~ **the mark** essere di qualità scadente.

belt, *n.* cintura.

bench, *n.* **1** banco. **2 the Bench** (*leg.*) la magistratura.

bencher, *n.* (*leg.*) membro anziano d'uno dei quattro «Inns of Court».

bend, *n.* curva.

benefice, *n.* (*leg.*) beneficio (*ecclesiastico*).

beneficial, *a.* che dà beneficio, benefico, vantaggioso. // ~ **interest** (*leg.*) diritti d'un beneficiario; ~ **owner** (*leg.*) beneficiario.

beneficiary, *n.* beneficiario. // **the** ~ **of an insurance policy** (*ass.*) il beneficiario d'una polizza d'assicurazione.

benefit[1], *n.* **1** vantaggio, utile. **2** (*leg.*) beneficio. **3** (*pers., sind.*) indennità, sussidio. // ~ **club** società di beneficienza; ~ **fund** (*org. az.*) fondo utili; «~ **of a fall» clause** (*leg.*) clausola di parità.

benefit[2], *v. i.* beneficiare, trarre profitto (*da qc.*).

benign, *a.* benigno, benevolo; favorevole. // ~ **neglect** (*econ.*) benevolo disinteresse.

bequeath, *v. t.* (*leg.*) legare per testamento, lasciare in eredità.

bequeather, *n.* (*leg.*) testatore di beni immobili.

bequest, *n.* (*leg.*) legato, lascito testamentario.

berry, *n.* (*slang USA*) dollaro.

berth[1], *n.* **1** (*fig.*) impiego, posto. **2** (*trasp. mar.*) luogo d'approdo o d'ancoraggio (*di una nave*); attracco, posto di ormeggio. **3** (*trasp. mar.*) cabina. **4** (*trasp. mar.*) cuccetta. // ~ **freighting** (*trasp. mar.*) nolo a cuccetta; ~ **terms** (*trasp. mar.*) clausola (*su una polizza di carico*) secondo la quale il consegnatario s'impegna a ritirare quel quantitativo di merce che il capitano è in grado di consegnargli giornalmente; **two-berths compartment** (*trasp. ferr.*) scompartimento a due letti.

berth[2], *v. t.* (*trasp. mar.*) ancorare, attraccare. *v. i.* (*trasp. mar.*) ancorarsi, attraccare.

berthage, *n.* (*trasp. mar.*) diritto d'ancoraggio, diritto d'ammaraggio.

berthing, *n.* (*trasp. mar.*) attracco.

bespeak, *v. t.* (*pass.* **bespoke,** *part. pass.* **bespoken**) ordinare (*merci*); prenotare.

bespoke, *a.* ordinato in anticipo, su misura. // ~ **boots** (*market., USA*) scarpe fatte su misura.

best, *a.* (il) migliore. *pron.* (la) cosa migliore. // ~ **profit equilibrium** (*econ.*) punto d'incontro dei costi e dei ricavi marginali; ~ **quantity** (*org. az.*) quantità ottimale; to **sell at** ~ (*fin.*) vendere al meglio.

bestow, *v. t.* **1** conferire. **2** (*leg.*) estendere (*un provvedimento e sim.*).

bet, *v. t.* e *i.* (*pass.* e *part. pass.* **bet**) scommettere.

beta, *n.* beta. // ~ **plus** (*market.*) (*di un articolo*) di qualità intermedia fra la seconda e la prima.

better[1], *a.* migliore. // ~ **-quality** di qualità migliore; ~ **-quality oils** le qualità migliori d'olio.

better[2], *v. t.* e *i.* migliorare, far migliorare; diventare migliore.

bettering, *n. V.* **betterment.**

betterment, *n.* miglioramento, miglioria.

beyond, *prep.* di là di. *avv.* in eccesso. // ~ **the sea** oltremare.

bid[1], *n.* **1** proposta. **2** offerta (*a una vendita all'asta*); licitazione. **3** offerta d'appalto. **4** (*Borsa, fin.*) quotazione d'acquisto. **5** (*leg.*) somma offerta (*specialm. a un'asta*). **6** (*leg.*) offerta d'iscrizione a una società. // ~ **-and-ask spread** (*Borsa, fin.*) margine del «remisier»; ~ **bond** cauzione per concorrere a una licitazione (*o* a una gara d'appalto); ~ **price and offer price** (*fin.*) denaro e lettera.

bid[2], *v. t.* (*pass.* e *part. pass.* **bid**) **1** offrire, fare un'offerta. **2** (*USA*) licitare, fare un'offerta d'appalto. // to ~ **at an auction-sale** fare offerte a una vendita all'asta; ~ **-for company** (*fin.*) società da rilevare; to ~ **in** fare salire il prezzo (*a un'asta*); to ~ **up** fare un'offerta superiore (*a un'asta*).

bidder, *n.* **1** offerente (*a un'asta*); partecipante a un'asta; astante. **2** concorrente, offerente (*a una gara di appalto*). // **to the highest** ~ al miglior offerente.

bidding, *n.* offerta (*a un'asta*). *a.* offerente. // ~ **company** (*fin.*) società offerente.

big, *a.* grande, grosso, importante. // **the** ~ **board** (*Borsa, slang USA*) la Borsa di New York; ~ **business** (*fin.*) grossi affari; **a** ~ **fall** (*market.*) una forte diminuzione (*di prezzi*); ~ **one** (*slang USA*) biglietto da mille dollari; **a** ~ **rise** (*market.*) un forte aumento (*di prezzi*); **the** ~ **slump** (*econ.*) il grande crollo; ~ **supermarket** (*econ., market.*) ipermercato (*più grande e meglio attrezzato d'un supermercato*); ~ **thing** (*market.*) articolo che va moltissimo, oggetto di gran moda; **the Big Three** (*fin., USA*) le tre grandi società produttrici di automobili negli Stati Uniti (*General Motors, Ford, Chrysler*).

bigness, *n.* grandezza.

bilateral, *a.* bilaterale. // ~ **agreement** accordo bilaterale; ~ **contract** (*leg.*) contratto bilaterale, contratto sinallagmatico; ~ **monopoly** (*econ.*) monopolio bilaterale; ~ **swapping** (*fin.*) «swap» bilaterale; ~ **trade policies** (*comm. est.*) politiche commerciali bilaterali.

bill[1], *n.* **1** effetto, cambiale, tratta. **2** fattura, conto, specifica. **3** (*dog.*) bolla, bolletta. **4** (*leg.*) disegno di legge, progetto di legge. **5** (*pubbl.*) cartellone pubblicitario, manifesto (*murale*). **6** (*USA*) banconota. **7** (*slang USA*) biglietto da cento dollari. **8 bills,** *pl.* denaro in banconote. // **bills and notes** (*cred.*) strumenti negoziabili; ~ **at sight** (*cred.*) cambiale a vista; ~ **board** (*pubbl.*) cartellone pubblicitario; ~ **book** (*rag.*) registro delle fatture, scadenzario; ~ **-broker** (*fin.*) agente di sconto; ~ **case** (*banca, rag.*) portafoglio-effetti; ~ **clerk** (*pers.*) impiegato addetto alla fatturazione; ~ **collection** (*rag.*) incasso di fatture; ~ **collector** (*pers.*) esattore; **bills department** (*banca*) portafoglio; ufficio portafoglio; servizio portafoglio-effetti; ~ **diary** (*rag.*) scadenzario delle fatture; ~ **file** (*org. az.*) archivio delle fatture; ~ **-filing clerk** (*pers.*) impiegato addetto alla fatturazione; ~ **for collection** (*banca*) effetto all'incasso; **bills for collection account** (*rag.*) conto effetti da esigere; ~ **form** modulo per cambiale; ~ **head** (*rag.*) intestazione di fattura; ~ **heading** (*rag.*) intestazione di fattura; **bills in hand** (*banca, fin.*) portafoglio; ~ **in a set** (*rag.*) fattura in una serie d'esemplari; **bills in a set** (*cred.*) cambiali in copia; ~ **noted for non-acceptance** (*cred.*) tratta con annotazione per mancata accettazione; ~ **of costs** parcella d'avvocato; (*leg.*) nota di spese giudiziarie; ~ **of debt** (*leg.*) riconoscimento di un debito; ~ **of entry** (*dog.*) bolletta d'entrata doganale; ~ **of exchange** (*cred.*) cambiale, tratta, effetto; **bills of exchange** (*banca*) portafoglio, portafoglio-effetti; ~ **of health** (*trasp. mar.*) patente (*o* certificato) di sanità; certificato sanitario; ~ **of lading** (*trasp. mar.*) polizza di carico; ~ **of lading accompanied by draft and insurance policy** (*trasp. mar.*) polizza di carico più tratta e polizza d'assicurazione; ~ **of lading attached to the following documents...** (*trasp. mar.*) polizza di carico annessa ai seguenti documenti...; ~ **of lading clause** (*trasp. mar.*) clausola della polizza di carico; ~ **of lading form** (*trasp. mar.*) modulo di polizza di carico; ~ **of lading to bearer** (*trasp. mar.*) polizza di carico al portatore; ~ **of lading to hand, but not in order** (*trasp. mar.*) (ci è) pervenuta la polizza di carico, ma non è regolare; ~ **of lading to order** (*trasp. mar.*) polizza di carico all'ordine; ~ **of sight** (*dog.*) certificato d'ispezione, richiesta di visita preventiva; ~ **of store** (*comm. est.*) certificato d'esportazione temporanea; ~ **of sufferance** (*dog.*) lettera di esenzione doganale; ~ **on demand** (*cred.*) cambiale a vista; **bills payable** (*rag.*) effetti passivi; **bills payable account** (*banca, rag.*) conto effetti passivi; **bills payable book** (*rag.*) registro degli effetti passivi; **bills payable journal** (*rag.*) giornale degli effetti passivi; **a ~ payable thirty days after sight** una cambiale pagabile a trenta giorni vista; ~ **payable to bearer** (*cred.*) cambiale pagabile al portatore; ~ **-posting** (*pubbl.*) affissione di manifesti; **bills receivable** (*rag.*) cambiali attive, effetti attivi; **bills receivable account** (*rag.*) conto effetti attivi; **bills receivable book** (*rag.*) registro degli effetti attivi; **bills receivable journal** (*rag.*) giornale degli effetti attivi; **bills received register** (*banca*) registro d'entrata degli effetti; ~ **stamp** bollo cambiario; ~ **to drawer** (*cred.*) cambiale a favore del traente; **bills unpaid** (*banca*) effetti non pagati.

bill², *v. t.* **1** fatturare. **2** (*USA*) inviare fatture a (*q.*).

billed, *a.* (*rag.*) fatturato.

biller, *n.* (*pers.*) impiegato addetto alla fatturazione.

billhead, *n.* (*rag., USA*) modulo di fattura.

billing, *n.* **1** (*rag.*) fatturazione. **2** (*rag.*) fatturato. // ~ **clerk** (*pers.*) impiegato addetto alla fatturazione; ~ **department** (*org. az.*) reparto fatturazione; ~ **machine** (*macch. uff.*) macchina per fatturazione, fatturatrice.

billion, *n.* **1** (*ingl.*) seconda potenza d'un milione (*un 1 seguito da 12 zeri; corrisponde dunque a un nostro trilione*). **2** (*USA*) bilione, miliardo.

billionaire, *n.* (*USA*) miliardario.

bimetalism, *n. V.* **bimetallism.**

bimetalist, *n. V.* **bimetallist.**

bimetalistic, *a. V.* **bimetallistic.**

bimetallic, *a.* (*econ., fin.*) bimetallico.

bimetallism, *n.* (*econ., fin.*) bimetallismo.

bimetallist, *n.* (*econ., fin.*) bimetallista.

bimetallistic, *a.* (*econ., fin.*) bimetallista.

bimonthly, *n.* (*giorn.*) pubblicazione bimestrale. *avv.* ogni due mesi.

bin card, *n.* (*org. az.*) scheda posizione.

bind, *v. t.* (*pass.* e *part. pass.* **bound**) **1** legare. **2** obbligare, impegnare, vincolare. **3** essere obbligatorio, vincolante per (*q.*). **4** consolidare. **5** rilegare. // to ~ **a contract** (*leg.*) ratificare un contratto; to ~ **out** (*pers.*) vincolare con contratto di apprendistato; to ~ **over** (*leg.*) obbligare legalmente; to ~ **a person by oath** (*leg.*) vincolare una persona con giuramento.

binder, *n.* **1** caparra. **2** (*ass.*) polizza provvisoria.

binding, *a.* obbligatorio, impegnativo, vincolante, obbligante. // ~ **offer** offerta vincolante.

bind oneself, *v. rifl.* impegnarsi, obbligarsi, vincolarsi. // to ~ **jointly and severally** (*fin.*) obbligarsi in solido.

binomial, *a.* binomiale. *n.* binomio. // ~ **distribution** distribuzione binomiale.

bipartite, *a.* bipartito. // ~ **board** (*org. az., sind.*) comitato paritetico.

birth, *n.* nascita. // ~ **certificate** atto (*o* certificato) di nascita; estratto d'atto di nascita; fede di nascita; ~ **control** (*econ.*) controllo delle nascite; ~ **rate** (*econ.*) indice di natalità.

birthplace, *n.* luogo di nascita.

bi-weekly, *a.* (*giorn.*) quindicinale. *n.* (*giorn.*) pubblicazione quindicinale.

bi-yearly, *a.* (*giorn.*) semestrale. *avv.* (*giorn.*) semestralmente.

biz, *n.* (*slang USA*) affari. // ~ **man** (*slang USA*) commerciante.

black, *a.* **1** nero. **2** tetro, truce, orribile. *n.* negro. // ~ **-coat worker** (*pers.*) impiegato; ~ **interest** (*rag.*) interessi neri, interessi passivi; ~ **list** lista nera; (*cred., fin.*) lista delle persone o ditte insolvibili o comunque non raccomandabili per rapporti commerciali, lista dei fallimenti, bollettino dei protesti; (*trasp. mar.*) lista dei disastri marittimi; ~ **market** mercato nero, borsa nera; ~ **money** (*fin.*) denaro «sporco»; ~ **products** (*rag.*) numeri neri; to **be in the** ~ (*banca*) essere in credito; avere un saldo attivo; (*slang USA*) avere successo negli affari.

blackleg, *n.* (*sind.*) crumiro.

blame[1]**,** *n.* colpa, responsabilità.

blame[2]**,** *v. t.* dare la colpa a, incolpare.

blank, *a.* bianco, in bianco, vuoto. *n.* **1** spazio in bianco, lacuna. **2** modulo. // ~ **acceptance** (*banca, cred.*) accettazione in bianco; ~ **bill** (*banca, cred.*) cambiale in bianco; ~ **cheque** (*banca, cred.*) assegno in bianco; ~ **credit** (*banca, cred.*) credito in bianco, credito libero, credito allo scoperto; ~ **deal** (*banca, cred.*) operazione in bianco; ~ **endorsement** (*banca, cred.*) girata in bianco; ~ **form** modulo in bianco; ~ **paper** carta bianca; ~ **signature** firma in bianco; ~ **space** spazio in bianco; ~ **transaction** operazione in bianco; ~ **transfer** (*leg.*) trasferimento a titolo di garanzia; **in** ~ in bianco.

blanket[1]**,** *n.* coperta. // ~ **insurance policy** (*ass.*) polizza (d'assicurazione) generale; ~ **mortgage** (*leg.*) ipoteca generale.

blanket[2]**,** *v. t.* (*fin.*) livellare, applicare in modo uniforme (*tasse, regolamenti, ecc.*).

bleed, *v. i.* (*pass.* e *part. pass.* **bled**) (*anche fig.*) sanguinare.

blend[1]**,** *n.* miscela.

blend[2]**,** *v. t.* miscelare, mescolare, fondere.

blending, *n.* **1** mescolatura. **2** miscela.

blind test, *n.* (*market.*) prova di preferenza del consumatore su due prodotti diversi ma presentati in confezioni identiche.

bloc, *n.* (*francese*) (*econ., fin.*) blocco (*politico, economico, finanziario*). // **en** ~ in blocco.

block[1]**,** *n.* **1** blocco, lotto, pacco. **2** (*giorn.*) zoccolo (*del cliché*). **3** (*giorn.*) zincotipia. **4** (*trasp.*) ingorgo (*del traffico*). // ~ **exemption** (*fin.*) esenzione per categorie; ~ **of shares** (*Borsa*) partita di titoli; ~ **of stock** (*Borsa*) pacchetto d'azioni; ~ **offer** offerta in blocco; **in** ~ **form** (*di una lettera commerciale*) a paragrafi spaziati, ma senza rientri a capolinea; to **be on the** ~ essere messo all'asta; essere in vendita.

block[2]**,** *v. t.* **1** bloccare. **2** ostacolare. // to ~ **an account** (*banca, cred.*) bloccare un conto; to ~ **the traffic** (*trasp. aut.*) bloccare il traffico.

blockade, *n.* blocco, assedio.

blocked account, *n.* (*banca*) conto bloccato.

blocked sterling, *n.* (*fin.*) unità monetaria con cui gli stranieri possono acquistare titoli in Gran Bretagna.

bloomer, *n.* (*slang USA*) affare andato male.

blotter, *n.* **1** (*rag.*) prima nota. **2** (*rag.*) brogliaccio.

blotting case, *n.* (*attr. uff.*) tampone di carta assorbente.

blotting dabber, *n.* (*attr. uff.*) tampone di carta assorbente.

blotting pad, *n.* (*attr. uff.*) tampone di carta assorbente.

blotting paper, *n.* (*attr. uff.*) carta assorbente.

blue, *a.* **1** blu, azzurro. **2** triste, severo. // ~ **book** (*fin.*) pubblicazione ufficiale del governo britannico (*in genere, rapporto di una commissione d'inchiesta*); ~ **chips** (*fin.*) azioni sicure e di tutta tranquillità, titoli a largo flottante, valori d'élite; ~ **collar** (*sind.*) operaio, uomo di fatica; ~ **-collar worker** (*pers.*) operaio; ~ **-collar workers** ceto operaio; ~ **cross** (*pers., USA*) mutua (*per l'assistenza medica*); ~ **law** (*leg.*) legge severa; ~ **pencil** (*attr. uff.*) matita blu; ~ **riband** (*attr. uff.*) nastro azzurro; ~ **ribbon** (*attr. uff.*) nastro azzurro; ~ **train** (*trasp. ferr.*) treno azzurro.

board[1]**,** *n.* **1** bordo (*di nave*). **2** cartellone pubblicitario. **3** (*amm., org. az.*) ufficio. **4** (*amm., org. az.*) comitato. **5** (*amm., org. az.*) ministero. **6** (*amm., org. az.*) ente. **7** (*tur.*) vitto. // ~ **-chairman** (*org. az.*) presidente del consiglio d'amministrazione; ~ **foot** unità di misura per cataste di legna (*equivale a 144 pollici cubici*); ~ **minutes** (*org. az.*) verbale d'adunanza; ~ **of arbitrators** (*sind.*) collegio arbitrale; ~ **of Customs and Excise** Ministero dei Dazi e delle Dogane; ~ **of directors** (*org. az.*) consiglio d'amministrazione; ~ **of Inland Revenue** Ministero dei Tributi Diretti e Indiretti; ~ **of inquiry** (*amm., leg.*) comitato d'inchiesta; ~ **of management** (*org. az.*) direzione (*di una fabbrica*); ~ **of trade** (*USA*) camera di commercio, associazione d'uomini d'affari; ~ **of Trade** (*G.B.*) divisione del «Department of Trade» (*che si occupa specialm. del commercio estero*); ~ **wages** (*pers.*) supplemento di salario per spese di vitto non corrisposto; **free on** ~ franco a bordo; **on** ~ (*trasp. aer., trasp. mar.*) a bordo, a bordo di; **on** ~ **bill of lading** (*trasp. mar.*) polizza di carico controfirmata dal capitano della nave o dal suo incaricato e attestante che le merci sono state effettivamente caricate a bordo.

board[2], *v. t.* 1 (*trasp. mar.*) abbordare. 2 (*trasp. mar.*) salire a bordo di (*una nave*). *v. i.* (*trasp. mar.*) bordeggiare. // to ~ **a ship** imbarcarsi.

boarding-house, *n.* (*tur.*) pensione.

boarding school, *n.* collegio.

boat, *n.* 1 (*trasp. mar.*) barca, imbarcazione, battello. 2 (*trasp. mar.*) nave, naviglio. // ~ **train** (*trasp. ferr., ingl.*) treno in coincidenza con un battello (*che attraversa la Manica*).

bob, *n.* (*pl. inv.*) 1 (*slang*) scellino. 2 (*slang USA*) dollaro. 3 (*slang USA*) denaro.

body, *n.* 1 corpo. 2 (*amm., org. az.*) ente. 3 (*giorn.*) corpo (*dei caratteri di stampa*). 4 (*trasp.*) carrozzeria (*d'autoveicolo*). 5 (*trasp. mar.*) scafo (*di nave*). // ~ **builder** (*trasp. aut.*) carrozziere, carrozzaio; ~ **corporate** (*leg.*) persona giuridica, ente morale; ~ **of creditors** (*leg.*) massa dei creditori; ~ **of laws** (*leg.*) corpo di leggi, raccolta di leggi; ~ **responsible for unemployment benefits** (*sind.*) Cassa Integrazione Guadagni.

boffo, *n.* (*slang USA*) dollaro.

bogie, *n.* (*trasp. ferr.*) carrello ferroviario.

bogus, *a.* falso, finto, contraffatto.

boiler, *n.* 1 bollitore. 2 caldaia.

bolt, *n.* misura lineare usata talvolta per i tessili (*corrispondente a 40 iarde*).

bona fide, *locuz. avv.* (*leg.*) in buona fede. *a. attr.* 1 (*leg.*) che è in buona fede. 2 (*leg.*) fatto in buona fede. // ~ **holder** (*leg.*) detentore in buona fede, terzo di buona fede; ~ **purchaser** (*leg.*) acquirente in buona fede; to **act** ~ (*leg.*) agire in buona fede.

bond[1], *n.* 1 (*anche fig.*) legame, obbligo, vincolo. 2 (*dog.*) cauzione, garanzia, dichiarazione di cauzione. 3 (*fin.*) titolo del debito pubblico, buono del Tesoro. 4 (*fin., USA*) obbligazione. 5 (*leg.*) cauzione, garanzia. // ~ **issue** (*fin., USA*) emissione obbligazionaria, aumento gratuito di capitale; ~ **note** (*dog.*) bolletta di cauzione; ~ **paper** carta uso bollo; ~ **to bearer** (*fin.*) obbligazione al portatore; ~ **yield** (*fin., USA*) reddito obbligazionario; **in** ~ (*dog.*) in magazzino doganale, soggetto a vincolo doganale, da sdoganare.

bond[2], *v. t.* 1 (*leg.*) assumere un impegno scritto per (*q.*). 2 (*leg.*) ipotecare. 3 (*leg.*) cauzionare. 4 (*trasp.*) porre (*merci*) in magazzino doganale.

bonded, *a.* 1 (*fin.*) (*di debito*) garantito da obbligazioni. 2 (*leg.*) vincolato. // ~ **goods** (*dog.*) merce in deposito nei magazzini doganali; ~ **shed** (*dog.*) capannone doganale; ~ **store** (*dog.*) magazzino doganale; ~ **warehouse** (*dog.*) magazzino doganale (*in regime di punto franco*), deposito doganale.

bonder, *n.* depositante (*di merci: nei magazzini doganali*).

bondholder, *n.* 1 (*fin.*) possessore di buoni del Tesoro. 2 (*fin., USA*) obbligazionista.

bonding, *n.* (*dog.*) deposito (*di merci: nei magazzini doganali*).

bone, *n.* (*slang USA*) dollaro.

bonnet, *n.* (*trasp. aut.*) cofano.

bonus, *n.* 1 (*fin.*) dividendo extra (*agli azionisti*). 2 (*pers., sind.*) pagamento straordinario, gratifica, premio. 3 (*pers., sind.*) indennità. // ~ **issue** (*fin.*) emissione riservata gratuita (*d'azioni*); ~ **shares** (*fin.*) azioni gratuite; ~ **systems** (*org. az., pers.*) sistemi di gratifiche in aggiunta al salario (*per rendimento, ecc.*); **Christmas** ~ (*org. az., pers.*) gratifica natalizia.

book[1], *n.* 1 libro. 2 blocchetto (*di biglietti, buoni, ecc.*). 3 (*banca, ecc.*) libretto. 4 (*Borsa*) posizione. 5 (*rag.*) registro. 6 **books,** *pl.* (*rag.*) libri contabili. // ~ **credit** (*rag.*) partita a credito; ~ **debit** (*rag.*) partita a debito; ~ **debt** (*leg., rag.*) credito chirografario, debito attivo; ~ **entry** (*rag.*) scrittura contabile; ~ **fair** (*market.*) fiera del libro; **books of account** (*rag.*) libri contabili; ~ **of accounts** (*rag.*) registro contabile; ~ **of entries** (*rag.*) libro giornale; ~ **of original entry** (*rag.*) libro giornale; ~ **profits** (*rag.*) utili contabili; ~ **ticket** (*trasp.*) libretto di biglietti; ~ **token** (*market.*) buono per acquisto di libri; ~ **trade** editoria; ~ **value** (*rag.*) valore contabile; (*fin., rag.*) valore di bilancio, valore d'inventario, valore di carico; **on the books** (*rag.*) registrato.

book[2], *v. t.* 1 registrare. 2 annotare, elencare (*per iscritto*). 3 (*rag.*) mettere a libro, registrare (*una partita*). 4 (*tur.*) prenotare, fissare. // to ~ **a room in a hotel** prenotare una stanza all'albergo; to ~ **a telephone call** prenotare una telefonata; to ~ **a transaction** (*rag.*) registrare un'operazione.

bookcase, *n.* (*attr. uff.*) armadietto per libri, libreria.

booketeria, *n.* (*market.*) libreria self-service.

bookie, *n.* (*slang*) allibratore.

booking, *n.* 1 (*rag.*) registrazione. 2 (*tur.*) prenotazione. // ~ **clerk** (*pers., trasp.*) impiegato alla biglietteria, bigliettaio; ~ **fee** (*leg.*) tassa di registrazione; ~ **office** (*trasp.*) ufficio prenotazioni; biglietteria.

bookkeeper, *n.* (*pers.*) contabile, computista.

bookkeeping, *n.* (*rag.*) contabilità, computisteria, tenuta dei libri. // ~ **difficulties** (*rag.*)

difficoltà contabili; ~ **error** (*rag.*) errore contabile; ~ **machine** (*macch. uff.*) macchina contabile; ~ **voucher** (*rag.*) pezza giustificativa contabile.

booklet, *n.* (*pubbl.*) libretto, opuscolo.

bookmaker, *n.* allibratore.

bookmaking, *n.* attività d'allibratore.

bookseller, *n.* libraio. // ~ **'s order form** cedola di commissione libraria.

bookshop, *n.* (*market.*) libreria.

boom[1], *n.* **1** (*econ.*) boom; congiuntura assai favorevole, congiuntura alta; improvviso e rapido aumento d'attività. **2** (*econ., market.*) rialzo dei prezzi. **3** (*slang USA*) aumento dei prezzi (*in Borsa*). // ~ **year** (*fin.*) esercizio finanziario eccezionalmente prospero.

boom[2], *v. i.* espandersi, fiorire, andare a gonfie vele. *v. t.* **1** far espandere, far prosperare. **2** (*pubbl.*) lanciare, far la pubblicità a (*un articolo*).

boomflation, *n.* (*econ.*) boom associato a inflazione (*è il contrario di «stagflation»*).

booming, *a.* (*econ.*) fiorente, dinamico.

boon, *n.* beneficio, dono, vantaggio.

boost[1], *n.* **1** spinta. **2** aiuto. **3** (*econ.*) spinta (*al rilancio*). **4** (*market.*) lancio pubblicitario. **5** (*slang USA*) aumento dei prezzi (*in Borsa*). // ~ **given to consumption** (*econ.*) spinta impressa ai consumi.

boost[2], *v. t.* **1** gonfiare (*fig.*). **2** (*market.*) lanciare (*un prodotto*). // to ~ **the value of a share** (*fin.*) gonfiare il valore di una azione.

booster, *n.* **1** (*econ.*) rilancio. **2** (*pubbl., slang USA*) pubblicitario. // ~ **measures** (*econ.*) «pacchetto» di misure anticongiunturali (*o* per il rilancio dell'economia).

boot[1], *n.* **1** scarpa alta, stivale, scarpa. **2** pedata, calcio. **3** (*sind.*) licenziamento. **4** (*trasp. aut.*) bagagliaio. // to **get the** ~ (*sind.*) essere licenziato; to **give the** ~ (*sind.*) licenziare; **to** ~ per giunta, per soprammercato.

boot[2], *v. t.* (*sind.*) licenziare.

bootlegger, *n.* (*slang USA*) contrabbandiere di liquori.

bootlegging, *n.* (*slang USA*) contrabbando di liquori.

bordereau, *n.* (*pl.* **bordereaux**) borderò, «bordereau».

borrow, *v. t.* **1** prendere a prestito, mutuare. **2** (*Borsa*) prendere a riporto, riportare.

borrower, *n.* (*cred.*) chi prende a prestito, percettore di un prestito, mutuatario.

borrowing, *a.* (*cred.*) mutuatario. *n.* (*cred.*) assunzione di prestito. // ~ **abroad by an Italian resident** assunzione di prestiti all'estero effettuata da un residente italiano; ~ **company** (*fin.*) società mutuataria; ~ **rate (of interest)** (*fin.*) tasso passivo; (*banca*) tasso di raccolta; ~ **short to lend long** (*cred.*) incorrere in passività a breve per acquistare attività a lungo termine; ~ **transactions** (*banca*) operazioni passive.

borrowings, *n. pl.* (*banca, fin.*) indebitamento.

boss[1], *n.* (*slang.*) capo, capufficio, dirigente, padrone. // ~ **man** (*sind., slang USA*) capo, capufficio, padrone.

boss[2], *v. t.* (*slang*) dare ordini a (*q.*).

both, *a.* e *pron. pl.* entrambi. // ~ **ends** (*trasp. mar.*) entrambe le fasi (*cioè, caricazione e discarica*).

bottom, *n.* **1** fondo. **2** (*trasp. mar.*) carena (*di nave*). **3** (*trasp. mar.*) nave. *a. attr.* l'ultimo. // ~ **left-hand corner** angolo inferiore sinistro; ~ **price** (*Borsa*) prezzo minimo; ~ **right-hand corner** angolo inferiore destro; **at** ~ in calce.

bottomry, *n.* (*trasp. mar.*) cambio marittimo, prestito a cambio marittimo. // ~ **bond** (*leg.*) contratto di prestito a cambio marittimo; ipoteca su di una nave, contratta dal capitano per far fronte a spese impreviste; ~ **loan** (*trasp. mar.*) prestito a cambio marittimo.

bought, *a.* acquistato, comprato. // ~ **account** (*rag.*) conto d'acquisto (*a provvigione*); ~ **book** (*rag.*) libro acquisti; ~ **contract** (*banca, fin.*) borderò d'acquisto, corso acquisto, corso denaro; (*Borsa*) distinta d'acquisto; ~ **day book** (*rag.*) registro giornaliero degli acquisti; ~ **for the account** (*Borsa*) acquistato a termine; ~ **journal** (*rag.*) registro acquisti; ~ **ledger** (*rag.*) mastro acquisti; ~ **note** (*Borsa*) fissato bollato; (*market.*) conto acquisti (*a provvigione*), distinta d'acquisto.

bounce, *v. t.* (*sind.*) licenziare.

bouncing cheque, *n.* (*banca*) assegno a vuoto.

bound, *a.* **1** legato. **2** obbligato, impegnato, tenuto, vincolato. **3** consolidato. // ~ **for** (*trasp. mar.*) diretto a; ~ **under oath** (*leg.*) sotto il vincolo del giuramento.

bounty, *n.* **1** premio. **2** (*sind.*) premio d'incoraggiamento. // ~ **on export** (*fin.*) premio all'esportazione; ~ **on production** (*sind.*) premio per la produzione.

bourbon, *n.* bourbon (*whisky distillato dal granoturco e dalla segala*).

bourse, *n.* (*francese*) Borsa Valori.

bow, *n.* (*trasp. mar.*) prora. // **at the** ~ (*trasp. mar.*) a prora.

box[1], *n.* **1** scatola. **2** cassa. **3** dono, mancia, regalia. **4** (*fin.*) portafoglio. **5** (*leg.*) banco della giuria. 6 (*leg.*) banco dei testimoni. 7 (*trasp. ferr.*) cabina di segnalazione. // ~ **car** (*trasp. ferr., USA*) vagone merci (*chiuso*); ~ **wagon** (*trasp. ferr.*) vagone merci (*chiuso*).

box², *v. t.* (*anche* to **box up**) mettere in scatole o casse, imballare (*in casse*), incassare, inscatolare.

boxing, *n.* imballaggio (*in casse*), inscatolamento. // ~ **machine** inscatolatrice.

Boxing day, *n.* (*in G.B.*) il 26 dicembre (*Santo Stefano*).

boy, *n.* giovane, fattorino.

boycott¹, *n.* boicottaggio.

boycott², *v. t.* boicottare.

boycotting, *n.* boicottaggio.

bracket, *n.* 1 (*econ.*) fascia (*di reddito, ecc.*). 2 (*econ.*) forcella. // **middle income** ~ (*econ.*) fascia media di reddito; **the target price** ~ **of the two producing Member States** la forcella dei prezzi indicativi dei due Stati Membri produttori.

Bradshaw, *n.* (*trasp. ferr.*) (*in G.B.*) orario ferroviario generale (*dal nome del primo stampatore*).

brain, *n.* cervello. // ~ **drain** (*econ.*) fuga dei cervelli.

brainwashing, *n.* (*market., pubbl.*) lavaggio del cervello (*per mezzo della propaganda, ecc.*).

brake¹, *n.* freno.

brake², *v. t.* frenare.

braking effect, *n.* (*econ.*) effetto frenante.

branch¹, *n.* 1 ramo, ramificazione. 2 (*org. az.*) filiale, succursale. // ~ **account** (*rag.*) conto succursale; ~ **banking** sistema bancario consistente in poche banche che operano attraverso filiali (*come in Italia e in Inghilterra*); ~ **house** (*org. az.*) succursale; ~ **manager** (*org. az., pers.*) direttore di filiale; **the branches of industry** (*econ.*) i rami dell'industria; ~ **office** (*org. az.*) filiale, succursale; ~ **post-office** succursale d'ufficio postale.

branch², *v. i.* ramificarsi. *v. t.* ramificare. // to ~ **out** (*market.*) ampliare il proprio giro d'affari.

brand¹, *n.* 1 marchio. 2 marca. 3 qualità, tipo. // ~ **loyalty** (*market.*) fedeltà alla marca; ~ **manager** (*market., org. az.*) direttore di marca, direttore di prodotto; ~ **name** (*market.*) marca; ~ **-new** nuovo di zecca; ~ **-position analysis** (*market.*) analisi della posizione concorrenziale.

brand², *v. t.* (*market.*) marcare.

branded goods, *n. pl.* articoli di marca.

branded pharmaceuticals, *n. pl.* specialità farmaceutiche.

brass, *n.* ottone. // ~ **nuts** (*slang USA*) direttore.

breach, *n.* 1 (*leg.*) infrazione, rottura, violazione. 2 (*leg.*) inadempimento. // ~ **of the conditions** (*leg.*) infrazione alle condizioni; ~ **of contract** (*leg.*) inadempimento di contratto, inadempienza contrattuale, rottura di contratto; ~ **of the peace** (*leg.*) turbamento dell'ordine pubblico; ~ **of promise** (*leg.*) rottura di promessa; ~ **of the provisions of the law** (*leg.*) infrazione alle disposizioni di legge; ~ **of regulations** (*leg.*) infrazione ai regolamenti; ~ **of trust** (*leg.*) abuso di fiducia; ~ **of warranty** (*leg.*) violazione di garanzia.

bread, *n.* 1 pane. 2 (*slang USA*) denaro. // ~ **and butter** pane e burro; (*market.*) mezzi di sussistenza; (*slang USA*) spese vive; ~ **-winner** chi guadagna il pane per sé e la famiglia.

breadth, *n.* larghezza.

break¹, *n.* 1 rottura. 2 interruzione. 3 intervallo, pausa. 4 (*econ., market.*) diminuzione, calo (*di prezzi, ecc.*). // ~ **-down** crollo; (*org. az.*) scomposizione (*di grandi gruppi*) in sottoclassi (*più agevolmente trattabili*); (*trasp. mar.*) avaria; ~ **-even** (*fin.*) chiusura in pareggio; pareggio (*dei conti*); ~ **of bulk** (*trasp. mar.*) inizio della discarica; ~ **of continuity** soluzione di continuità; ~ **of professional secrecy** (*leg.*) violazione del segreto professionale; ~ **-up** svendita, realizzo; ~ **-up value** (*market.*) valore di realizzo.

break², *v. t.* (*pass.* **broke**, *part. pass.* **broken**) 1 rompere. 2 cambiare (*una banconota o moneta: per avere denaro spicciolo*); spicciolare. 3 (*leg.*) infrangere, violare, venir meno a. *v. i.* 1 andare in rovina. 2 (*leg.*) fallire. // to ~ **an agreement** (*leg.*) rompere un contratto, violare un patto, non rispettare un accordo; to ~ **bulk** (*trasp. mar.*) cominciare a scaricare, cominciare lo scarico; to ~ **a contract** (*leg.*) rompere un contratto; to ~ **an engagement** (*leg.*) non tener fede a un impegno; to ~ **even** (*fin.*) chiudere in pareggio; pareggiare i conti; to ~ **one's journey** (*trasp.*) interrompere il viaggio; to ~ **off one's career** (*pers.*) lasciare la carriera; to ~ **off connections** sospendere le relazioni; to ~ **open** (*leg.*) forzare; to ~ **up** frazionare; cessare l'attività; liquidare (*un'azienda*).

breakable, *a.* fragile.

breakage, *n.* rottura. // ~ **risk** (*ass., trasp.*) rischio di rottura.

breakdown, *n.* 1 rottura. 2 interruzione. 3 ripartizione. 4 (*stat.*) quota. // ~ **car** (*trasp. aut.*) carro attrezzi; **the** ~ **of negotations** l'interruzione dei negoziati; **the** ~ **of State enterprise**

on total (*stat.*) la quota delle imprese pubbliche rispetto al totale.

breaker, *n.* (*leg.*) violatore.

breaking, *n.* rottura. // ~ **of seals** (*leg.*) violazione di sigilli; ~ **the stowage** (*trasp. mar.*) scaricamento (*d'una nave*).

brew[1]**,** *n.* processo di fermentazione della birra.

brew[2]**,** *v. t.* fabbricare (*la birra e altre bevande fermentate*).

brewer, *n.* fabbricante di birra.

bribe[1]**,** *n.* (*leg.*) dono; somma di denaro per corrompere; «bustarella».

bribe[2]**,** *v. t.* (*leg.*) corrompere, «comprare».

bribery, *n.* (*leg.*) corruzione (*a mezzo di denaro, doni, ecc.*).

bridge[1]**,** *n.* (*trasp. mar.*) ponte di comando, plancia. // « ~ **law**» (*econ.*) «legge-ponte».

bridge[2]**,** *v. t.* superare.

brief[1]**,** *a.* breve. *n.* **1** (*leg.*) difesa giudiziaria, comparsa. **2** (*leg., USA*) conclusioni presentate alla Corte. **3** (*leg., USA*) verbale d'un processo. // ~ **-bag** borsa da legale, cartella.

brief[2]**,** *v. t.* **1** riassumere. **2** (*anche leg.*) dare istruzioni a (*q.*).

briefing, *n.* (*org. az.*) istruzioni per lo svolgimento d'una attività (*date nel corso d'una riunione*). // ~ **session** (*org. az.*) conferenza informativa.

bright, *a.* **1** brillante. **2** (*Borsa, market.*) (*dell'attività commerciale*) vivace.

brightness, *n.* (*Borsa, market.*) buon andamento, vivacità. // **the** ~ **of a share** il buon andamento di un'azione.

bring, *v. t.* (*pass.* e *part. pass.* **brought**) **1** portare, prendere con sé. **2** (*leg.*) addurre, produrre (*argomenti, prove*). // to ~ **about** causare, determinare; to ~ **about sb.'s failure** dissestare q.; to ~ **about a ship** (*trasp. mar.*) invertire la rotta d'una nave; to ~ **the accounts up to date** (*rag.*) aggiornare i conti; to ~ **an action against sb.** (*leg.*) far causa a q., intentare causa (*o* lite) contro q.; to ~ **a charge against sb.** (*leg.*) muovere un'accusa contro q.; to ~ **down** (*market.*) abbassare, far calare; (*rag.*) portare (*in diminuzione*); to ~ **evidence** (*leg.*) fornire prove; to ~ **forward** (*rag.*) riportare (*p. es., un totale dal fondo della pagina precedente*); to ~ **in** apportare; fruttare, rendere; (*trasp. mar.*) portare in porto; to ~ **in capital** apportare capitali; to ~ **inflation under control** (*econ., fin.*) tenere l'inflazione sotto controllo; to ~ **the interested parties together** mettere in contatto gli interessati; to ~ **into** apportare; to ~ **into account** (*rag.*) mettere in conto; to ~ **into force** (*leg.*) mettere in vigore; to ~ **off a coup on the stock exchange** (*Borsa*) fare un colpo in Borsa; to ~ **out** (*market.*) lanciare (*p. es., titoli sul mercato*); to ~ **the rates to level time** (*market.*) portare i prezzi a un livello normale; to ~ **the rates to the same level** (*market.*) livellare i prezzi; to ~ **a task off** portare a termine un incarico; to ~ **up** (*fin., market.*) aumentare, far crescere (*prezzi, ecc.*); to ~ **st. up to date** aggiornare qc.

bringing forward, *n.* (*rag.*) riporto.

bringing out, *n.* (*market.*) lancio (*p. es., sul mercato*).

bringing up to date, *n.* aggiornamento; il mettere al corrente.

brink, *n.* bordo, orlo.

brisk, *a.* attivo, intenso, vivace.

briskness, *n.* animazione, vivacità.

British National Export Council, *n.* Organismo Cooperativo Nazionale Inglese (*fondato nel 1964 per guidare e assistere gli esportatori*).

broadcast[1]**,** *n.* (*comun.*) trasmissione (*per radio*), programma.

broadcast[2]**,** *v. t.* (*pass.* e *part. pass.* **broadcast**) (*comun.*) trasmettere (*per radio*); diffondere (*una notizia*).

broadcasting, *a.* (*comun.*) emittente. *n.* (*comun.*) emissione (*via radio*). // ~ **station** (*comun.*) stazione radiotrasmittente, emittente.

broadside, *n.* **1** (*pubbl.*) pieghevole. **2** (*trasp. mar.*) fiancata.

brochure, *n.* (*pubbl.*) fascicolo, opuscolo, pieghevole.

broke[1]**,** *a.* **1** (*slang*) fallito. **2** (*slang*) destituito, licenziato, silurato. // to **go** ~ (*slang*) andare in rovina, far fallimento.

broke[2]**,** *v. i.* (*ingl.*) fare il mediatore.

brokee, *n.* (*slang USA*) persona (*o* ditta) fallita.

broken, *a.* infranto, rotto. // ~ **money** (denari) spiccioli; ~ **time** (*org. az., sind.*) riduzione dell'orario (*dovuta a interruzioni*); ~ **week** settimana interrotta da una festa.

broker, *n.* **1** intermediario, mediatore, sensale. **2** (*Borsa*) (= **stockbroker**) agente di cambio. // ~ **'s account** (*Borsa*) conto di liquidazione; **brokers' account** (*Borsa*) conto di liquidazione; ~ **'s contract** (*Borsa*) contratto di commissione; ~ **'s contract note** bolletta del contratto di mediazione; ~ **'s note** distinta di senseria.

brokerage, *n.* **1** mediazione, senseria. **2** provvigione. **3** (*fin.*) brokeraggio.

broking, *n.* lavoro di mediatore, attività di sensale.

«brought forward», *a.* (*rag.*) «riporto».

brown, *a.* bruno, marrone, castano scuro, giallo scuro. // ~ **paper** carta da pacchi; ~ **ware** terraglie comuni.

brush off, *v. t.* (*sind.*) licenziare.

bubble, *n.* 1 (*fin.*) gonfiatura, montatura. 2 (*fin., leg.*) frode, truffa.

buck, *n.* 1 (*slang*) secchio. 2 (*slang USA*) dollaro. // ~ **-passing** (*org. az.*) «scaricabarile»; to **be in the bucks** (*slang USA*) essere in soldi.

bucket shop, *n.* 1 (*Borsa, slang USA*) agenzia di cambio illegale. 2 (*trasp. aer., fam.*) agenzia di viaggi che pratica forti sconti.

budge, *v. i.* (*econ.*) muoversi (*di prezzi*).

budget[1], *n.* 1 (*fin., rag.*) bilancio (*di previsione; specialm. quello dello Stato*), preventivo. 2 (*pubbl.*) stanziamento pubblicitario. // ~ **committee** (*fin., org. az.*) comitato del bilancio; ~ **deficit** (*fin., rag.*) disavanzo di bilancio, deficit di bilancio; ~ **estimate** (*fin., rag.*) previsione di bilancio; ~ **matters** (*fin., rag.*) problemi di bilancio; ~ **policy** (*econ., rag.*) politica di bilancio; **a ~ showing a deficit** (*o* **a loss**) (*fin., rag.*) un bilancio deficitario; ~ **surplus** (*fin., rag.*) avanzo di bilancio; ~ **target** (*econ., fin.*) obiettivo di bilancio; ~ **variance** (*fin., rag.*) scostamento dalle cifre di bilancio.

budget[2], *v. t.* 1 (*econ., rag.*) mettere in bilancio, programmare. 2 (*fin., rag.*) stanziare (*una somma*) in bilancio. *v. i.* (*econ., rag.*) impostare un bilancio.

budgetary, *a.* (*fin., rag.*) pertinente a bilancio, «buggetario», «budgetario», di bilancio «budgetario». // ~ **control** (*fin., rag.*) controllo a bilancio, controllo «budgetario»; ~ **deficit** (*fin., rag.*) *V.* **budget deficit;** ~ **surplus** (*fin., rag.*) *V.* **budget surplus.**

budgeted, *a.* (*fin., rag.*) iscritto nel «budget» (*q. V.*).

budgeting, *n.* (*fin., rag.*) preparazione del bilancio (*di previsione*); «budgeting». // ~ **control** (*fin., rag.*) *V.* **budgetary control.**

budlaing, *n. V.* **budla operation.**

budla operation, *n.* (*Borsa, fin.*) operazione di vendita a contanti contro riacquisto a termine.

buffer, *n.* (*fin.*) stock di riserva. // ~ **stock** (*econ.*) «stock-tampone».

build, *v. t.* (*pass.* e *part. pass.* **built**) costruire, erigere, fabbricare. // to ~ **up** costruire, costruirsi; to ~ **up a fortune** farsi una fortuna; to ~ **up reserves (stock)** costituire riserve (scorte).

builder, *n.* costruttore.

building, *n.* costruzione, edificio, fabbricato, fondo urbano, immobile. // ~ **contractor** imprenditore edile; ~ **land** terreno da costruzione; ~ **-lease** (*leg.*) affitto di terreno con obbligo di costruzione; ~ **port** (*trasp. mar.*) porto per costruzioni navali; **the ~ sector** il settore edilizio; ~ **-site** area fabbricabile; ~ **society** (*fin.*) società di finanziamento per l'acquisto o la costruzione di case; ~ **trade** (*econ.*) industria delle costruzioni; ~ **yard** cantiere edile.

build-up, *n.* (*pubbl.*) lancio pubblicitario.

built, *a.* costruito. // ~ **-in flexibility** (*fin.*) flessibilità automatica (*dei tassi di cambio*); ~ **-in stabilizers** (*econ.*) stabilizzatori automatici.

bulge, *n.* (*slang USA*) aumento dei prezzi (*in Borsa*).

bulk, *n.* 1 massa, quantità, volume. 2 (*trasp. mar.*) stiva. 3 (*trasp. mar.*) carico; carico alla rinfusa; carico secco. // ~ **buying** (*market.*) acquisto in massa; ~ **carrier** (*trasp. mar.*) nave per carichi secchi; ~ **load** (*trasp. mar.*) carico alla rinfusa; ~ **selling** (*market.*) vendita all'ingrosso; ~ **supply tariff** (*comm. est.*) tariffa preferenziale per merce alla rinfusa; **in ~** (*trasp. mar.*) alla rinfusa.

bull[1], *n.* (*Borsa*) rialzista, giocatore al rialzo. *a. attr.* (*Borsa*) rialzista. // ~ **account** (*Borsa*) posizione al rialzo; ~ **campaign** (*Borsa*) campagna al rialzo, campagna rialzista; ~ **point** (*Borsa*) punto a favore dei rialzisti; ~ **purchase** (*Borsa*) acquisto allo scoperto; ~ **run** (*Borsa*) (tendenza al) rialzo; ~ **transaction** (*Borsa*) operazione al rialzo.

bull[2], *v. i.* (*Borsa*) giocare, speculare al rialzo. // to ~ **the market** (*Borsa*) comprare allo scoperto.

bulletin, *n.* bollettino.

bullion, *n.* (*fin.*) oro o argento in verghe o lingotti // ~ **point** (*fin.*) punto dell'oro, punto metallico; ~ **reserve** (*fin.*) riserva metallica; ~ **trade** (*fin.*) commercio dell'oro e dell'argento.

bullionism, *n.* (*econ., fin.*) bullionismo.

bullionist, *n.* (*econ., fin.*) fautore del bullionismo.

bullish, *a.* (*Borsa*) di, da rialzista; orientato al rialzo; tendente al rialzo. // ~ **tendency** (*Borsa*) tendenza al rialzo; ~ **transaction** (*Borsa*) operazione al rialzo.

bullishness, *n.* (*Borsa*) tendenza al rialzo. // **eleven consecutive days of ~** (*Borsa*) undici sedute consecutive di rialzo.

bummaree, *n.* (*slang*) facchino (*al mercato della carne di Londra*).

bump, *v. t.* battere.

bumper, *n.* (*slang*) cosa di eccezionale grandezza o abbondanza. // **a ~ sale** (*market.*) una vendita straordinaria.

bunch, *n.* mazzo.

bunco, *n.* (*slang USA*) imbroglio, truffa.

bundle, *n.* **1** fascio, involto. **2** grande quantità.

bunker, *n.* (*trasp. mar.*) carbonile. // ~ **coal** (*trasp. mar.*) carbone per piroscafo.

bunkering, *n.* (*trasp. mar.*) caricamento dei carbonili. // ~ **station** (*trasp. mar.*) stazione di rifornimento.

buoy[1], *n.* (*trasp. mar.*) boa, gavitello. // ~ **dues** (*trasp. mar.*) diritti di gavitello.

buoy[2], *v. t.* appoggiare, sostenere.

buoyancy, *n.* **1** galleggiabilità. **2** (*fin.*) elasticità, esuberanza, capacità di ricupero. **3** (*market.*) tendenza al rialzo.

burden[1], *n.* **1** peso, onere. **2** (*trasp. mar.*) stazza, stazzatura, tonnellaggio. // ~ **of proof** (*leg.*) onere della prova; ~ **of proving** (*leg.*) onere della prova; ~ **of taxation** (*fin.*) carico tributario.

burden[2], *v. t.* **1** gravare. **2** tassare.

burdened estate, *n.* (*leg.*) proprietà con vincolo della prova.

bureau, *n.* **1** (*org. az.*) ufficio. **2** (*org. az.*) agenzia. // ~ **of the Budget** (*USA*) Ufficio del Bilancio.

bureaucracy, *n.* apparato amministrativo.

burglar, *n.* ladro, scassinatore.

burglary, *n.* (*leg.*) violazione di domicilio. // ~ **insurance** (*ass.*) assicurazione contro furto e scasso.

bursar, *n.* (*pers.*) economo, tesoriere. // ~ **'s office** economato (*l'ufficio*).

bursarship, *n.* economato (*la carica*).

burthen, *n. V.* **burden.**

bus, *n.* (*trasp.*) autobus, torpedone.

bushel, *n.* staio (*misura di capacità per aridi; pari a litri 36,36*).

business, *n.* **1** affare, affari. **2** compito, funzione. **3** commercio. **4** lavoro, occupazione. **5** azienda, compagnia, ditta, impresa. // ~ **address** indirizzo d'ufficio, recapito; ~ **agent** (*pers.*) agente (*o* rappresentante) di commercio; ~ **assistance** (*banca, comm.*) assistenza negli affari; ~ **card** biglietto di visita; ~ **centre** (*fin.*) centro d'affari; ~ **climate** (*econ.*) situazione congiunturale; ~ **combine** (*econ.*) concentrazione, fusione d'aziende; ~ **connections** relazioni d'affari, rapporti d'affari; ~ **consultant** commercialista; ~ **corporation** (*fin., USA*) società commerciale; ~ **correspondence** corrispondenza commerciale; ~ **cycle** (*econ.*) ciclo dell'attività commerciale; ciclo economico; ciclo congiunturale; ~ **day** (*org. az.*) giorno lavorativo; ~ **deal** transazione commerciale; **a ~ dip** (*econ., USA*) una lieve recessione; «~ **done**» (*Borsa*) «corsi praticati»; ~ **economics** (*econ.*) economia aziendale; ~ **English** (lingua) inglese commerciale; ~ **enterprise** impresa commerciale; ~ **entity** impresa commerciale; ~ **executive** (*pers.*) dirigente commerciale; ~ **field** (*econ.*) settore d'attività; ~ **game** (*org. az.*) gestione simulata; ~ **hours** (*org. az.*) ore d'ufficio; ~ **house** casa commerciale; ~ **letter** lettera d'affari; ~ **man** uomo d'affari; ~ **management** economia aziendale; ~ **manager** (*org. az.*) direttore commerciale; ~ **mathematics** (*rag.*) computisteria; ~ **name** nome dell'azienda, ragione sociale; ~ **papers** incartamenti d'affari; ~ **premises** (*comm.*) locali; ~ **recovery** (*econ.*) ripresa dell'attività commerciale; ~ **reply card** (*comun.*) cartolina con risposta pagata; ~ **report** informazioni commerciali; ~ **survey** (*econ., market.*) indagine congiunturale, inchiesta congiunturale; ~ **transaction** transazione commerciale; (*rag.*) operazione; ~ **trends** (*econ.*) evoluzione della congiuntura; ~ **trip** viaggio d'affari; ~ **visitor** (*market.*) operatore (*in una mostra o fiera*); ~ **year** (*rag.*) anno sociale, esercizio; **in** ~ in affari; **on** ~ per affari.

businessman, *n.* (*pl.* **businessmen**) uomo d'affari.

businesswoman, *n.* (*pl.* **businesswomen**) donna d'affari.

bust, *n.* (*econ.*) stasi dell'attività economica.

busy, *a.* impegnato, occupato.

butt, *n.* matrice.

butter, *n.* burro. // ~ **-making** fabbricazione del burro.

buttock, *n.* (*trasp. mar.*) giardinetto.

button, *v. t.* eseguire (*un'ordinazione*).

buy[1], *n.* **1** acquisto, compera, compra, spesa. **2** cosa in vendita. // ~ **order** (*Borsa*) ordine di acquisto.

buy[2], *v. t.* (*pass.* e *part. pass.* **bought**) acquistare, comprare. // to ~ **st. at an auction** comprare qc. a una vendita all'asta; to ~ **at best** (*fin.*) comprare al meglio; to ~ **cash** comprare a contanti; to ~ **cheap** comprare a buon mercato; to ~ **for forward delivery** comprare per futura consegna; to ~ **in** riscattare; to ~ **into a company** (*fin.*) comprare titoli d'una società; to ~ **off** corrompere (*col denaro o con doni*); to ~ **on credit** comprare a credito; to ~ **on easy terms** comprare a rate; to ~ **on instalment** (*o* **on the instalment plan,** *o* **by instalments**) acquistare a rate; to ~ **on term** (*Borsa*) comprare a termine; to ~ **out** rilevare (*un negozio, un'azienda e sim.*); (*fin.*) comprare (*un intero pacchetto* *azionario*), acquistare il pacchetto di maggioranza di (*una società*); to ~ **out a partner** rilevare la parte d'un socio; to ~ **over** corrompere (*col denaro o con doni*); to ~ **a season ticket** (*trasp.*) abbonarsi; to ~ **through loans** effettuare acquisti mediante mutui; to ~ **up** accaparrare, incettare, fare incetta di; to ~ **wholesale** (*market.*) comprare all'ingrosso.

buyable, *a.* acquistabile, comprabile.

buyer, *n.* **1** acquirente, compratore, committente. **2** (*pers.*) direttore dell'ufficio acquisti. // ~ **Countries** (*econ.*) Paesi acquirenti; **buyers' market** (*econ.*) mercato dell'acquirente, mercato al ribasso; ~ **'s monopoly** (*econ.*) monopsonio (*monopolio del compratore*); ~ **of a call option** (*Borsa*) compratore d'un «dont»; ~ **'s option** (*Borsa*) premio per il compratore; **«buyers over»** (*Borsa*) «eccedenza di compratori»; **buyers' strike** (*market.*) sciopero di consumatori (*in attesa d'una diminuzione dei prezzi*); ~ **-up** accaparratore, incettatore; **at (the)** ~ **'s risk** (*leg.*) a rischio (e pericolo) del compratore.

buying, *a.* acquirente. *n.* compera, acquisto. // ~ **and selling** (*market.*) compravendita; ~ **brokerage** mediazione per acquisti; ~ **commission** provvigione per acquisti; ~ **habit** (*market.*) abitudine di acquisto; ~ **in and selling out** (*Borsa*) transazione in Borsa; ~ **in or selling out** (*Borsa*) transazione in Borsa; ~ **-in price** prezzo di riacquisto; ~ **interest** (*Borsa*) interessamento del pubblico; ~ **offices** (*comm. est.*) uffici d'acquisto; ~ **order** ordine di acquisto; ~ **out a partner** rilevamento della parte d'un socio; ~ **policy** (*org. az.*) politica degli acquisti; ~ **power** (*econ.*) potere d'acquisto; (*market.*) potenziale d'acquisto; ~ **(*o* purchasing) agent** agente per gli acquisti; ~ **rate** (*banca*) cambio d'acquisto (*al quale la banca è disposta ad acquistare divise*); ~ **syndicate** (*fin.*) «sindacato» di compratori (*a costituzione volontaria*); ~ **-up** (*econ., market.*) accaparramento, incetta.

by, *prep.* per mezzo di. // ~ **Act of Parliament** (*ingl.*) per legge; ~ **air** (*trasp. aer.*) per via aerea; ~ **air mail** (*comun.*) per via aerea; ~ **banker** a mezzo banca; ~ **the day** (*org. az.*) a giornata; ~ **description** (*market.*) su descrizione; ~ **direct steamer** (*trasp. mar.*) tramite vapore diretto; ~ **the dozen** a dozzine; ~ **goods train** (*trasp. ferr.*) a piccola velocità; ~ **hand** a mano; ~ **the hour** (*org. az.*) a ore; ~ **land** (*trasp.*) per terra; ~ **measure** (*market.*) sciolto, sfuso; ~ **order of the board** per ordine del consiglio d'amministrazione; ~ **passenger train** (*trasp. ferr.*) a grande velocità; ~ **post** per posta; ~ **the pound** (*market.*) a libbre; ~ **proxy** (*leg.*) per procura; ~ **rail** (*trasp. ferr.*) per ferrovia; ~ **return of mail** a stretto giro di posta; ~ **right** (*leg.*) di diritto, secondo giustizia; ~ **sample** (*market.*) su campione; ~ **sea** (*trasp. mar.*) per mare; ~ **show of hands** per alzata di mano.

by-bidder, *n.* chi fa salire i prezzi (*a un'asta*) con offerte fittizie.

by-bidding, *n.* offerte all'asta (*d'accordo col banditore*) per raggiungere prezzi elevati.

by-business, *n.* attività collaterale.

bye, *n.* cosa di scarsa importanza, cosa secondaria. // ~ **-law** (*leg.*) *V.* **by-law.**

by-law, *n.* **1** (*leg.*) leggina. **2** (*leg.*) regolamento. **3** (*leg.*) statuto.

by-pass, *n.* (*trasp. aut.*) tangenziale.

by-product, *n.* (*org. az.*) sottoprodotto.

C

cab, *n.* (*trasp.*) carrozza di piazza.

cabbage, *n.* (*slang USA*) denaro. // ~ **leave** (*slang USA*) banconota.

cabin, *n.* (*trasp. aer., trasp. mar.*) cabina. // ~ **class** (*trasp. mar.*) seconda classe; ~ **passenger** (*trasp.*) passeggero di cabina.

cabinet, *n.* **1** (*amm.*) Gabinetto (*ministero*). **2** (*attr. uff.*) armadietto, stipo. **3** (*org. az.*) gabinetto. // ~ **edition** (*market.*) edizione corrente; **the** ~ **Office** la Presidenza del Consiglio.

cable[1], *n.* **1** (*comun.*) cablogramma. **2** (*cred.*) rimessa telegrafica. **3** (*trasp. mar.*) cavo, fune, gomena. **4** (*trasp. mar.*) unità di misura equivalente a 608 piedi (*per misurare la profondità dei cavi sottomarini*). // ~ **address** (*comun.*) indirizzo cablografico; ~ **'s length** (*trasp. mar.*) misura di lunghezza pari a 608 piedi; ~ **transfer** (*comun., cred.*) bonifico telegrafico, rimessa telegrafica.

cable[2], *v. t.* e *i.* **1** (*comun.*) cablografare, cablare, trasmettere (*qc.*) con un telegramma. **2** (*comun.*) mandare un telegramma.

cablegram, *n.* (*comun.*) cablogramma, cablo.

caboose, *n.* (*trasp. mar.*) cambusa, cucina di bordo.

cabotage, *n.* (*trasp. mar.*) cabotaggio.

ca'canny, *locuz.* (*scozz.*) sii prudente!; procedi con cautela! // ~ **strike** (*sind.*) sciopero bianco.

cadastral, *a.* catastale. // ~ **estimate** (*leg.*) stima catastale; ~ **survey** stima catastale.

caddis, *n.* tessuto di lana grezza.

cadres, *n. pl.* (*pers.*) quadri.

cafeteria, *n.* **1** ristorante in cui i clienti si servono da soli. **2** (*org. az.*) mensa aziendale.

cage, *n.* gabbia. // ~ **man** (*slang USA*) cassiere; ~ **woman** (*slang USA*) cassiera.

calculate, *v. t.* e *i.* (*rag.*) valutare.

calculating, *a. attr.* calcolatore. // ~ **machine** (*macch. uff.*) (macchina) calcolatrice.

calculation, *n.* **1** opinione. **2** previsione. **3** (*mat.*) calcolo, conteggio.

calculator, *n.* **1** (*attr. uff.*) prontuario per fare i calcoli. **2** (*macch. uff.*) (macchina) calcolatrice. **3** (*pers.*) computista.

calculus, *n.* (*pl.* **calculi** e *reg.*) (*mat.*) calcolo.

calendar[1], *n.* **1** calendario. **2** (*attr. uff.*) annuario. **3** (*attr. uff.*) registro. **4** (*org. az.*) lista. // ~ **day** giorno del calendario; ~ **month** mese solare; ~ **year** anno solare.

calendar[2], *v. t.* **1** (*org. az.*) registrare. **2** (*org. az.*) ordinare, schedare (*documenti, ecc.*). **3** (*org. az.*) includere in un elenco o in una lista.

calender, *n.* pressa.

call[1], *n.* **1** chiamata, telefonata. **2** ordine, richiesta di pagamento. **3** (*econ.*) richiesta. **4** (*fin.*) richiamo dei decimi (*sulle azioni sottoscritte*). **5** (*trasp. ferr.*) fermata (*di treno*). **6** (*trasp. mar.*) scalo (*di nave*). // ~ **-box** (*comun.*) cabina telefonica; ~ **charge** (*comun.*) importo d'una conversazione telefonica; ~ **for bids** (*o* **for tenders**) concorso d'appalto, bando di gara d'appalto; ~ **for funds** (*fin.*) richiesta di fondi; ~ **for manpower** (*econ.*) offerta di lavoro; **calls for public tender** (*fin.*) offerte per un appalto pubblico; ~ **letter** (*fin.*) lettera di domanda di pagamento di decimi; ~ **-loan** (*banca*) prestito bancario rimborsabile a vista, col preavviso d'un giorno; ~ **money** (*banca*) prestito rimborsabile a domanda; controvalore oggetto d'un prestito; (*cred.*) credito esigibile in qualsiasi momento; (*fin.*) denaro investito a brevissima scadenza (*per pochi giorni, specialm. in operazioni di Borsa*); ~ **number** (*comun.*) numero telefonico; (*rag.*) numero di schedario ; ~ **of more** (*Borsa*) diritto d'aggiunta, diritto d'ulteriore acquisto allo stesso prezzo; contratto con il quale il compratore acquista il diritto – contro il pagamento di un premio – di richiedere alla scadenza il doppio del quantitativo di titoli pattuito; ~ **of three times more** (*Borsa*) diritto d'aggiunta tripla; ~ **of twice more** (*Borsa*) diritto d'aggiunta doppia; ~ **office attendant** (*pers.*) gerente di posto telefonico pubblico; ~ **on the guarantor** (*leg.*) chiamata in garanzia; ~ **price** (*Borsa*) prezzo del contratto «dont»; ~ **receipt** (*cred.*) ricevuta di versamento per una richiesta di fondi; **calls risk** (*ass. mar.*) rischio negli scali; ~ **sign** (*trasp. mar.*) nominativo; ~ **-slip** (*market.*) tagliando che conferma l'avvenuta visita d'un piazzista a un cliente; ~ **stock** (*fin.*) azione redimibile; **«no calls»** (*trasp. mar.*) «senza scali intermedi»; **on** ~ (*cred.*) pagabile a richiesta.

call[2], *v. t.* **1** convocare, indire (*una riunione, ecc.*). **2** chiamare. **3** dare nome a, nominare. *v. i.* **1** venire (*nel senso di «far visita», «passare»*). **2** (*trasp. mar.*) fare scalo. // to ~ **at** andare, passare da (*un luogo*); to ~ **at intermediate ports** (*trasp. mar.*) fare scalo in porti intermedi; to ~ **at a named port** (*trasp. mar.*) fare scalo in un porto nominato; to ~ **sb.'s attention to st.** richiamare l'attenzione di q. su qc.; to ~ **bonds** (*fin.*) rimborsare delle obbligazioni; to ~ **a case** (*leg.*) fissare un'udienza; to ~ **the exchange** (*comun.*) chiamare il centralino (*telefonico*); to ~ **for bids** (*leg.*) fare un'offerta cauzionale per un'aggiudicazione; to ~ **for subscribed capital** (*fin.*) richiamare i decimi; to ~ **for tenders** bandire (*o* indire) una gara d'appalto; to ~ **in** ritirare; richiedere il pagamento di; (*cred.*) richiedere (*denaro prestato*); to ~ **off** disdire, revocare; to ~ **off a strike** (*sind.*) revocare uno sciopero; to ~ **on** far appello a; to ~ **on sb.** passare da q., fare una breve visita a q.; to ~ **on domestic savings** ricorrere al risparmio interno; to ~ **on a guarantee** (*leg.*) far appello a una garanzia; to ~ **the operator** (*comun.*) chiamare la centralinista; to ~ **the roll** (*pers.*) fare l'appello; to ~ **to revictual** (*trasp. mar.*) far scalo per rifornirsi di vettovaglie; to ~ **up** (*comun.*) chiamare al telefono.

callable bond, *n.* (*fin.*) obbligazione redimibile.

called bond, *n.* (*fin.*) obbligazione rimborsata, obbligazione estratta.

called-up capital, *n.* (*fin.*) capitale richiamato, capitale richiesto.

caller, *n.* visitatore.

calling, *n.* **1** convocazione. **2** chiamata. **3** invito. **4** visita. // ~ **-card** (*USA*) biglietto di visita; ~ **clause** (*trasp. mar.*) clausola relativa agli scali; ~ **for orders bill of lading** (*trasp. mar.*) polizza di carico all'ordine; ~ **together** convocazione: ~ **the shareholders together** convocazione degli azionisti; ~ **-up** richiamo: ~ **-up of the final instalment** richiamo dell'ultimo versamento; ~ **upon the underwriters** (*fin.*) invito ai sottoscrittori.

cambist, *n.* **1** (*fin.*) cambista. **2** (*fin., trasp.*) manuale per la conversione di misure, pesi e valute di differenti Paesi.

camera, *n.* **1** macchina fotografica. **2** (*leg.*) ufficio (*di un giudice*). // **in** ~ (*leg.*) nell'ufficio di un giudice.

cameralism, *n.* (*econ.*) cameralismo.

cameralist, *n.* (*econ.*) cameralista.

campaign, *n.* campagna (*militare, politica, pubblicitaria*). // ~ **planning** (*pubbl.*) pianificazione d'una campagna pubblicitaria.

can[1], *n.* **1** bidone, recipiente, scatola (*specialm. di latta*). **2** (*market., USA*) scatoletta (*di generi alimentari conservati*).

can[2], *v. t.* **1** (*market., USA*) mettere (*generi alimentari*) in scatola (*di latta*); inscatolare. **2** (*slang USA*) licenziare.

canal, *n.* canale (*in molti sensi; cfr.* **channel**). // ~ **boat** (*trasp.*) chiatta; ~ **harbour** (*trasp. mar.*) porto canale; ~ **service dues** (*trasp.*) diritti di canale.

cancel, *v. t.* **1** cancellare (*facendo una croce o tirando un frego*). **2** disdire, revocare, annullare (*un impegno, un'ordinazione, ecc.*). **3** (*leg.*) rescindere (*un contratto*). **4** (*leg.*) abrogare (*una legge*). **5** (*pubbl.*) omettere, sopprimere. // to ~ **an agreement** annullare un accordo; to ~ **a cause from the cause list** (*leg.*) cancellare una causa dal ruolo; to ~ **a charter party** (*leg.*) annullare un contratto di noleggio; to ~ **a contract** (*leg.*) annullare un contratto; to ~ **the customs duty on st.** (*dog.*) sgravare qc. dei diritti doganali; to ~ **a deed** (*leg.*) annullare un atto (*legale, notarile, ecc.*); to ~ **each other** (*rag.*) annullarsi, bilanciarsi; to ~ **a flight** (*trasp. aer.*) cancellare un volo; to ~ **an order** stornare (*o* annullare) un'ordinazione; to ~ **out** (*rag.*) bilanciare, neutralizzare; annullarsi; to ~ **a revenue stamp** annullare una marca da bollo.

cancelable, *a. V.* **cancellable.**

cancelation, *n. V.* **cancellation.**

canceling stamp, *n. V.* **cancelling stamp.**

cancellable, *a.* annullabile, risolvibile, rescindibile.

cancellation, *n.* **1** cancellazione, cancellatura; annullamento (*d'un impegno, ecc.*); revoca (*d'un'ordinazione, ecc.*). **2** (*leg.*) annullamento (*di contratto o atto*). **3** (*leg.*) risoluzione, rescissione (*d'un contratto*). **4** (*leg.*) abrogazione (*d'una legge*). **5** (*market.*) annullamento di disdetta (*d'un ordine*). **6** (*pubbl.*) omissione. // ~ **clause** (*leg.*) clausola di rescissione; ~ **date** data d'annullamento; ~ **of a debt** (*cred.*) estinzione d'un debito; ~ **of a flight** (*trasp. aer.*) cancellazione di un volo; ~ **of a licence** (*leg.*) ritiro d'una patente (*o* d'una licenza); ~ **of an order** storno (*o* annullamento) d'un ordine.

cancelling price, *n.* (*leg.*) indennità di rescissione (*d'un contratto, ecc.*).

cancelling stamp, *n.* timbro d'annullamento.

candidacy, *n.* (*USA*) candidatura.

candidate, *n.* (*pers.*) candidato; concorrente (*a un posto, ecc.*). // to **be a ~ for listing on the stock market** (*Borsa*) essere quotabile in Borsa.

candidature, *n.* candidatura.

candle, *n.* candela. // **~ -auction** asta basata sul consumo d'una candela.

candy, *n.* **1** candito. **2** (*USA*) caramella. **3** (*USA*) confetto. // **~ -store** (*USA*) negozio di caramelle, cioccolatini, ecc.

canister, *n.* scatola metallica (*per tè, caffè, tabacco, ecc.*).

canned goods, *n. pl.* (*market., USA*) scatolame.

cannery, *n.* stabilimento per la produzione d'alimenti in scatola.

canning, *n.* (*market., USA*) inscatolamento. // **~ industry** industria conserviera; **~ machine** inscatolatrice.

canny, *a.* circospetto.

canteen, *n.* (*org. az.*) posto di ristoro, mensa aziendale.

canvas, *n.* canovaccio.

canvass, *v. t.* **1** esaminare a fondo. **2** (*market.*) sollecitare (*ordinazioni commerciali, ecc.*). *v. i.* **1** (*market.*) fare propaganda, fare il piazzista. **2** (*pubbl.*) propagandare in modo capillare. // to **~ the town** (*market.*) battere la piazza.

canvasser, *n.* **1** (*pers.*) piazzista. **2** (*pubbl.*) propagandista «capillare».

canvassing, *n.* **1** (*market.*) attività di piazzista. **2** (*pubbl.*) propaganda (fatta in modo) capillare.

capability, *n.* **1** capacità, facoltà (*di fare qc.*). **2** idoneità. **3** possibilità.

capable, *a.* abile; (*di persona*) capace.

capacity, *n.* **1** capacità. **2** funzione, posizione, qualità, ufficio, veste (*fig.*). **3** (*leg.*) capacità, potere. **4** (*org. az.*) capacità (*degli impianti*), rendimento, massima capacità produttiva (*d'uno stabilimento, ecc.*). // **~ costs** (*rag.*) costi fissi; **~ of the U.S. economy** potenzialità dell'economia statunitense; **~ test** (*pers.*) test attitudinale; **~ to act** (*leg.*) capacità d'agire; **~ to contract** (*leg.*) capacità di contrarre, capacità giuridica; **~ -utilization rate** (*org. az.*) indice di utilizzazione della capacità (*degli impianti*); **~ variance** (*rag.*) scostamento dalle cifre iscritte nel budget per quanto riguarda la capacità produttiva; **in the ~ of** (*leg.*) in veste di.

capital, *n.* **1** (*econ.*) capitale. **2** (*rag.*) capitale. // **~ account** (*rag.*) conto capitale; **~ and reserves** (*ass.*) capitale e riserve patrimoniali; **~ appropriation** (*rag.*) impegno di capitale; **~ asset** (*econ.*) attività capitale; **~ assets** (*rag.*) capitale fisso, capitale immobilizzato; **~ at venture** (*fin.*) capitale a fondo perduto; **~ bearing 4% interest** (*fin.*) capitale che frutta un interesse del 4%; **~ bearing no interest** (*fin.*) capitale non fruttifero; **~ budget** (*rag.*) budget del fabbisogno di capitali; **~ charges** (*rag.*) spese di capitale; **~ coefficient** (*fin.*) *V.* **~ -output ratio**; **~ consumption allowance** (*econ.*) ammortamento degli investimenti; **~ contribution** (*fin.*) versamento alla massa sociale; **~ duty** (*fin.*) diritto di costituzione, tassa di bollo pagata su ogni azione emessa da una società; **~ equipment** (*rag.*) capitale investito (*in impianti e macchinari*), capitale immobilizzato; **~ expenditure** (*rag.*) investimento di capitali, immobilizzazioni; **~ expenditure account** (*rag.*) conto immobilizzazioni; **~ export restrictions** (*fin.*) restrizioni alle esportazioni di capitali; **~ flight** (*econ., fin.*) fuga di capitali; **~ flows** (*fin.*) movimenti di capitali; **~ fully paid up** (*fin.*) capitale interamente versato; **~ gain** utile di capitale, plusvalenza; **~ gains** (*econ., fin.*) utili di capitale, incrementi di capitale; maggiorazioni del valore di Borsa dei capitali investiti; **~ gains tax** (*fin.*) imposta sulle plusvalenze, cedolare, ritenuta d'acconto; **~ gearing** (*fin.*) rapporto fra i diversi tipi di capitale nella stessa società; **~ goods** (*econ.*) beni capitali, beni strumentali, beni d'investimento; **~ increase** (*fin., rag.*) aumento di capitale; **~ inflation** (*econ.*) inflazione da capitali; **a ~ injection** (*fin.*) un'iniezione di capitale; **~ -intensive** (*econ., fin.*) ad alto impiego di capitali; **~ invested** (*fin.*) capitale investito; **~ levy** (*fin.*) imposta patrimoniale, imposta sul patrimonio; **~ lying idle** (*fin.*) capitale infruttifero; **~ market** (*fin.*) mercato dei capitali, mercato finanziario; **~ movements** (*econ.*) movimenti di capitali; **~ offence** (*leg.*) reato passibile di pena capitale; **~ operations** (*fin.*) operazioni di capitale; **~ -output ratio** (*fin.*) rapporto tra il capitale investito negli impianti e il valore lordo della produzione; **~ owned** (*rag.*) capitale netto; **~ partly paid up** (*fin.*) capitale parzialmente versato; **~ profit** (*fin.*) utile derivante dalla vendita d'attività che non erano state acquistate per essere rivendute; **~ recovery** (*rag.*) ricupero di capitale; **~ redemption reserve fund** (*fin.*) fondo di riserva per i rimborsi di capitale; **~ reserve** (*rag.*) riserva statutaria; **~ stock** (*fin., USA*) capitale azionario; **~ structure** (*fin.*) struttura finanziaria, struttura del capitale (*tipo e numero delle azioni emesse o da* *emettere*); ~ **sum** (*rag.*) capitale; ~ **surplus** (*fin., USA*) «surplus» di capitale (*ammontare pagato dagli azionisti in eccedenza al valore nominale delle azioni*); ~ **transactions** (*fin.*) operazioni di capitale; ~ **transfer** (*fin.*) trasferimento di capitali, trasferimento finanziario; ~ **value** (*rag.*) valore in capitale.

capitalism, *n.* (*econ.*) capitalismo.

capitalist, *n.* (*econ.*) capitalista.

capitalistic, *a.* (*econ.*) capitalistico. // ~ **system** (*econ.*) sistema capitalistico.

capitalizable, *a.* (*rag.*) capitalizzabile.

capitalization, *n.* **1** (*rag.*) capitalizzazione. **2** (*rag.*) capitale complessivo (*d'una società*). // ~ **/ deposit ratio** (*banca*) rapporto tra capitalizzazione e depositi; ~ **issue** (*fin., rag.*) aumento gratuito di capitale; ~ **of interests** (*fin.*) capitalizzazione degli interessi; ~ **of profits** (*fin.*) capitalizzazione degli utili.

capitalize, *v. t.* **1** (*cred., fin.*) finanziare (*un'impresa*). **2** (*giorn.*) scrivere maiuscolo (*o* in maiuscolo). **3** (*rag.*) capitalizzare. **4** (*rag.*) immobilizzare. **5** (*rag.*) valutare il capitale complessivo (*d'una società*). **6** (*rag.*) realizzare il valore attuale di (*un'annualità, una rendita, ecc.*). // to ~ **on st.** trarre vantaggio da qc.

capitalized value, *n.* (*rag.*) valore capitalizzato.

capitation, *n.* (*leg.*) pagamento «pro capite», testatico. // ~ **tax** (*fin.*) imposta personale.

captain, *n.* (*pers., trasp. mar.*) capitano. // ~ **'s copy** (*trasp. mar.*) copia del capitano (*d'una polizza di carico*); ~ **'s entry** (*trasp. mar.*) dichiarazione del capitano (*della nave*) per la dogana; ~ **of foreign-going vessel** (*trasp. mar.*) capitano di lungo corso; ~ **'s protest** (*trasp. mar.*) testimoniale d'avaria, protesta del capitano (*della nave*) per danni subiti dalla nave o dal carico (*prende la forma d'una dichiarazione ufficiale*); ~ **'s report** (*trasp. mar.*) rapporto del capitano.

captainship, *n.* **1** comando, guida. **2** (*trasp. mar.*) grado di capitano.

captation, *n.* (*leg.*) captazione.

capture¹, *n.* **1** presa di possesso. **2** (*leg.*) arresto.

capture², *v. t.* **1** impadronirsi di (*qc.*). **2** (*leg.*) arrestare. // to ~ **the market** (*econ.*) conquistare il mercato.

car, *n.* **1** carro. **2** (*trasp.*) (= **motor-car**) automobile, auto, macchina, vettura. **3** (*trasp. ferr., USA*) vagone ferroviario, carrozza. // ~ **card** (*pubbl.*) manifesto per tram, autobus, metropolitana; ~ **hire** (*trasp.*) noleggio d'automobili; ~ **-maker** costruttore d'automobili; ~ **rental** (*trasp.*) *V.* ~ **hire;** ~ **sharing** uso collettivo di una sola automobile (*per andare al lavoro e tornare a casa*); ~ **stylist** carrozziere, carrozzaio; ~ **tax** (*fin.*) imposta sulle automobili (nuove) (*in G.B.*); ~ **worker** operaio dell'industria automobilistica.

carat, *n.* carato (*unità di misura usata in gioielleria ed equivalente a 2 decigrammi*).

carbon, *n.* **1** carbonio. **2** copia carbone. **3** (*attr. uff.*) foglio di carta carbone. // ~ **copy** copia su carta carbone, copia carbone; ~ **paper** (*attr. uff.*) carta carbone.

card, *n.* **1** biglietto, cartolina, cartoncino. **2** cartellino, tessera. **3** scheda (*per ufficio, biblioteca, o meccanografica*). **4** (*pers.*) libretto (*di marche assicurative*). **5** (*pubbl.*) contrassegno di riconoscimento. // ~ **compiler** (*pers.*) schedatore; ~ **-file** (*attr. uff.*) schedario; ~ **-holder** (*attr. uff.*) schedario; ~ **index** (*attr. uff.*) schedario «cardex» (*mobili e sistema per la conservazione e la schedatura dei documenti*); ~ **-index cabinet** (*attr. uff.*) schedario; ~ **-ledger** (*attr. uff.*) partitario a schede; ~ **money order** (*cred.*) mandato di pagamento; ~ **of admission** biglietto d'entrata, invito; ~ **punch** (*elab. elettr.*) perforatrice di schede.

cardboard, *n.* **1** cartone. **2** (*pubbl.*) cartoncino. // ~ **box** scatola di cartone.

care, *n.* cura, attenzione. // «~ **of general delivery**» (*USA*) «fermo (in) posta»; «**with** ~» (*scritto su una cassa*) «(fare) attenzione», «fragile».

careen¹, *n.* (*trasp. mar.*) sbandata.

careen², *v. t.* **1** (*trasp. mar.*) carenare. **2** (*trasp. mar.*) far sbandare.

careenage, *n.* (*trasp. mar.*) (spese di) carenaggio.

careening, *n.* **1** (*trasp. mar.*) carenamento. **2** (*trasp. mar.*) carenaggio.

career, *n.* carriera. // ~ **brief** (*pers.*) profilo professionale; ~ **-man** (*USA*) carrierista; ~ **opportunity** (*pers.*) possibilità di carriera.

careerism, *n.* carrierismo, arrivismo.

careerist, *n.* carrierista, arrivista.

caretaker, *n.* (*pers.*) guardiano, custode, sorvegliante. // ~ **Cabinet** Governo d'affari.

cargo, *n.* (*pl.* **cargoes** e *reg.*) **1** (*trasp. mar.*) carico (*d'una nave*). **2** (*trasp. mar.*) cargo, nave mercantile. // ~ **and passenger steamer** (*trasp. mar.*) piroscafo per il trasporto di merci e passeggeri; ~ **and passenger vessel** (*trasp. mar.*) nave per il trasporto di merci e passeggeri; ~ **boat** (*trasp. mar.*) nave da carico; ~ **book** (*org. az.*) registro dei carichi; ~ **in bulk** (*trasp. mar.*)

carico alla rinfusa; ~ **insurance** (*ass. mar.*) assicurazione marittima sulle merci; ~ **liner** (*trasp. mar.*) nave mercantile; **a ~ of timber** (*trasp. mar.*) un carico di legname; ~ **passage** (*trasp. mar.*) traversata su nave da carico; ~ **-plane** (*trasp. aer.*) aereo da carico; ~ **policy** (*ass. mar.*) polizza marittima sulle merci; ~ **service** (*trasp. mar.*) servizio su navi da carico; ~ **-ship** (*trasp. mar.*) nave da carico; ~ **steamer** (*trasp. mar.*) vapore da carico, nave da carico; ~ **summary** (*trasp. mar.*) manifesto di bordo; ~ **under-writer** (*ass. mar.*) assicuratore del carico; ~ **vessel** (*trasp. mar.*) nave da carico.

carman, *n.* (*pl.* **carmen**) (*pers.*) camionista. // ~ **'s delivery sheet** (*trasp. aut.*) nota di consegna a domicilio.

carnet, *n.* (*dog.*) permesso temporaneo d'importazione (*d'un automezzo: in esenzione di dazio*).

carriage, *n.* **1** trasporto (*di cose e persone*). **2** porto, spese di trasporto. **3** (*attr. uff.*) carrello (*di macchina da scrivere o contabile*). **4** (*trasp.*) carrozza, vettura. **5** (*trasp. ferr.*) carrozza ferroviaria. // ~ **by land** (*trasp.*) trasporto terrestre; ~ **by rail** (*trasp. ferr.*) trasporto per ferrovia; ~ **by sea** (*trasp.*) trasporto marittimo; ~ **charges** (*trasp.*) spese di trasporto; ~ **company** (*trasp.*) società di trasporti; ~ **forward** spese (di trasporto) a carico del destinatario, porto assegnato, pagabile alla consegna; ~ **free** franco di porto; ~ **lever** (*attr. uff.*) leva d'interlinea (*o* di spaziatura); ~ **note** (*trasp. aut.*) bolletta di spedizione, bolletta di trasporto; ~ **paid** spese (di trasporto) a carico del mittente, porto pagato; franco di porto, porto franco; ~ **rates** (*trasp.*) tariffe dei trasporti.

carried forward, *locuz.* (*rag.*) a riportare.

carrier, *n.* **1** (*trasp.*) imprenditore di trasporti, spedizioniere. **2** (*trasp.*) corriere, vettore, trasportatore. // ~ **'s risk rate** (*trasp. ferr.*) tariffa a rischio del vettore, tariffa generale.

carry[1], *n.* (*mat.*) riporto. // ~ **-back** (*fin., USA*) perdita o utile inutilizzato (*d'un esercizio passato*) detraibile dall'imponibile; ~ **over** residuo, rimanenza; (*Borsa*) riporto; (*fin.*) riporto; (*rag.*) riporto; ~ **-over day** (*Borsa*) primo giorno (dei riporti); ~ **-over of securities** (*banca*) riporto; ~ **-over rate** (*Borsa*) tasso del riporto, premio di riporto.

carry[2], *v. t.* **1** portare, trasportare. **2** (*leg.*) approvare, far passare. **3** (*market.*) trattare, vendere. // to ~ **forward** (*rag.*) riportare a nuovo, riportare (*in fin di pagina*); to ~ **forward the balance of the profit and loss account** (*rag.*) portare a nuovo il saldo del conto profitti e perdite; to ~ **interest** (*rag.*) dare interesse, essere fruttifero; to ~ **on** condurre, mandare avanti (*un'azienda*); esercitare (*un mestiere, un commercio*); to ~ **on trade** esercitare il commercio; to ~ **out** portare a termine, eseguire (*un lavoro, un'ordinazione*); condurre a buon fine (*un piano, ecc.*); to ~ **out the balance of interest in the principal column** (*rag.*) riportare il saldo interessi nella colonna capitali; to ~ **out one's engagements** adempiere ai propri impegni; to ~ **out an enterprise** dar corso a un'impresa; to ~ **out a negotiation** concludere una trattativa; to ~ **out an order** (*market.*) dar corso a un'ordinazione; eseguire, evadere un ordine; to ~ **over** (*Borsa*) fare un riporto; (*fin.*) riportare; (*rag.*) portare a nuovo, riportare (*una cifra ad altra colonna, pagina, libro*); to ~ **over a total** (*rag.*) riportare un totale; to ~ **a piece of news** (*giorn.*) riportare una notizia; to ~ **a resolution** adottare una deliberazione; to ~ **stock** (*Borsa*) riportare titoli, prendere titoli a riporto; to ~ **a sum of money about oneself** portare con sé una somma di denaro; to ~ **to account** (*rag.*) mettere in conto.

carrying, *n.* **1** trasporto. **2** (*leg.*) approvazione (*di una legge, ecc.*). **3** (*rag.*) immobilizzo. // ~ **capacity** (*trasp. mar.*) capacità di carico, portata; ~ **charges** (*rag.*) costi d'immobilizzo; ~ **costs** (*rag.*) spese d'immobilizzo; ~ **forward** (*rag.*) riporto; ~ **out** esecuzione, evasione (*d'un'ordinazione, ecc.*); ~ **over** (*rag.*) riporto: **the ~ over of losses to subsequent years** il riporto delle perdite.

cart[1], *n.* (*trasp.*) carro, carretta. // ~ **note** (*dog.*) lasciapassare.

cart[2], *v. t.* (*trasp.*) trasportare con un carro.

cartage, *n.* **1** (*trasp.*) trasporto (*a mezzo di carro*). **2** (*trasp.*) spese di trasporto. // ~ **contractor** (*trasp.*) spedizioniere; ~ **service** (*trasp.*) servizio di trasporto a domicilio.

cartel, *n.* (*econ.*) «cartello», consorzio; accordo per sostenere prezzi o ripartire mercati. // **a ~ of banks** (*fin.*) un cartello bancario.

cartelization, *n.* (*econ.*) formazione d'un «cartello».

cartelize, *v. t.* e *i.* (*econ.*) formare un «cartello».

carter, *n.* carrettiere.

carting, *n. V.* **cartage.**

carton, *n.* (*market.*) scatola di cartone, «cartone».

cartoon, *n.* (*pubbl.*) cartone animato, disegno animato, vignetta, «fumetto».

carve, *v. t.* incidere, intagliare. // to ~ **up** suddividere.

case[1], *n.* 1 cassa (*da imballaggio*). 2 caso. 3 (*leg.*) causa, processo. // **the ~ at bar** (*leg.*) la causa in discussione; **~ discussion** (*pers., sind.*) discussione di casi; **~ for counsel** (*leg.*) consulenza legale; **~ history** (*pers.*) caso; **~ -law** (*leg.*) giurisprudenza; **~ note** (*slang USA*) dollaro; **~ of need** (*cred.*) bisogno (*per una cambiale*); **~ -study method** (*pers.*) casistica; **in ~ of inevitable accidents** in casi di forza maggiore; **in ~ of need** (*banca, cred.*) al bisogno, occorrendo; **in ~ of rescission** (*leg.*) in caso di rescissione.

case[2], *v. t.* mettere in una cassa, in un astuccio, ecc.

cash[1], *n.* 1 denaro contante, contanti, denaro liquido, finanze, numerario. 2 (*rag.*) cassa, contanti. *avv.* e *a. attr.* in contanti, per contanti. // **~ account** (*rag.*) conto cassa; **~ accounting** (*rag.*) contabilità in contanti; **~ adjustment** (*rag.*) conguaglio in contanti; **a ~ advance** un anticipo in contanti; **~ against documents** pagamento contro documenti; **~ and carry** pagamento in contanti; centro grossisti, self-service all'ingrosso, supermercato per dettaglianti; **~ -and-carry** (*di merce, ecc.*) comprata (*o* venduta) per pagamento in contanti; **~ assets** (*rag.*) attivo liquido, attivo facilmente liquidabile; **~ at the bank** (*fin., rag.*) liquido in banca; **~ balance** (*rag.*) rimanenza di cassa, saldo di cassa; **~ basis method** (*rag.*) metodo di rilevazione contabile in cui la registrazione viene effettuata nel momento in cui si verifica la manifestazione numeraria; **~ bid** (*fin.*) offerta pubblica d'acquisto in contanti; **~ bond** (*fin.*) buono di cassa; **~ book** (*rag.*) libro (di) cassa, cassa; **~ bookkeeping** (*rag.*) contabilità in contanti; **~ box** cassetta per il (denaro) contante; **~ budget** (*rag.*) preventivo di cassa; **~ capital** (*rag.*) capitale in contanti; **~ -clerk** (*pers.*) cassiere; **~ column** (*rag.*) colonna di cassa; **~ control** (*amm.*) controllo di cassa; **~ -credit** (*banca*) apertura di credito; (*rag.*) credito di cassa, credito allo scoperto; **~ deal** operazione in contanti; **~ deficit** (*fin., rag.*) disavanzo di cassa; **~ department** (*org. az.*) ufficio cassa, cassa; **~ desk** (*org. az.*) cassa, sportello di cassa; **~ difference** (*rag.*) differenza di cassa; **~ disbursements journal** (*rag.*) giornale delle uscite di cassa; **~ discount** sconto per contanti, sconto di cassa; **~ dispenser** distributore automatico di moneta; **~ distribution** (*fin.*) conguaglio in contanti; **~ distribution plan** (*pers., sind.*) partecipazione agli utili con distribuzione in contanti; **~ down** per denaro contante, pronta cassa; **~ -down sale** vendita in (*o* per) contanti; **~ drawings** prelievi di cassa; **~ flow** (*org. az.*) insieme delle disponibilità finanziarie utilizzabili (*in un'azienda*); (*rag.*) movimento di cassa; **~ flow statement** (*rag.*) relazione sui movimenti di cassa; **~ forecast** (*rag.*) previsione di cassa; **~ grant** (*fin., rag.*) sovvenzione; **~ holdings** (*econ., fin.*) liquidità; **~ in hand** giacenza (*o* disponibilità) di cassa; liquido (*o* denaro) in cassa, fondo di cassa; **~ inspection** (*rag.*) verifica di cassa; **~ instructions** (*fin.*) istruzioni per l'incasso; **~ journal** (*rag.*) giornale di cassa, libro cassa; **~ market** (*fin.*) mercato a contanti; **~ on account** (*rag.*) contanti in conto; **~ on delivery** (*market.*) contro assegno; pagamento alla consegna, pagamento contro assegno; **~ on delivery fee** tassa per spedizione contro assegno; **~ on delivery parcel** pacco contro assegno; **~ on delivery sale** vendita contro assegno; **~ on hand** *V.* **~ in hand; ~ outlay** (*rag.*) esborso; **~ payment** pagamento in contanti, pagamento a pronti; **~ price** prezzo per contanti; **~ ratio** (*rag.*) rapporto di cassa (*rapporto fra disponibilità di cassa e crediti esigibili e passività correnti*); **~ receipts journal** (*rag.*) giornale delle entrate di cassa; **~ receipts and payments** (*rag.*) entrate e uscite di cassa; **~ register** (*macch. uff.*) registratore di cassa, quietanzatrice; **~ requirement** (*banca*) previsione di cassa; **~ sale** (*market.*) vendita per contanti; **~ settlement** regolamento in contanti; **~ shorts and overs** (*rag.*) ammanchi ed eccedenze di cassa; **~ statement** (*rag.*) situazione di cassa; **~ supply** scorta di contanti, dotazione di cassa; **~ tender** (*fin., USA*) offerta pubblica d'acquisto in contanti; **~ to balance** contanti per il saldo; «**~ value**» (*banca*) «valuta in contanti»; **~ voucher** buono di cassa, scontrino di cassa; **~ warrant** mandato di riscossione; **~ with bank** (*rag.*) capitali in banca; **~ with order** pagamento all'ordinazione; **for ~** in contanti, per contanti, a pronti; **in ~** in contanti, per contanti; **on a ~ basis** (*rag.*) col criterio per cassa.

cash[2], *v. t.* incassare, riscuotere, introitare, convertire in denaro. // to **~ a bill** (*cred.*) incassare una tratta; to **~ a cheque** (*cred.*) incassare un assegno; to **~ in on** st. ricavare un profitto da qc.

cashable, *a.* incassabile, riscuotibile, esigibile.

cashed, *a.* (*cred.*) incassato.

cashier, *n.* (*pers.*) cassiere, cassiera. // **~ and bookkeeper** (*pers.*) cassiere contabile; **~ 's check** (*cred., USA*) assegno circolare; **~ 's desk** (*org. az.*) ufficio cassa, cassa; **~ 's office** (*org. az.*) ufficio cassa, cassa.

cashomat, *n.* (*USA*) distributore automatico

di moneta (*quando viene inserita una tessera d'identità*).

cask, *n.* 1 fusto (*di legno*). 2 barile.

cassation, *n.* (*leg.*) cassazione, annullamento (*d'una sentenza*).

cast[1], *n.* getto, lancio, tiro.

cast[2], *v. t.* (*pass.* e *part. pass.* **cast**) buttare, gettare, lanciare. // to ~ **anchor** (*trasp. mar.*) gettare l'ancora; to ~ **away** (*trasp. mar.*) buttare a mare; to ~ **overboard part of the cargo** (*trasp. mar.*) buttare a mare una parte del carico; to ~ **a vote** dare un voto.

casual, *a.* casuale, accidentale, incerto. // ~ **labour** (*sind.*) lavoro temporaneo; ~ **profit** provento incerto; ~ **sample** (*market.*) campione casuale; ~ **vacancy** (*pers.*) vacanza accidentale; ~ **worker** (*sind.*) lavoratore avventizio, avventizio.

casualty, *n.* 1 disastro. 2 (*ass.*) incidente, sinistro. 3 (*ass.*) responsabilità civile «diversi» (*R.C. diversi*). // ~ **insurance** (*ass.*) assicurazione contro i sinistri, assicurazione infortuni.

catalog[1], *n.* (*USA*) catalogo.

catalog[2], *v. t.* (*USA*) catalogare.

cataloging, *n.* (*USA*) catalogazione.

catalogue[1], *n.* catalogo.

catalogue[2], *v. t.* catalogare, mettere in catalogo.

cataloguing, *n.* catalogazione.

catch[1], *n.* presa. // ~ **-phrase** (*pubbl.*) motto pubblicitario, slogan; ~ **-up** (*econ.*) ripresa.

catch[2], *v. t.* (*pass.* e *part. pass.* **caught**) prendere, afferrare. // to ~ **up** (*econ.*) riprendere, far registrare una ripresa; to **be caught short** (*Borsa*) essere allo scoperto.

catching-up, *n.* (*fin.*) ripresa.

catchword, *n.* (*pubbl.*) slogan.

categories of expenditure, *n. pl.* (*fin.*) categorie di spese.

categories of income, *n. pl.* (*fin.*) categorie di entrate.

cats and dogs, *n. pl.* (*Borsa, slang USA*) titoli di scarso valore.

cattle, *n.* bestiame (*specialm. bovini*). // ~ **-dealer** negoziante di bestiame; ~ **market** mercato del bestiame; ~ **prices** prezzi delle carni bovine; ~ **-show** esposizione di bestiame; ~ **truck** (*trasp.*) vagone bestiame; ~ **wagon** (*trasp.*) vagone bestiame.

causa proxima, *n.* (*trasp. mar.*) causa immediata.

causa remota, *n.* (*trasp. mar.*) causa remota.

cause[1], *n.* 1 causa, motivo, ragione. 2 (*leg.*) causa, processo. // ~ **beyond control** forza maggiore; ~ **-effect relationship** (*org. az.*) rapporto causa-effetto; ~ **-list** (*leg.*) elenco delle cause a ruolo; ~ **of action** (*leg.*) diritto posto a fondamento della propria azione.

cause[2], *v. t.* causare, produrre. // to ~ **to retire** (*pers.*) mettere in pensione, porre in quiescenza.

causeless, *a.* (*leg.*) senza causa.

caution, *n.* (*leg.*) cauzione. // «~ — **level crossing**» (*trasp. aut.*) «attenzione — passaggio a livello»; ~ **money** (*leg.*) cauzione, garanzia.

caveat, *n.* (*leg.*) ammonimento, avvertimento, diffida, intimazione. // ~ **emptor** (*leg., latino*) a rischio dell'acquirente.

cede, *v. t.* 1 cedere. 2 (*leg.*) cedere (*un diritto, un territorio, ecc.*).

ceiling, *n.* 1 soffitto. 2 (*fin.*) livello massimo (*di prezzi, salari, ecc.*). 3 (*fin.*) cielo (*del tunnel monetario*). // ~ **price** (*econ., fin.*) prezzo massimo; calmiere.

censurable, *a.* censurabile, sindacabile.

censure, *v. t.* censurare, sindacare.

census[1], *n.* (*stat.*) censimento. // ~ **of population** (*stat.*) censimento della popolazione; ~ **of production** (*econ., stat.*) censimento della produzione; ~ **paper** (*market.*) modulo per censimenti; ~ **taker** (*stat.*) censitore; ~ **tract** (*market., USA*) settore d'area urbana di 4.000 abitanti circa.

census[2], *v. t.* (*stat.*) censire.

cent, *n.* centesimo (*di dollaro*). // **per** ~ per cento; percentuale (*a.*).

centage, *n.* percentuale.

centime, *n.* centesimo (*di franco, di lira, ecc.*).

centimeter, *n. V.* **centimetre.**

centimetre, *n.* centimetro.

central[1], *a.* centrale. // ~ **bank** (*fin.*) banca centrale; ~ **European time** ora dell'Europa Centrale; ~ **(exchange) rates** (*fin.*) parità centrali (fra cambi).

central[2], *n.* 1 (*USA*) centrale telefonica, centralino. 2 (*USA*) telefonista di centralino, centralinista.

centralization, *n.* (*org. az.*) accentramento, centralizzazione.

centralize, *v. t.* (*org. az.*) accentrare, centralizzare.

centralized, *a.* (*org. az.*) centralizzato. // ~ **files** (*org. az.*) archivio centralizzato; ~ **planning** (*econ.*) pianificazione coercitiva.

centralizer, *n.* accentratore.

centralizing, *a.* accentratore.

centrally-planned economy, *n.* (*econ.*) economia dirigista.

centre, *n.* centro. // ~ **of production**

(*market.*) centro di produzione.

century, *n.* (*slang USA*) cento dollari.

cereals, *n. pl.* (*market.*) cereali.

certain, *a.* 1 certo. 2 certo, alcuno, qualche. // ~ **exchange** (*fin.*) cambio certo.

certifiable, *a.* certificabile, attestabile.

certificate[1], *n.* 1 certificato, attestato, diploma. 2 (*fin.*) cartella (*d'azioni, d'obbligazioni, ecc.*). 3 (*fin.*) titolo. // ~ **book** registro dei certificati; ~ **of airworthiness** (*trasp. aer.*) certificato di navigabilità; ~ **of analysis** (*comm. est.*) certificato d'analisi; ~ **of clearing inwards** (*dog.*) certificato d'arrivo; ~ **of clearing outwards** (*dog.*) certificato d'uscita; ~ **of damage** (*ass. mar.*) certificato d'avaria; ~ **of good character** (*leg.*) certificato di buona condotta; ~ **of incorporation** (*fin.*) certificato attestante l'esistenza legale d'una società, certificato di «registrazione» (*d'una società anonima*); ~ **of insurance** (*ass.*) certificato d'assicurazione; ~ **of issue** (*cred.*) ricevuta di versamento (*d'un vaglia postale*); ~ **of measurement** (*trasp. mar.*) certificato di stazzatura; ~ **of a notary public** (*leg.*) certificato notarile; ~ **of origin** (*comm. est.*) certificato d'origine; ~ **of pratique** (*dog.*) certificato d'ispezione doganale; ~ **of registry** (*trasp. mar.*) certificato d'immatricolazione (*d'una nave*); ~ **of satisfaction** (*leg.*) certificato di radiazione (*d'un'ipoteca*); ~ **of seaworthiness** (*trasp. mar.*) certificato di navigabilità; ~ **of shipment** (*trasp. mar.*) certificato d'imbarco; ~ **of survey** (*trasp. mar.*) certificato d'avaria; ~ **to commence business** certificato che autorizza l'inizio delle attività sociali (*d'una società anonima*).

certificate[2], *v. t.* 1 certificare, attestare. 2 (*leg.*) autorizzare per mezzo di certificati. 3 (*leg.*) abilitare.

certification, *n.* 1 certificazione, attestazione. 2 (*leg.*) autenticazione, legalizzazione, vidimazione. // ~ **mark** (*market.*) marchio d'origine.

certified, *a.* 1 autenticato, attestato. 2 (*leg.*) legalizzato, autenticato, vidimato. // ~ **advertisement** (*pubbl.*) annuncio pubblicitario riguardante la ricerca di personale o l'offerta di lavoro; ~ **broker** sensale autorizzato; ~ **copy** (*leg.*) copia legalizzata, copia autentica; ~ **copy of a deed** (*leg.*) copia autenticata d'un atto; ~ **public accountant** (*pers., USA*) revisore contabile; ragioniere iscritto all'albo; ragioniere (*che esercita la professione secondo le leggi dello Stato che gli ha rilasciato autorizzazione con certificato*); ~ **transfer of stock** (*fin.*) cessione documentata di titoli; ~ **true copy** (*leg.*) copia autentica conforme all'originale, copia conforme.

certify, *v. t.* 1 certificare, attestare. 2 (*leg.*) autenticare, legalizzare, vidimare. 3 garantire (*un assegno, ecc.: da parte di una banca*). // to ~ **a copy of a deed** (*leg.*) legalizzare la copia d'un atto; to ~ **a deed** (*leg.*) legalizzare un atto.

certitude, *n.* attendibilità.

cessation, *n.* cessazione, arresto. // ~ **from work** (*sind.*) sospensione del lavoro.

cesser, *n.* (*leg.*) cessazione.

cession, *n.* (*leg.*) cessione. // ~ **of property** (*leg.*) cessione di proprietà.

cessionary, *n.* (*leg.*) cessionario.

chaffer[1], *n.* mercanteggiamento.

chaffer[2], *v. i.* mercanteggiare, tirare sul prezzo.

chaffering, *n.* mercanteggiamento.

chain, *n.* 1 catena. 2 misura lineare usata in topografia (*equivalente a 1/10 di furlong o 20 metri circa*). // ~ **-reaction** reazione a catena; ~ **rule** (*mat., rag.*) regola catenaria, regola congiunta; ~ **store** (*market., USA*) grande negozio (*appartenente a una «catena»*), grande «magazzino», grandi magazzini.

chair[1], *n.* 1 sedia. 2 **the chair** (*slang USA*) (*per* **chairman**) presidente. // to **be in the** ~ (*org. az.*) avere la presidenza, presiedere.

chair[2], *v. t.* 1 (*org. az.*) insediare, installare. 2 (*fam.*) presiedere.

chairman, *n.* (*pl.* **chairmen**) (*org. az.*) presidente. // ~ **of the board** (*org. az.*) presidente del consiglio d'amministrazione; ~ **of directors** (*org. az.*) presidente del consiglio d'amministrazione.

chairmanship, *n.* (*org. az.*) presidenza.

chairwoman, *n.* (*pl.* **chairwomen**) (*org. az.*) presidentessa.

chalk up, *v. t.* (*fin.*) conseguire, ottenere. // to ~ **a gain of three marks** (*Borsa*) guadagnare tre punti.

challenge[1], *n.* (*leg.*) eccezione.

challenge[2], *v. t.* (*leg.*) fare opposizione a, impugnare.

chamber, *n.* 1 (*leg.*) ufficio di giudice (*presso il tribunale*). 2 (*leg.*) studio d'avvocato. // ~ **of Commerce** Camera di Commercio.

chambers, *n. pl.* 1 gabinetto, studio. 2 (*leg.*) studio d'avvocato. 3 (*leg.*) ufficio privato del giudice. // ~ **of a barrister** studio d'un avvocato.

Chancellor of the Exchequer, *n.* (*ingl.*) Cancelliere dello Scacchiere.

chancery division, *n.* (*leg.*) «chancery division» (*delle tre divisioni di cui è composta la*

«High Court of Justice» è quella che ha la competenza in materia di trust, vendita e ipoteche di immobili, fallimenti, società, diritti d'autore, brevetti, ecc.).

change[1], *n.* **1** cambiamento, cambio, mutamento, modifica, alterazione, trasformazione, variazione. **2** moneta spicciola, spiccioli, resto. **3** **'change** (*Borsa, fam.*) Borsa Valori. **4** (*rag.*) variazione. **5** (*slang USA*) denaro. // ~ **for the better** (*Borsa*) cambiamento al rialzo; ~ **for the worse** (*Borsa*) cambiamento al ribasso; ~ **in the bank rate** (*fin.*) cambiamento del tasso ufficiale di sconto; ~ **in demand and supply** (*econ.*) variazione nella domanda e nell'offerta; ~ **in gearing** (*fin.*) mutamento della composizione del portafoglio; ~ **of address** cambio d'indirizzo; ~ **of class** (*trasp. ferr.*) cambio di classe; ~ **of course** (*trasp. mar.*) *V.* ~ **of route;** ~ **of investments** (*fin.*) arbitraggio (di portafogli); ~ **of route** (*trasp. mar.*) cambiamento di rotta, dirottamento; ~ **of venue** (*leg.*) rinvio (*per incompetenza*) di una causa a un altro tribunale; **on the 'change** (*Borsa, fam.*) alla Borsa Valori, in Borsa.

change[2], *v. t.* **1** cambiare, mutare, modificare, alterare, trasformare. **2** cambiare (*denaro, banconote, ecc.*). // to ~ **one's course** (*o* **one's route**) (*trasp. mar.*) cambiare rotta, dirottare; to ~ **investments** (*fin.*) arbitrare; to ~ **one stock for another** (*fin.*) cambiare un titolo contro un altro; to ~ **trains** (*trasp. ferr.*) cambiare treno, trasbordare; to ~ **U.S. dollars into liras** cambiare dollari in lire.

changer, *n.* (*fin.*) cambiavalute.

channel, *n.* **1** (*pubbl.*) canale (*della televisione*). **2** (*ric. op.*) stazione. **3** (*trasp. mar.*) canale (*passaggio naturale marittimo*). // ~ **of distribution** (*market.*) canale di distribuzione.

Channel port, *n.* porto sulla Manica.

Channel tunnel, *n.* tunnel sotto la Manica.

chapman, *n.* (*pl.* **chapmen**) venditore ambulante.

chapter, *n.* capitolo.

charabanc, *n.* (*trasp.*) giardiniera, torpedone.

char-a-banc, *n.* *V.* **charabanc.**

character, *n.* **1** condotta. **2** (*elab. elettr.*) carattere. **3** (*pers.*) attestato di servizio; benservito (*per un domestico*). **4** (*pubbl.*) carattere di stampa. **5** (*trasp. mar.*) classe (*d'una nave*).

characterize, *v. t.* caratterizzare.

chare, *n.* lavoro fatto quando capita, lavoro a giornata.

charge[1], *n.* **1** carico, onere, dovere, obbligo, impegno, incarico. **2** custodia, cura. **3** costo, prezzo, prezzo richiesto, spesa. **4** (*banca*) fascio (*di biglietti o buoni*); plico. **5** (*leg.*) accusa, capo d'accusa, addebito, incriminazione, imputazione. **6** (*leg.*) privilegio; privilegio speciale (*su un bene*). **7** (*rag.*) addebito, conteggio, imputazione. // ~ **-account** (*market.*) conto aperto presso un negozio (*e utilizzabile per acquisti*); ~ **-account customer** (*market.*) cliente che utilizza un «charge-account»; ~ **and discharge** (*rag.*) carico e scarico; ~ **for call** (*comun.*) prezzo per una chiamata telefonica; **charges for carriage** (*trasp.*) spese di trasporto; ~ **for collection** (*trasp. ferr.*) tariffa per ritiro a domicilio; **charges for custody of securities** (*banca*) diritti di custodia per titoli; ~ **for delivery** (*trasp. ferr.*) tariffa per consegna a domicilio; **charges for freight** (*trasp. mar.*) spese di nolo; ~ **for redirection** (*comun.*) tassa di rispedizione (postale); **charges for telephone calls** (*comun.*) spese per comunicazioni telefoniche; **the** ~ **for a three minutes' conversation** (*comun.*) la tariffa per tre minuti di conversazione; **charges forward** spese assegnate, pagamento posticipato delle spese; **charges in closing a current account** (*banca*) competenze di chiusura; **charges levied on imports** (*fin.*) imposizioni all'importazione; ~ **of costs** (*leg.*) addebito di spese giudiziali; **charges on discount of bills** (*banca*) competenze per sconto d'effetti; ~ **-sheet** (*leg.*) elenco delle cause a ruolo; **at one's own** ~ a proprie spese; to **be in** ~ (*leg.*) essere in stato d'arresto; **without charges** (*banca, cred.*) senza spese.

charge[2], *v. t.* **1** caricare. **2** incaricare. **3** affidare. **4** attribuire, ascrivere (*ad altri*). **5** far pagare, addebitare, mettere in conto, conteggiare. **6** (*fin.*) tassare. **7** (*leg.*) accusare, imputare, incolpare, incriminare. **8** (*rag.*) imputare. **9** (*rag.*) considerare (*qc.*) come perdita, mettere al passivo. // to ~ **an account** (*rag.*) imputare a un conto, addebitare un conto; to ~ **an account with interest** (*rag.*) caricare interessi su un conto; to ~ **by the pound** (*fin.*) tassare a un tanto per libbra; to ~ **the postage to the customer** addebitare al cliente le spese postali; to ~ **a price** chiedere un prezzo; to ~ **to sb.'s account** segnare sul conto di q.; to ~ **with customs duty** (*dog.*) tassare di dazio doganale.

chargeable, *a.* **1** affidabile. **2** ascrivibile, attribuibile. **3** addebitabile, conteggiabile. **4** (*fin.*) imponibile, tassabile. **5** (*leg.*) incriminabile, imputabile. **6** (*rag.*) imputabile. // ~ **lands** (*fin.*) terreni tassabili; ~ **with duty** (*dog.*) tassabile, soggetto a dazio; to **be** ~ **to sb.** (*market., rag.*) essere a carico di q.

charged, *a.* (*leg.*) accusato.

charging, *n.* 1 (*fin.*) prelievo. 2 (*fin.*) tassazione. 3 (*leg.*) imputazione. 4 (*rag.*) imputazione, addebito, conteggio. // ~ **order** (*leg.*) ordine di sequestro (*dei beni di un debitore*).

charitable, *a.* caritatevole, filantropico. // ~ **donations** beneficenza; ~ **institution** (*leg.*) opera pia.

charity, *n.* (*leg.*) opera pia.

chart, *n.* 1 foglio con diagramma, quadro (*per informazioni*), tabella. 2 (*org. az.*) diagramma, grafico, schema. 3 (*trasp. mar.*) carta nautica. // ~ **of accounts** (*rag.*) piano dei conti.

charter[1], *n.* 1 carta, documento di concessione (*governativa o reale*), concessione esclusiva, privilegio, privativa, statuto. 2 (*leg.*) carta costitutiva (*d'una società*), atto istitutivo, statuto (*d'una società*). 3 (*trasp. mar.*) contratto di noleggio, nolo. // ~ **broker** (*trasp. mar.*) sensale di noli; ~ **flight** (*trasp. aer.*) volo charter; ~ **market** (*trasp. mar.*) mercato dei noli; ~ **member** (*fin., USA*) socio fondatore; ~ **-party** (*trasp. mar.*) contratto di nolo, contratto di noleggio, noleggio; ~ **service** (*trasp.*) servizio noleggio; **by Royal** ~ (*leg.*) per decreto reale.

charter[2], *v. t.* (*trasp.*) noleggiare (*navi o aerei*).

charterage, *n.* (*trasp. mar.*) nolo.

chartered, *a.* che gode di certi privilegi (*come concessioni esclusive, ecc.*). // ~ **accountant** ragioniere professionista, ragioniere iscritto all'Ordine, ragioniere membro dell'« Institute of Accountants »; ~ **company** (*fin.*) società commerciale istituita (*in G.B.*) con statuto reale, società commerciale che gode di speciali privilegi conferiti dal sovrano o dal Parlamento; ~ **freight** (*trasp. mar.*) nolo stabilito per contratto; ~ **public accountant** (*org. az., pers.*) ragioniere iscritto all'albo; ~ **vessel** (*trasp. mar.*) nave noleggiata.

charterer, *n.* (*trasp.*) noleggiatore (*di navi o d'aerei*), noleggiante.

chartering, *n.* (*trasp. aer., trasp. mar.*) nolo, noleggio. // ~ **agent** (*trasp. mar.*) mediatore di noli marittimi (*che cerca navi per il carico*); ~ **market** (*trasp. mar.*) *V.* **charter market.**

chattels, *n. pl.* (*leg.*) beni mobili e taluni beni reali (*V. sotto*). // ~ **personal** (*leg.*) beni mobili (*denaro, merci, mobilio, ecc.*); ~ **real** (*leg.*) beni reali non in proprietà assoluta (*un affitto, un raccolto in erba, ecc.; cfr.* «real estate»).

chauffeur, *n.* (*pers.*) autista, conducente.

chauffeuse, *n.* (*pers.*) conducente (*d'auto; donna*).

cheap, *a.* 1 a buon mercato, di poco prezzo, poco costoso, economico, dozzinale. 2 conveniente (*di un prezzo*). 3 (*di negoziante, negozio*) che vende a basso prezzo. *avv.* a buon prezzo, a basso prezzo, economicamente. // ~ **and nasty** di basso costo e di cattiva qualità; ~ **money** (*econ.*) denaro a buon mercato; (*fin.*) credito facile; ~ **sale** (*market.*) vendita a buon mercato; ~ **stuff** (*market.*) roba a buon mercato; **on the** ~ economicamente, a basso (*o* a poco) prezzo: **Italy on the** ~ (*tur.*) l'Italia a poco prezzo.

cheapen, *v. t.* diminuire il prezzo di (*qc.*), deprezzare. *v. i.* calare, diminuire (*di prezzo*).

cheapish, *a.* piuttosto a buon mercato, abbastanza conveniente, alquanto dozzinale.

cheaply, *avv.* a buon mercato, a buon prezzo.

cheapness, *n.* basso prezzo; convenienza (*d'una merce, d'un articolo*); modicità.

cheat[1], *n.* 1 frode, imbroglio, truffa. 2 imbroglione, truffatore.

cheat[2], *v. t.* imbrogliare, truffare. // to ~ **with false pretence** (*leg.*) truffare con raggiri.

check[1], *n.* 1 freno, impedimento. 2 controllo, esame, verifica, riscontro. 3 contrassegno, contromarca, scontrino. 4 (*banca, USA*) *V.* **cheque.** 5 (*USA*) conto (*di trattoria, ecc.*). 6 (*slang USA*) dollaro. *a. attr.* di controllo. // ~ **-book** (*banca, USA*) libretto d'assegni; ~ **certifier** (*banca, macch. uff., USA*) stampigliatrice per certificare la copertura d'un assegno bancario (*che acquista così la validità d'un assegno circolare*); ~ **circuit** (*elab. elettr.*) circuito di controllo; ~ **clerk** (*pers.*) revisore; ~ **endorsing machine** (*macch. uff.*) macchina per effettuare la girata di assegni bancari (*con matrici speciali, per prevenire contraffazioni della firma*); ~ **-in desk** banco d'accettazione (*d'aeroporto*); ~ **-ins** (*tur.*) arrivi (*in un albergo*); ~ **list** (*org. az.*) lista di controllo; ~ **number** numero di controllo; ~ **on delivery** controllo alla consegna; ~ **on ledger postings** (*rag.*) controllo delle registrazioni a mastro; ~ **-out counter** (*market.*) cassa (*di supermercato e sim.*); ~ **-out time** (*tur.*) ora in cui si deve lasciar libera una camera (*in albergo, ecc.*); ~ **-outs** (*tur.*) partenze (*in un albergo*); ~ **protector** (*macch. uff.*) macchina per stampare le cifre di un assegno bancario; ~ **-room** (*USA*) deposito bagagli; ~ **signer** (*macch. uff.*) macchina per firmare assegni bancari (*mediante matrici speciali, per prevenire la contraffazione della firma*); ~ **stub** (*banca, USA*) matrice d'assegno; ~ **survey** (*org. az.*) perizia di controllo; ~ **-till** (*macch. uff.*) registratore di cassa; ~ **-up** (*rag.*) verifica dei conti; ~ **-weigher** verificatore del peso.

check[2], *v. t.* **1** frenare, impedire. **2** controllare, esaminare, verificare, spuntare, riscontrare, sindacare. **3** contrassegnare. **4** (*USA*) depositare (*bagagli, ecc.*). *v. i.* **1** concordare. **2** (*banca, USA*) emettere un assegno bancario. // to ~ **an account** (*rag.*) controllare un conto; to ~ **competition** (*market.*) frenare la concorrenza; to ~ **in** (*trasp. ferr.*) depositare il bagaglio alla stazione; (*tur.*) registrare; registrarsi, registrarsi presso il «receptionist» (*d'un albergo*); to ~ **the luggage** (*trasp. ferr.*) depositare il bagaglio; to ~ **off** spuntare; to ~ **off items** spuntare articoli; to ~ **out** (*tur.*) lasciare libera una stanza (*in albergo*); saldare il conto (*d'un albergo*) e andarsene.

checkable deposit, *n.* (*banca, USA*) deposito traibile.

checker, *n.* **1** chi controlla, esamina, verifica, ecc. **2** (*pers.*) cassiera (*di supermercato*).

checking, *n.* controllo, verifica. // ~ **account** (*banca, USA*) conto corrente; ~ **copy** (*pubbl.*) giustificativo pubblicitario; ~ **slip** (*Borsa*) impegno.

checkoff, *n.* (*sind.*) trattenuta.

checkout, *n.* (*slang USA*) articolo che si vende bene.

checkwriter, *n. V.* **check protector.**

cheerful, *a.* allegro. // to **have a** ~ **aspect** (*Borsa, fin.*) avere una buona disposizione, avere un andamento favorevole.

chemical, *a.* chimico. // ~ **manipulations** (*market.*) manipolazioni chimiche.

chemist, *n.* **1** chimico. **2** (*in G.B.*) farmacista.

cheque, *n.* (*banca*) assegno bancario. // ~ **book** (*banca*) libretto d'assegni; ~ **card** (*banca*) carta assegni (*fino a una certa somma*); ~ **crossed generally** (*banca*) assegno con sbarratura generale; ~ **crossed «not negotiable»** (*banca*) assegno sbarrato con la dicitura «non negoziabile»; ~ **crossed specially** (*banca*) assegno con sbarratura qualificata; ~ **form** (*banca*) modulo d'assegno; ~ **guarantee card** (*banca*) *V.* ~ **card;** ~ **protector** (*macch. uff.*) macchina per stampare le cifre d'un assegno bancario; ~ **stamp** (*banca*) bollo dell'assegno; ~ **to be credited (to sb.'s account)** (*banca, cred.*) assegno per accreditamento; ~ **to bearer** assegno al portatore; ~ **to order** assegno all'ordine; **cheques unpaid** (*banca*) effetti non pagati; ~ **with receipt form attached** assegno con annesso talloncino di versamento.

chief, *a.* **1** principale, più importante, primo (*per importanza*). **2** più elevato (*in grado*). *n.* **1** capo. **2** (il) principale. // ~ **accountant** (*pers.*) ragioniere capo; ~ **clerk** (*pers.*) capoufficio, capufficio; ~ **creditor** creditore principale; ~ **exception** (*leg.*) eccezione principale; ~ **executive officer** (*pers.*) direttore generale; ~ **inspector** (*pers.*) ispettore generale; ~ **of the advertising department** (*pers.*) direttore della pubblicità.

child, *n.* (*pl.* **children**) bambino. // ~ **bounty** (*sind.*) assegni familiari; ~ **'s half-fare ticket** (*trasp.*) biglietto a riduzione per bambini.

chip, *n.* (*slang ingl.*) moneta metallica.

chipboard, *n.* (*pubbl.*) cartone di legno.

chirographary, *a.* (*leg.*) chirografario. // ~ **credit** credito chirografario; ~ **creditor** creditore chirografario; ~ **debenture** obbligazione chirografaria; ~ **debt** *V.* ~ **credit.**

choice, *n.* **1** scelta, assortimento. // ~ **goods** merce scelta, merce di prima scelta; ~ **paper** (*banca*) effetti di prim'ordine.

choosy, *a.* difficile da accontentare, esigente.

Christian name, *n.* nome di battesimo.

Christmas card, *n.* biglietto natalizio.

chronic, *a.* cronico. // ~ **inflation** (*econ.*) inflazione cronica; ~ **unemployment** (*sind.*) disoccupazione cronica.

chronometer, *n.* (*trasp. mar.*) cronometro.

chunnel, *n.* (*trasp.*) (*parola composta di* **channel** *e* **tunnel**) tunnel sotto la Manica.

cipher[1], *n.* **1** cifra. **2** cifrario. **3** (*mat.*) zero. // ~ **code** codice cifrato; ~ **-key** chiave di cifra, cifrario.

cipher[2], *v. t.* cifrare. // to ~ **out** calcolare; to ~ **out a sum** calcolare una somma.

circle, *n.* **1** ambiente. **2** (*trasp.*) circolare. // ~ **line** (*trasp.*) circolare.

circuit, *n.* circuito.

circuitous, *a.* tortuoso.

circular, *a.* e *n.* circolare. // ~ **letter** (*pubbl.*) circolare; ~ **letter of credit** (*banca*) lettera di credito circolare; ~ **note** (*banca*) assegno circolare; biglietto circolare; lettera circolare di credito (*simile al «travellers' cheque»*); ~ **ticket** (*trasp.*) biglietto circolare; ~ **tour ticket** (*trasp.*) libretto di biglietti per un viaggio circolare.

circularize, *v. t.* mandare circolari a (*q.*).

circulate, *v. i.* circolare. *v. t.* far circolare. // to ~ **capital** (*fin.*) far circolare capitali.

circulating, *a.* circolante. // ~ **assets** (*fin.*) capitali circolanti, capitali fluttuanti, capitali mobili, capitali mobiliari; ~ **capital** (*fin.*) capitale circolante; ~ **capitals** (*fin.*) capitali circolanti, capitali mobili, capitali fluttuanti, capitali mobiliari; ~ **medium** (*fin.*) moneta corrente, circolante.

circulation, *n.* **1** circolazione, movimento. **2**

(*econ.*) circolazione. **3** (*fin.*) corso. **4** (*mat.*) circuitazione. **5** (*pubbl.*) tiratura. // ~ **audit** (*pubbl.*) controllo della diffusione; ~ **of funds** (*rag.*) giro di capitali; ~ **of money** (*fin.*) circolazione monetaria; ~ **of paper** (*fin.*) circolazione cartacea.

circulator, *n.* (*mat.*) numero periodico.

circumstance, *n.* **1** circostanza. **2** condizione finanziaria.

circumstantial, *a.* (*leg.*) indiziario. // ~ **evidence** (*leg.*) indizi di prova, prove indiziarie; **a** ~ **report** un rapporto circostanziato.

citation, *n.* **1** (*anche leg.*) citazione. **2** (*leg.*) ordine di comparizione.

cite, *v. t.* **1** (*anche leg.*) citare. **2** (*leg.*) chiamare in giudizio.

city[1], *n.* città. // ~ **boundary** cinta daziaria; ~ **clerk** (*pers.*) segretario comunale; ~ **council** consiglio municipale; ~ **employee** (*pers.*) impiegato comunale; ~ **-owned enterprise** (*econ.*) azienda municipalizzata; ~ **-plan** piano regolatore.

City[2] **(the),** *n.* (*fin.*) il centro economico e finanziario di Londra. // ~ **editor** (*giorn.*) redattore finanziario (*d'un quotidiano o d'un settimanale*); ~ **man** (*fin.*) banchiere, commerciante, uomo d'affari della City (*del centro bancario e commerciale di Londra*).

civil, *a.* civile. // ~ **action** (*leg.*) causa civile; ~ **code** (*leg.*) codice civile; ~ **Court** (*leg.*) tribunale civile; ~ **division** (*leg.*) sezione civile; ~ **law** (*leg.*) diritto civile, diritto privato; ~ **rights** (*leg.*) diritti civili; ~ **servant** (*pers.*) impiegato statale, funzionario statale; ~ **service** amministrazione statale; ~ **suit** (*leg.*) causa civile, azione civile; ~ **year** anno civile (*365 giorni*).

civilian, *a.* e *n.* civile. *n.* (*leg.*) civilista. // ~ **spending** (*fin.*) investimenti civili.

civilist, *n.* (*leg.*) civilista.

civilly, *avv.* (*leg.*) civilmente. // ~ **liable** (*leg.*) responsabile civilmente.

clacker, *n.* (*slang USA*) dollaro.

claim[1], *n.* **1** domanda, domanda d'indennizzo, richiesta, pretesa. **2** reclamo. **3** credito. **4** (*ass.*) indennità, indennizzo. **5** (*leg.*) affermazione (*d'un diritto*); domanda (*di riconoscimento d'un diritto*); diritto (*di cui si chiede il riconoscimento*). **6** (*leg.*) eccezione, istanza, ricorso. // **claims (against a business)** (*rag.*) partite di debito; ~ **agent** (*ass. mar., trasp. mar.*) commissario d'avaria; **claims and defences** (*leg.*) azioni ed eccezioni; **claims book** registro dei reclami; ~ **for damages** (*leg.*) reclamo per danni, domanda di danni; ~ **for discharge** (*fin.*) domanda di sgravio; ~ **for indemnity** domanda d'indennizzo; ~ **for losses or damage** (*trasp. mar.*) reclamo per perdita o avaria; ~ **for relief** (*fin.*) domanda di sgravio; ~ **for repayment of duties** (*dog.*) ricorso per rimborso di dazio; ~ **form** modulo per ricorsi; **claims reserve** (*ass.*) riserva per sinistri da liquidare; ~ **secured by bond** (*leg.*) credito privilegiato; ~ **secured by mortgage** (*leg.*) credito garantito da ipoteca; **no** ~ **bonus** (*ass., trasp. aut.*) abbuono in assenza di sinistri.

claim[2], *v. t.* **1** affermare, asserire, sostenere (*d'aver fatto qc.*). **2** chiedere, pretendere, reclamare. **3** (*leg.*) reclamare, esigere (*il riconoscimento d'un diritto, la restituzione di qc., ecc.*). // to ~ **back** reclamare, ripetere; to ~ **damages** (*ass.*) pretendere il risarcimento dei danni.

claimable, *a.* esigibile.

claimant, *n.* **1** chi fa un ricorso (*per ottenere qc.*); ricorrente. **2** (*leg.*) attore (*in giudizio*).

claimer, *n.* *V.* **claimant.**

claiming back, *n.* reclamo.

clam, *n.* (*slang USA*) dollaro.

clandestine, *a.* clandestino. // ~ **trade** commercio clandestino.

clash, *n.* conflitto, urto.

class[1], *n.* **1** classe, categoria. **2** (*trasp.*) classe.

class[2], *v. t.* **1** classificare, assegnare a una classe. **2** (*market.*) cernere. // **«not classed»** (*nelle mostre*) «fuori concorso».

classical economics, *n. pl.* (*col v. al sing.*) (*econ.*) economia classica.

classification, *n.* **1** classificazione, classifica. **2** (*org. az.*) classificazione. **3** (*pers.*) graduatoria. **4** (*rag.*) imputazione. // ~ **certificate** (*trasp. mar.*) certificato di classifica; ~ **clause** (*trasp. mar.*) clausola di classifica; ~ **of goods** classificazione delle merci; ~ **of ships** (*trasp. mar.*) classificazione delle navi.

classified advertisement, *n.* (*giorn.*) inserzione fatta in una rubrica di giornale.

classified advertisements, *n. pl.* (*giorn., pubbl.*) annunci divisi per categorie, piccola pubblicità.

classify, *v. t.* **1** classificare. **2** (*rag.*) imputare.

classing, *n.* classificazione, classifica.

clause, *n.* **1** clausola, articolo. **2** (*leg.*) clausola. // **clauses governing a sale** condizioni di vendita; ~ **of a will** (*leg.*) disposizione testamentaria.

claused bill of lading, *n.* (*trasp. mar.*) polizza di carico recante girate.

claw, *v. t.* **1** artigliare. **2** afferrare. // to ~ **back** (*anche Borsa*) ricuperare.

claw-back, *n.* (*anche Borsa*) ricupero (*di de-*

naro pagato in eccesso).

clawing back, *n.* (*Borsa*) ricupero.

clean[1], *a.* pulito. // ~ **acceptance** (*banca, cred.*) accettazione incondizionata; ~ **bill** (*banca, cred.*) cambiale «netta», tratta libera, tratta non documentata; ~ **bill of health** (*trasp. mar.*) certificato sanitario «pulito»; ~ **bill of lading** (*trasp. mar.*) polizza di carico «pulita» (*esente da eccezioni e/o riserve*); ~ **charter** (*trasp. mar.*) contratto di noleggio senza riserva; ~ **copy** bella copia, buona copia; ~ **credit** (*banca, cred.*) credito non documentario; ~ **ship** (*trasp. mar.*) nave indenne; ~ **-up** (*slang USA*) svendita per cessazione d'esercizio.

clean[2], *v. t.* pulire. // to ~ **up a balance-sheet** (*rag.*) risanare un bilancio (*con l'eliminazione di crediti inesigibili, ecc.*).

clear[1], *a.* **1** libero. **2** netto. // ~ **-cut revival** (*econ.*) netta ripresa; ~ **days** (*leg.*) giorni effettivi (*in un contratto, ecc.*) escluso il primo e l'ultimo; ~ **of ice** (*trasp. mar.*) libero dai ghiacci; ~ **profit** (*rag.*) utile netto; ~ **system of accounts** (*rag.*) contabilità chiara; ~ **title** (*leg.*) titolo incontestabile.

clear[2], *v. t.* **1** chiarire, chiarificare. **2** liberare. **3** fare un guadagno netto di (*una somma*). **4** (*dog.*) svincolare, sdoganare (*merce*). **5** (*fin.*) passare (*un assegno, ecc.*) alla stanza di compensazione. **6** (*trasp. mar.*) dare via libera a (*una nave*). *v. i.* **1** (*fin.*) effettuare operazioni di compensazione. **2** (*trasp. mar.*) entrare in porto (*dopo le formalità doganali*). // to ~ **a bill** (*banca, cred.*) ritirare una cambiale; to ~ **correspondence** (*comun.*) evadere la corrispondenza; to ~ **a debt** (*cred.*) liberarsi da un debito (*pagandolo*); to ~ **the line** (*trasp. ferr.*) dare via libera; to ~ **off the correspondence** sbrigare la corrispondenza; to ~ **oneself from a debt** (*cred.*) liberarsi da un debito; to ~ **out** (*dog., trasp. mar.*) spedire (*una nave*) in dogana; to ~ **outwards** (*dog., trasp. mar.*) spedire (*una nave*) in dogana; to ~ **a parcel of goods** liquidare una partita di merci; to ~ **a ship inwards** (*dog.*) fare l'entrata in dogana d'una nave; to ~ **through the customs** (*dog.*) sdoganare.

clearance, *n.* **1** (*dog.*) sdoganamento (*di merce*), svincolo. **2** (*dog.*) pratica di sdoganamento (*di nave: per entrare in porto o salpare*). **3** (*fin.*) compensazione (*di debiti e crediti: con scambio d'assegni, ecc.*). **4** (*trasp. mar.*) libera pratica. // ~ **house** (*fin.*) stanza di compensazione; ~ **inwards** (*dog., trasp. mar.*) dichiarazione d'entrata, lasciapassare; ~ **papers** (*dog.*) documenti di sdoganamento, documenti di libera pratica, lasciapassare; ~ **sale** (*market.*) vendita di realizzo, (vendita di) liquidazione, svendita; ~ **through the customs** (*dog.*) sdoganamento.

cleared, *a.* (*dog.*) sdoganato, sdaziato, svincolato.

clearer, *n.* (*fam.*) *V.* **clearing bank.**

clearing, *n.* **1** il liberare, lo sgombrare. **2** liquidazione. **3** (*banca*) operazione di compensazione. **4** (*dog.*) sdoganamento, svincolo. **5** (*fin.*) compensazione. **6** (*rag.*) giro di partita, storno. // ~ **account** (*rag.*) partita di giro; ~ **agent** (*banca, fin.*) «agente» di compensazione; ~ **bank** (*banca, fin.*) «clearing bank»; banca che partecipa al sistema della compensazione (*aderendo alla stanza di compensazione di Londra*); ~ **banker** (*banca, fin.*) banca che aderisce alla stanza di compensazione; ~ **department** (*banca, fin.*) ufficio delle compensazioni (*della Banca d'Inghilterra*); ~ **house** (*Borsa*) cassa di liquidazione; (*fin.*) stanza di compensazione; ~ **-in book** (*fin.*) registro degli effetti attivi (*alla stanza di compensazione*); ~ **inwards** (*dog., trasp. mar.*) dichiarazione d'entrata; ~ **-out book** (*fin.*) registro degli effetti passivi (*alla stanza di compensazione*); ~ **sheet** (*Borsa*) foglio di liquidazione; ~ **transaction** (*rag.*) partita di giro; ~ **-up sale** (*market.*) liquidazione delle rimanenze, liquidazione.

clerical, *a.* d'ufficio, impiegatizio. // ~ **duties** (*pers.*) mansioni d'impiegato; ~ **staff** (*pers.*) impiegati, personale; ~ **work** (*org. az.*) lavoro d'ufficio, lavoro impiegatizio.

clerk, *n.* (*pers.*) impiegato. // ~ **of the Court** (*leg.*) cancelliere di tribunale; ~ **of the works** (*pers.*) sovrintendente ai lavori.

clerkdom, *n.* **1** ceto impiegatizio. **2** lavoro d'impiegato.

clerkship, *n.* (*leg.*) ufficio di cancelliere (*di tribunale*).

client, *n.* **1** cliente. **2** (*leg.*) cliente (*di avvocato*). **3 clients,** *pl. collett.* clientela. // ~ **industries** (*econ.*) settori utilizzatori; **clients' ledger** (*rag.*) libro mastro dei clienti.

clientage, *n.* clientela.

clientèle, *n.* clientela.

climate, *n.* (*anche fig.*) clima.

clipped coin, *n.* moneta tosata.

clipping, *n.* (*giorn., pubbl.*) ritaglio di stampa. // ~ **bureau** (*giorn., pubbl.*) ufficio che fornisce ritagli di giornali relativi a una persona, a un prodotto, ecc.

clique, *n.* cricca.

cloak room, *n.* (*trasp. ferr.*) deposito bagagli. // ~ **fee** (*trasp. ferr.*) tariffa per il deposito dei bagagli; ~ **ticket** (*trasp. ferr.*) scontrino di deposito.

clock, *n.* orologio da muro, orologio a pendolo. // ~ **card** (*org. az.*) cartellino di presenza, cartellino segnatempo, cartellino d'entrata e uscita degli operai.

clock in (*o* on), *v. t.* (*pers.*) timbrare il cartellino (*di presenza*) all'entrata.

clock out (*o* off), *v. t.* (*pers.*) timbrare il cartellino (*di presenza*) all'uscita.

close[1], *a.* 1 chiuso. 2 fitto. 3 (*fin.*) difficile (*a ottenersi*); scarso. *n.* 1 fine, conclusione. 2 (*Borsa*) chiusura. // ~ **corporation** (*fin., USA*) società per azioni a costituzione simultanea (*cfr. ingl.* **private limited company**); ~ **-cut price** (*market.*) prezzo ristrettissimo; ~ **of the fiscal year** (*fin., rag.*) chiusura dell'anno finanziario, chiusura dell'esercizio; ~ **-out sale** vendita di liquidazione per cessazione d'esercizio; ~ **port** (*trasp.*) porto interno, porto fluviale; ~ **price** (*market.*) prezzo ristretto; **at the** ~ (*Borsa, fin.*) in chiusura.

close[2], *v. t.* chiudere. *v. i.* finire. // to ~ **an account** (*rag.*) chiudere un conto; to ~ **one's accounts once a year** (*rag.*) chiudere i conti una volta all'anno; to ~ **a bankruptcy** (*leg.*) chiudere un fallimento; to ~ **a bargain** concludere un contratto; to ~ **a current account** (*banca, cred.*) chiudere un conto corrente; to ~ **doors** (*banca*) chiudere gli sportelli; to ~ **a letter** chiudere una lettera; to ~ **the meeting** togliere la seduta; to ~ **out an account** (*rag.*) bilanciare un conto; to ~ **the sitting** (*leg.*) togliere l'udienza; to ~ **a transaction** (*Borsa*) liquidare un'operazione; to ~ **up an account** (*rag.*) chiudere un conto; to ~ **up shop** chiudere bottega (*fig.*); to ~ **with an arrangement** accordarsi, mettersi d'accordo; to ~ **with a heavy deficit** (*fin., rag.*) accusare un disavanzo notevole.

closed, *a.* chiuso. // ~ **company** (*fin.*) società a carattere familiare; ~ **corporation** (*fin.*) società a carattere familiare; **a** ~ **-door session** (*leg.*) una seduta a porte chiuse; ~ **economy** (*econ.*) economia chiusa; ~ **-end fund** (*fin.*) fondo «chiuso» (*cioè, a capitale fisso*); ~ **-end investment fund** (*fin.*) fondo d'investimento «chiuso» (*cioè, a capitale fisso*); ~ **shop** (*sind.*) stabilimento in cui possono essere assunti solo gli appartenenti a un certo sindacato; ~ **system** (*econ.*) sistema economico chiuso; ~ **union** (*sind.*) sindacato che richiede ai propri aderenti il possesso di determinati requisiti professionali.

closely, *avv.* in sommo grado.

closest price, *n.* ultimo prezzo.

closing, *n.* 1 chiusura. 2 (*Borsa*) liquidazione, realizzazione. 3 (*rag.*) chiusura (*di conti*). // ~ **balance** (*rag.*) bilancio di chiusura; ~ **entry** (*rag.*) scrittura di chiusura; ~ **of the application list** (*fin.*) chiusura della sottoscrizione; ~ **price** (*Borsa*) prezzo di chiusura; ~ **procedures** (*rag.*) procedimenti di chiusura; ~ **quotation** (*Borsa*) quotazione di chiusura; ~ **rate** (*Borsa*) corso di chiusura, cambio di chiusura; ~ **speech** discorso di chiusura; ~ **stock** (*org. az.*) giacenza finale; (*rag.*) stock computato alla chiusura dell'esercizio; ~ **time** ora di chiusura (*di negozi, ecc.*); « ~ **time!** » «si chiude!».

closure, *n.* 1 chiusura. 2 conclusione (*di una discussione in un'adunanza, ecc.*).

cloth, *n.* panno. // ~ **bags** sacchi di tela.

clothier, *n.* 1 fabbricante di stoffe. 2 merciaio.

clothing, *n.* abbigliamento. // ~ **trade** commercio di articoli di vestiario.

club[1], *n.* associazione, società. // ~ **car** (*trasp. ferr., USA*) carrozza salone; ~ **trading** (*market.*) vendita a rate con piccoli versamenti mensili (*da parte di persone considerate quasi come soci d'un circolo*).

club[2], *v. t.* offrire (*denaro o altro: per un fine comune*). // to ~ **together** associarsi (*per raccogliere fondi o promuovere attività*).

clue, *n.* indizio.

clumsy, *a.* goffo, malfatto. // **a** ~ **distribution system** (*econ.*) un sistema distributivo poco efficiente.

coach[1], *n.* 1 (*pers.*) istruttore. 2 (*trasp.*) corriera, torpedone. 3 (*trasp. ferr.*) carrozza ferroviaria, vagone, vettura. // ~ **-builder** carrozziere; ~ **repairer** carrozziere.

coach[2], *v. t.* (*pers.*) istruire, addestrare.

coachbuilder, *n.* carrozziere. // ~ **'s shop** carrozzeria (*l'officina*).

coachbuilding, *n.* lavori di carrozzeria.

coaching, *n.* (*pers.*) addestramento, formazione.

coaction, *n.* (*leg.*) coazione, coercizione.

coactive, *a.* (*leg.*) coattivo.

coadjutor, *n.* collaboratore.

coadventurer, *n.* (*leg.*) cointeressato.

coal[1], *n.* carbone (*fossile*). // ~ **bunker** (*trasp. mar.*) carbonile; ~ **exchange** (*fin.*) Borsa del carbone; ~ **-field** bacino carbonifero; ~ **-mine** miniera di carbone; ~ **-pit** miniera di carbone; ~ **port** (*trasp. mar.*) porto carbonifero; ~ **shares** (*fin.*) azioni carbonifere; ~ **ship** (*trasp. mar.*) nave carboniera; ~ **-tar** catrame di carbon fossile; ~ **truck** (*trasp. ferr.*) vagone per il trasporto del carbone; ~ **wagon** (*trasp. ferr.*) vagone per il trasporto del carbone; ~ **wharf** (*trasp. mar.*) molo per il caricamento e lo scaricamento del carbone.

coal[2], *v. t.* (*trasp. mar.*) rifornire (*una nave, ecc.*) di carbone. *v. i.* (*trasp. mar.*) rifornirsi di carbone, far carbone.

coaler, *n.* 1 commerciante di carbone. 2 (*trasp. ferr.*) vagone per il trasporto del carbone. 3 (*trasp. mar.*) carboniera.

coaling, *n.* (*trasp. mar.*) rifornimento di carbone. // ~ **station** (*trasp. mar.*) scalo per rifornimento di carbone.

coalmining, *n.* attività carbonifera.

coast[1], *n.* costa, litorale. // ~ **-defence ship** (*trasp. mar.*) nave guardacoste; ~ **-guard** guardia costiera di finanza; ~ **line** (*trasp. mar.*) linea costiera; ~ **police** polizia costiera; ~ **port** (*trasp. mar.*) porto costiero.

coast[2], *v. t.* e *i.* 1 (*trasp. mar.*) costeggiare. 2 (*trasp. mar.*) fare il commercio costiero, fare il piccolo cabotaggio.

coaster, *n.* (*trasp. mar.*) nave costiera, nave di cabotaggio.

coasting, *n.* (*trasp. mar.*) cabotaggio. // ~ **cargo** (*trasp. mar.*) carico di cabotaggio, merce di cabotaggio; ~ **manifest** (*trasp. mar.*) manifesto di cabotaggio; ~ **navigation** (*trasp. mar.*) navigazione costiera; ~ **port** (*trasp. mar.*) porto di cabotaggio; ~ **ship** (*trasp. mar.*) nave da cabotaggio; ~ **trade** (*trasp. mar.*) commercio costiero, commercio di piccolo cabotaggio, cabotaggio; ~ **vessel** (*trasp. mar.*) nave di cabotaggio.

coastways, *avv.* e *a.* *V.* **coastwise.**

coastwise, *avv.* e *a.* (*trasp. mar.*) lungo la costa. // ~ **navigation** (*trasp. mar.*) navigazione costiera, navigazione di cabotaggio; ~ **trade** (*trasp. mar.*) *V.* **coasting trade.**

coat[1], *n.* 1 giacca. 2 strato superficiale, mano (*di vernice, ecc.*).

coat[2], *v. t.* ricoprire, rivestire.

coated paper, *n.* (*pubbl.*) carta patinata.

coating, *n.* rivestimento, mano (*di vernice, ecc.*).

cocontractant, *n.* (*leg.*) contraente in solido.

cocontracting, *a.* (*leg.*) contraente in solido.

cocreditor, *n.* (*leg.*) creditore in solido.

code[1], *n.* codice (*in ogni senso, eccetto quello di manoscritto antico*); cifrario, cifra. // ~ **address** (*comun.*) indirizzo convenuto; ~ **number** (*comun.*) numero di codice; prefisso (*telefonico*); ~ **of accounts** (*rag., USA*) piano dei conti; ~ **word** (*comun.*) parola in codice.

code[2], *v. t.* codificare, mettere in cifra.

codebtor, *n.* (*leg.*) debitore in solido.

co-defendant, *n.* (*leg.*) coimputato.

codicil, *n.* (*leg.*) codicillo.

codicillary, *a.* (*leg.*) codicillare.

co-director, *n.* (*pers.*) condirettore.

coefficient, *n.* (*mat.*) coefficiente. // ~ **of acceleration** (*econ.*) coefficiente d'accelerazione; ~ **of elasticity** (*econ.*) coefficiente d'elasticità.

coemption, *n.* (*market.*) accaparramento.

coercion, *n.* 1 (*leg.*) coercizione, coazione. 2 (*sind.*) coercizione.

coercitive, *a.* (*leg.*) coercitivo, coattivo.

coffer, *n.* 1 cassa, forziere. 2 **coffers,** *pl.* (*fin.*) riserve (*di valuta o di preziosi*). // **the coffers of the State** le casse dello Stato.

cogestion, *n.* (*econ.*) cogestione.

cognizable, *a.* (*leg.*) soggetto alla giurisdizione di un dato tribunale.

cognizance, *n.* 1 conoscenza. 2 (*leg.*) competenza, giurisdizione. // ~ **of the subject matter** (*leg.*) competenza sulla questione in discussione; ~ **ratione loci** (*leg.*) competenza territoriale; ~ **ratione materiae** (*leg.*) competenza per materia.

cognizant, *a.* 1 che è al corrente (*di qc.*). 2 (*leg.*) competente.

cognomen, *n.* soprannome.

coheir, *n.* (*leg.*) coerede (*uomo*).

coheiress, *n.* (*leg.*) coerede (*donna*).

coin[1], *n.* moneta (*metallica*); denaro. // **coins and currency** (*rag.*) denaro liquido; ~ **holder** (*attr. uff.*) portaspiccioli; ~ **no longer in circulation** moneta fuori corso; ~ **wrapper** (*banca*) fascetta sagomata per avvolgere monete; **in** ~ in contanti, effettivo.

coin[2], *v. t.* coniare. // to ~ **money** coniar monete, batter moneta; (*fig.*) arricchire alla svelta.

coinage, *n.* 1 coniazione, coniatura, conio. 2 sistema monetario in corso. 3 denaro, valuta. // ~ **offence** (*leg.*) reato di falsificazione di moneta.

coincide, *v. i.* coincidere.

coincidence, *n.* coincidenza.

coincidental, *a.* casuale. // ~ **telephone method** (*pubbl.*) metodo di indagine telefonica per il calcolo degli indici di gradimento dei programmi radiotelevisivi.

coiner, *n.* 1 coniatore. 2 falsario.

coinheritance, *n.* (*leg.*) coeredità.

coinsurance, *n.* (*ass.*) coassicurazione.

coinsured, *a.* e *n.* (*ass.*) coassicurato, assicurato in solido.

colessee, *n.* (*leg.*) prenditore in solido.

collaborate, *v. i.* collaborare.

collaboration, *n.* collaborazione.

collaborator, *n.* collaboratore.

collapse[1], *n.* caduta, collasso (*di prezzi, ecc.*). // ~ **of prices** (*econ.*) crollo dei prezzi.

collapse[2], *v. i.* cadere, crollare (*di prezzi, ecc.*).

collar-and-tie worker, *n.* (*sind., slang USA*) impiegato.

collate, *v. t.* (*leg.*) collazionare.

collateral, *a.* 1 collaterale, aggiuntivo. 2 (*leg.*) garantito (*con ipoteca*). *n. collett.* (*cred., fin.*) garanzie reali. // ~ **evidence** (*leg.*) prove aggiuntive; ~ **loan** (*banca, cred.*) prestito garantito; ~ **relation** (*leg.*) linea collaterale; ~ **security** (*banca, cred.*) garanzia aggiuntiva, garanzia collaterale; garanzia reale.

collation, *n.* 1 confronto. 2 (*leg.*) collazione.

colleague, *n.* (*pers.*) collega.

collect, *v. t.* 1 raccogliere. 2 ritirare, ricuperare. 3 riscuotere, incassare. // to ~ **bad debts** ricuperare crediti inesigibili; to ~ **a cheque** (*banca, cred.*) incassare un assegno; to ~ **a debt** riscuotere un credito; to ~ **a dividend** (*fin.*) riscuotere un dividendo; to ~ **an outstanding credit** esigere un credito in sospeso; to ~ **taxes** (*fin.*) riscuotere le imposte.

collectable, *a.* 1 ritirabile. 2 esigibile, riscuotibile, incassabile, ricuperabile. // ~ **credit** credito esigibile.

collected, *a.* incassato, esatto.

collectible, *a. V.* **collectable.**

collecting bank, *n.* banca esattrice.

collecting clerk, *n.* (*pers.*) esattore.

collecting department, *n.* (*banca*) ufficio incassi.

collection, *n.* 1 collezione, raccolta. 2 ricupero. 3 levata (*delle lettere dalle cassette*). 4 riscossione, incasso, esazione. // ~ **at residence** (*trasp.*) presa a domicilio; ~ **at the source** (*fin.*) esazione alla fonte; ~ **charges** (*banca, rag.*) spese d'incasso; ~ **department** (*org. az.*) ufficio incassi; ~ **fees** (*banca*) diritti di riscossione; ~ **of debts** esazione di crediti; **a** ~ **of letters** un carteggio; ~ **of taxes** (*fin.*) esazione delle imposte; ~ **on delivery** pagamento alla consegna, contro assegno; ~ **order** (*rag.*) reversale; ~ **voucher** (*rag.*) reversale.

collective, *a.* collettivo. *n.* collettivo. // ~ **bargaining** (*sind.*) contrattazione collettiva, trattative sindacali collettive; ~ **bargaining agreement** (*sind.*) contratto collettivo di lavoro; ~ **farm** (*econ.*) fattoria collettiva; ~ **goods** (*econ.*) beni pubblici; ~ **labour agreement** (*sind.*) contratto collettivo di lavoro; ~ **ownership** (*econ.*) proprietà collettiva; ~ **training** (*pers.*) tirocinio collettivo; ~ **wage agreements** (*sind.*) contratti collettivi.

collector, *n.* (*pers.*) esattore, ricevitore. // ~ **of customs** (*dog.*) ricevitore delle dogane; ~ **of taxes** (*fin.*) esattore delle imposte; ~ **'s office** esattoria.

collectorate, *n.* (*fin.*) ufficio di esattore delle imposte.

collectorship, *n. V.* **collectorate.**

college, *n.* (*USA*) piccola università. // ~ **graduate** (*pers.*) laureato.

colliding ship, *n.* (*trasp. mar.*) nave investitrice.

collier, *n.* (*trasp. mar.*) (nave) carboniera.

collision, *n.* 1 collisione. 2 conflitto (*d'interessi, ecc.*). 3 (*trasp. mar.*) abbordo, abbordaggio. // ~ **clause** (*trasp. mar.*) clausola d'abbordaggio, clausola relativa alle collisioni; ~ **regulations** (*trasp. mar.*) regolamenti intesi a prevenire le collisioni (*delle navi*); ~ **risk** (*trasp. mar.*) rischio d'abbordaggio.

collusion, *n.* (*leg.*) collusione.

collusive, *a.* (*leg.*) collusivo. // ~ **tendering** (*leg.*) collusione in una gara d'appalto.

collusively, *avv.* (*leg.*) collusivamente.

collusory, *a. V.* **collusive.**

colonial, *a.* coloniale. // ~ **trade** commercio coloniale.

colony, *n.* colonia.

color, *n.* e *composti* (*USA*) *V.* **colour** e *composti.*

colour, *n.* vernice. // ~ **addition** (*pubbl.*) mescolanza di colori; ~ **matching** (*pubbl.*) armonizzazione cromatica; ~ **scale** (*pubbl.*) scala di colori; ~ **slide** (*pubbl.*) diapositiva a colori; ~ **transparency** (*pubbl.*) fotocolor.

column, *n.* 1 colonna. 2 (*giorn.*) rubrica. // ~ **of advertisements** (*pubbl.*) colonna di annunci pubblicitari.

columnist, *n.* (*giorn.*) articolista.

combat, *v. t.* combattere. // to ~ **inflation** (*econ.*) combattere (*o* lottare contro) l'inflazione.

combination, *n.* 1 combinazione. 2 associazione, lega. 3 (*econ., fin.*) fusione, concentrazione, incorporazione (*d'aziende, ecc.*). 4 (*econ., fin.*) *V.* **combine,** *def. 3.* 5 (*leg.*) associazione per delinquere. // ~ **in plain language, code and/or cipher** (*comun.*) linguaggio misto formato da parole comuni e/o cifrate (*per telegrammi*); ~ **in restraint of trade** (*econ., fin.*) accordo (*illegale*) per la restrizione del commercio; ~ **of workers** (*sind.*) lega operaia; ~ **offer** (*market.*) offerta a premio.

combine[1], *n.* 1 accordo. 2 lega, unione. 3 (*fin.*) concentrazione, incorporazione (*d'aziende*); cartello, trust, sindacato.

combine[2], *v. t.* 1 combinare, unire. 2 (*econ., fin.*) concentrare, incorporare, fondere. *v. i.* 1 accordarsi. 2 (*econ., fin.*) fondersi, concentrarsi, incorporarsi.

combined, *a.* combinato. // ~ **demand and supply curve** (*econ.*) curva combinata della domanda e dell'offerta; ~ **entry** (*rag.*) articolo composto; ~ **journal and ledger** (*rag., USA*) giornale americano; ~ **rate** (*trasp.*) tariffa combinata; ~ **ticket** (*trasp.*) biglietto combinato.

come[1], *n.* (*nei composti*). // ~ **-again** proroga, rinvio; ~ **-back** ritorno in auge; ~ **-down** «crollo».

come[2], *v. i.* (*pass.* **came**, *part. pass.* **come**) 1 venire, giungere, arrivare. 2 pervenire. 3 venir bene. 4 venire a costare, ammontare (a). // to ~ **alongside** (*trasp. mar.*) accostare, accostarsi, affiancarsi; to ~ **down** calare (*di prezzi, ecc.*); to ~ **in** rientrare (*di denaro*); to ~ **into collision with another ship** (*trasp. mar.*) entrare in collisione con un'altra nave; to ~ **into force** (*leg.*) entrare in vigore; to ~ **into operation** essere applicato; (*fin.*) diventare fruttifero; to ~ **of age** (*leg.*) uscire di minorità, diventare maggiorenne; to ~ **on demurrage** (*trasp. mar.*) incorrere nelle controstallie; to ~ **on offer** essere offerto; to ~ **out** uscire; (*giorn., pubbl.*) venire fuori, essere pubblicato; to ~ **to** ammontare a, costare; to ~ **to an agreement** raggiungere un accordo, mettersi d'accordo, transigere; to ~ **to anchor** (*trasp. mar.*) ancorarsi; to ~ **to an arrangement** venire a un accordo; to ~ **to sb.'s assistance** venire in aiuto di q.; to ~ **to a conciliation** addivenire a una riconciliazione; to ~ **to a conclusion** venire a una conclusione; to ~ **to an end** finire, terminare; to ~ **to terms** venire a patti, mettersi d'accordo, addivenire a un accordo; to ~ **under sb.'s jurisdiction** (*leg.*) rientrare nell'ambito della giurisdizione di q.; to ~ **within** rientrare in.

comfortable, *a.* 1 comodo. 2 bastevole, soddisfacente.

comics, *n. pl.* (*pubbl.*) fumetti.

comic strip, *n.* (*pubbl.*) fumetto.

coming, *a.* entrante, futuro, venturo. *n.* venuta. // ~ **alongside** (*trasp. mar.*) accostamento; **the** ~ **campaign** (*pubbl.*) la campagna futura; ~ **down** discesa, calo (*di prezzi*); ~ **of age** (*leg.*) raggiungimento dell'età maggiore; ~ **out** (*Borsa*) emissione; ~ **-out price** (*fin.*) prezzo di emissione (*di nuove azioni*); **the** ~ **season** la stagione entrante; **the** ~ **thing** la cosa di domani (*che si sta affermando*), la cosa di moda.

comma, *n.* virgola.

command[1], *n.* comando. // ~ **directed economy** (*econ.*) economia dirigistica; ~ **directing** (*econ.*) dirigismo.

command[2], *v. t.* comandare, intimare.

commander, *n.* 1 comandante. 2 (*trasp. mar.*) comandante (*di una nave, ecc.*).

commence, *v. t.* e *i.* 1 cominciare, incominciare, iniziare. 2 (*leg.*) intentare (*una causa*). // to ~ **proceedings against a debtor** (*leg.*) intentare un'azione contro un debitore.

commencement, *n.* inizio. // ~ **and end of a risk** (*ass.*) inizio e fine d'un rischio.

commencing salary, *n.* (*pers.*) stipendio iniziale.

commend, *v. t.* 1 affidare. 2 raccomandare.

commensurate, *a.* proporzionato.

comment, *v. t.* commentare. // to ~ **on st.** commentare qc., fare commenti su qc.

commerce, *n.* commercio (*in generale, o fatto su larga scala, o fra città o Paesi lontani*). // ~ **technique** tecnica commerciale.

commercial, *a.* commerciale, mercantile. *n.* «stacco» **pubblicitario** (*alla radio o alla televisione*); carosello pubblicitario. // ~ **artist** (*pubbl.*) disegnatore pubblicitario; ~ **attaché** addetto commerciale; ~ **bank** (*banca*) banca commerciale; banca di credito ordinario; ~ **bookkeeping** (*rag.*) contabilità commerciale; ~ **code** (*leg.*) codice commerciale; ~ **concern** impresa commerciale; ~ **correspondence** corrispondenza commerciale; ~ **Court** (*leg.*) tribunale commerciale; ~ **credit** credito commerciale; ~ **credit company** (*fin.*) società finanziaria specializzata nell'acquisto di contratti di vendita rateale, nello sconto di cambiali e nel ricupero di crediti; ~ **defence** difesa commerciale; ~ **directory** indicatore commerciale; ~ **envelope** (*attr. uff.*) busta commerciale; ~ **farm** (*econ.*) azienda agricola; ~ **house** casa di commercio; ~ **intelligence** informazioni commerciali; ~ **intelligence department** ente ministeriale britannico che ha il compito di fornire informazioni ai commercianti (*è un organo del «Board of Trade»*); ~ **law** (*leg.*) diritto commerciale; ~ **lira** (*econ., fin.*) lira commerciale; ~ **marine** (*trasp. mar.*) marina mercantile; ~ **mark** marchio commerciale; ~ **par** (*fin.*) pari commerciale; ~ **policy** politica commerciale; ~ **traveller** (*market., pers.*) commesso viaggiatore, rappresentante di commercio, viaggiatore di commercio, piazzista; ~ **treaty** trattato commerciale; ~ **usage** uso commerciale; ~ **vehicles** autoveicoli industriali.

commercialism, *n.* mercantilismo (*comportamento o spirito da mercante*).

commercialist, *n.* affarista.

commerciality, *n.* carattere commerciale.

commercialization, *n.* commercializzazione.

commercialize, *v. t.* commercializzare, rendere commerciale.

commercially, *avv.* commercialmente.

commersh, *a.* (*slang USA*) commerciale.

comminate, *v. t.* (*leg.*) comminare.

commination, *n.* (*leg.*) comminazione.

comminatory, *a.* (*leg.*) comminatorio.

commission[1], *n.* 1 commissione, provvigione. 2 mandato. 3 (*Borsa*) rimessa. 4 (*leg.*) autorizzazione; autorità, potere (*di fare qc.*). 5 (*leg.*) strumento che conferisce autorità. 6 (*leg.*) commissione, esecuzione (*d'un reato, ecc.*). 7 (*org. az.*) commissione, comitato. // ~ **account** conto provvigioni; ~ **agent** (*market.*) agente commissionario, commissionario; ~ **contract** (*leg.*) contratto di commissione; ~ **for collection of bills** (*banca*) provvigione per l'incasso d'effetti; ~ **house** casa commissionaria; ~ **manufacturer** industriale che produce su commissione; ~ **merchant** (*market.*) commissionario; ~ **note** lettera di garanzia di commissione; ~ **of inspection** (*leg.*) commissione di vigilanza (*nel fallimento*), delegazione di sorveglianza; ~ **of peace** (*leg.*) autorità conferita ai giudici di pace; ~ **on contangoes** (*Borsa*) provvigione sui riporti; ~ **on purchases** provvigione sugli acquisti; ~ **on sales** provvigione sulle vendite; ~ **order** copia commissioni; ~ **order form** copia commissioni; ~ **rates** tariffe di mediazione; **in** ~ (*di persona*) autorizzato, delegato; **out of** ~ (*trasp. mar.*) in disarmo.

commission[2], *v. t.* 1 commissionare, ordinare. 2 autorizzare, delegare, incaricare. *v. i.* dare una commissione.

commissionaire, *n.* 1 (*comm. est.*) commissionario. 2 (*ingl.*) fattorino.

commissioner, *n.* 1 (*leg.*) membro d'una commissione, commissario. 2 (*leg.*) sovrintendente. // ~ **of audit** (*leg.*) consigliere referendario della Corte dei Conti; ~ **of customs** (*dog.*) sovrintendente alle dogane; **the Commissioners of Inland Revenue** (*fin.*) il Fisco.

commissoria lex, *n.* (*leg.*) clausola commissoria.

commit, *v. t.* commettere. // to ~ **a crime** (*leg.*) commettere (*o* consumare) un delitto; to ~ **sb. for trial** (*leg.*) rinviare q. a giudizio; to ~ **a fraud** (*leg.*) frodare; to ~ **money to a bank** depositare denaro in banca; to ~ **an offence** (*leg.*) commettere una colpa (*o* un reato); to ~ **to memory** affidare alla memoria; to ~ **to writing** mettere per iscritto.

commitment, *n.* impegno. // ~ **for trial** (*leg.*) detenzione preventiva.

commit oneself, *v. rifl.* assumere un impegno.

committally, *avv.* in modo impegnativo.

committee, *n.* 1 comitato. 2 (*leg.*) comitato, commissione. // ~ **of creditors** (*leg.*) comitato dei creditori; ~ **of inquiry** (*amm., leg.*) commissione d'inchiesta; ~ **of inspection** (*leg.*) commissione di vigilanza; delegazione di sorveglianza (*delle operazioni fallimentari*); ~ **on credentials** commissione per la verifica dei poteri.

commodatum, *n.* (*pl.* **commodata**) (*leg.*) comodato.

commoditization, *n.* mercificazione.

commodity, *n.* 1 prodotto (agricolo), derrata. 2 merce, articolo (*in genere*). 3 prodotto di base, materia prima, risorsa. // ~ **credits** crediti commerciali; ~ **-currency** (*fin.*) valuta in natura; ~ **Exchange** (*fin.*) Borsa Merci; **commodities intended for home consumption** prodotti destinati al consumo interno; ~ **market** mercato delle materie prime, mercato dei prodotti di base; ~ **prices** corsi commerciali.

common, *a.* 1 comune, ordinario. 2 (*Borsa*) ordinario. *n.* 1 terreno di proprietà comune. 2 (*leg.*) servitù. // ~ **average** (*ass. mar.*) avaria particolare; ~ **carrier** (*trasp.*) corriere, vettore; agenzia di trasporti; (*trasp. aut.*) autotrasportatore; ~ **consumer products** prodotti di grande consumo; ~ **customs tariff** (*dog.*) tariffa doganale comune; ~ **external tariff of the Community** tariffa comune nei confronti dei Paesi terzi; ~ **law** (*leg.*) diritto «comune» (*non esiste in Italia*); legge non scritta; ~ **plea** (*leg.*) causa civile; ~ **policy** (*ass.*) polizza tipo; ~ **pricing market** (*market.*) allineamento dei prezzi (*fra venditori concorrenti*); ~ **stock** (*fin., USA*) azione ordinaria, azioni ordinarie; (*fin.*) titoli ordinari; **by** ~ **consent** di comune accordo.

commonly, *avv.* comunemente.

Commons (the), *n. pl.* (la) Camera dei Comuni.

Commonwealth (the), *n.* (il) «Commonwealth» (*libera associazione di Paesi indipendenti, di lingua ufficiale inglese*). // ~ **preference Countries** (*comm. est.*) Paesi beneficiari delle preferenze del «Commonwealth».

communal, *a.* 1 pertinente a un comune. 2 pubblico. // ~ **land** suolo pubblico; ~ **tenure** (*leg.*) godimento in comune.

communicate, *v. t.* e *i.* comunicare, informare. // to ~ **one's approval to the seller of the goods** comunicare il proprio benestare al venditore della merce; to ~ **by telephone** comunicare per telefono.

communication, *n.* comunicazione. // ~ **axis** (*trasp.*) asse di comunicazione.

communiqué, *n.* 1 comunicato. 2 bollettino (*ufficiale*).

community, *n.* 1 comunità. 2 **the Community** la Comunità (*Economica Europea*). // ~ **financing** finanziamento comunitario; ~ **food aid** aiuti alimentari della Comunità; ~ **law** (*leg.*) diritto comunitario, ordinamento giuridico comunitario; ~ **refunds** (*comm. est.*) restituzioni comunitarie.

commutable, *a.* commutabile. // ~ **punishment** (*leg.*) pena commutabile.

commutation, *n.* commutazione (*di pena, di forma di pagamento, ecc.*). // ~ **ticket** (*trasp.*) biglietto d'abbonamento, abbonamento ferroviario.

commutative, *a.* commutativo. // ~ **contract** (*leg.*) contratto commutativo, contratto bilaterale.

commutor, *n.* (*trasp. ferr.*) pendolare, abbonato ferroviario. // ~ **services** (*trasp. ferr.*) servizi per i pendolari.

comodate, *n.* (*leg.*) comodato.

compact, *n.* accordo, alleanza, convenzione, patto. // ~ **car** automobile di piccole dimensioni.

company, *n.* 1 compagnia, impresa, società. 2 (*leg.*) persona giuridica, società legalmente riconosciuta. 3 (*leg.*) società di capitali. 4 (*leg.*) (= **limited company**) società per azioni. 5 (*trasp. mar.*) equipaggio, ciurma. // **companies act** (*leg.*) legge sulle società per azioni; ~ **'s assets** (*rag.*) attivo sociale; ~ **bid for** (*fin.*) società da rilevare; ~ **bookkeeping** (*rag.*) contabilità sociale; **the ~ 's books** (*fin., rag.*) i libri sociali; ~ **'s capital** (*fin.*) capitale sociale; ~ **'s cash on hand** (*fin.*) cassa sociale; ~ **climate** (*sind.*) clima aziendale; ~ **deeds** atti della società, atti sociali; ~ **director** (*pers.*) amministratore d'una società; ~ **economist** (*econ.*) economista aziendale; ~ **'s fiscal year** anno sociale, esercizio sociale; ~ **goal** (*org. az.*) obiettivo aziendale; ~ **growth** (*org. az.*) sviluppo aziendale; ~ **hierarchy** (*pers.*) gerarchia aziendale; ~ **income tax** (*fin.*) imposta sul reddito delle società per azioni; ~ **law** (*leg.*) legge sulle società, legislazione sulle società; diritto delle società, diritto societario; ~ **loyalty** (*pers.*) fedeltà all'azienda; ~ **policy** (*pers.*) politica aziendale; ~ **profits tax** (*fin.*) *V.* ~ **tax**; ~ **promotor** (*fin.*) socio promotore, socio fondatore; **companies' register office** ufficio del registro per le società per azioni; ~ **report** (*rag.*) relazione di bilancio; ~ **'s risk** (*trasp.*) rischio a carico del vettore; ~ **tax** (*fin.*) imposta societaria (*o* sulle società); ~ **title** (*amm.*) ragione sociale; ~ **union** (*sind.*) sindacato dipendente dall'impresa, sindacato giallo; ~ **with liability limited by guarantee** società a responsabilità limitata «da garanzia» (*non ha equivalente in Italia*); ~ **with liability limited by shares** società a responsabilità limitata dalle azioni (*corrisponde alla «società per azioni» italiana*).

comparable, *a.* paragonabile.

comparative, *a.* comparativo. // ~ **advantages** (*econ.*) vantaggi comparati; ~ **balance** (*rag.*) bilancio comparato; ~ **cost method** (*econ.*) metodo del calcolo della convenienza economica; ~ **studies of competitive products** (*market.*) studi comparativi di prodotti concorrenziali; ~ **study** studio comparativo.

compare, *v. t.* 1 paragonare. 2 (*leg.*) collazionare.

comparing, *n.* 1 paragone, raffronto. 2 (*leg.*) collazione.

compartment, *n.* 1 compartimento, scompartimento. 2 (*trasp. ferr.*) scompartimento.

compass, *n.* (*trasp. mar.*) bussola. // ~ **compensation** (*trasp. mar.*) compensazione della bussola.

compel, *v. t.* costringere, forzare, obbligare.

compendium, *n.* compendio, sunto, specchietto.

compensate, *v. t.* 1 compensare. 2 indennizzare, risarcire.

compensating error, *n.* (*rag.*) errore di compensazione, sbaglio compensativo.

compensating feedback, *n.* (*elab. elettr.*) retroazione a compensazione.

compensation, *n.* 1 compensazione. 2 compenso. 3 risarcimento, indennizzo, indennità. 4 (*pers.*) retribuzione. // ~ **for accident** (*ass.*) indennità per sinistro; ~ **for damages** (*ass.*) risarcimento di danni; ~ **for disability** (*ass.*) risarcimento per invalidità; ~ **for loss of office** (*pers.*) indennità di buonuscita (*data a un amministratore che lascia una società*); ~ **in case of delay** (*trasp.*) indennizzo in caso di ritardo; ~ **in case of dismissal** (*sind.*) indennità (in caso) di licenziamento; ~ **on retirement** (*pers.*) indennità per cessazione d'attività; ~ **stock** (*fin.*) obbligazioni usate come mezzo d'indennizzo per i possessori d'azioni di società nazionalizzate (*in G.B.*); ~ **trade** commercio in compensazione.

compensational, *a.* 1 di (*o* per) compensazione. 2 (*pers.*) retributivo.

compensatory, *a.* compensativo. // ~ **amounts** (*comm. est., econ.*) importi compensativi; ~ **measure** provvedimento compensativo.

compete, *v. i.* competere, concorrere. // to ~ **for** concorrere per; to ~ **for a vacancy** (*pers.*) concorrere a un posto vacante; to ~ **with** far concorrenza a (*qc.*), sostenere la concorrenza di (*q.*); to ~ **with one another** farsi concorrenza.

competence, *n.* **1** competenza, capacità. **2** mezzi di sussistenza. **3** (*leg.*) competenza (*di giudice, di pubblico ufficio, ecc.*). **4** (*leg.*) capacità (*di testimoniare, di testare*). **5** (*leg.*) ammissibilità (*di prova*). **6** (*rag.*) entrata, rendita. // ~ **clause** (*leg.*) clausola di giurisdizione; ~ **of persons** (*leg.*) capacità civile delle persone.

competent, *a.* **1** competente, capace, qualificato. **2** adeguato. **3** (*leg.*) competente. // ~ **Court** (*leg.*) tribunale competente; ~ **judge** (*leg.*) giudice competente; ~ **understanding of the law** (*leg.*) adeguata comprensione della legge.

competing, *a.* concorrente, concorrenziale. // ~ **goods** prodotti in concorrenza; ~ **industries** industrie concorrenti.

competish, *n.* (*slang USA*) concorrenza.

competition, *n.* **1** competizione, concorso, gara. **2** concorrenza. // ~ **among the majors** (*econ.*) lotta oligopolistica; ~ **law** (*comm., leg.*) diritto della concorrenza; ~ **policy** (*econ.*) politica della concorrenza; **not for** ~ fuori concorso.

competitive, *a.* **1** concorrenziale, competitivo. **2** in concorrenza. // ~ **advertising** (*pubbl.*) pubblicità concorrenziale (*pubblicità commerciale diretta a controbattere l'azione pubblicitaria dei concorrenti*); ~ **demand** (*econ.*) domanda concorrenziale; ~ **exam** (*pers.*) esame di concorso; ~ **firms** ditte in concorrenza; **a** ~ **framework** un quadro concorrenziale; ~ **market** mercato concorrenziale; **a** ~ **position** una situazione concorrenziale; **the** ~ **position of the company products** (*market.*) la posizione concorrenziale dei prodotti dell'azienda; ~ **price** (*market.*) prezzo concorrenziale; ~ **products** (*market.*) prodotti concorrenziali; ~ **supply** (*econ.*) offerta concorrenziale, offerta competitiva; ~ **system** (*econ.*) sistema concorrenziale.

competitiveness, *n.* competitività, capacità concorrenziale.

competitor, *n.* **1** concorrente, competitore. **2 competitors,** *pl.* (la) concorrenza.

compilation, *n.* compilazione.

compile, *v. t.* compilare.

complain, *v. i.* **1** lamentarsi, lagnarsi, reclamare. **2** (*leg.*) far causa, muovere querela.

complainant, *n.* **1** chi reclama, reclamante, ricorrente. **2** (*leg.*) querelante, attore, parte civile.

complaint, *n.* **1** lagnanza. **2** reclamo, protesta. **3** disturbo. **4** (*leg.*) querela, denuncia. // **complaints expressed by the customers** lagnanze manifestate dalla clientela; ~ **letter** lettera di reclamo.

complementary, *a.* complementare. // ~ **commodity** (*econ.*) bene complementare; ~ **demand** (*econ.*) domanda complementare; ~ **goods** (*econ.*) beni complementari.

complete[1], *a.* completo, integrale, perfetto.

complete[2], *v. t.* completare, finire, portare a termine, ultimare. // to ~ **a work** ultimare un lavoro.

completely, *avv.* completamente, integralmente.

completion, *n.* completamento, perfezionamento, ultimazione. // ~ **of mandate** (*leg.*) termine del mandato.

complex, *a.* composto, complicato. // ~ **fraction** (*mat.*) frazione complessa.

complexity, *n.* complessità.

compliance, *n.* conformità, osservanza, obbedienza, acquiescenza. // **in** ~ **with the law** (*leg.*) in osservanza alla legge; **in** ~ **with the provisions of Italian law** (*leg.*) in conformità alle disposizioni della legge italiana; **in** ~ **with your orders** in osservanza dei vostri ordini.

complicity, *n.* (*leg.*) complicità.

compliment[1], *n.* omaggio. // **«compliments of the manager»** «omaggio del direttore»; **«with the compliments of the firm»** «con gli omaggi della ditta».

compliment[2], *v. t.* complimentare. // to ~ **sb. on st.** complimentarsi con q. per qc.; to ~ **sb. with st.** fare omaggio a q. di qc.

complimentary, *a.* d'omaggio, in omaggio, di favore. // ~ **close (of a business letter)** chiusura con i convenevoli (d'una lettera commerciale); ~ **copy** copia in omaggio (*d'un libro, ecc.*); ~ **ticket** biglietto di favore.

comply, *v. i.* **1** attenersi (*a una regola, ecc.*), osservare (*una legge, ecc.*). **2** accondiscendere; aderire (*a una richiesta*). // to ~ **with certain common rules as regards production and marketing** conformarsi a un certo numero di norme comuni di produzione e commercializzazione; to ~ **with the clauses of an agreement** (*leg.*) rispettare le clausole d'un contratto.

component, *a.* e *n.* componente. // ~ **part** pezzo (*staccato: di macchina, ecc.*).

compose, *v. t.* **1** comporre. **2** (*sind.*) comporre (*una vertenza, ecc.*).

composite, *a.* composto. // ~ **carriage**

(*trasp. ferr.*) carrozza mista; ~ **credit appraisal** (*banca*) valutazione del fido concedibile; ~ **office** (*ass.*) ufficio che garantisce diversi rami assicurativi; ~ **train** (*trasp. ferr.*) treno misto (*passeggeri e merci*).

composition, *n.* 1 composizione, accomodamento, accordo. 2 (*leg.*) concordato, transazione. 3 (*pubbl.*) composizione (*tipografica*). // ~ **before bankruptcy** (*leg.*) concordato preventivo (*al fallimento*); ~ **deed** (*leg.*) atto di concordato (*tra debitore e creditori*); ~ **for stamp duty** (*fin.*) abbonamento al bollo; **a** ~ **of so much in the pound** (*cred.*) un concordato d'un tanto per sterlina; **a** ~ **of 10 cents in the dollar** (*cred.*) un accordo sulla base di 10 centesimi per dollaro; ~ **with creditors** (*leg.*) concordato fallimentare.

compound[1], *a.* composto. *n.* composto. // ~ **arbitrage** (*fin.*) arbitraggio indiretto; arbitraggio composto; ~ **fraction** (*mat.*) frazione composta; ~ **interest** (*mat., rag.*) interesse composto; ~ **ratio** (*mat., rag.*) proporzione composta, rapporto composto; **the** ~ **rule of three** (*mat.*) la regola del tre composto.

compound[2], *v. t.* 1 comporre. 2 saldare (*un debito: concordando un pagamento inferiore*). 3 (*leg.*) transigere (*una lite*). *v. i.* 1 venire a un accomodamento, accordarsi. 2 (*leg.*) venire a una transazione, fare un concordato. // to ~ **for stamp duty** (*fin.*) abbonarsi al bollo; to ~ **with one's creditors** (*cred.*) accordarsi coi propri creditori.

comprehend, *v. t.* comprendere.

comprehension, *n.* comprensione.

comprehensive, *a.* 1 comprensivo. 2 completo, globale. 3 esauriente. // **a** ~ **competition policy** una politica globale di concorrenza; ~ **policy** (*ass.*) polizza mista.

compressibility, *n.* comprimibilità.

compressible, *a.* comprimibile.

compression, *n.* compressione.

comprise, *v. t.* comprendere, contenere, includere.

compromise[1], *n.* compromesso, convenzione, transazione.

compromise[2], *v. t.* compromettere, accomodare, comporre (*una vertenza*), risolvere (*una questione*) con un compromesso. *v. i.* venire a un compromesso, venire a una transazione. // to ~ **one's share in a transaction** rinunciare alla propria parte in un affare.

comptometer, *n.* (*macch. uff.*) macchina calcolatrice.

compulsion, *n.* coercizione, costrizione, obbligo.

compulsoriness, *n.* obbligatorietà.

compulsory, *a.* coattivo, coercitivo, forzato, forzoso, obbligatorio. // ~ **administration** (*leg.*) amministrazione coattiva; ~ **arbitration** (*leg.*) arbitrato coercitivo; (*sind.*) arbitrato forzato, arbitrato obbligatorio (*imposto dalla legge*); ~ **purchase** (*econ.*) espropriazione per pubblica utilità; ~ **reserve** (*fin.*) riserva obbligatoria; ~ **sale** vendita forzosa; (*leg.*) liquidazione forzata (*di merce*); ~ **settlement** (*leg.*) liquidazione coattiva; ~ **winding up** (*leg.*) liquidazione forzata (*d'una società*), liquidazione disposta dall'autorità giudiziaria.

computable, *a.* computabile.

computation, *n.* computo, calcolo, stima.

compute, *v. t.* computare, calcolare, stimare. // to ~ **an arbitrage** (*Borsa*) calcolare un arbitraggio; to ~ **a bill** (*banca*) calcolare la scadenza d'una cambiale.

computed tare, *n.* tara convenuta.

computer, *n.* 1 (*elab. elettr.*) calcolatore, elaboratore (*elettronico*). 2 (*macch. uff.*) calcolatore, computatore; computatrice (*macchina calcolatrice*).

computerization, *n.* (*elab. elettr., org. az.*) computerizzazione.

computerize, *v. t.* (*elab. elettr., org. az.*) computerizzare.

computerized, *a.* (*elab. elettr., org. az.*) computerizzato. // ~ **tax register** (*fin.*) anagrafe tributaria computerizzata.

con[1], *avv.* e *n.* (il) contro.

con[2], *n.* (*slang USA*) truffa, truffa all'americana. // ~ **man** (*o* **artist**) truffatore, truffaldino.

conceal, *v. t.* 1 occultare (*prove, ecc.*). 2 sopprimere, sottrarre (*prove, ecc.*). 3 sottacere (*fatti*).

concealer, *n.* (*leg.*) occultatore.

concealment, *n.* 1 occultamento. 2 soppressione, sottrazione (*di prove, ecc.*). // ~ **of assets** (*leg.*) sottrazione d'attività (*in un fallimento*); ~ **of profits** (*leg.*) occultamento di utili.

concede, *v. t.* 1 concedere. 2 accogliere. 3 ammettere. // to ~ **claims** accogliere reclami; to ~ **a right** (*leg.*) concedere un diritto.

conceive, *v. t.* ideare.

concentrate, *v. t.* concentrare. *v. i.* concentrarsi.

concentration, *n.* concentrazione (*anche di società, ecc.*).

concern[1], *n.* 1 azienda, ditta, impresa, società. 2 interesse, cointeressenza, partecipazione.

concern[2], *v. t.* concernere. // to ~ **oneself with st.** interessarsi di qc.

concerning, *a.* concernente. // ~ **employers**

(*org. az., sind.*) datoriale (*relativo ai datori di lavoro*); ~ **industrial accidents** (*leg.*) infortunistico; ~ **a patent** (*leg.*) brevettuale.

concessible, *a.* concedibile. // ~ **lands** terreni da dare in concessione.

concession, *n.* 1 concessione, facilitazione. 2 accoglimento. 3 ammissione.

concessionaire, *n.* concessionario.

concessionary, *a.* concessionario. *n.* (*leg.*) concessionario. // ~ **company** società concessionaria.

concessioner, *n.* (*leg.*) concessionario.

conciliate, *v. t.* conciliare.

conciliation, *n.* conciliazione.

conciliator, *n.* (*sind.*) arbitro.

conclude, *v. t.* concludere. // to ~ **a bargain** concludere un affare.

conclusion, *n.* conclusione, chiusa. // ~ **by judgement** (*leg.*) decisione giudiziaria.

conclusive, *a.* 1 conclusivo, decisivo, finale. 2 perentorio. // ~ **evidence** (*leg.*) prova conclusiva, prova decisiva, prova perentoria.

concrete, *a.* concreto, solido.

concur, *v. i.* 1 concorrere. 2 coincidere.

concurrence, *n.* 1 concorso (*di fattori, ecc.*). 2 coincidenza. // ~ **of circumstances** (*leg.*) concorso di circostanze.

concurrent, *a.* 1 coesistente. 2 simultaneo. // « ~ **with discharge** » (*trasp. mar.*) clausola secondo la quale il nolo deve essere pagato in proporzione della quantità di merce scaricata di volta in volta, fino al completamento delle operazioni di scaricamento.

concussion, *n.* (*leg.*) concussione.

condemn, *v. t.* condannare. // to ~ **for default** (*leg.*) condannare in contumacia; to ~ **in costs** (*leg.*) condannare alle spese (giudiziali); to ~ **a ship** (*trasp. mar.*) dichiarare una nave inservibile, radiare una nave.

condemnation, *n.* (*leg.*) condanna, sentenza di condanna. // ~ **by default** (*leg.*) condanna in contumacia.

condensed, *a.* condensato, sintetico. // ~ **balance** (*rag.*) bilancio sintetico; ~ **balance-sheet** (*rag.*) bilancio sintetico.

condition[1], *n.* 1 condizione, stato. 2 (*leg.*) clausola condizionale (*in un contratto*). // **the conditions of a contract** (*leg.*) le condizioni d'un contratto; **the ~ of the market** la condizione (lo stato) del mercato; **conditions of sale** (*market.*) condizioni di vendita; ~ **precedent** (*leg.*) condizione sospensiva; ~ **subsequent** (*leg.*) condizione risolutiva; **on ~ that...** a condizione che..., a patto che...

condition[2], *v. t.* 1 condizionare, regolare. 2 pattuire, stabilire, stipulare. 3 esaminare, verificare la condizione di (*una merce*).

conditional, *a.* 1 condizionale. 2 condizionato. // ~ **acceptance** (*banca, cred.*) accettazione condizionata; ~ **amnesty for tax-evaders** (*fin.*) condono fiscale; ~ **clause** (*leg.*) clausola restrittiva; ~ **discharge** (*leg.*) libertà provvisoria; ~ **provision** (*leg.*) clausola sotto condizione; ~ **sale** (*market.*) vendita condizionata; ~ **sale agreement** (*leg.*) patto di riservato dominio; ~ **upon the deposit of the bills in advance** (*cred.*) subordinato al deposito preliminare degli effetti.

conditionally, *avv.* 1 subordinatamente. 2 (*leg.*) con la condizionale. // to **be ~ discharged for six months** essere prosciolto con la condizionale per sei mesi; ~ **to delivery being made within the end of the season** subordinatamente al fatto che la consegna sia eseguita prima della fine della stagione.

condonation, *n.* condono.

condone, *v. t.* condonare.

conducive to, *a.* che favorisce, che promuove, tendente a.

conduct[1], *n.* 1 condotta, comportamento. 2 modo di condurre (*affari, ecc.*); gestione. // ~ **of business** gestione degli affari.

conduct[2], *v. t.* 1 condurre, dirigere, guidare. 2 amministrare, gestire (*un'azienda, ecc.*). // to ~ **one's affairs in conformity with the laws of the Country** condurre i propri affari in conformità con le leggi del Paese; to ~ **business** occuparsi d'affari; to ~ **a business** trattare un affare; dirigere un'azienda; to ~ **a case** (*leg.*) trattare una causa; to ~ **the correspondence of a firm** sbrigare la corrispondenza d'una ditta.

conductor, *n.* 1 (*pers.*) conduttore, controllore. 2 (*pers.*) guida. 3 (*pers.*) bigliettaio, bigliettario (*di treno, tram o autobus*). 4 (*pers., USA*) controllore ferroviario. 5 (*pers., USA*) capotreno.

confection, *n.* (*market.*) confezione (*abito bell'e fatto*).

confederacy, *n.* confederazione.

confederation, *n.* confederazione.

confer, *v. t.* e *i.* conferire. // to ~ **full powers** conferire pieni poteri; to ~ **with one's lawyer** conferire col proprio avvocato.

conference, *n.* 1 conferenza, convegno. 2 consultazione. 3 discussione. 4 (*org. az.*) riunione. 5 (*pers.*) discussione libera. 6 (*pers.*) discussione guidata. // ~ **room** sala riunioni.

conferment, *n.* conferimento. // ~ **of a right** (*leg.*) conferimento d'un diritto.

confession, *n.* (*anche leg.*) confessione.

confide, *v. t.* e *i.* 1 aver fiducia. 2 affidare.

confidence, *n.* fiducia. // ~ **coefficient** (*market.*) coefficiente di fiducia; ~ **crisis** (*econ.*) crisi di fiducia; ~ **crook** (*leg.*) truffatore; ~ **game** (*leg.*) truffa all'americana; ~ **man** (*leg.*) truffatore; ~ **trick** (*leg.*) truffa all'americana.

confidential, *a.* confidenziale, riservato, segreto. // ~ **clerk** (*pers.*) segretario particolare, segretario privato; ~ **data** dati riservati; ~ **information** informazioni riservate; ~ **report** informazioni confidenziali, informazioni riservate.

confiding, *a.* fiducioso.

confine¹, *n.* (*di solito, al pl.*) confine, frontiera.

confine², *v. t.* limitare. // to ~ **oneself to sb.'s instructions** limitarsi alle istruzioni ricevute.

confined, *a.* limitato, ristretto.

confinement, *n.* limitazione, restrizione.

confirm, *v. t.* 1 confermare, convalidare, omologare. 2 approvare, ratificare. 3 (*leg.*) confermare (*una sentenza, ecc.*); sancire (*una norma, ecc.*). // to ~ **in writing** confermare per iscritto; to ~ **an order** confermare un'ordinazione.

confirmation, *n.* 1 conferma. 2 approvazione, convalida, ratifica. 3 (*leg.*) omologazione. // ~ **of an act** (*leg.*) convalida d'un atto; ~ **of a bankruptcy composition** (*leg.*) omologazione d'un concordato fallimentare; ~ **of a judgment** (*leg.*) conferma d'una sentenza; ~ **of the news** conferma delle notizie.

confirmative, *a.* confermativo.

confirmed, *a.* 1 confermato. 2 approvato, ratificato. // ~ **banker's credit** (*banca*) credito bancario confermato, credito all'esportazione; ~ **credit** (*cred.*) credito confermato, apertura di credito autorizzata; ~, **irrevocable banker's credit** (*banca, cred.*) credito bancario confermato e irrevocabile; ~ **letter of credit** (*cred.*) lettera di credito confermata; ~ **opening of credit** (*cred.*) apertura di credito autorizzata.

confiscable, *a.* (*leg.*) confiscabile, requisibile, sequestrabile.

confiscate, *v. t.* (*leg.*) confiscare, requisire, sequestrare.

confiscation, *n.* (*leg.*) confisca, requisizione, sequestro. // ~ **of falsely entered goods** (*leg.*) confisca di merci registrate in base a falsa dichiarazione; ~ **of property** (*leg.*) confisca di beni.

conflict, *n.* 1 conflitto. 2 (*sind.*) conflittualità. // ~ **of jurisdiction** (*leg.*) conflitto di giurisdizione; ~ **of powers** (*leg.*) conflitto d'attribuzioni; ~ **situation** (*ric. op.*) situazione concorrenziale.

conform, *v. t.* adattare. *v. i.* adeguarsi. // to ~ **to the provisions of the law** attenersi alle disposizioni di legge.

conformable, *a.* conforme.

conforming entry, *n.* (*rag.*) registrazione conforme.

conformity, *n.* conformità. // **in** ~ **with** in conformità di, conformemente a; ai sensi di.

confront, *v. t.* 1 essere di fronte a. 2 mettere a confronto, raffrontare. 3 affrontare.

confrontation, *n.* raffronto. // **the** ~ **of economic budgets** il raffronto dei bilanci economici.

confusion, *n.* confusione. // ~ **of goods** (*leg.*) confusione di beni; ~ **of rights** (*leg.*) confusione di diritti.

congress, *n.* 1 congresso. 2 **the Congress** il Congresso (*degli U.S.A.*).

conjunction, *n.* congiunzione. // **in** ~ **with** d'accordo con.

connect, *v. t.* 1 collegare. 2 associare. 3 mettere in comunicazione (*al telefono*), mettere in linea. 4 (*trasp.*) (*di treno, ecc.*) essere in coincidenza con.

connected, *a.* congiunto. // ~ **with the current economic situation** (*econ.*) congiunturale.

connection, *n.* 1 collegamento. 2 corrispondenza, corrispondente, relazione, rapporto. 3 clientela. 4 (*trasp.*) coincidenza. // **in** ~ **with** a proposito di.

connivance, *n.* (*leg.*) connivenza.

connive, *v. i.* (*leg.*) essere connivente.

conniver, *n.* (*leg.*) connivente.

conniving, *a.* (*leg.*) connivente.

connoisseur, *n.* intenditore.

conquer, *v. t.* conquistare.

consanguinity, *n.* (*leg.*) consanguineità.

conscience money, *n.* (*fin.*) pagamento anonimo d'una somma dovuta al fisco da un contribuente che si pente d'una precedente evasione (*il termine non trova riscontro nella lingua italiana*).

consecutive, *a.* consecutivo, successivo. // **on** ~ **days** in giorni successivi.

consensual, *a.* (*leg.*) consensuale. // ~ **contract** (*leg.*) contratto consensuale.

consent¹, *n.* consenso, accordo, adesione. // ~ **in writing** consenso scritto; ~ **of the Court** (*leg.*) omologazione del tribunale; ~ **of the parties** (*leg.*) consenso delle parti; ~ **to contract** (*leg.*) consenso nel contratto.

consent², *v. i.* consentire, acconsentire, essere d'accordo. // to ~ **to an arrangement** (*leg.*)

acconsentire a un accomodamento; to ~ **to a proposal** acconsentire a una proposta; to ~ **to a purchase** acconsentire a un acquisto.

consenting, *a.* consenziente.

consequential, *a.* che consegue. // ~ **damage** (*leg.*) danno emergente; ~ **damages** (*ass.*) danni indiretti.

conservancy, *n.* (*trasp. mar.*) commissione di controllo (*d'un porto, ecc.*).

conservatism, *n.* (*econ.*) conservatorismo.

conservative, *a.* moderato. *n.* (*econ.*) conservatore.

conservator, *n.* (*leg.*) tutore.

conservatory act, *n.* (*leg.*) atto conservativo.

conservatory seizure, *n.* (*leg.*) sequestro conservativo.

consider, *v. t.* esaminare, stimare. *v. i.* riflettere.

considerable, *a.* considerevole. // **a** ~ **proposal** una proposta degna di considerazione.

consideration, *n.* **1** importanza, interesse. **2** compenso, indennità, retribuzione, provvigione. **3** corrispettivo (*in un contratto*). **4** (*fin.*) copertura. **5** (*fin.*) prezzo d'acquisto d'un titolo azionario, esclusa la tassa di bollo e la mediazione. **6** (*leg.*) beneficio, vantaggio. **7** (*leg.*) causa, causale. // ~ **for sale** prezzo di vendita; ~ **money** prezzo, rimunerazione, indennità; ~ **money for a transfer** (*fin.*) prezzo d'un trasferimento (*di titoli*); **under** ~ in esame; **without** ~ a titolo gratuito.

considering, *avv.* dato, visto (*che*). // ~ **the small amount of capital at his disposal** dati i modesti capitali a sua disposizione.

consign, *v. t.* **1** consegnare, affidare, rilasciare. **2** spedire. **3** spedire in conto deposito. // to ~ **goods to an agent** spedire merce a un agente in conto deposito (*perché ne curi la vendita*); to ~ **a ship to the charterer's agents** (*trasp. mar.*) appoggiare una nave presso i raccomandatari di un noleggiatore.

consignation, *n.* **1** pagamento (*di una somma di denaro*) all'incaricato della riscossione. **2** (*raro*) consegna.

consignee, *n.* **1** consegnatario, depositario. **2** destinatario (*di merci*). // ~ **of a cargo** (*trasp. mar.*) consegnatario d'un carico; ~ **of the ship** (*trasp. mar.*) consegnatario della nave; **at the** ~ **'s risk** (*trasp.*) a rischio del destinatario.

consigner, *n.* **1** chi invia merce in conto deposito, committente. **2** mittente (*di merce*).

consignment, *n.* **1** invio, spedizione, rimessa. **2** consegna in conto deposito. **3** merce spedita, partita (*di merce*). **4** merce inviata in conto deposito. **5** (*trasp. mar.*) carico (*d'una nave*). // ~ **account** conto consegna; conto della merce spedita in deposito; ~ **note** nota di consegna; (*trasp. ferr.*) lettera di vettura, bollettino di spedizione, distinta di carico; ~ **sale** vendita in commissione; **on** ~ (*di merce*) in deposito; **on** ~ **basis** in conto deposito.

consignor, *n.* *V.* **consigner.**

consistency, *n.* **1** solidità. **2** concordanza, accordo.

consistent, *a.* **1** solido. **2** costante. **3** congruo. // ~ **behaviour** condotta coerente.

consociate[1], *a.* consociato, associato. *n.* consocio, socio.

consociate[2], *v. t.* consociare, associare. *v. i.* consociarsi, associarsi.

consociation, *n.* consociazione, associazione.

consol, *n.* **1** (*fin.*) prestito consolidato. **2** (*fin.*) titolo del (prestito) consolidato.

consolidate, *v. t.* **1** consolidare, rafforzare. **2** (*econ., fin.*) fondere, unificare. *v. i.* consolidarsi, rafforzarsi. // to ~ **banks** (*fin.*) fondere banche; to ~ **a debt** (*fin.*) unificare un debito pubblico.

consolidated, *a.* (*fin., rag.*) consolidato, unificato. // ~ **annuities** (*fin.*) titoli del debito pubblico, titoli consolidati, (il) consolidato; ~ **balance** (*rag.*) bilancio consolidato; ~ **balance-sheet** (*rag.*) bilancio unico (*d'una società madre e delle affiliate*); ~ **debt** (*fin.*) debito consolidato; ~ **Fund** (*fin.*) fondo del Tesoro (*presso la Banca d'Inghilterra*); ~ **loan** (*fin.*) prestito consolidato; ~ **stock** (*fin.*) *V.* **consols.**

consolidation, *n.* **1** consolidamento, rafforzamento. **2** (*econ., fin.*) fusione, unificazione, concentrazione (*di aziende, ecc.*). **3** (*fin.*) consolidazione (*del debito pubblico*). **4** (*leg.*) riunione (*d'azioni giudiziarie*). // ~ **act** (*leg.*) legge coordinata (*del Parlamento britannico*); testo unico; ~ **of agricultural holdings** ricomposizione fondiaria; ~ **of the floating debt** (*fin.*) consolidamento del debito fluttuante.

consols, *n. pl.* (*fin.*) titoli del debito pubblico consolidato; titoli del (prestito) consolidato; prestito consolidato; titoli consolidati; (il) consolidato.

consortium, *n.* (*pl.* **consortia**) (*market.*) consorzio.

conspicuous consumption, *n.* (*econ.*) consumi intesi come mezzo per ostentare una ricchezza inesistente.

constable, *n.* guardia, poliziotto.

constant, *a.* costante. // ~ **costs** (*econ.*)

costi costanti; ~ **dollars** (*econ., fin.*) dollari costanti (*in valuta reale, non inflazionata*).

constituency, *n.* abbonati (*a un giornale, ecc.*).

constituent meeting, *n.* (*fin., org. az.*) riunione costitutiva.

constitute, *v. t.* 1 costituire, fondare. 2 comporre, formare, dare un ordinamento a (*un'assemblea*). 3 eleggere, nominare. 4 (*leg.*) costituire. // to ~ **a committee** costituire un comitato; to ~ **a company** (*leg.*) formare una società (*di capitali*).

constitute oneself, *v. rifl.* costituirsi.

constitution, *n.* 1 costituzione, fondazione. 2 composizione, formazione. 3 nomina. 4 (*leg.*) costituzione.

constitutional, *a.* 1 costituzionale. 2 (*leg.*) costituzionale. // ~ **law** (*leg.*) diritto costituzionale.

constitutive, *a.* costitutivo.

construct, *v. t.* costruire.

constructed, *a.* costruito.

construction, *n.* 1 costruzione. 2 (*leg.*) interpretazione, senso. // ~ **firm** impresa di costruzioni.

constructional, *a.* di struttura. // ~ **defect** difetto di costruzione.

constructive, *a.* 1 costruttivo. 2 efficace. 3 dedotto, implicito, presunto. 4 (*leg.*) indiziario. // ~ **industry** (*econ.*) industria edile; ~ **measures** provvedimenti efficaci; ~ **possession** (*leg.*) possesso relativo; ~ **total loss** (*ass. mar.*) perdita totale relativa, perdita totale presunta; ~ **value** (*rag.*) valore presunto.

constructor, *n.* costruttore.

construe, *v. t.* interpretare.

consuetudinary, *a.* consuetudinario. // ~ **law** (*leg.*) diritto consuetudinario.

consul, *n.* console. // ~ **general** console generale.

consulage, *n.* (*comm. est.*) diritti consolari (*che si pagano per ottenere l'emissione d'una fattura consolare*).

consular, *a.* consolare. // ~ **agent** (*pers.*) agente consolare; ~ **charges** diritti consolari; ~ **declaration** (*comm. est.*) dichiarazione consolare; ~ **invoice** (*comm. est.*) fattura consolare; ~ **regulations** disposizioni consolari; ~ **report** rapporto consolare.

consulate, *n.* consolato.

consult, *v. t.* e *i.* 1 consultare. 2 deliberare. // to ~ **a counsel** (*leg.*) consultare un avvocato; to ~ **one's own interests** perseguire il proprio interesse; to ~ **a price list** consultare un listino prezzi.

consultant, *n.* 1 consulente, esperto. 2 (*pers.*) consulente.

consultation, *n.* 1 consultazione. 2 consulenza. 3 consulto.

consultative, *a.* consultivo, consultativo.

consulting counsel, *n.* (*leg.*) avvocato consulente.

consumable, *a.* consumabile.

consumables, *n. pl.* 1 (*market.*) beni di consumo. 2 (*market.*) derrate alimentari.

consume, *v. t.* consumare.

consumer, *n.* 1 consumatore, utente. 2 (*market.*) consumatore. // ~ **behaviour research** (*market.*) ricerca del comportamento del consumatore; ~ **boom** (*econ.*) «boom» dei consumi; ~ **contest** (*pubbl.*) concorso a premi; ~ (*o* **consumers'**) **co-operative** (*market.*) cooperativa di consumo; ~ **Country** Paese consumatore; ~ **credit** (*fin.*) credito al consumatore; ~ **durables** (*econ.*) beni di consumo durevoli; ~ **goods** (*econ.*) beni di consumo; (*market.*) articoli di largo consumo; ~ **'s** (*o* **consumers'**) **goods** (*econ.*) beni di consumo; ~ **groups** associazioni di consumatori; ~ **index** (*market.*) barometro delle marche; ~ **inventory** (*market.*) barometro delle marche; ~ **jury** (*market.*) giuria dei consumatori; ~ **-led boom** (*econ.*) boom alimentato dall'espansione dei consumi; **consumers' organizations** (*market.*) organizzazioni dei consumatori; ~ **panel** (*market.*) comitato di consumatori-pilota; ~ **preference** (*market.*) preferenze del consumatore; ~ **price index** (*econ., USA*) indice mensile del costo della vita compilato dall'«U.S. Bureau of Labor Statistics»; ~ **prices** prezzi al consumo; ~ **spending** spese di consumo; ~ **subsidies** sovvenzioni al consumo; ~ **'s surplus** (*econ.*) rendita del consumatore; **consumers' survey** (*market.*) indagine congiunturale presso i consumatori; ~ **trading area** (*market.*) area commerciale; ~ **trends** (*market.*) dinamica dei consumi; **consumers' union** (*market.*) unione dei consumatori.

consumerism, *n.* (*market.*) consumismo.

consuming Country, *n.* Paese consumatore.

consumption, *n.* 1 consumo. 2 (*econ.*) consumo. // ~ **goods** (*econ.*) beni di consumo; ~ **tax** (*fin.*) imposta sui consumi.

consumptive, *a.* (*econ.*) relativo al consumo (*o* ai consumi).

contact[1], *n.* contatto. // ~ **man** intermediario; (*pers.*) persona alla quale è affidata la rappresentanza d'una ditta (*nei contatti ad alto livello*).

contact[2], *v. t.* 1 mettersi in contatto con (*q.*);

contattare. **2** rivolgersi a (*q.*).

contain, *v. t.* **1** contenere, comprendere, includere. **2** contenere, frenare, reprimere.

container, *n.* **1** contenitore, recipiente. **2** (*trasp.*) «container» (*grande cassone di misura standard*). // ~ **terminal** (*trasp.*) «terminal-container».

containership, *n.* (*trasp. mar.*) (nave) portacontainers.

containment, *n.* contenimento.

contango[1], *n.* **1** (*Borsa*) riporto, contratto di riporto, operazione di riporto. **2** (*fin.*) riporto, interesse di riporto, premio di riporto. // ~ **day** giorno di riporto, giorno dei riporti (*il primo giorno dei tre dedicati alle transazioni in Borsa*); ~ **operation** (*fin.*) operazione a riporto; ~ **rate** (*Borsa*) tasso di riporto.

contango[2], *v. t.* e *i.* (*Borsa*) fare un riporto, riportare. // to ~ **a book from one settlement to the next** (*Borsa*) riportare una posizione da una liquidazione alla successiva.

contangoable, *a.* (*Borsa*) riportabile. // ~ **stocks** (*Borsa*) titoli riportabili.

contangoing, *n.* (*Borsa*) riporto.

contemplate, *v. t.* **1** contemplare. **2** aver in animo di (*fare qc.*); considerare, progettare. // to ~ **a journey** progettare un viaggio.

contempt, *n.* disprezzo. // ~ **of Court** (*leg.*) inosservanza delle disposizioni dell'autorità giudiziaria.

contend, *v. i.* e *t.* contendere, litigare, lottare.

contending, *a.* contendente, litigante. // ~ **parties** (*leg.*) parti litiganti (*in giudizio*).

content, *n.* contenuto.

contention, *n.* **1** controversia. **2** contestazione, reclamo.

contentious, *a.* **1** controverso. **2** (*leg.*) contenzioso. // ~ **clause in a contract** clausola controversa in un contratto; ~ **jurisdiction** (*leg.*) il contenzioso; ~ **procedure** (*leg.*) il contenzioso; ~ **proceedings** (*leg.*) meccanismi contenziosi.

contents, *n. pl.* contenuto. // ~ **of a bill of exchange** importo d'una cambiale; ~ **slip** (*org. az.*) tagliando di controllo; «~ **unknown**» (*trasp. mar.*) «contenuto ignoto» (*in una polizza di carico*).

contest[1], *n.* **1** controversia. **2** contestazione. **3** competizione, concorso, gara. **4** (*leg.*) impugnazione. **5** (*pubbl.*) concorso (*a premi, ecc.*).

contest[2], *v. t.* e *i.* **1** contendere, contrastare. **2** contestare. **3** (*leg.*) impugnare. // to ~ **a claim** (*leg.*) contestare un diritto; to ~ **a contract** (*leg.*) contestare un contratto; to ~ **a will** (*leg.*) contestare un testamento.

contestable, *a.* contestabile.

contestation, *n.* **1** controversia. **2** contestazione, discussione. // **in** ~ in discussione.

contingence, *n.* *V.* **contingency.**

contingency, *n.* **1** congiuntura, circostanza, evenienza. **2** possibilità. **3** caso, occasione. // ~ **budget** (*rag.*) bilancio di riserva; ~ **fund** (*rag.*) fondo di previdenza; ~ **reserve** (*rag.*) riserva di previdenza.

contingent, *a.* **1** contingente. **2** casuale. **3** (*leg.*) soggetto a condizione, condizionato, vincolato. // ~ **damages** (*ass.*) danni contingenti; ~ **fee** (*leg.*) parcella condizionata (*al buon esito della causa patrocinata*); ~ **order** (*Borsa*) ordine vincolato; ~ **profit** (*rag.*) utile aleatorio; ~ **reversibility** reversibilità contingente.

continuable, *a.* (*Borsa*) riportabile. // ~ **stocks** titoli riportabili.

continual, *a.* continuo. // ~ **conflict** (*sind.*) conflittualità permanente; ~ **labor unrest** (*sind.*) conflittualità permanente.

continuance, *n.* **1** durata. **2** (*leg.*) proroga, rinvio.

continuation, *n.* **1** prosecuzione. **2** (*Borsa*) riporto. **3** (*fin.*) riporto. **4** (*leg.*) proroga, rinvio, aggiornamento. // ~ **account** (*Borsa*) riporto; ~ **clause** (*ass. mar.*) clausola che prevede una proroga della validità dell'assicurazione fino al raggiungimento del porto di destino quando la cosa assicurata si trova ancora in mare allo scadere della polizza; ~ **contract** (*Borsa*) contratto di riporto; ~ **day** (*Borsa*) giorno dei riporti; ~ **on foreign exchanges** (*fin.*) riporti su divise; ~ **rate** (*Borsa*) prezzo del riporto, tasso del riporto, corso del riporto.

continue, *v. i.* e *t.* **1** proseguire. **2** (*Borsa*) fare un riporto, riportare. **3** (*leg.*) prorogare, rimandare, rinviare, aggiornare. // to ~ **sb. in office** mantenere q. in carica.

continuing partner, *n.* socio che manda avanti un'azienda (*dopo che gli altri si sono ritirati*).

continuous, *a.* ininterrotto. // ~ **discharge** (*trasp. mar.*) scarico senza interruzione; ~ **process** (*pers.*) processo di produzione a ciclo continuo, lavorazione a catena.

contra[1], *n.* contropartita. // ~ **account** (*rag.*) conto di contropartita, giroconto; ~ **entry** (*rag.*) scrittura inversa; registrazione per storno; **as per** ~ (*rag.*) *V.* **per** ~; **per** ~ (*rag.*) a fianco, a storno, in contropartita.

contra[2], *v. t.* (*rag.*) annullare, stornare. // to ~ **an entry** (*rag.*) stornare una registrazione, stornare una scrittura.

contraband, *n.* contrabbando. // ~ **goods**

merce di contrabbando.

contrabandist, *n.* contrabbandiere.

contract[1]**,** *n.* 1 contratto, convenzione, patto, trattato. 2 appalto. *a. attr.* per contratto, a forfait, forfettario. // ~ **and non-** ~ **rate system** (*trasp. mar.*) sistema delle tariffe differenziate (*fra quelli che hanno un contratto con la «Conferenza» e quelli che non l'hanno*); ~ **freight** (*trasp. mar.*) nolo contrattuale; nolo a tariffa ridotta; ~ **labour** (*sind.*) manodopera contrattuale; manodopera temporanea; ~ **limitation of liability** (*leg.*) limitazione contrattuale di responsabilità; ~ **note** (*Borsa*) nota di contratto; (*fin.*) fissato bollato; (*market.*) modulo di contratto, distinta di compravendita; ~ **of affreightment** (*trasp. mar.*) contratto di trasporto marittimo delle merci; ~ **of carriage** (*trasp.*) contratto di trasporto; ~ **of employment** (*pers.*) contratto di lavoro; ~ **of indemnity** contratto d'indennizzo; ~ **of marine insurance** (*ass. mar.*) contratto d'assicurazione marittima; ~ **of sale** contratto di vendita; ~ **of trust** (*leg.*) contratto di procura; ~ **price** prezzo forfettario; ~ **stamp** (*fin.*) bollo del fissato; ~ **system of wage payment** (*sind.*) sistema di pagamento per lavori a cottimo; ~ **under seal** (*leg.*) contratto mediante atto pubblico; ~ **void and null** (*leg.*) contratto nullo, contratto senza valore; ~ **work** lavoro a contratto; (*amm.*) lavoro d'appalto.

contract[2]**,** *v. t.* (*leg.*) contrarre. *v. i.* contrarsi. // to ~ **debts** (*cred.*) contrarre debiti; to ~ **a loan** (*cred.*) contrarre un mutuo; to ~ **(oneself) out of an engagement** svincolarsi da un impegno.

contractable, *a.* (*leg.*) contraibile.

contractant, *n.* (*leg.*) contraente.

contracting, *a.* (*leg.*) contraente. // **the** ~ **parties** le parti contraenti; ~ **party** parte contraente, parte in causa.

contraction, *n.* contrazione.

contractor, *n.* 1 contraente (*in un contratto*). 2 imprenditore, impresario. 3 appaltatore; aggiudicatario di un appalto.

contractual, *a.* (*leg.*) contrattuale. // ~ **obligation** obbligo contrattuale.

contractually, *avv.* 1 contrattualmente. 2 a forfait.

contradiction, *n.* contraddizione. // ~ **of interests** (*leg.*) conflitto d'interessi.

contradictory, *a.* contraddittorio.

contraing, *n.* (*rag.*) annullamento, storno.

contrary, *a.* contrario. // ~ **evidence** prova contraria; (*leg.*) controprova; ~ **to** contrariamente a; ~ **to our agreements** contrariamente ai nostri accordi; **unless advised to the** ~ salvo contrario avviso; **unless we hear to the** ~ salvo contrordini; **unless instructions to the** ~ **be given** salvo contrarie istruzioni.

contravene, *v. t.* contravvenire a, violare. // to ~ **a law** (*leg.*) trasgredire una legge.

contravention, *n.* (*leg.*) contravvenzione, infrazione, violazione.

contributable, *a.* contribuibile, pagabile come contributo.

contribute, *v. i.* 1 contribuire. 2 collaborare. *v. t.* apportare. // to ~ **an amount of money to a partnership** (*fin.*) conferire una somma di denaro a una società; to ~ **one third** contribuire per un terzo; to ~ **towards the costs** (*leg.*) contribuire alle spese processuali.

contributing, *a.* 1 contribuente. 2 che collabora. // ~ **interests and values** (*ass. mar.*) massa debitrice, massa passiva; ~ **values** (*ass. mar.*) massa debitrice, massa passiva.

contribution, *n.* 1 contribuzione, elargizione, contributo, apporto. 2 quota, quotaparte. 3 (*fin.*) concorso, conferimento (*di capitali*). 4 (*giorn.*) collaborazione. 5 (*pers.*) contributo previdenziale (*o* sociale). // ~ **margin** (*rag.*) margine lordo; ~ **of capital** (*fin.*) apporto di capitale; ~ **to the expenses** (*leg.*) contributo alle spese.

contributive, *a.* contributivo.

contributor, *n.* 1 collaboratore. 2 (*giorn., pubbl.*) collaboratore.

contributory, *a.* contributivo. // ~ **cause** (*leg.*) causa concomitante; ~ **mass** (*ass. mar.*) massa debitrice, massa passiva; ~ **negligence** (*leg.*) concorso di colpa; ~ **pension plans** (*sind.*) piani di pensionamento che prevedono contributi da parte sia del datore di lavoro sia dei dipendenti.

contrivance, *n.* 1 espediente, artificio. 2 macchinazione.

control[1]**,** *n.* 1 controllo. 2 (*org. az.*) controllo. // ~ **account** (*rag.*) conto sintetico; ~ **area** (*org. az.*) area di controllo; ~ **number** (*org. az.*) numero di controllo; ~ **of the cash** (*rag.*) controllo della cassa; ~ **scheme** (*econ.*) regime vincolistico; ~ **survey** (*leg.*) perizia in contraddittorio.

control[2]**,** *v. t.* controllare, tenere sotto il proprio dominio. // to ~ **by regulations** (*leg.*) regolamentare; to ~ **expenditures** contenere le spese.

controllable, *a.* controllabile.

controlled, *a.* controllato. // ~ **circulation** (*pubbl.*) diffusione guidata; ~ **floating** (*econ., fin.*) fluttuazione controllata (*d'una moneta*); ~ **rents** affitti bloccati.

controller, *n.* 1 (*org. az.*) controllore. 2

(*pers.*) controllore. **3** (*pers.*) chi rivede conti; economo. **4** (*pers., USA*) direttore amministrativo. // ~ **of the Mint** (*fin.*) controllore della Zecca.

controlling, *a.* di controllo. // ~ **account** (*rag.*) conto di controllo; ~ **corporation** (*fin., USA*) società dominante; ~ **group** (*econ., fin.*) gruppo di controllo; ~ **interest** (*fin.*) partecipazione di maggioranza; ~ **syndicate** (*econ., fin.*) sindacato di controllo.

controversy, *n.* **1** controversia. **2** (*leg.*) vertenza.

contumacious, *a.* (*leg.*) contumace.

contumacy, *n.* (*leg.*) contumacia.

conurbation, *n.* conurbazione.

convene, *v. t.* **1** convocare, adunare. **2** (*leg.*) convenire, citare (*q.*) in giudizio. *v. i.* convenire, adunarsi. // to ~ **an assembly** convocare un'assemblea; to ~ **sb. before the Court** (*leg.*) citare q. davanti al tribunale; to ~ **a meeting** convocare un'assemblea.

convenience, *n.* convenienza, interesse, utilità. // **for internal** ~ (*org. az.*) per ragioni d'ordine interno.

convenient, *a.* conveniente, comodo, adatto.

convening, *n.* convocazione (*d'assemblea, ecc.*).

convention, *n.* **1** convenzione. **2** (*USA*) convegno, congresso, assemblea. **3 conventions,** *pl.* convenzioni (sociali).

conventional, *a.* convenzionale.

conventionally, *avv.* convenzionalmente.

conversant, *a.* **1** che ha dimestichezza (*con q.*). **2** al corrente (*di qc.*).

converse, *n.* (*mat.*) inverso.

conversion, *n.* **1** conversione, trasformazione. **2** (*fin.*) conversione. **3** (*leg.*) appropriazione indebita. // ~ **costs** (*econ.*) costi di trasformazione (*dalla materia prima al prodotto finito*); ~ **into cash** (*fin., rag.*) realizzo, realizzazione in contanti; ~ **loan** (*cred.*) prestito di conversione; **the** ~ **of a firm** (*fin.*) la trasformazione d'un'azienda; ~ **of a gold currency** (*fin.*) conversione d'una valuta aurea; ~ **of goods** conversione di beni; ~ **of registered securities to bearer** (*fin.*) conversione di titoli nominativi in titoli al portatore; ~ **of securities into cash** (*fin.*) realizzazione di titoli in contante; **a** ~ **project** un progetto di riconversione; ~ **stock** (*fin.*) titoli del debito pubblico, emessi per sostituirne altri già giunti a scadenza.

convert, *v. t.* **1** convertire, trasformare. **2** (*fin.*) convertire. // to ~ **a bank-note into cash** spicciolare un biglietto di banca; to ~ **into cash** (*fin.*) realizzare.

convertibility, *n.* (*fin.*) convertibilità.

convertible, *a.* (*fin.*) convertibile. // ~ **debenture** (*fin.*) obbligazione convertibile; ~ **into cash** (*fin.*) convertibile in contanti, realizzabile; ~ **loan stock** (*fin.*) obbligazioni convertibili (*in azioni*); prestito obbligazionario convertibile (*in azioni*); ~ **preference shares** (*fin.*) azioni privilegiate convertibili (*in azioni ordinarie, della stessa società, a condizioni prefissate*); ~ **securities** (*fin.*) titoli convertibili; ~ **value** (*rag.*) valore di riscatto.

convey, *v. t.* **1** trasportare, portare, convogliare. **2** (*fin.*) trasferire, cedere. **3** (*leg.*) cedere, trasmettere, trasferire (*proprietà ad altri*). // to ~ **goods by rail** trasportare merci per ferrovia; to ~ **goods to a common pool** conferire merci all'ammasso; to ~ **the goods to the place of their destination** trasportare la merce al luogo di destinazione.

conveyance, *n.* **1** trasporto. **2** mezzo di trasporto. **3** (*fin.*) trasferimento, cessione. **4** (*leg.*) cessione, trasferimento, passaggio, trapasso (*di proprietà*). **5** (*leg.*) atto di trasmissione, atto di cessione (*di proprietà*). // ~ **by motor lorries** (*trasp. aut.*) trasporto a mezzo di autocarri; ~ **by sea** trasporto marittimo; ~ **duty** (*leg.*) diritti di trapasso; ~ **of actual chattels** (*leg.*) apporto effettivo; ~ **of goods to a common pool** conferimento di merci all'ammasso; ~ **of a patent** (*leg.*) cessione d'un brevetto; ~ **of property** (*leg.*) passaggio di proprietà; **through** ~ (*trasp.*) trasporto cumulativo.

conveyancing, *n.* (*leg.*) compilazione degli atti e dei documenti necessari per un passaggio di proprietà.

conveyer, *n.* **1** chi trasporta, trasportatore. **2** mezzo di trasporto. **3** latore. **4** (*org. az.*) trasportatore (*macchina per il trasporto di materiali*).

conveying, *n.* (*leg.*) trapasso.

conveyor, *n.* *V.* **conveyer.**

convict[1], *n.* (*leg.*) detenuto, condannato.

convict[2], *v. t.* (*leg.*) condannare.

conviction, *n.* (*leg.*) condanna.

convincing, *a.* convincente. // ~ **evidence** (*leg.*) prova convincente.

convocation, *n.* convocazione.

convoke, *v. t.* convocare.

convoy[1], *n.* **1** (*trasp.*) convoglio. **2** (*trasp.*) scorta. // **under** ~ (*trasp.*) sotto scorta.

convoy[2], *v. t.* (*trasp.*) scortare.

convoying, *n.* **1** (*trasp.*) convoglio. **2** (*trasp.*) scorta.

cool, *v. t.* raffreddare. // to ~ **down** (*fig.*)

raffreddare; raffreddarsi.

cooling, *n.* raffreddamento. // ~ **down** (*anche fig.: dell'economia*) raffreddamento; ~ **off** (*econ.*) flessione (*p. es., nella domanda*); ~ **-off period** (*sind., USA*) periodo in cui (*per effetto d'un'ingiunzione governativa prevista da una legge speciale*) i lavoratori devono astenersi dallo sciopero e i datori di lavoro dalla serrata.

coop, *n. V.* **co-op.**

co-op, *n.* (*econ.*) cooperativa. // ~ **advertising** (*pubbl.*) pubblicità a nome del venditore; **the** ~ **Bank** (*fin., G.B.*) la Banca Cooperativa (*di primaria importanza*); ~ **share** azione d'una cooperativa.

co-operate, *v. i.* **1** cooperare, collaborare. **2** (*sind.*) collaborare. // to ~ **in an enterprise** cooperare a un'impresa.

co-operation, *n.* **1** cooperazione, collaborazione. **2** (*sind.*) collaborazione.

co-operative, *a.* **1** cooperativo. **2** (*amm.*) cooperativo. *n.* (*econ.*) cooperativa. // ~ **advertising** (*pubbl.*) pubblicità a nome del rivenditore; ~ **association** (*econ.*) società cooperativa; ~ **bank** (*banca*) banca cooperativa; ~ **marketing** (*market.*) catena d'acquisti; **the** ~ **movement** (*econ.*) il movimento cooperativo, la cooperazione; ~ **society** (*econ.*) società cooperativa; ~ **store** (*market.*) cooperativa di consumo.

co-operator, *n.* **1** collaboratore. **2** (*pers.*) cooperatore.

co-opt, *v. t.* cooptare, eleggere per cooptazione. // to ~ **a director** eleggere un amministratore per cooptazione.

co-optate, *v. t. V.* **co-opt.**

co-optation, *n.* **1** cooptazione. **2** elezione (*d'un nuovo membro*).

co-option, *n. V.* **co-optation.**

co-ordinate, *v. t.* coordinare.

co-ordination, *n.* **1** coordinamento. **2** (*org. az.*) coordinamento, coordinazione. // **the** ~ **of national regional policies** il coordinamento delle politiche regionali dei singoli Paesi.

co-owner, *n.* **1** contitolare. **2** (*fin., leg.*) comproprietario.

copartner, *n.* consocio, socio, cointeressato, associato.

copartnership, *n.* **1** consociazione. **2** compartecipazione (*agli utili*).

cope with, *v. i.* far fronte a (*una situazione difficile, ecc.*).

copier, *n.* **1** imitatore. **2** (*pers.*) copista.

copper, *n.* (*slang USA*) centesimo di dollaro. // ~ **etching** (*pubbl.*) acquaforte; **the** ~ **market** (*fin.*) il mercato del rame; ~ **or nickel coin** moneta di rame o di nickel; ~ **shares** (*fin.*) azioni delle miniere di rame, azioni cuprifere.

coppers, *n. pl.* **1** monete di rame; spiccioli. **2** (*fin.*) *V.* **copper shares.**

coproprietor, *n.* comproprietario.

copy[1]**,** *n.* **1** copia, imitazione, trascrizione. **2** (*giorn., pubbl.*) testo. **3** (*giorn., pubbl.*) manoscritto (*da stampare*). // ~ **holder** (*attr. uff.*) copialettere; ~ **letter book** (*attr. uff.*) libro copialettere; ~ **of memorandum of satisfaction (of a mortgage)** (*leg.*) certificato di cancellazione (d'un'ipoteca); ~ **testing** (*pubbl.*) controllo dell'efficacia di testi pubblicitari.

copy[2]**,** *v. t.* **1** copiare, imitare, riprodurre, trascrivere. **2** (*pubbl.*) redigere (*testi pubblicitari*). // to ~ **a letter (a document, etc.)** copiare una lettera (un documento, ecc.).

copyhold, *n.* (*leg.*) proprietà d'un terreno, basata su una copia di antichi documenti di concessione feudale.

copying, *a. attr.* copiativo. *n.* copiatura, trascrizione. // ~ **clerk** (*pers.*) copista; ~ **pencil** (*attr. uff.*) matita copiativa; ~ **press** (*attr. uff.*) copialettere; ~ **ribbon** (*attr. uff.*) nastro copiativo (*per macchine da scrivere*).

copyist, *n.* (*pers.*) copista.

copyright[1]**,** *n.* (*leg.*) diritto d'autore, diritti d'autore. *a. attr.* (*leg.*) tutelato da diritto d'autore. // ~ **office** (*leg.*) ufficio per la tutela dei diritti d'autore.

copyright[2]**,** *v. t.* (*leg.*) tutelare (*un libro, ecc.*) in base alle leggi sui diritti d'autore.

copywriter, *n.* (*pubbl.*) copywriter, «creativo» (*chi dirige un testo pubblicitario, chi inventa uno slogan, ecc.*).

cord, *n.* misura inglese di volume, corrispondente a 3,60 metri cubi circa.

cordial, *a.* cordiale.

cordially, *avv.* cordialmente. // «~ **Yours**» Vostro cordialmente (*in chiusura d'una lettera commerciale, soprattutto americana*).

co-respondent, *n.* (*leg.*) correo, coimputato.

corn, *n.* **1** grano, frumento. **2** mais. // ~ **-dealer** grossista in granaglie; ~ **Exchange** (*Borsa*) Borsa dei cereali; ~ **-factor** commerciante in granaglie; ~ **market** (*market.*) mercato dei cereali.

corner[1]**,** *n.* **1** accaparramento, incetta. **2** (*leg.*) imboscamento (*di merce*). // ~ **man** accaparratore, incettatore.

corner[2]**,** *v. t.* **1** accaparrare (*merce*); accaparrarsi; incettare, fare incetta di (*qc.*). **2** mettere in difficoltà. **3** (*leg.*) imboscare (*merce*). // to ~ **the market** accaparrarsi il mercato.

cornerer, *n. V.* **corner man.**

cornering, *n.* incetta; imboscamento (*di merci*). // ~ **the market** (*market.*) accaparramento.

coroner, *n.* (*leg.*) «coroner» (*magistrato inquirente nei casi di morte non naturale*). // ~ **'s jury** giuria che assiste il «coroner» (*e che decide se vi sia causa a procedere in giudizio*).

corporate, *a.* 1 unito. 2 (*USA*) sociale, societario. // ~ **body** società costituita, persona giuridica, ente giuridico; **the ~ books** (*fin.*, *rag.*, *USA*) i libri sociali; ~ **capital** (*fin.*, *USA*) capitale sociale; ~ **cash generation** (*fin.*, *USA*) autofinanziamento (d'una società); ~ **charter** (*fin.*, *USA*) atto costitutivo di società; ~ **climate** (*sind.*, *USA*) clima aziendale; ~ **farm** (*USA*) grossa azienda agricola (*sul modello delle grandi società industriali*); ~ **financial planning** (*fin.*, *USA*) elaborazione di piani di finanziamento per le imprese; ~ **goal** (*org. az.*, *USA*) obiettivo aziendale; ~ **growth** (*org. az.*, *USA*) sviluppo aziendale; ~ **image** (*pubbl.*, *USA*) immagine aziendale; ~ **income tax** (*fin.*, *USA*) imposta sul reddito delle società per azioni; ~ **law** (*leg.*, *USA*) diritto delle società, diritto societario; ~ **merger** (*fin.*, *USA*) fusione d'imprese; ~ **name** (*leg.*, *USA*) nome sociale, ragione sociale; ~ **policy** (*org. az.*, *USA*) politica aziendale; ~ **profitability** (*econ.*, *USA*) profittabilità delle imprese; ~ **profits** (*econ.*, *USA*) utili delle imprese; ~ **property** proprietà d'una corporazione (d'un ente, ecc.); ~ **purpose** (*leg.*, *USA*) scopo della società, oggetto sociale; ~ **responsibility** responsabilità collegiale; ~ **saving** (*fin.*, *USA*) autofinanziamento; ~ **seal** (*leg.*, *USA*) sigillo sociale; ~ **secretary** (*org. az.*, *USA*) segretario del consiglio d'amministrazione; ~ **stock** (*fin.*, *USA*) azioni sociali; ~ **structure** (*org. az.*, *USA*) organizzazione aziendale; ~ **symbol** (*pubbl.*, *USA*) marchio (*d'una società*); ~ **tax** (*fin.*, *USA*) imposta sulle società, imposta societaria.

corporation, *n.* 1 consiglio municipale. 2 (*storico*) corporazione. 3 (*leg.*) ente morale, ente giuridico, ente pubblico; società di servizi pubblici. 4 (*leg.*, *USA*) società legalmente costituita; persona giuridica. 5 (*leg.*, *USA*) compagnia, società di capitali. 6 (*leg.*, *USA*) società per azioni. // ~ **aggregate** (*fin.*, *USA*) persona giuridica (*costituita da più individui*); ~ **image** (*pubbl.*, *USA*) immagine aziendale; ~ **net-income tax** (*fin.*, *USA*) imposta sulle società; ~ **stocks** (*fin.*) titoli di prestito municipali; ~ **tax** (*fin.*, *USA*) imposta sulle società, imposta societaria.

corporatism, *n.* (*econ.*) corporativismo.

corporatist, *a.* (*econ.*) corporativistico.

corporative, *a.* corporativo. // ~ **state** (*econ.*) stato corporativo.

corporativism, *n.* (*econ.*) corporativismo.

corpus delicti, *n.* (*leg.*) corpo del reato.

correct[1], *a.* corretto, esatto.

correct[2], *v. t.* correggere, rettificare.

correcting, *a.* rettificativo, di rettifica, di verifica. // ~ **entry** (*rag.*) registrazione di verifica, scrittura di verifica.

correction, *n.* correzione, rettifica. // ~ **of an account** (*rag.*) rettifica d'un conto; ~ **of assessed income** (*fin.*) rettifica del reddito accertato; ~ **of prices** (*Borsa*) rettifica dei corsi.

corrective, *a.* correttivo. // ~ **maintenance** (*org. az.*) manutenzione correttiva; ~ **measures** misure correttive.

correctly, *avv.* correttamente, esattamente.

correctness, *n.* correttezza, esattezza.

corrector, *n.* 1 correttore. 2 censore, critico.

correspond, *v. i.* corrispondere. // to ~ **with a firm** corrispondere con una ditta.

correspondence, *n.* corrispondenza. // ~ **clerk** (*pers.*) addetto alla corrispondenza, corrispondente; ~ **department** (*org. az.*) reparto corrispondenza.

correspondent, *a.* e *n.* (*pers.*) corrispondente. *n.* (*giorn.*) inviato. // ~ **bank** (*fin.*) banca corrispondente.

corresponding, *a.* corrispondente, conforme. // ~ **clerk** (*pers.*) corrispondente; ~ **member** socio corrispondente; ~ **period** periodo corrispondente; ~ **secretary** (*pers.*) segretario incaricato della corrispondenza.

corridor, *n.* corridoio. // ~ **carriage** (*trasp. ferr.*) carrozza con corridoio.

corrugated, *a.* ondulato. // ~ **cardboard** cartone ondulato; ~ **plates** lamiere ondulate.

corrupt, *v. t.* corrompere.

corruption, *n.* corruzione.

cosignatory, *n.* (*leg.*) cofirmatario (*firmatario insieme con altri*).

cosmopolitan, *a.* cosmopolita.

cost[1], *n.* 1 costo, onere, spesa. 2 (*econ.*) prezzo. 3 (*rag.*) costo. 4 **costs**, *pl.* (*leg.*) spese processuali. // ~ **account** (*rag.*) conto (relativo al) costo di lavorazione; ~ **accountant** (*pers.*) analizzatore dei costi (*in un'azienda*); ~ **accounting** (*rag.*) analisi dei costi, contabilità (relativa ai) costi di lavorazione, contabilità industriale; ~ **allocation** (*rag.*) distribuzione dei costi, imputazione dei costi; ~ **analysis** (*rag.*) analisi dei costi; **costs and fees** (*leg.*) spese e competenze (*d'una causa*); ~ **and freight** (*trasp. mar.*) costo e nolo; ~ **-book** (*rag.*) libro contabile dei profitti e delle perdite; ~ **center** (*org.*

az., USA) *V.* ~ **centre;** ~ **centre** (*org. az.*) centro di costo, centro di responsabilità; **costs charged to the loser** (*leg.*) spese a carico della parte soccombente; ~ **clerk** (*pers.*) *V.* ~ **accountant;** ~ **control** (*org. az.*) controllo dei costi; ~ **control account** (*rag.*) conto relativo al controllo dei costi di lavorazione; ~ **curve** (*econ.*) curva dei costi; ~ **cutting** (*org. az.*) riduzione dei costi, riduzione delle spese; ~ **estimating** (*rag.*) preventivo delle spese; ~ **free** franco di spese; « ~, **freight, and insurance** » (*trasp. mar.*) «costo, assicurazione e nolo»; ~ **-induced inflation** (*econ.*) inflazione indotta dai costi; ~ **inflation** (*econ.*) inflazione da (eccessivo aumento dei) costi; « ~, **insurance and freight, port of discharge** » (*trasp. mar.*) «costo, assicurazione e nolo al porto d'arrivo»; « ~, **insurance, freight** » (*trasp. mar.*) «costo, assicurazione e nolo»; **the costs of the action** (*leg.*) le spese processuali; ~ **of labour** (*rag.*) costo della manodopera; ~ **of living** (*econ.*) costo della vita; ~ **-of-living adjustment** (*econ.*) adeguamento (*dei salari*) al costo della vita (*secondo i punti della «contingenza»*); ~ **-of-living allowance** (*pers.*) (indennità di) carovita, (indennità di) contingenza; ~ **-of-living bonus** (*pers.*) (indennità di) carovita, (indennità di) contingenza; ~ **-of-living figure** (*stat.*) indice del costo della vita; ~ **-of-living index** (*econ.*) indice del costo della vita; ~ **-of-living wage escalator** (*econ., sind.*) scala mobile (*che attua un aggancio fra salari e costo della vita*); ~ **of the premises** (*rag.*) costo dei locali (*d'un'azienda*); ~ **of upkeep and repairs** (*rag.*) spese di manutenzione e riparazione; ~ **plus** quotazione basata sul prezzo d'acquisto, più una percentuale (*spesso determinata da regolamentazioni governative*); ~ **price** (*rag.*) prezzo di costo, prezzo d'acquisto, valore d'acquisto, corso d'acquisto; ~ **push** (*econ.*) spinta dei prezzi, dei costi; ~ **-push inflation** (*econ.*) inflazione da costi; ~ **reduction** (*rag.*) riduzione dei costi, riduzione delle spese; ~ **-revenue balance** (*econ.*) equilibrio costi-ricavi; ~ **unit** (*rag.*) unità di costo; **at** ~ a prezzo di costo; **below** ~ sotto costo; «**with costs**» (*leg.*) «condannato alle spese» (*quando la parte soccombente in una causa legale è condannata alle spese di giudizio*).

cost[2], *v. i.* (*pass.* e *part. pass.* **cost**) **1** costare. **2** (*rag.*) determinare, valutare i costi. *v. t.* **1** stabilire il costo di (*qc.*). **2** preventivare il costo di (*una merce, un articolo, ecc.*).

costing, *n.* (*rag.*) determinazione dei costi, valutazione dei costi.

costly, *a.* costoso, caro, dispendioso.

cosurety, *n.* (*leg.*) garante in solido.

cotenant, *n.* (*leg.*) coaffittuario.

cottage industry, *n.* (*econ.*) lavoro a domicilio (*nelle campagne*).

cotton, *n.* cotone. // **the** ~ **Belt** (*USA*) la zona del cotone; **the** ~ **Exchange** (*fin.*) la Borsa del Cotone; **the** ~ **market** (*market.*) il mercato cotoniero.

coulisse, *n.* (*fin.*) Borsa non ufficiale; fuoriborsa; «mercatino», borsino (*fam.*).

council, *n.* consiglio (*adunanza di persone*). // ~ **-chamber** camera di consiglio; ~ **hall** sala del consiglio; ~ **house** (*ingl.*) casa popolare; ~ **-man** (*USA*) consigliere; **the** ~ **of the Bar** (*leg.*) il Consiglio dell'Ordine degli Avvocati; ~ **of Economic Advisers** (*USA*) Consiglio dei Consulenti Economici; **the** ~ **of Europe** il Consiglio d'Europa; ~ **of judges** (*leg.*) consiglio giudiziario.

councillor, *n.* consigliere (*membro d'un consiglio*).

counsel[1], *n.* **1** consiglio, parere. **2** consultazione, consulenza. **3** (*leg.*) consulente legale, avvocato patrocinante, patrocinatore. // ~ **'s advice** (*leg.*) parere legale; ~ **appointed by the Court** (*leg.*) difensore d'ufficio; ~ **'s fees** (*leg.*) parcella d'avvocato; ~ **for the defence** (*leg.*) avvocato difensore; ~ **for the defendant** (*leg.*) avvocato del convenuto, avvocato difensore; ~ **for the plaintiff** (*leg.*) avvocato della parte lesa, avvocato di parte civile; ~ **'s opinion** (*leg.*) parere legale.

counsel[2], *v. t.* consigliare. *v. i.* consultarsi (*con q.*).

counsellor, *n.* **1** consigliere. **2** consulente. **3** (*leg.*) esperto legale che non esercita la professione nei tribunali, ma dà pareri ai clienti. **4** (*leg., USA*) avvocato patrocinante, patrono. // ~ **appointed by the Court** (*leg., USA*) difensore d'ufficio; ~ **-at-law** (*leg., USA*) avvocato patrocinante.

count[1], *n.* **1** conto, calcolo, conteggio. **2** (*leg.*) capo d'accusa. // ~ **of indictment** (*leg.*) capo d'accusa.

count[2], *v. t.* contare, calcolare, conteggiare. // to ~ **down** (*org. az.*) fare il conto alla rovescia; to ~ **from** con decorrenza da, a partire da: **to** ~ **from the first of this month** con decorrenza dal primo del mese in corso; to ~ **on** contare su, fare assegnamento su; to ~ **up** contare; to ~ **upon** contare su, fare affidamento su.

countdown, *n.* (*org. az.*) conto alla rovescia.

counter[1], *avv.* contro, in senso contrario, in opposizione (a). *a. attr.* contrario, opposto. //

~ **-action** (*leg.*) azione riconvenzionale; ~ **-charge** (*leg.*) domanda riconvenzionale; ~ **-claim** controrichiesta; (*leg.*) domanda riconvenzionale, riconvenzione, controquerela; ~ **-cyclical action** (*econ.*) azione anticiclica; ~ **-declaration** (*leg.*) controdichiarazione; ~ **-form** duplicato di modulo; ~ **-instructions** (*amm.*) controistruzioni; ~ **-list** duplicato d'elenco; ~ **-offer** controfferta; ~ **-order** contrordine; ~ **-proof** (*leg.*) controprova; ~ **-proposal** controproposta; ~ **-proposition** controproposta; ~ **-security** (*cred.*) controgaranzia, cauzione sussidiaria; ~ **-surety** (*cred.*) controgaranzia, cauzione sussidiaria.

counter[2], *n.* 1 contatore (*l'apparecchio*). 2 gettone (*per giochi, ecc.*). 3 (*pers.*) contatore.

counter[3], *n.* 1 banco (*di negozio*). 2 sportello (*di banca, ecc.*). 3 cassa. // ~ **cash book** (*banca*) brogliaccio di cassa; ~ **displays** (*pubbl.*) elementi di richiamo per banco di vendita; **over the** ~ al banco; alla cassa; in un ufficio privato; (*market.*) al dettaglio; **over-the-** ~ **sales** (*market.*) vendite al banco, vendite al dettaglio, vendite al minuto; **under the** ~ sottobanco; **under-the-** ~ **goods** roba di sottobanco.

counter[4], *v. t.* 1 controbattere; agire in opposizione, opporsi a (*q.*). 2 difendersi da, respingere (*un attacco, ecc.*). // to ~ **inflation** difendersi dall'inflazione.

counteraction, *n.* 1 antagonismo, resistenza. 2 (*leg.*) azione d'opposizione.

counterbond, *n.* (*cred.*) controgaranzia.

counterfeit[1], *a.* (*leg.*) contraffatto, falsificato, simulato. n. (*leg.*) contraffazione, falsificazione. // ~ **bank-notes** banconote false; ~ **bill** (*cred., leg.*) cambiale falsa; ~ **coin** moneta falsa.

counterfeit[2], *v. t.* (*leg.*) contraffare, falsificare, simulare. // to ~ **a signature** (*leg.*) falsificare una firma.

counterfeiter, *n.* (*leg.*) contraffattore, falsificatore, falsario.

counterfeiting, *n.* (*leg.*) contraffazione, falsificazione.

counterfoil, *n.* matrice, «madre» (*di registro, libretto, ecc.*). // ~ **book** libro (*o* registro) a «madre» e «figlia»; **the** ~ **of a cheque book** (*banca*) la matrice di un libretto d'assegni; ~ **of receipt** matrice di ricevuta.

countermand[1], *n.* 1 annullamento, revoca (*d'un ordine*). 2 contrordine. // ~ **of payment** (*banca, cred.*) revoca dell'ordine di pagamento.

countermand[2], *v. t.* e *i.* 1 annullare, revocare (*un ordine*). 2 dare un contrordine.

countermark, *n.* contromarca, contrassegno, segno aggiuntivo.

countermeasure, *n.* contromisura.

counterpart, *n.* 1 copia, duplicato. 2 «figlia» (*opposto a «madre», matrice*). 3 controparte. 4 contropartita. // ~ **of a deed** (*leg.*) duplicato d'un atto; ~ **sample** (*market.*) controcampione.

countersign[1], *n.* 1 contrassegno. 2 controfirma, firma d'autenticazione. 3 (*leg.*) legalizzazione (*d'un documento, ecc.*).

countersign[2], *v. t.* 1 controfirmare, autenticare. 2 (*leg.*) legalizzare (*un documento, ecc.*).

countersignature, *n.* 1 controfirma. 2 (*leg.*) firma di legalizzazione, firma d'autenticazione.

countervail, *v. t.* 1 bilanciare. 2 compensare, equilibrare.

countervailing charge, *n.* (*fin.*) tassa di compensazione.

countervailing credit, *n.* (*cred.*) controcredito.

countervailing duty, *n.* 1 (*dog.*) dazio doganale protettivo; ritorsione doganale. 2 (*econ.*) diritto compensatore.

countervalue, *n.* controvalore. // ~ **of securities applied for** (*banca*) controvalore dei titoli sottoscritti.

counting, *n.* 1 conto, calcolo, computo. 2 conteggio. // ~ **from** con decorrenza da, a decorrere da, a datare da; ~ **house** (*org. az.*) ufficio amministrativo; (*rag.*) (ufficio di) contabilità, (ufficio di) ragioneria; ~ **room** (*rag., USA*) (ufficio di) contabilità, (ufficio di) amministrazione, (ufficio di) ragioneria.

country, *n.* 1 campagna. 2 nazione, Paese, regione, Stato. *a. attr.* di Paese, di provincia. // ~ **bank** banca di provincia; (*fin., ingl.*) banca che non ha filiali a Londra; (*fin., USA*) banca che non ha sede in una città dove esiste un ufficio del «Federal Reserve System»; ~ **estate** fondo rustico; **Countries with excess production** (*econ.*) Paesi eccedentari.

countryside, *n.* campagna.

county, *n.* contea. // ~ **council** (*amm.*) consiglio amministrativo di contea; ~ **Courts** (*leg.*) tribunali locali di contea.

coup, *n.* colpo maestro, mossa brillante. // **a** ~ **on the Stock Exchange** (*Borsa*) un colpo in Borsa.

coupon, *n.* 1 buono, scontrino, tagliando. 2 (*fin.*) cedola, tagliando. 3 (*pubbl.*) buono. // ~ **bond** (*fin.*) obbligazione al portatore; ~ **in arrear** (*fin.*) cedola scaduta; ~ **sheet** (*fin.*) cartella di cedole; **ex** ~ **stock** (*fin.*) titolo secco (*senza cedola*).

courier, *n.* (*tur.*) accompagnatore turistico,

guida.

course, *n.* 1 corso, direzione, procedimento. 2 indirizzo, linea di condotta, condotta. 3 direttiva. 4 (*trasp. mar.*) rotta. // ~ **of exchange** (*fin.*) corso del cambio; ~ **of prices** (*market.*) andamento dei prezzi; **in the ~ of** nel corso di, durante; **in the ~ of one or two years** nel corso d'un anno o due.

court, *n.* 1 (*leg.*) Corte, Corte di giustizia, tribunale. 2 (*leg.*) autorità giudiziaria, magistratura. // ~ **of Admiralty** (*leg.*) Tribunale dell'Ammiragliato; ~ **of Appeal** (*leg.*) Corte d'Appello; ~ **of Appeals** (*leg., USA*) Corte d'Appello; ~ **of arbitration** (*leg.*) collegio arbitrale; ~ **of Assize** (*leg.*) Corte d'Assise; ~ **of bankruptcy** (*leg.*) tribunale fallimentare; ~ **of common pleas** (*leg.*) tribunale per processi comuni; ~ **of conciliation** (*leg.*) ufficio d'un giudice conciliatore; ~ **of equity** (*leg.*) tribunale civile; ~ **of inquiry** (*leg.*) consiglio d'inchiesta; ~ **of Justice** (*leg.*) Corte di Giustizia; ~ **of records** (*leg.*) tribunale di giurisdizione; ~ **record** (*leg.*) verbale d'un processo; **out of ~** (*leg.*) in via amichevole; in via stragiudiziale.

covenant[1], *n.* 1 accordo solenne, convenzione, patto. 2 (*leg.*) contratto solenne, contratto formale. 3 (*leg.*) garanzia. // ~ **of quiet enjoyment** (*leg.*) garanzia di pacifico godimento.

covenant[2], *v. t.* e *i.* convenire, accordarsi, pattuire.

cover[1], *n.* 1 copertina (*di libro*). 2 busta (*di lettera*). 3 involucro (*di pacco*), plico. 4 (*anche ass.*) copertura. 5 (*Borsa, fin.*) margine. 6 (*fin.*) rapporto fra gli utili d'una società e quelli distribuiti. 7 (*leg.*) cauzione, garanzia, somma depositata in garanzia. 8 (*pubbl.*) copertina. 9 (*slang USA*) polizza d'assicurazione. // ~ **for the day** (*banca*) previsione di cassa; ~ **for documentary credit** (*banca*) copertura di credito documentato; ~ **girl** (*pubbl.*) cover girl (*ragazza la cui foto appare sulle copertine dei periodici*); ~ **note** (*ass.*) certificato di copertura (*del rischio*); (*ass. mar.*) polizza provvisoria; (*banca, cred.*) nota di copertura; ~ **photo** (*giorn.*) foto di copertina; ~ **ratio** (*fin.*) tasso di copertura; **with ~** (*fin.*) con copertura, al coperto; **without ~** (*fin.*) senza copertura, allo scoperto.

cover[2], *v. t.* e *i.* 1 (*anche ass.*) coprire, proteggere. 2 (*fin.*) fornire la copertura di. 3 (*giorn.*) riferire per esteso. 4 (*leg.*) depositare (*a cauzione, in garanzia, a titolo di caparra*); garantire. 5 (*trasp.*) percorrere (*una certa distanza, un numero di miglia, ecc.*). // to ~ **one's expenses** coprire le spese; to ~ **oneself by buying back** (*Borsa*) mettersi al coperto tramite ricompera; to ~ **one's requirements** coprire il proprio fabbisogno; to ~ **a short account** (*Borsa*) coprire uno scoperto; to ~ **a small order** evadere un piccolo ordinativo.

coverage, *n.* 1 (*anche ass.*) copertura. 2 (*giorn.*) ampiezza di trattazione (*d'una notizia*). 3 (*giorn.*) inchiesta. 4 (*pubbl.*) copertura. // ~ **for the amount of the credit** copertura per l'importo del credito.

covered, *a.* (*anche ass.*) coperto, protetto. // ~ **arbitrage** (*Borsa, fin.*) arbitraggio coperto; ~ **truck** (*trasp. ferr.*) vagone coperto, vagone chiuso; ~ **van** (*trasp. ferr.*) vagone coperto, vagone chiuso; ~ **wagon** (*trasp. ferr.*) vagone coperto, vagone chiuso.

covering, *n.* (*anche ass.*) copertura, protezione. // ~ **letter** (*trasp.*) lettera d'accompagnamento; ~ **note** (*ass.*) polizza provvisoria; (*trasp.*) nota di copertura; ~ **of land risks** (*ass.*) copertura dei rischi terrestri.

crackdown, *n.* (*econ.*) giro di vite (*fig.*); provvedimenti drastici.

craft, *n.* 1 abilità. 2 arte, mestiere. 3 (*trasp. mar.*) (*pl.* **craft**) imbarcazione, nave, naviglio. // ~ **risk** (*ass. mar.*) rischio di chiatta, rischio d'alleggio; ~ **union** (*sind.*) sindacato di categoria (*V. anche* **closed union**).

craftsman, *n.* (*pl.* **craftsmen**) 1 (*pers.*) artigiano. 2 (*pers.*) artista. 3 (*pers.*) operaio.

craftsmanship, *n.* abilità d'artigiano o d'artista; arte.

cranage, *n.* (*trasp.*) diritto di gru.

crane, *n.* (*trasp.*) gru.

crash[1], *n.* 1 schianto. 2 crollo, fallimento. 3 (*trasp. aut.*) investimento. // ~ **-landing** (*trasp. aer.*) atterraggio d'emergenza (*con urto sul suolo*).

crash[2], *v. i.* 1 schiantarsi. 2 crollare, andare in rovina, fallire. 3 (*trasp.*) urtarsi.

crate[1], *n.* (*trasp.*) gabbia (*di legno: per imballaggi*).

crate[2], *v. t.* imballare in «gabbie».

crawling peg, *n.* (*fin.*) parità mobile (*nei cambi*).

create, *v. t.* creare. // to ~ **a new series of shares** (*fin.*) creare una nuova serie d'azioni.

creation, *n.* creazione. // ~ **register** (*org. az.*) registro dei nuovi documenti.

creative, *a.* creativo. // ~ **group** (*pubbl.*) gruppo creativo.

creator, *n.* creatore.

credentials, *n. pl.* credenziali.

credibility, *n.* credibilità.

credible, *a.* credibile.

credit[1], *n.* 1 credito. 2 fiducia, stima. 3

(*banca*) fido. **4** (*rag.*) accreditamento. **5** (*rag.*) somma registrata a credito. **6** (*rag.*) «avere», colonna dell'«avere». *a. attr.* **1** a credito, a termine. **2** di credito, creditizio. **3** (*rag.*) creditore. // «~ **abated**» (*banca*) «credito esaurito»; ~ **accommodations** (*fin.*) facilitazioni di credito; ~ **account** conto aperto (*presso un negozio, ecc.*); (*rag.*) conto creditore; ~ **advice** nota di accredito; ~ **at the bank** credito bancario; ~ **balance** (*rag.*) differenza a credito, saldo a credito, saldo creditore, saldo attivo, saldo «avere»; ~ **bank** banca di credito; ~ **Bureau** (*USA*) ufficio d'informazioni commerciali; ~ **card** (*banca, fin., market.*) carta di credito, «creditcarta», tessera rilasciata da un'organizzazione che seleziona i propri soci fra persone notoriamente solvibili e che dà diritto ad acquistare a credito; ~ **circulation** (*fin.*) circolazione fiduciaria; ~ **collection** (*fin.*) incasso di crediti; ~ **column** (*rag.*) colonna dei crediti, colonna creditrice, colonna dell'avere; ~ **company** (*fin.*) società creditrice; ~ **department** (*org. az.*) ufficio crediti, ufficio fidi; ~ **entry** (*rag.*) scrittura d'accredito, registrazione a credito; ~ **facilities** facilitazioni di credito; ~ **guaranteed by mortgage** (*fin.*) credito immobiliare; ~ **inflation** (*econ.*) inflazione da (eccessiva espansione dei) crediti; ~ **institution** (*banca*) istituto di credito; ~ **instrument** titolo di credito; ~ **insurance** (*ass.*) assicurazione per i crediti inesigibili, assicurazione-crediti; ~ **interest rates** (*banca*) tassi d'interesse «creditori»; ~ **investigation** (*fin.*) valutazione dei creditori; ~ **item** (*rag.*) partita a credito; ~ **ledger** (*rag.*) libro mastro degli acquisti; ~ **limit** (*fin.*) fido; ~ **line** (*banca*) cifra di fido, castelletto, «plafond»; ~ **losses** (*rag.*) perdite su crediti; ~ **management** (*fin.*) gestione dei crediti; ~ **maneuver** (*fin.*) manovra del credito; ~ **memo** (*rag.*) nota d'accreditamento, nota d'accredito; ~ **note** (*rag.*) nota d'accreditamento, nota d'accredito; ~ **numbers** (*banca*) numeri creditori; ~ **on real property** credito immobiliare; ~ **opening** (*fin.*) apertura di credito; ~ **policy** (*fin.*) politica creditizia; ~ **purchase** (*market., rag.*) acquisto a credito; ~ **rationing** (*fin.*) restrizione del credito; ~ **report** informazioni commerciali; ~ **reporting service** servizio informazioni commerciali; ~ **sale** (*market., rag.*) vendita a credito; ~ **settlement** (*market., rag.*) regolamento a termine; ~ **side** (*rag.*) credito, «avere» (*d'un conto*); ~ **slip** (*banca*) distinta di versamento; ~ **squeeze** (*fin.*) stretta creditizia, compressione creditizia, restrizione del credito; ~ **standing** credito (*di cui gode una ditta*); ~ **status** credito (*di cui uno gode*); ~ **-status information** informazioni commerciali; ~ **-status inquiry service** servizio informazioni commerciali; ~ **system** (*fin.*) sistema creditizio; **a** ~ **transaction** (*cred.*) un'operazione a credito; ~ **transfer** (*fin.*) bonifico; ~ **with the bank** credito bancario; **on** ~ a credito, a termine; **on a** ~ **basis** a credito; **upon** ~ a credito, a termine.

credit[2], *v. t.* **1** accreditare. **2** (*rag.*) accreditare, bonificare. **3** (*rag.*) registrare nella colonna dell'«avere». // to ~ **an account with a sum** (*rag.*) accreditare un conto d'una somma; to ~ **an amount to sb.** accreditare una somma a q.; to ~ **sb. with an amount** accreditare q. d'una somma, segnare una somma a credito di q.

«credited», *locuz.* (*rag.*) «avere».

credited party, *n.* (l')accreditato.

crediting, *a.* accreditante. *n.* (*banca, rag.*) accreditamento, accredito. // ~ **entry** (*rag.*) scrittura d'accreditamento; ~ **of bills value at maturity date** (*banca*) accredito d'effetti valuta scadenza; **the** ~ **party** l'accreditante; ~ **to sb.'s (current) account** (*banca*) accreditamento in conto a q.

creditor, *n.* **1** creditore. **2** (*rag.*) colonna dell'«avere», l'attivo (*d'un conto*). // ~ **account** (*rag.*) conto creditore; **creditors' ledger** (*rag.*) partitario fornitori; ~ **nation** (*econ.*) nazione creditrice; ~ **on mortgage** (*leg.*) creditore su ipoteca; ~ **side** (*rag.*) «avere»; ~ **'s suit** (*leg.*) azione legale per il ricupero di crediti.

creditworthiness, *n.* (*fin.*) l'essere degno di credito.

creditworthy, *a.* (*fin.*) degno di credito; cui si può fare credito.

creeping inflation, *n.* (*econ.*) inflazione strisciante.

creeping recovery, *n.* (*econ.*) ripresa strisciante.

crew, *n.* (*trasp. aer., trasp. mar.*) equipaggio, ciurma. // ~ **and cargo** (*trasp. mar.*) corpo e beni; ~ **list** (*trasp. mar.*) ruolo d'equipaggio.

crime, *n.* (*leg.*) crimine, delitto, illecito penale, reato.

criminal, *a.* (*leg.*) criminale, penale. *n.* (*leg.*) criminale. // ~ **case** (*leg.*) causa penale; ~ **code** (*leg.*) codice penale; ~ **law relating to economic transactions** (*leg.*) diritto penale dell'economia; ~ **lawyer** (*leg.*) avvocato penalista, penalista; ~ **offence** (*leg.*) reato penale; ~ **records** (*leg.*) casellario penale.

criminalist, *n.* criminalista.

criminality, *n.* criminalità.

criminologist, *n.* (*leg.*) esperto del diritto

penale, penalista.

crippling strike, *n.* (*sind.*) sciopero paralizzante.

crisis, *n.* (*pl.* **crises**) **1** crisi. **2** (*econ.*) crisi.

critic, *n.* critico.

critical, *a.* critico.

crofter, *n.* piccolo affittuario.

crook, *n.* truffatore, truffaldino.

crooked, *a.* disonesto, truffaldino, losco. // **a ~ land deal** un losco affare di terreni; **a ~ man** un uomo disonesto.

crookedness, *n.* disonestà.

crop[1], *n.* raccolto.

crop[2], *v. t.* **1** tagliare. **2** raccogliere.

cross[1], *a. attr.* **1** che interseca, obliquo, trasversale. **2** di rimando. *n.* incrocio. // **~ action** (*leg.*) azione impugnativa, azione riconvenzionale, domanda riconvenzionale, riconvenzione; **~ book** (*Borsa*) speculazione mista; **~ claim** (*leg.*) domanda riconvenzionale; **~ complaint** (*leg.*) controquerela; **~ credit relief** (*fin.*) deduzione reciproca (*d'imposte*); **~ -demand** (*leg.*) domanda in contraddittorio; **~ entry** (*rag.*) trasferimento d'una somma ad altro conto; **~ -examination** (*leg.*) interrogatorio in contraddittorio; to **~ -examine** (*leg.*) interrogare in contraddittorio; **~ firing** tiro incrociato; (*cred.*) tiraggio reciproco (*di tratte*); **~ participation** (*fin.*) partecipazione (*azionaria*) incrociata; **~ -question** (*leg.*) domanda in contraddittorio; to **~ -question** (*leg.*) interrogare in contraddittorio, interrogare a fondo; **~ rate** (*fin.*) cambio incrociato, cambio indiretto, cambio calcolato attraverso una terza valuta (*detto anche «indirect parity»*); **~ rates of exchange** (*econ., fin.*) parità indirette, parità relative (dei cambi); **~ reference** richiamo (*in un libro, ecc.*); **~ -roads** crocevia, crocicchio, incrocio; **~ -section analysis** (*econ.*) analisi dei settori rappresentativi; **~ -subsidy** (*fin.*) sussidio incrociato; sussidio indiretto; **~ summons** (*leg.*) riconvenzione.

cross[2], *v. t.* e *i.* **1** traversare. **2** incrociare, incrociarsi. **3** cancellare (*tirando un frego*). **4** (*banca*) sbarrare. // to **~ a cheque** (*banca*) sbarrare un assegno bancario; to **~ generally** (*banca*) sbarrare (*un assegno*) con sbarratura semplice; to **~ out** cancellare, eliminare.

crossed cheque, *n.* (*banca*) assegno sbarrato.

crossed warrant, *n.* (*fin.*) mandato di riscossione sbarrato (*vincolato a una persona; delle Poste britanniche*).

crossing, *n.* **1** incrocio. **2** cancellatura (*mediante un frego*). **3** (*banca*) sbarratura. **4** (*Borsa*) applicazione. **5** (*trasp. aer., trasp. mar.*) traversata. // **~ out** cancellatura, cancellazione, eliminazione.

crosstalk, *n.* (*comun.*) diafonia (*al telefono*).

crowd[1], *n.* moltitudine.

crowd[2], *v. t.* **1** affollare. *v. i.* affollarsi.

crowding, *n.* affollamento. // **~ round the ticket windows** (*trasp.*) affollamento alla biglietteria.

crown, *n.* corona. // **~ debt** (*ingl.*) debito dello Stato; **~ lands** (*ingl.*) terreni demaniali; **~ law** (*ingl.*) diritto penale.

crucial, *a.* critico, decisivo. // **~ stage** fase cruciale.

crude, *a.* grezzo. // **~ oil** petrolio grezzo, (petrolio) greggio.

cruise[1], *n.* (*trasp. mar.*) crociera.

cruise[2], *v. i.* **1** (*trasp. aer.*) volare a velocità di crociera. **2** (*trasp. mar.*) (*di nave*) incrociare. **3** (*trasp. mar.*) (*di persona*) andare in crociera, fare una crociera.

crumble, *v. t.* sbriciolare. *v. i.* **1** sbriciolarsi. **2** crollare, andare in rovina.

crumbling, *n.* (*Borsa*) crollo (*di prezzi, corsi, ecc.*).

crunch, *n.* (*fin.*) stretta. // **a credit ~** una stretta creditizia.

cry[1], *n.* grido.

cry[2], *v. t.* e *i.* **1** gridare. **2** proclamare.

cubage, *n.* cubaggio.

cube, *n.* (*mat.*) cubo. // **~ -root** (*mat.*) radice cubica.

cubic, *a.* cubico, cubo. // **~ metre** metro cubo, stero.

cubit, *n.* misura lineare per tessili, pari a 18 pollici.

culpability, *n.* (*leg.*) colpevolezza, colpa.

culpable, *a.* (*leg.*) colpevole.

culprit, *n.* (*leg.*) colpevole.

cultivation, *n.* coltura.

«cum», *prep.* con. // **~ coupon** (*fin.*) col dividendo; **~ dividend** (*fin.*) col dividendo; **~ drawing** (*Borsa*) con estrazione (*o* estrazione compresa); **~ new** (*Borsa*) col nuovo (*compresa la nuova emissione*); **~ rights** (*fin.*) col diritto, incluso il diritto d'opzione.

cumulate, *v. t.* accumulare, cumulare. *v. i.* accumularsi, cumularsi.

cumulation, *n.* accumulazione.

cumulative, *a.* cumulativo. // **~ dividend** (*fin.*) dividendo cumulativo; **~ preference shares** (*fin.*) azioni privilegiate cumulative; **~ preferred stock** (*fin.*) azioni privilegiate cumulative; **~ stock** (*fin.*) titoli a dividendo cumulativo; **~ turnover tax** (*fin.*) imposta cumulativa sulla cifra d'affari.

curator, *n.* 1 (*leg.*) curatore (*di minorenne, d'incapace, ecc.*); tutore. 2 (*leg.*) amministratore.

curatorship, *n.* (*leg.*) curatela (*di minorenne*).

curb[1], *n.* 1 (*fig.*) freno. 2 (*Borsa, USA*) mercatino. 3 (*econ., fin.*) contenimento. // ~ **market** (*Borsa, USA*) mercatino (*dei titoli non quotati*); **a ~ on inflation** (*econ., fin.*) il contenimento dell'inflazione; **on the ~** (*USA, di titolo*) non quotato (*ufficialmente*).

curb[2], *v. t.* 1 tenere a freno, trattenere. 2 contenere, reprimere. // to ~ **the expansion of savings** (*fin.*) paralizzare il risparmio; to ~ **inflation** (*fin.*) tenere a freno l'inflazione; to ~ **inflationary pressures** (*fin.*) contenere le spinte inflazionistiche.

curbist, *n.* (*Borsa, slang USA*) agente di cambio.

curiosity, *n.* curiosità.

currency, *n.* 1 (*econ.*) moneta circolante, moneta corrente (*in un Paese*). 2 (*fin.*) circolazione monetaria. 3 (*fin.*) valuta, divisa. 4 (*fin.*) decorrenza. 5 (*fin.*) validità (*di moneta, ecc.*). // ~ **act** (*fin.*) legge valutaria; ~ **adjustment** (*fin.*) allineamento valutario, conguaglio monetario; ~ **alignment** (*fin.*) allineamento delle valute; ~ **appreciation** (*econ.*) rivalutazione; ~ **circulation** (*econ.*) circolazione monetaria; ~ **convertibility** (*fin.*) convertibilità della valuta; ~ **depreciation** (*econ.*) svalutazione, devalutazione; ~ **devaluation** (*fin.*) svalutazione monetaria; ~ **exchange rates** (*fin.*) parità di cambio, parità valutaria; ~ **fluctuations** (*econ.*) fluttuazione delle monete; ~ **notes** (*fin.*) banconote, biglietti di Stato a corso forzoso; ~ **of an insurance** (*ass.*) validità d'un'assicurazione; ~ **parity** (*econ.*) parità monetaria; ~ **rate** (*fin.*) cambio certo per incerto; ~ **reform** (*econ.*) riforma monetaria, cambio della moneta; ~ **regulations** (*fin.*) norme valutarie; ~ **transactions** (*fin.*) manovre sulle valute.

current, *a.* 1 corrente, d'uso corrente, del giorno. 2 valevole, valido. 3 (*market.*) (*di modello*) di serie. // ~ **account** (*banca*) conto corrente; (*fin.*) bilancia commerciale, bilancia delle partite correnti, bilancia delle operazioni (*o* dei pagamenti) correnti; ~ **accounts** (*fin.*) partite correnti; ~ **assets** (*rag.*) attività correnti, disponibilità, capitale circolante; ~ **balance** (*econ.*) bilancia dei conti correnti (*bilancia dei pagamenti, incluse le partite invisibili, ma esclusi i movimenti di capitale*); ~ **budget** (*rag.*) entrate e uscite ordinarie (*bilancio di previsione*); **the ~ business situation** (*econ.*) la congiuntura; ~ **interests** (*rag.*) interessi correnti, interessi in corso; ~ **items** (*fin.*) partite correnti; ~ **liabilities** (*rag.*) passività correnti, debiti correnti, passività a breve scadenza; ~ **money** (*fin.*) moneta corrente; **the ~ month** il mese corrente; (*Borsa*) per consegna entro il mese; ~ **premium** (*ass.*) premio corrente; ~ **price** (*market.*) prezzo corrente; ~ **price list** (*market.*) listino dei prezzi correnti; ~ **quality** (*market.*) qualità corrente; ~ **rate of exchange** (*fin.*) cambio del giorno; ~ **ratio** (*econ., rag.*) rapporto tra attività e passività correnti; indice di liquidità; ~ **settlement** (*Borsa*) liquidazione corrente; ~ **spending** (*fin.*) spese correnti; **holder of a ~ account** (*banca*) correntista.

curriculum, *n.* (*pl.* **curricula**) (*pers.*) corso di studi. // ~ **vitae** (*pers.*) «curriculum vitae», curricolo.

curtail, *v. t.* 1 decurtare, diminuire, ridurre. 2 limitare, contingentare. // to ~ **an allowance of money** decurtare un assegno in denaro; to ~ **the output of metals** (*econ.*) contingentare la produzione di metalli; to ~ **wages** (*sind.*) ridurre i salari.

curtailing, *n.* 1 decurtazione, diminuzione, riduzione. 2 (*econ.*) limitazione, contingentamento.

curtailment, *n. V.* **curtailing.** // ~ **of output** (*econ.*) contingentamento della produzione.

curve, *n.* (*mat., trasp. aut.*) curva. // ~ **of absolute equality** (*econ.*) curva d'uguaglianza assoluta; ~ **of absolute inequality** (*econ.*) curva d'ineguaglianza assoluta.

cushion, *n.* (*org. az.*) cuscinetto, giacenza di sicurezza, «stock di riserva».

cuss, *n.* (*slang USA*) cliente.

custodian, *n.* (*pers.*) custode (*specialm. d'un edificio pubblico*).

custody, *n.* 1 custodia, protezione. 2 (*fin.*) custodia. 3 (*leg.*) custodia, tutela. 4 (*leg.*) detenzione. // ~ **bill of lading** (*trasp. mar.*) polizza di carico provvisoria; ~ **fees** (*fin.*) diritti di custodia; ~ **of the law** (*leg.*) custodia legale; **in ~** in buone mani; (*leg.*) sotto buona guardia, in stato d'arresto.

custom, *n.* 1 consuetudine, abitudine, uso, usanza. 2 clientela. 3 il servirsi (*presso un negozio*). 4 (*leg.*) consuetudine, uso. *a. attr.* 1 (*dog.*) doganale (*per i composti e le locuzioni, V. anche* **customs**). 2 (*USA*) che lavora su ordinazione. 3 (*USA*) fatto su misura, fatto su ordinazione. // ~ **-built** (*org. az.*) fatto su ordinazione, costruito a richiesta, fuori serie; ~ **-built body** carrozzeria fuori serie; ~ **collector** (*dog.*) esattore delle dogane; ~ **-house** (*dog.*) edificio della dogana, ufficio della dogana, dogana; ~ **-house broker** (*dog.*) agente doganale; ~ **-made** fatto su misura; ~ **of trade** uso commerciale; ~ **-surveyor** (*dog.*) ispettore doganale; ~ **watcher** (*dog.*) sorvegliante doganale.

customable, *a.* (*dog.*) soggetto a dazio doganale.

customary, *a.* **1** consueto, abituale. **2** convenzionale, ordinario. **3** (*leg.*) consuetudinario. // ~ **clause** clausola d'uso; ~ **route** (*trasp. mar.*) rotta ordinaria; ~ **tare** (*market.*) tara convenzionale, tara d'uso; **as ~ at the port of New York** (*trasp. mar.*) secondo gli usi del porto di New York.

customer, *n.* **1** cliente, avventore. **2 customers,** *pl.* clientela. // ~ **assistance** (*market.*) servizio accessorio (*fornito da un rivenditore ai suoi clienti*); ~ **code** (*banca*) codice cliente; **customers' ledger** (*rag.*) mastro dei clienti.

customs, *n. pl.* **1** (*dog.*) dogana, ufficio doganale. **2** (*dog.*) diritti doganali, dazi doganali. *a. attr.* (*dog.*) doganale. // ~ **agency** (*dog.*) agenzia doganale; ~ **agent** (*dog.*) agente doganale; (*dog., pers.*) spedizioniere doganale, depositario doganale; ~ **barriers** (*comm. est.*) barriere doganali; ~ **bill of entry** (*dog.*) dichiarazione doganale; ~ **bond** (*dog.*) cauzione doganale; ~ **charges** (*dog.*) diritti doganali, spese di dogana; ~ **clearance** (*dog.*) spedizione in dogana, sdoganamento; ~ **code** (*dog.*) codice doganale; ~ **debenture** (*dog.*) polizza (doganale) di rimborso; ~ **declaration** (*dog.*) dichiarazione doganale; ~ **division** (*dog.*) sezione doganale; ~ **drawback** (*dog.*) rimborso dei diritti doganali (*pagati per merce che viene riesportata*); ~ **duties** (*dog.*) dazi doganali; ~ **duty** (*dog.*) diritto di dogana, dazio doganale; dazio, dogana (*i diritti*); ~ **entry** (*dog.*) dichiarazione doganale, bolletta doganale; ~ **entry form** (*dog.*) modulo di dichiarazione doganale; ~ **examination** (*dog.*) controllo doganale; ~ **examination of baggage** (*dog., USA*) ispezione doganale del bagaglio; ~ **expenses** (*dog.*) spese di dogana; ~ **formalities** (*dog.*) formalità doganali; ~ **franchise** (*dog., fin.*) franchigia doganale; ~ **legislation** (*leg.*) legislazione doganale; ~ **manifest** (*dog.*) manifesto di dogana; ~ **nomenclature** (*dog.*) nomenclatura doganale; ~ **officer** (*dog.*) funzionario di dogana, doganiere; ~ **permit** (*dog.*) permesso doganale; ~ **receipts** (*dog.*) entrate doganali; ~ **regulations** (*dog.*) regolamenti doganali; ~ **report** (*dog.*) dichiarazione doganale; ~ **service** (*dog.*) servizio doganale; ~ **specification** (*dog.*) documento doganale richiesto a fini statistici; ~ **square** (*dog.*) piazzale doganale; ~ **station** (*dog.*) posto di dogana; ~ **store** (*dog.*) magazzino doganale; ~ **tariff** (*dog.*) tariffa doganale; ~ **union** (*comm. est.*) unione doganale; ~ **valuation** (*dog.*) valutazione doganale; ~ **value** (*dog.*) valore in dogana; ~ **warehouse** (*dog.*) magazzino doganale.

cut[1], *n.* **1** taglio. **2** diminuzione, limitazione, riduzione. **3** (*market.*) calo, ribasso (*di prezzi*). **4** (*market.*) riduzione (*delle ordinazioni*). **5** (*pubbl.*) stacco (*in televisione*). **6** (*slang USA*) dividendo, interesse. // ~ **-back** (*fin.*) riduzione; **a ~ in prices** (*market.*) una diminuzione di prezzi, un ribasso di prezzi; ~ **-out panel envelope** (*attr. uff.*) busta commerciale a finestra; ~ **-throat competition** aspra concorrenza.

cut[2], *v. t.* (*pass.* e *part. pass.* **cut**). **1** diminuire, limitare, ridurre. **2** (*market.*) calare, ribassare (*prezzi*). **3** (*market.*) ridurre (*ordinazioni*). **4** (*pubbl.*) montare (*un film*). // to ~ **back the cash deficit** (*rag.*) ridurre il disavanzo di cassa; to ~ **back a contract** (*leg.*) risolvere un contratto o ridurne i termini (*di tempo, quantità, ecc.*); to ~ **the discount rate** (*fin.*) ridurre il tasso di sconto; to ~ **down** ridurre; (*econ.*) diminuire (*prezzi, ecc.*); to ~ **down production** (*org. az.*) ridurre la produzione; to ~ **in** ribassare; (*trasp. aut.*) tagliare la strada; to ~ **in prices** (*market.*) ribassare i prezzi; to ~ **off** tagliar via, staccare; (*comun.*) interrompere (*una conversazione telefonica*); to ~ **out** (*Borsa*) compensare.

cut-price, *a. attr.* (*di un negozio, ecc.*) che pratica forti sconti.

cutting, *n.* **1** taglio. **2** diminuzione, limitazione, riduzione. **3** (*market.*) calo, ribasso (*di prezzi*). **4** (*market.*) riduzione (*delle ordinazioni*). // ~ **limit order** (*Borsa*) ordine stop; ~ **out** (*Borsa*) compensazione.

cybernated, *a.* (*elab. elettr.*) cibernetizzato. // **a ~ plant** uno stabilimento cibernetizzato.

cybernation, *n.* (*elab. elettr.*) cibernetizzazione.

cybernetics, *n. pl.* (*col verbo al sing.*) cibernetica.

cycle, *n.* ciclo.

cyclical, *a.* ciclico. // ~ **fluctuation** (*econ.*) fluttuazione ciclica, oscillazione ciclica; ~ **fluctuations of prices** (*econ.*) oscillazioni cicliche dei prezzi; ~ **malaise** (*econ.*) crisi congiunturale; ~ **movements** (*econ.*) movimenti ciclici; ~ **unemployment** (*econ.*) disoccupazione ciclica.

cyclostyle[1], *n.* (*attr. uff.*) ciclostile.

cyclostyle[2], *v. t.* ciclostilare.

cylinder, *n.* (*attr. uff.*) rullo (*di macchina da scrivere*).

cypher, *n. V.* **cipher.**

cypher out, *v. t. V.* **cipher out.**

D

dabble, *v. t.* **1** bagnare, tuffare. **2** agitare (*in un liquido*). *v. i.* diguazzare, sguazzare. // to ~ **in** (*o* **at**) dilettarsi di; to ~ **in statistics** occuparsi a tempo perso di statistica; to ~ **on the Stock Exchange** (*Borsa*) fare piccole operazioni di Borsa.

daily, *a.* quotidiano, giornaliero. *n.* (*giorn.*) quotidiano, giornale quotidiano. // ~ **allowance (for expenses)** (*pers.*) indennità giornaliera, diaria; ~ **loan** (*cred.*) prestito giornaliero; ~ **money** (*cred.*) prestito giornaliero; ~ **output** (*org. az.*) rendimento giornaliero; ~ **paper** (*giorn.*) quotidiano, giornale quotidiano; ~ **rate** (*pers.*) paga giornaliera; ~ **report** (*pubbl.*) notiziario giornaliero; ~ **sales** (*market.*) vendite giornaliere; ~ **schedule** (*org. az.*) programma giornaliero; ~ **wage** (*pers.*) paga giornaliera.

damage[1], *n.* **1** danno, danneggiamento, perdita. **2** (*trasp. mar.*) avaria. **3 damages,** *pl.* (*ass.*) danni. **4 damages,** *pl.* (*leg.*) danni; risarcimento dei danni, indennizzo. // ~ **by act of God** (*leg., trasp. mar.*) danno dovuto a forza maggiore; ~ **due to gross negligence** (*leg.*) danno dovuto a negligenza grave; ~ **in discharging** (*ass. mar.*) danni dovuti allo scarico; ~ **in loading** (*ass. mar.*) danni dovuti alla caricazione; ~ **in transit** (*ass., trasp.*) danno avvenuto durante il trasporto; ~ **report** (*ass. mar.*) certificato d'avaria; ~ **survey** (*ass.*) perizia dei danni; (*ass. mar.*) perizia d'avaria; ~ **to ship** (*trasp. mar.*) avaria alla nave.

damage[2], *v. t.* **1** danneggiare, recare danno a (*q. o qc.*). **2** avariare.

damageable, *a.* danneggiabile.

damaged, *a.* **1** danneggiato. **2** avariato. // ~ **goods** merci avariate; ~ **party** (*leg.*) parte lesa.

damp, *v. t.* **1** inumidire. **2** scoraggiare.

dampen, *v. t.* (*econ.*) raffreddare, allentare. // to ~ **domestic demand** (*econ.*) raffreddare la domanda interna.

dampener, *n.* (*econ.*) ammortizzatore.

dampening, *n.* (*econ.*) raffreddamento.

dampened inflation, *n.* (*econ.*) inflazione attenuata, inflazione decrescente.

dandy note, *n.* (*dog.*) ordine di consegna.

danger, *n.* pericolo, rischio. // ~ **angle** (*trasp. mar.*) angolo di pericolo; ~ **money** (*pers.*) indennità di rischio; **the dangers of the road** (*trasp. aut.*) i pericoli della strada; ~ **signal** (*trasp.*) segnale di pericolo.

dangerous, *a.* pericoloso, rischioso. // ~ **goods** (*trasp.*) merci pericolose; ~ **occupations** (*sind.*) mestieri pericolosi; ~ **trades** (*sind.*) mestieri pericolosi.

dash, *n.* (*comun.*) linea, lineetta.

data, *n. pl.* **1** dati. **2** (*elab. elettr.*) dati.

datable, *a.* databile.

date[1], *n.* data. // ~ **as postmark** (*comun.*) data del timbro postale; ~ **bill** cambiale a data prefissata; ~ **-line** (*giorn.*) linea che porta la data d'un articolo; ~ **of a bill** data (di scadenza) d'una cambiale; ~ **of issue** (*banca, fin.*) data d'emissione; ~ **of maturity** data di scadenza; ~ **of registry** (*trasp. mar.*) data d'immatricolazione (*d'una nave*); **the** ~ **of sailing** (*trasp. mar.*) la data di partenza; ~ **on which a tax becomes applicable** (*fin.*) decorrenza d'un'imposta (*o* d'una tassa); ~ **schedule** (*pubbl.*) calendario delle scadenze; ~ **stamp** (*attr. uff.*) timbro per data, timbro a data; **down-to-** ~ *V.* **up-to-** ~; **out-of-** ~ passato di moda, antiquato; to ~ sino ad oggi, a tutt'oggi; **up-to-** ~ d'attualità, alla moda, moderno, aggiornato, (compilato) a tutt'oggi.

date[2], *v. t.* datare (*una lettera, un documento, ecc.*). *v. i.* essere datato. // to ~ **back** retrodatare; to ~ **forward** postdatare.

dateable, *a. V.* **datable.**

dated, *a.* datato. // **a** ~ **and stamped document** un documento recante data e bollo.

dateless, *a.* privo di data. // ~ **letter** lettera senza data.

dater, *n.* (*attr. uff.*) timbro per data, datario.

dation, *n.* (*leg.*) dazione. // ~ **in payment** (*leg.*) dazione in pagamento.

datum, *n.* (*pl.* **data**) dato.

daughter, *n.* figlia.

day, *n.* **1** giorno, giornata. **2** (*Borsa*) giorno di Borsa. // **the** ~ **after tomorrow** domani l'altro, dopodomani; ~ **before** giorno precedente, vigilia; ~ **before the settlement** (*Borsa*) vigilia della liquidazione; ~ **book** (*rag.*) brogliaccio; ~ **charge** (*comun.*) tariffa (*telefonica*) diurna; ~ **'s close** (*Borsa, fin.*) quotazione di chiusura; ~ **control** (*org. az.*) controllo giornaliero; ~ **'s journey** (*trasp.*) giornata di viaggio; ~ **labour** (*pers.*) manodopera a giornata; (*sind.*) lavoro a giornata; ~ **labourer** (*pers.*) lavoratore a giornata, giornaliero; ~ **letter** (*comun.*) telegramma diurno (*costa meno e viaggia più lento*); ~ **letter telegram** (*comun.*) telegramma lettera; ~ **man** (*pers.*) lavoratore a giornata, giornaliero; **days of grace** (*cred.*) giorni di grazia, giorni di tolleranza; dilazione (di pagamento); ~ **of rest** (*pers.*) giorno di riposo; ~ **off** (*pers.*) giorno di libertà, giornata libera; **the ~ prior to maturity** (*cred.*) il giorno precedente la scadenza; ~ **rate** (*sind.*) paga giornaliera; ~ **shift** (*pers.*) turno di giorno; ~ **'s sight** (*cred.*) a certo tempo vista; ~ **'s spread** (*Borsa, fin.*) scarto del giorno; ~ **ticket** (*trasp. ferr., ingl.*) biglietto ferroviario valido un solo giorno; ~ **-to- ~ loan** (*cred.*) prestito giornaliero, prestito rimborsabile su domanda; ~ **-to- ~ money** (*cred.*) prestito rimborsabile su domanda, prestito giornaliero; ~ **train** (*trasp. ferr.*) treno diurno; ~ **wages** (*sind.*) paga giornaliera, «giornata»; ~ **'s work** (*sind.*) lavoro giornaliero; **on the ~ it falls due** (*banca, cred.*) il giorno della scadenza; **this ~ week** oggi a otto; **two days before** antivigilia.

daybook, *n.* (*rag.*) prima nota.

daylight, *n.* luce del giorno. // ~ **saving** (*USA*) ora legale, ora estiva; ~ **saving time** (*USA*) ora legale, ora estiva (*V. ingl.* **summer time**); ~ **time** (*USA*) ora legale, ora estiva; ~ **train** (*trasp. ferr.*) *V.* **day train.**

dayside, *n.* (*giorn., pers.*) personale pomeridiano.

daywork, *n.* (*sind.*) lavoro d'una giornata.

dead, *a.* morto (*anche fig.*), estinto. // ~ **account** (*rag.*) conto estinto, conto fittizio; ~ **assets** (*rag.*) attività fittizie; ~ **beat** (*slang USA*) chi non riesce a far fronte ai propri impegni finanziari; ~ **book** (*fam.*) registro delle società che hanno cessato l'attività; ~ **calm** (*trasp. mar.*) bonaccia; ~ **cargo** (*trasp. mar.*) carico sopra coperta; ~ **end** (*trasp. ferr.*) termine d'una diramazione di linea ferroviaria; ~ **-end job** (*sind.*) impiego senza sbocchi di carriera; ~ **freight** (*trasp. mar.*) nolo «vuoto per pieno»; ~ **letter** (*comun.*) lettera giacente (*non ritirata o non consegnata, per irreperibilità del destinatario*); ~ **loss** (*rag.*) perdita netta, perdita secca; ~ **money** (*fin.*) denaro infruttifero; ~ **postal packet** (*comun.*) pacco giacente; ~ **season** (*market.*) stagione morta; ~ **stock** (*econ.*) scorte morte; (*fin.*) capitale (azionario) inutilizzato; (*market.*) giacenza di merce difficile a vendersi; ~ **weight** (*trasp. mar.*) portata lorda; ~ **-weight capacity** (*trasp. mar.*) portata lorda; ~ **-weight charter** (*trasp. mar.*) noleggio al lordo; ~ **-weight tonnage** (*trasp. mar.*) portata lorda.

deadhead, *n.* chi viaggia senza pagare il biglietto, chi va a teatro senza pagare il biglietto, «portoghese».

deadline, *n.* **1** scadenza; ora (data, ecc.) di scadenza. **2** (*pubbl.*) termine ultimo.

deadlock, *n.* punto morto.

deadweight, *n.* (*trasp. mar.*) portata. // ~ **debt** (*fin.*) debito non garantito.

deal[1]**,** *n.* **1** quantità. **2** negoziazione, trattativa. **3** compromesso. **4** affare. **5** affare losco. **6** (*fam.*) trattamento. **7** (*comm.*) operazione, «transazione».

deal[2]**,** *v. i.* (*pass.* e *part. pass.* **dealt**) **1** fare affari. **2** negoziare. **3** (*Borsa*) negoziare, operare. // to ~ **for the account** (*Borsa*) negoziare a termine; to ~ **for cash** (*Borsa*) negoziare per contanti; to ~ **for a fall** (*Borsa*) operare al ribasso; to ~ **for money** (*Borsa*) negoziare per contanti; to ~ **for a rise** (*Borsa*) operare al rialzo; to ~ **for the settlement** (*Borsa*) negoziare a termine; to ~ **in** occuparsi di; commerciare in, trattare (*un articolo, ecc.*); (*Borsa*) trattare (*titoli, ecc.*); to ~ **on credit** comprare a credito, vendere a credito; to ~ **with** fare affari con (*q.*); occuparsi di (*qc.*); trattare (*q.* o *qc.*).

dealable, *a.* **1** negoziabile. **2** (*comm.*) commerciabile, trattabile.

dealer, *n.* **1** commerciante, commerciante al minuto, negoziante, venditore, rivenditore. **2** (*Borsa*) operatore di Borsa. **3** (*Borsa, ingl.*) *V.* **jobber, stock jobber. 4** (*comm.*) operatore. // ~ **help** (*market.*) assistenza «promozionale»; **a ~ in dry goods** un commerciante in cereali; (*USA*) un commerciante in tessuti; **a ~ in stocks** un operatore di Borsa; ~ **network** (*market.*) rete delle vendite; ~ **'s spread** (*Borsa, fin., USA*) margine del «remisier»; **authorized dealers** (*leg.*) rivenditori autorizzati.

dealing, *n.* **1** contrattazione, trattativa. **2** rapporto d'affari. **3** operazione, «transazione». **4** comportamento, modo d'agire. **5** (*Borsa, comm.*) negoziazione, operazione. // ~ **for the account** (*Borsa*) negoziazione a termine; **dealings for the account** (*Borsa*) operazioni a termine; ~ **for cash** (*Borsa*) negoziazione per contanti; ~ **for a fall** (*Borsa*) operazione al ribasso; ~ **for money** (*Borsa*) negoziazione per contanti; ~ **for a rise** (*Borsa*) operazione al rialzo; ~ **for the settlement** (*Borsa*) negoziazione a termine; ~ **in shares for the coming out** (*Borsa*) operazione in azioni ancora da emettere.

deaner, *n.* 1 (*slang ingl.*) scellino. 2 (*slang USA*) decima parte di dollaro.

dear, *a.* 1 caro, costoso, dispendioso. 2 (*nell'introduzione a una lettera commerciale*) egregio, gentile, stimatissimo. *avv.* caro, a caro prezzo. // ~ **money** (*econ., fin.*) denaro caro; ~ **Sir** Egregio Signore (*introduzione a una lettera commerciale*).

dearly, *avv.* a caro prezzo.

dearness, *n.* l'esser caro, l'esser dispendioso, alto prezzo. // **the ~ of credit nowadays** (*cred.*) l'alto prezzo del credito al giorno d'oggi.

dearth, *n.* carestia.

death, *n.* morte. // ~ **-bed will** (*leg.*) testamento fatto in punto di morte; ~ **certificate** (*leg.*) certificato di morte; ~ **duty** (*leg.*) imposta di successione, tassa di successione; ~ **grant** (*pers.*) assegno per morte (*di un lavoratore assistito*); ~ **tax** (*leg., USA*) imposta di successione; **accidental ~** (*leg.*) morte accidentale.

debar, *v. t.* 1 escludere (*da un diritto, ecc.*). 2 (*leg.*) prescrivere. // to **be debarred** (*leg.*) cadere in prescrizione; to **be debarred from an action** (*leg.*) decadere da un'azione.

debarment, *n.* 1 esclusione (*da un diritto, ecc.*). 2 (*leg.*) prescrizione. // ~ **from a right** (*leg.*) decadenza da un diritto.

debase, *v. t.* (*econ.*) deprezzare, svalutare (*monete, ecc.*).

debasement, *n.* 1 abbassamento (*di valore*). 2 (*econ.*) deprezzamento, svalutazione (*di monete, ecc.*). // ~ **of the coinage** (*econ.*) svalutazione della moneta.

debatable, *a.* 1 discutibile. 2 discusso, messo in dubbio.

debate[1], *n.* 1 dibattimento, discussione. 2 (*leg.*) discussione.

debate[2], *v. t.* discutere. // to ~ **a suit** (*leg.*) discutere una causa.

debated, *a.* dibattuto, controverso. // ~ **clause** (*leg.*) clausola controversa.

debenture, *n.* 1 (*dog.*) polizza di rimborso del dazio. 2 (*fin.*) obbligazione, titolo obbligazionario. 3 (*fin.*) titolo del Debito Pubblico. // ~ **bond** (*fin.*) obbligazione; ~ **capital** (*fin.*) capitale obbligazionario; ~ **certificate** (*fin.*) cartella obbligazionaria; ~ **debt** (*fin.*) debito obbligazionario; ~ **holder** (*fin.*) obbligazionista; ~ **loan** (*fin.*) prestito obbligazionario; ~ **payable to bearer** (*banca, cred.*) obbligazione pagabile al portatore; ~ **stock** (*fin.*) obbligazione, obbligazioni irredimibili; ~ **yield** (*fin.*) reddito obbligazionario.

debit[1], *n.* 1 (*rag.*) addebito. 2 (*rag.*) «dare», colonna del «dare». *a. attr.* (*rag.*) debitore, a debito. // ~ **account** (*rag.*) conto debitore, conto a debito; ~ **advice** (*rag.*) nota d'addebito; ~ **and credit** (*rag.*) «dare» e «avere», entrata e uscita; ~ **balance** (*rag.*) saldo debitore, saldo a debito, saldo passivo, saldo «dare»; ~ **column** (*rag.*) colonna del «dare», colonna debitrice; ~ **entry** (*rag.*) registrazione a debito; ~ **interest** (*banca*) interessi debitori; ~ **interest rates** (*banca*) tassi d'interesse «debitori»; ~ **item** (*rag.*) partita a debito; ~ **ledger** (*rag.*) (libro) mastro delle vendite; ~ **memo** (*rag.*) nota d'addebito, nota d'addebitamento; ~ **memorandum** (*rag.*) *V.* ~ **memo;** ~ **note** (*rag.*) nota d'addebito; ~ **numbers** (*banca*) numeri debitori; **the ~ of an account** (*rag.*) il «dare» d'un conto; ~ **side** (*rag.*) «dare» (*d'un conto*).

debit[2], *v. t.* 1 (*rag.*) addebitare. 2 (*rag.*) registrare nella colonna del «dare». // to ~ **an account** (*rag.*) addebitare un conto.

debt, *n.* 1 (*cred.*) debito. 2 (*rag.*) debito. // ~ **and rights** (*cred.*) credito; ~ **collecting** (*cred.*) ricupero dei crediti; ~ **collecting agency** (*cred.*) agenzia per il ricupero dei crediti; ~ **collection** (*cred.*) ricupero dei crediti; ~ **collection agency** (*cred.*) agenzia per il ricupero dei crediti; ~ **collector** (*cred.*) agente per il ricupero dei crediti, esattore dei crediti; ~ **extinguished by lapse of time** (*leg.*) debito prescritto; ~ **proved in bankruptcy** (*leg.*) credito ammesso al passivo del fallimento; ~ **recovery** (*cred.*) ricupero dei crediti; ~ **recovery agency** (*cred.*) agenzia per il ricupero dei crediti; ~ **to net worth ratio** (*rag.*) rapporto fra le passività totali d'una ditta e il suo valore patrimoniale; **bad ~** credito inesigibile; to **be in ~** essere indebitato.

debtor, *n.* 1 (*cred.*) debitore. 2 (*rag.*) (intestazione della colonna del) «dare». *a. attr.* (*rag.*) debitore. // **a ~ able to pay** un debitore in grado di pagare; ~ **account** (*rag.*) conto debitore; ~ **and creditor** (*rag.*) «dare» e «avere»; ~ **company** (*cred.*) società debitrice; **debtors' ledger** (*rag.*) partitario clienti; ~ **in arrears** debitore in mora; ~ **on mortgage** (*cred.*) debitore ipotecario; ~ **side** (*rag.*) (colonna del) «dare».

decadence, *n.* decadenza.

decagram(me), *n.* decagrammo.

decaliter, *n.* (*USA*) decalitro.

decalitre, *n.* decalitro.

decameter, *n.* (*USA*) decametro.

decametre, *n.* decametro.

decasualisation, *n.* (*econ.*) «decasualizzazione» (*attività legislativa e organizzativa prevista dal piano Beveridge, mirante a rendere stabile e sicuro, non «casuale», il lavoro*).

decay[1]**,** *n.* decadenza.

decay[2]**,** *v. i.* decadere.

deceased, *a.* morto.

deceit, *n.* 1 frode, truffa. 2 (*leg.*) dolo.

deceitful person, *n.* persona disonesta.

deceive, *v. t.* frodare, truffare.

deceiver, *n.* imbroglione.

decentralization, *n.* (*org. az.*) decentramento, decentralizzazione.

decentralize, *v. t.* (*org. az.*) decentrare.

decide, *v. t.* decidere, risolvere (*una questione, una lite, ecc.*). *v. i.* decidersi. // to ~ **a controversy** (*leg.*) decidere una controversia; to ~ **in chambers** (*leg.*) deliberare in camera di consiglio; to ~ **the issue** tagliare la testa al toro (*fig.*).

decided, *a.* 1 deciso, definito. 2 fermo, netto. // **a ~ difference between the two totals** (*rag.*) una netta differenza fra i due totali; **a ~ recovery of the market** (*market.*) una decisa ripresa del mercato.

decigram, *n.* decigrammo.

deciliter, *n.* (*USA*) decilitro.

decilitre, *n.* decilitro.

decimal, *a.* e *n.* (*mat.*) decimale. // ~ **coinage** (*econ.*) sistema monetario decimale; ~ **currency** (*econ.*) moneta decimale, sistema monetario decimale; ~ **notation** (*mat.*) numerazione decimale; ~ **number** (*mat.*) numero decimale; ~ **system** (*mat.*) sistema decimale.

decimalization, *n.* 1 (*econ.*) «decimalizzazione», adozione del sistema monetario decimale. 2 (*mat.*) «decimalizzazione», riduzione al sistema decimale.

decimalize, *v. t.* 1 (*econ.*) «decimalizzare», adottare il sistema decimale. 2 (*mat.*) «decimalizzare», ridurre al sistema decimale. // to ~ **the currency** (*econ.*) decimalizzare la moneta.

decimate, *v. t.* diminuire fortemente.

decimeter, *n.* (*USA*) decimetro.

decimetre, *n.* decimetro.

decision, *n.* 1 decisione, risoluzione. 2 (*leg.*) decisione, sentenza. 3 (*org. az.*) decisione. // ~ **by default** (*leg.*) sentenza in assenza della parte; ~ **making** (*org. az.*) processo decisorio; ~ **-making power** (*org. az.*) potere decisionale; **by ~ of the Court** (*leg.*) per decisione della Corte.

decisional, *a.* decisionale.

decisive, *a.* decisivo.

deck, *n.* 1 (*elab. elettr., USA*) pacco (*di schede perforate*). 2 (*trasp.*) piano (*di nave, d'autobus, ecc.*). 3 (*trasp. mar.*) ponte, coperta. // ~ **cargo** (*trasp. mar.*) carico di coperta; ~ **-cargo premium** (*trasp. mar.*) premio per il carico di coperta; ~ **-cargo risk** (*ass. mar.*) rischio per il carico di coperta; ~ **load** (*trasp. mar.*) carico di coperta; ~ **loading clause** (*ass. mar.*) clausola della caricazione sopra coperta; ~ **passenger** (*trasp. mar.*) passeggero che viaggia sopra coperta; **on ~** (*pers., fam.*) pronto; **on ~ bill of lading** (*trasp. mar.*) polizza di carico emessa per certe merci che per la loro infiammabilità, deperibilità o altro debbono essere trasportate sul ponte della nave anziché nella stiva.

declarable, *a.* 1 dichiarabile. 2 (*dog.*) dichiarabile.

declarant, *n.* (*dog., leg.*) dichiarante.

declaration, *n.* 1 dichiarazione. 2 (*ass., leg.*) dichiarazione. 3 (*Borsa*) risposta (*ai premi*). 4 (*dog.*) dichiarazione, denuncia. // ~ **attested by a notary** (*leg.*) dichiarazione autenticata da un notaio; ~ **fire policy** (*ass.*) polizza aperta (*o* d'abbonamento) contro l'incendio; ~ **inwards** (*dog.*) dichiarazione d'entrata; ~ **of mortgage** (*leg.*) dichiarazione d'ipoteca; ~ **of option** (*Borsa*) risposta premi; ~ **of solvency** (*leg.*) dichiarazione di solvibilità (*d'una società commerciale*); ~ **of the value of the goods** (*ass.*) dichiarazione del valore delle merci; ~ **on oath** (*ass. mar., leg.*) dichiarazione giurata; ~ **outwards** (*dog.*) dichiarazione d'uscita; ~ **policy** (*ass.*) polizza aperta (*o* d'abbonamento); (*ass. mar.*) polizza flottante.

declaratory, *a.* (*anche leg.*) dichiaratorio, dichiarativo.

declare, *v. t.* 1 dichiarare. 2 (*ass., leg.*) dichiarare. 3 (*Borsa*) rispondere a (*un premio*). 4 (*dog.*) dichiarare, denunciare. // to ~ **a meeting closed** dichiarare tolta la seduta; to ~ **off** ritirarsi (*da un impegno, ecc.*); to ~ **off a contract** recedere da un contratto; to ~ **an option** (*Borsa*) rispondere ai premi.

declared, *a.* dichiarato. // ~ **value** (*dog.*) valore dichiarato.

declare oneself, *v. rifl.* dichiararsi.

declination, *n.* 1 (*trasp. mar.*) declinazione (*della bussola*). 2 (*USA*) rifiuto.

decline[1]**,** *n.* 1 declino, diminuzione, carenza, flessione. 2 (*comm.*) diminuzione, calo, ribasso (*di prezzi, ecc.*). 3 (*fin.*) ribasso. // **a ~ in stocks** (*Borsa*) un ribasso nei titoli; ~ **of business activity** (*econ.*) indebolimento congiunturale.

decline[2]**,** *v. i.* 1 diminuire, essere in diminuzione. 2 (*comm.*) diminuire, calare, abbassarsi, ribassare (*di prezzi, ecc.*). *v. t.* 1 declinare, rifiutare. 2 (*leg.*) declinare. // to ~ **any liability** (*leg.*) declinare ogni responsabilità; to ~ **an invitation** declinare un invito.

declining, *a.* decrescente. // ~ **-marginal-efficiency-of-capital theory** (*econ.*) teoria (*Keynesiana*) della produttività marginale decrescente del capitale.

decontrol[1], *n.* abolizione dei controlli, liberalizzazione, sblocco. // **the ~ of domestic oil prices** la liberalizzazione dei prezzi interni dei prodotti petroliferi.

decontrol[2], *v. t.* abolire i controlli su (*qc.*), liberalizzare, sbloccare. // to ~ **rents** sbloccare gli affitti.

decrease[1], *n.* 1 diminuzione, calo, ribasso, decremento. 2 (*econ.*) flessione. 3 (*rag.*) scostamento in meno riscontrato fra le cifre iscritte nel budget e quelle del consuntivo. // **a ~ in income** un decremento del reddito; **a ~ in prices** (*market.*) un ribasso dei prezzi; **a ~ in receipts** (*fin., rag.*) una diminuzione delle entrate; **on the ~** in diminuzione.

decrease[2], *v. i.* e *t.* decrescere, diminuire, calare, far calare.

decreasing, *a.* decrescente. // ~ **charges** (*rag.*) quote (*d'ammortamento*) decrescenti; ~ **cost** (*econ.*) costo decrescente; ~ **function** (*econ., mat.*) funzione decrescente; ~ **marginal cost** (*econ.*) costo marginale decrescente.

decree[1], *n.* 1 (*leg.*) decreto, deliberazione, ordine. 2 (*leg.*) provvedimento giudiziario (*o* amministrativo). 3 (*leg.*) sentenza. // ~ **for specific performance** (*leg.*) sentenza d'esecuzione specifica; ~ **in bankruptcy** (*leg.*) dichiarazione giudiziale di fallimento; ~ **of injunction** (*leg.*) decreto d'ingiunzione.

decree[2], *v. t.* (*leg.*) decretare, deliberare, ordinare, sancire, statuire.

decry, *v. t.* 1 screditare. 2 deprezzare. 3 (*econ.*) svalutare ufficialmente. // to ~ **a coin** (*econ.*) svalutare ufficialmente una moneta.

deduce, *v. t.* dedurre.

deducible, *a.* deducibile.

deduct[1], *n.* 1 detrazione, defalco. 2 (*sind.*) trattenuta.

deduct[2], *v. t.* dedurre, detrarre, defalcare, scontare. // to ~ **the income tax** (*fin.*) dedurre l'imposta sul reddito; to ~ **the weight of packing** detrarre il peso dell'imballaggio.

deductible, *a.* (*market.*) detraibile, deducibile. *n.* 1 (*ass.*) clausola di franchigia. 2 (*ass.*) oggetto di franchigia (*breve periodo di tempo, piccolo ammontare di danni, ecc.*).

deduction, *n.* 1 deduzione, detrazione, defalco, sconto. 2 (*fin.*) ritenuta d'acconto. 3 (*sind.*) trattenuta. // **a ~ from the salary** (*sind.*) una trattenuta sullo stipendio; **a ~ from one's taxable income** (*fin.*) una detrazione dal proprio (reddito) imponibile.

deed[1], *n.* 1 atto, azione. 2 (*amm.*) atto, strumento. 3 (*leg.*) atto, atto solenne, scrittura pubblica o privata (*che ha effetto legale*), scrittura notarile, rogito. // **a ~ attested by a notary** (*leg.*) atto rogato da un notaio, un rogito notarile; ~ **directly enforceable** (*leg.*) titolo esecutivo; ~ **form** (*leg.*) modulo per un atto legale; ~ **of arrangement** (*leg.*) accordo, concordato; atto col quale viene ufficialmente registrato un accordo fra un debitore e i suoi creditori sulla base d'un pagamento parziale del debito; ~ **of assignment** (*leg.*) atto di cessione; ~ **of association** atto costitutivo (*d'una società*); ~ **of covenant** (*ingl.*) atto col quale una parte s'impegna a compiere annualmente e per almeno sette anni una donazione a una associazione benefica o culturale senza fini di lucro; ~ **of gift** (*leg.*) atto di donazione; ~ **of guaranty** (*leg.*) dichiarazione di garanzia; ~ **of indemnity** (*leg.*) sanatoria; ~ **of partnership** (*leg.*) contratto d'associazione, contratto di società; ~ **of sale** (*leg.*) atto di compravendita; ~ **of transfer** (*leg.*) atto di cessione, atto di trasmissione; atto di permuta; ~ **of trust** (*leg.*) atto fiduciario, fidecommesso; ~ **poll** (*leg.*) atto unilaterale; ~ **under private seal** (*leg.*) scrittura privata.

deed[2], *v. t.* (*leg.*) trasferire per mezzo d'un atto legale.

deem, *v. t.* e *i.* credere, pensare.

deemer, *n.* (*slang USA*) decima parte di dollaro.

deep, *a.* profondo. // ~ **sea** alto mare; ~ **-sea captain** (*trasp. mar.*) capitano di lungo corso; ~ **-sea master** (*trasp. mar.*) capitano di lungo corso.

de facto, *locuz. avv.* di fatto.

defalcate, *v. t.* e *i.* (*cred.*) ridurre (*un debito*) per compensazione.

defalcation, *n.* 1 (*cred.*) riduzione di debito per compensazione. 2 (*leg.*) appropriazione indebita.

defamation, *n.* (*leg.*) diffamazione, calunnia.

defamatory, *a.* (*leg.*) diffamatorio, calunnioso.

defame, *v. t.* (*leg.*) diffamare, calunniare.

defamer, *n.* (*leg.*) diffamatore, calunniatore.

default[1], *n.* 1 difetto, mancanza. 2 (*comm.*)

inadempienza. 3 (*leg.*) assenza (*d'una delle due parti*); contumacia. 4 (*leg.*) inadempienza d'un obbligo. // ~ **of loan terms** (*leg.*) inadempienza delle condizioni d'un prestito; ~ **price** (*Borsa*) prezzo di rescissione; ~ **summons** (*leg.*) citazione per contumacia; **by** ~ (*leg.*) contumaciale; **in** ~ **of** in difetto di, in mancanza di; **in** ~ **of agreement** in mancanza d'accordo.

default[2], *v. i.* 1 essere in difetto, venir meno a un impegno. 2 (*comm.*) essere inadempiente, non pagare. 3 (*leg.*) non comparire in tribunale, essere contumace. 4 (*leg.*) essere inadempiente a un obbligo. *v. t.* (*leg.*) condannare in contumacia. // to ~ **a loan** (*leg.*) non restituire l'ammontare d'un prestito.

defaulter, *n.* 1 chi vien meno a un impegno, inadempiente. 2 (*leg.*) contumace. 3 (*leg.*) chi non adempie un'obbligazione.

defaulting, *a.* inadempiente. // ~ **debtor** debitore moroso; **the** ~ **party** (*leg.*) la parte inadempiente.

defeasance, *n.* 1 annullamento. 2 (*leg.*) risoluzione. 3 (*leg.*) clausola risolutoria. // ~ **clause** (*leg.*) clausola risolutoria (*d'un atto o contratto*).

defeasibility, *n.* 1 annullabilità. 2 (*leg.*) risolubilità.

defeasible, *a.* 1 annullabile. 2 (*leg.*) risolubile.

defeat, *v. t.* battere, respingere. // to ~ **the law** (*leg.*) eludere la legge.

defect, *n.* 1 difetto, imperfezione. 2 mancanza. 3 (*leg.*) difetto, vizio. // ~ **in property sold** (*leg.*) vizio della cosa venduta; ~ **of title** (*leg.*) titolo di proprietà difettoso.

defective, *a.* difettoso, imperfetto. // ~ **goods** (*market.*) merci difettose; ~ **title** (*leg.*) titolo di proprietà viziato; ~ **title insurance** (*ass.*) assicurazione per titoli di proprietà viziati.

defence, *n.* (*leg.*) difesa.

defend, *v. t.* difendere. // to ~ **a case** (*leg.*) difendere una causa.

defendant, *n.* e *a. attr.* (*leg.*) citato in giudizio, convenuto, accusato, querelato, imputato. // **the** ~ **company** (*leg.*) la società convenuta; ~ **'s domicile** (*leg.*) domicilio del convenuto.

defender, *n.* difensore.

defend oneself, *v. rifl.* difendersi.

defense, *n.* (*USA*) difesa. // ~ **attorney** (avvocato) difensore; (la) difesa.

defensive reaction, *n.* (*econ.*) reazione difensiva (*a un processo inflazionistico*).

defer, *v. t.* differire, posticipare, procrastinare, posporre, rimandare, rinviare. // to ~ **a meeting** rinviare una seduta; to ~ **payments** (*leg.*) differire i pagamenti.

deferment, *n.* 1 differimento, posticipazione, rinvio. 2 (*leg.*) proroga. // ~ **of payment** (*leg.*) proroga di pagamento.

deferrable, *a.* differibile, rinviabile, rimandabile, posticipabile, procrastinabile.

deferred, *a.* 1 differito, posticipato, procrastinato, rimandato, rinviato. 2 (*fin.*) postergato. // ~ **annuity** (*ass.*) annualità differita, rendita vitalizia differita; (*econ.*) rendita differita; ~ **asset** (*rag.*) costo anticipato; ~ **charge** (*rag.*) costo anticipato, risconto attivo; ~ **charges** (*rag.*) risconti attivi; ~ **delivery** (*Borsa*) consegna differita; ~ **income** (*rag.*) risconto passivo, risconti passivi; ~ **pay** (*sind.*) ritenuta sulla paga; ~ **share** (*fin.*) azione postergata; ~ **stock** (*fin.*) azioni postergate.

deficiency, *n.* 1 deficienza, mancanza. 2 (*fin., rag.*) differenza (*in meno*), disavanzo. // ~ **bill** (*fin.*) prestito provvisorio per scarsità d'introiti (*concesso dalla Banca d'Inghilterra al Governo britannico*).

deficient, *a.* deficiente, manchevole. // to **be** ~ difettare.

deficit, *n.* 1 deficienza, scarsità. 2 (*fin., rag.*) deficit, disavanzo, passivo, saldo passivo, sbilancio. // ~ **financing** (*econ.*) accettazione deliberata del deficit d'uno Stato come mezzo per mettere in moto meccanismi di ripresa economica attraverso la dilatazione della spesa pubblica, ricorso al prestito pubblico per finanziare spese statali; **a** ~ **in the balance of payments** (*fin.*) un disavanzo nella bilancia dei pagamenti; ~ **to be expected** passivo prevedibile.

define, *v. t.* definire.

definite, *a.* definito. // ~ **and clear cut responsibilities** (*org. az.*) responsabilità chiare e definite; ~ **slip** (*ass. mar.*) polizzetta definitiva.

definition, *n.* definizione.

definitive, *a.* definitivo, decisivo, finale, ultimo. // **the** ~ **offer** l'ultima offerta.

deflate, *v. t.* (*econ.*) deflazionare.

deflation, *n.* 1 sgonfiamento. 2 (*econ.*) deflazione. // ~ **of credit** (*econ.*) deflazione creditizia.

deflationary, *a.* (*econ.*) deflazionistico, deflatorio. // ~ **effect** (*fin.*) effetto deflazionistico; ~ **gap** (*econ.*) deficit deflazionistico, divario deflazionistico; ~ **measures** (*econ.*) misure deflazionistiche; ~ **policy** (*econ.*) politica deflazionistica.

deflection of customs revenue, *n.* (*dog.*) deviazione d'introiti doganali.

deflection of trade, *n.* (*econ.*) diversione dei traffici.

defraud, *v. t.* (*leg.*) defraudare, frodare, truffare. // to ~ **with false pretences** (*leg.*) truffare con raggiri.

defray, *v. t.* 1 pagare (*il costo di qc.*). 2 sostenere (*spese*).

defunct company, *n.* (*amm.*) società liquidata, società sciolta.

degree, *n.* 1 grado. 2 laurea. 3 (*mat.*) grado. 4 (*mat.*) potenza. // ~ **of inability** (*pers.*) grado d'invalidità; ~ **of intelligence** (*pers.*) grado d'intelligenza; ~ **of kindred** (*leg.*) grado di parentela; ~ **of latitude** (*trasp. mar.*) grado di latitudine.

de jure, *locuz. avv.* di diritto.

dekagram, *n.* decagrammo.

dekaliter, *n.* (*USA*) decalitro.

dekalitre, *n.* decalitro.

dekameter, *n.* (*USA*) decametro.

dekametre, *n.* decametro.

delay[1], *n.* 1 indugio, ritardo. 2 dilazione, proroga, rinvio. 3 (*comm.*) dilazione, «respiro». 4 (*leg.*) mora. 5 (*org. az.*) ritardo. // ~ **in the execution of an order** ritardo nell'esecuzione d'un ordine; **without** ~ senza indugio; **without further** ~ senza ulteriore dilazione.

delay[2], *v. t.* 1 ritardare. 2 rimandare, rinviare, posporre, procrastinare. 3 trattenere. 4 (*cred.*) prorogare. *v. i.* indugiare. // to ~ **meeting an account** rimandare un pagamento, tirare in lungo un pagamento; to ~ **a payment** rinviare un pagamento.

delayable, *a.* 1 rimandabile, rinviabile. 2 (*cred.*) prorogabile.

delayed payment, *n.* pagamento ritardato.

delayed retirement, *n.* (*pers.*) pensionamento posticipato.

delaying, *a.* dilatorio. // **a** ~ **action** (*leg.*) un'azione dilatoria; ~ **practices** (*leg.*) espedienti dilatori.

del credere, *n.* e *a. attr.* (*comm., leg.*) star del credere. // ~ **agent** (*market.*) agente del credere; ~ **agreement** (*leg.*) contratto del credere; ~ **commission** (*market.*) commissione (*o* provvigione) del credere.

delegant, *n.* (*leg.*) delegante.

delegate[1], *n.* (*pers.*) delegato, incaricato.

delegate[2], *v. t.* 1 delegare, deputare. 2 (*org. az.*) delegare.

delegated debtor, *n.* (*leg.*) debitore delegato.

delegated law, *n.* (*leg.*) legge delega.

delegatee, *n.* (*leg.*) delegatario.

delegation, *n.* 1 (*leg.*) delegazione. 2 (*leg.*) delega. 3 (*org. az.*) delega. 4 (*org. az., sind.*) delegazione, deputazione, rappresentanza. // ~ **of authority** (*org. az.*) delega d'autorità; ~ **of powers** (*org. az.*) delega di potere; ~ **of responsibility** (*org. az.*) delega di responsabilità.

delegator, *n.* (*leg.*) delegante.

delete, *v. t.* cancellare, eliminare. // to ~ **an item from the catalogue** (*market.*) eliminare un articolo dal catalogo.

deletion, *n.* cancellatura, cancellazione, eliminazione.

deliberate[1], *a.* 1 intenzionale, voluto. 2 ponderato.

deliberate[2], *v. t.* 1 deliberare, discutere. 2 calcolare, ponderare.

deliberation, *n.* 1 deliberazione, discussione. 2 ponderatezza. 3 (*leg.*) deliberazione.

delinquent, *a.* 1 colpevole (*anche d'una negligenza*). 2 in arretrato, moroso. // ~ **debtor** (*leg.*) debitore moroso; ~ **taxes** (*leg.*) arretrati d'imposte.

deliver, *v. t.* 1 consegnare, recapitare, rilasciare. 2 distribuire. 3 (*trasp. mar.*) sbarcare (*merce: da una nave, ecc.*). // to ~ **goods** (*market.*) consegnare merce; to ~ **letters** (*comun.*) distribuire la corrispondenza; to ~ **stock** (*fin.*) consegnare titoli.

delivered prices, *n. pl.* prezzi franchi.

deliver oneself up, *v. rifl.* (*leg.*) costituirsi.

delivery, *n.* 1 consegna, rilascio, recapito. 2 distribuzione. 3 (*leg.*) consegna (*anche d'un atto o contratto*), tradizione. // ~ **area** (*comun.*) zona di distribuzione (*della posta, ecc.*); ~ **at the port of discharge** (*market.*) consegna al porto d'arrivo; ~ **book** (*trasp. ferr.*) bollettario di consegna; ~ **charges** (*rag.*) spese di consegna; ~ **costs** (*market.*) costi di distribuzione; ~ **ex-warehouse** (*trasp.*) consegna dal magazzino; ~ **free on rail** (*trasp. ferr.*) consegna franco rotaia; ~ **free on truck** (*trasp. ferr.*) consegna franco vagone; ~ **made in security of a debt** (*leg.*) consegna fatta a garanzia d'un debito; ~ **man** (*pers.*) addetto alle consegne; fattorino; ~ **note** (*org. az.*) bolla di consegna; (*trasp. ferr.*) nota di consegna, bolletta; ~ **of the ship** (*trasp. mar.*) consegna della nave; ~ **on term** (*market.*) consegna a termine; ~ **order** (*trasp.*) ordine di consegna; (*trasp. mar.*) buono di consegna; ~ **outside prescribed boundaries** (*trasp. ferr.*) servizio di rispedizione; ~ **schedule** (*org. az.*) tabella di previsione delle consegne; ~ **spot** (*market.*) consegna sopra luogo; ~ **terms** (*market.*) condizioni di consegna; ~ **to arrive** (*trasp. mar.*) consegna all'arrivo (*della nave*); ~ **under ship's tackle** (*trasp. mar.*) consegna sotto paranco; ~ **van** (*trasp. aut.*) furgone; **non-** ~ (*market.*) mancata consegna.

de-man, *v. t.* (*econ.*) ridurre il personale di (*un'industria, un'azienda, ecc.*). *v. i.* effettuare una riduzione di personale.

demand[1], *n.* **1** domanda, richiesta. **2** esigenza, pretesa. **3** (*econ.*) domanda. // ~ **analysis** (*market.*) analisi della domanda; ~ **and supply** (*econ.*) domanda e offerta; ~ **bill** (*banca*) tratta a vista; ~ **conditions** (*econ.*) situazione della domanda; ~ **curve** (*econ.*) curva della domanda; ~ **deposit** (*banca*) deposito a vista; (*fin., USA*) deposito in conto corrente di corrispondenza; ~ **draft** (*banca*) tratta a vista; ~ **inflation** (*econ.*) inflazione da (eccesso di) domanda; ~ **loan** (*cred.*) prestito (rimborsabile) a vista; ~ **pass** (*trasp. mar.*) patente mercantile; ~ **pull** (*econ.*) spinta della domanda; ~ **-push inflation** (*econ.*) inflazione da domanda; ~ **rate** (*fin.*) corso a vista, tasso a vista; **the** ~ **trend** (*econ.*) l'andamento della domanda; to **be in** ~ essere richiesto; **on** ~ (*banca, cred.*) a richiesta, a vista.

demand[2], *v. t.* **1** domandare, chiedere, richiedere. **2** esigere, pretendere.

demandable, *a.* esigibile.

demandant, *n.* (*leg.*) attore, richiedente.

de-manning, *n.* (*econ.*) riduzione del personale (*in un'azienda, ecc.*).

demesne, *n.* (*leg.*) proprietà (*d'immobili*).

demise[1], *n.* **1** (*leg.*) cessione. **2** (*leg.*) trasferimento (*di diritti*). **3** (*leg.*) traslazione di proprietà. // ~ **charter** (*trasp. mar.*) noleggio di scafo nudo.

demise[2], *v. t.* **1** (*leg.*) cedere (*specialm. in affitto*). **2** (*leg.*) trasferire (*diritti*).

demonetization, *n.* (*econ.*) demonetizzazione.

demonetize, *v. t.* (*econ.*) demonetizzare (*un metallo, ecc.*).

demonstrate, *v. t.* **1** dimostrare. **2** (*pubbl.*) dimostrare (*un articolo o un prodotto a un cliente potenziale*).

demonstration, *n.* **1** dimostrazione. **2** (*pubbl.*) dimostrazione (*d'un articolo o d'un prodotto a un cliente potenziale*).

demonstrator, *n.* **1** (*pers., pubbl.*) dimostratore. **2** (*pubbl.*) articolo (*o* prodotto) usato per una dimostrazione.

demur[1], *n.* **1** esitazione. **2** (*leg.*) eccezione, obiezione.

demur[2], *v. i.* **1** esitare. **2** temporeggiare. **3** (*leg.*) eccepire, obiettare, sollevare una obiezione.

demurrable, *a.* che può essere contestato.

demurrage, *n.* **1** (*trasp.*) ritardo (*di nave, carro merci, ecc.*). **2** (*trasp.*) diritto di sosta. **3** (*trasp. mar.*) controstallia, controstallie. // ~ **charges** (*trasp. mar.*) diritti di controstallia; ~ **club** (*trasp. mar.*) sezione controstallie; ~ **days** (*trasp. mar.*) giorni di controstallie.

demurrer, *n.* (*leg.*) eccezione.

denationalization, *n.* (*econ.*) denazionalizzazione, snazionalizzazione, privatizzazione.

denationalize, *v. t.* (*econ., fin.*) denazionalizzare, snazionalizzare, privatizzare.

denial, *n.* smentita.

denomination, *n.* **1** nome (*d'una classe di cose*). **2** unità di misura. **3** valore (*d'una moneta*). **4** taglio (*di biglietti di banca, ecc.*).

denominational value, *n.* (*econ.*) valore nominale (*d'una moneta, banconota, titolo, ecc.*).

denominator, *n.* (*mat.*) divisore.

denounce, *v. t.* (*anche leg.*) denunciare, denunziare.

dense, *a.* denso, fitto.

densely, *avv.* densamente.

density, *n.* **1** densità. **2** (*pubbl.*) opacità (*d'una negativa*). // ~ **of freight traffic** (*trasp.*) densità del traffico merci; ~ **of passenger traffic** (*trasp.*) densità del traffico passeggeri.

denunciable, *a.* denunciabile.

denunciation, *n.* (*anche leg.*) denuncia, denunzia.

deny, *v. t.* e *i.* **1** negare. **2** rifiutare. **3** non riconoscere, smentire. // to ~ **a charge** (*leg.*) negare un'accusa; to ~ **one's word** non tener fede alla parola.

depart, *v. i.* partire. *v. t.* lasciare. // to ~ **from** allontanarsi da, abbandonare; to ~ **from one's promise** non tener fede a una promessa.

departing clause, *n.* (*leg.*) clausola derogatoria.

department, *n.* **1** dipartimento, dicastero, ministero. **2** (*org. az.*) reparto, compartimento, sezione, ufficio, servizio. // ~ **head** (*pers.*) capo reparto; ~ **of Agriculture** (*USA*) Ministero dell'Agricoltura; ~ **of Commerce** (*USA*) Ministero del Commercio; ~ **of Defense** (*USA*) Ministero della Difesa; ~ **of Economic Affairs** Ministero degli Affari Economici; ~ **of Education and Science** Ministero della Pubblica Istruzione e della Ricerca Scientifica; ~ **of Health, Education and Welfare** (*USA*) Ministero della Sanità, della Pubblica Istruzione e del Benessere; ~ **of the Interior** (*USA*) Ministero dell'Interno; ~ **of Labor** (*USA*) Ministero del Lavoro; ~ **of Trade** (*G.B.*) Ministero del Commercio; ~ **of the Treasury**

(*USA*) Ministero del Tesoro; ~ **store** (*market.*) grande negozio, grande emporio, grandi magazzini; ~ **stores** (*market.*) grandi magazzini.

departmental, *a.* 1 dipartimentale. 2 diviso in reparti, sezioni, uffici, ecc. // ~ **costs** (*rag.*) costi diretti.

departure, *n.* 1 partenza. 2 allontanamento, deviazione, infrazione. // ~ **from the law** (*leg.*) deroga alla legge; **a** ~ **from official procedure** una deroga alla procedura ufficiale; ~ **lounge** (*trasp. aer.*) sala partenze; **on** ~ (*trasp.*) al momento della partenza.

depend, *v. i.* 1 dipendere. 2 fare assegnamento, contare (*su*); fidarsi (*di*).

dependability, *n.* fidatezza.

dependable, *a.* fidato, fido. // **a** ~ **employee** (*pers.*) un impiegato fidato.

dependant, *n.* (*sind.*) persona a carico.

dependence, *n.* 1 dipendenza. 2 sostegno, mezzo di sostentamento. 3 l'essere a carico (*di q.*). // ~ **effect** (*econ.*) effetto di dipendenza.

dependencies, *n. pl.* crediti probabili.

dependent, *a.* 1 dipendente, che dipende da (*q.*). 2 a carico di (*q.*). *n. V.* **dependant.** // ~ **variable** (*mat.*) variabile dipendente.

deplete, *v. t.* esaurire (*una miniera, un pozzo petrolifero*).

depletion, *n.* 1 esaurimento. 2 (*rag.*) riduzione di valore. // ~ **of capital** (*rag.*) svalutazione del capitale.

depone, *v. t.* (*leg.*) deporre, testimoniare, dichiarare sotto giuramento.

deponent, *n.* (*leg.*) chi fa una deposizione, testimone, testimonio.

depose, *v. t.* (*leg.*) deporre, testimoniare, dichiarare sotto giuramento.

deposer, *n.* (*leg.*) chi fa una deposizione, testimone, testimonio.

deposit[1], *n.* 1 deposito, versamento. 2 (*banca*) deposito, versamento. 3 (*dog.*) deposito, consegna (*di merci, ecc.*). 4 (*leg.*) deposito cauzionale, caparra. // ~ **account** (*banca*) conto di deposito, conto vincolato; ~ **account passbook** (*banca*) libretto di conto vincolato; ~ **at call** (*banca*) deposito (rimborsabile) a vista; ~ **at notice** (*banca*) deposito (rimborsabile) con preavviso; ~ **bank** (*banca*) banca di deposito; ~ **book** (*banca*) libretto (di deposito) nominativo; ~ **of cash** (*banca*) deposito di numerario; ~ **of dutiable goods** (*dog.*) consegna delle merci soggette a dazio (*doganale*); ~ **of stock** (*banca, fin.*) deposito di titoli; ~ **on current account** (*banca*) deposito in conto corrente; ~ **payable on demand** (*banca*) deposito esigibile a vista; ~ **receipt** (*banca*) buono di cassa; (*Borsa, fin.*) ricevuta di deposito; (*dog.*) ricevuta di consegna; ~ **slip** (*banca*) distinta (*o* modulo) di versamento; ~ **society** (*fin., ingl.*) tipo di società mutua che accetta piccoli versamenti periodici da parte dei soci; ~ **warrant** (*dog.*) certificato di deposito; **on** ~ (*banca*) in conto vincolato.

deposit[2], *v. t.* 1 depositare. 2 (*banca*) depositare, versare. 3 (*dog.*) depositare, consegnare (*merci, ecc.*). 4 (*leg.*) pagare (*una somma di denaro*) in anticipo; depositare in cauzione; pagare come caparra. // to ~ **st. as security** (*leg.*) depositare qc. in garanzia; to ~ **documents with the Court** (*leg.*) depositare documenti in tribunale; to ~ **money in the bank** (*banca*) depositare denaro in banca.

depositary, *a.* depositario. *n.* 1 (*leg.*) depositario. 2 (*market.*) depositario. // ~ **agent** (*pers.*) agente depositario.

deposition, *n.* (*leg.*) deposizione. // ~ **under oath** (*leg.*) deposizione giurata.

depositor, *n.* (*banca, leg.*) depositante. // ~**'s book** (*banca*) libretto del depositante, libretto nominativo.

depot, *n.* 1 (*org. az.*) deposito, magazzino. 2 (*trasp. ferr., USA*) stazione ferroviaria.

depreciate, *v. t.* 1 deprezzare, svalutare (*merci, ecc.*). 2 (*fin.*) svalutare. *v. i.* 1 deprezzarsi (*di merci, ecc.*). 2 (*fin.*) svalutarsi (*di monete, ecc.*).

depreciation, *n.* 1 deprezzamento (*di merci, ecc.*). 2 (*fin.*) deprezzamento (*di una valuta*), svalutazione. 3 (*fin., rag.*) ammortamento degli impianti. 4 (*rag.*) ammortamento, deprezzamento, svalutazione, obsolescenza. // ~ **allowance** (*fin.*) ammortamenti fiscali; ~ **charge** (*rag.*) aliquota d'ammortamento; ~ **fund** (*rag.*) fondo di deprezzamento, fondo d'ammortamento; ~ **of capital** (*econ.*) ammortamento di capitale; ~ **of a plant** (*rag.*) obsolescenza d'un impianto; ~ **of securities** (*fin.*) svalutazione di titoli; ~ **reserve ratio** (*org. az.*) rapporto fra il totale del fondo ammortamento e il costo originario d'un immobilizzo.

depress, *v. t.* 1 deprimere. 2 abbassare, ridurre (*il volume d'affari, i prezzi, ecc.*).

depressed, *a.* 1 depresso. 2 (*di volume d'affari, prezzo, ecc.*) abbassato, ridotto. // ~ **areas** (*econ.*) zone depresse; ~ **trade** commercio fiacco.

depressing, *a.* deprimente.

depression, *n.* 1 depressione. 2 abbassamento, riduzione (*del volume d'affari, dei prezzi, ecc.*). 3 (*econ.*) depressione, crisi (*commerciale, ecc.*). // **a** ~ **in trade** una crisi commerciale.

deprive, *v. t.* (*leg.*) privare.

depth, *n.* **1** profondità. **2** (*pubbl.*) altezza (*di un'inserzione, d'un carattere tipografico*). // ~ **interview** (*pers.*) intervista in profondità.

deputy, *n.* **1** sostituto, incaricato, interino. **2** (*leg.*) sostituto, delegato. **3** (*pers.*) sostituto, aggiunto, vice, facente funzione. // ~ **chairman** (*pers.*) vicepresidente; ~ **editor** (*giorn.*) vicedirettore; (*giorn., USA*) viceredattore; ~ **manager** (*pers.*) vicedirettore; **by** ~ (*leg.*) per procura.

derail, *v. t.* (*trasp. ferr.*) far deragliare.

derate, *v. t.* (*fin.*) diminuire (*o* eliminare) il carico d'imposta su (*qc.*).

deregulate, *v. t.* (*econ.*) liberalizzare, sbloccare (*prezzi, affitti, ecc.*).

deregulation, *n.* (*econ.*) liberalizzazione, sblocco (*di prezzi, affitti, ecc.*).

derelict, *a.* abbandonato. *n.* (*leg.*) cosa abbandonata (*dal proprietario*). // **a** ~ **ship** (*leg., trasp. mar.*) una nave abbandonata (un relitto).

derestrict, *v. t.* (*econ., fin.*) togliere restrizioni a, liberalizzare.

derivable, *a.* deducibile.

derive, *v. t.* e *i.* dedurre (*idee, ecc.*), ricavare, trarre, ottenere.

derived demand, *n.* (*econ.*) domanda derivata.

derived value, *n.* (*econ.*) valore derivato.

derogate, *v. i.* derogare. // to ~ **from the rule** derogare alla regola.

derogation, *n.* deroga. // ~ **of** (*o* **to**) **a contract** (*leg.*) deroga a un contratto; ~ **of** (*o* **to**) **a law** (*leg.*) deroga a una legge.

derogatory, *a.* (*leg.*) derogatorio. // ~ **clause** (*leg.*) clausola derogatoria.

descendant, *n.* (*leg.*) discendente.

descent, *n.* **1** discesa. **2** (*leg.*) discendenza.

describe, *v. t.* descrivere.

description, *n.* **1** descrizione. **2** (*banca, rag.*) causale. // ~ **column** (*rag.*) colonna delle causali; ~ **of goods** descrizione della merce; ~ **of shares** (*fin.*) descrizione delle azioni.

descriptive, *a.* descrittivo.

desert, *v. t.* abbandonare, lasciare (*per sempre*).

design[1], *n.* **1** disegno. **2** piano, progetto, disegno (industriale). **3** design. **4** (*org. az.*) progetto, progettazione. **5** (*org. az.*) disegno, modello. // **the** ~ **for a new plant** il progetto per un nuovo stabilimento; ~ **of manufacturing systems** (*org. az.*) progettazione d'impianti; ~ **patent** (*leg.*) brevetto industriale.

design[2], *v. t.* **1** disegnare, modellare. **2** progettare. *v. i.* **1** (*pers.*) fare il designer, fare il modellista. **2** (*pers.*) fare il progettista, far progetti.

designer, *n.* **1** (*pers.*) designer, disegnatore industriale, modellista, progettista. **2** (*pubbl.*) grafico.

desire[1], *n.* **1** desiderio. **2** invito, richiesta. // **at the** ~ **of Mr Brown** per invito di Mr Brown, su richiesta di Mr Brown.

desire[2], *v. t.* **1** desiderare. **2** chiedere, invitare.

desist, *v. i.* desistere.

desistance, *n.* desistenza. // ~ **from a suit** (*leg.*) remissione di causa; ~ **of injured party** (*leg.*) remissione di parte lesa.

desk, *n.* (*giorn., USA*) ufficio redazionale. // ~ **calendar** (*attr. uff.*) calendario da tavolo; ~ **clerk** (*tur., USA*) «receptionist», addetto al ricevimento; ~ **diary** (*attr. uff.*) agenda; ~ **jockey** (*slang USA*) impiegato d'ufficio; ~ **secretary** (*pers., USA*) segretario d'ufficio; ~ **-top computer** (*elab. elettr.*) elaboratore da tavolo; ~ **work** (*sind.*) lavoro fatto a tavolino, lavoro d'ufficio.

despatch, *n.* e *v. t. V.* **dispatch.**

destination, *n.* **1** destinazione, meta. **2** (*leg.*) destinazione. // ~ **for a legacy** (*leg.*) destinazione per un legato; ~ **station** (*trasp. ferr.*) stazione di destinazione.

destine, *v. t.* destinare.

destruction, *n.* soppressione. // ~ **of correspondence** (*leg.*) soppressione di corrispondenza.

detach, *v. t.* staccare. // to ~ **a coupon** (*fin.*) staccare una cedola.

detail[1], *n.* **1** particolare, dettaglio. **2** descrizione minuziosa. **3 details,** *pl.* (*leg.*) estremi. // **the details of a plan** i particolari d'un progetto; **in** ~ nei particolari.

detail[2], *v. t.* dettagliare, descrivere minutamente.

detailed, *a.* particolareggiato. // ~ **description** descrizione minuziosa; **a** ~ **list** (*fin., leg., market.*) una specifica; **a** ~ **report on market trends** (*market.*) una relazione particolareggiata sulle tendenze di mercato.

detain, *v. t.* **1** trattenere, non restituire. **2** (*leg.*) trattenere (*in stato di fermo*); detenere. // to **be detained (in custody) by the police** (*leg.*) essere detenuto dalla polizia.

detainee, *n.* (*leg.*) detenuto.

detainer, *n.* **1** (*leg.*) detentore. **2** (*leg.*) detenzione, detenzione illegale (*di persona o cosa*).

detect, *v. t.* scorgere.

detective, *n.* investigatore.

détente, *n.* distensione (*fig.*).

detention, *n.* 1 l'esser trattenuto. 2 (*anche leg.*) detenzione; fermo (*di polizia*); carcerazione preventiva. 3 (*trasp. mar.*) ritardo. // ~ **of a ship** (*trasp. mar.*) detenzione d'una nave.

determinable, *a.* determinabile. // **at a ~ future time** (*banca, cred.*) a data futura (determinabile).

determination, *n.* 1 determinazione. 2 (*econ.*) tendenza. 3 (*leg.*) decisione, conclusione, risoluzione. // ~ **clause** (*leg.*) clausola risolutiva; **the ~ of capital towards investment in transport industries** la tendenza del capitale verso gli investimenti nel settore dei trasporti.

determine, *v. t.* 1 determinare, causare. 2 (*leg.*) decidere, risolvere, mettere fine a. // to ~ **a contract** (*leg.*) risolvere un contratto.

determined, *a.* determinato.

detinue, *n.* (*leg.*) detenzione illegale (*di cosa dovuta ad altri*).

detrimental, *a.* dannoso.

deuce, *n.* (*slang USA*) banconota da due dollari.

devalorize, *v. t.* (*econ.*) svalutare.

devaluate, *v. t.* (*econ.*) svalutare.

devaluation, *n.* (*econ.*) svalutazione, devalutazione. // **the ~ rate** (*econ.*) il tasso (*o* saggio) di svalutazione.

devalue, *v. t.* (*econ.*) svalutare.

develop, *v. t.* 1 sviluppare, promuovere lo sfruttamento di. 2 (*mat.*) sviluppare (*un'equazione, ecc.*). 3 (*pubbl.*) sviluppare (*una pellicola*). *v. i.* 1 svilupparsi. 2 (*USA*) emergere. // to ~ **one's business** (*amm.*) sviluppare la propria azienda; to ~ **the competitive capacity of European firms** sviluppare la capacità concorrenziale delle imprese europee; to ~ **an equation** (*mat.*) sviluppare un'equazione; to ~ **a tendency** manifestare a poco a poco una tendenza; **developing and printing** (*pubbl.*) sviluppo e stampa.

developed, *a.* sviluppato. // ~ **Countries** (*econ.*) Paesi industrializzati.

developing, *a.* in via di sviluppo. // ~ **Countries** (*econ.*) Paesi in via di sviluppo.

development, *n.* 1 sviluppo, evoluzione. 2 (*mat.*) sviluppo (*d'un'equazione, ecc.*). 3 (*pubbl.*) sviluppo (*fotografico*). // ~ **area** (*econ.*) area di sviluppo, area depressa (*da sviluppare*); **the ~ of industry** (*econ.*) lo sviluppo industriale.

deviate, *v. i.* deviare.

deviation, *n.* 1 deviazione. 2 (*econ., fin., rag.*) scarto. 3 (*trasp. aer., trasp. mar.*) deviazione dalla rotta. // ~ **clause** (*ass. mar.*) clausola di deviazione; ~ **risk** (*ass. mar.*) rischio di deviazione.

device, *n.* 1 congegno, aggeggio. 2 accorgimento; piano, progetto. 3 (*leg.*) artificio.

devisable, *a.* (*leg.*) trasmissibile in eredità.

devise[1], *n.* (*leg.*) assegnazione testamentaria.

devise[2], *v. t.* 1 ideare. 2 (*leg.*) lasciare (*beni immobili*) in eredità.

devisee, *n.* (*leg.*) legatario.

devisor, *n.* (*leg.*) testatore, testatore di beni immobili.

devolution, *n.* (*anche leg.*) devoluzione.

devolve, *v. t.* 1 devolvere (*un diritto, ecc.*). 2 affidare, delegare. *v. i.* passare (*per competenza*). // to ~ **one's work on a subordinate** (*org. az.*) affidare il proprio lavoro a un dipendente.

devote, *v. t.* offrire.

dews, *n.* (*slang USA*) dieci dollari.

dexterous, *a.* abile.

diagram, *n.* diagramma, grafico, schema.

dial[1], 1 quadrante (*d'un orologio, d'una bilancia automatica, ecc.*). 2 (*comun.*) disco combinatore (*del telefono*). // ~ **lock** serratura «a combinazione»; ~ **tone** (*comun.*) segnale acustico di «linea libera» (*al telefono*).

dial[2], *v. t.* (*comun.*) comporre, fare, formare (*un numero telefonico*). // to ~ **direct to Italy** (*comun.*) chiamare l'Italia in teleselezione; to ~ **a number** (*comun.*) comporre un numero (*al telefono*).

diary, *n.* (*attr. uff.*) diario, agenda.

dib, *n.* 1 (*slang USA*) dollaro. 2 (*slang USA*) denaro.

dibs, *n. pl.* (*slang USA*) denaro.

Dictaphone, *n.* (*marchio*) (*attr. uff.*) dittafono.

dictate, *v. t.* dettare. // to ~ **a letter to the secretary** dettare una lettera alla segretaria.

dictating equipment, *n.* (*attr. uff.*) dittafono.

dictation, *n.* dettatura.

die, *n.* (*pubbl.*) fustella. // ~ **-cut** (*pubbl.*) fustellato.

differ, *v. i.* differire, essere diverso (*da*).

difference, *n.* 1 differenza, diversità. 2 (*leg.*) vertenza, contestazione. // ~ **between the debit and credit of an account** (*rag.*) differenza fra il dare e l'avere d'un conto; ~ **in the cash** (*rag.*) differenza di cassa; **the ~ in the exchange rate in the debtor's favour** (*fin.*) la differenza di cambio a favore del debitore; ~ **in price** (*market.*) differenza di prezzo; ~ **of exchange**

(*fin.*) differenza di cambio; ~ **of opinion** diversità d'opinioni.

different, *a.* differente, diverso.

differential, *a.* differenziale. // ~ **cost** (*o* **profit**) **analysis** (*fin.*) analisi marginale; ~ **rates on a railway** (*trasp. ferr.*) tariffe ferroviarie differenziali; ~ **tariffs** (*comm. est.*) tariffe differenziali.

difficult, *a.* difficile. // ~ **of access** di difficile accesso.

difficulty, *n.* difficoltà.

diffuse, *v. t.* diffondere.

dilatation, *n.* dilatazione.

dilate, *v. t.* dilatare. *v. i.* dilatarsi.

dilatory plea, *n.* (*leg.*) eccezione dilatoria.

dime, *n.* (*USA*) moneta degli Stati Uniti, del valòre di 10 centesimi di dollaro; decima parte di dollaro. // ~ **-note** (*slang USA*) banconota da dieci dollari; ~ **store** (*market.*) grande magazzino (*che, originariamente, vendeva solo articoli al prezzo d'un «dime», dieci centesimi di dollaro*).

dimension, *n.* dimensione.

diminish, *v. i.* diminuire, decrescere, scemare.

diminishing marginal utility, *n.* (*econ.*) utilità marginale decrescente.

diminishing returns, *n. pl.* (*econ.*) produttività decrescente.

dimmer, *n.* (*slang USA*) decima parte di dollaro.

dimmo, *n.* (*slang USA*) decima parte di dollaro.

dinar, *n.* dinaro.

dine, *v. i.* pranzare, desinare.

diner, *n.* (*trasp. ferr.*) vettura ristorante.

dinero, *n.* (*slang USA*) denaro.

dingbat, *n.* (*slang USA*) denaro.

dining-car, *n.* (*trasp. ferr.*) carrozza (*o* vagone, vettura) ristorante.

dip[1], *n.* (*Borsa, fin., market.*) calo modesto, lieve caduta (*di prezzi, ecc.*).

dip[2], *v. t.* **1** tuffare. **2** abbassare. *v. i.* **1** tuffarsi. **2** abbassarsi (*improvvisamente*). **3** (*fin., market.*) scendere, diminuire (*di valore*). // to ~ **into reserves** (*fin., rag.*) fare ricorso alle riserve.

diploma, *n.* diploma.

diplomatic, *a.* diplomatico. // ~ **immunity** (*dog.*) franchigia diplomatica.

diplomatist, *n.* diplomatico.

direct[1], *a.* diretto. *avv.* direttamente. // ~ **action** (*sind.*) azione diretta; ~ **advertising** (*pubbl.*) pubblicità diretta; ~ **arbitrage** (*fin.*) arbitraggio diretto; ~ **call** (*trasp. mar.*) scalo diretto; ~ **charge** (*rag.*) costo diretto; ~ **control** (*fin.*) controllo di maggioranza; ~ **cost** (*rag.*) costo diretto, costo variabile; ~ **costing** (*rag.*) contabilità a costi diretti; ~ **discount** (*rag.*) sconto del capitale; ~ **evidence** (*leg.*) prova testimoniale diretta; ~ **exchange** (*fin.*) cambio diretto, cambio fisso; ~ **exchange line** (*comun.*) linea (telefonica) diretta; ~ **expenses** (*rag.*) spese dirette, spese proporzionali; ~ **importation** (*comm. est.*) importazione diretta; ~ **incentive** (*pers.*) incentivo diretto; ~ **initiative** (*leg.*) iniziativa diretta; ~ **insurance** (*ass.*) assicurazione diretta; ~ **investments** (*econ.*) investimenti diretti; ~ **investor** (*fin.*) investitore diretto; ~ **labor** (*pers.*) manodopera diretta; ~ **labor hours allowed per unit** (*org. az.*) ore di lavoro diretto imputabili a ciascuna unità di prodotto; ~ **mail** (*pubbl.*) pubblicità diretta; ~ **mail coordinator** (*pubbl.*) dirigente il servizio di pubblicità; ~ **mail house** (*pubbl.*) ditta di pubblicità; ~ **material** (*org. az.*) materiale diretto; ~ **sale** (*market.*) vendita all'ingrosso; ~ **salesman** (*pers.*) piazzista; ~ **selling** (*market.*) vendita diretta; ~ **services** (*market.*) servizi non collegati con il processo di distribuzione delle merci; ~ **tax** (*fin.*) imposta diretta; ~ **taxation** (*fin.*) imposizione (*o* fiscalità) diretta; ~ **Taxation Office** (*fin.*) Ufficio delle Imposte Dirette; ~ **trade** (*market.*) commercio all'ingrosso; ~ **trader** (*market.*) commerciante all'ingrosso, grossista; ~ **user** (*econ.*) utente diretto.

direct[2], *v. t.* **1** dirigere. **2** dare istruzioni a (*q.*), comandare. **3** assegnare (*fondi, ecc.*). **4** richiamare (*l'attenzione di q., ecc.*). // to ~ **a letter** indirizzare una lettera; **as directed** secondo le direttive ricevute.

directed economy, *n.* (*econ.*) economia dirigistica.

direction, *n.* **1** direzione. **2** (*org. az.*) direzione, guida dell'attività corrente. **3** (*org. az.*) consiglio d'amministrazione. **4 directions,** *pl.* istruzioni, direttive.

directive, *n.* direttiva.

directly, *avv.* direttamente. // ~ **productive investments** (*banca, fin.*) impieghi direttamente produttivi.

director, *n.* **1** (*amm.*) direttore, direttore d'azienda. **2** (*amm.*) amministratore, consigliere d'amministrazione. **3 directors,** *pl.* (*amm.*) consiglio d'amministrazione. // **directors' fees** (*rag.*) compenso agli amministratori; ~ **general** (*amm.*) direttore generale (*specialm. in un ministero e sim.*); **directors' meeting** (*amm.*) riunione del consiglio d'amministrazione; **directors' report** (*amm.*) relazione del consiglio d'amministrazione.

directorate, *n.* 1 (*amm.*) carica di direttore, amministratore, ecc. 2 (*amm.*) consiglio d'amministrazione.

directorial, *a.* (*amm.*) direzionale.

directorship, *n.* (*amm.*) carica di direttore, amministratore, ecc.

directory, *n.* 1 annuario, elenco nominativo. 2 (*amm., USA*) consiglio d'amministrazione. 3 (*attr. uff.*) guida del telefono. // ~ **enquiry** (*comun.*) servizio informazioni (*telefoniche*); **a ~ of manufactures** un annuario dei fabbricanti.

dirigisme, *n.* (*econ.*) dirigismo.

dirt cheap, *a.* e *avv.* a prezzo bassissimo.

dirty, *a.* sporco, sudicio. // ~ **bill of lading** (*trasp. mar.*) polizza di carico con riserva.

disability, *n.* 1 (*leg.*) incapacità, infermità, invalidità. 2 (*sind.*) invalidità (*al lavoro*). // ~ **benefits** (*sind.*) assegni d'invalidità; ~ **clause** (*sind.*) clausola d'invalidità; ~ **insurance** (*sind.*) assicurazione sulla invalidità; ~ **pension** (*sind.*) pensione d'invalidità.

disabled, *a.* 1 (*leg.*) inabile, interdetto. 2 (*sind.*) invalido (*al lavoro*). // ~ **person** (*leg.*) inabile, interdetto; (*sind.*) inabile (*al lavoro*).

disablement, *n.* 1 (*leg.*) inabilità. 2 (*sind.*) invalidità (*al lavoro*). // ~ **insurance** (*ass., sind.*) assicurazione contro l'invalidità.

disadvantage[1], *n.* danno.

disadvantage[2], *v. t.* danneggiare.

disaffection, *n.* disaffezione.

disagree, *v. i.* discordare, dissentire, non concordare.

disagreement, *n.* dissenso.

disallow, *v. t.* respingere.

disallowance, *n.* (*leg.*) rigetto (*d'una richiesta, d'un'istanza*).

disarmament, *n.* disarmo.

disaster, *n.* disastro.

disbar, *v. t.* (*leg.*) cancellare, espellere (*un avvocato*) dall'albo.

disbarment, *n.* (*leg.*) cancellazione.

disburse, *v. t.* 1 sborsare, esborsare (*denaro, ecc.*). 2 (*cred., fin.*) erogare.

disbursement, *n.* 1 sborso, esborso (*di denaro, ecc.*). 2 pagamento, spesa. 3 (*cred., fin.*) erogazione (*di denaro, ecc.*). // ~ **approval** (*rag.*) delibera di spesa.

discharge[1], *n.* 1 scarico, scaricamento. 2 (*fin.*) pagamento, estinzione. 3 (*leg.*) adempimento (*d'un'obbligazione*). 4 (*leg.*) scarico, sgravio. 5 (*leg.*) assoluzione. 6 (*rag.*) scarico. 7 (*sind.*) licenziamento. 8 (*trasp. mar.*) discarica. // ~ **for cause** (*leg., pers.*) licenziamento per giusta causa; **the ~ of an attachment** (*leg.*) la levata d'un sequestro; **the ~ of a bankrupt** (*leg.*) la riabilitazione d'un fallito; ~ **of a bill** estinzione d'una cambiale; **the ~ of a clerk** (*sind.*) il licenziamento d'un impiegato; **the ~ of a debt** (*cred.*) il pagamento d'un debito; **the ~ of a ship** (*trasp. mar.*) lo scaricamento d'una nave.

discharge[2], *v. t.* 1 scaricare. 2 adempiere (*un dovere, ecc.*). 3 pagare. 4 (*leg.*) adempiere (*un'obbligazione*); liberarsi di (*un'obbligazione, un debito, ecc.*). 5 (*leg.*) assolvere. 6 (*sind.*) destituire, dimettere, licenziare. 7 (*trasp. mar.*) scaricare. // to ~ **an account** (*rag.*) liquidare un conto; to ~ **ballast** (*trasp. mar.*) scaricare la zavorra; to ~ **a bankrupt** (*leg.*) riabilitare un fallito; to ~ **a bill** estinguere una cambiale; to ~ **a cargo** (*trasp. mar.*) scaricare un carico; to ~ **a debt** (*cred.*) pagare un debito; to ~ **sb. from an obligation** (*leg.*) liberare q. da un obbligo; to ~ **a ship** (*trasp. mar.*) scaricare una nave; to ~ **the staff** (*sind.*) licenziare il personale.

discharged, *a.* 1 (*cred.*) estinto (*di debito e sim.*). 2 (*pers., sind.*) dimesso, destituito, licenziato.

discharged bankrupt, *n.* (*leg.*) fallito riabilitato.

discharging berth, *n.* (*trasp. mar.*) posto di scarico (*d'una nave*).

discharging port, *n.* (*trasp. mar.*) porto di discarica.

disciplinary, *a.* disciplinare. // ~ **action** (*pers.*) provvedimento disciplinare; ~ **layoff** (*pers.*) sospensione disciplinare; ~ **rules** (*leg.*) norme disciplinari.

discipline, *n.* (*org. az.*) disciplina.

disclaim, *v. t.* 1 (*leg.*) negare (*un'accusa, ecc.*). 2 (*leg.*) rinunciare a un diritto (*di proprietà, ecc.*).

disclaimer, *n.* (*leg.*) rinunzia a un diritto (*di proprietà, ecc.*); rinuncia formale. // ~ **of a contract** (*leg.*) denuncia d'un contratto.

discontinuance, *n.* 1 interruzione, cessazione. 2 (*leg.*) interruzione. 3 (*leg.*) estinzione (*d'un procedimento giudiziario*). // ~ **from a suit** (*leg.*) desistenza da una causa; ~ **of business** cessazione (*o* interruzione) dell'attività commerciale.

discontinue, *v. t.* 1 interrompere, abbandonare, cessare, sospendere. 2 (*leg.*) lasciare estinguere (*un procedimento giudiziario*). // to ~ **a subscription** non rinnovare un abbonamento.

discount[1], *n.* 1 sconto, abbuono, ribasso, riduzione. 2 detrazione (*da un conto, ecc.*). 3

(*banca, fin.*) sconto. // **discounts and advances** (*rag.*) sconti e anticipazioni; ~ **bank** (*fin.*) *V.* **discounting house;** ~ **broker** (*fin.*) scontista; ~ **charges** (*banca*) spese di sconto; ~ **day** (*banca*) giorno di sconto; ~ **for cash** sconto per (pagamento in) contanti; ~ **house** (*fin.*) *V.* **discounting house;** (*market.*) casa di sconto, magazzino a prezzo ridotto; ~ **market** (*fin.*) mercato degli sconti; ~ **of bills on Italy** (*banca*) «sconto effetti Italia»; ~ **of foreign bills** (*banca*) «sconto d'effetti sull'estero»; ~ **on purchases** sconto sugli acquisti; ~ **on sales** sconto sulle vendite; ~ **rate** (*banca, fin.*) tasso di sconto; ~ **rate of the open market** (*fin.*) tasso di sconto del mercato libero; ~ **store** (*market., USA*) casa di sconto; **at a** ~ sotto prezzo; (*fin.*) sotto la pari; **less** ~ (*banca, fin.*) dedotto lo sconto.

discount², *v. t.* 1 scontare. 2 detrarre (*da un conto, ecc.*). 3 (*banca, fin.*) scontare. 4 (*market.*) vendere sottocosto. // to ~ **a bill** (*banca*) scontare un effetto; to ~ **a bill of exchange** (*banca*) scontare una cambiale.

discountable, *a.* scontabile.

discounted-cash-flow method, *n.* (*fin., org. az.*) metodo per determinare la convenienza d'un investimento, basato sulla valutazione, in termini d'interessi, del reddito futuro scontato al valore attuale.

discounter, *n.* (*fin.*) scontista.

discounting, *n.* (*banca, cred.*) sconto (*l'operazione*). // ~ **bills of exchange** (*banca*) sconto delle cambiali; ~ **house** (*fin.*) istituto di sconto, banca di sconto; ~ **of credits from the sale of real estate** sconto di crediti derivanti da vendite d'immobili; ~ **of notes** sconto di effetti bancari.

discourage, *v. t.* 1 ostacolare. 2 (*econ.*) disincentivare. *v. i.* scoraggiarsi.

discover, *v. t.* rivelare.

discovery, *n.* 1 rivelazione. 2 (*leg.*) comunicazione. // ~ **of documents** (*leg.*) comunicazione di documenti.

discreet, *a.* discreto.

discrepancy, *n.* 1 discrepanza, diversità. 2 dissenso.

discretion, *n.* discrezione, giudizio, facoltà (*di decidere, ecc.*). // **at** ~ a discrezione, liberamente.

discretional, *a.* *V.* **discretionary.**

discretionary, *a.* discrezionale. // ~ **bonus** (*pers.*) gratifica discrezionale; ~ **expenses** (*rag.*) costi flessibili; ~ **powers** (*leg.*) poteri discrezionali.

discriminate, *v. t.* discriminare, distinguere, far differenza fra. // to ~ **in favour of certain Countries** (*comm. est.*) discriminare in favore di certi Paesi.

discriminating, *a.* 1 che discrimina, acuto, fine. 2 discriminatorio, di favore. // ~ **duty** (*dog.*) dazio discriminatorio; ~ **tariffs** (*comm. est.*) tariffe differenziali; ~ **treatment** trattamento di favore.

discriminatory, *a.* discriminatorio. // ~ **discharge** (*pers.*) licenziamento discriminatorio.

discuss, *v. t.* discutere.

discussion, *n.* 1 discussione. 2 (*leg.*) discussione.

disease, *n.* malattia, infermità.

diseconomic, *a.* (*econ.*) non economico.

diseconomy, *n.* (*econ.*) diseconomia.

disembark, *v. t.* e *i.* (*trasp. mar.*) sbarcare (*passeggeri ed equipaggi*); scendere a terra.

disembarkation, *n.* (*trasp. mar.*) sbarco.

disembarking, *n.* (*trasp. mar.*) sbarco.

disembarkment, *n.* (*trasp. mar.*) sbarco.

disentitle, *v. t.* togliere un titolo a, rimuovere (*q.*). // to ~ **a solicitor** (*leg.*) rimuovere un procuratore legale dall'esercizio della professione.

disequilibrium, *n.* (*pl.* **disequilibria** e *reg.*) 1 squilibrio. 2 (*econ.*) instabilità (*economica, ecc.*).

disguise, *v. t.* travestire, mascherare.

disguised unemployment, *n.* (*pers.*) disoccupazione mascherata.

dishonest, *a.* disonesto.

dishonesty, *n.* disonestà.

dishonour¹, *n.* 1 disonore. 2 (*cred., leg.*) mancata accettazione (*d'una cambiale, ecc.*). 3 (*cred., leg.*) mancato pagamento (*d'una cambiale, ecc.*). // ~ **by non-acceptance** (*cred., leg.*) mancata accettazione; ~ **by non-payment** (*cred., leg.*) mancato pagamento.

dishonour², *v. t.* 1 disonorare. 2 (*cred., leg.*) lasciare andare in protesto (*una cambiale, ecc.*). 3 (*cred., leg.*) rifiutare di pagare (*un assegno, ecc.*). // to ~ **a bill** «disonorare» una cambiale, lasciare insoluta una cambiale.

dishonoured check, *n.* (*fin.*) assegno a vuoto.

disincentive, *n.* 1 disincentivo, freno. 2 (*econ.*) disincentivo.

disinflate, *v. t.* (*econ.*) disinflazionare.

disinflation, *n.* (*econ.*) disinflazione.

disinflationary, *a.* (*econ.*) disinflazionistico.

disinherit, *v. t.* diseredare.

disinheritance, *n.* diseredazione.

disinterested, *a.* disinteressato.

disinvest, *v. t.* (*econ.*) disinvestire.

disinvestment, *n.* 1 (*econ.*) disinvestimento. 2 (*econ.*) vendita d'un investimento, smobilizzazione d'un investimento. 3 (*econ.*) consumo di capitale.

disjoined signature, *n.* (*amm.*) firma disgiunta.

disloyal, *a.* sleale.

disloyalty, *n.* slealtà.

dismal science, *n.* (*econ.*) scienza delle delusioni (*definizione dell'economia politica data da Thomas Carlyle*).

dismantling, *n.* smantellamento.

dismiss, *v. t.* 1 (*leg.*) rigettare, respingere. 2 (*pers.*) destituire, dimettere, licenziare, rimuovere (*da un grado*). // to ~ **an assembly** (*org. az.*) sciogliere un'assemblea; to ~ **a bankruptcy petition** rigettare un'istanza di fallimento; to ~ **a case** (*leg.*) archiviare un processo.

dismissal, *n.* 1 (*leg.*) rigetto. 2 (*pers.*) destituzione, rimozione (*da un grado*); licenziamento. // ~ **for cause** (*leg., pers.*) licenziamento per giusta causa; **the ~ of a case** (*leg.*) l'archiviazione d'una causa; ~ **wage** (*sind., USA*) indennità di licenziamento, liquidazione (*al lavoratore licenziato senza sua colpa*); ~ **without notice** (*sind.*) licenziamento senza preavviso, licenziamento in tronco.

disorder, *n.* disordine.

disparity, *n.* disparità.

dispatch[1], *n.* 1 invio, spedizione. 2 dispaccio, messaggio. 3 (*trasp.*) servizio di spedizioni per espresso. // ~ **clerk** (*pers.*) addetto alle spedizioni; ~ **days** (*trasp. mar.*) giorni d'acceleramento; ~ **money** (*trasp. mar.*) premio d'acceleramento, riscatto di stallia; ~ **note** (*comun.*) bollettino di spedizione; **the ~ of goods** la spedizione di merci; **the ~ of telegrams** (*comun.*) l'invio di telegrammi; **with ~** con prontezza.

dispatch[2], *v. t.* 1 inviare, mandare, spedire. 2 sbrigare. 3 (*amm.*) evadere (*una pratica, ecc.*). // to ~ **business** sbrigare affari.

dispatcher, *n.* (*org. az.*) organizzatore del lavoro d'officina.

dispatching, *n.* 1 spedizione. 2 (*org. az.*) lancio della produzione, «dispacciamento». // ~ **office** (*comun.*) ufficio spedizioni (*postali*).

dispense, *v. t.* dispensare, esimere, esentare. // to ~ **from an obligation** dispensare da un obbligo; to ~ **justice** (*leg.*) amministrare la giustizia; to ~ **with st.** fare a meno di qc.

dispersion, *n.* dispersione.

displace, *v. t.* 1 spostare, rimuovere, trasferire. 2 destituire, deporre (*q. da un ufficio, ecc.*). 3 sostituire. 4 (*trasp. mar.*) dislocare.

displacement, *n.* 1 spostamento, rimozione, trasferimento. 2 destituzione, deposizione. 3 sostituzione. 4 (*trasp. mar.*) dislocamento, spostamento. // ~ **of funds** (*fin.*) trasferimento di capitali; **the ~ of an unjust law** (*leg.*) la rimozione d'una legge ingiusta; ~ **ton** (*trasp. mar.*) tonnellata di dislocamento.

display[1], *n.* mostra, esposizione, esibizione. // ~ **artist** (*pers.*) vetrinista; ~ **card** (*pubbl.*) cartello da vetrina; ~ **window** (*market.*) vetrina per esposizione (*della merce*).

display[2], *v. t.* 1 mettere in mostra, mostrare, esporre, esibire. 2 (*pubbl.*) stampare a grandi caratteri.

displayman, *n.* (*pl.* **displaymen**) (*pers.*) vetrinista.

disposable, *a.* 1 disponibile, di cui si può disporre (*liberamente*). 2 (*di contenitore, ecc.*) che si può gettare, da gettare dopo l'uso, non «a rendere». 3 (*leg.*) cedibile, vendibile. // ~ **income** (*fin.*) reddito disponibile, reddito netto (*da imposta*); ~ **portion** (*leg.*) beni disponibili (*in un testamento*).

disposal, *n.* 1 disposizione. 2 (*leg.*) cessione, vendita. // **at the ~ of** a disposizione di.

dispose, *v. t.* disporre, collocare, sistemare. *v. i.* **dispose of** 1 disporre di. 2 (*leg.*) cedere, vendere. // to ~ **by will** (*leg.*) disporre per testamento.

disposition, *n.* (*anche leg.*) disposizione.

dispossess, *v. t.* 1 privare, spogliare (*d'ogni avere*). 2 (*leg.*) espropriare. 3 (*leg.*) sfrattare.

dispossessed, *a.* (*leg.*) sfrattato.

dispossession, *n.* 1 (*leg.*) espropriazione. 2 (*leg.*) sfratto.

dispossess notice, *n.* (*leg.*) avviso di sfratto.

dispossessor, *n.* (*leg.*) chi dà lo sfratto.

dispossessory warrant, *n.* (*leg.*) decreto di sfratto.

disputable, *a.* 1 discutibile. 2 contestabile. // **a ~ claim** (*leg.*) un diritto contestabile; **a ~ statement** un'affermazione opinabile.

dispute[1], *n.* 1 controversia, lite, vertenza. 2 discussione, contestazione. 3 (*leg.*) causa. 4 (*sind.*) controversia, vertenza. // **without ~** indiscutibilmente.

dispute[2], *v. t.* e *i.* 1 discutere. 2 mettere in discussione, contestare. // to ~ **a claim** (*leg.*) contestare un diritto.

disputed claims office, *n.* (*leg.*) ufficio del contenzioso.

disputed credit, *n.* (*leg.*) credito contestato.

disqualification, *n.* 1 squalificazione (*raro*).

2 (*leg.*) incapacità, incapacità legale, mancanza dei requisiti necessari, interdizione.

disqualified, *a.* (*leg.*) inabilitato, incapace.

disqualify, *v. t.* **1** inabilitare. **2** (*leg.*) inabilitare, interdire, dichiarare incapace.

disreputable, *a.* di dubbia onestà.

dissatisfaction, *n.* insoddisfazione.

dissatisfied, *a.* insoddisfatto.

dissaving, *n.* **1** (*econ.*) spesa dei risparmi accumulati. **2** (*econ.*) spesa in eccesso del reddito, risparmio negativo.

dissect, *v. t.* **1** sezionare. **2** analizzare, esaminare minutamente. // to ~ **an account** (*rag.*) analizzare un conto.

dissection, *n.* analisi, esame particolareggiato. // **the ~ of last year's balance** (*rag.*) l'analisi del bilancio dell'esercizio passato.

dissent[1], *n.* (*anche leg.*) dissenso. // **~ of the parties** (*leg.*) dissenso delle parti.

dissent[2], *v. i.* dissentire.

dissequester[1], *n.* (*leg.*) dissequestro.

dissequester[2], *v. t.* (*leg.*) dissequestrare.

dissequestration, *n. V.* **dissequester**[1].

disservice, *n.* **1** cattivo servizio. **2** (*org. az.*) disservizio.

dissolution, *n.* **1** scioglimento. **2** (*leg.*) dissoluzione. **3** (*leg.*) risoluzione (*d'un contratto*). // **~ of a partnership** scioglimento d'una società.

dissolve, *v. t.* **1** dissolvere, sciogliere. **2** (*leg.*) sciogliere (*una società*). **3** (*leg.*) risolvere (*un contratto*). // to ~ **a partnership** (*fin.*) sciogliere una società.

distance, *n.* distanza. // **~ freight** (*trasp. mar.*) nolo proporzionale alla distanza.

distant, *a.* distante, lontano. // **~ block signal** (*trasp. ferr.*) segnale a distanza; **~ signal** (*trasp. ferr.*) segnale a distanza.

distension, *n.* distensione (*in senso concreto*).

distinct, *a.* distinto, netto.

distinction, *n.* distinzione.

distinctly, *avv.* distintamente.

distinguish, *v. t.* distinguere.

distinguished, *a.* distinto, egregio.

distort, *v. t.* **1** distorcere. **2** falsare. // to ~ **the results** (*market.*) interpretare i risultati in modo sbagliato.

distortions of competition, *n. pl.* (*market.*) distorsioni della concorrenza.

distract, *v. t.* (*anche fig.*) distrarre.

distrain, *v. t.* (*leg.*) pignorare, sequestrare. // to ~ **personal chattels** (*leg.*) pignorare beni mobili; to ~ **upon sb.'s goods for rent** (*leg.*) sequestrare i beni di q. per il mancato pagamento d'un fitto.

distrainable, *a.* (*leg.*) pignorabile, sequestrabile. // **~ chattels** (*leg.*) beni soggetti a pignoramento, beni soggetti a sequestro.

distrainor, *n.* (*leg.*) usciere (*giudiziario*).

distraint, *n.* (*leg.*) pignoramento, sequestro.

distress[1], *n.* **1** bisogno. **2** difficoltà, pericolo. **3** (*leg.*) sequestro. **4** (*leg.*) beni sequestrati. **5** (*trasp. mar.*) pericolo. // **~ call** (*comun.*) segnale di pericolo, S.O.S.; **~ goods** (*market.*) merce (venduta) sottocosto; **~ on bankrupt's estate** (*leg.*) sequestro dei beni del fallito; **~ sale** (*market.*) vendita (di merce) sottocosto; **~ signal** (*trasp. mar.*) segnale di pericolo.

distress[2], *v. t.* mettere in difficoltà.

distressed, *a.* in difficoltà. // **~ area** (*econ.*) area disastrata; **a ~ ship** (*trasp. mar.*) una nave in pericolo.

distributable, *a.* distribuibile, ripartibile.

distribute, *v. t.* **1** distribuire, ripartire. **2** (*comun.*) smistare. **3** (*pubbl.*) scomporre (caratteri di stampa). // to ~ **dividends** (*fin.*) distribuire dividendi; to ~ **justice** (*leg.*) amministrare la giustizia; to ~ **profits among the members** (*rag.*) ripartire gli utili fra i soci.

distributed income, *n.* (*rag.*) utili distribuiti.

distributing centre, *n.* (*org. az.*) centro di smistamento.

distribution, *n.* **1** ripartizione. **2** (*comun.*) smistamento. **3** (*econ.*) distribuzione (*del reddito, della ricchezza, ecc.*). **4** (*market.*) distribuzione (*delle merci dal produttore al consumatore*). **5** (*pubbl.*) scomposizione (*di caratteri di stampa*). // **~ costs** (*market.*) costi di distribuzione; **the ~ machinery** (*market.*) l'apparato della distribuzione; **~ of customs receipts** (*dog.*) ripartizione dei proventi doganali; **the ~ of goods** (*econ.*) la distribuzione dei beni; **~ of income** (*econ.*) distribuzione del reddito; **the ~ of profits** (*rag.*) la ripartizione degli utili; **~ of type** (*pubbl.*) scomposizione; **~ problems** (*econ.*) problemi della distribuzione; **~ system** (*econ.*) sistema di distribuzione, sistema distributivo.

distributive, *a.* distributivo. // **~ justice** (*econ.*) giustizia distributiva; **the ~ trades** (*market.*) la distribuzione; (*trasp.*) i trasporti.

distributor, *n.* **1** (*giorn., pubbl.*) scompositore. **2** (*market.*) distributore. **3 distributors,** *pl.* (*market.*) il settore della distribuzione, gli addetti alla distribuzione.

district, *n.* **1** distretto, circoscrizione, regione, zona. **2** (*ingl.*) distretto (*suddivisione di contea*). **3** (*USA*) circoscrizione elettorale (*rap-*

presentata da un membro della Camera dei Rappresentanti). // ~ **attorney** (*leg., USA*) procuratore distrettuale; ~ **council** (*leg.*) consiglio distrettuale; ~ **Court** (*leg., USA*) tribunale di prima istanza; ~ **judge** (*leg., USA*) giudice distrettuale; ~ **manager** (*pers.*) direttore di zona; ~ **representative** (*pers.*) rappresentante di zona.

disturb, *v. t.* turbare, mettere in disordine. // to ~ **the peace** (*leg.*) turbare la quiete pubblica.

disturbance, *n.* **1** turbamento. **2** disordine. **3** (*leg.*) turbativa. // ~ **of possession** (*leg.*) turbativa di possesso.

disutility, *n.* (*econ.*) disutilità.

ditto, *a.* **1** predetto, suddetto, «idem» (*nelle fatture, negli inventari, ecc.*). **2** (*rag.*) detto. *avv.* come sopra, nello stesso modo.

div, *n.* **1** (*Borsa, slang USA*) dividendo. **2** (*Borsa, slang USA*) interesse.

divergence, *n.* divergenza.

divergency, *n.* divergenza.

diversification, *n.* **1** (*econ.*) diversificazione. **2** (*market.*) differenziazione. // ~ **of products** (*org. az.*) diversificazione dei prodotti; ~ **of trade** (*comm. est.*) la diversificazione degli scambi commerciali.

diversified, *a.* differenziato. // ~ **investment fund** (*fin.*) fondo d'investimento a portafoglio differenziato.

diversify, *v. t.* diversificare.

diversion, *n.* **1** deviazione. **2** storno, diversione; (*fig.*) dirottamento. // ~ **of demand** (*econ.*) dirottamento della domanda (*su altri beni*); ~ **of public funds** (*leg.*) storno di denaro pubblico; **diversions of trade** (*market.*) deviazioni del traffico.

divert, *v. t.* **1** deviare. **2** stornare; dirottare (*fig.*).

divest, *v. t.* (*leg.*) disinvestire, privare, spossessare.

dividable, *a.* divisibile.

divide, *v. t.* dividere, ripartire, distribuire. *v. i.* dividersi, ripartirsi. // to ~ **a joint property** (*leg.*) dividere una comproprietà.

divided payments, *n. pl.* (*market.*) pagamenti rateali.

dividend, *n.* **1** (*fin., rag.*) dividendo. **2** (*market.*) «omaggio». **3** (*mat.*) dividendo. // ~ **-bearing share** (*fin.*) azione di godimento; ~ **coupon** (*fin.*) cedola; ~ **crop** (*Borsa*) campagna dividendi; ~ **days** (*fin.*) giorni di ripartizione del dividendo; ~ **off** (*fin., USA*) (*di titolo*) senza cedola; ~ **on** (*fin., USA*) (*di titolo*) con cedola; «~ **payable**» (*fin.*) «godimento»; ~ **warrant** (*fin.*) cedola, assegno emesso da una società in favore d'un azionista per l'importo che gli compete quale dividendo sulle azioni possedute.

divisibility, *n.* divisibilità.

divisible, *a.* divisibile, ripartibile. // ~ **profits** (*rag.*) utili ripartibili.

division, *n.* **1** divisione, ripartizione. **2** (*mat.*) divisione. **3** (*org. az.*) reparto, sezione. // ~ **into instalments** (*market.*) rateazione; ~ **of labour** (*org. az.*) divisione del lavoro; ~ **of powers** (*amm.*) divisione dei poteri; ~ **of profits** (*rag.*) ripartizione degli utili; ~ **of work** (*org. az.*) divisione del lavoro, ripartizione del lavoro, specializzazione dei compiti.

divisional, *a.* (*mat.*) frazionario.

divisor, *n.* (*mat.*) divisore.

divvy[1], *n.* (*slang USA*) dividendo.

divvy[2] **up,** *v. i.* (*slang USA*) distribuire dividendi.

Dix, *n.* (*slang USA*) banconota da dieci dollari.

do[1], *n.* (*pl.* **dos** o **do's**) ciò che si può (*o* si deve) fare; comando o preghiera di fare qualcosa. // **the do's and don'ts** ciò che si può (*o* si deve) fare e ciò che non si può (*o* non si deve) fare; i «comandamenti».

do[2], *v. t.* (*pass.* **did,** *part. pass.* **done**) fare, agire. // to ~ **away with** abolire, eliminare, sopprimere: to ~ **broking** (*Borsa*) fare il mediatore; to ~ **business** fare affari; to ~ **the correspondence** (*org. az.*) sbrigare la corrispondenza; to ~ **one's duty** fare il proprio dovere; to ~ **oneself well** (*USA*) aver successo; to ~ **the place** (*market.*) battere la piazza; to ~ **one's shopping** (*market.*) fare acquisti (*o* compere); fare la spesa; to ~ **a subtraction** (*mat.*) fare una sottrazione; to ~ **st. to the best of one's ability** fare del proprio meglio; to ~ **one's training** (*pers.*) fare il (*proprio*) tirocinio; to ~ **with sb.** trattare con q.; to ~ **without st.** fare a meno di qc.

dock[1], *n.* **1** (*leg.*) banco degli accusati. **2** (*trasp. ferr.*) piattaforma di carico (*alla fine d'un binario*). **3** (*trasp. mar.*) bacino. **4** (*trasp. mar., USA*) banchina, molo, scalo d'approdo. **5** **docks,** *pl.* (*trasp. ferr.*) «docks». **6** **docks,** *pl.* (*trasp. mar.*) cantiere navale; arsenale. **7** **docks,** *pl.* (*trasp. mar.*) magazzini generali (*traducente improprio*). // ~ **authorities** (*trasp. mar.*) autorità portuali; ~ **dues** (*trasp. mar.*) spese di «dock»; ~ **labour** (*pers.*) manodopera portuale; ~ **receipt** (*trasp. mar.*) ricevuta del custode del «dock»; ~ **-warrant** (*dog.*) fede di deposito doganale; ~ **workers** (*pers.*) lavoratori portuali, portuali.

dock², *v. i.* 1 (*di nave*) entrare in bacino. 2 (*trasp. mar., USA*) accostare alla banchina, attraccare. *v. t.* 1 (*fam.*) diminuire, ridurre. 2 (*trasp. mar.*) mettere in bacino (*una nave*). 3 (*trasp. mar., USA*) attraccare (*una nave*). // to ~ **an employee's salary** (*sind.*) ridurre lo stipendio d'un impiegato.

dockage, *n.* (*trasp. mar.*) spese di «dock», spese di bacino.

docker, *n.* (*pers.*) scaricatore di porto, portuale.

docket¹, *n.* 1 (*dog.*) scontrino doganale. 2 (*fin.*) cedola. 3 (*leg.*) verbale (*nei procedimenti giudiziari*). 4 (*leg.*) lista delle cause da discutere. 5 (*leg.*) attergato. 6 (*org. az.*) ordine del giorno, agenda (*dei lavori d'una commissione, ecc.*).

docket², *v. t.* 1 (*leg.*) attergare (*una pratica*). 2 (*leg.*) registrare (*una sentenza*).

dockhand, *n.* (*pers.*) scaricatore di porto.

docking, *n.* 1 (*pers.*) multa. 2 (*trasp. mar.*) attracco.

dockmaster, *n.* (*pers.*) direttore di bacino.

dockyard, *n.* (*trasp. mar.*) cantiere navale, arsenale, darsena. // ~ **hands** (*pers.*) maestranze d'un cantiere navale.

doctor, *n.* dottore, medico. // **on a ~ 's panel** (*pers.*) (*di paziente*) mutuato.

doctrine, *n.* dottrina.

document¹, *n.* documento, certificato, attestato, titolo. // **documents against acceptance** (*market.*) documenti contro accettazione; **documents against payment** (*market.*) documenti contro pagamento; ~ **bill** (*cred.*) tratta documentaria; ~ **credit** credito documentario; **documents in support** pezze d'appoggio; **documents of credit** (*cred.*) titoli di credito; ~ **of title** (*leg.*) titolo di proprietà; **documents of title** (*leg.*) documenti rappresentativi (*delle merci*); **documents of value** documenti di valore.

document², *v. t.* 1 documentare, attestare, provare. 2 (*trasp. mar.*) immatricolare, iscrivere (*una nave*). // to ~ **a bill of exchange** (*cred.*) documentare una cambiale.

documentary, *a.* documentario, documentato. *n.* documentario. // ~ **bill** (*cred.*) tratta documentaria; ~ **credit** (*comm. est.*) credito documentario (*o* documentato); ~ **draft** (*cred.*) tratta documentaria; ~ **evidence** (*leg.*) prova documentata, prova scritta; ~ **stamp** (*leg.*) marca da bollo per documenti.

documentation, *n.* documentazione.

dodge, *v. t.* e *i.* 1 eludere, schivare (*le responsabilità*). 2 usare sotterfugi. // to ~ **taxes** (*fin.*) sottrarsi al fisco, evadere (le imposte).

dodger, *n.* 1 imbroglione. 2 (*leg.*) evasore fiscale. 3 (*pubbl., USA*) foglietto pubblicitario.

dog, *n.* (*slang USA*) pagherò cambiario.

doldrums, *n. pl.* (*econ.*) stato di inattività, stato di stagnazione, crisi.

dole, *n.* (*sind.*) sussidio di disoccupazione.

dollar, *n.* dollaro. // ~ **area** (*econ., fin.*) area del dollaro; ~ **diplomacy** (*econ.*) politica dell'infiltrazione economica come mezzo di potere politico; ~ **efficiency** (*pubbl.*) efficacia pubblicitaria riferita a dollaro di spesa; ~ **gap** (*fin.*) mancanza di dollari; ~ **glut** (*fin.*) abbondanza di dollari; ~ **of account** (*Borsa, ingl.*) dollaro contabile; ~ **parity** (*fin.*) parità in dollari; ~ **shortage** (*fin.*) *V.* ~ **gap**; ~ **standard** (*fin.*) tipo dollaro.

dolly, *n.* (*pubbl.*) carrello (*su cui è posta la macchina da presa, cinematografica o televisiva*).

domestic, *a.* 1 domestico, nazionale, interno. 2 (*market., USA*) nostrano. // ~ **bill** (*cred.*) cambiale pagabile all'interno; ~ **corporation** (*fin., USA*) società nazionale; ~ **credit market** (*fin.*) mercato creditizio interno; ~ **demand** (*econ.*) domanda interna; ~ **equilibrium** (*econ.*) equilibrio interno; ~ **goods** (*market.*) prodotti nazionali; ~ **law** (*leg.*) diritto interno (*d'un singolo Paese*); ~ **liquidity** (*fin.*) liquidità interna; **a ~ loan** (*cred.*) un prestito nazionale; ~ **product** (*econ.*) prodotto nazionale; ~ **system** (*econ.*) sistema industriale basato sul lavoro a domicilio; ~ **trade** commercio interno, commercio nazionale.

domestics, *n. pl.* (*market., USA*) (articoli) casalinghi. // ~ **department** (*market., USA*) reparto (articoli) casalinghi.

domicile¹, *n.* 1 domicilio. 2 (*leg.*) domicilio, residenza stabile.

domicile², *v. t.* 1 (*cred.*) domiciliare (*una cambiale*). 2 (*leg.*) stabilire la residenza di (*q. in un posto*). // to ~ **a bill** (*cred.*) domiciliare una cambiale.

domiciled bill, *n.* (*cred.*) cambiale domiciliata, tratta domiciliata.

domiciliary, *a.* domiciliare.

donate, *v. t.* donare.

donation, *n.* (*leg.*) donazione, dono, elargizione di denaro.

donee, *n.* (*leg.*) donatario.

donor, *n.* (*leg.*) donatore, donante.

don't, *n.* (*pl.* **don'ts**) ciò che non si può (*o* non si deve) fare; comando o preghiera di non fare qualcosa.

door, *n.* porta. // ~ **opener** (*market.*) omaggio (*dono di poco prezzo offerto da un* *piazzista per ingraziarsi la persona che ha aperto la porta*); ~ **-to-** ~ **distribution** (*market.*) distribuzione porta a porta; ~ **-to-** ~ **sale** (*market.*) vendita a domicilio; ~ **-to-** ~ **sales approach** (*market.*) forma di vendita diretta porta a porta; ~ **-to-** ~ **salesman** (*market.*) venditore a domicilio; ~ **-to-** ~ **service** (*market.*) servizio a domicilio.

dormant, *a.* addormentato, inattivo. // ~ **account** (*banca*) conto inattivo; ~ **partner** (*leg.*) socio di capitali.

dormitory towns, *n. pl.* città «dormitorio» (*comunità residenziali alle quali i lavoratori pendolari ritornano dopo la loro giornata di lavoro nelle grandi città*).

dose, *n.* (*econ.*) dose, unità.

dossier, *n.* (*leg.*) «dossier», incartamento.

dot[1], *n.* punto, segno. // **dots and dashes** (*comun.*) punti e linee (*del telegrafo*).

dot[2], *v. t.* punteggiare.

dotal property, *n.* (*leg.*) beni dotali.

double[1], *a.* doppio, duplice. *n.* (*il*) doppio. *avv.* due volte. // ~ **application** (*rag.*) registrazione (*contabile*) doppia; ~ **-barrelled quotation** (*Borsa, fin.*) quotazione doppia; ~ **counting** (*market.*) conteggio doppio; to ~ **-cross** (*fam.*) fare il doppio gioco con (q.), ingannare; ~ **daylight saving time** (*USA*) ora legale doppia (*in anticipo di due ore su quella solare*); ~ **-decker** (*trasp.*) autobus a due piani; (*trasp. mar.*) nave a due ponti; ~ **declining balance method** (*rag.*) metodi (*d'ammortamento*) a quote variabili decrescenti; ~ **entry** (*rag.*) partita doppia; ~ **-entry bookkeeping** (*rag.*) contabilità a partita doppia, tenuta dei libri a partita doppia; ~ **-entry system** (*rag.*) metodo della partita doppia; ~ **freight** (*trasp. mar.*) doppio nolo; ~ **insurance** (*ass.*) assicurazione cumulativa; ~ **-leaded** (*in tipografia*) a spaziatura doppia fra riga e riga; ~ **option** (*Borsa*) «stellage», stellaggio; ~ **postcard** (*attr. uff.*) cartolina doppia; ~ **-saw** (*slang USA*) banconota da venti dollari, somma di venti dollari; ~ **sawbuck** (*slang USA*) banconota da venti dollari, somma di venti dollari; ~ **space** (*in dattilografia*) spazio doppio; to ~ **-space** scrivere (*a macchina*) lasciando uno spazio doppio; ~ **standard** (*econ.*) bimetallismo; ~ **summer time** ora legale doppia (*in anticipo di due ore su quella solare*); ~ **taxation** (*econ.*) imposizione doppia, tassazione doppia; **the** ~ **-tier system for the lira** (*econ.*) il sistema dei doppi cambi per la lira; ~ **track** (*trasp. ferr.*) doppio binario; ~ **will** (*leg.*) testamento congiuntivo e reciproco.

double[2], *v. t.* raddoppiare. // to ~ **one's income** raddoppiare le proprie entrate; to ~ **the price** raddoppiare il prezzo.

doubtful, *a.* discutibile, incerto. // ~ **debts** (*cred.*) crediti di dubbia (*o* d'incerta) esigibilità; **a** ~ **remedy** un rimedio discutibile.

Dow-Jones index, *n.* (*fin.*) indice Dow Jones.

down, *avv.* **1** giù, in giù. **2** in contanti. *a. attr.* (che va) in giù, in discesa, in pendenza. *n.* **1** basso, rovescio (*della sorte*). **2** (*market.*) periodo di crisi (*delle vendite, ecc.*). // ~ **grade** (*trasp. ferr.*) discesa; ~ **payment** pagamento in contanti, versamento della prima rata; ~ **platform** (*trasp. ferr.*) marciapiede di partenza o d'arrivo d'un «down train»; **a** ~ **train** (*trasp. ferr.*) un treno che dalla città principale porta in provincia.

downfall, *n.* (*econ., fin.*) caduta, flessione. // ~ **of bonds** (*o* **of shares**) (*Borsa, fin.*) cedenze.

downstairs, *avv.* al piano di sotto.

downswing, *n.* **1** (*econ.*) ribasso. **2** (*econ.*) fase di flessione, recessione improvvisa; congiuntura sfavorevole.

downtime, *n.* (*org. az.*) periodo d'inattività (*d'una macchina, d'una fabbrica o d'un reparto*).

downtown, *avv.* verso il centro commerciale (*d'una grande città*). *n.* centro commerciale (*d'una grande città*). // ~ **store** (*market.*) negozio del centro.

downtrend, *n.* **1** (*Borsa*) fase di flessione. **2** (*econ.*) tendenza al ribasso.

downturn, *n.* (*econ.*) tendenza al ribasso, flessione.

downward, *avv.* e *a.* in discesa. // ~ **price stickiness** (*econ.*) vischiosità dei prezzi; ~ **sloping trend** (*econ.*) tendenza al ribasso; ~ **stickiness** (*econ.*) vischiosità; **the** ~ **stickiness of wages** (*econ.*) la vischiosità dei salari; ~ **trend** (*econ.*) tendenza al ribasso.

dowry, *n.* (*leg.*) dote.

dozen, *n.* dozzina.

drachma, *n.* (*pl.* **drachmae** e *reg.*) (*econ.*) unità monetaria greca (*si suddivide in 100 lepta*).

draft[1], *n.* **1** abbozzo, bozzetto, schizzo. **2** copia, brutta copia, minuta. **3** disegno, progetto, schema. **4** (*cred.*) cambiale, tratta, cambiale tratta. **5** (*cred.*) ordine di pagamento. **6** (*rag.*) abbuono per «calo peso», abbuono per «corpi estranei». **7** (*trasp. mar.*) pescaggio. // ~ **agreement** (*amm.*) schema di accordo; ~ **allowance** (*rag.*) abbuono per «calo peso», abbuono per «corpi estranei»; ~ **articles** (*amm.*) progetto di statuto; ~ **at sight** (*cred.*)

tratta a vista; ~ **budget** (*fin.*) progetto di bilancio, bilancio preventivo di massima; ~ **contract** (*amm.*) schema di contratto; **the ~ of a letter** la minuta d'una lettera; ~ **package of requests** (*econ.*) piattaforma comune di richieste; ~ **payable at sight** (*cred.*) tratta a vista; ~ **regulation** (*org. az.*) proposta di regolamento.

draft[2], *v. t.* 1 disegnare. 2 abbozzare; fare uno schema di (qc.). 3 elaborare. // to ~ **a contract** (*amm.*) preparare lo schema d'un contratto.

drafter, *n.* (*leg.*) estensore (*d'un documento*).

drafting, *n.* elaborazione. // **the ~ of a program** (*org. az.*) l'elaborazione d'un programma.

draftsman, *n.* (*pl.* **draftsmen**) 1 (*pers.*) disegnatore, disegnatore tecnico. 2 (*pers.*) progettista.

drain[1], *n.* (*fig.*) esaurimento. // **a ~ of dollars** (*fin.*) un esaurimento di dollari.

drain[2], *v. t.* (*fig.*) esaurire, logorare. // to ~ **the wealth of a nation** (*econ.*) esaurire le risorse d'una nazione.

dram, *n.* dramma (*misura di peso corrispondente a 1,7718 grammi*).

drastic, *a.* drastico.

draught, *n. V.* **draft**[1].

draw, *v. t.* (*pass.* **drew,** *part. pass.* **drawn**) 1 tirare, trarre. 2 estrarre. 3 disegnare. 4 attingere, ottenere. 5 richiamare. 6 (*banca*) trarre, prelevare (*denaro*). 7 (*cred.*) spiccare (*una tratta*). 8 (*fin.*) estrarre (*obbligazioni*). 9 (*leg.*) redigere (*un documento*). 10 (*sind.*) ricevere, percepire (*uno stipendio*). *v. i.* (*cred.*) trarre, spiccare tratta. // to ~ **a bill of exchange** (*cred.*) spiccare una tratta, spiccare una cambiale; to ~ **a cheque** (*cred.*) «staccare» un assegno; to ~ **a contract** stendere un contratto; to ~ **a deed** (*leg.*) redigere un atto legale; to ~ **in** fare economia; to ~ **lots for** (*fin.*) estrarre a sorte; to ~ **near** (*trasp. mar.*) avvicinarsi; to ~ **on sb.** spiccar tratta su q.; to ~ **on an account** (*banca*) trarre su un conto; to ~ **a plan** formulare un piano; to ~ **a profit** trarre un profitto; to ~ **one's salary** (*pers.*) tirare lo stipendio, tirare la paga; to ~ **together** (*trasp. mar.*) (*di navi*) avvicinarsi, accostarsi; to ~ **two salaries** (*pers.*) cumulare due stipendi; to ~ **st. up** redigere qc.; (*leg.*) rogare; to ~ **up an accusation** (*leg.*) stendere un'accusa; to ~ **up an agreement** stipulare un contratto; to ~ **up a balance-sheet** (*fin., rag.*) redigere un bilancio; to ~ **up a bill of lading** (*trasp. mar.*) redigere una polizza di carico; to ~ **up a contract** stendere un contratto; to ~ **up a deed** (*leg.*) redigere un atto; to ~ **up a statement of account** (*banca*) redigere un estratto-conto; **«your securities drawn»** (*banca*) «vostri titoli estratti».

drawback, *n.* 1 (*dog.*) rimborso dei dazi, restituzione di dazio, premio all'esportazione. 2 (*dog.*) dazio doganale rimborsato (*quando la merce è riesportata*). 3 (*fin.*) ristorno.

drawee, *n.* (*cred.*) trattario, trassato.

drawer, *n.* (*cred.*) traente, emittente. // **the ~ of a bill of exchange** (*cred.*) il traente d'una cambiale; **the ~ of a cheque** (*cred.*) l'emittente d'un assegno bancario.

drawing, *n.* 1 disegno. 2 estrazione, sorteggio. 3 (*banca*) prelevamento, prelievo. 4 (*pubbl.*) disegno. // ~ **account** (*banca*) deposito in conto corrente, conto corrente, conto prelevamenti; ~ **deposit** (*banca*) deposito traibile; ~ **of samples** (*market., stat.*) prelevamento di campioni; ~ **on a current account** (*banca*) prelevamento su un conto corrente; ~ **power** (*pers.*) capacità di richiamare clientela; ~ **right** (*fin.*) diritto di prelievo (*ammontare di valute pregiate che un Paese può acquistare dal Fondo Monetario Internazionale in cambio di propria valuta*); ~ **up** (*leg.*) stesura, stipulazione, stipula; **the ~ up of a contract** (*leg.*) la stesura d'un contratto.

drawn and payable, *a.* (*banca, cred.*) emesso e pagabile.

drawn bond, *n.* (*fin.*) titolo estratto.

drawn ticket, *n.* (*fin.*) estratto.

drawn upon, *a.* (*cred.*) trassato.

dress[1], *n.* abito da donna.

dress[2], *v. t.* (*pubbl.*) allestire (*una vetrina*).

dressing, *n.* (*pubbl.*) allestimento (*d'una vetrina*).

drift[1], *n.* 1 spostamento. 2 inclinazione, direzione. 3 tendenza. 4 (il) lasciar andare le cose per conto loro; (il) lasciar correre; inazione. 5 (*trasp. mar.*) deriva. 6 (*trasp. mar.*) percorso. // ~ **angle** (*trasp. mar.*) angolo di deriva; **the ~ from the land** (*econ.*) la fuga dai campi; **the ~ of population from country to city** (*stat.*) lo spostamento della popolazione dalla campagna alla città; **a ~ towards centralization of power** una tendenza alla centralizzazione del potere.

drift[2], *v. i.* 1 andare alla deriva (*anche fig.*). 2 (*trasp. mar.*) andare alla deriva.

drill, *v. t.* trapanare.

drive[1], *n.* 1 viaggio in (*o* alla guida di una) automobile. 2 iniziativa. 3 (*market., USA*) campagna (*commerciale*). 4 (*trasp. aut.*) trazione. // ~ **-in** (*market.*) «drive-in» (*sistema di* *vendita che consente l'accesso diretto al negozio da parte di clienti in automobile, senza che le operazioni d'acquisto rendano necessario abbandonare il posto di guida*); ~ **-in window** (*banca*) sportello (*di banca*) cui si accede in automobile.

drive², *v. t.* e *i.* (*pass.* **drove**, *part. pass.* **driven**) **1** guidare. **2** andare (*guidando un veicolo*). // to ~ **a bargain with sb.** concludere un affare con q.; to ~ **down** (*market.*) far diminuire, abbassare (*prezzi, ecc.*); to ~ **a good bargain** fare un buon affare; to ~ **prices down** (*econ.*) esercitare una pressione sui prezzi; to ~ **a roaring trade** fare affari d'oro.

driver, *n.* (*trasp. aut.*) guidatore, conduttore, conducente.

driving, *n.* (*trasp. aut.*) guida. // ~ (*o* **driver's) licence** (*trasp. aut.*) patente di guida.

drop¹, *n.* **1** caduta. **2** (*fin.*) ribasso, flessione. **3** (*market.*) caduta, flessione, diminuzione, contrazione (*dei prezzi*). // **a ~ in distribution costs** (*econ.*) una riduzione dei costi di distribuzione; **drops in Italian exports** flessioni dell'export italiano; **a ~ in net exports** (*comm. est.*) un regresso delle esportazioni; **a ~ in overall domestic demand** (*econ.*) un calo della domanda globale interna; **a ~ in state revenues** (*fin.*) una flessione del gettito fiscale; ~ **shipment** (*market., USA*) spedizione (*di merci*) fatta dal produttore direttamente al dettagliante (*e non dal grossista che ha effettuato la vendita*).

drop², *v. i.* **1** cadere. **2** (*fin.*) diminuire (*di valore*). // to ~ **anchor** (*trasp. mar.*) gettare l'ancora.

drug, *n.* sostanza medicinale. // ~ **in the market** (*market.*) articolo poco richiesto, prodotto invendibile; ~ **on the market** *V.* ~ **in the market.**

drugstore, *n.* (*market., USA*) farmacia (*dove sono venduti anche cosmetici, tabacco, gelati, libri, ecc.*).

drum, *v. i.* suonare il tamburo.

drummer, *n.* (*market., USA*) viaggiatore di commercio.

dry, *a.* secco. // ~ **cargo** (*trasp. mar.*) carico secco; ~ **cargo ships** (*trasp. mar.*) navi per il trasporto di cereali; ~ **dock** (*trasp. mar.*) bacino a secco, bacino di carenaggio; to ~ **-dock** (*trasp. mar.*) carenare, immettere (*una nave*) nel bacino di carenaggio; mettere a secco lo scafo; ~ **-docking** (*trasp. mar.*) carenaggio; carenamento; ~ **goods** merci solide; (*trasp. mar.*) carichi secchi; aridi; (*USA*) mercerie; ~ **measure** misura per merci solide, misura per cereali; ~ **run** (*pubbl.*) numero zero.

dub, *v. t.* (*pubbl.*) doppiare.

dubbing, *n.* (*pubbl.*) doppiaggio.

duck, *n.* (*Borsa, slang*) debitore moroso.

dud, *a.* falso, che non vale nulla. *n.* persona che non riesce a cavare un ragno da un buco. // ~ **cheque** (*banca*) assegno a vuoto.

due, *a.* **1** dovuto (*a*), causato (*da*). **2** (*leg.*) dovuto, spettante, esigibile, pagabile, che scade. **3** (*trasp.*) atteso, in arrivo. **4** (*trasp. mar.*) in direzione (*di*). *n.* **1** ciò che è dovuto (*a q.*). **2** **dues**, *pl.* (*dog.*) dazi. **3** **dues**, *pl.* (*leg.*) diritti. **4** **dues**, *pl.* (*sind.*) contributi sindacali. // ~ **care** (*leg.*) normale diligenza; ~ **date** (*cred.*) scadenza, data di scadenza (*d'un debito*); (*rag.*) data di scadenza; ~ **date of coupon** (*fin.*) godimento della cedola; **dues for lighthouse** (*trasp. mar.*) diritti di faro; ~ **notice** (*leg.*) avviso dato nei termini richiesti; ~ **register** (*attr. uff.*) scadenzario; **after ~ consideration** dopo adeguata riflessione; **by ~ process of law** (*leg.*) con regolare processo; **in ~ course** a tempo debito; **in ~ time** a tempo debito; **not yet** ~ (*cred.*) non ancora scaduto; **with ~ care** con la debita cura.

dull, *a.* fiacco, inerte. // ~ **market** (*market.*) mercato fiacco; ~ **season** (*market.*) stagione morta.

dullness, *n.* inerzia.

dulness, *n.* *V.* **dullness.**

duly, *avv.* **1** debitamente, adeguatamente. **2** a tempo debito, puntualmente.

dummy, *a.* falso, finto, fittizio, di comodo. *n.* **1** uomo di paglia. **2** (*leg.*) prestanome. // **a ~ corporation** una società commerciale fittizia; ~ **dollar** (*fin.*) quotazione di comodo del dollaro (*alla Borsa Valori di Londra*); ~ **name** nome fittizio.

dump, *v. t.* (*market.*) vendere sottocosto, svendere (*prodotti, specialm. all'estero*).

dumping, *n.* (*econ.*) «dumping» (*consiste nel fissare prezzi di esportazione inferiori a quelli praticati sul mercato interno*); vendita sottocosto (*di merce, specialm. all'estero*).

dun¹, *n.* **1** insistente richiesta di pagamento. **2** (*cred.*) creditore insistente. **3** (*cred.*) esattore di crediti.

dun², *v. t.* sollecitare (*il pagamento d'un debito*).

dunnage, *n.* (*trasp. mar.*) fondo della stiva.

dunning letter, *n.* (*comun.*) lettera di sollecitazione, sollecitatoria, sollecito.

duopoly, *n.* (*econ.*) duopolio.

duopsony, *n.* (*econ.*) duopsonio.

dupe, *n.* (*slang USA*) copia, copia carbone, duplicato.

duplicate[1], *a.* doppio, in duplice copia. *n.* duplicato, seconda copia. // the ~ **of a deed** la copia d'un atto; **in** ~ in duplice copia.

duplicate[2], *v. t.* **1** duplicare, fare una seconda copia di (*un documento, ecc.*). **2** ciclostilare (*lettere, ecc.*). // **duplicating and copying methods** (*attr. uff.*) metodi di duplicazione e riproduzione.

duplicating equipment, *n.* (*macch. uff.*) duplicatore.

duplicating machine, *n.* (*macch. uff.*) duplicatrice.

duplicating set, *n.* (*macch. uff.*) duplicatore.

duplication, *n.* **1** duplicazione. **2** duplicato, copia. **3** (*pubbl.*) duplicazione.

duplicator, *n.* (*macch. uff.*) ciclostile, duplicatore.

durable, *a.* durevole, duraturo. // ~ **consumer goods** (*econ.*) beni di consumo durevoli; ~ **goods** (*econ.*) beni durevoli.

durables, *n. pl.* (*econ., market.*) beni durevoli, articoli durevoli.

duration, *n.* durata.

during, *prep.* durante.

Dutch auction, *n.* asta al ribasso, asta olandese (*in cui si parte da un prezzo massimo e si scende per gradi fino a trovare un compratore*).

dutiable, *a.* (*dog., fin.*) soggetto a dazio, daziabile. // ~ **goods** (*dog., fin.*) merce soggetta a dazio.

duty, *n.* **1** dovere. **2** compito, funzione, mansione. **3** (*dog., fin.*) dazio, dogana. **4** (*fin.*) imposta, tassa, diritto. **5** (*pers.*) turno (*di lavoro*). // ~ **-free** (*dog., fin.*) franco di dazio, esente da dazio, in franchigia doganale; ~ **-free entry** (*dog., fin.*) ammissione (*o* importazione) in franchigia doganale; ~ **-free goods** (*dog., fin.*) merce franca di dazio; ~ **-free shop** (*dog., trasp. aer.*) negozio esente da dazio; **the duties of a bookkeeper** (*pers.*) le mansioni d'un ragioniere; ~ **-paid** (*dog., fin.*) sdoganato, sdaziato; ~ **-paid entry** (*dog., fin.*) dichiarazione di avvenuto pagamento del dazio; ~ **unpaid** (*dog., fin.*) dazio escluso (*da pagare*); **off** ~ (*pers.*) fuori servizio; **on** ~ (*pers.*) in servizio.

dwelling place, *n.* luogo di residenza.

dynamic, *a.* dinamico. // ~ **economics** (*econ.*) economia dinamica.

dynamics, *n. pl.* (*col verbo al sing.*) dinamica.

dynamiter, *n.* (*slang USA*) commerciante dinamico e intraprendente.

E

eagle, *n.* (*USA*) antica moneta d'oro da dieci dollari. // ~ **day** (*slang USA*) giorno di paga.

ear, *n.* **1** orecchio. **2 ears,** *pl.* rettangoli disponibili per la pubblicità accanto alla testata d'un quotidiano.

early, *a.* prossimo, vicino (*nel tempo*). *avv.* presto, per tempo. // ~ **closing** (*market.*) chiusura anticipata, chiusura pomeridiana (*dei negozi*); ~ **-closing day** (*market.*) giorno di chiusura anticipata, giorno di chiusura pomeridiana (*dei negozi*); ~ **retirement** (*pers.*) prepensionamento, pensionamento anticipato.

earmark, *v. t.* accantonare, destinare, mettere da parte (*per un particolare scopo*).

earmarking, *n.* accantonamento.

earn, *v. t.* guadagnare, ottenere. *v. i.* (*fin.*) rendere, produrre interesse. // to ~ **a bare living** guadagnare appena (tanto) da vivere; to ~ **a great reputation on the market** (*market.*) ottenere una grande rinomanza sul mercato; to ~ **a high interest** (*fin.*) ottenere un alto interesse; to ~ **one's living** guadagnarsi la vita; to ~ **a profit** (*fin., rag.*) realizzare un utile.

earned income, *n.* (*fin.*) redditi di lavoro.

earned surplus, *n.* (*rag.*) fondo di riserva.

earnest, *a.* serio, zelante. *n.* caparra. // ~ **money** caparra.

earning capacity, *n.* (*pers.*) capacità di guadagno.

earnings, *n. pl.* **1** guadagni, profitti. **2** (*pers.*) salario, stipendio. **3** (*rag.*) utile. // **an ~ -related pension** (*pers.*) una pensione agganciata allo stipendio (*o* al salario) già percepito (*dal lavoratore*).

earphone, *n.* (*attr. uff.*) telefono a cuffia.

ease[1], *n.* **1** facilità. **2** (*market.*) (*di prezzi*) tendenza al ribasso.

ease[2], *v. i.* **1** placarsi. **2** (*Borsa*) (*di prezzi, quotazioni, ecc.*) scendere. *v. t.* alleviare.

easement, *n.* **1** alleggerimento. **2** (*leg.*) servitù. // ~ **appurtenant** (*leg.*) servitù fondiaria; ~ **in gross** (*leg.*) diritto d'uso.

easily, *avv.* agevolmente, facilmente. // ~ **cashable** (*o* **cashed**) (*cred.*) di facile realizzo.

easiness, *n.* facilità. // **the ~ of money** (*fin.*) la facilità del denaro.

east, *n.* est, oriente. // ~ **European Time** *V.* **Eastern European Time.**

eastern, *a.* orientale. // ~ **European Time** (*comun.*) ora dell'Europa orientale.

easy, *a.* facile. // **an ~ customer** (*market.*) un cliente facile; ~ **make** (*slang USA*) cliente facile (da accontentare); ~ **money** (*econ.*) denaro facile; to **be in ~ circumstances** essere di agiata condizione.

eatable, *a.* mangiabile.

eatables, *n. pl.* viveri.

econ, *n.* (*slang USA*) economia.

econometric, *a.* (*econ.*) econometrico.

econometrician, *n.* (*econ.*) econometrista.

econometrics, *n. pl.* (*col verbo al sing.*) (*econ.*) econometria.

economic, *a.* (*econ.*) economico. // ~ **activity** (*econ.*) attività economica, congiuntura; ~ **activity of consumption** (*econ.*) attività di consumo; ~ **adviser** (*econ.*) consigliere economico; ~ **and Social Committee (ESC)** Comitato Economico e Sociale (*CÉS*); ~ **cycle** (*econ.*) ciclo economico; ~ **development** (*econ.*) sviluppo economico; ~ **ends** (*econ.*) fini economici; ~ **expansion** (*econ.*) espansione economica; ~ **-financial crisis** (*econ., fin.*) crisi economico-finanziaria; ~ **freedom** (*econ.*) libertà economica (*termine usato soltanto da A. Marshall e dalla sua scuola*); ~ **geography** geografia economica; ~ **good** (*econ.*) bene economico; ~ **growth** (*econ.*) sviluppo economico; ~ **imbalance** (*econ.*) squilibrio economico; ~ **indicator** (*econ.*) indicatore economico; ~ **infrastructures** (*econ.*) infrastrutture economiche; ~ **laws** (*econ.*) leggi economiche; ~ **miracle** (*econ.*) miracolo economico; ~ **order quantity** (*org. az.*) quantità ottimale; ~ **outlook** (*econ.*) congiuntura; ~ **planning** (*econ.*) programmazione economica; ~ **policy** (*econ.*) politica congiunturale; (*econ., org. az.*) politica economica; ~ **potential** (*econ.*) potenziale economico; ~ **recovery** (*econ.*) ripresa economica; ~ **revival** (*econ.*) ripresa economica; ~ **sanctions** (*econ.*) sanzioni economiche; ~ **situation** (*econ.*) situazione economica, congiuntura; ~ **statistics** (*econ., stat.*) statistica economica; ~ **stock** (*org. az.*) stock economico; ~ **survey** (*econ.*) relazione sullo stato dell'economia; ~ **system** (*econ.*) sistema economico; ~ **trend** (*econ.*) congiuntura, evoluzione della congiuntura; ~ **union** (*econ.*) unione economica; ~ **welfare** (*econ.*) benessere economico.

economical, *a.* 1 economico, parsimonioso, economo, che fa risparmiare. 2 (*econ.*) economico. // ~ **speed** (*trasp. mar.*) velocità economica.

economically, *avv.* economicamente.

economics, *n. pl.* (*col verbo al sing.*) (*econ.*) economia (*la scienza*); economia politica.

economist, *n.* 1 economo, persona economa. 2 (*econ.*) economista.

economization, *n.* economia, risparmio.

economize, *v. t.* economizzare, risparmiare, fare economia di (*qc.*).

economy, *n.* 1 economia, parsimonia. 2 (*econ.*) economia, sistema economico. 3 (*trasp. aer.*) classe economica. // ~ **class** (*trasp. aer.*) classe economica; ~ **of scale** (*econ.*) economia di massa.

edge, *n.* 1 bordo. 2 (*fin.*) punto estremo (*d'una fascia d'oscillazione dei tassi di cambio*).

edit, *v. t.* (*giorn.*) dirigere (*giornali, riviste, ecc.*).

edition, *n.* (*giorn.*) edizione.

editor, *n.* 1 (*giorn.*) direttore (*di giornale, rivista, ecc.*). 2 (*giorn.*) redattore d'articoli di fondo. // ~ **in chief** (*giorn., USA*) direttore (*di giornale, rivista, ecc.*).

editorial, *a.* 1 (*giorn.*) editoriale. 2 (*giorn.*) del direttore (*d'un giornale*); direttoriale. // ~ **matter** (*giorn.*) testo; ~ **work** (*giorn.*) lavoro editoriale; ~ **writer** (*giorn., USA*) articolista.

editorship, *n.* (*giorn.*) direzione (*di giornale, rivista, ecc.*).

education, *n.* istruzione.

educational qualifications, *n. pl.* titoli di studio.

effect[1], *n.* 1 effetto, incidenza. 2 senso, significato, tenore. 3 (*leg.*) vigore. // **the effects of industrial combination on the economy and on competition** gli effetti della concentrazione sull'economia e sulla concorrenza; «**no effects**» (*banca*) «privo di fondi» (*scritto su un assegno emesso allo scoperto*); **to the** ~ **that** (*di documento*) attestante che.

effect[2], *v. t.* effettuare. // to ~ **a composition** (*leg.*) giungere a una transazione; to ~ **a delivery** (*market.*) fare una consegna; to ~ **the insurance of the goods** (*ass.*) curare l'assicurazione della merce; to ~ **a payment** effettuare, eseguire, fare un pagamento; to ~ **a policy** (*ass.*) sottoscrivere una polizza d'assicurazione.

effective, *a.* 1 effettivo. 2 efficiente. 3 efficace. // ~ **measures to curb inflation** (*econ.*) provvedimenti efficaci per tenere a freno l'inflazione.

effectiveness, *n.* 1 efficienza. 2 efficacia. 3 (*org. az.*) rendimento (*specialm. della manodopera*).

efficiency, *n.* 1 efficienza. 2 efficacia. 3 (*cronot.*) efficienza, produttività, rendimento. // ~ **engineer** (*o* **expert**) (*org. az.*) esperto di problemi d'efficienza.

efficient, *a.* efficiente. // **an** ~ **secretary** (*pers.*) un segretario efficiente.

egalitarianism, *n.* (*econ.*) tendenza a ridurre la disuguaglianza dei redditi.

eight, *num.* otto. // ~ **-hour working day** (*org. az.*) giornata lavorativa d'otto ore.

eject, *v. t.* 1 (*leg.*) espellere. 2 (*leg.*) sfrattare.

ejectment, *n.* 1 (*leg.*) esproprio forzato. 2 (*leg.*) sfratto.

elaborator, *n.* elaboratore.

elastic, *a.* elastico. // ~ **currency** (*econ.*) circolazione monetaria elastica.

elasticity, *n.* elasticità, adattabilità. // ~ **of demand** (*econ.*) elasticità della domanda; ~ **of supply** (*econ.*) elasticità dell'offerta.

elect, *v. t.* eleggere. // to ~ **a member of the board** eleggere un membro del consiglio d'amministrazione; to ~ **sb. president** eleggere q. presidente.

election, *n.* elezione. // **by-** ~ elezione suppletiva.

elective, *a.* elettivo. // **an** ~ **assembly** un'assemblea elettiva; **an** ~ **office** una carica elettiva.

electric, *a.* elettrico. // ~ **sign** (*pubbl.*) insegna luminosa; ~ **typewriter** (*macch. uff.*) macchina da scrivere elettrica.

electronic, *a.* elettronico. // ~ **computer** (*elab. elettr.*) calcolatore (*o* elaboratore) elettronico.

electronics, *n. pl.* (*col verbo al sing.*) elettronica.

eleemosynary, *a.* gratuito. // ~ **corporation** (*fin., USA*) società di beneficenza.

elegant, *a.* elegante.

element, *n.* elemento. // ~ **of proof** (*leg.*) mezzo di prova.

elementary, *a.* elementare.

elevated railroad, *n.* (*trasp. ferr., USA*) ferrovia elevata.

elevated train, *n.* (*trasp. ferr., USA*) treno della (ferrovia) elevata.

elevation, *n.* elevazione.

elevator, *n.* (*trasp.*) elevatore.

eligibility, *n.* **1** l'essere adatto; l'avere i requisiti necessari (*per qc.*). **2** (*leg.*) eleggibilità. **3** (*rag.*) imputabilità.

eligible, *a.* **1** adatto, atto. **2** (*leg.*) eleggibile. **3** (*leg.*) che ha diritto (*a qc.*). **4** (*rag.*) imputabile. // ~ **paper** (*cred., fin.*) carta bancabile, titoli di credito con buoni requisiti di bancabilità; to **be ~ for a pension** (*leg.*) avere diritto a una pensione; to **be ~ for a position** (*pers.*) avere i requisiti per un impiego.

eliminate, *v. t.* eliminare, rimuovere. // to ~ **fiscal frontiers** (*fin.*) rimuovere le frontiere fiscali; to ~ **measures likely to distort conditions of competition** (*market.*) eliminare le misure che tendono a falsare le condizioni di concorrenza.

elimination, *n.* eliminazione, rimozione. // ~ **of tariffs** (*dog., econ.*) abolizione delle tariffe.

elusion, *n.* elusione.

em, *n.* (*pubbl., USA*) misura tipografica rappresentata da un quadrato di lato pari a sei punti.

emancipate, *v. t.* emancipare.

emancipation, *n.* (*leg.*) emancipazione.

embarcation, *n.* (*trasp. aer., trasp. mar.*) imbarco.

embargo[1], *n.* **1** (*fig.*) divieto. **2** (*leg.*) divieto d'esportazione (*di talune merci*). **3** (*leg., trasp. mar.*) embargo; fermo o sequestro di nave mercantile, requisizione.

embargo[2], *v. t.* (*leg., trasp. mar.*) requisire, sequestrare (*navi, merci*); mettere l'embargo su (*navi, merci*).

embark, *v. t.* (*trasp. aer., trasp. mar.*) imbarcare. *v. i.* imbarcarsi (*anche fig.*).

embarkation, *n.* (*trasp. aer., trasp. mar.*) imbarco. // ~ **card** (*trasp. aer., trasp. mar.*) carta d'imbarco.

embarkment, *n.* (*trasp. aer., trasp. mar.*) imbarco.

embarrass, *v. t.* imbarazzare.

embarrassment, *n.* imbarazzo.

embezzle, *v. t.* (*leg.*) appropriarsi indebitamente di (*denaro o altri beni*).

embezzlement, *n.* (*leg.*) appropriazione indebita, prevaricazione.

emblements, *n. pl.* (*leg.*) prodotti della terra.

emboss, *v. t.* punzonare, targhettare (*indirizzi*).

embossed, *a.* in rilievo. // ~ **(metal) plate** (*attr. uff.*) targhetta (*per indirizzi*); ~ **stamp** (*attr. uff.*) timbro a secco.

embossing plate, *n.* (*attr. uff.*) punzone.

emcee[1], *n.* (*pubbl., fam.*) presentatore (*di spettacoli*).

emcee[2], *v. t.* (*pubbl., fam.*) presentare (*spettacoli*).

emerge, *v. i.* emergere.

emergency, *n.* emergenza, congiuntura. // ~ **fund** (*rag.*) fondo d'emergenza, fondo di riserva; ~ **landing field** (*trasp. aer.*) campo di fortuna; ~ **runaway** (*o* **strip**) (*trasp. aer.*) pista d'emergenza.

emigrant, *n.* (*econ.*) emigrante.

emigrate, *v. i.* (*econ.*) emigrare.

emigration, *n.* (*econ.*) emigrazione.

eminent, *a.* egregio. // ~ **domain** (*leg.*) potere d'espropriazione per motivi d'interesse generale.

emolument, *n.* (*sind.*) emolumento, retribuzione.

emphyteusis, *n.* (*pl.* **emphyteuses**) (*leg.*) enfiteusi.

emphyteuta, *n.* (*pl.* **emphyteutae**) enfiteuta.

emphyteutic, *a.* (*leg.*) enfiteutico.

employ[1], *n.* (*pers.*) impiego, occupazione. // to **be in the ~ of sb.** (*pers.*) essere alle dipendenze di q.

employ[2], *v. t.* **1** impiegare. **2** (*pers.*) impiegare, dare lavoro a (*q.*), occupare. // to ~ **money** (*fin.*) investire denaro.

employe, *n. V.* **employee.**

employee, *n.* **1** (*pers.*) prestatore d'opera, impiegato, dipendente. **2 the employees,** *pl.* (*pers.*) le maestranze. // ~ **benefit plan** (*sind.*) sistema previdenziale; ~ **communications** (*org. az.*) comunicazioni col personale, comunicazioni interne; ~ **cooperation** (*pers.*) collaborazione del personale; ~ **health service** (*pers.*) assistenza sanitaria interna; **employees' manual** (*pers.*) manuale d'accoglimento; **employees on payroll** (*pers.*) operai in forza; **an ~ on the regular staff** un impiegato fisso; ~ **rating chart** (*pers.*) scheda personale; ~ **shareholding** (*pers.*) azionariato operaio; to **be in the ~ roll** (*pers.*) essere in ruolo.

employer, *n.* (*amm.*) datore di lavoro, principale, padrone (*d'un'azienda*). *a. attr.* (*org. az.*) datoriale (*relativo ai datori di lavoro*). // **employers' association** (*sind.*) associazione di datori di lavoro, unione industriale, sindacato padronale; ~ **'s liability** (*ass.*) responsabilità civile del datore di lavoro; ~ **'s liability insurance** (*ass.*) assicurazione (*stipulata dal datore di lavoro*) contro gli infortuni sul lavoro.

employment, *n.* **1** impiego. **2** (*econ.*)

occupazione; lavoro subordinato. 3 (*pers.*) impiego. // ~ **agency** (*pers., USA*) agenzia, ufficio di collocamento; ~ **bureau** (*pers.*) ufficio di collocamento; ~ **card** (*pers.*) libretto di lavoro; **the ~ function** (*econ.*) la funzione dell'occupazione; ~ **in agriculture** (*econ.*) l'occupazione agricola; ~ **increase** (*econ.*) aumento dell'occupazione; ~ **index** (*econ.*) indice dell'occupazione; ~ **interview** (*pers.*) intervista d'assunzione, intervista preliminare; **the ~ of capital in industry** (*econ.*) l'impiego di capitali nell'industria; **the ~ of women** (*econ.*) l'occupazione femminile; **the ~ problems** (*econ.*) i problemi dell'occupazione; ~ **rate** (*econ.*) tasso d'occupazione; **the ~ trend** (*econ.*) l'evoluzione dell'occupazione.

emporium, *n.* (*pl.* **emporia** e *reg.*) (*market.*) emporio, centro o base commerciale.

empty, *a.* vuoto. *n.* (*market.*) recipiente vuoto, vuoto. // ~ **journey** (*trasp. ferr.*) percorso a (vagone) vuoto; **out- ~ and return-loaded services** (*market.*) servizi nei quali il viaggio di andata è effettuato a veicolo vuoto e il viaggio di ritorno a veicolo carico.

en, *n.* (*pubbl. USA*) misura tipografica pari a un mezzo «em».

enact, *v. t.* 1 (*leg.*) stabilire per legge, statuire. 2 (*leg.*) emanare (*un decreto, una legge*). // to ~ **regulations** (*leg., org. az.*) emanare regolamenti.

enamel, *n.* vernice. // ~ **paper** (*pubbl.*) carta patinata.

encash, *v. t.* 1 incassare. 2 convertire in contanti; realizzare (*un credito, ecc.*). 3 (*cred., fin., rag.*) introitare.

encashable, *a.* 1 incassabile. 2 convertibile in contanti; (*d'un credito, ecc.*) realizzabile.

encashment, *n.* 1 incasso. 2 conversione in contanti; realizzazione (*d'un credito, ecc.*), realizzo.

enclose, *v. t.* (*comm.*) accludere, allegare.

enclosed, *a.* accluso, allegato, annesso.

enclosure, *n.* (*com.*) allegato.

encroachment, *n.* 1 usurpazione. 2 (*leg.*) lesione (*del diritto di proprietà altrui*).

encroach on, *v. t.* (*leg.*) ledere (*il diritto di proprietà altrui*).

encumber, *v. t.* (*fin., leg.*) gravare.

encumbered, *a.* (*fin., leg.*) gravato.

encumberment, *n. V.* **encumbrance.**

encumbrance, *n.* 1 (*leg.*) gravame. 2 (*leg.*) carico ipotecario. 3 (*pers.*) carico (*anche di famiglia*). 4 (*pers.*) persona a carico.

end[1]**,** *n.* 1 fine, estremità, fondo. 2 fine, scopo. // ~ **current account** (*Borsa*) fine corrente (mese); ~ **-item** (*org. az.*) prodotto finito; ~ **next** (*Borsa*) fine prossimo (mese); ~ **next account** (*Borsa*) fine prossimo (mese); ~ **-of-contract strike** (*sind.*) sciopero al momento del rinnovo d'un contratto collettivo; **the ~ of the fiscal year** (*fin.*) la fine dell'anno finanziario; ~ **product** (*org. az.*) prodotto finito; ~ **this** (*Borsa*) fine corrente (mese); ~ **this account** (*Borsa*) fine corrente (mese); ~ **-year rebate** (*market.*) abbuono di fine d'anno (*calcolato sul fatturato*).

end[2]**,** *v. t.* e *i.* finire. // to ~ **up** finire, concludersi.

endanger, *v. t.* mettere in pericolo, compromettere.

ending inventory, *n.* (*rag.*) rimanenze finali.

endorsable, *a.* (*cred.*) girabile. // **an ~ instrument** (*cred.*) un titolo girabile.

endorse, *v. t.* 1 approvare, vistare. 2 (*cred.*) firmare a tergo, attergare, girare. // to ~ **a bill of lading** (*trasp. mar.*) girare una polizza di carico; to ~ **a cheque** (*cred.*) girare un assegno; to ~ **in blank** (*cred.*) girare in bianco.

endorsee, *n.* (*cred.*) giratario.

endorsement, *n.* 1 approvazione, parere favorevole, visto. 2 (*cred.*) girata, attergato. // ~ **in blank** (*cred.*) girata in bianco; ~ **without recourse** (*cred.*) girata «senza rivalsa» (*o* «senza regresso»).

endorser, *n.* 1 chi approva, chi esprime parere favorevole (*su qc.*). 2 (*cred.*) girante.

endow, *v. t.* dotare, assegnare, sovvenzionare.

endowed, *a.* dotato.

endowment, *n.* 1 dotazione, assegnazione, sovvenzione. 2 dote. // ~ **fund** (*rag.*) fondo di dotazione; ~ **insurance** (*ass.*) assicurazione mista; ~ **policy** (*ass.*) polizza d'assicurazione con capitalizzazione dei premi.

endurance, *n.* (*trasp. mar.*) autonomia, percorrenza.

endure, *v. t.* e *i.* resistere, tollerare.

enface, *v. t.* 1 scrivere, stampare (*qc.*) su una cambiale, un assegno, ecc. 2 munire (*una cambiale, un assegno, ecc.*) di una dicitura a mano o a stampa.

enforce, *v. t.* 1 rafforzare. 2 imporre, applicare, rendere esecutivo, far osservare. // to ~ **the award** (*leg.*) eseguire il lodo; to ~ **a judgment** (*leg.*) dare esecuzione a una sentenza; to ~ **a law** (*leg.*) applicare una legge; to ~ **a right** (*leg.*) far valere un diritto.

enforceability, *n.* (*leg.*) applicabilità, esecutività, esecutorietà. // **the ~ of a contract** (*leg.*)

l'esecutorietà d'un contratto.

enforceable, *a.* (*leg.*) applicabile, esecutivo, esecutorio. // ~ **judgment** (*leg.*) sentenza esecutiva.

enforcement, *n.* 1 rafforzamento. 2 imposizione, applicazione. 3 (*leg.*) esecuzione. // **the** ~ **of the law** (*leg.*) l'esecuzione della legge.

engage, *v. t.* 1 impegnare. 2 occupare. 3 impiegare, ingaggiare, assumere. 4 noleggiare. *v. i.* impegnarsi, obbligarsi. // to ~ **an employee** (*pers.*) assumere un impiegato; to ~ **in business** mettersi in affari; to ~ **a taxi** noleggiare un taxi.

engaged, *a.* 1 impegnato. 2 occupato. // ~ **tone** (*comun.*) segnale di linea occupata.

engagement, *n.* 1 impegno, obbligo. 2 (*pers.*) assunzione, occupazione, ingaggio.

engine, *n.* 1 motore. 2 (*trasp. ferr.*) locomotiva, motrice. 3 (*trasp. mar.*) motrice, macchina. // ~ **driver** (*trasp. ferr.*) macchinista; ~ **failure** (*trasp. mar.*) avaria in macchina; ~ **-room** (*trasp. mar.*) sala macchine; ~ **shed** (*trasp. ferr.*) deposito locomotive.

engineer[1], *n.* 1 (*pers.*) perito industriale. 2 (*pers.*) progettatore d'impianti. 3 (*pers.*) tecnico specializzato. 4 (*trasp. ferr., USA*) macchinista. 5 (*trasp. mar.*) capitano di macchina, ufficiale di macchina, macchinista, motorista. // ~ **'s cab** (*trasp. ferr.*) cabina di comando.

engineer[2], *v. t.* preparare, organizzare.

engineering, *n.* (*org. az.*) progettazione d'impianti.

English, *a.* inglese. *n.* inglese (*la lingua*). // ~ **ell** misura lineare per tessili (*pari a 1 iarda e 1/4*).

Englishman, *n.* (*pl.* **Englishmen**) inglese (*uomo*).

Englishwoman, *n.* (*pl.* **Englishwomen**) inglese (*donna*).

engrave, *v. t.* (*pubbl.*) incidere.

engraver, *n.* (*pubbl.*) incisore.

engraving, *n.* (*pubbl.*) incisione.

engross, *v. t.* 1 assorbire completamente. 2 (*econ.*) accaparrare, incettare (*merci, prodotti, ecc.*). 3 (*leg.*) redigere (*un atto legale*).

engrosser, *n.* (*econ.*) accaparratore, incettatore.

engrossing, *n.* (*econ.*) accaparramento.

engrossment, *n.* (*econ.*) accaparramento (*di merci, prodotti, ecc.*), incetta.

enhance, *v. t.* accrescere, aumentare. // to ~ **the price** (*market.*) aumentare (*o* crescere) il prezzo.

enhancement, *n.* accrescimento, aumento. // **an** ~ **of price** (*market.*) un aumento di prezzo.

enjoin, *v. t.* (*leg.*) comandare, imporre, ingiungere, intimare, diffidare.

enjoy, *v. t.* godere. // to ~ **the esteem of the principal** (*pers.*) godere della stima del principale; to ~ **in usufruct** (*leg.*) usufruire; to ~ **a right** (*leg.*) godere (di) un diritto, fruire di un diritto.

enjoyment, *n.* godimento. // **the** ~ **of civic rights** (*leg.*) il godimento dei diritti civili.

enlarge, *v. t.* ampliare.

enlarged, *a.* ampliato. // **the** ~ **Common Market** il Mercato Comune allargato; l'Europa dei Dieci.

enlargement, *n.* ampliamento.

enormous, *a.* enorme, ingente.

enquire, *n.* e *derivati V.* **inquire** e *derivati.*

enrich, *v. t.* arricchire.

enrichment, *n.* arricchimento.

enroll, *v. t.* 1 elencare. 2 registrare.

enroll oneself, *v. rifl.* iscriversi.

enrolment, *n.* 1 elencazione. 2 (*leg.*) registrazione. 3 (*trasp. mar., USA*) certificato d'idoneità (*per navi cabotiere*). // **the** ~ **of a decree** (*leg.*) la registrazione d'una sentenza.

ensue, *v. i.* seguire, risultare.

ensuing, *a.* successivo. // **the** ~ **account** (*Borsa*) la liquidazione successiva; **the** ~ **settlement** (*Borsa*) la liquidazione successiva.

ensure, *v. t.* assicurare, garantire. // to ~ **that growers get a fair income** (*econ.*) garantire un reddito equo ai produttori.

entail, *v. t.* (*leg.*) lasciare in eredità (*terre, ecc.*) con vincolo d'inalienabilità.

entailment, *n.* 1 (*leg.*) conseguenza inevitabile. 2 (*leg.*) lascito soggetto a vincoli d'inalienabilità.

entente, *n.* intesa (*politica*).

enter, *v. t.* e *i.* 1 entrare (in). 2 mettere in elenco, iscrivere. 3 (*rag.*) registrare, scrivere. // to ~ **an action against sb.** (*leg.*) intentare una causa a q.; to ~ **an action in the cause list** (*leg.*) iscrivere a ruolo una causa; to ~ **a bid at an auction** fare un'offerta all'asta; to ~ **evidence** (*leg.*) presentare prove; to ~ **goods for transit** (*dog.*) dichiarare merci in transito; to ~ **into agreement with sb.** concludere un accordo con q.; to ~ **into business connections** iniziare relazioni d'affari; to ~ **into force** (*leg.*) entrare in vigore; to ~ **into partnership** (*fin.*) associarsi; to ~ **into possession** (*leg.*) entrare in possesso; to ~ **inwards** (*trasp. mar.*) fare dichiarazione d'entrata; to ~ **one's name** iscriversi; to ~ **on the credit side** (*rag.*) registrare a credito; to ~ **on the debit side** (*rag.*) registrare a debito; to ~

outwards (*trasp. mar.*) fare dichiarazione d'uscita; to ~ **a ship** (*trasp. mar.*) registrare una nave alla dogana; to ~ **a suit in the cause list** (*leg.*) iscrivere una causa a ruolo; to ~ **a transaction** (*rag.*) registrare un'operazione; to ~ **up** (*rag.*) finire di registrare; to ~ **upon an inheritance** (*leg.*) entrare in possesso d'un'eredità.

entering, *n.* (*leg.*) dichiarazione. // ~ **for non suit** (*leg.*) dichiarazione di non luogo a procedere.

enterprise, *n.* 1 impresa, progetto. 2 intraprendenza, iniziativa.

enterprising, *a.* intraprendente.

entertain, *v. t.* 1 ricevere. 2 prendere in considerazione, considerare. // to ~ **correspondence with sb.** tenersi in corrispondenza con q.; to ~ **a customer at** (*o* **to) dinner** avere un cliente a pranzo; to ~ **an offer** considerare un'offerta; to ~ **a proposal** prendere in considerazione una proposta.

entertaining expenses, *n. pl.* (*rag.*) spese di rappresentanza.

entertainment, *n.* 1 trattenimento, ricevimento. 2 spettacolo. // ~ **allowance** (*rag.*) assegno, indennità per spese di rappresentanza; **entertainments duty** (*fin.*) tassa sugli spettacoli.

entire, *a.* intero.

entirely, *avv.* interamente.

entitle, *v. t.* 1 intitolare. 2 (*leg.*) dare un diritto a (*q.*). // **entitled to succeed** (*leg.*) successibile.

entitling, *n.* intitolazione.

entrance, *n.* 1 entrata. 2 (*pers.*) assunzione (*dal punto di vista della persona da assumere*). // ~ **channel** (*trasp. mar.*) canale d'accesso; ~ **test** (*pers.*) test d'assunzione.

entrant, *n.* (*pers.*) candidato all'assunzione.

entreat, *v. t.* implorare, sollecitare.

entreaty, *n.* 1 implorazione, sollecitazione. 2 sollecito.

entrepôt, *n.* 1 (*dog.*) punto franco (*per merci in transito*). 2 (*dog.*) deposito doganale, magazzino doganale. // ~ **trade** (*comm. est.*) commercio di transito, commercio di riesportazione.

entrepreneur, *n.* (*econ.*) imprenditore. // ~ **-executive** (*econ.*) imprenditore-manager; ~ **-owner** (*econ.*) imprenditore-proprietario.

entrepreneurial, *a.* (*econ.*) imprenditoriale. // ~ **class** (*econ.*) classe imprenditoriale; ~ **skills** (*pers.*) capacità imprenditoriali.

entrust, *v. t.* 1 affidare. 2 aggiudicare (*lavori in appalto*). // to ~ **a case** (*leg.*) affidare una causa; to ~ **a matter** affidare un incarico.

entry, *n.* 1 entrata. 2 annotazione. 3 (*leg.*) entrata in possesso (*d'una proprietà, d'un immobile, ecc.*). 4 (*leg.*) inserzione (*d'un atto*) in un pubblico registro. 5 (*rag.*) registrazione, voce (*contabile*); scrittura (*a partita doppia*); rilevazione, partita. // ~ **for dutiable goods** (*dog.*) dichiarazione per merce schiava di dazio; ~ **for free goods** (*dog., ingl.*) dichiarazione per merci esenti da dazio, bolletta d'entrata di merce esente da dazio; ~ **for home use** (*dog., ingl.*) dichiarazione per merci soggette a diritti doganali; bolletta d'entrata di merce per consumo interno; ~ **for warehousing** (*dog.*) bolletta d'accompagnamento in deposito doganale; ~ **into force** (*leg.*) entrata in vigore; ~ **inwards** (*dog.*) bolletta doganale d'entrata; ~ **of an action** (*o* **of a suit) in the list of cases** (*leg.*) iscrizione d'una causa a ruolo; ~ **outwards** (*dog.*) bolletta doganale d'uscita; ~ **to the profession** (*leg.*) accesso alla professione; ~ **visa** (*comm. est., tur.*) visto d'ingresso; «**no** ~» (*trasp. aut.*) «senso vietato».

envelope, *n.* (*attr. uff.*) busta, plico. // ~ **stuffer** (*pubbl.*) materiale pubblicitario (*per pubblicità diretta*).

environment, *n.* ambiente; condizioni (ambientali).

environmental, *a.* ambientale, dell'ambiente.

epoch, *n.* epoca.

equal[1], *a.* 1 uguale, medesimo. 2 equo, giusto. // ~ **competitive footing** (*market.*) parità concorrenziale; ~ **conditions of competition** (*market.*) parità concorrenziale; ~ **laws** (*leg.*) leggi eque; ~ **marginal utility** (*econ.*) utilità marginale comparata; ~ **pay for ~ work** (*sind.*) parità salariale.

equal[2], *v. t.* uguagliare.

equality, *n.* uguaglianza. // ~ **of starting points** (*econ.*) uguaglianza dei punti di partenza; ~ **of treatment** uguaglianza di trattamento; ~ **of votes** parità di voti.

equalization, *n.* parificazione, pareggiamento, equiparazione, perequazione, livellamento. // ~ **of financing methods** (*fin.*) parificazione dei sistemi di finanziamento; **the ~ of taxes** (*fin.*) la perequazione delle imposte.

equalize, *v. t.* pareggiare, parificare, perequare, equiparare, livellare. // to ~ **incomes** (*fin.*) livellare i redditi, perequare i redditi; to ~ **taxes** (*fin.*) perequare le imposte.

equally, *avv.* ugualmente.

equation, *n.* 1 (*mat.*) equazione. // **the ~ of demand and supply** il livellamento della domanda e dell'offerta; ~ **of second degree** (*mat.*)

equazione di secondo grado.

equilibrium, *n.* (*pl.* **equilibria** e *reg.*) equilibrio. // ~ **price** (*econ.*) prezzo d'equilibrio, prezzo di mercato; ~ **rate of interest** (*econ.*) tasso d'interesse d'equilibrio (*si ha quando il risparmio naturale è uguagliato dagli investimenti*); ~ **theory** (*econ.*) teoria dell'equilibrio (*economico*).

equip, *v. t.* **1** equipaggiare, dotare. **2** (*trasp. mar.*) allestire, armare (*una nave*).

equipment, *n.* **1** equipaggiamento, apparecchiatura, attrezzatura, corredo. **2** (*trasp. ferr.*) materiale rotabile. **3** (*trasp. mar.*) armamento, materiale d'armamento. // ~ **design** (*org. az.*) progettazione d'impianti; ~ **goods** attrezzature; ~ **of cargo ships** (*trasp. mar.*) dotazione d'armamento delle navi da carico; ~ **repairs and maintenance** (*rag.*) manutenzione e riparazione attrezzature.

equitable, *a.* equo, giusto. // **an** ~ **price** (*market.*) un prezzo equo.

equitably, *avv.* equamente.

equity, *n.* **1** equità, giustizia. **2** (*fin.*) azione ordinaria. **3** (*leg.*) «equità» (*corpo di norme emanate dal «Lord Chancellor» a modifica e integrazione della «common law»*). **4** (*leg.*) valore d'una proprietà al netto d'ipoteche. **5** (*rag.*) capitale netto. // ~ **capital** (*fin.*) capitale azionario (*specialm. di società fondata da poco*); ~ **interests** (*fin.*) partecipazioni azionarie; ~ **of redemption** (*leg.*) diritto di riscatto (*d'ipoteca*); ~ **participations** (*fin.*) partecipazioni azionarie; ~ **securities** (*fin.*) azioni e titoli a interesse variabile.

equivalence, *n.* equivalenza.

equivalent, *a.* e *n.* equivalente.

era, *n.* epoca.

erasable, *a.* cancellabile.

erase, *v. t.* cancellare.

eraser, *n.* (*attr. uff.*) gomma.

erasure, *n.* cancellatura.

erect, *v. t.* erigere.

erode, *v. t.* erodere.

erosion, *n.* erosione.

err, *v. i.* errare.

errand, *n.* commissione. // ~ **-boy** (*pers.*) fattorino.

error, *n.* errore. // **errors and omissions excepted** salvo errori e omissioni; **errors excepted** salvo errori; ~ **in** (*o* **of**) **fact** (*leg.*) errore di fatto, errore di diritto; **an** ~ **of judgment** un errore di giudizio; ~ **of sampling** (*market.*) errore di campionamento.

escalation, *n.* (*sind.*) adeguamento delle retribuzioni alle variazioni del costo della vita.

escalator, *n.* scala mobile. // ~ **clause** (*sind.*) clausola di scala mobile; ~ **provision** (*sind.*) clausola di scala mobile.

escape[1]**,** *n.* fuga, evasione. // ~ **clause** (*econ., USA*) clausola (*di trattato commerciale*) che prevede la revisione o la rescissione d'un accordo se questo può turbare la stabilità d'un settore industriale, clausola d'aggancio a una scala mobile; ~ **contract** (*sind.*) contratto agganciato a una scala mobile.

escape[2]**,** *v. i.* fuggire, evadere.

escheat, *v. t.* (*leg.*) indemaniare. *v. i.* (*leg.*) essere indemaniato.

escort[1]**,** *n.* **1** (*pers.*) accompagnatore. **2** (*trasp.*) scorta.

escort[2]**,** *v. t.* accompagnare, scortare.

escrow, *v. t.* (*leg.*) depositare in garanzia.

espionage, *n.* spionaggio.

essential, *a.* essenziale.

establish, *v. t.* **1** stabilire, fondare, impiantare, instaurare. **2** nominare. **3** dimostrare, provare, far riconoscere, rendere accetto. // **to** ~ **objectives** (*org. az.*) stabilire degli obiettivi, porre degli obiettivi; **to** ~ **one's residence** (*leg.*) stabilire la propria residenza.

establishing a norm, *locuz. a.* (*leg.*) normativo.

establishment, *n.* **1** stabilimento, azienda, fabbrica. **2** fondazione, istituzione, instaurazione. **3** (*econ.*) unità produttiva. // ~ **charges** (*rag.*) spese di costituzione; **the** ~ **of the Common Market** (*econ.*) l'instaurazione del Mercato Comune.

estate, *n.* **1** proprietà (*specialm. terriera*), tenuta, patrimonio, averi, beni. **2** podere, fondo rustico. **3** (*leg.*) asse patrimoniale. // ~ **agency** (*fin.*) agenzia immobiliare; ~ **agent** (*pers.*) agente immobiliare, mediatore di case e terreni, sovrintendente (*d'azienda agricola*); ~ **and property** (*leg.*) asse patrimoniale; ~ **duty** (*fin., ingl.*) tassa di successione (*su beni immobili*); ~ **in abeyance** (*leg.*) successione vacante; ~ **in inheritance** (*leg.*) patrimonio proveniente da eredità; ~ **left by the deceased** (*leg.*) asse ereditario; **the** ~ **of a bankrupt** (*leg.*) la situazione contabile d'un fallito; ~ **tax** (*fin., USA*) tassa di successione (*su beni immobili*).

esteem[1]**,** *n.* stima, apprezzamento.

esteem[2]**,** *v. t.* considerare, apprezzare.

esteemed, *a.* stimato, apprezzato. // **your** ~ **letter** la vostra stimata lettera.

estimate[1]**,** *n.* **1** (*rag.*) stima, estimo, preventivo, stato di previsione, valutazione. **2** (*stat.*) stima. **3 the Estimates,** *pl.* (*fin.*) il bilancio preventivo dello Stato. // ~ **of costs** (*rag.*)

preventivo dei costi, calcolo delle spese (da sostenere).

estimate[2], *v. t.* (*rag.*) stimare, preventivare, valutare. // to ~ **damages** (*ass.*) periziare i danni; to ~ **expenditures** (*rag.*) fare il preventivo delle spese.

estimated, *a.* (*rag.*) stimato, preventivato. // ~ **costs** (*rag.*) costi stimati; ~ **expenditure** (*fin.*, *rag.*) spesa presunta, presuntivo; ~ **financial strength** (*fin.*) forza finanziaria stimata; ~ **value** (*rag.*) valore approssimativo.

estimation, *n.* (*rag.*) stima, preventivo, valutazione, stato di previsione.

estimative, *n.* (*rag.*) estimativo, preventivo.

estimator, *n.* stimatore, perito in preventivi.

estrangement, *n.* disaffezione.

estreat[1], *n.* (*leg.*) estratto, copia.

estreat[2], *v. t.* (*leg.*) fare un estratto, fare una copia di (*un documento, ecc.*).

etch, *v. t.* (*pubbl.*) incidere.

etcher, *n.* (*pubbl.*) incisore.

etching, *n.* (*pubbl.*) incisione.

eurobond, *n.* (*fin.*) euroemissione, euro-obbligazione. // **the ~ market for long-term transactions** (*fin.*) il mercato delle euroemissioni per le operazioni a lungo termine.

eurocheque, *n.* (*fin.*) «eurocheque», euroassegno.

Euro-clear, *n.* (*fin.*) eurocompensazione.

eurocurrency, *n.* (*fin.*) euro-divisa. // **the ~ market for short-term transactions** (*fin.*) il mercato delle euro-divise per le operazioni a breve termine.

eurodollar, *n.* (*fin.*) eurodollaro. // ~ **loans** (*fin.*) prestiti in eurodollari; **the ~ market** (*fin.*) il mercato dell'eurodollaro.

euroequity, *n.* (*fin.*) euroazione.

euromarket, *n.* (*fin.*) euromercato.

Europe, *n.* Europa.

European, *a.* europeo. // **the ~ capital market** (*fin.*) il mercato Europeo dei capitali; **the ~ Common Market** (*econ.*) il Mercato Comune Europeo; **the ~ Community** (*econ.*) la Comunità Europea; **the ~ economic integration** (*econ.*) l'integrazione economica dell'Europa; **the ~ Free Trade Association** (*econ.*) l'Associazione Europea di Libero Scambio; **the ~ Investment Bank (E.I.B.)** (*fin.*) la Banca Europea per gli Investimenti (*B.E.I.*).

evade, *v. t.* e *i.* 1 evadere. 2 eludere, evitare, sottrarsi a. // to ~ **one's income tax** (*leg.*) sottrarsi all'imposta sui redditi.

evader, *n.* evasore.

evaluate, *v. t.* valutare, calcolare, quotare. // to ~ **results** (*org. az.*) valutare i risultati.

evaluation, *n.* valutazione, calcolo. // ~ **interview** (*pers.*) intervista di valutazione.

evaluator, *n.* (*pers.*) valutatore, analista.

evasion, *n.* evasione, elusione.

even, *a.* 1 pari, alla pari. 2 esatto, preciso. 3 equo, giusto. 4 (*Borsa*) alla pari. *avv.* perfino. // **an ~ exchange** (*market.*) uno scambio equo; ~ **money** cifra tonda; ~ **numbers** (*mat.*) numeri pari; **of ~ date** in pari data, della stessa data.

event, *n.* evento.

eventuality, *n.* eventualità.

evergreen, *n.* 1 sempreverde. 2 (*market.*) articolo non soggetto a obsolescenza.

everybody, *pron.* ognuno.

evict, *v. t.* 1 (*leg.*) escomiare, espellere, sfrattare. 2 (*leg.*) evincere (*una proprietà mediante un processo*).

evictee, *n.* (*leg.*) chi è escomiato, chi è sfrattato.

eviction, *n.* 1 (*leg.*) escomio, espulsione, sfratto. 2 (*leg.*) evizione (*d'una proprietà mediante un processo*). // ~ **of a tenant** (*leg.*) sfratto d'un inquilino.

evictor, *n.* (*leg.*) chi dà l'escomio, chi dà lo sfratto.

evidence[1], *n.* 1 traccia. 2 (*leg.*) prova, deposizione, testimonianza, testimoniale. // ~ **for the accused** (*leg.*) prova a discarico; ~ **for the prosecution** (*leg.*) prova a carico; ~ **to the contrary** (*leg.*) prova in contrario; to **be** ~ (*leg.*) far fede; **on** ~ (*market.*) (*di merce*) «come si trova».

evidence[2], *v. t.* (*leg.*) attestare, comprovare, testimoniare, provare.

evident, *a.* manifesto, ovvio.

evil, *a.* cattivo, dannoso. *n.* danno. // ~ **-doer** (*leg.*) malfattore.

evolution, *n.* evoluzione, sviluppo. // **the ~ of trade** lo sviluppo dell'attività commerciale.

ex, *avv.* ex-, già, un tempo. *prep.* 1 (*Borsa*) (*di titolo*) senza. 2 (*market.*) (*di merce*) fuori di, su. 3 (*market.*) (*di merce*) franco. // ~ **-all** (*Borsa*) (*di titolo*) senza privilegi o riserve; ~ **allotment** (*Borsa*) (*di titolo*) senza ripartizione (*di nuove azioni*); ~ **ante** ad anteriori, preventivo; ~ **bond** (*dog.*) (*di merce*) sdoganata; ~ **bonus** (*Borsa*) (*di titolo*) senza riparti straordinari d'utili; ~ **capitalization** (*Borsa*) (*di titolo*) al netto d'aumento o di distribuzione gratuita d'azioni; ~ **coupon** (*Borsa*) (*di titolo*) ex-cedola; ~ **dividend** (*Borsa*) (*di titolo*) senza dividendi, ex-cedola; ~ **drawing** (*Borsa*) (*di titolo*) senza diritto all'estrazione; ~ **factory** (*market.*) (*di merce*) franco fabbrica; ~ **interest** (*Borsa*) (*di titolo*) senza interessi; ~ **new** (*Borsa*)

V. ~ **rights**; ~ **officio** (*leg.*) d'ufficio; ~ **officio proceedings** (*leg.*) procedimento d'ufficio; ~ **post** a posteriori, consuntivo; ~ **president** (*pers.*) ex-presidente; ~ **quay** (*market., trasp. mar.*) (*di merce*) sulla banchina; ~ **refinery** (*market.*) (*di merce*) franco raffineria; ~ **rights** (*Borsa*) (*di titolo*) ex-diritti (*quotazione senza diritto d'opzione*); ~ **ship** (*market., trasp. mar.*) (*di merce*) fuori della nave, franco nave; ~ **steamer** (*market., trasp. mar.*) (*di merce*) franco nave; ~ **store** (*market.*) (*di merce*) franco magazzino; ~ **warehouse** (*market.*) (*di merce*) dal magazzino; ~ **wharf** (*market., trasp. mar.*) (*di merce*) sulla banchina, franco banchina; ~ **works** (*market.*) (*di merce*) dall'officina, franco officina.

exact[1], *a.* esatto. // ~ **weight** peso esatto.

exact[2], *v. t.* esigere, richiedere. // to ~ **payment of a debt** (*cred.*) esigere il pagamento d'un debito; to ~ **a tax** (*fin.*) esigere un tributo.

exactable, *a.* esigibile.

exacting, *a.* esigente, difficile. // **an** ~ **job** (*pers.*) un lavoro difficile; **an** ~ **principal** un principale esigente.

exaction, *n.* 1 esazione (*di denaro*). 2 (*leg.*) estorsione.

exactly, *avv.* esattamente.

exactness, *n.* esattezza.

exaggerate, *v. t.* esagerare.

exaggerated, *a.* esagerato.

exaggeratedly, *avv.* esageratamente.

exaggeration, *n.* esagerazione.

exam, *n.* esame.

examination, *n.* 1 esame, indagine. 2 interrogatorio. 3 (*dog.*) visita, ispezione. 4 (*leg.*) escussione. // ~ **in chief** (*leg.*) interrogatorio dei propri testimoni; ~ **of the accused** (*leg.*) interrogatorio dell'imputato; **an** ~ **of business accounts** (*rag.*) una verifica dei conti; **the** ~ **of a sample** (*market.*) l'esame d'un campione; ~ **of witnesses for the defence** (*leg.*) escussione di testi a difesa; ~ **of witnesses for the prosecution** (*leg.*) escussione di testi d'accusa.

examine, *v. t.* 1 esaminare, indagare. 2 interrogare. 3 (*dog.*) visitare. 4 (*leg.*) escutere. // to ~ **the accounts** (*rag.*) verificare i conti; to ~ **a proposal** prendere in esame una proposta.

excavate, *v. t.* estrarre (*minerali*).

excavating, *n.* estrazione (*di minerali*).

exceed, *v. t.* eccedere.

exceeding, *a.* 1 eccedente. 2 eccessivo, straordinario, estremo. // **the** ~ **disorder of the accounts** (*rag.*) l'estremo disordine della situazione contabile.

exceedingly, *avv.* eccessivamente, straordinariamente, estremamente.

excellent, *a.* eccellente, sopraffino.

except[1], *prep.* eccetto, eccettuato, a eccezione di, salvo.

except[2], *v. t.* e *i.* 1 eccettuare, escludere. 2 eccepire, obiettare, sollevare obiezioni.

exception, *n.* 1 eccezione, esclusione, obiezione. 2 (*leg.*) eccezione. 3 **exceptions,** *pl.* (*dog., econ.*) «eccezioni» (*prodotti esclusi dalle riduzioni o abolizioni delle tariffe doganali*).

exceptional, *a.* eccezionale.

exceptionally, *avv.* eccezionalmente.

excess, *n.* 1 eccesso. 2 (*rag.*) eccedenza, rimanenza, supero. *a. attr.* aggiuntivo, addizionale, in eccedenza. // ~ **baggage** (*trasp., USA*) bagaglio in eccedenza; ~ **charge** (*market.*) soprapprezzo; ~ **corporate profit** (*rag.*) utile aziendale addizionale; ~ **fare** (*trasp. ferr.*) supplemento di tariffa; ~ **insurance** (*ass. mar.*) assicurazione con franchigia; ~ **luggage** (*trasp.*) bagaglio in eccedenza; **the** ~ **of assets over liabilities** (*rag.*) l'eccedenza dell'attivo sul passivo; **an** ~ **of exports over imports** (*econ.*) un'eccedenza delle esportazioni sulle importazioni; ~ **postage** (*comun.*) affrancatura aggiuntiva (*d'una lettera*), soprattassa; ~ **price** (*rag.*) sovrapprezzo; ~ **profits** (*rag.*) sovrapprofitti; ~ **-profits duty** (*o* **tax**) (*fin.*) tassa sui sovrapprofitti.

excessive, *a.* eccessivo.

exchange[1], *n.* 1 cambio, scambio, baratto, permuta. 2 (*comun.*) centrale, centralino. 3 (*fin.*) Borsa. 4 (*fin.*) (*anche* **Stock Exchange**) Borsa Valori. // ~ **bank** (*banca, fin.*) banca di cambio; ~ **bid** (*fin.*) offerta pubblica di scambio; ~ **broker** (*fin.*) agente di cambio; cambiavalute; ~ **charge** (*banca*) provvigione di incasso (*per effetti fuori piazza*); ~ **contract** (*Borsa*) borderò di cambio; ~ **control** (*fin.*) controllo dei cambi; ~ **for forward delivery** (*fin.*) operazioni di cambio a termine; ~ **for spot delivery** (*fin.*) operazioni di cambio per contanti; **the** ~ **list** (*fin.*) il bollettino dei cambi; ~ **of correspondence** (*comun.*) scambio di corrispondenza; ~ **of goods** scambio di merci; ~ **of views** scambio d'opinioni; ~ **offer** (*fin., USA*) offerta pubblica di scambio; ~ **office** (*fin.*) ufficio di cambio; ~ **operator** (*comun.*) centralinista; ~ **rate** (*fin.*) corso (*o* tasso) del cambio; ~ **-rate guarantee** (*fin.*) garanzia dei corsi dei cambi; ~ **rate stability** (*fin.*) stabilità dei tassi di cambio; ~ **rates** (*fin.*) rapporti di cambio; ~ **regulations** (*fin.*) regolamentazione dei cambi; ~ **restrictions** (*fin.*) restrizioni di cambio, restrizioni valutarie; ~ **transactions**

(*fin.*) operazioni di cambio; ~ **value** (*econ.*) controvalore; ~ **values** (*fin.*) valori di cambio.

exchange[2], *v. t.* scambiare, barattare. *v. i.* (*fin.*) (*di moneta*) cambiarsi.

exchequer, *n.* **1** (*fin.*) fondi, riserve monetarie. **2** (*fin., ingl.*) erario, tesoro. // ~ **bond** (*fin., ingl.*) buono del tesoro.

excisable, *a.* **1** (*fin.*) soggetto a imposta di fabbricazione. **2** (*fin.*) soggetto a dazio di consumo.

excise[1], *n.* **1** (*fin.*) imposta indiretta. **2** (*fin.*) imposta di fabbricazione. **3** (*fin.*) dazio di consumo. **4 the Excise** (*fin.*) l'ufficio delle imposte. **5 the Excise** (*fin.*) il Dazio. // ~ **duty** (*fin.*) imposta di consumo, dazio di consumo; ~ **law** (*leg., USA*) legge sulla produzione e la vendita degli alcoolici; ~ **licence** (*leg.*) permesso amministrativo (*ottenuto mediante il pagamento d'una tassa*); ~ **officer** (*fin.*) esattore del dazio, daziere, guardia daziaria.

excise[2], *v. t.* (*fin.*) tassare.

exciseman, *n.* (*pl.* **excisemen**) **1** (*pers.*) agente delle imposte. **2** (*pers.*) esattore del dazio, daziere.

exclude, *v. t.* escludere, eccettuare.

exclusion, *n.* esclusione. // ~ **clause** (*ass.*) clausola d'esclusione (*di talune perdite o rischi, dalla copertura*); **to the** ~ **of** a esclusione di.

exclusive, *a.* **1** (*leg., market.*) esclusivo, unico. **2** (*market., USA*) (*d'articolo, negozio, ecc.*) di prima qualità, di prima scelta. *n.* **1** (*giorn.*) servizio in esclusiva, esclusiva. **2** (*leg.*) diritto esclusivo, esclusiva. // ~ **agency** (*market.*) concessione esclusiva, rappresentanza esclusiva; ~ **agency agreement** (*market.*) contratto di concessione esclusiva; ~ **agency selling** (*market.*) vendita in esclusiva; ~ **agent** (*market.*) agente esclusivo, rappresentante esclusivo, esclusivista; ~ **dealer** (*market.*) concessionario in esclusiva; ~ **dealing** (*market.*) esclusiva; ~ **dealing agreements** (*market.*) accordi d'esclusiva; ~ **distributor** (*leg., market.*) concessionario; ~ **of** eccetto; ~ **privilege** (*leg.*) privilegio esclusivo, privativa; **an** ~ **right** (*leg.*) un diritto esclusivo, un'esclusiva; **an** ~ **shop** (*fam.*) un negozio caro; ~ **title** (*leg.*) diritto esclusivo.

exclusively, *avv.* esclusivamente.

exclusivist, *n.* (*anche econ.*) esclusivista.

excuse[1], *n.* giustificazione.

excuse[2], *v. t.* **1** giustificare. **2** esentare, esonerare, dispensare. **3** condonare. // to ~ **an absence** giustificare un'assenza.

execute, *v. t.* **1** eseguire, mettere in esecuzione. **2** (*leg.*) eseguire (*una sentenza*). **3** (*leg.*) redigere. **4** (*leg.*) perfezionare. // to ~ **a contract** (*leg.*) perfezionare un contratto; to ~ **a law** (*leg.*) mettere in esecuzione una legge; to ~ **an order** (*market.*) eseguire (*o* evadere, dar corso a) un'ordinazione; to ~ **a plan** mettere in esecuzione un disegno; to ~ **a policy** (*ass.*) emettere una polizza.

execution, *n.* **1** esecuzione. **2** (*leg.*) esecuzione (*d'una sentenza*). **3** (*leg.*) perfezionamento. // **the** ~ **of a judgment** (*leg.*) l'esecuzione d'una sentenza; **the** ~ **of the national budget** (*fin.*) la gestione del bilancio dello Stato; **the** ~ **of an order** (*market.*) l'esecuzione (*o* l'evasione) d'un ordine.

executive, *a.* esecutivo, amministrativo, direttivo, direzionale. *n.* **1** (*pers.*) dirigente, capo (*d'un servizio, ecc.*). **2 the executive** (*politica*) l'esecutivo. **3 the executives,** *pl.* (*pers.*) il personale direttivo. // ~ **ability** capacità direttiva; ~ **cadres** (*pers.*) quadri direttivi, quadri dirigenti; ~ **coaching** formazione dei dirigenti; ~ **committee** comitato esecutivo; ~ **control** (*org. az.*) controllo esecutivo; ~ **game** (*amm.*) gestione simulata; ~ **Office of the President** (*USA*) Ufficio della Presidenza (*della Repubblica e del Consiglio, insieme*); ~ **power** potere esecutivo; ~ **secretary** (*pers.*) segretario di direzione; ~ **training** (*org. az.*) addestramento dei dirigenti.

executor, *n.* **1** esecutore. **2** (*leg.*) esecutore testamentario. // ~ **of a will** (*leg.*) esecutore testamentario.

executory, *a.* esecutorio, esecutivo. // ~ **judgment** (*leg.*) giudizio esecutivo.

executrix, *n.* (*pl.* **executrices**) **1** esecutrice. **2** (*leg.*) esecutrice testamentaria.

exemplar, *n.* modello.

exemplary, *a.* tipico.

exempt[1], *a.* esente. *n.* (*fin.*) persona esente (*specialm. da imposte*). // ~ **from stamp duty** (*fin.*) esente da bollo; ~ **private company** (*fin., ingl.*) società non obbligata alla presentazione annuale del bilancio.

exempt[2], *v. t.* esentare, esimere, esonerare, dispensare.

exempted, *a.* esonerato, dispensato.

exemption, *n.* **1** esenzione, esonero, dispensa. **2** (*fin.*) franchigia. // ~ **from taxation** (*fin.*) esenzione dalle imposte, esonero fiscale.

exercise[1], *n.* esercizio. // **the** ~ **of a right** (*leg.*) l'esercizio d'un diritto.

exercise[2], *v. t.* esercitare. // to ~ **a function** esercitare una funzione; to ~ **an option** (*Borsa*) esercitare un'opzione.

exercise oneself, *v. rifl.* esercitarsi.

exhaust, *v. t.* esaurire, consumare, vuotare. // to ~ **a bank account** (*banca*) esaurire un conto in banca.

exhausted, *a.* esaurito.

exhaustion, *n.* esaurimento, svuotamento. // **the ~ of funds** (*rag.*) l'esaurimento dei fondi.

exhaustive, *a.* esauriente, completo. // **an ~ inquiry** un'indagine esauriente.

exhaust oneself, *v. rifl.* esaurirsi.

exheredate, *v. t.* diseredare.

exheredation, *n.* (*leg.*) diseredazione.

exhibit[1]**,** *n.* 1 esposizione, mostra. 2 (*leg.*) documento esibito, documento prodotto; prova esibita, prova prodotta. 3 (*market.*) oggetto in mostra. 4 **exhibits,** *pl.* (*market.*) materiale da esposizione.

exhibit[2]**,** *v. t.* 1 esporre, mostrare. 2 (*leg.*) esibire, produrre (*documenti, prove, ecc.*). // to ~ **documents in Court** (*leg.*) produrre documenti in tribunale.

exhibition, *n.* 1 esposizione, mostra. 2 (*leg.*) esibizione, produzione di documenti. 3 (*market.*) esposizione, mostra. // ~ **hall** (*market.*) salone da esposizione; ~ **of documents** (*leg.*) produzione di documenti.

exhibitor, *n.* (*market.*) espositore, ditta espositrice.

exigency, *n.* esigenza.

exist, *v. i.* esistere.

existence, *n.* esistenza.

existing, *a.* esistente.

exit, *n.* uscita. // ~ **visa** (*comm. est., tur.*) visto d'uscita.

exonerate, *v. t.* 1 esonerare, dispensare, sgravare. 2 (*leg.*) discolpare. // to ~ **sb. from his duties** esonerare q. dai propri doveri.

exoneration, *n.* 1 esonero, dispensa, sgravio. 2 (*leg.*) discolpa.

expand, *v. t.* 1 espandere, ampliare, sviluppare. 2 (*mat.*) sviluppare (*un'equazione, ecc.*). *v. i.* espandersi, ampliarsi, svilupparsi.

expanding, *a.* in espansione. // ~ **economy** (*econ.*) economia in via d'espansione; ~ **industries** industrie in espansione.

expansion, *n.* 1 ampliamento, allargamento, aumento, sviluppo. 2 (*mat.*) sviluppo (*d'una equazione, ecc.*). // **the ~ of currency** (*fin.*) l'aumento della circolazione monetaria; **the ~ of home demand** (*econ.*) la dilatazione della domanda interna; **the ~ of lending** (*banca*) l'aumento delle aperture di credito; **the ~ of trade** (*market.*) il moltiplicarsi degli scambi.

expansionism, *n.* (*econ.*) espansionismo.

expansionist, *n.* espansionista. // ~ **policy** (*org. az.*) politica d'espansione.

expatriate, *a.* e *n.* espatriato. // ~ **enterprise** (*org. az.*) impresa all'estero.

expect, *v. t.* e *i.* 1 aspettare, attendere. 2 presumere, prevedere.

expectation, *n.* 1 attesa. 2 previsione. // ~ **of life** (*mat. attuariale*) vita presunta.

expedite, *v. t.* accelerare, sollecitare, sbrigare.

expediting, *n.* (*org. az.*) sollecitazione delle consegne.

expel, *v. t.* espellere, estromettere.

expenditure, *n.* 1 spesa, spese. 2 (*fin., rag.*) uscita, uscite. // ~ **of the public authorities** (*fin.*) spese pubbliche; **the ~ of the State** (*fin.*) la spesa statale.

expense[1]**,** *n.* 1 spesa, carico. 2 **expenses,** *pl.* (*banca*) spese. // ~ **account** (*pers.*) nota spese (*da rimborsarsi a un dipendente*); ~ **account per diem** (*pers.*) diaria; **expenses of selling** (*rag.*) spese di vendita; «**expenses to be debited to you** (*o* **charged to your account**)» (*market., rag.*) «spese a carico del vostro conto»; **at sb.'s ~** (*rag.*) a carico di q.; **at our ~** (*rag.*) a nostre spese.

expense[2]**,** *v. t.* far pagare spese.

expensive, *a.* costoso, dispendioso, caro.

experience[1]**,** *n.* esperienza, pratica, prova.

experience[2]**,** *v. t.* fare esperienza di, provare, incontrare, subire. // to ~ **a loss** (*rag.*) subire una perdita.

experienced, *a.* esperto, competente. // **an ~ accountant** (*pers.*) un contabile esperto.

experiment, *n.* esperimento.

experimental, *a.* sperimentale. // ~ **method** (*market.*) metodo dell'esperimento.

expert, *a.* e *n.* 1 esperto, competente, versato. 2 (*leg.*) perito. // ~ **appointed by the Court** (*leg.*) perito nominato dal tribunale; ~ **evidence** (*leg.*) testimonianza di perito; ~ **in commercial law** (*leg.*) commercialista; **an ~ opinion** il parere d'un competente.

expertise, *n.* competenza, perizia.

expertize, *v. i.* dare un parere professionale, dare un parere d'esperto.

expiration, *n.* scadenza, termine. // ~ **of an option** (*Borsa*) scadenza d'un'opzione; **the ~ of a team of office** (*amm.*) lo scadere d'una permanenza in carica; ~ **of the time limit for appearance before the Court** (*leg.*) scadenza del termine utile per comparire davanti al tribunale.

expire, *v. i.* scadere.

expired, *a.* (*d'ufficio, carica, ecc.*) scaduto.

expiry, *n.* (*banca, cred.*) scadenza. // **before the ~** (*banca, cred.*) prima della scadenza.

explain, *v. t.* manifestare.

exploit, *v. t.* sfruttare, servirsi di. // to ~ **natural resources** sfruttare le risorse naturali.

exploitation, *n.* sfruttamento. // ~ **company** società di ricerca; ~ **of the working classes** (*sind.*) sfruttamento delle classi lavoratrici.

exploiter, *n.* sfruttatore, utilizzatore.

exploration, *n.* investigazione, indagine, esame. // **an** ~ **of supply resources** un esame delle fonti d'approvvigionamento.

explore, *v. t.* indagare, investigare, esaminare.

export[1]**,** *n.* 1 (*comm. est.*) esportazione. 2 (*comm. est.*) merce d'esportazione, prodotto d'esportazione. // ~ **agent** (*comm. est.*) agente esportatore, esportatore su commissione; ~ **bounty** (*comm. est.*) sovvenzione (*o* premio) all'esportazione; ~ **commission agent** (*comm. est.*) agente esportatore, esportatore su commissione; ~ **credit insurance** (*comm. est.*) assicurazione dei crediti all'esportazione; ~ **credits** (*comm. est.*) crediti all'esportazione; ~ **duty** (*dog.*) dazio d'esportazione; ~ **goods** (*comm. est.*) merce d'esportazione; ~ **-induced inflation** (*econ.*) inflazione indotta dalle esportazioni; ~ **insurance** (*ass.*) assicurazione all'esportazione; ~ **insurance techniques** (*ass.*) tecniche d'assicurazione all'esportazione; ~ **-led boom** (*econ.*) boom alimentato dalle esportazioni; ~ **licence** (*comm. est.*) licenza d'esportazione; ~ **merchant** (*comm. est.*) esportatore in proprio; ~ **of capitals** (*fin.*) esportazione di capitali; **exports of goods and services** (*comm. est.*) esportazione di beni e servizi; ~ **permit** (*comm. est.*) permesso d'esportazione; ~ **rebate** (*comm. est.*) *V.* ~ **bounty;** ~ **receipts** (*fin.*) proventi delle esportazioni; ~ **refunds** (*fin.*) restituzioni all'esportazione; ~ **specification** (*dog.*) dichiarazione d'esportazione; ~ **tax** (*dog.*) dazio d'esportazione; ~ **trade** (*comm. est.*) commercio d'esportazione; ~ **winner** (*comm. est.*) articolo d'esportazione di prim'ordine.

export[2]**,** *v. t.* (*comm. est.*) esportare. // to ~ **again** (*comm. est.*) riesportare.

exportable, *a.* (*comm. est.*) esportabile.

exportation, *n.* 1 (*comm. est.*) esportazione. 2 (*comm. est.*) merce d'esportazione, prodotto d'esportazione. // **the** ~ **voucher (of a pass sheet)** (*dog.*) il foglio d'uscita (in un «trittico»).

exporter, *n.* 1 (*comm. est.*) esportatore. 2 (*comm. est.*) Paese esportatore.

exporting, *a.* (*comm. est.*) esportatore. *n.* l'esportare, esportazione. // ~ **country** (*comm. est.*) Paese esportatore.

expose, *v. t.* esporre.

expose oneself, *v. rifl.* esporsi.

exposure, *n.* esposizione (*anche fotografica*).

expound, *v. t.* esporre (*una teoria, le proprie idee, ecc.*).

express[1]**,** *a.* espresso, manifesto. *n.* 1 (*trasp., USA*) servizio di spedizioni per espresso. 2 (*trasp. ferr.*) treno espresso, direttissimo. *avv.* per espresso. // ~ **agreement** (*leg.*) accordo espresso, accordo esplicito; ~ **company** (*trasp., USA*) agenzia di spedizioni per espresso; ~ **delivery** (*market.*) consegna per espresso; ~ **fee** (*comun.*) sovrattassa per (lettera) espresso; **an** ~ **highway** (*trasp., USA*) un'autostrada; ~ **letter** (*comun.*) (lettera) espresso; ~ **mail** (*comun.*) posta espresso; **an** ~ **train** (*trasp. ferr.*) un treno espresso, un treno rapido; ~ **warranty** (*ass. mar.*) garanzia espressa, condizione esplicita.

express[2]**,** *v. t.* 1 esprimere, dichiarare, manifestare. 2 (*comun.*) spedire (*una lettera*) per espresso.

expressage, *n.* 1 (*trasp.*) trasporto di pacchi per espresso. 2 (*trasp.*) spese di trasporto di pacchi per espresso.

expression, *n.* (*anche mat.*) espressione.

expropriate, *v. t.* (*leg.*) espropriare.

expropriation, *n.* (*leg.*) espropriazione, esproprio.

expulsion, *n.* espulsione.

expunge, *v. t.* cancellare, togliere.

extend, *v. t.* 1 estendere, ampliare. 2 (*cred.*) dilazionare, prorogare (*il pagamento d'un debito*). 3 (*rag.*) riportare a nuovo; trasferire (*cifre, totali, ecc.*) da una colonna a un'altra. *v. i.* estendersi. // to ~ **the maturity of a bill** (*cred.*) differire la scadenza d'una cambiale; to ~ **the time of payment of a bill** (*cred.*) prorogare la scadenza d'una cambiale; to ~ **the time of payment of a debt** (*cred.*) prolungare la scadenza d'un debito.

extended, *a.* 1 esteso, ampliato. 2 (*cred.*) (*d'un pagamento*) dilazionato, prorogato. 3 (*rag.*) (*di cifra, di totale, ecc.*) riportato a nuovo. // ~ **coverage** (*ass.*) copertura estesa; ~ **credit** (*banca*) credito superiore a sei mesi (*che, in via eccezionale, una banca concede a un esportatore*); ~ **medium-term** (*cred.*) medio termine prolungato; ~ **medium-term purchasers** (*cred.*) acquirenti a medio termine prolungato.

extendible, *a.* (*cred.*) prorogabile.

extensible, *a.* (*cred.*) prorogabile.

extension, *n.* 1 estensione, ampliamento. 2 (*comun.*) (numero telefonico) interno. 3 (*cred.*) dilazione, proroga. 4 (*rag.*) riporto a nuovo, somma riportata a nuovo. // ~ **of payment** (*cred.*) dilazione di pagamento; **the** ~ **of a railway** (*trasp. ferr.*) il prolungamento d'una ferrovia.

extensive, *a.* esteso, estensivo, esauriente.

extent, *n.* **1** estensione. **2** grado, limite. **3** (*leg.*) ordine di confisca. // **to the ~ of** fino all'ammontare di, fino alla concorrenza di.

extenuate, *v. t.* attenuare, ridurre.

extenuating, *a.* attenuante. // **an ~ circumstance** (*leg.*) una circostanza attenuante.

extenuation, *n.* attenuazione.

external, *a.* **1** esterno, esteriore. **2** estero. // **~ auditing** (*rag.*) revisione contabile «esterna» (*eseguita da ditte specializzate che svolgono le funzioni attribuite in Italia al collegio sindacale*); **~ convertibility** (*fin.*) convertibilità esterna; **~ evidence** (*leg.*) prove esterne; **~ exchange** (*fin.*) cambio estero; **~ relations** (*pubbl.*) rapporti col pubblico; **~ trade** (*comm. est.*) scambi esteri.

extinction, *n.* estinzione. // **~ of a debt** (*cred.*) estinzione d'un debito.

extinguish, *v. t.* estinguere. // to **~ a mortgage** (*leg.*) radiare un'ipoteca.

extinguished, *a.* (*leg.*) estinto.

extort, *v. t.* (*anche leg.*) estorcere.

extortion, *n.* (*anche leg.*) estorsione.

extra, *a.* «extra», addizionale, aggiuntivo, supplementare, straordinario. *n.* **1** «extra», aggiunta, supplemento. **2** spesa aggiuntiva. **3** (*giorn.*) edizione straordinaria (*d'un giornale*). **4** (*pers.*) extra; lavoratore (*impiegato, operaio, ecc.*) straordinario. *avv.* «extra», straordinariamente. // **~ charge** (*rag.*) spesa supplementare; (*trasp. ferr.*) supplemento, soprattassa; **~ fine quality** (*market.*) qualità «extrafina», qualità superiore; **~ freight** (*trasp. mar.*) nolo supplementare, soprannolo; **~ holiday train** (*trasp. ferr.*) treno festivo; **~ pay** (*pers.*) compenso aggiuntivo (*o* straordinario); supplemento; **~ premium** (*ass.*) premio supplementare; **~ -special** (*giorn.*) ultimissima edizione (*d'un giornale della sera*); **~ tax** (*fin.*) soprattassa; **~ work** (*pers.*) lavoro straordinario; **no ~** (*market.*) senza supplementi, tutto compreso.

extract[1], *n.* estratto (*di carne, ecc.*).

extract[2], *v. t.* estrarre.

extraction, *n.* estrazione.

extradite, *v. t.* (*leg.*) estradare.

extradition, *n.* (*leg.*) estradizione.

extrajudicial, *a.* (*leg.*) stragiudiziale, estraprocessuale. // **an ~ investigation** (*leg.*) un'indagine stragiudiziale; **an ~ transaction** (*leg.*) una transazione stragiudiziale.

extralegal, *a.* (*leg.*) estralegale.

extraordinary, *a.* straordinario, eccezionale. // **~ expenses** (*rag.*) spese straordinarie; **~ general meeting** (*amm.*) assemblea straordinaria; **an ~ influx of foreign capital to Italy** (*fin.*) un forte afflusso di capitali esteri in Italia; **~ meeting** (*amm.*) assemblea straordinaria; **~ powers** (*leg.*) poteri straordinari; **~ reserve** (*rag.*) riserva straordinaria.

extraterritorial, *a.* estraterritoriale. // **~ jurisdiction** (*leg.*) giurisdizione estraterritoriale.

extreme, *a.* estremo, ultimo. // **~ values** (*market.*) valori estremi.

extremely, *avv.* estremamente.

extremes, *n. pl.* **1** (*market.*) valori estremi. **2** (*mat.*) (gli) estremi.

extremity, *n.* estremità.

extrinsic, *a.* estrinseco. // **the ~ value of a coin** (*fin.*) il valore estrinseco d'una moneta.

eye, *n.* occhio. // **~ -catcher** (*pubbl.*) oggetto (*o* articolo, prodotto, ecc.) che attira la vista; **~ -catching** (*pubbl.*) vistoso; **an ~ -catching ad** (*pubbl.*) un annuncio pubblicitario vistoso; **~ -witness** (*leg.*) testimone oculare.

eyewitness, *n.* (*leg.*) testimone oculare.

F

face[1], *n.* 1 viso. 2 superficie. 3 (*d'un documento*) recto. 4 (*pubbl.*) carattere (*tipografico*). // **the faces of a problem** (*org. az.*) gli aspetti d'un problema; **the ~ of a stock certificate** (*fin.*) il recto d'un certificato azionario; **~ value** (*fin.*) valore facciale, valore nominale (*d'una moneta, banconota, ecc.*); **the ~ value of a share** (*fin.*) il valore nominale d'un'azione.

face[2], *v. t.* affrontare, fronteggiare, far fronte a.

facia, *n.* insegna di negozio.

facilitate, *v. t.* facilitare.

facilitation, *n.* facilitazione.

facilities, *n. pl.* 1 (*econ.*) infrastrutture. 2 (*org. az.*) attrezzature, mezzi, impianti, servizi. // **~ of payment** (*cred.*) facilitazioni di pagamento; **the ~ of a suburban community** le infrastrutture d'un centro suburbano.

facility, *n.* 1 facilità. 2 facilitazione, agevolazione.

facsimile[1], *n.* facsimile, copia esatta. // **~ signature** (*leg.*) facsimile di firma.

facsimile[2], *v. t.* fare un facsimile di (*qc.*); riprodurre esattamente (*qc.*).

fact, *n.* 1 fatto, fatto reale. 2 **the facts,** *pl.* (*leg.*) i fatti. // **~ finder** (*amm., leg.*) inquirente; **~ -finding** che indaga sui fatti; **~ -finding board** (*amm., leg.*) commissione d'inchiesta.

factor, *n.* 1 fattore, elemento. 2 (*fin., USA*) organizzazione specializzata nell'incasso di crediti per conto di terzi. 3 (*leg.*) mandatario commerciale (*cui vengono affidate le merci di cui ha la piena disponibilità*). 4 (*market.*) agente depositario, depositario; grossista. 5 (*mat.*) fattore, coefficiente. // **~ comparison** (*pers.*) raffronto per fattore; **~ cost** (*econ.*) prezzo pagato dal consumatore, al netto d'ogni tassa o dazio incluso nel prezzo di vendita; **~ of expansion** (*comm. est.*) fattore d'espansione; **a ~ of production** (*org. az.*) un fattore produttivo; **the factors of production** (*econ.*) i fattori della produzione.

factorage, *n.* 1 (*fin.*) commissione, provvigione (*di commissionario*). 2 (*fin., USA*) compenso percentuale (*V.* **factoring**).

factorial, *a.* fattoriale. *n.* (*mat.*) fattoriale.

factoring, *n.* (*fin., USA*) «factoring» (*finanziamento aziendale basato sulla cessione di crediti a organizzazioni, dette «factors», le quali provvedono all'incasso per un compenso percentuale detto «factorage»*). // **~ firm** (*fin.*) società di «factoring».

factorize, *v. t.* (*mat.*) scomporre in fattori.

factory, *n.* (*org. az.*) fabbrica, stabilimento, opificio, manifattura. // **~ cost** (*rag.*) costo di produzione; **~ indirect expenses** (*rag.*) spese generali di produzione; **~ -owner** proprietario d'una fabbrica, manifatturiere; **~ price** (*rag.*) prezzo di fabbrica.

factotum, *n.* (*pers.*) factotum, impiegato tuttofare.

facultative, *a.* facoltativo.

faculty, *n.* 1 facoltà, abilità, capacità. 2 (*econ.*) condizioni finanziarie. // **~ theory** (*econ.*) teoria della capacità contributiva.

fade, *v. t.* affievolire, far svanire. *v. i.* affievolirsi, svanire.

fail[1], *n.* fallo, errore. // **without ~** senza fallo, certamente.

fail[2], *v. i.* 1 fallire, non riuscire, mancare. 2 (*leg.*) fallire, andar fallito. // to **~ to meet an obligation** (*leg.*) contravvenire a un impegno (*o* a un obbligo).

failing, *prep.* venendo meno, in mancanza di. // **~ specific instructions** in mancanza d'istruzioni specifiche.

failure, *n.* 1 fallimento, insuccesso, fiasco, mancanza, insufficienza. 2 (*econ., fin.*) fallimento, dissesto, rovina. 3 (*elab. elettr.*) avaria. 4 (*leg.*) inadempienza, omissione. 5 (*leg.*) fallimento. // **~ of evidence** (*leg.*) mancanza di prove; **~ of issue** (*leg.*) mancanza d'eredi; **~ to appear** (*leg.*) mancata comparizione in giudizio, contumacia; **~ to perform** (*leg.*) mancata esecuzione; **~ to produce documents** (*leg.*) mancata produzione di documenti; **~ to protest a bill** (*leg.*) mancato protesto di cambiale.

fair[1], *a.* 1 equo, giusto. 2 onesto. 3 giustificato. // **~ average quality** (*market.*)

qualità buona media; ~ **competition** (*market.*) concorrenza leale; ~ **copy** bella copia, buona copia (*di documento, ecc.*); **a ~ exchange** uno scambio equo; **a ~ price** (*market.*) un prezzo equo; ~ **trade practices** (*market.*) correttezza commerciale; **a ~ wage** (*pers.*) una paga giusta.

fair², *n.* (*market.*) fiera, mostra, mercato.

fair³, *v. t.* fare la bella copia di.

fairly, *avv.* equamente.

faith, *n.* fede.

faithful, *a.* fedele. // **the ~ copy of a document** la copia fedele d'un documento; to **be ~ to one's word** essere fedele alla parola data.

faithfully, *avv.* fedelmente.

faithfulness, *n.* fedeltà.

fall¹, *n.* **1** caduta, crollo. **2** calo, abbassamento, ribasso. **3** (*USA*) autunno. // ~ **clause** (*leg.*) clausola di parità; ~ **fashions** (*market.*) modelli autunnali (*d'abiti per l'autunno*); **a ~ in exports** (*comm. est.*) una diminuzione delle esportazioni; **a ~ in prices** (*market.*) un ribasso dei prezzi.

fall², *v. i.* (*pass.* **fell**, *part. pass.* **fallen**) **1** cadere, crollare. **2** calare, abbassarsi. // to ~ **behind** essere in ritardo, restare indietro; to ~ **down** (*market.*) (*di prezzi*) crollare; to ~ **due** scadere, giungere a scadenza, maturare; to ~ **foul of** (*trasp. mar.*) investire (*una nave, ecc.*); to ~ **into abeyance** cadere in disuso; to ~ **off** (*market.*) (*di prezzi, ecc.*) diminuire, contrarsi; (*di qualità*) scadere, peggiorare; to ~ **short of** essere insufficiente rispetto a, diventare insufficiente rispetto a (*qc.*); to ~ **within the competence of sb.** essere di competenza di q., competere a q.; «**as they ~ due**» (*cred.*) (*di cambiali*) in ordine di scadenza.

falling, *n.* caduta. // ~ **of goods overboard** (*ass. mar.*) caduta in mare di merci; ~ **-off** (*market.*) (*di prezzi, ecc.*) flessione; ~ **-off in quality** (*market.*) calo di qualità; **a ~ trend** (*econ.*) una tendenza al ribasso.

falloff, *n.* **1** (*econ., fin., market.*) declino (*di prezzi, ecc.*). **2** (*market.*) diminuzione, contrazione. // **a ~ in exports** (*comm. est.*) una contrazione delle esportazioni.

false, *a.* **1** falso, falsificato, contraffatto. **2** errato. // **a ~ coin** una moneta falsa; ~ **evidence** (*leg.*) prova falsa; ~ **medium-term securities** (*Borsa, leg.*) buoni di «cassa» falsificati; ~ **oath** (*leg.*) falso giuramento; ~ **pretences** (*leg.*) dichiarazioni false, millantato credito; ~ **statement** (*leg.*) falsa dichiarazione; **a ~ verdict** (*leg.*) un verdetto errato.

falsehood, *n.* falsità; (il) falso; finzione.

falsification, *n.* falsificazione, contraffazione. // ~ **of accounts** (*leg.*) falsificazione delle scritture contabili.

falsifier, *n.* (*leg.*) falsificatore, contraffattore, falsario.

falsify, *v. t.* (*leg.*) falsificare, falsare, contraffare. // to ~ **documents** (*leg.*) falsificare documenti; to ~ **a signature** (*leg.*) falsificare una firma.

fame, *n.* fama.

familiar, *a.* familiare.

family, *n.* famiglia. // ~ **allowance** (*pers.*) assegni familiari; ~ **budget** bilancio familiare; ~ **fare** (*trasp.*) tariffa (ridotta) per famiglie; ~ **income** (*econ.*) reddito familiare; ~ **-run company** (*org. az.*) società a base familiare; ~ **wage** (*econ.*) reddito familiare; **one- ~ farm** (*econ.*) azienda agricola a conduzione familiare.

famine, *n.* carestia.

famous, *a.* famoso.

fancy, *n.* **1** capriccio. *a. attr.* **1** (di) fantasia, di vario colore. **2** elaborato, elegante. **3** d'affezione. **4** (*market., USA*) di qualità superiore. // ~ **goods** (*market.*) articoli vari; **a ~ price** (*market.*) un prezzo d'affezione; **a ~ shop** (*market.*) un negozio di lusso.

far, *avv.* lontano. // ~ **-away**, ~ **-off** lontano (*avv. e a.*).

fare, *n.* **1** (*trasp.*) prezzo del biglietto, prezzo della corsa. **2** (*trasp.*) tariffa. **3** (*trasp.*) passeggero (*di mezzo pubblico*).

farm¹, *n.* **1** fattoria, fondo rustico, podere, azienda agricola, tenuta. **2** casa colonica. // ~ **-house** fattoria (*l'edificio*); ~ **incomes** (*econ.*) redditi agricoli; ~ **labourer** (*pers.*) bracciante agricolo; ~ **price** (*econ.*) prezzo agricolo; ~ **-price support** (*econ.*) sostegno dei prezzi agricoli; ~ **products** prodotti agricoli; ~ **subsides** (*econ.*) sussidi all'agricoltura; ~ **surpluses** (*econ.*) surplus agricoli.

farm², *v. t.* **1** coltivare. **2** (*leg.*) appaltare, dare in appalto. *v. i.* fare l'agricoltore. // to ~ **out** (*leg.*) appaltare, dare in appalto (*un lavoro*); to ~ **a tax** (*leg.*) appaltare l'esazione d'un'imposta.

farmer, *n.* **1** agricoltore. **2** (*leg.*) appaltatore (*d'imposte*). // **farmers' union** consorzio agrario.

farmhand, *n.* (*pers.*) bracciante agricolo.

farming, *n.* agricoltura.

fashion, *n.* moda, voga.

fast, *a.* **1** veloce. **2** fermo. // **a ~ train** (*trasp. ferr.*) un (treno) diretto.

fate, *n.* fato, destino, sorte. // **the ~ of a bill** (*cred.*) l'esito d'una cambiale.

father, *n.* padre. // ~ **'s name** (*leg.*) paternità.

fathom, *n.* «fathom» (*misura di profondità*

marina equivalente a sei piedi).

fatigue, *n.* fatica, stanchezza.

fault, *n.* 1 colpa. 2 errore, sbaglio. // **with all faults** (*market.*) a rischio del compratore.

faulty, *a.* difettoso. // ~ **articles** (*market.*) articoli difettosi; ~ **stowage** (*trasp. mar.*) stivaggio difettoso.

favour[1], *n.* 1 favore. 2 (*comun.*) (*nella corrispondenza commerciale*) gradita lettera.

favour[2], *v. t.* favorire.

favourable, *a.* favorevole. // **a ~ answer** una risposta favorevole; **a ~ balance of trade** (*econ.*) bilancia commerciale attiva; ~ **trend** (*econ.*) congiuntura favorevole, alta congiuntura.

favoured, *a.* favorito. // **most ~ nation clause** (*comm. est.*) clausola di nazione più favorita.

favourite, *a.* e *n.* favorito.

fear[1], *n.* paura.

fear[2], *v. t.* e *i.* aver paura (di).

feasibility, *n.* l'essere fattibile. // ~ **study** (*org. az.*) calcolo di convenienza economica.

feasible, *a.* fattibile, possibile.

feature[1], *n.* 1 caratteristica. 2 (*giorn.*) articolo importante. // ~ **film** (*pubbl.*) film a soggetto.

feature[2], *v. t.* (*giorn.*) mettere in evidenza (*una notizia, ecc.*), dare risalto a (*una notizia, ecc.*); dare risalto agli aspetti principali di (*qc.*).

Federal, *a.* (*USA*) Federale. // ~ **property** (*amm.*) demanio; ~ **property office** (*amm.*) il demanio (*l'ufficio*).

fee[1], *n.* 1 rimunerazione, compenso, emolumento, onorario. 2 (*fin.*) tassa, diritto, quota. 3 (*pubbl.*) compenso d'agenzia. // **fees and costs** (*leg.*) competenze e spese; ~ **bill** (*leg.*) lista delle spese (*sostenute per una causa legale*); tariffario degli onorari (*degli avvocati, ecc.*); ~ **farm** (*leg.*) terreno in enfiteusi; ~ **for clearance through customs** (*dog.*) tassa di sdoganamento; ~ **for registration** (*comun.*) tassa per (lettera) raccomandata; ~ **simple** (*leg.*) proprietà assoluta; ~ **tail** (*leg.*) possesso con limitazioni riguardo alla successione.

fee[2], *v. t.* pagare, rimunerare (*un professionista*). // to ~ **a lawyer** pagare un avvocato.

feed[1], *n.* 1 mangime. 2 (*elab. elettr.*) alimentazione.

feed[2], *v. t.* (*pass.* e *part. pass.* **fed**). 1 alimentare, cibare, nutrire. 2 (*elab. elettr.*) alimentare.

feedback, *n. m.* (*elab. elettr.*) «feedback»; retroazione.

feeder, *n.* 1 (*elab. elettr.*) alimentatore. 2 (*trasp. ferr.*) raccordo. // ~ **line** (*trasp. ferr.*) binario di raccordo.

feedforward, *n.* (*elab. elettr.*) «feedforward», preazione.

feeding, *n.* 1 alimentazione. 2 (*elab. elettr.*) alimentazione, avanzamento.

feign, *v. t.* falsificare, contraffare. *v. i.* fingere.

fellow, *n.* individuo, compagno, collega. // ~ **clerk** (*pers.*) collega d'ufficio; ~ **heir** (*leg.*) coerede; ~ **subsidiary** (*fin.*) (società) consociata; ~ **worker** (*pers.*) compagno di lavoro.

felony, *n.* (*leg.*) delitto (grave).

female, *a.* femminile. // ~ **labour** (*pers.*) manodopera femminile.

ferry[1], *n.* 1 (*leg.*) diritto di traghetto. 2 (*trasp. mar.*) traghetto, barca per traghetti. // ~ **port** (*trasp. mar.*) scalo traghetti, porto traghetti.

ferry[2], *v. t.* (*trasp. mar.*) traghettare.

ferryboat, *n.* (*trasp. mar.*) (nave) traghetto.

ferryman, *n.* (*pl.* **ferrymen**) (*trasp. mar.*) traghettatore.

fetch, *v. t.* (*market.*) raggiungere (*un prezzo*); essere venduto per. // to ~ **a price** (*market.*) spuntare un prezzo.

«fiasco», *n.* fiasco (*fig.*); fallimento.

fiat, *n.* 1 approvazione. 2 comando, decreto (*dell'autorità*). // ~ **money** (*fin.*) moneta a corso forzoso; ~ **paper money** (*fin.*) moneta a corso forzoso; ~ **standard** (*fin.*) tipo a corso forzoso.

fictitious, *a.* fittizio, falso, inventato. // ~ **act** (*leg.*) atto fittizio; ~ **assets** (*rag.*) attività fittizie; ~ **name** (*leg.*) nome fittizio; ~ **payee** (*leg.*) beneficiario fittizio.

fidei-commissum, *n.* (*leg.*) fidecommesso.

fidejussion, *n.* (*leg.*) fideiussione.

fidejussor, *n.* (*leg.*) fideiussore.

fidelity, *n.* fedeltà, esattezza. // ~ **insurance** (*ass.*) assicurazione contro i danni provocati dalla disonestà dei dipendenti.

fiduciary, *a.* e *n.* fiduciario. // ~ **circulation** (*econ.*) corso fiduciario (*di carta moneta*); ~ **currency** (*econ.*) moneta che ha corso fiduciario; ~ **heir** (*leg.*) erede fiduciario; ~ **issue** (*econ.*) emissione fiduciaria (*di carta moneta*); ~ **loan** (*fin.*) prestito fiduciario; ~ **money** (*econ.*) denaro a corso fiduciario.

field, *n.* campo (*anche fig.*); settore. // ~ **investigation** (*market.*) ricerca esterna; ~ **manager** (*market.*) ispettore di zona; ~ **research** (*market.*) ricerca esterna; ~ **salesman** (*market.*) commesso viaggiatore; ~ **staff** (*pers.*) impiegati esterni; ~ **supervisor** (*market.*) ispettore di zona; ~ **warehousing** (*fin., USA*) forma di finanziamento consistente nella cessione in garanzia delle merci depositate nel proprio magazzino. (*Queste ultime vengono commerciate sotto il controllo d'una persona di fiducia del finanziatore*).

fieldwork, *n.* (*market.*) raccolta di dati tramite interviste e sperimentazioni all'esterno dell'azienda.

fifty, *a.* e *n.* cinquanta.

fight, *v. t.* e *i.* (*pass.* e *part. pass.* **fought**) lottare.

figure[1], *n.* **1** figura, immagine, aspetto. **2** (*mat.*) numero.

figure[2], *v. t.* e *i.* **1** figurare, raffigurare, adornare di disegni. **2** (*mat., rag.*) far di conto, fare calcoli, calcolare. // to ~ **expenses** (*rag.*) calcolare le spese; to ~ **out** calcolare, risolvere col calcolo; to ~ **up** (*mat., rag.*) calcolare l'ammontare di; to ~ **up at** (*mat., rag.*) ammontare a.

figurehead, *n.* (*leg.*) uomo di paglia, prestanome.

file[1], *n.* **1** (*attr. uff.*) fascicolo, incartamento. **2** (*attr. uff.*) raccolta, collezione (*di documenti, giornali, ecc.*). **3** (*attr. uff.*) casellario, schedario, archivio, protocollo. // ~ **card** (*attr. uff.*) scheda, cartellino; ~ **holder** (*attr. uff.*) raccoglitore; ~ **material** (*attr. uff.*) materiale d'archivio; **on** ~ (*di documento*) registrato, schedato.

file[2], *v. t.* **1** schedare. **2** archiviare, protocollare. **3** (*leg.*) presentare, depositare, produrre (*un documento, ecc.*). **4** (*leg.*) passare agli atti. // to ~ **the award** (*leg.*) depositare il lodo; to ~ **a bankruptcy petition** (*leg.*) presentare istanza di fallimento; to ~ **a claim** (*leg.*) presentare un reclamo; to ~ **a petition for bankruptcy** (*leg.*) chiedere il fallimento, presentare istanza di fallimento; to ~ **a suit against sb.** (*leg.*) far causa a q.

filibuster, *v. i.* fare ostruzionismo.

filing, *n.* **1** schedatura. **2** archiviazione. // ~ **cabinet** (*attr. uff.*) casellario, mobile a scomparti per schedario; ~ **clerk** (*pers.*) archivista, schedatore; ~ **cupboard** (*attr. uff.*) scaffale da archivio.

fill, *v. t.* **1** riempire, colmare. **2** occupare (*un posto, un impiego, ecc.*). // to ~ **in one's name** scrivere il proprio nome in un modulo; to ~ **in the tax form** compilare il modulo per la dichiarazione dei redditi; to ~ **an order** eseguire (*o* evadere, dar corso a) un'ordinazione; to ~ **out documents** completare documenti; to ~ **the tank** (*o* to ~ **up**) **with petrol** (*trasp. aut.*) fare il pieno; to ~ **a vacancy** (*pers.*) occupare un posto vacante.

filling, *n.* **1** riempimento, ecc. (*V.* **fill**). **2** (*market.*) esecuzione, evasione (*di un ordine*). // ~ **station** (*trasp. aut., USA*) distributore di benzina.

film[1], *n.* (*pubbl.*) film. // **the** ~ **industry** (*econ.*) l'industria cinematografica.

film[2], *v. t.* e *i.* (*pubbl.*) filmare, girare un film.

filmslide, *n.* (*pubbl.*) diapositiva.

filmstrip, *n.* (*pubbl.*) filmina.

final, *a.* finale, ultimo. *n.* (*giorn.*) ultima edizione (*d'un giornale*). // ~ **balance** (*rag.*) (bilancio) consuntivo; **a** ~ **decree** (*leg.*) un decreto irrevocabile; ~ **instalment** (*fin.*) (*di azioni*) versamento (di decimi) a liberazione; ~ **invoice** (*market.*) fattura definitiva; **a** ~ **judgment** (*leg.*) una sentenza definitiva; **the** ~ **offer** (*market.*) l'ultima parola; ~ **payment** (*fin.*) (*di azioni*) versamento (di decimi) a liberazione; ~ **product** (*org. az.*) prodotto finale; ~ **proof** (*pubbl.*) bozza di stampa; ~ **report** (*org. az.*) rapporto finale; ~ **statement of a case** (*leg.*) comparsa conclusionale, conclusionale; ~ **utility** (*econ.*) utilità marginale (*termine usato da Marshall e Jevons*).

finance[1], *n.* **1** (*fin.*) finanza, finanze. **2** (*fin.*) finanziamento. // ~ **bill** (*fin., leg.*) progetto di legge finanziaria; ~ **company** (*fin.*) società di finanziamento; società specializzata nella concessione di piccoli mutui a privati; ~ **house** (*fin., ingl.*) società finanziaria specializzata nel finanziamento delle vendite rateali; ~ **shares** (*fin.*) azioni finanziarie; ~ **stamp** (*fin.*) bollo sui titoli.

finance[2], *v. t.* finanziare.

financial, *a.* (*fin.*) finanziario. // ~ **accounting** (*rag.*) contabilità finanziaria; ~ **advertising** (*pubbl.*) pubblicità finanziaria; ~ **aid** (*fin.*) assistenza finanziaria; ~ **analyst** (*fin.*) analista finanziario; ~ **backer** (*fin.*) finanziatore, sovventore; ~ **bill** (*fin., leg.*) progetto di legge finanziaria; ~ **charges** (*rag.*) oneri finanziari; **the** ~ **circles** (*fin.*) gli ambienti finanziari; ~ **combination** (*fin.*) combinazione finanziaria; ~ **control** (*econ.*) controllo finanziario; ~ **credits** (*cred.*) crediti finanziari; **a** ~ **crisis** (*fin.*) una crisi finanziaria; ~ **department store** (*fin., USA*) supermercato finanziario; ~ **establishments** (*fin.*) istituti finanziari; ~ **incentive** (*pers.*) incentivo monetario, incentivo diretto; ~ **know-how** (*fin.*) esperienza finanziaria; ~ **leasing** «leasing» finanziario; ~ **lira** (*econ., fin.*) lira finanziaria; ~ **market** (*fin.*) mercato finanziario; **the ~ policymakers** (*fin.*) i responsabili della politica finanziaria; **~ position** (*fin.*) situazione finanziaria; **~ ratios** (*fin.*) indici finanziari; **~ relations** (*fin.*) relazioni finanziarie; **~ report** (*fin.*) rapporto finanziario; **~ resources** (*fin.*) mezzi finanziari, finanze; **~ standing** (*banca, cred.*) posizione finanziaria; **~ status** (*fin.*) situazione finanziaria; **~ upheaval** (*fin.*) terremoto finanziario; **~ year** (*fin.*) anno finanziario, esercizio finanziario, esercizio.

financier, *n.* 1 (*fin.*) finanziere. 2 (*fin.*) finanziatore.

financing, *n.* (*fin.*) finanziamento. // **~ by corporate saving** (*fin.*) autofinanziamento.

find, *v. t.* (*pass.* e *part. pass.* **found**) 1 trovare, reperire. 2 (*leg.*) giudicare, dichiarare. 3 (*leg.*) emettere (*un verdetto*). // to **~ one's account in st.** trovare il proprio tornaconto in qc.; to **~ a common level** livellarsi; to **~ favour with sb.** incontrare il favore di q.; to **~ sb. guilty (not guilty)** (*leg.: della giuria*) dichiarare q. colpevole (innocente); to **~ a job** trovare un lavoro, un impiego; impiegarsi; to **~ a job for sb.** trovare lavoro per q.; to **~ money** (*cred., fin.*) reperire capitali; to **~ a verdict** (*leg.*) emettere un verdetto; to **~ work** *V.* to **~ a job.**

finding, *n.* 1 reperimento. 2 (*leg.*) sentenza. 3 (*leg.*) verdetto.

fine[1], *a.* 1 bello, buono. 2 fine. // **~ bill** (*cred.*) cambiale scontabile al tasso minimo; **~ paper** (*cred.*) effetto di buona firma; **~ trade bill** (*cred.*) effetto di buona firma; **~ trade paper** (*cred.*) carta commerciale di prim'ordine; **the finest rate of discount** (*fin.*) il più basso tasso di sconto, il minimo tasso di sconto.

fine[2], *n.* (*leg.*) ammenda, contravvenzione, multa, pena pecuniaria.

fine[3], *v. t.* 1 (*leg.*) multare, fare la contravvenzione a (*q.*). 2 (*trasp. aut.*) multare, fare la multa a (*q.*). // to **be fined** essere dichiarato in multa.

fineness, *n.* titolo (*di monete*).

finish[1], *n.* finitura, completamento, ultimo tocco. // **at the ~** (*Borsa*) in chiusura.

finish[2], *v. t.* e *i.* 1 finire. 2 completare. // to **~ the printing** (*giorn., pubbl.*) ultimare la stampa.

finished, *a.* 1 finito, terminato. 2 completato. // **~ goods** (*org. az.*) pezzi finiti; **~ goods storehouse** (*org. az.*) magazzino pezzi finiti; **~ product** (*org. az.*) prodotto finito.

finishing touch, *n.* tocco finale, finitura.

finite, *a.* (*mat.*) finito.

fire[1], *n.* incendio. // **~ department** (*ass., ingl.*) ufficio incendi (*in una compagnia d'assicurazioni*); **~ insurance** (*ass.*) assicurazione contro l'incendio; **~ insurance company** (*ass.*) società d'assicurazione contro gli incendi; **~ insurance policy** (*ass.*) polizza d'assicurazione contro gli incendi; **~ office** (*ass.*) ufficio di società d'assicurazione contro gli incendi; **~ policy** (*ass.*) polizza d'assicurazione contro gli incendi; **~ risk** (*ass.*) rischio d'incendio.

fire[2], *v. t.* 1 dar fuoco a, incendiare. 2 (*pers.*) licenziare.

firm[1], *a.* 1 fermo, saldo, sicuro. 2 stabile. // **a ~ bargain** (*Borsa*) un contratto fermo; **a ~ currency** (*fin.*) una valuta forte; **a ~ market** (*fin.*) un mercato sostenuto; **a ~ offer** (*market.*) un'offerta stabile; **a ~ pound sterling** (*fin.*) una sterlina forte; **~ prices** (*market.*) prezzi stabili.

firm[2], *n.* ditta, azienda, casa commerciale, impresa; esercizio (commerciale). // **~ name** ragione sociale.

firm[3], *v. t.* consolidare, fermare, rassodare. *v. i.* consolidarsi, rassodarsi. // to **~ up** consolidarsi, rassodarsi.

firmness, *n.* fermezza.

first, *a.* 1 primo. 2 primario, principale. // **~ call** (*fin.*) primo richiamo (*della somma parziale dovuta come versamento iniziale per l'assegnazione delle azioni*); **~ class** (*trasp.*) prima classe; *a. attr.* di prima classe, di prima qualità, eccellente, sopraffino; **~ -class carriage** (*trasp. ferr.*) vettura di prima classe; **a ~ class compartment** (*trasp. ferr.*) uno scompartimento di prima classe; **~ class paper** (*fin.*) effetto di buona firma; **~ -class passenger** (*trasp. ferr.*) viaggiatore di prima classe; **a ~ class ticket** (*trasp.*) un biglietto di prima classe; **~ cost** (*rag.*) costo primo; **~ -grade** (*market.*) di prima qualità, sopraffino; **~ half** (*fin.*) primo semestre (*d'anno finanziario*); **~ in, ~ out (FIFO)** (*rag.*) procedimento contabile per il calcolo dell'inventario consistente nel considerare la prima merce entrata in magazzino come la prima uscitane; **~ -line** di prima qualità; **~ -line supervisor** (*pers.*) capo intermedio; **~ meeting of creditors** (*leg.*) prima adunanza dei creditori; **~ mortgage** (*leg.*) ipoteca di primo grado; **~ name** nome di battesimo; **~ of exchange** (*fin.*) prima di cambio, prima copia di cambiale; **~ quarter** (*fin.*) primo trimestre (*d'anno finanziario*); **~ -rate** di prima qualità, di prim'ordine; **a ~ -rate article** (*market.*) un articolo di prima qualità; **~ shift** (*pers.*) turno di giorno.

fisc, *n.* (*fin.*) (*storico: dei Romani*) erario pubblico.

fiscal, *a.* (*fin.*) fiscale, erariale, tributario. //

the ~ **cases** (*leg.*) il contenzioso tributario; ~ **charges** (*fin.*) oneri fiscali; ~ **deductions** (*fin.*) detrazioni fiscali; ~ **drag** (*fin.*) salasso fiscale, onere tributario (*dovuto al gioco delle aliquote progressive e dell'inflazione*); ~ **duties** (*dog.*) dazi fiscali; ~ **monopoly** (*fin.*) monopolio fiscale; ~ **policy** (*fin.*) politica fiscale; ~ **reform** (*fin.*) riforma tributaria; ~ **year** (*fin.*) anno finanziario, esercizio finanziario, periodo d'imposta.

fiscality, *n.* fiscalismo.

fisherman, *n.* (*pl.* **fishermen**) **1** pescatore. **2** (*trasp. mar.*) peschereccio.

fishing, *a.* peschereccio. *n.* pésca, il pescare. // ~ **-boat** (*trasp. mar.*) peschereccio; ~ **-vessel** (*trasp. mar.*) peschereccio.

fit[1], *a.* adatto, idoneo.

fit[2], *v. t.* adattare, preparare, rendere idoneo a. // to ~ **out** attrezzare; to ~ **out a ship** (*trasp. mar.*) armare una nave, allestire una nave, equipaggiare una nave.

fitness, *n.* idoneità.

fitting, *n.* **1** preparazione. **2** montaggio. **3** **fittings,** *pl.* apparecchiature, impianti. // **fittings and fixtures** (*rag.*) apparecchiature e impianti; ~ **department** (*org. az.*) reparto montaggio; ~ **-out** (*trasp. mar.*) armamento, allestimento, equipaggiamento.

five, *num.* cinque. // ~ **-and-dime** (*market., USA*) *V.* ~ **-and-ten**; ~ **-and-ten** (*market., USA*) grandi magazzini che vendono solo articoli al prezzo di cinque o dieci dollari; ~ **-day week** (*pers., sind.*) settimana (lavorativa) di cinque giorni, settimana «corta»; ~ **-for-sixer** (*slang USA*) prestatore di denaro; ~ **sheets of paper** (*attr. uff.*) quinterno; ~ **-spot** (*slang USA*) banconota da cinque dollari; ~ **-year plan** (*econ.*) piano quinquennale.

fiver, *n.* (*slang USA*) banconota da cinque dollari.

fix, *v. t.* **1** fissare, stabilire. **2** (*fam., USA*) saldare i conti con (*q.*). // to ~ **the amount of damages to be allowed** (*ass.*) fissare l'ammontare dei danni da pagare; to ~ **a ceiling price for st.** (*econ.*) calmierare qc.; to ~ **a date** fissare una data; to ~ **prices** (*market.*) fissare i prezzi; to ~ **a quota for st.** (*econ.*) contingentare qc.

fixed, *a.* fisso. // ~ **allowance** (*econ.*) razione; ~ **assets** (*rag.*) attività fisse, capitali fissi, immobilizzazioni tecniche, immobilizzi, immobili, immobili e impianti; ~ **capital** (*rag.*) capitale fisso; ~ **charges** (*rag.*) spese fisse; ~ **costs** (*rag.*) costi fissi, spese generali; ~ **date** (*leg.*) data certa; ~ **debenture** (*fin.*) obbligazione garantita da ipoteca su un immobile specifico; ~ **deposit** (*banca*) deposito vincolato a scadenza determinata; ~ **deposit account** (*banca*) conto vincolato a scadenza determinata; ~ **depreciation** (*rag.*) ammortamento fisso; ~ **exchange** (*fin.*) cambio fisso, cambio certo per l'incerto; ~ **exchange-rate system** (*fin.*) sistema del corso dei cambi fisso; ~ **income** (*rag.*) reddito fisso; ~ **-income securities** (*banca*) titoli a reddito fisso; ~ **interest** (*fin.*) reddito fisso; ~ **-interest market** (*fin.*) mercato del reddito fisso; ~ **-interest securities** (*fin.*) titoli a reddito fisso; ~ **liabilities** (*rag.*) debiti a lunga scadenza; ~ **number** (*mat.*) numero fisso; ~ **parity** (*fin.*) parità fissa; ~ **plants** (*org. az.*) impianti fissi; ~ **prices** (*market., rag.*) prezzi fissi; ~ **property** (*econ.*) beni immobili; ~ **shift** (*pers.*) turno fisso; ~ **trust** (*fin.*) fondo d'investimento a capitale fisso; **at a** ~ **date** (*banca, cred.*) a data fissa.

fixing, *n.* **1** fissazione. **2** (*Borsa*) fixing. // ~ **of boundaries** (*leg.*) regolamento di confini; **the** ~ **of the new parities** (*fin.*) la fissazione delle nuove parità; **the** ~ **of prices** (*econ.*) la fissazione dei prezzi.

fixtures, *n. pl.* infissi. // ~ **and fittings** (*rag.*) impianti fissi, immobili e impianti.

flag, *n.* bandiera. // ~ **carrier** (*trasp. aer., trasp. mar.*) compagnia di bandiera, linea di bandiera; ~ **clause** (*trasp. mar.*) clausola della bandiera; ~ **discrimination** (*trasp. mar.*) discriminazione di bandiera; ~ **of convenience** (*trasp. mar.*) bandiera di convenienza, bandiera di comodo; ~ **surtax** (*trasp. mar.*) soprattassa di bandiera.

flagrancy, *n.* (*leg.*) flagranza.

flagrant, *a.* (*leg.*) flagrante.

flash, *n.* **1** bagliore, lampo. **2** sprazzo. **3** (*giorn.*) notizia-lampo (*trasmessa per radio o per telegrafo*). *a. attr.* **1** abbagliante. **2** falso. // ~ **check** (*banca, USA*) assegno senza copertura, assegno «cabriolet»; ~ **money** moneta falsa; ~ **notes** banconote false.

flask, *n.* fiasco.

flat, *a.* **1** piano, piatto. **2** fisso, rigido. **3** uguale. **4** netto, reciso. **5** (*market.*) (*di prezzo, mercato*) inattivo, rigido. *n.* **1** (*Borsa*) «tel quel», tale quale. **2** (*trasp. ferr., USA*) carro merci senza sponde. // ~ **advertising rate** (*pubbl.*) tariffa pubblicitaria fissa (*cioè, indipendente dallo spazio occupato*); ~ **cost** (*rag.*) costo di produzione; ~ **organization structure** (*org. az.*) struttura organizzativa orizzontale; ~ **rate** (*fin.*) reddito effettivo; (*market.*) prezzo a forfait; (*trasp.*) tariffa fissa (*cioè, indipendente* *dalla distanza percorsa*); **a ~ rate** un importo fisso; **~ -rate taxation of imports** (*fin.*) tassazione forfettaria delle importazioni; **~ truck** *V. ~ n., def. 2.*

flatcar, *n.* (*trasp. ferr., USA*) carro merci senza sponde.

flatten, *v. t.* **1** appiattire. **2** abbattere. *v. i.* **1** appiattirsi. **2** rallentarsi. // to **~ out** appiattire, appiattirsi, rallentare.

flattening, *n.* (*anche di prezzi, salari, ecc.*) appiattimento.

flaw, *n.* **1** difetto. **2** errore. **3** (*leg.*) vizio. // **~ chart** (*org. az.*) schema di flusso che evidenzia i difetti riscontrati nella successione delle operazioni.

flection, *n.* flessione (*in senso proprio*).

fleet, *n.* **1** (*org. az.*) gruppo (*d'autobus, autocarri, ecc., della stessa azienda*). **2** (*trasp. mar.*) flotta, naviglio.

flexibility, *n.* (*anche fig.*) flessibilità.

flexible, *a.* flessibile, elastico. // **~ budget** (*org. az.*) budget variabile, bilancio preventivo variabile; **~ exchange rate** (*fin.*) cambio a corso libero; **a ~ income-tax structure** (*fin.*) un sistema flessibile d'imposte sul reddito; **~ planning** (*org. az.*) pianificazione scorrevole; **~ tariff** (*trasp.*) tariffa flessibile.

flexion, *n.* flessione (*in senso proprio*).

flight, *n.* **1** fuga. **2** (*trasp. aer.*) volo, viaggio aereo. // **~ of capital** (*econ.*) fuga di capitali all'estero.

flimsy, *n.* (*attr. uff.*) (carta) velina.

float[1], *n.* (*econ., fin.*) fluttuazione (*d'una moneta*).

float[2], *v. i.* **1** fluttuare, oscillare, variare. **2** (*econ., fin.*) (*di moneta*) fluttuare. **3** (*trasp. mar.*) galleggiare. *v. t.* **1** (*comm.*) lanciare, promuovere. **2** (*trasp. mar.*) far galleggiare. // to **~ bonds** (*fin.*) emettere obbligazioni; to **~ exchange rate** (*econ., fin.*) far fluttuare il tasso di cambio; to **~ a loan** (*cred.*) lanciare un prestito; to **~ the yen** (*econ.*) permettere la fluttuazione dello yen; **floating rate loan** (*cred.*) prestito a saggio d'interesse fluttuante.

floatation, *n.* **1** (*comm.*) lancio (*d'un'impresa o società commerciale*). **2** (*trasp. mar.*) galleggiamento.

floater, *n.* **1** (*comm.*) promotore (*d'una società commerciale*). **2** (*fin.*) buono del Tesoro.

floating, *a.* **1** fluttuante, oscillante, variabile. **2** (*econ., fin.*) (*di moneta*) fluttuante. **3** (*trasp. mar.*) galleggiante. // **~ assets** (*rag.*) attività variabili, capitale circolante; **~ balance** (*fin.*) saldo attivo fluttuante; **~ capital** (*rag.*) capitale circolante; **~ clause** (*ass. mar.*) clausola nave sempre a galla; **~ currency** (*econ.*) moneta oscillante; **~ debt** (*fin.*) debito fluttuante; **~ devaluation** (*econ.*) svalutazione fluttuante; **~ dock** (*trasp. mar.*) bacino galleggiante; **~ exchange rate** (*fin.*) cambio fluttuante; **~ fire policy** (*ass.*) polizza flottante contro l'incendio; **~ policy** (*ass. mar.*) polizza aperta, polizza flottante, polizza valida per nave non nominata ma per rotta specificata; **~ rate** (*fin.*) cambio fluttuante, cambio a corso libero; **~ -rate** (*fin.*) (*di titolo*) indicizzato; **~ -rate bond** (*fin.*) obbligazione indicizzata; **~ supply** (*fin.*) numero d'azioni (*d'una società*) in circolazione sul mercato.

floating of a loan, *locuz. n.* (*fin.*) emissione d'un prestito.

flood[1], *n.* inondazione.

flood[2], *v. t.* inondare.

flooded, *a.* inondato, allagato, sommerso.

floor, *n.* **1** pavimento. **2** base. **3** (*Borsa*) sala (delle) contrattazioni, recinto alle grida, «corbeille», «parquet». **4** (*econ., fin.*) fondo (*del tunnel monetario*). **5** (*fin., market.*) livello minimo (*di prezzi, quotazioni, ecc.*), quotazione minima, prezzo minimo, il minimo. // **~ boy** (*pers.*) fattorino; **~ broker** (*Borsa*) agente (di cambio) di sala; **~ price** (*fin., market.*) prezzo minimo; **~ trader** (*Borsa*) membro che agisce in proprio sul «floor»; **~ -walker** (*pers.*) *V.* **floorwalker.**

floorwalker, *n.* (*pers.*) ispettore di reparto (*di grande magazzino, ecc.*).

flop, *n.* (*fam.*) insuccesso.

flourish, *v. i.* fiorire.

flourishing, *a.* fiorente, florido.

flow[1], *n.* **1** flusso. **2** (*fin.*) afflusso. **3** (*trasp. mar.*) flusso (*di marea*); portata (*di fiume*). // **~ of funds** (*econ.*) flusso finanziario; **~ of materials** (*org. az.*) flusso di materiali; **the ~ of tourists** (*tur.*) il movimento turistico; **the ~ of trade** (*comm. est.*) le correnti di scambio; **~ process** (*org. az.*) dinamica del lavoro.

flow[2], *v. i.* fluire, scorrere. // to **~ in** affluire.

fluctuant, *a.* fluttuante, oscillante. // **a ~ exchange rate** (*fin.*) un corso dei cambi fluttuante.

fluctuate, *v. i.* fluttuare, oscillare.

fluctuating, *a.* fluttuante, oscillante. // **~ overdraft** (*banca*) «scoperto» di conto, assistito da «fido»; «castelletto»; **~ prices** (*market.*) prezzi oscillanti; **~ values** (*Borsa*) corsi oscillanti.

fluctuation, *n.* fluttuazione, oscillazione. // **~ bands of currencies** (*fin.*) margini di fluttuazione delle monete; **fluctuations in exchange rates** (*comm. est., fin.*) variazioni dei cambi, oscillazioni di cambio; **fluctuations of exchange** (*fin.*) oscillazioni di cambio.

fluid, *a.* (*anche fig.*) fluido.

fluidity, *n.* fluidità, fluidezza (*raro*). // ~ **of labour** (*econ.*) mobilità del lavoro.

fluvial, *a.* (*trasp.*) fluviale.

fly[1], *n.* **1** volo. **2** distanza percorsa a volo. // ~ **sheet** (*pubbl.*) foglio volante, volantino.

fly[2], *v. i.* (*pass.* **flew,** *part. pass.* **flown**) **1** volare. **2** (*trasp. aer.*) andare in aeroplano. *v. t.* (*trasp. mar.*) battere (*una bandiera*). // to ~ **a kite** (*cred.*) prendere denaro a prestito con cambiali di comodo; emettere un assegno scoperto; to ~ **low** (*trasp. aer.*) volare a bassa quota.

fold, *v. t.* piegare, ripiegare.

folder, *n.* **1** (*attr. uff.*) cartella (*di cartone: per tenervi fogli*); carpetta. **2** (*pubbl.*) opuscolo pieghevole, pieghevole, dépliant.

folding, *a.* pieghevole. // ~ **money** (*USA*) grossa somma di denaro.

foliate, *v. t. V.* **folio**[2].

folio[1], *n.* **1** (*pubbl.*) numero (*di pagina*). **2** (*rag.*) foglio intero.

folio[2], *v. t.* **1** numerare i fogli di (*un libro, ecc.*). **2** (*leg.*) numerare progressivamente i fogli di (*una «comparsa», ecc.*).

follow[1], *n.* il seguire. // ~ **-up** seguito (*d'un'azione, ecc.*); (*comun.*) lettera di sollecitazione, sollecito, sollecitatoria; (*pers.*) aggiornamento, periodo d'addestramento; *a. attr.* successivo; ~ **-up instructions** istruzioni successive.

follow[2], *v. t.* seguire. // to ~ **up** perseguire.

following, *a.* successivo. *prep.* in seguito a, successivamente a. // ~ **settlement** (*Borsa*) liquidazione successiva.

food, *n.* **1** alimento, cibo. **2** (*tur.*) trattamento. // ~ **aid** (*econ.*) aiuti alimentari; ~ **controller** (*amm.*) controllore annonario (*o* degli approvvigionamenti); ~ **for human consumption** (*econ.*) prodotti destinati all'alimentazione umana; ~ **industry** (*econ.*) industria alimentare; ~ **legislation** (*leg.*) legislazione sui prodotti alimentari; ~ **prices** (*econ.*) prezzi dei prodotti alimentari; ~ **products** (*econ.*) prodotti alimentari.

foodstuffs, *n. pl.* (*econ.*) prodotti alimentari, generi alimentari, derrate alimentari, alimentari.

foolscap, *n.* (*attr. uff.*) carta protocollo.

foot[1], *n.* (*pl.* **feet**) **1** piede. **2** piede (*misura di lunghezza pari a cm 30,48*). // ~ **page** (*pers.*) fattorino; **at** ~ in calce.

foot[2], *v. t.* fare il «piede» a (*una calza, un calzino, ecc.*). // to ~ **the bill** pagare il conto; to ~ **up an account** fare la somma (delle varie voci) d'un conto; to ~ **up to** ammontare a.

footage, *n.* lunghezza in «piedi».

footboy, *n.* (*pers.*) fattorino.

footing, *n.* **1** punto d'appoggio, appiglio. **2** posizione (*fig.*). **3** relazione, rapporto. **4** (l') addizione, (il) totale che risulta da un'addizione. // ~ **-up** (l') addizione, (il) totale che risulta da un'addizione; to **be on a friendly** ~ **with sb.** essere in rapporti d'amicizia con q.

footnote, *n.* nota a piè di pagina.

for, *prep.* per. // ~ **the account** (*Borsa*) a termine; ~ **and on behalf of sb.** a nome e per conto di q.; « ~ **deposit only**» **cheque** (*banca*) assegno sbarrato; ~ **hire** a nolo, a noleggio; ~ **money** (*fin.*) per contanti; ~ **sale** (*market.*) in vendita; ~ **want of funds** per mancanza di fondi.

forbid, *v. t.* (*pass.* **forbade,** *part. pass.* **forbidden**) proibire, vietare.

forbiddance, *n.* divieto.

force[1], *n.* **1** forza. **2** vigore, validità. // ~ **majeure** (*leg.*) forza maggiore; **in** ~ (*leg.*) in vigore; vigente (*a. pred.*); **into** ~ (*leg.*) in vigore.

force[2], *v. t.* forzare, costringere, obbligare. // to ~ **the bidding** far salire le offerte (*a un'asta*); to ~ **down** (*market.*) far calare (*prezzi, quotazioni, ecc.*); to ~ **down the cost of credit** (*fin.*) ridurre il costo del denaro; to ~ **sales** (*market.*) spingere le vendite; to ~ **up** (*market.*) far aumentare, far crescere (*prezzi, quotazioni, ecc.*).

forced, *a.* **1** forzato, costretto, obbligato. **2** forzoso. // ~ **circulation** (*fin.*) corso forzoso; ~ **currency paper** (*fin.*) banconote a corso forzoso; ~ **heir** (*leg.*) erede necessario; legittimario; ~ **loan** (*fin.*) prestito forzoso; ~ **sale** (*leg.*) vendita coatta; ~ **saving** (*econ.*) risparmio forzato.

forcibly, *avv.* a (viva) forza.

forcing, *n.* (*market.*) spinta (*delle vendite*).

forecast[1], *n.* previsione, predizione. // **forecasts covering several years** previsioni pluriennali.

forecast[2], *v. t.* (*pass.* e *part. pass.* **forecast** o *reg.*) prevedere, predire.

foreclose, *v. t.* escludere.

foreclosure, *n.* **1** esclusione. **2** (*leg.*) vendita giudiziaria.

foredate, *v. t.* antedatare.

foreign, *a.* (*ingl., USA*) estero. // ~ **adjustment** (*ass. mar.*) liquidazione (d'avaria) all'estero; ~ **affairs** (*econ., fin.*) affari esteri; ~

aids (*econ.*) aiuti ai Paesi esteri; ~ **bill** (*cred.*) cambiale estera; ~ **bills** (*banca*) portafoglio estero; ~ **borrowings** (*banca, fin.*) provvista in valuta estera; ~ **company** (*fin.*) società estera; ~ **corporation** (*fin., USA*) società estera; ~ **correspondent** (*comm. est.*) corrispondente all'estero; (*pers.*) corrispondente estero, corrispondente in lingue estere; ~ **currency** (*fin.*) divisa estera, valuta estera; ~ **-currency account** (*rag.*) conto in valuta estera; ~ **demand** (*econ.*) domanda estera; ~ **exchange** (*fin.*) cambio estero; ~ **-exchange broker** (*fin.*) cambiavalute; ~ **-exchange market** (*fin.*) mercato delle valute; ~ **-exchange positions** (*fin.*) posizioni valutarie; ~ **-exchange rate** (*fin.*) corso dei cambi; **a** ~ **finance group** (*econ.*) un gruppo finanziario estero; ~ **investments** (*econ.*) investimenti esteri; ~ **jurisdiction** (*leg.*) giurisdizione straniera; ~ **languages correspondent** (*pers.*) corrispondente estero, corrispondente in lingue estere; ~ **manpower** (*pers.*) manodopera straniera; ~ **markets** (*comm. est.*) i mercati esteri; ~ **money order** (*banca, cred.*) vaglia per l'estero; **the** ~ **Office** (*ingl.*) il Ministero degli Esteri; **the** ~ **press** (*giorn.*) la stampa estera; ~ **relations** (*econ.*) relazioni internazionali; ~ **Secretary** (*ingl.*) Ministro degli Esteri; ~ **securities** (*fin.*) titoli esteri; ~ **services editor** (*giorn.*) inviato speciale; ~ **stocks** (*fin.*) titoli esteri; ~ **trade** (*comm. est.*) commercio estero, commercio con l'estero; ~ **-trade zone** (*dog., trasp., USA*) punto franco; ~ **trader** (*comm. est.*) commerciante straniero; ~ **trader's identity card** (*comm. est.*) tessera di commerciante straniero.

foreman, *n.* (*pl.* **foremen**). **1** (*leg.*) capo della giuria. **2** (*pers.*) capo intermedio. **3** (*pers.*) caposquadra, capo (*d'operai*).

forensic, *a.* (*leg.*) forense. // ~ **medicine** (*leg.*) medicina legale.

foresee, *v. t.* (*pass.* **foresaw,** *part. pass.* **foreseen**) prevedere.

foresight, *n.* previsione.

forestall, *v. t.* **1** precedere. **2** (*market.*) accaparrare (*merci, ecc.*). // to ~ **competitors** (*market.*) prevenire i concorrenti.

forestaller, *n.* (*market.*) accaparratore (*di merci, ecc.*).

forestallment, *n.* (*market.*) accaparramento (*di merci, ecc.*).

forewoman, *n.* (*pl.* **forewomen**) (*leg.*) capo d'una giuria femminile.

forfaitement, *n.* (*comm. est., cred.*) forfettaggio (*tecnica di credito all'esportazione*).

forfeit[1], *n.* **1** (*leg.*) ammenda, multa, penalità. **2** (*leg.*) cosa confiscata.

forfeit[2], *v. t.* **1** (*leg.*) essere privato di (*qc., per confisca*), perdere (*un diritto*) per confisca. **2** (*leg.*) perdere (*un diritto*) per inadempimento, perdere (*un diritto*) per violazione d'una norma. // to ~ **one's bail** (*leg.*) non comparire al processo (*dopo aver ottenuto la libertà provvisoria su cauzione*).

forfeiture, *n.* **1** (*leg.*) penalità, penale. **2** (*leg.*) confisca. **3** (*leg.*) perdita (*d'un diritto*) per confisca. **4** (*leg.*) perdita (*d'un diritto*) per inadempimento, perdita (*d'un diritto*) per violazione d'una norma. // **the** ~ **of a right** (*leg.*) la decadenza da un diritto.

forge, *v. t.* (*leg.*) falsare, falsificare, contraffare. // to ~ **a signature** (*leg.*) contraffare una firma; to ~ **a will** (*leg*) falsificare un testamento.

forged, *a.* falso, contraffatto. // ~ **bill** (*cred., leg.*) cambiale falsa; ~ **document** (*leg.*) documento falso; ~ **signature** (*leg.*) firma falsa.

forger, *n.* (*leg.*) falsario, contraffattore.

forgery, *n.* **1** (*leg.*) falsificazione, contraffazione. **2** (*leg.*) falso, documento falso, firma falsa.

forgive, *v. t.* (*pass.* **forgave,** *part. pass.* **forgiven**) condonare (*una pena, una colpa, ecc.*). // to ~ **a debt** (*cred.*) condonare un debito.

forgotten, *a.* dimenticato. // **a** ~ **man** (*fam.*) un disoccupato.

form[1], *n.* **1** forma. **2** formula. **3** modulo, scheda, stampato. **4** circolare, lettera circolare. **5** (*leg.*) forma. **6** (*pubbl.*) forma. // ~ **letter** circolare, lettera circolare; **a** ~ **of application** un modulo di domanda (d'impiego); ~ **of application for stocks** (*fin.*) modulo di sottoscrizione per azioni; ~ **of a bill of lading** (*trasp. mar.*) modulo di polizza di carico; **forms of business organization** forme d'organizzazione commerciale; ~ **of material transfer** (*org. az.*) buono di passaggio; ~ **of a telegram** (*comun.*) modulo di telegramma; ~ **of transfer** (*fin.*) modulo di trasferimento (*di titoli*).

form[2], *v. t.* **1** formare. **2** formulare. // to ~ **a company** (*fin.*) costituire una società (di capitali); to ~ **a plan** formulare un piano.

forma, *n.* (*pl.* **formae** e *reg.*) forma.

formal, *a.* formale, ufficiale. // ~ **contract** (*leg.*) contratto formale; ~ **defects** (*leg.*) difetti formali; **a** ~ **denial** una smentita ufficiale; ~ **notice** (*leg.*) intimazione; (*pers.*) comunicazione scritta; ~ **protest** (*leg.*) protesto.

formality, *n.* formalità, modalità.

formation, *n.* formazione, costituzione. //

~ **expenses** (*rag.*) spese di costituzione; ~ **of a partnership** (*fin.*) costituzione d'una società (di persone).

former, *a.* già; ex.

formerly, *avv.* già; un tempo.

formula, *n.* (*pl.* **formulae** e *reg.*) (*mat.*) formula.

formulate, *v. t.* formulare.

formulation, *n.* formulazione.

forthcoming, *a.* **1** che sta per apparire, futuro. **2** disponibile.

fortnight, *n.* quindicina, quindici giorni, due settimane. // **a** ~ **to-day** oggi a quindici.

fortnightly, *a.* quindicinale, bimensile. *avv.* ogni quindici giorni, ogni due settimane. *n.* (*giorn.*) quindicinale, pubblicazione quindicinale. // **a** ~ **meeting** (*org. az.*) un'assemblea quindicinale.

fortuitous, *a.* accidentale, casuale. // ~ **event** (*leg.*) evento fortuito.

forward[1], *avv.* innanzi. *a.* **1** d'avanguardia, avanzato. **2** (*comm.*) futuro, a tempo, a termine. // ~ **call** (*trasp. mar.*) scalo diretto; **a** ~ **contract** (*market.*) un contratto a tempo; ~ **cover** (*Borsa, fin.*) copertura a termine; ~ **delivery** (*market.*) consegna a termine, futura consegna; ~ **draught** (*trasp. mar.*) pescaggio a riva; ~ **exchange market** (*fin.*) mercato a termine delle valute; ~ **-looking** previdente; ~ **market** (*fin.*) mercato a termine; ~ **marketing** (*fin.*) contrattazione a termine; ~ **opinions** idee avanzate; ~ **prices** (*Borsa, fin.*) prezzi per futura consegna; (*market.*) prezzi futuri; ~ **rates** (*fin.*) corsi per operazioni a termine; ~ **sale** (*Borsa, fin.*) vendita per futura consegna, vendita a termine; **a** ~ **school of advertising** (*pubbl.*) una scuola pubblicitaria d'avanguardia; ~ **shifting** (*econ.*) traslazione (*d'imposta*) in avanti (*cioè, sul consumatore*); ~ **slip** (*ass. mar.*) polizzetta definitiva.

forward[2], *v. t.* **1** inoltrare, inviare, spedire. **2** favorire, promuovere. **3** aiutare, appoggiare. **4** (*rag.*) riportare (*un totale, un saldo*) a nuovo. // to ~ **again** (*comun., trasp.*) rispedire; to ~ **a balance** (*rag.*) riportare un saldo; to ~ **goods** (*trasp.*) spedire merce (*specialm. per via di terra*); to ~ **goods by passenger** (*o* **fast**) **train** (*trasp. ferr.*) spedire merci a grande velocità; to ~ **goods by slow train** (*trasp. ferr.*) spedire merci a piccola velocità; to ~ **a letter to a new address** (*comun.*) inoltrare una lettera a un nuovo indirizzo; «to **be forwarded**» (*comun.*) «far proseguire».

forwarder, *n.* **1** speditore, spedizioniere. **2** fautore, promotore. **3** (*trasp.*) mittente (*di merce*).

forwarding, *n.* (*trasp.*) spedizione, invio (*specialm. per via di terra*). // ~ **agent** (*trasp.*) spedizioniere (*specialm. per via di terra*); ~ **agents** (*trasp.*) spedizionieri, agenzia di spedizioni; ~ **and shipping agent** (*trasp., trasp. mar.*) spedizioniere (per spedizioni terrestri e marittime); ~ **by rail** (*trasp. ferr.*) spedizione per ferrovia; ~ **charges** (*trasp.*) spese di spedizione; ~ **department** (*org. az.*) ufficio spedizioni; ~ **merchant** (*trasp. ferr.*) spedizioniere (*specialm. per via di terra*); ~ **station** (*trasp. ferr.*) stazione di partenza (*della merce*).

forwards, *avv.* *V.* **forward**[1].

foster, *v. t.* animare, promuovere.

foul[1], *a.* **1** sporco. **2** brutto, cattivo. *n.* (*trasp. mar.*) collisione. // ~ **berth** (*trasp. mar.*) cattivo ormeggio; ~ **bill of health** (*trasp. mar.*) certificato sanitario «sporco»; ~ **bill of lading** (*trasp. mar.*) polizza di carico «sporca» (*emessa, cioè, con riserve o eccezioni alle clausole generali*); ~ **copy** brutta copia, mala copia, minuta; ~ **play** condotta sleale.

foul[2], *v. t.* **1** sporcare. **2** (*trasp. mar.*) investire. *v. i.* (*trasp. mar.*) entrare in collisione.

found, *v. t.* fondare, costituire, instaurare. // to **be founded** fondarsi.

foundation, *n.* **1** fondazione, costituzione, instaurazione. **2** fondamento. // ~ **member** (*fin., ingl.*) socio promotore (*d'una società per azioni*); **the** ~ **of a company** (*fin.*) la costituzione d'una società.

founder, *n.* **1** fondatore. **2** (*fin.*) promotore (*d'una società per azioni*). // **founders' shares** (*fin.*) azioni devolute ai promotori (*d'una società per azioni*).

four, *num.* quattro. // ~ **bits** (*slang USA*) cinquanta centesimi di dollaro.

fours, *n. pl.* (*fin.*) azioni al 4% (d'interesse), titoli al 4% (d'interesse).

fourth, *ord.* quarto. // **a** ~ un quarto, una quarta parte; ~ **cover** (*giorn.*) quarta di copertina.

fraction[1], *n.* **1** frazione, parte (*d'un tutto*). **2** (*mat.*) frazione. // **for every 100 dollars or** ~ **of 100 dollars** per ogni frazione indivisibile di cento dollari.

fraction[2], *v. t.* frazionare.

fractional, *a.* **1** esiguo, piccolo. **2** (*mat.*) frazionario. // ~ **currency** (*econ.*) moneta divisionale.

fractioning, *n.* frazionamento.

fragile, *a.* fragile.

frame[1], *n.* **1** quadro (*fig.*). **2** composizione, struttura, forma. // **the** ~ **of distribution**

(*market.*) la struttura distributiva.

frame², *v. t.* formare, formulare, elaborare.

framework, *n.* composizione, struttura.

franc, *n.* (*econ.*) franco (*moneta francese, svizzera e belga*).

franchise, *n.* **1** (*ass.*) franchigia, valore (*di danni*) in franchigia. **2** (*leg.*) franchigia; diritto, privilegio (*conferito da un'autorità*). **3** (*leg.*) appalto (*specialm. di lavori o servizi pubblici*). // **a ~ for a bus service** (*trasp.*) un appalto per un servizio d'autobus; **~ holder** (*leg.*) *V.* **franchisee**; **~ stamp** francobollo (celebrativo) in franchigia.

franchisee, *n.* (*leg.*) appaltatore (*specialm. di lavori o di servizi pubblici*).

«franco», *avv.* (*trasp.*) «franco», «senza spese».

frank¹, *a.* franco, sincero.

frank², *v. t.* **1** (*comun.*) affrancare (*una lettera, ecc.*). **2** (*cred., leg.*) affrancare, esimere (*da un pagamento*). **3** (*fin.*) esentare (*da un tributo*). // to **~ a letter** (*comun.*) affrancare una lettera; spedire una lettera in franchigia.

franked, *a.* **1** (*comun.*) affrancato. **2** (*comun.*) spedito in franchigia. **3** (*cred., leg.*) affrancato, reso esente. **4** (*fin.*) con franchigia fiscale.

franking, *n.* **1** (*comun.*) affrancatura (*d'una lettera, ecc.*). **2** (*cred., leg.*) affrancamento. **3** (*fin.*) franchigia fiscale. // **~ machine** (*macch. uff.*) affrancatrice, macchina affrancatrice.

fraud, *n.* **1** (*leg.*) frode, truffa. **2** (*leg.*) dolo. **3** (*leg.*) truffatore. // **the ~ Squad** (*G.B.*) la Squadra contro le frodi industriali (*alimentari, ecc.; cfr. ital. N.A.S.*).

fraudulence, *n.* (*leg.*) fraudolenza.

fraudulent, *a.* **1** (*leg.*) fraudolento, truffaldino. **2** (*leg.*) doloso. // **~ act** (*leg.*) atto fraudolento, atto doloso; **~ concealment** (*leg.*) occultamento doloso (*di fatti, ecc.*); **~ conversion** (*leg.*) distrazione dolosa (*di fondi, ecc.*); **~ conveyance** (*leg.*) trasferimento doloso (*di beni: a danno dei creditori*).

free¹, *a.* **1** libero. **2** (*comm.*) gratuito. **3** (*comm.*) franco, esente. **4** (*trasp.*) libero (*di posto*). *avv.* gratis, gratuitamente. // **~ admission** (*o* **admittance**) entrata libera; **~ allowance** (*trasp.*) franchigia (*di peso*) per il bagaglio; «**~ alongside ship**» **(FAS)** (*trasp. mar.*) «FAS partenza», «franco sotto bordo»; «**~ alongside vessel**» (*trasp. mar.*) «FAS» partenza, «franco sotto bordo»; **~ and open market** (*Borsa*) mercato libero e aperto; **~ baggage** (*trasp., USA*) bagaglio in franchigia; **~ bonds** (*Borsa*) obbligazioni trattate più di frequente; **~ capital** (*fin., rag.*) capitale liquido, capitale disponibile (*per investimenti*); **~ capital reserve** (*econ., rag.*) riserva straordinaria disponibile; **~ commodities** (*dog.*) merci esenti da dogana; **~ competition** (*econ.*) libera concorrenza; «**~ docks**» (*trasp. mar.*) «franco docks»; **~ economy** (*econ.*) economia di mercato; **~ enterprise** (*econ.*) libera iniziativa, libertà economica; **~ enterprise economy** (*econ.*) economia libera; **~ enterprise system** (*econ.*) sistema liberistico, liberismo; **~ entry** (*dog.*) bolla di merce esente (da dazio); **~ exchange rate** (*fin.*) cambio a corso libero, cambio libero; **~-for-all**, *a.* aperto a tutti; privo di regole, privo di restrizioni; *n.* (*fig.*) disordine; **~ from any encumbrance** (*leg.*) libero da ogni vincolo; **~ good** (*econ.*) bene non economico; **~ goods** (*comm. est.*) merci franche di dazio; (*market., pubbl.*) prodotti (offerti) in omaggio, «omaggi»; **~ gratis**, *avv.* gratis, gratuitamente; *a.* gratuito; **~ imports** (*comm. est.*) importazioni esenti da dogana; **~ labour** (*sind.*) operai non iscritti ai sindacati; **~-lance**, *a.* libero, indipendente; *n.* (*giorn., pubbl.*) giornalista indipendente; **~ list** (*comm. est.*) lista d'articoli d'importazione libera; **~ luggage** (*trasp.*) bagaglio in franchigia; **~ market** (*econ.*) mercato di libera concorrenza, libero scambio, liberismo, liberoscambismo; **~ marketeer** (*econ.*) liberoscambista; **the ~ movement of goods** (*market.*) la libera circolazione delle merci; **the ~ movement of workers** (*pers., sind.*) la libera circolazione della manodopera; «**~ of average**» (*ass. mar.*) «franco d'avaria»; «**~ of charge**» (*trasp.*) «franco», «senza spese», «franco di spese», «franco a domicilio»; (*leg.*) a titolo gratuito; «**~ of commission**» (*market.*) «franco provvigione»; **~ of duty** (*dog.*) esente da dazio; «**~ of general average**» (*ass. mar.*) «franco d'avaria generale»; **~ of mortgage** (*leg.*) libero da ipoteche; «**~ of particular average**» **(FPA)** (*ass. mar.*) «franco d'avaria particolare»; «**~ of port charges**» (*trasp. mar.*) «franco di spese portuali»; «**~ of total loss**» (*ass. mar.*) «franco di perdita totale»; **~ offer** (*market.*) offerta gratuita (*d'un prodotto*); **~ on application** (*market.*) gratis a richiesta; «**~ on board**» **(FOB)** (*trasp. mar.*) «FOB partenza», «franco a bordo»; «**~ on rail**» **(FOR)** (*trasp. ferr.*) «franco stazione (ferroviaria)», «franco vagone» (*alla stazione di partenza*); «**~ on truck**» **(FOT)** (*trasp.*) «franco vagone» (*alla stazione di partenza*); «**~ on waggon**» (*trasp. ferr.*) «franco vagone» (*alla stazione di partenza*); «**~ overside**» (*trasp. mar.*) «sotto paranco», «FOB destino»; ~ **pass** (*trasp. ferr.*) biglietto di libera circolazione; ~ **port** (*dog., trasp.*) porto franco; (*dog., trasp., USA*) *V.* **foreign-trade zone;** ~ **rate of exchange** (*fin.*) cambio a corso libero, cambio libero; ~ **reserves** (*fin., rag.*) riserve disponibili; ~ **sample** (*market.*) campione (in) omaggio; « ~ **to the receiving station**» (*trasp. ferr.*) «franco stazione d'arrivo»; ~ **trade** (*econ.*) libertà dei traffici, libero scambio; liberismo, liberoscambismo; ~ **-trade minded** (*econ.*) favorevole al liberismo, liberista; ~ **trader** (*econ.*) liberoscambista, liberista; (*trasp. mar.*) nave contrabbandiera; ~ **zone** (*dog.*) zona franca; **on** ~ **approval** (*o* **trial**) gratis in prova.

free[2], *v. t.* **1** liberare, affrancare. **2** liberalizzare. **3** esonerare (*da vincoli, ecc.*). // to ~ **movements of capital within the Community** (*econ.*) liberalizzare i movimenti di capitale nell'ambito della Comunità.

freedom, *n.* libertà. // ~ **of choice of the consumer** (*market.*) libertà di scelta del consumatore; ~ **of contract** (*leg.*) libertà contrattuale; ~ **of navigation** (*leg.*) libertà di navigazione; ~ **to supply services** (*leg.*) libera prestazione di servizi.

freehold, *n.* **1** (*leg.*) proprietà assoluta d'un terreno. **2** (*leg.*) terreno tenuto in proprietà assoluta.

freeholder, *n.* (*leg.*) chi possiede (terreni) in proprietà assoluta.

freeing, *n.* liberazione, affrancamento.

freely, *avv.* **1** liberamente. **2** gratuitamente, gratis.

free oneself, *v. rifl.* liberarsi.

freeze[1], *n.* **1** congelamento. **2** blocco. // ~ **on hiring** (*econ.*) blocco delle assunzioni; ~ **-out** (*market.*) boicottaggio, eliminazione (*d'un concorrente, ecc.*).

freeze[2], *v. t.* (*pass.* **froze,** *part. pass.* **frozen**) **1** congelare, irrigidire. **2** bloccare. *v. i.* congelarsi, irrigidirsi. // to ~ **credit** (*fin.*) congelare i crediti; to ~ **sb. out** (*market.*) eliminare, escludere, boicottare, tagliar fuori q.; to ~ **prices** (*market.*) congelare i prezzi, bloccare i prezzi; to ~ **wages** (*sind.*) bloccare i salari.

freezing, *n.* **1** congelamento, irrigidimento. **2** (*banca, fin.*) congelamento.

freight, *n.* **1** (*trasp., USA*) trasporto terrestre, carico terrestre. **2** (*trasp., USA*) spese di trasporto (*in genere*), «porto». **3** (*trasp. aer., ingl., USA*) trasporto aereo, carico aereo. **4** (*trasp. mar., ingl., USA*) trasporto marittimo, carico marittimo. **5** (*trasp. mar., ingl., USA*) noleggio (*di nave*). **6** (*trasp. mar., ingl., USA*) nolo (*prezzo del trasporto marittimo*). // ~ **booking** (*trasp. mar.*) prenotazione del nolo; ~ **-booking note** (*trasp. mar.*) registro di prenotazione dei noli; ~ **broker** (*trasp. mar.*) sensale di noli; ~ **brokerage** (*trasp. mar.*) provvigione di noleggio; ~ **bureau** (*trasp. mar., USA*) «Conferenza» della Navigazione; ~ **by measure** (*trasp. mar.*) nolo a tonnellate; ~ **by weight** (*trasp. mar.*) nolo a peso; ~ **car** (*trasp. ferr., USA*) carro merci; ~ **charges** (*trasp. mar.*) spese di nolo; ~ **clause** (*trasp. mar.*) clausola di noleggio; ~ **club** (*ass. mar.*) sezione noli (*per il rimborso dei noli perduti*); ~ **collision clause** (*trasp. mar.*) clausola assicurativa per il rimborso delle spese pagate per il nolo, in seguito a danni dovuti a collisione; ~ **compensation between enterprises** (*trasp. mar.*) compensazione interaziendale dei noli; ~ **conference** (*trasp. mar., USA*) «Conferenza» della Navigazione; ~ **contract** (*trasp. mar.*) contratto di noleggio; ~ **depot** (*trasp. ferr., USA*) scalo merci; ~ **earned** (*trasp. mar.*) nolo non rimborsabile; ~ **forward** (*trasp. ferr., USA*) porto assegnato; (*trasp. mar.*) nolo pagato a destinazione, nolo posticipato; ~ **in advance** (*trasp. mar.*) nolo anticipato; ~ **index** (*trasp. mar.*) indice dei noli; ~ **insurance** (*ass. mar.*) assicurazione sul nolo; ~ **market** (*trasp. mar.*) mercato dei noli; « ~ **not repayable**» (*trasp. mar.*) «nolo non rimborsabile»; ~ **note** (*trasp. mar.*) polizza di noleggio; ~ **out and home** (*trasp. mar.*) nolo d'andata e ritorno; ~ **payable on sailing** (*trasp. mar.*) nolo da pagarsi alla partenza; ~ **pro rata** (*trasp. mar.*) nolo «pro rata» (*cioè, in proporzione al tratto di viaggio percorso*); ~ **rate** (*trasp. ferr., USA*) tariffa di trasporto (*di merci*); (*trasp. mar.*) rata di nolo, tariffa di nolo; ~ **release** (*trasp. mar.*) «rilascio carico», mandato di scarico, quietanza per nolo; ~ **ton** (*trasp. mar.*) tonnellata di noleggio; ~ **train** (*trasp. ferr., USA*) treno merci; ~ **-yard** (*trasp. ferr., USA*) scalo merci.

freightage, *n. V.* **freight.**

freighter, *n.* **1** (*trasp., USA*) consegnatario (*di merci per trasporto via terra*). **2** (*trasp. aer.*) aereo per trasporto merci. **3** (*trasp. ferr., USA*) vagone merci. **4** (*trasp. mar.*) nave da carico. **5** (*trasp. mar., ingl., USA*) spedizioniere. **6** (*trasp. mar., ingl., USA*) noleggiatore marittimo.

frequency, *n.* frequenza. // ~ **of purchase** (*market.*) frequenza d'acquisto.

fresh, *a.* **1** fresco. **2** recente. // ~ **food** (generi) alimentari freschi (*non surgelati*); ~ **off the press** (*giorn.*) fresco di stampa; **a** ~ **supply** (*org. az.*) una nuova provvista, un nuovo rifornimento, una nuova ordinazione.

friction, *n.* 1 frizione.

frictional, *a.* di frizione.

friendly, *a.* amichevole. // ~ **arbitrator** (*leg.*) arbitro (amichevole) compositore; **a ~ arrangement** un accomodamento amichevole; **a ~ composition** (*leg.*) una transazione amichevole; **a ~ settlement** (*leg.*) un concordato amichevole.

fringe, *n.* margine. // ~ **benefits** (*pers.*) addizionali; ~ **body** (*amm., G.B.*) ente parastatale, ente quasi autonomo.

front, *n.* fronte (*quasi in ogni senso*); parte anteriore, (il) davanti. // ~ **-loaded wage settlement** (*econ., sind.*) accordo salariale che prevede i maggiori aumenti entro il primo anno (*dalla sua stipulazione*); ~ **page** (*giorn.*) prima pagina (*di giornale*); to ~ **-page** (*giorn.*) mettere (*una notizia, ecc.*) in prima pagina; ~ **-page news** (*giorn.*) notizie di (*o* da) prima pagina; **the ~ page of a paper** (*giorn.*) la prima pagina d'un giornale; ~ **-wheel drive** (*trasp. aut.*) trazione anteriore; **in ~ of** di fronte a, davanti.

frontier, *n.* frontiera. // ~ **area** (*comm. est.*) zona frontaliera; ~ **crossing** (*comm. est.*) posto di frontiera, posto di confine; ~ **formalities** (*comm. est.*) formalità di frontiera; ~ **guard** (*dog.*) guardia di frontiera; finanziere (*in Italia*).

frozen, *a.* 1 gelato, ghiacciato. 2 (*comm.*) congelato. // ~ **accounts** (*fin.*) conti congelati; ~ **credit** (*cred.*) credito «congelato»; ~ **food** surgelati; ~ **funds** (*fin.*) capitali congelati.

fruit, *n.* frutto.

fruitless, *a.* infruttifero (*in senso proprio*).

frustrate, *v. t.* battere, vincere.

frustration, *n.* 1 insuccesso. 2 (*leg.*) impossibilità d'esecuzione (*d'un contratto*).

fuel, *n.* combustibile, carburante.

fulfil, *v. t.* 1 adempiere, eseguire. 2 (*market.*) far fronte a (*un'ordinazione, una richiesta, ecc.*). // to ~ **expectations** rispettare le previsioni; to ~ **an obligation** (*leg.*) sciogliere un obbligo.

fulfill, *v. t.* (*USA*) *V.* **fulfil.**

fulfillment, *n.* (*USA*) *V.* **fulfilment.**

fulfilment, *n.* adempimento, esecuzione. // **the ~ of a contract** (*leg.*) l'esecuzione d'un contratto.

full, *a.* pieno (*in ogni senso*), intero, completo. *avv.* pienamente, interamente, completamente. // ~ **-aged** (*leg.*) maggiorenne; ~ **cargo** (*trasp. mar.*) carico completo; ~ **coverage** (*ass.*) copertura totale; ~ **display** (*pubbl.*) affissione piena; ~ **employment** (*econ.*) pieno impiego, piena occupazione; ~ **endorsement** (*cred.*) girata completa, girata in pieno; ~ **fare** (*trasp.*) tariffa intera; ~ **-form insurance** (*ass. mar.*) assicurazione sulla perdita totale e parziale; ~ **freight** (*trasp. mar.*) nolo intero; ~ **gold standard** (*econ.*) monometallismo aureo; ~ **load** (*trasp.*) pieno carico, carico completo; ~ **load displacement tonnage** (*trasp. mar.*) tonnellaggio a pieno carico normale; ~ **name** (*leg.*) nome e cognome; ~ **of debts** pieno di debiti, dissestato; ~ **-page** (*pubbl.*) a pagina intera; ~ **-page advertisement** (*pubbl.*) un annuncio pubblicitario su tutta una pagina; ~ **-paid stock** (*fin., USA*) azioni interamente liberate; ~ **pay** (*pers.*) paga intera (*senza detrazioni*); ~ **payment** (*cred.*) pagamento a saldo, pagamento totale, saldo; ~ **power of attorney** (*leg.*) procura generale; ~ **powers** pieni poteri; ~ **rate** (*comun.*) tariffa (*telegrafica, ecc.*) intera; (*dog.*) tariffa intera; ~ **showing** (*pubbl.*) affissione piena; ~ **silver standard** (*econ.*) monometallismo argenteo; «~ **speed ahead**» (*trasp. mar.*) «avanti a tutta forza!»; ~ **time** (*pers., sind.*) full time, tempo pieno; **a ~ -time job** (*pers., sind.*) un impiego a tempo pieno; ~ **weight** (*market.*) peso abbondante; **in ~ balance** (*cred.*) a saldo completo; **in ~ settlement** (*cred.*) a saldo completo.

fully, *avv.* pienamente, interamente, completamente. // ~ **paid** interamente pagato; ~ **paid capital** (*fin.*) capitale interamente versato; ~ **paid stock** (*fin.*) azioni interamente liberate; ~ **paid-up capital** (*fin.*) capitale interamente versato.

function[1], *n.* 1 funzione. 2 (*mat.*) funzione. 3 (*pers.*) compito, mansione.

function[2], *v. i.* 1 funzionare. 2 fungere (*da*).

functional, *a.* funzionale. // ~ **middleman** (*market.*) agente mediatore; ~ **structure** (*org. az.*) struttura funzionale.

functionary, *n.* (*pers.*) funzionario, impiegato statale.

functioning, *n.* funzionamento.

fund[1], *n.* (*rag.*) fondo, provvista, riserva, stanziamento. // «**no funds**» (*banca, cred.*) «mancanza di fondi» (*o* di corrispettivo); **out of funds** privo di fondi.

fund[2], *v. t.* 1 (*fin.*) consolidare (*un debito*). 2 (*fin.*) investire (*denaro*) in titoli di Stato.

fundamental, *a.* fondamentale, basilare, essenziale. // ~ **research** (*org. az.*) ricerca di base.

funded, *a.* (*fin.*) consolidato. // ~ **bond** (*fin.*) obbligazione consolidata; ~ **debt** (*Borsa*) mercato a lunga; (*fin.*) debito consolidato;

(*rag.*) debito a lunga scadenza; ~ **liability** (*fin.*) debito consolidato; (*rag.*) debito a lunga scadenza.

fundholder, *n.* (*fin.*) possessore di titoli di Stato, possessore di titoli del debito pubblico.

funding, *n.* **1** (*banca, fin.*) assegnazione di fondi. **2** (*fin.*) consolidamento (*d'un debito*). // ~ **loan** (*fin.*) prestito consolidato.

funds, *n. pl.* (*rag.*) disponibilità. // **the funds** (*fin.*) i titoli di Stato, i titoli del debito pubblico.

fungible, *a.* (*econ.*) fungibile. *n.* (*econ.*) bene fungibile.

furlough[1], *n.* (*pers., USA*) congedo, permesso, licenza.

furlough[2], *v. t.* (*pers., USA*) concedere un congedo a, concedere un permesso a (*q.*).

furnish, *v. t.* **1** (*market.*) fornire, rifornire, provvedere. **2** (*market.*) arredare, ammobiliare.

furnisher, *n.* (*market.*) fornitore.

furnishing, *n.* (*market.*) arredamento.

furnishings, *n. pl.* **1** (*market.*) mobili e infissi. **2** (*market.*) mobilia. **3** (*market., USA*) articoli per la casa.

furniture, *n.* **1** mobilia, mobili. **2** arredamento. // ~ **and fittings** mobili e arredi.

further[1], *a.* ulteriore, aggiuntivo, nuovo. *avv.* ulteriormente, inoltre. // ~ **hearing** (*leg.*) udienza aggiornata (*che completa un'udienza definitiva*); ~ **information** ulteriori informazioni; ~ **proceedings** (*leg.*) udienza aggiornata (*che completa un'udienza non definitiva*); ~ **to** in seguito a, facendo seguito a; **till** ~ **notice** fino a nuovo avviso.

further[2], *v. t.* **1** promuovere, agevolare. **2** appoggiare. // to ~ **a new enterprise** promuovere una nuova impresa.

future, *a.* futuro, venturo. *n.* futuro. // ~ **delivery** (*market.*) futura consegna; ~ **prospects** prospettive per l'avvenire.

futures, *n. pl.* (*Borsa, fin.*) operazioni a termine, contratti per consegne a termine. // ~ **market** (*Borsa, fin.*) mercato a termine.

G

gage¹, *n.* (*leg.*) pegno, arra, caparra, garanzia.

gage², *v. t.* (*leg.*) dare in pegno, impegnare, dare in garanzia.

gain¹, *n.* **1** guadagno, lucro. **2** aumento. **3** (*rag.*) profitto, provento, utile, ricavo. // **a ~ of 2% over last year** (*rag.*) un aumento del 2% rispetto allo scorso anno.

gain², *v. t.* guadagnare, lucrare, ricavare. *v. i.* aumentare. // to ~ **a good reputation on the market** guadagnarsi una buona reputazione sul mercato; to ~ **ground** (*anche fig.*) guadagnare terreno; to ~ **one's living** guadagnarsi da vivere; to ~ **popularity** guadagnare popolarità; to ~ **strength** rafforzarsi; to ~ **a suit at law** (*leg.*) vincere una causa.

gainful, *a.* profittevole, lucrativo, remunerativo. // **a ~ job** (*pers.*) un'occupazione remunerativa, un lavoro retribuito.

galley, *n.* **1** (*pubbl.*) vantaggio. **2** (*trasp. mar.*) cambusa, cucina di bordo.

gallon, *n.* **1** gallone (*misura di capacità per liquidi e aridi pari a litri 4,545*). **2** (*USA*) gallone (*misura di capacità per liquidi pari a litri 3,785*).

gallop, *v. i.* galoppare.

galloping, *a.* galoppante. // **~ inflation** (*fin.*) inflazione galoppante.

Gallup poll, *locuz. n.* (*stat.*) indagine demoscopica.

gamble¹, *n.* **1** gioco d'azzardo. **2** rischio.

gamble², *v. i.* **1** giocare d'azzardo. **2** (*Borsa*) speculare. // to ~ **on the Stock Exchange** (*Borsa*) speculare in Borsa, giocare in Borsa.

gambler, *n.* **1** giocatore d'azzardo. **2** (*Borsa*) speculatore.

gang, *n.* (*pers.*) squadra (*d'operai*).

ganger, *n.* (*pers.*) caposquadra.

gangplank, *n.* (*trasp. mar.*) barcarizzo.

gangway, *n.* **1** passaggio. **2** (*trasp. mar.*) barcarizzo.

gap, *n.* **1** divario, differenza, squilibrio. **2** lacuna. **3** (*elab. elettr.*) spazio (compreso) fra più registrazioni. **4** (*fin.*) saldo passivo; deficit; disavanzo. **5** (*stat.*) saldo. // **the population ~** il saldo demografico; **the trade ~** il deficit della bilancia commerciale.

garage, *n.* (*trasp. aut.*) autorimessa, rimessa, garage.

garnish, *v. t.* (*leg.*) citare (*come testimone, ecc.*).

garnishee¹, *n.* **1** (*leg.*) terzo pignorato. **2** (*leg.*) chi detiene beni o denaro del «convenuto», ma non può disporne, in attesa della sentenza. // **~ order** (*leg.*) ordine di pignoramento presso terzi.

garnishee², *v. t.* (*leg.*) mettere il fermo su (*beni, ecc.*).

garnisher, *n.* (*leg.*) sequestrante, sequestratore.

garnishment, *n.* **1** (*leg.*) citazione come teste. **2** (*leg.*) pignoramento presso terzi. **3** (*leg., pers.*) effettuato dal datore di lavoro a un creditore.

gas¹, *n.* (*fam., USA*) benzina. // **~ station** (*trasp. aut.*) distributore di benzina.

gas² **up**, *v. i.* (*trasp. aut., USA*) far benzina.

gate, *n.* **1** cancello. **2** (*ric. op.*) stazione. **3** (*trasp. aer.*) cancello, uscita (*d'aeroporto*). **4** (*trasp. ferr.*) barriera, cancello di passaggio a livello.

gather, *v. t.* **1** raccogliere. **2** dedurre, capire. *v. rifl.* raccogliersi. // to ~ **documents on st.** documentarsi su qc.; to ~ **information** assumere informazioni; to ~ **taxes** (*fin.*) riscuotere imposte.

gathering, *n.* raccolta. // **~ of intelligence** raccolta d'informazioni; **~ of statistical data** (*fin.*) rilevazioni statistiche.

gazette¹, *n.* **1** (*giorn.*) gazzetta. **2** (*giorn.*) gazzetta ufficiale (*che pubblica anche il bollettino dei fallimenti e altri atti ufficiali*).

gazette², *v. t.* (*giorn.*) pubblicare su una gazzetta ufficiale.

gear¹, *n.* meccanismo.

gear², *v. t.* innestare (*un congegno*). // to ~ **production to demand** (*econ.*) modificare la produzione secondo le esigenze della domanda; to ~ **up** accelerare; to ~ **up production** (*org. az.*) accelerare la produzione.

gearing, *n.* (*fin.*) differenziazione del portafoglio (*da parte di un fondo d'investimento; anche* ~ **of capital**).

general, *a.* **1** generale, comune. **2** collettivo, pubblico. // ~ **acceptance** (*cred.*) accettazione incondizionata, accettazione senza riserve; ~ **accounting** (*rag.*) contabilità generale; ~ **agency** (*ass.*) agenzia generale; (*leg.*) mandato generale; ~ **agent** (*ass., pers.*) agente generale; ~ **Agreement on Tariffs and Trade (GATT)** (*comm. est., dog.*) accordo generale sulle tariffe doganali e il commercio (*GATT*); ~ **assignment** (*leg.*) cessione generale (*di beni ai creditori*); ~ **average** (*ass. mar.*) avaria generale, avaria totale; ~ **average bond** (*ass. mar.*) compromesso d'avaria generale; ~ **average clause** (*ass. mar.*) clausola d'avaria generale; ~ **average contribution** (*ass. mar.*) contributo d'avaria generale; ~ **average loss** (*ass. mar.*) perdita per avaria generale; ~ **average payable as per foreign adjustment or per York-Antwerp Rules** (*ass. mar.*) avaria generale pagabile secondo la liquidazione all'estero o secondo i Regolamenti di York-Anversa; ~ **average statement** (*ass. mar.*) regolamento d'avaria generale; ~ **balance-sheet** (*rag.*) bilancio generale; ~ **bill of lading** (*trasp. mar.*) polizza di carico collettiva; «~ **business**» (*org. az.*) «varie ed eventuali» (*ultima voce d'un ordine del giorno*); ~ **cargo** (*trasp. mar.*) carico misto, carico a collettame; ~ **charges** (*rag.*) spese generali; **the** ~ **crossing of a cheque** (*banca*) la sbarratura semplice d'un assegno; ~ **dealer** (*market.*) commerciante in generi diversi, negoziante in generi diversi; **a** ~ **economic squeeze** (*econ.*) un giro di vite a tutta l'economia; ~ **editor** (*giorn.*) direttore generale; **a** ~ **election** un'elezione generale; ~ **endorsement** (*cred.*) girata in bianco; ~ **expenses** (*rag.*) spese generali; ~ **grant** (*econ., ingl.*) sussidio governativo agli Enti locali; ~ **ledger** (*rag.*) libro mastro generale; ~ **legacy** (*leg.*) legato generale; ~ **management** (*org. az.*) direzione generale; ~ **manager** (*pers.*) direttore generale; ~ **meeting** (*fin.*) assemblea generale (*degli azionisti*); ~ **mortgage** (*leg.*) ipoteca generale; ~ **mortgage bond** (*leg.*) obbligazione ipotecaria; ~ **partner** (*fin.*) socio accomandatario; ~ **partnership** (*fin.*) società in nome collettivo; ~ **power (of attorney)** (*leg.*) procura generale; ~ **property tax** (*fin., USA*) tassa proporzionale a favore degli Enti locali (*che colpisce la ricchezza individuale sotto qualsiasi forma*); ~ **proxy** (*leg.*) procura generale; procuratore generale; ~ **-purpose** concepito per due o più usi; ~ **-purpose sample** (*market.*) campione per tutte le necessità; ~ **Registry of Stocks and Shares** (*fin., leg.*) Schedario Generale dei Titoli Azionari; ~ **report** (*rag.*) relazione generale; ~ **reserve** (*rag.*) riserva statutaria; ~ **sales manager** (*pers.*) direttore generale alle vendite; ~ **store** (*market., USA*) negozio di generi vari; **a** ~ **strike** (*sind.*) uno sciopero generale; ~ **warehouse** (*dog.*) magazzino generale.

generalized, *a.* generalizzato. // ~ **tariff preferences** (*comm. est.*) preferenze tariffarie generalizzate; ~ **tariff quotas** (*dog.*) preferenze tariffarie generalizzate.

gentleman, *n.* (*pl.* **gentlemen**) gentiluomo, signore. // **a** ~ **'s agreement** un accordo sulla parola, un accordo leale; **a** ~ **at large** (*slang USA*) un disoccupato.

genuine, *a.* genuino.

geographic(al), *a.* geografico. // ~ **coverage** (*giorn., pubbl.*) copertura geografica.

geography, *n.* geografia.

Germany, *n.* Germania.

get, *v. t.* (*pass.* e *part. pass.* **got**) **1** ottenere, ricevere. **2** comprare. **3** guadagnare. **4** persuadere, far (*fare qc. a q.*). *v. i.* diventare, divenire, farsi. // to ~ **an advance of money** (*cred., market.*) ottenere un anticipo di denaro; to ~ **afloat** (*trasp. mar.*) disincagliare, disincagliarsi; (*fig.*) lanciare; to ~ **a business afloat** (*market.*) lanciare una azienda; to ~ **the air** (*slang USA*) essere licenziato; to ~ **along** farcela; to ~ **the ax** (*pers., slang USA*) essere licenziato, farsi licenziare; to ~ **st. back** farsi restituire qc.; to ~ **a bill discounted** (*banca, cred.*) farsi scontare una cambiale; to ~ **the boot** (*slang USA*) essere licenziato, farsi licenziare; to ~ **dearer** (*market.*) diventare più caro, diventare più costoso, rincarare; to ~ **one's degree** laurearsi; to ~ **the gate** (*pers., slang USA*) essere licenziato, farsi licenziare; to ~ **a good position (o job)** ottenere un buon impiego; to ~ **in** entrare, introdursi; arrivare; to ~ **in on the ground floor** (*slang USA*) comprare al prezzo minimo; to ~ **in touch with sb.** mettersi in contatto con q., entrare in relazione con q., contattare q.; to ~ **into** entrare, introdursi; to ~ **into arrears** (*cred.*) essere in ritardo (*con un pagamento*), diventare moroso; to ~ **into debt** (*cred.*) indebitarsi, contrarre debiti; to ~ **a job** trovar lavoro, impiegarsi; to ~ **on in the world** far fortuna; to ~ **st. out of** ottenere qc. da, ricavare qc. da; to ~ **out of debt** (*cred.*) liberarsi dai debiti; to ~ **st. out of pawn** disimpegnare qc. (*dal monte dei pegni*); to ~ **out of the red** (*banca, cred.*) sdebitarsi; to ~ **rich** arricchire; to ~ **the sack** (*pers., fam.*) essere licenziato, farsi licenziare; to ~ **a**

situation (*pers.*) ottenere un impiego; to ~ **a situation for sb.** (*pers.*) ottenere un impiego per q.; to ~ **through** (*leg.*) far approvare (*un disegno di legge, un provvedimento, ecc.*); to ~ **time** (*cred.*) ottenere una dilazione (*di pagamento*).

giant, *n.* gigante. *a. attr.* di gigante, gigantesco. // ~ **corporation** (*fin.*) grande società.

giffen goods, *n. pl.* (*econ.*) merci povere (*per le quali si verifica il fenomeno dell'aumento della domanda all'aumento del prezzo; sembra che il primo a richiamare l'attenzione degli esperti su questo fenomeno fosse Sir Robert Giffen*).

gift, *n.* **1** dono, regalo, presente. **2** (*leg.*) donazione. // ~ **causa mortis** (*leg.*) donazione fatta in punto di morte («*donatio mortis causa*»); ~ **stamps** (*market.*) bolli premio, bollini; ~ **tax** (*fin.*) imposta sulle donazioni; ~ **token** (*fin., ingl.*) assegno dono in tagli fissi (*venduto dagli uffici postali*).

gill, *n.* **1** «gill» (*misura di capacità per liquidi e aridi pari a metri cubi 0,142*). **2** (*USA*) «gill» (*misura di capacità per liquidi pari a litri 0,118*).

gilt, *a.* dorato. // ~ **-edged** (*o* ~ **-edge**) col bordo dorato; (*fig.*) della migliore qualità, di prima qualità; ~ **-edged** (*o* ~ **-edge**) **securities** (*fin.*) titoli di prim'ordine, titoli sicurissimi, titoli primari.

gilts, *n. pl.* (*fin., fam.*) *V.* **gilt-edged securities.**

girl, *n.* **1** ragazza, giovane. **2** (*pers.*) impiegata. **3** (*pers.*) segretaria. // ~ **courier** (*tur.*) accompagnatrice turistica; guida (*donna*); ~ **Friday** (*pers.*) *V.* ~ **friday;** ~ **friday** (*pers.*) segretaria tuttofare, factotum.

giro, *n.* **1** (*cred.*) giroconto (*bancario o postale*). **2** (*cred.*) postagiro. **3** (*fin., G.B.*) *V.* **National Girobank.** // ~ **slip** (*G.B.*) modulo d'accredito in giroconto (*sostituisce l'assegno*).

give, *v. t.* (*pass.* **gave,** *part. pass.* **given**) **1** dare, donare. **2** consegnare. **3** accordare, assegnare. **4** pagare. // to ~ **an allowance** (*o* **a bonus**) **to sb.** (*pers.*) gratificare q.; to ~ **st. as security** (*leg.*) dare qc. in garanzia; to ~ (*o* to **render**) **assistance to sb.** dare (*o* prestare) aiuto a q.; to ~ **back** restituire; to ~ **the bulk of one's business to sb.** concentrare i propri acquisti presso q.; to ~ **change for a dollar** cambiare un dollaro, dare il resto di un dollaro; to ~ **one's confidence** concedere la propria fiducia; to ~ **credit** (*cred.*) far credito; to ~ **sb. credit for a sum of money** (*cred.*) accreditare una somma di denaro a q.; to ~ **an earnest** dare una caparra; to ~ **effective guarantees** dare garanzie effettive; to ~ **employment to** (*pers.*) dare lavoro a, impiegare; to ~ **evidence** (*leg.*) testimoniare, rendere testimonianza; to ~ **false testimony** (*leg.*) deporre il falso; to ~ **for the call** (*Borsa*) comprare a premio, comprare il «dont»; to ~ **for the call of more** (*Borsa*) comprare con diritto d'aggiunta; to ~ **for the call of twice more** (*Borsa*) comprare con diritto d'aggiunta doppia; to ~ **for the put** (*Borsa*) vendere a premio, vendere con facoltà d'opzione; to ~ **for the put and call** (*Borsa*) comprare a doppia opzione, comprare lo «stellage»; to ~ **for a put of more** (*Borsa*) vendere con facoltà di doppia consegna; to ~ **for a song** (*market.*) vendere a basso prezzo, «regalare»; to ~ **sb. the gate** (*pers., slang USA*) licenziare q.; to ~ **good returns** (*fin.: d'un investimento*) fruttare bene; to ~ **an interest to sb.** (*fin.*) interessare q. (*in un'azienda e sim.*); to ~ **legal notice** (*leg.*) dare avviso legale; to ~ **notice** informare; dare il preavviso, dare la disdetta; to ~ **notice of st.** denunciare qc.; to ~ **notice of damage to the shipowner** (*ass. mar.*) denunciare l'avaria all'armatore; to ~ **notice to sb.** (*leg.*) dare la disdetta a q.; (*pers.*) dar a q. il preavviso di licenziamento, licenziare q.; to ~ **notice to one's employer** (*pers.*) licenziarsi, dimettersi; to ~ **notice to quit** (*leg.*) dare disdetta di sfratto; to ~ **on** (*Borsa*) farsi riportare; to ~ **on stock** (*Borsa*) dare titoli a riporto; to ~ **oneself up** (*leg.*) costituirsi; to ~ **an order for goods** (*market.*) fare un'ordinazione di merci; to ~ **out** annunciare, pubblicare; to ~ **the rate** (*Borsa*) farsi riportare; to ~ **the rate on stock** (*Borsa*) dare titoli a riporto; to ~ **(a) receipt** dare ricevuta, rilasciare (una) ricevuta; to ~ **a rise** (*pers.*) concedere un aumento (*di salario*); to ~ **rise to** causare, cagionare; to ~ **sb. the sack** (*pers., fam.*) licenziare q.; to ~ **security** (*leg.*) fornire cauzione, prestar garanzia; to ~ **sb. a share in st.** (*fin.*) interessare q. a qc.; to ~ **unsecured credit** (*banca, cred.*) concedere crediti senza garanzie; to ~ **st. up** abbandonare qc., rinunciare a qc.; to ~ **way** cedere, rompersi, spezzarsi; to ~ **way to a ship** (*trasp. mar.*) lasciar libera la rotta a una nave; to ~ **one's word** dare la propria parola.

giveaway, *n.* (*market.*) articolo dato in regalo, articolo in omaggio, omaggio.

given, *a.* **1** donato. **2** fissato, prestabilito. **3** (*leg.*) dato, certo. *cong.* supposto che, ammesso che. // ~ **name** (*USA*) nome di battesimo, prenome.

giver, *n.* **1** datore, donatore. **2** (*fin.,*

market.) venditore.

gladly, *avv.* lietamente, felicemente.

glamour stocks, *n. pl.* (*Borsa*) titoli «affascinanti» (*fra i più richiesti in una data Borsa*).

glassware, *n.* (*market.*) articoli di vetro.

global, *a.* globale, complessivo. // ~ **free trade** (*econ.*) totale libertà dei traffici.

glossy, *a.* liscio. // ~ **paper** (*giorn., pubbl.*) carta patinata.

glue, *n.* (*attr. uff.*) colla.

glut[1], *n.* **1** sazietà. **2** (*econ.*) saturazione. // **oil** ~ saturazione dei prodotti petroliferi; saturazione petrolifera.

glut[2], *v. t.* **1** saziare. **2** (*econ.*) saturare (*un mercato, ecc.*).

go[1], *n.* **1** l'andare, moto, movimento. **2** (*fam.*) animazione, attività. **3** (*econ., fin.*) ripresa. **4** (*market.*) moda, voga. // ~ **-slow** sciopero bianco.

go[2], *v. i.* (*pass.* **went,** *part. pass.* **gone**) andare. // to ~ **aboard** (*trasp. mar.*) imbarcarsi; to ~ **about st.** occuparsi di qc.; to ~ **alongside a ship** (*trasp. mar.*) accostarsi (*o* affiancarsi) a una nave; to ~ **ashore** (*trasp. mar.*) approdare, sbarcare; to ~ **away** andar via, allontanarsi; to ~ **back** (*fig.*) far marcia indietro; to ~ **back on** (*o* **upon**) **one's word** non mantenere la parola; to ~ **bail for sb.** (*leg.*) pagare (*o* versare) la cauzione per (*ottenere la libertà provvisoria di*) q.; farsi garante per q. (*per ottenergli la libertà provvisoria*); to ~ **bankrupt** (*leg.*) fallire, far fallimento; to ~ **a bear** (*Borsa*) speculare al ribasso; to ~ **better** migliorare; (*fin., market.*) aumentare (*o* crescere) di valore; to ~ **beyond** eccedere; to ~ **a bull** (*Borsa*) speculare al rialzo; to ~ **by car** andare in automobile; to ~ **by plane** andare in aeroplano; to ~ **by ship** andare in nave; to ~ **cheap** (*market.*) (*di un articolo*) essere venduto a basso prezzo; to ~ **down** (*market.*) calare, diminuire (*di prezzo, ecc.*); (*market.*) (*di prezzo, ecc.*) essere ribassato; to ~ **halves** fare a mezzo, dividere le spese; to ~ **in for** intraprendere (*una professione e sim.*); to ~ **industrial** (*econ.*) passare all'industria; to ~ **into** entrare in; andare al fondo di, approfondire (*qc.*); to ~ **into an account** (*rag.*) esaminare un conto; to ~ **into business** entrare in affari, mettersi in affari, mettersi in commercio; to ~ **into dry dock** (*trasp. mar.*) entrare in bacino di carenaggio; to ~ **into the evidence** (*leg.*) approfondire l'esame delle prove; to ~ **into liquidation** (*fin.*) mettersi in liquidazione; to ~ **into a matter** esaminare una pratica, esaminare una questione; «~ **it alone**» (*econ.*) politica autarchica; to ~ **long in a given currency** (*Borsa, fin.*) detenere troppa valuta di una certa moneta; to ~ **multinational** (*fin.: di una società*) diventare multinazionale; to ~ **off** (*market.*) andare, vendersi; (*market.*) scadere di qualità; to ~ **off duty** (*pers.*) «staccare»; to ~ **off the rails** (*trasp. ferr.*) deragliare; to ~ **on a cruise** (*trasp. mar.*) andare in crociera; to ~ **on a holiday** (*pers.*) andare in ferie; to ~ **on a journey** (*tur.*) fare un viaggio (*per via di terra*); to ~ **one better** (*market., sind.*) offrire un prezzo più alto; to ~ **out** andare fuori, uscire; to ~ **out of dry dock** (*trasp. mar.*) uscire dal bacino di carenaggio; to ~ **out of fashion** (*market.*) passar di moda; to ~ **out (on strike)** (*pers., sind.*) mettersi in sciopero; to ~ **public** (*fin.*) diventare pubblico; to ~ **slow** (*sind.*) rallentare il lavoro; fare uno sciopero bianco; to ~ **strong** andar forte, «tirare»; to ~ **surety for sb.** (*leg.*) farsi garante per q.; to ~ **through** esaminare attentamente; to ~ **through an account** (*rag.*) spulciare un conto; to ~ **through one's correspondence** fare lo spoglio della propria corrispondenza; to ~ **to the Bar** (*leg.*) darsi alla professione forense, diventare avvocato; to ~ **to the bottom** (*trasp. mar.*) andare a fondo, colare a picco; to ~ **to Court** (*leg.*) adire il tribunale, ricorrere alla giustizia; to ~ **to protest** (*cred., leg.*) andare in protesto; to ~ **up** andar su; (*market.*) aumentare, crescere (*di prezzo, ecc.*), rincarare; (*market.*) (*di prezzo, ecc.*) essere in aumento, salire, lievitare; to ~ **worse** (*fin., market.*) diminuire di valore, deprezzarsi.

goal, *n.* **1** meta, scopo, fine. **2** (*org. az.*) obiettivo, scopo.

going, *a.* **1** che va. **2** che va bene. **3** (*market.*) corrente. *n.* **1** andata, partenza. **2** (*trasp.*) andatura, moto, velocità. // **a** ~ **concern** (*econ.*) un'azienda bene avviata, un'azienda in attività; ~ **price** (*market.*) prezzo corrente; ~ **value** (*market.*) valore corrente.

gold, *n.* oro. *a. attr.* aureo. // **a** ~ **bar** un lingotto d'oro; ~ **bullion standard** (*fin.*) tipo a cambio in verghe auree; ~ **clause** (*leg.*) clausola (di contratto, che prevede il pagamento in) oro; ~ **cover** (*econ., fin.*) copertura aurea; ~ **currency** (*econ., fin.*) valuta aurea; ~ **-exchange standard** (*econ., fin.*) sistema monetario basato sulla libera convertibilità delle monete rispetto a una moneta «base» a parità aurea; ~ **francs** (*econ., fin.*) franchi-oro; ~ **inflation** (*econ.*) inflazione da (eccesso di produzione di) oro; ~ **money** (*econ., fin.*) valuta aurea; ~ **points** (*econ., fin.*) punti dell'oro, punti metallici; ~ **pool** (*fin.*) «pool» dell'oro; ~ **reserve** (*banca,* *econ., fin.*) riserva aurea; ~ **standard** (*econ., fin.*) sistema (monometallico) aureo, parità aurea, valuta aurea; **in** ~ (*fin.*) in valuta aurea, in oro.

golden, *a. attr.* aureo. // ~ **handshake** (*fin.*) buonuscita (*al direttore uscente d'una società*).

gone, *part. pass. di* to **go.** // «**gone!**» (*in una vendita all'asta*) «aggiudicato!».

good, *a.* buono. *n.* **1** bene, beneficio, pro. **2** (*econ.*) bene economico. // ~ **appearance** (*pers.*) bella presenza; ~ **average quality** (*market.*) qualità buona media; **a** ~ **bargain** un buon affare; ~ **behaviour** (*leg.*) buona condotta; ~ **cause** (*leg.*) buona causa; ~ **debts** (*cred.*) crediti sicuri; ~ **delivery** (*Borsa*) buona consegna, consegna valida (*di titoli*); ~ **faith** (*leg.*) buona fede; ~ **-for** (*slang USA*) pagherò cambiario; ~ **for 50 dollars** (*cred., market.*) del valore di 50 dollari; **a** ~ **man** (*comm.*) un uomo reputato solido, un uomo solvibile; ~ **offices** impegno, interessamento; ~ **paper** (*cred.*) buona carta, effetti sicuri; **a** ~ **security** (*leg.*) una buona cauzione; ~ **standing** (*econ.*) alto tenore di vita; ~ **till cancelled order** (*Borsa*) ordine valido a revoca.

goods, *n. pl.* **1** beni mobili. **2** merci, merce. **3** prodotti. **4** (*rag.*) conto merci. // ~ **account** (*rag.*) conto merci; ~ **afloat** (*trasp.*) merci flottanti; ~ **and chattels** (*leg.*) beni mobili, beni personali; ~ **entrance** ingresso merci; ~ **for home use** (*dog.*) merci per uso (*o* consumo) interno; ~ **for private consumption** (*market.*) prodotti destinati al consumo privato; ~ **for temporary admission** (*comm. est.*) merce in transito; ~ **in apparent good order and condition** (*market.*) merce che sembra in ordine e in buone condizioni; ~ **in bond** (*dog.*) merce schiava di dazio; ~ **in consignment** (*market.*) merce in deposito; ~ **in process** (*org. az.*) prodotti in corso di lavorazione, semilavorati, prodotti semilavorati; ~ **in stock** (*org. az.*) merce in magazzino; ~ **loan** (*cred.*) anticipazione su merci; ~ **lying at the railway station** merce giacente in stazione; ~ **lying in customs** (*dog.*) merci in dogana; ~ **on hand** (*org. az.*) merce in magazzino; ~ **rates** (*trasp.*) tariffe per il trasporto delle merci; ~ **station** (*trasp. ferr.*) scalo merci; ~ **stored ashore** (*trasp. mar.*) merce immagazzinata a terra; ~ **traffic** (*trasp.*) movimento merci; ~ **train** (*trasp. ferr.*) treno merci; ~ **transport** (*trasp.*) trasporto di merci; ~ **truck** (*trasp. ferr.*) vagone merci; ~ **wagon** (*trasp. ferr.*) vagone merci; **by** ~ **train** (*trasp. ferr.*) a piccola velocità.

goodwill, *n.* **1** buona volontà. **2** (*rag.*) avviamento (*d'un'azienda, d'un negozio, ecc.*). // ~ **money** buonuscita (*pagata a un negoziante, ecc.*).

govern, *v. t.* **1** governare, condurre, dirigere. **2** amministrare. **3** controllare, tenere a freno.

governed, *a.* **1** governato, condotto, diretto. **2** controllato, tenuto a freno. // ~ **economy** (*econ.*) economia controllata.

government, *n.* **1** governo, amministrazione, ministero. **2** (*org. az.*) amministrazione, gestione. // ~ **bank** (*banca*) banca di Stato; ~ **bonds** (*fin.*) obbligazioni dello Stato, buoni del Tesoro, cartelle del debito pubblico; ~ **concession tax** (*fin.*) tassa sulle concessioni governative; ~ **corporation** (*fin., USA*) società pubblica (*che esercita funzioni d'interesse pubblico*); ~ **depository** (*banca*) banca (che svolge funzioni) di Tesoreria per lo Stato; ~ **expenditure** (*fin.*) spesa pubblica; ~ **-inflation** (*econ.*) inflazione controllata dal governo; ~ **loan** (*econ.*) prestito pubblico; ~ **monopolies** (*econ.*) monopoli di Stato, monopoli nazionali (*a carattere commerciale*); ~ **office** ente governativo, ente pubblico; ~ **purchasers** (*econ.*) acquirenti pubblici; ~ **revenue** (*fin.*) entrate pubbliche; ~ **securities** (*fin.*) titoli di Stato, titoli pubblici; ~ **securities are advancing steadily** i titoli di Stato sono in continuo aumento; ~ **stock** (*fin.*) titoli pubblici; ~ **tax on secured loans** (*fin.*) tassa erariale sulle operazioni garantite.

governor, *n.* **1** governatore. **2** amministratore. // ~ **-general** (*ingl.*) governatore generale; **the** ~ **of the Bank of England** (*banca, ingl.*) il Governatore della Banca d'Inghilterra.

grace, *n.* grazia. // ~ **period** (*ass.*) mora, moratoria.

gradation, *n.* gradazione.

grade¹, *n.* **1** grado. **2** (*market.*) categoria, classe. **3** (*market.*) standard qualitativo, qualità, varietà. // ~ **crossing** (*trasp. ferr., USA*) passaggio a livello; **on the up** ~ in ascesa; (*fin., market.*) in rialzo, in via di miglioramento; **up to** ~ (*market.*) di qualità buona media.

grade², *v. t.* **1** graduare. **2** (*market.*) classificare, cernere.

grading, *n.* (*market.*) classificazione, cernita.

gradual, *a.* graduale.

graduate¹, *n.* **1** laureato, laureata. **2** (*USA*) diplomato, diplomata. // ~ **in economics** laureato in economia.

graduate², *v. t.* **1** graduare. **2** (*soprattutto USA*) conferire la laurea a, laureare. **3** (*USA*) rilasciare un diploma a, diplomare. *v. i.* **1**

laurearsi, conseguire la laurea. **2** (*USA*) diplomarsi, conseguire il diploma. // to ~ **taxes** (*fin.*) graduare le imposte.

graduated, *a.* graduato. // ~ **prices** (*market.*) prezzi differenziali; ~ **tax** (*fin.*) imposta progressiva.

graduation, *n.* graduazione.

graft[1], *n.* **1** (*fam.*) «bustarella». **2** (*leg.*) concussione, prevaricazione.

graft[2], *v. i.* (*leg.*) prevaricare. *v. t.* (*leg.*) procurarsi (*denaro, cariche, ecc.*) con mezzi illeciti.

grafter, *n.* (*leg.*) prevaricatore.

grain, *n.* (*ingl.*) grano (*misura di peso pari a 0,0648 grammi*).

gram, *n.* grammo.

gramme, *n.* grammo.

grand, *a.* **1** grande, importante, principale. **2** complessivo, totale. // ~ **jury** (*leg.*) giuria speciale (*che decide se q. debba essere rinviato a giudizio*); ~ **total** (*rag.*) somma complessiva, totale generale.

grandee, *n.* (*fin.*) magnate.

grant[1], *n.* **1** concessione. **2** ammissione. **3** (*fin.*) sovvenzione; (*USA*) borsa di studio. **4** (*leg.*) concessione, cessione, assegnazione, trasferimento (*di beni, diritti, proprietà*). // ~ **-in aid** (*fin.*) contributo statale (*agli Enti pubblici*); **the ~ of a patent** (*leg.*) il rilascio d'un brevetto.

grant[2], *v. t.* **1** accordare, concedere. **2** ammettere, riconoscere. **3** (*fin.*) sovvenzionare. **4** (*leg.*) concedere, cedere, assegnare, trasferire (*beni, diritti, proprietà*). // to ~ **sb. an audience** concedere un'udienza a q.; to ~ **clean credits** (*banca, cred.*) concedere un credito di cassa; to ~ (*sb.*) **a diploma** diplomare; to ~ **a discount** (*market.*) concedere uno sconto; to ~ **an extension of payment** concedere una dilazione di pagamento; to ~ **the know-how** (*leg.*) cedere il «know-how» (*q. V.*); to ~ **sb. a leave** (*pers.*) concedere un congedo (*o* un permesso) a q.; to ~ **a loan** (*cred.*) concedere un prestito; to ~ **loans on favourable terms** (*cred.*) concedere prestiti a condizioni di favore; to ~ **an overdraft** (*banca, cred.*) concedere uno scoperto; to ~ **a patent** (*leg.*) concedere un brevetto; to ~ **a request** accogliere una richiesta.

grantee, *n.* (*leg.*) cessionario, concessionario, assegnatario, beneficiario.

grantor, *n.* **1** (*leg.*) cedente, concedente. **2** (*leg.*) garante, avallante.

graphic, *a.* grafico.

graphical, *a. V.* **graphic.**

grasp[1], *n.* **1** presa. **2** comprensione. // **beyond one's ~** (*d'un problema, ecc.*) che non si riesce a capire (*o* a risolvere); **within one's ~** (*d'un problema, ecc.*) che si riesce a capire (*o* a risolvere).

grasp[2], *v. t.* **1** afferrare, agguantare, impugnare. **2** comprendere, capire.

grateful, *a.* grato.

gratefully, *avv.* con gratitudine.

gratefulness, *n.* gratitudine.

gratifying, *a.* gratificante.

gratis, *avv.* gratis, gratuitamente. *a.* gratuito.

gratuitous, *a.* gratuito.

gratuity, *n.* **1** gratificazione, gratifica, regalia. **2** «bustarella». **3** (*pers.*) indennità di buonuscita, liquidazione (*in G.B.: in genere, a militari o impiegati dello Stato*).

grave, *a.* grave.

graveyard, *n.* cimitero, camposanto. // ~ **shift** (*pers.*) turno di notte; operai del turno di notte.

graving, *n.* (*trasp. mar.*) carenaggio. // ~ **-dock** (*trasp. mar.*) bacino di carenaggio.

gravy, *n.* **1** sugo, salsa. **2** (*slang USA*) fonte di profitti illegali. // ~ **job** (*fam., ingl.*) occupazione oltremodo redditizia; ~ **train** (*slang USA*) occupazione oltremodo redditizia.

gray, *a. V.* **grey.**

grease, *n.* grasso, unto.

greasy, *a.* grasso, untuoso. // ~ **crayon** (*attr. uff.*) matita grassa.

great, *a.* grande, grosso, importante. // **the ~ Depression** la Grande Crisi (*o* Depressione) (*quella del 1929, in U.S.A.*); ~ **gross** quantità pari a dodici grosse (*cioè, 1.728 unità*); **the greatest common factor** (*mat.*) il massimo comun divisore.

greatness, *n.* grandezza.

green, *a.* inesperto. *n.* (*USA*) denaro cartaceo. // ~ **goods** (*USA*) banconote false; ~ **money** (*USA*) denaro cartaceo.

greenback, *n.* (*USA*) biglietto di banca.

greenbacks, *n. pl.* (*USA*) dollari.

Greenwich, *n. pr.* Greenwich (*presso Londra*). // ~ **civil time** *V.* ~ **(mean) time;** ~ **(mean) time (G.M.T.)** ora (solare misurata sul meridiano di) Greenwich.

grey, *a.* grigio. // ~ **market** (*econ.*) mercato «grigio» (*situazione simile a quella del mercato nero, ma non altrettanto apertamente illegale*).

grievance, *n.* **1** lagnanza, reclamo. **2** offesa. **3** (*sind.*) lagnanza, reclamo. // ~ **committee** (*sind.*) commissione interna (*per la discussione delle lagnanze del personale*).

groceries, *n. pl.* (*market.*) coloniali.

gross, *a.* 1 grossolano, grezzo. 2 grosso, grave. 3 (*comm.*) complessivo, totale. 4 (*comm.*) lordo. *n.* grossa (*dodici dozzine*). // ~ **amount** ammontare complessivo; importo lordo; ~ **average** (*ass. mar.*) avaria generale; ~ **cash flow** (*rag.*) somma degli utili lordi e degli ammortamenti; ~ **commodities** (*market.*) derrate grezze; ~ **earnings** (*rag.*) entrate lorde; ~ **fixed assets** (*rag.*) capitale fisso lordo; «~ **for net**» (*market.*) «lordo per netto» (*non si computa la tara*); ~ **freight** (*trasp. mar.*) nolo lordo; ~ **income** (*rag.*) entrata lorda; reddito complessivo; reddito lordo; ~ **margin** (*rag.*) margine lordo; ~ **national product (GNP)** (*econ.*) prodotto nazionale lordo (*PNL*); ~ **negligence** (*leg.*) negligenza grave; ~ **operating profits** (*fin., rag.*) risultati lordi di gestione; ~ **output** (*fin., rag.*) prodotto lordo; ~ **premium** (*ass.*) premio lordo, premio «di tariffario»; ~ **price** (*market.*) prezzo lordo; ~ **product** (*fin., rag.*) prodotto lordo; reddito lordo; ~ **profit** (*o* ~ **profits**) (*rag.*) utile lordo; ~ **receipts** (*rag.*) incasso lordo; ~ **tonnage** (*trasp. mar.*) tonnellaggio lordo; stazza lorda; ~ **trading profits** (*fin., rag.*) margini lordi di utile commerciale; ~ **weight** peso lordo.

ground[1], *n.* 1 terreno, suolo. 2 fondamento. 3 causa, motivo, ragione. 4 (*leg.*) causa, motivo. 5 (*trasp. mar.*) fondo (*del mare, ecc.*). // ~ **of appeal** (*leg.*) motivo d'appello; **the grounds of a judgment** (*leg.*) la motivazione d'una sentenza; **the ~ of an objection** (*leg.*) il motivo d'un'eccezione; ~ **of suspicion** (*leg.*) causa di sospetto.

ground[2], *v. t.* 1 fondare, motivare. 2 (*trasp. aer.*) costringere all'atterraggio. 3 (*trasp. mar.*) incagliare, fare arenare. *v. i.* (*trasp. mar.*) incagliarsi, arenarsi.

groundage, *n.* (*trasp. mar.*) diritto di porto, diritto portuale, diritto d'ancoraggio.

groundless, *a.* infondato, ingiustificato. // ~ **objection** (*leg.*) eccezione infondata.

group, *n.* gruppo. // ~ **insurance** (*ass.*) assicurazione collettiva, assicurazione popolare; ~ **interview** (*market., pubbl.*) intervista di gruppo; ~ **work** (*pers.*) lavoro di gruppo.

grow, *v. i.* (*pass.* **grew**, *part. pass.* **grown**) 1 crescere, aumentare. 2 svilupparsi, progredire. *v. t.* 1 far crescere. 2 produrre. // to ~ **old** invecchiare.

grower, *n.* produttore.

growing, *a.* crescente, in aumento. *n.* produzione. // **the ~ interpenetration of the Member States' economies** (*econ.*) la sempre maggiore interpenetrazione delle economie degli Stati Membri; ~ **reserves** (*fin., rag.*) riserve in aumento.

growth, *n.* 1 crescita, accrescimento, aumento, incremento. 2 sviluppo. 3 produzione. 4 (*econ.*) espansione economica. // ~ **area** (*econ.*) area di sviluppo; ~ **company** (*fin.*) società in via di sviluppo; ~ **fund** (*fin.*) fondo (d'investimento) di sviluppo; ~ **in value** (*fin.*) incremento in valore; ~ **of productivity** (*econ.*) incremento produttivo; ~ **rate** (*econ., fin.*) tasso di sviluppo, tasso d'incremento, incremento; ~ **stock** (*fin.*) titolo d'azienda in espansione.

guarantee[1], *n.* 1 garanzia. 2 (*cred., fin.*) avallo, malleveadoria, cauzione, sicurtà. 3 (*cred., fin.*) avallante. 4 (*leg.*) garanzia. 5 (*leg.*) garante. // ~ **commission** (*fin.*) del credere; ~ **fund** (*fin.*) fondo di garanzia, fondo di cauzione; ~ **of payment** (*cred.*) garanzia di pagamento; ~ **of quality** (*market.*) garanzia di qualità.

guarantee[2], *v. t.* 1 garantire. 2 (*cred., fin.*) avallare, far da mallevadore a (*q.*), farsi mallevadore di (*q.*). 3 (*leg.*) garantire. // to ~ **a bill** (*cred.*) avallare una cambiale; to ~ **an endorsement** (*cred.*) avallare una girata.

guaranteed, *a.* 1 garantito. 2 (*cred., fin.*) avallato. 3 (*leg.*) garantito. // ~ **annual wage** (*pers.*) retribuzione annuale garantita; ~ **bond** (*fin.*) obbligazione garantita; ~ **rate** (*pers.*) paga (minima) garantita (*indipendentemente dalla quantità prodotta*); ~ **stock** (*fin.*) azioni a dividendo garantito.

guarantor, *n.* 1 (*cred., fin.*) avallante. 2 (*leg.*) garante. // **the ~ of a bill of exchange** l'avallante di una cambiale.

guaranty, *n. V.* **guarantee[1].**

guard[1], *n.* 1 guardia, custodia. 2 (*pers.*) guardiano, custode, sorvegliante. 3 (*trasp. ferr.*) conduttore, controllore, capotreno.

guard[2], *v. t.* custodire, fare la guardia a (*q. o qc.*).

guardian, *n.* (*leg.*) tutore. *a. attr.* (*leg.*) tutelare.

guardianship, *n.* (*leg.*) tutela, curatela (*di un minore*).

guardrail, *n.* (*trasp. aut.*) «guardrail».

guardsman, *n.* (*pl.* **guardsmen**) guardia.

guest, *n.* 1 (*market.*) cliente, consumatore. 2 (*tur.*) cliente. // ~ **currencies** (*fin.*) valute ospiti.

guidance, *n.* guida, direzione, orientamento.

guide[1], *n.* 1 guida, orientamento, regola. 2 (*pers., tur.*) guida. // ~ **board** (*trasp.*) cartello segnaletico (*stradale*); ~ **-book** guida (*libro*); ~ **price** (*market.*) prezzo d'orientamento.

guide², *v. t.* guidare, regolare, orientare.

guideline, *n.* linea direttrice, orientamento.

guidepost, *n.* (*trasp.*) indicatore stradale.

guild, *n.* **1** (*fin.*) corporazione, associazione (*d'arti e mestieri*). **2** (*fin.*) associazione (*di mutuo soccorso, ecc.*). **3** (*fin.*) consorzio.

guilder, *n.* fiorino (*olandese*).

guilt, *n.* (*leg.*) colpa, colpevolezza.

guilty, *a.* (*leg.*) colpevole. // **a verdict of «~»** (*leg.*) un verdetto di colpevolezza; **a verdict of «not~»** (*leg.*) un verdetto d'innocenza.

guinea, *n.* (*ingl.*) ghinea (*moneta di conto pari a 21 scellini, non più in corso, ma usata per onorari, per certi articoli di lusso, ecc.*).

gum, *n.* (*pubbl.*) colla (*per manifesti*).

H

habeas corpus, *n.* (*leg.*) mandato di comparizione (*dell'arrestato*) davanti al magistrato (*che decide della legalità dell'arresto*).

haberdasher, *n.* merciaio; confezionista.

habit, *n.* abitudine.

haggle[1], *n.* **1** litigio. **2** (*market.*) mercanteggiamento.

haggle[2], *v. t.* e *i.* **1** litigare. **2** (*market.*) mercanteggiare, contrattare.

haggling, *n.* mercanteggiamento, contrattazione.

hail, *n.* grandine. // ~ **insurance** (*ass.*) assicurazione contro la grandine; ~ **storms** (*ass.*) grandine.

hair, *n. collett.* **1** capelli, capigliatura, chioma. **2** capello, pelo.

half, *n.* (*pl.* **halves**) **1** metà, mezzo. **2** (*USA*) mezzo dollaro, cinquanta centesimi di dollaro, moneta da mezzo dollaro. **3** (*trasp. ferr.*) biglietto a metà prezzo. *a.* mezzo, semi-. // to ~ **-adjust** (*elab. elettr.*) arrotondare; ~ **-and-** ~ mezz'e mezzo; ~ **-and-** ~ **policy** (*amm.*) politica del compromesso; ~ **brother** (*leg.*) fratellastro; ~ **a C** (*slang USA*) banconota da cinquanta dollari; ~ **-commission** (*Borsa*) mezza commissione, mezza provvigione (*compenso generalmente spettante al remissore*); ~ **-commission man** (*Borsa*) remissore (*procacciatore d'ordini a un agente di cambio*); ~ **-dollar** (*USA*) mezzo dollaro, moneta da mezzo dollaro, cinquanta centesimi di dollaro; ~ **fare** (*trasp.*) tariffa dimezzata, tariffa ridotta; ~ **-fare ticket** (*trasp.*) biglietto a tariffa ridotta; ~ **-holiday** (*pers., sind.*) mezza festa; ~ **per cent** mezzo per cento; ~ **a pound** mezza libbra; ~ **(-)price** a metà prezzo; ~ **showing** (*pubbl.*) affissione di media intensità; ~ **year** semestre; ~ **-yearly** semestrale, semestralmente; ~ **-yearly** (*o* ~ **year's) dividend** (*fin.*) dividendo semestrale; **at** ~ **price** (*market.*) a metà prezzo; **on** ~ **pay** (*pers.*) a mezza paga.

halftone, *n.* (*pubbl.*) illustrazione a mezza tinta. *a. attr.* (*pubbl.*) a mezza tinta. // ~ **block** (*pubbl.*) cliché a mezza tinta.

hall, *n.* **1** sala, salone. **2** ingresso (*il locale*).

hallmark[1], *n.* **1** (*market., pubbl.*) marchio di garanzia sull'oro e sull'argento. **2** (*market., pubbl.*) marchio (*di garanzia, d'origine, ecc. su un prodotto*). **3** (*market., pubbl., ingl.*) marchio ufficiale di garanzia sull'oro e sull'argento.

hallmark[2], *v. t.* (*market., pubbl.*) marchiare, marcare.

halt[1], *n.* **1** arresto, fermata. **2** (*trasp. ferr.*) fermata.

halt[2], *v. t.* arrestare, fermare. *v. i.* arrestarsi, fermarsi.

halve, *v. t.* dividere per metà.

hammer[1], *n.* martello, mazzuolo (*anche di banditore d'asta*).

hammer[2], *v. t.* e *i.* **1** martellare (*anche fig.*), picchiare con il martello. **2** (*Borsa, ingl.*) estromettere, espellere (*un agente di cambio o un «jobber»*) per indegnità professionale o per debiti insoluti.

hand[1], *n.* **1** mano. **2** (*leg.*) firma. **3** (*pers.*) operaio. // ~ **baggage** (*trasp., USA*) bagaglio a mano; ~ **labour** (*pers.*) lavoro (fatto) a mano, lavoro manuale; ~ **luggage** (*trasp.*) bagaglio a mano; ~ **-me-down** (*market.*) bell'e fatto; (*d'indumento*) di seconda mano; abito bell'e fatto; abito di seconda mano; ~ **money** caparra; ~ **-to-mouth** alla giornata, precario; ~ **-to-mouth finances** (*fin.*) finanze precarie; **in** ~ per le mani, fra mano, intrapreso; in serbo, in riserva; **on** ~ (*market.: di merce*) esistente, a disposizione, disponibile.

hand[2], *v. t.* **1** dare. **2** consegnare, rimettere. **3** passare. // to ~ **down** (*leg.*) annunciare (*un verdetto, ecc.*); to ~ **in** dare, presentare, rassegnare; to ~ **in one's notice** (*pers.*) licenziarsi; to ~ **in one's resignation** (*pers.*) dare le dimissioni, rassegnare le dimissioni; to ~ **over to sb.** (*pers.*) dare le consegne a q.; to ~ **over** (*o* **on**) **st. to sb.** consegnare, passare qc. a q.; to ~ **sb. over to justice** (*leg.*) deferire q. alla giustizia (*o* in giudizio).

handbill, *n.* (*pubbl.*) volantino, foglietto pubblicitario, pieghevole, manifestino (*distribuito a mano*).

handbook, *n.* (*attr. uff.*) manuale, annuario, prontuario.

handcar, *n.* (*trasp. ferr., USA*) carrello di servizio.

handicap[1], *n.* ostacolo.

handicap[2], *v. t.* mettere in condizione d'inferiorità, ostacolare.

handicraft, *n.* 1 (*econ.*) mestiere (*manuale*). 2 (*econ.*) artigianato. // ~ **products** (*econ.*) *V.* **handicrafts.**

handicrafts, *n. pl.* (*econ.*) prodotti fabbricati a mano, prodotti dell'artigianato.

handicraftsman, *n.* (*pl.* **handicraftsmen**) (*pers.*) artigiano.

handle, *v. t.* 1 maneggiare, manipolare, toccare. 2 trattare (*q.*). 3 fare affari con (*q.*). 4 occuparsi di (*qc.*). 5 (*market.*) trattare (*un articolo, ecc.*), commerciare in (*qc.*). 6 (*trasp. mar.*) manovrare. // to ~ **a ship** (*trasp. mar.*) manovrare una nave.

handling, *n.* 1 manipolazione, maneggio, trattamento. 2 (*org. az.*) trasporti interni. 3 (*trasp. mar.*) manovra. // ~ **charges** (*rag.*) spese di manutenzione; ~ **costs** (*org. az., rag.*) spese di trasporto interno.

handmade, *a.* (*market.*) fatto a mano, fabbricato a mano, lavorato a mano.

handout, *n.* (*giorn., pubbl.*) comunicato, comunicato stampa.

hands, *n. pl.* 1 (*pers.*) mano d'opera, maestranze. 2 (*trasp. mar.*) equipaggio, ciurma.

handsel, *n.* caparra.

handsome, *a.* 1 bello, avvenente. 2 considerevole, grande. // **a** ~ **fortune** un bel (*o* un gran) patrimonio; **a** ~ **price** (*market.*) un bel prezzo, un prezzo alto.

handwork, *n.* 1 lavorazione a mano. 2 (*market.*) lavoro (eseguito) a mano, manufatto. 3 (*pers.*) lavoro (fatto) a mano, lavoro manuale.

handwrite, *v. t.* (*pass.* **handwrote,** *part. pass.* **handwritten**) scrivere a mano.

handwriting, *n.* 1 scrittura, grafia. 2 manoscritto.

handwritten, *a.* manoscritto.

handyman, *n.* (*pl.* **handymen**) factotum.

hangar, *n.* (*trasp. aer.*) aviorimessa, hangar.

happen, *v. i.* accadere.

happening, *n.* evento.

happily, *avv.* felicemente.

happy, *a.* felice.

harbor, *n.* (*USA*) *V.* **harbour.**

harbour, *n.* (*trasp. mar.*) porto. // ~ **authorities** (*trasp. mar.*) autorità portuali; ~ **basin** (*trasp. mar.*) bacino del porto, bacino portuale; ~ **channel** (*trasp. mar.*) canale del porto, canale portuale; ~ **dues** (*trasp. mar.*) diritti portuali; ~ **entrance** (*trasp. mar.*) bocca del porto, imboccatura del porto; ~ **equipment** (*trasp. mar.*) attrezzature portuali; ~ **fees** (*trasp. mar.*) diritti portuali; ~ **master** (*trasp. mar.*) capitano di porto; ~ **of refuge** (*trasp. mar.*) porto di rifugio, porto di rilascio forzato; ~ **office** (*trasp. mar.*) capitaneria di porto; ~ **service** (*trasp. mar.*) servizio di porto, servizio portuale; ~ **works** (*trasp. mar.*) opere portuali, opere portuarie.

hard, *a.* 1 fermo, rigido, saldo. 2 faticoso, oneroso. 3 (*fin.: di una moneta*) forte; sostenuto. *avv.* fortemente, intensamente, forte. // ~**-and-fast** rigido; **a** ~ **bargain** un affare a condizioni inique, un affare a condizioni poco vantaggiose; ~ **cash** denaro in contanti, moneta metallica; ~ **core** nucleo duro (*o* resistente); «~ **-core**» **tariffs** (*dog., econ.*) tariffe «dure», tariffe «irriducibili», tariffe di più difficile riduzione (*o* abolizione); ~ **currency** (*econ.*) moneta solida, moneta forte, valuta forte; **a** ~ **customer** (*market.*) un cliente difficile; ~ **goods** (*market.*) merci d'uso durevole; **a** ~ **job** (*pers.*) un lavoro duro, un lavoro gravoso; ~ **merchandise** (*market.*) merce durevole; ~ **money** (*USA*) denaro metallico; ~ **prices** (*market.*) prezzi alti; ~ **sell** (*market.*) tecnica di vendita basata sull'insistenza nell'offerta della merce; metodo «duro» di vendita; ~ **to sell** (*market.*) difficile a collocarsi.

harden, *v. t.* irrigidire, rassodare, rafforzare. *v. i.* indurirsi, irrigidirsi, rassodarsi, rafforzarsi.

hardware, *n. collett.* (*market.*) articoli di ferro.

harm[1], *n.* danno.

harm[2], *v. t.* danneggiare.

harmful, *a.* dannoso.

harmonized, *a.* armonizzato. // ~ **statistics** (*stat.*) statistiche armonizzate.

harsh, *a.* aspro.

hat, *n.* cappello. // ~ **money** (*trasp. mar.*) cappa, diritto di cappa.

hatch, *n.* (*trasp. mar.*) boccaporto. // **under hatches** (*trasp. mar.*) sotto coperta.

hatchway, *n.* (*trasp. mar.*) boccaporto.

haul[1], *n.* 1 il tirare, il trascinare. 2 (*trasp.*) distanza percorsa (*da un carico*). 3 (*trasp.*) quantità di merce trasportata.

haul[2], *v. t.* 1 tirare, trascinare. 2 trainare. 3 (*trasp. mar.*) alare. 4 (*trasp. mar.*) far cambiar rotta a (*una nave*).

haulage, *n.* 1 (*trasp.*) trasporto, convogliamento. 2 (*trasp. mar.*) alaggio. 3 (*trasp. mar.*) prezzo del trasporto. // ~ **contractor** (*trasp.*)

trasportatore; ~ **trade** (*trasp.*) trasporto delle merci.

hauler, *n.* (*USA*) *V.* **haulier.**

haulier, *n.* (*trasp.*) chi fa trasporti, trasportatore, vettore.

have, *v. t.* (*pass.* e *part. pass.* **had**) **1** avere, possedere. **2** ottenere, ricevere. **3** avere da, dovere. **4** (*seguito da un complemento oggetto e da un part. pass.*) fare. // to ~ **authority over sb.** avere autorità su q.; to ~ **a balance of payments surplus** (*fin.*) trovarsi con una bilancia dei pagamenti favorevoli; to ~ **a bill discounted** (*banca*) farsi scontare una cambiale; to ~ **a bill protested** (*leg.*) far protestare una cambiale; to ~ **a charge on the personal property of a debtor** (*leg.*) avere un privilegio sui beni d'un debitore; to ~ **a holiday** (*pers.*) far vacanza; to ~ **important economic implications** (*econ.*) avere notevole incidenza economica; to ~ **in stock** (*market.*) disporre di (*merce, ecc.*); to ~ **an interest (o a share) in a concern (a firm, etc.)** essere interessato in un'azienda (una ditta, ecc.); to ~ **a letter translated** far tradurre una lettera; to ~ **money in the bank** avere denaro in banca; to ~ **a right of access to a document** (*leg.*) avere il diritto di prendere visione di un documento; to ~ **a talk with sb.** avere un colloquio con q.; to ~ **a tonnage of** (*trasp. mar.*) (*di nave*) stazzare.

haven[1], *n.* **1** (*fig.*) asilo. **2** (*trasp. mar.*) ancoraggio, rada.

haven[2], *v. i.* (*trasp. mar.*) rifugiarsi in un porto.

hawk, *v. t.* vendere (*merce*) di casa in casa, vendere (*merce*) per la strada.

hawker, *n.* venditore ambulante, ambulante.

hawking, *n.* (*market.*) commercio ambulante, ambulantato.

hawser, *n.* (*trasp. mar.*) gomena, cavo d'ormeggio.

hazard, *n.* pericolo, rischio.

hazardous, *a.* azzardato, pericoloso, rischioso. // ~ **activity** (*pers.*) attività pericolosa; ~ **occupation** (*pers.*) occupazione pericolosa; ~ **speculation** (*fin.*) speculazione azzardata.

head[1], *n.* **1** capo, testa. **2** capo. **3** (*trasp. mar.*) prora. *a. attr.* principale, primo. // ~ **clerk** (*pers.*) capo ufficio; ~ **money** quota individuale; (*fin.*) imposta personale; **the ~ of a family** il capo d'una famiglia, il capofamiglia; **the ~ of planning** (*pers.*) il responsabile della pianificazione; **the ~ of research** (*pers.*) il responsabile della ricerca; ~ **office** (*org. az.*) ufficio principale, centro direttivo, centrale; sede principale; ~ **office manager** (*pers.*) direttore di sede; ~ **tax** (*fin.*) imposta personale.

head[2], *v. t.* **1** capeggiare, capitanare, guidare. **2** intestare, intitolare. *v. i.* **1** dirigersi. **2** (*trasp. mar.*) fare rotta per.

headache, *n.* mal di testa, mal di capo.

headacher, *n.* (*pers., slang USA*) direttore.

headed, *a.* intestato, intitolato. // ~ **letter-paper** (*attr. uff.*) carta da lettere intestata.

header card, *n.* (*elab. elettr.*) scheda principale.

heading, *n.* **1** titolo, voce. **2** (*rag.*) intitolazione (*di un conto*). // ~ **for the settlement** (*Borsa*) arbitraggio a termine; **the ~ of a business letter** l'intestazione d'una lettera commerciale.

headline, *n.* (*giorn.*) titolo.

headphone, *n.* (*attr. uff.*) ricevitore telefonico.

headquarters, *n. pl.* (*spesso col verbo al sing.*) (*org. az.*) centro amministrativo (*o* direttivo) d'un'impresa, centrale, sede principale degli affari.

health, *n.* sanità. // ~ **and welfare plan** (*pers., sind.*) sistema previdenziale; ~ **certificate** (*pers.*) certificato medico; ~ **inspection** controllo sanitario; ~ **insurance** (*ass., sind.*) assicurazione contro le malattie; ~ **insurance association** (*pers.*) mutua (*per l'assistenza medica*); ~ **-officer** ufficiale sanitario.

healthy, *a.* sano, che gode buona salute. // **a ~ economy** (*econ.*) un'economia sana.

heap, *n.* cumulo.

hear, *v. t.* (*pass.* e *part. pass.* **heard**) **1** udire. **2** apprendere, ricevere (*una notizia*). **3** (*leg.*) ascoltare, giudicare, esaminare. *v. i.* ricevere notizie (*da q.*). // to ~ **both cases** (*leg.*) udire entrambe le parti (*in giudizio*); to ~ **a case** (*leg.*) discutere una causa, giudicare una causa; to ~ **the evidence** (*leg.*) ascoltare le testimonianze; to ~ **the witnesses** (*leg.*) udire i testimoni.

hearing, *n.* **1** ascolto, udienza. **2** (*leg.*) udienza. // ~ **in Chambers** (*leg.*) udienza a porte chiuse; ~ **in open Court** (*leg.*) udienza a porte aperte.

hearsay, *n.* sentito dire, diceria, pettegolezzo, voce. // ~ **evidence** (*leg.*) testimonianza fondata su dicerie.

hearty, *a.* cordiale.

heat[1], *n.* riscaldamento. // ~ **-proof** (*market.*) resistente al calore; ~ **-resisting** (*market.*) *V.* ~ **-proof.**

heat[2], *v. t.* scaldare. *v. i.* riscaldarsi, scaldarsi.

heavily, *a.* pesantemente. // ~ **mortgaged** (*leg.*) gravato da ipoteche.

heavy, *a.* (*fin.*) caratterizzato dalla diminuzione dei prezzi. // **a ~ buyer** (*market.*) un grosso acquirente; **~ expenses** forti spese; **~ goods** (*market.*) merci pesanti; **~ industry** (*econ.*) industria pesante; **~ sea** (*trasp. mar.*) mare grosso; **~ stocks** (*fin.*) titoli «pesanti»; **~ traffic** traffico pesante, traffico intenso; **~ work** (*pers.*) un lavoro pesante, un lavoro gravoso.

hectare (ha), *n.* ettaro.

hectogram, *n.* *V.* **hectogramme.**

hectogramme (hg), *n.* ettogrammo.

hectoliter, *n.* *V.* **hectolitre.**

hectolitre (hl), *n.* ettolitro.

hectometer, *n.* *V.* **hectometre.**

hectometre (hm), *n.* ettometro.

hedge[1], *n.* **1** siepe. **2** (*fig.*) barriera, protezione. **3** (*fin.*) copertura (*dai rischi di perdite finanziarie*). **4** (*fin.*) acquisto effettuato non per ricavarne principalmente un profitto ma per proteggersi da un certo rischio (*o* da fluttuazioni di mercato). // **~ contract** (*Borsa*) contratto a termine; **~ funds** (*Borsa, fin.*) fondi di copertura, fondi di protezione.

hedge[2], *v. t.* (*fin.*) coprirsi da, mettersi al riparo da (*rischi di perdite finanziarie*). *v. i.* (*fin.*) proteggersi finanziariamente. // **to ~ against loss due to price fluctuations** (*fin.*) proteggersi dalle perdite derivanti da oscillazioni nei prezzi.

hedging, *n.* (*Borsa, fin.*) copertura, riporto staccato.

hedonistic, *a.* edonistico.

height, *n.* altezza.

heir, *n.* (*leg.*) erede (*maschio*). // **heirs and assignees** (*leg.*) eredi e aventi diritto; **~ apparent** (*leg.*) erede legittimo; **~ -at-law** (*leg.*) erede legittimo; **~ general** (*leg.*) erede legittimo; **~ presumptive** (*leg.*) presunto erede.

heiress, *n.* (*leg.*) erede (*donna*), ereditiera.

heirless, *a.* (*leg.*) privo d'eredi.

heliport, *n.* (*trasp. aer.*) eliporto.

helm, *n.* (*trasp. mar.*) timone.

help[1], *n.* **1** aiuto, assistenza. **2** (*pers.*) impiegato, operaio. // **~ -wanted column** (*giorn.*) «offerte di lavoro».

help[2], *v. t.* aiutare, assistere. // **to ~ industrial development** (*econ.*) favorire lo sviluppo industriale.

hereby, *avv.* (*leg.*) con il presente (*atto, documento, ecc.*), con la presente (*scrittura, dichiarazione, ecc.*); per mezzo di ciò.

hereditable, *a.* (*leg.*) ereditabile, ereditario. *n.* (*leg.*) bene d'asse ereditario.

hereditament, *n.* (*leg.*) eredità, beni mobili trasmissibili per eredità, massa ereditaria.

hereditary, *a.* (*leg.*) ereditario. // **~ rights** (*leg.*) diritti ereditari; **~ succession** (*leg.*) successione ereditaria.

herein, *avv.* (*leg.*) qui. // **~ enclosed** qui accluso.

hereinabove, *avv.* (*leg.*) sopra, in precedenza.

hereinafter, *avv.* (*leg.*) sotto, in seguito. // **as ~ specified** (*leg.*) come (è) specificato più avanti.

hereinbefore, *avv.* (*leg.*) sopra, in precedenza.

hereinbelow, *avv.* (*leg.*) sotto.

hereunder, *avv.* **1** (*leg.*) sotto. **2** (*leg.*) in virtù del presente (*atto, documento, ecc.*).

herewith, *avv.* qui. // **~ enclosed** qui accluso.

heritable, *a.* (*leg.*) ereditabile, ereditario.

heritage, *n.* (*leg.*) eredità, asse ereditario, patrimonio derivante da eredità.

hesitate, *v. t.* esitare.

hesitation, *n.* esitazione.

hidden, *a.* occulto, celato, riposto. // **~ assets** (*rag.*) attività occulte; **~ capital movements** (*econ.*) movimenti occulti di capitali; **~ defect** (*leg.*) vizio occulto; **~ persuaders** (*pubbl.*) persuasori occulti; **~ reserve** (*rag.*) riserva occulta; **~ tax** (*fin.*) imposta indiretta; **~ unemployment** (*econ., sind.*) disoccupazione occulta.

hide, *v. t.* (*pass.* **hid**, *part. pass.* **hidden**) occultare.

hiding, *n.* (*leg.*) occultamento.

hierarchic, *a.* *V.* **hierarchical.**

hierarchical, *a.* gerarchico. // **~ structure** (*org. az.*) struttura gerarchica.

hierarchy, *n.* (*org. az.*) gerarchia.

higgle, *v. i.* (*market.*) mercanteggiare, tirare sul prezzo.

higgling, *n.* (*market.*) mercanteggiamento.

high, *a.* **1** alto, elevato. **2** (*Borsa, fin.*) massimo. **3** (*market.*) costoso, caro. *n.* (*Borsa, fin.*) prezzo massimo, quotazione massima, (il) massimo. *avv.* (*anche fig.*) in alto, in alto grado. // **highs and lows** (*Borsa, fin.*) massimi e minimi, prezzi massimi e minimi, quotazioni massime e minime; **~ -class** (*market.*) di prim'ordine; **~ -class goods** (*market.*) merce di prim'ordine; **~ cost of living** carovita, caroviveri; **~ Court of Justice** (*leg.*) Alta Corte di Giustizia; **a ~ debit level** (*fin.*) un livello d'indebitamento assai elevato; **a ~ deficit** (*fin., rag.*) un forte disavanzo; **~ -duty articles** (*dog., fin.*) articoli pesantemente tassati; **~ farming**

(*econ.*) agricoltura intensiva; ~ **finance** (*fin.*) alta finanza; ~ **-grade** (*market.*) di qualità superiore; ~ **-grade securities** (*fin.*) titoli di prim'ordine; ~ **ground** altura; ~ **-level conference** conferenza ad alto livello, «vertice»; ~ **-level staff** (*pers.*) personale ad alto livello; ~ **-leverage trust** (*fin., USA*) fondo (d'investimento) con forte indebitamento; ~ **price** (*fin., market.*) alto prezzo; **the** ~ **seas** (*trasp. mar.*) l'alto mare, il mare aperto, le acque extraterritoriali; ~ **-tax Country** (*fin.*) Paese soggetto a forte pressione fiscale; ~ **-technology industries** (*econ.*) industrie a tecnologia avanzata; ~ **wages** (*pers.*) salari elevati; ~ **water** (*trasp. mar.*) acqua alta, alta marea; **higher bid** rilancio, maggiore offerta (a un'asta); **higher education** istruzione superiore; **higher mathematics** (*mat.*) matematica superiore; **the highest bidder** l'aggiudicatario.

highflier, *n. V.* **highflyer.**

highflyer, *n.* (*Borsa*) titolo «che va forte».

highlight[1], *n.* momento di maggior interesse.

highlight[2], *v. t.* (*giorn.*) mettere in evidenza.

highly, *avv.* altamente, estremamente, molto, assai. // ~ **geared trust** (*fin.*) fondo (*d'investimento*) con forte indebitamento; ~ **industrialized Countries** (*econ.*) Paesi altamente industrializzati.

highway, *n.* (*trasp. aut.*) strada statale, statale. // **the** ~ **Code** il Codice della strada.

hijack, *v. t.* (*leg., trasp.*) dirottare.

hijacker, *n.* (*leg., trasp.*) dirottatore.

hijacking, *n.* (*leg., trasp.*) dirottamento.

hint[1], *n.* accenno.

hint[2], *v. i.* accennare.

hire[1], *n.* 1 (*leg.*) nolo, noleggio. 2 (*pers.*) assunzione. 3 (*pers.*) impiego. 4 (*pers.*) salario. // ~ **purchase** (*market.*) vendita a rate; ~ **-purchase system** (*market.*) sistema delle vendite a rate; ~ **-purchase terms** (*market.*) condizioni di vendita rateale; **for** (*o* **on**) ~ (*market.*) da nolo; (*pers.*) che si può assumere, disponibile; **for** ~ **or reward** (*market.*) per conto terzi.

hire[2], *v. t.* 1 (*leg.*) noleggiare; prendere a nolo, dare a nolo. 2 (*pers.*) assumere. // to ~ **out** (*leg.*) noleggiare, dare a nolo; to ~ **st. out on tender** (*leg.*) dare qc. in appalto.

hired, *a.* 1 (*leg.*) noleggiato; preso a nolo, preso in affitto; dato a nolo, affittato. 2 (*pers.*) assunto. // ~ **person** (*leg., pers.*) prestatore d'opera.

hirer, *n.* (*leg.*) noleggiatore, noleggiante.

hiring, *n.* (*pers.*) assunzione, assunzioni.

historical, *a.* 1 storico. 2 reale. // ~ **cost** (*rag.*) costo reale, costo originario.

hit[1], *n.* 1 colpo, botta, urto. 2 (*market.*) successo, prodotto di grande successo.

hit[2], *v. t.* (*pass.* e *part. pass.* **hit**) 1 colpire (*anche fig.*); battere, urtare contro. 2 azzeccare. // ~ **-and-run driver** (*trasp. aut.*) pirata della strada.

hoard[1], *n.* ammasso, cumulo.

hoard[2], *v. t.* 1 ammassare, accumulare. 2 accaparrare, incettare, fare incetta di, tesaurizzare, tesoreggiare. 3 (*econ.*) tesaurizzare. // to ~ **food** (*econ.*) accaparrare generi alimentari; to ~ **gold** (*econ.*) tesaurizzare oro.

hoarder, *n.* incettatore.

hoarding, *n.* 1 accaparramento, incetta. 2 (*econ.*) tesaurizzazione, tesoreggiamento.

hoist a flag, *locuz. v.* (*trasp. mar.*) alzare una bandiera.

hold[1], *n.* (*trasp. mar.*) stiva.

hold[2], *v. t.* (*pass.* e *part. pass.* **held**) 1 tenere. 2 trattenere, mantenere. 3 possedere, avere. 4 detenere, occupare. *v. i.* resistere, reggere, «tenere». // to ~ **back** trattenere; to ~ **a brief for sb.** (*leg.*) patrocinare q.; to ~ **down** (*fig.*) tenere a freno, frenare; to ~ **down consumption** (*econ.*) deprimere i consumi; to ~ **down the prices-wages spiral** (*econ.*) frenare la spirale dei prezzi e dei salari; to ~ **down rates** (*fin.*) mantenere un livello di tassi basso; to ~ **in custody** (*leg.*) tenere in custodia; to ~ **land** possedere terreni; to ~ **the line** (*comun.*) restare in linea; (*econ.*) contenere i prezzi entro un certo limite; to ~ **office** (*amm.*) essere in carica; to ~ **out** tener duro, resistere; to ~ **st. over** mettere da parte, accantonare qc.; to ~ **several offices** (*pers.*) cumulare diversi uffici; to ~ **shares in a business enterprise** (*fin.*) possedere azioni d'una società commerciale; to ~ **sb. to bail** (*leg.*) vincolare q. col versamento d'una cauzione; to ~ **up** assaltare, rapinare; (*Borsa, fin.*) «tenere», difendersi bene.

holdback, *n.* 1 impedimento, ostacolo. 2 (*pers.*) trattenuta. // ~ **pay** (*pers.*) trattenuta.

holder, *n.* 1 possessore. 2 (*cred., fin.*) detentore, portatore, titolare, tenutario, tenitore. // ~ **in due course** (*leg.*) possessore di buona fede (*d'un titolo di credito*); **the** ~ **of an account** (*rag.*) il titolare d'un conto; **the** ~ **of a bill of exchange** (*cred.*) il portatore d'una cambiale; ~ **of a current account** (*banca, cred.*) correntista; ~ **of a diploma** diplomato.

holding, *n.* 1 proprietà, bene. 2 (*fin.*) società controllata (*da una «holding company» q. V.*). 3 (*rag.*) portafoglio; azioni, titoli. 4 **holdings,** *pl.* (*fin.*) partecipazioni. // ~ **commission** (*banca*) commissione richiesta per la presa in consegna della merce; ~ **company** (*fin.*) (società) finanziaria, società controllante, società di portafoglio, (società) holding, gruppo finanziario di controllo; società capogruppo (*che possiede titoli d'un'altra, generalm. sotto forma di partecipazioni di controllo*); ~ **company stocks** (*Borsa*) finanziari.

hold-up, *n.* assalto, rapina.

hole, *n.* foro.

holiday, *n.* 1 festa, vacanza, giorno festivo. 2 **holidays,** *pl.* (*pers.*) ferie, vacanze. // ~ **camp** (*pers.*) colonia (*per i dipendenti e/o i loro familiari*); **holidays with pay** (*pers.*) ferie pagate, vacanze retribuite.

holograph, *n.* (*leg.*) olografo; documento olografo, testamento olografo. *a.* (*leg.*) olografo.

holographic, *a.* (*leg.*) olografo. // ~ **will** (*o* **testament**) (*leg.*) testamento olografo.

holographical, *a. V.* **holographic.**

home, *n.* 1 casa (*dove si abita*); casa (natale). 2 (*org. az.*) sede, sede principale. *a. attr.* 1 domestico, familiare. 2 nazionale, interno, nostrano. // ~ **affairs** affari interni; ~ **consumption** (*econ.*) consumo interno; ~ **currency** (*fin.*) moneta nazionale, valuta nazionale; ~ **delivery** (*market.*) consegna a domicilio; ~ **-grown** (*market.*) nostrano; ~ **manufacturing** (*org. az.*) lavoro a domicilio; ~ **market** (*econ.*) mercato nazionale, mercato interno; ~ **office** (*org. az.*) sede principale (*degli affari*); ~ **Office** (*ingl.*) Ministero dell'Interno; ~ **port** (*trasp. mar.*) porto d'origine, porto di registrazione (*d'una nave*), porto d'armamento; ~ **-produced goods** (*comm. est., market.*) prodotti nazionali; ~ **producers** (*comm. est., market.*) produttori nazionali; ~ **products** (*comm. est., market.*) prodotti nazionali; ~ **Secretary** (*ingl.*) Ministro dell'Interno; ~ **securities** (*fin.*) titoli nazionali; ~ **stocks** (*fin.*) titoli nazionali; ~ **trade** commercio interno, commercio nazionale; ~ **-trade bill** (*cred.*) cambiale per l'interno; ~ **-use entry** (*dog., ingl.*) dichiarazione per merci soggette a diritti doganali; **at** ~ a casa; (*market.*) sul mercato interno.

homemade, *a.* (*market.*) per uso domestico.

homestead, *n.* casa colonica, fattoria.

homesteader, *n.* agricoltore, proprietario di fattoria.

homeward, *a. attr.* e *avv.* 1 verso la patria. 2 (*trasp. mar.*) di ritorno. // ~ **bill of lading** (*trasp. mar.*) polizza di carico per il viaggio di ritorno; ~ **-bound** (*trasp. mar.*) diretto in patria; ~ **-bound ship** (*trasp. mar.*) nave «verso casa» (*in viaggio di ritorno*); ~ **cargo** (*trasp. mar.*) carico di ritorno; ~ **journey** (*trasp. mar.*) viaggio di ritorno; ~ **passage** (*trasp. mar.*) viaggio di ritorno.

homewards, *avv. V.* **homeward.**

homework, *n.* (*org. az.*) lavoro a domicilio.

homologate, *v. t.* (*leg.*) omologare.

homologation, *n.* (*leg.*) omologazione.

honest, *a.* onesto. // ~ **profits** guadagni onesti; ~ **weight** (*market.*) peso onesto, peso giusto.

honestly, *avv.* onestamente, sinceramente.

honesty, *n.* onestà.

honor, *n. V.* **honour.**

honorarium, *n.* (*pl.* **honoraria** e *reg.*) (*leg.*) onorario, compenso, emolumento, parcella.

honorary, *a.* onorario, onorifico. // ~ **member** socio onorario; ~ **office** carica onorifica; ~ **president** presidente onorario.

honour[1], *n.* onore. // **for** ~ **supra protest** (*banca, cred.*) per intervento.

honour[2], *v. t.* 1 onorare, fare onore a. 2 (*comm.*) onorare, fare onore a; accettare; pagare. // to ~ **a bill of exchange** (*cred.*) onorare una cambiale.

hood, *n.* (*USA*) cofano (*d'automobile*).

hopeful, *a.* fiducioso.

horizontal, *a.* orizzontale. // ~ **agreements** (*comm. est.*) accordi orizzontali, intese orizzontali; ~ **combination** (*econ., fin.*) concentrazione (*o* integrazione) orizzontale; ~ **coordination** (*org. az.*) coordinamento orizzontale; ~ **expansion** (*org. az.*) espansione orizzontale; ~ **integration** (*org. az.*) integrazione orizzontale; **a** ~ **merger** (*econ.*) una fusione orizzontale; ~ **organizational structure** (*org. az.*) struttura organizzativa orizzontale; **the** ~ **spread of buying power** (*econ.*) l'espansione globale del potere d'acquisto.

hot, *a.* rovente. // ~ **money** (*fin.*) capitali vaganti, moneta che scotta, «denaro caldo» (*fondi di proprietà straniera depositati o investiti al fine di evitare la svalutazione e soggetti a repentini prelevamenti*).

hotchpot, *n.* (*leg.*) collazione.

hotchpotch, *n. V.* **hotchpot.**

hotel, *n.* albergo. *a. attr.* alberghiero. // ~ **business** (*econ.*) attività alberghiera.

hour, *n.* 1 ora. 2 **hours,** *pl.* ore, orario, orario di lavoro. // **hours lost through strikes** (*econ.*) ore (*di lavoro*) perdute a causa di scioperi.

hourage, *n.* (*sind.*) tempo complessivo di lavoro in ore.

hourly, *a.* orario, d'ogni ora. *avv.* ogni ora. // ~ **output** (*org. az.*) produzione oraria; ~

rate (*pers.*) paga oraria; ~ **-rated** (*pers.*) (*di lavoro*) retribuito a ore.

house[1], *n.* 1 casa, edificio, fondo urbano, immobile. 2 (*comm.*) casa commerciale, ditta. 3 **the House** (*fin.*, *fam.*) la Borsa Valori. // ~ **-agent** agente immobiliare, mediatore di case; ~ **-flag** (*trasp. mar.*) bandiera di una società (*di navigazione*); **the** ~ **of Commons** (*ingl.*) la Camera dei Comuni; **the** ~ **of Lords** (*ingl.*) la Camera dei Lord; **the** ~ **of Representatives** (*USA*) la Camera dei Rappresentanti (*dei deputati*); ~ **organ** (*giorn.*) giornale aziendale, organo aziendale; ~ **phone** telefono interno; ~ **tax** (*fin.*) imposta sui fabbricati; ~ **-to-** ~ di casa in casa; (*market.*) a domicilio: ~ **-to-** ~ **selling** (*market.*) vendita a domicilio; ~ **-to-** ~ **service** servizio a domicilio; « ~ **to let** » (*avviso*) « affittasi », « appigionasi ».

house[2], *v. t.* dare una casa a, alloggiare.

housebreaking, *n.* (*leg.*) violazione di domicilio.

household, *n.* famiglia, casa. // ~ **department** (*market.*) reparto (articoli) casalinghi; ~ **saving** (*econ.*) risparmio familiare.

householder, *n.* padrone di casa, capofamiglia.

housewife, *n.* (*pl.* **housewives**) padrona di casa. // **the** ~ **'s shopping basket** (*econ.*) il paniere dei consumi privati.

housing, *n.* 1 alloggio, casa. 2 (*econ.*, *stat.*) abitazioni. // ~ **costs** (*rag.*) spese di magazzino; **the** ~ **problem** (*econ.*) la crisi degli alloggi; **the** ~ **shortage** (*econ.*) la crisi degli alloggi.

hovercraft, *n.* (*trasp. mar.*) « hovercraft », nave a cuscino d'aria, aeronave.

hoverferry, *n.* (*trasp. mar.*) aeronave-traghetto.

how, *avv.* (*interrogativo*) come.

huge, *a.* ingente.

hull, *n.* (*trasp. mar.*) carena, scafo. // ~ **insurance** (*ass. mar.*) assicurazione sullo scafo (*della nave*), assicurazione sulla nave.

human, *a.* umano. // ~ **capital** (*org. az.*) capitale umano; ~ **relationist** (*pers.*) esperto in relazioni umane; ~ **relations** (*pers.*) relazioni umane.

hundred, *a.* e *n.* cento.

hundredth, *a.* e *n.* centesimo.

hundredweight (cwt.), *n.* 1 (*ingl.*) « hundredweight » (*misura di peso pari a 50,80 kg*). 2 (*USA*) « hundredweight » (*misura di peso pari a 45,36 kg*). // **long** ~ *V.* ~, *def. 1*; **short** ~ *V.* ~, *def. 2*.

hurt, *v. t.* (*pass.* e *part. pass.* **hurt**) ledere.

hurtful, *a.* dannoso.

hygiene, *n.* igiene.

hygienic, *a.* igienico.

hygienical, *a.* igienico.

hyperinflation, *n.* (*fin.*) inflazione inarrestabile, inflazione galoppante, inflazione eccessiva, iperinflazione.

hypermarket, *n.* (*econ.*, *market.*) ipermercato.

hyphen, *n.* (*giorn.*) lineetta (*corta*), trattino d'unione.

hypothec, *n.* (*leg.*: *nel diritto romano*) ipoteca.

hypothecary, *a.* (*leg.*) ipotecario.

hypothecate, *v. t.* (*leg.*) ipotecare (*specialm. nel diritto romano e in quello della navigazione*). // to ~ **stocks** (*Borsa*) dare titoli a cauzione.

hypothecation, *n.* 1 (*Borsa*) dazione di titoli a cauzione. 2 (*leg.*) l'ipotecare, ipoteca.

I

idea, *n.* idea, opinione, proposito. // ~ **man** (*fin., pers.*) «uomo-idea» (*persona dotata d'un'eccezionale capacità d'immaginare e formulare nuove tecniche, nuovi prodotti o soluzioni a problemi*).

idem, *avv.* e *pron.* idem.

identical, *a.* identico.

identity, *n.* 1 identità. 2 (*mat.*) identità. // ~ **card** carta d'identità.

idle[1], *a.* ozioso, inattivo, pigro. // ~ **capitals** (*fin.*) capitali inattivi; ~ **machines** (*org. az.*) macchine inattive; ~ **money** (*fin.*) capitali inattivi; ~ **stocks** (*fin.*) titoli inattivi (*per i quali non c'è richiesta*).

idle[2], *v. i.* oziare, essere ozioso. *v. t.* rendere inattivo.

idleness, *n.* ozio, inazione.

if, *cong.* se. // ~ **duly paid** (*cred.*) salvo buon fine.

ignore, *v. t.* 1 fingere di non conoscere. 2 passare sotto silenzio.

ill, *a.* 1 cattivo. 2 dannoso, nocivo. 3 infermo. *n.* 1 danno. 2 difficoltà, disordine, guaio. // ~ **fame** cattiva fama; ~ **management** (*amm.*) cattiva amministrazione (*degli affari, ecc.*); ~ **repute** cattiva reputazione.

illegal, *a.* (*leg.*) illegale, illecito. // ~ **contract** (*leg.*) contratto illegale; ~ **partnership** (*leg.*) società (costituita) per scopi illeciti; ~ **strike** (*sind.*) sciopero illegale, sciopero «a gatto selvaggio»; ~ **trade** (*leg.*) commercio illecito.

illegality, *n.* (*leg.*) illegalità.

illegalization, *n.* (*leg.*) dichiarazione d'illegalità.

illegalize, *v. t.* (*leg.*) dichiarare illegale.

illegally, *avv.* illegalmente.

illegible, *a.* illeggibile.

illegitimacy, *n.* (*leg.*) illegittimità.

illegitimate[1], *a.* (*leg.*) illegittimo, illecito. *n.* (*leg.*) illegittimo.

illegitimate[2], *v. t.* (*leg.*) dichiarare illegittimo.

illegitimation, *n.* (*leg.*) dichiarazione d'illegittimità.

illicit, *a.* (*leg.*) illecito, illegale. // ~ **consideration** (*leg.*) causa illecita.

illness, *n.* malattia, infermità.

illuminated, *a.* illuminato. // ~ **sign** (*pubbl., ingl.*) insegna luminosa.

illustrate, *v. t.* 1 illustrare. 2 (*giorn., pubbl.*) illustrare. // to ~ **text-books** illustrare libri di testo.

illustrated, *a.* illustrato, arricchito d'illustrazioni, delucidato, spiegato.

illustration, *n.* 1 illustrazione. 2 (*giorn., pubbl.*) illustrazione.

illustrative, *a.* illustrativo. // ~ **material** (*market., pubbl.*) materiale illustrativo.

image, *n.* immagine.

imbalance, *n.* 1 squilibrio. 2 (*econ.*) squilibrio, sbilancio. // ~ **between supply and demand** (*econ.*) squilibrio fra l'offerta e la domanda.

imitate, *v. t.* 1 imitare. 2 (*market.*) imitare.

imitation, *n.* 1 imitazione. 2 (*market.*) imitazione, contraffazione. *a. attr.* (*market.*) imitato, artificiale, falso, finto. // ~ **leather** (*market.*) finto cuoio, finta pelle; ~ **of a trade-mark** (*leg.*) imitazione di marchio.

imitator, *n.* (*market.*) imitatore.

immediate, *a.* immediato. // ~ **annuity** (*fin.*) rendita immediata; ~ **cause** (*ass.*) causa immediata (*d'un sinistro*); ~ **delivery** consegna immediata; ~ **holding company** (*fin.*) società controllante; ~ **notice** (*leg.*) avviso immediato; ~ **or cancel order** (*Borsa*) ordine a esecuzione immediata.

immediately, *avv.* immediatamente.

immigrant, *n.* (*econ.*) immigrante. // ~ **remittances** (*econ.*) rimesse degli emigranti.

immigrate, *v. i.* (*econ.*) immigrare.

immigration, *n.* (*econ.*) immigrazione. // ~ **quota** (*econ.*) quota d'immigrazione.

imminent, *a.* imminente, prossimo. // ~ **peril** (*trasp. mar.*) pericolo imminente.

immobile, *a.* immobile.

immobilism, *n.* immobilismo.

immobilization, *n.* 1 immobilizzazione. 2 (*fin., rag.*) immobilizzazione, immobilizzo.

immobilize, *v. t.* 1 immobilizzare. 2 (*fin.,*

rag.) immobilizzare (*convertire capitali circolanti in capitali fissi*).

immoral, *a.* immorale.

immovable, *a.* 1 immobile; inamovibile. 2 (*leg.*) immobile. // ~ **property** (*leg.*) beni immobili.

immovables, *n. pl.* (*leg.*) beni immobili, immobili. // ~ **by destination** (*leg.*) immobili per destinazione.

immoveable, *a. V.* **immovable.**

immune, *a.* (*leg.*) immune.

immunity, *n.* 1 (*leg.*) immunità. 2 (*leg.*) esenzione. // ~ **from distraint** (*leg.*) esenzione da pignoramento; ~ **from fines** (*leg.*) tutela contro l'erogazione di ammende; ~ **from taxation** (*fin.*) esenzione dalle imposte.

impact, *n.* 1 forza d'urto; (*anche fig.*) impatto. 2 forte influsso; effetto; incidenza.

impasse, *n.* 1 «punto morto». 2 (*econ.*) fase di stanchezza.

impeach, *v. t.* 1 (*leg.*) accusare, denunciare, incriminare, mettere in stato d'accusa. 2 (*leg.*) impugnare.

impeachable, *a.* (*leg.*) accusabile, denunziabile, incriminabile.

impeachment, *n.* (*leg.*) accusa, incriminazione, messa in stato d'accusa. // **without ~ of waste** (*leg.*) esente da azione legale per danni (*arrecati da un affittuario ai fondi che egli ha in affitto*).

impede, *v. t.* impedire, impacciare.

impediment, *n.* 1 impedimento, ostacolo. 2 (*leg.*) impedimento; ostacolo alla stipulazione d'un contratto (*per incapacità d'una delle parti*).

imperfect, *a.* 1 imperfetto. 2 (*leg.*) imperfetto, mancante di qualche requisito essenziale, risolubile. // competition (*econ.*) concorrenza imperfetta.

imperial, *a.* sovrano. // ~ **bushel** (*ingl.*) «bushel» imperiale (*o* britannico) (*misura di capacità pari a litri 36,36*); ~ **gallon** (*ingl.*) gallone imperiale (*o* britannico) (*misura di capacità pari a litri 4,54*); ~ **pint** (*ingl.*) pinta imperiale (*o* britannica) (*misura di capacità pari a litri 0,57*); ~ **preference** (*ingl.*) trattamento tariffario di favore (*accordato ai Paesi membri del Commonwealth britannico*); ~ **quart** (*ingl.*) «quart» imperiale (*o* britannico) (*misura di capacità pari a litri 1,14*).

impersonal, *a.* impersonale. // ~ **account** (*rag.*) conto non intestato a persona fisica o a ditta.

implement¹, *n.* (*org. az.*) attrezzo, apparecchio, strumento.

implement², *v. t.* 1 adempiere. 2 effettuare. 3 (*leg.*) perfezionare (*un contratto*). // to ~ **an engagement** adempiere a un impegno.

implementation, *n.* 1 adempimento. 2 effettuamento. 3 (*leg.*) perfezionamento (*d'un contratto*). // **the ~ of a treaty** l'applicazione (*o* l'esecuzione) d'un trattato.

implicate, *v. t.* implicare.

implication, *n.* implicazione.

implicit, *a.* (*leg.*) implicito.

implied, *a.* (*leg.*) implicito, tacito. // ~ **condition** (*leg.*) condizione implicita; ~ **contract** (*leg.*) contratto implicito; ~ **powers** (*leg.*) poteri impliciti; ~ **terms** (*leg.*) condizioni implicite (*in un contratto, ecc.*); ~ **waiver** (*leg.*) rinuncia implicita; ~ **warranty** (*leg.*) garanzia tacita.

imply, *v. t.* implicare, importare, avere in sé.

import¹, *n.* (*comm. est.*) importazione, merce d'importazione, prodotto d'importazione. // ~ **agent** (*comm. est.*) agente importatore; ~ **commission agent** (*comm. est.*) importatore su commissione; ~ **credits** (*comm. est.*) crediti all'importazione; ~ **duty** (*dog.*) dazio d'importazione; ~ **-export movements** (*comm. est., fin.*) interscambio; ~ **goods** (*comm. est.*) merce d'importazione; ~ **-induced inflation** (*econ.*) inflazione indotta dalle importazioni; ~ **licence** (*comm. est.*) licenza d'importazione; ~ **merchant** (*comm. est.*) importatore in proprio; ~ **of capitals** (*fin.*) importazione di capitali; ~ **permit** (*comm. est.*) permesso d'importazione; ~ **prohibition** (*econ.*) divieto d'importazione; ~ **quotas** (*comm. est.*) contingenti d'importazione; ~ **specification** (*dog.*) dichiarazione d'importazione; ~ **surcharge** (*comm. est., fin.*) soprattassa sulle importazioni; ~ **tax** (*dog.*) dazio d'importazione; ~ **trade** (*comm. est.*) commercio d'importazione.

import², *v. t.* (*comm. est.*) importare.

importable, *a.* (*comm. est.*) importabile.

importance, *n.* importanza.

important, *a.* importante.

importation, *n.* 1 (*comm. est.*) importazione. 2 (*comm. est.*) merce d'importazione, prodotto d'importazione. // **the ~ voucher (of a pass sheet)** (*dog.*) il foglio d'entrata (in un «trittico»).

importer, *n.* 1 (*comm. est.*) importatore. 2 (*comm. est.*) Paese importatore.

importing, *a. attr.* (*comm. est.*) importatore. // ~ **country** (*comm. est.*) paese importatore.

impose, *v. t.* 1 imporre. 2 (*fin.*) imporre, riscuotere. 3 (*giorn.*) mettere in macchina.

imposition, *n.* 1 imposizione. 2 (*fin.*) imposta, tassa. // **the ~ of new taxes** (*fin.*)

l'imposizione di nuovi balzelli.

impossibility, *n.* impossibilità. // ~ **of performance** (*leg.*) impossibilità d'esecuzione (*d'un contratto*).

impossible, *a.* impossibile.

impost[1], *n.* 1 (*dog.*) dazio d'importazione. 2 (*fin.*) imposta, tassa, tributo.

impost[2], *v. t.* (*dog.*) classificare (*le importazioni*) per fissare il dazio d'importazione.

imprescriptibility, *n.* (*leg.*) imprescrittibilità.

imprescriptible, *a.* (*leg.*) imprescrittibile.

impress, *v. t.* 1 stampare. 2 fissare (*nella memoria, ecc.*). 3 colpire, provocare un'impressione su (*q.*). 4 (*leg.*) confiscare (*denaro, beni, ecc.*). 5 (*leg.*) requisire (*merci: per uso pubblico*). // to ~ **sb. favourably (unfavourably)** fare una buona (una cattiva) impressione a q.

impressed, *a.* 1 stampato. 2 fissato (*nella memoria, ecc.*). // ~ **stamp** bollo stampato (*su una busta, un documento, ecc.*).

impression, *n.* (*giorn., pubbl.*) stampa, tiratura. // **an ~ of 15,000 copies** (*giorn., pubbl.*) una tiratura di 15.000 copie.

impressment, *n.* 1 (*leg.*) confisca. 2 (*leg.*) requisizione.

imprest, *n.* 1 (*cred.*) anticipazione (*di denaro*). 2 (*leg.*) prestito (*dello Stato a un privato: per permettergli di far fronte ai suoi debiti*). // ~ **fund** (*rag.*) fondo cassa per piccole spese.

imprint[1], *n.* segno. // ~ **stamp** bollo stampato (*su una busta, un documento, ecc.*).

imprint[2], *v. t.* 1 stampare. 2 applicare, apporre. // to ~ **a postmark on a letter** applicare un francobollo a una lettera.

imprinted, *a.* 1 stampato. 2 applicato, apposto. // ~ **form** modulo a stampa.

imprison, *v. t.* (*leg.*) imprigionare.

imprisonment, *n.* (*leg.*) detenzione, reclusione.

improper, *a.* erroneo. // ~ **stowage** (*trasp. mar.*) negligenza nello stivaggio.

improve, *v. t.* e *i.* 1 migliorare, perfezionare. 2 valorizzare, far migliorie a (*un terreno, ecc.*). 3 (*comm.*) aumentare, essere in rialzo. // to ~ **on st.** migliorare una cosa; to ~ **on the prices offered** (*market.*) migliorare i prezzi offerti.

improvement, *n.* 1 miglioramento, perfezionamento. 2 miglioria, valorizzazione (*d'un terreno, ecc.*). 3 (*comm.*) aumento, rialzo. // ~ **in bookkeeping terms** (*rag.*) miglioramento contabile.

improver, *n.* (*pers.*) apprendista, praticante d'ufficio (*che accetta lavoro per acquisirne esperienza, pur non essendo retribuito*).

improvised, *a.* improvvisato.

impugn, *v. t.* (*leg.*) impugnare. // to ~ **the clause of a contract** (*leg.*) impugnare una clausola contrattuale.

impugnable, *a.* (*leg.*) impugnabile.

impugnment, *n.* (*leg.*) impugnazione.

impulse, *n.* impulso, spinta. // ~ **buying** (*market.*) acquisti (fatti) per impulso; ~ **purchase** (*market.*) acquisto (fatto) per impulso.

imputability, *n.* 1 (*leg.*) imputabilità. 2 (*rag.*) imputabilità.

imputable, *a.* 1 (*leg.*) imputabile. 2 (*rag.*) imputabile, addebitabile, ascrivibile, attribuibile.

imputation, *n.* 1 (*leg.*) imputazione. 2 (*rag.*) imputazione, attribuzione.

impute, *v. t.* 1 (*leg.*) imputare. 2 (*rag.*) imputare, addebitare, ascrivere, attribuire.

imputed, *a.* 1 (*leg.*) imputato. 2 (*rag.*) imputato, addebitato, ascritto, attribuito.

in, *prep.* e *avv.* in, entro, dentro. *a.* 1 interno. 2 di moda, in voga. 3 (*fam.*) in attivo di. 4 (*trasp.*) in arrivo. // ~ **-and-out** (*Borsa*) «dentro e fuori» (*relativo ad acquisto e vendita dello stesso titolo in un breve periodo*); ~ **-and-out trading** (*Borsa*) contrattazione «dentro e fuori»; **the ~ boat** (*trasp. mar.*) il battello in arrivo; ~ **-clearing** (*banca, ingl.*) insieme degli assegni, ecc., spiccati su una banca e da questa presentati alla Stanza di compensazione; ~ **fashion** (*market.*) alla moda, in voga; ~ **-flight** (*trasp. aer.*) effettuato in volo; ~ **-flight movie** (*trasp. aer.*) film proiettato durante il volo; ~ **-house** (*org. az.*) interno, ristretto; ~ **-house meetings** (*org. az.*) riunioni ristrette; ~ **kind** (*leg.*) in natura; ~ **the long run** (*econ., fin.*) a lungo termine; ~ **-plant** (*org. az.*) interno; ~ **-plant training programme** (*org. az.*) piano d'addestramento interno; ~ **-print** (*giorn., pubbl.*) titolo in corso di stampa; ~ **-process** (*org. az.*) in corso di lavorazione; ~ **-season** (*tur.*) stagionale; ~ **-season accommodation** (*tur.*) ricettività stagionale; ~ **the short run** (*econ., fin.*) a breve termine; ~ **-transit** (*trasp.*) di transito; ~ **-transit freight rates** (*trasp.*) tariffa per noli di transito; ~ **-transit goods** (*trasp.*) merci di transito; ~ **-tray** (*attr. uff.*) cassetta della corrispondenza in arrivo; **payment ~ kind** (*comm.*) pagamento in natura.

inability, *n.* 1 (*leg.*) inabilità, incapacità. 2 (*pers.*) invalidità. // ~ **to meet one's debts** (*leg.*) incapacità di far fronte ai propri impegni; ~ **to work** (*pers.*) inabilità, incapacità al lavoro.

inaccurate, *a.* inesatto. // ~ **accounts** (*rag.*) conti inesatti.

inaction, *n.* inazione, inattività.

inactive, *a.* inattivo, inoperoso. // **an** ~ **contract** (*leg.*) un contratto che non è in vigore; **an** ~ **machinery** (*org. az.*) un macchinario inoperoso; ~ **post** (*Borsa*) recinto grida inattivo; ~ **stocks** (*Borsa*) titoli inattivi, titoli a scarso flottante.

inactivity, *n.* inattività.

inadequacy, *n.* insufficienza.

inadequate, *a.* insufficiente. // ~ **consideration** corrispettivo inadeguato (*alla prestazione*).

inadmissibility, *n.* (*anche leg.*) inammissibilità.

inadmissible, *a.* (*anche leg.*) inammissibile.

inalienability, *n.* (*leg.*) inalienabilità.

inalienable, *a.* (*leg.*) inalienabile. // ~ **rights** (*leg.*) diritti inalienabili.

inbalance, *n. V.* **imbalance.**

incapable, *a.* incapace.

incapacitate, *v. t.* (*leg.*) inabilitare.

incapacitation, *n.* (*leg.*) inabilitazione; il rendere inabile, il rendere incapace; l'essere reso inabile, l'essere reso incapace.

incapacity, *n.* (*leg.*) incapacità, inabilità.

incentive, *n.* incentivo, incitamento. // ~ **pay** (*pers.*) cottimo; ~ **wage** (*pers.*) salario a cottimo.

inch, *n.* pollice (*misura lineare pari a cm 2,54*).

inchmaree clause, *n.* (*ass. mar.*) clausola che prevede la copertura dei rischi non derivanti necessariamente da incidenti marittimi (*p. es.: i rischi per danni al carico quando la nave è nel porto*).

incidence, *n.* incidenza. // **the** ~ **of a tax on the consumer** (*fin.*) l'incidenza d'un'imposta sul consumatore.

incident, *a.* (*leg.*) inerente, congiunto, dipendente. *n.* (*leg.*) diritto accessorio, privilegio.

incidental, *a.* incidentale, accessorio. // ~ **cause** (*leg.*) causa incidentale; ~ **expenses** (*rag.*) spese accessorie; spese impreviste; costi imprevisti; ~ **incomes** (*rag.*) entrate accessorie; entrate impreviste; ricavi imprevisti.

incite, *v. t.* incitare, istigare.

incitement, *n.* incitamento, istigazione.

inclination, *n.* inclinazione.

incline, *v. t.* inclinare.

inclose, *v. t. V.* **enclose.**

inclosure, *n. V.* **enclosure.**

include, *v. t.* includere, comprendere, contenere, racchiudere.

included, *a.* incluso, compreso.

inclusive, *a.* comprensivo, complessivo. // ~ **price** (*market.*) «tutto compreso»; ~ **terms** (*tur.*) «tutto compreso».

income, *n.* **1** (*econ., fin.*) entrata, entrate. **2** (*econ., fin.*) reddito. **3** (*econ., fin.*) rendita, utile. **4** (*rag.*) parte «entrate» (*di un bilancio*). // ~ **account** (*rag.*) conto profitti e perdite; **incomes accruing to the factors of production** (*econ.*) redditi ascrivibili ai fattori della produzione; ~ **available for distribution** (*rag.*) utile da distribuire; ~ **bond** (*Borsa, fin.*) obbligazione di partecipazione; ~ **bracket** (*fin.*) gruppo di reddito, categoria di contribuenti (*raggruppati secondo il reddito*); ~ **classes** (*fin.*) classi di reddito; ~ **deflation** (*econ.*) deflazione da redditi; ~ **derived from the self-employment of private individuals** (*fin.*) reddito di lavoro autonomo di persone fisiche; ~ **determination** (*fin.*) determinazione del reddito; ~ **distribution** (*fin.*) distribuzione del reddito; ~ **earner** (*fin.*) percettore di reddito; ~ **estimation** (*econ.*) valutazione del reddito; ~ **for life** (*ass., fin.*) rendita vitalizia, vitalizio; ~ **for the year** (*rag.*) utile d'esercizio; ~ **from capital** (*fin.*) reddito di capitale; ~ **from employed persons** (*fin.*) reddito di lavoro subordinato; ~ **from employment** (*fin.*) reddito di lavoro subordinato; ~ **from farms** (*fin.*) reddito terriero; ~ **groups** (*fin., stat.*) gruppi di reddito; ~ **inflation** (*econ.*) inflazione da redditi; ~ **items** (*fin.*) categorie di redditi; ~ **liable to tax** (*fin.*) reddito tassabile; **incomes package** (*fin.*) «pacchetto» di misure di politica dei redditi; **incomes policy** (*econ.*) politica dei redditi; ~ **profits** (*fin.*) redditi di lavoro; ~ **range** (*fin.*) classe di reddito; **incomes restraint** (*econ.*) freno all'aumento dei redditi (*o* dei salari); ~ **splitting** (*fin.*) «splitting» dei redditi (*equa distribuzione del reddito complessivo fra i membri di una famiglia, ai fini fiscali; non è ancora ammesso in Italia*); ~ **statement** (*rag.*) conto profitti e perdite; conto economico; ~ **surtax** (*fin.*) imposta complementare sul reddito; ~ **tax** (*fin.*) imposta sul reddito; imposta di ricchezza mobile; ~ **-tax return** (*fin.*) dichiarazione dei redditi.

incoming, *a. attr.* **1** entrante, subentrante. **2** in arrivo. // ~ **letters** (*comun.*) corrispondenza in arrivo; ~ **mail** (*comun.*) corrispondenza in arrivo; ~ **profits** (*rag.*) profitti in via di maturazione; **the** ~ **tenants** (*leg.*) gli affittuari subentranti.

incompatibility, *n.* (*leg.*) incompatibilità.

incompatible, *a.* (*leg.*) incompatibile.

incompetence, *n.* (*leg.*) incompetenza, incapacità.

incompetent, *a.* (*leg.*) incompetente, incapace.

inconsumable, *a.* 1 inconsumabile. 2 (*econ.*) (*di bene, ecc.*) non di consumo; strumentale.

incontestability, *n.* (*leg.*) incontestabilità, inconfutabilità.

incontestable, *a.* (*leg.*) incontestabile, inconfutabile. // ~ **clause** (*ass.*) clausola d'incontestabilità (*d'una polizza*); ~ **evidence** (*leg.*) prova inconfutabile.

incontrovertibility, *n.* (*leg.*) incontrovertibilità, inconfutabilità, inoppugnabilità.

incontrovertible, *a.* (*leg.*) incontrovertibile, inconfutabile, inoppugnabile. // ~ **evidence** (*leg.*) prova inconfutabile.

inconvenience, *n.* inconveniente.

inconvenient, *a.* che reca disagio. // **an ~ arrangement** un accordo svantaggioso.

inconvertibility, *n.* (*econ.*) inconvertibilità.

inconvertible, *a.* (*econ.*) inconvertibile. // ~ **circulation** (*econ.*) corso forzoso; ~ **currency** (*econ.*) valuta non convertibile; ~ **paper money** (*econ.*) banconote a corso forzoso.

incorporate[1], *a.* (*leg.*) (*di ditta, ecc.*) associato.

incorporate[2], *v. t.* 1 (*leg.*) erigere in ente giuridico, morale o pubblico. 2 (*leg.*) costituire (*una società*); «registrare» (*ditte, ecc.*). 3 (*leg.*) associare, fondere (*ditte, ecc.*). *v. i.* (*leg.*) (*di ditte, ecc.*) associarsi, fondersi.

incorporation, *n.* 1 (*leg.*) costituzione, «registrazione» (*di ditte, ecc.*). 2 (*leg.*) associazione, fusione (*di ditte, ecc.*). // **the ~ of a company** (*leg.*) la costituzione d'una società.

incorporator, *n.* (*leg.*) socio fondatore.

incorporeal, *a.* (*leg.*) incorporeo. // ~ **chattel** (*leg.*) bene mobile di cui non si ha possesso ma ripetibile con una causa.

incorrect, *a.* errato, erroneo.

incoterms, *n. pl.* (*comm. est., comun.*) «incoterms» (*norme internazionali per l'interpretazione dei termini commerciali, edite a cura della Camera di Commercio Internazionale*).

increase[1], *n.* 1 aumento, accrescimento, maggiorazione, crescita. 2 (*econ., fin.*) crescita, dilatazione, rialzo, lievitazione, dinamica (*dei prezzi, ecc.*). 3 (*mat.*) incremento. 4 (*pers.*) aumento, scatto (*di salario*). // **the ~ and decrease of economic activity** (*econ.*) le fluttuazioni della congiuntura; **an ~ in consumption demand** (*econ.*) un aumento della domanda di consumi; **an ~ in population** (*econ., stat.*) un aumento della popolazione; ~ **in prices and costs** (*market.*) «lievitazione» dei prezzi e dei costi; ~ **of capital** (*fin., rag.*) aumento di capitale; ~ **of the risk** (*ass.*) aggravamento del rischio; ~ **of wages according to ages** (*pers.*) scatto salariale per anzianità.

increase[2], *v. t.* e *i.* 1 aumentare, incrementare, accrescere, crescere. 2 (*econ., fin.: di prezzi*) dilatarsi, lievitare. // to ~ **in price** (*market.*) aumentare di prezzo; to ~ **prices** (*market.*) elevare i prezzi, rincarare; to ~ **total supply** (*econ.*) aumentare l'offerta globale.

increasing, *a.* crescente, in aumento. // ~ **costs** (*econ.*) costi crescenti; ~ **returns** (*econ.*) produttività crescente.

increment, *n.* 1 aumento, accrescimento. 2 (*mat.*) incremento. 3 (*pers.*) aumento (*di stipendio*).

incriminate, *v. t.* (*leg.*) incriminare.

incrimination, *n.* (*leg.*) incriminazione.

incumbrance, *n. V.* **encumbrance.**

incur, *v. t.* 1 incorrere in, esporsi a. 2 contrarre, fare. // to ~ **debts** contrarre debiti; esporsi (*finanziariamente*); to ~ **a risk** correre un rischio.

indebted, *a.* 1 (*fig.*) grato, obbligato. 2 (*cred.*) indebitato.

indebtedness, *n.* 1 (*cred.*) indebitamento, debito, situazione debitoria. 2 (*fin.*) gratitudine, obbligo. 3 (*rag.*) passività, passivo.

indefeasibility, *n.* 1 (*leg.*) inalienabilità. 2 (*leg.*) imprescrittibilità. 3 (*leg.*) inoppugnabilità.

indefeasible, *a.* 1 (*leg.*) inalienabile. 2 (*leg.*) imprescrittibile. 3 (*leg.*) inoppugnabile. // ~ **claims** (*leg.*) richieste inoppugnabili; ~ **rights** (*leg.*) diritti inalienabili.

indefinite, *a.* indefinito.

indemnifiable, *a.* risarcibile.

indemnification, *n.* (*ass.*) indennizzo, risarcimento, reintegrazione.

indemnify, *v. t.* 1 garantire, tutelare (*contro perdite, danni, ecc.*). 2 (*ass.*) indennizzare, risarcire, reintegrare.

indemnify oneself, *v. rifl.* garantirsi, tutelarsi.

indemnitee, *n.* (*leg.*) chi è (*o* ha diritto a essere) indennizzato; chi è (*o* ha diritto a essere) risarcito.

indemnitor, *n.* 1 (*leg.*) chi indennizza, chi risarcisce. 2 (*leg.*) chi è tenuto a indennizzare, chi è tenuto a risarcire.

indemnity, *n.* 1 assicurazione, garanzia (*contro perdite, danni, ecc.*). 2 (*ass.*) indennizzo, risarcimento. 3 (*leg.*) indennità. // ~ **club** (*ass. mar.*) sezione avarie.

indent[1], *n.* 1 (*comm.*) ordinazione di merce

(*soprattutto all'estero*). 2 (*leg., ingl.*) requisizione ufficiale.

indent[2], *v. t.* 1 far rientrare (*l'inizio d'una riga*) dal margine della pagina. 2 compilare, redigere (*un documento*) in duplice copia. 3 (*comm.*) ordinare (*merce, soprattutto all'estero*). *v. i.* compilare documenti in duplice copia. // to ~ **the first word of a paragraph** far rientrare la prima parola d'un paragrafo; to ~ **upon sb. for st.** (*leg., ingl.*) spiccare su q. un ordine di requisizione.

indenture, *n.* 1 (*Borsa, USA*) contratto obbligazionario (*che illustra dettagliatamente le condizioni d'emissione d'un prestito obbligazionario*). 2 (*leg.*) accordo scritto; contratto bilaterale.

independence, *n.* indipendenza.

independent, *a.* indipendente, libero. // ~ **audit** (*fin.*) revisione contabile esterna; ~ **contractor** appaltatore libero (*nella scelta dei mezzi e dei metodi di lavorazione*); ~ **unions** (*sind.*) sindacati liberi, sindacati non confederali; ~ **variable** (*mat.*) variabile indipendente.

index[1], *n.* (*pl.* **indices** e *reg.*) 1 indice analitico (*d'un libro*). 2 (*econ., fin., stat.*) indice (*del costo della vita, ecc.*). // ~ **-linked** (*econ., fin.*) indicizzato; ~ **-linking** (*econ., fin.*) indicizzazione; ~ **number** (*stat.*) numero indice; **the ~ numbers of industrial production** (*econ., stat.*) i numeri indici della produzione industriale; ~ **of economic well-being** indice di benessere economico; ~ **of productivity** (*econ.*) indice della produttività; ~ **of retail prices** (*market.*) indice dei prezzi al minuto, indice dei prezzi al dettaglio; ~ **of stock rotation** (*org. az.*) indice di rotazione delle scorte; ~ **of wholesale prices** (*market.*) indice dei prezzi all'ingrosso.

index[2], *v. t.* (*econ., fin.*) indicizzare. // to ~ **incomes** indicizzare i redditi.

indexation, *n.* (*econ., fin.*) indicizzazione.

indicate, *v. t.* indicare.

indication, *n.* indicazione.

indicator, *n.* (*econ., fin., stat.*) indicatore, indice.

indict, *v. t.* (*leg.*) accusare, incriminare, mettere in stato d'accusa.

indictable, *a.* 1 (*leg.*) accusabile, incriminabile. 2 (*leg.*) perseguibile, passibile di pena. // ~ **offence** (*leg.*) infrazione passibile di pena.

indictee, *n.* (*leg.*) chi è accusato, chi è incriminato, chi è messo in stato d'accusa.

indicter, *n. V.* **indictor.**

indictment, *n.* (*leg.*) accusa scritta, incriminazione, messa in stato d'accusa.

indictor, *n.* (*leg.*) accusatore, chi accusa, chi incrimina, chi mette in stato d'accusa.

indifference, *n.* indifferenza. // ~ **curve** (*econ.*) curva d'indifferenza.

indirect, *a.* indiretto. // ~ **arbitrage** (*fin.*) arbitraggio indiretto; ~ **call** (*trasp. mar.*) scalo intermedio; ~ **charge** (*rag.*) costo indiretto; ~ **cost** (*rag.*) costo indiretto, costo fisso; ~ **dealings** trattative «sotto banco»; ~ **exchange** (*fin.*) cambio indiretto, cambio «incerto per certo»; ~ **expenses** (*rag.*) spese indirette, spese generali; ~ **incentive** (*pers.*) incentivo indiretto; ~ **initiative** (*leg.*) iniziativa indiretta; ~ **labour** (*pers.*) manodopera indiretta; ~ **parities** (*fin.*) parità indirette (*cambi calcolati attraverso una terza valuta*); ~ **tax** (*fin.*) imposta indiretta; ~ **taxation** (*fin.*) imposizione indiretta, fiscalità indiretta.

indiscriminate, *a.* indiscriminato.

indispensable, *a.* indispensabile.

individual, *a.* individuale. *n.* 1 individuo. 2 (*leg.*) persona fisica. // ~ **person** (*leg.*) persona fisica; ~ **policy** (*ass.*) polizza individuale; ~ **rate** (*pers.*) paga individuale.

individually, *avv.* individualmente.

indorsable, *a. V.* **endorsable.**

indorse, *v. t. V.* **endorse.**

indorsee, *n. V.* **endorsee.**

indorsement, *n. V.* **endorsement.**

indorser, *n. V.* **endorser.**

induce, *v. t.* 1 indurre, persuadere. 2 incitare, spingere a. 3 (*leg.*) istigare.

induced, *a.* indotto.

inducement, *n.* 1 persuasione, incitamento. 2 (*leg.*) istigazione. // ~ **to invest** (*econ.*) incentivo all'investimento.

induction, *n.* induzione.

indulgence, *n.* indulgenza.

industrial, *a.* industriale. *n.* 1 (*fin.*) impresa industriale. 2 **industrials,** *pl.* (*fin.*) azioni, titoli, valori (d'imprese) industriali. // ~ **accident** (*pers.*) infortunio sul lavoro; ~ **accident and health insurance** (*ass., pers.*) assicurazione contro le malattie e gli infortuni sul lavoro; ~ **action** (*sind.*) agitazione sindacale; ~ **advertising** (*pubbl.*) pubblicità industriale; ~ **area** (*econ.*) zona industriale; ~ **combination** (*econ.*) concentrazione d'imprese; ~ **communications** (*org. az.*) comunicazioni aziendali, comunicazioni interne; ~ **concern** impresa industriale; ~ **Countries** (*econ.*) Paesi industriali; ~ **Court** (*leg., ingl.*) tribunale che giudica sulle controversie in materia di lavoro; ~ **design** (*org. az., pubbl.*) «industrial design», disegno industriale; ~ **designer** (*org. az., pubbl.*) «industrial designer», disegnatore industriale; ~ **development pole** (*econ.*) polo di sviluppo industriale; ~ **disease** (*pers.*) malattia professionale; ~ **disputes** (*econ.*) vertenze sindacali, conflitti di lavoro; ~ **disputes tribunal** (*leg.*) *V.* ~ **Court**; ~ **espionage** (*leg.*) spionaggio industriale; ~ **goods** (*econ.*) beni strumentali; ~ **health and medicine** (*pers., sind.*) igiene e medicina del lavoro; ~ **injury** (*pers.*) incidente (*o* infortunio) sul lavoro; ~ **injury legislation** (*leg.*) legislazione infortunistica; ~ **management** (*org. az.*) direzione aziendale; ~ **medicine** (*org. az., pers.*) medicina del lavoro; ~ **package** (*econ.*) «pacchetto industriale»; ~ **peace** (*sind.*) tregua sindacale; ~ **production** (*econ.*) produzione industriale; ~ **production index** (*econ.*) indice della produzione industriale; ~ **property rights** (*leg.*) diritti di privativa industriale; ~ **purchasing** (*org. az.*) approvvigionamento; ~ **relations** (*market., pers.*) relazioni industriali; (*pers., sind.*) relazioni professionali; ~ **reorganization** (*econ.*) riconversione industriale; ~ **review** (*econ.*) rassegna industriale; ~ **site** (*econ.*) zona industriale; ~ **training** (*pers.*) istruzione professionale; ~ **wages** (*pers.*) paghe industriali; ~ **workers** (*pers.*) lavoratori dell'industria, operai dell'industria.

industrialism, *n.* (*econ.*) industrialismo.

industrialist, *n.* industriale, fabbricante.

industrialization, *n.* (*econ.*) industrializzazione.

industrialize, *v. t.* (*econ.*) industrializzare.

industry, *n.* (*econ.*) industria, manifattura.

ineffective, *a.* inefficiente, inefficace.

ineffectiveness, *n.* inefficienza, inefficacia.

ineffectual, *a.* inefficiente, inefficace.

ineffectualness, *n.* inefficienza, inefficacia.

inefficacious, *a.* inefficace.

inefficaciousness, *n.* inefficacia.

inefficacity, *n.* inefficacia.

inelastic, *a.* 1 non elastico, mancante d'elasticità. 2 rigido.

inelasticity, *n.* 1 mancanza d'elasticità. 2 rigidità. // ~ **of demand** (*econ.*) rigidità della domanda; ~ **of supply** (*econ.*) rigidità dell'offerta.

inequality, *n.* 1 disparità, sperequazione. 2 irregolarità. // ~ **of income** (*econ.*) sperequazione dei redditi.

inequitable, *a.* iniquo, ingiusto, non equo. // **an** ~ **division of an estate among the heirs** (*leg.*) un'iniqua distribuzione dei beni fra gli eredi.

inequity, *n.* mancanza d'equità, ingiustizia.

inert, *a.* inerte.

inertia, *n.* inerzia.

inestimable, *a.* inapprezzabile.

inevitable, *a.* inevitabile. // ~ **damage** (*ass., leg.*) danno inevitabile.

inexact, *a.* inesatto.

inexistent, *a.* inesistente.

inexpensive, *a.* di poco prezzo, a buon mercato.

inexpensiveness, *n.* basso costo, economicità.

inexperienced, *a.* inesperto; che non ha esperienza.

inexpert, *a.* inesperto (*in un lavoro*).

infant, *n.* (*leg.*) minorenne. *a.* (*fig.*) nuovo. // ~ **industry** (*econ.*) industria «bambina»; **our** ~ **rubber industry** (*econ.*) la nostra nascente industria della gomma.

infer, *v. t.* dedurre.

inferable, *a.* deducibile.

inference, *n.* 1 deduzione. 2 (*stat.*) inferenza.

inferior, *a.* inferiore. *n.* (*pers.*) subalterno, subordinato. // **an** ~ **Court of law** (*leg.*) un tribunale (di grado) inferiore; ~ **quality** (*market.*) qualità inferiore.

inferred, *a.* dedotto.

infirmity, *n.* infermità.

inflate, *v. t.* 1 gonfiare. 2 (*econ.*) alzare (*i prezzi*). 3 (*econ.*) inflazionare. *v. i.* 1 gonfiarsi. 2 (*econ.*) ricorrere all'inflazione. // **to** ~ **a currency** (*econ.*) inflazionare una moneta.

inflating, *n.* (*trasp. aut.*) gonfiatura (*delle gomme*).

inflation, *n.* 1 gonfiamento. 2 (*econ.*) inflazione. // ~ **policy** (*econ.*) politica inflazionistica; ~ **rate** (*econ.*) tasso inflazionistico.

inflationary, *a.* (*econ.*) inflazionistico. // ~ **gap** (*econ.*) «gap» (*o* divario, *o* vuoto) inflazionistico; ~ **pressure** (*econ.*) pressione inflazionistica; ~ **spiral** (*econ.*) spirale inflazionistica; ~ **strains** (*econ.*) tendenze inflazionistiche; ~ **tendencies** (*econ.*) tendenze inflazionistiche, spinte inflazionistiche; ~ **wage rises** (*econ.*) aumenti inflazionistici dei salari; ~ **wage settlement** (*econ.*) accordo salariale con conseguenze inflazionistiche.

inflationism, *n.* (*econ., fin.*) inflazionismo.

inflationist, *n.* (*econ., fin.*) inflazionista, fautore dell'inflazione economica.

inflow, *n.* 1 afflusso. 2 **inflows,** *pl.* (*fin.*) «ricuperi». // ~ **of bank deposits** (*banca*) afflusso di depositi bancari; ~ **of capital** (*econ.*) afflusso di capitali, entrata di capitali, apporto di capitali.

influence[1], *n.* 1 influenza, influsso. 2 ascendente, autorità.

influence[2], *v. t.* influenzare, influire su.

influential, *a.* influente.

influx, *n. V.* **inflow.**

inform, *v. t.* informare, avvertire, ragguagliare; dare informazioni, dar notizie a. // to ~ **in advance** preavvisare.

informal, *a.* non ufficiale, ufficioso. // **an ~ agreement** un accordo di massima; **an ~ meeting** (*org. az.*) una riunione non ufficiale.

informatics, *n. pl.* (*col verbo al sing.*) informatica.

information, *n. collett.* informazione, informazioni; l'informare; notizia, notizie; ragguagli. // ~ **bureau** (*org. az.*) ufficio informazioni; ~ **desk** (*org. az.*) ufficio (*o* banco) informazioni; ~ **gathering** (*market., org. az.*) raccolta di dati; ~ **methods** (*giorn.*) mezzi d'informazione; ~ **on forecast** (*market.*) informazioni previsionali; ~ **on past trends** (*market.*) informazioni retrospettive; ~ **science** scienza dell'informazione.

informative, *a.* informativo.

infrangibility, *n.* (*specialm. fig.*) infrangibilità.

infrangible, *a.* infrangibile.

infrastructure, *n.* (*econ.*) infrastruttura. // ~ **costs** (*econ.*) costi infrastrutturali.

infringe, *v. t.* (*leg.*) infrangere, trasgredire, contravvenire a. // to ~ **a contract (a treaty)** (*leg.*) contravvenire a un contratto (a un trattato); to ~ **a copyright** (*leg.*) violare la legge sul diritto d'autore.

infringement, *n.* **1** (*leg.*) infrazione, violazione, trasgressione, contravvenzione. **2** (*leg.*) uso illecito dell'altrui ragione sociale. // ~ **of the law** (*leg.*) violazione della legge; ~ **of a right** (*leg.*) violazione d'un diritto; ~ **of the trade marks** (*leg.*) contraffazione dei marchi di fabbrica.

infringer, *n.* **1** (*leg.*) contravventore, violatore, trasgressore. **2** (*leg.*) chi usa illegalmente l'altrui marchio di fabbrica. **3** (*leg.*) chi usa illegalmente l'altrui ragione sociale.

ingot, *n.* lingotto; verga (*d'oro, ecc.*).

inhabit, *v. t.* abitare in (*un luogo*).

inhabitancy, *n.* (*leg.*) sede principale degli affari (*d'una società commerciale, d'un'associazione, ecc.*).

inherent, *a.* inerente, intrinseco. // ~ **vice** (*leg.*) vizio intrinseco.

inherit, *v. t.* (*leg.*) ricevere in eredità.

inheritable, *a.* (*leg.*) ereditabile, ereditario.

inheritance, *n.* (*leg.*) eredità, patrimonio (*proveniente da eredità*). // ~ **tax** (*fin.*) imposta (*o* tassa) di successione.

initial[1], *a.* iniziale, primo. *n.* **initials,** *pl.* (lettere) iniziali (*d'un nome e d'un cognome*). // ~ **allowance** (*rag.*) ammortamento iniziale; ~ **capital** (*fin.*) capitale iniziale, capitale d'avviamento; ~ **reserve** (*ass.*) riserva iniziale.

initial[2], *v. t.* apporre le iniziali a.

initiate, *v. t.* iniziare, avviare, introdurre. // to ~ **a change in fashion** (*pubbl.*) avviare un cambiamento nella moda; to ~ **a work** (*org. az.*) iniziare un lavoro.

initiative, *n.* iniziativa, intraprendenza. // **on one's own ~** (*amm., leg.*) d'ufficio.

initiator, *n.* iniziatore.

injection, *n.* iniezione.

injunction, *n.* (*leg.*) ingiunzione, imposizione, comando, ordine, ordinanza.

injunctive, *a.* (*leg.*) ingiuntivo.

injure, *v. t.* (*leg.*) danneggiare, ledere. // to ~ **sb.'s reputation** (*leg.*) ledere la reputazione di q.

injured, *a.* (*leg.*) danneggiato, leso, offeso. // **the ~ party** (*leg.*) la parte lesa, la parte danneggiata.

injurious, *a.* dannoso.

injury, *n.* **1** (*leg.*) danno, lesione. **2** (*leg.*) atto illecito. **3** (*pers.*) incidente, infortunio (*sul lavoro*). // ~ **benefit** (*pers.*) assegno d'invalidità (*o* di malattia).

injustice, *n.* ingiustizia.

ink, *n.* (*attr. uff.*) inchiostro. // ~ **eraser** (*attr. uff.*) gomma da inchiostro; ~ **-pad** (*attr. uff.*) tampone per timbri, cuscinetto per timbri; ~ **roller** (*attr. uff.*) nastro inchiostratore.

inked, *a.* inchiostrato. // ~ **ribbon** (*attr. uff.*) nastro dattilografico.

inland, *a. attr.* **1** situato nell'entroterra, situato nel retroterra. **2** (*comm.*) interno. // ~ **bill** (*cred.*) cambiale pagabile all'interno; ~ **bills** (*banca*) portafoglio interno; ~ **duty** (*fin.*) dazio interno; ~ **navigation** (*trasp.*) navigazione interna, navigazione fluviale, navigazione per idrovie; ~ **revenue** (*fin.*) imposte e dazi interni, fisco, erario; ~ **revenue stamp** (*fin.*) bollo fiscale; **an ~ town** una città dell'entroterra; ~ **trade** commercio interno; ~ **water transport** (*trasp.*) navigazione fluviale, navigazione interna; ~ **waterway vessel** (*trasp.*) battello fluviale; ~ **waterways** (*trasp.*) vie navigabili, vie fluviali.

in-laws, *n. pl.* (*fam.*) affini.

innavigable, *a.* (*trasp.*) non navigabile, innavigabile.

inner, *a. attr.* interno, intimo, segreto. // ~ **band** (*fin.*) fascia interna; ~ **port** (*trasp.*) porto interno; ~ **reserve** (*rag.*) riserva occulta.

innocence, *n.* innocenza.

innocent, *a.* innocente.

innovation, *n.* innovazione.

inobservance, *n.* (*leg.*) inosservanza.

inofficial, *a.* non ufficiale, ufficioso.

inoperative, *a.* (*leg.*) non operante, inoperante, inefficace. // **an ~ plant** (*org. az.*) uno stabilimento non operante (*che è, cioè, inutilizzato*).

inoperativeness, *n.* (*leg.*) inefficacia.

in-plant, *a. attr.* in fabbrica; nell'ambito di uno stabilimento; aziendale. // **~ courses** corsi aziendali.

input, *n.* **1** (*econ.*) fattore produttivo (*p. es., il lavoro, le materie prime, ecc.*). **2** (*elab. elettr.*) entrata, ingresso.

inquire, *v. t.* e *i.* **1** informarsi, informarsi di, domandare. **2** indagare, investigare, fare ricerche. // to **~ about** (*o* **after**) **the market trend** (*market.*) informarsi sulla tendenza del mercato; to **~ for st.** (*market.*) chiedere qc. (*per comprare, procurarsi, ecc.*); to **~ into** fare indagini su, esaminare; to **~ sb.'s name** domandare il nome di q.

inquiry, *n.* **1** richiesta d'informazioni. **2** indagine, inchiesta. **3** (*leg.*) inchiesta. // **~ office** (*org. az.*) ufficio informazioni.

inquisitorial, *a.* (*leg.*) inquisitorio.

inroad, *n.* **1** incursione, irruzione. **2** (*fin.*) prelievo.

inscribe, *v. t.* **1** inscrivere. **2** (*fin., ingl.*) registrare (*il nome del detentore di titoli*).

inscribed stock, *n. collett.* (*fin., ingl.*) titoli nominativi, azioni nominative.

inscription, *n.* **1** iscrizione. **2** (*fin., ingl.*) iscrizione di titoli nei registri; trascrizione di titoli.

insert¹, *n.* (*giorn., pubbl.*) inserto; supplemento.

insert², *v. t.* inserire.

insertion, *n.* **1** inserzione, inserimento. **2** (*giorn., pubbl.*) inserzione, avviso pubblicitario.

inset, *n.* (*giorn., pubbl.*) inserto; supplemento; fascicolo (*inserito in un giornale*).

inside, *avv.* e *prep.* dentro. *n.* **1** (il) didentro, parte interna, (l')interno. **2** (*fam.*) informazioni confidenziali, informazioni riservate. *a. attr.* **1** interno, interiore. **2** intimo, segreto. // **~ -back cover** (*giorn.*) terza di copertina; **~ -front cover** (*giorn.*) seconda di copertina; **~ information** informazioni confidenziali, informazioni riservate; **~ stuff** (*slang USA*) informazioni confidenziali, informazioni riservate.

insider, *n.* **1** «addetto ai lavori». **2** (*pers.*) chi ha accesso a informazioni riservate.

insinuate, *v. t.* insinuare.

insist, *v. i.* insistere.

insistence, *n.* insistenza.

insistent, *a.* insistente.

insolvency, *n.* (*leg.*) insolvenza. // **~ law** (*leg.*) diritto fallimentare.

insolvent, *a.* (*leg.*) insolvente, insolvibile. *n.* (*leg.*) debitore insolvente. // **an ~ debtor** (*leg.*) un debitore insolvente.

inspect, *v. t.* **1** ispezionare, verificare. **2** (*leg.*) esaminare, visitare. **3** (*org. az.*) controllare. // to **~ the books** (*leg.*) esaminare i libri (contabili); to **~ the luggage** (*dog.*) ispezionare il bagaglio.

inspection, *n.* **1** ispezione, verifica. **2** (*leg.*) esame, visita. **3** (*org. az.*) controllo. // **~ of documents** (*leg.*) esame di documenti; **~ order** (*dog.*) ordine d'ispezione (*dei bagagli*).

inspector, *n.* **1** (*leg.*) ispettore. **2** (*org. az.*) controllore, verificatore. // **~ general** (*leg.*) ispettore generale; **~ of pavements** (*slang USA*) disoccupato; **~ 's office** ispettorato (*l'ufficio*).

inspectorate, *n.* (*leg.*) ispettorato.

inspectorship, *n.* (*leg.*) ispettorato (*durata in carica*); carica d'ispettore.

instability, *n.* instabilità.

instal, *v. t. V.* **install.**

install, *v. t.* (*org. az.*) installare, insediare.

installation, *n.* (*org. az.*) installazione, insediamento, messa in opera; impianto.

installment, *n. V.* **instalment.**

instalment, *n.* **1** rata. **2** anticipo, acconto. **3** (*giorn.*) dispensa. // **~ buying** (*market.*) acquisti a rate; **~ loan** (*cred.*) prestito rimborsabile a rate; **~ plan** (*market.*) (programma di) vendita a rate; **~ selling** (*market.*) vendita rateale; **by instalments** (*market.*) rateale; **on the ~ plan** (*market.*) rateale.

instance, *n.* (*leg.*) istanza, petizione. // **at the ~ of** (*leg.*) su istanza di.

instant, *a.* **1** istantaneo, immediato. **2** presente, corrente. *n.* istante.

instantaneous, *a.* istantaneo, immediato.

instigate, *v. t.* istigare. // to **~ workers to stop work** (*pers., sind.*) istigare gli operai ad abbandonare il lavoro.

instigation, *n.* istigazione. // **~ to commit a crime** (*leg.*) istigazione a delinquere.

institute¹, *n.* (*leg.*) istituto, istituzione.

institute², *v. t.* **1** istituire, fondare. **2** nominare, insediare. // to **~ proceeding against sb.** (*leg.*) intentare un'azione legale contro q.

institution, *n.* **1** istituzione, l'istituire. **2** (*leg.*) istituzione; istituto (*pubblico, assistenziale, ecc.*); ente morale, associazione, organizzazione. // ~ **of heir** (*leg.*) istituzione d'erede; **the ~ of laws and customs** (*leg.*) l'istituzione di leggi e consuetudini.

institutional, *a.* istituzionale. // ~ **investors** (*fin.*) investitori istituzionali.

instruct, *v. t.* 1 istruire, ammaestrare. 2 (*leg.*) istruire, dare istruzioni a. // to ~ **the jury** (*leg.*) dare istruzioni alla giuria.

instruction, *n.* 1 istruzione, ammaestramento. 2 **instructions,** *pl.* istruzioni, direttive, consegne, consigli. // ~ **card** (*org. az., pers.*) foglio d'istruzioni; ~ **code** (*elab. elettr.*) codice operativo; **instructions for use** (*market., pubbl.*) istruzioni per l'uso.

instructor, *n.* (*pers.*) istruttore.

instrument, *n.* 1 strumento. 2 (*leg.*) documento formale, atto pubblico, atto notarile, strumento. // ~ **of credit** (*leg.*) titolo di credito; ~ **of transfer** (*leg.*) atto di cessione.

instrumental, *a.* strumentale. // ~ **goods** (*econ., org. az.*) beni strumentali.

insufficiency, *n.* insufficienza.

insufficient, *a.* insufficiente, deficitario.

insult, *n.* ingiuria.

insurable, *a.* (*ass.*) assicurabile. // ~ **interest** (*ass.*) interesse assicurabile; ~ **value** (*ass.*) valore assicurabile.

insurance, *n.* (*ass.*) assicurazione. // ~ **adjuster** (*ass.*) liquidatore, perito; ~ **against loss by fire** (*ass.*) assicurazione contro l'incendio; ~ **agency** (*ass.*) agenzia d'assicurazioni; ~ **agent** (*ass.*) agente d'assicurazioni, produttore (*d'assicurazioni*); ~ **broker** (*ass.*) agente d'assicurazione (*per lo più marittima*); ~ **certificate** (*ass. mar.*) certificato d'assicurazione; ~ **company** (*ass.*) compagnia d'assicurazione, società di assicurazione; ~ **for participation in overseas trade fairs** (*ass.*) assicurazione-fiera; ~ **of advertising and promotional expenses** (*ass.*) assicurazione-prospezione; ~ **of hull and cargo** (*ass. mar.*) assicurazione su corpo e carico; ~ **policy** (*ass.*) polizza d'assicurazione; ~ **premium** (*ass.*) premio d'assicurazione; ~ **rates** (*ass.*) tariffe d'assicurazione; ~ **salesman** (*ass.*) produttore; ~ **shares** (*fin.*) titoli (*azionari*) assicurativi; ~ **stamp** (*leg., pers.*) «marchetta» (*della «mutua»*); ~ **stocks** (*fin.*) (titoli) assicurativi.

insurant, *n.* (*ass.*) assicurato.

insure, *v. t.* (*ass.*) assicurare. *v. i.* (*ass.*) assicurarsi. // to ~ **again** (*ass.*) riassicurare; to ~ **against a risk** (*ass.*) assicurarsi contro un rischio; to ~ **a letter** assicurare una lettera; to ~ **one's life** (*ass.*) assicurarsi sulla vita.

insured, *a.* (*ass.*) assicurato. *n.* (*ass.*) assicurato. // ~ **capital** (*ass.*) capitale assicurato; ~ **property** (*ass.*) cosa assicurata; ~ **value** (*ass.*) valore assicurato.

insurer, *n.* (*ass.*) assicuratore.

intact, *a.* intatto.

intake, *n.* (*trasp. mar.*) quantitativo di merce caricata a bordo. // ~ **measurement** (*trasp. mar.*) cubaggio della merce caricata a bordo, peso della merce caricata a bordo.

intangible, *a.* incorporeo. *n.* (*rag.*) attività immateriale, attività invisibile. // ~ **assets** (*rag.*) attività immateriali, attività invisibili.

integral, *a.* integrale.

integrally, *avv.* integralmente.

integrate, *v. t.* integrare.

integration, *n.* integrazione.

integrative, *a.* integrativo.

intelligence, *n.* 1 intelligenza. 2 (*comm.*) informazioni, notizie.

intelligent, *a.* intelligente.

intend, *v. i.* intendere, aver l'intenzione di, voler dire.

intendant, *n.* intendente.

intense, *a.* intenso.

intensely, *avv.* intensamente.

intensification, *n.* 1 intensificazione. 2 potenziamento. // ~ **of research** (*econ.*) potenziamento della ricerca.

intensify, *v. t.* intensificare. *v. i.* intensificarsi.

intensive, *a.* 1 intensivo. 2 concentrato. // ~ **agriculture** (*econ.*) agricoltura intensiva.

intent, *n.* (*leg.*) intenzione.

intention, *n.* intenzione.

intentional, *a.* intenzionale. // ~ **damage** (*leg.*) danno intenzionale.

intentionality, *n.* intenzionalità.

intentionally, *avv.* intenzionalmente.

interact, *v. i.* interagire.

interaction, *n.* 1 interazione, azione reciproca, influsso reciproco. 2 (*stat.*) interazione.

interagency, *n.* intermediazione.

interagent, *n.* intermediario, agente intermediario.

interbank, *a. attr.* (*banca*) interbancario. // ~ **deposits** (*banca*) depositi interbancari; ~ **lira market** (*fin.*) mercato della lira interbancaria.

interchange[1], *n.* scambio. // **the ~ of currency between nations** (*econ.*) lo scambio di valuta fra nazioni.

interchange[2], *v. t.* scambiare. *v. i.* scambiarsi.

interchangeability, *n.* intercambiabilità.

interchangeable, *a.* intercambiabile.

interchangeably, *avv.* scambievolmente.

intercom, *n.* (*attr. uff.*) citofono, interfonico.

intercompany, *a. attr.* (*org. az.*) interaziendale.

intercorporate, *a.* (*org. az., USA*) interaziendale.

interdict, *v. t.* (*leg.*) interdire, vietare.

interdiction, *n.* (*leg.*) interdizione, divieto.

interdictory, *a.* (*leg.*) interdittorio, che interdice. // ~ **decree** (*leg.*) sentenza d'interdizione.

inter-enterprise, *a. attr.* (*org. az.*) interaziendale. // ~ **cooperation agreements** (*comm.*) accordi di cooperazione tra imprese.

interest[1], *n.* **1** interesse, vantaggio. **2** (*fin., rag.*) interesse, interessi; frutto (*del denaro*), utile. **3** (*leg.*) diritto soggettivo. // ~ **account** (*rag.*) conto interessi; ~ **accruing from a certain date** (*rag.*) interesse decorrente da una certa data; ~ **and commission** (*banca*) interessi e commissioni; ~ **-bearing** (*rag.*) fruttifero; ~ **-bearing account** (*rag.*) conto fruttifero; ~ **-bearing deposit** (*banca*) deposito fruttifero; ~ **book** (*rag.*) libro interessi; ~ **coupon** (*rag.*) cedola d'interesse; ~ **in arrears** (*rag.*) interessi di mora; ~ **in black** (*banca*) interessi sui numeri neri; ~ **in red** (*banca*) interessi sui numeri rossi; ~ **-induced inflation** (*econ.*) inflazione indotta dagli interessi; **the** ~ **on a loan** (*cred.*) gli interessi su un prestito; ~ **rates** (*fin.*) tassi d'interesse; ~ **subsidies** (*fin., rag.*) abbuoni d'interesse; ~ **table** (*rag.*) prontuario degli interessi; « ~ **to run from April 12th** » (*banca*) «valuta 12 aprile»; to **have an** ~ **in a business** (*fin.*) essere cointeressati in un'azienda; **non-** ~ **-bearing Government notes** (*fin.*) buoni del tesoro infruttiferi.

interest[2], *v. t.* interessare. // to ~ **a banker in a loan** (*cred.*) interessare un banchiere a un mutuo.

interested, *a.* interessato. // **the** ~ **parties** (*leg.*) le parti interessate.

interesting, *a.* interessante.

interest oneself, *v. rifl.* interessarsi. // to ~ **in st.** interessarsi di (a) qc.

interfere, *v. i.* interferire.

interference, *n.* interferenza, ingerenza.

interfirm, *a.* (*org. az.*) interaziendale.

intergovernmental, *a.* intergovernativo. // ~ **transactions** (*dog., fin.*) transazioni intergovernative.

interim, *a.* (*comm.*) provvisorio. // ~ **certificate** (*fin.*) certificato provvisorio (*di titoli azionari, ecc.*); ~ **dividends** (*fin.*) dividendi provvisori, dividendi in acconto; ~ **receiver** (*leg.*) curatore (fallimentare) provvisorio; ~ **report** relazione provvisoria, relazione interinale.

interindustrial, *a.* (*org. az.*) infraindustriale.

interior, *a.* **1** interiore, interno. **2** *n.* (l')interno.

interlock, *v. t.* collegare.

interlocking, *a.* che collega, che connette. // ~ **director** (*amm.*) amministratore comune (*di più società*).

interlocutory, *a.* (*leg.*) interlocutorio. // ~ **judgement** (*leg.*) sentenza interlocutoria.

intermediary, *a.* **1** intermedio. **2** intermediario. *n.* intermediario, mediatore. // **the intermediaries in trade** gli intermediari del commercio.

intermediate, *a.* intermedio. *n.* intermediario, mediatore. // **the** ~ **cadres** (*pers.*) i quadri intermedi; ~ **carrier** (*trasp.*) vettore intermedio; ~ **goods** (*org. az.*) beni strumentali; ~ **port** (*trasp. mar.*) scalo intermedio; ~ **station** (*trasp. ferr.*) stazione intermedia.

intermediation, *n.* intermediazione.

intermittent, *a.* intermittente. // ~ **strike** (*sind.*) sciopero a singhiozzo.

intern[1], *n.* (*pers.*) (medico) interno.

intern[2], *v. t.* (*leg.*) mandare al confino.

internal, *a.* interno. // ~ **audit** (*fin.*) controllo contabile interno, revisione contabile interna; ~ **auditing** (*fin.*) *V.* ~ **audit**; ~ **check** (*rag.*) controllo (contabilistico) interno; ~ **combustion engine** (*trasp.*) motore a combustione interna, motore a scoppio; ~ **commerce** commercio interno; ~ **compensation** (*rag.*) giroconto; ~ **navigation** (*trasp.*) navigazione interna, navigazione fluviale; ~ **revenue tax** (*fin.*) imposta indiretta, imposta di fabbricazione; dazio di consumo; **for** ~ **convenience** per ragioni d'ordine interno.

internally, *avv.* internamente. // ~ **generated cash resources** (*fin.*) autofinanziamento.

international, *a.* internazionale. // ~ **arbitration** (*comm. est.*) arbitrato internazionale; ~ **Bureau of Weights and Measures** Ufficio Internazionale dei Pesi e delle Misure; ~ **Chamber of Commerce (ICC)** Camera di Commercio Internazionale (*CCI*); **an** ~ **Court** (*leg.*) un tribunale internazionale; ~ **financial group** (*fin.*) gruppo finanziario internazionale; **the** ~ **haulage trade** (*trasp.*) i trasporti internazionali; ~ **Labour Organization (ILO)** Organizzazione Internazionale del Lavoro (*OIL*); ~ **law** (*leg.*) diritto internazionale; ~ **legislation** (*leg.*) legislazione internazionale; ~ **liquidity** (*fin.*)

liquidità internazionale; ~ **Monetary Fund (IMF)** Fondo Monetario Internazionale (*FMI*); ~ **money order** (*cred.*) vaglia internazionale; ~ **private law** (*leg.*) diritto privato internazionale; ~ **stock** (*Borsa, fin.*) titolo a mercato internazionale; ~ **trade** (*comm. est.*) commercio internazionale.

interoffice, *a. attr.* (*org. az.*) fra gli uffici (*d'una ditta, ecc.*); interno. // ~ **memo** (*org. az.*) promemoria interno, nota interna; ~ **telephone** (*attr. uff.*) telefono interno.

interpenetrate, *v. recipr.* interpenetrarsi.

interpenetration, *n.* (*econ.*) interpenetrazione (*di mercati*).

interphone, *n.* (*attr. uff.*) interfonico, citofono.

interplant, *a.* (*org. az.*) interno. // ~ **transfers of materials** (*org. az.*) passaggi interni di materie.

interpret, *v. t.* interpretare. // to ~ **a contract** (*leg.*) interpretare un contratto.

interpretation, *n.* interpretazione. // ~ **clause** (*leg.*) clausola interpretativa; **the ~ of a law** (*leg.*) l'interpretazione d'una legge; ~ **of markets** (*market.*) interpretazione dei mercati.

interpretative, *a.* interpretativo.

interpreter, *n.* (*pers.*) interprete.

interrogate, *v. t.* interrogare.

interrogation, *n.* interrogazione.

interrogatory, *n.* (*leg.*) interrogatorio.

interrupt, *v. t.* interrompere.

interruption, *n.* interruzione.

interstate, *a.* (*USA*) interstatale. // ~ **commerce** (*USA*) commercio interstatale (*fra Stati dell'Unione*).

interurban, *a.* (*trasp.*) interurbano.

interval, *n.* intervallo.

intervene, *v. i.* intervenire. // to ~ **in a dispute** intervenire in una disputa.

intervener, *n.* (*leg.*) interveniente.

intervening, *a.* (*leg.*) interveniente.

intervenor, *n. V.* **intervener.**

intervention, *n.* 1 intervento. 2 interposizione. 3 mediazione. // ~ **in a suit** (*leg.*) intervento in causa; ~ **point** (*fin.*) punto d'intervento (*dello SME, ecc.*); ~ **prices** (*econ.*) prezzi d'intervento.

interview[1], *n.* (*market., pers.*) intervista, colloquio.

interview[2], *v. t.* (*market., pers.*) intervistare; avere un colloquio, abboccarsi con (*q.*). // to ~ **housewives about their preferences** (*market.*) intervistare le massaie sulle loro preferenze; to ~ **job applicants** (*pers.*) intervistare gli aspiranti a un impiego.

interviewee, *n.* (*market., pers.*) intervistato.

interviewer, *n.* (*market., pers.*) intervistatore.

interwoven, *a.* intrecciato. // ~ **holdings** (*fin.*) partecipazioni incrociate; ~ **participations** (*fin.*) partecipazioni incrociate.

intestate, *a.* (*leg.*) intestato, senza aver fatto testamento.

intimate, *a.* intimo.

intimation, *n.* (*leg.*) intimazione, notificazione.

intimidate, *v. t.* intimidire.

intimidation, *n.* intimidazione.

into, *prep.* dentro.

intra-Community, *a.* intracomunitario. // ~ **duties** (*comm. est.*) dazi intracomunitari.

intracompany, *a.* (*org. az.*) che si svolge nell'ambito d'una società.

intrinsic, *a.* intrinseco. // ~ **value** (*econ.*) valore intrinseco.

introduce, *v. t.* 1 introdurre, immettere, inserire. 2 presentare, far conoscere. 3 (*pubbl.*) presentare (*un articolo, ecc.*). // to ~ **arrangements for «upping» incomes** introdurre il principio della integrazione dei redditi; to ~ **a bill** (*leg.*) presentare un progetto di legge; to ~ **new manufacturing processes** (*org. az.*) introdurre nuovi metodi di lavorazione.

introduction, *n.* 1 introduzione, immissione, inserimento, inserzione. 2 presentazione. 3 (*pubbl.*) presentazione (*d'un articolo, ecc.*).

introductive, *a.* introduttivo.

introductory, *a.* introduttivo.

intrust, *v. t. V.* **entrust.**

inure, *v. i.* (*leg.*) entrare in vigore, avere effetto, cominciare.

invade, *v. t.* (*leg.*) invadere, infrangere, violare.

invalid[1], *a.* 1 invalido, infermo, inabile. 2 (*leg.*) invalido, non valido. *n.* invalido. // ~ **workmen** (*pers.*) operai invalidi.

invalid[2], *v. t.* inabilitare. *v. i.* diventare invalido.

invalidate, *v. t.* (*leg.*) invalidare. // to ~ **a will** (*leg.*) invalidare un testamento.

invalidation, *n.* (*leg.*) invalidazione.

invalidity, *n.* 1 invalidità. 2 (*leg.*) invalidità. // ~ **pension** (*pers.*) pensione d'invalidità (al lavoro).

invaluable, *a.* inapprezzabile.

invasion, *n.* (*leg.*) invasione, infrazione, violazione.

invent, *v. t.* inventare.

invention, *n.* invenzione.

inventor, *n.* inventore.

inventory[1], *n.* 1 (*org. az.*) assortimento, stock; scorta, scorte; merci in magazzino; rimanenze. 2 (*rag.*) inventario. // ~ **adjustment** (*org. az.*) adeguamento delle scorte; ~ **and valuation of stocks** (*rag.*) rilevazione e stima delle scorte; ~ **balance** (*rag.*) saldo di chiusura; ~ **by quantity** (*org. az.*) inventario quantitativo; ~ **control** (*org. az.*) controllo delle giacenze, controllo (*o* gestione) delle scorte, controllo di magazzino; ~ **costs** (*rag.*) spese di magazzino; ~ **increase** (*org. az.*) accrescimento degli stock; ~ **items** (*rag.*) scorte; ~ **management** (*org. az.*) gestione dei materiali; ~ **of the cargo** (*trasp. mar.*) inventario del carico; ~ **pricing** (*rag.*) valutazione delle scorte; ~ **reduction** (*org. az.*) riduzione delle scorte; ~ **turnover** (*org. az.*) ricambio del magazzino; ~ **variations** (*rag.*) variazione degli stock.

inventory[2], *v. t.* (*rag.*) inventariare, fare l'inventario di (*prodotti, articoli, ecc.*). // to ~ **at** (*rag.*) avere un valore d'inventario pari a.

inverse, *a.* inverso, contrario, opposto.

inversion, *n.* inversione.

invert, *v. t.* invertire.

invertible, *a.* invertibile.

invest, *v. t.* (*fin.*) investire, impiegare (*denaro*). *v. i.* (*fin.*) fare investimenti, investire denaro. // to ~ **in shares** (*fin.*) investire in azioni; to ~ **sb. with full powers** (*leg.*) investire q. di pieni poteri.

investigate, *v. t.* (*leg.*) investigare, indagare, fare indagini su (*q.*).

investigating, *a.* (*leg.*) inquirente. // ~ **magistrate** (*leg.*) giudice istruttore.

investigation, *n.* (*leg.*) investigazione, indagine, accertamento, sopralluogo.

investigational, *a.* (*leg.*) investigativo.

investigative, *a.* (*leg.*) investigativo. // ~ **power** (*leg.*) potere investigativo.

investigator, *n.* 1 investigatore. 2 (*ass.*) liquidatore, perito.

investigatory, *n.* (*leg.*) investigativo.

investing, *a.* (*fin.*) che investe; investitore (*agg.*). // **the** ~ **company** la società investitrice.

investment, *n.* (*fin.*) investimento, impiego (*di denaro*). // ~ **adviser** (*fin.*) esperto finanziario; ~ **analysis** (*fin.*) analisi degli investimenti; ~ **bank** (*fin., ingl.*) «investment bank» (*società finanziaria tipica del mercato dei capitali inglese*); ~ **banking** (*fin., ingl.*) «investment banking» (*attività finanziaria tipica del mercato dei capitali inglese*); ~ **company** (*fin.*) società per investimenti finanziari, società d'investimenti mobiliari; ~ **counsellor** (*fin.*) *V.* ~ **adviser;** ~ **dealer** (*fin.*) collocatore (*di fondi d'investimento*); ~ **fund** (*fin.*) fondo comune d'investimento; ~ **goods** (*econ., fin.*) beni d'investimento; **an** ~ **in common stocks** (*fin.*) un investimento in azioni ordinarie; ~ **in fixed assets** (*fin.*) investimenti in beni immobili; ~ **in movable assets** (*fin.*) investimenti in beni mobili; ~ **-led boom** (*econ.*) boom alimentato dagli investimenti; ~ **management** (*banca*) servizio-Borsa; (*fin.*) gestione di portafogli azionari; ~ **policy** (*econ., fin.*) politica degli investimenti; ~ **portfolio** (*rag.*) portafoglio titoli; ~ **trends** (*fin.*) dinamica degli investimenti; ~ **trust** (*fin.*) fondo comune d'investimento.

investor, *n.* (*fin.*) investitore, risparmiatore.

invisible, *a.* invisibile. // ~ **exports** (*comm. est., econ.*) esportazioni invisibili, entrate invisibili; ~ **imports** (*comm. est., econ.*) importazioni invisibili, uscite invisibili; ~ **items** (*econ.*) partite invisibili (*della bilancia dei pagamenti*); ~ **tariffs** (*econ.*) tariffe invisibili.

invisibles, *n. pl. V.* **invisible items.**

invitation, *n.* invito. // ~ **card** (biglietto di) invito.

invite, *v. t.* invitare. // to ~ **tenders** (*fin.*) sollecitare offerte cauzionali per un'aggiudicazione, bandire (*o* indire) una gara d'appalto.

invocation, *n.* invocazione.

invoice[1], *n.* 1 fattura. 2 (*trasp. mar.*) polizza di carico. // ~ **book** (*rag.*) libro fatture; libro acquisti; ~ **clerk** (*pers.*) fatturista; ~ **control** (*rag.*) controllo fatturazione; ~ **department** (*org. az.*) reparto fatturazione; ~ **price** prezzo di fattura.

invoice[2], *v. t.* 1 (*market., USA*) inviare fatture a (*q.*). 2 (*rag.*) fatturare. 3 (*trasp.*) spedire (*una partita di merce, ecc.*).

invoiced, *a.* (*rag.*) fatturato.

invoicing, *n.* (*rag.*) fatturazione. // ~ **machine** (*macch. uff.*) (macchina) fatturatrice.

invoke, *v. t.* invocare.

involuntary, *a.* 1 involontario. 2 obbligatorio, forzato. // ~ **bankruptcy** (*leg.*) fallimento dichiarato su istanza dei creditori; ~ **saving** (*econ.*) risparmio forzato; ~ **unemployment** (*econ., sind.*) disoccupazione forzata.

involve, *v. t.* implicare. // to ~ **great expenditure** richiedere spese enormi.

inward, *a.* 1 interno. 2 (*trasp.*) di ritorno. // ~ **bound vessel** (*trasp. mar.*) nave «in entrata»; ~ **bound voyage** (*trasp. mar.*) viaggio di ritorno; ~ **freight** (*trasp. mar.*) nolo d'entrata.

IOU, *n.* (*abbr. di* **I owe you**) (*cred.*) «IOU», riconoscimento scritto di un debito.

iron, *n.* ferro. *a. attr.* ferreo. // ~ **and steel** (*econ.*) siderurgico; ~ **and steel industry** (*econ.*)

industria siderurgica; ~ **-metallurgy** (*econ.*) siderurgia; ~ **-worker** (*pers.*) (operaio) metallurgico.

irrecoverable, *a.* 1 irrecuperabile. 2 irreparabile. // ~ **debt** (*o* **credit**) (*cred.*) credito inesigibile; ~ **losses** perdite irreparabili.

irredeemable, *a.* irredimibile. // ~ **debenture** (*fin.*) obbligazione irredimibile; ~ **paper money** (*fin.*) carta moneta non convertibile (*in moneta metallica*).

irrefutability, *n.* inconfutabilità.

irrefutable, *a.* inconfutabile. // ~ **evidence** (*leg.*) prova certa.

irregular, *a.* irregolare. // ~ **payments** pagamenti irregolari; **an** ~ **worker** (*pers.*) un lavoratore saltuario.

irregularity, *n.* irregolarità.

irregulars, *n. pl.* (*market.*) merci difettose, merci di qualità inferiore a quella normale (*generalm. vendute senza marca e con forti sconti*).

irremovable, *a.* (*pers.*) inamovibile.

irreparable, *a.* irreparabile.

irresponsibility, *n.* irresponsabilità.

irresponsible, *a.* irresponsabile.

irrevocability, *n.* irrevocabilità.

irrevocable, *a.* irrevocabile. // ~ **and confirmed credit** (*banca*) credito irrevocabile e confermato; ~ **credit** (*cred.*) credito irrevocabile; ~ **judgement** (*leg.*) sentenza irrevocabile; ~ **letter of credit** (*banca*) lettera di credito irrevocabile.

isolate, *v. t.* isolare.

isolation, *n.* isolamento.

issuance, *n.* 1 (*fin., USA*) emissione, rilascio. 2 (*giorn., USA*) pubblicazione.

issue[1], *n.* 1 emissione, distribuzione, consegna, rilascio. 2 (*giorn.*) pubblicazione, stampa, tiratura. 3 (*giorn.*) edizione, numero (*d'un giornale*); fascicolo (*d'una rivista, ecc.*). 4 (*leg.*) discendenza. 5 (*leg.*) questione, problema. // ~ **expressed in dollars** (*fin.*) emissione in dollari; ~ **market** (*fin.*) mercato delle emissioni; **an** ~ **of bonds** (*fin.*) un'emissione di titoli; ~ **of fact** (*leg.*) questione di fatto; **the** ~ **of import and export licences** (*comm. est.*) il rilascio delle licenze d'importazione e d'esportazione; ~ **of law** (*leg.*) questione di diritto; **the** ~ **of a loan** (*fin.*) l'emissione d'un prestito; **the** ~ **of new coinage** l'emissione di nuove monete; ~ **of shares** (*fin.*) emissione azionaria; ~ **price** (*fin.*) prezzo d'emissione; ~ **to shareholders only** (*fin.*) emissione di azioni riservate ai vecchi azionisti.

issue[2], *v. t.* 1 emettere, distribuire, rilasciare, consegnare. 2 (*cred.*) emettere, trarre, spiccare. 3 (*giorn.*) pubblicare, mettere in circolazione. *v. i.* (*giorn.*) (*di giornale*) essere pubblicato, uscire. // to ~ **bank-notes** (*fin.*) emettere banconote; to ~ **a bill of exchange** (*cred.*) trarre una cambiale; to ~ **a bill of lading** (*trasp. mar.*) emettere una polizza di carico; to ~ **a cheque** (*cred.*) emettere un assegno; to ~ **a directive** dare una direttiva; to ~ **a financial paper** (*giorn.*) pubblicare un foglio finanziario.

issued capital, *n.* (*fin.*) capitale emesso.

issuer, *n.* 1 (*banca, cred.*) emittente (*della lettera di credito*). 2 (*fin.*) emittente (*d'azioni, obbligazioni, ecc.*).

issuing house, *n.* (*fin.*) «società promotrice» (*società finanziaria che si occupa del lancio di società per azioni*).

Italian, *a.* e *n.* italiano.

item, *n.* 1 (*comm.*) articolo, «voce» (*d'elenco, bilancio, ecc.*). 2 (*rag.*) capo, capitolo, partita. // ~ **-by-** ~ **haggling** (*econ.*) mercanteggiamento sulle singole «voci» (*sui singoli prodotti*); **the items of a balance sheet** (*rag.*) le poste d'un bilancio; **the items of a catalogue** (*market.*) le «voci» d'un catalogo; ~ **of expenditure** (*econ., fin.*) capo (*o* capitolo) di spesa.

itemize, *v. t.* specificare, scrivere (qc.) dando i particolari. // to ~ **all expenses** (*rag.*) specificare tutte le spese.

itemized, *a.* specificato.

itinerant salesman, *n.* (*pl.* **itinerant salesmen**) (*pers.*) viaggiatore di commercio.

itinerary, *n.* (*trasp.*) itinerario.

J

jail, *n.* carcere.

jargon, *n.* gergo.

Jason clause, *n.* (*ass. mar.*) clausola di negligenza (*nell'avaria generale*).

jeopardize, *v. t.* mettere in pericolo.

jerque, *v. t.* e *i.* (*dog.*) ispezionare (*i documenti e il carico d'una nave*).

jerry building, *n.* (*econ.*) speculazione edilizia (*caratterizzata dalla fretta e dall'impiego di materiali scadenti*).

jetsam, *n.* (*trasp. mar.*) gettito, scarico in mare.

jettison[1], *n.* (*trasp. mar.*) getto del carico (*o di parte di esso: per alleggerire la nave in pericolo*).

jettison[2], *v. t.* (*trasp. mar.*) gettare a mare (*il carico o parte di esso: per alleggerire la nave in pericolo*). // to ~ **ballast** (*trasp. mar.*) gettare la zavorra; **jettisoned cargo** (*o* **goods**) (*trasp. mar.*) gettito.

jetty, *n.* (*trasp. mar.*) gettata, banchina, molo.

jingle, *n.* (*pubbl.*) canzonetta (*in radio o TV*).

job[1], *n.* (*pers.*) lavoro, mestiere, mansione, occupazione, ufficio. // ~ **analysis** (*org. az.*) analisi del lavoro; ~ **classification** (*org. az.*) classificazione del lavoro; ~ **-classification method** (*org. az.*) metodo di classificazione del lavoro; ~ **description** (*org. az.*) descrizione del lavoro; ~ **enlargement** (*org. az.*) diversificazione del lavoro; ~ **-enrichment** (*org. az.*) «job-enrichment»; ~ **evaluation** (*org. az.*) valutazione del lavoro, valutazione delle mansioni; ~ **-hopper** (*pers.*) chi passa da un'occupazione all'altra, chi cambia mestiere di continuo; ~ **-hopping** (*pers.*) passaggio da un'occupazione all'altra; ~ **lot** (*market.*) partita di merci disparate; **the** ~ **market** (*econ., pers.*) il mercato del lavoro; ~ **offers** (*econ.*) offerte di lavoro; ~ **opportunities** (*econ.*) possibilità d'impiego; ~ **order** (*org. az.*) ordine di lavorazione, buono di lavorazione; **jobs package** (*econ.*) pacchetto di misure contro la disoccupazione; ~ **production** (*econ.*) produzione su commessa, produzione su ordine; ~ **rating** (*org. az.*) valutazione del lavoro; ~ **rotation** (*org. az.*) rotazione delle mansioni; ~ **sharing** (*econ.*) riduzione della produttività individuale; ~ **sheet** (*org. az.*) foglio d'istruzioni; ~ **work** (*pers.*) lavoro a cottimo; **in** ~ **lots** (*market.*) alla rinfusa; to **be out of** ~ (*pers.*) essere disoccupato.

job[2], *v. i.* **1** (*Borsa, ingl.*) essere un «jobber», fare lo speculatore «professionista». **2** (*market.*) comprare all'ingrosso, fare il grossista. **3** (*pers.*) lavorare a cottimo. *v. t.* (*leg.*) subappaltare, dare in subappalto (*lavori*). // to ~ **out work** dare lavoro a cottimo.

jobber, *n.* **1** (*Borsa*) aggiotatore. **2** (*Borsa, ingl.*) «jobber», «remisier», speculatore «professionista» (*non esiste in Italia*). **3** (*market.*) grossista. **4** (*pers.*) lavoratore a cottimo, cottimista. // ~ **'s turn** (*Borsa, ingl.*) margine del «remisier».

jobbing, *n.* (*pers.*) lavorazione a cottimo, lavorazione su commessa. // ~ **contract** (*pers.*) cottimo; ~ **in contangoes** (*Borsa*) arbitraggio dei riporti; ~ **profits** (*fin.*) utili d'intermediazione.

jobless, *a.* disoccupato. // ~ **rate** (*econ.*) tasso di disoccupazione.

joint, *a.* **1** congiunto, unito. **2** collegiale, collettivo, comune, paritetico. // ~ **account** (*rag.*) conto in partecipazione, conto sociale; ~ **adventure** (*leg.*) associazione in partecipazione; ~ **and several liability** (*leg.*) responsabilità congiunta e solidale; ~ **association** (*leg.*) associazione in partecipazione; ~ **cause** (*leg.*) concausa; ~ **committee** (*pers., sind.*) commissione mista, comitato misto (*p. es.: di rappresentanti dei lavoratori e dei datori di lavoro*); ~ **commodity** (*econ.*) bene complementare; ~ **consultation** (*pers., sind.*) consultazione mista; ~ **debtor** (*leg.*) debitore solidale; **a** ~ **declaration** una dichiarazione congiunta; ~ **demand** (*econ.*) domanda complementare; ~ **director** (*amm.*) condirettore; ~ **European float** (*econ.*) fluttuazione comune delle monete europee; ~ **financing** (*fin.*) finanziamento comune; ~

floating of European currencies (*econ., fin.*) fluttuazione comune delle monete europee; ~ **liability** (*leg.*) responsabilità solidale, solidarietà; ~ **management** (*amm.*) condirezione; ~ **manager** (*amm.*) condirettore; ~ **obligation** (*leg.*) obbligazione solidale; ~ **owner** (*leg.*) comproprietario; ~ **ownership** (*leg.*) proprietà indivisa, comproprietà; ~ **partner** (*leg.*) comproprietario, cointeressato; ~ **property** (*leg.*) comproprietà; **a** ~ **property** (*leg.*) una proprietà comune; ~ **proprietor** (*leg.*) comproprietario; ~ **responsibility** (*leg.*) responsabilità collegiale, responsabilità collettiva; ~ **signatures** firme abbinate; ~ **stock** (*fin.*) capitale sociale, capitale azionario; ~ **-stock bank** (*banca*) banca a capitale azionario, banca di credito ordinario; ~ **-stock company** (*fin.*) società di capitali, società a capitale variabile; (*di solito*) società per azioni, società anonima; ~ **-stock company limited by guarantee** (*leg.*) società per azioni a responsabilità limitata al capitale sottoscritto e inoltre fino a una data cifra oltre il capitale sociale (*non esiste in Italia, e, di solito, non ha fini di lucro*); ~ **-stock company limited by shares** (*fin.*) società anonima a responsabilità limitata al capitale azionario, società per azioni; ~ **-stock limited company** (*fin.*) società a responsabilità limitata dalle azioni, società per azioni; ~ **tariffs** (*trasp.*) tariffe cumulative (*su cui si accordano due o più vettori*); ~ **venture** (*econ.*) iniziativa imprenditoriale associata; (*leg.*) associazione in partecipazione.

jointly, *avv.* 1 insieme, solidalmente. 2 collegialmente, collettivamente, comunemente. // ~ **and severally** (*leg.*) solidalmente; ~ **interested** cointeressato; ~ **liable** (*o* **responsible**) (*leg.*) responsabile in solido, solidale.

jot, *v. t.* annotare in fretta (*appunti, ecc.*), buttar giù (*note frettolose, ecc.*). // to ~ **down** scribacchiare (*note, ecc.*).

jotting, *n.* annotazione frettolosa, breve appunto.

journal, *n.* 1 (*giorn.*) quotidiano. 2 (*giorn.*) periodico. 3 (*rag.*) libro giornale, giornale. 4 (*trasp. mar.*) giornale di bordo. // ~ **entry** (*rag.*) registrazione a giornale; ~ **of forward transactions and transactions for the account** (*fin., rag.*) libro (per l'annotazione giornaliera) delle operazioni a termine e di riporto.

journalism, *n.* (*giorn.*) giornalismo.

journalist, *n.* (*giorn.*) giornalista.

journalistic, *a.* (*giorn.*) giornalistico.

journalize, *v. t.* (*rag.*) registrare a giornale. *v. i.* (*rag.*) tenere un (libro) giornale.

journey[1], *n.* (*trasp.*) viaggio (*specialm. per via di terra*), tragitto, percorso. // ~ **by land** (*trasp.*) viaggio di terra; ~ **by plane** (*trasp. aer.*) viaggio aereo; ~ **empty** (*trasp. ferr.*) percorso a vuoto; ~ **loaded** (*trasp. ferr.*) percorso con carico.

journey[2], *v. i.* (*trasp.*) viaggiare, fare un viaggio.

journeyman, *n.* (*pl.* **journeymen**) (*pers.*) operaio giornaliero, giornaliero.

judge[1], *n.* (*leg.*) giudice, magistrato. // ~ **delegate** (*leg.*) giudice delegato; ~ **-made law** (*leg.*) giurisprudenza (*diritto creato dai giudici stessi, basato sul «precedente» giudiziario*).

judge[2], *v. t.* 1 (*leg.*) giudicare. 2 (*leg.*) appianare (*una vertenza*). // to ~ **a case** (*leg.*) giudicare una causa legale.

judgement, *n.* 1 giudizio. 2 (*leg.*) giudizio, sentenza. 3 (*leg.*) decreto penale. // ~ **book** (*leg.*) registro delle sentenze; ~ **by default** (*leg.*) giudizio contumaciale; ~ **creditor** (*leg.*) creditore giudiziario; ~ **debt** (*leg.*) debito portato in giudizio; ~ **debtor** (*leg.*) debitore giudiziario; ~ **of first instance** (*leg.*) giudizio di primo grado; ~ **of last resort** (*leg.*) giudizio d'ultima istanza.

judgeship, *n.* (*leg.*) ufficio di giudice.

judgment, *n.* *V.* **judgement.**

judicature, *n.* 1 (*leg.*) ordinamento giudiziario, magistratura. 2 (*leg.*) giurisdizione. 3 (*leg.*) ufficio di giudice. 4 (*leg.*) tribunale.

judicial, *a.* (*leg.*) giudiziale, giudiziario. // ~ **act** (*leg.*) atto giudiziale, atto giudiziario; ~ **admission** (*leg.*) confessione giudiziale; ~ **attachment** (*leg.*) sequestro giudiziario; ~ **confession** (*leg.*) confessione giudiziale; ~ **controversy** (*leg.*) vertenza giudiziaria; ~ **inquiry** (*leg.*) istruttoria; ~ **power** (*leg.*) potere giudiziario; ~ **proceedings** (*leg.*) azione legale, vie legali; ~ **register** (*leg.*) casellario giudiziario; ~ **sale** (*leg.*) vendita giudiziale.

judiciary, *a.* (*leg.*) giudiziario. *n.* (*leg.*) potere giudiziario, magistratura, ordinamento giudiziario.

jumble, *n.* 1 confusione, miscuglio. 2 (*market., ingl.*) articoli spaiati, articoli di poco prezzo. // ~ **sale** (*market., ingl.*) vendita d'articoli di poco prezzo.

jump[1], *n.* balzo. // **a** ~ **in prices** (*market.*) un aumento improvviso dei prezzi.

jump[2], *v. i.* 1 balzare. 2 (*fin., market.*) (*di prezzi*) aumentare improvvisamente. *v. t.* scavalcare. // to ~ **at an offer** affrettarsi ad accettare un'offerta.

junction, *n.* 1 (*trasp.*) incrocio, nodo stradale. 2 (*trasp. ferr.*) nodo ferroviario.

junior, *a.* junior, iuniore. *n.* 1 (*pers.*)

impiegato di grado inferiore; subalterno. **2** (*pers.*) operaio di grado inferiore. // ~ **partner** (*fin.*) socio di minore importanza, socio di data più recente.

junta, *n.* (*amm.*) giunta.

juridical, *a.* (*leg.*) giuridico, legale. // ~ **act** (*leg.*) atto giuridico; ~ **days** (*leg.*) giorni d'udienza; ~ **person** (*leg.*) persona giuridica.

jurisdiction, *n.* (*leg.*) giurisdizione.

jurisdictional, *a.* (*leg.*) giurisdizionale.

jurisprudence, *n.* (*leg.*) giurisprudenza.

jurisprudential, *a.* (*leg.*) giurisprudenziale.

jurist, *n.* (*leg.*) giurista.

juristic, *a.* (*leg.*) giuristico, giuridico, legale. // ~ **act** (*leg.*) atto giuridico; ~ **person** (*leg.*) persona giuridica.

juror, *n.* (*leg.*) giurato, membro di giuria.

jury, *n.* (*leg.*) giuria, giurì. // ~ **foreman** presidente della giuria; ~ **list** albo dei giurati.

juryman, *n.* (*pl.* **jurymen**) (*leg.*) giurato, membro di giuria.

jus relictae, *n.* (*leg.: in Scozia*) legittima.

just¹, *a.* giusto.

just², *avv.* appena, da poco.

justice, *n.* **1** (*leg.*) giustizia. **2** (*leg., ingl.*) giudice (*della Corte Suprema*). // ~ **of the Peace** (*leg.*) giudice di pace, giudice conciliatore.

justiceship, *n.* (*leg.*) ufficio di giudice.

justification, *n.* (*giorn., pubbl.*) allineamento (*d'una riga*); giustificazione.

justified, *a.* giustificato.

justify, *v. t.* **1** (*giorn., pubbl.*) allineare, giustificare. **2** (*leg.*) addurre (*un mezzo*) a difesa. // to ~ **a line** (*giorn., pubbl.*) allineare una riga.

juvenile, *a.* (*leg.*) minorile.

K

keel, *n.* 1 (*trasp. mar.*) chiglia, carena. 2 (*trasp. mar.*) chiatta; barcone (*a fondo piatto*).

keelage, *n.* (*trasp. mar.*) diritti d'entrata in porto, diritto d'ancoraggio, diritto d'ormeggio.

keen, *a.* 1 acuto, forte. 2 (*market.*) (*di prezzo*) conveniente, basso, favorevole all'acquirente. // **a ~ competition** (*market.*) una concorrenza vivace.

keenness, *n.* (*market.*) convenienza (*di prezzo*).

keep, *v. t.* (*pass.* e *part. pass.* **kept**) 1 tenere, trattenere. 2 mantenere, custodire. // to ~ **an account alive** (*rag.*) tenere acceso un conto; to ~ **an account with sb.** (*rag.*) tenere un conto aperto presso q.; to ~ **accounts** (*rag.*) tenere i conti (*o* la contabilità); to ~ **sb. advised about st.** tenere q. al corrente di qc.; to ~ **an appointment** mantenere un appuntamento; to ~ **back** trattenere; to ~ **bills afloat** (*cred.*) tenere in circolazione degli effetti; to ~ **the books** (*rag.*) tenere i libri contabili, tenere la contabilità, tenere i conti; to ~ **the books by double entry** (*rag.*) tenere la contabilità a partita doppia; to ~ **the books up to date** (*rag.*) tenere aggiornati i conti; to ~ **a business** mandare avanti una azienda; to ~ **one's business going** mandare avanti la baracca (*fam.*); «~ **cool**» (*market.*) «tenere al fresco» (*scritto su scatole, ecc.*); to ~ **st. down** tenere qc. a freno, limitare qc.; «~ **dry**» (*market.*) «tenere all'asciutto»; to ~ **an engagement** tener fede a un impegno; to ~ **a firm's accounts** (*rag.*) tenere la contabilità d'un'azienda; to ~ **a firm's books** (*rag.*) tenere la contabilità d'una ditta; to ~ **the law** (*leg.*) osservare la legge, rispettare la legge; to ~ **prices down** (*econ., market.*) tener bassi i prezzi; to ~ **prices steady** (*econ., market.*) mantenere stabili i prezzi, stabilizzare i prezzi; to ~ **the sea** (*trasp. mar.*) tenere il mare; to ~ **a shop** (*market.*) esercire un negozio; to ~ **silent** far silenzio; to ~ **up the price of certain goods** (*market.*) mantenere alto il prezzo di talune merci; to ~ **up prices** (*econ.*) sostenere i prezzi; to ~ **up with the times** andar di pari passo coi tempi, essere moderno.

keeper, *n.* (*pers.*) custode, guardiano, sorvegliante.

keeping, *n.* custodia, guardia, sorveglianza.

Kennedy round, *n.* (*comm. est.*) «Kennedy round» (*appello, lanciato nel 1963 dal presidente J.F. Kennedy, per la riduzione globale dei dazi doganali*). // ~ **negotiations** (*comm. est.*) negoziati per il «Kennedy round»; ~ **tariff cuts** (*comm. est.*) riduzioni tariffarie (previste negli accordi) del «Kennedy round».

key, *n.* chiave. *a. attr.* importante, principale, chiave. // ~ **bargain** (*sind.*) insieme delle condizioni «chiave» (*d'un accordo collettivo di lavoro, che costituiscono un precedente per altre aziende*); ~ **box** (*tur.*) buchetta per le chiavi (*in un albergo*); **a ~ industry** (*econ.*) un'industria «chiave»; **a ~ job** (*pers.*) una mansione «chiave»; ~ **money** buonuscita (*a un inquilino uscente*); **a ~ position** (*pers.*) un posto chiave.

keyboard, *n.* (*elab. elettr.*) tastiera. // ~ **operator** (*elab. elettr.*) tastierista.

Keynesian, *a.* (*econ.*) keynesiano.

kick¹, *n.* 1 calcio, pedata. 2 (*fig.*) licenziamento. // to **get the ~** (*pers.*) essere licenziato.

kick², *v. t.* e *i.* calciare, tirar calci, dare calci a, prendere a calci, prendere a pedate. // to ~ **out** (*pers.*) licenziare.

kickback, *n.* (*market.*) abbuono sottobanco, sconto sottobanco, tangente.

kickout, *n.* (*pers.*) licenziamento.

kidnap, *v. t.* (*leg.*) sequestrare (*q. a scopo di ricatto*); rapire.

kidnapping, *n.* (*leg.*) sequestro.

kilogram, *n.* *V.* **kilogramme.**

kilogramme, *n.* chilogrammo.

kilometer, *n.* *V.* **kilometre.**

kilometre, *n.* chilometro.

kind¹, *n.* genere, qualità, tipo, varietà. // **in ~** in natura.

kind², *a.* 1 gentile, cordiale. 2 (*di lettera, scritto*) gradito.

kindness, *n.* gentilezza.

kitchen, *n.* cucina. // ~ **aids** accessori (*articoli, piccoli elettrodomestici, ecc.*) per la cucina.

kite[1], *n.* 1 (*fam.*) cambiale di comodo, cambiale di favore. 2 (*fam.*) assegno senza copertura, assegno «cabriolet». // ~ **flying** (*fam.*) emissione di cambiali di comodo; emissione di assegni allo scoperto.

kite[2], *v. t.* 1 (*fam.*) emettere (*una cambiale di comodo*). 2 (*fam.*) spiccare (*un assegno allo scoperto*). *v. i.* (*fam.*) ottenere denaro per mezzo d'una cambiale di comodo.

knock, *v. t.* battere, colpire, percuotere, picchiare. // to ~ **down** abbattere, atterrare, gettare a terra; aggiudicare (*un oggetto venduto all'asta*); (*fin., pers.*) guadagnare; to ~ **sb. down 4%** (*fam.*) strappare a q. una riduzione del 4% (*su un prezzo*); to ~ **off** smontare (*dal lavoro*), «staccare»; (*market.*) detrarre, defalcare; to ~ **off business** (*fam.*) sbrigare affari.

knockdown, *n.* (*market.*) abbassamento (*di prezzi*). *a. attr.* (*market.*) (*di prezzo*) ridotto, minimo. // **a ~ offer** un'offerta minima; **a ~ rate** (*fin.*) un tasso minimo.

knocking down, *n.* aggiudicazione (*in una vendita all'asta*).

knot, *n.* (*trasp. mar.*) nodo (*misura di velocità pari a un miglio marino, o 1.853 metri, all'ora*).

know, *v. t.* (*pass.* **knew**, *part. pass.* **known**) conoscere.

know-how, *n.* abilità tecnica; complesso di cognizioni tecniche (*non brevettate*); «know-how».

knowledge, *n.* conoscenza. // **without our ~** a nostra insaputa.

know-what, *n.* chiarezza d'idee.

L

lab, *n.* (*fam.*) laboratorio (*scientifico*).

label[1], *n.* 1 (*market.*) cartellino, etichetta. 2 (*market.*) marca di registrazioni discografiche. 3 (*market.*) casa produttrice di registrazioni discografiche. 4 (*trasp.*) cartellino (*sul bagaglio*).

label[2], *v. t.* 1 (*market.*) contrassegnare con un cartellino, mettere un'etichetta a, etichettare. 2 (*trasp.*) contrassegnare (*il bagaglio*) con un cartellino.

labeling, *n. V.* **labelling.**

labelling, *n.* (*market.*) etichettatura.

labor, *n.* e *v. t. V.* **labour.**

laboratory, *n.* laboratorio (*scientifico*).

laborer, *n. V.* **labourer.**

labour[1], *n.* 1 lavoro. 2 fatica. 3 (*econ.*) lavoro, attività lavorativa. 4 (*econ., pers.*) manodopera, lavoratori. // ~ **and capital** (*econ.*) il lavoro e il capitale; ~ **contract** (*pers., sind.*) contratto di lavoro; ~ **copartnership** (*sind.*) compartecipazione agli utili aziendali; ~ **costs** (*econ., rag.*) costo del lavoro, oneri salariali; ~ **day** festa del lavoro; ~ **dispute** (*sind.*) controversia sindacale, vertenza sindacale; ~ **engagement form** (*pers.*) modulo d'assunzione (*al lavoro*); ~ **exchange** (*sind., ingl.*) ufficio di collocamento; ~ **-exchange official** (*pers.*) collocatore (*funzionario d'ufficio di collocamento*); ~ **-intensive** (*econ.*) ad alto impiego di manodopera; ~ **-intensive products** (*org. az.*) prodotti che richiedono un largo impiego di manodopera; ~ **leader** (*sind.*) sindacalista; ~ **legislation** (*leg.*) legislazione in materia di lavoro, diritto del lavoro; ~ **market** (*econ., sind.*) mercato del lavoro; ~ **movement** (*sind.*) movimento sindacale; ~ **negotiation** (*sind.*) trattativa sindacale; ~ **organization** (*sind.*) organizzazione sindacale; **the** ~ **question** (*sind.*) la questione operaia; ~ **relations** (*pers., sind.*) rapporti sindacali, rapporti tra la direzione e le maestranze; ~ **-saving** (*org. az.*) che fa risparmiare lavoro; ~ **-saving appliance** (*org. az.*) attrezzatura che fa risparmiare lavoro; ~ **-saving devices** (*org. az.*) accorgimenti tendenti a risparmiare manodopera; ~ **shortage** (*econ.*) carenza di manodopera; ~ **situation** (*pers.*) situazione del (mercato del) lavoro, «clima» sindacale; ~ **skate** (*slang USA*) iscritto a un sindacato; ~ **turnover** (*org. az.*) ricambio (*o* mobilità) della manodopera; ~ **union** (*sind.*) sindacato; ~ **unionism** (*sind.*) sindacalismo; ~ **unit** (*econ.*) unità di lavoro.

labour[2], *v. i.* 1 faticare, lavorare, operare. 2 *v. t.* elaborare.

labourer, *n.* 1 lavoratore. 2 (*pers.*) lavorante, operaio non qualificato. 3 (*pers.*) bracciante, manovale.

laches, *n.* (*pl. inv.*) (*leg.*) negligenza, morosità, ritardo.

lack[1], *n.* mancanza, carenza. // ~ **of balance** mancanza d'equilibrio, squilibrio; ~ **of diversification** (*econ.*) mancanza di diversificazione; ~ **of evidence** (*leg.*) mancanza di prove; ~ **of funds** (*fin.*) mancanza di fondi; ~ **of jurisdiction** (*leg.*) mancanza di giurisdizione; ~ **of title** (*leg.*) mancanza di titolo.

lack[2], *v. t.* mancare di, difettare di, esser privo di (*qc.*).

lacking, *a.* che manca, mancante. // to **be** ~ mancare, far difetto; to **be** ~ **in** esser privo di.

lade, *v. t.* (*part. pass.* **laden**) (*trasp. mar.*) caricare. // to ~ **a vessel** (*trasp. mar.*) caricare una nave.

laden, *a.* carico.

lading, *n.* (*trasp. mar.*) caricamento, carico. // ~ **port** (*trasp. mar.*) porto di caricamento.

lady, *n.* signora. // ~ **president** presidentessa.

lag[1], *n.* 1 ritardo, indugio, l'indugiare, l'attardarsi. 2 intervallo.

lag[2], *v. i.* 1 attardarsi, indugiare, restare indietro. 2 (*fig.*) ristagnare.

laggard, *n.* (*Borsa, fin.*) titolo il cui prezzo non ha subito variazioni (*a differenza di quello d'altri titoli dello stesso tipo sul mercato*).

laissez-faire, *n.* (*econ.*) «laissez-faire», liberismo. *a. attr.* (*econ.*) liberistico. // ~ **economics** (*econ.*) liberismo; **a** ~ **policy** (*econ.*) una politica liberistica.

laissez-faireism, *n.* (*econ.*) dottrina del

«laissez-faire» (*q. V.*).

lame, *a.* 1 zoppo, zoppicante. 2 (*fig.*) che non regge. 3 (*econ., fin.*) (*di moneta*) debole. // ~ **duck** (*Borsa, fin.*) speculatore insolvente; industria improduttiva.

lamp, *n.* lampada, fanale.

land[1], *n.* 1 terreno, suolo. 2 (*rag.*) terreni (*voce di bilancio*). // ~ **agency** (*econ., ingl.*) agenzia fondiaria; mansione di mediatore di terreni, lavoro di fattore; ~ **agent** (*econ., ingl.*) agente fondiario, mediatore di terreni; agente agricolo, fattore; ~ **bank** (*banca*) banca di credito agricolo; ~ **broker** (*econ., ingl.*) agente immobiliare; ~ **carriage** (*trasp.*) trasporto per via di terra; ~ **credit** (*cred.*) credito immobiliare; ~ **freeze** (*econ.*) congelamento delle vendite di terreni; ~ **improvement** (*econ.*) miglioramento fondiario; ~ **jobber** (*fin.*) speculatore di beni immobili; ~ **-mark** pietra di confine, limite; ~ **office** (*fin.*) ufficio del catasto; ~ **-office business** affari fiorenti e rapidi; ~ **-owner** (*econ.*) proprietario terriero; ~ **reform** (*econ.*) riforma fondiaria; ~ **Register** (*o* **Registry**) Catasto; ~ **route** (*trasp.*) via di terra; ~ **tax** (*fin.*) imposta fondiaria.

land[2], *v. i.* 1 (*trasp. aer.*) atterrare. 2 (*trasp. mar.*) sbarcare, approdare, toccare terra. *v. t.* 1 (*trasp. aer., trasp. mar.*) scaricare. 2 (*trasp. aer., trasp. mar.*) sbarcare. // to ~ **the cargo** (*trasp. aer., trasp. mar.*) sbarcare il carico; to ~ **passengers and goods** (*trasp. aer., trasp. mar.*) sbarcare passeggeri e scaricare merce.

landed, *a.* (*econ.*) terriero, agricolo, fondiario. // ~ **estate** (*econ.*) proprietà fondiaria, beni fondiari; ~ **property** (*econ.*) proprietà fondiaria, proprietà terriera; (*rag.*) terreni (*voce di bilancio*); beni fondiari; **a** ~ **proprietor** (*econ.*) un proprietario terriero; ~ **weight** (*trasp. mar.*) peso allo sbarco, peso sbarcato.

landholder, *n.* (*econ.*) proprietario terriero.

landing, *n.* 1 (*trasp. aer.*) atterraggio, scalo. 2 (*trasp. aer., trasp. mar.*) sbarco, approdo, scalo. // ~ **book** (*trasp. mar.*) registro di sbarco; ~ **card** (*trasp. mar.*) carta di sbarco (*per passeggeri*); ~ **certificate** (*trasp. mar.*) certificato di sbarco, certificato di scarico; ~ **charges** (*trasp. mar.*) spese di sbarco (*per merci*); ~ **-gear** (*trasp. aer.*) carrello; ~ **officer** (*dog.*) ufficiale doganale; ~ **order** (*trasp. mar.*) permesso di sbarco; ~ **place** (*trasp. aer.*) scalo aereo; (*trasp. mar.*) approdo, imbarcadero; ~ **stage** (*trasp. mar.*) imbarcadero; ~ **strip** (*trasp. aer.*) pista d'atterraggio; ~ **ticket** (*trasp. mar.*) permesso di sbarco; ~ **waiter** (*dog., ingl.*) *V.* **landwaiter;** ~ **weight** (*trasp. mar.*) peso sbarcato, peso (accettato) allo sbarco.

landlord, *n.* (*leg.*) concedente; locatore (*d'immobili*); locatore (*di case*); proprietario di casa.

landowner, *n.* (*econ.*) proprietario terriero.

landwaiter, *n.* (*dog., ingl.*) ufficiale doganale.

landworker, *n.* (*pers.*) bracciante agricolo.

lane, *n.* (*trasp. aut.*) corsia. // ~ **closures** chiusure di corsia (in autostrada); **a two-** ~ **highway** (*trasp. aut.*) una strada a due corsie.

language, *n.* lingua, linguaggio.

lapse[1], *n.* 1 periodo (*di tempo*). 2 intervallo, interruzione. 3 (*ass.*) cessazione di copertura (*per mancato pagamento di premi*). 4 (*leg.*) decadenza, prescrizione.

lapse[2], *v. i.* 1 (*anche leg.*) passare. 2 (*leg.*) cadere in prescrizione, decadere.

larceny, *n.* (*ass.*) furto (*più o meno grave*).

large, *a.* grande, grosso, ampio. // ~ **bond** (*fin., USA*) obbligazione del valore nominale di oltre 1.000 dollari; **the** ~ **businesses** (*fin.*) le grandi imprese; **the** ~ **companies** (*fin.*) le grandi imprese; ~ **expenditures** forti spese; **a** ~ **increase in consumption** (*econ.*) una cospicua dilatazione dei consumi; ~ **paper edition** (*pubbl.*) edizione di lusso (*di un libro*); ~ **-scale** in grande; (*fig.*) forte; **a** ~ **-scale corporation** (*fin., USA*) una grande società; ~ **-scale economies** (*econ.*) economie di scala; ~ **-scale production** (*econ.*) produzione su grande scala; ~ **-scale structural changes** (*org. az.*) ingenti variazioni strutturali.

last[1], *a.* passato, scorso, ultimo. // ~ **in, first out (LIFO)** (*rag.*) procedimento contabile per il calcolo dell'inventario consistente nel considerare l'ultima merce entrata in magazzino come la prima uscitane; **the** ~ **thing** (*market., pubbl.*) l'ultima novità, l'ultimo «grido»; ~ **will** (*leg.*) ultime volontà; **the** ~ **word** (*market., pubbl.*) l'ultima novità, l'ultimo «grido».

last[2], *n.* 1 «lasta» (*misura di capacità per granaglie pari a 80 «bushels»*). 2 «lasta» (*misura di peso pari a circa 4.000 libbre*).

last[3], *v. i.* durare, protrarsi, andare per le lunghe.

lasting, *a.* duraturo, durevole.

late, *avv.* in ritardo. *a.* 1 in ritardo. 2 precedente, ex. // ~ **in the season** (*market.*) a stagione inoltrata; ~ **partner** (*fin.*) ex socio; ~ **penalty** (*leg.*) multa per ritardo, multa a carico dei ritardatari; **of** ~ di recente, recentemente, ultimamente.

lately, *avv.* recentemente, ultimamente, di recente.

latent, *a.* latente, nascosto, occulto. // ~ **defects** (*leg.*) vizi occulti; ~ **faults** (*leg.*) vizi occulti.

later, *avv.* poi. *a. attr.* più tardo, posteriore, successivo. // ~ **on** in seguito; **at a** ~ **date** in data posteriore; **not** ~ **than** non più tardi di.

latest, *a.* (il) più recente, recentissimo, ultimo. *n.* (*market., pubbl.*) ultima novità, ultimo «grido». // **the** ~ **edition** (*giorn.*) l'ultima edizione; **the** ~ **news** (*giorn.*) le ultime notizie, le «ultimissime»; **the** ~ **quotations** (*fin.*) le ultime quotazioni.

launch[1], *n.* (*trasp. mar.*) varo.

launch[2], *v. t.* **1** (*market., pubbl.*) lanciare. **2** (*trasp. mar.*) varare. // to ~ **an enterprise** (*fin.*) varare un'impresa; to ~ **a new product** (*market., pubbl.*) lanciare un nuovo prodotto; to ~ **a ship** (*trasp. mar.*) varare una nave.

launching, *n.* **1** (*market., pubbl.*) lancio. **2** (*trasp. mar.*) varo.

law, *n.* **1** (*leg.*) legge, ordinanza. **2** (*leg.*) diritto, giurisprudenza. // ~ **-agent** (*leg.*) procuratore legale; ~ **costs** (*leg.*) spese giudiziarie; ~ **-Court** (*leg.*) tribunale; ~ **-day** (*leg.*) giorno d'udienza (*di corte giudiziaria*); ~ **expenses** (*leg.*) spese giudiziarie, spese processuali; ~ **list** (*leg.*) albo degli avvocati e dei procuratori; ~ **-lords** (*leg., ingl.*) lord (nominati) a vita; ~ **merchant** (*leg., ingl.*) diritto commerciale; ~ **of diminishing returns** (*econ.*) legge della produttività decrescente; ~ **of down-sloping demand** (*econ.*) legge della domanda decrescente; ~ **of the flag** (*leg., trasp. mar.*) legge del Paese di bandiera; ~ **of nations** (*leg.*) diritto delle genti; **the** ~ **of supply and demand** (*econ.*) la legge della domanda e dell'offerta; ~ **office** (*leg.*) ufficio legale; **the** ~ **Officers** (*leg.*) l'«Attorney General» e il «Solicitor General» (*in G.B.*); ~ **proper** (*leg.*) diritto positivo; ~ **provision** (*leg.*) disposizione di legge; ~ **relating to economic activities** (*leg.*) diritto dell'economia; ~ **relating to sales** (*leg.*) diritto in materia di vendite; ~ **suit** (*leg.*) querela; ~ **terms** (*leg.*) termini di legge; ~ **-way** (*leg.*) tradizione (*praticamente con forza di legge*); to **be at** ~ (*leg.*) essere in causa (*legale*); **by** ~ (*leg.*) per legge; **by-** ~ (*leg.*) «leggina»; regolamento locale.

lawbreaker, *n.* (*leg.*) violatore della legge.

lawbreaking, *n.* (*leg.*) violazione della legge.

lawful, *a.* **1** (*leg.*) legale, legittimo. **2** (*leg.*) lecito, permesso. // ~ **acts** (*leg.*) azioni lecite, atti leciti; ~ **age** (*leg.*) età legale (*per compiere taluni atti regolati dalla legge*); ~ **debts** (*leg.*) crediti riconosciuti dalla legge; ~ **money** (*leg.*) moneta legale; ~ **owner** (*leg.*) proprietario legittimo.

lawfulness, *n.* (*leg.*) legalità, legittimità.

lawgiver, *n.* (*leg.*) legislatore.

lawless, *a.* (*leg.*) illegale, illecito. // ~ **acts** (*leg.*) azioni illegali.

lawmaker, *n.* (*leg.*) legislatore.

lawsuit, *n.* (*leg.*) causa, azione (*legale*), lite, processo; querela.

lawyer, *n.* **1** (*leg.*) avvocato, legale. **2** (*leg.*) giurista.

lay[1], *n.* **1** disposizione, posizione. **2** (*fam.*) ramo d'affari, occupazione. **3** (*fam.*) prezzo. **4** (*pers.*) cointeressenza, partecipazione agli utili. // ~ **-days** (*trasp. mar.*) stallie; ~ **-up** (*trasp. mar.*) messa in disarmo (*d'una nave*); ~ **-up refund** (*ass. mar.*) rimborso (*di parte del premio*) per nave in disarmo (*e quindi non soggetta a rischi di mare*).

lay[2], *v. t.* (*pass.* e *part. pass.* **laid**) collocare, mettere, porre. // to ~ **aside** mettere da parte, risparmiare; to ~ **aside money** (*rag.*) mettere da parte denaro; to ~ **one's case before a commission** sottoporre il proprio caso a una commissione; to ~ **a case before the Court** (*leg.*) presentare una causa al tribunale; to ~ **damages at a certain sum** (*leg.*) fissare una data somma come risarcimento di danni; to ~ **down** metter giù, deporre; stabilire, disporre; (*trasp. mar.*) mettere in cantiere, impostare (*una nave*); to ~ **down an exacting time-table** (*org. az.*) stabilire un calendario rigoroso; to ~ **a duty on st.** (*dog., fin.*) daziare qc.; to ~ **the embargo on a ship** (*trasp. mar.*) mettere l'embargo su una nave; to ~ **in supplies** approvvigionarsi; to ~ **off** (*org. az.*) sospendere (*il lavoro*); (*pers.*) sospendere (*dal lavoro*); (*pers., USA*) licenziare (*per mancanza d'attività dell'azienda*); to ~ **out money** (*fin.*) investire denaro; to ~ **over** posticipare, rimandare, rinviare; to ~ **taxes** (*fin.*) imporre tributi; to ~ **up** (*trasp. mar.*) disarmare; to ~ **up a ship** (*trasp. mar.*) mettere in disarmo una nave.

laying, *n.* installazione. // ~ **-down** (*trasp. mar.*) messa in cantiere, impostazione (*d'una nave*); ~ **on the stocks** (*trasp. mar.*) impostazione (*d'una nave*); ~ **-up** (*trasp. mar.*) disarmo (*d'una nave*).

layoff, *n.* **1** (*org. az.*) periodo d'inattività, stagione morta. **2** (*org. az.*) sospensione (*del lavoro*). **3** (*pers.*) sospensione (*dal lavoro*). **4** (*pers., USA*) licenziamento (*per mancanza d'attività dell'azienda*). **5 layoffs,** *pl.* (*econ.*) procedure di ridimensionamento aziendale.

layout, *n.* 1 disposizione, posizione. 2 (*pubbl.*) impaginatura. // **the ~ of a modern office** la disposizione dei locali di un ufficio moderno.

laziness, *n.* pigrizia.

lazy, *a.* pigro.

lead[1], *n.* 1 direzione, guida. 2 posizione di testa, primo posto, avanguardia. 3 vantaggio (*in una gara*). 4 (*comm. est.*) anticipo (*di pagamento*). 5 (*giorn.*) articolo di fondo. // **leads and lags** (*comm. est., econ., fin.*) anticipi e dilazioni; **~ time** (*org. az.*) intervallo fra progettazione e produzione (*d'un articolo, prodotto, ecc.*); (*market., org. az.*) intervallo fra ordinazione e consegna, tempo d'approvvigionamento, tempo di consegna; to **have the ~ over one's rivals** (*market.*) essere in posizione di testa su tutti i concorrenti.

lead[2], *v. t.* (*pass.* e *part. pass.* **led**) 1 condurre, dirigere, essere a capo di. 2 guidare. // to **~ the fashion** (*market., pubbl.*) dettare la moda.

leader, *n.* 1 guida, capo, leader, comandante. 2 (*econ.*) *V.* **leading indicator.** 3 (*giorn.*) editoriale. 4 (*leg.*) avvocato principale. 5 (*market.*) articolo di valore offerto a un prezzo conveniente (*per dare impulso alle vendite*). 6 (*pers.*) capo intermedio, caposquadra, capo (*d'operai*).

leadership, *n.* 1 comando, direzione. 2 attitudine al comando, capacità di comando.

leading, *a.* principale. // **~ article** (*giorn.*) articolo di fondo; **~ case** (*leg.*) caso (*giudiziario*) che costituisce un «precedente», decisione giurisdizionale che fa testo; **a ~ concern** (*econ.*) un'azienda primaria; **~ indicator** (*econ.*) indice «guida», lampeggiatore; **~ question** (*leg.*) domanda tendenziosa; **the ~ sectors** (*econ., market.*) i settori di «punta».

leaflet, *n.* (*pubbl.*) dépliant, pieghevole, volantino, manifestino.

league, *n.* lega (*politica*).

leak[1], *n.* 1 crepa, fenditura, fessura. 2 (*trasp. mar.*) falla, via d'acqua.

leak[2], *v. t.* e *i.* 1 colare, perdere (*liquido*). 2 (*anche fig.*) spandersi. 3 (*trasp. mar.*) imbarcare acqua.

leakage, *n.* 1 perdita (*di liquido*). 2 (*market., trasp.*) calo (*di liquidi*). 3 (*trasp. mar.*) colaggio, dispersione, fuga, spillatura. 4 (*trasp. mar.*) abbuono per colaggio, abbuono per dispersione.

lean, *a.* (*anche fig.*) magro. // **a ~ harvest** (*econ.*) un magro raccolto; **a ~ year** (*econ.*) un'annata magra.

leap[1], *n.* 1 balzo. 2 sbalzo, aumento improvviso. // **~ year** (*banca, cred.*) anno bisestile.

leap[2], *v. i.* (*pass.* e *part. pass.* **leapt**) 1 balzare. 2 sbalzare, aumentare improvvisamente. // **leaping inflation** (*econ.*) inflazione che procede a balzi.

learn, *v. i.* (*pass.* e *part. pass.* **learnt**) 1 imparare. 2 apprendere, avere notizia, venire a sapere.

learner, *n.* (*pers.*) apprendista.

lease[1], *n.* 1 (*leg.*) contratto d'affitto, affittanza, locazione, noleggio. 2 (*leg.*) proprietà affittata, terreno affittato. 3 (*leg., trasp. mar.*) affitto. // **on ~** (*leg.*) in affitto.

lease[2], *v. t.* (*leg.*) affittare, dare in affitto, concedere in affitto, prendere in affitto, noleggiare.

leaseback, *n.* (*leg., USA*) vendita di proprietà terriera con successiva affittanza al venditore in base a un canone che permetterà all'acquirente d'ammortizzare l'investimento.

leased, *a.* affittato, noleggiato.

leasehold, *n.* 1 (*leg.*) affittanza, conduzione, locazione. 2 (*leg.*) terreni affittati, terreni tenuti in affitto.

leaseholder, *n.* (*leg.*) affittuario, locatario.

leasing, *n.* (*fin., org. az.*) locazione (*di macchinari, ecc.*); «leasing». // **~ company** società di «leasing»; **~ of industrial machinery and equipment** locazione di macchinari ed attrezzature.

least, *a.* (il) più piccolo, minimo. // **~ common denominator** (*mat.*) minimo comune denominatore; **~ common multiple** (*mat.*) minimo comune multiplo.

leave[1], *n.* 1 permesso, consenso, facoltà. 2 (*pers.*) congedo, licenza, aspettativa, permesso. // **~ of absence** (*pers.*) permesso (d'assentarsi), congedo, licenza; **~ with pay** (*pers.*) permesso retribuito, congedo retribuito; to **be on ~** (*pers.*) essere in congedo, essere in licenza, essere in permesso.

leave[2], *v. t.* (*pass.* e *part. pass.* **left**) 1 lasciare, abbandonare. 2 affidare. 3 (*leg.*) lasciare in eredità. // to **~ by will** (*leg.*) legare per testamento; to **~ the chair** togliere la seduta; (*amm.*) lasciare la presidenza; to **~ one's job** (*pers.*) lasciare il proprio impiego; to **~ off** cessare, sospendere; to **~ off work** (*org. az.*) sospendere il lavoro; to **~ out** omettere; to **~ over** rimandare, rinviare; to **~ over a matter** rinviare una faccenda; to **~ port** (*trasp. mar.*) uscire dal porto; to **~ the rails** (*trasp. ferr.*) deragliare; to **~ the road** (*trasp. aut.*) uscire di strada; to ~ **word with sb.** lasciar detto a q.; to **be left broke** rimanere al verde; to **be left till called for** (*comun.*) fermo posta (*di lettera, ecc.*).

leaven[1], *n.* (*anche fig.*) lievito.

leaven[2], *v. i.* lievitare.

leavening, *n.* lievitazione.

ledge, *n.* sporgenza, orlo.

ledger, *n.* (*rag.*) mastro, libro mastro, partitario. // ~ **account** (*rag.*) conto di mastro; ~ **balances** (*rag.*) saldi di mastro; ~ **heading** (*rag.*) intestazione di mastro.

lee, *n.* **1** protezione. **2** (*trasp. mar.*) lato sottovento.

leeward, *n.* (*trasp. mar.*) lato sottovento.

leeway, *n.* **1** (*anche fig.*) margine di sicurezza, tolleranza. **2** (*fig.*) perdita di tempo (*da ricuperare*). **3** (*fig.*) perdita di denaro (*da ricuperare*). **4** (*trasp. aer.*) angolo di deriva. **5** (*trasp. aer., trasp. mar.*) deriva.

left[1], *a.* **1** lasciato, abbandonato. **2** affidato. // ~ **-luggage office** (*trasp. ferr., ingl.*) deposito bagagli.

left[2], *a.* sinistro, a sinistra, mancino. // **the** ~ **wing of a party** l'ala sinistra d'un partito; **the** ~ **wing of a union** (*sind.*) la corrente di sinistra d'un sindacato.

legacy, *n.* (*leg.*) lascito. // ~ **duty** (*leg.*) tassa di successione; ~ **tax** (*leg., USA*) tassa di successione.

legal, *a.* **1** (*leg.*) legale, legittimo, giuridico. **2** (*leg.*) perseguibile per legge. // ~ **action** (*leg.*) azione legale; ~ **action against delinquent debtors** (*leg.*) azioni legali contro debitori morosi; ~ **acts** (*leg.*) atti legali; ~ **adviser** (*leg.*) consulente legale; ~ **age** (*leg.*) età legale (*per compiere taluni atti regolati dalla legge*); ~ **aid** (*leg.*) assistenza legale (*in giudizio*); ~ **assessor** (*leg.*) consulente legale; ~ **assets** (*leg.*) asse (*o* patrimonio) ereditario, massa ereditaria; ~ **assistance** (*leg.*) assistenza legale; ~ **cap** (*leg.*) carta per uso legale, foglio protocollo (*per uso bollo*); ~ **capacity** (*leg.*) capacità legale; ~ **capital** (*fin., leg.*) capitale legale; ~ **consideration** (*leg.*) causa lecita (*in un contratto*); ~ **costs** (*leg.*) spese legali; ~ **department** (*org. az.*) (ufficio del) contenzioso (*d'un'azienda e sim.*); ~ **disability** (*leg.*) incapacità legale; ~ **expenses** (*leg.*) spese legali, spese di giudizio; ~ **fees** (*leg.*) spese legali, spese di giudizio; ~ **heir** (*leg.*) erede legittimo; ~ **holiday** (*leg.*) giorno festivo legale; ~ **incapacity** (*leg.*) incapacità giuridica; ~ **interest** (*fin., leg.*) interesse legale; ~ **medicine** (*leg.*) medicina legale; ~ **offenses** (*leg.*) reati perseguibili a termini di legge; ~ **office** (*org. az.*) ufficio legale, contenzioso (*d'una ditta*); ~ **owner** (*leg.*) proprietario legittimo; ~ **person** (*leg.*) persona giuridica; ~ **power of attorney** (*leg.*) procura legale; ~ **presumption** (*leg.*) presunzione legale; ~ **proceedings** (*leg.*) vie legali; ~ **profession** (*leg.*) professione legale, avvocatura; ~ **rate of interest** (*fin., leg.*) interesse legale; ~ **redress** (*leg.*) risarcimento legale; ~ **representation** (*leg.*) rappresentanza legale, patrocinio; ~ **representative** (*leg.*) rappresentante legale; ~ **reserve** (*ass., leg., rag.*) riserva legale; ~ **residence** (*leg.*) residenza legale, domicilio (*legale*); ~ **rights** (*leg.*) diritti stabiliti dalla legge; ~ **status** (*leg.*) personalità (*giudirica*); ~ **steps** (*leg.*) vie legali; ~ **system** (*leg.*) ordinamento giuridico; ~ **tender** (*econ., fin.*) (moneta a) corso legale; ~ **tender currency** (*econ., fin.*) moneta a corso legale; ~ **transaction** (*leg.*) negozio giuridico; ~ **usufruct** (*leg.*) usufrutto legale; ~ **weight** (*comm. est., leg.*) peso netto (*comprendente l'eventuale involucro interno della merce*).

legality, *n.* (*leg.*) legalità, legittimità.

legalization, *n.* (*leg.*) legalizzazione, legittimazione, autenticazione. // **the** ~ **of a document** (*leg.*) la legalizzazione d'un documento.

legalize, *v. t.* (*leg.*) legalizzare, legittimare, autenticare.

legatee, *n.* (*leg.*) legatario.

legislate, *v. i.* (*leg.*) legiferare.

legislation, *n.* (*leg.*) legislazione.

legislative, *a.* (*leg.*) legislativo. // ~ **power** (*leg.*) potere legislativo.

legislator, *n.* (*leg.*) legislatore.

legislature, *n.* (*leg.*) corpo legislativo, assemblea legislativa.

legitim, *n.* (*leg.*) legittima (*in Scozia*).

legitimacy, *n.* (*leg.*) legittimità.

legitimate[1], *a.* (*leg.*) legittimo, lecito.

legitimate[2], *v. t.* (*leg.*) legittimare.

legitimation, *n.* (*leg.*) legittimazione.

legitimization, *n.* (*leg.*) legittimazione.

legitimize, *v. t.* (*leg.*) legittimare.

leisure time, *n.* (*pers.*) tempo libero.

lend, *v. t.* (*pass. e part. pass.* **lent**) (*cred.*) prestare, imprestare, dare a prestito, dare a mutuo, mutuare. *v. i.* (*cred.*) concedere un prestito. // to ~ **at the rate of 6%** (*cred.*) concedere un prestito al (tasso del) 6%; to ~ **money on contango** (*Borsa*) prestare capitali a riporto; to ~ **on collateral** (*cred.*) imprestare su garanzia; to ~ **stock** (*Borsa, fin.*) dare titoli a riporto.

lender, *n.* (*cred.*) prestatore, mutuante. //

«~ **of last resort**» (*fin.*) «prestatrice d'ultimo appello» (*detto della Banca d'Inghilterra*).

lending, *n.* (*cred.*) prestito. // ~ **rate (of interest)** (*fin.*) tasso attivo; (*banca*) tasso d'impiego; ~ **short** (*fin.*) finanziamento a breve; ~ **transactions** (*banca*) operazioni di prestito, operazioni attive; (*cred.*) operazioni di prestito.

length, *n.* 1 lunghezza. 2 (*market.*) lunghezza (*di stoffa*). // **a ~ of material** (*market.*) un taglio di stoffa; ~ **of service** (*pers.*) anzianità di servizio; ~ **of service increases** (*pers.*) scatti per anzianità (*di servizio*).

lesion, *n.* lesione.

less, *a., avv.* e *n.* meno, di meno. *prep.* meno, ad eccezione di, escludendo. // ~ **discount** meno lo sconto.

lessee, *n.* (*leg.*) affittuario, locatario, conduttore.

lessen, *v. t.* 1 diminuire, ridurre. 2 attenuare. *v. i.* 1 diminuire, ridursi. 2 attenuarsi.

lessening, *n.* 1 diminuzione, riduzione. 2 attenuazione. // ~ **of Government controls** (*econ.*) allentamento dei controlli governativi; ~ **of strain** (*sind.*) distensione.

lessor, *n.* (*leg.*) locatore, concedente, chi dà in affitto.

let, *v. t.* (*pass.* e *part. pass.* **let**) 1 lasciare, permettere. 2 (*leg.*) affittare, dare in affitto, concedere, locare, appigionare. 3 (*leg.*) noleggiare, dare a nolo. 4 (*leg.*) dare in appalto (*un lavoro*). 5 (*leg.*) assegnare (*un contratto*). *v. i.* (*leg.*) appigionarsi. // «**to** ~» (*avviso*) «affittasi»; to ~ **sb. in** lasciar entrare q.; to ~ **sb. know** (*comun.*) far sapere a q., informare q.; to ~ **lands** (*leg.*) dare terreni in affitto; to ~ **an office for 5 years** (*leg.*) appigionare un ufficio per 5 anni; to ~ **sb. out** lasciar uscire q.; to ~ **sb. out on bail** (*leg.*) accordare a q. la libertà provvisoria su cauzione; to ~ **out (on contract)** (*leg.*) appaltare, dare in appalto; to **be no longer let** (*leg.*) spigionarsi.

letter, *n.* 1 (*comun.*) lettera. 2 (*pubbl.*) lettera, carattere (*di stampa*). // ~ **basket** (*attr. uff.*) cestino per la corrispondenza; ~ **-book** (*attr. uff.*) copialettere; ~ **-box** cassetta per le lettere, buca delle lettere; **letters credential** credenziale; ~ **gadget** (*pubbl.*) omaggio (*di scarso valore*) in busta; ~ **of acknowledgement** «accusa» di ricevuta; ~ **of advice** lettera d'avviso, notificazione; (*cred., USA*) lettera di notifica dell'emissione d'una tratta; ~ **of allotment** (*fin.*) avviso di ripartizione (*d'una sottoscrizione azionaria ed obbligazionaria*); ~ **of application** (*pers.*) lettera di domanda d'assunzione; ~ **of attorney** (*leg.*) lettera di procura; ~ **of credence** credenziale; ~ **of credit** (*banca, cred.*) lettera di credito; ~ **of delegation** lettera di delega; ~ **of indemnity** (*comm. est.*) lettera di garanzia d'indennizzo (*per eventuali danni alla merce*); ~ **of indication** (*banca, cred.*) lettera d'identificazione; ~ **of intention** (*fin.*) lettera d'intenti (*per ottenere un prestito del Fondo Monetario Internazionale*); ~ **of introduction** (*pers.*) lettera di presentazione, lettera di raccomandazione; **the ~ of the law** (*leg.*) la lettera della legge, il testo della legge; ~ **of recommendation** (*pers.*) lettera di raccomandazione, lettera di presentazione; ~ **of revolving credit** (*banca, cred.*) lettera di credito rotativo; ~ **opener** (*attr. uff.*) tagliacarte; **letters overt** (*leg.*) brevetto (*d'invenzione*); ~ **-paper** (*attr. uff.*) carta da lettere; **letters patent** (*leg.*) brevetto (*d'invenzione*); ~ **rate** tariffa (*postale*) per lettere; **letters rogatory** (*leg.*) rogatoria; ~ **sheet** biglietto postale (*pieghevole, e che non abbisogna di busta*); ~ **telegram** telegramma-lettera; ~ **tray** (*attr. uff.*) cestino per la corrispondenza.

letterhead, *n.* 1 intestazione (*di lettera*). 2 foglio di carta intestata.

letterheading, *n.* 1 intestazione (*di lettera*). 2 foglio di carta intestata.

letterpress, *n.* 1 (*attr. uff.*) copialettere (*di tipo antiquato*). 2 (*giorn., pubbl., ingl.*) testo (*distinto dalle illustrazioni*).

letterspace, *v. t.* (*pubbl.*) spaziare (*le lettere d'una parola, ecc.*).

letterspacing, *n.* (*pubbl.*) spaziatura (*delle lettere d'una parola, ecc.*).

letting value, *n.* (*fin.*) valore locativo.

level[1], *n.* livello. *a.* a livello, orizzontale. // ~ **crossing** (*trasp. ferr., ingl.*) passaggio a livello; **the ~ of private capital investments** (*econ., fin.*) il livello degli investimenti privati di capitale; ~ **premium** (*ass.*) premio costante.

level[2], *v. t.* 1 livellare, spianare. 2 uguagliare, rendere uguale, appianare. 3 (*econ., fin., market.*) appiattire (*prezzi, salari, ecc.*). *v. i.* livellarsi. // to ~ **down** *V.* ~, *def. 3*; to ~ **off** stabilizzarsi, equilibrarsi; to ~ **out** *V.* ~, *def. 3*; to ~ **prices** (*econ., market.*) livellare i prezzi.

leveling, *n.* (*USA*) *V.* **levelling.**

levelling, *n.* livellamento. // ~ **down (*o* out)** (*econ., fin., market.*) appiattimento (*di prezzi, salari, ecc.*).

lever, *n.* 1 (*anche fig.*) leva. 2 (*fig.*) mezzo, strumento. // **the levers of economic power** le leve del potere economico.

leverage, *n.* 1 (*anche fig.*) autorità, potere,

influsso. 2 (*Borsa, fin.*) «leva» finanziaria (*forte effetto speculativo delle fluttuazioni finanziarie sui titoli ordinari d'una società*). 3 (*fin., USA*) differenziazione del portafoglio (*da parte di un fondo d'investimento*). // ~ **funds** (*Borsa, fin.*) fondi con «effetto leva»; ~ **ratio** (*fin.*) rapporto di leva finanziaria; rapporto tra indebitamento e mezzi propri.

levy[1], *n.* 1 (*fin.*) imposizione, esazione (*di tasse, tributi, ecc.*); prelievo. 2 (*fin.*) imposta, tassa. 3 (*leg.*) esecuzione forzata, pignoramento. // **levies charged on imports from non-member Countries** (*econ., fin.*) prelievi riscossi nei confronti dei Paesi terzi; **the ~ system** (*econ., fin.*) il regime dei prelievi.

levy[2], *v. t.* 1 (*fin.*) imporre, riscuotere (*tasse, tributi, ecc.*). 2 (*leg.*) far pagare (*una multa*). // to ~ **the attachment** (*leg.*) imporre il sequestro; to ~ **a distress** (*leg.*) fare un sequestro; to ~ **on sb.'s property** (*leg.*) agire esecutivamente sui beni di q.; to ~ **a tax** (*fin.*) riscuotere un tributo; to ~ **taxes on imports** (*fin.*) stabilire imposizioni all'importazione.

liabilities, *n. pl.* (*rag.*) passività, passivo, valori passivi, debiti, impegni. // **the ~ side** (*rag.*) la parte (*o* sezione) dell'«avere».

liability, *n.* 1 (*leg.*) responsabilità. 2 (*leg.*) obbligazione, l'essere soggetto (*a qc., a fare qc.*). 3 (*leg.*) debito. 4 (*rag.*) passività. // ~ **insurance** (*ass.*) assicurazione di responsabilità civile; **the ~ of the carrier** (*leg., trasp.*) la responsabilità del vettore; **the ~ of the employer** (*leg., pers.*) la responsabilità del datore di lavoro; ~ **to accidents** (*ass.*) sinistrosità; sinistrabilità; **the ~ to pay taxes** (*fin.*) l'essere soggetto al pagamento d'imposte.

liable, *a.* 1 (*leg.*) responsabile, passibile. 2 (*leg.*) soggetto (*a qc., a fare qc.*). // ~ **for damages** (*leg.*) responsabile per danni, tenuto a risarcire i danni; ~ **for gross negligence** (*leg.*) responsabile di negligenza grave; ~ **to audit** (*fin., leg.*) verificabile, sindacabile; ~ **to deferment** (*leg.*) prorogabile; ~ **to inspection** (*fin., leg.*) verificabile, sindacabile; to **be ~ to a fine** (*leg.*) essere passibile di multa.

liaise, *v. i.* allacciare una relazione, mettersi in contatto, stabilire un contatto (*con q.*).

liaison, *n.* collegamento, contatto, relazione.

libel, *n.* (*leg.*) reato di stampa.

liberal, *a.* liberale.

liberalization, *n.* 1 il rendere liberale. 2 (*comm. est., econ.*) liberalizzazione. // **the ~ of trade** (*comm. est.*) la liberalizzazione degli scambi.

liberalize, *v. t.* 1 rendere liberale. 2 (*comm. est., econ.*) liberalizzare. // to ~ **foreign trade** liberalizzare il commercio estero.

liberalized, *a.* (*comm. est., econ.*) liberalizzato.

liberation, *n.* liberazione.

liberty, *n.* libertà. // ~ **of calling at any port** (*trasp. mar.*) libertà di fare scalo in qualsiasi porto; ~ **of contract** (*econ.*) libertà contrattuale; ~ **of the press** (*giorn.*) libertà di stampa; **at ~** (*slang USA*) disoccupato.

Libor, *n.* (*fin.*) tasso base (*d'interesse*) londinese.

licence, *n.* 1 (*leg.*) licenza, permesso, autorizzazione. 2 (*leg.*) brevetto, patente. // ~ **bond** (*market.*) deposito cauzionale per licenza di commercio; ~ **plate** (*trasp. aut.*) bollo di circolazione; (*USA*) targa; ~ **tag** (*trasp. aut.*) bollo di circolazione; ~ **tax** (*fin.*) imposta di licenza.

license[1], *n.* (*USA*) *V.* **licence.** // ~ **fee** (*fin., USA*) tassa di licenza; ~ **tax** (*fin., USA*) imposta di licenza.

license[2], *v. t.* (*leg.*) dar licenza a, permettere, autorizzare.

licensee, *n.* 1 (*leg.*) concessionario di licenza, detentore di permesso, licenziatario. 2 (*leg.*) detentore di brevetto, detentore di patente.

lie, *v. i.* (*pass.* **lay,** *part. pass.* **lain**) 1 giacere. 2 essere situato, trovarsi. 3 (*leg.*) essere fondato. // to ~ **off** (*pers.*) sospendere momentaneamente il lavoro; (*trasp. mar.*) stare (*alla fonda*) al largo; to ~ **over** essere rimandato, essere rinviato; (*di debito*) non essere pagato dopo la scadenza; to ~ **to** (*trasp. mar.*) essere alla cappa; to ~ **up** (*trasp. mar.*) essere in porto, rimanere in porto (*per riparazioni, ecc.*).

lien, *n.* 1 (*leg.*) garanzia, pegno. 2 (*leg.*) diritto di pegno, diritto di garanzia, diritto di riservato dominio; privilegio, ipoteca. // ~ **creditor** (*leg.*) creditore privilegiato.

lienee, *n.* (*leg.*) proprietario di bene gravato da pegno, proprietario di bene gravato da privilegio, proprietario di bene ipotecato.

lienholder, *n.* (*leg.*) detentore di pegno su un bene altrui, detentore d'ipoteca su un bene altrui.

lienor, *n.* (*leg.*) detentore di pegno su un bene altrui, detentore di privilegio su un bene altrui, detentore d'ipoteca su un bene altrui.

life, *n.* (*pl.* **lives**) vita. // ~ **annuitant** (*ass.*) chi gode di un vitalizio; ~ **annuity** (*ass.*) rendita vitalizia, rendita perpetua, vitalizio; ~ **annuity fund** (*ass.*) riserva matematica; ~ **assurance** (*ass.*) assicurazione sulla vita; ~ **expectancy**

(*ass.*) durata media della vita residua; ~ **insurance** (*ass.*) assicurazione sulla vita; ~ **-insurance company** (*ass.*) compagnia d'assicurazioni sulla vita; ~ **-insurance policy** (*ass.*) polizza d'assicurazione sulla vita; ~ **office** (*ass.*) agenzia d'assicurazioni sulla vita; ~ **policy** (*ass.*) polizza d'assicurazione sulla vita; ~ **sentence** (*leg.*) condanna a vita; ~ **tenancy** (*leg.*) usufrutto a vita; ~ **tenant** (*leg.*) usufruttuario vita natural durante, usufruttuario a vita.

lifeless, *a.* inerte.

lifelessness, *n.* inerzia.

lift[1]**,** *n.* **1** abolizione, soppressione. **2** (*econ., market.*) rialzo, aumento (*di prezzi, ecc.*).

lift[2]**,** *v. t.* **1** alzare. **2** abolire, sopprimere. **3** (*cred., leg.*) pagare, saldare (*un debito, ecc.*). **4** (*cred., leg.*) estinguere (*un'obbligazione, ecc.*). **5** (*econ., market.*) aumentare (*prezzi, ecc.*). // to ~ **the embargo** (*econ.*) togliere l'embargo; to ~ **a mortgage** (*cred., leg.*) togliere un'ipoteca; to ~ **prices** (*market.*) esagerare nel prezzo.

lifting, *n.* abolizione, soppressione.

light[1]**,** *a.* leggero, lieve. // ~ **displacement** (*trasp. mar.*) dislocamento (*di nave*) a vuoto; ~ **displacement tonnage** (*trasp. mar.*) tonnellaggio a nave scarica; **the** ~ **industry** (*econ.*) l'industria leggera; ~ **railway** (*trasp. ferr.*) ferrovia a scartamento ridotto.

light[2]**,** *n.* **1** luce. **2** (*trasp. mar.*) fanale. // ~ **bill** (*trasp. mar.*) ricevuta di pagamento dei diritti di faro; ~ **dues** (*trasp. mar.*) diritti di fanalaggio, diritti di faro; ~ **duties** (*trasp. mar.*) diritti di fanalaggio, diritti di faro; ~ **list** (*trasp. mar.*) elenco dei fari e fanali.

lighten, *v. t.* alleggerire. // to ~ **a ship** (*trasp. mar.*) alleggerire (il carico di) una nave.

lightening, *n.* **1** alleggerimento, alleviamento. **2** (*trasp. mar.*) aleggio.

lighter[1]**,** *n.* (*trasp. mar.*) chiatta, zattera.

lighter[2]**,** *v. t.* (*trasp. mar.*) caricare (*merce*) su chiatte, trasportare (*merce*) con chiatte, zatteraggio.

lighterage, *n.* **1** (*trasp. mar.*) trasporto su chiatte. **2** (*trasp. mar.*) spese di trasporto su chiatte.

lighterman, *n.* (*pl.* **lightermen**) (*trasp. mar.*) chiattaiolo.

lighthouse, *n.* (*trasp. mar.*) faro.

lightning, *n.* lampo, baleno, fulmine. // ~ **strike** (*pers., sind.*) sciopero senza preavviso.

lightship, *n.* (*trasp. mar.*) nave faro.

like[1]**,** *a.* uguale.

like[2]**,** *n.* ciò che piace, simpatia, preferenza. // **the likes and dislikes of the public** (*market.*) i gusti del pubblico.

like[3]**,** *v. t.* gradire.

liking, *n.* gradimento.

limit[1]**,** *n.* **1** limite, limitazione. **2** (*mat.*) limite. // ~ **of liability** (*ass.*) ammontare massimo di responsabilità (*per l'assicuratore*); ~ **order** (*Borsa*) ordine d'acquisto (*di titoli*) a un prezzo massimo; ordine di vendita (*di titoli*) a un prezzo minimo.

limit[2]**,** *v. t.* limitare, ridurre. // to ~ **expenses** (*econ.*) limitare le spese.

limitation, *n.* **1** limitazione, limite, restrizione. **2** (*ass.*) limitazione, limite (*di copertura*). **3** (*leg.*) limite di tempo (*per far valere un diritto*).

limited, *a.* limitato, esiguo. // ~ **company** (*fin., ingl.*) società a responsabilità limitata dalle azioni (*è diversa dalla s.r.l. italiana*), società per azioni; ~ **edition** (*giorn., pubbl.*) edizione numerata (*di pubblicazione*); ~ **flexibility** (*fin.*) flessibilità limitata; ~ **liability** (*leg.*) responsabilità limitata; ~ **-liability company** (*fin., ingl.*) *V.* ~ **company;** ~ **order** (*Borsa*) ordine d'acquisto (*di titoli*) a un prezzo massimo; ordine di vendita (*di titoli*) a un prezzo minimo; ~ **partner** (*fin.*) accomandante, socio accomandante; ~ **partnership** (*fin.*) accomandita, società in accomandita semplice; ~ **-payment life insurance** (*ass.*) assicurazione «vita intera a premi limitati»; ~ **policy** (*ass.*) polizza con limitazioni di copertura.

limit oneself, *v. rifl.* limitarsi.

limping standard, *n.* (*fin.*) bimetallismo zoppo.

linage, *n.* **1** (*giorn., pubbl.*) numero di righe (*di testo a stampa*). **2** (*giorn., pubbl.*) pagamento a un tanto la riga.

line[1]**,** *n.* **1** linea; fila; (*fig.*) indirizzo, linea di condotta. **2** (*ass.*) limite massimo, massimale. **3** (*banca, cred.*) castelletto. **4** (*comm.*) genere, ramo, settore (*d'affari*). **5** (*giorn., pubbl.*) segno (*grafico*). **6** (*market.*) classe di merci; «linea» (*di prodotti*); gamma, serie (*di prodotti*); articoli. **7** (*org. az.*) linea (*di produzione*). **8** (*org. az., pers.*) personale direttivo. **9** (*trasp.*) linea. **10** (*trasp. mar.*) linea di navigazione. **11** (*trasp. mar.*) gomena. // ~ **card** (*ass.*) fascicolo (*relativo a un cliente*); ~ **of business** genere d'affari, settore d'attività; ~ **of credit** (*banca, cred.*) castelletto, «plafond»; ~ **of flight** (*trasp. aer.*) linea di volo; ~ **of flotation** (*trasp. mar.*) linea di galleggiamento, linea d'immersione; ~ **production** (*org. az.*) lavorazione a catena; ~ **sheet** (*ass.*) guida (*che descrive le condizioni assicurative*).

line[2]**,** *v. t.* allineare. // to ~ **up** allinearsi.

lineal, *a.* 1 lineare. 2 (*leg.*) (discendente) in linea retta, diretto. // **a ~ heir** (*leg.*) un erede diretto.

linear, *a.* lineare.

liner, *n.* 1 (*trasp. aer.*) aereo di linea. 2 (*trasp. mar.*) nave di linea, transatlantico. // **~ freighting** (*trasp. mar.*) noleggio a collettame.

link[1], *n.* collegamento.

link[2], *v. t.* collegare. // to **~ up** *V.* **~.**

liquid, *a.* liquido. // **~ assets** (*rag.*) attività liquide, disponibilità liquide, liquidità; **~ measure** unità di misura per liquidi; **~ ratio** (*fin., rag.*) tasso di liquidità (*rapporto tra attività e passività correnti*).

liquidate, *v. t.* 1 (*ass., leg.*) liquidare. 2 (*cred., fin.*) liquidare, mettere in liquidazione. 3 (*rag.*) convertire (*attività di bilancio*) in liquidità, stralciare. *v. i.* (*fin.*) (*di società*) andare in liquidazione. // to **~ a corporation** (*fin., USA*) liquidare una società; to **~ damages** (*ass., leg.*) liquidare danni; to **~ a firm** (*fin.*) stralciare una azienda; to **~ the national debt** (*fin.*) liquidare il debito nazionale.

liquidating dividend, *n.* (*fin.*) dividendo di liquidazione.

liquidation, *n.* 1 (*ass., leg.*) liquidazione (*di danni, ecc.*). 2 (*cred., fin.*) liquidazione, messa in liquidazione, stralcio. 3 (*fin., leg.*) liquidazione (*di società di capitali*). 4 (*rag.*) conversione (*d'attività*) in liquidità.

liquidator, *n.* (*ass., fin., leg.*) liquidatore.

liquidity, *n.* (*rag.*) liquidità. // **~ preference** (*fin., rag.*) preferenza alla liquidità; **~ ratio** (*fin.*) tasso di liquidità.

lira, *n.* lira (*unità monetaria italiana*).

list[1], *n.* 1 lista, elenco. 2 (*Borsa, fin.*) listino, bollettino. 3 (*comm.*) nota, distinta, specifica. 4 (*market.*) listino, catalogo. 5 (*pers.*) graduatoria. 6 (*trasp. mar.*) sbandata. // **the ~ of bills for collection** (*banca*) la distinta (degli) effetti all'incasso; **the ~ of bills for discount** (*banca*) la distinta (degli) effetti allo sconto, il borderò di sconto; **the ~ of the crew** (*trasp. aer., trasp. mar.*) il ruolo dell'equipaggio; **the ~ of passengers** (*trasp. aer., trasp. mar.*) l'elenco dei passeggeri; **~ of questions** (*market.*) questionario; **~ price** (*market.*) prezzo di listino.

list[2], *n.* (*trasp. mar.*) inclinazione, sbandamento.

list[3], *v. t.* 1 mettere in lista, mettere in elenco, elencare. 2 (*Borsa, fin.*) inserire (*titoli*) in un listino ufficiale. 3 (*fin.*) iscrivere (*beni*) nei ruoli d'imposta. 4 (*market.*) mettere (*articoli, ecc.*) in listino; inserire (*articoli, ecc.*) in catalogo. // to **~ at** (*market.*) essere in catalogo al prezzo di.

list[4], *v. i.* (*trasp. mar.*) inclinarsi.

listable, *a.* (*fin.*) soggetto a imposta, imponibile.

listed, *a.* incluso in una lista (o *un listino*). // **~ security** (*Borsa*) titolo quotato; **~ shares** (*Borsa*) valori del listino; **~ stock** (*Borsa*) azione iscritta a listino.

listen, *v. i.* ascoltare.

listener, *n.* ascoltatore.

listing, *n.* elencazione.

liter, *n. V.* **litre.**

literal, *a.* alla lettera. *n.* (*giorn., pubbl.*) errore di stampa. // **the ~ meaning** il senso letterale.

literally, *avv.* letteralmente, alla lettera.

literary, *a.* letterario. // **~ page** (*giorn.*) terza pagina.

literature, *n.* (*market., pubbl.*) materiale illustrativo, opuscoli a stampa.

litigant, *a.* e *n.* (*leg.*) litigante, contendente, parte in causa.

litigate, *v. i.* (*leg.*) litigare. *v. t.* (*leg.*) contestare.

litigation, *n.* (*leg.*) lite, controversia, vertenza, causa.

litigious, *a.* (*leg.*) litigioso.

litigiousness, *n.* (*leg.*) litigiosità.

litre, *n.* litro.

littoral, *n.* litorale.

livability, *n.* (*econ.*) abitabilità, «livability».

live[1], *a. attr.* vivente. // **~ load** (*trasp.*) carico utile; peso dei passeggeri, peso del carico.

live[2], *v. i.* vivere, abitare.

liveability, *n. V.* **livability.**

liveliness, *n.* vivacità, animazione.

lively, *a.* vivace, animato, attivo. // **a ~ trade** un commercio attivo.

livestock products, *n. pl.* (*econ.*) prodotti zootecnici.

living, *n.* 1 (il) vivere, vita. 2 (*econ.*) mezzi di sussistenza. // **the ~ and working conditions** (*econ.*) le condizioni di vita e di lavoro; **a ~ wage** (*pers.*) un salario sufficiente per vivere.

Lloyd's, *n.* (*ass. mar., ingl.*) Compagnia del Lloyd (*di Londra*). // **~ list** (*ass. mar., ingl.*) bollettino del Lloyd.

load[1], *n.* 1 carico, peso, onere. 2 (*trasp.*) carico, carico trainato. 3 (*trasp. mar.*) misura per carichi di legname, pari a 50 piedi cubici. // **~ displacement** (*trasp. mar.*) dislocamento a pieno carico; **~ draught** (*trasp. mar.*) pescaggio a carico; **~ line** (*trasp. mar.*) linea di carico; **~ line certificate** (*trasp. mar.*) certificato della linea di carico; **~ waterline** (*trasp. mar.*) *V.* **~**

line.

load², *v. t.* 1 caricare. 2 (*ass.*) aggiungere un'addizionale al (*premio*). 3 (*fin., market.*) «caricare» (*un prezzo, ecc.*) per coprire le spese e trarne un profitto. 4 (*trasp.*) caricare. *v. i.* (*trasp.*) fare il carico. // to ~ **the cargo** (*trasp. mar.*) imbarcare il carico; to ~ **goods aboard a ship** (*trasp. mar.*) caricare merci a bordo d'una nave.

loaded, *a.* (*trasp.*) carico. // ~ **journey** (*trasp. ferr.*) percorso a (vagone) carico; **out-** ~ **return-empty services** (*trasp.*) servizi con andata a (veicolo) carico e ritorno a (veicolo) vuoto.

loader, *n.* (*pers.*) caricatore.

loading, *n.* 1 (*ass.*) addizionale (*di premio*). 2 (*trasp.*) caricamento, carico. 3 (*trasp. mar.*) caricazione. // ~ **aboard** (*trasp. mar.*) messa a bordo, caricamento a bordo; ~ **and unloading charges** (*trasp. mar.*) spese di carico e scarico; ~ **and unloading operations** (*trasp. mar.*) operazioni di carico e scarico; ~ **area** (*trasp. mar.*) zona di carico, piazzale di carico; ~ **broker** (*trasp. mar.*) sensale di carichi; ~ **charges** (*trasp. mar.*) spese di carico, spese d'imbarco; ~ **day** (*trasp. mar.*) giorno di caricamento; ~ **dock** (*trasp. mar.*) banchina di carico; ~ **guarantee** (*trasp. mar.*) garanzia di caricazione; ~ **place** (*trasp.*) luogo di caricamento; (*trasp. mar.*) posto di caricazione; ~ **platform** (*trasp. ferr.*) piattaforma di carico, piano caricatore (*o* di caricamento); ~ **port** (*trasp. mar.*) porto di caricamento, porto d'imbarco; ~ **risk** (*trasp. mar.*) rischio di carico.

loan¹, *n.* (*cred.*) prestito, imprestito, finanziamento, mutuo. // ~ **account** (*cred., fin.*) conto anticipazioni, scoperto di conto corrente; ~ **agreements** (*cred.*) contratti di prestito; ~ **at call** (*banca*) prestito rimborsabile su richiesta; ~ **at interest** (*cred.*) prestito a interesse; ~ **capital** (*cred., fin.*) capitale mutuato; ~ **certificate** (*cred.*) certificato di prestito, cartella di prestito; **loans denominated in Euro-dollars** (*fin.*) prestiti stilati in eurodollari; ~ **holder** (*cred.*) detentore d'obbligazioni; creditore ipotecario; ~ **interest** (*cred.*) interesse di prestito; ~ **office** (*cred.*) ufficio prestiti; ~ **on mortgage** (*cred.*) prestito ipotecario; ~ **on overdraft** (*cred.*) prestito allo scoperto; ~ **on one's salary** (*pers.*) cessione di stipendio; ~ **on stock** (*cred.*) finanziamento su titoli; **loans outstanding** (*banca, fin.*) operazione di finanziamento in essere; ~ **shark** (*cred.*) strozzino; ~ **stock** (*cred., fin.*) capitale obbligazionario; **loans to finance productive investment** (*cred.*) crediti destinati a finanziare investimenti produttivi; ~ **value** (*ass.*) valore (massimo) di credito (*che un assicurato sulla vita può ottenere, su garanzia del valore effettivo della polizza*); valore redimibile.

loan², *v. t.* 1 (*cred., USA*) prestare, imprestare (*denaro*) a interesse, dare a mutuo, mutuare. 2 (*fam., USA*) prendere a prestito. *v. i.* (*cred., USA*) prestare denaro a interesse.

lobby, *n.* (*USA*) gruppo di pressione politica (*dedito a manovre di corridoio*).

lobster, *n.* aragosta. // ~ **shift** (*giorn., pers., USA*) turno di notte; ~ **trick** (*giorn., pers., USA*) turno di notte.

local, *a.* locale, del luogo. *n.* 1 (*giorn.*) notizia d'interesse locale, notizia di cronaca cittadina. 2 (*sind.*) sezione locale (*d'un sindacato*). 3 (*trasp. ferr.*) treno locale. // ~ **acceptance** (*cred.*) accettazione condizionata del luogo di pagamento; ~ **agent** (*ass., pers.*) agente di zona; ~ **authorities** enti locali; ~ **call** (*comun.*) telefonata (*o* chiamata) urbana; ~ **customs** (*leg.*) consuetudini locali, usi locali; ~ **finance** (*fin.*) finanza locale; ~ **freight** (*trasp. ferr., USA*) treno merci locale; ~ **news** (*giorn.*) notizie d'interesse locale, notizie di cronaca cittadina; **the** ~ **press** (*giorn.*) la stampa locale; ~ **station** (*trasp. ferr.*) stazione locale; ~ **taxes** (*fin.*) imposte locali; ~ **time** ora locale; ~ **traffic** (*trasp. ferr.*) traffico locale; ~ **train** (*trasp. ferr.*) treno locale; ~ **transit** (*trasp.*) trasporti urbani; ~ **union** (*sind.*) sindacato locale, sezione locale di sindacato; ~ **usance** (*banca*) consuetudine locale, uso di piazza.

locality, *n.* località.

localization, *n.* localizzazione.

localize, *v. t.* localizzare.

localizer, *n.* (*trasp. aer.*) localizzatore.

locate, *v. t.* fissare, stabilire. *v. i.* stabilirsi, domiciliarsi. // to **be located** essere situato, essere ubicato, trovarsi.

locatio conductio, *n.* (*leg.*) locazione-conduzione.

location, *n.* 1 posizione, posto. 2 (*econ.*) localizzazione. 3 (*leg.*) locazione.

locator, *n.* (*econ.*) localizzatore.

lock¹, *n.* 1 serratura. 2 (*trasp.*) chiusa (*di fiume, canale, ecc.*).

lock², *v. t.* chiudere a chiave. // to ~ **the controls** (*trasp. aer.*) bloccare i comandi; to ~ **out** (*pers., sind.*) sospendere dal lavoro (*i lavoratori: per ottenere concessioni*); to ~ **up** chiudere a chiave; (*fin.*) immobilizzare, impegnare, vincolare, investire (*denaro*); to ~ **up capital** (*fin.*) investire capitale.

lock-away, *n.* (*fin.*) titolo da cassetto.

lock-in, *n.* (*sind., USA*) protesta con asserragliamento nel posto di lavoro.

lockout, *n.* (*pers., sind.*) serrata.

lockup, *n.* (*fin.*) immobilizzazione, immobilizzo, investimento (*di denaro*). // **a ~ of capital** un'immobilizzazione di capitale; **~ investment** (*Borsa, fin.*) investimento di cassetta.

locomotive, *n.* (*trasp. ferr.*) locomotiva.

loco price, *n.* (*market.*) prezzo «sopra luogo», prezzo «franco al punto di partenza».

locum-, *pref.* luogo. // **~ -tenency** (*leg., org. az.*) ufficio di facente funzioni, ufficio di sostituto, ufficio di supplente, supplenza; **~ tenens** (*leg., org. az.*) luogotenente, interino, supplente, sostituto, facente funzioni.

lodge, *v. t.* e *i.* **1** alloggiare, albergare. **2** (*fin.*) depositare (*denaro, valori, ecc.*). **3** (*leg.*) presentare. // to **~ accusations** (*leg.*) sporgere denunce; to **~ an appeal** (*leg.*) fare un ricorso; to **~ a complaint** (*leg.*) presentare un reclamo; to **~ money with a bank** (*fin.*) depositare denaro in banca; to **~ securities** (*fin.*) depositare titoli; to **~ stock as cover** (*fin.*) depositare titoli a garanzia.

lodgement, *n. V.* **lodgment.**

lodgment, *n.* **1** alloggio. **2** (*fin.*) deposito, versamento (*di denaro, ecc.*). **3** (*leg.*) presentazione. // **the ~ of complaints** (*leg.*) la presentazione di reclami.

log, *n.* (*trasp. mar.*) giornale di bordo.

logarithm, *n.* (*mat.*) logaritmo. // **~ tables** (*mat.*) tavole dei logaritmi.

logbook, *n.* (*trasp. mar.*) giornale di bordo.

Lombard, *a.* lombardo. *n.* (*fin., fig.*) prestatore di denaro, banchiere. // **~ Street** «Lombard Street» (*strada di Londra in cui hanno sede molte banche che un tempo appartenevano a banchieri italiani*); (*fin., fig.*) il mercato finanziario.

London, *n.* Londra. // **~ Bankers' Clearing House** (*banca, fin., ingl.*) Stanza di Compensazione di Londra; **~ clause** (*trasp. mar.*) clausola di Londra (*clausola in base alla quale le spese di «dock» devono essere sostenute dal caricatore*); **~ Discount Houses Association** (*fin.*) Associazione londinese degli Istituti di Sconto; **the ~ Stock Exchange** la Borsa Valori di Londra.

long[1], *a.* lungo, esteso. *n.* (*Borsa, fin.*) rialzista, speculatore al rialzo. // **~ bill** (*banca, cred.*) effetto a lunga scadenza; **~ bond** (*fin.*) obbligazione ventennale (*o* ultraventennale); **~ credit** (*cred.*) credito a lunga scadenza; **~ -dated bill** (*banca, cred.*) effetto a lunga scadenza; **~ -dated paper** (*banca, cred.*) effetto a lunga scadenza; **~ -distance** lontano; (*comun.*) interurbano, in interurbana; **~ distance** (*comun.*) comunicazione interurbana; **~ -distance call** (*comun.*) chiamata interurbana; **~ -distance night rates** (*comun.*) tariffe (per) interurbane notturne; **~ -established industries** (*econ.*) industrie tradizionali; **~ green** (*slang USA*) moneta cartacea, denaro, soldi; **~ hundredweight** «hundredweight» inglese (*misura di peso pari a kg 50,80*); **~ -range** lungo, a lungo termine; **~ -range forecasts** (*org. az.*) previsioni a lungo termine; **~ ream** (*pubbl.*) risma (*unità di misura di fogli di carta pari a 20 mazzette di 25 fogli l'una*); **~ -run** a lungo termine; **a ~ run** (*giorn.*) una tiratura forte; **~ -run trend** tendenza a lungo termine; (*stat.*) «trend» (*q. V.*) a lungo termine; **~ -standing** vecchio; **a ~ -standing family firm** una vecchia azienda familiare; **~ -term** a lungo termine, a lungo, nel lungo periodo, a lunga scadenza; (*fin., rag.*) (*di profitti, perdite, operazioni, ecc.*) a lungo termine (*generalm. più di 10 anni*); (*d'attività di capitale*) a lungo termine (*generalm. più di 6 mesi*); **~ -term credit** (*cred.*) credito a lungo termine, credito a lungo; **~ -term expectation** (*econ.*) aspettativa a lungo termine; **~ -term investor** (*Borsa, fin.*) cassettista; **~ -term liabilities** (*fin., rag.*) passività a lungo termine; passività consolidate; debiti a lungo termine; **~ -term loans** (*cred.*) mutui a lunga scadenza; **~ ton** tonnellata inglese (*pari a kg 1.016 circa*); **for a ~ time** a lungo; **in the ~ run** a lungo andare, alla lunga; **in the ~ term** nel lungo periodo, a lungo termine; to **be on the ~ side of the market** (*Borsa, fin.*) operare al rialzo.

long[2], *avv.* a lungo.

longevity, *n.* longevità. // **~ pay** (*pers.*) indennità d'anzianità.

look, *v. i.* parere, avere l'aspetto di. // to **~ at** guardare; to **~ for** cercare; to **~ forward** guardare avanti, pensare al futuro; to **~ into st.** esaminare qc., indagare su qc.; to **~ out** fare attenzione; to **~ over the correspondence** guardare la corrispondenza; to **~ up** guardare su, alzare lo sguardo; (*comm.*) andar meglio, migliorare.

loop, *n.* occhiello.

loose, *a.* sciolto, slegato, allentato, lento. // **~ cash** denari spiccioli, spiccioli; **~ change** denari spiccioli, spiccioli; **~ funds** (*fin., rag.*) fondi privi di qualsiasi destinazione, fondi liberi; **~ -leaf bookkeeping systems** (*rag.*) sistemi di contabilità a fogli mobili; **~ -leaf ledger** (*attr. uff.*) mastro a fogli staccati.

Lord, *n.* (*ingl.*) lord, pari d'Inghilterra. //

the Lords (*ingl.*) i Lord, la Camera dei Lord; ~ **Chancellor** (*ingl.*) Presidente della Camera dei Lord; **the** ~ **Chief Justice** (*ingl.*) il magistrato inglese di più alto grado; ~ **Privy Seal** (*ingl.*) Lord del Sigillo Privato.

lorry, *n.* (*trasp. aut., ingl.*) autocarro, camion. // ~ **driver** camionista, autotrasportatore, «padroncino».

lose, *v. t.* (*pass.* e *part. pass.* **lost**) perdere, smarrire. // to ~ **one's berth** (*o* **job**) (*pers.*) perdere l'impiego; to ~ **a lawsuit** (*leg.*) perdere una causa; to ~ **one's reputation** perdere la (propria) reputazione; to ~ **a right** (*leg.*) perdere un diritto, decadere da un diritto; to **be lost** perdersi, smarrirsi, andare smarrito.

loss, *n.* **1** perdita, smarrimento. **2** (*ass.*) perdita, danno. **3** (*rag.*) deficit, disavanzo, perdita, rimessa, sbilancio. // ~ **-and-gain account** (*rag.*) conto profitti e perdite, conto perdite e profitti; ~ **by leakage** (*ass. mar.*) perdita per colaggio; ~ **in process** (*org. az.*) perdita di lavorazione; **a** ~ **in weight** (*market.*) un calo di peso (*della merce, ecc.*); ~ **leader** (*market.*) articolo venduto in perdita per attirare clienti, articolo civetta; **the** ~ **of a right** (*leg.*) la perdita d'un diritto, la decadenza da un diritto; **the** ~ **of the ship** (*ass. mar.*) la perdita della nave; ~ **on exchange** (*fin.*) perdita (per oscillazioni) di cambio; ~ **reserve** (*ass.*) riserva per sinistri; **at a** ~ (*comm.*) in perdita.

lossmaker, *n.* **1** (*econ.*) azienda in deficit (*o* in perdita). **2** (*econ.*) industria decotta.

lossmaking, *a.* (*econ.*) in deficit, in passivo; in perdita; decotto. // ~ **industries** industrie decotte.

lot[1], *n.* **1** (*comm.*) lotto (*di merce: a un'asta*). **2** (*econ.*) lotto, appezzamento (*di terreno*). **3** (*fin.*) pacchetto, partita (*di titoli*). **4** (*market.*) partita, assortimento (*di merci*). **5** (*trasp. aut.*) area di parcheggio. // ~ **money** (*econ.*) diritti d'asta (*destinati al banditore*); **a** ~ **of shares** (*fin.*) una partita di titoli (azionari); **a** ~ **of shoes** (*market.*) una partita di calzature; ~ **tolerance per cent defective** (*org. az.*) tolleranza percentuale di scarti per lotto.

lot[2], *v. t.* **1** (*econ.*) dividere (*terreni*) in lotti, lottizzare. **2** (*fin.*) dividere (*titoli*) in pacchetti. **3** (*market.*) dividere (*merci*) in partite. // to ~ **out** lottizzare; to ~ **out goods in parcels** (*market.*) dividere merci in partite.

lottery, *n.* lotteria. // ~ **bond** (*fin.*) obbligazione a premio.

lotting, *n.* lottizzazione.

lounge car, *n.* (*trasp. ferr.*) carrozza salone.

low, *a.* **1** basso. **2** (*Borsa, fin.*) minimo. **3** (*market.*) a basso prezzo, a buon mercato. *n.* (*Borsa, fin.*) prezzo minimo, quotazione minima, (il) minimo. *avv.* (*anche fig.*) in basso. // ~ **-class** (*market.*) di qualità inferiore, scadente; ~ **-class goods** (*market.*) merce di qualità inferiore; ~ **cost** basso costo; ~ **-cost** (*fin., market.*) a buon mercato; ~ **-cost money** (*fin.*) denaro a buon mercato; ~ **-duty articles** (*dog., fin.*) articoli tassati moderatamente; ~ **-end** (*market.*) di qualità inferiore, scadente; (*di fabbrica, ditta, ecc.*) che produce articoli di qualità inferiore; ~ **-geared trust** (*fin.*) fondo (d'investimento) con basso indebitamento; ~ **-grade** (*market.*) di qualità inferiore, scadente; ~ **-leverage trust** (*fin., USA*) fondo (d'investimento) con basso indebitamento; ~ **-price** basso prezzo; ~ **wages** (*pers.*) salari bassi; ~ **water** (*trasp. mar.*) acqua bassa, bassa marea; **a lower ceiling on aids** (*econ.*) un massimale di aiuti più basso; **lower court judge** (*leg.*) pretore; **lower deck** (*trasp. mar.*) sottocoperta; **lowest common denominator** (*mat.*) minimo comune denominatore; **lowest common multiple** (*mat.*) minimo comune multiplo; **the lowest price** (*market.*) l'ultimo prezzo.

lower, *v. t.* abbassare, diminuire, ridurre. *v. i.* abbassarsi, calare, diminuire, ridursi. // to ~ **duties** (*dog., fin.*) ridurre i dazi.

lowering, *n.* abbassamento, calo, diminuzione, riduzione. // **a** ~ **of trade restrictions** (*comm. est.*) una riduzione delle limitazioni agli scambi commerciali.

loyal, *a.* fedele.

loyally, *avv.* fedelmente.

loyalty, *n.* fedeltà.

lucrative, *a.* lucrativo, lucroso, profittevole, remunerativo. // **a** ~ **investment** un investimento remunerativo; **a** ~ **job** (*pers.*) un'occupazione redditizia.

lucrativeness, *n.* l'essere lucrativo, proficuità.

lucre, *n.* lucro, guadagno, profitto.

luggage, *n.* (*trasp.*) bagaglio. // «~ **in transit**» **insurance** (*ass.*) assicurazione per il bagaglio personale; ~ **ticket** (*trasp.*) scontrino di bagaglio; ~ **van** (*trasp. ferr.*) carro bagagli, bagagliaio.

lump, *n.* mucchietto, piccola massa. // ~ **charter** (*trasp. mar.*) contratto di noleggio a corpo; ~ **freight** (*trasp. mar.*) nolo «a corpo», nolo «a massa»; ~ **sum** somma pagata tutta in una volta, forfait; **a** ~ **-sum payment** un pagamento in soluzione unica, un pagamento forfettario; **in the** ~ in massa, in blocco; (*comm.*) all'ingrosso; **on a** ~ **-sum basis** a forfait.

lumper, *n.* (*pers.*) scaricatore di porto.

lunch, *n.* pasto di mezzogiorno. // ~ **-bag** (*tur.*) centino da viaggio; ~ **wagon** (*trasp. ferr.*) vagone ristorante.

luncheon, *n.* seconda colazione. // ~ **vouchers** (*pers.*) buoni mensa.

luster, *n.* (*USA*) *V.* **lustre.**

lustre[1], *n.* lucentezza.

lustre[2], *n.* (*raro*) lustro (*periodo di cinque anni*).

luxurious, *a.* lussuoso.

luxury, *n.* lusso, fasto, sfarzo. // ~ **articles** (*market.*) articoli di lusso; **a** ~ **shop** (*market.*) un negozio di lusso; ~ **tax** (*fin.*) imposta sugli articoli di lusso.

lying, *a.* giacente.

M

machine[1], *n.* macchina. // ~ **-load card** (*org. az.*) scheda di macchina; ~ **-made** (*market.*) fatto a macchina; ~ **shop** (*org. az.*) officina meccanica; ~ **tender** (*pers.*) addetto a una macchina.

machine[2], *v. t.* **1** fare a macchina, eseguire a macchina. **2** stampare, tirare (*un giornale, ecc.*).

machinery, *n. collett.* **1** (*org. az.*) macchinario, macchine. **2** (*org. az.*) apparato. // ~ **and equipment** (*org. az.*) macchine e impianti.

machining, *n.* (*org. az.*) lavorazione a macchina.

macroeconomic, *a.* (*econ.*) macroeconomico. // ~ **decisions** (*econ.*) decisioni macroeconomiche, scelte macroeconomiche.

macroeconomics, *n. pl.* (*col verbo al sing.*) (*econ.*) macroeconomia.

made, *a.* fatto, fabbricato, prodotto, costruito, composto, confezionato, eseguito. // ~ **in Japan** (*market.*) fabbricato in Giappone; **a** ~ **man** (*fig.*) un uomo «arrivato»; ~ **-on-order** (*market.*) fatto su ordinazione; ~ **-to-order** (*market.*) fatto su ordinazione; **a self-** ~ **man** un uomo che s'è fatto da sé.

magazine, *n.* (*giorn.*) periodico. // ~ **advertising** (*giorn., pubbl.*) pubblicità (sulla) stampa.

magistrate, *n.* **1** (*leg.*) magistrato. **2** (*leg.*) giudice di pace, giudice conciliatore. // **magistrates' bench** (*leg.*) banco dei magistrati; ~ **'s Court** (*leg.*) «pretura», corte di giustizia di primo grado.

magistrateship, *n.* (*leg.*) carica di magistrato, magistratura.

magistrature, *n.* (*leg.*) magistratura.

magnate, *n.* (*fin.*) magnate.

magnetic, *a.* magnetico. // ~ **compass** (*trasp. mar.*) bussola magnetica; ~ **declination** (*trasp. mar.*) declinazione magnetica; ~ **deviation** (*trasp. mar.*) declinazione magnetica; ~ **recording** registrazione magnetica; ~ **tape recorder** (*macch. uff.*) registratore a nastro magnetico; ~ **variation** (*trasp. mar.*) declinazione magnetica.

maiden, *n.* fanciulla, vergine. // **the** ~ **voyage** (*trasp. mar.*) il viaggio inaugurale (*d'una nave*).

mail[1], *n. collett.* **1** posta, corrispondenza, lettere, pacchi. **2** sacco postale. **3 the mail** il servizio postale (*d'uno Stato*). **4** (*trasp.*) mezzo (*di trasporto*) postale. **5 the mails,** *pl.* il servizio postale (*d'uno Stato*). // ~ **-bag** sacco postale; ~ **car** (*trasp. ferr.*) vagone postale; ~ **carriage** (*trasp. ferr.*) vagone postale; ~ **clerk** (*pers.*) impiegato (*di ditta privata o ente pubblico*) addetto alla corrispondenza; ~ **order** (*market.*) ordinazione (*di merci*) fatta (ed eseguita) per corrispondenza; ~ **-order business** (*market.*) ditta che commercia (col sistema delle ordinazioni) per corrispondenza; ~ **-order catalogue** (*market.*) catalogo per vendite per corrispondenza; ~ **-order department** (*org. az.*) reparto per le ordinazioni per posta; ~ **-order firm** (*market.*) *V.* ~ **-order business;** ~ **-order house** (*market.*) *V.* ~ **-order business;** ~ **room** (*org. az.*) ufficio spedizioni; ~ **service** servizio postale; ~ **-steamer** (*trasp. mar.*) postale, nave postale, vapore postale; ~ **survey** (*market.*) indagine postale, inchiesta per corrispondenza; ~ **-train** (*trasp. ferr.*) treno postale, postale; ~ **-van** (*trasp. aut.*) furgone postale; **by** ~ (*comun.*) per posta; **in-coming** ~ (*comun.*) posta in arrivo; **out-going** ~ (*comun.*) posta in partenza.

mail[2], *v. t.* **1** mandare per posta, spedire per posta. **2** impostare, imbucare.

mailbox, *n.* (*USA*) cassetta della posta, buca da lettere.

mailing, *n.* **1** materiale postale. **2** (*comun.*) impostazione. // ~ **list** (*comun.*) lista di spedizione, elenco d'indirizzi (*per l'inoltro di materiale pubblicitario, ecc.*), indirizzario.

main, *a.* principale, più importante, essenziale. // ~ **line** (*trasp. ferr.*) linea principale; strada principale, strada statale, statale; ~ **station** (*trasp. ferr.*) stazione principale; ~ **stem** (*trasp. ferr.*) linea principale.

mainmast, *n.* (*trasp. mar.*) albero maestro.

mainsail, *n.* (*trasp. mar.*) vela di maestra.

mainspring, *n.* **1** molla principale (*d'un*

meccanismo). 2 (*fig.*) motivo principale.

maintain, *v. t.* 1 mantenere. 2 sostenere, affermare. // to ~ **a certain standard of living** (*econ.*) mantenere un certo tenore di vita.

maintenance, *n.* 1 mantenimento. 2 (*leg.*) aiuto illecito (*a una parte in causa*). 3 (*org. az.*) manutenzione, lavoro di manutenzione. // ~ **charges** (*rag.*) spese di manutenzione; ~ **costs** (*rag.*) costi di manutenzione; ~ **handbook** (*org. az.*) manuale di manutenzione; ~ **man** (*pers.*) addetto alla manutenzione.

major, *a.* 1 più grande. 2 più anziano. 3 principale. 4 (*leg.*) maggiorenne. *n.* chi è superiore (*in un gruppo: per importanza, potere, ecc.*).

majority, *n.* maggioranza. // ~ **control** (*amm.*) controllo di maggioranza; **a** ~ **resolution** (*amm.*) una delibera presa a maggioranza; **a** ~ **verdict** (*leg.*) un verdetto emesso a maggioranza (*dei giurati*).

make[1], *n.* 1 fabbricazione, produzione, fattura. 2 (*market.*) marca (*di prodotto, ecc.*); tipo (*d'articolo, ecc.*). 3 (*market.*) (*d'abito*) taglio. // ~ **-do** improvvisato; espediente temporaneo, rimedio provvisorio; **a** ~ **-do policy** (*amm.*) una politica improvvisata; ~ **-up** (*Borsa, ingl.*) compensazione; (*giorn.*) impaginatura; ~ **-up price** (*Borsa, ingl.*) prezzo di compensazione.

make[2], *v. t.* (*pass.* e *part. pass.* **made**) fare, fabbricare, produrre, costruire, confezionare, creare, comporre, eseguire. // to ~ **accounts agree** (*rag.*) far quadrare i conti; to ~ **an allotment** (*leg.*) fare una distribuzione; to ~ **allowance for** tener conto di (*qc.*); to ~ **allowance for fluctuations in exchange** (*fin., rag.*) tener conto delle oscillazioni di cambio; to ~ **an alteration** (*org. az.*) apportare una modifica; (*rag.*) fare una correzione; to ~ **an apology to sb.** fare le proprie scuse a q.; to ~ **appeal to** fare appello a; to ~ **an appeal to** rivolgersi a; to ~ **an appointment with sb.** prendere un appuntamento con q.; to ~ **an appropriation for the payment of debts** accantonare del denaro per il pagamento di debiti; to ~ **appropriations** (*fin., rag.*) accantonare denaro, stanziare somme; to ~ **an arrangement with sb.** raggiungere un accomodamento con q.; to ~ **arrangements for** dare disposizioni per; to ~ **an attachment on the debtor's property** (*leg.*) eseguire un pignoramento sui beni del debitore; to ~ **one's authority felt** far sentire la propria autorità; to ~ **st. available to sb.** mettere qc. a disposizione di q.; to ~ **a bid** fare un'offerta (*a un'asta*); to ~ **by hand** fare a mano; to ~ **by machine** fare a macchina; to ~ **a call** far (una breve) visita; (*trasp. mar.*) far scalo; to ~ **a call to short-end funds** (*fin.*) far ricorso alle risorse monetarie; to ~ **a complaint against sb.** (*leg.*) muovere un'accusa a q., querelare q.; to ~ **a deal over st.** contrattare qc.; to ~ **a delivery** (*market.*) fare una consegna; to ~ **an entry** (*rag.*) fare una registrazione; to ~ **an estimate of** preventivare; to ~ **fast** (*trasp. mar.*) dar volta a (un cavo); to ~ **for** (*trasp. mar.*) far rotta per; to ~ **a fortune** farsi una fortuna; to ~ **one's fortune** far fortuna; to ~ **good** (*ass.*) indennizzare, risarcire; to ~ **a good bargain** fare un buon affare; to ~ **good sb.'s loss** (*ass.*) risarcire q. d'una perdita subita; to ~ **harsher** (*o* **stricter**) inasprire; **to** ~ **inquiries** chiedere informazioni, fare indagini; to ~ **an inventory of** (*rag.*) inventariare; to ~ **it** farcela, riuscire; to ~ **a journey** (*tur.*) fare un viaggio (*per via di terra*); to ~ **laws** (*leg.*) fare leggi, legiferare; to ~ **a loss** (*fin.*) subire una perdita; to ~ **an offer** fare un'offerta; to ~ **out** compilare (*una lista, ecc.*); to ~ **out a list** compilare un elenco; to ~ **out a receipt** compilare una ricevuta, rilasciare una ricevuta; to ~ **over** passare, trasferire; to ~ **a payment** (*cred.*) fare un pagamento; to ~ **a price** (*market.*) fare un prezzo, praticare un prezzo; to ~ **a profit** (*fin.*) fare un guadagno; to ~ **st. profitable** (*fin.*) consentire un margine d'utile per qc.; to ~ **a protest** (*leg.*) fare un protesto; to ~ **protest of a bill** (*leg.*) far protestare una cambiale; to ~ **the punishment fit the crime** (*leg.*) commisurare la pena al delitto; to ~ **purchases** (*market.*) fare acquisti; to ~ **a return of one's income** (*fin.*) fare la dichiarazione dei redditi; to ~ **a sale** (*market.*) fare una vendita; to ~ **sb. a subscriber** (*giorn.*) abbonare q.; to ~ **a tender** fare un'offerta (*per un appalto*); to ~ **a transfer** (*leg.*) fare una cessione (*o* un passaggio) di proprietà; to ~ **up** compilare, redigere; (*econ., fin.*) integrare; mettere in colonna; to ~ **up one's accounts once every six months** (*rag.*) fare l'inventario una volta ogni sei mesi; to ~ **up a balance-sheet** (*rag.*) redigere un bilancio; to ~ **up differences** appianare divergenze; to ~ **up for** compensare, ricuperare; to ~ **up a parcel** (*market.*) fare un pacco (*o* un pacchetto); to ~ **up a quarrel** (*leg.*) comporre una lite, conciliare una lite; to ~ **a voyage** fare un viaggio (*per mare*); fare una traversata; to ~ **one's will** (*leg.*) far testamento; to ~ **st. worthwhile** (*econ., fin.*) rendere qc. retributivo; to **be made payable** essere (reso) pagabile.

maker, *n.* 1 creatore, esecutore. 2 chi

costruisce, costruttore, fabbricante, produttore. 3 (*cred.*) emittente (*d'un pagherò cambiario*). // ~ **-up** (*market., ingl.*) confezionista.

makeup, *n.* (*USA*) *V.* **make-up.**

making, *n.* **1** fattura, fabbricazione, costruzione, produzione, creazione, composizione, confezione, esecuzione. **2 the makings,** *pl.* (*econ., fin.*) i guadagni, i profitti, i ricavi, gli utili. // ~ **-up day** (*Borsa, ingl.*) giorno di riporto; ~ **-up price** (*Borsa, ingl.*) prezzo di compensazione.

maladministration, *n.* (*amm.*) cattiva amministrazione.

mala fide, *avv.* (*leg.*) in mala fede. *a. attr.* **1** (*leg.*) che è in mala fede. **2** (*leg.*) fatto in mala fede. // **a** ~ **possessor** (*leg.*) un possessore in mala fede.

maldistribution, *n.* cattiva distribuzione.

male, *a.* maschio, maschile. *n.* maschio.

malefactor, *n.* (*leg.*) malfattore.

malfeasance, *n.* **1** (*leg.*) condotta disonesta, condotta illecita. **2** (*leg.*) azione disonesta, azione illecita.

malfeasant, *a.* (*leg.*) disonesto. *n.* (*leg.*) persona disonesta.

malice, *n.* **1** malevolenza, cattiveria. **2** (*leg.*) intenzione criminosa, dolo, dolosità.

malicious, *a.* **1** malevolo, cattivo. **2** (*leg.*) criminoso, doloso.

malpractice, *n.* **1** prevaricazione. **2** (*leg.*) negligenza (*nell'esercizio professionale*).

man¹, *n.* (*pl.* **men**). **1** uomo. **2** (*pers.*) operaio, lavorante. **3** (*pers., fam.*) agente, rappresentante, «uomo». // **«men at work»** (*trasp. aut.: segnale stradale*) «lavori in corso»; ~ **Friday** (*pers.*) uomo di fiducia, impiegato tuttofare; ~ **-hours lost due to strikes** ore perdute per conflitti di lavoro; **the** ~ **in the street** l'uomo della strada, l'uomo qualunque; ~ **-made** fatto dall'uomo; **a** ~ **of average ability** un uomo di medie capacità; **the** ~ **of the house** l'uomo di casa; ~ **of straw** (*leg.*) prestanome; **the** ~ **on the street** *V.* **the** ~ **in the street.**

man², *v. t.* **1** fornire d'uomini. **2** (*trasp. mar.*) armare (*una nave*). // to ~, **equip and supply a ship** (*trasp. mar.*) armare ed equipaggiare una nave.

manage, *v. t.* e *i.* **1** destreggiarsi, manovrare. **2** (*fam.*) farcela. **3** (*amm.*) amministrare, controllare, dirigere, avere la direzione di, gestire, governare, reggere. **4** (*amm.*) condurre gli affari, dirigere gli affari. // to ~ **a business** (*fin.*) amministrare un'azienda.

managed, *a.* (*amm.*) controllato, diretto, gestito, governato, retto. // **a** ~ **currency** (*fin.*) una valuta controllata (*nel suo potere d'acquisto: dalle autorità monetarie*); **a** ~ **economy** (*econ.*) un'economia controllata; ~ **flexibility** (*fin.*) flessibilità manovrata; ~ **floating** (*econ., fin.*) fluttuazione controllata (*d'una moneta*); ~ **money** (*fin.*) *V.* ~ **currency;** ~ **standard** (*econ., fin.*) sistema monetario manovrato.

management, *n.* **1** (*amm.*) amministrazione, conduzione, controllo, direzione (*l'attività direttiva*), direzione aziendale, gestione, «management». **2** (*amm.*) direzione (*il corpo direttivo*). **3** (*econ.*) politica. // ~ **accountancy** (*amm., rag.*) contabilità direzionale; ~ **accounting** (*amm., rag.*) contabilità direzionale; ~ **advisory committee** (*amm., pers., sind.*) comitato di consultazione mista; ~ **appraisal** (*amm.*) rilevazione dello stato organizzativo; ~ **by objectives** (*org. az.*) direzione (*od* organizzazione) per obiettivi; ~ **company** (*fin.*) società di gestione; ~ **consultant** (*amm.*) consulente d'organizzazione aziendale; ~ **consulting** (*amm.*) consulenza organizzativa; ~ **control** (*amm.*) controllo manageriale, controllo direzionale; ~ **evaluation** (*amm.*) rilevazione dello stato organizzativo; ~ **expenses** (*rag.*) spese di gestione; ~ **functions** (*amm.*) funzioni manageriali, funzioni direttive, mansioni dirigenziali; ~ **selection and training** (*pers.*) sviluppo e formazione manageriale; ~ **structure** (*org. az.*) struttura direzionale; ~ **techniques** (*amm.*) tecniche di direzione aziendale; ~ **tools** (*amm.*) tecniche di direzione aziendale.

manager, *n.* (*amm.*) amministratore, direttore (*d'azienda*), dirigente, gerente, gestore, manager. // ~ **development** (*pers.*) formazione dei dirigenti; **the** ~ **-owner relationship** (*org. az.*) il rapporto manager-imprenditore.

manageress, *n.* (*amm.*) amministratrice, direttrice (*d'azienda*), dirigente, gerente.

managerial, *a.* (*amm.*) di direttore (*d'azienda*), della direzione (*d'affari*), direttivo, direttoriale, direzionale, dirigenziale, gestionale, manageriale. // ~ **ability** (*amm.*) capacità manageriale, capacità direttiva; ~ **innovations** (*amm.*) innovazioni gestionali; ~ **problems** (*amm.*) problemi di direzione.

managership, *n.* (*amm.*) autorità di direttore, posizione di direttore, doveri di direttore (*V.* **manager**).

managing, *a.* (*amm.*) direttivo, dirigente, gerente. // ~ **activity** (*amm.*) attività direttiva; ~ **committee** (*amm.*) comitato direttivo, (il) direttivo; ~ **director** (*amm.*) consigliere delegato, amministratore delegato; ~ **editor** (*amm.*, *giorn.*) direttore editoriale, direttore amministrativo; ~ **partner** (*amm.*) socio gerente.

mandamus[1], *n.* (*leg.*) mandato, ordinanza (*del giudice a un pubblico ufficiale*).

mandamus[2], *v. t.* (*leg.*) obbligare per mezzo di un «mandamus» (*q. V.*).

mandant, *n.* (*leg.*) mandante.

mandatary, *n.* (*leg.*) mandatario.

mandate, *n.* (*leg.*) mandato.

mandatee, *n.* (*leg.*) mandatario.

mandator, *n.* (*leg.*) mandante.

mandatory, *a.* (*leg.*) imperativo, obbligatorio, vincolante. *n.* (*leg.*) *V.* **mandatary.**

manifest[1], *a.* manifesto. *n.* **1** (*trasp. aer., trasp. mar.*) manifesto (*di carico*), nota di carico. **2** (*trasp. ferr., USA*) treno rapido (*per merci deperibili, bestiame, ecc.*).

manifest[2], *v. t.* manifestare.

manifold[1], *a.* molteplice, vario.

manifold[2], *v. t.* **1** moltiplicare, rendere molteplice. **2** (*giorn., pubbl.*) poligrafare.

manipulate, *v. t.* **1** manipolare, maneggiare. **2** (*fig.*) manovrare. **3** (*leg.*) manipolare. // to ~ **the bank rate** (*fin.*) manovrare il tasso di sconto; to ~ **prices** (*econ.*) manovrare i prezzi.

manipulation, *n.* **1** manipolazione, il maneggiare. **2** (*fig.*) manovra. **3** (*leg.*) manipolazione. **4** (*market.*) manipolazione (*delle merci*). // **the** ~ **of the bank rate** (*fin.*) la manovra del tasso di sconto.

mannequin, *n.* (*market., pubbl.*) indossatrice.

manning, *n.* assunzione e impiego del personale.

manoeuver[1], *n. V.* **manoeuvre**[1].

manoeuver[2], *v. t. V.* **manoeuvre**[2].

manoeuvre[1], *n.* manovra.

manoeuvre[2], *v. t.* manovrare.

manpower, *n.* (*econ., stat.*) manodopera, forze di lavoro. // ~ **problems** (*pers., sind.*) problemi della manodopera; ~ **training** (*org. az., pers.*) addestramento della manodopera.

manual, *a.* manuale. *n.* manuale, prontuario, guida, trattato. // ~ **delivery** (*leg.*) trasferimento manuale, tradizione manuale; ~ **dexterity** (*pers.*) abilità manuale; ~ **labour** (*econ.*) lavoro manuale; ~ **workers** (*pers.*) lavoratori manuali.

manufactory, *n.* (*org. az.*) manifattura, fabbrica, opificio.

manufacture[1], *n.* **1** (*market.*) manufatto, prodotto manufatto. **2** (*org. az.*) manifattura, fabbricazione, produzione, industria, lavorazione (*della lana, dei metalli, ecc.*).

manufacture[2], *v. t.* (*org. az.*) fabbricare, produrre, lavorare (*lana, metalli, ecc.*), confezionare (*capi d'abbigliamento, ecc.*). // to ~ **shirts** (*org. az.*) confezionare camicie.

manufactured articles, *n. pl.* (*org. az.*) manufatture, manufatti.

manufactured goods, *n. pl.* (*market.*) manufatti, prodotti lavorati.

manufacturer, *n.* fabbricante, produttore, industriale. // ~ **'s certificate** (*market.*) certificato di garanzia.

manufacturing, *a.* (*org. az.*) manifatturiero, industriale. *n.* attività industriale, fabbricazione, produzione. // **a** ~ **city** (*econ.*) una città industriale; ~ **cost** (*rag.*) costo di lavorazione, costo industriale; ~ **cycle** (*cronot.*) ciclo di lavorazione; ~ **industry** (*econ.*) industria manifatturiera; ~ **licence** (*leg.*) licenza di fabbricazione; ~ **overhead cost** (*rag.*) spese generali di produzione; ~ **overheads** (*rag.*) spese generali di produzione; ~ **process** (*org. az.*) processo di fabbricazione, processo produttivo.

manuscript, *n.* manoscritto.

map[1], *n.* carta geografica, carta topografica.

map[2], *v. t.* fare una mappa di (*una regione, ecc.*). // to ~ **out** fare un piano, tracciare un piano.

margin[1], *n.* **1** margine. **2** (*econ., rag.*) margine, margine lordo, differenza, scarto. // ~ **call** (*Borsa, fin.*) richiesta di copertura; **the** ~ **of a page** il margine d'una pagina.

margin[2], *v. t.* fare annotazioni in margine di (*una pagina, ecc.*). // to ~ **up** (*Borsa, fin.*) completare la copertura di (*titoli, ecc.*).

marginal, *a.* marginale, in margine. // ~ **analysis** (*econ.*) analisi marginale; ~ **buyer** (*econ.*) compratore marginale; ~ **cost** (*econ.*) costo marginale; ~ **costing** (*econ.*) accertamento del costo (*di produzione*) d'un'unità marginale; **the** ~ **efficiency of capital** (*econ.*) l'efficienza marginale del capitale; ~ **notes** annotazioni in margine, postille; ~ **product** (*econ.*) prodotto marginale; ~ **productivity** (*econ.*) produttività marginale; ~ **profit** (*econ.*) reddito marginale, utile marginale; ~ **propensity to consume** (*econ.*) propensione marginale al consumo; ~ **propensity to save** (*econ.*) propensione marginale al risparmio; ~ **unity** (*econ.*) unità marginale; ~ **utility** (*econ.*) utilità marginale.

marine, *a.* **1** marino. **2** (*trasp. mar.*) marittimo, nautico, navale. *n.* (*trasp. mar.*) marina. // ~ **adventure** (*trasp. mar.*) spedizione marittima, viaggio di mare; ~ **casualties** (*ass. mar.*) rischi marittimi imprevisti; ~ **insurance** (*ass. mar.*) assicurazione marittima; ~ **insur-**

ance broker (*ass. mar.*) sensale d'assicurazioni marittime; ~ **insurance company** (*ass. mar.*) compagnia d'assicurazione marittima; ~ **insurance policy** (*ass. mar.*) polizza d'assicurazione marittima; ~ **interest** (*ass. mar.*) interesse su cambio marittimo; ~ **law** (*leg.*) diritto marittimo, diritto della navigazione; ~ **perils** (*ass. mar., trasp. mar.*) rischi di mare, rischi e pericoli della navigazione; ~ **risks** (*ass. mar., trasp. mar.*) rischi di mare, rischi e pericoli della navigazione; ~ **stores** (*trasp. mar.*) magazzini navali.

maritime, *a.* (*trasp. mar.*) marittimo, navale. // ~ **contract** (*leg.*) contratto di navigazione; ~ **credit** (*cred.*) credito navale; ~ **insurance** (*ass. mar.*) assicurazione marittima; ~ **interest** (*ass. mar.*) interesse su cambio marittimo; ~ **law** (*leg.*) diritto marittimo, diritto della navigazione; ~ **lien** (*leg.*) pegno marittimo, privilegio marittimo; ~ **loan** (*ass. mar.*) cambio marittimo; ~ **perils** (*ass. mar., trasp. mar.*) rischi di mare, rischi e pericoli della navigazione.

mark[1]**,** *n.* **1** (*Borsa*) punto. **2** (*fin.*) marco (*unità monetaria tedesca*). **3** (*market.*) contrassegno (*del prezzo, ecc.*). **4** (*market.*) marchio di fabbrica, marca. // ~ **-on** (*market.*) margine di profitto (*aggiunto al costo per ottenere il prezzo di vendita*).

mark[2]**,** *v. t.* **1** marcare, segnare. **2** (*banca*) vistare (*titoli di credito, ecc.*). **3** (*market.*) mettere il cartellino del prezzo a (*articoli in vendita*). **4** (*market.*) contrassegnare (*con un marchio, una marca, ecc.*). // to ~ **an article** (*market.*) mettere il cartellino (*del prezzo*) a un articolo; to ~ **down** annotare, registrare, segnare; (*market.*) abbassare il prezzo di (*articoli, merci, ecc.*); to ~ **a price** (*Borsa, fin.*) quotare un corso; (*market.*) quotare un prezzo; to ~ **time** (*anche fig.*) segnare il passo, non fare progressi; to ~ **up** (*market.*) alzare il prezzo di (*articoli, merci, ecc.*).

markdown, *n.* **1** (*market.*) ribasso di prezzo, diminuzione di prezzo. **2** (*market.*) ammontare della diminuzione di prezzo.

marked, *a.* **1** marcato, segnato. **2** (*banca*) vistato. **3** (*market.*) contrassegnato. // ~ **cheques** (*banca*) assegni vistati; ~ **shares** (*fin.*) azioni stampigliate.

marker, *n.* **1** (*cred., USA*) pagherò cambiario. **2** (*cred., USA*) *V.* **IOU.** **3** (*trasp. ferr.*) segnale.

market[1]**,** *n.* **1** mercato. **2** (*Borsa, fin.*) operazioni (*di Borsa*); Borsa; quotazione (*di titolo*). **3** (*comm.*) piazza. **4** (*econ.*) sbocco commerciale. **5** (*econ.*) prezzo di mercato. **6** (*econ., market.*) domanda, richiesta. **7** (*market.*) smercio, vendita. // ~ **analysis** (*market.*) analisi di mercato; ~ **analyst** (*market.*) analista di mercato, analizzatore del mercato; ~ **conditions** (*econ., market.*) condizioni di mercato; ~ **crisis** (*Borsa*) crisi della Borsa; ~ **day** (*market.*) giorno di mercato; ~ **demand prorationing system** (*econ., USA*) sistema del razionamento della domanda di mercato; ~ **economy** (*econ.*) economia di mercato; ~ **gardener** (*econ.*) ortofrutticoltore; ~ **gardening** (*econ.*) ortofrutticoltura; ~ **jobbery** (*Borsa*) aggiotaggio; ~ **leaders** (*econ., market.*) aziende leader; ~ **-list** (*econ.*) mercuriale; ~ **mechanisms** (*econ., market.*) meccanismi di mercato; ~ **news** (*giorn.*) Borse e Mercati (*titolo di rubrica, colonna, ecc.*); ~ **order** (*Borsa, fin.*) ordine (d'acquisto) al meglio, ordine (di vendita) al meglio; ~ **outlets** (*econ., market.*) sbocchi di mercato; ~ **potential** (*econ.*) potenziale di mercato; ~ **price** (*econ., market.*) prezzo di mercato; ~ **report** (*econ., market.*) rassegna di mercato, mercuriale; ~ **requirements** (*econ., market.*) esigenze di mercato; ~ **research** (*econ., market.*) ricerca di mercato, indagine di mercato; ~ **stage** (*econ., market.*) fase di mercato; ~ **supply** (*econ.*) offerta di mercato; ~ **-supply curve** (*econ.*) curva dell'offerta di mercato; ~ **support** (*econ., market.*) intervento sul mercato; ~ **-support agencies** (*econ., market.*) organismi d'intervento sul mercato; ~ **syndicate** (*Borsa*) sindacato di Borsa; ~ **target price** (*econ.*) prezzo indicativo di mercato; ~ **trend** (*econ., market.*) tendenza di mercato; ~ **value** (*econ., market.*) valore di mercato; **at the** ~ (*Borsa*) al prezzo prevalente; **in the** ~ (*market.*) in vendita; **on the** ~ (*market.*) in vendita.

market[2]**,** *v. t.* (*market.*) smerciare, mettere in vendita, vendere, porre in commercio. *v. i.* **1** (*market.*) fare acquisti. **2** (*market.*) fare vendite.

marketability, *n.* (*market.*) commerciabilità, negoziabilità.

marketable, *a.* (*market.*) commerciabile, negoziabile, commercializzabile, smerciabile, vendibile. // ~ **securities** (*fin.*) titoli trasferibili; ~ **titles** (*leg.*) titoli trasferibili.

marketeer, *n.* (*market.*) chi vende al mercato. // **free** ~ (*econ.*) liberoscambista.

marketer, *n.* **1** (*market.*) chi vende al mercato. **2** (*market.*) chi compra al mercato.

marketing, *n.* **1** (*market.*) commercializzazione, marketing, distribuzione, compravendita, smercio. **2** (*market.*) marketing, tecnica delle ricerche di mercato, studio e analisi dei mercati. // ~ **assistance to customers** (*market.*) assistenza di marketing alla clientela; ~ **centres** (*market.*) centri di commercializzazione; ~ **cost** (*econ., market.*) costo di distribuzione; ~ **director** (*pers.*) direttore del marketing; ~ **manager** (*pers.*) direttore del marketing; **the ~ of commodities** (*econ.*) la commercializzazione dei prodotti; ~ **research** (*econ., market.*) ricerca di marketing, indagine di mercato; ~ **year** (*market.*) campagna (*di vendita: in un dato anno*).

marking, *n.* (*Borsa*) registrazione e pubblicazione giornaliera dei prezzi quotati.

markup, *n.* **1** (*Borsa, fin.*) rialzo (*di prezzi, quotazioni, ecc.*). **2** (*market.*) aumento di prezzo; rincaro (*di prezzi*). **3** (*market.*) margine di profitto (*aggiunto al costo per ottenere il prezzo di vendita*); utile.

marriage, *n.* matrimonio. // ~ **leave** (*pers.*) congedo per matrimonio.

marshal[1], *n.* **1** maresciallo. **2** (*leg., USA*) ufficiale giudiziario.

marshal[2], *v. t.* **1** mettere in ordine, ordinare (*secondo certi criteri di priorità*). **2** (*leg.*) ordinare (*le attività patrimoniali*) riguardo alla disponibilità per la soddisfazione d'obbligazioni. **3** (*leg.*) ordinare (*i creditori, gli aventi diritto, ecc.*) in vista della soddisfazione dei crediti nei confronti d'un debitore insolvente.

mass, *n.* massa, grande quantità. // ~ **advertising** (*pubbl.*) pubblicità di massa; ~ **-circulation press** (*giorn.*) stampa a grande tiratura; ~ **communication media** (*giorn., pubbl.*) mezzi di comunicazione di massa; ~ **distribution** (*econ.*) distribuzione (*delle merci*) in grandissime quantità; ~ **man** (*pubbl.*) uomo medio; ~ **medium** (*giorn., pubbl.*) mezzo di comunicazione di massa; ~ **picketing** (*sind.*) picchettaggio di massa; to ~ **-produce** (*econ.*) produrre (*o* costruire) in serie, standardizzare; ~ **-produced** (*org. az.*) prodotto (*o* costruito) in serie, standardizzato; ~ **-producer** (*market.*) chi attua una produzione di massa; ~ **production** (*org. az.*) produzione di massa, produzione in serie, fabbricazione in serie, standardizzazione.

mast[1], *n.* (*trasp. mar.*) albero (*di nave*).

mast[2], *v. t.* (*trasp. mar.*) alberare (*una nave*).

master[1], *n.* **1** padrone. **2** (*pers.*) capo, datore di lavoro. **3** (*trasp. mar.*) capitano (*di mercantile*), comandante. // ~ **catalogue** (*market.*) catalogo generale; ~ **'s certificate** (*trasp. mar.*) brevetto di capitano; ~ **in chancery** (*leg.*) assistente di giudice; ~ **mariner** (*trasp. mar.*) capitano di (nave) mercantile; **the ~ of the house** il capofamiglia; **at the ~ 's option** (*trasp. mar.*) a scelta del capitano (*della nave*).

master[2], *v. t.* essere padrone di, conoscere a fondo.

mastery, *n.* conoscenza approfondita.

matching, *n.* (*fin., rag.*) concordanza (*di elementi, scadenze, ecc.*).

mate, *n.* **1** compagno. **2** (*pers.*) compagno di lavoro. **3** (*trasp. mar.*) comandante in seconda (*di mercantile*). // ~ **'s receipt** (*trasp. mar.*) ricevuta provvisoria d'imbarco.

material, *a.* **1** materiale. **2** (*leg.*) importante, essenziale. *n.* materiale, materia, sostanza. // **materials control** (*org. az.*) controllo dei materiali; ~ **facts** (*leg.*) fatti importanti; **materials handling** (*org. az.*) maneggio dei materiali, trasporto (*interno*) dei materiali; ~ **needs** (*econ.*) bisogni materiali; **a ~ piece of evidence** (*leg.*) una prova essenziale.

materialize, *v. t.* ridurre a condizione materiale, materializzare. *v. i.* materializzarsi, realizzarsi.

maternal, *a.* materno. // ~ **welfare** (*leg., pers.*) tutela della maternità.

maternity, *n.* maternità. // ~ **leave** (*pers.*) congedo per maternità, congedo per gravidanza e puerperio.

math, *n.* (*fam., USA*) matematica.

mathematic, *a.* *V.* **mathematical.**

mathematical, *a.* (*mat.*) matematico.

mathematician, *n.* matematico.

mathematics, *n. pl.* (*col verbo al sing.*) (*mat.*) matematica.

maths, *n.* (*fam.*) matematica.

matriculate, *v. t.* immatricolare.

matriculation, *n.* immatricolazione.

matrix, *n.* (*pl.* **matrices** e *reg.*) **1** (*mat.*) matrice. **2** (*pubbl.*) matrice (*di stampa*).

matter[1], *n.* **1** materia, sostanza. **2** argomento, contenuto, oggetto, soggetto. **3** affare, questione, problema. // ~ **in controversy** (*leg.*) oggetto della controversia, oggetto della lite; ~ **in deed** (*leg.*) materia di fatto, motivo di fatto; **a ~ of complaint** un motivo di lagnanza; **matters of concern to consumers** (*comm., comm. est.*) questioni interessanti i consumatori; **the ~ of the dispute** (*leg.*) l'oggetto della controversia, l'oggetto della lite; ~ **of fact** (*leg.*) materia di fatto, motivo di fatto; ~ **of law** (*leg.*) materia di diritto, motivo di diritto; **a ~ of priority** un problema che ha precedenza assoluta; **as a ~ of course** (*amm., leg.*) d'ufficio.

matter[2], *v. i.* avere importanza, importare, interessare.

mature[1], *a.* **1** (*anche fig.*) maturo. **2** (*cred.*)

(*di cambiale, ecc.*) in scadenza, scaduto.

mature², *v. t.* 1 maturare, portare a maturità. 2 (*fig.*) maturare (*un'idea, un piano*). *v. i.* 1 maturare, maturarsi. 2 (*cred.*) (*di cambiale, ecc.*) giungere a scadenza, scadere.

matureness, *n. V.* **maturity**.

maturity, *n.* 1 maturazione. 2 (*cred.*) (*di cambiale, ecc.*) scadenza. // **at** (*o* **on**) ~ (*cred.*) alla scadenza; **before** ~ (*cred.*) prima della scadenza.

maximal, *a.* massimale.

maximation, *n. V.* **maximization**.

maximization, *n.* 1 (*econ.*) massimizzazione, aumento spinto al massimo. 2 (*mat.*) massimizzazione.

maximize, *v. t.* 1 (*econ.*) massimizzare. 2 (*mat.*) massimizzare (*una funzione, ecc.*); trovare il valore massimo di (*una funzione, ecc.*).

maximum, *n.* 1 (il) massimo. 2 (*mat.*) valore massimo (*d'una funzione, ecc.*). *a. attr.* massimo. // ~ **axle load** (*trasp.*) carico massimo per assale, peso massimo per assale; ~ **load** (*trasp.*) carico massimo, peso massimo; ~ **overdraft** (*banca, cred.*) massimo scoperto; ~ **rate** (*ass.*) massimale; ~ **risk** (*ass.*) rischio massimo; ~ **wage** (*pers.*) salario massimo.

mayor, *n.* sindaco (*di città*).

mayoral, *a.* di sindaco (*di città*), sindacale.

mean¹, *a.* medio, intermedio. *n.* 1 via di mezzo. 2 (*mat., stat.*) media. 3 **means**, *pl.* (*spesso col verbo al sing.*) mezzo, espediente, modo, modalità, maniera, (*fig.*) strumento. 4 **means**, *pl.* (*fin.*) mezzi (*di sussistenza*), averi, denari, proprietà. // ~ **life** (*ass.*) vita media; **means of conveyance** (*trasp.*) mezzo (*o* mezzi) di trasporto; **a means of speeding up public spending** (*fin.*) uno strumento d'accelerazione della spesa pubblica; **means of transportation** mezzo di trasporto; ~ **price** (*market.*) prezzo medio; ~ **price difference** (*market.*) scarto medio dei prezzi; ~ **proportional** (*mat.*) media proporzionale; **a** ~ **quantity** una quantità media; **by means of** per mezzo di, mediante.

mean², *v. t.* (*pass.* e *part. pass.* **meant**) intendere, avere l'intenzione di. // to ~ **business** fare sul serio.

meaning, *n.* senso.

measurable, *a.* misurabile.

measure¹, *n.* 1 misura. 2 (*fig.*) misura, provvedimento, precauzione. 3 (*leg.*) via (legale). 4 (*mat.*) divisore. // **measures aimed at boosting the economy** (*econ.*) provvedimenti di rilancio economico; ~ **of damage** (*ass., leg.*) metodo di valutazione dei danni; **measures taken for the safety of the ship** (*trasp. mar.*) provvedimenti presi per la salvezza della nave; **measures taken to stem the recession** (*econ.*) provvedimenti anticongiunturali; **measures taken to support prices** (*econ.*) misure di sostegno dei prezzi.

measure², *v. t.* 1 misurare. 2 giudicare, valutare. *v. i.* misurare, fare misurazioni, avere una (certa) misura. // to ~ **the tonnage of** (*trasp. mar.*) stazzare.

measurement, *n.* 1 misurazione, il misurare. 2 misura. 3 (*trasp. mar.*) stazzatura. // ~ **brief** (*trasp. mar.*) certificato di stazza; ~ **cargo** (*trasp. mar.*) merci a cubatura; ~ **freight** (*trasp. mar.*) merci a cubatura; ~ **goods** (*trasp. mar.*) merci a cubatura; ~ **rate** (*trasp. mar.*) rata (di nolo) a cubaggio.

meat, *n.* (*market.*) carne. // ~ **centre** centro delle carni.

mechanic, *a.* meccanico. *n.* (*pers.*) meccanico.

mechanical, *a.* meccanico. // ~ **aptitude test** (*pers.*) test d'attitudine meccanica; ~ **drawing** (*pubbl.*) disegno tecnico; ~ **engineering** (*econ.*) industrie meccaniche; ~ **handling** (*org. az.*) trasporti (*interni*) meccanizzati; ~ **technology** (*org. az.*) tecnologia meccanica; ~ **transport** (*trasp.*) trasporto motorizzato.

mechanism, *n.* meccanismo.

mechanization, *n.* meccanizzazione.

mechanize, *v. t.* 1 meccanizzare. 2 (*org. az.*) fornire di macchinari.

mechanized, *a.* meccanizzato. // ~ **silo** (*org. az.*) silo meccanizzato.

media, *n. pl.* (*pubbl.*) mezzi tecnici d'informazione, mezzi pubblicitari. // ~ **buyer** (*pubbl.*) «media buyer» (*chi acquista spazio su un giornale o tempo alla radio e TV per fare la pubblicità a un prodotto*); ~ **department** (*pubbl.*) reparto mezzi pubblicitari; ~ **man** (*pubbl.*) esperto in mezzi pubblicitari, esperto pubblicitario, pubblicitario; ~ **research** (*org. az., pubbl.*) ricerca dei mezzi d'informazione.

median, *a.* mediano, di mezzo.

mediate¹, *a.* mediato. // **a** ~ **testimony** (*leg.*) una testimonianza per procura.

mediate², *v. i.* fare da mediatore, fare da intermediario. *v. t.* ottenere con la propria mediazione. // to ~ **a settlement** ottenere un accomodamento esercitando la mediazione.

mediation, *n.* mediazione.

mediator, *n.* mediatore (*di liti, ecc.*).

medical, *a.* medico. // ~ **assistance** (*pers.*) assistenza medica; ~ **examiner** (*ass., pers.*) medico legale; ~ **inspection of passengers** (*leg., trasp.*) controllo sanitario dei passeggeri; ~

jurisprudence (*leg.*) medicina legale; ~ **officer** (*leg.*) ufficiale sanitario.

medicine, *n.* medicina.

medium, *n.* **1** mezzo, espediente, modo, strumento, (*fig.*) tramite. **2** (*econ.*) mezzo di scambio. **3** (*pubbl.*) mezzo tecnico d'informazione, mezzo pubblicitario. *a. attr.* medio, intermedio. // **a ~ of communication** (*comun.*) un mezzo di comunicazione; **a ~ of exchange** (*econ.*) un mezzo di scambio; **~ -sized** medio; **the ~ -sized companies** (*fin.*) le medie imprese; **a ~ -sized enterprise** (*fin.*) una media impresa; **~ -term** a medio termine, a medio, a media scadenza, nel medio periodo; (*fin., rag.*) (*di profitti, perdite, operazioni, ecc.*) a medio termine (*più d'un anno ma meno di dieci anni*); **~ term credit** (*cred.*) credito a medio (termine), mediocredito; **~ -term economic outlook** (*econ.*) prospettive economiche a medio termine; **~ -term economic policy** (*econ.*) politica economica a medio termine; **~ -term investment policy** (*econ.*) politica d'investimenti a medio termine; **a ~ -term loan** (*cred.*) un finanziamento a medio termine; **a ~ -term plan** (*econ.*) un piano poliennale; **in the ~ term** a medio termine, a media scadenza, nel medio periodo.

meet, *v. t.* (*pass.* e *part. pass.* **met**) **1** incontrare, conoscere, fare la conoscenza di, essere presentato a. **2** (*anche fig.*) andare incontro a, venire incontro a. **3** far fronte a, fronteggiare, affrontare. **4** soddisfare. **5** (*cred.*) far onore a, onorare (*una cambiale, ecc.*); pagare. *v. i.* incontrarsi, trovarsi. // **to ~ a bill of exchange** (*cred.*) onorare una cambiale, pagare una cambiale; **to ~ sb. by appointment** incontrare q. su appuntamento; **to ~ competition** (*market.*) sostenere la concorrenza; **to ~ the customers' requirements** (*market.*) corrispondere alle esigenze dei clienti; **to ~ a debt** (*cred.*) far fronte a un debito; **to ~ a demand** soddisfare una richiesta; **to ~ the demand** (*econ.*) essere all'altezza della domanda, essere pari alla domanda; **to ~ one's engagements** (*leg.*) soddisfare i propri impegni; **to ~ an expense** sostenere una spesa; **to ~ with** incontrarsi con, incontrare; **to ~ with appreciation** essere apprezzato; **to ~ with sb.'s approval** incontrare l'approvazione di q., essere approvato da q.

meeting, *n.* **1** incontro, riunione, convegno. **2** (*leg.*) assemblea, adunanza. // **the ~ of the board of directors** (*amm.*) l'adunanza del consiglio d'amministrazione; **the ~ of creditors** (*leg.*) l'assemblea dei creditori; **the ~ of shareholders** (*fin.*) l'assemblea degli azionisti.

megabuck, *n.* (*slang USA*) (un) milione di dollari.

melt, *v. t.* fondere. *v. i.* fondersi.

melting, *n.* fusione (*in senso proprio*).

member, *n.* **1** membro. **2** (*fin.*) associato, socio. **3** (*sind.*) iscritto. // **~ corporation** (*Borsa, USA*) società aderente alla Borsa Valori di New York; **a ~ of the Bar association** (*leg.*) un iscritto all'ordine degli avvocati; **the members of the crew** (*trasp. mar.*) i membri dell'equipaggio; to **be a ~ of** essere membro di.

membership, *n.* **1** condizione di membro. **2** (*fin.*) condizione di socio; appartenenza (*a una società, ecc.*). **3** (*fin.*) numero di soci. **4** (*sind.*) l'essere iscritto, appartenenza (*a un sindacato*). **5** (*sind.*) numero di iscritti.

memo[1], *n.* **1** (*az. org., fam.*) memorandum, promemoria, nota, annotazione, appunto. **2** (*org. az., fam.*) comunicazione, comunicazione di servizio. // **~ book** (*attr. uff.*) memorandum, agenda, taccuino.

memo[2], *v. t.* **1** (*org. az., fam.*) fare un memorandum di (*qc.*), fare un'annotazione di (*qc.*). **2** (*org. az., fam.*) inviare una comunicazione (di servizio) a (*q.*).

memorandum[1], *n.* (*pl.* **memoranda** e *reg.*) **1** memorandum, promemoria, nota, appunto. **2** (*org. az.*) comunicazione, comunicazione di servizio. **3** (*trasp. mar.*) duplicato di polizza di carico. // **~ book** (*attr. uff.*) memorandum, agenda, taccuino; **~ of association** (*fin., ingl.*) atto costitutivo (*d'una società di capitali*); **as a ~** come promemoria.

memorandum[2], *v. t.* fare un memorandum di (*qc.*).

memorial, *n.* **1** memoriale, memorandum, promemoria, nota, petizione. **2** (*leg.*) estratto.

memory, *n.* **1** memoria. **2** (*elab. elettr.*) memoria. // **~ book** (*attr. uff.*) memorandum, agenda, taccuino.

mend, *v. t.* accomodare, aggiustare.

mending, *n.* aggiustamento.

mensualisation, *n.* (*pers., sind.*) mensualizzazione (*dei salari*).

mental, *a.* mentale. // **~ capacity** (*leg.*) capacità d'intendere e di volere; **~ competence** (*leg.*) capacità d'intendere e di volere; **~ disease** (*leg.*) malattia mentale, infermità mentale; **~ powers** (*leg.*) facoltà mentali.

mention[1], *n.* menzione, accenno, citazione, indicazione.

mention[2], *v. t.* menzionare, far menzione di, accennare a, citare, indicare. // **mentioned above** predetto, suddetto.

mercantile, *a.* mercantile, commerciale. // ~ **agency** (*leg.*) agenzia, rappresentanza di commercio; agenzia d'informazioni commerciali; ~ **agent** (*leg.*) agente di commercio; titolare d'un'agenzia d'informazioni commerciali; ~ **credit** (*cred.*) credito mercantile; ~ **law** (*leg.*) diritto commerciale; ~ **marine** (*trasp. mar.*) marina mercantile; ~ **paper** (*banca, cred.*) carta commerciale, effetti commerciali; ~ **system** (*econ.*) mercantilismo; ~ **theory** (*econ.*) teoria mercantilistica.

mercantilism, *n.* (*econ.*) mercantilismo.

mercantilist, *n.* (*econ.*) mercantilista, fautore del mercantilismo. *a.* (*econ.*) mercantilista.

mercantilistic, *a.* (*econ.*) mercantilistico, mercantilista.

merchandise[1], *n. collett.* (*market.*) mercanzia, merce, derrate. // ~ **traffic** (*trasp.*) movimento (delle) merci; ~ **train** (*trasp. ferr.*) treno merci.

merchandise[2], *v. i.* (*market.*) commerciare, fare affari. *v. t.* **1** (*market.*) commerciare in (*un articolo, ecc.*), trattare (*un articolo, ecc.*), occuparsi di (*un certo articolo, un ramo d'affari, ecc.*). **2** (*market.*) promuovere le vendite di (*un articolo, ecc.*). **3** (*pubbl.*) reclamizzare (*un prodotto, ecc.*).

merchandising, *n.* (*pubbl.*) complesso d'attività promozionali di vendita.

merchandize, *v. t.* e *i. V.* **merchandise.**

merchant[1], *n.* **1** mercante, commerciante. **2** (*USA*) negoziante, bottegaio. *a. attr.* mercantile, commerciale. // ~ **bank** (*fin., ingl.*) «banca d'affari»; ~ **banker** (*fin.*) «banchiere d'affari»; ~ **banking** (*fin., ingl.*) «merchant banking» (*V.* ~ **bank**); ~ **flag** (*trasp. mar.*) bandiera di (nave) mercantile; ~ **fleet** (*trasp. mar.*) flotta mercantile; ~ **law** (*leg.*) diritto commerciale; ~ **marine** (*trasp. mar.*) marina mercantile; ~ **navy** (*trasp. mar., ingl.*) marina mercantile; ~ **service** (*trasp. mar.*) marina (*o* flotta) mercantile; **a** ~ **ship** (*trasp. mar.*) una nave mercantile, un mercantile.

merchant[2], *v. t.* (*market.*) commerciare in (*un articolo, ecc.*), trattare (*un articolo, ecc.*), occuparsi di (*un articolo, un certo ramo d'affari, ecc.*).

merchantable, *a.* (*market.*) commerciabile.

merchantman, *n.* (*pl.* **merchantmen**) (*trasp. mar.*) mercantile, nave mercantile.

mercy, *n.* (*leg.*) grazia.

merge, *v. t.* **1** mescolare. **2** (*fin.*) incorporare, concentrare, fondere (*aziende, ecc.*). **3** (*leg.*) confondere (*redditi, interessi, ecc.*). *v. i.* **1** mescolarsi. **2** (*fin.*) (*di aziende, ecc.*) fondersi, concentrarsi, incorporarsi. **3** (*fin.*) (*d'azienda, ente, ecc.*) essere assorbito o incorporato (*da un altro*). **4** (*leg.*) (*interessi, ecc.*) confondersi.

merger, *n.* **1** (*fin.*) fusione, concentrazione, incorporazione (*d'aziende*). **2** (*fin.*) assorbimento (*d'una o più aziende da parte d'un'altra*). **3** (*leg.*) confusione (*d'interessi, ecc.*). // **a** ~ **deal** (*fin.*) un'operazione di fusione.

merit, *n.* **1** pregio, valore. **2** **merits,** *pl.* (*leg.*) diritti strettamente legali delle parti. // ~ **pay** (*pers.*) salario a incentivo; ~ **rating** (*pers.*) valutazione del merito, valutazione del personale; ~ **rating in terms of activities** (*pers.*) valutazione in termini di risultati.

message[1], *n.* **1** (*comun.*) messaggio, comunicazione, dispaccio. **2** (*pubbl.*) slogan, parole usate per reclamizzare un prodotto; «stacco». // **the messages of TV commercials** (*pubbl.*) gli slogan dei caroselli televisivi.

message[2], *v. t.* (*comun.*) comunicare, trasmettere.

messenger, *n.* **1** messaggero. **2** (*banca, pers.*) commesso. **3** (*pers.*) fattorino. // ~ **-boy** (*pers.*) fattorino.

metal[1], *n.* **1** metallo. **2** **metals,** *pl.* (*trasp. ferr., ingl.*) binario.

metal[2], *v. t.* dare un rivestimento metallico a.

metallic, *a.* metallico. // ~ **circulation** (*fin.*) circolazione (monetaria) metallica; ~ **clause** (*ass. mar.*) clausola in base alla quale l'assicuratore non risponde dei danni e delle perdite dovute alla normale usura cui è soggetta la nave durante il viaggio; ~ **currency** (*fin.*) moneta metallica, valuta metallica; ~ **reserve** (*banca*) riserva metallica.

metallurgic, *a.* (*econ.*) metallurgico.

metallurgical, *a. V.* **metallurgic.**

metallurgy, *n.* (*econ.*) metallurgia.

metalware, *n.* (*market.*) articoli in metallo.

metalworker, *n.* (*pers.*) operaio metallurgico, metallurgico.

metalworking, *n.* (*econ.*) metallurgia.

métayage, *n.* (*econ.*) mezzadria.

métayer, *n.* (*econ.*) mezzadro. // ~ **system** (*econ.*) mezzadria.

mete, *n.* limite. // **metes and bounds** (*leg.*) confini e limiti (*d'una proprietà*).

meter[1], *n.* **1** strumento misuratore. **2** contatore. **3** (*macch. uff.*) macchina affrancatrice. **4** (*USA*) *V.* **metre.** // ~ **slogan** (*comun., pubbl.*) slogan (*pubblicitario*) compreso nel timbro postale (*sulla corrispondenza affrancata mediante affrancatrice*).

meter[2], *v. t.* **1** misurare. **2** (*di macch. uff.*) affrancare (*lettere, ecc.*) mediante una (macchina) affrancatrice.

metering, *n.* (*di macch. uff.*) affrancatura (*di lettere, ecc.*) mediante (macchina) affrancatrice.

method, *n.* metodo, modo. // ~ **of packing** (*market.*) metodo d'imballaggio.

methodological, *a.* metodologico.

methodology, *n.* metodologia.

metre, *n.* metro.

metric, *a.* metrico. // ~ **equivalent** equivalente (secondo il sistema metrico) decimale; **the ~ system** il sistema metrico decimale; ~ **ton** tonnellata metrica, tonnellata.

metrical, *a.* *V.* **metric.**

metrication, *n.* (*mat.*) riduzione al sistema metrico (*decimale*).

metropolis, *n.* 1 metropoli. 2 **the Metropolis** (*ingl.*) Londra.

metropolitan, *a.* metropolitano. // ~ **area** (*econ.*) area metropolitana.

microeconomics, *n. pl.* (*col verbo al sing.*) (*econ.*) microeconomia.

microfilm[1], *n.* (*pubbl.*) microfilm.

microfilm[2], *v. t.* (*pubbl.*) fotografare su microfilm.

mid, *a.* medio, di mezzo. *n.* mezzo. // ~ **Europe Time** *V.* ~ **European Time;** ~ **European Time (M.E.T.)** ora dell'Europa Centrale; ~ **-September** metà settembre, il quindici di settembre.

middle, *a.* medio, intermedio, di mezzo. *n.* mezzo, metà, punto medio. // **the ~ class** (*econ.*) la classe media, il ceto medio; ~ **-of-the-road** centrale; ~ **price** (*econ.*) prezzo medio; ~ **-sized** di grandezza media, medio (*di grandezza*); ~ **-sized industries** (*econ.*) medie industrie.

middleman, *n.* (*pl.* **middlemen**) (*market.*) intermediario, mediatore.

middling, *a.* (*market.*) di media qualità, di seconda qualità, mediocre. // ~ **goods** (*market.*) merce di seconda qualità.

migrant, *n.* 1 (*econ.*) emigrante. 2 (*econ.*) emigrante interno (*chi cambia residenza in cerca di lavoro, specialm. stagionale*). // ~ **workers** (*econ.*) lavoratori migranti.

migrate, *v. i.* 1 (*econ.*) emigrare, migrare. 2 (*econ.*) cambiare residenza in cerca di lavoro (*specialm. stagionale*).

migration, *n.* 1 (*econ.*) emigrazione. 2 (*econ.*) emigrazione interna.

migrator, *n.* 1 (*econ.*) emigrante. 2 (*econ.*) emigrante interno.

migratory, *n.* 1 (*econ.*) emigrante. 2 (*econ.*) emigrante interno. // ~ **workers** (*econ.*) lavoratori migranti.

milage, *n.* 1 (*pers.*) indennità di viaggio (*a un tanto al miglio*). 2 (*trasp.*) distanza (percorsa) in miglia. 3 (*trasp.*) costo per miglio, spesa per miglio.

mild, *a.* mite. // ~ **recession** (*econ.*) lieve ristagno.

mile, *n.* miglio (*misura di lunghezza pari a km 1.609*).

mileage, *n.* *V.* **milage.**

militancy, *n.* 1 il militare. 2 combattività, pugnacità.

militant, *a.* 1 che milita. 2 combattivo, pugnace. *n.* militante. // ~ **trade unionism** (*sind.*) sindacalismo combattivo.

mill[1], *n.* 1 molino. 2 (*org. az.*) fabbrica, opificio, stabilimento. // ~ **-hand** (*pers.*) operaio di fabbrica.

mill[2], *n.* (*fin., USA*) millesimo di dollaro (*unità monetaria usata nei calcoli*).

milliard, *n.* (*ingl.*) miliardo, bilione, mille milioni.

milligram, *n.* milligrammo.

milligramme, *n.* *V.* **milligram.**

milliliter, *n.* millilitro.

millilitre, *n.* millilitro.

millimeter, *n.* millimetro.

millimetre, *n.* millimetro.

million, *n.* milione.

mimeo, *n.* pubblicazione ciclostilata.

mimeograph[1], *n.* (*macch. uff.*) ciclostile.

mimeograph[2], *v. t.* ciclostilare.

mimeographed, *a.* ciclostilato. // **a ~ form** un modulo ciclostilato.

mine[1], *n.* miniera.

mine[2], *v. t.* estrarre (*minerali*).

mini-convertibility, *n.* (*fin.*) mini-convertibilità. // **dollar inconvertibility and ~** l'inconvertibilità e la mini-convertibilità del dollaro.

minimax, *n.* (*mat., ric. op.*) minimax (*perdita minima in un insieme di perdite massime: nella teoria dei giochi*), minimomassimo.

minimization, *n.* 1 riduzione al minimo, attenuazione; minimizzazione.

minimize, *v. t.* 1 ridurre al minimo, attenuare. 2 (*mat.*) trovare il valore minimo di (*una funzione, ecc.*). // **to ~ expenses** (*amm.*) ridurre al minimo le spese; to ~ **the risk** (*ric. op.*) minimizzare i rischi.

minimum, *n.* 1 (il) minimo. 2 (*mat.*) valore minimo. *a. attr.* minimo. // ~ **goals** (*org. az.*) obiettivi minimi; ~ **Lending Rate** (*fin.*) (*abbr.* **M.L.R.**) tasso ufficiale di sconto (*in G.B.*); ~

pay (*pers.*) paga minima, minimo di paga; **the ~ penalty** (*leg.*) il minimo della pena; **~ price guaranteed to producer** (*comm., econ.*) prezzo minimo garantito al produttore; **~ rates** (*fin.*) tassi minimi; **the ~ rates of interest paid on deposits by banks** (*fin.*) i tassi minimi debitori delle banche; **~ stock** (*org. az.*) giacenza minima; **~ value** (*mat.*) (valore) minimo (*d'una funzione, ecc.*); **~ wage** (*pers.*) salario minimo.

mining, *n.* estrazione (*di minerali*).

minister, *n.* (*ingl.*) ministro.

ministerial, *a.* ministeriale.

ministry, *n.* (*ingl.*) ministero, dicastero. // **~ of Agriculture, Fisheries and Food** Ministero dell'Agricoltura, della Pesca e dell'Alimentazione; **~ of the Civil Service** Ministero per la riforma della Pubblica Amministrazione; **~ of Health** Ministero della Sanità; **~ of Housing and Local Government** Ministero per l'Edilizia Popolare e le Autonomie Locali; **~ of Labour** Ministero del Lavoro; **~ of Land and Natural Resources** Ministero per la Conservazione dell'Ambiente e le Risorse Naturali; **~ of Overseas Developments** Ministero per lo Sviluppo dei Rapporti Economici con i Paesi d'Oltremare; **~ of Power** Ministero per l'Energia; **~ of Social Security** Ministero della Sicurezza Sociale; **~ of Technology** Ministero per la Tecnologia.

minor, *a.* minore, di second'ordine, poco importante. *n.* (*leg.*) minore, minorenne. // **a ~ damage** (*ass.*) un danno di lieve entità.

minority, *n.* **1** minoranza. **2** (*leg.*) minorità, età minore. // **~ control** (*fin.*) controllo di minoranza; **~ group** (*fin.*) gruppo di minoranza; **~ shareholder** (*fin.*) azionista di minoranza.

mint[1], *n.* (*fin.*) zecca. // **~ charge** (*fin.*) tassa di coniatura; **~ -mark** (impronta fatta con il) conio; **~ par of exchange** (*fin.*) parità di cambio.

mint[2], *v. t.* (*fin.*) coniare (*monete*). *v. i.* (*fin.*) battere moneta.

mintage, *n.* **1** (*fin.*) coniatura, conio. **2** (*fin.*) tassa di coniatura.

minting-die, *n.* conio (*punzone per coniare*).

mintmark, *n.* (*fin.*) conio.

mintmaster, *n.* (*fin.*) sovrintendente alla zecca.

minus, *prep.* (*mat.*) meno. *a.* (*mat.*) negativo. *n.* (*mat.*) «meno». // **~ discount** (*market.*) meno lo sconto.

minuscule, *a.* (*pubbl.*) minuscolo. *n.* (*pubbl.*) minuscola, carattere minuscolo.

minute[1], *n.* minuto, minuto primo. // **up to the ~** (*market.*) aggiornatissimo, modernissimo, all'ultimissima moda.

minute[2], *n.* **1** minuta, bozza. **2** nota, promemoria. **3 minutes,** *pl.* (*leg.*) verbale, processo verbale. // **~ book** (*leg.*) libro dei verbali, registro dei verbali; **the minutes of the shareholders' meeting** il verbale dell'assemblea degli azionisti.

minute[3], *v. t.* **1** stendere la minuta di (*qc.*); minutare. **2** (*leg.*) stendere il verbale di (*una riunione, ecc.*); verbalizzare, mettere a verbale (*gli interventi in un'assemblea, ecc.*). // to **~ the proceedings of a meeting** (*leg.*) verbalizzare gli atti d'una seduta.

misaddress, *v. t.* (*comun.*) indirizzare erroneamente (*corrispondenza, ecc.*). // to **~ a letter** (*comun.*) indirizzare erroneamente una lettera.

misadventure, *n.* (*leg.*) disgrazia, morte accidentale.

misapplication, *n.* **1** uso erroneo. **2** (*leg.*) uso abusivo (*di denaro altrui*); distrazione (*di denaro altrui*).

misapply, *v. t.* **1** usare malamente, fare un uso errato di (*qc.*). **2** (*leg.*) usare abusivamente, distrarre (*denaro altrui*).

misappropriate, *v. t.* (*leg.*) appropriarsi indebitamente di (*denaro altrui*).

misappropriation, *n.* (*leg.*) appropriazione indebita. // **a ~ of trade marks** (*leg.*) un uso abusivo di marchio di fabbrica.

miscalculate, *v. i.* fare male i propri calcoli. *v. t.* calcolare male.

miscalculation, *n.* calcolo sbagliato, calcolo errato, errore di calcolo.

miscarriage, *n.* **1** (*comun.*) disguido (*di corrispondenza*). **2** (*leg.*) errore giudiziario. **3** (*trasp.*) smarrimento (*di merce, ecc.*). // **~ of justice** (*leg.*) errore giudiziario.

miscarry, *v. t.* (*comun.*) smarrire (*corrispondenza, merce, ecc.*). *v. i.* (*comun.*) (*di corrispondenza, merce, ecc.*) andare smarrita, smarrirsi.

miscellaneous, *a.* **1** eterogeneo. **2** (*econ., giorn.*) (*nei grafici*) varie. **3** (*market.*) misto, assortito. // **~ expenses** (*rag.*) spese varie.

misconduct[1], *n.* **1** cattiva condotta, comportamento indegno. **2** (*amm.*) cattiva amministrazione.

misconduct[2], *v. t.* (*amm.*) dirigere male.

misdeliver, *v. t.* (*comun.*) consegnare (*corrispondenza, ecc.*) per errore.

misdelivery, *n.* (*comun.*) consegna errata (*di corrispondenza, ecc.*).

misdemeanour, *n.* **1** (*leg.*) cattiva condotta.

2 (*leg.*) infrazione, trasgressione; reato.

misdirect, *v. t.* 1 dare istruzioni erronee a (*q.*). // to ~ **the jury** (*leg.*) dare istruzioni erronee alla giuria.

misdirection, *n.* 1 istruzione erronea, indicazione sbagliata. 2 (*comun.*) indirizzo sbagliato (*d'una lettera, ecc.*).

misinform, *v. t.* informare male, dare informazioni sbagliate a (*q.*), fuorviare.

misinformation, *n.* informazioni sbagliate.

mislead, *v. t.* (*pass.* e *part. pass.* **misled**) fuorviare.

mismanage, *v. t.* 1 (*amm.*) dirigere male (*un'azienda, ecc.*). 2 (*amm.*) condurre (*gli affari, ecc.*) in modo disonesto.

mismanagement, *n.* 1 (*amm.*) cattiva amministrazione. 2 (*amm.*) amministrazione disonesta.

misprint[1], *n.* (*giorn., pubbl.*) errore di stampa.

misprint[2], *v. t.* (*giorn., pubbl.*) stampare (*qc.*) male, stampare (*qc.*) con errori.

misrepresent, *v. t.* e *i.* 1 (*leg.*) fare una dichiarazione erronea. 2 (*leg.*) dichiarare (*qc.*) falsamente; fare una dichiarazione falsa. // to ~ **one's income** (*leg.*) dichiarare falsamente i propri redditi.

misrepresentation, *n.* 1 (*leg.*) dichiarazione erronea. 2 (*leg.*) dichiarazione falsa.

miss, *v. t.* perdere, non afferrare, fare tardi a, mancare a. // to ~ **an appointment** perdere un appuntamento, mancare a un appuntamento; to ~ **a bargain** lasciarsi scappare un affare; to ~ **the bus** (*fig., fam.*) perdere il treno, perdere un'occasione (favorevole); to ~ **an opportunity** perdere un'occasione; to ~ **the stays** (*trasp. mar.*) non riuscire a virare di bordo; to ~ **a train** perdere un treno.

missing, *a.* mancante, smarrito. // to **be** ~ mancare.

mission, *n.* (*comm. est.*) missione, missione commerciale.

mistake[1], *n.* sbaglio, errore, fallo. // **a ~ in calculation** un errore di calcolo; **a ~ of fact** (*leg.*) un errore di fatto; **a ~ of law** (*leg.*) un errore di diritto; **by** ~ per errore, per sbaglio.

mistake[2], *v. t.* e *i.* (*pass.* **mistook,** *part. pass.* **mistaken**) errare, fare uno sbaglio.

mistaken, *a.* errato. // to **be** ~ errare.

mistrial, *n.* (*leg.*) processo nullo per vizio di procedura.

mistrust, *n.* mancanza di fiducia.

misunderstand, *v. t.* (*pass.* e *part. pass.* **misunderstood**) capire male, fraintendere.

misunderstanding, *n.* malinteso.

misuse, *n.* cattivo uso. // ~ **of power** (*leg.*) abuso (*o* eccesso) di potere.

mitigate, *v. t.* alleviare, attenuare.

mitigating, *a.* 1 che mitiga, che allevia, che attenua. 2 (*leg.*) attenuante. // ~ **circumstances** (*leg.*) attenuanti, circostanze attenuanti.

mitigation, *n.* attenuazione, alleviamento.

mittimus, *n.* 1 (*fam., ingl.*) licenziamento. 2 (*fam., ingl.*) magistrato. 3 (*leg.*) mandato d'arresto.

mix, *v. t.* mescolare, mischiare, miscelare.

mixed, *a.* 1 mescolato. 2 misto, di diverse specie. // ~ **accounts** (*rag.*) conti misti; ~ **bag** (*market.*) assortimento; ~ **cargo** (*trasp. mar.*) carico misto; ~ **economy** (*econ.*) economia di tipo misto; ~ **income** (*econ.*) reddito misto; ~ **policy** (*ass.*) polizza mista; ~ **traffic** (*trasp.*) traffico misto; ~ **train** (*trasp. ferr.*) treno misto (*per passeggeri e merci*).

mixing, *n.* mescolatura, miscelatura.

mixture, *n.* miscela.

mobile, *a.* mobile. // **a ~ shop** (*market.*) un autocarro attrezzato per la vendita.

mobility, *n.* mobilità. // **the ~ of labour** (*econ., pers.*) la mobilità del lavoro, la mobilità della manodopera; **the ~ of workers** (*econ., pers.*) la mobilità professionale.

mobilization, *n.* (*fin.*) mobilizzazione, mobilitazione. // **the ~ of wealth** (*fin.*) la mobilizzazione della ricchezza.

mobilize, *v. t.* (*fin.*) mobilizzare, mobilitare. // to ~ **capital** (*econ.*) mobilizzare il capitale.

mock, *a.* finto, falso, contraffatto, imitato, simulato.

mode, *n.* 1 modo, maniera. 2 (*market.*) moda.

model[1], *n.* 1 modello, tipo. 2 (*market., pubbl.*) indossatore, indossatrice. // ~ **contract** (*leg.*) contratto tipo; **~-maker** modellista; **the ~ of consumer action** (*market.*) il modello di comportamento del consumatore.

model[2], *v. t.* modellare.

moderate, *a.* mite, modico. // ~ **costs** (*econ.*) costi moderati; **a ~ income** (*econ.*) un reddito modesto; ~ **prices** (*market.*) prezzi modici.

moderateness, *n.* modicità.

modernization, *n.* modernizzazione, ammodernamento. // **the ~ of the tax structure** (*fis.*) l'ammodernamento della struttura (d'imposizione) fiscale.

modernize, *v. t.* modernizzare, ammodernare.

modification, *n.* 1 modificazione, modifica. 2 (*org. az.*) modifica.

modify, *v. t.* modificare. // to ~ **the distribution of basic quotas** (*comm. est.*) modificare la ripartizione dei contingenti di base; to ~ **the terms of a contract** (*leg.*) modificare le condizioni d'un contratto.

modular, *a.* (*org. az.*) modulare. // ~ **design** (*org. az.*) progettazione modulare.

moment, *n.* momento, istante.

monetarist, *n.* (*econ.*) fautore dell'adozione di misure monetarie (*per regolare l'economia di un Paese*).

monetary, *a.* monetario, pecuniario, valutario. // ~ **agreement** (*fin.*) accordo monetario; ~ **area** (*fin.*) area monetaria; **the** ~ **authorities** (*fin.*) le autorità monetarie; **the** ~ **field** (*fin.*) il settore monetario; ~ **inflation** (*fin.*) inflazione monetaria; ~ **liquidity** (*fin.*) liquidità finanziaria; ~ **management** (*fin.*) politica monetaria; ~ **policy** (*fin.*) politica monetaria; ~ **regulations** (*fin.*) norme valutarie; ~ **reserves** (*fin.*) riserve monetarie; ~ **snake** (*econ.*) serpente monetario; ~ **system** (*fin.*) sistema monetario; ~ **tunnel** (*econ.*) tunnel monetario; ~ **union** (*fin.*) unione monetaria; ~ **unit** (*fin.*) unità monetaria; ~ **upheaval** (*fin.*) terremoto monetario.

money, *n.* 1 moneta, denaro; soldi (*fam.*). 2 (*fin.*) fondi, valuta, ricchezza. // ~ **at call** (*fin.*) denaro (rimborsabile) a vista; ~ **at short notice** (*fin.*) denaro (rimborsabile) a vista; ~ **-back guarantee** (*fin., market.*) garanzia di rimborso; ~ **bill** (disegno di) legge finanziaria; ~ **-box** salvadanaro; ~ **changer** (*fin.*) cambiavalute; ~ **convention** (*fin.*) convenzione monetaria; ~ **-grubber** (*cred.*) strozzino; ~ **-grubbing** (*cred.*) strozzinaggio; ~ **lender** (*cred., fin.*) prestatore di denaro, finanziatore; ~ **market** (*Borsa, fin.*) mercato monetario; ~ **-market intelligence** (*fin.*) informazioni finanziarie; ~ **of account** (*fin.*) moneta di conto, valuta di conto; ~ **of exchange** (*fin.*) moneta di cambio; ~ **order** (*fin.*) ordine di pagamento, mandato (*di pagamento*); vaglia postale; **a** ~ **squeeze** (*fin.*) una grave restrizione del credito, una stretta creditizia; **the** ~ **supply** (*fin.*) la disponibilità di capitali; ~ **transfer** (*banca, cred.*) bonifico bancario, bancogiro, giroconto; ~ **value** (*fin.*) valore monetario; **for** ~ in contanti; **for a** ~ **consideration** (*comm.*) per un corrispettivo in denaro; (*leg.*) a titolo oneroso.

moneyed, *a.* 1 danaroso, ricco. 2 (*fin.*) finanziario. // ~ **capital** (*fin.*) capitale finanziario (*investito o reinvestito per trarne profitto*); ~ **resources** (*fin.*) risorse finanziarie.

moneyquake, *n.* (*slang USA*) terremoto monetario, terremoto finanziario.

monometallic, *a.* (*econ.*) monometallico.

monometallism, *n.* (*econ.*) monometallismo.

monopolist, *n.* (*econ.*) monopolista. // **the** ~ **'s profit** (*econ.*) la rendita del monopolista.

monopolistic, *a.* (*econ.*) monopolistico. // ~ **competition** (*econ.*) concorrenza monopolistica.

monopolization, *n.* (*econ.*) monopolizzazione.

monopolize, *v. t.* (*econ.*) monopolizzare.

monopolizer, *n.* (*econ.*) monopolista, monopolizzatore.

monopoly, *n.* (*econ.*) monopolio, privativa. // ~ **control** (*econ.*) controllo monopolistico; ~ **(-determined) price** (*econ.*) prezzo monopolistico, prezzo di monopolio; **a** ~ **system** (*econ.*) un regime monopolistico; **under a** ~ **system** (*econ.*) in regime di monopolio.

monopsony, *n.* (*econ.*) monopsonio (*monopolio del compratore*).

monotype, *n.* (*giorn., pubbl.*) monotype.

montage, *n.* (*pubbl.*) montaggio, fotomontaggio.

month, *n.* mese, mesata. // ~ **'s pay** (*pers.*) paga mensile.

monthly, *a.* mensile. *n.* (*giorn.*) mensile, pubblicazione mensile, periodico mensile. *avv.* mensilmente, ogni mese, al mese. // ~ **allowance** (*pers.*) mesata, mensile, mese; ~ **instalment** (*market.*) rata mensile, mensilità; **a** ~ **magazine** (*giorn.*) un mensile; ~ **pay** (*pers.*) paga mensile, mensilità, mensile, mesata; ~ **report** (*amm., rag.*) relazione mensile, rapporto mensile, notiziario mensile; **a** ~ **statement of account** (*rag.*) un estratto (di) conto mensile; ~ **wage** (*pers.*) paga mensile.

mood, *n.* stato d'animo.

moonlight, *n.* chiaro di luna.

moonlighter, *n.* (*USA*) chi si dedica contemporaneamente a due professioni.

moor, *v. t.* (*trasp. mar.*) attraccare. *v. i.* (*trasp. mar.*) attraccare. // to ~ **along a quay** (*trasp. mar.*) attraccare alla banchina.

moorage, *n.* (*trasp. mar.*) diritti d'ormeggio.

mooring, *n.* 1 (*trasp. mar.*) attracco. 2 **moorings,** *pl.* (*trasp. mar.*) attracco (*il luogo*). // ~ **line** cavo d'ormeggio.

mopping up, *n.* prosciugamento.

mop up, *v. t.* asciugare. // to ~ **the part of disposable money available by the introduction of rationing** (*econ.*) ritirare dalla circolazione quella parte dei redditi che non può essere spesa a causa del razionamento.

mora, *n.* (*leg.*) mora.

moratorium, *n.* (*pl.* **moratoria** e *reg.*) (*comm., leg.*) moratoria.

moratory, *a.* (*comm., leg.*) moratorio.

morning, *n.* mattina, mattino.

mortgage¹, *n.* 1 (*leg.*) ipoteca. 2 (*fin., fam.*) mutuo ipotecario. // ~ **bond** (*fin.*) obbligazione ipotecaria; ~ **creditor** (*cred., leg.*) creditore ipotecario; ~ **debenture** (*fin.*) obbligazione ipotecaria; ~ **debt** (*cred., leg.*) debito ipotecario; ~ **debtor** (*cred., leg.*) debitore ipotecario; ~ **deed** (*leg.*) contratto d'ipoteca; ~ **duty** (*leg.*) tasse ipotecarie; ~ **loan** (*cred., leg.*) prestito ipotecario; ~ **market** (*fin.*) mercato ipotecario; ~ **registrar** (*leg.*) conservatore delle ipoteche; ~ **registry** (*leg.*) conservatoria delle ipoteche; ~ **tax** (*fin.*) imposta ipotecaria.

mortgage², *v. t.* (*leg.*) ipotecare, gravare (*qc.*) d'ipoteca.

mortgageable, *a.* (*leg.*) ipotecabile.

mortgagee, *n.* (*leg.*) creditore ipotecario.

mortgager, *n.* (*leg.*) debitore ipotecario.

mortgagor, *n. V.* **mortgager.**

most, *avv.* e *a.* (il) più. // **the ~ favoured nation** (*econ.*) la nazione (più) favorita; ~ **-favoured-nation (MFN)** (*econ.*) di nazione (più) favorita, di nazione preferita; ~ **-favoured-nation clause** (*econ.*) clausola di nazione (più) favorita; ~ **-favoured-nation treatment** (*econ.*) trattamento di nazione preferita.

motel, *n.* (*trasp. aut.*) autostello, motel.

mother, *n.* madre.

motion, *n.* 1 movimento. 2 (*leg.*) mozione, istanza. // **on ~ of** (*leg.*) su istanza di; **on ~ of the plaintiff's lawyer** (*leg.*) su istanza del legale dell'attore.

motionless, *a.* immobile.

motivate, *v. t.* 1 motivare, dare motivo a. 2 incitare; (*fig.*) spingere, spronare.

motivation, *n.* 1 motivazione. 2 motivo, causa. 3 incitamento; (*fig.*) spinta, sprone. 4 (*market., pubbl.*) motivazione.

motivational, *a.* (*market., pubbl.*) motivazionale. // ~ **factors** (*market., pubbl.*) fattori motivazionali; ~ **research** (*market., pubbl.*) ricerca motivazionale, indagine motivazionale.

motive, *n.* motivo.

motor, *n.* 1 motore. 2 (*trasp. aut.*) motrice. // ~ **banking** (*banca, trasp. aut.*) operazioni di sportello bancario per clienti che le compiono senza scendere dall'automobile; ~ **-boat** (*trasp.*) motobarca; ~ **-car** (*trasp. aut.*) automobile, macchina, vettura; ~ **-coach** (*trasp. aut.*) torpedone; ~ **court** (*trasp. aut., USA*) autostello, motel; ~ **insurance** (*ass.*) assicurazione automobilistica (*o* per autoveicoli); ~ **-lorry** (*trasp. aut., ingl.*) autocarro, camion; ~ **patrol vessel** (*trasp.*) motovedetta; ~ **-ship** (*trasp. mar.*) motonave; ~ **transport** (*trasp. aut.*) trasporto automobilistico; ~ **-trawler** (*trasp. mar.*) motopeschereccio; ~ **-van** (*trasp. aut.*) motofurgone, motocarro; ~ **-vehicle** (*trasp. aut.*) veicolo a motore, motoveicolo, autoveicolo, automezzo; ~ **-vehicle tax** (*fin., trasp. aut.*) tassa di circolazione.

motorcar, *n. V.* **motor-car.**

motoring, *n.* automobilismo. // ~ **map** (*trasp. aut.*) carta automobilistica.

motorization, *n.* (*trasp. aut.*) motorizzazione.

motorize, *v. t.* (*trasp. aut.*) motorizzare. *v. rifl.* (*trasp. aut.*) motorizzarsi.

motortruck, *n.* (*trasp. aut., USA*) autocarro, camion.

motorway, *n.* (*trasp. aut.*) autostrada.

mouth, *n.* bocca. // **the ~ of a harbour** (*trasp. mar.*) l'entrata di un porto.

movable, *a.* 1 mobile. 2 (*leg., rag.*) mobiliare. // ~ **band** (*fin.*) fascia mobile; ~ **exchange** (*fin.*) cambio indiretto, cambio «incerto per certo»; ~ **goods** (*econ.*) beni mobili, mobili.

movables, *n. pl.* (*econ.*) mobili, beni mobili.

move¹, *n.* 1 movimento, moto. 2 trasferimento. 3 mossa, manovra.

move², *v. t.* e *i.* 1 muovere, muoversi. 2 trasferire, trasferirsi. 3 (*fin.*) (*di quotazioni, ecc.*) oscillare. 4 (*market.*) (*di prezzi, ecc.*) muoversi. // to ~ **ahead** andare avanti, procedere; (*econ., fig.*) conquistare posizioni.

moveable, *a. V.* **movable.**

movement, *n.* 1 movimento, moto, mossa. 2 (*fin.*) oscillazione (*di quotazioni, ecc.*). 3 (*market.*) movimento (*di prezzi, ecc.*). // **movements of capital** (*fin., rag.*) movimenti di capitali, movimenti di conto; **movements of freight** (*econ., fin.*) movimenti di merci.

mover, *n.* (*leg.*) proponente (*d'una mozione, in una assemblea*).

moving staircase, *n.* scala mobile (*per trasportare persone*).

mulct¹, *n.* (*leg.*) multa, penalità.

mulct², *v. t.* (*leg.*) multare.

multiannual, *a.* pluriennale. // **a ~ programme** un programma pluriennale.

multilateral, *a.* multilaterale. // ~ **commercial relations** (*comm. est.*) relazioni commerciali multilaterali; ~ **guarantees** (*comm. est.*) garanzie multilaterali; ~ **tariff negotiations**

(*comm. est.*) negoziati tariffari multilaterali; ~ **trade** (*comm. est.*) commercio multilaterale.

multi-millionaire, *n.* miliardario.

multinational, *a.* (*comm. est., org. az.*) multinazionale. // ~ **companies** le multinazionali; **a** ~ **organization** un'impresa multinazionale.

multiple, *a.* molteplice, vario. *n.* **1** (*market., fam.*) *V.* ~ **store. 2** (*mat.*) multiplo. // ~ **-branch bank** (*fin.*) banca che copre (*con le sue filiali*) il territorio nazionale; ~ **currency system** (*fin.*) sistema delle valute multiple; ~ **equilibrium** (*econ.*) equilibrio multiplo; ~ **shop** (*market.*) negozio appartenente a una «catena», grande magazzino; ~ **store** (*market., fam.*) negozio appartenente a una «catena».

multiplicand, *n.* (*mat.*) moltiplicando.

multiplication, *n.* (*mat.*) moltiplicazione.

multiplicator, *n.* (*mat.*) moltiplicatore.

multiplier, *n.* **1** (*econ.*) moltiplicatore. **2** (*mat.*) moltiplicatore. // ~ **effect** (*econ.*) effetto moltiplicatore.

multiply, *v. t.* **1** moltiplicare. **2** (*mat.*) moltiplicare. // to ~ **by four** quadruplicare; to ~ **expenses** (*amm.*) moltiplicare le spese.

municipal, *a.* comunale. // ~ **customs office** ufficio daziario, dazio; ~ **customs rate** (*fin.*) tariffa daziaria; ~ **office of rates** (*fin.*) esattoria comunale.

municipality, *n.* comune.

must, *n.* (*fam.*) (una) cosa che si deve fare, (una) cosa che si deve conoscere.

muster roll, *n.* (*trasp. mar.*) ruolo dell'equipaggio.

mutual, *a.* mutuo, reciproco, scambievole. // ~ **agreement** (*leg.*) mutuo consenso; ~ **aid association** società di mutuo soccorso, mutua; ~ **consent** (*leg.*) mutuo consenso; ~ **engagement** (*leg.*) impegno reciproco; ~ **fund** (*fin.*) fondo comune di investimento (del tipo «aperto», cioè, a capitale variabile); ~ **savings bank** (*fin., USA*) cassa cooperativa di risparmio; **on** ~ **terms** (*comm.*) su basi di reciprocità.

mystic testament, *n.* (*leg.*) testamento segreto.

mystify, *v. t.* (*leg.*) mistificare.

N

nail[1], *n.* chiodo. // **on the ~** (*fam.*) immediatamente, in contanti.

nail[2], *v. t.* 1 (*anche fig.*) inchiodare. 2 (*fam.*) afferrare, acchiappare, prendere al volo. // to ~ **a bargain** (*fam.*) assicurarsi un affare.

naked, *a.* 1 nudo. 2 sguarnito. // **a ~ contract** (*leg.*) un contratto non valido (*per mancanza di qualche requisito essenziale*); ~ **debentures** (*fin., leg.*) obbligazioni non garantite da ipoteca.

name[1], *n.* 1 nome. 2 rinomanza, fama. *a. attr.* (*market.*) di (buona) qualità, di marca, pregiato. // ~ **day** (*Borsa, ingl.*) giorno di spunta (*in cui gli agenti di cambio forniscono ai venditori i nominativi dei compratori*); ~ **merchandise** (*market.*) merce di (buona) qualità; **the ~ of an account** (*rag.*) l'intestazione d'un conto; **the ~ of a firm** (*fin.*) la ragione sociale d'una ditta; **in one's ~** per proprio conto; **in the ~ of the law** (*leg.*) in nome della legge.

name[2], *v. t.* 1 nominare. 2 designare, eleggere. 3 (*market.*) fissare, stabilire, stipulare (*un prezzo, ecc.*).

named, *a.* 1 nominato. 2 designato. 3 (*market.*) fissato, stabilito, stipulato. // ~ **policy** (*ass. mar.*) polizza relativa a una nave designata; **the ~ price** (*market.*) il prezzo stipulato; **the ~ ship** (*trasp. mar.*) la nave designata; **the above-** ~ il suddetto, il summenzionato.

narrow[1], *a.* 1 stretto, angusto. 2 limitato, esiguo. 3 preciso. 4 (*market.*) (*di mercato, ecc.*) fiacco. // ~ **-gage railway** (*trasp. ferr., USA*) *V.* ~ **-gauge railway**; ~ **-gaged railway** (*trasp. ferr., USA*) *V.* ~ **-gauge railway**; **a ~ -gauge railway** (*trasp. ferr.*) una ferrovia a scartamento ridotto; **a ~ inspection of the firm's books** (*rag.*) un esame accurato dei libri contabili; ~ **market** (*market.*) mercato fiacco, periodo di scarsa attività del mercato; to **be in ~ circumstances** avere scarsità di mezzi.

narrow[2], *v. t.* 1 restringere. 2 delimitare, ridurre.

nation, *n.* nazione.

national, *a.* nazionale, nostrano. *n.* compatriota. // ~ **accounts** (*econ.*) contabilità nazionale; ~ **advertising** (*pubbl.*) pubblicità su tutto il territorio nazionale; **a ~ bank** (*fin.*) una banca nazionale; ~ **budget** (*fin.*) bilancio dello Stato; ~ **company** (*fin.*) società nazionale; ~ **currency** (*econ., fin.*) moneta nazionale; ~ **day** (*pers.*) giornata nazionale, festa nazionale; ~ **debt** (*fin.*) debito nazionale, debito pubblico, debito dello Stato; **the ~ health service** (*pers.*) le mutue (*organizzate dallo Stato*); ~ **holiday** (*pers.*) festa nazionale; ~ **income** (*econ.*) reddito nazionale; ~ **income accounting** (*fin., rag.*) contabilità pubblica; ~ **interest bank** banca di interesse nazionale; ~ **laws** (*leg.*) legislazioni nazionali; ~ **planning** (*econ.*) politica di programmazione; ~ **product** (*econ.*) prodotto nazionale; ~ **revenue** (*fin.*) fisco, erario; **the ~ Savings Bank** (*fin., in G.B.*) la Cassa di Risparmio Nazionale (*già* **Post Office Savings Bank,** *tuttora gestita dal Ministero delle Poste*); ~ **union** (*sind.*) sindacato nazionale; ~ **warehouse** (*dog.*) magazzino nazionale; ~ **wealth** (*econ.*) ricchezza nazionale.

nationality, *n.* nazionalità.

nationalization, *n.* (*econ.*) nazionalizzazione, statizzazione.

nationalize, *v. t.* (*econ.*) nazionalizzare, statizzare.

nationwide, *a.* di dimensioni nazionali, a carattere nazionale, nazionale. // **a ~ strike** (*sind.*) uno sciopero a carattere nazionale.

natural, *a.* naturale. // ~ **causes** (*leg.*) cause naturali; **a ~ child** (*leg.*) un figlio naturale; ~ **harbour** (*o* **port**) (*trasp. mar.*) porto naturale; **a ~ person** (*leg.*) una persona fisica; **the ~ rate of interest** (*fin.*) il tasso d'interesse naturale (*quello per cui si ha uguaglianza fra domanda di fondi e offerta di risparmio*); ~ **resources** (*econ.*) risorse naturali.

naturalization, *n.* acquisizione della cittadinanza.

nature, *n.* 1 natura. 2 genere, qualità. // **the ~ of contents** (*dog.*) la natura del contenuto (*d'una valigia, d'un pacco, ecc.*).

naught, *n.* (*elab. elettr., mat.*) zero.

nautical, *a.* (*trasp. mar.*) nautico, navale, marino. // ~ **mile** (*trasp. mar.*) miglio nautico, miglio marino (*unità di misura pari a 1.853 metri*); ~ **science** (*trasp. mar.*) nautica.

naval, *a.* (*trasp. mar.*) navale, marittimo.

navicert, *n.* (*abbr. di* **navigation certificate**) (*trasp. mar., ingl.*) permesso di navigazione (*rilasciato da un'autorità consolare, ecc. a navi non soggette a perquisizione da parte della Guardia di Finanza*).

navigability, *n.* 1 (*trasp.*) navigabilità (*d'un fiume, ecc.*). 2 (*trasp. aer., trasp. mar.*) navigabilità (*d'aereo, nave, ecc.*).

navigable, *a.* (*trasp. aer., trasp. mar.*) navigabile. // ~ **airspace** (*trasp. aer.*) spazio aereo navigabile; **a** ~ **canal** (*trasp.*) un canale (artificiale) navigabile; **a** ~ **river** (*trasp.*) fiume navigabile; ~ **waters** (*trasp.*) acque navigabili.

navigate, *v. i.* (*trasp. aer., trasp. mar.*) navigare. *v. t.* (*trasp. mar.*) governare (*una nave*). // to ~ **with caution** (*trasp. mar.*) navigare con cautela.

navigation, *n.* 1 (*trasp. aer., trasp. mar.*) navigazione. 2 (*trasp. mar.*) traffico marittimo, commercio marittimo. 3 (*trasp. mar.*) nautica. // ~ **bounty** (*trasp. mar.*) sovvenzione (*governativa*) alla marina mercantile; ~ **company** (*trasp. mar.*) compagnia di navigazione; ~ **dues** (*trasp. mar.*) diritti di navigazione; ~ **lights** (*trasp. mar.*) fanali di via; ~ **permit** (*trasp. mar.*) permesso di navigazione.

navy, *n.* (*trasp. mar.*) marina, flotta. // ~ **yard** (*trasp. mar.*) arsenale marittimo.

near[1], *avv.* dappresso. *prep.* accanto a. *a.* vicino. // ~ **-money** (*fin.*) attività a breve (termine), attività liquide; ~ **-stagnation** (*econ.*) quasi «stagnazione», quasi ristagno.

near[2], *v. t.* avvicinarsi a, accostarsi a. *v. i.* avvicinarsi.

nearly, *avv.* quasi.

necessary, *a.* necessario, occorrente, indispensabile, obbligatorio. *n.* 1 (il) necessario. 2 cosa necessaria, bene di prima necessità. 3 (*spesso pl.*) (il) necessario (*alla vita*); (i) generi di prima necessità; (i) beni di prima necessità. // **the** ~ **steps to obtain a patent** (*leg.*) le pratiche brevettuali.

necessity, *n.* 1 necessità, bisogno, occorrenza. 2 cosa necessaria. // **for the** ~ **of the ship and cargo** (*trasp. mar.*) per la salvezza della nave e del carico.

need[1], *n.* bisogno, necessità.

need[2], *v. t.* abbisognare di, avere bisogno di, avere necessità di. // to ~ **st. badly** avere un gran bisogno di qc.

needy, *a.* bisognoso.

negation, *n.* negazione.

negative[1], *a.* negativo. *n.* 1 negazione. 2 risposta negativa. 3 (*mat.*) quantità negativa. // ~ **business cycle** (*econ.*) congiuntura negativa; ~ **easement** (*leg.*) servitù negativa; ~ **evidence** (*leg.*) prova negativa; ~ **income tax scheme** (*fin., sind.*) progetto di riduzione dell'imposta sul reddito (per gli scioperanti); ~ **investment** (*econ.*) disinvestimento, consumo di capitale; ~ **servitude** (*leg.*) servitù negativa; **in the** ~ negativamente.

negative[2], *v. t.* respingere.

negatively, *avv.* negativamente.

neglect[1], *n. V.* **negligence.**

neglect[2], *v. t.* negligere.

negligence, *n.* 1 (*leg.*) negligenza. 2 (*leg.*) colpa. // ~ **of the master** (*trasp. mar.*) colpa del capitano.

negotiability, *n.* 1 (*cred.*) negoziabilità. 2 (*trasp. aut.*) transitabilità.

negotiable, *a.* 1 (*cred.*) negoziabile. 2 (*trasp. aut.*) transitabile. // **a** ~ **document** (*cred.*) un documento (*o* titolo) negoziabile; **a** ~ **instrument** (*cred.*) un titolo (di credito) negoziabile, uno strumento negoziabile; ~ **papers** (*cred.*) titoli negoziabili; ~ **securities** (*fin.*) titoli negoziabili.

negotiate, *v. i.* 1 (*comm.*) negoziare, contrattare. 2 (*comm.*) mercanteggiare. *v. t.* 1 (*comm.*) negoziare. 2 (*comm.*) amministrare, condurre (*affari, ecc.*). 3 (*comm.*) prendere accordi per (*una compravendita, ecc.*). // to ~ **a bill** (*cred.*) negoziare una cambiale; to ~ **securities** (*fin.*) negoziare titoli.

negotiation, *n.* 1 (*comm.*) negoziazione, contrattazione. 2 (*comm.*) negoziato, trattativa. // **negotiations of foreign currency** (*fin.*) negoziazioni di divise estere.

negotiator, *n.* negoziatore.

neoclassic, *a.* neoclassico.

neoclassical, *a.* neoclassico. // ~ **economics** (*econ.*) economia neoclassica.

net[1], *a.* (*comm.*) netto. *n.* 1 (*market.*) peso netto. 2 (*market.*) prezzo netto. 3 (*rag.*) guadagno netto. // ~ **amount** (*market.*) importo netto; ~ **assets** (*rag.*) attivo netto, patrimonio netto; ~ **bonded debt** (*fin.*) indebitamento obbligazionario netto; ~ **cash** (*rag.*) contante netto; ~ **cash flow** (*rag.*) somma degli utili non distribuiti e degli ammortamenti effettuati da un'azienda; ~ **commercial (industrial) income** (*fin.*) reddito commerciale (industriale) netto; ~ **earnings** (*rag.*) reddito netto, utile netto (*d'esercizio*); ~ **freight** (*trasp. mar.*) nolo netto; ~

income (*rag.*) reddito netto, utile netto (*d'esercizio*); ~ **loss** (*rag.*) perdita netta; ~ **national product (NNP)** (*econ.*) prodotto nazionale netto; ~ **premium** (*ass.*) premio netto; ~ **price** (*market.*) prezzo netto; ~ **proceeds** (*rag.*) proventi netti; ~ **profit** (*rag.*) utile netto; ~ **receipts** (*rag.*) incasso netto; ~ **registered tonnage** (*trasp. mar.*) stazza netta registrata; ~ **sales** (*market.*) vendite nette; ~ **ton** tonnellata netta; ~ **tonnage** (*trasp. mar.*) tonnellaggio netto, stazza netta; ~ **weight** (*market.*) peso netto; peso netto (*della merce, compreso il peso dell'involucro interno della medesima*); ~ **worth** (*rag.*) attivo netto, patrimonio netto.

net², *n.* rete.

net³, *v. t.* 1 guadagnare, ricavare. 2 dare un utile di; rendere (*una certa somma*) come guadagno.

nett, *a.* (*ingl.*) *V.* **net¹**.

network, *n.* 1 lavoro a rete. 2 (*fig.*) rete, sistema. // ~ **of canals** (*trasp.*) rete di canali (*artificiali*); ~ **of roads** (*trasp. aut.*) rete stradale, viabilità.

new, *a.* nuovo, moderno, recente. // ~ **-day** (*market., pubbl.*) aggiornato, di moda, moderno; **the ~ edition of a magazine** (*giorn.*) la nuova edizione d'una rivista; **the ~ entrants** (*pers.*) le «nuove leve» (*di lavoratori*); **the ~ fashion** (*market., pubbl.*) la nuova moda; ~ **Issue Market** (*fin.*) Mercato dell'Emissione di Nuovo Capitale; **a ~ issue of stock** (*fin.*) una nuova emissione azionaria; **a ~ look** (*market., pubbl.*) un nuovo «stile», una nuova «linea»; **the ~ look** (*market., pubbl.*) la nuova moda; ~ **management methods** (*amm.*) nuovi metodi di gestione; ~ **money market** (*fin.*) mercato euromonetario; **a ~ order** (*market.*) una nuova ordinazione; ~ **-product demand** (*market.*) domanda d'un nuovo prodotto; ~ **-product demand estimate** (*market.*) stima della domanda d'un nuovo prodotto.

newly, *avv.* di recente, di fresco, appena.

newness, *a.* novità (*l'esser nuovo*).

news, *n. pl.* (*col verbo al sing.*) notizia, notizie, informazioni, novità. // ~ **agency** (*giorn., pubbl.*) agenzia d'informazioni, agenzia di stampa; ~ **broadcasts** (*giorn.*) giornali radio; telegiornali; ~ **bulletin** (*giorn.*) notiziario; giornale radio; ~ **conference** (*giorn.*) conferenza stampa; ~ **dealer** (*giorn., market.*) giornalaio, edicolante; ~ **editor** (*giorn.*) capo cronista; ~ **item** (*giorn.*) notizia; **the ~ of the accident** (*ass.*) la notizia del sinistro; ~ **service** (*giorn., pubbl.*) agenzia d'informazioni, agenzia di stampa; ~ **vendor** (*giorn., market.*) giornalaio, edicolante.

newscast, *n.* 1 (*giorn.*) notiziario. 2 (*giorn.*) giornale radio. 3 (*giorn.*) telegiornale.

newsletter, *n.* (*comm.*) notiziario, bollettino d'informazioni.

newsman, *n.* (*pl.* **newsmen**) (*giorn., USA*) giornalista.

newspaper, *n.* 1 (*giorn.*) giornale, gazzetta. 2 (*giorn.*) periodico, settimanale. // ~ **advertising** (*giorn., pubbl.*) pubblicità (a mezzo) stampa; ~ **rate** (*giorn.*) tariffa (*postale*) per giornali e periodici.

newspaperman, *n.* (*pl.* **newspapermen**) (*giorn.*) giornalista, cronista.

newspaperwoman, *n.* (*pl.* **newspaperwomen**) (*giorn.*) giornalista, cronista (*donna*).

newspaporial, *a.* (*giorn.*) giornalistico.

newsstand, *n.* (*giorn., market.*) edicola, chiosco.

newsweekly, *a.* (*giorn.*) settimanale.

next, *a.* 1 (il) più vicino. 2 successivo. *avv.* 1 in seguito, poi. 2 (*fin.*) (il) mese prossimo. // ~ **account** (*Borsa*) liquidazione prossima; ~ **friend** (*leg.*) tutore (*di minore, ecc.*); ~ **month** (*fin.*) (il) mese prossimo; ~ **settlement** (*Borsa*) liquidazione prossima.

nickel, *n.* 1 nickel. 2 (*USA*) moneta da cinque centesimi (*di dollaro*).

night, *n.* notte. // ~ **-boat** (*trasp. mar.*) nave-traghetto che fa servizio notturno; ~ **letter** (*comun.*) telegramma notturno (*a tariffa ridotta*); ~ **lettergram** (*comun.*) telegramma notturno (*a tariffa ridotta*); ~ **man** (*pers.*) operaio che fa turni di notte; guardiano notturno, sorvegliante notturno; ~ **safe** (*banca*) cassa continua; ~ **shift** (*pers.*) turno di notte, servizio notturno; operai del turno di notte; **nights spent** (*tur.*) pernottamenti; ~ **train** (*trasp. ferr.*) treno notturno; ~ **watchman** (*pers.*) guardiano notturno, custode notturno, sorvegliante notturno; ~ **work** (*pers.*) lavoro notturno.

nightside, *n.* (*giorn.*) personale che lavora all'edizione del mattino (*d'un quotidiano*).

nil, *n.* niente, nulla, zero. *a.* nullo, inesistente. // ~ **duties** (*dog.*) dazi nulli; ~ **profits** (*rag.*) guadagni inesistenti; **with ~ duties** (*dog.*) in esenzione.

nine, *a.* e *n.* nove. // **the Nine** (*econ., fin.*) i «Nove» (*cioè, i Paesi della CEE allargata*).

no, *avv.* no. *n.* (*pl.* **noes**). 1 no. 2 votante contrario. // ~ **advice** (*banca*) senza avviso; ~ **agents** (*comm.*) intermediari esclusi, inintermediari; ~ **changes** (*Borsa*) nessuna variazione (*nella quotazione d'un titolo*); ~ **entry** (*trasp.*

aut.) divieto d'accesso; ~ **funds (N.F.)** (*banca*) (*di conto*) senza fondi; mancanza di copertura; ~ **noting** (*cred., leg.*) (*su una cambiale*) senza spese; ~ **-par** (*fin.*) senza valore nominale; ~ **-par shares** (*fin.*) azioni senza valore nominale; ~ **-par value** (*fin.*) senza valore nominale; ~ **thoroughfare** (*trasp. aut.*) strada chiusa, vicolo cieco; divieto di transito.

noise, *n.* rumore, frastuono.

nolle prosequi, *n.* (*leg.*) remissione di querela.

nomenclature, *n.* nomenclatura.

nominal, *a.* 1 nominale; di nome (*ma non di fatto*). 2 nominativo. // ~ **capital** (*fin.*) capitale nominale; ~ **list** elenco nominativo; ~ **partner** (*fin.*) socio nominale; **a** ~ **price** un prezzo nominale; (*market.*) un prezzo teorico; **a** ~ **rate** (*fin.*) un tasso nominale; **a** ~ **rent** (*leg.*) un affitto nominale, un affitto irrisorio; **a** ~ **roll** un elenco nominativo; ~ **value** (*fin.*) valore nominale; ~ **wage** (*pers.*) salario teorico.

nominate, *v. t.* nominare.

nomination, *n.* 1 nomina. 2 presentazione come candidato, candidatura.

nominative, *a.* nominativo. // ~ **shares** (*fin.*) azioni nominative.

nominee, *n.* 1 persona nominata (*a occupare un ufficio*). 2 persona designata (*a un ufficio*). 3 persona proposta (*ad assumere un ufficio*).

non-acceptance, *n.* (*cred.*) mancata accettazione (*d'una cambiale*).

non-age, *n.* (*leg.*) età minore, minorità.

non-agricultural products, *n. pl.* (*econ.*) prodotti non agricoli.

non-aligned, *a.* (*di Stato*) non allineato.

non-alignment, *n.* non allineamento (*d'uno Stato*); disimpegno (*d'uno Stato, nelle scelte politico-economiche*).

non-appearance, *n.* (*leg.*) mancata comparizione, assenza (*d'imputato o di teste*); contumacia.

non-arrival, *n.* (*trasp.*) mancato arrivo.

non-assessable, *a.* (*fin.*) non accertabile, non imponibile, non tassabile. // ~ **stock** (*fin.*) capitale azionario non tassabile.

non-attendance, *n.* (*leg.*) mancata comparizione, assenza (*d'imputato o di teste*); contumacia.

non-committal, *a.* non impegnativo. // **a** ~ **statement** una dichiarazione non impegnativa.

non-competing, *a.* (*market.*) non concorrenziale.

non-compliance, *n.* (*leg.*) inadempienza.

non-cumulative, *a.* (*fin.*) non cumulativo. // ~ **dividend** (*fin.*) dividendo non cumulativo.

non-current liabilities, *n. pl.* (*rag.*) passività inesigibili.

non-dealable, *a.* (*cred.*) non negoziabile.

non-deductible, *a.* non deducibile. // ~ **losses** (*fin.*) perdite non deducibili (*agli effetti fiscali*).

non-delivery, *n.* (*comm.*) mancata consegna.

non-diversified, *a.* indifferenziato. // ~ **investment fund** (*fin.*) fondo d'investimento a portafoglio indifferenziato.

non-dollar, *a.* (*econ.*) (*di nazione, ecc.*) fuori dell'«area del dollaro». // **the** ~ **Countries** (*econ.*) i Paesi fuori dell'area del dollaro.

non-durable goods, *n. pl.* (*econ.*) beni di consumo non durevoli.

non-durables, *n. pl.* (*econ.*) beni di consumo non durevoli.

non-existent, *a.* inesistente.

non-feasance, *n.* (*leg.*) omissione.

non-food products, *n. pl.* (*econ.*) prodotti non alimentari.

non-fulfilment, *n.* (*leg.*) inadempienza, inadempimento, inesecuzione.

non-instalment credit, *n.* (*fin.*) prestito (rimborsabile) in un'unica soluzione.

non-interest bearing, *a.* (*fin., rag.*) non fruttifero, infruttifero. // ~ **accounts** (*fin., rag.*) conti non fruttiferi.

non-liability, *n.* (*leg.*) non responsabilità. // ~ **clause** (*leg.*) clausola di non responsabilità.

non-marine, *a.* (*ass.*) terrestre. // ~ **risk** (*ass.*) rischio di terra, rischio terrestre.

non-marketable, *a.* (*fin.*) non negoziabile. // ~ **securities** (*fin.*) titoli non negoziabili.

non-negative, *a.* (*mat.*) maggiore di, o uguale a, zero.

non-negotiable, *a.* (*cred.*) (*di documento, titolo, ecc.*) non negoziabile.

non-observance, *n.* (*leg.*) inosservanza.

non-payment, *n.* 1 (*comm.*) mancato pagamento. 2 (*comm.*) rifiuto di pagare.

non-pecuniary, *a.* (*leg.*) non pecuniario.

non-performance, *n.* (*leg.*) inadempienza, inadempimento, inesecuzione.

non-perishable, *a.* non deperibile. // ~ **goods** (*market.*) merci non deperibili.

non-productive, *a.* (*econ.*) improduttivo.

non-profit, *a.* (*econ.*) che non ha scopi di lucro, disinteressato. // **a** ~ **organization** (*econ.*) un ente senza scopi di lucro.

non-quotation, *n.* (*Borsa*) mancanza di quotazione, mancata quotazione.

non-recurring, *a.* non ricorrente. // ~

expenses (*rag.*) spese non ricorrenti.

non-representative, *a.* non rappresentativo. // ~ **of the majority** non rappresentativo della maggioranza.

non-returnable, *a.* (*market.*) da non restituire, non rimborsabile, «a perdere». // ~ **bottles** (*market.*) bottiglie (*vuote*) «a perdere».

non-selling, *a.* (*org. az.*) (*di reparto, ecc.*) non adibito alla vendita.

non-shipment, *n.* (*trasp.*) mancato imbarco, mancata spedizione.

non-stock, *a.* (*fin., USA*) senza capitale azionario. // **a** ~ **corporation** (*fin., USA*) una società senza capitale azionario.

non-stop, *a.* 1 (*trasp.*) (*di viaggio*) senza fermate, ininterrotto. 2 (*trasp. aer.*) (*di volo aereo*) senza scalo. 3 (*trasp. aut.*) (*d'autobus*) diretto. 4 (*trasp. ferr.*) (*di treno*) diretto. *n.* 1 (*trasp. aut.*) autobus diretto. 2 (*trasp. ferr.*) treno diretto. *avv.* 1 (*trasp. aer.*) senza scalo. 2 (*trasp. aut., trasp. ferr.*) senza fermate (intermedie). // ~ **flights** (*trasp. aer.*) voli senza scalo; voli diretti.

non-sufficient funds cheques, *n. pl.* (*banca, USA*) assegni scoperti.

nonsuit, *n.* (*leg.*) «non luogo a procedere». // ~ **judgment** (*leg.*) sentenza di «non luogo a procedere».

non-tariff, *a.* (*comm. est.*) non tariffario. // ~ **barriers (NTB's)** (*dog.*) barriere non tariffarie.

non-taxable, *a.* (*fin.*) non tassabile, non imponibile. // ~ **income** (*fin.*) reddito non tassabile.

non-union, *a.* (*pers., sind.*) (*d'operaio, ecc.*) non iscritto a un sindacato. // ~ **shop** (*sind.*) stabilimento nel quale il datore di lavoro non riconosce alcun sindacato ed esclude ogni dipendente iscrittovi.

non-utilized, *a.* (*econ.*) non utilizzato.

non-voting, *a.* senza diritto di voto. // ~ **shares** (*fin.*) azioni senza diritto di voto.

norm, *n.* 1 norma, regola. 2 modello, tipo. // ~ **price** (*econ.*) prezzo d'obiettivo.

normal, *a.* normale. // ~ **price** (*econ.*) prezzo d'equilibrio.

normalization, *n.* normalizzazione. // **the** ~ **of international relations** la normalizzazione dei rapporti internazionali.

normalize, *v. t.* normalizzare, rendere normale.

normative, *a.* normativo. // ~ **currency** (*econ.*) sistema valutario la cui unità è basata su uno standard metallico; ~ **judgment** (*leg.*) sentenza normativa; **a** ~ **law** (*leg.*) una legge normativa, una normativa.

north, *n.* nord, settentrione. *avv.* 1 a nord. 2 verso nord.

northbound, *a.* (*trasp.*) diretto verso il nord. // ~ **traffic** traffico (diretto) verso il nord.

not, *avv.* non. // ~ **entered** (*dog.*) (*di un articolo, ecc.*) non dichiarato; ~ **exceeding** non eccedente, non superiore a; non oltre, fino alla concorrenza di; ~ **guilty** (*leg.*) innocente; ~ **negotiable** (*cred.*) (*di documento, titolo, ecc.*) non negoziabile; ~ **repayable** (*comm.*) non rimborsabile, da non restituire; ~ **returnable** (*comm.*) non rimborsabile; (*market.*) da non restituire, «a perdere»; ~ **sufficient** insufficiente; « ~ **sufficient funds**» (*banca*) «fondi insufficienti» (*nel conto d'un cliente: per coprire un assegno*); «scoperto».

notarial, *a.* (*leg.*) notarile. // ~ **charges** (*leg.*) spese notarili; ~ **deed** (*leg.*) atto notarile, rogito; ~ **documents** (*leg.*) documenti notarili.

notarization, *n.* (*leg.*) certificazione notarile (*apposta a un documento*), autenticazione notarile, legalizzazione notarile.

notarize, *v. t.* (*leg.*) (*detto di notaio*) autenticare, legalizzare (*un documento, ecc.*).

notary, *n.* (*leg.*) notaio. // **under a** ~ **'s hand** (*leg.*) per mano di notaio.

notaryship, *n.* (*leg.*) funzione di notaio, ufficio di notaio.

notation, *n.* 1 (*mat.*) numerazione. 2 (*mat.*) simbolo.

note[1], *n.* 1 nota, annotazione, appunto, promemoria. 2 biglietto. 3 (*banca*) banconota, biglietto (di banca). 4 (*comm.*) bolletta, bolla. 5 (*cred.*) distinta. 6 (*fin.*) buono. 7 (*trasp.*) bollettino. // ~ **broker** (*fin., USA*) agente di cambio che tratta titoli negoziabili a breve termine; ~ **-issuing bank** (*fin.*) istituto d'emissione; ~ **of counsel's fees** (*leg.*) parcella d'avvocato; ~ **of expenses** (*rag.*) nota spese; ~ **of hand** (*comm.*) lettera di cambio, pagherò (cambiario), vaglia cambiario; **a** ~ **of thanks** un biglietto di ringraziamento; ~ **-paper** carta da lettere; ~ **payable** (*banca, rag.*) effetto passivo; **notes payable** (*banca, rag.*) conto effetti passivi, distinta effetti passivi; ~ **receivable** (*banca, rag.*) effetto all'incasso; **notes receivable** (*banca, rag.*) conto effetti all'incasso, distinta effetti all'incasso.

note[2], *v. t.* 1 notare, osservare, fare attenzione a. 2 notare, annotare, prender nota di. // to **have a bill noted** (*banca, cred.*) far protestare una cambiale in via preliminare.

notebook, *n.* taccuino.

notehead, *n.* intestazione (*su un foglietto di*

carta da lettere).

noteheading, *n.* intestazione (*su un foglietto di carta da lettere*).

nothing, *pron. indef.* nulla.

notice[1], *n.* 1 annuncio, comunicazione, avviso, manifesto. 2 preavviso, notifica. 3 (*fin.*) avviso (di convocazione) d'assemblea. 4 (*leg.*) disdetta. 5 (*pers.*) preavviso di licenziamento. // ~ **-board** albo (per avvisi); ~ **of abandonment** (*ass. mar.*) avviso di abbandono, dichiarazione d'abbandono (*della nave e/o del carico*); ~ **of dishonour** (*leg.*) avviso di mancata accettazione (*d'una cambiale*); avviso di mancato pagamento (*d'una cambiale*); ~ **of dismissal** (*pers.*) notifica di licenziamento; ~ **of meeting** (*fin.*) avviso (di convocazione) d'assemblea; ~ **of payment** (*cred.*) avviso di pagamento; **a** ~ **of withdrawl** (*banca*) un preavviso di prelevamento (*di fondi*); ~ **period** (*leg.*) termine di preavviso; ~ **to quit** (*leg.*) disdetta (*di contratto di locazione*); notifica di sfratto; escomio (*la notifica*); **at short** ~ con breve preavviso, entro breve tempo; to **give** ~ comunicare; **till further** ~ fino a nuovo avviso; **without** ~ senza preavviso.

notice[2], *v. t.* 1 notare, osservare, accorgersi di, rilevare. 2 (*leg.*) dare disdetta a (*un inquilino*).

notification, *n.* 1 notificazione, comunicazione. 2 (*leg.*) notifica.

notify, *v. t.* 1 avvisare, informare, comunicare a. 2 (*leg.*) notificare a. // to ~ **the police** informare la polizia.

noting, *n.* (*leg.*) protesto preliminare. // ~ **charges** (*leg.*) competenze per il protesto preliminare.

notoriety, *n.* notorietà.

notorious, *a.* notorio, noto.

notwithstanding, *avv.* tuttavia.

now, *avv.* adesso.

nowadays, *avv.* oggigiorno, oggi.

nude, *a.* nudo, ignudo. // ~ **contract** (*leg.*) contratto privo di tutela giuridica.

nuisance, *n.* 1 molestia. 2 (*leg.*) infrazione (*di legge*), turbativa.

null[1], *a.* (*leg.*) nullo, non valido. *n.* zero. // ~ **and void** (*leg.*) nullo.

null[2], *v. t.* (*leg.*) annullare, invalidare.

nullification, *n.* (*leg.*) annullamento.

nullify, *v. t.* (*leg.*) annullare, invalidare.

nullity, *n.* (*leg.*) nullità.

number[1], *n.* 1 numero, cifra. 2 (*trasp. aut.*) numero di targa. // ~ **of accidents** (*ass.*) sinistrosità; ~ **of copies** (*giorn.*) tiratura; **the** ~ **of packages** (*trasp.*) il numero dei colli; ~ **of passengers** (*trasp.*) numero dei passeggeri trasportati; ~ **of readers** (*giorn.*) numero di lettori; ~ **-plate** (*trasp. aut.*) targa.

number[2], *v. t.* numerare, dare un numero a.

numbering, *n.* numerazione. // ~ **machine** (*macch. uff.*) numeratrice.

numeral, *a.* e *n.* numerale.

numeration, *n.* (*mat.*) numerazione.

numerator, *n.* (*mat.*) numeratore.

numeric, *a.* (*mat.*) numerico.

numerical, *a.* (*mat.*) numerico. // ~ **rating** (*org. az.*) valutazione mediante punteggio.

nuncupative, *a.* (*leg.*) nuncupativo. // ~ **will** (*leg.*) testamento nuncupativo.

O

oath, *n.* (*leg.*) giuramento. // **~ breaking** (*leg.*) violazione di giuramento; **on ~** (*leg.*) sotto giuramento; **under ~** (*leg.*) sotto giuramento; **upon ~** (*leg.*) sotto giuramento.

obedience, *n.* ubbidienza. // **in ~ to the law** (*leg.*) in ossequio alla legge.

obey, *v. t.* ubbidire a.

object[1], *n.* **1** oggetto. **2** argomento, materia. **3** obiettivo, scopo.

object[2], *v. i.* obiettare. // to **~ to** opporsi a (*qc.*).

objection, *n.* **1** obiezione. **2** (*leg.*) obiezione, contestazione.

objective, *a.* obiettivo. *n.* **1** obiettivo. **2** (*org. az.*) obiettivo, scopo. // **~ data** dati oggettivi.

obligate, *v. t.* (*leg.*) obbligare.

obligation, *n.* **1** obbligo, impegno, dovere. **2** (*leg.*) obbligazione. // **an ~ without consideration** (*leg.*) un'obbligazione senza causa, un'obbligazione senza controprestazione.

obligative, *a.* obbligatorio. // **an ~ contract** (*leg.*) un contratto obbligatorio.

obligator, *n.* **1** *V.* **obliger. 2** (*leg.*) *V.* **obligor.**

obligatory, *a.* obbligatorio. // **an ~ contribution** (*leg.*) un contributo obbligatorio.

oblige, *v. t.* **1** obbligare, costringere. **2** fare una cortesia, fare un favore a (*q.*). // to **~ oneself by oath** (*leg.*) impegnarsi con giuramento.

obligee, *n.* (*leg.*) obbligatario, creditore.

obliger, *n.* obbligante.

obligor, *n.* (*leg.*) obbligato, debitore, stipulante.

obliterate, *v. t.* cancellare.

obliteration, *n.* cancellatura.

observance, *n.* (*leg.*) osservanza. // **in ~ of the law** (*leg.*) in ossequio alla legge.

observant, *a.* (*leg.*) che osserva (*leggi, prescrizioni, ecc.*).

observation, *n.* osservazione. // **~ car** (*trasp. ferr.*) carrozza belvedere; **the ~ of price trends** (*market.*) la rilevazione dei prezzi.

observational, *a.* che è frutto d'osservazioni. // **the ~ method** (*market.*) il metodo del sopralluogo.

observe, *v. t.* **1** osservare. **2** (*leg.*) osservare. // to **~ a clause** (*leg.*) rispettare una clausola; to **~ the laws** (*leg.*) osservare le leggi.

observer, *n.* osservatore.

obsession, *n.* ossessione.

obsolesce, *v. i.* (*di macchine e sim.*) diventare obsoleto, invecchiare.

obsolescence, *n.* **1** il cader in disuso. **2** invecchiamento. **3** (*org. az.*) obsolescenza. // **the ~ of machinery** (*org. az.*) l'obsolescenza dei macchinari.

obsolescent, *a.* obsolescente.

obsolete, *a.* **1** antiquato. **2** (*org. az.*) obsoleto. // **~ prices** prezzi non più validi, prezzi scaduti.

obstacle, *n.* ostacolo.

obstinate, *a.* ostinato.

obstruct, *v. t.* impedire, ostacolare. *v. i.* fare ostruzionismo. // to **~ the traffic** (*trasp.*) ostacolare il traffico.

obstruction, *n.* impedimento, ostacolo.

obtain, *v. t.* ottenere, conseguire, ricavare. // to **~ the agency of a firm** (*market.*) ottenere la rappresentanza d'una ditta; to **~ a diploma** diplomarsi; to **~ an extension of time for payment** (*cred.*) ottenere una dilazione di pagamento; to **~ a footing in the market** (*market.*) affermarsi sul mercato.

obtainable, *a.* **1** conseguibile. **2** (*fin., market.*) disponibile.

obtainment, *n.* ottenimento.

occasion, *n.* occasione.

occupancy, *n.* (*leg.*) occupazione.

occupant, *n.* **1** (*leg.*) occupante, affittuario, locatario. **2** (*pers.*) titolare (*di posto, impiego, ecc.*).

occupation, *n.* **1** (*pers.*) occupazione, impiego, lavoro, professione. **2 occupations,** *pl.* (*tur.*) presenze (*in alberghi, ecc.*).

occupational, *a.* (*pers.*) occupazionale, professionale. // **~ diseases** (*pers.*) malattie professionali, malattie del lavoro; **~ levels** (*econ.*) livelli d'occupazione.

occupier, *n.* 1 (*leg., ingl.*) occupante. 2 (*leg., ingl.*) affittuario, conduttore, locatario.

occupy, *v. t.* 1 occupare. 2 essere il proprietario di (*una casa, ecc.*). 3 (*leg., ingl.*) avere in affitto, avere in locazione.

ocean, *n.* oceano. // ~ **cargo insurance** (*ass. mar.*) assicurazione del vettore marittimo; ~ **-going** (*trasp. mar.*) (*di nave, ecc.*) oceanico, di lungo corso, d'altura, alturiero; **an** ~ **-going ship** (*trasp. mar.*) una nave di lungo corso; ~ **lane** (*trasp. mar.*) rotta atlantica; ~ **liner** (*trasp. mar.*) nave di linea transoceanica, transatlantico; ~ **tramp** (*trasp. mar.*) nave da carico, nave rinfusiera, «carretta».

octavo, *a. attr.* (*pubbl.*) in ottavo.

octodecimo, *n.* (*pubbl.*) formato in diciottesimo.

octroi, *n.* casello daziario.

odd, *a.* 1 strano. 2 (*mat.*) dispari. // **the** ~ **change** il resto, gli spiccioli; ~ **jobs** (*pers.*) lavori occasionali, lavori saltuari; ~ **lot** (*Borsa*) spezzatura (*numero d'azioni in quantità inferiore all'unità di contrattazione*); ~ **-lot broker** (*Borsa*) speculatore che tratta in spezzature; ~ **-lotter** (*Borsa*) speculatore che tratta in spezzature; **the** ~ **money** il resto, gli spiccioli.

oddments, *n. pl.* 1 pezzi spaiati, oggetti scompagnati. 2 (*market.*) rimanenze. // **an** ~ **sale** (*market.*) una vendita di rimanenze.

off, *avv.* e *prep.* 1 fuori (di). 2 lontano (da). 3 al largo di. *a.* 1 (*fin.*) (*di guadagno, ecc.*) scarso. 2 (*market.*) inattivo, di stasi, morto. // ~ **-board** (*Borsa, fin.*) non ufficiale; **the** ~ **-board market for securities** (*Borsa, fin.*) il mercato azionario non ufficiale; **an** ~ **day** (*pers.*) un giorno libero, un giorno di vacanza; ~ **duty** (*pers.*) fuori servizio; ~ **-list** (*market.*) (*d'articolo, ecc.*) comprato a un prezzo inferiore a quello di listino; ~ **-print** (*giorn.*) estratto (*d'articolo, di rivista, ecc.*); ~ **-the-record** (*giorn.*) (*di notizia*) non ufficiale; **the** ~ **-season** (*market.*) la stagione morta; ~ **shore** (*trasp. mar.*) in mare aperto; ~ **-shore navigation** (*trasp. mar.*) navigazione in mare aperto; ~ **-shore purchases** (*market., USA*) acquisti (fatti) all'estero; ~ **time** (*pers.*) tempo libero; to **be** ~ (*fin.*) (*di titoli in Borsa*) essere «sotto»; to **give the staff a day** ~ (*pers.*) dare una giornata di vacanza ai propri dipendenti.

offence, *n.* (*leg.*) contravvenzione, trasgressione, illecito penale, delitto, reato. // **an** ~ **against the law** (*leg.*) una trasgressione alla legge; ~ **committed without malice** (*leg.*) delitto colposo.

offend, *v. i.* (*leg.*) commettere una colpa, commettere un reato. // to ~ **against the law** (*leg.*) violare la legge.

offended, *a.* 1 offeso. 2 (*leg.*) leso. // **the** ~ **party** (*leg.*) la parte lesa.

offender, *n.* (*leg.*) contravventore, trasgressore, colpevole.

offer[1], *n.* 1 offerta. 2 proposta. // ~ **prices** (*fin., market.*) prezzi d'offerta; ~ **subject to goods being unsold** offerta «salvo venduto»; **on** ~ (*market.*) in vendita.

offer[2], *v. t.* 1 offrire. 2 proporre. *v. i.* (*ingl.*) diventare disponibile. // to ~ **goods on sale** (*market.*) mettere in vendita della merce.

offerer, *n.* offerente.

office, *n.* 1 ufficio, gabinetto, studio; recapito. 2 (*pers.*) ufficio, agenzia, sede, succursale. 3 (*pers.*) carica, incarico, dovere, funzione, mansione, incombenza. // ~ **appliances** arredamento d'ufficio; ~ **-bearer** (*pers.*) chi ha una carica, chi tiene un ufficio, funzionario; ~ **-boy** (*pers.*) fattorino; ~ **copy** (*leg.*) copia autentica (*d'un atto legale, ecc.*); ~ **equipment** (*attr. uff.*) attrezzature per ufficio; ~ **expenses** (*rag.*) spese d'ufficio; ~ **furnishings** forniture per ufficio; ~ **furniture** (*attr. uff.*) mobili per ufficio; ~ **-holder** (*pers.*) chi tiene un ufficio, chi ha una carica, funzionario; ~ **hours** (*org. az.*) ore d'ufficio, orario d'ufficio; ~ **machines** (*macch. uff.*) macchine per ufficio; ~ **mechanization** (*org. az.*) meccanizzazione del lavoro d'ufficio; **the** ~ **of chairman** (*amm.*) le funzioni di presidente; ~ **personnel** (*pers.*) personale d'ufficio; ~ **premium** (*ass.*) premio lordo, premio «di tariffario»; ~ **staff** (*pers.*) personale d'ufficio; ~ **work** (*org. az.*) lavoro d'ufficio; ~ **workers** (*pers.*) operai del settore del commercio.

officer, *n.* 1 (*pers.*) funzionario, dirigente. 2 (*trasp. mar., ecc.*) ufficiale. // **an** ~ **of a bank** (*pers.*) un funzionario di banca; ~ **of customs** (*dog.*) funzionario di dogana; ~ **of health** (*leg.*) ufficiale sanitario.

official, *a.* 1 ufficiale. 2 d'un ufficio. *n.* (*pers.*) funzionario, impiegato. // ~ **action** (*leg.*) atto amministrativo; **an** ~ **appraisal** (*leg.*) una perizia ufficiale; ~ **assets** (*rag.*) averi ufficiali; ~ **character** ufficialità; ~ **intervention point** (*fin.*) punto d'intervento ufficiale (*nei tassi di cambio*); ~ **list** (*Borsa*) listino ufficiale, listino di chiusura; ~ **list of prices** (*econ.*) calmiere (*il listino prezzi*); ~ **Log Book** (*trasp. mar.*) giornale di bordo; ~ **net reserves** (*fin.*) riserve ufficiali nette; ~ **rate** (*fin.*) tasso ufficiale; ~ **rate of exchange** (*comm. est.*) cambio ufficiale; ~ **rate of interest** (*fin.*) tasso legale d'interesse;

~ **receiver** (*leg.*) amministratore, liquidatore, curatore provvisorio, curatore «ad interim» (*d'un fallimento*); ~ **responsibilities** (*pers.*) responsabilità pertinenti a un ufficio; **in one's ~ capacity** (*leg.*) in veste ufficiale.

officially, *avv.* ufficialmente.

officious, *a.* ufficioso.

offing, *n.* (*trasp. mar.*) (il) largo, mare aperto. // **in the ~** (*trasp. mar.*) al largo.

offset[1], *n.* compensazione. // ~ **print** (*giorn., pubbl.*) stampa offset (*il risultato*); ~ **printing** (*giorn., pubbl.*) stampa offset (*il procedimento*); (*giorn., pubbl.*) stampa offset.

offset[2], *v. t.* (*pass.* e *part. pass.* **offset**) 1 compensare. 2 (*giorn., pubbl.*) stampare in offset, stampare in fotolito.

offshore, *avv.* e *a.* (*trasp. mar.*) al largo. // ~ **fund** (*fin.*) fondo (d'investimento) operante all'estero.

oil, *n.* petrolio. // **oils and fats** materie grasse; ~ **and natural gas** idrocarburi; ~ **companies** (*fin.*) società petrolifere; **the ~ market** (*fin.*) il mercato petrolifero; ~ **-pipeline** oleodotto; ~ **-tanker** (*trasp. mar.*) petroliera; ~ **-vessel** (*trasp. mar.*) petroliera; ~ **worker** (*pers.*) petroliere (*addetto alla lavorazione del petrolio*).

old, *a.* vecchio. // ~ **age** anzianità; ~ **-age and survivors insurance** (*ass.*) assicurazione di vecchiaia e per i sopravvissuti; ~ **-age insurance** (*ass.*) assicurazione contro la vecchiaia; ~ **-fashioned** antiquato; **the ~ Lady (of Threadneedle Street)** (*fam., ingl.*) la Banca d'Inghilterra.

oleaginous, *a.* oleaginoso.

oligopoly, *n.* (*econ.*) oligopolio.

oligopsony, *n.* (*econ.*) oligopsonio.

omission, *n.* omissione, il tralasciare, il trascurare. // **errors and omissions excepted (E.&.O.E.)** salvo errori ed omissioni (*S.E.O.)*.

omnibus, *a.* che serve a più scopi. *n.* (*trasp. aut.*) autobus. // **an ~ clause** (*ass.*) clausola onnicomprensiva (*comprensiva d'ogni rischio*); (*leg.*) una clausola riguardante vari argomenti; **an ~ train** (*trasp. ferr.*) un treno omnibus.

on, *avv.* e *prep.* 1 sopra. 2 vicino (a), presso. 3 (*comm.*) contro, dietro. *a.* (*fin.*) (*di titolo, ecc.*) alto, in rialzo. // ~ **-and-offer** (*slang USA*) lavoratore temporaneo; ~ **approval** (*market.*) salvo prova, salvo vista e verifica; in esame, in visione; ~ **arrival** (*trasp.*) all'arrivo, al momento dell'arrivo; ~ **behalf of** per conto di; ~ **board** (*trasp. mar.*) a bordo; ~ **change** (*Borsa, fam.*) alla Borsa Valori; ~ **the cheap** (*market.*) a buon mercato; ~ **-coming** che s'avvicina, prossimo; **the ~ -coming year** l'anno prossimo, l'anno entrante; ~ **consignment** (*market.*) in conto deposito; ~ **delivery** (*market.*) alla consegna, all'atto della consegna; ~ **demand** (*comm.*) a vista; ~ **duty** (*pers.*) in servizio; ~ **hand** (*giorn., pubbl.*) in corso di stampa; (*market.*) (*d'ordinazioni*) in corso (d'esecuzione); (*org. az.*) (*di merce, ecc.*) in magazzino; ~ **-the-job training** (*org. az., pers.*) addestramento sul lavoro; ~ **loan** (*cred.*) in prestito; ~ **-off strike** (*sind.*) sciopero a singhiozzo; ~ **passage** (*trasp.*) (*di merce, ecc.*) in viaggio, in transito; ~ **sale** (*market.*) in vendita; ~ **sale or return** (*market.*) da vendere o rimandare; in deposito; ~ **term** (*cred., market.*) a termine; ~ **trial** (*market.*) in prova; ~ **-year** (*econ.*) anno buono, anno favorevole, buona annata; to **be ~ a committee** far parte di una commissione; to **be ~ the jury** (*leg.*) far parte della giuria; to **be ~ the regular staff** (*pers.*) essere in pianta stabile, essere di ruolo; to **be ~ the staff** (*pers.*) fare parte del personale; **interest ~ capital** (*fin.*) gli interessi del capitale; to **retire ~ a pension** (*pers.*) andare in pensione; **a tax ~ luxury articles** (*fin.*) una tassa sugli articoli di lusso; **a village ~ the frontier** un paese vicino alla frontiera.

once, *avv.* 1 una sola volta. 2 una volta, un tempo. *cong.* non appena, quando.

oncost, *n.* (*rag., ingl.*) spese generali, spese indirette.

one, *n.* (*USA*) banconota da un dollaro. // ~ **-class liner** (*trasp. mar.*) piroscafo a classe unica; ~ **-man business** (*org. az.*) ditta individuale; «~ **off» production** (*org. az.*) produzione d'un articolo secondo le particolari richieste del cliente; ~ **-price** (*market.*) a prezzo unico; «~ **price only**» (*market.*) «prezzi fissi»; ~ **-sided** (*leg.*) unilaterale; ~ **-sidedness** (*leg.*) unilateralità; **a ~ -track railway** (*trasp. ferr.*) una ferrovia a binario unico; ~ **-way callable stock** (*fin.*) titoli irredimibili da parte del detentore (*e la cui redimibilità è lasciata alla discrezione dell'organismo emittente*).

onerous, *a.* 1 oneroso. 2 (*leg.*) oneroso. // ~ **contract** (*leg.*) contratto a titolo oneroso; ~ **property** (*leg.*) proprietà a titolo oneroso.

only, *a.* solo. *avv.* solamente.

onshore, *avv.* e *a.* (*trasp. mar.*) sulla terraferma; presso (*o* verso) la terraferma. // ~ **fund** (*fin.*) fondo (d'investimento) operante in patria (*in origine, negli U.S.A.*).

onus, *n.* onere, peso. // ~ **of proof** (*leg.*) onere della prova; ~ **probandi** (*leg.*) onere della prova.

open[1], *a.* 1 aperto. 2 disponibile, libero,

vacante. // ~ **account terms** (*market.*) condizioni d'acquisto a credito; ~ **audience** (*leg.*) udienza pubblica; **an** ~ **cheque** (*cred., ingl.*) un assegno bancario non sbarrato e senza girate; ~ **Court** (*leg.*) udienza a porte aperte; ~ **cover** (*ass.*) copertura in abbonamento; ~ **credit** (*cred.*) credito aperto; (*anche*) credito allo scoperto, credito in bianco, credito non documentario; **an** ~ **-door trade policy** (*comm. est.*) una politica di libertà dei traffici; ~ **-end fund** (*fin.*) fondo «aperto», fondo a capitale variabile; ~ **-end investment fund** (*fin.*) fondo d'investimento «aperto», fondo d'investimento a capitale variabile; ~ **inflation** (*econ.*) inflazione incontrollata; ~ **market** (*fin.*) mercato aperto, mercato libero; ~ **market operations** (*fin.*) operazioni sul mercato aperto; ~ **policy** (*ass. mar.*) polizza aperta, polizza flottante; **an** ~ **port** (*trasp. mar.*) un porto franco; ~ **sea** (*trasp. mar.*) mare aperto, altura; ~ **shop** (*sind., USA*) azienda che accoglie anche operai non iscritti ai sindacati; ~ **union** (*sind.*) sindacato aperto (*a tutti, senza discriminazioni di razza, sesso, ecc.*); to **be** ~ (*org. az.*) (*di reparto, ufficio, ecc.*) fare servizio; to **be** ~ **to an offer** esser disposto a prendere in considerazione un'offerta; **in** ~ **Court** (*leg.*) in presenza del pubblico, in pubblica udienza.

open^2, *v. t.* e *i.* **1** aprire, aprirsi. **2** aprire i battenti, cominciare, iniziare. **3** (*rag.*) aprire, accendere, impostare (*un conto*). // to ~ **an account at the bank** (*cred.*) aprire un conto in banca; to ~ **an account in sb.'s name** (*banca, cred.*) intestare un conto a q.; to ~ **an account with sb.** aprire un conto con q.; to ~ **at par** (*Borsa*) (*di titoli, ecc.*) aprire alla pari; to ~ **the books** (*fin.*) dare inizio alla sottoscrizione (*di nuovi titoli, ecc.*); to ~ **a business** intraprendere un'attività commerciale; to ~ **a case** (*leg.*) (*detto d'avvocato*) cominciare a perorare una causa; to ~ **a credit with a bank** (*banca, cred.*) aprire un credito presso una banca; to ~ **the door** (*fig.*) aprire la strada (*a negoziati, ecc.*); to ~ **a law practice** aprire uno studio legale; to ~ **a meeting** aprire una seduta; to ~ **a new advertising campaign** dare inizio a una nuova campagna pubblicitaria; to ~ **port** (*trasp. mar.*) giungere in vista del porto; to ~ **unduly** (*leg.*) aprire indebitamente, manomettere; to ~ **up** aprire.

opener, *n.* **1** chi apre. **2** (*cred.*) persona che «apre» il credito.

opening, *n.* **1** apertura. **2** inizio, principio. **3** prospettiva. **4** (*comm.*) sbocco. **5** (*leg.*) apertura d'udienza, inizio della perorazione. **6** (*pers.*) posto vacante. **7** (*rag.*) apertura, impostazione (*d'un conto; anche:* ~ **of an account**). // ~ **balance** (*rag.*) bilancio d'apertura; ~ **capital** (*fin.*) capitale iniziale, capitale d'impianto; ~ **entry** (*rag.*) scrittura d'apertura, rilevazione d'apertura; ~ **of credit** (*banca, cred.*) apertura di credito; ~ **price** (*Borsa*) prezzo d'apertura, quotazione d'apertura; ~ **rate (of exchange)** (*fin.*) cambio d'apertura; ~ **speech** discorso d'apertura; ~ **stock** (*rag.*) giacenza iniziale, rimanenza iniziale; ~ **time** (*market.*) orario d'apertura.

operant, *a.* operante.

operate, *v. t.* **1** operare, agire. **2** far funzionare. **3** (*amm.*) condurre, gestire (*un'impresa*). **4** (*Borsa, fin.*) operare, speculare. *v. i.* (*di macchine e sim.*) funzionare. // to ~ **for a fall** (*Borsa, fin.*) speculare al ribasso; to ~ **for a rise** (*Borsa, fin.*) speculare al rialzo; to ~ **on a market** (*fin.*) operare su un mercato.

operating, *a.* **1** operativo. **2** (*org. az.*) esecutivo, produttivo. *n.* **1** funzionamento. **2** (*amm.*) gestione, conduzione (*d'impresa*). // ~ **accounts** (*rag.*) conti di gestione; ~ **activity** (*org. az.*) attività esecutiva; ~ **capacity** (*org. az.*) capacità produttiva; ~ **costs** (*rag.*) costi di gestione, costi d'esercizio; ~ **cycle** (*org. az.*) ciclo operativo; ~ **expenses** (*rag.*) spese di gestione, spese d'esercizio; ~ **profit** (*rag.*) utili diretti (*derivanti, cioè, dall'attività volta a perseguire il fine principale dell'azienda*); utile lordo sulle vendite; ~ **revenue** (*rag.*) ricavo d'esercizio; ~ **statement** (*rag.*) conto profitti e perdite; ~ **unit** (*org. az.*) unità operativa.

operation, *n.* **1** operazione. **2** funzionamento. **3** (*amm.*) gestione, conduzione (*d'impresa*). **4** (*Borsa, fin.*) operazione, speculazione. **5** (*mat.*) operazione. // ~ **cause** (*banca*) causale d'un'operazione; ~ **list** (*org. az.*) distinta delle operazioni; **in** ~ in funzione; (*leg.*) in vigore.

operational, *a.* **1** operativo. **2** (*amm.*) gestionale, di gestione, d'esercizio. // ~ **costs** (*rag.*) costi d'esercizio.

operative, *a.* **1** operativo. **2** efficace. **3** (*leg.*) operante. *n.* (*pers.*) lavorante, operaio.

operator, *n.* **1** operatore. **2** (*amm.*) gestore (*d'impresa*). **3** (*Borsa, fin.*) operatore, speculatore. **4** (*comun.*) centralinista, telefonista. **5** (*pers.*) operaio (*addetto a una macchina*).

opinion, *n.* **1** opinione, parere, avviso. **2** (*leg.*) parere. // ~ **former** (*pubbl.*) leader d'opinione, formatore d'opinione; ~ **leader** (*o* **maker**) (*pubbl.*) *V.* ~ **former**; ~ **poll** (*market.*) indagine d'opinione, sondaggio d'opinione, indagine demoscopica; ~ **survey** (*market.*) *V.* ~

poll.

opponent, *n.* 1 antagonista, avversario. 2 (*comm.*) concorrente.

opportunity, *n.* occasione, possibilità. // ~ **cost** (*rag.*) costo dell'opportunità, costo alternativo.

oppose, *v. t.* opporre. *v. rifl.* opporsi.

opposite, *a.* opposto, inverso. // **the** ~ **party** (*leg.*) la controparte.

oppress, *v. t.* opprimere, vessare.

oppression, *n.* oppressione, vessazione.

oppressive, *a.* oppressivo, vessatorio.

optimal, *a.* ottimale, ottimo. // ~ **size** (*econ.*) dimensioni ottimali.

optimum, *n.* «optimum». *a. attr.* ottimale. // ~ **efficiency** (*org. az.*) efficienza ottimale; ~ **growth** (*econ.*) sviluppo ottimale; ~ **population** (*econ., stat.*) popolazione ottimale.

option, *n.* 1 scelta, facoltà di scelta, libertà di scelta. 2 (*Borsa, fin.*) opzione, diritto d'opzione, operazione a premio. // ~ **bargain** (*Borsa, fin.*) contratto a premio; ~ **day** (*Borsa, fin.*) giorno della risposta premi; ~ **dealings** (*Borsa, fin.*) operazioni a premio; ~ **declaration day** (*Borsa, fin.*) giorno della risposta premi; ~ **market** (*Borsa, fin.*) mercato a termine; **options settlement** (*Borsa, fin.*) risposta premi.

optional, *a.* opzionale, facoltativo, a scelta.

opulence, *n.* opulenza.

opulent, *a.* opulento.

oral, *a.* verbale. // ~ **contract** (*leg.*) contratto verbale; ~ **evidence** (*leg.*) prova orale; ~ **reprimand** (*pers.*) ammonizione orale.

orally, *avv.* verbalmente.

order[1], *n.* 1 ordine, comando. 2 (*comm.*) ordinazione, ordinativo, ordine, commessa, commissione. 3 (*leg.*) ordinanza, mandato. // ~ **bill of lading** (*trasp. mar.*) polizza di carico all'ordine; ~ **-book** (*org. az.*) libro (*o* registro) delle ordinazioni (*o* delle commissioni); copiacommissione; ~ **cheque** (*cred.*) assegno bancario all'ordine; ~ **-clerk** (*pers.*) impiegato che registra le ordinazioni; **an** ~ **for payment** (*rag.*) un ordine di pagamento, un mandato di pagamento; ~ **form** (*market.*) modulo d'ordinazione; **an** ~ **from catalogue** (*market.*) un'ordinazione su catalogo; ~ **of business** ordine del giorno (*d'un'assemblea, ecc.*); ~ **of the day** ordine del giorno; ~ **of discharge** (*leg.*) ordinanza di riabilitazione (*d'un fallito*); ~ **of magnitude** (*mat.*) ordine di grandezza; **an** ~ **to pay** (*rag.*) un ordine di pagamento, un mandato di pagamento; ~ **to view** permesso di visita (*a un appartamento e sim.*); **on** ~ (*market.*) su ordinazione, su commessa; **to** ~ (*cred.*) (*di titolo di credito*) all'ordine; (*market.*) su ordinazione; **up to the** ~ (*market.*) (*di merce, ecc.*) conforme all'ordinazione.

order[2], *v. t.* 1 ordinare, comandare, intimare. 2 ordinare, riordinare, mettere in ordine. 3 (*comm.*) ordinare, commissionare (*merce*). // to ~ **goods from (*o* of) sb.** ordinare merce a q.; to ~ **sb. to pay the costs** (*leg.*) condannare q. al pagamento delle spese (processuali).

ordinance, *n.* (*leg.*) ordinanza.

ordinary, *a.* 1 ordinario, comune, mediocre. 2 ordinario, consueto, normale. // ~ **charges** (*rag.*) spese ordinarie; **the** ~ **course of business** la prassi commerciale; ~ **life insurance** (*ass.*) assicurazione «vita intera»; ~ **loans** (*cred.*) prestiti per operazioni ordinarie; **an** ~ **meeting** (*amm.*) un'assemblea ordinaria; ~ **prudence** (*leg.*) diligenza ordinaria; ~ **rate** (*comun., trasp.*) tariffa ordinaria; ~ **shares** (*fin.*) azioni ordinarie.

ordinate, *n.* (*mat.*) ordinata.

organ, *n.* (*anche fig.*) organo.

organic, *a.* organico.

organization, *n.* 1 organizzazione, organismo. 2 (*org. az.*) organizzazione. // ~ **chart** (*org. az.*) organigramma; ~ **manual** (*org. az.*) manuale d'organizzazione; ~ **structure** (*org. az.*) struttura organizzativa; **the** ~ **theory** (*org. az.*) la teoria dell'organizzazione.

organizatory, *a.* organizzativo.

organize, *v. t.* organizzare. *v. i.* organizzarsi. // to ~ **a strike** (*sind.*) organizzare uno sciopero.

organizer, *n.* 1 organizzatore. 2 (*sind.*) attivista, sindacalista.

orient, *v. t.* orientare.

orientation, *n.* orientamento.

origin, *n.* origine.

original, *a.* originale, originario. *n.* (l')originale. // ~ **entry** (*rag.*) rilevazione (contabile) originaria; ~ **goods** (*econ.*) beni naturali; ~ **invoice** (*market.*) fattura originale; ~ **jurisdiction** (*leg.*) giurisdizione di prima istanza; ~ **slip** (*ass. mar.*) polizzetta provvisoria.

originate, *v. t.* originare, dare origine a. *v. i.* originare, aver origine. // to **be originated** avere inizio.

orthographic, *a.* ortografico.

orthographical, *a.* ortografico.

oscillate, *v. i.* oscillare.

oscillation, *n.* oscillazione.

other, *a.* e *pron.* altro. // «~ **things being equal**» (*econ.*) a parità di condizioni.

ounce, *n.* oncia (*unità di peso*). // ~ **avoirdupois** oncia «avoirdupois» (*unità di peso* *pari a 28,35 grammi*); ~ **troy** oncia «troy» (*unità di peso pari a 31,1 grammi*).

oust, *v. t.* estromettere, prendere il posto di.

ouster, *n.* (*leg.*) spodestamento, esproprio.

ousting, *n.* (*leg.*) spossessamento, esproprio, espropriazione.

out, *avv.* fuori. *a.* **1** esterno. **2** fuori moda, passato di moda, non più in voga. **3** (*trasp.*) in partenza. // ~ **-clearing** (*banca, ingl.*) insieme degli assegni, ecc. pagabili a una banca e presentati alla stanza di compensazione; ~ **-loaded return-empty services** (*trasp.*) servizi nei quali il viaggio d'andata è effettuato a veicolo carico e il viaggio di ritorno a veicolo vuoto; ~ **of** fuori di (*o* da); (*trasp. mar.*) al largo di; ~ **of commission** (*trasp. mar.*) (*di nave*) in disarmo; ~ **-of-date** (*market.*) passato di moda, antiquato; ~ **of fashion** (*market.*) fuori moda; ~ **of money** a corto di quattrini; ~ **of order** (*org. az.*) (*di macchinario*) fuori servizio, fuori uso; ~ **of pocket** privo di fondi; ~ **-of-pocket expenses** (*rag.*) spese che prevedono un'immediata uscita di numerario; ~ **-of-print** (*giorn., pubbl.*) (*di libro, ecc.*) esaurito, in ristampa; ~ **of sale** (*market.*) (*d'articolo, ecc.*) non in vendita, esaurito; ~ **of work** (*pers.*) disoccupato, a spasso (*fam.*); **the** ~ **train** (*trasp. ferr.*) il treno in partenza; ~ **-tray** (*attr. uff.*) cassetta della corrispondenza in partenza; ~ **-turn** (*econ.*) risultato effettivo.

outbid, *v. t.* (*pass.* e *part. pass.* **outbid**) (*comm.*) offrire di più di (*q.*) (*a un'asta, ecc.*).

outboard, *avv.* (*trasp. mar.*) fuori bordo. *a.* e *n.* (*trasp. mar.*) fuoribordo. // ~ **motor** fuoribordo (*il motore*).

outbound, *a.* (*trasp. mar.*) diretto all'estero. // ~ **for** (*trasp. mar.*) in rotta per; ~ **traffic** (*trasp. mar.*) traffico diretto all'estero.

outburst, *n.* impeto, impulso.

outcome, *n.* esito, risultato.

outdated, *a.* (*market.*) antiquato, passato di moda.

outdoor, *a. attr.* esterno, all'aperto. // ~ **advertising** (*pubbl.*) pubblicità esterna.

outer, *a.* esterno, esteriore. // ~ **band** (*fin.*) fascia esterna; ~ **harbour** (*trasp. mar.*) avamporto; **the** ~ **Seven** (*econ.*) i Paesi dell'EFTA (*European Free Trade Association*) (*geograficamente «esterni» rispetto alla CEE*).

outfit, *n.* attrezzatura, corredo.

outfitter, *n.* (*market.*) confezionista.

outflow[1], *n.* efflusso. // ~ **of capital** (*fin.*) fuga di capitali.

outflow[2], *v. i.* effluire.

outgo[1], *n.* (*econ., rag.*) uscita, spesa.

outgo[2], *v. i.* (*pass.* **outwent,** *part. pass.* **outgone**) uscire, effluire.

outgoing, *a. attr.* **1** in partenza. **2** (*pers.*) uscente, dimissionario. // ~ **mail** (*comun.*) corrispondenza in partenza; **an** ~ **ship** (*trasp. mar.*) una nave in partenza.

outgoings, *n. pl.* (*econ., rag.*) uscite, spese.

outgrow, *v. t.* (*pass.* **outgrew,** *part. pass.* **outgrown**) crescere più di.

outlaw[1], *a.* (*leg.*) illegale. // **an** ~ **strike** (*sind.*) uno sciopero illegale.

outlaw[2], *v. t.* **1** (*leg.*) bandire, proscrivere. **2** (*leg.*) dichiarare illegale, rendere illegale.

outlay[1], *n.* (*econ., rag.*) uscita, sborso, spesa. // ~ **on salesmanship** (*pers.*) spese per l'addestramento dei venditori.

outlay[2], *v. t.* (*pass.* e *part. pass.* **outlaid**) (*econ., rag.*) sborsare.

outlet, *n.* **1** (*comm.*) sbocco. **2** (*market.*) punto di vendita, negozio al dettaglio.

outline[1], *n.* abbozzo, schema. // ~ **law** (*leg.*) legge quadro; **the outlines of a wage settlement** (*sind.*) i punti principali d'un accordo salariale; ~ **provisions** (*leg.*) normativa quadro; ~ **regulation** (*leg.*) normativa quadro.

outline[2], *v. t.* abbozzare, delineare; descrivere per sommi capi. // ~ **provisions** (*leg.*) normativa quadro; ~ **regulation** (*leg.*) normativa quadro.

outlook, *n.* prospettiva, prospettive.

outmode, *v. t.* (*market.*) rendere obsoleto, far passare di moda. *v. i.* (*market.*) diventare antiquato, diventare obsoleto, passare di moda, invecchiare (*fig.*).

outport, *n.* **1** (*trasp. mar.*) porto secondario. **2** (*trasp. mar.*) porto alla foce d'un fiume. **3** (*trasp. mar.*) porto fuori della sede d'armamento.

output, *n.* **1** (*econ.*) produzione. **2** (*econ.*) rendimento, resa. **3** (*elab. elettr.*) uscita. // ~ **circuit** (*elab. elettr.*) circuito d'uscita; **the** ~ **per man-hour** (*org. az.*) la produzione per ora lavorativa.

outrage[1], *n.* (*leg.*) insulto.

outrage[2], *v. t.* (*leg.*) oltraggiare, insultare.

outright, *a.* **1** completo, integrale. **2** immediato. *avv.* **1** interamente. **2** immediatamente. // **an** ~ **payment** un pagamento integrale; un pagamento immediato.

outsell, *v. t.* (*pass.* e *part. pass.* **outsold**) **1** (*market.*) vendere più di (*un collega, un concorrente, ecc.*). **2** (*market.*) (*di merce*) vendersi più di (*un'altra*).

outside, *avv.* fuori, di fuori. *prep.* fuori di, all'esterno di. *n.* (il) di fuori, parte esterna, (l')esterno. *a. attr.* **1** esterno, esteriore. **2** (*fin.*) di massima. // ~ **broker** (*fin.*) operatore estraneo alla Borsa Valori, agente di cambio senza riconoscimento ufficiale; ~ **consultant** (*amm., org. az.*) consulente esterno; **an ~ estimate** (*fin.*) un preventivo di massima; ~ **market** (*fin., USA*) mercato finanziario al di fuori della Borsa Valori di New York; ~ **shareholders** (*fin.*) terzi azionisti.

outsider, *n.* **1** osservatore esterno. **2** estraneo, profano, «non addetto ai lavori». **3** **the outsiders,** *pl.* i terzi.

outstanding, *a.* **1** arretrato, in arretrato, in sospeso. **2** (*cred.*) in pendenza, non pagato, insoluto, arretrato. **3** (*fin.*) (*d'assegno bancario, cambiale, ecc.*) in circolazione, in sofferenza. **4** (*org. az.*) in sospeso, in arretrato. // ~ **account** (*banca, cred.*) conto insoluto; conto scoperto, pendenza; ~ **bills** (*cred.*) cambiali non pagate, cambiali in circolazione, effetti in sofferenza; ~ **cheques** (*cred.*) assegni in circolazione; ~ **coupons** (*fin.*) cedole non pagate; ~ **debts** (*cred.*) debiti insoluti; ~ **matter** (*leg.*) pendenza.

outward, *a.* **1** esterno. **2** (*trasp.*) d'andata. // ~ **bill of lading** (*trasp. mar.*) polizza di carico per il viaggio d'andata; ~ **-bound** (*trasp. mar.*) (*di nave o passeggero*) in partenza, diretto a un porto straniero; ~ **-bound ship** (*trasp. mar.*) nave «in uscita», nave in viaggio d'andata; ~ **-bound voyage** (*trasp. mar.*) *V.* ~ **voyage;** ~ **bounder** (*trasp. mar.*) nave in partenza, nave in viaggio d'andata; ~ **cargo** (*trasp. mar.*) carico d'andata; ~ **freight** (*trasp. mar.*) nolo d'andata; ~ **journey** (*trasp. mar.*) viaggio d'andata; ~ **manifest** (*trasp. mar.*) manifesto d'uscita; ~ **passage** (*trasp. mar.*) viaggio d'andata; ~ **voyage** (*trasp. mar.*) viaggio d'andata.

outwork, *n.* (*org. az.*) lavoro a domicilio.

over, *avv.* e *prep.* **1** sopra, di sopra. **2** al di sopra. **3** nei confronti di. // ~ **and above** in aggiunta a, oltre a; to ~ **-capitalize** (*fin.*) accumulare eccessive riserve di capitale in (*un'azienda*); dare un eccessivo valore nominale al capitale di (*una società*); ~ **-the-counter** (*fin.*) (*di titolo, ecc.*) non trattato in una Borsa ufficiale; ~ **-the-counter market** (*fin.*) mercato «ristretto», fuori borsa; ~ **-entry certificate** (*dog.*) rettifica di dichiarazione errata per eccesso; ~ **-issue** (*fin.*) emissione eccessiva (*d'azioni, obbligazioni, ecc.*); to ~ **-issue** (*fin.*) emettere (*azioni, obbligazioni, ecc.*) in eccesso; to ~ **-produce** (*econ.*) produrre in eccesso; ~ **-production** (*econ.*) sovrapproduzione; to **be** ~ (*di lavoro, ecc.*) essere finito.

overall, *a.* complessivo, globale, totale. // ~ **demand** (*econ.*) domanda globale; ~ **efficiency** (*org. az.*) rendimento totale; ~ **income** (*fin.*) reddito globale; ~ **production** (*org. az.*) produzione complessiva; ~ **surpluses** (*econ., fin.*) eccedenze globali; **in ~ economic terms** (*econ.*) dal punto di vista economico generale.

overassessment, *n.* (*fin.*) eccessiva tassazione.

overbalance[1], *n.* eccedenza.

overbalance[2], *v. t.* **1** sbilanciare. **2** superare in importanza. // to ~ **the cash budget** (*rag.*) sbilanciare il (bilancio) preventivo.

overbid, *v. t.* (*pass.* e *part. pass.* **overbid**) **1** (*comm.*) fare un'offerta superiore a (*quella di q. altro*). **2** (*comm.*) offrire di più di (*q. altro*). *v. i.* (*comm.*) offrire troppo.

overboard, *avv.* (*trasp. mar.*) fuori bordo, in mare.

overbuy, *v. t.* (*pass.* e *part. pass.* **overbought**) (*market.*) comprare (*qc.*) in quantità eccessiva (*rispetto al fabbisogno*). *v. i.* (*market.*) comprare troppa merce.

overcall, *v.t.* e *i. V.* **overbid.**

overceiling, *a. attr.* oltre il livello massimo (*previsto, consentito, ecc.*).

overcharge[1], *n.* prezzo eccessivo, eccedenza di prezzo, addebito eccessivo, somma superiore al giusto. // ~ **claim** (*trasp. mar.*) reclamo per addebito eccessivo.

overcharge[2], *v. t.* far pagare troppo caro. *v. i.* far prezzi troppo alti.

overcome, *v. t.* (*pass.* **overcame,** *part. pass.* **overcome**) **1** sopraffare. **2** vincere.

overcoming, *n.* **1** sopraffazione, sconfitta. **2** vittoria.

overdraft, *n.* **1** (*banca*) emissione per una somma eccedente il proprio conto. **2** (*banca*) somma tratta allo scoperto. **3** (*banca*) «scoperto» di conto corrente. **4** (*banca*) «scoperto» di conto, assistito da fido. // ~ **costs** (*fin.*) costi dello scoperto (*o* del fido) bancario; ~ **credit** (*banca*) credito in conto corrente; ~ **on current account** (*banca*) «scoperto» di conto corrente, assistito da fido bancario.

overdraw, *v. t.* (*pass.* **overdrew,** *part. pass.* **overdrawn**) (*banca*) emettere assegni per una somma eccedente (*il proprio conto*). *v. i.* (*banca*) trarre allo «scoperto».

overdrawn, *a.* **1** (*banca*) (*di conto*) «scoperto». **2** (*banca*) (*di correntista*) allo «scoperto». // ~ **account** (*banca*) conto «scoperto»; to **be** ~ essere allo «scoperto».

overdue, *a.* **1** (*cred.*) (*di titolo*) scaduto, in sofferenza. **2** (*trasp.*) (*di treno, nave, ecc.*) in ritardo. // ~ **interests** (*cred.*) interessi di mora.

overemployment, *n.* (*econ.*) sovraoccupazione.

overestimate[1], *n.* sopravvalutazione.

overestimate[2], *v. t.* sopravvalutare.

overflooded, *a.* inondato. // ~ **with money** (*fin.*) inondato di valuta.

overfreight, *n.* **1** (*trasp. mar.*) eccedenza di carico. **2** (*trasp. mar.*) eccedenza di nolo.

overfull, *a.* troppo pieno, strabocchevole. // ~ **employment** (*econ.*) sovraoccupazione.

overhaul[1], *n.* (*org. az.*) revisione (*dei macchinari, ecc.*).

overhaul[2], *v. t.* (*org. az.*) «revisionare».

overhead, *a. attr.* (*comm.*) complessivo, generale. // ~ **charges** (*rag.*) spese generali; ~ **costs** (*rag.*) costi fissi; ~ **expenses** (*rag.*) spese generali; ~ **price** (*market.*) prezzo globale.

overheads, *n. pl.* (*rag.*) spese generali.

overheat, *v. t.* (*anche fig.*) surriscaldare. *v. i.* (*anche fig.: dell'economia*) surriscaldarsi.

overheating, *n.* (*anche fig.*) surriscaldamento. // **the ~ of the economy** (*econ.*) l'eccessiva espansione congiunturale.

overinsurance, *n.* (*ass.*) assicurazione per un valore superiore a quello di realizzo della cosa assicurata.

overland, *a.* e *avv.* (*trasp.*) per via di terra. // ~ **shipment** (*trasp., USA*) spedizione per via di terra; ~ **trade** commercio per via di terra; ~ **transport** (*trasp.*) trasporti per via di terra.

overleaf, *avv.* a tergo, sul retro.

overload[1], *n.* sovraccarico.

overload[2], *v. t.* sovraccaricare. // to ~ **a ship** (*trasp. mar.*) sovraccaricare una nave.

overloaded, *a.* sovraccarico.

overlook, *v. t.* lasciarsi sfuggire.

overman[1], *n.* (*pl.* **overmen**) (*pers.*) capo, caposquadra.

overman[2], *v. t.* (*org. az.*) impiegare troppo personale per le necessità di (*un reparto, un'attività, ecc.*); avere troppo personale da adibire a (*un reparto, un'attività, ecc.*).

overmanned, *a.* (*econ., org. az.*) che ha un eccesso di manodopera. // an ~ **industry** (*econ., org. az.*) un'industria con eccessiva manodopera.

overnight stay, *n.* (*tur.*) pernottamento.

overplus, *n.* sovrappiù, eccesso, rimanenza.

overpopulation, *n.* (*econ., stat.*) eccesso di popolazione; sovrappopolazione.

overprice, *n.* (*market.*) soprapprezzo.

overproduction, *n.* (*econ.*) sovrapproduzione, eccesso di produzione, superproduzione.

override[1], *n.* (*pers.*) premio «d'operosità» (*V.* **override**[2]).

override[2], *v. t.* (*pass.* **overrode,** *part. pass.* **overridden**) (*anche fig.*) passare sopra a, non tenere in nessun conto.

overrule, *v. t.* (*leg.*) capovolgere (*una sentenza*).

overrun[1], *n.* **1** straripamento. **2** superamento.

overrun[2], *v. t.* e *i.* (*pass.* **overran,** *part. pass.* **overrun**) **1** straripare, traboccare. **2** eccedere. **3** (*giorn.*) stampare copie supplementari di (*una pubblicazione, un inserto speciale, ecc.*).

oversaving, *n.* (*econ.*) eccesso di risparmio.

overseas, *avv.* oltremare, all'estero. *a. attr.* d'oltremare, estero. // **the ~ markets** (*comm. est.*) i mercati d'oltremare, i mercati esteri; ~ **trade** (*comm. est.*) traffici d'oltremare, commercio con l'estero.

overseeing, *n.* sorveglianza (*il sorvegliare*).

overseer, *n.* (*pers.*) sorvegliante.

oversell, *v. t.* (*pass.* e *part. pass.* **oversold**) (*market.*) vendere più (*merce, ecc.*) di quanta se ne abbia in magazzino. *v. i.* (*market.*) vendere troppo.

overside, *a.* e *avv.* (*trasp. mar.*) a fianco della nave.

oversight, *n.* **1** omissione. **2** (*amm.*) sorveglianza, supervisione, direzione.

overspending, *n.* (*econ.*) eccesso di spesa (*in rapporto alla produzione e al reddito nazionale*).

overstate, *v. t.* (*rag.*) sopravvalutare, supervalutare.

overstock[1], *n.* (*org. az.*) eccesso di merce (*in giacenza, in negozio, ecc.*).

overstock[2], *v. t.* (*org. az.*) approvvigionare all'eccesso. // to **be overstocked with goods** (*org. az.*) aver troppa merce (*in magazzino, in negozio, ecc.*).

overstow, *v. t.* e *i.* (*trasp. mar.*) «imbarazzare» (*il carico*).

overtax, *v. t.* (*fin.*) gravare d'imposte.

overtaxation, *n.* (*fin.*) eccessiva tassazione, imposizione troppo gravosa.

overtaxed, *a.* (*fin.*) soggetto a un eccessivo carico fiscale, eccessivamente gravato da imposte.

overtime, *n.* (*pers., sind.*) lavoro «straordinario», «straordinario». // ~ **pay** (*pers., sind.*) indennità di lavoro «straordinario», «straordinario»; ~ **work** (*pers., sind.*) lavoro «straordinario», «straordinario»; to **be on** ~ (*pers., sind.*) fare lo «straordinario».

overtrade, *v. i.* (*market.*) commerciare oltre i limiti delle proprie disponibilità.

overvaluation, *n.* (*fin.*) eccesso di valutazione.

overweight, *n.* 1 (*market.*) sovrappeso, eccedenza di peso. 2 (*market.*) peso «abbondante». *a.* (*trasp.*) (*di bagaglio*) che eccede il peso consentito. // ~ **coin** (*fin.*) moneta forte.

overwork, *n.* eccesso di lavoro.

owe, *v. t.* e *i.* dovere.

owing, *a.* 1 dovuto, ancora da pagare. 2 arretrato, scaduto. // ~ **to** a causa di, a motivo di.

own[1], *a.* proprio. // ~ **funds** (*fin.*) fondi propri; ~ **-initiative** di propria iniziativa.

own[2], *v. t.* possedere, avere.

owner, *n.* 1 proprietario, possessore, padrone. 2 (*leg.*) titolare, tenutario. 3 (*trasp. mar.*) (= **shipowner**) armatore. // ~ **-occupier** (*leg.*) proprietario di casa abitata dal medesimo; ~ **'s risk rate** (*trasp. ferr.*) tariffa speciale; **at** ~ **'s risk** (*market.*) a rischio e pericolo del committente, a rischio e pericolo del destinatario.

ownership, *n.* (*leg.*) proprietà.

P

pace¹, *n.* 1 andatura. 2 tasso di sviluppo.

pace², *v. i.* andare al passo.

pack¹, *n.* 1 pacco. 2 (*market.*) balla (*di lana, ecc.*). 3 (*market.*) imballaggio, incarto. 4 (*market.*) materiale per imballaggio. 5 (*market.*) metodo d'imballaggio. // ~ **-house** stabilimento per la preparazione di cibi in scatola.

pack², *v. t.* 1 impaccare. 2 (*market.*) imballare. 3 (*market.*) mettere in casse. 4 (*market.*) mettere in scatola. // to ~ **in bales** (*market.*) imballare; to ~ **in boxes** imballare in scatole, inscatolare; to ~ **in cans** (*o* **in tins**) inscatolare (*in scatole di latta*); to ~ **in cases** incassare; to ~ **in crates** imballare in «gabbie».

package¹, *n.* 1 (*market.*) pacco, collo. 2 (*market.*) balla. 3 (*market.*) cassa. 4 (*market.*) imballaggio, imballo, incarto, confezione (*d'un prodotto, ecc.*). 5 (*econ., fin.*) «pacchetto». 6 **packages**, *pl.* (*trasp. mar.*) collettame. 7 (*tur.*) combinazione. // ~ **advertising** (*pubbl.*) pubblicità posta sulla confezione della merce venduta; ~ **deal** (*econ., fin.*) «pacchetto»; ~ **to be returned** (*market.*) imballaggio a rendere; ~ **tour** (*tur.*) viaggio «tutto compreso».

package², *v. t.* 1 (*market.*) impaccare. 2 (*market.*) imballare. 3 (*market.*) confezionare (*un prodotto, ecc.*).

packaging, *n.* (*market.*) impaccaggio, imballaggio, imballo, confezione (*d'un prodotto, ecc.*). // **the** ~ **of foodstuffs** (*market.*) l'imballaggio delle derrate alimentari.

packer, *n.* 1 (*org. az.*) macchina per impaccare, impacchettatrice. 2 (*org. az.*) imballatrice. 3 (*pers.*) impaccatore. 4 (*pers.*) imballatore. // **packers' can** (*market.*) scatoletta per cibi conservati.

packet, *n.* 1 pacchetto, involto. 2 (*pers., ingl.*) busta paga. 3 (*pers., ingl.*) paga, salario, stipendio. 4 (*trasp. mar.*) «postale», nave postale. // ~ **-boat** (*trasp. mar.*) «postale», nave postale; ~ **-ship** (*trasp. mar.*) «postale», nave postale.

packing, *n.* 1 (*market.*) impaccaggio, imballaggio, imballo. 2 (*market.*) confezionamento di cibi (*in scatola, ecc.*). // ~ **and despatch department** (*org. az.*) reparto imballaggio e spedizioni; ~ **-box** (*market.*) cassa da imballaggio; ~ **-case** (*market.*) cassa da imballaggio; ~ **charges** (*market.*) spese d'imballaggio; ~ **expenses** (*rag.*) spese d'imballaggio; ~ **free** (*market.*) franco d'imballaggio, imballo gratis; ~ **house** (*org. az.*) stabilimento per la preparazione di cibi in scatola; ~ **list** (*trasp.*) distinta della merce; ~ **-paper** (*market.*) carta da imballaggio; ~ **plant** (*org. az.*) stabilimento per la preparazione di cibi in scatola.

pact, *n.* (*leg.*) patto, accordo, convenzione.

pad, *n.* cuscinetto, tampone.

page¹, *n.* pagina. // ~ **number** (*pubbl.*) numero di pagina.

page², *v. t.* numerare le pagine di (*un libro, ecc.*).

paginate, *v. t.* numerare le pagine di (*un libro, ecc.*).

pagination, *n.* impaginatura.

paid, *a.* 1 pagato. 2 (*cred.*) saldato. 3 (*pers.*) rimunerato, retribuito. // ~ **holidays** (*pers.*) ferie pagate; ~ **-in capital** (*fin.*) capitale versato; ~ **-up capital** (*fin.*) capitale versato; ~ **-up policy value** (*ass.*) valore di riduzione (*del capitale assicurato*); ~ **-up shares** (*fin.*) azioni liberate.

panel, *n.* 1 elenco, lista. 2 (*ingl.*) (i) «mutuati» 4 (*market.*) «panel» (*gruppo di persone selezionate allo scopo di registrarne le opinioni su uno o più prodotti*). // **a** ~ **doctor** (*ingl.*) un medico «convenzionato», un medico mutualistico; to **be on the** ~ (*ingl.*) (*di medico*) essere «convenzionato» con una «mutua».

paper, *n.* 1 carta. 2 appunto, documento, scritto. 3 (*banca, cred.*) titolo di credito, effetto, valore (*assegno, cambiale, ecc.*). 4 (*fin.*) carta moneta, carta monetata, biglietti di banca, banconote. 5 (*giorn.*) giornale. 6 **papers**, *pl.* (*leg.*) documenti, carteggio, incartamento. // ~ **-bag** (*market.*) sacchetto di carta; ~ **-clip** (*attr. uff.*) serracarte; ~ **currency** (*fin.*) carta moneta, carta monetata, moneta cartacea, valuta cartacea, biglietti di banca, banconote; **a** ~ **edition** (*pubbl.*) un'edizione in brossura; ~

holdings (*fin.*) titoli fiduciari, valori di portafoglio, portafoglio; ~ **-knife** (*attr. uff.*) tagliacarte; ~ **money** (*fin.*) carta moneta, carta monetata, moneta cartacea, biglietti di banca, banconote; ~ **money inflation** (*econ.*) inflazione della carta moneta; ~ **profits** (*rag.*) utili figurativi, profitti ipotetici; ~ **securities** (*fin.*) titoli fiduciari, valori di portafoglio, portafoglio; ~ **standard** (*econ., fin.*) sistema monetario basato su carta moneta non convertibile; ~ **-weight** (*attr. uff.*) fermacarte; **on** ~ (*fig.*) in teoria.

paperback, *n.* (*pubbl.*) libro in brossura.

paperbook, *n.* (*pubbl.*) libro in brossura.

par, *n.* (*fin.*) parità, pari. // ~ **of exchange** (*fin.*) parità di cambio, cambio alla pari; ~ **value** (*fin.*) valore nominale; **above** ~ (*fin.*) sopra la pari; **at** ~ (*fin.*) alla pari; **below** ~ (*fin.*) sotto la pari.

paragraph¹, *n.* 1 paragrafo. 2 (*giorn.*) trafiletto. 3 (*leg.*) comma. 4 (*pubbl.*) alinea.

paragraph², *v. t.* 1 dividere in paragrafi. 2 (*giorn.*) trattare (*un argomento*) in un trafiletto.

paralyse, *v. t.* (*anche fig.*) paralizzare.

paralysis, *n.* (*pl.* **paralyses**) (*anche fig.*) paralisi.

paralyze, *v. t.* (*USA*) V. **paralyse.**

paramount, *a.* sommo, capitale.

paraphernal, *a.* (*leg.*) parafernale.

parcel¹, *n.* 1 pacco, pacchetto, collo, involto. 2 (*leg.*) parcella fondiaria, particella catastale, lotto di terreno. 3 (*market.*) partita (*di merce posta in vendita*). // **a** ~ **of goods** (*market.*) una partita di merci; ~ **of shares** (*fin.*) pacchetto azionario; **parcels office** (*trasp.*) ufficio (*spedizione e/o distribuzione*) pacchi; ~ **post** (*trasp.*) messaggeria, messaggerie; servizio dei pacchi postali; **parcels rate** (*trasp. ferr.*) tariffa per (la spedizione di) colli; **by** ~ **post** (*comun.*) per pacco postale.

parcel², *v. t.* 1 impaccare, impacchettare, involtare. 2 lottizzare (*terreni*). // **to** ~ **purchases** impacchettare gli acquisti.

parcellation, *n.* lottizzazione (*di terreni*).

parcenary, *n.* (*leg.*) coeredità, l'essere coerede.

parcener, *n.* (*leg.*) coerede.

pardon, *n.* (*leg.*) grazia, indulto.

parent, *n.* 1 madre. 2 (*fig.*) origine, fonte, causa. // ~ **company** (*fin., org. az.*) società madre, casa madre; ~ **corporation** (*fin., org. az., USA*) società madre, casa madre.

parental, *a.* paterno, materno.

parenthesis, *n.* (*pl.* **parentheses**) parentesi.

parity, *n.* 1 parità, uguaglianza. 2 (*econ., fin.*) parità. // ~ **band** (*fin.*) fascia d'oscillazione (*dei tassi di cambio, ecc.*), banda (*o* fascia) di parità; **the** ~ **between two rates of exchange** (*fin.*) la parità fra due tassi di cambio; **parities of exchange** (*fin.*) parità cambiarie; **at a** ~ **of votes** a parità di voti.

parking, *n.* (*trasp. aut.*) posteggio. // ~ **meter** (*trasp. aut.*) parcometro; «**no** ~» (*avviso*) «divieto di parcheggio».

Parkinson's law, *n.* 1 legge di Parkinson (*secondo la quale il numero dei dipendenti cresce in maniera fissa a prescindere dalla quantità di lavoro prodotto*). 2 legge di Parkinson (*secondo la quale il lavoro aumenta tanto da occupare tutto il tempo disponibile per il suo svolgimento*).

parliamentary, *a.* (*leg., ingl.*) parlamentare. // ~ **committee** (*leg., ingl.*) commissione parlamentare; ~ **law** (*leg., ingl.*) legge parlamentare.

parlor, *n.* 1 (*market., USA*) «salone», negozio. 2 (*USA*) salotto, salottino. // ~ **-car** (*trasp. ferr., USA*) carrozza (di) lusso, carrozza salone.

parlour, *n.* 1 salotto, salottino. 2 (*market.*) «salone», negozio.

parol, *n.* (*leg.*) dichiarazione orale. *a. attr.* (*leg.*) verbale. // ~ **contract** (*leg.*) contratto verbale; ~ **evidence** (*leg.*) prove (*testimoniali*) verbali.

part¹, *n.* parte, aliquota. // ~ **and parcel** parte integrante; ~ **cargo charter** (*trasp. mar.*) noleggio parziale; ~ **-owner** (*leg.*) comproprietario; ~ **-ownership** (*leg.*) comproprietà; (*trasp. mar.*) caratura; ~ **payment** (*cred.*) pagamento parziale, acconto; ~ **time** (*pers.*) orario ridotto, tempo definito (*di lavoro, ecc.*); ~ **-time job** (*pers.*) lavoro a orario ridotto; ~ **-time work** (*org. az.*) lavoro a orario ridotto; ~ **-time worker** (*pers.*) operaio (che lavora) a orario ridotto; ~ **-timer** (*pers.*) chi lavora a orario ridotto; **on the** ~ **of** da parte di.

part², *v. t.* dividere. // **to** ~ **with st.** cedere qc.; **to** ~ **with one's right to vote** (*amm., fin.*) cedere il proprio diritto di voto.

partial, *a.* 1 parziale. 2 parziale, ingiusto. // ~ **customs exemption** (*dog.*) esenzione doganale parziale; ~ **disability** (*pers.*) invalidità parziale; ~ **loss** (*ass.*) perdita parziale; ~ **monopoly** (*econ.*) monopolio parziale; ~ **verdict** (*leg.*) verdetto parziale.

participant, *n.* partecipante.

participate, *v. i.* partecipare, essere partecipe di. // **to** ~ **in** prendere parte a; condividere.

participating, *a.* compartecipe. // ~ **shares**

(*fin.*) quote di partecipazione.

participation, *n.* 1 partecipazione. 2 (*fin.*) partecipazione agli utili.

particular, *a.* particolare, peculiare. *n.* 1 particolare, particolarità, dettaglio. 2 dato, ragguaglio. 3 **particulars,** *pl.* (*leg.*) particolari, estremi (*d'una domanda, ecc.*). // ~ **average** (*ass. mar.*) avaria particolare; **a** ~ **lien** (*leg.*) un privilegio speciale; ~ **partnership** (*fin.*) associazione in partecipazione; **with** ~ **average (W.P.A.)** (*ass. mar.*) avaria particolare inclusa.

partition¹, *n.* 1 partizione, ripartizione. 2 (*leg.*) divisione patrimoniale. // **the** ~ **of power** (*leg.*) la divisione dei poteri.

partition², *v. t.* dividere in parti, ripartire.

partly, *avv.* parzialmente, in parte. // ~ **-finished goods** (*org. az.*) prodotti in corso di lavorazione, semilavorati; ~ **-paid capital** (*fin.*) capitale versato in parte; ~ **-paid shares** (*fin.*) azioni parzialmente liberate.

partner, *n.* (*fin.*) socio, associato. // ~ **by estoppel** (*fin.*) quasi socio, socio nominale.

partnership, *n.* 1 (*leg.*) società di persone. 2 (*leg.*) (= **general partnership**) società in nome collettivo. *a. attr.* (*leg.*) sociale. // **the** ~ **assets** (*fin.*) l'attivo sociale; ~ **deed** (*fin.*) contratto di società (di persone); ~ **funds** (*fin.*) fondi sociali.

party, *n.* 1 gruppo. 2 (*leg.*) parte, parte contraente, parte in causa. // **the** ~ **concerned** (*leg.*) la parte interessata, l'interessato, gli interessati; **the** ~ **entitled** (*leg.*) gli aventi diritto; ~ **-line** (*comun.*) duplex, telefono in duplex; **the** ~ **named** (*cred.*) l'accreditato (*in una lettera di credito, ecc.*); ~ **ticket** (*trasp. ferr.*) biglietto collettivo, biglietto cumulativo; **the parties to the case** (*leg.*) le parti in causa; ~ **-wire** (*comun.*) duplex, telefono in duplex; **the third** ~ (*leg.*) i terzi.

pass¹, *n.* 1 lasciapassare. 2 (*trasp.*) biglietto gratuito. 3 (*trasp. mar.*) passaggio marittimo. // ~ **-book** (*banca*) libretto di deposito; ~ **-money** (*trasp. mar.*) prezzo del passaggio marittimo; ~ **-sheet** (*trasp. aut.*) trittico.

pass², *v. i.* 1 passare. 2 (*econ.*) (*di monete, ecc.*) circolare. 3 (*leg.*) passare (*di proprietà*). 4 (*leg.*) (*di disegno di legge, ecc.*) essere approvato, passare. *v. t.* 1 (*leg.*) approvare, passare (*un disegno di legge, ecc.*). 2 (*leg.*) promuovere, sanzionare (*una legge, ecc.*). 3 (*leg.*) essere approvato da (*un'assemblea legislativa*). // to ~ **the articles of association** (*fin.*) approvare lo statuto societario; to ~ **a customs entry** (*dog.*) fare una dichiarazione in dogana; to ~ **judgement on an accused man** (*leg.*) giudicare un imputato; to ~ **a law** (*leg.*) varare una legge; to ~ **one's oath** (*leg.*) impegnarsi con giuramento, giurare; to ~ **an order on sb.** (*comun., market.*) trasmettere un'ordinazione a q.; to ~ **a resolution** (*leg.*) approvare una deliberazione; to ~ **sentence on an accused man** (*leg.*) giudicare un imputato; to ~ **a transfer** (*rag.*) registrare uno «storno»; to ~ **one's word** dare la propria parola, impegnarsi; to **have passed the chair** (*amm.*) aver lasciato la presidenza, non essere più presidente.

passable, *a.* (*trasp.*) (*di luogo, strada e sim.*) transitabile.

passage, *n.* 1 (*leg.*) approvazione (*di un disegno di legge, ecc.*). 2 (*trasp.*) passaggio, tragitto. 3 (*trasp. aer., trasp. mar.*) passaggio, traversata, viaggio. 4 (*trasp. aer., trasp. mar.*) prezzo del viaggio. // ~ **broker** (*trasp. mar.*) sensale di passeggeri; ~ **days** (*trasp. mar.*) durata del viaggio; ~ **home** (*trasp. mar.*) viaggio di ritorno; ~ **money** (*trasp. aer., trasp. mar.*) prezzo della traversata; ~ **out** (*trasp. mar.*) viaggio d'andata.

passenger, *n.* (*trasp.*) passeggero, viaggiatore. // ~ **and goods train** (*trasp. ferr.*) treno misto (*per merci e passeggeri*); ~ **car** (*trasp. ferr.*) carrozza viaggiatori; ~ **-kilometre** (*stat., trasp.*) viaggiatore-chilometro; ~ **liner** (*trasp. mar.*) nave di linea per passeggeri; ~ **list** (*trasp. aer., trasp. mar.*) elenco (dei) passeggeri; ~ **-mile** (*stat., trasp.*) «viaggiatore-miglio»; ~ **traffic** (*trasp.*) movimento (di) viaggiatori; ~ **train** (*trasp. ferr.*) treno viaggiatori; ~ **transport** (*trasp.*) trasporto (di) persone.

passive, *a.* passivo. // **a** ~ **balance of trade** (*econ.*) una bilancia commerciale passiva; ~ **change** (*rag.*) variazione passiva; ~ **debt** (*cred.*) debito passivo (*senza interessi*); credito infruttifero; ~ **reaction** (*econ.*) reazione passiva (*al processo inflazionistico*).

passport, *n.* (*tur.*) passaporto.

past, *a.* passato, scorso, ultimo. *n.* (il) passato. *avv.* oltre, al di là di. // ~ **-due** (*cred.*) scaduto; (*trasp.*) (*di treno, ecc.*) in ritardo; ~ **week** la settimana scorsa; ~ **year** l'anno scorso; (*fin., rag.*) l'esercizio trascorso.

paste, *n.* (*pubbl.*) colla (*per manifesti*).

patch¹, *n.* (*anche fig.*) pezza, rattoppo.

patch², *v. t.* (*anche fig.*) rattoppare. // to ~ **up** (*anche fig.*) rattoppare.

patent¹, *n.* (*leg.*) brevetto, patente. 2 (*leg.*) procedimento brevettato, invenzione brevettata. 3 (*leg.*) diritto di brevetto, esclusiva. *a. attr.* 1 (*leg.*) brevettato. 2 (*leg.*) fabbricato su brevetto. // ~ **law** (*leg.*) diritto sui brevetti; ~ **-licensing**

contracts (*leg.*) contratti di licenze per brevetti; ~ **Office** (*leg.*) ufficio brevetti; ~ **rights** (*leg.*) diritti di privativa industriale, proprietà industriale, brevetti.

patent², *v. t.* 1 (*leg.*) brevettare (*un'invenzione, un procedimento, ecc.*). 2 (*leg.*) concedere a (*q.*) un diritto di brevetto; concedere a (*q.*) un'esclusiva.

patentable, *a.* (*leg.*) brevettabile.

patentee, *n.* (*leg.*) concessionario di brevetto, titolare di brevetto.

patentor, *n.* (*leg.*) *V.* **patentee.**

paternity, *n.* paternità.

pathological, *a.* patologico. // ~ **income** (*econ.*) rendita patologica.

patrimonial, *a.* patrimoniale.

patrimony, *n.* patrimonio, averi.

patron, *n.* (*market.*) avventore, cliente abituale (*d'un negozio*).

patronage, *n.* 1 (*leg.*) patrocinio. 2 (*market.*) clientela (*d'un negozio*).

patronize, *v. t.* 1 (*leg.*) patrocinare. 2 (*market.*) essere cliente abituale di (*un negozio*).

patronizing, *a.* patrocinante.

pattern¹, *n.* 1 campione. 2 modello (*anche fig.*). 3 (*market.*) disegno (*di stoffa, ecc.*). // ~ **bargaining** (*sind.*) trattativa basata su un modello di contratto di lavoro ritenuto valido; ~ **-book** (*market.*) campionario (*di tessuti, carta, ecc.*).

pattern², *v. t.* 1 modellare (*anche fig.*). 2 copiare da un campione.

patterned, *a.* 1 modellato. 2 copiato da un campione. // ~ **interview** (*market.*) intervista guidata.

pawn¹, *n.* 1 (*comm., leg.*) pegno. 2 (*comm., leg.*) caparra, garanzia. // ~ **-ticket** (*comm., leg.*) polizza di pegno.

pawn², *v. t.* 1 (*comm., leg.*) impegnare, dare in pegno, pignorare. 2 (*comm., leg.*) dare in garanzia.

pawnable, *a.* (*comm., leg.*) che si può dare in pegno, pignorabile.

pawnbroker, *n.* (*comm., leg.*) prestatore su pegno. // ~ **'s shop** (*comm., leg.*) agenzia (*o* banco) di prestiti su pegno, «Monte di Pegno», «Monte di Pietà».

pawnee, *n.* 1 (*comm., leg.*) chi impegna qc.; chi costituisce un pegno. 2 (*comm., leg.*) chi ha ricevuto qc. in pegno.

pawnshop, *n.* (*comm., leg.*) agenzia di prestiti su pegno, «Monte di Pegno», «Monte di Pietà».

pay¹, *n.* (*pers.*) paga, retribuzione, salario, stipendio. *a. attr.* (*pers.*) salariale. // ~ **-day** (*Borsa*) giorno di liquidazione; (*pers.*) giorno di paga; ~ **-envelope** (*pers.*) busta paga; ~ **-load** (*trasp. aer.*) carico pagante; ~ **-off** (*pers.*) pagamento; paga; ~ **-office** (*org. az.*) ufficio paga; ~ **-out ratio** (*fin.*) rapporto tra il valore delle uscite per il pagamento dei dividendi e il valore dei profitti (*d'una società*); ~ **-packet** (*pers., ingl.*) busta paga; ~ **pause** (*econ., sind.*) tregua salariale; ~ **phone** (*comun.*) telefono a pagamento, telefono a gettoni (*in G.B.,* a monete metalliche); ~ **-raise** (*pers., USA*) aumento salariale, aumento di stipendio; ~ **restraint** (*econ.*) compressione dei salari; ~ **restraint policy** (*econ.*) politica di compressione dei salari; ~ **-roll** (*org. az.*) personale (che è) nei libri paga; (*rag.*) libro paga, somma necessaria a pagare i dipendenti; ~ **-roll tax** (*rag.*) contributi (*basati sui libri paga*), contributi «sociali»; ~ **-roller** (*pers.*) chi riceve una retribuzione; ~ **-sheet** (*pers., ingl.*) *V.* ~ **-roll;** ~ **slip** (*pers.*) striscia (*di carta*) sulla quale sono indicati dettagliatamente i conteggi relativi al salario (*o* stipendio) netto; to **be on the** ~ **-roll** (*pers.*) essere nei libri paga (*di un datore di lavoro*); to **be on sb.'s** ~ **-roll** (*pers.*) essere alle dipendenze di q.

pay², *v. t.* e *i.* (*pass.* e *part. pass.* **paid**) 1 pagare, fare un pagamento. 2 (*cred.*) saldare. 3 (*econ., fin.*) fruttare, rendere. 4 (*pers.*) (*d'occupazione*) rendere. // ~ **-as-you-earn (P.A.Y.E.)** (*fin.*) ritenuta alla fonte (*del debito d'imposta: in G.B.*); sistema di tassazione per mezzo di ritenute sul salario (*o* sullo stipendio); ~ **-as-you-earn taxpayer** (*fin.*) contribuente soggetto alla ritenuta d'acconto; ~ **-as-you-go** (*fin., USA*) sistema di tassazione sul reddito mediante trattenute al momento in cui esso è conseguito; (*market., USA*) pagare i conti alla scadenza; to ~ **back** restituire (*denaro*); to ~ **back in advance** rimborsare anticipatamente; to ~ **the balance** saldare la rimanenza; to ~ **a bill at maturity** (*cred.*) pagare una cambiale alla scadenza; to ~ **by instalments** pagare a rate; to ~ **cash** pagare in contanti; to ~ **cash on delivery** (*market.*) pagare alla consegna; to ~ **the customs duties (on)** (*dog.*) sdaziare; to ~ **one's debts** (*cred.*) sdebitarsi; to ~ **a dividend** (*fin.*) pagare un dividendo; to ~ **down** (*market.*) pagare in contanti; versare (*la prima rata*); to ~ **(sb.'s) expenses** spesare; to ~ **a fine** (*leg.*) pagare (*o* conciliare) una multa; to ~ **for the goods** pagare la merce; to ~ **in** (*banca*) versare (*denaro*); to ~ **in advance** pagare in anticipo; to ~ **in driblets** pagare in piccole somme, pagare «col contagocce»; to ~ **in full**

pagare a saldo; to ~ **in kind** pagare in natura; to ~ **into** (*banca*) versare (*denaro*); to ~ **money back to sb.** rimborsare q.; to ~ **money on account** (*cred.*, *rag.*) versare denaro in acconto; to ~ **money out** (*fin.*) (*di banca*) versare denaro (*a un cliente*); to ~ **off** (*cred.*) liquidare, saldare, tacitare (*un creditore, ecc.*); estinguere, scalare (*un debito, ecc.*); to ~ **off a loan** (*cred.*) estinguere un prestito; to ~ **off a mortgage** (*cred.*) estinguere un'ipoteca; to ~ **on demand** pagare a vista; to ~ **on the nail** pagare a tamburo battente; to ~ **out** pagare, sborsare, versare; to ~ **a salary (to)** (*pers.*) stipendiare, salariare; ~ **self** (*banca*) (*su un assegno*) pagate al mio ordine, pagate a me medesimo (*M.M.*); to ~ **through the nose** pagare un occhio della testa; to ~ **to bearer** (*cred.*) pagare al portatore; to ~ **to the last penny** pagare fino all'ultimo centesimo; to ~ **toll** (*trasp.*) pagare il pedaggio; to ~ **up** (*cred.*) pagare totalmente, saldare; to ~ **wages (to)** (*pers.*) salariare.

payable, *a.* **1** pagabile, esigibile. **2** (*econ.*, *fin.*) (*d'un investimento, ecc.*) redditizio, rimunerativo. **3** (*pers.*) (*d'un lavoro, ecc.*) redditizio. // ~ **against invoice** (*market.*) pagabile contro fattura; ~ **at maturity** (*cred.*) pagabile alla scadenza; ~ **at sight** (*cred.*) pagabile a vista; ~ **in monthly instalments** pagabile a rate mensili; ~ **on delivery** (*market.*) pagabile alla consegna; ~ **on demand** (*cred.*) pagabile a richiesta, pagabile a vista; ~ **to bearer** (*cred.*) pagabile al portatore; ~ **to order** (*cred.*) pagabile all'ordine.

payables, *n. pl.* (*rag.*) debiti complessivi (*d'un'azienda*).

paycheck, *n.* (*pers.*, *USA*) assegno paga, paga, salario, stipendio.

payee, *n.* **1** (*ass.*) beneficiario. **2** (*cred.*) beneficiario, portatore (*d'un assegno e sim.*); prenditore.

payer, *n.* chi paga, chi è tenuto a pagare; pagatore.

paying, *a.* **1** che paga, pagante, pagatore. **2** (*econ.*, *fin.*) fruttifero, lucrativo, redditizio, rimunerativo. **3** (*pers.*) (*di lavoro, ecc.*) rimunerativo. *n.* pagamento, versamento. // **the** ~ **banker** la banca pagatrice; ~ **counter** (*banca*) cassa pagamenti; ~ **-in** (*banca*) versamento; ~ **-in book** (*banca, ingl.*) libretto per i versamenti; ~ **-in slip** (*banca, ingl.*) distinta di versamento, modulo di versamento; ~ **office** (*org. az.*) ufficio pagamenti.

paymaster, *n.* **1** chi prepara gli stipendi. **2** (*pers.*, *ingl.*) ufficiale pagatore (*nelle Forze Armate*). // ~ **general** (*amm.*) capo della Ragioneria dello Stato, Ragioniere Capo (*dello Stato*); (*pers.*, *USA*) ufficiale pagatore (*delle Forze Armate*).

payment, *n.* pagamento, versamento, somma pagata, rata. // ~ **accommodations** (*market.*) facilitazioni di pagamento; ~ **against documents** (*cred.*) pagamento contro documenti; ~ **at the debtor's domicile** (*cred.*) pagamento al domicilio del debitore; ~ **before due date** (*cred.*) pagamento anticipato; ~ **by cheque** (*banca, cred.*) pagamento mediante assegno bancario; ~ **by instalments** (*market.*) pagamento a rate; «~ **counterdemanded**» (*banca*) «ordine di pagamento revocato»; **payments deficit** (*econ.*) deficit della bilancia dei pagamenti; ~ **for honour** (*banca, cred.*) pagamento «per l'onore di firma», pagamento per intervento; ~ **in advance** pagamento anticipato; acconto, caparra; ~ **in driblets** pagamento in piccole somme, pagamento «col contagocce»; ~ **in full** pagamento a saldo; saldo; ~ **in kind** (*cred.*) pagamento in natura; **a** ~ **into the bank** (*banca*) un versamento in banca; ~ **of bills** (*banca*) ritiro (di) effetti; ~ **of losses** (*ass.*) rimborso delle perdite; ~ **of your cheque No 365532** (*banca*) pagamento (del) vostro assegno n° 365532; ~ **on account** acconto; ~ **on current account** (*banca, cred.*) pagamento in conto corrente; ~ **on delivery** (*market.*) pagamento alla consegna; ~ **on place agreed** (*cred.*) pagamento al luogo convenuto; ~ **order** (*banca*) ordine di bonifico; ~ **overdue** (*cred.*) pagamento arretrato; ~ **per intervention** (*banca, cred.*) pagamento per intervento; **payments situation** (*econ.*) situazione dei pagamenti; ~ **supra protest** (*banca, cred.*) pagamento «per intervento»; **payments surplus** (*econ.*) eccedenza della bilancia dei pagamenti; **against** ~ **of** dietro pagamento di; **for** ~ **of** dietro pagamento di; **in-** ~ (*banca*) versamento; **non-** ~ (*comm.*) mancato pagamento; rifiuto di pagare.

payola, *n.* (*USA*) bustarella.

payor, *n.* *V.* **payer.**

peak[1], *n.* **1** vetta. **2** (*fig.*) valore massimo, (il) massimo. **3** (*mat.*, *ric. op.*) valore massimo (*d'una funzione, ecc.*). *a. attr.* massimo, di punta. // ~ **efficiency** (*org. az.*) rendimento massimo; ~ **hours** (*comun.*, *trasp.*) ore di punta; (*market.*) ore di punta; ~ **level** (*Borsa*, *fin.*) rialzo massimo (*di quotazioni, ecc.*); ~ **load** (*comun.*, *trasp.*) carico massimo; (*org. az.*) carico massimo (*dei macchinari, ecc.*); ~ **productivity** (*econ.*) produttività massima, il massimo della produttività; ~ **season** (*market.*) alta stagione.

peak[2], *v. t.* portare (*qc.*) al massimo.

peck, *n.* 1 «peck» (*misura per cereali pari a 9,09 litri*). 2 recipiente della capacità d'un «peck». 3 (*USA*) «peck» (*misura per cereali pari a 8,8 litri*).

peculate, *v. i.* (*leg.*) commettere peculato, prevaricare. *v. t.* (*leg.*) appropriarsi indebitamente di (*denaro, specialm. pubblico*).

peculation, *n.* (*leg.*) appropriazione indebita, prevaricazione.

peculator, *n.* (*leg.*) prevaricatore.

pecuniary, *a.* pecuniario, finanziario, monetario. // ~ **needs** (*fin.*) necessità finanziarie; ~ **offence** (*leg.*) reato passibile di pena pecuniaria; ~ **penalty** (*leg.*) pena pecuniaria; ~ **punishment** (*leg.*) pena pecuniaria; ~ **unit** (*econ.*) unità monetaria.

peddle, *v. i.* (*market.*) fare il venditore ambulante.

peddler, *n. V.* **pedlar.**

peddling, *n.* (*market.*) commercio ambulante.

pedlar, *n.* (*market.*) venditore ambulante.

peg[1], *n.* 1 picchetto, piuolo. 2 (*fin.*) punto d'intervento, tasso d'intervento, parità. // ~ **-adjustments** (*fin.*) adeguazioni delle parità.

peg[2], *v. t.* 1 infiggere con picchetti. 2 fissare. 3 (*Borsa, fin.*) stabilizzare il prezzo di (*titoli, ecc.*). 4 (*market.*) fissare (*prezzi, quotazioni, ecc.*).

pen, *n.* penna.

penal, *a.* (*leg.*) penale. // ~ **action** (*leg.*) azione penale, causa penale; ~ **code** (*leg.*) codice penale; ~ **law** (*leg.*) diritto penale; ~ **offence** (*leg.*) reato perseguibile a termini di legge; ~ **reform** (*leg.*) riforma (del diritto) penale; ~ **suit** (*leg.*) azione penale, causa penale.

penalty, *n.* 1 (*leg.*) penalità. 2 (*leg.*) pena, sanzione penale. 3 (*leg.*) penale, multa. // ~ **clause** (*comm.*) penale, clausola penale (*in un contratto, ecc.*); ~ **for delay** (*leg.*) penalità per ritardo; **under** ~ **of** sotto pena di.

pence, *n. pl.* «pence». // ~ **rate** (*fin., ingl.*) cambio incerto per certo.

pencil, *n.* matita. // ~ **sharpener** (*attr. uff.*) temperamatite, temperalapis.

pendent, *a.* 1 pendente, sospeso. 2 (*leg.*) (*di causa, ecc.*) pendente, in sospeso, non ancora giudicato.

pending, *a.* 1 pendente, non risolto, indeciso. 2 (*leg.*) (*di causa, ecc.*) pendente, in sospeso. *prep.* in attesa di, durante, fino a. // ~ **dealings** trattative in corso; ~ **further information** in attesa d'ulteriori informazioni; ~ **our negotiations** durante i nostri negoziati; **a** ~ **suit** (*leg.*) una questione (legale) pendente, una pendenza; ~ **your acceptance** in attesa della vostra accettazione.

penny, *n.* 1 (*ingl.*) (*pl.* **pence** o **pennies**) penny (*moneta pari a 1/100 di sterlina*). 2 (*USA*) (*pl.* **pennies**) centesimo (*di dollaro*). // ~ **pincher** (*market., fam.*) oggetto (*articolo, automezzo, ecc.*) che ha un prezzo assai conveniente; ~ **stock** (*Borsa, USA*) azioni in vendita a meno di 1 dollaro l'una e quotate in cent; **a pretty** ~ (*fig.*) una bella somma di denaro, un sacco di soldi; to **turn an honest** ~ (*fig.*) guadagnarsi la vita in modo onesto.

pennyworth, *n.* (il) valore di un penny. // **a bad** ~ (*fig.*) un cattivo affare; **a good** ~ (*fig.*) un buon affare.

penologist, *n.* (*leg.*) penalista (*esperto del diritto penale*).

pension[1], *n.* 1 pensione (*assegno fisso percepito da un pensionato*). 2 (*tur.*) pensione. // ~ **contributions** (*pers., rag.*) contributi al fondo pensioni; ~ **fund** (*pers., rag.*) fondo pensioni; ~ **plan** (*pers., rag.*) piano di pensionamento; to **retire on a** ~ (*pers.*) andare in pensione.

pension[2], *v. t.* pensionare, assegnare una pensione a (*q.*). // to ~ **sb. off** (*pers.*) mandar q. in pensione.

pensionable, *a.* (*pers., rag.*) pensionabile, che ha diritto a pensione, che dà diritto a pensione. // ~ **age** (*pers., rag.*) età pensionabile; ~ **disability** (*pers., rag.*) invalidità che dà diritto a pensione; ~ **salary** (*pers., rag.*) stipendio pensionabile.

pensionary, *n.* (*pers.*) pensionato.

pensioner, *n.* (*pers.*) pensionato.

people, *n. collett.* (*col verbo al pl.*) gente.

peppercorn, *n.* granello di pepe nero (*anticamente usato come pagamento d'un affitto nominale*). // ~ **rent** (*leg.*) affitto nominale.

per, *prep.* 1 per, a. 2 per mezzo di, mediante. // ~ **annum** all'anno; ~ **capita** (*econ., stat.*) «pro capite», per persona, a testa; ~ **capita consumption** (*econ.*) consumo «pro capite»; ~ **capita income** (*econ.*) reddito «pro capite»; ~ **capita net national income** (*econ.*) reddito nazionale netto «pro capite»; ~ **capita net national product** (*econ.*) prodotto nazionale netto «pro capite»; ~ **cent** per cento; ~ **goods train** (*trasp. ferr.*) a piccola velocità; ~ **head** per persona; ~ **list price** (*market.*) prezzo come da listino; ~ **Mr Roberts** per il tramite di Mr Roberts; ~ **passenger train** (*trasp. ferr.*) a grande velocità; ~ **post** (*comun.*) per posta; ~ **pro** (*leg.*) per procura; ~ **procuration** (*leg.*) per procura; « ~ **procurationem** » (*leg.*) per procura; ~ **rail** (*trasp. ferr.*) per ferrovia; ~ **thousand** per mille; **as** ~ **invoice** (*market.*) come da fattura.

percent, *a.* e *n.* percentuale. // ~ **variations in cost of living** (*econ.*) variazioni percentuali del costo della vita; ~ **variations in retail prices** (*market.*) variazioni percentuali dei prezzi al consumo.

percentage, *n.* percentuale. // ~ **of precious metal** (*fin.*) titolo (*dell'oro, dell'argento*); **a** ~ **of the proceeds** una percentuale sugli utili; ~ **on sales** (*market.*) percentuale sulle vendite, interessenza; ~ **shop** (*sind.*) stabilimento nel quale (*in base ad accordi fra il sindacato delle maestranze e il datore di lavoro*) una percentuale dei dipendenti deve essere assunta fra gli appartenenti al sindacato stesso; ~ **tare** (*market.*) tara percentuale.

peremptory, *a.* perentorio. // ~ **exception** (*leg.*) eccezione perentoria; ~ **plea** (*leg.*) istanza perentoria; ~ **term** (*leg.*) termine perentorio; **a** ~ **writ** (*leg.*) una citazione a comparire.

perfect[1]**,** *a.* perfetto. // ~ **competition** (*econ.*) concorrenza perfetta; ~ **usufruct** (*leg.*) usufrutto perfetto.

perfect[2]**,** *v. t.* perfezionare, migliorare.

perfect oneself, *v. rifl.* perfezionarsi.

perforated, *a.* perforato.

perforator, *n.* (*attr. uff.*) punzonatrice, punzone. // **check** ~ (*banca, USA*) perforatrice per assegni.

perform, *v. t.* **1** fare, effettuare, eseguire. **2** adempiere (a), assolvere. **3** fornire, provvedere. *v. i.* (*org. az.*) (*di macchina, ecc.*) funzionare. // to ~ **calculations** eseguire dei calcoli; to ~ **a contract** (*leg.*) eseguire un contratto; to ~ **a duty** assolvere un dovere; to ~ **a promise** adempiere una promessa; to ~ **a task** eseguire un lavoro, adempiere un compito.

performance, *n.* **1** effettuazione, esecuzione. **2** adempimento. **3** (*market.*) indice delle vendite (*d'un prodotto*). **4** (*org. az.*) (*di macchina, ecc.*) prestazione, rendimento. // ~ **appraisal** (*pers.*) valutazione del merito, valutazione del personale; **the** ~ **of the stock market** (*Borsa*) l'andamento del mercato azionario; ~ **test** (*pers.*) test di rendimento.

peril, *n.* pericolo. // **perils of the sea** (*ass. mar.*) pericoli del mare, rischi attinenti alla navigazione; **at one's** ~ a proprio rischio e pericolo.

perilous, *a.* pericoloso. // ~ **seas** mari pericolosi.

period, *n.* periodo, lasso di tempo. // **the** ~ **after the war** il periodo dopo la guerra; ~ **bill** (*cred.*) cambiale a data fissa (*o* a data futura determinabile); ~ **costs** (*rag.*) spese di periodo; **a** ~ **of financial squeeze** (*fin.*) un periodo di restrizioni finanziarie; ~ **of limitation** (*leg.*) prescrizione contrattuale (*ha la durata di sei anni per i contratti semplici e di venti per quelli formali*); termine di prescrizione; **a** ~ **of rising prices** (*market.*) un periodo di prezzi crescenti; **off** ~ (*elab. elettr.*) tempo d'interdizione; **on the** ~ **the bill has yet to run** (*banca, cred.*) dalla decorrenza della cambiale.

periodic, *a.* periodico. // ~ **number** (*mat.*) numero periodico.

periodical, *a.* periodico. *n.* (*giorn.*) periodico, pubblicazione periodica. // ~ **statement** (*banca*) estratto periodico.

peripheral, *a.* periferico. // ~ **region** (*econ.*) regione periferica.

peripheric, *a.* periferico.

perish, *v. i.* **1** perire, andare distrutto. **2** (*market.*) (*di merce*) deperire, deteriorarsi.

perishable, *a.* (*market.*) (*di merce*) deperibile, deteriorabile. // ~ **goods** (*market.*) merci deperibili; ~ **products** (*market.*) merci deperibili.

perishables, *n. pl.* (*market.*) merci deperibili.

perjury, *n.* **1** (*leg.*) falsa dichiarazione giurata. **2** (*leg.*) falsa testimonianza.

perks, *n. pl.* (*fam.*) *V.* **perquisites.**

permanent, *a.* durevole, stabile. // ~ **assets** (*rag.*) capitali fissi, capitali immobilizzati; ~ **conflict** (*sind.*) conflittualità permanente; ~ **disablement** (*leg.*) invalidità permanente; ~ **income** (*econ.*) reddito permanente; **a** ~ **position** (*pers.*) un posto stabile, un posto di ruolo; ~ **staff** (*pers.*) personale di ruolo; to **be on the** ~ **staff** (*pers.*) essere in pianta stabile, essere di ruolo.

permission, *n.* permesso, autorizzazione, licenza.

permissive, *a.* che permette, concessivo. // ~ **wage-adjustment clause** (*sind.*) clausola che prevede la revisione del contratto di lavoro (*quando, p. es., si siano avute variazioni nel costo della vita, ecc., durante il periodo di validità del contratto stesso*).

permit[1]**,** *n.* permesso, licenza, patente, nullaosta.

permit[2]**,** *v. t.* permettere, consentire, concedere a. // to ~ **access to the records** consentire l'accesso ai documenti.

permutable, *a.* permutabile.

permutation, *n.* (*leg.*) permuta.

perpetual, *a.* perpetuo, eterno. // ~ **annuity** (*fin.*) rendita perpetua; ~ **calendar** (*attr. uff.*) calendario perpetuo; ~ **debt** (*fin.*) prestito irredimibile; ~ **inventory** (*fin.*) inventario permanente; ~ **lease** (*leg.*) affittanza perpetua; ~ **loan** (*fin.*) prestito irredimibile; ~ **right-of-way** (*leg.*) diritto di passaggio perpetuo.

perquisites, *n. pl.* guadagni occasionali; incerti.

persist, *v. i.* insistere.

person, *n.* **1** persona. **2** (*leg.*) persona giuridica. // ~ **aggrieved** (*leg.*) chi ha motivo di ricorrere in appello; ~ **entitled to succeed** (*leg.*) successibile; **the** ~ **in charge** il responsabile; **per** ~ a (*o* per) persona.

personal, *a.* **1** personale, individuale. **2** particolare, privato. **3** (*leg., rag.*) mobiliare. // ~ **accident insurance** (*ass.*) assicurazione contro gli infortuni; ~ **accounts** (*rag.*) conti intestati a persone fisiche; conti intestati a ditte; ~ **action** (*leg.*) azione personale; ~ **advertisement** (*giorn., pubbl.*) annuncio personale (*nella «piccola pubblicità»*); ~ **agency** (*pubbl.*) studio pubblicitario; ~ **belongings** (*leg.*) oggetti personali; ~ **chattels** (*leg.*) beni mobili (*denaro, mobilio, merci, ecc.*); ~ **column** (*giorn., pubbl.*) colonna degli annunci personali; ~ **credit** (*cred., fin.*) credito personale; ~ **effects** (*leg.*) effetti personali; ~ **estate** (*leg.*) beni mobili, patrimonio personale; ~ **income** (*econ.*) reddito personale; ~ **income tax** (*fin.*) imposta sul reddito delle persone fisiche; ~ **injury** (*leg.*) lesione personale; danno personale; ~ **loan** (*cred.*) credito personale; ~ **property** (*leg.*) patrimonio personale, beni mobili, patrimonio mobiliare, ricchezza mobile; ~ **qualifications** (*pers.*) qualifiche personali; ~ **right** (*leg.*) diritto personale; ~ **selling assistance** (*market.*) assistenza del personale di vendita; ~ **servitude** (*leg.*) servitù personale; ~ **shopper** (*market., pers.*) assistente dei clienti (*che li aiuta negli acquisti*); ~ **tax** (*fin.*) imposta personale.

personality, *n.* personalità. // ~ **test** (*pers.*) test di personalità, test caratterologico.

personation, *n.* **1** personificazione, l'impersonare. **2** (*leg.*) sostituzione di persona.

personnel, *n.* (*pers.*) personale, impiegati e operai, organico. // ~ **administration** (*org. az.*) direzione del personale, organizzazione del personale; ~ **bureau** (*org. az.*) ufficio (del) personale; ~ **communications** (*org. az.*) comunicazioni interne; ~ **department** (*org. az.*) ufficio (del) personale; ~ **management** (*org. az.*) direzione del personale, organizzazione del personale; ~ **manager** (*pers.*) direttore del personale, capo del personale; ~ **selection** (*pers.*) selezione del personale.

perspective, *a.* (*pubbl.*) in prospettiva. *n.* (*pubbl.*) prospettiva.

persuade, *v. t.* persuadere.

persuader, *n.* persuasore. // **the hidden persuaders** (*pubbl.*) i persuasori occulti.

persuasion, *n.* persuasione.

pertinent, *a.* pertinente. // ~ **facts** (*leg.*) fatti pertinenti.

peruse, *v. t.* esaminare accuratamente.

petition[1], *n.* **1** (*leg.*) petizione, istanza, esposto. **2** (*leg.*) ricorso. // ~ **for intervention** (*leg.*) istanza per intervento; ~ **in bankruptcy** (*leg.*) istanza di fallimento; ~ **of creditors** (*leg.*) istanza dei creditori.

petition[2], *v. i.* **1** (*leg.*) fare una petizione, fare un'istanza. **2** (*leg.*) fare un ricorso, ricorrere. *v. t.* **1** (*leg.*) presentare una petizione a (*q.*), presentare un'istanza a (*q.*). **2** (*leg.*) presentare un ricorso a (*q.*).

petitionee, *n.* chi è chiamato a rispondere a un'istanza.

petitioner, *n.* **1** (*leg.*) istante, richiedente. **2** (*leg.*) chi fa un ricorso, ricorrente.

petrodollar, *n.* (*econ., fin.*) petrodollaro.

petrol, *n.* benzina. // ~ **coupon** (*trasp. aut.*) buono per benzina; ~ **pump** (*trasp. aut.*) distributore di benzina; ~ **station** (*trasp. aut.*) stazione di rifornimento.

petroleum, *n.* petrolio.

petroliferous, *a.* petrolifero.

petrosterling, *n.* (*fin.*) petrosterlina.

petty, *a.* piccolo, di poca importanza. // ~ **cash** (*rag.*) piccola cassa, piccole entrate; piccole spese, fondo di cassa per le piccole spese; ~ **-cash book** (*rag.*) libro (di) piccola cassa; ~ **-cash voucher** (*rag.*) buono di piccola spesa; ~ **jury** (*leg.*) giuria ordinaria (*che emette il verdetto alla fine d'un processo; cfr.* **coroner's jury, grand jury**); ~ **larceny** (*leg.*) furto di poca entità; ~ **offence** (*leg.*) reato minore; ~ **producers** (*econ.*) piccoli produttori; ~ **shopkeepers** (*market.*) piccoli negozianti, piccoli bottegai.

phase, *n.* fase.

phenomenon, *n.* (*pl.* **phenomena**) fenomeno.

Phillips curve, *n.* (*econ.*) (*dal nome dell'economista inglese A.W.H. Phillips*) legge di Phillips (*rappresentazione grafica della relazione esistente fra l'inflazione e la disoccupazione*).

phone[1], *n.* (*comun., fam.*) telefono. // to **be**

on the ~ essere al telefono; (*anche*) essere in elenco (telefonico).

phone², *v. t.* (*comun.*) telefonare a (*q.*); fare una telefonata a (*q.*).

photo¹, *n.* (*giorn., pubbl.*) fotografia, foto (*il risultato*).

photo², *v. t.* (*giorn., pubbl.*) fotografare.

photocopy¹, *n.* (*giorn., pubbl.*) fotocopia (*il risultato*).

photocopy², *v. t.* (*giorn., pubbl.*) fotocopiare.

photograph¹, *n.* (*giorn., pubbl.*) fotografia, foto (*il risultato*).

photograph², *v. t.* (*giorn., pubbl.*) fotografare.

photographer, *n.* (*pers.*) fotografo.

photographic, *a.* (*giorn., pubbl.*) fotografico.

photographical, *a.* (*giorn., pubbl.*) fotografico.

photography, *n.* (*giorn., pubbl.*) fotografia (*il procedimento*).

photomontage, *n.* (*giorn., pubbl.*) fotomontaggio (*il procedimento e il risultato*).

photoprint, *n.* (*giorn., pubbl.*) stampa fotografica (*il risultato*).

photoprinting, *n.* (*giorn., pubbl.*) stampa fotografica (*il procedimento*).

photostat¹, *n.* **1** copia fotostatica. **2** (*macch. uff.*) apparecchio fotostatico.

photostat², *v. t.* fare una copia fotostatica di (*documenti, ecc.*).

physical, *a.* fisico. // ~ **stock** (*org. az.*) stock fisico; ~ **transfers of securities** (*econ., fin.*) movimenti materiali di titoli.

physiocracy, *n.* (*econ.*) fisiocrazia.

physiocrat, *n.* (*econ.*) fisiocrate.

physiocratic, *a.* (*econ.*) fisiocratico.

pick¹, *n.* **1** selezione, scelta. **2** cosa migliore. **3** parte migliore. // ~ **-up** (*econ.*) recupero, ripresa (*d'attività*); (*rag.*) totale a riportarsi, saldo a riportarsi; (*trasp.*) articolo preso in consegna da un vettore (*per essere spedito*).

pick², *v. t.* **1** raccogliere. **2** cernere. // to ~ **up** raccogliere; (*econ.*) (*d'attività commerciale, ecc.*) riprendere, riprendere slancio, riprendere vigore; (*trasp.*) far salire; to ~ **up a bargain** fare un buon affare.

picket¹, *n.* **1** (*sind.*) picchetto (*di scioperanti*). **2** (*sind.*) picchettatore. // ~ **line** fila di picchettatori.

picket², *v. t.* (*sind.*) picchettare (*una fabbrica, ecc.*), circondare (*una fabbrica, ecc.*) di picchetti di scioperanti.

picketing, *n.* (*sind.*) picchettaggio.

picking, *n.* (*market.*) scelta, cernita.

pickled, *a.* (*market.*) conservato sotto sale.

pickpocket, *n.* ladro, borsaiolo.

picture postcard, *n.* (*comun.*) cartolina illustrata.

piece, *n.* **1** pezzo, parte. **2** (*market.*) pezza (*di stoffa*). // **a** ~ **of business** un affare; **a** ~ **of evidence** (*leg.*) un mezzo di prova; **a** ~ **of information** (*comun.*) un'informazione; **a** ~ **of news** (*giorn.*) una notizia; ~ **rate** (*pers.*) retribuzione a pezzo, retribuzione a cottimo; ~ **wage** (*pers.*) salario a cottimo; ~ **-work** (*org. az.*) cottimo, lavoro a cottimo; ~ **-worker** (*pers.*) cottimista; **by the** ~ (*market.*) al pezzo; a pezze; (*pers.*) a cottimo.

pier, *n.* (*trasp. mar.*) banchina, gettata, molo. // ~ **dues** (*trasp. mar.*) diritti di banchina; ~ **face** (*trasp. mar.*) fronte del molo; «**ex** ~» (*trasp. mar.*) «franco molo».

pierage, *n. collett.* (*trasp. mar.*) diritti di banchina.

pigeon-hole¹, *n.* (*attr. uff.*) casella (*di casellario*).

pigeon-hole², *v. t.* insabbiare (*una pratica e sim.*).

pilfering, *n.* (*leg.*) furto di poca entità.

pillage, *v. t.* (*leg.*) svaligiare.

pilot¹, *n.* (*trasp. aer., trasp. mar.*) pilota. // ~ **master** (*trasp. mar.*) capo pilota; ~ **plant** (*org. az.*) impianto pilota, impianto sperimentale.

pilotage, *n.* **1** (*trasp. mar.*) pilotaggio. **2** (*trasp. mar.*) compenso dato al pilota. // ~ **dues** (*trasp. mar.*) diritti di pilotaggio.

pint, *n.* **1** (*ingl.*) pinta (*misura per liquidi, pari a litri 0.57*). **2** (*USA*) pinta (*misura per liquidi, pari a litri 0.47 e, per aridi, pari a litri 0,55*).

pit, *n.* **1** buca, fossa. **2** (*fin., USA*) sala (delle) contrattazioni, recinto alle grida, «corbeille», «parquet»; settore (*d'una Borsa*) riservato a una determinata merce.

pitch¹, *n.* **1** (*market., ingl.*) quantità di merce esposta per la vendita. **2** (*trasp. aer., trasp. mar.*) beccheggio.

pitch², *v. i.* **1** (*trasp. aer.*) impennarsi, picchiare. **2** (*trasp. aer., trasp. mar.*) beccheggiare.

placard¹, *n.* **1** (*pubbl.*) cartello, cartellone. **2** (*pubbl.*) manifesto.

placard², *v. t.* **1** (*pubbl.*) annunciare (*qc.*) con cartelloni. **2** (*pubbl.*) coprire di manifesti, affiggere manifesti su (*un muro, ecc.*).

place¹, *n.* **1** posto, luogo, località. **2** (*pers.*) posto, posizione, impiego, ufficio. // ~ **of**

jurisdiction (*leg.*) Foro competente; ~ **of birth** luogo di nascita; ~ **of business** (*pers.*) posto di lavoro; ~ **of call** (*trasp. mar.*) scalo; ~ **of delivery** (*market.*) luogo di consegna; ~ **of destination** (*trasp. mar.*) luogo di destinazione; ~ **of payment** (*banca, cred.*) piazza di pagamento (*d'un effetto, ecc.*); ~ **of residence** (*leg.*) luogo di residenza; **in** ~ **of** in luogo di, al posto di, invece di; to **keep sb. in his** ~ (*fig.*) far stare q. al suo posto; to **know one's** ~ (*fig.*) saper stare al proprio posto.

place², *v. t.* **1** collocare, mettere, porre, disporre. **2** (*fin.*) investire (*denaro*). **3** (*giorn., pubbl.*) trovare un editore per (*un manoscritto, ecc.*). **4** (*market.*) dare, conferire, passare, piazzare (*un'ordinazione*). **5** (*market.*) collocare (*merci, prodotti, ecc.*). **6** trovare lavoro per (*q.*). // to ~ **a bond issue** (*fin.*) collocare un'emissione obbligazionaria; to ~ **an order for st.** (*market.*) commissionare qc.; to ~ **a telephone call** (*comun.*) prenotare una chiamata telefonica.

placement, *n.* **1** collocamento, il mettere, il porre. **2** (*comun.*) prenotazione (*d'una chiamata telefonica*). **3** (*fin.*) investimento (*di denaro*). **4** (*market.*) piazzamento (*d'un'ordinazione*). **5** (*market.*) collocamento (*di merci, prodotti, ecc.*). **6** (*pers.*) collocamento. // **the** ~ **of domestic products on foreign markets** (*comm. est.*) il collocamento di prodotti nazionali sui mercati esteri; **the** ~ **of labour** (*pers.*) il collocamento della manodopera.

place oneself, *v. rifl.* porsi in ordine.

placing of an order, *locuz. n.* (*market.*) conferimento di un ordine.

plaint, *n.* (*leg.*) atto scritto di difesa (*dell'attore*).

plaintiff, *n.* (*leg.*) attore, querelante, parte civile, richiedente, ricorrente. // ~ **'s attorney** (*leg.*) avvocato di parte civile; ~ **'s domicile** (*leg.*) domicilio dell'attore; ~ **in a civil suit** (*leg.*) attore in una causa civile.

plan¹, *n.* piano, progetto, programma.

plan², *v. t.* **1** pianificatore, progettare, programmare. **2** studiare (*qc.*) nei particolari. **3** (*econ.*) pianificare, programmare. // to ~ **production** (*org. az.*) programmare la produzione.

plane¹, *n.* (*trasp. aer.*) aereo, aeroplano, apparecchio.

plane², *v. i.* (*trasp. aer.*) planare.

planetary, *a.* planetario.

planned, *a.* **1** pianificato, progettato, programmato. **2** (*econ.*) pianificato, programmato, dirigistico. // ~ **economy** (*econ.*) economia pianificata; ~ **obsolescence** (*org. az.*) obsolescenza programmata.

planner, *n.* **1** pianificatore, progettista, programmatore. **2** (*econ.*) pianificatore, programmatore.

planning, *n.* **1** pianificazione, progettazione, programmazione. **2** (*econ.*) pianificazione, programmazione. // ~ **board** comitato per la programmazione; **the** ~ **of production** (*org. az.*) la programmazione produttiva.

plant, *n.* (*econ.*) impianto, fabbrica, stabilimento. // ~ **assets** (*rag.*) attività fisse; ~ **bargaining** (*sind.*) trattative (salariali) a livello aziendale; ~ **inventory** (*org. az.*) inventario di fabbrica; ~ **location** (*org. az.*) localizzazione degli impianti; ~ **manager** (*pers.*) direttore di stabilimento; ~ **replacement** (*org. az.*) sostituzione d'impianti.

plate, *n.* (*trasp. aut.*) targa. // ~ **number** (*trasp. aut.*) numero di targa.

platen, *n.* (*di macch. uff.*) rullo (*di macchina da scrivere*).

platform, *n.* **1** piattaforma. **2** (*sind.*) piattaforma (*rivendicativa, ecc.*). **3** (*trasp. ferr.*) banchina. // ~ **-car** (*trasp. ferr.*) carro merci senza sponde; ~ **for lorries** (*trasp. aut.*) banchina per autocarri; ~ **-roofing** (*trasp. ferr.*) pensilina.

play¹, *n.* gioco.

play², *v. i.* e *t.* giocare. // to ~ **the market** (*Borsa, fin.*) giocare in Borsa, speculare in Borsa; to ~ **on the Stock Exchange** (*Borsa, fin.*) giocare in Borsa.

player, *n.* **1** giocatore. **2** (*Borsa, fin.*) speculatore in Borsa.

plea, *n.* **1** giustificazione, scusa. **2** (*leg.*) argomento di difesa, dichiarazione della difesa, istanza. **3** (*leg.*) dichiarazione dell'imputato. **4** (*leg.*) eccezione. // ~ **in abatement** (*leg.*) eccezione d'annullamento; ~ **in bar** (*leg.*) eccezione perentoria.

plead, *v. i.* **1** (*leg.*) (*d'avvocato*) patrocinare una causa. **2** (*leg.*) dichiararsi, riconoscersi (*colpevole o innocente*). *v. t.* **1** accampare, addurre, eccepire, invocare (*a giustificazione, a discolpa*). **2** (*leg.*) patrocinare, difendere. // to ~ **an alibi** (*leg.*) invocare un alibi; to ~ **a case** (*leg.*) difendere una causa.

pleader, *n.* (*leg.*) patrocinatore, patrocinante, avvocato patrocinante, avvocato difensore.

pleading, *n.* **1** (*leg.*) discussione d'una causa. **2** (*leg.*) arringa, difesa. **3 pleadings**, *pl.* (*leg.*) difese scritte delle parti in causa, «comparse».

please, *v. i.* piacere. *v. t.* far piacere a, soddisfare. // «~ **forward**» (*comun.*) «far proseguire».

pleased, *a.* compiaciuto, soddisfatto.

pledge[1], *n.* (*leg.*) pegno, garanzia. // **goods lying in** ~ (*comm.*) merce data in pegno; to **put st. in** ~ dare qc. in pegno; **securities in** ~ titoli offerti (*o* dati) in garanzia; to **take st. out of** ~ disimpegnare qc.

pledge[2], *v. t.* (*leg.*) impegnare, costituire in pegno, dare come pegno.

pledgee, *n.* (*leg.*) chi ha ricevuto qc. in pegno.

pledger, *n.* (*leg.*) chi ha dato qc. in pegno.

plenary, *a.* plenario.

plenum, *n.* (*pl.* **plena** o *reg.*) (*leg.*) «plenum», assemblea plenaria.

plomb, *v. t.* (*leg.*) piombare, apporre un sigillo di piombo a.

plot[1], *n.* appezzamento, lotto (*di terreno*); area. // **a building** ~ un'area fabbricabile.

plot[2], *v. t.* **1** rilevare. **2** (*mat.*) rappresentare graficamente (*una funzione*) per mezzo d'una curva. **3** (*trasp. mar.*) tracciare (*la rotta*).

plough[1], *n.* (*ingl.*) terreno arato.

plough[2], *v. t.* arare (*il terreno*). // to ~ **back** sotterrare (*erba, trifoglio*) con l'aratro; (*fin., fam.*) reinvestire (*profitti*) in un'impresa; (*d'impresa*) autofinanziarsi.

plug, *n.* **1** (*pubbl., slang USA*) annuncio pubblicitario. **2** (*slang USA*) raccomandazione, «spinta».

plunder, *n.* (*leg.*) svaligiamento.

plunderer, *n.* (*leg.*) svaligiatore.

plunge[1], *n.* **1** tuffo. **2** (*fin., fam.*) investimento avventato. // **the** ~ **in prices** (*fin., market.*) la caduta dei prezzi.

plunge[2], *v. i.* **1** tuffarsi. **2** (*trasp. mar.*) (*di nave*) beccheggiare. *v. t.* tuffare. // to ~ **into debt** ingolfarsi nei debiti.

plurality, *n.* **1** pluralità. **2** (*leg.*) maggioranza relativa. // ~ **of offices** (*pers.*) cumulo d'incarichi.

pluriannual, *a.* pluriennale. // ~ **forecasts** (*econ.*) previsioni pluriennali.

plus, *n.* **1** aggiunta, quantità in più, (un) extra. **2** (*mat.*) «più». *a. attr.* **1** aggiuntivo, extra. **2** (*mat.*) positivo.

ply, *v. t.* e *i.* **1** esercitare (*un mestiere*). **2** (*trasp. mar.*) (*di nave, ecc.*) fare servizio regolare.

pneumatic, *a.* pneumatico. // ~ **dispatch** (*comun.*) posta pneumatica (*sistema di tubi ad aria compressa*); ~ **post** (*comun.*) posta pneumatica (*trasmissione della corrispondenza con un sistema di tubi ad aria compressa*).

pocket[1], *n.* **1** tasca; (*fig.*) sacca. **2** (*fin.*) mezzi finanziari, risorse finanziarie. *a. attr.* tascabile. // ~ **book** agenda, taccuino; (*fin.*) reddito, risorse finanziarie, borsa (*fig.*); (*pubbl.*) libro tascabile; ~ **edition** (*pubbl.*) edizione tascabile; ~ **expenses** piccole spese personali; ~ **money** denaro per le piccole spese, spiccioli; **pockets of underdevelopment** (*econ.*) sacche di sottosviluppo; ~ **size** (*pubbl.*) tascabile; **a** ~ **-size book** (*pubbl.*) un libro tascabile; **in** ~ (*fin.*) (*d'un individuo*) provvisto di fondi.

pocket[2], *v. t.* **1** intascare, mettersi in tasca, appropriarsi di. **2** (*leg.*) sottrarre.

point[1], *n.* **1** punto. **2** punto essenziale. **3** (*Borsa, fin.*) punto (*unità di misura per la quotazione dei titoli*). **4** (*cred.*) percentuale del valore attuale d'un mutuo (*spesso aggiunta come compenso di collocazione*). **5** (*giorn.*) punto (*tipografico*). **6** (*mat.*) virgola. **7 points,** *pl.* (*trasp. ferr.*) scambi. // **the points of the compass** (*trasp. mar.*) i punti della bussola; ~ **of indifference** (*econ.*) punto d'indifferenza; **the** ~ **of intersection** (*mat.*) il punto d'intersezione (*di due rette, ecc.*); ~ **of no return** (*econ.*) punto dal quale non si torna indietro; **a** ~ **of order** (*leg.*) una mozione d'ordine, una questione di procedura; ~ **of purchase** (*market.*) punto d'acquisto; ~ **of sale** (*market.*) punto di vendita; ~ **system** (*pers.*) sistema del punteggio (*per la valutazione del lavoro*); **in** ~ **of** con riferimento a, in materia di; **in** ~ **of law** (*leg.*) in materia di legge.

point[2], *v. t.* fare la punta a, affilare. // to ~ **out** additare, indicare, mostrare; mettere in evidenza, far notare, far rilevare.

pointer, *n.* **1** cosa che indica. **2** indicazione, suggerimento. **3** (*econ., fin.*) indice, indicatore (*economico, ecc.*).

pointsman, *n.* (*pl.* **pointsmen**) (*trasp. ferr.*) scambista.

pole, *n.* polo. // ~ **of development** (*econ.*) polo di sviluppo.

police, *n.* polizia, forza pubblica.

policeman, *n.* (*pl.* **policemen**) poliziotto, guardia.

policy, *n.* **1** (*ass.*) polizza. **2** (*econ.*) politica, linea di condotta, piano d'azione. // ~ **-holder** (*ass.*) titolare d'una polizza, assicurato; ~ **loan** (*ass.*) prestito su polizza; **the** ~ **of full employment** (*econ., sind.*) la politica del pieno impiego; ~ **on cargo** (*trasp. mar.*) polizza sul carico; ~ **on freight** (*trasp. mar.*) polizza sul nolo; ~ **-owner** (*ass.*) titolare d'una polizza, assicurato; ~ **period** (*ass.*) periodo di copertura;

~ **stamp** (*ass.*) bollo della polizza; ~ **to bearer** (*ass.*) polizza al portatore; ~ **to a named person** (*ass.*) polizza nominativa; ~ **to order** (*ass.*) polizza all'ordine; **a ~ towards individual industries** (*econ.*) una politica settoriale.

polite, *a.* educato, cortese.

political, *a.* politico. // ~ **economy** (*econ.*) economia politica; ~ **rights** (*leg.*) diritti politici.

politics, *n.* politica (*arte del governare uno Stato*).

poll[1], *n.* (*giorn., market.*) inchiesta (*d'opinione*), indagine demoscopica, indagine su campione, sondaggio. // ~ **tax** (*fin.*) capitazione.

poll[2], *v. t.* (*giorn., market.*) intervistare, sondare.

pollee, *n.* (*giorn., market.*) intervistato.

poller, *n.* (*giorn., market.*) intervistatore.

pollster, *n.* (*pubbl.*) «pollster» (*chi esegue sondaggi d'opinione pubblica*).

pollute, *v. t.* insudiciare.

polynomial, *a.* (*mat.*) di polinomio.

polypoly, *n.* (*econ.*) polipolio.

pool[1], *n.* **1** (*econ.*) ammasso (*specialm. governativo*). **2** (*fin.*) «pool» (*accordo fra imprese che operano nello stesso settore*); consorzio (*d'imprese*), sindacato, cartello. **3** (*fin.*) fondo monetario comune. // ~ **swap** (*fin.*) «pool swap» (*fondo di valute di riserva, manovrato dalla Banca dei Regolamenti Internazionali*).

pool[2], *v. t.* (*fin.*) consorziare, mettere in comune (*fondi, risorse, ecc.*). *v. i.* (*fin.*) (*d'imprese, ecc.*) consorziarsi, mettersi insieme. // to ~ **the revenue from custom duties** (*comm. est.*) mettere in comune i proventi doganali.

pooling arrangements, *n. pl.* (*fin.*) accordi di «pool».

poor, *a.* **1** povero. **2** cattivo, mediocre, scadente. // **a ~ harvest** (*econ.*) un raccolto scarso; ~ **quality** (*market.*) cattiva qualità.

popular, *a.* **1** alla moda, in voga. **2** (*market.*) a buon mercato. // to **be** ~ (*market.: di un prodotto*) incontrare; **a ~ magazine** (*giorn.*) un periodico popolare; **at ~ prices** (*market.*) a prezzi popolari.

port, *n.* **1** (*trasp. aer.*) *V.* **airport. 2** (*trasp. mar.*) porto. **3** (*trasp. mar.*) fianco sinistro (*di nave*). // ~ **area** (*trasp. mar.*) zona portuale; ~ **charges** (*trasp. mar.*) spese portuali, diritti di porto; ~ **dues** (*trasp. mar.*) diritti di porto; ~ **facilities** (*trasp. mar.*) attrezzature portuali; ~ **of arrival** (*trasp. mar.*) porto d'arrivo, porto d'entrata, porto d'indoganamento; ~ **of call** (*trasp. mar.*) scalo, porto di scalo; ~ **of delivery** (*trasp. mar.*) porto di sbarco, porto di scarico; ~ **of departure** (*trasp. mar.*) porto di partenza, porto d'imbarco; ~ **of destination** (*trasp. mar.*) porto di destinazione, porto di destino; ~ **of entry** (*trasp. mar.*) porto d'entrata (*di merce importata*); ~ **of exit** (*trasp. mar.*) porto d'imbarco; ~ **of loading** (*trasp. mar.*) porto di caricazione, porto d'imbarco; ~ **of origin** (*trasp. mar.*) porto d'origine, porto di provenienza, porto d'armamento; ~ **of Registry** (*trasp. mar.*) porto d'immatricolazione; ~ **of survey** (*trasp. mar.*) porto di perizia (*d'una nave*); ~ **regulations** (*trasp. mar.*) regolamenti portuali; ~ **sanitary authority** (*trasp. mar.*) autorità sanitaria portuale, sanità di porto; ~ **speed** (*trasp. mar.*) velocità di manipolazione del carico; ~ **warden** (*trasp. mar., ingl.*) ispettore del carico e dello stivaggio; **the ~ workers** (*trasp. mar.*) i lavoratori portuali, le maestranze portuali, i portuali.

portable, *a.* portabile.

porter, *n.* **1** (*trasp.*) facchino. **2** (*trasp. ferr., USA*) inserviente (*di vagone letto, ecc.*).

porterage, *n.* **1** (*trasp.*) facchinaggio. **2** (*trasp.*) spese di facchinaggio.

portfolio, *n.* **1** cartella (*generalm. di cuoio*). **2** (*ass.*) portafoglio. **3** (*banca, fin.*) portafoglio. // ~ **investment** (*fin.*) investimento di portafoglio.

portion[1], *n.* **1** parte. **2** (*fin.*) porzione, quota, rata, tangente.

portion[2], *v. t.* dividere, ripartire. // to ~ **out** assegnare, distribuire.

position, *n.* **1** posizione, condizione, situazione, stato. **2** (*pers.*) impiego, posto (*di lavoro*). **3** (*pers.*) funzione. **4 positions,** *pl.* (*banca*) posizioni. // ~ **analysis** (*org. az.*) analisi del lavoro; **the positions of the customers' accounts** (*banca*) le posizioni dei conti dei clienti; **the ~ of the market** (*fin., market.*) la situazione del mercato.

positive, *a.* positivo. *n.* (*pubbl.*) stampa (*fotografica: il risultato*). // ~ **easement** (*leg.*) servitù positiva; **a ~ proof** (*leg.*) una prova certa, una prova fondata (*sui fatti*); ~ **servitude** (*leg.*) servitù positiva.

possess, *v. t.* **1** possedere, avere. **2** conoscere profondamente, possedere (*una lingua straniera, un'abilità, ecc.*). **3** (*leg.*) possedere, avere il possesso di (*qc.*).

possession, *n.* **1** possesso. **2** conoscenza approfondita, possesso (*d'una lingua, d'un'abilità, ecc.*). **3** (*leg.*) possesso. **4 possessions,** *pl.* beni, proprietà.

possessor, *n.* **1** possessore, chi possiede. **2**

(*leg.*) possessore.

possessory, *a.* (*leg.*) possessorio, relativo al possesso. // **a ~ action** (*leg.*) un'azione possessoria; **~ interest** (*leg.*) interesse possessorio.

possibility, *n.* possibilità (*l'esser possibile*). // **~ of transit** (*trasp.*) transitabilità.

possible, *a.* possibile, eventuale. *n.* (il) possibile.

possibly, *avv.* possibilmente.

post-[1], *pref.* post-. // **~ -date** data posteriore (*a quella reale*); to **~ -date** postdatare (*un documento, ecc.*); to **~ -date a cheque** (*cred.*) postdatare un assegno; **~ -entry** (*dog.*) rettifica di dichiarazione errata per difetto; (*rag.*) scrittura rettificativa.

post[2], *n.* **1** (*comun.*) posta, corrispondenza; levata della posta; tariffa postale; ufficio postale. **2** (*pers.*) posto, posto di lavoro, impiego. **3** (*pers.*) carica, funzione. // **~ -bag** (*comun.*) sacco postale; **~ -boat** (*comun.*) postale, battello postale; **~ -box** (*comun.*) cassetta della posta, buca da lettere; **~ -card** (*comun.*) cartolina postale; **~ -free** (*comun.*) franco di posta, in franchigia postale; **~ -man** (*comun.*) postino; **~ office** (*comun.*) ufficio postale; **~ Office** (*comun., ingl.*) Ministero delle Poste; **~ -office box** (*comun.*) casella postale; **~ -office car** (*trasp. ferr.*) vagone postale; **~ Office Department** (*comun., USA*) Ministero delle Poste; **~ -office order** (*banca, cred.*) vaglia postale (*fino a un certo ammontare*); **~ -office savings-bank** (*banca, cred.*) cassa di risparmio postale (*in G.B., fino al 1968; ora* **National Savings Bank**); **~ -paid** (*comun.*) porto pagato; **~ parcel** pacco postale; **by ~** (*comun.*) per posta, a mezzo posta.

post[3], *v. t.* **1** (*comun.*) impostare, imbucare. **2** (*comun.*) spedire per posta. **3** (*pubbl.*) affiggere, attaccare (*un manifesto, ecc.*). **4** (*pubbl.*) coprire (*un muro, ecc.*) di manifesti. **5** (*rag.*) passare, registrare (*una partita*) a mastro. // to **~ up** (*pubbl.*) affiggere, attaccare (*un manifesto, ecc.*); (*rag.*) passare, registrare (*una partita*) a mastro; to **~ up the general ledger** (*rag.*) aggiornare il (libro) mastro generale.

postage, *n.* (*comun.*) affrancatura, tariffa postale. // «**~ due**» (*comun.*) «affrancatura insufficiente»; **~ -due stamp** (*comun.*) segnatasse; **~ meter** (*macch. uff.*) macchina affrancatrice; **~ stamp** (*comun.*) francobollo.

postal, *a.* (*comun.*) postale. // **~ area** (*comun.*) distretto postale; **~ car** (*trasp. ferr.*) vagone postale; **~ charges** (*comun.*) spese postali; **~ clerk** (*comun.*) impiegato postale; **~ delivery zone** (*comun.*) distretto postale; **~ giro** (*cred.*) conto corrente postale; **~ meter** (*macch. uff.*) macchina affrancatrice; **~ money order** (*banca, cred.*) vaglia postale (*fino a un certo ammontare*); **~ note** (*cred., ingl.*) *V.* **~ order**; **~ order** (*cred., ingl.*) vaglia postale (*con un diverso limite della somma*); **~ service** (*comun.*) servizio postale; **~ tariff** (*comun.*) tariffa postale; **~ union** (*comun.*) unione postale (*fra Stati*); **~ zone** (*comun.*) distretto postale.

postbus, *n.* (*abbr. fam. di* **Post Office minibus**) piccolo autobus delle Poste (*per corrispondenza e per passeggeri, nelle zone rurali ingl.*).

postcard, *n.* (*comun.*) cartolina.

postcode[1], *n.* (*comun.*) codice d'avviamento postale (*abbr. C.A.P.*).

postcode[2], *v. t.* (*comun.*) mettere il codice d'avviamento postale su (*una busta, ecc.*).

poster[1], *n.* (*pubbl.*) affisso, avviso, cartello, cartellone, manifesto. // **~ advertising** (*pubbl.*) pubblicità a mezzo affissione; **~ designer** (*pubbl.*) cartellonista; **~ panel** (*pubbl.*) tabellone pubblicitario (*sul quale si affiggono manifesti*).

poster[2], *v. t.* (*pubbl.*) coprire (*un muro, ecc.*) di manifesti; affiggere manifesti (*e sim.*) su (*un muro, ecc.*).

poste restante, *n.* **1** (*comun.*) fermo (in) posta. **2** (*comun.*) ufficio delle fermo (in) posta.

posting, *n.* **1** (*comun.*) impostazione (*della corrispondenza*). **2** (*pubbl.*) affissione (*di manifesti e sim.*). **3** (*rag.*) registrazione (*d'una partita*) a mastro. // **~ box** (*comun., ingl.*) cassetta della posta, buca da lettere; **~ reference** (*rag.*) riferimento a mastro.

postmark[1], *n.* (*comun.*) bollo postale, timbro postale. // **~ advertising** (*pubbl.*) pubblicità a mezzo timbro postale.

postmark[2], *v. t.* (*comun.*) bollare, timbrare (*una lettera*).

postmaster, *n.* (*comun.*) ufficiale postale (*uomo*). // **~ General** (*ingl., USA*) Ministro delle Poste.

postmistress, *n.* (*comun.*) ufficiale postale (*donna*).

postpone, *v. t.* **1** posticipare, prorogare, differire, dilazionare, aggiornare, rimandare, rinviare, procrastinare, posporre. **2** (*fin., leg.*) postergare. // to **~ a mortgage** (*leg.*) postergare un'ipoteca.

postponement, *n.* posticipazione, differimento, dilazione, aggiornamento, proroga, sospensiva, rinvio.

postscript, *n.* (*comun.*) poscritto.

postscriptum, *n.* (*pl.* **postscripta**) (*comun.*) poscritto.

potential, *a.* potenziale. *n.* (il) potenziale, risorse potenziali. // **~ analysis** (*org. az.*) valutazione potenziale; **a ~ buyer** (*market.*) un acquirente potenziale; **~ demand** (*econ.*) domanda potenziale; **the ~ market** (*market.*) il mercato potenziale; **~ profit** (*econ.*) reddito potenziale.

potentiality, *n.* potenzialità, (il) potenziale, risorse potenziali.

potentiate, *v. t.* potenziare.

potentiation, *n.* potenziamento.

pound, *n.* **1** libbra (*unità di peso pari a 453 grammi circa*). **2** (*ingl.*) sterlina, lira sterlina. // **~ sterling** (*ingl.*) lira sterlina, sterlina.

poundage, *n.* **1** peso in libbre. **2** (*pers.*) provvigione calcolata a un tanto la sterlina (*o* la libbra).

pour, *v. t.* **1** versare (*un liquido*). **2** fornire (*qc.*) in abbondanza. *v. i.* riversarsi. // **to ~ in** (*fig.: di capitali, ecc.*) affluire, arrivare.

poverty, *n.* povertà.

power, *n.* **1** potere, potenza, forza. **2** capacità, facoltà. **3** (*mat.*) potenza. // **~ -boat** (*trasp. mar.*) motobarca; **~ of attorney** (*leg.*) «procura» (*l'autorità conferita*); procura (*documento — più formale della lettera — che ne conferisce l'autorità*); **the ~ of the law** (*leg.*) la forza della legge; **~ -plant** centrale elettrica; **~ -station** centrale elettrica.

practicable, *a.* effettuabile, fattibile.

practice, *n.* **1** pratica, esercizio, abitudine, uso. **2** pratica (*professionale*). **3** (*leg.*) procedura. // **practices in restraint of competition** (*market.*) le pratiche che limitano la concorrenza; **the ~ of law** (*leg.*) l'esercizio della professione legale; **commercial ~** la tecnica commerciale.

practicing, *a.* che esercita una professione, praticante. // **a ~ barrister** (*leg.*) un avvocato che esercita la professione.

practise, *v. i.* **1** far pratica, esercitarsi. **2** esercitare una professione. *v. t.* praticare.

practitioner, *n.* chi esercita una professione, professionista. // **general ~** medico generico.

praise, *v. t.* elogiare.

pratique, *n.* (*trasp. mar.*) pratica, libera pratica. // **~ boat** (*trasp. mar.*) battello della sanità di porto; **~ certificate** (*trasp. mar.*) certificato di libera pratica.

praxis, *n.* (*pl.* **praxes**) **1** prassi, pratica, abitudine. **2** (*org. az.*) prassi.

pre-, *pref.* pre-. // **to ~ -empt** (*leg.*) acquistare (*qc.*) valendosi del diritto di prelazione; **~ -emption** (*leg.*) acquisto fatto esercitando il diritto di prelazione, diritto di prelazione, prelazione; **~ -emption right** (*leg.*) diritto di prelazione; **~ -emptive** (*leg.*) di prelazione; **~ -emptive right** (*fin.*) diritto di prelazione (*d'azionisti: all'acquisto di nuove azioni*), diritto d'opzione; **~ -war** dell'anteguerra.

precaution, *n.* precauzione.

precautionary, *a.* precauzionale.

precede, *v. t.* e *i.* precedere, venire prima.

precedence, *n.* precedenza, priorità.

precedent[1], *n.* (*leg.*) precedente (*giudiziario*). *a.* (*leg.*) sospensivo. // **conditions ~** (*leg.*) condizioni sospensive (*di un contratto*).

precedent[2], *v. t.* (*leg.*) giustificare (*una sentenza, ecc.*) con un precedente.

preceding, *a.* precedente, previo.

precept, *n.* **1** massima, norma. **2** (*fin., ingl.*) ingiunzione di pagamento (*d'un'imposta locale*). **3** (*leg.*) intimazione.

precious, *a.* prezioso.

precise, *a.* esatto.

precision, *n.* esattezza. // **~ finish** (*org. az.*) finiture di precisione; **~ instruments** (*org. az.*) strumenti di precisione.

predate, *v. t.* antidatare.

predominance, *n.* predominanza.

predominant, *a.* predominante.

prefer, *v. t.* **1** preferire. **2** (*cred.*) accordare la priorità a (*un creditore, ecc.*). **3** (*leg.*) avanzare, presentare, sporgere.

preference, *n.* **1** preferenza. **2** (*comm. est.*) trattamento di favore (*accordato da un Governo a certi Paesi, in materia di tariffe, ecc.*). *a. attr.* preferenziale, privilegiato. // **~ margins** (*comm. est.*) preferenze contrattuali; **~ shareholder** (*fin.*) detentore d'azioni privilegiate, azionista privilegiato; **~ shares** (*fin.*) azioni preferenziali, azioni privilegiate; **~ stock** (*fin.*) azioni preferenziali, azioni privilegiate.

preferential, *a.* **1** preferenziale, di preferenza, privilegiato. **2** (*leg.*) privilegiato. // **~ credit** (*leg.*) credito privilegiato; **~ creditor** (*leg.*) creditore privilegiato; **~ rediscount rate** (*banca, cred.*) tasso di risconto privilegiato; **~ shop** (*sind.*) stabilimento nel quale è accordata una preferenza, nelle assunzioni, agli iscritti a un sindacato; **~ tariffs** (*comm. est.*) tariffe preferenziali; **~ treatment** (*comm. est.*) trattamento privilegiato (*che un Governo accorda a un altro, in materia di tariffe, ecc.*).

preferred, *a.* **1** preferito. **2** (*fin., leg.*) privilegiato. // **~ creditor** (*leg.*) creditore privilegiato; **~ debt** (*cred.*) credito privilegiato; **~ shares** (*fin.*) azioni preferenziali, azioni privilegiate; ~ **stock** (*fin.*) azioni preferenziali, azioni privilegiate.

prejudice, *v. t.* (*leg.*) ledere.

prejudicial, *a.* (*leg.*) lesivo.

preliminary, *a.* preliminare, preventivo. *n.* preliminare, esame preliminare. // **a ~ agreement to sell** (*market.*) un preliminare di vendita, un compromesso di vendita; ~ **economic budget** (*econ.*) bilancio economico preliminare; ~ **investigation (of a case)** (*leg.*) istruttoria; (*market.*) studio preliminare; ~ **proof** (*ass.*) prova preliminare (*di danno subito*).

premier, *a.* primario, primo, (il) più importante.

premise[1], *n.* premessa.

premise[2], *v. t.* premettere.

premises, *n. pl.* **1** fabbricati, locali, terreni. **2** (*leg.*) immobili, sede degli affari (*d'un'impresa*). **3** (*leg.*) premesse (*d'un contratto*). // ~ **and conclusions** (*leg.*) le premesse e le conclusioni.

premium, *n.* **1** premio, pagamento straordinario. **2** (*ass.*) premio. **3** (*fin.*) aggio (*nel cambio valutario*). **4** (*market.*) «omaggio», articolo dato in omaggio. **5** (*pers.*) gratifica. *a. attr.* (*market.*) di primissima qualità. // ~ **gasoline** (*trasp. aut., USA*) benzina «super»; ~ **notice** (*ass.*) avviso di pagamento del premio (*notificato all'assicurato*); ~ **of insurance** (*ass.*) premio d'assicurazione; ~ **of shares** (*fin.*) premio d'emissione azionaria; ~ **offer** (*market.*) offerta premio; ~ **pay** (*pers.*) retribuzione a premio; ~ **products** (*market.*) prodotti di primissima qualità; ~ **rates** (*ass.*) tariffa dei premi; ~ **sales** (*market.*) vendite a premio; ~ **stamps** (*market.*) punti «qualità»; ~ **system** (*pers.*) sistema della retribuzione a premio; **at a ~** (*Borsa, fin.*) sopra la pari; **at a ~ to be arranged** (*ass.*) per un premio da convenirsi.

prepacked, *a.* (*market.*) (già) confezionato, in confezione.

prepaid, *a.* **1** pagato in anticipo. **2** (*trasp.*) franco (*di porto*). // ~ **expenses** (*rag.*) risconti attivi; ~ **freight charges** (*trasp. mar.*) spese di nolo anticipate; ~ **interests** (*rag.*) risconti attivi su interessi; ~ **rent** (*rag.*) risconti attivi su fitti; ~ **reply** (*comun.*) risposta pagata.

preparation, *n.* **1** preparazione. **2** (*market.*) preparato.

preparatory, *a.* preliminare. // ~ **measures** provvedimenti preliminari.

prepare, *v. t.* **1** preparare, disporre, elaborare. **2** (*leg.*) redigere (*un contratto, ecc.*). *v. i.* prepararsi, far preparativi. // to ~ **a new strategy for the launching of a product** (*market., pubbl.*) elaborare una nuova strategia per il lancio d'un prodotto.

prepay, *v. t.* (*pass.* e *part. pass.* **prepaid**) pagare in anticipo. // to ~ **the interest on a loan** (*cred.*) pagare in anticipo gli interessi su un prestito; to ~ **the postage on correspondence** (*comun.*) affrancare la corrispondenza.

prepayment, *n.* pagamento anticipato. // **the ~ of freight** (*trasp. mar.*) il pagamento anticipato del nolo.

prerequisite, *a.* indispensabile, essenziale. *n.* requisito indispensabile.

prerogative, *n.* **1** qualità speciale. **2** (*leg.*) prerogativa.

prescribe, *v. t.* **1** prescrivere. **2** (*leg.*) prescrivere. **3** (*leg.*) usucapire, acquisire per usucapione. **4** (*market.*) fissare (*prezzi*). *v. i.* (*leg.*) prescriversi, andare in prescrizione, cadere in prescrizione.

prescription, *n.* **1** prescrizione. **2** (*leg.*) prescrizione. **3** (*leg.*) prescrizione acquisitiva, usucapione. **4** (*market.*) fissazione (*di prezzi*).

presell, *v. t.* (*pass.* e *part. pass.* **presold**) (*market., pubbl.*) precondizionare (*merce o clienti*) alla vendita.

presence, *n.* presenza.

present[1], *a.* presente, corrente. *n.* **1** (il) presente, (il) tempo presente. **2** dono, presente, regalo. // ~ **-day** contemporaneo; ~ **discounted value** (*mat.*) valore attuale; **the ~ month** il mese corrente; ~ **value** (*mat.*) valore attuale; ~ **worth** (*mat.*) valore attuale; **at ~** al presente; **for the ~** per il momento.

present[2], *v. t.* **1** presentare, offrire. **2** consegnare. **3** donare, regalare. // to ~ **the accounts** (*rag.*) presentare i conti; to ~ **one's apologies** presentare le proprie scuse; to ~ **a bill for acceptance** (*cred.*) presentare una cambiale all'accettazione; to ~ **a cheque** (*banca*) presentare un assegno (*per l'incasso*); to ~ **a complaint** (*leg.*) presentare un reclamo.

presentation, *n.* **1** presentazione. **2** offerta. **3** consegna. **4** dono, regalo. // **a ~ copy** (*pubbl.*) una copia (*di libro, ecc.*) in omaggio; ~ **for acceptance** (*cred.*) presentazione per l'accettazione; **the ~ of a customs entry** (*dog.*) la presentazione d'una dichiarazione doganale; **on ~** su presentazione, contro presentazione.

presenter, *n.* (*cred., fin.*) presentatore.

presentment, *n.* **1** presentazione. **2** (*leg.*) dichiarazione d'una giuria. // **the ~ of a matured bill of exchange** (*cred.*) la presentazione d'una cambiale maturata.

present oneself, *v. rifl.* presentarsi. // to ~ **for trial** (*leg.*) comparire in giudizio.

preserve[1], *n.* marmellata.

preserve[2], *v. t.* (*market.*) mettere in conserva.

preserved, *a.* (*market.*) conservato in scatola.

preserving agents, *n. pl.* (*market.*) conservanti.

preside, *v. i.* presiedere, presiedere a.

presidency, *n.* **1** presidenza. **2 the Presidency** (*USA*) la Presidenza.

president, *n.* **1** presidente. **2** (*amm.*) amministratore delegato. **3** (*amm., USA*) direttore generale (*d'una società*). **4** (*banca, USA*) presidente. **5** (*USA*) Presidente (*della Confederazione*).

press[1], *n.* **1** (*giorn.*) stampa. **2** (*giorn.*) giornalismo. // ~ **-agency** (*giorn.*) agenzia di stampa, agenzia d'informazioni (*per la stampa*); ~ **-agent** (*giorn., pubbl.*) «press-agent», addetto stampa, agente pubblicitario; to ~ **-agent** (*giorn., pubbl.*) fare il «press-agent», fare l'addetto stampa, fare l'agente pubblicitario; pubblicizzare, fare il «press-agent» per (*q.*); ~ **campaign** (*giorn.*) campagna di stampa; ~ **conference** (*giorn.*) conferenza stampa; ~ **-photographer** (*giorn.*) fotoreporter; ~ **proofs** (*giorn.*) ultime bozze di stampa (*prima di andare in macchina*); ~ **releases** (*giorn.*) comunicati stampa; ~ **secretary** addetto stampa (*di un uomo politico*).

press[2], *v. t.* comprimere.

pressing, *a.* pressante, incalzante, urgente. // ~ **demand** (*econ.*) domanda pressante; ~ **expenses** (*rag.*) spese urgenti.

pressman, *n.* (*pl.* **pressmen**) (*giorn.*) giornalista.

pressure, *n.* **1** pressione, costrizione, insistenza. **2** (*econ.*) pressione. // ~ **cabin** (*trasp. aer.*) cabina pressurizzata; ~ **group** (*econ.*) gruppo di pressione; ~ **of business** affari urgenti; **the** ~ **of taxation** (*fin.*) la pressione fiscale; **under the** ~ **of competition** (*market.*) sotto lo stimolo della concorrenza.

presswoman, *n.* (*pl.* **presswomen**) (*giorn., ingl.*) giornalista.

presume, *v. t.* presumere.

presumption, *n.* **1** presunzione. **2** (*leg.*) presunzione. // ~ **of death** (*leg.*) presunzione di morte; ~ **of fact** (*leg.*) presunzione di fatto; ~ **of guilt** (*leg.*) presunzione di colpa; ~ **of innocence** (*leg.*) presunzione d'innocenza; ~ **of law** (*leg.*) presunzione legale, presunzione legittima.

presumptive, *a.* (*leg.*) presuntivo, presunto, indiziario. // ~ **evidence** (*leg.*) prove indiziarie; ~ **heir** (*leg.*) erede presuntivo, presunto erede.

pretence, *n.* finzione, simulazione.

pretend, *v. t.* fingere, simulare.

pretension, *n.* pretesa.

prêt-nom, *n.* (*leg.*) prestanome.

prevaricate, *v. t.* e *i.* (*leg.*) prevaricare, abusare del potere per trarne vantaggi personali.

prevarication, *n.* (*leg.*) prevaricazione.

prevaricator, *n.* (*leg.*) prevaricatore.

prevent, *v. t.* impedire, ostacolare. // to ~ **the gap in the balance of payments from becoming much wider** (*econ., fin.*) contenere il disavanzo della bilancia dei pagamenti.

prevention, *n.* impedimento, ostacolo.

preventive, *a.* preventivo. // ~ **attachment** (*leg.*) sequestro conservativo; ~ **auditing** (*leg.*) controllo preventivo; ~ **detention** (*leg.*) detenzione preventiva; ~ **medicine** medicina preventiva.

previous, *a.* precedente, antecedente, previo. // **the** ~ **balance** (*rag.*) il saldo precedente.

prevision, *n.* previsione.

price[1], *n.* **1** prezzo. **2** (*Borsa, fin.*) prezzo, corso. **3** (*econ., market.*) prezzo, corso. // **prices account** (*econ.*) mercuriale; ~ **adjustment** (*econ.*) movimento di prezzo; (*market.*) adattamento dei prezzi; ~ **after hours** (*Borsa*) prezzo del dopoborsa; ~ **at origin** (*market.*) prezzo all'origine; **prices bubble** (*econ., market.*) «bolla» dei prezzi (*improvviso aumento, subito dopo un periodo di congelamento*); ~ **by the job** (*market.*) prezzo a forfait; **a** ~ **-calming factor** (*market.*) un ruolo calmieratore dei prezzi; ~ **control** (*econ.*) controllo dei prezzi, calmiere; **prices current** (*econ.*) listino dei prezzi correnti, listino dei prezzi di mercato; ~ **cuttings** (*market.*) riduzioni di prezzo; ~ **differences** (*market.*) differenze nei prezzi, divari nei prezzi; ~ **-earnings ratio** (*econ.*) rapporto prezzo-utili; (*fin.*) rapporto fra gli utili (*annuali*) d'un'azione e la sua quotazione (*in un dato momento*); ~ **fall** (*market.*) crollo dei prezzi, discesa dei prezzi; ~ **-fixing** (*econ.*) fissazione dei prezzi; ~ **follower** (*econ., market.*) imitatore del prezzo, imitatrice del prezzo; **the** ~ **for current account** (*Borsa*) prezzo per la corrente liquidazione; ~ **formation** (*econ.*) formazione dei prezzi; ~ **freeze** (*econ.*) «congelamento» dei prezzi, irrigidimento dei prezzi, blocco dei prezzi; **the** ~ **front** (*fin.*) il fronte dei prezzi; **the prices in force in the Community** (*econ.*) i prezzi in vigore nella Comunità; **the** ~ **increase** (*econ.*) l'aumento dei prezzi, la dinamica dei prezzi; ~ **index** (*econ., stat.*) prezzo indice; ~ **inflation** (*econ.*) inflazione da prezzi; ~ **level** (*econ.*) livello dei prezzi, indice dei prezzi; ~ **-list** (*econ.*) listino (dei) prezzi (*d'una ditta*); ~ **maintenance** (*market.*) mantenimento (*da parte del rivenditore*) del prezzo di vendita fissato dal produttore; ~ **mechanism** (*econ.*) meccanismo dei prezzi; ~ **of issue** (*fin.*) prezzo d'emissione; **the ~ of money** (*cred., fin.*) il prezzo del denaro (*tasso d'interesse per denaro preso a prestito*); **prices on importation** (*comm. est.*) prezzi all'importazione; ~ **policy** (*econ.*) politica dei prezzi; ~ **rise** (*market.*) rialzo dei prezzi; ~ **rises** (*econ.*) dinamica dei prezzi; ~ **spiral** (*econ.*) spirale dei prezzi; ~ **stability** (*econ.*) stabilità dei prezzi; ~ **stickiness** (*econ.*) vischiosità dei prezzi; ~ **support** (*econ.*) sostegno dei prezzi; ~ **system** (*econ.*) sistema dei prezzi, regime dei prezzi; ~ **-tag** (*market.*) cartellino del prezzo; **prices to the consumer** (*econ.*) prezzi al consumo; ~ **trends** (*econ.*) andamento dei prezzi, evoluzione dei prezzi; ~ **war** (*econ.*) guerra dei prezzi (*periodo di spietata concorrenza*); **under ~** (*market.*) sottocosto.

price², *v. t.* **1** (*Borsa, fin.*) fissare il prezzo, fissare il corso di (*qc.*). **2** (*econ., market.*) fissare il prezzo, fissare il corso di (*qc.*). **3** (*market.*) segnare il prezzo su (*merce, ecc.*). // **to ~ -mark** (*market.*) segnare il prezzo (*al dettaglio*) su (*articoli, ecc.*); **to ~ oneself out of the market** (*market.*) praticare prezzi proibitivi (*escludendosi, così, dal mercato*).

pricing, *n.* **1** (*Borsa, fin.*) determinazione del prezzo. **2** (*econ., market.*) determinazione del prezzo. // **the ~ policy** (*econ.*) la politica dei prezzi.

prima facie, *locuz. avv.* a prima vista. // ~ **evidence** (*leg.*) prova incontestabile.

primage, *n.* (*trasp. mar.*) cappa, soprannolo.

primary, *a.* principale, fondamentale. // ~ **deposit** (*banca*) deposito primario; ~ **economic activities** (*econ.*) attività economiche fondamentali; ~ **evidence** (*leg.*) prova incontestabile; **the ~ factors of production** (*econ.*) i fattori produttivi primari; ~ **obligation** (*leg.*) obbligazione principale; ~ **products** (*econ.*) prodotti di base; ~ **reserve** (*banca*) riserva primaria.

prime, *a.* **1** primo, primario, principale. **2** (*market.*) di prima qualità, eccellente, ottimo. *n.* **1** (il) meglio, (la) parte migliore (*di qc.*). **2** (*mat.*) numero primo. // ~ **cost** (*rag.*) costo primo (*costo della materia prima più le spese dirette di lavorazione*); ~ **entry** (*dog.*) bolletta d'entrata; ~ **number** (*mat.*) numero primo; ~ **rate** (*fin., USA*) tasso primario; ~ **warrant** (*dog.*) «fede di deposito» provvisoria.

principal, *a.* principale. *n.* **1** (*fin., rag.*) capitale (*contrapposto a «interessi»*). **2** (*leg.*) committente, mandante, rappresentato. **3** (*leg.*) imputato principale. **4** (*org. az.*) principale, datore di lavoro, padrone, capo, direttore. // ~ **and interest** (*fin.*) capitale e interessi; ~ **costs** (*fin., rag.*) costi di capitale; ~ **creditor** (*cred.*) creditore principale; ~ **debtor** (*cred.*) debitore principale.

principle, *n.* principio, norma, regola, orientamento. // **principles of administration** (*amm.*) principi di direzione; **the principles of assessment for VAT purposes** (*fin.*) i principi di valutazione dell'IVA; **the ~ of comparative costs** (*econ.*) il principio dei costi comparati; **the ~ of good faith** (*ass., leg.*) il principio della buona fede; **the ~ of indemnity** (*ass.*) il principio dell'indennizzo; **the ~ of insurable interest** (*ass.*) il principio dell'interesse assicurabile; **principles of management** (*amm.*) principi di direzione, regole «manageriali».

print¹, *n.* **1** (*giorn.*) stampa (*il risultato*). **2** (*giorn.*) stampato. **3** (*pubbl.*) stampa, positivo. **4** **prints**, *pl.* (*giorn.*) opuscoli stampati, pubblicazioni, riviste. // **in ~** (*giorn.*) (*di libro e sim.*) stampato, in stampa, in circolazione; **out of ~** (*giorn.*) (*di libro, ecc.*) esaurito, fuori commercio, fuori stampa.

print², *v. t.* **1** scrivere in stampatello. **2** (*giorn.*) stampare, pubblicare, tirare (*copie*). **3** (*pubbl.*) stampare (*copie fotografiche*). // **to ~ banknotes** (*fin.*) stampare banconote; **to ~ the edition of a newspaper** (*giorn.*) stampare l'edizione d'un quotidiano.

printed, *a.* **1** a stampa. **2** (*giorn.*) stampato, dato alle stampe. // ~ **form** modulo a stampa; ~ **matter** (*giorn.*) stampe, stampati; ~ **publications** (*giorn.*) stampati.

printer, *n.* **1** (*elab. elettr.*) stampante. **2** (*giorn.*) stampatore, poligrafico. // ~ **'s ink** (*giorn., fig.*) (la) stampa, (il) giornalismo; ~ **'s reader** (*giorn.*) correttore di bozze; ~ **'s ream** (*giorn.*) risma (*di 516 fogli*).

printing, *a.* che stampa, stampante. *n.* **1** (*giorn.*) stampa, pubblicazione (*il procedimento*). **2** (*giorn.*) tiratura, numero di copie stampate. **3** (*pubbl.*) stampa (*fotografica: il procedimento*). // ~ **and engraving expert** (*pers.*) grafico; ~ **-machine** stampatrice; ~ **-office** (*giorn.*) stamperia; ~ **-paper** (*giorn.*) carta da stampa; ~ **plant** (*giorn.*) poligrafico (*l'impianto*); ~ **-press** (*giorn.*) stampatrice; ~ **works** (*giorn.*) stabilimento tipografico, stamperia.

priority, *n.* priorità, precedenza. // ~ **objectives** obiettivi prioritari; **a ~ of claim** (*leg.*) una priorità di diritto; **the ~ of an invention** (*leg.*) la priorità d'un'invenzione.

prison, *n.* carcere.

prisoner, *n.* (*leg.*) carcerato, detenuto.

private, *a.* privato, personale, particolare. // ~ **act** (*leg.*) scrittura privata; ~ **address** indirizzo privato; **a ~ arrangement** (*leg.*) una composizione amichevole; **a ~ bank** (*fin.*) una banca privata; **the ~ banking system** (*fin.*) il sistema bancario privato; ~ **carrier** (*trasp.*) vettore privato; **a ~ citizen** (*leg.*) un privato; ~ **company** (*fin., ingl.*) *V.* ~ **limited company;** ~ **consumer expenditure** (*econ., stat.*) il consumo privato; ~ **consumer goods** (*econ., stat.*) beni destinati al consumo privato; ~ **consumption** (*econ., stat.*) consumo privato; ~ **contract** (*leg.*) scrittura privata; ~ **corporation** (*fin.*) società privata; (*USA*) *V.* ~ **limited company;** ~ **corporations** (*fin.*) grandi operatori privati; ~ **finance holding company** (*fin.*) holding finanziaria privata; **a ~ individual** (*leg.*) una persona fisica; ~ **law** (*leg.*) diritto privato; ~ **limited company** (*fin., ingl.*) società per azioni a costituzione simultanea (*e con un numero massimo di 50 soci*); ~ **placement** (*fin.*) collocazione privata (*di titoli, ecc.*); ~ **practice** libera professione; ~ **property** (*leg.*) proprietà privata; ~ **savings** (*banca, fin.*) risparmio privato; ~ **secretary** (*pers.*) segretario particolare, segretario privato; **the ~ sector** (*econ.*) il settore privato; ~ **treaty** trattativa privata; ~ **wrong** (*leg.*) illecito privato; **under ~ seal** (*leg.*) sotto sigillo privato.

privilege[1], *n.* (*anche leg.*) privilegio, prerogativa.

privilege[2], *v. t.* (*anche leg.*) privilegiare, accordare un privilegio a (*q.*).

privileged, *a.* (*anche leg.*) privilegiato. // **the ~ classes** (*econ.*) le classi privilegiate; ~ **communication** (*leg.*) notizia (*strettamente*) confidenziale; ~ **debt** (*cred.*) credito privilegiato.

prize, *n.* premio. // ~ **bond** (*fin.*) obbligazione a premio; **a ~ contest** (*giorn., pubbl.*) un concorso a premi.

pro-[1], *pref.* **1** pro-, filo-, in favore di, favorevole a. **2** che fa le veci di, facente funzione di. // ~ **-consul** proconsole; **a ~ -Soviet policy** una politica filosovietica; ~ **-treasurer** facente funzione di cassiere.

pro[2], *avv.* pro, in modo favorevole, in favore. *prep.* pro, in favore di. *a. attr.* favorevole. *n.* **1** pro, ragione in favore di (*qc.*). **2** chi è favorevole, chi vota a favore. // ~ **and con** pro e contro; (il) pro e (il) contro: **the pros and cons of a certain market policy** (*market.*) i pro e i contro d'una certa politica di mercato; to ~ **-and-con** discutere (*qc.*); ~ **forma** «pro forma»; **a ~ forma financial statement** (*fin.*) una relazione finanziaria «pro forma»; ~ **forma invoice** (*market.*) fattura «pro forma», fattura simulata; ~ **rata** «pro rata», in proporzione; ~ **rata freight** (*trasp. mar.*) nolo «pro rata»; ~ **tempore** «pro tempore», temporaneamente; interino; ~ **tempore office** (*amm.*) interinato.

probability, *n.* (*mat.*) probabilità.

probate[1], *n.* (*leg.*) copia autenticata (*di testamento*). // ~ **duty** (*fin., ingl.*) tassa di successione.

probate[2], *v. t.* (*leg.*) autenticare (*un testamento*).

probation, *n.* **1** (*leg.*) condizionale, sospensione condizionale (*della pena*); condanna condizionale, libertà vigilata. **2** (*pers.*) periodo di prova, tirocinio. // ~ **year** (*pers.*) anno di (*o* in) prova (*per es., di un insegnante*); **on ~** (*leg.*) in libertà vigilata; (*pers.*) in prova; **an officer on ~** (*pers.*) un funzionario in prova.

probationary, *a.* **1** (*pers.*) di tirocinio. **2** (*pers.*) in prova. // ~ **appointment** (*pers.*) nomina soggetta a un periodo di prova; ~ **employees** (*pers.*) impiegati in prova; ~ **period** (*pers.*) periodo di prova; ~ **salary** (*pers.*) stipendio del periodo di prova.

probatory, *a.* (*leg.*) probatorio. // ~ **evidence** (*leg.*) testimonianza probatoria.

problem, *n.* problema. // **problems of adjustment** (*org. az.*) problemi d'adeguamento; **the ~ of plant capacity utilization** (*org. az.*) il problema dei margini d'utilizzazione degli impianti; **problems of quotas** (*econ.*) problemi di contingentamento; **problems of a technical nature** (*org. az.*) problemi d'ordine tecnico.

procedural, *a.* (*leg.*) procedurale. // ~ **details** (*leg.*) dettagli procedurali.

procedure, *n.* **1** procedimento. **2** (*leg.*) procedura.

proceed, *v. i.* **1** procedere, andare avanti, avanzare. **2** (*leg.*) procedere, agire, condurre un'azione legale.

proceeding, *n.* **1** procedimento, modo d'agire, condotta, azione. **2 proceedings,** *pl.* (*amm.*) atti (*d'un congresso, ecc.*); verbali (*di un'assemblea, ecc.*). **3 proceedings,** *pl.* (*leg.*) procedimento, azione giudiziaria, processo. **4 proceedings,** *pl.* (*leg.*) procedura. // **proceedings at law** (*leg.*) procedura legale; **proceedings in bankruptcy** (*leg.*) procedura fallimentare.

proceeds, *n. pl.* 1 (*banca*) somma incassata (*per un assegno e sim.*) al netto di sconti (*o provvigioni, ecc.*). 2 (*fin.*) gettito. 3 (*rag.*) incassi, introiti, proventi, profitto, ricavato, ricavo. // «~ **of bills collected for your account**» (*banca*) «ricavo (dei) vostri effetti all'incasso»; **the ~ of loans in 1984** (*fin.*) il gettito dei prestiti nel 1984; «~ **of our remittance for collection**» (*banca*) «ricavo della nostra rimessa (di) effetti all'incasso»; ~ **of sales** (*market.*) fatturato.

process[1], *n.* 1 (*leg.*) azione legale, procedimento legale. 2 (*leg.*) mandato di comparizione. 3 (*org. az.*) processo (*produttivo*); metodo, sistema (*di lavorazione*). // ~ **analysis** (*org. az.*) analisi del processo produttivo, studio della produzione; ~ **average quality** (*org. az.*) qualità media della produzione; ~ **cost** (*rag.*) costo di produzione; ~ **rules** (*org. az.*) norme di lavorazione; ~ **-server** (*leg.*) ufficiale giudiziario (*cui compete la notifica di citazione al «convenuto»*); ~ **standards** (*org. az.*) norme di lavorazione; **in ~ of construction** (*org. az.*) in costruzione.

process[2], *v. t.* 1 (*leg.*) citare (*q.*) in giudizio. 2 (*org. az.*) sottoporre (*una materia prima, ecc.*) a un processo; lavorare (*materie prime, ecc.*); trasformare. 3 (*pubbl.*) trattare (*una pellicola*).

processed commodities, *n. pl.* (*org. az.*) prodotti trasformati.

processing, *n.* 1 (*econ.*) industria di trasformazione. 2 (*elab. elettr.*) elaborazione. 3 (*org. az.*) lavorazione, trattamento, trasformazione. 4 (*org. az.*) sistema di lavorazione. 5 (*pubbl.*) trattamento (*d'una pellicola*). // ~ **industries** (*econ.*) industrie trasformative; **the ~ industry** (*econ.*) l'industria di trasformazione; ~ **techniques** (*org. az.*) metodi di lavorazione.

proclaim, *v. t.* bandire, indire (*un concorso e sim.*).

procuration, *n.* 1 il procurare. 2 (*cred.*) procacciamento (*di prestiti a favore di terzi*). 3 (*leg.*) «procura» (*l'autorità conferita*). 4 (*leg.*) procura (*documento — più formale della lettera di procura — che ne conferisce l'autorità*). // ~ **fee** (*cred.*) mediazione pagata per aver ottenuto un prestito; ~ **money** (*cred.*) *V.* ~ **fee.**

procure, *v. t.* 1 procacciare, procacciarsi, reperire. 2 (*org. az.*) approvvigionarsi di (*materie prime, ecc.*).

procurement, *n.* 1 procacciamento, reperimento. 2 (*org. az.*) approvvigionamento (*di materie prime, ecc.*). // **the ~ of a loan** (*cred.*) il conseguimento d'un prestito.

produce[1], *n.* (*econ.*) prodotto (*specialm. agricolo o minerario*); produzione (*specialm. agricola o mineraria*); prodotti agricoli. // ~ **-broker** (*fin.*) mediatore di prodotti; ~ **exchange** (*fin.*) borsa merci; **the ~ market** (*econ.*) il mercato dei prodotti (*specialm. agricoli*); ~ **not intended for export** (*econ.*) prodotti non destinati all'esportazione; «~ **of China**» (*market.*) «prodotto in Cina».

produce[2], *v. t.* 1 (*econ.*) produrre. 2 (*leg.*) produrre, presentare, esibire. // to ~ **a document** (*leg.*) esibire un documento; to ~ **evidence** (*leg.*) presentare prove; to ~ **for export** (*econ.*) produrre per l'esportazione; to ~ **witnesses** (*leg.*) produrre testimoni.

producer, *n.* 1 (*econ.*) produttore. 2 (*econ.*) Paese produttore. // ~ **coefficient** (*econ.*) coefficiente di produzione; ~ **co-operative** (*econ.*) cooperativa di produzione; ~ **Country** (*econ.*) Paese produttore; ~ **goods** (*econ.*) beni capitali; **producers goods** (*econ.*) beni strumentali; ~ **'s surplus** (*econ.*) rendita del produttore; **from the ~ to the consumer** (*market.*) dal produttore al consumatore.

product, *n.* 1 prodotto, risultato. 2 (*econ., market.*) prodotto. 3 (*mat.*) prodotto. // ~ **development** (*market.*) sviluppo del prodotto; ~ **diversification** (*org. az.*) diversificazione produttiva; ~ **image** (*pubbl.*) immagine del prodotto; ~ **line** (*org. az.*) linea di prodotti, assortimento di articoli (*d'un'azienda*); ~ **manager** (*market., org. az.*) direttore di prodotto; ~ **sector** (*econ.*) settore economico; ~ **simplification** (*org. az.*) semplificazione produttiva; ~ **tests** (*org. az.*) prove sul prodotto; **by-** ~ (*org. az.*) sottoprodotto.

production, *n.* 1 (*econ.*) produzione. 2 (*leg.*) produzione (*di prove, ecc.*); esibizione (*di documenti, ecc.*). 3 (*org. az.*) produzione. // ~ **bonus** (*pers.*) gratifica di bilancio, premio di produzione; ~ **control** (*org. az.*) pianificazione produttiva; ~ **cost** (*rag.*) costo di produzione; ~ **cycle** (*org. az.*) ciclo produttivo; ~ **for stock** (*org. az.*) produzione per il magazzino; ~ **function** (*econ.*) funzione della produzione; ~ **goods** (*econ.*) beni strumentali; ~ **increase** (*econ.*) aumento della produzione; ~ **machinery** (*econ., org. az.*) apparato produttivo; ~ **management** (*org. az.*) organizzazione della produzione; (*org. az.*) direttore della produzione; **the ~ of documents for the prosecution** (*leg.*) l'esibizione di documenti per l'accusa; **the ~ of a witness** (*leg.*) la produzione d'un testimone; ~ **optimum** (*econ.*) «optimum» produttivo; ~ **recovery** (*econ.*) ripresa produttiva; ~ **run** (*org. az.*) fase di fabbricazione; ~

standard (*org. az.*) standard produttivo; ~ **subsidies** (*econ.*) sovvenzioni alla produzione; ~ **targets** (*econ.*) obiettivi di produzione; ~ **unit** (*org. az.*) unità produttiva; ~ **volume** (*org. az.*) volume produttivo.

productive, *a.* (*econ.*) produttivo. // ~ **cycle** (*org. az.*) ciclo produttivo; ~ **investments** (*fin.*) investimenti produttivi; ~ **labour** (*econ.*) lavoro produttivo; (*pers.*) manodopera diretta; ~ **sector** (*econ.*) settore produttivo; ~ **soil** (*econ.*) terreno produttivo.

productivity, *n.* (*econ.*) produttività. // ~ **measurement** (*org. az.*) misura della produttività.

profert, *n.* (*leg.*) presentazione d'un atto (*o* di un documento, *ecc.*) in tribunale.

profession, *n.* **1** professione, mestiere. **2 the profession** i membri d'una professione. **3 professions,** *pl.* libere professioni. // **the ~ of a lawyer** la professione d'avvocato; **by ~** di professione, di mestiere.

professional, *a.* **1** professionale, di (una) professione, di (un) mestiere. **2** professionistico, professionista. *n.* professionista. // ~ **earnings** (*fin.*) redditi professionali; **a ~ man** un professionista, un libero professionista; ~ **rights** (*leg.*) diritti professionali; ~ **training** (*pers.*) addestramento professionale, istruzione professionale.

proficiency test, *n.* (*pers.*) test di rendimento.

profit[1]**,** *n.* **1** profitto, beneficio. **2** (*econ., fin., rag.*) profitto, guadagno, lucro, utile, reddito. // ~ **and loss** (*rag.*) conto profitti e perdite; ~ **and loss account** (*rag.*) conto economico; ~ **and loss statement** (*rag.*) conto profitti e perdite; ~ **deflation** (*econ.*) deflazione da profitti; ~ **index** (*econ.*) indice di profitto; ~ **-induced inflation** (*econ.*) inflazione indotta dai profitti; ~ **inflation** (*econ.*) inflazione da profitti; ~ **-making** proficuo, lucrativo; ~ **margins** (*econ.*) margini degli utili; ~ **maximation** (*econ.*) massimizzazione dei profitti; **the ~ on sales** (*rag.*) l'utile sulle vendite; ~ **push** (*econ.*) spinta dei profitti; ~ **-push inflation** (*econ.*) inflazione da profitti; ~ **seeking** (*econ.*) ricerca del profitto; ~ **-sharing** (*fin.*) *a.* che partecipa agli utili, cointeressato; *n.* compartecipazione agli utili, cointeressenza, interessenza; ~ **squeeze** (*econ.*) riduzione degli utili; ~ **system** (*econ.*) libertà economica, libera iniziativa; **non- ~** che non ha fini di lucro; **non- ~ corporation** (*fin., USA*) ente morale che non può esercitare attività commerciali con fini di lucro.

profit[2]**,** *v. i.* approfittare (*di q.*); trarre profitto (*da qc.*).

profitability, *n.* (*econ., fin., rag.*) redditività, profitto. // ~ **index** (*econ.*) indice di profitto.

profitable, *a.* **1** vantaggioso, utile. **2** (*econ., fin., rag.*) lucrativo, lucroso, rimunerativo, redditizio.

profiteer[1]**,** *n.* (*econ.*) affarista.

profiteer[2]**,** *v. i.* (*econ.*) fare guadagni esorbitanti.

program[1]**,** *n.* (*USA*) *V.* **programme**[1]**.**

program[2]**,** *v. t.* (*USA*) *V.* **programme**[2]**.**

programmatic, *a.* programmatico.

programme[1]**,** *n.* programma, progetto, piano. // **a ~ of budgetary austerity** (*amm.*) un programma d'austerità di bilancio.

programme[2]**,** *v. t.* programmare, mettere in programma, progettare, pianificare.

programmed, *a.* programmato, progettato, pianificato. // ~ **check** (*elab. elettr.*) controllo programmato; ~ **instruction** istruzione programmata.

progress[1]**,** *n.* **1** (il) progredire, (il) procedere; avanzamento. **2** (*econ.*) tendenza ascensoriale. // ~ **chart** (*org. az.*) grafico d'avanzamento; ~ **clerk** (*org. az.*) controllore dell'avanzamento (*d'un processo produttivo*); **in ~** in via d'esecuzione, in corso.

progress[2]**,** *v. i.* far progressi, procedere, avanzare.

progression, *n.* (il) progredire, (il) procedere; avanzamento.

progressive, *a.* progressivo. // ~ **tax** (*fin.*) imposta progressiva.

prohibit, *v. t.* **1** proibire, impedire, vietare. **2** (*leg.*) vietare.

prohibited, *a.* impedito. // ~ **agreements** (*leg.*) accordi vietati.

prohibition, *n.* **1** proibizione, divieto. **2** (*leg.*) divieto.

prohibitive, *a.* proibitivo. // ~ **tariffs** (*comm., econ.*) tariffe proibitive.

project[1]**,** *n.* progetto, programma, piano.

project[2]**,** *v. t.* progettare, programmare, pianificare.

projection, *n.* progettazione, il progettare.

projective test, *n.* (*pers.*) test proiettivo.

prolong, *v. t.* prolungare. // **to ~ a bill** (*cred.*) prorogare la scadenza d'una cambiale.

prolonged, *a.* prolungato.

prominence, *n.* **1** prominenza. **2** (*fig.*) importanza.

promise[1]**,** *n.* promessa. // **a ~ to pay** (*cred.*) una promessa di pagamento; **a ~ to sell**

(*market.*) un preliminare di vendita.

promise[2], *v. t.* e *i.* promettere, fare una promessa.

promisee, *n.* (*leg.*) chi riceve una promessa.

promisor, *n.* (*leg.*) chi fa una promessa.

promissory, *a.* che ha il carattere d'una promessa. // ~ **note** (*cred.*) pagherò (*cambiario*), vaglia cambiario.

promo, *a.* (*abbr. fam. di* **promotional**) (*pubbl.*) promozionale.

promote, *v. t.* 1 promuovere, favorire, far progredire. 2 (*fin.*) promuovere (*una società, ecc.*). 3 (*market., pubbl.*) promuovere la vendita di (*prodotti, ecc.*). 4 (*pers.*) promuovere, far avanzare (*nella carriera*). // to ~ **an article** (*market., pubbl.*) promuovere la vendita d'un articolo; to ~ **a new company** (*fin.*) farsi promotore di una nuova società; to ~ **sales** (*market., pubbl.*) promuovere le vendite.

promoter, *n.* 1 promotore, fautore, iniziatore. 2 (*fin.*) fondatore (*d'una società*).

promotion, *n.* 1 promozione, (il) favorire, (l')incoraggiare, (il) promuovere. 2 (*fin.*) fondazione (*d'una società*). 3 (*market., pubbl.*) «promotion», promozione, sviluppo. 4 (*pers.*) promozione, avanzamento. // ~ **exams** (*pers.*) esami di promozione; ~ **in order of age** (*pers.*) promozione per anzianità.

promotional, *a.* 1 (*market., pubbl.*) promozionale, relativo alla promozione delle vendite. 2 (*pers.*) di promozione, d'avanzamento. // ~ **activities** (*market., pubbl.*) attività promozionali; ~ **campaign** (*market., pubbl.*) campagna promozionale; ~ **possibilities** (*pers.*) prospettive d'avanzamento; ~ **sale** (*market., pubbl.*) vendita di propaganda.

prompt, *a.* 1 pronto, sollecito. 2 (*comm.*) immediato. *n.* (*comm.*) termine di tempo per il saldo (*d'un pagamento*). // ~ **cash** (*market.*) pronta cassa; ~ **day** (*comm.*) giorno in cui si saldano i conti; **the ~ delivery of goods** (*market.*) la consegna immediata di merci; ~ **goods** (*market.*) merci pronte (*per la consegna*); ~ **note** (*market.*) promemoria di pagamento (*rilasciato da un venditore al cliente, e contenente l'indicazione dell'ammontare del debito e la scadenza del medesimo*); ~ **payment** (*cred.*) pagamento immediato; **for ~ cash** (*market.*) a pronta cassa, in contanti.

promptly, *avv.* sollecitamente.

promptness, *n.* prontezza.

pronounce, *v. t.* 1 (*leg.*) dichiarare. 2 (*leg.*) emettere (*una sentenza*). // to ~ **the meeting adjourned** (*leg.*) dichiarare il rinvio della seduta.

proof, *n.* 1 prova, dimostrazione, verifica. 2 (*giorn.*) bozza. 3 (*leg.*) prova. 4 (*mat.*) prova. // ~ **correcting** (*giorn.*) correzione di bozze; ~ **of debts** (*leg.*) verifica dei crediti (*nella procedura fallimentare*); ~ **of loss** (*ass.*) pezza giustificativa di perdita (*subita*); ~ **of ownership** (*leg.*) titolo giustificativo di proprietà; ~ **-pulling** (*giorn.*) tiratura delle bozze; ~ **reader** (*giorn.*) revisore; ~ **-sheet** (*giorn.*) bozza di prova.

propaganda, *n.* (*pubbl.*) propaganda.

propagandist, *n.* (*pers.*) propagandista.

propagandize, *v. t.* (*pubbl.*) propagandare.

propagate, *v. i.* propagarsi.

propensity, *n.* propensione, inclinazione, tendenza. // ~ **to consume** (*econ.*) propensione al consumo; ~ **to invest** (*econ.*) propensione agli investimenti; ~ **to save** (*econ.*) propensione al risparmio.

proper, *a.* 1 proprio. 2 adatto, conveniente, giusto, pertinente. 3 decoroso, per bene. // ~ **behaviour** comportamento decoroso; ~ **fraction** (*mat.*) frazione propria; **the ~ tool for a job** lo strumento adatto per un lavoro; to **do st. the ~ way** fare qc. come si deve.

property, *n.* 1 proprietà, patrimonio, tenuta, avere, beni. 2 (*leg.*) proprietà. // ~ **abroad** (*leg.*) beni all'estero; ~ **damage insurance** (*ass.*) assicurazione di responsabilità civile (*per danni causati ai beni altrui*); ~ **dividend** (*fin.*) dividendo in beni; ~ **-increment tax** (*fin.*) imposta sull'incremento di valore dei beni immobili; ~ **right** (*leg.*) diritto di proprietà; ~ **speculator** speculatore edile (*p. es., palazzinaro, ecc.*); ~ **tax** (*fin.*) imposta sul patrimonio, imposta patrimoniale, imposta di valore locativo, imposta fondiaria.

proportion[1], *n.* 1 proporzione, quota parte, quota, percentuale. 2 (*mat.*) proporzione. // **the ~ of gross to net load** (*trasp. mar.*) il coefficiente di carico.

proportion[2], *v. t.* proporzionare, dividere in parti eque. // to ~ **one's expenditure to one's income** proporzionare le spese ai redditi.

proportional, *a.* 1 proporzionale, proporzionato. 2 percentuale. 3 in proporzione (*a*). 4 (*mat.*) proporzionale. // **a ~ system of immigration quotas** (*econ.*) un sistema proporzionale di contingenti d'immigrazione; ~ **tax** (*fin.*) imposta proporzionale.

proportionality, *n.* proporzionalità.

proportionate, *a.* proporzionale, proporzionato. // ~ **tax** (*fin.*) imposta proporzionale.

proposal, *n.* proposta, offerta. // **a ~ for a compromise** (*leg.*) una proposta di transazione; **a ~ of composition** (*leg.*) proposta di concordato (*che deve essere vagliata dai creditori*); **a ~**

of insurance (*ass.*) una proposta d'assicurazione.

propose, *v. t.* proporre, offrire. // to ~ **favourable terms** proporre condizioni favorevoli.

proposition[1]**,** *n.* 1 proposta. 2 (*mat.*) problema.

proposition[2]**,** *v. t.* fare una proposta a (*q.*).

proprietary, *a.* (*leg.*) di proprietà riservata, brevettato, patentato. *n.* 1 (*leg.*) proprietario. 2 (*market.*) specialità medicinale. // ~ **articles** (*market.*) articoli in esclusiva; ~ **company** (*fin., ingl.*) società per azioni a costituzione simultanea; (*fin., USA*) società controllante; ~ **medicines** (*market.*) specialità medicinali; ~ **right of manufacture** (*leg.*) diritto di fabbricazione in esclusiva, brevetto di fabbricazione; ~ **rights** (*leg.*) diritti di proprietà riservata, brevetti.

proprietor, *n.* 1 padrone. 2 (*leg.*) proprietario, tenutario, titolare.

proprietorship, *n.* (*leg.*) proprietà, condizione di proprietario, diritto di proprietà.

proprietress, *n.* 1 padrona. 2 proprietaria, tenutaria, titolare.

prorate, *v. t.* ripartire, distribuire proporzionalmente.

prosecutable, *a.* (*leg.*) perseguibile.

prosecute, *v. t.* (*leg.*) perseguire (*a termini di legge*); far causa a, querelare. // to ~ **the charge** (*leg.*) sostenere l'accusa; to ~ **a claim** (*leg.*) far valere un diritto per vie legali; to ~ **a crime** (*leg.*) perseguire un reato; to ~ **in a civil case** (*leg.*) costituirsi parte civile.

prosecution, *n.* 1 (*leg.*) procedimento giudiziario, processo. 2 **the prosecution** (*leg.*) l'accusa.

prosecutor, *n.* 1 (*leg.*) querelante. 2 (*leg.*) accusatore.

prospect[1]**,** *n.* 1 prospettiva, previsione, aspettativa. 2 (*market.*) cliente potenziale. 3 **prospects,** *pl.* (*fin.*) prospettive finanziarie.

prospect[2]**,** *v. t.* (*econ.*) fare ricerche minerarie in (*una regione, ecc.*). // to ~ **for gold** (*econ.*) andare alla ricerca dell'oro.

prospective, *a.* eventuale, sperato. // **a ~ client** (*market.*) un cliente potenziale; ~ **customers** (*market.*) clientela potenziale.

prospectus, *n.* (*fin.*) programma (*d'una nuova società*); documento che descrive i dettagli d'una nuova emissione (*di titoli*).

protect, *v. t.* 1 proteggere, difendere, tutelare. 2 (*fig.*) sostenere. 3 (*cred.*) far fronte a (*una cambiale, ecc.*); preparare i fondi per il pagamento di (*una tratta, ecc.*). // to ~ **a bill** (*cred.*) curare il pagamento d'una cambiale; to ~ **one's interest** tutelare i propri interessi.

protection, *n.* 1 protezione, difesa, tutela. 2 (*fig.*) sostegno. 3 (*econ.*) protezionismo.

protectionism, *n.* (*econ.*) protezionismo.

protectionist, *n.* (*econ.*) protezionista. *a. attr.* (*econ.*) protezionista, protezionistico. // ~ **barriers** (*econ.*) barriere protezionistiche; ~ **measures** (*econ.*) misure protezionistiche; ~ **pressures** (*econ.*) pressioni protezionistiche; ~ **trends** (*econ.*) tendenze protezionistiche.

protective, *a.* 1 protettivo. 2 (*econ.*) protezionistico. // ~ **duties** (*dog.*) dazi protettivi; ~ **policy** (*econ.*) politica protezionistica; ~ **system** (*econ.*) sistema protezionistico; ~ **tariffs** (*econ.*) tariffe protezionistiche.

protest[1]**,** *n.* 1 protesta. 2 (*leg.*) protesto, protesto cambiario. // ~ **charges** (*leg.*) spese di protesto; ~ **for non-acceptance** (*leg.*) protesto per mancata accettazione; ~ **for non-payment** (*leg.*) protesto per mancato pagamento; «**supra** ~» (*leg.*) «per intervento».

protest[2]**,** *v. t.* e *i.* 1 protestare. 2 (*leg.*) protestare (*una cambiale*). // to **be protested** (*cred., fin.: di un effetto*) andare in protesto.

protester, *n.* 1 chi protesta. 2 (*leg.*) creditore che fa eseguire il protesto.

protestor, *n. V.* **protester.**

protocol, *n.* (*leg.*) protocollo.

protocolar, *a.* (*leg.*) protocollare.

protocolary, *a. V.* **protocolar.**

prove, *v. t.* 1 provare, dimostrare, verificare. 2 (*leg.*) provare, dimostrare l'autenticità di (*qc.*). // to ~ **by documents** (*leg.*) documentare; to ~ **by witnesses** (*leg.*) provare per mezzo di testi; to ~ **a debt in a bankruptcy** (*leg.*) insinuare un credito in un fallimento; to ~ **a loss** (*ass.*) fornire le prove d'un sinistro; to ~ **the value of the thing insured** (*ass.*) provare il valore della cosa assicurata.

proved credit, *n.* (*leg.*) credito verificato (*e ammesso al passivo d'un fallimento*).

proven, *a.* (*leg.*) provato. // **to be found not** ~ (*leg.*) essere assolto per insufficienza di prove (*in Scozia*).

provide, *v. i.* 1 provvedere, procacciare, fornire, munire. 2 (*leg.*) (*di contratto, legge, ecc.*) prevedere, disporre, stipulare, stabilire, contemplare. // to ~ **against** premunirsi contro, prepararsi a, prendere provvedimenti in vista di; to ~ **against a fall** (*Borsa*) prepararsi a un ribasso; to ~ **against a rise** (*Borsa*) prepararsi a un rialzo; to ~ **the basic materials for industry** provvedere le materie prime per l'industria; to ~ **a bill with acceptance** (*cred.*) curare l'accettazione di una cambiale; **unless otherwise provided** (*leg.*) salvo convenzione contraria.

provident, *a.* prudente. // ~ **funds** (*fin.*) fondi di previdenza.

province, *n.* **1** distretto, regione. **2** (*fig.*) campo, competenza.

provision[1], *n.* **1** provvedimento, misura. **2** provvista. **3** (*leg.*) disposizione, disposto, convenzione, condizione, stipulazione, norma, clausola. **4 provisions,** *pl.* disposizioni, disposto. // ~ **account for bad debts** (*rag.*) fondo svalutazione crediti; ~ **account for depreciation** (*rag.*) fondo svalutazione (*merci, titoli, ecc.*); ~ **account for income taxes** (*rag.*) fondo imposte da liquidare; ~ **accounts** (*rag.*) fondi rischi; **the provisions of the articles of association** (*fin.*) le norme statutarie; **the ~ of capital** (*fin.*) la provvista di fondi; **the provisions of a contract** (*leg.*) le norme contrattuali.

provision[2], *v. t.* approvvigionare. // to ~ **a ship** (*trasp. mar.*) approvvigionare una nave.

provisional, *a.* provvisorio. // ~ **accounts** (*rag.*) conti provvisori; ~ **appointment** (*amm., pers.*) nomina provvisoria; ~ **arrest** (*leg.*) fermo (di polizia); ~ **certificate** (*Borsa, fin.*) certificato provvisorio (*di titoli*); **a ~ contract** (*leg.*) un contratto provvisorio; ~ **detention** (*leg.*) fermo (di polizia); ~ **insurance** (*ass.*) assicurazione provvisoria; ~ **invoice** (*market.*) fattura provvisoria.

provisionary, *a.* *V.* **provisional.**

provisions, *n. pl.* (*market.*) provviste.

proviso, *n.* (*pl.* **provisoes** e *reg.*) (*leg.*) condizione, clausola condizionale.

provisory, *a.* **1** (*leg.*) condizionale. **2** (*leg.*) soggetto a una clausola condizionale.

proximate, *a.* prossimo. // **the ~ cause** (*leg.*) la causa immediata.

proximity, *n.* prossimità, vicinanza.

proximo, *a.* (*abbr.* **prox.**) (*comm.*) prossimo, prossimo venturo, del mese venturo.

proxy, *n.* **1** (*fin.*) procura, delega (*concessa da un azionista a una terza persona perché voti in sua vece*). **2** (*leg.*) procura, delega. **3** (*leg.*) procuratore, mandatario. // **by ~** (*leg.*) per procura.

prudent, *a.* avveduto. // ~ **man** (*leg.*) buon padre di famiglia.

public, *a.* pubblico. *n.* (*market., pubbl.*) pubblico, clientela. // ~ **accountant** (*rag.*) ragioniere professionista; ~ **acquisition offer** (*Borsa, fin.*) offerta pubblica d'acquisto; ~ **assistance** (*leg.*) assistenza pubblica; ~ **body** (*leg.*) ente pubblico; ~ **-controlled financial institutes** (*econ.*) società finanziarie a controllo pubblico; ~ **corporation** (*fin.*) impresa pubblica, azienda a partecipazione statale; **the ~ debt** (*fin.*) il debito pubblico; ~ **defender** (*leg.*) difensore d'ufficio; **the ~ domain** (*leg.*) le proprietà demaniali, i beni demaniali, il (pubblico) demanio; ~ **employment office** (*sind., USA*) ufficio (di) collocamento; ~ **expenditure policy** (*fin.*) politica della spesa pubblica; ~ **expenditures** (*amm., fin.*) spese pubbliche; ~ **finance** (*fin.*) finanza pubblica; ~ **funds** (*fin.*) fondi pubblici; ~ **hearing** (*leg.*) udienza pubblica; ~ **holiday** (*leg.*) festa nazionale; **the ~ image** (*pubbl.*) l'immagine aziendale; ~ **law** (*leg.*) diritto pubblico; ~ **limited company** (*fin.*) società per azioni costituita tramite pubblica sottoscrizione; ~ **opinion** l'opinione pubblica; ~ **-opinion poll** (*market., pubbl.*) sondaggio della pubblica opinione; ~ **prosecution** (*leg.*) pubblica accusa; ~ **purchase offer** (*Borsa, fin.*) offerta pubblica d'acquisto; ~ **-relations man** (*pubbl.*) esperto in pubbliche relazioni; ~ **revenue** (*fin.*) entrate pubbliche, erario, fisco; **the ~ sector** (*econ.*) il settore pubblico; ~ **-service corporation** (*leg., USA*) azienda di servizi pubblici; ~ **services** (*econ.*) settore pubblico; ~ **statute** (*leg.*) norma di diritto pubblico; ~ **-supply contracts** (*econ.*) appalti pubblici di forniture; ~ **telephone** (*comun.*) telefono pubblico; ~ **utility** (*amm.*) azienda di servizi pubblici; ~ **utility service** (*econ.*) servizio pubblico; ~ **waters** (*leg.*) acque pubbliche; ~ **works** (*amm., leg.*) lavori pubblici, opere pubbliche; ~ **-works contracts** (*econ.*) pubblici appalti.

publication, *n.* **1** pubblicazione. **2** (*giorn.*) pubblicazione. // ~ **date** (*giorn.*) data di pubblicazione.

publicist, *n.* **1** (*giorn.*) pubblicista, giornalista. **2** (*leg.*) pubblicista, esperto di diritto pubblico (*o* internazionale).

publicity, *n.* (*pubbl.*) pubblicità, propaganda. // ~ **campaign** (*pubbl.*) campagna pubblicitaria; **a ~ stunt** (*pubbl.*) una montatura pubblicitaria.

publicize, *v. t.* (*giorn., pubbl.*) pubblicizzare; dare pubblicità, fare pubblicità a (*qc.*).

publicly, *avv.* pubblicamente.

publish, *v. t.* (*giorn., pubbl.*) pubblicare, stampare. // to **be published** (*giorn., pubbl.*) essere pubblicato, «venir fuori».

publisher, *n.* (*giorn., pubbl.*) editore, casa editrice.

publishing, *n.* (*econ.*) editoria. // ~ **house** (*giorn., pubbl.*) casa editrice.

pull[1], *n.* (*pubbl.*) capacità di attirare il

pubblico, richiamo. // ~ **force** (*econ.*) forza d'attrazione.

pull², *v. t.* 1 tirare. 2 (*giorn.*) stampare. // to ~ **down** tirare giù; (*fin., market.*) far crollare (*prezzi, quotazioni e sim.*); to ~ **in** (*trasp. ferr.*) (*di treno*) entrare in stazione; to ~ **out** estrarre; to ~ **up** (*trasp. aut.: d'autoveicolo*) fermarsi.

punch¹, *n.* (*macch. uff.*) punzonatrice.

punch², *v. t.* 1 punzonare, forare. 2 (*elab. elettr.*) perforare. // to ~ **in** (*pers.*) timbrare il cartellino di presenza (*nell'apposita macchina*) all'inizio del lavoro; to ~ **out** (*pers.*) timbrare il cartellino di presenza (*nell'apposita macchina*) alla cessazione del lavoro.

punched, *a.* punzonato, forato. // ~ **card** (*elab. elettr.*) scheda perforata; ~ **form** modulo perforato.

punching, *n.* 1 punzonatura. 2 (*elab. elettr.*) perforazione.

punishment, *n.* pena.

punitive, *a.* punitivo. // ~ **measures** (*leg.*) misure punitive; ~ **taxes** (*fin.*) imposte severe.

pupil, *n.* (*leg., scozz.*) minorenne.

purchasable, *a.* (*market.*) acquistabile.

purchase¹, *n.* 1 (*market.*) acquisto, compera, compra. 2 (*org. az.*) approvvigionamento. // **purchases account** (*rag.*) conto acquisti; ~ **book** (*rag.*) libro acquisti; ~ **confirmation** (*Borsa, fin.*) fissato bollato; ~ **contract** (*market.*) contratto d'acquisto; ~ **department** (*org. az.*) servizio acquisti; ~ **for the account** (*Borsa*) acquisto a termine; ~ **for cash** (*market.*) acquisto (con pagamento) in contanti; ~ **for money** (*market.*) acquisto (con pagamento) in contanti; ~ **for the settlement** (*Borsa*) acquisto a termine; ~ **invoice** (*market.*) fattura d'acquisto; ~ **journal** (*rag.*) giornale acquisti; ~ **money** (*market.*) prezzo d'acquisto (*specialm. d'immobili*); **the** ~ **of shares** (*fin.*) l'acquisto d'azioni; ~ **on credit** (*market.*) acquisto (*o* compera) a credito; ~ **on term** (*market.*) acquisto (*o* compera) a scadenza; ~ **order** (*fin., market.*) ordine d'acquisto; ~ **price** (*market.*) prezzo d'acquisto; ~ **returns and allowances** (*rag.*) resi e abbuoni sugli acquisti; ~ **tax** (*fin., ingl.*) imposta generale sull'entrata (*ora sostituita dalla «value added tax», q.V.*).

purchase², *v. t.* (*market.*) acquistare, comprare, comperare. // to ~ **merchandise (real estate, etc.)** acquistare merce (beni immobili, ecc.).

purchaser, *n.* (*market.*) acquirente, compratore, committente.

purchasing, *a.* 1 acquirente, che acquista, che compra. 2 di acquisto, relativo ad acquisti. // ~ **agent** (*market.*) commissionario; (*pers.*) responsabile degli acquisti; ~ **bureau** (*org. az.*) ufficio acquisti; ~ **conditions and terms of sale and delivery** (*market.*) condizioni di vendita e di consegna; ~ **department** (*org. az.*) ufficio acquisti; ~ **manager** (*pers.*) responsabile degli acquisti; ~ **office** (*org. az.*) ufficio acquisti; **the** ~ **party** (*leg.*) la parte acquirente; ~ **period** (*org. az.*) periodo d'approvvigionamenti; ~ **power** (*econ.*) potere d'acquisto; ~ **power parity** (*econ.*) parità del potere d'acquisto (*di due monete*).

pure, *a.* puro. // ~ **competition** (*econ.*) concorrenza pura; ~ **endowment insurance** (*ass.*) assicurazione «in caso di vita»; ~ **premium** (*ass.*) premio netto.

purser, *n.* (*trasp. mar.*) commissario di bordo.

pursuance, *n.* 1 ricerca. 2 adempimento, esecuzione. // **the** ~ **of truth** (*leg.*) la ricerca della verità; **the** ~ **of your orders** l'esecuzione delle vostre ordinazioni; **in** ~ **of** (*leg.*) in esecuzione di, in applicazione di, conformemente a.

pursuant, *a.* che segue, che consegue. // ~ **to** facendo seguito a, aderendo a, in conformità con; (*leg.*) ai sensi di.

pursue, *v. t.* perseguire, andare in cerca di, cercare, ricercare.

pursuit, *n.* ricerca, perseguimento. // **the** ~ **of profit** (*econ.*) la ricerca del profitto.

purview, *n.* (*leg.*) portata, testo (*d'una legge*).

push¹, *n.* 1 (*anche fig.*) spinta. 2 (*pubbl.*) sostenuta campagna di promozione delle vendite (*d'un articolo, ecc.*). // ~ **force** (*econ.*) forza respingente; ~ **money** (*market.*) percentuale pagata (*da un fabbricante a un venditore*) per l'incentivazione delle vendite d'un prodotto.

push², *v. t.* 1 (*anche fig.*) spingere, premere. 2 (*market.*) cercare d'imporre (*un articolo, ecc.*) al pubblico. 3 (*pubbl.*) propagandare (*merce, ecc.*); fare pubblicità a (*un prodotto, ecc.*). // to ~ **the sale of a product** (*market., pubbl.*) incrementare la vendita d'un prodotto; to ~ **sales** (*market.*) incentivare le vendite.

put¹, *n.* (*Borsa*) opzione di vendita (*diritto del compratore di consegnare i titoli a una data futura, o di non consegnarli*). // ~ **of more** (*Borsa*) diritto di vendere il doppio; ~ **of three times more** (*Borsa*) diritto di vendere il quadruplo; ~ **of twice more** (*Borsa*) diritto di vendere il triplo; ~ **option** (*Borsa*) vendita a premio; ~ **price** (*Borsa*) prezzo della vendita a premio.

put², *v. t.* (*pass.* e *part. pass.* **put**) **1** mettere, porre, collocare. **2** apporre. // to ~ **advertisements in a paper** (*pubbl.*) mettere annunci su un giornale; to ~ **one's affairs in order** mettere ordine nei propri affari; to ~ **one's balance of payments on an even keel** (*econ., fin.*) aggiustare i propri conti con l'estero; to ~ **by** mettere da parte; to ~ **by money** (*fin.*) mettere da parte denaro; to ~ **a clause in a contract** (*leg.*) inserire una clausola in un contratto; to ~ **a company into liquidation** (*fin.*) mettere in liquidazione una società; to ~ **down** deporre; to ~ **an embargo on a ship** (*trasp. mar.*) mettere l'embargo su una nave; to ~ **forward** avanzare, mettere avanti, preporre; to ~ **forward a proposal** avanzare una proposta; to ~ **goods ashore** (*trasp. mar.*) sbarcare merci; to ~ **goods on the market** (*market.*) immettere merci in un mercato; to ~ **in** presentare, proporre; to ~ **in evidence** (*leg.*) fornire prove; to ~ **into port** (*trasp. mar.*) entrare in porto; to ~ **a new catalogue out every six months** (*market., pubbl.*) pubblicare un catalogo nuovo ogni sei mesi; to ~ **off** rimandare, rinviare, differire, dilazionare, aggiornare; to ~ **off a meeting** rimandare una riunione; to ~ **off payments** (*cred.*) differire i pagamenti; to ~ **on** mettere su, aggiungere; indossare; to ~ **it on** (*d'albergo, ecc.*) aumentare i prezzi (*indebitamente*); to ~ **on extra trains** (*trasp. ferr.*) aggiungere treni straordinari; to ~ **out** (*giorn.*) pubblicare; (*org. az.*) produrre; to ~ **petrol into one's tank** (*trasp. aut.*) far benzina; to ~ **a question to the vote** porre ai voti una questione; to ~ **one's savings into shares** (*fin.*) investire i propri risparmi in azioni; to ~ **one's signature on a document** apporre la (propria) firma a un documento; to ~ **a special tax on luxuries** (*fin.*) imporre un tributo speciale sugli articoli di lusso; to ~ **through** (*comun.*) mettere in comunicazione (*telefonica*); to ~ **up** mettere su, alzare, aumentare; (*di turista, ecc.*) scendere (*a un albergo, ecc.*); to ~ **st. up for auction** mettere all'asta qc., mettere qc. all'incanto; to ~ **up one's goods for sale** (*market.*) mettere in vendita la propria merce; to ~ **up prices after every wage increase** (*market.*) alzare i prezzi dopo ogni aumento salariale; to ~ **up the shutters** abbassare le serrande; (*fig.*) ritirarsi dagli affari, «chiuder bottega»; to ~ **upon wages** (*pers.*) salariare; to ~ **the veto on a proposal** (*leg.*) porre il veto a una proposta; to ~ **work out** (*org. az.*) dare del lavoro a domicilio; to **be put on the employee roll** (*pers.*) passare in ruolo; to **be put on the sick-list** (*pers.*) essere collocato a riposo (*per malattia*).

putting into port, *locuz. v.* (*trasp. mar.*) entrata in porto (*d'una nave*).

pyramider, *n.* (*Borsa, fin.*) speculatore che reinveste i suoi utili in nuovi titoli.

pyramiding, *n.* (*Borsa, fin.*) reinvestimento degli utili in nuovi titoli.

Q

quadratic, *n.* (*mat.*) equazione di secondo grado. // ~ **equation** (*mat.*) equazione di secondo grado.

quadrillion, *n.* (*USA*) quadrilione.

quadruple[1], *n.* (*mat.*) quadruplo.

quadruple[2], *v. t.* (*mat.*) quadruplicare.

quadruplicate[1], *a.* **1** quadruplicato, quadruplo. **2** (*di documento*) in quattro copie.

quadruplicate[2], *v. t.* **1** quadruplicare. **2** fare quattro copie di (*un documento*).

qualification, *n.* **1** qualità. **2** (*banca, cred.*) condizione, condizione restrittiva, restrizione. **3** (*leg.*) limitazione, restrizione. **4** (*leg.*) abilitazione (*all'esercizio d'una professione*), qualificazione. **5** (*leg., pers.*) qualifica, requisito, titolo. // ~ **shares** (*fin.*) azioni (depositate) in garanzia.

qualified, *a.* **1** condizionato, condizionale, con restrizioni, con riserve. **2** (*leg.*) abilitato, qualificato. **3** (*leg., pers.*) dotato dei requisiti richiesti. // ~ **acceptance** (*banca, cred.*) accettazione condizionata, accettazione restrittiva; ~ **endorsement** (*banca, cred.*) girata condizionata; ~ **property** (*leg.*) proprietà soggetta a restrizioni.

qualify, *v. t.* **1** condizionare, sottoporre (*qc.*) a condizioni. **2** (*leg.*) limitare. **3** (*leg.*) abilitare, qualificare. **4** (*leg., pers.*) avere i requisiti (*per svolgere una mansione, esercitare una professione, ecc.*). *v. i.* (*leg.*) abilitarsi.

qualitative, *a.* qualitativo.

quality, *n.* qualità. // ~ **control** (*org. az.*) controllo della qualità, controllo qualitativo; ~ **standards** (*market.*) norme conformi di qualità, standard qualitativi; **in** ~ **of** (*leg.*) in qualità di, in veste di; **in the** ~ **of** (*leg.*) in qualità di, in veste di.

quantitative, *a.* quantitativo. // ~ **derogations** (*comm. est.*) deroghe quantitative; ~ **import restrictions** (*comm. est.*) restrizioni quantitative all'importazione.

quantity, *n.* quantità, quantitativo. // ~ **production** (*org. az.*) produzione in grande quantità; ~ **theory of money** (*econ.*) teoria quantitativa della moneta (*sviluppata dall'economista americano I. Fisher*).

quarantine[1], *n.* (*trasp. mar.*) quarantena. // ~ **anchorage** (*trasp. mar.*) ancoraggio di quarantena, posto di quarantena; ~ **fees** (*trasp. mar.*) diritti di quarantena; ~ **risk** (*trasp. mar.*) rischio di quarantena; to **be in** ~ (*trasp. mar.*) essere in quarantena; **out of** ~ (*trasp. mar.*) fuori quarantena.

quarantine[2], *v. t.* (*trasp. mar.*) tenere in quarantena.

quarrel[1], *n.* lite, litigio.

quarrel[2], *v. i.* litigare.

quarrelsome, *a.* litigioso.

quart, *n.* quarto di «gallone» (*misura per liquidi pari a litri 1,14 circa*).

quarter, *n.* **1** quarto. **2** quarto di «hundredweight» (*misura di peso pari a kg 12,70*). **3** «quarter» (*misura per cereali pari a ettolitri 2,90 circa*). **4** (*trasp. mar.*) giardinetto. **5** (*USA*) quarto di dollaro; moneta da 25 centesimi (*di dollaro*). **6** (*USA*) quarto di «hundredweight» (*misura di peso pari a kg 11,34*). // ~ **dollar** (*USA*) moneta da 25 centesimi (*di dollaro*); ~ **sessions** (*leg., ingl.*) udienze trimestrali.

quarterage, *n.* pagamento trimestrale (*d'imposta, pensione, salario, ecc.*).

quarterly, *a.* **1** trimestrale. **2** (*giorn.*) trimestrale. *n.* (*giorn.*) (pubblicazione) trimestrale. *avv.* trimestralmente. // **a** ~ **meeting** un'assemblea trimestrale; ~ **payments** pagamenti trimestrali.

quash, *v. t.* (*leg.*) annullare, cassare, invalidare. // to ~ **a conviction** (*leg.*) annullare una condanna; to ~ **a decision** (*leg.*) annullare una sentenza; to ~ **a verdict** (*leg.*) annullare un verdetto.

quashed, *a.* (*leg.*) annullato, cassato, invalidato.

quasi, *avv.* e *a.* quasi, pressoché, come se. // ~ **-contract** (*leg.*) quasi contratto; ~ **income** (*econ.*) quasi rendita; ~ **partner** (*fin.*) «quasi socio», socio nominale; ~ **-usufruct** (*leg.*) quasi usufrutto, usufrutto imperfetto.

quay, *n.* (*trasp. mar.*) molo, banchina d'attracco.

quayage, *n.* (*trasp. mar.*) diritti di banchina.

question[1], *n.* 1 domanda, quesito, interrogazione. 2 questione, controversia, problema. // ~ **of competence** (*leg.*) questione di competenza; ~ **of fact** (*leg.*) questione di fatto; ~ **of law** (*leg.*) questione di diritto.

question[2], *v. t.* interrogare, fare domande a (*q.*).

questionnaire, *n.* (*market.*) questionario.

queue[1], *n.* coda, fila.

queue[2], *v. i.* fare la coda, fare la fila. // to ~ **up** fare la coda, fare la fila.

quick, *a.* svelto, veloce. // ~ **assets** (*rag.*) attività a vista, attività a breve (termine); ~ **assets ratio** (*rag.*) rapporto fra le attività a breve e le passività correnti; ~ **profits** (*fin.*) profitti rapidi (*riguardo al realizzo*); ~ **ratio** (*rag.*) *V.* **acid test ratio.**

quicken, *v. t.* affrettare, sollecitare.

quickie strike, *n.* (*sind.*) sciopero a gatto selvaggio, sciopero illegale.

quickness, *n.* fretta.

quiescence, *n.* quiescenza.

quiescency, *n.* quiescenza.

quietus, *n.* 1 ricevuta (*di pagamento*). 2 estinzione (*d'un debito*).

quintal, *n.* 1 quintale. 2 «hundredweight» (*pari a 100 libbre in U.S.A. e a 112 in Gran Bretagna*).

quintillion, *n.* (*USA*) quintilione.

quintuple[1], *a.* e *n.* quintuplo.

quintuple[2], *v. t.* quintuplicare.

quintuplicate[1], *a.* 1 quintuplicato. 2 (*di documento*) in cinque copie.

quintuplicate[2], *v. t.* 1 quintuplicare. 2 fare cinque copie di (*un documento*).

quit[1], *n.* 1 (il) lasciare, abbandono. 2 (*pers.*) abbandono del posto di lavoro.

quit[2], *v. t.* abbandonare, lasciare. // to ~ **a debt** (*cred.*) pagare un debito; to ~ **a job** (*pers.*) abbandonare un impiego.

quitclaim[1], *n.* (*leg.*) rinuncia a un diritto.

quitclaim[2], *v. t.* (*leg.*) rinunciare a (*un diritto*).

quittance, *n.* quietanza, ricevuta.

quorum, *n.* (*leg.*) «quorum», numero legale. // **the** ~ **of creditors** (*leg.*) il numero legale dei creditori.

quota, *n.* 1 quota, aliquota, parte, rata. 2 (*econ.*) contingente. 3 (*fin.*) tangente. // ~ **sample** (*market.*) campione stratificato; ~ **system** (*econ.*) contingentamento, sistema del contingentamento.

quotable, *a.* (*fin.*) quotabile.

quotation, *n.* 1 citazione. 2 (*fin., market.*) quotazione, prezzo corrente. // ~ **for the account** (*Borsa*) quotazione a termine; **quotations for cash** (*Borsa*) quotazioni a contanti; **quotations for freight** (*trasp. mar.*) quotazioni di nolo; ~ **in the list** (*fin.*) quotazioni in Borsa; **the** ~ **of prices** (*fin., market.*) la quotazione dei prezzi.

quote, *v. t.* 1 citare. 2 (*fin., market.*) quotare, indicare il prezzo corrente di (*azioni, merci, ecc.*). // to ~ **fixed exchange** (*fin.*) quotare il «certo per l'incerto»; to ~ **the freight** (*trasp. mar.*) quotare il nolo; to ~ **movable exchange** (*fin.*) quotare l'«incerto per il certo»; to ~ **prices** (*fin., market.*) quotare prezzi; **quoted investments** (*rag.*) investimenti azionari, investimenti obbligazionari.

quoted, *a.* (*fin.*) quotato.

quotient, *n.* (*mat.*) quoziente.

R

rack, *n.* 1 rastrelliera. 2 (*market.*) «display» per esposizione (e distribuzione) nel punto di vendita. // ~ **rent** affitto esageratamente alto.

radical, *a.* integrale, profondo. // ~ **sign** (*mat.*) segno di radice.

radio, *n.* 1 apparecchio radio, radiofonia. 2 (*trasp. mar.*) radiogramma. // ~ **and television advertising** (*pubbl.*) pubblicità radio-televisiva; ~ **broadcast** (*comun.*) trasmissione radiofonica; ~ **broadcasting** (*comun.*) trasmissione radiofonica (*il trasmettere*); ~ **communications** (*trasp. mar.*) comunicazioni radio; ~ **distress signal** (*trasp. mar.*) segnale di soccorso via radio; ~ **set** radio; ~ **-telephone** (*comun.*) radiotelefono; ~ **-telephony** (*comun.*) radiotelefonia.

radiophone, *n.* (*comun.*) radiotelefono.

radius, *n.* (*pl.* **radii** e *reg.*) (*mat.*) raggio. // ~ **clause** (*pers., sind.*) clausola (*di contratto di lavoro*) in base alla quale l'impiegato in fase d'addestramento s'impegna a non cercare lavoro presso un altro datore per un certo tempo.

raft, *n.* zattera.

raging inflation, *n.* (*econ.*) inflazione che imperversa.

rail[1], *n.* 1 (*trasp. ferr.*) (*abbr. di* **railway, railroad**) ferrovia. 2 **rails,** *pl.* (*Borsa*) azioni ferroviarie, titoli ferroviari. // ~ **carrier** (*trasp. ferr.*) vettore ferroviario; ~ **traffic** (*trasp. ferr.*) traffico ferroviario; ~ **transport** (*trasp. ferr.*) trasporti ferroviari; **free on** ~ **(F.O.R.)** (*trasp. ferr.*) «franco vagone» (*alla stazione di partenza*).

rail[2], *v. t.* (*trasp. ferr., ingl.*) spedire per ferrovia.

railroad[1], *n.* 1 (*fin., specialm. USA*) società ferroviaria. 2 (*trasp. ferr., specialm. USA*) ferrovia. 3 **railroads,** *pl.* (*Borsa, specialm. USA*) azioni ferroviarie, titoli ferroviari. // ~ **company** (*fin.*) società ferroviaria; ~ **rates** (*trasp. ferr.*) tariffe ferroviarie; ~ **shares** (*Borsa, specialm. USA*) azioni di compagnia ferroviaria; ~ **station** (*trasp. ferr.*) stazione ferroviaria.

railroad[2], *v. t.* (*trasp. ferr., specialm. USA*) trasportare per ferrovia.

railway, *n.* (*trasp. ferr.*) ferrovia. // ~ **accident** (*trasp. ferr.*) incidente ferroviario; ~ **carriage** (*trasp. ferr.*) carrozza, vagone, vettura; ~ **company** (*fin.*) società ferroviaria; ~ **engine** (*trasp. ferr.*) locomotiva; ~ **junction** (*trasp. ferr.*) raccordo ferroviario; ~ **line** (*trasp. ferr.*) linea ferroviaria; ~ **network** (*trasp. ferr.*) rete ferroviaria; ~ **platform** (*trasp. ferr.*) banchina ferroviaria; ~ **rates** (*trasp. ferr.*) tariffe ferroviarie; ~ **section** (*trasp. ferr.*) tronco ferroviario; ~ **shares** (*Borsa*) azioni ferroviarie, titoli ferroviari; ~ **siding** (*trasp. ferr.*) raccordo ferroviario; ~ **station** (*trasp. ferr.*) stazione ferroviaria; ~ **system** (*trasp. ferr.*) rete ferroviaria; ~ **ticket** (*trasp. ferr.*) biglietto ferroviario; ~ **track** (*trasp. ferr.*) binario; ~ **traffic** (*trasp. ferr.*) traffico ferroviario; ~ **yard** (*trasp. ferr.*) scalo ferroviario, sistema di binari per deposito (*smistamento, ecc.*).

raincoat, *n.* (*market.*) impermeabile.

raise[1], *n.* 1 (*pers., specialm. USA*) aumento di stipendio. 2 (*specialm. USA*) elevazione. 3 (*specialm. USA*) aumento.

raise[2], *v. t.* 1 alzare, elevare. 2 aumentare. 3 (*fin.*) raccogliere (*fondi, ecc.*). 4 (*mat.*) elevare. // to ~ **anchor** (*trasp. mar.*) alzare l'ancora; to ~ **the bank rate** (*fin.*) aumentare il tasso di sconto; to ~ **the blockade** (*trasp. mar.*) togliere il blocco; to ~ **a claim** presentare un reclamo; to ~ **custom duties** (*dog., fin.*) aumentare (*o* crescere) i dazi doganali; to ~ **the discount rate** (*fin.*) aumentare il tasso di sconto; to ~ **duties** (*dog.*) aumentare i dazi; to ~ **a loan on an insurance policy** (*cred.*) ottenere un prestito su una polizza d'assicurazione; to ~ **an objection** sollevare un'obiezione; (*leg.*) sollevare un'eccezione; to ~ **the price of** (*market.*) rincarare; to ~ **prices** (*market.*) aumentare i prezzi; to ~ **real wages** (*pers.*) aumentare i salari reali; to ~ **the standard of living** (*econ.*) elevare il tenore di vita; to ~ **a tax** (*fin.*) esigere un tributo.

raising, *n.* alzata.

rally[1], *n.* 1 adunanza, riunione. 2 (*Borsa, fin.*) rafforzamento delle quotazioni (*di titoli, ecc.*) dopo un crollo. 3 (*Borsa, fin., market.*) (*di titoli, ecc.*) ricupero, ripresa.

rally², *v. t.* 1 raccogliere, adunare. 2 (*Borsa, fin.*) rafforzare le quotazioni di (*titoli, ecc.*) dopo un crollo. 3 (*fin., market.*) favorire la ripresa di (*un mercato, ecc.*). *v. i.* 1 adunarsi. 2 (*Borsa, fin.*) (*di titoli, ecc.*) riprendersi, ricuperare.

rampant inflation, *n.* (*econ.*) inflazione «rampante».

range¹, *n.* 1 fila, serie. 2 (*econ., fin., rag.*) scarto. 3 (*market.*) assortimento, gamma (*di prodotti*). 4 (*trasp. aer.*) autonomia (*d'un aereo*). // **the ~ of prices** (*market.*) la gamma dei prezzi, la scala dei prezzi.

range², *v. i.* estendersi, andare (*da ... a*).

rank¹, *n.* 1 linea, fila, riga. 2 grado, ceto, posizione, rango. *a. attr.* troppo alto (*nell'ammontare*); eccessivo. // **the ~ and file** i militari di truppa; (*org. az., fig.*) la «truppa», le maestranze, gli operai; (*sind., fig.*) la «base»; **the ~ of a mortgage** (*leg.*) il grado d'un'ipoteca; **the ranks of the unemployed** (*sind.*) le file dei disoccupati; **a ~ rate of interest** (*fin.*) un tasso d'interesse eccessivo; **from the ranks** (*pers.*) dalla «gavetta».

rank², *v. t.* mettere in riga. *v. i.* occupare una certa posizione.

ratable, *a.* 1 stimabile, valutabile. 2 proporzionale. 3 (*fin., ingl.*) imponibile. // **the ~ distribution of profits** la distribuzione proporzionale dei profitti; **the ~ value of a property** (*fin., ingl.*) il valore imponibile d'una proprietà, il valore locativo d'una proprietà.

ratably, *avv.* proporzionalmente, in proporzione.

rate¹, *n.* 1 aliquota, percentuale. 2 indice. 3 costo, prezzo, tariffa. 4 (*fin.*) saggio, tasso. 5 (*fin.*) corso. 6 (*fin., ingl.*) imposta comunale, tassa locale. 7 (*trasp. mar.*) rata di nolo. // **~ at par** (*fin.*) cambio alla pari; **~ basis** base tariffaria; **~ -bracket system** (*fin.*) sistema di tariffe a forcelle; **~ collector** (*pers.*) esattore comunale; **~ cutting** riduzione delle tariffe; **the ~ for printed matter** (*comun.*) la tariffa per (la spedizione degli) stampati; **~ of commission** tariffa di mediazione; **the ~ of conversion of a currency** (*econ.*) il tasso di conversione d'una valuta; **the ~ of corporate profits** (*fin., rag.*) la percentuale degli utili sociali; **the rates of countervailing charges on imports** (*comm. est.*) le aliquote delle imposte compensative all'importazione; **the ~ of depreciation** (*econ.*) il saggio di svalutazione, tasso d'ammortamento; **~ of discount** (*fin.*) tasso (*o* saggio) di sconto; **~ of exchange** (*fin.*) tasso di cambio, cambio; **~ of growth** (*econ.*) tasso di sviluppo; **the ~ of increase in the gross national product** (*econ.*) il saggio di crescita del prodotto nazionale lordo; **the ~ of inflation** (*econ.*) il tasso inflazionistico; **the ~ of interest** (*fin.*) il tasso d'interesse; **~ of pay** (*pers.*) paga; **~ of premium** (*ass.*) aliquota del premio; **the rates of refunds on exports** (*comm. est.*) le aliquote dei rimborsi all'esportazione; **the ~ of return** (*rag.*) tasso di remunerazione (*del capitale*); **the ~ of return of capital investment** (*fin.*) il tasso di remunerazione degli investimenti; **~ of turnover** (*rag.*) tasso di rotazione delle scorte; **~ payer** (*fin., ingl.*) contribuente; **~ war** (*comm. est., fig.*) guerra tariffaria.

rate², *v. t.* 1 apprezzare, stimare, valutare. 2 (*ass.*) fissare l'ammontare del premio per (*un certo rischio*). 3 (*fin., ingl.*) stabilire l'imponibile di (*un bene*). 4 (*market.*) quotare, fare il prezzo a. 5 (*pubbl.*) misurare l'indice d'ascolto (*radiofonico o televisivo*) di (*q. o qc.*). 6 (*trasp. mar.*) classificare (*una nave*). // to **~ goods** (*trasp.*) fissare le tariffe per il trasporto delle merci.

rateable, *a. V.* **ratable.**

rated, *a.* (*fin.*) quotato.

ratification, *n.* (*leg.*) ratificazione, ratifica, sanzione, omologazione. // **the ~ of a treaty** (*leg.*) la ratifica d'un trattato.

ratify, *v. t.* (*leg.*) ratificare, sanzionare, omologare, sancire. // to **~ a contract** (*leg.*) ratificare un contratto; to **~ a nomination** (*leg.*) sancire una nomina.

rating, *n.* 1 apprezzamento, stima, valutazione. 2 (*cred., fin.*) valutazione del credito (*di cui gode un individuo o una ditta*). 3 (*fin., leg.*) estimo. 4 (*market.*) quotazione (*del prezzo d'un prodotto, ecc.*). 5 (*pubbl.*) indice d'ascolto (*radiofonico o televisivo*). 6 (*trasp. mar.*) classificazione, rango (*d'una nave*).

ratio, *n.* (*mat.*) proporzione, rapporto. // **the ~ between stock prices and dividends** (*fin.*) il rapporto fra il prezzo delle azioni e i dividendi.

ration¹, *n.* (*econ.*) razione.

ration², *v. t.* (*econ.*) razionare, contingentare.

rational, *a.* razionale.

rationalization, *n.* 1 (*mat.*) razionalizzazione. 2 (*org. az.*) razionalizzazione, organizzazione razionale (*del lavoro*).

rationalize, *v. t.* 1 (*mat.*) razionalizzare. 2 (*org. az.*) razionalizzare, organizzare razionalmente (*il lavoro*). // to **~ the industrial process** (*org. az.*) razionalizzare il processo produttivo.

rationing, *n.* (*econ.*) razionamento, contingentamento. // **the ~ of gasoline** (*econ., USA*) il razionamento della benzina; **~ system** (*econ.*)

sistema di razionamento.

raw, *a.* greggio, grezzo. // **~ materials** (*econ.*) materiali grezzi, materie prime; **~ petroleum** petrolio greggio, (il) greggio.

reabsorption, *n.* riassorbimento. // **the ~ of workers leaving the land** (*econ., pers.*) la riconversione dei lavoratori che abbandonano l'agricoltura.

reach, *v. t.* raggiungere, giungere a. // to **~ sb. by phone** (*comun.*) mettersi in contatto con q. per telefono; to **~ harbour** (*trasp. mar.*) giungere in porto; **~ -me-down** (*market., ingl.*) (*d'abito*) confezionato; (*market., ingl.*) abito confezionato.

reaction, *n.* reazione. // **a ~ in stock prices** (*Borsa*) una reazione nelle quotazioni (*dei titoli*); **~ index** (*pubbl.*) indice di gradimento.

reactivate, *v. t.* **1** riattivare, rimettere in funzione. **2** rilanciare (*fig.*).

reactivation, *n.* **1** riattivazione. **2** rilancio (*fig.*). // **the ~ of the economic and monetary union** (*econ.*) il rilancio dell'unione economica e monetaria.

reactor, *n.* (*econ.*) reattivo.

read, *v. t.* (*pass.* e *part. pass.* **read**) leggere. *v. i.* (*di documento e sim.*) dire (*alla lettura*).

reader, *n.* **1** lettore. **2** (*giorn.*) lettore.

readership, *n.* (*giorn., stat.*) numero di lettori.

reading, *n.* lettura, (il) leggere.

readjust, *v. t.* (*fin., market., trasp.*) ritoccare (*prezzi, tariffe, ecc.*).

readjustment, *n.* (*fin., market., trasp.*) ritocco (*di prezzi, tariffe, ecc.*).

ready, *a.* **1** pronto, sollecito. **2** rapido. // **~ assets** (*rag.*) disponibilità liquide; **~ cash** (*market.*) pronta cassa; **~ for sea** (*trasp. mar.*) (*di nave, battello, ecc.*) pronto a prendere il mare; **~ -for-wear** (*market.*) *V.* **~ -made; ~ -made** (*market.*) (*d'abito, ecc.*) confezionato; **~ -made clothes** (*market.*) abiti confezionati, confezioni; **~ -made shop** (*market.*) negozio d'abiti confezionati; **~ money** denaro contante, contanti; **~ reckoner** (*attr. uff.*) prontuario di calcoli; **~ -to-wear** (*market.*) (*d'abito*) confezionato, bell'e fatto.

real, *a.* **1** reale, effettivo. **2** (*fin., leg.*) immobiliare, immobile. **3** (*market.*) naturale (*opposto a «finto», artificiale, ecc.*). **4** (*mat.*) reale. // **~ accounts** (*rag.*) conti numerari (*alle attività e passività*); **~ agent** (*fin.*) V. **~ -estate agent; ~ assets** (*fin., leg.*) immobili, beni immobili; **~ capital** (*rag.*) capitale d'immobilizzo; **~ chattels** (*fin., leg.*) beni reali (*non in proprietà assoluta: un affitto, un raccolto in erba, ecc.*); **~ contract** (*leg.*) contratto reale; **~ cost** (*rag.*) costo reale; **~ estate** (*fin., leg.*) beni immobili; **~ -estate agency** (*fin.*) agenzia immobiliare (*o* fondiaria); **~ -estate agent** (*fin.*) agente immobiliare; **the ~ -estate market** (*fin.*) il mercato immobiliare; **~ estate register** (*amm.*) libro catastale; **the ~ -estate sector** (*fin.*) il settore degli affari immobiliari; **~ exchange** (*fin.*) cambio reale; **the ~ gross national product** (*econ.*) il prodotto nazionale lordo in termini reali; **~ income** (*econ.*) reddito in termini reali; **~ money** moneta corrente, contanti; **~ national income** (*econ.*) reddito nazionale in termini reali; **~ partner** (*fin.*) socio effettivo; **the ~ party in interest** (*leg.*) la parte in causa; **~ property** (*fin., leg.*) proprietà immobiliare, patrimonio immobiliare; **the ~ rate of interest on loans** (*cred.*) l'effettivo tasso d'interesse sui prestiti; **~ rights** (*leg.*) diritti reali; **~ tare** (*market.*) tara reale; **~ wages** (*pers.*) salario effettivo, salario reale (*considerando il potere d'acquisto della moneta*).

realignment, *n.* (*econ., fin.*) riassetto.

realizable, *a.* (*econ., fin.*) realizzabile, convertibile in contanti. // **~ value** (*fin., rag.*) valore venale.

realization, *n.* **1** realizzazione, effettuazione. **2** (*econ., fin.*) realizzo, conversione in contanti. // **~ and liquidation account** (*rag.*) bilancio di liquidazione, stato patrimoniale di liquidazione; **~ of a bankrupt's estate** (*leg.*) realizzo della proprietà d'un fallito; **the ~ of a profit** (*rag.*) l'ottenimento d'un utile.

realize, *v. t.* **1** realizzare, effettuare. **2** (*econ., fin.*) realizzare, convertire in contanti. **3** (*market.*) ottenere (*un prezzo*). // to **~ a credit** (*cred.*) realizzare un credito; to **~ a profit** (*rag.*) ottenere un utile.

realtor, *n.* (*fin., USA*) agente immobiliare, agente fondiario, mediatore di case e terreni.

realty, *n.* (*fin., leg.*) proprietà immobiliare, beni immobili.

ream, *n.* (*pubbl.*) risma (*480 o 500 fogli di carta da scrivere*).

reappraisal, *n.* (*rag.*) rivalutazione.

reappraise, *v. t.* (*rag.*) rivalutare.

re-arrange, *v. t.* (*econ., fin.*) riassettare.

re-arrangement, *n.* (*econ., fin.*) riassetto.

reason¹, *n.* ragione, motivo. // **reasons of procedure** (*leg.*) motivi procedurali.

reason², *v. i.* e *t.* ragionare, discorrere.

reasonable, *a.* (*market.*) a buon mercato, non caro. // **a ~ price** (*market.*) un prezzo ragionevole; **a ~ request** una richiesta ragionevole.

reassess, *v. t.* 1 (*ass.*) valutare di nuovo (*un danno, ecc.*). 2 (*fin.*) fissare di nuovo (*un'imposta, un imponibile, ecc.*).

reassessment, *n.* 1 (*ass.*) nuova valutazione (*d'un danno, ecc.*). 2 (*fin.*) nuova determinazione d'imposta.

reassurance, *n.* (*ass.*) riassicurazione.

reassure, *v. t.* (*ass.*) riassicurare.

rebate[1], *n.* 1 (*cred., fin.*) rimborso (*di parte degli interessi pagati per una somma prestata e che viene restituita in anticipo*). 2 (*market.*) ribasso, riduzione, deduzione, detrazione, defalco, sconto. // **a ~ of freight** (*trasp. mar.*) un rimborso del nolo; **~ of income taxes** (*fin., sind.*) riduzione delle imposte sul reddito (per gli scioperanti); **a ~ of premium** (*ass.*) uno sconto sul premio; **the ~ on bills not due** (*banca*) risconto di portafoglio.

rebate[2], *v. t.* (*cred., fin.*) rimborsare (*parte degli interessi pagati per una somma prestata e che viene restituita in anticipo*). *v. i.* (*market.*) praticare ribassi, concedere sconti.

rebound, *n.* ristorno.

rebuild, *v. t.* (*pass.* e *part. pass.* **rebuilt**) riedificare.

rebut, *v. t.* 1 rifiutare, respingere. 2 (*leg.*) respingere, rigettare (*un addebito, ecc.*). 3 (*leg.*) confutare (*prove, ecc.*). // **to ~ a charge** (*leg.*) respingere un'accusa; **to ~ sb.'s proposals** respingere le proposte di q.

rebuttable presumption, *n.* (*leg.*) presunzione relativa.

rebuttal, *n.* 1 rifiuto, ripulsa. 2 (*leg.*) rigetto (*d'un addebito, ecc.*). 3 (*leg.*) confutazione.

rebutter, *n.* 1 chi rifiuta. 2 (*leg.*) chi respinge (*un addebito, ecc.*).

recapitulation, *n.* ricapitolazione.

recaption, *n.* (*leg.*) ripresa di possesso di beni sottratti illecitamente.

recede, *v. i.* 1 recedere, ritirarsi, rinunziare (a). 2 (*fin., market.*) (*di prezzi, quotazioni, ecc.*) calare, diminuire. // **to ~ from a contract** (*leg.*) recedere da un contratto.

receipt[1], *n.* 1 ricevimento, ricezione, ricevuta, riscontro. 2 (*comm.*) ricevuta, quietanza, «giustificativo». 3 **receipts,** *pl.* (*rag.*) entrate, introiti, proventi, profitti, ricavi. // **~ book** registro delle ricevute, bollettario; **a ~ for the balance** una ricevuta a saldo; **a ~ for payment** una ricevuta di pagamento; **~ form** modulo di ricevuta; **a ~ in full** una ricevuta a saldo; **a ~ on account** una ricevuta in conto; **~ stamp** bollo per ricevuta; to **be in ~ of** (*comm.*) avere ricevuto.

receipt[2], *v. t.* 1 (*comm.*) quietanzare (*un conto, una fattura, ecc.*). 2 (*comm.*) accusare ricevuta di (*merci*). // **to ~ a bill of lading** (*trasp. mar.*) quietanzare una polizza di carico; **to ~ an invoice** (*market.*) quietanzare una fattura.

receivable, *a.* 1 ricevibile. 2 (*comm.*) esigibile. 3 (*leg.*) accettabile, ammissibile. // **~ accounts** (*rag.*) conti attivi.

receivables, *n. pl.* (*rag.*) esposizione (*complesso dei crediti d'un'azienda*).

receive, *v. t.* 1 ricevere, accogliere. 2 (*pers.*) ricevere, percepire (*un salario, ecc.*). // **to ~ money on deposit** (*fin.*) ricevere denaro in deposito; **to ~ notice to quit** (*leg.*) ricevere l'ordine di sfratto; **to ~ one's pay** (*pers.*) riscuotere la paga.

received, *a.* ricevuto, accolto. // **«~ for shipment» bill of lading** (*trasp. mar.*) polizza «ricevuto per l'imbarco»; **~ stamp** timbro di ricevuta.

receiver, *n.* 1 chi riceve. 2 (*comun., trasp.*) ricevitore, destinatario. 3 (*fin.*) cassiere, tesoriere; prenditore. 4 (*leg.*) (= **receiver of stolen goods**) ricettatore. 5 (*leg., ingl.*) amministratore fiduciario; curatore (*di minore, d'interdetto, ecc.*). 6 (*leg., ingl.*) custode giudiziario di beni, liquidatore; curatore (*di fallimento*). // **~ in bankruptcy** (*leg., ingl.*) curatore fallimentare.

receivership, *n.* 1 (*leg., ingl.*) curatela (*di minore, interdetto, ecc.*). 2 (*leg., ingl.*) curatela, amministrazione (*fallimentare*).

receiving, *a.* che riceve, ricevente. *n.* ricevimento, ricezione, (il) ricevere. // **~ order** (*leg., ingl.*) ordinanza di trapasso delle attività (*del debitore al curatore fallimentare*). // **~ stolen goods** (*leg.*) ricettazione.

recent, *a.* recente.

reception, *n.* 1 ricevimento, ricezione; (il) ricevere; accoglienza. 2 (*market., pers.*) segreteria d'accoglimento (*dei visitatori, nelle mostre, fiere, e sim.*). // **~ desk** (*tur.*) bureau, ricezione.

receptionist, *n.* (*market., pers.*) segretario (*d'accoglimento dei visitatori nelle mostre, fiere, ecc.*).

receptivity, *n.* ricettività.

recession, *n.* (*econ.*) recessione, congiuntura negativa.

recessionary, *a.* (*econ.*) recessivo. // **~ trends** tendenze recessive.

recidive, *n.* (*leg.*) recidiva.

recidivism, *n.* (*leg.*) recidiva, condizione del recidivo.

recidivist, *n.* (*leg.*) recidivo.

reciprocal, *a.* 1 reciproco. 2 (*mat.*) reciproco. // **~ demand** (*econ.*) domanda reciproca (*di prodotti: fra due persone o due comunità*); ~ **quantities** (*mat.*) quantità reciproche (*il cui prodotto è uguale a 1*); ~ **ratio** (*mat.*) rapporto inverso; ~ **trade agreements** (*comm. est.*) accordi commerciali bilaterali.

reciprocity, *n.* 1 reciprocità. 2 (*comm. est.*) reciprocità. // ~ **in trade** (*comm. est.*) reciprocità di trattamento commerciale.

reckon, *v. t.* e *i.* calcolare, computare, contare, far di conto.

reckoner, *n.* 1 (= **ready reckoner**) prontuario dei calcoli. 2 (*pers.*) contabile, computista.

reckoning, *n.* 1 (il) far di conto. 2 calcolo, computo. 3 conto (*da pagare*). // ~ **from today** a contare da oggi, a partire da oggi.

re-claim[1], *v. t.* (*leg.*) pretendere la restituzione di (*qc.*).

reclaim[2], *v. t.* e *i.* 1 reclamare, protestare. 2 ricuperare. 3 (*econ.*) bonificare, risanare.

reclaiming, *n.* (*econ.*) bonifica, risanamento.

reclamation, *n.* 1 reclamo; protesta. 2 ricupero. 3 (*econ.*) risanamento.

recoal, *v. t.* (*trasp. mar.*) rifornire (*una nave e sim.*) di carbone. *v. i.* (*trasp. mar.*) (*di nave e sim.*) rifornirsi di carbone.

recognition, *n.* 1 riconoscimento, ammissione. 2 accettazione, accoglimento (*d'un reclamo e sim.*).

recognizance, *n.* (*leg.*) cauzione, garanzia.

recognize, *v. t.* 1 riconoscere, ammettere, riconoscere la giustizia di (*qc.*). 2 accettare, accogliere. // to ~ **a claim** accogliere un reclamo.

recommend, *v. t.* raccomandare, consigliare.

recommendable, *a.* consigliabile.

recommendation, *n.* raccomandazione, consiglio.

recompense[1], *n.* 1 rimunerazione. 2 (*leg.*) risarcimento (*d'un danno*).

recompense[2], *v. t.* 1 rimunerare. 2 (*leg.*) risarcire (*un danno*).

reconcile, *v. t.* 1 (*leg.*) conciliare (*le parti contendenti*). 2 (*leg.*) comporre (*una lite*). 3 (*rag.*) far quadrare (*conti, ecc.*); far quadrare le cifre di (*un conto: con quelle d'un altro*); spuntare (*cifre, voci d'un conto, ecc.*). // to ~ **the accounts** (*rag.*) far quadrare i conti.

reconciliation, *n.* 1 (*leg.*) conciliazione (*fra le parti contendenti*). 2 (*leg.*) composizione (*d'una lite*). 3 (*leg.*) spunta (*di cifre, di voci d'un conto, ecc.*).

reconduction, *n.* (*leg.*) rinnovo del contratto d'affitto, riconduzione.

reconfirm, *v. t.* riconfermare.

reconfirmation, *n.* riconferma.

reconvention, *n.* (*leg.*) azione riconvenzionale.

reconversion, *n.* (*econ.*) riconversione (*d'industrie belliche in industrie di pace*).

reconvert, *v. t.* (*econ.*) (*d'industrie*) riconvertire. *v. i.* (*econ.*) (*d'industrie*) riconvertirsi.

reconvey, *v. t.* 1 (*trasp.*) trasportare indietro. 2 (*trasp.*) rispedire.

reconveyance, *n.* 1 (*leg.*) restituzione (*d'una proprietà al possessore precedente*). 2 (*trasp.*) rispedizione.

record[1], *n.* 1 record, primato. 2 registrazione, nota, memoria, documento, documentazione, protocollo. 3 (*leg.*) verbale. 4 (*pers.*) carriera (trascorsa), stato di servizio, curriculum, curricolo. 5 (*rag.*) registrazione, scrittura (contabile). 6 **records,** *pl.* (*leg.*) atti ufficiali. 7 **records,** *pl.* (*leg.*) archivio. *a. attr.* da primato, straordinario, record. // ~ **-breaking** record, da record, da primato; **a ~ -breaking production** (*econ.*) una produzione da record; **records centre** (*org. az.*) archivio; **a ~ crop** (*econ.*) un raccolto record (*abbondantissimo*); **records detention** (*org. az.*) archiviazione; **the ~ of an applicant** (*pers.*) lo stato di servizio d'un aspirante (*a un posto*); **the records of a company** (*rag.*) le scritture (*contabili*) d'una società; **the records of the Court of law** (*leg.*) i verbali del tribunale; ~ **of payments to third parties** (*fin.*) libro dei compensi a terzi; **the ~ of service** (*pers.*) lo stato di servizio; **the Records Office** l'Archivio di Stato; ~ **prices** (*market.*) prezzi imbattibili; **of ~** (*leg.*) (*di fatto, atto, ecc.*) documentato, provato; **off the ~** (*giorn.*) (*di dichiarazione, intervista, e sim.*) da non pubblicarsi, non ufficiale; (*leg.*) ufficiosamente.

record[2], *v. t.* 1 registrare, prender nota di, protocollare. 2 (*leg.*) mettere a verbale, «verbalizzare», trascrivere. 3 (*leg.*) archiviare. 4 (*market.*) incidere, registrare (*su dischi, «cassette», ecc.*). 5 (*rag.*) registrare (*scritture contabili*). // to ~ **in protocol** (*leg.*) protocollare; to ~ **the proceedings of a congress** (*leg.*) verbalizzare gli atti d'un congresso; to ~ **a vote** (*leg.*) mettere a verbale una votazione.

recordation, *n.* (*leg.*) registrazione.

recorder, *n.* 1 chi registra, chi prende nota. 2 (*leg.*) archivista. 3 (*leg.*) cancelliere. 4 (*leg., ingl.*) magistrato (*in certe città*). 5 (*market.*) registratore (*a nastro magnetico o a «cassette»*), magnetofono.

recording, *n.* 1 il registrare (il prender nota,

ecc., *V.* **record**[2]). 2 registrazione, incisione (*su dischi, nastri magnetici, «cassette», ecc.*). 3 (*leg.*) verbalizzazione, trascrizione.

re-count[1], *n.* nuovo computo.

re-count[2], *v. t.* contare di nuovo.

recoup, *v. t.* e *i.* 1 ricuperare. 2 (*leg.*) trattenere (*parte d'una somma dovuta*). 3 (*leg.*) rimborsare, risarcire, indennizzare. 4 (*leg.*) ricuperare (*qc.*); farsi risarcire (*un danno*). // to ~ **sb. for damages** (*leg.*) risarcire q. per danni.

recoupment, *n.* 1 ricupero. 2 (*leg.*) trattenuta (*di parte d'una somma dovuta*). 3 (*leg.*) rimborso, risarcimento, indennizzo.

recourse, *n.* 1 ricorso. 2 (*cred.*) regresso (*cambiario*); azione di regresso, azione di rivalsa. // to **have** ~ **to the law** (*leg.*) ricorrere alla legge, adire le vie legali; **without** ~ (*cred.*) senza regresso, senza rivalsa.

recover, *v. t.* 1 ricuperare. 2 compensare. 3 (*leg.*) ottenere (*qc., dal tribunale*). *v. i.* 1 (*anche fig.*) riaversi, riprendersi, ristabilirsi, rimettersi (*in salute*). 2 (*Borsa, fin.*) (*di titoli, ecc.*) essere in ripresa. 3 (*econ.*) (*di situazione economica*) essere in ripresa. // to ~ **costs** (*leg.*) ricuperare le spese (*d'una causa*); to ~ **damages** (*leg.*) ottenere il risarcimento dei danni; to ~ **a debt at law** (*leg.*) ricuperare un credito mediante un'azione giudiziaria; to ~ **expenses** ricuperare le spese; to ~ **judgment against the defendant** (*leg.*) ottenere una sentenza contro il convenuto; to ~ **a loss** compensare una perdita.

recoverable, *a.* ricuperabile.

recovery, *n.* 1 ricupero. 2 (*anche fig.*) ripresa. 3 (*Borsa, fin.*) (*detto di titoli, ecc.*) ripresa. 4 (*econ.*) ripresa, risanamento. 5 (*leg.*) ottenimento (*di qc., dal tribunale*). // **a** ~ **in production** (*econ.*) una ripresa produttiva; **the** ~ **of cash** (*rag.*) il realizzo del contante; **the** ~ **of a credit** (*cred.*) il ricupero d'un credito; ~ **package** (*econ.*) piano di risanamento.

recreation, *n.* svago.

recruit, *v. t.* 1 reclutare. 2 (*pers.*) assumere. // to ~ **skilled workers** (*econ., pers.*) reclutare manodopera qualificata.

recruiting, *n.* 1 reclutamento. 2 (*pers.*) assunzione. // **the** ~ **of personnel** (*econ., pers.*) il reclutamento di personale; ~ **office** (*pers.*) ufficio assunzioni.

recruitment, *n.* 1 reclutamento. 2 (*pers.*) assunzione. // **a** ~ **plan** (*pers.*) un programma d'assunzione.

rectification, *n.* rettificazione, rettifica, correzione. // **the detection and** ~ **of misprints** (*giorn.*) la correzione degli errori di stampa.

rectify, *v. t.* rettificare, correggere. // to ~ **a figure** (*rag.*) rettificare una cifra.

recurrent, *a.* ricorrente, periodico.

recyclable, *a.* (*econ.*) riciclabile.

recycle, *v. t.* (*econ.*) reciclare, riciclare.

recycling, *n.* (*econ.*) reciclaggio, riciclaggio, riciclo.

red, *a.* rosso. *n.* (il) rosso, color rosso. // ~ **interest** (*banca, rag.*) interessi sui numeri rossi; ~ **products** (*banca, rag.*) numeri rossi; to **be in the** ~ (*banca, cred., rag.*) essere in deficit, essere allo scoperto, essere «sotto».

redeem, *v. t.* 1 redimere. 2 (*fin.*) convertire in denaro contante, rimborsare (*obbligazioni*). 3 (*fin., leg.*) affrancare, liberare. 4 (*fin., leg.*) ricuperare, riscattare. 5 (*fin., leg.*) estinguere (*un'ipoteca, ecc.*). // to ~ **an estate** (*leg.*) svincolare una proprietà; to ~ **an inheritance** (*leg.*) affrancare un'eredità; to ~ **a mortgage** (*leg.*) estinguere un'ipoteca; to ~ **mortgaged land** (*leg.*) riscattare terreni ipotecati; to ~ **a pledge** (*leg.*) riscattare un pegno; to ~ **pledged goods** (*leg.*) ritirare oggetti dati in pegno; to ~ **one's rights** (*leg.*) ricuperare i propri diritti (*cioè, esservi reintegrato*).

redeemability, *n.* (*fin., leg.*) redimibilità, convertibilità in contanti.

redeemable, *a.* (*fin., leg.*) redimibile, ricuperabile, riscattabile, convertibile in contanti. // ~ **bonds** (*fin.*) obbligazioni redimibili; ~ **loan** (*cred.*) prestito redimibile; ~ **stock** (*fin.*) rendite ammortizzabili; ~ **stocks** (*fin.*) titoli redimibili.

redeemableness, *n.* (*fin., leg.*) redimibilità.

redemption, *n.* 1 disimpegno (*di una cosa data in pegno*). 2 (*fin.*) rimborso (*d'obbligazioni*). 3 (*fin., leg.*) ricupero, riscatto. 4 (*fin., leg.*) svincolo, liberazione (*da un impegno*). 5 (*fin., leg.*) estinzione (*d'un'ipoteca, ecc.*). // ~ **coupon** (*market.*) buono omaggio, buono sconto; ~ **date** (*cred.*) data prevista per il rimborso (*d'un prestito*); ~ **fund** (*fin.*) fondo d'ammortamento; **the** ~ **of mortgages** (*fin.*) l'estinzione (*o* la liberazione) d'ipoteche; **the** ~ **of a promissory note** (*cred.*) l'estinzione d'un pagherò.

redhibitory, *a.* (*leg.*) redibitorio. // ~ **action** (*leg.*) azione redibitoria.

redirect, *v. t.* (*comun.*) reindirizzare, rispedire (*una lettera*) a un nuovo indirizzo.

rediscount[1], *n.* (*banca, cred.*) risconto. // ~ **accounts** (*banca, cred.*) risconti; ~ **rate** (*banca, cred.*) tasso di risconto.

rediscount[2], *v. t.* (*banca, cred.*) riscontare, scontare di nuovo (*titoli di credito*).

redistribute, *v. t.* ridistribuire.

redistribution, *n.* ridistribuzione. // **the** ~

of income (*econ.*) la ridistribuzione del reddito.

redraft, *n.* **1** (*cred., leg.*) rivalsa. **2** (*cred., leg.*) cambiale di rivalsa.

redress[1], *n.* (*leg.*) risarcimento (*di danni, ecc.*). // to **get legal** ~ (*leg.*) ottenere giustizia.

redress[2], *v. t.* (*leg.*) risarcire (*danni, ecc.*). // to ~ **a damage** (*leg.*) risarcire un danno; to ~ **a wrong** (*leg.*) riparare un torto.

reduce, *v. t.* **1** ridurre, diminuire. **2** (*market.*) ribassare (*prezzi, ecc.*). **3** (*mat.*) ridurre (*una frazione, ai minimi termini*). // to ~ **a deficit** (*fin., rag.*) ridurre un disavanzo; to ~ **the discount rate** (*fin.*) ridurre il tasso di sconto; to ~ **dividends** (*fin.*) ridurre i dividendi; to ~ **the level of minimum reserves** (*fin.*) diminuire il livello delle riserve minime; to ~ **prices** (*market.*) ribassare i prezzi; to ~ **the staff** (*org. az.*) ridurre il personale.

reduced, *a.* ridotto, diminuito. // ~ **-rate** (*trasp.*) a tariffa ridotta; ~ **-rate ticket** (*trasp.*) biglietto a tariffa ridotta; ~ **rates** tariffe ridotte; **at** ~ **prices** (*market.*) a prezzi ribassati; to **be in** ~ **circumstances** essere in ristrettezze.

reduction, *n.* **1** riduzione, diminuizione. **2** (*market.*) ribasso (*di prezzi, ecc.*). **3** (*mat.*) riduzione (*d'una frazione: ai minimi termini*). // **a** ~ **in working hours** (*sind.*) una diminuzione delle ore di lavoro; **a** ~ **of capital** (*rag.*) una riduzione di capitale; **the** ~ **of the discount rate** (*banca, cred.*) la riduzione del tasso di sconto.

redundancy, *n.* **1** (*econ.*) esuberanza (*di personale, di manodopera*). **2** (*sind.*) (*di personale*) l'essere in soprannumero. // ~ **fund** (*sind., ingl.*) fondo per le indennità di licenziamento (*fondo previsto dalla legge inglese del 1965 e costituito col contributo dello Stato e dei datori di lavoro; in G.B. non esiste la Cassa integrazione guadagni*); ~ **money** (*o* **pay**) (*sind.*) liquidazione, indennità di licenziamento (*a manodopera esuberante*).

redundant, *a.* **1** ridondante. **2** (*sind.*) (*di personale*) esuberante, soprannumerario, in soprannumero. // to **be made** ~ (*sind., ingl.*) (*di dipendente*) essere dichiarato esuberante; essere licenziato perché in soprannumero.

re-embark, *v. t.* (*trasp. mar.*) reimbarcare, rimbarcare. *v. i.* (*trasp. mar.*) reimbarcarsi, rimbarcarsi.

re-embarkation, *n.* (*trsp. mar.*) reimbarco, rimbarco.

re-employ, *v. t.* **1** reimpiegare, rimpiegare, impiegare di nuovo. **2** (*pers.*) assumere di nuovo, riassumere.

re-employment, *n.* reimpiego. // **the** ~ **and readaptation of workers** (*sind.*) il reimpiego e il riadattamento dei lavoratori.

re-enact, *v. t.* rimettere (*una legge*) in vigore.

re-enactment, *n.* (*leg.*) rimessa in vigore (*d'una legge*).

re-enter, *v. t.* e *i.* **1** (*leg.*) rientrare (*in possesso di qc.*). **2** (*rag.*) registrare di nuovo (*scritture, ecc.*).

re-entry, *n.* **1** (*leg.*) il rientrare in possesso (*di qc.*). **2** (*rag.*) nuova registrazione (*di scritture, ecc.*).

re-establish, *v. t.* restaurare. // to ~ **the budget on a sound footing** (*rag.*) risanare il bilancio.

re-establishment, *n.* restaurazione.

re-estimate, *v. t.* (*rag.*) rivalutare.

re-estimation, *n.* (*rag.*) rivalutazione.

re-examination, *n.* riesame.

re-examine, *v. t.* riesaminare.

re-export[1], *n.* **1** (*comm. est.*) riesportazione. **2** (*comm. est.*) merce riesportata.

re-export[2], *v. t.* (*comm. est.*) riesportare.

re-exportation, *n.* **1** (*comm. est.*) riesportazione. **2** (*comm. est.*) merce riesportata.

re-exporter, *n.* (*comm. est.*) riesportatore.

refer, *v. t.* **1** deferire, rinviare. **2** affidare, rimettere. **3** indirizzare, dire a (*q.*) di rivolgersi (*a q. altro*). **4** (*pers.*) indirizzare per referenze, dare a (*q.*) il nome (*di q. altro*) come referenza. *v. i.* **1** accennare, riferirsi, fare riferimento. **2** rivolgersi (*per aiuto, informazioni, ecc.*). // to ~ **a case to a law-Court** (*leg.*) deferire una causa al tribunale; to ~ **to st.** concernere qc.; to ~ **to the award of the arbitrators** (*leg.*) rimettersi al lodo degli arbitri; to ~ **to a dictionary (a graph, etc.)** consultare un dizionario (un diagramma, ecc.); «~ **to drawer**» **(R/D)** (*banca, cred.*) «rivolgersi al traente» (*formula con la quale una banca rifiuta il pagamento d'un assegno scoperto*).

referee[1], *n.* **1** (*banca, cred.*) *V.* ~ **in case of need.** **2** (*leg.*) arbitro (*d'una lite*). **3** (*pers., ingl.*) chi è chiamato a dare referenze (*su q.*). // ~ **in bankruptcy** (*leg.*) giudice fallimentare; ~ **in case of need** (*banca, cred.*) bisognatario.

referee[2], *v. i.* (*leg.*) arbitrare, agire come arbitro. *v. t.* (*leg.*) arbitrare (*una lite, ecc.*).

reference[1], *n.* **1** riferimento, rinvio. **2** accenno. **3** consultazione. **4** (*leg.*) deferimento (*d'una lite*) a un arbitro. **5** (*leg.*) compromesso arbitrale. **6** (*pers.*) referenza, attestato, benservito. **7** (*pers.*) raccomandazione. **8** (*pers.*) chi è chiamato a dare referenze (*su q.*). // ~ **checking** (*pers.*) controllo delle referenze; ~ **currencies** (*fin.*) valute di riferimento; ~ **number** numero di riferimento; ~ **price** (*fin., market.*) prezzo di riferimento; ~ **tariffs** tariffe di riferimento; **in** (*o* **with**) ~ **to** in riferimento a, in relazione a.

reference[2], *v. t.* (*pers.*) fornire (*q.*) di referenze.

referendum, *n.* referendum.

referring, *n.* (*leg.*) deferimento (*di una causa a un tribunale*).

referring to, *prep.* in riferimento a. // ~ **our telephone conversation** in riferimento alla nostra conversazione telefonica.

re-finance, *v. t.* (*fin.*) finanziare di nuovo.

refitting yard, *n.* (*trasp. mar.*) cantiere di raddobbo.

reflate, *v. t.* (*econ.*) reflazionare, aumentare nuovamente il volume di (*credito, valuta, ecc.*). *v. i.* adottare misure reflazionistiche; provocare una reflazione.

reflation, *n.* (*econ.*) reflazione.

reflationary, *a.* (*econ.*) reflazionistico. // **a** ~ **budget** (*econ.*) un bilancio reflazionistico.

reforest, *v. t.* (*econ.*) rimboschire.

reforestation, *n.* (*econ.*) rimboschimento.

reform[1], *n.* riforma, miglioramento. // **the** ~ **of the international monetary system** (*econ.*) la riforma del sistema monetario internazionale.

reform[2], *v. t.* riformare, migliorare.

reforward, *v. t.* (*comun., trasp.*) rispedire.

reforwarding, *a.* (*comun., trasp.*) rispedizione.

refresher, *n.* (*leg., ingl.*) parcella supplementare (*pagata a un avvocato in una causa lunga*).

refrigerate, *v. t.* refrigerare, mettere (*qc.*) in frigorifero.

refrigeration, *n.* refrigerazione.

refrigerator, *n.* refrigeratore. // ~ **car** (*trasp. ferr.*) vagone frigorifero; ~ **van** (*trasp. aut.*) autocarro frigorifero; ~ **warehouse** (*market.*) magazzino frigorifero.

refuge, *n.* asilo.

refugee, *n.* profugo. // ~ **capitals** (*econ.*) capitali vaganti.

refund[1], *n.* **1** rifusione, restituzione. **2** rimborso (*di spese, ecc.*). **3** risarcimento, reintegrazione (*di danni, ecc.*). // **the** ~ **and remission of custom duties and of dues charges treated** (*comm. est.*) il rimborso e il ricupero dei dazi doganali e dei diritti assimilati; **refunds on exports** (*comm. est.*) restituzioni (all'esportazione).

refund[2], *v. t.* e *i.* **1** rifondere, restituire. **2** rimborsare (*spese, ecc.*); fare un rimborso. **3** risarcire, reintegrare (*danni, ecc.*). // to ~ **expenses** rimborsare le spese; to ~ **taxes on exports** (*comm. est.*) restituire tasse alla esportazione.

refunding, *n.* (*fin.*) conversione del debito pubblico.

refusal, *n.* **1** rifiuto. **2** (*comm.*) scelta, opzione, diritto d'opzione.

refuse, *v. t.* e *i.* rifiutare, rifiutarsi, respingere.

regain, *v. t.* ricuperare. // to ~ **one's footing** rimettersi in piedi (*dopo una caduta; anche fig.*).

regard[1], *n.* ossequio, rispetto. // **in** ~ **to** riguardo a, in quanto a; **without** ~ **to** senza tener conto di.

regard[2], *v. t.* **1** riguardare. **2** tenere in considerazione. // **as regards** quanto a.

regardless, *a.* sbadato. // ~ **of** a dispetto di; ~ **of expenses** senza badare a spese.

region, *n.* regione, provincia, zona.

regional, *a.* regionale, provinciale, zonale. // ~ **economic problems** (*econ.*) problemi economici regionali; ~ **edition** (*giorn.*) edizione regionale; ~ **exchanges** (*Borsa, USA*) Borse (valori) regionali (*che, cioè, hanno sede fuori New York*); ~ **policy** politica regionale.

register[1], *n.* **1** registro. **2** (*rag.*) registro, libro contabile. **3** (*trasp. mar.*) *V.* ~ **tonnage.** // **the** ~ **of Companies** (*fin., leg.*) il Registro delle Società; ~ **of credits** (*banca, cred.*) libro dei fidi; **the** ~ **of debenture-holders** (*fin.*) il registro degli obbligazionisti; **the** ~ **of directors** (*fin., leg.*) il registro degli amministratori; **the** ~ **of members** (*fin.*) il registro dei soci; **the** ~ **of patents** (*leg.*) il registro dei brevetti; **the** ~ **of shareholders** (*fin.*) il registro degli azionisti; **the** ~ **of shipping** (*trasp. mar.*) il registro marittimo, il registro navale; ~ **of stocks and shares** (*fin., rag.*) libro delle obbligazioni; ~ **office** (*amm.*) ufficio dello Stato Civile, anagrafe; ~ **ton** (*trasp. mar.*) tonnellata di registro, tonnellata di stazza; ~ **tonnage** (*trasp. mar.*) tonnellaggio di registro, tonnellaggio di stazza.

register[2], *v. t.* **1** registrare, prendere nota di (*qc.*). **2** (*comun.*) raccomandare (*una lettera*). **3** (*fin.*) registrare (*titoli*) a nome del detentore. **4** (*leg.*) intestare; depositare (*un brevetto, un marchio di fabbrica*). **5** (*trasp.*) spedire (*bagaglio*) assicurato. **6** (*trasp. aer., trasp. aut.*) immatricolare, iscrivere (*una nave, un'automobile*). // to ~ **a deed** (*leg.*) registrare un atto; to ~ **a law** (*leg.*) trascrivere una legge; to ~ **a mortgage charge** (*leg.*) registrare un privilegio ipotecario; to ~ **a parcel** (*comun.*) raccomandare un pacco; to ~ **shares (bonds, etc.) in sb.'s name** (*cred., fin.*) intestare azioni (titoli, ecc.) a q.; to ~ **a trade-mark** (*leg.*) depositare un marchio di fabbrica.

registered, *a.* 1 registrato. 2 (*fin.*) (*di titolo*) nominativo. 3 (*leg.*) intestato; (*di brevetto, marchio di fabbrica, ecc.*) depositato. 4 (*trasp.*) (*di bagaglio*) assicurato. 5 (*trasp. aer., trasp. aut.*) (*d'automobile, naviglio, ecc.*) immatricolato. // ~ **bond** (*fin.*) obbligazione nominativa; ~ **capital** (*fin.*) capitale nominale, capitale sociale (*autorizzato dal Conservatore del Registro delle Società*); ~ **company** (*fin., ingl.*) società costituita mediante registrazione (*ai sensi delle leggi sulle società di capitali*); ~ **holder** (*fin., leg.*) intestatario; ~ **letter** (*comun.*) raccomandata, lettera raccomandata; ~ **mail** (*comun.*) posta raccomandata; ~ **office** (*fin.*) sede legale (*d'una società*); (*leg.*) domicilio legale; ~ **parcels** (*trasp.*) pacchi raccomandati; ~ **pattern** (*leg.*) modello depositato; ~ **securities** (*fin.*) titoli nominativi; ~ **shares** (*fin.*) azioni nominative; ~ **tonnage** (*trasp. mar.*) *V.* **register tonnage;** ~ **trade-mark** (*leg.*) marchio registrato.

registrar, *n.* 1 (*amm.*) ufficiale di Stato Civile. 2 (*amm.*) archivista. 3 (*leg.*) cancelliere. // **the** ~ **of Companies** (*fin., ingl.*) il Conservatore del Registro delle Società; **the** ~ **of Mortgages** (*leg.*) il Conservatore delle Ipoteche.

registration, *n.* 1 registrazione, annotazione. 2 (*comun.*) (*di lettere*) raccomandazione. 3 (*fin.*) registrazione (*di titoli*) a nome del detentore. 4 (*leg.*) intestazione; deposito (*di brevetti, marchi di fabbrica, ecc.*). 5 (*trasp.*) spedizione assicurata (*di bagaglio*). 6 (*trasp. aer., trasp. mar.*) immatricolazione (*di nave, automobile, ecc.*). // ~ **certificate** (*trasp. mar.*) certificato di registrazione; ~ **fee** (*comun.*) tassa per (lettera) raccomandata; **the** ~ **of business names** (*fin., leg.*) la registrazione delle ditte; ~ **of a mortgage** (*leg.*) iscrizione ipotecaria; ~ **of a transfer deed** (*leg.*) voltura; ~ **statement** (*fin., USA*) documento che descrive i dettagli d'una nuova emissione (*di titoli*); ~ **under the Companies Act** (*fin., ingl.*) registrazione ai sensi delle leggi sulle società.

registry, *n.* *V.* **registration.** // ~ **fee** (*comun., USA*) *V.* **registration fee;** ~ **office** (*amm.*) anagrafe, ufficio di stato civile.

regress, *n.* regresso.

regression, *n.* regresso.

regressive, *a.* regressivo. // ~ **tax** (*fin.*) imposta regressiva.

regret[1], *n.* rimpianto.

regret[2], *v. t.* rimpiangere; dispiacere.

regular, *a.* 1 regolare, normale, regolamentare. 2 solito, usuale. 3 (*pers.: d'impiegato*) effettivo, titolare. // **a** ~ **customer** (*market.*) un cliente abituale, un cliente fisso; **a** ~ **job** (*pers.*) un lavoro stabile, un lavoro fisso; ~ **lot** (*Borsa, fin.*) unità normale di contrattazione (*di titoli*); **the** ~ **procedure** la procedura usuale, la prassi; ~ **stop** (*trasp.*) fermata obbligatoria; **on the** ~ **staff** (*pers.*) in pianta stabile, effettivo.

regularity, *n.* regolarità. // **the** ~ **of a deed** (*leg.*) la regolarità d'un atto.

regularization, *n.* regolarizzazione.

regularize, *v. t.* regolarizzare. // to ~ **markets** (*econ.*) regolarizzare i mercati.

regulate, *v. t.* 1 regolare, ordinare, regolarizzare. 2 (*leg.*) regolamentare. // to ~ **freight rates** (*trasp. mar.*) regolamentare le tariffe di nolo.

regulated company, *n.* (*econ.*) società a economia controllata (*dallo Stato*).

regulation, *n.* 1 regolazione, regolarizzazione. 2 (*leg.*) regolamentazione, ordinamento. 3 (*leg.*) regola, regolamento, norma. // **the regulations in force** (*leg.*) le disposizioni vigenti; **the** ~ **of affairs** la regolamentazione degli affari.

rehabilitate, *v. t.* 1 (*leg.*) riabilitare. 2 (*leg.*) reintegrare (*q.*) nei suoi diritti. 3 (*leg.*) rimettere (*q.*) in carica. // to ~ **a company financially** (*fin.*) rimettere in piedi una società (finanziariamente).

rehabilitation, *n.* (*leg.*) riabilitazione. // **the** ~ **of an insolvent debtor** (*leg.*) la riabilitazione d'un debitore insolvente.

rehear, *v. t.* (*pass.* e *part. pass.* **reheard**) 1 udire di nuovo, riudire. 2 (*leg.*) riesaminare, giudicare di nuovo (*una causa*).

rehearing, *n.* (*leg.*) riesame (*d'una causa*); revisione.

reimbursable, *a.* rimborsabile, restituibile, risarcibile. // ~ **expenses** spese rimborsabili.

reimburse, *v. t.* rimborsare, rifondere, risarcire, restituire.

reimbursement, *n.* rimborso, risarcimento, rifusione, restituzione. // **a** ~ **of expenses** un rimborso (delle) spese.

reimport[1], *n.* 1 (*comm. est.*) reimportazione. 2 (*comm. est.*) merce reimportata.

reimport[2], *v. t.* (*comm. est.*) reimportare, importare di nuovo.

reimportation, *n.* 1 (*comm. est.*) reimportazione. 2 (*comm. est.*) merce reimportata.

reinstate, *v. t.* (*leg.*) riabilitare. // to **be reinstated in one's rights** (*leg.*) rientrare nei propri diritti.

reinstatement, *n.* (*leg.*) riabilitazione.

reinsurance, *n.* (*ass.*) riassicurazione. // ~ **company** (*ass.*) compagnia di riassicurazioni.

reinsure, *v. t.* (*ass.*) riassicurare.

reinsured, *a.* (*ass.*) riassicurato.

reinsurer, *n.* (*ass.*) riassicuratore.

reinvest, *v. t.* (*fin.*) reinvestire, reimpiegare, rimpiegare (*capitali*). *v. i.* (*fin.*) fare un reinvestimento.

reinvestment, *n.* (*fin.*) reinvestimento, reimpiego (*di capitali*). // **a ~ of capitals** (*fin.*) un reinvestimento di capitali.

reissue[1], *n.* (*fin.*) nuova emissione (*di titoli*).

reissue[2], *v. t.* **1** (*fin.*) emettere di nuovo (*titoli*). **2** (*giorn., pubbl.*) ristampare (*libri, giornali, ecc.*).

reject[1], *n.* (*market.*) rifiuto, scarto, oggetto di scarto.

reject[2], *v. t.* **1** rifiutare, respingere. **2** gettar via, scartare. // to ~ **a claim** respingere un reclamo; to ~ **a defective specimen** scartare un esemplare difettoso; to ~ **an offer** respingere un'offerta; **rejected material** (*market.*) scarto.

rejection, *n.* rigetto (*burocratico*); rifiuto, reiezione. // **the ~ of a petition** (*leg.*) il rigetto d'una istanza.

rejoin, *v. t.* (*leg.*) controreplicare.

rejoinder, *n.* **1** risposta. **2** (*leg.*) controreplica.

relabel, *v. t.* (*market.*) mettere una nuova etichetta a (*qc.*).

relate, *v. t.* **1** mettere in relazione, collegare. **2** riferire, raccontare. // to **be related (with)** essere connesso (con); **relating to procedure** (*leg.*) procedurale.

relation, *n.* **1** relazione, rapporto, collegamento. **2 relations,** *pl.* relazioni, rapporti; ambiente, clima (*fig.*). // **in ~ to** riferendosi a.

relationship, *n.* **1** relazione, rapporto. **2** (*leg.*) parentela. // ~ **by collateral line** (*leg.*) parentela in linea collaterale.

relative, *a.* relativo, connesso, rispettivo. *n.* congiunto. // **the relatives-in-law** (*leg.*) gli affini; ~ **to** in relazione con.

relax, *v. t.* allentare, diminuire, ridurre. *v. i* **1** rilassarsi. **2** attenuarsi, diminuire. // to ~ **discipline** allentare la disciplina.

relaxation, *n.* **1** rilassamento, rilassatezza. **2** allentamento, diminuzione. // **the ~ of a fine** (*leg.*) la remissione d'un'ammenda; **the ~ of a law** (*leg.*) l'attenuazione d'una legge.

relaxed, *a.* allentato, diminuito, ridotto. // ~ **restrictions on imports** (*comm. est.*) ridotte restrizioni all'importazione.

release[1], *n.* **1** liberazione. **2** (*giorn.*) permesso di pubblicazione (*d'una notizia*). **3** (*leg.*) rilascio (*d'un detenuto*). **4** (*leg.*) liberazione (*da un obbligo*), svincolo. **5** (*leg.*) cessione (*di proprietà*); atto di cessione (*d'un diritto*). **6** (*leg.*) abbandono (*d'un diritto*). **7** (*leg.*) remissione (*d'un debito*). // ~ **from seizure** (*leg.*) dissequestro; ~ **on bail** (*leg.*) rilascio sotto cauzione.

release[2], *v. t.* **1** liberare. **2** (*giorn.*) rendere pubblica (*una notizia*). **3** (*leg.*) rilasciare, prosciogliere (*un prigioniero*). **4** (*leg.*) liberare (*da un obbligo*). **5** (*leg.*) abbandonare (*un diritto*). **6** (*leg.*) cedere (*una proprietà*). **7** (*leg.*) rimettere (*un debito*). // to ~ **from seizure** (*leg.*) dissequestrare; to ~ **a right** (*leg.*) rinunciare a un diritto.

releasee, *n.* (*leg.*) cessionario (*chi ottiene la cessione d'una proprietà*).

releasement, *n.* liberazione (*V. anche* **release**[1]).

releaser, *n. V.* **releasor.**

releasor, *n.* (*leg.*) cedente (*chi cede un diritto o una proprietà*).

relessee, *n. V.* **releasee.**

relet, *v. t.* (*pass.* e *part. pass.* **relet**) (*leg.*) subaffittare.

reletting, *n.* (*leg.*) subaffitto.

relevant, *a.* **1** importante. **2** attinente, pertinente. // **a ~ testimony** (*leg.*) una deposizione pertinente.

reliability, *n.* attendibilità, credibilità, fidatezza.

reliable, *a.* attendibile, credibile, fidato.

reliance, *n.* **1** affidamento, assegnamento. **2** fiducia, fede. // to **place ~ on st.** fare ricorso a qc.

relief, *n.* **1** ristoro. **2** aiuto, assistenza. **3** (*comm., fin., market.*) agevolazione. **4** (*fin.*) esenzione, sgravio (*da una tassa, ecc.*). **5** (*leg.*) condono. **6** (*pers.*) cambio (*che si dà a un collega, alla fine d'un turno di lavoro*). // ~ **for expenses** (*fin.*) deduzione (*o* detrazione) per spese sostenute (*concessa dal fisco*); ~ **for vacant property** (*fin.*) sgravio (fiscale) per sfitto; ~ **funds** fondi d'assistenza; ~ **train** (*trasp. ferr.*) treno straordinario, treno supplementare; to **be on ~** (*sind.*) (*di lavoratore*) percepire il sussidio di disoccupazione.

relieve, *v. t.* **1** ristorare, sollevare, dar sollievo a. **2** alleviare. **3** assistere, aiutare. **4** (*fin.*) esentare, sgravare (*da una tassa, ecc.*). **5** (*pers.*) dare il cambio a (*un collega*). // to ~ **sb. of all responsibility** (*leg.*) alleggerire q. da ogni responsabilità.

relinquish, *v. t.* **1** abbandonare, lasciare. **2** cedere, rinunciare a. // to ~ **one's claim to an**

inheritance (*leg.*) rinunciare il proprio diritto a un'eredità; to ~ **a right** (*leg.*) cedere un diritto.

relinquishment, *n.* 1 abbandono. 2 cessione, rinuncia.

reload[1], *n.* (*trasp.*) ricaricamento.

reload[2], *v. t.* (*trasp.*) ricaricare.

relocation, *n.* (*leg.*) rinnovo del contratto d'affitto, riconduzione.

rely, *v. t.* contare (*su*), fidarsi (*di*).

remain, *v. i.* rimanere, restare. // to ~ **in force** (*leg.*) (*di contratto, patto, ecc.*) restare in vigore; to ~ **in office** rimanere in carica; to ~ **vacant** (*leg.*) (*di locale, ecc.*) restare spigionato, restare sfitto.

remainder[1], *n.* 1 resto, residuo, rimanente, avanzo. 2 (*market.*) rimanenza, giacenza. 3 (*mat.*) resto, residuo. // **the ~ of the goods** (*market.*) il rimanente della merce; ~ **prices** (*market.*) prezzi delle rimanenze.

remainder[2], *v. t.* liquidare (*merce invenduta*); svendere (*rimanenze*). *v. i.* (*market.*) liquidare le rimanenze.

remainders, *n. pl.* (*market.*) giacenze (*o* rimanenze, fondi) di magazzino.

remaining, *a.* rimanente, restante.

remand[1], *n.* (*leg.*) rinvio in carcere (*per un supplemento d'istruttoria*). // to **be on** ~ (*leg.*) (*d'imputato*) essere trattenuto in carcere.

remand[2], *v. t.* 1 (*leg.*) rinviare (*una causa a un tribunale inferiore*). 2 (*leg.*) rinviare (*un imputato in carcere*).

remanet, *n.* (*leg.*) causa rinviata (*a nuova udienza*).

remedy[1], *n.* 1 cura. 2 provvedimento. 3 (*leg.*) azione giudiziaria.

remind, *v. t.* ricordare a (*q.*).

reminder, *n.* 1 promemoria, «memento». 2 (*comm.*) lettera di sollecitazione, sollecito, sollecitatoria. // ~ **of due date** (*comm.*) promemoria di scadenza.

remint, *v. t.* (*fin.*) coniare di nuovo (*monete*).

remise[1], *n.* (*leg.*) rinuncia (*a un diritto*). // **the ~ of a claim** (*leg.*) l'abbandono d'una pretesa; **the ~ of a right** (*leg.*) la rinuncia a un diritto.

remise[2], *v. t.* 1 (*leg.*) rinunciare a (*un diritto*). 2 (*leg.*) cedere (*una proprietà*).

remission, *n.* 1 (*leg.*) remissione, condono. 2 (*leg.*) cessione (*di proprietà*). // **the ~ of a case** (*leg.*) il rinvio d'una causa (*a un altro tribunale*); **the ~ of a claim** (*leg.*) la rinuncia a far valere un diritto; **the ~ of a debt** (*cred.*) la remissione d'un debito; **the ~ of an offence** (*leg.*) la remissione d'un delitto.

remit, *v. t.* 1 affidare, demandare. 2 (*comun.*) mandare, inviare, spedire. 3 (*leg.*) rimettere, condonare. 4 (*leg.*) rinviare (*una causa*) a un altro tribunale. *v. i.* (*comm.*) fare una rimessa, inviare denaro. // to ~ **a debt** (*cred.*) rimettere un debito; to ~ **a penalty** (*leg.*) condonare una pena; to ~ **a sentence** (*leg.*) sospendere una sentenza.

remittal, *n. V.* **remission.**

remittance, *n.* 1 (*comm.*) rimessa (*in denaro, ecc.*); invio (*di denaro, ecc.*). 2 (*comm.*) denaro spedito. // **a ~ in settlement** (*cred.*) una rimessa a saldo; **a ~ of cheques subject to payment** (*banca*) rimessa d'assegni salvo buon fine; «**our ~ of bills**» (*banca*) «nostra rimessa d'effetti».

remittee, *n.* (*comm.*) destinatario d'una rimessa (*di denaro, ecc.*).

remitter, *n.* (*comm.*) chi effettua una rimessa (*di denaro, ecc.*).

remnant, *n.* 1 resto, avanzo, rimanenza. 2 (*market.*) ritaglio (*di stoffa*). // **a ~ sale** (*market.*) una vendita di scampoli.

remote, *a.* remoto, lontano, distante. // ~ **control** (*comun.*) telecomando, telecontrollo; ~ **damages** (*leg.*) danni remoti, danni indiretti.

removal, *n.* 1 spostamento, trasferimento. 2 (*dog., econ.*) disarmo. 3 (*pers.*) destituzione; allontanamento (*da un ufficio*); rimozione (*da un grado*); sospensione (*dal lavoro*). // **a ~ agency** un'agenzia di traslochi; **the ~ of a cause** (*leg.*) il rinvio d'una causa (*a un altro giudice*); **the ~ of distrained chattels** (*leg.*) la sottrazione di beni pignorati; **the ~ of quotas and customs barriers** (*comm. est., dog.*) il disarmo dei dazi e dei contingenti; **the ~ of seals** (*leg.*) la rimozione dei sigilli; ~ **under bond** (*dog.*) ritiro sotto cauzione; ~ **van** (*trasp. aut.*) furgone per traslochi.

remove, *v. t.* 1 rimuovere, levare, togliere; allontanare, trasferire. 2 (*pers.*) destituire; allontanare (*q., da un ufficio*); rimuovere (*q., da un grado*); sospendere (*dal lavoro*). *v. i.* trasferirsi. // to ~ **all barriers to trade** (*comm. est.*) sopprimere tutti gli ostacoli agli scambi; to ~ **an article from the catalogue** (*market.*) stralciare un articolo dal catalogo; to ~ **the attachment** (*leg.*) togliere il sequestro; to ~ **sb. from office** (*pers.*) rimuovere q. dalla carica; dimettere, licenziare q.; to ~ **goods from the customs** (*dog.*) ritirare merci dalla dogana.

remover, *n.* (*ingl.*) proprietario d'un'agenzia di traslochi.

remunerate, *v. t.* rimunerare, retribuire, pagare. // to ~ **expenses** rimborsare le spese.

remuneration, *n.* rimunerazione, pagamento, retribuzione. // ~ **for salvage** (*trasp. mar.*) indennità di salvataggio, premio di salvataggio.

remunerative, *a.* rimunerativo, rimuneratorio, lucrativo, redditizio. // **a ~ business** un'azienda redditizia; ~ **jobs** (*pers.*) lavori rimunerativi; **a ~ salary** (*pers.*) uno stipendio rimunerativo.

render, *v. t.* 1 rendere, restituire. 2 sottoporre (*un documento*). 3 (*market.*) presentare (*un conto: a un cliente, ecc.*). // to ~ **an account of one's actions** render conto delle proprie azioni; to ~ **a service** rendere un servizio, fare un favore; to ~ **void** (*leg.*) rendere nullo; «**account rendered**» «conto presentato» (*ma non ancora saldato*); «to **be rendered**» (*market.*) «a rendere».

renew, *v. t.* rinnovare, rimettere a nuovo, sostituire. // to ~ **a bill** (*banca, cred.*) rinnovare una cambiale; to ~ **a contract** (*leg.*) rinnovare un contratto; to ~ **the staff** (*org. az.*) rinnovare il personale.

renewal, *n.* 1 rinnovamento, sostituzione. 2 (*comm.*) rinnovo. // **the ~ of a bill** (*banca, cred.*) il rinnovo d'una cambiale; **the ~ of a contract** (*leg.*) il rinnovo d'un contratto; **the ~ of a copyright** (*leg.*) il rinnovo d'un diritto d'autore; ~ **of lease** (*leg.*) riconduzione; ~ **premium** (*ass.*) premio di rinnovo.

renounce, *v. t.* rinunciare a, cedere, abbandonare. // to ~ **a claim** abbandonare una pretesa; to ~ **a right** (*leg.*) rinunciare a un diritto.

renouncement, *n.* rinuncia, cessione, abbandono.

renown, *n.* rinomanza, fama, notorietà. // **the ~ of our products** la rinomanza dei nostri prodotti.

renowned, *a.* rinomato, famoso.

rent[1], *n.* 1 (*econ.*) rendita. 2 (*leg.*) affitto, canone d'affitto, prezzo della locazione. 3 (*leg.*) (*di macchinario, ecc.*) nolo. // ~ **agreement** (*leg.*) contratto d'affitto; ~ **control** (*econ.*) blocco degli affitti; ~ **-free** (*leg.*) (*d'alloggio*) gratuito; ~ **in advance** (*leg.*) affitto anticipato; ~ **in arrears** (*leg.*) affitto in arretrato; ~ **-roll** (*fin.*) ruolo dei censi, ammontare delle rendite dei propri terreni; ~ **-service** (*leg.*) servizi resi in luogo del canone d'affitto; «**for** ~» (*USA*) «a nolo», «affittasi».

rent[2], *v. t.* 1 (*leg.*) affittare. 2 (*leg.*) prendere in affitto, avere in affitto. 3 (*leg.*) locare, dare in affitto.

rentable, *a.* (*leg.*) affittabile.

rental, *n.* 1 (*econ.*) reddito di fabbricati, reddito dominicale. 2 (*leg.*) canone d'affitto. 3 (*leg.*) valore locativo. 4 (*leg.*) proprietà data in affitto. // ~ **value** (*leg.*) valore locativo; ~ **-value insurance** (*ass.*) assicurazione sul valore locativo.

renter, *n.* 1 (*leg.*) locatario, inquilino. 2 (*leg.*) affittuario, fittavolo. // ~ **of a safe-deposit box** (*banca*) cassettista (*chi ha in affitto una cassetta di sicurezza*).

renunciation, *n.* rinuncia, abbandono, cessione.

reopen, *v. t.* 1 riaprire. 2 riprendere (*una discussione, ecc.*). *v. i.* 1 ricominciare. 2 (*market.*) (*di negozio, ecc.*) riaprire. // to ~ **an account** (*rag.*) riaprire un conto.

reopening, *n.* 1 riapertura. 2 ripresa (*d'una discussione, ecc.*). 3 (*market.*) (*di negozio*) riapertura. // ~ **clause** (*sind.*) clausola che prevede la riapertura d'un contratto collettivo di lavoro; **the ~ of the books** (*rag.*) la riapertura dei libri (contabili).

reorder[1], *n.* (*market.*) nuova ordinazione (*delle stesse merci ordinate precedentemente*).

reorder[2], *v. t.* 1 rimettere in ordine. 2 (*market.*) ordinare (*merci*) di nuovo. 3 (*org. az.*) riorganizzare. *v. i.* (*market.*) fare nuove ordinazioni.

reordering, *n.* (*org. az.*) riorganizzazione.

reorganization, *n.* 1 riorganizzazione. 2 (*org. az.*) riorganizzazione. // **the ~ of the staff** (*org. az.*) la riorganizzazione del personale.

reorganize, *v. t.* 1 riorganizzare. 2 (*org. az.*) riorganizzare. *v. i.* 1 riorganizzarsi. 2 (*org. az.*) riorganizzarsi.

rep, *n.* (*abbr. di* **representative**) (*pers., USA*) rappresentante.

repair[1], *n.* (*trasp. mar.*) raddobbo. // **repairs and upkeep** (*org. az., rag.*) manutenzioni e riparazioni; ~ **charges** (*rag.*) spese di riparazione; ~ **ship** (*trasp. mar.*) nave officina; **under ~** in riparazione.

repair[2], *v. t.* 1 aggiustare. 2 metter riparo a, risarcire. // to ~ **a loss** (*leg.*) risarcire una perdita.

repairing, *n.* aggiustamento. // ~ **basin** (*trasp. mar.*) bacino di raddobbo, bacino di carenaggio.

reparable, *a.* 1 riparabile. 2 rimediabile, risarcibile. // **a ~ damage** un danno riparabile.

reparation, *n.* 1 riparazione (*di danni, torti, ecc.*). 2 **reparations,** *pl.* riparazioni, restauri.

repay, *v. t.* (*pass.* e *part. pass.* **repaid**) 1 restituire, rendere. 2 rimborsare, reintegrare. // to ~ **creditors** (*cred.*) rimborsare i creditori; to

~ **sb. for his services** ricompensare q. per i suoi servigi.

repayable, *a.* rimborsabile, restituibile. // ~ **at call** (*cred.*) rimborsabile a vista; ~ **costs** (*leg.*) spese (*di causa*) ripetibili.

repayment, *n.* rimborso, restituzione, resa. // ~ **of VAT on exportation** (*fin.*) restituzione dell'IVA all'esportazione.

repeal[1], *n.* (*leg.*) abrogazione, annullamento, revoca. // **the** ~ **of a law** (*leg.*) l'abrogazione d'una legge; **the** ~ **of a provision** (*leg.*) la revoca d'una disposizione.

repeal[2], *v. t.* (*leg.*) abrogare, annullare, revocare.

repealable, *a.* (*leg.*) abrogabile, annullabile, revocabile.

repeat[1], *n.* **1** rinnovo. **2** (*comm.*) rinnovo. // ~ **order** (*market.*) ordinazione rinnovata.

repeat[2], *v. t.* rinnovare, rifare, ridire. // to ~ **an order** (*market.*) rinnovare un'ordinazione.

repeater, *n.* **1** chi ripete. **2** (*mat.*) numero periodico.

repel, *v. t.* respingere, ricacciare.

repetend, *n.* (*mat.*) periodo (*di decimale periodico*).

replace, *v. t.* **1** riporre. **2** sostituire. **3** (*amm., pers.*) subentrare a (*q.*).

replaceable, *a.* **1** sostituibile, soppiantabile. **2** (*econ.*) fungibile, surrogabile. // ~ **goods** (*econ.*) beni fungibili.

replacement, *n.* **1** soppiantamento, sostituzione. **2** (*amm., pers.*) successione, subentro. // ~ **cost** (*org. az.*) costo di sostituzione (*d'un'attività fissa con un'altra altrettanto valida*); ~ **value** (*econ.*) valore di sostituzione.

repleader, *n.* **1** (*leg.*) diritto di replica. **2** (*leg.*) riapertura d'un processo (*per scoperta d'un vizio*).

replenish, *v. t.* **1** riempire. **2** (*org. az.*) rifornire (*il magazzino*). **3** (*org. az.*) completare (*le scorte*). **4** (*trasp. mar.*) rifornire. *v. i.* (*trasp. mar.*) rifornirsi. // to ~ **a ship at sea** (*trasp. mar.*) rifornire una nave in mare.

replenishment, *n.* **1** riempimento. **2** (*org. az.*) rifornimento (*del magazzino*). **3** (*org. az.*) completamento (*delle scorte*); ristabilimento (*delle giacenze*). **4** (*trasp. mar.*) rifornimento. // **a** ~ **at sea** (*trasp. mar.*) un rifornimento in mare.

replevin[1], *n.* (*leg.*) reintegrazione (*sotto cauzione*) di beni mobili.

replevin[2], *v. t. V.* **replevy.**

replevy, *v. t.* (*leg.*) ricuperare sotto cauzione (*beni mobili*).

replication, *n.* risposta.

reply[1], *n.* risposta. // ~ **card** (*comun.*) cartolina con risposta pagata; ~ **-paid telegram** (*comun.*) telegramma con risposta pagata; ~ **postal card** (*comun.*) cartolina con risposta pagata; ~ **sheet** (*market., pubbl.*) foglio per le risposte (*in un questionario, ecc.*); **a** ~ **to a letter of application** (*comun.*) la risposta a una domanda d'assunzione.

reply[2], *v. t.* e *i.* rispondere. // to ~ **in writing** (*comun.*) rispondere per iscritto.

report[1], *n.* **1** rapporto, relazione, resoconto. **2** annuncio, comunicazione. **3** (*giorn.*) servizio, pezzo di cronaca. // **the** ~ **of the auditors** (*leg.*) la relazione dei revisori dei conti; **the** ~ **of the whole cargo** (*trasp. mar.*) la dichiarazione generale (*in dogana*); ~ **on a clerk** (*pers.*) note informative; **on** ~ (*org. az., pers.*) a rapporto.

report[2], *v. t.* **1** riportare, riferire, «relazionare». **2** annunciare, comunicare, dichiarare. **3** fare rapporto contro (*q.*); deferire, denunciare. *v. i.* presentarsi. // to ~ **an accident** denunciare un incidente; to ~ **the cargo** (*trasp. mar.*) dichiarare il carico (*in dogana*); to ~ **an employee to the management** fare rapporto alla direzione contro un dipendente.

reportage, *n.* (*giorn.*) cronaca giornalistica.

reporter, *n.* **1** chi riferisce, rapportatore. **2** (*giorn.*) cronista, redattore, reporter.

reporting, *n.* **1** (*giorn.*) servizio d'informazioni. **2** (*giorn.*) giornalismo.

report oneself, *v. rifl.* presentarsi (a rapporto).

repossess, *v. t.* **1** (*leg.*) rientrare in possesso di (*qc.*). **2** (*leg.*) reintegrare (*q.*) nel possesso di qc. **3** (*market.*) ricuperare (*un oggetto venduto a rate, ma non pagato del tutto*) senza adire le vie legali.

repossession, *n.* **1** (*leg.*) (il) rientrare in possesso. **2** (*leg.*) il reintegrare (*q.*) nel possesso di qc. **3** (*market.*) ricupero pacifico (*d'un oggetto venduto a rate, ma non pagato interamente*).

represent, *v. t.* **1** rappresentare, simboleggiare. **2** (*leg.*) rappresentare. **3** (*market., pers.*) fare il rappresentante per (*q.*). // to ~ **the parties** (*leg.*) rappresentare le parti contendenti (*davanti al tribunale*).

representation, *n.* **1** rappresentazione. **2** (*leg.*) rappresentazione (*nel diritto di successione*). **3** (*leg.*) rappresentanza.

representational, *a.* rappresentativo.

representative, *a.* rappresentativo. *n.* **1** rappresentante. **2** (*pers.*) (= **representative agent**) rappresentante, agente, venditore. // ~ **agent** (*pers.*) rappresentante, venditore; ~ **firm**

(*market.*) azienda tipo; **a ~ Government** un sistema (di Governo) rappresentativo; **the representatives of the press** (*giorn.*) i rappresentanti della stampa.

repressed inflation, *n.* (*econ.*) inflazione controllata (*dal Governo*).

reprice, *v. t.* (*market.*) stabilire un nuovo prezzo per (*articoli, merci, ecc.*).

reprieve[1]**,** *n.* (*leg.*) sospensione dell'esecuzione (*d'una sentenza*).

reprieve[2]**,** *v. t.* (*leg.*) sospendere l'esecuzione di (*una sentenza*).

reprimand[1]**,** *n.* (*pers.*) ammonizione.

reprimand[2]**,** *v. t.* (*pers.*) ammonire.

reprisal, *n.* (*leg.*) rappresaglia, ritorsione.

reprise, *n.* (*fin.*) detrazione annuale (*sul reddito agrario, per pagamento di annualità, imposte, ecc.*). // **above all reprises** (*fin.*) al netto di tutte le detrazioni.

reproduce, *v. t.* riprodurre. *v. i.* essere riprodotto, essere copiato.

reproductive, *a.* di riproduzione. // **~ industries** (*econ.*) industrie di riproduzione.

repudiate, *v. t.* **1** ricusare. **2** rifiutare di riconoscere, misconoscere. // to **~ a debt** (*cred.*) rifiutare di riconoscere un debito.

repudiation, *n.* misconoscimento, rifiuto di riconoscere (*un debito, ecc.*).

repurchase[1]**,** *n.* ricompera, riscatto. // **~ clause** (*leg.*) clausola di riacquisto.

repurchase[2]**,** *v. t.* riscattare.

reputable, *a.* rispettabile, stimabile. // **~ conduct** una condotta rispettabile.

reputation, *n.* fama, nome, buon nome, stima.

repute[1]**,** *n.* fama, nome, buon nome.

repute[2]**,** *v. t.* credere, giudicare, stimare.

reputed owner, *n.* (*leg.*) proprietario presunto.

reputed ownership, *n.* (*leg.*) proprietà presunta.

request[1]**,** *n.* richiesta, domanda, istanza, sollecitazione, sollecito. // **~ for bids** (*o* **for tenders**) concorso (*o* gara) d'appalto; **a ~ for credit** (*banca, cred.*) una richiesta d'accreditamento; **a ~ for a loan** (*cred.*) una domanda di mutuo; **~ stop** (*trasp.*) fermata a richiesta; **at ~** a richiesta, su invito; **by ~** a richiesta, su invito; to **be in ~** (*market.*) (*di prodotto, ecc.*) essere richiesto; **on ~** su richiesta; **upon ~** su richiesta.

request[2]**,** *v. t.* richiedere, chiedere, domandare, sollecitare. // to **~ a delay** (*market.*) chiedere una dilazione.

require, *v. t.* **1** richiedere, chiedere, domandare. **2** abbisognare, aver bisogno di (*qc.*). **3** esigere, volere. **4** volerci. // to **~ the payment of a debt** (*cred.*) esigere il pagamento d'un debito; **the required books** (*rag.*) i libri (contabili) obbligatori.

requirement, *n.* **1** bisogno, fabbisogno. **2** esigenza, necessità. **3** requisito, qualità richiesta, richiesta. **4 requirements,** *pl.* (*fin., rag.*) parte fabbisogni (*d'un bilancio*).

requisite, *a.* richiesto, necessario, indispensabile. *n.* **1** requisito. **2** fabbisogno, (il) necessario, (l')occorrente.

requisition[1]**,** *n.* **1** richiesta (*generalm. scritta*), istanza, domanda. **2** requisito, qualità richiesta. **3** (*leg.*) requisizione. // **the requisitions for admission** (*pers.*) i requisiti d'ammissione; **the ~ of file material** (*org. az.*) il prelievo di materiale d'archivio.

requisition[2]**,** *v. t.* **1** (*leg.*) requisire. **2** (*leg.*) imporre una requisizione a (*q. o qc.*); costringere (*q.*) a consegnare qc.

reroute, *v. t.* **1** avviare di nuovo. **2** (*econ., fin.*) dirottare. // to **~ investments** (*econ., fin.*) dirottare gli investimenti.

resalable, *a. V.* **resaleable.**

resale, *n.* (*market.*) rivendita, il rivendere; nuova vendita, vendita di seconda mano. // **~ price** (*market.*) prezzo di rivendita; prezzo raccomandato, prezzo imposto (*dal produttore al dettagliante*).

resaleable, *a.* (*market.*) rivendibile.

rescale, *v. t.* **1** (*econ.*) formulare (*piani, ecc.*) su scala ridotta. **2** (*econ.*) pianificare (*qc.*) su scala minore. **3** (*econ.*) ridimensionare (*le spese, ecc.*).

rescaling, *n.* (*econ.*) pianificazione su scala ridotta, ridimensionamento.

rescind, *v. t.* (*leg.*) rescindere, abrogare, annullare, risolvere, sopprimere. // to **~ a contract** (*leg.*) rescindere un contratto.

rescindable, *a.* (*leg.*) rescindibile, abrogabile, annullabile.

rescission, *n.* (*leg.*) rescissione, abrogazione, annullamento, soppressione.

rescissory, *a.* (*leg.*) rescissorio. // **~ action** (*leg.*) azione rescissoria.

rescue[1]**,** *n.* salvataggio, soccorso.

rescue[2]**,** *v. t.* salvare, soccorrere.

research[1]**,** *n.* ricerca, inchiesta, indagine, studio (*scientifico*). // **~ and development** (*econ.*) ricerca e sviluppo; **~ and development policy** (*econ.*) politica di ricerca e di sviluppo; **~ expenses** (*org. az., rag.*) spese per la ricerca; **~ facilities** (*market.*) apparato di ricerca; **~ programme** (*org. az.*) programma di ricerca; ~

worker ricercatore.

research², *v. t.* investigare. *v. i.* far ricerche, fare indagini.

researcher, *n.* ricercatore, investigatore.

resell, *v. t.* (*pass.* e *part. pass.* **resold**) (*market.*) rivendere, vendere di nuovo.

reseller, *n.* (*market.*) rivenditore.

reselling, *n.* (*market.*) rivendita (*il rivendere*).

reservation, *n.* 1 riserva, restrizione, eccezione. 2 (*trasp., tur.*) prenotazione (*in albergo, aereo, ecc.*). // **the ~ of a right** (*leg.*) la riserva d'un diritto; **the ~ of a seat on a plane** (*trasp. aer.*) la prenotazione d'un posto su un aereo; **without ~** senza alcuna riserva, senza condizioni, incondizionatamente.

reserve¹, *n.* 1 riserva, serbo. 2 (*banca, fin., rag.*) riserva. 3 (*banca, fin., rag.*) (= **reserve account**) fondo di riserva. // **~ account** (*rag.*) conto (di) riserva; **~ account for bad debts** (*rag.*) fondo svalutazione crediti; **~ account for depreciation** (*rag.*) fondo svalutazione (*merci, titoli, ecc.*); **~ account for income taxes** (*rag.*) fondo imposte da liquidare; **~ accounts** (*rag.*) fondi rischi; **~ bank** (*banca, USA*) banca centrale; **~ district** (*banca, USA*) zona sottoposta alla giurisdizione d'una «reserve bank» (*q. V.*); **~ for depreciation** (*rag.*) fondo d'ammortamento; **~ for obsolescence** (*rag.*) riserva per obsolescenza (*d'attività fisse*); **~ fund** (*rag.*) fondo di riserva; **~ price** (*comm.*) prezzo minimo (*a un'asta pubblica*); **~ ratio** (*banca*) rapporto fra le riserve in contanti e le passività; **with all (due) reserves** con tutte le (dovute) riserve; **without ~** senza alcuna riserva, senza condizioni, incondizionatamente.

reserve², *v. t.* 1 riservare, riservarsi. 2 (*trasp., tur.*) prenotare (*una camera d'albergo, un posto in aereo, ecc.*). // to **~ the right to do st.** riservarsi il diritto di fare qc.

reserved, *a.* impegnato.

reset, *v. i.* (*pass.* e *part. pass.* **reset**) (*leg., scozz.*) fare il ricettatore.

reship, *v. t.* 1 (*trasp., USA*) spedire (*qc.*) di nuovo, rispedire. 2 (*trasp. mar.*) spedire di nuovo (*qc.*) via mare; rimbarcare. 3 (*trasp. mar.*) trasbordare (*merce*). // to **~ bonded merchandise** (*trasp. mar.*) trasbordare merce da sdoganare.

reshipment, *n.* 1 (*trasp., USA*) rispedizione. 2 (*trasp. mar.*) nuova spedizione via mare, rimbarco. 3 (*trasp. mar.*) trasbordo (*di merci*) da una nave all'altra.

reshipping, *n. V.* **reshipment.**

reshuffle¹, *n.* rimescolata.

reshuffle², *v. t.* 1 rimescolare, mescolare di nuovo. 2 fare un rimpasto di (*un Governo, ecc.*).

reside, *v. i.* abitare, vivere, trovarsi.

residence, *n.* 1 abitazione. 2 (*leg.*) domicilio fiscale. // **~ permit** (*tur.*) permesso di soggiorno.

residential, *a.* (*leg.*) che obbliga alla residenza. // **~ requirement** (*leg.*) obbligo della residenza.

residual, *a.* residuo, residuale, rimanente. *n.* (*mat.*) resto (*d'una sottrazione*); differenza. // **~ product** (*org. az.*) sottoprodotto.

residuary, *a.* residuo, rimanente. // **~ estate** (*leg.*) proprietà residua (*dopo il pagamento di debiti e legati*); **~ right of ownership** (*leg.*) nuda proprietà.

residue, *n.* 1 residuo, resto, rimanente. 2 (*leg.*) parte residua (*d'eredità: dopo il pagamento di debiti e legati*).

resign¹, *v. t.* abbandonare, cedere, lasciare, rinunciare a. *v. i.* (*pers.*) rassegnare (*o* dare) le dimissioni, dimettersi, licenziarsi. // to **~ as manager** (*amm.*) dare le dimissioni da direttore; to **~ the chairmanship** (*amm.*) lasciare la presidenza; to **~ a position** (*pers.*) lasciare un posto.

re-sign², *v. t.* firmare di nuovo.

resignation, *n.* 1 abbandono, cessione, rinuncia. 2 (*pers.*) dimissioni.

resignee, *n.* 1 colui in favore del quale q. rinuncia a qc. 2 (*pers.*) dimissionario.

resigner, *n.* 1 chi abbandona (*qc.*), chi rinuncia (*a qc.*). 2 (*pers.*) dimissionario.

resigning, *a.* (*pers.*) dimissionario.

resist, *v. t.* e *i.* opporsi a; respingere.

resolution, *n.* 1 risoluzione, soluzione (*d'un problema*). 2 decisione, deliberazione, delibera. 3 (*leg.*) risoluzione (*d'un contratto*). // **the ~ of a legal doubt** (*leg.*) la soluzione d'un dubbio legale.

resolutive, *a.* (*leg.*) risolutorio, risolutivo.

resolutory, *a.* (*leg.*) risolutorio, risolutivo. // **~ clause** (*leg.*) clausola risolutiva; **~ condition** (*leg.*) condizione risolutiva.

resolvable, *a.* risolvibile, risolubile.

resolve, *v. t.* 1 risolvere. 2 deliberare, decidere.

resort¹, *n.* 1 ricorso, il ricorrere. 2 (*tur.*) località, stazione (*balneare, climatica e sim.*). // **without ~ to force** senza far ricorso alla forza.

resort², *v. i.* ricorrere, fare ricorso (*a.*). // to **~ to legal proceedings** (*leg.*) ricorrere alle vie legali.

resource, *n.* 1 risorsa. 2 mezzo, espediente.

3 **resources,** *pl.* (*econ., fin.*) risorse, fonti di reddito. // ~ **allocation** (*econ.*) distribuzione (*o* impiego) delle risorse.

resourceful, *a.* pieno di risorse, intraprendente.

respect[1], *n.* rispetto. // **with** ~ **to** rispetto a, quanto a; (*comun.*) con riferimento a, facendo riferimento a; **without** ~ **to** senza riguardo a, senza curarsi di.

respect[2], *v. t.* rispettare. // to ~ **the law** (*leg.*) rispettare la legge.

respectable, *a.* (*di somma, ecc.*) considerevole.

respectfully, *avv.* rispettosamente. // ~ **Yours** (*comun.*) con osservanza.

respite[1], *n.* 1 (*cred.*) proroga, dilazione (*d'un pagamento, ecc.*), mora. 2 (*leg.*) sospensione (*d'una sentenza*).

respite[2], *v. t.* 1 (*fig.*) dare respiro a (*q.*). 2 (*cred.*) concedere una dilazione a (*un debitore, ecc.*). 3 (*cred.*) differire (*un pagamento*). 4 (*leg.*) sospendere (*una condanna*).

respond, *v. i.* rispondere.

respondent, *n.* 1 chi risponde, chi reagisce. 2 (*leg.*) convenuto.

respondentia, *n.* (*trasp. mar.*) prestito a cambio marittimo (*con garanzia sul carico*).

response, *n.* risposta, reazione.

responsibility, *n.* responsabilità. // **the** ~ **of one seeking a loan** (*cred.*) la fidatezza di chi cerca un mutuo; **on one's own** ~ (*leg.*) sotto la propria responsabilità.

responsible, *a.* 1 responsabile. 2 (*di carica, ufficio, ecc.*) di grande responsabilità.

rest[1], *n.* riposo. // ~ **day** (*pers.*) giorno di riposo; ~ **period** (*pers.*) intervallo.

rest[2], *v. i.* 1 riposarsi. 2 appoggiare, poggiare, essere basato, fondarsi.

rest[3], *n.* 1 resto, (il) restante, residuo, rimanente, avanzo. 2 (*banca, fin., ingl.*) riserva (*costituita dagli utili indivisi che restano dopo il pagamento dei dividendi*). 3 (*rag.*) saldo passivo.

rest[4], *v. i.* stare, restare. // to ~ **assured** star certo; to ~ **with** essere affidato a, essere di competenza di, essere la prerogativa di.

restaff, *v. t.* (*org. az., pers.*) fornire (*un'azienda, ecc.*) di nuovo personale.

restaur, *n.* 1 (*ass.*) ricorso fra assicuratori. 2 (*ass. mar.*) ricorso (*della compagnia d'assicurazioni*) contro il capitano (*quando il danno è dovuto a negligenza di quest'ultimo*).

restaurant, *n.* ristorante. // ~ **car** (*trasp. ferr.*) carrozza ristorante.

restock, *v. t.* (*org. az.*) rifornire. *v. i.* (*org. az.*) rifornirsi.

restocking, *n.* (*org. az.*) rifornimento.

restor, *n.* *V.* **restaur.**

restoration, *n.* 1 restaurazione, reintegrazione. 2 (*trasp. mar.*) reintegrazione (*d'una nave*) nella classe di registro.

restore, *v. t.* reintegrare. // to ~ **sb. to his rights** (*leg.*) reintegrare q. nei suoi diritti.

restow, *v. t.* (*trasp. mar.*) stivare di nuovo (*il carico*).

restrain, *v. t.* limitare, porre un freno a, frenare (*fig.*), contenere.

restraint, *n.* limitazione, restrizione, freno (*fig.*) contenimento. // ~ **of trade** (*econ.*) limitazione al libero commercio.

restrict, *v. t.* limitare.

restriction, *n.* limitazione, restrizione. // **restrictions on exportation** (*comm. est.*) restrizioni alle esportazioni; **restrictions on trade** limitazione degli scambi; ~ **scheme** (*econ.*) regime vincolistico.

restrictive, *a.* restrittivo, limitativo. // ~ **covenants** (*leg., pers.*) clausole (*contrattuali*) sulla concorrenza sleale; **a** ~ **endorsement** (*banca, cred.*) una girata restrittiva; ~ **measures** misure restrittive; **a** ~ **price and terms of sale agreement** (*market.*) un'intesa ristretta in materia di prezzi e di condizioni di vendita; ~ **regulations** (*leg.*) regolamenti restrittivi; ~ **tariffs** tariffe restrittive.

result[1], *n.* 1 risultato, risultanza, esito, conclusione. 2 (*mat.*) risultato. // **without** ~ senza alcun risultato, infruttuoso.

result[2], *v. i.* 1 risultare, risolversi, finire. 2 (*leg.*) (*di beni, ecc.*) andare, spettare (*a q.*) per riversione.

resume, *v. t.* 1 riprendere. 2 riassumere, fare il riassunto di. // to ~ **possession** (*leg.*) rientrare in possesso (*di qc.*), riprendersi (*qc.*); to ~ **work** (*org. az.*) riprendere il lavoro.

resummon, *v. t.* (*leg.*) citare di nuovo, chiamare di nuovo.

resummons, *n.* (*leg.*) nuova chiamata, nuova citazione.

resumption, *n.* ripresa. // **the** ~ **of possession** (*leg.*) la ripresa di possesso.

retail[1], *n.* (*market.*) dettaglio, minuto. *a.* e *avv.* (*market.*) al minuto, al dettaglio, al consumo. // ~ **credit** (*market.*) credito al consumatore; ~ **department** (*market.*) reparto vendite al minuto; ~ **merchant** (*market.*) commerciante al minuto, dettagliante; ~ **outlet** (*market.*) punto di vendita al dettaglio; ~ **-price trend** (*econ., market.*) l'evoluzione dei prezzi al consumo; ~ **prices** (*market.*) prezzi al dettaglio, prezzi al minuto, prezzi al consumo; ~ **sale** (*market.*) vendita al dettaglio, vendita al minuto; ~ **shop** (*market.*) negozio al dettaglio (*o* al minuto), rivendita; ~ **trade** (*market.*) commercio al dettaglio, commercio al minuto; ~ **trading zone** (*market.*) zona di vendita al dettaglio; **at** ~ (*market.*) a un prezzo (richiesto normalmente) da (un) dettagliante; **by** ~ (*market.*) al dettaglio, al minuto.

retail[2], *v. t.* (*market.*) vendere (*merce*) al minuto (*o* al dettaglio); dettagliare, rivendere. *v. i.* (*market.*) (*di merce*) vendersi al minuto.

retailer, *n.* (*market.*) commerciante al minuto, dettagliante, rivenditore.

retain, *v. t.* 1 mantenere, trattenere. 2 (*leg.*) ritenere. // to ~ **a bill of lading** (*trasp. mar.*) trattenere una polizza di carico; to ~ **an employee for another six months** (*pers.*) confermare un dipendente per altri sei mesi.

retained earnings, *n. pl.* (*rag.*) utili non distribuiti.

retainer, *n.* 1 (*pers.*) assunzione, ingaggio. 2 (*pers.*) impiego.

retaliate, *v. t.* 1 (*leg.*) restituire (*un'offesa, ecc.*). 2 ritorcere (*un'accusa*). *v. i.* (*leg.*) rivalersi, fare rappresaglie. // to ~ **against a transgressor** (*leg.*) rivalersi su un trasgressore.

retaliation, *n.* (*leg.*) rappresaglia, ritorsione, rivalsa, restituzione (*d'un'offesa*). // **by way of** ~ per ritorsione, per rappresaglia.

retaliatory, *a.* (*leg.*) di ritorsione, di rappresaglia. // ~ **duties** (*comm. est.*) *V.* ~ **tariffs**; ~ **measures** provvedimenti adottati per rappresaglia; ~ **tariffs** (*comm. est.*) tariffe adottate per rappresaglia (*da un Paese nei confronti d'un altro, affinché quest'ultimo accordi privilegi di reciprocità*).

retire, *v. i.* 1 ritirarsi, andarsene. 2 (*amm., pers.*) ritirarsi dagli affari, mandare in pensione, dimettersi, congedarsi. *v. t.* 1 (*amm., pers.*) congedare, far dimettere, mandare in pensione, porre in quiescenza, mettere (*o* collocare) a riposo, pensionare. 2 (*comm.*) ritirare (*merce e sim.*). 3 (*fin.*) ritirare (*circolante e sim.*). // to ~ **a bill** (*banca, cred.*) richiamare una cambiale; to ~ **from business** ritirarsi dagli affari, «chiudere bottega»; to ~ **stocks** (*fin.*) ritirare titoli.

retired, *a.* 1 ritirato. 2 (*pers.*) (collocato) a riposo. 3 (*pers.*) (*di ex dipendente*) pensionato, in pensione. // **a** ~ **civil servant** (*amm., pers.*) un pensionato statale; ~ **pay** (*pers.*) pensione, trattamento di quiescenza; ~ **pension** (*pers.*) pensione, trattamento di quiescenza; **the** ~ **personnel** (*pers.*) i pensionati.

retirement, *n.* 1 ritiro. 2 (*pers.*) congedo, andata in pensione, andata a riposo, pensionamento. 3 (*pers.*) congedo, pensionamento, collocamento a riposo. // ~ **date** (*pers.*) data del pensionamento; ~ **pension** (*pers.*) pensione ordinaria (*per raggiunti limiti d'età*); ~ **plan** (*pers.*) piano di pensionamento.

retiring, *a.* 1 (*amm., pers.*) che va in pensione; (*di dipendente*) che lascia il posto. 2 (*amm., pers.*) (*di dipendente, d'organo, ecc.*) uscente. // ~ **allowance** (*pers.*) premio di buonuscita; **the** ~ **personnel** (*pers.*) il personale uscente.

retort[1], *n.* (*leg.*) ritorsione (*d'un'accusa*).

retort[2], *v. t.* (*leg.*) ritorcere (*un'accusa*).

retract, *v. t.* 1 ritirare, tirare indietro. 2 revocare, disdire. 3 (*leg.*) ritrattare, rimangiarsi. // to ~ **an offer** revocare un'offerta; to ~ **a promise** ritirare la parola data.

retraction, *n.* 1 revoca. 2 (*leg.*) ritrattazione.

retrench, *v. t.* 1 limitare, ridurre (*le spese*); decurtare. 2 (*giorn.*) omettere, tagliare (*parti d'un articolo, libro, ecc.*). *v. i.* ridurre le spese, fare economie, economizzare. // to ~ **expenses** ridurre le spese; to ~ **privileges** (*leg.*) ridurre i privilegi.

retrenchment, *n.* 1 riduzione delle spese. 2 economia (*l'economizzare*); risparmio (*il risparmiare*). 3 (*econ., fin.*) taglio (*nelle spese previste in bilancio*). 4 (*giorn.*) omissione (*di parte d'un articolo, libro, ecc.*), taglio (*in un articolo, libro, ecc.*).

retroactive, *a.* retroattivo. // ~ **effect** (*leg.*) effetto retroattivo; ~ **laws** (*leg.*) norme retroattive; ~ **pay** (*pers.*) (gli) arretrati (di stipendio); ~ **tax** (*fin.*) imposta retroattiva.

retroactivity, *n.* (*leg.*) retroattività.

retrospective, *a.* (*leg.*) retroattivo. // ~ **exemption** (*fin.*) esenzione retroattiva; ~ **laws** (*leg.*) norme retroattive.

return[1], *n.* 1 ritorno, viaggio di ritorno. 2 (*comm.*) prospetto, rendiconto. 3 (*cred.*) restituzione, resa. 4 (*fin.*) (= **tax return**) dichiarazione dei redditi. 5 (*fin., rag.*) guadagno, profitto, provento, ricavo, remunerazione. 6 (*leg.*) relazione, rapporto. 7 (*stat.*) statistiche. 8 (*trasp., ingl.*) (= **return ticket**) biglietto d'andata e ritorno. 9 **returns,** *pl.* (*giorn.*) resa (*all'editore: di libri, ecc., invenduti*). 10 **returns,** *pl.* (*pubbl.*) posta ricevuta in seguito alla pubblicazione (*o* trasmissione radiotelevisiva) d'un annuncio pubblicitario. 11 **returns,** *pl.* (*rag.*) incassi, introiti. // ~ **address** (*comun.*) indirizzo del mittente; **returns book** (*rag.*) giornale delle (merci) rese; ~ **cargo** (*trasp.*) carico (del viaggio) di ritorno; ~ **envelope** (*comun.*) busta (*generalm. affran-*

cata e indirizzata) per la risposta; ~ **freight** (*trasp. mar.*) nolo (del viaggio) di ritorno; **returns inwards** (*rag.*) rese dai clienti; **the ~ of damaged merchandise** (*market.*) il rinvio (al fornitore) di merci avariate; **a ~ of expenses** (*comm.*) un prospetto delle spese; **the ~ of income** (*fin.*) la denuncia dei redditi; **the ~ of premium** (*ass.*) la restituzione del premio; **the ~ of taxes** (*fin.*) il rimborso d'imposte (*pagate in più del dovuto*); **the ~ on capital** (*econ., fin.*) il reddito (*o* il frutto, il profitto) del capitale (*investito*); **returns outwards** (*rag.*) rese al fornitore; ~ **receipt** (*comun.*) ricevuta di ritorno; ~ **ticket** (*trasp., ingl.*) biglietto d'andata e ritorno; **returns to scale of plant** (*econ.*) rapporto fra la quantità di merce prodotta e quella dei fattori produttivi impiegati; ~ **trip** (*trasp., ingl.*) viaggio d'andata e ritorno; **by ~ of mail** (*comun.*) a giro di posta, a volta di corriere; **by ~ of post** (*comun.*) *V.* **by ~ of mail; in ~ for** in cambio di, in compenso di.

return², *v. i.* ritornare. *v. t.* **1** (*comun.*) rimandare, rinviare, rispedire, respingere. **2** (*cred.*) restituire, rendere. **3** (*leg.*) dichiarare, fare (una) denuncia di. // to ~ **the details of one's income** (*fin.*) fare una denuncia dettagliata dei (propri) redditi; to ~ **goods of poor quality** (*market.*) respingere merci di qualità scadente; to ~ **a letter** (*comun.*) respingere una lettera; to ~ **a profit** (*fin., rag.*) dare (un) frutto, fruttare; «to **be returned**» (*market.*) «a rendere».

returnable, *a.* **1** restituibile. **2** rimborsabile. **3** da restituire, da rendere. // ~ **containers** (*market.*) recipienti a rendere; ~ **deposits** (*cred.*) depositi rimborsabili.

returning, *n.* rinvio.

revalorization, *n.* **1** rivalutazione. **2** (*fin., rag.*) rivalutazione.

revalorize, *v. t.* **1** rivalutare. **2** (*fin., rag.*) rivalutare (*una moneta, ecc.*); valutare di nuovo. // to ~ **the assets on a balance-sheet** (*rag.*) rivalutare le attività di bilancio; to ~ **a currency** (*fin.*) rivalutare una moneta.

revaluate, *v. t.* (*fin., rag.*) rivalutare (*una moneta, ecc.*); valutare di nuovo.

revaluation, *n.* (*fin., rag.*) rivalutazione. // **the ~ of the lira in terms of the dollar** (*fin.*) la rivalutazione della lira sul dollaro; **the ~ of a property** (*fin.*) la rivalutazione d'una proprietà.

revalue, *v. t.* (*fin., rag.*) rivalutare, valutare di nuovo. // to ~ **the premises** (*rag.*) rivalutare gli stabili.

revenue, *n.* **1** (*econ., fin., rag.*) entrata, reddito, rendita, ricavi. **2** (*fin.*) (= **Inland Revenue**) fisco, erario. // ~ **account** (*rag.*) conto profitti e perdite; ~ **act** (*leg.*) legge fiscale; ~ **and expenditures** (*rag.*) entrate e spese; **the ~ authorities** (*fin.*) il fisco; ~ **-bearing** (*fin.*) produttivo di reddito; ~ **claim** (*fin.*) credito fiscale; ~ **duties** (*fin.*) diritti erariali; **the ~ from taxation** (*fin.*) il gettito tributario; ~ **inspector** (*fin.*) ispettore delle finanze; ~ **receipts** (*fin.*) entrate erariali; ~ **reserve** (*rag.*) riserva disponibile; ~ **stamp** (*fin.*) marca da bollo; ~ **tax** (*fin.*) imposta fiscale, imposta erariale, tributo fiscale.

revenues, *n. pl.* (*fin.*) introiti erariali (*o* fiscali).

reversal, *n.* **1** inversione. **2** (*leg.*) riforma, revoca (*d'una sentenza*). **3** (*rag.*) storno (*di scritture a partita doppia*). // **a ~ of entry** (*rag.*) uno storno di scrittura; **a ~ of trend** un'inversione di tendenza; **in ~** (*rag.*) a storno.

reverse, *v. t.* **1** invertire. **2** (*leg.*) riformare, revocare, cassare (*una sentenza*). **3** (*rag.*) stornare (*una scrittura a partita doppia*). // to ~ **an entry** (*rag.*) stornare una registrazione, stornare una scrittura; to ~ **the procedure** (*leg.*) capovolgere la procedura.

reversibility, *n.* **1** invertibilità, l'essere rovesciabile (*anche fig.*). **2** (*leg.*) reversibilità. **3** (*leg.*) revocabilità.

reversible, *a.* **1** invertibile. **2** (*leg.*) reversibile. **3** (*leg.*) revocabile, cassabile.

reversion, *n.* **1** (*ass.*) capitale assicurato (*da pagarsi in caso di morte*). **2** (*leg.*) reversione. **3** (*leg.*) proprietà reversibile, beni reversibili.

reversional, *a. V.* **reversionary.**

reversionary, *a.* (*leg.*) reversibile. // ~ **annuity** (*leg.*) pensione reversibile [illegible] ione di reversibilità.

revert, *v. i.* (*leg.*) andare (*a q.*) per reversione, spettare (*a q.*) per reversione.

reverter, *n. V.* **reversion.**

review¹, *n.* **1** rassegna, esame. **2** (*giorn.*) rivista, pubblicazione. **3** (*leg.*) revisione, riesame. // **a ~ clause** (*leg.*) una clausola di revisione.

review², *v. t.* **1** riesaminare, passare in rassegna. **2** (*leg.*) riesaminare (*una causa, ecc.*); sottoporre (*una causa, ecc.*) a revisione.

revise, *v. t.* **1** correggere, revisionare. **2** (*market., trasp.*) ritoccare (*prezzi, tariffe, ecc.*). // to ~ **tariffs** ritoccare le tariffe.

reviser, *n.* revisore.

revision, *n.* **1** revisione, correzione. **2** (*market., trasp.*) ritocco (*di prezzi, tariffe, ecc.*).

revisionary, *a.* di revisione. // ~ **bonus** (*ass.*) premio di partecipazione agli utili.

revisor, *n.* revisore.

revival, *n.* (*leg.*) (*di leggi, ecc.*) ritorno in vigore.

revive, *v. t.* 1 ravvivare. 2 (*leg.*) rimettere in vigore (*una legge, ecc.*), ridare validità a (*una legge, ecc.*). *v. i.* risvegliarsi (*fig.*).

revocable, *a.* (*leg.*) revocabile, abrogabile, annullabile. // **a ~ credit** (*cred.*) un credito revocabile; **a ~ privilege** (*leg.*) un privilegio revocabile.

revocableness, *n.* (*leg.*) revocabilità, abrogabilità, annullabilità.

revocation, *n.* (*leg.*) revoca, revocazione, abrogazione, annullamento. // **the ~ of a license** (*leg.*) il ritiro d'una licenza; **the ~ of a provision** (*leg.*) la revoca d'una disposizione; **the ~ of a will** (*leg.*) la revoca d'un testamento.

revoke, *v. t.* (*leg.*) revocare, abrogare, annullare. // to **~ a grant** (*leg.*) revocare una concessione.

revokeable, *a. V.* **revocable.**

revolt, *n.* rivolta.

revolving, *a.* rotante, girevole. // **~ credit** (*banca*) credito rotativo; **~ fund** (*cred., fin.*) fondo rotativo; **~ letter of credit** (*banca, cred.*) lettera di credito rotativo.

reward, *n.* 1 premio. 2 (*leg.*) taglia.

rewarding, *a.* gratificante.

ribbon, *n.* (*di macch. uff.*) nastro (*di macchina da scrivere, ecc.*).

rich, *a.* ricco.

richness, *n.* ricchezza.

rider, *n.* (*leg.*) clausola addizionale, codicillo, postilla.

rig[1], *n.* (*trasp. mar.*) attrezzatura, armamento (*d'una nave*).

rig[2], *v. t.* (*trasp. mar.*) attrezzare, armare, equipaggiare (*una nave*).

rig[3], *n.* 1 (*leg.*) aggiotaggio. 2 (*market.*) maneggiamento (*di prezzi, ecc.*); manovra (*per far salire i prezzi*). 3 (*market.*) controllo disonesto (*del mercato*).

rig[4], *v. t.* 1 (*market.*) maneggiare, manovrare (*prezzi, ecc.*). 2 (*market.*) controllare disonestamente (*il mercato*). // to **~ the market** (*fin.*) speculare senza scrupoli mediante la pressione di massicce vendite (*o* acquisti); to **~ prices** (*market.*) manovrare i prezzi; to **~ the stock market** (*fin.*) manovrare il mercato dei titoli.

rigger, *n.* (*leg.*) aggiotatore.

rigging, *n.* (*trasp. mar.*) armamento, attrezzatura.

rigging the market, *n.* (*leg.*) aggiotaggio.

right[1], *a.* 1 diritto. 2 corretto, giusto. // **~-center** centrodestra (*governativo, ecc.*); **~-hand** di destra, a mano destra; **the ~ heir** (*leg.*) l'erede legittimo; **a ~-winger** un uomo della destra (*politica*).

right[2], *n.* 1 (il) giusto, giustizia. 2 (*leg.*) diritto, pretesa, titolo. // **rights and duties** (*leg.*) diritti e doveri; **~ and wrong** (*leg.*) la ragione e il torto; **rights issue** (*Borsa, fin.*) emissione riservata sotto costo; **~ of action** (*leg.*) diritto d'agire in giudizio; **~ of application** (*fin.*) diritto di sottoscrizione (*di titoli, ecc.*); **~ of assembly** (*leg., sind.*) diritto di riunione; **~ of association** (*leg., sind.*) diritto d'associazione; **~ of blockade** (*trasp. mar.*) diritto di blocco; **~ of coinage** (*leg.*) diritto di batter moneta; **~ of convoy** (*trasp. mar.*) diritto di scorta; **~ of mooring** (*trasp. mar.*) diritto d'ancoraggio; **~ of option** (*fin.*) diritto d'opzione; **~ of preemption** (*leg.*) diritto di prelazione; **~ of recourse** (*cred., leg.*) diritto di regresso; **~ of redemption** (*leg.*) diritto di riscatto; **~ of veto** (*leg.*) diritto di veto; **~ of voting** (*leg.*) diritto di voto; **~-of-way** (*leg.*) diritto di passaggio, diritto di transito; (*trasp. aut.*) diritto di precedenza; **~ to withdraw** (*fin., leg.*) diritto di recesso (*da una società, ecc.*); **the ~ to work** (*leg., sind.*) il diritto al lavoro; **by ~** (*leg.*) in via di diritto, di diritto; **1-for-3 rights issue** (*Borsa, fin.*) emissione d'un'azione nuova ogni tre possedute.

right[3], *v. t.* 1 rettificare, correggere. 2 aggiustare (*fig.*). // to **~ a mistake** correggere un errore.

rightful, *a.* 1 (*leg.*) giusto, equo, onesto. 2 (*leg.*) legittimo. // **a ~ claim** una richiesta legittima; **a ~ heir** (*leg.*) un erede legittimo; **a ~ inheritance** (*leg.*) un'eredità legittima.

rightfulness, *n.* 1 giustizia, equità, onestà. 2 (*leg.*) legittimità.

rigid, *a.* 1 rigido. // **~ Government controls** severi controlli governativi; **~ parity** (*fin.*) parità rigida.

rigidity, *n.* rigidità.

ring[1], *n.* 1 cerchio. 2 cricca (*di speculatori*). 3 (*fin., market.*) «catena», «cerchio» (*di acquirenti e di venditori: in una Borsa Merci*); recinto alle grida. // **~-road** (*trasp. aut., ingl.*) raccordo anulare.

ring[2], *n.* suono (*di campana*).

ring[3], *v. i.* (*pass.* **rang,** *part. pass.* **rung**) squillare. // to **~ in** (*pers.*) segnare l'ora d'entrata, «marcare» l'ora; to **~ out** (*pers.*) segnare l'ora d'uscita; to **~ sb. up** telefonare, fare una telefonata a q.

rise[1], *n.* 1 ascesa. 2 aumento, crescita, rialzo. 3 (*fin., market.*) ascesa, aumento, rialzo, lievitazione, «dinamica» (*di prezzi, quotazioni*). 4 (*pers.*) aumento (*di stipendio*). // **a ~ in the bank rate** (*fin.*) un aumento del tasso di sconto; **the ~ in the cost of living** (*econ.*) l'aumento del costo della vita; **the ~ in prices** l'aumento (*o* la crescita, il rincaro) dei prezzi; to **be on the ~** (*market.*) (*di prezzi*) essere in aumento.

rise[2], *v. i.* (*pass.* **rose**, *part. pass.* **risen**) 1 aumentare, crescere. 2 (*fin., market.*) (*di prezzi, ecc.*) aumentare, essere in aumento, crescere, gonfiarsi, lievitare. // to **~ in price** (*market.*) (*di merce*) rincarare.

rising, *a.* che aumenta, crescente. // **a ~ market** (*econ.*) un mercato al rialzo; **~ prices** (*market.*) prezzi crescenti; **a ~ trend** (*econ., fin.*) una tendenza al rialzo.

risk[1], *n.* 1 rischio, pericolo. 2 (*ass.*) rischio. // **~ bearer** (*ass.*) chi corre un rischio; **~, contingency and policy reserves** (*ass.*) riserve tecniche per danni e riporto premi; **~ of breakage** (*trasp.*) rischio di rottura; **~ of craft** (*ass. mar.*) rischio d'alleggio; **~ of damage for exposure to weather** (*ass.*) rischio di danno per esposizione alle intemperie; **~ of fire** (*ass.*) rischio d'incendio; **~ premium** (*ass.*) premio netto; **all risks** (*ass.*) assicurazione contro rischi vari; **at the ~ of the owners of the goods** (*market.*) a rischio dei proprietari della merce; **at the ~ of the shippers** (*market.*) a rischio dello spedizioniere.

risk[2], *v. t.* e *i.* rischiare. // to **~ one's fortune in an enterprise** rischiare la propria fortuna in un'impresa.

risky, *a.* rischioso. // **a ~ investment** (*fin.*) un investimento azzardoso.

river, *n.* fiume. // **~ -basin** (*trasp.*) bacino fluviale; **~ dues** (*trasp.*) diritti di navigazione fluviale; **~ navigation** navigazione fluviale; **~ port** (*trasp.*) porto fluviale; **~ traffic** (*trasp.*) traffico fluviale; **~ works** (*trasp.*) opere fluviali.

road, *n.* 1 via. 2 (*trasp. ferr., USA*) (= **railroad**) ferrovia. 3 (*trasp. mar.*) rada. 4 **roads,** *pl.* (*trasp. aut.*) rete stradale, viabilità. // **~ accident** incidente stradale, investimento; **~ block** (*trasp. aut.*) blocco stradale; **~ conditions** (*trasp. aut.*) viabilità; **~ crossing** (*trasp. aut.*) crocevia, crocicchio; **~ directory** (*trasp. aut.*) guida (*o* indicatore) stradale; **~ fork** (*trasp. aut.*) bivio stradale; **~ haulage** (*trasp. aut.*) trasporto stradale, trasporto di merce su strada; **~ haulier** (*trasp. aut.*) trasportatore (*di merci*) su strada, vettore; **~ junction** (*trasp. aut.*) nodo stradale; **~ network** (*trasp. aut.*) rete stradale; **~ section** (*trasp. aut.*) tronco stradale; **~ -sign** (*trasp. aut.*) indicatore stradale; **~ signal** (*trasp. aut.*) segnale stradale; **~ tax** (*fin., trasp. aut.*) imposta di circolazione; **~ traffic** (*trasp. aut.*) circolazione stradale; **~ transport** (*trasp. aut.*) trasporti su strada; **~ yard** cantiere stradale.

robber, *n.* ladro.

robbery, *n.* (*ass., leg.*) furti.

rock, *n.* roccia. // **~ -bottom prices** (*market.*) prezzi ridottissimi.

rocket[1], *n.* razzo, missile.

rocket[2], *v. i.* alzarsi a razzo.

rogatory letter, *n.* (*leg.*) rogatoria.

roll[1], *n.* 1 elenco, lista; «organico» (*del personale*). 2 registro. 3 (*leg.*) ruolo (*di cause, ecc.*). 4 (*leg.*) albo. 5 (*leg.*) verbale. 6 (*trasp. aer., trasp. mar.*) rullio. 7 **the Rolls,** *pl.* (*leg.*) l'Albo degli avvocati. // to **be on the ~** (*pers.*) essere in organico.

roll[2], *v. i.* 1 rotolare. 2 (*trasp. aer., trasp. mar.*) rullare. *v. t.* 1 arrotolare. 2 roteare (*gli occhi*). // to **~ back the price of** (*econ., market.*) calmierare.

rollback, *n.* (*econ., market.*) riduzione (*dei prezzi, ecc.*) ottenuta mediante interventi statali, calmiere. // **a ~ of prices** (*econ., market.*) una riduzione dei prezzi.

rolling, *n.* 1 rotolamento. 2 arrotolamento. 3 (*trasp. aer., trasp. mar.*) rullio. // **~ -stock** (*trasp. ferr.*) materiale rotabile.

Roman, *a.* romano. // **~ law** (*leg.*) diritto romano; **~ numerals** (*o* **figures**) (*mat.*) numeri romani.

room, *n.* camera, stanza.

root, *n.* (*anche mat.*) radice.

rope, *n.* 1 fune. 2 (*trasp. mar.*) gomena.

rotary, *a.* 1 rotante, girevole. 2 rotatorio. // **~ adding machine** (*macch. uff.*) addizionatrice a lettura immediata; **~ file** (*attr. uff.*) schedario rotante.

rotate, *v. t.* e *i.* 1 ruotare, roteare. 2 succedersi regolarmente. 3 (*econ.*) fare la rotazione di (*raccolti*), avvicendare (*colture*). 4 (*pers.*) (*di dipendenti*) avvicendarsi (*nelle diverse mansioni*).

rotating shifts, *n. pl.* (*org. az., pers.*) turni rotatori.

rotation, *n.* 1 rotazione. 2 (*econ.*) rotazione agraria; avvicendamento delle colture. 3 (*pers.*) rotazione (*delle cariche*); avvicendamento (*nelle mansioni*). // **the ~ of crops** (*econ.*) il sistema rotativo agrario; **by ~** in successione; **in ~** in successione.

rough, *a.* 1 greggio, grezzo. 2 rozzo, rude. 3 grossolano, approssimativo (*fig.*). // **~ and ready** approssimativo, grossolano; **~ and ready**

calculations calcoli approssimativi; ~ **copy** brutta copia, minuta; ~ **draft** abbozzo, minuta; ~ **justice** (*leg.*) giustizia sommaria.

round[1], *a.* rotondo. // ~ **brackets** parentesi tonde; ~ **chartering** (*trasp. mar.*) noleggio d'andata e ritorno; ~ **figure** cifra tonda; ~ **house** (*trasp. ferr.*) deposito locomotive; ~ **lot** (*Borsa, fin.*) unità di contrattazione (*generalm. 100 azioni*), quantitativo minimo trattabile (*di titoli*); ~ **table** (*fin., market.*) (i) partecipanti a una «tavola rotonda»; argomento discusso in una «tavola rotonda»; ~ **trip** (*trasp., USA*) viaggio d'andata e ritorno; ~ **-trip ticket** (*trasp., USA*) biglietto d'andata e ritorno; **as a** ~ **figure** in cifra tonda; **in** ~ **figures** in cifra tonda; **in** ~ **numbers** in cifra tonda.

round[2], *n.* 1 giro (*d'ispezione, ecc.*). 2 (*market.*) giro (*di visite ai clienti*). // **the** ~ **of one's customers** (*market.*) il giro dei (propri) clienti.

round[3], *avv.* 1 in tondo. 2 attorno, all'intorno. *prep.* intorno a. // ~ **the corner** girato l'angolo.

round[4], *v. t.* 1 (*anche mat.*) arrotondare. 2 (*trasp. mar.*) doppiare (*un promontorio e sim.*). // to ~ **a figure** arrotondare una cifra; to ~ **off one's career** (*pers.*) completare la carriera.

rounding, *n.* (*mat.*) arrotondamento.

roup[1], *n.* (*scozz.*) vendita all'asta.

roup[2], *v. t.* (*scozz.*) vendere all'asta.

route[1], *n.* 1 itinerario, percorso, via. 2 (*comun.*) linea telefonica. 3 (*market.*) itinerario di vendita. 4 (*trasp. aer., trasp. mar.*) rotta. // ~ **card** (*org. az.*) scheda di ciclo di lavorazione; ~ **-map** (*trasp. aut.*) carta stradale; **en** ~ (*trasp.*) in viaggio.

route[2], *v. t.* 1 (*comun.*) inoltrare, spedire (*documenti, ecc.*). 2 (*trasp.*) avviare, instradare (*merci, ecc.*).

routine, *n.* 1 abitudine, consuetudine. 2 monotonia, routine. 3 (*org. az.*) ordinaria amministrazione. // ~ **duties** doveri abituali, compiti abituali; **a** ~ **job** (*pers.*) un compito d'ordinaria amministrazione; ~ **mail** (*comun.*) corrispondenza ordinaria; ~ **maintenance** (*org. az.*) manutenzione ordinaria.

row, *n.* fila.

royal, *a.* reale, regale. // ~ **demesne** (*in G.B.*) demanio reale.

royalty, *n.* 1 sovranità. 2 **royalties**, *pl.* (*econ., leg.*) diritti di sfruttamento (*d'una miniera*). 3 **royalties**, *pl.* (*leg.*) diritti di brevetto, diritti di licenza, diritti d'autore.

rubber, *n.* gomma. // ~ **stamp** (*attr. uff.*) timbro di gomma.

rubbish, *n.* 1 rifiuti, immondizie. 2 (*market.*) merce di scarto.

ruin[1], *n.* dissesto.

ruin[2], *v. t.* dissestare.

ruined, *a.* dissestato.

rule[1], *n.* 1 regola. 2 (*giorn., pubbl.*) filetto. 3 (*leg.*) regolamento, norma, legge. 4 (*leg.*) decisione, ordinanza, ordine. 5 (*mat.*) regolo (*calcolatore*). // **rules for the enforcement of the law** (*leg.*) regolamenti esecutivi; **a** ~ **of law** (*leg.*) una norma di legge; **the rules of navigation** (*trasp. mar.*) le regole della navigazione; **the rules of the road** (*trasp. aut.*) il codice della strada.

rule[2], *v. t.* 1 regolare. 2 (*leg.*) decidere, dichiarare, ordinare, riconoscere. *v. i.* 1 (*market.*) (*di prezzo*) praticarsi, essere praticato. 2 (*market.*) (*di prezzi*) mantenersi (*a un certo livello*). // to ~ **off one's accounts** (*comm.*) regolare i conti.

ruler, *n.* (*attr. uff.*) regolo.

rummage[1], *n. collett.* 1 (*market.*) articoli spaiati, fondi di magazzino. 2 (*market., USA*) *V.* ~ **sale.** // ~ **sale** (*market.*) vendita di magazzino.

rummage[2], *v. t.* 1 frugare. 2 perquisire. *v. i.* (*trasp. mar.*) stivare il carico. // to ~ **a ship** (*trasp. mar.*) perquisire una nave.

rummaging, *n.* (*trasp. mar.*) perquisizione doganale.

run[1], *n.* 1 (*banca, fin., market.*) assalto (*fig.*), corsa (*fig.*), domanda forte e insistente (*da parte di risparmiatori, creditori, clienti*). 2 (*giorn.*) tiratura. 3 (*market.*) andamento (*del mercato, ecc.*). 4 (*market.*) successo, voga. 5 (*trasp. aut.*) corsa (*d'un autobus, ecc.*). // ~ **duration** (*org. az.*) durata d'esecuzione (*d'un ciclo di lavorazione*); **the** ~ **of the stock market** (*fin.*) l'andamento del mercato dei titoli; **a** ~ **on Swiss securities** (*fin.*) una corsa ai titoli svizzeri; ~ **-up** (*market.*) balzo, impennata (*dei prezzi*); **with a** ~ improvvisamente.

run[2], *v. i.* (*pass.* **ran**, *part. pass.* **run**) 1 correre; incorrere; funzionare. 2 (*comm.*) decorrere. 3 (*leg.*) (*di contratto, legge, ecc.*) essere in vigore, durare. 4 (*trasp.*) (*di veicolo, nave, ecc.*) circolare, funzionare, far servizio, far la spola, transitare. *v. t.* 1 condurre, dirigere, esercire, gestire (*un'azienda e sim.*). 2 far funzionare. 3 (*trasp.*) effettuare corse di (*treni, ecc.*). // to ~ **aground** (*trasp. mar.*) arenarsi, incagliarsi; arenare, far incagliare; to ~ **ashore** (*trasp. mar.*) arenarsi, incagliarsi; arenare, far incagliare; to ~ **at a deficit** (*fin., rag.*) presentare una gestione passiva; to ~ **away** correr via, fuggire; to ~ **away up the inflationary spiral** (*econ.*) essere preso nella spirale inflazionistica; to ~ **a bill at a shop** (*market.*) avere un conto corrente con un negozio; to ~ **a business** condurre un'azienda; to ~ **down** (*trasp. aut.*) investire (*una persona*); to ~ **foul** (*trasp. mar.*) (*di navi*) entrare in collisione; to ~ **high** crescere; to ~ **into** (*trasp. aut.*) investire (*un ostacolo fisso o un altro veicolo*); to ~ **into debts** indebitarsi; to ~ **off** (*giorn., pubbl.*) stampare, tirare; to ~ **off the rails** (*trasp. ferr.*) «deragliare»; to ~ **off the road** (*trasp. aut.*) uscire di strada; to ~ **out** esaurirsi, finire; to ~ **out of stock** (*market.*) finire le scorte, rimanere sprovvisti (di merce); to ~ **over** (*trasp. aut.*) investire (*una persona*); to ~ **short** (*market.: di scorte*) esaurirsi, finire; to ~ **short of** rimanere a corto di (*qc.*); to ~ **up** (*market.*) (*di prezzi*) balzare, impennarsi (*fig.*).

runaway, *a. attr.* **1** che fugge. **2** (*market.*) (*di prezzo*) soggetto a repentini cambiamenti (*generalm. in aumento*). // ~ **inflation** (*econ.*) inflazione galoppante; ~ **prices** (*market.*) prezzi in rapido aumento; ~ **shop** (*econ., org. az.*) stabilimento industriale trasferito dal proprietario in altro luogo (*per sfuggire ai regolamenti sindacali, ecc.*).

rundown, *n.* riduzione.

runner, *n.* **1** podista. **2** (*pers.*) sollecitatore (*d'ordinazioni, ecc.*); propagandista; «piazzista».

running, *a.* corrente. *n.* (il) correre; funzionamento. // ~ **account** (*banca, cred.*) conto corrente; ~ **aground** (*o* **ashore**) (*trasp. mar.*) incaglio; ~ **balance** (*rag.*) saldo parziale; ~ **costs** (*rag.*) costi variabili; ~ **days** giorni consecutivi; ~ **-down clause** (*ass. mar.*) clausola relativa all'abbordaggio; ~ **expenses** (*rag.*) spese correnti, spese d'esercizio; ~ **inventory** (*rag.*) inventario perpetuo; ~ **time** (*trasp. ferr.*) durata della corsa.

runway, *n.* (*trasp. aer.*) pista (*d'atterraggio o di decollo*).

rural, *a.* rurale.

rush[1], *n.* **1** traffico, trambusto. **2** affollamento, ressa. // **a** ~ **of business** una quantità d'affari; **a** ~ **order** (*market.*) un'ordinazione urgente; **the** ~ **season** (*market., trasp., tur.*) l'alta stagione.

rush[2], *v. t.* e *i.* **1** affrettarsi, affrettare, fare (*qc.*) in fretta. **2** (*market.*) sbrigare (*ordinazioni, ecc.*).

rye, *n.* segale, segala.

S

sack[1], *n.* **1** (*market.*) sacco, sacchetto, sacchetto di carta. **2** (*market.*) contenuto d'un sacco. **3** (*pers., fam.*) licenziamento; benservito (*fig., fam.*). // **a ~ of flour** un sacco di farina; to **get the ~** (*pers., fam.*) essere licenziato, farsi licenziare; to **give sb. the ~** (*pers., fam.*) licenziare q., mandare q. «a spasso».

sack[2], *v. t.* **1** (*market.*) mettere (*merce*) in sacchi, insaccare. **2** (*pers., fam.*) licenziare, mandare «a spasso». **3** (*USA*) incassare, guadagnare, fare (*profitti, ecc.*).

sacking, *n.* (*pers., fam.*) licenziamento.

sacrifice[1], *n.* (*comm.*) perdita, scapito. // **at a ~** (*comm.*) in perdita.

sacrifice[2], *v. t.* (*comm.*) vendere (*articoli*) in perdita, vendere (*articoli*) sotto costo.

saddle[1], *n.* sella.

saddle[2], *v. t.* (*fig.*) accollare, appioppare, caricare.

safe[1], *a.* **1** salvo, in salvo; al sicuro; fuor di pericolo. **2** intatto. **3** attendibile. // **~ and sound** sano e salvo; **~ arrival** (*trasp.*) arrivo in buono stato (*di merci, ecc.*); **~ custody** (*banca*) custodia in cassette di sicurezza; (*leg.*) custodia; **~ deposit** (*banca*) deposito in cassette di sicurezza; **~ -deposit box** (*banca*) cassetta di sicurezza; **a ~ investment** (*fin.*) un investimento privo di rischi; **~ -keeping** (*banca*) custodia; **a ~ port** (*trasp. mar.*) un porto sicuro.

safe[2], *n.* (*attr. uff.*) cassaforte.

safeguard[1], *n.* custodia, difesa, protezione. // **the ~ of small industries** (*fin.*) la protezione delle piccole imprese.

safeguard[2], *v. t.* custodire, difendere, proteggere. // to **~ one's reputation** difendere la propria reputazione.

safely, *avv.* **1** in salvo, al sicuro, felicemente. **2** con sicurezza. // **~ into harbour** (*trasp. mar.*) felicemente in porto; **~ into port** (*trasp. mar.*) felicemente in porto.

safety, *n.* salvezza. // **~ allowance** (*org. az.*) livello di sicurezza, limite di guardia, giacenza minima; **~ -belt** (*trasp. aer., trasp. aut.*) cintura di sicurezza; **~ equipment** (*org. az., pers.*) corredo antinfortunistico; **~ level** (*org. az.*) livello di sicurezza, limite di guardia; **~ margin** (*Borsa, fin.*) scarto di garanzia; **~ margins (on contango operations** (*Borsa, fin.*) scarti di garanzia nelle operazioni a riporto; **~ rail** (*trasp. aut.*) «guardrail», guardavia; **~ valve** (*anche fig.*) valvola di sicurezza.

sag[1], *n.* **1** abbassamento, cedimento. **2** (*comm.*) calo, diminuzione, flessione, declino, crollo (*dei prezzi, ecc.*).

sag[2], *v. i.* **1** abbassarsi, cedere. **2** (*comm.*) (*di prezzi, ecc.*) calare, diminuire, subire una flessione, crollare.

sagging, *n. V.* **sag**[1].

said, *a.* detto, predetto, suddetto, summenzionato.

sail, *v. i.* **1** (*trasp. mar.*) far vela (*verso una destinazione*), far rotta (*per*), imbarcarsi. **2** (*trasp. mar.*) navigare. *v. t.* (*trasp. mar.*) navigare, percorrere. // to **~ against the wind** (*trasp. mar.*) navigare contro vento, bordeggiare; to **~ along the coast** (*trasp. mar.*) costeggiare; to **~ before the wind** (*trasp. mar.*) avere il vento in poppa; to **~ for** (*trasp. mar.*) far rotta, partire, essere diretto a (*un porto, ecc.*); to **~ from** (*trasp. mar.*) partire da (*un porto, ecc.*); to **~ in ballast** (*trasp. mar.*) navigare in zavorra, andare in zavorra; to **~ laden** (*trasp. mar.*) navigare in carico; to **~ the seas** (*trasp. mar.*) navigare i mari; to **~ up a river** (*trasp. mar.*) risalire un fiume; **about to ~** (*trasp. mar.*) (*di nave*) in partenza.

sailable, *a.* (*trasp. mar.*) navigabile.

sailer, *n.* (*trasp. mar.*) veliero.

sailing, *n.* **1** (*trasp. mar.*) imbarco; (*di nave*) partenza. **2** (*trasp. mar.*) navigazione, arte del navigare. // **sailings board** (*trasp. mar.*) quadro delle partenze, tabella delle partenze; **~ day** (*trasp. mar.*) giorno di partenza; **~ orders** (*trasp. mar.*) ordini di partenza; **~ ship** (*o* **vessel)** (*trasp. mar.*) veliero.

sailor, *n.* (*trasp. mar.*) navigante, navigatore.

salable, *a. V.* **saleable.**

salaried, *a.* (*pers.*) stipendiato. // **a ~ person** (*pers.*) uno stipendiato; **a ~ position**

(*pers.*) un posto stipendiato.

salary[1], *n.* (*pers.*) stipendio, retribuzione. // ~ **cut** (*pers.*) riduzione di stipendio; ~ **rise** (*pers.*) aumento di salario.

salary[2], *v. t.* (*pers.*) stipendiare.

sale, *n.* **1** (*market.*) vendita, smercio. **2** (*market.*) vendita di liquidazione, liquidazione, svendita, saldo. **3 sales,** *pl.* (*rag.*) vendite, fatturato. // **sales account** (*rag.*) conto vendite; **sales agent** (*pers.*) agente di vendita; **sales analysis** (*market.*) analisi delle vendite; ~ **-and-leaseback** (*fin., leg.*) *V.* **leaseback;** ~ **and return** (*market.*) retrovendita; ~ **at best** (*fin., market.*) vendita al meglio; **sales book** (*rag.*) libro (delle) vendite; **sales budget** (*org. az., rag.*) bilancio preventivo delle vendite, previsione delle vendite; ~ **by auction** vendita all'asta, vendita all'incanto; **a** ~ **by inch of candle** una vendita all'ultimo offerente (*in un'asta*); ~ **by instalments** (*market.*) vendita a rate; ~ **by lots** (*market.*) vendita a lotti; ~ **by order of the Court** (*leg.*) vendita giudiziaria; ~ **by private treaty** (*leg.*) vendita privata; ~ **by retail** (*market.*) vendita al dettaglio, vendita al minuto; ~ **by sample** (*market.*) vendita su campione; ~ **confirmation** (*Borsa, fin.*) fissato bollato; **sales consortia** (*market.*) consorzi di vendita; ~ **contract** (*Borsa*) distinta di vendita; (*leg.*) contratto di vendita, contratto di compravendita; **sales day book** (*rag.*) libro (delle) vendite; ~ **delivered ex-ship** (*trasp. mar.*) vendita allo sbarco; **sales department** (*org. az.*) servizio vendite, ufficio vendite; **sales discounts** (*rag.*) sconti su vendite; **sales finance company** (*fin., USA*) società finanziaria (*specializzata nell'acquisto di contratti di vendita a rate, nello sconto di cambiali e nel ricupero dei crediti dei dettaglianti*); ~ **for the account** (*Borsa*) vendita a termine; ~ **for future delivery** (*fin.*) vendita per futura consegna; ~ **for the settlement** (*Borsa*) vendita a termine; **sales forecast** (*market.*) previsione delle vendite; **sales incentives** (*market.*) incentivi di vendita; **sales journal** (*rag.*) libro (delle) vendite; **sales letter** (*comun.*) lettera di vendita; **sales manager** (*pers.*) direttore (delle) vendite, direttore commerciale; **sales manual** (*org. az.*) manuale di vendita; ~ **note** (*market.*) distinta di vendita; **sales of assets** (*rag.*) smobilizzi e realizzi; ~ **of goods afloat** (*trasp. mar.*) vendita di merce flottante; **a** ~ **of real property** (*fin.*) una vendita immobiliare; **sales officer** (*pers.*) funzionario (addetto alle) vendite; **sales offices** (*market.*) punti di vendita; ~ **on approval** (*market.*) vendita salvo prova; ~ **on ex-ship terms** (*trasp. mar.*) vendita allo sbarco; ~ **on landed terms** (*trasp. mar.*) vendita allo sbarco; ~ **or return** (*market.*) *V.* ~ **and return; sales organization** (*market.*) organizzazione di vendita; **sales outlet** (*market.*) sbocco di vendita, centro di vendita, punto di vendita; **sales point** (*market.*) punto di vendita; **sales policy** (*market.*) politica di vendita; **sales potential** (*market.*) potenziale di vendita; ~ **price** (*market.*) prezzo di vendita; **sales promotion** (*pubbl.*) promozione delle vendite, incentivazione delle vendite, sviluppo (delle) vendite, «promotion»; **sales register** (*macch. uff.*) registratore di cassa; **sales representative** (*pers.*) rappresentante; **sales returns** (*rag.*) resi su vendite; ~ **-ring** cricca di compratori (*a una vendita all'asta*); ~ **room** (*org. az.*) sala (delle) vendite; **sales supervisor** (*pers.*) ispettore (delle) vendite; **sales talk** (*market., pubbl.*) discorsino tenuto a un cliente potenziale (*per indurlo all'acquisto*); **sales tax** (*fin.*) imposta sull'entrata; **sales territory** (*market.*) zona di vendita (*d'un viaggiatore, ecc.*); **sales ticket** (*market.*) scontrino di vendita; ~ **to arrive** (*market.*) vendita salvo arrivo (*della merce*); **a** ~ **to the highest bidder** (*market.*) una vendita al miglior offerente; ~ **with option to repurchase** (*leg.*) vendita con diritto di riscatto; **a** ~ **with right of redemption** (*leg.*) una vendita con patto di riscatto; «**for** ~» (*market.*) «in vendita», «vendesi»; «**on** ~» (*market.*) «in vendita», «vendesi»; to **be on** ~ (*market.*) (*d'articolo*) essere in vendita, essere in commercio; **on** ~ **and return** (*market.*) *V.* **on** ~ **or return; on** ~ **or return** (*market.*) salvo vista e verifica; (*di merce*) in conto deposito, in deposito.

saleable, *a.* vendibile, smerciabile, alienabile.

salesclerk, *n.* **1** (*pers.*) commesso (*di negozio*). **2** (*pers.*) commessa (*di negozio*).

salesgirl, *n. V.* **saleswoman.**

saleslady, *n. V.* **saleswoman.**

salesman, *n.* (*pl.* **salesmen**) **1** (*pers.*) commesso (*di negozio*). **2** (*pers.*) commesso viaggiatore, viaggiatore di commercio, piazzista, propagandista, venditore.

salesmanship, *n.* (*market.*) arte del vendere, capacità di vendere.

salespeople, *n. collett.* (*pers.*) addetti alle vendite, personale di vendita, venditori.

salesperson, *n. V.* **salesclerk.**

saleswoman, *n.* (*pl.* **saleswomen**) **1** (*pers.*) commessa (*di negozio*). **2** (*pers.*) viaggiatrice di commercio, propagandista.

saloon, *n.* **1** salone. **2** (*trasp. aut.*) berlina. **3** (*trasp. mar.*) sala di prima classe. **4** (*tur.*) sala (*d'albergo, ecc.*). // ~ **car** (*trasp. aut.*) berlina; ~ **-car** (*trasp. ferr.*) vettura salone, vagone salotto; ~ **-carriage** (*trasp. ferr.*) vettura salone, vagone salotto; ~ **-passenger** (*trasp. mar.*) viaggiatore di prima classe.

salt[1], *n.* sale marino. *a. attr.* salato. // **a ~ bill** (*fam.*) un conto salato.

salt[2], *v. t.* salare. // **to ~ an account** (*comm., fam.*) calcar la mano su un conto, presentare un conto salato; **to ~ away money** (*fam.*) *V.* **to ~ down money; to ~ the books of a business** (*comm., fam.*) alterare le cifre della contabilità d'un'impresa; **to ~ down money** (*fam.*) mettere da parte denaro.

salutation, *n.* (*comun.*) formula iniziale (*nelle lettere: p. es., «Dear Sir»*); «vocativo» (*nelle lettere*).

salvage[1], *n.* **1** (*ass.*) materiale ricuperato. **2** (*org. az.*) materiale di ricupero. **3** (*trasp. mar.*) salvataggio (*della nave, del carico, ecc.*); ricupero, operazioni di ricupero. **4** (*trasp. mar.*) materiale ricuperato (*da un naufragio, ecc.*). **5** (*trasp. mar.*) compenso pagato per il ricupero marittimo, compenso di salvataggio. // ~ **agreement** (*trasp. mar.*) contratto di salvataggio, contratto di ricupero; ~ **apparatus** (*trasp. mar.*) apparecchio di salvataggio; ~ **award** (*trasp. mar.*) compenso di salvataggio; ~ **charges** (*trasp. mar.*) spese di ricupero, diritti di salvataggio; ~ **company** (*trasp. mar.*) società di ricuperi marittimi; ~ **corps** (*ass.*) uomini addetti al salvataggio (*per conto di società d'assicurazione*) di beni minacciati dal fuoco; ~ **-dealer** (*comm.*) commerciante in materiali di ricupero; ~ **gear** (*trasp. mar.*) attrezzature di salvataggio, mezzi di salvataggio; ~ **loss** (*ass.*) perdita con ricupero, perdita al netto del valore della merce ricuperata; ~ **money** (*trasp. mar.*) compenso pagato per il ricupero marittimo, compenso di salvataggio; ~ **operations** (*trasp. mar.*) operazioni di salvataggio; ~ **service** (*trasp. mar.*) servizio di salvataggio; ~ **value** (*rag.*) valore di ricupero; ~ **vessel** (*trasp. mar.*) nave di salvataggio.

salvage[2], *v. t.* ricuperatore (*un carico, ecc.*).

salvaged materials, *n. pl.* **1** (*org. az.*) materiali di ricupero. **2** (*trasp. mar.*) materiali di ricupero.

salvager, *n.* (*trasp. mar.*) ricuperatore, addetto ai ricuperi marittimi.

salve, *v. t.* (*trasp. mar.*) ricuperare (*un carico, ecc.*).

salvor, *n.* (*trasp. mar.*) ricuperatore, addetto ai ricuperi marittimi.

same, *a.* medesimo, identico. *pron.* **1** (lo) stesso, (la) stessa cosa. **2** (*comm.*) (= **the same**) il medesimo, lo stesso. **the same,** *avv.* allo stesso modo, nella medesima maniera.

sample[1], *n.* (*market.*) campione, modello, saggio. // ~ **-card** (*market.*) cartella di campioni; ~ **check** (*market.*) controllo su campione; ~ **collection** (*market.*) campionario; ~ **fair** (*market., pubbl.*) fiera campionaria; **samples on collection** (*market.*) campioni su richiesta; «**samples only**» (*comun.*) «campione senza valore»; ~ **rate** (*comun.*) tariffa (postale) per la spedizione di campioni; ~ **room** (*market., pubbl.*) sala (adibita alla mostra) dei campioni; ~ **survey** (*stat.*) indagine campionaria; **as per ~** come da campione; **by ~** (*market.*) (*di vendita*) su campione.

sample[2], *v. t.* (*market.*) campionare; saggiare la qualità di (*merci, ecc.*).

sampleman, *n.* (*pl.* **samplemen**) *V.* **sampler.**

sampler, *n.* (*market.*) campionatore, campionarista.

sampling, *n.* (*market.*) campionamento, campionatura. // ~ **inspection** (*org. az.*) ispezione su campione; ~ **order** (*market.*) ordine di prova, ordine di saggio.

sanction[1], *n.* **1** (*leg.*) sanzione, approvazione, ratifica. **2** (*leg.*) pena.

sanction[2], *v. t.* (*leg.*) sanzionare, approvare, ratificare, sancire. // **to ~ a law** (*leg.*) sancire una legge.

sanctioned rights, *n. pl.* (*leg.*) diritti sanzionati.

sand[1], *n.* sabbia, rena. // ~ **-bank** (*trasp. mar.*) banco di sabbia; ~ **-bar** (*trasp. mar.*) banco di sabbia.

sand[2], *v. t.* cospargere di sabbia, insabbiare.

sanding-up, *n.* (*trasp. mar.*) insabbiamento.

sandwich, *n.* sandwich, panino imbottito, tramezzino. // ~ **man** (*pubbl.*) uomo sandwich (*stretto fra due cartelloni pubblicitari che porta in giro*).

sane, *a.* (*leg.*) sano (*di mente*).

sanitary, *a.* sanitario, igienico. // ~ **certificate** (*dog.*) certificato sanitario, certificato d'igiene; ~ **inspection** (*leg.*) visita sanitaria; ~ **ware** apparecchi sanitari.

«sans frais», *locuz. avv.* (*cred.*) senza spese.

«sans recours», *locuz. avv.* (*cred.*) senza ricorso.

satisfaction, *n.* **1** soddisfazione, soddisfacimento, appagamento, gradimento. **2** (*cred.*) soddisfazione (*d'un debito*). **3** (*leg.*) soddisfazione. **4** (*leg.*) adempimento, esecuzione (*di un'obbligazione*). // **the ~ of a mortgage** (*leg.*)

l'esecuzione d'un'ipoteca, la liberazione da un'ipoteca; **in ~ of** (*leg.*) a risarcimento di.

satisfactory, *a.* soddisfacente.

satisfied, *a.* 1 soddisfatto. 2 (*leg.*) (*d'obbligo, ecc.*) adempiuto, eseguito. // **a ~ mortgage** (*leg.*) un'ipoteca liberata.

satisfy, *v. t.* 1 soddisfare, appagare. 2 rispondere, essere conforme a (*requisiti, ecc.*). 3 (*cred.*) tacitare (*un creditore*). 4 (*leg.*) soddisfare, soddisfare a. 5 (*leg.*) adempiere, eseguire (*un'obbligazione*). // to **~ a debt** (*cred.*) pagare un debito; to **~ a lien** (*leg.*) revocare un pegno; to **~ one's needs** (*econ.*) soddisfare i propri bisogni; to **~ an obligation** adempiere (a) un dovere.

saturation, *n.* saturazione. // **~ point** (*anche fig.*) punto di saturazione.

save[1], *v. t.* 1 salvare. 2 risparmiare. *v. i.* risparmiare, fare economia, economizzare. // to **~ up** risparmiare, fare economia.

save[2], *prep.* salvo, eccetto, eccettuato.

saver, *n.* 1 risparmiatore, economizzatore. 2 (*banca, fin.*) risparmiatore.

saving, *a.* 1 che salva. 2 che risparmia, economo. 3 che fa risparmiare. *n.* 1 risparmio, economia. 2 (*org. az.*) riduzione degli sprechi. 3 **savings,** *pl.* risparmi. // **savings account** (*banca*) conto di deposito fruttifero; (*banca, USA*) deposito vincolato; **savings bank** (*banca*) cassa di risparmio; **savings-bank depositor's book** (*banca*) libretto di risparmio; **a ~ clause** (*leg.*) una riserva di legge, un'eccezione; **savings deposit** (*banca*) deposito a risparmio; **savings motivated by caution** (*econ.*) risparmi cautelativi; **savings ratio** (*econ., fin.*) rapporto tra il reddito disponibile e quello risparmiato; **savings shares** (*fin.*) azioni di risparmio.

say[1], *n.* opinione, voce in capitolo.

say[2], *v. t.* (*pass.* e *part. pass.* **said**) dire, affermare, asserire, dichiarare.

scab[1], *n.* (*sind.*) crumiro.

scab[2], *v. i.* (*sind.*) fare il crumiro.

scalar, *a.* (*mat.*) scalare. // **~ process** (*org. az.*) processo scalare; **~ product** (*mat.*) prodotto scalare.

scale[1], *n.* 1 piatto della bilancia. 2 scala, gamma. 3 grado. 4 (*sind.*) tariffa. // **~ charges** prezzi tariffari; **~ -down** riduzione progressiva; **~ of priority** scala di priorità; **a ~ of taxation** (*fin.*) una gamma d'imposte; **~ rates** *V.* **~ charges; ~ -up** aumento progressivo.

scale[2], *v. t.* graduare, misurare con una scala. // to **~ down** ridurre (*qc.*) progressivamente, scalare; to **~ up** aumentare (*qc.*) progressivamente; to **~ up imports** (*econ.*) aumentare progressivamente le importazioni.

scales, *n. pl.* bilancia. // **the ~ of justice** (*fig.*) la bilancia della giustizia.

scalp, *v. i.* fare il bagarinaggio.

scantiness, *n.* insufficienza.

scantling, *n.* (*trasp. mar.*) dimensioni (*delle parti strutturali d'una nave*).

scanty, *a.* inadeguato, insufficiente, magro. // **a ~ crop** (*econ.*) un magro raccolto.

scarce, *a.* inádeguato, insufficiente.

scarcity, *n.* scarsezza, carenza.

schedule[1], *n.* 1 distinta, elenco, lista. 2 prospetto, specchietto, tabella. 3 (*leg.*) elenco dell'attivo e del passivo fallimentare. 4 (*org. az.*) programma (*di lavoro, delle consegne, ecc.*). 5 (*trasp., USA*) orario (*dei treni, ecc.*). // **a ~ of freight rates** (*trasp. mar.*) una tabella dei noli; **~ rate** (*ass.*) tariffa tabellare; **behind ~** (*org. az.*) in ritardo (*col lavoro, con le consegne, ecc.*); **on ~** (*org. az.*) in orario, a tempo; **two-column ~** prospetto a due colonne.

schedule[2], *v. t.* 1 elencare, mettere in lista. 2 mettere in programma, fissare, stabilire. // to **~ new trains** (*trasp. ferr.*) istituire nuovi treni.

scheduled flight, *n.* (*trasp. aer.*) volo di linea.

scheme[1], *n.* 1 schema, disegno, piano, progetto, programma. 2 (*leg., ingl.*) piano governativo. // **a ~ of work** (*org. az.*) un piano di lavoro.

scheme[2], *v. t.* e *i.* progettare, pianificare, disegnare, far piani.

science, *n.* scienza.

scienter, *avv.* (*leg.*) intenzionalmente.

scientific, *a.* scientifico. // **~ management** (*org. az.*) organizzazione scientifica; **~ research** (*econ.*) ricerca scientifica.

scope, *n.* 1 ambito, campo (*d'azione*), portata (*fig.*), sfera (*fig.*). 2 scopo.

scrap[1], *n.* 1 pezzo, pezzetto. 2 (*org. az.*) scarto, scarti. // **~ book** brogliaccio; **~ recovery** (*org. az.*) ricupero degli scarti.

scrap[2], *v. t.* scartare, gettar via.

scrapyard, *n.* (*trasp. mar.*) cantiere di demolizione.

screen[1], *n.* 1 schermo. 2 (*pubbl.*) industria cinematografica.

screen[2], *v. t.* passare al vaglio, selezionare.

screening, *n.* (*pers.*) selezione preliminare.

screenwriter, *n.* (*pubbl.*) sceneggiatore.

scrip, *n.* (*fin.*) certificato (*azionario*) provvisorio.

script, *n.* 1 (*leg.*) documento originale. 2 (*pubbl.*) copione, testo (*radiotelevisivo*).

scrivener, *n.* (*leg.*) notaio.

scruple, *n.* scrupolo (*misura di peso pari a 20 grani o 1,296 grammi*).

scrutinize, *v. t.* scrutare, esaminare attentamente, investigare, spulciare. // to ~ **economic policies in the light of guidelines of the programme** vagliare le politiche economiche in rapporto agli orientamenti programmatici.

sea, *n.* mare. // ~ **accident** (*trasp. mar.*) incidente di mare, sinistro marittimo; ~ **and land carriage** (*trasp., trasp. mar.*) trasporto misto; ~ **area** (*trasp. mar.*) area marittima; ~ **assurance** (*ass. mar.*) assicurazione marittima; ~ **bed** (*trasp. mar.*) fondo marino, alveo marino; ~ **-borne** marittimo; ~ **-borne goods** (*trasp. mar.*) merci trasportate via mare; ~ **-borne trade** (*trasp. mar.*) commercio marittimo, traffici marittimi; ~ **camp** (*org. az., pers.*) colonia marina; ~ **charts** (*trasp. mar.*) carte nautiche; ~ **-damaged** (*trasp. mar.*) (*di carico*) danneggiato dall'acqua di mare; ~ **-gauge** (*trasp. mar.*) pescaggio (*della nave*); ~ **-going** (*trasp. mar.*) d'alto mare, di lungo cabotaggio; ~ **-going vessel** (*trasp. mar.*) naviglio d'alto mare; ~ **insurance** (*ass. mar.*) assicurazione marittima; ~ **journal** (*trasp. mar.*) giornale di bordo; ~ **-kindliness** (*trasp. mar.*) (*d'imbarcazione*) attitudine al mare, tenuta del mare; ~ **law** (*leg.*) diritto marittimo; ~ **level** (*trasp. mar.*) livello del mare; ~ **mile** (*trasp. mar.*) miglio marittimo; **a ~ of debt** (*fig.*) un mare di debiti; ~ **passage** (*trasp. mar.*) passaggio marittimo; ~ **perils** (*ass. mar.*) rischi marittimi; ~ **risks** (*ass. mar.*) rischi marittimi; ~ **road** (*trasp. mar.*) rotta navale; ~ **traffic** (*trasp. mar.*) traffico marittimo; **at ~** in mare; **by ~** per mare.

seacraft, *n.* (*trasp. mar.*) naviglio d'alto mare.

seakeeping, *a.* (*trasp. mar.*) (*di nave*) che tiene bene il mare.

seal[1], *n.* 1 sigillo, bollo. 2 (*leg.*) sigillo. // **under ~** (*leg.*) (*d'atto*) recante la firma e il sigillo di chi lo redige.

seal[2], *v. t.* 1 sigillare. 2 (*leg.*) sigillare, apporre i sigilli, piombare. // to ~ **a letter** sigillare una lettera; to ~ **with lead** (*leg.*) sigillare con piombini, piombare.

sealed, *a.* 1 sigillato. 2 (*leg.*) sigillato, piombato. // **a ~ bid** (*o* **tender**) (*comm.*) un'offerta (*d'appalto, ecc.*) sigillata, un'offerta (*d'appalto, ecc.*) in busta chiusa; **a ~ verdict** (*leg.*) una sentenza sigillata; ~ **will** (*leg.*) testamento segreto.

sealing, *n.* 1 sigillatura. 2 (*leg.*) sigillatura, piombatura.

seaman, *n.* (*pl.* **seamen**) (*trasp. mar.*) marittimo, navigante, navigatore.

seamen, *n. pl.* (*trasp. mar.*) marittimi, gente di mare.

seaport, *n.* (*trasp. mar.*) porto di mare.

search[1], *n.* 1 ricerca, indagine. 2 (*leg.*) perquisizione, ispezione. 3 (*trasp. mar.*) visita di controllo. // ~ **and rescue** (*trasp. mar.*) operazione (*aeronavale*) di salvataggio.

search[2], *v. t.* e *i.* 1 indagare, fare ricerche. 2 (*leg.*) perquisire, ispezionare, visitare. // to ~ **a ship** (*leg.*) perquisire una nave.

searching, *n.* 1 ricerca, indagine. 2 (*leg.*) perquisizione. // **the ~ for new markets** (*econ.*) la ricerca di nuovi mercati.

seaside, *n.* spiaggia. // **a ~ resort** (*tur.*) una stazione balneare.

season, *n.* stagione. // ~ **employment** (*pers.*) impiego stagionale; ~ **ticket** (*trasp.*) abbonamento (*ferroviario, ecc.*), tessera (*ferroviaria, ecc.*); ~ **-ticket holder** (*trasp.*) abbonato; ~ **unemployment** (*sind.*) disoccupazione stagionale; ~ **work** (*pers.*) lavoro stagionale.

seasonal, *a.* stagionale, di stagione. // ~ **adjustment** (*market.*) adattamento stagionale; ~ **down** (*econ.*) crisi stagionale; ~ **employment** (*pers.*) impiego stagionale; ~ **industry** (*econ.*) industria stagionale; ~ **occupations** (*pers.*) lavori stagionali; ~ **rates** tariffe stagionali; ~ **unemployment** (*sind.*) disoccupazione stagionale; ~ **worker** (*pers.*) (lavoratore) stagionale.

seat[1], *n.* 1 sedile, posto (a sedere). 2 (*econ.*) centro (*di produzione, ecc.*). 3 (*org. az.*) sede, sede degli affari. 4 (*trasp.*) posto (a sedere). // ~ **belt** (*trasp. aer., trasp. aut.*) cintura (di sicurezza); **the ~ of a company** (*fin.*) la sede d'una società.

seat[2], *v. t.* 1 avere posti a sedere per (*un certo numero di persone*). 2 (*org. az.*) installare.

seaward, *a.* (*trasp. mar.*) diretto verso il mare, rivolto verso il mare.

seaway, *n.* (*trasp. mar.*) rotta oceanica.

seaworthiness, *n.* (*trasp. mar.*) (*d'una nave*) navigabilità, capacità di tenere il mare.

seaworthy, *a.* (*trasp. mar.*) (*di nave*) capace di tenere il mare, atto (*o* idoneo) alla navigazione, navigabile.

second[1], *n.* 1 minuto secondo. 2 **seconds,** *pl.* (*market.*) merci di seconda qualità. // ~ **ballot** (*leg.*) ballottaggio; ~ **-class** inferiore, mediocre, di qualità scadente, di seconda qualità; (*trasp.*) seconda classe, seconda; di seconda classe, in seconda classe; ~ **-class carriage** (*trasp. ferr.*) vettura di seconda classe; ~ **-class passengers** (*trasp.*) viaggiatori di seconda classe; ~ **-class**

tickets (*trasp.*) biglietti di seconda classe; ~ **cover** (*giorn.*) seconda di copertina; ~ **half** (*fin.*) *V.* ~ **half-year;** ~ **half-year** (*fin.*) secondo semestre; ~ **-hand** di seconda mano, usato; **a** ~ **-hand car** un'automobile di seconda mano; ~ **-hand sale** (*market.*) vendita di seconda mano; ~ **mortgage** (*leg.*) ipoteca di secondo grado; ~ **of exchange** (*fin.*) seconda di cambio; ~ **-rate** di seconda qualità, dozzinale; ~ **shift** (*pers.*) turno pomeridiano; ~ **via** (*fin.*) seconda di cambio.

second[2], *v. t.* **1** essere secondo a. **2** assecondare, appoggiare, sostenere.

secondary, *a.* **1** accessorio. **2** (*pers.*) subalterno, subordinato, delegato. // ~ **evidence** (*leg.*) prova accessoria (*p. es., la copia d'un contratto quando l'originale sia andato smarrito*); ~ **strike** (*sind.*) sciopero di solidarietà.

secrecy, *n.* **1** segretezza. **2** segreto. // **the banking** ~ il segreto bancario.

secret, *a.* occulto. // ~ **agreement** accordo segreto; ~ **partner** (*fin.*) socio occulto; ~ **profits** (*rag.*) profitti occulti; ~ **reserve** (*rag.*) riserva occulta.

secretarial, *a.* (*pers.*) di segretario, da segretario, di segreteria.

secretariat, *n.* **1** (*pers.*) segretariato. **2** (*pers.*) personale di segreteria. **3** (*pers.*) segreteria (*mansioni di segretario*).

secretariate, *n.* *V.* **secretariat.**

secretary, *n.* **1** (*pers.*) segretario, segretaria. **2** (*pers.*) direttore amministrativo (*d'una società per azioni e sim.*). // ~ **-general** segretario generale; ~ **'s office** (*org. az.*) segreteria; ~ **-treasurer** (*giorn.*) direttore amministrativo; **Under-** ~ Sottosegretario.

secretaryship, *n.* segretariato (*carica o mansioni di segretario*).

section[1], *n.* **1** sezione, divisione, parte. **2** categoria, classe, gruppo (*di persone*). **3** quartiere (*di città*). **4** (*giorn.*) paragrafo. **5** (*giorn.*) rubrica. **6** (*leg.*) paragrafo. **7** (*market.*) reparto (*di negozio, ecc.*). **8** (*trasp. ferr.*) tronco (*ferroviario*), tratto. **9** (*USA*) «sezione» (*unità di misura di superficie pari a un miglio quadrato*). // ~ **manager** (*market.*) ispettore di reparto (*di grande magazzino, ecc.*).

section[2], *v. t.* sezionare.

sectional, *a.* settoriale, locale.

sector, *n.* (*econ.*) settore. // ~ **-by-** ~ **negotiations** (*econ.*) negoziati settoriali.

sectorial, *a.* settoriale, di settore. // ~ **policies** (*econ.*) politiche di settore.

secular, *a.* secolare.

secure[1], *a.* certo, al sicuro, fiducioso, tranquillo.

secure[2], *v. t.* **1** assicurare, mettere al sicuro. **2** assicurarsi. **3** (*leg.*) garantire.

secured, *a.* **1** assicurato. **2** (*leg.*) garantito, privilegiato. // ~ **advance** (*banca*) anticipazione su garanzia; ~ **creditor** (*banca*) creditore privilegiato; ~ **credits** (*cred.*) crediti privilegiati; ~ **loan** (*banca*) mutuo garantito.

secure oneself, *v. rifl.* assicurarsi, garantirsi, premunirsi. // to ~ **against exchange-rate fluctuations** (*fin.*) premunirsi contro fluttuazioni nei tassi di cambio.

security, *n.* **1** certezza. **2** (*leg.*) garanzia, cauzione, pegno, mallevadoria, sicurtà. **3** (*leg.*) garante. **4** **securities,** *pl.* (*Borsa, fin.*) obbligazioni, titoli, valori. // ~ **department** (*banca*) ufficio titoli, portafoglio titoli; ~ **for costs** (*leg.*) garanzia per le spese giudiziarie; **the** ~ **given by an employee** (*pers.*) la cauzione versata da un dipendente; **the securities market** (*fin.*) il mercato mobiliare; **securities owned** (*fin.*) titoli di proprietà; **without** ~ (*cred.*) senza garanzia, allo scoperto.

sedan, *n.* (*trasp. aut.*) «berlina», automobile chiusa.

see, *v. t.* (*pass.* **saw,** *part. pass.* **seen**) **1** esaminare. **2** consultare. **3** provvedere, fare in modo (che). // to ~ **about st.** occuparsi di qc.; to ~ **into** esaminare, indagare; to ~ **to** occuparsi di, provvedere a; to **be seeing sb.** andare a trovare q., essere a colloquio con q.

seed, *n.* seme. // ~ **-time** (*econ.*) tempo della semina.

seek, *v. t.* (*pass.* e *part. pass.* **sought**) **1** cercare, ricercare. **2** chiedere, richiedere. // to ~ **a situation** (*pers.*) cercare un impiego.

seem, *v. i.* parere. // **as it seems** a quanto pare.

segment, *n.* settore, sezione, parte.

segmentize, *v. t.* segmentare.

segregate, *v. t.* segregare, isolare, separare.

segregation, *n.* segregazione, isolamento, separazione. // **the** ~ **of extraordinary expenses in the budget** (*rag.*) l'isolamento delle spese straordinarie nel preventivo.

seizable, *a.* (*leg.*) confiscabile, pignorabile, sequestrabile. // ~ **chattels** (*leg.*) beni pignorabili.

seize, *v. t.* **1** (*leg.*) confiscare, pignorare, sequestrare, mettere (*qc.*) sotto sequestro. **2** (*leg.*) acquistare il possesso di (*qc.*). // to ~ **contraband goods** (*leg.*) sequestrare merce di contrabbando.

seizure, *n.* **1** (*leg.*) confisca, pignoramento, sequestro. **2** (*leg.*) acquisto di possesso (*di qc.*).

// **a ~ by order of the Court** (*leg.*) un sequestro giudiziario; **~ of incomes** (*leg.*) pignoramento di rendite.

select, *v. t.* **1** selezionare. **2** (*leg.*) eleggere (*con votazione*). // to **~ a sample** (*market.*) scegliere un campione.

selected, *a.* selezionato, scelto. // **~ quality** (*market.*) qualità selezionata.

selection, *n.* **1** selezione, scelta. **2** (*market.*) assortimento. **3** (*pers.*) selezione.

selective, *a.* **1** selettivo. **2** (*market.*) (*di cliente*) esigente. // **~ assembly** (*org. az.*) assemblaggio selettivo; **~ control** (*org. az.*) controllo selettivo; **~ employment tax (S.E.T.)** (*fin., ingl.*) imposta (*introdotta nel 1966*) sulle ditte, commisurata proporzionalmente al numero dei dipendenti; **a ~ monetary control** (*econ.*) un controllo monetario selettivo; **a ~ revaluation of one's monetary parity with the dollar** (*econ.*) un riallineamento selettivo della propria parità monetaria col dollaro.

self[1], *n.* sé, se stesso. // **«pay to ~»** (*comm.*) (*su un assegno*) «pagate a me medesimo».

self-[2], *pref.* **1** auto-; autonomo; automatico. **2** di sé; in sé; personale. // **~ -addressed** (*comun.*) preindirizzato, munito dell'indirizzo del mittente; **~ -advertiser** (*pubbl.*) reclamista; **~ -defence** (*leg.*) legittima difesa; **~ -determination** autodeterminazione; **~ -employed** (*org. az.*) indipendente, per conto proprio; **~ -employed activities** (*org. az.*) attività non salariate; **~ -employed activities in retail trade** (*org. az.*) attività di commercio al dettaglio per conto proprio; **~ -employed workers** (*econ.*) lavoratori indipendenti; **~ -employment** (*econ.*) lavoro indipendente, lavoro autonomo, lavoro in proprio; **~ -financing** (*fin.*) autofinanziamento; **~ -injurer** autolesionista; **~ -insurance** (*rag.*) autoassicurazione; **~ -made man** uomo che s'è fatto da sé; **~ -mailer** (*pubbl.*) pieghevole (*che può essere spedito senza bisogno di busta*); **~ -service** (*market.*) self-service, servizio fatto per sé dal cliente stesso; **~ -service store (*o* shop)** (*market.*) self-service, negozio self-service; **~ -sufficiency** (*econ.*) autosufficienza, autarchia; (*org. az.*) autoapprovvigionamento; **~ -sufficiency policy** (*econ.*) politica autarchica; **~ -sufficient** (*econ.*) autosufficiente, autarchico; **~ -sufficient nation** (*econ.*) nazione autosufficiente; **~ -taxation** (*fin.*) autotassazione; **~ -trimmer** (*trasp. mar.*) autostivante, nave autostivante.

sell, *v. t.* (*pass.* e *part. pass.* **sold**) **1** (*leg.*) alienare. **2** (*market.*) vendere, cedere, smerciare. **3** (*market.*) far vendere, promuovere la vendita di (*qc.*). *v. i.* (*market.*) vendersi, trovare smercio. // to **~ at any price** (*market.*) vendere per vendere; to **~ at bargain prices** (*market.*) vendere a stralcio; to **~ at best** (*fin., market.*) vendere al meglio; to **~ at a loss** (*market.*) vendere in perdita; to **~ at a sacrifice** (*market.*) vendere in perdita; to **~ below cost price** (*market.*) vendere sotto costo; to **~ by auction** vendere all'asta, vendere all'incanto; to **~ by inch of candle** vendere all'ultimo offerente (*in un'asta*); to **~ by instalments** (*market.*) vendere a rate; to **~ by lots** (*market.*) vendere a lotti; to **~ by the metre** (*market.*) vendere al metro; to **~ by retail** (*market.*) vendere al dettaglio (*o* al minuto); dettagliare; to **~ by weight** (*market.*) vendere a peso; to **~ cash on delivery** (*market.*) vendere contro assegno; to **~ cheaply** (*market.*) vendere a buon mercato; to **~ door-to-door** (*market.*) vendere a domicilio; to **~ ex-ship** (*trasp. mar.*) vendere allo sbarco; to **~ for** (*market.*) costare; to **~ for the account** (*o* **for the settlement**) (*Borsa*) vendere a termine; to **~ for the call** (*Borsa*) vendere a premio con facoltà d'opzione (*per il compratore*); to **~ for cash** (*market.*) vendere a contanti; to **~ for forward delivery** (*fin.*) vendere per futura consegna; to **~ for a song** (*slang USA*) vendere a buon mercato, vendere «per una cicca»; to **~ goods on approval** (*market.*) vendere merce salvo prova, vendere merce salvo vista e verifica; to **~ house-to-house** (*market.*) vendere di casa in casa, vendere a domicilio; to **~ in bulk** (*market.*) vendere all'ingrosso; to **~ insurance** (*ass.*) stipulare contratti di assicurazione, fare l'assicuratore; to **~ off** (*fin., market.*) subire un calo nei prezzi di vendita; (*market.*) svendere, liquidare, smerciare; to **~ on the black market** (*market.*) vendere a mercato nero; to **~ on commission** (*market.*) vendere per conto terzi; to **~ on credit** (*market.*) vendere a credito; to **~ on easy terms** (*market.*) vendere praticando facilitazioni (*di pagamento*); to **~ on hire purchase** (*market.*) vendere a rate; to **~ out** (*market.*) vendere, svendere, cedere, liquidare; to **~ out one's share of a business** (*fin.*) cedere la propria parte in un'azienda; to **~ over the counter** (*market.*) vendere al dettaglio (*o* al minuto), dettagliare; to **~ a pig in a poke** (*fig.*) vendere a scatola chiusa; to **~ retail** (*market.*) *V.* to **~ by retail**; to **~ second-hand** (*market.*) vendere di seconda mano; to **~ short** (*Borsa*) (*di ribassista*) vendere titoli senza averne la disponibilità, vendere allo scoperto; to **~ to the highest bidder** (*market.*) vendere al miglior offerente; to **~ under the counter** (*market.*) vendere sotto banco; to ~ **sb. up** (*leg.*) mettere in liquidazione i beni di q. (*che è fallito*); to ~ **wholesale** (*market.*) vendere all'ingrosso; to ~ **with option to repurchase** (*leg.*) vendere con patto di riscatto; to ~ **with right of redemption** (*leg.*) vendere con patto di riscatto; to **be sold by quantity** (*di merce*) andare a numero; to **be sold by weight** (*di merce*) andare a peso.

seller, *n.* 1 (*market.*) venditore. 2 (*market.*) negoziante. // **sellers' market** (*market.*) mercato favorevole alle vendite; **the ~ of a call option** (*Borsa*) il venditore d'un (contratto) «dont»; **the ~ of a put option** (*Borsa*) il venditore d'un premio indiretto; ~ **'s option** (*Borsa*) premio per il venditore (*di titoli*); ~ **'s option double** (*Borsa*) diritto del venditore di raddoppiare; «**sellers over**» (*Borsa, fin.*) i venditori sono in numero superiore ai compratori.

selling, *n.* (*market.*) vendita. // ~ **agent** (*market.*) commissionario; ~ **and administrative expenses** (*rag.*) spese generali (*voce di bilancio*); ~ **brokerage** mediazione di vendita; ~ **commission** commissione di vendita; ~ **department** (*org. az.*) reparto di vendita; ~ **expenses** (*rag.*) spese di vendita; ~ **licence** (*leg.*) licenza di vendita; ~ **-off** (*market.*) liquidazione, svendita, vendita totale (*delle rimanenze*); ~ **order** (*market.*) ordinazione di vendita; ~ **-out** (*market.*) *V.* ~ **-off;** ~ **policy** (*market.*) politica delle vendite; ~ **power** (*market.*) potenziale di vendita; ~ **-price** (*market.*) prezzo di vendita; (*rag.*) valore venale; ~ **rate** (*banca*) cambio di vendita; ~ **-up** (*leg.*) vendita forzosa (*dei beni d'un debitore insolvente*); **non-** ~ **department** (*org. az.*) reparto non addetto alla vendita.

sell-off, *n.* (*Borsa, fin.*) crollo dei prezzi dei titoli.

sellout, *n.* (*market.*) esaurimento delle scorte d'un articolo (*a causa della domanda eccezionalmente alta*).

semester, *n.* semestre.

semestral, *a.* semestrale.

semi-, *pref.* semi-, mezzo. // ~ **-annual** semestrale; ~ **-annually** semestralmente; ~ **-inflation** (*econ.*) quasi inflazione; ~ **-monthly** quindicinale; (*giorn.*) quindicinale, pubblicazione quindicinale; ~ **-official** semiufficiale, ufficioso; ~ **-weekly** due volte la settimana; (*giorn.*) pubblicazione bisettimanale; ~ **-yearly** *V.* ~ **-annual.**

semifinished, *a.* (*org. az.*) semilavorato. // ~ **products** (*org. az.*) prodotti semilavorati, semilavorati.

semimanufactured, *a.* *V.* **semifinished.**

semimanufactures, *n. pl.* (*org. az.*) semilavorati, prodotti semilavorati.

send, *v. t.* (*pass.* e *part. pass.* **sent**) **1** inviare, mandare, spedire, rimettere. **2** (*comun.*) trasmettere. // to ~ **again** (*comun., trasp.*) rinviare, rispedire; to ~ **away** inviare, mandare, spedire; (*pers.*) mandare via, licenziare; to ~ **back** rimandare, rinviare, rispedire, respingere; to ~ **by air-mail** (*comun.*) spedire per posta aerea; to ~ **by book-post** (*comun.*) spedire in busta aperta; to ~ **by sample-post** (*comun.*) spedire come campione; to ~ **cash on delivery** (*comun.*) spedire contro assegno; to ~ **down** far calare, far scendere; to ~ **down prices** (*fin., market.*) far calare i prezzi; to ~ **for** (*market.*) mandare a prendere, ordinare: to ~ **for st. on approval** (*market.*) ordinare qc. in esame; to ~ **goods by rail** (*trasp. ferr.*) spedire merce per ferrovia; to ~ **goods on approval** (*market.*) inviare merce in esame, inviare merce in visione; to ~ **in** inviare, mandare, spedire; to ~ **in one's papers** (*amm.*) presentare le dimissioni; to ~ **in one's resignation** (*amm.*) presentare le dimissioni; to ~ **a message** (*comun.*) trasmettere un messaggio; to ~ **money** (*comun.*) rimettere denaro; to ~ **on** inoltrare; to ~ **out** far circolare, emanare; to ~ **a remittance** (*comun.*) inviare una rimessa; to ~ **round** far circolare, diffondere, inviare; to ~ **under cover** (*comun.*) spedire sotto fascia; to ~ **up** (*fin., market.*) far aumentare, far crescere, far salire; to ~ **up prices** (*fin., market.*) far salire i prezzi.

sender, *n.* mittente, speditore. // ~ **'s name and address** (*comun.*) nome e indirizzo del venditore.

sending, *n.* **1** invio, spedizione, rimessa. **2** (*comun.*) trasmissione.

senior, *a.* seniore, più anziano, anziano. // **the ~ partner** (*amm.*) il socio più anziano (*d'una ditta*); ~ **securities** (*fin.*) titoli di priorità; ~ **vicepresident** (*amm.*) vicepresidente anziano.

seniority, *n.* (*pers.*) anzianità di servizio. // ~ **list** (*amm., pers.*) ruolo d'anzianità; ~ **rights** (*pers.*) diritti d'anzianità.

sentence[1], *n.* **1** (*leg.*) sentenza, giudizio. **2** (*leg.*) condanna, pena. // **a ~ of the Court** (*leg.*) una sentenza del tribunale; ~ **of death** (*leg.*) condanna a morte.

sentence[2], *v. t.* (*leg.*) emettere una sentenza contro (*q.*), condannare. // to ~ **sb. by default** (*leg.*) condannare q. in contumacia.

sentimental value, *n.* valore d'affezione.

separate[1], *a.* distinto, diviso. *n.* (*giorn., pubbl.*) estratto (*d'articolo, ecc.*). // ~ **accounts**

(*rag.*) conti distinti; ~ **estate** (*leg.*) beni parafernali; ~ **policy** (*ass.*) polizza distinta; ~ **signature** (*leg.*) firma singola; **under** ~ **cover** (*comun.*) in plico separato.

separate[2], *v. t.* **1** distinguere, dividere. **2** (*comun.*) smistare. **3** (*pers.*) licenziare. // to ~ **the mail** smistare la corrispondenza.

separation, *n.* **1** distinzione, divisione. **2** (*comun.*) smistamento (*della corrispondenza*). **3** (*pers.*) licenziamento. // **the** ~ **of powers** (*leg.*) la divisione dei poteri.

sequence[1], *n.* sequela, successione.

sequence[2], *v. t.* mettere in successione.

sequential, *a.* in successione, in serie ininterrotta.

sequester, *v. t.* (*leg.*) sequestrare, mettere sotto sequestro, confiscare.

sequestrate, *v. t.* (*leg.*) sequestrare, metter sotto sequestro, confiscare.

sequestration, *n.* (*leg.*) sequestro, confisca.

sequestrator, *n.* **1** (*leg.*) sequestrante. **2** (*leg.*) sequestratario.

serial, *a.* **1** di serie, in serie. **2** (*giorn.*) (*di pubblicazione, opuscolo, ecc.*) periodico. // ~ **bond** (*fin.*) obbligazione (appartenente a una serie) a scadenza periodica; ~ **number** numero di serie (*di biglietti di banca, ecc.*); ~ **production** (*org. az.*) produzione in serie.

series, *n.* **1** serie, successione. **2** (*fin.*) serie (*di monete, ecc.*). **3** (*mat.*) serie. // **in** ~ in serie.

serious, *a.* serio, grave. // **a** ~ **damage** (*leg.*) un danno grave.

serve, *v. t.* **1** essere al servizio di (*q.*). **2** (*leg.*) intimare, notificare, presentare. **3** (*leg.*) scontare (*una condanna*). **4** (*leg., scozz.*) dichiarare (*q.*) erede. **5** (*market.*) servire (*i clienti*). *v. i.* **1** (*market.*) servire i clienti. **2** (*trasp. mar.*) (*di marea*) essere favorevole. // to ~ **one's apprenticeship with sb.** (*pers.*) fare l'apprendistato presso q.; to ~ **an attachment** (*leg.*) intimare un arresto; notificare un sequestro; to ~ **in an acting capacity** (*leg.*) prestare servizio come interino; to ~ **an office** (*amm.*) tenere una carica fino al termine; to ~ **a paper** (*leg.*) notificare un atto; to ~ **a summons on sb.** (*leg.*) intimare a q. un mandato di comparizione; citare q. in giudizio; to ~ **sb. with a summons** (*leg.*) intimare a q. un mandato di comparizione; citare q. in giudizio.

service, *n.* **1** servigio, prestazione (*professionale*). **2** (*leg.*) citazione, notificazione, notifica. **3** (*market.*) servizio, assistenza, manutenzione. **4 services,** *pl.* (*econ.*) (i) servizi, attività terziarie, attività di prestazione di servizi. // ~ **at sea** (*trasp. mar.*) servizio a bordo; ~ **charge** (*banca*) percentuale per un particolare servizio (*reso alla clientela*); ~ **department** (*org. az.*) ufficio assistenza; ~ **industry** (*econ.*) industria di servizi, industria del settore «terziario»; ~ **life** (*org. az.*) durata di vita utile (*d'un macchinario, ecc.*); **the** ~ **of a decree** (*leg.*) la notifica d'un decreto; **the** ~ **of a judgment** (*leg.*) la notifica d'una sentenza; **the** ~ **of a loan** (*cred.*) il servizio di un prestito; **services rendered** servizi resi, prestazioni; **the services sector** (*econ.*) il settore terziario, il «terziario», le attività «terziarie», il settore della distribuzione; ~ **shopping** (*market.*) raccolta di notizie sull'attività della concorrenza attuata per mezzo di «falsi clienti»; ~ **station** (*trasp. aut.*) stazione di servizio.

serviceable, *a.* utile.

servitude, *n.* *V.* **easement.**

session, *n.* **1** (*leg.*) riunione. **2** (*leg.*) udienza.

set[1], *n.* **1** insieme (*di cose affini*); assortimento. **2** gruppo (*di persone*). **3** (*comun.*) apparecchio (*radiofonico, televisivo, ecc.*). **4** (*pers.*) squadra (*d'operai*). // ~ **-back** regresso; ostacolo; (*market.*) ribasso (*che riporta i prezzi al livello precedente il loro aumento*); **a** ~ **of articles** (*market.*) un assortimento d'articoli; ~ **of books** (*rag.*) impianto contabile; ~ **of exchange** (*cred.*) prima, seconda e terza di cambio; ~ **of rules** (*leg.*) normativa; ~ **of samples** (*market.*) campionario; **a** ~ **of tyres** (*trasp. aut.*) un treno di gomme; ~ **-off** compenso, contropartita; (*cred.*) compensazione (*di debito*); (*leg.*) domanda riconvenzionale; ~ **-out** (*market.*) esposizione, mostra (*di merci*); ~ **-up** (*org. az.*) fondazione, organizzazione, impianto (*d'un'impresa*).

set[2], *v. t.* (*pass.* e *part. pass.* **set**) **1** collocare, mettere, porre. **2** stabilire, fissare. **3** regolare, tarare (*uno strumento e sim.*). **4** (*giorn., pubbl.*) comporre (*tipograficamente*). // to ~ **one's affairs in order** mettere in ordine i propri affari; to ~ **afloat** far galleggiare; (*fig.*) varare, lanciare (*un'impresa*); to ~ **apart** mettere da parte; (*rag.*) stanziare (*una somma*); to ~ **ashore** (*trasp. mar.*) sbarcare (*merci, passeggeri*); to ~ **aside** mettere da parte; (*leg.*) annullare (*un verdetto, ecc.*); (*rag.*) accantonare; to ~ **back** ritardare; ostacolare; to ~ **down** fissare, stabilire; (*trasp. aut.*) far scendere (*un passeggero*); to ~ **the fashion** (*market.*) fare la moda; to ~ **fire to st.** incendiare qc.; to ~ **free** lasciare libero, liberare; rilasciare (*un detenuto*); to ~ **one's hand to a document** (*leg.*) firmare un documento; to ~ **in** (*trasp. mar.*) (*della marea*) avanzare; to ~ **money free** (*fin.*) rimettere denaro in circolazione; to ~ **objectives** (*org. az.*) formulare degli obiettivi, stabilire degli obiettivi; to ~ **off** compensare; to ~ **off a debt** (*cred.*) compensare un debito; to ~ **on** (*pers.*) mettere al lavoro, impiegare; to ~ **out** impostare (*un problema*); (*market.*) esporre, mettere in mostra (*merce in vendita*); (*rag.*) impostare (*un conto*); to ~ **out for display** (*market.*) mettere in mostra, disporre (*merce in vendita*); to ~ **a price on goods** (*market.*) fare il prezzo alla merce; to ~ **quotas** (*market.*) stabilire quote (*di vendita*); to ~ **sail** (*trasp. mar.*) alzare le vele; to ~ **one's signature to a paper** apporre la propria firma a un documento; to ~ **up** erigere; fondare, impiantare, installare, instaurare, istituire, avviare; (*giorn., pubbl.*) comporre (*tipograficamente*); to ~ **up a committee** fondare un comitato; to ~ **up a machine** (*org. az.*) installare una macchina; to ~ **up shop** (*market.*) «aprir bottega», mettere su un negozio; to ~ **up a stand** (*market., pubbl.*) allestire uno stand.

set[3], *a.* fermo, fisso, saldo. // **a ~ form of enquiry** (*comun.*) una forma fissa di richiesta d'informazioni; ~ **wages** (*pers.*) salari fissi; ~ **working hours** (*org. az.*) ore di lavoro fisse.

setting-out, *n.* 1 impostazione (*d'un problema, ecc.*). 2 (*rag.*) impostazione (*di un conto*).

setting-up, *n.* fondazione, installazione, impianto, instaurazione, istituzione.

settle, *v. t.* 1 decidere, fissare, risolvere, stabilire. 2 definire (*una faccenda*). 3 (*cred.*) pagare, saldare, estinguere (*un debito*). 4 (*leg.*) assegnare, intestare. 5 (*leg.*) comporre (*una vertenza*). 6 (*rag.*) chiudere (*conti, ecc.*). *v. i.* (*cred.*) pagare un conto, saldare un debito. // to ~ **an account** (*cred.*) saldare un conto; to ~ **one's affairs** (*leg.*) far testamento; to ~ **an annuity** (*fin.*) costituire una rendita vitalizia; to ~ **an argument** (*leg.*) decidere una controversia; to ~ **a bill** (*cred.*) pagare una fattura; to ~ **a dispute** (*leg.*) appianare una lite; to ~ **a fine out of Court** (*leg.*) conciliare una multa; to ~ **sb. in business** avviare q. negli affari; to ~ **a matter** (*amm.*) evadere una pratica; to ~ **a price** (*market.*) (*di venditore e acquirente*) fissare un prezzo, accordarsi su un prezzo.

settled, *a.* 1 fermo, fisso, saldo. 2 (*cred.*) pagato, saldato, estinto. 3 (*rag.: di conto*) chiuso. // ~ **in full** (*cred.*) pagato a saldo, saldato; ~ **prices** (*market.*) prezzi fissi (*imposti dal fabbricante*).

settlement, *n.* 1 (*Borsa*) liquidazione periodica. 2 (*cred.*) pagamento, estinzione (*d'un debito*), saldo. 3 (*leg.*) accomodamento, composizione (*d'una vertenza*), compromesso, transazione. 4 (*rag.*) conguaglio, chiusura (*di conti*). // ~ **bargain** (*Borsa*) vendita allo scoperto, mercato a termine; ~ **day** (*Borsa*) giorno di liquidazione; **the ~ of accounts** (*Borsa*) la liquidazione dei conti; **the ~ of an annuity on sb.** (*fin.*) la costituzione d'una rendita per q.; **the ~ of a controversy** (*leg.*) la composizione d'una controversia; **the ~ of a dispute** (*leg.*) la definizione d'una lite (*o* di una vertenza); ~ **out of Court** (*leg.*) transazione stragiudiziale; ~ **price** (*Borsa*) prezzo di compenso; **in full ~ of your account** (*rag.*) a saldo del vostro (*o* di ogni vostro) avere.

settling, *n.* 1 (*fin.*) liquidazione. 2 (*leg.*) accomodamento. 3 (*rag.*) chiusura, conguaglio (*di conti*). // ~ **-day** (*Borsa*) giorno di liquidazione; ~ **-up** (*fin.*) liquidazione, regolamento dei conti.

seven, *a.* e *n.* sette.

sever, *v. t.* dividere, distinguere.

several, *a.* 1 distinto, separato. 2 individuale, particolare, singolo. 3 (*leg.*) solidale. // ~ **covenant** (*leg.*) solidarietà passiva; ~ **liability** (*leg.*) responsabilità individuale; ~ **responsibility** (*leg.*) responsabilità individuale.

severally, *avv.* 1 distintamente. 2 individualmente, singolarmente.

severalty, *n.* (*leg.*) proprietà individuale (*di beni non condivisi con altri*).

severance, *n.* (*pers.*) rescissione (*d'un contratto d'impiego, ecc.*). // ~ **pay** (*pers.*) indennità di licenziamento (*o* di buonuscita), liquidazione (*pagata al dipendente licenziato senza sua colpa*).

shade[1], *n.* sfumatura.

shade[2], *v. i.* cambiare per gradi, mutare lentamente.

shady, *a.* (*fig.*) disonesto. // **a ~ transaction** un affare equivoco.

shake, *v. t.* (*pass.* **shook,** *part. pass.* **shaken**) agitare. // to ~ **down** (*fig.*) adattarsi; to ~ **up** agitare, mescolare; (*fig.*) destare; (*org. az.*) riorganizzare (*un'azienda*).

shake-out, *n.* (*market.*) lieve diminuzione dell'attività commerciale (*dopo un periodo inflazionistico, ecc.*).

shake-up, *n.* 1 mescolamento. 2 (*fig.*) scuotimento. 3 (*org. az.*) riorganizzazione (*d'un'azienda*). 4 (*org. az., pers.*) movimento (*di funzionari*).

sham[1], *n.* 1 imitazione. 2 (*leg.*) finzione, simulazione. 3 (*leg.*) frode. 4 (*market.*) imitazione (*d'un altro articolo*). *a. attr.* falso, finto, fittizio. // ~ **dividends** (*fin., rag.*) dividendi fittizi.

sham[2], *v. t.* e *i.* (*leg.*) fingere, simulare, mistificare.

shammer, *n.* (*leg.*) simulatore, mistificatore.

shape[1], *n.* forma.

shape[2], *v. t.* formare.

share[1], *n.* **1** parte. **2** quota parte. **3** (*fin.*) partecipazione. **4** (*fin.*) azione, titolo azionario. **5** (*trasp. mar.*) caratura. // ~ **capital** (*fin.*) capitale azionario; ~ **certificate** (*fin.*) certificato azionario (*provvisorio*), cartella azionaria; ~ **in the profits** (*fin.*) partecipazione agli utili; ~ **index** (*fin.*) numero indice delle azioni, indice finanziario; ~ **investment** (*fin.*) investimento azionario; ~ **issue** (*fin.*) emissione azionaria; ~ **ledger** (*fin.*) *V.* ~ **register**; ~ **-list** (*Borsa*) listino «valori»; ~ **market** (*fin.*) mercato azionario; ~ **of stock** (*fin.*) partecipazione (*al capitale azionario*); ~ **premium** (*fin.*) plusvalore (azionario); ~ **prices** (*fin.*) corsi delle azioni; ~ **pushing** (*fin.*) collocamento clandestino d'azioni; ~ **qualification** (*fin.*) cauzione in titoli azionari; ~ **register** (*fin.*) registro degli azionisti; ~ **transfer** (*fin.*) trasferimento azionario; ~ **warrant** (*fin.*) certificato azionario.

share[2], *v. t.* **1** dividere (*in parti uguali*), ripartire, distribuire (*equamente*). **2** condividere, sostenere insieme. // to ~ **in** partecipare a; to ~ **in the management** (*amm.*) partecipare alla gestione; to ~ **in the profits** (*fin.*) partecipare agli utili; to ~ **profits** (*fin.*) partecipare agli utili.

sharebroker, *n.* (*fin.*) agente di cambio.

sharecropper, *n.* (*econ., USA*) mezzadro.

sharecropping, *n.* (*econ., USA*) mezzadria.

shareholder, *n.* **1** (*fin.*) azionista. **2** (*fin.*) **shareholders**, *pl.* azionariato (*sing., collett.*). // **shareholders' equity** (*fin.*) capitale netto (*d'una società per azioni*); **shareholders in arrears with calls** (*fin.*) azionisti in ritardo coi versamenti (*per azioni sottoscritte*); **shareholders' meeting** (*fin.*) assemblea degli azionisti.

shareholding, *n.* (*fin.*) azionariato.

sharing, *a.* compartecipe. *n.* partecipazione, compartecipazione. // ~ **of profits** (*fin.*) partecipazione agli utili.

sharp, *a.* **1** marcato, netto. **2** disonesto. // **a** ~ **trader** (*market.*) un commerciante disonesto.

shatter, *v. t.* infrangere.

sheer[1], *n.* (*trasp. mar.*) cambio di rotta.

sheer[2], *v. i.* (*trasp. mar.*) deviare dalla rotta.

sheet, *n.* **1** foglio (*di carta, ecc.*). **2** (*giorn.*) pubblicazione, giornale.

shelf, *n.* (*pl.* **shelves**) (*attr. uff.*) scaffale a muro. // **on the** ~ (*fig.*) a riposo.

shelter[1], *n.* difesa, protezione. // ~ **goods** (*econ.*) beni di rifugio.

shelter[2], *v. t.* **1** dare rifugio a. **2** difendere, proteggere. // to ~ **trade** (*econ.*) proteggere gli scambi (*dalla concorrenza straniera, ecc.*).

shelve, *v. t.* **1** mettere su una mensola, mettere su uno scaffale. **2** (*fig.*) mettere da parte, accantonare (*un problema, ecc.*); rimandare (*una discussione, ecc.*); insabbiare (*fig.*). **3** (*pers.*) collocare a riposo. **4** (*pers.*) licenziare. // to **be shelved** (*d'un problema, ecc.*) essere accantonato, rimandato; insabbiarsi.

sheriff, *n.* (*leg.*) sceriffo (*primo magistrato della Contea, nominato dalla Corona*).

shift[1], *n.* **1** cambiamento, avvicendamento, sostituzione, spostamento. **2** (*econ.*) raccolto ottenuto per rotazione. **3** (*pers.*) turno (*di lavoro*). **4** (*pers.*) squadra (*di turno*). // ~ **boss** (*pers.*) capo della squadra di turno; **shifts in international capital movements** (*fin.*) spostamenti nei movimenti internazionali di capitali; ~ **in portfolio** (*fin.*) mutamento della composizione del portafoglio; ~ **-lock** (*di macch. uff.*) «arresto» delle maiuscole (*di macchina da scrivere*); **the** ~ **of crops** (*econ.*) la rotazione dei raccolti; **a** ~ **of responsibility** un passaggio di responsabilità; ~ **worker** (*pers.*) turnista.

shift[2], *v. t.* **1** cambiare, sostituire, avvicendare. **2** spostare. *v. i.* (*trasp. mar.*) (*del carico*) spostarsi, scorrere. // to ~ **the burden of proof** (*leg.*) scaricare l'onere della prova; to ~ **the responsibility** scaricare la responsabilità.

shiftable parity, *n.* (*fin.*) parità mobile.

shifting, *n.* **1** cambiamento, sostituzione, avvicendamento. **2** (*trasp. mar.*) spostamento, scorrimento (*del carico*). *a.* variabile, incostante, instabile. // ~ **of tax** (*econ., fin.*) traslazione d'imposta.

shiftman, *n.* (*pl.* **shiftmen**) *V.* **shift boss.**

shilling, *n.* scellino.

shining, *a.* splendente.

ship[1], *n.* **1** (*trasp. mar.*) nave, bastimento, naviglio, vascello. **2** (*trasp. mar.*) (= **steamship**) piroscafo. // ~ **abandoned at sea** (*trasp. mar.*) nave abbandonata in mare; ~ **'s agent** (*trasp. mar.*) raccomandatario; ~ **aground** (*trasp. mar.*) nave arenata, nave incagliata; ~ **'s articles** (*trasp. mar.*) clausole d'ingaggio, contratto d'arruolamento; ~ **'s books** (*trasp. mar.*) libri di bordo; ~ **-broker** (*trasp. mar.*) agente marittimo, sensale marittimo, mediatore di noleggi marittimi; ~ **-canal** (*trasp.*) canale navigabile; ~ **'s certificate of registry** (*trasp. mar.*) certificato di registro della nave; ~

-chandler (*trasp. mar.*) fornitore navale; ~ **-chandlery** (*trasp. mar.*) forniture navali; ~ **'s company** (*trasp. mar.*) equipaggio (*esclusi gli ufficiali*); ~ **'s days** (*trasp. mar.*) stallie; ~ **'s husband** (*trasp. mar.*) capitano d'armamento, raccomandatario; ~ **in ballast** (*trasp. mar.*) nave in zavorra; ~ **in commission** (*trasp. mar.*) nave in armamento; ~ **in distress** (*trasp. mar.*) nave in pericolo; ~ **in every way fitted to the voyage** (*trasp. mar.*) nave sotto tutti i riguardi atta al viaggio; ~ **loading** (*trasp. mar.*) nave sotto carico; ~ **'s manifest** (*trasp. mar.*) manifesto di bordo; ~ **-master** (*trasp. mar.*) capitano di nave, padrone; ~ **on order** (*trasp. mar.*) nave in commessa; ~ **'s papers** (*trasp. mar.*) carte di bordo, documenti di bordo; ~ **'s protest** (*trasp. mar.*) protesto marittimo (*dichiarazione giurata dal capitano e dall'equipaggio d'una nave danneggiata, riguardante i danni subiti, le loro cause, ecc.*); ~ **ready for sea** (*trasp. mar.*) nave pronta a prendere il mare; ~ **'s register** (*trasp. mar.*) certificato d'immatricolazione; ~ **'s report** (*trasp. mar.*) dichiarazione di bordo; ~ **riding at anchor** (*trasp. mar.*) nave all'ancora, nave alla fonda; ~ **'s stores** forniture di bordo, forniture navali; ~ **under average** (*trasp. mar.*) nave in stato d'avaria; **ships under convoy** (*trasp. mar.*) navi in convoglio, navi scortate; ~ **under repair** (*trasp. mar.*) nave in raddobbo; **at ~ 's rail** (*trasp. mar.*) sotto paranco; **ex ~** (*trasp. mar.*) sotto paranco, F.O.B. destino; **under ~ 's derrick** (*trasp. mar.*) sotto paranco, F.O.B. destino; **under ~ 's tackle** (*trasp. mar.*) sotto paranco, F.O.B. destino.

ship[2], *v. t.* **1** (*trasp., trasp. mar., USA*) inviare, spedire, trasportare. **2** (*trasp. mar.*) imbarcare, caricare, inviare, spedire, trasportare. // to ~ **water (o a heavy sea)** (*trasp. mar.*) imbarcare acqua.

shipbuilding, *n.* (*trasp. mar.*) costruzioni navali. // ~ **group** (*trasp. mar.*) gruppo cantieristico; ~ **labour** (*trasp. mar.*) manodopera del settore cantieristico; ~ **yard** (*trasp. mar.*) cantiere navale.

shipload, *n.* (*trasp. mar.*) carico completo (*d'una nave*).

shipmaster, *n.* (*trasp. mar.*) capitano (*di mercantile*).

shipment, *n.* **1** (*trasp., USA*) spedizione (*l'atto di spedire, in genere*). **2** (*trasp., USA*) spedizione (*la merce spedita, in genere*). **3** (*trasp. mar.*) imbarco, operazioni di carico. **4** (*trasp. mar.*) spedizione (*l'atto di spedire*). **5** (*trasp. mar.*) spedizione (*la merce spedita*).

shipowner, *n.* (*trasp. mar.*) armatore. // ~ **'s club** (*trasp. mar.*) consorzio armatoriale; **shipowners' company** (*trasp. mar.*) società armatrice; ~ **'s lien** (*trasp. mar.*) privilegio dell'armatore (*sul nolo e le altre spese attinenti al carico*).

shipped bill of lading, *n.* (*trasp. mar.*) polizza di carico per merce imbarcata.

shipped weight, *n.* (*trasp. mar.*) peso imbarcato.

shipper, *n.* **1** (*trasp., USA*) spedizioniere. **2** (*trasp. mar.*) spedizioniere, caricatore. **3** (*trasp. mar.*) consegnatario, destinatario (*del carico*); ricevitore. **4** (*trasp. mar.*) merce spedita, merce da carico. // ~ **'s letter of instructions** (*trasp. aer.*) lettera d'istruzione dello speditore; ~ **'s papers** (*trasp. mar.*) documenti di spedizione.

shipping, *n.* **1** (*trasp., USA*) spedizione (*in genere*). **2** (*trasp. mar.*) spedizione marittima, imbarco. **3** (*trasp. mar.*) navigazione, traffico marittimo. **4** (*trasp. mar.*) marina mercantile, naviglio. // ~ **-advice notice** (*trasp. mar.*) nota d'imbarco; ~ **agency** (*trasp. mar.*) agenzia marittima; ~ **agent** (*trasp. mar.*) spedizioniere marittimo, agente di compagnia di navigazione; (*trasp., USA*) spedizioniere (*in genere*); ~ **and forwarding charges** (*trasp. mar.*) spese d'imbarco e di spedizione; ~ **-articles** (*trasp. mar.*) clausole d'ingaggio, contratto d'imbarco; ~ **bill** (*dog., trasp. mar.*) bolletta di sortita; ~ **business** (*trasp. mar.*) commercio marittimo; ~ **charges** (*trasp. mar.*) spese d'imbarco, diritti d'imbarco; ~ **company** (*trasp. mar.*) società di navigazione; ~ **date** (*trasp. mar.*) data di spedizione; ~ **department** (*org. az.*) ufficio spedizioni; ~ **documents** (*trasp. mar.*) documenti di spedizione; ~ **Exchange** (*trasp. mar.*) Borsa dei Noli; ~ **expenses** (*trasp. mar.*) spese di caricazione, spese d'imbarco; diritti d'imbarco; ~ **firm** (*trasp. mar.*) società d'armamento; ~ **industry** (*trasp. mar.*) industria navale, (industria dell') armamento; ~ **instructions** (*trasp. mar.*) istruzioni per l'imbarco (*delle merci*); ~ **law** (*leg.*) diritto marittimo; ~ **line** (*trasp. mar.*) compagnia di navigazione, linea di navigazione; ~ **link** (*trasp. mar.*) collegamento marittimo; ~ **market** (*trasp. mar.*) mercato marittimo; ~ **-master** (*trasp. mar.*) commissario di bordo; ~ **note** (*trasp. mar.*) ordine d'imbarco, buono d'imbarco; ~ **order** (*trasp. mar.*) ordinativo d'imbarco, buono d'imbarco; ~ **papers** (*trasp. mar.*) documenti di spedizione; ~ **port** (*trasp. mar.*) porto d'imbarco; ~ **ton** (*trasp. mar.*) tonnellata di portata lorda; ~ **tonnage** (*trasp. mar.*) tonnellaggio di spedizione;

~ **trade** (*trasp. mar.*) commercio marittimo; (industria dell') armamento; ~ **weight** (*trasp. mar.*) peso (*del carico*) all'imbarco.

shipwreck[1], *n.* 1 (*fig.*) naufragio. 2 (*trasp. mar.*) naufragio.

shipwreck[2], *v. i.* (*trasp. mar.*) naufragare. *v. t.* (*fig.*) far naufragare, mandare in rovina, far fallire. // to **be shipwrecked** (*trasp. mar.*: *di persone*) naufragare, fare naufragio.

shipyard, *n.* (*trasp. mar.*) cantiere navale, arsenale, darsena. // ~ **activities** (*trasp. mar.*) attività cantieristiche.

shoal, *n.* (*trasp. mar.*) secca.

shock[1], *n.* colpo, urto. // ~ **-workers** (*sind.*) lavoratori «d'assalto».

shock[2], *v. t.* colpire, urtare.

shoot, *v. t.* (*pass.* e *part. pass.* **shot**) 1 lanciare, scagliare. 2 sparare. // to ~ **a film** (*pubbl.*) girare un film; to ~ **up** (*fin., market.*) (*di prezzi*) balzare.

shop, *n.* 1 (*market.*) bottega, negozio, esercizio, fondo urbano. 2 (*org. az.*) (= **workshop**) officina, stabilimento. 3 (*org. az.*) (= **workshop**) reparto (*di fabbrica*). // ~ **-assembly** (*org. az.*) montaggio in officina; ~ **-assistant** (*pers.*) commesso, commessa; ~ **-boy** (*pers.*) giovane di negozio; ~ **card** (*sind.*) manifesto di fabbrica (*affisso, a cura d'un sindacato, in uno stabilimento, per mostrare che in questo il lavoro è svolto secondo le norme previste dal contratto*); **shops' closing-hours** (*market.*) orari di chiusura dei negozi; ~ **committee** (*pers., sind.*) commissione interna (*d'una fabbrica*); ~ **foreman** (*pers.*) capo officina; ~ **-girl** (*pers.*) commessa (*di negozio*); ~ **-lifter** (*leg.*) taccheggiatore; ladro (*in un negozio*); ~ **-lifting** (*leg.*) taccheggiamento; furto in un negozio; ~ **-management** (*org. az.*) organizzazione di fabbrica; ~ **-order** (*org. az.*) ordine di fabbricazione; ~ **paper** (*market.*) carta sottile per avvolgere la merce; ~ **stewart** (*pers., sind.*) membro della commissione interna, delegato di fabbrica; ~ **-window** (*market.*) vetrina.

shopkeeper, *n.* (*market.*) bottegaio, negoziante, esercente, dettagliante.

shopman, *n.* (*pl.* **shopmen**) 1 (*pers.*) commesso. 2 (*pers.*) operaio d'officina.

shoppe, *n.* (*market.*) bottega, negozio.

shopper, *n.* (*market.*) acquirente, compratore, cliente.

shopping, *n.* (*market.*) acquisti, compere (*effettuate nei negozi*); spesa. // ~ **area** (*market., USA*) *V.* ~ **centre;** ~ **center** (*market., USA*) *V.* ~ **centre;** ~ **centre** (*market.*) centro per acquisti; zona di negozi, area suburbana di empori e negozi; ~ **goods** (*market.*) beni di consumo acquistati dopo attento esame e confronto fra le qualità, i prezzi, ecc., offerti da altri negozianti; ~ **mall** (*market., USA*) *V.* ~ **centre;** ~ **plaza** (*market., USA*) *V.* ~ **centre;** ~ **precinct** (*market.*) centro per acquisti pedonalizzato.

shopwalker, *n.* (*pers.*) ispettore di reparto (*di grande magazzino, ecc.*).

shore, *n.* (*trasp. mar.*) litorale. // **sailors on** ~ **leave** (*trasp. mar.*) marinai in franchigia.

short, *a.* 1 breve. 2 insufficiente. 3 (*cred.*) a breve scadenza. 4 (*rag.*) parziale. *n.* 1 (*Borsa, fin.*) speculatore al ribasso, ribassista. 2 (*pubbl.*) cortometraggio; carosello (*televisivo*). 3 (*rag.*) somma parziale, totale parziale. 4 **shorts,** *pl.* (*Borsa, fin.*) impegni a breve (termine). // ~ **article** (*giorn.*) trafiletto; **a** ~ **bill** (*cred.*) cambiale a breve scadenza; ~ **covering** (*Borsa, fin.*) acquisto (*di titoli*) a copertura; **a** ~ **-dated bill** (*cred.*) una cambiale a breve scadenza; **a** ~ **film** (*pubbl.*) un cortometraggio; ~ **-handed** (*org. az.*) (*di datore di lavoro*) a corto di manodopera; (*trasp. mar.*) (*di nave*) con equipaggio incompleto; ~ **hundredweight** «hundredweight» americano (*misura di peso pari a 1/20 di «ton» o 45,36 kg*); ~ **interest** (*Borsa, fin.*) insieme di titoli (*o* merci) venduti allo scoperto a una certa data; to ~ **-land** (*trasp. mar.*) scaricare meno di quanto dichiarato nel manifesto; ~ **-paid** (*comun.*) (*di lettera, ecc.*) recante affrancatura insufficiente; ~ **period** (*econ.*) periodo breve, breve (termine); ~ **position** (*Borsa, fin.*) *V.* ~ **interest;** ~ **range** (*econ.*) periodo breve, breve (termine); ~ **-range forecast** (*econ.*) previsione a breve termine; ~ **ream** (*giorn., pubbl.*) risma di 480 fogli; ~ **run** (*econ.*) periodo breve, breve (termine); (*giorn.*) piccola tiratura; ~ **-run planning** (*econ.*) programmazione a breve termine; ~ **sale** (*Borsa, fin.*) vendita allo scoperto; ~ **sale against the box** (*Borsa, fin.*) vendita allo scoperto di titoli in possesso di chi opera (*e che non desidera impugnarli*); ~ **seller** (*Borsa, fin.*) venditore allo scoperto; ~ **selling** (*Borsa, fin.*) vendita allo scoperto; ~ **-shipped** (*trasp. mar.*) (*di merce, carico, ecc.*) imbarcato in meno (*di quanto accordato*); ~ **-staffed** (*org. az.*) (*d'azienda, ecc.*) a corto di personale; ~ **-term** (*econ., fin.*) a breve termine, a breve, congiunturale; ~ **-term action** (*econ.*) interventi a breve (termine); ~ **-term bank debt** (*fin.*) indebitamento a breve verso banche; ~ **-term borrowing** (*cred.*) finanziamento a (breve) termine; ~

-term changes (*econ.*) variazioni congiunturali; ~ **-term credit** (*cred.*) credito a breve (termine); ~ **-term economic policy** (*econ.*) politica congiunturale; ~ **-term expectation** (*econ.*) aspettativa a breve termine; ~ **-term financing** (*cred.*) finanziamento a breve (termine); ~ **-term funds** (*fin.*) capitali a breve, risorse monetarie a breve; ~ **-term liabilities** (*fin.*, *rag.*) debiti a breve (termine); ~ **-term loans** (*cred.*) mutui a breve scadenza, denaro a breve; ~ **-term paper** (*cred.*) titolo di credito a breve termine; ~ **-term recovery** (*econ.*) ripresa a breve termine; ~ **-term saving** (*econ.*) risparmio a breve termine; ~ **-term statistics** (*stat.*) statistiche congiunturali; ~ **-time** (*org. az.*) orario ridotto; ~ **ton** tonnellata americana (*misura di peso pari a 2.000 libbre o 907 kg*); ~ **weight** (*market.*) peso scarso; to ~ **-weight** (*market.*) dare il peso scarso; to **be** ~ **in one's payments** (*cred.*) essere in arretrato coi pagamenti, essere moroso; to **be** ~ **of** mancare di; **at** ~ **notice** (*comun.*) con breve preavviso, entro breve termine; **at** ~ **range** a breve termine; **in the** ~ **run** (*o* **term**) a breve termine; **in** ~ **supply** (*market.*) (*di merce*) scarseggiante.

shortage, *n.* **1** deficienza, carenza, insufficienza, mancanza. **2** (*econ.*, *fin.*, *rag.*) ammanco, deficit. // **a** ~ **in cash** (*rag.*) un ammanco di cassa.

shortcoming, *n.* deficienza, difetto, imperfezione, manchevolezza.

shortfall, *n.* (*econ.*, *fin.*, *rag.*) ammanco, deficit, saldo passivo.

shorthand[1], *n.* stenografia. *a. attr.* stenografico. // ~ **typewriting** stenodattilografia; ~ **-typist** (*pers.*) stenodattilografo; stenodattilografa; ~ **-writer** (*pers.*) stenografo; stenografa.

shorthand[2], *v. t.* stenografare.

show[1], *n.* **1** mostra, esibizione. **2** (*leg.*) produzione (*di documenti, ecc.*). **3** (*market.*, *pubbl.*) mostra, esposizione, fiera. **4** (*market.*, *pubbl.*) dimostrazione. **5** (*pubbl.*) spettacolo, programma. // ~ **-how** (*market.*) dimostrazione (*d'un metodo, d'una procedura, ecc.*); **a** ~ **of documents** (*leg.*) una produzione di documenti; ~ **-room** (*market.*, *pubbl.*) sala d'esposizione; ~ **-window** (*market.*) mostra (*di negozio*), vetrina; **by** ~ **of hands** (*di votazione*) per alzata di mano.

show[2], *v. t.* (*pass.* **showed,** *part. pass.* **shown**) **1** mostrare, esibire. **2** (*leg.*) produrre (*documenti, ecc.*). **3** (*market.*, *pubbl.*) presentare a una mostra, mettere in mostra, esporre. // to ~ **a balance** (*rag.*) presentare un saldo; to ~ **cause** (*leg.*) provare il proprio diritto; to ~ **one's passport** (*tur.*) mostrare il passaporto; to ~ **up** smascherare; to ~ **up a fraud** (*leg.*) mettere a nudo una frode.

showing, *a.* che mostra, che esibisce. *n.* **1** esibizione. **2** presentazione (*di documenti e sim.*). **3** esposizione. **4** (*fin.*) situazione, stato (*degli affari, ecc.*). // ~ **a deficit** (*o* **a loss**) (*fin.*, *rag.*) deficitario; ~ **of evidence** (*leg.*) presentazione di prove.

shrink, *v. i.* (*pass.* **shrank,** *part. pass.* **shrunk**) **1** contrarsi. **2** diminuire, ridursi, rimpicciolire.

shrinkage, *n.* **1** contrazione, restringimento. **2** diminuzione, riduzione. **3** (*market.*, *trasp.*) calo (*di peso, ecc.: della merce*). // **a** ~ **in prices** (*market.*) una contrazione dei prezzi; **a** ~ **in sales** (*market.*) una contrazione delle vendite; **a** ~ **of the export trade** (*comm. est.*) una contrazione del commercio con l'estero.

shunt[1], *n.* **1** (*trasp. ferr.*) scambio. **2** (*trasp. ferr.*) deviazione, instradamento, smistamento (*d'un treno*).

shunt[2], *v. t.* (*trasp. ferr.*) deviare, instradare, smistare (*un treno*). *v. i.* **1** (*fig.*) fare la spola (*fra due località*). **2** (*trasp. ferr.*) (*di treno*) cambiare binario, essere smistato.

shunter, *n.* (*trasp. ferr.*) deviatore, manovratore di scambi, scambista.

shunting, *n.* (*trasp. ferr.*) instradamento, smistamento, manovra. // ~ **locomotive** (*trasp. ferr.*) locomotiva da manovra; ~ **station** (*trasp. ferr.*) stazione di smistamento.

shut[1], *n.* chiusura. // ~ **-down** (*org. az.*) chiusura temporanea (*d'una fabbrica*), interruzione del lavoro.

shut[2], *v. t.* (*pass.* e *part. pass.* **shut**) chiudere, serrare. // to ~ **the door upon an offer** (*fig.*) rifiutare un'offerta; to ~ **down** (*org. az.*) chiudere (*una fabbrica, ecc.*); (*d'azienda, ecc.*) chiudere, «chiuder bottega»; to ~ **down a factory for shortage of personnel** (*org. az.*) chiudere una fabbrica per scarsità di personale; to ~ **up** (*fam.*) far silenzio; to ~ **up shop** (*fig.*) sospendere ogni attività, «chiuder bottega».

shuttle[1], *n.* spoletta. // ~ **service** (*trasp. ferr.*) servizio a navetta, servizio locale (*fra due stazioni*); ~ **train** (*trasp. ferr.*) treno che fa la spola fra due stazioni.

shuttle[2], *v. i.* far la spola, andare avanti e indietro.

sick, *a.* (*anche fig.*) malato, infermo. // ~ **-benefit** (*pers.*) *V.* **sickness benefit; a** ~ **economy** (*econ.*, *fig.*) un'economia malata; ~ **-insurance** (*ass.*, *pers.*) assicurazione per malattie; ~ **-leave** (*pers.*) congedo per malattia; ~

pay (*pers.*) retribuzione per il periodo di congedo per malattia; to **be on ~ -leave** (*pers.*) essere in mutua.

sickness, *n.* malattia. // **~ benefit** (*pers.*) sussidio di malattia (*o* d'invalidità).

side[1], *n.* fianco, lato, parte. // **~ -car** (*trasp.*) «sidecar»; **~ -line** (*market.*) «linea» di prodotti secondaria (*rispetto a quella che costituisce oggetto principale di vendita*); (*org. az.*) attività secondaria, ramo d'affari meno importante; **a ~ road** (*trasp. aut.*) una laterale; **~ -slip** (*trasp. aut.*) sbandata; **~ -track** (*trasp. ferr.*) binario di raccordo; **on the credit ~** (*rag.*) a credito; **on the debit ~** (*rag.*) a debito; **«this ~ down»** (*trasp.*) «basso» (*scritto su un collo di merci*); **«this ~ up»** (*trasp.*) «alto», «tenere diritto» (*scritto su un collo di merci*).

side[2], *v. i.* prendere le parti (*di q.*); appoggiare, sostenere.

siding, *n.* (*trasp. ferr.*) raccordo, binario di raccordo. // **~ track** (*trasp. ferr.*) *V.* **~.**

sight[1], *n.* **1** vista. **2 sights,** *pl.* (*tur.*) curiosità d'un luogo. **3 sights,** *pl.* (*tur.*) luoghi d'interesse turistico. // **~ bill** (*cred.*) cambiale a vista; **~ draft** (*cred.*) tratta a vista; **at ~** a vista.

sight[2], *v. t.* **1** giungere in vista di. **2** (*cred.*) presentare (*una cambiale*) per il pagamento.

sightsee, *v. i.* (*tur.*) fare un giro turistico.

sightseeing, *n.* (*tur.*) visita alle curiosità d'un luogo. // **~ bus** (*tur.*) autobus per gite turistiche; **~ tour** (*tur.*) giro turistico; **~ trip** (*tur.*) gita turistica.

sign[1], *n.* **1** indicazione. **2** (*market.*) insegna (*di negozio*). **3** (*trasp.*) cartello (*stradale, ecc.*). // **~ -board** (*market.*) insegna (*di negozio*); **~ -post** (*trasp.*) cartello (*o* indicatore) stradale.

sign[2], *v. t.* **1** firmare. **2** (*leg.*) ratificare, sanzionare. **3** (*pers.*) assumere (*q., facendolo firmare*). **4** (*trasp.*) mettere segnali lungo (*una strada, ecc.*). *v. i.* firmare. // to **~ away** (*leg.*) alienare formalmente, cedere formalmente (*una proprietà, un diritto, ecc.*); to **~ in** (*pers.*) timbrare il cartellino (*arrivando sul posto di lavoro*); (*tur.*) firmare il registro delle presenze (*all'albergo, ecc.*), registrarsi (*all'arrivo, ecc.*); to **~ the mail** (*comun.*) firmare la corrispondenza; to **~ on** (*pers.*) far la firma, assumere; (*trasp. mar.*) arruolarsi, imbarcarsi; arruolare: to **~ on for another five years** (*pers.*) far la firma per altri cinque anni; to **~ out** (*pers.*) timbrare il cartellino (*abbandonando il posto di lavoro*); (*tur.*) registrarsi (*alla partenza*); to **~ over** (*leg.*) *V.* to **~ away;** to **~ a street intersection** (*trasp. aut.*) mettere segnali a un incrocio stradale; to **~ a treaty** (*leg.*) ratificare un trattato; to **~ up** *V.* to **~ on;** to **~ a will** (*leg.*) firmare un testamento.

signal[1], *n.* **1** segnale. **2** (*trasp. ferr., trasp. mar.*) segnale. // **~ -box** (*trasp. ferr.*) cabina di comando dei segnali; **~ lamp** (*trasp. mar.*) fanale da segnali; **~ -man** (*trasp. ferr.*) addetto ai segnali, manovratore; **~ tower** (*trasp. ferr., USA*) *V.* **~ -box.**

signal[2], *v. t.* e *i.* far segnalazioni, far segnali a (*q.*).

signatory, *a.* e *n.* (*leg.*) firmatario, segnatario.

signature[1], *n.* **1** firma. **2** (*leg.*) vidimazione. // **~ book** (*banca*) libro delle firme (*dei clienti d'un istituto di credito*); **~ loan** (*cred.*) prestito senza garanzia.

signature[2], *v. t.* (*leg.*) autenticare (*un documento, ecc.*) mediante la firma.

signee, *n.* (*leg.*) firmatario.

signer, *n.* (*leg.*) firmatario.

significance, *n.* **1** senso. **2** importanza, peso (*fig.*), portata (*fig.*).

significant, *a.* importante.

signify, *v. t.* annunciare, comunicare.

silent, *a.* silenzioso. // **~ partner** (*fin., leg.*) socio di capitali; (*anche*) socio occulto; to **be ~** far silenzio; to **be ~ about (***o* **on)** passar sotto silenzio.

silly, *a.* sciocco, stupido. // **the ~ season** (*giorn.*) la stagione morta (*quando i giornali, per mancanza di notizie, si trovano costretti a pubblicare racconti, servizi di scarso interesse, ecc.*).

silo, *n.* (*org. az.*) silo.

silver, *n.* argento. // **~ bullion** (*econ.*) argento monetabile; **a ~ coin** una moneta d'argento; **~ currency** (*econ.*) valuta argentea; **~ standard** (*econ.*) standard argenteo, circolazione (monetaria) argentea.

simple, *a.* (*mat.*) semplice. // **~ arbitrage** (*fin.*) arbitraggio semplice; **~ bond** (*leg.*) obbligazione incondizionata; **~ contract** (*leg.*) contratto semplice, contratto verbale; **~ credit** (*cred.*) credito non confermato; **~ debenture** (*fin.*) obbligazione chirografaria; **~ interest** (*mat., rag.*) interesse semplice; **~ majority** (*leg.*) maggioranza semplice; **~ obligation** (*leg.*) obbligazione incondizionata; **the ~ rule of three** (*mat.*) la regola del tre semplice.

simplex, *n.* (*mat.*) simplesso. // **~ system** (*comun.*) sistema (telefonico) simplex.

simplified, *a.* semplificato. // **~ index of productivity** (*org. az.*) indice di produttività semplificato.

simplify, *v. t.* semplificare. // to **~ a**

manufacturing process (*org. az.*) semplificare un processo di lavorazione.

simulate, *v. t.* (*leg.*) simulare, fingere.

simulation, *n.* (*leg.*) finzione, simulazione. // ~ **of offence** (*leg.*) simulazione di reato.

simulator, *n.* (*anche leg.*) simulatore.

simultaneous, *a.* simultaneo.

since, *cong.* (*tempo*) da quando, dacché.

sine, *avv.* (*latino*) senza. // ~ **die** (*leg.*) «sine die»; a tempo indeterminato, a data da determinarsi.

sinecure, *n.* (*pers.*) sinecura.

sinecurist, *n.* (*pers.*) chi gode d'una sinecura.

single, *a.* semplice, individuale. *n.* **1** (*trasp.*) biglietto d'andata. **2** (*ingl.*) banconota da una sterlina. **3** (*USA*) banconota da un dollaro. // ~ **-decker** (*trasp. mar.*) nave a un ponte; ~ **entry** (*rag.*) partita semplice; ~ **-entry bookkeeping** (*rag.*) contabilità a partita semplice; **a** ~ **European monetary front** (*econ.*) un fronte monetario europeo unico; ~ **issue** (*o* **number**) (*giorn.*) numero unico (*di rivista, ecc.*); ~ **market** (*econ.*) mercato unico; **a** ~ **market for agricultural products** (*econ.*) un mercato unico per i prodotti agricoli; ~ **-member constituency** (*leg.*) collegio uninominale; ~ **-name paper** (*cred.*) pagherò cambiario recante la sola firma dell'emittente (*e nessuna girata*); ~ **payment** pagamento in soluzione unica, pagamento «una tantum»; ~ **premium** (*ass.*) premio unico; ~ **price** (*market.*) prezzo unico; ~ **standard** (*econ.*) monometallismo; ~ **ticket** (*trasp.*) biglietto d'andata; **a** ~ **-track railway** (*trasp. ferr.*) una ferrovia a un solo binario; ~ **-use goods** (*econ.*) capitale circolante (*beni che si esauriscono completamente in un solo processo produttivo*).

sink, *v. t.* (*pass.* **sank,** *part. pass.* **sunk**) **1** (*cred.*) ammortare, ammortizzare, saldare (*un debito*). **2** (*fin.*) investire (*denaro*). **3** (*fin.*) perdere (*denaro: in investimenti azzardati*). *v. i.* (*trasp. mar.*) affondare, andare a picco.

sinkable, *a.* **1** (*cred., fin., rag.*) ammortabile, ammortizzabile. **2** (*trasp. mar.*) affondabile.

sinking, *n.* **1** (*cred.*) ammortamento (*d'un mutuo, ecc.*); estinzione (*d'un debito, ecc.*). **2** (*trasp. mar.*) affondamento. // ~ **fund** (*rag.*) fondo d'ammortamento; ~ **plan** (*rag.*) piano d'ammortamento.

sister, *n.* sorella. // ~ **ships** (*trasp. mar.*) navi gemelle.

sistership, *n.* l'essere sorelle. // ~ **clause** (*ass. mar.*) clausola che regola la collisione fra due navi appartenenti allo stesso armatore.

sit, *v. i.* (*pass.* e *part. pass.* **sat**) **1** sedersi, essere seduto. **2** (*leg.*) avere un seggio. **3** (*leg.*) tenere udienza. // to ~ **for an exam** sostenere un esame; to ~ **on** (*leg.*) essere membro di; to ~ **on the board of directors** (*amm.*) far parte del consiglio d'amministrazione; to ~ **on a committee** far parte d'una commissione.

sit-down, *n.* (*sind.*) *V.* ~ **strike.** // ~ **strike** (*sind.*) sciopero con occupazione del posto di lavoro.

sit-in, *n. V.* **sit-down strike.**

sitting, *n.* adunanza, udienza. // **a** ~ **of the Court** (*leg.*) un'udienza del tribunale.

situation, *n.* **1** situazione. **2** (*econ.*) congiuntura. **3** (*pers.*) posto (*di lavoro*), impiego. // ~ **analysis** (*market.*) analisi della situazione; «**situations vacant**» (*giorn., pubbl.*) «offerte d'impiego», «cercasi»; «**situations wanted**» (*giorn., pubbl.*) «domande d'impiego», «offresi».

six, *a.* e *n.* sei.

size, *n.* **1** dimensione, grandezza, misura. **2** ammontare, volume (*fig.*). **3** (*market.*) numero (*di scarpe*); taglia (*d'indumento*). // ~ **of business** (*org. az.*) dimensioni d'impresa; **the** ~ **of an order** (*market.*) l'ammontare d'un'ordinazione.

skeleton, *n.* scheletro. // ~ **staff** (*org. az.*) personale ridotto al minimo.

sketch[1], *n.* disegno, vignetta.

sketch[2], *v. t.* disegnare.

skew[1], *a.* obliquo, sbilenco, sghembo.

skew[2], *v. t.* rendere obliquo, far deviare.

skid[1], *n.* (*trasp.*) slittamento, sbandata.

skid[2], *v. i.* (*trasp.*) slittare.

skilful, *a.* abile, esperto, «finito», qualificato.

skill, *n.* **1** abilità. **2** (*pers.*) operai qualificati.

skilled, *a.* **1** abile. **2** (*pers.*) (*d'operaio*) qualificato, specializzato. // ~ **labour** (*pers.*) manodopera qualificata; ~ **work** (*pers.*) lavoro specializzato.

skipper, *n.* (*trasp. mar.*) capitano (*di piccolo mercantile*).

sky, *n.* cielo. // ~ **-sign** (*pubbl.*) insegna (*luminosa*) su un edificio.

skyway, *n.* (*trasp. aer.*) rotta aerea.

slack, *a.* **1** lento, allentato. **2** debole, fiacco. **3** inerte. *n.* (*market.*) periodo d'inattività, periodo di ristagno. // **a** ~ **domestic demand** (*econ.*) una debole domanda interna; **a** ~ **employee** (*pers.*) un impiegato indolente; **the** ~ **season** (*market.*) la stagione morta.

slacken, *v. t.* e *i.* **1** allentare, allentarsi. **2** calare, diminuire, ridursi. // to ~ **discipline**

(*org. az.*) allentare la disciplina.

slackening, *n.* 1 allentamento. 2 (*econ., fin., market.*) calo, diminuzione, riduzione, declino.

slackness, *n.* 1 fiacchezza, debolezza. 2 lentezza, l'essere allentato. 3 inerzia. // ~ **in business** (*econ.*) lentezza nell'attività commerciale.

slander[1], *n.* (*leg.*) calunnia, diffamazione.

slander[2], *v. t.* (*leg.*) calunniare, diffamare.

slanderer, *n.* (*leg.*) calunniatore, diffamatore.

slanderous, *a.* (*leg.*) calunnioso, diffamatorio. // **a ~ statement** (*leg.*) un'affermazione calunniosa.

slash[1], *n.* 1 (*anche fig.*) taglio. 2 (*econ., fin.*) riduzione (*di fondi, spese, ecc.*).

slash[2], *v. t.* 1 (*anche fig.*) tagliare. 2 (*econ., fin.*) apportare «tagli» a (*un bilancio*); ridurre drasticamente (*fondi, spese, ecc.*).

slaughter[1], *n.* macellazione.

slaughter[2], *v. t.* 1 macellare. 2 (*fig.*) far strage di. 3 (*fin.*) vendere (*titoli*) in perdita.

sleep, *v. i.* (*pass.* e *part. pass.* **slept**) dormire. *v. t.* (*tur.*) (*d'albergo, ecc.*) dar da dormire a (*un certo numero di persone*); aver letti per (*un certo numero di persone*).

sleeper, *n.* 1 chi dorme, dormiente. 2 (*Borsa, fin.*) titolo apparentemente ignorato dagli speculatori (*e che perciò ha una quotazione troppo bassa rispetto al resto del mercato*). 3 (*market.*) articolo che si vende con difficoltà (*o con lentezza*). 4 (*trasp. ferr.*) vagone letto.

sleeping, *a.* dormiente, addormentato. // ~ **berth** (*trasp.*) cuccetta, letto; ~ **-car** (*trasp. ferr.*) carrozza con letti, vagone letto; ~ **-carriage** (*trasp. ferr.*) *V.* ~ **-car;** ~ **partner** (*fin., leg.*) socio di capitali; ~ **rent** (*econ.*) rendita fissa.

slice[1], *n.* parte; (*anche fig.*) porzione, fetta.

slice[2], *v. t.* 1 affettare, tagliare, tagliar via. 2 eliminare (*tagliando*); ridurre (*come tagliando con un coltello*).

slide, *n.* 1 scivolone. 2 (*pubbl.*) diapositiva. // ~ **rule** (*attr. uff.*) regolo calcolatore.

sliding, *a.* scorrevole, mobile. *n.* (*anche fig.*) slittamento. // ~ **rule** (*attr. uff.*) regolo calcolatore; ~ **scale** (*econ.*) scala mobile (*dei salari, ecc.*); ~ **wage-scale** (*econ., sind.*) scala mobile dei salari.

slight, *a.* esiguo, leggero, lieve. // ~ **damages** (*leg.*) danni lievi; ~ **negligence** (*leg.*) negligenza lieve.

slip[1], *n.* 1 scivolone. 2 errore. 3 foglietto. 4 (*banca*) distinta. 5 (*banca*) talloncino. 6 (*trasp. mar.*) scalo d'alaggio. 7 (*trasp. mar.*) polizzetta. // **a ~ in spelling** un errore d'ortografia.

slip[2], *v. i.* (*market.*) (*di vendite, ecc.*) diminuire. // to ~ **back** scivolare indietro.

slipway, *n.* 1 (*trasp. mar.*) scalo d'alaggio. 2 (*trasp. mar.*) scalo di costruzione.

slogan, *n.* (*pubbl.*) slogan.

sloganeer, *n.* (*pubbl., USA*) chi inventa slogan.

slow[1], *a.* 1 lento, pigro. 2 (*econ.*) (*di mercato, ecc.*) fiacco. // **a ~ month** (*market.*) un mese «morto» (*in cui non si fanno affari*).

slow[2], *v. t.* e *i.* (*fig.*) frenare.

slowdown, *n.* (*pers., sind.*) sciopero bianco (*che si attua con un rallentamento del lavoro*).

slowness, *n.* lentezza.

slug, *n.* (*giorn.*) zeppa.

sluggish, *a.* 1 (*anche fig.*) lento, pigro, inerte. 2 (*econ., market.*) (*di prezzo, ecc.*) fermo. // **a ~ market** (*econ.*) un mercato inerte.

sluggishness, *n.* pigrizia, inerzia.

sluice, *n.* (*trasp.*) canale con chiusa. // ~ **-gate** (*trasp.*) chiusa; ~ **-gate prices** (*econ.*) prezzi limite.

slump[1], *n.* 1 (*econ.*) crisi, depressione, recessione, congiuntura bassa. 2 (*econ., fin., market.*) caduta, crollo, ribasso improvviso (*di prezzi, ecc.*). // **a ~ in prices** (*Borsa*) una flessione nelle quotazioni; (*market.*) un crollo dei prezzi; **a ~ on the Stock Exchange** (*fin.*) una crisi della Borsa; ~ **symptoms** (*econ.*) nodi congiunturali.

slump[2], *v. i.* (*econ., fin., market.*) (*di prezzi, ecc.*) crollare, ribassare all'improvviso, subire una forte flessione.

slumpflation, *n.* (*econ.*) inflazione più recessione.

slush funds, *n. pl.* (*fin.*) fondi neri.

small, *a.* piccolo, esiguo, scarso, basso. // ~ **bankruptcy** (*leg.*) piccolo fallimento; ~ **basket** cestino; ~ **bond** (*fin., USA*) obbligazione del valore nominale di 10, 25 o 50 dollari; ~ **business** (*econ.*) piccola industria; ~ **-business financing** (*fin.*) finanziamento alla piccola industria; ~ **case** cassetta; ~ **change** moneta spicciola, spiccioli, spicciolame; ~ **claim** (*leg., USA*) *V.* ~ **debt;** ~ **-claims Court** (*leg., USA*) *V.* ~ **-debts Court;** ~ **companies** (*econ.*) piccole imprese; ~ **debt** (*leg.*) debito di lieve entità; ~ **-debts Court** (*leg.*) tribunale speciale in cui vengono giudicate le controversie derivanti dagli «small debt» (*q. V.*); **a ~ farmer** (*econ.*) un piccolo proprietario, un colono; ~ **gross** (*comm.*) dieci dozzine; ~ **holder** (*econ.*) piccolo proprietario, piccolo affittuario; ~ **holding** (*econ.*) piccola azienda agricola; ~ **industry** (*econ.*) piccola industria; ~ **money** *V.* ~ **change**; ~ **-scale** su piccola scala, piccolo; ~ **-scale industry** (*econ.*) piccola industria; ~ **taxes** (*fin.*) imposte esigue; **a** ~ **tradesman** (*market.*) piccolo commerciante.

smart, *a.* 1 abile, accorto. 2 bello, elegante. // ~ **appearance** (*pers.*) bella presenza; **a** ~ **deal** un buon affare, un affarone; **a** ~ **investment** (*fin.*) un investimento accorto; ~ **money** (*pers., sind.*) indennizzo (*pagato da un datore di lavoro*) a un dipendente infortunato; **a** ~ **price** (*market.*) un prezzo alto, un bel prezzo.

smash[1], *n.* 1 rottura, l'andare in frantumi. 2 (*fig.*) disastro. 3 (*econ., fin.*) crollo; fallimento, bancarotta. 4 (*USA*) moneta falsa. 5 (*USA*) moneta, monete. 6 (*slang USA*) denaro. *a. attr.* straordinario, fantastico. // **a** ~ **success** un successo strepitoso.

smash[2], *v. t.* infrangere. *v. i.* 1 (*anche fig.*) andare in pezzi. 2 (*econ., fin., fig.*) andare in rovina, subire un tracollo, fallire, far bancarotta. // to ~ **up** (*econ., fin., fig.*) andare in rovina, fallire.

smuggle, *v. t.* (*leg.*) contrabbandare; esportare (*merce*) di contrabbando; importare (*merce*) di contrabbando. *v. i.* (*leg.*) fare il contrabbando. // to ~ **in** (*leg.*) importare di contrabbando; to ~ **out** (*leg.*) esportare di contrabbando.

smuggler, *n.* 1 (*leg.*) contrabbandiere. 2 (*leg.*) nave contrabbandiera.

smuggling, *n.* (*leg.*) contrabbando.

snake, *n.* serpente. // **the «~ in the tunnel»** (*econ., neol.*) il «serpente nel tunnel».

snapback, *n.* improvvisa ripresa.

social, *a.* sociale. // ~ **activities** (*org. az.*) attività sociali; ~ **and economic disequilibria** (*econ.*) squilibri sociali ed economici; ~ **charges** (*pers.*) oneri sociali; ~ **class** (*econ.*) classe sociale; **a** ~ **climber** un arrivista; ~ **justice** (*econ.*) giustizia sociale; ~ **legislation** (*leg.*) legislazione sociale; ~ **mobility** (*econ.*) mobilità sociale; ~ **net product** (*econ.*) prodotto netto sociale; ~ **policy** (*econ.*) politica sociale; ~ **-security agencies** (*pers.*) istituti di previdenza sociale; ~ **-security plan** (*pers.*) sistema previdenziale; ~ **-security taxes** (*fin.*) contributi sociali, oneri sociali; ~ **worker** (*pers.*) assistente sociale.

socialist, *a.* e *n.* (*econ.*) socialista. // ~ **economy** (*econ.*) economia socialista.

society, *n.* 1 società. 2 (*leg.*) associazione. // **a** ~ **of lawyers** (*leg.*) un'associazione d'avvocati.

socioeconomic, *a.* (*econ.*) socio-economico.

sociometric test, *n.* (*pers.*) test sociometrico.

soft, *a.* 1 molle, soffice. 2 (*fam.*) leggero. 3 (*fam.*) facile. // ~ **currency** (*econ.*) valuta debole, moneta non convertibile (*in oro*); ~ **goods** (*econ.*) beni non durevoli; ~ **money** (*fin.*) moneta cartacea; moneta debole; ~ **sell** (*market., pubbl.*) uso della suggestione o della persuasione nelle tecniche di vendita.

soggy, *a.* (*fin.*) debole, fiacco. // **the** ~ **dollar** il dollaro fiacco.

sola, *n.* (*cred.*) sola di cambio, cambiale in unico originale. // ~ **bill** (*cred.*) *V.* ~.

sold, *a.* venduto. // ~ **contract** (*banca, fin.*) corso lettera, corso vendita; ~ **note** (*Borsa, fin.*) fissato bollato (*di vendita*); (*market.*) conto vendite (*a provvigione*); ~ **out** (*market.*) (*d'articolo*) esaurito.

sole, *a.* esclusivo, unico. // ~ **agency** (*market.*) esclusiva (*di vendita, ecc.*), rappresentanza esclusiva; ~ **agent** (*market.*) agente esclusivo, agente unico, rappresentante esclusivo, esclusivista; ~ **director** (*amm.*) amministratore unico; ~ **distributor** (*market.*) concessionario; ~ **heir** (*leg.*) erede universale; ~ **legatee** (*leg.*) legatario universale; ~ **proprietor** (*leg.*) unico proprietario; ~ **right** (*leg.*) diritto esclusivo; ~ **trader** (*org. az.*) commerciante in proprio.

solemn, *a.* 1 formale. 2 pubblico. // **a** ~ **will** (*leg.*) un testamento pubblico.

solicit, *v. t.* 1 sollecitare, chiedere, invitare. 2 (*leg.*) agire come procuratore legale di (*q.*). // to ~ **orders** sollecitare ordinazioni.

solicitation, *n.* sollecitazione, sollecito.

solicitor, *n.* 1 (*leg.*) procuratore legale; avvocato (*che tratta coi clienti, ma normalmente non discute in tribunale*). 2 (*market., USA*) procacciatore d'affari. // **the** ~ **of the defendant** (*leg.*) il procuratore del convenuto; ~ **'s office** (*leg.*) studio legale.

solid, *a.* 1 (*market.*) (*di stoffa*) a tinta unita. 2 (*mat.*) cubico. *n.* (*mat.*) solido. // **a** ~ **firm** una ditta solida; ~ **inch** «pollice» cubico; ~ **measures** misure cubiche.

solidarity, *n.* solidarietà.

solution, *n.* soluzione. // ~ **of continuity** soluzione di continuità; **the** ~ **of a problem** (*anche mat.*) la soluzione d'un problema.

solvable, *a.* risolubile, risolvibile.

solve, *v. t.* risolvere, sciogliere. // to ~ **a problem** (*anche mat.*) risolvere un problema.

solvency, *n.* (*cred.*) solvibilità.

solvent, *a.* (*cred.*) solvibile. // **a ~ debtor** (*cred.*) un debitore solvibile; **a ~ merchant** (*cred.*) un commerciante solvibile.

some, *a.* e *pron.* del, dello, dei, degli, delle, alcuni, alcune.

son, *n.* figlio.

sophisticate, *v. t.* (*leg.*) sofisticare, falsificare, fatturare.

sophisticated, *a.* 1 «sofisticato». 2 (*leg.*) sofisticato, falsificato. // **a ~ wine** (*market.*) un vino sofisticato.

sophistication, *n.* 1 «sofisticazione». 2 (*leg.*) sofisticazione, falsificazione.

sophisticator, *n.* (*leg.*) sofisticatore.

sort[1], *n.* classe, genere, tipo.

sort[2], *v. t.* 1 cernere, ordinare. 2 (*comun.*) smistare (*lettere, pacchi, ecc.*). 3 (*market.*) smistare, assortire (*merci*). // to **~ the mail** (*comun.*) smistare la corrispondenza, fare la cernita (*o* lo spoglio) della corrispondenza.

sortation, *n.* 1 cernita. 2 (*comun., market.*) smistamento. // **the ~ of mail** (*comun.*) lo smistamento (*o* la cernita) della corrispondenza.

sorting, *n.* 1 cernita, ordinamento. 2 (*comun.*) smistamento. 3 (*market.*) smistamento, assortimento (*di merci*).

sound[1], *a.* 1 sano. 2 buono, in buone condizioni. 3 (*cred.*) solvibile. 4 (*leg.*) valido. // **a ~ bank** (*banca*) una banca solida; **a ~ currency** (*econ.*) una moneta sana; **a ~ economy** (*econ.*) un'economia sana; **a ~ investment** (*fin.*) un investimento sicuro; **~ money** (*econ.*) moneta stabile; **~ paper** (*fin.*) effetti sicuri, effetti di buona firma; **a ~ ship** (*trasp. mar.*) una nave in buone condizioni.

sound[2], *n.* rumore. // **~ -film** (*pubbl.*) film sonoro.

sound[3], *v. t.* (*trasp. mar.*) sondare.

sounding, *n.* (*trasp. mar.*) sondaggio.

source, *n.* 1 fonte. 2 (*giorn.*) fonte. // **~ material** (*econ.*) materia prima; **~ of income** (*econ., fin.*) fonte di reddito, cespite; **a ~ of information** (*giorn.*) una fonte d'informazioni.

space[1], *n.* 1 spazio. 2 spazio di tempo, intervallo. 3 (*comun., pubbl.*) tempo (*a disposizione di chi fa pubblicità radiotelevisiva*). 4 (*giorn., pubbl.*) spazio (*per la pubblicità sulla stampa*). // **~ -bar** (*di macch. uff.*) barra spaziatrice (*di macchina da scrivere*); **~ -key** (*di macch. uff.*) *V.* **~ -bar;** **~ man** (*giorn.*) *V.* **~ writer;** **~ writer** (*giorn.*) pubblicista pagato a un tanto la riga.

space[2], *v. t.* (*giorn., pubbl.*) spaziare, spazieggiare (*in tipografia*).

spaced payment, *n.* (*market.*) pagamento rateale, pagamento frazionato.

spacing, *n.* (*giorn.*) spaziatura.

spare[1], *n.* (*org. az.*) ricambio, parte di ricambio, pezzo di ricambio. *a. attr.* 1 di ricambio, di scorta. 2 d'avanzo, disponibile. // **~ cash** (*rag.*) denaro disponibile, riserva di denaro; **~ hand** (*pers.*) operaio di riserva (*adibito a lavori saltuari o alla sostituzione d'un operaio «regolare»*); **~ parts** (*org. az.*) pezzi di ricambio, parti di ricambio, ricambi.

spare[2], *v. t.* risparmiare, economizzare. // **enough and to ~** d'avanzo e da vendere.

speak, *v. t.* e *i.* (*pass.* **spoke,** *part. pass.* **spoken**) 1 parlare. 2 (*trasp. mar.*) far segnali a. // to **~ on the telephone** (*comun.*) parlare al telefono; to **~ a passing ship** (*trasp. mar.*) far segnali a una nave che si sta incrociando.

speaker, *n.* 1 chi parla, oratore. 2 portavoce.

special, *a.* particolare, straordinario. *n.* 1 (*giorn.*) edizione straordinaria. 2 (*market.*) (*di modello*) fuori serie. 3 (*trasp. ferr.*) treno straordinario. // **~ act** (*leg.*) legge speciale; **~ agent** (*ass.*) agente di zona; **~ bonuses** (*leg.*) diritti casuali; **~ carrier** (*trasp.*) vettore privato; **~ contract** (*leg.*) contratto formale; **~ correspondent** (*giorn.*) inviato speciale; **~ Court** (*leg.*) tribunale speciale; **~ crossing** (*cred.*) sbarratura particolare (*d'assegno*); **~ delivery** (*comun., USA*) consegna per espresso; **~ -delivery letter** (*comun., USA*) espresso; **~ -delivery service** (*comun., USA*) servizio di consegna per espresso; **~ drawing rights** (*fin.*) diritti speciali di prelievo; **the ~ edition of a newspaper** (*giorn.*) l'edizione straordinaria d'un giornale; **~ endorsement** (*cred.*) girata speciale; **~ number** (*giorn.*) numero unico; **~ partner** (*fin.*) socio accomandante (*di società in accomandita semplice*); **~ partnership** (*fin.*) società in accomandita semplice, associazione in partecipazione; **~ power (of attorney)** (*leg.*) procura speciale; **~ price** (*market.*) prezzo di favore; **~ settlement** (*Borsa*) liquidazione speciale; **~ train** (*trasp. ferr.*) treno straordinario.

specialization, *n.* (*econ., org. az.*) specializzazione. // **the ~ of industry** (*econ.*) la specializzazione industriale.

specialize, *v. t.* 1 specializzare. 2 specificare. *v. i.* (*org. az.*) specializzarsi, essere specializzato.

specialized, *a.* specializzato. // **~ assistance** (*market.*) assistenza di personale specializzato; **~ worker** (*pers.*) operaio specializzato.

specialty, *n.* 1 (*fin.*) titolo che si sottrae alle fluttuazioni del mercato (*per talune caratteristiche particolari*). 2 (*leg.*) contratto solenne. 3

(*market.*) specialità, prodotto speciale. // ~ **contract** (*leg.*) contratto formale (*o* solenne); ~ **dealer** (*market.*) rivenditore specializzato; ~ **goods** (*market.*) prodotti speciali, specialità; **the ~ of the house** (*market., tur.*) la specialità della Casa; ~ **shops** (*market.*) negozi specializzati.

specie, *n.* (*fin.*) numerario, moneta metallica. // ~ **points** (*econ., fin.*) punti dell'oro, punti metallici.

specific, *a.* specifico, preciso, esatto. // ~ **cost** (*rag.*) costo diretto; ~ **duties** (*dog.*) dazi specifici; ~ **legacy** (*leg.*) legato particolare; ~ **lien** (*leg.*) privilegio speciale; ~ **rate** (*ass.*) tariffa tabellare; ~ **weight** peso specifico.

specification, *n.* **1** specificazione, descrizione particolareggiata. **2** (*dog.*) dichiarazione d'imbarco. **3** (*leg.*) specificazione (*modo d'acquisto della proprietà d'una cosa ricavata dall'utilizzazione di materie altrui, quando il valore della materia impiegata non sia di molto superiore a quello della manodopera*). **4** (*leg.*) descrizione dell'invenzione (*in un brevetto*). **5 specifications,** *pl.* (*leg.*) capitolato. // **the ~ of materials** (*org. az.*) la distinta dei materiali.

specify, *v. t.* **1** specificare, descrivere nei particolari. **2** (*leg.*) indicare nel capitolato.

specimen, *n.* campione, modello, saggio. // ~ **copy** (*giorn., pubbl.*) copia in saggio (*di libro*); **the ~ of a signature** (*banca*) il facsimile d'una firma; ~ **uniform agreement** (*leg.*) contratto tipo.

spectacular, *a.* spettacoloso, straordinario.

speculate, *v. i.* (*fin.*) speculare, fare speculazioni.

speculation, *n.* (*fin.*) speculazione.

speculative, *a.* **1** (*d'affare*) rischioso. **2** (*fin.*) speculativo, di speculazione. // **a ~ enterprise** un'impresa rischiosa; ~ **manoeuvres** (*fin.*) manovre speculative; **a ~ situation on the exchange** (*fin.*) una situazione speculativa in Borsa; **a ~ stock** (*fin.*) un titolo che invita alla speculazione; **a ~ trader** (*fin.*) uno speculatore.

speculator, *n.* (*Borsa, fin.*) speculatore: aggiotatore, giocatore di Borsa.

speech, *n.* discorso.

speed[1], *n.* velocità. // ~ **limit** (*trasp. aut.*) limite (massimo) di velocità.

speed[2], *v. t.* e *i.* (*pass.* e *part. pass.* **sped**) **1** accelerare. **2** (*trasp. aut.*) andare a tutta velocità. // to ~ **up** accelerare; to ~ **up deliveries** (*org. az.*) accelerare le consegne.

speeding, *n.* (*trasp. aut.*) eccesso di velocità.

speedometer, *n.* (*trasp. aut.*) tachimetro.

speedway, *n.* (*trasp. aut., USA*) autostrada.

speedy, *a.* veloce, svelto, sollecito. // **a ~ recovery of the market** (*econ.*) una rapida ripresa del mercato.

spell[1], *n.* **1** periodo. **2** (*pers.*) turno (*di lavoro, di servizio, ecc.*). // **a ~ of unemployment** (*econ.*) un periodo di disoccupazione.

spell[2], *v. t.* (*pass.* e *part. pass.* **spelt** o *reg.*) pronunciare (*o* scrivere) lettera per lettera. *v. i.* (*pers.*) lavorare a turno.

spend, *v. t.* (*pass.* e *part. pass.* **spent**) impiegare, passare (*il tempo*).

spending, *n.* spesa, spese. // ~ **cut-backs** riduzione nelle spese; ~ **money** soldi per le piccole spese; ~ **spree** (*econ.*) corsa agli acquisti (*conseguente a una riduzione delle imposte*).

spillover inflation, *n.* (*econ.*) inflazione dovuta a eccesso della spesa pubblica.

spinster, *n.* (*leg.*) nubile.

spiral[1], *n.* spirale. // **the ~ of prices** (*econ.*) la spirale dei prezzi.

spiral[2], *v. i.* muoversi a spirale. // to ~ **upward** (*econ.*) (*di prezzi, ecc.*) aumentare vertiginosamente.

spirited, *a.* animato, vivace.

split[1], *n.* **1** divisione, scissione, separazione. **2** (*fin.*) divisione del capitale azionario (*con l'emissione di due o più azioni nuove per ogni azione vecchia*). // ~ **-down** (*fin.*) diminuzione del numero delle azioni (*d'una società*); ~ **-off** (*fin.*) trasferimento di parte delle attività (*d'una società*) a un'altra società, contro pagamento in azioni; ~ **-up** (*fin.*) trasferimento di parte delle attività (*d'una società*) a un'altra società, e del rimanente a una terza, contro pagamento in azioni; interruzione della vita d'una società (*per ragioni legali, ecc.*).

split[2], *v. t.* (*pass.* e *part. pass.* **split**) **1** dividere. **2** (*fin.*) dividere (*il capitale d'una società*) per mezzo del frazionamento d'ogni azione (*in due o più azioni*). // to ~ **the difference** (*comm.*) fare a metà; tagliare a metà (*la differenza fra il prezzo richiesto e quello offerto*); to ~ **off** dividere; to ~ **up** frazionare; to ~ **up a train** (*trasp. ferr.*) scomporre un treno.

split[3], *a.* **1** diviso, scisso, separato. **2** (*Borsa, fin.*) (*di quotazione*) data in sedicesimi anziché in ottavi. **3** (*fin.*) (*di titolo azionario*) frazionato. // **a ~ exchange system** (*econ., fin.*) un doppio regime dei cambi; ~ **order to buy** (*fin.*) ordine d'acquisto (*di titoli*) frazionato (*circa il tempo dell'operazione e il prezzo*); ~ **order to sell** (*fin.*) ordine di vendita frazionato; **a ~ run** (*giorn.*) una tiratura frazionata; ~ **shares** (*fin.*) azioni frazionate.

splitting, *n.* frazionamento.

spoilage, *n.* (*giorn., pubbl.*) scarto (*carta sciupata nel processo di stampa*).

spokesman, *n.* (*pl.* **spokesmen**) portavoce, rappresentante.

sponsor¹, *n.* 1 patrocinatore. 2 (*fin.*) società specializzata nel collocamento delle azioni d'un fondo comune d'investimento mobiliare. 3 (*leg.*) garante.

sponsor², *v. t.* 1 patrocinare. 2 (*leg.*) garantire, far da mallevadore a (*q.*). 3 (*pubbl.*) finanziare, «offrire» (*un programma radiotelevisivo*).

spoon¹, *n.* cucchiaio. // to ~ **-feed** nutrire col cucchiaino.

spoon², *v. t.* prender su col cucchiaio.

sport, *n.* sport. // **sports magazine** (*giorn.*) periodico sportivo.

spot, *n.* 1 luogo, posto, punto. 2 **spots,** *pl.* (*market.*) merce venduta a contanti. *a. attr.* 1 (*market.*) (*di merce, articolo, ecc.*) per consegna immediata. 2 (*market.*) (*di pagamento*) in contanti, alla consegna. // ~ **broadcast** (*comun.*) emissione (radiotelevisiva) locale; ~ **cash** (*market.*) pagamento a contanti, pagamento «a tamburo battente»; ~ **contract** (*market.*) contratto a pronti; ~ **delivery** (*market.*) consegna immediata; ~ **goods** (*market.*) merce pronta per consegna immediata; ~ **market** (*market.*) mercato a contanti; ~ **news** (*giorn.*) recentissime, notizie recentissime, ultimissime; ~ **price** (*market.*) prezzo per contanti, prezzo «sopra luogo», prezzo «franco al luogo di partenza»; ~ **transaction** (*market.*) operazione a contanti.

spread¹, *n.* 1 diffusione, espansione. 2 (*econ., market.*) differenza fra il costo di produzione e il prezzo di vendita. 3 (*econ., market.*) differenza fra il prezzo massimo e quello minimo (*per un prodotto, in un dato periodo*). 4 (*fin.*) margine rispetto al tasso base d'interesse. 5 (*fin.*) condizione che si verifica quando, nelle operazioni d'arbitraggio, la differenza di prezzo per la stessa merce (*o* per lo stesso titolo) in due mercati è superiore al normale. 6 (*market.*) differenza fra i prezzi di due articoli simili. // **the** ~ **of risk** (*ass.*) il frazionamento del rischio.

spread², *v. t.* (*pass.* e *part. pass.* **spread**) diffondere, distribuire, spargere. *v. i.* diffondersi, spargersi.

spread³, *a.* diffuso, propagato, sparso, distribuito. // ~ **investment** (*fin.*) «giardinetto».

spreading, *n.* diffusione.

spurt¹, *n.* 1 scatto, «volata». 2 (*econ.*) improvviso aumento (*dell'attività commerciale*). // **a** ~ **in sales** (*market.*) un improvviso aumento delle vendite.

spurt², *v. i.* 1 fare uno scatto. 2 (*econ.*) (*d'attività commerciale*) aumentare improvvisamente.

squandering, *n.* dissipazione.

square¹, *a.* (*anche mat.*) quadro. // ~ **bracket** parentesi quadra; **a** ~ **foot** un «piede» quadrato; ~ **root** (*mat.*) radice quadrata.

square², *v. t.* 1 quadrare, far quadrare, pareggiare. 2 (*cred.*) regolare, pagare, saldare. 3 (*mat.*) elevare al quadrato. 4 (*rag.*) quadrare (*i conti*). // to ~ **accounts** (*cred.*) regolare i conti; to ~ **figures** far quadrare le cifre.

squeezability, *n.* (*econ.*) comprimibilità.

squeezable, *a.* (*econ.*) comprimibile.

squeeze¹, *n.* 1 stretta, compressione. 2 (*fig.*) restrizione; (*fig.*) giro di vite. 3 (*econ.*) blocco, difficoltà economica.

squeeze², *v. t.* 1 stringere; (*anche fig.*) comprimere. 2 (*fig.*) mettere (*q.*) in difficoltà economiche. 3 (*econ.*) far diminuire (*i profitti di q. o qc.*). // **that can be squeezed** (*econ.*) comprimibile.

stability, *n.* 1 stabilità, fermezza, saldezza. 2 (*econ.*) equilibrio. // **the** ~ **of personnel tenure** (*org. az.*) la stabilità del personale (*nel posto di lavoro*).

stabilization, *n.* stabilizzazione, consolidamento. // **the** ~ **of wages** (*econ., sind.*) la stabilizzazione dei salari.

stabilize, *v. t.* stabilizzare, rendere stabile, consolidare. *v. i.* stabilizzarsi. // to ~ **a currency** (*econ.*) render stabile una moneta; to ~ **markets** (*econ.*) stabilizzare i mercati.

stabilizer, *n.* (*econ.*) stabilizzatore.

stable, *a.* 1 stabile, fermo. 2 (*fin.*) (*di prezzo, ecc.*) sostenuto. // **a** ~ **economy** (*econ.*) un'economia solida; **a** ~ **money** (*econ.*) una moneta stabile; ~ **personnel** (*org. az.*) personale stabile.

staff¹, *n.* (*org. az.*) personale, dipendenti, organico, impiegati, funzionari, staff. // ~ **assistant** (*pers.*) assistente del personale; ~ **cards** (*pers.*) schede del personale; ~ **employee** (*pers.*) impiegato di concetto; ~ **manager** (*amm.*) direttore del personale; ~ **secretary** (*giorn.*) segretario di redazione; ~ **structure** (*org. az.*) struttura funzionale; ~ **turnover** (*org. az.*) ricambio del personale.

staff², *v. t.* (*org. az.*) provvedere (*una ditta, ecc.*) di personale. // **over-staffed** (*org. az.*) con eccedenza di personale; **under-staffed** (*org. az.*) con personale insufficiente.

staffer, *n.* (*pers.*) membro del personale, membro dello staff.

stag[1]**,** *n.* (*Borsa*) speculatore che compra nuovi titoli al prezzo d'apertura per rivenderli dopo breve tempo, premista.

stag[2]**,** *v. i.* (*Borsa*) fare lo «stag» (*q. V.*).

stage, *n.* stadio, fase, periodo, punto. // ~ **of development** (*econ.*) fase di sviluppo; **a** ~ **of inactivity** un periodo d'inattività.

stagflation, *n.* (*econ.*) stagflazione (*recessione e inflazione a un tempo*).

stagflationary, *a.* (*econ.*) recessivo e inflattivo a un tempo (*V.* **stagflation**).

stagger, *v. t.* (*fig.*) scaglionare, distribuire nel tempo.

staggered shift, *n.* (*org. az.*) turno a scacchi.

stagnant, *a.* (*anche fig.*) stagnante, in ristagno, fermo, inattivo. // **a** ~ **market** (*econ.*) un mercato stagnante.

stagnate, *v. i.* stagnare, ristagnare, essere inattivo. *v. t.* far ristagnare, rendere inattivo.

stagnation, *n.* **1** ristagno, stasi, inattività. **2** (*econ.*) stagnazione.

stake[1]**,** *n.* **1** posta (*al gioco*). **2** scommessa. // **at** ~ in gioco.

stake[2]**,** *v. t.* **1** rischiare. **2** (*fin.*) finanziare, sostenere (*q.*) finanziariamente. // to ~ **a claim** (*leg.*) accampare diritti, avanzare una pretesa.

stale, *a.* **1** stantio, vecchio. **2** (*leg.*) scaduto, in prescrizione. // **a** ~ **cheque** (*banca, cred.*) assegno vecchio (*assegno emesso da più di sei mesi e non ancora incassato*).

stall, *n.* (*market.*) bancarella, chiosco, edicola. // ~ **-holder** (*market.*) venditore con bancarella.

stallage, *n.* tassa pagata per acquisire il diritto d'occupare suolo pubblico con bancarelle (*chioschi, edicole, ecc.*).

stamp[1]**,** *n.* **1** bollo. **2** (*attr. uff.*) timbro, stampiglia. **3** (*comun.*) (= **postage-stamp**) francobollo. **4** (*fin.*) (= **revenue-stamp**) marca da bollo. **5** (*market.*) marchio di fabbrica, marca. **6** (*pers.*) «marchetta» assicurativa, «marchetta» della mutua. // ~ **charges** (*fin.*) spese di bollo; ~ **dues** (*fin.*) spese di bollo; ~ **duty** (*fin.*) diritto di bollo, tassa di bollo; ~ **-office** (*fin.*) ufficio del bollo; **the** ~ **on a coin** il conio (*l'impronta*) su una moneta; ~ **-paper** (*fin.*) carta bollata; ~ **-tax** (*fin.*) *V.* ~ **duty.**

stamp[2]**,** *v. t.* **1** bollare, timbrare, stampigliare. **2** (*comun.*) affrancare (*una lettera, ecc.*). **3** (*market.*) marcare, marchiare. // to ~ **a letter** (*comun.*) affrancare una lettera.

stamped, *a.* **1** bollato, timbrato, stampigliato. **2** (*comun.*) affrancato. // **a** ~ **envelope** (*comun.*) una busta affrancata; ~ **paper** (*fin.*) carta bollata (*o* da bollo), cancelleria bollata.

stampede[1]**,** *n.* fuga precipitosa, fuggi fuggi.

stampede[2]**,** *v. i.* (*anche fig.*) darsi a fuga precipitosa.

stamping machine, *n.* (*macch. uff.*) stampigliatrice.

stand[1]**,** *n.* **1** arresto, fermata, sosta. **2** (*market.*) stand, bancarella, banco d'esposizione, chiosco, edicola. // ~ **attendant** (*market.*) standista; ~ **-by credit** (*fin.*) credito di sostegno; credito aperto (*per un certo numero di anni*); ~ **designer** (*market.*) standista; ~ **space** (*market.*) area di posteggio (*per uno stand, in una fiera campionaria*).

stand[2]**,** *v. i.* (*pass.* e *part. pass.* **stood**) stare, essere, trovarsi. // to ~ **at a discount** (*fin.*) (*di titoli*) essere sotto la pari; to ~ **at a premium** (*fin.*) (*di titoli*) essere sopra la pari; to ~ **by** star pronto; stare a (*un patto*), osservare (*un accordo*); to ~ **by the anchor** (*trasp. mar.*) tenersi pronti a salpare; to ~ **by the terms** stare ai patti; to ~ **by one's word** mantenere la parola; to ~ **convicted of an offence** (*leg.*) essere riconosciuto colpevole d'un reato; to ~ **down** (*leg.*) lasciare il banco dei testimoni; to ~ **for** (*trasp. mar.*) (*di nave*) far rotta per, dirigersi verso; to ~ **sb. off** tener lontano q., allontanare q.; to ~ **off and on** (*trasp. mar.*) (*di nave*) bordeggiare; to ~ **off a creditor** (*cred.*) tenere a bada un creditore; to ~ **on** (*trasp. mar.*) mantenere la rotta; to ~ **surety for sb.** (*leg.*) farsi garante per q., pagare la cauzione per q.; to ~ **to** stare a, mantenere, tener fede a; to ~ **to the terms** stare ai patti; to ~ **up to competition** (*market.*) sostenere la concorrenza.

standard, *n.* **1** campione, modello, norma, regola, standard. **2** grado, livello, qualità. *a. attr.* standard, normale, corrente, tipo. // ~ **charge** tariffa fissa, tariffa forfettaria; ~ **cost per unit** (*org. az., rag.*) costo standard per unità di prodotto, costo standard unitario; ~ **costing** (*rag.*) determinazione dei costi standard, valutazione a costi standard; ~ **-hour plan** (*org. az.*) sistema dell'ora standard; ~ **insurance policy** (*ass.*) polizza assicurativa tipo; **the** ~ **model of a vehicle** (*trasp.*) il modello di serie d'un veicolo; ~ **money** (*econ.*) valuta ufficiale, valuta legale; **standards of quality** (*market.*) norme di qualità, standard qualitativi; **standards of weight and measure** pesi e misure tipo; ~ **prices** (*market.*) prezzi normali; ~ **quality** (*market.*) qualità corrente; ~ **rate** (*pers.*) paga base; ~ **sample** (*market.*) campione unificato; ~ **subsidy** (*econ.*)

aiuto forfettario; ~ **tax** (*fin.*) tassazione forfettaria; ~ **time** ora ufficiale, ora solare.

standardization, *n.* **1** standardizzazione, normalizzazione, tipificazione, tipizzazione, unificazione. **2** (*econ.*) costruzione in serie. // **the ~ of the basis for assessment of VAT (Value Added Tax)** (*fin.*) l'unificazione della base imponibile dell'IVA (Imposta sul Valore Aggiunto).

standardize, *v. t.* **1** standardizzare, normalizzare, tipificare, tipizzare, unificare. **2** (*econ.*) costruire in serie. // to ~ **production** (*org. az.*) standardizzare la produzione.

standardized legal systems, *n. pl.* (*leg.*) codici unificati.

standardized test, *n.* (*pers.*) test standardizzato.

standholder, *n.* (*market.*) standista (*chi allestisce e/o lavora a uno «stand», q. V.*).

standing[1], *n.* **1** posizione, condizione, situazione. **2** grado, durata. **3** buona reputazione.

standing[2], *a.* fisso, stabile, stabilito. // ~ **charges** (*rag.*) spese generali; **a ~ committee** (*amm., org. az.*) una commissione permanente; ~ **expenses** (*rag.*) spese generali; **a ~ order** (*market.*) un'ordinazione fatta una volta per sempre (*che s'intende rinnovata tacitamente*); **by ~ order** (*banca*) per ordine e conto (*di un cliente*).

standstill, *n.* **1** arresto, fermata, sosta. **2** battuta d'arresto, punto morto, ristagno.

staple[1], *a. attr.* principale, più importante. *n.* **1** (*econ.*) materia prima, materiale grezzo. **2** (*market.*) merce a domanda costante (*indipendentemente dalle fluttuazioni economiche*). // ~ **commodities** (*econ.*) merci di prima necessità; ~ **industry** (*econ.*) industria fondamentale, industria di base.

staple[2], *n.* (*attr. uff.*) graffa, graffetta, punto metallico.

staple[3], *v. t.* graffare.

stapler, *n.* (*attr. uff.*) graffatrice.

start[1], *n.* principio, inizio.

start[2], *v. t.* e *i.* **1** cominciare, incominciare, iniziare, intraprendere. **2** fondare, (*anche fig.*) avviare, (*fig.*) impostare, (*fig.*) impiantare. **3** (*pers.*) assumere. // to ~ **from scratch** partire da zero (*fig.*); to ~ **a shop** (*market.*) aprir bottega.

starting, *n.* **1** inizio. **2** (*anche fig.*) avviamento. // ~ **capital** (*rag.*) capitale iniziale; ~ **entries** (*rag.*) scritture d'apertura (*dell'esercizio*); ~ **-up** (*econ.*) avviamento; ~ **-up aids to growers' associations** (*econ.*) aiuti d'avviamento alle associazioni di produttori.

starvation, *n.* fame. // ~ **wages** (*pers.*) salari da fame.

starve, *v. i.* morir di fame, essere affamato. *v. t.* far morir di fame, affamare.

state[1], *n.* **1** stato, condizione, situazione. **2** Stato, nazione. **3 the State** (*econ.*) l'operatore pubblico. *a. attr.* di Stato, dello Stato, statale. // ~ **agency** (*econ., leg.*) ente pubblico; **a ~ bank** (*fin.*) una banca dello Stato; ~ **border** (*amm.*) confine di Stato; ~ **capitalism** (*econ.*) capitalismo di Stato; ~ **-controlled** (*econ.*) controllato dallo Stato, a controllo statale, a partecipazione statale, dirigistico; ~ **-controlled enterprise** (*econ.*) azienda a partecipazione statale; ~ **-controlled price** (*econ.*) prezzo di calmiere; ~ **-controlled purchase** (*econ.*) consumi pubblici; **the ~ Department** (*USA*) il Dipartimento di Stato (*il Ministero degli Esteri*); ~ **enterprise** (*econ.*) azienda a partecipazione statale; ~ **finance** (*econ.*) finanza statale, finanza pubblica; **a ~ holding company** (*fin.*) una finanziaria pubblica; ~ **-owned** (*econ.*) di proprietà dello Stato; ~ **-owned agencies** (*econ.*) enti pubblici; ~ **-owned enterprise** (*econ.*) azienda di Stato; ~ **-papers** documenti di Stato; **the ~ participation system** (*econ.*) il sistema delle partecipazioni statali; ~ **-planned economy** (*econ.*) economia pianificata; ~ **property** (*amm.*) demanio; ~ **property office** il demanio (*l'ufficio*); ~ **-room** (*trasp. mar.*) cabina di lusso; ~ **-run organizations** (*econ.*) enti statali e parastatali; ~ **-trading Countries** (*econ.*) Paesi a commercio di Stato; ~ **-trading monopolies** (*econ.*) monopoli nazionali a carattere commerciale; **the ~ Treasury** (*fin.*) la Tesoreria dello Stato.

state[2], *v. t.* **1** affermare, asserire, dichiarare. **2** esporre, esprimere. **3** determinare, stabilire. // to ~ **an account in dollars** (*rag.*) esprimere un conto in dollari; to ~ **the facts of a case** (*leg.*) esporre i fatti d'un processo; to ~ **on oath** (*leg.*) dichiarare sotto giuramento; to ~ **reasons for a judgment** (*leg.*) motivare una sentenza; «~ **salary required**» (*pers.*) (*nelle offerte di impiego*) «indicare le pretese».

stated, *a.* **1** asserito. **2** determinato, stabilito, fissato, fisso. **3** (*fin., rag.*) quotato. // ~ **account** (*cred.*) conto approvato (*dal debitore*); (*rag.*) conto liquidato; ~ **capital** (*fin.*) capitale dichiarato.

statement, *n.* **1** affermazione, asserzione, dichiarazione. **2** esposizione, espressione. **3** (*comm., leg.*) rapporto, relazione, rendiconto. **4** (*leg.*) verbale (*resoconto fatto alla polizia*). // ~ **of account** (*rag.*) estratto conto; rendiconto; ~ **of accumulated profits** (*rag.*) conto economico;

~ **of affairs** (*leg.*) dichiarazione relativa alla situazione finanziaria (*di un'impresa in via di fallimento*); ~ **of assets and liabilities** (*rag.*) stato patrimoniale; **a** ~ **of expenses** (*rag.*) un rendiconto delle spese; ~ **of financial position** (*rag.*) prospetto della situazione finanziaria; ~ **of liabilities** (*leg.*) stato del passivo; ~ **of net proceeds** (*rag.*) conto di netto ricavo; ~ **of redeemable income** (*fin., rag.*) prospetto dei cespiti ammortizzabili.

station, *n.* **1** (*comun.*) stazione ricetrasmittente. **2** (*econ.*) stazione, centrale, impianto. **3** (*trasp. ferr.*) stazione. // ~ **-calendar** (*trasp. ferr.*) tabella delle partenze dei treni; ~ **-master** (*trasp. ferr.*) capostazione; ~ **of arrival** (*trasp. ferr.*) stazione d'arrivo; ~ **of departure** (*trasp. ferr.*) stazione di partenza; ~ **of destination** (*trasp. ferr.*) stazione di destinazione; ~ **-roof** (*trasp. ferr.*) pensilina; ~ **wagon** (*trasp. aut.*) giardinetta, giardiniera, familiare.

stationary, *a.* fermo, fisso.

stationery, *n.* (*attr. uff.*) cancelleria, articoli di cancelleria. // ~ **department** (*market.*) reparto (articoli di) cancelleria.

statistic[1], *a.* *V.* **statistical.**

statistic[2], *n.* (*stat.*) statistica (*dato statistico*).

statistical, *a.* (*stat.*) statistico. // ~ **department** (*org. az.*) reparto statistico, ufficio statistico; ~ **sample** (*stat.*) campione statistico.

statistician, *n.* (*stat.*) «statistico», studioso di statistica.

statistics, *n. pl.* (*col verbo al sing.*) (*stat.*) statistica (*la scienza*).

status, *n.* **1** situazione, condizione speciale, status. **2** (*leg.*) stato giuridico. // ~ **inquiry** (*banca, cred.*) richiesta d'informazioni sulla solvibilità (*d'un cliente potenziale*); ~ **inquiry agency** ufficio informazioni commerciali; ~ **quo** status quo; ~ **symbol** (*econ., pubbl.*) «status symbol», simbolo di successo.

statute, *n.* (*leg.*) statuto, legge (*del Parlamento*). // ~ **-barred** (*leg.*) prescritto: **a** ~ **-barred debt** (*leg.*) un debito prescritto; ~ **-book** (*leg.*) raccolta di leggi; codice; ~ **law** (*leg.*) diritto statutario, legge parlamentare; ~ **mile** miglio ufficiale (*pari a metri 1.610 circa*); ~ **of limitations** (*leg.*) «statuto delle restrizioni», legge sulla prescrizione; ~ **of repose** (*leg.*) *V.* ~ **of limitations;** ~ **-roll** (*leg.*) raccolta di leggi, codice.

statutory, *a.* **1** (*leg.*) statutario, fissato dalla legge. **2** (*leg.*) legale, regolamentare. // ~ **books** (*leg., rag.*) libri (contabili) obbligatori; **a** ~ **company** (*fin., ingl.*) società costituita con legge speciale; ~ **holiday** (*leg.*) giorno festivo legale; ~ **meeting** (*fin.*) assemblea generale per l'approvazione dello statuto (*d'una società anonima*); ~ **period** (*leg.*) periodo di prescrizione; ~ **reserve** (*rag.*) riserva statutaria.

stay[1], *n.* (*leg.*) sospensione. // ~ **-in** (*sind.*) *V.* ~ **-in strike;** ~ **-in strike** (*sind.*) sciopero con occupazione del posto di lavoro; ~ **law** (*leg.*) legge moratoria; ~ **-low prices** (*market.*) prezzi tenuti bassi; **a** ~ **of execution** (*leg.*) una sospensione dell'esecuzione della condanna.

stay[2], *v. i.* stare, restare, rimanere. *v. t.* (*leg.*) differire, rimandare, rinviare, sospendere. // to ~ **at a hotel** (*tur.*) alloggiare in (*un*) albergo; to ~ **judgment** (*leg.*) sospendere la sentenza; to ~ **proceedings** (*leg.*) sospendere il procedimento.

steady[1], *a.* **1** costante, fermo, fisso, regolare. **2** stabile. **3** (*fin., market.*) (*di quotazione, prezzo, ecc.*) sostenuto. // **a** ~ **job** (*pers.*) un lavoro fisso, un'occupazione stabile; **a** ~ **market** (*fin., market.*) un mercato sostenuto; ~ **seller** (*market.*) «steady seller» (*libro, o altro oggetto, che ha una vendita costante*).

steady[2], *v. t.* consolidare, rendere fermo, stabilizzare. *v. i.* consolidarsi, diventare fermo, stabilizzarsi.

steam, *n.* vapore. // ~ **collier** (*trasp. mar.*) nave carboniera; ~ **-engine** macchina a vapore; (*trasp. ferr.*) locomotiva a vapore; ~ **navigation** (*trasp. mar.*) navigazione a vapore.

steamboat, *n.* (*trasp. mar.*) piroscafo, vapore.

steamer, *n.* (*trasp. mar.*) vapore, nave a vapore, piroscafo, vaporetto.

steamship, *n.* (*trasp. mar.*) vapore, nave a vapore, piroscafo, vaporetto. // ~ **line** (*trasp. mar.*) linea di navigazione a vapore.

steer, *v. t.* (*trasp. mar.*) dirigere (*una nave*).

steerage, *n.* (*trasp. mar.*) ponte di terza classe. // ~ **passengers** (*trasp. mar.*) passeggeri di terza classe.

steering, *n.* **1** (*fig.*) amministrazione, direzione. **2** (*trasp. mar.*) governo (*della nave*). // ~ **committee** (*org. az.*) comitato direttivo.

stencil[1], *n.* (*attr. uff.*) matrice (*per ciclostile*).

stencil[2], *v. t.* ciclostilare, riprodurre (*lettere, disegni, ecc.*) con uno stampino.

stenograph[1], *n.* **1** stenogramma. **2** (*macch. uff.*) macchina per stenografare.

stenograph[2], *v. t.* stenografare.

stenographer, *n.* (*pers.*) stenografo, stenografa.

stenographic, *a.* stenografico.

stenographical, *a.* stenografico.

stenography, *n.* stenografia.

stenotypist, *n.* (*pers.*) stenodattilografo, stenodattilografa.

stenotypy, *n.* stenotipia.

step[1], *n.* 1 misura, provvedimento. 2 (*pers.*) avanzamento, promozione. // ~ **-down** calo, diminuzione, riduzione; ~ **-up** aumento, accrescimento.

step[2], *v. i.* fare un passo. // to ~ **down** (*fig.*) rinunciare, dimettersi; to ~ **down from a position** (*pers.*) rinunciare a un posto; to ~ **in** entrare; (*fig.*) intervenire; to ~ **into a good job** (*fig.*) ottenere un buon impiego; to ~ **up** aumentare, accrescere, intensificare, crescere, intensificarsi; (*amm.*) concedere un avanzamento, dare una promozione a (*un dipendente*); promuovere; essere promosso, ricevere una promozione; to ~ **up production** (*org. az.*) accrescere la produzione; to ~ **up savings** (*econ.*) aumentare i risparmi.

stepbrother, *n.* (*leg.*) fratellastro.

stepwise inflation, *n.* (*econ.*) inflazione graduale.

stere, *n.* stero.

sterile, *a.* sterile.

sterling, *a.* genuino, di buona lega. *n.* (*ingl.*) moneta inglese a corso legale. // **the** ~ **area** (*econ.*) l'area della sterlina; **the** ~ **bloc** (*econ.*) l'area della sterlina; **the** ~ **exchange** (*fin.*) il cambio della sterlina; ~ **prices** (*fin., market.*) prezzi in sterline; ~ **quality** (*market.*) qualità genuina; ~ **silver** argento puro (*925 parti d'argento e 75 di rame*); **pound** ~ lira sterlina.

stevedore[1], *n.* (*trasp. mar.*) stivatore, scaricatore di porto.

stevedore[2], *v. t.* (*trasp. mar.*) lavorare al carico (*o* allo scarico) di (*una nave*).

steward[1], *n.* 1 fattore agricolo. 2 (*trasp. aer., trasp. mar.*) steward, cameriere di bordo. 3 (*trasp. mar.*) cambusiere.

steward[2], *v. i.* 1 (*trasp. aer.*) fare la hostess. 2 (*trasp. aer., trasp. mar.*) fare lo steward. 3 (*trasp. mar.*) fare il cambusiere.

stewardess, *n.* 1 (*trasp. aer.*) hostess. 2 (*trasp. mar.*) cameriera di bordo.

stick, *v. t.* (*pass.* e *part. pass.* **stuck**) attaccare, affiggere. // to ~ **out** tener duro, rifiutarsi di giungere a un accordo; (*pers., sind.*) scioperare; to ~ **out for a higher price** (*market.*) cercar di strappare un prezzo più alto; to ~ **a stamp on a letter** attaccare un francobollo a una lettera; to ~ **to** attenersi a, tener fede a; to ~ **to one's word** mantenere la parola data.

sticker, *n.* (*market.*) tagliando da incollare, etichetta.

stickiness, *n.* (*econ.*) vischiosità, rigidezza (*di domanda, prezzo, ecc.*).

stick-out, *n.* (*pers., sind.*) sciopero, sciopero bianco.

sticky, *a.* 1 appiccicaticcio. 2 (*di credito*) di difficile realizzo. 3 (*econ.*) (*di domanda, prezzo, ecc.*) rigido, vischioso. 4 (*market.*) (*d'articolo, ecc.*) difficile da vendere. // **a** ~ **customer** (*market.*) un cliente difficile (*da accontentare*); ~ **prices** (*econ.*) prezzi vischiosi.

stiff, *a.* 1 rigido. 2 (*fin., market.*) (*di mercato, prezzo, ecc.*) sostenuto, tendente al rialzo. 3 (*fin., market.*) (*di prezzo*) salato. *n.* 1 (*slang USA*) titolo di credito. 2 (*slang USA*) denaro. 3 (*slang USA*) assegno falso. 4 (*slang USA*) cambiale falsa. 5 (*slang USA*) operaio.

stiffen, *v. t.* 1 irrigidire. 2 (*fin., market.*) aumentare, crescere (*i prezzi, ecc.*). *v. i.* indurirsi, irrigidirsi. // to ~ **the market** (*econ.*) irrigidire il mercato.

stiffening, *n.* 1 irrigidimento. 2 (*fin., market.*) aumento (*di prezzi, ecc.*).

stiffness, *n.* rigidità.

stimulant, *n.* stimolante, incentivo.

stimulate, *v. t.* incitare, incentivare. // to ~ **a convention** convenzionarsi; to ~ **production** (*econ.*) incentivare la produzione.

stimulation, *n.* incitamento, incentivazione.

stimulus, *n.* (*pl.* **stimuli**) incitamento, incentivo. // **a** ~ **to competition** (*market.*) un incentivo alla concorrenza.

stipulate, *v. t.* (*leg.*) stipulare, convenire, pattuire, accordarsi su, esigere come condizione essenziale. // to ~ **a contract** (*leg.*) stipulare un contratto; to ~ **a guarantee** (*leg.*) pattuire una garanzia.

stipulated damages, *n. pl.* (*ass.*) danni liquidati.

stipulation, *n.* 1 (*leg.*) stipulazione, stipula. 2 (*leg.*) clausola essenziale, condizione essenziale. // **under the** ~ **that...** (*leg.*) a condizione che...

stipulator, *n.* (*leg.*) stipulante.

stochastic, *a.* aleatorio. // ~ **variable** (*stat.*) variabile stocastica.

stock[1], *n.* 1 (*econ.*) (= **live stock**) scorte vive, bestiame. 2 (*fin.*) (= **joint-stock**) capitale azionario; azioni, titoli, valori. 3 (*org. az.*) stock, giacenza, provvista, scorta, assortimento, merci in magazzino. 4 (*org. az.*) materia prima, materiale grezzo. 5 **stocks,** *pl.* (*fin.*) azioni; obbligazioni. 6 **stocks,** *pl.* (*fin.*) buoni del Tesoro, titoli di Stato. // ~ **-account** (*rag.*) conto inventari; ~ **accounting** (*rag.*) contabilità di magazzino; **stocks and shares** (*fin.*) valori mobiliari; ~ **arbitrage** (*fin.*) arbitraggio su titoli; **stocks bid for** (*fin.*) titoli di cui vi è richiesta; ~ **bonus** (*fin.*) gratifica in azioni (*concessa da una società ai suoi dipendenti*); ~ **-book** (*rag.*) libro inventari, libro magazzino; ~ **borrowed** (*Borsa*) titoli riportati; ~ **-broker** (*Borsa*) agente di cambio, scambista; ~ **-broking** (*Borsa*) mediazione nella compravendita di titoli, lavoro d'agente di cambio; ~ **capital** (*fin.*) capitale sociale; ~ **-car** (*trasp. ferr.*) carro bestiame; ~ **-card** (*org. az.*) scheda di magazzino; ~ **certificate** (*fin.*) certificato azionario; ~ **clerk** (*pers.*) magazziniere; ~ **company** (= **joint-stock company**) (*fin.*) società per azioni; ~ **corporation** (*fin., USA*) società per azioni; ~ **department** (*banca*) ufficio titoli; ~ **dividend** (*fin.*) distribuzione di dividendi in azioni (*della società stessa*); azioni distribuite come dividendo, dividendo capitale; ~ **-Exchange** (*fin.*) Borsa Valori: to **be on the ~ Exchange** (*Borsa, ingl.*) essere membro dell'associazione della Borsa Valori di Londra; **the ~ Exchange list** (*fin.*) il bollettino della Borsa (Valori); ~ **-farm** (*econ.*) fattoria per l'allevamento del bestiame; ~ **-in-trade** (*org. az.*) merce in magazzino; (*rag.*) capitale in commercio, capitale impiegato nell'attività commerciale; ~ **issue** (*fin.*) emissione azionaria; ~ **ledger** (*fin., USA*) libro dei soci; ~ **-list** (*fin.*) listino di Borsa, listino «valori»; ~ **management** (*org. az.*) gestione dei materiali; ~ **market** (*fin.*) mercato azionario, mercato dei titoli finanziari, Borsa Valori; ~ **market crash** (*fin.*) crollo dei prezzi in Borsa; **a ~ of goods** (*org. az.*) uno stock di merci; ~ **on hand** (*org. az.*) giacenza, scorte; ~ **option** (*fin.*) opzione; ~ **photo** (*giorn.*) foto d'archivio; ~ **record account** (*rag.*) registro di carico e scarico; ~ **reduction** (*org. az.*) riduzione delle giacenze; ~ **right** (*fin.*) diritto d'opzione; ~ **room** (*org. az.*) magazzino; ~ **split** (*fin.*) frazionamento azionario; ~ **-taking** (*org. az.*) inventario, operazioni d'inventario; ~ **ticker** (*Borsa, fin.*) «teleborsa»; ~ **to bearer** (*fin.*) titolo al portatore; ~ **-turn** (*org. az.*) indice di rotazione delle scorte (*in un dato periodo: generalm. un anno*); ~ **turnover** (*org. az.*) ricambio del magazzino, rotazione delle scorte; ~ **volume** (*org. az.*) volume delle giacenze; ~ **-withdrawal order** (*org. az.*) bolla di prelievo; **in ~** (*market.: di merce*) esistente in magazzino; **out of ~** (*org. az.*) (*d'articolo, ecc.*) esaurito.

stock², *v. t.* **1** (*org. az.*) approvvigionare, fornire, rifornire. **2** (*org. az.*) essere provvisto di (*certa merce, ecc.*); tenere (*certa merce, ecc.*). // to ~ **a shop with goods** (*org. az.*) rifornire un negozio di merci; to ~ **up** (*org. az.*) depositare in magazzino, immagazzinare, far provvista di (*merce, ecc.*).

stockbroker, *n.* (*Borsa*) agente di cambio, operatore di Borsa, scambista. // ~ **'s contract** (*fin.*) borderò di Borsa.

stockbrokerage, *n. V.* **stockbroking.**

stockbroking, *n.* (*Borsa*) mediazione nella compravendita di titoli; lavoro d'agente di cambio.

stockholder, *n.* (*fin.*) azionista. // **stockholders' committee** (*fin.*) comitato esecutivo; **stockholders' equity** (*fin.*) totale del capitale sociale (*iscritto al valore nominale*) più gli utili non distribuiti; **stockholders' proxies** (*fin.*) deleghe degli azionisti.

stockist, *n.* (*market.*) grossista, depositario, fornitore.

stockjobber, *n.* **1** (*Borsa*) aggiotatore, «remisier». **2** (*Borsa, ingl.*) speculatore «professionista» (*non esiste in Italia*).

stockjobbing, *n.* **1** (*Borsa*) aggiotaggio. **2** (*Borsa, ingl.*) lavoro di «stockjobber» (*q. V.*).

stockpile¹, *n.* (*org. az.*) riserva (*di materie prime, merci, ecc.*).

stockpile², *v. t.* (*org. az.*) formare riserve di (*materie prime, merci, ecc.*).

stone, *n.* «stone» (*misura di peso pari a kg 6,350 circa*).

stoneware, *n.* articoli di gres.

stop¹, *n.* **1** arresto, fermata. **2** interruzione. **3** (*comun.*) «stop» (*nei telegrammi, ecc.*). **4** (*trasp.*) fermata. // ~ **-and-go policy** (*econ.*) politica alterna, di freni e stimoli (*della produzione, ecc.*); ~ **news** (*giorn.*) (notizie) recentissime; ~ **on request** (*trasp.*) fermata facoltativa; ~ **payment** (*banca*) ordine di fermo (*su un assegno*); ~ **press** (*giorn., ingl.*) notizie dell'ultima ora, recentissime; ~ **-press corrections** (*giorn.*) ritocchi dell'ultimo minuto; ~ **-press news** (*giorn.*) *V.* ~ **press;** ~ **sign** (*trasp. aut.*) segnale di «stop».

stop², *v. t.* **1** arrestare, fermare. **2** interrompere, sospendere. **3** (*pers.*) trattenere (*parte dello stipendio*). *v. i.* **1** arrestarsi, fermarsi. **2** cessare. // to ~ **a cheque** (*banca*) bloccare un assegno, mettere il fermo su un assegno; to ~ **the payment of a cheque** (*banca*) *V.* to ~ **a cheque;** to ~ **payments** (*banca*) chiudere gli sportelli; to ~ **a plant** (*org. az.*) chiudere una fabbrica; to ~ **sb.'s salary** (*pers.*) sospendere q. dallo stipendio, trattenere a q. lo stipendio; to ~ **talking** far silenzio, tacere; to ~ **work** (*org. az., pers.*) finire il lavoro, finire (di lavorare), staccare.

stopgap, *n.* **1** soluzione provvisoria. **2**

(*pers.*) sostituto temporaneo.

stoppage, *n.* 1 arresto, fermata. 2 interruzione, sospensione. 3 sosta. 4 (*dog.*, *leg.*) fermo. 5 (*pers.*) trattenuta, ritenuta (*sulla paga*). 6 (*sind.*) sciopero, interruzione del lavoro. // ~ **at source** (*fin.*) esazione alla fonte.

stopping, *n.* arresto, fermata. // ~ **in transit** (*trasp. mar.*) servizio del vettore che consente al caricatore di scaricare parte della merce durante il viaggio e spedire il resto del carico a destinazione a tariffa forfettaria.

stopwatch, *n.* cronometro.

storage, *n.* 1 (*elab. elettr.*, *USA*) memoria. 2 (*org. az.*) ammasso, deposito. 3 (*org. az.*) l'immagazzinare, magazzinaggio, immagazzinaggio, stoccaggio. 4 (*org. az.*) magazzinaggio, prezzo del magazzinaggio. // ~ **bin** (*org. az.*) silo; ~ **charges** (*rag.*) spese di magazzinaggio; ~ **costs** (*rag.*) costi di magazzinaggio; ~ **in transit** (*trasp.*) deposito (*di merci*) in transito; ~ **operations** (*org. az.*) operazioni di magazzinaggio; ~ **track** (*trasp. ferr.*, *USA*) binario di deposito.

store[1], *n.* 1 provvista, riserva, scorta. 2 (*elab. elettr.*) memoria. 3 (*market.*, *USA*) bottega, negozio. 4 (*org. az.*) deposito, magazzino. 5 **stores,** *pl.* (*market.*) grandi magazzini. 6 **stores,** *pl.* (*trasp. mar.*) dotazioni di bordo, provviste di bordo, rifornimenti di bordo. // ~ **block** (*elab. elettr.*) blocco di memoria; **a ~ for cheese seasoning** (*org. az.*) un magazzino per la stagionatura dei formaggi; **stores ledger** (*org. az.*) inventario perpetuo di magazzino; ~ **loyalty** (*market.*) fedeltà al negozio; ~ **order** (*org. az.*) ordine di magazzino; ~ **sign** (*market.*) insegna di negozio; ~ **-yard** (*org. az.*) piazzale d'immagazzinaggio.

store[2], *v. t.* 1 accumulare, far provvista di (*qc.*). 2 (*org. az.*) immagazzinare, mettere in magazzino.

storekeep, *v. i.* (*market.*, *USA*) fare l'esercente.

storekeeper, *n.* 1 (*market.*, *USA*) bottegaio, negoziante, esercente. 2 (*org. az.*) magazziniere.

storeman, *n.* (*pl.* **storemen**) (*org. az.*) magazziniere.

storing charges, *n. pl.* (*rag.*) spese di magazzinaggio.

storing expenses, *n. pl. V.* **storing charges.**

story, *n.* (*giorn.*) servizio.

stow, *v. t.* (*trasp. mar.*) stivare. // to ~ **goods in bulk** (*trasp. mar.*) stivare merci alla rinfusa.

stowage, *n.* 1 (*trasp. mar.*) stivaggio. 2 (*trasp. mar.*) spese di stivaggio. 3 (*trasp. mar.*) capacità di stivaggio. // ~ **certificate** (*trasp. mar.*) certificato di stivaggio; ~ **in bulk** (*trasp. mar.*) stivaggio alla rinfusa.

stowaway, *n.* (*trasp. aer.*, *trasp. mar.*) (passeggero) clandestino.

stower, *n.* (*trasp. mar.*) stivatore.

straddle, *n.* (*Borsa*) opzione; «doppio privilegio» (*operazione composta d'un «put» — q.V. — e d'un «call» — q.V. —, esercitabili tuttavia allo stesso prezzo, che è di regola quello del mercato al momento della stipulazione*).

straight, *a.* 1 diritto. 2 diretto. 3 giusto, onesto. 4 (*mat.*) retto. *avv.* 1 dritto, in linea retta. 2 direttamente. // **a ~ bill of lading** (*trasp. mar.*) una polizza di carico diretta; **a ~ businessman** un commerciante onesto; **a ~ course** (*trasp.*) un itinerario diretto; ~ **life annuity** (*ass.*) vitalizio, assegno vitalizio; ~ **life insurance** (*ass.*) assicurazione «vita intera»; ~ **-line** (*mat.*) in linea retta; (*rag.*) (*d'ammortamento*) a quote costanti; ~ **-line depreciation** (*rag.*) ammortamento a quote costanti; ~ **-line method** (*rag.*) metodo (*d'ammortamento*) a quote costanti; ~ **paper** (*cred.*, *fin.*) titolo di credito trasferibile firmato (*o* girato) da una sola persona; ~ **time** (*org. az.*, *pers.*) orario normale (*di lavoro: con esclusione degli straordinari, ecc.*).

straightaway, *a.* 1 rettilineo. 2 diretto. *avv.* 1 direttamente. 2 immediatamente. // **a ~ flight** (*trasp. aer.*) un volo diretto (*senza deviazioni di rotta*).

straighten, *v. t.* drizzare. // to ~ **out** rettificare, correggere; mettere in ordine, ordinare; to ~ **up** *V.* to ~ **out.**

straightforward, *a.* 1 diritto, rettilineo. 2 onesto.

strain[1], *n.* sforzo. // **the ~ of modern life** il logorio della vita moderna.

strain[2], *v. t.* 1 tendere, forzare. 2 distorcere. // to ~ **one's authority** (*leg.*) abusare della propria autorità; to ~ **the law** (*leg.*) fare uno strappo alla legge, violare la legge; to ~ **one's power** (*leg.*) eccedere i propri poteri; to ~ **the truth** (*leg.*) distorcere la verità.

strand, *v. t.* (*trasp. mar.*) arenare, incagliare. *v. i.* (*trasp. mar.*) (*di nave*) arenarsi, incagliarsi.

stranding, *n.* (*trasp. mar.*) arenamento, incaglio.

strap, *n.* (*Borsa*, *USA*) combinazione di due «call» (*q.V.*) e d'un «put» (*q.V.*).

stratification, *n.* stratificazione.

stratified sample, *n.* campione stratificato.

straw, *n.* paglia. *a. attr.* (*anche fig.*) di

paglia. // ~ **ballot** (*USA*) *V.* ~ **vote;** ~ **bond** (*leg.*) obbligazione con garanzie prive di valore; ~ **boss** (*pers.*) vice caposquadra; ~ **man** (*leg.*) uomo di paglia; ~ **vote** (*USA*) sondaggio dell'opinione pubblica.

stream, *n.* (*anche fig.*) corrente, flusso, afflusso.

street, *n.* **1** via. **2 the Street** (*fin., USA*) (= **Wall Street**) Wall Street (*strada che è simbolo del mercato monetario americano*). **3 the Street** (*fin., USA*) chi opera in Wall Street. **4 the Street** (*giorn., ingl.*) (= **Fleet Street**) Fleet Street (*strada in cui hanno sede molti giornali*). **5 the Street** (*giorn., ingl.*) chi lavora in Fleet Street. // ~ **broker** (*fin.*) agente di cambio che lavora fuori della Borsa; ~ **-car** (*trasp., USA*) tram, tranvai; ~ **-car line** (*trasp., USA*) tranvia; ~ **-car operator** (*trasp., USA*) tranviere; ~ **-island** (*trasp. aut.*) isola pedonale; ~ **market** (*fin.*) «dopoborsa», fuori borsa, mercatino, «borsino»; ~ **price** (*fin.*) prezzo del dopoborsa; ~ **trader** ambulante.

strength, *n.* **1** forza, vigore. **2** risorsa. **3** (*econ.*) vigore della domanda. **4** (*econ.*) tendenza dei prezzi al rialzo.

strengthen, *v. t.* rafforzare, consolidare, rinvigorire, potenziare. *v. i.* rafforzarsi, rinvigorirsi, consolidarsi, potenziarsi.

strengthening, *n.* rafforzamento, consolidamento, potenziamento.

stress¹, *n.* **1** sollecitazione, spinta. **2** (*anche fig.*) accento.

stress², *v. t.* **1** mettere l'accento su, accentare. **2** accentuare.

stretch¹, *n.* **1** allungamento, stiramento. **2** periodo ininterrotto (*di tempo*). **3** (*pers.*) periodo (passato) alle dipendenze (*di q.*). **4** (*trasp. ferr.*) tratta. // **a** ~ **of authority** (*leg.*) un abuso di potere; **at a** ~ di filato.

stretch², *v. t.* tendere, tirare, allungare (*tirando*). // to ~ **a budget** (*fin.*) ampliare un bilancio; to ~ **the law** (*leg.*) fare uno strappo alla legge; to ~ **one's powers** (*leg.*) abusare del proprio potere.

strict, *a.* rigido. // **a** ~ **construction** (*leg.*) un'interpretazione restrittiva (*della legge*).

strictly, *avv.* rigorosamente, rigidamente, severamente. // ~ **in confidence** in via riservatissima.

strife, *n.* (*sind.*) conflittualità.

strike¹, *n.* (*sind.*) sciopero. // ~ **ban** (*econ.*) proibizione di scioperare, precettazione; ~ **benefit** (*sind.*) *V.* ~ **pay;** ~ **-breaker** (*org. az.*) chi è assunto per sostituire uno scioperante; (*sind.*) crumiro; ~ **epidemics** (*sind.*) conflittualità permanente; ~ **pay** (*sind.*) sussidio (*pagato dai sindacati, ecc.*) durante uno sciopero; sussidio agli scioperanti; ~ **to the last** (*sind.*) sciopero a oltranza; to **be on** ~ (*sind.*) essere in sciopero; to **go on** ~ (*sind.*) mettersi in sciopero.

strike², *v. t.* (*pass.* e *part. pass.* **struck**) **1** battere, colpire, percuotere. **2** (*fin.*) battere (*moneta*); coniare (*monete*). *v. i.* **1** (*sind.*) scioperare. **2** (*trasp. mar.*) (*di nave*) andare in secco, incagliarsi. // to ~ **a balance** (*rag.*) fare il bilancio, tirare le somme, chiudere i conti, far quadrare i conti; to ~ **a bargain** concludere un affare; fare un buon affare; to ~ **coins** (*fin.*) coniare monete; to ~ **a docket** (*fam., ingl.*) insinuare un credito (*nel passivo d'un fallimento*); to ~ **down** (*trasp. mar.*) calare (*un carico*) nella stiva; to ~ **work** (*sind.*) scioperare.

strikebound, *a.* (*sind.*) (*di stabilimento, ecc.*) fermo per sciopero.

striker, *n.* (*sind.*) scioperante.

string, *n.* **1** stringa, spago, legaccio. **2** (*market., org. az.*) catena (*di negozi, ecc.*). **3 strings,** *pl.* (*leg., USA*) condizioni accessorie. // **a** ~ **of shops** (*market.*) una catena di negozi.

stringency, *n.* (*fin.*) difficoltà (*dovuta alla mancanza di denaro*).

stringent, *a.* **1** rigido, severo. **2** (*fin.*) (*di mercato, ecc.*) difficile, sostenuto (*per mancanza di denaro*). // ~ **laws** (*leg.*) disposizioni rigide, leggi severe.

strip¹, *n.* **1** (*giorn.*) striscia (*a fumetti*). **2** (*trasp. aer.*) pista. // to ~ **-crop** (*econ.*) terrazzare (*terreni*); ~ **-cropping** (*econ.*) terrazzamento (*di terreni*); ~ **-farming** (*econ.*) *V.* ~ **-cropping.**

strip², *v. t.* strappare, togliere. // to ~ **a ship** (*trasp. mar.*) disarmare una nave.

stroke, *n.* **1** colpo, botta, percossa. **2** battuta (*dattilografica*). // **a** ~ **of business** un buon affare, un affarone; **a** ~ **of genius** un lampo di genio, un'idea geniale; **two-(four-)** ~ **engine** (*trasp.*) motore a due (a quattro) tempi.

strong, *a.* **1** forte, robusto, vigoroso, saldo. **2** (*fin., market.*) alto, sostenuto. *avv.* forte, vigorosamente. // ~ **-box** (*attr. uff.*) cassaforte, forziere; **a** ~ **currency** (*fin.*) una valuta forte; **a** ~ **economy** (*econ.*) un'economia sana; ~ **prices** (*market.*) prezzi alti; ~ **-room** (*attr. uff., banca*) camera di sicurezza, camera blindata; to **be going** ~ essere ancora vigoroso, (*fam.*) andar forte, «tirare».

structural, *a.* strutturale. // ~ **inflation** (*econ.*) inflazione «strutturale»; ~ **malaise** (*econ.*) crisi strutturale; ~ **modernization** (*org.*

az.) ammodernamento delle strutture; ~ **policy** (*econ.*) politica strutturale; **a ~ policy in specific industries** (*econ.*) una politica settoriale; ~ **shortcomings** (*econ.*) inefficienze strutturali; ~ **unemployment** (*econ.*) disoccupazione strutturale.

structure, *n.* struttura. // ~ **by objectives** (*org. az.*) struttura per obiettivi.

struggle[1], *n.* lotta.

struggle[2], *v. i.* lottare.

stub, *n.* (*USA*) «madre», matrice (*di libretto d'assegni*).

stubborn, *a.* ostinato.

study[1], *n.* 1 studio. 2 esame, indagine. // **a ~ by sector** una ricerca (di carattere) settoriale; ~ **of industrial accidents** (*leg.*) infortunistica.

study[2], *v. t.* esaminare, indagare.

stumer, *n.* (*fam., ingl.*) assegno falso, assegno senza valore.

stumour, *n. V.* **stumer.**

stump, *n.* (*rag.*) matrice (*di registro, libretto e sim.*).

style[1], *n.* 1 modo. 2 appellativo, nome, titolo. 3 (*leg.*) ragione sociale, nome commerciale (*d'una ditta*). 4 (*market.*) modello (*alla moda*). 5 (*market.*) foggia, taglio, linea (*d'abiti, ecc.*).

style[2], *v. t.* 1 appellare, dare il titolo di. 2 (*pubbl., USA*) disegnare, modellare. // to ~ **a new product** (*pubbl., USA*) disegnare un nuovo prodotto.

stylist, *n.* (*pubbl., USA*) disegnatore.

sub[1], *n.* (*pers., fam.*) sostituto, supplente, vice.

sub[2], *v. i.* (*org. az., fam.*) far le veci. // to ~ **for sb.** far le veci di q.; (*org. az., fam.*) sostituire, supplire q.

subaccount, *n.* (*rag.*) sottoconto.

subagency, *n.* (*org. az.*) subagenzia.

subagent, *n.* (*org. az.*) subagente.

subaltern, *a.* subalterno.

subcommission, *n.* (*leg., org. az.*) sottocommissione.

subcommissioner, *n.* (*leg., org. az.*) vicecommissario.

subcommittee, *n.* (*leg., org. az.*) sottocommissione, sottocomitato.

subcompany, *n.* (*leg.*) società sussidiaria, consociata.

subcontract[1], *n.* (*leg.*) subappalto.

subcontract[2], *v. t.* (*leg.*) subappaltare.

subcontractor, *n.* (*leg.*) subappaltatore.

subdivide, *v. i.* suddividersi.

subedit, *v. t.* (*giorn.*) essere il vicedirettore di (*un giornale*).

subeditor, *n.* 1 (*giorn.*) vicedirettore. 2 (*giorn.*) redattore capo.

subemployed, *a.* (*econ.*) sottoccupato.

subemployment, *n.* (*econ.*) sottoccupazione.

subheading, *n.* (*giorn., rag.*) sottovoce (*d'articolo, conto, ecc.*).

subject[1], *a.* soggetto, sottomesso, sottoposto. *n.* 1 soggetto. 2 oggetto, argomento. // **a ~ for taxation** (*fin.*) un soggetto tassabile; ~ **-matter** argomento, contenuto, materia; (*ass.*) oggetto; **the ~ -matter insured** (*ass.*) l'oggetto assicurato; **the ~ -matter of the action** (*leg.*) l'oggetto della causa; **the ~ -matter of a business letter** (*comun.*) l'oggetto d'una lettera commerciale; **the ~ -matter of the risk** (*ass.*) l'oggetto del rischio; ~ **to** salvo; ~ **to our approval** salvo approvazione da parte nostra; ~ **to collection** (*cred.*) salvo incasso, salvo buon fine; ~ **to a condition** (*leg.*) soggetto a condizione; ~ **to goods being unsold** (*market.*) salvo venduto; ~ **to sale** (*market.*) salvo venduto.

subject[2], *v. t.* sottoporre. // to ~ **goods to a duty** (*dog., fin.*) daziare merce.

subjective, *a.* soggettivo. // ~ **utility** (*econ.*) utilità soggettiva (*d'un bene*).

subject oneself, *v. rifl.* sottoporsi.

sublease[1], *n.* (*leg.*) subaffitto, sublocazione.

sublease[2], *v. t.* (*leg.*) subaffittare, sublocare, prendere (*un locale, ecc.*) in subaffitto.

sublessee, *n.* (*leg.*) subaffittuario, sublocatario.

sublessor, *n.* (*leg.*) subaffittante.

sublet, *v. t.* (*pass.* e *part. pass.* **sublet**) 1 (*leg.*) subaffittare, sublocare. 2 (*leg.*) subappaltare.

subliminal, *a.* subliminale. // ~ **advertising** (*pubbl.*) pubblicità invisibile; **the ~ techniques in TV advertising** le tecniche subliminali della pubblicità televisiva.

submarine, *a.* sottomarino.

submission, *n.* 1 sottomissione. 2 presentazione (*di qc. a q., perché venga esaminata, ecc.*). 3 (*leg.*) compromesso arbitrale. // **the ~ of important papers to a Court** (*leg.*) la presentazione di documenti importanti a un tribunale.

submit, *v. t.* 1 sottoporre, presentare, rimettere. 2 affermare. 3 (*leg.*) demandare. // to ~ **a case to a law-Court** (*leg.*) deferire una causa a un tribunale; to ~ **a matter to arbitration** (*leg.*) sottoporre una questione ad arbitrato.

submitting, *n.* (*leg.*) deferimento (*d'una causa*).

subordinate[1], *a.* subordinato, soggetto, subalterno, sottoposto. *n.* (*pers.*) subordinato, subalterno, dipendente, sottoposto.

subordinate[2], *v. t.* subordinare, assoggettare, sottoporre.

subordination, *n.* (*leg.*) subordinazione.

suborn, *v. t.* (*leg.*) corrompere (*testimoni, ecc.*).

subpena, *n.* e *v. t. V.* **subpoena.**

subpoena[1], *n.* (*leg.*) citazione in giudizio, mandato di comparizione.

subpoena[2], *v. t.* (*leg.*) citare (*q.*) in giudizio, notificare un mandato di comparizione a (*q.*).

subquality, *n.* (*market.*) qualità inferiore. *a. attr.* (*market.*) di qualità inferiore. // ~ **products** (*market.*) prodotti di qualità inferiore.

subrogate, *v. t.* **1** surrogare. **2** (*leg.*) applicare le norme sulla surrogazione a (*q.*).

subrogation, *n.* (*leg.*) surrogazione, rapporto di surrogazione.

subscribe, *v. t.* **1** sottoscrivere, firmare. **2** versare. *v. i.* **1** aderire. **2** (*giorn.*) abbonarsi, prenotarsi. // to ~ **for shares** (*fin.*) sottoscrivere azioni; to ~ **a loan** (*fin.*) sottoscrivere un prestito; to ~ **official documents** (*leg.*) firmare documenti ufficiali; to ~ **to an agreement** approvare un accordo.

subscribed, *a.* sottoscritto. // ~ **capital** (*fin.*) capitale sottoscritto.

subscriber, *n.* **1** sottoscrittore. **2** (*giorn.*) abbonato. // **subscribers' list** (*fin.*) elenco dei sottoscrittori; (*giorn.*) elenco degli abbonati.

subscription, *n.* **1** sottoscrizione. **2** firma. **3** quota (*di denaro, ecc.*) versata (*o* da versare). **4** (*giorn.*) abbonamento. // ~ **rates** (*giorn.*) quote d'abbonamento; ~ **to an issue** (*fin.*) sottoscrizione di un'emissione (*azionaria, ecc.*); ~ **warrant** (*fin.*) ricevuta di sottoscrizione; (*giorn.*) ricevuta d'abbonamento.

subsequent buyer, *n.* (*leg.*) terzo acquirente.

subsidiary, *a.* sussidiario, accessorio, supplementare. *n.* (*fin.*) società sussidiaria, società collegata, società controllata, consociata. // ~ **account** (*rag.*) sottoconto; **a** ~ **company** (*fin.*) una società controllata, una società collegata, una consociata; ~ **journal** (*rag.*) giornale ausiliario; ~ **ledger** (*rag.*) registro ausiliario, mastro sussidiario.

subsidize, *v. t.* sussidiare, sovvenzionare.

subsidy, *n.* sussidio, sovvenzione, aiuto finanziario.

subsist, *v. t.* **1** vivere. **2** sostenersi, tenersi in vita.

subsistence, *n.* **1** vita. **2** mezzi di sussistenza. **3** (*econ.*) minimo vitale. // ~ **allowance** (*pers.*) indennità di trasferta, diaria; (*anche*) indennità integrativa; ~ **money** (*pers.*) indennità di trasferta.

substantial, *n.* effettivo, reale, considerevole. // ~ **damages** (*ass.*) danni reali; ~ **evidence** (*leg.*) prove sostanziali; **a** ~ **firm** (*econ.*) una ditta solida; ~ **orders** (*market.*) ordinazioni considerevoli; **a** ~ **proof** (*leg.*) una prova sostanziale; ~ **right** (*leg.*) diritto materiale; **a** ~ **rise in prices** (*market.*) un forte incremento dei prezzi.

substantiate, *v. t.* (*leg.*) convalidare, provare, addurre valide prove per (*qc.*). // to ~ **a charge** (*leg.*) provare un'accusa; to ~ **a claim** (*leg.*) convalidare un diritto.

substantiation, *n.* (*leg.*) convalidazione, convalida, prova.

substantive, *a.* effettivo, reale. // ~ **law** (*leg., USA*) diritto sostanziale.

substitute[1], *n.* **1** (*econ., market.*) surrogato, succedaneo. **2** (*pers.*) sostituto, supplente, interino.

substitute[2], *v. t.* sostituire, usare invece di.

substitution, *n.* **1** sostituzione. **2** (*leg.*) surrogazione. // **the** ~ **of out-dated marketing techniques** (*market.*) la sostituzione di tecniche distributive antiquate.

subtenancy, *n.* (*leg.*) subaffitto.

subtenant, *n.* (*leg.*) subaffittuario.

subtotal[1], *n.* (*mat.*) importo parziale.

subtotal[2], *v. t.* (*mat.*) determinare l'importo parziale di (*un numero di cifre*). // to ~ **a column** (*mat.*) determinare l'importo parziale d'una colonna.

subtract, *v. t.* e *i.* (*mat.*) sottrarre, fare una sottrazione.

subtraction, *n.* (*mat.*) sottrazione. // **a** ~ **mark** (*mat.*) *V.* ~ **sign; a** ~ **sign** (*mat.*) un «meno».

sub-units, *n. pl.* (*fin.*) quote di partecipazione.

subway, *n.* (*trasp. ferr., USA*) ferrovia sotterranea, metropolitana.

succeed, *v. i.* **1** aver successo. **2** subentrare. *v. t.* succedere, subentrare a (*q.*).

success, *n.* successo. // to **be a** ~ aver successo; (*market.: d'un articolo*) incontrare.

successful, *a.* riuscito. // to **be** ~ aver successo; (*market.: d'un articolo*) incontrare.

succession, *n.* **1** successione, serie. **2** (*leg.*) successione. **3** (*leg.*) discendenti, eredi. // ~ **duty** (*leg.*) imposta di successione; **the** ~ **of crops** (*econ.*) la rotazione delle colture; ~ **tax** (*leg., USA*) imposta di successione.

successive, *a.* successivo.

successor, *n.* successore.

sudden, *a.* improvviso.

suddenly, *avv.* improvvisamente.

sue, *v. t.* (*leg.*) citare, chiamare in giudizio; intentare (*o* muovere) lite, intentar causa a (*q.*). // to ~ **at law** (*leg.*) adire le vie legali; to ~ **in a civil case** (*leg.*) costituirsi parte civile.

sue and labour clause, *locuz. n.* (*ass. mar.*) clausola che autorizza alle misure conservative.

suffer, *v. t.* subire. // to ~ **losses** (*rag.*) subire perdite.

sufferance, *n.* (*leg.*) acquiescenza, tacito consenso.

sufficiency, *n.* **1** adeguatezza. **2** quantità sufficiente. // **a ~ of basic materials** (*org. az.*) una quantità sufficiente di materie prime.

sufficient, *a.* adeguato.

suggest, *v. t.* consigliare, proporre.

suggestion, *n.* consiglio, proposta. // ~ **box** (*org. az.*) cassetta dei suggerimenti; ~ **case** (*org. az.*) cassetta dei suggerimenti; ~ **committee** (*org. az.*) comitato di studio dei suggerimenti.

suit, *n.* (*leg.*) azione legale, causa, lite, processo; querela. // ~ **at law** (*leg.*) *V.* ~.

suitor, *n.* (*leg.*) attore, parte in giudizio.

sum[1], *n.* **1** somma, ammontare, somma di denaro. **2** (*mat.*) somma, totale. // **sums allocated** (*fin.*) stanziamenti; **the sums allocated for administrative expenditure** (*amm.*) gli stanziamenti per le spese amministrative; **the ~ total** la somma, il totale.

sum[2], *v. t.* **1** sommare. **2** (*mat.*) sommare. // to ~ **into** assommare a, ammontare a; to ~ **to** *V.* to ~ **into.**

summary, *a.* sommario, per sommi capi, sintetico. *n.* specchietto. // ~ **procedure** (*leg.*) procedura sommaria; ~ **trial** (*leg.*) giudizio sommario.

summation, *n.* (*mat.*) sommatoria.

summer, *n.* estate. // ~ **camp** (*org. az., pers.*) colonia estiva; ~ **resort** (*tur.*) stazione di villeggiatura estiva; ~ **time** ora (legale) estiva.

summing-up, *n.* (*leg.*) conclusioni.

summit, *n.* **1** sommità, vetta. **2** (*amm.*) vertice, riunione al vertice. // ~ **conference** conferenza al vertice; ~ **meeting** incontro al vertice, vertice.

summon, *v. t.* (*leg.*) citare (*q.*) in giudizio, chiamare (*q.*) a comparire. // to ~ **Parliament** (*leg.*) convocare il Parlamento; to ~ **witnesses** (*leg.*) citare testimoni.

summons[1], *n.* (*leg.*) citazione in giudizio, decreto di citazione, mandato di comparizione, notifica.

summons[2], *v. t. V.* **summon.**

sumptuary tax, *n.* (*fin.*) imposta (*o* tassa) restrittiva dei consumi.

Sunday, *n.* domenica. // ~ **supplement** (*giorn.*) supplemento domenicale.

sundries, *n. pl.* **1** oggetti di vario genere. **2** (*market.*) articoli diversi. **3** (*rag.*) «diversi». // ~ **column** (*rag.*) colonna dei «diversi».

sundry, *a.* diversi, vari. // ~ **creditors** (*rag.*) creditori diversi; ~ **debtors** (*rag.*) debitori diversi; ~ **goods and services** (*rag.*) beni e servizi diversi; ~ **payments** (*rag.*) pagamenti diversi.

super, *a.* sopraffino, eccellente. *n.* **1** (*market.*) qualità superiore. **2** (*market.*) prodotto di qualità superiore.

superabundance, *n.* eccesso.

superabundant, *a.* eccessivo. // ~ **crops** (*econ.*) raccolti sovrabbondanti.

superannuate, *v. t.* **1** mettere (*un dipendente*) in pensione; pensionare. **2** (*org. az.*) scartare (*un macchinario*) perché antiquato.

superannuated, *a.* **1** (*org. az.*) (*di macchinario*) antiquato, obsoleto. **2** (*pers.*) pensionato, inabile al lavoro (*per raggiunti limiti d'età*).

superannuation, *n.* **1** (*org. az.*) obsolescenza. **2** (*pers.*) collocamento a riposo, andata in pensione (*per raggiunti limiti d'età*). **3** (*pers.*) pensione (*di vecchiaia*).

superannuitant, *n.* (*pers.*) pensionato (*per raggiunti limiti d'età*).

superfine, *a.* (*market.*) (*d'articolo, ecc.*) sopraffino, finissimo.

superintend, *v. t.* soprintendere, dirigere, sorvegliare. // to ~ **the works** (*org. az.*) dirigere i lavori.

superintendence, *n.* soprintendenza, direzione, sorveglianza.

superintendent, *n.* **1** (*pers.*) soprintendente, intendente, direttore, supervisore, sorvegliante. **2** (*pers.*) responsabile di settore.

superior, *a.* (*market.*) di qualità superiore, di prima qualità, ottimo.

superiority, *n.* supremazia, primato.

supermarket, *n.* (*market.*) supermarket, supermercato, grande magazzino, grande emporio.

supernumerary, *a.* soprannumerario, soprannumero. *n.* soprannumero.

supersede, *v. t.* (*org. az.*) sostituire, scartare (*macchine, impianti, ecc.*).

supertax, *n.* (*fin.*) soprattassa, addizionale, imposta addizionale.

supervise, *v. t.* (*org. az.*) sorvegliare,

dirigere, soprintendere a. // to ~ **works** (*org. az.*) dirigere i lavori.

supervision, *n.* (*org. az.*) supervisione, sorveglianza, soprintendenza, direzione.

supervisor, *n.* (*pers.*) supervisore, sorvegliante, soprintendente, direttore.

supervisory, *a.* (*org. az.*) di sorveglianza, direttivo. // ~ **personnel** (*pers.*) personale direttivo; **a ~ position** (*org. az.*) compiti (*o* mansioni) di sorveglianza.

supplement[1], *n.* **1** supplemento, aggiunta. **2** (*giorn.*) supplemento. **3** (*mat.*) supplemento.

supplement[2], *v. t.* completare, integrare, fare aggiunte a. // to ~ **one's income** arrotondare lo stipendio (*o* il salario).

supplementary, *a.* supplementare, suppletivo, suppletorio, addizionale, integrativo. // ~ **budget** (*rag.*) bilancio suppletivo.

suppletory, *a.* (*leg.*) suppletorio, suppletivo. // ~ **oath** (*leg.*) giuramento suppletorio.

supplier, *n.* **1** (*econ., market.*) fornitore, approvvigionatore. **2** (*econ., market.*) Paese fornitore, Paese produttore.

supply[1], *n.* **1** approvvigionamento, fornitura, rifornimento. **2** (*econ.*) offerta. **3** (*org. az.*) provvista, riserva, scorta. // ~ **and demand trends** (*econ.*) evoluzione dell'offerta e della domanda; ~ **balance-sheet** (*rag.*) bilancio d'approvvigionamento; ~ **conditions** (*econ.*) situazione dell'offerta; ~ **curve** (*econ.*) curva dell'offerta; **supplies on hand** (*rag.*) rimanenze finali; ~ **sources** (*org. az.*) fonti d'approvvigionamento, fonti di rifornimento; ~ **structures** (*econ.*) strutture dell'approvvigionamento.

supply[2], *v. t.* **1** approvvigionare, fornire, rifornire, provvedere. **2** supplire. // to ~ **a vacancy** (*pers.*) occupare un posto vacante; to ~ **sb. with funds** (*fin.*) rifornire q. di fondi, finanziare q.

support[1], *n.* aiuto, patrocinio, (*anche fig.*) appoggio, sostegno. // ~ **arrangements** (*econ.*) meccanismi d'intervento (*governativo, ecc.*); ~ **limit** (*fin.*) punto d'intervento ufficiale (*nei tassi di cambio*); ~ **measures** (*econ.*) interventi (*governativi, ecc.*); ~ **point** (*fin.*) *V.* ~ **limit**; ~ **tariffs** (*econ.*) tariffe di sostegno.

support[2], *v. t.* **1** appoggiare, aiutare, sostenere, patrocinare. **2** mantenere. // to ~ **a cause** appoggiare una causa; to ~ **a charge** (*leg.*) convalidare un'accusa; to ~ **prices** (*econ.*) sostenere i prezzi; to ~ **retail prices** (*econ.*) sostenere i prezzi al dettaglio.

supporter, *n.* sostenitore, difensore.

supporting documents, *n. pl.* (*leg.*) documenti giustificativi; «pezze d'appoggio» (*fam.*).

suppress, *v. t.* sopprimere, abolire, annullare, omettere. // to ~ **evidence** (*leg.*) far scomparire prove; to ~ **news from publication** (*giorn.*) omettere la pubblicazione di notizie.

suppressed inflation, *n.* (*econ.*) inflazione controllata (*mediante il differimento delle spese per beni di consumo*).

suppression, *n.* soppressione, abolizione, annullamento, omissione. // ~ **of news** (*giorn.*) omissione della pubblicazione di notizie; **the ~ of a publication** (*giorn.*) la soppressione d'una pubblicazione.

supranational, *a.* soprannazionale, supernazionale. // ~ **company** (*fin.*) soprannazionale, società soprannazionale.

supraprotest, *n.* **1** (*cred.*) accettazione (*d'una cambiale*) per intervento. **2** (*cred.*) pagamento (*d'una cambiale*) per intervento.

supreme, *a.* altissimo, massimo. // **the ~ Court** (*leg., USA*) la Corte Suprema.

surcharge[1], *n.* **1** (*fin.*) soprattassa. **2** (*market.*) soprapprezzo, supplemento, maggiorazione (*di prezzo*). **3** (*trasp.*) sovraccarico.

surcharge[2], *v. t.* **1** (*fin.*) applicare una soprattassa a (*q. o qc.*). **2** (*market.*) far pagare di più, maggiorare il prezzo di (*qc.*). **3** (*trasp.*) sovraccaricare.

surety, *n.* **1** (*leg.*) cauzione, garanzia, fideiussione, mallevadoria. **2** (*leg.*) garante. // ~ **bond** (*leg.*) cauzione, garanzia (*scritta*).

surface, *n.* superficie. // ~ **mail** (*comun.*) posta normale (*che viaggia via terra o via mare, ma non per via aerea*).

surplus, *n.* **1** soprappiù, eccedenza, eccesso. **2** (*econ., fin.*) «surplus», avanzo, eccedenza, rimanenza, supero, residuo attivo, saldo attivo, riserva (*di capitale*). // ~ **balance** (*econ., rag.*) saldo attivo; **a ~ of assets over liabilities** (*rag.*) un'eccedenza delle attività sulle passività; **a ~ on current account** (*econ.*) un saldo attivo della bilancia dei pagamenti correnti; ~ **produce** (*econ.*) eccedenze agricole; ~ **products** (*econ.*) eccedenze industriali; ~ **reserve** (*rag.*) riserva straordinaria; ~ **stock** (*market.*) rimanenze; ~ **value** (*econ.*) plusvalore.

surprise counts, *n. pl.* controlli (*di cassa, ecc.*) a sorpresa.

surrender[1], *n.* **1** resa, l'arrendersi. **2** (*ass.*) riscatto (*d'una polizza*). **3** (*leg.*) cessione, abbandono. // **the ~ of an estate by a bankrupt** (*leg.*) la cessione d'una proprietà da parte d'un fallito; **the ~ of a right** (*leg.*) l'abbandono d'un diritto; **the ~ value of a policy** (*ass.*) il valore di riscatto d'una polizza.

surrender[2], *v. t.* **1** rendere. **2** (*ass.*) riscattare (*una polizza*). 3 (*leg.*) cedere, abbandonare. *v. i.* arrendersi. // to ~ **oneself to justice** (*leg.*) costituirsi all'autorità giudiziaria; to ~ **a policy** (*ass.*) riscattare una polizza; to ~ **a privilege** (*leg.*) cedere un privilegio.

surrenderee, *n.* (*leg.*) cessionario (*V. anche* **surrender**[2]).

surrenderor, *n.* (*leg.*) cedente (*V. anche* **surrender**[2]).

surreptitious, *a.* (*leg.*) surrettizio.

surtax[1], *n.* 1 (*fin.*) soprattassa, sovrattassa; (imposta) addizionale. 2 (*fin.*) imposta complementare.

surtax[2], *v. t.* (*fin.*) gravare (*q.*) con soprattassa, soprattassare.

survey[1], *n.* 1 esame, indagine, studio, rilevazione. 2 ispezione, verifica, perizia; rilevamento (*topografico*). 3 (*giorn.*) inchiesta. 4 (*market., pubbl.*) inchiesta, indagine. 5 (*trasp. mar.*) visita (*effettuata dagli istituti di classificazione, per l'assegnazione, conservazione o cambiamento di classe delle navi mercantili*). // ~ **certificate** (*trasp. mar.*) certificato di visita; ~ **report** (*trasp. mar.*) perizia, relazione di perizia.

survey[2], *v. t.* 1 esaminare, indagare. 2 ispezionare, verificare, fare la perizia di (*qc.*). 3 (*market., pubbl.*) fare un'inchiesta, fare un'indagine su (*qc.*). // to ~ **the ship and cargo** (*trasp. mar.*) ispezionare la nave e il carico.

surveyor, *n.* 1 ispettore, controllore, verificatore. 2 (*ass.*) perito. 3 (*dog., USA*) doganiere. // **a** ~ **of customs** (*dog.*) un ispettore doganale; **a** ~ **of weights and measures** (*leg.*) un controllore dei pesi e delle misure.

survival, *n.* (*ass.*) sopravvivenza. // ~ **rate** (*ass.*) tasso di sopravvivenza.

survive, *v. i.* (*ass.*) sopravvivere.

surviving, *a.* sopravvissuto, superstite.

survivor, *n.* (*ass.*) sopravvissuto, superstite.

survivorship, *n.* (*leg.*) sopravvivenza. // ~ **annuity** (*ass.*) vitalizio (*corrisposto al beneficiario*) in caso di morte (*dell'assicurato*); (*pers.*) pensione di reversibilità.

suspect, *n.* (*leg.*) persona sospetta.

suspected, *a.* sospetto. // ~ **bill of health** (*trasp. mar.*) certificato sanitario sospetto.

suspend, *v. t.* 1 sospendere, interrompere. 2 (*pers.*) sospendere (*dal lavoro*). // to ~ **sb. from office** (*pers.*) sospendere q. dall'ufficio; to ~ **judgement** (*leg.*) sospendere il giudizio; to ~ **sentence** (*leg.*) concedere la condizionale.

suspended, *a.* (*pers.*) sospeso (*dal lavoro*).

suspense, *n.* sospensione. // ~ **account** (*rag.*) conto sospeso, conto d'ordine; ~ **entry** (*rag.*) scrittura d'ordine.

suspension, *n.* 1 sospensione, interruzione. 2 (*pers.*) sospensione (*dal lavoro*). // **the** ~ **of payments** la sospensione dei pagamenti.

suspensive, *a.* sospensivo, dilatorio. // ~ **condition** (*leg.*) condizione sospensiva.

suspicion, *n.* (*leg.*) suspicione.

sustain, *v. t.* 1 sostenere, subire. 2 mantenere. 3 (*leg.*) appoggiare, accogliere. // to ~ **a claim** (*leg.*) appoggiare una rivendicazione; to ~ **objections** (*leg.*) accogliere eccezioni.

sustenance, *n.* mantenimento.

swap, *n.* 1 baratto. 2 (*fin.*) «swap», riporto valutario, riporto in cambi, riporto su divise. // ~ **agreements** (*fin.*) accordi di «swap»; ~ **of currency** (*fin.*) riporto valutario; ~ **rates** (*fin.*) saggi di riporto valutario.

swear, *v. t.* e *i.* (*pass.* **swore,** *part. pass.* **sworn**) 1 (*leg.*) giurare, prestare giuramento. 2 (*leg.*) far giurare, sottoporre (*q.*) a giuramento. // to ~ **an affidavit** (*leg.*) fare una dichiarazione giurata; to ~ **a charge against sb.** (*leg.*) muovere un'accusa formale contro q.; to ~ **in a jury** (*leg.*) insediare una giuria; to ~ **an oath** (*leg.*) fare (*o* prestare) giuramento.

sweat[1], *n.* 1 sudore. 2 (*fam.*) grave fatica. // ~ **-shop** (*org. az., fam.*) azienda che sfrutta le maestranze.

sweat[2], *v. i.* sudare. *v. t.* (*pers., fam.*) sfruttare (*dipendenti*).

sweeten, *v. t.* 1 (*anche fig.*) addolcire, dolcificare. 2 (*fin.*) migliorare le condizioni di (*un'emissione di titoli*) per facilitarne il collocamento.

sweetheart, *n.* innamorato, innamorata; amoroso, amorosa. // ~ **agreement** (*sind., USA*) contratto di lavoro negoziato fra un datore di lavoro e un sindacato (*e contenente clausole favorevoli al primo*) stipulato senza la partecipazione degli iscritti al sindacato stesso.

swell[1], *n.* (*fig.*) aumento, crescita, dilatazione. // **a** ~ **in population** (*stat.*) un aumento della popolazione.

swell[2], *v. i.* (*pass.* **swelled,** *part. pass.* **swollen**) 1 (*anche fig.*) gonfiarsi, dilatarsi. 2 (*anche fig.*) aumentare, crescere. 3 (*fin., market.: di prezzi*) gonfiarsi, lievitare. *v. t.* 1 gonfiare, dilatare. 2 accrescere, far aumentare.

swindle[1], *n.* imbroglio, truffa.

swindle[2], *v. t.* imbrogliare, truffare.

swindler, *n.* imbroglione, truffatore, truffaldino.

swing[1], *n.* 1 dondolio. 2 (*anche fig.*) fluttuazione, oscillazione. // **the** ~ **of prices** (*market.*) il fluttuare dei prezzi; ~ **shift** (*pers.*)

turno (*di lavoro*) dalle ore 16 alle 24, turno pendolare.

swing[2], *v. i.* (*pass. e part. pass.* **swung**) **1** dondolare. **2** (*anche fig.*) fluttuare, oscillare.

switch[1], *n.* **1** commutatore. **2** (*trasp. ferr.*) scambio. // ~ **-back** (*trasp. ferr.*) regresso; ~ **-board** (*tur.*) centralino (*d'albergo e sim.*); ~ **-signal** (*trasp. ferr., USA*) segnale dello scambio.

switch[2], *v. t.* **1** girare l'interruttore di (*un circuito elettrico, ecc.*). **2** (*fin.*) rinviare (*un contratto a termine*) da un mese al mese successivo (*in una Borsa merci*). **3** (*trasp. ferr.*) instradare, smistare (*un treno*). *v. i.* (*trasp. ferr.*) (*di treno*) essere smistato. // to ~ **on** (*elab. elettr.*) inserire.

switchman, *n.* (*pl.* **switchmen**) (*trasp. ferr., USA*) deviatore, manovratore, scambista.

swop, *n.* (*fin.*) riporto in cambi.

sworn, *a.* giurato. // ~ **broker** (*fin., leg.*) mediatore giurato; ~ **statement** (*leg.*) dichiarazione giurata; ~ **witness** (*leg.*) testimone giurato.

sympathetic, *a.* che prova simpatia, comprensivo, amichevole. // ~ **strike** (*sind.*) sciopero di solidarietà.

synallagmatic, *a.* (*leg.*) bilaterale. // **a** ~ **contract** (*leg.*) un contratto sinallagmatico.

synchronous, *a.* sincrono, simultaneo.

syndical, *a.* (*sind.*) sindacale.

syndicalism, *n.* (*sind.*) sindacalismo.

syndicalist, *n.* (*sind.*) sindacalista, fautore del sindacalismo.

syndicate[1], *n.* **1** (*econ.*) cartello. **2** (*econ., fin.*) gruppo monopolistico. **3** (*fin.*) sindacato, associazione (*di banchieri, finanzieri, ecc.*). **4** (*giorn.*) agenzia di stampa.

syndicate[2], *v. t.* **1** (*fin.*) associare in sindacato (*V.* **syndicate**[1]). **2** (*giorn.*) controllare (*un certo numero di giornali*). *v. i.* (*fin.*) costituirsi in sindacato (*V.* **syndicate**[1]).

syndicated bid, *n.* (*fin.*) offerta consorziata.

synopsis, *n.* (*pl.* **synopses**) sinossi, compendio, specchietto, sunto.

system, *n.* **1** sistema, metodo. **2** (*mat.*) sistema. **3** (*org. az.*) sistema. // **the** ~ **of generalized preferences** (*econ.*) il sistema delle preferenze generalizzate; **a** ~ **of Government** un sistema di Governo; **the** ~ **of import and export certificates** (*comm. est.*) il regime per i titoli d'importazione e d'esportazione; **a** ~ **of national accounts** (*rag.*) un sistema di contabilità nazionale; **the** ~ **of trade** (*comm. est.*) il regime degli scambi.

T

tab, *n.* **1** striscetta (*di carta, stoffa, ecc.*). **2** (*fam.*) prezzo. **3** (*attr. uff.*) linguetta sporgente (*di scheda di casellario, ecc.*).

table¹, *n.* tabella, prospetto. // ~ **of contents** indice (*di libro*); ~ **of weights and measures** tabella dei pesi e delle misure; **on the** ~ (*fig.*) sul tavolo, in tavola; **under the** ~ (*fig.*) sottobanco.

table², *v. t.* **1** mettere su una tavola. **2** ordinare (*dati, ecc.*) su una tabella. **3** (*leg.*) rimandare (*una mozione, ecc.*) «sine die». **4** (*org. az.*) mettere (*un argomento, ecc.*) all'ordine del giorno.

tabloid, *a.* per sommi capi. *n.* (*giorn.*) «tabloid», giornale popolare (*con molte fotografie e poche notizie condensate*).

tabular, *a.* **1** di tabella. **2** classificato in tavole. // ~ **values** valori tabellari.

tabulate, *v. t.* disporre in tavole.

tabulator, *n.* (*di macch. uff.*) tabulatore (*di macchina da scrivere*).

tachymeter, *n.* (*trasp. aut.*) tachimetro.

tacit, *a.* tacito, implicito. // ~ **agreement** (*leg.*) tacito accordo; ~ **consent** (*leg.*) tacito consenso.

tack, *v. t.* **1** attaccare (*un nastro, ecc.*) con punti lunghi. **2** (*fig.*) aggiungere, allegare.

tacking, *n.* (*leg.*) priorità (*d'una terza ipoteca quando la seconda non è stata notificata*).

tackle¹, *n.* **1** (*org. az.*) attrezzatura, attrezzi, arnesi, strumenti. **2** (*trasp. mar.*) paranco.

tackle², *v. t.* affrontare, fronteggiare, venire alle prese con (*una difficoltà, ecc.*).

tag¹, *n.* **1** (*market.*) cartellino segnaprezzo, etichetta. **2** (*trasp. aut., USA*) multa. // ~ **line** (*pubbl.*) slogan.

tag², *v. t.* **1** (*market.*) fornire (*articoli, ecc.*) di cartellino segnaprezzo. **2** (*market.*) fissare il prezzo di (*qc.*). **3** (*trasp. aut., USA*) multare (*un'automobile, ecc.*).

tail, *n.* (*anche fig.*) coda, estremità, fine. // ~ **-light** (*trasp.*) fanale di coda.

tailor¹, *n.* sarto. // ~ **-made** (*market.*) (*d'abito*) fatto su misura; (*d'articolo*) fatto su ordinazione.

tailor², *v. t.* **1** (*fig.*) adattare, aggiustare. **2** (*market.*) fare (*un abito*) su misura. **3** (*market.*) fare (*un articolo*) su ordinazione.

tailored, *a.* **1** (*market.*) (*d'abito*) fatto su misura. **2** (*market.*) (*d'articolo*) fatto su ordinazione.

take¹, *n.* **1** incasso, introito, entrata, entrate. **2** guadagno, profitto, ricavo, resa. **3** (*fin.*) gettito. // ~ **-home** (*pers.*) *V.* ~ **-home pay;** ~ **-home pay** (*pers.*) paga netta, salario netto, stipendio netto; ~ **-home pay-packet** (*pers.*) *V.* ~ **-home pay;** ~ **-home wages** (*pers.*) salario netto; ~ **-off** (*econ.*) decollo; (*trasp. aer.*) decollo; ~ **-off strip** (*trasp. aer.*) pista di decollo; ~ **-over** (*fin.*) assorbimento, rilevamento (*d'un'azienda*); concentrazione, fusione; ~ **-over bid** (*fin.*) offerta pubblica d'acquisto (*OPA*); ~ **-over bidder** (*fin.*) società offerente; ~ **-over company** (*fin.*) società offerente; ~ **-over deal** (*fin.*) accordo di fusione (*di aziende*); ~ **-over scheme** (*fin.*) schema di fusione; ~ **-up** accaparramento, incetta.

take², *v. t.* (*pass.* **took,** *part. pass.* **taken**) **1** prendere, pigliare. **2** accettare, accogliere. **3** prendere (con sé), portare. **4** portar via, togliere. **5** impiegare, metterci. **6** intendere, supporre. **7** (*fam.*) ricevere (*come retribuzione*), guadagnare. *v. impers.* richiedere, volerci. // to ~ **aboard** (*trasp. mar.*) (*di vettore*) imbarcare; to ~ **advantage of** avvantaggiarsi di; to ~ **an affidavit** (*leg.*) ricevere una dichiarazione giurata; to ~ **st. as read** dare qc. per letto (*in un'assemblea e sim.*); to ~ **the average between the highest and lowest price** (*econ., market.*) fare la media fra il prezzo più alto e quello più basso; to ~ **away** levare, togliere; to ~ **back** prendere indietro, riprendere; disdire; to ~ **back an article** (*market.*) riprendere un articolo (*restituendo al cliente il prezzo che aveva pagato*); to ~ **bribes** (*leg.*) farsi corrompere; to ~ **care** fare attenzione, stare attento; to ~ **care of** sorvegliare; curare, prendersi cura di; to ~ **care of oneself** curarsi, aver cura di sé; to ~ **the chair** (*amm.*) assumere la presidenza (*d'una* *società, ecc.*); presiedere (*una società, ecc.*); dare inizio ai lavori (*d'un'assemblea, ecc.*); to ~ **one's chance** stare al gioco (*fig.*); to ~ **charge of st.** (*org. az.*) prendere in consegna qc., occuparsi di qc.; to ~ **one's degree** laurearsi; to ~ **delivery of securities** (*fin.*) ritirare titoli; to ~ **down** prender nota di, registrare, trascrivere; to ~ **down a speech in shorthand** stenografare un discorso; to ~ **an engagement** (*leg.*) prendere un impegno; to ~ **an examination** dare (*sostenere*) un esame; to ~ **for the call** (*Borsa, fin.*) vendere a premio; to ~ **goods on account** (*market.*) prendere merce a credito; to ~ **goods out of bond** (*dog.*) sdoganare merci; to ~ **in** (*giorn.*) ricevere regolarmente (*una pubblicazione, ecc.*), essere abbonato a (*un giornale, ecc.*); (*market.*) incassare, introitare; to ~ **in ballast** (*trasp. mar.*) imbarcare zavorra, zavorrare; to ~ **in coal** (*trasp. mar.*) caricare carbone, fare (rifornimento di) carbone; to ~ **in stocks** (*Borsa, fin.*) riportare titoli; to ~ **an interest in st.** interessarsi di qc.; to ~ **an interest in an enterprise** partecipare a un'impresa; to ~ **into custody** (*leg.*) prendere in custodia; to ~ **sb. into partnership** prendere q. come socio in affari, ammettere q. in una società; to ~ **an inventory** (*rag.*) procedere a un inventario; to ~ **a job** (*pers.*) occupare un posto; to ~ **one's leave from sb.** licenziarsi (*o* accomiatarsi) da q.; to ~ **legal action** (*leg.*) adire le vie legali; to ~ **legal advice** (*leg.*) consultare un avvocato; to ~ **legal steps** (*leg.*) adire le vie legali, agire; to ~ **a letter** scrivere una lettera sotto dettatura; to ~ **the liberty** prendersi la libertà, permettersi; to ~ **minutes** (*leg.*) mettere a verbale, verbalizzare; to ~ **the minutes of a meeting** (*amm.*) tenere il verbale d'un'assemblea; to ~ **a mortgage on a property** (*leg.*) accendere un'ipoteca su una proprietà; to ~ **no further action on a matter** (*leg.*) archiviare una pratica; to ~ **an oath** (*leg.*) fare un giuramento, prestare giuramento; to ~ **off** togliere, sopprimere; «tirare» (*copie; da un originale*); riprodurre (*documenti, ecc.*); (*market.*) dedurre, detrarre, scontare; (*rag.*) calcolare (*una quantità*) con una macchina calcolatrice; (*trasp. aer.*) decollare; to ~ **off the embargo on a ship** (*trasp. mar.*) togliere l'embargo su una nave; to ~ **off a tax** (*fin.*) togliere un'imposta, abolire un'imposta; to ~ **off a total** (*rag.*) fare un totale; to ~ **office** (*amm.*) assumere una carica, insediarsi; to ~ **out** togliere, cavare; sottoscrivere; to ~ **out an insurance policy** (*ass.*) sottoscrivere una polizza d'assicurazione; to ~ **out loans** (*cred.*) fare mutui; esporsi (*finanziariamente*); to ~ **out a patent** (*leg.*) prendere un brevetto; to ~ **over** subentrare, succedere; (*amm.*) insediarsi; (*fin.*) assorbire, acquistare il controllo di (*una società*); to ~ **over a business** (*fin.*) rilevare un'azienda, assorbire un'impresa; to ~ **a partner into the business** prendere un (nuovo) socio nell'azienda; to ~ **place** aver luogo; to ~ **the place of sb.** subentrare a q.; to ~ **a poll** (*market.*) fare un'inchiesta; to ~ **possession of st.** (*leg.*) prendere possesso di qc.; appropriarsi, impadronirsi di qc.; to ~ **precautions** premunirsi; to ~ **proceedings** (*leg.*) adire le vie legali; to ~ **a share in the profits** (*fin.*) partecipare agli utili; to ~ **stock** (*org. az.*) fare l'inventario; to ~ **time off** (*pers.*) far vacanza; to ~ **up** sollevare; fare incetta di, accaparrare, accaparrarsi; (*trasp.*) far salire; to ~ **up a bill** (*banca, cred.*) ritirare una cambiale; (*cred.*) onorare una cambiale; to ~ **up contributions** raccogliere sottoscrizioni; to ~ **up one's domicile** (*o* **residence**) domiciliarsi; to ~ **up a loan** (*cred.*) sottoscrivere un mutuo.

taken, *a.* impegnato, riservato.

taker, *n.* **1** chi prende, chi riceve (*V. anche* **take²**). **2** (*Borsa*) riportatore. **3** (*cred., fin.*) prenditore. // ~ **for a call** (*Borsa*) venditore d'un «dont»; ~ **for a put** (*Borsa*) compratore d'un premio indiretto; ~ **-in** (*Borsa*) persona disposta a compiere operazioni di riporto in sostituzione d'un rialzista (*che in un dato momento non vuole, o non può, pagare certi titoli*); ~ **of the rate** (*Borsa*) ricevitore del premio.

taking-over, *n.* **1** (*amm.*) insediamento; (il) subentrare. **2** (*fin.*) assorbimento, rilevamento (*d'un'azienda*).

takings, *n. pl.* (*cred., fin., rag.*) incassi, introiti, profitti.

tale quale, *locuz. a. V.* **tel quel.**

tales, *n. pl.* (*leg.*) giurati supplenti.

talesman, *n.* (*pl.* **talesmen**) (*leg.*) giurato supplente.

talk¹, *n.* **1** discorso. **2** abboccamento, colloquio. **3** negoziato, trattativa. **4** voce.

talk², *v. i.* discorrere, parlare. *v. t.* parlare di, discutere di.

talkie, *n.* (*pubbl.*) film sonoro.

talking film, *n. V.* **talkie.**

talking picture, *n. V.* **talkie.**

tall, *a.* **1** alto, elevato. **2** (*market.*) (*di prezzo, ecc.*) altissimo, esagerato. // ~ **organization** (*org. az.*) struttura organizzativa verticale.

tallness, *n.* altezza.

tally¹, *n.* **1** conto. **2** (*cred.*) annotazione, registrazione (*di credito, ecc.*). **3** (*market.*)

tagliando di riscontro («*madre*» o «*figlia*»). // ~ **card** (*market.*) *V.* ~ **sheet;** ~ **clerk** (*pers.*) controllore (*alla consegna di merci*); ~ **sheet** (*market.*) foglio di riscontro.

tally[2], *v. t.* 1 calcolare, computare. 2 (*cred.*) annotare, registrare (*crediti, ecc.*). 3 (*trasp. mar.*) controllare (*la merce ricevuta in consegna*); fare la «spunta» di (*un carico: articolo per articolo*). *v. i.* coincidere, corrispondere. // to ~ **a load** (*trasp. mar.*) controllare un carico.

tallyman, *n.* (*pl.* **tallymen**) (*trasp. mar.*) controllore (*del carico*); spuntatore.

talon, *n.* 1 talloncino. 2 (*fin.*) cedola (*di titolo al portatore, utilizzabile per richiedere un nuovo certificato azionario*).

tame, *v. t.* 1 addomesticare. 2 (*anche fig.*) domare. // to ~ **inflation** (*econ.*) bloccare l'inflazione.

tamper, *v. i.* interferire. // to ~ **with st.** (*leg.*) manomettere, falsificare; to ~ **with documents** (*leg.*) falsificare documenti, manomettere documenti; to ~ **with foodstuffs** (*leg.*) adulterare generi alimentari.

tamperer, *n.* (*leg.*) corruttore, falsificatore.

tampering, *n.* (*leg.*) manomissione, falsificazione, subornazione.

tandem increase, *n.* (*pers.*) aumento abbinato.

tangent, *a.* e *n.* (*mat.*) tangente. // ~ **line** (*mat.*) tangente.

tangential, *a.* (*mat.*) tangenziale.

tangible, *a.* manifesto, sicuro. // ~ **assets** (*rag.*) beni reali; **a** ~ **gain** un guadagno concreto; ~ **net worth** (*rag.*) attività totali nette, valore patrimoniale, patrimonio fisico; **a** ~ **proof** (*leg.*) una prova sicura; ~ **property** (*leg.*) beni corporali, beni materiali.

tank, *n.* cisterna, vasca. // ~ **-car** (*trasp. ferr.*) carro cisterna; ~ **engine** (*trasp. ferr.*) locomotiva; ~ **-steamer** (*trasp. mar.*) nave cisterna; ~ **truck** (*trasp. aut.*) autobotte, autocisterna.

tanker, *n.* 1 (*trasp. aer.*) aerocisterna. 2 (*trasp. aut.*) autobotte. 3 (*trasp. mar.*) nave cisterna. 4 (*trasp. mar.*) petroliera.

tankship, *n.* (*trasp. mar.*) nave cisterna.

tape[1], *n.* 1 nastro. 2 nastro magnetico. // ~ **-machine** (*Borsa*) teleborsa (*strumento elettronico che registra e trasmette istantaneamente a tutto il mondo i prezzi e il volume delle contrattazioni in titoli*); to ~ **-record** registrare (*qc.*) su nastro (magnetico); ~ **recorder** (*macch. uff.*) registratore a nastro, magnetofono.

tape[2], *v. t.* registrare (*su nastro magnetico*).

tap issue, *n.* (*Borsa, fin.*) emissione «a rubinetto».

tardy, *a.* 1 pigro, lento. 2 in ritardo. 3 (*cred., leg.*) moroso. // **a** ~ **debtor** (*cred.*) un debitore moroso.

tare[1], *n.* (*market.*) tara. // ~ **allowance** (*market.*) abbuono per tara; ~ **weight** (*market., trasp.*) peso a vuoto (*d'un veicolo, d'un contenitore, ecc.*).

tare[2], *v. t.* (*market.*) tarare; calcolare la tara di (*merci, ecc.*); fare la tara a (*merci, ecc.*).

target[1], *n.* 1 bersaglio. 2 (*anche fig.*) obiettivo, meta, scopo. // **a** ~ **of economic development** (*econ.*) un obiettivo di sviluppo economico; ~ **price** (*econ., market.*) prezzo indicativo.

target[2], *v. t.* (*fig.*) porre (*qc.*) come obiettivo, porre (*qc.*) come traguardo. // to ~ **a price** (*econ.*) fissare un prezzo.

tariff[1], *n.* 1 (*comm. est., econ.*) tariffa. 2 (*tur.*) tariffa (*alberghiera*); prezzo (*fatto pagare in un albergo, ecc.*). // ~ **adjustments** (*comm. est., econ.*) movimenti tariffari; ~ **agreement** (*comm. est., econ.*) accordo tariffario; ~ **arrangement** (*comm. est., econ.*) accordo tariffario; ~ **barriers** (*comm. est., econ.*) barriere tariffarie; ~ **concessions** (*comm. est., econ.*) concessioni tariffarie; ~ **countermeasures** (*comm. est., econ.*) contromisure tariffarie; ~ **cut** (*comm. est., econ.*) riduzione tariffaria; ~ **-cutting negotiations** (*comm. est., econ.*) negoziati tendenti alla riduzione delle tariffe, negoziati tariffari; ~ **disarmament** (*comm. est., econ.*) disarmo tariffario; ~ **headings** (*comm. est., econ.*) voci tariffarie (*di bilancia commerciale, ecc.*); ~ **increases** (*comm. est., econ.*) rialzi tariffari; ~ **negotiations** (*comm. est., econ.*) negoziati tariffari; ~ **quotas** (*comm. est., econ.*) contingenti tariffari, contingenti doganali; ~ **reductions** (*comm. est., econ.*) riduzioni tariffarie; ~ **subheading** (*comm. est., econ.*) sottovoce tariffaria (*di bilancia commerciale, ecc.*); ~ **union** (*comm. est.*) unione tariffaria; ~ **wall** (*comm. est., econ.*) barriera tariffaria; ~ **war** (*comm. est., econ.*) guerra tariffaria.

tariff[2], *v. t.* (*comm. est., econ.*) «tariffare» (*merci, servizi, ecc.*); sottoporre (*merci, servizi, ecc.*) a tariffa.

tariffless, *a.* (*comm. est., econ.*) privo di tariffe, non soggetto a tariffe, liberalizzato.

task[1], *n.* compito, dovere, lavoro, incarico, mansione. // ~ **-and-bonus system** (*org. az.*) sistema di incentivi sul lavoro; ~ **bond** (*pers.*) indennità per prestazioni speciali; ~ **setting** (*org. az.*) assegnazione degli incarichi, distribuzione dei compiti; ~ **-wage** (*pers.*) salario a cottimo; ~ **-work** (*org. az.*) lavoro a cottimo.

task[2], *v. t.* assegnare un compito a (*q.*).

taste, *n.* gusto, predilezione, preferenza.

tax[1], *n.* (*fin.*) imposta, tassa, tributo, contributo, dazio. // ~ **alleviation** (*fin.*) sgravi fiscali; ~ **allowance** (*fin.*) detrazione fiscale, sgravio fiscale; ~ **and credit inducements** (*fin.*) facilitazioni fiscali e creditizie; ~ **assessment** (*fin.*) valutazione (*d'un bene*) ai fini della determinazione dell'imponibile; cartella delle tasse; ~ **at source** (*fin.*) imposta alla fonte; ~ **avoidance** (*fin.*) l'evitare di pagare le tasse; ~ **bill** (*fin.*) imposte da pagare; (*la*) «cartella» (*fam.*); ~ **book** (*fin.*) *V.* ~ **roll;** ~ **burden** (*fin.*) carico fiscale, onere fiscale; ~ **collector** (*fin.*) esattore delle imposte; ~ **collector's office** (*fin.*) agenzia delle tasse; ~ **credit** (*fin.*) credito d'imposta; ~ **cut** (*fin.*) sgravio fiscale; ~ **-deduction card** (*amm., fin.*) modulo (*compilato dal datore di lavoro*) per le detrazioni delle imposte (*da stipendi e salari*); ~ **discrimination** (*fin.*) discriminazione d'ordine fiscale; ~ **dodger** (*fin.*) evasore fiscale; ~ **dodging** (*fin.*) *V.* ~ **evasion;** ~ **drawbacks** (*fin.*) ristorni d'imposta; ~ **equity** (*fin.*) giustizia fiscale; ~ **evader** (*fin.*) evasore fiscale; ~ **evasion** (*fin.*) evasione fiscale; ~ **-exempt** (*fin.*) esente da imposta; obbligazione esente da imposta; ~ **-exempt bond** (*fin.*) obbligazione esente da imposta; ~ **-exempt general and special reserves** (*fin.*) riserve e accantonamenti esenti da imposta; ~ **-exempt security** (*fin.*) titolo (*a interesse*) esente da imposta; ~ **exemption** (*fin.*) esenzione fiscale, franchigia fiscale; ~ **expert** (*fin.*) fiscalista; ~ **facilities** (*fin.*) agevolazioni fiscali; ~ **-free** (*fin.*) esente da imposte, libero da imposte (*o* da tasse); **a** ~ **-free interest** (*fin.*) un interesse esente da imposta; ~ **harmonization** (*fin.*) armonizzazione fiscale; ~ **in kind** (*fin.*) imposta in natura; ~ **incentives** (*fin.*) incentivazioni che prevedono sgravi fiscali; ~ **incidence** incidenza fiscale; ~ **list** (*fin.*) *V.* ~ **roll;** ~ **loophole** (*fin.*) «scappatoia» offerta al contribuente (*per effetto d'un errore nella legge, o per il dichiarato proposito di concedere una facilitazione fiscale*); ~ **office** (*fin.*) ufficio (delle) imposte, fisco; ~ **on agricultural income** (*fin.*) imposta sul reddito agrario; ~ **on bonds** (*fin.*) imposta sulle obbligazioni; **taxes on consumer goods** (*fin.*) imposte di consumo; ~ **on dividend warrants** (*fin.*) (imposta) cedolare; ~ **on income** (*fin.*) imposta sul reddito; ~ **on income from land** (*fin.*) imposta sul reddito dominicale (*dei terreni*); ~ **on the income of corporate bodies** (*fin.*) imposta sul reddito delle persone giuridiche; ~ **on revenue from buildings** (*fin.*) imposta sul reddito dei fabbricati; **taxes paid** (*fin.*) onere tributario; ~ **-payer** (*fin.*) contribuente; ~ **-paying group** (*fin.*) gruppo di contribuenti; ~ **rates** (*fin.*) aliquote di imposta; ~ **receipts** (*fin.*) introiti fiscali; ~ **reduction** (*fin.*) riduzione delle imposte; ~ **reform** (*fin.*) riforma fiscale; ~ **register** (*fin.*) anagrafe tributaria; ~ **regulations** (*fin.*) regime fiscale (*o* tributario); ~ **relief** (*fin.*) abbuono fiscale, esonero fiscale, sgravio fiscale; ~ **return** (*fin.*) denuncia delle imposte (*o* delle tasse); cartella delle tasse; ~ **return form** (*fin.*) modulo della dichiarazione delle imposte (*o* delle tasse); ~ **revenue** (*fin.*) gettito fiscale; ~ **roll** (*fin.*) ruolo dei contribuenti; ~ **selling** (*fin.*) vendita concordata di titoli a fine anno (*per la determinazione di perdite e profitti ai fini della dichiarazione dell'imposta sul reddito*); ~ **treatment** (*fin.*) regime fiscale (*o* tributario).

tax[2], *v. t.* (*fin.*) tassare; imporre tributi a (*q.*); imporre tributi su (*qc.*). // to ~ **luxury articles** (*fin.*) tassare gli articoli di lusso.

taxable, *a.* (*fin.*) soggetto a imposta, imponibile; soggetto a tassazione, tassabile. *n.* **1** (*fin.*) soggetto tassabile. **2** (*fin.*) proprietà soggetta a imposta. // ~ **ability** (*fin.*) capacità contributiva; ~ **basis** (*fin.*) oggetto d'imposta; ~ **bond** (*fin.*) obbligazione tassabile; ~ **capacity** (*fin.*) capacità contributiva; ~ **company profits** (*fin.*) utili d'impresa soggetti a imposta; ~ **income** (*fin.*) reddito imponibile; ~ **property** (*fin.*) proprietà soggetta a imposta; ~ **value** (*fin.*) imponibile, valore imponibile; **the** ~ **year** (*fin.*) l'anno fiscale.

taxation, *n.* **1** (*fin.*) imposizione, tassazione. **2** (*fin.*) fiscalità, regime fiscale (*o* tributario). **3** (*fin.*) imposta, tassa. // ~ **at source** (*fin.*) ritenuta alla fonte; ~ **consultant** (*fin.*) fiscalista; ~ **in agriculture** (*fin.*) il regime fiscale in agricoltura; ~ **law** (*leg.*) diritto tributario; ~ **policy** (*fin.*) politica fiscale; **the** ~ **system** (*fin.*) il sistema tributario.

taxi, *n.* (*trasp. aut.*) taxi.

taxing authority, *n.* (*fin.*) autorità fiscale.

taxpayer, *n.* (*fin.*) contribuente. // **a** ~ **in arrears** (*fin.*) un contribuente moroso.

team, *n.* **1** (*pers.*) gruppo (*di lavoro*). **2** (*pers.*) squadra (*d'operai, ecc.*). // ~ **-work** (*org. az.*) lavoro di gruppo, lavoro d'équipe.

teamster, *n.* (*trasp. aut., USA*) camionista.

teamwork, *n.* (*org. az.*) lavoro di gruppo, lavoro d'équipe.

technical, *a.* tecnico. // ~ **assistance** (*market.*) assistenza tecnica; ~ **education** istruzione tecnica; ~ **language** linguaggio tecnico.

technician, *n.* (*pers.*) tecnico, perito.

technicist, *n. V.* **technician.**

technique, *n.* tecnica, abilità, metodo, modo.

technocracy, *n.* (*econ.*) tecnocrazia.

technocrat, *n.* (*econ.*) tecnocrate.

technologic, *a. V.* **technological.**

technological, *a.* (*org. az.*) tecnologico. // ~ **gap** (*econ., org. az.*) divario tecnologico; ~ **unemployment** (*pers.*) disoccupazione tecnologica.

technology, *n.* (*econ., org. az.*) tecnologia.

technosophe, *n.* (*econ., neol.*) «tecnosofo» (*autorevole esperto in problemi tecnologici*).

technostructure, *n.* **1** (*econ., neol.*) «tecnostruttura». **2** (*fin.*) tecnostruttura, società di grandi dimensioni.

telecamera, *n.* (*comun.*) telecamera.

telecast[1]**,** *n.* (*comun.*) trasmissione televisiva.

telecast[2]**,** *v. t.* (*pass.* e *part. pass.* **telecast**) (*comun.*) trasmettere per televisione.

telecommunications, *n. pl.* (*comun.*) telecomunicazioni.

telecontrol, *n.* (*comun.*) telecomando.

telegram[1]**,** *n.* (*comun.*) telegramma. // ~ **form** (*comun.*) modulo per telegramma; **a ~ via wireless** (*comun.*) un telegramma via radio; **as per your ~** (*comun.*) come da vostro telegramma.

telegram[2]**,** *v. t.* (*comun.*) telegrafare.

telegraph[1]**,** *n.* **1** (*comun.*) telegrafo. **2** (*comun., USA*) telegramma. // ~ **form** (*comun.*) modulo telegrafico; ~ **line** (*comun.*) linea telegrafica; ~ **-office** (*comun.*) ufficio del telegrafo; ~ **-operator** (*comun.*) telegrafista; ~ **rate** (*comun.*) tariffa per telegrammi.

telegraph[2]**,** *v. t.* **1** (*comun.*) telegrafare (*qc.*); trasmettere (*qc.*) per mezzo del telegrafo. **2** (*comun.*) telegrafare a (*q.*); mandare un telegramma a (*q.*).

telegraphic, *a.* (*comun.*) telegrafico. // ~ **address** (*comun.*) indirizzo telegrafico; ~ **code** (*comun.*) codice telegrafico; ~ **money order** (*comun., cred.*) vaglia telegrafico; ~ **transfer** (*comun., cred.*) bonifico telegrafico; ~ **transfer rates** (*fin.*) cambi telegrafici.

telegraphist, *n.* (*comun.*) telegrafista.

telegraphy, *n.* (*comun.*) telegrafia.

telematics, *n. pl.* (*col verbo al sing.*) (*comun., elab. elettr.*) telematica.

telephone[1]**,** *n.* (*comun.*) telefono. // ~ **book** (*comun., USA*) elenco degli abbonati; ~ **box** (*comun.*) cabina telefonica; ~ **call** (*comun.*) chiamata telefonica, telefonata; ~ **directory** (*comun.*) elenco telefonico, elenco degli abbonati; ~ **exchange** (*comun.*) centrale telefonica, centralino telefonico; ~ **line** (*comun.*) linea telefonica; ~ **number** (*comun.*) numero telefonico; ~ **operator** (*comun.*) telefonista, centralinista; ~ **receiver** (*comun.*) ricevitore telefonico; ~ **service** (*comun.*) telefono (*il servizio pubblico*); ~ **subscriber** (*comun.*) abbonato al telefono; ~ **system** (*o* **network**) (*comun.*) rete telefonica; **by ~** per telefono.

telephone[2]**,** *v. t.* **1** (*comun.*) telefonare (*qc.*); trasmettere (*qc.*) per telefono. **2** (*comun.*) telefonare a (*q.*); fare una telefonata a (*q.*).

telephonic, *a.* (*comun.*) telefonico. // ~ **connection** (*comun.*) collegamento telefonico.

telephonist, *n.* (*comun.*) telefonista, centralinista.

teleplay, *n.* (*comun.*) sceneggiato televisivo.

teleprinter, *n.* (*macch. uff.*) telescrivente.

teletypewriter, *n.* (*macch. uff.*) telescrivente.

teletypist, *n.* (*pers.*) operatore di telescrivente, telescriventista.

televise, *v. t.* (*comun.*) trasmettere per televisione.

television, *n.* (*comun.*) televisore. // ~ **newsreel** (*comun.*) telegiornale.

telex[1]**,** *n.* (*comun.*) telex.

telex[2]**,** *v. t.* (*comun.*) trasmettere a mezzo telex.

tell, *v. t.* (*pass.* e *part. pass.* **told**) **1** dire. **2** contare (*denaro*).

teller, *n.* **1** (*banca*) impiegato di sportello, sportellista. **2** (*banca*) cassiere. // ~ **in** (*banca*) cassiere allo sportello dei versamenti; ~ **out** (*banca*) cassiere allo sportello dei pagamenti.

tel quel, *locuz. a.* (*fin.*) «tel quel», tale quale. // ~ **quotation** (*fin.*) *V.* ~ **rate;** ~ **rate** (*fin.*) corso «tel quel», corso «tale quale».

temper, *v. t.* **1** temprare. **2** temperare, attenuare, frenare.

temporary, *a.* **1** transitorio, passeggero. **2** (*amm., pers.*) interinale, interino. *n.* (*pers.*) avventizio, supplente. // ~ **account** (*rag.*) conto provvisorio; ~ **admission** (*comm. est.*) importazione temporanea; ~ **annuity** (*leg.*) rendita temporanea; ~ **balance** (*rag.*) bilancio provvisorio; ~ **combine** (*fin.*) accordo temporaneo; ~ **exports** (*comm. est.*) merci esportate temporaneamente; ~ **laws** (*leg.*) disposizioni transitorie; ~ **office** (*amm.*) interinato; ~ **post** (*pers.*) supplenza; ~ **staff** (*pers.*) avventizi, impiegati non di ruolo; ~ **substitution** (*pers.*) supplenza; ~ **warehousing** (*dog.*) custodia doganale temporanea.

ten, *a.* e *n.* dieci. *n.* 1 (*fam.*) biglietto da dieci sterline. 2 (*fam., USA*) biglietto da dieci dollari. // ~ **-cent** (*fam., USA*) dozzinale, meschino; ~ **-cent store** (*market., USA*) grandi magazzini che vendono solo articoli al prezzo di cinque o dieci dollari.

tenancy, *n.* 1 (*leg.*) affittanza, affitto, locazione. 2 (*leg.*) durata dell'affitto, durata della locazione. 3 (*leg.*) proprietà data in affitto. // ~ **at sufferance** (*leg.*) locazione rinnovata tacitamente; ~ **at will** (*leg.*) affitto a tempo indeterminato (*con diritto di disdetta da parte del locatore*); ~ **for life** (*leg.*) usufrutto perpetuo.

tenant[1], *n.* 1 (*leg.*) affittuario, locatario, inquilino, conduttore (*d'un appartamento*). 2 (*leg.*) affittuario, fittavolo, conduttore (*d'un fondo*). // ~ **-farmer** (*leg.*) fittavolo; ~ **right** (*leg.*) diritto d'affittanza.

tenant[2], *v. t.* (*leg.*) tenere in affitto, occupare come inquilino.

tenantry, *n.* 1 (*leg.*) affittanza, durata dell'affitto, durata della locazione. 2 (*leg.*) (gli) inquilini (*d'una casa*).

tendency, *n.* 1 tendenza, inclinazione, propensione. 2 (*econ., fin.*) andamento, evoluzione, «dinamica». // **a ~ for business conditions to weaken** (*econ.*) un indebolimento congiunturale; **the ~ of the money market** (*fin.*) l'andamento del mercato monetario.

tender[1], *n.* 1 (*cred.*) offerta (*di pagamento d'un debito, ecc.*). 2 (*econ.*) denaro, moneta, valuta. 3 (*fin., USA*) offerta pubblica d'acquisto (*di titoli, ecc.*). 4 (*leg.*) offerta reale. 5 (*leg.*) offerta d'appalto, gara d'appalto, licitazione. 6 (*leg.*) capitolato (*d'appalto*). 7 (*trasp. ferr.*) «tender».

tender[2], *v. t.* 1 (*cred.*) offrire (*denaro, ecc.*) in pagamento d'un debito. 2 (*fin., USA*) offrire (*titoli, ecc.: al pubblico*). *v. i.* 1 (*leg.*) fare un'offerta. 2 (*leg.*) fare un'offerta per un contratto, concorrere a un appalto. // to ~ **bail** (*leg.*) offrire garanzia; to ~ **for a contract** (*leg.*) fare un'offerta per un contratto; to ~ **one's resignation** (*pers.*) presentare le dimissioni.

tenemental, *a.* (*leg.*) d'affitto, d'enfiteusi.

tenementary, *a. V.* **tenemental.**

tenner, *n.* 1 (*fam.*) banconota da dieci sterline. 2 (*fam., USA*) banconota da dieci dollari.

tenor, *n.* 1 andamento, corso. 2 (*cred.*) (*d'una cambiale*) termine (*periodo di tempo che va dalla data d'emissione — o d'accettazione — a quella di scadenza*).

tentative, *a.* di prova, sperimentale. // ~ **specification** (*leg.*) bozza di capitolato.

tenth, *a.* e *n.* decimo.

tenure, *n.* 1 (*leg.*) occupazione, possesso, tenuta. 2 (*leg.*) diritto di possesso. 3 (*leg.*) durata (*d'un possesso*).

term, *n.* 1 termine. 2 trimestre; periodo di tempo, durata. 3 termine, parola. 4 (*ass.*) durata. 5 (*mat.*) termine. 6 **terms,** *pl.* accordo, patto, patti. 7 **terms,** *pl.* (*fin., market.*) clausole, condizioni. 8 **terms,** *pl.* (*market., tur.*) prezzo, tariffa, tariffe. // **the terms agreed upon** (*leg.*) le condizioni contrattuali; ~ **day** (*cred., leg.*) giorno di scadenza; ~ **insurance** (*ass.*) assicurazione «temporanea» (*in caso di morte*); **the terms of a contract** (*leg.*) le condizioni contrattuali; **terms of delivery** (*market.*) condizioni di consegna; **the terms of a geometrical progression** (*mat.*) i termini d'una progressione geometrica; ~ **of office** (*leg.*) periodo di permanenza in carica; **terms of payment** (*market.*) condizioni di pagamento; **the terms of repayment of a loan** (*cred.*) le condizioni di rimborso d'un prestito; **terms of sale** (*market.*) condizioni di vendita; **terms of trade** (*comm. est.*) ragione di scambio; **terms of underwriting** (*fin.*) clausole di sottoscrizione; **the terms of a will** (*leg.*) le clausole d'un testamento; ~ **policy** (*ass., USA*) polizza assicurativa (*su beni di proprietà*) a tariffa ridotta (*e per un periodo dai tre ai cinque anni*); ~ **rate** (*ass., USA*) tariffa ridotta (*da applicarsi a una «~ policy»*); ~ **settlement** (*Borsa*) liquidazione periodica; **under the terms** (*leg.*) secondo le clausole (*d'un contratto*).

terminable, *a.* 1 terminabile, cui si può porre termine. 2 (*leg.*) (*di contratto*) a termine. // **a ~ bond** (*fin.*) un'obbligazione a termine, un'obbligazione riscattabile; ~ **contracts** (*leg.*) rendita annua a termine fisso.

terminal, *a.* 1 terminale, estremo, finale. 2 trimestrale; periodico. *n.* 1 terminale. 2 (*trasp.*) città capolinea (*di servizio d'autotrasporti, ecc.*). 3 (*trasp. aer.*) terminal (*aerostazione urbana collegata all'aeroporto con mezzi di trasporto*). 4 (*trasp. ferr.*) capolinea, stazione di testa. // ~ **accounts** (*rag.*) rendiconto trimestrale; ~ **market** (*market.*) borsa-mercato (*dei prodotti agricoli*); borsa-mercato (*del bestiame*); ~ **payments** (*rag.*) pagamenti periodici; ~ **reserve** (*ass.*) riserva netta finale (*alla chiusura dell'esercizio*); ~ **station** (*trasp. ferr.*) capolinea, stazione di testa.

terminate[1], *a.* limitato, finito.

terminate[2], *v. t.* 1 porre termine a, finire, concludere. 2 (*leg.*) rescindere. // to ~ **sb.'s**

employment (*pers.*) rescindere il contratto d'impiego con q.

termination, *n.* 1 terminazione, conclusione, fine. 2 (*leg.*) rescissione. // **the ~ of a contract** (*leg.*) la rescissione d'un contratto; **the ~ of the insured risk** (*ass.*) la fine del rischio assicurato; **the ~ of a lease** (*leg.*) la cessazione d'una locazione.

terminus, *n.* (*trasp. ferr.*) capolinea, stazione di testa.

termor, *n.* 1 (*leg.*) usufruttuario a termine. 2 (*leg.*) usufruttuario a vita.

territorial, *a.* territoriale. // **~ jurisdiction** (*leg.*) giurisdizione territoriale; **~ law** (*leg.*) diritto territoriale; **~ sea** (*leg., trasp. mar.*) mare territoriale; **~ waters** (*leg., trasp. mar.*) acque territoriali.

territoriality, *n.* territorialità.

territory, *n.* 1 territorio. 2 (*market.*) distretto, zona. // **~ to which the tax applies** (*fin.*) territorialità dell'imposta.

test[1], *n.* esame, prova, esperimento, saggio, saggiatura, test. // **~ campaign** (*pubbl.*) campagna di prova; **~ case** (*leg.*) causa legale che serve a creare un precedente; **~ check** (*amm.*) controllo particolare; **~ expert** (*pers.*) testista (*esperto di prove psicologiche per valutare le capacità dei candidati a un posto di lavoro*); **~ market** (*market., stat.*) mercato di prova; **~ marketing** (*market.*) marketing di prova; **~ of clerical aptitude** (*pers.*) test d'attitudine al lavoro di ufficio; **~ of manual dexterity** (*pers.*) test di destrezza; **~ track** (*trasp. aut.*) pista di prova.

test[2], *v. t.* 1 esaminare, mettere alla prova, provare, saggiare. 2 (*market., pers.*) sottoporre a un test; testare (*neol.*).

testament, *n.* (*leg.*) testamento.

testamental, *a.* (*leg.*) testamentario.

testamentary, *a.* (*leg.*) testamentario. // **~ capacity** (*leg.*) capacità a testare; **~ donation** (*leg.*) donazione testamentaria; **~ heir** (*leg.*) erede testamentario; **~ succession** (*leg.*) successione testamentaria.

testate, *a.* 1 (*leg.*) (*di persona deceduta*) che ha fatto testamento. 2 (*leg.*) (*di bene, ecc.*) nominato nel testamento. *n.* (*leg.*) testatore.

testator, *n.* (*leg.*) testatore.

testatrix, *n.* (*pl.* **testatrices**) (*leg.*) testatrice.

testifiable, *a.* (*leg.*) testimoniabile, attestabile.

testify, *v. t.* 1 (*leg.*) testimoniare, deporre. 2 (*leg.*) attestare, esser prova di. // to **~ before a committee** (*leg.*) deporre davanti a una commissione.

testimonial, *n.* 1 (*leg.*) attestato di buona condotta. 2 (*pers.*) certificato di servizio, benservito, referenza. 3 (*pers.*) lettera di presentazione. // **~ evidence** (*leg.*) prova testimoniale.

testimony, *n.* 1 (*leg.*) testimonianza, deposizione. 2 (*leg.*) attestazione, dichiarazione, prova. // **in ~ whereof** (*leg.*) in fede di ciò.

testing, *n.* collaudo. // **~ department** (*org. az.*) reparto collaudi.

text, *n.* testo. // **the ~ of an insurance policy** (*ass.*) il testo d'una polizza d'assicurazione.

textile, *a.* tessile. *n.* **textiles,** *pl.* (*econ.*) prodotti tessili, tessili. // **~ worker** (*pers.*) operaio tessile, tessile.

thank, *v. t.* ringraziare. // **thanking you beforehand** ringraziandovi anticipatamente; **thanking you in advance** ringraziandovi anticipatamente.

thankful, *a.* grato.

thankfulness, *n.* gratitudine.

thanks, *n. pl.* ringraziamenti, ringraziamento. // **thanks!** grazie!; **~ to** grazie a, mercè.

theft, *n.* (*leg.*) furto, ladrocinio. // **~ insurance** (*ass.*) assicurazione contro i furti; **~ risk** (*ass.*) rischio di furto.

theftproof, *a.* a prova di furto. // **~ lock** serratura a prova di scasso; **~ strongbox** (*attr. uff.*) cassaforte a prova di furto.

theory, *n.* teoria, dottrina. // **the ~ of the business cycle** (*econ.*) la teoria del ciclo economico; **the ~ of comparative costs** (*econ.*) la teoria dei costi comparati; **the ~ of monopolistic competition** (*econ.*) la teoria della concorrenza monopolistica, la teoria dei monopoli; **the ~ of prices** (*econ.*) la teoria dei prezzi; **the ~ of probability** (*mat., stat.*) la teoria della probabilità; **the ~ of surplus value** (*econ.*) la teoria del plusvalore; **the ~ of taxation** (*econ., fin.*) la teoria delle imposte; **the theories of the trade cycle** (*econ.*) la teoria del ciclo economico; **the theories of value** (*econ.*) le teorie del valore; **the theories of wages** (*econ.*) le teorie dei salari.

thick, *a.* fitto.

thief, *n.* (*pl.* **thieves**) ladro.

thieving, *a.* disonesto.

thin, *a.* 1 sottile, esile, magro. 2 (*market.*) (*di mercato*) caratterizzato dalla scarsità dell'offerta. // **a ~ market** (*fin., market.*) un mercato ristretto.

thing, *n.* 1 cosa, oggetto. 2 (*market., pubbl.*) moda, grido. // **the ~ insured** (*ass.*) la cosa assicurata; **things personal** (*leg.*) beni mobili; **things real** (*leg.*) beni immobili.

think, *v. t.* (*pass.* e *part. pass.* **thought**) credere, considerare, giudicare.

third, *a.* terzo. *n.* **1** (*mat.*) terzo. **2** (*trasp., fam.*) terza (classe). // ~ **class** (*trasp.*) terza (classe); ~ **-class** (*market.*) di qualità scadente; (*trasp.*) di terza (classe); **a ~ -class carriage** (*trasp. ferr.*) una carrozza di terza (classe); ~ **cover** (*giorn.*) terza di copertina; ~ **mortgage** (*leg.*) ipoteca di terzo grado; ~ **of exchange** (*cred.*) terza di cambio; **a ~ party** (*leg.*) una terza persona, un terzo; ~ **-party auto insurance** (*ass., trasp. aut.*) Responsabilità Civile Auto (*RCA*); ~ **-party insurance** (*ass.*) assicurazione contro terzi, assicurazione di responsabilità civile (*RC*); ~ **-party risks** (*ass.*) rischi contro terzi; ~ **shift** (*pers.*) turno di notte; **the ~ world** il terzo mondo.

thirty, *a.* e *n.* trenta. // **at ~ days after date** (*cred.*) a trenta giorni (dalla) data.

this, *a.* e *pron.* (*pl.* **these**) questo. // ~ **day** oggi; ~ **day month** oggi a un mese; ~ **day week** oggi a otto.

thorough, *a.* **1** completo, intero. **2** profondo. // ~ **changes in the economic structure** (*econ.*) mutamenti radicali nella struttura economica.

thoroughfare, *n.* strada, via. // «**no ~**» (*trasp. aut.*) «circolazione vietata».

thousand, *n.* mille. // (*ingl.*) **one ~ billions** quadrilione; (*ingl.*) **one ~ millions** bilione, miliardo.

thread, *n.* filo.

three, *a.* e *n.* tre. // **the ~ C's** (*market., pubbl.*) le tre C (*car, colour TV, air conditioning*); ~ **-course system** (*econ.*) *V.* ~ **-field system**; ~ **-field system** (*econ.*) sistema (*agricolo*) a tre colture (*alternate*).

threshold, *n.* soglia. // ~ **price** (*econ.*) prezzo d'entrata; to **be below the ~ of VAT** (*fin.*) essere esenti dall'IVA.

thrift, *n.* economia, parsimonia, risparmio. // ~ **account** (*banca*) conto di deposito a risparmio; ~ **shop** (*market.*) negozio d'articoli usati; ~ **society** (*fin.*) consorzio di risparmiatori.

thrifty, *a.* economo, parsimonioso.

thrive, *v. i.* (*pass.* **throve,** *part. pass.* **thriven** o *reg.*) fiorire (*fig.*).

thriving, *a.* prosperoso, fiorente, florido. // **a ~ business** un'azienda florida; **a ~ tourist centre** un fiorente centro turistico.

through[1], *avv.* e *prep.* **1** da parte a parte. **2** completamente. **3** per il tramite di, per mezzo di, mediante. **4** (*trasp.*) direttamente. // ~ **official channels** (*leg.*) per tramite gerarchico, per via gerarchica; ~ **train** (*trasp. ferr.*) treno diretto; to **be ~** (*comun.*) essere in comunicazione (telefonica), essere in linea; to **go ~** esaminare, controllare, verificare.

through[2], *a. attr.* diretto. // ~ **bill of lading** (*trasp. mar.*) polizza di carico diretta, polizza di carico cumulativa; **a ~ carriage** (*trasp. ferr.*) una vettura diretta; ~ **freight** (*trasp. mar.*) nolo a forfait; **a ~ passenger** (*trasp. ferr.*) un viaggiatore di (treno) diretto; ~ **rates** (*trasp.*) tariffe cumulative, tariffe per trasporti in servizio cumulativo; ~ **ticket** (*trasp.*) biglietto cumulativo; **a ~ train** (*trasp. ferr.*) un (treno) diretto.

throughput, *n.* **1** (*econ., USA*) produzione. **2** (*elab. elettr.*) «output». **3** (*org. az.*) quantità di materia prima messa in lavorazione (*in una certa unità di tempo*).

throw[1], *n.* getto, lancio.

throw[2], *v. t.* (*pass.* **threw,** *part. pass.* **thrown**) **1** scagliare. **2** (*anche fig.*) buttare, gettare, lanciare. // to ~ **away** gettar via; to ~ **down one's tools** deporre gli attrezzi; (*fam.*) scioperare; to ~ **good money after bad** buttare altro denaro per tentare di ricuperare quello perduto; to ~ **st. into the bargain** dare qc. per soprammercato; to ~ **out** buttar fuori, respingere; to ~ **sb. out of employment** (*pers.*) lasciare q. senza lavoro; licenziare q. (*dal lavoro*); to **be thrown out of work** (*pers.*) rimanere senza lavoro, restare disoccupato.

throwaway, *n.* (*pubbl., USA*) foglietto pubblicitario, manifestino, «volantino».

throwing, *n.* getto, lancio.

thumb, *n.* pollice.

tick[1], *n.* spunta (*segno usato per operazioni di controllo di conti, prospetti contabili, ecc.*).

tick[2] **(off),** *v. t.* spuntare (*una cifra, una voce, ecc.*); fare una spunta a fianco di (*una cifra, una voce, ecc.*). // to ~ **off invoices** (*rag.*) spuntare le fatture; to ~ **off the items in a catalogue** (*market.*) spuntare le voci d'un catalogo.

ticker, *n.* (*Borsa*) teleborsa (*strumento elettronico che registra e trasmette istantaneamente, a tutto il mondo, i prezzi e il volume delle contrattazioni in titoli*).

ticket[1], *n.* **1** biglietto. **2** biglietto di visita. **3** etichetta. **4** scontrino, tessera. **5** (*market.*) cartellino (*del prezzo*). **6** (*pers.*) cartellino. **7** (*trasp.*) biglietto. **8** (*trasp. aut., USA*) multa. // ~ **-agent** titolare d'agenzia per la vendita di biglietti; ~ **-collector** (*trasp. ferr.*) bigliettaio, controllore; ~ **-day** (*Borsa*) vigilia di liquidazione; ~ **inspection** (*trasp.*) controllo dei biglietti; ~ **-office** (*trasp. ferr.*) biglietteria; ~ **-window** (*trasp.*) sportello (*di biglietteria*).

ticket[2], *v. t.* 1 (*market.*) apporre il cartellino (*del prezzo*) su (*articoli, ecc.*). 2 (*trasp. aut., USA*) multare.

tickler, *n.* (*attr. uff.*) scadenzario.

tidal, *a.* (*trasp. mar.*) soggetto alla marea. // ~ **basin** (*trasp. mar.*) bacino di marea; ~ **current** (*trasp. mar., USA*) *V.* ~ **stream;** ~ **dock** (*trasp. mar.*) *V.* ~ **basin;** ~ **harbour** (*trasp. mar.*) porto accessibile soltanto con l'alta marea; ~ **stream** (*trasp. mar.*) corrente di marea; ~ **waters** (*trasp. mar.*) acque soggette a marea.

tide, *n.* (*trasp. mar.*) marea. // ~ **indicator** (*trasp. mar.*) indicatore di marea; ~ **-mark** (*trasp. mar.*) limite di marea; ~ **-signal** (*trasp. mar.*) segnale di marea; ~ **-waiter** (*trasp. mar.*) doganiere (*che sale a bordo*).

tie[1], *n.* 1 (*anche fig.*) legame, nodo. 2 (*fig.*) vincolo, impedimento. // ~ **-in sale** (*market.*) vendita (*d'un articolo, effettuata soltanto se*) abbinata (*alla vendita d'un altro prodotto*); ~ **-up** (*sind.*) cessazione del lavoro (*per sciopero, serrata, ecc.*); (*trasp.*) arresto del traffico, ingorgo.

tie[2], *v. t.* 1 (*anche fig.*) legare, annodare. 2 (*fig.*) vincolare, impegnare. // to ~ **sb. down to a contract** (*leg.*) impegnare q. con un contratto; to ~ **up money** (*comm., fin.*) immobilizzare (*o* impegnare) denaro; to ~ **up a parcel** (*market.*) legare un pacco; to ~ **up properties** (*leg.*) vincolare proprietà.

tight, *a.* serrato, chiuso. // ~ **credit** (*fin.*) credito difficile; ~ **money** (*fin.*) denaro scarso; **a policy of** ~ **credit** (*o* **money**) (*econ., fin.*) una politica che provoca una stretta creditizia.

tighten, *v. t.* serrare. *v. i.* stringersi, serrarsi. // to ~ **one's belt** fare economie; to ~ **up** inasprire; to ~ **up restrictions** (*econ.*) inasprire le restrizioni.

tightening-up, *n.* inasprimento.

till[1], *n.* 1 (*fig.*) contante, denaro contante. 2 (*market.*) cassa. // ~ **money** (*market.*) denaro in cassa.

till[2], *v. t.* 1 (*market.*) mettere (*denaro*) in cassa. 2 (*market.*) incassare (*denaro*).

till[3], *prep.* (*di tempo*) fino a.

tiller, *n.* (*trasp. mar.*) sbarra, barra del timone.

tilt, *v. t.* inclinare.

time, *n.* 1 tempo; epoca, periodo; durata. 2 ora; (*ingl.*) ora prevista dalla legge per la chiusura (*d'un pub*). 3 momento. 4 (*comun.*) numero delle «unità» (*d'una conversazione telefonica*). 5 (*trasp.*) orario. // ~ **bargain** (*Borsa*) vendita allo scoperto; mercato a termine; ~ **bill** (*cred.*) cambiale a termine; (*trasp.*) orario (*ferroviario, ecc.*); ~ **-book** (*pers.*) registro delle ore di lavoro, registro di presenza; ~ **buying** (*comun., pubbl.*) acquisto di tempo (*per la pubblicità radiotelevisiva*); ~ **card** (*pers.*) cartellino di presenza; ~ **charter** (*trasp. mar.*) noleggio a tempo, nolo a tempo; ~ **charter party** (*trasp. aer., trasp. mar.*) contratto di nolo a tempo; ~ **clerk** (*pers.*) controllore delle ore di lavoro; ~ **clock** (*pers.*) orologio «marcatempo»; ~ **deposit** (*banca*) deposito vincolato; ~ **draft** (*cred.*) tratta a termine; ~ **freight** (*trasp. mar.*) nolo a tempo; ~ **limit** (*leg.*) termine, termine ultimo; ~ **limit for appearance** (*leg.*) termine di comparizione (*in giudizio*); ~ **loan** (*cred.*) prestito a termine; ~ **note** (*cred.*) effetto a termine; **the** ~ **of payment** (*cred.*) il termine di scadenza, la scadenza; ~ **payment** (*cred.*) pagamento dilazionato; (*market.*) pagamento rateale; ~ **-penalty clause** (*trasp. mar.*) clausola del ritardo; ~ **policy** (*ass. mar.*) polizza a tempo; ~ **purchase** (*market.*) acquisto (con pagamento) rateale; ~ **sale** (*market.*) vendita (con pagamento) «a respiro»; ~ **saving** (*org. az.*) risparmio di tempo; ~ **-saving** che fa risparmiare tempo; ~ **-sharing** (*comun.*) servizio (*telefonico*) d'elaborazione elettronica delle informazioni; ~ **-sheet** (*pers.*) foglio di presenza; ~ **signal** (*comun.*) segnale orario; ~ **study engineer** (*o* **expert**) (*pers.*) cronotecnico; ~ **-table** (*trasp.*) orario (*ferroviario, ecc.*); ~ **ticket** (*pers.*) cartellino di presenza; ~ **-work** (*org. az.*) lavoro (retribuito) a ore, lavoro «in economia»; ~ **-worker** (*pers.*) operaio (retribuito) a ore; ~ **zone** fuso orario; **at the same** ~ insieme; **behind** ~ in ritardo.

timekeeper, *n.* (*pers.*) controllore delle ore di lavoro; cronometrista.

timekeeping, *n.* (*org. az.*) rilevamento dei tempi (*di lavoro*).

timetable, *n. V.* **time-table.**

tin[1], *n.* scatola (*di latta*).

tin[2], *v. t.* inscatolare (*cibarie*).

tinned, *a.* in scatola. // ~ **goods** (*market.*) scatolame.

tinning, *n.* inscatolamento.

tire, *n.* (*trasp. aut.*) «gomma». // ~ **-chains** (*trasp. aut.*) catene da neve.

tissue paper, *n.* (*attr. uff.*) carta velina, velina.

tithe, *n.* (*fin., leg.*) decima.

title, *n.* 1 (*anche fig.*) titolo. 2 (*fig.*) diritto, merito. 3 (*nella corrispondenza, nei moduli, ecc.*) appellativo (Mr, Mrs, Miss e Ms: *premesso a un cognome o a un nome e cognome*). // ~

-deed (*leg.*) documento comprovante un diritto di proprietà; **the ~ of gold** (*econ.*) il titolo dell'oro (*espresso in carati*).

tobacconist's (shop), *n.* rivendita di tabacchi, privativa.

today, *avv.* e *n.* oggi, oggigiorno. // **~ week** oggi a otto.

todayish, *a.* 1 (*fam.*) d'oggi, del giorno d'oggi. 2 (*fam.*) corrente, alla moda, moderno.

together, *avv.* insieme.

token, *n.* 1 simbolo. 2 contrassegno, contromarca, gettone. // **~ coins** (*econ.*) monete divisionarie; **~ currency** (*econ.*) circolante divisionario; **~ money** (*econ.*) moneta simbolica; **~ payment** (*cred.*) pagamento simbolico.

tolerance, *n.* 1 tolleranza, indulgenza. 2 (*market.*) tolleranza. // **~ for loss of weight** (*market.*) tolleranza per diminuzione di peso; **~ of weight** (*market.*) tolleranza di peso.

toll[1], *n.* 1 (*fin.*) dazio, imposta. 2 (*trasp.*) pedaggio. // **~ -bar** (*trasp.*) barriera di pedaggio; **~ -call** (*comun.*) telefonata interurbana; **~ collector** (*fin.*) esattore (*di dazi, imposte, ecc.*); **~ -gate** casello daziario; **~ -gates** cinta daziaria (*d'una città*); **~ -house** casello daziario; **~ -line** (*comun.*) linea interurbana.

toll[2], *v. t.* e *i.* 1 (*fin.*) esigere un tributo. 2 (*trasp.*) far pagare un pedaggio. 3 (*trasp.*) pagare un pedaggio.

tollage, *n.* 1 (*fin.*) dazio, pagamento di dazio, riscossione di dazio. 2 (*trasp.*) pedaggio, pagamento di pedaggio, riscossione di pedaggio.

tollbooth, *n.* (*trasp.*) ufficio del dazio, esattoria del dazio.

toller, *n. V.* **toll collector.**

tollgate, *n.* (*trasp. aut.*) casello (*d'autostrada, ecc.*).

tollhouse, *n.* (*trasp. aut.*) casello (*d'autostrada, ecc.*).

tomorrow, *avv.* domani.

ton, *n.* 1 (= **long ton**) tonnellata (*misura di peso pari a kg 1.016 circa*). 2 (= **metric ton**) tonnellata metrica. 3 (*USA*) (= **short ton**) tonnellata (*misura di peso pari a kg 907 circa*). // **~ burden** (*trasp. mar.*) tonnellata di portata (*unità di misura della portata d'una nave mercantile*); **~ capacity** (*trasp. mar.*) tonnellata di stazza; **~ dead weight** (*trasp. mar.*) tonnellata di portata lorda; **~ displacement** (*trasp. mar.*) tonnellata di dislocamento.

tongue, *n.* 1 lingua. 2 (*di scarpa*) linguetta.

tonnage, *n.* 1 (*trasp. mar.*) tonnellaggio. 2 (*trasp. mar.*) stazza, stazzatura. 3 (*trasp. mar.*) naviglio mercantile (*d'una nazione o d'un porto, nel complesso*). // **~ admeasurement** (*trasp. mar.*) stazzatura; **~ broken up** (*trasp. mar.*) tonnellaggio demolito; **~ dues** (*trasp. mar.*) diritti di tonnellaggio; diritti di stazza; **~ -measurer** (*trasp. mar.*) stazzatore; **~ rules** (*trasp. mar.*) regole di stazzatura; **~ tax** (*trasp. mar.*) tassa sulla stazza; **~ under deck** (*trasp. mar.*) tonnellaggio sotto il ponte.

tool, *n.* 1 arnese, attrezzo. 2 (*anche fig.*) strumento. 3 (*org. az.*) (= **machine tool**) macchina utensile. // **~ -room** (*org. az.*) sala (degli) attrezzi.

top[1], *n.* 1 sommità, vetta, apice, vertice. 2 (la) parte scelta, (il) meglio. *a. attr.* 1 che sta in cima. 2 primo, principale, massimo. 3 (*market.*) di prima qualità, di prima scelta, eccellente. // **~ executive** (*amm.*) alto dirigente; **~ -level** ad alto livello, di grande importanza, d'ottima qualità; **~ -level management** (*amm.*) alta dirigenza; **~ management** (*amm.*) alta dirigenza; **~ manager** (*amm.*) alto dirigente; **the ~ of the market** (*fin., market.*) l'apice del mercato (*il momento, cioè, in cui le quotazioni hanno raggiunto il livello più alto*); **~ prices** (*market.*) prezzi massimi; **~ priority** (*org. az.*) precedenza assoluta; **~ rate** (*fin.*) tasso (*d'interesse*) praticato (*dalle banche*) ai clienti meno favoriti; **~ -selling** (*market.*) più venduto; (che è) in cima alle vendite.

top[2], *v. t.* sorpassare.

topic, *n.* argomento, soggetto.

tort, *n.* (*leg.*) atto illecito, reato (*civile*).

total[1], *a.* totale, intero, completo, complessivo. *n.* totale, somma totale. // **~ account** (*rag.*) conto collettivo; **~ assets** (*rag.*) attività totali, totale delle attività; **~ balance** (*rag.*) saldo totale; **~ cost** (*rag.*) costo complessivo; **~ current accounts** (*fin., rag.*) totale partite correnti; **~ customs exemption** (*dog.*) esenzione doganale totale; **~ disability** (*pers.*) invalidità totale; **~ loss** (*ass. mar.*) perdita totale; **~ loss with abandonment** (*ass. mar.*) perdita totale con abbandono (*della nave*); **~ utility** (*econ.*) utilità totale.

total[2], *v. t.* 1 sommare. 2 ammontare a, raggiungere il numero di. *v. i.* (*di macchina calcolatrice*) calcolare i totali (*fino a un certo numero*).

touch[1], *n.* contatto, relazione, rapporto. // **a ~ -and-go business** un affare incerto, un affare rischioso; **~ -down** (*trasp. aer.*) appoggio (*del carrello*).

touch[2], *v. t.* toccare. // to **~ at a port** (*trasp. mar.*) far scalo a un porto; to **~ bottom** (*fin.*) (*di prezzi, ecc.*) raggiungere il (livello) minimo;

to ~ **down** (*trasp. aer.*) atterrare; to ~ **up** (*pubbl.*) ritoccare.

tour[1], *n.* (*tur.*) giro, gita, escursione, viaggio.

tour[2], *v. i.* (*tur.*) viaggiare, fare una gita. *v. t.* (*tur.*) viaggiare in (*un Paese*). // to ~ **sb.** guidare q. in visita (*a qc.*).

touring, *n.* (*tur.*) turismo. *a. attr.* (*tur.*) da turismo. // **a** ~ **car** (*tur.*) un'auto da turismo.

tourism, *n.* (*tur.*) turismo.

tourist, *n.* (*tur.*) turista. *a. attr.* (*tur.*) turistico, di turismo. // **a** ~ **agency** (*tur.*) un'agenzia turistica; ~ **class** (*trasp.*) classe turistica, classe economica, seconda classe; ~ **court** (*tur.*) motel; ~ **expenditures** (*fin.*) spese per il turismo (*partita «invariabile» della bilancia dei pagamenti*); **the** ~ **industry** (*econ.*) il turismo; ~ **office** (*tur.*) ufficio turistico; **a** ~ **ticket** (*trasp., tur.*) un biglietto turistico.

tout[1], *n.* sollecitatore d'ordinazioni, propagandista, piazzista.

tout[2], *v. i.* sollecitare ordinazioni, andare in cerca di clienti, fare il propagandista, fare il piazzista, fare la piazza.

touter, *n. V.* **tout**[1].

tow[1], *n.* (*trasp. aut., trasp. mar.*) il rimorchiare, l'essere rimorchiato. // ~ **-barge** (*trasp. mar.*) chiatta; ~ **car** (*trasp. aut.*) carro attrezzi, autogru; ~ **-rope** (*trasp. aut.*) cavo di traino; ~ **truck** (*trasp. aut.*) *V.* ~ **car.**

tow[2], *v. t.* **1** (*trasp. aut., trasp. mar.*) trainare. **2** (*trasp. mar.*) alare.

towage, *n.* **1** (*trasp. aut., trasp. mar.*) spese di rimorchio. **2** (*trasp. mar.*) alaggio. // ~ **fees** (*trasp. aut., trasp. mar.*) spese di rimorchio; ~ **service** (*trasp. aut., trasp. mar.*) servizio di rimorchio.

towaway zone, *n.* (*trasp. aut.*) zona (*di divieto di sosta*) dalla quale le automobili vengono rimosse (*con autogru, ecc.*).

towing, *n.* (*trasp. mar.*) alaggio.

town, *n.* città. // ~ **clerk** segretario comunale; ~ **council** consiglio comunale; ~ **councillor** consigliere comunale; ~ **-lights** (*trasp. aut.*) luci da città, luci di posizione; ~ **mayor** sindaco (*d'una città*); ~ **-traveller** (*pers.*) piazzista.

trace, *v. t.* (*anche fig.*) rintracciare, trovare.

track[1], *n.* **1** orma. **2** (*trasp. ferr.*) binario.

track[2], *v. t.* **1** (*trasp. ferr.*) (*di vagone*) avere uno scartamento di. **2** (*trasp. mar.*) alare (*un natante*).

trackage, *n. V.* **towage.**

traction, *n.* (*trasp.*) trazione.

tractor, *n.* trattore.

trade[1], *n.* **1** commercio, traffico, traffici, scambi. **2** (*econ.*) industria. **3** (*market.*) clientela, clienti. **4** (*org. az.*) azienda, ditta. **5** (*pers.*) lavoro, mestiere, occupazione. **6 the trade** (*collett.*) gli esercenti. // ~ **acceptance** (*cred.*) cambiale (*o* tratta) recante l'accettazione del debitore; ~ **agreement** (*comm. est.*) accordo commerciale, trattato commerciale; ~ **area** (*market.*) zona commerciale; ~ **balance** (*econ.*) bilancia commerciale; ~ **barriers** (*comm. est.*) barriere commerciali, barriere al libero scambio; ~ **bill** (*cred.*) cambiale (*o* tratta) commerciale; ~ **by barter** (*econ.*) commercio di scambio; ~ **channels** (*market.*) canali di distribuzione (*dei prodotti*); **the** ~ **circles** gli ambienti commerciali; ~ **cycle** (*econ.*) ciclo economico; ~ **deficit** (*econ.*) deficit della bilancia commerciale; ~ **discount** (*market.*) sconto commerciale; ~ **dispute** (*sind.*) vertenza sindacale; ~ **fair** (*market., pubbl.*) fiera commerciale, fiera campionaria; ~ **gap** (*econ.*) disavanzo della bilancia commerciale; ~ **guild** (*sind.*) sindacato; ~ **-in** articolo accettato (*dal venditore*) in pagamento (*parziale o totale*) d'un acquisto; ~ **liberalization** (*econ.*) liberalizzazione dei traffici; ~ **-mark** (*leg.*) marchio di fabbrica; to ~ **-mark** (*leg.*) depositare il marchio di fabbrica di (*un articolo, ecc.*); apporre un marchio di fabbrica su (*un articolo, ecc.*); ~ **-mark infringement** (*leg.*) violazione di marchio di fabbrica, uso illecito dell'altrui marchio di fabbrica; ~ **-name** (*leg.*) nome commerciale (*d'una ditta*); nome depositato (*d'un prodotto*); to ~ **-name** (*leg.*) dare un nome commerciale a (*una ditta*); dare un nome a (*un prodotto*); ~ **policy** (*econ.*) politica commerciale; ~ **practice** usi in materia commerciale; ~ **price** (*market.*) prezzo al rivenditore; ~ **relations** rapporti commerciali; ~ **report** bollettino commerciale; ~ **route** (*trasp. mar.*) rotta commerciale; ~ **talks** (*comm. est.*) negoziati commerciali; ~ **treaty** (*comm. est.*) trattato commerciale; ~ **-union** (*sind.*) sindacato; **trades-union** (*sind.*) sindacato; ~ **-union enforced wages** (*sind.*) salari d'imposizione sindacale; ~ **-union militancy** (*sind.*) il militare in un sindacato (*V.* **a** ~ **union militant**); **a** ~ **union militant** (*sind.*) un militante d'un sindacato; ~ **-unionism** (*sind.*) sindacalismo; **trades-unionism** (*sind.*) *V.* ~ **-unionism;** **-unionist** (*sind.*) iscritto a un sindacato; sindacalista; ~ **war** (*econ.*) guerra commerciale.

trade[2], *v. t.* e *i.* **1** commerciare, fare affari, negoziare. **2** (*market.*) fare acquisti, far spese. // to ~ **in** cedere (*un oggetto usato*) in pagamento parziale; to ~ **up** (*market.*) promuovere la vendita d'articoli più cari; persuadere (*un *cliente*) ad acquistare un articolo di prezzo più alto.

trademark, *n.* e *v. t. V.* **trade-mark.**

trader, *n.* 1 commerciante. 2 (*trasp. mar.*) nave mercantile.

tradesman, *n.* (*pl.* **tradesmen**) commerciante, negoziante, bottegaio, esercente.

tradespeople, *n. pl.* (*market.*) esercenti.

trading, *a.* commerciale, mercantile. *n.* commercio, compravendita, negozio (*il negoziare*), traffici, scambi. // ~ **account** (*rag.*) stato patrimoniale; ~ **area** (*market.*) *V.* **trade area; the ~ balance** (*econ.*) la bilancia commerciale; **a ~ centre** un centro commerciale; ~ **estate** (*econ.*) zona industriale; ~ **loss** (*rag.*) perdita d'esercizio; **a ~ nation** (*econ.*) una nazione commerciale; ~ **profit** (*rag.*) utile d'esercizio; ~ **results** (*rag.*) risultati d'esercizio; ~ **stamps** (*market.*) bolli premio, bollini; **a ~ transaction** un'operazione commerciale; ~ **vessel** (*trasp. mar.*) mercantile, nave mercantile; **the ~ volume** (*Borsa*) il volume delle contrattazioni; ~ **year** (*fin., rag.*) anno finanziario, esercizio finanziario.

tradition, *n.* 1 tradizione. 2 (*leg.*) trasmissione, consegna, tradizione.

traffic, *n.* 1 traffico, movimento, commercio. 2 (*trasp.*) traffico; numero dei passeggeri trasportati; volume delle merci trasportate. // ~ **block** (*trasp. aut.*) ingorgo stradale; ~ **control** (*trasp. aut.*) controllo del traffico; ~ **density** (*trasp.*) densità del movimento merci; ~ **divider** (*trasp. aut.*) «guardrail»; ~ **island** (*trasp. aut.*) spartitraffico; ~ **jam** (*trasp. aut.*) *V.* ~ **block;** ~ **manager** (*trasp. ferr.*) dirigente del movimento; ~ **unit** (*trasp.*) unità di movimento (*di merci o passeggeri*).

trafficators, *n. pl.* (*trasp. aut.*) lampeggiatori.

train[1], *n.* (*trasp. ferr.*) treno. // ~ **-ferry** (*trasp. ferr.*) nave traghetto; ~ **-load** (*trasp. ferr.*) passeggeri trasportati; merci trasportate; **down ~** (*fam., ingl.*) treno diretto in provincia (*specialm. in partenza da Londra*); **the in ~** (*trasp. ferr.*) il treno in arrivo; **up ~** (*fam., ingl.*) treno diretto in città (*specialm. a Londra*).

train[2], *v. t.* addestrare, esercitare, istruire. *v. i.* esercitarsi.

trainee, *n.* (*pers.*) persona sottoposta ad addestramento, tirocinante.

trainer, *n.* 1 (*pers.*) istruttore. 2 (*pers.*) *V.* **trainee.**

training, *n.* 1 addestramento, istruzione, formazione. 2 (*org. az.*) tirocinio. *a.* (*pers.*) tirocinante. // ~ **programme** (*org. az.*) programma d'addestramento.

tram, *n.* (*trasp.*) tram, tranvai. // ~ **-conductor** tranviere (*bigliettaio*); ~ **-driver** tranviere (*conducente*).

tramp, *n.* (*trasp. mar.*) «carretta», nave rinfusiera, nave da carico non di linea. // ~ **ship** (*trasp. mar.*) *V.* ~; ~ **steamer** (*trasp. mar.*) *V.* ~.

tramway, *n.* (*trasp.*) tranvia.

transact, *v. t.* trattare, sbrigare. // to ~ **a bargain** sbrigare un affare; to ~ **business** fare affari.

transaction, *n.* 1 trattazione. 2 affare, operazione. 3 (*leg.*) transazione, accomodamento, accordo, compromesso. // ~ **for the account** (*Borsa*) operazione a termine; **a ~ for cash** un'operazione a contanti; ~ **for the settlement** (*Borsa*) operazione a termine; **the transactions of a bank** (*banca*) le operazioni d'una banca; **a ~ on credit** (*cred.*) un'operazione a credito; **a ~ on the Stock Exchange** (*Borsa*) un'operazione di Borsa.

transactor, *n.* 1 agente economico, operatore economico. 2 negoziatore.

transatlantic, *a.* transatlantico.

transcribe, *v. t.* 1 (*comun.*) registrare (*un programma radiotelevisivo*). 2 (*comun.*) trasmettere (*un programma radiotelevisivo registrato*). 3 (*elab. elettr.*) trascrivere.

transcribing machine, *n.* (*macch. uff.*) fonoriproduttore.

transcript, *n.* 1 trascrizione. 2 (*leg.*) copia (*a verbale di causa*).

transcription, *n.* 1 (*comun.*) registrazione (*di programma radiotelevisivo*). 2 (*leg.*) copia (*a verbale di causa*).

transfer[1], *n.* 1 trasferimento. 2 (*banca, fin.*) bonifico, rimessa. 3 (*leg.*) trasferimento, tradizione, trasmissione, cessione, passaggio di proprietà, trapasso. 4 (*pers.*) trasferimento, trasferta (*l'andare in servizio fuori della propria residenza*). 5 (*rag.*) storno. 6 (*trasp.*) (= **transfer ticket**) biglietto cumulativo. 7 (*trasp. ferr.*) trasbordo. 8 (*trasp. mar.*) traghetto. 9 (*trasp. mar.*) nave-traghetto. // ~ **agent** (*fin., USA*) agenzia incaricata del trasferimento di titoli; ~ **-book** (*fin., leg.*) registro delle cessioni (*d'azioni, ecc.*); libro dei soci; ~ **deed** (*Borsa*) atto di trasferimento, contratto di cessione; (*leg.*) atto di cessione; ~ **duty** (*leg.*) *V.* ~ **tax;** ~ **entry** (*rag.*) scrittura di storno; ~ **house** (*trasp. ferr.*) stazione di trasbordo; **the ~ of an entry** (*rag.*) lo storno d'una scrittura; **the ~ of an estate** (*leg.*) la tradizione d'una proprietà; ~ **of funds** (*fin.*) trasferimento di capitali; ~ **of**

mortgage (*leg.*) trapasso d'ipoteca; ~ **of property** (*leg.*) passaggio di proprietà; **a** ~ **of shares** (*fin.*) un trasferimento d'azioni; ~ **of title** (*leg.*) passaggio di proprietà; ~ **tax** (*fin.*) imposta di successione; ~ **track** (*trasp. ferr.*) binario di trasbordo.

transfer[2], *v. t.* **1** trasferire. **2** (*leg.*) trasferire, trasmettere, cedere. **3** (*pers.*) trasferire. **4** (*rag.*) stornare. **5** (*trasp. ferr.*) trasbordare. *v. i.* **1** trasferirsi. **2** (*trasp.*) trasbordare, fare un trasbordo. // to ~ **a balance to profit and loss account** (*rag.*) girare un saldo al conto perdite e profitti; to ~ **a bill by endorsement** (*cred.*) trasmettere una cambiale per mezzo della girata; to ~ **a property** (*leg.*) cedere una proprietà.

transferable, *a.* (*leg.*) trasferibile, cedibile, trasmissibile. // **a** ~ **credit** (*cred.*) un credito trasferibile; **a** ~ **right** (*leg.*) un diritto trasmissibile; ~ **stock** (*fin.*) azioni negoziabili, azioni al portatore.

transferance, *n.* (*leg.*) trasferimento, tradizione.

transferee, *n.* (*leg.*) cessionario.

transferer, *n. V.* **transferor.**

transferor, *n.* (*leg.*) cedente.

transferrer, *n.* (*leg.*) *V.* **transferor.**

transferror, *n. V.* **transferor.**

transform, *v. t.* trasformare.

transformation, *n.* trasformazione.

transgress, *v. t.* (*leg.*) trasgredire, violare, contravvenire a. // to ~ **the law** (*leg.*) trasgredire la (*o* alla) legge; to ~ **a treaty** violare un trattato.

transgression, *n.* (*leg.*) trasgressione, violazione, il contravvenire a (*una legge, ecc.*).

transgressor, *n.* (*leg.*) trasgressore, contravventore, violatore.

tranship, *v. t. V.* **transship.**

transhipment, *n. V.* **transshipment.**

transit[1], *n.* (*trasp.*) transito, passaggio. // ~ **duty** (*dog.*) dazio doganale di transito; ~ **entry** (*dog.*) dichiarazione di transito; ~ **goods** (*comm. est.*) merce di transito; ~ **manifest** (*dog.*) manifesto di transito; ~ **trade** (*comm. est.*) commercio di transito; **in** ~ (*trasp.*) in viaggio, durante il viaggio.

transit[2], *v. i.* (*trasp.*) transitare, passare. *v. t.* (*trasp.*) lasciar transitare, far passare.

transition, *n.* transizione.

transitoriness, *n.* transitorietà.

transitory, *a.* transitorio, passeggero.

translator, *n.* (*pers.*) interprete.

transmissible, *a.* trasmissibile.

transmission, *n.* **1** (*comun.*) trasmissione. **2** (*leg.*) trasmissione. // ~ **by descent** (*leg.*) trasmissione per successione.

transmit, *v. t.* (*comun.*) trasmettere.

transmitter, *n.* (*comun.*) trasmettitore.

transmitting, *a.* (*comun.*) trasmittente. // ~ **station** (*comun.*) (stazione) trasmittente.

transport[1], *n.* trasporto, (i) trasporti. // ~ **agent** (*trasp.*) spedizioniere; ~ **by rail** (*trasp. ferr.*) i trasporti ferroviari; ~ **charges** (*trasp.*) (prezzo del) trasporto; ~ **company** (*trasp.*) società di trasporti, messaggerie; **the** ~ **industry** (*econ.*) il settore dei trasporti; **the** ~ **market** (*econ.*) il mercato dei trasporti; ~ **rates** (*trasp.*) tariffe dei trasporti; ~ **rates and conditions** (*trasp.*) prezzi e condizioni di trasporto; **the** ~ **sector** (*econ.*) il settore (dei) trasporti.

transport[2], *v. t.* trasportare.

transportal, *n. V.* **transportation,** *def. 1.*

transportation, *n.* **1** trasporto. **2** costo del trasporto, prezzo del trasporto. **3** mezzo di trasporto. **4** (i) trasporti. // ~ **by air** trasporti aerei; ~ **facilities** (*trasp.*) mezzi di trasporto; ~ **insurance** (*ass. mar.*) assicurazione marittima.

transportational, *a.* dei trasporti, relativo ai trasporti. // ~ **organizations** le organizzazioni dei trasporti; ~ **routes** vie di trasporto.

transporter, *n.* (*trasp.*) trasportatore, vettore.

transship, *v. t.* e *i.* (*trasp. mar.*) trasbordare.

transshipment, *n.* (*trasp. mar.*) trasbordo. // ~ **entry** (*trasp. mar.*) dichiarazione per il trasbordo; ~ **expenses** (*trasp. mar.*) spese di trasbordo; ~ **note** (*trasp. mar.*) nota di trasbordo; ~ **permit** (*trasp. mar.*) permesso di trasbordo; ~ **platform** (*trasp. mar.*) banchina di trasbordo; ~ **risk** (*ass. mar.*) rischio di trasbordo (*in G.B., per il piccolo cabotaggio*).

transshipping port, *n.* (*trasp. mar.*) porto di trasbordo.

trap, *n.* trappola.

travel[1], *n.* **1** viaggio. **2** (il) viaggiare, (i) viaggi. // ~ **agency** (*tur.*) agenzia di viaggi; ~ **agent** (*tur.*) titolare d'agenzia di viaggio; ~ **bureau** (*tur.*) *V.* ~ **agency;** ~ **tickets** (*tur.*) biglietti di viaggio.

travel[2], *v. i.* **1** viaggiare, fare un viaggio. **2** (*pers.*) viaggiare, fare il commesso viaggiatore, fare il rappresentante. *v. t.* **1** viaggiare in (*un Paese, ecc.*); percorrere. **2** (*pers.*) viaggiare in (*una zona*); lavorare su (*una piazza*).

traveler, *n.* (*USA*) *V.* **traveller.**

traveling, *n.* (*USA*) *V.* **travelling.**

traveller, *n.* **1** viaggiatore, viaggiatrice, passeggero, passeggera. **2** (*pers.*) viaggiatore (di commercio); commesso viaggiatore. // ~ **'s** (*o*

travellers') cheque (*cred.*) traveller's cheque, assegno turistico; ~ **'s letter of credit** (*banca, cred.*) lettera di credito circolare.

travelling, *a.* di viaggio, da viaggio. // ~ **allowance** (*pers.*) indennità di viaggio; indennità di missione (*o* di trasferta); ~ **clerk** (*pers.*) viaggiatore (di commercio), commesso viaggiatore; ~ **exhibit** (*market., pubbl.*) mostra itinerante; ~ **expenses** spese di viaggio, indennità di trasferta; ~ **indemnity** indennità di trasferta; ~ **man** (*pers.*) *V.* ~ **salesman;** ~ **salesman** (*pers.*) viaggiatore di commercio, commesso viaggiatore.

traverse[1], *n.* (*leg.*) negazione.

traverse[2], *v. t.* **1** traversare. **2** (*leg.*) contestare, negare.

treasure[1], *n.* tesoro. // ~ **trove** (*leg.*) tesoro trovato.

treasure[2], *v. t.* (*econ.*) tesoreggiare, tesaurizzare. // to ~ **gold and silver** (*econ.*) tesaurizzare oro e argento.

treasurer, *n.* (*fin.*) tesoriere, cassiere.

treasurership, *n.* (*fin.*) carica di tesoriere, ufficio di tesoriere; carica di cassiere, ufficio di cassiere.

treasury, *n.* **1** (*fin.*) tesoreria, cassa. **2 the Treasury** (*amm.*) il Tesoro, il Ministero del Tesoro. **3 the Treasury** (*fin.*) l'Erario. // ~ **bill** (*fin.*) buono del Tesoro; ~ **bond** (*fin.*) buono del Tesoro; ~ **borrowings** (*fin.*) indebitamento del Tesoro; ~ **certificate** (*fin., USA*) buono fruttifero del Tesoro (*con scadenza fino a un anno*); ~ **note** (*fin.*) biglietto di banca; **the** ~ **officers** (*fin.*) il Fisco, i funzionari del Fisco; ~ **stock** (*fin.*) titoli di proprietà (*d'una società*); azioni di portafoglio.

treat, *v. t.* trattare, discutere, negoziare.

treatise, *n.* trattato (*esposizione d'una dottrina*).

treatment, *n.* **1** trattamento. **2** trattazione (d'un argomento).

treaty, *n.* (*leg.*) trattato, accordo, patto. // ~ **port** (*trasp. mar.*) porto franco; ~ **reinsurance** (*ass. mar.*) riassicurazione in abbonamento.

treble[1], *a.* triplice. // ~ **damages** (*leg.*) danni triplici.

treble[2], *v. t.* triplicare.

trend[1], *n.* (*anche econ., fin.*) tendenza, andamento, indirizzo, evoluzione, «dinamica», orientamento, «trend». // **the** ~ **of activity** (*econ.*) l'evoluzione congiunturale; **the** ~ **of the stock market** (*Borsa, fin.*) l'andamento del mercato dei titoli.

trend[2], *v. i.* tendere, dirigersi, volgere.

trespass[1], *n.* **1** trasgressione, contravvenzione, infrazione. **2** (*leg.*) violazione di proprietà, sconfinamento. **3** (*leg.*) abuso, prevaricazione, violazione.

trespass[2], *v. i.* **1** trasgredire, contravvenire (*a un divieto, ecc.*). **2** (*leg.*) sconfinare, entrare abusivamente. **3** (*leg.*) abusare (*di qc.*). // to ~ **on a private property** (*leg.*) introdursi abusivamente in una proprietà privata; to ~ **upon sb.'s rights** (*leg.*) violare i diritti di q.; «**No trespassing!**» «proprietà privata».

trespasser, *n.* **1** (*leg.*) trasgressore. **2** (*leg.*) contravventore (*a un divieto d'accesso*); violatore di confini (*V. anche* **trespass**[2]).

trespassing, *n.* **1** contravvenzione (*a un divieto*). **2** (*leg.*) sconfinamento.

trial, *n.* **1** prova, esperimento. **2** (*leg.*) processo, giudizio. // ~ **at bar** (*leg.*) udienza plenaria; ~ **balance** (*rag.*) bilancio di verifica; ~ **based on circumstantial evidence** (*leg.*) processo indiziario; ~ **Court** (*leg.*) tribunale di prima istanza; ~ «**in camera**» (*leg.*) udienza a porte chiuse; ~ **list** (*leg.*) ruolo delle cause da discutere; ~ **order** (*market.*) ordinazione di prova; ~ **sample** (*market.*) campione di prova, campione di saggio; ~ **trip** (*trasp. mar.*) viaggio di prova; to **be on** ~ (*leg.*) subire un processo.

tribunal, *n.* (*leg.*) tribunale, Corte di giustizia.

tribute, *n.* tributo.

trigger, *n.* «scatto».

trillion, *n.* **1** (*ingl.*) quintilione. **2** (*USA*) trilione.

trim, *v. t.* **1** aggiustare, assettare, rassettare, mettere in ordine. **2** spuntare, tagliare. **3** (*trasp. mar.*) livellare (*il carico*). // to ~ **the budget** (*econ.*) apportare «tagli» al bilancio; to ~ **the cargo** (*trasp. mar.*) assettare il carico; to ~ **holds** (*trasp. mar.*) stivare; to ~ **a ship** (*trasp. mar.*) assettare una nave.

trimmer, *n.* (*trasp. mar.*) stivatore.

trimming, *n.* (*trasp. mar.*) assetto, livellamento (*del carico*). // ~ **and bagging** (*trasp. mar.*) stivaggio e caricazione in sacchi; ~ **charges** (*trasp. mar.*) spese di stivaggio.

trip, *n.* **1** (*trasp.*) viaggio, viaggetto, gita. **2** (*trasp.*) tragitto, percorso.

tripartite, *a.* (*leg.*) (*di documento*) in tre copie. // ~ **agreement** accordo tripartito; ~ **board** (*sind.*) commissione tripartita (*che emette il lodo arbitrale*).

triple[1], *a.* triplice.

triple[2], *v. t.* triplicare. *v. i.* triplicarsi.

triplicate[1], *a.* **1** triplice. **2** (*di documento*) in triplice copia. **3** (*di copia*) terza. *n.* **1** triplice copia. **2** terza copia (*di documento*).

triplicate[2], *v. t.* 1 triplicare, moltiplicare per tre. 2 redigere l'originale e due copie di (*un documento*). 3 riprodurre (*un originale*) due volte.

trolley, *n.* (*trasp. ferr.*) carrello di servizio. // ~ **-bus** (*trasp. aut.*) filobus; ~ **car** (*trasp., USA*) tram, tranvai.

trouble[1], *n.* 1 molestia. 2 agitazione, tumulto (*popolare*), disordine. // ~ **man** (*pers., USA*) *V.* **troubleshooter.**

trouble[2], *v. t.* molestare, seccare, turbare.

troubleshooter, *n.* (*pers., USA*) operaio che scopre e localizza i guasti (*d'un macchinario, ecc.*).

trough, *n.* 1 cavo (*dell'onda*). 2 (*econ.*) punto più basso (*d'un ciclo economico*); fondo (*d'una congiuntura*). 3 (*mat.*) valore minimo (*d'una funzione, ecc.*).

trover, *n.* (*leg.*) ricupero di beni mobili.

troy, *n.* «troy» (*sistema di peso per metalli preziosi e medicinali*). // ~ **pound** libbra «troy» (*unità di peso pari a grammi 373,24*); ~ **weight** *V.* ~.

truck, *n.* 1 baratto, scambio. 2 (*pers.*) (= **truck system**) sistema di pagamento (*degli operai*) in natura. 3 (*trasp.*) carro, vagone. 4 (*trasp. aut., USA*) autocarro, camion. 5 (*trasp. ferr.*) carrello (*di locomotiva o di carrozza ferroviaria*). 6 (*trasp. ferr.*) carro merci aperto, pianale. // ~ **-driver** (*trasp. aut., USA*) «autotrasportatore», camionista; ~ **farmer** (*econ., USA*) ortofrutticoltore; ~ **farming** (*econ., USA*) ortofrutticoltura; ~ **gardener** (*econ., USA*) *V.* ~ **farmer;** ~ **gardening** (*econ., USA*) *V.* ~ **farming;** ~ **load** (*trasp. ferr.*) vagone completo; ~ **-load consignments** (*trasp. ferr.*) spedizioni a caricazione completa (*di vagone*); ~ **load rates** (*trasp. ferr.*) tariffe per vagoni completi; ~ **owner-operator** (*trasp. aut.*) padroncino (*camionista proprietario del camion*); ~ **system** (*pers.*) sistema di pagamento in natura.

truckage, *n.* 1 (*trasp.*) trasporto mediante carro (*o* autocarro). 2 (*trasp.*) spese di porto (*V. anche* **truck**).

trucker, *n.* (*econ., USA*) ortofrutticoltore.

truckman, *n.* (*pl.* **truckmen**) *V.* **truck-driver.**

true, *a.* 1 effettivo, reale. 2 fedele, preciso. // ~ **airspeed** (*trasp. aer.*) velocità effettiva; ~ **bill** (*leg.*) incriminazione; ~ **copy** (*leg.*) copia autentica, copia conforme; ~ **discount** (*mat.*) sconto razionale; **the** ~ **heir** (*leg.*) l'erede legittimo; ~ **to the original** conforme all'originale; to **be** ~ **to one's word** tener fede alla parola data.

truly, *avv.* 1 realmente. 2 sinceramente. 3 fedelmente.

trunk, *n.* tronco. // ~ **-call** (*comun.*) chiamata (*telefonica*) interurbana; ~ **-exchange** (*comun.*) centrale (*telefonica*) interurbana; ~ **-line** (*comun.*) linea (*telefonica*) interurbana; (*trasp. ferr.*) linea principale; ~ **-road** (*trasp. aut.*) strada principale.

trust[1], *n.* 1 fiducia, fede, responsabilità. 2 (*fin.*) trust, consorzio monopolistico (*fra imprese*), monopolio. 3 (*fin.*) fondo (comune) d'investimento. 4 (*leg.*) amministrazione fiduciaria (*di beni altrui*). 5 (*leg.*) lascito (*in proprietà fiduciaria*); fidecommesso. // ~ **company** (*fin.*) società di gestione del portafoglio; ~ **deed** (*leg.*) atto fiduciario; ~ **estate** (*leg.*) proprietà tenuta in amministrazione fiduciaria; ~ **letter** (*banca, cred.*) ricevuta attestante l'avvenuta consegna dei documenti; ~ **property** (*leg.*) proprietà tenuta in amministrazione fiduciaria; ~ **receipt** (*banca, cred.*) *V.* ~ **letter;** ~ **without any gearing** (*o, USA,* **without any leverage**) (*fin.*) fondo (d'investimento) con sole azioni ordinarie; **on** ~ (*market.*) a credito.

trust[2], *v. t.* e *i.* 1 aver fiducia in (*q.*); fidarsi di (*q.*); fare assegnamento su (*q.*). 2 affidare, consegnare. 3 nutrire fiducia. 4 (*market.*) far credito, vendere a credito, concedere prestiti. // to ~ **sb. with st.** affidare qc. a q.

trustee[1], *n.* 1 (*amm.*) membro del consiglio d'amministrazione (*d'un ente pubblico, d'una scuola, d'un ospedale, ecc.*). 2 (*leg.*) fiduciario, amministratore fiduciario. 3 (*leg.*) (= **trustee in bankruptcy**) curatore (fallimentare). // ~ **company** (*fin.*) società fiduciaria (*o* depositaria), ente fiduciario; ~ **deed** (*fin., leg.*) atto fiduciario; **a** ~ **in bankruptcy** (*leg.*) un curatore fallimentare; ~ **Savings Bank** (*banca*) Cassa di Risparmio fiduciario.

trustee[2], *v. t.* (*leg.*) affidare (*beni*) in amministrazione (*o* gestione) fiduciaria.

trusteeship, *n.* 1 (*leg.*) amministrazione fiduciaria, gestione fiduciaria. 2 (*leg.*) curatela.

trustful, *a.* fiducioso.

trustworthiness, *n.* fidatezza.

trustworthy, *a.* fidato, credibile.

try, *v. t.* 1 cercare. 2 (*leg.*) giudicare, processare. // to ~ **sb. for theft** (*leg.*) processare q. per furto.

tube, *n.* 1 tubo. 2 (*econ., fin.*) «tunnel» (*monetario europeo*).

tumble[1], *n.* (*econ., fin., market.*) crollo.

tumble[2], *v. i.* crollare (*di solito,* to ~ **down**).

tuning band, *n.* (*comun.*) gamma di

sintonia.

tunnel, *n.* 1 tunnel. 2 (*econ., fin.*) tunnel (*monetario europeo*).

turn[1], *n.* 1 giro, rotazione. 2 curva (*anche fig.*). 3 (*econ.*) inversione di tendenza. 4 (*fin.*) operazione (*d'acquisto e vendita*) in titoli. 5 (*fin., rag.*) *V.* **turnover.** 6 (*pers.*) turno. 7 (*trasp. aer., trasp. mar.*) accostata. // **a ~ for the better (for the worse)** un cambiamento in meglio (in peggio); **a ~ in a road** (*trasp. aut.*) una curva in una strada; **the ~ of the tide** (*trasp. mar.*) il cambiamento della marea; **a ~ of work** (*pers.*) un turno di lavoro; **~ -out** *V.* **turnout; ~ -over** *V.* **turnover.**

turn[2], *v. i.* 1 girare. 2 volgersi. 3 rivolgersi, fare ricorso. 4 diventare (*all'improvviso*). 5 (*trasp. mar.*) (*di marea*) girare, cambiare. *v. t.* cambiare, convertire. // to **~ about** (*trasp. mar.: di nave*) invertire la rotta; to **~ a banknote into cash** (*fin.*) cambiare una banconota in spiccioli; to **~ down an offer** rifiutare un'offerta; to **~ in** consegnare; (*rag.*) (*di conto, ecc.*) dare (*un certo saldo, ecc.*), registrare, far registrare; to **~ in an expense account** consegnare un conto spese; to **~ off** (*pers.*) licenziare; to **~ out** (*econ., org. az.*) produrre; (*leg.*) sfrattare; (*pers.*) licenziare, mettere (*q.*) alla porta; to **~ over** consegnare, inoltrare; avere un volume d'affari di; to **~ a partnership into a limited company** (*fin.*) trasformare una società in nome collettivo in una società anonima; to **~ a profit** (*rag.*) ricavare un utile; to **~ st. to account** valorizzare qc.

turnabout, *n.* 1 cambiamento repentino. 2 (*econ.*) cambiamento di tendenza, inversione di tendenza. 3 (*trasp. mar.*) inversione di rotta.

turnaround, *n.* 1 (*econ.*) inversione di tendenza. 2 (*econ.*) aggiustamento.

turndown, *n.* rifiuto. // **the ~ of an offer** il rifiuto d'un'offerta.

turning, *a.* girevole.

turning out, *n.* 1 (*leg.*) sfratto. 2 (*pers.*) licenziamento.

turnout, *n.* 1 (*org. az.*) produzione (*ottenuta*). 2 (*pers.*) licenziamento. 3 (*sind.*) sciopero. 4 (*sind.*) scioperante.

turnover, *n.* 1 (*fin.*) giro d'affari, volume d'affari. 2 (*market.*) volume delle vendite, fatturato. 3 (*org. az.*) ricambio, rotazione delle giacenze. 4 (*pers.*) avvicendamento. // **~ rate** (*org. az.*) tasso di rotazione del magazzino, indice di rotazione delle giacenze; **~ tax** (*fin.*) imposta sulla cifra d'affari, imposta sugli affari.

turnpike, *n.* (*trasp. aut., USA*) autostrada.

tutelary, *a.* (*leg.*) tutorio.

tutor, *n.* (*leg.*) tutore.

tutorship, *n.* (*leg.*) tutela.

two, *a.* e *n.* due. // **~ bits** (*slang USA*) venticinque centesimi di dollaro; **~ by ~** a due a due; **a ~ -master** (*trasp. mar.*) un due-alberi; **~ -tier** doppio, duplice; **a ~ -tier exchange system** (*econ., fin.*) un doppio regime dei cambi; **~ -tier market** (*econ.*) doppio mercato valutario; **by twos** a due a due.

tycoon, *n.* (*fin., USA*) gran finanziere, magnate.

type[1], *n.* 1 tipo. 2 (*giorn., pubbl.*) tipo, carattere tipografico, carattere di stampa. // **~ -setting** (*giorn., pubbl.*) composizione (*tipografica*).

type[2], *v. t.* scrivere a macchina, dattilografare; battere (*fam.*).

typescript, *n.* dattiloscritto.

typewrite, *v. t.* (*pass.* **typewrote,** *part. pass.* **typewritten**) scrivere a macchina, dattilografare.

typewriting, *n.* (lo) scrivere a macchina, dattilografia. // **~ ribbon** (*attr. uff.*) nastro dattilografico.

typical, *a.* tipico.

typification, *n.* tipificazione, tipizzazione.

typify, *v. t.* tipificare, tipizzare.

typing mistake, *n.* errore di battuta (*di macchina da scrivere*).

typist, *n.* (*pers.*) dattilografo, dattilografa.

typographer, *n.* (*giorn.*) stampatore.

U

ullage, *n.* 1 (*dog.*) quantità effettiva (*in barili, botti, ecc.*). 2 (*market.*) calo, «colaggio», quantità mancante (*in barili, botti, ecc.*). 3 (*market.*) abbuono per calo, abbuono per «colaggio».

ultimate, *a.* 1 ultimo, definitivo, finale. 2 basilare. // ~ **buyer** (*econ.*) ultimo compratore; ~ **consumer** (*econ.*) ultimo consumatore; ~ **purchaser** (*econ.*) ultimo compratore.

ultimatum, *n.* (*pl.* **ultimata** e *reg.*) ultimatum.

ultimo, *a.* (*abbr.* **ult.**) (*comm.*) scorso, ultimo scorso, del mese scorso.

ultra vires, *locuz. a.* e *avv.* (*leg.*) in eccesso di potere. // **an** ~ **contract** (*leg.*) un contratto «ultra vires».

umpirage, *n.* (*leg., sind.*) arbitrato, arbitraggio, arbitramento, decisione arbitrale.

umpire[1], *n.* (*leg., sind.*) arbitratore, arbitro, arbitro unico.

umpire[2], *v. t.* (*leg., sind.*) arbitrare, decidere (*una controversia*) in qualità d'arbitro. *v. i.* (*leg., sind.*) fare da arbitro.

unable, *a.* incapace, inabile. // ~ **to work** (*pers.*) inabile al lavoro; to **be** ~ non essere in grado, non potere.

unabridged, *a.* (*giorn., pubbl.*) (*d'articolo, volume, ecc.*) completo, integrale.

unabsorbed, *a.* non assorbito.

unacceptance, *n.* (*cred.*) mancanza d'accettazione.

unaccepted, *a.* (*cred.*) non accettato. // ~ **bills** (*cred.*) cambiali non accettate.

unaddressed, *a.* (*comun.*) privo d'indirizzo, senza indirizzo. // **an** ~ **envelope** (*comun.*) una busta senza indirizzo.

unalienable, *a.* (*leg.*) inalienabile.

unaltered, *a.* costante.

unanchor, *v. t.* (*trasp. mar.*) disancorare. *v. i.* (*trasp. mar.*) levare l'ancora.

unanimous, *a.* concorde. // ~ **consent** consenso unanime.

unanswerability, *n.* (*leg.*) irresponsabilità.

unanswerable, *a.* 1 incontestabile. 2 (*leg.*) irresponsabile, non responsabile. // **an** ~ **argument** un argomento irrefutabile.

unanswered, *a.* 1 senza risposta. 2 (*comun.*) inevaso. // **an** ~ **letter** (*comun.*) una lettera inevasa.

unappealable, *a.* inappellabile. // **an** ~ **decision** una decisione inappellabile.

unappropriated, *a.* (*fin.*) (*di fondo*) non assegnato, non stanziato. // ~ **profits** (*fin.*) dividendi non distribuiti.

unassignable, *a.* (*leg.*) non trasferibile.

unauthorized, *a.* non autorizzato, abusivo, arbitrario.

unavailable, *a.* 1 non disponibile. 2 inefficace, inutile. 3 (*market.*) (*d'articolo*) non in vendita, esaurito.

unavoidable, *a.* inevitabile. // ~ **accident** (*ass.*) incidente inevitabile; ~ **casualty** (*ass.*) incidente inevitabile.

unbalance[1], *n.* mancanza d'equilibrio, squilibrio, sbilancio, scompenso.

unbalance[2], *v. t.* sbilanciare, scompensare. // to ~ **a budget** (*econ., rag.*) scompensare un bilancio.

unbalanced, *a.* sbilanciato, scompensato. // **an** ~ **account** (*rag.*) un conto scompensato; **an** ~ **budget** (*econ., rag.*) un bilancio scompensato.

unballast, *v. i.* (*trasp. mar.*) scaricare la zavorra. *v. t.* (*trasp. mar.*) alleggerire della zavorra.

unbankable, *a.* (*banca*) non bancabile. // ~ **papers** (*banca*) effetti non bancabili.

unbind, *v. t.* (*pass.* e *part. pass.* **unbound**) slegare, sciogliere.

unbinding, *a.* non vincolante, non impegnativo, non obbligatorio. // **an** ~ **offer** un'offerta non vincolante.

unbreakable, *a.* infrangibile.

uncalled, *a.* non chiamato. // ~ **capital** (*fin.*) capitale non richiamato; ~ **for** (*comun.*) (*di lettera e sim.*) giacente alla posta.

uncashable, *a.* (*cred.*) non riscuotibile.

uncertain, *a.* incerto, indeciso.

uncertainty, *n.* incertezza, non prevedibilità.

unchartered, *a.* 1 (*amm.*) privo di speciali privilegi (*come concessioni esclusive, ecc.*). 2 (*trasp. aer., trasp. mar.*) (*di nave, aereo, ecc.*) non noleggiato.

unclaimed, *a.* non reclamato; (*leg.*) giacente. // **an ~ dividend** (*fin.*) dividendo prescritto.

unclean, *a.* sporco. // **~ bill of lading** (*trasp. mar.*) polizza di carico «con riserva».

uncleared, *a.* (*dog.*) (*d'articolo*) non sdoganato.

uncollected, *a.* (*cred.*) non incassato, non riscosso, non pagato, inesatto. // **an ~ debt** (*cred.*) un credito non riscosso; **an ~ tax** (*fin.*) un tributo inesatto.

uncollectible, *a.* (*cred.*) non incassabile, non riscuotibile, inesigibile. *n.* (*cred.*) credito inesigibile. // **~ credit** (*cred.*) credito inesigibile; **~ debt** (*cred.*) credito inesigibile.

unconditional, *a.* 1 senza condizioni, senza riserve, incondizionato. 2 netto, pieno.

unconditionally, *avv.* incondizionatamente.

unconfirmed, *a.* non confermato. // **~ letter of credit** (*banca, cred.*) lettera di credito non confermata; **~ rumours** voci non confermate.

unconstitutional, *a.* (*leg.*) incostituzionale.

unconstitutionality, *n.* (*leg.*) incostituzionalità.

unconvertible, *a.* (*fin.*) inconvertibile, non convertibile. // **~ securities** (*fin.*) titoli inconvertibili.

uncovered, *a.* 1 scoperto. 2 (*ass.*) (*di rischio*) non assicurato, non coperto, scoperto. 3 (*banca, cred.*) allo scoperto, scoperto. // **~ advance** (*banca*) anticipazione allo scoperto; **~ arbitrage** (*Borsa, fin.*) arbitraggio scoperto; **~ cheque** (*banca, cred.*) assegno scoperto (*o* senza copertura).

uncustomed, *a.* 1 (*dog.*) non sdoganato, non sdaziato. 2 (*dog.*) esente da dogana, esente da dazio.

undamaged, *a.* (*ass., trasp.*) non danneggiato, non avariato, indenne, in buone condizioni.

undated, *a.* senza data. // **an ~ letter** (*comun.*) una lettera non datata.

undecided, *a.* indeciso.

undefined, *a.* indefinito, irrisolto.

undelivered, *a.* non consegnato, non recapitato, giacente.

undeniable, *a.* innegabile.

under, *avv.* e *prep.* 1 sotto. 2 in corso di. 3 a meno di. *a. attr.* inferiore, subalterno. // **~ -agent** (*pers.*) subagente; **~ arrest** (*leg.*) in stato d'arresto; **~ -clerk** (*pers.*) impiegato in sottordine, subordinato; **~ construction** in costruzione; **~ control** (*trasp. mar.*) (*di nave*) in governo; **~ -the counter** (*market.*) (*di vendita*) sottobanco; **~ discussion** in discussione, in esame; **~ (full) age** (*leg.*) minorenne; **~ the law** (*leg.*) ai sensi della legge; **~ -lease** (*leg.*) subaffitto; **~ no circumstance** in nessun caso; **~ oath** (*leg.*) sotto giuramento; **~ quarantine** (*trasp. mar.*) in quarantena; **~ -secretary** sottosegretario, vicesegretario; **~ separate cover** (*comun.*) sotto fascia, in plico a parte; **~ ship's derrick** (*trasp. mar.*) *V.* **~ ship's tackle**; **~ ship's tackle** (*trasp. mar.*) sotto paranco; **~ this contract** (*leg.*) in virtù di questo contratto; to **be ~ age** essere minorenne.

underbid, *v. t.* (*pass.* e *part. pass.* **underbid**) 1 (*market.*) offrire meno di (*un concorrente*). 2 (*market.*) offrire merce (servizi, ecc.) a un prezzo inferiore a quello di (*un concorrente*).

undercarriage, *n.* (*trasp. aer.*) carrello (*d'atterraggio*).

undercharge, *v. t.* (*market.*) far pagare a (*q.*) meno del giusto (*o* del solito).

undercut, *v. t.* (*pass.* e *part. pass.* **undercut**) (*market.*) vendere a un prezzo inferiore a quello di (*un concorrente*).

underdeck, *n.* (*trasp. mar.*) sottocoperta. // **~ tonnage** (*trasp. mar.*) stazza sotto ponte.

underdeveloped, *a.* (*econ.*) sottosviluppato, depresso. // **~ Countries** (*econ.*) Paesi sottosviluppati.

underdevelopment, *n.* (*econ.*) sottosviluppo. // **the ~ of industrial resources** (*econ.*) il sottosviluppo delle risorse industriali.

underemployed, *a.* (*sind.*) sottoccupato, non occupato a tempo pieno.

underemployment, *n.* (*sind.*) sottoccupazione.

underestimate[1], *n.* 1 valutazione inadeguata. 2 preventivo troppo basso.

underestimate[2], *v. t.* fare un preventivo troppo basso per (*un lavoro*).

undergo, *v. t.* (*pass.* **underwent,** *part. pass.* **undergone**) subire, sopportare, essere sottoposto a (*prove e sim.*). // to **~ an examination** (*leg.*) subire un interrogatorio; to **~ repairs** (*org. az.*) (*di macchinario*) andare in riparazione; (*trasp. mar.*) (*di nave*) andare ai lavori.

underground, *avv.* sotterra. *n.* (*trasp. ferr.*) ferrovia sotterranea, metropolitana. // **~ premises** (*org. az.*) depositi interrati; **~ railway** (*trasp. ferr.*) (ferrovia) metropolitana; **~ station** (*trasp. ferr.*) stazione della metropolitana.

undergrounder, *n.* (*trasp. ferr.*) chi si serve

della metropolitana.

underhanded, *a.* (*org. az.*) (*di fabbrica*) con manodopera insufficiente.

underinsurance, *n.* (*ass.*) assicurazione per un valore insufficiente (*a coprire i danni*).

underlease[1], *n.* (*leg.*) subaffitto.

underlease[2], *v. t.* (*leg.*) subaffittare.

underlessee, *n.* (*leg.*) subaffittuario.

underlet, *v. t.* (*pass.* e *part. pass.* **underlet**) **1** (*leg.*) subaffittare. **2** (*leg.*) affittare (*locali e sim.*) a un prezzo inferiore al giusto.

underline, *v. t.* (*anche fig.*) mettere in evidenza.

undermanned, *a.* (*org. az.*) (*di fabbrica*) con manodopera insufficiente, con pochi operai.

undermentioned, *a.* sottomenzionato, sottoindicato.

underpay, *v. t.* (*pass.* e *part. pass.* **underpaid**) (*pers.*) retribuire inadeguatamente.

underprice, *v. t.* **1** (*market.*) porre un prezzo a (*un articolo e sim.*) inferiore a quello corrente. **2** (*market.*) battere (*un concorrente*) nei prezzi.

underproduction, *n.* (*econ., org. az.*) sottoproduzione, produzione insufficiente.

underproductive, *a.* (*econ., org. az.*) sottoproduttivo.

undersecretary, *n.* sottosegretario, vicesegretario.

undersecretaryship, *n.* sottosegretariato.

undersell, *v. t.* (*pass.* e *part. pass.* **undersold**) **1** (*market.*) «svendere» (*merce*), vendere (*merce*) sottocosto. **2** (*market.*) vendere a prezzi più bassi di (*altri prodotti similari*). **3** (*market.*) vendere a un prezzo inferiore a quello di (*un concorrente*).

underselling, *n.* (*market.*) vendita sottocosto.

undersign, *v. t.* sottoscrivere, firmare in calce (*un documento, una lettera, ecc.*).

undersigned, *a.* sottoscritto. // **the ~** il sottoscritto.

understand, *v. t.* (*pass.* e *part. pass.* **understood**) **1** capire, comprendere, intendere. **2** apprendere, venire a sapere. **3** credere, immaginare, pensare. // to **~ each other** (*o* **one another**) capirsi, intendersi.

understanding, *n.* **1** comprensione. **2** accordo, intesa. // **on this ~** a questa condizione; **on the ~ that** a condizione che, a patto che.

understate, *v. t.* attenuare; sottovalutare. // to **~ one's taxable income** (*fin.*) dichiarare un (reddito) imponibile inferiore a quello reale.

understock[1], *n.* (*market., org. az.*) scorta insufficiente (*di merci, materie prime, ecc.*).

understock[2], *v. t.* (*market., org. az.*) approvvigionare (*un negozio, uno stabilimento, ecc.*) d'una quantità insufficiente di merce. // **to be understocked with certain goods** (*org. az.*) avere poca merce d'un certo tipo (*in magazzino, in negozio, ecc.*).

understood, *a.* compreso, capito, inteso.

undertake, *v. t.* (*pass.* **undertook,** *part. pass.* **undertaken**) **1** intraprendere. **2** assumere. **3** assumersi l'impegno di, impegnarsi a. // to **~ legal proceedings against sb.** (*leg.*) procedere per vie legali contro q.; to **~ on contract** (*leg.*) prendere in appalto, appaltare; to **~ a responsibility** assumersi una responsabilità.

undertaker, *n.* **1** imprenditore. **2** appaltatore. **3** impresario di pompe funebri.

undertaking, *n.* **1** impresa, azienda. **2** impegno, promessa.

undertone, *n.* **1** tono basso, tono sommesso. **2** (*Borsa, fin.*) tendenza di base (*d'un mercato e sim.*).

underuse, *v. t.* (*econ.*) non sfruttare adeguatamente.

undervaluation, *n.* (*econ.*) svalutazione, deprezzamento.

undervalue, *v. t.* (*econ.*) svalutare, deprezzare.

undervalued, *a.* **1** sottovalutato. **2** svalutato, deprezzato.

underwrite, *v. t.* (*pass.* **underwrote,** *part. pass.* **underwritten**) **1** (*anche fig.*) sottoscrivere. **2** (*ass.*) assicurare (*specialm. una nave*). **3** (*ass.*) emettere (*una polizza, specialm. d'assicurazione marittima*). **4** (*fin.*) sottoscrivere (*un'emissione di titoli*); acquistare (*azioni, titoli*). **5** (*fin.*) finanziare, sostenere finanziariamente (*un'impresa e sim.*). // to **~ stock** (*fin.*) sottoscrivere capitale azionario.

underwriter, *n.* **1** (*ass.*) assicuratore (*specialm. marittimo*). **2** (*fin.*) sottoscrittore (*di titoli*). **3** (*fin.*) finanziatore. **4** (*fin.*) società gestrice di fondi (comuni) d'investimento.

underwriting, *n.* **1** (*ass.*) assicurazione (*specialm. marittima*). **2** (*ass., fin.*) «underwriting». **3** (*fin.*) sottoscrizione (*di titoli*). **4** (*fin.*) finanziamento.

undischarged, *a.* **1** non scaricato, ancora carico. **2** (*cred.*) non saldato, insoluto. // **~ bankrupt** (*leg.*) fallito non riabilitato; **an ~ debt** (*cred.*) un debito insoluto.

undisclosed, *a.* non svelato, non reso noto, occulto.

undisputed, *a.* non contestato. // **an ~ credit** (*cred.*) un credito non contestato.

undistributed, *a.* non distribuito. // ~ **profits** (*fin.*) utili non distribuiti.

undivided, *a.* indiviso, intero. // ~ **profits** (*fin.*) utili indivisi; ~ **responsibility** responsabilità indivisa.

undock, *v. t.* (*trasp. mar.*) far uscire (*una nave*) dal bacino. *v. i.* (*trasp. mar.*) uscire dal bacino.

undue, *a.* 1 indebito. 2 (*cred.*) non dovuto, non ancora scaduto. // **an** ~ **debt** (*cred.*) un debito non ancora scaduto; ~ **influence** (*leg.*) ingerenza illegale, captazione.

unearned, *a.* non guadagnato. // ~ **income** (*econ.*) reddito non di lavoro, rendita; ~ **increment** (*econ.*) plusvalore; ~ **premium** (*ass.*) parte di premio rimborsabile in caso di disdetta anticipata (*della polizza*); ~ **revenue** (*econ.*) *V.* ~ **income.**

uneconomic, *a.* 1 (*econ.*) antieconomico. 2 (*econ.*) improduttivo. // ~ **industries** (*econ.*) industrie improduttive; **an** ~ **method of production** (*econ.*) un metodo di produzione antieconomico.

uneconomical, *a. V.* **uneconomic.**

unemployed, *a.* 1 (*econ.*) (*di denaro*) non investito, inutilizzato. 2 (*sind.*) disoccupato. 3 **the unemployed** (*sind.*) i disoccupati. // ~ **capital** (*econ.*) capitale inutilizzato, inattivo.

unemployment, *n.* (*sind.*) disoccupazione. // ~ **benefit** (*sind.*) sussidio di disoccupazione; ~ **benefits** (*sind.*) cassa integrazione (guadagni); ~ **compensation** (*sind.*) *V.* ~ **benefit;** ~ **insurance** (*ass.*) assicurazione contro la disoccupazione; ~ **level** (*sind.*) livello di disoccupazione; ~ **rate** (*sind.*) indice di disoccupazione, tasso di disoccupazione.

unendorsed, *a.* (*cred.*) non girato, senza girata. // **an** ~ **cheque** (*banca, cred.*) un assegno non girato.

uneven, *a.* 1 irregolare. 2 (*mat.*) dispari. // ~ **earnings** (*rag.*) guadagni irregolari; ~ **numbers** (*mat.*) numeri dispari.

unevenness, *n.* disuguaglianza.

unexcused, *a.* non scusato, ingiustificato. // ~ **absences** (*pers.*) assenze ingiustificate.

unexpected, *a.* imprevisto, improvviso. // **an** ~ **circumstance** (*o* **event**) un imprevisto.

unexpectedly, *avv.* improvvisamente.

unexpensive, *a.* non dispendioso, a buon mercato.

unexpired, *a.* (*leg.*) non (ancora) scaduto. // **an** ~ **lease** (*leg.*) un affitto non ancora scaduto; ~ **time** (*cred.*) tempo mancante alla scadenza (*di un effetto e sim.*).

unexpressed, *a.* non espresso, inespresso, tacito.

unfair, *a.* ingiusto, iniquo, disonesto, sleale. // ~ **competition** (*leg., market.*) concorrenza sleale; **an** ~ **judgment** (*leg.*) una sentenza iniqua; ~ **practice** (*leg., market.*). *V.* ~ **competition.**

unfairness, *n.* ingiustizia.

unfashionable, *a.* fuori moda.

unfavourable, *a.* contrario. // ~ **answer** risposta negativa; **an** ~ **balance of trade** (*econ.*) una bilancia commerciale passiva; **an** ~ **business climate** un «clima» non propizio agli scambi; **an** ~ **economic trend** (*econ.*) una congiuntura sfavorevole, una congiuntura avversa; **an** ~ **exchange** (*econ.*) un cambio sfavorevole.

unfeasible, *a.* non fattibile.

unfilled, *a.* 1 non riempito, vuoto. 2 (*org. az.*) (*di posto*) libero, non occupato, vacante. // **the** ~ **spaces** gli spazi in bianco (*d'un modulo e sim.*); ~ **vacancy** (*org. az.*) posto di lavoro non occupato.

unfinished, *a.* 1 non finito. 2 (*org. az.*) (*di prodotto*) semilavorato. // ~ **products** (*org. az.*) prodotti semilavorati, semilavorati.

unfit, *a.* disadatto.

unforeseeable, *a.* imprevedibile.

unforeseen, *a.* imprevisto.

unfounded, *a.* infondato, ingiustificato. // **an** ~ **accusation** (*leg.*) un'accusa infondata; **an** ~ **claim** (*leg.*) una pretesa ingiustificata; **an** ~ **rumour** una voce infondata.

unfranked, *a.* (*fin.*) senza franchigia fiscale.

unfreeze, *v. t.* (*pass.* **unfroze,** *part. pass.* **unfrozen**) 1 sgelare. 2 (*econ.*) liberalizzare (*prezzi*); liberare (*i prezzi*) dai regolamenti (dai controlli, ecc); sbloccare (*prezzi, fondi, ecc.*). 3 (*econ.*) smobilizzare (*capitali*).

unfreezing, *n.* 1 (*econ.*) liberalizzazione (*dei prezzi*); sblocco (*di prezzi, fondi, ecc.*). 2 (*econ.*) smobilizzo (*di capitali*).

unfruitful, *a.* infruttifero (*in senso proprio*).

unfunded, *a.* (*fin.*) (*di debito pubblico*) non consolidato, fluttuante. // ~ **debt** (*fin.*) debito (pubblico) fluttuante.

unification, *n.* unificazione.

unified, *a.* unificato, reso uniforme. // **a** ~ **currency** (*econ.*) una moneta comune; ~ **debt** (*fin.*) debito consolidato.

unify, *v. t.* unificare.

unilateral, *a.* (*leg.*) unilaterale. // ~ **contract** (*leg.*) contratto unilaterale.

unilaterality, *n.* (*leg.*) unilateralità.

unindorsed, *a.* (*cred.*) non girato, senza girata. // **an** ~ **cheque** (*cred.*) un assegno non girato.

uninominal, *a.* uninominale.

uninsured, *a.* (*ass.*) non assicurato.

uninterrupted, *a.* ininterrotto.

uninvested, *a.* (*fin.*) giacente (*non investito*).

union, *n.* 1 unione, alleanza, confederazione. 2 (*sind.*) (= **trade union, labor union**) sindacato. // **unions' actions** (*sind.*) manifestazioni sindacali; ~ **card** (*sind.*) tessera del sindacato; ~ **headquarters** (*sind.*) centrale sindacale; ~ **leader** (*sind.*) dirigente sindacale; **a** ~ **member** (*sind.*) un iscritto a un sindacato; ~ **militancy** (*sind.*) attivismo sindacale, il militare in un sindacato; ~ **militant** (*sind.*) chi milita nelle file d'un sindacato, attivista sindacale; ~ **officer** (*sind.*) sindacalista; ~ **policy** (*sind.*) politica sindacale; ~ **representative** (*sind.*) sindacalista; ~ **shop** (*sind., USA*) stabilimento in cui tutti gli operai sono tenuti ad aderire a un sindacato; ~ **steward** (*sind.*) dirigente sindacale.

unionism, *n.* (= **trade unionism, labor unionism**) (*sind.*) sindacalismo.

unique, *a.* unico. // ~ **selling proposition** (*pubbl.*) proposta unica di vendita.

unissued stock, *n.* (*fin.*) capitale non emesso.

unit, *n.* 1 unità. 2 (*econ., org. az.*) unità produttiva, azienda. 3 (*mat.*) unità. // ~ **banking** (*banca, USA*) sistema bancario caratterizzato dalla presenza di molte piccole banche locali (*e non da poche grandi banche che operano attraverso filiali*); ~ **cost** (*rag.*) costo unitario; ~ **of account (u.a.)** (*econ., fin.*) unità di conto (*U.C.*); ~ **of account issues** (*fin.*) emissioni in unità di conto; ~ **of assessment** (*fin., leg.*) unità (*di misura*) usata ai fini della determinazione dell'imponibile; ~ **of length** unità di lunghezza; ~ **of measurement** unità di misura; ~ **of value** unità di valore; (*fig.*) metro di valutazione; (*fig., leg.*) *V.* ~ **of assessment;** ~ **of weight** unità di peso; ~ **price** (*econ., market.*) prezzo unitario; ~ **trusts** (*fin.*) fondi comuni d'investimento.

unitary, *a.* unitario.

united, *a.* unito, riunito, congiunto. // **the** ~ **Kingdom** il Regno Unito; **the** ~ **Nations** le Nazioni Unite.

unity, *n.* 1 unità. 2 (*mat.*) unità. // ~ **of command** (*org. az.*) unità di comando; ~ **of direction** (*org. az.*) unità di direzione; ~ **of supervision** (*org. az.*) unità di controllo.

universal, *a.* universale. // ~ **agent** (*pers.*) agente universale, agente generale; ~ **legacy** (*leg.*) legato universale; ~ **succession** (*leg.*) successione universale.

universe, *n.* universo.

unjust, *a.* 1 ingiusto, iniquo. 2 (*leg.*) indebito. // ~ **enrichment** (*leg.*) indebito (*o* illecito) arricchimento.

unjustified, *a.* ingiustificato.

unknown, *a.* ignoto, sconosciuto. *n.* (*mat.*) incognita. // ~ **person** (*leg.*) ignoto.

unlawful, *a.* (*leg.*) illegale, illecito, illegittimo, abusivo. // **the** ~ **consideration of a contract** (*leg.*) la causa illecita d'un contratto; ~ **measures** (*leg.*) misure illecite; ~ **son** (*leg.*) figlio illegittimo, figlio naturale.

unlawfulness, *n.* (*leg.*) illegalità, illiceità, illegittimità.

unlimited, *a.* illimitato. // ~ **company** (*fin.*) società in nome collettivo; ~ **flexibility** (*fin.*) flessibilità illimitata; ~ **liability** (*fin.*) responsabilità illimitata; ~ **partnership** (*fin.*) società in nome collettivo; ~ **policy** (*ass.*) polizza che copre tutti i rischi (*d'un ramo*).

unlisted, *a.* che non figura in un elenco. // ~ **security** (*fin.*) titolo non quotato (*in Borsa*).

unload[1], *n.* (*trasp. mar.*) merce scaricata, merce sbarcata.

unload[2], *v. t.* 1 (*fin., market.*) svendere (*titoli, merci, ecc.*). 2 (*trasp.*) scaricare (*una nave, un carico, ecc.*); sbarcare (*un carico*). *v. i.* 1 (*fin., market.*) svendere titoli o merci (*avendo previsto un crollo dei prezzi*). 2 (*trasp.*) (*di nave*) scaricare.

unloader, *n.* (*pers.*) scaricatore.

unloading, *n.* 1 (*trasp.*) scarico, scaricamento. 2 (*trasp. mar.*) discarico, sbarco. // ~ **charges** (*trasp. mar.*) spese di sbarco; ~ **operations** (*trasp.*) operazioni di scarico; ~ **risk** (*trasp. mar.*) rischio di sbarco.

unmanaged flexibility, *n.* (*fin.*) flessibilità libera.

unmanufactured, *a.* (*market.*) (*di prodotto*) non lavorato, greggio, grezzo.

unmarked, *a.* non marcato, non contrassegnato. // ~ **shares** (*fin.*) azioni non stampigliate.

unmarketable, *a.* (*market.*) non commerciabile, invendibile.

unmarried, *a.* (*leg.*) nubile.

unmerchantable, *a.* (*market.*) non commerciabile, invendibile. // ~ **goods** (*market.*) merce invendibile.

unmoor, *v. t.* (*trasp. mar.*) disormeggiare. *v. i.* (*trasp. mar.*) togliere gli ormeggi.

unmooring, *n.* (*trasp. mar.*) disormeggio.

unmortgaged, *a.* (*leg.*) non gravato da

ipoteca, non ipotecato. // **an ~ estate** (*leg.*) un immobile non gravato da ipoteca.

unnavigable, *a.* (*trasp., trasp. mar.*) non navigabile, innavigabile.

unofficial, *a.* non ufficiale, ufficioso. // **~ character** ufficiosità; **an ~ estimate** una stima non ufficiale; **~ stoppage** (*sind.*) *V.* **~ strike**; **~ strike** (*sind.*) sciopero «selvaggio».

unofficially, *avv.* ufficiosamente.

unpack, *v. t.* **1** disimballare, spacchettare. **2** (*market., trasp.*) sballare.

unpacking, *n.* (*market., trasp.*) sballatura.

unpaid, *a.* **1** non pagato. **2** (*cred.*) non saldato, insoluto. **3** (*pers.*) non retribuito, irremunerato. // **an ~ bill** (*cred.*) una cambiale insoluta, una cambiale in sofferenza; **~ invoices** (*market.*) fatture insolute; **an ~ position** (*pers.*) un impiego non retribuito.

unpatented, *a.* (*leg.*) non brevettato. // **~ inventions** (*leg.*) invenzioni non brevettate.

unpaying, *a.* che non paga.

unpredictable, *a.* imprevedibile.

unproductive, *a.* improduttivo, sterile. // **~ consumption** (*econ.*) (i) consumi improduttivi.

unproductiveness, *n.* (*econ.*) improduttività.

unprofitable, *a.* **1** non redditizio, infruttuoso. **2** (*rag.*) passivo.

unquestionable, *a.* incontestabile. // **~ evidence** (*leg.*) prove incontestabili.

unquoted, *a.* (*fin.*) (*di titolo*) non quotato (*nel listino ufficiale di Borsa*).

unreadable, *a.* illeggibile.

unrealizable, *a.* irrealizzabile, di (assai) difficile realizzo. // **an ~ asset** (*econ., rag.*) un'attività di difficile realizzo.

unrecorded, *a.* non registrato. // **an ~ deed to property** (*leg.*) un atto di proprietà non registrato.

unrecoverable, *a.* irrecuperabile. // **an ~ debt** (*o* **credit**) (*cred.*) un credito irrecuperabile.

unredeemable, *a.* irredimibile, non riscattabile. // **~ bank-notes** (*fin.*) banconote non convertibili (*in moneta metallica*); **an ~ loan** (*fin.*) un prestito irredimibile.

unregistered, *a.* **1** (*fin.*) (*di titolo*) non nominativo, al portatore. **2** (*leg.*) non registrato, non iscritto. // **~ letters** (*comun.*) lettere non raccomandate; **~ mortgage** (*leg.*) ipoteca non accesa; **~ trademark** (*leg.*) marchio (di fabbrica) non registrato.

unremunerative, *a.* non remunerativo, tutt'altro che lucrativo, infruttuoso.

unrest, *n.* **1** agitazione. **2** sommossa, tumulto.

unsafe, *a.* pericoloso, rischioso.

unsalability, *n.* invendibilità.

unsalable, *a.* invendibile, inalienabile.

unsaleability, *n. V.* **unsalability.**

unsaleable, *a. V.* **unsalable.**

unsatisfactory, *a.* insoddisfacente.

unsatisfied, *a.* insoddisfatto, non soddisfatto. // **~ applications for jobs** (*pers.*) domande di lavoro non soddisfatte; **an ~ demand** (*econ.*) una domanda insoddisfatta.

unseal, *v. t.* togliere i sigilli a.

unseat, *v. t.* dimettere (*q.*) da una carica.

unseaworthy, *a.* (*trasp. mar.*) (*di nave*) non idoneo alla navigazione.

unsecured, *a.* (*cred.*) non garantito, senza garanzia, allo scoperto. // **~ advances** (*cred.*) anticipazioni allo scoperto, anticipi allo scoperto; **~ bond** (*cred.*) un'obbligazione senza garanzia; **~ credit** (*leg.*) credito chirografario; **~ creditor** (*leg.*) creditore chirografario; **~ debt** (*leg.*) credito chirografario; **~ loan** (*cred.*) prestito non garantito.

unsettle, *v. t.* agitare, turbare.

unsettled, *a.* **1** agitato, turbato. **2** (*cred.*) non pagato, non saldato, insoluto.

unship, *v. t.* (*trasp. mar.*) sbarcare, scaricare (*merci*).

unsinkable, *a.* (*trasp. mar.*) (*di nave*) inaffondabile, insommergibile.

unskilled, *a.* **1** inesperto. **2** (*pers.*) non specializzato. // **~ labour** (*pers.*) manodopera non qualificata, manovalanza; **~ worker** (*pers.*) operaio non qualificato, manovale.

unsold, *a.* (*market.*) invenduto. // **~ goods** (*market.*) l'invenduto, le giacenze di magazzino.

unson, *v. t.* (*leg.*) non riconoscere (*q.*) come figlio.

unsophisticated, *a.* non sofisticato, genuino.

unstable, *a.* instabile, incerto.

unstableness, *n.* instabilità, incertezza.

unstamped, *a.* **1** (*comun.*) (*di lettera*) non affrancato, senza francobollo. **2** (*leg.*) (*di documento*) senza bollo. // **~ paper** carta libera; **~ shares** (*fin.*) azioni non stampigliate.

unsteadiness, *n.* instabilità, irregolarità.

unsteady, *a.* instabile, irregolare, variabile. // **an ~ economic system** (*econ.*) un sistema economico instabile; **~ prices** (*market.*) prezzi instabili.

unstow, *v. t.* (*trasp. mar.*) distivare, disistivare, scaricare (*merce già stivata*). // **to ~ a ship** (*trasp. mar.*) scaricare una nave.

unstowing, *n.* (*trasp. mar.*) disistivaggio,

discarico (*di merce già stivata*).

unsuccessful, *a.* 1 che non ha (avuto) successo, sfortunato, non riuscito, fallito. 2 inutile. // **the ~ party** (*leg.*) la parte soccombente (*in giudizio*).

unsuitable, *a.* disadatto.

untax, *v. t.* (*fin.*) esentare (*q.* o *qc.*) dalle imposte, detassare.

untaxed, *a.* 1 (*fin.*) esente da imposte, non tassato. 2 (*fin.*) esentasse, detraibile. // **an ~ property** (*fin.*) una proprietà non soggetta a imposta.

untaxing, *n.* (*fin.*) detassazione.

until, *prep.* sino a. *cong.* fino al momento che, finché non. // **~ further advice** fino a nuovo avviso.

untouched, *a.* intatto.

untransferable, *a.* (*leg.*) non trasferibile, non cedibile. // **an ~ right** (*leg.*) un diritto inalienabile.

untrue, *a.* non vero, falso, menzognero.

unused, *a.* 1 non usato, non adoperato, inutilizzato. 2 non ancora usato. 3 in disuso.

unvalued, *a.* non valutato. // **~ policy** (*ass.*) polizza priva dell'indicazione del valore assicurato.

unwritten, *a.* tradizionale. // **the ~ laws** (*leg.*) la legge non scritta.

up[1], *avv.* e *prep.* in su, in alto. *a.* 1 che va in su, ascendente. 2 (*anche fig.*) alto. 3 (*econ.*) (*di domanda, prezzo, ecc.*) in aumento, in ripresa. *n.* alto (*nell'espressione «gli alti e i bassi»*); periodo buono, periodo di prosperità, periodo di successo. // **~ -to-date** al corrente, aggiornato; (*market., pubbl.*) alla moda, moderno; to **be ~ to** (*di cosa*) essere conforme a, corrispondere a; (*di cosa e di persona*) essere all'altezza di; (*di persona*) stare tramando.

up[2], *v. t.* 1 alzare. 2 aumentare, far aumentare, far salire. 3 (*pers.*) promuovere. *v. i.* 1 alzarsi. 2 aumentare, crescere.

update, *v. t.* ammodernare, rinnovare.

updating, *n.* ammodernamento, rinnovamento. // **the ~ of managers** (*pers.*) l'adeguamento dei quadri direttivi.

upgrade, *v. t.* 1 (*market.*) migliorare la qualità di (*un prodotto*). 2 (*market.*) sostituire (*un prodotto di qualità inferiore*) con un prodotto migliore (*per ottenere un prezzo più alto*). 3 (*pers.*) promuovere (*un dipendente*).

upkeep, *n.* 1 mantenimento. 2 (*org. az.*) manutenzione. 3 (*rag.*) spese di manutenzione. // **~ expenses** (*rag.*) spese di manutenzione.

upon, *avv.* e *prep.* 1 sopra. 2 a, all'atto di, al momento di. // **~ collection** alla riscossione; (*banca, cred.*) salvo incasso, salvo buon fine; **~ receipt of your letter** (*comun.*) al ricevimento della vostra lettera; **~ request** su richiesta, a richiesta.

upper, *a.* più elevato. // **the ~ class** (*econ.*) la nobiltà, la «crema» (*della società*); **the ~ House** (*ingl.*) la Camera dei Lord.

upset[1], *n.* 1 (*anche fig.*) capovolgimento. 2 (*anche fig.*) turbamento.

upset[2], *v. t.* (*pass.* e *part. pass.* **upset**) 1 (*anche fig.*) capovolgere. 2 (*anche fig.*) turbare.

upset[3], *a.* 1 (*anche fig.*) capovolto, rovesciato. 2 (*anche fig.*) agitato, turbato. // **the ~ price** il prezzo (*minimo*) d'apertura (*in una vendita all'asta*).

upsurge[1], *n.* 1 aumento, crescita, incremento. 2 (*Borsa, market.*) rialzo improvviso, «impennata» (*delle quotazioni, dei prezzi, ecc.*). // **an ~ of wage claims** (*sind.*) un'«impennata» delle richieste salariali.

upsurge[2], *v. i.* aumentare, crescere, rialzarsi, avere un incremento.

upswing, *n.* 1 aumento improvviso, crescita subitanea. 2 (*Borsa*) fase di rialzo. 3 (*Borsa, econ.*) ripresa. 4 (*Borsa, market.*) «impennata» (*di prezzi, ecc.*). 5 (*econ.*) espansione, tendenza all'espansione.

uptrend, *n.* (*Borsa, fin.*) fase di rialzo; tendenza al rialzo.

upturn, *n.* (*econ.*) tendenza al rialzo, espansione, tendenza all'espansione. // **an ~ in the standard of living** (*econ.*) un miglioramento del tenore di vita; **an exceptional ~ of strikes** (*sind.*) un'ondata eccezionale di scioperi.

upvaluation, *n.* (*fin.*) sopravvalutazione.

upvalue, *v. t.* (*fin.*) sopravvalutare.

upward, *a.* diretto verso l'alto. // **an ~ movement** (*econ.*) un rialzo; **~ phase** (*econ.*) fase d'espansione, fase positiva; **~ tendency** (*econ.*) *V.* **~ trend; ~ trend** (*econ.*) tendenza al rialzo (*dei prezzi*).

urge[1], *n.* incitamento, sollecitazione.

urge[2], *v. t.* incitare, sollecitare. *v. i.* insistere. // to **~ payments** (*cred.*) sollecitare i pagamenti.

urgency, *n.* insistenza.

urgent, *a.* insistente. // **an ~ creditor** (*cred.*) un creditore insistente; **~ messages** (*comun.*) messaggi urgenti; **~ rate** (*comun.*) tariffa per telegrammi urgenti.

usage, *n.* uso, consuetudine, usanza. // **~ and abusage** uso e abuso.

usance, *n.* 1 (*cred., leg.*) tempo concesso per il pagamento delle cambiali estere (*secondo la consuetudine locale*). 2 (*leg.*) usanza, consuetudine.

use[1], *n.* 1 uso, impiego. 2 uso, usanza, consuetudine. 3 (*leg.*) uso, utenza, godimento. // ~ **and wont** uso e costume; ~ **tax** (*fin.*) tassa sull'uso (*d'un certo articolo*).

use[2], *v. t.* usare, impiegare, far uso di. // to ~ **up** consumare, esaurire.

used, *a.* usato. // ~ **cars** automobili di seconda mano; to **be** ~ **to** essere abituato a.

useful, *a.* utile. // to **be** ~ esser utile.

usefulness, *n.* utilità.

useless, *a.* inutile, disutile.

uselessness, *n.* inutilità, disutilità.

user, *n.* 1 chi usa (*qc.*), utente, fruitore. 2 (*econ., market.*) consumatore. 3 (*leg.*) diritto d'uso. // **right of** ~ (*leg.*) servitù.

usher, *n.* (*pers.*) usciere.

usual, *a.* abituale, consueto. // ~ **tare** (*market.*) tara d'uso; **as** ~ al solito, come di consueto.

usucapion, *n. V.* **usucaption.**

usucaption, *n.* (*leg.*) usucapione.

usufruct, *n.* (*leg.*) usufrutto.

usufructuary, *a.* (*leg.*) di usufrutto, pertinente a usufrutto. *n.* (*leg.*) usufruttuario.

usurer, *n.* strozzino.

usury, *n.* strozzinaggio.

utilities, *n. pl.* (*fin., USA*) titoli d'aziende di servizi pubblici.

utility, *n.* 1 utilità. 2 (*econ.*) utilità. 3 (*fin., USA*) servizio pubblico. 4 (*fin., USA*) azienda di servizio pubblico. // ~ **companies** (*fin., USA*) società di servizi pubblici (*del gas, dei trasporti, ecc.*); ~ **man** (*pers., USA*) fattorino; **the** ~ **theory of value** (*econ.*) la teoria utilitaristica del valore.

utilization, *n.* utilizzo. // **the** ~ **of plant facilities** (*org. az.*) lo sfruttamento degli impianti.

V

vacancy, *n.* 1 (*leg.*) vacanza (*d'eredità*). 2 (*leg., pers.*) vacanza, posto vacante, impiego vacante. // ~ **clause** (*ass.*) clausola che prevede il mantenimento della copertura di locali non occupati; ~ **permit** (*ass.*) *V.* ~ **clause.**

vacant, *a.* 1 (*leg.*) (*d'appartamento e sim.*) sfitto. 2 (*leg.*) (*di proprietà, di terreno*) senza proprietario, vacante. 3 (*leg., pers.*) vacante. 4 (*pers.*) (*di posto*) libero, non occupato; scoperto. // **a** ~ **estate** (*leg.*) una proprietà abbandonata; **a** ~ **house** una casa sfitta; ~ **land** (*leg.*) terreno non occupato, terreno non utilizzato (*non coltivato, ecc.*); **a** ~ **post** (*o* **situation**) (*pers.*) un posto (*o* un impiego) vacante; ~ **succession** (*leg.*) eredità giacente (*o* vacante).

vacate, *v. t.* 1 lasciar vuoto, lasciar libero, sfittare, sgomberare. 2 (*leg.*) annullare, cassare. 3 (*pers.*) dimettersi, dare le dimissioni da (*una carica e sim.*). *v. i.* (*pers.*) dimettersi, dare le dimissioni. // to ~ **a charter** (*leg.*) annullare uno statuto; to ~ **a position** (*pers.*) liberare un posto (di lavoro).

vacation[1], *n.* 1 sgombero (*da una casa a un'altra, ecc.*). 2 (*pers.*) vacanza, ferie. 3 (*pers.*) dimissione, rinuncia. // **on** ~ (*pers.*) in ferie; in villeggiatura.

vacation[2], *v. i.* 1 (*pers., USA*) far vacanza, andare in ferie. 2 (*USA*) passare le vacanze.

vade-mecum, *n.* vademecum, taccuino, prontuario.

vague, *a.* vago, incerto.

valid, *a.* (*anche leg.*) valido, fondato. // **a** ~ **claim** (*leg.*) una pretesa fondata; ~ **consent** (*leg.*) consenso valido; **a** ~ **contract** (*leg.*) un contratto valido; **a** ~ **title** (*leg.*) un titolo legittimo.

validate, *v. t.* 1 (*leg.*) convalidare, riconoscere la validità di (*qc.*). 2 (*leg.*) omologare. 3 (*leg.*) dichiarare (*q.*) eletto. // to ~ **a treaty** (*leg.*) omologare un trattato.

validation, *n.* 1 (*leg.*) convalidazione, convalida. 2 (*leg.*) omologazione. // **the** ~ **of a contract** (*leg.*) la convalida d'un contratto.

validity, *n.* (*anche leg.*) validità, fondatezza. // **the** ~ **of a claim** (*leg.*) la fondatezza d'una pretesa; **the** ~ **of a deed** (*leg.*) la validità d'un atto; **the** ~ **of a railway ticket** (*trasp. ferr.*) la validità d'un biglietto ferroviario.

valorization, *n.* (*econ.*) valorizzazione (*d'un prodotto*).

valorize, *v. t.* (*econ.*) valorizzare (*un prodotto*).

valuable, *a.* 1 valutabile. 2 (*anche fig.*) di gran valore, prezioso. // ~ **articles** *V.* ~ **goods;** ~ **goods** merci preziose, valori, preziosi; **for a** ~ **consideration** (*leg.*) a titolo oneroso.

valuables, *n. pl.* 1 valori. 2 preziosi, merci preziose.

valuation, *n.* 1 valutazione, apprezzamento. 2 (*ass.*) determinazione del valore attuale (*d'una polizza sulla vita*). 3 (*econ.*) prezzo (*d'un bene*) determinato secondo la stima del valore di mercato. 4 (*fin., leg., rag.*) estimo, valutazione, perizia, stima. // ~ **accounts** (*rag.*) fondi rischi; **the** ~ **for customs purposes** (*dog.*) la fissazione del valore in dogana; **the** ~ **of a property** (*rag.*) la stima d'una proprietà; **the** ~ **of a risk** (*ass.*) la valutazione d'un rischio.

valuator, *n.* (*ass., leg.*) stimatore, perito.

value[1], *n.* 1 valore, pregio. 2 (*banca, fin., rag.*) valuta. 3 (*econ.*) valore, prezzo. 4 (*mat.*) valore. // ~ **added** (*econ.*) valore aggiunto; ~ **-added tax (VAT)** (*fin.*) imposta sul valore aggiunto (*IVA*); **VAT-free** (*fin.*) esente da IVA; **VAT-inclusive price** (*market.*) prezzo IVA inclusa; ~ **-added tax rates** (*fin.*) aliquote dell'imposta sul valore aggiunto; ~ **analysis** (*org. az., rag.*) analisi valutativa; ~ **date** (*banca, fin.*) giorno di valuta, valuta al; **the** ~ **declared** (*ass.*) il valore dichiarato; ~ **goods** valori, preziosi, merci preziose; ~ **in account** (*banca*) valuta in conto; ~ **in exchange** (*econ.*) potere d'acquisto; «~ **on account**» (*banca*) «valuta in conto»; ~ **parcel** (*comun.*) pacco (di) valori, pacco assicurato; **values to be made good** (*ass. mar.*) massa attiva, massa creditizia (*d'avaria generale*); **at** ~ (*market.*) al prezzo corrente di mercato; **(for)** ~ **received** (*banca*) per valuta ricevuta.

value², *v. t.* valutare, apprezzare, stimare. // to ~ **at cost** (*rag.*) valutare al costo; to ~ **at market price** (*rag.*) valutare al prezzo di mercato; to ~ **on sb.** (*cred.*) rivalersi su q. (*spiccando una tratta*); to ~ **a property** (*rag.*) stimare una proprietà.

valued, *a.* valutato, apprezzato, pregiato, stimato. // ~ **goods** (*market.*) merci pregiate; ~ **policy** (*ass.*) polizza valutata, polizza con valore dichiarato.

valuer, *n.* stimatore, perito.

van¹, *n.* 1 (*trasp. aut.*) furgone, autofurgone. 2 (*trasp. ferr.*) bagagliaio. 3 (*trasp. ferr.*) vagone. 4 (*trasp. ferr.*) carro merci.

van², *v. t.* (*trasp. aut.*) trasportare (*merci*) con un furgone.

variable, *a.* variabile, mutevole. *n.* (*mat.*) variabile. // ~ **costs** (*rag.*) costi variabili; ~ **exchange** (*fin.*) (l')incerto (*nelle locuzioni: «quotare il certo per l'incerto», ecc.*); ~ **-rate loan** (*fin.*) prestito (*o* mutuo) a tasso (d'interesse) variabile; **a** ~ **yield** (*rag.*) un reddito variabile; ~ **-yield** (*fin., rag.*) a reddito variabile; ~ **-yield securities** (*fin.*) titoli a reddito variabile.

variance, *n.* 1 variazione. 2 differenza, discrepanza. 3 (*mat., rag.*) deviazione, scostamento.

variation, *n.* variazione, cambiamento, modifica, mutamento. // ~ **of compulsory reserve** (*banca, fin.*) variazione della riserva obbligatoria.

varied, *a.* vario, svariato.

variety, *n.* 1 varietà. 2 (*market.*) varietà, assortimento, gamma. 3 (*market., USA*) *V.* ~ **store.** // **a** ~ **of apples** (*market.*) una varietà di mele; ~ **shop** (*market., USA*) negozio (per la vendita al dettaglio) di articoli vari; ~ **store** (*market., USA*) negozio (per la vendita al dettaglio) di articoli vari.

vary, *v. t.* cambiare, modificare, mutare, diversificare. *v. i.* 1 cambiare, modificarsi, mutare, diversificarsi. 2 differire. // to ~ **from the law** (*leg.*) trasgredire alla legge.

vault, *n.* 1 volta (*architettonica*). 2 (*banca*) camera blindata.

vector, *n.* (*mat.*) vettore.

vehicle, *n.* 1 (*fig.*) veicolo, mezzo, strumento. 2 (*trasp.*) veicolo, vettura, mezzo di trasporto.

velocity, *n.* velocità. // **the** ~ **of circulation** (*econ.*) la velocità di circolazione (*della moneta*); **the** ~ **of money** (*econ.*) la velocità di circolazione della moneta.

vend, *v. t.* (*market.*) vendere. *v. i.* (*market.*) (*d'articolo*) vendersi, essere scambiato, diventare oggetto di scambio.

vendee, *n.* (*market.*) acquirente, compratore.

vender, *n.* 1 (*market.*) venditore. 2 (*market.*) distributore automatico (*d'articoli*).

vending machine, *n.* (*market.*) distributore automatico (*d'articoli*).

vendor, *n.* 1 (*market.*) venditore. 2 (*market.*) distributore automatico (*d'articoli*). // ~ **'s lien** (*leg.*) privilegio del venditore (*di terreni*); ~ **'s shares** (*fin.*) azioni di fondazione (*d'una società*).

vendue, *n.* (*USA*) asta pubblica. // ~ **crier** (*USA*) banditore (*d'asta*); ~ **master** (*USA*) banditore (*d'asta*).

venture¹, *n.* 1 pericolo, rischio. 2 impresa rischiosa. 3 (*econ.*) iniziativa imprenditoriale. 4 (*fin.*) speculazione. // ~ **capital** «venture capital» (*tipo assai complesso di «investment banking», q. V.*); capitale di rischio; ~ **-capital company** (*fin.*) società specializzata nel «venture capital».

venture², *v. t.* rischiare. // to ~ **one's capital** (*fin.*) mettere a repentaglio il proprio capitale.

venturer, *n.* (*fin.*) chi rischia denaro, speculatore.

verbal, *a.* verbale. // ~ **agreement** (*leg.*) accordo verbale; **a** ~ **contract** (*leg.*) un contratto verbale; ~ **evidence** (*leg.*) prova orale, testimonianza orale.

verbally, *avv.* verbalmente, oralmente.

verdict, *n.* (*leg.*) verdetto. // ~ **for the plaintiff** (*leg.*) verdetto di condanna, verdetto di colpevolezza; ~ **of guilty** (*leg.*) verdetto di colpevolezza (*o* di condanna); ~ **of not guilty** (*leg.*) verdetto d'assoluzione.

verifiable, *a.* verificabile, controllabile.

verification, *n.* 1 verificazione, verifica, accertamento, controllo, riscontro. 2 (*leg.*) ratifica, sanzione. 3 (*leg.*) autenticazione (*di documenti*). // ~ **of facts** (*leg.*) verifica dei fatti.

verifier, *n.* (*pers.*) verificatore, controllore.

verify, *v. t.* 1 verificare, accertare, controllare, riscontrare. 2 (*leg.*) ratificare, sanzionare. 3 (*leg.*) autenticare (*documenti*). // to ~ **the contents of a packet** (*dog.*) verificare il contenuto d'un pacco.

versus, *prep.* (*abbr.* **v.**) (*leg.*) contro.

vertical, *a.* (*anche fig.*) verticale. // **a** ~ **business organization** (*econ., org. az.*) un'organizzazione commerciale verticale; ~ **combination** (*econ., org. az.*) *V.* ~ **integration;** ~ **combine** (*econ., org. az.*) gruppo economico verticale; ~ **expansion** (*org. az.*) espansione verticale; ~ **file** (*attr. uff.*) schedario verticale, archivio verticale; ~ **integration** (*econ., org. az.*) integrazione verticale, concentrazione verticale; ~ **labour union** (*sind.*) sindacato d'operai appartenenti a un'intera industria; ~ **merger** (*econ., org. az.*) fusione verticale; ~ **organizational structure** (*econ., org. az.*) struttura organizzativa verticale; ~ **trust** (*econ.*) monopolio verticale.

very, *avv.* assai. // ~ **dear** (*market.*) (*di articolo*) carissimo; **the ~ last thing(s)** (*market.*) le ultimissime novità.

vessel, *n.* (*trasp. mar.*) vascello, bastimento, nave. // ~ **aground** (*trasp. mar.*) nave in secco; ~ **discharging** (*trasp. mar.*) nave in discarica; ~ **entering in ballast** (*trasp. mar.*) nave che entra (in porto) in zavorra.

vest, *v. t.* 1 assegnare, attribuire, conferire. 2 (*fin.*) investire (*capitali*). *v. i.* (*leg.*) (*di diritto*) essere conferito, andare. // to ~ **sb. with the power to do st.** (*leg.*) investire q. dell'autorità (della facoltà, ecc.) di fare qc.

vested, *a.* (*leg.*) assegnato legalmente, acquisito, fissato, legittimo. // ~ **interests** (*leg.*) interessi acquisiti; **a ~ right** (*leg.*) un diritto acquisito.

veto[1]**,** *n.* veto.

veto[2]**,** *v. t.* mettere il veto a. // to ~ **a proposal** porre il veto a una proposta.

vexation, *n.* (*leg.*) vessazione.

vexatious, *a.* (*leg.*) vessatorio. // **a ~ suit at law** (*leg.*) un'azione legale vessatoria.

via[1]**,** *prep.* 1 per via di, mediante. 2 (*trasp.*) via, per la via di.

via[2]**,** *n.* (*cred.*) copia di cambiale, duplicato di cambiale.

viability, *n.* 1 vitalità. 2 (*econ., fin.*) solvibilità (*d'uno Stato*).

viable, *a.* (*econ., fin.*) (*d'uno Stato*) solvibile.

vice[1]**,** *n.* (*anche leg.*) vizio, difetto.

vice-[2]**,** *pref.* vice-. // ~ **-chairman** (*amm.*) vicepresidente; ~ **-treasurer** (*pers.*) vicetesoriere.

vice[3]**,** *n.* (*fam.*) vice (*abbr. di «vicedirettore» e sim.*).

victual[1]**,** *n.* vitto.

victual[2]**,** *v. t.* rifornire di viveri, approvvigionare. *v. i.* (*trasp. mar.*) (*di nave*) rifornirsi di viveri, approvvigionarsi.

victualer, *n.* (*USA*) *V.* **victualler.**

victualler, *n.* 1 approvvigionatore, fornitore (*di viveri*). 2 (*trasp. mar.*) nave (di) rifornimento.

victualling, *n.* approvvigionamento. // ~ **bill** (*trasp. mar.*) permesso (*doganale*) di provvigione a bordo (*elenco delle provviste in esenzione doganale*); ~ **ship** (*trasp. mar.*) nave (di) rifornimento; ~ **yard** (*trasp. mar.*) magazzino viveri.

videomaster, *n.* (*Borsa*) «videomaster».

view[1]**,** *n.* 1 vista. 2 opinione. 3 ispezione, sopralluogo. 4 fine, scopo. // **in ~** in vista; (*market.*) in mostra, aperto al(la vista del) pubblico; **in ~ of** in vista di; **on ~** (*market.*) in mostra, aperto al(la vista del) pubblico; **with a ~ to profit** a scopo di lucro.

view[2]**,** *v. t.* 1 guardare, osservare. 2 esaminare, ispezionare, prendere in considerazione, giudicare. // to ~ **evidence** (*leg.*) esaminare le prove.

vindicate, *v. t.* (*leg.*) convalidare, provare, sanzionare (*un diritto*).

vindication, *n.* (*leg.*) convalida, prova (*d'un diritto*), sanzione. // **the ~ of a man falsely convicted** (*leg.*) il proscioglimento d'un uomo accusato falsamente.

violate, *v. t.* (*leg.*) violare; contravvenire, trasgredire a (*una norma*). // to ~ **a law** (*leg.*) violare una legge.

violation, *n.* (*leg.*) violazione, contravvenzione, infrazione, trasgressione. // ~ **of the peace** (*leg.*) turbamento dell'ordine pubblico; **the ~ of a promise** la violazione d'una promessa.

violator, *n.* (*leg.*) violatore, contravventore, trasgressore.

virtual, *a.* effettivo, di fatto, in pratica.

virtually, *avv.* di fatto.

visa[1]**,** *n.* 1 visto, benestare. 2 (*tur.*) vidimazione, visto (*di passaporto e sim.*).

visa[2]**,** *v. t.* 1 (*tur.*) (*detto d'un'autorità consolare, ecc.*) vidimare, vistare, mettere il visto su (*un passaporto e sim.*). 2 (*tur.*) (*detto d'un'autorità consolare, ecc.*) concedere il passaporto a (*q.*).

vis-à-vis, *locuz. avv.* «vis-à-vis», dirimpetto. *prep.* (*anche fig.*) di fronte a; a fronte di.

visible, *a.* visibile. **visibles,** *n. pl.* (*econ.*) partite visibili. // ~ **and invisible items** (*econ.*) partite visibili e invisibili; **the ~ items in the balance of payments** (*econ.*) le partite visibili della bilancia dei pagamenti; ~ **supply** (*econ., org. az.*) scorte disponibili.

visit[1]**,** *n.* 1 visita. 2 (*trasp. mar.*) visita, ispezione (*doganale*).

visit[2]**,** *v. t.* 1 visitare, far visita a (*una persona o un luogo*). 2 (*trasp. mar.*) ispezionare; sottoporre (*una nave*) a visita doganale.

visiter, *n. V.* **visitor.**

visitor, *n.* 1 visitatore. 2 (*market.*) cliente. 3 (*tur.*) turista.

vital, *a.* 1 vivo. 2 essenziale, indispensabile.

vitiate, *v. t.* 1 viziare, corrompere. 2 (*leg.*) invalidare.

vocation, *n.* mestiere, professione. // ~: **joiner** (*su un modulo*) mestiere o professione: falegname.

vocational, *a.* 1 di vocazione, attitudinale. 2 di mestiere, professionale. // ~ **bureau** (*pers., sind.*) *V.* ~ **office**; ~ **education** istruzione professionale; ~ **guidance** (*pers.*) orientamento professionale; ~ **interest** (*pers.*) corredo attitudinale; ~ **-interest test** (*pers.*) test vocazionale, test d'interesse; ~ **office** (*pers., sind.*) ufficio (di) collocamento (*che inoltre offre assistenza per l'orientamento professionale*); ~ **training** (*pers.*) formazione professionale.

vogue, *n.* (*market.*) voga, moda. // **in** ~ (*market.*) in voga, alla moda.

void[1], *a.* (*leg.*) nullo, inefficace, non valido.

void[2], *v. t.* (*leg.*) annullare, rendere nullo, invalidare. // to ~ **a contract** (*leg.*) annullare un contratto; to ~ **a deed** (*leg.*) invalidare un atto; to ~ **a form** annullare un modulo.

voidable, *a.* (*leg.*) annullabile, invalidabile.

voidness, *n.* (*leg.*) inefficacia, nullità.

volatile, *a.* (*fig.*) volubile, mutevole. // **a** ~ **market** (*econ.*) un mercato soggetto a forti oscillazioni (*dei prezzi*); ~ **stocks** (*fin.*) titoli che hanno oscillazioni (*di valore*) molto ampie.

volume, *n.* 1 volume, capacità, massa, quantità. 2 (*giorn.*) volume, libro. 3 (*giorn.*) annata (*raccolta di giornali e sim.*). // **the** ~ **of a container** (*market.*) la capacità d'un recipiente; **the** ~ **of imports** (*comm. est.*) il volume delle importazioni; ~ **production** (*econ.*) produzione in massa, produzione in grandi quantità.

voluntary, *a.* intenzionale. // ~ **bankruptcy** (*leg.*) fallimento su istanza del fallito; ~ **checkoff** (*pers., sind.*) trattenuta volontaria; **a** ~ **confession** (*leg.*) una confessione spontanea; ~ **conveyance** (*leg.*) cessione a titolo gratuito; ~ **sale** (*leg.*) vendita volontaria; ~ **stranding to avoid wreck** (*ass. mar.*) arenamento volontario per evitare il naufragio; ~ **winding up** liquidazione volontaria (*d'una società*).

volunteer, *n.* (*leg.*) donatario.

vote[1], *n.* 1 numero di voti. 2 (*leg.*) diritto di voto. 3 (*leg.*) scheda di votazione.

vote[2], *v. t.* e *i.* dare il voto, approvare (*una mozione e sim.*) votando. // to ~ **a bill through** (*leg.*) approvare un disegno di legge; to ~ **a candidate in** (*leg.*) eleggere un candidato, nominare un candidato (*con votazione*); to ~ **down a motion** respingere una mozione (*votando contro*).

voter, *n.* elettore.

voting, *n.* votazione. // ~ **arrangements** procedura di votazione; ~ **right** (*leg.*) diritto di voto; ~ **stock** (*fin.*) azioni con diritto di voto; ~ **trust** (*fin.*) sindacato azionario.

vouch, *v. t.* 1 (*leg.*) attestare, comprovare, provare. 2 (*leg.*) garantire. *v. i.* (*leg.*) dichiararsi mallevadore (*per q.*); rispondere (*di q. o qc.*).

voucher[1], *n.* 1 (*leg.*) garante. 2 (*leg., pers.*) documento giustificativo, pezza d'appoggio. 3 (*market.*) buono, scontrino. 4 (*market.*) ricevuta, quietanza; buono di consegna. // ~ **cheque** (*cred.*) assegno con annotazione degli estremi della fattura; ~ **payable** (*rag.*) saldo debitore (*d'un conto corrente*).

voucher[2], *v. t.* 1 autenticare, vidimare. 2 (*leg., pers.*) provvedere di documento giustificativo (*o* di pezza d'appoggio). 3 (*market.*) munire d'un buono (*o* d'uno scontrino).

voyage[1], *n.* 1 (*trasp., trasp. aer., trasp. mar.*) viaggio (*fluviale, aereo, o di mare*). 2 (*trasp. aer., trasp. mar.*) passaggio, traversata. // ~ **charter** (*trasp., trasp. aer., trasp. mar.*) noleggio a viaggio; ~ **charter party** (*trasp., trasp. aer., trasp. mar.*) contratto di nolo a viaggio; ~ **freight** (*trasp., trasp. aer., trasp. mar.*) nolo a viaggio; ~ **policy** (*ass. mar.*) polizza a viaggio; **homeward** ~ (*trasp. mar.*) viaggio di ritorno; **on the** ~ **home** (*trasp. mar.*) nel viaggio di ritorno; **on the** ~ **out** (*trasp. mar.*) nel viaggio d'andata; **outward** ~ (*trasp. mar.*) viaggio d'andata.

voyage[2], *v. i.* 1 (*trasp., trasp. aer., trasp. mar.*) viaggiare, fare un viaggio (*per via d'acqua o aerea*). 2 (*trasp. aer., trasp. mar.*) fare una traversata. *v. t.* (*trasp., trasp. aer., trasp. mar.*) navigare, percorrere (*laghi, oceani, ecc.*).

voyager, *n.* (*specialm. trasp. mar.*) viaggiatore.

W

wage, *n.* (*generalm. al pl.*) (*pers.*) paga, retribuzione, salario. // ~ **advances** (*pers.*) aumenti salariali; ~ **and salaries** (*pers.*) retribuzioni; ~ **and salary control** (*amm.*) controllo (del livello) delle retribuzioni; **wages and terms of employment** (*pers., sind.*) salari e condizioni di lavoro; ~ **automatic adjustment** (*econ.*) scala mobile (*dei salari: in Italia*); ~ **awards** (*pers.*) aumenti salariali; ~ **bargaining** (*sind.*) contrattazione (per ottenere un aumento) salariale; ~ **bill** (*econ.*) «costo» degli aumenti salariali; (*econ., rag.*) «conto» salari; ~ **-boosting power** (*econ., sind.*) potere (*dei sindacati*) d'ottenere grossi aumenti salariali; ~ **claims** (*sind.*) richieste d'aumenti salariali; ~ **-cost spiral** (*econ.*) spirale (dei) costi (e dei) salari; ~ **costs** (*econ.*) costi salariali; ~ **dividend** (*pers.*) quota di dividendo pagato ai dipendenti; ~ **drift** (*econ.*) slittamento salariale (*divario fra i livelli retributivi previsti dai contratti collettivi e quelli effettivi aziendali*); ~ **-earner** (*pers.*) salariato, salariata; **the** ~ **-earners** (*pers.*) il salariato (*sing. collett.*); ~ **escalation** (*econ.*) aumento dei salari (*per agganciamento agli indici del costo della vita*); ~ **-freeze** (*sind.*) congelamento salariale, blocco dei salari; **wages fund** (*econ.*) fondo salari; ~ **-fund theory** (*econ.*) teoria dei salari (*secondo John Stuart Mill, il livello dei salari dipende dal rapporto fra il numero dei lavoratori e l'ammontare del capitale impiegato nella loro retribuzione; di conseguenza il solo modo per aumentare i salari è o quello di ridurre il numero dei lavoratori o quello d'aumentare il fondo destinato a retribuirli*); **wages-fund theory** (*econ.*) *V.* ~ **-fund theory;** ~ **increases** (*pers.*) aumenti salariali; ~ **indexation** (*econ.*) indicizzazione dei salari (*in Italia: la «scala mobile»*); ~ **inflation** (*econ.*) inflazione da (aumento eccessivo dei) salari; ~ **level** (*econ.*) livello salariale; ~ **pause** (*econ., sind.*) tregua salariale; **wages policy** (*econ.*) politica salariale; ~ **-price spiral** (*econ.*) spirale (dei) prezzi (e dei) salari; ~ **-push inflation** spinta inflazionistica da salari; ~ **rate** (*pers.*) paga base (*per unità di tempo o per unità di prodotto*); ~ **rise** (*pers.*) aumento di salario, aumento salariale; ~ **scale** (*sind.*) tabella (base) dei salari; ~ **-sheet** (*pers.*) foglio paga; ~ **structure** (*econ., sind.*) struttura dei salari; ~ **surrender** (*sind.*) cedimento alle rivendicazioni salariali; ~ **talk** (*sind.*) discussione per ottenere miglioramenti salariali; ~ **unit** (*econ.*) unità di salario; ~ **-worker** (*pers.*) *V.* ~ **-earner.**

wager[1], *n.* **1** scommessa. **2** posta (*d'una scommessa*). // ~ **policy** (*ass. mar.*) polizza che copre beni per cui l'assicurato non può dimostrare un interesse assicurabile.

wager[2], *v. t.* e *i.* fare una scommessa.

wagering contract, *n.* (*leg.*) contratto aleatorio.

wages, *n. pl. V.* **wage.**

waggon[1], *n.* **1** (*trasp.*) carro. **2** (*trasp. aut.*) (= **station waggon**) giardiniera, giardinetta, familiare. **3** (*trasp. ferr.*) vagone, carro merci, carro.

waggon[2], *v. t.* (*trasp.*) trasportare (*merci*) con un carro (*V. anche* **waggon**[1]). *v. i.* (*trasp.*) viaggiare su un carro (*V. anche* **waggon**[1]).

wagon, *n.* e *v. V.* **waggon.**

waif, *n.* oggetto smarrito, relitto. // **waifs and strays** (*leg.*) oggetti smarriti.

wait[1], *n.* attesa, indugio. // ~ **list** lista d'attesa.

wait[2], *v. i.* aspettare, attendere, indugiare; essere (*o* restare) in attesa. // to ~ **out the stock market** (*fin.*) aspettare un miglioramento del mercato dei titoli.

waiter, *n.* **1** chi aspetta, chi attende (*V. anche* **wait**[2]). **2** (*dog., ingl.*) ufficiale doganale. **3** (*fin., ingl.*) commesso (*della Borsa Valori di Londra*). **4** (*pers.*) cameriere.

waiting, *n.* attesa. // ~ **-berth clause** (*trasp. mar.*) clausola del tempo d'attesa per l'attracco; ~ **list** lista d'attesa; ~ **room** (*trasp. ferr.*) sala d'attesa, sala d'aspetto; **no** ~ (*trasp. aut.*) divieto di sosta, sosta vietata.

waitress, *n.* (*pers.*) cameriera.

waive, *v. t.* abbandonare, rinunciare a, fare a meno di. // to ~ **collateral** (*cred., fin.*) rinunciare a garanzie reali; to ~ **the customary**

formalities abbandonare le formalità d'uso; to ~ **fulfilment of certain provisions of a contract** (*leg.*) rinunciare all'esecuzione di talune clausole contrattuali; to ~ **a right** (*leg.*) rinunciare a un diritto.

waiver, *n.* (*leg.*) abbandono (*d'una pretesa*); rinunzia (*a un diritto*). // ~ **clause** (*ass. mar.*) clausola di rinunzia, clausola di recessione; **the** ~ **of a contract provision** (*leg.*) l'abbandono d'una clausola contrattuale; ~ **of premium** (*ass.*) clausola che (*in certe circostanze*) prevede la copertura ininterrotta (*del rischio*) anche senza pagamento del premio.

walk[1], *n.* passeggiata. // ~ **-clerk** (*banca*) commesso; ~ **-out** (*sind., fam.*) sciopero; sciopero non autorizzato.

walk[2], *v. i.* andare a piedi, passeggiare. // to ~ **off with** (*di ladro*) portarsi via; guadagnare; to ~ **out** uscire; (*sind., fam.*) scioperare.

walkie-talkie, *n.* (*comun.*) radiotelefono (*ricetrasmittente*) portatile.

walking, *a.* che cammina, che passeggia. *n.* il camminare, il passeggiare. // ~ **boss** (*pers.*) capo (*d'operai*), caposquadra; ~ **delegate** (*sind.*) sindacalista viaggiante (*che visita operai e stabilimenti per controllare l'applicazione delle norme previste dai contratti collettivi di lavoro*); ~ **orders** (*sind., fam.*) *V.* ~ **papers**; ~ **papers** (*sind., fam.*) notifica di licenziamento; ~ **ticket** (*sind., fam.*) *V.* ~ **papers**; ~ **-tour** (*tur.*) giro turistico a piedi; ~ **-way** passaggio pedonale.

walky-talky, *n. V.* **walkie-talkie.**

wall, *n.* parete. // ~ **calendar** (*attr. uff.*) calendario murale; ~ **clock** (*attr. uff.*) orologio da muro; ~ **newspaper** (*giorn.*) giornale murale; ~ **Street** Wall Street (*strada di New York*); (*fig., USA*) il mercato finanziario americano, i finanzieri di New York; ~ **Streeter** (*fin., USA*) operatore finanziario di Wall Street.

wallet, *n.* portafoglio.

want[1], *n.* 1 deficienza, mancanza, ristrettezza. 2 (*anche econ.*) bisogno, necessità, esigenza. // ~ **ad** (*giorn., pubbl.*) annunzio pubblicitario (*richiesta od offerta di lavoro*); ~ **creation** (*econ., pubbl.*) creazione dei bisogni (*nei consumatori*); ~ **of competence** incompetenza; ~ **of evidence** (*leg.*) mancanza di prova; ~ **of jurisdiction** (*leg.*) mancanza di giurisdizione.

want[2], *v. t.* 1 aver bisogno, abbisognare di. 2 volere, desiderare.

wanted, *a.* 1 (*giorn., pubbl.*) (*negli annunzi pubblicitari*) cercasi, cercansi. 2 (*leg.*) ricercato.

wanting, *a.* 1 che ha bisogno, bisognoso. 2 che vuole, ecc. // to **be** ~ difettare.

war, *n.* (*anche fig.*) guerra, lotta. // ~ **-damage compensation** (*econ.*) risarcimento dei danni di guerra; ~ **-damages** (*econ.*) danni di guerra; ~ **debt** (*econ., fin.*) debito di guerra; ~ **-loan** (*econ., fin.*) prestito di guerra; ~ **pension** (*econ.*) pensione di guerra.

ward[1], *n.* 1 (*leg.*) custodia, tutela (*di minorenne e sim.*). 2 (*leg.*) minore.

ward[2], *v. t.* difendere, proteggere, custodire.

warden, *n.* (*pers.*) custode, guardiano.

wardship, *n.* (*leg.*) custodia, tutela (*di minorenne e sim.*). // to **be under** ~ (*leg.*) essere sotto tutela.

ware, *n.* 1 (*market.*) merce, mercanzia, articoli, oggetti. 2 (*market.*) (*generalm. nei composti: p. es.,* **chinaware** *porcellane,* **hardware** *ferramenta,* **earthenware** *terraglie, ecc.*).

warehouse[1], *n.* 1 (*dog.*) (= **bonded warehouse**) magazzino doganale, deposito franco. 2 (*market.*) emporio, grande negozio, negozio. 3 (*org. az.*) magazzino, deposito. // ~ **bond** (*org. az.*) buono di carico (*di magazzino*); ~ **book** (*org. az.*) libro di (carico e scarico del) magazzino; ~ **charges** (*rag.*) spese di magazzinaggio; ~ **dues** (*dog., trasp.*) (spese di) magazzinaggio; ~ **-keeper** (*pers.*) magazziniere; ~ **-keeper's certificate** (*dog.*) certificato del magazziniere; ~ **-keeper's order** (*dog.*) ordine di scarico della bolletta di cauzione; ~ **-keeper's receipt** (*dog.*) ricevuta del magazziniere; ~ **-to-** ~ **insurance** (*ass. mar.*) assicurazione (*della merce*) da magazzino a magazzino (*dal magazzino del venditore a quello del destinatario*); ~ **warrant** (*dog.*) fede di deposito; **ex** ~ (*market., trasp.*) franco magazzino.

warehouse[2], *v. t.* 1 (*dog.*) mettere (*merci*) in magazzino doganale. 2 (*org. az.*) depositare in magazzino, immagazzinare (*merci, ecc.*).

warehouseman, *n.* (*pl.* **warehousemen**) 1 (*market.*) commerciante all'ingrosso, grossista. 2 (*pers.*) magazziniere.

warehouser, *n.* (*pers.*) magazziniere.

warehousing, *n.* 1 (*dog., org. az.*) immagazzinamento, immagazzinaggio, magazzinaggio, deposito (*di merci*). 2 (*org. az.*) costituzione delle scorte. // ~ **charges** (*rag.*) spese di magazzinaggio.

wareroom, *n.* 1 (*market.*) negozio. 2 (*market.*) sala di mostra (*delle merci*).

warn, *v. t.* 1 avvertire, avvisare. 2 ammonire, mettere in guardia. 3 (*leg.*) diffidare.

warning, *n.* 1 avvertimento, avviso. 2 ammonimento, ammonizione. 3 (*leg.*) diffida. 4

(*leg.*) preavviso (*di disdetta di contratto di locazione, ecc.*). **5** (*pers.*) preavviso di licenziamento; (gli) «otto giorni». // ~ **to shipping** (*trasp. mar.*) avviso ai naviganti; **gale** ~ (*trasp. mar.*) avviso di burrasca.

warrant[1], *n.* **1** autorità, diritto, motivo valido. **2** garanzia. **3** (*dog.*) fede di deposito, nota di pegno, «warrant». **4** (*fin.*) diritto (*concesso a un azionista*) d'acquisto di titoli a un prezzo stabilito (*tale diritto è assai più lungo di quello del «right», q.V., ed è offerto congiuntamente a nuove azioni od obbligazioni per facilitarne il collocamento*). **5** (*leg.*) mandato, ordinanza, ordine. // ~ **for attachment** (*leg.*) ordinanza di sequestro conservativo; ~ **for delivery** buono di consegna; ~ **for payment** (*banca, cred.*) mandato di pagamento; ~ **of attorney** (*leg.*) procura, atto di procura.

warrant[2], *v. t.* **1** assicurare, attestare. **2** (*anche leg.*) garantire. **3** (*leg.*) autorizzare; dare autorità a (*q.*); dare mandato a (*q.*).

warrantee, *n.* (*leg.*) chi riceve una garanzia.

warranter, *n. V.* **warrantor.**

warrantor, *n.* (*leg.*) garante.

warranty, *n.* (*leg.*) garanzia. // ~ **deed** (*leg.*) garanzia (*il documento*); ~ **for hidden defects** (*leg.*) garanzia per vizi occulti; ~ **of seaworthiness** (*trasp. mar.*) garanzia di navigabilità.

wash[1], *n.* **1** lavatura, lavata. **2** (*trasp. aut.*) lavaggio (*d'automobili, ecc.*). // ~ **-and-wear** (*market.*) (*di tessuto*) «lava e indossa» (*che non necessita di stiratura*); «wash-and-wear»; ~ **'n'wear** (*market.*) *V.* ~ **-and-wear.**

wash[2], *v. t.* lavare. *v. i.* lavarsi. // to ~ **one's hands of st.** lavarsi le mani di qc.

washer, *n.* lavatrice.

washing, *n.* lavatura, lavaggio. // ~ **machine** lavatrice, macchina lavatrice.

waste[1], *n.* **1** (*leg.*) danneggiamento. **2** (*market., org. az.*) scarto; rifiuti. *a. attr.* di scarto. // ~ **-basket** (*attr. uff.*) cestino per la carta straccia; ~ **-book** (*rag.*) brogliaccio; ~ **-control** (*org. az.*) riduzione degli sprechi; ~ **paper** carta straccia; ~ **-paper basket** (*attr. uff.*) cestino per la carta straccia; ~ **products** (*market., org. az.*) prodotti di scarto, rifiuti.

waste[2], *v. t.* (*leg.*) trascurare (*una proprietà e sim.*). // to ~ **a golden opportunity** sciupare un'occasione d'oro; to ~ **one's time** perdere tempo.

watch[1], *n.* **1** guardia, sorveglianza, custodia. **2** orologio (*da tasca o da polso*). **3** (*trasp. mar.*) personale di guardia. // ~ **ashore** (*trasp. mar.*) guardia franca a terra; ~ **below** (*trasp. mar.*) guardia franca.

watch[2], *v. t.* **1** guardare, osservare. **2** sorvegliare. // to ~ **TV** guardare la TV.

watcher, *n.* (*pers.*) sorvegliante.

watchman, *n.* (*pl.* **watchmen**) (*pers.*) sorvegliante, guardia giurata, guardia.

water[1], *n.* **1** acqua. **2** (*trasp. mar.*) marea. // ~ **ballast** (*trasp. mar.*) zavorra d'acqua; ~ **boat** (*trasp. mar.*) nave cisterna; ~ **-borne** (*trasp.*) trasportato per via d'acqua; ~ **-bus** (*trasp.*) vaporetto (*in servizio di linea su un lago, ecc.*); ~ **carriage** (*trasp., trasp. mar.*) trasporto per via d'acqua; mezzi di trasporto per via d'acqua; ~ **carrier** (*trasp.*) vettore fluviale; (*trasp. mar.*) vettore marittimo; ~ **gate** (*trasp.*) cateratta (*di chiusa*); ~ **guard** (*trasp. mar.*) guardia di finanza portuale; ~ **level** (*trasp. mar.*) livello del mare; ~ **rate** tariffa per la fornitura idrica; ~ **rent** *V.* ~ **rate;** ~ **supply** (*org. az.*) approvvigionamento idrico; rifornimento idrico; ~ **transportation** (*trasp.*) trasporti per via d'acqua; **above** ~ sopra il livello dell'acqua; (*anche fig.*) a galla; **by** ~ (*trasp.*) per via fluviale; (*trasp., trasp. mar.*) per via d'acqua; (*trasp. mar.*) per mare; **in deep water(s)** (*fig.*) in difficoltà, nei guai; **in low water(s)** in secca; (*fig.*) a corto di quattrini, al verde; **on the** ~ (*trasp. mar.*) (*di merce*) in viaggio; **upon the** ~ (*trasp. mar.*) (*di merce*) in viaggio.

water[2], *v. t.* **1** innaffiare. **2** (*fin.*) gonfiare artificiosamente (*il capitale nominale*).

waterage, *n.* **1** (*trasp.*) trasporto per via d'acqua. **2** (*trasp.*) spese di trasporto per via d'acqua.

waterfront, *n.* (*trasp. mar.*) fronte del molo.

watering, *n.* innaffiamento.

waterline, *n.* (*trasp. mar.*) linea di galleggiamento.

waterproof[1], *a.* (*market.*) (*di stoffa*) impermeabile, «waterproof». *n.* (*market.*) impermeabile.

waterproof[2], *v. t.* impermeabilizzare.

watertight, *a.* impermeabile all'acqua, stagno. // ~ **compartments** (*trasp. mar.*) compartimenti stagni.

waterway, *n.* (*trasp.*) corso d'acqua navigabile, via di navigazione, via d'acqua, canale navigabile.

waterworks, *n. pl.* acquedotto.

watt, *n.* watt. // ~ **-hour** wattora; ~ **-hour meter** wattometro.

wave, *n.* (*anche fig.*) ondata. // ~ **-band** (*comun.*) gamma di lunghezze d'onda; ~ **-length** (*comun.*) lunghezza d'onda; **a** ~ **of**

falling prices (*econ.*) un'ondata di ribasso; **a ~ of speculation** (*econ.*) un'ondata speculativa.

way, *n.* **1** via. **2** mezzo, modo. **3** (*leg.*) (= **right of way**) diritto di passaggio. **4 ways,** *pl.* (*trasp. mar.*) scalo di costruzione. // **ways and means** (*fin.*) metodo (*specialm. di reperire fondi*); **~ -bill** (*trasp.*) lista dei passeggeri; (*trasp. ferr.*) lettera di vettura; **ways-end** (*trasp. mar.*) avanscalo, avantiscalo, antiscalo; **~ freight** (*trasp. ferr., USA*) treno merci locale; **~ in** entrata; **~ -leave** (*leg.*) permesso di passaggio; **~ out** uscita; sbocco (*anche fig.*); **~ point** (*trasp. ferr., USA*) *V.* **~ station; ~ station** (*trasp. ferr., USA*) stazione secondaria, stazione intermedia; **~ traffic** (*trasp. ferr., USA*) traffico locale, movimento (*merci o passeggeri*) locale; **~ train** (*trasp. ferr., USA*) locale, treno locale; **by ~ of** (*trasp., tur.*) via, passando per; **by ~ of exception** in via eccezionale; **by ~ of trial** (*market.*) a titolo di prova, in saggio; to **be under ~** (*trasp. mar.*) far rotta, navigare.

waybill, *v. t.* (*trasp. ferr.*) spedire (*merci*) con accompagnamento della lettera di vettura.

weak, *a.* **1** debole, fiacco. **2** (*econ., fin., market.*) (*di merce, titolo, ecc.*) a debole domanda, tendente a una diminuzione di prezzo. // **a ~ crew** (*trasp. mar.*) un equipaggio insufficiente; **~ currency** (*fin.*) valuta debole.

weaken, *v. t.* indebolire. *v. i.* **1** indebolirsi. **2** calare, scemare.

weakening, *n.* indebolimento.

weakness, *n.* debolezza, fiacchezza.

wealth, *n.* ricchezza, censo, averi.

wealthy, *a.* ricco, agiato, danaroso.

wear[1], *n.* **1** uso. **2** consumo, logoramento; logorio (*di macchine, ecc.*). **3** (*market.*) vestiario, vestiti, abiti. // **~ and tear** logorio, logoramento, deterioramento; (*org. az.*) deprezzamento (*d'un macchinario, ecc.*) per l'uso (*cui è stato sottoposto*); **~ -out** (*org. az., rag.*) deprezzamento (*d'un macchinario, ecc.*) per l'uso (*cui è stato sottoposto*).

wear[2], *v. t.* (*pass.* **wore,** *part. pass.* **worn**) **1** consumare, logorare. **2** indossare, portare. *v. i.* **1** consumarsi, logorarsi. **2** (*trasp. mar.*) bordeggiare. // to **~ out** consumare, logorare, esaurire; consumarsi, logorarsi, esaurirsi; to **~ oneself out** (*di persona*) logorarsi.

weather, *n.* tempo (*atmosferico*). // **~ board** (*trasp. mar.*) lato sopravvento; **~ -bound** (*trasp. mar.*) (*di naviglio*) trattenuto (*in porto*) dal maltempo; **~ bureau** ufficio meteorologico; **~ cast** *V.* **~ forecast; ~ conditions** condizioni meteorologiche; **~ forecast** previsioni del tempo; **~ -ship** (*trasp. mar.*) nave del servizio meteorologico; **~ side** (*trasp. mar.*) lato sopravvento; **~ signal** (*trasp. mar.*) segnale meteorologico; **~ warning** (*trasp. mar.*) avviso di cattivo tempo.

week, *n.* settimana. // **~ -end** fine settimana, week-end; **~ 's pay** (*o* **wages**) (*pers.*) paga d'una settimana, settimanale, settimana; **by the ~** (*pers.*) (*di retribuzione*) alla settimana, settimanalmente; **today ~** oggi a otto; **tomorrow ~** domani a otto.

weekday, *n.* **1** giorno feriale. **2** (*pers.*) giornata lavorativa.

weekly, *a.* settimanale. *avv.* settimanalmente, ogni settimana. *n.* (*giorn.*) (un) settimanale, pubblicazione settimanale, periodico settimanale. // **a ~ pay** (*pers.*) una paga settimanale; **the ~ periodicals** (*giorn.*) i (periodici) settimanali; **a ~ report** (*giorn.*) un notiziario settimanale; **~ time schedules** (*org. az.*) orari settimanali.

weigh, *v. t.* **1** pesare. **2** (*fig.*) valutare. *v. i.* **1** essere pesante, avere il peso di. **2** (*trasp. mar.*) levare l'àncora. // to **~ anchor** (*trasp. mar.*) levare l'àncora.

weighage, *n.* (*trasp., ingl.*) tassa di pesatura.

weighing, *n.* pesa. // **~ machine** bilancia.

weighmaster, *n.* verificatore del peso (*delle merci*).

weight[1], *n.* (*anche fig.*) peso; (*fig.*) carico, gravame, onere; (*fig.*) importanza, valore. // **~ allowed free** (*trasp.*) peso in franchigia; franchigia di peso; **weights and measures** pesi e misure; **~ cargo** (*trasp. aer., trasp. mar.*) merce pesante; **~ delivered** (*trasp. mar.*) peso allo sbarco; **~ draft** (*market.*) abbuono per il peso; **~ goods** (*trasp.*) merce pesante; **~ note** (*trasp. mar.*) bolletta dei pesi, distinta dei pesi; **~ or measurement** (*trasp. mar.*) peso o volume; **by ~** (*market.*) (*di sistema di vendita, valutazione, ecc.*) a peso.

weight[2], *v. t.* gravare.

weighted, *a.* gravato.

weighting, *n.* peso, ciò che è usato come peso. // **~ allowance** (*sind., ingl.*) indennità di grande sede.

welcome, *a.* gradito. *n.* benvenuto.

welfare, *n.* benessere. // **~ contributions** (*econ., sind.*) oneri previdenziali; **~ economics** (*econ.*) economia del benessere; **the ~ of a nation** (*econ.*) il benessere d'una nazione; **~ officer** (*sind.*) assistente sociale; **the ~ State** (*econ.*) lo Stato sociale, lo Stato assistenziale; **~ worker** (*sind.*) assistente sociale; **~ works** (*econ.*) servizi sociali.

well, *avv.* bene. // ~ **-heeled** (*fig.*) bene organizzato, ben strutturato; ~ **-known** notorio, noto; ~ **-organized** (*org. az.*) bene organizzato, ben strutturato; ~ **-to-do** agiato, ricco, danaroso.

west, *n.* 1 ponente, occidente, ovest. 2 **the West** (*USA*) il West, l'Ovest (*il territorio a ovest del Mississippi*). *a. attr.* di ponente. *avv.* a ovest, all'ovest, verso occidente, verso ponente. // ~ **Europe Time** *V.* ~ **European Time;** ~ **European Time** ora dell'Europa occidentale.

western, *a.* occidentale, di ponente, dell'ovest. // **the** ~ **bloc** il blocco (dei Paesi) dell'Occidente; ~ **European Time** *V.* **West European Time; the** ~ **European Union (WEU)** l'Unione dell'Europa Occidentale (*UEO*).

wet, *a.* bagnato. // ~ **basin** (*trasp. mar.*) darsena; ~ **dock** (*trasp. mar.*) darsena idrostatica, bacino a livello d'acqua costante; ~ **goods** merci liquide.

wharf[1], *n.* (*pl.* **wharves** e *reg.*) (*trasp. mar.*) banchina, calata, molo interno, scalo. // ~ **dues** (*trasp. mar.*) diritti di banchina, diritti di sbarco; ~ **for fuel-oil bunkering** (*trasp. mar.*) stazione di rifornimento nafta; **free on** ~ **(F.O.W.)** (*trasp. mar.*) franco banchina.

wharf[2], *v. t.* 1 (*trasp. mar.*) attraccare, ormeggiare (*una nave*) al molo. 2 (*trasp. mar.*) scaricare (*merce*) a un molo.

wharfage, *n.* 1 (*trasp. mar.*) uso d'un molo (*per caricare e/o scaricare merce*). 2 (*trasp. mar.*) diritti di banchina.

wharfing, *n.* (*trasp. mar.*) complesso delle banchine (*d'un porto*).

wharfinger, *n.* 1 (*trasp. mar.*) proprietario di banchina. 2 (*trasp. mar.*) custode di scalo. // ~ **'s receipt** (*trasp. mar.*) ricevuta del custode dello scalo.

wharfman, *n.* (*pl.* **wharfmen**) (*trasp. mar.*) sorvegliante di banchina, portuale addetto a una banchina.

wharfmaster, *n. V.* **wharfinger.**

wheat, *n.* (*market.*) grano.

wheel, *v. t.* far girare, far ruotare.

wheeler-dealer, *n.* (*slang USA*) speculatore in grande stile.

whereas, *cong.* (*leg.*) premesso che, considerato che (*forma introduttiva d'un contratto, e sim.*).

white, *a.* bianco. // ~ **-collar** (*pers.*) impiegatizio; **the** ~ **-collar families** (*pers.*) le famiglie degli impiegati; ~ **-collar worker** (*pers.*) chi lavora in ufficio, impiegato, funzionario; ~ **-collar workers** il ceto impiegatizio; ~ **paper** (*amm.*) libro bianco, rapporto governativo.

whole, *a.* tutto, intero, completo. // ~ **life** (*ass.*) vita intera; ~ **-life insurance** (*ass.*) assicurazione «vita intera».

wholesale[1], *n.* (*market.*) vendita all'ingrosso. *a. attr.* (*market.*) all'ingrosso. *avv.* 1 in massa. 2 (*market.*) all'ingrosso. // **a** ~ **dealer** (*market.*) un commerciante all'ingrosso, un grossista; ~ **manufacture** (*org. az.*) fabbricazione all'ingrosso; ~ **market** (*market.*) mercato all'ingrosso; ~ **prices** (*market.*) prezzi all'ingrosso, corsi sul mercato all'ingrosso; ~ **trade** (*market.*) commercio all'ingrosso; ~ **warehousing** (*market.*) operazioni di magazzinaggio nel commercio all'ingrosso; **at** ~ (*market., USA*) all'ingrosso; **by** ~ (*market.*) all'ingrosso.

wholesale[2], *v. t.* (*market.*) vendere (*qc.*) all'ingrosso. *v. i.* 1 (*market.*) vendere all'ingrosso, fare il grossista. 2 (*market.*) (*d'articolo*) vendersi all'ingrosso.

wholesaler, *n.* (*market.*) commerciante all'ingrosso, grossista.

wholly, *avv.* interamente.

wide, *a.* 1 ampio, esteso, largo. 2 (*fin., market.*) (*di fluttuazione di prezzi, ecc.*) considerevole. // **a** ~ **margin** (*fin.*) un ampio margine.

widow, *n.* (*leg.*) vedova.

widowed, *a.* (*leg.*) vedovile.

widower, *n.* (*leg.*) vedovo.

widowhood, *n.* (*leg.*) vedovanza.

width, *n.* ampiezza, larghezza.

wild, *a.* 1 selvaggio, selvatico. 2 barbaro, feroce.

wildcat, *n.* 1 gatto selvatico. 2 (*pers.*) (= **wildcat strike**) sciopero «selvaggio». *a. attr.* 1 (*fin.*) (*d'impresa, ecc.*) insolvibile. 2 (*leg.*) illegale, illecito. // **a** ~ **bank** (*fin.*) una banca insolvibile; ~ **strike** (*pers.*) sciopero «selvaggio»; **a** ~ **work stoppage** (*pers.*) un'interruzione arbitraria del lavoro (*senza il consenso dei sindacati*).

wildcatter, *n.* (*fin., leg.*) speculatore senza scrupoli.

wilful, *a.* 1 (*leg.*) intenzionale. 2 (*leg.*) doloso. // ~ **and malicious offence** (*leg.*) delitto doloso; ~ **damage** (*leg.*) danneggiamento doloso.

wilfully, *avv.* (*leg.*) intenzionalmente.

wilfulness, *n.* 1 (*leg.*) intenzionalità. 2 (*leg.*) dolosità.

will, *n.* 1 (il) volere. 2 (*leg.*) ultime volontà, testamento. // ~ **and testament** (*leg.*) testamento, ultime volontà; **at** ~ (*leg.*) (*di contratto d'affitto, d'affittuario, ecc.*) a tempo indeterminato; **by** ~ (*leg.*) per testamento; **last** ~ **and testament** (*leg.*) *V.* ~ **and testament.**

willful, *a.* (*USA*) *V.* **wilful.**

willing, *a.* spontaneo. // to **be** ~ **to do st.** essere disposto a far qc.

willingly, *avv.* volentieri, di buon grado.

win, *v. t.* e *i.* (*pass.* e *part. pass.* **won**) **1** vincere, essere vittorioso. **2** guadagnarsi, ottenere. // to ~ **one's bread** guadagnarsi il pane; to ~ **a case** (*leg.*) vincere una causa; to ~ **competition** (*market.*) vincere la concorrenza.

wind[1], *n.* vento. // ~ **bound** (*trasp. mar.*) (*di naviglio*) trattenuto (*in porto*) dal vento contrario; ~ **-chart** (*trasp. mar.*) carta dei venti; **on the** ~ (*trasp. mar.*) controvento.

wind[2], *n.* avvolgimento. // ~ **-up** (*fin., rag.*) liquidazione (*d'una società, dei conti, ecc.*).

wind[3], *v. t.* (*pass.* e *part. pass.* **wound**) **1** far girare. **2** caricare (*un orologio e sim.*). *v. i.* **1** avvolgersi. **2** girare. // to ~ **up** (*fin.*) (*di società, di ente*) esser messo in liquidazione; (*fin., rag.*) liquidare (*una società, i conti, ecc.*); to ~ **up one's business affairs** (*fin.*) liquidare i propri affari; to ~ **up a business company** (*fin.*) liquidare una società commerciale.

windfall, *n.* (*fam.*) colpo di fortuna, guadagno inatteso, bazza. // ~ **gain** (*econ.*) guadagno accidentale; ~ **loss** (*econ.*) perdita accidentale.

winding, *n.* avvolgimento. // ~ **-up** (*fin.*) liquidazione, scioglimento, stralcio (*d'una società*).

windmill, *n.* (*cred., fam.*) cambiale di comodo, effetto di comodo.

window, *n.* **1** (*banca, org. az.*) sportello. **2** (*market.*) (= **shop-window**) vetrina (*di negozio*). // ~ **-card** (*market.*) cartellino pubblicitario da vetrina (*di negozio*); ~ **display** (*market.*) esposizione (*di merce*) in vetrina; ~ **-dresser** (*pers.*) vetrinista; ~ **-dressing** (*fig.*) presentazione (*d'uno stato patrimoniale, ecc.*) in modo da fare una buona impressione (*sul pubblico, ecc.*); (*market.*) allestimento della vetrina (*o* delle vetrine), arte del vetrinista, arte del disporre la merce in vetrina; ~ **-envelope** (*attr. uff., comun.*) busta a finestra (*con una finestrella*).

windowman, *n.* (*pl.* **windowmen**) (*pers.*) sportellista.

windward, *n.* (*trasp. mar.*) direzione del vento. // ~ **side** (*trasp. mar.*) lato sopravvento; **to** ~ (*trasp. mar.*) in direzione del vento.

wipe, *v. t.* **1** strofinare. **2** pulire (*strofinando*). // to ~ **off** pulire strofinando; spazzare via; cancellare; (*cred.*) pagare, liquidare (*un debito, ecc.*); to ~ **out** *V.* to ~ **off.**

wire[1], *n.* **1** filo (*metallico*). **2** (*comun.*) telegramma. // ~ **recorder** (*macch. uff.*) magnetofono a filo; ~ **recording** registrazione su filo; **by** ~ (*comun.*) tramite telegramma, per telegrafo.

wire[2], *v. t.* (*comun.*) telegrafare, trasmettere (*qc.*) per telegrafo.

wireless[1], *n.* (*comun.*) radiotelegrafia. // ~ **installation** (*comun.*) impianto radiotelegrafico; ~ **message** (*comun.*) radiogramma; ~ **service** (*comun.*) servizi radio (*telegrafici*); **a** ~ **set** un apparecchio radio; ~ **telegraphy** (*comun.*) telegrafia senza fili, radiotelegrafia; ~ **telephony** (*comun.*) radiotelefonia; **over the** ~ (*comun.*) alla radio.

wireless[2], *v. t.* (*comun.*) radiotelegrafare, trasmettere per radio.

with, *prep.* con. // ~ **coupon** (*fin.*) (*di titolo*) con la cedola, col dividendo; ~ **dividend** (*fin.*) (*di titolo*) col dividendo; ~ **particular average (WPA)** (*ass. mar.*) con avaria particolare; ~ **prejudice** (*leg.*) con riserve; ~ **rights** (*fin.*) (*di titolo*) coi diritti, col nuovo.

withdraw, *v. t.* e *i.* (*pass.* **withdrew,** *part. pass.* **withdrawn**) **1** ritirare, ritirarsi. **2** fare una ritrattazione. **3** (*banca*) prelevare (*fondi*); ritirare (*denaro*). // to ~ **a charge** (*leg.*) ritirare un'accusa; to ~ **a complaint** (*leg.*) ritirare una denuncia; to ~ **an order** annullare un ordine.

withdrawal, *n.* **1** ritiro. **2** (*banca*) prelevamento (*di fondi*). **3** (*leg.*) remissione. // **withdrawals from the special reserve** (*fin., rag.*) storni alla riserva speciale; ~ **notice** (*banca*) preavviso di prelevamento; **the** ~ **of an action** (*leg.*) la remissione d'una querela; **the** ~ **of a partner** (*fin.*) il ritiro d'un socio (*da una società*); ~ **warrant** (*banca*) benestare di prelevamento (*di fondi, da un conto di risparmio*); (*dog., fin.*) benestare di prelevamento (*di merce*).

withhold, *v. t.* (*pass.* e *part. pass.* **withheld**) **1** trattenere. **2** rifiutare (*di dare*), negare (*qc. a q.*). // to ~ **one's consent** (*leg.*) negare il proprio consenso; to ~ **payment** rifiutarsi di pagare; to ~ **permission** negare un permesso.

withholding, *n.* (*fin.*) ritenuta alla fonte (*l'azione*). // ~ **tax** (*fin.*) ritenuta alla fonte, ritenuta (*o* trattenuta) d'acconto; ~ **-tax system** (*fin.*) sistema di ritenuta alla fonte.

within, *avv.* e *prep.* **1** dentro, fra (*di tempo*). **2** (*leg.*) nel presente atto, qui. *a. attr.* (*leg.*) accluso, incluso, presente. // ~ **board** (*trasp. mar.*) a bordo; **the** ~ **complaint** (*leg.*) l'accluso reclamo; **the** ~ **indictment** (*leg.*) la presente incriminazione; ~ **the law** (*leg.*) nell'ambito della legge; ~ **a month** (*cred.*) (*di pagamento, ecc.*) a un mese; ~ **sight of the port** (*trasp. mar.*) in vista del porto.

without, *prep.* senza. // ~ **date** (*leg.*) «sine die»; ~ **delay** senza indugio; (*market., trasp.*) senza ritardo; ~ **engagement** senza impegno; ~ **prejudice** (*leg.*) senza riserve.

witness[1], *n.* 1 (*anche leg.*) testimonianza, dimostrazione, prova. 2 (*leg.*) teste, testimone, testimonio. // ~ **-box** (*leg.*) banco dei testimoni; ~ **for the defence** (*leg.*) teste a discarico, testimone a difesa; ~ **for the prosecution** (*leg.*) testimone d'accusa, teste a carico; **in** ~ **thereof** (*leg.*) in fede di ciò, in fede di che.

witness[2], *v. t.* e *i.* 1 essere presente a, assistere a, vedere. 2 (*anche leg.*) dimostrare, provare, essere prova di. 3 (*leg.*) testimoniare, attestare, fare da testimone, deporre come teste. 4 (*leg.*) sottoscrivere (*un documento e sim.*) come testimone. // to ~ **against sb.** (*leg.*) deporre contro q., deporre a carico di q.; to ~ **for sb.** (*leg.*) deporre in favore di q., deporre a discarico di q.

witnessing, *n.* (*leg.*) testimonianza.

woman, *n.* (*pl.* **women**) 1 donna. 2 (*pers.*) lavorante (*donna*). // ~ **journalist** (*giorn., USA*) giornalista (*donna*).

woollens, *n. pl.* (*market.*) articoli di lana.

word[1], *n.* 1 parola, termine. 2 informazione, notizia, notizie. // ~ **for** ~ parola per parola, alla lettera; ~ **of honour** parola d'onore; **by** ~ **of mouth** verbalmente; **in words** in parole, in lettere; **the last** ~ **in** (*market., fig.*) l'ultima novità in fatto di.

word[2], *v. t.* mettere in parole, esprimere, formulare, redigere, stilare.

wording, *n.* 1 formulazione. 2 stesura. // **the** ~ **of an insurance policy** (*ass.*) il testo d'una polizza assicurativa.

work[1], *n.* 1 lavoro, attività, occupazione, mestiere. 2 (*org. az.*) (= **workpiece**) pezzo (da lavorare). // «**works ahead**» (*trasp. aut.*) «lavori in corso» (*segnale stradale*); ~ **by the day** (*org. az.*) lavoro a giornata, lavoro in economia; ~ **by the piece** lavoro a cottimo; ~ **cost** (*rag.*) costo del lavoro; ~ **-day** giorno lavorativo, giorno feriale; ~ **environment** ambiente di lavoro; ~ **force** (*econ., org. az.*) forza (di) lavoro; ~ **group** (*pers.*) gruppo di lavoro; ~ **in hand** (*org. az.*) lavoro in corso; ~ **in process** (*org. az.*) lavoro in corso; ~ **in progress** (*org. az.*) lavoro in corso; ~ **load** (*pers.*) carico di lavoro, quantità di lavoro (*assegnata a un operaio*), tempo assegnato (*a un operaio*) per eseguire un certo lavoro; ~ **order** (*org. az.*) buono di lavorazione, commessa (*di lavorazione*); ~ **-people** (*pers.*) lavoratori, operai, manodopera; ~ **permit** (*pers.*) permesso di lavoro; ~ **-place** luogo di lavoro, sede di lavoro; ~ **stoppage** (*sind.*) interruzione del lavoro; ~ **ticket** (*org. az.*) buono di lavorazione, commessa (*di lavorazione*); ~ **-week** settimana lavorativa; **at** ~ al lavoro; **in** ~ (*USA*) in lavorazione; to **be in regular** ~ avere un lavoro fisso; to **be out of** ~ essere disoccupato.

work[2], *v. i.* 1 lavorare, fare un lavoro. 2 (*anche fig.*) (*di macchinario e sim.*) funzionare, andare. *v. t.* 1 lavorare, manipolare, plasmare. 2 far funzionare, manovrare. 3 (*econ.*) coltivare, sfruttare (*una miniera e sim.*). // to ~ **an area** (*pers.*) *V.* to ~ **a district**; to ~ **a district** (*pers.*) (*di commesso viaggiatore*) lavorare in una zona, «fare» una zona; to ~ **an engine** (*trasp. ferr.*) manovrare una locomotiva; to ~ **full-time** lavorare a tempo pieno; to ~ **half-time** lavorare a mezzo tempo, lavorare a orario ridotto; to ~ **in shifts** (*pers.*) lavorare a turno; to ~ **iron** lavorare il ferro (*forgiarlo*); to ~ **off** sbrigare; (*market.*) vendere, svendere; to ~ **off a debt** (*cred.*) pagare un debito (*col ricavato del proprio lavoro*); to ~ **on contract** (*pers.*) lavorare a contratto; to ~ **out** elaborare, calcolare; risolvere; (*mat., rag.*) (*d'un conto, d'una somma, ecc.*) venire; to ~ **out a financial problem** risolvere un problema finanziario; to ~ **out the interests** (*rag.*) calcolare gli interessi; to ~ **overtime** (*pers.*) fare lavoro straordinario, fare lo straordinario; to ~ **part-time** lavorare a mezzo tempo; to ~ **a patent** (*leg.*) sfruttare un brevetto; to ~ **a ship** (*trasp. mar.*) manovrare una nave; to ~ **to rule** (*sind.*) fare uno sciopero bianco.

workable, *a.* 1 fattibile. 2 (*econ.*) (*di miniera e sim.*) sfruttabile.

workbook, *n.* manuale (*d'istruzioni, ecc.*).

workday, *n.* giornata lavorativa, giorno feriale.

worker, *n.* (*pers.*) lavoratore, operaio, operaia.

workhand, *n.* (*pers.*) prestatore di lavoro, dipendente, operaio.

working, *a.* 1 che lavora, attivo. 2 funzionante, operante. 3 (*pers.: di giorno, periodo di tempo*) lavorativo, feriale. *n.* 1 lavorazione, lavoro. 2 funzionamento (*d'una macchina, ecc.*). // ~ **assets** (*rag.*) attività non di capitale; ~ **capital** (*rag.*) capitale d'esercizio, capitale liquido; ~ **-capital requirements** (*amm., rag.*)

esigenze di gestione; ~ **class** (*econ.*) classe operaia; ~ **conditions** (*pers.*) condizioni di lavoro; ~ **costs** (*rag.*) spese d'esercizio; ~ **day** giornata lavorativa, giorno feriale; ~ **expenses** (*rag.*) spese d'esercizio; ~ **hours** (*org. az.*) ore lavorative, orario di lavoro; ~ **hours lost** (*econ.*) ore lavorative perdute; ~ **-man** (*pers.*) *V.* **worker**; ~ **-out** elaborazione; esecuzione; calcolo; risoluzione; ~ **party** (*sind.*) commissione di studio (*dei problemi del lavoro*); ~ **population** (*econ.*) popolazione attiva; ~ **time** (*org. az.*) orario di lavoro; ~ **to rule** (*sind.*) sciopero bianco (*applicazione rigida dei regolamenti, con conseguente rallentamento della produzione*); ~ **week** settimana lavorativa; **in** ~ **order** (*di macchinario*) in grado di funzionare, in buono stato.

workless, *a.* senza lavoro, disoccupato.

workman, *n.* (*pl.* **workmen**) **1** lavoratore; chi lavora (*in un certo modo*). **2** (*pers.*) operaio. // **workmen's compensation** (*ass.*) indennità per infortuni sul lavoro e malattie professionali.

workmanship, *n.* **1** abilità tecnica. **2** esecuzione, lavorazione, fattura.

workroom, *n.* stanza di lavoro, laboratorio.

works, *n. pl.* (*col verbo al pl.* o *al sing.*) (*org. az.*) fabbrica, impianto, officina, opificio, stabilimento. // ~ **committee** (*org. az., sind.*) commissione mista; ~ **council** (*org. az., sind.*) consiglio di gestione; ~ **manager** (*pers.*) direttore (dei) lavori, capo del reparto produzione; to **be at the** ~ (*pers.*) essere in fabbrica, essere in officina; **ex** ~ (*market., trasp.*) franco stabilimento; **in the** ~ (*USA*) in (via di) preparazione, allo studio; (*org. az., USA*) in corso di lavorazione.

workshop, *n.* **1** bottega artigiana. **2** (*org. az.*) officina, laboratorio, opificio, stabilimento, reparto. // ~ **of a coach repairer** (*trasp. aut.*) carrozzeria (*l'officina*).

workweek, *n.* settimana lavorativa.

workwoman, *n.* (*pl.* **workwomen**) (*pers.*) operaia.

world, *n.* mondo. // **the** ~ **Bank** (*fin.*) la Banca Mondiale; **the** ~ **trade** il commercio mondiale.

worn out, *a.* **1** consunto, logoro. **2** (*di persona*) esaurito.

worth, *a.* che vale, del valore di. *n.* **1** valore, pregio. **2** patrimonio (*personale*), ricchezze. // to **be** ~ (*di cosa*) costare; (*di persona*) che ha (*un certo patrimonio*), in possesso di.

worthless, *a.* privo di valore, senza valore. // **a** ~ **currency** (*econ.*) una moneta priva di valore.

wound, *n.* ferita, lesione.

wrap, *v. t.* (*market.*) incartare, impaccare; involtare (*fam.*). // to ~ **up** (*market.*) incartare, impaccare; to ~ **up a parcel** (*market.*) fare un pacchetto.

wrappage, *n. V.* **wrapping.**

wrapper, *n.* **1** (*giorn.*) fascia, fascetta (*di rivista, ecc.*). **2** (*market.*) incarto, involto, involucro. // **under** ~ sottofascia.

wrapping, *n.* **1** avvolgimento, incartata. **2** materiale da imballaggio (*o* da imballo). **3** (*market.*) incarto, involto, involucro, impaccaggio. // ~ **paper** (*market.*) carta da pacchi, carta da imballo; ~ **-up** incartata; (*market.*) impaccaggio.

wrap-up, *n.* **1** (*comun., USA*) riepilogo delle notizie trasmesse, breve «giornale radio». **2** (*slang USA*) articolo che si vende bene.

wreck[1]**,** *n.* **1** (*trasp.*) disastro, sinistro (*automobilistico e sim.*). **2** (*trasp. mar.*) (= **shipwreck**) naufragio. **3** (*trasp. mar.*) nave naufragata.

wreck[2]**,** *v. t.* **1** (*anche fig.*) far naufragare. **2** (*fig.*) mandare in rovina. *v. i.* **1** (*trasp.*) (*d'auto, treni, ecc.*) subire un incidente. **2** (*trasp. mar.*) (*di nave*) naufragare, fare naufragio.

wreckage, *n.* **1** (*anche fig.*) naufragio. **2** (*trasp.*) disastro, sinistro (*automobilistico e sim.*). **3** (*trasp.*) rottami (*d'un disastro aereo, stradale, ecc.*). **4** (*trasp. mar.*) relitti (*d'un naufragio*).

wrecker, *n.* **1** (*trasp. aut.*) carro attrezzi, autogru, carro gru. **2** (*trasp. mar.*) nave di soccorso, nave per ricuperi.

wrecking, *n.* (*trasp. mar.*) servizio di ricupero, servizio di salvataggio. // ~ **car** (*trasp. aut.*) carro attrezzi, autogru, carro gru; ~ **crew** (*trasp. mar.*) equipaggio addetto ai ricuperi.

writ, *n.* (*leg.*) decreto, mandato, ordine, ordinanza. // ~ **of attachment** (*leg.*) ordine di sequestro; ~ **of detinue** (*leg.*) ordine di ricupero di cose immobili illegalmente possedute; ~ **of execution** (*leg.*) titolo esecutivo; ~ **of subpoena** (*leg.*) mandato di comparizione; ~ **of summons** (*leg.*) citazione; **a** ~ **served on a defendant** (*leg.*) una citazione notificata al convenuto.

write[1]**,** *n.* (*giorn., pubbl.*) caratteri (*tipografici o di macchina da scrivere*). // ~ **-down** (*fin.*) svalutazione; ~ **-off** (*cred.*) annullamento, cancellazione; (*fin., rag.*) svalutazione, deprezzamento; (*fig., fam.*) cosa (*o* oggetto) che non vale (più) nulla; **a** ~ **-off for amortization** (*rag.*) una svalutazione a fini d'ammortamento; **the** ~ **-off of a bad debt** (*cred.*) la cancellazione d'un credito inesigibile; ~ **-up** aggiornamento; (*fin., rag.*) rivalutazione; **the ~ -up of machinery** (*rag.*) la rivalutazione del macchinario.

write², *v. t.* (*pass.* **wrote**, *part. pass.* **written**) scrivere. // to ~ **a cheque** compilare un assegno; to ~ **down** annotare, prender nota di, registrare; (*fin., rag.*) ridurre il valore nominale di (*titoli*); svalutare (*attività, titoli, ecc.*); (*market.*) ribassare (*merci*); to ~ **down an asset** (*rag.*) svalutare un'attività; to ~ **down expenses** (*rag.*) notare le spese; to ~ **in shorthand** stenografare; to ~ **off** (*cred.*) annullare, cancellare; (*fin., rag.*) svalutare, deprezzare; to ~ **off the copy of a contract** (*leg.*) redigere la còpia d'un contratto; to ~ **off a debt** (*cred.*) cancellare un debito; to ~ **out** scrivere per esteso, trascrivere; compilare, redigere; to ~ **up** aggiornare, completare; (*fin., rag.*) rivalutare; to ~ **up one's accounts** (*rag.*) aggiornare i (propri) conti.

writer, *n.* (*comun.*) scrivente. // **the ~ of a document** (*leg.*) l'estensore d'un documento.

writing, *n.* **1** (lo) scrivere, scrittura, grafia. **2** (*anche leg.*) documento scritto. // ~ **-off** (*cred.*) cancellazione; (*fin., rag.*) svalutazione; ~ **-paper** (*attr. uff.*) carta da scrivere, carta da lettere; **in ~** (*d'atto, accordo, e sim.*) fatto per iscritto.

written, *a.* (*leg.*) codificato. // ~ **agreement** (*leg.*) accordo scritto; ~ **communications** (*org. az.*) comunicazioni scritte; ~ **evidence** (*leg.*) prova scritta; ~ **law** (*leg.*) legge scritta; ~ **reprimand** (*pers.*) ammonizione scritta; ~ **telephone message** (*comun.*) fonogramma.

wrong¹, *a.* errato. *n.* **1** (*leg.*) azione disonesta, atto illecito, ingiustizia, ingiuria. **2** (*leg.*) danno. // **a ~ entry** (*rag.*) una scrittura (*a partita doppia*) sbagliata; to **be ~** essere in errore; to **be in the ~** aver torto; **on the ~ side of the road** (*trasp.*) contro mano.

wrong², *v. t.* (*leg.*) far torto a.

wrongdoer, *n.* (*leg.*) malfattore, trasgressore.

wrongdoing, *n.* (*leg.*) atto illecito, infrazione, trasgressione.

wrongful, *a.* (*leg.*) ingiusto, iniquo, illegale, illecito, criminoso. // ~ **abstraction** (*leg., pers.*) sottrazione indebita di beni del datore di lavoro (*da parte d'un dipendente*); **a ~ act** (*leg.*) un atto lesivo; ~ **dismissal** (*leg., pers.*) licenziamento non per giusta causa; **a ~ heir** (*leg.*) un erede illegittimo; **the ~ occupation of a property** (*leg.*) l'occupazione illegale d'una proprietà.

X

x, *n.* **1** (*mat.*) incognita, quantità incognita. **2** (*mat.*) x (*variabile indipendente*). **3** (*mat.*) ascissa, asse delle x, coordinata delle x.

xerographic, *a.* (*giorn., pubbl.*) xerografico.

xerography, *n.* (*giorn., pubbl.*) xerografia.

Xmas, *n.* (*abbr. di* **Christmas**) (il) Natale. // **at ~** a Natale; **on ~ day** il giorno di Natale.

Y

y, *n.* **1** (*mat.*) y, seconda quantità incognita. **2** (*mat.*) y (*variabile dipendente*). **3** (*mat.*) ordinata, asse delle y, coordinata delle y. // ~ **-axis** (*mat.*) ordinata; ~ **-coordinate** (*mat.*) ordinata.

yard[1], *n.* iarda, yard (*misura di lunghezza pari a m 0,914*). // ~ **-measure** misura pari a una iarda; (*slang USA*) cento dollari.

yard[2], *n.* **1** cortile, recinto; cantiere. **2** (*trasp. ferr.*) (= **railway-yard**) scalo ferroviario, «piazzale» (*di stazione*), sistema di binari per deposito (smistamento, ecc.). **3 the Yard** (*ingl.*) (= **Scotland Yard**) Scotland Yard (*a Londra: sede centrale della polizia*). // ~ **-locomotive** (*trasp. ferr.*) locomotiva di manovra, locomotiva da manovra; ~ **-man** (*trasp. ferr.*) manovratore; ~ **-master** (*trasp. ferr.*) capo d'uno scalo.

yardage[1], *n.* lunghezza in iarde.

yardage[2], *n.* **1** uso d'un recinto (*come deposito, ecc.*). **2** prezzo d'affitto d'un recinto (*o* d'un deposito).

yardstick, *n.* **1** verga d'una iarda (*strumento per misurare*). **2** (*fig.*) metro di valutazione, unità di misura, parametro.

year, *n.* **1** anno, annata. **2** (*fin., rag.*) esercizio, esercizio finanziario, esercizio sociale. // ~ **end** fine d'anno; ~ **-end** (*econ., fin., rag.*) di fine d'anno, di fine esercizio, di chiusura (*dell'esercizio*); ~ **-end adjustments** (*rag.*) rettifiche di fine esercizio; ~ **-end bonus** (*pers.*) tredicesima; ~ **-end closing entries** (*rag.*) scritture di fine esercizio, scritture di chiusura; **the** ~ **-end position** (*rag.*) la situazione con cui s'è chiusa l'annata; ~ **-end profit and loss picture** (*rag.*) risultato economico di fine esercizio; **the** ~ **of assessment** (*fin.*) l'anno d'imposizione (fiscale); ~ **'s purchase** (*econ., fin.*) rendita annua (*d'un terreno, d'un'impresa, ecc.*).

yearly, *a.* annuale, annuo. *avv.* annualmente. // ~ **income** (*fin.*) reddito annuale; ~ **interest** (*fin.*) annualità d'interessi; **a** ~ **rent** (*fin.*) una rendita annuale; ~ **wage** (*pers.*) salario annuo.

yellow, *a.* giallo. // ~ **dog** (*fam.*) persona spregevole; ~ **flag** (*trasp. mar.*) bandiera gialla, bandiera di quarantena; **the** ~ **press** (*giorn.*) la stampa scandalistica, la stampa «sensazionale».

yen, *n.* yen (*unità monetaria giapponese*).

yield[1], *n.* **1** raccolto. **2** prodotto, produzione. **3** rendimento, resa. **4** (*econ.*) frutto, reddito, rendita. **5** (*fin.*) gettito (*d'imposte, tasse, ecc.*). // **the** ~ **of taxes** (*fin.*) il gettito d'imposta, il gettito delle imposte; **the** ~ **on investments** (*fin.*) la resa degli investimenti; **the** ~ **on shares** (*fin.*) la rendita derivante da titoli azionari; ~ **to maturity** (*fin.*) reddito netto (*d'un'obbligazione*).

yield[2], *v. t.* **1** (*econ., fin.*) dare, fruttare, produrre, rendere. **2** (*fin.*) (*d'imposta, tassa, ecc.*) dare il gettito di (*una certa somma*). // to ~ **an interest** (*fin.*) produrre interesse; to ~ **no profit** essere infruttifero.

yielder, *n.* **1** (*econ., fin.*) cosa che produce. **2** (*econ., fin.*) cosa che rende, fonte di guadagno, cespite.

yielding, *a.* (*econ., fin.*) produttivo (*d'interesse*).

yours, *pron. poss.* **1** vostro, Vostro. **2** tuo. // ~ **faithfully** (*o* **sincerely,** *o* **truly,** *o* **cordially**) distinti saluti (*nella corrispondenza commerciale*).

Z

z, *n.* (*mat.*) z.

zeggist, *n.* (*econ.*) «zegista» (*fautore dello «sviluppo economico zero»*).

zero, *n.* **1** zero. **2** (*mat.*) zero, nullo. *a. attr.* «*zero*». // ~ **economic growth (ZEG)** (*econ.*) «sviluppo economico zero»; ~ **hour** (*anche fig.*) l'ora «zero»; ~ **inflation** (*econ.*) inflazione «zero»; ~ **rate of growth** (*econ.*) tasso di sviluppo nullo, tasso di crescita zero.

zincotype, *n.* (*giorn., pubbl.*) zincotipia.

zincotypist, *n.* (*giorn., pubbl.*) zincotipista.

zip code[1], *n.* (*abbr. di* **zone improvement plan**) (*comun., USA*) codice d'avviamento postale (*CAP*).

zip-code[2], *v. t.* (*comun., USA*) fornire di codice d'avviamento postale.

zip number, *n. V.* **zip code**[1].

zone, *n.* zona, area, regione. // ~ **time** ora locale.

zoom[1], *n.* **1** rapido (e subitaneo) movimento verso l'alto. **2** (*econ., market.*) balzo, impennata (*dei prezzi, ecc.*). **3** (*giorn., pubbl.*) zumata.

zoom[2], *v. i.* **1** (*econ., market.*) (*di prezzi, ecc.*) balzare, impennarsi, andare alle stelle. **2** (*giorn., pubbl.*) zumare (*variare il campo d'immagine cinematografica con un obiettivo a lunghezza focale variabile*). // to ~ **up** (*econ., market.*) (*di prezzi, ecc.*) balzare, andare alle stelle.

ABBREVIATIONS, SYMBOLS AND TABLES
ABBREVIATIONI, SIMBOLI E TAVOLE

ABBREVIATIONS, ACRONYMS AND SYMBOLS COMMONLY USED IN COMMERCIAL ENGLISH

a. 1 **acre** acro. 2 (*cred., fin.*) **accepted** accettato. 3 (*pers.*) **acting** facente funzione.

A. (*trasp. mar.*) **first-class** di prima classe.

A.A. 1 **Advertising Association** Associazione Pubblicitaria. 2 **Automobile Association** Automobile Club (*in G.B.*). 3 (*trasp. mar.*) **always afloat** sempre a galla.

A.A.A. **American Accounting Association** Associazione Americana di Ragioneria.

A.A.A.A. **American Association of Advertising Agents** Associazione Americana degli Agenti Pubblicitari.

A.A.C.C.A. **Associate of the Association of Certified and Corporate Accountants** Membro dell'Associazione dei Ragionieri «Certificati e Incorporati» (*in G.B.*).

A.A. of A. **Automobile Association of America** Automobile Club d'America.

a.a/r (*o* **A.a.r., a.a/R**) (*ass.*) **against all risks** contro tutti i rischi.

A.A.S.O. **Association of American Shipowners** Associazione degli Armatori Americani.

A.B. (*rag.*) **account bought** conto vendite.

A.B.A. **American Bankers' Association** Associazione dei Banchieri Americani.

A.B.C. 1 **Aerated Bread Company** catena di ristoranti economici (*in G.B.*). 2 **American Broadcasting Company** Compagnia Americana di Radiodiffusione.

A.B.C.C. **Association of British Chambers of Commerce** Associazione delle Camere di Commercio Britanniche.

A.B.P. **Associated Business Publications** Pubblicazioni Commerciali Associate.

A.B.S. **American Bureau of Shipping** Registro Navale Americano.

a/c (*rag.*) **account** conto.

A.C. 1 (*leg.*) **Appeal Court** Corte d'Appello. 2 (*macch. uff.*) **Automatic Computer** Calcolatore Automatico.

A/C (*banca, cred.*) **account current** conto corrente.

A.C.B. **Advertising Checking Bureau** Ufficio per il Controllo della Pubblicità.

A.C.B. of A. **Associated Credit Bureaus of America** Uffici Associati Americani per il Credito.

acc. 1 (*cred., fin.*) **acceptance** accettazione. 2 (*cred., fin.*) **accepted** accettato. 3 (*rag.*) **account** conto.

A.C.I.B. **Associate of the Corporation of Insurance Brokers** Membro della Corporazione dei Mediatori d'Assicurazione (*in G.B.*).

A.C.I.S. **Associate of the Chartered Institute of Secretaries** Membro dell'Istituto dei Segretari e delle Segretarie.

A.C.M. **Association for Computing Machinery** Associazione per le Macchine Calcolatrici (*in U.S.A.*).

A.C.M.E. **Association of Consulting Management Engineers** Associazione dei Consulenti d'Organizzazione Aziendale.

A.C.W.A. **Associate of the Institute of Cost and Works Accountants** Membro dell'Istituto degli Esperti di Analisi dei Costi e Contabilità Industriale (*in G.B.*).

a/d (*cred.*) **after date** «data».

A.D. **Anno Domini** Dopo Cristo.

ad. (*o* **advt.**) (*pubbl.*) **advertisement** annuncio pubblicitario.

add. (*comun.*) **address** indirizzo.

Adm **Administrator** Amministratore.

A.D.P. **Automatic Data Processing** Elaborazione Automatica dei Dati.

ad val. (*dog., fin.*) **ad valorem** ad valorem.

A.E.A. 1 **American Economic Association** Associazione Economica Americana. 2 **Atomic Energy Authority** Autorità per l'Energia Atomica (*in G.B.*).

A.E.C. **Atomic Energy Commission** Commissione per l'Energia Atomica.

A.E.S. **American Economic Society** Società degli Economisti Americani.

a.f. (*trasp. mar.*) **advance freight** nolo anticipato.

A.F.A. 1 **Advertising Federation of America** Federazione Pubblicitaria Americana. 2 **American Finance Association** Associazione Finanziaria Americana.

A.F.I.P.S. **American Federation of Infor-**

mation Processing Societies Federazione Americana delle Società per l'Elaborazione delle Informazioni.

A.F.L.-C.I.O. **American Federation of Labor and Congress of Industrial Organizations** Sindacato Unificato dei Lavoratori USA.

A.F. of L. **American Federation of Labor** Federazione Americana del Lavoro.

A.G.M. (*amm., fin.*) **Annual General Meeting** Assemblea Generale Annuale.

Agt. (*leg., market.*) **Agent** Agente, Rappresentante.

Agy. (*leg., market.*) **Agency** Agenzia, Rappresentanza.

A.H.U.A. **American Hull Underwriters Association** Associazione degli Assicuratori Americani su Corpo.

A.I.A. **Associate of the Institute of Actuaries** Membro dell'Istituto degli Attuari (*in G.B.*).

A.I.B. **Associate of the Institute of Bankers** Membro dell'Istituto dei Banchieri (*in G.B.*).

A.I.C.A. **Associate of the Institute of Company Accountants** Membro dell'Istituto dei Contabili di Società (*in G.B.*).

A.I.C.P.A. **American Institute of Certified Public Accountants** Istituto Americano dei Ragionieri Iscritti all'Albo.

A.I.C.S. **Associate of the Institute of Chartered Shipbrokers** Membro dell'Istituto dei Mediatori di Noli (*in G.B.*).

A.I.D. **Agency for International Development** Ente per lo Sviluppo Internazionale (*in U.S.A.*).

A.I.M. **American Institute of Management** Istituto Americano d'Organizzazione Aziendale.

Ala. **Alabama** Alabama.

Alask. **Alaska** Alaska.

ALGOL (*elab. elettr.*) **Algorithmic Language** Linguaggio Algoritmico.

Am. (*o* **Amer.**) 1 **America** America. 2 **American** americano.

A.M. (*comun.*) **Air Mail** Posta Aerea.

A.M. (*o* **a.m.**) **ante meridiem** prima di mezzogiorno.

A.M.A. **American Marketing Association** Associazione Americana di Marketing.

A.M.B.I.M. **Associate Member of the British Institute of Management** Membro dell'Istituto Britannico d'Organizzazione Aziendale.

A.M.C. **Advanced Management Course** Corso Progredito d'Organizzazione Aziendale.

A.M.S. **Agricultural Marketing Service** Servizio di Marketing per l'Agricoltura (*in U.S.A.*).

amt. (*rag.*) **amount** ammontare, somma.

A.N.A. **Association of National Advertisers** Associazione Nazionale dei Pubblicitari (*in U.S.A.*).

ans. (*comun.*) **answer** risposta.

a/o (*rag.*) **account of** in conto di.

Ap. (*o* **Apl., Apr.**) **April** aprile.

A.P. 1 (*ass. mar.*) **additional premium** premio supplementare. 2 (*giorn.*) **Associated Press** Federazione (della) Stampa.

A.P.C. **Average Propensity to Consume** Tendenza Media ai Consumi.

appro. (*market.*) **approval** approvazione.

approx. 1 **approximate** approssimativo. 2 **approximately** approssimativamente.

A.P.S. **Average Propensity to Save** Tendenza Media al Risparmio.

A.R. 1 (*ass. mar.*) **all risks** qualsiasi rischio, pieno rischio. 2 (*comun.*) **Advice of Receipt** Avviso di Ricevuta. 3 (*rag.*) **Annual Return** Introito Annuo, Entrate Annue.

ar. (*o* **arr.**) 1 **arrive** arrivano. 2 **arrives** arriva. 3 **arrival** arrivo. 4 **arranged** concordato, fissato, stabilito.

Ariz. **Arizona** Arizona.

Ark. **Arkansas** Arkansas.

arr. *V.* **ar.**

A/S (*rag.*) **account sales** conto vendite.

A.S.A. 1 **American Standards Association** Associazione Americana per la Normalizzazione (*di misure, ecc.*). 2 **American Statistical Association** Associazione Statistica Americana, Associazione Americana di Statistica.

A.S.C.S. **American Society of Corporate Secretaries** Società Americana dei Direttori Amministrativi di Società.

A.S.E. **American Stock Exchange** Borsa Valori Americana.

A.S.Q.C. **American Society for Quality Control** Società Americana per i Controlli Qualitativi.

Ass. (*o* **Assn., Assoc.**) **Association** Associazione.

A.S.S.D. **Association of Stock and Share Dealers** Associazione degli Operatori di Borsa (*in G.B.*).

Asst. (*pers.*) **Assistant** Assistente, Vice.

A.S.T. **Atlantic Standard Time** Ora Standard dell'Oceano Atlantico.

A.T.A. 1 **Actual Time of Arrival** Ora Effettiva d'Arrivo. 2 **Air Transport Association of America** Associazione Americana per i Trasporti Aerei.

A.T. & T. **American Telegraph and Tele-**

phone Telegrafi e Telefoni Americani.

A.T.D. **Actual Time of Departure** Ora Effettiva di Partenza.

att. (*comun.*) **attached** allegato.

Att. (*o* **Atty.**) (*leg.*) **Attorney** Procuratore.

Att.-Gen. (*leg.*) **Attorney-General** Procuratore Generale.

Atty. *V.* **Att.**

Aug. **August** agosto.

aut. **1 automatic** automatico. **2** (*trasp. aut.*) **automobile** automobile.

auth. **1 authorization** autorizzazione. **2 authorized** autorizzato.

av. (*mat., stat.*) **average** media, medio.

A/V (*ass. mar.*) **Average** Avaria.

avdp. (*o* **avoir.**) **avoirdupois.**

Ave. **Avenue** via, viale.

avoir. *V.* **avdp.**

B. (*o* **Brit.**) **1 Britain** Gran Bretagna. **2 British** britannico.

B.A. **Bachelor of Arts** laureato in lettere.

B.A.B.S. (*trasp. aer.*) **Beam Approach Beacon System** Sistema d'Avvicinamento con Radar Faro.

bal. (*rag.*) **balance** bilancio, saldo.

bar. (*o* **bbl., bl.**) **barrel** barile.

Bar. (*leg.*) **Barrister** avvocato.

B.B.C. (*comun.*) **British Broadcasting Corporation** Ente Radiofonico (e Televisivo) Britannico.

bbl. *V.* **bar.**

B.C. **1 Before Christ** Avanti Cristo. **2** (*leg.*) **Bankruptcy Court** Tribunale Fallimentare.

BCN (*trasp. mar.*) **Beacon** Radiofaro.

B.Com(m). **Bachelor of Commerce** laureato in commercio.

B. Com. Sc. **Bachelor of Commercial Science** Laureato in Scienze Commerciali.

B.C.S. **British Computer Society** Società Britannica dei Calcolatori.

B/D (*banca, cred.*) **bank draft** (*o* **banker's draft**) tratta bancaria; assegno circolare.

b.d.i. (*ass. mar.*) **both days included** entrambi i giorni inclusi.

B/E (*cred.*) **Bill of Exchange** cambiale, tratta.

bef. **before** prima.

Benelux **Belgium, the Netherlands and Luxemburg** Benelux.

B.E.P.O. **British Empire Producers' Organization** Organizzazione dei Produttori dell'Impero Britannico.

B.E.S. **Bureau of Employment Security** Ufficio per la Sicurezza del Lavoro (*in U.S.A.*).

B.E.T.R.O. **British Export Trade Research Organization** Organizzazione per le Ricerche sul Commercio d'Esportazione Britannico.

b/f (*rag.*) **brought forward** riportato.

B.F.C.U. **Bureau of Federal Credit Unions** Ufficio delle Unioni Federali di Credito (*in U.S.A.*).

B/G (*dog.*) **bonded goods** merci in punto franco (*o* in porto franco).

B.I.A.T.A. **British Independent Air Transport Association** Associazione Britannica delle Compagnie Aeree Indipendenti.

B.I.F. **British Industries Fair** Fiera delle Industrie Britanniche.

B.I.M. **British Institute of Management** Istituto Britannico per l'Organizzazione Aziendale.

B.I.S. **Bank for International Settlements** Banca dei Regolamenti Internazionali (*in Svizzera*).

bkcy. (*fin., leg.*) **bankruptcy** fallimento.

bkg. **1** (*banca*) **banking** attività bancaria. **2** (*tur.*) **booking** prenotazione.

bkrpt. (*fin., leg.*) **bankrupt** fallito.

bl. *V.* **bar.**

B/L (*trasp. mar.*) **Bill of Lading** Polizza di Carico.

B.L.S. **Bureau of Labor Statistics** Ufficio per le Statistiche del Lavoro (*in U.S.A.*).

blst. (*trasp. mar.*) **ballast** zavorra.

B.M.C. **British Motor Corporation** Società Britannica Motori (*fabbrica d'automobili*).

B.M.R.B. **British Market Research Bureau** Ufficio Britannico per le Ricerche di Mercato.

B.N. (*fin.*) **banknote** banconota.

B.N.E.C. **British National Export Council** Consiglio Nazionale Britannico per le Esportazioni.

b.o. **1** (*market.*) **buyer's option** opzione dell'acquirente. **2** (*org. az.*) **branch office** ufficio di filiale.

B. of A. **Bank of America** Banca d'America.

B. of E. **Bank of England** Banca d'Inghilterra.

bot. (*o* **bt.**) (*market.*) **bought** acquistato, comprato.

b.p. **1** (*cred., rag.*) **bill payable** cambiale passiva. **2** (*cred., rag.*) **bills payable** cambiali passive.

B.P. **British Petroleum** (*società petrolifera*).

B.P.A. **Business Publication Audit of Circulation** Attestato sulla Tiratura delle Pubblicazioni Commerciali (*in U.S.A.*).

B.P.C. 1 **British Petroleum Company** Società Petrolifera Britannica. 2 **British Productivity Council** Consiglio Britannico per la Produttività.

B.P.I. (*econ.*) **Buying Power Index** Indice del Potere d'Acquisto.

B.P.R. **Bureau of Public Roads** Ente delle Strade Nazionali (*in U.S.A.*).

br. (*org. az.*) **branch** filiale.

B.R. 1 **British Railways** Ferrovie Britanniche. 2 (*fin.*) **Bank Rate** Tasso di Sconto.

b. rec. (*cred., rag.*) **bills receivable** cambiali attive.

Brit. 1 **Britain** Gran Bretagna. 2 **British** britannico.

Bros. **Brothers** Fratelli.

B.R.S. **British Road Services** Servizi Stradali Britannici, Servizio Nazionale Britannico dei Trasporti su Strada.

B.R.T. **Brotherhood of Railroad Trainmen** (*sindacato dei ferrovieri americani*).

B/S (*leg., market.*) **Bill of Sale** Contratto di Vendita.

B. Sc. **Bachelor of Science** Laureato in Scienze.

B. Sc. (Econ.) **Bachelor of Science in the Faculty of Economics** Laureato in Economia.

B. Sc. (Soc.) **Bachelor of Science in the Faculty of Sociology** Laureato in Sociologia.

B.S.T. 1 **British Standard Time** Tempo Standard Britannico, Ora Standard Britannica, Ora Ufficiale Britannica. 2 **British Summer Time** Ora Estiva Inglese.

bt. *V.* **bot.**

B.T.C. **British Transport Commission** Commissione dei Trasporti Britannici.

B.T.H.A. **British Travel and Holidays Association** Associazione Britannica per i Viaggi e le Vacanze.

B.T.U. **Board of Trade Unit** Unità del Ministero del Commercio (*in G.B.*).

bu. **bushel, bushels** (*misura*).

bul. **bulletin** bollettino.

B.U.P. **British United Press** Stampa Associata Britannica (*agenzia di stampa*).

bus. *V.* **bu.**

bush. *V.* **bu.**

B.W. (*dog.*) **Bonded Warehouse** Magazzino Doganale, Punto Franco.

C. 1 **Canada** Canada. 2 **Canadian** canadese. 3 **Captain** Capitano. 4 **Celsius** Celsius. 5 **Centigrade** Centigrado.

C.A. 1 **Central America** America Centrale. 2 **Commercial Agent** Agente di Commercio. 3 (*leg.*) **Court of Appeal** Corte d'Appello. 4 (*pers., rag.*) **Chartered Accountant** Ragioniere Iscritto all'Albo.

C/A 1 **Commercial Agent** Agente di Commercio. 2 (*fin., rag.*) **Capital Account** Conto Capitale.

c. & f. (*market.*) **cost and freight** costo e nolo.

Cal. **California** California.

Calif. *V.* **Cal.**

Can. 1 **Canada** Canada. 2 **Canadian** canadese.

Capt. **Captain** Capitano.

car. **carat** carato.

Cash. (*banca, pers.*) **Cashier** Cassiere.

cat. (*market.*) **catalogue; catalog** (*USA*) catalogo.

C.A.T. **College of Advanced Technology** Istituto Superiore di Tecnologia.

C.B.D. (*market.*) **Cash Before Delivery** Pagamento Prima della Consegna.

C.B.I. **Confederation of British Industries** Confederazione delle Industrie Britanniche.

c.c. 1 **cubic centimetre** centimetro cubo. 2 **cubic centimetres** centimetri cubi.

C.C. 1 **Chamber of Commerce** Camera di Commercio. 2 (*amm.*) **City Council** Consiglio Comunale. 3 (*amm.*) **County Council** Consiglio di Contea. 4 (*leg.*) **Circuit Court** Tribunale Distrettuale.

c.d. 1 (*fin.*) **cum dividend** (*with dividend*) con dividendo. 2 (*market.*) **cash discount** sconto cassa.

c/d (*rag.*) **carried down** riportato.

C.D. 1 **Certificate of Deposit** Certificato di Deposito. 2 **Consular Declaration** Dichiarazione Consolare.

C/D *V.* **c/d.**

C.E. 1 **Chancellor of the Exchequer** Cancelliere dello Scacchiere. 2 (*dog.*) **Customs and Excise** Dogana e Dazio.

C.E.A. 1 **Commodity Exchange Authority** Ente degli Scambi Commerciali (*in U.S.A.*). 2 **Council of Economic Advisers** Consiglio dei Consulenti Economici (*in U.S.A.*).

C.E.C. **Canadian Economic Council** Consiglio Canadese per l'Economia.

C.E.D. **Committee for Economic Development** Comitato per lo Sviluppo Economico.

Cel. **Celsius** Celsius.

cen. 1 **central** centrale. 2 **century** secolo.

cent. 1 *V.* **cen.** 2 *V.* **cent.**

cent **centum** cento.

cert. 1 **certificated, certified** certificato (*a.*), autenticato, vidimato. 2 **certificate** certificato (*n.*).

certif. *V.* **cert.**

C.E.S. **Committee of European Shipowners** Comitato degli Armatori Europei.

c/f (*rag.*) **carried forward** riportato.

C/F *V.* **c/f.**

c. f. & i. (*market.*) **cost, freight and insurance** costo, nolo e assicurazione.

cg. 1 **centigram** centigrammo. 2 **centigrams** centigrammi.

C.G. 1 (*amm.*) **Consul General** Console Generale. 2 (*dog.*) **Coast Guard** Guardia Costiera.

ch. 1 **chairman** presidente. 2 (*rag.*) **charge** addebito.

C.H. (*dog.*) **Customs House** Dogana.

chq. (*cred., fin.*) **cheque** assegno bancario.

C.I. 1 (*ass., leg.*) **Compulsory Insurance** Assicurazione Obbligatoria. 2 (*comm. est.*) **Consular Invoice** Fattura Consolare.

C.I.A. **Controllers' Institute of America** Istituto dei Controllori Americani.

C.I.B. **Corporation of Insurance Brokers** Associazione dei Mediatori di Assicurazioni Marittime.

c.i.f. (*market.*) **cost, insurance, freight** costo, assicurazione, nolo.

C.I.F.C.I. (*market., trasp. mar.*) **cost, insurance, freight, commission and interest** costo, assicurazione, nolo, provvigione e interesse.

C.I.F.E. (*market., trasp. mar.*) **cost, insurance, freight and exchange** costo, assicurazione, nolo e commissione.

C.I.F.L.T. (*market., trasp. mar.*) **cost, insurance and freight, London terms** costo, assicurazione e nolo, clausola di Londra.

C.I.O. **Congress of Industrial Organizations** (*sindacato lavoratori USA*).

cl. 1 **centilitre** centilitro. 2 **centilitres** centilitri.

cm. 1 **centimetre** centimetro. 2 **centimetres** centimetri.

C.N. (*o* **C/N**) (*rag.*) **Credit Note** Nota di Accredito.

c/o 1 (*comun.*) **care of** presso. 2 (*rag.*) **carried over** riportato.

Co. 1 (*amm.*) **County** Contea. 2 (*fin.*) **Company** Società (*di capitali*).

C.O.A. (*trasp. mar.*) **contract of affreightment** contratto di trasporto marittimo.

COBOL (*elab. elettr.*) **Common Business Oriented Language** Linguaggio Orientato alle Procedure Amministrative Correnti (*COBOL*).

C.O.D. (*market.*) **Cash On Delivery** Pagamento alla Consegna (*o* Contro Assegno).

Col. **Colorado** Colorado.

coll. 1 **colleague** collega. 2 (*ass. mar., trasp. mar.*) **collision** collisione.

com. 1 **commerce** commercio. 2 **commercial** commerciale. 3 **commission** commissione.

Com. 1 **Commissioner** Commissario. 2 **Committee** Comitato. 3 **Commonwealth.**

CO.M.ECON **Council for Mutual Economic Aid** Consiglio di Mutua Assistenza Economica (*a Mosca*).

comm. *V.* **com.**

comp. 1 **compound** composto. 2 **comprehensive** comprensivo, inclusivo. 3 (*elab. elettr.*) **computer** elaboratore (*o* calcolatore) elettronico.

Cong. **Congress** Congresso (*in U.S.A.*).

Conn. **Connecticut** Connecticut.

Cons. 1 (*amm.*) **Consul** Console. 2 (*fin.*) **Consolidated** Consolidato. 3 (*fin.*) *V.* **Consols.**

consgt. (*market., trasp.*) **consignment** spedizione.

Consols (*fin.*) **Consolidated Annuities** (*o* **Funds**) Annualità Consolidate, Fondi Consolidati (*titoli di Stato*).

cont. (*o* **contd.**) **continued** continua.

contr. **controller** controllore.

Co-op. 1 **Co-operation** Cooperazione. 2 (*fin.*) **Co-operative** Cooperativa.

Corp. (*fin.*) **Corporation** Ente Pubblico (*in G.B.*); Società (*di capitali: in U.S.A.*).

cos. 1 **countries** Paesi. 2 (*amm.*) **counties** contee. 3 (*fin.*) **companies** società (*di capitali*).

c.p. (*market.*) **carriage paid** porto pagato, franco di porto.

C.P. (*o* **C/P**) 1 (*market.*) **Carriage Paid** Porto Pagato, Trasporto Incluso. 2 (*trasp. mar.*) **Charter Party** Contratto di Nolo (*o* di Noleggio).

C.P.A. **Certified Public Accountant** Ragioniere Iscritto all'Albo (*in U.S.A.*).

cr. *V.* **Cr.**

Cr. 1 (*fin., rag.*) **Credit** Credito, Avere. 2 (*fin., rag.*) **Creditor** Creditore.

C.S. 1 (*amm.*) **Civil Service** Amministrazione Statale, Pubblica Amministrazione. 2 (*pers.*) **Chief of Staff** Capo del Personale.

C.S.C.A. **Civil Service Clerical Association** Associazione dei Dipendenti della Pubblica Amministrazione.

C.S.E. **Certificate of Secondary Education** Diploma di Scuola secondaria (*di primo grado*).

C.S.I.R. **Council for Scientific and Industrial Research** Consiglio per la Ricerca Scientifica e Industriale (*in G.B.*).

C.S.O. **Central Statistics Office** Ufficio Centrale di Statistica (*in G.B.*).

ct. 1 **carat** carato. 2 (*fin.*) **cent** centesimo.

Ct. *V.* **Conn.**

C.T.A. **Council for Technological Advancement** Consiglio per il Progresso della Tecnologia (*in U.S.A.*).

C.T.C. **Central Training Council** Consiglio Centrale per l'Addestramento al Lavoro.

C.T.L. (*ass. mar.*) **constructive total loss** perdita totale presunta.

C.T.L.O. (*ass. mar.*) **constructive total loss only** soltanto con perdita totale presunta.

cts. (*fin.*) **cents** centesimi.

cu (*o* cub.) **cubic** cubico, cubo.

C.U. 1 **Consumers' Union** Unione Consumatori (*in U.S.A.*). 2 **Credit Union** Unione di Credito (*in U.S.A.*).

cum. pref. shares (*fin.*) **cumulative preference shares** azioni privilegiate cumulative.

C.U.N.A. **Credit Unions National Association** Associazione Nazionale delle Unioni di Credito (*in U.S.A.*).

C.W.O. (*market.*) **Cash With Order** Pagamento all'Ordinazione.

C.W.S. **Co-operative Wholesale Society** Società delle Cooperative di Consumo (*in G.B.*).

cwt. **hundredweight** (*misura inglese o americana*).

d. 1 **penny** penny. 2 **pence** penny (*pl.*).

d/a (*cred., fin.*) **days after acceptance** giorni dall'accettazione.

D/A 1 (*banca, cred.*) **Deposit Account** Conto di Deposito, Conto Vincolato. 2 (*market.*) **Documents Against Acceptance** Documenti Contro Accettazione.

D.A.A. (*market.*) **Documents Against Acceptance** Documenti Contro Accettazione.

D.A.C. **Development Assistance Committee** Comitato per l'Assistenza Economica.

dbk (*fin.*) **drawback** rimborso di dazio (*all'esportazione*).

dbt 1 (*fin., rag.*) **Debit** Debito, Dare. 2 (*fin., rag.*) **Debtor** Debitore.

D.C. 1 **District of Columbia** Distretto di Columbia (*in U.S.A.*). 2 (*leg.*) **District Court** Tribunale Distrettuale.

D.C.F. method **Discounted-Cash-Flow method** metodo per determinare la convenienza di un investimento, basato sulla valutazione, in termini d'interessi, del reddito futuro scontato al valore attuale.

d.d. (*o* **d/d**) 1 (*comun.*) **dated** datato. 2 (*cred., fin.*) **days after date** giorni data.

D.D. 1 (*leg.*) **Death Duty** Imposta di Successione. 2 (*trasp.*) **Delayed Delivery** Consegna Ritardata. 3 (*trasp. mar.*) **Delivered at Docks** Consegnato sulle Banchine.

dec. **declaration** dichiarazione.

Dec. **December** dicembre.

decl. **declaration** dichiarazione.

deg. 1 **degree** grado. 2 **degrees** gradi.

del. **delegate** delegato.

Del. **Delaware** Delaware.

dely. (*market.*) **delivery** consegna.

dep. (*trasp.*) **departure** partenza.

dept. 1 **deputy** sostituto, vice. 2 (*amm.*) **department** dicastero. 3 (*org. az.*) **department** reparto.

dft. (*cred., fin.*) **draft** tratta.

dg. 1 **decigram(me)** decigrammo. 2 **decigram(me)s** decigrammi.

D.I. (*econ.*) **Disposable Income** Reddito Disponibile.

dict. (*attr. uff.*) **dictaphone** dittafono.

diff. 1 **difference** differenza. 2 **different** differente.

Dip. Techn. **Diploma in Technology** Diploma in Tecnologia.

dir. 1 **direct** diretto. 2 (*comun.*) **directory** elenco telefonico. 3 (*fin.*) *V.* **Dir.**

Dir. (*fin.*) **Director** Amministratore, Consigliere (*membro di Consiglio d'Amministrazione*).

disc. (*market.*) **discount** sconto.

div. 1 (*fin., mat.*) **dividend** dividendo. 2 (*mat.*) **division** divisione.

divd. (*fin., mat.*) **dividend** dividendo.

dkl. 1 **dekalitre** decalitro. 2 **dekalitres** decalitri.

dkm. 1 **dekametre** decametro. 2 **dekametres** decametri.

dl. 1 **decilitre** decilitro. 2 **decilitres** decilitri.

D.L.H. (*org. az.*) **Direct Labour Hours** Ore di Lavoro Effettive.

dm. 1 **decimetre** decimetro. 2 **decimetres** decimetri.

D.M.A.A. **Direct Mail Advertising Association** Associazione della Pubblicità Diretta per Posta (*in U.S.A.*).

D.N. (*o* **D/N**) (*rag.*) **Debit Note** Nota di Addebito.

do. **ditto** (*the same*) idem (*il medesimo*).

D/O (*market., trasp.*) **Delivery Order** Ordine di Consegna.

doct. **document** documento.

dols. (*fin.*) **dollars** dollari.

doz. 1 **dozen** dozzina, dozzine. 2 **dozens** dozzine.

D.P. 1 **Data Processing** Elaborazione dei Dati. 2 (*dog.*) **Duty Paid** Dazio Pagato.

D/P (*market.*) **Documents against Payment** Documenti contro Pagamento.

dpt. *V.* **dept.**

dr. 1 **dram** dramma (*peso*). 2 (*cred.*) **debtor** debitore. 3 (*cred.*) **drawer** traente.

Dr. 1 **Doctor** Dottore. 2 (*rag.*) **Debit** Dare. 3 (*trasp. aut.*) **Driver** Autista, Conducente.

d.s. (*o* **d/s**) (*cred., fin.*) **days after sight** giorni vista.

D.S. 1 (*amm.*) **Department of State** Dipartimento di Stato (*Ministero degli Esteri: in U.S.A.*). 2 (*pers.*) **Deputy Secretary** Vicesegretario.

d.w. (*trasp. mar.*) **dead weight** portata lorda.

D.W. (*dog.*) **Dock Warrant** Fede di Deposito Doganale.

D/W *V.* **D.W.**

d.w.c. (*trasp. mar.*) **dead weight capacity** esponente di carico, portata lorda.

d.w.t. (*trasp. mar.*) **dead weight tonnage** portata lorda.

d/y *V.* **dely.**

D.Y. (*trasp. mar.*) **Dockyard** Cantiere Navale.

E. 1 **East** Est. 2 (*trasp. mar.*) **second-class** di seconda classe.

E. & O.E. (*anche rag.*) **Errors and Omissions Excepted** Salvo Errori e Omissioni.

E.B. (*trasp. aer.*) **Excess Baggage** Bagaglio in Eccesso.

E.B.I. **European Bank of Investment** Banca Europea degli Investimenti.

E.B.U. **European Broadcasting Union** Unione Europea delle Radiodiffusioni (*in Svizzera*).

E.C.A. 1 **Economic Commission for Africa** Commissione Economica per l'Africa (*in Etiopia*). 2 **Economic Cooperation Administration** Ente per la Cooperazione Economica.

E.C.A.F.E. **Economic Commission for Asia and the Far East** Commissione Economica per l'Asia e l'Estremo Oriente (*in Thailandia*).

E.C.E. **Economic Commission for Europe** Commissione Economica per l'Europa (*in Svizzera*).

E.C.L.A. **Economic Commission for Latin America** Commissione Economica per l'America Latina (*in Cile*).

E.C.M. **European Common Market** Mercato Comune Europeo.

ECO.SO.C. **Economic and Social Council** Consiglio Economico e Sociale (*all'ONU*).

E.C.S.C. **European Coal and Steel Community** Comunità Europea del Carbone e dell'Acciaio (*C.E.C.A.*).

E.C.U. **European Customs Union** Unione Doganale Europea.

e.c.u. (*fin.*) **European currency unit** unità monetaria europea.

E.D.P. (*elab. elettr.*) **Electronic Data Processing** Elaborazione Elettronica dei Dati.

E.E. 1 (*pers.*) **Employment Exchange** Ufficio del Lavoro, Agenzia di Collocamento. 2 (*rag.*) **Errors Excepted** Salvo Errori.

E.E.C. **European Economic Community** Comunità Economica Europea (*C.E.E.*).

E.F.O.G.A. **European Fund for the Orientation and Guarantee of Agriculture** Fondo Europeo d'Orientamento e Garanzia Agricola (*F.E.O.G.A.*).

E.F.T.A. **European Free Trade Association** Associazione Europea di Libero Scambio (*E.F.T.A.*).

e.g. **exempli gratia** (*for example*) per esempio.

E.I.A. **Electronic Industries Association** Associazione delle Industrie Elettroniche (*in U.S.A.*).

E.I.B. **European Investment Bank** Banca Europea degli Investimenti (*B.E.I.*).

E.M.A. **European Monetary Agreement** Accordo Monetario Europeo.

Emb. **Embassy** Ambasciata.

E.M.S. (*fin.*) **European Monetary System** Sistema Monetario Europeo (*S.M.E.*).

encl. 1 **enclosed** allegato (*a.*). 2 **enclosure** allegato (*n.*).

E.N.E.A. **European Nuclear Energy Authority** Agenzia Europea per l'Energia Nucleare (*in Francia*).

Eng. 1 **England** Inghilterra. 2 **English** inglese (*a.*).

E.N.I.A.C. (*elab. elettr.*) **Electronic Numerical Integrator and Computer** Integratore ed Elaboratore Numerico Elettronico.

e.o. (*leg.*) **ex officio** d'ufficio.

E.O.E.C. **European Organization for Economic Cooperation** Organizzazione Europea per la Cooperazione Economica (*O.E.C.E.*).

E.P.A. **European Productivity Agency** Ente Europeo per la Produttività.

E.P.T. (*fin.*) **Excess Profits Tax** Imposta

sugli Extraprofitti.

E.P.T.A. **Expanded Program for Technical Assistance** Programma Ampliato d'Assistenza Tecnica.

E.P.U. **European Payments Union** Unione Europea dei Pagamenti.

E.R.P. **European Recovery Program** Piano di Ricostruzione Europea.

E.S. **Econometric Society** Società di Econometria (*in U.S.A.*).

E.S.O.M.A.R. **European Society for Opinion Surveys and Market Research** Società Europea per lo Studio dell'Opinione Pubblica e dei Mercati (*in Belgio*).

esp. **especially** specialmente.

espec. *V.* **esp.**

Esq. **Esquire** Signor.

Esqr. *V.* **Esq.**

est. **1 established** stabilito, fondato. **2 estimated** calcolato, preventivato.

e.t.a. *V.* **E.T.A.**

E.T.A. (*trasp.*) **Estimated Time of Arrival** Ora Prevista d'Arrivo.

etc. **et cetera** (*and the others*) eccetera.

e.t.d. *V.* **E.T.D.**

E.T.D. (*trasp.*) **Estimated Time of Departure** Ora Prevista di Partenza.

EURATOM **European Atomic Energy Community** Comunità Europea per l'Energia Atomica.

Eurovision **European Television** Televisione Europea (Eurovisione).

ex. **1 esamined** esaminato, ispezionato. **2 example** esempio. **3 exception** eccezione. **4 export** esportazione.

Ex. (*fin.*) **Exchange** Borsa.

exec. (*pers.*) **executive** dirigente.

EXIMBANK **Export-Import Bank** Banca per l'Esportazione e l'Importazione (*a Washington*).

exp. **1 expense** spesa. **2 export** esportazione. **3** (*comun., trasp. ferr.*) **express** expresso.

ext. **1 extra** extra. **2 extract** estratto. **3** (*comun.*) **extension** derivazione; interno (*n.*).

F. **1 Fahrenheit** Fahrenheit. **2 Fellow** Membro, Socio. **3 Finance** Finanza. **4** (*mat.*) **Function** Funzione.

Fa. **Florida** Florida.

f.a.a. (*ass. mar.*) **free of all average** franco d'avaria (*generale e particolare*).

F.A.C.C.A. **Fellow of the Association of Certified and Corporate Accountants** Membro dell'Associazione dei Ragionieri Iscritti all'Albo.

F.A.F. **Financial Analysts Federation** Federazione degli Analisti Finanziari.

Fahr. **Fahrenheit** Fahrenheit.

F. and D. (*trasp. mar.*) **freight and demurrage** nolo e controstallie.

F.A.O. **Food and Agricolture Organization** Organizzazione per l'Alimentazione e l'Agricoltura (*dell'ONU: a Roma*).

F.A.Q. (*market.*) **Fair Average Quality** Buona Qualità Media.

f. a. s. (*trasp. mar.*) **free along-side ship** franco sotto bordo, franco sotto banda.

F.B. **1 Fire Brigade** Vigili del Fuoco. **2** (*trasp. aer.*) **Free Baggage** Bagaglio in Esenzione.

F.C.A. **Farm Credit Administration** Ente per il Credito Agricolo (*in U.S.A.*).

f.c. & s. (*ass. mar.*) **free of capture and seizure** franco di cattura e di sequestro.

f.d. (*market.*) **free delivery** consegna franco di spese.

F.D. **1** (*fin.*) **Federal Debt** Debito Federale. **2** (*org. az.*) **Factory Department** Reparto di Fabbrica.

Feb. **February** febbraio.

F. Econ. **Fellow of the Royal Economic Society** Membro della Reale Società d'Economia.

Fed. **Federal** Federale.

F.E.I. **Financial Executives Institute** Istituto dei Dirigenti Finanziari (*in U.S.A.*).

f.f.a. (*market., trasp. mar.*) **free from alongside** franco banchina a destinazione.

f.g.a. (*ass. mar.*) **free of general average** franco d'avaria generale.

F.I.A. **Fellow of the Institute of Actuaries** Membro dell'Istituto degli Attuari.

f.i.b. **1** (*market., trasp. mar.*) **free into barge** franco su chiatta. **2** (*market., trasp. mar.*) **free into bunkers** franco carbonili.

FIFO (*rag.*) **First In, First Out** (*procedimento contabile*).

f.i.o. (*market., trasp. mar.*) **free in and out** carico e scarico franco di spese.

f.i.s. (*pers.*) **family income supplement** integrazione salariale per assegni di famiglia.

Fla. *V.* **Fa.**

Flor. *V.* **Fa.**

fm. **1 fathom** (*misura*). **2 fathoms** (*misura*). **3 form** modulo.

F.N.C.B. **First National City Bank** (*in U.S.A.*).

F.N.M.A. **Federal National Mortgage Association** Associazione Federale Nazionale per le Ipoteche (*in U.S.A.*).

f.o. (*market.*) **firm offer** offerta valida.

F.O. (*amm.*) **Foreign Office** Ministero degli Esteri (*in G.B.*).

F.O.A. **Foreign Operations Administration** Amministrazione per le Operazioni all'Estero.

f.o.b. (*market., trasp. mar.*) **free on board** franco a bordo.

f.o.c. (*market., trasp. ferr.*) **free on car** franco vagone.

f.o.d. (*ass. mar.*) **free of damage** franco di avarie.

f.o.q. (*market., trasp. mar.*) **free on quay** franco sulla banchina.

f.o.r. (*trasp. ferr.*) **free on rail** franco stazione ferroviaria.

F.O.R. (*ass.*) **Fire Risk Only** Soltanto per il Rischio d'Incendio.

FORTRAN (*elab. elettr.*) **Formula Translation** Traduzione di Formule.

f.o.s. (*market., trasp. mar.*) **free overside ship** franco fuori bordo, franco sotto paranco.

f.o.t. *V.* **F.O.T.**

F.O.T. (*trasp. ferr.*) **Free On Truck** Franco Vagone.

F.P. (*ass.*) **Floating Policy** Polizza Flottante.

f. p. a. (*ass. mar.*) **free of particular average** franco d'avaria particolare.

F.R.B. **Federal Reserve Bank** (*o* **Banks**) Banca (*o* Banche) di Riserva Federale (*in U.S.A.*).

Fri. **Friday** venerdì.

F.R.S. **Federal Reserve System** Sistema Federale di Riserva (*in U.S.A.*).

frt. (*trasp. mar.*) **freight** nolo.

ft. **1 foot** piede (*misura*). **2 feet** piedi (*misura*).

F.T. **Financial Times** Times Finanziario.

F.T.C. **Federal Trade Commission** Commissione Federale per il Commercio (*in U.S.A.).*

fth. *V.* **fm.**

fthm. *V.* **fm.**

fur. **1 furlong** (*misura*). **2 furlongs** (*misura*).

fwd. **1 forward** avanti. **2** (*market.*) **forward** assegnato. **3** (*rag.*) **forward** riportato.

g. **1 gram(me)** grammo. **2 gram(me)s** grammi.

G. (*leg.*) **Guardian** Tutore.

Ga. **Georgia** Georgia.

g.a. (*ass. mar.*) **general average** avaria generale.

G.A. **General Assembly** Assemblea Generale.

G.A. and S. (*ass. mar.*) **General Average and Salvage** Avaria Generale e Salvataggio.

gall. **1 gallon** gallone (*misura*). **2 gallons** galloni (*misura*).

G.A.O. **General Accounting Office** Ufficio di Contabilità Generale (*in U.S.A.*).

G.A.T.T. **General Agreement on Tariffs and Trade** Accordo Generale sulle Tariffe e il Commercio (*G.A.T.T.*).

G.B. **Great Britain** Gran Bretagna.

G.C.E. **General Certificate of Education** Diploma di Scuola secondaria (*di secondo grado*).

G.D.P. (*econ.*) **Gross Domestic Product** Prodotto Interno Lordo.

G.E. **General Electric** (*società americana*).

gent. **1 gentleman** signore. **2 gentlemen** signori.

Geo. *V.* **Ga.**

gm. *V.* **g.**

G.M. (*pers.*) **General Manager** Direttore Generale.

G.M.T. (*comun., trasp.*) **Greenwich Mean Time** Ora di Greenwich.

gn. (*fin.*) **1 guinea** ghinea. **2 guineas** ghinee.

gnp. *V.* **G.N.P.**

G.N.P. (*econ.*) **Gross National Product** Prodotto Nazionale Lordo.

Gov. **1** (*amm.*) **Government** Governo. **2** (*amm.*) **Governor** Governatore.

Govt. (*amm.*) **Government** Governo.

G.P. **Gallup Poll** Sondaggio Gallup.

G.P.O. **1 Government Printing Office** Poligrafici di Stato (*in U.S.A.*). **2** (*comun.*) **General Post Office** Posta Centrale.

gr. **1** *V.* **g. 2** (*market.*) **gross** lordo.

G.R. (*fin.*) **Gold Reserve** Riserva Aurea.

Grad. **Graduate** Laureato.

Gr.T. (*trasp. mar.*) **Gross Ton** Tonnellata di Stazza.

G.R.T. (*trasp. mar.*) **Gross Register Ton** Tonnellaggio Lordo di Registro, Stazza Lorda di Registro.

gr.wt. **gross weight** peso lordo.

G.S. **General Secretary** Segretario Generale.

G.V. (*trasp. ferr.*) **Grande Vitesse** Grande Velocità.

H. (*trasp. mar.*) **Harbour** Porto.

ha. **1 hectare** ettaro. **2 hectares** ettari.

h. and c. water (*tur.*) **hot and cold water**

acqua calda e fredda.

H.B.M. **Her** (*o* **His**) **Britannic Majesty** Sua Maestà Britannica.

H.C. (*leg.*) **High Court** Alta Corte.

hg. 1 **hectogram(me)** ettogrammo. 2 **hectogram(me)s** ettogrammi.

hhd. **hogshead** misura per liquidi (*USA*).

H.M.C. (*dog.*) **Her** (*o* **His**) **Majesty's Customs** la Dogana Britannica.

H.M.S. (*trasp. mar.*) **Her** (*o* **His**) **Majesty's Ship** Nave Britannica.

H.M.S.O. **Her** (*o* **His**) **Majesty's Stationery Office** Poligrafici di Stato (*in G.B.*).

H.O. 1 (*amm.*) **Home Office** Ministero dell'Interno. 2 (*org. az.*) **Head Office** Sede Centrale.

Hon. 1 **Honorable** Onorevole. 2 **Honorary** Onorario.

H.P. 1 (*amm.*) **Houses of Parliament** il Parlamento, le Camere. 2 (*market.*) **Hire Purchase** (Sistema di) Acquisti a Rate.

H.Q. (*org. az.*) **Headquarters** Sede centrale.

hr. **hour** ora.

H.R. 1 **Human Relations** Relazioni Umane. 2 (*amm.*) **House of Representatives** Camera dei Deputati (*in U.S.A.*).

hrs. **hours** ore.

H.S. 1 **High School** Scuola Secondaria. 2 (*amm.*) **Home Secretary** Ministro dell'Interno. 3 (*trasp. mar.*) **Harbour Service** Servizio Portuale.

H.W. (*trasp. mar.*) **High Water** Alta Marea, Acqua Alta.

I. 1 **Ireland** Irlanda. 2 **Irish** irlandese (*a.*).

Ia. **Iowa** Iowa.

I.A.E.A. **International Atomic Energy Agency** Ente Internazionale per l'Energia Atomica.

I.A.T.A. **International Air Transport Association** Associazione Internazionale Trasporti Aerei (*in Canada*).

ib. **ibidem** (*in the same place*) ibidem.

I.B. 1 **Institute of Bankers** Istituto dei Banchieri. 2 **International Bank** Banca Internazionale. 3 (*dog.*) **In Bond** Soggetto a Dazio. 4 (*trasp. mar.*) **Inboard** a Bordo.

I.B.A. **Investment Bankers Association** Associazione degli «Investment Bankers» (*in U.S.A.*).

ibid. *V.* **ib.**

I.B.M. **International Business Machines** Macchine Contabili Internazionali (*società americana*).

I.B.R.D. **International Bank for Reconstruction and Development** Banca Internazionale per la Ricostruzione e lo Sviluppo (*in U.S.A.*).

I.C.A. **International Cooperative Alliance** Alleanza Cooperativa Internazionale.

I.C.A.O. **International Civil Aviation Organization** Organizzazione Internazionale per l'Aviazione Civile (*in Canada*).

I.C.C. **Interstate Commerce Commission** Commissione Interstatale per il Commercio (*in U.S.A.*).

I.C.C.A. **International Consumer Credit Association** Associazione Internazionale per il Credito ai Consumatori.

I.C.F.C. **Industrial and Commercial Finance Corporation** Ente Finanziario per l'Industria e il Commercio.

I.C.F.T.U. **International Confederation of Free Trade Unions** Confederazione Internazionale dei Sindacati Liberi.

I.C.I. **Imperial Chemical Industries** (*società britannica*).

id. **idem** (*the same*) idem.

Id. **Idaho** Idaho.

I.D.A. **International Development Association** Associazione Internazionale per lo Sviluppo.

I.D.A.C. **Import Duties Advisory Committee** Comitato di Consulenza per i Dazi alle Importazioni.

I.D.P. (*elab. elettr.*) **Integrated Data Processing** Elaborazione Integrata dei Dati.

i.e. **id est** (*that is*) cioè.

I.F.A.L.P.A. **International Federation of Air Line Pilots Associations** Federazione Internazionale delle Associazioni dei Piloti di Linee Aeree.

I.F.A.P. **International Federation of Agricultural Producers** Federazione Internazionale dei Produttori Agricoli.

I.F.C. **International Finance Corporation** Società Finanziaria Internazionale.

I.L.A. 1 **International Law Association** Associazione Internazionale del Diritto (*in G.B.*). 2 **International Longshoremen's Association** Sindacato Internazionale degli Scaricatori di Porto (*in U.S.A.*).

I.L.I. **Institute of Life Insurance** Istituto per l'Assicurazione sulla Vita (*in U.S.A.*).

Ill. **Illinois** Illinois.

I.L.O. **International Labour Organization** Organizzazione Internazionale del Lavoro (*in Svizzera*).

I.L.U. **Institute of London Underwriters** Istituto degli Assicuratori Marittimi di Londra.

I.M. **Imperial Measure** Misura Imperiale.

I.M.C.O. **Inter-Governmental Maritime Consultative Organization** Organizzazione Consultiva Intergovernativa Marittima.

I.M.F. **International Monetary Fund** Fondo Monetario Internazionale (*in U.S.A.*).

I.M.O. (*cred., fin.*) **International Money Order** Vaglia Internazionale.

imp. **1 import** importazione. **2 imported** importato. **3 importer** importatore.

in. **1 inch** pollice (*misura*). **2 inches** pollici (*misura*).

Inc. (*fin.*) **Incorporated** Registrato.

incl. **1 included** incluso. **2 including** incluso. **3 inclusive** comprensivo, inclusivo.

Incorp. *V.* **Inc.**

Ind. **Indiana** Indiana.

inf. **information** informazione, informazioni.

ins. **1 inches** pollici (*misura*). **2** (*ass.*) **insurance** assicurazione.

inst. **1 instant** presente. **2 institute** istituto. **3 institution** istituzione.

int. **1 international** internazionale. **2** (*fin.*) **interest** interesse. **3** (*tur.*) **interpreter** interprete.

in trans. (*dog., trasp.*) **in transit** in transito, durante il viaggio.

inv. **1 inventory** inventario. **2** (*market.*) **invoice** fattura.

I.O.C.S. **1** (*econ., org. az.*) **Input-Output Control System** Sistema di Controllo basato sul rapporto fra i Fattori Produttivi e la Produzione. **2** (*elab. elettr.*) **Input Output Control System** Sistema di Controllo di Entrata e Uscita (*dei dati*).

I.O.M. **Isle of Man** Isola di Man.

I.O.U. (*cred.*) **I Owe You** (*riconoscimento scritto di un debito*).

I.O.W. **Isle of Wight** Isola di Wight.

I.P.A. **Institute of Practitioners in Advertising** Istituto degli Agenti Pubblicitari (*in G.B.*).

I.P.I. **International Press Institute** Istituto Internazionale per la Stampa.

I.P.U. **Interparliamentary Union** Unione Interparlamentare.

I.Q. **Intelligence Quotient** Quoziente d'Intelligenza.

I.R.C. **Industrial Reorganization Corporation** Ente per la Riorganizzazione Industriale.

Ire. **1 Ireland** Irlanda. **2 Irish** irlandese (*a.*).

I.R.S. **Internal Revenue Service** Servizio delle Imposte Interne (*in U.S.A.*).

I.S.A. **International Federation of the National Standardizing Associations** Federazione Internazionale delle Associazioni Nazionali di Unificazione (*delle misure, ecc.*).

I.S.B.A. **Incorporated Society of British Advertisers** Società dei Pubblicitari Britannici.

I.S.F. **International Shipping Federation** Federazione Internazionale degli Armatori.

I.S.O. **International Organization for Standardization** Organizzazione Internazionale per l'Unificazione (*delle misure, ecc.*).

It. **1 Italian** italiano. **2 Italy** Italia.

I.T. (*tur*). **Inclusive Tours** Viaggi Tutto Compreso.

I.T.A. **Independent Television Authority** Autorità della Televisione Indipendente (*in G.B.*).

I.T.O. **1 International Trade Organization** Organizzazione Internazionale per il Commercio. **2** (*fin.*) **Income Tax Office** Ufficio delle Imposte Dirette.

I.T.S. **Industrial Training Service** Servizio d'Addestramento al Lavoro nell'Industria (*in G.B.*).

I.T.U. **International Telecommunications Union** Unione Internazionale delle Telecomunicazioni.

J. **1** (*leg.*) **Judge** Giudice. **2** (*leg.*) **Justice** Giudice.

Jan. **January** gennaio.

J.C. **1** (*leg.*) **Justice Clerk** Cancelliere. **2** (*leg.*) **Juvenile Court** Tribunale dei Minorenni.

Jr. **Junior** Junior.

Jun. *V.* **Jr.**

Junr. *V.* **Jr.**

K (*trasp. mar.*) **Knot** Nodo (*misura*).

K. **Kansas** Kansas.

Kan. **Kansas** Kansas.

K.C. **1 Kansas City. 2** (*leg.*) **Kings' Counsel** (*titolo onorifico per avvocati*).

Ken. **Kentucky** Kentucky.

kg. **1 kilogram(me)** chilogrammo. **2 kilogram(me)s** chilogrammi.

Kil. **Kilogram(me)** chilogrammo.

kilo. *V.* **kg.**

Kl. **Kilometre** chilometro.

km. **1 kilometre** chilometro. **2 kilometres** chilometri.

kw **1 kilowatt** chilowatt. **2 kilowatts** chilowatt (*pl.*).

kwh. **1 kilowatt hour** chilowattora. **2 kilowatt hours** chilowattore.

Ky. **Kentucky** Kentucky.

l. **1 league** lega (*misura*). **2 litre** litro. **3 litres** litri.

L. **1 Labour** Lavoro, Manodopera. **2** (*trasp. aut.*) **Learner** Principiante. **3** (*trasp. mar.*) **Liner** Nave di Linea.

La. **Louisiana** Louisiana.

L.A. **1 Los Angeles. 2** (*amm.*) **Legislative Assembly** Assemblea Legislativa. **3** (*amm.*) **Local Authority** Autorità Locale. **4** (*leg.*) **Law Association** Ordine Forense.

Lab. **1 Labour** Lavoro, Manodopera. **2 Labrador** Labrador.

L.A.F.T.A. **Latin American Free Trade Association** Associazione Latino Americana di Libero Scambio.

lang. **language** lingua, linguaggio.

lb. **1 pound** (*libra*) libbra. **2 pounds** libbre.

lbt. **pound troy** (*libra troy*) libbra troy.

L.C. **1** (*amm.*) **Lord Chancellor** il Lord Cancelliere. **2** (*trasp. mar.*) **London Clause** Clausola di Londra.

L/C (*fin.*) **Letter of Credit** Lettera di Credito.

L.C.C. **1 London Chamber of Commerce** Camera di Commercio di Londra. **2** (*amm.*) **London County Council** Consiglio della Contea di Londra.

L.D. **1 Doctor of Letters** Dottore in Lettere (*in U.S.A.*). **2** (*trasp. mar.*) **London Docks** Bacini di Londra.

l.d.d. (*ass. mar.*) **loss during discharge** perdita durante la discarica.

Ldg. (*trasp. mar.*) **loading** carico, caricazione.

l.d.l. (*ass. mar.*) **loss during loading** perdita durante il carico (*o* la caricazione).

leg. **1 legal** legale. **2 legate** legato.

L.E.S.S. **Least Cost Estimating and Scheduling** Calcolo e Programmazione del Costo Minimo.

L.G. (*trasp. aer.*) **Landing Ground** Campo d'Atterraggio.

lgth. **length** lunghezza.

lg. tn. **long ton** tonnellata inglese, di 2.240 libbre (*kg. 1.016*).

L.H. (*trasp. mar.*) **Lighthouse** Faro.

L.H.D. (*trasp. aut.*) **Left-Hand Drive** Guida a Sinistra (*su un cartello stradale*).

liq. **liquid** liquido.

L.J. (*leg.*) **Lord Justice.**

L.L. (*fin.*) **Limited Liability** Responsabilità Limitata.

LL.B. **Bachelor of Law** Laureato in Legge.

LL.D. **Doctor of Law** Dottore in Legge.

Llds. (*ass. mar.*) **Lloyd's** Lloyd.

L.O. (*econ.*) **Lock-Out** Serrata.

Lond. **London** Londra.

L.P.T.B. **London Passenger Transport Board** Azienda Trasporto Passeggeri di Londra.

L.R. **1** (*ass. mar.*) **Lloyd's Register** Registro del Lloyd (*di Londra*). **2** (*leg.*) **Law Reports** Atti Giudiziari.

L.S. (*leg.*) **Law Society** Società Forense.

l.t. *V.* **lg. tn.**

L.T. **1** (*fin.*) **Legal Tender** Moneta a Corso Legale. **2** (*trasp.*) *V.* **L.P.T.B.**

Ltd. (*fin.*) **Limited** a responsabilità limitata; per azioni.

ltge. (*trasp. mar.*) **lighterage** alleggio, spese d'alleggio.

ltr. **litre** litro.

L.W. (*trasp. mar.*) **Low Water** Bassa Marea, Acqua Bassa.

m. **1 metre** metro. **2 metres** metri. **3 mile** miglio. **4 miles** miglia. **5 month** mese.

M. (*trasp. aut.*) **Motorway** Autostrada.

M. **1 Magistrate** Magistrato. **2 Member** Membro, Socio. **3 Monday** lunedì.

M.A. **1 Master of Arts** Dottore in Lettere. **2** (*amm.*) **Ministry of Agriculture** Ministero dell'Agricoltura.

M/A (*banca, rag.*) **My Account** a Me Medesimo, a Mio Favore.

mach. **machinery** macchinario.

mag. (*giorn.*) **magazine** rivista illustrata.

mar. **maritime** marittimo.

Mar. **March** marzo.

Mass. **Massachusetts** Massachusetts.

M.B. (*trasp. mar.*) **Motor Boat** Motobarca, Motoscafo.

M.B.D. (*trasp. mar.*) **Machinery Breakdown** Avaria alle Macchine.

M.b.O. (*org. az.*) **Management by Objectives** Direzione (*od* Organizzazione) per Obiettivi.

M.C. (*amm.*) **1 Member of Congress** Membro del Congresso (*in U.S.A.*). **2 Ministry of Commerce** Ministero del Commercio.

M.C.A. **Management Consultants' Association** Associazione dei Consulenti d'Organizzazione Aziendale.

Mchy Dge (*trasp. mar.*) **Machinery Damage** Avaria alle Macchine.

M.D. **1 Managing Director** Consigliere Delegato. 2 **Market Day** Giorno di Mercato.

Md. **Maryland** Maryland.

m/d (*cred.*) **months after date** mesi data.

M. Dk. (*trasp. mar.*) **Main Deck** Ponte Principale.

Me. **Maine** Maine.

mem. 1 **member** membro. 2 *V.* **memo.**

memo **memorandum** memorandum, promemoria, nota.

Messrs **Messieurs** Signori.

mfd. **manufactured** fabbricato.

mfg. **manufacturing** fabbricante (*a.*).

mfrs. **manufacturers** fabbricanti.

mg. 1 **milligram(me)** milligrammo. 2 **milligram(me)s** milligrammi.

mgm. *V.* **mg.**

mgr. *V.* **mg.**

Mgr. **Manager** Direttore (*di un'azienda*).

mi. **mile** miglio.

Mi. **Mississippi** Mississippi.

Mich. **Michigan** Michigan.

min. 1 **minimum** minimo. 2 **minute** minuto. 3 **minutes** minuti.

Minn. **Minnesota** Minnesota.

M.I.P. (*ass. mar.*) **Marine Insurance Policy** Polizza d'Assicurazione Marittima.

Miss. *V.* **Mi.**

M.I.T. **Massachusetts Institute of Technology** Istituto di Tecnologia del Massachusetts.

ml. 1 **millilitre** millilitro. 2 **millilitres** millilitri.

mm. 1 **millimetre** millimetro. 2 **millimetres** millimetri.

M.M. 1 **Mercantile Marine** Marina Mercantile. 2 (*fin.*) **Money Market** Mercato Monetario.

M.N. **Merchant Navy** Marina Mercantile.

mo. **month** mese.

Mo. **Missouri** Missouri.

M.O. (*cred.*) **Money Order** Vaglia.

M.O.H. **Medical Officer of Health** Ufficiale Sanitario Marittimo.

mon. (*fin.*) **monetary** monetario.

Mon. **Monday** lunedì.

Mont. **Montana** Montana.

M.P. **Member of Parliament** Membro del Parlamento (*in G.B.*).

M.P. & C. **Management Planning and Control** Controllo e Programmazione Manageriale.

M.P.C. (*econ.*) **Marginal Propensity to Consume** Propensione Marginale al Consumo.

m.p.h. **miles per hour** miglia all'ora.

M.P.S. (*econ.*) **Marginal Propensity to Save** Propensione Marginale al Risparmio.

Mr **Mister** Signor.

M.R. (*trasp. mar.*) **Mate's Receipt** Ricevuta d'Imbarco.

Mrs **Mistress** Signora.

m.s. *V.* **m/s.**

m/s 1 (*cred.*) **months after sight** mesi vista. 2 (*trasp. mar.*) **motor ship** motonave.

Ms 1 **Miss** Signorina. 2 *V.* **Mrs.**

MS **Manuscript** Manoscritto.

M.S. 1 **Master of Science** Dottore in Scienze. 2 **Metric System** Sistema Metrico. 3 **Ministry of Shipping** Ministero della Marina. 4 (*trasp. mar.*) **Mail Steamer** (Piroscafo) Postale.

M.T. 1 **Mean Time** Tempo Medio, Ora Media. 2 **Measurement Ton** Tonnellata di Cubaggio (*o* d'Ingombro). 3 **Metric Ton** Tonnellata Metrica (*o* di Peso). 4 **Ministry of Transport** Ministero dei Trasporti. 5 **Motor Transport** Trasporto con Veicoli a Motore.

M/T 1 (*cred.*) **Mail Transfer** Bonifico per Posta. 2 (*trasp. mar.*) **Motor Tanker** Motocisterna.

mth. **month** mese.

M.T.M. (*org. az.*) **Methods and Time Measurement** Misura Metodi e Tempi.

n. 1 **name** nome. 2 **number** numero.

N. 1 **Navigation** Navigazione. 2 **North** Nord. 3 (*trasp. aer., trasp. mar.*) **Navigator** Ufficiale di Rotta.

N.A. **North America** America Settentrionale.

n. a. a. (*trasp. mar.*) **not always afloat** non sempre a galla.

N.A.A. **National Association of Accountants** Associazione Nazionale dei Ragionieri (*in U.S.A.*).

N.A.B. **National Association of Broadcasters** Associazione Nazionale dei Radiotrasmettitori (*in U.S.A.*).

N.A.B.E. **National Association of Business Economists** Associazione Nazionale degli Economisti Aziendali (*in U.S.A.*).

N.A.F.T.A. **New Zealand-Australia Free Trade Agreement** Accordo di Libero Scambio fra la Nuova Zelanda e l'Australia.

N.A.M. **National Association of Manufacturers** Associazione Nazionale degli Industriali (*in U.S.A.*).

N.A.M.C. **National Association of Credit Management** Associazione Nazionale di Gestione dei Crediti (*in U.S.A.*).

N.A.P.A. **National Association of Purchasing Agents** Associazione Nazionale dei Commissionari (*in U.S.A.*).

NASA **National Aeronautic and Space Administration** Ente Aeronautico e Spaziale Americano.

N.A.S.D. **National Association of Security Dealers** Associazione Nazionale degli Operatori di Borsa (*in U.S.A.*).

N.A.T.O. **North Atlantic Treaty Organization** Organizzazione del Trattato Nord-Atlantico.

nav. **1 navigation** navigazione. **2** (*trasp. aer., trasp. mar.*) **navigator** ufficiale di rotta.

navig. *V.* **nav.**

N.B.C. **National Broadcasting Corporation** Ente Radiofonico Nazionale (*in U.S.A.*).

N.B.E.R. **National Bureau of Economic Research** Ufficio Nazionale per la Ricerca Economica (*in U.S.A.*).

N.B.S. **National Bureau of Standards** Ufficio Nazionale delle Misure (*in U.S.A.*).

N.C. **North Carolina** Carolina del Nord.

N.C.B. **National Coal Board** Ente Nazionale per il Carbone (*in G.B.*).

N.D. **1 Nord Dakota** Dakota del Nord. **2** (*econ., fin.*) **National Debt** Debito Pubblico.

N. Dak. **North Dakota** Dakota del Nord.

N.E. **1 New England** Nuova Inghilterra. **2** (*market.*) **National Exhibition** Esposizione Nazionale.

Neb. *V.* **Nebr.**

Nebr. **Nebraska** Nebraska.

N.E.C. **National Economic Council** Consiglio Nazionale dell'Economia (*in U.S.A.*).

Ned *V.* **N.E.D.C.**

N.E.D.C. **National Economic Development Council** Consiglio Nazionale per lo Sviluppo Economico (*in G.B.*).

Nev. **Nevada** Nevada.

New M. **New Mexico** Nuovo Messico.

N.F. **1 Newfoundland** Terranova. **2** (*trasp. aer.*) **Night Flight** Volo Notturno.

N.F.U. **National Farmers'Union** Unione Nazionale degli Agricoltori (*in G.B. e in U.S.A.*).

N.G.A. **National Graphical Association** Unione Nazionale dei Poligrafici (*in G.B.*).

N.H. **New Hampshire** Nuovo Hampshire.

N.H.I. **National Health Insurance** Assicurazione Nazionale contro le Malattie (*in G.B.*).

N.H.S. **National Health Service** Servizio Nazionale contro le Malattie (*in G.B.*).

N.I. **1 Northern Ireland** Irlanda Settentrionale. **2** (*econ.*) **National Income** Reddito Nazionale.

N.I.C. **National Income Commission** Commissione Nazionale sui Redditi (*in G.B.*).

N.J. **New Jersey** Nuovo Jersey.

N.L.R.B. **National Labor Relations Board** Ufficio Nazionale per le Relazioni Sindacali (*in U.S.A.*).

N.M. *V.* **New M.**

N. Mex. *V.* **New M.**

N.N.P. (*econ.*) **Net National Product** Prodotto Nazionale Netto.

no. **number** numero.

No. **Number** Numero.

nos. **numbers** numeri.

Nos. **Numbers** Numeri.

Nov. **November** novembre.

N.P. (*leg.*) **Notary Public** Pubblico Notaio.

N.R.C. **National Research Council** Consiglio Nazionale delle Ricerche (*in U.S.A.*).

N.R.M.A **National Retail Merchants' Association** Associazione Nazionale dei Dettaglianti (*in U.S.A.*).

N.S. (*trasp. mar.*) **Nuclear Ship** Nave a Propulsione Nucleare.

N.T.S.C. **National Television System Committee** Comitato Nazionale per la Televisione a Colori (*in U.S.A.*).

N.U.M. **1 National Union of Manufacturers** Unione Nazionale degli Industriali (*in G.B.*). **2** (*sind.*) **National Union of Mineworkers** Sindacato Nazionale dei Minatori.

N.U.R. **National Union of Railwaymen** Sindacato Nazionale dei Ferrovieri (*in G.B.*).

N.Y. **New York** Nuova York.

N.Y.C. **New York City** Città di Nuova York.

N.Y.S.E. **New York Stock Exchange** Borsa Valori di Nuova York.

O. **Ohio** Ohio.

o/a (*cred.*) **on account** in conto.

O.A.E.C. **Organization of Asian Economic Cooperation** Organizzazione per la Collaborazione Economica Asiatica.

O.A.S. **Organization of American States** Organizzazione degli Stati Americani.

O.B. **Ordinary Business** Affari d'Ordinaria Amministrazione.

O.B.E. **1 Office of Business Economics** Ufficio d'Economia Aziendale (*in U.S.A.*). **2** **Order of the British Empire** Ordine dell'Impero Britannico.

Oc. B/L (*trasp. mar.*) **Ocean Bill of Lading** Polizza di Carico per Trasporti Oceanici.

Oct. **October** ottobre.

O. Dk. (*trasp. mar.*) **Observation Deck**

Ponte Osservazioni Astronomiche, (Ponte di) Casseretto.

O.E.C.D. **Organization for Economic Cooperation and Development** Organizzazione per la Cooperazione e lo Sviluppo Economico (*O.C.S.E.*).

O.E.E.C. **Organization for European Economic Cooperation** Organizzazione Europea per la Cooperazione Economica (*O.E.C.E.*).

off. **official** ufficiale (*a.*).

O.H.M.S. **On Her** (*o* **His**) **Majesty's Service** Al Servizio di Sua Maestà.

O.K. **all correct** bene, benissimo.

Okla. **Oklahoma** Oklahoma.

op. *V.* **opp.**

O.P. (*ass. mar.*) **Open Policy** Polizza d'Abbonamento (*o* Non Valutata).

OPEC **Organization of Petroleum Exporting Countries** Organizzazione dei Paesi Esportatori di Petrolio (*OPEC*).

opp. **opposite** opposto, di fronte.

Or. *V.* **Ore.**

O.R. 1 **Operations Research, Operational Research** Ricerca Operativa. 2 (*trasp.*) **Owner's Risk** a Rischio del Proprietario, a Rischio e Pericolo del Destinatario.

Ore. **Oregon** Oregon.

Oreg. *V.* **Ore.**

org. 1 **organization** organizzazione. 2 **organized** organizzato.

O.S. (*market.*) **On Sample** Su Campione.

o.t. (*pers.*) **overtime** (lavoro) straordinario.

O.T. **Overseas Trade** Commercio Estero.

oz. 1 **ounce** oncia. 2 **ounces** once.

p **new penny** nuovo penny, nuovi penny.

p. **page** pagina.

P (*trasp.*) **Parking** Parcheggio.

p.a. **per annum** all'anno.

Pa. **Pennsylvania** Pennsylvania.

P.A. 1 **Press Association** Associazione della Stampa. 2 **Publishers' Association** Associazione degli Editori.

PANAM **Pan American World Airways** Linee Aeree Americane per Tutti i Continenti.

Parl. 1 **Parliament** Parlamento. 2 **Parliamentary** Parlamentare.

pat. 1 **patent** brevetto. 2 **patented** brevettato.

Pat. Off. **Patent Office** Ufficio Brevetti.

P.A.Y.E. **Pay As Your Earn** Ritenuta alla fonte (*in G.B.*).

payt. **payment** pagamento, versamento.

P.B. (*trasp. mar.*) **Permanent Bunkers** Carbonili Fissi.

P.B.R. **Payment By Results** Pagamento Secondo i Risultati.

pc. *V.* **p.c.**

p.c. 1 (*comun.*) **postcard** cartolina postale. 2 (*mat.*) **per cent** per cento.

p./c. 1 (*market.*) **prices current** listino dei prezzi correnti. 2 (*rag.*) **petty cash** «piccola cassa».

P.C. **Police Constable** Agente di Polizia.

P./C. *V.* **p./c.**

pd. **paid** pagato.

P.D. 1 (*comun.*) **Post District** Distretto Postale. 2 (*org. az.*) **Personnel Department** Reparto del Personale. 3 (*trasp. mar.*) **Port Dues** Diritti Portuali.

Penn. *V.* **Pa.**

P.E.P. **Political and Economical Planning** Pianificazione Politica ed Economica.

per cent. (*mat.*) **per centum** per cento.

per ct. *V.* **per cent.**

perf. 1 (*leg.*) **performance** esecuzione. 2 (*org. az.*) **performance** rendimento.

per pro. (*leg.*) **per procurationem** (*by proxy*) per procura.

pers. **personal** personale (*a.*).

Pers. **Persian** persiano.

P.E.R.T. (*org. az.*) **Problem Evaluation and Review Technique** Tecnica di Valutazione e Revisione dei Programmi, Metodo P.E.R.T.

P.I. (*econ.*) **Personal Income** Reddito Personale.

pk. **peck** peck (*misura*).

Pk. **Park** Parco (*negli indirizzi*).

pl. **plan** piano, progetto.

Pl. **Place** (*negli indirizzi*).

P.L.A. **Port of London Authority** Autorità del Porto di Londra.

pm. (*ass.*) **premium** premio.

P.M. 1 **post meridiem** di pomeriggio, di sera. 2 (*amm.*) **Prime Minister** Primo Ministro. 3 (*comun.*) **Postmaster** Ufficiale Postale. 4 (*leg.*) **Police Magistrate** Pretore. 5 (*org. az.*) **Preventive Maintenance** Manutenzione Preventiva.

P.M.G. **Postmaster General** Ministro delle Poste.

P/N (*cred., fin.*) **Promissory Note** Pagherò.

P.O. 1 (*comun.*) **Post Office** Ufficio Postale. 2 (*cred.*) **Postal Order** Vaglia Postale. 3 (*trasp. aer.*) **Pilot Officer** Ufficiale Pilota.

p.o.b. *V.* **P.O.B.**

P.O.B. (*comun.*) **Post Office Box** Casella Postale.

p.o.c. (*trasp. mar.*) **port of call** porto di

scalo.

P.O.D. (*market.*) **Pay On Delivery** Pagate Alla Consegna.

pop. **population** popolazione.

P.O.S.B. **Post Office Savings Bank** Cassa di Risparmio presso un Ufficio Postale.

pp. **pages** pagine.

p.p. 1 *V.* **per pro.** 2 (*comun.*) **parcel post** pacco postale. 3 (*market.*) **post paid** franco di posta.

P.P. (*comun.*) **Parcel Post** Pacco Postale.

pr. 1 **pair** paio, coppia. 2 (*market.*) **price** prezzo.

Pr. **Priority** Precedenza.

P.R. 1 **Public Relations** Pubbliche Relazioni. 2 (*comun.*) **Poste Restante** Fermo Posta.

P.R.C. **Price Regulation Committee** Comitato di Controllo dei Prezzi.

Pres. **President** Presidente.

Pro. **Professional** Professionale.

P.R.O. **Public Relations Officer** Addetto alle Pubbliche Relazioni.

prof. **profession** professione.

prop. 1 **proprietor** proprietario. 2 (*trasp. mar.*) **propeller** elica.

pro tem. **pro tempore** interino, interinalmente.

prox. **proximo** (*next*) prossimo.

P.R.S.A. **Public Relations Society of America** Società Americana di Pubbliche Relazioni.

P.S. **Post Scriptum** Poscritto.

P/S **Public Sale** Vendita Pubblica.

pt. 1 **payment** pagamento, versamento. 2 **pint** pinta. 3 **pints** pinte.

P.T. 1 (*comm. est.*) **Preferential Tariffs** Tariffe Preferenziali. 2 (*fin.*) **Purchase Tax** Imposta sugli Acquisti (*cfr. ital. I.V.A.*).

P.T.O. **Please Turn Over** Voltare Pagina.

pty. (*leg.*) **proprietary** di proprietà, in esclusiva.

pub. 1 **publisher** editore. 2 **publishing** editoriale (*a.*), editrice (*a.*).

P.V. (*trasp. ferr.*) **Petite Vitesse** Piccola Velocità.

q **quintal** quintale.

Q. **Queen** Regina.

Q.C. (*leg.*) **Queen's Counsel** (*titolo onorifico conferito ad avvocati*).

ql. 1 **quintal** quintale. 2 **quintals** quintali.

qr. 1 **quarter** quarto. 2 **quarters** quarti.

qt. **quart** quarto (*misura*).

qts. **quarts** quarti (*misura*).

quot. 1 **quotation** citazione. 2 (*market.*) **quotation** quotazione.

r. 1 **railway** ferrovia. 2 **river** fiume. 3 **road** strada.

R. 1 **Railway** Ferrovia. 2 **Reserved** Riservato. 3 **River** Fiume. 4 (*fin.*) **Registered** «Registrato».

R.A.B. **Radio Advertising Bureau** Ufficio per la Pubblicità Radiofonica (*in U.S.A.*).

R. & D. **Research and Development** Ricerca e Sviluppo.

R.C. **Royal Commission** Commissione Reale.

r. d. (*trasp. mar.*) **running days** giorni consecutivi.

Rd. **Road** Strada, Via (*negli indirizzi*).

R.D. **Road Department** Reparto Viabilità.

R/D (*banca*) **Refer to Drawer** Mancano i Fondi (*per pagare un assegno*).

re. 1 **reference** riferimento. 2 **with reference to** con (*o* in) riferimento a.

recd. **received** ricevuto.

recpt. **receipt** ricevuta.

reg. 1 **registered** registrato. 2 (*comun.*) **registered** raccomandato.

Reg. *V.* **reg.**

rem. 1 **remainder** rimanente (*n.*). 2 (*fin.*) **remittance** rimessa.

rept. *V.* **recpt.**

retd. 1 **retired** ritirato; ritiratosi, in pensione. 2 **returned** restituito.

R.F.C. **Reconstruction Finance Corporation** Società Finanziaria per la Ricostruzione (*in U.S.A.*).

R.F.S. (*trasp. mar.*) **Ready For Sea** Pronto a Prendere il Mare.

R.I. (*ass.*) **Reinsurance** Riassicurazione.

R.I.C.A. **Research Institute for Consumers' Affairs** Istituto di Ricerca Relativo ai Consumatori.

Rit. (*tur.*) **Rail inclusive tours** Itinerari ferroviari tutto compreso.

Rly. **Railway** Ferrovia.

R.M. 1 **Royal Mail** Regie Poste. 2 **Royal Mint** Regia Zecca.

R.N.R. **Royal Navy Reserve** Riserva della Regia Marina.

R.P. 1 (*comun.*) **Rates of Postage** Tariffe Postali. 2 (*comun.*) **Reply Paid** Risposta Pagata.

R/P (*comun.*) **Return of Post** Giro di Posta.

R.P.M. 1 **Revolutions Per Minute** Giri al

Minuto (*di un motore*). 2 (*market.*) **Resale Price Maintenance** Mantenimento dei Prezzi di Rivendita.

R.S.V.P. **Répondez, s'il vous plaît** (*reply, if you please*) È gradita una risposta.

RT (*trasp.*) **Round Trip** Viaggio d'Andata e Ritorno.

R.V. (*fin.*) **Ratable Value** Valore Imponibile.

R.W. (*trasp. aut.*) **Right of Way** Diritto di Precedenza.

Ry. *V.* **Rly.**

S. 1 **Secretary** Segretario. 2 **Society** Società. 3 **South** Sud.

s/a (*market.*) **subject to approval** salvo approvazione.

s.a. (*trasp. mar.*) **safe arrival** felice arrivo.

Sa. *V.* **Sat.**

S.A.E. (*comun.*) **Stamped Addressed Envelope** Busta Affrancata e Indirizzata.

S.A.L.E. (*elab. elettr.*) **Simple Alphabetic Language for Engineers** Linguaggio Alfabetico Semplice per Tecnici.

S.A.M. **Society for the Advancement of Management** Società per il Progresso dell'Organizzazione Aziendale.

S. and S.C. (*trasp. mar.*) **Salvage and Salvage Charges** Salvataggio e Spese di Salvataggio.

S.A.N.S. (*elab. elettr.*) **Simultaneous Alphabetic and Numeric Sequencing** Ordinamento (in Sequenza) Simultaneo Alfabetico e Numerico.

Sat. **Saturday** sabato.

S.A.Y.E. (*fin.*) **Save as You Earn** (*piano di versamenti mensili per*) risparmio indicizzato ed esentasse (*in G.B.*).

S.B. (*fin.*) **Savings Bank** Cassa di Risparmio.

S.C. 1 *V.* **S. Car.** 2 (*leg.*) **Supreme Court** Corte Suprema.

S/C (*trasp. mar.*) **Salvage Charges** Spese di Salvataggio.

S. Car. **South Carolina** Carolina del Sud.

S.C.I.T. **Special Commissioners of Income Tax** Commissari Speciali per l'Imposta sui Redditi.

Scot. 1 **Scotland** Scozia. 2 **Scottish** scozzese (*a.*).

S.D. 1 *V.* **S. Dak.** 2 (*market.*) **Supply Depot** Magazzino Rifornimenti.

S/D 1 (*cred., fin.*) **Sight Draft** Tratta a Vista. 2 (*trasp. mar.*) **Sea Damaged** Danneggiato dal Mare.

S. Dak. **South Dakota** Dakota del Sud.

S.D.R. (*fin.*) **Special Drawing Rights** Diritti Speciali di Prelievo.

sec. 1 **second** secondo. 2 **seconds** secondi.

Sec. **Secretary** Segretario, Segretaria.

Secy. *V.* **Sec.**

Sep. *V.* **Sept.**

Sept. **September** settembre.

serv. **service** servizio.

S.E.T. (*fin.*) **Selective Employment Tax** Imposta Calcolata in Base al Numero dei Dipendenti (*in G.B.*).

S.F. (*fin.*) **Sinking Fund** Fondo d'Ammortamento.

S.G. (*leg.*) **Solicitor General** (*in G.B.*).

sgd. **signed** firmato.

S/H.E. (*trasp. mar.*) **Sundays and Holidays Excepted** Eccettuate le Domeniche e i Giorni Festivi.

Shl. Dk. (*trasp. mar.*) **Shelter Deck** Ponte di Riparo.

sh. tn. **short ton** tonnellata americana, di 2.000 libbre (*kg 907*).

S.I.A.M. **Society for Industrial and Applied Mathematics** Società per la Matematica Industriale e Applicata (*in U.S.A.*).

S.I.C. **Standard Industrial Classification System** Sistema di Classificazione Industriale Standard (*in U.S.A.*).

sig. **signature** firma.

sim. 1 **similar** simile. 2 **similarly** similmente.

sld. (*trasp. mar.*) **sailed** salpato.

S.L.T. (*elab. elettr.*) **Solid Logic Technology** Tecnologia dello Stato Solido.

S.M. (*fin.*) **Stock Market** Mercato Azionario, Mercato dei titoli.

S/N (*trasp. mar.*) **Shipping Note** Buono (*o* Ordine) d'Imbarco.

s.o. (*market.*) **sellers' option** opzione del venditore.

S/O (*trasp. mar.*) **Shipowner** Armatore.

Soc. **Society** Società.

Sol. (*leg.*) **Solicitor** Avvocato.

S.O.L. (*trasp. mar.*) **Shipowner's Liability** Responsabilità dell'Armatore.

Sol. Gen. (*leg.*) **Solicitor General** (*in G.B.*).

Solr. *V.* **Sol.**

SO.N.A.R. (*trasp. mar.*) **Sound Navigation and Ranging** Navigazione e Misurazione per mezzo del Suono.

S.O.S. (*trasp. mar.*) «**Save Our Souls**» (*o* «**Save Our Ship**») (*distress call*) S.O.S.

S.P. (*comun.*) **Sample Post** Campione senza Valore.

S.P.A. (*ass. mar.*) **Subject to Particular Average** Soggetto ad Avaria Particolare.

spec. 1 **specification** specificazione. 2 **specimen** esemplare, campione.

Sq. **Square** Piazza (*negli indirizzi*).

S.Q.C. **Statistical Quality Control** Controllo Statistico della Qualità.

Sr. **Senior** Seniore, Anziano.

S.R.I. **Stanford Research Institute** Istituto di Ricerca della Stanford University.

S.S. 1 (*market.*) **Same Size** Stessa Misura. 2 (*trasp. mar.*) **Screw Steamer** Piroscafo a Elica. 3 (*trasp. mar.*) **Steamship** Vapore, Nave a Vapore.

S.S.A. **Social Security Administration** Amministrazione della Sicurezza Sociale (*in U.S.A.*).

st. **stone** stone (*peso*).

St. 1 **Strait** Stretto (*di mare*). 2 **Street** Strada, Via (*negli indirizzi*).

stb. (*trasp. mar.*) **starboard** dritta.

S.T.D. (*comun.*) **Subscriber Trunk Dialling** Teleselezione (*in G.B.*).

std. **standard** standard, tipo (*a.*).

ster. **sterling** (*a.*) sterlina (*nella locuzione «lira sterlina»*).

St. Ex. *V.* **St. Exch.**

St. Exch. (*fin.*) **Stock Exchange** Borsa Valori.

stg. *V.* **ster.**

str. (*trasp. mar.*) **steamer** vapore, nave a vapore.

sub. (*giorn.*) **subscription** abbonamento.

S.U.B. (*pers.*) **Supplemental Unemployment Benefit** Sussidio Supplementare di Disoccupazione (*in U.S.A.*).

sub-ed. (*giorn.*) **sub-editor** vicedirettore.

subst. (*pers.*) **substitute** sostituto, vice.

Sun. **Sunday** domenica.

sup. *V.* **suppl.**

supp. *V.* **suppl.**

suppl. 1 **supplement** supplemento. 2 **supplementary** supplementare.

S.V. (*trasp. mar.*) **Sailing Vessel** Nave a Vela.

S.W. (*trasp. mar.*) **Sea Water** Acqua di Mare.

S.W.I.F.T. (*banca, fin.*) **Society for World-Wide Interbank Telecommunication** Associazione Interbancaria per lo Scambio di Ordini di Pagamento Internazionali (*mediante un sistema elettronico*).

syst. **system** sistema.

t 1 **ton** tonnellata. 2 **tons** tonnellate.

T.A. (*comun.*) **Telegraphic Address** Indirizzo Telegrafico.

T.A.B. **Traffic Audit Bureau** Ufficio per il Controllo del Traffico (*in U.S.A.*).

T.A.M. **Television Audience Measurement** Misurazione del Gradimento dei Programmi Televisivi.

T.B. (*rag.*) **Trial Balance** Bilancio di Prova.

T.B.A. **Television Bureau of Advertising** Ufficio per la Pubblicità Televisiva (*in U.S.A.*).

T.C. 1 **Technical College** Istituto Superiore di Tecnologia. 2 **Town Councillor** Consigliere Comunale. 3 **Training Centre** Centro d'Addestramento. 4 (*amm.*) **Town Clerk** Segretario Comunale. 5 (*comun.*) **Telegram(me) in Code** Telegramma in Codice.

T.C.W.U. **Teamsters' Union** Sindacato dei Camionisti (*in U.S.A.*).

T.Dks. (*trasp. mar.*) **'Tweendecks** Interponte.

T.D.R. **Treasury Deposit Receipts** Ricevute di Deposito del Tesoro.

techn. 1 **technical** tecnico. 2 **technology** tecnologia.

T.E.E. (*trasp. ferr.*) **Trans Europe Express** Trans-Europa Express.

tel. 1 (*comun.*) **telephone** telefono. 2 (*comun.*) *V.* **teleg.**

teleg. 1 (*comun.*) **telegram** telegramma. 2 (*comun.*) **telegraph** telegrafo. 3 (*comun.*) **telegraphic** telegrafico.

TELEX (*comun.*) **Teleprinter Exchange** Trasmissione per Telescrivente.

temp. (*pers.*) **temporary** temporaneo; avventizio (*a.* e *n.*).

Ten. *V.* **Tenn.**

Tenn. **Tennessee** Tennessee.

Terr. 1 **Terrace** (*negli indirizzi*). 2 **Territory** Territorio.

Tex. **Texas** Texas.

T.G.W.U. **Transport and General Workers' Union** Sindacato dei Lavoratori delle Aziende di Trasporto (*in G.B.*).

Th. *V.* **Thur.**

Thur. **Thursday** giovedì.

T.L. (*ass. mar.*) **Total Loss** Perdita Totale.

tlg. *V.* **teleg.**

T.M.O. (*cred.*) **Telegraphic Money Order** Vaglia Telegrafico.

T.N. **Telephone Number** Numero Telefonico.

T.O. 1 **Telegraph Office** Ufficio del Telegrafo. 2 **Telephone Office** Ufficio del Telefono.

Tonn. (*trasp. mar.*) **Tonnage** Tonnellaggio.

T.R. (*trasp. mar.*) **Tons Registered** Tonnellate di Registro (*o* di Stazza).

trans. **1 transaction** operazione commerciale. **2 translation** traduzione. **3 translator** traduttore. **4** (*fin., leg.*) **transfer** trasferimento.

transf. (*fin., leg.*) **transferred** trasferito.

Treas. **1 Treasurer** Tesoriere. **2 Treasury** Tesoro.

T/S (*trasp. mar.*) **Turbine Ship, Turboship** Turbonave.

T.T. (*cred.*) **Telegraphic Transfer** Bonifico Telegrafico.

Tu. *V.* **Tues.**

T.U. **Trade Union** Sindacato Lavoratori.

T.U.C. **Trade Unions Congress** Congresso delle «Trade Unions» (*in G.B.*).

Tues. **Tuesday** martedì.

TV. *V.* **T.V.**

T.V. (*comun.*) **Television** Televisione.

T.W.A. **Trans World Airlines** Linee Aeree Intercontinentali.

U.A.B. **Unemployment Assistance Board** Comitato d'Assistenza ai Disoccupati.

U.A.W. **United Auto Workers** Sindacato dei Lavoratori dell'Automobile (*in U.S.A.*).

U.D. **1 Urban District** Distretto Urbano. **2** (*trasp. mar.*) **Upper Deck** Ponte Superiore.

U.D.C. **Universal Decimal Classification** Classificazione Decimale Universale.

U.Dk. (*trasp. mar.*) **Upperdeck** Ponte Superiore (*o* di Coperta).

U.K. **United Kingdom** Regno Unito.

ult. **ultimo** (*last*) scorso.

U.M.W. **United Mine Workers** Sindacato dei Minatori (*in U.S.A.*).

U.N. **United Nations** Nazioni Unite.

U.N.C.T.A.D. **United Nations Committee for Trade and Development** Comitato delle Nazioni Unite per il Commercio e lo Sviluppo.

U.N.D.P. **United Nations Development Program** Programma delle Nazioni Unite per lo Sviluppo.

U.N.E.P.T.A. **United Nations Expanded Program of Technical Assistance for the Economic Development of Underdeveloped Countries** Programma Ampliato delle Nazioni Unite d'Assistenza Tecnica per lo Sviluppo Economico dei Paesi Sottosviluppati.

U.N.E.S.C.O. **United Nations Educational, Scientific, and Cultural Organization** Organizzazione delle Nazioni Unite per l'Educazione, la Scienza e la Cultura (*in Francia*).

U.N.I.D.O. **United Nations Industrial Development Organization** Organizzazione delle Nazioni Unite per lo Sviluppo Industriale.

U.N.I.T.A.R. **United Nations Institute for Training and Research** Istituto di Formazione e di Ricerca delle Nazioni Unite.

Univ. **University** Università.

UNIVAC (*elab. elettr.*) **Universal Automatic Computer** Calcolatore Automatico Universale.

U.N.O. **United Nations Organization** Organizzazione delle Nazioni Unite (*O.N.U.*).

U.N.R.R.A. **United Nations Relief and Rehabilitation Administration** Amministrazione dei Soccorsi delle Nazioni Unite.

U.P. **United Press** (*agenzia di stampa U.S.A.*).

U/R (*trasp. mar.*) **Under Repairs** In Raddobbo.

u/s *V.* **u.s.**

u.s. **1 unserviceable** fuori uso. **2 useless** inutile.

U.S. **United States** Stati Uniti.

U.S.A. **United States of America** Stati Uniti d'America.

U.S.W.A. **United Steel Workers of America** Sindacato dei Metallurgici Americani.

Ut. **Utah** Utah.

U/W (*ass. mar.*) **Underwriter** Assicuratore Marittimo.

v. **1 volume** volume. **2** (*leg.*) **versus** (*against*) contro.

Va. **Virginia** Virginia.

V.A.C. **Verified Audit Circulation Corp.** Società per il Controllo delle Tirature (*in U.S.A.*).

val. **value** valore.

V.A.T. (*fin.*) **Value Added Tax** Imposta sul Valore Aggiunto (*I.V.A.*).

V.C. **1 Vice-Chairman** Vicepresidente. **2 Vice-Consul** Viceconsole.

V.F.R. (*trasp. aer.*) **Visual Flight Rules** Regole del Volo a Vista.

V.I.P. **Very Important Person** Persona Assai Importante.

Virg. *V.* **Va.**

viz. **videlicet** (*namely*) cioè.

V.K. (*trasp. mar.*) **Vertical Keel** Chiglia Verticale, Paramezzale Centrale.

Vt. **Vermont** Vermont.

W. **West** Ovest.

W.A. (*ass. mar.*) **With Average** Con

Avaria.

Wash. **Washington** Washington.

w/b **1** (*trasp.*) **way-bill** lista dei passeggeri. **2** (*trasp. ferr.*) **way-bill** lettera di vettura.

W.B. **1** *V.* **w./b. 2** (*rag.*) **Warehouse Book** Libro Magazzino. **3** (*trasp. mar.*) **Water Ballast** Zavorra d'Acqua.

W.C. **1 water-closet** ritirata, gabinetto. **2 West Central** (*distretto postale*).

W.D.F. (*trasp. mar.*) **Wireless Direction-Finder** Radiogoniometro.

We. *V.* **Wed.**

W.E.A. **Workers' Educational Association** Associazione Culturale dei Lavoratori (*in G.B.*).

Wed. **Wednesday** mercoledì.

W.F. **Work Factor** Fattore Lavoro.

W.F.S. **Work Factor System** Sistema del Fattore Lavoro.

W.H.O. **World Health Organization** Organizzazione Mondiale della Sanità.

Wis. **Wisconsin** Wisconsin.

wk. **week** settimana.

W.P.A. (*ass. mar.*) **With Particular Average** Con Avaria Particolare (*C.A.P.*).

W.R.O. (*ass. mar.*) **War Risks Only** Soltanto Rischi di Guerra.

wt. **weight** peso.

W.T. (*comun.*) **Wireless Telegraphy** Radiotelegrafia.

W.T.A.O. **World Touring and Automobile Organization** Organizzazione Mondiale del Turismo e dell'Automobile (*in G.B.*).

W/W (*dog.*) **Warehouse Warrant** Fede di Deposito Doganale.

W.W.D. (*trasp. mar.*) **Weather Working Days** Giorni Lavorativi Tempo Permettendo.

Wy. **Wyoming** Wyoming.

Xmas **Christmas** Natale.

Y (*tur.*) **Economy Class** Classe Turistica (*o* Economica).

Y.A.R. (*ass. mar.*) **York-Antwerp Rules** Regolamenti di York-Anversa.

Y.A. Rules (*ass. mar.*) **York-Antwerp Rules** Regolamenti di York-Anversa.

Y.B. **Year Book** Annuario.

yd. **1 yard** iarda. **2 yards** iarde.

YH (*tur.*) **Economy-High Season** Classe Turistica (*o* Economica)-Alta Stagione.

Y.H.A. **Youth Hostels Association** Associazione degli Ostelli della Gioventù.

YO (*tur.*) **Economy-Off Peak** Classe Turistica (*o* Economica)-Bassa Stagione.

yr. **1 year** anno. **2 years** anni. **3 your** vostro. **4 younger** più giovane.

ZIP (*comun.*) **Zone Improvement Plan** Codice d'Avviamento Postale (*CAP*).

Z.T. (*trasp. mar.*) **Zone Time** Tempo (*o* Ora) del Fuso.

SYMBOLS: COMMERCE, FINANCE, LAW AND MATHEMATICS
SIMBOLI: COMMERCIO, FINANZA, LEGGE E MATEMATICA

I. Commerce, Finance, Law

& **ampersand** (*leggasi* **and**) «e» commerciale.

$ **1 dollar** dollaro. **2 dollars** dollari.

¢ **1 cent** centesimo. **2 cents** centesimi (*di dollaro*).

£ **1 pound sterling** sterlina. **2 pounds sterling** sterline.

© **copyrighted** tutelato da diritto d'autore.

@ **at** (*a given price*) a (*un certo prezzo*).

% **per cent** per cento.

& C. **et cetera** eccetera.

number (*before a figure*) numero (*davanti a una cifra*).

II. Mathematics

+ **plus** più.

— **minus** meno.

±, ∓ **plus or minus** più o meno.

× **multiplied by** (moltiplicato) per.

÷ **divided by** diviso (per).

= **is equal to** (*o* **equals**) uguale a.

≠ **is not equal to** diverso da.

> **is greater than** maggiore di.

< **is less than** minore di.

≮, ≥, ≥ **is not less than; is equal to or greater than** maggiore o uguale a.

≯, ≤, ≤ **is not greater than; is equal to or less than** minore o uguale a.

≡ **is identical with** identico a.

≎ **is equivalent to** equivalente a.

~ **approximately** approssimativamente.

∝ **is directly proportional to** direttamente proporzionale a.

∺ **geometric proportion** proporzione geometrica.

: **is to** sta a.

∞ **infinity** infinito.

!, ⌊ **the factorial of** fattoriale di.

∴ **therefore** perciò.

∵ **since** dato che.

... **and so on** eccetera.

√‾, √ **radical sign, root** radicale, radice.

^{1}, ^{2}, ^{3} **exponents** esponenti.

′, ″, ‴ **prime, double** (*o* **second**) **prime, triple** (*o* **third**) **prime** prima, seconda, terza.

( ) **parentheses** parentesi tonde.

[ ] **brackets** parentesi quadre.

{ } **braces** parentesi graffe.

f, F **function, function of** funzione, funzione di.

d **differential of** differenziale di.

∫ **integral, integral of** integrale, integrale di.

$\int_a^b$ **definite integral** integrale definito.

Σ **sum, algebric sum** somma, sommatoria, somma algebrica.

TABLES-TAVOLE

MONEY / LA MONETA

BRITISH SYSTEM: £ p (*POUNDS AND PENCE*) 1 *POUND* (£ 1) = 100 *PENCE* (100 p)

amount	[valore]	coins [monete metalliche]
½ p	*a halfpenny, half a penny*	*a halfpenny*
1 p	*a penny; one p* (fam.)	*a penny*
2 p	*twopence, two pence; two p* (fam.)	*a twopenny piece*
5 p	*five pence*	*a fivepenny piece*
10 p	*ten pence*	*a tenpenny piece*
50 p	*fifty pence*	*a fifty pence piece*
		notes [banconote]
£ 1	*a pound; a quid* (fam.)	*a pound note*
£ 5	*five pounds; five quid* (fam.)	*a five-pound note; a fiver* (fam.)
£ 10	*ten pounds; ten quid* (fam.)	*a ten-pound note; a tenner* (fam.)
£ 20	*twenty pounds; twenty quid* (fam.)	*a twenty-pound note*

U.S. SYSTEM: $ ¢ (*DOLLARS AND CENTS*) 1 *DOLLAR* ($ 1) = 100 *CENTS* (100 ¢)

amount	[valore]	coins [monete metalliche]
1 ¢	*a cent*	*a penny*
5 ¢	*five cents*	*a nickel*
10 ¢	*ten cents*	*a dime*
25 ¢	*twenty-five cents*	*a quarter*
50 ¢	*half a dollar; half a buck* (fam.)	*a half-dollar*
		notes [banconote]
$ 1	*a dollar; a buck* (fam.)	*a dollar bill*
$ 5	*five dollars; five bucks* (fam.)	*five-dollar bill*
$ 10	*ten dollars; ten bucks* (fam.)	*ten-dollar bill*
$ 20	*twenty dollars; twenty bucks* (fam.)	*twenty-dollar bill*

a.s.o. up to $ 1,000
e così via fino a $ 1.000

WEIGHTS AND MEASURES / PESI E MISURE

METRIC SYSTEM / SISTEMA METRICO DECIMALE

LINEAR MEASURES / MISURE LINEARI

10 millimetri	= 1 centimetro	=	*0,3937*	*inch**
10 centimetri	= 1 decimetro	=	*3,937*	*inches*
10 decimetri	= 1 metro	=	*39,37*	*inches (3,28 feet)*
10 metri	= 1 decametro	=	*393,7*	*inches*
10 decametri	= 1 ettometro	=	*328*	*feet 1 inch*
10 ettometri	= 1 kilometro	=	*0,621*	*mile*
10 kilometri	= 1 miriametro	=	*6,21*	*miles*

SQUARE MEASURES / MISURE QUADRATE

100 millimetri²	= 1 centimetro²	=	*0,1549*	*sq. inch*
100 centimetri²	= 1 decimetro²	=	*15,499*	*sq. inches*
100 decimetri²	= 1 metro²	=	*1.549*	*sq. inches (1,196 sq. yards)*
100 metri²	= 1 decametro²	=	*119,6*	*sq. yards*
100 decametri²	= 1 ettometro²	=	*2,471*	*acres*
100 ettometri²	= 1 kilometro²	=	*0,386*	*sq. mile*

LAND MEASURES / MISURE AGRICOLE

1 metro²	= 1 centiara	=	*1.549,9*	*sq. inches*
100 centiare	= 1 ara	=	*119,6*	*sq. yards*
100 are	= 1 ettaro	=	*2,471*	*acres*
100 ettari	= 1 kilometro²	=	*0,386*	*sq. mile*

* *For decimal figures and for 4-digit numbers the continental system was employed. Therefore a comma stands for a point, and a point for a comma.*

Per i decimali e per i numeri di 4 cifre si è usato il sistema continentale; perciò la virgola sta al posto del punto e viceversa.

VOLUME MEASURES / MISURE DI VOLUME

1.000 millimetri³	=	1 centimetro³	=	*0,06102*	*cubic inch*
1.000 centimetri³	=	1 decimetro³	=	*61,02*	*cubic inches*
1.000 decimetri³	=	1 metro³	=	*35,314*	*cubic feet*

CAPACITY MEASURES / MISURE DI CAPACITÀ

10 millilitri	=	1 centilitro	=	*0,338*	*fluid ounce*
10 centilitri	=	1 decilitro	=	*3,38*	*fluid ounces*
10 decilitri	=	1 litro	=	*1,0567*	*liquid quarts (0,9081 dry quart)*
10 litri	=	1 decalitro	=	*2,64*	*gallons (0,284 bushel)*
10 decalitri	=	1 ettolitro	=	*26,418*	*gallons (2,838 bushels)*
10 ettolitri	=	1 kilolitro	=	*264,18*	*gallons (35,315 cubic feet)*

WEIGHTS / PESI

10 milligrammi	=	1 centigrammo	=	*0,1543*	*grain*
10 centigrammi	=	1 decigrammo	=	*1,5432*	*grains*
10 decigrammi	=	1 grammo	=	*15,432*	*grains*
10 grammi	=	1 decagrammo	=	*0,3527*	*ounce*
10 decagrammi	=	1 ettogrammo	=	*3,5274*	*ounces*
10 ettogrammi	=	1 kilogrammo	=	*2,2046*	*pounds*
10 kilogrammi	=	1 miriagrammo	=	*22,046*	*pounds*
10 miriagrammi	=	1 quintale	=	*220,46*	*pounds*
10 quintali	=	1 tonnellata metrica	=	*2.204,6*	*pounds*

BRITISH AND AMERICAN SYSTEM / SISTEMA BRITANNICO E AMERICANO

LINEAR MEASURES / MISURE LINEARI

1 inch			=	2,54	centimetri
12 inches	=	*1 foot*	=	30,48	centimetri
3 feet	=	*1 yard*	=	0,914	metri
5½ yards (16½ feet)	=	*1 rod*	=	5,029	metri
40 rods	=	*1 furlong*	=	201,18	metri
8 furlongs (1,760 yards; 5,280 feet)	=	*1 (statute) mile*	=	1.609,3	metri
3 miles	=	*1 (land) league*	=	4,83	kilometri

SQUARE MEASURES / MISURE QUADRATE

1 square inch		=	6,452 centimetri^2
144 square inches	= *1 square foot*	=	929 centimetri^2
9 square feet	= *1 square yard*	=	0,8361 metri^2
30¼ square yards	= *1 square rod*	=	25,29 metri^2
160 square rods (*4,840 square yards; 43,560 square feet*)	= *1 acre*	=	0,4047 ettari
640 acres	= *1 square mile*	=	259 ettari (2,59 kilometri^2)

CUBIC MEASURES / MISURE CUBICHE

1	*cubic inch*		=	16,387 centimetri^3
1,728	*cubic inches*	= *1 cubic foot*	=	0,0283 metri^3
27	*cubic feet*	= *1 cubic yard*	=	0,7646 metri^3
16	*cubic feet*	= *1 cord foot*	=	0,4528 metri^3
8	*cord feet*	= *1 cord*	=	3,625 metri^3

AVOIRDUPOIS WEIGHTS / PESI « AVOIRDUPOIS »

1 dram (27.34 grains)		=	1,772 grammi
16 drams (437.5 grains)	= *1 ounce*	=	28,3495 grammi
16 ounces (7,000 grains)	= *1 pound*	=	453,59 grammi
*100 pounds**	= *1 hundredweight*	=	45,36 kilogrammi
2,000 pounds	= *1 ton*	=	907,18 kilogrammi

TROY WEIGHTS / PESI « TROY »

*3.086 grains***	= *1 carat*	=	200 milligrammi
24 grains	= *1 pennyweight*	=	1,5552 grammi
20 pennyweights (480 grains)	= *1 ounce*	=	31,1035 grammi
12 ounces (5,760 grains)	= *1 pound*	=	373,24 grammi

* *In Great Britain, 14 pounds (6.35 kilogrammes) = 1 stone; 112 pounds (50.80 kilogrammes) = 1 hundredweight, and 2,240 pounds (1,016.05 kilogrammes) = 1 long ton.*
In Gran Bretagna 14 pound (6,35 kilogrammi) = 1 stone; 112 pound (50,80 kilogrammi) = 1 hundredweight e 2.240 pound (1.016,05 kilogrammi) = 1 long ton.

** *The grain, equal to 0.0648 gramme, is the same in both tables of weight.*
Il grain, pari a 0,0648 grammi, è il medesimo in entrambe le tavole dei pesi.

DRY MEASURES / MISURE PER ARIDI				
1 pint		*= 33.60 cubic inches*	= 0,55 litri
2 pints	*= 1 quart*	*= 67.20 cubic inches*	= 1,10 litri
8 quarts	*= 1 peck*	*= 537.61 cubic inches*	= 8,80 litri
4 pecks	*= 1 bushel*	*= 2,150.42 cubic inches*	= 35,23 litri
1 British dry quart	*= 1.032 U.S. dry quarts*		

LIQUID MEASURES / MISURE PER LIQUIDI			
1 gill	*= 4 fluid ounces*	*= 7.219 cubic inches*	= 0,118 litri
4 gills	*= 1 pint*	*= 28.875 cubic inches*	= 0,473 litri
2 pints	*= 1 quart*	*= 57.75 cubic inches*	= 0,946 litri
4 quarts	*= 1 gallon*	*= 231 cubic inches*	= 3,785 litri

CONVERSION FACTORS / MOLTIPLICATORI PER LA CONVERSIONE

TO CHANGE PER TRASFORMARE	*TO* IN	*MULTIPLY BY** MOLTIPLICARE PER
bushels (U.S.)	*hectolitres*	0,3524
centimetres	*inches*	0,3937
cubic feet	*cubic metres*	0,0283
cubic metres	*cubic feet*	35,3145
cubic metres	*cubic yards*	1,3079
cubic yards	*cubic metres*	0,7646
feet	*metres*	0,3048
gallons (U.S.)	*litres*	3,7853
grains	*grams*	0,0648
grams	*grains*	15,4324
grams	*ounces avdp.*	0,0353
hectares	*acres*	2,4710
hectolitres	*bushels (U.S.)*	2,8378

* *For decimal figures the continental system was employed. Therefore a comma stands for a point.*
Per i decimali si è usato il sistema continentale; perciò la virgola sta al posto del punto.

TO CHANGE PER TRASFORMARE	*TO* IN	*MULTIPLY BY* MOLTIPLICARE PER
inches	*millimetres*	25,4000
inches	*centimetres*	2,5400
kilogrammes	*pounds troy*	2,6792
kilogrammes	*pounds avdp.*	2,2046
kilometres	*miles*	0,6214
litres	*gallons (U.S.)*	0,2642
litres	*pecks*	0,1135
litres	*pints (dry)*	1,8162
litres	*pints (liquid)*	2,1134
litres	*quarts (dry)*	0,9081
litres	*quarts (liquid)*	1,0567
metres	*feet*	3,2808
metres	*yards*	1,0936
metric tons	*tons (long)*	0,9842
metric tons	*tons (short)*	1,1023
miles	*kilometres*	1,6093
millimetres	*inches*	0,0394
ounces avdp.	*grams*	28,3495
pecks	*litres*	8,8096
pints (dry)	*litres*	0,5506
pints (liquid)	*litres*	0,4732
pounds troy	*kilogrammes*	0,3732
pounds avdp.	*kilogrammes*	0,4536
quarts (dry)	*litres*	1,1012
quarts (liquid)	*litres*	0,9463
square feet	*square metres*	0,0929
sq. kilometres	*sq. miles*	0,3861
sq. metres	*sq. feet*	10,7639
sq. metres	*sq. yards*	1,1960
sq. miles	*sq. kilometres*	2,5900
sq. yards	*sq. metres*	0,8361
tons (long)	*metric tons*	1,0160
tons (short)	*metric tons*	0,9072
yards	*metres*	0,9144

CONVERSION TABLES FOR SIZES OF WEAR AND SHOES / TAVOLE DI CONVERSIONE DELLE MISURE DEGLI ARTICOLI D'ABBIGLIAMENTO E DELLE CALZATURE

MEN'S SUITS ABITI PER UOMO	G.B.	36	38	40	42	44	46
	U.S.A.	36	38	40	42	44	46
	ITALY	46	48	50	52	54	56

LADIES' DRESSES ABITI PER SIGNORA	G.B.	32	34	36	38	40	42	44
	U.S.A.	8	10	12	14	16	18	20
	ITALY	38	40	42	44	46	48	50

SHIRTS CAMICIE DA UOMO	G.B.	14	14½	15	15½	15¾	16	16½	16¾	17
	U.S.A.	14	14½	15	15½	15¾	16	16½	16¾	17
	ITALY	36	37	38	39	40	41	42	43	44

MEN'S SHOES SCARPE DA UOMO	G.B.	7	8	9	10
	U.S.A.	7½	8½	9½	10½
	ITALY	41	42	43	44

LADIES' SHOES SCARPE DA DONNA	G.B.	3	4	5	6	7
	U.S.A.	4½	5½	6½	7½	8½
	ITALY	35½	36½	38	39½	40½

SOCKS CALZINI	G.B.	10	10½	11	11½	12	12½
	U.S.A.	10	10½	11	11½	12	12½
	ITALY	40	41	42	43	44	45

STOCKINGS CALZE	G.B.	8½	9	9½	10	10½	11
	U.S.A.	8½	9	9½	10	10½	11
	ITALY	36	37	38	39	40	41

TELEPHONE SPELLING KEY / PAROLE CHIAVE PER LA COMPITAZIONE TELEFONICA

	ITALY	*G.B.-U.S.A.*	*INTERNATIONAL*
A	Ancona	*Alfred*	*Amsterdam*
B	Bologna	*Benjamin*	*Baltimore*
C	Como	*Charles*	*Casablanca*
D	Domodossola	*David*	*Danemark*
E	Empoli	*Edward*	*Edison*
F	Firenze	*Frederick*	*Florida*
G	Genova	*George*	*Gallipoli*
H	Hotel	*Harry*	*Havana*
I	Imola	*Isaac*	*Italia*
J	Jersey	*Jack*	*Jérusalem*
K	Kursaal	*King*	*Kilogramme*
L	Livorno	*London*	*Liverpool*
M	Milano	*Mary*	*Madagascar*
N	Napoli	*Nellie*	*New York*
O	Otranto	*Oliver*	*Oslo*
P	Palermo	*Peter*	*Paris*
Q	Quaderno	*Queen*	*Québec*
R	Roma	*Robert*	*Roma*
S	Savona	*Samuel*	*Santiago*
T	Torino	*Tommy*	*Tripoli*
U	Udine	*Uncle*	*Uppsala*
V	Venezia	*Victor*	*Valencia*
W	Washington	*William*	*Washington*
X	Xanthia	*X-ray*	*Xantippe*
Y	York	*Yellow*	*Yokohama*
Z	Zara	*Zebra*	*Zürich*

TIME / IL TEMPO

HOW TO TELL THE TIME / *COME INDICARE L'ORA*

COMMON USAGE* *USO COMUNE*		FOR TIME-TABLES, etc. *PER GLI ORARI, ecc.*	ITALIAN *ITALIANO*
ten o'clock; ten A.M.	10.00	ten hundred hours	*le dieci*
five past ten	10.05	ten oh five	*le dieci e cinque*
a quarter past ten	10.15	ten fifteen	*le dieci e un quarto*
twenty-five past ten	10.25	ten twenty-five	*le dieci e venticinque*
half past ten	10.30	ten thirty	*le dieci e mezzo;* *le dieci e trenta*
twenty-five to eleven	10.35	ten thirty-five	*le dieci e trentacinque;* *venticinque minuti alle undici*
a quarter to eleven	10.45	ten forty-five	*le dieci e tre quarti;* *un quarto alle undici*
ten to eleven	10.50	ten fifty	*le dieci e cinquanta;* *dieci minuti alle undici*
twelve o'clock; twelve noon	12.00	twelve hundred hours	*le dodici; mezzogiorno*
four o'clock P.M.	4.00; 16.00	sixteen hundred hours	*le sedici;* *le quattro del pomeriggio*
twelve o'clock P.M.; midnight	12.00; 24.00	twenty-four hundred hours	*le ventiquattro;* *mezzanotte*

* In the U.S.A. *after* is often used instead of *past*, and *of* instead of *to*.
Negli Stati Uniti s'usano spesso after *al posto di* past *e* of *al posto di* to.

THE DAYS OF THE WEEK / *I GIORNI DELLA SETTIMANA*

Sunday	(Sun.)	1. *domenica*	Thursday	(Thur.)	5. *giovedì*
Monday	(Mon.)	2. *lunedì*	Friday	(Fri.)	6. *venerdì*
Tuesday	(Tues.)	3. *martedì*	Saturday	(Sat.)	7. *sabato*
Wednesday	(Wed.)	4. *mercoledì*			

THE MONTHS OF THE YEAR / *I MESI DELL'ANNO*

January	(Jan)	1. *gennaio*	July	(July)	7. *luglio*
February	(Feb)	2. *febbraio*	August	(Aug)	8. *agosto*
March	(Mar)	3. *marzo*	September	(Sept)	9. *settembre*
April	(Apr)	4. *aprile*	October	(Oct)	10. *ottobre*
May	(May)	5. *maggio*	November	(Nov)	11. *novembre*
June	(Jun)	6. *giugno*	December	(Dec)	12. *dicembre*

HOW TO WRITE THE DATE / *COME SI SCRIVE LA DATA*

ENGLISH**					ENGLISH & *ITALIANO*
1 (st)	April,	1984	1 Apr	84	1. 4.84
2 (nd)	May,	1984	2 May	84	2. 5.84
3 (rd)	June,	1984	3 Jun	84	3. 6.84
4 (th)	July,	1984	4 July	84	4. 7.84
11 (th)	August,	1984	11 Aug	84	11. 8.84
12 (th)	September,	1984	12 Sept	84	12. 9.84
13 (th)	October,	1984	13 Oct	84	13.10.84
20 (th)	November,	1984	20 Nov	84	20.11.84
21 (st)	December,	1984	21 Dec	84	21.12.84
22 (nd)	January,	1984	22 Jan	84	22. 1.84
23 (rd)	February,	1984	23 Feb	84	23. 2.84
31 (st)	March,	1984	31 Mar	84	31. 3.84

ITALIANO		U.S.A.			
1 aprile	*1984*	April	1,	1984	4. 1.84
2 maggio	*1984*	May	2,	1984	5. 2.84
3 giugno	*1984*	June	3,	1984	6. 3.84
4 luglio	*1984*	July	4,	1984	7. 4.84
11 agosto	*1984*	August	11,	1984	8.11.84
12 settembre	*1984*	September	12,	1984	9.12.84
13 ottobre	*1984*	October	13,	1984	10.13.84
20 novembre	*1984*	November	20,	1984	11.20.84
21 dicembre	*1984*	December	21,	1984	12.21.84
22 gennaio	*1984*	January	22,	1984	1.22.84
23 febbraio	*1984*	February	23,	1984	2.23.84
31 marzo	*1984*	March	31,	1984	3.31.84

** The letters in brackets are optional. So you can either write 1st April, 1984 or 1 April, 1984.

Le lettere fra parentesi sono facoltative. Perciò si può scrivere 1st April, 1984 o 1 April, 1984.

ITALIANO - INGLESE

A

abbandonare, *v. t.* **1** to abandon, to depart from, to discontinue, to give★ up, to leave★, to quit, to relinquish. **2** (*ass. mar., trasp. mar.*) to abandon. **3** (*leg.*) to abandon, to renounce, to resign, to surrender, to waive. **4** (*leg.*) (*un diritto*) to release. // ~ **un'azione** (*leg.*) to abandon prosecution; ~ **le formalità d'uso** to waive the customary formalities; ~ **un impiego** (*pers.*) to quit a job; ~ **un'impresa (una nave, ecc.)** to abandon an undertaking (a ship, etc.); ~ **una pretesa** (*leg.*) to renounce a claim.

abbandono, *n. m.* **1** abandonment, relinquishment, quit. **2** (*ass. mar., trasp. mar.*) abandonment. **3** (*leg.*) abandonment, renouncement, renunciation, resignation, surrender, waiver. **4** (*leg.*) (*d'un diritto*) release. // ~ **del posto di lavoro** (*pers.*) quit; ~ **della merce in dogana** (*dog.*) abandonment of goods in customs; ~ **d'un'azione** (*leg.*) abandonment of an action; **lo** ~ **d'una clausola contrattuale** (*leg.*) the waiver of a contract provision; ~ **di cosa assicurata** (*ass.*) abandonment of insured property; **l'** ~ **d'un diritto** (*leg.*) the surrender of a right; **l'** ~ **d'una nave** (*ass. mar.*) the abandonment of a ship; **l'** ~ **d'una pretesa** (*leg.*) the remise of a claim.

abbassamento, *n. m.* **1** lowering, depression, fall, sag. **2** (*di valore*) debasement. **3** (*market.*) (*di prezzi, anche*) knockdown.

abbassare, *v. t.* **1** to lower, to depress, to dip. **2** (*market.*) to bring★ down, to drive★ down. // ~ **il prezzo di** (*articoli, merci, ecc.*) (*market.*) to mark down; ~ **le serrande** to put up the shutters.

abbassarsi, *v. rifl.* **1** to lower, to dip, to fall★, to go★ down, to sag. **2** (*comm.*) (*di prezzi, ecc.*) to decline.

abbattere, *v. t.* to beat★ down, to flatten, to knock down.

abbattimento, *n. m.* **1** beating down, flattening, knocking down. **2** (*di prezzi*) abatement. // ~ **alla base** (*d'un reddito imponibile*) (*fin.*) basic abatement.

abbisognare, *v. i.* to need, to require, to want.

abboccamento, *n. m.* talk, interview.

abboccarsi, *v. rifl.* to have a talk (with sb.), to interview (sb.).

abbonamento, *n. m.* **1** (*giorn.*) subscription. **2** (*trasp.*) (*ferroviario, ecc.*) season ticket. // ~ **al bollo** (*fin.*) composition for stamp duty; ~ **ferroviario** (*trasp., USA*) commutation ticket.

abbonare, *v. t.* **1** to allow. **2** (*giorn.*) to make★ (sb.) a subscriber.

abbonarsi, *v. rifl.* **1** (*giorn.*) to subscribe. **2** (*trasp.*) to buy★ a season ticket. // ~ **al bollo** (*fin.*) to compound for stamp duty.

abbonato, *n. m.* **1** (*giorn.*) subscriber. **2** (*trasp.*) season-ticket holder. **3 abbonati,** *pl.* (*a un giornale, ecc.*) constituency. // ~ **al telefono** (*comun.*) telephone subscriber; ~ **ferroviario** (*trasp. ferr.*) commuter; **essere** ~ **a** (*un giornale, ecc.*) (*giorn.*) to take in.

abbondante, *a.* abundant.

abbondanza, *n. f.* abundance. // ~ **di dollari** (*fin.*) dollar glut.

abbordaggio, *n. m.* (*trasp. mar.*) collision.

abbordare, *v. t.* (*trasp. mar.*) to board.

abbordo, *n. m.* (*trasp. mar.*) collision.

abbozzare, *v. t.* to draft, to outline.

abbozzato, *a.* drafted, outlined.

abbozzo, *n. m.* draft, rough draft, outline.

abbuono, *n. m.* allowance, discount. // ~ **di fine d'anno** (*calcolato sul fatturato*) (*market.*) end-year rebate; **abbuoni d'interesse** (*fin., rag.*) interest subsidies; ~ **fiscale** (*fin.*) tax relief; ~ **globale** (*market.*) aggregate rebate; ~ **in assenza di sinistri** (*ass.*) no claim bonus; ~ **per calo** (*market.*) ullage; ~ **per «calo peso»** (*market.*) draft allowance, draft; ~ **per colaggio** (*trasp. mar.*) leakage, ullage; ~ **per «corpi estranei»** (*market.*) draft allowance, draft; ~ **per dispersione** (*trasp. mar.*) leakage; ~ **per il peso** (*market.*) weight draft; ~ **per scarto di qualità** (*market.*) allowance for difference of quality; ~ **per tara** (*market.*) allowance for tare, tare allowance; ~ **sottobanco** (*market.*) kickback.

abile, *a.* able, capable, skilled, smart. // ~ **al lavoro** fit for the job.

abilità, *n. f. inv.* ability, craft, faculty, skill, technique. // ~ **d'artigiano** (*o* **d'artista**) craftsmanship; ~ **manuale** (*pers.*) manual dexterity; ~ **tecnica** know-how, workmanship.

abilitare, *v. t.* (*leg.*) to certificate, to qualify.

abilitarsi, *v. rifl.* (*leg.*) to qualify.

abilitato, *a.* (*leg.*) qualified.

abilitazione, *n. f.* (*leg.*) (*all'esercizio d'una professione*) qualification.

abitabilità, *n. f.* (*econ.*) livability, liveability.

abitare, *v. i.* to live, to reside. *v. t.* to inhabit.

abitazione, *n. f.* 1 abode, dwelling, house, residence. 2 **abitazioni,** *pl.* (*econ.*) (*termine usato nei grafici, ecc.*) housing.

abito, *n. m.* 1 (*da uomo*) suit. 2 (*da donna*) dress. 3 **abiti,** *pl.* (*da uomo e da donna*) clothes. 4 **abiti,** *pl.* (*market.*) wear (*sing.*). // ~ **bell'e fatto** (*market.*) hand-me-down; ~ **confezionato** (*market., ingl.*) reach-me-down; **abiti confezionati** (*market.*) ready-made clothes; ~ **di seconda mano** (*market.*) hand-me-down.

abituale, *a.* customary, habitual, usual.

abitudine, *n. f.* 1 habit, custom. 2 practice, praxis★, routine. // ~ **d'acquisto** (*market.*) buying habit.

abolire, *v. t.* to abolish, to suppress, to do★ away with. // ~ **i controlli su** (*qc.*) to decontrol; ~ **un dazio doganale** to abolish a customs duty; ~ **un'imposta** (*fin.*) to take off a tax.

abolizione, *n. f.* abolition, suppression, lifting. // ~ **dei controlli** decontrol; ~ **delle tariffe** (*dog., econ.*) elimination of tariffs.

abrogabile, *a.* (*leg.*) repealable, rescindable, revocable.

abrogare, *v. t.* (*leg.*) to abrogate, to cancel, to repeal, to rescind, to revoke.

abrogazione, *n. f.* (*leg.*) abrogation, cancellation, repeal, rescission, revocation.

abusare, *v. i.* 1 to abuse. 2 (*leg.*) to trespass. // ~ **del proprio potere** (*leg.*) to stretch one's powers; ~ **della propria autorità** (*leg.*) to strain one's authority.

abusivo, *a.* 1 unauthorized. 2 (*leg.*) abusive, unlawful.

abuso, *n. m.* 1 abuse. 2 (*leg.*) abuse, trespass. // ~ **d'assegno in bianco** (*leg.*) abuse of blank cheque; ~ **d'autorità** (*leg.*) abuse of power; ~ **di bianco segno** (*leg.*) abuse of blank signature; ~ **d'un diritto** (*leg.*) abuse of right; ~ **di fiducia** (*leg.*) abuse of confidence, breach of trust; **un** ~ **di potere** (*leg.*) a stretch of authority.

accampare, *v. t.* 1 (*a giustificazione, a discolpa*) to plead. 2 (*leg.*) to advance. // ~ **un diritto** (*o* **una pretesa**) (*leg.*) to advance a claim, to stake a claim.

accantonamento, *n. m.* 1 earmarking. 2 (*fin., rag.*) allocation, appropriation.

accantonare, *v. t.* 1 to earmark, to hold★ over, to shelve. 2 (*fin., rag.*) to allocate, to appropriate. 3 (*rag.*) to set★ aside. // ~ **denaro** (*fin., rag.*) to make appropriations; ~ **denaro per il pagamento di debiti** to make an appropriation for the payment of debts; ~ **materiali per un progetto** to allocate materials for a project.

accaparramento, *n. m.* (*econ., market.*) buying-up, coemption, corner, cornering (the market), engrossing, engrossment, forestallment, hoarding, take-up. // **l'** ~ **di generi alimentari** the hoarding of food; **l'** ~ **d'un mercato** the forestallment of a market.

accaparrare, *v. t.* (*econ., market.*) to buy★ up, to corner, to engross, to forestall, to hoard, to take★ up. // ~ **generi alimentari** to hoard food; **accaparrarsi un mercato** to engross a market.

accaparrarsi, *v. t. V.* **accaparrare.**

accaparratore, *n. m.* (*econ., market.*) buyer-up, corner man★, cornerer, engrosser, forestaller.

accedere, *v. i.* 1 to have access, to reach. 2 (*acconsentire, aderire*) to accede, to agree.

accelerare, *v. t.* to accelerate, to expedite, to gear up, to speed★, to speed★ up. // ~ **le consegne** (*org. az.*) to speed up deliveries; ~ **la produzione** (*org. az.*) to gear up production.

acceleratore, *n. m.* (*econ.*) accelerator.

accelerazione, *n. f.* (*econ.*) acceleration.

accendere, *v. t.* to light★. // ~ **un conto** (*rag.*) to open an account; ~ **un'ipoteca su una proprietà** (*leg.*) to take a mortgage on a property.

accennare, *v. i.* to hint (at), to mention, to refer.

accenno, *n. m.* hint, mention, reference. // **fare un** ~ **a qc.** to make a hint at st., to mention st., to refer to st.

accentare, *v. t.* to stress.

accento, *n. m.* (*anche fig.*) stress.

accentramento, *n. m.* (*org. az.*) centralization.

accentrare, *v. t.* (*org. az.*) to centralize.

accentratore, *n. m.* (*org. az.*) centralizer. *a.* (*org. az.*) centralizing.

accentuare, *v. t.* to stress.

accentuarsi, *v. rifl.* (*fig.: aumentare*) to gain strength, to grow★.

accertabile, *a.* 1 ascertainable, verifiable. 2 (*fin.*) assessable. // **non** ~ (*fin.*) non-assessable.

accertamento, *n. m.* 1 ascertainment, verification. 2 (*fin.*) assessment. 3 (*leg.*) investigation. // ~ **dei redditi** (*fin.*) assessment on income; ~ **del costo (di produzione) d'una unità marginale** (*econ.*) marginal costing; **l'** ~ **dell'importo (di un conto)** the agreeing of an account; ~ **d'ufficio** (*fin.*) arbitrary assessment.

accertare, *v. t.* 1 to ascertain, to verify. 2 (*fin.*) to assess. // ~ **i danni dopo un incidente** (*ass.*) to assess damages after an accident; ~ **l'entità del danno** (*ass.*) to ascertain the extent of the damage; ~ **il valore d'una proprietà agli effetti fiscali** (*fin.*) to appraise property for taxation.

accertarsi, *v. rifl.* to ascertain, to make* sure.

accessibile, *a.* 1 approachable. 2 (*trasp. aut.*) accessible.

accessione, *n. f.* accession.

accesso, *n. m.* access. // ~ **al mercato** access to the market; ~ **alla professione** (*leg.*) entry to the profession; ~ **libero** (*a un locale, a uno spettacolo, ecc.*) free admittance; **chi ha** ~ **a informazioni riservate** (*pers.*) insider.

accessorio, *a.* accessory, accessary, accessorial, ancillary, incidental, secondary, subsidiary. *n. m.* accessory, accessary. // **gli accessori di un'automobile** the accessories of a motor-car; **accessori per la cucina** kitchen aids.

accettabile, *a.* 1 acceptable. 2 (*leg.*) receivable.

accettabilità, *n. f.* acceptability, acceptableness.

accettante, *a.* accepting. *n. m.* e *f.* (*banca, cred.*) acceptor. // ~ **per intervento** acceptor for honour; acceptor supra protest.

accettare, *v. t.* 1 to accept, to agree to, to assume, to recognize, to take*. 2 (*comm.*) to honour. 3 (*fin., rag.*) (*una dichiarazione, un conto, ecc.*) to agree. // ~ **un arbitrato** (*leg.*) to agree to an arbitration; ~ **una cambiale** (*cred.*) to accept a bill of exchange; ~ **un concordato** to accept a composition, to agree to an arrangement; ~ **le condizioni di q.** to accept sb.'s terms; ~ **impegni precisi** to accept firm commitments; ~ **una parte del rischio da coprire** (*ass.*) to accept a part of the risk to be covered; ~ **le scuse di q.** to accept sb.'s apologies; ~ **un suggerimento** to accept a suggestion; «**accettato**» (*formula di accettazione d'una cambiale*) «accepted».

accettato, *a.* accepted. // **non** ~ (*cred.*) unaccepted.

accettazione, *n. f.* 1 acceptance, acceptation, assumption, recognition. 2 (*banca, cred.*) (*nel senso di cambiale recante la dicitura «accettato»*) acceptance. // ~ **bancaria** (*banca, cred.*) acceptance of a bill by a bank, banker's acceptance; (*la cambiale*) bank acceptance; ~ **cambiaria** (*cred.*) acceptance of a bill; ~ **condizionata** (*banca, cred.*) conditional acceptance, qualified acceptance; ~ **condizionata del luogo di pagamento** (*banca, cred.*) local acceptance; ~ **condizionata quanto al tempo** (*banca, cred.*) acceptance qualified as to time; ~ **contro documenti** (*banca, cred.*) acceptance against documents; ~ **di comodo** (*banca, cred.*) accommodation acceptance; ~ (*espressa o tacita*) **d'un contratto** (*leg.*) affirmation of a contract; **l'** ~ **d'un obbligo** the assumption of an obligation; ~ **d'un'offerta d'appalto** (*comm.*) acceptance of a bid; ~ **d'una sentenza** (*leg.*) acceptance of a judgment; ~ **in bianco** (*banca, cred.*) blank acceptance; ~ **incondizionata** (*banca, cred.*) clean acceptance, general acceptance; ~ **per conto d'un cliente** (*da parte d'una banca*) acceptance on account of a customer; ~ **per intervento** (*di una cambiale*) (*banca, cred.*) acceptance for honour, acceptance under protest, acceptance supra protest, supraprotest; ~ **restrittiva** (*banca, cred.*) qualified acceptance; ~ **senza riserve** (*banca, cred.*) general acceptance; **mancata** ~ (*banca, cred.*) non-acceptance, dishonour by non-acceptance, dishonour.

accidentale, *a.* accidental, casual, fortuitous.

acclamazione, *n. f.* acclamation.

accludere, *v. t.* 1 to attach. 2 (*comm.*) to enclose.

accluso, *a.* 1 (*comm.*) enclosed, inclosed. 2 (*leg.*) within (*attr.*). // **l'** ~ **reclamo** (*leg.*) the within complaint; **come da acclusa fattura** as per enclosed invoice.

accoglienza, *n. f.* reception.

accogliere, *v. t.* 1 to receive. 2 to accept, to allow, to concede, to recognize. 3 (*leg.*) to sustain. 4 (*tur.*) to accommodate. // ~ **eccezioni** (*leg.*) to sustain objections; ~ **un reclamo** to allow a claim, to admit a claim, to concede a claim, to recognize a claim; ~ **una richiesta** to grant a request; ~ **un ricorso** (*leg.*) to admit a claim.

accoglimento, *n. m.* 1 acceptation, concession. 2 (*d'un reclamo e sim.*) recognition. // **l'** ~ **d'un reclamo** the acceptance of a complaint; **lo** ~ **d'una richiesta** the granting of a request; **l'** ~ **d'un ricorso** the recognition of a claim.

accomandante, *n. m.* e *f.* 1 (*fin., leg.*) (*di*

società in accomandita) limited partner. 2 (*fin., leg.*) (*improprio*) sleeping partner.

accomandatario, *n. m.* 1 (*fin., leg.*) (*di società in accomandita*) general partner. 2 (*fin., leg.*) (*improprio*) active partner.

accomandita, *n. f.* (*fin., leg.*) limited partnership.

accomodamento, *n. m.* 1 accommodation, arrangement, settlement, settling. 2 (*leg.*) (*con i creditori*) composition. 3 (*leg.*) transaction (*nel diritto romano*).

accomodare, *v. t.* (*sistemare, comporre*) to arrange, to compound, to compromise, to settle.

accompagnare, *v. t.* to accompany, to escort.

accompagnatore, *n. m.* 1 attendant. 2 (*pers.*) escort. 3 (*tur.*) courier.

accompagnatrice turistica, *locuz. n.* (*tur.*) girl courier.

accondiscendere, *v. i.* to comply. // ~ **ai desideri di q.** to comply with sb.'s wishes.

acconsentire, *v. i.* to assent, to consent, to accede. // ~ **a un accomodamento** to consent to an arrangement; ~ **a un acquisto** to consent to a purchase; ~ **a una proposta** to accede to a proposal, to consent to a proposal; ~ **a vendere** to agree to a sale.

acconto, *n. m.* 1 advance, payment in advance, payment on account, part payment. 2 (*cred., rag.*) (*rata*) instalment, installment. // **come** ~ (*cred., rag.*) by way of account; **in** ~ (*cred., rag.*) on account.

accordare, *v. t.* 1 to allow, to grant, to give*. 2 to accord, to adjudge. // ~ **un indennizzo a q.** (*leg.*) to adjudge legal damages to sb.; ~ **l'interesse del 6% sui depositi** to allow 6% interest on deposits; ~ **la priorità a** (*un creditore, ecc.*) (*cred.*) to prefer; ~ **un privilegio a q.** (*anche leg.*) to privilege (sb.).

accordarsi, *v. recipr.* 1 (*raggiungere un accordo*) to agree, to come* to an agreement, to reach an agreement. 2 (*stringere un patto*) to combine, to covenant. 3 (*leg.*) (*con i creditori*) to compound. // ~ **per** to agree on; ~ **su** (*leg.*) to stipulate for; ~ **su una concessione** to agree to a concession; ~ **su un prezzo** (*market.*) (*di venditore e acquirente*) to settle a price.

accordo, *n. m.* 1 agreement, arrangement, understanding. 2 (*accomodamento*) composition, settlement, transaction. 3 (*patto*) compact, combination, combine, treaty. 4 (*consenso*) consent, concert, accord. 5 (*coerenza*) consistency. 6 (*leg.*) deed of arrangement. // **un** ~ **amichevole** an amicable settlement; ~ **bilaterale** bilateral agreement; ~ **commerciale** (*comm. est.*) trade agreement; **accordi commerciali bilaterali** (*comm. est.*) reciprocal trade agreements; ~ **d'apprendistato** articles of apprenticeship; **accordi d'associazione** association agreements; **accordi di cooperazione tra imprese** (*comm.*) inter-enterprise cooperation agreements; **accordi d'esclusiva** (*market.*) exclusive dealing agreements; ~ **di fusione** (*econ., fin.*) amalgamation agreement, takeover deal; **un** ~ **di massima** an informal agreement; **accordi di «pool»** (*fin.*) pooling arrangements; **accordi di «swap»** (*q. V.*) (*fin.*) swap agreements; ~ **esplicito** (*leg.*) express agreement; ~ **espresso** (*leg.*) express agreement; ~ **generale sulle tariffe doganali e il commercio (GATT)** (*comm. est., dog.*) General Agreement on Tariffs and Trade (*GATT*); ~ **(illegale) per la restrizione del commercio** (*econ., fin.*) combination in restraint of trade; **un** ~ **leale** a gentleman's agreement; ~ **monetario** (*fin.*) monetary agreement; **accordi orizzontali** (*comm. est.*) horizontal agreements; ~ **salariale che prevede i maggiori aumenti entro il primo anno** (*dalla sua stipulazione*) (*econ., sind.*) front-loaded wage settlement; **un** ~ **salariale con conseguenze inflazionistiche** (*econ.*) an inflationary wage settlement; ~ **scritto** written agreement; (*leg.*) indenture; ~ **segreto** secret agreement; ~ **solenne** covenant; **un** ~ **sulla parola** a gentleman's agreement; **un** ~ **svantaggioso** an inconvenient arrangement; ~ **tariffario** (*comm. est., econ.*) tariff arrangement; ~ **temporaneo** (*fin.*) temporary combine; ~ **tripartito** tripartite agreement; ~ **verbale** verbal agreement; **accordi vietati** (*leg.*) prohibited agreements; **contrariamente ai nostri accordi** contrary to our agreements; **essere d'** ~ to be agreeable, to agree, to consent; **secondo gli accordi (presi)** as agreed upon.

accorgimento, *n. m.* device. // **accorgimenti tendenti a risparmiare manodopera** (*org. az.*) labour-saving devices.

accostamento, *n. m.* (*trasp. mar.*) coming alongside.

accostare, *v. i.* (*trasp. mar.*) to come* alongside. // ~ **alla banchina** (*trasp. mar., USA*) to dock.

accostarsi, *v. rifl.* (*trasp. mar.*) to come* alongside. *v. recipr.* (*trasp. mar.*) to draw* together. // ~ **a una nave** (*trasp. mar.*) to go alongside a ship.

accostata, *n. f.* (*trasp. aer., trasp. mar.*) turn.

accreditamento, *n. m.* (*banca, rag.*) crediting, credit. // ~ **in conto a q.** (*banca, cred.*) crediting to sb.'s (current) account.

accreditante, *a.* crediting. *n. m.* e *f.* (the) crediting party.

accreditare, *v. t.* 1 to credit. 2 (*cred., rag.*) to accredit, to credit. // ~ **un conto d'una somma** (*rag.*) to credit an account with a sum; ~ **q. d'una somma** to credit sb. with an amount; ~ **una somma a q.** to credit an amount to sb., to give sb. credit for a sum of money.

accreditato, *a.* (*cred., rag.*) accredited. *n. m.* (*cred., rag.*) accreditee, (the) accredited party, (the) credited party.

accredito, *n. m.* (*banca, rag.*) crediting. // « ~ **di effetti valuta scadenza** » (*banca*) «crediting of bills value at maturity date».

accrescere, *v. t.* to increase, to augment, to enhance, to step up. // ~ **la produzione** (*org. az.*) to step up production.

accrescimento, *n. m.* 1 increase, increment, enhancement, growth, step-up. 2 (*leg.*) accretion. // ~ **degli stock** (*org. az.*) inventory increase; ~ **fra coeredi** (*leg.*) accretion among coheirs; ~ **per alluvione** (*leg.*) accretion by alluvion.

accumulare, *v. t.* to accumulate, to cumulate, to amass, to hoard, to store (up). // ~ **eccessive riserve di capitale in un'azienda** (*fin.*) to over-capitalize a business; ~ **merci in un magazzino** to store up goods in a warehouse; ~ **perdite (su perdite)** to accumulate losses; ~ **ricchezze** to accumulate wealth, to amass riches.

accumularsi, *v. rifl.* 1 to accumulate. 2 (*fin.*) to accrue.

accumulato, *a.* 1 accumulated. 2 (*fin.*) accrued.

accumulazione, *n. f.* 1 accumulation, cumulation. 2 (*fin.*) accrual.

accusa, *n. f.* 1 (*leg.*) accusation, charge, impeachment. 2 **l'accusa** (*leg.*) the prosecution. // ~ **di ricevuta** acknowledgment of receipt; letter of acknowledgment; **un'** ~ **infondata** (*leg.*) an unfounded accusation; ~ **scritta** (*leg.*) indictment.

accusabile, *a.* (*leg.*) impeachable, indictable.

accusare, *v. t.* (*leg.*) to accuse, to charge, to impeach, to indict. // ~ **un disavanzo notevole** (*fin., rag.*) to close with a heavy deficit; ~ **ricevuta** to acknowledge receipt; ~ **ricevuta di merci** (*comm.*) to receipt goods.

accusato, *a.* (*leg.*) accused, charged. *n. m.* (*leg.*) defendant, indictee.

accusatore, *n. m.* 1 (*leg.*) indictor, indicter. 2 (*leg.*) (= **pubblico accusatore**) prosecutor.

accusatorio, *a.* (*leg.*) accusatorial.

acqua, *n. f.* water. // ~ **alta** (*trasp. mar.*) high water; ~ **bassa** (*trasp. mar.*) low water; **le acque extraterritoriali** (*trasp. mar.*) the high seas; **acque navigabili** (*trasp.*) navigable waters; **acque pubbliche** (*leg.*) public waters; **acque soggette a marea** (*trasp. mar.*) tidal waters; **acque territoriali** (*trasp. mar.*) territorial waters.

acquaforte, *n. f.* (*pubbl.*) copper etching.

acquedotto, *n. m.* waterworks.

acquiescenza, *n. f.* 1 compliance. 2 (*leg.*) sufferance.

acquirente, *a.* (*market.*) buying, purchasing. *n. m.* e *f.* 1 (*market.*) buyer, purchaser, vendee. 2 (*market.*) (*in un negozio*) shopper. // **acquirenti a medio termine prolungato** (*cred.*) extended medium-term purchasers; **l'** ~ **d'un premio indiretto** (*Borsa*) the seller of a put option; ~ **in buona fede** (*leg.*) bona fide purchaser; **un** ~ **potenziale** (*market.*) a potential buyer; **acquirenti pubblici** (*econ.*) Government purchasers.

acquisire, *v. t.* to acquire. // ~ **un documento a un processo** (*leg.*) to admit a document as evidence in a trial; ~ **per usucapione** (*leg.*) to prescribe.

acquisito, *a.* (*leg.*) (*di un diritto*) vested.

acquisizione, *n. f.* acquisition. // ~ **della cittadinanza** (*d'un Paese*) (*leg.*) naturalization.

acquistabile, *a.* (*market.*) buyable, purchasable.

acquistare, *v. t.* 1 (*acquisire*) to acquire. 2 (*fin.*) to underwrite★. 3 (*market.*) to buy★, to purchase. // ~ **a rate** to buy on instalment (*o* by instalments); ~ **il controllo d'una società** (*fin.*) to take over a company; ~ **merce (beni immobili, ecc.)** to purchase merchandise (real estate, etc.); ~ **il pacchetto di maggioranza di una società** (*fin.*) to buy out a company; ~ **il possesso di qc.** (*leg.*) to seize st.; ~ **(qc.) valendosi del diritto di prelazione** (*leg.*) to pre-empt.

acquistato, *a.* (*market.*) bought, purchased. // ~ **a termine** (*Borsa*) bought for the account.

acquisto, *n. m.* 1 (*acquisizione*) acquisition. 2 (*market.*) buy, buying, purchase. 3 **acquisti,** *pl.* (*market.*) shopping. // ~ (*di titoli*) **a copertura** (*Borsa, fin.*) short covering; ~ **a credito** (*market., rag.*) credit purchase; **acquisti a rate** (*market.*) instalment buying; ~ **a termine** (*Borsa*) purchase for the account, purchase for the settlement; ~ **allo scoperto** (*Borsa*) bull purchase; ~ **(con pagamento) in contanti** (*market.*) purchase for cash, purchase for money; ~ **(con pagamento) rateale** (*market.*) time purchase; **l'** ~ **d'azioni** (*fin.*) the purchase of shares; ~ **di possesso** (*di qc.*) (*leg.*) seizure; ~ **di tempo** (*per la pubblicità radiotelevisiva*) (*comm., pubbl.*) time buying; ~ **effettuato per proteggersi da un**

rischio o da fluttuazioni di mercato (*e non a fini esclusivi di lucro*) (*fin.*) hedge; **acquisti (fatti) all'estero** (*market., USA*) off-shore purchases; ~ **fatto esercitando il diritto di prelazione** (*leg.*) pre-emption; ~ **(fatto) per impulso** (*market.*) impulse purchase; **acquisti (fatti) per impulso** (*market.*) impulse buying; ~ **in massa** (*market.*) bulk buying.

acro, *n. m.* acre.

acuto, *a.* **1** (*acuminato*) sharp. **2** (*fig.*) keen, discriminating.

adattabile, *a.* adaptable.

adattabilità, *n. f.* adaptability, elasticity.

adattamento, *n. m.* accommodation, adaptation, adjustment. // ~ **dei prezzi** (*market.*) price adjustment; ~ **stagionale** (*market.*) seasonal adjustment.

adattare, *v. t.* **1** to accommodate, to adapt, to adjust, to conform, to fit. **2** to tailor (*fig.*). // ~ **una nave da carico per il trasporto di emigranti** (*trasp. mar.*) to accommodate a cargo ship for the carriage of emigrants.

adatto, *a.* **1** fit, suitable, right, eligible. **2** appropriate, convenient, proper.

addebitabile, *a.* **1** chargeable. **2** (*rag.*) imputable, chargeable.

addebitare, *v. t.* **1** to charge. **2** (*rag.*) to debit, to charge, to impute. // ~ **al cliente le spese postali** to charge the postage to the customer; ~ **un conto** (*rag.*) to charge an account, to debit an account.

addebito, *n. m.* **1** (*leg.*) charge. **2** (*rag.*) debit. // ~ **di spese giudiziali** (*leg.*) charge of costs; ~ **eccessivo** overcharge.

addestramento, *n. m.* (*pers.*) training, coaching. // ~ **dei dirigenti** (*org. az.*) executive training; ~ **della manodopera** (*org. az., pers.*) manpower training; ~ **professionale** (*pers.*) professional training; ~ **sul lavoro** (*org. az., pers.*) on-the-job training.

addestrare, *v. t.* (*pers.*) to train, to coach.

addetto, *n. m.* (*nella carriera diplomatica*) attaché. // « ~ **ai lavori** » insider; ~ **ai ricuperi marittimi** (*trasp. mar.*) salvager, salvor; ~ **ai segnali** (*trasp. ferr.*) signal-man; ~ **al ricevimento** (*tur.*) receptionist; ~ **all'accettazione** (*di telegrammi*) (*comun.*) accepting officer; ~ **alla corrispondenza** (*pers.*) correspondence clerk; **gli addetti alla distribuzione** (*market.*) distributors; ~ **alla manutenzione** (*pers.*) maintenance man; ~ **alle consegne** (*pers.*) delivery man; ~ **alle spedizioni** (*pers.*) dispatch clerk; **addetti alle vendite** (*pers.*) salespeople; ~ **commerciale** commercial attaché; ~ **stampa** (*giorn., pubbl.*) press-agent; (*di un uomo politico*) press-secretary; « **non** ~ **ai lavori** » outsider.

addivenire, *v. i.* to come* to, to reach. // ~ **a un accordo** to come to terms; ~ **a una riconciliazione** to come to a conciliation.

addizionale, *a.* additional, supplementary; excess, extra (*attr.*). *n. f.* **1** (*spesa addizionale*) additional charge. **2** (*ass.*) (*di premio*) loading. **3** (*fin.*) (*imposta*) addition. **4** (*fin.*) (*imposta addizionale*) additional tax, supertax. **5 addizionali,** *pl.* (*pers.*) fringe benefits.

addizionatrice, *n. f.* (*macch. uff.*) adding machine, adder. // ~ **a lettura immediata** (*macch. uff.*) rotary adding machine; ~ **-sottrattrice** (*macch. uff.*) adding-subtracting machine.

addurre, *v. t.* **1** to allege. **2** (*a giustificazione, a discolpa*) to plead. // ~ (*un mezzo*) **a difesa** (*leg.*) to justify; ~ **argomenti** (*leg.*) to bring arguments; ~ **valide prove per qc.** (*leg.*) to substantiate st.

adeguamento, *n. m.* adjustment, adaptation. // **l'** ~ **dei quadri direttivi** (*pers.*) the updating of managers; ~ **(dei salari) al costo della vita** (*secondo i punti della «contingenza»*) (*econ.*) cost-of-living adjustment; ~ **delle retribuzioni alle variazioni del costo della vita** (*sind.*) escalation; ~ **delle scorte** (*org. az.*) inventory adjustment.

adeguare, *v. t.* to adjust, to adapt.

adeguarsi, *v. rifl.* to conform (oneself).

adeguatamente, *avv.* adequately, duly.

adeguatezza, *n. f.* adequacy, sufficiency.

adeguato, *a.* adequate, appropriate, competent, sufficient. // **adeguata comprensione della legge** (*leg.*) competent understanding of the law; **dopo adeguata riflessione** after due consideration.

adeguazioni delle parità, *n. pl.* (*fin.*) peg adjustments.

adempiere, *v. t.* e *i.* **1** to fulfil; to fulfill (*USA*); to implement, to perform, to discharge. **2** (*leg.*) (*un'obbligazione*) to discharge, to satisfy. // ~ **a un impegno** to implement an engagement; ~ **(a) un obbligo** to satisfy an obligation; ~ **ai propri impegni** to carry out one's engagements; ~ **un compito** to perform a task; ~ **una promessa** to perform a promise.

adempimento, *n. m.* **1** fulfilment; fulfillment (*USA*); implementation, performance, pursuance. **2** (*leg.*) (*d'un'obbligazione*) discharge, satisfaction.

adempiuto, *a.* (*leg.*) (*d'obbligo, ecc.*) satisfied.

aderire, *v. i.* **1** to accede. **2** (*sottoscrivere*) to subscribe. // ~ **a un invito** to accept an invitation; ~ **a una richiesta** to comply with a request.

adesione, *n. f.* (*fig.*) consent. // **l' ~ a un invito** the acceptance of an invitation.

adesivo, *a.* e *n. m.* adhesive.

adire, *v. t.* (*nelle seguenti locuz.*) ~ **il tribunale** (*leg.*) to go to Court; ~ **le vie legali** (*leg.*) to have recourse to the law, to take legal action (*o* legal steps), to take proceedings; ~ **le vie legali contro q.** (*leg.*) to sue sb. at law.

adottante, *n. m.* e *f.* (*leg.*) adopter.

adottare, *v. t.* (*anche leg.*) to adopt. // ~ **una deliberazione** to carry a resolution; ~ **misure reflazionistiche** (*econ.*) to reflate; ~ **il sistema decimale per una moneta** (*econ.*) to decimalize a currency.

adottato, *n. m.* (*leg.*) adoptee.

adottivo, *a.* (*leg.*) adoptive.

adozione, *n. f.* (*leg.*) adoption. // ~ **del sistema monetario decimale** (*econ.*) decimalization.

adrema, *n. f.* (*macch. uff., neol.*) (*macchina per indirizzi, targhettatrice*) addressing machine, addresser.

adunanza, *n. f.* **1** meeting, sitting, rally. **2** (*le persone adunate*) assembly. // ~ **del consiglio d'amministrazione** board meeting.

adunare, *v. t.* to assemble, to convene, to rally.

adunarsi, *v. rifl.* to assemble, to convene, to rally.

aereo, *a.* aerial. *n. m.* (*trasp. aer.*) plane, aircraft. // ~ **da carico** (*trasp. aer.*) cargo-plane; ~ **da trasporto** (*trasp. aer.*) air freighter; ~ **di linea** (*trasp. aer.*) airliner, liner; ~ **per trasporto merci** (*trasp. aer.*) freighter.

aerocisterna, *n. f.* (*trasp. aer.*) tanker.

aerodromo, *n. m.* (*trasp. aer.*) airdrome (*USA*).

aerografo, *n. m.* (*pubbl.*) airbrush.

aerogramma, *n. m.* (*comun.*) aerogram.

aeronautica, *n. f.* aeronautics.

aeronautico, *a.* aeronautic, aeronautical.

aeronave, *n. f.* (*trasp. mar.*) hovercraft. // ~ **-traghetto** (*trasp. mar.*) hoverferry.

aeroplano, *n. m.* **1** (*trasp. aer.*) aeroplane; airplane (*USA*); plane, aircraft. **2 aeroplani,** *collett.* (*trasp. aer.*) aircraft.

aeroporto, *n. m.* (*trasp. aer.*) airport, port. // ~ **di arrivo** (*per merci*) airport of delivery; ~ **di partenza** (*per merci*) airport of lading.

aerotrasportato, *a.* (*trasp. aer.*) airborne.

affamare, *v. t.* (*anche fig.*) to starve. // **essere affamato** to starve, to be starving.

affare, *n. m.* **1** business (*solo al sing.*). **2** (*singola operazione*) piece of business, deal, transaction. **3** (*buon affare*) bargain. **4** (*faccenda*) affair, matter. **5 affari,** *pl.* business (*solo al sing.*), affairs; biz, beeswax (*slang USA*). // **un ~ a condizioni inique** a hard bargain; **un ~ a condizioni poco vantaggiose** a hard bargain; **un ~ a termine** (*Borsa*) a bargain for the account; ~ **andato male** bloomer (*slang USA*); **affari conclusi alla Borsa Valori di Londra** (*Borsa*) bargains; **affari di Stato** affairs of State; **un ~ equivoco** a shady transaction; **affari esteri** (*econ., fin.*) foreign affairs; **un ~ favorevole** a bargain; **affari fiorenti e rapidi** land-office business; **un ~ incerto** a touch-and-go business; **affari interni** home affairs; **un ~ losco** a deal; **un ~ per contanti** a bargain for cash; **un ~ rischioso** a touch-and-go business; **essere in affari** to be in business; **per affari** on business; **un affarone** a smart deal, a stroke of business.

affarista, *n. m.* e *f.* profiteer, commercialist.

affermare, *v. t.* **1** (*asserire*) to affirm, to assert, to state. **2** (*dire*) to say★. **3** (*sostenere*) to claim, to maintain. // ~ **la propria innocenza** (*leg.*) to assert one's innocence.

affermarsi, *v. rifl.* to assert oneself. // ~ **sul mercato** (*market.*) (*di merce*) to obtain a footing in the market.

affermazione, *n. f.* **1** affirmation, assertion, statement. **2** (*leg.*) (*d'un diritto*) claim. // **un' ~ calunniosa** (*leg.*) a slanderous statement; **un' ~ opinabile** a disputable statement.

afferrare, *v. t.* **1** to catch★; to nail (*fam.*). **2** (*anche, fig., capire*) to grasp. **3** (*artigliare*) to claw.

affiancarsi, *v. rifl.* (*trasp. mar.*) to come★ alongside. // ~ **a una nave** (*trasp. mar.*) to go alongside a ship.

affidamento, *n. m.* **1** reliance. **2** (*leg.*) (*di figli minorenni*) awarding. // **un impiegato che dà ~** (*pers.*) a reliable clerk.

affidare, *v. t.* **1** to entrust, to intrust, to trust. **2** (*confidare*) to confide. **3** (*consegnare*) to consign. **4** (*raccomandare*) to commend. **5** (*indirizzare, rinviare*) to refer, to remit. **6** (*leg.*) (*i figli minorenni; in caso di divorzio*) to award. **7** (*trasp. mar.*) to address. // ~ **alla memoria** to commit to memory; ~ **una causa** (*leg.*) to entrust a case; ~ **un compito a q.** to charge sb. with a task, to devolve a duty to (*o* on) sb.; ~ **una faccenda a q.** to leave a matter in sb.'s hands; ~ (*beni*) **in amministrazione** (*o* **gestione**) **fiduciaria** (*leg.*) to trustee; ~ **il proprio lavoro a un dipendente** (*org. az.*) to devolve one's work on a subordinate; ~ **una missione importante a**

q. to charge sb. with an important mission.

«affidavit», *n. m.* (*leg., ingl.*) affidavit.

affiggere, *v. t.* (*pubbl.*) to stick★, to post (up). // ~ **manifesti su** (*un muro, ecc.*) (*pubbl.*) to placard, to poster.

affiliare, *v. t.* (*leg.*) to affiliate.

affiliato, *a.* (*leg.*) affiliated.

affiliazione, *n. f.* (*leg.*) affiliation.

affini, *n. pl.* (*leg.*) relatives-in-law; in-laws (*fam.*).

affissione, *n. f.* (*pubbl.*) posting. // ~ **di manifesti** (*pubbl.*) bill-posting; ~ **di media intensità** (*pubbl.*) half showing; ~ **piena** (*pubbl.*) full display, full showing.

affisso, *n. m.* (*pubbl.*) poster.

affittabile, *a.* (*leg.*) rentable.

affittanza, *n. f.* **1** (*leg.*) leasehold, tenancy, tenantry. **2** (*leg.*) (*contratto d'affitto*) lease. // ~ **perpetua** (*leg.*) perpetual lease.

affittare, *v. t.* **1** (*leg.*) (*dare in affitto*) to lease, to let★, to rent. **2** (*leg.*) (*prendere, tenere in affitto*) to lease, to rent. // ~ (*locali e sim.*) **a un prezzo inferiore al giusto** (*leg.*) to underlet; **essere da** ~ to be let, to be for rent; **«affittasi»** «to let»; «for rent» (*USA*).

affittato, *a.* (*leg.*) leased, let.

affitto, *n. m.* **1** (*leg.*) lease, rent. **2** (*leg.*) (*affittanza*) tenancy. // ~ **a tempo indeterminato** (*con diritto di disdetta da parte del locatore*) (*leg.*) tenancy at will; ~ **anticipato** (*leg.*) rent in advance; ~ **arretrato** back rent; **affitti bloccati** controlled rents; ~ **di terreno con obbligo di costruzione** (*leg.*) building-lease; ~ **esageratamente alto** rack rent; ~ **in arretrato** (*leg.*) rent in arrears, arrears of rent; **un** ~ **irrisorio** a nominal rent; **un** ~ **nominale** (*leg.*) a nominal rent, a peppercorn rent (*fam.*); **un** ~ **non ancora scaduto** (*leg.*) an unexpired lease; **d'** ~ (*leg.*) tenemental; **in** ~ (*leg.*) on lease; **chi dà in** ~ (*leg.*) lessor.

affittuario, *n. m.* (*leg.*) leaseholder, lessee, occupant, occupier, renter, tenant. // **gli affittuari subentranti** (*leg.*) the incoming tenants.

affluire, *v. i.* to flow in, to pour in.

afflusso, *n. m.* inflow, influx, flow, stream (*fig.*). // ~ **di depositi bancari** (*banca*) inflow of bank deposits; **un forte** ~ **di capitali esteri in Italia** (*fin.*) an extraordinary flow (*o* inflow, influx) of foreign capital to Italy.

affollamento, *n. m.* crowding, rush. // ~ **alla biglietteria** (*trasp.*) crowding round the ticket windows.

affollare, *v. t.* to crowd.

affollarsi, *v. rifl.* to crowd.

affondabile, *a.* (*trasp. mar.*) sinkable.

affondamento, *n. m.* (*trasp. mar.*) sinking.

affondare, *v. t.* e *i.* (*trasp. mar.*) to sink★.

affrancamento, *n. m.* **1** (*liberazione*) freeing. **2** (*cred., leg.*) (*da un pagamento*) franking.

affrancare, *v. t.* **1** (*liberare*) to free. **2** (*comun.*) (*una lettera, ecc.*) to frank, to stamp. **3** (*cred., leg.*) (*da un pagamento*) to frank. **4** (*fin., leg.*) (*riscattare*) to redeem. // ~ **la corrispondenza** (*comun.*) to prepay the postage on correspondence; ~ **un'eredità** (*leg.*) to redeem an inheritance; ~ **una lettera** (*comun.*) to frank a letter, to stamp a letter; ~ (*lettere, ecc.*) **mediante una** (*macchina*) **affrancatrice** (*di macch. uff.*) to meter.

affrancato, *a.* **1** (*comun.*) franked, stamped. **2** (*cred., leg.*) franked. // **non** ~ (*comun.*) (*di lettera*) unstamped.

affrancatrice, *n. f.* (*macch. uff.*) franking machine.

affrancatura, *n. f.* **1** (*comun.*) (*d'una lettera, ecc.*) franking. **2** (*comun.*) (*i francobolli applicati*) postage. // ~ **aggiuntiva** (*d'una lettera*) (*comun.*) excess postage; « ~ **insufficiente**» (*comun.*) «postage due»; ~ (*di lettere, ecc.*) **mediante** (*macchina*) **affrancatrice** metering; **recante** ~ **insufficiente** (*comun.*) (*di lettera, ecc.*) short-paid.

affrettare, *v. t.* to rush, to speed★ up.

affrettarsi, *v. rifl.* to rush, to speed★ up. // ~ **ad accettare un'offerta** to jump at an offer.

affrontare, *v. t.* to confront, to face, to meet★, to tackle.

agenda, *n. f.* **1** appointment book, pocket book. **2** (*attr. uff.*) diary, desk diary, memorandum book, memory book, memo book. **3** (*org. az.*) (*dei lavori d'una commissione, ecc.*) docket.

agente, *n. m.* (*pers.*) agent, representative agent, representative; man★ (*fam.*). // ~ **agricolo** (*econ., ingl.*) land agent; ~ **commissionario** (*pers.*) commission agent; ~ **consolare** (*pers.*) consular agent; ~ **del credere** (*pers.*) del credere agent; ~ **delle imposte** (*pers.*) exciseman★, assessor; ~ **depositario** (*pers.*) depositary agent, factor; ~ **d'assicurazione** (*ass.*) insurance agent; insurance broker (*per lo più marittima*); ~ **di cambio** (*Borsa*) stock-broker, stockbroker, broker; (*fin.*) exchange broker, sharebroker; curbist (*slang USA*); ~ **di cambio che lavora fuori della Borsa** (*fin.*) street broker; ~ **di cambio che tratta titoli negoziabili a breve termine** (*fin., USA*) note broker; ~ **di cambio senza riconoscimento ufficiale** (*fin.*) outside broker; ~ **di commercio** (*leg.*) mercantile agent;

(*pers.*) business agent; ~ **di compagnia di navigazione** (*trasp. mar.*) shipping-agent; ~ **di pubblicità** (*pubbl.*) advertising agent; ~ (*di cambio*) **di sala** (*Borsa*) floor broker; ~ **di sconto** (*fin.*) bill-broker; ~ **di vendita** (*pers.*) sales agent; ~ **di zona** (*ass., pers.*) local agent, special agent; ~ **doganale** (*dog.*) customs agent, custom house broker; ~ **economico** transactor; ~ **esclusivo** exclusive (*o* sole) agent; ~ **esportatore** (*comm. est.*) export agent, export commission agent; ~ **fondiario** land agent (*ingl.*); realtor (*USA*); ~ **generale** (*ass., pers.*) general agent; (*pers.*) universal agent; ~ **immobiliare** (*econ.*) land broker (*ingl.*); real-estate agent, estate agent, house-agent; realtor (*USA*); ~ **importatore** (*comm. est.*) import agent; ~ **intermediario** interagent; ~ **marittimo** (*trasp. mar.*) ship-broker; ~ **mediatore** (*market.*) functional middleman; ~ **per gli acquisti** buying (*o* purchasing) agent; ~ **per il ricupero dei crediti** (*cred.*) debt collector; ~ **pubblicitario** (*giorn., pubbl.*) press-agent; (*pubbl.*) advertising agent, advertising man, adman; ~ **universale** (*pers.*) universal agent.

agenzia, *n. f.* **1** (*leg.*) (*l'impresa e l'incarico*) agency, mercantile agency. **2** (*org. az.*) (*l'ufficio*) bureau, office. // ~ **delle tasse** (*fin.*) tax collector's office; ~ **d'assicurazioni** (*ass.*) insurance agency; ~ **d'assicurazioni sulla vita** (*ass.*) life office; ~ **di cambio illegale** (*Borsa*) bucket shop (*slang USA*); ~ **di collocamento** employment bureau; employment agency (*USA*); ~ **d'informazioni** (*giorn., pubbl.*) news agency, press-agency, news service; ~ **d'informazioni commerciali** mercantile agency; ~ **di prestiti su pegno** (*comm., leg.*) pawnbrokers' shop, pawnshop; ~ **di pubblicità** (*pubbl.*) advertising agency, advertising bureau; ~ **di spedizioni** (*trasp.*) forwarding agents; shipping agents (*USA*); ~ **di spedizioni marittime** (*trasp.*) shipping agents; ~ **di spedizioni per espresso** (*trasp.*) express company (*USA*); ~ **di stampa** (*giorn., pubbl.*) news agency, press-agency, news service, syndicate; **un'** ~ **di traslochi** a removal agency; ~ **di trasporti** (*trasp.*) common carrier; ~ **di viaggi** (*tur.*) travel agency, travel bureau; ~ **doganale** (*dog.*) customs agency; ~ **fondiaria** land agency (*ingl.*); real estate agency (*USA*); ~ **generale** (*ass.*) general agency; ~ **immobiliare** estate agency; ~ **incaricata del trasferimento di titoli** (*fin., USA*) transfer agents; ~ **marittima** (*trasp. mar.*) shipping agency; ~ **per il ricupero dei crediti** (*cred.*) debt collecting agency, debt collection agency, debt recovery agency; ~ **turistica** (*tur.*) tourist agency.

agevolare, *v. t.* (*favorire*) to accommodate, to facilitate, to further.

agevolazione, *n. f.* **1** accommodation, facility. **2** (*comm., fin., market.*) relief. // **agevolazioni fiscali** (*fin.*) tax facilities.

aggio, *n. m.* (*fin.*) agio, premium.

aggiornamento, *n. m.* **1** (*il differire*) adjournment, postponement. **2** (*il mettere al corrente*) bringing up to date. **3** (*leg.*) continuation. **4** (*pers.*) follow-up. **5** (*rag.*) write-up.

aggiornare, *v. t.* **1** (*differire*) to adjourn, to postpone, to put* off. **2** (*mettere al corrente*) to bring* up to date. **3** (*leg.*) to continue. **4** (*rag.*) to write* up. // ~ **il (libro) mastro generale** (*rag.*) to post up the general ledger.

aggiornarsi, *v. rifl.* **1** (*interrompere i lavori*) to adjourn. **2** (*mettersi al corrente*) to bring* oneself up to date.

aggiornato, *a.* **1** up-to-date, down-to-date. **2** (*market., pubbl.*) new-day (*attr.*).

aggiotaggio, *n. m.* **1** (*Borsa*) agiotage, stockjobbing, market jobbery. **2** (*leg.*) rigging the market, rig.

aggiotatore, *n. m.* **1** (*Borsa*) stockjobber, jobber, speculator. **2** (*leg.*) rigger (of the market).

aggiudicabile, *a.* allottable, awardable.

aggiudicare, *v. t.* **1** to adjudge, to adjudicate. **2** (*assegnare*) to allot, to award. **3** (*concedere in appalto*) to entrust. **4** (*in una vendita all'asta*) to knock down. // ~ **un premio a q.** to adjudge (to adjudicate, to award) a prize to sb.; «**aggiudicato!**» (*in una vendita all'asta*) «gone!».

aggiudicatario, *n. m.* **1** (*assegnatario*) allottee. **2** (*d'un appalto*) contractor. **3** (*all'asta*) highest bidder.

aggiudicazione, *n. f.* **1** adjudication. **2** (*assegnazione*) allotment, award. **3** (*all'asta*) knocking down. // **l'** ~ **d'un contratto** the award of a contract.

aggiungere, *v. t.* **1** to add, to add back, to put* on, to tack (*fig.*). **2** (*per iscritto*) to append. // ~ **un'addizionale al premio** (*ass.*) to load the premium; ~ **una clausola a un contratto** to append a clause to a treaty; ~ **il nolo al valore della merce** to add freight to the value of the goods; ~ **un poscritto a una lettera** to add a postscript to a letter; ~ **treni straordinari** (*trasp. ferr.*) to put on extra trains.

aggiunta, *n. f.* addition, supplement, extra, plus. // **in** ~ additionally; **in** ~ **a** over and above.

aggiuntivo, *a.* collateral, further, excess, extra, plus. // **salario** ~ (*pers.*) extra pay.

aggiunto, *a.* (*pers.*) deputy.

aggiustamento, *n. m.* 1 mending, repairing. 2 (*regolamento*) settlement. 3 (*fin.*) alteration, turnaround. // ~ **automatico dei salari** (*econ., org. az.*) automatic wage adjustment; **l'~ dei conti** the settlement of accounts.

aggiustare, *v. t.* 1 (*accomodare*) to mend, to repair, to trim; to tailor (*fig.*). 2 (*correggere, sistemare*) to correct, to right, to settle. // ~ **i conti** (*rag.*) to settle accounts; ~ **i propri conti con l'estero** (*fin.*) to put one's balance of payments on an even keel.

aggiustarsi, *v. rifl.* (*accordarsi*) to agree, to come★ to an agreement, to reach an agreement.

aggravamento, *n. m.* aggravation. // **l'~ del rischio** (*ass.*) the aggravation of the risk, the increase of the risk.

aggressione, *n. f.* (*leg.*) assault.

agiato, *a.* wealthy, well-to-do. // **essere di agiata condizione** to be in easy circumstances.

agire, *v. t.* 1 to act, to do★, to operate. 2 (*leg.*) to proceed, to take★ legal steps. // ~ **come arbitro** (*leg.*) to referee; ~ **come procuratore legale di q.** (*leg.*) to solicit for sb.; ~ **esecutivamente sui beni di q.** (*leg.*) to levy on sb.'s property; ~ **in buona fede** (*leg.*) to act bona fide; ~ **in malafede** to act in bad faith; ~ **in opposizione** to counter; ~ **per bassi motivi** to act from base motives; ~ **per conto di q.** to act on behalf of sb.

agitare, *v. t.* 1 to shake★, to shake★ up. 2 (*disturbare*) to trouble, to unsettle.

agitato, *a.* unsettled, upset (*anche fig.*).

agitazione, *n. f.* trouble, unrest. // ~ **sindacale** labour trouble, industrial action.

agrario, *a.* agrarian, agricultural.

agricolo, *a.* agricultural, agrarian; landed (*attr.*).

agricoltore, *n. m.* farmer, homesteader.

agricoltura, *n. f.* agriculture, farming. // ~ **intensiva** (*econ.*) intensive agriculture, high farming.

aiutare, *v. t.* 1 to aid, to help, to assist, to relieve, to support. 2 (*promuovere*) to forward, to further. // ~ **q. a fare qc.** to assist sb. in doing st.

aiuto, *n. m.* 1 aid, help, assistance, relief, support. 2 (*assistente*) assistant. // **aiuti ai Paesi esteri** (*econ.*) foreing aids; **aiuti ai Paesi in via di sviluppo** (*econ.*) aids to developing Countries; **aiuti alimentari della Comunità** Community food aid; **aiuti alle esportazioni** (*comm. est.*) aids for exports; ~ **contabile** (*pers.*) assistant accountant; **aiuti d'avviamento alle associazioni di produttori** (*econ.*) starting-up aids to growers' associations; ~ **finanziario** subsidy, aid disbursement; ~ **forfettario** (*econ.*) standard subsidy; ~ **illecito** (*a una parte in causa*) (*leg.*) maintenance; ~ **reciproco** mutual aid; **aiuti settoriali** (*econ.*) aids to individual industries.

ala, *n. f.* (*anche fig.*) wing. // **l'~ sinistra d'un partito (d'un sindacato, ecc.)** the left wing of a party (of a trade union, etc.).

alaggio, *n. m.* (*trasp. mar.*) haulage, towage, towing.

alare, *v. t.* (*trasp. mar.*) to haul, to tow, to track.

alberare, *v. t.* (*trasp. mar.*) (*una nave*) to mast.

alberghiero, *a.* (*tur.*) hotel (*attr.*).

albergo, *n. m.* (*tur.*) hotel.

albero, *n. m.* 1 tree. 2 (*trasp. mar.*) (*di nave*) mast. // ~ **maestro** (*trasp. mar.*) mainmast.

albo, *n. m.* 1 (*per avvisi*) notice-board. 2 (*per foto, francobolli, ecc.*) album. 3 (*leg.*) roll. // **l'~ degli avvocati** (*leg.*) the Rolls; ~ **degli avvocati e dei procuratori** (*leg.*) law list; ~ **dei giurati** (*leg.*) jury list.

alibi, *n. m.* (*leg.*) alibi.

alienabile, *a.* 1 saleable. 2 (*leg.*) alienable.

alienabilità, *n. f.* (*leg.*) alienability.

alienare, *v. t.* 1 to sell★. 2 (*leg.*) to alienate. // ~ **formalmente** (*una proprietà, un diritto, ecc.*) (*leg.*) to sign away.

alienazione, *n. f.* (*leg.*) alienation.

alimentare, *v. t.* 1 to feed★. 2 (*elab. elettr.*) to feed★.

alimentari, *n. pl.* (*market.*) foodstuffs. // ~ **freschi** (*non surgelati*) fresh food.

alimentatore, *n. m.* (*elab. elettr.*) feeder.

alimentazione, *n. f.* 1 feeding. 2 (*elab. elettr.*) feeding, feed.

alimento, *n. m.* 1 food. 2 **alimenti,** *pl.* (*leg.*) allowance. 3 **alimenti,** *pl.* (*leg.*) (*in una causa di separazione o divorzio*) alimony. // **alimenti a seguito di separazione legale** (*leg.*) allowance for separate maintenance.

alinea, *n. f.* (*pubbl.*) paragraph.

aliquota, *n. f.* 1 part, quota, rate. 2 (*fin.*) tax rate. // **le aliquote dei rimborsi all'esportazione** (*comm. est.*) the rates of refunds on exports; ~ **del premio** (*ass.*) rate of premium; **aliquote dell'imposta sul valore aggiunto** (*fin.*) value-added tax rates; **le aliquote delle imposte compensative all'importazione** (*comm. est.*) the rates of countervailing charges on imports; ~ **d'ammortamento** (*rag.*) depreciation charge; **aliquote d'imposta** (*fin.*) tax rates.

alleanza, *n. f.* alliance, compact, union.

allegare, *v. t.* 1 (*anche leg.*) to allege. 2 (*accludere*) to enclose, to inclose, to attach, to append; to tack (*fig.*). // ~ **un documento a una lettera** to attach a document to a letter.

allegato, *n. m.* (*comm.*) enclosure, inclosure.

allegazione, *n. f.* (*anche leg.*) allegation.

alleggerimento, *n. m.* easement, lightening.

alleggerire, *v. t.* to ease, to lighten. // ~ **(il carico di) una nave** (*trasp. mar.*) to lighten a ship; ~ **q. da ogni responsabilità** (*leg.*) to relieve sb. of all responsibility; ~ **una nave della zavorra** (*trasp. mar.*) to unballast a ship.

alleggio, *n. m.* (*trasp. mar.*) lightening.

allentamento, *n. m.* relaxation, slackening. // ~ **dei controlli governativi** (*econ.*) lessening of Government controls.

allentare, *v. t.* 1 to relax, to slacken. 2 (*econ.*) (*la domanda, ecc.*) to dampen. // ~ **la disciplina** (*org. az.*) to slacken discipline, to relax discipline.

allentarsi, *v. rifl.* to relax, to slacken.

allentato, *a.* loose, relaxed, slack.

allestimento, *n. m.* 1 (*pubbl.*) (*di una vetrina*) dressing (of a window). 2 (*trasp. mar.*) fitting-out. // ~ **delle vetrine** (*market.*) window-dressing.

allestire, *v. t.* 1 (*pubbl.*) to dress. 2 (*trasp. mar.*) to equip, to fit out. // ~ **una nave** (*trasp. mar.*) to fit out a ship; ~ **uno stand** (*market., pubbl.*) to set up a stand; ~ **una vetrina** (*pubbl.*) to dress a shop-window.

alleviamento, *n. m.* alleviation, lightening, mitigation, relief.

alleviare, *v. t.* to ease, to alleviate, to mitigate, to relieve.

allibratore, *n. m.* bookmaker; bookie (*slang*).

allineamento, *n. m.* 1 alignment, adjustment. 2 (*giorn., pubbl.*) (*d'una riga*) justification. // ~ **dei prezzi** (*econ.*) adjustment of prices; (*market.*) (*fra venditori concorrenti*) common pricing market; ~ **delle valute** (*fin.*) currency alignment; ~ **valutario** (*fin.*) currency adjustment; **non** ~ (*d'uno Stato*) non-alignment.

allineare, *v. t.* 1 to align, to line. 2 (*giorn., pubbl.*) to justify. // ~ **una riga** (*giorn., pubbl.*) to justify a line; **non allineato** (*di Stato*) non-aligned.

allinearsi, *v. rifl.* to align oneself, to line up. // ~ **sulla tariffa doganale comune** to align oneself on the common customs tariff.

allocuzione, *n. f.* address.

alloggiare, *v. t.* to house, to lodge. *v. i.* to stay.

alloggio, *n. m.* 1 (*l'alloggiare*) housing, lodging, lodgment, lodgement. 2 (*casa, appartamento*) house, flat.

allontanamento, *n. m.* 1 (*partenza*) departure. 2 (*pers.*) (*da un ufficio*) removal.

allontanare, *v. t.* 1 (*definitivamente*) to remove. 2 (*temporaneamente*) to stand* off. 3 (*un pericolo e sim.*) to prevent, to ward off. // ~ **q. da un ufficio** (*pers.*) to remove sb. from office; ~ **un dipendente** to stand off an employee.

allontanarsi, *v. rifl.* 1 (*andar via*) to go* away. 2 (*discostarsi*) to depart.

allunga, *n. f.* (*banca, cred.*) (*di cambiale*) allonge.

alluvione, *n. f.* (*leg.*) alluvion.

alterare, *v. t.* to alter, to change. // ~ **le cifre della contabilità d'un'impresa** (*comm.*) to salt the books of a business (*fam.*); ~ **una scrittura contabile** (*rag.*) to alter an entry.

alterazione, *n. f.* alteration, change. // **l'~ d'un atto ufficiale** (*leg.*) the alteration of a deed; **l'~ d'una scrittura contabile** (*rag.*) the alteration of an entry.

altezza, *n. f.* 1 height, tallness. 2 (*pubbl.*) (*di un'inserzione, di un carattere tipografico*) depth. // **essere all'~ della domanda** (*econ.*) to meet the demand.

alto, *a.* 1 high, tall. 2 (*anche fig.*) up. 3 (*fin.*) (*di titolo, ecc.*) on. 4 (*fin., market.*) (*di prezzo*) strong. *n. m.* (*nell'espressione «gli alti e i bassi»*) up. // **«alto»** (*trasp.*) (*scritto su un collo di merci*) «this side up»; **alta congiuntura** (*econ.*) favourable trend; **Alta Corte di Giustizia** (*leg.*) High Court of Justice; ~ **dirigente** (*amm.*) top executive, top manager; **alta dirigenza** (*amm.*) top management, top-level management; **alta finanza** (*fin.*) high finance; **l'~ mare** (*trasp. mar.*) the high seas, the deep sea; **alta marea** (*trasp. mar.*) high water; ~ **prezzo** (*fin., market.*) high price, tall price, strong price, dearness; **l'~ prezzo del credito al giorno d'oggi** (*cred.*) the dearness of credit nowadays; **l'alta stagione** (*market., trasp., tur.*) the rush season, the peak season; ~ **tenore di vita** (*econ.*) good standing; **ad ~ livello** top-level; **d'~ mare** (*trasp. mar.*) sea-going; **in ~ grado** (*anche fig.*) high; **altissimo** very high, supreme; (*market.*) (*di prezzo, ecc.*) tall.

altura, *n. f.* 1 high ground. 2 (*collina*) hill. 3 (*trasp. mar.*) open sea. // **d'~** (*trasp. mar.*) (*di nave, ecc.*) ocean-going.

alturiero, *a.* (*trasp. mar.*) (*di nave, ecc.*) ocean-going.

alzare, *v. t.* 1 to raise, to put* up, to up. 2 (*sollevare*) to lift, to hoist. // ~ **l'àncora** (*trasp.*

mar.) to raise anchor; ~ **una bandiera** (*trasp. mar.*) to hoist a flag; ~ **i prezzi** (*econ.*) to inflate prices; ~ **il prezzo di** (*articoli, merci, ecc.*) (*market.*) to mark up; ~ **lo sguardo** to look up.

alzata, *n. f.* 1 raising. 2 (*sollevamento*) lifting, hoisting. // **per ~ di mano** (*di votazione*) by show of hands; **per ~ e seduta** (*di votazione*) by standing or remaining seated.

ambasciata, *n. f.* (*messaggio*) errand.

ambientale, *a.* environmental.

ambiente, *n. m.* 1 environment, background. 2 **ambienti,** *pl.* circles, relations. // **gli ambienti commerciali** the trade circles; ~ **di lavoro** work environment; **gli ambienti finanziari** (*fin.*) the financial circles.

àmbito, *n. m.* scope. // **che si svolge nell'~ d'una società** (*org. az.*) intracompany; **nell'~ della legge** (*leg.*) within the law.

ambulantato, *n. m.* (*market.*) hawking.

ambulante, *n. m.* e *f.* (*market.*) street trader, hawker.

ammaestramento, *n. m.* (*pers.*) instruction.

ammaestrare, *v. t.* (*pers.*) to instruct.

ammanco, *n. m.* (*econ., fin., rag.*) shortage, shortfall. // **un ~ di cassa** (*rag.*) a shortage in cash; **ammanchi ed eccedenze di cassa** (*rag.*) cash shorts and overs.

ammassare, *v. t.* 1 to hoard. 2 (*immagazzinare*) to store. 3 (*portare all'ammasso*) to pool. // ~ **denaro** to hoard money; ~ **mobili vecchi in un magazzino** to store old furniture in a warehouse.

ammasso, *n. m.* 1 hoard. 2 (*econ.*) (*governativo*) pool. 3 (*org. az.*) storage.

ammenda, *n. f.* 1 (*fig.*) amends (*pl.*). 2 (*leg.*) (*pena pecuniaria*) fine, forfeit.

ammesso, *a.* 1 admitted. 2 (*permesso*) allowed. // ~ **che** given; (*supponendo che*) supposing that.

ammettere, *v. t.* 1 to admit. 2 (*permettere*) to allow. 3 (*consentire*) to admit of, to allow of. 4 (*riconoscere*) to acknowledge, to admit, to concede, to recognize. // ~ **un credito al passivo d'un fallimento** (*leg.*) to admit proof of debt in a bankruptcy; ~ **q. in una società** to take sb. into partnership; ~ **un reclamo** (*o* **un ricorso**) to grant (*o* to concede) a claim.

amministrare, *v. t.* 1 to administer, to conduct, to govern, to manage. 2 (*comm.*) (*affari, ecc.*) to negotiate. // ~ **la giustizia** (*leg.*) to administer (*o* to dispense, to distribute) justice.

amministrativamente, *avv.* administratively.

amministrativo, *a.* administrative, executive.

amministrato, *a.* administered. // **prezzi amministrati** (*econ., fin.*) administered prices.

amministratore, *n. m.* 1 administrator, governor, manager. 2 (*fin.*) (*membro di un consiglio d'amministrazione*) director. 3 (*leg.*) curator. // ~ **comune** (*di più società*) (*fin.*) interlocking director; ~ **dei beni d'un fallito** (*leg.*) assignee in bankruptcy; ~ **delegato** (*fin.*) managing director; president; ~ **d'una società** (*fin.*) company director; ~ **fiduciario** (*leg.*) trustee; (*in un fallimento*) receiver, official receiver.

amministratrice, *n. f.* (*amm., fin.*) manageress.

amministrazione, *n. f.* 1 administration, government, management; steering (*fig.*). 2 (*org. az.*) government. 3 (*org. az., rag.*) (*l'ufficio*) accounting department; counting-room (*USA*). // ~ **coattiva** (*leg.*) compulsory administration; **l'~ della giustizia** the administration of justice; ~ **disonesta** (*amm.*) mismanagement; ~ **fiduciaria** (*leg.*) trusteeship; (*in un fallimento*) receivership; **l'~ statale** the civil service.

ammissibile, *a.* 1 admissible. 2 (*leg.*) (*di ricorso e sim.*) receivable.

ammissibilità, *n. f.* 1 admissibility. 2 (*leg.*) (*di prova*) competence.

ammissione, *n. f.* 1 admission, admittance. 2 (*concessione*) concession, grant. 3 (*riconoscimento*) acknowledgment, admission, recognition. // ~ **alla quotazione (di titoli)** (*Borsa*) admission to quotation (of stocks and shares); ~ **di credito insinuato al fallimento** (*leg.*) admission of proofs; ~ **di prova** (*leg.*) admission of evidence; ~ **in franchigia** (*dog., fin.*) duty-free entry; ~ **temporanea** (*di merci da riesportare dopo lavorazione parziale*) (*dog.*) «admission temporaire».

ammobiliare, *v. t.* (*market.*) to furnish.

ammodernamento, *n. m.* modernization, updating. // **l'~ della struttura (d'imposizione) fiscale** (*fin.*) the modernization of the tax structure; ~ **delle strutture** (*org. az.*) structural modernization.

ammodernare, *v. t.* to modernize, to update.

ammonimento, *n. m.* 1 warning. 2 (*leg.*) caveat.

ammonire, *v. t.* 1 to warn. 2 (*pers.*) to reprimand.

ammonizione, *n. f.* 1 warning. 2 (*pers.*) reprimand. // ~ **orale** (*pers.*) oral reprimand; ~ **scritta** (*pers.*) written reprimand.

ammontare[1], *n. m.* amount, size, sum. // ~ **complessivo** gross amount; ~ **della diminuzione di prezzo** (*market.*) markdown; ~ **delle rendite**

dei propri terreni (*fin.*) rent-roll; **l'~ d'un'ordinazione** (*market.*) the size of an order; **~ massimo di responsabilità** (*per l'assicuratore*) (*ass.*) limit of liability; **fino all'~ di** to the amount of, to the extent of.

ammontare[2], *v. i.* **1** to amount, to come★ (to), to foot up (to), to sum (to *o* into), to total. **2** (*mat., rag.*) to figure up (at).

ammortabile, *a.* (*rag.*) amortizable, sinkable.

ammortamento, *n. m.* (*rag.*) amortization, amortizement, depreciation, sinking. // **~ a quote costanti** (*rag.*) straight-line depreciation; **~ case operaie** (*fin., rag.*) amortization of workers' housing; **~ degli impianti** (*fin., rag.*) depreciation; **~ degli investimenti** (*econ.*) capital consumption allowance; **~ dei crediti inesigibili** (*rag.*) bad debts reserve; **~ di capitale** (*rag.*) depreciation of capital; **l'~ d'un prestito (d'un debito, ecc.)** the amortization of a loan (a debt, etc.); **~ fiscale** (*fin.*) depreciation allowance; **~ fisso** (*rag.*) fixed depreciation; **~ iniziale** (*rag.*) initial allowance; **~ per deprezzamento** (*rag.*) amount written off.

ammortare, *v. t.* (*rag.*) to amortize, to amortise, to sink★. // **~ un debito** (*rag.*) to amortize a debt.

ammortizzabile, *a.* (*rag.*) amortizable, sinkable.

ammortizzamento, *n. m.* (*rag.*) amortizement, amortization.

ammortizzare, *v. t.* (*rag.*) to amortize, to sink★.

ampiezza, *n. f.* width. // **~ di trattazione** (*d'una notizia*) (*giorn.*) coverage.

ampio, *a.* large, wide. // **un ~ margine** (*fin.*) a wide margin.

ampliamento, *n. m.* enlargement, expansion, extension.

ampliare, *v. t.* to enlarge, to expand, to extend. // **~ un bilancio** (*fin.*) to stretch a budget; **~ il proprio giro d'affari** (*market.*) to branch out.

ampliarsi, *v. rifl.* (*espandersi*) to expand.

anagrafe, *n. f.* (*amm.*) registry office, register office. // **~ tributaria** (*fin.*) tax register; **~ tributaria computerizzata** (*elab. elettr., fin.*) computerized tax register.

analisi, *n. f.* analysis★, dissection. // **~ degli investimenti** (*fin.*) investment analysis; **l'~ dei capitoli di spesa** the analysis of expenses items; **~ dei costi** (*rag.*) cost accounting, cost analysis; **~ dei rapporti fra i fattori produttivi e la produzione** (*econ., org. az.*) input-output analysis; **~ dei settori rappresentativi** (*econ.*) cross-section analysis; **~ del lavoro** (*org. az.*) job analysis, position analysis; **~ del processo produttivo** (*org. az.*) process analysis; **~ dell'accettazione d'un prodotto nuovo** (*market.*) analysis of customer acceptance of a new product; **~ della diffusione** (*giorn., pubbl.*) analysis of circulation; **~ della domanda** (*market.*) demand analysis; **~ della posizione concorrenziale** (*market.*) brand-position analysis; **~ della situazione** (*market.*) situation analysis; **~ delle dimensioni di mercato** (*market.*) analysis of market size; **~ delle interdipendenze settoriali** (*econ.*) input-output analysis; **~ delle vendite** (*market.*) sales analysis; **~ di mercato** (*market.*) market analysis; **~ marginale** (*econ.*) marginal analysis; (*fin.*) differential cost (*o* profit) analysis; **~ valutativa** (*org. az., rag.*) value analysis.

analista, *n. m.* e *f.* **1** analyst. **2** (*pers.*) evaluator. // **~ di mercato** (*market.*) market analyst; **~ finanziario** (*fin.*) financial analyst.

analiticamente, *avv.* analytically.

analitico, *a.* analytic, analytical.

analizzabile, *a.* analysable, analyzable, analizable.

analizzare, *v. t.* to analyse, to analyze, to analise, to analize, to dissect. // **~ un conto** (*rag.*) to dissect an account; **~ un conto (un'operazione commerciale, ecc.)** to analyse an account (a transaction, etc.); **~ l'evoluzione economica** to analyse the economic trend.

analizzatore, *n. m.* analyzer, analyst. // **~ dei costi** (*in un'azienda*) (*pers.*) cost accountant, cost clerk; **~ del mercato** (*market.*) market analyst.

anche, *avv.* also, as well, too. // **~ se** even if.

àncora, *n. f.* (*trasp. mar.*) anchor.

ancoraggio, *n. m.* **1** (*trasp. mar.*) (*l'ancorarsi*) anchoring. **2** (*trasp. mar.*) (*il luogo*) anchorage, berth. **3** (*trasp. mar.*) (*porto*) haven. // **~ di quarantena** (*trasp. mar.*) quarantine anchorage.

ancorare, *v. t.* (*trasp. mar.*) to anchor, to berth.

ancorarsi, *v. rifl.* (*trasp. mar.*) to anchor, to berth, to come★ to anchor.

andamento, *n. m.* **1** (*econ., fin.*) (*della congiuntura, ecc.*) tendency, trend. **2** (*market.*) (*del mercato, ecc.*) run. // **~ dei prezzi** (*econ.*) price trends; (*market.*) course of prices; **l'~ del mercato azionario** (*Borsa, fin.*) the performance of the stock market; **l'~ del mercato dei titoli** (*Borsa, fin.*) the trend of the stock market, the run of the stock market; **l'~ del mercato monetario** (*fin.*) the tendency of the money market;

l' ~ **della domanda** (*econ.*) the demand trend.

andare, *v. i.* 1 to go★. 2 (*guidando un veicolo*) to drive★. 3 (*a far visita*) to call (at, on). 4 (*estendersi, variare*) to range, to work. 5 (*di macchinario e sim.*) to run★. 6 (*andar bene, convenire*) to suit. 7 (*al passivo: essere*) to be, to get★. 8 (*dovere*) to be to; must (*al presente*); should (*al condizionale*). 9 (*leg.*) (*di diritto*) to vest. 10 (*market.*) (*vendersi*) to go★ off. // ~ **a fondo** (*trasp. mar.*) to go to the bottom; ~ **a gonfie vele** to boom; ~ **a numero** (*di merce*) to be sold by quantity; ~ **a peso** (*di merce*) to be sold by weight; ~ **a picco** (*trasp. mar.*) to sink; ~ **a piedi** to walk; ~ **a ruba** (*di merce*) to sell like hot cakes; ~ **a trovare q.** (*anche*) to be seeing sb.; ~ **a tutta velocità** (*trasp. mar.*) to speed; ~ **ai lavori** (*trasp. mar.*) (*di nave*) to undergo repairs; ~ **al fondo di qc.** to go into st.; ~ **al passo** to pace; ~ **alla deriva** (*trasp. mar. e fig.*) to drift; ~ **alla ricerca dell'oro** (*econ.*) to prospect for gold; ~ **alle stelle** (*econ., market.*) (*di prezzi, ecc.*) to zoom, to zoom up; ~ **avanti** to move ahead, to proceed; ~ **avanti e indietro** (*trasp.*) to shuttle; ~ **bene negli affari** to do well in business; ~ **di pari passo coi tempi** to keep up with the times; ~ **distrutto** to perish; ~ **fallito** to fail; ~ **forte** (*fam.*) to be going strong, to go strong; ~ **fuori** to go out; ~ **giù** to go down; ~ **in aereo** (*o* **in aeroplano**) (*trasp. aer.*) to go by plane, to fly; ~ **in auto** (*o* **in automobile**) (*trasp. aut.*) to go by car, to drive; ~ **in cerca di** to pursue; ~ **in cerca di clienti** to tout; ~ **in cerca di guai** to ask for trouble; ~ **in crociera** (*trasp. mar.*) to cruise, to go on a cruise; ~ **in ferie** (*pers.*) to go on (a) holiday; to vacation (*USA*); ~ **in liquidazione** (*fin.*) (*di società*) to liquidate; ~ **in nave** (*trasp. mar.*) to go by ship; ~ **in pensione** (*pers.*) to retire on a pension, to retire; ~ **in pezzi** (*anche fig.*) to smash; ~ **in prescrizione** (*leg.*) to prescribe; ~ **in protesto** (*cred., leg.*) to go to protest, to be protested; ~ **in riparazione** (*org. az.*) (*di macchinario*) to undergo repairs; ~ **in rovina** to break, to crash, to crumble, to smash, to smash up; ~ **in secco** (*trasp. mar.*) (*di nave*) to strike; ~ **in zavorra** (*trasp. mar.*) to sail in ballast; ~ **incontro a** (*anche fig.*) to meet; ~ **male** (*d'affari e sim.*) to be bad; ~ **meglio** (*d'affari e sim.*) to look up; ~ **per i propri affari** to go about one's business; ~ (*a q.*) **per reversione** (*leg.*) to revert, to result; ~ **smarrita** (*comun.*) (*di corrispondenza, merce, ecc.*) to miscarry.

andata, *n. f.* going. // ~ **a riposo** (*pers.*) retirement; ~ **in pensione** (*pers.*) retirement; (*per raggiunti limiti d'età*) superannuation; **d'** ~ (*trasp.*) outward (*attr.*).

andatura, *n. f.* 1 (*trasp.*) going. 2 (*trasp.*) (*velocità*) pace, speed.

angolo, *n. m.* 1 corner. 2 (*mat.*) angle. // ~ **di deriva** (*trasp. aer.*) leeway; (*trasp. mar.*) drift angle; ~ **di pericolo** (*trasp. mar.*) danger angle; ~ **inferiore destro** bottom right-hand corner; ~ **inferiore sinistro** bottom left-hand corner; **girato l'** ~ round the corner.

animare, *v. t.* to give★ (new) life to, to foster, to activate. // ~ **il commercio (i traffici)** to foster trade.

animato, *a.* 1 lively, brisk, spirited. 2 (*pubbl.*) animated.

animazione, *n. f.* 1 animation, liveliness, briskness; go (*fam.*). 2 (*pubbl.*) animation.

annata, *n. f.* 1 year. 2 (*giorn.*) (*raccolta di giornali e sim.*) volume. // **un'** ~ **magra** (*econ.*) a lean year.

annesso, *a.* 1 (*comm.*) (*accluso, allegato*) attached, enclosed. 2 (*leg.*) appurtenant. *n. m.* 1 (*comm.*) (*allegato*) enclosure. 2 **(gli) annessi,** *pl.* (*leg.*) appurtenances.

annettere, *v. t.* (*comm.*) (*accludere, allegare*) to attach, to enclose.

anno, *n. m.* 1 year. 2 (*in talune locuz.*) annum. // ~ **bisestile** (*banca, cred.*) leap year; ~ **buono** (*econ.*) on year; ~ **civile** (*365 giorni*) civil year; **l'** ~ **d'imposizione (fiscale)** (*fin.*) the year of assessment; ~ **di** (*o* **in**) **prova** (*pers.*) probation year; **l'** ~ **entrante** the on-coming year; ~ **favorevole** (*econ.*) on year; ~ **finanziario** (*fin.*) financial year, fiscal year, trading year; **l'** ~ **fiscale** (*fin.*) the taxable year; **l'** ~ **prossimo** next year, the on-coming year; **l'** ~ **scorso** last year, the past year; ~ **sociale** company's fiscal year; (*rag.*) business year; ~ **solare** calendar year; **all'** ~ per annum (*p.a.*).

annotare, *v. t.* 1 to note, to mark down, to write★ down. 2 (*registrare*) to book. 3 (*cred.*) (*crediti, ecc.*) to tally. // ~ **in fretta** (*appunti, ecc.*) to jot (down).

annotazione, *n. f.* 1 note. 2 (*registrazione*) registration, entry. 3 (*cred.*) (*di credito, ecc.*) tally. 4 (*org. az.*) memo (*fam.*). // ~ **frettolosa** jotting; **annotazioni in calce** foot notes; **annotazioni in margine** marginal notes.

annuale, *a.* annual, yearly.

annualità, *n. f.* annuity. // ~ **a rimborso d'un debito** annuity in redemption of a debt; ~ **d'interessi** (*fin.*) yearly interest; ~ **differita** (*ass.*) deferred annuity.

annualmente, *avv.* annually, yearly.

annuario, *n. m.* 1 directory, annual. 2 (*attr. uff.*) calendar, handbook. // **un** ~ **dei fabbri-**

canti a directory of manufacturers.

annullabile, *a.* 1 annullable, cancellable, cancelable, defeasible. 2 (*leg.*) avoidable, repealable, rescindable, revocable, voidable.

annullabilità, *n. f.* defeasibility.

annullamento, *n. m.* 1 annulment, defeasance, suppression. 2 (*di un impegno, di un'ordinazione, ecc.*) cancellation, cancelation. 3 (*di un ordine*) countermand. 4 (*cred.*) write-off. 5 (*leg.*) avoidance, abatement, nullification. 6 (*leg.*) (*di contratto o atto*) cancellation, rescission. 7 (*leg.*) (*d'una sentenza*) cassation. 8 (*leg.*) (*revoca*) revocation, repeal. 9 (*rag.*) contraing. // ~ **di causa** (*leg.*) abatement at law; ~ **di matrimonio** annulment of marriage; ~ **di un'ordinazione** cancellation of an order.

annullare, *v. t.* 1 to annul, to suppress. 2 (*un impegno, un'ordinazione, ecc.*) to cancel. 3 (*un ordine*) to countermand. 4 (*cred.*) to write★ off. 5 (*leg.*) to abate, to avoid, to null, to nullify, to quash, to vacate, to void. 6 (*leg.*) (*rescindere*) to rescind. 7 (*leg.*) (*revocare*) to revoke, to repeal, to rescind. 8 (*leg.*) (*una sentenza, un verdetto, ecc.*) to set★ aside. 9 (*rag.*) to contra. // ~ **un accordo** to cancel an agreement; ~ **un atto** (*legale, notarile, ecc.*) (*leg.*) to cancel a deed; ~ **una condanna** (*leg.*) to quash a conviction; ~ **un contratto** (*leg.*) to cancel a contract, to void a contract; ~ **un contratto di noleggio** (*leg.*) to cancel a charter party; ~ **una marca da bollo** to cancel a revenue stamp; ~ **un matrimonio** (*leg.*) to annul a marriage; ~ **un modulo** to void a form; ~ **un'ordinazione** to cancel an order; ~ **un ordine** (*un comando*) to countermand (*o* to withdraw) an order; ~ **una sentenza** (*leg.*) to quash a decision; ~ **uno statuto** (*leg.*) to vacate a charter; ~ **un verdetto** (*leg.*) to quash a verdict.

annullarsi, *v. recipr.* (*rag.*) to cancel each other, to cancel out.

annunciare, *v. t.* 1 to announce, to give★ out, to report, to signify. 2 (*leg.*) (*un verdetto, ecc.*) to hand down. 3 (*pubbl.*) (*un prodotto nuovo*) to advertise. // ~ (*qc.*) **con cartelloni** (*pubbl.*) to placard; ~ **il pagamento d'un tagliando** (*fin.*) to announce the payment of a coupon.

annunciatore, *n. m.* announcer.

annuncio, *n. m.* announcement, notice, report. // **un** ~ **di matrimonio** an announcement of marriage; **l'**~ **di una vendita** the advertisement of a sale; **annunci divisi per categorie** (*pubbl.*) classified advertisements; ~ **giudiziario** (*leg.*) advertisement required by law; ~ **personale** (*nella «piccola pubblicità»*) (*giorn., pubbl.*) personal advertisement; ~ **pubblicitario** (*pubbl.*) advertisement, advertizement, ad; advert, plug (*slang USA*); (*richiesta od offerta di lavoro*) want ad; **annunci pubblicitari divisi in rubriche** (*giorn., pubbl.*) classified advertisements; ~ **pubblicitario riguardante la ricerca di personale o l'offerta di lavoro** (*pubbl.*) certified advertisement; **un** ~ **pubblicitario su tutta una pagina** (*pubbl.*) a full-page advertisement; **un** ~ **pubblicitario vistoso** (*pubbl.*) an eye-catching ad.

annunziare, *v. t. V.* **annunciare.**

annunziatore, *n. m. V.* **annunciatore.**

annunzio, *n. m. V.* **annuncio.**

annuo, *a.* annual, yearly.

antagonismo, *n. m.* 1 antagonism. 2 (*rivalità*) rivarly. 3 (*resistenza*) counteraction.

antagonista, *n. m.* e *f.* 1 antagonist, opponent. 2 (*rivale*) rival.

antagonistico, *a.* antagonistic.

antecedente, *a.* previous.

anti-, *pref.* anti-. // «~ **-dumping**» (*econ.*) anti-dumping, antidumping; «~ **-trust**» (*econ.*) anti-trust, antitrust.

anticipare, *v. t.* 1 to anticipate. 2 (*banca, cred.*) to advance. // ~ **la spedizione della merce** to send goods in advance; «**pagamento anticipato**» (*market.*) payment in advance.

anticipatamente, *avv.* beforehand, in advance.

anticipazione, *n. f.* 1 (*banca, cred.*) advance. 2 (*cred.*) (*prestito*) imprest, loan. // ~ **allo scoperto** (*banca*) uncovered advance; **anticipazioni allo scoperto** (*cred.*) unsecured advances; ~ **su garanzia** (*banca*) advance against security, secured advance; ~ **su merci** (*cred.*) goods loan.

anticipo, *n. m.* 1 anticipation. 2 (*pagamento anticipato*) payment in advance, instalment. 3 (*banca, cred.*) advance. 4 (*comm. est., fin.*) (*di pagamento*) lead. // **anticipi allo scoperto** (*cred.*) unsecured advances; **l'**~ **d'un pagamento** the anticipation of a payment; **anticipi e dilazioni** (*comm. est., econ., fin.*) leads and lags; **un** ~ **in contanti** a cash advance; ~ **in conto corrente** (*banca*) advance on current account; ~ **in conto prestito** (*banca*) advance on loan account; **in** ~ in advance, beforehand.

anticoncorrenziale, *a.* (*econ.*) anti-competitive.

anticongiunturale, *a.* (*econ.*) counter-cyclical, antislump. // **una misura** ~ an antislump measure.

antidata, *n. f.* 1 antedate. 2 (*l'antidatare*) antedating.

antidatare, *v. t.* to antedate, to foredate, to predate. // ~ **un contratto** (*leg.*) to antedate a contract.

antieconomico, *a.* (*econ.*) uneconomic, uneconomical.

antimonopolistico, *a.* (*econ.*) anti-trust.

antinflazionistico, *a.* (*econ.*) anti-inflationary.

antinfortunistica, *n. f.* (*pers.*) accident prevention.

antiquato, *a.* **1** obsolete, out-of-date. **2** (*market.*) out-of-date, outdated. **3** (*org. az.*) (*di macchinario*) superannuated.

antiscalo, *n. m.* (*trasp. mar.*) ways-end.

anzianità, *n. f.* **1** (*vecchiaia*) old age. **2** (*pers.*) *V.* ~ **di servizio.** // ~ **di servizio** (*pers.*) length of service.

anziano, *a.* **1** elderly; (*vecchio*) old. **2** (*pers.*) senior. *n. m.* (*pers.*) senior. // **più** ~ senior, major.

aperto, *a.* open. // ~ **a tutti** free-for-all; ~ **al(la vista del) pubblico** (*market.*) in view, on view; **all'** ~ in the open; out of doors.

apertura, *n. f.* opening. // ~ **di credito** (*banca, cred.*) opening of credit, credit opening, cash-credit; ~ **di credito autorizzata** (*cred.*) confirmed opening of credit, confirmed credit; ~ **d'udienza** (*leg.*) opening.

appaltare, *v. t.* **1** (*leg.*) (*dare in appalto*) to let* out (on contract), to farm out; to auction off (*USA*). **2** (*leg.*) (*prendere in appalto*) to undertake* on contract. // ~ **l'esazione d'un'imposta** (*leg.*) to farm a tax.

appaltatore, *n. m.* **1** (*leg.*) contractor, farmer, undertaker. **2** (*leg.*) (*specialm. di lavori o servizi pubblici*) franchise holder, franchisee. // **l'** ~ **dell'esazione d'una imposta** (*leg.*) the farmer of a tax; ~ **di pubblicità** (*pubbl.*) advertising contractor; ~ **libero** (*nella scelta dei mezzi e dei metodi di lavorazione*) independent contractor.

appalto, *n. m.* **1** (*leg.*) contract. **2** (*leg.*) (*specialm. di lavori o servizi pubblici*) franchise. // **un** ~ **per un servizio d'autobus** (*trasp.*) a franchise for a bus service; **appalti pubblici di forniture** (*econ.*) public-supply contracts.

apparato, *n. m.* apparatus, machinery. // ~ **amministrativo** bureaucracy; **l'** ~ **della distribuzione** (*market.*) the distribution machinery; ~ **di ricerca** (*market.*) research facilities; ~ **produttivo** (*econ., org. az.*) production machinery.

apparecchiatura, *n. f.* **1** equipment. **2 apparecchiature,** *pl.* fittings. // **apparecchiature e impianti** (*rag.*) fittings and fixtures.

apparecchio, *n. m.* **1** (*comm.*) set. **2** (*org. az.*) implement. **3** (*trasp. aer.*) plane. // ~ **di salvataggio** (*trasp. mar.*) salvage apparatus; ~ **fotostatico** (*macch. uff.*) photostat; ~ **radio** radio set, radio, wireless set; **apparecchi sanitari** sanitary ware.

apparente, *a.* **1** apparent. **2** (*leg.*) apparent.

apparentemente, *avv.* apparently.

apparenza, *n. f.* appearance.

apparire, *v. t.* to appear. // **che sta per** ~ (*di pubblicazione*) forthcoming.

apparizione, *n. f.* appearance.

appartenenza, *n. f.* **1** belonging. **2** (*fin.*) (*a una società, ecc.*) membership. **3** (*sind.*) (*a un sindacato*) membership.

appartenere, *v. i.* to belong.

appellabile, *a.* (*leg.*) appealable.

appellabilità, *n. f.* (*leg.*) appealability.

appellante, *n. m.* e *f.* (*leg.*) appellant.

appellare, *v. t.* (*chiamare*) to call, to style. *v. i.* (*leg.*) *V.* **appellarsi.**

appellarsi, *v. rifl.* (*leg.*) to appeal. // ~ **all'autorità giudiziaria superiore** to appeal to a higher Court; ~ **contro una sentenza** to appeal against a judgement.

appellativo, *n. m.* **1** style. **2** (*nella corrispondenza, nei moduli, ecc.*) title (Mr, Mrs, Miss, Ms: *premesso a un cognome o a un nome e cognome*).

appellato, *n. m.* (*leg.*) appellee.

appello, *n. m.* **1** (*nominale*) roll-call. **2** (*leg.*) appeal. // **l'** ~ **contro una sentenza** an appeal from a decision.

appianare, *v. t.* **1** to level. **2** (*leg.*) (*una vertenza*) to judge. // ~ **divergenze** to make up differences; ~ **una lite** (*leg.*) to settle a dispute.

appiattimento, *n. m.* (*di prezzi, salari, ecc.*) flattening (out), levelling (out, down).

appiattire, *v. t.* (*prezzi, salari, ecc.*) to flatten, to flatten out, to level (out, down).

appiattirsi, *v. rifl.* (*di prezzi, salari, ecc.*) to flatten, to flatten out, to level (out, down).

appigionare, *v. t.* (*leg.*) to let*. // ~ **un ufficio per 5 anni** to let an office for 5 years.

appigionarsi, *v. rifl.* (*leg.*) to let*. // **«appigionasi»** (*avviso*) «house to let».

applicabile, *a.* **1** applicable. **2** (*fin.*) assessable. **3** (*leg.*) enforceable.

applicabilità, *n. f.* **1** applicability. **2** (*leg.*) enforceability.

applicare, *v. t.* **1** to apply. **2** (*fin.*) (*un'imposta, una multa, ecc.*) to assess. **3** (*leg.*) (*una legge*) to enforce. // ~ **un francobollo a una lettera** to imprint a postmark on a letter; ~ **in modo uniforme** (*tasse, regolamenti, ecc.*) (*fin.*) to blanket; ~ **una legge** (*leg.*) to enforce a law;

~ **le norme della surrogazione a** (*q.*) (*leg.*) to subrogate; ~ **il regolamento a un caso nuovo** to apply the rules to a new case; ~ **una soprattassa a** (*q. o qc.*) (*fin.*) to surcharge; **essere applicato** (*di regolamento e sim.*) to come into operation.

applicarsi, *v. rifl.* 1 to apply oneself. 2 (*riferirsi*) to apply.

applicazione, *n. f.* 1 application. 2 (*Borsa*) crossing. 3 (*leg.*) enforcement. // **l'~ d'un trattato** (*leg.*) the application (*o* the implementation) of a treaty; **in ~ di** (*leg.*) in pursuance of.

appoggiare, *v. t.* e *i.* 1 to rest. 2 (*sostenere*) to back (up), to support. 3 (*favorire, promuovere*) to forward, to further. 4 (*incoraggiare, assecondare*) to buoy (up), to second. 5 (*prendere le parti di*) to side with. 6 (*leg.*) to sustain. // ~ **una causa** to support a cause, to further a cause; ~ **una nave presso i raccomandatari d'un noleggiatore** (*trasp. mar.*) to consign a ship to the charterer's agents; ~ **una rivendicazione** (*leg.*) to sustain a claim.

appoggio, *n. m.* 1 backing, support. 2 (*aiuto*) assistance, help. 3 (*persona o cosa su cui contare*) stand-by. 4 (*trasp. aer.*) (*del carrello*) touch-down.

apporre, *v. t.* 1 to affix, to append, to put★. 2 (*un francobollo e sim.*) to imprint. // ~ **il cartellino (del prezzo) su** (*articoli, ecc.*) (*market.*) to ticket; ~ **la firma** to append one's signature; ~ **la (propria) firma a un documento** to put one's signature on a document, to affix one's signature to a document, to set one's signature to a paper; ~ **le iniziali a qc.** to initial st.; ~ **un marchio di fabbrica su** (*un articolo, ecc.*) (*leg.*) to trade-mark; ~ **i sigilli a un documento** (*leg.*) to seal a document.

apportare, *v. t.* 1 to bring★ in, to bring★ into, to contribute. 2 (*fare*) to make★. // ~ **capitale** to bring in (*o* to contribute) capital; ~ **una modifica** (*org. az.*) to make an alteration; ~ **«tagli» al bilancio** (*econ., fin.*) to trim the budget; (*più drasticamente*) to slash the budget.

apporto, *n. m.* 1 contribution. 2 (*fin.*) (*dato a un'azienda*) assets brought in. // ~ **a un'azienda** (*fin.*) assets brought into a business, assets transferred to a company; ~ **di capitale** (*fin.*) contribution of capital; ~ **di capitali** (*econ.*) inflow of capital.

apposizione, *n. f.* (*l'apporre*) affixing, appending. // **l'~ dei sigilli a un documento legale** the affixing of seals to a legal document.

apprendere, *v. t.* 1 (*imparare*) to learn★. 2 (*una notizia*) to hear★, to learn★, to understand★.

apprendista, *n. m.* e *f.* 1 (*chi apprende*) learner, improver. 2 (*pers.*) apprentice.

apprendistato, *n. m.* (*pers.*) apprenticeship. // **(contratto di) ~** articles (of apprenticeship).

apprezzabile, *a.* appreciable.

apprezzamento, *n. m.* 1 (*riconoscimento del valore*) appreciation. 2 (*stima*) esteem. 3 (*valutazione*) rating, valuation.

apprezzare, *v. t.* 1 to appreciate, to value. 2 (*stimare*) to esteem. 3 (*valutare il prezzo*) to rate, to value.

apprezzato, *a.* esteemed, valued. // **essere ~** to meet with appreciation.

approccio, *n. m.* approach.

approdare, *v. i.* (*trasp. mar.*) to go★ ashore, to land.

approdo, *n. m.* 1 (*trasp. mar.*) (*l'approdare*) landing. 2 (*trasp. mar.*) (*il luogo*) landing-place.

approfittare, *v. i.* to profit (by); to avail oneself, to take★ advantage (of).

approfondire, *v. t.* (*fig.*) to go★ into. // ~ **l'esame delle prove** (*leg.*) to go into the evidence.

appropriarsi, *v. rifl.* 1 to take★ possession (of st.). 2 (*intascare*) to pocket. 3 (*leg.*) to appropriate. // ~ **d'una somma di denaro** (*leg.*) to appropriate a sum of money (to oneself); ~ **indebitamente di** (*denaro altrui*) (*leg.*) to misappropriate; (*denaro o altri beni*) to embezzle; (*denaro, specialm. pubblico*) to peculate.

appropriazione, *n. f.* (*leg.*) appropriation. // **l'~ d'oggetti smarriti** (*leg.*) the appropriation of lost property; ~ **indebita** (*leg.*) conversion, defalcation, embezzlement, misappropriation, peculation (*V.* **appropriarsi**).

approssimativamente, *avv.* approximately.

approssimativo, *a.* 1 approximate, rough, rough and ready. 2 (*Borsa*) (*di prezzo*) about (*attr.*).

approssimato, *a.* approximate.

approssimazione, *n. f.* approximation.

approvare, *v. t.* 1 to approve, to approve of, to confirm, to endorse. 2 (*sancire*) to sanction. 3 (*leg.*) to carry. 4 (*leg.*) (*un disegno di legge, ecc.*) to pass. // ~ **un accordo** to subscribe to an agreement; ~ **un bilancio** to adopt a balance; ~ **una deliberazione** (*leg.*) to pass a resolution; ~ **un disegno di legge** (*leg.*) to vote a bill through; ~ **una proposta** to approve a proposal; ~ **lo statuto societario** (*fin.*) to pass the articles of association; ~ (*una mozione e sim.*) **votando** to vote; **essere approvato** (*leg.*) (*di disegno di legge, ecc.*) to pass; **essere approvato da q.** to meet with sb.'s approval.

approvazione, *n. f.* 1 approval, approbation, confirmation, endorsement. 2 (*assenso*) assent. 3 (*leg.*) fiat. 4 (*leg.*) (*sanzione*) sanction. 5 (*leg.*) (*di una legge, ecc.*) carrying. 6 (*leg.*) (*di un disegno di legge, ecc.*) passage. // **l'~ del verbale dell'adunanza** the adoption of the report of the meeting; **salvo ~ da parte nostra** subject to our approval.

approvvigionamento, *n. m.* 1 (*fornitura*) supply. 2 (*di viveri*) victualling. 3 (*org. az.*) purchase, industrial purchasing. 4 (*org. az.*) (*di materie prime, ecc.*) procurement. 5 **approvvigionamenti,** *pl.* (*provviste*) supplies; provisions. // **~ idrico** (*org. az.*) water supply.

approvvigionare, *v. t.* 1 to provision, to supply. 2 (*di viveri*) to victual. 3 (*org. az.*) to stock. // **~ all'eccesso** (*market., org. az.*) to overstock; **~** (*un negozio, uno stabilimento, ecc.*) **d'una quantità insufficiente di merce** (*market., org. az.*) to understock; **~ una nave** (*trasp. mar.*) to provision a ship.

approvvigionarsi, *v. rifl.* 1 to lay★ in supplies. 2 (*org. az.*) (*di materie prime, ecc.*) to procure. 3 (*trasp. mar.*) (*di nave*) to victual.

approvvigionatore, *n. m.* 1 (*fornitore*) supplier. 2 (*di viveri*) victualler.

appuntamento, *n. m.* appointment.

appunto, *n. m.* 1 note. 2 (*promemoria*) memorandum★; memo (*fam.*).

aprire, *v. t.* e *i.* to open, to open up. // **~ alla pari** (*Borsa*) (*di titoli, ecc.*) to open at par; **~ i battenti** to open; **~ bottega** (*market.*) to start a shop, to set up shop; **~ un conto con q.** to open an account with sb.; **~ un conto in banca** (*cred.*) to open an account at the bank; **~ un credito presso una banca** (*banca, cred.*) to open a credit with a bank; **~ una seduta** to open a meeting; **~ la strada** (*a negoziati, ecc.*) (*fig.*) to open the door; **~ uno studio legale** to open a law practice.

aprirsi, *v. rifl.* to open.

ara, *n. f.* (*misura di superficie*) are.

arbitraggio, *n. m.* 1 (*Borsa*) arbitrage, arbitraging, arbitration of exchange. 2 (*fin.*) (*di portafoglio*) change of investments. 3 (*leg., sind.*) umpirage, arbitration. // **~ a termine** (*Borsa*) heading for the settlement; **~ composto** (*Borsa, fin.*) compound arbitrage; **~ coperto** (*Borsa, fin.*) covered arbitrage; **~ dei riporti** (*Borsa*) jobbing in contangoes; **~ diretto** (*fin.*) direct arbitrage; **~ indiretto** (*fin.*) indirect (*o* compound) arbitrage; **~ scoperto** (*Borsa, fin.*) uncovered arbitrage; **~ semplice** (*Borsa, fin.*) simple arbitrage; **~ su titoli** (*fin.*) stock arbitrage.

arbitrale, *a.* arbitral; arbitration (*attr.*).

arbitramento, *n. m.* (*leg., sind.*) umpirage, arbitration.

arbitrare, *v. t.* 1 to arbitrate. 2 (*leg.*) (*una lite, ecc.*) to referee. 3 (*leg., sind.*) to umpire. *v. i.* (*fin.*) to change investments.

arbitrariamente, *avv.* arbitrarily.

arbitrario, *a.* arbitrary, unauthorized.

arbitrato, *n. m.* (*leg., sind.*) arbitration, umpirage. // **~ coercitivo** (*leg.*) compulsory arbitration; **~ forzato** (*imposto dalla legge*) (*leg., sind.*) compulsory arbitration; **~ internazionale** (*comm. est.*) international arbitration; **~ obbligatorio** (*imposto dalla legge*) (*leg., sind.*) compulsory arbitration.

arbitratore, *n. m.* (*leg., sind.*) umpire.

arbitro, *n. m.* 1 arbiter. 2 (*leg.*) (*d'una lite*) referee. 3 (*leg., sind.*) arbitrator, umpire. 4 (*sind.*) conciliator. // **~ (amichevole) compositore** (*leg.*) friendly arbitrator; **~ unico** umpire.

archiviare, *v. t.* 1 to file. 2 (*leg.*) to record. // **~ una pratica** (*leg.*) to take no further action on a matter; **~ un processo** (*leg.*) to dismiss a case.

archiviazione, *n. f.* 1 filing. 2 (*org. az.*) records detention. // **l'~ d'una causa** (*leg.*) the dismissal of a case.

archivio, *n. m.* 1 (*attr. uff.*) file; files (*pl.*). 2 (*leg.*) records (*pl.*). 3 (*org. az.*) records centre. // **~ centralizzato** (*org. az.*) centralized files; **~ degli arretrati** (*attr. uff.*) back file; **~ delle fatture** (*org. az.*) bill file; **~ di Stato** archives (*pl.*); Records Office; **~ verticale** (*attr. uff.*) vertical file.

archivista, *n. m.* e *f.* 1 archivist. 2 (*amm.*) registrar. 3 (*leg.*) recorder. 4 (*pers.*) filing clerk.

area, *n. f.* 1 area, zone. 2 (*di terreno edificabile, ecc.*) plot, lot. // **~ commerciale** (*market.*) consumer trading area; **l'~ del dollaro** (*econ., fin.*) the dollar area; **l'~ della sterlina** (*econ., fin.*) the sterling area, the sterling bloc; **~ depressa** (*da sviluppare*) (*econ.*) development area; **~ di controllo** (*org. az.*) area of control, control area; **~ di parcheggio** (*trasp. aut.*) parking lot; **~ di posteggio** (*per uno stand, in una fiera campionaria*) (*market.*) stand space; **~ di sviluppo** (*econ.*) development area, growth area; **~ disastrata** (*econ.*) distressed area; **~ fabbricabile** building lot; building plot; building site; **~ marittima** (*trasp. mar.*) sea area; **~ metropolitana** (*econ.*) metropolitan area; **~ monetaria** (*fin.*) monetary area; **~ suburbana di empori e negozi** (*market.*) shopping centre; **fuori dell'« ~ del dollaro »** (*econ.*) (*di nazione, ecc.*) non-dollar (*attr.*).

arenamento, *n. m.* (*trasp. mar.*) stranding, beaching. // **~ accidentale** (*ass. mar., trasp.

mar.) accidental stranding; ~ **volontario per evitare il naufragio** (*ass. mar.*) voluntary stranding to avoid wreck.

arenare, *v. t.* (*trasp. mar.*) to strand, to beach, to run* aground, to run* ashore.

arenarsi, *v. rifl.* (*trasp. mar.*) (*di nave*) to strand, to beach, to ground, to run* aground, to run* ashore.

argento, *n. m.* silver. // ~ **monetabile** (*econ.*) silver bullion; ~ **puro** (*925 parti d'argento e 75 di rame*) sterling silver.

argomento, *n. m.* **1** argument. **2** (*materia, oggetto*) matter, subject-matter, object, subject, topic. // ~ **di difesa** (*leg.*) plea; ~ **discusso in una «tavola rotonda»** (*fin., market.*) round table; **un** ~ **irrefutabile** an unanswerable argument.

aria, *n. f.* **1** (*anche fig.*) air. **2** (*fig.*) (*sensazione*) feeling.

aridi, *n. pl.* (*trasp. mar.*) dry goods.

armadietto, *n. m.* (*attr. uff.*) cabinet. // ~ **per libri** (*attr. uff.*) bookcase.

armamento, *n. m.* **1** (*trasp. mar.*) equipment, fitting-out, rigging, rig. **2** (*trasp. mar.*) (*industria dell'armamento*) shipping industry (*o* trade).

armare, *v. t.* **1** (*trasp. mar.*) (*una nave*) to equip, to fit out, to rig. **2** (*trasp. mar.*) (*equipaggiare*) to man. // ~ **ed equipaggiare una nave** (*trasp. mar.*) to man, equip and supply a ship.

armatore, *n. m.* (*trasp. mar.*) shipowner.

armonizzazione, *n. f.* harmonization. // ~ **cromatica** (*pubbl.*) colour matching; ~ **fiscale** (*fin.*) tax harmonization.

arnese, *n. m.* **1** tool, implement. **2 arnesi,** *pl.* (*org. az.*) tackle.

arra, *n. f.* (*leg.*) gage.

arredamento, *n. m.* (*market.*) furnishing. // ~ **d'ufficio** office appliances.

arredare, *v. t.* (*market.*) to furnish.

arrestare, *v. t.* **1** to halt, to stop. **2** (*anche leg.*) to arrest. **3** (*leg.*) to capture.

arrestarsi, *v. rifl.* to halt, to stop.

arresto, *n. m.* **1** halt, stop, stoppage, stopping, standstill, stand. **2** (*cessazione*) cessation. **3** (*elab. elettr.*) halt, shut-down. **4** (*anche leg.*) arrest. **5** (*leg.*) capture, arrestment; caption (*scozz.*). // ~ **del traffico** (*trasp.*) tie-up; ~ **delle maiuscole** (*di macchina da scrivere*) shift-lock.

arretrati, *n. pl.* **1** arrears, arrearages. **2** (*pers.*) (*del salario, dello stipendio*) back pay, retroactive pay. // ~ **dei pagamenti** arrears in payments; ~ **di corrispondenza** arrears of correspondence; ~ **d'imposte** (*leg.*) delinquent taxes; ~ **di salario** arrears of wages.

arretrato, *a.* **1** back, outstanding. **2** (*di Paese, ecc.*) backward. **3** (*cred.*) outstanding, owing. *n. m.* (*di lavoro o affari*) backlog. // **in** ~ (*di persona*) in arrears, behind, behindhand; (*di cosa*) in arrears, outstanding; **essere in** ~ **coi pagamenti** (*cred.*) to be short in one's payments.

arricchimento, *n. m.* enrichment. // ~ **illecito** (*leg.*) unjust enrichment.

arricchire, *v. t.* to enrich. *v. i.* to get* rich. // ~ **alla svelta** to get rich quickly; to coin money (*fig.*).

arringa, *n. f.* (*leg.*) pleading.

arrivare, *v. i.* **1** to arrive (*anche fig.*); to come*, to get* in. **2** (*fig.*) to pour in. // ~ **in buone condizioni** (*di merce*) to arrive safely; ~ **in un porto** (*o* **in porto**) to arrive at a port (*o* in harbour); ~ **sano e salvo** (*di persona*) to arrive safely.

arrivismo, *n. m.* careerism.

arrivista, *n. m.* e *f.* careerist, social climber.

arrivo, *n. m.* **1** arrival. **2 arrivi,** *pl.* (*tur.*) arrivals. **3 arrivi,** *pl.* (*tur.*) (*in un albergo*) check-ins. // ~ **in buono stato** (*trasp.*) (*di merci, ecc.*) safe arrival; **all'**~ (*trasp.*) on arrival; **in** ~ incoming; (*trasp.*) due; «**salvo** ~» (*market., trasp. mar.*) «to arrive».

arrotondamento, *n. m.* (*mat.*) rounding.

arrotondare, *v. t.* (*anche mat.*) to round. // ~ **una cifra** to round a figure; ~ **lo stipendio** (*o* **il salario**) (*fig.*) to supplement one's income.

arruolare, *v. t.* (*trasp. mar.*) to sign on.

arruolarsi, *v. rifl.* (*trasp. mar.*) to sign on.

arsenale, *n. m.* (*trasp. mar.*) dockyard, shipyard; docks (*pl.*). // ~ **marittimo** (*trasp. mar.*) navy yard.

arte, *n. f.* art, craft, craftsmanship. // ~ **del disporre la merce in vetrina** (*market.*) window-dressing; ~ **del navigare** (*trasp. mar.*) sailing; ~ **del vendere** (*market.*) salesmanship; ~ **del vetrinista** (*market.*) window-dressing.

articolista, *n. m.* e *f.* (*giorn.*) columnist; editorial writer (*USA*).

articolo, *n. m.* **1** (*in genere*) article. **2** (*merce*) commodity. **3** (*comm., rag.*) (*d'elenco, bilancio, ecc.*) item, entry. **4** (*leg.*) article, clause. **5 articoli,** *pl.* (*market.*) line, ware. // ~ **accettato** (*dal venditore*) **in pagamento** (*parziale o totale*) **d'un acquisto** trade-in; ~ **che si vende bene** checkout; wrap-up (*slang USA*); ~ **che si vende con difficoltà** (*o* **con lentezza**) (*market.*) sleeper; ~ **che va moltissimo** (*market.*) big thing; ~ **civetta** (*market.*) loss leader; ~ **composto** (*rag.*) combined entry; **un** ~ **confezionato male** a badly made article; ~ **dato in omaggio** (*market.*) premium; ~ **dato in regalo** (*market.*)

giveaway; **un ~ della Costituzione** (*leg.*) an article of the Constitution; **articoli di cancelleria** (*attr. uff.*) stationery; **articoli di consumo corrente** (*market.*) articles of everyday consumption; **~ d'esportazione di prim'ordine** (*comm. est.*) export winner; **articoli di ferro** (*market.*) hardware; **~ di fondo** (*giorn.*) leading article, leader, lead; **articoli di gres** (*market.*) stoneware; **articoli di lana** (*market.*) woolens; **articoli di largo consumo** (*market.*) consumer goods; **~ articoli di lusso** (*market.*) luxury articles; **articoli di marca** (*market.*) branded goods; **articoli di poco prezzo** (*market.*) jumble (*ingl.*); **un ~ di prima qualità** (*market.*) a first-rate article; **~ di qualità scadente** abortion (*slang USA*); **~ di valore offerto a un prezzo conveniente** (*per dare impulso alle vendite*) (*market.*) leader; **articoli di vestiario** (*market.*) articles of clothing; **articoli di vetro** (*market.*) glassware; **articoli difettosi** (*market.*) faulty articles; **articoli diversi** (*market.*) sundries; **articoli in esclusiva** (*market.*) proprietary articles; **articoli in metallo** (*market.*) metalware; **~ in omaggio** (*market.*) giveaway; **~ non soggetto a obsolescenza** (*market.*) evergreen; **articoli per la casa** (*market.*) furnishings (*USA*); **articoli pesantemente tassati** (*dog., fin.*) high-duty articles; **~ poco richiesto** (*market.*) drug in the market; **~ preso in consegna da un vettore** (*per essere spedito*) (*trasp.*) pick-up; **articoli spaiati** (*market.*) rummage; jumble (*ingl.*); **articoli tassati moderatamente** (*dog., fin.*) low-duty articles; **~ usato per una dimostrazione** (*pubbl.*) demonstrator; **articoli vari** (*market.*) fancy goods; **~ venduto in perdita** (*per attirare i clienti*) (*market.*) loss leader.

artificiale, *a.* 1 artificial. 2 (*market.*) (*del cuoio, ecc.*) imitation (*attr.*).

artificio, *n. m.* 1 (*espediente*) contrivance. 2 (*leg.*) device.

artigianato, *n. m.* 1 handicraft. 2 (*abilità d'artigiano*) craftsmanship.

artigiano, *n. m.* artisan, craftsman★, handicraftsman★.

artista, *n. m.* 1 artist. 2 (*artigiano*) craftsman★.

ascendente, *a.* 1 ascending; up (*attr.*). 2 (*ammontante*) amounting. *n. m.* ascendance, ascendancy, influence.

ascendere, *v. i.* 1 to ascend, to rise★. 2 (*ammontare*) to amount.

ascesa, *n. f.* 1 ascent, rise. 2 (*fin., market.*) rise. // **in ~** on the up grade.

ascoltare, *v. t.* 1 to listen (to sb., to st.). 2 (*leg.*) to hear★. // **~ le testimonianze** (*leg.*) to hear the evidence.

ascoltatore, *n. m.* 1 listener. 2 **ascoltatori,** *pl.* (*uditorio*) audience (*sing.*). // **ascoltatori potenziali** (*pubbl.*) available audience.

ascolto, *n. m.* (*leg.*) hearing.

ascrivere, *v. t.* 1 to ascribe; (*qc. di brutto*) to charge. 2 (*rag.*) to impute.

ascrivibile, *a.* 1 ascribable; chargeable. 2 (*rag.*) imputable.

aspettare, *v. t.* 1 to wait, to await. 2 (*aspettarsi*) to expect. // **~ un miglioramento del mercato dei titoli** (*fin.*) to wait out the stock market.

aspettativa, *n. f.* 1 anticipation, expectation, prospect. 2 (*pers.*) (*congedo temporaneo*) leave. // **~ a breve termine** (*econ.*) short-term expectation; **~ a lungo termine** (*econ.*) long-term expectation.

aspetto, *n. m.* 1 aspect, appearance. 2 (*figura*) figure. 3 (*portamento*) bearing. // **gli aspetti d'un problema** (*org. az.*) the faces of a problem.

aspirante, *a.* 1 aspiring. 2 (*che si presenta candidato*) acceding. *n. m.* e *f.* applicant, candidate. // **un ~ a una nomina** a candidate for an appointment.

aspro, *a.* 1 harsh, rough. 2 (*di concorrenza e sim.*) keen; cut-throat.

assaltare, *v. t.* 1 to assault. 2 (*rapinare*) to hold★ up. // **~ una banca** to hold up a bank.

assalto, *n. m.* 1 (*banca, fin., market., fig.*) run. 2 (*leg.*) assault. 3 (*leg.*) (*rapina*) hold-up.

asse, *n. m.* (*mat.*) axis★. // **~ di comunicazione** (*trasp.*) communication axis; **~ ereditario** (*leg.*) heritage; estate left by the deceased; **~ patrimoniale** (*leg.*) estate.

assegnabile, *a.* 1 assignable. 2 allottable. 3 awardable (*V.* **assegnare**).

assegnamento, *n. m.* 1 assignment. 2 (*attribuzione*) allotment, allowance. 3 (*aggiudicazione*) award. 4 (*affidamento, fiducia*) reliance (*V. anche* **assegnare**).

assegnare, *v. t.* 1 to assign. 2 (*attribuire*) to allot, to allow. 3 (*aggiudicare*) to award. 4 (*dare*) to give★. 5 (*dotare*) to endow. 6 (*ripartire*) to apportion, to portion out. 7 (*fin.*) (*destinare fondi, ecc.*) to direct. 8 (*fin., rag.*) to allocate, to appropriate. 9 (*leg.*) (*beni, diritti, proprietà*) to grant, to vest. 10 (*leg.*) (*un contratto*) to let★. // **~ a una classe** to class; **~ compiti a un impiegato** (*anche*) to allocate duties to a clerk; **~ un compito a q.** to task sb.; **~ una pensione** to assign a pension; **~ una pensione a q.** to pension sb.; **~ tutte le azioni sottoscritte** to allot the shares in full; **non assegnato** (*fin.*) (*di fondo*) unappropriated.

assegnatario, *n. m.* (*leg.*) assignee, allottee,

grantee.

assegnazione, *n. f.* 1 (*di persone, a un lavoro, ecc.*) assignment. 2 (*attribuzione*) allotment, allowance. 3 (*aggiudicazione*) award. 4 (*dotazione*) endowment. 5 (*ripartizione*) apportionment. 6 (*fin., rag.*) allocation, appropriation. 7 (*leg.*) (*di beni, diritti, proprietà*) grant. 8 (*org. az., pers.*) (*del lavoro*) allocation. // ~ **degli incarichi** (*org. az.*) task setting; ~ **di fondi** (*banca, fin.*) funding; ~ **di quote** (*econ., fin.*) allocation of quotas; ~ **di tutte le azioni sottoscritte** (*fin.*) allotment in full; ~ **testamentaria** (*leg.*) devise.

assegno, *n. m.* 1 (*banca, cred.*) cheque; check (*USA*). 2 (*pers.*) allowance. // ~ **a vuoto** (*banca, cred.*) dishonoured check; bad cheque, bouncing cheque; dud cheque (*fam.*); ~ **al portatore** (*banca, cred.*) cheque to bearer, bearer cheque; bearer check (*USA*); ~ **all'ordine** (*banca, cred.*) cheque to order; ~ **annuale** annuity; ~ **bancario** (*banca, cred.*) cheque, bank cheque; check, bank check (*USA*); ~ **bancario all'ordine** (*banca, cred.*) order cheque; **un ~ bancario non sbarrato e senza girate** (*banca, cred.*) an open cheque; ~ **«cabriolet»** (*fam.*) kite; flash check (*USA*); ~ **circolare** (*banca, cred.*) «assegno circolare» (*nell'uso, ma non nella forma, corrisponde all'ingl. «bank draft» o «banker's draft»*); circular note; cashier's check (*USA*); ~ **con annesso talloncino di versamento** (*banca, cred.*) cheque with receipt form attached; ~ **con annotazione degli estremi della fattura** (*banca, cred.*) voucher cheque; ~ **con sbarratura generale** (*banca, cred.*) cheque crossed generally; ~ **con sbarratura qualificata** (*banca, cred.*) cheque crossed specially; **assegni d'invalidità** (*pers.*) disability benefits; ~ **d'invalidità (o di malattia)** (*pers.*) injury benefit; ~ **dono in tagli fissi** (*venduto dagli uffici postali*) (*fin., ingl.*) gift token; ~ **falso** stumer (*fam., ingl.*); stiff (*slang USA*); **assegni familiari** (*pers.*) family allotment cheques; family allowance (*sing.*); child bounty (*fam.*); ~ **in bianco** (*banca, cred.*) blank cheque; **assegni in circolazione** (*cred.*) outstanding cheques; **un ~ non girato** (*banca, cred.*) an unendorsed cheque, an unindorsed cheque; ~ **paga** (*pers.*) paycheck (*USA*); ~ **per accreditamento** (*banca, cred.*) cheque to be credited (to sb.'s account); ~ **per morte** (*di un lavoratore assistito*) (*pers.*) death grant; ~ **sbarrato** (*banca, cred.*) crossed cheque, «for deposit only» cheque; ~ **sbarrato con la dicitura «non negoziabile»** (*banca, cred.*) cheque crossed «not negotiable»; ~ **scoperto** (*banca, cred.*) *V.* ~ **senza copertura;** ~ **senza copertura** (*banca, cred.*) uncovered cheque; non-sufficient funds cheque; kite (*fam.*); flash check (*fam., USA*); ~ **senza valore** stumer, stumour (*fam., ingl.*); ~ **turistico** (*cred.*) traveller's cheque; **un ~ vecchio** (*emesso da più di sei mesi e non ancora incassato*) (*banca, cred.*) a stale cheque; **assegni vistati** (*banca*) marked cheques; ~ **vitalizio** (*ass.*) straight life annuity; **contro ~** cash on delivery, collection on delivery.

assemblaggio, *n. m.* assembly. // ~ **selettivo** (*org. az.*) selective assembly.

assemblea, *n. f.* assembly, meeting; convention (*USA*). // **l'~ degli azionisti** (*fin.*) the meeting of shareholders, the shareholders' meeting; **l'~ dei creditori** (*leg.*) the meeting of creditors, the creditors' meeting; ~ **dei soci** (*d'una società per azioni*) (*fin.*) shareholders' meeting; **un' ~ elettiva** an elective assembly; ~ **generale** (*degli azionisti*) (*fin.*) general meeting; ~ **generale annuale** (*fin.*) annual general meeting; ~ **generale per l'approvazione dello statuto** (*d'una società anonima*) (*fin.*) statutory meeting; ~ **legislativa** (*leg.*) legislature; **un'~ ordinaria** (*fin.*) an ordinary meeting; ~ **plenaria** (*leg.*) plenum; **un'~ quindicinale** (*org. az.*) a fortnightly meeting; ~ **straordinaria** (*fin.*) extraordinary meeting; **un'~ trimestrale** a quarterly meeting.

assenteismo, *n. m.* (*econ., sind.*) absenteeism.

assenza, *n. f.* 1 absence. 2 (*leg.*) (*d'una delle due parti*) default. 3 (*leg.*) (*d'imputato o di teste*) non-appearance, non-attendance. // **assenze ingiustificate** (*pers.*) unexcused absences.

asserire, *v. t.* 1 to assert, to affirm, to claim, to say★, to state. 2 (*a discolpa*) to allege. // ~ **un diritto** to claim a right; ~ **la propria innocenza** to assert one's innocence; ~ **la verità** to affirm the truth.

asserzione, *n. f.* 1 assertion, affirmation, statement. 2 (*a discolpa*) allegation.

assettare, *v. t.* to trim. // ~ **il carico** (*trasp. mar.*) to trim the cargo; ~ **una nave** (*trasp. mar.*) to trim a ship.

assetto, *n. m.* (*trasp. mar.*) (*del carico*) trimming.

assicurabile, *a.* (*ass.*) insurable; assurable (*USA o sulla vita*).

assicurare, *v. t.* 1 (*dare assicurazioni*) to assure; to warrant. 2 (*procurare*) to assure, to ensure. 3 (*rendere sicuro, non farsi sfuggire*) to secure. 4 (*ass.*) to insure; to assure (*USA o, per lo più, sulla vita*). 5 (*ass.*) (*specialm. una nave*) to underwrite★. // ~ **una lettera** to insure a letter.

assicurarsi, *v. rifl.* 1 (*accertarsi*) to assure oneself, to make★ sure. 2 (*non farsi sfuggire*) to secure. 3 (*premunirsi*) to secure oneself. 4 (*ass.*) to insure (oneself). // ~ **un affare** to nail a bargain (*fam.*); ~ **contro un rischio** (*ass.*) to insure against a risk; ~ **sulla vita** (*ass.*) to insure one's life.

assicurativi, *n. pl.* (*fin.*) insurance stocks.

assicurato, *a.* 1 assured. 2 ensured. 3 secured. 4 (*ass.*) insured; assured (*USA o, per lo più, sulla vita*). 5 (*trasp.*) (*di bagaglio*) registered. *n. m.* 1 (*ass.*) insured; assured (*USA o, per lo più, sulla vita*); insurant. 2 (*ass.*) (*detentore di polizza*) policy-holder, policy-owner. // ~ **in solido** (*ass.*) coinsured; **non** ~ (*ass.*) uninsured; (*di rischio*) uncovered.

assicuratore, *n. m.* 1 (*ass.*) insurer; assurer (*specialm. USA*). 2 (*ass.*) (*specialm. marittimo*) underwriter. // ~ **del carico** (*ass. mar.*) cargo underwriter; **fare l'** ~ to sell insurance.

assicurazione, *n. f.* 1 assurance. 2 (*ass.*) insurance; assurance (*USA o, per lo più, sulla vita*). 3 (*ass.*) (*specialm. marittima*) underwriting. // ~ **all'esportazione** (*ass., comm. est.*) export insurance; ~ **automobilistica** (*o* **per autoveicoli**) (*ass.*) motor insurance; ~ **collettiva** (*ass.*) group insurance; ~ **con franchigia** (*ass. mar.*) excess insurance; ~ **contro i danni provocati dalla disonestà dei dipendenti** (*ass.*) fidelity insurance; ~ **contro la disoccupazione** (*ass., pers.*) unemployment insurance; ~ **contro i furti** (*ass.*) theft insurance; ~ **contro furto e scasso** (*ass.*) burglary insurance; ~ **contro la grandine** (*ass.*) hail insurance; ~ **contro l'incendio** (*ass.*) fire insurance, insurance against loss by fire; ~ **contro gli infortuni** (*ass.*) personal accident insurance; ~ (*stipulata dal datore di lavoro*) **contro gli infortuni sul lavoro** (*ass.*) employer's liability insurance; ~ **contro l'invalidità** (*ass., pers.*) disablement insurance; ~ **contro le malattie** (*ass., pers.*) health insurance; ~ **contro le malattie e gli infortuni sul lavoro** (*ass., pers.*) industrial accident and health insurance; ~ **contro rischi vari** (*ass.*) all risks (insurance); ~ **contro i sinistri** (*ass.*) casualty insurance; ~ **contro terzi** (*ass., trasp. aut.*) third-party insurance; ~ **contro la vecchiaia** (*ass., pers.*) old-age insurance; ~ **-crediti** (*ass.*) credit insurance; ~ **cumulativa** (*ass.*) double insurance; ~ (*della merce*) **da magazzino a magazzino** (*dal magazzino del venditore a quello del destinatario*) (*ass. mar.*) warehouse-to-warehouse insurance; ~ **dei crediti all'esportazione** (*ass., comm. est.*) export credit insurance; ~ **del vettore aereo per merci** (*ass.*) aircraft cargo insurance; ~ **del vettore aereo per passeggeri** (*ass.*) aircraft passenger insurance; ~ **del vettore marittimo** (*ass. mar.*) ocean cargo insurance; ~ **di responsabilità civile** (*ass.*) liability insurance, third-party insurance; (*per danni causati ai beni altrui*) property damage insurance; ~ **di vecchiaia e per i sopravvissuti** (*ass., pers.*) old-age and survivors insurance; ~ **diretta** (*ass.*) direct insurance; ~ **-fiera** (*ass.*) insurance for participation in overseas trade fairs; ~ **«in caso di vita»** (*ass.*) pure endowment insurance; ~ **infortuni** (*ass., pers.*) accident insurance, casualty insurance; ~ **marittima** (*ass. mar.*) maritime insurance, sea insurance; transportation insurance, sea assurance (*USA*); ~ **marittima sulle merci** (*ass. mar.*) cargo insurance; ~ **mista** (*ass.*) endowment insurance; ~ **per il bagaglio personale** (*ass.*) «luggage in transit» insurance; ~ **per i crediti inesigibili** (*ass.*) credit insurance; ~ **per malattie** (*ass., pers.*) sick-insurance; ~ **per titoli di proprietà viziati** (*ass.*) defective title insurance; ~ **per un valore insufficiente** (*a coprire i danni*) (*ass.*) underinsurance; ~ **per un valore superiore a quello di realizzo della cosa assicurata** (*ass.*) overinsurance; ~ **popolare** (*ass.*) group insurance; ~ **-prospezione** (*ass.*) insurance of advertising and promotional expenses; ~ **provvisoria** (*ass.*) provisional insurance; ~ **sociale** social insurance; ~ **su corpo e carico** (*ass. mar.*) insurance of hull and cargo; ~ **sui depositi bancari** (*contro perdite derivanti da fallimento, ecc.*) (*ass., banca*) bank guaranty; ~ **sul nolo** (*ass. mar.*) freight insurance; ~ **sul valore locativo** (*ass.*) rental-value insurance; ~ **sulla invalidità** (*ass., pers.*) disability insurance; ~ **sulla nave** (*ass. mar.*) hull insurance; ~ **sulla perdita totale e parziale** (*ass. mar.*) full-form insurance; ~ **sulla vita** (*ass.*) life insurance, life assurance; ~ **sull'incasso dei crediti** (*ass.*) accounts receivable insurance; ~ **sullo scafo** (*della nave*) (*ass. mar.*) hull insurance; ~ **«temporanea»** (*in caso di morte*) (*ass.*) term insurance; ~ **«vita intera»** (*ass.*) ordinary life insurance, straight life insurance, whole-life insurance; ~ **«vita intera a premi limitati»** (*ass.*) limited-payment life insurance.

assise, *n. f. inv.* (*leg.*) assizes (*pl.*). // **l'** ~ **di Londra** the Assize Court of London.

assistente, *n. m.* e *f.* (*pers.*) assistant. // ~ **dei clienti** (*chi li aiuta negli acquisti*) (*market., pers.*) personal shopper; ~ **del consigliere delegato** (*pers.*) assistant to the managing director; ~ **del personale** (*pers.*) staff assistant; ~ **di giudice** (*leg.*) master in chancery; ~ **di volo** (*trasp. aer.*) air-hostess; ~ **sociale** (*pers.*) social worker, welfare worker, welfare officer.

assistenza, *n. f.* 1 assistance, aid, help. 2

(*sollievo*) relief. **3** (*market.*) service. // ~ **alla clientela** (*market.*) after-sales service; ~ **del personale di vendita** (*market.*) personal selling assistance; ~ **di marketing alla clientela** (*market.*) marketing assistance to customers; ~ **di personale specializzato** (*market.*) specialized assistance; ~ **finanziaria** (*fin.*) financial aid; ~ **legale** (*leg.*) legal assistance; (*in giudizio*) legal aid; ~ **medica** (*pers.*) medical assistance; ~ **negli affari** (*banca, comm.*) business assistance; ~ **«promozionale»** (*market.*) dealer help; ~ **pubblica** public assistance; ~ **sanitaria interna** (*pers.*) employee health service; ~ **tecnica** (*market.*) technical assistance.

assistere, *v. t.* **1** to assist, to aid, to help. **2** (*dare sollievo a*) to relieve. *v. i.* (*presenziare*) to be present (at); to attend, to witness. // ~ **a un processo** to attend a trial.

associare, *v. t.* **1** to associate, to consociate. **2** (*collegare*) to associate, to connect. **3** (*leg.*) (*ditte, ecc.*) to incorporate. // ~ **in sindacato** (*fin.*) to syndicate.

associarsi, *v. rifl.* **1** to associate (oneself), to consociate, to affiliate. **2** (*per raccogliere fondi o promuovere attività*) to club together. **3** (*fin.*) to enter into partnership. **4** (*leg.*) (*di ditte, ecc.*) to incorporate.

associato, *a.* **1** associate, consociate. **2** (*leg.*) (*di ditta, ecc.*) incorporate. *n. m.* **1** associate, consociate. **2** (*fin.*) (*di una società in nome collettivo o in accomandita*) partner, copartner. **3** (*fin.*) (*di una società per azioni*) member (of a company).

associazione, *n. f.* **1** association, club. **2** (*l'associarsi*) association, combination, consociation. **3** (*d'arti e mestieri*) guild. **4** (*fin.*) (*di mutuo soccorso, ecc.*) guild. **5** (*fin.*) (*di banchieri, finanzieri, ecc.*) syndicate. **6** (*leg.*) society, institution. **7** (*leg.*) (*di società per azioni*) incorporation. // **un'**~ **d'avvocati** (*leg.*) a society of lawyers; **associazioni di consumatori** consumer groups; ~ **di datori di lavoro** (*sind.*) employers' association; **associazioni di produttori agricoli** agricultural producers' groups; ~ **d'uomini d'affari** board of trade (*USA*); **l'**~ **Europea di Libero Scambio** (*econ.*) the European Free Trade Association; ~ **in partecipazione** (*fin.*) particular partnership, special partnership; (*leg.*) joint association, joint adventure, joint venture; ~ **per delinquere** (*leg.*) combination.

assoluzione, *n. f.* (*leg.*) absolution, acquittal, discharge. // ~ **d'un imputato** acquittal of a defendant; ~ **per insufficienza di prove** (*leg.*) (*non esiste in G.B.*) acquittal for lack of evidence.

assolvere, *v. t.* **1** (*compiere*) to perform. **2** (*leg.*) to absolve, to acquit, to discharge. // ~ **bene un compito** to acquit oneself well; ~ **q. da un'accusa** (*leg.*) to acquit sb. of a charge; ~ **un dovere** to perform a duty; ~ **per amnistia** (*leg.*) to acquit under amnesty.

assommare, *v. i.* to sum into, to amount.

assorbimento, *n. m.* **1** absorption. **2** (*fin.*) (*di un'azienda*) take-over. **3** (*fin.*) (*d'una o più aziende da parte d'un'altra*) merger.

assorbire, *v. t.* **1** to absorb. **2** (*completamente*) to engross. **3** (*fin.*) to take★ over. // **essere assorbito** (*da un altro*) (*fin.*) (*d'azienda, ente, ecc.*) to merge; **non assorbito** unabsorbed.

assortimento, *n. m.* (*market.*) **1** assortment. **2** (*market.*) (*scelta*) selection, choice. **3** (*market.*) (*gamma*) range, mixed bag, variety. **4** (*market.*) (*complesso*) lot, set. **5** (*market.*) (*l'assortire*) sorting. **6** (*org. az.*) stock, inventory. // **un** ~ **d'articoli** (*market.*) a set of articles; ~ **d'articoli** (*d'un'azienda*) (*org. az.*) product line.

assortire, *v. t.* (*market.*) (*merci*) to sort.

assortito, *a.* (*market.*) assorted, miscellaneous.

assumere, *v. t.* **1** to assume, to undertake★. **2** (*pers.*) to engage, to hire, to recruit, to start. **3** (*pers.*) (*q., facendolo firmare*) to sign, to sign on. // ~ **una carica** to assume office, to take office; ~ **la direzione di un'azienda** to assume the direction of a business; ~ **un impegno** to commit oneself; ~ **un impegno scritto per q.** (*leg.*) to bond sb.; ~ **un impiegato** (*pers.*) to engage an employee; ~ **informazioni** to gather information; ~ **una nuova forma** to reshape; ~ **un nuovo nome** to assume a new name; ~ **la presidenza** (*d'una società, ecc.*) (*fin.*) to take the chair; **assumersi un debito** to assume a debt; **assumersi l'impegno di fare qc.** to undertake to do st.; **assumersi una responsabilità** to undertake a responsibility.

assunzione, *n. f.* **1** assumption; (*di un impegno*) undertaking. **2** (*pers.*) engagement, hire, hiring, recruiting, recruitment, retainer. **3** (*pers.*) (*dal punto di vista della persona da assumere*) entrance. **4** (*pers.*) **assunzioni,** *pl.* hiring. // **l'**~ **del potere** the assumption of power; ~ **di prestito** (*cred.*) borrowing; ~ **di rischi** (*ass.*) assumption of risks; ~ **e impiego del personale** (*org. az.*) manning.

asta, *n. f.* (*licitazione*) auction; vendue (*USA*). // ~ **al ribasso** Dutch auction; ~ **basata sul consumo d'una candela** candle-auction; ~

olandese (*in cui si parte da un prezzo massimo e si scende per gradi fino a trovare un compratore*) Dutch auction; ~ **pubblica** auction; vendue (*USA*).

astante, *n. m.* e *f.* (*partecipante a un'asta*) bidder (at an auction).

astinenza, *n. f.* (*econ.*) abstinence.

attaccare, *v. t.* **1** (*assalire, aggredire*) to attack. **2** (*congiungere, fissare, unire*) to attach, to affix, to stick*. **3** (*pubbl.*) (*un manifesto, ecc.*) to post, to post up. // ~ **a ogni articolo il cartellino del prezzo** to attach the price tags on each article; ~ (*un nastro, ecc.*) **con punti lunghi** to tack; ~ **un francobollo** (*anche*) to affix a stamp.

attacco, *n. m.* **1** (*assalto*) attack. **2** (*di un apparecchio*) attachment. // ~ **dei ribassisti** (*Borsa*) bear raid.

attendere, *v. t.* **1** (*aspettare*) to wait for, to await, to expect. **2** (*aspettarsi*) to expect. *v. i.* **1** (*aspettare*) to wait. **2** (*badare a, occuparsi di*) to attend (to).

attendibile, *a.* **1** (*di persona*) reliable, trustworthy. **2** (*di cosa, anche*) safe. // **una valutazione ~ del comportamento dei consumatori** a safe estimate of the consumers' behaviour.

attendibilità, *n. f.* reliability, trustworthiness. // **l'~ delle notizie** the reliability of the news; **l'~ di un'informazione** the certitude of a piece of information.

attenersi, *v. rifl.* to abide* (by), to comply (with), to stick* (to). // ~ **alle disposizioni di legge** to conform to the provisions of the law.

attenuante, *a.* (*leg.*) extenuating, mitigating.

attenuanti, *n. pl.* (*leg.*) mitigating circumstances.

attenuare, *v. t.* **1** to extenuate, to attenuate, to lessen, to mitigate, to temper. **2** (*minimizzare*) to minimize, to understate.

attenuarsi, *v. rifl.* to lessen, to relax.

attenuazione, *n. f.* **1** extenuation, attenuation, lessening, mitigation. **2** (*minimizzazione*) minimization. // **l'~ d'una legge** (*leg.*) the relaxation of a law.

attenzione, *n. f.* attention, care. // **«attenzione!»** (*trasp.*) (*scritto su un collo, pacco, ecc.*) «(handle) with care»; «~: **porcellane**» (*trasp.*) «chinaware, with care»; «~: **passaggio a livello**» (*trasp. aut.*) «caution, level crossing»; **«all'~ di Mr X.Y.»** «attention of Mr X.Y.».

attergare, *v. t.* **1** (*cred.*) to endorse, to indorse. **2** (*leg.*) (*una pratica*) to docket.

attergato, *n. m.* **1** (*cred.*) endorsement, indorsement. **2** (*leg.*) docket.

atterraggio, *n. m.* (*trasp. aer.*) landing. // ~ **d'emergenza** (*con urto sul suolo*) (*trasp. aer.*) crash landing.

atterrare, *v. t.* (*abbattere*) to knock down. *v. i.* (*trasp. aer.*) to land, to touch down.

attesa, *n. f.* **1** wait, waiting. **2** (*aspettazione*) expectation. // **in ~ della vostra accettazione** pending your acceptance; **in ~ d'ulteriori informazioni** pending further information; **essere in ~ di** to wait for, to await.

atteso, *a.* **1** waited for, awaited. **2** (*trasp.*) due. // ~ **a lungo** long-awaited; ~ **che...** considering that...

attestabile, *a.* **1** attestable. **2** warrantable. **3** certifiable. **4** documentable. **5** (*leg.*) testifiable.

attestante, *a.* (*di documento*) to the effect. // **un certificato ~ che...** a certificate to the effect that...

attestare, *v. t.* **1** to attest. **2** (*affermare, asserire*) to vouch (for), to warrant. **3** (*certificare*) to certificate, to certify. **4** (*documentare*) to document. **5** (*leg.*) (*comprovare*) to evidence. **6** (*leg.*) (*testimoniare*) to testify, to witness. // ~ **un fatto** to attest a fact.

attestato, *n. m.* **1** certificate, document. **2** (*pers.*) reference. // ~ **di buona condotta** (*leg.*) testimonial; ~ **di servizio** (*pers.*) character.

attestazione, *n. f.* **1** attestation. **2** (*certificazione*) certification. **3** (*prova*) evidence. **4** (*leg.*) (*testimonianza*) testimony. // ~ **ufficiale** (*leg.*) affidavit.

attitudinale, *a.* vocational. // **test ~** vocational test.

attitudine, *n. f.* aptitude. // ~ **al comando** leadership; ~ **al mare** (*trasp. mar.*) (*d'imbarcazione*) sea kindliness; ~ **alla navigazione aerea** (*trasp. aer.*) airworthiness.

attivamente, *avv.* actively.

attivismo, *n. m.* activism. // ~ **sindacale** (*sind.*) union militancy.

attivista, *n. m.* e *f.* **1** activist. **2** (*sind.*) organizer. // **un ~ sindacale** (*sind.*) a union militant.

attività, *n. f. inv.* **1** activity, work; go (*fam.*). **2 attività,** *pl.* (*rag.*) assets. // **attività a breve (termine)** (*fin., rag.*) near-money, quick assets; **attività a vista** (*rag.*) quick assets; ~ **agricola** agricultural industry; ~ **alberghiera** hotel business; **attività ausiliari del commercio** (*assicurazioni, banche, trasporti, ecc.*) ancillaries to trade; ~ **bancaria** banking, banking business; **attività cantieristiche** (*trasp. mar.*) shipyard activities; ~ **capitale** (*econ.*) capital asset; ~ **carbonifera** coalmining; ~ **collaterale** by-business; **attività correnti** (*rag.*) current assets; ~ **d'allibratore** bookmaking; **attività di commercio al dettaglio per conto proprio** (*org. az.*) self-employed activities in retail trade; ~ **di consumo** (*econ.*) economic activity of consumption; **un'** ~ **di difficile realizzo** (*econ., rag.*) an unrealizable asset; ~ **di piazzista** (*market.*) canvassing; ~ **di prestazione di servizi** (*econ.*) services; ~ **di sensale** broking; ~ **direttiva** (*amm.*) managing activity; ~ **economica** (*econ.*) economic activity; **attività economiche fondamentali** (*econ.*) primary economic activities; ~ **esecutiva** (*org. az.*) operating activity; **attività fisse** (*rag.*) fixed assets; plant assets; **attività fittizie** (*rag.*) fictitious assets, dead assets; ~ **immateriale** (*rag.*) intangible; **attività immateriali** (*rag.*) intangible assets; ~ **industriale** manufacturing; ~ **invisibile** (*rag.*) intangible; **attività invisibili** (*rag.*) intangible assets; ~ **lavorativa** (*econ.*) labour; **attività liquide** (*fin., rag.*) near-money, liquid assets; **attività non di capitale** (*rag.*) working assets; **attività non salariate** (*org. az.*) self-employed activities; **attività occulte** (*rag.*) hidden assets; ~ **pericolosa** (*pers.*) hazardous activity; **attività promozionali** (*market., pubbl.*) promotional activities; **attività ricreative** (*pers.*) recreational activities; ~ **secondaria** (*org. az.*) side-line; **attività sociali** (*org. az.*) social activities; **le attività «terziarie»** (*econ.*) the services sector, the services; **attività totali** (*rag.*) total assets; **attività totali nette** (*rag.*) tangible net worth; **attività variabili** (*rag.*) floating assets; **essere in** ~ **di servizio** (*pers.*) to be in active service.

attivo, *a.* 1 active, brisk, lively. 2 (*econ.*) (*che lavora*) working. *n. m.* 1 (*rag.*) assets (*pl.*). 2 (*rag.*) (*di un conto*) creditor. // ~ **del fallimento** (*leg.*) bankruptcy assets; ~ **e passivo** (*rag.*) assets and liabilities; ~ **fisso** (*rag.*) fixed assets; ~ **liquido** (*o facilmente liquidabile*) (*rag.*) cash assets; ~ **netto** (*rag.*) net assets, net worth; **l'** ~ **sociale** (*fin.*) the partnership's assets; the company's assets; **essere in** ~ (*banca, fam.*) to be in the black.

atto¹, *n. m.* 1 act, action, deed. 2 (*amm.*) deed. 3 (*leg.*) deed. 4 **atti,** *pl.* (*amm.*) (*d'un congresso, ecc.*) proceedings. // ~ **amministrativo** (*leg.*) official action; **un** ~ **arbitrario** (*leg.*) an arbitrary action; ~ **autorizzato** authorized act; ~ **conservativo** (*leg.*) conservatory act; ~ **costitutivo** (*di una società*) deed of association; (*d'una società di capitali*) (*fin.*) memorandum of association (*ingl.*); corporate charter (*USA*); **atti della società** company deeds; ~ **di cessione** (*di una proprietà*) (*leg.*) deed of assignment, deed of transfer, transfer deed, instrument of transfer; (*d'un diritto*) release; ~ **di compravendita** (*leg.*) deed of sale; ~ **di concordato** (*tra debitore e creditori*) (*leg.*) composition deed; ~ **di delega** (*leg.*) instrument of delegation of powers; ~ **di donazione** (*leg.*) deed of gift; « ~ **di fallimento** » (*leg., ingl.*) (*ogni cessazione dei pagamenti da parte del debitore, sia egli un commerciante o no*) act of bankruptcy; **atti di guerra** acts of war; ~ **di nascita** birth certificate; ~ **di notorietà** (*leg.*) attested affidavit; ~ **di ordinaria amministrazione** authorized act; ~ **di permuta** (*leg.*) deed of transfer; ~ **di procura** (*leg.*) warrant of attorney; **un** ~ **di proprietà non registrato** (*leg.*) an unrecorded deed to property; ~ **d'un sovrano** act of a prince; ~ **di trasferimento** (*Borsa*) transfer deed; ~ **di trasmissione** (*leg.*) deed of transfer, conveyance; ~ **doloso** (*leg.*) fraudulent act; « ~ **fallimentare** » (*leg., ingl.*) bankruptcy act; ~ **fiduciario** (*leg.*) deed of trust; (*fin., leg.*) trust deed; ~ **fittizio** (*leg.*) fictitious act; ~ **fraudolento** (*leg.*) fraudulent act; ~ **giudiziale** (*leg.*) judicial act; ~ **giudiziario** (*leg.*) judicial act; ~ **giuridico** (*leg.*) juridical act, juristic act; ~ **illecito** (*leg.*) injury; (*civile*) tort, wrong, wrong-doing; ~ **istitutivo** (*leg.*) charter; **atti leciti** (*leg.*) lawful acts; **atti legali** (*leg.*) legal acts; **un** ~ **lesivo** (*leg.*) a wrongful act; ~ **notarile** (*leg.*) notarial deed, instrument; ~ **notorio** (*leg.*) attested affidavit; **atti processuali** (*leg.*) acts and judicial proceedings; ~ **pubblico** (*leg.*) instrument; **un** ~ **retrodatato** (*leg.*) an antedated deed; **un** ~ **rogato da un notaio** (*leg.*) a deed attested by a notary; ~ **scritto di difesa** (*dell'attore*) (*leg.*) plaint; **atti sociali** company deeds; ~ **solenne** (*leg.*) deed; **atti ufficiali** (*leg.*) records; ~ **unilaterale** (*leg.*) deed poll; **all'** ~ **di** on, upon: **all'** ~ **della consegna** (*market.*) on delivery.

atto², *a.* 1 (*adatto*) fit, suitable. 2 (*capace*) able, capable. 3 (*per coprire una carica, per un ufficio, ecc.*) eligible. // ~ **alla navigazione** (*trasp. mar.*) seaworthy; ~ **alla navigazione aerea** (*trasp. aer.*) airworthy.

attore, *n. m.* 1 (*leg.*) (*in giudizio*) claimant, claimer, complainant, demandant, plaintiff, suitor. 2 (*leg.*) (*spesso in giudizio come principale teste a carico*) prosecutor. // ~ **in una causa civile** (*leg.*) plaintiff in a civil suit.

attraccare, *v. t.* e *i.* (*trasp. mar.*) to berth, to moor; to dock (*USA*). // ~ (*una nave*) **al molo** (*trasp. mar.*) to wharf; ~ **alla banchina** (*trasp. mar.*) to moor along a quay.

attracco, *n. m.* 1 (*trasp. mar.*) (*l'attraccare*) berthing, mooring; docking (*USA*). 2 (*trasp. mar.*) (*il luogo*) berth; moorings (*pl.*).

attrezzare, *v. t.* 1 (*arredare*) to fit out. 2 (*equipaggiare*) to equip. 3 (*fornire di attrezzi*) to tool. 4 (*trasp. mar.*) (*una nave*) to rig.

attrezzatura, *n. f.* **1** equipment, outfit. **2** (*org. az.*) tackle. **3** (*trasp. mar.*) (*d'una nave*) rigging, rig. **4** **attrezzature,** *pl.* appointments, accommodations, equipment goods. **5** **attrezzature,** *pl.* (*org. az.*) facilities. // ~ **che fa risparmiare lavoro** (*org. az.*) labour-saving appliance; **attrezzature della nave** (*alberi, vele, ancore, ecc.*) (*trasp. mar.*) apparel; **attrezzature di salvataggio** (*trasp. mar.*) salvage gear; **attrezzature per ufficio** (*attr. uff.*) office equipment; **attrezzature portuali** (*trasp. mar.*) harbour equipment, port facilities.

attrezzo, *n. m.* **1** (*org. az.*) implement, tool. **2** (*trasp. mar.*) article of (the ship's) gear. **3** **attrezzi,** *pl.* (*org. az.*) tackle. // **attrezzi agricoli** agricultural implements.

attribuibile, *a.* **1** attributable, assignable. **2** (*imputabile*) chargeable. **3** (*rag.*) imputable.

attribuire, *v. t.* **1** to attribute, to assign, to attach. **2** (*imputare*) to charge. **3** (*rag.*) to impute. // ~ **un premio** to award a prize.

attribuzione, *n. f.* **1** attribution, assignment. **2** (*rag.*) imputation. // **l'~ d'un premio** the award of a prize.

audimetro, *n. m.* (*pubbl.*) audimeter.

aumentare, *v. t.* **1** to augment, to increase, to raise, to advance, to put★ up, to up. **2** (*econ.*) (*la produzione, ecc.*) to enhance, to step up. **3** (*econ., market.*) (*prezzi, ecc.*) to lift, to stiffen. *v. i.* **1** to augment, to increase, to rise★, to advance. **2** (*in fretta*) to upsurge, to swell. **3** (*per gradi*) to grow★. **4** (*econ.*) (*della domanda, ecc.*) to improve. **5** (*fin., market.*) (*di prezzi, ecc.*) to rise★, to go★ up, to up. // ~ **gli affitti in modo iniquo** to advance rents unfairly; ~ **i dazi** (*dog.*) to raise duties; ~ **di prezzo** to advance in price, to increase in price, to appreciate; ~ **di valore** (*fin., market.*) to go better; (*fin., rag.*) to appreciate; ~ **improvvisamente** (*econ.*) (*d'attività commerciale*) to spurt; (*fin., market.*) to jump, to leap; ~ **nuovamente il volume di** (*credito, valuta, ecc.*) (*econ.*) to reflate; ~ **l'offerta globale** (*econ.*) to increase total supply; ~ **i prezzi** (*market.*) to raise prices, to enhance prices; ~ **il prezzo della benzina** to advance the price of petrol; ~ (*qc.*) **progressivamente** to scale up; ~ **i risparmi** (*econ.*) to step up savings; ~ **i salari reali** (*pers.*) to raise real wages; ~ **il tasso di sconto** (*fin.*) to raise the discount rate; ~ **il tasso ufficiale di sconto** (*fin.*) to raise the bank rate; ~ **vertiginosamente** (*econ.*) (*di prezzi, ecc.*) to spiral upward.

aumento, *n. m.* **1** augmentation (*raro*), increase, increment, rise, raise (*specialm. USA*), advance, enhancement. **2** (*repentino*) upsurge, swell. **3** (*graduale*) growth. **4** (*econ.*) (*espansione*) expansion. **5** (*econ.*) (*della produzione, ecc.*) step-up. **6** (*econ.*) (*della domanda*) improvement. **7** (*econ., market.*) (*di prezzi, ecc.*) lift, rise. **8** (*pers.*) (*di salario*) increase, increment, advance, rise. // ~ **abbinato** (*pers.*) tandem increase; **un ~ annuale dei redditi** an annual boost in income; ~ **automatico del salario** (*pers.*) automatic pay increase; ~ **dei prezzi** (*econ.*) price increase; (*in Borsa*) boom, boost, bulge; ballooning (*slang USA*); ~ **dei salari** (*per agganciamento agli indici del costo della vita*) (*econ.*) wage escalation; ~ **del capitale** (*con il concorso dell'interesse capitalizzato o degli utili reinvestiti*) (*fin.*) accumulation; **l'~ del costo della vita** (*econ., stat.*) the rise in the cost of living; **un ~ del 2% rispetto allo scorso anno** (*rag.*) a gain of 2% over last year; **un ~ del tasso ufficiale di sconto** (*fin.*) a rise in the bank rate; **l'~ della circolazione monetaria** (*fin.*) the expansion of currency; **un ~ della domanda di consumi** (*econ.*) an increase in consumption demands; ~ **dell'occupazione** (*econ.*) employment increase; **un ~ della popolazione** (*stat.*) an increase in population, a swell in population; ~ **della produzione** (*econ.*) production increase; **l'~ delle aperture di credito** (*banca*) the expansion of lending; **un ~ demografico** (*stat.*) an increase in population; ~ **di capitale** (*fin., rag.*) increase of capital, capital increase; ~ **di prezzo** (*market.*) advance in price, enhancement of price, markup; ~ **di salario** (*pers.*) wage rise; pay-raise (*USA*); ~ **di stipendio** (*pers.*) salary rise; pay-raise, raise (*USA*); ~ **di valore** (*fin., rag.*) appreciation; ~ **gratuito di capitale** (*fin., rag.*) capitalization issue; bond issue (*USA*); ~ **improvviso** (*di prezzi*) (*fin., market.*) jump, leap, upswing; **aumenti inflazionistici dei salari** (*econ.*) inflationary wage rises; ~ **progressivo** scale-up; ~ **salariale** (*pers.*) wage rise; pay-raise (*USA*); **aumenti salariali** (*pers.*) wage increases, wage advances, wage awards; ~ **spinto al massimo** maximization; **in ~** increasing, growing; **essere in ~** (*econ.*) (*di domanda, prezzo, ecc.*) to be up; (*fin., market.*) (*di prezzi, ecc.*) to rise, to be on the rise; to increase, to be on the increase, to advance.

aureo, *a.* gold, golden.

austerità, *n. f.* austerity.

autarchia, *n. f.* (*econ.*) autarchy, autarky, self-sufficiency.

autarchico, *a.* (*econ.*) autarchic, autarchical, autarkic, autarkical, self-sufficient.

autenticare, *v. t.* **1** to countersign, to voucher. **2** (*leg.*) to authenticate, to legalize. **3**

(*leg.*) (*attestare*) to attest, to certify. **4** (*leg.*) (*verificare*) to verify. **5** (*leg.*) (*detto di notaio*) to notarize. **6** (*leg.*) (*un testamento*) to probate. // ~ **un certificato** (*leg.*) to authenticate a certificate; ~ **una firma** (*leg.*) to attest a signature; ~ (*un documento, ecc.*) **mediante la firma** (*leg.*) to signature.

autenticazione, *n. f.* **1** (*leg.*) authentication, legalization. **2** (*leg.*) (*certificazione*) certification. **3** (*leg.*) (*verifica*) verification. // ~ **notarile** (*leg.*) notarization.

autenticità, *n. f.* authenticity.

autentico, *a.* **1** authentic. **2** (*originale*) original. **3** (*genuino*) genuine. **4** (*leg.*) (*di copia: conforme all'originale*) attested, certified.

auto-[1], *pref.* self-. // **autodeterminazione** self-determination; **autolesionista** self-injurer; **autosufficienza** self-sufficiency.

auto-[2], *pref.* auto-, motor-. // **autoambulanza** (*o* **autolettiga**) motor-ambulance; **autoraduno** auto-rally.

auto[3], *n. f.* (*abbr. di* **automobile**) (*trasp.*) car, motorcar. // **un'** ~ **da turismo** (*tur.*) a touring car.

autoapprovvigionamento, *n. m.* (*org. az.*) self-sufficiency.

autoassicurazione, *n. f.* (*rag.*) self-insurance.

autobotte, *n. f.* (*trasp. aut.*) tank truck, tanker.

autobus, *n. m.* (*trasp.*) bus; omnibus (*raro*). // ~ **a due piani** (*trasp.*) double-decker; ~ **diretto** (*trasp. aut.*) non-stop; ~ **per gite turistiche** (*tur.*) sightseeing bus.

autocarro, *n. m.* (*trasp. aut.*) motor-lorry, lorry (*ingl.*); motortruck, truck (*USA*). // **un** ~ **attrezzato per la vendita** (*market.*) a mobile shop; ~ **frigorifero** (*trasp. aut.*) refrigerator van; ~ **per il trasporto di automobili nuove** (*trasp.*) haulaway.

autocisterna, *n. f.* (*trasp. aut.*) tank truck.

autodeterminazione, *n. f.* self-determination. // ~ **dell'imponibile** (*da parte delle aziende*) (*fin.*) self-assessment.

autofinanziamento, *n. m.* (*fin.*) self-financing; internally generated cash resources; (financing by) corporate saving, corporate cash generation (*USA*).

autofurgone, *n. m.* (*trasp. aut.*) van.

autogrù, *n. f. inv.* (*trasp. aut.*) tow car, tow truck, wrecking car, wrecker.

automezzo, *n. m.* (*trasp. aut.*) motor-vehicle.

automobile, *n. f.* (*trasp. aut.*) motor-car, motorcar, car; automobile (*USA*). // ~ **chiusa** (*trasp. aut.*) sedan; ~ **di piccole dimensioni** compact car; **un'** ~ **di seconda mano** a second-hand car; **automobili di seconda mano** used cars; ~ **utilitaria** baby car.

autonomia, *n. f.* **1** autonomy. **2** (*trasp. aer.*) range. **3** (*trasp. mar.*) endurance.

autonomo, *a.* autonomous.

autorità, *n. f. inv.* **1** authority, influence, leverage, warrant. **2** (*leg.*) (*di fare qc.*) commission. // ~ **conferita ai giudici di pace** (*leg.*) commission of peace; ~ **di direttore** (*amm.*) managership; ~ **fiscale** (*fin.*) taxing authority; **l'** ~ **giudiziaria** (*leg.*) the Court; **le autorità monetarie** (*fin.*) the monetary authorities; **autorità portuali** (*trasp. mar.*) harbour authorities; dock authorities; ~ **sanitaria portuale** (*trasp. mar.*) port sanitary authority; **d'** ~ by authority.

autorizzare, *v. t.* **1** to authorize, to commission. **2** (*leg.*) to license, to warrant. // ~ **il pagamento delle spese di viaggio** to authorize the payment of travelling expenses; ~ **per mezzo di certificati** (*leg.*) to certificate; ~ **la spesa di 100.000 sterline per la nuova sede** to authorize the spending of £. 100,000 on new premises.

autorizzato, *a.* **1** authorized. **2** (*di persona*) in commission (*V.* **autorizzare**). // **non** ~ unauthorized.

autorizzazione, *n. f.* **1** authorization, authority. **2** (*permesso*) permission, allowance. **3** (*leg.*) commission, licence. // ~ **a procedere** (*leg.*) authorization to proceed; ~ **delle reimportazioni in franchigia di merci in precedenza esportate** (*dog.*) authorization for the duty-free reimport of returned goods.

autostello, *n. m.* (*trasp. aut.*) motel; motor court (*USA*).

autostivante, *n. f.* (*trasp. mar.*) self-trimmer.

autostrada, *n. f.* (*trasp. aut.*) motorway; express highway, speedway (*USA*); (*a pagamento*) turnpike (*USA*).

autosufficiente, *a.* (*econ.*) self-sufficient.

autosufficienza, *n. f.* (*econ.*) self-sufficiency.

autotassazione, *n. f.* (*fin.*) self-taxation.

autotrasportatore, *n. m.* **1** (*trasp. aut.*) common carrier. **2** (*trasp. aut.*) («*padroncino*») lorry-driver; truck-driver (*USA*).

autoveicolo, *n. m.* (*trasp. aut.*) motor-vehicle. // **autoveicoli industriali** commercial vehicles.

avallante, *n. m.* e *f.* (*cred., fin.*) guarantor, backer, guarantee, grantor (*raro*). // **l'** ~ **d'una cambiale** the guarantor (*o* backer) of a bill of exchange.

avallare, *v. t.* (*cred., fin.*) to guarantee, to back. // ~ **una cambiale** (*cred.*) to guarantee a bill; ~ **una girata** (*cred.*) to guarantee an endorsement.

avallato, *a.* (*cred., fin.*) guaranteed, backed.

avallo, *n. m.* (*cred., fin.*) guarantee.

avamborsa, *n. m.* (*Borsa, fin.*) before hours.

avamporto, *n. m.* (*trasp. mar.*) outer harbour.

avanscalo, *n. m.* (*trasp. mar.*) ways-end.

avantiscalo, *n. m.* (*trasp. mar.*) ways-end.

avanzamento, *n. m.* **1** advancement. **2** (*progressi*) progress, progression. **3** (*elab. elettr.*) feeding. **4** (*pers.*) promotion, step.

avanzare[1], *v. i.* **1** to advance, to proceed. **2** (*progredire*) to progress. **3** (*trasp. mar.*) (*della marea*) to set★ in. *v. t.* **1** to advance, to put★ forward. **2** (*leg.*) to prefer. **3** (*pers.*) (*promuovere*) to advance, to promote. // ~ **una domanda** (*scritta*) to submit an application; ~ **una pretesa** to advance a claim; (*leg.*) to stake a claim.

avanzare[2], *v. i.* (*rimanere*) to remain, to be left. *v. t.* (*essere creditore di*) to be in credit of.

avanzo, *n. m.* **1** remainder, remnant, rest. **2** (*econ., fin.*) surplus. // ~ **di bilancio** (*fin., rag.*) budget surplus, budgetary surplus; ~ **di cassa** (*rag.*) cash on hand.

avaria, *n. f.* **1** (*ass. mar.*) average. **2** (*elab. elettr.*) failure, fault. **3** (*trasp. mar.*) damage, break-down. // ~ **alla nave** (*trasp. mar.*) damage to ship; ~ **generale** (*ass. mar.*) general average, gross average; ~ **particolare** (*ass. mar.*) particular average, common average; ~ **particolare inclusa** (*ass. mar.*) with particular average (*W.P.A.*); ~ **totale** (*ass. mar.*) general average; **con** ~ **particolare** (*ass. mar.*) with particular average (*W.P.A.*).

avariare, *v. t.* to damage.

avariato, *a.* damaged. // **non** ~ (*ass., trasp.*) undamaged.

avente causa, *n. m.* e *f.* (*leg.*) assign, assignee.

avente diritto, *n. m.* e *f.* (*leg.*) assign, assignee.

avere[1], *n. m.* **1** property, estate; (*patrimonio*) patrimony; (*ricchezza*) wealth. **2** (*fin., rag.*) assets (*pl.*). **3** (*rag.*) (*nelle imputazioni*) «credit», «credited». **4** (*rag.*) (*d'un conto*) credit side, creditor side. **5 averi,** *pl.* belongings, possessions. **6 averi,** *pl.* (*fin.*) means. // **averi ufficiali** (*fin., rag.*) official assets; **a saldo del vostro** (*o* **d'ogni vostro**) ~ (*rag.*) in (full) settlement of your account.

avere[2], *v. t.* **1** to have; (*possedere*) to own, to possess; (*valere*) to be worth. **2** (*v. ausiliare*) to have. **3** (*ottenere*) to obtain, to get★. **4** (*guadagnare*) to earn. // ~ **un andamento favorevole** (*Borsa, fin.*) to have a cheerful aspect; ~ **l'aspetto di** to look; ~ **autorità su q.** to have authority over sb.; ~ **bisogno di** to need, to require, to want; ~ **una buona disposizione** (*Borsa, fin.*) to have a cheerful aspect; ~ **un cliente a pranzo** to entertain a customer at (*o* to) dinner; ~ **un colloquio con q.** to have a talk with sb.; (*market., pers.*) to interview sb.; ~ **un conto corrente con un negozio** (*market.*) to run a bill at a shop; ~ **una conversazione con q.** to hold a conversation with sb.; ~ **denaro in banca** to have money in the bank; ~ **la direzione di** (*amm.*) to manage; ~ **diritto a qc.** to be entitled to st.; to be eligible for st.; ~ **il diritto di prendere visione di** (*qc.*) (*leg.*) to have a right of access to; ~ **effetto** (*leg.*) to attach, to inure; ~ **un effetto deleterio su** to affect; ~ **effetto su** to affect; ~ **fiducia** to confide; ~ **fiducia in q.** to trust sb.; ~ **un gran bisogno di qc.** to need st. badly; ~ **importanza** to matter; ~ **in affitto** (*leg.*) to rent; to occupy (*ingl.*); ~ **in animo di fare qc.** to contemplate doing st.; ~ **in locazione** (*leg.*) to occupy; ~ **inizio** to begin, to commence, to start; to be originated; ~ **un lavoro fisso** to be in regular work; ~ **letti per** (*un certo numero di persone*) (*tur.: d'albergo*) to sleep; ~ **luogo** to take place; ~ **una** (*certa*) **misura** to measure; ~ **necessità di** to need; ~ **notevole incidenza economica** (*econ.*) to have important economic implications; ~ **notizia** (*apprendere*) to learn, to hear; ~ **origine** to originate; ~ **un** (*certo*) **peso** to weigh; ~ **poca merce d'un certo tipo** (*in magazzino, in negozio, ecc.*) (*org. az.*) to be understocked with certain goods; ~ **il possesso di qc.** (*leg.*) to possess st.; ~ **posti a sedere per** (*un certo numero di persone*) (*trasp.*) (*di mezzo di trasporto*) to seat; ~ **posti in piedi per** (*un certo numero di persone*) (*trasp.*) (*di mezzo di trasporto*) to stand; ~ **la presidenza** (*org. az.*) to be in the chair; ~ **un privilegio sui beni d'un debitore** to have a charge on the personal property of a debtor; ~ **i requisiti** (*per svolgere una mansione, esercitare una professione, ecc.*) (*leg., pers.*) to qualify; ~ **i requisiti per un impiego** (*pers.*) to be eligible for a position; ~ **scarsità di mezzi** to be in narrow circumstances; ~ **uno scartamento di** (*trasp. ferr.*) (*di vagone*) to track; ~ **un seggio in Parlamento** (*leg.*) to sit in Parliament; ~ **stima di** to esteem; ~ **successo** (*di cosa*) to be a success; (*di persona e di cosa*) to be successful;

(*di persona*) to succeed; to do oneself well (*USA*); ~ **torto** to be wrong, to be in the wrong; ~ **troppa merce** (*in magazzino, in negozio, ecc.*) (*org. az.*) to be overstocked with goods; ~ **un valore d'inventario pari a** (*rag.*) to inventory at; ~ **il vento in poppa** (*trasp. mar.*) to sail before the wind; ~ **un volume d'affari di** to turn over.

aviorimessa, *n. f.* (*trasp. aer.*) hangar.

«avoirdupois», *n. m.* (*sistema di pesi inglesi, la cui unità è la libbra*) avoirdupois.

avvantaggiare, *v. t.* to advantage, to benefit, to favour. // **essere avvantaggiato da qc.** to be advantaged by st.

avvantaggiarsi, *v. rifl.* to take★ advantage.

avventizio, *a.* (*pers.*) casual, temporary. *n. m.* 1 (*pers.*) casual worker, temporary. 2 **avventizi,** *pl.* temporary staff; (*operai*) casual workers.

avventore, *n. m.* (*market.*) customer, patron.

avvertimento, *n. m.* 1 warning. 2 (*leg.*) caveat.

avvertire, *v. t.* 1 to inform, to let★ know, to notify. 2 (*ammonire*) to warn.

avviamento, *n. m.* 1 (*anche fig.*) starting. 2 (*econ.*) (*di un'impresa, ecc.*) starting-up. 3 (*rag.*) (*d'un'azienda, d'un negozio, ecc.*) goodwill. // **capitale d'** ~ initial capital.

avviare, *v. t.* 1 (*anche fig.*) to start; to initiate, to set★ up. 2 (*trasp.*) (*merci, ecc.*) to route. // ~ **un cambiamento nella moda** (*pubbl.*) to initiate a change in fashion; ~ **di nuovo** (*merci, ecc.*) (*trasp.*) to reroute; ~ **q. negli affari** to start (*o* to set up, to settle) sb. in business; **un'azienda (ben) avviata** a going concern.

avvicendamento, *n. m.* 1 alternation, shifting, shift. 2 (*econ.*) (*delle colture*) rotation. 3 (*pers.*) turnover. 4 (*pers.*) (*nelle mansioni*) rotation.

avvicendare, *v. t.* 1 to alternate, to shift. 2 (*econ.*) (*colture*) to rotate.

avvicendarsi, *v. rifl.* 1 to alternate. 2 (*pers.*) (*di dipendenti: nelle diverse mansioni*) to rotate.

avvicinare, *v. t.* to approach.

avvicinarsi, *v. rifl.* 1 to near, to come★ near. 2 (*trasp. mar.*) to draw★ near. *v. recipr.* (*trasp. mar.*) (*di navi*) to draw★ together.

avvisare, *v. t.* 1 to advise, to inform, to notify. 2 (*ammonire*) to warn.

avviso, *n. m.* 1 advice, notice. 2 (*ammonimento*) warning. 3 (*parere*) opinion. 4 (*annunzio*) announcement. 5 (*annuncio pubblicitario*) advertisement, ad. 6 (*pubbl.*) (*cartellone*) poster. 7 (*trasp. ferr.*) advice note. // ~ **ai naviganti** (*trasp. mar.*) warning to shipping; ~ **dato nei termini richiesti** (*leg.*) due notice; ~ **d'abbandono** (*della nave e/o del carico*) (*ass. mar.*) notice of abandonment; ~ **d'appalto** (*comm.*) advertisement for bids; ~ **di burrasca** (*trasp. mar.*) gale warning; ~ **di cattivo tempo** (*trasp. mar.*) weather warning; ~ **di consegna** (*trasp.*) advice of delivery; ~ **(di convocazione) d'assemblea** (*fin.*) notice of meeting, notice; ~ **di mancata accettazione** (*d'una cambiale*) (*leg.*) notice of dishonour; ~ **di mancato pagamento** (*d'una cambiale*) (*leg.*) notice of dishonour; ~ **d'operazione compiuta** (*Borsa*) advice of deal; ~ **di pagamento** (*cred.*) notice of payment, advice of payment; ~ **di pagamento del premio** (*notificato all'assicurato*) (*ass.*) premium notice; ~ **di ricevuta** advice of receipt; ~ **di ripartizione** (*d'una sottoscrizione azionaria ed obbligazionaria*) (*fin.*) letter of allotment, allotment letter; ~ **di sfratto** (*leg.*) dispossess notice; ~ **di spedizione** (*trasp.*) advice of shipment; ~ **immediato** (*leg.*) immediate notice; ~ **pubblicitario** (*giorn., pubbl.*) advertisement, ad, insertion; **come da** ~ as per advice; **fino a nuovo** ~ till further notice; **salvo contrario** ~ unless advised to the contrary; «**senza** ~» (*banca*) «no advice».

avvocato, *n. m.* 1 (*leg.*) (*in genere*) lawyer; attorney (*USA*); advocate (*in Scozia*). 2 (*leg.*) (*procuratore legale*) attorney-at-law. 3 (*leg.*) (*che discute le cause in tribunale*) attorney. 4 (*leg.*) (*che tratta coi clienti, ma normalmente non discute in tribunale*) solicitor. // **un** ~ **che esercita la professione** (*leg.*) a practicing barrister; **un** ~ **consulente** (*leg.*) a consulting counsel; ~ **del convenuto** (*leg.*) counsel for the defendant; ~ **della parte lesa** (*leg.*) counsel for the plaintiff; ~ **di parte civile** (*leg.*) counsel for the plaintiff, plaintiff's attorney; ~ **d'ufficio** (*leg.*) counsel appointed by the Court; ~ **difensore** (*leg.*) counsel for the defendant, counsel for the defence, pleader; ~ **patrocinante** (*leg.*) barrister, barrister-at-law, counsel, pleader; counsellor, counsellor-at-law (*USA*); ~ **principale** (*leg.*) leader.

avvocatura, *n. f.* 1 (*leg.*) (*professione legale*) legal profession, (the) Bar. 2 (*leg.*) (*complesso degli avvocati*) (the) Bar. 3 (*leg.*) (*in Scozia*) advocacy. // **l'** ~ **di Stato** (*leg.*) the Law Officers.

azienda, *n. f.* 1 business, concern, establishment, firm, undertaking. 2 (*econ., org. az.*) unit. 3 (*org. az.*) trade. // ~ **a partecipazione statale** (*econ.*) state-controlled enterprise, state enterprise, public corporation; ~ **agricola** farm, commercial farm; ~ **agricola a conduzione familiare** (*econ.*) one-family farm; ~ **bancaria** banking concern; **un' ~ bene avviata** a going concern; ~ **che accoglie anche operai non iscritti ai sindacati** (*sind., USA*) open shop; ~ **che sfrutta le maestranze** (*org. az.*) sweat-shop (*fam.*); ~ **decotta** (*econ.*) lossmaker; **l' ~ dello Stato** the State administration; ~ **di servizi pubblici** (*amm.*) public utility; utility, public-service corporation (*USA*); ~ **di Stato** (*econ.*) State-owned enterprise; **un' ~ florida** a thriving business; **un' ~ in attività** (*econ.*) a going concern; ~ **in deficit** (*o* **in perdita**) (*econ.*) lossmaker; ~ **individuale** one-man business; **aziende leader** (*econ., market.*) market leaders; ~ **municipalizzata** (*amm.*) city-owned enterprise; **un' ~ primaria** a leading concern; **un' ~ redditizia** a remunerative business; ~ **tipo** (*market., stat.*) representative firm; **grossa ~ agricola** (*econ.*) corporate farm (*USA*).

aziendale, *a.* **1** business, concern (*attr.*) **2** (*nell'ambito di un'azienda*) in-plant (*attr.*). // **conti aziendali** business accounts; **corsi aziendali** in-plant courses; **organizzazione ~** (*materia di studio*) business administration.

azionariato, *n. m.* **1** (*fin.*) shareholding. **2** (*fin.*) (*complesso degli azionisti*) shareholders. // ~ **operaio** employee shareholding.

azionario, *a.* (*fin.*) share, stock (*attr.*). // **capitale ~** (*fin.*) share capital; capital shares (*ingl.*); capital stock (*USA*).

azione, *n. f.* **1** action, deed, proceeding. **2** (*fin.*) share. **3** (*leg.*) action, lawsuit. **4 azioni,** *pl.* (*fin.*) stock (*sing.*); shares (*ingl.*); stocks (*USA*). **5 azioni,** *pl.* (*rag.*) holding (*sing.*). // **azioni a dividendo garantito** (*fin.*) guaranteed stock; **azioni al portatore** (*fin.*) bearer shares, transferable stock; **azioni al 4% (d'interesse)** (*fin.*) fours; ~ **anticiclica** (*econ.*) countercyclical action; **azioni bancarie** (*fin.*) bank shares; ~ **cambiaria** (*leg.*) action upon a bill; **azioni carbonifere** (*fin.*) coal shares; ~ **civile** (*leg.*) civil action, civil suit; **azioni con diritto di voto** (*fin.*) voting stock; **azioni cuprifere** (*fin.*) copper shares; **azioni delle miniere di rame** (*fin.*) copper shares; **azioni devolute ai promotori** (*d'una società per azioni*) (*fin.*) founders' shares; **azioni di compagnia ferroviaria** (*Borsa, specialm. USA*) railroad shares; **azioni d'una cooperativa** co-op shares; **azioni di fondazione** (*d'una società*) (*fin.*) vendor's shares; ~ **di godimento** (*fin.*) dividend-bearing share; ~ **d'indennizzo per inadempienza contrattuale** (*leg.*) action of covenant; ~ **d'opposizione** (*leg.*) counteraction; **azioni di portafoglio** (*fin.*) treasury stock; ~ **di regresso** (*cred.*) recourse; **azioni di risparmio** (*fin.*) savings shares; ~ **di rivalsa** (*cred.*) recourse; ~ **di rivendica** (*leg.*) action for recovery; **un' ~ dilatoria** (*leg.*) a delaying action; ~ **diretta** (*sind.*) direct action; ~ **disonesta** (*leg.*) malfeasance, wrong; **azioni distribuite come dividendo** (*fin.*) stock dividend; **azioni e titoli a interesse variabile** (*fin.*) equity securities; **azioni ferroviarie** (*Borsa*) railway shares, rails; railroads (*USA*); **azioni finanziarie** (*fin.*) finance shares; **azioni frazionate** (*fin.*) split shares; ~ **giudiziaria** (*leg.*) proceedings (*pl.*), remedy; **azioni gratuite** (*fin.*) bonus shares; ~ **illecita** (*leg.*) malfeasance; **azioni illegali** (*leg.*) lawless acts; ~ **impugnativa** (*leg.*) cross action; **azioni** (*depositate*) **in garanzia** (*fin.*) qualification shares; **azioni** (*d'imprese*) **industriali** (*fin.*) industrials; ~ **intempestiva per decorrenza del termine** (*leg.*) action barred by lapse of time; **azioni interamente liberate** (*fin.*) fully paid stock; full-paid stock (*USA*); **azioni iscritte a listino** (*Borsa*) listed stock; **azioni lecite** (*leg.*) lawful acts; ~ **legale** (*leg.*) action at law, legal action, judicial proceedings, process, suit at law, lawsuit, suit; ~ **legale contro debitori morosi** (*leg.*) legal action against delinquent debtors; ~ **legale per il ricupero di crediti** (*leg.*) creditor's suit; **un' ~ legale vessatoria** (*leg.*) a vexatious suit at law; **azioni liberate** (*fin.*) paid-up shares; **azioni negoziabili** (*fin.*) transferable stock; **azioni nominative** (*fin.*) nominative shares, registered shares; inscribed stock (*ingl.*); **azioni non stampigliate** (*fin.*) unstamped shares, unmarked shares; **azioni o eccezioni** (*leg.*) claims and defences; ~ **ordinaria** (*fin.*) equity; common stock (*USA*); **azioni ordinarie** (*fin.*) ordinary shares; common stock (*USA*); **azioni parzialmente liberate** (*fin.*) partly-paid shares; ~ **penale** (*leg.*) penal action, penal suit; ~ **per annullamento di contratto** (*leg.*) action for avoidance of contract; ~ **personale** (*leg.*) personal action; ~ **petitoria** (*leg.*) petitory action; **un' ~ possessoria** (*leg.*) a possessory action; ~ **postergata** (*fin.*) deferred share; **azioni postergate** (*fin.*) deferred stock; **azioni preferenziali** (*fin.*) preference shares, preferred shares, preference stock, preferred stock; **azioni privilegiate** (*fin.*) preference shares, preferred shares, preference stock, preferred stock; **azioni privilegiate convertibili** (*in azioni ordinarie, della stessa società, a condizioni prefissate*) (*fin.*) convertible preference shares; **azioni privilegiate cumulative** (*fin.*) cumulative preference shares, cumulative preferred stock; ~ **reciproca** interaction; ~ **redibitoria** (*leg.*) redhibitory action; **azioni redimibili** (*fin.*) call stock; ~ **rescissoria** (*leg.*) rescissory action; ~ **riconvenzionale** (*leg.*) counteraction, cross action, reconvention; **azioni senza diritto di voto** (*fin.*) non-voting shares; **azioni senza valore nominale** (*fin.*) no-par shares; **azioni sicure e di tutta tranquillità** (*fin.*) blue chips; **azioni sociali** (*fin., USA*) corporate stock; **azioni stampigliate** (*fin.*) marked shares.

azionista, *n. m.* e *f.* (*fin.*) shareholder, stockholder. // ~ **di minoranza** (*fin.*) minority shareholder; **azionisti in ritardo coi versamenti** (*per azioni sottoscritte*) (*fin.*) shareholders in arrears with calls; ~ **privilegiato** (*fin.*) preference shareholder.

B

bacino, *n. m.* (*trasp. mar.*) basin, dock. // ~ **a livello d'acqua costante** (*trasp. mar.*) wet dock; ~ **a secco** (*trasp. mar.*) dry dock; ~ **carbonifero** coal-field; ~ **del porto** (*trasp. mar.*) harbour basin; ~ **di carenaggio** (*trasp. mar.*) dry dock, graving-dock, repairing basin; ~ **di marea** (*trasp. mar.*) tidal basin, tidal dock; ~ **di raddobbo** (*trasp. mar.*) repairing basin; ~ **fluviale** (*trasp.*) river-basin; ~ **galleggiante** (*di carenaggio*) (*trasp. mar.*) floating dock; ~ **portuale** (*trasp. mar.*) harbour basin.

bagagliaio, *n. m.* **1** (*trasp. aut.*) boot. **2** (*trasp. ferr.*) luggage van, van.

bagaglio, *n. m.* (*trasp.*) luggage; baggage (*USA*). // ~ **a mano** (*trasp.*) hand luggage; hand baggage (*USA*); ~ **appresso** (*trasp.*) accompanied luggage; ~ **in eccedenza** (*trasp.*) excess luggage; excess baggage (*USA*); ~ **in franchigia** (*trasp.*) free luggage; free baggage (*USA*).

balla, *n. f.* **1** bale. **2** (*market.*) package; (*di lana, ecc.*) pack.

ballottaggio, *n. m.* (*leg.*) second ballot.

balzare, *v. i.* **1** to jump, to leap★, to skip. **2** (*market.*) (*di prezzi*) to run★ up, to shoot★ up, to zoom, to zoom up.

balzo, *n. m.* **1** jump, leap, skip. **2** (*market.*) (*dei prezzi*) run-up, zoom.

banca, *n. f.* (*cred.*) bank. // ~ **a capitale azionario** (*banca*) joint-stock bank; ~ **centrale** (*fin.*) central bank; ~ **che aderisce alla stanza di compensazione** (*fin.*) clearing bank, clearing banker; ~ **che copre** (*con le sue filiali*) **il territorio nazionale** (*fin.*) multiple-branch bank; ~ **che non ha filiali a Londra** (*fin., ingl.*) country bank; ~ **che partecipa al sistema della compensazione** (*aderendo alla stanza di compensazione di Londra*) (*fin.*) clearing bank; ~ **commerciale** commercial bank; ~ **cooperativa** co-operative bank; ~ **corrispondente** correspondent bank; **la** ~ **dei Regolamenti Internazionali (B.R.I.)** the Bank of International Settlements (*B.I.S.*); ~ **del commercio** bank of commerce; ~ **dell'agricoltura** agricultural bank; **la** «~ **delle banche**» (*la banca centrale*) the bankers' bank; **la** ~ **dello Stato** the bank of State; ~ **d'affari** «banque d'affaires»; merchant bank (*ingl.*); ~ **di cambio** (*fin.*) exchange bank; ~ **di credito** credit bank; ~ **di credito agricolo** agricultural credit bank, land bank; ~ **di credito ordinario** commercial bank, joint-stock bank; ~ **di deposito** bank of deposit, deposit bank; ~ **d'emissione** bank of issue, bank of circulation; **la** ~ **d'Inghilterra** the Bank of England, the Bank; the Old Lady (of Threadneedle Street); ~ **d'interesse nazionale** national interest bank; ~ **di provincia** country bank; ~ **di sconto** (*fin.*) bank of discount, discount bank, discounting house, discount house; **la** ~ **di Stato** the bank of State; the Government bank; ~ (*che svolge funzioni*) **di Tesoreria per lo Stato** Government depository; ~ **esattrice** collecting bank; **la** ~ **Europea per gli Investimenti (B.E.I.)** (*fin.*) the European Investment Bank (*E.I.B.*); **una** ~ **insolvibile** (*fin.*) a wildcat bank; **la** ~ **Mondiale** (*fin.*) the World Bank; **una** ~ **nazionale** (*fin.*) a national bank; **la** ~ **pagatrice** the paying banker; **una** ~ **privata** (*fin.*) a private bank; **una** ~ **solida** a sound bank; **a mezzo** ~ by banker.

bancabile, *a.* (*cred.*) bankable. // **non** ~ unbankable.

bancarella, *n. f.* (*market.*) stall, stand.

bancario, *a.* banking, bank (*attr.*). **1** (*pers.*) *n. m.* bank clerk, bank employee. **2 bancari,** *pl.* (*fin.*) (*titoli*) bank stocks.

bancarotta, *n. f.* **1** (*fig.*) (*disastro finanziario*) smash. **2** (*leg.*) «bancarotta» (*bankruptcy due either to misdemeanour or a fraudulent act on the part of the insolvent debtor*). // ~ **fraudolenta** «bancarotta fraudolenta» (*bankruptcy due to a fraudulent act on the part of the insolvent debtor*); ~ **semplice** «bancarotta semplice» (*bankruptcy due to misdemeanour on the part of the insolvent debtor*).

bancarottiere, *n. m.* (*leg.*) «bancarottiere» (*one who has committed «bancarotta», q.V.*).

banchiere, *n. m.* banker; bankster (*slang USA*). // ~ **accreditato** (*fin.*) accredited banker; ~ **della City di Londra** (*fin.*) City man; «~ **d'affari**» (*fin.*) merchant banker.

banchina, *n. f.* **1** (*trasp. ferr.*) platform. **2**

(*trasp. mar.*) jetty, pier, wharf★; dock (*USA*). // ~ **d'attracco** (*trasp. mar.*) quay; ~ **di carico** (*trasp. mar.*) loading dock; ~ **di trasbordo** (*trasp. mar.*) transshipment platform; ~ **ferroviaria** (*trasp. ferr.*) railway platform; ~ **per autocarri** (*trasp. aut.*) platform for lorries; **sulla** ~ (*market., trasp. mar.*) (*di merce*) ex quay, ex wharf.

banco, *n. m.* 1 bench. 2 (*di negozio*) counter. 3 (*storico*) banco. 4 (*trasp. mar.*) (*di sabbia, ecc.*) bank. // ~ **degli accusati** (*leg.*) dock; **il** ~ **dei magistrati** (*leg.*) the magistrates' bench; ~ **dei testimoni** (*leg.*) witness-box, box; ~ **della giuria** (*leg.*) box; ~ **d'accettazione** (*d'aeroporto*) (*trasp. aer.*) check-in desk; ~ **d'esposizione** (*market.*) stand; ~ **di prestiti su pegno** pawnbroker's (shop); ~ **di sabbia** (*trasp. mar.*) sand-bank, sand-bar; ~ **di saggio** assay office; **al** ~ over the counter; **roba di sotto** ~ under-the-counter goods; **sotto** ~ (*fig.*) under the counter; **vendita al** ~ over-the-counter sale; **vendita sotto** ~ under-the-counter sale.

bancogiro, *n. m.* (*banca, cred.*) money transfer.

banconota, *n. f.* 1 bank-note, note; bill (*USA*). 2 **banconote,** *pl.* (*fin.*) currency notes, paper currency, paper money, paper. // **banconote a corso forzoso** (*fin.*) forced currency paper, inconvertible paper money; **una** ~ **da cinquanta dollari** a fifty-dollar note (*o, USA,* bill); half a C (*slang USA*); **una** ~ **da cinque dollari** a five-dollar note (*o* bill); a five-spot, a fiver (*slang USA*); **una** ~ **da dieci dollari** a ten-dollar note (*o* bill); a tenner (*fam., USA*); a Dix, a dime-note (*slang USA*); **una** ~ **da dieci sterline** a ten-pound note; a tenner (*fam.*); **una** ~ **da due dollari** a two-dollar note (*o* bill); a deuce (*slang USA*); **una** ~ **da un dollaro** a one-dollar note (*o* bill); a single, a one (*fam., USA*); an ace (*slang USA*); **una** ~ **da una sterlina** a one-pound note; a single (*fam., ingl.*); **una** ~ **da venti dollari** a twenty-dollar note (*o* bill); a double-saw, a double sawbuck (*slang USA*); **una** ~ **di grosso taglio** a large bank-note; **banconote false** counterfeit bank-notes, flash notes; green goods (*fam., USA*); **banconote non convertibili** (*in moneta metallica*) (*fin.*) unredeemable bank-notes.

banda, *n. f.* band. // ~ **di parità** (*fin.*) parity band.

bandiera, *n. f.* flag. // ~ **di comodo** (*trasp. mar.*) flag of convenience; ~ **di convenienza** (*trasp. mar.*) flag of convenience; ~ **di (nave) mercantile** (*trasp. mar.*) merchant flag; ~ **di quarantena** (*trasp. mar.*) yellow flag; ~ **d'una società** (*di navigazione*) (*trasp. mar.*) house-flag; ~ **gialla** (*trasp. mar.*) yellow flag.

bandire, *v. t.* 1 (*proclamare*) to proclaim, to announce, to publish. 2 (*leg.*) (*mettere al bando*) to ban, to banish, to outlaw. // ~ **un concorso** to announce (*o* to publish) a competition; ~ **una gara d'appalto** to call for tenders; to invite to submit tenders.

banditore, *n. m.* (*di vendita all'asta*) auctioneer; vendue crier, vendue master (*USA*).

bando, *n. m.* 1 ban, proclamation. 2 (*leg.*) banishment. // ~ **di gara d'appalto** (*comm.*) ask (*o* call) for bids; invitation to tender.

barattare, *v. t.* 1 to barter. 2 (*scambiarsi*) to exchange; to swap (*fam.*).

baratteria, *n. f.* (*leg.*) (*atto o comportamento doloso di chi ha la responsabilità di un trasporto marittimo*) barratry.

baratto, *n. m.* 1 barter, truck. 2 (*scambio*) exchange; swap (*fam.*).

barca, *n. f.* (*trasp. mar.*) boat. // ~ **di salvataggio** (*trasp. mar.*) life-boat; ~ **per traghetti** ferry.

barcarizzo, *n. m.* (*trasp. mar.*) accommodation ladder, gangplank, gangway.

barcone, *n. m.* 1 (*trasp. mar.*) barge. 2 (*trasp. mar.*) (*a fondo piatto*) keel.

barile, *n. m.* 1 (*anche misura*) barrel. 2 cask.

barometro, *n. m.* (*anche fig.*) barometer. // ~ **congiunturale** (*econ.*) economic barometer; ~ **delle marche** (*market.*) consumer index, consumer inventory.

barra, *n. f.* (*alla foce d'un fiume*) bar. // ~ **spaziatrice** (*di macch. uff.*) space-bar, space-key.

«barrel», *n. m.* (*misura inglese di capacità per liquidi, pari a litri 163,45*) barrel.

barriera, *n. f.* 1 (*anche fig.*) barrier. 2 (*fig.*) hedge. 3 (*trasp. ferr.*) gate. // **barriere al libero scambio** (*comm. est.*) trade barriers; **barriere commerciali** (*comm. est.*) trade barriers; ~ **di pedaggio** (*trasp.*) tollbar; **barriere doganali** (*comm. est.*) customs barriers; **barriere non tariffarie** (*dog.*) non-tariff barriers (*NTB's*); **barriere protezionistiche** (*econ.*) protectionist barriers; ~ **tariffaria** (*comm. est., econ.*) tariff barrier, tariff wall.

base, *n. f.* 1 base, basis★, floor. 2 **la «base»** (*sind., fig.*) the rank and file. 3 **basi,** *pl.* (*anche*) footing. // **la** ~ **dell'accertamento** (*dell'imponibile*) the basis of assessment; **la** ~ **d'un contratto** (*leg.*) the basis of a contract; ~ **tariffaria** rate basis; **di** ~ basic; **in** ~ **alla legge** according to the law; **su basi di reciprocità** (*comm.*) on mutual terms; **sulla** ~ **d'un'analisi per campio-**

namento (*market.*) by analysing a sample.

basilare, *a.* basic, fundamental, ultimate.

basso, *a.* 1 low, small. 2 (*fig.*) (*vile, spregevole*) base. 3 (*market.*) (*di prezzo, anche*) keen. *n. m.* (*nell'espressione «gli alti e i bassi»*) down. // «**basso**» (*trasp.*) (*scritto su un collo di merci*) «this side down»; ~ **costo** low cost; inexpensiveness; **bassa marea** (*trasp. mar.*) low water; ~ **prezzo** low price; cheapness; ~ **tenore di vita** bad standing; **a** ~ **prezzo** (*market.*) low, cheap; **che vende a** ~ **prezzo** (*di negoziante, negozio*) cheap; **di** ~ **costo e di cattiva qualità** cheap and nasty; **in** ~ (*anche fig.*) low.

bastimento, *n. m.* (*trasp. mar.*) ship, vessel.

battello, *n. m.* (*trasp. mar.*) boat. // ~ **della sanità di porto** (*trasp. mar.*) pratique boat; ~ **fluviale** (*trasp.*) inland waterway vessel; **il** ~ **in arrivo** (*trasp. mar.*) the in boat; ~ **postale** (*comun.*) post-boat.

battere, *v. t.* 1 (*colpire*) to beat★, to knock, to strike★, to hit★, to bump. 2 (*sconfiggere*) to beat★, to defeat, to frustrate. 3 (*fam.*) (*scrivere a macchina*) to type. 4 (*fin.*) (*moneta*) to strike★. 5 (*trasp. mar.*) (*una bandiera*) to fly★. // ~ **cassa** (*fam.*) to ask for money; ~ **moneta** (*fin., anche*) to coin money, to mint; ~ (*un concorrente*) **nei prezzi** (*market.*) to underprice; ~ **la piazza** (*market.*) to canvass the town; to do the place (*fam.*); ~ **un primato** to beat a record, to break a record.

battuta, *n. f.* 1 beat, beating. 2 (*dattilografica*) stroke. // ~ **d'arresto** standstill.

beccheggiare, *v. i.* 1 (*trasp. aer., trasp. mar.*) to pitch. 2 (*trasp. mar.*) (*di nave*) to plunge.

beccheggio, *n. m.* (*trasp. aer., trasp. mar.*) pitch.

bello, *a.* (*anche fig.*) fine, fair, handsome; smart (*fig.*). // **bella copia** (*di documento, ecc.*) fair copy, clean copy; **bell'e fatto** (*d'abito*) (*market.*) ready-to-wear, hand-me-down; **un bel patrimonio** a handsome fortune; **bella presenza** (*pers.*) good appearance, smart appearance; **un bel prezzo** (*market.*) a handsome price, a smart price.

bene[1], *n. m.* 1 (*econ.*) good. 2 **beni,** *pl.* (*econ.*) possessions, goods; property, estate (*sing.*). 3 **beni,** *pl.* (*leg.*) assets. // **beni all'estero** (*leg.*) property abroad; **beni capitali** (*econ.*) capital goods, producer goods; ~ **complementare** (*econ.*) complementary commodity, joint commodity; **beni complementari** (*econ.*) complementary goods; **beni corporali** (*leg.*) tangible property; **i beni demaniali** (*leg.*) the public domain; **beni destinati al consumo privato** (*econ.*) private consumer goods; **beni d'asse ereditario** (*leg.*) hereditables; **beni di consumo** (*econ.*) consumer goods, consumer's goods, consumers' goods, consumption goods, consumables; **beni di consumo durevoli** (*econ.*) durable consumer goods, consumer durables; **beni di consumo non durevoli** (*econ.*) non-durable goods, non-durables; **beni d'investimento** (*econ., fin.*) investment goods, capital goods; **beni di prima necessità** necessaries; **beni di rifugio** (*econ.*) shelter goods; **i beni disponibili** (*leg.*) (*in un testamento*) the disposable portion; **beni dotali** (*leg.*) dotal property; **beni durevoli** (*econ.*) durable goods; **beni e servizi diversi** (*rag.*) sundry goods and services; ~ **economico** (*econ.*) economic good; **beni fondiari** (*econ.*) landed estate, landed property; ~ **fungibile** (*econ.*) fungible; **beni fungibili** (*econ.*) replaceable goods; **beni immobili** (*econ.*) fixed property, immovable property, immovables, real assets, things real; (*fin., leg.*) real estate, realty; **beni materiali** (*econ.*) tangible property; **beni mobili** (*econ.*) movable goods, goods, movables; (*denaro, mobilio, merci, ecc.*) chattels, chattels personal, things personal, goods and chattels; **beni mobili trasmissibili per eredità** (*leg.*) hereditament; **beni naturali** (*econ.*) original goods; **beni non durevoli** (*econ.*) soft goods; ~ **non economico** (*econ.*) free good; **beni parafernali** (*leg.*) separate estate; **beni personali** (*econ.*) goods and chattels, personal property, personal estate; **beni pignorabili** (*leg.*) seizable chattels; **beni principali** (*leg.*) chattels; **beni pubblici** (*econ.*) collective goods; **beni reali** (*fin., rag.*) tangible assets; (*leg.*) (*non in proprietà assoluta: un affitto, un raccolto in erba, ecc.*) chattels real; **beni reversibili** (*leg.*) reversion; **beni sequestrati** (*leg.*) distress; **beni soggetti a pignoramento** (*leg.*) distrainable chattels; **beni soggetti a sequestro** (*leg.*) distrainable chattels; **beni strumentali** (*econ.*) capital goods, industrial goods, instrumental goods, intermediate goods, auxiliary goods, producer goods, production goods; **beni strumentali essenziali** (*econ.*) basic capital goods; ~ **surrogabile** (*econ.*) alternative commodity.

bene[2], *avv.* 1 well. 2 (*rettamente*) rightly. // ~ **organizzato** (*o* **strutturato**) (*org. az.*) well-organized; well-heeled (*fig.*).

beneficiare, *v. i.* to benefit, to profit (by).

beneficiario, *n. m.* 1 beneficiary. 2 (*ass.*) payee. 3 (*cred.*) (*d'un pagamento*) payee. 4 (*leg.*) beneficial owner, grantee. // **il** ~ **d'una polizza d'assicurazione** (*ass.*) the beneficiary of an insurance policy; ~ **d'un vitalizio** annuitant; ~ **fittizio** (*leg.*) fictitious payee.

beneficio, *n. m.* **1** benefit, advantage, boon, good. **2** (*fin.*) profit, gain. **3** (*leg.*) benefit, consideration. **4** (*leg.*) (*ecclesiastico*) benefice.

benefico, *a.* beneficial, advantageous, profitable.

benessere, *n. m.* welfare. // **il ~ d'una nazione** (*econ.*) the welfare of a nation; **~ economico** (*econ.*) economic welfare; affluence.

benestante, *a.* (*econ.*) affluent, well-off, well-to-do. *n. m.* e *f.* wealthy person.

benestare, *n. m.* **1** approval. **2** (*visto*) visa. // **~ bancario** bank clearance; **~ di prelevamento** (*di fondi, da un conto di risparmio*) (*banca*) withdrawl warrant.

benevolo, *a.* benevolent, benign. // **~ disinteresse** (*econ.*) benign neglect.

benservito, *n. m.* **1** (*pers.*) reference, testimonial. **2** (*pers.*) (*per un domestico*) character. **3** (*pers., fig.*) (*licenziamento*) sack.

berlina, *n. f.* (*trasp. aut.*) saloon car, saloon, sedan.

bianco, *a.* **1** white. **2** (*non scritto*) blank. // **in ~** in blank, blank.

bidone, *n. m.* **1** can, bin. **2** (*fig., fam.*) (*imbroglio*) swindle.

bigliettaio, *n. m.* **1** (*pers., trasp.*) (*nelle stazioni*) booking-clerk. **2** (*pers., trasp.*) (*di treno, tram, o autobus*) conductor. **3** (*pers., trasp. ferr.*) ticket-collector.

bigliettario, *n. m. V.* **bigliettaio.**

biglietteria, *n. f.* (*trasp.*) booking office, ticket-office.

biglietto, *n. m.* **1** card, note, ticket. **2** (*trasp.*) ticket. // **~ a metà prezzo** (*per bambini e cani*) (*trasp.*) half; **~ a riduzione per bambini** (*trasp.*) child's half-fare ticket; **~ a tariffa ridotta** (*trasp.*) reduced-rate ticket; **~ a tariffa ridotta del 50%** (*trasp.*) half-fare ticket; **~ circolare** (*banca*) circular note; (*trasp.*) circular ticket; **~ collettivo** (*trasp. ferr.*) party ticket; **~ combinato** (*trasp.*) combined ticket; **~ cumulativo** (*trasp. ferr.*) party ticket, through ticket, transfer ticket, transfer; **~ da cento dollari** hundred-dollar bill; bill (*slang USA*); **~ da cinque dollari** five-dollar bill; Abe's cabe (*slang USA*); **~ da dieci dollari** ten-dollar bill; ten (*fam., USA*); **~ da dieci sterline** ten-pound note; ten (*fam.*); **~ da mille dollari** thousand-dollar bill; big one (*slang USA*); **~ da visita** *V.* **~ di visita**; **~ d'abbonamento** (*trasp.*) commutation ticket; **~ d'aereo** aeroplane ticket, air ticket; **~ d'andata** (*trasp.*) single ticket, single; **~ d'andata e ritorno** (*trasp., ingl.*) return ticket, return; round-trip ticket (*USA*); **~ di banca** bank-note, treasury note, note; bank bill, bill (*USA*); **biglietti di banca** (*fin.*) paper currency, paper money, paper (*sing.*); **~ d'entrata** entrance ticket, admission ticket, card of admission; **~ di favore** complimentary ticket; **~ d'ingresso** admission ticket, entrance ticket; **~ d'invito** invitation card; **~ di libera circolazione** (*trasp. ferr.*) free pass; **un ~ di prima classe** (*trasp.*) a first-class ticket; **un ~ di ringraziamento** a note of thanks; **un ~ di seconda classe** (*trasp.*) a second-class ticket; **biglietti di Stato a corso forzoso** (*fion.*) currency notes; **biglietti di viaggio** (*tur.*) travel tickets; **~ di visita** visiting card, business card, ticket; calling-card (*USA*); **~ ferroviario** (*trasp. ferr.*) railway ticket; **~ ferroviario valido un solo giorno** (*trasp. ferr.*) day ticket (*ingl.*); **~ gratuito** (*trasp.*) pass; **~ natalizio** Christmas card; **~ per posta aerea** (*comun.*) air letter; **~ postale** (*pieghevole, e che non abbisogna di busta*) letter sheet; **un ~ turistico** (*trasp., tur.*) a tourist ticket.

bilancia, *n. f.* **1** (*lo strumento*) weighing machine; scales (*pl.*); pair of scales. **2** (*econ., fin.*) balance, account. // **~ commerciale** (*econ., fin.*) balance of trade, trade balance, trading balance, current account; **una ~ commerciale attiva** (*econ., fin.*) an active balance of trade, a favourable balance of trade; **una ~ commerciale deficitaria** (*econ., fin.*) an adverse trade balance, an unfavourable balance of trade; **una ~ commerciale passiva** (*econ., fin.*) a passive balance of trade, an adverse trade balance; **~ dei conti** (*econ., fin.*) balance of indebtedness; **~ dei conti correnti** (*econ., fin.*) (*bilancia dei pagamenti, incluse le partite invisibili, ma esclusi i movimenti di capitale*) current balance; **~ dei pagamenti** (*econ., fin.*) balance of payments; **la ~ dei pagamenti internazionali** (*econ., fin.*) the balance of international payments; **la ~ della giustizia** (*fig.*) the scales of justice; **la ~ delle operazioni** (*o* **dei pagamenti**) **correnti** (*econ., fin.*) the current account; the balance on current account; **la ~ delle partite correnti** (*econ., fin.*) the current account.

bilanciare, *v. t.* **1** (*tenere in equilibrio*) to balance. **2** (*compensare*) to balance, to countervail, to offset★. **3** (*fin., rag.*) to balance, to balance up. **4** (*rag.*) to cancel out, to close out. // **~ un conto** (*fin., rag.*) to balance an account; (*rag.*) to close out an account.

bilanciarsi, *v. recipr.* **1** (*fin., rag.*) to balance each other. **2** (*rag.*) to cancel each other.

bilancio, *n. m.* **1** (*fin., rag.*) balance. **2** (*fin., rag.*) (*di previsione; specialm. quello dello Stato*) budget. **3** (*rag.*) (*prospetto del dare e dell'avere*) balance-sheet. // **~ amministrativo** (*rag.*) administrative budget; ~ **annuale** (*rag.*) balance-sheet; ~ **«budgetario»** (*fin., rag.*) budget; ~ **(chiuso) al 31 dicembre 1983** balance-sheet made up to (*o* as at) December 31st 1983; ~ **commerciale** (*rag.*) balance-sheet; ~ **comparato** (*rag.*) comparative balance; ~ **consolidato** (*rag.*) consolidated balance; ~ **consuntivo** (*rag.*) final balance, appropriation account; ~ **dello Stato** (*econ.*) national budget; ~ **d'apertura** (*rag.*) opening balance; ~ **d'approvvigionamento** (*rag.*) supply balance-sheet; ~ **di chiusura** (*rag.*) closing balance; ~ **di funzionamento** (*rag.*) operating budget; ~ **di liquidazione** (*rag.*) realization and liquidation account; ~ **di previsione** (*rag.*) anticipatory account, budget; ~ **di riserva** (*rag.*) contingency budget; ~ **di verifica** (*rag.*) trial balance; ~ **economico** (*fin., rag.*) balance of indebtedness; ~ **economico preliminare** (*fin., rag.*) preliminary economic budget; ~ **familiare** family budget; **bilanci finanziari** (*fin., rag.*) balance-sheets; ~ **generale** (*rag.*) general balance-sheet; ~ **preventivo delle vendite** (*org. az., rag.*) sales budget; **il ~ preventivo dello Stato** (*fin.*) the national budget; the estimates (*pl.*); ~ **preventivo di massima** (*fin.*) draft budget; ~ **preventivo variabile** (*fin.*) flexible budget; ~ **provvisorio** (*rag.*) temporary balance; **un ~ reflazionistico** (*econ., fin.*) a reflationary budget; ~ **rettificativo** (*rag.*) rectifying budget, amended budget; **un ~ scompensato** (*fin., rag.*) an unbalanced budget; ~ **sintetico** (*rag.*) condensed balance, condensed balance-sheet; ~ **statale** (*econ.*) *V.* ~ **dello Stato**; ~ **suppletivo** (*rag.*) supplementary budget; ~ **unico** (*d'una società madre e delle affiliate*) (*rag.*) consolidated balance-sheet; **di ~ «budgetario»** (*fin., rag.*) budgetary.

bilaterale, *a.* **1** bilateral. **2** (*leg.*) synallagmatic.

bilione, *n. m.* (*un 1 seguito da 9 zeri*) billion (*USA*); one thousand millions, milliard (*ingl.*).

bimetallico, *a.* (*econ., fin.*) bimetallic.

bimetallismo, *n. m.* (*econ., fin.*) bimetallism, bimetalism, double standard. // ~ **zoppo** (*fin.*) limping standard.

bimetallista, *a.* (*econ., fin.*) bimetallistic, bimetalistic. *n. m.* e *f.* (*econ., fin.*) bimetallist, bimetalist.

binario, *n. m.* (*trasp. ferr.*) railway track, track; metals (*pl., ingl.*). // ~ **di deposito** (*trasp. ferr.*) storage track; ~ **di raccordo** (*trasp. ferr.*) side-track, siding track, siding, feeder line; ~ **di trasbordo** (*trasp. ferr.*) transfer track.

bisognatario, *n. m.* (*banca, cred.*) referee in case of need; referee.

bisogno, *n. m.* **1** need, necessity, requirement, distress. **2** (*anche econ.*) want. **3** (*cred.*) (*per una cambiale*) case of need. // **bisogni fittizi** fictitious needs; **bisogni materiali** (*econ.*) material needs; **bisogni reali** real needs; **al ~** (*banca, cred.*) in case of need.

bivio stradale, *n. m.* (*trasp. aut.*) road fork.

bloccare, *v. t.* to block, to freeze★. // ~ **un assegno** (*banca, cred.*) to stop a cheque; ~ **un conto** (*banca, cred.*) to block an account; ~ **l'inflazione** (*econ.*) to tame inflation; ~ **i prezzi** (*market.*) to freeze prices; ~ **i salari** (*sind.*) to freeze wages; ~ **il traffico** (*trasp. aut.*) to block the traffic.

blocchetto, *n. m.* (*di biglietti, buoni, ecc.*) book.

blocco, *n. m.* **1** block, blockade, freeze, squeeze. **2** (*econ., fin.*) (*politico, economico, finanziario*) bloc (*francese*). // ~ **degli affitti** (*econ.*) rent control; **il ~ (dei Paesi) dell'Occidente** the Western bloc; ~ **dei prezzi** (*econ.*) price freeze; ~ **dei salari** (*sind.*) wage-freeze; ~ **delle assunzioni** (*econ.*) freeze on hiring; ~ **di memoria** (*elab. elettr.*) store block; ~ **stradale** (*trasp. aut.*) road block; **in ~** (*market.*) en bloc, in the bulk, in the lump.

boa, *n. f.* (*trasp. mar.*) buoy. // ~ **luminosa** (*trasp. mar.*) beacon.

bocca del porto, *n. f.* (*trasp. mar.*) harbour entrance.

boccaporto, *n. m.* (*trasp. mar.*) hatch, hatchway.

boicottaggio, *n. m.* **1** boycott, boycotting. **2** (*market.*) freeze-out.

boicottare, *v. t.* **1** to boycott. **2** (*market.*) to freeze★ out.

bolla, *n. f.* **1** (*comm.*) bill, note. **2** (*dog.*) bill of entry, entry. // ~ **con richiesta di visita preventiva** (*dog.*) bill of sight; ~ **dei prezzi** (*improvviso aumento subito dopo un periodo di congelamento*) (*econ., market.*) prices bubble; ~ **di consegna** (*org. az.*) delivery note; ~ **di merce esente** (*da dazio*) (*dog.*) free entry; ~ **di prelievo** (*org. az.*) stock-withdrawal order.

bollare, *v. t.* **1** to stamp. **2** (*comun.*) (*una lettera*) to postmark. // **carta bollata** stamped paper.

bolletta, *n. f.* **1** (*comm.*) note, bill. **2** (*dog.*) bill of entry, entry. **3** (*trasp. ferr.*) delivery note. // ~ **dei pesi** (*trasp. mar.*) weight note; ~ **del contratto di mediazione** broker's contract note; **la ~ del gas** the gas bill; ~ **d'accompagnamento in deposito doganale** (*dog.*) entry for warehousing; ~ **di cauzione** (*dog.*) bond note; ~ **di consegna** (*trasp.*) delivery note; ~ **d'entrata**

(*dog.*) prime entry; ~ **d'entrata di merce esente da dazio** (*dog.*) entry for free goods, free entry; ~ **d'entrata di merce per consumo interno** (*dog.*) entry for home use; ~ **d'entrata doganale** (*dog.*) bill of entry; ~ **di sortita** (*dog., trasp. mar.*) shipping bill; ~ **di spedizione** (*trasp. aut.*) carriage note; ~ **di spedizione ferroviaria** (*trasp. ferr.*) consignment note; ~ **di trasporto** (*trasp. aut.*) carriage note; ~ **di trasporto aereo** (*trasp. aer.*) air consignment note, air waybill, air bill; ~ **doganale** (*dog.*) customs entry; ~ **doganale d'entrata** (*dog.*) entry inwards; ~ **doganale d'uscita** (*dog.*) entry outwards.

bollettario, *n. m.* receipt book. // ~ **a madre e figlia** counterfoil book; stub book (*USA*); ~ **di consegna** (*trasp. ferr.*) delivery book.

bollettino, *n. m.* 1 bulletin. 2 (*ufficiale*) communiqué. 3 (*banca, Borsa, cred.*) list. 4 (*trasp.*) note. // ~ **commerciale** trade report; **il ~ commerciale dei prezzi correnti** the current price list; **il ~ dei cambi** (*Borsa*) the Exchange list; ~ **dei protesti** (*cred., fin.*) black list; **il ~ del Lloyd** (*ass. mar.*) the Lloyd's list; **il ~ della Borsa** the Stock Exchange list; **un ~ d'informazioni** an advisory bulletin; (*comm.*) a newsletter; ~ **di spedizione** (*trasp.*) dispatch note; (*trasp. ferr.*) consignment note; ~ **metereologico** weather forecast.

bollino, *n. m.* (*market.*) trading stamp, gift stamp.

bollo, *n. m.* 1 stamp. 2 (*sigillo*) seal. // ~ **ad valorem** ad valorem stamp; ~ **cambiario** bill stamp; ~ **del fissato** (*fin.*) contract stamp; ~ **della polizza** (*ass.*) policy stamp; ~ **dell'assegno** (*banca*) cheque stamp; ~ **di circolazione** (*trasp. aut.*) licence plate, licence tag; ~ **fiscale** (*fin.*) inland revenue stamp; ~ **per ricevuta** receipt stamp; ~ **postale** (*comun.*) postmark; **bolli premio** (*market., pubbl.*) trading stamps, gift stamps; ~ **stampato** (*su una busta, un documento, ecc.*) impressed stamp, imprint stamp; ~ **sui titoli** (*fin.*) finance stamp; **carta da ~** stamped paper; **senza ~** (*leg.*) (*di documento*) unstamped.

bonaccia, *n. f.* (*trasp. mar.*) dead calm.

bonificare, *v. t.* 1 (*abbuonare, scontare*) to allow, to discount. 2 (*banca, cred.*) to credit. 3 (*econ.*) (*un terreno, ecc.*) to reclaim.

bonifico, *n. m.* 1 (*abbuono, sconto*) allowance, discount. 2 (*banca, cred.*) transfer, credit transfer. // ~ **bancario** (*banca, cred.*) money transfer; ~ **telegrafico** (*comun., cred.*) telegraphic transfer, cable transfer.

boom, *n. m.* (*econ.*) boom. // ~ **alimentato dagli investimenti** (*econ.*) investment-led boom; ~ **alimentato dall'espansione dei consumi** (*econ.*) consumer-led boom; ~ **alimentato dalle esportazioni** (*econ.*) exported boom; ~ **associato a inflazione** (*econ.*) boomflation; ~ **dei consumi** (*econ.*) consumer boom.

bordeggiare, *v. i.* (*trasp. mar.*) to board, to sail against the wind, to stand★ off and on, to wear★.

borderò, *n. m.* (*comm.*) bordereau★, list, note. // ~ **d'acquisto** (*fin.*) bought note (*o* contract); ~ **di Borsa** (*fin.*) stockbroker's contract; ~ **di cambio** (*Borsa*) Exchange contract; ~ **di sconto** (*banca, cred.*) list of bills for discount.

bordo, *n. m.* 1 (*orlo*) edge, brink. 2 (*di nave*) board. // **a ~** (*trasp. aer., trasp. mar.*) on board; (*trasp. mar.*) on board, aboard, within board; **a ~ di** (*trasp. aer., trasp. mar.*) on board, aboard; **fuori ~** (*trasp. mar.*) overboard; (*di motore*) outboard; **sotto ~** (*trasp. mar.*) alongside.

borsa, *n. f.* 1 (*fin.*) Exchange. 2 (*fin.*) (*Borsa Valori*) (Stock) Exchange, stock market, market. // **la ~ dei cereali** the Corn Exchange; **la ~ dei Noli** (*trasp. mar.*) the Shipping Exchange; **la ~ dei Noli Marittimi e dei Cereali** (*a Londra*) (*fin., trasp. mar.*) the Baltic Mercantile and Shipping Exchange, the Baltic Exchange, the Baltic; **la ~ del Carbone** (*fin.*) the Coal Exchange; **la ~ del Cotone** (*fin.*) the Cotton Exchange; **la ~ di New York** the New York Stock Exchange; the big board (*slang USA*); «**Borse e Mercati**» (*giorn.*) (*titolo di rubrica, colonna, ecc.*) market news; ~ **-mercato** (*market.*) (*del bestiame e dei prodotti agricoli*) terminal market; ~ **Merci** (*fin.*) Commodity Exchange, Produce Exchange; ~ **nera** black market; ~ **non ufficiale** (*fin.*) coulisse; ~ **Valori** (*fin.*) Stock Exchange, Exchange; (the) 'change, (the) House (*fam.*); stock market; bourse (*francese*); **la ~ Valori di Londra** the London Stock Exchange; **alla ~ Valori** on the Exchange; on the 'change, on 'change (*fam.*); **in ~** on the 'change (*fam.*).

borsino, *n. m.* (*Borsa*) coulisse; street market (*a Londra*).

bottega, *n. f.* 1 (*market.*) shop; store (*USA*). 2 (*azienda*) business, concern. // ~ **artigiana** workshop.

bottegaio, *n. m.* (*market.*) shopkeeper, tradesman★; storekeeper, merchant (*USA*).

bozza, *n. f.* 1 minute, draft. 2 (*giorn.*) proof. // ~ **di capitolato** (*leg.*) tentative specifications; ~ **di prova** (*giorn.*) proof-sheet; ~ **di stampa** (*pubbl.*) final proof.

bracciante, *n. m.* (*pers.*) labourer; laborer (*USA*). // ~ **agricolo** (*pers.*) farm labourer, farm hand, land worker.

breve, *a.* brief, short. *n. m.* (*econ.*) *V.* ~ **termine.** // ~ **appunto** jotting; ~ **termine** (*econ.*) short period, short range, short run, short term; **a** ~ (*econ., fin.*) short-term; **a** ~ **scadenza** (*cred.*) short-dated, short; **a** ~ **termine** (*econ., fin.*) in the short run; short-term (*attr.*); **con** ~ **preavviso** at short notice; **entro** ~ **tempo** at short notice; **entro** ~ **termine** at short notice; **entro il più** ~ **termine possibile** as soon as possible.

brevettabile, *a.* (*leg.*) patentable.

brevettare, *v. t.* (*leg.*) (*un'invenzione, un procedimento, ecc.*) to patent.

brevettato, *a.* (*leg.*) patent (*attr.*), proprietary. // **non** ~ (*leg.*) unpatented.

brevetto, *n. m.* **1** (*leg.*) patent, licence. **2** (*leg.*) (*d'invenzione*) letters patent, letters overt (*pl.*). **3 brevetti,** *pl.* (*leg.*) (*diritti*) patent rights, proprietary rights. // ~ **di capitano** (*trasp. mar.*) master's certificate; ~ **di fabbricazione** (*leg.*) proprietary right of manufacture; ~ **industriale** (*leg.*) design patent.

brevettuale, *a.* (*leg.*) concerning a patent.

brogliaccio, *n. m.* **1** scrap book. **2** (*rag.*) day book, waste-book, blotter. // ~ **di cassa** (*banca*) counter cash book.

brokeraggio, *n. m.* (*fin.*) brokerage.

brutto, *a.* bad, foul, ugly. // **un** ~ **affare** a bad job (*fam.*); **brutta copia** foul copy, draft; ~ **tempo** bad weather.

buca, *n. f.* pit. // ~ **da lettere** (*comun.*) post-box, letter-box, posting box; mailbox (*USA*).

buchetta per le chiavi, *locuz. n.* (*tur.*) (*in un albergo*) key box.

budget, *n. m.* (*fin., rag.*) budget. // ~ **(del fabbisogno) dei capitali** capital budget; ~ **variabile** flexible budget.

budgetario, *a.* (*fin., rag.*) budgetary.

budgeting, *n. m.* (*fin., rag.*) budgeting.

buggetario, *a.* (*fin., rag.*) budgetary.

bullionismo, *n. m.* (*econ., fin.*) bullionism.

buono[1], *a.* good, fine, sound. // **un buon affare** a good bargain, a bargain, a smart deal, a stroke of business; a good pennyworth (*fam.*); **buon andamento** (*Borsa, market.*) brightness; **buona annata** (*econ.*) on-year; **buona carta** (*cred.*) good paper; **buona causa** (*leg.*) good cause; **una buona cauzione** (*leg.*) a good security; **buona condotta** (*leg.*) good behaviour; **buona consegna** (*di titoli*) (*Borsa*) good delivery; **buona copia** (*di documento, ecc.*) fair copy, clean copy; **buona fede** (*leg.*) good faith; **buon nome** (good) reputation, repute; **buon padre di famiglia** (*leg.*) prudent man; **buona qualità media** (*market.*) good average quality; **buona reputazione** good reputation, standing; **buona volontà** good-will; **a buon mercato** cheap, low-cost, inexpensive, unexpensive (*aggettivi*); cheaply, cheap, on the cheap, low (*avverbi*); **a buon prezzo** cheap (*a.*); cheaply, cheap (*avverbi*); **di buon grado** willingly; **di buona lega** (*di metallo prezioso*) sterling; **in buone condizioni** sound; (*ass., trasp.*) undamaged; **in buona fede** (*leg.*) bona fide; **in** ~ **stato** (*di macchinario*) in working order; **piuttosto a buon mercato** cheapish; **sotto buona guardia** (*leg.*) in custody.

buono[2], *n. m.* **1** (*tagliando*) coupon, voucher. **2** (*fin.*) bill, bond, note. **3** (*market.*) voucher. **4** (*pubbl.*) coupon. **5** (*rag.*) voucher. // ~ **del Tesoro** (*fin.*) Treasury bill; (*poliennale*) Treasury bond, Exchequer bond, bond; **buoni del Tesoro** (*fin.*) Government bonds, stocks; **buoni del Tesoro infruttiferi** (*fin.*) non-interest-bearing Government notes; ~ **d'anticipazione** (*banca, cred.*) advance note; ~ **d'avaria** (*ass. mar.*) average bond; ~ **di carico** (*di magazzino*) (*org. az.*) warehouse bond; ~ **di cassa** cash voucher; (*banca*) deposit receipt; (*fin.*) cash bond; **buoni di «cassa» falsificati** (*Borsa, leg.*) false medium-term securities; ~ **di consegna** warrant for delivery, voucher; (*trasp. mar.*) delivery order; ~ **d'imbarco** (*trasp. mar.*) shipping order, shipping note; ~ **di lavorazione** (*org. az.*) job order, work order, work ticket; ~ **di passaggio** (*org. az.*) form of material transfer; ~ **di piccola cassa** (*rag.*) petty-cash voucher; ~ **fruttifero del Tesoro** (*con scadenza fino a un anno*) (*fin., USA*) Treasury certificate; **buoni mensa** (*pers.*) luncheon vouchers; ~ **omaggio** (*market.*) redemption coupon; ~ **per acquisto di libri** (*market.*) book token; ~ **per benzina** (*trasp. aut.*) petrol coupon; ~ **sconto** (*market.*) redemption coupon.

buonuscita, *n. f.* **1** (*a un inquilino uscente*) key money. **2** (*a un negoziante, ecc.: per l'avviamento*) good-will money. **3** (*fin.*) (*al direttore uscente d'una società*) golden handshake. **4** (*leg., pers.*) (*indennità di fine lavoro pagata a un dipendente*) retirement bonus (*non esiste in G.B.*).

bureau, *n. m.* (*tur.*) reception desk.

bussola, *n. f.* (*trasp. mar.*) compass. // ~ **magnetica** magnetic compass.

busta, *n. f.* **1** envelope. **2** (*comun.*) cover. // ~ **a finestra** (*comun.*) window-envelope; **una** ~ **affrancata** (*comun.*) a stamped envelope; ~ **commerciale** (*comun.*) commercial envelope; ~

commerciale a finestra (*comun.*) cut-out panel envelope; ~ **paga** (*pers.*) pay-envelope; pay-packet, packet (*ingl.*); ~ (*generalm. affrancata e indirizzata*) **per la risposta** (*comun.*) return envelope; **una ~ senza indirizzo** (*comun.*) an unaddressed envelope.

«bustarella», *n. f.* **1** (*mancia*) gratuity. **2** (*leg.*) bribe; payola (*USA*).

buttare, *v. t.* (*anche fig.*) to throw*, to fling*, to cast*. // ~ **a mare** (*trasp. mar.*) to cast away; ~ **a mare una parte del carico** (*trasp. mar.*) to cast overboard part of the cargo; ~ **altro denaro per tentare di ricuperare quello perduto** to throw good money after bad; ~ **fuori** to throw out; ~ **giù** (*note frettolose, ecc.*) to jot (down); ~ **giù il mercato** (*provocando un forte ribasso dei prezzi*) (*fin.*) to bang the market; ~ **via il denaro** to throw away one's money.

C

cabina, *n. f.* **1** (*trasp. aer., trasp. mar.*) cabin. **2** (*trasp. mar.*) berth. // ~ **di comando** (*di locomotiva, ecc.*) (*trasp. ferr.*) engineer's cab; ~ **di comando dei segnali** (*trasp. ferr.*) signal-box; signal tower (*USA*); ~ **di lusso** (*trasp. mar.*) state-room; ~ **di segnalazione** (*trasp. ferr.*) box; ~ **pressurizzata** (*trasp. aer.*) pressure cabin; ~ **telefonica** (*comun.*) call-box, telephone box (*o* booth).

cablare, *v. t.* (*comun.*) to cable.

cablo, *n. m.* (*comun.*) cablegram, cable.

cablografare, *v. t.* (*comun.*) to cable.

cablogramma, *n. m.* (*comun.*) cablegram, cable.

cabotaggio, *n. m.* (*trasp. mar.*) cabotage; coasting trade.

cadere, *v. i.* **1** (*anche fig.*) to fall★, to drop. **2** (*di prezzi, ecc.*) to collapse. // ~ **in disuso** (*leg.*) to fall into abeyance; ~ **in perenzione** (*o* **in prescrizione**) (*leg.*) to prescribe, to lapse; to be debarred (by the statute of limitations).

caduta, *n. f.* **1** (*anche fig.*) fall, falling, drop. **2** (*di prezzi, ecc.*) collapse, plunge, slump, downfall. // ~ **in mare di merci** (*ass. mar.*) falling of goods overboard; **una lieve** (*e spesso temporanea*) ~ **dei prezzi** (*Borsa, fin., market.*) a dip in prices.

calare, *v. i.* **1** to decrease, to fall★, to drop, to decline, to diminish (in value), to lower (in value), to slacken, to weaken. **2** (*di prezzi, ecc.*) to come★ down, to go★ down, to sag. **3** (*fin., market.*) (*di prezzi, quotazioni, ecc.*) to recede. *v. t.* **1** to lower. **2** (*i prezzi*) to cut★. // ~ **di prezzo** (*di merce*) to cheapen; ~ (*un carico*) **nella stiva** (*trasp. mar.*) to strike down; **far** ~ **il prezzo di** to cheapen.

calata, *n. f.* (*trasp. mar.*) quay, wharf★.

calce, *n. f.* (*comm.*) (*nella locuz.*) **in** ~ at foot, at bottom, below.

calcolare, *v. t.* **1** (*computare, contare*) to compute, to count. **2** (*farsi un'idea di*) to reckon, to figure out. **3** (*controllare*) to tally. **4** (*stimare*) to evaluate. **5** (*mat.*) to calculate, to cast★, to cipher out, to cypher out, to figure, to work out. // ~ **l'ammontare di** (*mat., rag.*) to figure up; ~ **un arbitraggio** (*Borsa*) to compute an arbitrage; ~ (*una quantità*) **con una macchina calcolatrice** (*rag.*) to take off; ~ **gli interessi** (*rag.*) to work out the interests; ~ **male** to miscalculate; ~ **la scadenza d'una cambiale** (*banca*) to compute a bill; ~ **una somma** to cipher out a sum; ~ **le spese** (*rag.*) to figure expenses; ~ **la tara di** (*merci, ecc.*) (*market.*) to tare; ~ **i totali** (*di macchina calcolatrice*) to total.

calcolatore, *a.* calculating. *n. m.* **1** (*elab. elettr.*) computer. **2** (*macch. uff.*) computer. // ~ **elettronico** (*elab. elettr.*) electronic computer.

calcolatrice, *n. f.* (*macch. uff.*) calculating machine, calculator.

calcolo, *n. m.* **1** (*conteggio*) count, counting; (*computo*) computation. **2** (*idea approssimativa*) reckoning, working-out. **3** (*stima*) evaluation. **4** (*mat.*) calculation, calculus★, cast. // **calcoli approssimativi** rough and ready calculations; ~ **delle spese** (*da sostenere*) estimate of costs; ~ **di convenienza economica** (*org. az.*) feasibility study; ~ **errato** miscalculation; **un** ~ **esatto** an accurate calculation; ~ **sbagliato** miscalculation.

calendario, *n. m.* calendar. // ~ **da tavolo** (*attr. uff.*) desk calendar; ~ **delle scadenze** (*pubbl.*) date schedule; ~ **murale** (*attr. uff.*) wall calendar; ~ **perpetuo** (*attr. uff.*) perpetual calendar.

calmierare, *v. t.* (*econ.*) to fix a ceiling price for, to roll back the price of.

calmiere, *n. m.* **1** (*econ.*) price control, rollback (of prices). **2** (*econ.*) (*il listino prezzi*) official list of prices. **3** (*econ.*) (*prezzo massimo*) ceiling price.

calo, *n. m.* **1** decrease, fall, drop, decline, lowering, slackening, step-down. **2** (*di prezzi, ecc.*) decline, break, cut, cutting, coming down, sag. **3** (*market., trasp.*) (*di peso o volume: della merce*) shrinkage. **4** (*market., trasp.*) (*di liquidi*) leakage, ullage. // **un** ~ **di peso** (*della merce, ecc.*) (*market.*) a loss in weight; ~ **di qualità** (*market.*) falling-off in quality; **un** ~ **moderato** (*e spesso temporaneo*) **dei prezzi** (*Borsa, fin.,* *market.*) a dip in prices.

calunnia, *n. f.* (*leg.*) defamation, slander.

calunniare, *v. t.* (*leg.*) to defame, to slander.

calunniatore, *n. m.* (*leg.*) defamer, slanderer.

calunnioso, *a.* (*leg.*) defamatory, slanderous.

cambiale, *n. f.* (*cred.*) bill of exchange, bill, draft. // **una ~ a breve scadenza** (*cred.*) a short bill, a short-dated bill; **~ a data fissa (o a data futura determinabile)** (*cred.*) period bill; **~ a data prefissata** date bill; **~ a favore del traente** (*cred.*) bill to drawer; **~ a lunga scadenza** (*cred.*) long-dated bill; **~ a termine** (*cred.*) time bill; **~ a vista** (*cred.*) bill at sight, sight bill, bill on demand; **~ accettata** (*banca, cred.*) acceptance; **cambiali all'incasso** (*banca*) accounts receivable; **cambiali attive** (*rag.*) bills receivable; **cambiali avallate** (*cred.*) backed bills; **~ commerciale** (*cred.*) trade bill; **~ di comodo** (*banca, cred.*) accommodation bill, accommodation note, accommodation paper; windmill, kite (*fam.*); **~ di favore** (*banca, cred.*) *V.* **~ di comodo; ~ di rivalsa** (*cred., leg.*) redraft; **~ domiciliata** (*cred.*) domiciled bill; **~ estera** (*cred.*) foreign bill; **~ falsa** (*cred., leg.*) forged bill, counterfeit bill (of exchange); stiff (*slang USA*); **~ in bianco** (*banca, cred.*) blank bill; **cambiali in circolazione** (*cred.*) outstanding bills; **cambiali in copia** (*cred.*) bills in a set; **cambiali in pagamento** (*banca*) accounts payable; **~ in sofferenza** (*cred.*) unpaid bill; **~ in unico originale** (*cred.*) sola, sola bill; **una ~ insoluta** (*cred.*) an unpaid bill; **~ «netta»** (*banca, cred.*) clean bill; **cambiali non accettate** (*cred.*) unaccepted bills; **cambiali non pagate** (*cred.*) outstanding bills; **una ~ pagabile a trenta giorni vista** a bill payable thirty days after sight; **~ pagabile al portatore** (*cred.*) bill payable to bearer; **~ pagabile all'interno** (*cred.*) domestic bill, inland bill; **~ per l'interno** (*cred.*) hometrade bill; **~ recante l'accettazione del debitore** (*cred.*) trade acceptance; **~ scontabile al tasso minimo** (*cred.*) fine bill; **~ tratta** (*cred.*) draft.

cambiamento, *n. m.* **1** change, alteration, variation. **2** (*spostamento*) shift, shifting. **3** (*repentino*) turnabout. // **~ al rialzo** (*Borsa*) change for the better; **~ al ribasso** (*Borsa*) change for the worse; **~ del tasso ufficiale di sconto** (*fin.*) change in the bank rate; **il ~ della marea** (*trasp. mar.*) the turn of the tide; **~ di rotta** (*trasp. mar.*) change of route; **~ di tendenza** (*econ.*) turnabout; **un ~ in meglio (in peggio)** a turn for the better (for the worse).

cambiamonete, *n. m.* e *f. inv. V.* **cambiavalute.**

cambiare, *v. t.* e *i.* **1** to change, to alter, to turn, to vary. **2** (*spostarsi*) to shift. **3** (*denaro, banconote, ecc.*) to change, to give★ change for, to break★. **4** (*trasp. mar.*) (*di marea*) to turn. // **~ una banconota in spiccioli** (*fin.*) to turn a bank-note into cash; **~ binario** (*trasp. ferr.*) (*di treno*) to shunt; **~ dollari in lire** to change U.S. dollars into liras; **~ un dollaro** to give change for a dollar; **~ un titolo contro un altro** (*fin.*) to change one stock for another; **~ treno** (*trasp. ferr.*) to change trains.

cambiarsi, *v. rifl.* (*fin.*) (*di moneta*) to exchange.

cambiavalute, *n. m.* e *f. inv.* (*fin.*) money changer, changer, foreign-exchange broker, exchange broker.

cambio, *n. m.* **1** change. **2** (*scambio*) exchange. **3** (*fin.*) exchange. **4** (*fin.*) (*tasso di cambio*) rate (of exchange). **5** (*pers.*) (*che si dà a un collega, alla fine d'un turno di lavoro*) relief. // **~ a corso libero** (*fin.*) flexible exchange rate, floating rate, free rate of exchange, free exchange rate; **~ alla pari** (*fin.*) rate at par; par of exchange; **~ calcolato attraverso una terza valuta** (*fin.*) cross rate; (*talora*) indirect parity; **~ certo** (*fin.*) certain exchange; **~ «certo per l'incerto»** (*fin.*) fixed exchange; (*fin.*) currency rate; **~ del giorno** (*fin.*) current rate of exchange; **il ~ della moneta** (*econ.*) the currency reform; **il ~ della sterlina** (*fin.*) the sterling exchange; **~ d'acquisto** (*al quale la banca è disposta ad acquistare divise*) (*banca*) buying rate; **~ d'apertura** (*fin.*) opening rate (of exchange); **~ di chiusura** (*fin.*) closing rate (of exchange); **~ di classe** (*trasp. ferr.*) change of class; **~ d'indirizzo** change of address; **~ di rotta** (*trasp. mar.*) sheer; **~ di vendita** (*banca*) selling rate; **~ diretto** (*fin.*) direct exchange; **~ estero** (*fin.*) foreign exchange, external exchange; **~ fisso** (*fin.*) fixed exchange, direct exchange; **~ fluttuante** (*fin.*) floating exchange rate, floating rate; **~ in divise auree** (*fin.*) gold exchange standard; **~ «incerto per certo»** (*fin.*) indirect exchange, movable exchange; pence rate (*in G.B.*); **~ incrociato** (*fin.*) cross rate; **~ indiretto** (*fin.*) indirect exchange, movable exchange, cross rate; **~ libero** (*fin.*) free rate of exchange, free exchange rate; **~ marittimo** (*trasp. mar.*) bottomry, maritime loan; **~ reale** (*fin.*) real exchange; **un ~ sfavorevole** (*econ.*) an unfavourable exchange; **cambi telegrafici** (*fin.*) telegraphic transfer rates; **~ ufficiale** (*comm. est.*)

official rate of exchange; **in ~ di** in return for.

cambista, *n. m.* e *f. V.* **cambiavalute.**

cambusa, *n. f.* (*trasp. mar.*) caboose, galley.

cambusiere, *n. m.* (*trasp. mar.*) steward.

camera, *n. f.* room, chamber. // **~ blindata** (*attr. uff., banca*) strong-room, vault; **la ~ dei Comuni** the House of Commons (*ingl.*), the Commons; **la ~ dei Lord** the House of Lords (*ingl.*), the Lords; **la ~ dei Rappresentanti** (*dei deputati*) the House of Representatives (*USA*); **~ di Commercio** Chamber of Commerce; Board of Trade (*USA*); **~ di Commercio Internazionale (CCI)** International Chamber of Commerce (*ICC*); **~ di consiglio** council-chamber; **~ di sicurezza** (*attr. uff., banca*) strong-room.

cameralismo, *n. m.* (*econ.*) cameralism.

cameralista, *n. m.* e *f.* (*econ.*) cameralist.

cameriera, *n. f.* (*pers.*) waitress. // **~ di bordo** (*trasp. mar.*) stewardess.

cameriere, *n. m.* (*pers.*) waiter. // **~ di bordo** (*trasp. aer., trasp. mar.*) steward.

camion, *n. m.* (*trasp. aut.*) motor-lorry, lorry; motortruck, truck (*USA*).

camionista, *n. m.* (*trasp. aut.*) lorry driver; truck driver, truckman★, teamster (*USA*).

campagna, *n. f.* **1** country; countryside. **2** (*militare, politica, pubblicitaria*) campaign. **3** (*market.*) (*commerciale*) drive. **4** (*market.*) (*di vendita: in un dato anno*) marketing year. // **~ al rialzo** (*Borsa*) bull campaign; **~ al ribasso** (*Borsa*) bear campaign; **~ di prova** (*pubbl.*) test campaign; **~ di stampa** (*giorn.*) press campaign; **~ di vendita speciale** (*market.*) bargain campaign; **~ dividendi** (*Borsa*) dividend crop; **la ~ futura** (*pubbl.*) the coming campaign; **~ per la prevenzione degli infortuni** anti-accident campaign; **~ promozionale** (*market., pubbl.*) promotional campaign; **~ pubblicitaria** (*pubbl.*) advertising campaign, publicity campaign; **~ rialzista** (*Borsa*) bull campaign; **~ ribassista** (*Borsa*) bear campaign.

campionamento, *n. m.* (*market.*) sampling. // **~ su un'area** (*market.*) area sampling.

campionare, *v. t.* (*market.*) to sample.

campionario, *a.* sample, trade (*attr.*). *n. m.* **1** (*market.*) sample collection, set of samples. **2** (*market.*) (*di tessuti, carta, ecc.*) pattern-book.

campionarista, *n. m.* e *f.* (*market.*) sampler.

campionatore, *n. m.* (*market.*) sampler, sampleman★.

campionatura, *n. f.* (*market.*) sampling.

campione, *n. m.* **1** specimen. **2** (*di stoffe, carta da parati e sim.*) pattern. **3** (*market.*) sample. *a. attr.* standard. // **~ casuale** (*market.*) random sample; **~ di prova** (*market.*) trial sample; **~ di saggio** (*market.*) trial sample; **~ (in) omaggio** (*market.*) free sample; **~ per tutte le necessità** (*market.*) general-purpose sample; « **~ senza valore** » (*comun.*) « samples only »; **~ statistico** (*stat.*) statistical sample; **~ stratificato** (*market.*) quota sample, stratified sample; **campioni su richiesta** (*market.*) samples on collection; **~ unificato** (*market.*) standard sample; **come da ~** as per sample; **su ~** (*market.*) (*di vendita*) by sample.

campo, *n. m.* **1** (*anche fig.*) field. **2** (*campo d'azione*) scope; province (*fig.*). **3** (*estensione*) extent. // **~ d'atterraggio** (*trasp. aer.*) airstrip; **~ d'aviazione** (*trasp. aer.*) airfield; **~ di fortuna** (*trasp. aer.*) emergency landing field; **in ~ agricolo** in the agricultural sector.

canale, *n. m.* **1** (*in molti sensi; anche, « canale artificiale »*) canal. **2** (*pubbl.*) (*della televisione*) channel. **3** (*trasp. mar.*) (*passaggio naturale marittimo*) channel. // **~ con chiusa** (*trasp.*) sluice; **~ del porto** (*trasp. mar.*) harbour channel; **~ d'accesso** (*trasp. mar.*) entrance channel; **~ di distribuzione** (*market.*) channel of distribution; **canali di distribuzione** (*dei prodotti*) (*market.*) trade channels; **un ~** (*artificiale*) **navigabile** (*trasp.*) a navigable canal, a ship-canal; **~ portuale** (*trasp. mar.*) harbour channel.

cancellabile, *a.* erasable.

cancellare, *v. t.* **1** (*facendo una croce o tirando un frego*) to cancel, to cross, to cross out. **2** (*con la gomma*) to erase. **3** (*con cimosa o straccio*) to wipe off. **4** (*in genere*) to delete, to expunge, to obliterate. **5** (*cred.*) to write★ off. // **~ una causa dal ruolo** (*leg.*) to cancel a cause from the cause list; **~** (*un avvocato*) **dall'albo** (*leg.*) to disbar; **~ un debito** (*cred.*) to write off a debt; **~ un volo** (*trasp. aer.*) to cancel a flight.

cancellatura, *n. f.* **1** (*con una croce o un frego*) cancellation, crossing, crossing out. **2** (*con la gomma*) erasure. **3** (*in genere*) deletion, obliteration.

cancellazione, *n. f.* **1** (*con una croce o un frego*) cancellation, crossing (out). **2** (*in genere*) deletion, obliteration. **3** (*cred.*) write-off, writing off. // **~** (*d'un avvocato*) **dall'albo** (*leg.*) disbarment; **la ~ d'un credito inesigibile** (*cred.*) the write-off of a bad debt; **~ di un volo** (*trasp. aer.*) cancellation of a flight.

cancelleria, *n. f.* (*attr. uff.*) stationery.

cancelliere, *n. m.* (*leg.*) recorder, registrar. // **~ dello Scacchiere** (*ingl.*) Chancellor of the Exchequer; **~ di tribunale** (*leg.*) clerk of the Court.

cancello, *n. m.* 1 gate. 2 (*trasp. aer.*) (*di aeroporto*) gate. // ~ **di passaggio a livello** (*trasp. ferr.*) gate.

candidato, *a.* acceding. *n. m.* (*pers.*) candidate, applicant. // ~ **all'assunzione** (*pers.*) entrant.

candidatura, *n. f.* candidature; candidacy (*USA*).

canone, *n. m.* (*d'affitto*) rent, rental.

cantiere, *n. m.* 1 yard. 2 (*trasp. mar.*) shipyard, yard. // ~ **di demolizione** (*trasp. mar.*) scrapyard; ~ **di raddobbo** (*trasp. mar.*) refitting yard; ~ **edile** building yard; ~ **navale** (*trasp. mar.*) shipyard, shipbuilding yard, dockyard; docks (*pl.*); ~ **stradale** road yard.

capace, *a.* 1 able, capable, competent. 2 (*spazioso*) capacious, roomy. // ~ **di tenere il mare** (*trasp. mar.*) (*di nave*) seaworthy; **essere ~ di fare qc.** to be able to do st.

capacità, *n. f. inv.* 1 ability, capability, capacity, competence. 2 (*facoltà, potere*) faculty, power. 3 (*capienza*) capacity. 4 (*volume*) volume. 5 (*leg.*) capacity, competence. 6 (*org. az.*) (*degli impianti*) capacity. // ~ **a testare** (*leg.*) testamentary capacity; ~ **civile delle persone** (*leg.*) competence of persons; ~ **concorrenziale** competitiveness; ~ **contributiva** (*fin.*) taxable capacity, taxable ability; ~ **d'agire** (*leg.*) capacity to act; ~ **d'attirare il pubblico** (*pubbl.*) pull; ~ **di carico** (*trasp. mar.*) carrying capacity; ~ **di comando** leadership; ~ **di contrarre** (*leg.*) capacity to contract; ~ **di guadagno** (*pers.*) earning capacity; ~ **d'intendere e di volere** (*leg.*) mental capacity, mental competence; **la ~ d'un recipiente** (*market.*) the volume of a container; ~ **di richiamare clientela** (*market., pers.*) drawing power; ~ **di ricupero** (*fin.*) buoyancy; ~ **di stivaggio** (*trasp. mar.*) stowage; ~ **di stoccaggio** (*org. az.*) storage capacity; ~ **di tenere il mare** (*trasp. mar.*) (*di nave*) seaworthiness; ~ **di vendere** (*market.*) salesmanship; ~ **direttiva** (*amm.*) managerial ability, executive ability; ~ **giuridica** (*leg.*) capacity to contract; **capacità imprenditoriali** (*pers.*) entrepreneurial skills; ~ **legale** (*leg.*) legal capacity; ~ **manageriale** (*amm.*) managerial ability; ~ **produttiva** production capacity; (*org. az.*) operating capacity.

capannone doganale, *n. m.* (*dog.*) bonded shed.

caparra, *n. f.* 1 earnest money, earnest, hand money, handsel, payment in advance. 2 (*comm., leg.*) (*pegno*) pawn. 3 (*leg.*) (*deposito*) deposit, gage.

capire, *v. t.* to understand★, to gather, to grasp. // ~ **male** to misunderstand; **che non si riesce a ~** (*d'un problema, ecc.*) beyond one's grasp; **che si riesce a ~** (*d'un problema, ecc.*) within one's grasp.

capitale¹, *a.* 1 capital, paramount. 2 (*leg.*) capital. // **un crimine passibile di pena ~** (*leg.*) a capital crime.

capitale², *n. m.* 1 (*econ.*) capital. 2 (*fin., rag.*) (*contrapposto a «interessi»*) principal. 3 (*rag.*) capital sum, capital. 4 **capitali,** *pl.* (*econ.*) (*beni strumentali*) capital goods. // **capitali a breve** (*fin.*) short-term funds; ~ **a fondo perduto** (*fin.*) capital at venture; ~ **assicurato** (*ass.*) insured capital, reversion; ~ **azionario** (*fin.*) share capital, joint stock, stock; capital shares (*ingl.*); capital stock (*USA*); (*specialm. di società fondata da poco*) equity capital; ~ **azionario non tassabile** (*fin.*) non-assessable stock; ~ **che frutta un interesse del 4%** capital bearing 4% interest; ~ **circolante** (*econ.*) (*beni che si esauriscono completamente in un solo processo produttivo*) single-use goods; (*fin.*) circulating capital, floating capital; (*rag.*) floating assets, current assets; **capitali circolanti** (*fin.*) circulating capitals, circulating assets; ~ **complessivo** (*d'una società*) (*rag.*) capitalization; **capitali congelati** (*fin.*) frozen funds; ~ **d'esercizio** (*rag.*) working capital; ~ **d'immobilizzo** (*rag.*) real capital; ~ **d'impianto** (*fin.*) opening capital; ~ **di rischio** (*fin.*) venture capital; ~ **dichiarato** (*fin.*) stated capital; ~ **disponibile** (*per investimenti*) (*fin., rag.*) free capital; ~ **e interessi** (*fin.*) principal and interest; ~ **e riserve patrimoniali** (*ass.*) capital and reserves; ~ **emesso** (*fin.*) issued capital; ~ **finanziario** (*investito o reinvestito per trarne profitto*) moneyed capital; **capitali fissi** (*rag.*) fixed assets, permanent assets; ~ **fisso** (*rag.*) fixed capital, capital assets; ~ **fisso lordo** (*fin., rag.*) gross fixed assets; **capitali fluttuanti** (*fin.*) circulating assets, circulating capitals; ~ **immobilizzato** (*rag.*) capital equipment, capital assets; **capitali immobilizzati** (*rag.*) permanent assets; ~ **impiegato nell'attività commerciale** (*rag.*) stock-in-trade; **capitali in banca** (*rag.*) cash with bank; ~ **in commercio** (*rag.*) stock-in-trade; ~ **in contanti** (*rag.*) cash capital; **capitali inattivi** (*fin.*) idle capitals, idle money; ~ **iniziale** (*fin.*) initial capital, opening capital, starting capital; ~ **interamente versato** (*fin.*) capital fully paid up, fully paid-up capital, fully paid capital; ~ **inutilizzato** (*econ.*) unemployed capital; (*fin.*) (*azionario*) dead stock; ~ **investito** (*in genere*) amount of money invested; (*fin.*) capital invested; (*rag.*) (*in impianti e macchinari*) capital equipment; ~ **legale** (*fin., leg.*) legal capital; ~ **liquido** (*fin., rag.*) free capital, working capital; **capitali mobili** (*fin.*) circulating capitals, circulating assets; **capitali mobiliari** (*fin.*) circulating capitals, circulating assets; ~ **mutuato** (*cred., fin.*) loan capital; ~ **netto** (*d'una società per azioni*) (*fin.*) shareholders' equity; (*rag.*) capital owned, equity; ~ **nominale** (*fin.*) nominal capital, authorized capital, registered capital; ~ **non emesso** (*fin.*) unissued stock; ~ **non fruttifero** (*fin.*) capital bearing no interest; ~ **non richiamato** (*fin.*) uncalled capital; ~ **obbligazionario** (*fin.*) debenture capital, loan stock; ~ **parzialmente versato** (*fin.*) capital partly paid up; ~ **richiamato** (*fin.*) called-up capital; ~ **richiesto** (*fin.*) called-up capital; ~ **sociale** (*fin.*) company's capital, registered capital, stock capital, joint stock; corporate capital (*USA*); ~ **sottoscritto** (*fin.*) subscribed capital; ~ **strumentale** (*econ., fin.*) auxiliary capital; ~ **umano** (*org. az.*) human capital; **capitali vaganti** (*fin.*) refugee capitals, hot money; ~ **versato** (*fin.*) paid-up capital, paid-in capital; ~ **versato in parte** (*fin.*) partly-paid capital; **ad alto impiego di capitali** (*econ., fin.*) capital-intensive.

capitalismo, *n. m.* (*econ.*) capitalism. // ~ **di Stato** (*econ.*) Statc capitalism.

capitalista, *n. m.* e *f.* (*econ.*) capitalist.

capitalistico, *a.* (*econ.*) capitalistic.

capitalizzabile, *a.* (*rag.*) capitalizable.

capitalizzare, *v. t.* (*rag.*) to capitalize.

capitalizzazione, *n. f.* (*rag.*) capitalization. // ~ **degli interessi** (*fin.*) capitalization of interests; ~ **degli utili** (*fin.*) capitalization of profits.

capitaneria di porto, *n. f.* (*trasp. mar.*) harbour office.

capitano, *n. m.* 1 (*anche fig.*) captain. 2 (*trasp. mar.*) captain. 3 (*trasp. mar.*) (*di mercantile*) master, shipmaster. 4 (*trasp. mar.*) (*di piccolo mercantile*) skipper. // ~ **d'armamento** (*trasp. mar.*) ship's husband; ~ **di lungo corso** (*trasp. mar.*) captain of foreign-going vessel, deep-sea captain; deep-sea master; ~ **di (nave) mercantile** (*trasp. mar.*) master mariner, shipmaster; ~ **di porto** (*trasp. mar.*) harbour master.

capitazione, *n. f.* (*fin.*) poll tax.

capitolato, *n. m.* 1 (*leg.*) specifications (*pl.*). 2 (*leg.*) (*d'appalto*) tender.

capitolo, *n. m.* 1 chapter. 2 (*rag.*) item. // **capitoli del bilancio** (*rag.*) balance-sheet items; ~ **di spesa** (*fin.*) item of expenditure; **capitoli di spesa iscritti nel budget** (*fin., rag.*) budgeted (standard) prices.

capo, *n. m.* 1 (*chi comanda*) chief, head, master, principal; boss (*fam.*); leader. 2 (*singolo oggetto*) article, item. 3 (*pers.*) (*d'un servizio, ecc.*) executive, manager. 4 (*pers.*) (*d'operai*) foreman★, overman★, walking boss; boss man★ (*slang USA*). 5 (*rag.*) item. // ~ **del personale** (*pers.*) personnel manager, staff manager; ~ **del reparto produzione** (*pers.*) works manager; ~ **della giuria** (*leg.*) foreman; ~ **della squadra di turno** (*pers.*) shift boss, shiftman; ~ **d'accusa** (*leg.*) article of accusation, charge, count of indictment, count; **il** ~ **d'una famiglia** the head of a family; ~ **d'una giuria femminile** (*leg.*) forewoman; ~ **d'uno scalo** (*trasp. ferr.*) yard-master; ~ **di spesa** (*fin.*) item of expenditure; **un** ~ **di vestiario** an article of clothing; ~ **intermedio** (*pers.*) leader, first-line supervisor, foreman; ~ **officina** (*pers.*) shop foreman; ~ **operaio** (*pers.*) foreman; ~ **pilota** (*trasp. mar.*) pilot master; ~ **reparto** (*pers.*) department head; ~ **ufficio** (*pers.*) head clerk, chief clerk; boss (*fam.*); boss man (*slang USA*).

capofamiglia, *n. m.* e *f. inv.* head of a family, householder. // **il** ~ the master (*o* the man) of the house.

capolinea, *n. m. inv.* (*trasp.*) terminal station, terminal, terminus.

caposquadra, *n. m. inv.* (*pers.*) foreman★, overman★, leader, walking boss.

capostazione, *n. m.* (*trasp. ferr.*) stationmaster.

capotreno, *n. m.* (*trasp. ferr.*) guard; conductor (*USA*).

capoufficio, *n. m.* e *f.* (*pers.*) chief clerk, head clerk; boss (*fam.*); boss man★ (*slang USA*).

capovolgere, *v. t.* 1 (*anche fig.*) to upset★. 2 (*leg.*) to overrule, to reverse. // ~ **la procedura** (*leg.*) to reverse the procedure; ~ **una sentenza** (*leg.*) to overrule a sentence.

capovolgimento, *n. m.* (*anche fig.*) upset.

cappa, *n. f.* (*trasp. mar.*) primage, hat money. // **essere alla** ~ (*trasp. mar.*) (*di nave*) to lie to.

captazione, *n. f.* (*leg.*) captation, undue influence.

capufficio, *n. m. inv. V.* **capoufficio.**

carato, *n. m.* 1 (*unità di misura usata in gioielleria ed equivalente a 2 decigrammi*) carat. 2 (*trasp. mar.*) (*24ª parte di comproprietà di nave*) one twenty-fourth (of the value of a ship). 3 (*per estensione: quota parte in un'azienda*) share (in a firm).

carattere, *n. m.* 1 character. 2 (*di stampa*) type, face (*sempre sing.*); character, letter. // ~ **maiuscolo** (*giorn., pubbl.*) upper case, capital;

~ **minuscolo** (*giorn., pubbl.*) lower case, minuscule; ~ **tipografico** (*giorn., pubbl.*) type (*sempre sing.*); character, letter, face; **a ~ nazionale** nation-wide.

caratteristica, *n. f.* characteristic, feature.

caratteristico, *a.* characteristic.

caratterizzare, *v. t.* to characterize. // **caratterizzato dalla diminuzione dei prezzi** (*fin.*) (*di mercato, ecc.*) heavy; **caratterizzato dalla scarsità dell'offerta** (*fin.*) (*di mercato*) thin.

caratura, *n. f.* **1** (*trasp. mar.*) part-ownership. **2** (*per estensione: quota parte in un'azienda*) share (in a firm).

carbone, *n. m.* **1** (*fossile*) coal. **2** (*di legna*) charcoal. // ~ **per piroscafo** (*trasp. mar.*) bunker coal.

carboniera, *n. f.* (*trasp. mar.*) coaler, collier.

carbonile, *n. m.* (*trasp. mar.*) coal bunker, bunker.

carcere, *n. m.* prison, jail. // ~ **preventivo** (*leg.*) detention.

cardex, *n. m.* (*attr. uff., neol.*) (*mobili e sistema per la conservazione e la schedatura dei documenti*) card index.

carena, *n. f.* (*trasp. mar.*) hull, keel, bottom.

carenaggio, *n. m.* **1** (*trasp. mar.*) careening, dry-docking, graving. **2** (*trasp. mar.*) (*spese di carenaggio*) careenage.

carenamento, *n. m.* (*trasp. mar.*) careening, dry-docking, graving.

carenare, *v. t.* (*trasp. mar.*) to careen, to dry-dock.

carenza, *n. f.* **1** lack, shortage, scarcity. **2** (*econ.*) (*della domanda e sim.*) decline. // ~ **di manodopera** (*econ.*) labour shortage.

carestia, *n. f.* **1** famine. **2** (*fig.*) dearth, scarcity.

cargo, *n. m.* (*trasp. mar.*) cargo.

carica, *n. f.* **1** (*pers.*) (*ufficio*) office. **2** (*pers.*) (*impiego*) post. // ~ **di cassiere** (*fin.*) treasurership; ~ **di direttore (amministratore,** ecc.) (*fin.*) directorship, directorate; ~ **d'ispettore** (*leg.*) inspectorship; ~ **di magistrato** (*leg.*) magistrateship; ~ **di tesoriere** (*fin.*) treasurership; **una ~ elettiva** an elective office; **una ~ onorifica** an honorary office; **chi ha una ~** (*pers.*) office-bearer, office-holder; **essere in ~** (*amm.*) to hold office.

caricamento, *n. m.* **1** (*trasp.*) loading. **2** (*trasp. mar., anche*) lading. // ~ **a bordo** (*trasp. mar.*) loading aboard; ~ **dei carbonili** (*trasp. mar.*) bunkering.

caricare, *v. t.* **1** to charge, to load. **2** (*un orologio e sim.*) to wind*. **3** (*trasp.*) to load. **4** (*trasp. mar., anche*) to lade*, to ship. *v. i.* (*trasp. mar.*) to load. // ~ **una batteria** to charge an accumulator; ~ **carbone** (*trasp. mar.*) to take in coal; ~ **interessi su un conto** (*rag.*) to charge an account with interest; ~ **merci a bordo d'una nave** (*trasp. mar.*) to load goods aboard a ship; ~ **una nave** (*trasp. mar.*) to lade a vessel; ~ **un prezzo** (*per coprire le spese e trarne un profitto*) (*fin., market.*) to load a price; ~ (*merce*) **su chiatte** (*trasp. mar.*) to lighter.

caricatore, *n. m.* **1** (*pers.*) loader. **2** (*trasp. mar.*) shipper.

caricazione, *n. f.* (*trasp., trasp. mar.*) loading.

carico, *a.* **1** (*anche fig.*) laden. **2** (*trasp.*) loaded. *n. m.* **1** charge, load. **2** (*fig.*) weight, burden, load. **3** (*fig.*) (*aggravio, spesa*) charge, expense. **4** (*trasp.*) load, consignment. **5** (*trasp.*) (*caricamento*) loading. **6** (*trasp. mar.*) cargo, bulk, load, shipment. **7** (*trasp. mar.*) (*caricamento*) loading, lading. // ~ **a collettame** (*trasp. mar.*) general cargo; ~ **aereo** (*trasp. aer.*) freight; ~ **alla rinfusa** (*trasp. mar.*) cargo in bulk, bulk load, bulk; ~ **completo** (*trasp.*) full load; (*trasp. mar.*) shipload, full cargo; ~ **d'andata** (*trasp. mar.*) outward cargo; ~ **di cabotaggio** (*trasp. mar.*) coasting cargo; ~ **di coperta** (*trasp. mar.*) deck cargo, deck load; ~ **di famiglia** (*pers.*) encumbrance; ~ **di lavoro** (*pers.*) work load; **un ~ di legname** (*trasp. mar.*) a cargo of timber; ~ **di ritorno** (*trasp. mar.*) homeward cargo, return cargo; ~ **e scarico** (*rag.*) charge and discharge; ~ **fiscale** (*fin.*) tax burden; ~ **ipotecario** (*leg.*) encumbrance; ~ **marittimo** (*trasp. mar.*) freight; ~ **massimo** (*comun., trasp.*) peak load; (*org. az.*) (*dei macchinari, ecc.*) peak load; (*trasp.*) maximum load; ~ **massimo per assale** (*trasp.*) maximum axle load; ~ **misto** (*trasp. mar.*) mixed cargo, general cargo; ~ **pagante** (*trasp. aer.*) pay-load; ~ **secco** (*trasp. mar.*) dry cargo, bulk; **carichi secchi** (*trasp. mar.*) dry goods; ~ **sopra coperta** (*trasp. mar.*) dead cargo; ~ **terrestre** (*trasp.*) carriage; freight (*USA*); ~ **trasportato su di un aereo** (*trasp. aer.*) air cargo; ~ **tributario** (*fin.*) burden of taxation; ~ **utile** (*trasp.*) live load; **a ~ di q.** (*market., rag.*) chargeable to sb.; at sb.'s expense; (*pers.*) dependent on sb.; **l'essere a ~** (*di q.*) (*pers.*) dependence; **persone a ~** (*pers.*) dependants; «**spese a ~ del vostro conto**» (*market., rag.*) «expenses to be debited to you» (*o* charged to your account).

carne, *n. f.* meat. // **centro carni** (*market.*)

meat centre.

caro, *a.* (*market.*) dear, costly, expensive, high. *n. m.* high cost, high price. *avv.* dear, dearly. // **l'esser ~** dearness; **a ~ prezzo** dearly, dear; **non ~** (*market.*) (*d'articolo*) inexpensive; (*di prezzo*) reasonable.

carosello pubblicitario, *n. m.* commercial.

carosello televisivo, *n. m.* (*pubbl.*) short.

carovita, *n. m.* 1 high cost of living. 2 (*pers.*) (*indennità*) cost-of-living allowance, cost-of-living bonus.

caroviveri, *n. m. V.* **carovita.**

carpetta, *n. f.* (*attr. uff.*) folder.

carrello, *n. m.* 1 (*attr. uff.*) (*di macchina da scrivere o contabile*) carriage. 2 (*pubbl.*) (*su cui è posta la macchina da presa, cinematografica o televisiva*) dolly. 3 (*trasp. aer.*) (*d'atterraggio*) undercarriage, landing gear. 4 (*trasp. ferr.*) (*di locomotiva o di carrozza ferroviaria*) truck. // **~ di servizio** (*trasp. ferr.*) trolley; handcar (*USA*); **~ ferroviario** (*telaio di carro*) (*trasp. ferr.*) bogie.

carretta, *n. f.* 1 (*trasp.*) cart. 2 (*trasp. mar.*) tramp, ocean tramp.

carrettiere, *n. m.* carter.

carriera, *n. f.* 1 career. 2 (*pers.*) (*trascorsa*) record.

carrierismo, *n. m.* careerism.

carrierista, *n. m.* careerist; career-man*.

carro, *n. m.* 1 (*trasp.*) cart, truck, waggon, wagon. 2 (*trasp.*) (*contenuto di un carro*) cart-load. 3 (*trasp. ferr.*) waggon; (*senza sponde*) truck; car (*USA*). // **~ attrezzi** (*trasp. aut.*) breakdown car, tow car, wrecking car, wrecker; **~ bagagli** (*trasp. ferr.*) luggage van; baggage car (*USA*); **~ bestiame** (*trasp. ferr.*) stock car; **~ cisterna** (*trasp. ferr.*) tank-car; **~ (di) soccorso** (*o* **~ gru**) (*trasp. aut.*) wrecking car, wrecker; **~ merci** (*coperto*) (*trasp. ferr.*) waggon, van; freight car (*USA*); **~ merci aperto** (*trasp. ferr.*) truck; **~ merci senza sponde** (*trasp. ferr.*) (flat) truck; platform-car; flatcar, flat (*USA*).

carrozza, *n. f.* 1 (*trasp.*) carriage, coach. 2 (*trasp. ferr.*) railway carriage, carriage, coach; car (*USA*). // **~ belvedere** (*trasp. ferr.*) observation car; **~ con corridoio** (*trasp. ferr.*) corridor carriage; **~ con letti** (*trasp. ferr.*) sleeping-car; **~ (di) lusso** (*trasp. ferr., USA*) parlor car, club car, lounge car; **~ di piazza** (*trasp.*) cab; **una ~ di seconda (classe)** (*trasp. ferr.*) a second-class carriage; **~ ferroviaria** (*trasp. ferr.*) carriage, coach; car, coach (*USA*); **~ mista** (*trasp. ferr.*) composite carriage; **~ ristorante** (*trasp. ferr.*) restaurant car (*ingl.*); dining-car (*ingl. e USA*); **~ salone** (*trasp. ferr., USA*) club car, lounge car, parlor car; **~ viaggiatori** carriage, coach; passenger car (*USA*).

carrozzeria, *n. f.* 1 (*trasp.*) (*d'autoveicolo*) body. 2 (*trasp. aut.*) (*officina di chi fa carrozzerie*) coach builder's workshop. 3 (*trasp. aut.*) (*officina di chi le ripara*) workshop of a coach repairer. // **~ fuori serie** custom-built body; **lavori di ~** coachbuilding; coach repairing.

carrozziere, *n. m.* 1 (*chi fa carrozzerie*) coachbuilder, coach-builder, body builder, car stylist. 2 (*chi le ripara*) coach repairer.

carta, *n. f.* 1 paper. 2 (*statuto*) charter. 3 **carte,** *pl.* (*documenti*) papers, documents. // **~ assegni** (*banca*) cheque guarantee card, cheque card; **~ assorbente** (*attr. uff.*) blotting paper; **~ automobilistica** (*trasp. aut.*) motoring map; **~ bancabile** (*fin.*) eligible paper; **~ bianca** (*non scritta*) blank paper; (*fig.*) «carte blanche», free hand; **~ bollata** (*fin.*) stamped paper, stamp-paper; **~ carbone** (*attr. uff.*) carbon paper; **~ commerciale** (*banca, cred.*) mercantile paper; **~ commerciale di prim'ordine** (*cred.*) fine trade paper; **~ costitutiva** (*d'una società*) (*leg.*) charter; **~ da bollo** (*fin.*) *V.* **~ bollata; ~ da imballaggio** (*market.*) packing-paper, wrapping-paper; **~ da lettere** (*attr. uff.*) letter-paper, writing-paper, note-paper; **~ da lettere intestata** (*attr. uff.*) headed letter-paper; **~ da pacchi** (*market.*) wrapping-paper, packing-paper, brown paper; **~ da scrivere** (*attr. uff.*) writing-paper; **~ da stampa** (*giorn.*) printing-paper; **~ dei venti** (*trasp. mar.*) wind-chart; **carte di bordo** (*trasp. mar.*) ship's papers; **~ di credito** (*banca, fin.*) credit card; **~ d'identità** identity card; **~ d'imbarco** (*per passeggeri*) (*trasp. mar.*) embarkation card; **~ di sbarco** (*per passeggeri*) (*trasp. mar.*) landing card; **~ geografica** map; **~ intestata** (*attr. uff.*) headed letter-paper; **~ libera** (*esente da bollo*) unstamped paper; **~ moneta** (*fin.*) paper currency, paper money, paper; **~ moneta non convertibile** (*in moneta metallica*) (*fin.*) irredeemable paper money; **~ monetata** (*fin.*) paper currency, paper money, paper; **~ nautica** (*trasp. mar.*) chart, sea chart; **~ patinata** (*giorn., pubbl.*) glossy paper, coated-paper, enamel paper; **~ per uso legale** (*leg.*) legal cap; **~ sottile per avvolgere la merce** (*market.*) shop paper; **~ straccia** waste paper; **~ stradale** (*trasp. aut.*) route-map; **~ topografica** map; **~ uso bollo** bond paper.

cartaceo, *a.* paper (*attr.*). // **moneta cartacea** (*fin.*) paper currency, paper money.

carteggio, *n. m.* 1 (*corrispondenza*) correspondence. 2 (*raccolta di lettere*) collection of letters. **3** (*leg.*) (*documenti*) papers (*pl.*).

cartella, *n. f.* **1** (*per documenti*) briefcase. **2** (*per documenti legali*) brief bag (*ingl.*). **3** (*generalm. di cuoio*) portfolio. **4** (*attr. uff.*) (*di cartone: per tenervi fogli*) folder. **5** (*fin.*) (*di azioni, di obbligazioni, ecc.*) certificate. // ~ **azionaria** (*fin.*) share certificate; ~ **del debito pubblico** (*fin.*) Government bond; ~ **delle imposte** (*o* **delle tasse**) (*fin.*) tax assessment, tax return; ~ **delle tasse** (*l'importo*) (*fin.*) tax bill; ~ **di campioni** (*market.*) sample-card; ~ **di cedole** (*fin.*) coupon sheet; ~ **di prestito** (*o* **di mutuo**) (*cred.*) loan certificate; ~ **obbligazionaria** (*fin.*) debenture certificate.

cartellino, *n. m.* **1** card. **2** (*attr. uff.*) file card. **3** (*market.*) label, ticket; (*a ciondolo*) tag. **4** (*pers.*) card, ticket. **5** (*trasp.*) (*etichetta sul bagaglio*) label, (*a ciondolo*) tag. // ~ **del prezzo** (*market.*) price-tag; ~ **d'entrata e uscita degli operai** (*org. az.*) clock card; ~ **di presenza** (*org. az.*) clock card, time card, time ticket; ~ **pubblicitario da vetrina** (*di negozio*) (*market.*) window-card; ~ **segnaprezzo** (*market.*) tag; ~ **segnatempo** (*org. az.*) clock card.

cartello, *n. m.* **1** (*manifesto*) bill, placard, poster. **2** (*econ., fin.*) cartel, combine, pool, syndicate. **3** (*pubbl.*) poster, placard, bill; billboard (*USA*). **4** (*trasp.*) (*stradale, ecc.*) sign. // **un** ~ **bancario** (*fin.*) a cartel of banks; ~ **da vetrina** (*pubbl.*) display card; ~ **pubblicitario** (*pubbl.*) *V.* ~, *def. 3*; ~ **segnaletico** (*stradale*) (*trasp.*) guide board; ~ **stradale** (*trasp. aut.*) road-sign.

cartellone, *n. m.* (*pubbl.*) poster, placard, bill; billboard, board (*USA*). // ~ **pubblicitario** (*pubbl.*) *V.* ~.

cartellonista, *n. m.* e *f.* (*pubbl.*) poster designer.

cartolina, *n. f.* (*comun.*) postcard, card. // ~ **con risposta pagata** (*comun.*) reply postal card, business reply card, reply card; ~ **doppia** double postcard; ~ **illustrata** picture postcard; ~ **postale** (*comun.*) postcard.

cartoncino, *n. m.* **1** (*biglietto*) card. **2** (*pubbl.*) cardboard.

cartone, *n. m.* **1** cardboard. **2** (*market.*) (*imballaggio di cartone*) cartoon. // ~ **animato** (*pubbl.*) (animated) cartoon; ~ **di legno** (*pubbl.*) chipboard; ~ **forte** (*o* **grosso**) millboard; ~ **ondulato** corrugated cardboard.

casa, *n. f.* **1** house. **2** (*dove si abita*) home. **3** (*natale*) home. **4** (*unità familiare*) household. **5** (*azienda, ditta*) (business) house; firm. // ~ **colonica** farm, farmhouse, homestead; ~ **commerciale** business house, house, firm; ~ **commissionaria** commission house; ~ **di commercio** commercial house; ~ **di sconto** (*market.*) discount house; discount store (*USA*); ~ **editrice** (*giorn., pubbl.*) publishing house, publisher; ~ **madre** (*fin., org. az.*) parent company; parent corporation (*USA*); ~ **popolare** council house (*ingl.*); **una** ~ **sfitta** a vacant house; **a** ~ at home; **di** ~ **in** ~ (*market., pubbl.*) house-to-house (*attr.*).

casella, *n. f.* (*di casellario*) pigeon-hole. // ~ **postale** (*comun.*) post-office box.

casellario, *n. m.* (*attr. uff.*) filing cabinet; files (*pl.*). // ~ **giudiziario** (*leg.*) judicial register; ~ **penale** (*leg.*) criminal records (*pl.*).

casello, *n. m.* (*trasp. aut.*) (*d'autostrada, ecc.*) toll-house, tollgate. // ~ **daziario** toll-house.

cash and carry, *locuz. n.* (*market.*) cash and carry.

casistica, *n. f.* (*pers.*) case-study method.

caso, *n. m.* **1** case; (*circostanza*) circumstance, contingency. **2** (*sorte*) chance. **3** (*pers.*) case history. // ~ (*giudiziario*) **che costituisce un «precedente»** (*leg.*) leading case; ~ **di bisogno** (*cred.*) case of need; **«in** ~ **di bisogno, presso Mr C. Parish»** (*avviso su una cambiale*) «in case of need, apply to Mr C. Parish»; **un** ~ **di coscienza** a case of conscience; **casi di forza maggiore** (*ass., leg.*) acts of God; **in casi di forza maggiore** in case of inevitable accidents; **in nessun** ~ under no circumstance; **secondo il** ~ according to circumstances.

cassa, *n. f.* **1** (*da imballaggio*) case, box, package. **2** (*forziere*) coffer. **3** (*dove sta il cassiere o la cassiera*) cash desk, cashier's desk; till; (*banco, «sportello»*) counter. **4** (*banca, fin.*) bank. **5** (*fin.*) treasury. **6** (*market.*) (*di supermercato e sim.*) check-out counter. **7** (*org. az.*) (*l'ufficio, il reparto*) cashier's office, cash department. **8** (*rag.*) (*contante*) cash, cash on hand. **9** (*rag.*) (*libro «cassa»*) cash book. // ~ **continua** (*banca*) night safe; ~ **cooperativa di risparmio** (*fin.*) mutual savings bank; ~ **da imballaggio** (*market.*) packing-case, packing-box; **le casse dello Stato** the coffers of the State; ~ **di liquidazione** (*Borsa*) clearing house; ~ **di pensione** (*fin.*) pension fund; ~ **di risparmio** (*banca*) savings bank; ~ **di risparmio postale** (*banca, cred.*) post-office savings-bank; ~ **integrazione (guadagni)** (*pers., sind.*) body responsible for unemployment state-subsidised benefits (*in Italia*); ~ **pagamenti** (*banca*) paying counter; ~ **sociale** (*fin.*) company's cash on hand; **andare** (*o* **essere messo**) **in** ~ **integrazione** (*pers., sind.*) to go on state-subsidised lay-off (*in Italia*); **di-**

pendente messo in ~ integrazione *V.* **cassintegrato; pagamenti della ~ integrazione** state-subsidised lay-off pay (*in Italia*).

cassabile, *a.* (*leg.*) reversible (*V.* **cassare**).

cassaforte, *n. f.* **1** (*attr. uff.*) strong-box. **2** (*attr. uff.*) safe. **3** (*banca*) (*camera blindata*) strong room. **//** ~ **a prova di furto** (*attr. uff.*) theftproof strong-box.

cassare, *v. t.* (*leg.*) (*una sentenza*) to reverse, to quash, to vacate; to cass (*scozz.*).

cassazione, *n. f.* (*leg.*) (*d'una sentenza*) cassation.

cassetta, *n. f.* box, (small) case. **//** ~ **dei suggerimenti** (*org. az.*) suggestion box, suggestion case; ~ **della corrispondenza in arrivo** (*attr. uff.*) in-tray; ~ **della corrispondenza in partenza** (*attr. uff.*) out-tray; ~ **della posta** (*comun.*) post-box; posting box (*ingl.*); mailbox (*USA*); ~ **di sicurezza** (*banca*) safe-deposit box; ~ **per il (denaro) contante** cash box; ~ **per le lettere** letter-box; **investimento di** ~ (*Borsa, fin.*) lock-up investment.

cassettista, *n. m.* e *f.* **1** (*banca*) renter of a safe-deposit box. **2** (*Borsa, fin.*) long-term investor.

cassiera, *n. f.* **1** (*banca*) cashier; cage woman★ (*slang USA*). **2** (*pers.*) (*di negozio*) cash clerk, cashier. **3** (*pers.*) (*di supermercato*) checker.

cassiere, *n. m.* **1** (*banca*) cashier, teller; cage man★ (*slang USA*). **2** (*fin.*) (*tesoriere*) treasurer, receiver. **3** (*pers.*) (*di negozio*) cash-clerk, cashier. **4** (*pers.*) (*di supermercato*) checker. **//** ~ **allo sportello dei pagamenti** (*banca*) teller out; ~ **allo sportello dei versamenti** (*banca*) teller in; ~ **contabile** (*pers.*) cashier and bookkeeper; ~ **in sott'ordine** (*pers.*) assistant cashier.

cassintegrato, *n. m.* (*pers., sind.*) worker on state-subsidised lay-off (*in Italia*).

castelletto, *n. m.* **1** (*banca*) (*scoperto di conto, assistito da fido*) fluctuating overdraft. **2** (*banca, cred.*) line of credit, credit line, line.

casuale, *a.* casual, accidental, coincidental, contingent, fortuitous. **// diritti casuali** (*leg.*) special bonuses.

catalogare, *v. t.* to catalogue; to catalog (*USA*).

catalogazione, *n. f.* cataloguing; cataloging (*USA*).

catalogo, *n. m.* **1** (*anche market.*) catalogue; catalog (*USA*). **2** (*market.*) (*lista*) list. **//** ~ **generale** (*market.*) master catalogue; ~ **per vendite per corrispondenza** (*market.*) mail-order catalogue; **essere in** ~ **al prezzo di** (*market.*) to list at.

categoria, *n. f.* **1** category, class, section. **2** (*market.*) grade. **//** ~ **di contribuenti** (*raggruppati secondo il reddito*) (*fin.*) income bracket; **categorie d'entrate** (*fin.*) categories of income; **categorie di redditi** (*fin.*) income items; **categorie di spese** (*fin.*) categories of expenditure.

catena, *n. f.* **1** (*anche fig.*) chain. **2** (*market.*) (*di acquirenti e di venditori: in una Borsa Merci*) ring. **3** (*market., org. az.*) (*di negozi, ecc.*) string. **// catene da neve** (*trasp. aut.*) tire-chains; ~ **d'acquisti** (*market.*) cooperative marketing; ~ **di montaggio** assembly line; **una** ~ **di negozi** (*market.*) a string of shops.

cateratta, *n. f.* (*trasp.*) (*di chiusa*) water gate.

cattivo, *a.* bad, foul, ill, malicious, poor. **// cattiva amministrazione** (*amm.*) maladministration; (*degli affari, ecc.*) ill management, mismanagement, misconduct; **cattiva condotta** misconduct; (*leg.*) misdemeanour; **cattiva distribuzione** maldistribution; **cattiva fama** ill fame; **cattive notizie** bad news; ~ **ormeggio** (*trasp. mar.*) foul berth; **cattiva qualità** (*market.*) poor quality; **cattiva reputazione** ill repute; ~ **servizio** disservice; **una cattiva speculazione** (*fin.*) a bad speculation.

causa, *n. f.* **1** cause, ground, motivation, motive. **2** (*leg.*) cause, case. **3** (*leg.*) (*lite*) action, lawsuit, suit, dispute, litigation. **4** (*leg.*) (*motivo*) ground. **5** (*leg.*) (*corrispettivo*) consideration. **//** ~ **accessoria** (*leg.*) accessory action; ~ **annullata** (*leg.*) abated suit; ~ **che serve a creare un precedente** (*leg.*) test case; ~ **civile** (*leg.*) civil action, civil suit, common plea; ~ **concomitante** (*leg.*) contributory cause; ~ **d'esproprio** (*leg.*) action for ejectment; ~ **di sospetto** (*leg.*) ground for suspicion; ~ **illecita** (*leg.*) illicit consideration; **la** ~ **illecita d'un contratto** (*leg.*) the unlawful consideration of a contract; ~ **immediata** (*d'un sinistro*) (*ass.*) immediate cause; (*leg.*) proximate cause; (*trasp. mar.*) causa proxima; **la** ~ **in discussione** (*leg.*) the case at bar; ~ **incidentale** (*leg.*) incidental cause; ~ **lecita** (*in un contratto*) (*leg.*) legal consideration; **cause naturali** (*leg.*) natural causes; ~ **penale** (*leg.*) penal action, penal suit; criminal case; ~ **per danni** (*leg.*) action for damages; ~ **per esecuzione di contratto** (*leg.*) action for enforcement of contract; ~ **per truffa** (*leg.*) action for fraud; ~ **per violazione di contratto** (*leg.*) action for breach of contract; ~ **remota** (*trasp. mar.*) causa remota; ~ **rinviata** (*a nuova udienza*) (*leg.*) remanent; **a** ~ **di** owing to, because of, due to; **essere in** ~ **(legale)** (*leg.*) to be at law; **senza** ~ (*leg.*) causeless.

causale, *n. f.* 1 (*banca, rag.*) description. 2 (*leg.*) consideration. // ~ **d'un'operazione** (*banca*) operation cause.

causare, *v. t.* to cause, to bring★ about, to determine, to give★ rise to.

cauzionare, *v. t.* (*leg.*) to bail, to bond.

cauzione, *n. f.* 1 (*cred., fin.*) guarantee, security, surety. 2 (*cred., fin.*) (*in denaro*) caution money, caution, cover. 3 (*dog.*) bond. 4 (*leg.*) bail, bailment, bond, bail-bond, recognizance. // ~ **doganale** (*dog.*) customs bond; ~ **in titoli azionari** (*fin.*) share qualification; ~ **per concorrere a una licitazione (*o* gara d'appalto)** bid bond; ~ **scritta** (*leg.*) surety bond; ~ **sussidiaria** (*cred.*) counter-security, counter-surety; **la ~ versata da un dipendente** (*pers.*) the security given by an employee; **sotto ~** (*leg.*) on bail.

cavo, *n. m.* (*comun., trasp.*) cable, rope. // ~ **d'ormeggio** (*trasp. mar.*) mooring line, hawser; ~ **di traino** (*trasp. aut.*) tow-rope.

cedente, *n. m.* e *f.* 1 (*leg.*) (*specialm. di beni*) alienor, surrenderor, transferor, transferror, transferer, transferrer. 2 (*leg.*) (*specialm. di diritti*) assignor, grantor. 3 (*leg.*) (*di beni o di diritti*) releasor, releaser.

cedenze, *n. pl.* (*Borsa, fin.*) downfall of bonds (*o* of shares).

cedere, *v. i.* 1 to cede, to give★ way, to sag. 2 (*arrendersi*) to give★ in, to give★ up, to surrender. *v. t.* 1 to relinquish, to renounce, to resign, to part with (st.). 2 (*leg.*) (*un diritto, un bene, un territorio, ecc.*) to cede, to assign, to convey, to grant, to release, to remise, to surrender, to transfer. 3 (*market.*) (*vendere*) to sell★, to dispose of; (*svendere*) to sell★ out. // ~ **la direzione di un'azienda** to hand over the management of a business; ~ **un diritto** (*leg., anche*) to relinquish a right; ~ **formalmente** (*una proprietà, un diritto, ecc.*) (*leg.*) to sign away, to sign over; ~ **in affitto** (*leg.*) to demise; ~ **in cambio** to barter; ~ (*un oggetto usato*) **in pagamento parziale** to trade in; ~ **il «know-how»** (*leg.*) to grant the know-how; ~ **la propria parte in un'azienda** (*fin.*) to sell out one's share of a business; ~ **un privilegio** (*leg.*) to surrender a privilege; ~ **le redini a q.** (*fig.*) to hand over to sb.

cedibile, *a.* (*leg.*) assignable, disposable, grantable, transferable (*V.* **cedere**). // **non ~** (*leg.*) untransferable.

cedimento, *n. m.* 1 (*anche fig.*) sag. 2 (*resa*) giving in, surrender. // ~ **alle rivendicazioni salariali** (*sind.*) wage surrender.

cedola, *n. f.* 1 (*fin.*) coupon, dividend coupon, dividend warrant, docket. 2 (*fin.*) (*di titolo al portatore, utilizzabile per richiedere un nuovo certificato azionario*) talon. // ~ **di commissione libraria** bookseller's order form; ~ **d'interesse** (*fin.*) interest coupon; **cedole non pagate** (*fin.*) outstanding coupons; ~ **scaduta** (*fin.*) coupon in arrear; **con la ~** (*fin.*) (*di titolo*) with coupon; dividend on (*USA*); **senza ~** (*fin.*) (*di titolo*) dividend off (*USA*).

cedolare, *n. f.* (*fin.*) tax on dividend warrants, capital gains tax. // **imposta ~** (*fin.*) *V.* ~.

censire, *v. t.* (*fin.*) (*a scopo fiscale*) to assess.

censo, *n. m.* wealth, estate.

centesimo, *num. ord.* hundredth. *n. m.* 1 (a, one) hundredth. 2 (*fin.*) (*di dollaro*) cent; penny★ (*fam., USA*); copper (*slang USA*). 3 (*fin.*) (*di franco, di lira, ecc.*) centime.

centimetro, *n. m.* centimetre; centimeter (*USA*).

cento, *num. card.* a (*o* one) hundred. // ~ **dollari** a hundred dollars; a century, a yard-measure (*slang USA*); **per ~** per cent.

centrale, *a.* 1 central. 2 (*principale*) main; head (*attr.*). *n. f.* 1 (*comun.*) exchange. 2 (*econ.*) (*centro di produzione di beni e servizi*) plant, station. 3 (*org. az.*) (*centro direttivo*) head office; headquarters. // ~ **elettrica** (*econ.*) power-station, power-plant; ~ (*telefonica*) **interurbana** (*comun.*) trunk-exchange; long-distance exchange (*USA*); ~ **sindacale** (*sind.*) union headquarters; ~ **telefonica** (*comun.*) telephone exchange; central (*USA*).

centralinista, *n. m.* e *f.* (*comun.*) telephone operator, exchange operator, operator, telephonist.

centralino, *n. m.* 1 (*comun.*) exchange; central (*USA*). 2 (*tur.*) (*d'albergo e sim.*) switchboard. // ~ **automatico** (*comun.*) automatic exchange; ~ **telefonico** (*comun.*) telephone exchange.

centralizzare, *v. t.* (*org. az.*) to centralize.

centralizzato, *a.* (*org. az.*) centralized.

centralizzazione, *n. f.* (*org. az.*) centralization.

centro, *n. m.* 1 centre; center (*USA*). 2 (*commerciale, di una grande città*) downtown. 3 (*econ.*) (*di produzione, ecc.*) seat. // ~ **amministrativo** (*di un'impresa*) (*org. az.*) headquarters; **un ~ commerciale** a trading centre, an emporium; ~ **degli acquisti** (*market.*) shopping centre; shopping center, shopping mall, shopping plaza, shopping area (*USA*); ~ **d'affari** (*fin.*) business centre; **centri di commercializzazione** (*market.*) marketing centres; ~ **di costo** (*org. az.*) cost centre; cost center (*USA*); ~ **di**

produzione (*market.*) centre of production; ~ **di responsabilità** (*org. az.*) cost centre; ~ **di smistamento** (*org. az.*) distributing centre; ~ **di vendita** (*market.*) sales outlet; ~ **grossisti** (*market.*) cash and carry; ~ **per acquisti** *V.* ~ **degli acquisti**; ~ **per acquisti pedonalizzato** (*market.*) shopping precinct.

cercare, *v. t.* **1** to look for, to seek★. **2** (*sforzarsi d'ottenere*) to pursue. **3** (*chiedere di q.*) to call. *v. i.* **1** (*tentare*) to try; to endeavour. **2** (*sforzarsi*) to strive★. // ~ **di farsi dei clienti** to prospect for customers; ~ **d'imporre** (*un articolo, ecc.*) **al pubblico** (*market.*) to push; ~ **di strappare un prezzo più alto** (*market.*) to stick out for a higher price; ~ **un impiegato mediante inserzioni** to advertise for a clerk; ~ **un impiego** (*pers.*) to seek a situation; «**cercansi**» (*giorn., pubbl.*) «wanted»; «**cercasi**» (*giorn., pubbl.*) «situations vacant», «wanted».

cerchio, *n. m.* **1** ring. **2** (*market.*) (*d'acquirenti e di venditori: in una Borsa Merci*) ring.

cernere, *v. t.* (*market.*) to grade, to class, to sort (out), to pick.

cernita, *n. f.* (*market.*) grading, sorting (out), sortation, picking. // **fare la** ~ **della corrispondenza** (*comun.*) to sort the mail.

certificabile, *a.* certifiable.

certificare, *v. t.* to certify, to certificate. // **copia certificata** (*conforme all'originale*) (*leg.*) certified copy.

certificato, *n. m.* certificate. // ~ **attestante l'esistenza legale d'una società** (*fin.*) certificate of incorporation; ~ **azionario** (*fin.*) share warrant; ~ **azionario provvisorio** (*fin.*) share certificate, stock certificate; ~ **che autorizza l'inizio delle attività sociali** (*d'una società anonima*) certificate to commence business; ~ **del magazziniere** (*dog.*) warehouse-keeper's certificate; ~ **della linea di carico** (*trasp. mar.*) load line certificate; ~ **d'analisi** (*comm. est.*) certificate of analysis; ~ **d'arrivo** (*dog.*) certificate of clearing inwards; ~ **d'assicurazione** (*ass.*) certificate of insurance; (*ass. mar.*) insurance certificate; ~ **d'avaria** (*ass. mar.*) certificate of damage, certificate of survey, damage report; ~ **di buona condotta** (*leg.*) certificate of good character; ~ **di cancellazione (d'un'ipoteca)** (*leg.*) copy of memorandum of satisfaction (of a mortgage); ~ **di classifica** (*trasp. mar.*) classification certificate; ~ **di copertura** (*del rischio*) (*ass.*) cover note; ~ **di deposito** (*dog.*) deposit warrant; ~ **d'esportazione temporanea** (*comm. est.*) bill of store; ~ **di garanzia** (*market.*) manufacturer's certificate; ~ **d'idoneità** (*per navi cabotiere*) (*trasp. mar., USA*) enrolment; ~ **d'igiene** (*dog.*) sanitary certificate; ~ **d'imbarco** (*trasp. mar.*) certificate of shipment; ~ **d'immatricolazione** (*d'una nave*) (*trasp. mar.*) certificate of registry, ship's register; ~ **d'ispezione** (*dog.*) bill of sight; ~ **di libera pratica** (*trasp. mar.*) pratique certificate, certificate of pratique; ~ **di liquidazione d'avaria** (*ass. mar.*) average statement; ~ **di morte** (*leg.*) death certificate; ~ **di nascita** (*leg.*) birth certificate; ~ **di navigabilità** (*trasp. aer.*) certificate of airworthiness; (*trasp. mar.*) certificate of seaworthiness; ~ **d'origine** (*comm. est.*) certificate of origin; ~ **di prestito** (*cred.*) loan certificate; ~ **di radiazione** (*d'una ipoteca*) (*leg.*) certificate of satisfaction; ~ **di «registrazione»** (*d'una società anonima*) (*fin.*) certificate of incorporation; ~ **di registrazione** (*trasp. mar.*) registration certificate; ~ **di registro della nave** (*trasp. mar.*) ship's certificate of registry; ~ **di sbarco** (*trasp. mar.*) landing certificate; ~ **di scarico** (*trasp. mar.*) landing certificate; ~ **di servizio** (*pers.*) testimonial; ~ **di stazza** (*trasp. mar.*) measurement brief; ~ **di stazzatura** (*trasp. mar.*) certificate of measurement; ~ **di stivaggio** (*trasp. mar.*) stowage certificate; ~ **d'uscita** (*dog.*) certificate of clearing outwards; ~ **di visita** (*trasp. mar.*) survey certificate; ~ **medico** (*pers.*) health certificate; ~ **provvisorio** (*di titoli*) (*Borsa, fin.*) provisional certificate, interim certificate, scrip; ~ **sanitario** (*dog.*) sanitary certificate; (*trasp. mar.*) bill of health; ~ **sanitario «pulito»** (*trasp. mar.*) clean bill of health; ~ **sanitario sospetto** (*trasp. mar.*) suspected bill of health; ~ **sanitario «sporco»** (*trasp. mar.*) foul bill of health.

certificazione, *n. f.* certification, certifying. // ~ **di bilancio** (*org. az., rag.*) auditor's opinion on the fairness of balance-sheet presentation; ~ **notarile** (*apposta a un documento*) (*leg.*) notarization.

certo, *a.* certain, sure. // **a** ~ **tempo vista** (*banca*) (*di cambiali*) after sight; **data certa** (*leg.*) fixed date; **prova certa** (*leg.*) irrefutable evidence.

cespite, *n. m.* (*econ., fin.*) source of income, yielder.

cessare, *v. i.* to cease, to discontinue, to leave★ off, to stop. // ~ **l'attività** to break up; ~ **da un ufficio (da una carica, ecc.)** to retire from office; ~ **dal commercio** to go out of business.

cessazione, *n. f.* **1** cessation, discontinuance. **2** (*leg.*) cesser. // ~ **del lavoro** (*per sciopero, serrata, ecc.*) (*sind.*) tie-up; ~ **dell'attività commerciale** discontinuance of business; ~ **di**

copertura (*per mancato pagamento di premi*) (*ass.*) lapse; ~ **d'una locazione** (*leg.*) termination of a lease.

cessionario, *n. m.* 1 (*leg.*) (*specialm. di beni*) alienee, surrenderee, transferee. 2 (*leg.*) (*specialm. di diritti*) assignee, assign, grantee. 3 (*leg.*) (*di beni o diritti*) cessionary, releasee, relessee. // ~ **dei diritti di proprietà** (*ass. mar.*) (*assicuratore marittimo cui è ceduta la nave, il relitto, o il carico ricuperato in un naufragio*) abandonee.

cessione, *n. f.* 1 (*abbandono, rinuncia*) relinquishment, resignation, renouncement, renunciation. 2 (*leg.*) (*di diritti, di beni o di territorio*) cession, assignment, conveyance, disposal, grant, release, remission, surrender, transfer. // ~ **a titolo gratuito** (*leg.*) voluntary conveyance; ~ **di beni ai creditori** (*leg.*) assignment of property to creditors; ~ **d'un brevetto** (*leg.*) assignment of a patent, conveyance of a patent; ~ **di credito** (*leg.*) assignment of credit; ~ **di proprietà** (*leg.*) cession of property; **la ~ d'una proprietà da parte d'un fallito** (*leg.*) the surrender of an estate by a bankrupt; ~ **di quota** (*fin.*) assignment of share; ~ **di stipendio** (*pers.*) loan on one's salary; ~ **d'usufrutto** (*leg.*) assignment of interest; ~ **documentata di titoli** (*fin.*) certified transfer of stock; ~ **generale** (*di beni ai creditori*) (*leg.*) general assignment.

cestino, *n. m.* small basket. // ~ **da viaggio** (*tur.*) lunch-bag; ~ **per la carta straccia** (*attr. uff.*) waste-paper basket, waste-basket; ~ **per la corrispondenza** (*attr. uff.*) letter basket, letter tray.

ceto, *n. m.* 1 rank, status. 2 (*gruppo sociale*) social group, class. // ~ **impiegatizio** clerkdom; white-collar workers (*pl.*); **il ~ medio** the middle class; ~ **operaio** blue-collar workers (*pl.*).

chiamare, *v. t.* to call. // ~ (*q.*) **a comparire** (*leg.*) to summon, to summons; ~ **al telefono** (*comun.*) to call up; ~ **la centralinista** (*comun.*) to call the operator; ~ **il centralino** (*telefonico*) (*comun.*) to call the exchange; ~ **di nuovo** (*leg.*) to resummon; ~ **in giudizio** (*leg.*) to sue, to cite; ~ **l'Italia in teleselezione** (*comun.*) to dial direct to Italy.

chiamata, *n. f.* call, calling. // ~ **in garanzia** (*leg.*) call on the guarantor; ~ (*telefonica*) **interurbana** (*comun.*) trunk-call; long-distance call (*USA*); ~ **telefonica** (*comun.*) telephone call; ~ **urbana** (*comun.*) local call.

chiatta, *n. f.* 1 (*trasp.*) canal boat. 2 (*trasp. mar.*) barge, tow-barge, lighter, keel.

chiattaiolo, *n. m.* (*trasp. mar.*) bargee, bargeman*, lighterman*.

chiedere, *v. t.* 1 (*per sapere*) to ask; (*con autorità*) to demand. 2 (*per avere o comprare*) to ask for. 3 (*richiedere*) to require, to request, to demand; (*insistentemente*) to solicit; (*esigere*) to claim. 4 (*market.*) (*un prezzo*) to ask. 5 (*market.*) (*per avere informazioni su un articolo*) to inquire for. // ~ **a q. informazioni su qc.** to ask sb. about st.; ~ **consiglio** to ask (for) advice, to seek advice; ~ **di q.** (*di vedere, parlare con q.*) to ask (*o* call, *o* inquire) for sb.; ~ **una dilazione** (*market.*) to request a delay; ~ **il fallimento** (*leg.*) to file a petition for bankruptcy; ~ **un favore a q.** to ask a favour of sb.; ~ **informazioni** to make inquiries; ~ **informazioni su qc.** to inquire about (*o* upon) st.; ~ **notizie di q.** to ask after sb.; ~ **un prezzo** (*anche*) to charge a price; ~ **referenze** to ask for references.

chiglia, *n. f.* (*trasp. mar.*) keel.

chilogrammo, *n. m.* kilogramme, kilogram.

chilometro, *n. m.* kilometre, kilometer.

chiodo, *n. m.* nail.

chiosco, *n. m.* 1 (*di giornali*) news-stand. 2 (*market.*) stall, stand.

chiudere, *v. t.* e *i.* 1 to close, to shut*. 2 (*concludere*) to close, to conclude. 3 (*org. az.*) (*una fabbrica, ecc.*) to shut* down. 4 (*rag.*) (*un conto*) to balance. // ~ **a chiave** to lock, to lock up; ~ **bottega** to put up the shutters; (*fig.*) to shut up shop, to close up shop, to retire from business; (*org. az., fam.*) (*d'azienda, ecc.*) to shut down; ~ **i conti** (*rag.*) to close one's accounts, to strike a balance; ~ **un conto** (*rag.*) to balance an account, to close (up) an account; ~ **un conto corrente** (*banca, cred.*) to close a current account; ~ **un fallimento** (*leg.*) to close a bankruptcy; ~ **in pareggio** (*fin.*) to break even, to balance; ~ **una lettera** to close a letter; ~ **gli sportelli** (*banca*) to close doors.

chiusa, *n. f.* 1 (*conclusione*) close, conclusion. 2 (*sbarramento*) dam, dyke, weir. 3 (*trasp.*) (*di fiume, canale, ecc.*) lock, sluice-gate.

chiuso, *a.* 1 closed, shut. 2 (*stretto*) tight. 3 (*rag.*) (*di conto*) balanced, settled.

chiusura, *n. f.* 1 closing, shutting. 2 (*di un dibattito*) closure. 3 (*conclusione*) close, conclusion. 4 (*Borsa*) close. 5 (*org. az.*) (*di un'azienda*) shut-down. 6 (*rag.*) (*di conti*) closing, settling, settlement. // ~ **anticipata** (*market.*) (*di negozi*) early closing; ~ **con i convenevoli** (*di una lettera commerciale*) complimentary close; ~ **della sottoscrizione** (*fin.*) closing of the application list; ~ **dell'anno finanziario** (*fin., rag.*) close of the fiscal year; ~ **dell'esercizio** (*fin., rag.*) close of the fiscal year; **chiusure di corsie** (*d'auto-*

strada) (*trasp. aut.*) lane closures; ~ **in pareggio** (*fin.*) break-even; ~ **pomeridiana** (*dei negozi*) (*market.*) early closing; ~ **temporanea** (*d'una fabbrica: per sciopero, serrata, ecc.*) (*org. az.*) shut-down; **di** ~ (*dell'esercizio*) (*econ., fin., rag.*) year-end (*attr.*); **in** ~ (*Borsa, fin.*) at the close, at the finish.

cibare, *v. t.* to feed★.

cibernetica, *n. f.* cybernetics.

cibernetizzato, *a.* (*elab. elettr.*) cybernated.

cibernetizzazione, *n. f.* (*elab. elettr.*) cybernation.

cibo, *n.* food.

ciclico, *a.* cyclical.

ciclo, *n. m.* cycle. // ~ **congiunturale** (*econ.*) business cycle; ~ **dell'attività commerciale** (*econ.*) business cycle; ~ **di lavorazione** manufacturing cycle; ~ **economico** (*econ.*) economic cycle, business cycle; trade cycle (*ingl.*); ~ **operativo** (*org. az.*) operating cycle; ~ **produttivo** (*org. az.*) productive cycle, production cycle.

ciclostilare, *v. t.* to cyclostyle, to duplicate, to mimeograph, to stencil.

ciclostile, *n. m.* (*attr. uff.*) cyclostyle, duplicator, mimeograph.

cielo, *n. m.* **1** sky. **2** (*fin.*) (*del tunnel monetario*) ceiling.

cifra, *n. f.* **1** (*numero*) number, numeral. **2** (*somma di denaro*) amount, figure, sum. **3** (*segno convenzionale*) cipher, cypher, code. // ~ **di «castelletto»** (*banca, cred.*) credit line; ~ **di deprezzamento** (*rag.*) amount written off; ~ **tonda** round figure, even money; **in** ~ **tonda** as a round figure, in round figures, in round numbers.

cifrare, *v. t.* to cipher, to cypher.

cifrario, *n. m.* **1** cipher, cypher, code. **2** (*chiave del cifrario*) cipher-key.

cinquanta, *num. card.* fifty. // ~ **centesimi di dollaro** fifty cents, half-dollar; half (*fam., USA*); four bits (*slang USA*).

cinque, *num. card.* five. // **in** ~ **copie** (*di documento*) quintuplicate.

cintura, *n. f.* **1** belt. **2** (*trasp. aer., trasp. aut.*) safety belt, seat belt. // ~ **di salvataggio** (*trasp. mar.*) life-belt; ~ **di sicurezza** (*trasp.*) *V.* ~, *def.* 2.

circolante, *a.* circulating. *n. m.* (*fin.*) circulating medium, currency. // ~ **divisionario** (*econ.*) token currency.

circolare[1], *a.* circular. *n. f.* **1** (*comm.*) circular letter, circular, form letter, form. **2** (*trasp.*) circle line, circle.

circolare[2], *v. i.* **1** to circulate. **2** (*fin.*) (*di monete: essere accettate*) to pass. **3** (*trasp.*) to run★.

circolazione, *n. f.* **1** (*anche giorn.*) circulation. **2** (*econ.*) circulation. **3** (*trasp. aut.*) traffic. // ~ (*monetaria*) **argentea** (*econ.*) silver standard; ~ (*monetaria*) **aurea** (*econ., storico*) gold standard; ~ **cartacea** (*fin.*) circulation of paper; ~ **effettiva** (*econ., fin.*) active circulation; ~ **fiduciaria** (*fin.*) credit circulation; ~ (*monetaria*) **metallica** (*fin.*) metallic circulation; ~ **monetaria** (*fin.*) circulation of money, currency circulation, currency; ~ **monetaria elastica** (*econ.*) elastic currency; ~ **stradale** (*trasp. aut.*) road traffic; «~ **vietata**» (*trasp. aut.*) (*cartello*) «no thoroughfare»; **in** ~ (*in giro*) about; (*banca*) (*d'effetti*) afloat; (*fin.*) (*d'assegno bancario, cambiale, ecc.*) outstanding.

circoscrizione, *n. f.* (*amm.*) district. // ~ **elettorale** constituency (*in G.B.*); district (*in U.S.A.*); ~ **giudiziaria** (*leg.*) area of jurisdiction.

circostanza, *n. f.* **1** circumstance. **2** (*imprevista*) contingency. // ~ **aggravante** (*leg.*) aggravating circumstance; ~ **attenuante** (*leg.*) extenuating (*o* mitigating) circumstance.

circuitazione, *n. f.* (*mat.*) circulation.

circuito, *n. m.* circuit. // ~ **di controllo** (*elab. elettr.*) check circuit; ~ **d'uscita** (*elab. elettr.*) output circuit.

citare, *v. t.* **1** to quote. **2** (*menzionare*) to mention. **3** (*anche leg.*) to cite. **4** (*leg.*) (*come testimone, ecc.*) to garnish, to summon, to summons, to subpoena, to subpena. **5** (*leg.*) (*perseguire in giudizio*) to sue, to convene, to process. // ~ **q. davanti al tribunale** (*leg.*) to convene sb. before the Court; ~ **q. in giudizio** (*leg., anche*) to serve sb. with a summons, to serve a summons on sb.

citazione, *n. f.* **1** quotation. **2** (*menzione*) mention. **3** (*anche leg.*) citation. **4** (*leg.*) (*come teste, ecc.*) garnishment, summons, writ of summons, subpoena, subpena. // **una** ~ **a comparire** (*leg.*) a peremptory writ; **una** ~ **notificata al convenuto** (*leg.*) a writ served on a defendant; ~ **per contumacia** (*leg.*) default summons.

citofono, *n. m.* (*attr. uff.*) intercom; interphone.

città, *n. f. inv.* town; (*grande*) city. // ~ **capolinea** (*di servizio d'autotrasporti, ecc.*) (*trasp.*) terminal; **una** ~ **dell'entroterra** an inland town; **città «dormitorio»** (*comunità residenziali alle quali i lavoratori pendolari ritornano dopo la loro giornata di lavoro nelle grandi città*) dormitory towns; **una** ~ **industriale** (*econ.*) a manufacturing city.

ciurma, *n. f.* crew, company; hands (*pl.*).

civile, *a.* (*anche leg.*) civil. *n. m.* (*borghese*) civilian.

civilista, *n. m.* e *f.* (*leg.*) civilian, civilist.

civilmente, *avv.* (*anche leg.*) civilly.

clandestino, *a.* clandestine. *n. m.* (*trasp. aer., trasp. mar.*) stowaway. // **passeggero ~** *V.* **~**, *n. m.*

classe, *n. f.* **1** class. **2** (*della società, anche*) section. **3** (*categoria*) class, category, sort. **4** (*market.*) (*di merce*) grade, line. **5** (*trasp.*) class. **6** (*trasp. mar.*) (*d'una nave*) character, rating. // **~ di reddito** (*fin.*) income class, income range; **la ~ dirigente** the ruling class; **~ economica** (*trasp.*) tourist class; (*trasp. aer.*) economy class, economy; **la ~ imprenditoriale** (*econ.*) the entrepreneurial class; **la ~ media** (*econ.*) the middle class; **la ~ operaia** (*econ.*) the working class, the proletariat; **le classi privilegiate** (*econ.*) the privileged classes; **~ sociale** (*econ.*) social class; **~ turistica** (*trasp.*) tourist class.

classifica, *n. f.* **1** classification, classing. **2** (*market.*) (*della merce*) grading.

classificare, *v. t.* **1** to classify, to class. **2** (*market.*) (*merci*) to grade. **3** (*trasp. mar.*) (*una nave*) to rate.

classificazione, *n. f.* **1** classification, classing. **2** (*market.*) (*di merce*) grading. **3** (*org. az.*) classification. **4** (*trasp. mar.*) (*d'una nave*) rating. // **~ del lavoro** (*org. az.*) job classification; **~ delle merci** (*anche*) classification of goods; **~ delle navi** (*trasp. mar., anche*) classification of ships.

clausola, *n. f.* **1** clause, article. **2** (*leg.*) clause, provision. **3 clausole,** *pl.* (*fin., market.*) terms. // **~ addizionale** (*o* **aggiuntiva**) (*a un atto*) (*leg.*) additional clause, rider; **~ arbitrale** (*leg.*) arbitration clause; **~ commissoria** (*leg.*) commissoria lex; **~ compromissoria** (*leg.*) arbitration agreement, arbitration clause; **~ condizionale** (*leg.*) condition, proviso; **~ contrattuale** (*leg.*) agreement clause; **~ controversa** (*leg.*) debated clause, contentious clause; **~ del ritardo** (*trasp. mar.*) time-penalty clause; **~ del tempo d'attesa per l'attracco** (*trasp. mar.*) waiting-berth clause; **~ del valore stabilito** (*ass. mar.*) agreed valuation clause; **~ della bandiera** (*trasp. mar.*) flag clause; **~ della caricazione sopra coperta** (*trasp. mar.*) deck loading clause; **~ della polizza di carico** (*trasp. mar.*) bill of lading clause; **~ derogatoria** (*leg.*) derogatory clause, departing clause; **~ d'abbordaggio** (*ass. mar.*) collision clause; **~ d'aggancio a una scala mobile** (*sind.*) escalator clause (*o* provision); **~ d'avaria** (*ass. mar.*) average clause; **~ d'avaria generale** (*ass. mar.*) general average clause; **~ di deviazione** (*dalla rotta*) (*ass. mar.*) deviation clause; **~ d'esclusione** (*di talune perdite o rischi: dalla copertura*) (*ass.*) exclusion clause; **~ di franchigia** (*ass.*) deductible; **~ di giurisdizione** (*leg.*) competence clause; **~ d'incontestabilità** (*d'una polizza*) (*ass.*) incontestable clause; **clausole d'ingaggio** (*trasp. mar.*) ship's articles, shipping articles; **~ d'invalidità** (*pers.*) disability clause; **~ di nazione favorita** (*econ.*) most-favoured-nation clause; **~ di negligenza** (*nell'avaria generale*) (*ass. mar.*) Jason clause; **~ di noleggio** (*trasp. mar.*) freight clause; **~ di non responsabilità** (*leg.*) non-liability clause; **~ di parità** (*leg.*) «benefit of a fall» clause, fall clause; **~ di raccomandazione** (*in un contratto di noleggio*) (*trasp. mar.*) address clause; **~ di recessione** (*ass. mar.*) waiver clause; **~ di rescissione** (*leg.*) cancellation clause; **~ di revisione** (*leg.*) review clause; **~ di riacquisto** (*leg.*) repurchase clause; **~ di rinunzia** (*ass. mar.*) waiver clause; **~ di scala mobile** (*sind.*) escalator clause, escalator provision; **clausole di sottoscrizione** (*di azioni*) (*fin.*) terms of underwriting; **le clausole d'un testamento** (*leg.*) the terms of a will; **~ d'uso** (*leg.*) customary clause; **~ essenziale** (*leg.*) stipulation; **~ interpretativa** (*leg.*) interpretation clause; **~ nave sempre a galla** (*ass., trasp. mar.*) floating clause; **~ onnicomprensiva** (*comprensiva d'ogni rischio*) (*ass.*) omnibus clause; **~ penale** (*in un contratto, ecc.*) (*leg.*) penalty clause; **~ relativa agli scali** (*trasp. mar.*) calling clause; **~ relativa alle collisioni** (*trasp. mar.*) collision clause; **~ relativa all'abbordaggio** (*ass. mar.*) running-down clause, collision clause; **~ restrittiva** (*leg.*) conditional clause; **una ~ riguardante vari argomenti** (*leg.*) an omnibus clause; **~ risolutiva** (*leg.*) resolutory clause, avoidance clause, determination clause; **~ risolutoria** (*d'un atto o contratto*) (*leg.*) defeasance clause, defeasance; **~ sotto condizione** (*leg.*) conditional provision; **clausole** (*contrattuali*) **sulla concorrenza sleale** (*leg., pers.*) restrictive covenants; **secondo le clausole** (*d'un contratto*) (*leg.*) under the terms; **la suddetta ~** the above clause.

cliente, *n. m.* e *f.* **1** (*d'un negozio, d'un'azienda*) customer; cuss (*slang USA*). **2** (*specialm. d'un professionista*) client. **3** (*leg.*) (*d'avvocato*) client. **4** (*market.*) shopper, visitor. **5** (*tur.*) guest. **6 clienti,** *pl.* (*market.*) trade (*sing. collett.*). // **un ~ abituale** (*market.*) a regular customer, a patron; **un ~ difficile** (*market.*) a hard customer, a sticky customer; **un ~ facile** (*market.*) an easy customer; an easy make (*slang*

USA); **un ~ fisso** (*market.*) a regular customer; **un ~ potenziale** (*market.*) a prospective client, a prospect; **essere ~ abituale d'un negozio** (*market.*) to patronize a shop; **essere ~ di** (*una banca*) to bank with.

clientela, *n. f.* **1** clientele, clientage, trade; customers, clients (*pl.*). **2** (*rapporti d'affari*) connection. **3** (*market.*) (*l'esser clienti*) custom; (*d'un negozio*) patronage. **4** (*market., pubbl.*) clientele, public. **5** (*tur.*) clientele; guests (*pl.*). // **~ potenziale** (*market.*) prospective customers.

clima, *n. m.* **1** (*anche fig.*) climate. **2** (*fig.*) relations (*pl.*). // **~ aziendale** (*sind.*) company climate; corporate climate (*USA*); **un ~ non propizio agli scambi** an unfavourable business climate; **~ sindacale** (*sind.*) labour situation.

coaffittuario, *n. m.* (*leg.*) cotenant.

coassicurato, *a.* e *n. m.* (*ass.*) coinsured.

coassicurazione, *n. f.* (*ass.*) coinsurance.

coattivo, *a.* **1** compulsory, coercitive. **2** (*leg.*) coactive.

coazione, *n. f.* (*leg.*) coaction.

coda, *n. f.* **1** (*anche fig.*) tail. **2** (*di gente in attesa*) queue. **3** (*banca, cred.*) (*di cambiale*) allonge. // **far la ~** (*la fila*) to form a queue; to queue up.

codice, *n. m.* **1** (*in ogni senso, eccetto quello di manoscritto antico*) code. **2** (*leg., anche*) statute-book; statute-roll. // **~ cifrato** cipher code; **~ civile** (*leg.*) civil code; **~ cliente** (*banca*) customer code; **~ commerciale** (*leg.*) commercial code; **il ~ della strada** (*trasp. aut.*) the Highway Code, the rules of the road; **~ d'avviamento postale (CAP)** (*comun.*) postcode; zip code (*USA*) (*abbr. di* zone improvement plan); **~ doganale** (*dog.*) customs code; **~ fiscale** (*fin.*) fiscal code number (*in Italia*); **~ penale** (*leg.*) penal code, criminal code; **~ telegrafico** (*comun.*) telegraphic code; **mettere il ~ d'avviamento postale su** (*una busta, ecc.*) to postcode.

codicillare, *a.* (*leg.*) codicillary.

codicillo, *n. m.* (*leg.*) codicil, rider.

codificare, *v. t.* **1** to code. **2** (*leg.*) to codify.

codificazione, *n. f.* (*leg.*) codification.

coefficiente, *n. m.* (*mat.*) coefficient, factor. // **~ d'accelerazione** (*econ.*) coefficient of acceleration; **il ~ di carico** (*trasp. mar.*) the proportion of gross to net load; **~ d'elasticità** (*econ.*) coefficient of elasticity; **~ di fiducia** (*market.*) confidence coefficient; **~ di produzione** (*econ.*) production coefficient.

coercitivo, *a.* **1** compulsory. **2** (*leg.*) coercitive.

coercizione, *n. f.* **1** compulsion. **2** (*leg.*) coercion, coaction. **3** (*sind.*) coercion. // **~ fisica** (*leg.*) actual coercion.

coerede, *n. m.* e *f.* (*leg.*) fellow heir, parcener. *n. m.* (*uomo*) (*leg.*) coheir. *n. f.* (*donna*) (*leg.*) coheiress.

coeredità, *n. f.* (*leg.*) coinheritance, parcenary.

cofano, *n. m.* (*trasp. aut.*) bonnet; hood (*USA*).

cofirmatario, *n. m.* (*leg.*) cosignatory.

cogestione, *n. f.* (*econ.*) cogestion.

coimputato, *n. m.* (*leg.*) co-defendant, corespondent.

coincidenza, *n. f.* **1** coincidence, concurrence. **2** (*trasp.*) connection. // **essere in ~ con** (*trasp.*) (*di treno, ecc.*) to connect with.

coincidere, *v. i.* to coincide, to concur, to tally.

cointeressato, *a.* **1** jointly interested. **2** (*econ., fin.*) (*che partecipa ai profitti*) profit-sharing. *n. m.* **1** (*leg.*) coadventurer. **2** (*leg.*) (*consocio*) co-partner, joint partner. // **essere ~ in un'azienda** (*fin.*) to have an interest in a business.

cointeressenza, *n. f.* **1** concern. **2** (*fin.*) (*partecipazione agli utili*) profit-sharing. **3** (*pers.*) lay.

colaggio, *n. m.* (*trasp. mar.*) leakage, ullage.

colare, *v. i.* **1** to leak. **2** (*gocciolare*) to drip, to drop. // **~ a picco** (*trasp. mar.*) to go to the bottom.

colla, *n. f.* **1** (*attr. uff.*) glue. **2** (*pubbl.*) (*per manifesti*) gum, paste.

collaborare, *v. t.* **1** to collaborate, to cooperate. **2** (*giorn.*) to contribute. **3** (*sind.*) to cooperate.

collaboratore, *n. m.* **1** collaborator, cooperator, coadjutor. **2** (*giorn., pubbl.*) contributor. **3** (*pers.*) assistant. // **~ d'affari** associate in business.

collaborazione, *n. f.* **1** collaboration, cooperation. **2** (*giorn.*) contribution. **3** (*sind.*) cooperation. // **~ del personale** (*pers.*) employee cooperation.

collasso, *n. m.* (*econ.*) collapse.

collaterale, *a.* collateral. // **parentela in linea ~** (*leg.*) relationship by collateral line.

collazionare, *v. t.* (*leg.*) to collate, to compare.

collazione, *n. f.* **1** collation, comparing. **2** (*leg.*) (*di beni, per una spartizione fra eredi*) hotchpot, hotchpotch.

collega, *n. m.* e *f.* (*pers.*) colleague. // **~ d'ufficio** (*pers.*) fellow clerk.

collegamento, *n. m.* **1** connection, connexion; (*associazione d'idee*) association; (*rap-

porto) relation. **2** (*cosa che collega*) link, liaison. // **il ~ della moda con la realtà industriale** (*market.*) the association of fashion with industrial reality; **~ marittimo** (*trasp. mar.*) shipping link; **~ telefonico** (*comun.*) telephonic connection.

collegare, *v. t.* **1** to connect; (*associare*) to associate, to relate. **2** to link (up), to interlock.

collegiale, *a.* joint.

collegialmente, *avv.* jointly.

collegio, *n. m.* **1** boarding school. **2** (*universitario*) college. **3** (*comitato*) board, committee. // **~ arbitrale** (*leg.*) arbitration board, court of arbitration; arbitrators (*pl.*); (*sind.*) board of arbitrators; **~ dei revisori contabili** (*fin., rag.*) auditors' committee; **un ~ di periti** a group of appraisers.

collettame, *n. m.* (*trasp.*) packages (*pl.*). // **noleggio a ~** (*trasp. mar.*) liner freighting; **trasporto a ~** (*trasp. mar.*) general cargo service.

collettivamente, *avv.* jointly, collectively.

collettivo, *a.* collective, joint. *n. m.* collective. // **in nome ~** (*di società*) general.

collezione, *n. f.* **1** collection. **2** (*attr. uff.*) (*di documenti, giornali, ecc.*) file.

collisione, *n. f.* **1** (*trasp.*) collision. **2** (*trasp. mar., anche*) foul. // **~ accidentale** (*trasp.*) accidental collision.

collo, *n. m.* **1** (*market.*) (*pacco*) package, parcel. **2** (*market.*) (*balla*) bale.

collocamento, *n. m.* **1** placement; (*sistemazione*) settlement. **2** (*market.*) (*di merci, prodotti, ecc.*) placement. **3** (*pers.*) placement, employment. // **~ a riposo** (*pers.*) retirement, superannuation; **~ clandestino di azioni** (*fin.*) share pushing; **il ~ della manodopera** (*pers.*) the placement of labour; **il ~ di prodotti nazionali sui mercati esteri** (*comm. est.*) the placement of domestic products on foreign markets; **agenzia** (*o* **ufficio**) **di ~** (*pers., sind.*) employment agency.

collocare, *v. t.* **1** to place; (*disporre*) to dispose; (*sistemare*) to settle; (*mettere*) to set★; (*posare*) to lay★. **2** (*market.*) (*merci, prodotti, ecc.*) to place. // **~ a riposo** (*pers.*) to retire, to shelve; **~** (*q.*) **come apprendista** (*sind.*) to apprentice; **~ un'emissione obbligazionaria** (*fin.*) to place a bond issue.

collocatore, *n. m.* **1** (*fin.*) (*di fondi d'investimento*) investment dealer. **2** (*pers.*) (*funzionario d'ufficio di collocamento*) labour-exchange official.

collocazione, *n. f.* **1** placement; (*sistemazione*) arrangement, settlement. **2** (*posto occupato da q.*) position, post. // **~ privata** (*di titoli, ecc.*) (*fin.*) private placement.

colloquio, *n. m.* **1** talk. **2** (*market., pers.*) interview.

collusione, *n. f.* (*leg.*) collusion. // **~ in una gara d'appalto** (*leg.*) collusive tendering.

collusivamente, *avv.* (*leg.*) collusively.

collusivo, *a.* (*leg.*) collusive, collusory.

colonia, *n. f.* **1** colony. **2** (*pers.*) (*per i dipendenti e/o i loro familiari*) holiday camp. // **~ estiva** (*org. az., pers.*) summer camp; **~ marina** (*org. az., pers.*) sea camp.

coloniale, *a.* colonial. // **commercio ~** colonial trade; **generi coloniali** (*market.*) *V.* **coloniali.**

coloniali, *n. pl.* (*market.*) groceries.

colonna, *n. f.* column. // **~ creditrice** (*rag.*) credit column; **~ debitrice** (*rag.*) debit column; **~ degli annunci personali** (*giorn., pubbl.*) personal column; **~ dei crediti** (*rag.*) credit column; **~ dei «diversi»** (*rag.*) sundries column; **~ del «dare»** (*rag.*) debit column, debtor side, debit; **la ~ delle attività** (*rag.*) the assets side; **~ delle causali** (*rag.*) description column; **la ~ delle cifre** (*rag.*) the amount column; **~ dell'«avere»** (*rag.*) credit column, credit, creditor; **~ d'annunci pubblicitari** (*giorn.*) column of advertisements; **~ di cassa** (*rag.*) cash column.

colpa, *n. f.* **1** fault; (*talora*) blame. **2** (*leg.*) guilt. **3** (*leg.*) (*negligenza*) negligence. // **~ del capitano** (*trasp. mar.*) negligence of the master.

colpevole, *a.* (*leg.*) guilty, culpable. *n. m.* e *f.* **1** (*leg.*) culprit, offender. **2** (*leg.*) (*anche d'una negligenza*) delinquent.

colpevolezza, *n. f.* (*leg.*) guilt, culpability. // **~ di complice** (*leg.*) accessorial guilt.

colpire, *v. t.* **1** to hit★, to knock, to strike★. **2** (*far colpo su*) to impress; (*avere un effetto su*) to affect; (*urtare*) to shock.

colpo, *n. m.* **1** hit, knock, stroke. **2** (*impressione*) impression. **3** (*choc*) shock. **4** (*Borsa*) coup (*francese*). // **un ~ di fortuna** a stroke of good luck; a windfall (*fam.*); **un ~ in Borsa** (*Borsa*) a coup on the Stock Exchange; **~ maestro** coup.

comandante, *n. m.* **1** commander, leader. **2** (*trasp. mar.*) commander, master. // **~ in seconda** (*di mercantile*) (*trasp. mar.*) mate.

comandare, *v. t.* **1** to command, to order, to direct. **2** (*leg.*) to enjoin. *v. i.* to be in authority.

comando, *n. m.* **1** command, order; (*dell'autorità*) fiat. **2** (*posizione di comando*) leadership. **3** (*leg.*) injunction. **4** (*trasp. mar.*) captainship.

combinare, *v. t.* to combine. // **~ un affare**

to bring off (*o* to put through) a business deal; ~ **un buon affare** to make (*o* to strike) a bargain.

combinazione, *n. f.* **1** combination. **2** (*caso*) chance; (*coincidenza*) coincidence. **3** (*tur.*) package. // ~ **di due «call»** (*q. V.*) **e d'un «put»** (*q. V.*) (*Borsa, USA*) strap; ~ **finanziaria** (*fin.*) financial combination; **per** ~ by chance.

come, *avv.* **1** as. **2** (*a somiglianza di*) like. **3** (*interrogativo*) how. // ~ **da** as per; ~ **da campione** as per sample; ~ **di consueto** as customary, as usual; ~ **segue...** as follows...; «~ **si trova**» (*market.*) (*di merce*) «on evidence»; ~ **sopra** as above; (*comm.*) ditto.

cominciare, *v. t.* e *i.* **1** to begin*, to commence, to open, to start. **2** (*leg.*) to inure. // ~ **a perorare una causa** (*leg.*) (*d'avvocato*) to open a case; ~ **a scaricare** (*trasp. mar.*) to break bulk; ~ **un dibattito** to open a debate; ~ **lo scarico** (*trasp. mar.*) to break bulk.

comitato, *n. m.* **1** committee. **2** (*amm., org. az.*) board. **3** (*leg.*) committee. **4** (*org. az.*) commission. // ~ **consultivo** (*org. az.*) advisory committee; ~ **dei creditori** (*leg.*) committee of creditors; ~ **del bilancio** (*fin., org. az.*) budget committee; ~ **di consultazione mista** (*amm., pers., sind.*) management advisory committee; ~ **di consumatori-pilota** (*market.*) consumer panel; ~ **di controllo dei conti** (*fin., rag.*) audit committee; ~ **d'inchiesta** (*amm., leg.*) board of inquiry; ~ **di studio dei suggerimenti** (*org. az.*) suggestion committee; ~ **direttivo** (*org. az.*) managing committee, steering committee; ~ **Economico e Sociale (CES)** Economic and Social Committee (*ESC*); ~ **esecutivo** executive committee; (*fin.*) stockholders' committee; ~ **misto** (*p. es., di rappresentanti dei lavoratori e dei datori di lavoro*) (*pers., sind.*) joint committee; ~ **paritetico** (*org. az., sind.*) bipartite board; ~ **per la programmazione** (*econ.*) planning board; ~ **permanente** (*amm., org. az.*) standing committee; **essere in un** ~ to be on a committee.

comma, *n. m.* (*leg.*) paragraph.

commerciabile, *a.* (*market.*) dealable, merchantable, marketable. // **non** ~ (*market.*) unmerchantable, unmarketable.

commerciabilità, *n. f.* (*market.*) marketability.

commerciale, *a.* commercial, mercantile, trading; merchant (*attr.*); commersh (*slang USA*).

commercialista, *n. m.* e *f.* **1** (*dottore in Economia e Commercio*) graduate in economics and commerce. **2** (*consulente*) business consultant. **3** (*leg.*) (*specialista in diritto commerciale*) expert in commercial law.

commercializzabile, *a.* (*market.*) marketable.

commercializzare, *v. t.* **1** to commercialize. **2** (*market.*) to market.

commercializzazione, *n. f.* **1** commercialization. **2** (*market.*) marketing. // **la** ~ **dei prodotti** (*econ.*) the marketing of commodities.

commercialmente, *avv.* commercially.

commerciante, *n. m.* e *f.* **1** dealer, trader; merchant (*di solito, nei composti*). **2** (*uomo d'affari*) businessman*; biz man* (*slang USA*). **3** (*negoziante*) tradesman*. **4 commercianti,** *pl. collett.* (*negozianti*) tradespeople, tradesfolk. // ~ **al dettaglio** (*market.*) *V.* ~ **al minuto;** ~ **al minuto** (*market.*) retail merchant, retail dealer, retailer; ~ **all'ingrosso** (*market.*) wholesale dealer, wholesaler, direct trader, warehouseman; ~ **della City di Londra** (*fin.*) City man; ~ **di carbone** coal-merchant, coaler; ~ **di ferramenta** ironmonger; ~ **di vini** wine-merchant; **un** ~ **disonesto** (*market.*) a sharp trader; **un** ~ **in cereali** a dealer in dry goods; ~ **in generi diversi** general dealer; ~ **in granaglie** (*anche*) cornfactor; ~ **in proprio** (*market.*) sole trader; **un** ~ **in tessuti** a dealer in dry goods (*USA*); **un** ~ **onesto** a straight businessman; **un** ~ **solvibile** (*cred.*) a solvent merchant; **un** ~ **straniero** (*comm. est.*) a foreign trader.

commerciare, *v. i.* to trade, to carry on trade; to deal* (in); to handle, to merchant, to merchandise. // ~ **oltre i limiti delle proprie disponibilità** (*market.*) to overtrade.

commercio, *n. m.* **1** (*in generale, o fatto su larga scala, o fra città o Paesi lontani*) commerce. **2** (*lo scambio delle merci*) trade, trading; (*i traffici*) traffic. **3** (*di solito nei composti*) business. // ~ **al dettaglio** (*market.*) retail trade; ~ **al minuto** (*market.*) retail trade; ~ **all'ingrosso** (*market.*) wholesale trade, direct trade; ~ **ambulante** (*market.*) hawking, peddling; **un** ~ **attivo** a lively trade; ~ **clandestino** clandestine trade; ~ **coloniale** colonial trade; ~ **con l'estero** foreign trade, overseas trade; ~ **costiero** (*trasp. mar.*) coasting trade; ~ **dei prodotti agricoli** agricultural trade; **il** ~ **dei vini** the wine trade; **il** ~ **del carbone** the coal trade; **il** ~ **del cotone** the cotton trade; ~ **dell'oro e dell'argento** (*fin.*) bullion trade; ~ **d'articoli di vestiario** clothing trade; ~ **d'esportazione** (*comm. est.*) export trade; ~ **d'importazione** (*comm. est.*) import trade; ~ **di piccolo cabotaggio** (*trasp. mar.*) coasting trade, coastwise trade; ~ **di rappresentanza** agency trade; ~ **di riesportazione** (*comm. est.*) entrepôt trade; ~ **di scambio**

(*econ.*) trade by barter; ~ **di transito** (*comm. est.*) entrepôt trade, transit trade; ~ **estero** foreign trade; ~ **fiacco** depressed trade; ~ **illecito** (*leg.*) illegal trade; back-door trade (*fam.*); ~ **in compensazione** compensation trade; ~ **internazionale** international trade; ~ **interno** domestic trade, home trade, inland trade, internal commerce; ~ **interstatale** (*fra Stati dell'Unione*) interstate commerce (*USA*); ~ **marittimo** (*trasp. mar.*) shipping trade, shipping business, seaborne trade, navigation; **il** ~ **mondiale** the world trade; ~ **multilaterale** (*comm. est.*) multilateral trade; ~ **nazionale** domestic trade, home trade; ~ **per via di terra** overland trade; **esser fuori** ~ (*market.*) (*d'articolo*) to be out of sale; (*d'un libro*) to be out of print; **essere in** ~ (*market.*) (*d'articolo*) to be on the market, to be on sale; **il Ministero del** ~ (*amm.*) the Board of Trade (*in G.B.*); the Department of Commerce (*in U.S.A.*).

commessa[1], *n. f.* **1** (*comun., market.*) (*ordinazione*) order. **2** (*org. az.*) (*di lavorazione*) work order, work ticket. // **produzione su** ~ (*market.*) production on order.

commessa[2], *n. f.* (*pers.*) (*di negozio*) saleswoman★, saleslady, salesgirl, shop-girl, shop-assistant; salesclerk.

commesso, *n. m.* **1** (*banca, pers.*) messenger, walk-clerk. **2** (*fin., ingl.*) (*della Borsa Valori di Londra*) waiter. **3** (*pers.*) (*di negozio*) shop-assistant, shopman★, salesman★; salesclerk, clerk (*USA*). // ~ **viaggiatore** (*market., pers.*) commercial traveller, traveller, travelling clerk, travelling salesman, field salesman, salesman.

commettere, *v. t.* **1** (*fare, eseguire*) to commit, to perform. **2** (*affidare*) to commit, to entrust. // ~ **una colpa** (*leg.*) to commit an offence, to offend; ~ **un errore** to make a mistake; ~ **peculato** (*leg.*) to peculate; ~ **un reato** (*leg.*) to commit an offence, to offend.

comminare, *v. t.* (*leg.*) to comminate.

comminatorio, *a.* (*leg.*) comminatory.

comminazione, *n. f.* (*leg.*) commination.

commissario, *n. m.* **1** commissary. **2** (*leg.*) commissioner. // ~ **d'avaria** (*ass. mar., trasp. mar.*) claim agent; ~ **di bordo** (*trasp. mar.*) purser, shipping-master.

commissionare, *v. t.* **1** to commission. **2** (*market.*) (*ordinare*) to order, to place an order for.

commissionario, *n. m.* **1** (*comm. est.*) commissionaire. **2** (*market.*) commission agent, commission merchant; consignee; factor; selling agent; purchasing agent. // ~ **di Borsa** (*in Italia*) «commissionario di Borsa» (*chi acquista o vende titoli per conto di un committente; cfr. ingl.* **jobber**).

commissione, *n. f.* **1** (*comitato*) commission, committee, board. **2** (*incarico*) errand, commission, assignment, task. **3** (*leg.*) (*d'agente commerciale*) commission. **4** (*leg.*) (*di commissionario*) factorage. **5** (*market.*) (*ordinazione*) order; order form. **6** (*org. az.*) commission. // ~ **bancaria** bank commission; **commissioni bancarie** bank charges; ~ **del credere** (*market.*) del credere commission; ~ **di controllo** (*d'un porto, ecc.*) (*trasp. mar.*) conservancy; ~ **di controllo dei conti** (*fin., rag.*) audit board; ~ **d'inchiesta** (*amm., leg.*) committee of inquiry, fact-finding board; ~ **di raccomandazione** (*in un contratto di noleggio*) (*trasp. mar.*) address commission; ~ **di studio** (*dei problemi del lavoro*) (*sind.*) working party; ~ **di vendita** (*market.*) selling commission; ~ **di vigilanza** (*nel fallimento*) (*leg.*) commission of inspection, committee of inspection; ~ **interna** (*d'una fabbrica*) (*pers., sind.*) shop committee; (*per la discussione delle lagnanze del personale*) grievance committee; ~ **mista** joint committee; (*org. az., sind.*) works committee; ~ **parlamentare** (*leg.*) parliamentary committee; ~ **per la verifica dei poteri** (*amm., fin.*) committee on credentials; **una** ~ **permanente** a standing committee; ~ **tripartita** (*che emette il lodo arbitrale*) (*sind.*) tripartite board.

committente, *n. m.* e *f.* **1** (*leg., market.*) consigner, consignor, principal. **2** (*market.*) (*acquirente*) buyer, purchaser, customer.

comodante, *n. m.* e *f.* (*leg.*) bailer, bailor.

comodatario, *n. m.* (*leg.*) bailee.

comodato, *n. m.* (*leg.*) bailment, commodatum★.

comodo, *a.* **1** comfortable. **2** (*conveniente*) convenient.

compagnia, *n. f.* **1** company. **2** (*fin., leg.*) (*società*) company; corporation (*USA*). **3** (*market.*) (*azienda, ditta*) business, concern, firm. // **la** ~ **del Lloyd** (*di Londra*) (*ass. mar., ingl.*) the Lloyd's; ~ **d'assicurazione** (*ass.*) insurance company; assurance company (*sulla vita o USA*); ~ **d'assicurazione marittima** (*ass. mar.*) marine insurance company; ~ **d'assicurazioni sulla vita** (*ass.*) life-insurance company; ~ **di bandiera** (*trasp. aer., trasp. mar.*) flag carrier; ~ **di navigazione** (*trasp. mar.*) navigation company, shipping line; ~ **di riassicurazioni** (*ass.*) reinsurance company.

compagno, *n. m.* fellow, mate. // ~ **di lavoro** (*pers.*) fellow-worker, mate.

comparente, *n. m.* e *f.* (*leg.*) appearer, appearing party.

comparire, *v. i.* to appear. // ~ **in giudizio** (*leg.*) to appear at the Bar, to appear before the Court, to present oneself for trial; **non ~ al processo** (*dopo aver ottenuto la libertà provvisoria su cauzione*) (*leg.*) to forfeit one's bail; **non ~ in tribunale** (*leg.*) to default.

comparizione, *n. f.* appearance. // ~ **in giudizio** (*leg.*) appearance before the Court, attendance in Court.

comparsa, *n. f.* **1** (*comparizione*) appearance. **2** (*leg.*) (*atto scritto di parte*) brief, pleading, statement. // **la ~ conclusionale** (*leg.*) the final statement of the case.

compartecipazione, *n. f.* (*leg.*) copartnership. // ~ **agli utili** (*fin.*) profit sharing; ~ **agli utili aziendali** (*sind.*) labour copartnership.

compartecipe, *a.* partecipating; sharing. // ~ **agli utili** profit-sharing.

compartimento, *n. m.* **1** compartment. **2** (*org. az.*) department. // **compartimenti stagni** (*trasp. mar.*) watertight compartments.

compensare, *v. t.* **1** (*ricompensare, rimunerare*) to recompense, to reward. **2** (*bilanciare*) to compensate, to recover, to make★ up (for). **3** (*controbilanciare*) to countervail, to set★ off, to offset★. **4** (*Borsa*) to cut★ out. // ~ **un debito** (*cred.*) to set off a debt; ~ **una perdita** to recover a loss.

compensarsi, *v. recipr.* (*bilanciarsi*) to balance each other.

compensativo, *a.* compensatory.

compensazione, *n. f.* **1** compensation, offset. **2** (*Borsa*) cutting out; make up. **3** (*cred.*) (*di debito*) set-off. **4** (*fin.*) (*di debiti e crediti: con scambio d'assegni, ecc.*) clearance, clearing. // ~ **della bussola** (*trasp. mar.*) compass compensation; ~ **interaziendale dei noli** (*trasp. mar.*) freight compensation between enterprises.

compenso, *n. m.* **1** compensation. **2** (*in denaro, anche*) consideration. **3** (*ricompensa*) recompense, reward. **4** (*retribuzione*) pay; (*salario*) wages; (*stipendio*) salary. **5** (*onorario*) fee, honorarium. **6** (*ciò che serve a controbilanciare*) set-off, offset. // ~ **aggiuntivo** (*oltre la paga*) (*pers.*) extra pay; ~ **agli amministratori** (*rag.*) directors' fees; ~ **dato al pilota** (*trasp. mar.*) pilotage; ~ **d'agenzia** (*leg., market.*) agency commission; (*pubbl.*) fee; ~ **di salvataggio** (*trasp. mar.*) salvage award; ~ **forfettario** agreed consideration; ~ **pagato per il ricupero marittimo** (*trasp. mar.*) salvage, salvage money; ~ **percentuale** (*fin., USA*) factorage (*V.* **factoring**); ~ **simbolico** token payment; ~ **straordinario** (*pers.*) extra pay; **in ~ di** in return for.

compera, *n. f.* **1** (*market.*) purchase, buying; buy (*fam.*). **2 compere,** *pl.* (*market.*) (*effettuate nei negozi*) shopping (*collett.*). // ~ **a credito** purchase on credit; ~ **a scadenza** purchase on term; **una ~ di seconda mano** a second-hand purchase.

competente, *a.* **1** competent, experienced, expert. **2** (*atto, adeguato*) competent, appropriate. **3** (*leg.*) competent, cognizant.

competenza, *n. f.* **1** competence, expertise. **2** (*fig.*) (*campo*) province. **3** (*leg.*) competence, cognizance. **4 competenze,** *pl.* (*spese*) charges, fees. // **competenze di chiusura** (*banca*) charges in closing a current account; **competenze e spese** (*leg.*) fees and costs; ~ **per materia** (*leg.*) cognizance ratione materiae; **competenze per il protesto preliminare** (*leg.*) noting charges; **competenze per sconto d'effetti** (*banca*) charges on discount of bills; ~ **sulla questione in discussione** (*leg.*) cognizance of the subject-matter; ~ **territoriale** (*leg.*) cognizance ratione loci; **essere di ~ di q.** to fall within the competence of sb., to rest with sb.

competere, *v. i.* **1** to compete. **2** (*leg.*) (*essere di competenza, spettare a*) to be (*o* to fall★) within the competence (of).

competitività, *n. f.* competitiveness.

competitivo, *a.* competitive.

competitore, *n. m.* competitor.

competizione, *n. f.* competition.

compilare, *v. t.* **1** to compile. **2** (*un documento*) to make★ up, to draw★ up. **3** (*una lista, ecc.*) to make★ out, to write★ out. **4** (*un modulo*) to fill in (*o* up, *o* out). // ~ **un assegno** to write a cheque; ~ **un elenco** to make out a list; ~ (*un documento*) **in duplice copia** to indent; ~ **un modulo** to fill in a form; ~ **il modulo per la dichiarazione dei redditi** to fill in the tax form; ~ **una ricevuta** to make out a receipt.

compilazione, *n. f.* compilation (*V. anche* **compilare**). // ~ **degli atti e dei documenti necessari per un passaggio di proprietà** (*leg.*) conveyancing.

compito, *n. m.* **1** assignment, business, duty, task. **2** (*pers.*) (*mansione*) function. // **compiti abituali** routine duties; **un ~ d'ordinaria amministrazione** (*pers.*) a routine job; **compiti di sorveglianza** (*org. az.*) a supervisory position (*sing.*).

complessità, *n. f.* complexity.

complessivo, *a.* **1** aggregate, global, inclusive, overall, total. **2** (*comm.*) gross, overhead. **3** (*rag.*) grand.

complesso, *a.* complex, complicated. *n. m.*

1 aggregate, set, batch. 2 (*industriale*) plant, unit. // ~ **delle banchine** (*d'un porto*) (*trasp. mar.*) wharfing; ~ **d'attività promozionali di vendita** (*pubbl.*) merchandising; ~ **di cognizioni tecniche** (*non brevettate*) know-how.

completamente, *avv.* completely, fully.

completamento, *n. m.* completion, conclusion, finishing, finish. // **il** ~ **delle scorte** (*org. az.*) the replenishment of the stock.

completare, *v. t.* 1 to complete, to conclude, to finish. 2 (*integrare*) to supplement. 3 (*compilare*) to fill in (*o* up, *o* out), to write★ up. 4 (*org. az.*) (*le scorte*) to replenish. // ~ **la carriera** (*pers.*) to round off one's career; ~ **la copertura di** (*titoli, ecc.*) (*Borsa, fin.*) to margin up; ~ **documenti** to fill out documents.

completo, *a.* 1 complete, comprehensive, full, whole. 2 (*assoluto*) outright, thorough. 3 (*esauriente*) exhaustive.

complice, *n. m.* e *f.* (*leg.*) accomplice, accessary, accessory. // ~ **in un delitto** (*leg.*) accessary (*o* accessory) to a crime; **di** ~ (*leg.*) accessorial.

complicità, *n. f.* (*leg.*) complicity.

comporre, *v. t.* 1 to compose, to constitute, to make★ (up). 2 (*comun.*) (*un numero telefonico*) to dial. 3 (*giorn., pubbl.*) (*tipograficamente*) to set★, to set★ up. 4 (*leg.*) (*una vertenza*) to compound, to compromise, to reconcile, to settle. 5 (*sind.*) (*una vertenza, ecc.*) to compose. // ~ **una lite** (*leg., anche*) to accommodate a quarrel, to make up a quarrel; ~ **un numero** (*al telefono*) (*comun.*) to dial a number.

comportamento, *n. m.* 1 behaviour, conduct. 2 (*market.*) behaviour. // ~ **decoroso** proper behaviour; ~ **indegno** misconduct.

composizione, *n. f.* 1 composition, constitution, frame, framework, making. 2 (*giorn., pubbl.*) (*tipografica*) type-setting, composition. 3 (*leg.*) (*d'una lite, d'una vertenza, ecc.*) composition, agreement, settlement, reconciliation. // **una** ~ **amichevole** (*leg.*) a private arrangement; **la** ~ **d'una controversia** (*leg.*) the settlement of a controversy.

composto, *a.* composite. *n. m.* compound, complex.

compra, *n. f. V.* **compera.**

comprabile, *a.* buyable, purchaseable, purchasable.

comprare, *v. t.* 1 to buy★; to purchase (*meno usato*); to get★ (*fam.*). 2 (*fin.*) (*un intero pacchetto azionario*) to buy★ out. 3 (*leg.*) (*corrompere*) to bribe, to buy★ up. // ~ **a buon mercato** to buy cheap; ~ **a contanti** to buy cash; ~ **a credito** to buy on credit, to deal on credit; ~ **a doppia opzione** (*Borsa*) to give for the put and call; ~ **a premio** (*Borsa*) to give for the call; ~ **a rate** (*market.*) to buy on easy terms; to buy on the instalment plan; ~ **a termine** (*Borsa*) to buy on term; ~ **al meglio** (*fin.*) to buy at best; ~ **al prezzo minimo** to buy at the lowest price; to get in on the ground floor (*slang USA*); ~ **all'asta** (*o* **all'incanto**) to buy at an auction; ~ **all'ingrosso** (*market.*) to buy wholesale, to job; ~ **allo scoperto** (*Borsa*) to bull the market; ~ **con diritto d'aggiunta** (*Borsa*) to give for the call of more; ~ **con diritto d'aggiunta doppia** (*Borsa*) to give for the call of twice more; ~ **il «dont»** (*Borsa*) to give for the call; ~ (*qc.*) **in quantità eccessiva** (*rispetto al fabbisogno*) (*market.*) to overbuy; ~ **per futura consegna** to buy for forward delivery; ~ **lo «stellage»** (*Borsa*) to give for the put and call; ~ **titoli d'una società** (*fin.*) to buy into a company; ~ **troppa merce** (*market.*) to overbuy.

comprato, *a.* bought. // ~ **a un prezzo inferiore a quello di listino** (*market.*) (*d'articolo, ecc.*) off-list.

compratore, *n. m.* 1 buyer, purchaser. 2 (*leg.*) (*specialm. di beni immobili*) vendee. 3 (*market.*) (*in un negozio e sim.*) shopper, customer. 4 (*org. az.*) (*addetto agli acquisti*) buyer. // ~ **d'un «dont»** (*Borsa*) buyer of a call option; ~ **d'un premio indiretto** (*Borsa*) taker for a put; ~ **marginale** (*econ.*) marginal buyer.

compravendita, *n. f.* 1 (*fin., market.*) trading, buying and selling. 2 (*leg.*) (*il contratto*) contract of sale. 3 (*market.*) marketing.

comprendere, *v. t.* 1 (*contenere*) to comprise, to comprehend, to contain, to include. 2 (*capire*) to understand★, to comprehend, to grasp.

comprensione, *n. f.* understanding, comprehension, grasp.

comprensivo, *a.* 1 comprehensive, inclusive. 2 (*che dimostra comprensione*) understanding, sympathetic.

compreso, *a.* (*incluso*) included, inclusive. // **tutto** ~ (*market.*) (*di prezzo*) all-inclusive; «**tutto** ~» (*market.*) «no extra», «all in».

compressione, *n. f.* 1 compression. 2 (*stretta*) squeeze. // ~ **creditizia** (*fin.*) credit squeeze; ~ **dei salari** (*econ.*) pay restraint.

comprimere, *v. t.* 1 to press. 2 (*anche fig.*) to squeeze.

comprimibile, *a.* 1 compressible. 2 (*econ.*) (*della domanda*) squeezable, that can be squeezed.

comprimibilità, *n. f.* 1 compressibility. 2 (*econ.*) squeezability.

compromesso, *n. m.* **1** compromise, deal. **2** (*leg.*) settlement, transaction, ad referendum. **3** (*leg.*) (*patto di futura vendita*) agreement to sell. // ~ **arbitrale** (*leg.*) arbitration agreement, reference, submission; ~ **d'avaria generale** (*ass. mar.*) general average bond; **un ~ di vendita** (*market.*) a preliminary agreement to sell.

compromettere, *v. t.* to compromise, to endanger.

comproprietà, *n. f.* (*leg.*) part-ownership, joint ownership, joint property.

comproprietario, *n. m.* (*leg.*) part-owner, co-owner, joint owner, coproprietor, joint proprietor.

comprovare, *v. t.* (*leg.*) to evidence, to vouch.

computabile, *a.* computable.

computare, *v. t.* to compute, to reckon, to tally.

computatore, *n. m.* (*macch. uff.*) computer.

computatrice, *n. f.* (*macch. uff.*) computer.

computerizzare, *v. t.* (*elab. elettr., org. az.*) to computerize.

computerizzato, *a.* (*elab. elettr., org. az.*) computerized.

computerizzazione, *n. f.* (*elab. elettr., org. az.*) computerization.

computista, *n. m.* e *f.* **1** (*pers.*) calculator, reckoner. **2** (*pers.*) (*contabile*) bookkeeper.

computisteria, *n. f.* **1** (*mat.*) business mathematics. **2** (*rag.*) (*contabilità*) bookkeeping.

computo, *n. m.* computation, counting, reckoning.

comune, *a.* **1** (*generale, condiviso*) common, general, joint. **2** (*ordinario, normale*) common, ordinary, normal. // **di ~ accordo** by common consent.

comunemente, *avv.* **1** (*in comune*) commonly, jointly. **2** (*in genere, di solito*) usually, normally.

comunicare, *v. t.* e *i.* to communicate, to announce, to give★ notice, to notify, to report, to signify. // ~ **il proprio benestare al venditore della merce** to communicate one's approval to the seller of the goods.

comunicato, *n. m.* **1** notice. **2** (*ufficiale*) «communiqué». **3** (*giorn., pubbl.*) handout. // ~ **stampa** (*giorn., pubbl.*) handout; **comunicati stampa** (*giorn.*) press releases.

comunicazione, *n. f.* **1** communication. **2** (*annunzio, avviso*) announcement, notification, notice. **3** (*messaggio*) message. **4** (*rapporto, relazione*) report. **5** (*leg.*) (*trasmissione di documenti*) discovery (of documents). **6** (*org. az.*) memorandum★; memo (*fam.*). // **comunicazioni aziendali** (*org. az.*) industrial communications; **comunicazioni col personale** (*org. az.*) employee communications; ~ **di servizio** (*org. az.*) memorandum; memo (*fam.*); **comunicazioni interne** (*org. az.*) personnel communications, employee communications, industrial communications; ~ **interurbana** trunk call; long-distance call (*USA*); **comunicazioni radio** (*trasp. mar.*) radio communications; ~ **scritta** (*pers.*) formal notice; **comunicazioni scritte** (*org. az.*) written communications; ~ **telefonica** telephone call; **essere in ~** (*telefonica*) (*comun.*) to be through; to be connected (*USA*).

concausa, *n. f.* (*leg.*) joint cause.

concedente, *n. m.* e *f.* **1** (*leg.*) grantor. **2** (*leg.*) (*specialm. d'un immobile in affitto*) lessor, landlord.

concedere, *v. t.* **1** to concede, to accord, to allow, to award, to grant. **2** (*ammettere*) to concede, to admit, to own. **3** (*leg.*) (*beni, diritti, proprietà*) to grant, to concede. **4** (*leg.*) (*in affitto*) to let★ (out), to lease. // ~ **a q. di fare qc.** to permit sb. to do st.; ~ **un aumento** (*di salario*) (*pers.*) to give a rise; ~ **un avanzamento a** (*un dipendente*) (*amm.*) to step up; ~ **un brevetto** (*leg.*) to grant a patent; ~ **un congedo a q.** (*pers.*) to grant sb. a leave; to furlough sb. (*USA*); ~ **crediti di cassa** (*banca, cred.*) to grant clean credits; ~ **crediti senza garanzie** (*banca, cred.*) to give unsecured credit; ~ **una dilazione a un debitore** (*cred.*) to respite a debtor; ~ **una dilazione di pagamento** (*anche*) to grant an extension of payment; ~ **un diritto di brevetto a q.** (*leg.*) to patent sb.; ~ **un'esclusiva a q.** (*leg.*) to patent sb.; ~ **la propria fiducia** to give one's confidence; ~ **il passaporto a q.** (*tur.*) (*detto d'un'autorità consolare, ecc.*) to visa sb.; ~ **un permesso a q.** (*pers.*) to grant sb. a leave; to furlough sb. (*USA*); ~ **prestiti a condizione di favore** (*cred.*) to grant loans on favourable terms; ~ **un prestito** (*cred.*) to grant a loan, to agree to a loan; ~ **un prestito al (tasso del) 6%** (*cred.*) to lend at the rate of 6%; ~ **un privilegio a una società** (*amm., fin.*) to charter a company; ~ **sconti** (*market.*) to rebate; ~ **uno sconto** (*market.*) to grant a discount; ~ **uno sconto del 3% sull'importo d'una fattura** to allow a discount of 3% on the amount of an invoice; ~ **uno scoperto** (*banca, cred.*) to grant an overdraft; ~ **un'udienza a q.** to grant sb. an audience.

concedibile, *a.* concessible, allowable, grantable (*V.* **concedere**).

concentrare, *v. t.* **1** to concentrate. **2** (*cen-

tralizzare) to centralize. 3 (*econ., fin.*) (*aziende, imprese, ecc.*) to combine, to amalgamate, to merge. // ~ **i propri acquisti presso q.** to give the bulk of one's business to sb.

concentrarsi, *v. rifl.* 1 to concentrate. 2 (*essere centralizzato*) to be centralized. *v. recipr.* (*econ., fin.*) (*d'aziende, imprese, ecc.*) to combine, to amalgamate, to merge.

concentrazione, *n. f.* 1 concentration. 2 (*econ., fin.*) (*d'aziende, ecc.*) combination, amalgamation, consolidation, business combine, combine, merger. 3 (*econ., fin.*) (*quando un'azienda maggiore rileva le minori*) take-over. // ~ **d'imprese** (*econ.*) industrial combination; ~ **orizzontale** (*econ., fin.*) horizontal combination; ~ **verticale** (*econ., fin.*) vertical combination.

concessionario, *a.* (*leg.*) concessionary. *n. m.* 1 (*leg.*) concessionaire, concessioner, concessionary. 2 (*leg.*) (*di beni, diritti, proprietà*) grantee. // ~ **di brevetto** (*leg.*) patentee, patentor; ~ **di licenza** (*leg.*) licensee; ~ **in esclusiva** (*market.*) exclusive dealer, exclusive (*o* sole) distributor.

concessione, *n. f.* 1 concession, allowance, grant. 2 (*leg.*) concession. 3 (*leg.*) (*di beni, diritti, proprietà*) grant. // ~ **esclusiva** (*da parte d'un sovrano e sim.*) (*amm., leg.*) charter; (*market.*) exclusive agency; **concessioni tariffarie** (*comm. est., econ.*) tariff concessions.

conciliare, *v. t.* 1 to conciliate. 2 (*leg.*) (*le parti contendenti*) to reconcile. // ~ **una lite** (*leg.*) to make up a quarrel; ~ **una multa** (*leg.*) to settle a fine out of Court; to pay a fine.

conciliazione, *n. f.* 1 conciliation. 2 (*leg.*) (*fra le parti contendenti*) reconciliation.

concludere, *v. t.* (*condurre a termine*) to conclude, to carry out, to terminate. // ~ **un accordo con q.** to enter into agreement with sb.; ~ **un affare con q.** to conclude a bargain with sb., to close a bargain with sb., to drive a bargain with sb., to strike a bargain with sb.; ~ **una trattativa** to carry out a negotiation.

conclusionale, *n. f.* (*leg.*) final statement (of a case).

conclusione, *n. f.* 1 conclusion, end, termination. 2 (*chiusa, chiusura*) close; (*d'una discussione in un'adunanza, ecc.*) closure. 3 (*risultato*) result, issue. 4 (*leg.*) (*d'una causa*) determination. 5 **conclusioni,** *pl.* (*leg.*) summing up; brief (*USA*).

conclusivo, *a.* conclusive.

concordanza, *n. f.* 1 accordance, agreement, consistency. 2 (*fin., rag.*) (*di elementi, scadenze, ecc.*) matching.

concordare, *v. i.* to agree, to consist. *v. t.* 1 (*opinioni discordi, ecc.*) to reconcile. 2 (*stabilire di comune accordo*) to agree on (*o* upon). 3 (*controllare: conti e sim.*) to check.

concordato, *n. m.* 1 (*politico-religioso*) concordat. 2 (*leg.*) composition, arrangement, agreement, settlement. 3 (*leg.*) (*il documento*) deed of arrangement. // ~ **amichevole** (*leg.*) friendly settlement; ~ **con i creditori** (*leg.*) arrangement with creditors, composition with creditors, adjustment of creditors' claims; ~ **fallimentare** (*leg.*) *V.* ~ **con i creditori;** ~ **fiscale** (*fin.*) arrangement with the Revenue Office; ~ **preventivo** (*al fallimento*) (*leg.*) composition before bankruptcy; ~ **stragiudiziale** (*leg.*) *V.* ~ **amichevole;** ~ **tributario** (*fin.*) *V.* ~ **fiscale.**

concorrente, *a.* (*market.*) competing. *n. m.* 1 competitor, opponent, rival. 2 (*candidato a un posto, ecc.*) candidate, applicant. 3 (*a una gara d'appalto*) bidder, tenderer.

concorrenza, *n. f.* 1 (*econ., market.*) competition; competish (*slang USA*). 2 **la concorrenza,** *collett.* competitors (*pl.*). // ~ **imperfetta** (*econ.*) imperfect competition; ~ **leale** (*market.*) fair competition; ~ **monopolistica** (*econ.*) monopolistic competition; ~ **perfetta** (*econ.*) perfect competition; ~ **pura** (*econ.*) pure competition; ~ **sleale** (*leg., market.*) unfair competition, unfair practice; **una** ~ **vivace** (*market.*) a keen competition; **fino alla** ~ **di** to the amount of, up to the amount of, to the extent of, not exceeding; **sotto lo stimolo della** ~ (*market.*) under the pressure of competition.

concorrenziale, *a.* competitive, competing. // **mercato** ~ competitive market; **regime** ~ competitive system.

concorrere, *v. i.* 1 (*contribuire*) to concur, to contribute; to share (in); to take* part (in). 2 (*aspirare a un posto e sim.*) to compete, to apply (for). 3 (*econ., market.*) to compete. // ~ **a un appalto** to tender; ~ **a un posto vacante** (*pers.*) to compete for a vacancy.

concorso, *n. m.* 1 (*di fattori, ecc.*) concurrence. 2 (*afflusso*) concourse, attendance. 3 (*assistenza, aiuto*) assistance, aid, help. 4 (*competizione, gara, esame*) competition, contest. 5 (*pubbl.*) (*a premi, ecc.*) contest. // **un** ~ **a premi** (*giorn., pubbl.*) a prize contest, a consumer contest; ~ **d'appalto** call (*o* request) for bids (*o* for tenders); ~ **di circostanze** (*leg.*) concurrence of circumstances; ~ **di colpa** (*leg.*) contributory negligence; **esame di** ~ competitive exam; **fuori** ~ not for competition; «**fuori** ~» (*nelle mostre*) «not classed».

concussione, *n. f.* (*leg.*) concussion, graft.

condanna, *n. f.* (*leg.*) condemnation, conviction, sentence. // ~ **a morte** (*leg.*) sentence of death; ~ **a vita** (*leg.*) life sentence; ~ **condizionale** (*leg.*) probation; ~ **in contumacia** (*leg.*) condemnation by default.

condannare, *v. t.* (*leg.*) to condemn, to convict, to sentence. // ~ **q. al pagamento delle spese (processuali)** (*leg.*) to order sb. to pay the costs; ~ **alle spese (giudiziali)** (*leg.*) to condemn in costs; ~ **in contumacia** (*leg.*) to condemn for default, to default; «**condannato alle spese**» (*leg.*) (*di chi perde una causa*) «with costs»; **essere condannato all'insuccesso** (*fig.*) to be doomed to failure.

condannato, *n. m.* (*leg.*) convict.

condirettore, *n. m.* **1** (*amm.*) joint director, codirector, joint manager. **2** (*giorn., pers.*) associate editor.

condirezione, *n. f.* (*amm.*) joint management.

condividere, *v. t.* to share, to participate in.

condizionale, *a.* **1** conditional. **2** (*restrittivo*) qualified. **3** (*leg.*) provisory. *n. f.* (*leg.*) probation. // **con la** ~ (*leg.*) conditionally: **essere prosciolto con la** ~ **per sei mesi** to be conditionally discharged for six months; **concedere la** ~ (*leg.*) to suspend sentence.

condizionare, *v. t.* **1** to condition. **2** (*sottoporre a condizioni*) to qualify.

condizionato, *a.* **1** conditional, qualified. **2** (*leg.*) contingent. // **accettazione condizionata** (*d'una cambiale*) (*banca, cred.*) qualified acceptance.

condizione, *n. f.* **1** condition. **2** (*posizione, stato*) position, standing, state. **3** (*banca, cred.*) qualification. **4** (*leg.*) provision, proviso★. **5 condizioni,** *pl.* (*ambientali*) environment. **6 condizioni,** *pl.* (*fin., market.*) terms. // **condizioni accessorie** (*leg., USA*) strings; **le condizioni contrattuali** (*leg.*) the terms of a contract, the terms agreed upon; **la** ~ (*lo stato*) **del mercato** the condition of the market; ~ **del recidivo** (*leg.*) recidivism; **condizioni d'acquisto a credito** (*market.*) open account terms; **condizioni di consegna** (*market.*) terms of delivery, delivery terms; **le condizioni d'un contratto** (*leg.*) the conditions of a contract; **condizioni di lavoro** (*pers.*) working conditions; ~ **di membro** (*d'una società, ecc.*) membership; **condizioni di mercato** (*econ., market.*) market conditions; **condizioni di pagamento** (*market.*) terms of payment; ~ **di proprietario** (*leg.*) proprietorship; **le condizioni di rimborso d'un prestito** (*cred.*) the terms of repayment of a loan; ~ **di socio** (*fin.*) membership; **condizioni di vendita** (*market.*) conditions of sale, terms of sale; **condizioni di vendita e di consegna** (*market.*) purchasing conditions and terms of delivery; **condizioni di vendita rateale** (*market.*) hire-purchase terms; **le condizioni di vita e di lavoro** (*econ.*) the living and working conditions; ~ **esplicita** (*ass. mar.*) express warranty; ~ **essenziale** (*leg.*) stipulation; ~ **finanziaria** financial standing, circumstance; ~ **implicita** (*leg.*) implied condition, implied term; **condizioni meteorologiche** weather conditions; ~ **restrittiva** (*banca, cred.*) qualification; ~ **risolutiva** (*leg.*) resolutory condition, condition subsequent; ~ **sospensiva** (*leg.*) suspensive condition, condition precedent; **a** ~ **che...** on condition that..., on the understanding that...; (*leg.*) under the stipulation that...; **a questa** ~ on this understanding; **senza condizioni** without reservation, without reserve; unconditional (*a.*).

condonare, *v. t.* **1** to condone, to forgive★, to excuse. **2** (*leg.*) to remit. // ~ **un debito** (*cred.*) to forgive a debt; ~ **una pena** (*leg.*) to remit a penalty.

condono, *n. m.* **1** condonation. **2** (*leg.*) remission, relief. // ~ **fiscale** (*fin.*) conditional amnesty for tax-evaders.

condotta, *n. f.* **1** (*comportamento*) conduct, character, behaviour. **2** (*modo di condurre*) conduct, management. **3** (*procedimento*) proceeding, course. // ~ **coerente** consistent behaviour; ~ **disonesta** (*leg.*) malfeasance; ~ **illecita** (*leg.*) malfeasance; ~ **rispettabile** reputable conduct; ~ **sleale** foul play.

conducente, *n. m.* e *f.* **1** chauffeur (*m.*); chauffeuse (*f.*); driver. **2** (*leg.*) *V.* **conduttore.**

condurre, *v. t.* **1** (*guidare*) to lead★. **2** (*un veicolo*) to drive★. **3** (*accompagnare*) to accompany, to take★. **4** (*gestire*) to conduct, to manage, to carry on, to govern. **5** (*un'azienda e sim., anche*) to run★, to operate. **6** (*affari, ecc., anche*) to negotiate. // ~ **a buon fine** (*un piano, ecc.*) to carry out; ~ **un'azione legale** (*leg.*) to proceed; ~ (*gli affari, ecc.*) **in modo disonesto** to mismanage.

conduttore, *n. m.* **1** (*guidatore d'un veicolo*) driver. **2** (*leg.*) lessee; (*d'un appartamento, d'un fondo*) tenant; occupier (*ingl.*). **3** (*trasp. aut.*) (*di tram, d'autobus, ecc.*) driver. **4** (*trasp. ferr.*) guard; conductor (*USA*).

conduzione, *n. f.* **1** (*gestione*) management, operation, operating. **2** (*leg.*) leasehold. // **locazione-** ~ (*leg.*) «locatio conductio».

confederazione, *n. f.* **1** confederation, confederacy. **2** (*di sindacati, ecc.*) union.

conferenza, *n. f.* **1** conference. **2** (*discorso*) lecture. // ~ **ad alto livello** high-level conference; ~ **al vertice** summit conference; ~ **della**

Navigazione (*trasp. mar., USA*) freight conference, freight bureau; ~ **informativa** (*org. az.*) briefing session; ~ **stampa** (*giorn.*) press conference, news conference.

conferimento, *n. m.* 1 conferment, award, grant, bestowal. 2 (*fin.*) (*apporto di capitale*) contribution. // **il ~ d'un diritto** (*leg.*) the conferment of a right; **il ~ di merci all'ammasso** (*market.*) the conveyance of goods to a common pool; **il ~ d'un ordine** (*market.*) the placing of an order; **il ~ d'un premio** the award of a prize.

conferire, *v. t.* 1 to confer, to award, to bestow, to grant. 2 (*dare, aggiungere*) to give★, to lend★. 3 (*leg.*) (*diritti, onori, ecc.*) to vest. *v. i.* (*avere un colloquio*) to confer (with); to consult. // ~ **merci all'ammasso** to convey goods to a common pool; ~ **una ordinazione** (*market.*) to place (*o* to give) an order; ~ **una somma di denaro a una società** (*fin.*) to contribute an amount of money to a partnership.

conferma, *n. f.* 1 confirmation. 2 (*leg.*) confirmation, affirmation. // ~ **delle notizie** confirmation of the news; **la ~ d'un giudizio** (*leg.*) the affirmation of a decision; **la ~ d'una sentenza** (*leg.*) the confirmation of a judgment.

confermare, *v. t.* 1 to confirm. 2 (*provare*) to bear★ out, to prove. 3 (*leg.*) to confirm, to affirm. // ~ **un dipendente per altri sei mesi** (*pers.*) to retain an employee for another six months; ~ **un'ordinazione** (*market.*) to confirm an order; ~ **per iscritto** to confirm in writing.

confermativo, *a.* confirmative.

confermato, *a.* confirmed. // **non ~** unconfirmed.

confessione, *n. f.* 1 confession. 2 (*leg.*) confession. 3 (*leg.*) (*in cause civili, salvo quelle di divorzio*) admission. // ~ **giudiziale** (*leg.*) judicial confession; judicial admission; **una ~ spontanea** (*leg.*) a voluntary confession.

confezionamento, *n. m.* 1 making. 2 (*fabbricazione*) manufacture, manufacturing. // **il ~ di cibi** (*in scatola, ecc.*) (*market.*) the packing of food.

confezionare, *v. t.* 1 to make★. 2 (*market.*) (*imballare: un prodotto, ecc.*) to package. 3 (*org. az.*) (*capi d'abbigliamento, ecc.*) to manufacture. // ~ **camicie** (*org. az.*) to manufacture shirts.

confezionato, *a.* 1 made. 2 (*fabbricato*) manufactured. 3 (*market.*) (*già confezionato*) prepacked. 4 (*market.*) (*d'abito, ecc.*) ready-made, ready-for-wear, ready-to-wear; reach-me-down (*ingl.*).

confezione, *n. f.* 1 making. 2 (*fabbricazione*) manufacture, manufacturing. 3 (*fattura*) workmanship. 4 (*market.*) (*imballaggio: d'un prodotto, ecc.*) package, packaging. 5 (*market.*) confection; ready-made suit (*o* dress). // **confezioni da donna** ready-made dresses; confections; **confezioni da uomo** ready-made suits; **in ~** (*market.*) prepacked.

confezionista, *n. m.* e *f.* (*market.*) haberdasher, outfitter; maker-up (*ingl.*).

confisca, *n. f.* (*leg.*) confiscation, forfeiture, impressment, seizure, sequestration. // ~ **di beni** (*leg.*) confiscation of property; ~ **di merci registrate in base a falsa dichiarazione** (*dog.*) confiscation of falsely entered goods.

confiscabile, *a.* (*leg.*) confiscable, forfeitable, seizable.

confiscare, *v. t.* (*leg.*) to confiscate, to forfeit, to impress, to seize, to sequestrate, to sequester.

conflitto, *n. m.* 1 conflict. 2 (*d'interessi, ecc.*) collision, clash. // ~ **d'attribuzioni** (*leg.*) conflict of powers; ~ **di giurisdizione** (*leg.*) conflict of jurisdiction; ~ **d'interessi** (*leg.*) conflict (*o* clash) of interests; **conflitti di lavoro** (*sind.*) industrial disputes; **interessi in ~** conflicting interests.

conflittualità, *n. f.* (*sind.*) conflict, strife. // ~ **permanente** permanent conflict, continual conflict, continual labour unrest; (*scioperi a catena*) strike epidemics.

confondere, *v. t.* (*leg.*) (*interessi, ecc.*) to merge.

confondersi, *v. rifl.* (*leg.*) (*di interessi, ecc.*) to merge.

conformarsi, *v. rifl.* to conform; to comply (with).

conforme, *a.* 1 conformable, conforming, corresponding, agreeable. 2 (*di copia e sim.*) true (to the original). // **essere ~ a** (*market.*) (*di merce*) to be up to; **essere ~ ai requisiti richiesti** to satisfy (*o* to meet) the requirements.

conformemente, *avv.* accordingly. // ~ **a** agreeably to, in conformity with; (*leg.*) in pursuance of.

conformità, *n. f.* conformity, compliance, accordance. // **in ~** accordingly; **in ~ a (di, con)** in conformity with, in compliance with; agreeably to (*avv.*); agreeable to (*a.*); (*leg.*) in pursuance of, pursuant to.

confusione, *n. f.* 1 confusion. 2 (*disordine*) disorder, muddle, jumble. 3 (*leg.*) (*d'interessi, ecc.*) merger. // ~ **di beni** (*leg.*) confusion of goods; ~ **di diritti** (*leg.*) confusion of rights.

confutare, *v. t.* (*leg.*) (*prove, ecc.*) to rebut.

confutazione, *n. f.* (*leg.*) rebuttal.

congedare, *v. t.* 1 (*amm., pers.*) (*licenziare*)

to dismiss, to discharge. **2** (*amm., pers.*) (*mandare in pensione*) to retire, to discharge; (*smobilitare*) to demobilize.

congedarsi, *v. rifl.* (*amm., pers.*) to retire.

congedo, *n. m.* **1** (*pers.*) leave of absence, leave; furlough (*USA*). **2** (*pers.*) (*licenziamento*) dismissal, discharge. **3** (*pers.*) (*pensionamento*) retirement, discharge. // ~ **per gravidanza e puerperio** (*pers.*) maternity leave; ~ **per malattia** (*pers.*) sick-leave; ~ **per maternità** (*pers.*) maternity leave; ~ **per matrimonio** (*pers.*) marriage leave; ~ **retribuito** (*pers.*) leave with pay; **essere in** ~ (*pers.*) to be on leave.

congelamento, *n. m.* freeze, freezing. // ~ **dei prezzi** (*econ.*) price freeze; ~ **delle vendite di terreni** (*econ.*) land freeze; ~ **salariale** (*sind.*) wage-freeze.

congelare, *v. t.* to freeze★. // ~ **i crediti** (*fin.*) to freeze credit; ~ **i prezzi** (*market.*) to freeze prices.

congelarsi, *v. rifl.* to freeze★.

congelato, *a.* (*econ., fin.*) frozen. // **conto** ~ (*banca, cred.*) frozen account; **credito** ~ (*banca, fin.*) frozen account; **credito** ~ (*banca, fin.*) frozen credit.

congiunto, *a.* **1** connected, united. **2** (*solidale*) joint. **3** (*leg.*) incident. *n. m.* (*parente*) relative.

congiuntura, *n. f.* **1** (*situazione critica*) contingency, emergency. **2** (*econ.*) (*situazione economica*) economic situation, current business situation, situation, (economic) background, economic activity. **3** (*econ.*) (*ciclo*) business cycle. **4** (*econ.*) (*tendenza*) economic trend; (*prospettiva*) economic outlook. **5** (*econ.*) (*congiuntura sfavorevole*) slump; (*come tendenza*) downswing. // ~ **alta** (*econ.*) boom; **una** ~ **avversa** (*econ.*) an unfavourable economic trend; ~ **bassa** (*econ.*) slump; ~ **favorevole** (*econ.*) favourable trend; ~ **molto favorevole** (*econ.*) boom; ~ **negativa** (*econ.*) negative business cycle; recession; **una** ~ **sfavorevole** (*econ.*) an unfavourable economic trend, an adverse economic trend.

congiunturale, *a.* **1** (*econ.*) connected with the current economic (*o* business) situation. **2** (*econ.*) (*ciclico*) cyclical. **3** (*econ.*) (*a breve termine*) short-term (*attr.*). **4** (*econ.*) (*di provvedimento: contro la congiuntura*) counter-cyclical.

congresso, *n. m.* **1** congress; convention (*USA*). **2 il Congresso** (*degli U.S.A.*) the Congress.

congruo, *a.* adequate, consistent.

conguagliare, *v. t.* (*fin., rag.*) to balance, to adjust.

conguaglio, *n. m.* (*fin., rag.*) balance, adjustment, settlement. // ~ **in contanti** (*rag.*) cash adjustment, cash distribution; ~ **monetario** (*fin.*) currency adjustment.

coniare, *v. t.* **1** (*anche fig.*) to coin. **2** (*fin.*) (*monete*) to mint, to strike★. // ~ **di nuovo** (*monete*) (*fin.*) to remint.

coniatore, *n. m.* coiner.

coniatura, *n. f.* **1** (*anche fig.*) coinage. **2** (*fin.*) mintage.

coniazione, *n. f. V.* **coniatura.**

conio, *n. m.* **1** (*punzone per coniare*) minting-die. **2** (*impronta fatta col conio*) mintmark; stamp (on a coin). **3** (*fin.*) (*coniatura*) coinage, mintage.

connivente, *a.* (*leg.*) conniving. *n. m.* e *f.* (*leg.*) conniver, accomplice. // **essere** ~ (*leg.*) to connive.

connivenza, *n. f.* (*leg.*) connivance.

conoscente, *n. m.* e *f.* acquaintance.

conoscenza, *n. f.* **1** (*il sapere*) knowledge. **2** (*il conoscere q.; la persona conosciuta*) acquaintance. **3** (*leg.*) cognizance. // ~ **approfondita** (*di qc.*) mastery, possession; **essere a** ~ **di** to be acquainted with.

conoscere, *v. t.* **1** (*sapere*) to know★, to be acquainted with. **2** (*fare la conoscenza di*) to meet★. // ~ **a fondo** to master; ~ **profondamente** to possess.

conquistare, *v. t.* to conquer. // ~ **un mercato** (*econ.*) to capture a market; ~ **posizioni** (*econ., fig.*) to move ahead.

consanguineità, *n. f.* (*leg.*) consanguinity.

consecutivo, *a.* consecutive, running.

consegna, *n. f.* **1** delivery. **2** (*anche la merce consegnata*) consignment. **3** (*dog.*) (*di merce, ecc.*) deposit. **4** (*leg.*) (*anche d'un atto, contratto o documento*) delivery, tradition. **5 consegne,** *pl.* (*ordini, istruzioni*) instructions, orders. // ~ **a domicilio** (*market.*) delivery at the buyer's domicile, home delivery; ~ **a termine** (*market.*) delivery on term, forward delivery; ~ **al porto d'arrivo** (*market.*) delivery at the port of discharge; ~ **all'arrivo** (*della nave*) (*trasp. mar.*) delivery to arrive; ~ **dal magazzino** (*trasp.*) delivery ex warehouse; ~ **della merce in cattivo stato** bad delivery of the goods; ~ **della nave** (*trasp. mar.*) delivery of the ship; ~ **delle merci soggette a dazio** (*dog.*) deposit of dutiable goods; ~ **differita** (*Borsa*) deferred delivery; ~ **errata** (*di corrispondenza, ecc.*) (*comun.*) misdelivery; ~ **fatta a garanzia d'un debito** (*leg.*) delivery made in security of a debt; ~ **franco rotaia** (*trasp. ferr.*) delivery free on rail; ~ **franco vagone** (*trasp. ferr.*) delivery free on truck; ~ **immediata** (*market.*) spot delivery, immediate delivery, prompt delivery; ~ **in conto deposito** consignment; ~ **per espresso** (*comun., market.*) express delivery; special delivery (*USA*); «~ **sopra luogo**» (*market.*) «delivery spot»; ~ **sotto paranco** (*trasp. mar.*) delivery under ship's tackle; ~ **valida** (*di titoli*) (*Borsa*) good delivery; **alla** ~ (*market.*) on delivery; (*di pagamento*) spot; **dare le consegne a q.** (*pers.*) to hand over to sb; **per** ~ **entro il mese** (*Borsa*) the current month; **per** ~ **immediata** (*market.*) (*di merce, articolo, ecc.*) spot; **salvo** ~ (*Borsa*) against delivery.

consegnare, *v. t.* **1** (*dare*) to give★, to hand, to present, to turn in, to turn over. **2** (*affidare*) to consign, to commit, to trust. **3** (*dog.*) (*merci, ecc.*) to deposit. **4** (*market.*) (*di merci*) to deliver; (*specialm. in deposito*) to consign. // ~ **un conto spese** to turn in an expense account; ~ **titoli** (*fin.*) to deliver stock.

consegnatario, *n. m.* **1** (*leg.*) consignee. **2** (*trasp.*) (*di merci, per trasporto via terra*) carrier; freighter (*USA*). **3** (*trasp. mar.*) (*del carico*) shipper; freighter (*USA*). // **il** ~ **della nave** (*trasp. mar.*) the consignee of the ship; **il** ~ **d'un carico** (*trasp. mar., anche*) the consignee of a cargo.

consegnato, *a.* (*market.*) delivered. // **non** ~ undelivered.

conseguibile, *a.* attainable, obtainable.

conseguimento, *n. m.* attainment, achievement. // **il** ~ **d'un prestito** (*cred.*) the procurement of a loan.

conseguire, *v. t.* **1** to attain, to achieve, to obtain. **2** (*fin.*) (*profitti e sim.*) to chalk up. // ~ **il diploma** to get one's diploma; to graduate (*USA*); ~ **la laurea** to graduate; to get one's degree.

consenso, *n. m.* **1** consent, assent. **2** (*permesso*) leave. // ~ **delle parti** (*leg.*) consent of the parties; ~ **nel contratto** (*leg.*) consent to contract; ~ **scritto (o per iscritto)** consent in writing; ~ **unanime** unanimous consent; ~ **valido** (*leg.*) valid consent.

consensuale, *a.* (*leg.*) consensual.

consentire, *v. t.* to consent (to); to allow, to permit. // ~ **l'accesso ai documenti** to permit access to the records; ~ **un maggior coordinamento** to allow closer co-ordination; ~ **un margine d'utile per qc.** (*fin.*) to make st. profitable.

consenziente, *a.* consenting (with), agreeable (to).

conservanti, *n. pl.* (*market.*) preserving agents.

conservato, *a.* (*market.*) preserved.

conservatore, *n. m.* (*econ.*) conservative. // **il** ~ **del Registro delle Società** (*fin.*) the Registrar of Companies; **il** ~ **delle Ipoteche** (*leg.*) the Registrar of Mortgages.

conservatoria delle ipoteche, *n. f.* (*leg.*) mortgage registry.

conservatorismo, *n. m.* (*econ.*) conservatism.

considerevole, *a.* **1** considerable, remarkable, substantial. **2** (*di somma, ecc., anche*) respectable, handsome. **3** (*fin., market.*) (*di fluttuazione di prezzi, ecc.*) wide.

consigliabile, *a.* advisable.

consigliare, *v. t.* to advise, to counsel, to recommend, to suggest.

consigliere, *n. m.* **1** (*membro di consiglio*) councillor, councilman★. **2** (*amm., org. az.*) adviser, advisor, counsellor. // ~ **comunale** town councillor; ~ **delegato** (*fin.*) managing director; ~ **d'amministrazione** (*fin.*) director; ~ **economico** (*econ.*) economic adviser; ~ **supplente** (*in una «limited company», q.V.*) (*fin.*) alternate director.

consiglio, *n. m.* **1** advice, counsel, recommendation, suggestion. **2** (*adunanza di persone*) council. **3** **consigli,** *pl.* instructions, suggestions; advice (*sing.*). // ~ **amministrativo di contea** (*amm.*) county council; ~ **comunale** (*amm.*) town council; **il** ~ **dei Ministri** (*amm.*) the Council of Ministers; the Cabinet (*in G.B.*); **il** ~ **dell'Ordine degli Avvocati** (*leg.*) the Council of the Bar; ~ **d'amministrazione** (*fin.*) board of directors, direction, directors; directorate, directory (*USA*); **il** ~ **d'Europa** the Council of Europe; ~ **di gestione** (*org. az., sind.*) works council; ~ **d'inchiesta** (*leg.*) Court of inquiry; **il** ~ **di Stato** (*leg.*) the Council of State; ~ **distrettuale** (*leg.*) district council; ~ **giudiziario** (*leg.*) council of judges; ~ **municipale** city council, corporation.

consociare, *v. t.* to consociate.

consociarsi, *v. recipr.* to consociate.

consociata, *n. f.* (*fin.*) subsidiary company, fellow subsidiary, subsidiary, subcompany.

consociato, *a.* consociate.

consociazione, *n. f.* consociation, copartnership.

consocio, *n. m.* consociate, copartner.

consolare, *a.* consular.

consolato, *n. m.* consulate.

console, *n. m.* consul. // ~ **generale** consul general.

consolidamento, *n. m.* **1** consolidation, stabilization. **2** (*fin.*) (*d'un debito, anche*) funding. // ~ **del debito fluttuante** (*fin.*) consolidation of the floating debt.

consolidare, *v. t.* 1 to consolidate, to firm, to stabilize, to strengthen, to steady. 2 (*fin.*) (*un debito, anche*) to fund.

consolidarsi, *v. rifl.* to consolidate, to firm, to firm up, to steady.

consolidato, *a.* (*fin., rag.*) consolidated, funded. *n. m.* (*fin.*) consolidated annuities, consols (*pl.*). // **non** ~ (*fin.*) (*di debito pubblico*) unfunded.

consolidazione, *n. f. V.* **consolidamento.**

consorziare, *v. t.* (*fin.*) (*fondi, risorse, ecc.*) to pool.

consorziarsi, *v. recipr.* (*fin.*) (*d'imprese, ecc.*) to pool.

consorzio, *n. m.* 1 (*fin.*) (*d'imprese*) pool. 2 (*fin.*) (*monopolistico*) trust, cartel. 3 (*fin., market.*) consortium★. // ~ **agrario** farmers' union; ~ **armatoriale** (*trasp. mar.*) shipowner's club; ~ **di risparmiatori** (*fin.*) thrift society; **consorzi di vendita** (*market.*) sales consortia.

constatare, *v. t.* to ascertain, to assess.

constatazione, *n. f.* ascertainment, assessment.

consueto, *a.* customary, ordinary, usual. // **come di** ~ as customary, as usual.

consuetudinario, *a.* 1 customary, habitual. 2 (*leg.*) consuetudinary.

consuetudine, *n. f.* 1 custom, habit, usage, usance, use. 2 routine. 3 (*leg.*) custom. // ~ **locale** (*banca*) local usance; **consuetudini locali** (*leg.*) local customs; **secondo le consuetudini** according to usage, according to custom.

consulente, *n. m.* e *f.* 1 consultant, counsellor. 2 (*amm., org. az.*) adviser, advisor, consultant. // ~ **d'organizzazione aziendale** (*amm.*) management consultant; ~ **esterno** (*amm., org. az.*) outside consultant; ~ **legale** (*leg.*) legal adviser, legal assessor, counsel.

consulenza, *n. f.* consultation, counsel. // ~ **legale** (*leg.*) case for counsel; ~ **organizzativa** (*amm.*) management consulting.

consultare, *v. t.* to consult, to see★, to advise (with). // ~ **un avvocato** (*leg.*) to consult a lawyer, to take legal advice; ~ **un dizionario (un diagramma, ecc)** to refer to a dictionary (a graph, etc.); ~ **un listino prezzi** to consult a price list.

consultarsi, *v. rifl.* to counsel, to take★ counsel, to confer.

consultazione, *n. f.* 1 consultation, counsel. 2 (*bibliografica*) reference. 3 (*riunione*) conference, meeting. // ~ **mista** (*pers., sind.*) joint consultation.

consultivo, *a.* consultative, advisory.

consulto, *n. m.* consultation.

consumabile, *a.* consumable.

consumare, *v. t.* 1 to consume, 2 (*esaurire*) to exhaust, to use up. 3 (*logorare*) to wear★, to wear★ out. // ~ **un delitto** (*leg.*) to commit a crime; ~ **tempo ed energia** to spend time and energy.

consumarsi, *v. rifl.* (*di cosa*) to wear★ (out).

consumatore, *n. m.* 1 (*econ., market.*) consumer. 2 (*econ., market.*) (*fruitore*) user. 3 (*market.*) (*cliente di bar o ristorante*) customer, guest.

consumismo, *n. m.* (*market.*) consumerism.

consumo, *n. m.* 1 consumption, wear. 2 (*econ., market.*) consumption. // ~ **di capitale** (*econ.*) negative investment, disinvestment; **(i) consumi improduttivi** (*econ.*) unproductive consumption; ~ **interno** (*econ.*) home consumption; ~ **privato** (*econ., stat.*) private consumption, private consumer expenditure; ~ **«pro capite»** (*econ.*) per capita consumption; **consumi pubblici** (*econ.*) state-controlled purchase; **al** ~ (*market.*) retail; **cooperativa di** ~ consumer cooperative; **non di** ~ (*econ.*) (*di bene, ecc.*) inconsumable.

consuntivo, *a.* (*rag.*) ex post (*attr.*). *n. m.* (*rag.*) final balance, aggregate.

contabile, *a.* (*rag.*) accountable. *n. m.* e *f.* 1 (*pers.*) bookkeeper, reckoner. 2 (*pers.*) (*ragioniere*) accountant, accounting officer. // **un** ~ **esperto** (*pers.*) an experienced accountant; **una macchina** ~ (*macch. uff.*) an accounting machine.

contabilità, *n. f. inv.* 1 (*rag.*) bookkeeping. 2 (*rag.*) (*ragioneria*) accounting, accountancy. 3 (*rag.*) (*i conti*) accounts (*pl.*). 4 (*rag.*) (*l'ufficio*) accounts department; counting-house; counting-room (*USA*). // ~ **a costi diretti** (*rag.*) direct costing; ~ **a partita doppia** (*rag.*) double-entry bookkeeping; ~ **a partita semplice** (*rag.*) single-entry bookkeeping; ~ **chiara** (*rag.*) clear system of accounts; ~ **commerciale** (*rag.*) commercial bookkeeping; ~ (*relativa ai*) **costi di lavorazione** (*rag.*) cost accounting; ~ **di bilancio** (*fin., rag.*) budget accounts; ~ **di magazzino** (*rag.*) stock accounting; ~ **direzionale** (*amm., rag.*) management accountancy, management accounting; ~ **finanziaria** (*rag.*) financial accounting; ~ **generale** (*rag.*) general accounting; ~ **in contanti** (*rag.*) cash bookkeeping, cash accounting; ~ **industriale** (*rag.*) cost accounting; ~ **nazionale** (*econ.*) national accounts; ~ **pubblica** (*fin., rag.*) national income accounting; ~ **sociale** (*rag.*) company bookkeeping; **reparto** ~ accounts department.

«container», *n. m.* (*trasp.*) (*grande cassone metallico di misura standard, per il trasporto delle merci*) container.

contante, *n. m.* **1** ready money, cash; till (*fig.*); dough (*slang USA*). **2 contanti,** *pl.* ready money, real money, cash. // **contanti in conto** (*rag.*) cash on account; ~ **netto** (*rag.*) net cash; **contanti per il saldo** (*rag.*) cash to balance; **a contanti** (*o* **in contanti**) (*market.*) for prompt cash, for cash, in cash, cash down, down, for money, in coin; on the nail (*fam.*); **pagamento in** (*o* **per**) **contanti** (*market.*) spot payment; **per contanti** (*market.*) *V.* **in contanti; prezzo in** (*o* **per**) **contanti** (*market.*) cash price.

contare, *v. t.* e *i.* **1** to count, to count up, to reckon. **2** (*denaro, anche*) to tell*. **3** (*fare assegnamento*) to count, to depend, to rely. **4** (*intendere, aspettarsi*) to intend, to propose, to expect; to reckon (*USA*). // ~ **alla rovescia** to count down; ~ **di nuovo** to re-count, to count again; **a** ~ **da oggi** reckoning from today.

contatore, *n. m.* **1** (*l'apparecchio*) counter, meter. **2** (*pers.*) (*chi conta*) counter. // ~ **del gas** gas meter; ~ **Geiger** Geiger counter.

contattare, *v. t.* to contact, to get* in touch with.

contatto, *n. m.* **1** contact, touch. **2** (*collegamento*) liaison.

contea, *n. f.* (*amm.*) county (*in G.B.*).

conteggiabile, *a.* (*addebitabile*) chargeable.

conteggiare, *v. t.* e *i.* **1** to count, to calculate. **2** (*addebitare*) to charge.

conteggio, *n. m.* **1** count, counting, calculation. **2** (*addebito*) charge, charging. // ~ **d'avaria** (*ass. mar.*) average bill; ~ **doppio** (*market.*) double counting.

contemplare, *v. t.* **1** to contemplate. **2** (*leg.*) (*di contratto, legge, ecc.*) to provide for.

contendente, *a.* contending. *n. m.* e *f.* **1** contender, contestant. **2** (*leg.*) litigant.

contendere, *v. t.* e *i.* **1** to contend, to contest. **2** (*gareggiare*) to compete.

contenere, *v. t.* **1** to contain, to comprise, to include, to hold*. **2** (*frenare, reprimere*) to contain, to check, to control, to curb, to restrain. // ~ **il disavanzo della bilancia dei pagamenti** (*econ., fin.*) to prevent the gap in the balance of payments from becoming much wider; ~ **i prezzi entro un certo limite** (*econ., market.*) to hold the line (*fig.*); ~ **le spese** (*fin.*) to control expenditures; ~ **le spinte inflazionistiche** (*econ.*) to curb inflationary pressures.

contenimento, *n. m.* containment, check, control, curb, restraint. // **il** ~ **della spesa pubblica** (*econ., fin.*) the restraint of public expenditure; **un** ~ **dell'inflazione** (*econ., fin.*) a curb on inflation.

contenitore, *n. m.* container.

contenuto, *n. m.* **1** contents (*pl.*). **2** (*argomento*) content, matter, subject-matter. **3** (*sostanza*) content, substance. // «~ **ignoto**» (*trasp. mar.*) (*in una polizza di carico*) «contents unknown»; ~ **patrimoniale d'una società** (*riferito a un titolo*) (*Borsa, fin.*) asset value.

contenzioso, *a.* **1** (*leg.*) contentious. **2** (*org. az.*) legal. *n. m.* **1** (*leg.*) (*la giurisdizione*) contentious jurisdiction. **2** (*leg.*) (*il procedimento*) contentious procedure. **3** (*leg.*) (*il complesso delle cause*) (the) cases (*pl.*). **4** (*org. az.*) (*ufficio o reparto*) legal department; legal office. // **il** ~ **amministrativo** the administrative cases; **il** ~ **tributario** the fiscal cases.

contestabile, *a.* contestable, challengeable, disputable, questionable.

contestare, *v. t.* **1** (*anche leg.*) to contest, to challenge, to dispute, to question. **2** (*leg.*) to litigate, to traverse. // ~ **un contratto** (*leg.*) to contest a contract; ~ **un diritto** (*leg.*) to contest a claim, to dispute a claim; ~ **un testamento** (*leg.*) to contest a will.

contestazione, *n. f.* **1** (*anche leg.*) (*il contestare*) contestation. **2** (*anche leg.*) (*contesa*) contest, contention, dispute, difference. **3** (*anche leg.*) (*obiezione*) objection.

contingentamento, *n. m.* **1** (*econ.*) (*il contingentare*) curtailing, curtailment. **2** (*econ.*) (*il sistema*) quota system. **3** (*econ.*) (*razionamento*) rationing. // **il** ~ **della produzione** (*org. az.*) the curtailment of output.

contingentare, *v. t.* **1** (*econ.*) to curtail, to fix a quota for (st.). **2** (*econ.*) (*razionare*) to ration. // ~ **la produzione di metalli** (*econ.*) to curtail the output of metals.

contingente, *n. m.* **1** contingent. **2** (*econ.*) quota. // **contingenti d'importazione** (*comm. est.*) import quotas; **contingenti doganali** (*o* **tariffari**) (*comm. est., econ.*) tariff quotas.

contingenza, *n. f.* **1** contingency, contingence. **2** (*pers.*) (*indennità di contingenza*) cost-of-living allowance (*o* bonus).

contitolare, *n. m.* e *f.* (*fin., leg.*) co-owner.

conto, *n. m.* **1** (*conteggio, calcolo*) count, counting, reckoning, tally. **2** (*da pagare*) reckoning, bill; check (*USA*). **3** (*rag.*) account. // ~ **a debito** (*rag.*) debit account; ~ **acquisti** (*rag.*) purchases account; (*a provvigione*) bought note; ~ **alla rovescia** (*org. az.*) countdown; ~ **anticipazioni** (*cred., fin.*) loan account; ~ **aperto** (*presso un negozio, ecc.*) (*market.*) credit account, charge-account; ~ **approvato** (*dal debi-*

tore) (*cred.*) stated account, account stated; **conti arretrati** (*rag.*) outstanding accounts; **un ~ attivo** (*banca*) an active account; **conti attivi** (*rag.*) credit accounts, receivable accounts; **conti aziendali** (*rag.*) accounts of the business; **un ~ bancario** (*banca*) a bank account; **~ bloccato** (*banca*) blocked account; **~ capitale** (*rag.*) capital account; **~ cassa** (*rag.*) cash account; **~ collettivo** (*rag.*) total account, balance account; **conti collettivi** (*fin.*) allocation accounts; **conti con l'estero** (*fin.*) balance of payments; **conti «congelati»** (*fin.*) frozen accounts; **~ consegna** consignment account; **~ corrente** (*banca, cred.*) current account, account current, drawing account; checking account (*USA*); **~ corrente di corrispondenza** (*cred.*) running account; **~ corrente fruttifero** (*banca*) account current with interest; **~ corrente postale** (*cred.*) postal giro; **~** (*relativo al*) **costo di lavorazione** (*rag.*) cost account; **~ creditore** (*rag.*) credit account, creditor account; **~ debitore** (*rag.*) debit account, debtor account; **~ della merce spedita in deposito** consignment account; **~ delle spese bancarie** (*su di una cambiale protestata*) banker's ticket; **~ d'acquisto** (*rag.*) account of goods purchased; (*a provvigione*) bought account (*o* note); **~ d'un'agenzia** (*rag.*) agency account; **~ di** (*o* **in**) **banca** bank account, banking account; **conti di bilancio** (*fin., rag.*) balance-sheet accounts; **~ di controllo** (*rag.*) controlling account; **~ di contropartita** (*rag.*) contra account; **~ di deposito** (*banca*) deposit account; **~ di deposito a risparmio** (*banca*) thrift account; **~ di deposito fruttifero** (*banca*) savings account; **~ di gestione** (*rag.*) operating account; account for revenue and expenditure; **~ di liquidazione** (*Borsa*) broker's account, brokers' account; **~ di mastro** (*rag.*) ledger account; **~ di netto ricavo** (*rag.*) statement of net proceeds; **~ d'ordine** (*rag.*) suspense account; **~ di ripartizione** (*rag.*) averaging account; **conti distinti** (*rag.*) separate accounts; **~ economico** (*rag.*) income statement, profit and loss account, statement of accumulated profits; **~ effetti all'incasso** (*banca, rag.*) notes receivable (account); **~ effetti attivi** (*banca, rag.*) bills receivable account; **~ effetti da esigere** (*banca, rag.*) bills for collection account; **~ effetti passivi** (*banca, rag.*) bills payable account, notes payable (account); **~ estinto** (*banca, rag.*) dead account; **~ fittizio** (*banca, rag.*) dead account; **~ fruttifero** (*banca, rag.*) interest-bearing account; **~ generale** (*rag.*) adjustment account; **~ immobilizzazioni** (*rag.*) capital expenditure account; **~ in partecipazione** (*rag.*) joint account; **~ in valuta estera** (*banca, rag.*) foreign-currency account; **~ inattivo** (*banca*) dormant account; **conti inesatti** (*rag.*) inaccurate accounts; **~ insoluto** (*banca, cred.*) outstanding account; **~ interessi** (*rag.*) interest account; **conti intestati a ditte** (*rag.*) personal accounts; **conti intestati a persone fisiche** (*rag.*) personal accounts; **~ inventari** (*rag.*) stock-account; **~ liquidato** (*rag.*) stated account; «**~ liquidato**» (*rag.*) «account stated»; **~ merci** (*rag.*) goods account; «**~ merci**» (*rag.*) «goods»; **conti misti** (*rag.*) mixed accounts; **conti non fruttiferi** (*fin., rag.*) non-interest bearing accounts; **~ non intestato a persona fisica o a ditta** (*rag.*) impersonal account; **conti numerari** (*alle attività e passività*) (*rag.*) real accounts; **un ~ particolareggiato** (*rag.*) an itemized account; **conti passivi** (*rag.*) debit accounts, payable accounts; **~ perdite e profitti** (*rag.*) *V.* **~ profitti e perdite**; **~ prelevamenti** (*pers., sind.*) drawing account; **~ profitti e perdite** (*rag.*) profit and loss account, loss-and-gain account, profit and loss statement, income account, income statement, operating statement, revenue account; **~ provvigioni** (*rag.*) commission account; **conti provvisori** (*rag.*) temporary accounts, provisional accounts, suspense accounts; **~ relativo al controllo dei costi di lavorazione** (*rag.*) cost control account; **~** (*di*) **riserva** (*rag.*) reserve account; **~ salari** (*econ., rag.*) wage bill; **un ~ salato** (*fam.*) a salt bill; **~ saldato** account settled; **un ~ scompensato** (*rag.*) an unbalanced account; **~ «scoperto»** (*banca*) overdrawn account; (*banca, cred.*) outstanding account; **~ sintetico** (*rag.*) control account; **~ sociale** (*rag.*) joint account; **~ sospeso** (*rag.*) suspense account; **~ succursale** (*rag.*) branch account; **~ vendite** (*rag.*) sales account; (*a provvigione*) sold note; **~ vincolato** (*banca*) deposit account; **~ vincolato a scadenza determinata** (*banca*) fixed deposit account; **chi rivede conti** (*pers.*) controller; **estratto ~** (*banca, rag.*) statement of account; **in ~** (*rag.*) on account; **in ~ deposito** (*market.*) (*di merce*) on consignment, on sale or return; **incidere su un ~** (*rag.*) to affect an account; **lavorare per ~ proprio** to be self-employed; **mettersi (in affari) per proprio ~** to set up (in business) for oneself; **per proprio ~** for one's own account; in one's name; **per ~ di** on behalf of; **per ~ terzi** (*leg.*) on behalf of a third party; (*market.*) (*di merce venduta*) for hire or reward.

contrabbandare, *v. t.* (*leg.*) to smuggle.

contrabbandiere, *n. m.* (*leg.*) smuggler, contrabandist. // **~ di liquori** bootlegger (*slang USA*).

contrabbando, *n. m.* (*leg.*) smuggling, contraband. // ~ **di liquori** bootlegging (*slang USA*); **esportare (importare) qc. di** ~ to smuggle st. out (in).

contraddittorio, *a.* contradictory. *n. m.* (*leg.*) (*di testimoni*) cross-examination. // **domanda in** ~ (*leg.*) cross-demand; **interrogatorio in** ~ (*leg.*) cross-examination.

contraente, *a.* (*leg.*) contracting. *n. m.* e *f.* (*leg.*) contractant, contractor; (contracting) party; party (to a contract). // ~ **in solido** (*leg.*) cocontracting (*a.*); cocontractant (*n.*).

contraffare, *v. t.* **1** (*leg.*) (*monete, scritti, firme, ecc.*) to counterfeit, to forge; (*documenti in genere*) to falsify. **2** (*leg.*) (*sofisticare*) to adulterate.

contraffatto, *a.* **1** false; mock, bogus (*attr.*). **2** (*leg.*) counterfeit.

contraffattore, *n. m.* **1** (*leg.*) counterfeiter, forger, falsifier. **2** (*leg.*) (*sofisticatore*) adulterer.

contraffazione, *n. f.* **1** (*leg.*) counterfeit, counterfeiting, forgery, falsification. **2** (*leg.*) (*sofisticazione*) adulteration. **3** (*market.*) (*imitazione*) imitation. // ~ **dei marchi di fabbrica** (*leg.*) infringement of the trade marks.

contraibile, *a.* (*leg.*) contractable.

contrariamente (a), *prep.* contrary to. // ~ **alle nostre istruzioni** contrary to our instructions.

contrario, *a.* **1** contrary, opposite; counter (*attr.*). **2** (*inverso*) inverse. **3** (*sfavorevole*) unfavourable, adverse. *n. m.* (*voto o votante contrario*) no. // **al** ~ on the contrary; **in caso** ~ (*altrimenti*) otherwise; **in senso** ~ (*fig.*) to the contrary; **salvo contrarie istruzioni** unless instructions to the contrary be given.

contrarre, *v. t.* (*leg.*) to contract. // ~ **debiti** (*cred.*) to contract debts, to incur debts, to get into debt; ~ **un mutuo** (*cred.*) to contract a loan; ~ **un obbligo** (*leg.*) to contract an obligation.

contrarsi, *v. rifl.* **1** (*restringersi, diminuire*) to contract, to shrink★. **2** (*econ.*) (*della domanda, ecc.*) to fall★ off. **3** (*econ., market.*) (*di prezzi, ecc.*) to fall★, to decline, to drop.

contrassegnare, *v. t.* **1** to check, to earmark. **2** (*market.*) (*con un marchio, una marca, ecc.*) to mark. // ~ **con un cartellino** (*market.*) (*un articolo*) to label; (*trasp.*) (*il bagaglio*) to label.

contrassegnato, *a.* (*market.*) marked. // **non** ~ unmarked.

contrassegno, *n. m.* **1** countersign, countermark, check, token. **2** (*market.*) (*del prezzo, ecc.*) mark. // ~ **di riconoscimento** (*pubbl.*) card.

contrattare, *v. t.* e *i.* **1** to negotiate; to bargain (over st.) to make★ a deal (over st.). **2** (*mercanteggiare*) to bargain; to haggle (*fam.*).

contrattazione, *n. f.* **1** negotiation, bargaining, dealing. **2** (*mercanteggiamento*) bargaining; haggling (*fam.*). // ~ **a termine** (*fin.*) forward marketing; ~ **collettiva** (*sind.*) collective bargaining; ~ **«dentro e fuori»** (*Borsa*) in-and-out trading; ~ **(per ottenere un aumento) salariale** (*sind.*) wage bargaining.

contratto, *n. m.* (*leg.*) **1** contract, bargain, deed. **2** (*leg.*) (*accordo*) agreement. **3** (*leg.*) (*solenne*) covenant. // ~ **a premio** (*Borsa, fin.*) option bargain; ~ **a pronti** (*market.*) spot contract; **un** ~ **a tempo** (*market.*) a forward contract; ~ **a termine** (*Borsa, fin.*) futures contract, bargain for the account, hedge contract; ~ **a titolo gratuito** (*leg.*) bare contract; ~ **a titolo oneroso** (*leg.*) onerous contract; ~ (*di lavoro*) **agganciato a una scala mobile** (*sind.*) escalator contract; ~ **aleatorio** (*leg.*) wagering contract; ~ **bilaterale** (*leg.*) bilateral contract, commutative contract, indenture; **un** ~ **che non è in vigore** (*leg.*) an inactive contract; ~ **collettivo di lavoro** (*sind.*) collective labour agreement, collective wage agreement; ~ **commutativo** (*leg.*) commutative contract; ~ **consensuale** (*leg.*) consensual contract; ~ **del credere** (*leg.*) del credere agreement; ~ **d'acquisto** (*market.*) purchase contract; ~ **d'affitto** (*leg.*) lease, rent agreement; ~ **d'arruolamento** (*trasp. mar.*) ship's articles, articles; ~ **d'assicurazione marittima** (*ass. mar.*) contract of marine insurance; ~ **d'associazione** (*leg.*) deed of partnership; ~ **di cessione** (*Borsa*) transfer deed; ~ **di commissione** (*Borsa*) broker's contract; (*leg.*) commission contract; ~ **di comodato** (*leg.*) bare contract; ~ **di compravendita** (*leg.*) sale contract, contract of sale; ~ **di concessione esclusiva** (*market.*) exclusive agency agreement; ~ **d'imbarco** (*trasp. mar.*) shipping-articles; ~ **d'indennizzo** contract of indemnity; ~ **d'ipoteca** (*leg.*) mortgage deed; ~ **di lavoro** (*pers.*) contract of employment; (*pers., sind.*) labour contract; **contratti di licenza per brevetti** (*leg.*) patent-licensing contracts; ~ **di navigazione** (*leg.*) maritime contract; ~ **di noleggio** (*trasp. mar.*) freight contract, charter party, charter; ~ **di noleggio a corpo** (*trasp. mar.*) lump charter; ~ **di noleggio della sola nave** (*trasp. mar.*) bareboat charter; ~ **di noleggio senza riserve** (*trasp. mar.*) clean charter; ~ **di nolo** (*trasp. mar.*) *V.* ~ **di noleggio;** ~ **di nolo a tempo** (*trasp. aer., trasp. mar.*) time charter party; ~ **di nolo a viaggio**

(*trasp. aer., trasp. mar.*) voyage charter party; **contratti di prestito** (*cred.*) loan agreements; ~ **di prestito a cambio marittimo** (*leg.*) bottomry bond; ~ **di procura** (*leg.*) contract of trust; ~ **di rappresentanza** (*leg.*) agency contract, agency agreement; ~ **di ricupero** (*trasp. mar.*) salvage agreement; ~ **di riporto** (*Borsa*) continuation contract, contango; ~ **di salvataggio** (*trasp. mar.*) salvage agreement; ~ **di società** (*di persone*) (*fin.*) partnership deed, deed of partnership; ~ **di trasporto** (*trasp.*) contract of carriage; ~ **di trasporto marittimo** (*delle merci*) (*trasp. mar.*) contract of affreightment; ~ **di vendita** (*leg.*) contract of sale, sale contract, agreement for sale; **un ~ fermo** (*Borsa*) a firm bargain; ~ **formale** (*leg.*) formal contract, special contract, specialty contract; ~ **illegale** (*leg.*) illegal contract; ~ **implicito** (*leg.*) implied contract; ~ **mediante atto pubblico** (*leg.*) contract under seal; **un ~ non valido** (*per mancanza di qualche requisito essenziale*) (*leg.*) a naked contract; ~ **nullo** (*leg.*) contract void and null; **un ~ obbligatorio** (*leg.*) an obligative contract; **contratti per consegne a termine** (*Borsa*) futures; ~ **privo di tutela giuridica** (*leg.*) nude contract; **un ~ provvisorio** (*leg.*) a provisional contract; **un ~ provvisorio di vendita** (*leg.*) an agreement to sell; ~ **reale** (*leg.*) real contract; ~ **scritto** (*leg.*) agreement in writing; ~ **semplice** (*leg.*) simple contract; ~ **senza valore** (*leg.*) contract void and null; ~ **sinallagmatico** (*leg.*) synallagmatic contract, bilateral contract; ~ **solenne** (*leg.*) covenant, specialty contract; ~ **tipo** (*leg.*) model contract, specimen uniform agreement; **un ~ «ultra vires»** (*leg.*) an ultra vires contract; ~ **unilaterale** (*leg.*) unilateral contract; **un ~ valido** (*leg.*) a valid contract; ~ **verbale** (*leg.*) verbal contract, oral contract, parol contract; **lavorare a ~** to work on contract; **rottura di ~** (*leg.*) breach of contract; **stabilire per ~ di fare qc.** to contract to do st.

contrattuale, *a.* (*leg.*) contractual, of (a) contract. // **inadempienza ~** (*leg.*) breach of contract; non-performance.

contrattualmente, *avv.* contractually.

contravvenire, *v. i.* to contravene, to infringe, to transgress, to violate. // ~ **a un contratto (a un trattato)** (*leg.*) to infringe a contract (a treaty); ~ **a un impegno (a un obbligo)** (*leg.*) to fail to meet an obligation.

contravventore, *n. m.* 1 (*leg.*) infringer, offender, transgressor, violator. 2 (*leg.*) (*a un divieto d'accesso*) trespasser.

contravvenzione, *n. f.* 1 (*leg.*) contravention, infringement, offence, transgression, violation. 2 (*leg.*) (*multa*) fine. 3 (*leg.*) (*a un divieto d'accesso, ecc.*) trespass. // **essere dichiarato in ~** (*trasp. aut.*) to be fined; **fare la ~ a q.** (*trasp. aut.*) to fine sb.

contrazione, *n. f.* 1 contraction. 2 (*econ., market.*) shrinkage, decline, drop, falloff. // **una ~ dei prezzi** (*anche*) a shrinkage in prices; **una ~ delle esportazioni** (*comm. est.*) a falloff in exports; **una ~ delle vendite** (*market.*) a shrinkage in sales.

contribuente, *a.* contributing, contributory. *n. m.* e *f.* 1 (*fin.*) (*per le imposte statali*) taxpayer, taxpayer. 2 (*fin.*) (*per le imposte locali*) rate payer. // **un ~ moroso** (*fin.*) a taxpayer in arrears; **un ~ soggetto alla ritenuta d'acconto** (*fin.*) a pay-as-you-earn taxpayer.

contribuibile, *a.* contributable.

contribuire, *v. i.* to contribute. // ~ **alle spese processuali** (*leg.*) to contribute towards the costs; ~ **per un terzo** to contribute one third.

contributivo, *a.* contributive, contributory. // **capacità contributiva** (*econ., fin.*) faculty (*o* ability) to pay taxes; **teoria della capacità contributiva** (*econ., fin.*) faculty theory.

contributo, *n. m.* 1 contribution. 2 (*aiuto, assistenza*) aid, assistance, subsidy. 3 (*ass. mar.*) contribution. 4 (*fin.*) (*imposta o tassa*) tax. 5 (*pers.*) (*della Previdenza Sociale*) contribution. // **contributi al fondo pensioni** (*pers., rag.*) pension contributions; ~ **alle spese** (*leg.*) contribution to the expenses; **contributi basati sui libri paga** (*pers., rag.*) pay-roll tax; **« ~ concesso »** (*fin.*) «aid granted»; ~ **d'avaria generale** (*ass. mar.*) general average contribution; **un ~ obbligatorio** (*leg.*) an obligatory contribution; **contributi previdenziali** (*pers.*) contributions; **contributi sindacali** (*sind.*) dues; **contributi sociali** (*pers., rag.*) contributions, social-security taxes, pay-roll tax; ~ **statale** (*agli Enti pubblici*) (*fin.*) grant-in-aid.

contribuzione, *n. f.* contribution.

contro, *prep.* 1 against, counter to. 2 (*comm.*) against; on. 3 (*leg.*) versus (*abbr.* v.). *n. m.* (*nella locuz.* «*il pro e il contro*») con. // ~ **assegno** (*market.*) cash on delivery; **« ~ tutti i rischi »** (*ass.*) «against all risks» (*a.a.r.*); **Everett ~ Young** (*causa giudiziaria*) Everett versus Young; **pagamento ~ documenti** (*market.*) payment against documents.

controcampione, *n. m.* (*market.*) counterpart sample.

controcredito, *n. m.* (*cred.*) countervailing credit.

controdichiarazione, *n. f.* (*leg.*) counterdeclaration.

controfferta, *n. f.* counter-offer.

controfirma, *n. f.* **1** countersignature. **2** (*per autenticazione*) countersign.

controfirmare, *v. t.* to countersign.

controgaranzia, *n. f.* (*cred.*) counterbond, countersecurity, counter-surety.

controistruzioni, *n. pl.* (*amm.*) counter-instructions.

controllabile, *a.* controllable.

controllare, *v. t.* **1** to control, to check, to go* through, to verify. **2** (*amm., fin.*) (*avere il controllo di*) to control, to syndicate. **3** (*amm., org. az.*) (*reggere, dirigere*) to govern, to manage. **4** (*amm., org. az., rag.*) (*i conti: ufficialmente*) to audit. **5** (*org. az.*) to control, to inspect. **6** (*trasp. mar.*) (*la merce ricevuta in consegna*) to tally. // ~ **un carico** (*trasp. mar.*) to tally a load; ~ **un conto** (*rag.*) to check (*o* to control) an account; ~ **disonestamente il mercato** (*market.*) to rig the market.

controllato, *a.* **1** controlled. **2** (*diretto*) governed, managed. // ~ **dallo Stato** (*econ.*) State-controlled; **economia controllata** (*econ.*) managed economy.

controllo, *n. m.* **1** control, check, checking, verification. **2** (*amm., fin.*) control. **3** (*amm., org. az.*) (*direzione*) management. **4** (*amm., org. az., rag.*) (*ufficiale: dei conti*) audit, auditing. **5** (*org. az.*) control, inspection. // ~ **a bilancio** (*rag.*) budgetary control; **controlli** (*di cassa*) **a sorpresa** (*fin., rag.*) surprise counts; ~ **alla consegna** check on delivery; ~ **budgetario** (*fin., rag.*) budgetary control, budgeting control; ~ **contabile interno** (*fin., rag.*) internal audit; ~ **dei biglietti** (*trasp.*) ticket inspection; ~ **dei cambi** (*fin.*) exchange control; ~ **dei conti** (*amm., org. az., rag.*) audit; ~ **dei costi** (*org. az.*) cost control; ~ **dei materiali** (*org. az.*) materials control; ~ **dei prezzi** (*econ.*) price control; ~ **del traffico** (*trasp. aut.*) traffic control; ~ **della cassa** (*rag.*) control of the cash; ~ **della diffusione** (*pubbl.*) circulation audit; ~ **dell'efficacia di testi pubblicitari** (*pubbl.*) copy testing; ~ **della qualità** (*org. az.*) quality control; ~ **delle giacenze** (*org. az.*) inventory control; ~ **delle referenze** (*pers.*) reference checking; ~ **delle registrazioni a mastro** (*rag.*) check on ledger postings; ~ (*del livello*) **delle retribuzioni** (*pers.*) wage and salary control; ~ **delle scorte** (*org. az.*) inventory control; ~ **di cassa** (*rag.*) cash control; ~ **di magazzino** (*org. az.*) inventory control; ~ **di maggioranza** (*fin.*) majority control, direct control; ~ **di minoranza** (*fin.*) minority control; ~ **di qualità** (*org. az.*) quality control; ~ **direzionale** (*fin.*) management control; ~ **disonesto** (*del mercato*) (*market.*) rig; ~ **doganale** (*dog.*) customs examination; ~ **esecutivo** (*org. az.*) executive control; ~ **fatturazione** (*rag.*) invoice control; ~ **finanziario** (*econ.*) financial control; ~ **giornaliero** (*org. az.*) day control; ~ (*contabile*) **interno** (*rag.*) internal check; ~ **manageriale** (*fin.*) management control; **un** ~ **monetario selettivo** (*econ., fin.*) a selective monetary control; ~ **monopolistico** (*econ.*) monopoly control; ~ **particolare** (*org. az.*) test check; ~ **preventivo** (*leg.*) preventive auditing; ~ **qualitativo** *V.* ~ **della qualità;** ~ **sanitario** health inspection; ~ **sanitario dei passeggeri** (*leg., trasp.*) medical inspection of passengers; ~ **selettivo** (*org. az.*) selective control; ~ **su campione** (*market.*) sample check; **a** ~ **statale** (*econ.*) state-controlled; **di** ~ controlling; governing: **organismo di** ~ controlling (*o* governing) body.

controllore, *n. m.* **1** (*pers.*) controller, comptroller, inspector, surveyor, verifier. **2** (*trasp. aut.*) conductor. **3** (*trasp. ferr.*) ticket-collector, guard; conductor (*USA*). **4** (*trasp. mar.*) (*del carico*) tallyman*, tally clerk. // ~ **annonario** (*o* **degli approvvigionamenti**) (*amm.*) food controller; ~ **dei conti** (*amm., org. az., rag.*) auditor; **un** ~ **dei pesi e delle misure** (*leg.*) a surveyor of weights and measures; ~ **della Zecca** (*fin.*) controller of the Mint; ~ **delle ore di lavoro** (*pers.*) time clerk, timekeeper; ~ **dell'avanzamento** (*d'un processo produttivo*) (*org. az.*) progress clerk; ~ **ferroviario** (*pers.*) guard; conductor (*USA*).

contromarca, *n. f.* countermark, check, token.

contromisura, *n. f.* countermeasure. // **contromisure tariffarie** (*comm. est., econ.*) tariff countermeasures.

controparte, *n. f.* **1** counterpart. **2** (*leg.*) opposite party, (the) other party. // **le controparti sociali** (*econ.*) employers and labour.

contropartita, *n. f.* **1** counterpart. **2** (*rag.*) contra, set-off. // **in** ~ (*rag.*) per contra; **fondi (franchi, lire,** ecc.) **in** ~ counterpart funds (francs, lire, etc.).

controproposta, *n. f.* counter-proposal, counter-proposition.

controprova, *n. f.* (*leg.*) contrary evidence, counterproof.

controquerela, *n. f.* (*leg.*) cross complaint, counter-claim.

contrordine, *n. m.* counter-order, countermand. // **salvo contrordini** unless we hear to the contrary.

controreplica, *n. f.* (*leg.*) rejoinder.

controreplicare, *v. t.* (*leg.*) to rejoin.

controrichiesta, *n. f.* (*leg.*) counter-claim.

controstallia, *n. f.* 1 (*trasp. mar.*) demurrage. 2 **controstallie,** *pl.* (*trasp. mar.*) demurrage days, demurrage.

controvalore, *n. m.* 1 countervalue, equivalent. 2 (*econ.*) exchange value, value in exchange. // ~ **dei titoli sottoscritti** (*banca*) countervalue of securities applied for; ~ **oggetto d'un prestito** (*banca*) call money.

controvento, *avv.* (*trasp. mar.*) on the wind, into the wind; windward.

controversia, *n. f.* 1 controversy, contention, contest, dispute, question. 2 (*leg.*) litigation. 3 (*sind.*) dispute. // ~ **di lavoro (*o* sindacale)** (*sind.*) labour dispute.

controverso, *a.* 1 controversial, contentious. 2 (*dibattuto, discusso*) debated. 3 (*dubbio*) doubtful.

contumace, *a.* (*leg.*) contumacious. *n. m.* e *f.* (*leg.*) defaulter. // **essere** ~ (*leg.*) to default.

contumacia, *n. f.* (*leg.*) default, contumacy, non-attendance, non-appearance, failure to appear, absence to appear, absence. // **condannare q. in** ~ (*leg.*) to sentence sb. by default; **giudizio in** ~ (*leg.*) judgment by default.

contumaciale, *a.* (*leg.*) by default. // **giudizio (*o* sentenza)** ~ judgment by default.

convalida, *n. f.* 1 confirmation. 2 (*leg.*) validation, substantiation. 3 (*leg.*) (*d'un diritto*) vindication. // ~ **d'un atto** (*leg.*) confirmation of an act; **la** ~ **d'un contratto** (*leg.*) the validation of a contract.

convalidare, *v. t.* 1 to confirm. 2 (*leg.*) to validate, to substantiate. 3 (*leg.*) (*un diritto*) to vindicate. // ~ **un'accusa** (*leg.*) to support a charge; ~ **un diritto** (*leg.*) to substantiate a claim.

convalidazione, *n. f. V.* **convalida.**

convegno, *n. m.* 1 meeting, conference; convention (*USA*). 2 (*appuntamento*) appointment, rendez-vous.

conveniente, *a.* 1 convenient, proper. 2 (*market.*) (*di prezzo*) keen, low. 3 (*market.*) (*d'un articolo*) cheap. // **abbastanza** ~ (*market.*) (*d'articolo, ecc.*) cheapish.

convenienza, *n. f.* 1 convenience. 2 (*market.*) (*di prezzo*) keenness. 3 (*market.*) (*d'un articolo*) cheapness.

convenire, *v. i.* 1 (*adunarsi*) to convene, to assemble, to gather. 2 (*accordarsi, essere d'accordo*) to agree, to be agreed. 3 (*essere appropriato*) to suit, to become*. 4 (*tornare utile*) to be convenient, to be worth while; to suit. 5 (*essere opportuno, necessario*) to be better, to be necessary. *v. t.* 1 (*accordarsi su*) to agree on, to establish, to fix. 2 (*consentire, ammettere*) to admit, to allow, to grant. 3 (*leg.*) (*convocare*) to convene. 4 (*leg.*) (*pattuire*) to stipulate, to covenant. // **secondo quanto convenuto** as agreed upon.

convenuto, *n. m.* (*leg.*) defendant, respondent.

convenzionale, *a.* 1 conventional. 2 (*usuale*) customary, traditional. 3 (*leg.*) (*stabilito per accordo*) agreed upon.

convenzionalmente, *avv.* conventionally.

convenzionarsi, *v. rifl.* to stipulate a convention; to sign an agreement.

convenzionato, *a.* 1 (*pers.*) (*di medico, d'ospedale, ecc.*) operating (*o* working) within the national health service. 2 (*pers.*) (*di medico, anche*) on the panel.

convenzione, *n. f.* 1 (*leg.*) convention, covenant, compact. 2 (*leg.*) (*patto, contratto*) agreement, contract. 3 (*leg.*) (*clausola*) provision. 4 **convenzioni,** *pl.* conventions. // ~ **monetaria** (*fin.*) money convention; **salvo** ~ **contraria** (*leg.*) unless otherwise provided.

conversione, *n. f.* 1 conversion. 2 (*fin.*) conversion. // ~ **del debito pubblico** (*fin.*) refunding; ~ **di beni** (*leg.*) conversion of goods; ~ **di titoli nominativi in titoli al portatore** (*fin.*) conversion of registered securities to bearer; ~ **d'una valuta aurea** (*fin.*) conversion of a gold currency; ~ **in contanti** (*econ., fin.*) realization; (*rag.*) encashment; ~ (*d'attività*) **in liquidità** (*rag.*) liquidation.

convertibile, *a.* (*fin.*) convertible. // ~ **in contanti** (*econ., fin.*) realizable; (*fin., leg.*) redeemable; (*rag.*) encashable; **non** ~ (*fin.*) unconvertible.

convertibilità, *n. f.* (*fin.*) convertibility. // ~ **della valuta** (*fin.*) currency convertibility; ~ **esterna** (*fin.*) external convertibility; ~ **in contanti** (*fin., leg.*) redeemability.

convertire, *v. t.* 1 to convert; to turn. 2 (*fin.*) to convert. // ~ **in contanti** (*econ., fin.*) to realize; (*fin., leg.*) to redeem; (*rag.*) to encash; ~ (*un vaglia, ecc.*) **in denaro** to cash; ~ **in denaro contante** (*econ., fin.*) *V.* ~ **in contanti;** ~ (*attività di bilancio*) **in liquidità** (*rag.*) to liquidate.

convocare, *v. t.* to convoke, to convene, to call, to summon. // ~ **un'assemblea** to convene an assembly, to convene a meeting; ~ **il Parlamento** (*leg.*) to convoke (*o* to summon) Parliament.

convocazione, *n. f.* convocation, convening, calling, calling together, summons. // ~

degli azionisti calling the shareholders together.

convogliamento, *n. m.* (*trasp.*) haulage, conveyance.

convogliare, *v. t.* (*trasp.*) to convey, to haul.

convoglio, *n. m.* **1** (*trasp.*) convoy. **2** (*trasp.*) (*l'azione, anche*) convoying.

cooperare, *v. i.* to co-operate, to collaborate. // ~ **a un'impresa** to co-operate in an enterprise.

cooperativa, *n. f.* (*econ.*) co-operative, co-op, coop. // ~ **di consumo** (*market.*) consumers' co-operative, co-operative store; ~ **di produzione** (*econ.*) producer co-operative.

cooperativo, *a.* (*econ.*) co-operative. // **società cooperativa** co-operative society; **spaccio** ~ co-operative store.

cooperatore, *n. m.* (*pers.*) co-operator, collaborator.

cooperazione, *n. f.* **1** co-operation, collaboration. **2 la** ~ (*econ.*) the co-operative movement.

cooptare, *v. t.* to co-opt, to co-optate.

cooptazione, *n. f.* co-optation, co-option.

coordinamento, *n. m.* **1** co-ordination. **2** (*org. az.*) co-ordination. // **il** ~ **delle politiche regionali dei singoli Paesi** the coordination of national regional policies; ~ **orizzontale** (*org. az.*) horizontal coordination.

coordinare, *v. t.* (*anche org. az.*) to co-ordinate.

coordinazione, *n. f.* (*anche org. az.*) co-ordination.

coperta, *n. f.* **1** blanket. **2** (*trasp. mar.*) (*d'una nave*) deck. // **sotto** ~ (*trasp. mar.*) under hatches.

copertina, *n. f.* (*di libro*) cover. // ~ **mobile** jacket.

coperto, *a.* (*anche ass.*) covered. // **al** ~ (*fin.*) with cover; **non** ~ (*ass.*) (*di rischio*) uncovered.

copertura, *n. f.* **1** (*anche ass.*) cover, coverage, covering. **2** (*Borsa, fin.*) hedging. **3** (*fin.*) (*d'una cambiale, ecc.*) consideration. **4** (*fin.*) (*d'un'emissione di banconote*) backing. **5** (*fin.*) (*dai rischi di perdite finanziarie*) hedge. **6** (*pubbl.*) coverage. // ~ **a termine** (*Borsa, fin.*) forward cover; ~ **aurea** (*econ., fin.*) gold cover; ~ **dei rischi terrestri** (*ass.*) covering of land risks; ~ **di credito documentato** (*banca, cred.*) cover for documentary credit; ~ **estesa** (*ass.*) extended coverage; ~ **geografica** (*giorn., pubbl.*) geographical coverage; ~ **in abbonamento** (*ass.*) open cover; ~ **per l'importo del credito** (*banca, cred.*) coverage for the amount of the credit; ~ **totale** (*ass.*) full coverage; **con** ~ (*fin.*) with cover; «**mancanza di** ~» (*banca, cred.*) «no funds».

copia, *n. f.* **1** copy, duplicate, duplication; dupe (*slang USA*). **2** (*mala copia, abbozzo*) rough copy, draft. **3** (*esatta riproduzione*) counterpart. **4** (*leg.*) (*a verbale di causa*) transcript, transcription, estreat. // ~ **autentica** (*d'un documento*) (*leg.*) authenticated copy, certified copy, attested copy, true copy; (*d'un atto legale, ecc.*) office copy; ~ **autentica conforme all'originale** (*leg.*) certified true copy; ~ **autenticata d'un atto** (*leg.*) certified copy of a deed; ~ **autenticata d'un testamento** (*leg.*) probate; ~ **carbone** carbon copy, carbon; dupe (*slang USA*); ~ **commissioni** commission order form, commission order; ~ **conforme** (*leg.*) true copy, certified true copy; ~ **del capitano** (*d'una polizza di carico*) (*trasp. mar.*) captain's copy; **la** ~ **d'un atto** (*leg.*) the duplicate of a deed; ~ **di cambiale** (*cred.*) via; ~ **esatta** facsimile; **la** ~ **fedele d'un documento** the faithful copy of a document; ~ **fotostatica** photostat; ~ **in omaggio** (*di un libro, ecc.*) (*giorn., pubbl.*) complimentary copy, presentation copy; ~ **in saggio** (*d'un libro, ecc.*) (*giorn., pubbl.*) specimen copy; ~ **legalizzata** (*leg.*) certified copy; ~ **notarile** (*leg.*) certificate of a notary public; ~ **su carta carbone** carbon copy; ~ **vidimata** attested copy.

copiacommissione, *n. m. inv.* (*org. az.*) order book.

copialettere, *n. m. inv.* **1** (*attr. uff.*) (*registro*) letter-book, copy holder. **2** (*attr. uff.*) (*macchina*) copying press; (*di tipo antiquato*) letterpress.

copiare, *v. t.* to copy. // ~ **una lettera (un documento, ecc.)** to copy a letter (a document, etc.).

copiativo, *a.* copying.

copiatura, *n. f.* **1** copying. **2** (*leg.*) (*d'un atto legale*) engrossment.

copione, *n. m.* (*pubbl.*) (*radiotelevisivo*) script.

copista, *n. m.* e *f.* (*pers.*) copyist, copier, copying clerk.

coprire, *v. t.* (*anche ass.*) to cover. // ~ (*un muro, ecc.*) **di manifesti** (*pubbl.*) to post, to poster, to placard; ~ **il proprio fabbisogno** to cover one's requirements; ~ **uno scoperto** (*Borsa*) to cover a short account; ~ **le spese** to cover one's expenses.

coprirsi, *v. rifl.* **1** (*Borsa*) to cover oneself. **2** (*fin.*) (*da rischi di perdite finanziarie*) to hedge.

copywriter, *n. m.* (*pubbl.*) (*chi redige un*

testo pubblicitario, chi inventa uno slogan, ecc.) copywriter.

«corbeille», *n. f.* (*Borsa*) floor; pit (*USA*).

cordiale, *a.* cordial, hearty, kind. // **«cordiali saluti»** (*comun.*) (*nelle lettere commerciali*) «sincerely Yours».

cordialmente, *avv.* cordially. // **«vostro ~»** (*in chiusura d'una lettera commerciale, soprattutto americana*) «cordially Yours».

«coroner», *n. m.* (*leg.*) (*magistrato inquirente nei casi di morte non naturale*) coroner (*in G.B.*).

corpo, *n. m.* **1** body. **2** (*giorn., pubbl.*) (*tipografico*) type-size; point size (*USA*). // **~ del reato** (*leg.*) «corpus delicti»; **~ di leggi** (*leg.*) body of laws; **~ e beni** (*trasp. mar.*) crew and cargo; **~ insegnante** teaching staff; **~ legislativo** (*leg.*) legislature.

corporativismo, *n. m.* (*econ.*) corporativism, corporatism.

corporativistico, *a.* (*econ.*) corporatist.

corporativo, *a.* (*econ.*) corporative.

corporazione, *n. f.* **1** (*storico*) corporation. **2** (*fin.*) guild.

corredo, *n. m.* equipment, outfit. // **~ antinfortunistico** (*org. az., pers.*) safety equipment; **~ attitudinale** (*pers.*) vocational interest.

correggere, *v. t.* to correct, to adjust, to alter, to rectify, to revise, to right, to straighten out. // **~ un errore** to right a mistake; **~ un manoscritto** to revise a manuscript; **~ squilibri fondamentali** (*econ., fin.*) to adjust fundamental imbalances.

corrente, *a.* **1** current, instant, running. **2** (*presente*) present; todayish (*fam.*). **3** (*fin.*) (*di capitolo d'entrata o spesa di bilancio*) above-the-line, above-line. **4** (*market.*) (*di qualità*) going, standard. *n. f.* (*anche fig.*) stream, current. // **~ alternata** alternating current; **~ continua** direct current; **~ di marea** (*trasp. mar.*) tidal stream; tidal current (*USA*); **le correnti di scambio** (*comm. est.*) the flow of trade; **la ~ di sinistra d'un sindacato** (*sind.*) the left wing of a union; **al ~** (*di persona e di cosa*) up-to-date; (*di persona*) conversant (with st.); (*anche leg.*) cognizant.

correntista, *n. m.* e *f.* (*banca, cred.*) holder of a current account; depositor.

correo, *n. m.* (*leg.*) co-respondent.

correre, *v. i.* e *t.* to run★. // **~ un rischio** to run a risk; to incur a risk; **~ via** to run away.

correttamente, *avv.* correctly.

correttezza, *n. f.* correctness. // **~ commerciale** (*market.*) fair trade practices.

correttivo, *a.* corrective.

corretto, *a.* correct, right.

correttore, *n. m.* corrector.

correzione, *n. f.* correction, alteration, rectification, revision. // **~ di bozze** (*giorn.*) proof-correcting, proof-reading.

corriera, *n. f.* (*trasp.*) coach.

corriere, *n. m.* (*trasp.*) carrier, common carrier. // **a volta di ~** (*comun.*) by return of mail.

corrispettivo, *n. m.* (*leg.*) consideration. // **~ inadeguato** (*alla prestazione*) inadequate consideration; **per un ~ in denaro** (*comm.*) for a money consideration.

corrispondente, *a.* corresponding. *n. m.* e *f.* **1** (*market.*) connection. **2** (*pers.*) correspondent, correspondence clerk, corresponding clerk. // **~ all'estero** (*comm. est.*) foreign correspondent; **~ estero** (*pers.*) foreign correspondent, foreign languages correspondent; **~ in lingue estere** (*pers.*) foreign languages correspondent, foreign correspondent.

corrispondenza, *n. f.* **1** correspondence; (*relazione, rapporto*) connection, connexion. **2** (*comun.*) (*posta*) correspondence, post, mail. // **~ commerciale** commercial correspondence, business correspondence; **~ in arretrato** arrears of correspondence; **~ in arrivo** (*comun.*) incoming letters, incoming mail; **~ in partenza** (*comun.*) outgoing letters, outgoing mail; **~ ordinaria** (*comun.*) routine mail; **~ per via aerea** (*comun.*) airmail correspondence.

corrispondere, *v. i.* **1** to correspond, to agree, to tally. **2** (*comun.*) to correspond. *v. t.* (*pagare*) to pay★, to pay★ out; to give★. // **~ al campione** (*market.*) (*di merce*) to be up to sample; **~ alle aspettative di q.** to come up to sb.'s expectations; **~ alle esigenze dei clienti** (*market.*) to meet the customers' requirements.

corrompere, *v. t.* **1** to corrupt, to vitiate. **2** (*leg.*) to bribe, to buy★ off, to buy★ over. **3** (*leg.*) (*testimoni, ecc.*) to suborn.

corruzione, *n. f.* **1** corruption. **2** (*leg.*) (*a mezzo di denaro, doni, ecc.*) bribery.

corsa, *n. f.* **1** run. **2** (*banca, fin., market.*) run. **3** (*trasp. aut.*) (*d'un autobus, ecc.*) run. // **~ agli acquisti** (*conseguente a una riduzione delle imposte*) (*econ.*) spending spree; **una ~ ai titoli svizzeri** (*fin.*) a run on Swiss securities; **~ alle vendite** (*Borsa*) bear stampede.

corso, *n. m.* **1** course. **2** (*Borsa, fin.*) price. **3** (*econ., market.*) price. **4** (*fin.*) (*circolazione*) circulation. **5** (*fin.*) (*tasso*) rate. // **~ a vista** (*fin.*) demand rate; **~ acquisto** (*banca, fin.*) bought contract; **corsi commerciali** (*market.*) commodity prices; **~ dei cambi** (*fin.*) foreign-exchange rate; **un ~ dei cambi fluttuante** (*fin.*) a fluctuant exchange rate; ~ **del cambio** (*fin.*) course of exchange, exchange rate; ~ **del riporto** (*Borsa*) continuation rate; **corsi delle azioni** (*fin.*) share prices; ~ **denaro** (*banca, fin.*) bought contract; ~ **d'acqua navigabile** (*trasp.*) waterway; ~ **d'acquisto** (*rag.*) cost price; ~ **di chiusura** (*Borsa*) closing rate; ~ **di studi** (*pers.*) curriculum; ~ **fiduciario** (*di carta moneta*) (*fin.*) fiduciary circulation; ~ **forzoso** (*fin.*) forced circulation, inconvertible circulation; ~ **legale** (*fin.*) legal tender; ~ **lettera** (*banca, fin.*) sold contract; **corsi oscillanti** (*Borsa*) fluctuating values; **corsi per operazioni a termine** (*fin.*) forward rates; «**corsi praticati**» (*Borsa*) «business done», «bargains done»; **corsi sul mercato all'ingrosso** (*market.*) wholesale prices; ~ «**tale quale**» (*o* «**tel quel**») (*fin.*) tel quel rate, tel quel quotation; ~ **vendita** (*banca, fin.*) sold contract; **dar ~ a un'ordinazione** to carry out (*o* to execute, to fill) an order; **in ~** (*d'un lavoro, ecc.*) in progress, in hand; **in ~ di costruzione** under construction; **in ~ d'esecuzione** (*market.*) (*d'ordinazioni*) on hand; **in ~ di lavorazione** (*org. az.*) in process; in the works (*USA*); **nel ~ d'un anno o due** in the course of one or two years.

corte, *n. f.* (*leg.*) court. // ~ **Costituzionale** (*leg.*) Constitutional Court (*in Italia*); ~ **dei Conti** (*leg.*) State Audit Court (*in Italia*); ~ **d'Appello** (*leg.*) Court of Appeal; Appellate Court, Court of Appeals (*USA*); ~ **d'Assise** (*leg.*) Court of Assize; ~ **di Cassazione** (*leg.*) Court of Cassation (*in Italia*); High Court of Justice (*in G.B.*); ~ **di Giustizia** (*leg.*) Court of Justice, law-Court, Court, tribunal; ~ **di Giustizia di primo grado** (*leg.*) magistrate's Court (*in G.B.*); **la ~ Suprema** (*leg., USA*) the Supreme Court.

cosa, *n. f.* **1** thing. **2** (*faccenda*) matter. // ~ **abbandonata** (*dal proprietario*) (*leg.*) derelict; **la ~ assicurata** (*ass.*) the thing insured, the insured property; ~ **che indica** pointer; ~ **che non vale (più) nulla** (*fig., fam.*) write-off; ~ **che produce** (*o* **che rende**) (*econ., fin.*) yielder; **una ~ che si deve fare** a must (*fam.*); ~ **confiscata** (*leg.*) forfeit; **la ~ di domani** (*pubbl.*) (*il prodotto che si sta affermando*) the coming thing; **la ~ di moda** (*pubbl.*) the coming thing; ~ **in vendita** buy (*fam.*); **la ~ migliore** (the) best thing, best; pick (*fam.*); ~ **necessaria** necessity, necessary.

costa, *n. f.* coast. // **lungo la ~** (*trasp. mar.*) coastwise, coastways.

costante, *a.* constant, steady, unaltered, consistent.

costare, *v. i.* **1** to cost★ (*anche fig.*); to come★ to, to sell★ for; to be (*fam.*). **2** (*valere*) to be worth.

costeggiare, *v. i.* (*trasp. mar.*) to coast, to sail along the coast. *v. t.* (*trasp. mar.*) to coast (*o* to sail).

costiero, *a.* (*trasp. mar.*) coasting. // **commercio ~** coasting trade.

costituire, *v. t.* **1** to constitute, to form, to make★ up. **2** (*fondare*) to found, to set★ up. **3** (*leg.*) to constitute. **4** (*leg.*) (*una società di capitali*) to incorporate. // ~ **un comitato** to constitute a committee; ~ **in pegno** (*leg.*) to pledge; ~ **reato** (*leg.*) to amount to an offence (*o* to a crime); ~ **una rendita vitalizia** (*fin.*) to settle an annuity; ~ **riserve (scorte)** to build up reserves (stock); ~ **una società (di capitali)** (*fin.*) to form a company; ~ **una società (di persone)** (*fin.*) to form a partnership.

costituirsi, *v. rifl.* **1** to constitute oneself. **2** (*leg.*) to deliver (*o* to give★) oneself up. // ~ **all'autorità giudiziaria** (*leg.*) to surrender oneself to justice; ~ **in giudizio** (*leg.*) to appear before the Court; ~ **in sindacato** (*fin.*) to syndicate; ~ **parte civile** (*leg.*) to prosecute, to sue (in a civil case).

costitutivo, *a.* **1** constitutive. **2** (*fin., leg.*) of association.

costituzionale, *a.* constitutional.

costituzione, *n. f.* **1** constitution, formation. **2** (*fondazione*) foundation, setting up. **3** (*leg.*) constitution. **4** (*leg.*) (*di società di capitali*) incorporation. // ~ **delle scorte** (*org. az.*) warehousing; **la ~ d'una rendita per q.** (*fin.*) the settlement of an annuity on sb.; **la ~ d'una società (di capitali)** (*fin.*) the foundation of a company, the incorporation of a company; **la ~ d'una società (di persone)** (*fin.*) the formation of a partnership; ~ **in giudizio** (*leg.*) appearance before the Court.

costo, *n. m.* **1** cost. **2** (*spesa*) charge, expense. **3** (*tariffa*) rate. **4** (*rag.*) cost. // ~ **alternativo** (*rag.*) alternative cost, opportunity cost; ~ **anticipato** (*rag.*) deferred charge, deferred asset; «~, **assicurazione e nolo**» (*trasp. mar.*) «cost, freight and insurance», «cost, insurance, freight» (*c.i.f.*); ~ **complessivo** (*econ., market.*) all-in cost; (*rag.*) total cost; **costi costanti** (*econ.*) constant costs; **costi crescenti** (*econ.*) increasing costs; **costi decrescenti** (*econ.*) decreasing costs; ~ **degli aumenti salariali** (*econ.*) wage bill; ~ **dei locali** (*d'un'azienda*) (*rag.*) cost of the premises; ~ **del lavoro** (*econ., rag.*) labour costs; (*rag.*) work cost; ~ **del trasporto** carriage; transportation (*USA*); ~ **della manodopera** (*rag.*) cost of labour; ~ **dell'op-**

portunità (*econ.*) opportunity cost; ~ **della vita** (*econ.*) cost of living; **costi dello scoperto** (*o* **del fido**) **bancario** (*fin.*) overdraft costs; **costi d'amministrazione** (*rag.*) administrative cost; **costi di capitale** (*fin.*, *rag.*) principal costs; **costi di distribuzione** (*econ.*) distribution costs, marketing costs; (*market.*) delivery costs; **costi d'esercizio** (*rag.*) operating costs; operational costs, operating expenses; **costi di gestione** (*rag.*) operating costs; **costi d'immobilizzo** (*rag.*) carrying charges; ~ **di lavorazione** (*rag.*) manufacturing cost; **costi di magazzinaggio** (*rag.*) storage costs; **costi di manutenzione** (*rag.*) maintenance costs; ~ **di produzione** (*rag.*) production cost, process cost, factory cost, flat cost; ~ **di sostituzione** (*d'un'attività fissa con un'altra altrettanto valida*) (*org. az.*) replacement cost; **costi di trasformazione** (*dalla materia prima al prodotto finito*) (*econ.*) conversion costs; ~ **diretto** (*rag.*) direct cost, direct charge, specific cost; «~ **e nolo**» (*trasp. mar.*) cost and freight (*c. & f.*); **costi fissi** (*rag.*) fixed costs, indirect costs, capacity costs, overhead costs; **costi flessibili** (*rag.*) discretionary expenses; ~ **indiretto** (*rag.*) indirect cost, indirect charge; ~ **industriale** (*rag.*) manufacturing cost; **costi infrastrutturali** (*econ.*) infrastructure costs; ~ **marginale** (*econ.*) marginal cost; ~ **marginale decrescente** (*econ.*) decreasing marginal cost; ~ **medio** (*econ.*) average cost; **costi moderati** (*econ.*) moderate costs; ~ **originario** (*rag.*) historical cost; ~ **per miglio** (*trasp.*) milage; ~ **primo** (*rag.*) (*costo della materia prima più le spese dirette di lavorazione*) prime cost, first cost; ~ **reale** (*rag.*) real cost, historical cost; **costi salariali** (*econ.*) wage costs; ~ **standard per unità di prodotto** (*org. az.*, *rag.*) standard cost per unit; ~ **standard unitario** (*org. az.*, *rag.*) standard cost per unit; **costi stimati** (*rag.*) estimated costs; ~ **unitario** (*rag.*) unit cost; **costi variabili** (*rag.*) variable costs, running costs, direct costs; **sotto** ~ below cost.

costoso, *a.* **1** costly, expensive, dear. **2** (*market.*, *anche*) high. // **poco** ~ cheap, inexpensive.

costringere, *v. t.* to compel, to force, to oblige. // ~ (*q.*) **a consegnare qc.** (*leg.*) to requisition; ~ **all'atterraggio** (*trasp. aer.*) to ground.

costrizione, *n. f.* **1** compulsion, pressure. **2** (*leg.*) (*coercizione*) coercion.

costruire, *v. t.* to construct, to build*, to build* up, to make*. // ~ **in serie** (*econ.*) to mass-produce, to standardize.

costruito, *a.* constructed, built, made. // ~ **a richiesta** (*org. az.*) custom-built; ~ **in serie** (*org. az.*) mass-produced.

costruttivo, *a.* constructive.

costruttore, *n. m.* builder, constructor, maker. // ~ **d'automobili** (*trasp. aut.*) carmaker.

costruzione, *n. f.* building, construction, making. // ~ **in serie** (*econ.*) mass-production, standardization; **costruzioni navali** (*trasp. mar.*) shipbuilding; **in** ~ (*org. az.*) under construction, in process of construction.

cottimista, *n. m.* e *f.* (*pers.*) piece-worker, jobber.

cottimo, *n. m.* **1** (*org. az.*) piece-work. **2** (*pers.*) (*il contratto*) jobbing contract. **3** (*pers.*) (*la retribuzione*) incentive pay. // **a** ~ (*pers.*) by the piece; **dare lavoro a** ~ to job out work; **lavoro a** ~ work by the piece; piecework.

cover girl, *n. f.* (*pubbl.*) (*ragazza la cui foto appare sulle copertine dei periodici*) cover girl.

creare, *v. t.* **1** to create, to make*. **2** (*fondare*) to found, to set* up. **3** (*causare, determinare*) to cause, to determine. // ~ **difficoltà** to make difficulties; ~ **una nuova serie di azioni** (*fin.*) to create a new series of shares.

creativo, *a.* creative. *n. m.* (*pubbl.*) copywriter.

creatore, *n. m.* creator, maker.

creazione, *n. f.* creation, making. // ~ **dei bisogni** (*nei consumatori*) (*econ.*, *pubbl.*) want creation.

credenziale, *n. f.* (*banca, cred.*) bank draft, banker's draft.

credenziali, *n. pl.* credentials; letter credential, letter of credence (*sing.*).

credere, *v. t.* e *i.* **1** (*prestar fede*) to believe. **2** (*reputare, ritenere*) to think*, to believe, to deem, to repute. // ~ **a un testimone** to believe a witness.

credibile, *a.* **1** believable, credible. **2** (*di persona*) (*degno di fede*) reliable, trustworthy.

credibilità, *n. f.* **1** believableness, credibility. **2** (*di persona*) reliability, trustworthiness.

«creditcarta», *n. f.* (*banca, cred., fin.*) credit card.

creditizio, *a.* credit (*attr.*). // **la stretta creditizia** (*econ.*, *fin.*) the credit squeeze.

credito, *n. m.* **1** credit; (*talora*) claim. **2** (*fiducia, reputazione*) credit, credence, reputation. **3** (*di cui gode una ditta*) credit standing, credit status. **4** (*rag.*) (*d'un conto*) credit; (*lato dell'avere*) credit side. // **crediti a breve scadenza** (*rag.*) account receivable; ~ **a breve (termine)** (*cred.*) short-term credit; ~ **a lunga scadenza** (*cred.*) long credit; ~ **a lungo (termine)** (*cred.*) long-term credit; ~ **a medio (termine)** (*cred.*) medium-term credit; ~ **agrario** agricultural credit; ~ **al consumatore** (*fin., market.*) consumer credit, retail credit; ~ **all'esportazione** (*banca*) confirmed banker's credit; **crediti all'esportazione** (*comm. est.*) export credits; **crediti all'importazione** (*comm. est.*) import credits; ~ **allo scoperto** (*banca, cred.*) bank credit, open credit; (*rag.*) cash credit; ~ **aperto** (*fin.*) open credit; (*per un certo numero d'anni*) stand-by credit; ~ **bancario** credit at the bank, credit with the bank, bank credit; ~ **bancario confermato** (*banca, cred.*) confirmed banker's credit; ~ **bancario confermato e irrevocabile** (*banca, cred.*) confirmed, irrevocable banker's credit; ~ **chirografario** (*leg.*) chirographary credit (*o* debt); unsecured credit (*o* debt), book debt; **crediti commerciali** commercial credits, commodity credits; ~ **confermato** (*cred.*) confirmed credit; ~ **«congelato»** (*cred.*) frozen credit; ~ **contestato** (*leg.*) disputed credit; **crediti destinati a finanziare investimenti produttivi** (*cred.*) loans to finance productive investment; ~ **d'accettazione** (*banca, cred.*) acceptance credit; ~ **di cassa** (*rag.*) cash credit; **crediti di dubbia esigibilità** (*cred.*) doubtful debts; ~ **d'imposta** (*fin.*) tax credit; **crediti d'incerta esigibilità** (*cred.*) doubtful debts; ~ **di sostegno** (*fin.*) stand-by credit; ~ **difficile** (*fin.*) tight credit; **un** ~ **difficile da ricuperare** a bad debt; ~ **documentario** (*comm. est.*) documentary credit, document credit; ~ **documentato** (*comm. est.*) *V.* ~ **documentario;** ~ **esaurito** (*banca*) credit abated; ~ **esigibile** (*cred.*) collectable credit, collectible credit; ~ **esigibile in qualsiasi momento** (*cred.*) call-money; ~ **facile** (*fin.*) cheap money; **crediti finanziari** (*cred.*) financial credits; ~ **fiscale** (*fin.*) revenue claim; ~ **garantito da ipoteca** (*leg.*) claim secured by mortgage; ~ **immobiliare** (*cred.*) land credit, credit on real property; ~ **in bianco** (*banca, cred.*) blank credit, open credit; ~ **in conto corrente** (*banca*) overdraft credit; **un** ~ **inesigibile** (*cred.*) an uncollectible credit, an uncollectible debt, an uncollectible, a bad debt; ~ **infruttifero** (*cred.*) passive debt; **un** ~ **irrecuperabile** (*cred.*) an irrecoverable credit (*o* debt), an unrecoverable credit (*o* debt); ~ **irrevocabile** (*banca, cred.*) irrevocable credit; ~ **irrevocabile e confermato** (*banca, cred.*) irrevocable and confirmed credit; ~ **libero** (*banca, cred.*) blank credit; ~ **-locazione** (*fin.*) leasing; ~ **mercantile** (*cred.*) mercantile credit; ~ **navale** (*cred.*) maritime credit; ~ **non confermato** (*cred.*) simple credit; **un** ~ **non contestato** (*cred.*) an undisputed credit; ~ **non documentario** (*banca, cred.*) clean credit; open credit; **un** ~ **non riscosso** (*cred.*) an uncollected debt; ~ **personale** (*cred., fin.*) personal credit, personal loan; ~ **prescritto** (*cred.*) barred credit; ~ **privilegiato** (*cred.*) preferential credit, secured credit, claim secured by bond, privileged debt, preferred debt; **crediti probabili** (*cred.*) dependencies; **un** ~ **revocabile** (*cred.*) a revocable credit; **crediti riconosciuti dalla legge** (*leg.*) lawful debts; ~ **rotativo** (*banca*) revolving credit; **crediti sicuri** (*cred.*) good debts; ~ **superiore a sei mesi** (*che, in via eccezionale, una banca concede a un esportatore*) (*banca*) extended credit; **un** ~ **trasferibile** (*cred.*) a transferable credit; ~ **verificato** (*e ammesso al passivo d'un fallimento*) (*leg.*) proved credit; **a** ~ on credit, upon credit, on a credit basis, on trust; (*rag.*) on the credit side; credit (*a. attr.*); **di** ~ credit (*attr.*); **titolo di** ~ credit instrument.

creditore, *n. m.* **1** creditor. **2** (*leg., anche*) obligee. **3** (*rag.*) creditor, credit, credit side. // ~ **che fa eseguire il protesto** (*leg.*) protester, protestor; ~ **chirografario** (*leg.*) chirographary creditor, unsecured creditor; **creditori diversi** (*rag.*) sundry creditors; ~ **giudiziario** (*leg.*) judgement creditor; ~ **in solido** (*leg.*) co-creditor; **un** ~ **insistente** (*cred.*) an urgent creditor; a dun (*fam.*); ~ **ipotecario** (*cred., leg.*) mortgage creditor, mortgagee, loan holder; ~ **principale** (*cred.*) principal creditor, chief creditor; ~ **privilegiato** (*leg.*) preferential creditor, preferred creditor, lien creditor, secured creditor; ~ **su ipoteca** (*leg.*) creditor on mortgage.

crescente, *a.* growing, increasing, rising.

crescere, *v. t.* **1** (*aumentare*) to increase, to augment, to raise, to advance, to put★ up, to up. **2** (*allevare, educare*) to bring★ up, to rear. **3** (*coltivare*) to grow★. **4** (*econ., market.*) (*i prezzi, ecc., anche*) to lift, to stiffen. *v. i.* **1** (*svilupparsi*) to grow★, to grow★ up. **2** (*aumentare*) to grow★, to increase, to augment, to advance, to rise★, to go★ up, to step up. **3** (*in fretta*) to swell, to upsurge. **4** (*fin., market.*) (*di prezzi, ecc.*) to rise★, to go★ up, to up. // ~ **come un fungo** to mushroom; ~ **i dazi doganali** (*dog.*) to raise custom duties; ~ **di prezzo** to advance (*o* to increase) in price, to appreciate; ~ **di valore** (*fin., market.*) to appreciate, to go better; ~ **improvvisamente** (*fin., market.*) (*di prezzi, ecc.*) to jump, to leap; ~ **i prezzi** (*market., anche*) to raise prices, to enhance prices; ~ **il prezzo della benzina** to advance the price of petrol; ~ **vertiginosamente** (*econ.*) (*di prezzi, ecc.*) to spiral upward; **far** ~ **i prezzi** (*fin., market.*) to force up prices.

crescita, *n. f.* **1** growth. **2** (*aumento*) growth, increase, rise, advance. **3** (*repentina*) upsurge, upswing, swell. 4 (*econ.*, *market.*) (*di costi, prezzi, ecc.*) lift, increase, rise. 5 (*pers.*) (*di salario*) advance, increase, increment, rise; raise (*USA*). // **la ~ dei prezzi** (*econ.*) the price increase; the rise in prices; **~ di valore** (*fin.*, *rag.*) appreciation; **~ economica zero** (*econ.*) zero economic growth; **~ improvvisa (dei prezzi)** (*fin.*, *market.*) jump, leap, upswing (in prices).

cricca, *n. f.* clique. // **~ di compratori** (*a una vendita all'asta*) sale-ring; **~ di speculatori** (*fin.*) ring.

criminale, *a.* e *n. m.* e *f.* (*leg.*) criminal.

criminalista, *n. m.* e *f.* (*leg.*) criminalist.

criminalità, *n. f.* 1 (*leg.*) criminality. 2 (*crimine*) crime.

crimine, *n. m.* (*leg.*) crime. // **~ passibile di pena capitale** (*leg.*) capital offence.

criminoso, *a.* (*leg.*) malicious, wrongful.

crisi, *n. f. inv.* 1 crisis★. 2 (*econ.*) crisis★, depression, slump; doldrums (*pl.*). // **~ congiunturale** (*econ.*) cyclical malaise; **la ~ degli alloggi** (*econ.*) the housing shortage, the housing problem; **la ~ del 1929** (*in U.S.A.*) the Great Depression; **~ della Borsa** (*fin.*) slump on the Stock Exchange, market crisis; **~ di fiducia** (*econ.*) confidence crisis; **~ economico-finanziaria** (*econ.*, *fin.*) economic-financial crisis; **una ~ finanziaria** (*fin.*) a financial crisis; **~ stagionale** (*econ.*) seasonal down; **~ strutturale** (*econ.*) structural malaise.

criterio, *n. m.* criterion★, principle, rule. // **col ~ della competenza (economica)** (*fin.*, *rag.*) on an accrual basis; **col ~ per cassa** (*fin.*, *rag.*) on a cash basis.

critico, *a.* critical, crucial. *n. m.* critic; (*correttore*) corrector.

crocevia, *n. m. inv.* (*trasp. aut.*) road crossing; cross-roads (*col verbo al sing.*).

crocicchio, *n. m.* (*trasp. aut.*) road crossing; cross-roads (*col verbo al sing.*).

crociera, *n. f.* (*trasp. mar.*, *tur.*) cruise.

crollare, *v. i.* 1 to collapse, to fall★ down, to crumble up, to tumble down. 2 (*fig.*) (*andare in rovina*) to collapse, to crash, to fall★ to pieces. 3 (*econ.*, *fin.*, *market.*) (*di prezzi, ecc.*) to collapse, to crumble, to fall★, to sag, to slump.

crollo, *n. m.* 1 (*anche fig.*) collapse, crumbling, downfall, fall. 2 (*fisico e morale: d'una persona*) break-down. 3 (*econ.*, *fin.*, *market.*) collapse, crash, come-down, crumbling, fall, sag, slump, smash, tumble. // **~ dei prezzi** (*econ.*, *fin.*, *market.*) collapse of prices; sag (*o* slump) in prices; price fall; **~ dei prezzi dei titoli** (*Borsa*, *fin.*) sell-off; **~ dei prezzi in Borsa** stock market crash.

cronometrista, *n. m.* e *f.* (*pers.*) timekeeper. // **~ analista (*o* industriale)** (*pers.*) *V.* **cronotecnico.**

cronometro, *n. m.* 1 stopwatch, watch. 2 (*trasp. mar.*) chronometer.

cronotecnico, *n. m.* (*pers.*) (*tecnico che annota e studia i tempi di lavorazione in un'azienda*) time-study engineer, time-study expert.

crumiro, *n. m.* (*sind.*) blackleg, scab, strike-breaker.

cubaggio, *n. m.* cubage. // **~ della merce caricata a bordo** (*trasp. mar.*) intake measurement.

cubico, *a.* (*mat.*) cubic, solid.

cubo, *a.* (*mat.*) cubic. *n. m.* (*mat.*) cube. // **metro ~** (*mat.*) cubic metre.

cuccetta, *n. f.* 1 (*trasp.*) sleeping berth. 2 (*trasp. mar.*) berth.

cucina, *n. f.* kitchen. // **~ di bordo** (*trasp. mar.*) caboose, galley.

cumulare, *v. t.* to cumulate, to accumulate, to heap up, to hoard. // **~ diversi uffici** (*pers.*) to hold several offices; **~ due stipendi** (*pers.*) to draw two salaries.

cumularsi, *v. rifl.* 1 to cumulate, to accumulate. 2 (*fin.*) (*d'interessi*) to accrue.

cumulativo, *a.* (*anche fig.*) cumulative, accumulative. // **non ~** (*fin.*) non-cumulative.

cumulo, *n. m.* heap; (*di denaro*) hoard. // **~ d'incarichi** (*pers.*) plurality of offices; **~ di pene** (*leg.*) accumulative judgment (*o* sentence).

cura, *n. f.* 1 (*premura*) care. 2 (*attenzione*) care, carefulness, accuracy, attention. 3 (*medicamento*) care, treatment, remedy. 4 (*responsabilità di q.*) charge.

curare, *v. t.* 1 (*prendersi cura di*) to take★ care of, to attend to, to see★ to. 2 (*medicare*) to treat. 3 (*guarire*) to cure. // **~ l'accettazione d'una cambiale** (*cred.*) to provide a bill with acceptance; **~ l'assicurazione della merce** (*ass.*) to effect (the) insurance of the goods; **~ l'incasso d'una cambiale** (*cred.*) to attend to the collection of a bill; **~ il pagamento d'una cambiale** (*cred.*) to protect a bill.

curarsi, *v. rifl.* 1 (*aver cura di sé*) to take★ care of oneself. 2 (*occuparsi di*) to take★ care of, to attend to, to look after, to see★ to, to mind. 3 (*essere in cura*) to be under treatment.

curatela, *n. f.* 1 (*leg.*) trusteeship. 2 (*leg.*) (*d'un minore, ecc.*) curatorship (*in Italia*); guardianship (*in G.B. e in U.S.A.*). 3 (*leg.*) (*di minore, interdetto, ecc.*) receivership (*in G.B.*). 4 (*leg.*) (*fallimentare*) receivership (*in G.B.*). // **~ d'un fallimento** (*leg.*, *anche*) administration of a bankrupt's estate.

curatore, *n. m.* **1** (*leg.*) trustee; administrator. **2** (*leg.*) (*di minorenne, d'incapace, ecc.*) curator (*in Italia*); receiver (*in G.B.*). **3** (*leg.*) (*fallimentare*) trustee in bankruptcy, trustee; receiver (*in G.B.*). // ~ **«ad interim»** (*d'un fallimento*) (*leg.*) official receiver (*in G.B.*); ~ **d'un alienato** (*leg.*) administrator for an insane person; ~ **d'eredità giacente** (*leg.*) administrator for vacant succession; ~ **d'un fallimento** (*leg.*) assignee in bankruptcy; ~ **d'un interdetto** (*leg.*) administrator for a disabled person; ~ **fallimentare** (*leg.*) trustee in bankruptcy; receiver in bankruptcy (*in G.B.*); ~ **provvisorio** (*d'un fallimento*) (*leg.*) official receiver, interim receiver.

curricolo, *n. m.* (*pers.*) «curriculum★ vitae», record.

curriculum, *n. m.* (*pers.*) «curriculum★ vitae», record. // « ~ **vitae**» (*pers.*) «curriculum vitae».

curva, *n. f.* **1** bend, curve, turn. **2** (*mat.*) curve. // ~ **combinata della domanda e dell'offerta** (*econ.*) combined demand and supply curve; ~ **dei costi** (*econ.*) cost curve; ~ **della domanda** (*econ.*) demand curve; ~ **dell'offerta** (*econ.*) supply curve; ~ **dell'offerta di mercato** (*econ.*) market-supply curve; ~ **d'indifferenza** (*econ.*) indifference curve; ~ **d'ineguaglianza assoluta** (*econ.*) curve of absolute inequality; ~ **d'uguaglianza assoluta** (*econ.*) curve of absolute equality; **una ~ in una strada** (*trasp. aut.*) a turn in a road.

cuscinetto, *n. m.* **1** (*imbottitura, tampone*) pad. **2** (*org. az.*) cushion. // ~ **per timbri** (*attr. uff.*) ink-pad.

custode, *n. m.* e *f.* **1** (*pers.*) keeper, warden, caretaker, guard. **2** (*pers.*) (*d'un edificio pubblico*) custodian. // ~ **di scalo** (*trasp. mar.*) wharfinger; ~ **giudiziario di beni** (*leg.*) receiver (*in G.B.*); ~ **notturno** (*pers.*) night watchman.

custodia, *n. f.* **1** custody, charge, safeguard. **2** (*lavoro di custode*) keeping, guard, watch. **3** (*banca*) safe-keeping, safe custody. **4** (*fin.*) custody. **5** (*leg.*) custody. **6** (*leg.*) (*di minorenne e sim.*) ward, wardship. // ~ **di cassette di sicurezza** (*banca*) safe custody, safe-keeping; ~ **doganale temporanea** (*dog.*) temporary warehousing; ~ **legale** (*leg.*) custody of the law.

custodire, *v. t.* **1** (*conservare, serbare*) to keep★, to guard, to safeguard. **2** (*sorvegliare*) to watch. **3** (*aver cura di*) to take★ care of; to look after. **4** (*leg.*) to hold★ in custody, to ward. // ~ **un segreto** to keep a secret.

D

danaro, *n. m. V.* **denaro.**

danaroso, *a.* wealthy, rich; well-to-do, moneyed.

danneggiabile, *a.* damageable.

danneggiamento, *n. m.* **1** damage, injure. **2** (*sciupio*) spoiling, waste. //; ~ **doloso** wilful damage.

danneggiare, *v. t.* **1** to damage, to injure. **2** (*sciupare*) to spoil, to waste. **3** (*svantaggiare*) to disadvantage, to affect. **4** (*nuocere a*) to harm.

danneggiato, *a.* damaged, injured. *n. m.* (*leg.*) (the) injured party. // ~ **dall'acqua di mare** (*trasp. mar.*) (*di carico*) sea-damaged; **non** ~ (*ass., trasp.*) undamaged; **la parte danneggiata** (*leg.*) the injured party.

danno, *n. m.* **1** (*anche leg.*) damage. **2** (*svantaggio*) disadvantage. **3** (*nocumento*) harm, ill. **4** (*ass.*) damage. **5** (*leg.*) injury, wrong. **6 danni,** *pl.* (*ass., leg.*) damages, losses. // ~ **accidentale** (*leg.*) accidental damage; ~ **avvenuto durante il trasporto** (*ass., trasp.*) damage in transit; **danni contingenti** (*ass.*) contingent damages; **danni d'avaria** (*ass. mar.*) average damage; **danni di guerra** (*econ.*) war-damages; **un** ~ **di lieve entità** (*ass.*) a minor damage; ~ **dovuto a forza maggiore** (*leg., trasp. mar.*) damage by act of God; ~ **dovuto a negligenza grave** (*leg.*) damage due to gross negligence; **danni dovuti alla caricazione** (*ass. mar.*) damage in loading; **danni dovuti allo scarico** (*ass. mar.*) damage in discharging; ~ **emergente** (*leg.*) consequential damage; **un** ~ **evidente** an apparent damage; **un** ~ **grave** (*leg.*) a serious damage; **danni indiretti** (*ass.*) consequential damages, remote damages; ~ **inevitabile** (*ass., leg.*) inevitable damage; ~ **intenzionale** (*leg.*) intentional damage; **danni lievi** (*leg.*) slight damages; **danni liquidati** (*ass.*) stipulated damages; ~ **personale** (*leg.*) personal injury; **danni reali** (*ass.*) substantial damages; **danni remoti** (*leg.*) remote damages; **un** ~ **riparabile** a reparable damage; **danni triplici** (*leg.*) treble damages.

dannoso, *a.* detrimental, harmful, hurtful, injurious.

dare[1], *n. m.* **1** (*cred.*) (*debito*) debt. **2** (*rag.*) debit, debit side; debtor, debtor side. // **il** ~ **d'un conto** (*rag.*) the debit of an account; ~ **e avere** (*rag.*) debit and credit; debtor and creditor; **la colonna del** ~ (*rag.*) the debit column.

dare[2], *v. t.* **1** to give*. **2** (*porgere, consegnare*) to hand; (*rassegnare*) to hand in. **3** (*concedere*) to allow, to award, to grant. **4** (*econ., fin.*) to yield, to bear*. **5** (*market.*) (*un'ordinazione*) to place. **6** (*rag.*) (*di conto, ecc.: un certo saldo*) to turn in. // ~ **a nolo** (*leg.*) to hire, to hire out, to let; ~ **a q. il nome di q. altro come referenza** (*pers.*) to refer sb. to sb. else; ~ **a prestito** (*cred.*) to lend; ~ **aiuto a q.** to give assistance to sb.; ~ **atto di qc.** to acknowledge st.; ~ **autorità a q.** (*leg.*) to warrant sb., to empower sb.; ~ **avviso legale** (*leg.*) to give legal notice; ~ **il benvenuto a q.** to welcome sb.; ~ **il cambio a** (*un collega*) (*pers.*) to relieve; ~ **una caparra** to give an earnest; ~ **la colpa a q.** to blame sb.; ~ **come pegno** (*leg.*) to pledge; ~ **un contrordine** to countermand; ~ **corso a un'impresa** to carry out an enterprise; ~ **da dormire a** (*un certo numero di persone*) (*tur.: d'albergo, ecc.*) to sleep; ~ **le dimissioni** (*pers.*) to hand in one's resignation, to resign; ~ **le dimissioni da** (*una carica, e sim.*) (*pers.*) to vacate; ~ **le dimissioni da direttore** (*amm.*) to resign as manager; ~ **una direttiva** to issue a directive; ~ **un diritto a** (*q.*) (*leg.*) to entitle; ~ **la disdetta** (*leg.*) to give notice; ~ **la disdetta a q.** (*leg.*) to give notice to sb.; ~ **disdetta di sfratto** (*leg.*) to give notice to quit; ~ **disposizioni per qc.** to make arrangements for st.; ~ **un eccessivo valore nominale al capitale di** (*una società*) (*fin.*) to over-capitalize; ~ **un esame** (*pers.*) to take an examination; ~ **esecuzione a una sentenza** (*leg.*) to enforce a judgment; ~ **(un) frutto** (*fin., rag.*) to return a profit; ~ **garanzie effettive** to give effective guarantees; ~ **il gettito di** (*una certa somma*) (*fin.*) (*d'imposta, tassa, ecc.*) to yield; ~ **in affitto** (*leg.*) to lease, to let, to rent; ~ **in appalto** (*leg.*) to farm, to farm out, to job, to let, to hire out on tender; ~ **in garanzia** (*leg.*) to give as security, to gage, to pawn; ~ **in pegno** to put in pledge, to gage, to pawn; ~ **informazioni** to give information; ~ **informazioni a q.** to inform sb.; ~ **informazioni sbagliate a q.** to misinform sb.; ~ **inizio a una nuova campagna pubblicitaria** (*pubbl.*) to open a new advertising campaign; ~ **inizio ai lavori** (*d'un'assemblea, ecc.*) (*amm.*) to take the chair; ~ **inizio alla sottoscrizione** (*di nuovi titoli, ecc.*) (*fin.*) to open the books; ~ **istruzioni a q.** to instruct, to direct, to brief sb.; ~ **istruzioni alla giuria** (*leg.*) to instruct the jury; ~ **istruzioni erronee a q.** to misdirect sb.; ~ **istruzioni erronee alla giuria** (*leg.*) to misdirect the jury; ~ **lavoro a** (*q.*) (*pers.*) to employ; ~ **lavoro a domicilio** (*org. az.*) to put work out; ~ **licenza a q.** (*leg.*) to license sb.; ~ **mandato a q.** (*leg.*) to warrant sb.; ~ **motivo a** to motivate; ~ **nome a** to call; ~ **un nome a** (*un prodotto*) (*leg.*) to trade-name; ~ **un nome commerciale a** (*una ditta*) (*leg.*) to trade-name; ~ **notizie a q.** to inform sb.; ~ **un numero a** to number; ~ **origine a** to originate; ~ **un parere di esperto** to expertize; ~ **un parere professionale** to expertize; ~ **la propria parola** to give one's word, to pass one's word; ~ **qc. per letto** (*in un'assemblea e sim.*) to take st. as read; ~ **qc. per soprammercato** to throw st. into the bargain; ~ **il peso scarso** (*market.*) to short-weight; ~ **il preavviso** to give notice; ~ **il preavviso di licenziamento a q.** (*pers.*) to give notice to sb.; ~ **una promozione a un dipendente** (*amm.*) to step up an employee; ~ **pubblicità a qc.** (*giorn., pubbl.*) to publicize st.; ~ **respiro a q.** (*fig.*) (*concedergli una dilazione*) to respite sb.; ~ **il resto d'un dollaro** to give change for a dollar; ~ **ricevuta** to give (a) receipt; ~ **rifugio a q.** to shelter sb.; ~ **sollievo a** to relieve; ~ **terreni in affitto** (*leg.*) to let lands; ~ **titoli a cauzione** (*Borsa*) to hypothecate stocks; ~ **titoli a riporto** (*Borsa*) to give the rate on stock, to give on stock, to lend stock; ~ **il titolo di** to style; ~ **un utile di** (*fin.*) to net; ~ **via libera** (*trasp. ferr.*) to clear the line; ~ **via libera a una nave** (*trasp. mar.*) to clear a ship; ~ **un voto** to cast a vote; ~ **il voto a** (*o* **per**) **q.** to vote for sb.; **darsi alla latitanza** (*leg.*) to abscond from justice, to abscond; **darsi alla professione forense** (*leg.*) to go to the bar; **non** ~ **alcun utile** (*fin.*) to yield no profit.

darsena, *n. f.* **1** (*trasp. mar.*) wet basin, wet dock. **2** (*trasp. mar.*) (*cantiere navale*) dockyard, shipyard.

data, *n. f.* date. // ~ **del pensionamento** (*pers.*) retirement date; ~ **del timbro postale** (*comun.*) date as postmark; ~ **d'annullamento** cancellation date; ~ **d'attracco** (*trasp. mar.*) alongside-date; ~ (*di scadenza*) **d'una cambiale** (*cred.*) date of a bill; ~ **d'emissione** (*banca, fin.*) date of issue; ~ **d'immatricolazione** (*d'una nave*) (*trasp. mar.*) date of registry; **la** ~ **di partenza** (*trasp. mar.*) the date of sailing; ~ **di pubblicazione** (*giorn.*) publication date; ~ **di registrazione** (*rag.*) accounting date; ~ **di scadenza** (*d'una cambiale*) (*cred.*) date of maturity; (*cred.*) (*d'un debito*) due date; (*rag.*) due date; ~ **di spedizione** (*trasp. mar.*) shipping date; ~ **posteriore** (*a quella reale*) post-date; ~ **prevista per il rimborso** (*d'un prestito*) (*cred.*) redemption date; **a** ~ **da determinarsi** (*o* **da fissare**) (*leg.*) sine die; **a** ~ **fissa** (*banca, cred.*) at a fixed date; **a** ~ **futura (determinabile)** (*banca, cred.*) at a determinable future time; **a certo tempo** ~ (*banca*) (*di cambiali*) after date; **della stessa** ~ of even date; **in** ~ **d'oggi** under today's date; today; **in** ~ **posteriore** at a later date; **mettere la** ~ **a** (*un documento, ecc.*) to date; **senza** ~ undated.

databile, *a.* datable, dateable.

datare, *v. t.* (*una lettera, un documento, ecc.*) to date. // **a** ~ **da** beginning from, starting from, counting from.

datario, *n. m.* (*attr. uff.*) dater.

dato, *a.* **1** given; (*certo*) certain, particular. **2** (*leg.*) given. *n. m.* **1** datum★. **2 dati,** *pl.* data. **3 dati,** *pl.* (*elab. elettr.*) data. // ~ **(che)** considering (that); (*poiché*) since; **dati contabili** (*rag.*) accounting data; **data in sedicesimi** (*anziché in ottavi*) (*Borsa, fin.: di quotazione*) split; **dati oggettivi** objective data; **dati riservati** confidential data.

datore, *n. m.* giver. // ~ **di lavoro** (*econ.*) employer; (*org. az.*) principal; (*pers.*) master; boss (*fam.*).

datoriale, *a.* (*org. az., sind.*) (*relativo ai datori di lavoro*) concerning employers; employer (*attr.*).

dattilografa, *n. f.* (*pers.*) typist. // **una** ~ **perfetta** an accomplished typist.

dattilografare, *v. t.* to typewrite★, to type.

dattilografia, *n. f.* typewriting.

dattilografo, *n. m.* (*pers.*) typist.

dattiloscritto, *n. m.* typescript.

davanti, *avv.* before; in front. **davanti (a),** *prep.* before, in front of. **(il) davanti,** *n. m.* (the) front.

daziabile, *a.* (*dog., fin.*) dutiable.

daziare, *v. t.* (*dog., fin.*) to subject to a duty; to lay★ a duty on.

daziario, *a.* (*fin.*) excise, toll (*attr.*). // **casello** ~ toll-gate; octroi; **cinta daziaria** toll-gates (*pl.*); city boundary; **guardia daziaria** excise officer, exciseman; **tariffa daziaria** municipal customs rate; **ufficio** ~ municipal customs office.

daziere, *n. m.* (*fin.*) excise officer, exciseman★.

dazio, *n. m.* **1** (*dog.*) customs duty; customs (*col verbo al sing.*). **2** (*dog., fin.*) duty. **3** (*fin.*) (*di consumo*) excise duty, excise, toll, tollage; municipal customs; tax. **4 il Dazio** (*fin.*) the Excise. **5** (*fin.*) (*l'ufficio*) municipal customs office. **6 dazi,** *pl.* (*dog., anche*) dues. // ~ **ad valorem** (*dog.*) ad valorem duty; ~ **di base** basic duty; ~ **di consumo** (*fin.*) excise duty, excise, internal revenue tax; ~ **d'esportazione** (*dog.*) export duty, export tax; ~ **d'importazione** (*dog.*) import duty, import tax, impost; ~ **discriminatorio** (*dog.*) discriminating duty; **dazi doganali** (*dog.*) customs duties, customs; ~ **doganale «anti-dumping»** (*dog.*) anti-dumping duty; ~ **doganale di transito** (*dog.*) transit duty; ~ **doganale protettivo** (*dog.*) countervailing duty; ~ **doganale rimborsato** (*quando la merce è riesportata*) (*dog.*) drawback; ~ **escluso** (*cioè da pagare*) (*dog., fin.*) duty unpaid; **dazi fiscali** (*dog.*) fiscal duties; ~ **interno** (*fin.*) inland duty; **dazi intracomunitari** (*comm. est.*) intra-Community duties; **dazi nulli** (*dog.*) nil duties; **dazi protettivi** (*dog.*) protective duties; **dazi specifici** (*dog.*) specific duties.

dazione, *n. f.* (*leg.*) dation. // ~ **di titoli a cauzione** (*Borsa*) hypothecation; ~ **in pagamento** (*leg.*) dation in payment.

debitamente, *avv.* duly.

debito¹, *n. m.* **1** (*cred.*) debt. **2** (*cred.*) (*indebitamento*) indebtedness. **3** (*leg.*) debt, liability. **4** (*rag.*) (*d'un conto*) debit; (*lato del dare*) debit side. // **debiti a breve scadenza** (*rag.*) accounts payable; **debiti a breve (termine)** (*fin., rag.*) short-term liabilities; **debiti a lunga scadenza** (*rag.*) funded debts, funded liabilities, fixed liabilities; **debiti a lungo (termine)** (*fin., rag.*) long-term liabilities; ~ **ammesso al passivo del fallimento** (*leg.*) debt proved in bankruptcy; ~ **attivo** (*leg., rag.*) book debt; ~ **chirografario** (*leg.*) chirographary debt, book debt; **debiti complessivi** (*d'un'azienda*) (*rag.*) payables; ~ **complessivo del fallito** (*leg.*) bankrupt's indebtedness; ~ **consolidato** (*fin.*) consolidated debt, funded debt, funded liability, unified debt; **debiti correnti** (*fin., rag.*) current liabilities; ~ **dello Stato** (*fin.*) national debt; Crown debt (*ingl.*); ~ **di guerra** (*econ., fin.*) war debt; **un** ~ **di lieve entità** (*leg.*) a small debt; a small claim (*USA*); ~ **fluttuante** (*fin.*) floating debt, unfunded debt; **un** ~ **insoluto** (*cred.*) an undischarged debt, an outstanding debt; ~ **ipotecario** (*cred., leg.*) mortgage debt; ~ **nazionale** (*fin.*) national debt; **un** ~ **non ancora scaduto** (*cred.*) an undue debt; ~ **non garantito** (*fin.*) deadweight debt; ~ **obbligazionario** (*fin.*) debenture debt; ~ **passivo** (*cioè senza interessi*) (*cred.*) passive debt; ~ **portato in giudizio** (*leg.*) judgement debt; **un** ~ **prescritto** (*per legge*) (*leg.*) a statute-barred debt; (*per decorrenza del tempo*) a debt extinguished by lapse of time; **il** ~ **pubblico** (*fin.*) the public debt, the national debt; **a** ~ (*market.*) on credit; (*rag.*) on the debit side; debit (*a. attr.*).

debito², *a.* due. // **a tempo** ~ in due time; **nel modo** ~ in the proper (*o* right) way.

debitore, *n. m.* **1** (*cred.*) debtor. **2** (*leg., anche*) obligor. **3** (*rag.*) debtor, debit, debit side. // ~ **delegato** (*leg.*) delegated debtor; **debitori diversi** (*rag.*) sundry debtors; ~ **giudiziario** (*leg.*) judgement debtor; **un** ~ **in grado di pagare** a debtor able to pay; ~ **in mora** debtor in arrears; ~ **in solido** (*leg.*) co-debtor; **un** ~ **insolvente** (*leg.*) an insolvent debtor; ~ **ipotecario** (*cred., leg.*) debtor on mortgage, mortgage debtor, mortgager, mortgagor; **un** ~ **moroso** (*cred.*) a tardy debtor, a defaulting debtor, a delinquent debtor; (*Borsa*) a duck (*slang.*); ~ **principale** (*cred.*) principal debtor; ~ **solidale** (*leg.*) joint debtor; **un** ~ **solvibile** (*cred.*) a solvent debtor; **essere** ~ **verso q.** to be indebted to sb.

debitorio, *a.* (*cred., leg.*) debt, debit (*attr.*). // **situazione debitoria** indebtedness.

debole, *a.* **1** weak, feeble. **2** (*econ.*) (*della domanda, ecc.*) slack. **3** (*econ., fin.*) (*di moneta, anche*) lame, soggy. // **a** ~ **domanda** (*econ., market.*) weak.

debolezza, *n. f.* **1** weakness, feebleness. **2** (*econ.*) (*della domanda, ecc.*) slackness.

decadenza, *n. f.* **1** decadence, decay, decline. **2** (*leg.*) lapse. // **la** ~ **da un diritto** (*leg.*) the forfeiture of a right, the debarment from a right, the loss of a right.

decadere, *v. i.* **1** to decline, to decay. **2** (*leg.*) to lapse. // ~ **da un'azione** (*leg.*) to be debarred from an action; ~ **da un diritto** (*leg.*) to lose a right, to forfeit one's right.

decagrammo, *n. m.* decagramme, dekagramme; decagram, dekagram (*USA*).

decalitro, *n. m.* decalitre, dekalitre; decaliter, dekaliter (*USA*).

decametro, *n. m.* decametre, dekametre; decameter, dekameter (*USA*).

decentralizzazione, *n. f.* (*org. az.*) decentralization.

decentramento, *n. m.* (*org. az.*) decentralization.

decentrare, *v. t.* (*org. az.*) to decentralize.

decidere, *v. t.* **1** to decide, to resolve, to settle. **2** (*leg.*) to decide, to determine, to rule. **3** (*leg.*) (*in qualità d'arbitro*) to umpire. // ~ **una controversia** (*leg.*) to decide a controversy, to settle an argument; ~ **una controversia in qualità d'arbitro** (*leg., sind.*) to umpire a controversy; ~ **una lite mediante arbitrato** (*leg.*) to arbitrate a quarrel.

decidersi, *v. rifl.* to decide; to make* up one's mind.

decigrammo, *n. m.* decigram.

decilitro, *n. m.* decilitre; deciliter (*USA*).

decima, *n. f.* (*fin., leg.*) tithe.

decimale, *a.* e *n. m.* (*mat.*) decimal.

«decimalizzare», *v. t.* (*mat.*) to decimalize. // ~ **la moneta** (*econ., fin.*) to decimalize the currency.

«decimalizzazione», *n. f.* (*mat.*) decimalization.

decimetro, *n. m.* decimetre; decimeter (*USA*).

decimi, *n. pl.* (*fin.*) arrears (of subscribed capital) (*in Italia*).

decimo, *num. ord.* tenth. // **decima parte di dollaro** dime; dimmer, dimmo, deaner, deemer (*slang USA*).

decina, *n. f.* about ten.

decisionale, *a.* decisional, decision-making.

decisione, *n. f.* **1** decision, resolution. **2** (*leg.*) decision, determination, judgement, rule. **3** (*org. az.*) decision. // ~ **arbitrale** (*leg., sind.*) umpirage; (*lodo*) award; ~ **giudiziaria** (*leg.*) conclusion by judgement; ~ **giurisdizionale che fa testo** (*leg.*) leading case; **una** ~ **inappellabile** (*leg.*) an unappealable decision; **decisioni macroeconomiche** (*econ.*) macroeconomic decisions; **per** ~ **della Corte** (*leg.*) by decision of the Court.

decisivo, *a.* **1** decisive, conclusive. **2** (*definitivo*) definitive, final. **3** (*cruciale*) crucial.

deciso, *a.* decided. // **una decisa ripresa del mercato** (*market.*) a decided recovery of the market.

declinare, *v. t.* **1** to decline. **2** (*leg.*) to decline. *v. i.* (*diminuire*) to decline, to fall* off, to wane. // ~ **un invito** to decline an invitation; ~ **ogni responsabilità** (*leg.*) to decline any liability.

declinazione, *n. f.* **1** (*grammatica*) declension. **2** (*trasp. mar.*) declination. // ~ **magnetica** (*trasp. mar.*) magnetic declination (*o* deviation, *o* variation).

declino, *n. m.* **1** decline. **2** (*econ., fin., market.*) (*di prezzi, ecc., anche*) falloff, sag, sagging, slackening.

decollare, *v. i.* (*trasp. aer.*) to take* off.

decollo, *n. m.* **1** (*econ.*) take-off. **2** (*trasp. aer.*) take off.

decorrenza, *n. f.* **1** (*cred., fin.*) currency; period (a bill has yet to run). **2** (*leg.*) attachment. // ~ **della copertura del rischio** (*ass.*) attachment of the risk; ~ **d'un'imposta** (*o* **d'una tassa**) (*fin.*) date on which a tax becomes applicable; **con** ~ **da** counting from, to count from; **con** ~ **dal primo del mese in corso** to count from the first of this month; **dalla** ~ **della cambiale** (*banca, cred.*) on the period the bill has yet to run.

decorrere, *v. i.* **1** (*comm.*) to run*. **2** (*fin.*) (*d'interessi, anche*) to accrue. **3** (*leg.*) to attach, to have effect. //**a** ~ **da** counting from.

decotto, *a.* (*econ.*) (*d'industria, complesso, ecc.*) lossmaking.

decremento, *n. m.* **1** decrease, diminution. **2** (*mat.*) decrement. // **un** ~ **del reddito** a decrease in income.

decrescente, *a.* decreasing, declining.

decrescere, *v. i.* to decrease, to diminish.

decretare, *v. t.* (*leg.*) to decree.

decreto, *n. m.* **1** (*leg.*) decree, order, warrant, writ. **2** (*leg.*) (*dell'autorità politica*) fiat. // ~ **di citazione** (*in giudizio*) (*leg.*) summons; ~ **d'ingiunzione** (*leg.*) decree of injunction; ~ **di sfratto** (*leg.*) dispossessory warrant; **un** ~ **irrevocabile** (*leg.*) a final decree; ~ **legge** (*leg.*) order of the executive; ~ **penale** (*leg.*) judgement; **per** ~ **reale** (*leg.*) by Royal Charter.

decurtare, *v. t.* to curtail, to cut*, to reduce, to retrench. // ~ **un assegno in denaro** to curtail an allowance of money; ~ **il salario** (**lo stipendio**) **di q.** to retrench (*o* to dock) sb.'s wages (salary).

decurtazione, *n. f.* curtailing, cut, reduction.

dedotto, *a.* (*leg.*) inferred, constructive.

deducibile, *a.* **1** deducible, derivable. **2** (*leg.*) inferable. **3** (*market.*) (*detraibile*) deductible, allowable. // **non** ~ (*market.*) non-deductible.

dedurre, *v. t.* **1** to deduce, to derive, to gather. **2** (*leg.*) to infer. **3** (*market.*) (*detrarre*) to take* off, to deduct, to allow. // ~ **l'imposta sul reddito** (*fin.*) to deduct the income tax.

deduzione, *n. f.* **1** deduction. **2** (*leg.*) inference. **3** (*market.*) (*detrazione*) deduction, allowance, rebate. // ~ **per spese sostenute** (*concessa dal fisco*) (*fin.*) relief for expenses; ~ **reciproca** (*d'imposte*) (*fin.*) cross credit relief.

defalcare, *v. t.* to deduct, to allow, to take* off, to knock off.

defalcazione, *n. f. V.* **defalco.**

defalco, *n. m.* deduction, deduct, allowance, rebate.

deferimento, *n. m.* (*leg.*) referring, submitting. // ~ (*d'una lite*) **a un arbitro** (*leg.*) reference.

deferire, *v. t.* to refer, to report, to submit. // ~ **q. alla giustizia (*o* in giudizio)** (*leg.*) to hand over sb. to justice; ~ **una causa al tribunale** to refer (*o* to submit) a case to a law-Court; ~ **un giuramento** (*leg.*) to administer an oath.

deficienza, *n. f.* **1** deficiency, deficit, shortcoming. **2** (*scarsità*) shortage. **3** (*mancanza*) lack, want.

deficit, *n. m. inv.* **1** (*fin., rag.*) deficit, shortage, shortfall, gap. **2** (*rag.*) (*perdita*) loss. // ~ **deflazionistico** (*econ.*) deflationary gap; ~ **della bilancia commerciale** (*econ.*) trade deficit, trade gap; ~ **della bilancia dei pagamenti** (*econ.*) payments deficit; ~ **di bilancio** (*fin., rag.*) budget deficit; **essere in** ~ (*banca, cred., rag.*) to be in the red.

deficitario, *a.* **1** (*insufficiente*) insufficient. **2** (*fin., rag.*) deficit (*attr.*); showing a deficit (*o* a loss). // **un bilancio** ~ (*fin., rag.*) a budget showing a deficit.

definire, *v. t.* **1** to define. **2** (*risolvere, sistemare*) to settle.

definitivo, *a.* definitive, final, ultimate.

definito, *a.* definite, decided.

definizione, *n. f.* **1** definition. **2** (*sistemazione*) settlement. // **la ~ d'una lite (d'una vertenza)** (*leg.*) the settlement of a dispute.

deflatorio, *a.* (*econ.*) deflationary.

deflazionare, *v. t.* (*econ.*) to deflate.

deflazionario, *a.* (*econ.*) deflationary.

deflazione, *n. f.* (*econ.*) deflation. // ~ **creditizia** (*econ.*) deflation of credit; ~ **da profitti** (*econ.*) profit deflation; ~ **da redditi** (*econ.*) income deflation.

deflazionistico, *a.* (*econ.*) deflationary.

defraudare, *v. t.* (*leg.*) to defraud, to cheat. // ~ **q. del denaro** to swindle money out of sb.

del credere, *locuz. n.* (*fin., leg.*) del credere, guarantee commission.

delega, *n. f.* **1** delegation. **2** (*fin.*) (*concessa da un azionista a una terza persona perché voti in sua vece*) proxy. **3** (*leg.*) delegation, proxy. **4** (*org. az.*) delegation. // **deleghe degli azionisti** (*fin.*) stockholders' proxies; ~ **d'autorità** (*org. az.*) delegation of authority; ~ **di potere** (*org. az.*) delegation of powers; ~ **di responsabilità** (*org. az.*) delegation of responsibility; **legge** ~ delegated law.

delegante, *n. m.* e *f.* (*leg.*) delegant, delegator.

delegare, *v. t.* **1** to delegate (*anche leg.*); to devolve, to commission. **2** (*org. az., sind.*) to delegate.

delegatario, *n. m.* (*leg.*) delegatee.

delegato, *n. m.* e *a.* **1** delegate. **2** (*leg.*) deputy, proxy. **3** (*pers.*) delegate, secondary. // ~ **di fabbrica** (*sind.*) shop steward; **amministratore (*o* consigliere)** ~ (*fin.*) managing director.

delegazione, *n. f.* **1** (*leg.*) delegation. **2** (*org. az., sind.*) delegation. // ~ **di sorveglianza** (*delle operazioni fallimentari*) (*leg.*) committee of inspection, commission of inspection.

delibera, *n. f.* deliberation, resolution. // ~ **di spesa** (*rag.*) disbursement approval; **una ~ presa a maggioranza** (*amm.*) a majority resolution.

deliberare, *v. t.* **1** to deliberate, to consult. **2** (*decidere*) to resolve, to decide. **3** (*leg.*) to decree. // ~ **in camera di consiglio** (*leg.*) to decide in chambers.

deliberazione, *n. f.* **1** deliberation. **2** (*decisione*) resolution. **3** (*leg.*) deliberation. **4** (*leg.*) decree.

delitto, *n. m.* **1** (*leg.*) crime. **2** (*leg.*) (*assai grave*) felony. **3** (*leg.*) (*reato*) offence. **4** (*leg.*) (*piuttosto lieve*) misdemeanour. // ~ **colposo** (*leg.*) offence committed without malice; ~ **doloso** (*leg.*) willful and malicious offence.

demandare, *v. t.* **1** to remit, to refer. **2** (*leg.*) to submit, to refer.

demaniale, *a.* State-owned; State (*attr.*); Federal (*attr., USA*). // **beni demaniali** State property; Federal lands (*in U.S.A.*).

demanio, *n. m.* **1** (*amm.*) State property (*in Italia, in G.B., e in un singolo Stato in U.S.A.*); Federal property (*in U.S.A.*). **2** (*amm.*) (*l'ufficio*) State property office; Federal property office (*in U.S.A.*). // ~ **reale** (*in G.B.*) Royal Demesne.

demonetizzare, *v. t.* (*econ.*) (*un metallo, ecc.*) to demonetize.

demonetizzazione, *n. f.* (*econ.*) demonetization.

denaro, *n. m.* **1** money. **2** (*contante*) cash. **3** (*econ., fin.*) (*a corso legale*) tender. **4 denari,** *pl.* (*monete metalliche*) coins, coinage. **5 denari,** *pl.* (*fin.*) (*mezzi finanziari*) means. // ~ **a breve** (*cred.*) short-term loans; ~ **a buon mercato** (*econ., fin.*) cheap money, low-cost money; ~ **a corso fiduciario** (*econ.*) fiduciary money; ~ (*rimborsabile*) **a vista** (*fin.*) money at call, money at short notice; ~ **caldo** (*fin.*) hot money; ~ **caro** (*econ., fin.*) dear money; ~ **car-**

taceo (*fin.*) paper money; green money, green (*fam., USA*); ~ **contante** ready money, cash; till (*fig.*); ~ **disponibile** (*rag.*) spare cash; ~ **e lettera** (*fin.*) bid price and offer price; ~ **facile** (*econ., fin.*) easy money; ~ **in banconote** (*fin.*) bank-notes; bills (*USA*); ~ **in cassa** cash in hand, till money; ~ **in contanti** hard cash; ~ **infruttifero** (*fin.*) dead money; ~ **investito a brevissima scadenza** (*per pochi giorni, specialm. in operazioni di Borsa*) (*fin.*) call money; ~ **liquido** cash; (*rag.*) coins and currency; ~ **metallico** (*fin.*) coinage, coins; hard money (*USA*); ~ **per le piccole spese** pocket money; ~ **scarso** (*econ., fin.*) tight money; ~ **spedito** (*comm.*) remittance; **denari spiccioli** loose cash, loose change, change; ~ **«sporco»** (*fin.*) black money; **in** (*o* **per**) ~ **contante** for cash, cash down.

denazionalizzare, *v. t.* (*econ.*) to denationalize.

denazionalizzazione, *n. f.* (*econ.*) denationalization.

densamente, *avv.* densely.

densità, *n. f.* density. // ~ **del movimento merci** (*trasp.*) traffic density; ~ **del traffico merci** (*trasp.*) density of freight traffic; ~ **del traffico passeggeri** (*trasp.*) density of passenger traffic.

denso, *a.* dense, thick.

dentro, *avv.* e *prep.* **1** (*luogo*) inside, in, within. **2** (*moto a luogo*) into. **3** (*tempo*) by; within. // « ~ **e fuori**» (*Borsa*) (*d'acquisto e vendita dello stesso titolo in un breve periodo*) in-and-out.

denuncia, *n. f.* **1** (*anche leg.*) denunciation, notification, notice. **2** (*dog.*) declaration. **3** (*fin.*) (*dei redditi*) return (of income). **4** (*leg.*) complaint, accusation. // ~ **dei redditi** (*fin.*) return of income; ~ **delle imposte** (*o* **delle tasse**) (*fin.*) tax return; ~ **d'un contratto** (*leg.*) disclaimer of a contract.

denunciabile, *a.* (*leg.*) impeachable.

denunciare, *v. t.* **1** (*anche leg.*) to denounce, to give★ notice of, to report. **2** (*dog.*) to declare. **3** (*leg.*) to accuse, to impeach. // ~ **l'avaria all'armatore** (*ass. mar.*) to give notice of damage to the shipowner; ~ **un incidente** to report an accident.

deperibile, *a.* (*market.*) (*di merce*) perishable. // **non** ~ (*market.*) (*di merce*) unperishable.

deperire, *v. i.* (*market.*) (*di merce*) to perish, to be perishable.

dépliant, *n. m.* (*pubbl.*) leaflet, folder.

deporre, *v. t.* **1** (*posare*) to put★ down, to lay★ down, to throw★ down. **2** (*specialm. un sovrano*) to depose. **3** (*licenziare*) to remove (*sb.*) from office, to dismiss, to displace. **4** (*leg.*) (*testimoniare*) to depose, to depone, to testify, to bear★ witness. // ~ **a carico di q.** (*leg.*) to witness against sb.; ~ **a discarico di q.** (*leg.*) to witness for sb.; ~ **gli attrezzi** to throw down one's tools; ~ **come teste** (*leg.*) to witness; ~ **contro q.** (*leg.*) to witness against sb.; ~ **davanti a una commissione** (*leg.*) to testify before a committee; ~ **il falso** (*leg.*) to bear false witness; to give false testimony; ~ **in favore di q.** (*leg.*) to witness for sb.

deporto, *n.* (*Borsa, fin.*) backwardation, backwardization. // **a** ~ (*Borsa, fin.*) backwardized (*attr.*).

depositante, *n. m.* e *f.* **1** (*banca, leg.*) depositor. **2** (*dog.*) (*di merci: nei magazzini doganali*) bonder. **3** (*leg.*) (*di merci, a garanzia*) bailor, bailer.

depositare, *v. t.* **1** to deposit; (*bagagli, ecc.*) to check (*USA*). **2** (*banca*) to deposit. **3** (*dog.*) (*merci, ecc.*) to deposit. **4** (*fin.*) (*denaro, valori, ecc., anche*) to lodge. **5** (*leg.*) (*a cauzione, in garanzia, a titolo di caparra*) to cover. **6** (*leg.*) (*merci, a garanzia*) to bail. **7** (*leg.*) (*un documento, ecc.*) to file. **8** (*leg.*) (*un brevetto, un marchio di fabbrica*) to register. // ~ **il bagaglio** (*trasp. ferr.*) to check the luggage; ~ **il bagaglio alla stazione** (*trasp. ferr.*) to check in; ~ **denaro in banca** (*banca*) to deposit money in the bank, to lodge money with a bank; ~ **documenti in tribunale** (*leg., anche*) to deposit documents with the Court; ~ (*denaro*) **in banca** to bank; ~ **in cauzione** (*leg.*) to deposit; ~ **qc. in garanzia** (*leg.*) to deposit st. as security; to escrow st.; ~ **in magazzino** (*merce, ecc.*) to store, to warehouse, to stock; ~ **il lodo** (*leg.*) to file the award; ~ **un marchio di fabbrica** (*leg.*) to register a trade-mark; ~ **il marchio di fabbrica di** (*un articolo, ecc.*) (*leg.*) to trade-mark, to trademark; ~ **titoli** (*fin.*) to lodge securities; ~ **titoli a garanzia** (*fin.*) to lodge stock as cover.

depositario, *a.* depositary. *n. m.* **1** (*leg.*) depositary. **2** (*leg.*) (*di merci, a garanzia*) bailee. **3** (*market.*) consignee, factor, stockist; depositary (agent). // ~ **doganale** (*dog.*) customs agent; **agente** ~ (*market.*) depositary agent.

depositato, *a.* (*leg.*) (*di brevetto, marchio di fabbrica, ecc.*) registered.

deposito, *n. m.* **1** deposit. **2** (*banca*) deposit. **3** (*dog.*) (*di merci, ecc.*) deposit. **4** (*dog.*) (*il depositare merci*) warehousing; (*nei magazzini doganali*) bonding. **5** (*fin.*) (*di denaro, ecc.: anche*) lodgment. **6** (*leg.*) (*di brevetti, marchi di fab-

brica, ecc.) registration. **7** (*org. az.*) depot, store, warehouse. **8** (*org. az.*) (*l'immagazzinaggio*) storage, warehousing. // ~ **a garanzia** (*in genere*) (*leg.*) bailment; ~ **a risparmio** (*banca*) savings deposit; **depositi a termine** (*banca*) fixed-period (*o* time) deposits; ~ **a vista** (*banca*) demand deposit, deposit at call; ~ **bagagli** (*trasp. ferr.*) cloak room, left-luggage office (*ingl.*); check-room (*USA*); ~ **bancario** bank deposit; ~ **cauzionale** (*leg.*) deposit; ~ **cauzionale per licenza di commercio** (*market.*) licence bond; ~ (*rimborsabile*) **con preavviso** (*banca*) deposit at notice; ~ **di numerario** (*banca*) deposit of cash; ~ **di titoli** (*banca, fin.*) deposit of stock; ~ **doganale** (*dog.*) bonded warehouse, entrepôt; ~ **franco** (*dog.*) bonded warehouse, warehouse; ~ **fruttifero** (*banca*) interest-bearing deposit; ~ **in cassette di sicurezza** (*banca*) safe deposit; ~ **in contanti** (*fin.*) bar depot; ~ **in conto corrente** (*banca*) deposit on current account, drawing account; ~ **in conto corrente di corrispondenza** (*fin.*) demand deposit; ~ (*di merci*) **in transito** (*trasp.*) storage in transit; **depositi interbancari** (*banca*) interbank deposits; **depositi interrati** (*org. az.*) underground premises; ~ **locomotive** (*trasp. ferr.*) engine-shed, round house; ~ **primario** (*banca*) primary deposit; **depositi rimborsabili** (*cred.*) returnable deposits; ~ **traibile** (*banca*) drawing deposit; checkable deposit (*USA*); ~ **vincolato** (*banca*) time deposit; savings account (*USA*); ~ **vincolato a scadenza determinata** (*banca*) fixed deposit; **in** ~ (*banca*) on deposit; (*market.*) on consignment, on sale or return; **denaro in** ~ money on deposit.

deposizione, *n. f.* **1** deposition. **2** (*da una carica*) removal (from office); displacement. **3** (*leg.*) (*dichiarazione solenne*) deposition. **4** (*leg.*) (*testimonianza*) testimony, evidence. // ~ **giurata** (*leg.*) deposition under oath, affidavit; **una** ~ **pertinente** (*leg.*) a relevant testimony; **chi fa una** ~ (*leg.*) deponent, deposer.

depressione, *n. f.* **1** depression. **2** (*econ.*) depression, slump.

depresso, *a.* **1** depressed. **2** (*econ.*) underdeveloped.

deprezzamento, *n. m.* **1** (*econ., fin.*) depreciation, undervaluation. **2** (*econ., fin.*) (*di monete, ecc.: anche*) debasement. **3** (*fin., rag.*) depreciation, write-off. **4** (*market.*) (*di merci, ecc.*) depreciation. **5** (*org. az.*) (*d'un macchinario, ecc.: per l'uso*) wear and tear, wear-out.

deprezzare, *v. t.* **1** (*econ., fin.*) to depreciate, to undervalue. **2** (*econ., fin.*) (*monete, ecc., anche*) to debase; to decry (*anche fig.*). **3** (*fin., rag.*) to depreciate, to write★ off. **4** (*market.*) (*merci, ecc.*) to depreciate, to cheapen.

deprezzarsi, *v. rifl.* **1** (*econ., fin.*) to depreciate, to go★ worse. **2** (*market.*) to depreciate.

deprimente, *a.* depressing.

deprimere, *v. t.* to depress. // ~ **i consumi** (*econ.*) to hold down consumption.

deputare, *v. t.* to delegate.

deputazione, *n. f.* delegation.

deragliare, *v. i.* (*trasp. ferr.*) to go★ off the rails, to run★ off the rails, to leave★ the rails.

deriva, *n. f.* **1** (*trasp. aer., trasp. mar.*) leeway. **2** (*trasp. mar.*) drift.

deroga, *n. f.* derogation. // ~ **a un contratto** (*leg.*) derogation of (*o* to) a contract; ~ **a una legge** (*leg.*) derogation of (*o* to) a law; ~ **alla legge** (*leg.*) departure from the law; **una** ~ **alla procedura ufficiale** a departure from official procedure; **deroghe quantitative** (*comm. est.*) quantitative derogations.

derogare, *v. i.* to derogate. // ~ **alle regole** to derogate (*o* to depart) from the rules.

derogatorio, *a.* (*leg.*) derogatory.

derrata, *n. f.* **1** (*market.*) commodity. **2 derrate,** *pl.* (*market.*) merchandise. // **derrate alimentari** foodstuffs, consumables; **derrate grezze** gross commodities.

descrittivo, *a.* descriptive.

descrivere, *v. t.* to describe. // ~ **dettagliatamente** (*o* **minutamente**) to detail; ~ **nei particolari** to specify; ~ **per sommi capi** to outline.

descrizione, *n. f.* description, account. // ~ **del lavoro** (*org. az.*) job description; ~ **dell'invenzione** (*in un brevetto*) (*leg.*) specification; ~ **della merce** description of the goods; ~ **delle azioni** (*fin.*) description of the shares; ~ **minuziosa** detailed description, detail; ~ **particolareggiata** specification; **su** ~ (*market.*) (*di merce venduta*) by description.

desiderare, *v. t.* to desire, to wish, to want.

desiderio, *n. m.* desire, wish.

design, *n. m.* design.

designer, *n. m.* (*pers.*) designer.

desistenza, *n. f.* **1** desistance. **2** (*leg.*) abandonment. // ~ **da un'azione** (*leg.*) abandonment of action; ~ **da una causa** (*leg.*) discontinuance from a suit.

desistere, *v. i.* to desist. // ~ **da** (*leg.*) to abandon.

destinare, *v. t.* to destine, to allocate, to appropriate, to assign, to earmark. // ~ **q. a un compito** (**a un lavoro**) (*org. az.*) to assign sb. to a task; ~ **fondi al riscatto di un'annualità** to appropriate funds for the redemption of an annuity; ~ **stanziamenti** to allocate sums (of money).

destinatario, *n. m.* **1** receiver. **2** (*d'una lettera e sim.*) addressee. **3** (*di merci*) consignee. **4** (*trasp. mar.*) (*del carico*) shipper. // ~ **d'una rimessa** (*di denaro, ecc.*) (*comm.*) remittee.

destinazione, *n. f.* **1** destination; (*assegnazione*) allocation, appropriation. **2** (*leg.*) destination. **3** (*org. az.*) (*a un compito*) assignment. // ~ **per un legato** (*leg.*) destination for a legacy; **con** ~ (*trasp. mar.*) bound for; **una nave con** ~ **Melbourne** a ship bound for Melbourne.

destituire, *v. t.* (*pers.*) to dismiss, to displace, to remove.

destituzione, *n. f.* (*pers.*) dismissal, displacement, removal.

detassare, *v. t.* (*fin.*) to untax.

detassazione, *n. f.* (*fin.*) untaxing.

detenere, *v. t.* **1** to hold★. **2** (*leg.*) to detain. // ~ **armi illegalmente** to hold arms illegally; ~ **troppa valuta d'una certa moneta** (*Borsa, fin.*) to go long in a given currency; **essere detenuto dalla polizia** (*leg.*) to be detained (in custody) by the police.

detentore, *n. m.* **1** (*comm.*) holder. **2** (*leg.*) detainer. // ~ **d'azioni privilegiate** (*fin.*) preference shareholder; ~ **di brevetto** (*leg.*) licensee; ~ **d'ipoteca su un bene altrui** (*leg.*) lienholder, lienor; ~ **d'obbligazioni** (*cred.*) loan holder; (*fin.*) debenture holder; ~ **di patente** (*leg.*) licensee; ~ **di pegno su un bene altrui** (*leg.*) lienholder, lienor; ~ **di permesso** (*leg.*) licensee; ~ **in buona fede** (*leg.*) bona fide holder.

detenuto, *n. m.* **1** (*leg.*) detainee. **2** (*leg.*) (*carcerato*) convict, prisoner.

detenzione, *n. f.* **1** (*anche leg.*) detention. **2** (*leg.*) custody, detainer, imprisonment. // ~ **d'una nave** (*trasp. mar.*) detention of a ship; ~ **illegale** (*leg.*) (*di persona o cosa*) detainer; (*di cosa dovuta ad altri*) detinue; ~ **preventiva** (*leg.*) preventive detention, commitment for trial.

deteriorabile, *a.* (*market.*) (*di merce*) perishable.

deterioramento, *n. m.* **1** deterioration. **2** (*per l'uso*) wear and tear.

deteriorarsi, *v. rifl.* (*market.*) (*di merce*) to perish, to go★ bad.

determinabile, *a.* **1** determinable. **2** (*fin.*) (*d'imponibile*) assessable.

determinare, *v. t.* **1** to determine, to state. **2** (*causare, anche*) to bring★ about. **3** (*fin.*) (*l'imponibile*) to assess. // ~ **l'ammontare dei danni** (*ass.*) to assess the amount of damages; ~ **i costi** (*rag.*) to cost; ~ **l'importo parziale d'una colonna** (*mat.*) to subtotal a column.

determinato, *a.* **1** determined, stated. **2** (*ass., fin.*) (*di danno, ecc.*) assessed.

determinazione, *n. f.* **1** determination. **2** (*ass., fin.*) (*d'un danno, dell'imponibile*) assessment. // ~ **dei costi** (*rag.*) costing; ~ **dei costi standard** (*rag.*) standard costing; ~ **del prezzo** (*Borsa, fin.*) pricing; (*econ., market.*) pricing; ~ **del reddito** (*fin.*) income determination; ~ **del valore attuale** (*d'una polizza sulla vita*) (*ass.*) valuation.

detraibile, *a.* **1** deductible, allowable. **2** (*fin.*) untaxed.

detrarre, *v. t.* to deduct, to discount, to allow, to knock off, to take★ off. // ~ **il peso dell'imballaggio** (*market.*) to deduct the weight of packing.

detrazione, *n. f.* deduction, deduct, discount, allowance, rebate. // **detrazioni ammesse nella denuncia dei redditi** (*fin.*) allowable income-tax deductions; **una** ~ **dal proprio (reddito) imponibile** (*fin.*) a deduction from one's taxable income; ~ **fiscale** (*fin.*) tax allowance; **detrazioni fiscali** (*fin.*) fiscal deductions; ~ **per spese** allowance for expenses.

dettagliante, *n. m.* e *f.* (*market.*) retailer, retail merchant, retail trader, shopkeeper.

dettagliare, *v. t.* e *i.* **1** to detail, to go★ into details. **2** (*market.*) to retail, to sell★ by retail.

dettaglio, *n. m.* **1** detail, particular. **2** (*market.*) retail. // **dettagli procedurali** (*leg.*) procedural details; **al** ~ (*market.*) by retail, retail, over the counter.

dettare, *v. t.* to dictate. // ~ **una lettera alla segretaria** to dictate a letter to one's secretary; ~ **la moda** (*market., pubbl.*) to lead the fashion.

dettatura, *n. f.* dictation.

detto, *a.* **1** said. **2** (*suddetto*) above-mentioned; above-named; above. **3** (*rag.*) ditto.

devalutazione, *n. f.* (*econ.*) devaluation, depreciation. // ~ **della moneta** (*fin.*) currency depreciation.

deviare, *v. i.* to deviate. *v. t.* (*trasp. ferr.*) (*un treno*) to shunt. // ~ **dalla rotta** (*trasp. mar.*) to sheer.

deviatore, *n. m.* (*trasp. ferr.*) shunter; switchman★ (*USA*).

deviazione, *n. f.* **1** deviation, departure, diversion. **2** (*mat., rag.*) variance. **3** (*trasp. ferr.*) (*d'un treno*) shunt. // ~ **dalla rotta** (*trasp. aer., trasp. mar.*) deviation; **deviazioni dei traffici** (*market.*) diversions of trade; ~ **d'introiti doganali** (*dog.*) deflection of customs revenue.

devoluzione, *n. f.* **1** (*anche leg.*) devolution. **2** (*assegnazione*) allocation, assignment.

devolvere, *v. t.* **1** (*un diritto, ecc.*) to devolve. **2** (*assegnare*) to assign, to allocate. // ~ **una somma in beneficienza** to allocate a sum of money for benefaction.

diafonia, *n. f.* (*comun.*) (*al telefono*) cross-talk.

diapositiva, *n. f.* (*pubbl.*) filmslide, slide. // ~ **a colori** (*pubbl.*) colour slide.

diaria, *n. f.* (*pers.*) expense account per diem; daily allowance (for expenses); subsistence allowance.

diario, *n. m.* (*attr. uff.*) diary, day-book.

dicastero, *n. m.* (*amm.*) ministry; department (*USA*).

dichiarabile, *a.* **1** declarable. **2** (*dog.*) declarable (*V.* **dichiarare**).

dichiarante, *n. m.* e *f.* (*dog., leg.*) declarant.

dichiarare, *v. t.* e *i.* **1** to declare, to state, to express, to report, to say*. **2** (*a discolpa*) to allege. **3** (*ass., leg.*) to declare. **4** (*dog.*) to declare. **5** (*leg.*) to pronounce, to rule. **6** (*leg.*) (*riconoscere*) to find*, to return. // ~ **la propria buona fede** to allege one's good faith; ~ **il carico** (*in dogana*) (*trasp. mar.*) to report the cargo; ~ **q. colpevole (innocente)** (*leg.*) (*della giuria*) to find sb. guilty (not guilty); ~ **un dividendo straordinario** (*fin.*) to declare an extra dividend; ~ (*q.*) **eletto** (*leg.*) to validate; ~ (*qc.*) **erroneamente** (*leg.*) to misrepresent; ~ **q. fallito** (*leg.*) to adjudicate sb. bankrupt; ~ **falsamente i propri redditi** (*leg.*) to misrepresent one's income; ~ **illegale** (*leg.*) to illegalize, to outlaw; ~ **illegittimo** (*leg.*) to illegitimate; ~ **un imponibile inferiore a quello reale** (*fin.*) to understate one's taxable income; ~ **incapace** (*leg.*) to incapacitate, to disqualify; ~ **merci in transito** (*dog.*) to enter goods for transit; ~ **una nave inservibile** (*trasp. mar.*) to condemn a ship; ~ **il rinvio della seduta** (*leg.*) to pronounce the meeting adjourned; ~ **sotto giuramento** (*leg.*) to state on oath, to depose, to depone; ~ **tolta la seduta** to declare a meeting closed.

dichiararsi, *v. rifl.* **1** to declare oneself; to declare. **2** (*leg.*) (*d'imputato: colpevole o innocente*) to plead. // ~ **contrario a q. (a qc.)** to declare against sb. (against st.); ~ **favorevole a q. (a qc.)** to declare for sb. (for st.); ~ **mallevadore per q.** (*leg.*) to vouch for sb.

dichiarativo, *a.* (*anche leg.*) declaratory.

dichiaratorio, *a.* (*anche leg.*) declaratory.

dichiarazione, *n. f.* **1** declaration, statement. **2** (*a discolpa*) allegation. **3** (*ass., leg.*) declaration. **4** (*dog.*) declaration. **5** (*leg.*) (*testimonianza*) testimony. // ~ **autenticata da un notaio** (*leg.*) declaration attested by a notary; **una** ~ **congiunta** a joint declaration; ~ **consolare** (*comm. est.*) consular declaration; ~ **dei redditi** (*fin.*) return of income, income-tax return; ~ **del capitano** (*della nave*) **per la dogana** (*trasp. mar.*) captain's entry; ~ **del valore delle merci** (*ass.*) declaration of the value of the goods; ~ **della difesa** (*leg.*) plea; ~ **dell'imputato** (*leg.*) plea; ~ **d'abbandono** (*della nave e/o del carico*) (*ass. mar.*) notice of abandonment; ~ **d'avvenuto pagamento del dazio** (*dog., fin.*) duty-paid entry; ~ **di bordo** (*trasp. mar.*) ship's report; ~ **di cauzione** (*dog.*) bond; **la** ~ **d'un dividendo straordinario** (*fin.*) the declaration of an extra dividend; ~ **d'entrata** (*dog.*) declaration inwards, clearance inwards, clearing inwards; ~ **d'esportazione** (*dog.*) export specification; ~ **di fallimento** (*leg.*) adjudication of (*o* in) bankruptcy; ~ **di garanzia** (*leg.*) deed of guaranty; ~ **d'una giuria** (*leg.*) presentment; ~ **d'illegalità** (*leg.*) illegalization; ~ **d'illegittimità** (*leg.*) illegitimation; ~ **d'imbarco** (*dog.*) specification; ~ **d'importazione** (*dog.*) import specification; ~ **d'ipoteca** (*leg.*) declaration of mortgage; ~ **di non luogo a procedere** (*leg.*) entering for non suit; ~ **di solvibilità** (*d'una società commerciale*) (*leg.*) declaration of solvency; ~ **di transito** (*dog.*) transit entry; ~ **d'uscita** (*dog.*) declaration outwards; ~ **doganale** (*dog.*) customs declaration, customs report, customs entry, customs bill of entry; ~ **erronea** (*leg.*) misrepresentation; ~ **falsa** (*leg.*) misrepresentation; **dichiarazioni false** (*leg.*) false pretences (*anche*); **la** ~ **generale** (*in dogana*) (*trasp. mar.*) the report of the whole cargo; ~ **giudiziale di fallimento** (*leg.*) decree in bankruptcy; ~ **giurata** (*leg.*) sworn statement, affidavit; (*ass. mar., leg.*) declaration on oath; **una** ~ **non impegnativa** a non-committal statement; ~ **orale** (*leg.*) parol; ~ **per merce schiava di dazio** (*dog.*) entry for dutiable goods; ~ **per merci esenti da dazio** (*dog.*) entry for free goods; ~ **per merci soggette a diritti doganali** (*dog.*) entry for home use, home-use entry; ~ **per il trasbordo** (*trasp. mar.*) transshipment entry; ~ **relativa alla situazione finanziaria** (*d'un'impresa in via di fallimento*) (*leg.*) statement of affairs.

dieci, *num. card.* ten. // ~ **dollari** ten dollars; dews (*slang USA*); ~ **dozzine** ten dozen; (*comm.*) small gross.

dietro, *avv.* e *prep.* **1** after, behind. **2** (*comm.*) against; on. **3** (*trasp. mar.*) aft. // ~ **pagamento d'una somma** against (*o* on) payment of a sum; ~ **ricevuta** against receipt; ~ **richiesta** on request; on application.

difendere, *v. t.* **1** to defend, to protect, to safeguard, to shelter, to ward. **2** (*leg.*) to defend. // ~ **una causa** (*leg.*) to defend a case, to plead a case; ~ **la propria reputazione** to safeguard one's reputation.

difendersi, *v. rifl.* to defend oneself; to be on the defensive. // ~ **bene** (*Borsa, fin.*) (*d'un titolo*) to hold up; ~ **dall'inflazione** to counter inflation.

difensore, *n. m.* **1** defender. **2** (*sostenitore*) advocate, supporter. **3** (*leg.*) (*avvocato difensore*) counsel for the defence; defense attorney (*USA*). // ~ **d'ufficio** (*leg.*) public defender; counsel (*o* counsellor) appointed by the Court.

difesa, *n. f.* **1** defence; defense (*USA*); protection, safeguard, shelter. **2** (*leg.*) defence. **3** (*leg.*) (*perorazione*) plea, pleading. **4** (*leg.*) (*avvocato difensore*) counsel for the defence; defense attorney (*USA*). // ~ **commerciale** commercial defence; ~ **giudiziaria** (*leg.*) brief; **difese scritte delle parti in causa** (*leg.*) pleadings.

difettare, *v. i.* to be deficient; to be lacking (*o* wanting); to lack.

difetto, *n. m.* **1** (*mancanza*) deficiency, lack, want. **2** (*imperfezione*) defect, fault, flaw, shortcoming. **3** (*anche leg.*) vice, defect. // ~ **di costruzione** constructional defect; **un** ~ **evidente** an apparent defect; **difetti formali** (*leg.*) formal defects; **essere in** ~ to default; **in** ~ **di** (*in mancanza di*) in default of.

difettoso, *a.* defective, faulty.

diffalcare, *v. t. V.* **defalcare.**

diffalco, *n. m. V.* **defalco.**

diffamare, *v. t.* (*leg.*) to defame, to slander.

diffamatore, *n. m.* (*leg.*) defamer, slanderer.

diffamatorio, *a.* (*leg.*) defamatory, slanderous.

diffamazione, *n. f.* (*leg.*) defamation, slander.

differente, *a.* different.

differenza, *n. f.* **1** difference, gap; (*discrepanza*) discrepancy, variance. **2** (*econ., rag.*) margin. **3** (*fin., rag.*) (*in meno*) deficiency. // ~ **a credito** (*rag.*) credit balance; ~ **a saldo** (*fin., rag.*) balance; ~ **di cambio** (*fin.*) difference of exchange; ~ **di cassa** (*rag.*) difference in the cash, cash difference; ~ **di prezzo** (*market.*) difference in price; ~ **fra il costo di produzione e il prezzo di vendita** (*econ., market.*) spread; ~ **fra il dare e l'avere d'un conto** (*rag.*) difference between the debit and credit of an account; ~ **fra i prezzi di due articoli simili** (*market.*) spread; ~ **fra il prezzo massimo e quello minimo** (*per un prodotto, in un dato periodo*) (*econ., market.*) spread; **differenze nei prezzi** (*market.*) price differences.

differenziazione, *n. f.* (*market.*) diversification. // ~ **del portafoglio** (*da parte d'un fondo d'investimento*) (*fin.*) gearing (of capital); leverage (*USA*).

differibile, *a.* deferrable, postponable, adjournable.

differimento, *n. m.* deferment, postponement, adjournment.

differire, *v. t.* **1** to defer, to postpone, to put★ off, to adjourn. **2** (*cred.*) (*un pagamento*) to respite. **3** (*leg.*) to stay. *v. i.* to differ, to vary, to be different (from). // ~ **i pagamenti** (*cred.*) to put off payments, to defer payments; ~ **una riunione** to postpone (*o* to put off) a meeting; (*se già in corso*) to adjourn a meeting; ~ **la scadenza d'una cambiale** (*cred.*) to extend the maturity of a bill.

differito, *a.* (*cred., fin.*) deferred.

difficile, *a.* **1** difficult. **2** (*a ottenersi*) close. **3** (*esigente*) exacting. **4** (*fin.*) (*di mercato, ecc.: per mancanza di denaro*) stringent. // ~ **a collocarsi** (*market.*) hard to sell; ~ **da accontentare** hard to please; ~ **da vendere** (*market.*) (*d'articolo, ecc.*) hard to sell, sticky; **di** ~ **accesso** difficult of access; **di** ~ **realizzo** (*di credito*) sticky; **di assai** ~ **realizzo** (*fin.*) unrealizable.

difficoltà, *n. f. inv.* **1** difficulty; (*situazione di disagio*) distress; (*male*) ill. **2** (*fin.*) (*dovuta alla mancanza di denaro*) stringency. // **difficoltà contabili** (*rag.*) bookkeeping difficulties; ~ **economica** (*econ.*) squeeze.

diffida, *n. f.* (*leg.*) warning, caveat.

diffidare, *v. t.* (*leg.*) to enjoin, to warn. *v. i.* to distrust; to mistrust; to have no faith (in st.).

diffondere, *v. t.* **1** to spread★, to diffuse, to send★ round. **2** (*notizie*) to circulate, to propagate. **3** (*comun.*) (*una notizia, per radio*) to broadcast★; (*per televisione*) to telecast★.

diffondersi, *v. rifl.* to spread★.

diffusione, *n. f.* **1** diffusion, spread. **2** (*di notizie, anche*) circulation, propagation. // ~ **guidata** (*pubbl.*) controlled circulation.

dilatamento, *n. m. V.* **dilatazione.**

dilatare, *v. t.* **1** to dilate; to swell★ (*anche fig.*). **2** (*espandere*) to expand. **3** (*econ., fin.*) (*aumentare*) to increase.

dilatarsi, *v. rifl.* **1** to dilate; to swell★ (*anche fig.*). **2** (*espandersi*) to expand. **3** (*econ., fin.*) (*aumentare*) to increase.

dilatazione, *n. f.* **1** dilatation; swelling (*anche fig.*). **2** (*espansione*) expansion. **3** (*econ.,* *fin.*) (*aumento*) increase. // **la ~ della domanda interna** (*econ.*) the expansion of home demand; **una cospicua ~ dei consumi** (*econ.*) a large increase in consumption.

dilatorio, *a.* (*leg.*) dilatory, delaying, suspensive.

dilazionare, *v. t.* **1** (*ritardare*) to delay. **2** (*posporre*) to postpone, to put★ off. **3** (*cred.*) (*il pagamento d'un debito*) to extend.

dilazionato, *a.* (*cred.*) (*d'un pagamento*) extended.

dilazione, *n. f.* **1** (*indugio*) delay. **2** (*rinvio*) postponement. **3** (*comm.*) (*ritardo*) delay. **4** (*cred.*) (*d'un pagamento*) extension, respite. // **~ di pagamento** (*cred.*) extension of payment; (*per una cambiale*) days of grace; **senza ulteriore ~** without further delay.

dimensione, *n. f.* **1** dimension, size. **2 dimensioni,** *pl.* (*trasp. mar.*) (*delle parti strutturali d'una nave*) scantling. // **dimensioni d'impresa** (*org. az.*) size of business; **dimensioni ottimali** (*econ.*) optimal size; **di dimensioni nazionali** nationwide.

dimettere, *v. t.* **1** (*licenziare*) to dismiss; to remove (from office); to unseat. **2** (*anche leg.*) to discharge.

dimettersi, *v. rifl.* (*pers.*) to resign, to retire, to step down, to vacate. // **~ da** (*una carica, e sim.*) (*amm., fin.*) to vacate.

diminuire, *v. i.* **1** to decrease, to diminish, to decline, to drop, to fall★, to lessen, to relax, to shrink★, to slacken. **2** (*di prezzi, ecc., anche*) to come★ down, to go★ down, to fall★ off, to sag. **3** (*fin., market.*) (*di prezzi, quotazioni, vendite, ecc., anche*) to recede; (*di poco, e per breve tempo*) to dip; (*per gradi*) to slip. *v. t.* to decrease, to diminish, to curtail, to cut★, to cut★ down, to lessen, to lower, to reduce. // **~ il carico d'imposta su** (*qc.*) (*fin.*) to derate; **~ di prezzo** (*market.*) to cheapen; **~ di valore** (*fin., market., anche*) to go worse, to lower in value; **~ il livello delle riserve minime** (*fin.*) to reduce the level of minimum reserves; **~ il prezzo di** (*qc.*) to cheapen; to cut.

diminuzione, *n. f.* **1** decrease, diminution, decline, curtailing, curtailment, drop, fall, lessening, lowering, reduction, relaxation, shrinkage, slackening, stepdown. **2** (*di prezzi, ecc., anche*) decline, break, cut, cutting, drop, falloff, sag. // **~ del numero delle azioni** (*d'una società*) (*fin.*) split-down; **una ~ delle entrate** (*fin., rag.*) a decrease in receipts; **una ~ delle esportazioni** (*comm. est.*) a fall in exports; **una ~ delle ore di lavoro** (*sind.*) a reduction in working hours; **una ~ di prezzi** (*market.*) a cut in prices; **~ di prezzo** (*market., anche*) markdown; **una ~ moderata** (*e spesso temporanea*) **dei prezzi** (*Borsa, fin., market.*) a dip in prices; **in ~** on the decrease.

dimissionario, *a.* (*pers.*) resigning, outgoing. *n. m.* (*pers.*) resigner, resignee.

dimissioni, *n. pl.* (*pers.*) resignation, vacation (*sing.*).

dimostrare, *v. t.* **1** to demonstrate, to establish, to prove. **2** (*anche leg.*) to witness. **3** (*pubbl.*) (*un articolo o un prodotto a un cliente potenziale*) to demonstrate. *v. i.* (*sind.*) to demonstrate. // **~ l'autenticità di qc.** (*leg.*) to prove st.

dimostratore, *n. m.* (*pers., pubbl.*) demonstrator.

dimostrazione, *n. f.* **1** demonstration, proof. **2** (*anche leg.*) witness. **3** (*market.*) (*d'un metodo, d'una procedura, ecc.*) show-how. **4** (*pubbl.*) (*d'un articolo o d'un prodotto a un cliente potenziale*) demonstration, show.

dinamica, *n. f.* **1** dynamics (*pl., col verbo al sing.*). **2** (*econ.*) (*tendenza*) tendency, trend. **3** (*econ.*) (*rialzo*) increase, rise. **4** (*org. az.*) (*processo*) process. // **~ degli investimenti** (*fin.*) investment trends; **~ dei consumi** (*market.*) consumer trends; **la ~ dei prezzi** (*econ.*) the price increase; price rises (*pl.*); **~ del lavoro** (*org. az.*) flow process.

dinamico, *a.* **1** (*anche di persona*) dynamic. **2** (*econ.*) (*fiorente, attivo*) booming.

dinaro, *n. m.* dinar.

dipartimentale, *a.* departmental.

dipartimento, *n. m.* department. // **il ~ di Stato** (*il Ministero degli Esteri in U.S.A.*) the State Department.

dipendente, *a.* **1** dependent. **2** (*leg.*) incident. *n. m.* e *f.* **1** (*pers.*) employee, subordinate. **2** (*pers.*) (*operaio*) workhand. **3 dipendenti,** *pl.* (*pers.*) personnel, staff (*collett.*).

dipendenza, *n. f.* dependence. // **essere alle dipendenze di q.** (*pers.*) to be in the employ of sb., to be on sb.'s pay-roll.

dipendere, *v. i.* to depend, to be dependent (on).

diploma, *n. m.* diploma, certificate.

diplomare, *v. t.* to grant (sb.) a diploma; to graduate (*USA*).

diplomarsi, *v. rifl.* to obtain a diploma; to graduate (*USA*).

diplomatico, *a.* diplomatic. *n. m.* diplomatist.

diplomato, *n. m.* holder of a diploma; graduate (*USA*).

dire, *v. t.* **1** to say★. **2** (*raccontare, riferire*) to tell★. 3 (*di documento e sim.*) to read★. // ~ **a q. di rivolgersi a q. altro** to refer sb. to sb. else; ~ **di no** to say no; to refuse; ~ **di sì** to say yes; to accept, to agree; ~ **la verità** to tell (*o* to speak) the truth.

direttamente, *avv.* 1 directly, direct, straight, straightaway. 2 (*trasp., anche*) through.

direttissimo, *n. m.* (*trasp. ferr.*) express.

direttiva, *n. f.* 1 directive, direction, instruction. 2 (*linea di condotta*) course (of action).

direttivo, *a.* 1 (*amm.*) managerial, managing, executive. 2 (*org. az., anche*) supervisory. *n. m.* (*amm.*) managing committee.

diretto, *a.* 1 direct, straight, straightaway, through. 2 (*leg.*) lineal. 3 (*trasp. aut.*) (*d'autobus*) non-stop. 4 (*trasp. ferr.*) (*di treno*) non-stop. *n. m.* (*trasp. ferr.*) fast train, through train. // ~ **a** (*trasp. mar.*) bound for; ~ **a un porto straniero** (*trasp. mar.*) (*di nave o passeggero*) outward-bound; ~ **all'estero** (*trasp. mar.*) outbound; ~ **in patria** (*trasp. mar.*) homeward-bound; ~ **verso il mare** (*trasp. mar.*) seaward; ~ **verso il nord** (*trasp.*) northbound; **essere ~ a** (*un porto, ecc.*) (*trasp. mar.*) to sail for; **treno ~** (*trasp. ferr.*) fast (*o* through, *o* non-stop) train.

direttore, *n. m.* 1 (*amm.*) (*d'azienda*) manager, director. 2 (*giorn.*) (*di giornale, rivista, ecc.*) editor; editor in chief (*USA*). 3 (*org. az.*) principal, superintendent, supervisor. // ~ **alle vendite di zona** (*pers.*) area sales manager; ~ **amministrativo** (*giorn.*) managing editor, secretary-treasurer; (*pers.*) administrative director, secretary; controller (*USA*); ~ **artistico** (*d'un'agenzia pubblicitaria*) (*pers.*) art director; (*di teatro*) art director; (*di giornale*) art editor; ~ **commerciale** (*pers.*) sales manager, business manager; ~ **(dei) lavori** (*pers.*) works manager; ~ **del marketing** (*pers.*) marketing director, marketing manager; ~ **del personale** (*pers.*) personnel manager, staff manager; ~ **della produzione** (*pers.*) production manager; ~ **della pubblicità** (*pers.*) advertising manager, chief of the advertising department; ~ **(delle) vendite** (*pers.*) sales manager; ~ **dell'ufficio acquisti** (*pers.*) buyer; ~ **d'azienda** (*pers.*) director; ~ **di bacino** (*pers., trasp. mar.*) dockmaster; ~ **di banca** bank manager; ~ **di filiale** (*org. az., pers.*) branch manager; ~ **di marca** (*market., org. az.*) brand manager; ~ **di prodotto** (*market., org. az.*) product manager, brand manager; ~ **di sede** (*pers.*) head-office manager; ~ **di stabilimento** (*pers.*) plant manager; ~ **di zona** (*pers.*) district manager, area manager; ~ **editoriale** (*amm., giorn.*) managing editor; ~ **generale** (*amm.*) (*specialm. in un ministero e sim.*) director general; (*giorn.*) general editor; (*pers.*) (*d'una società*) general manager, chief executive officer; president (*USA*); ~ **generale alle vendite** (*pers.*) general sales manager; **del ~** (*d'un giornale*) editorial; (*d'un'azienda*) managerial.

direttoriale, *a.* 1 (*giorn.*) editorial. 2 (*pers.*) managerial. // **ufficio ~** manager's office.

direttrice, *n. f.* (*pers.*) (*d'azienda*) manageress.

direzionale, *a.* (*pers.*) managerial, executive, directorial.

direzione, *n. f.* 1 direction, course, drift. 2 (*guida*) guidance; steering (*fig.*). 3 (*comando*) lead, leadership. 4 (*amm.*) (*l'attività direttiva*) management, direction. 5 (*amm.*) (*il corpo direttivo*) management. 6 (*giorn.*) (*di giornale, rivista, ecc.*) editorship. 7 (*org. az.*) supervision, superintendence, oversight. 8 (*org. az.*) (*d'una fabbrica*) board of management. // ~ **aziendale** (*amm.*) management; (*org. az.*) industrial management; ~ **del personale** (*org. az.*) personnel administration, personnel management; ~ **generale** (*org. az.*) general management; ~ **operativa** administration; **della ~** (*d'affari*) (*amm.*) managerial; **in ~ del vento** (*trasp. mar.*) to windward; **in ~ di** (*trasp. mar.*) (*di nave*) bound for.

dirigente, *a.* (*amm.*) managing. *n. m.* e *f.* (*pers.*) executive, officer. *n. m.* (*pers.*) manager. *n. f.* (*pers.*) manageress. // ~ **commerciale** (*pers.*) business executive; ~ **del movimento** (*trasp. ferr.*) traffic manager; ~ **del servizio di pubblicità** (*pubbl.*) direct mail coordinator; ~ **sindacale** (*sind.*) union leader, union steward.

dirigenziale, *a.* (*amm.*) managerial, executive.

dirigere, *v. t.* 1 to direct, to conduct, to govern. 2 (*guidare*) to lead★. 3 (*amm.*) to manage, to run★. 4 (*giorn.*) (*giornali, riviste, ecc.*) to edit. 5 (*org. az.*) to supervise, to superintend. 6 (*trasp. mar.*) (*una nave*) to steer. // ~ **gli affari** (*amm.*) to manage; ~ **un'azienda** (*anche*) to conduct a business; ~ **i lavori** (*org. az.*) to supervise the works, to superintend the works; ~ **male** (*un'azienda, ecc.*) (*amm.*) to mismanage, to misconduct.

dirigersi, *v. rifl.* 1 to head (for). 2 (*rivolgersi a*) to turn (to).

dirigibile, *n. m.* (*trasp. aer.*) airship.

dirigismo, *n. m.* (*econ.*) dirigisme; command directing.

dirigista, *n. m.* e *f.* (*econ.*) advocate of dirigisme. *a.* (*econ.*) *V.* **dirigistico.**

dirigistico, *a.* (*econ.*) State-controlled, planned. // ~ **un'economia dirigistica** a planned economy.

diritto[1], *a.* straight, upright, straightforward.

diritto[2], *n. m.* **1** right. **2** (*giurisprudenza*) law. **3** (*fin.*) fee, duty. **4** (*leg.*) (*ciò che spetta*) right; (*su un bene immobile*) title. **5** (*leg.*) (*ciò di cui si chiede il riconoscimento*) claim. **6** (*leg.*) (*conferito da un'autorità*) franchise, warrant. **7** **diritti,** *pl.* (*fin.*) dues, duties, charges. // ~ **accessorio** (*leg.*) incident; **un ~ acquisito** (*leg.*) a vested right; **il ~ al lavoro** (*leg., sind.*) the right to work; ~ **amministrativo** (*leg.*) administrative law; ~ **civile** (*leg.*) civil law; **i diritti civili** (*leg.*) civil rights; ~ **commerciale** (*leg.*) commercial law, mercantile law, merchant law; law merchant (*ingl.*); ~ **compensatore** (*econ.*) countervailing duty; «~ **comune**» (*leg.*) common law (*in G.B.*); ~ **comunitario** (*leg.*) Community law; **diritti consolari** (*comm. est.*) consular charges, consulage; ~ **consuetudinario** (*leg.*) consuetudinary law; **un ~ contestabile** (*leg.*) a disputable claim; ~ **costituzionale** (*leg.*) constitutional law; ~ **da far valere** (*leg.*) claim; ~ **del lavoro** (*leg.*) labour legislation; ~ **del venditore di raddoppiare** (*fin.*) seller's option to double; ~ **della concorrenza** (*comm., leg.*) competition law; ~ **dell'economia** (*leg.*) law relating to economic activities; ~ **della navigazione** (*leg.*) marine law, maritime law; Admiralty law (*in G.B.*); **il ~ delle genti** (*leg.*) the law of nations; ~ **delle società** (*leg.*) company law; corporate law (*USA*); ~ **d'affittanza** (*leg.*) tenant right; ~ **d'aggiunta** (*Borsa*) call of more; ~ **d'aggiunta doppia** (*Borsa*) call of twice more; ~ **d'aggiunta tripla** (*Borsa*) call of three times more; ~ **d'agire in giudizio** (*leg.*) right of action; ~ **(*o* diritti) d'ancoraggio** (*trasp. mar.*) anchorage, berthage, groundage, keelage, right of mooring; **diritti d'anzianità** (*pers.*) seniority rights; **diritti d'arbitrato** (*leg.*) arbitration fees; ~ **d'associazione** (*leg., sind.*) right of association; **diritti d'asta** (*destinati al banditore*) (*market.*) lot money; **diritti d'autore** (*leg.*) (*proprietà letteraria*) copyright; (*ciò che spetta all'autore*) royalties; (*su uno spettacolo; computati in percentuale del prezzo*) admission tax; **diritti di banchina** (*trasp. mar.*) pier dues, pierage, wharf dues, wharfage; quayage; ~ **di batter moneta** (*leg.*) right of coinage; **diritti d'un beneficiario** (*leg.*) beneficial interest; ~ **di blocco** (*trasp. mar.*) right of blockade; ~ **di bollo** (*fin.*) stamp duty; ~ **di brevetto** (*leg.*) patent; **diritti di brevetto** (*leg.*) (*le competenze*) royalties; **diritti di canale** (*trasp.*) canal service dues; ~ **di cappa** (*trasp. mar.*) hat money; **diritti di controstallia** (*trasp. mar.*) demurrage charges; ~ **di costituzione** (*fin.*) capital duty; **diritti di custodia** (*fin.*) custody fees; **diritti di custodia per titoli** (*banca*) charges for custody of securities; ~ **di dogana** (*dog.*) customs duty; **diritti d'entrata in porto** (*trasp. mar.*) keelage; ~ **di fabbricazione in esclusiva** (*leg.*) proprietary right of manufacture; **diritti di fanalaggio** (*trasp. mar.*) light dues, light duties; ~ **di faro** (*trasp. mar.*) beaconage; **diritti di faro** (*trasp. mar.*) dues for lighthouse, light dues, light duties; ~ **di garanzia** (*leg.*) lien; **diritti di gavitello** (*trasp. mar.*) buoy dues; ~ **di gru** (*trasp.*) cranage; **diritti d'imbarco** (*trasp. mar.*) shipping charges, shipping expenses; **diritti di licenza** (*leg.*) royalties; **diritti di navigazione** (*trasp. mar.*) navigation dues; **diritti di navigazione fluviale** (*trasp.*) river dues; ~ **d'opzione** (*fin.*) right of option, option, pre-emptive right, stock right; (*market.*) refusal; ~ **(*o* diritti) d'ormeggio** (*trasp. mar.*) keelage, moorage; ~ **di passaggio** (*leg.*) right-of-way; ~ **di passaggio perpetuo** (*leg.*) perpetual right-of-way; ~ **di pegno** (*leg.*) lien; **diritti di pilotaggio** (*trasp. mar.*) pilotage dues; ~ **di porto** (*trasp. mar.*) groundage; **diritti di porto** (*trasp. mar.*) port charges, port dues; ~ **di possesso** (*leg.*) tenure; ~ **di precedenza** (*trasp. aut.*) right-of-way; ~ **di prelazione** (*leg.*) preemption right, pre-emption; (*fin.*) (*d'azionisti: all'acquisto di nuove azioni*) pre-emptive right; ~ **di prelievo** (*fin.*) (*ammontare di valute pregiate che un Paese può acquistare dal Fondo Monetario Internazionale in cambio di propria valuta*) drawing right; **diritti di privativa industriale** (*leg.*) industrial property rights, patent rights; ~ **di proprietà** (*leg.*) property right, proprietorship; ~ **di proprietà assoluto** (*leg.*) absolute title; **diritti di proprietà riservata** (*leg.*) proprietary rights; **diritti di quarantena** (*trasp. mar.*) quarantine fees; ~ **di recesso** (*da una società, ecc.*) (*fin., leg.*) right to withdraw; ~ **di regresso** (*cred., leg.*) right of recourse; ~ **di replica** (*leg.*) repleader; ~ **di riscatto** (*leg.*) right of redemption; (*d'ipoteca*) equity of redemption; **diritti di riscossione** (*banca*) collection fees; ~ **di riservato dominio** (*leg.*) lien; ~ **di riunione** (*leg., sind.*) right of assembly; **diritti di salvataggio** (*trasp. mar.*) salvage charges; **diritti di sbarco** (*trasp. mar.*) wharf dues; ~ **di scorta** (*trasp. mar.*) right of convoy; **diritti di sfruttamento** (*d'una miniera*) (*econ., leg.*) royalties; ~ **di sosta** (*trasp.*) demurrage; ~ **di sottoscrizione** (*di titoli, ecc.*)

(*fin.*) right of application, application right; **diritti di stazza** (*trasp. mar.*) tonnage dues; **diritti di tonnellaggio** (*trasp. mar.*) tonnage dues; ~ **di traghetto** (*leg.*) ferry; ~ **di transito** (*leg.*) right-of-way; **diritti di trapasso** (*di proprietà*) (*leg.*) conveyance duty; ~ **d'ulteriore acquisto allo stesso prezzo** (*Borsa*) call of more; ~ **d'uso** (*leg.*) user; easement in gross; ~ **di vendere il doppio** (*Borsa*) put of more; ~ **di vendere il quadruplo** (*Borsa*) put of three times more; ~ **di vendere il triplo** (*Borsa*) put of twice more; ~ **di voto** (*leg.*) right of voting, voting right, vote; **diritti doganali** (*dog.*) customs charges, customs; **diritti e doveri** (*leg.*) rights and duties; **diritti erariali** (*fin.*) revenue duties; ~ **esclusivo** (*leg.*) exclusive right, sole right, exclusive title; ~ **fallimentare** (*leg.*) bankruptcy law, insolvency law; ~ **in materia di vendite** (*leg.*) law relating to sales; **un** ~ **inalienabile** (*leg.*) an untrasferable right; **diritti inalienabili** (*leg.*) inalienable rights, indefeasible rights; **un** ~ **incontestabile** (*leg.*) an absolute right; ~ **internazionale** (*leg.*) international law; ~ **interno** (*d'un singolo Paese*) (*leg.*) domestic law; ~ **marittimo** (*leg.*) maritime law, marine law, shipping law, sea law; ~ **materiale** (*leg.*) substantial right; ~ **penale** (*leg.*) penal law, criminal law; Crown law (*in G.B.*); ~ **personale** (*leg.*) personal right; **diritti politici** (*leg.*) political rights; ~ **portuale** (*trasp. mar.*) groundage; **diritti portuali** (*trasp. mar.*) harbour dues, harbour fees; ~ **positivo** (*leg.*) law proper; ~ **posto a fondamento della propria azione** (*leg.*) cause of action; ~ **privato** (*leg.*) private law, civil law; ~ **privato internazionale** (*leg.*) international private law; **diritti professionali** (*leg.*) professional rights; ~ **pubblico** (*leg.*) public law; **diritti reali** (*leg.*) real rights; ~ **romano** (*leg.*) Roman law; **diritti sanzionati** (*leg.*) sanctioned rights; ~ **societario** (*leg.*) company law; corporate law (*USA*); ~ **soggettivo** (*leg.*) interest; ~ **sostanziale** (*leg., USA*) substantive law; **diritti speciali di prelievo** (*fin.*) special drawing rights; **diritti stabiliti dalla legge** (*leg.*) legal rights; ~ **statutario** (*leg.*) statute law; **diritti strettamente legali delle parti** (*leg.*) merits; ~ **sui brevetti** (*leg.*) patent law; ~ **territoriale** (*leg.*) territorial law; **un** ~ **trasmissibile** (*leg.*) a transferable right; ~ **tributario** (*leg.*) taxation law; **col** ~ (*o* **coi diritti**) (*fin.*) (*d'un titolo*) cum rights, with rights; **di** ~ (*leg.*) by right, de jure; **ex-diritti** (*Borsa*) (*quotazione di titolo senza diritto d'opzione*) ex rights, ex new; **senza** ~ **all'estrazione** (*Borsa*) (*di titoli*) ex drawing; **senza** ~ **di voto** non-voting (*attr.*).

dirottamento, *n. m.* **1** (*fig.*) diversion. **2** (*leg., trasp. aer., trasp. mar.*) hijacking. **3** (*trasp. mar.*) (*mutamento di rotta*) change of course. // **il** ~ **della domanda** (*su altri beni*) (*econ.*) the diversion of demand.

dirottare, *v. t.* **1** (*fig.*) to divert. **2** (*econ., fin.*) to reroute. **3** (*leg., trasp. aer., trasp. mar.*) to hijack. *v. i.* (*trasp. mar.*) (*di nave*) to alter (*o* to change) one's course. // ~ **gli investimenti** (*econ., fin.*) to reroute investments.

dirottatore, *n. m.* (*leg., trasp. aer., trasp. mar.*) hijacker.

disaffezione, *n. f.* **1** disaffection, estrangement. **2** (*pers.*) alienation.

disancorare, *v. t.* (*trasp. mar.*) to unanchor.

disarmare, *v. t.* (*trasp. mar.*) (*una nave*) to lay★ up, to strip.

disarmo, *n. m.* **1** disarmament. **2** (*dog., econ.*) removal. **3** (*trasp. mar.*) (*d'una nave*) laying-up. // **il** ~ **dei dazi e dei contingenti** (*comm. est., dog.*) the removal of quotas and customs barriers; ~ **tariffario** (*comm. est., econ.*) tariff disarmament; **in** ~ (*trasp. mar.*) (*di nave*) out of commission.

disastro, *n. m.* **1** disaster; smash (*fig.*). **2** (*grave incidente*) serious accident, casualty. **3** (*trasp.*) wreck, wreckage.

disavanzo, *n. m.* **1** (*fin., rag.*) deficit, deficiency, gap. **2** (*rag.*) (*perdita*) loss. // ~ **complessivo** (*rag.*) aggregate deficit; ~ **della bilancia commerciale** (*econ.*) trade gap; ~ **di bilancio** (*fin., rag.*) budget deficit, budgetary deficit; ~ **di cassa** (*fin., rag.*) cash deficit; **un** ~ **nella bilancia dei pagamenti** (*fin.*) a deficit in the balance of payments.

discarica, *n. f.* (*trasp. mar.*) discharge, unloading.

discarico, *n. m.* **1** (*trasp. mar.*) unloading, discharge. **2** (*trasp. mar.*) (*di merce già stivata*) unstowing.

discendente, *n. m.* e *f.* **1** (*leg.*) descendant. **2 discendenti,** *pl.* (*leg.*) descendants; succession (*sing.*).

discendenza, *n. f.* **1** (*leg.*) descent. **2** (*leg.*) (*i discendenti*) issue.

discesa, *n. f.* **1** descent. **2** (*fin., market.*) (*di prezzi*) coming down, fall. **3** (*trasp. ferr.*) down grade.

disciplina, *n. f.* (*anche org. az.*) discipline.

disciplinare, *a.* disciplinary.

discolpa, *n. f.* (*leg.*) exoneration.

discolpare, *v. t.* (*leg.*) to exonerate.

discordare, *v. i.* to disagree.

discorrere, *v. i.* to talk, to speak★, to

reason.

discorso, *n. m.* **1** talk. **2** (*di tono più elevato*) speech. // ~ **d'apertura** opening speech; ~ **di chiusura** closing speech; ~ **ufficiale** address; **discorsino tenuto a un cliente potenziale** (*per indurlo all'acquisto*) (*market., pubbl.*) sales talk.

discrepanza, *n. f.* discrepancy, variance. // ~ **contabile** (*rag.*) accounts variance.

discreto, *a.* **1** (*che ha discrezione*) discreet. **2** (*abbastanza buono*) fairly good. **3** (*moderato*) moderate. **4** (*adeguato*) adequate.

discrezionale, *a.* (*anche leg.*) discretionary, discretional.

discrezione, *n. f.* discretion. // **a** ~ at discretion.

discriminare, *v. t.* to discriminate. // ~ **in favore di certi Paesi** (*comm. est.*) to discriminate in favour of certain Countries; **che discrimina** discriminating.

discriminatorio, *a.* discriminatory, discriminating.

discriminazione, *n. f.* **1** discrimination. **2** (*misura discriminatoria*) discriminatory measure. // ~ **di bandiera** (*trasp. mar.*) flag discrimination; ~ **d'ordine fiscale** (*fin.*) tax discrimination.

discussione, *n. f.* **1** discussion, debate. **2** (*deliberazione*) deliberation, conference. **3** (*disputa*) dispute, argument. **4** (*leg.*) discussion, debate. // **una** ~ **amichevole** an amicable discussion; ~ **di casi** (*pers., sind.*) case discussion; ~ **d'una causa** (*leg., anche*) pleading; ~ **guidata** (*pers.*) conference; ~ **libera** (*pers.*) conference; ~ **per ottenere miglioramenti salariali** (*sind.*) wage talk; **in** ~ under discussion; (*in contestazione*) in contestation.

discusso, *a.* (*discutibile*) debatable.

discutere, *v. t.* e *i.* **1** to discuss, to debate, to argue, to dispute. **2** (*deliberare*) to deliberate. **3** (*ponderare*) to weigh, to pro-and-con. // ~ **una causa** (*leg.*) to debate a suit; (*da parte del giudice*) to hear a case.

discutibile, *a.* debatable, disputable, doubtful.

disdetta, *n. f.* **1** (*leg.*) notice to quit, notice. **2** (*market.*) (*annullamento*) cancellation.

disdire, *v. t.* **1** (*annullare*) to cancel, to call off. **2** (*ritrattare*) to retract.

diseconomia, *n. f.* (*econ.*) diseconomy.

disegnare, *v. t.* **1** to draw★. **2** (*progettare*) to plan, to draft, to scheme. **3** (*market., pubbl.*) to design; to style (*USA*). // ~ **un nuovo prodotto** (*pubbl.*) to style a new product.

disegnatore, *n. m.* **1** (*pers.*) draftsman★. **2** (*pubbl.*) (*progettista*) designer; stylist (*USA*). // ~ **industriale** (*pers., pubbl.*) industrial designer, designer; ~ **pubblicitario** (*pubbl.*) commercial artist; ~ **tecnico** (*pers.*) draftsman.

disegno, *n. m.* **1** drawing. **2** (*progetto*) plan, draft, scheme. **3** (*market.*) (*di stoffa, ecc.*) pattern. **4** (*market., pubbl.*) (*progettazione*) design. **5** (*org. az.*) (*progettazione*) design. **6** (*pubbl.*) drawing. // **disegni animati** (*pubbl.*) animated cartoons; ~ **di legge** (*leg.*) bill; **disegni di legge per stanziamenti in bilancio** (*amm., fin.*) appropriation bills; ~ **industriale** (*org. az., pubbl.*) industrial design, design; ~ **tecnico** (*pubbl.*) mechanical drawing.

diseredare, *v. t.* (*leg.*) to disinherit, to exheredate.

diseredazione, *n. f.* (*leg.*) disinheritance, exheredation.

disgrazia, *n. f.* (*leg.*) (*morte accidentale*) misadventure.

disguido, *n. m.* (*comun.*) (*di corrispondenza*) miscarriage.

disimballare, *v. t.* to unpack.

disimpegnare, *v. t.* **1** to get★ (st.) out of pawn, to take★ (st.) out of pledge. **2** (*liberare da un impiego*) to disengage, to free (sb.) from an engagement. **3** (*adempiere*) to carry out, to fulfil, to perform. // ~ **un compito (un incarico)** to carry out a duty; to perform a task.

disimpegno, *n. m.* **1** (*di cosa data in pegno*) redemption. **2** (*da un impegno*) disengagement. **3** (*adempimento*) fulfilment, performance. **4** (*econ.*) (*d'uno Stato, nelle scelte politico-economiche*) non-alignment.

disincagliare, *v. t.* (*trasp. mar.*) to get★ afloat.

disincagliarsi, *v. rifl.* (*trasp. mar.*) to get★ afloat.

disincentivare, *v. t.* (*econ.*) to discourage.

disincentivo, *n. m.* (*econ.*) disincentive.

disinflazionare, *v. t.* (*econ.*) to disinflate.

disinflazione, *n. f.* (*econ.*) disinflation.

disinflazionistico, *a.* (*econ.*) disinflationary.

disinteressato, *a.* **1** disinterested. **2** (*econ.*) non-profit (*attr.*).

disinvestimento, *n. m.* (*econ.*) disinvestment, negative investment.

disinvestire, *v. t.* (*econ.*) to disinvest.

disistivaggio, *n. m.* (*trasp. mar.*) unstowing.

disistivare, *v. t.* (*trasp. mar.*) to unstow.

dislocamento, *n. m.* (*trasp. mar.*) displacement. // ~ **a pieno carico** (*trasp. mar.*) load displacement; ~ (*di nave*) **a vuoto** (*trasp. mar.*)

light displacement.

dislocare, *v. t.* (*trasp. mar.*) to displace.

disoccupato, *a.* (*pers., sind.*) unemployed, jobless, workless; out of work; at liberty (*slang USA*). *n. m.* **1** (*pers., sind.*) unemployed person; forgotten man* (*fam.*); gentleman* at large, inspector of pavements (*slang USA*). **2 i disoccupati,** *pl.* (*sind.*) the unemployed. // **essere ~** to be out of work, to be out of job.

disoccupazione, *n. f.* (*econ., pers., sind.*) unemployment. // **~ ciclica** (*econ.*) cyclical unemployment; **~ cronica** (*econ.*) chronic unemployment; **~ forzata** (*econ., sind.*) involuntary unemployment; **~ mascherata** (*econ., sind.*) disguised unemployment; **~ occulta** (*econ., sind.*) hidden unemployment; **~ stagionale** (*econ., sind.*) season unemployment, seasonal unemployment; **~ strutturale** (*econ., sind.*) structural unemployment; **~ tecnologica** (*econ., org. az.*) technological unemployment.

disonestà, *n. f.* dishonesty, crookedness.

disonesto, *a.* **1** dishonest, crooked, unfair, shady, sharp. **2** (*leg.*) (*di persona*) malfeasant.

disonorare, *v. t.* (*anche comm.*) to dishonour.

disonore, *n. m.* dishonour.

disordine, *n. m.* **1** disorder. **2** (*dissesto, malanno*) disturbance, trouble, ill. **3** (*tumulto*) disorder, riot, uprising.

disorganizzare, *v. t.* to disorganize.

disorganizzazione, *n. f.* disorganization.

disormeggiare, *v. t.* (*trasp. mar.*) to unmoor.

disormeggio, *n. m.* (*trasp. mar.*) unmooring.

«dispacciamento», *n. m.* (*org. az.*) dispatching.

dispaccio, *n. m.* (*comun.*) dispatch, despatch, message.

dispari, *a.* (*mat.*) odd, uneven.

disparità, *n. f.* disparity, inequality. // **~ di grado (di posizione, di trattamento, ecc.)** disparity of rank (of position, of treatment, etc.).

dispendioso, *a.* expensive, costly, dear. // **l'esser ~** dearness, expensiveness; **non ~** unexpensive, cheap.

dispensa, *n. f.* **1** (*esenzione, esonero*) exemption, exoneration, dispensation. **2** (*giorn.*) instalment.

dispensare, *v. t.* (*esimere, esonerare*) to dispense, to exempt, to exonerate, to excuse. // **~ q. da un obbligo** to dispense sb. from an obligation.

dispersione, *n. f.* **1** dispersion. **2** (*trasp. mar.*) leakage.

dispiacere, *v. i. impers.* to be sorry, to regret.

disponibile, *a.* **1** disposable, available, on hand. **2** (*entro breve tempo*) forthcoming. **3** (*di riserva, in serbo*) spare. **4** (*disposto, pronto, aperto*) ready, open. **5** (*fin., market.*) obtainable. **6** (*pers.*) for (*o* on) hire. // **non ~** unavailable.

disponibilità, *n. f. inv.* **1** availability. **2 disponibilità,** *pl.* (*rag.*) available assets, current assets, available funds, ready assets; funds. // **la ~ di capitali** (*fin.*) the availability of capital, the money supply; **~ in cassa** (*rag.*) cash in hand; **disponibilità liquide** (*rag.*) liquid assets; **insieme delle disponibilità finanziarie utilizzabili** (*in un'azienda*) (*org. az.*) cash flow.

disporre, *v. t.* **1** (*sistemare, collocare*) to arrange, to place, to dispose. **2** (*preparare*) to prepare; to make* arrangements for. **3** (*comandare, decidere, ordinare*) to command, to order, to decide. **4** (*leg.*) to lay* down, to provide. **5** (*market.*) (*mettere in mostra*) to display, to set* out for display. *v. i.* **1** to dispose (of). **2** (*avere a disposizione*) to have at one's disposal; to have. **3** (*market.*) (*di merce*) to have in stock; to have. **4** (*tur.*) (*d'un albergo*) to have. // **~ per testamento** (*leg.*) to dispose by will; **di cui si può ~ (liberamente)** disposable.

disposizione, *n. f.* **1** disposal. **2** (*collocamento*) disposition, placing, arrangement. **3** (*sistemazione*) lay, layout. **4** (*ordine, istruzione*) direction, instruction, order, provision. **5** (*inclinazione, tendenza*) disposition, bent, turn. **6** (*leg.*) disposition, provision. **7 disposizioni,** *pl.* arrangements. // **disposizioni consolari** consular regulations; **la ~ dei locali d'un ufficio moderno** the layout of a modern office; **~ di legge** (*leg.*) law provision; **disposizioni rigide** (*leg.*) stringent laws (*o* regulations); **~ testamentaria** (*leg.*) clause of a will; **le disposizioni vigenti** (*leg.*) the regulations in force; **a ~ di** at the disposal of; (*market.*) (*di merce*) on hand.

disposto, *a.* **1** (*pronto*) prepared, ready, willing. **2** (*incline*) inclined. *n. m.* (*leg.*) provision, provisions. // **essere ~ a prendere in considerazione un'offerta** to be open to an offer.

disprezzo, *n. m.* contempt. // **«~ della Corte»** (*leg.*) contempt of Court.

dissenso, *n. m.* **1** disagreement, discrepancy. **2** (*anche leg.*) dissent. // **~ delle parti** dissent of the parties.

dissentire, *v. i.* to dissent (from); to disagree (with).

dissequestrare, *v. t.* (*leg.*) to dissequester, to release from seizure.

dissequestro, *n. m.* (*leg.*) dissequester, dissequestration; release from seizure.

disservizio, *n. m.* (*org. az.*) disservice.

dissestare, *v. t.* (*econ., fin.*) to ruin; to bring★ about the failure of.

dissestato, *a.* **1** (*econ., fin.*) ruined; full of debts. **2** (*econ., fin.*) (*insolvente*) insolvent.

dissesto, *n. m.* **1** (*econ., fin.*) failure, ruin. **2** (*leg.*) (*fallimento*) bankruptcy.

dissoluzione, *n. f.* (*leg.*) dissolution. // **la ~ d'una società di persone** the dissolution of a partnership.

dissolvere, *v. t.* (*anche leg.*) to dissolve.

distante, *a.* distant, remote.

distanza, *n. f.* distance. // **~** (*percorsa*) **in miglia** (*trasp.*) mileage, milage; **~ percorsa** (*da un carico*) (*trasp.*) haul; **~ percorsa a volo** (*trasp. aer.*) fly.

distensione, *n. f.* **1** distension. **2** (*fig.*) relaxation. **3** (*politica*) détente. **4** (*sind.*) lessening of strain.

distinguere, *v. t.* **1** to distinguish. **2** (*discriminare*) to discriminate. **3** (*separare*) to separate, to sever.

distinta, *n. f.* **1** list, note, schedule. **2** (*banca*) slip. **3** (*cred.*) note. // **la ~ (degli) effetti all'incasso** (*banca*) the list of bills for collection; **la ~ (degli) effetti allo sconto** (*banca*) the list of bills for discount; **la ~ dei materiali** (*org. az.*) the specification of materials; **la ~ dei prezzi** (*market.*) the price-list; **~ della merce** (*trasp.*) packing list; **~ delle operazioni** (*org. az.*) operation list; **~ d'acquisto** (*Borsa*) bought contract; (*market.*) bought note; **~ di carico** (*trasp. ferr.*) consignment note; **~ di compravendita** (*market.*) contract note; **~ di senseria** broker's note; **~ di vendita** (*Borsa*) sale contract; (*market.*) sales note; **~ di versamento** (*banca*) credit slip; paying-in slip (*ingl.*); deposit slip (*USA*); « **~ effetti all'incasso** » (*banca, rag.*) « notes receivable »; « **~ effetti passivi** » (*banca, rag.*) « notes payable ».

distintamente, *avv.* **1** distinctly. **2** severally.

distinto, *a.* **1** (*dignitoso, elegante*) distinguished. **2** (*netto, separato*) distinct, separate, several.

distinzione, *n. f.* **1** distinction. **2** (*discriminazione*) discrimination. **3** (*separazione*) separation.

distivare, *v. t.* (*trasp. mar.*) to unstow.

distorcere, *v. t.* to distort, to strain. // **~ la verità** (*leg.*) to strain the truth.

distorsione, *n. f.* distortion. // **distorsioni della concorrenza** (*market.*) distortions of competition.

distrarre, *v. t.* **1** to distract. **2** (*divertire*) to amuse, to entertain. **3** (*leg.*) (*denaro altrui*) to misapply.

distrazione, *n. f.* **1** absent-mindedness. **2** (*divertimento*) distraction, amusement, entertainment. **3** (*leg.*) (*di denaro altrui*) misapplication. // **~ dolosa** (*di fondi, ecc.*) (*leg.*) fraudulent conversion.

distretto, *n. m.* **1** district, province. **2** (*suddivisione di contea*) district (*in G.B.*). **3** (*market.*) territory. // **~ postale** (*comun.*) postal delivery zone, postal zone, postal area.

distribuibile, *a.* **1** distributable. **2** (*ripartibile*) apportionable.

distribuire, *v. t.* **1** to distribute. **2** (*diffondere*) to spread★. **3** (*consegnare*) to deliver. **4** (*dividere*) to divide. **5** (*equamente*) to share (out), to apportion, to portion out. **6** (*fin.*) (*assegnare*) to allot, to allocate. // **~ la corrispondenza** (*comun.*) to deliver letters; **~ dividendi** (*fin.*) to distribute dividends; to divvy up (*slang USA*); **~ nel tempo** to spread over a period of time; to stagger; **~ proporzionalmente** to prorate; **~ una somma di denaro a varie persone** to apportion a sum of money among several persons.

distribuito, *a.* **1** distributed. **2** (*nel tempo*) spread (*V.* **distribuire**). // **non ~** undistributed.

distributivo, *a.* distributive.

distributore, *n. m.* (*market.*) distributor. // **~ automatico** (*d'articoli*) (*market.*) vending machine, automatic vendor, vendor, vender; **~ automatico di moneta** (*quando viene inserita una tessera d'identità*) cash dispenser; cashomat (*USA*); **~ di benzina** (*trasp. aut.*) petrol pump; gas station, filling station (*USA*).

distribuzione, *n. f.* **1** distribution. **2** (*consegna*) delivery. **3** (*ripartizione*) apportionment. **4** (*assegnazione*) allotment, allocation. **5** (*econ.*) (*del reddito, della ricchezza, ecc.*) distribution. **6** (*market.*) (*delle merci dal produttore al consumatore*) distribution, marketing. **7** (*market.*) (*le attività terziarie*) the distributive trades (*pl.*). // **la ~ dei beni** (*econ.*) the distribution of goods; **~ dei compiti** (*org. az.*) task setting; **~ dei costi** (*rag.*) cost allocation; **la ~ dei dividendi** (*fin.*) the apportionment of dividends; **~ del reddito** (*econ.*) distribution of income, income distribution; **~ delle risorse** (*econ.*) resource allocation; **~ di dividendi in azioni** (*della società stessa*) (*fin.*) stock dividend; **~** (*delle merci*) **in grandissime quantità** (*econ.*) mass distribution; **~ porta a porta** (*market.*) door-to-door distribution.

disutile, *a.* **1** useless. **2** (*di persona*) unhelpful.

disutilità, *n. f.* **1** uselessness. **2** (*econ.*) disutility.

ditta, *n. f.* business, concern, firm, house, trade. // **~ che commercia** (*col sistema delle ordinazioni*) **per corrispondenza** (*market.*) mail-order business, mail-order firm, mail-order house; **~ di pubblicità** (*pubbl.*) direct mail house; **ditte espositrici** (*market.*) exhibitors; **una ~ familiare** a family business; **ditte in concorrenza** competitive firms, competing firms; **~ individuale** (*org. az.*) one-man business; **una ~ solida** a solid firm, a substantial firm; **Spett. ~** (*nella corrispondenza commerciale*) (*nell'indirizzo*) Messrs; (*nell'introduzione*) Dear Sirs.

dittafono, *n. m.* (*attr. uff.*) Dictaphone (*marchio*); dictating equipment.

divario, *n. m.* difference, gap. // **~ deflazionistico** (*econ.*) deflationary gap; **~ inflazionistico** (*econ.*) inflationary gap; **divari nei prezzi** (*market.*) price differences; **~ tecnologico** (*econ., org. az.*) technological gap.

divenire, *v. i. V.* **diventare.**

diventare, *v. i.* **1** to become★, to get★. **2** (*per gradi*) to grow★, to develop. **3** (*all'improvviso*) to turn. // **~ antiquato** (*market.*) to outmode; **~ avvocato** (*leg.*) to go to the bar; **~ disponibile** to offer (*ingl.*); **~ fermo** to steady (up); **~ fruttifero** (*fin.*) to come into value; **~ insufficiente rispetto a** (*qc.*) to fall short of (st.); **~ invalido** to invalid; **~ maggiorenne** (*leg.*) to come of age; **~ migliore** to better, to improve; **~ moroso** (*cred.*) to get into arrears; **~ multinazionale** (*fin.*) (*di società*) to go multinational; **~ obsoleto** (*market.*) to outmode; **~ oggetto di scambio** (*market.*) (*d'articolo*) to vend; **~ più caro** (*market.*) to get dearer; **~ più costoso** (*market.*) to get dearer; **~ pubblica** (*fin.*) (*di società*) to go public.

divergenza, *n. f.* **1** divergence, divergency. **2** (*pers., sind.*) (*vertenza*) dispute. // **~ d'opinioni** difference of opinion.

diversi, *a. pl.* sundry. *n. pl.* (*rag.*) sundries. // «**creditori ~**» (*rag.*) «sundry creditors».

diversificare, *v. t.* to diversify, to vary.

diversificarsi, *v. rifl.* to vary.

diversificazione, *n. f.* (*anche econ.*) diversification. // **la ~ degli scambi commerciali** (*comm. est.*) the diversification of trade; **~ dei prodotti** (*org. az.*) diversification of products; **~ del lavoro** (*org. az.*) job enlargement; **~ produttiva** (*org. az.*) product diversification.

diversione, *n. f.* diversion. // **~ dei traffici** (*econ.*) deflection of trade.

diversità, *n. f.* difference, discrepancy.

diverso, *a.* different. // **essere ~ (da)** to differ (from).

dividendo, *n. m.* **1** (*fin., rag.*) dividend; divvy, div, cut (*slang USA*). **2** (*mat.*) dividend. // **dividendi accumulati** (*fin.*) accrued dividends; **~ capitale** (*in azioni*) (*fin.*) stock dividend; **~ cumulativo** (*fin.*) cumulative dividend; **~ d'avaria** (*ass. mar., trasp. mar.*) average payment; **~ di liquidazione** (*fin.*) liquidating dividend; **~ extra** (*agli azionisti*) (*fin.*) bonus; **dividendi fittizi** (*fin., rag.*) sham dividends; **dividendi in acconto** (*fin.*) interim dividends; **~ in beni** (*fin.*) property dividend; **~ non cumulativo** (*fin.*) non-cumulative dividend; **dividendi non distribuiti** (*fin.*) unappropriated profits; **un ~ prescritto** (*fin.*) an unclaimed dividend; **dividendi provvisori** (*fin.*) interim dividends; **dividendi reinvestiti** (*fin.*) accumulative dividends; **~ semestrale** (*fin.*) half-yearly (*o* half year's) dividend; **col ~** (*Borsa, fin.*) (*di titolo*) with dividend, «cum» dividend, with coupon, «cum» coupon; **senza dividendi** (*Borsa, fin.*) (*di titolo*) ex dividend.

dividere, *v. t.* **1** to divide, to part, to portion (out), to split★, to split★ up, to split★ off. **2** (*in parti uguali*) to share. **3** (*separare*) to separate, to sever. // **~ una comproprietà** (*leg.*) to divide a joint property; **~** (*terreni*) **in lotti** (*econ.*) to lot; **~** (*titoli*) **in pacchetti** (*fin.*) to lot; **~ in paragrafi** to paragraph; **~ in parti** to partition; **~ in parti eque** to proportion; **~** (*merci*) **in partite** (*market.*) to lot; **~ merci in partite** (*market.*) to lot out goods in parcels; **~ per metà** to halve; **~ le spese** to go halves (*fam.*).

dividersi, *v. rifl.* **1** to divide, to be divided. **2** (*separarsi*) to part (from); to part company (with).

divieto, *n. m.* **1** prohibition; embargo (*fig.*). **2** (*leg.*) prohibition, interdiction, ban. // «**~ d'accesso**» (*trasp. aut.*) «no entry»; «**~ d'affissione**» «post no bills!», «stick no bills!»; **~ d'importazione** (*econ.*) import prohibition; embargo; «**~ di parcheggio**» (*trasp. aut.*) «no parking»; **~ di pubblicità** (*leg.*) ban on prospecting for customers; «**~ di sosta**» (*trasp. aut.*) «no waiting»; «**~ di transito**» (*trasp. aut.*) «no thoroughfare».

divisa, *n. f.* (*fin.*) currency. // **~ estera** (*fin.*) foreign currency.

divisibile, *a.* divisible, dividable.

divisibilità, *n. f.* divisibility.

divisione, *n. f.* **1** division, split, partition. **2** (*in parti uguali*) sharing-out. **3** (*sezione*) section. **4** (*separazione*) separation. **5** (*amm.*) division (*in Italia e in U.S.A.*). **6** (*leg.*) (*di beni, ecc.*) partition. **7** (*mat.*) division. // **la ~ dei poteri** (*amm.*)

the division of powers; (*leg.*) the separation of powers; **la ~ del lavoro** (*org. az.*) the division of labour, the division of work; **~ patrimoniale** (*leg.*) partition.

diviso, *a.* 1 divided, split. 2 (*separato*) separate. // **~ in reparti (sezioni, uffici, ecc.)** departmental.

divisore, *n. m.* (*mat.*) divisor, denominator, measure.

«dock», *n. m.* (*trasp. mar.*) dock.

documentare, *v. t.* 1 to document. 2 (*leg.*) to prove by documents. // **~ una cambiale** (*cred.*) to document a bill of exchange.

documentario, *a.* documentary. *n. m.* (*film.*) documentary. // **credito ~** (*cred.*) documentary credit.

documentarsi, *v. rifl.* to gather documents (on st.).

documentato, *a.* documentary.

documentazione, *n. f.* 1 documentation. 2 (*insieme di documenti*) record; documents (*pl.*). 3 (*leg.*) documentary evidence.

documento, *n. m.* 1 document, paper, record. 2 **documenti,** *pl.* (*leg.*) papers, documents. // **~ che descrive i dettagli d'una nuova emissione** (*di titoli*) (*fin.*) prospectus; registration statement (*USA*); **~ comprovante un diritto di proprietà** (*leg.*) title-deed, document of title; **documenti contro accettazione** (*market.*) documents against acceptance; **documenti contro pagamento** (*market.*) documents against payment; **documenti di bordo** (*trasp. mar.*) ship's papers; **~ di concessione** (*governativa o reale*) charter; **documenti di libera pratica** (*dog.*) clearance papers; **documenti di sdoganamento** (*dog.*) clearance papers; **documenti di spedizione** (*trasp. mar.*) shipping documents, shipping papers, shipper's papers; **documenti di Stato** State papers; **documenti di valore** documents of value; **~ doganale** (*dog.*) bill; **~ doganale richiesto a fini statistici** (*dog.*) customs specification; **~ esibito** (*leg.*) exhibit; **~ falso** (*leg.*) forged document, forgery; **~ formale** (*leg.*) instrument; **~ giustificativo** (*leg., pers.*) voucher; **documenti giustificativi** (*leg.*) supporting documents; **un ~ negoziabile** (*cred.*) a negotiable document; **documenti notarili** (*leg.*) notarial documents; **~ olografo** (*leg.*) holograph; **~ originale** original document; (*elab. elettr.*) source document; (*leg.*) script; **~ prodotto** (*leg.*) exhibit; **documenti rappresentativi** (*delle merci*) (*leg.*) documents of title; **un ~ recante data e bollo** a dated and stamped document; **~ scritto** written document; (*anche leg.*) writing.

dogana, *n. f.* 1 (*dog.*) customs. 2 (*dog.*) (*l'edificio*) custom-house. 3 (*dog., fin.*) (*dazio doganale*) customs duty; customs, duty.

doganale, *a.* (*dog.*) customs; custom (*attr.*). // **unione ~** (*comm. est.*) customs union.

doganiere, *n. m.* 1 (*dog.*) customs officer; surveyor (*USA*). 2 (*trasp. mar.*) (*che sale a bordo*) tidewaiter.

dollaro, *n. m.* 1 dollar; berry, bob, boffo, bone, buck, case note, check, clacker, clam, dib (*slang USA*). 2 **dollari,** *pl.* greenbacks (*fam., USA*). // **~ contabile** (*Borsa, ingl.*) dollar of account; **dollari costanti** (*econ., fin.*) (*in valuta reale, non inflazionata*) constant dollars; **~ d'argento** silver dollar.

dolo, *n. m.* 1 (*leg.*) malice, wilfulness. 2 (*leg.*) (*frode, inganno*) fraud, deceit.

dolosità, *n. f. V.* **dolo,** *def. 1.*

doloso, *a.* 1 (*leg.*) malicious, wilful. 2 (*leg.*) fraudolent, deceitful.

domanda, *n. f.* 1 (*orale, o d'esame*) question. 2 (*richiesta*) request; (*formale*) demand; (*di riconoscimento d'un diritto*) claim; (*burocratica*) requisition. 3 (*scritta*) application. 4 (*econ.*) demand. 5 (*econ., market.*) market. 6 (*leg.*) (*di riconoscimento d'un diritto*) claim. // **~ complementare** (*econ.*) complementary demand, joint demand; **~ complessiva** (*econ.*) aggregate demand; **~ concorrenziale** (*econ.*) competitive demand; **~ derivata** (*econ.*) derived demand; **una ~ d'assunzione** (*pers.*) an application for a situation; **domande di concorso (di contributo)** (*fin.*) applications for aid; **~ di danni** (*leg.*) claim for damages; **una ~ d'impiego** (*pers.*) an application for a situation, an application for employment; **«domande d'impiego»** (*giorn., pubbl.*) «situations wanted»; **~ d'indennizzo** claim for indemnity, claim; **domande di lavoro non soddisfatte** (*pers.*) unsatisfied applications for jobs; **una ~ di mutuo** (*cred.*) a request for a loan; **~ d'un nuovo prodotto** (*market.*) new-product demand; **domande di rimborso** applications for reimbursement; **~ di sgravio** (*fin.*) claim for discharge, claim for relief; **una ~ di sgravio fiscale** (*fin.*) an application for tax discharge; **~ e offerta** (*econ.*) demand and supply; **~ estera** (*econ.*) foreign demand; **~ forte e insistente** (*da parte di risparmiatori, creditori, clienti*) (*banca, fin., market.*) run; **~ globale** (*di capitali o beni di consumo, su un dato mercato*) (*econ.*) aggregate demand, overall demand; **~ in contraddittorio** (*leg.*) cross-question; **una ~ insoddisfatta** (*econ.*) an unsatisfied demand; **~ interna** (*econ.*) domestic demand; **~ potenziale** (*econ.*) potential demand; **~ pressante** (*econ.*) pressing demand; **~ reciproca** (*di* *prodotti: fra due persone o due comunità*) (*econ.*) reciprocal demand; ~ **riconvenzionale** (*leg.*) counter-claim, counterclaim, cross claim, cross action, counter-charge, set-off; ~ **tendenziosa** (*leg.*) leading question; **a** ~ (*market.*) on application, on request.

domandare, *v. t.* **1** (*per sapere*) to ask; to inquire; (*più formale*) to demand. **2** (*per ottenere*) to ask for. **3** (*richiedere*) to request, to require. // ~ **qc. a q.** to ask st. of sb.; ~ **il nome di q.** to inquire sb.'s name; ~ **notizie di q.** to ask (*o* to inquire) after sb.

domani, *avv.* tomorrow. // ~ **a otto** tomorrow week; ~ **l'altro** the day after tomorrow.

domenica, *n. f.* Sunday.

domestico, *a.* domestic; home (*attr.*).

domiciliare[1], *a.* domiciliary.

domiciliare[2], *v. t.* (*cred.*) to domicile. // ~ **una cambiale** (*cred.*) to domicile a bill.

domiciliarsi, *v. rifl.* to take★ up one's domicile (*o* residence); to locate.

domicilio, *n. m.* **1** domicile, residence. **2** (*leg.*) domicile. // ~ **del convenuto** (*leg.*) defendant's domicile; ~ **dell'attore** (*leg.*) plaintiff's domicile; ~ **fiscale** (*leg.*) residence; ~ **legale** (*leg.*) legal residence; (*d'una ditta*) registered office; **a** ~ (*market.*) house-to-house; **servizio a** ~ house-to-house service.

donante, *n. m.* e *f.* (*leg.*) donor.

donare, *v. t.* **1** to present, to give★. **2** (*leg.*) to donate.

donatario, *n. m.* (*leg.*) donee, volunteer.

donatore, *n. m.* **1** giver. **2** (*leg.*) donor.

donazione, *n. f.* (*leg.*) donation, gift. // ~ **fatta in punto di morte** (*leg.*) gift causa mortis; ~ **testamentaria** (*leg.*) testamentary donation.

donna, *n. f.* woman★. // ~ **d'affari** businesswoman.

dono, *n. m.* **1** present, presentation, gift. **2** (*mancia*) box. **3** (*fig.*) asset, boon. **4** (*leg.*) donation. **5** (*leg.*) (*bustarella*) bribe.

dopoborsa, *n. m. inv.* (*Borsa*) after hours; street market. // **prezzo del** ~ (*fin.*) price after hours.

doppiaggio, *n. m.* (*pubbl.*) dubbing.

doppiare, *v. t.* **1** (*pubbl.*) to dub. **2** (*trasp. mar.*) (*un promontorio e sim.*) to round.

doppio, *a.* **1** double, duplicate. **2** (*in due stadi*) two-tier. *n. m.* double; twice as much (*sing.*); twice as many (*pl.*). // ~ **binario** (*trasp. ferr.*) double track; ~ **mercato valutario** (*econ., fin.*) two-tier market; ~ **nolo** (*trasp. mar.*) double freight; « ~ **privilegio** » (*Borsa*) straddle; **un** ~ **regime dei cambi** (*econ., fin.*) a split exchange system, a two-tier exchange system; **doppia registrazione** (*rag.*) amount entered twice.

dorso, *n. m.* (*di documento e sim.*) back.

dosare, *v. t.* (*anche econ.*) to dose.

dose, *n. f.* (*anche econ.*) dose.

«dossier», *n. m.* (*leg.*) dossier.

dotare, *v. t.* **1** to endow. **2** (*attrezzare*) to equip.

dotato, *a.* **1** endowed. **2** (*attrezzato*) equipped. // ~ **dei requisiti richiesti** (*leg., pers.*) qualified.

dotazione, *n. f.* **1** endowment. **2** (*attrezzatura*) equipment. // ~ **d'armamento delle navi da carico** (*trasp. mar.*) equipment of cargo ships; **dotazioni di bordo** (*trasp. mar.*) stores; ~ **di cassa** (*fin., rag.*) cash supply.

dote, *n. f.* **1** endowment, asset. **2** (*leg.*) dowry.

dottrina, *n. f.* doctrine, theory. // ~ **del «laissez-faire»** (*econ.*) laissez-faireism.

dovere[1], *n. m.* **1** duty. **2** (*obbligo*) obligation. **3** (*compito*) charge, task. **4** (*pers.*) office. // **doveri abituali** routine duties; **doveri del direttore** managerial (*o* manager's) duties; managership.

dovere[2], *v. t.* **1** to have to, to be to; must (*al presente*); should, ought to (*al condizionale*). **2** (*essere debitore*) to owe. // ~ **arrivare** (*trasp.*) to be due; ~ **una somma di denaro a q.** to owe sb. a sum of money; **una cosa che si deve conoscere** (*o* **fare**) a must (*fam.*).

dovuto, *a.* **1** due. **2** (*cred.*) owing, due. **3** (*leg.*) due. *n. m.* (*cred.*) one's due; amount due. // **non** ~ (*cred.*) unduc; **più del** ~ (*cred.*) more than the amount due, more than is (*o* was) due (*o* worth).

dozzina, *n. f.* dozen. // **a dozzine** by the dozen.

dozzinale, *a.* second-rate, cheap; ten-cent (*fam., USA*). // **alquanto** ~ cheapish.

dramma, *n. f.* (*misura inglese di peso corrispondente a 1,7718 grammi*) dram.

«drive-in», *n. m.* (*market.*) (*sistema di vendita che consente l'accesso diretto al negozio da parte di clienti in automobile, senza che le operazioni d'acquisto rendano necessario abbandonare il posto di guida*) drive-in.

due, *num. card.* two. // **un** ~ **-alberi** (*trasp. mar.*) a two-master; ~ **volte** twice; ~ **volte tanto (tanti)** twice as much (as many); double; **a** ~ **a** ~ two by two, by twos.

«dumping», *n. m.* (*econ.*) (*pratica che consiste nel fissare prezzi d'esportazione inferiori a quelli praticati sul mercato interno*) dumping.

duopolio, *n. m.* (*econ.*) duopoly.

duopsonio, *n. m.* (*econ.*) duopsony.

duplex, *n. m.* (*comun.*) party-line, party-wire.

duplicare, *v. t.* to duplicate.

duplicato, *a.* duplicate. *n. m.* duplicate, duplication, counterpart; dupe (*slang USA*). // ~ **d'un atto** (*leg.*) counterpart of a deed; ~ **di cambiale** (*cred.*) via; ~ **d'elenco** counter-list; ~ **di modulo** counter-form; ~ **di polizza di carico** (*trasp. mar.*) memorandum.

duplicatore, *n. m.* (*macch. uff.*) duplicator, duplicating equipment, duplicating set.

duplicatrice, *n. f.* (*macch. uff.*) duplicating machine.

duplicazione, *n. f.* **1** duplication. **2** (*pubbl.*) duplication.

duplice, *a.* **1** duplicate, twofold. **2** (*doppio*) double. **3** (*a due stadi*) two-tier. // **in ~ copia** in duplicate.

durante, *prep.* during, in the course of, pending. // ~ **i nostri negoziati** pending our negotiations.

durare, *v. i.* **1** to last, to go★ on. **2** (*leg.*) (*di contratto, legge, ecc.*) to run★.

durata, *n. f.* **1** duration, continuance, standing, term, time. **2** (*ass.*) term. **3** (*leg.*) (*d'un possesso*) tenure. // ~ **del viaggio** (*trasp. mar.*) passage days; ~ **della corsa** (*trasp. ferr.*) running time; ~ **della locazione** (*leg.*) tenancy, tenantry; ~ **dell'affitto** (*leg.*) tenancy, tenantry; ~ **d'esecuzione** (*d'un ciclo di lavorazione*) (*org. az.*) run duration; ~ **di vita utile** (*d'un macchinario, ecc.*) (*org. az.*) service life; ~ **media della vita residua** (*ass.*) life expectancy.

duraturo, *a.* lasting, durable.

durevole, *a.* durable, lasting, permanent. // **articoli durevoli** (*econ., market.*) durables.

E

eccedente, *a.* exceeding; excess, surplus (*attr.*). *n. m.* excess, surplus. // **bagaglio ~ il peso** (*trasp.*) overweight luggage; **non ~** not exceeding.

eccedenza, *n. f.* 1 excess, surplus. 2 (*econ., fin.*) surplus, overbalance. 3 (*rag.*) excess, surplus. // **eccedenze agricole** (*econ.*) surplus produce; **~ della bilancia dei pagamenti** (*econ.*) payments surplus; **un' ~ delle attività sulle passività** (*rag.*) a surplus of assets over liabilities; **un' ~ delle esportazioni sulle importazioni** (*econ.*) an excess of esports over imports; **l' ~ dell'attivo sul passivo** (*rag.*) the excess of assets over liabilities; **~ di carico** (*trasp. mar.*) overfreight; «**~ di compratori o acquirenti**» (*Borsa*) «buyers over»; **~ di nolo** (*trasp. mar.*) overfreight; **~ di peso** (*market.*) overweight; **~ di prezzo** overcharge; **eccedenze globali** (*econ., fin.*) overall surpluses; **eccedenze industriali** (*econ.*) surplus products; **con ~ di personale** (*org. az.*) (*d'azienda, ecc.*) over-staffed (*a.*); **in ~** excess (*attr.*).

eccedere, *v. t.* to exceed, to go★ beyond, to overrun★. // **~ i propri poteri** (*leg.*) to strain one's power.

eccellente, *a.* 1 excellent, super. 2 (*market.*) prime, first-class; top (*attr.*).

eccepire, *v. t.* 1 to except. 2 (*obiettare*) to object. 3 (*leg.*) (*addurre in contrario*) to plead, to demur.

eccessivamente, *avv.* exceedingly.

eccessivo, *a.* 1 excessive, exceeding, rank. 2 (*sovrabbondante*) superabundant. // **l'eccessiva espansione congiunturale** (*econ.*) the overheating of the economy; **eccessiva tassazione** (*fin.*) overtaxation, overassessment.

eccesso, *n. m.* 1 (*sovrabbondanza*) superabundance. 2 (*anche econ., fin.*) excess, overplus, surplus. // **~ di merce** (*in giacenza, in negozio, ecc.*) (*org. az.*) overstock; **~ di potere** (*leg.*) misuse of power; action ultra vires; **~ di produzione** (*econ.*) overproduction; **~ di risparmio** (*econ.*) oversaving; **~ di spesa** (*in rapporto alla produzione e al reddito nazionale*) (*econ.*) overspending; **~ di valutazione** (*fin.*) overvaluation; **~ di velocità** (*trasp. aut.*) speeding; **che ha un ~ di manodopera** (*econ., org. az.*) overmanned; **in ~ di potere** (*leg.*) ultra vires.

eccetto, *prep.* except, except for, bar, barring, save.

eccettuare, *v. t.* to except, to exclude, to bar.

eccettuato, *a.* except, save, exclusive of.

eccezionale, *a.* exceptional, extraordinary. // **in via ~** as an exception; by way of exception.

eccezionalmente, *avv.* exceptionally.

eccezione, *n. f.* 1 exception. 2 (*obiezione*) objection. 3 (*leg.*) exception, challenge, claim, demur, demurrer, plea. 4 (*leg.*) (*riserva*) saving clause, reservation. // **~ d'annullamento** (*leg.*) plea in abatement; **~ dilatoria** (*leg.*) dilatory plea; **~ infondata** (*leg.*) groundless objection; **~ perentoria** (*leg.*) peremptory exception, plea in bar; **~ principale** (*leg.*) chief exception; **a ~ di** except, less.

economato, *n. m.* 1 (*la carica*) bursarship. 2 (*l'ufficio*) bursar's office.

econometria, *n. f.* (*econ.*) econometrics.

econometrico, *a.* (*econ.*) econometric.

econometrista, *n. m.* e *f.* (*econ.*) econometrician.

economia, *n. f.* 1 (*l'economizzare*) economy, economization, retrenchment; (*risparmio*) saving, thrift. 2 (*econ.*) (*d'un Paese, ecc.*) economy. 3 (*econ.*) (*la scienza*) economics. 4 **economie,** *pl.* (*risparmi*) savings. // **~ applicata** applied economics; **economie arretrate** backward economies; **~ aziendale** business economics, business management; **un' ~ chiusa** a closed economy; **~ classica** classical economics; **un' ~ controllata** a managed economy, a governed economy; **~ del benessere** welfare economics; **~ di massa** economy of scale; **~ di mercato** market economy, free economy; **economie di scala** large-scale economies; **un' ~ di tipo misto** a mixed economy; **~ dinamica** dynamic economics; **un' ~ dirigista** a centrally-planned economy, a command-directed economy, a directed economy; **~ dirigistica** *V.* **~**

dirigista; un' ~ in via d'espansione an expanding economy; **~ libera** free enterprise economy; **un' ~ malata** a sick economy; **~ neoclassica** neoclassical economics; **~ pianificata** state-planned economy, planned economy; **~ politica** political economy, economics; **un' ~ sana** a healthy economy, a sound economy, a strong economy; **~ socialista** socialist economy; **un' ~ solida** a stable economy; **~ «sommersa»** (*econ., anche*) «submerged» economy (*in Italia*).

economicamente, *avv.* economically; on the cheap (*fam.*).

economicità, *n. f.* inexpensiveness, cheapness.

economico, *a.* **1** (*che costa poco*) economical, inexpensive, cheap. **2** (*che fa economie*) economical, thrifty. **3** (*econ.*) economic, economical. // **un bene ~** (*econ.*) an economic good; **non ~** (*econ.*) diseconomic.

economista, *n. m.* e *f.* (*econ.*) economist. // **~ aziendale** (*econ.*) company economist.

economizzare, *v. t.* **1** (*risparmiare*) to economize, to save, to retrench. **2** (*non usare*) to spare.

economizzatore, *n. m.* saver.

economo, *a.* economical, saving, thrifty. *n. m.* **1** (*risparmiatore*) economist. **2** (*pers.*) bursar, controller.

edicola, *n. f.* (*giorn., market.*) newsstand, stand, stall.

edicolante, *n. m.* e *f.* (*giorn., market.*) news dealer, news vendor.

edificio, *n. m.* building, house. // **~ della dogana** (*dog.*) custom house.

editore, *n. m.* (*giorn., pubbl.*) publisher.

editoria, *n. f.* (*giorn., pubbl.*) publishing; book trade.

editoriale, *n. m.* (*giorn.*) editorial, leader.

edizione, *n. f.* **1** (*giorn.*) edition. **2** (*giorn.*) (*d'un giornale*) issue. // **~ corrente** (*market.*) cabinet edition; **~ di lusso** (*d'un libro*) (*pubbl.*) large paper edition; **un' ~ in brossura** (*pubbl.*) a paper edition; **~ numerata** (*di pubblicazione*) (*giorn., pubbl.*) limited edition; **~ regionale** (*giorn.*) regional edition; **~ straordinaria** (*d'un giornale*) (*giorn.*) special edition, special, extra; **~ tascabile** (*pubbl.*) pocket edition.

effettivamente, *avv.* actually, really.

effettivo, *a.* **1** actual, real. **2** (*vero*) true, virtual. **3** (*tangibile*) substantial, substantive. **4** (*efficace*) effective, active. **5** (*pers.*) regular, on the regular staff. // **l' ~ tasso d'interesse sui prestiti** (*cred.*) the real rate of interest on loans; **soci onorari e soci effettivi** honorary members and members.

effetto, *n. m.* **1** effect, impact. **2** (*banca, cred.*) paper; (*cambiale*) bill of exchange, bill; (*pagherò*) promissory note, note. // **~ a lunga scadenza** (*banca, cred.*) long-dated paper, long-dated bill, long bill; **~ a termine** (*cred.*) time note; **~ all'incasso** (*banca*) bill for collection; **~ attivo** (*banca, rag.*) note receivable; **effetti attivi** (*rag.*) bills receivable, accounts receivable; **effetti bancabili** (*cred.*) bankable bills; **effetti bancari** (*cred.*) bank bills; **~ cambiario** (*banca, cred.*) bill of exchange; **effetti commerciali** (*banca, cred.*) mercantile paper; **~ deflazionistico** (*fin.*) deflationary effect; **~ di buona firma** (*cred.*) fine paper, sound paper, first class paper, fine trade bill; **~ di comodo** (*cred.*) accommodation bill; windmill (*fam.*); **~ di dipendenza** (*econ.*) dependence effect; **effetti di prim'ordine** (*banca*) choice paper; **~ frenante** (*econ.*) braking effect; **effetti in sofferenza** (*cred.*) out-standing bills; **~ moltiplicatore** (*econ.*) multiplier effect; **un ~ negoziabile** (*cred.*) a negotiable paper; **effetti non bancabili** (*banca*) unbankable papers; **effetti non pagati** (*banca*) bills unpaid; (*anche*) cheques unpaid; **~ passivo** (*banca, rag.*) note payable; **effetti passivi** (*rag.*) bills payable, accounts payable; **effetti personali** (*leg.*) personal effects, personal belongings; **effetti sicuri** (*cred.*) good paper, sound paper.

effettuabile, *a.* practicable.

effettuare, *v. t.* **1** to effect, to implement, to realize. **2** (*eseguire*) to execute, to perform. // **~ acquisti mediante mutui** (*cred.*) to buy through loans; **~ corse** (*trasp.*) (*di treni, ecc.*) to run; **~ operazioni di compensazione** (*fin.*) to clear; **~ una rimessa** (*anche*) to remit.

effettuazione, *n. f.* **1** realization, implementation. **2** (*esecuzione*) execution, performance.

efficace, *a.* effective, constructive, operative.

efficacia, *n. f.* **1** effectiveness. **2** (*efficienza*) efficiency. // **~ pubblicitaria riferita a dollaro di spesa** (*pubbl.*) dollar efficiency.

efficiente, *a.* efficient, effective.

efficienza, *n. f.* efficiency, effectiveness. // **l' ~ marginale del capitale** (*econ.*) the marginal efficiency of capital; **~ ottimale** (*org. az.*) optimum efficiency.

effluire, *v. i.* to outflow, to outgo★.

efflusso, *n. m.* outflow, outflux.

egregio, *a.* **1** eminent, distinguished. **2** (*nell'introduzione a una lettera commerciale*) dear.

elaborare, *v. t.* to draft, to frame, to prepare, to work out. // ~ **una nuova strategia per il lancio d'un prodotto** (*market., pubbl.*) to prepare a new strategy for the launching of a product.

elaboratore, *n. m.* 1 elaborator. 2 (*elettronico*) computer. // ~ **da tavolo** (*elab. elettr.*) desk-top computer.

elaborazione, *n. f.* 1 drafting, working-out. 2 (*elab. elettr.*) processing. // ~ **automatica dei dati** (*elab. elettr.*) automatic data processing; ~ **di piani di finanziamento per le imprese** (*fin., USA*) corporate financial planning; **l'** ~ **d'un programma** (*org. az.*) the drafting of a program.

elargizione, *n. f.* contribution. // ~ **di denaro** (*leg.*) donation.

elasticità, *n. f.* elasticity, buoyancy. // ~ **della domanda** (*econ.*) elasticity of demand; ~ **dell'offerta** (*econ.*) elasticity of supply.

elastico, *a.* elastic, flexible. // **non** ~ inelastic.

elegante, *a.* 1 elegant, smart. 2 (*di articolo*) fancy.

eleggere, *v. t.* 1 to elect, to name. 2 (*un comitato e sim.*) to constitute. 3 (*leg.*) (*con votazione*) to select. // ~ **un candidato** (*leg.*) to vote a candidate in; ~ **per cooptazione** to co(-)opt; ~ **q. presidente** to elect sb. president.

eleggibile, *a.* (*leg.*) eligible.

eleggibilità, *n. f.* (*leg.*) eligibility.

elementare, *a.* elementary.

elemento, *n. m.* 1 element, factor. 2 (*d'un tutto*) component part. // ~ **ad valorem** ad valorem element; **elementi di richiamo per banco di vendita** (*pubbl.*) counter displays; ~ **mobile di richiamo** (*per la vetrina d'un negozio*) (*pubbl.*) animated display.

elencare, *v. t.* to list, to schedule, to book, to enrol.

elencazione, *n. f.* listing, enrolment.

elenco, *n. m.* list, panel, roll, schedule. // ~ **degli abbonati** (*comun.*) telephone directory; telephone book (*USA*); (*giorn.*) subscribers' list; ~ **dei fari e fanali** (*trasp. mar.*) light list; **l'** ~ **dei passeggeri** (*trasp. aer., trasp. mar.*) the list of passengers; ~ **dei sottoscrittori** (*fin.*) subscribers' list; ~ **del telefono** (*comun.*) telephone directory; ~ **delle cause a ruolo** (*leg.*) cause-list, charge-sheet; ~ **delle ordinazioni inevase** backlog of unfilled orders; ~ **dell'attivo e del passivo fallimentare** (*leg.*) schedule; ~ **d'indirizzi** (*per l'inoltro di materiale pubblicitario, ecc.*) (*comun.*) mailing list; ~ **nominativo** nominal list, nominal roll, directory; ~ **passeggeri** (*trasp. aer., trasp. mar.*) passenger list; **essere in** ~ (*telefonico*) to be on the phone.

elettivo, *a.* elective.

elettore, *n. m.* voter.

elettronica, *n. f.* electronics.

elettronico, *a.* electronic.

elevare, *v. t.* 1 to raise. 2 (*mat.*) to raise. // ~ **al quadrato** (*mat.*) to square; ~ **i prezzi** (*market.*) to increase prices; ~ **il tenore di vita** (*econ.*) to raise the standard of living.

elevato, *a.* high, tall. // **più** ~ upper; (*in grado*) chief (*attr.*).

elevatore, *n. m.* (*trasp.*) elevator.

elevazione, *n. f.* elevation; raise (*specialm. USA*).

elezione, *n. f.* 1 election. 2 (*d'un nuovo membro*) co(-)optation. // **un'** ~ **generale** a general election; ~ **suppletiva** by-election.

eliminare, *v. t.* 1 to eliminate, to do★ away with. 2 (*tagliando*) to slice. 3 (*cancellare*) to delete, to cross out. 4 (*market.*) to freeze★ (sb) out. // ~ **un articolo dal catalogo** (*market.*) to delete an item from the catalogue; ~ **il carico d'imposta su qc.** (*fin.*) to derate st.

eliminazione, *n. f.* 1 elimination. 2 (*cancellazione*) deletion, crossing out. 3 (*market.*) (*d'un concorrente, ecc.*) freeze-out.

eliporto, *n. m.* (*trasp. aer.*) heliport.

eludere, *v. t.* to dodge, to elude, to evade. // ~ **la legge** (*leg.*) to evade (*o* to defeat) the law.

elusione, *n. f.* elusion, evasion.

emanare, *v. t.* 1 to send★ out. 2 (*leg.*) to enact. // ~ **regolamenti** (*leg., org. az.*) to enact regulations.

emancipare, *v. t.* (*leg.*) to emancipate.

emancipazione, *n. f.* (*leg.*) emancipation.

embargo, *n. m.* 1 (*comm. est.*) embargo. 2 (*leg., trasp. mar.*) embargo.

emergenza, *n. f.* emergency. // **un fondo di** ~ (*fin.*) an emergency fund.

emergere, *v. i.* 1 to emerge. 2 (*risultare*) to come★ out; to develop (*USA*). 3 (*distinguersi*) to stand★ out.

emesso, *a.* (*banca, cred.*) issued; drawn. // ~ **e pagabile** (*banca, cred.*) drawn and payable.

emettere, *v. t.* 1 to issue. 2 (*una cambiale*) to draw★; (*una cambiale di comodo*) to kite (*fam.*). 3 (*ass.*) (*una polizza, specialm. d'assicurazione marittima*) to underwrite★. 4 (*leg.*) (*una sentenza*) to pronounce. 5 (*leg.*) (*un verdetto*) to find★. // ~ **assegni per una somma eccedente il proprio conto** (*banca*) to overdraw one's account; ~ **un assegno** (*cred.*) to issue a cheque; to check (*USA*); ~ **un assegno scoperto** (*cred.*) to fly a kite; ~ **banconote** (*fin.*) to issue bank-notes; ~ **di nuovo** (*titoli*) (*fin.*) to reissue; ~ (*azioni, obbligazioni, ecc.*) **in eccesso** (*fin.*) to over-issue; ~ **obbligazioni** (*fin.*) to float bonds; ~ **una polizza** (*ass.*) to execute a policy; ~ **una polizza di carico** (*trasp. mar.*) to issue a bill of lading; ~ **una sentenza contro q.** (*leg.*) to sentence sb.; ~ **un verdetto** (*leg.*) to find a verdict.

emigrante, *a.* (*econ.*) migrant, migratory. *n. m.* e *f.* (*econ.*) emigrant, migrator. // ~ **interno** (*chi cambia residenza in cerca di lavoro, specialm. stagionale*) (*econ.*) migrant, migrator.

emigrare, *v. i.* (*econ.*) to emigrate, to migrate.

emigrazione, *n. f.* (*econ.*) emigration, migration. // ~ **interna** (*econ.*) migration.

emissione, *n. f.* **1** issue. **2** (*Borsa*) coming out. **3** (*comun.*) (*via radio*) broadcasting. **4** (*fin.*) issue; issuance (*USA*). // ~ **«a rubinetto»** (*Borsa, fin.*) tap issue; ~ **allo scoperto** (*d'assegni*) bank overdraft; ~ **azionaria** (*fin.*) issue of shares, share issue, stock issue; ~ **d'assegni allo scoperto** kite flying (*fam.*); ~ **d'un'azione nuova ogni tre possedute** (*Borsa*) 1-for-3 rights issue; ~ **d'azioni riservate ai vecchi azionisti** (*fin.*) issue to shareholders only; ~ **di cambiali di comodo** issue of accommodation bills; kite flying (*fam.*); **l'** ~ **di nuove monete** the issue of new coinage; **l'** ~ **d'un prestito** (*fin.*) the issue of a loan, the floating of a loan; **un'** ~ **di titoli** (*fin.*) an issue of bonds; ~ **eccessiva** (*d'azioni, obbligazioni, ecc.*) (*fin.*) over-issue; ~ **fiduciaria** (*di cartamoneta*) (*econ.*) fiduciary issue; ~ **in dollari** (*fin.*) issue expressed in dollars; **emissioni in unità di conto** (*fin.*) unit of account issues; ~ (*radiotelevisiva*) **locale** (*comun.*) spot broadcast; ~ **obbligazionaria** (*fin.*) bond issue; ~ **per una somma eccedente il proprio conto** (*banca*) overdraft; ~ **riservata gratuita** (*d'azioni*) (*fin.*) bonus issue; ~ **riservata sotto costo** (*Borsa, fin.*) rights issue.

emittente, *a.* **1** (*banca, cred.*) issuing. **2** (*comun.*) (*via radio*) broadcasting. *n. m.* e *f.* **1** (*banca, cred.*) (*della lettera di credito*) issuer. **2** (*comun.*) broadcasting station. **3** (*cred.*) (*d'una cambiale e sim.*) drawer. **4** (*cred.*) (*d'un pagherò cambiario*) maker. **5** (*fin.*) (*d'azioni, obbligazioni, ecc.*) issuer. // **l'** ~ **d'un assegno bancario** (*cred.*) the drawer of a cheque.

emolumento, *n. m.* **1** emolument, fee. **2** (*leg.*) honorarium★.

emporio, *n. m.* **1** (*market.*) emporium★, department store. **2** (*market.*) (*magazzino*) warehouse.

enfiteusi, *n. f.* (*leg.*) emphyteusis★.

enfiteuta, *n. m.* (*leg.*) emphyteuta★.

enfiteutico, *a.* (*leg.*) emphyteutic.

ente, *n. m.* (*amm., org. az.*) board, body; (*pubblico o parastatale*) authority; agency (*USA*). // ~ **fiduciario** (*fin.*) trustee company; ~ **giuridico** (*leg.*) corporate body, corporation; ~ **governativo** Government office; agency (*USA*); **enti locali** local authorities; ~ **morale** (*leg.*) body corporate, corporation, institution; ~ **pubblico** (*leg.*) public body, corporation, Government office; State-owned agency, State agency (*USA*); **un** ~ **senza scopi di lucro** (*econ.*) a non-profit organization; **enti statali e parastatali** (*econ.*) State-run organizations.

entrambi, *a.* e *pron. pl.* both. // **entrambe le fasi** (*cioè, caricazione e discarica*) (*trasp. mar.*) both ends.

entrante, *a.* coming, incoming, next.

entrare, *v. i.* to enter, to get★ in, to get★ into, to step in, to step into; (*andare dentro*) to go★ in, to go★ into; (*venir dentro*) to come★ in, to come★ into. // ~ **abusivamente** (*leg.*) to trespass; ~ **in affari** (*anche*) to go into business; ~ **in applicazione** (*leg.*) to become applicable; ~ **in bacino** (*trasp. mar.*) to dock; ~ **in bacino di carenaggio** (*trasp. mar.*) to go into dry dock; ~ **in collisione** (*trasp. mar.*) to foul, to run foul; ~ **in collisione con un'altra nave** (*trasp. mar.*) to come into collision with another ship; ~ **in porto** (*trasp. mar.*) to put into port; (*dopo le formalità doganali*) to clear; ~ **in possesso di qc.** (*leg.*) to enter into possession of st.; ~ **in possesso d'un bene immobile** (*leg.*) to accede to an estate; ~ **in possesso d'un'eredità** (*leg.*) to enter upon an inheritance; ~ **in una professione** to enter a profession; ~ **in relazione con q.** to get in touch with sb.; ~ **in relazioni** (*o* **rapporti**) **d'affari con q.** to enter into business relations with sb.; ~ **in stazione** (*trasp. ferr.*) (*di treno*) to pull in; ~ **in vigore** (*leg.*) to come into force, to enter into force, to inure.

entrata, *n. f.* **1** entrance; (*più elevato*) entry. **2** (*accesso*) access, entry, way in. **3** admission, admittance. **4** (*atrio, ingresso*) hall. **5** (*econ., fin., rag.*) (*provento*) revenue; (*incasso*) take; (*guadagno*) earning; (*reddito*) income; (*rendita*) unearned income. **6** (*elab. elettr.*) input. **7** (*rag.*) competence. **8 entrate,** *pl.* (*econ., fin., rag.*) receipts, takings; revenue, income, take (*sing.*). // **entrate accessorie** (*rag.*) incidental incomes; ~ **di capitali** (*econ.*) inflow of capital; **l'** ~ **d'un porto** (*trasp. mar.*) the mouth of a harbour; **entrate doganali** (*dog.*) customs receipts; **entrate e spese** (*rag.*) revenue and expenditures; **entrate e spese straordinarie** (*fin.*) (*voci del bilancio del Governo britannico*) below-the-line payments and receipts; ~ **e uscita** (*rag.*) debit and credit; **entrate e uscite di cassa** (*rag.*) cash receipts and payments; **entrate e uscite ordinarie** (*bilancio di previsione*) (*rag.*) current budget; **entrate erariali** (*fin.*) revenue receipts; **entrate impreviste** *V.* **entrate accessorie; ~ in carica** entrance upon (*o* into) office, accession to office; **l'~ in porto** (*trasp. mar.*) putting into port; **~ in possesso** (*di un bene*) (*leg.*) assumption of ownership; entry; **~ in possesso d'un bene immobile** (*leg.*) accession to an estate; **~ in vigore** (*leg.*) entry into force; **entrate invisibili** (*comm. est., econ.*) invisible exports; **~ libera** free admission (*o* admittance); **~ lorda** (*rag.*) gross income; **entrate lorde** (*rag.*) gross earnings; **entrate pubbliche** (*fin.*) public revenue, Government revenue.

epoca, *n. f.* **1** epoch, age, era. **2** (*periodo*) period. // **~ d'inizio** (*in un conto corrente fruttifero*) (*banca*) base date.

equamente, *avv.* equitably, fairly.

equazione, *n. f.* (*mat.*) equation. // **un'~ algebrica** an algebraic equation; **~ di secondo grado** equation of second degree, quadratic equation, quadratic.

equilibrare, *v. t.* **1** to balance. **2** (*fare da contrappeso a*) to counterbalance, to countervail. **3** (*rag.*) to balance. // **~ il bilancio ordinario** to balance the ordinary budget.

equilibrarsi, *v. rifl.* to balance, to level off. *v. recipr.* (*rag.*) (*di conti*) to balance each other.

equilibrato, *a.* balanced, well-balanced.

equilibrio, *n. m.* **1** (*anche econ.*) balance, equilibrium★. **2** (*econ.*) (*stabilità*) stability. // **~ costi-ricavi** (*econ.*) cost-revenue balance; **l'~ delle forze (politiche)** the balance of powers; **~ interno** (*econ.*) domestic equilibrium; **~ multiplo** (*econ.*) multiple equilibrium.

equipaggiamento, *n. m.* **1** equipment. **2** (*trasp. mar.*) (*d'una nave*) fitting-out, rigging, rig.

equipaggiare, *v. t.* **1** to equip. **2** (*trasp. mar.*) (*una nave*) to rig, to fit out.

equipaggio, *n. m.* **1** (*trasp. aer.*) crew. **2** (*trasp. mar.*) crew. **3** (*trasp. mar.*) (*esclusi gli ufficiali*) ship's company, company; hands (*pl.*). // **~ addetto ai ricuperi** (*trasp. mar.*) wrecking crew; **un ~ insufficiente** (*trasp. mar.*) a weak crew; **con ~ incompleto** (*trasp. mar.*) (*di nave*) short-handed.

equiparare, *v. t.* **1** (*pareggiare*) to equalize. **2** (*confrontare*) to compare.

equiparazione, *n. f.* **1** (*pareggiamento*) equalization. **2** (*confronto*) comparison.

equità, *n. f.* **1** equity, fairness. **2** (*leg.*) (*corpo di norme emanate dal Lord Chancellor a modifica e integrazione della «common law»*) equity (*in G.B.*).

equivalente, *a.* e *n. m.* equivalent. // **~ decimale** (*secondo il sistema metrico decimale*) metric equivalent.

equivalenza, *n. f.* equivalence.

equo, *a.* **1** equitable, fair. **2** (*uguale*) equal, even. **3** (*leg.*) rightful. // **non ~** inequitable.

erariale, *a.* revenue (*attr.*); fiscal; of the treasury; of the exchequer. // **imposte erariali** (*fin.*) revenue taxes; **introiti erariali** (*fin.*) revenues.

erario, *n. m.* **1** (*fin.*) national revenue, inland revenue, revenue, exchequer, fisc. **2 l'Erario** (*fin.*) the Treasury; the Exchequer (*in G.B.*). // **l'~ pubblico** *V.* **~**, *def. 1*; **un impiegato dell'~** a revenue officer.

erede, *n. m.* (*leg.*) heir. *n. f.* (*leg.*) heiress. **eredi,** *pl.* (*leg., anche*) succession (*collett.*). // **~ assente** (*leg.*) absent heir; **un ~ diretto** (*leg.*) a lineal heir; **eredi e aventi diritto** (*leg.*) heirs and assignees; **~ fiduciario** (*leg.*) fiduciary heir; **un ~ illegittimo** (*leg.*) a wrongful heir; **~ legittimo** (*leg.*) legal heir, heir-at-law, rightful heir, true heir, heir apparent, heir general; **~ necessario** (*leg.*) forced heir; **~ presuntivo** (*leg.*) presumptive heir; **~ testamentario** (*leg.*) testamentary heir; **~ universale** (*leg.*) sole heir.

eredità, *n. f. inv.* (*leg.*) hereditament, heritage, inheritance. // **~ giacente** (*leg.*) vacant succession; **un'~ legittima** (*leg.*) a rightful inheritance.

ereditabile, *a.* (*leg.*) hereditable, inheritable, heritable.

ereditare, *v. t.* (*leg.*) to inherit. *v. i.* to come★ into an inheritance.

ereditario, *a.* **1** (*leg.*) hereditary. **2** (*leg.*) (*ereditabile*) hereditable, inheritable, heritable. // **asse (o patrimonio) ~** (*leg.*) legal assets (*pl.*); patrimony of a deceased person; **diritti ereditari** (*leg.*) hereditary rights.

ereditiera, *n. f.* (*leg.*) heiress.

erigere, *v. t.* **1** (*costruire*) to erect, to build★. **2** (*fondare*) to found, to set★ up. // **~ in ente giuridico, morale o pubblico** (*leg.*) to incorporate.

erodere, *v. t.* (*anche fig.*) to erode.

erogare, *v. t.* (*cred., fin.*) to disburse, to allocate.

erogazione, *n. f.* **1** (*cred., fin.*) (*di denaro, ecc.*) disbursement, allocation. **2 erogazioni,** *pl.* (*fin.*) aids.

erosione, *n. f.* (*anche fig.*) erosion. // **continua ~ dei salari reali** steady erosion of real earnings.

errare, *v. i.* (*sbagliare*) to err, to be mistaken, to be wrong, to mistake★.

errato, *a.* mistaken, incorrect, false, wrong.

erroneo, *a.* erroneous, incorrect, improper, mistaken, wrong.

errore, *n. m.* 1 error, mistake, blunder. 2 (*pecca, manchevolezza*) fail, fault, flaw. 3 (*svista*) oversight, slip. // ~ **contabile** (*rag.*) bookkeeping error; ~ **di battuta** (*scrivendo a macchina*) typing mistake; **un** ~ **di calcolo** a mistake in calculation, a miscalculation; ~ **di campionamento** (*market.*) error of sampling; ~ **di compensazione** (*rag.*) compensating error; ~ **di copiatura** clerical error; **un** ~ **di diritto** (*leg.*) an error in (*o* of) law, a mistake of law; **un** ~ **di fatto** (*leg.*) an error in (*o* of) fact, a mistake of fact; **un** ~ **di giudizio** an error of judgment; **un** ~ **d'ortografia** a slip in spelling, a spelling mistake; ~ **di stampa** (*giorn., pubbl.*) misprint, literal; ~ **giudiziario** (*leg.*) miscarriage of justice, miscarriage; **essere in** ~ to be wrong, to be mistaken; **per** ~ by mistake; **salvo errori** errors excepted; **salvo errori e omissioni** errors and omissions excepted.

esagerare, *v. t.* e *i.* to exaggerate. // ~ **nel prezzo** (*market.*) to ask too high a price; to lift prices.

esageratamente, *avv.* exaggeratedly.

esagerato, *a.* 1 exaggerated. 2 (*market.*) (*di prezzo, ecc.*) tall.

esagerazione, *n. f.* exaggeration.

esame, *n. m.* 1 examination, exam, test. 2 (*controllo*) control, checking, check. 3 (*indagine*) investigation. 4 (*studio, rassegna*) study, survey, review. 5 (*leg.*) inspection. // **un** ~ **accurato dei libri contabili** (*rag.*) a narrow inspection of the firm's books; **un** ~ **delle fonti d'approvvigionamento** an exploration of supply resources; **l'** ~ **d'un campione** (*market.*) the examination of a sample; **l'** ~ **di documenti** (*leg.*) the inspection of documents; **esami di promozione** (*pers.*) promotion exams; ~ **particolareggiato** dissection; ~ **preliminare** preliminary; **all'** ~ on examination; **in** ~ under discussion, under consideration; (*market.*) on approval.

esaminare, *v. t.* 1 to examine, to consider, to see★, to see★ into, to look into, to go★ through, to explore, to survey, to view. 2 (*controllare*) to control, to check. 3 (*indagare*) to investigate, to inquire into. 4 (*studiare*) to study. 5 (*leg.*) to inspect. 6 (*leg.*) (*testi, deposizioni*) to hear★. 7 (*pers.*) (*candidati*) to examine, to test. // ~ **a fondo** to canvass; ~ **accuratamente** to peruse; ~ **attentamente** to go through, to scrutinize; ~ **le condizioni di** (*una merce*) to condition; ~ **un conto** (*rag.*) to check an account, to go into an account; ~ **i libri (contabili)** (*leg.*) to inspect the books; ~ **minutamente** to dissect; ~ **una pratica** to go into a matter; ~ **le prove** (*leg.*) to view the evidence; ~ **una questione** to go into a matter.

esattamente, *avv.* 1 exactly, correctly. 2 (*accuratamente*) accurately.

esattezza, *n. f.* 1 exactness, exactitude, correctness. 2 (*accuratezza*) accuracy, precision. 3 (*fedeltà*) fidelity.

esatto, *a.* 1 exact, correct. 2 (*accurato, preciso*) accurate, precise, specific. 3 (*preciso, tondo*) even.

esattore, *n. m.* 1 (*fin.*) (*di dazi, imposte, ecc.*) toll collector, toller. 2 (*pers.*) collector, bill collector, collecting clerk. // ~ **comunale** (*pers.*) rate collector; ~ **dei crediti** (*cred.*) debt collector; dun; ~ **del dazio** (*fin.*) excise officer, exciseman; ~ **delle dogane** (*dog.*) custom collector; ~ **delle imposte** (*fin.*) collector of taxes, tax collector; ~ **delle tasse** (*fin.*) *V.* ~ **delle imposte.**

esattoria, *n. f.* collector's office. // ~ **comunale** (*fin.*) municipal office of rates; ~ **del dazio** (*trasp.*) toll-booth.

esauriente, *a.* exhaustive, extensive, comprehensive.

esaurimento, *n. m.* 1 exhaustion, drain. 2 (*di una miniera, un pozzo petrolifero, ecc.*) depletion. // **l'** ~ **dei fondi** (*rag.*) the exhaustion of funds; ~ **delle scorte d'un articolo** (*a causa della domanda eccezionalmente alta*) (*market.*) sellout; **un** ~ **di dollari** (*fin.*) a drain of dollars.

esaurire, *v. t.* 1 to exhaust, to drain, to use up, to wear★ out. 2 (*una miniera, un pozzo petrolifero, ecc.*) to deplete. 3 (*nel senso di «utilizzare»: una polizza di carico, ecc.*) to accomplish. // ~ **un conto in banca** (*banca*) to exhaust a bank account; ~ **le risorse d'una nazione** (*econ.*) to drain the wealth of a nation.

esaurirsi, *v. rifl.* 1 to become★ exhausted; to exhaust oneself. 2 to run★ out, to wear★ out. 3 (*giorn.*) (*d'un libro*) to be out of print. 4 (*market.*) (*di scorte*) to run★ short.

esaurito, *a.* 1 exhausted, worn out. 2 (*nel senso di «utilizzato»*) accomplished. 3 (*giorn.*) (*di libro, ecc.*) out of print. 4 (*market.*) (*d'articolo*) unavailable, sold out, out of stock.

esazione, *n. f.* 1 collection. 2 (*fin.*) (*di tasse, tributi, ecc.*) levy, exaction. // ~ **alla fonte** (*fin.*) collection at the source, stoppage at the source; ~ **delle imposte** (*fin.*) collection of taxes; ~ **delle tasse** (*fin.*) *V.* ~ **delle imposte;** ~ **di crediti** collection of debts.

esborsare, *v. t.* (*denaro, ecc.*) to disburse.

esborso, *n. m.* 1 (*di denaro, ecc.*) disbursement. 2 (*rag.*) cash outlay.

escludere, *v. t.* 1 to exclude, to bar, to foreclose. 2 (*eccettuare*) to except. 3 (*leg.*) (*da un diritto, ecc.*) to debar. 4 (*market.*) to freeze★ (sb.) out.

esclusione, *n. f.* 1 exclusion. 2 (*eccettuazione*) exception. 3 (*leg.*) (*da un diritto, ecc.*) debarment, foreclosure. // **l'~ d'un socio** the expulsion of a member.

esclusiva, *n. f.* 1 (*giorn.*) exclusive right, exclusive. 2 (*leg.*) exclusive right, exclusive; (*brevetto*) patent. 3 (*market.*) (*di vendita, ecc.*) sole agency, exclusive dealing; exclusive rights (*pl.*). // **~ di vendita** (*market.*) *V.* ~, *def. 3*; **diritto d'~** (*leg.*) exclusive right.

esclusivamente, *avv.* exclusively.

esclusivista, *n. m.* e *f.* 1 (*anche econ.*) exclusivist. 2 (*leg., market.*) exclusive agent; sole agent.

esclusivo, *a.* 1 (*giorn., leg.*) exclusive. 2 (*leg., market.*) (*di agente, ecc.*) exclusive, sole.

escomiare, *v. t.* (*leg.*) to evict. // **chi è escomiato** (*leg.*) evictee.

escomio, *n. m.* 1 (*leg.*) eviction. 2 (*leg.*) (*la notifica*) notice to quit. // **chi dà l'~** (*leg.*) evictor.

escursione, *n. f.* (*tur.*) tour, trip.

escussione, *n. f.* (*leg.*) examination. // **~ di testi a difesa** (*leg.*) examination of witnesses for the defence; **~ di testi d'accusa** (*leg.*) examination of witnesses for the prosecution.

escutere, *v. t.* (*leg.*) (*testimoni*) to examine.

esecutività, *n. f.* (*leg.*) enforceability.

esecutivo, *a.* 1 executive, executory. 2 (*leg.*) enforceable. 3 (*org. az.*) operating. *n. m.* (*politica*) (the) executive. // **il potere ~** the executive power.

esecutore, *n. m.* executor, maker. // **~ testamentario** (*leg.*) executor of a will, executor, administrator.

esecutorietà, *n. f.* (*leg.*) enforceability. // **l'~ d'un contratto** (*leg.*) the enforceability of a contract.

esecutorio, *a.* 1 executory. 2 (*leg.*) enforceable.

esecutrice, *n. f.* executrix★. // **~ testamentaria** (*leg.*) executrix (of a will).

esecuzione, *n. f.* 1 execution, carrying out, performance. 2 (*attuazione, compimento*) implementation, fulfilment. 3 (*fabbricazione*) making, working-out. 4 (*lavorazione, fattura*) workmanship. 5 (*leg.*) (*d'una legge*) enforcement. 6 (*leg.*) (*d'una sentenza*) execution. 7 (*leg.*) (*d'un'obbligazione*) satisfaction. 8 (*market.*) (*d'una ordinazione, ecc.*) carrying out, execution, fulfilment, pursuance. // **l'~ della legge** (*leg.*) the enforcement of the law; **l'~ d'un contratto** (*leg.*) the fulfilment of a contract; **l'~ d'un'ipoteca** (*leg.*) the satisfaction of a mortgage; **l'~ d'una sentenza** (*leg.*) the execution of a judgment; **l'~ d'un trattato** (*leg.*) the implementation of a treaty; **~ forzata** (*leg.*) levy; **in ~ di** (*leg.*) in pursuance of; **in via d'~** (*di lavoro*) in progress.

eseguire, *v. t.* 1 to execute, to carry out, to perform. 2 (*attuare, compiere*) to implement, to fulfil. 3 (*fare*) to make★, to do★. 4 (*leg.*) (*una sentenza*) to execute. 5 (*leg.*) (*un'obbligazione*) to satisfy. 6 (*market.*) to execute, to carry out, to fill, to button. // **~ a macchina** (*org. az.*) to machine; **~ un contratto** (*leg.*) to perform a contract; **~ dei calcoli** to perform calculations; **~ il lodo** (*leg.*) to enforce the award; **~ un pagamento** (*cred.*) to effect (*o* to make) a payment; **~ un pignoramento sui beni del debitore** (*leg.*) to make an attachment on the debtor's property.

eseguito, *a.* 1. executed. 2 (*fatto*) made. 3 (*leg.*) (*d'obbligo, ecc.*) satisfied.

esentare, *v. t.* 1 to exempt (from); to dispense (with); to excuse. 2 (*fin., anche*) to frank. // **~ (*q. o qc.*) dalle imposte** (*fin., anche*) to untax.

esente, *a.* (*anche fin.*) exempt, free. // **~ da bollo** (*fin.*) exempt from stamp duty; **~ da dazio** (*dog.*) free of duty, duty-free, uncustomed; **~ da dogana** (*dog.*) uncustomed; **~ da imposta (*o* da imposte)** (*fin.*) tax-exempt, tax-free, untaxed; **~ da IVA** (*fin.*) VAT-free.

esenzione, *n. f.* 1 (*anche fin.*) exemption. 2 (*fin.*) (*da una tassa, ecc.*) relief. 3 (*fin., leg.*) immunity. // **~ da pignoramento** (*leg.*) immunity from distraint; **~ dalle imposte** (*fin.*) exemption from taxation, immunity from taxation; **~ dalle tasse** (*fin.*) *V.* **~ dalle imposte; ~ doganale parziale** (*dog.*) partial customs exemption; **~ doganale totale** (*dog.*) total customs exemption; **~ fiscale** (*fin.*) tax exemption; **~ per categorie** (*fin.*) block exemption; **~ retroattiva** (*fin.*) retrospective exemption; **in ~** (*dog.*) with nil duties; **lettera d'~ doganale** (*dog.*) bill of sufferance.

esercente, *n. m.* e *f.* 1 (*market.*) tradesman★ (*m.*); shopkeeper; storekeeper (*USA*). 2 **gli esercenti,** *pl.* (*market.*) tradespeople; trade (*collett.*).

esercire, *v. t.* 1 (*un'azienda e sim.*) to run★, to operate. 2 *V.* **esercitare.** // **~ un negozio** (*market.*) to keep a shop.

esercitare, *v. t.* 1 to exercise. 2 (*un mestiere,*

un commercio) to carry on, to ply. **3** (*una professione*) to practise. **4** (*pers.*) (*addestrare*) to train. // **~ il commercio** to carry on trade; **~ una funzione** to exercise a function; **~ la propria influenza su q.** to exert one's influence on sb.; **~ un'opzione** (*Borsa, fin.*) to exercise an option; **~ una pressione sui prezzi** (*econ.*) to drive prices down.

esercitarsi, *v. rifl.* to exercise oneself, to practise.

esercizio, *n. m.* **1** exercise. **2** (*l'esercitarsi*) practice. **3** (*fin., rag.*) financial year, business year, year. **4** (*market.*) (*negozio, ecc.*) shop, business, firm, undertaking. **5** (*rag.*) accounting period, account. **6 esercizi,** *pl.* (*alberghieri ed extra-alberghieri*) (*tur.*) accommodation facilities. // **l'~ della professione legale** (*leg.*) the practice of law; **l'~ d'un diritto** (*leg.*) the exercise of a right, the assertion of a right; **~ finanziario** (*fin.*) financial year, fiscal year, trading year, year; **~ finanziario eccezionalmente prospero** (*fin.*) boom year; **~ sociale** (*fin.*) company's fiscal year, year; **l'~ trascorso** (*fin., rag.*) the past year; **costi d' ~** operational (*o* operation) costs.

esibire, *v. t.* **1** to exhibit, to show★. **2** (*leg.*) (*documenti, prove, ecc.*) to exhibit, to produce. **3** (*market.*) (*merci*) to display. // **~ un documento** (*leg.*) to produce a document.

esibizione, *n. f.* **1** exhibition, showing, show. **2** (*leg.*) (*di documenti*) exhibition, production. **3** (*market.*) (*di merce*) display. // **l'~ di documenti per l'accusa** (*leg.*) the production of documents for the prosecution.

esigente, *a.* **1** exacting, exigent. **2** (*market.*) (*di cliente*) selective; choosy (*fam.*).

esigenza, *n. f.* **1** exigency. **2** (*necessità, bisogno*) requirement, want. **3** (*richiesta, pretesa*) demand, claim. // **esigenze di gestione** (*amm., rag.*) working-capital requirements; **esigenze di mercato** (*econ., market.*) market requirements.

esigere, *v. t.* **1** to exact, to demand, to require. **2** (*cred., fin.*) (*riscuotere*) to collect, to cash. **3** (*leg.*) (*il riconoscimento d'un diritto, la restituzione di qc., ecc.*) to claim. // **~ come condizione essenziale** (*leg.*) to stipulate; **~ un credito in sospeso** (*cred.*) to collect an outstanding credit; **~ il pagamento d'un debito** (*cred.*) to exact payment of a debt, to require the payment of a debt; **~ un tributo** (*fin.*) to exact a tax, to raise a tax; to toll.

esigibile, *a.* **1** exactable, demandable. **2** (*cred., fin.*) (*riscuotibile*) collectable, cashable, receivable. **3** (*cred., fin.*) (*pagabile*) payable. **4** (*cred., fin.*) (*in scadenza*) due. **5** (*leg.*) claimable. // **deposito ~ a vista** (*banca*) deposit payable on demand.

esiguo, *a.* **1** small, limited, narrow, slight, fractional. **2** (*fin.*) (*di guadagno, ecc.*) off (*attr.*).

esimere, *v. t.* **1** to exempt (from), to dispense (with). **2** (*cred., leg.*) (*da un pagamento, anche*) to frank.

esistente, *a.* **1** existing. **2** (*di cosa*) extant. **3** (*market.*) (*di merce*) on hand; in stock.

esistenza, *n. f.* **1** existence. **2** (*vita*) life★. // **~ di cassa** (*rag.*) cash in (*o* on) hand.

esistere, *v. i.* to exist, to be.

esitare, *v. i.* to hesitate, to demur. *v. t.* (*market.*) (*vendere*) to sell★.

esitarsi, *v. rifl.* (*market.*) to sell★, to be sold.

esitazione, *n. f.* hesitation, demur.

esito, *n. m.* **1** outcome, result. **2** (*market.*) sale. // **l'~ d'una cambiale** (*cred.*) the fate of a bill.

esonerare, *v. t.* **1** to exonerate, to exempt, to excuse. **2** (*da vincoli, oneri, ecc.*) to free, to release, to relieve. // **~ q. dai propri doveri** to exonerate sb. from his duties.

esonero, *n. m.* **1** exoneration, exemption. **2** (*da oneri, vincoli, ecc.*) release, relief. // **~ fiscale** (*fin.*) exemption from taxation; tax relief.

espandere, *v. t.* to expand, to spread★.

espandersi, *v. rifl.* **1** to expand, to spread★. **2** (*econ., anche*) to boom.

espansione, *n. f.* **1** expansion, spread. **2** (*econ., anche*) upswing, upturn. // **~ economica** (*econ.*) economic expansion, growth; **l'~ globale del potere di acquisto** (*econ.*) the horizontal spread of buying power; **~ orizzontale** (*org. az.*) horizontal expansion; **~ verticale** (*org. az.*) vertical expansion; **in ~** expanding.

espansionismo, *n. m.* (*econ.*) expansionism.

espansionista, *n. m.* e *f.* (*econ.*) expansionist.

espediente, *n. m.* **1** contrivance, device. **2** (*mezzo*) means, medium. // **espedienti dilatori** (*leg.*) delaying practices; **~ temporaneo** make-do, makeshift.

espellere, *v. t.* **1** to expel, to eject. **2** (*Borsa di Londra*) to hammer. **3** (*leg.*) to evict. // **~** (*un avvocato*) **dall'albo** (*leg.*) to disbar.

esperienza, *n. f.* experience. // **~ finanziaria** (*fin.*) financial know-how.

esperimento, *n. m.* **1** experiment. **2** (*prova, esame*) test, trial.

esperto, *a.* experienced, expert. *n. m.* expert, consultant. // **~ di diritto pubblico** (*o* **internazionale**) (*leg.*) publicist; **~ finanziario** (*fin.*) investment adviser, investment counsellor; ~ **in mezzi pubblicitari** (*pubbl.*) media man; ~ **di problemi d'efficienza** (*org. az.*) efficiency engineer (*o* expert); ~ **in pubbliche relazioni** (*pubbl.*) public-relations man; ~ **in relazioni umane** (*pers.*) human relationist; ~ **pubblicitario** (*pubbl.*) media man.

esporre, *v. t.* **1** to expose. **2** (*esibire, mettere in mostra*) to exhibit. **3** (*una teoria, le proprie idee, ecc.*) to expound; to state. **4** (*market.*) to display, to expose, to set★ out, to show★. // ~ **un avviso** to stick up a notice; ~ **una bandiera** to put up a flag; ~ **i fatti d'un processo** (*leg.*) to state the facts of a case.

esporsi, *v. rifl.* **1** to expose oneself. **2** (*compromettersi*) to commit oneself. **3** (*cred.*) (*finanziariamente*) to incur debts; to take★ out loans. // ~ **a un rischio** (*anche*) to incur a risk.

esportabile, *a.* (*comm. est.*) exportable.

esportare, *v. t.* (*comm. est.*) to export. // ~ (*merce*) **di contrabbando** (*leg.*) to smuggle, to smuggle out.

esportatore, *n. m.* (*comm. est.*) exporter. *a.* (*comm. est.*) exporting. // ~ **in proprio** (*comm. est.*) export merchant; ~ **su commissione** (*comm. est.*) export agent, export commission agent; **paesi esportatori** (*comm. est.*) exporting countries.

esportazione, *n. f.* **1** (*comm. est.*) exportation, export. **2** (*comm. est.*) (*merce esporata*) export, exportation. // ~ **di beni e servizi** (*comm. est.*) exports of goods and services; ~ **di capitali** (*fin.*) export of capitals; **esportazioni invisibili** (*comm. est., econ.*) invisible exports; **merci d'** ~ exports.

espositore, *n. m.* (*market.*) exhibitor.

esposizione, *n. f.* **1** (*anche fotografica*) exposure. **2** (*mostra*) exhibition, exhibit. **3** (*di fatti, ecc.*) statement, exposition. **4** (*market.*) (*il mettere in mostra*) display, showing, set-out. **5** (*market.*) (*la mostra*) exhibition, exposition, show. **6** (*rag.*) (*complesso dei crediti d'una azienda*) receivables (*pl.*). // ~ **agricola** agricultural show; ~ **della situazione finanziaria** (*leg.*) statement of affairs; ~ **di bestiame** cattle-show; ~ **(di merce) in vetrina** (*market.*) window display.

esposto, *n. m.* **1** (*leg.*) account, statement. **2** (*leg.*) (*petizione*) petition.

espressione, *n. f.* **1** (*anche mat.*) expression. **2** (*dichiarazione*) statement.

espresso, *a.* **1** express. **2** (*esplicito*) explicit. *n. m.* (*comun.*) express letter; special-delivery letter (*USA*). // **non** ~ unexpressed; **per** ~ express.

esprimere, *v. t.* to express, to state, to word. // ~ **un conto in dollari** (*rag.*) to state an account in dollars.

espropriare, *v. t.* (*leg.*) to expropriate, to dispossess.

espropriazione, *n. f.* (*leg.*) expropriation, dispossession. // ~ **per pubblica utilità** (*econ.*) compulsory purchase.

esproprio, *n. m.* *V.* **espropriazione.**

espulsione, *n. f.* **1** expulsion. **2** (*leg.*) eviction.

essenziale, *a.* **1** essential, fundamental, main, prerequisite, vital. **2** (*leg.*) material.

essere, *v. i.* **1** to be; (*esistere*) to exist. **2** (*ausiliare nella voce passiva*) to be. **3** (*ausiliare nella voce attiva*) to have. **4** (*andare*) to be. **5** (*costare*) to be.

est, *n. m.* east. // **verso** ~ eastward.

estate, *n. f.* summer.

estendere, *v. t.* **1** to extend, to spread★ out. **2** (*leg.*) (*un provvedimento, ecc.*) to grant, to bestow, to give★. // ~ **la propria clientela** (*market.*) to increase the number of one's customers.

estendersi, *v. rifl.* **1** to extend, to range. **2** (*propagarsi*) to spread★.

estensione, *n. f.* **1** extension; extent. **2** (*espansione, aumento*) expansion, increase.

estensivo, *a.* extensive.

estensore, *n. m.* (*leg.*) writer (of a document); drafter.

esteriore, *a.* external; outer, outside (*attr.*).

esterno, *a.* **1** external; outer, outside, outward, out (*attr.*). **2** (*all'aperto*) outdoor. *n. m.* **(l')esterno** (the) outside. // **all'** ~ **di** outside.

estero, *a.* foreign, external; overseas (*attr.*). // **all'** ~ abroad, overseas; **dall'** ~ from abroad.

esteso, *a.* extended, extensive, long, wide.

estimativo, *a.* (*rag.*) estimative.

estimo, *n. m.* **1** (*fin., leg.*) estimate; valuation; rating. **2** (*fin., leg.*) (*a scopi fiscali*) assessment.

estinguere, *v. t.* **1** to extinguish. **2** (*cred.*) (*un debito, ecc., anche*) to pay★ off, to settle. **3** (*cred., leg.*) (*un'obbligazione, ecc.*) to lift. **4** (*fin., leg.*) (*un'ipoteca, ecc.*) to redeem. // ~ **una cambiale** (*cred.*) to discharge a bill; ~ **un'ipoteca** (*cred., anche*) to pay off a mortgage; ~ **un prestito** (*cred.*) to pay off a loan.

estinto, *a.* **1** dead. **2** (*cred.*) (*di debito e sim.*) discharged, settled.

estinzione, *n. f.* **1** extinction, extinguishment. **2** (*cred.*) (*d'un debito, ecc.*) settlement, discharge, sinking, quietus. **3** (*fin., leg.*) (*d'un'ipoteca, ecc.*) redemption. **4** (*leg.*) (*d'un procedi-*

mento giudiziario) discontinuance. // ~ **d'una cambiale** (*cred.*) discharge of a bill; ~ **d'un debito** (*cred.*) extinction of a debt, cancellation of a debt; **l'~ d'ipoteche** (*fin.*) the redemption of mortgages; **l'~ d'un pagherò** (*cred.*) the redemption of a promissory note.

estorcere, *v. t.* (*anche leg.*) to extort, to exact.

estorsione, *n. f.* (*anche leg.*) extortion, exaction.

estradare, *v. t.* (*leg.*) to extradite.

estradizione, *n. f.* (*leg.*) extradition.

estragiudiziale, *a.* (*leg.*) extrajudicial.

estralegale, *a.* (*leg.*) extralegal.

estraneo, *a.* alien; outside (*attr.*). *n. m.* outsider.

estrarre, *v. t.* **1** to extract, to pull out, to draw★ (out). **2** (*minerali*) to excavate, to mine. **3** (*fin.*) (*obbligazioni, ecc.*) to draw★. // ~ **a sorte** to draw lots; «**vostri titoli estratti**» (*banca*) «your securities drawn».

estratto, *n. m.* **1** (*di carne, ecc.*) extract. **2** (*riassunto*) abstract, summary. **3** (*fin.*) drawn ticket. **4** (*giorn.*) (*d'articolo, di rivista, ecc.*) off-print, separate. **5** (*leg.*) estreat. **6** (*leg.*) (*memoriale*) memorial. // ~ **conto** (*banca*) abstract of account, bank statement; (*rag.*) statement of account; ~ **d'atto di nascita** (*amm.*) birth certificate; ~ **di certificato di proprietà** (*leg.*) abstract of title; **un ~ (di) conto mensile** (*rag.*) a monthly statement of account; ~ **di documento** (*leg.*) abstract; ~ **di verbale** abstract of record; ~ **periodico** (*banca*) periodical statement.

estrazione, *n. f.* **1** extraction. **2** (*di minerale*) excavating; mining. **3** (*a sorte*) drawing. // **l'~ del carbone** coal-mining; **con ~** (*o* ~ **compresa**) (*Borsa*) «cum» drawing.

estremamente, *avv.* extremely, exceedingly, highly.

estremi, *n. pl.* **1** (*leg.*) data; particulars; details. **2** (*mat.*) extremes.

estremità, *n. f. inv.* **1** extremity. **2** (*parte estrema*) end, tail. **3** (*punta*) point, tip.

estremo, *a.* **1** extreme, exceeding. **2** (*il più lontano*) furthermost, farthest. **3** (*il più esterno*) outermost, terminal. // **l'~ disordine della situazione contabile** (*rag.*) the exceeding disorder of the accounts.

estrinseco, *a.* extrinsic.

estromettere, *v. t.* **1** to expel; to oust. **2** (*Borsa di Londra*) (*un agente di cambio o un «jobber»*) to hammer.

esuberante, *a.* (*econ.*) redundant. // **manodopera ~** (*econ.*) redundant manpower.

esuberanza, *n. f.* (*econ.*) redundancy (*di personale, di manodopera*).

età, *n. f. inv.* age. // ~ **legale** (*per compiere taluni atti regolati dalla legge*) (*leg.*) lawful age; ~ **maggiore** (*leg.*) full age; ~ **minore** (*leg.*) minority, non-age; ~ **pensionabile** (*pers., rag.*) pensionable age.

etichetta, *n. f.* **1** (*cartellino*) ticket. **2** (*market.*) label, tag, sticker. // ~ **con indirizzo** address label; ~ **del prezzo** (*market.*) price tag.

etichettare, *v. t.* (*market.*) to label.

etichettatura, *n. f.* (*market.*) labelling, labeling.

ettaro, *n. m.* hectare.

ettogrammo, *n. m.* hectogramme, hectogram.

ettolitro, *n. m.* hectolitre; hectoliter (*USA*).

ettometro, *n. m.* hectometre; hectometer (*USA*).

euroassegno, *n. m. V.* «**eurocheque**».

euroazione, *n. f.* (*fin.*) euroequity.

«**eurocheque**», *n. m.* (*fin.*) eurocheque.

eurocompensazione, *n. f.* (*fin.*) Euroclear.

eurodivisa, *n. f.* (*fin.*) eurocurrency.

eurodollaro, *n. m.* (*fin.*) eurodollar.

euroemissione, *n. f.* (*fin.*) eurobond.

euromercato, *n. m.* (*fin.*) euromarket.

euro-obbligazione, *n. f.* (*fin.*) euro-bond.

Europa, *n. f.* Europe. // **l'~ dei Dieci** the enlarged Common Market.

europeo, *a.* e *n. m.* European.

evadere, *v. i.* **1** (*dal carcere*) to escape. **2** (*fin.*) to evade (*o* to dodge) taxes. *v. t.* **1** (*amm.*) (*eseguire, sbrigare*) to dispatch, to settle. **2** (*comm.*) (*eseguire: un ordine*) to execute, to carry out, to fill. **3** (*comun.*) (*la corrispondenza*) to clear. **4** (*fin., leg.*) (*sottrarsi: al fisco*) to evade, to dodge.

evasione, *n. f.* **1** (*dal carcere*) escape. **2** (*comm.*) (*d'un'ordinazione*) execution, carrying-out, filling. **3** (*comun.*) (*della corrispondenza*) clearing. **4** (*fin., leg.*) evasion. // ~ **fiscale** (*fin.*) tax evasion, tax dodging; **dare ~ a un'ordinazione** to carry out (*o* to execute, to fill) an order.

evasore, *n. m.* (*fin., leg.*) evader, dodger. // ~ **fiscale** (*fin., leg.*) tax evader, tax dodger.

evento, *n. m.* event, happening. // ~ **fortuito** (*leg.*) fortuitous event.

eventuale, *a.* **1** (*possibile*) possible; eventual (*raro*). **2** (*probabile*) probable, prospective. **3** (*accidentale*) accidental, fortuitous. // «**eventuali e varie**» (*rag.*) «any other business».

eventualità, *n. f. inv.* **1** eventuality, possibility. **2** (*probabilità*) probability. **3** (*circostanza*) circumstance.

evincere, *v. t.* (*leg.*) (*una proprietà mediante un processo*) to evict.

evizione, *n. f.* (*leg.*) (*d'una proprietà mediante un processo*) eviction.

evoluzione, *n. f.* **1** evolution, progress. **2** (*sviluppo*) development. **3** (*tendenza*) tendency, trend. // **l'** ~ **congiunturale** (*econ.*) the trend of activity; ~ **dei prezzi** (*econ.*) price trends; **l'** ~ **dei prezzi al consumo** (*econ., market.*) retail-price trend; ~ **della congiuntura** (*econ.*) economic trend, business trend; **l'** ~ **dell'occupazione** (*econ.*) the employment trend; ~ **dell'offerta e della domanda** (*econ.*) supply and demand trends.

ex, *prep.* **1** ex, former, late. **2** (*se riferito a defunto*) late. // ~ **cedola** (*Borsa*) (*di titolo*) ex coupon, ex dividend; **l'** ~ **marito** (*di divorziata*) her former husband; (*di vedova*) her late husband; **l'** ~ **presidente** (*fin.*) the ex president; **il nostro** ~ **socio** (*fin.*) our late partner.

extra, *prep.* extra, plus. *a.* extra. *n. m. inv.* **1** extra, plus. **2** (*pers.*) extra; additional worker.

F

fabbisogno, *n. m.* requirement, requisite, need.

fabbrica, *n. f.* factory, manufactory; (*stabilimento*) establishment; (*impianto*) plant; mill, works (*specialm. nei composti*). // ~ **di mattoni** brick-works; **essere in** ~ (*pers.*) to be at the works; **in** ~ (*che avviene nell'ambito della fabbrica*) in-plant (*attr.*); **operaio di** ~ factory worker, mill-hand.

fabbricante, *n. m.* e *f.* manufacturer, maker; (*costruttore*) builder; (*industriale*) industrialist. // ~ **di birra** brewer; ~ **di stoffe** clothier.

fabbricare, *v. t.* 1 to manufacture, to make★. 2 (*costruire*) to build★. 3 (*la birra e altre bevande fermentate*) to brew.

fabbricato[1]**,** *a.* 1 manufactured, made. 2 (*costruito*) built. // ~ **a macchina** (*market.*) machine-made; ~ **a mano** (*market.*) handmade; ~ **in Giappone** (*market.*) made in Japan; ~ **su brevetto** (*leg.*) patent (*attr.*).

fabbricato[2]**,** *n. m.* 1 building. 2 (*casa*) house. 3 **fabbricati,** *pl.* (*anche*) premises.

fabbricazione, *n. f.* 1 manufacture, manufacturing, making, make. 2 (*costruzione*) building. // ~ **all'ingrosso** (*org. az.*) wholesale manufacture; ~ **del burro** butter-making; ~ **in serie** (*org. az.*) mass-production.

facchinaggio, *n. m.* (*trasp.*) porterage.

facchino, *n. m.* 1 (*trasp.*) porter. 2 (*trasp.*) (*al mercato della carne di Londra*) bummaree (*slang*).

facente, *part. pres.* (*nelle seguenti locuz.*) ~ **funzione** (*n. m.* e *f.*) (*leg., org. az.*) locum tenens; (*pers.*) deputy; ~ **funzione di** (*a.*) acting, pro-; ~ **funzione di cassiere** pro-treasurer; ~ **funzione di direttore** (*pers.*) acting manager, alternate manager.

facile, *a.* easy; soft (*fam.*).

facilità, *n. f.* 1 facility, easiness, ease. 2 (*attitudine*) aptitude. // **la** ~ **del denaro** (*fin.*) the easiness of money.

facilitare, *v. t.* to facilitate, to make★ easy (*o* easier).

facilitazione, *n. f.* 1 facilitation. 2 (*agevolazione*) facility, accommodation, concession. // **facilitazioni di credito** (*fin.*) credit accommodations, credit facilities; **facilitazioni di pagamento** (*cred.*) facilities of payment, accommodations for payment, payment accommodations; **facilitazioni fiscali e creditizie** (*fin.*) tax and credit inducements.

facoltà, *n. f. inv.* 1 (*mentale, ecc.*) faculty. 2 (*autorità, potere*) authority, power. 3 (*capacità*) capability. 4 (*di decidere, ecc.*) discretion. 5 (*permesso*) leave. // ~ **di scelta** option; **facoltà mentali** (*leg.*) mental powers.

facoltativo, *a.* facultative, optional.

facsimile, *n. m.* facsimile, specimen. // **il** ~ **d'una firma** (*banca*) the specimen of a signature; ~ **di firma** (*leg.*) facsimile signature.

«factoring», *n. m.* (*fin., USA*) factoring.

factotum, *n. m. inv.* (*pers.*) factotum, handyman★.

falla, *n. f.* (*trasp. mar.*) leak.

fallimento, *n. m.* 1 failure. 2 (*econ., fin.*) smash, crash. 3 (*leg.*) bankruptcy; failure (*meno comune*). // ~ **dichiarato su istanza dei creditori** (*leg.*) involuntary bankruptcy; ~ **su istanza del fallito** (*leg.*) voluntary bankruptcy.

fallire, *v. i.* 1 to fail. 2 (*econ., fin.*) to smash, to smash up, to crash. 3 (*leg.*) to become★ bankrupt, to go★ bankrupt, to be declared bankrupt; to fail, to break★.

fallito, *a.* 1 unsuccessful. 2 (*finanziariamente*) broke, stony-broke. 3 (*leg.*) bankrupt. *n. m.* 1 unsuccessful man★; failure. 2 (*leg.*) bankrupt. // ~ **non riabilitato** (*leg.*) undischarged bankrupt; ~ **riabilitato** (*leg.*) discharged bankrupt.

fallo, *n. m.* 1 fail, fault. 2 (*errore*) error, mistake.

falsare, *v. t.* 1 to distort, to alter. 2 (*leg.*) (*falsificare*) to falsify, to forge.

falsario, *n. m.* 1 (*di monete metalliche*) coiner. 2 (*leg.*) falsifier, counterfeiter, forger.

falsificare, *v. t.* 1 to falsify, to feign; to tamper (with st.). 2 (*leg.*) (*banconote, firme, ecc.*) to counterfeit, to forge. 3 (*leg.*) (*sofisticare*) to sophisticate, to adulterate. // ~ **docu-**

menti (*leg.*) to falsify documents, to tamper with documents; ~ **una firma** (*leg.*) to counterfeit a signature, to falsify a signature; ~ **la moneta** (*leg., anche*) to adulterate the coinage; ~ **un testamento** (*leg.*) to forge a will.

falsificato, *a.* 1 false. 2 (*leg.*) counterfeit. 3 (*leg.*) (*sofisticato*) sophisticated, adulterated.

falsificatore, *n. m.* 1 (*leg.*) falsifier, tamperer. 2 (*leg.*) (*di banconote, firme, ecc.*) counterfeiter, forger.

falsificazione, *n. f.* 1 falsification. 2 (*leg.*) (*di banconote, firme, ecc.*) counterfeiting, counterfeit, forgery. 3 (*leg.*) (*sofisticazione*) sophistication, adulteration. // ~ **della moneta** (*leg., anche*) adulteration of the coinage; ~ **delle scritture contabili** (*leg.*) falsification of accounts.

falso[1], *a.* 1 false, untrue; bogus, dummy, dud (*fam.*). 2 (*fittizio*) fictitious, flash. 3 (*market.*) (*d'imitazione*) imitation, sham, mock (*attr.*). // **falsa dichiarazione** (*leg.*) false statement; **falsa dichiarazione giurata** (*leg.*) perjury; ~ **giuramento** (*leg.*) false oath; **falsa testimonianza** (*leg.*) perjury.

falso[2], *n. m.* 1 (*falsità*) falsehood. 2 (*leg.*) forgery. 3 (*market.*) imitation.

fama, *n. f.* 1 fame, renown. 2 (*reputazione*) reputation, repute, name.

famiglia, *n. f.* family, household. // **le famiglie degli impiegati** (*pers.*) the white-collar families.

familiare, *a.* familiar; family, home (*attr.*). *n. f.* (*trasp. aut.*) station wagon, wagon.

familiarizzarsi, *v. rifl.* 1 to become★ familiar (with sb.). 2 to acquaint oneself (with st.).

famoso, *a.* famous, renowned.

fanale, *n. m.* 1 lamp. 2 (*trasp. mar.*) light. // ~ **da segnali** (*trasp. mar.*) signal lamp; ~ **di coda** (*trasp.*) tail-light; **fanali di via** (*trasp. mar.*) navigation lights.

fare, *v. t.* 1 (*agire, e in senso astratto*) to do★. 2 (*costruire, fabbricare, confezionare, manipolare, ecc.*) to make★. 3 (*agire*) to act. 4 (*eseguire*) to execute, to carry out, to perform. 5 (*nominare*) to make★. 6 (*percorrere*) (*a piedi*) to go★; (*in auto*) to drive★. 7 (*seguito da un infinito con valore causativo*) (*con senso attivo*) to make★ (*in genere, o con costrizione*); to get★ (*convincere*); to let★ (*consentire, permettere*); to cause (*causare*); (*con senso passivo*) to get★, to have. *v. i.* 1 (*essere*) to be. 2 (*essere adatto*) to suit. // ~ **a macchina** to make by machine, to machine; ~ **a mano** to make by hand; ~ **a meno di qc.** to do without st., to dispense with st.; (*rinunciare a*) to waive st.; ~ **a metà** (*o* **a mezzo**) (*comm.*) to split the difference, to go halves; ~ **acqua** (*trasp. mar.*) (*di nave*) to leak; ~ **acquisti** (*market.*) to make purchases, to do one's shopping; to market, to trade; ~ **un affare** to make (*o* to strike) a bargain; ~ **affari** to do business, to transact business, to deal, to trade, to merchandise; ~ **affari con** (*q.*) to deal with, to trade with, to handle; ~ **affari d'oro** to drive a roaring trade; ~ **affidamento su** to count upon, to rely on; ~ **aggio** (*Borsa*) to be above par; ~ **aggiunte a qc.** to supplement st.; ~ **l'agricoltore** to farm; ~ **ammenda di qc.** to make amends for st.; ~ **una annotazione di** (*qc.*) (*org. az., fam.*) to memo; ~ **annotazioni in margine di** (*una pagina, ecc.*) to margin; ~ **l'appello** (*pers.*) to call the roll; ~ **appello a** to make appeal to, to appeal to, to call on; (*leg.*) to appeal to; ~ **appello a una garanzia** (*leg.*) to call on a guarantee; ~ **l'apprendistato presso q.** (*pers.*) to serve one's apprenticeship with sb.; ~ **arenare** (*trasp. mar.*) to beach, to ground; ~ **assegnamento su** to count on, to depend on, to trust; ~ **un'assicurazione** (*stipularla*) (*ass.*) to take out an insurance; ~ **un'assicurazione sulla vita** to assure one's life; ~ **attenzione** (*stare attento*) to pay attention; to be attentive; « ~ **attenzione** » (*scritto su una cassa, ecc.*) «handle with care», «with care»; ~ **attenzione a** (*badare*) to take care of, to note; ~ **aumentare** (*prezzi, quotazioni, ecc.*) (*fin., market.*) to force up, to send up, to up; ~ **avanzare** (*nella carriera*) (*pers.*) to promote, to advance; ~ **il bagarinaggio** to scalp (*USA*); ~ **bancarotta** (*econ., fin.*) to smash, to crash; (*leg.*) to go (*o* to become) bankrupt; ~ **la bella copia di** (*un documento*) to fair; ~ **benzina** (*trasp. aut.*) to put petrol into one's tank; to gas up (*USA*); ~ **il bilancio** (*rag.*) to strike a balance; ~ **il bilancio dei libri contabili per l'anno d'esercizio** (*rag.*) to balance the books for the year; ~ **una breve visita a q.** to call on sb.; ~ **un buon affare** to make a good bargain, to drive a good bargain, to pick up a bargain, to strike a bargain; ~ **una buona (una cattiva) impressione a q.** to impress sb. favourably (unfavourably); ~ **calare** (*prezzi, quotazioni, ecc.*) (*market.*) to force down, to bring down, to send down, to decrease; ~ **calcoli** (*mat.*) to calculate, to figure; ~ **cambiar rotta a una nave** (*trasp. mar.*) to haul a ship; ~ **carbone** (*trasp. mar.*) to coal, to take in coal; ~ **il carico** (*trasp.*) to load; ~ **causa** (*leg.*) to complain, to take legal steps; ~ **causa a q.** (*leg.*) to bring an action against sb., to file a suit against sb., to prosecute sb.; ~ **una cessione** (*leg.*) to make a transfer; ~ **cinque copie di** (*un docu-*

mento) to quintuplicate; ~ **circolare** to circulate; (*una notizia, ecc., anche*) to send round, to send out; ~ **circolare capitali** (*fin.*) to circulate capital; ~ **la coda** to queue, to queue up; ~ **un colpo in Borsa** (*Borsa*) to bring off a coup on the stock exchange; ~ **commenti su qc.** to comment on st.; ~ **il commercio costiero** (*trasp. mar.*) to coast; ~ **il commesso viaggiatore** (*pers.*) to travel; ~ **compere** (*market.*) *V.* ~ **acquisti**; ~ **un concordato** (*leg.*) to compound; ~ **concorrenza a** (*qc. o q.*) to compete with; ~ **la conoscenza di q.** to meet sb., to get acquainted with sb.; ~ **conoscere qc.** to make st. known, to introduce st.; ~ **una consegna** (*market.*) to make (*o* to effect) a delivery; ~ **conti** (*mat.*) to calculate, to count, to cast; ~ **il conto alla rovescia** (*org. az.*) to count down; ~ **il contrabbando** (*leg.*) to smuggle; ~ **la contravvenzione a q.** (*leg.*) to fine sb.; ~ **un controllo di cassa** (*rag.*) to audit the cash in hand; ~ **una copia di** (*un documento, ecc.*) to make a copy of; (*leg.*) to estreat; ~ **una copia fotostatica di** (*documenti, ecc.*) to photostat; ~ **una correzione** (*rag.*) to make an alteration; ~ **una cortesia a q.** to oblige sb.; ~ **credito** (*cred.*) to give credit, to trust; ~ **crescere** to grow; (*fin., market.*) (*far aumentare: prezzi, ecc.*) to force up, to bring up, to send up; ~ **una crociera** (*trasp. mar.*) to cruise; ~ **crollare** (*prezzi, quotazioni e sim.*) (*fin., market.*) to pull down; ~ **il crumiro** (*sind.*) to scab; ~ **da arbitro** (*leg., sind.*) to arbitrate; to umpire; ~ **da intermediario** to mediate; ~ **da mallevadore a** (*q.*) (*cred., fin.*) to guarantee; (*leg.*) to sponsor; ~ **da mediatore** to mediate; ~ **da testimone** (*leg.*) to witness; ~ **debiti** to incur debts; ~ **decorrere le controstallie** (*trasp. mar.*) to attach demurrage; ~ **del proprio meglio** to do one's best, to do st. to the best of one's ability; ~ **una denuncia dettagliata dei (propri) redditi** (*fin.*) to return the details of one's income; ~ **deragliare** (*trasp. ferr.*) to derail; ~ **il designer** (*pers.*) to design; ~ **di conto** (*mat., rag.*) to reckon, to figure; ~ **la dichiarazione dei redditi** (*fin.*) to make a return of one's income; ~ **dichiarazione d'entrata** (*trasp. mar.*) to enter inwards; ~ **dichiarazione d'uscita** (*trasp. mar.*) to enter outwards; ~ **una dichiarazione erronea** (*o* **falsa**) (*leg.*) to misrepresent; ~ **una dichiarazione giurata** (*leg.*) to swear an affidavit; ~ **una dichiarazione in dogana** (*dog.*) to pass a customs entry; ~ **difetto** to be lacking; ~ **differenza fra** to discriminate; ~ **una digressione** to make a digression; ~ **dimettere** (*amm., pers.*) to retire, to dismiss; ~ **diminuire** (*i profitti di q. o qc.*) (*econ.*) to squeeze; (*market.*) (*prezzi, ecc.*) to drive down; ~ **una distribuzione** (*d'azioni, ecc.*) (*fin., leg.*) to make an allotment; ~ **una domanda** (*orale*) to ask a question; (*scritta*) to make (*o* to submit) an application; ~ **domanda di rappresentanza** to apply for an agency; ~ **domanda per un impiego (per una borsa di studio, ecc.)** to apply for a job (for a scholarship, etc.); ~ **domande a q.** to ask sb. questions, to question sb.; ~ **il doppio gioco con q.** to double-cross sb.; ~ **il proprio dovere** to do one's duty; ~ **economia** (*o* **economie**) to save, to save up, to economize; to draw in; to retrench; to tighten one's belt (*fam.*); ~ **entrare** (*una nave*) **in bacino** (*trasp. mar.*) to dock; ~ **l'entrata in dogana d'una nave** (*dog.*) to clear a ship inwards; ~ **l'esercente** (*market.*) to be a shopkeeper; to storekeep (*USA*); ~ **espandere** to expand, to boom; ~ **esperienza di qc.** to experience st.; ~ **un estratto di** (*un documento*) (*leg.*) to estreat; ~ **un facsimile di** (*qc.*) to facsimile; ~ **fallimento** (*leg.*) to go (*o* to become) bankrupt; to fail; to go broke (*slang*); ~ **fallire** (*leg.*) to bankrupt; (*detto del tribunale*) to declare (*sb.*) bankrupt; (*fig.*) to ruin, to shipwreck (*fig.*); ~ **un favore** to do a favour, to render a service; ~ **un favore a q.** to do sb. a favour, to oblige sb.; ~ **fede** (*leg.*) to be evidence; ~ **la fila** to queue, to queue up; ~ **la firma** (*d'ingaggio*) (*pers.*) to sign on, to sign up; ~ **fluttuare il tasso di cambio** (*econ., fin.*) to float the exchange rate; ~ **fortuna** to make one's fortune; to get on in the world; **farsi una fortuna** to make a fortune, to build up a fortune; ~ **fronte a** to face, to meet; (*market.*) (*un'ordinazione, una richiesta, ecc.*) to fulfil; ~ **fronte a una cambiale** (*cred.*) to protect a bill; ~ **fronte a un debito** (*cred.*) to meet a debt; ~ **fronte a una situazione difficile** to cope with a difficult situation; ~ **funzionare** to operate, to run, to work; ~ **funzione di (direttore, ecc.)** to act as (manager, etc.); ~ **galleggiare** (*trasp. mar.*) to float, to set afloat; ~ **girare** to wheel; (*avvolgere*) to wind; ~ **un giro turistico** (*tur.*) to sightsee; ~ **una gita** (*tur.*) to tour; ~ **un giuramento** (*leg.*) to take an oath, to swear an oath; ~ **giurare** (*i testimoni, ecc.*) (*leg.*) to swear; ~ **grandi spese** to incur great expense; ~ **il grossista** (*market.*) to wholesale, to job; ~ **guadagni esorbitanti** (*econ.*) to profiteer; ~ **un guadagno** (*fin.*) to make a profit; ~ **un guadagno netto di** (*una somma*) to clear; ~ **un guadagno onesto** to turn an honest penny; ~ **la guardia a** (*q. o qc.*) to guard, to watch; ~ **la hostess** (*trasp. aer.*) to be an air-hostess; to steward; ~ **qc. in fretta** to do st. in a hurry; to rush st.; ~ **in media otto ore al**

giorno (*di lavoro, di studio, ecc.*) to average eight hours a day; ~ **in media 300 miglia al giorno** to average 300 miles a day; ~ **incagliare** (*trasp. mar.*) to run aground, to run ashore; ~ **incetta di** (*qc.*) to corner, to buy up, to take up, to hoard; ~ **un'inchiesta** (*market.*) to take a poll; ~ **un'inchiesta (*o* un'indagine) su qc.** (*market., pubbl.*) to survey st.; ~ **indagini** to make inquiries, to research; ~ **indagini su q.** (*leg.*) to investigate sb.; ~ **indagini su qc.** to inquire into st.; ~ **inserzioni** (*su un giornale*) (*pubbl.*) to advertise; ~ **inserzioni per un posto d'impiegato** to advertise for a clerk; ~ **l'inventario** (*org. az.*) to take stock; ~ **l'inventario di** (*prodotti, articoli, ecc.*) (*rag.*) to inventory; ~ **l'inventario una volta ogni sei mesi** (*rag.*) to make up one's accounts once every six months; ~ **investimenti** (*fin.*) to invest; ~ **un investimento** (*fin.*) to make an investment; ~ **un'istanza** (*leg.*) to petition; ~ **istanza a q.** (*leg.*) to apply to sb.; ~ **istanza al tribunale** (*leg.*) to apply to the Court; ~ **lavoro straordinario** (*pers.*) to work overtime; ~ **leggi** (*leg.*) to make laws; ~ **male i propri calcoli** to miscalculate; ~ **marcia indietro** (*fig.*) to go back; ~ **una media** (*mat.*) to average, to average up; ~ **una media del prezzo degli acquisti** to average purchases; ~ **una media del prezzo delle vendite** to average sales; ~ **la media fra il prezzo più alto e quello più basso** (*econ., market.*) to take the average between the highest and lowest price; ~ **il mediatore** to be a broker; to broke (*ingl.*); (*Borsa*) to do broking; ~ **un memorandum di** (*qc.*) to memorandum; to memo (*fam.*); ~ **menzione di qc.** to mention st.; ~ **migliorare** to better, to improve; ~ **migliorie a** (*un terreno, ecc.*) to improve; ~ **misurazioni** to measure; ~ **la moda** (*market.*) to set the fashion; ~ **il modellista** (*pers.*) to design; ~ **morir di fame** to starve; ~ **naufragare** (*anche fig.*) to wreck, to shipwreck; ~ **naufragio** (*trasp. mar.*) (*di nave*) to wreck; (*di persone*) to be ship-wrecked; ~ **notare** to point out; ~ **il numero** (*al telefono*) (*comun.*) to dial; ~ **nuove ordinazioni** (*market.*) to reorder; ~ **un'offerta** to make an offer; (*a un'asta*) to make a bid, to bid; (*per un appalto*) to make a tender, to tender; ~ **un'offerta all'asta** (*anche*) to enter a bid at an auction; ~ **un'offerta cauzionale per un'aggiudicazione** (*leg.*) to call for bids; ~ **un'offerta d'appalto** to bid (*USA*); ~ **un'offerta per un contratto** (*leg.*) to tender for a contract, to tender; ~ **un'offerta superiore** (*a un'asta*) to bid up; ~ **un'offerta superiore a** (*quella di q. altro*) to overbid; to overcall; ~ **offerte a una vendita all'asta** to bid at an auction-sale; ~ **omaggio a q. di qc.** to compliment sb. with st.; ~ **onore a** to honour; ~ **onore ai propri impegni** (*cred.*) to meet one's obligations; ~ **opposizione a** (*leg.*) to challenge; ~ **un'ordinazione di merci** (*market.*) to give an order for goods; ~ **osservare** (*una legge, ecc.*) (*leg.*) to enforce; ~ **ostruzionismo** to obstruct, to filibuster; ~ **un pacco (*o* un pacchetto)** (*market.*) to make up a parcel, to wrap up a parcel; ~ **un pagamento** to make (*o* to effect) a payment; to pay; ~ **pagare** (*un articolo, un servizio, ecc.*) to charge for; ~ **pagare a q. meno del giusto (*o* del solito)** (*market.*) to undercharge sb.; ~ **pagare di più** (*market.*) to surcharge; ~ **pagare una multa** (*leg.*) to levy a fine; ~ **pagare un pedaggio** (*trasp.*) to toll; ~ **pagare spese** to charge expenses, to expense; ~ **pagare troppo caro** to overcharge; ~ **parte del consiglio d'amministrazione** (*amm.*) to sit on the board of directors; ~ **parte del personale** (*pers.*) to be on the staff; ~ **parte della giuria** (*leg.*) to be (*o* to sit) on the jury; ~ **parte d'una commissione** to be on a committee, to sit on a committee; ~ **un passaggio di proprietà** (*leg.*) to make a transfer (of property); ~ **passare** (*trasp.*) to transit; (*leg.*) (*una legge*) to carry; ~ **passare di moda** (*market.*) to outmode; ~ **un passo** to take a step, to step; ~ **il pendolare** (*trasp. ferr.*) to commute; ~ **la perizia di qc.** to survey st.; ~ **una petizione** (*leg.*) to petition; ~ **piacere a q.** to please sb.; ~ **piani** to make plans, to plan, to scheme; ~ **un piano** to make a plan, to map out; ~ **il piazzista** (*market.*) to canvass, to tout; ~ **il piccolo cabotaggio** (*trasp. mar.*) to coast; ~ **piccole operazioni di Borsa** to dabble on the Stock Exchange; ~ **il pieno** (*trasp. aut.*) to fill the tank (with petrol); to fill up; ~ **pratica** to practise; ~ **preparativi** to make preparations, to prepare; ~ **presente** to point out; ~ **il preventivo delle spese** (*rag.*) to estimate expenditures; ~ **un preventivo troppo basso per** (*un lavoro*) to underestimate; ~ **prezzi troppo alti** to overcharge; ~ **un prezzo** (*market.*) to make a price; ~ **il prezzo a** (*un articolo, ecc.*) (*market.*) to rate; ~ **il prezzo alla merce** (*market.*) to set a price on goods; ~ **progetti** to make plans; (*fare il progettista*) to design; ~ **il progettista** (*pers.*) to design; ~ **progredire** to advance, to promote; ~ **progressi** to make progress, to progress; ~ **una promessa** to make a promise, to promise; ~ **propaganda** (*market.*) to canvass; ~ **il propagandista** to tout; ~ **una proposta a q.** to make sb. a proposal, to propose sb., to proposition sb.; ~ **proseguire** (*lettere, merci, ecc.*) (*comun., trasp.*) to forward; ~ **prosperare** to boom; ~

protestare una cambiale (*leg.*) to have a bill protested, to make protest of a bill; ~ **protestare una cambiale in via preliminare** (*banca, cred.*) to have a bill noted; ~ **un protesto** (*leg.*) to make a protest; ~ **provvista di** (*merce, ecc.*) (*org. az.*) to stock up, to store; ~ **pubblicità** (*pubbl.*) to advertise, to advertize; ~ **pubblicità a** (*giorn., pubbl.*) to plublicize; to push, to boom (*fam.*); ~ **pubblicità alla radio** to advertise on the radio; ~ **pubblicità alla televisione** to advertise on television; ~ **la pubblicità su un giornale** to advertise in a newspaper; ~ **quadrare** to square; (*rag.*) (*conti, ecc.*) to reconcile; ~ **quadrare le cifre** to square figures; ~ **quadrare le cifre di** (*un conto: con quelle d'un altro*) (*rag.*) to reconcile; ~ **quadrare i conti** (*rag.*) to make accounts agree, to reconcile the accounts; to strike a balance; ~ **quattrini** to make money; ~ **quattro copie di** (*un documento*) to quadruplicate; ~ **rapporto alla direzione contro un dipendente** to report an employee to the management; ~ **rappresaglie** (*leg.*) to retaliate; ~ **il rappresentante** to act as an agent, to be an agent; ~ **il rappresentante per una ditta** (*market., pers.*) to represent a firm; ~ **registrare** (*rag.*) (*di conto, ecc.*) to turn in; ~ **registrare una ripresa** (*econ.*) to catch up; ~ **una registrazione** (*rag.*) to make an entry; ~ **un reinvestimento** (*fin.*) to reinvest; ~ **il riassunto di** to resume, to sum up; ~ **ricerche** to make researches, to research, to search, to inquire; ~ **richiesta di qc. a q.** to make a request to sb. for st.; ~ **un ricorso** (*leg.*) to lodge an appeal, to petition; ~ **ricorso a** to resort to, to turn to; ~ **ricorso alle riserve** (*fin., rag.*) to dip into reserves; ~ **ricorso alle risorse monetarie** (*fin.*) to make a call to short-end funds; ~ **rientrare** (*l'inizio d'una riga: dal margine della pagina*) to indent; ~ **riferimento a** to refer to; ~ **rilevare** to point out; ~ **un rimborso** to refund; ~ **una rimessa** (*comm.*) to remit; ~ **un rimpasto di** (*un Governo, ecc.*) to reshuffle; ~ **un riporto** (*Borsa*) to carry over, to contango, to continue; ~ **ristagnare** to stagnate; ~ **una ritrattazione** to retract, to recant, to withdraw; ~ **la rotazione di** (*raccolti*) (*econ.*) to rotate; ~ **rotta** (*trasp. mar.*) to be under way; ~ **rotta per** (*un porto, ecc.*) (*trasp. mar.*) to head for, to sail for, to stand for; ~ **ruotare** to wheel, to rotate; ~ **salire** to send up; (*fin., market.*) (*prezzi, quotazioni, ecc.*) to force up, to up; (*trasp.*) (*passeggeri*) to take up, to pick up; ~ **salire le offerte** (*a un'asta*) to force the bidding; ~ **salire il prezzo** (*a un'asta*) to bid in; ~ **sapere a q.** (*comun.*) to let sb. know; ~ **uno sbaglio** to make a mistake, to mistake; ~ **sbandare** (*una nave*) (*trasp. mar.*) to careen; ~ **scalo** (*trasp. mar.*) to make a call, to call; ~ **scalo a un porto** (*trasp. mar.*) to call at (*o* to touch at) a port; ~ **scalo in porti intermedi** (*trasp. mar.*) to call at intermediate ports; ~ **scalo in un porto nominato** (*trasp. mar.*) to call at a named port; ~ **scalo per rifornirsi di vettovaglie** (*trasp. mar.*) to call to revictual; ~ **scendere** to send down; (*fin., market.*) (*prezzi e sim.*) *V.* ~ **diminuire**; (*trasp. aut.*) (*un passeggero*) to set down; ~ **uno schema di** (*qc.*) to draft; ~ **uno sciopero bianco** (*sind.*) to work to rule; ~ **una scommessa** to make (*o* to lay) a wager; to wager; ~ **scomparire prove** (*leg.*) to suppress evidence; ~ **le proprie scuse a q.** to make an apology to sb.; ~ **una seconda copia di** (*un documento, ecc.*) to duplicate; ~ **segnalazioni** to signal; ~ **segnali a** (*q.*) to signal; (*trasp. mar.*) to speak; ~ **segnali a una nave che si sta incrociando** (*trasp. mar.*) to speak a passing ship; ~ **sentire la propria autorità** to make one's authority felt; ~ **sentire l'effetto (o gli effetti) su** to affect; ~ **un sequestro** (*leg.*) to levy a distress; ~ **servizio** (*trasp.*) (*di veicolo, nave, ecc.*) to run; ~ **servizio regolare** (*trasp. mar.*) (*di nave, ecc.*) to ply; ~ **silenzio** (*restare muto*) to be silent, to keep silent; (*ammutolire*) to stop talking; to shut up (*fam.*); ~ **la somma (delle varie voci) d'un conto** to foot up an account; ~ **una sottrazione** (*mat.*) to do a subtraction, to subtract; ~ **lo speculatore «professionista»** (*alla Borsa Valori di Londra*) to job; ~ **speculazioni** (*fin.*) to speculate; ~ **la spesa** (*market.*) to do one's shopping; ~ **spese** (*market.*) to trade; ~ **lo spoglio della corrispondenza** (*alla Posta*) (*comun.*) to sort the mail; ~ **lo spoglio della propria corrispondenza** to go through one's correspondence; ~ **la spola** to shuttle, to shunt; (*fare il pendolare*) to commute; (*trasp.*) (*di veicolo, nave, ecc.*) to run; (*trasp. mar.*) (*di nave, ecc.*) to ply; ~ **una spunta a fianco di** (*una cifra, una voce, ecc.*) to tick (off); ~ **la spunta di** (*un carico: articolo per articolo)* (*trasp. mar.*) to tally; ~ **lo «stag»** (*q. V.*) (*Borsa*) to stag; ~ **la stima dei danni** (*ass.*) to appraise damages; ~ **lo straordinario** (*pers.*) to work overtime, to be on overtime; ~ **uno strappo alla legge** (*leg.*) to strain the law, to stretch the law; ~ (*un abito*) **su misura** (*market.*) to tailor, to make to measure; ~ (*un articolo*) **su ordinazione** (*market.*) to tailor; ~ **sul serio** to be in earnest, to mean business; ~ **la tara a** (*merci, ecc.*) (*market.*) to tare; ~ **tardi** to be late; ~ **tardi a** (*una riunione, ecc.*) to miss; ~ **una telefonata a q.** (*comun.*) to telephone sb., to phone sb., to ring sb. up; ~ **testamento**

(*leg.*) to make one's will; to settle one's affairs; ~ **torto a** (*leg.*) to wrong; ~ **un totale** (*rag.*) to take off a total; ~ **un trasbordo** (*trasp.*) to transfer; ~ **trasloco** to move (to new premises); ~ **una traversata** (*trasp. aer., trasp. mar.*) to make a voyage, to voyage; ~ **uscire** (*una nave*) **dal bacino** (*trasp. mar.*) to undock; ~ **un uso errato di qc.** to misapply st., to misuse st.; ~ **vacanza** (*pers.*) to have a holiday; to take time off; to vacation (*USA*); ~ **valere i propri diritti** (*leg.*) to push one's claims; ~ **valere un diritto** (*leg.*) to enforce a right; ~ **valere un diritto per vie legali** (*leg.*) to prosecute a claim; ~ **le veci** (*org. az.*) to sub; ~ **le veci di q.** to act for sb., to sub for sb., to take sb.'s place; ~ **vela** (*verso una destinazione*) (*trasp. mar.*) to sail; ~ **vendere** (*market.*) to sell; ~ **una vendita** (*market.*) to make a sale; ~ **vendite** (*market.*) to market; ~ **il venditore ambulante** (*market.*) to peddle, to hawk; ~ **il viaggiatore di commercio** (*pers.*) to travel; ~ **un viaggio** (*per via di terra*) (*tur.*) to make (*o* to go on) a journey; to journey, to travel; (*per mare*) to make a voyage, to voyage; ~ **visita a** (*una persona o un luogo*) to visit; ~ **una visita a q.** to make a call on sb.; ~ **una zona** (*pers.*) (*di commesso viaggiatore*) to work a district; **farcela** (*fam.*) (*riuscire*) to make it, to succeed, to manage; (*tirar avanti*) to get along, to manage; **facendo riferimento a** (*comun.*) with respect to; **facendo seguito a** pursuant to, further to; **non** ~ **progressi** (*anche fig.*) to mark time.

faro, *n. m.* (*trasp. mar.*) lighthouse, beacon.

farsi, *v. rifl.* **1** (*diventare*) to become★, to get★; (*per gradi*) to grow★. **2** (*del tempo, ecc.*) to get★. **3** (*rendersi*) to make★ oneself. **4** (*far sì che*) to get★ oneself, to have oneself. // ~ **concorrenza** (*v. recipr.*) to compete with each other (*o* with one another); ~ **corrompere** (*leg.*) to take bribes; ~ **dare il conto (il listino dei prezzi, la ricevuta, ecc.)** to get one's bill (the price-list, the receipt, etc.); ~ **garante di qc.** to answer for st.; ~ **garante per q.** (*leg.*) to go surety for sb., to stand surety for sb.; (*per ottenergli la libertà provvisoria*) to go bail for sb.; ~ **licenziare** (*pers.*) to get the sack (*fam.*); to get the boot, to get the gate, to get the ax (*slang USA*); ~ **mallevadore di** (*q. o qc.*) (*cred., fin.*) to guarantee; ~ **prestare del danaro da q.** (*cred.*) to borrow some money from sb.; ~ **restituire qc.** to get st. back; ~ **riportare** (*Borsa*) to give on, to give the rate; ~ **risarcire** (*un danno e sim.*) (*leg.*) to recoup; ~ **scontare una cambiale** (*banca, cred.*) to get a bill discounted; ~ **strada** (*fig.*) to make one's way (in life); ~ **valere** to assert oneself.

fascetta, *n. f.* (*giorn.*) (*di rivista, ecc.*) wrapper. // ~ **sagomata per avvolgere monete** (*banca*) coin wrapper.

fascia, *n. f.* **1** band. **2** (*econ., fin.*) bracket. **3** (*giorn.*) (*di rivista, ecc.*) wrapper. // ~ **d'oscillazione** (*dei tassi di cambio, ecc.*) (*fin.*) band of fluctuation, parity band; ~ **di parità** (*fin.*) parity band; ~ **entro** ~ (*fin.*) band within band; ~ **esterna** (*fin.*) outer band; ~ **interna** (*fin.*) inner band; ~ **media di reddito** (*econ., fin.*) middle income bracket; ~ **mobile** (*fin.*) movable band; **sotto** ~ (*comun.*) under separate cover.

fascicolo, *n. m.* **1** (*ass.*) (*relativo a un cliente*) line card. **2** (*attr. uff.*) file. **3** (*giorn.*) (*d'una rivista, ecc.*) issue. **4** (*giorn., pubbl.*) (*inserito in un giornale*) inset. **5** (*pubbl.*) brochure.

fascio, *n. m.* **1** bundle. **2** (*banca*) (*di biglietti o buoni*) charge.

fase, *n. f.* phase, stage. // ~ **critica** critical stage; ~ **cruciale** crucial stage; ~ **depressiva** (*econ.*) downward phase; ~ **d'espansione** (*econ.*) upward phase; ~ **di fabbricazione** (*org. az.*) production run; ~ **di flessione** (*econ.*) downward phase, downswing, downtrend; ~ **di mercato** (*econ., market.*) market stage; ~ **di rialzo** (*Borsa, fin.*) upswing, uptrend; ~ **di stanchezza** (*econ.*) impasse; ~ **di sviluppo** (*econ.*) stage of development; ~ **negativa** (*econ.*) downward phase; ~ **positiva** (*econ.*) upward phase.

«FAS partenza», *locuz. avv.* (*trasp. mar.*) «free alongside ship» (*FAS*); «free alongside vessel».

«fathom», *n. m.* (*misura di profondità marina equivalente a sei piedi, e cioè a m 1,83*) fathom.

fatica, *n. f.* fatigue, labour, toil.

faticare, *v. i.* to labour, to toil.

faticoso, *a.* tiring, hard.

fattibile, *a.* feasible, practicable, workable. // **l'essere** ~ feasibility; **non** ~ unfeasible.

fatto[1], *a.* made. // ~ **a macchina** (*market.*) machine-made; ~ **a mano** (*market.*) handmade; ~ **dall'uomo** man-made; ~ **in buona fede** (*leg.*) bona fide (*attr.*); ~ **in mala fede** (*leg.*) mala fide (*attr.*); ~ **per iscritto** (*d'atto, accordo, e sim.*) in writing; ~ **su misura** (*market.*) made-to-measure; (*market.*) (*d'abito, e fig.*) tailor-made, tailored; custom-made, custom; ~ **su ordinazione** (*market.*) made-to-order, tailor-made; tailored, custom-built, custom (*USA*).

fatto[2], *n. m.* **1** fact. **2 i fatti,** *pl.* (*leg.*) the facts. // **un** ~ **compiuto** an accomplished fact; **fatti importanti** (*leg.*) material facts; **fatti perti-**

nenti (*leg.*) pertinent facts; ~ **reale** fact; **che indaga sui fatti** fact-finding; **di** ~ de facto; virtually (*avv.*); virtual (*a.*); **sul** ~ (*leg.*) in the act.

fattore, *n. m.* **1** factor. **2** (*agricolo*) steward; land agent (*ingl.*); (*d'una grande tenuta*) bailiff. **3** (*mat.*) factor. // **i fattori della produzione** (*econ.*) the factors (*o* agents) of production; ~ **d'espansione** (*econ.*) factor of expansion; **fattori motivazionali** (*market., pubbl.*) motivational factors; ~ **produttivo** (*p. es., il lavoro, le materie prime, ecc.*) (*econ.*) input; **i fattori produttivi primari** (*econ.*) the primary factors of production.

fattoria, *n. f.* **1** farm. **2** (*l'edificio*) farmhouse, homestead. // ~ **collettiva** (*econ.*) collective farm; ~ **per l'allevamento del bestiame** stock-farm.

fattoriale, *a.* (*mat.*) factorial. *n. m.* (*mat.*) factorial.

fattorino, *n. m.* **1** (*pers.*) (*in genere*) errand-boy, messenger-boy, messenger, footboy, foot page; commissionaire (*ingl.*); utility man (*USA*). **2** (*pers.*) (*d'un'azienda*) floor boy. **3** (*pers.*) (*d'un ufficio*) office-boy. **4** (*pers.*) (*addetto alle consegne*) delivery man.

fattura, *n. f.* **1** make, workmanship; (*il fabbricare*) making, manufacture. **2** (*market.*) invoice; bill of sale, bill (*USA*). // ~ **consolare** (*comm. est.*) consular invoice; ~ **definitiva** (*market.*) final invoice; ~ **d'acquisto** (*market.*) purchase invoice; ~ **in una serie d'esemplari** (*market.*) bill in a set; **fatture insolute** (*market.*) unpaid invoices; ~ **originale** (*market.*) original invoice; ~ **«pro forma»** (*market.*) pro forma invoice; ~ **provvisoria** (*market.*) provisional invoice; **una** ~ **rettificata** an amended invoice; ~ **simulata** (*market.*) pro forma invoice; **come da** ~ (*market.*) as per invoice; **come da vostra** ~ as per your invoice.

fatturare, *v. t.* **1** (*leg.*) (*sofisticare*) to adulterate, to sophisticate. **2** (*rag.*) to invoice; to bill (*USA*).

fatturato, *a.* (*rag.*) invoiced; billed (*USA*). *n. m.* (*market.*) proceeds of sales, sales (*pl.*); (*giro d'affari*) turnover; billing (*USA*).

fatturatrice, *n. f.* (*macch. uff.*) invoicing machine; billing machine (*USA*).

fatturazione, *n. f.* (*rag.*) invoicing; billing (*USA*).

fatturista, *n. m.* e *f.* (*pers.*) invoice clerk.

fautore, *n. m.* advocate, forwarder, promoter. // ~ **del bullionismo** (*econ., fin.*) bullionist; **un** ~ **del liberismo** an advocate of Free Trade; ~ **del mercantilismo** (*econ.*) mercantilist.

favore, *n. m.* favour. // **a** ~ **di** on behalf of; **di** ~ (*in omaggio*) complimentary; (*di preferenza*) discriminating; **in** ~ pro (*avv.* e *a.*).

favorevole, *a.* favourable; pro (*attr.*). // ~ **a** pro-; ~ **all'acquirente** (*market.*) (*di prezzo*) keen; **essere** ~ (*trasp. mar.*) (*di marea*) to serve; **chi è** ~ pro.

favorire, *v. t.* **1** to favour. **2** (*promuovere, incoraggiare*) to advance, to forward, to promote, to be conducive to. // ~ **la ripresa di** (*un mercato, ecc.*) (*fin., market.*) to rally; ~ **lo sviluppo industriale** (*econ.*) to help industrial development.

favorito, *a.* favoured. *a.* e *n. m.* favourite. // **clausola di nazione più favorita** (*comm. est.*) most-favoured-nation clause.

fede, *n. f.* **1** faith. **2** (*fiducia, anche*) reliance, trust. **3** (*parola, anche*) word. **4** (*documento che fa fede*) warrant. // ~ **di deposito** (*dog.*) warehouse warrant, warrant; ~ **di deposito doganale** (*dog.*) dock-warrant; ~ **di deposito provvisoria** (*dog.*) prime warrant; ~ **di nascita** (*amm.*) birth certificate; **in** ~ **di che** (*leg.*) in witness thereof, in testimony whereof; **tener** ~ **a una promessa** to keep one's promise.

fedele, *a.* **1** faithful, loyal. **2** (*verace*) true; (*preciso*) accurate. // **essere** ~ **alla parola data** to be faithful to one's word.

fedelmente, *avv.* **1** faithfully, loyally. **2** (*veracemente*) truly; (*accuratamente*) accurately.

fedeltà, *n. f.* **1** faithfulness, fidelity, loyalty. **2** (*accuratezza*) accuracy. // ~ **al negozio** (*market.*) store loyalty; ~ **all'azienda** (*pers.*) company loyalty; ~ **alla marca** (*market.*) brand loyalty.

feedback, *n. m.* (*elab. elettr.*) feedback.

feedforward, *n. m.* (*elab. elettr.*) feedforward.

felice, *a.* **1** happy. **2** (*lieto*) glad.

felicemente, *avv.* **1** happily; gladly. **2** (*senza incidenti*) safely. // ~ **in porto** (*trasp. mar.*) safely (*o* into) harbour.

fenomeno, *n. m.* **1** phenomenon*. **2** (*caso*) case. // **fenomeni di «disaffezione» nel mondo imprenditoriale** cases of entrepreneurial alienation.

feriale, *a.* (*pers.*) week; (*di fabbrica, ecc.*) work, working; (*d'ufficio*) business (*tutti attr.*).

ferie, *n. pl.* (*pers.*) holidays; vacation (*sing.*); vacations (*USA*). // ~ **pagate** (*pers.*) paid holidays, holidays with pay; **in** ~ (*pers.*) on vacation, on leave.

fermacarte, *n. m. inv.* (*attr. uff.*) paperweight.

fermare, *v. t.* **1** (*rendere fermo, assicurare*) to firm, to fasten, to tighten. **2** (*arrestare*) to arrest, to halt, to stop. 3 (*leg.*) to arrest. // ~ **un assegno** (*banca*) to stop a cheque, to stop the payment of a cheque.

fermarsi, *v. rifl.* 1 to halt, to stop. 2 (*trasp. aut.*) (*di automezzo*) to pull up.

fermata, *n. f.* 1 halt, stop, stand. 2 (*arresto, interruzione*) stoppage, stopping, standstill. 3 (*trasp.*) stop. 4 (*trasp. ferr., anche*) halt, call. // ~ **facoltativa** (*trasp.*) stop on request, request stop; ~ **obbligatoria** (*trasp.*) regular stop; **senza fermate** (*intermedie*) (*trasp. aut., trasp. ferr.*) non-stop (*avv.* e *a.*).

fermezza, *n. f.* 1 (*anche fig.*) firmness. 2 (*stabilità*) stability, steadiness.

fermo[1], *a.* 1 (*anche fig.*) firm; (*risoluto*) resolute, decided. 2 (*solido, fissato fermamente*) fast, hard, set, settled. 3 (*stabile*) stable, steady. 4 (*stazionario*) stationary, stagnant. 5 (*econ., market.*) (*di prezzo, ecc.*) sluggish. // ~ **per sciopero** (*sind.*) (*di stabilimento, ecc.*) strike-bound; « ~ **posta** » (*comun.*) (*di lettera, ecc.*) «to be left till called for», «to await arrival», «poste restante»; «care of general delivery» (*USA*).

fermo[2], *n. m.* 1 (*dog., leg.*) stoppage. 2 (*leg.*) provisional arrest, detention. 3 (*leg., trasp. mar.*) (*di nave mercantile*) embargo. // ~ **di polizia** (*leg.*) *V.* ~, *def. 2*; **mettere il** ~ **a un assegno** (*banca*) to stop a cheque.

ferrovia, *n. f.* (*trasp. ferr.*) railway, rail; railroad, road (*USA*). // ~ **a binario unico** (*trasp. ferr.*) one-track railway; **una** ~ **a scartamento ridotto** (*trasp. ferr.*) a narrow-gauge railway, a light railway; a narrow-gage railway, a narrow-gaged railway (*USA*); **una** ~ **a un solo binario** (*trasp. ferr.*) a single-track railway; ~ **elevata** (*trasp. ferr., USA*) elevated railroad; ~ **sotterranea** (*trasp. ferr.*) underground railway, underground; **per** ~ (*trasp. ferr.*) by rail.

ferroviario, *a.* railway, rail; railroad (*USA*) (*tutti attr.*).

festa, *n. f.* holiday. // ~ **del lavoro** labour day; ~ **nazionale** (*leg.*) public holiday, national holiday, national day.

fiacca, *n. f.* 1 (*stanchezza*) tiredness. 2 (*pigrizia*) laziness; sluggishness (*anche fig.*). 3 (*fig.*) dullness.

fiacchezza, *n. f.* 1 (*debolezza*) weakness. 2 (*fig.*) dullness, slackness.

fiacco, *a.* 1 (*anche fig.*) weak. 2 (*fig.*) dull, slack. 3 (*econ.*) (*di mercato, ecc.*) slow, narrow.

fiancata, *n. f.* (*trasp. mar.*) broadside.

fianco, *n. f.* side. // ~ **destro** (*di nave*) (*trasp. mar.*) starboard; ~ **sinistro** (*di nave*) (*trasp. mar.*) port; **a** ~ (*rag.*) per contra, as per contra; **a** ~ **della nave** (*trasp. mar.*) overside; **a** ~ **di** alongside.

fiasco, *n. m.* 1 flask. 2 (*fig.*) failure, «fiasco».

fidarsi, *v. rifl.* to trust; to depend, to rely (on).

fidatezza, *n. f.* 1 trustworthiness, dependability, reliability. 2 (*cred.*) (*di chi chiede credito*) responsibility.

fidato, *a.* trustworthy, dependable, reliable.

fidecommesso, *n. m.* (*leg.*) fidei-commissum; (deed of) trust.

fideiussione, *n. f.* (*leg.*) fidejussion, guaranty, surety, bail.

fideiussore, *n. m.* (*leg.*) fidejussor.

fido[1], *a. V.* **fidato.**

fido[2], *n. m.* 1 (*banca, cred.*) credit. 2 (*banca, cred.*) (*cifra di fido*) credit line, credit limit.

fiducia, *n. f.* confidence, credit, reliance, trust.

fiduciario, *a.* (*anche fin., leg.*) fiduciary. *n. m.* (*leg.*) trustee, fiduciary.

fiducioso, *a.* 1 trustful, hopeful. 2 (*anche fig., del mercato e sim.*) confident, confiding.

fiera, *n. f.* (*market.*) fair, show. // ~ **campionaria** (*market., pubbl.*) sample fair, trade fair; ~ **commerciale** (*market., pubbl.*) trade fair; ~ **del libro** (*market.*) book fair.

figlia, *n. f.* 1 daughter. 2 (*opposto a «madre», matrice*) counterpart.

figlio, *n. m.* son. // ~ **illegittimo** (*leg.*) unlawful son; **un** ~ **naturale** (*leg.*) a natural child, an unlawful son.

figura, *n. f.* 1 figure. 2 (*illustrazione*) picture.

figurare, *v. t.* 1 to figure. 2 (*rappresentare*) to represent. *v. i.* (*rag.*) to appear.

fila, *n. f.* 1 line, row, range. 2 (*rango*) rank. 3 (*di persone in attesa*) queue. // **le file dei disoccupati** (*sind.*) the ranks of the unemployed.

filiale, *n. f.* (*org. az.*) branch, branch office. // ~ **di banca** bank branch; ~ **di provincia** country branch.

film, *n. m.* (*pubbl.*) film. // ~ **a soggetto** feature film; ~ **sonoro** sound-film, talking film, talking picture, talkie.

filmare, *v. t.* (*pubbl.*) to film.

filmina, *n. f.* (*pubbl.*) filmstrip.

filo[1], *n. m.* 1 thread. 2 (*metallico*) wire. // **il** ~ **del telefono** (**del telegrafo**) the telephone (telegraph) wire.

filo-[2], *pref.* pro-. // **filoamericano** pro-American; **filosovietico** pro-Soviet.

filobus, *n. m. inv.* (*trasp. aut.*) trolley-bus.

finale, *a.* 1 final, definitive, ultimate. 2 (*con-

clusivo) conclusive. **3** (*terminale*) terminal.

finanza, *n. f.* **1** (*fin.*) finance. **2 finanze,** *pl.* (*fin.*) finances, financial resources; (*d'un privato*) cash. // ~ **locale** local finance; **finanze precarie** hand-to-mouth finances; ~ **pubblica** public finance, State finance; ~ **statale** State finance.

finanziamento, *n. m.* **1** (*fin.*) financing, finance, underwriting. **2** (*fin.*) (*prestito, mutuo*) loan. // ~ **a breve (termine)** (*cred.*) short-term financing, lending short, short-term borrowing; **un** ~ **a medio termine** (*cred.*) a medium-term loan; ~ **alla piccola industria** (*fin.*) small-business financing; ~ **comune** (*fin.*) joint financing; ~ **comunitario** (*fin.*) community financing; **un** ~ **su titoli** (*cred.*) a loan on stock.

finanziare, *v. t.* **1** (*in genere*) to finance. **2** (*comun., pubbl.*) (*un programma radiotelevisivo*) to sponsor. **3** (*cred., fin.*) (*un'impresa, anche*) to capitalize, to underwrite★; to ante (*slang USA*). **4** (*fin.*) (*un privato*) to supply (sb.) with funds, to stake; to bankroll (*slang USA*). // ~ **di nuovo** (*fin.*) to re-finance.

finanziari, *n. pl.* (*Borsa*) holding company stocks.

finanziaria, *n. f.* (*fin.*) holding company. // **una** ~ **pubblica** a State holding company.

finanziario, *a.* (*fin.*) financial, pecuniary, moneyed.

finanziatore, *n. m.* **1** (*fin.*) financier, underwriter. **2** (*fin.*) (*prestatore di denaro*) money lender.

finanziere, *n. m.* **1** (*dog.*) customs officer. **2** (*dog.*) (*alla frontiera*) frontier guard. **3** (*fin.*) financier. // **i finanzieri di New York** Wall Street (*fig., USA*).

fine[1], *a.* **1** fine, delicate. **2** (*sottile*) thin, slender. **3** (*di persona*) fine, discriminating. // **finissimo** (*market.*) (*d'articolo, ecc.*) superfine.

fine[2], *n. f.* **1** end, close, termination; tail (*fig.*). **2** (*leg.*) (*d'una causa, anche*) determination. // ~ **corrente (mese)** (*Borsa*) end current account, end this account, end this; **la** ~ **del rischio assicurato** (*ass.*) the termination of the insured risk; **la** ~ **dell'anno finanziario** (*fin.*) the end of the fiscal year; ~ **d'anno** year end; ~ **prossimo (mese)** (*Borsa*) end next account, end next; ~ **settimana** week-end; **di** ~ **d'anno** (*econ., fin., rag.*) year-end (*a. attr.*); **di** ~ **esercizio** (*econ., fin., rag.*) year-end (*a. attr.*).

fine[3], *n. m.* **1** (*scopo*) end, aim, goal, object, view. **2** (*conclusione, risultato*) conclusion, result. // **fini economici** (*econ.*) economic ends; **fini sociali** social ends.

fingere, *v. t.* **1** to feign, to pretend, to assume. **2** (*leg.*) (*simulare*) to simulate. // ~ **di non conoscere** to ignore.

finire, *v. i.* **1** to end, to end up, to come★ to an end, to terminate; (*bene, male, ecc.*) to result. **2** (*cessare, smettere*) to cease, to stop. **3** (*market.*) (*di scorte*) to run★ out. **4** (*market.*) (*di merce*) to sell★ out. **5** (*org. az., pers.*) to stop work. *v. t.* **1** to finish, to end, to bring★ to an end, to close. **2** (*completare*) to complete. **3** (*concludere*) to conclude, to end by. **4** (*fin., market.*) (*esaurire: fondi, scorte e sim.*) to run★ out of, to run★ short of. // ~ **di registrare** (*rag.*) to enter up; **essere finito** (*di lavoro, ecc.*) to be over.

finito, *a.* **1** finished. **2** (*mat.*) finite, terminate. **3** (*pers.*) (*esperto*) accomplished, skilful. // **non** ~ unfinished.

finitura, *n. f.* **1** finish. **2** (*tocco finale*) finishing touch. // **finiture di precisione** (*org. az.*) precision finish.

finto, *a.* **1** false; mock, sham, dummy, bogus (*attr.*). **2** (*market.*) imitation. // ~ **cuoio** (*market.*) imitation leather; **finta pelle** (*market.*) imitation leather.

finzione, *n. f.* **1** falsehood; assumption, pretence. **2** (*leg.*) simulation, sham.

fiorente, *a.* **1** flourishing, thriving. **2** (*econ.*) booming. // **un** ~ **centro turistico** a thriving tourist centre.

fiorino, *n. m.* (*olandese*) guilder.

fiorire, *v. i.* **1** (*prosperare*) to flourish, to thrive★. **2** (*econ.*) to boom.

firma, *n. f.* **1** signature, subscription. **2** (*leg.*) hand. // **firme abbinate** (*amm.*) joint signatures; **una** ~ **autentica** an authentic signature; ~ **d'autenticazione** (*leg.*) countersignature, countersign; ~ **di legalizzazione** (*leg.*) countersignature; ~ **disgiunta** (*amm.*) disjoined signature; ~ **falsa** (*leg.*) forged signature, forgery; ~ **in bianco** blank signature; ~ **singola** (*amm.*) separate signature.

firmare, *v. t.* **1** to sign, to subscribe. **2** (*leg., anche*) to set★ one's hand to (a document). // ~ **a tergo** (*cred.*) to endorse; ~ **la corrispondenza** (*comun.*) to sign the mail; ~ **di nuovo** to re-sign; ~ **documenti ufficiali** (*leg.*) to subscribe official documents; ~ **in calce** (*un documento, una lettera, ecc.*) to undersign; ~ **il registro delle presenze** (*all'albergo, ecc.*) (*tur.*) to sign in; ~ **un testamento** (*leg.*) to sign a will.

firmatario, *n. m.* (*leg.*) signatory, signer, signee. *a.* (*leg.*) signatory.

fiscale, *a.* (*fin.*) fiscal; tax, revenue (*attr.*).

fiscalismo, *n. m.* (*fin.*) fiscality.

fiscalista, *n. m.* e *f.* (*fin.*) tax expert; taxation consultant.

fiscalità, *n. f.* 1 (*fin.*) taxation, system of taxation. 2 (*fin.*) (*fiscalismo*) fiscality. // ~ **diretta** (*fin.*) direct taxation; ~ **indiretta** (*fin.*) indirect taxation.

fiscalizzare, *v. t.* (*fin.*) to make★ (st.) fiscal. // (*dello stato italiano*) ~ **gli aumenti dei contributi (*o* degli oneri) sociali** (*econ.*) to pay the increases in contributions for social benefits (in industry).

fisco, *n. m.* 1 (*fin.*) (*erario*) national revenue, public revenue, inland revenue, revenue. 2 (*fin.*) (*l'ufficio delle imposte*) (the) tax office; (*in G.B.*) (the) Commissioners of Inland Revenue. 3 (*fin.*) (*chi ne cura le entrate*) (the) revenue authorities; (the) treasury officers. // **agente del** ~ tax officer, officer of inland revenue.

fisiocrate, *n. m.* (*econ.*) physiocrat.

fisiocratico, *a.* (*econ.*) physiocratic.

fisiocrazia, *n. f.* (*econ.*) physiocracy.

fissaggio, *n. m.* (*Borsa*) fixing.

fissare, *v. t.* 1 (*rendere fisso*) to fix, to set★. 2 (*fermare*) to fasten. 3 (*guardar fisso*) to fix one's eyes on (sb.); to stare at, to gaze at. 4 (*stabilire*) to fix, to appoint, to arrange, to assign, to set★ down, to settle, to schedule. 5 (*in un luogo*) to locate. 6 (*nella memoria, ecc.*) to impress. 7 (*fin.*) (*un'imposta, ecc.*) to assess. 8 (*fin., market.*) (*prezzi, quotazioni, ecc.*) to peg. 9 (*market.*) (*un prezzo, ecc., anche*) to name, to prescribe. 10 (*tur.*) (*prenotare*) to book. // ~ **l'ammontare dei danni da pagare** (*ass.*) to fix the amount of damages to be allowed; ~ **l'ammontare del premio per** (*un certo rischio*) (*ass.*) to rate; ~ **il corso di** (*qc.*) (*Borsa, fin.*) to price; (*econ., market.*) to price; ~ **una data** to fix a date; ~ **una data somma come risarcimento di danni** (*leg.*) to lay damages at a certain sum; ~ **di nuovo** (*un'imposta, un imponibile, ecc.*) (*fin.*) to reassess; ~ **il giorno del processo** (*leg.*) to assign a day for the trial; ~ **i prezzi** (*market.*) to fix prices; ~ **un prezzo** (*econ.*) to target a price; (*market.*) (*di venditore e acquirente*) to settle a price; ~ **il prezzo di** (*qc.*) (*Borsa, fin.*) to price; (*econ., market.*) to price; (*market.*) to tag; ~ **le tariffe per il trasporto delle merci** (*trasp.*) to rate goods; ~ **un'udienza** (*leg.*) to call a case.

fissato, *a.* 1 fixed (*V.* **fissare**). 2 (*dichiarato, dato*) stated, given. 3 (*nella memoria, ecc.*) impressed. 4 (*leg.*) vested. 5 (*market.*) (*di prezzo, anche*) prescribed. // ~ **bollato** (*Borsa, fin.*) contract note; (*d'acquisto*) bought note, purchase confirmation; (*di vendita*) sold note, sale confirmation; ~ **dalla legge** (*leg.*) statutory.

fissazione, *n. f.* 1 (*in genere*) fixing. 2 (*market.*) (*di prezzi, anche*) prescription. // **la** ~ **dei prezzi** (*econ.*) the fixing of prices, price-fixing; **la** ~ **del valore in dogana** (*dog.*) the valuation for customs purposes; **la** ~ **delle nuove parità** (*fin.*) the fixing of the new parities.

fisso, *a.* 1 fixed, set. 2 (*di prezzo, anche*) standing, flat. 3 (*stabilito, fissato*) settled, stated. 4 (*stazionario*) stationary, steady. // **un impiegato** ~ an employee on the regular staff.

fittizio, *a.* fictitious, dummy, sham.

fitto[1], *a.* thick, dense, close.

fitto[2], *n. m. V.* **affitto.**

fiume, *n. m.* river. // **un** ~ **navigabile** (*trasp.*) a navigable river.

fixing, *n. m.* (*Borsa*) fixing.

flagrante, *a.* flagrant. // **in** ~ (*leg.*) in the act.

flagranza, *n. f.* (*leg.*) flagrancy.

flessibile, *a.* (*anche fig.*) flexible.

flessibilità, *n. f.* (*anche fig.*) flexibility. // ~ **automatica** (*dei tassi di cambio*) (*fin.*) built-in flexibility; ~ **illimitata** (*fin.*) unlimited flexibility; ~ **libera** (*fin.*) unmanaged flexibility; ~ **limitata** (*fin.*) limited flexibility; ~ **manovrata** (*fin.*) managed flexibility.

flessione, *n. f.* 1 flection; flexion. 2 (*econ., fin.*) decrease, decline, drop, downswing, downfall, downturn. 3 (*econ., fin.*) (*p. es., della domanda*) cooling-off. 4 (*market.*) (*di prezzi, ecc.*) falling-off, sag. // **una** ~ **del gettito fiscale** (*fin.*) a drop in state revenues; **una** ~ **nelle quotazioni** (*Borsa*) a slump in prices.

florido, *a.* flourishing, thriving.

flotta, *n. f.* (*trasp. mar.*) fleet, navy. // ~ **mercantile** (*trasp. mar.*) merchant fleet, merchant navy.

flottante, *n. m.* (*nelle locuz.* **a largo** ~, **a scarso** ~) *V. sotto* **titolo.**

fluidità, *n. f.* (*anche fig.*) fluidity.

fluido, *a.* (*anche fig.*) fluid.

fluire, *v. i.* to flow.

flusso, *n. m.* 1 flow, stream. 2 (*trasp. mar.*) (*di marea*) flow. // ~ **di materiali** (*org. az.*) flow of materials; ~ **finanziario** (*econ.*) flow of funds.

fluttuante, *a.* 1 fluctuant, fluctuating, floating. 2 (*econ., fig.*) (*di moneta*) floating. 3 (*fin.*) (*di debito pubblico*) unfunded.

fluttuare, *v. i.* 1 to fluctuate, to float, to swing★ (*anche fig.*). 2 (*econ., fin.*) to float. // **il** ~ **dei prezzi** (*market.*) the swing of prices.

fluttuazione, *n. f.* 1 fluctuation, swing (*anche fig.*). 2 (*econ., fig.*) (*di una moneta*) floating, float. // ~ **ciclica** (*econ.*) cyclical fluctuation; ~ **comune delle monete europee** (*econ., *fin.*) joint floating of European currencies, joint European float; ~ **controllata** (*d'una moneta*) (*econ., fin.*) controlled floating, managed floating; **le fluttuazioni della congiuntura** (*econ.*) the increase and decrease of economic activity; **fluttuazioni delle monete** (*econ.*) currency fluctuations; ~ **verso l'alto** (*d'una moneta*) (*econ., fin.*) floating up; ~ **verso il basso** (*d'una moneta*) (*econ., fin.*) floating down.

fluviale, *a.* (*trasp.*) fluvial; river (*attr.*). // **navigazione** ~ river navigation; **vie fluviali** inland waterways.

F.O.B. destino, *locuz. avv.* (*trasp. mar.*) ex ship, free overside, under ship's derrick, under ship's tackle.

F.O.B. partenza, *locuz. avv.* (*trasp. mar.*) free on board.

foglietto, *n. m.* slip (of paper); (*volantino*) leaflet. // ~ **pubblicitario** (*pubbl.*) handbill; throwaway, dodger (*USA*).

foglio, *n. m.* 1 (*di carta, ecc.*) sheet. 2 (*giorn.*) (*giornale*) newspaper, paper. // ~ **delle presenze** (*pers.*) attendance sheet; ~ **di carta carbone** (*attr. uff.*) carbon; ~ **di carta intestata** letterhead, letterheading; **il** ~ **d'entrata** (*in un «trittico»*) (*dog.*) the importation voucher (*of a pass sheet*); ~ **d'istruzioni** (*org. az.*) job sheet, instruction card; ~ **di liquidazione** (*Borsa*) clearing sheet; ~ **di presenza** (*pers.*) time-sheet; ~ **di prolungamento** (*d'un documento*) allonge; ~ **di riscontro** (*market.*) tally sheet, tally card; ~ **di sottoscrizione e di ripartizione** (*d'azioni*) (*fin.*) application and allotment sheet; **il** ~ **d'uscita** (*in un «trittico»*) (*dog.*) the exportation voucher (*of a pass sheet*); ~ **intero** (*di libro mastro*) (*rag.*) folio; **fogli mobili d'aggiornamento** amendment sheets; ~ **paga** (*pers.*) wage-sheet; ~ **per le risposte** (*in un questionario, ecc.*) (*market., pubbl.*) reply sheet; ~ **protocollo** (*per uso bollo*) (*leg.*) legal cap; ~ **rosa** (*trasp. aut., fam.*) provisional licence; ~ **volante** (*pubbl.*) fly sheet, handbill.

fonda, *n. f.* (*trasp. mar.*) anchorage. // **essere alla** ~ (*trasp. mar.*) to be (*o* to lie, *o* to ride) at anchor.

fondamentale, *a.* fundamental, essential, primary.

fondamento, *n. m.* 1 (*anche fig.*) foundation, basis*. 2 (*motivo*) ground. // **senza** ~ (*d'un'accusa*) (*leg.*) groundless; unfounded.

fondare, *v. t.* 1 (*porre le fondamenta di, basare*) to found, to base, to ground. 2 (*costituire, formare*) to found, to constitute, to establish, to institute, to set* up, to start. // ~ **un comitato** to set up a committee.

fondarsi, *v. rifl.* 1 to be founded. 2 (*di persona*) to base oneself. 3 (*anche leg.*) to rest.

fondatezza, *n. f.* (*anche leg.*) validity. // **la** ~ **d'una pretesa** (*leg.*) the validity of a claim.

fondato, *a.* (*anche leg.*) valid. // **essere** ~ to be founded; (*leg., anche*) to lie, to rest.

fondatore, *n. m.* 1 founder. 2 (*fin.*) (*d'una società*) promoter.

fondazione, *n. f.* 1 foundation, constitution, establishment, set-up. 2 (*fin.*) (*d'una società*) promotion.

fondere, *v. t.* 1 (*metalli, ecc.*) to melt. 2 (*mescolare*) to blend. 3 (*econ., fin.*) to amalgamate, to combine, to consolidate, to incorporate, to merge. // ~ **banche** (*fin.*) to consolidate banks.

fondersi, *v. rifl.* 1 (*di neve e sim.*) to melt. 2 (*di colori, ecc.*) to dissolve. *v. recipr.* (*econ., fin.*) to amalgamate, to combine, to incorporate, to merge.

fondiario, *a.* (*econ.*) landed, land (*attr.*); agricultural. // **banca di credito** ~ agricultural bank; **imposta fondiaria** (*fin.*) land tax; **proprietà fondiaria** landed property.

fondo, *n. m.* 1 (*parte più bassa*) bottom. 2 (*estremità*) end. 3 (*parte posteriore*) back. 4 (*proprietà*) estate, property. 5 (*econ.*) (*d'una congiuntura*) trough. 6 (*econ., fin.*) (*del tunnel monetario*) floor. 7 (*fin., rag.*) fund. 8 (*trasp. mar.*) (*del mare, ecc.*) ground, bottom. 9 **fondi,** *pl.* (*fin., rag.*) funds; money, exchequer (*sing.*). // ~ **a capitale fisso** (*fin.*) closed-end fund; ~ **a capitale variabile** (*fin.*) open-end fund; ~ **«aperto»** (*fin.*) open-end fund; ~ **cassa per piccole spese** (*rag.*) imprest fund; ~ **«chiuso»** (*fin.*) closed-end fund; ~ **comune d'investimento** (*fin.*) investment fund, investment trust, unit trust; mutual fund (*USA*); ~ (*d'investimento*) **con basso indebitamento** (*fin.*) low-geared trust; low-leverage trust (*USA*); **fondi con «effetto leva»** (*Borsa, fin.*) leverage funds; ~ (*d'investimento*) **con forte indebitamento** (*fin.*) highly geared trust; high-leverage trust (*USA*); ~ (*d'investimento*) **con sole azioni ordinarie** (*fin.*) trust without any gearing; trust without any leverage (*USA*); ~ **del Tesoro** (*presso la Banca d'Inghilterra*) (*fin.*) Consolidated Fund; ~ **della stiva** (*trasp. mar.*) dunnage; ~ **d'ammortamento** (*fin., rag.*) sinking fund, depreciation fund, redemption fund; (*rag.*) allowance for depreciation, reserve for depreciation; **fondi d'assistenza** relief funds; ~ **di cassa** (*rag.*) cash in hand; ~ **di cassa per le piccole spese** (*rag.*) petty cash; ~ **di cauzione** (*fin.*) guarantee fund; **fondi di copertura** (*Borsa, fin.*) hedge funds; ~ **di deprezzamento** (*fin., rag.*) depreciation fund; ~ **di dotazione** (*rag.*) endowment fund; ~ **di garanzia** (*fin.*) guarantee fund; ~ **d'investimento a capitale fisso** closed-end investment fund, fixed trust; ~ **d'investimento a capitale variabile** (*fin.*) open-end investment fund; ~ **d'investimento a portafoglio differenziato** (*fin.*) diversified investment fund; ~ **d'investimento «aperto»** (*fin.*) open-end investment fund; ~ **d'investimento «chiuso»** (*fin.*) closed-end investment fund; ~ **d'investimento operante all'estero** (*in origine, fuori degli U.S.A.*) (*fin.*) offshore fund; ~ **d'investimento operante in patria** (*in origine, negli U.S.A.*) (*fin.*) onshore fund; **fondi di magazzino** (*market.*) remainders; rummage (*sing.*); ~ **di previdenza** (*pers., rag.*) provident fund, contingency fund; **fondi di protezione** (*Borsa, fin.*) hedge funds; ~ **di riserva** (*fin., rag.*) reserve fund, reserve, emergency fund, earned surplus; backlog (*slang USA*); ~ **di riserva per i rimborsi di capitale** (*fin.*) capital redemption reserve fund; **fondi disponibili** available funds; ~ (*d'investimento*) **di sviluppo** (*fin.*) growth fund; ~ **imposte da liquidare** (*rag.*) provision account for income taxes, reserve account for income taxes; «**fondi insufficienti**» (*nel conto d'un cliente: per coprire un assegno*) (*banca*) «not sufficient funds»; **fondi liberi** (*fin., rag.*) loose funds; ~ **marino** (*trasp. mar.*) sea bed; ~ **monetario comune** (*fin.*) pool; ~ **Monetario Internazionale (FMI)** International Monetary Fund (*IMF*); **fondi neri** (*fin.*) slush funds; ~ **pensioni** (*pers., rag.*) pension fund; **fondi privi di qualsiasi destinazione** (*fin., rag.*) loose funds; **fondi propri** (*fin.*) own funds; **fondi pubblici** (*fin.*) public funds; «**fondi rischi**» (*rag.*) provision accounts, reserve accounts, valuation accounts; ~ **rotativo** (*cred., fin.*) revolving fund; ~ **rustico** country estate, farm; ~ **salari** (*econ.*) wages fund; **fondi sociali** (*fin.*) partnership funds; ~ **svalutazione** (*merci, titoli, ecc.*) (*rag.*) provision account for depreciation, reserve account for depreciation; ~ **svalutazione crediti** (*rag.*) allowance for bad debts, allowance for dubious accounts, allowance for incollectible accounts, provision account for bad debts, reserve account for bad debts; «~ **tasse**» (*rag.*) «accrued taxes»; ~ **urbano** building; (*casa*) house; (*negozio*) shop; «~ **utili**» (*org. az.*) benefit fund; «**senza fondi**» (*banca*) (*di conto*) «no funds» (*N.F.*).

fonogramma, *n. m.* (*comun.*) written telephone message.

fonoriproduttore, *n. m.* (*macch. uff.*) transcribing machine.

fonte, *n. f.* **1** source. **2** (*giorn.*) source. // **fonti d'approvvigionamento** (*org. az.*) supply sources; **una ~ d'informazioni** (*giorn.*) a source of information; ~ **di profitti illegali** source of illegal profits; gravy (*slang USA*); ~ **di reddito** (*econ., fin.*) source of income; **fonti di reddito** (*econ., fin.*) resources; **fonti di rifornimento** (*org. az.*) supply sources.

forare, *v. t.* (*biglietti, ecc.*) to punch.

forcella, *n. f.* (*econ.*) bracket. // **la ~ dei prezzi indicativi dei due Stati Membri produttori** the target price bracket of the two producing Member States.

forense, *a.* (*leg.*) forensic.

forfait, *n. m.* lump sum. // **a ~** on a lump-sum basis; contractually (*avv.*); contract (*a. attr.*).

forfettaggio, *n. m.* (*comm. est., fin.*) forfaitement (*francese*) (*tecnica di credito all'esportazione*).

forfettario, *a.* contract (*attr.*). // **pagamento ~** lump-sum payment; **prezzo ~** contract price.

forma, *n. f.* **1** form, shape, frame. **2** (*leg.*) form. **3** (*pubbl.*) form. // **forme d'organizzazione commerciale** forms of business organization; ~ **di vendita diretta «porta a porta»** (*market.*) door-to-door sales approach.

formale, *a.* formal.

formalità, *n. f. inv.* formality. // **formalità di frontiera** (*comm. est.*) frontier formalities; **formalità doganali** (*dog.*) customs formalities.

formare, *v. t.* **1** to form, to constitute. **2** (*modellare*) to shape, to frame. // ~ **un «cartello»** (*econ.*) to cartelize; ~ **un numero** (*telefonico*) (*comun.*) to dial a number; ~ **riserve di** (*materie prime, merci, ecc.*) (*org. az.*) to stockpile; ~ **una società** (*leg.*) (*di persone*) to form a partnership; (*di capitali*) to constitute a company.

formatore d'opinione, *n. m.* (*market., pubbl.*) opinion leader, opinion maker.

formazione, *n. f.* **1** formation, constitution. **2** (*pers.*) (*addestramento*) coaching, training. // ~ **dei dirigenti** executive coaching, manager development; ~ **dei prezzi** (*econ.*) price formation; ~ **d'un «cartello»** (*econ.*) cartelization; ~ **professionale** (*pers.*) vocational training.

formula, *n. f.* **1** (*mat.*) formula★. **2** (*forma*) form. **3** (*dicitura*) wording. // ~ **iniziale** (*nelle lettere: p. es., Dear Sir*) (*comun.*) salutation.

formulare, *v. t.* **1** to formulate. **2** (*formare*) to form, to frame. **3** (*esprimere*) to express, to word. // ~ **degli obiettivi** (*org. az.*) to set objectives; ~ **un piano** to form a plan, to draw a plan; ~ (*piani, ecc.*) **su scala ridotta** (*econ.*) to rescale.

formulazione, *n. f.* **1** formulation, wording. **2** (*formazione*) formation, framing.

fornire, *v. t.* **1** to furnish, to provide; (*dare*) to give★, to contribute. **2** (*eseguire: una prestazione*) to perform. **3** (*market.*) to furnish; to supply (sb. with st.). **4** (*org. az.*) to stock. // ~ **cauzione** (*leg.*) to give security; ~ **la copertura per** (*banca, cred.*) to cover; ~ (*articoli, ecc.*) **di cartellino segnaprezzo** (*market.*) to tag; ~ **di codice d'avviamento postale** (*comun., USA*) to zip-code; ~ **di macchinari** (*org. az.*) to mechanize; ~ (*un'azienda, ecc.*) **di nuovo personale** (*org. az., pers.*) to restaff; ~ (*q.*) **di referenze** (*pers.*) to reference; ~ **d'uomini** to man; ~ **prove** (*leg.*) to bring evidence, to put in evidence; ~ **le prove d'un sinistro** (*ass.*) to prove a loss.

fornitore, *n. m.* **1** (*econ., market.*) supplier, furnisher, stockist. **2** (*market.*) (*di viveri*) victualler. // «~ (*o* **fornitori**) **della Casa Reale**» «by appointment to H.M. the Queen (*o* H.M. the King)»; ~ **navale** (*trasp. mar.*) ship-chandler.

fornitura, *n. f.* **1** supply; (*il fornire, anche*) supplying. **2 forniture,** *pl.* supplies, stores; (*attrezzature*) furnishings, fittings. // **forniture di bordo** (*trasp. mar.*) ship's stores; **forniture navali** ship's stores; (*l'azienda*) ship-chandlery; **forniture per ufficio** office furnishings.

foro[1], *n. m.* hole.

Foro[2], *n. m.* **1** (*leg.*) (*tribunale*) Court of justice; law-Court. **2** (*leg.*) (*l'avvocatura*) (the) Bar. // ~ **competente** (*leg.*) place of jurisdiction.

forte, *a.* **1** strong. **2** (*duro*) hard. **3** (*considerevole, grande*) big, high, remarkable, considerable, large; large-scale (*attr.*). **4** (*della concorrenza*) keen. **5** (*fin.*) (*di valuta*) strong; hard. // **una** ~ **diminuzione** (*di prezzi*) (*market.*) a big fall; **un** ~ **disavanzo** (*fin., rag.*) a high deficit; **un** ~ **guadagno** a large gain; **un** ~ **incremento dei prezzi** (*market.*) a substantial rise in prices; ~ **influsso** strong influence; impact; **una** ~ **perdita** a heavy loss; **forti spese** large expenditures, heavy expenses.

forza, *n. f.* **1** strength, force. **2** (*potenza*) power. **3** (*pubbl.*) (*del messaggio pubblicitario*) impact. // **forze del lavoro** (*econ.*) labour force, work force, manpower; **la** ~ **della legge** (*leg.*) the power of the law; ~ **d'attrazione** (*econ.*) pull force; ~ **d'urto** impact; ~ **finanziaria stimata** (*fin.*) estimated financial strength; ~ (*di*) **lavoro** (*econ., org. az.*) work force, manpower; ~ **maggiore** (*ass., leg.*) force majeure, act of God, cause beyond one's control; **la** ~ **pubblica** the police; ~ **respingente** (*econ.*) push force; **a tutta** ~ (*trasp. mar.*) at full speed.

forzare, *v. t.* **1** (*costringere*) to force, to compel. **2** (*sforzare*) to force, to strain. **3** (*leg.*) (*aprire con la forza*) to force (st.) open; to break★ (st.) open.

forzato, *a.* forced, compulsory, involuntary.

forziere, *n. m.* coffer, strong-box.

forzoso, *a.* forced, compulsory.

foto, *n. f. inv.* photo. // ~ **d'archivio** (*giorn.*) stock photo; ~ **di copertina** (*giorn.*) cover photo.

fotocolor, *n. m.* (*pubbl.*) colour transparency.

fotocopia, *n. f.* (*giorn., pubbl.*) photocopy.

fotocopiare, *v. t.* (*giorn., pubbl.*) to photocopy.

fotografare, *v. t.* (*giorn., pubbl.*) to photograph, to photo. // ~ **su microfilm** (*pubbl.*) to microfilm.

fotografia, *n. f.* **1** (*giorn., pubbl.*) (*il procedimento*) photography. **2** (*giorn., pubbl.*) (*il risultato*) photo.

fotografico, *a.* (*giorn., pubbl.*) photographic, photographical.

fotografo, *n. m.* (*pers.*) photographer.

fotomontaggio, *n. m.* (*giorn., pubbl.*) (*il procedimento e il risultato*) photomontage, montage.

fotoreporter, *n. m.* (*giorn.*) press-photographer.

fragile, *a.* fragile, breakable. // «**fragile**» (*su una cassa, ecc.*) «handle with care», «with care».

fraintendere, *v. t.* to misunderstand★.

franchigia, *n. f.* **1** (*ass.*) franchise. **2** (*fin.*) exemption. **3** (*leg.*) franchise. // ~ **di peso** (*trasp.*) weight allowed free; ~ **diplomatica** diplomatic immunity; ~ **doganale** (*dog., fin.*) custom franchise; ~ **fiscale** (*fin.*) tax exemption, franking; ~ (*di peso*) **per il bagaglio** (*trasp.*) free allowance; **bagaglio in** ~ (*trasp.*) free luggage; **con** ~ **fiscale** (*fin.*) (*di reddito*) franked; **in** ~ **doganale** (*dog., fin.*) duty-free; **in** ~ **postale** (*comun.*) post-free; **marinai in** ~ (*trasp. mar.*) sailors on shore leave; **senza** ~ **fiscale** (*fin.*) unfranked (*a.*).

franco[1], *a.* **1** frank, outspoken; (*leale*) loyal. **2** (*libero, aperto*) free, open. **3** (*market., trasp.*) free, ex. **4** (*market., trasp.*) (*esente da ogni spesa*) «franco», «free of charge». // «~ **a bordo**» (*trasp. mar.*) «free on board» (*FOB*); «~ **a domicilio**» (*trasp.*) «free of charge», «franco»; «~ **banchina**» (*trasp. mar.*) «free on wharf» (*FOW*), «ex wharf»; «~ **d'avaria**» (*ass. mar.*) «free of average»; «~ **d'avaria generale**» (*ass. mar.*) «free of general average»; «~ **d'avaria particolare**» (*ass. mar.*) «free of particular average» (*FPA*); «~ **di dazio**» (*dog., fin.*) «duty-free»; «~ **d'imballaggio**» (*market.*) «packing free»; «~ **di perdita totale**» (*ass. mar.*) «free of total loss»; «~ **di porto**» (*trasp.*) «carriage free», «carriage paid», «carriage prepaid»; «~ **di posta**» (*comun.*) «post-free»; «~ **di spese**» (*trasp.*) «free of charge», «cost free»; «~ **di spese portuali**» (*trasp. mar.*) «free of port charges»; «~ **di spese postali**» (*comun.*) *V.* «~ **di posta**»; «~ **docks**» (*trasp. mar.*) «free docks»; «~ **fabbrica**» (*trasp.*) «ex factory»; «~ **magazzino**» (*trasp.*) «ex store», «ex warehouse»; «~ **molo**» (*trasp. mar.*) «ex pier»; «~ **nave**» (*trasp. mar.*) «ex ship», «ex steamer»; «~ **officina**» (*trasp.*) «ex works»; «~ **provvigione**» (*market.*) «free of commission»; «~ **raffineria**» (*trasp.*) «ex refinery»; «~ **sotto bordo**» (*trasp. mar.*) «free alongside ship» (*FAS*), «free alongside vessel»; «~ **stabilimento**» (*trasp.*) «ex works»; «~ **stazione d'arrivo**» (*trasp. ferr.*) «free to the receiving station»; «~ **stazione (ferroviaria)**» (*trasp. ferr.*) «free on rail» (*FOR*); «~ **vagone**» (*alla stazione di partenza*) (*trasp. ferr.*) «free on rail» (*FOR*), «free on truck» (*FOT*), «free on waggon».

franco[2], *n. m.* (*fin.*) (*moneta francese, svizzera e belga*) franc. // **franchi-oro** (*econ., fin.*) gold francs.

francobollo, *n. m.* (*comun.*) postage stamp, stamp. // ~ **adesivo** adhesive stamp; ~ (*celebrativo*) **in franchigia** franchise stamp; **senza** ~ (*comun.*) (*di lettera*) unstamped.

fraudolento, *a.* (*leg.*) fraudulent.

fraudolenza, *n. f.* (*leg.*) fraudulence.

frazionamento, *n. m.* fractioning, splitting, split. // ~ **azionario** (*fin.*) stock split; **il** ~ **del rischio** (*ass.*) the spread of risk.

frazionare, *v. t.* to fraction, to split★ up, to break★ up.

frazionario, *a.* (*mat.*) fractional, divisional.

frazionato, *a.* (*fin.*) (*di titolo azionario*) split.

frazione, *n. f.* 1 fraction. 2 (*mat.*) fraction. // ~ **complessa** (*mat.*) complex fraction; ~ **composta** (*mat.*) compound fraction; **per ogni ~ indivisibile di cento dollari** for every 100 dollars or fraction of 100 dollars.

frenare, *v. t.* 1 to brake. 2 (*fig.*) to check, to curb, to hold★ down, to restrain, to temper. 3 (*rallentare*) to slow, to slow down. // ~ **la concorrenza** (*market.*) to check competition; ~ **l'inflazione** (*econ.*) to curb inflation; ~ **la spirale dei prezzi e dei salari** (*econ.*) to hold down the prices-wages spiral.

freno, *n. m.* 1 (*anche fig.*) brake. 2 (*fig.*) check, control, curb, restraint. 3 (*disincentivo*) disincentive. // ~ **all'aumento dei redditi** (*econ.*) incomes restraint.

frequentare, *v. t.* to attend.

frequentatore, *n. m.* (*market.*) regular customer (*o* client).

frequenza, *n. f.* 1 frequency. 2 (*a scuola, ecc.*) attendance. // ~ **d'acquisto** (*market.*) frequency of purchase; ~ **scolastica** attendance at school.

fresco, *a.* (*anche fig.*) fresh. // ~ **di stampa** (*giorn.*) fresh off the press.

frizione, *n. f.* (*anche fig.*) friction. // **di** ~ frictional.

frodare, *v. t.* 1 to deceive, to cheat, to swindle. 2 (*leg.*) to defraud. *v. i.* (*leg.*) to commit a fraud.

frode, *n. f.* 1 deceit, cheat, sham, swindle. 2 (*fin., leg.*) bubble. 3 (*leg.*) fraud.

fronte[1], *n. f.* 1 (*di persona*) forehead. 2 (*d'edificio*) front. // **di** ~ opposite; vis-à-vis; **di ~ a** in front of; **trovarsi di ~ a** (*fig.*) to be confronted with.

fronte[2], *n. m.* (*quasi in ogni senso*) front. // **il ~ dei prezzi** (*fin.*) the price front; ~ **del molo** (*trasp. mar.*) pier face, waterfront; **un ~ monetario europeo unico** (*econ.*) a single European monetary front.

fronteggiare, *v. t.* (*anche fig.*) to face; (*fig.*) to meet★, to tackle.

frontiera, *n. f.* frontier, border.

fruire, *v. i.* to use; to make★ use (of st.). // ~ **d'un diritto** (*leg.*) to enjoy (*o* to have) a right.

fruitore, *n. m.* user.

fruttare, *v. t.* (*econ., fin.*) to yield, to bear★, to bring★ in, to pay★. *v. i.* (*fin., rag.*) to return a profit. // ~ **bene** (*fin.*) (*d'investimento, ecc.*) to give good returns.

fruttifero, *a.* 1 (*econ., fin.*) paying. 2 (*fin., rag.*) (*di titolo*) interest-bearing. // **essere** ~ (*fin., rag., anche*) to carry interest; **non** ~ (*fin., rag.*) non-interest bearing.

frutto, *n. m.* 1 fruit. 2 (*econ., fin.*) yield; (*reddito*) income; (*rendita*) revenue. 3 (*fin., rag.*) (*del denaro*) interest. // ~ **del capitale** (*fin., rag.*) return on capital; interest.

fuga, *n. f.* 1 flight. 2 (*scampo*) escape. 3 (*trasp. mar.*) leakage. // **la ~ dai campi** (*econ.*) the drift from the land; ~ **dei cervelli** (*econ.*) brain drain; ~ **di capitali** (*econ., fin.*) capital flight, outflow of capital.

fuggi fuggi, *n. m. inv.* stampede.

fuggire, *v. i.* **1** to run★ away. **2** (*evadere, sottrarsi a*) to escape.

full time, *locuz. n.* (*pers., sind.*) full time.

fumetto, *n. m.* **1** (*pubbl.*) comic strip, cartoon. **2 fumetti,** *pl.* (*pubbl.*) comics.

fune, *n. f.* (*trasp. mar.*) cable, rope.

fungere, *v. i.* to act, to function.

fungibile, *a.* **1** (*econ.*) replaceable, fungible. **2** (*leg.*) fungible.

funzionale, *a.* functional.

funzionamento, *n. m.* **1** functioning, operation, operating. **2** (*d'una macchina, ecc., anche*) working.

funzionante, *a.* (*d'una macchina, ecc.*) working.

funzionare, *v. i.* **1** to function, to operate. **2** (*di macchinario e sim.*) to work (*anche fig.*); to perform, to run★.

funzionario, *n. m.* **1** (*pers.*) functionary, office-bearer, office-holder, officer, official, white-collar worker. **2 (i) funzionari,** *pl.* (*org. az.*) (the) staff (*collett.*). // ~ **(addetto) alle vendite** (*pers.*) sales officer; ~ **del fisco** assessor; ~ **d'un'agenzia pubblicitaria** (*il quale mantiene i contatti con i clienti*) (*pubbl.*) account executive; **un ~ di banca** (*pers.*) an officer of a bank; **un ~ di dogana** (*dog.*) an officer of customs, a customs officer; **un ~ di prima nomina** (*pers.*) a newly appointed officer; **un ~ in prova** (*pers.*) an officer on probation; ~ **statale** (*pers.*) civil servant (*in G.B.*); functionary (*in Italia*).

funzione, *n. f.* **1** function, business, duty. **2** (*qualità, condizione*) capacity. **3** (*mat.*) function. **4** (*pers.*) (*ufficio*) office. **5** (*pers.*) (*posto*) position, post. // ~ **decrescente** (*econ., mat.*) decreasing function; **la ~ dell'occupazione** (*econ.*) the employment function; **la ~ della produzione** (*econ.*) the production function; ~ **di notaio** (*leg.*) notaryship; ~ **d'offerta complessiva** (*econ.*) aggregate supply function; **le funzioni di presidente** (*amm.*) the office of chairman; **funzioni direttive** (*amm.*) management functions; **funzioni manageriali** (*amm.*) management functions; **in ~** (*di macchina, ecc.*) in operation.

fuori, *avv.* out, outside. *prep.* **fuori di** (*o* **da**) **1** out of, outside, off. **2** (*market.*) (*di merce*) ex. *n. m.* **(il) di fuori** (the) outside. // ~ **bordo** (*avv.*) (*trasp. mar.*) overboard; ~ **della nave** (*market., trasp. mar.*) (*di merce*) ex ship; **essere ~ moda** to be out of fashion, to be out; **di ~** outside.

fuoribordo, *n. m. inv.* (*trasp. mar.*) outboard motor; outboard (*anche la barca*).

fuoriborsa, *n. m.* (*Borsa*) over-the-counter market, street market; coulisse (*a Parigi*).

fuorviare, *v. t.* **1** to mislead★. **2** (*con informazioni erronee*) to misinform.

furgoncino, *n. m.* (*trasp. aut.*) small van; delivery van.

furgone, *n. m.* (*trasp. aut.*) van, delivery van. // ~ **per traslochi** (*trasp. aut.*) removal van; ~ **postale** (*trasp. aut.*) mail-van.

furto, *n. m.* **1** (*leg.*) theft, larceny. **2 furti,** *pl.* (*ass., leg.*) robbery. // ~ **con effrazione** (*o* **con scasso**) (*leg.*) burglary; ~ **di poca entità** petty larceny; pilfering; ~ **in un negozio** (*taccheggio*) (*leg.*) shop-lifting.

fusione, *n. f.* **1** melting. **2** (*di metalli*) smelting. **3** (*econ., fin.*) combination, amalgamation, consolidation, incorporation, merger. **4** (*econ., fin.*) (*rilevamento*) take-over. // ~ **d'aziende** (*econ., fin.*) business combine; ~ **d'imprese** (*econ., fin.*) company merger; corporate merger (*USA*); **la ~ di società commerciali** (*econ., fin.*) the amalgamation of companies; **una ~ orizzontale** (*econ.*) a horizontal merger; **una ~ verticale** (*econ.*) a vertical merger.

fuso, *n. m.* spindle. // ~ **orario** time zone.

fustella, *n. f.* (*pubbl.*) die.

fustellato, *a.* (*pubbl.*) die cut.

fusto, *n. m.* (*di legno*) cask.

futuro, *a.* **1** future. **2** (*prossimo*) forthcoming, coming. **3** (*comm., anche*) forward. *n. m.* future. // **futura consegna** (*market.*) future delivery, forward delivery.

G

gabbia, *n. f.* **1** cage. **2** (*trasp.*) (*di legno: per imballaggi*) crate.

gabinetto, *n. m.* **1** office; chambers (*pl.*). **2** (*di decenza*) toilet. **3** (*amm.*) (*Ministero*) Cabinet. **4** (*org. az.*) cabinet.

galla, *n. f.* (*nella locuz.*) **a ~** afloat; (*anche fig.*) above water.

galleggiabilità, *n. f.* (*anche fig.*) buoyancy.

galleggiamento, *n. m.* (*trasp. mar.*) floatation. // **linea di ~** (*trasp. mar.*) waterline.

galleggiante, *a.* (*trasp. mar.*) floating.

galleggiare, *v. i.* (*trasp. mar.*) to float.

gallone, *n. m.* **1** (*misura di capacità per liquidi e aridi pari a litri 4,545*) gallon. **2** (*USA*) (*misura di capacità per liquidi pari a litri 3,785*) gallon. // **~ imperiale (***o* **britannico)** (*misura di capacità pari a litri 4,545*) imperial gallon.

galoppante, *a.* galloping. // **inflazione ~** (*econ.*) galloping inflation.

galoppare, *v. i.* to gallop.

gamma, *n. f.* **1** range, scale. **2** (*market.*) (*di prodotti*) range, line, variety. // **la ~ dei prezzi** (*market.*) the range of prices; **una ~ d'imposte** (*fin.*) a scale of taxation; **~ di lunghezze d'onda** (*comun.*) wave-band; **~ di sintonia** (*comun.*) tuning band.

«gap», *n. m.* gap. // **~ inflazionistico** (*econ.*) inflationary gap; **~ tecnologico** technological gap.

gara, *n. f.* competition, contest. // **~ d'appalto** tender.

garante, *n. m.* e *f.* **1** (*leg.*) guarantor, sponsor, voucher; grantor, warrantor, warranter (*meno comuni*). **2** (*leg.*) (*chi offre cauzione per q.*) bailsman★. **3** (*leg.*) (*garanzia*) guarantee, guaranty, surety, security; bail. // **~ in solido** (*leg.*) cosurety.

garantire, *v. t.* **1** to guarantee, to warrant, to assure. **2** (*assicurare*) to ensure. **3** (*ass.*) (*contro perdite, danni, ecc.*) to indemnify. **4** (*banca*) (*un assegno, ecc., da parte d'una banca*) to certify. **5** (*cred., leg.*) to secure, to cover, to back. **6** (*leg.*) to guarantee, to sponsor, to vouch, to warrant. *v. i.* (*leg.*) (*offrire cauzione per q.*) to go★ bail (for sb.). // **~ una cambiale** to back a bill.

garantirsi, *v. rifl.* **1** (*assicurarsi*) to secure oneself. **2** (*ass.*) (*contro danni, rischi, ecc.*) to indemnify oneself.

garantito, *a.* **1** guaranteed. **2** (*cred., leg.*) secured, backed. **3** (*leg.*) guaranteed. // **~ con ipoteca** (*leg.*) collateral; **~ da obbligazioni** (*fin.*) (*di debito*) bonded; **non ~** (*cred.*) unsecured.

garanzia, *n. f.* **1** guarantee, warrant. **2** (*ass.*) (*contro perdite, danni, ecc.*) indemnity. **3** (*cred., leg.*) security, cover. **4** (*leg.*) guarantee, surety, security, warranty. **5** (*leg.*) (*scritta*) surety bond, warranty deed. **6** (*leg.*) (*cauzione*) bond, caution money, caution, recognizance. **7** (*leg.*) (*cauzione per un imputato*) bail, bailment. **8** (*leg.*) (*pegno*) pledge, pawn, gage. **9** (*leg., market.*) (*su merci*) lien. // **~ aggiuntiva** (*banca, cred.*) collateral security; **~ bancaria** (*rilasciata dalla banca d'un importatore, sulla solvibilità di quest'ultimo*) bank guarantee; **~ collaterale** (*banca, cred.*) collateral security; **~ dei corsi dei cambi** (*fin.*) exchange-rate guarantee; **~ di caricazione** (*trasp. mar.*) loading guarantee; **~ di navigabilità** (*trasp. mar.*) warranty of seaworthiness; **~ di pacifico godimento** (*leg.*) covenant of quiet enjoyment; **~ di pagamento** (*cred.*) guarantee of payment; **~ di qualità** (*market.*) guarantee of quality; **~ di rimborso** (*fin., market.*) money-back guarantee; **~ espressa** (*ass. mar.*) express warranty; **garanzie multilaterali** (*comm. est.*) multilateral guarantees; **~ per le spese giudiziarie** (*leg.*) security for costs; **~ per vizi occulti** (*leg.*) warranty for hidden defects; **~ reale** (*banca, cred.*) collateral security, collateral; **~ tacita** (*leg.*) implied warranty; **chi riceve una ~** (*leg.*) warrantee; **senza ~** (*cred.*) without security; unsecured (*a.*).

gavitello, *n. m.* **1** (*trasp. mar.*) buoy. **2** (*trasp. mar.*) (*luminoso*) beacon.

gazzetta, *n. f.* (*giorn.*) gazette, newspaper. // **~ ufficiale** (*che pubblica anche il bollettino dei fallimenti e altri atti ufficiali*) (*giorn.*) gazette.

generale, *a.* **1** general. **2** (*comm.*) overhead. // **spese generali** (*rag.*) overhead expenses.

genere, *n. m.* **1** kind, sort, nature. **2** (*comm.*)

(*d'affari*) line. // **generi alimentari** (*market.*) foodstuffs; food (*collett.*); ~ **d'affari** line of business; **generi di prima necessità** (*econ.*) necessaries; commodities.

gente, *n. f.* people (*col v. al pl.*). // ~ **di mare** (*trasp. mar.*) seamen.

gentile, *a.* 1 kind. 2 (*nell'introduzione a una lettera commerciale*) dear.

gentiluomo, *n. m.* gentleman★.

genuino, *a.* 1 genuine, unsophisticated. 2 (*puro*) sterling.

geografia, *n. f.* geography. // ~ **economica** economic geography.

geografico, *a.* geographic, geographical.

gerarchia, *n. f.* (*org. az.*) hierarchy. // ~ **aziendale** (*pers.*) company hierarchy.

gerarchico, *a.* hierarchical, hierarchic.

gerente, *a.* (*amm.*) managing. *n. m.* 1 (*amm.*) manager. 2 (*fin.*) (*socio attivo*) active partner. *n. f.* (*amm.*) manageress. // ~ **di posto telefonico pubblico** (*pers.*) call office attendant.

gergo, *n. m.* jargon. // ~ **burocratico** officialese.

Germania, *n. f.* Germany. // **la** ~ **Occidentale** West Germany; **la** ~ **Orientale** East Germany.

gestionale, *a.* (*amm.*) managerial, operational.

gestione, *n. f.* 1 conduct, direction, administration. 2 (*amm.*) management, operating, operation. 3 (*org. az.*) government. // ~ **degli affari** conduct of business; ~ **dei crediti** (*fin.*) credit management; ~ **dei materiali** (*org. az.*) stock management, inventory management; **la** ~ **del bilancio dello Stato** (*fin.*) the execution of the national budget; ~ **delle scorte** (*org. az.*) inventory control; ~ **di portafogli azionari** (*fin.*) investment management; ~ **fiduciaria** (*leg.*) trusteeship; ~ **simulata** (*amm.*) executive game, business game; **di** ~ (*amm.*) operational; operating, operation (*attr.*).

gestire, *v. t.* (*amm.*) to manage, to operate, to conduct, to run★.

gestore, *n. m.* (*amm.*) manager, operator.

gettare, *v. t.* 1 (*anche fig.*) to throw★, to cast★. 2 (*trasp. mar.*) *V.* ~ **a mare.** // ~ **a mare** (*il carico o parte di esso: per alleggerire la nave in pericolo*) (*trasp. mar.*) to jettison; ~ **a terra** to knock down; ~ **l'àncora** (*trasp. mar.*) to cast anchor; to drop anchor; ~ **via** to throw away, to reject, to scrap; **che si può** ~ (*di contenitore, ecc.*) disposable; **da** ~ **dopo l'uso** disposable.

gettata, *n. f.* (*trasp. mar.*) jetty, pier.

gettito, *n. m.* 1 (*fin.*) (*d'imposte, tasse, ecc.*) yield, take; proceeds, takings (*pl.*). 2 (*trasp. mar.*) jetsam; jettisoned cargo (*o* goods). // **il** ~ **dei prestiti nel 1974** (*fin.*) the proceeds of loans in 1974; **il** ~ **delle imposte** (*fin.*) the yield of taxes; **il** ~ **d'imposta** (*fin.*) the yield of taxes; ~ **fiscale** (*fin.*) tax revenue; **il** ~ **tributario** (*fin.*) the revenue from taxation, the tax revenue.

getto, *n. m.* 1 throw, cast. 2 (*trasp. mar.*) *V.* ~ **del carico.** // ~ **del carico** (*o di parte di esso: per alleggerire la nave in pericolo*) (*trasp. mar.*) jettison.

gettone, *n. m.* 1 token. 2 (*per giochi e sim.*) counter. // ~ **di presenza** (*pers.*) attendance-check; (*il compenso*) attendance fee.

ghinea, *n. f.* (*ingl.*) (*moneta di conto pari a 21 scellini, non più in corso, ma usata per onorari, per certi articoli di lusso, ecc.*) guinea.

già, *avv.* 1 already. 2 (*un tempo*) formerly (*avv.*); former (*a.*); ex (*pref.*).

giacente, *a.* 1 (*comun., market.*) undelivered. 2 (*fin.*) (*non investito*) uninvested. 3 (*leg.*) unclaimed. // ~ **alla posta** (*comun.*) (*di lettera e sim.*) uncalled for; **merce** ~ **in stazione** goods lying at the railway station.

giacenza, *n. f.* 1 (*fin., rag.*) cash in hand. 2 (*market.*) remainder. 3 (*org. az.*) stock, stock on hand. // **giacenze di magazzino** (*market.*) remainders; unsold goods; ~ **di merce difficile a vendersi** (*market.*) dead stock; ~ **di sicurezza** (*org. az.*) cushion; **giacenze disponibili** (*market.*) available stocks; ~ **finale** (*org. az.*) closing stock; ~ **iniziale** (*rag.*) opening stock; ~ **media** (*org. az.*) average stock; ~ **minima** (*org. az.*) minimum stock, safety allowance; **in** ~ *V.* **giacente.**

giacere, *v. i.* to lie★.

giardinetta, *n. f.* (*trasp. aut.*) station wagon, waggon.

giardinetto, *n. m.* 1 (*fin.*) spread investment. 2 (*trasp. mar.*) quarter; buttock.

giardiniera, *n. f.* (*trasp. aut.*) station wagon, waggon, char-a-banc, charabanc.

«gill», *n. m.* 1 (*ingl.*) (*misura di capacità per liquidi e aridi pari a litri 0,142*) gill. 2 (*USA*) (*misura di capacità per liquidi pari a litri 0,118*) gill.

giocare, *v. t.* e *i.* 1 to play. 2 (*d'azzardo*) to gamble. // ~ **al rialzo** (*Borsa*) to bull; ~ **al ribasso** (*Borsa*) to bear; ~ **d'azzardo** to gamble; ~ **in Borsa** (*Borsa*) to gamble on the Stock Exchange, to play on the Stock Exchange, to play the market.

giocatore, *n. m.* 1 player. 2 (*d'azzardo, o in Borsa*) gambler; (*in piccolo*) dabbler. // ~ **al**

rialzo (*Borsa*) bull; ~ **al ribasso** (*Borsa*) bear; ~ **d'azzardo** gambler; ~ **di Borsa** speculator.

gioco, *n. m.* play. // ~ **d'azzardo** gamble; ~ **di Borsa** gambling on the Stock Exchange; speculation; **in** ~ (*fig.*) at stake.

giornalaio, *n. m.* (*giorn., market.*) news dealer, news vendor.

giornale, *n. m.* **1** (*giorn.*) newspaper, paper, sheet. **2** (*rag.*) journal. // ~ **acquisti** (*rag.*) purchase journal; ~ **americano** (*rag., USA*) combined journal and ledger; ~ **ausiliario** (*rag.*) subsidiary journal; ~ **aziendale** (*giorn.*) house organ; ~ **degli effetti attivi** (*rag.*) bills receivable journal; ~ **degli effetti passivi** (*rag.*) bills payable journal; ~ **delle entrate di cassa** (*rag.*) cash receipts journal; ~ **delle (merci) rese** (*rag.*) returns book; ~ **delle uscite di cassa** (*rag.*) cash disbursement journal; ~ **di bordo** (*trasp. mar.*) sea journal, journal; (*trasp. mar.*) logbook, log; ~ **di cassa** (*rag.*) cash journal; ~ **murale** (*giorn.*) wall newspaper; ~ **popolare** (*con molte fotografie e poche notizie condensate*) (*giorn.*) tabloid; ~ **quotidiano** (*giorn.*) daily paper, daily; ~ **radio** (*giorn.*) news bulletin, news broadcast, newscast.

giornaliero, *a.* daily. *n. m.* (*pers.*) day labourer, day man★, journeyman★.

giornalismo, *n. m.* **1** (*giorn.*) journalism, reporting. **2** (*giorn.*) (*la stampa*) press. // ~ **popolare** popular journalism; ~ **scandalistico** scandal journalism.

giornalista, *n. m.* e *f.* (*giorn.*) journalist, publicist. *n. m.* (*giorn.*) newspaperman★, pressman★; newsman★ (*USA*). *n. f.* newspaperwoman★. // ~ **indipendente** (*giorn., pubbl.*) free lance.

giornalistico, *a.* (*giorn.*) journalistic, newspaporial.

giornata, *n. f.* **1** day. **2** (*pers.*) (*paga d'un giorno*) day's wages. **3** (*trasp.*) (*di viaggio*) day's journey. // ~ **lavorativa** working day, workday, weekday; ~ **lavorativa d'otto ore** (*org. az.*) eight-hour working day; ~ **libera** (*pers.*) day off; ~ **nazionale** (*pers.*) national day; **a** ~ (*org. az.*) by the day; **alla** ~ (*fig.*) hand-to-mouth.

giorno, *n. m.* day. // **giorni consecutivi** running days; ~ **dei riporti** (*il primo giorno dei tre dedicati alle transazioni in Borsa*) contango day, continuation day; ~ **del calendario** calendar day; ~ **della risposta premi** (*Borsa, fin.*) option declaration day, option day; **il** ~ **della scadenza** (*di cambiale e sim.*) (*banca, cred.*) on the day it falls due; **giorni d'acceleramento** (*trasp. mar.*) dispatch days; ~ **di Borsa** (*Borsa*) day; ~ **di caricamento** (*trasp. mar.*) loading day; ~ **di chiusura pomeridiana** (*dei negozi*) (*market.*) early-closing day; **giorni di controstallie** (*trasp. mar.*) demurrage days; **giorni di grazia** (*cred.*) days of grace; ~ **di libertà** (*pers.*) day off; ~ **di liquidazione** (*Borsa*) account day, pay-day, settlement day, settling-day; **giorni di liquidazione** (*Borsa*) account days; ~ **di mercato** (*market.*) market day; **il** ~ **di Natale** on Christmas day; on Xmas day (*fam.*); ~ **di paga** (*pers.*) pay-day; eagle day (*slang USA*); ~ **di partenza** (*trasp. mar.*) sailing day; **giorni di ripartizione del dividendo** (*fin.*) dividend days; ~ **di riporto** (*Borsa*) contango day, continuation day; making-up day (*ingl.*); ~ **di riposo** (*pers.*) day of rest, rest day; ~ **di scadenza** (*cred., leg.*) term day; ~ **di sconto** (*banca*) discount day; **giorni di tolleranza** (*cred.*) *V.* **giorni di grazia**; ~ **d'udienza** (*leg.*) law-day, juridical day; **un** ~ **di vacanza** (*pers.*) an off day; ~ **di valuta** (*banca, fin.*) value date, value; **giorni effettivi** (*in un contratto, ecc.: escluso il primo e l'ultimo*) (*leg.*) clear days; ~ **feriale** weekday, work-day, workday, working day; ~ **festivo** holiday; ~ **festivo legale** bank holiday; (*leg.*) legal holiday, statutory holiday; ~ **in cui si saldano i conti** (*comm.*) prompt day; ~ **infrasettimanale** weekday; ~ **lavorativo** work-day, working day; (*per gli uffici*) business day; **un** ~ **libero** (*pers.*) an off day; ~ **precedente** day before; **a giorni alterni** on alternate days; **a trenta giorni (dalla) data** (*banca*) (*di cambiali*) at thirty days after date; **del** ~ (*fin., rag.*) current; **del** ~ **d'oggi** today's; (*moderno*) up-to-date; todayish (*fam.*); **in giorni successivi** on consecutive days; **ultimi giorni prima del giorno di liquidazione** (*Borsa*) account days.

giovane, *a.* young. *n. m.* young man★; boy. *n. f.* young woman★; girl. // ~ **di negozio** (*pers.*) shop-boy.

girabile, *a.* (*cred.*) endorsable, indorsable.

girante, *n. m.* e *f.* (*cred.*) endorser, indorser. // ~ **di comodo** (*banca, cred.*) accommodation endorser.

girare, *v. t.* e *i.* **1** to turn. **2** (*avvolgere, avvolgersi*) to wind★. **3** (*cred.*) to endorse, to indorse. **4** (*trasp. mar.*) (*di marea*) to turn. // ~ **un assegno** (*cred.*) to endorse a cheque; ~ **un film** (*pubbl.*) to shoot a film; to film; ~ **in bianco** (*cred.*) to endorse in blank; ~ **una polizza di carico** (*trasp. mar.*) to endorse a bill of lading; ~ **un saldo a partita doppia** (*rag.*) to transfer a balance to profit and loss account; **non girato** (*cred.*) unendorsed, unindorsed.

girata, *n. f.* **1** turn. **2** (*passeggiata*) walk. **3** (*cred.*) endorsement, indorsement. // ~ **completa** (*cred.*) full endorsement; ~ **condizionata**

(*banca, cred.*) qualified endorsement; ~ **di comodo** (*o* **di favore**) (*cred.*) accommodation endorsement; ~ **in bianco** (*cred.*) endorsement in blank, blank endorsement, general endorsement; ~ **in pieno** (*cred.*) full endorsement; **una** ~ **restrittiva** (*banca, cred.*) a restrictive endorsement; ~ «**senza rivalsa**» (*o* «**senza regresso**») (*cred.*) endorsement without recourse; ~ **speciale** (*cred.*) special endorsement; **senza** ~ (*cred.*) unendorsed, unindorsed (*a.*).

giratario, *n. m.* (*cred.*) endorsee, indorsee.

girevole, *a.* turning, revolving, rotary.

giro, *n. m.* **1** turn. **2** (*d'ispezione, ecc.*) round. **3** (*market.*) (*di visite ai clienti*) round. **4** (*tur.*) tour, trip. // **il** ~ **dei (propri) clienti** (*market.*) the round of one's customers; ~ **d'affari** (*fin.*) turnover; ~ **di capitali** (*rag.*) circulation of funds; ~ **di partita** (*rag.*) clearing; ~ **di vite** turn of the screw; (*fig.*) squeeze; ~ **turistico** (*tur.*) tour, sightseeing tour; ~ **turistico a piedi** (*tur.*) walking-tour; **a stretto** ~ **di posta** (*comun.*) by return of mail.

giroconto, *n. m.* **1** (*banca, fin.*) money transfer. **2** (*cred.*) (*bancario o postale*) giro. **3** (*rag.*) contra account, internal compensation. // ~ **postale** (*cred., ingl.*) giro.

gita, *n. f.* (*tur.*) tour, trip. // ~ **turistica** (*tur.*) sightseeing trip.

giù, *avv.* **1** down. **2** (*al piano di sotto*) downstairs. // **in** ~ down, downwards.

giudicare, *v. t.* **1** (*reputare*) to think★, to consider, to judge, to repute, to view. **2** (*leg.*) to judge, to hear★. **3** (*leg.*) (*colpevole, innocente*) to find★. **4** (*leg.*) (*processare*) to try. // ~ **una causa legale** (*leg.*) to judge a case, to hear a case; ~ **di nuovo** (*una causa*) (*leg.*) to rehear; ~ **un imputato** (*leg.*) to pass judgement on an accused man, to pass sentence on an accused man; **non ancora giudicato** (*leg.*) (*di causa, ecc.*) pendent.

giudice, *n. m.* **1** (*leg.*) judge. **2** (*leg., ingl.*) (*della Corte Suprema*) justice. // ~ «**a latere**» (*leg.*) associate judge; ~ **competente** (*leg.*) competent judge; ~ **conciliatore** (*leg.*) Justice of the Peace, magistrate; ~ **delegato** (*leg.*) judge delegate; ~ **di pace** (*leg.*) Justice of the Peace, magistrate; ~ **distrettuale** (*leg., USA*) district judge; ~ **fallimentare** (*leg.*) referee in bankruptcy, bankruptcy judge; ~ **istruttore** (*leg.*) investigating magistrate.

giudiziale, *a.* (*leg.*) judicial.

giudiziario, *a.* (*leg.*) judicial, judiciary. // **il potere** ~ (*amm.*) the judiciary.

giudizio, *n. m.* **1** judgement, judgment, discretion. **2** (*stima di danni, ecc.*) assessment. **3** (*leg.*) judgement, judgment, sentence. **4** (*leg.*) (*processo*) trial. // ~ **arbitrale** (*leg.*) award; ~ **contumaciale** (*leg.*) judgement by default; ~ **di primo grado** (*leg.*) judgement of first instance; ~ **d'ultima istanza** (*leg.*) judgement of last resort; ~ **esecutivo** (*leg.*) executory judgment; ~ **sommario** (*leg.*) summary trial; **a mio** ~ in my judgement; (*secondo me*) in my opinion.

giungere, *v. t.* to come★, to arrive. // ~ **a** to reach; ~ **a una conclusione** to arrive at a conclusion; ~ **a scadenza** (*cred.*) (*di cambiale, ecc.*) to fall due, to mature; ~ **a una transazione** (*leg.*) to effect a composition; ~ **in porto** (*trasp. mar.*) to reach harbour; ~ **in vista del porto** (*trasp. mar.*) to open port.

giunta[1], *n. f.* (*amm.*) junta.

giunta[2], *n. f.* (*nella locuz.*) **per** ~ into the bargain, to boot.

giuoco, *n. m. V.* **gioco.**

giuramento, *n. m.* (*leg.*) oath. // ~ **suppletorio** (*leg.*) suppletory oath; **sotto** ~ (*leg.*) on oath, upon oath.

giurare, *v. t.* (*leg.*) to swear★. *v. i.* (*leg.*) to take★ an oath, to pass one's oath.

giurato, *n. m.* (*leg.*) juryman★, juror. // ~ **supplente** (*leg.*) talesman; **giurati supplenti** (*leg.*) tales.

giurì, *n. m. inv.* (*leg.*) jury.

giuria, *n. f.* (*leg.*) jury. // ~ **che assiste il** «**coroner**» (*e che decide se vi sia causa a procedere in giudizio*) (*leg.*) coroner's jury (*in G.B.*); ~ **dei consumatori** (*market.*) consumer jury; ~ **ordinaria** (*che emette il verdetto alla fine d'un processo*) (*leg.*) petty jury (*cfr.* **coroner's jury, grand jury**); ~ **speciale** (*che decide se qualcuno debba essere rinviato a giudizio*) (*leg.*) grand jury.

giuridico, *a.* (*leg.*) juridical, juristic, legal.

giurisdizionale, *a.* (*leg.*) jurisdictional.

giurisdizione, *n. f.* **1** (*leg.*) jurisdiction, judicature. **2** (*leg.*) (*competenza*) cognizance. // ~ **d'appello** (*leg.*) appellate jurisdiction; ~ **di prima istanza** (*leg.*) original jurisdiction; ~ **extraterritoriale** (*leg.*) extraterritorial jurisdiction; ~ **straniera** (*leg.*) foreign jurisdiction; ~ **territoriale** (*leg.*) territorial jurisdiction.

giurisprudenza, *n. f.* **1** (*leg.*) jurisprudence, law. **2** (*leg.*) (*diritto creato dai giudici stessi, basato sul* «*precedente*» *giudiziario*) judge-made law, case-law (*in G.B.*).

giurisprudenziale, *a.* (*leg.*) jurisprudential.

giurista, *n. m.* e *f.* (*leg.*) jurist, lawyer.

giuristico, *a.* (*leg.*) juristic.

giustificare, *v. t.* to justify, to excuse. // ~ **un'assenza** to excuse an absence; ~ (*una sen-*

tenza, ecc.) **con un precedente** (*leg.*) to precedent.

giustificativo, *n. m.* (*comm.*) voucher, receipt. // ~ **pubblicitario** (*pubbl.*) checking copy.

giustificato, *a.* justified, fair.

giustificazione, *n. f.* justification, excuse, plea.

giustizia, *n. f.* **1** justice, equity, right. **2** (*leg.*) justice. // ~ **distributiva** (*econ.*) distributive justice; ~ **fiscale** (*fin.*) tax equity; ~ **sociale** (*econ.*) social justice; ~ **sommaria** (*leg.*) rough justice.

giusto, *a.* **1** just, fair, equitable, equal, even, straight. **2** (*adatto*) proper, right. **3** (*leg.*) rightful, right. *n. m.* **(il) giusto 1** (*ciò che è giusto*) (the) right. **2** (*ciò che spetta a q.*) sb.'s due.

globale, *a.* global, aggregate, comprehensive, overall, all-round; all-around (*USA*).

godere, *v. i.* to enjoy. // ~ **(di) un diritto** (*leg.*) to enjoy a right.

godimento, *n. m.* **1** enjoyment. **2** (*leg.*) use. // **«godimento»** (*fin.*) «dividend payable»: « ~ **1° aprile 1° ottobre**» «dividend payable: 1st April and 1st October»; **il** ~ **dei diritti civili** (*leg.*) the enjoyment of civic rights; ~ **della cedola** (*fin.*) due date of coupon; ~ **in comune** (*leg.*) communal tenure.

gomena, *n. f.* (*trasp. mar.*) cable, hawser, line, rope.

gomma, *n. f.* **1** rubber. **2** (*attr. uff.*) eraser. **3** (*trasp. aut.*) tire. // ~ **da inchiostro** (*attr. uff.*) ink eraser.

gonfiamento, *n. m.* inflation.

gonfiare, *v. t.* **1** to inflate. **2** (*un fiume*) to swell★. **3** (*fig.*) to boost. // ~ **artificiosamente** (*il capitale nominale*) (*fin.*) to water; ~ **il valore d'un'azione** (*fin.*) to boost the value of a share.

gonfiarsi, *v. rifl.* **1** to inflate. **2** (*anche fig.*) to swell★. **3** (*fin., market.*) (*di prezzi, ecc.*) to rise★, to swell★.

gonfiatura, *n. f.* **1** (*montatura*) swelling. **2** (*fin.*) bubble. **3** (*trasp. aut.*) (*delle gomme*) inflating.

governare, *v. t.* **1** to govern. **2** (*amm.*) to manage. // ~ **una nave** (*trasp. mar.*) to steer; ~ **la rotta** (*trasp. aer., trasp. mar.*) to navigate.

governatore, *n. m.* governor. // **il** ~ **della Banca d'Inghilterra** (*banca, ingl.*) the Governor of the Bank of England; ~ **generale** governor-general.

governo, *n. m.* **1** government. **2** (*trasp. mar.*) (*della nave*) steering. // ~ **d'affari** Caretaker Cabinet; **in** ~ (*trasp. mar.*) (*di nave*) under control.

gradimento, *n. m.* **1** liking, satisfaction. **2** (*accettazione*) acceptance.

gradire, *v. t.* **1** to like. **2** (*accettare*) to accept.

gradito, *a.* **1** appreciated, welcome. **2** (*comun.*) (*di lettera*) kind.

grado, *n. m.* **1** grade, degree, standard. **2** (*gerarchico*) rank. **3** (*estensione, ampiezza*) extent, scale. **4** (*condizione*) standing. **5** (*mat.*) degree. // ~ **di capitano** (*trasp. mar.*) captainship; ~ **d'intelligenza** (*pers.*) degree of intelligence; ~ **d'invalidità** (*pers.*) degree of inability; **il** ~ **d'un'ipoteca** (*leg.*) the rank of a mortgage; ~ **di latitudine** (*trasp. mar.*) degree of latitude; ~ **di parentela** (*leg.*) degree of kindred; **essere in** ~ **di** to be able to; **in sommo** ~ greatly; **non essere in** ~ **di fare qc.** to be unable to do st.

graduale, *a.* gradual.

graduare, *v. t.* to grade, to graduate, to scale. // ~ **le imposte** (*fin.*) to graduate taxes.

graduatoria, *n. f.* (*pers.*) classification, list.

graduazione, *n. f.* graduation, scale.

graffa, *n. f.* *V.* **graffetta.**

graffare, *v. t.* to staple.

graffatrice, *n. f.* (*attr. uff.*) stapler.

graffetta, *n. f.* (*attr. uff.*) staple.

grafia, *n. f.* writing, handwriting.

grafico, *a.* graphic, graphical. *n. m.* **1** diagram. **2** (*org. az.*) chart. **3** (*pers.*) printing and engraving expert. **4** (*pubbl.*) designer. // ~ **d'avanzamento** (*org. az.*) progress chart.

grammo, *n. m.* gram, gramme.

grande, *a.* great, grand, big, large; handsome (*fam.*). // **il** ~ **crollo** (*econ.*) the big slump; ~ **emporio** (*market.*) department store, supermarket; ~ **finanziere** (*fin.*) tycoon (*USA*); **le grandi imprese** (*fin.*) the large businesses, the large companies; **un** ~ **magazzino** (*org. az.*) a large warehouse (*o* store); ~ **«magazzino»** (*market.*) multiple shop, supermarket; chain store (*USA*); **grandi magazzini** (*market.*) department store; chain-store (*USA*); department stores, stores; ~ **negozio** (*market.*) department store; warehouse (*ingl.*); chain store (*USA*); **i grandi operatori privati** (*fin.*) the private corporations; **una** ~ **quantità di** a large quantity of, a great deal of; a mass of, a bundle of (*fam.*); **una** ~ **società** (*fin.*) a giant corporation, a large-scale corporation (*USA*); **a** ~ **velocità** (*trasp. ferr.*) by passenger train, per passenger train; **di** ~ **responsabilità** (*di carica, ufficio, ecc.*) responsible; **di** ~ **valore** (*anche fig.*) valuable; **in** ~ large-scale (*a.*).

grandezza, *n. f.* **1** greatness, bigness. **2** (*dimensioni*) size. // **di** ~ **media** middle-sized (*a.*).

grandine, *n. f.* **1** hail. **2** (*ass.*) hail storms.

grano, *n. m.* **1** wheat, corn. **2** (*misura di peso pari a 0,0648 grammi*) (*ingl.*) grain.

gratifica, *n. f.* (*pers.*) allowance, bonus, gratuity, premium. // ~ **di bilancio** (*pers.*) production bonus; ~ **discrezionale** (*pers.*) discretionary bonus; ~ **in azioni** (*concessa da una società ai suoi dipendenti*) (*fin.*) stock bonus; ~ **natalizia** (*pers.*) Christmas bonus; **sistema di gratifiche in aggiunta al salario** (*per rendimento, ecc.*) (*org. az., pers.*) bonus system.

gratificante, *a.* gratifying, rewarding.

gratificare, *v. t.* (*pers.*) to give★ an allowance to (sb.); to give★ (sb.) a bonus.

gratis, *avv.* gratis, freely, free gratis; free (*anche a.*). // ~ **a richiesta** (*market.*) free on application; ~ **in prova** (*market.*) on free approval, on free trial.

gratitudine, *n. f.* gratefulness, thankfulness; indebtedness (*fig.*). // **con** ~ gratefully, thankfully.

grato, *a.* grateful, thankful; indebted (*fig.*).

gratuitamente, *avv.* gratis, freely, free gratis, free.

gratuito, *a.* **1** gratuitous, free gratis, gratis, eleemosynary. **2** (*comm.*) free. **3** (*leg.*) (*d'alloggio*) rent-free.

gravame, *n. m.* **1** (*fig.*) weight, burden. **2** (*fin.*) (*imposta*) tax. **3** (*leg.*) encumbrance, encumberment.

gravare, *v. t.* **1** to weight, to burden, to bear★ hard on. **2** (*fin., leg.*) to encumber. // ~ (*q.*) **con soprattassa** (*fin.*) to surtax; ~ **d'imposte** (*fin.*) to overtax; ~ (*qc.*) **d'ipoteca** (*leg.*) to mortgage.

gravato, *a.* **1** weighted, burdened. **2** (*fin., leg.*) encumbered. // **eccessivamente** ~ **da imposte** (*fin.*) overtaxed; **non** ~ **da ipoteca** (*leg.*) unmortgaged.

grave, *a.* **1** (*pesante*) heavy. **2** (*serio*) serious, bad, grave, gross, hard. // **un** ~ **errore** a bad mistake; ~ **fatica** hard toil; sweat (*fam.*); **una** ~ **restrizione del credito** (*fin.*) a money squeeze.

gravità, *n. f.* gravity; seriousness (*fig.*).

grazia, *n. f.* **1** grace. **2** (*leg.*) mercy; pardon. **3 grazie,** *pl.* (*ringraziamenti*) thanks. // **grazie!** thanks!; **grazie a** thanks to.

greggio, *a.* **1** raw, crude, gross, rough. **2** (*market.*) (*di prodotto*) unmanufactured. *n. m.* crude oil, raw petroleum.

grezzo, *a. V.* **greggio.**

gridare, *v. i.* to cry, to shout. *v. t.* (*un nome*) to call.

grido, *n. m.* **1** cry, shout. **2** (*market., pubbl.*) thing. // **l'ultimo** ~ the latest thing.

grossa, *n. f.* (*dodici dozzine*) gross.

grossista, *n. m.* e *f.* (*market.*) wholesaler, wholesale-dealer, direct trader, factor, jobber, stockist; warehouseman★ (*m.*). // ~ **in granaglie** corn-dealer.

grosso, *a.* big, large, great, gross. // **un** ~ **acquirente** (*market.*) a heavy buyer; **grossi affari** (*fin.*) big business; **un** ~ **errore** a bad blunder; **una grossa somma di denaro** a large sum of money; folding money (*USA*); **mare** ~ (*trasp. mar.*) heavy sea.

grossolano, *a.* **1** gross, rough. **2** (*approssimativo*) rough and ready.

gru, *n. f. inv.* (*trasp.*) crane.

gruppo, *n. m.* **1** group, batch. **2** (*di persone*) party, section, set. **3** (*org. az.*) (*d'autobus, autocarri, ecc., della stessa azienda*) fleet. **4** (*pers.*) (*di lavoro*) team. // ~ **cantieristico** (*trasp. mar.*) shipbuilding group; ~ **creativo** (*pubbl.*) creative group; ~ **di contribuenti** (*fin.*) tax-paying group; (*divisi in base al reddito*) income bracket; ~ **di controllo** (*econ., fin.*) controlling group; ~ **di lavoro** (*pers.*) work group, team; ~ **di minoranza** (*fin.*) minority group; ~ **di pressione** (*econ.*) pressure group; **gruppi di reddito** (*fin., stat.*) income groups, income brackets; ~ **economico verticale** (*econ., org. az.*) vertical combine; ~ **finanziario di controllo** (*fin.*) holding company; **un** ~ **finanziario estero** (*fin.*) a foreign finance group; **un** ~ **finanziario internazionale** (*fin.*) an international financial group; ~ **monopolistico** (*econ., fin.*) syndicate.

guadagnare, *v. t.* to gain, to earn, to get★; to take★, to net, to knock down (*fam.*); to sack (*fam., USA*). // ~ **appena (tanto) da vivere** to earn a bare living; ~ **popolarità** to gain popularity; ~ **terreno** (*anche fig.*) to gain ground; ~ **tre punti** (*Borsa*) to chalk up a gain of three marks; **guadagnarsi una buona reputazione sul mercato** to gain a good reputation on the market; **guadagnarsi da vivere** to gain one's living; **guadagnarsi il pane** to win one's bread; **guadagnarsi la vita** to earn one's living; **non guadagnato** unearned.

guadagno, *n. m.* **1** gain, take. **2** (*lucro*) lucre. **3** (*econ., fin., rag.*) profit, return. **4 guadagni,** *pl.* earnings, makings, takings. // ~ **accidentale** (*econ.*) windfall gain; **un** ~ **concreto** a tangible gain; **un** ~ **inatteso** an unexpected gain; a windfall (*fam.*); **guadagni inesistenti** (*rag.*) nil profits; **guadagni irregolari** (*rag.*) uneven earnings; ~ **netto** (*rag.*) net profit, net; **guadagni onesti** honest profits.

guardare, *v. t.* e *i.* **1** to look at. **2** (*osservare*) to watch, to view. // ~ **avanti** to look forward;

~ **la corrispondenza** to look over the correspondence; ~ **su** to look up; ~ **la TV** to watch TV.

guardavia, *n. f. inv.* (*trasp. aut.*) safety rail.

guardia, *n. f.* **1** guard, watch. **2** (*custodia*) keeping. **3** (*pers.*) guardsman★, watchman★. **4** (*pers.*) (*poliziotto*) constable, policeman★. // ~ **costiera di finanza** coast-guard; ~ **di finanza portuale** (*trasp. mar.*) water guard; ~ **franca** (*trasp. mar.*) watch below; ~ **franca a terra** (*trasp. mar.*) watch ashore; ~ **giurata** (*pers.*) watchman.

guardiano, *n. m.* (*pers.*) keeper, care-taker, guard, warden. // ~ **notturno** (*pers.*) night watchman.

«guardrail», *n. m.* (*trasp. aut.*) guardrail, safety rail, traffic divider.

guerra, *n. f.* (*anche fig.*) war. // ~ **commerciale** (*econ.*) trade war; ~ **dei prezzi** (*econ.*) (*periodo di spietata concorrenza*) price war; ~ **tariffaria** (*comm. est., fig.*) rate war, tariff war.

guida, *n. f.* **1** guide, guidance; lead, captainship. **2** (*libro*) guide-book, manual. **3** (*capo*) leader. **4** (*ass.*) (*che descrive le condizioni assicurative*) line sheet. **5** (*pers., tur.*) conductor, guide, courier; (*donna*) girl courier. **6** (*trasp. aut.*) driving. // ~ **del telefono** (*attr. uff.*) (telephone) directory; ~ **dell'attività corrente** (*org. az.*) direction.

guidare, *v. t.* **1** to guide, to conduct, to lead★, to head. **2** (*trasp. aut.*) to drive★. // ~ **q. in visita** (*a qc.*) to tour sb.; ~ **una nave** (*trasp. mar.*) to steer a ship.

guidatore, *n. m.* (*trasp. aut.*) driver.

gusto, *n. m.* **1** taste. **2 gusti,** *pl.* (*anche*) likes and dislikes. // **i gusti del pubblico** (*market.*) the likes and dislikes of the public.

H

hangar, *n. m.* (*trasp. aer.*) hangar.

holding, *n. f.* (*fin.*) holding company. // ~ **finanziaria privata** (*fin.*) private finance holding company.

hostess, *n. f.* (*trasp. aer.*) air-hostess, stewardess.

«hovercraft», *n. m.* (*trasp. mar.*) hovercraft.

«hundredweight», *n. m.* **1** (*ingl.*) (*misura di peso pari a 50,80 kg*) hundredweight (*cwt.*). **2** (*USA*) (*misura di peso pari a 45,36 kg*) hundredweight (*cwt.*). // ~ **americano** (*misura di peso pari a 1/20 di «ton» o 45,36 kg*) short hundredweight; ~ **inglese** (*misura di peso pari a 50,80 kg*) long hundredweight.

I

iarda, *n. f.* (*misura di lunghezza pari a m 0,914*) yard.

idea, *n. f.* **1** idea. **2** (*opinione*) opinion; mind. // **idee avanzate** forward opinions; **un'~ geniale** a stroke of genius.

ideare, *v. t.* to conceive, to devise.

idem, *pron.* e *avv.* **1** idem. **2** (*nelle fatture, negli inventari, ecc.*) ditto.

identico, *a.* identical; (the) same.

identità, *n. f.* **1** identity. **2** (*mat.*) identity.

idoneità, *n. f.* fitness, capability, qualification.

idoneo, *a.* fit, capable, qualified. // **~ alla navigazione** (*trasp. mar.*) (*di natante*) seaworthy; **non ~ alla navigazione** (*trasp. mar.*) (*di natante*) unseaworthy.

igiene, *n. f.* hygiene. // **~ e medicina del lavoro** (*pers., sind.*) industrial health and medicine.

igienico, *a.* hygienic, hygienical, sanitary.

ignoto, *a.* unknown. *n. m.* (*leg.*) unknown person.

illecito, *a.* **1** (*leg.*) illicit, illegitimate, illegal, lawless, unlawful, wrongful. **2** (*leg.*) (*di sciopero*) wildcat (*attr.*). // **~ civile** (*leg.*) tort; **~ d'agenzia** (*leg.*) agent's tort; **~ penale** (*leg.*) offense, crime; **~ privato** (*leg.*) private wrong.

illegale, *a.* **1** (*leg.*) illegal, lawless, illicit, unlawful, wrongful; outlaw (*attr.*). **2** (*leg.*) (*di sciopero*) wildcat.

illegalità, *n. f.* (*leg.*) illegality, unlawfulness.

illegalmente, *avv.* (*leg.*) illegally.

illeggibile, *a.* illegible, unreadable.

illegittimità, *n. f.* (*leg.*) illegitimacy, unlawfulness.

illegittimo, *a.* (*leg.*) illegitimate, unlawful.

illiceità, *n. f.* (*leg.*) unlawfulness.

illimitato, *a.* unlimited.

illustrare, *v. t.* **1** to illustrate. **2** (*giorn., pubbl.*) to illustrate. // **~ libri di testo** to illustrate text-books.

illustrativo, *a.* illustrative.

illustrato, *a.* illustrated.

illustrazione, *n. f.* **1** illustration. **2** (*giorn., pubbl.*) illustration. // **~ a mezza tinta** (*pubbl.*) halftone.

imballaggio, *n. m.* **1** (*market.*) (*l'imballare*) packaging, packing. **2** (*market.*) (*balla, pacco, ecc.*) package, pack. **3** (*market.*) (*in balle*) baling. **4** (*market.*) (*in casse*) boxing. // **~ a rendere** (*market.*) package to be returned; **l'~ delle derrate alimentari** (*market.*) the packaging of foodstuffs; **~ gratis** (*market.*) packing free.

imballare, *v. t.* **1** (*market.*) to package, to pack. **2** (*market.*) (*in balle*) to pack in bales, to bale. // **~ in casse** (*market.*) to pack in boxes, to box up; **~ in «gabbie»** (*market.*) to pack in crates, to crate.

imballatore, *n. m.* **1** (*pers.*) packer. **2** (*pers.*) (*di merce in balle*) baler.

imballatrice, *n. f.* **1** (*org. az.*) packer. **2** (*org. az.*) (*di merce in balle*) baler.

imballatura, *n. f. V.* **imballaggio.**

imballo, *n. m. V.* **imballaggio.**

imbarazzare, *v. t.* **1** to embarrass. **2** (*ingombrare*) to encumber. **3** (*trasp. mar.*) (*il carico*) to overstow.

imbarazzo, *n. m.* embarrassment. // **~ finanziario** financial difficulty.

imbarcadero, *n. m.* (*trasp. mar.*) landing place, landing stage.

imbarcare, *v. t.* **1** (*trasp. aer., trasp. mar.*) to embark. **2** (*trasp. mar.*) to take★ aboard. **3** (*trasp. mar.*) (*spedire*) to ship. // **~ acqua** (*trasp. mar.*) to ship water (*o* a heavy sea); to leak; **~ il carico** (*trasp. mar.*) to load the cargo; **imbarcato in meno** (*di quanto accordato*) (*trasp. mar.*) (*di merce, carico, ecc.*) short-shipped.

imbarcarsi, *v. rifl.* **1** (*trasp. aer., trasp. mar.* e *fig.*) to embark. **2** (*trasp. mar.*) to go★ aboard, to board a ship. **3** (*trasp. mar.*) (*partire*) to sail. **4** (*trasp. mar.*) (*come marinaio*) to sign on.

imbarcazione, *n. f.* (*trasp. mar.*) boat, craft★. // **~ di salvataggio** (*trasp. mar.*) lifeboat.

imbarco, *n. m.* **1** (*trasp. aer., trasp. mar.*) embarcation, embarkation, embarkment. **2** (*trasp. mar.*) shipping, shipment. **3** (*trasp. mar.*) (*partenza*) sailing.

imboccatura del porto, *n. f.* (*trasp. mar.*) harbour entrance.

imboscamento, *n. m.* (*leg.*) (*di merci*) corner, cornering.

imboscare, *v. t.* (*leg.*) (*merci*) to corner.

imbrogliare, *v. t.* to cheat, to swindle.

imbroglio, *n. m.* cheat, swindle; bunco (*slang USA*).

imbroglione, *n. m.* cheat, swindler, deceiver, dodger.

imbucare, *v. t.* (*impostare*) to mail, to post.

imitare, *v. t.* **1** to imitate; (*copiare*) to copy. **2** (*market.*) to imitate.

imitato, *a.* **1** imitation, mock (*attr.*). **2** (*falso*) fake (*attr.*).

imitatore, *n. m.* **1** imitator; (*copiatore*) copier. **2** (*market.*) imitator. // ~ **del prezzo** (*econ., market.*) price follower.

imitazione, *n. f.* **1** imitation, copy, sham. **2** (*market.*) imitation, sham. // ~ **di marchio** (*leg.*) imitation of a trade-mark.

immagazzinaggio, *n. m. V.* **immagazzinamento.**

immagazzinamento, *n. m.* (*dog., org. az.*) warehousing, storage.

immagazzinare, *v. t.* (*org. az.*) to stock up, to store, to warehouse.

immagine, *n. f.* **1** image. **2** (*figura*) figure. // **l'~ aziendale** (*pubbl.*) the public image; the corporation image (*USA*); ~ **del prodotto** (*pubbl.*) product image.

immatricolare, *v. t.* **1** to matriculate. **2** (*trasp.*) (*un aereo, una nave, un'automobile*) to register. **3** (*trasp. mar.*) (*una nave, anche*) to document (*USA*).

immatricolato, *a.* (*trasp.*) (*d'aereo, automobile, naviglio, ecc.*) registered.

immatricolazione, *n. f.* **1** matriculation. **2** (*trasp.*) (*d'aereo, di nave, d'automobile, ecc.*) registration.

immediatamente, *avv.* immediately, outright, straightaway; on the nail (*fam.*).

immediato, *a.* **1** immediate, instant, instantaneous, outright. **2** (*comm.*) (*di consegna*) prompt.

immettere, *v. t.* to introduce, to put★ (in, *o* on). // ~ **merci in un mercato** (*market.*) to put goods on the market; ~ (*una nave*) **nel bacino di carenaggio** (*trasp. mar.*) to dry-dock.

immigrante, *n. m.* e *f.* (*econ.*) immigrant.

immigrare, *v. i.* (*econ.*) to immigrate.

immigrazione, *n. f.* (*econ.*) immigration.

immissione, *n. f.* introduction.

immobile, *a.* **1** immobile; motionless; immovable. **2** (*leg.*) (*di bene*) immovable, immoveable, real. *n. m.* **1** (*leg.*) building; house. **2** **immobili,** *pl.* (*leg.*) immovables; (*locali*) premises. **3** **immobili,** *pl.* (*rag.*) fixed assets, real assets. // **immobili e impianti** (*rag.*) fixtures and fittings, fixed assets; **un ~ non gravato da ipoteca** (*leg.*) an unmortgaged estate; **immobili per destinazione** (*leg.*) immovables by destination.

immobiliare, *a.* (*fin., leg.*) real. // **credito ~** (*fin.*) credit guaranteed by mortgage; **proprietà ~** real estate.

immobilismo, *n. m.* immobilism.

immobilizzare, *v. t.* **1** to immobilize. **2** (*fin., rag.*) (*convertire capitali circolanti in capitali fissi*) to immobilize, to capitalize, to tie up, to lock up.

immobilizzazione, *n. f.* **1** immobilization. **2** (*fin., rag.*) immobilization, lockup. **3** **immobilizzazioni,** *pl.* (*rag.*) capital expenditure. // **un'~ di capitale** a lockup of capital; **immobilizzazioni tecniche** (*rag.*) fixed assets.

immobilizzo, *n. m.* **1** (*fin., rag.*) immobilization, lockup. **2** (*rag.*) carrying. **3** **immobilizzi,** *pl.* (*rag.*) fixed assets.

immune, *a.* (*leg.*) immune.

immunità, *n. f.* (*leg.*) immunity.

impaccaggio, *n. m.* (*market.*) packing, packaging; wrapping (up).

impaccare, *v. t.* **1** to pack, to parcel. **2** (*market.*) to package, to pack, to wrap, to wrap up.

impaccatore, *n. m.* (*pers.*) packer.

impaccatura, *n. f. V.* **impaccaggio.**

impacchettare, *v. t. V.* **impaccare.**

impacchettatore, *n. m. V.* **impaccatore.**

impacchettatrice, *n. f.* (*org. az.*) packer.

impadronirsi, *v. rifl.* **1** to take★ possession (of); to appropriate. **2** (*con la forza*) to seize, to capture.

impatto, *n. m.* (*anche fig.*) impact.

impedimento, *n. m.* **1** impediment, obstruction; tie (*fig.*). **2** (*freno*) check, curb, holdback. **3** (*prevenzione*) prevention. **4** (*leg.*) impediment, bar. // ~ **procedurale** (*leg.*) bar to action.

impedire, *v. t.* **1** to prevent. **2** (*impacciare*) to impede, to obstruct. **3** (*frenare*) to check, to curb. **4** (*proibire*) to prohibit, to bar, to forbid★.

impegnare, *v. t.* **1** (*vincolare*) to bind★, to tie. **2** (*ingaggiare*) to engage. **3** (*comm., fin.*) (*denaro, ecc.*) to tie up, to lock up. **4** (*comm., leg.*) (*dare in pegno*) to pawn, to pledge, to gage. // ~ **q. con un contratto** (*leg.*) to tie sb. down to a contract; **chi impegna qc.** (*comm., leg.*) pawnee.

impegnarsi, *v. rifl.* to engage, to undertake★; (*con la parola*) to pledge one's word, to pass one's word; (*più solenne*) to bind★ oneself. // ~ **con giuramento** (*leg.*) to oblige oneself by oath, to pass one's oath.

impegnativo, *a.* binding. // **non** ~ unbinding.

impegnato, *a.* **1** bound. **2** (*occupato*) busy, engaged. **3** (*riservato*) reserved, taken.

impegno, *n. m.* **1** engagement, undertaking. **2** (*obbligo*) obligation, commitment, charge. **3** (*cura, diligenza*) care, diligence. **4** (*Borsa*) checking slip. **5 impegni,** *pl.* (*fin., rag.*) liabilities. // **impegni a breve (termine)** (*Borsa, fin.*) shorts; ~ **di capitale** (*rag.*) capital appropriation; ~ **di spesa** (*rag.*) appropriation; ~ **reciproco** (*leg.*) mutual engagement; **chi vien meno a un** ~ defaulter; **senza** ~ without engagement, non committally.

impennarsi, *v. rifl.* **1** (*d'un cavallo*) to rear up. **2** (*market.*) (*di prezzi*) to run★ up, to zoom. **3** (*trasp. aer.*) (*d'aereo*) to pitch.

impennata, *n. f.* **1** (*di cavallo*) rearing. **2** (*Borsa, market.*) (*delle quotazioni, dei prezzi, ecc.*) upsurge, upswing. **3** (*market.*) (*dei prezzi*) run-up, zoom. // **un'** ~ **delle richieste salariali** (*sind.*) an upsurge of wage claims.

imperativo, *a.* (*leg.*) mandatory.

imperfetto, *a.* **1** imperfect, defective. **2** (*leg.*) imperfect.

imperfezione, *n. f.* imperfection, defect, shortcoming.

impermeabile, *a.* (*market.*) (*di stoffa*) waterproof. *n. m.* (*market.*) waterproof, raincoat. // ~ **all'acqua** (*trasp.*) watertight; ~ **all'aria** (*trasp.*) airtight.

impermeabilizzare, *v. t.* to waterproof.

impersonale, *a.* impersonal.

impiantare, *v. t.* (*fondare, avviare*) to establish, to set★ up, to start.

impianto, *n. m.* **1** (*l'impiantare*) setting up, set-up; (*installazione*) installation. **2** (*org. az.*) plant; works (*col verbo al sing.*). **3 impianti,** *pl.* (*org. az.*) facilities, fittings; equipment (*sing.*). // ~ **contabile** (*rag.*) set of books; **l'** ~ **d'una nuova fabbrica** the setting up of a new factory; **impianti fissi** (*org. az.*) fixed plants; (*rag.*) fixtures and fittings; ~ **pilota** (*org. az.*) pilot plant; ~ **radiotelegrafico** (*comun.*) wireless installation; ~ **sperimentale** (*org. az.*) pilot plant.

impiegare, *v. t.* **1** (*usare*) to employ, to use. **2** (*il tempo*) to spend★, to take★. **3** (*fin.*) (*denaro*) to invest. **4** (*pers.*) (*dar lavoro a*) to employ, to engage. **5** (*pers.*) (*adibire*) to set★ on. // ~ **di nuovo** to re-employ; ~ **male il proprio denaro (il proprio tempo)** to waste one's money (one's time); ~ **troppo personale per le necessità di** (*un reparto, un'attività, ecc.*) (*org. az.*) to overman.

impiegarsi, *v. rifl.* to get★ a job; to find★ a job.

impiegata, *n. f.* (*pers.*) employee; girl (*fam.*).

impiegatizio, *a.* clerical; white-collar (*attr.*). // **la classe impiegatizia** white-collar workers; **lavoro** ~ clerical work.

impiegato, *n. m.* **1** (*pers.*) (*in genere*) employee; employe (*USA*). **2** (*pers.*) (*d'ufficio*) clerk; white-collar worker; black-coat worker; collar-and-tie worker (*slang USA*). **3** (*pers.*) (*funzionario*) official. **4** (*pers.*) (*assistente*) help. **5 impiegati,** *pl. collett.* (*pers.*) clerical staff, staff. // ~ (*di ditta privata o ente pubblico*) **addetto alla corrispondenza** (*pers.*) mail clerk; ~ **addetto alla fatturazione** (*pers.*) bill-filing clerk, billing clerk, bill clerk, biller; ~ **alla biglietteria** (*pers., trasp.*) booking clerk; ~ **che registra le ordinazioni** (*pers.*) order-clerk; ~ **comunale** (*pers.*) city employee; ~ **di banca** (*pers.*) bank clerk; ~ **di concetto** (*pers.*) staff employee; ~ **di grado inferiore** (*pers.*) junior; ~ **di sportello** (*banca*) teller; ~ **d'ufficio** (*pers.*) clerk; desk jockey (*slang USA*); **impiegati e operai** (*pers.*) personnel, staff; **impiegati esterni** (*pers.*) field staff; **un** ~ **fidato** (*pers.*) a dependable employee; **impiegati in prova** (*pers.*) probationary employees; ~ **in sottordine** (*pers.*) underclerk; **un** ~ **indolente** (*pers.*) a slack employee; **impiegati non di ruolo** (*pers.*) temporary staff; ~ **postale** (*comun.*) postal clerk; ~ **statale** (*pers.*) functionary; civil servant (*in G.B.*); ~ **tuttofare** (*pers.*) factotum, man Friday.

impiego, *n. m.* **1** (*uso*) employment, use. **2** (*fin.*) (*di denaro*) investment. **3** (*pers.*) (*occupazione*) employment, employ, occupation, appointment, hire, retainer. **4** (*pers.*) (*posto di lavoro*) position, post, job, situation, place; berth (*fig.*). // **un** ~ **a tempo pieno** (*pers., sind.*) a full-time job; ~ **delle risorse** (*econ.*) resource allocation; **l'** ~ **di capitali nell'industria** (*econ.*) the employment of capital in industry; **impieghi direttamente produttivi** (*banca, fin.*) directly productive investments; **un** ~ **non retribuito** (*pers.*) an unpaid position; ~ **senza sbocchi di carriera** (*pers.*) dead-end job; ~ **stagionale** (*pers.*) season employment, seasonal employment; ~ **vacante** (*pers.*) vacant post (*o* situation, *ecc.*); vacancy.

implicare, *v. t.* **1** (*racchiudere, sottintendere*) to imply, to involve. **2** (*leg.*) to implicate.

implicazione, *n. f.* implication.

implicito, *a.* 1 implicit, constructive, tacit. 2 (*leg.*) implicit, implied.

imponibile, *a.* (*fin.*) assessable, taxable; ratable, chargeable, listable. *n. m.* (*fin.*) assessable income, taxable value; assessment. // ~ **accertato** (*fin.*) assessed taxes; ~ **fiscale** *V.* ~ *n.*; **non** ~ (*fin.*) non-assessable, non-taxable.

imporre, *v. t.* 1 to impose. 2 (*fin.*) (*tasse, tributi, ecc.*) to impose, to levy, to lay★. 3 (*leg.*) to enjoin, to enforce. // ~ **una requisizione a** (*q. o qc.*) (*leg.*) to requisition; ~ **il sequestro** (*leg.*) to levy the attachment; ~ **tributi a q.** (*fin.*) to tax sb.; ~ **tributi su qc.** (*fin.*) to tax st.; ~ **un tributo speciale sugli articoli di lusso** (*fin., anche*) to put a special tax on luxuries.

importabile, *a.* (*comm. est.*) importable.

importante, *a.* 1 important, big, great, grand, relevant, significant; key (*attr.*). 2 (*leg.*) material. // **il più** ~ the chief, the main, the premier; (*econ.*) the staple; **poco** ~ of little importance, minor.

importanza, *n. f.* importance, significance, consideration; weight (*fig.*). // **di grande** ~ of great importance; (*d'incontro e sim.*) top-level (*attr.*); **di nessuna** ~ of no importance; **di qualche** ~ of some importance.

importare, *v. i.* 1 (*avere importanza*) to matter (*impers.*); to care (*pers.*). 2 (*essere necessario*) to be necessary, to need. *v. t.* 1 (*implicare*) to imply, to involve. 2 (*comm. est.*) to import. // ~ (*merce*) **di contrabbando** (*leg.*) to smuggle, to smuggle in; ~ **di nuovo** (*comm. est.*) to reimport.

importatore, *n. m.* (*comm. est.*) importer. *a.* (*comm. est.*) importing. // ~ **in proprio** (*comm. est.*) import merchant; ~ **su commissione** (*comm. est.*) import (*o* commission) agent; **paesi importatori** (*comm. est.*) importing countries.

importazione, *n. f.* 1 (*comm. est.*) importation, import. 2 (*comm. est.*) (*merce importata*) import, importation. // ~ **di capitali** (*fin.*) import of capitals; ~ **diretta** (*comm. est.*) direct importation; **importazioni esenti da dogana** (*comm. est.*) free imports; ~ **in franchigia doganale** (*dog., fin.*) duty-free entry; ~ **temporanea** (*dog., fin.*) temporary admission; **merci d'** ~ imports.

importo, *n. m.* 1 amount. 2 (*somma di denaro*) sum (of money). // **importi compensativi** (*comm. est., econ.*) compensatory amounts; **l'** ~ **d'una cambiale** the contents of a bill of exchange; ~ **d'una conversazione telefonica** (*comun.*) call charge; **l'** ~ **d'una fattura** the amount of an invoice; **l'** ~ **fatturato** the amount invoiced; **un** ~ **fisso** a flat rate; ~ **lordo** (*market., rag.*) gross amount; ~ **netto** (*market., rag.*) net amount; ~ **pagato in anticipo** amount paid in advance; ~ **parziale** (*mat., rag.*) subtotal.

imposizione, *n. f.* 1 imposition. 2 (*fin.*) (*di tasse, tributi, ecc.*) levy, imposition. 3 (*fin.*) (*tassazione*) taxation. 4 (*fin.*) (*imposta, tassa, tributo*) tax, duty. 5 (*leg.*) injunction, enforcement. // ~ **addizionale** (*fin.*) additional assessment, additional taxation; **imposizioni all'importazione** (*fin.*) charges levied on imports; **l'** ~ **di nuovi balzelli** (*fin.*) the imposition of new taxes; ~ **diretta** (*fin.*) direct taxation; ~ **doppia** (*fin.*) double taxation; ~ **indiretta** (*fin.*) indirect taxation; ~ **troppo gravosa** (*fin.*) overtaxation.

impossessarsi, *v. rifl. V.* **impadronirsi.**

impossibile, *a.* impossible.

impossibilità, *n. f.* impossibility. // ~ **d'esecuzione** (*d'un contratto*) impossibility of performance.

imposta, *n. f.* 1 (*fin.*) tax; impost (*meno comune*); (*dazio, tributo*) duty, due, toll. 2 (*fin.*) (*imposizione*) imposition, levy. 3 (*fin.*) (*tassazione*) taxation, assessment. // ~ **addizionale** (*fin.*) additional tax, surtax, supertax; ~ **alla fonte** (*fin.*) tax at source; ~ **cedolare** (*fin.*) tax on dividend warrants, capital gains tax; ~ **complementare (di rivalsa)** (*fin.*) complementary income tax, surtax; ~ **complementare sul reddito** (*fin.*) income surtax; ~ **comunale** (*fin.*) rate (*ingl.*); ~ **comunale sull'incremento di valore degli immobili (INVIM)** (*fin.*) communal tax on increases in real estate value; ~ **cumulativa sulla cifra d'affari** (*fin.*) cumulative turnover tax; **imposte da pagare** (*la «cartella»*) (*fin.*) tax bill; ~ **di bollo** (*fin.*) stamp duty; ~ **di circolazione** (*fin., trasp. aut.*) road tax; ~ **di conguaglio per le importazioni** (*fin.*) adjustment tax on imports; ~ **di consumo** (*fin.*) excise duty, tax on consumer goods; ~ **di fabbricazione** (*fin.*) internal revenue tax, excise; ~ **di licenza** (*fin.*) licence tax; license tax (*USA*); ~ **di registro** (*fin.*) registration tax; ~ **di ricchezza mobile** (*fin.*) tax on movable wealth, income tax; ~ **di successione** (*leg.*) death duty, succession duty, inheritance tax, transfer duty, transfer tax; death tax, succession tax (*USA*); ~ **di valore locativo** (*fin.*) property tax; ~ **diretta** (*fin.*) direct tax; **imposte e dazi interni** (*fin.*) inland revenue; **imposte esigue** (*fin.*) small taxes; ~ **fiscale** (*fin.*) revenue tax; ~ **fondiaria** (*fin.*) land tax, property tax, assessment on landed property; ~ **forfettaria** (*fin.*) composition tax; ~ **generale sull'entrata** (*IGE; ora sostituita dall'IVA*) (*fin.*) purchase tax (*ingl.*); sales tax (*USA*); (*specialm. se riferita a servizi, o nel comm. est.*) turnover tax; ~ **in natura** (*fin.*) tax in kind; ~ **indiretta** (*fin.*) indirect tax, hidden tax, internal revenue tax, excise; ~ **ipotecaria** (*fin.*) mortgage tax; **imposte locali** (*fin.*) local taxes, rates; ~ **locale sui redditi patrimoniali** (*fin.*) local tax on income from all types of property; ~ **patrimoniale** (*fin.*) capital levy, property tax; ~ **personale** (*fin.*) personal tax, capitation tax, head tax, head money; ~ **progressiva** (*fin.*) progressive tax, graduated tax; ~ **proporzionale** (*fin.*) proportional tax, proportionate tax; ~ **regressiva** (*fin.*) regressive tax; ~ **retroattiva** (*fin.*) retroactive tax; **imposte severe** (*fin.*) punitive taxes; ~ **societaria** (*fin.*) company tax, company profits tax; corporation tax, corporate tax (*USA*); ~ **sugli affari** (*fin.*) turnover tax; ~ **sugli articoli di lusso** (*fin.*) luxury tax; ~ **sui consumi** (*fin.*) consumption tax; ~ **sui fabbricati** (*fin.*) house tax; ~ **sul patrimonio** (*fin.*) capital levy, property tax; ~ **sul reddito** (*fin.*) tax on income, income tax, assessment on income; ~ **sul reddito agrario** (*fin.*) tax on agricultural income; ~ **sul reddito dei fabbricati** (*fin.*) tax on revenue from buildings; ~ **sul reddito delle persone fisiche** (*fin.*) personal income tax; ~ **sul reddito delle persone giuridiche** (*fin.*) tax on the income of corporate bodies; ~ **sul reddito delle società per azioni** (*fin.*) company income tax; corporation net-income tax, corporate income tax (*USA*); ~ **sul reddito dominicale** (*dei terreni*) (*fin.*) tax on income from land; ~ **sul valore aggiunto (IVA)** (*fin.*) value-added tax (*VAT*); ~ **sul valore locativo** (*fin.*) property tax; ~ **sulla cifra d'affari** (*fin.*) turnover tax; ~ **sull'entrata** (*fin.*) *V.* ~ **generale sull'entrata;** ~ **sulle donazioni** (*fin.*) gift tax; ~ **sulle obbligazioni** (*fin.*) tax on bonds; ~ **sulle plusvalenze** (*fin.*) capital gains tax; ~ **sulle società** company tax, company profits tax; corporate tax, corporation tax; ~ **sull'incremento di valore dei beni immobili** (*fin.*) property-increment tax; ~ **sull'incremento di valore delle aree fabbricabili** (*fin.*) tax on increases in the value of building plots.

impostare[1], *v. t.* **1** (*un problema, ecc.*) to state, to set★ out. **2** (*progettare, stabilire*) to draw★; to plan; to set★ out. **3** (*fondare, avviare: un'azienda*) to set★ up; to establish, to start. **4** (*rag.*) (*un conto*) to set★ out, to open. **5** (*trasp. mar.*) (*una nave*) to lay★ down (on the stocks). // ~ **un bilancio** (*econ., rag.*) to budget.

impostare[2], *v. t.* (*comun.*) (*imbucare*) to post, to mail.

impostazione[1], *n. f.* **1** (*d'un problema*) stating, setting out. **2** (*progettazione*) planning, setting out. **3** (*fondazione, avviamento: d'un'azienda*) setting up, starting. **4** (*rag.*) (*d'un conto*) opening (of an account). **5** (*trasp. mar.*) (*d'una nave*) laying (on the stocks). // ~ **di un problema** (*anche*) approach to a problem.

impostazione[2], *n. f.* (*della corrispondenza*) (*comun.*) posting, mailing.

imprenditore, *n. m.* **1** (*econ.*) entrepreneur, undertaker. **2** (*econ.*) (*appaltatore*) contractor. // ~ **di trasporti** carrier; ~ **edile** building contractor; ~ **-manager** (*econ.*) entrepreneur-executive; ~ **-proprietario** (*econ.*) entrepreneur-owner.

imprenditoriale, *a.* (*econ.*) entrepreneurial.

impresa, *n. f.* **1** enterprise, undertaking. **2** (*azienda, ditta*) business, company, concern, firm. // ~ **all'estero** expatriate enterprise; ~ **commerciale** commercial concern, business enterprise, business entity; ~ **di costruzioni** *V.* ~ **edile;** ~ **edile** construction firm; builders, contractors (*pl.*); ~ **industriale** industrial concern, industrial; **un'** ~ **multinazionale** a multinational organization; ~ **pubblica** (*fin.*) public corporation; **un'** ~ **rischiosa** a speculative enterprise, a venture.

impresario, *n. m.* (*appaltatore*) contractor. // ~ **di pompe funebri** undertaker; ~ **di pubblicità** (*pubbl.*) advertising contractor.

imprescrittibile, *a.* (*leg.*) imprescriptible, indefeasible.

imprescrittibilità, *n. f.* (*leg.*) imprescriptibility, indefeasibility.

imprestare, *v. t.* (*cred.*) to lend★; to loan (*USA*). // ~ **su garanzia** (*cred.*) to lend on collateral.

imprestito, *n. m.* (*cred.*) loan.

imprevedibile, *a.* unforeseeable, unpredictable.

imprevisto, *a.* unforseen, unexpected. **1** *n. m.* unexpected event (*o* circumstance). **2 imprevisti,** *pl.* (*spese impreviste*) incidental expenses.

improduttività, *n. f.* (*econ.*) unproductiveness.

improduttivo, *a.* **1** (*econ.*) unproductive, non-productive. **2** (*econ.*) (*non economico*) uneconomic, uneconomical.

improvvisamente, *avv.* suddenly, unexpectedly.

improvvisato, *a.* improvised, make-do.

improvviso, *a.* sudden, unexpected. // ~ **aumento** (*dell'attività commerciale*) (*econ.*) spurt; **un** ~ **aumento delle vendite** (*market.*) a spurt in sales; ~ **e rapido aumento d'attività** (*econ.*) boom.

impugnabile, *a.* (*leg.*) impugnable.

impugnare, *v. t.* **1** (*stringere in pugno*) to grasp, to grip, to seize. **2** (*leg.*) to impugn, to impeach, to challenge, to contest. // ~ **una clausola contrattuale** (*leg.*) to impugn the clause of a contract.

impugnazione, *n. f.* (*leg.*) impugnment, contest.

impulso, *n. m.* impulse.

imputabile, *a.* **1** (*leg.*) imputable, chargeable. **2** (*rag.*) imputable, chargeable, eligible.

imputabilità, *n. f.* **1** (*leg.*) imputability. **2** (*rag.*) imputability, eligibility.

imputare, *v. t.* **1** (*leg.*) to impute, to charge, to accuse. **2** (*rag.*) to impute, to charge, to apply, to classify. // ~ **una somma a un conto** (*rag.*) to charge an account with a sum.

imputato, *n. m.* (*leg.*) accused person, defendant. // ~ **principale** (*leg.*) principal.

imputazione, *n. f.* **1** (*leg.*) imputation, charging. **2** (*leg.*) (*capo d'imputazione*) charge. **3** (*rag.*) imputation, charging, charge, application, classification. // ~ **dei costi** (*rag., anche*) cost allocation.

inabile, *a.* **1** (*incapace*) unable. **2** (*invalido*) invalid. **3** (*leg.*) disabled. *n. m.* e *f.* **1** (*leg.*) disabled person. **2** (*pers.*) (*al lavoro*) disabled person. // ~ **al lavoro** (*pers.*) unable to work; (*per raggiunti limiti d'età*) superannuated; **l'esser reso** ~ (*leg.*) incapacitation.

inabilità, *n. f. inv.* **1** inability, incapacity. **2** (*leg.*) disablement. // ~ **al lavoro** (*pers.*) inability to work.

inabilitare, *v. t.* **1** to invalid, to disqualify. **2** (*leg.*) to incapacitate, to disqualify.

inabilitazione, *n. f.* (*leg.*) incapacitation.

inadempiente, *a.* (*leg.*) defaulting. *n. m.* e *f.* (*leg.*) defaulter. // **essere** ~ (*a un obbligo*) (*leg.*) to default; **la parte** ~ (*leg.*) the defaulting party.

inadempienza, *n. f.* (*leg.*) default, failure, non-compliance, non-fulfilment, non-performance. // ~ **contrattuale** (*leg.*) breach of contract; ~ **delle condizioni d'un prestito** (*leg.*) default of loan terms; ~ **d'un obbligo** (*leg.*) default.

inadempimento, *n. m. V.* **inadempienza.**

inaffondabile, *a.* (*trasp. mar.*) (*di nave*) unsinkable.

inalienabile, *a.* **1** (*leg.*) inalienable, unalienable, indefeasible. **2** (*market.*) unsalable, unsaleable.

inalienabilità, *n. f.* (*leg.*) inalienability, indefeasibility.

inammissibile, *a.* (*anche leg.*) inadmissible.

inammissibilità, *n. f.* (*anche leg.*) inadmissibility.

inamovibile, *a.* **1** immovable. **2** (*pers.*) (*da un ufficio, ecc.*) irremovable.

inappellabile, *a.* (*leg.*) unappealable.

inapprezzabile, *a.* **1** (*inestimabile*) inestimable, invaluable. **2** (*insignificante*) negligible.

inasprimento, *n. m.* tightening up.

inasprire, *v. t.* to make★ harsher (*o* stricter); to tighten up.

inattività, *n. f.* inactivity, inaction, stagnation.

inattivo, *a.* **1** inactive, idle, stagnant. **2** (*leg.*) (*di un socio*) dormant. **3** (*market.*) (*di prezzo, mercato, anche*) flat. // **essere** ~ (*anche*) to stagnate; **capitale** ~ (*fin.*) unemployed capital.

inazione, *n. f.* inaction, idleness, drift.

incagliare, *v. t.* (*trasp. mar.*) to ground, to strand.

incagliarsi, *v. rifl.* (*trasp. mar.*) (*di nave*) to strand, to ground, to run★ aground, to run★ ashore, to strike★.

incaglio, *n. m.* (*trasp. mar.*) stranding, running aground (*o* ashore).

incameramento, *n. m.* **1** (*leg.*) appropriation. **2** (*leg.*) (*confisca*) confiscation.

incamerare, *v. t.* **1** (*leg.*) to appropriate. **2** (*leg.*) (*confiscare*) to confiscate.

incanto, *n. m.* (*market.*) auction sale, auction.

incapace, *a.* **1** (*anche leg.*) unable, incapable. **2** (*leg.*) incompetent, disabled, disqualified. // **l'esser reso** ~ (*leg.*) incapacitation.

incapacità, *n. f.* **1** (*anche leg.*) inability, incapacity. **2** (*leg.*) incompetence, disability, disqualification. // ~ **di far fronte ai propri impegni** (*leg.*) inability to meet one's debts; ~ **giuridica** (*leg.*) legal incapacity; ~ **legale** (*leg.*) legal disability, disqualification.

incaricare, *v. t.* **1** to assign, to charge, to commission, to entrust. **2** (*dare istruzioni a*) to instruct.

incaricato, *n. m.* **1** appointee, delegate, deputy, representative. **2** (*di qc. di preciso*) man★ in charge.

incarico, *n. m.* **1** assignment, appointment, charge, commission. **2** (*compito*) task. **3** (*pers.*) (*ufficio, carica*) office.

incartamento, *n. m.* **1** file. **2** (*leg.*) dossier; papers, documents (*pl.*). // **incartamenti d'affari** business papers.

incartare, *v. t.* (*market.*) to wrap, to wrap up (in paper).

incartata, *n. f. V.* **incarto,** *def. 1.*

incarto, *n. m.* **1** (*market.*) (*l'incartare*) wrapping, wrappage. **2** (*market.*) (*l'involucro*) wrapper, package.

incassabile, *a.* (*cred.*) cashable, encashable, collectable, collectible. // **non ~** (*cred.*) uncollectible.

incassare, *v. t.* **1** (*mettere in casse*) to pack into a case (*o* into cases); to box. **2** (*cred.*) to cash, to encash, to collect, to till. **3** (*market.*) to take★ in; to sack (*USA*). // **~ un assegno** (*cred.*) to cash a cheque, to collect a cheque; **~ una tratta** (*cred.*) to cash a bill.

incassato, *a.* (*cred.*) cashed, collected. // **non ~** (*cred.*) uncollected.

incasso, *n. m.* **1** (*cred.*) (*l'incassare*) collection, encashment. **2** (*cred.*) (*la somma incassata*) take. **3 incassi,** *pl.* (*rag.*) proceeds, returns, takings. // **~ di crediti** (*fin.*) credit collection; **~ di fatture** (*rag.*) bill collection; **~ lordo** (*rag.*) gross receipts; **~ netto** (*rag.*) net receipts.

incendiare, *v. t.* to fire, to set★ fire to (st.).

incendio, *n. m.* fire. // **~ doloso** (*ass., leg.*) arson.

incentivare, *v. t.* to stimulate, to enliven. // **~ la produzione** (*econ.*) to stimulate production; **~ le vendite** (*market., anche*) to push sales.

incentivazione, *n. f.* **1** stimulation. **2** (*incentivo*) incentive. // **incentivazioni che prevedono sgravi fiscali** (*fin.*) tax incentives; **~ delle vendite** (*market., org. az.*) sales promotion.

incentivo, *n. m.* incentive, stimulant, stimulus★. // **un ~ alla concorrenza** (*market.*) a stimulus to competition; **~ all'investimento** (*econ.*) inducement to invest; **incentivi di vendita** (*market.*) sales incentives; **~ diretto** (*pers.*) direct incentive, financial incentive; **~ indiretto** (*pers.*) indirect incentive; **~ monetario** (*pers.*) financial incentive.

incertezza, *n. f.* **1** uncertainty. **2** (*indecisione*) indecision, irresolution. **3** (*instabilità*) unstableness.

incerto, *a.* **1** uncertain, doubtful, vague. **2** (*indeciso*) undecided. **3** (*fortuito*) casual. **4** (*instabile*) unstable. *n. m.* **1** (the) uncertain. **2** (*fin.*) (*nelle locuzioni «quotare il certo per l'incerto», ecc.*) variable exchange. **3 incerti,** *pl.* (*lavori occasionali*) odd jobs. **4 incerti,** *pl.* (*guadagni occasionali*) perquisites; perks (*fam.*). // **gli incerti del mestiere** the risks inherent in one's job.

incetta, *n. f.* corner, cornering, engrossment, hoarding, take-up.

incettare, *v. t.* to corner, to buy★ up, to engross, to hoard.

incettatore, *n. m.* cornerer, corner man★, buyer-up, engrosser, hoarder.

inchiesta, *n. f.* **1** investigation, inquiry, enquiry. **2** (*giorn.*) survey, coverage. **3** (*giorn., market.*) (*d'opinione*) poll. **4** (*leg.*) inquiry. **5** (*market., pubbl.*) survey. // **~ congiunturale** (*econ., fin.*) business survey; **~ per corrispondenza** (*market.*) mail survey.

incidentale, *a.* incidental, occasional.

incidente, *n. m.* **1** (*ass.*) accident, casualty. **2** (*pers.*) (*sul lavoro*) injury. // **~ di mare** (*trasp. mar.*) sea accident; **un ~ di navigazione** (*trasp. mar.*) an accident of navigation; **un ~ ferroviario** (*trasp. ferr.*) a railway accident; **un ~ grave** a bad accident; **~ inevitabile** (*ass.*) unavoidable accident, unavoidable casualty; **un ~ marittimo** (*trasp. mar.*) an accident at sea (*o* of the sea); **~ sul lavoro** (*pers.*) industrial injury.

incidenza, *n. f.* incidence, impact, effect; effects (*pl.*). // **l'~ d'un'imposta sul consumatore** (*fin.*) the incidence of a tax on the consumer; **~ fiscale** tax incidence.

incidere[1], *v. t.* **1** to carve. **2** (*market., pubbl.*) (*su dischi, ecc.*) to record. **3** (*pubbl.*) to engrave, to etch.

incidere[2], *v. i.* to have an effect, to have repercussions, to bear★ heavily (on st.). // **~ su** to affect.

incisione, *n. f.* **1** (*market., pubbl.*) (*di dischi, nastri, ecc.*) recording. **2** (*pubbl.*) engraving, etching.

incisore, *n. m.* (*pubbl.*) engraver, etcher.

incitamento, *n. m.* **1** incitement, stimulation, motivation. **2** (*incentivo, stimolo*) incentive, inducement, stimulus★, urge. // **~ a delinquere** (*leg.*) instigation to commit a crime.

incitare, *v. t.* **1** to incite, to stimulate, to urge. **2** (*indurre, motivare*) to induce, to motivate.

inclinare, *v. t.* to incline, to tilt, to tip.

inclinarsi, *v. rifl.* (*trasp. mar.*) to list.

inclinazione, *n. f.* **1** (*anche fig.*) inclination. **2** (*fig.*) propensity, tendency, drift. **3** (*trasp. mar.*) list.

includere, *v. t.* **1** to include, to comprise, to contain. **2** (*allegare*) to enclose. // **~ in un elenco** (*o* **in una lista**) (*org. az.*) to calendar.

inclusivo, *a.* inclusive.

incluso, *a.* **1** included. **2** (*allegato*) enclosed. **3** (*leg.*) (*accluso*) within. // **~ il diritto d'opzione** (*fin.*) «cum» rights; **~ in una lista** (*o* **in un listino**) listed; **prezzo tutto ~** (*market.*) all-round price, all-in price.

incolpare, *v. t.* to blame (sb. for st.); to accuse (sb. of st.); to charge (sb. with st.).

incombenza, *n. f.* (*pers.*) office, duty, task.

incominciare, *v. t.* e *i.* to begin★, to commence, to start. // ~ **a lavorare** to start work; ~ **un lavoro nuovo** to begin (*o* to start on) a new job.

incompatibile, *a.* (*leg.*) incompatible.

incompatibilità, *a.* (*leg.*) incompatibility.

incompetente, *a.* (*leg.*) incompetent.

incompetenza, *n. f.* (*leg.*) incompetence.

incondizionatamente, *avv.* unconditionally.

incondizionato, *a.* unconditional.

inconfutabile, *a.* (*leg.*) irrefutable, incontestable, incontrovertible.

inconfutabilità, *n. f.* irrefutability, incontestability, incontrovertibility.

inconsumabile, *a.* inconsumable.

incontestabile, *a.* **1** unquestionable, unanswerable. **2** (*leg.*) incontestable.

incontestabilità, *n. f.* (*leg.*) incontestability.

incontrare, *v. t.* **1** to meet★. **2** (*davanti a un nome astratto*) to meet★ with; (*provare*) to experience. *v. i.* (*market.*) (*di un articolo, d'un modello, ecc.*) to be a success; to be successful; to be popular. // ~ **l'approvazione di q.** to meet with sb.'s approval; ~ **il favore di q.** to find favour with sb.; ~ **i gusti della clientela** (*market.*) to appeal to one's customers' tastes; ~ **q. su appuntamento** to meet sb. by appointment.

incontrarsi, *v. recipr.* to meet★ (each other). // ~ **con q.** to meet with sb.

incontro, *n. m.* meeting. // ~ **al vertice** summit meeting.

incontrovertibile, *a.* (*leg.*) incontrovertible.

incontrovertibilità, *n. f.* (*leg.*) incontrovertibility.

inconveniente, *n. m.* **1** inconvenience. **2** (*difficoltà*) difficulty. **3** (*ostacolo*) drawback, hindrance, obstacle, setback.

inconvertibile, *a.* (*econ., fin.*) inconvertible, unconvertible.

inconvertibilità, *n. f.* (*econ., fin.*) inconvertibility.

incorporare, *v. t.* **1** (*rilevare*) to take★ over. **2** (*fin.*) to amalgamate, to combine, to merge. // **essere incorporato** (*fin.*) (*d'azienda, ente, ecc.*) to merge, to be taken over.

incorporarsi, *v. recipr.* (*fin.*) to amalgamate, to combine, to merge.

incorporazione, *n. f.* (*fin.*) (*d'aziende*) amalgamation, combination, combine, merger.

incorporeo, *a.* (*leg.*) incorporeal, intangible.

incorrere, *v. i.* to run★, to fall★ (into); to incur (*v.t.*). // ~ **in passività a breve per acquistare attività a lungo termine** (*cred.*) borrowing short to lend long; ~ **nelle controstallie** (*trasp. mar.*) to come on demurrage.

incostituzionale, *a.* (*leg.*) unconstitutional.

incostituzionalità, *n. f.* (*leg.*) unconstitutionality.

incrementare, *v. t.* **1** (*aumentare*) to increase, to augment. **2** (*favorire, promuovere*) to promote, to foster, to forward. // ~ **la vendita d'un prodotto** (*market., pubbl.*) to push the sale of a product.

incremento, *n. m.* **1** increment. **2** (*aumento*) increase, growth, upsurge. **3** (*econ., fin.*) (*tasso di sviluppo*) growth rate. // **incrementi di capitale** (*fin.*) capital gains; ~ **in valore** (*fin.*) growth in value; ~ **produttivo** (*econ.*) growth of productivity.

incriminabile, *a.* (*leg.*) accusable, chargeable, impeachable, indictable.

incriminare, *v. t.* (*leg.*) to incriminate, to accuse, to charge, to impeach, to indict. // **chi incrimina** (*leg.*) indictor; **chi è incriminato** (*leg.*) indictee.

incriminazione, *n. f.* (*leg.*) incrimination, accusation, charge, impeachment, indictment, true bill.

incrociare, *v. t.* to cross. *v. i.* (*trasp. mar.*) to cruise.

incrociarsi, *v. recipr.* (*di lettere e sim.*) to cross.

incrocio, *n. m.* **1** (*di razze, ecc.*) cross. **2** (*trasp.*) crossing; cross-roads (*col verbo al sing.*); junction.

indagare, *v. t.* e *i.* **1** to inquire, to enquire, to search, to see★, to look (into st.). **2** (*esaminare*) to examine, to explore, to survey, to study. **3** (*leg.*) to investigate.

indagine, *n. f.* **1** inquiry, enquiry, survey, study. **2** (*ricerca*) search, searching, research. **3** (*esame*) examination, exploration. **4** (*leg.*) investigation. **5** (*market., pubbl.*) survey. // ~ **campionaria** (*market.*) sample survey; ~ **congiunturale** (*econ., market.*) business survey; ~ **congiunturale presso i consumatori** (*market.*) consumers' survey; ~ **demoscopica** (*market.*) opinion poll, Gallup poll, poll, opinion survey; ~ **di mercato** (*econ., market.*) market research, marketing research; ~ **d'opinione** (*market.*) opinion poll; **un'~ esauriente** an exhaustive inquiry; ~ **motivazionale** (*market., pubbl.*) motivational research; ~ **postale** (*market.*) mail survey; ~ **previsionale** (*market.*) anticipation survey; **un'~ stragiudiziale** (*leg.*) an extrajudicial investigation; ~ **su campione** (*market.*) poll.

indebitamento, *n. m.* **1** (*banca, fin.*) borrowings (*pl.*). **2** (*cred., fin.*) indebtedness. // ~ **a breve verso banche** (*fin.*) short-term bank debt;

~ **del Tesoro** (*fin.*) Treasury borrowings; ~ **obbligazionario netto** (*fin.*) net bonded debt.

indebitarsi, *v. rifl.* (*cred.*) to get★ into debt, to run★ into debt.

indebitato, *a.* (*cred.*) indebted. // **essere** ~ to be in debt.

indebito, *a.* 1 undue. 2 (*leg.*) unjust. // ~ **arricchimento** (*leg.*) unjust enrichment.

indebolimento, *n. m.* (*anche fig.*) weakening. // **un** ~ **congiunturale** (*econ.*) a decline of business activity, a tendency for business conditions to weaken.

indebolire, *v. t.* (*anche fig.*) to weaken.

indebolirsi, *v. rifl.* (*anche fig.*) to weaken.

indeciso, *a.* 1 undecided, uncertain, pending. 2 (*irresoluto*) irresolute.

indefinito, *a.* 1 indefinite. 2 (*irrisolto*) undefined.

indemaniare, *v. t.* (*leg.*) to escheat. // **essere indemaniato** (*leg.*) to escheat.

indenne, *a.* (*ass., trasp.*) undamaged.

indennità, *n. f. inv.* 1 indemnity, compensation, consideration, consideration money. 2 (*ass.*) claim. 3 (*leg.*) indemnity. 4 (*pers.*) allowance, benefit, bonus. // ~ **d'anzianità** (*pers.*) longevity pay; ~ **di buonuscita** (*pers.*) (*pagata a un dipendente licenziato senza sua colpa*) severance pay; dismissal wage (*USA*); (*a militari o impiegati dello Stato: in G.B.*) gratuity; (*data a un amministratore che lascia una società*) compensation for loss of office; ~ **di carovita** (*pers.*) cost-of-living allowance, cost-of-living bonus; ~ **di fine (del rapporto di) lavoro** (*per pensionamento*) (*pers.*) retirement bonus (*non esiste in G.B.*); ~ **di grande sede** (*pers.*) weighting allowance; ~ **di lavoro straordinario** (*pers.*) overtime pay; ~ **di licenziamento** (*pers.*) dismissal wage, compensation in case of dismissal, severance pay; ~ **di missione** (*amm., pers.*) travelling allowance; ~ **di rescissione** (*d'un contratto, ecc.*) (*leg.*) cancelling price; ~ **di rischio** (*pers.*) danger money; ~ **di salvataggio** (*trasp. mar.*) remuneration for salvage; ~ **di trasferta** (*pers.*) travelling allowance, subsistence allowance, subsistence money; ~ **di viaggio** (*pers.*) travelling allowance; (*a un tanto al miglio*) mileage; ~ **giornaliera** (*pers.*) daily allowance; ~ **integrativa** (*econ.*) subsistence allowance; ~ **per cessazione d'attività** (*pers.*) compensation on retirement; ~ **per infortuni sul lavoro e malattie professionali** (*ass.*) workmen's compensation; ~ **per prestazioni speciali** (*pers.*) task bond; ~ **per sinistro** (*ass.*) compensation for accident; ~ **per spese di rappresentanza** (*rag.*) entertainment allowance.

indennizzare, *v. t.* 1 (*anche ass.*) to indemnify, to compensate, to make★ good. 2 (*leg.*) to indemnify, to recoup. // ~ **un danno (una perdita)** (*ass.*) to indemnify a damage (a loss); **chi indennizza** (*leg.*) indemnitor; **chi è** (*o* **ha diritto a essere) indennizzato** (*leg.*) indemnitee; **chi è tenuto a** ~ (*leg.*) indemnitor.

indennizzo, *n. m.* 1 (*anche ass.*) indemnification, compensation. 2 (*anche ass.*) (*il denaro*) indemnity, allowance. 3 (*ass.*) (*domanda d'indennizzo*) claim. 4 (*leg.*) indemnification, indemnity, recoupment. // ~ (*pagato da un datore di lavoro*) **a un dipendente infortunato** (*pers., sind.*) smart money; ~ **in caso di ritardo** (*trasp.*) compensation in case of delay.

indicare, *v. t.* 1 to indicate; (*mostrare*) to show★, to point out. 2 (*menzionare, dichiarare*) to mention, to state. 3 (*citare*) to quote. // ~ **nel capitolato** (*leg.*) to specify; ~ **il prezzo corrente di** (*azioni, merci, ecc.*) (*fin., market.*) to quote; ~ **la strada** to show the way; ~ **la strada giusta** to indicate the right road.

indicatore, *n. m.* 1 indicator. 2 (*econ., fin.*) (*economico, ecc.*) pointer. // ~ **commerciale** commercial directory; **indicatori di direzione** (*econ.*) leading indicators; ~ **di marea** (*trasp. mar.*) tide indicator; ~ **economico** (*econ., anche*) economic indicator; ~ **stradale** (*trasp.*) (*guida*) road directory; (*cartello indicatore*) guide-post, sign-post, road sign.

indicazione, *n. f.* 1 indication, sign, pointer. 2 (*menzione*) mention. 3 (*istruzione*) direction. 4 (*suggerimento*) suggestion. // ~ **sbagliata** misdirection.

indice, *n. m.* 1 (*il dito*) forefinger. 2 (*indizio*) indication, sign. 3 (*di libro*) table of contents. 4 (*econ., fin., stat.*) pointer, index★, indicator. // ~ **analitico** (*d'un libro*) index; ~ **dei noli** (*trasp. mar.*) freight index; ~ **dei prezzi** (*econ.*) price level; ~ **dei prezzi al dettaglio** (*o* **al minuto**) (*market.*) index of retail prices; ~ **dei prezzi all'ingrosso** (*market.*) index of wholesale prices; ~ **del costo della vita** (*econ.*) cost-of-living index, cost-of-living figure; ~ **dell'occupazione** (*econ.*) employment index; ~ **della produttività** (*econ.*) index of productivity; ~ **della produzione industriale** (*econ.*) industrial production index; ~ **delle vendite** (*d'un prodotto*) (*market.*) performance; ~ **d'ascolto** (*radiofonico o televisivo*) (*pubbl.*) rating; ~ **di benessere economico** index of economic well-being; ~ **di disoccupazione** (*sind.*) unemployment rate; ~ **di gradimento** (*pubbl.*) reaction index; ~ **di liquidità** (*econ., rag.*) current ratio; ~ **di produtti-**

vità semplificato (*org. az.*) simplified index of productivity; ~ **di profitto** (*econ.*) profit index, profitability index; ~ **di rotazione delle giacenze** (*org. az.*) turnover rate; ~ **di rotazione delle scorte** (*org. az.*) index of stock rotation; (*in un dato periodo: generalm. un anno*) stock-turn; ~ **di utilizzazione della capacità** (*degli impianti*) (*org. az.*) capacity-utilization rate; ~ **Dow Jones** (*fin.*) Dow-Jones index; ~ **finanziario** (*fin., stat.*) share index; **indici finanziari** (*fin., anche*) financial ratios; ~ «**guida**» (*econ.*) leading indicator, leader; ~ **mensile del costo della vita** (*compilato dall'« U.S. Bureau of Labor Statistics»*) (*econ., USA*) consumer price index.

indicizzare, *v. t.* (*econ., fin.*) to index. // ~ **i redditi** to index incomes.

indicizzato, *a.* **1** (*econ., fin.*) index-linked. **2** (*fin.*) (*di titolo*) floating-rate (*attr.*).

indicizzazione, *n. f.* (*econ., fin.*) indexation. // ~ **dei salari** (*econ.*) wage indexation (*in Italia: la «scala mobile»*).

indietro, *avv.* **1** back, behind. **2** (*moto, anche*) backwards. **3** (*trasp. mar.*) astern. // « ~ **e/o avanti**» (*trasp. mar.*) (*clausola che consente alla nave di fare scalo in qualsiasi porto intermedio*) «backwards and/or forwards»; **all'** ~ backwards.

indipendente, *a.* **1** independent; free-lance (*attr.*). **2** (*org. az.*) self-employed.

indipendenza, *n. f.* independence.

indire, *v. t.* **1** to announce, to proclaim. **2** (*convocare*) to summon. **3** (*una riunione, ecc.*) to call. // ~ **una gara d'appalto** (*leg.*) to call for tenders.

indirizzare, *v. t.* **1** (*una lettera e sim.*) to address. **2** (*mandare q. da q. altro*) to refer, to direct, to send★. // ~ **erroneamente una lettera** (*comun.*) to misaddress a letter; ~ **per referenze** (*pers.*) to refer.

indirizzario, *n. m.* (*comun.*) mailing list, address book.

indirizzarsi, *v. rifl.* **1** (*rivolgere la parola a q.*) to address oneself (to sb.). **2** (*rivolgersi*) to apply (to sb.).

indirizzo, *n. m.* **1** (*postale*) address. **2** (*direzione, tendenza, piega*) direction, trend, turn. **3** (*linea di condotta, politica*) line (of conduct), course, policy. // ~ **cablografico** (*comun.*) cable address; ~ **convenuto** (*comun.*) code address; ~ **del mittente** (*comun.*) return address; ~ **d'ufficio** business address; ~ **privato** private address; ~ **sbagliato** (*d'una lettera, ecc.*) (*comun.*) misdirection; ~ **telegrafico** (*comun.*) telegraphic address, abbreviated address; **senza** ~ (*comun.*) (*di lettera, ecc.*) unaddressed.

indispensabile, *a.* indispensable, necessary, prerequisite, requisite, vital.

individuale, *a.* **1** individual, personal. **2** (*separato*) several, single.

individualmente, *avv.* **1** individually. **2** (*separatamente*) severally.

individuo, *n. m.* individual, fellow, person.

indiviso, *a.* undivided. // **proprietà indivisa** (*leg.*) joint ownership.

indiziario, *a.* (*leg.*) constructive, circumstantial, presumptive. // **processo** ~ (*leg.*) trial based on circumstantial evidence; **prova indiziaria** (*leg.*) circumstantial evidence.

indizio, *n. m.* **1** clue. **2** (*leg.*) circumstantial evidence. // **indizi di prova** (*leg.*) circumstantial evidence.

indossare, *v. t.* to wear★, to put★ on.

indossatrice, *n. f.* (*market., pubbl.*) mannequin; model.

indotto, *a.* induced.

indugiare, *v. i.* to delay, to lag, to wait.

indugio, *n. m.* delay, lag, wait. // **senza** ~ without delay.

indulgenza, *n. f.* indulgence, tolerance.

indulto, *n. m.* **1** (*leg.*) pardon. **2** (*leg.*) (*il provvedimento*) act of oblivion.

indurre, *v. t.* **1** to induce. **2** (*convincere*) to convince, to persuade. // ~ **q. in errore** to lead sb. into error.

industria, *n. f.* (*econ.*) industry, manufacture, trade. // **industrie a tecnologia avanzata** (*econ.*) high-technology industries; ~ **aerospaziale** (*econ.*) aerospace industry; ~ **alimentare** (*econ.*) food industry; **industrie arretrate** (*econ.*) backward industries; ~ «**bambina**» (*econ.*) infant industry; **un'** ~ «**chiave**» (*econ.*) a key industry; **l'** ~ **cinematografica** (*econ.*) the film industry, the screen; **un'** ~ **con eccessiva manodopera** (*econ., org. az.*) an overmanned industry; **industrie concorrenti** competing industries; ~ **conserviera** (*econ.*) canning industry; **l'** ~ **cotoniera** (*econ.*) the cotton trade; ~ **decotta** (*econ.*) lossmaking industry, lossmaker; ~ **del settore «terziario»** (*econ.*) service industry; ~ **delle costruzioni** (*econ.*) building trade; ~ **di base** (*econ.*) staple industry, basic industry; **industrie di riproduzione** (*econ.*) reproductive industries; ~ **di servizi** (*econ.*) service industry; **l'** ~ **di trasformazione** (*econ.*) the processing industry, processing; ~ **edile** (*econ.*) constructive industry; ~ **fondamentale** (*econ.*) staple industry; **industrie improduttive** (*econ.*) uneconomic industries; lame ducks (*fam.*); **industrie in espansione** expanding industries; **l'** ~ **leggera** (*econ.*) the light industry; ~ **manifatturiera** (*econ.*)

manufacturing industry; **industrie meccaniche** (*econ.*) mechanical engineering; ~ **navale** (*trasp. mar.*) shipping industry; ~ **pesante** (*econ.*) heavy industry; ~ **siderurgica** (*econ.*) iron and steel industry; ~ **stagionale** (*econ.*) seasonal industry; **industrie tradizionali** (*econ.*) long-established industries; **industrie trasformative** (*econ.*) processing industries.

industrial design, *n. m.* (*org. az., pubbl.*) industrial design.

industrial designer, *n. m.* (*org. az., pubbl.*) industrial designer.

industriale, *a.* industrial; manufacturing (*attr.*). *n. m.* e *f.* industrialist, manufacturer. // ~ **che produce su commissione** commission manufacturer.

industrialismo, *n. m.* (*econ.*) industrialism.

industrializzare, *v. t.* (*econ.*) to industrialize.

industrializzazione, *n. f.* (*econ.*) industrialization.

inefficace, *a.* 1 inefficacious, ineffective, ineffectual. 2 (*inutile*) useless, unavailing, unavailable. 3 (*leg.*) inoperative, void.

inefficacia, *n. f.* 1 inefficacity, inefficaciousness, ineffectiveness, ineffectualness. 2 (*leg.*) inoperativeness, voidness.

inefficiente, *a.* 1 (*di persona*) inefficient, ineffective; ineffectual (*USA*). 2 (*di cosa*) ineffectual.

inefficienza, *n. f.* 1 inefficiency, ineffectiveness. 2 (*difetto, manchevolezza*) shortcoming. // **inefficienze strutturali** (*econ.*) structural shortcomings.

inerente, *a.* 1 inherent. 2 (*leg.*) incident. // ~ **a** attendant, concerning; incident, incidental, pertaining to.

inerte, *a.* 1 inert; lifeless. 2 (*anche econ., fin.*) dull, slack, sluggish.

inerzia, *n. f.* 1 inertia; lifelessness. 2 (*anche econ., fin.*) dullness, slackness, sluggishness.

inesatto[1], *a.* (*scorretto*) inexact, inaccurate, incorrect.

inesatto[2], *a.* (*cred.*) (*non riscosso*) uncollected.

inesecuzione, *n. f.* (*leg.*) non-fulfilment, non-performance.

inesigibile, *a.* (*cred.*) uncollectible.

inesistente, *a.* 1 inexistent; non-existent. 2 (*dog., fin.*) (*di dazio e sim.*) nil (*attr.*).

inesperto, *a.* 1 (*che non ha esperienza*) inexperienced. 2 (*in un lavoro*) inexpert, unskilled.

inespresso, *a.* unexpressed.

inevaso, *a.* (*comun.*) (*di lettera, ecc.*) unanswered.

inevitabile, *a.* inevitable, unavoidable.

inferiore, *a.* 1 inferior; under (*attr.*). 2 (*di seconda qualità*) second-class (*attr.*). // **a un prezzo** ~ (*market.*) at a lower (*o* cheaper) price.

infermità, *n. f. inv.* 1 infirmity, disease, illness. 2 (*pers.*) (*inabilità al lavoro*) disability. // ~ **mentale** (*leg.*) mental disease.

infermo, *a.* 1 ill, sick, invalid. 2 (*pers.*) (*inabile al lavoro*) disable.

inflazionare, *v. t.* (*econ.*) to inflate. // ~ **una moneta** (*econ.*) to inflate a currency.

inflazione, *n. f.* (*econ.*) inflation. // ~ **attenuata** (*econ.*) dampened inflation; ~ **che imperversa** (*econ.*) raging inflation; ~ **che procede a balzi** (*econ.*) leaping inflation; ~ **controllata** (*mediante il differimento delle spese per beni di consumo*) (*econ.*) suppressed inflation; ~ **controllata dal Governo** (*econ.*) Government inflation, repressed inflation; ~ **cronica** (*econ.*) chronic inflation; ~ **da capitali** (*econ.*) capital inflation; ~ **da** (*eccessivo aumento dei*) **costi** (*econ.*) cost inflation, cost-push inflation; ~ **da** (*eccessiva espansione dei*) **crediti** (*econ.*) credit inflation; ~ **da** (*eccesso di*) **domanda** (*econ.*) demand inflation, demand-pull inflation, demand-push inflation; ~ **da** (*eccesso di produzione dell'*) **oro** (*econ.*) gold inflation; ~ **da** (*eccessivo aumento dei*) **prezzi** (*econ.*) price inflation; ~ **da profitti** (*econ.*) profit inflation, profit-push inflation; ~ **da redditi** (*econ.*) income inflation; ~ **da** (*aumento eccessivo dei*) **salari** (*econ.*) wage inflation; ~ **decrescente** (*econ.*) dampened inflation; ~ **del credito bancario** (*econ., fin.*) bank credit inflation; ~ **della cartamoneta** (*econ.*) paper money inflation; ~ **dovuta ad eccesso della spesa pubblica** (*econ.*) spillover inflation; ~ **eccessiva** (*econ.*) hyperinflation; ~ **effettiva** (*econ.*) actual inflation; ~ **galoppante** (*econ.*) galloping inflation, runaway inflation, hyperinflation; ~ **graduale** (*econ.*) stepwise inflation; ~ **inarrestabile** (*fin.*) hyperinflation; ~ **incontrollabile** (*econ.*) runaway inflation; ~ **incontrollata** (*econ.*) open inflation; ~ **indotta dagli interessi** (*econ.*) interest-induced inflation; ~ **indotta dai costi** (*econ.*) cost-induced inflation; ~ **indotta dai profitti** (*econ.*) profit-induced inflation; ~ **indotta dalle esportazioni** (*econ.*) export-induced inflation; ~ **indotta dalle importazioni** (*econ.*) import-induced inflation; ~ **intermittente** (*econ.*) intermittent inflation; ~ **monetaria** (*fin.*) monetary inflation; ~ «**rampante**» (*econ.*) rampant inflation; ~ **strisciante** (*econ.*) creeping inflation; ~ «**strutturale**» (*econ.*) structural inflation; ~ «**zero**» (*econ.*) zero inflation; **chi favorisce l' ~ economica** (*econ.*) inflationist.

inflazionismo, *n. m.* (*econ., fin.*) inflationism.

inflazionista, *n. m.* e *f.* (*econ., fin.*) inflationist.

inflazionistico, *a.* (*econ.*) inflationary.

influente, *a.* influential.

influenza, *n. f.* (*influsso*) influence, bearing.

influenzare, *v. t.* to influence, to affect.

influire, *v. i.* to exert an influence (on st.). // ~ **su** (*anche*) to influence, to affect.

influsso, *n. m.* influence, leverage. // ~ **reciproco** interaction.

infondato, *a.* unfounded, groundless.

informare, *v. t.* to inform, to acquaint, to communicate, to let★ (sb.) know, to notify, to give★ notice. // ~ **male** to misinform; ~ **la polizia** to notify the police.

informarsi, *v. rifl.* to inquire, to get★ information, to check up. // ~ **sulla tendenza del mercato** (*market.*) to inquire about (*o* after) the market trend.

informatica, *n. f.* informatics.

informativo, *a.* informative. // **un colloquio** ~ an informative talk; **note informative** (*pers.*) report (on a clerk).

informazione, *n. f.* **1** (*in genere*) information (*sing. collett.*). **2** (*singola notizia*) piece of information. **3 informazioni,** *pl.* information, intelligence, news (*tutti sing. collett.*). // **informazioni commerciali** commercial intelligence, business report; (*sulla solvibilità*) credit report, credit-status information; **informazioni confidenziali** confidential report, inside information; inside (*fam.*); inside stuff (*slang USA*); **informazioni finanziarie** (*fin.*) money-market intelligence; **informazioni previsionali** (*market.*) information on forecast; **informazioni retrospettive** (*market.*) information on past trends; **informazioni riservate** *V.* **informazioni confidenziali; informazioni sbagliate** misinformation.

infortunio, *n. m.* **1** (*ass.*) accident. **2** (*pers.*) (*sul lavoro, anche*) injury. // ~ **sul lavoro** (*pers.*) industrial accident, industrial injury.

infortunistica, *n. f.* (*leg.*) study of industrial accidents.

infortunistico, *a.* (*leg.*) councerning industrial accident; injury (*attr.*). // **legislazione infortunistica** (*leg.*) industrial injury legislation.

infraindustriale, *a.* (*org. az.*) interindustrial.

infrangere, *v. t.* **1** to break★, to shatter, to smash. **2** (*leg.*) to infringe, to break★, to invade.

infrangibile, *a.* umbreakable, infrangible.

infrangibilità, *n. f.* (*specialm. fig.*) infrangibility.

infrastruttura, *n. f.* **1** (*econ.*) infrastructure. **2 infrastrutture,** *pl.* (*econ.*) facilities. // **infrastrutture economiche** (*econ.*) economic infrastructures.

infrazione, *n. f.* **1** (*leg.*) infringement, breach, countravention, trespass, violation. **2** (*leg.*) (*reato lieve*) misdemeanour, nuisance, wrongdoing. // ~ **ai regolamenti** (*leg.*) breach of regulations; ~ **alle condizioni** (*leg.*) breach of the conditions; ~ **alle disposizioni di legge** (*leg.*) breach of the provisions of the law; ~ **passibile di pena** (*leg.*) indictable offence.

infruttifero, *a.* **1** unfruitful, fruitless. **2** (*fin., rag.*) non-interest bearing. // **essere** ~ (*fin.*) to yield no profit (*o* no interest); **capitale** ~ (*fin.*) capital lying idle.

infruttuoso, *a.* **1** unprofitable, unremunerative. **2** (*inutile, vano*) useless, unsuccessful, without result.

ingaggiare, *v. t.* (*pers.*) to engage.

ingaggio, *n. m.* (*pers.*) engagement, retainer.

ingente, *a.* enormous, huge; large-scale (*attr.*). // **ingenti variazioni strutturali** (*org. az.*) large-scale structural changes.

ingerenza, *n. f.* (*anche leg.*) interference. // ~ **illegale** (*leg.*) undue influence.

ingiungere, *v. t.* (*leg.*) to enjoin.

ingiuntivo, *a.* (*leg.*) injunctive.

ingiunzione, *n. f.* (*leg.*) injunction. // ~ **di pagamento** (*d'un'imposta locale*) (*fin.*) precept (*ingl.*); ~ **di riprendere il lavoro** (*sind.*) back-to-work injunction.

ingiuria, *n. f.* **1** insult, affront. **2** (*leg.*) (*torto*) wrong. **3** (*leg.*) (*diffamazione*) slander.

ingiustificato, *a.* unjustified, groundless, unfounded.

ingiustizia, *n. f.* **1** injustice, unfairness, inequity. **2** (*leg.*) (*torto*) wrong.

ingiusto, *a.* **1** unjust, inequitable, unfair, partial. **2** (*leg.*) wrongful, wrong.

inglese, *a.* English. *n. m.* **1** (*la lingua*) English. **2** (*uomo inglese*) Englishman★. *n. f.* Englishwoman★. // **l' ~ commerciale** business English.

ingolfarsi nei debiti, *locuz. verb.* to plunge into debt.

ingorgo, *n. m.* (*trasp.*) block, tie-up. // ~ **stradale** (*trasp. aut.*) traffic block, traffic jam.

ingresso, *n. m.* **1** admission, admittance. **2** (*il locale*) hall. **3** (*elab. elettr.*) input. // ~ (*delle*) **merci** (*market.*) goods entrance.

ingrosso, *n. m.* (*market.*) wholesale. // **all'** ~

(*market.*) by wholesale, wholesale; at wholesale (*USA*); in the lump.

iniezione, *n. f.* injection. // **un' ~ di capitale** (*fin.*) a capital injection; **un' ~ di contante** (*fin.*) an injection of cash.

«inintermediari», *n. pl.* (*pubbl.*) (*in un annuncio*) «no agents».

ininterrotto, *a.* **1** uninterrupted, continuous. **2** (*trasp.*) (*di viaggio*) non-stop.

iniquo, *a.* **1** unjust, inequitable, unfair. **2** (*leg.*) wrongful. // **un'iniqua distribuzione dei beni fra gli eredi** (*leg.*) an inequitable division of an estate among the heirs.

iniziale, *a.* initial. *n. f.* **1** (*d'un capitolo, ecc.*) initial. **2 iniziali,** *pl.* (*d'un nome e d'un cognome*) initials.

iniziare, *v. t.* to initiate, to begin★, to open, to start. // **~ un lavoro** (*org. az.*) to initiate a work; **~ relazioni d'affari** to enter into business connections.

iniziativa, *n. f.* initiative, enterprise, drive. // **~ diretta** (*leg.*) direct initiative; **~ imprenditoriale associata** (*econ.*) joint venture; **~ indiretta** (*leg.*) indirect initiative; **di propria ~** own-initiative (*a. attr.*).

iniziatore, *n. m.* **1** initiator. **2** (*promotore*) promoter.

inizio, *n. m.* beginning, commencement, opening, start, starting. // **l' ~ del nuovo esercizio sociale** the beginning of the new fiscal year; **~ della discarica** (*trasp. mar.*) break of bulk; **~ della perorazione** (*leg.*) opening; **~ e fine d'un rischio** (*ass.*) commencement and end of a risk.

innavigabile, *a.* (*trasp., trasp. mar.*) unnavigable, innavigable.

innocente, *a.* **1** innocent. **2** (*leg.*) (*in talune formule*) not guilty. // **dichiararsi ~ (colpevole)** to plead not guilty (guilty).

innocenza, *n. f.* innocence.

innovazione, *n. f.* innovation. // **innovazioni gestionali** (*amm.*) managerial innovations.

inoltrare, *v. t.* **1** to forward, to send★ on, to route, to turn over. **2** (*presentare: documenti e sim.*) to submit, to file. // **~ una domanda d'impiego** to submit an application; **~ un reclamo a q.** to lodge a complaint with sb.

inondare, *v. t.* to flood.

inondato, *a.* **1** flooded. **2** (*fig.*) overflooded. // **~ di valuta** (*fin.*) overflooded with money.

inondazione, *n. f.* flood.

inoperante, *a.* (*leg.*) inoperative.

inoperoso, *a.* inactive.

inoppugnabile, *a.* **1** incontrovertible. **2** (*leg.*) indefeasible.

inoppugnabilità, *n. f.* **1** incontrovertibility. **2** (*leg.*) indefeasibility.

inosservanza, *n. f.* (*leg.*) inobservance, non-observance. // **~ delle disposizioni dell'autorità giudiziaria** (*leg.*) contempt of Court.

inquilino, *n. m.* **1** (*leg.*) tenant, renter. **2 (gli) inquilini,** *pl.* (*leg.*) (*d'una casa*) tenantry (*sing. collett.*).

inquirente, *a.* (*amm., leg.*) investigating. *n. m.* e *f.* (*amm., leg.*) fact finder.

inquisitorio, *a.* (*leg.*) inquisitorial.

insabbiamento, *n. m.* (*trasp. mar.*) sanding-up. // **l' ~ d'una pratica (d'un disegno di legge, ecc.)** (*fig.*) the shelving of a matter (of a bill, etc.).

insabbiare, *v. t.* **1** to sand, to cover with sand. **2** (*fig.*) (*un progetto e sim.*) to shelve; to pigeon-hole.

insabbiarsi, *v. rifl.* **1** to be covered with sand; to become★ sanded up. **2** (*fig.: essere accantonato*) to be shelved; to be pigeon-holed.

insaccare, *v. t.* (*market.*) to sack.

insaputa, *n. f.* (*nella locuz.*) **a nostra ~** without our knowledge.

inscatolamento, *n. m.* **1** boxing. **2** (*in scatole di latta*) tinning (*ingl.*); canning (*USA*).

inscatolare, *v. t.* **1** to box, to pack in boxes. **2** (*in scatole di latta*) to tin (*ingl.*); to can (*USA*); to pack in tins (*o* in cans). // **carne inscatolata** tinned (*o* canned) meat.

inscatolatrice, *n. f.* **1** boxing machine. **2** (*per scatole di latta*) canning machine.

insediamento, *n. m.* (*amm.*) installation, taking over.

insediare, *v. t.* (*amm.*) to install, to institute, to chair. // **~ una giuria** (*leg.*) to swear in a jury.

insediarsi, *v. rifl.* (*amm.*) to take★ office, to take★ over.

insegna, *n. f.* (*market.*) (*di negozio*) sign, sign-board; facia (*USA*). // **~ di negozio** (*market.*) store sign; **~ luminosa** (*pubbl.*) electric sign; illuminated sign (*ingl.*); **~** (*luminosa*) **su un edificio** (*pubbl.*) sky-sign.

inserimento, *n. m.* insertion, introduction.

inserire, *v. t.* to insert, to introduce. // **~ una clausola in un contratto** (*leg.*) to put a clause in a contract; **~** (*articoli, ecc.*) **in catalogo** (*market.*) to list; **~** (*titoli*) **in un listino ufficiale** (*Borsa, fin.*) to list.

inserto, *n. m.* (*giorn., pubbl.*) insert, inset.

inserviente, *n. m.* e *f.* **1** attendant. **2** (*trasp. ferr.*) (*di vagone letto, ecc.*) porter.

inserzione, *n. f.* **1** insertion, introduction. **2** (*giorn., pubbl.*) insertion, advertisement; ad (*fam.*). // ~ **fatta in una rubrica di giornale** (*giorn.*) classified advertisement; ~ (*d'un atto*) **in un pubblico registro** (*leg.*) entry.

inserzionista, *n. m.* e *f.* (*pubbl.*) advertiser.

insieme[1], *avv.* **1** together; jointly. **2** (*nello stesso tempo*) at the same time.

insieme[2], *n. m.* aggregate, set. // ~ **degli assegni, ecc. pagabili a una banca e presentati alla stanza di compensazione** (*banca, ingl.*) out-clearing; ~ **degli assegni, ecc. spiccati su una banca e da questa presentati alla stanza di compensazione** (*banca, ingl.*) in-clearing; ~ **delle condizioni «chiave»** (*d'un accordo collettivo di lavoro, che costituiscono un precedente per altre aziende*) (*sind.*) key bargain; ~ **di titoli** (*o* **merci**) **venduti allo scoperto a una certa data** (*Borsa, fin.*) short interest, short position.

insinuare, *v. t.* to insinuate. // ~ **un credito in un fallimento** (*leg.*) to prove a debt in a bankruptcy; to strike a docket (*fam., ingl.*).

insistente, *a.* insistent, urgent. // ~ **richiesta di pagamento** dun.

insistenza, *n. f.* insistence, pressure, urgency.

insistere, *v. i.* to insist, to persist, to urge.

insoddisfacente, *a.* unsatisfactory.

insoddisfatto, *a.* unsatisfied, dissatisfied.

insoddisfazione, *n. f.* dissatisfaction.

insoluto, *a.* (*cred.*) unpaid, unsettled, undischarged, outstanding.

insolvente, *a.* (*leg.*) insolvent.

insolvenza, *n. f.* (*leg.*) insolvency.

insolvibile, *a.* **1** (*fin.*) (*d'impresa, ecc.*) wildcat (*attr.*). **2** (*leg.*) insolvent.

insommergibile, *a.* (*trasp. mar.*) (*di nave*) unsinkable.

instabile, *a.* unstable, unsteady.

instabilità, *n. f.* **1** instability, unstableness, unsteadiness. **2** (*econ.*) (*economica, ecc.*) disequilibrium.

installare, *v. t.* **1** (*insediare*) to install, to institute, to chair. **2** (*org. az.*) to install, to instal, to seat, to set★ up. // ~ **una macchina** (*org. az.*) to set up a machine.

installazione, *n. f.* **1** (*insediamento*) installation. **2** (*org. az.*) installation, laying, setting up.

instaurare, *v. t.* to establish, to found, to set★ up.

instaurazione, *n. f.* establishment, foundation. // **l'**~ **del Mercato Comune** (*econ.*) the establishment of the Common Market.

instradamento, *n. m.* (*trasp. ferr.*) (*d'un treno*) shunt, shunting.

instradare, *v. t.* **1** (*trasp.*) (*merci, ecc.*) to route. **2** (*trasp. ferr.*) (*un treno*) to shunt, to switch.

insuccesso, *n. m.* failure, frustration; flop (*fam.*).

insufficiente, *a.* **1** insufficient, not sufficient, scanty, scarce, short. **2** (*inadeguato*) inadequate. // **essere** ~ **rispetto a q.** to fall short of st.

insufficienza, *n. f.* **1** insufficiency, scantiness, shortage. **2** (*inadeguatezza*) inadequacy.

intatto, *a.* **1** intact, untouched. **2** (*indenne*) safe.

integrale, *a.* **1** integral, complete, outright. **2** (*radicale*) radical. **3** (*giorn., pubbl.*) (*d'articolo, ecc.*) unabridged.

integralmente, *avv.* integrally, completely.

integrare, *v. t.* **1** to integrate, to make★ up. **2** (*lo stipendio, ecc.*) to supplement.

integrativo, *a.* integrative, supplementary.

integrazione, *n. f.* integration. // **l'**~ **economica dell'Europa** (*econ.*) the European economic integration; ~ **orizzontale** (*econ., org. az.*) horizontal integration, horizontal combination; ~ **verticale** (*econ., org. az.*) vertical integration, vertical combination.

intelligente, *a.* intelligent.

intelligenza, *n. f.* intelligence.

intendente, *n. m.* intendant, superintendent. // ~ **di finanza** (*amm., fin.*) Chief Financial Officer (*in a province*).

intendere, *v. t.* **1** (*capire*) to understand★; to take★ it (*fam.*). **2** (*udire*) to hear★. **3** (*aver l'intenzione di, voler dire*) to intend, to mean★. // **s'intende che...** it is understood that...

intendersi, *v. rifl.* **1** (*raggiungere un accordo*) to come★ to (*o* to reach) an agreement. **2** (*essere conoscitore*) to know★ a lot (about st.); to understand★ (how st. works). *v. recipr.* to understand★ each other (*o* one another).

intenditore, *n. m.* expert; connoisseur.

intensamente, *avv.* intensely, hard.

intensificare, *v. t.* to intensify, to step up.

intensificarsi, *v. rifl.* to intensify, to step up.

intensificazione, *n. f.* intensification.

intensivo, *a.* intensive.

intenso, *a.* intense; (*forte*) strong; (*vivace*) brisk.

intentare, *v. t.* (*leg.*) to institute, to commence. // ~ **un'azione contro un debitore** (*leg.*) to commence proceedings against a debtor; ~ **un'azione legale contro q.** (*leg.*) to institute proceeding against sb.; ~ **causa contro q.** (*leg.*) to bring an action against sb., to enter an action against sb., to sue sb.

intenzionale, *a.* **1** intentional, deliberate,

voluntary. **2** (*leg.*) wilful; willful (*USA*).

intenzionalità, *n. f.* **1** intentionality. **2** (*leg.*) wilfulness.

intenzionalmente, *avv.* **1** intentionally. **2** (*leg.*) wilfully, scienter.

intenzione, *n. f.* **1** intention. **2** (*leg.*) intent. // ~ **criminosa** (*leg.*) malice; **senza** ~ unintentionally.

interagire, *v. i.* to interact.

interamente, *avv.* fully, full, entirely, wholly, outright. // ~ **pagato** fully paid.

interaziendale, *a.* (*org. az.*) intercompany, interenterprise, interfirm (*tutti attr.*); intercorporate (*USA*).

interazione, *n. f.* (*stat.*) interaction.

interbancario, *a.* (*banca*) interbank (*attr.*).

intercambiabile, *a.* interchangeable.

intercambiabilità, *n. f.* interchangeability.

interdetto, *a.* (*leg.*) disabled. *n. m.* (*leg.*) disabled person.

interdire, *v. t.* **1** (*leg.*) (*proibire*) to interdict, to forbid★. **2** (*leg.*) (*bandire*) to ban, to disable, to disqualify.

interdittorio, *a.* (*leg.*) interdictory.

interdizione, *n. f.* **1** (*leg.*) (*proibizione*) interdiction. **2** (*leg.*) (*bando*) disqualification.

interessamento, *n. m.* **1** (*interesse*) interest. **2** (*preoccupazione, premura*) concern, sympathy. **3** (*impegno*) good offices (*pl.*); trouble.

interessante, *a.* interesting.

interessare, *v. t.* **1** to interest. **2** (*riguardare*) to concern. **3** (*comm., fin.*) to give★ an interest (*o* a share) to (*sb.*). *v. i.* (*importare*) to matter, to be important, to be of importance. // ~ **un banchiere a un mutuo** (*cred.*) to interest a banker in a loan.

interessarsi, *v. rifl.* **1** to interest oneself; to take★ an interest; to be interested. **2** (*occuparsi di qc.*) to take★ care of, to see★ to, to look into. **3** (*badare a*) to look after; to mind. // ~ **di** (*o* **a**) **qc.** to interest oneself in st., to concern oneself with st.

interessato, *a.* interested, concerned. *n. m.* **1** (*leg.*) (the) party concerned. **2** (**gli**) **interessati,** *pl.* (*leg.*) (the) party concerned. // **essere** ~ **in un'azienda** (*comun., fin.*) to have an interest (*o* a share) in a concern; «**A tutti gli interessati**» (*in una circolare, una referenza, ecc.*) (*comun.*) «to whom it may concern».

interesse, *n. m.* **1** interest, concern. **2** (*convenienza*) convenience. **3** (*corrispettivo*) consideration. **4** (*fin., rag.*) interest. **5 interessi,** *pl.* (*affari*) affairs, business affairs; business (*sing.*). **6 interessi,** *pl.* (*fin., rag.*) interest (*sing.*). // **interessi acquisiti** (*leg.*) vested interests; ~ **assicurabile** (*ass.*) insurable interest; ~ **composto** (*mat., rag.*) compound interest; **interessi correnti** (*rag.*) current interests; **interessi da maturare** accruing interest; **interessi debitori** (*banca*) debit interest; ~ **decorrente da una certa data** (*rag.*) interest accruing from a certain date; **gli interessi del capitale** (*fin.*) interest on capital; **interessi di mora** (*cred.*) overdue interests, interest in arrears; ~ **di prestito** (*cred.*) loan interest; ~ **di riporto** (*Borsa, fin.*) contango; **interessi e commissioni** (*banca*) interest and commission; **un** ~ **esente da imposta** (*fin.*) a tax-free interest; **interessi in corso** (*rag.*) current interests; ~ **legale** (*fin., leg.*) legal interest, legal rate of interest; **interessi maturati** (*fin.*) accrued interest; **interessi neri** (*rag.*) black interest; **interessi passivi** (*rag.*) black interest; ~ **possessorio** (*leg.*) possessory interest; ~ **semplice** (*rag.*) simple interest; ~ **su cambio marittimo** (*ass. mar.*) marine interest, maritime interest; **gli interessi su un prestito** (*cred.*) the interest on a loan; **interessi sui numeri neri** (*banca*) interest in black; **interessi sui numeri rossi** (*banca*) interest in red, red interest; **nell'** ~ **di** on behalf of; **senza interessi** (*Borsa*) (*di titolo*) ex interest.

interessenza, *n. f.* **1** (*econ., fin.*) profit-sharing. **2** (*market.*) (*percentuale sulle vendite*) percentage on sales.

interferenza, *n. f.* interference.

interferire, *v. i.* to interfere, to meddle, to tamper.

interfonico, *n. m.* (*attr. uff.*) intercom.

interinale, *a. V.* **interino.**

interinato, *n. m.* (*amm.*) pro tempore (*o* temporary) office.

interino, *a.* (*amm.*) pro tempore, temporary. *n. m.* (*amm.*) locum tenens★, deputy, substitute.

interiore, *a.* interior, internal; inside (*attr.*).

interlocutorio, *a.* (*leg.*) interlocutory.

intermediario, *a.* intermediary, intermediate. *n. m.* **1** intermediary, interagent, contact man★. **2** (*market.*) middleman★; (*sensale*) broker. // **gli intermediari del commercio** (*market.*) the intermediaries in trade; «**intermediari esclusi**» (*comm.*) «no agents».

intermediazione, *n. f.* intermediation; interagency.

intermedio, *a.* intermediate, intermediary, mean, middle, medium.

internamente, *avv.* internally.

internazionale, *a.* international.

interno, *a.* **1** internal, inner, interior; inward, inside (*attr.*). **2** (*comm., econ.*) internal, domestic; inland, home (*attr.*). **3** (*org. az.*) in-house, in-plant (*attr.*). **4** (*org. az.*) interoffice, interplant (*attr.*). *n. m.* **1** inside, interior. **2** (*comun.*) (*telefono*) extension. **3** (*pers.*) (*medico interno*) intern.

intero, *a.* **1** entire, whole, undivided. **2** (*pieno, completo*) full, thorough, total.

interpenetrarsi, *v. recipr.* to interpenetrate.

interpenetrazione, *n. f.* (*econ.*) (*dei mercati, ecc.*) interpenetration.

interporre appello, *locuz. verb.* (*leg.*) to lodge an appeal, to appeal.

interpretare, *v. t.* **1** to interpret. **2** (*leg., anche*) to construe. // ~ **un contratto** to interpret a contract; ~ **i risultati in modo sbagliato** to distort the results.

interpretativo, *a.* interpretative.

interpretazione, *n. f.* **1** interpretation. **2** (*leg., anche*) construction. // **l'~ dei mercati** (*market.*) the interpretation of markets; **l'~ d'una legge** (*leg.*) the interpretation of a law; **un'~ restrittiva** (*della legge*) (*leg.*) a strict construction.

interprete, *n. m.* e *f.* (*pers.*) interpreter, translator.

interrogare, *v. t.* **1** to interrogate. **2** (*chiedere a*) to ask. **3** (*specialm. leg.*) to examine, to question. // ~ **a fondo** (*leg.*) to cross-question; ~ **in contraddittorio** (*leg.*) to cross-examine, to cross-question.

interrogatorio, *n. m.* (*leg.*) interrogatory, examination. // ~ **dei propri testimoni** (*leg.*) examination in chief; ~ **dell'imputato** (*leg.*) examination of the accused.

interrogazione, *n. f.* **1** (*anche leg.*) interrogation. **2** (*domanda*) question.

interrompere, *v. t.* **1** to interrupt, to break★ (off), to discontinue, to stop, to suspend. **2** (*comun.*) (*una conversazione telefonica*) to cut★ off. // ~ **il viaggio** (*trasp.*) to break one's journey.

interruzione, *n. f.* **1** interruption, break, breakdown, discontinuance, lapse, stop, stoppage, suspension. **2** (*d'un pubblico servizio, per un guasto*) breakdown. **3** (*leg.*) discontinuance. // **un'~ arbitraria del lavoro** (*senza il consenso dei sindacati*) (*pers.*) a wildcat work stoppage; **l'~ dei negoziati** the breakdown of negotiations; ~ **del lavoro** (*sind.*) work stoppage, stoppage, shut-down; ~ **della vita d'una società** (*per ragioni legali, ecc.*) (*fin.*) split-up.

interscambio, *n. m.* (*comm. est., fin.*) import-export movements (*pl.*).

interstatale, *a.* (*USA*) interstate (*attr.*).

interurbana, *n. f.* (*comun.*) trunk call; long-distance call (*USA*).

interurbano, *a.* **1** (*comun.*) trunk; long-distance (*USA*). **2** (*trasp.*) interurban. // **telefonata interurbana** (*comun.*) *V.* **interurbana.**

intervallo, *n. m.* **1** interval, break, lag, lapse, space. **2** (*pers.*) rest period. // ~ **fra ordinazione e consegna** (*market., org. az.*) lead time; ~ **fra progettazione e produzione** (*d'un articolo, prodotto, ecc.*) (*org. az.*) lead time.

interveniente, *a.* (*leg.*) intervening. *n. m.* e *f.* (*leg.*) intervener, intervenor.

intervenire, *v. i.* to intervene, to step in. // ~ **a una riunione** to attend a meeting; ~ **in una disputa** to intervene in a dispute.

intervento, *n. m.* **1** intervention. **2 interventi,** *pl.* (*econ.*) (*governativi, ecc.*) support measures. // **interventi a breve (termine)** (*econ.*) short-term action; ~ **in causa** (*leg.*) intervention in a suit; ~ **sul mercato** (*econ., market.*) market support; **«per ~»** (*leg.*) (*per una cambiale*) «supra protest», for honour supra protest.

intervista, *n. f.* (*market., pers.*) interview. // ~ **d'assunzione** (*pers.*) employment interview; ~ **di gruppo** (*market., pubbl.*) group interview; ~ **di valutazione** (*pers.*) evaluation interview, appraisal interview; ~ **guidata** (*market.*) patterned interview; ~ **in profondità** (*pers.*) depth interview; ~ **preliminare** (*pers.*) employment interview.

intervistare, *v. t.* **1** (*giorn., market.*) to poll. **2** (*market., pers.*) to interview. **3** (*pubbl.*) to poll. // ~ **gli aspiranti a un impiego** (*pers.*) to interview job applicants; ~ **le massaie sulle loro preferenze** (*market.*) to interview housewives about their preferences.

intervistato, *n. m.* **1** (*giorn., market.*) pollee. **2** (*market., pers.*) interviewee.

intervistatore, *n. m.* **1** (*giorn., market.*) poller. **2** (*market., pers.*) interviewer.

intesa, *n. f.* **1** understanding, agreement. **2** (*politica*) entente. // **intese orizzontali** (*comm. est.*) horizontal agreements; **un'~ ristretta in materia di prezzi e di condizioni di vendita** (*market.*) a restrictive price and terms of sale agreement.

inteso, *a.* (*convenuto*) understood, agreed upon.

intestare, *v. t.* **1** to head. **2** (*cred., fin.*) (*un assegno e sim.*) to make★ out. **3** (*leg.*) (*una proprietà*) to settle, to register. // ~ **azioni (titoli, ecc.) a q.** (*cred., fin.*) to register shares (bonds, etc.) in sb.'s name; ~ **un conto a q.** (*banca, cred.*) to open an account in sb.'s name.

intestatario, *n. m.* (*cred., fin.*) registered holder.

intestato[1], *a.* **1** headed. **2** (*leg.*) registered.

intestato², *a.* e *n. m.* (*leg.*) intestate.

intestazione, *n. f.* 1 heading. 2 (*di lettera*) letterheading, letterhead. 3 (*su un foglietto di carta da lettere*) noteheading, notehead. 4 (*leg.*) registration (*in sb.'s name*). // **~ della colonna del «dare»** (*rag.*) debtor; **l'~ d'un conto** (*rag.*) the name of an account; **~ di fattura** (*rag.*) bill heading, bill head; **l'~ d'una lettera commerciale** the heading of a business letter; **~ di mastro** (*rag.*) ledger heading.

intimare, *v. t.* 1 (*comandare*) to command, to order. 2 (*leg.*) to enjoin, to serve. // **~ un arresto** (*leg.*) to serve an attachment; **~ un mandato di comparizione a q.** (*leg.*) to serve a summons on sb., to serve sb. with a summons.

intimazione, *n. f.* (*leg.*) intimation, formal notice, precept, caveat.

intimidazione, *n. f.* (*specialm. leg.*) intimidation.

intimidire, *v. t.* (*specialm. leg.*) to intimidate.

intimo, *a.* 1 intimate. 2 (*interno*) inner, inside (*attr.*).

intitolare, *v. t.* 1 to entitle. 2 (*rag.*) (*un conto, ecc.*) to head.

intitolazione, *n. f.* 1 entitling. 2 (*rag.*) (*d'un conto*) heading.

intorno, *avv.* round, around. // **~ a** round; **all'~** round.

intracomunitario, *a.* intra-Community (*attr.*).

intraprendente, *a.* enterprising, resourceful.

intraprendenza, *n. f.* enterprise, initiative.

intraprendere, *v. t.* 1 to undertake*, to start. 2 (*una professione e sim.*) to take* up, to go* in for. // **~ un'attività commerciale** to start (*o* to open) a business.

intrinseco, *a.* 1 intrinsic. 2 (*inerente*) inherent.

introdurre, *v. t.* to introduce, to initiate. // **~ nuovi metodi di lavorazione** (*org. az.*) to introduce new manufacturing processes; **~ il principio dell'integrazione dei redditi** to introduce arrangements for «upping» incomes.

introdursi, *v. rifl.* to get* in (*o* into). // **~ abusivamente in una proprietà privata** (*leg.*) to trespass on a private property.

introduttivo, *a.* introductive, introductory.

introduzione, *n. f.* introduction.

introitare, *v. t.* (*cred., fin., rag.*) to cash, to encash; to take* in; to collect.

introito, *n. m.* 1 (*cred., fin., rag.*) take; (*profitto*) profit, yield. 2 **introiti,** *pl.* (*cred., fin., rag.*) proceeds, returns, takings, receipts. // **introiti fiscali** tax receipts.

inutile, *a.* useless, unsuccessful, unavailable.

inutilità, *n. f.* uselessness.

inutilizzato, *a.* 1 unused. 2 (*econ.*) (*di denaro*) unemployed.

invalidabile, *a.* (*leg.*) voidable.

invalidare, *v. t.* (*leg.*) to invalidate, to nullify, to null, to quash, to vitiate, to void. // **~ un atto** (*leg.*) to void a deed; **~ un testamento** (*leg.*) to invalidate a will.

invalidazione, *n. f.* (*leg.*) invalidation.

invalidità, *n. f. inv.* 1 invalidity. 2 (*leg.*) invalidity. 3 (*pers.*) inability, disability, disablement. // **~ che dà diritto a pensione** (*pers.*) pensionable disability; **~ parziale** (*pers.*) partial disability; **~ permanente** (*leg.*) permanent disablement; **~ totale** (*pers.*) total disability.

invalido, *a.* 1 invalid. 2 (*leg.*) invalid. 3 (*pers.*) (*al lavoro*) disabled. *n. m.* 1 invalid. 2 (*pers.*) (*al lavoro*) disabled person.

invecchiamento, *n. m.* 1 aging, ageing. 2 (*org. az.*) (*di macchine, ecc.*) obsolescence.

invecchiare, *v. i.* 1 to grow* old, to age. 2 (*org. az.*) (*di macchine, ecc.*) to obsolesce, to become* obsolete, to outmode.

invendibile, *a.* 1 unsalable, unsaleable. 2 (*market.*) unmarketable, unmerchantable.

invendibilità, *n. f.* unsal(e)ability.

invenduto, *a.* (*market.*) unsold.

inventare, *v. t.* to invent.

inventariare, *v. t.* (*rag.*) to inventory, to make* an inventory of, to take* stock of.

inventario, *n. m.* 1 (*rag.*) inventory, stocktaking. 2 (*rag.*) (*bilancio, conto profitti e perdite, conto d'esercizio, ecc.*) balance-sheet and schedules. // **~ del carico** (*trasp. mar.*) inventory of the cargo; **~ di fabbrica** (*org. az.*) plant inventory; **~ permanente** (*o* **perpetuo**) (*rag.*) perpetual inventory, running inventory; **~ perpetuo di magazzino** (*org. az.*) stores ledger; **~ quantitativo** (*org. az.*) inventory by quantity; **procedere a un ~** (*rag.*) to take an inventory.

inventore, *n. m.* inventor.

invenzione, *n. f.* invention. // **~ brevettata** (*leg.*) patent; **invenzioni non brevettate** (*leg.*) unpatented inventions.

inversione, *n. f.* inversion, reversal. // **~ di rotta** (*trasp. mar.*) turnabout; **~ di tendenza** (*econ.*) reversal of trend, turn, turnabout, turnaround.

inverso, *a.* 1 (*anche mat.*) inverse, converse. 2 (*opposto*) opposite. *n. m.* (the) inverse, reverse, opposite.

invertibile, *a.* invertible, reversible.

invertibilità, *n. f.* reversibility.

invertire, *v. t.* to invert, to reverse. // **~ la**

rotta (*trasp. mar.*) (*di nave*) to turn about; ~ **la rotta d'una nave** (*trasp. mar.*) to bring about a ship.

investigare, *v. t.* **1** to investigate, to inquire into, to explore, to research, to scrutinize. **2** (*leg.*) to investigate. *v. i.* to make★ inquiries.

investigativo, *a.* (*leg.*) investigative, investigatory, investigational.

investigatore, *n. m.* **1** investigator. **2** (*ricercatore*) researcher. **3** (*leg.*) detective.

investigazione, *n. f.* **1** investigation, exploration. **2** (*leg.*) investigation.

investimento, *n. m.* **1** (*fin.*) investment, placement, lockup. **2** (*trasp. aut.*) collision, crash, road accident. // **un ~ accorto** (*fin.*) a smart investment; **~ autonomo** (*fin., rag.*) autonomous investment; **~ avventato** (*fin.*) plunge (*fam.*); **~ azionario** (*fin.*) share investment; **investimenti azionari** (*rag.*) quoted investments; **un ~ azzardoso** (*fin.*) a risky investment; **investimenti civili** (*fin.*) civilian spending; **~ di capitali** (*rag.*) capital expenditure; **~ di portafoglio** (*fin.*) portfolio investment; **investimenti diretti** (*econ.*) direct investments; **investimenti esteri** (*econ.*) foreign investments; **un ~ in azioni ordinarie** (*fin.*) an investment in common stocks; **investimenti in beni immobili** (*fin.*) investment in fixed assets; **investimenti in beni mobili** (*fin.*) investment in movable assets; **investimenti obbligazionari** (*rag.*) quoted investments; **un ~ privo di rischi** (*fin.*) a safe investment; **investimenti produttivi** (*fin.*) productive investments; **un ~ remunerativo** a lucrative investment; **un ~ sicuro** (*fin.*) a sound investment.

investire, *v. t.* **1** (*fin.*) to invest, to place, to lock up, to sink★. **2** (*trasp. aut.*) (*una persona*) to run★ down, to run★ over; (*un altro veicolo*) to run★ into. **3** (*trasp. mar.*) to foul, to fall★ foul of. // **~ q. dell'autorità (della facoltà, ecc.) di fare qc.** (*leg.*) to vest sb. with the power to do st.; **~ denaro** (*fin.*) to employ (to lay out, to put) money; to invest; **~ q. di pieni poteri** (*leg.*) to invest sb. with full powers; **~ in azioni** (*fin.*) to invest in shares; **~** (*denaro*) **in titoli di Stato** (*fin.*) to fund; **~ i propri risparmi in azioni** (*fin.*) to put one's savings into shares; **non investito** (*econ.*) (*di denaro*) unemployed.

investitore, *n. m.* (*fin.*) investor. *a.* (*fin.*) investing. // **~ diretto** (*fin.*) direct investor; **investitori istituzionali** (*fin.*) institutional investors; **la società investitrice** (*fin.*) the investing company.

«investment bank», *n. f.* (*fin.*) investment bank.

«investment banking», *n. m.* (*fin.*) investment banking.

inviare, *v. t.* **1** to forward, to dispatch, to send★, to send★ away, to send★ in, to send★ round. **2** (*cred.*) (*denaro*) to remit. **3** (*trasp.*) to ship (*specialm. USA*). **4** (*trasp. mar.*) to ship. // **~ una comunicazione** (*di servizio*) **a q.** (*org. az.*) to memo sb. (*fam.*); **~ fatture a q.** (*market.*) to invoice sb.; to bill sb. (*USA*); **~ merce in esame** (*o* **in visione**) (*market.*) to send goods on approval; **~ una rimessa** (*comun.*) to send a remittance.

inviato, *n. m.* (*giorn.*) correspondent. // **~ speciale** (*giorn.*) special correspondent, foreign services editor.

invio, *n. m.* **1** forwarding, dispatch, sending. **2** (*di merce*) consignment. **3** (*cred.*) (*di denaro, ecc.*) remittance. **4** (*trasp.*) shipment (*specialm. USA*). **5** (*trasp. mar.*) shipment. // **l'~ di telegrammi** (*comun.*) the dispatch of telegrams.

invisibile, *a.* invisible.

invitare, *v. t.* **1** to invite, to ask, to desire. **2** (*sollecitare*) to solicit. // **~ q. a colazione** to ask sb. to lunch; **~ q. a entrare** to ask sb. in.

invito, *n. m.* **1** invitation. **2** (*biglietto*) card of admission, invitation card. // **~ ai sottoscrittori a ritirare le azioni** (*fin.*) calling on the underwriters to take up shares; **per ~ di Mr Brown** at the desire of Mr Brown; **su ~** at request, by request.

invocare, *v. t.* **1** to invoke. **2** (*fare appello a*) to call upon, to appeal to. **3** (*a giustificazione, a discolpa*) to plead. // **~ un alibi** (*leg.*) to plead an alibi.

invocazione, *n. f.* invocation. // **~ d'aiuto** call for help.

involontario, *a.* involuntary.

involtare, *v. t.* (*fam.*) to wrap up, to parcel.

involto, *n. m.* **1** (*fagotto*) bundle. **2** (*pacchetto*) packet, parcel. **3** (*market.*) wrapper, wrapping.

involucro, *n. m.* **1** (*di pacco*) cover. **2** (*market.*) wrapper, wrapping.

iperinflazione, *n. f.* (*econ.*) hyperinflation.

ipermercato, *n. m.* (*econ., market.*) (*più grande e meglio attrezzato d'un supermercato*) hypermarket, big supermarket.

ipoteca, *n. f.* **1** (*leg.*) mortgage, back-bond, lien. **2** (*leg.*) (*nel diritto romano*) hypothec. **3** (*leg.*) (*specialm. nel diritto della navigazione*) hypothecation. // **~ di primo grado** (*leg.*) first mortgage; **~ di secondo grado** (*leg.*) second mortgage; **~ di terzo grado** (*leg.*) third mortgage; **~ generale** (*leg.*) general mortgage, blanket mortgage; **un'~ liberata** (*leg.*) a satisfied mortgage; **~ non accesa** (*leg.*) unregistered mortgage; ~ **su beni mobili** (*leg.*) chattel mortgage; ~ **su d'una nave** (*contratta dal capitano per far fronte a spese impreviste*) (*leg.*) bottomry bond; **gravato da ipoteche** (*leg.*) heavily mortgaged.

ipotecabile, *a.* (*leg.*) mortgageable.

ipotecare, *v. t.* **1** (*leg.*) to mortgage, to bond. **2** (*leg.*) (*specialm. nel diritto romano e della navigazione*) to hypothecate. // **non ipotecato** (*leg.*) unmortgaged.

ipotecario, *a.* (*leg.*) mortgage (*attr.*); hypothecary. // **creditore** ~ (*leg.*) mortgagee; **debito** ~ (*leg.*) mortgage debt; **debitore** ~ mortgagor.

irrealizzabile, *a.* unrealizable.

irrecuperabile, *a.* irrecoverable, unrecoverable.

irredimibile, *a.* (*fin.*) irredeemable, unredeemable.

irregolare, *a.* **1** irregular. **2** (*del terreno, del tempo, ecc.*) uneven. **3** (*instabile*) unsteady.

irregolarità, *n. f. inv.* **1** irregularity, inequality. **2** (*del terreno*) unevenness. **3** (*instabilità*) unsteadiness.

irremunerato, *a.* (*pers.*) unpaid.

irreparabile, *a.* irreparable, irrecoverable.

irresponsabile, *a.* **1** irresponsible. **2** (*leg.*) unanswerable.

irresponsabilità, *n. f.* **1** irresponsibility. **2** (*leg.*) unanswerability.

irrevocabile, *a.* irrevocable.

irrevocabilità, *n. f.* irrevocability.

irrigidimento, *n. m.* stiffening. // ~ **dei prezzi** (*econ.*) price freeze.

irrigidire, *v. t.* **1** (*anche fig.*) to stiffen, to harden. **2** (*econ.*) (*prezzi, ecc.*) to freeze★. // ~ **il mercato** (*econ.*) to stiffen the market.

irrigidirsi, *v. rifl.* **1** (*anche fig.*) to stiffen, to harden. **2** (*econ.*) (*di prezzi, anche*) to freeze★.

iscritto, *n. m.* **1** member. **2** (*abbonato*) subscriber. **3** (*sind.*) member. // **un** ~ **a un sindacato** (*sind.*) a union member, a trade-unionist; a labour skate (*slang USA*); **un** ~ **all'ordine degli avvocati** (*leg.*) a member of the Bar association; **l'essere** ~ membership; **non** ~ (*leg.*) unregistered; **non** ~ **a un sindacato** (*pers., sind.*) (*d'operaio, ecc.*) non-union (*attr.*).

iscrivere, *v. t.* **1** to inscribe. **2** (*registrare*) to register, to enter. **3** (*trasp. mar.*) (*una nave*) to register; to document (*USA*). // ~ **a ruolo una causa** (*leg.*) to enter an action (*o* a suit) in the cause list; ~ **q. all'albo degli avvocati** to call sb. to the Bar; ~ (*beni*) **nei ruoli d'imposta** (*fin.*) to list; ~ **un nome in un elenco** to enter a name on a list.

iscriversi, *v. rifl.* **1** to enter one's name (for st.); to enroll oneself. **2** (*registrarsi*) to register.

iscrizione, *n. f.* **1** inscription. **2** (*registrazione*) registration, entry. // ~ **all'università** matriculation; ~ **d'una causa a ruolo** (*leg.*) entry of an action (*o* of a suit) in the list of cases; ~ **di titoli nei registri** (*fin.*) inscription; ~ **ipotecaria** (*leg.*) registration of a mortgage.

isolamento, *n. m.* (*anche fig.*) isolation, segregation. // **l'** ~ **delle spese straordinarie nel preventivo** (*rag.*) the segregation of extraordinary expenses in the budget.

isolare, *v. t.* (*anche fig.*) to isolate, to segregate.

ispettorato, *n. m.* **1** inspectorate. **2** (*durata in carica*) inspectorship. **3** (*l'ufficio*) inspector's office.

ispettore, *n. m.* inspector, surveyor. // ~ **del carico e dello stivaggio** (*trasp. mar., ingl.*) port warden; ~ **delle finanze** (*fin.*) revenue inspector; ~ **(delle) vendite** (*pers.*) sales supervisor; ~ **di reparto** (*di grande magazzino, ecc.*) (*market., pers.*) section manager; shopwalker, floorwalker, floor-walker; ~ **di zona** (*market.*) field manager, field supervisor; **un** ~ **doganale** (*dog.*) a surveyor of customs, a custom surveyor; ~ **generale** (*amm.*) inspector general; (*pers.*) chief inspector.

ispezionare, *v. t.* **1** to inspect, to survey, to view. **2** (*dog.*) (*i documenti e il carico d'una nave*) to jerque. **3** (*trasp. mar.*) (*una nave, anche*) to visit. // ~ **il bagaglio** (*dog.*) to inspect the luggage; ~ **la nave e il carico** (*trasp. mar.*) to survey the ship and cargo.

ispezione, *n. f.* **1** inspection, survey, view. **2** (*dog.*) examination. **3** (*trasp. mar., anche*) visit. // ~ **doganale del bagaglio** (*dog.*) customs examination of luggage; ~ **su campione** (*org. az.*) sampling inspection.

istantaneo, *a.* instantaneous, instant.

istante[1], *n. m.* instant, moment. // **all'** ~ on the instant; on the spot.

istante[2], *n. m.* e *f.* (*leg.*) petitioner.

istanza, *n. f.* **1** (*domanda*) request, application. **2** (*esigenza, aspirazione*) need, requirement; demand, request. **3** (*leg.*) application, petition, motion, claim, plea, instance. // ~ **dei creditori** (*leg.*) petition of creditors; ~ **di fallimento** (*leg.*) petition in bankruptcy, bankruptcy petition; ~ **fallimentare** (*leg.*) bankruptcy petition; ~ **per intervento** (*leg.*) petition for intervention; ~ **perentoria** (*leg.*) peremptory plea; **chi è chiamato a rispondere a un'** ~ (*leg.*) petitionee; **su** ~ **di** (*leg.*) at the instance of, on motion of: **su** ~ **del legale dell'attore** on motion of the plaintiff's lawyer.

istigare, *v. t.* **1** to instigate, to incite. **2** (*leg., anche*) to induce. // ~ **gli operai ad abbandonare il lavoro** (*pers., sind.*) to instigate the workers to stop work.

istigazione, *n. f.* **1** instigation, incitement. **2** (*leg., anche*) inducement. // ~ **a delinquere** (*leg.*) instigation (*o* incitement) to commit a crime.

istituire, *v. t.* to institute, to establish, to set★ up. // ~ **una commissione d'inchiesta** to institute a board of inquiry; ~ **q. erede** (*leg.*) to appoint sb. heir; ~ **nuovi treni** (*trasp. ferr.*) to schedule new trains.

istituto, *n. m.* **1** (*leg.*) institute. **2** (*leg.*) (*pubblico, assistenziale, ecc.*) institution, body; agency (*USA*). // ~ **bancario** banking company, banking establishment, banking firm, banking house, bank; ~ **d'accettazione bancaria** (*caratteristico del mercato monetario londinese*) (*fin.*) acceptance house, accepting house; ~ **di credito** (*banca*) credit institution, bank; ~ **d'emissione** (*fin.*) note-issuing bank; **istituti di previdenza sociale** (*pers.*) social-security agencies; ~ **di sconto** (*fin.*) discounting house, discount house; **istituti finanziari** (*fin.*) financial establishments.

istituzionale, *a.* institutional.

istituzione, *n. f.* **1** institution, establishment, setting-up. **2** (*leg.*) institution, institute. // ~ **d'erede** (*leg.*) institution of heir; **l'** ~ **di leggi e consuetudini** (*leg.*) the institution of laws and customs.

istruire, *v. t.* **1** to instruct. **2** (*leg.*) to instruct. **3** (*pers.*) (*addestrare*) to coach, to train.

istruttore, *n. m.* (*pers.*) instructor, coach, trainer.

istruttoria, *n. f.* (*leg.*) judicial inquiry; preliminary investigation (*of a case*).

istruzione, *n. f.* **1** instruction, education. **2** (*addestramento*) training. **3 istruzioni,** *pl.* instructions, directions. // ~ **erronea** misdirection; **istruzioni per l'imbarco** (*delle merci*) (*trasp. mar.*) shipping instructions; **istruzioni per l'incasso** (*fin.*) cash instructions; **istruzioni per lo svolgimento d'un'attività** (*date nel corso d'una riunione*) (*org. az.*) briefing; **istruzioni per l'uso** (*market., pubbl.*) instructions for use; ~ **professionale** (*pers.*) vocational education, vocational training, professional training, industrial training; ~ **programmata** programmed instruction; **istruzioni successive** follow-up instructions; ~ **superiore** higher education; ~ **tecnica** technical education; **secondo le istruzioni** as instructed; **secondo le vostre istruzioni** according to your instructions.

italiano, *a.* e *n. m.* Italian.

itinerario, *n. m.* (*trasp.*) itinerary, route. // ~ **di vendita** (*market.*) route; **un** ~ **diretto** (*trasp.*) a straight course.

iuniore, *a.* junior.

J

«jobber», *n. m.* (*Borsa, ingl.*) jobber. // **essere un ~** (*Borsa, ingl.*) to job.

«job-enrichment», *n. m.* (*org. az.*) job-enrichment.

«junior», *a.* junior.

K

«**Kennedy round**», *n. m.* (*comm. est.*) (*appello, lanciato nel 1963 dal presidente J.F. Kennedy, per la riduzione globale dei dazi doganali*) Kennedy round.

keynesiano, *a.* (*econ.*) Keynesian.

«**know-how**», *n. m.* know-how.

L

laboratorio, *n. m.* **1** (*scientifico*) laboratory; lab (*fam.*). **2** (*org. az.*) workshop, workroom.

lacuna, *n. f.* blank, gap.

ladro, *n. m.* **1** thief★. **2** (*scassinatore*) burglar. **3** (*borsaiolo*) pickpocket. **4** (*taccheggiatore*) shop-lifter.

ladrocinio, *n. m.* (*leg.*) theft.

lagnanza, *n. f.* **1** complaint, grievance. **2** (*sind.*) grievance.

lagnarsi, *v. rifl.* (*protestare*) to complain.

«laissez-faire», *locuz, verb.* (*econ.*) laissez-faire.

lamentarsi, *v. rifl.* (*protestare*) to complain.

lampeggiatori, *n. pl.* **1** (*econ.*) leading indicators. **2** (*trasp. aut.*) trafficators.

lampo, *n. m.* flash, lightning. // **un ~ di genio** a stroke of genius.

lanciare, *v. t.* **1** to throw (*anche fig.*); to shoot★; (*talora*) to cast★. **2** (*fig.*) (*un'impresa*) to set★ afloat, to get★ afloat, to float. **3** (*fin., market.*) (*p. es., titoli sul mercato*) to bring★ out. **4** (*market., pubbl.*) to launch, to boost, to boom. // **~ un'azienda** (*market.*) to get a business afloat; **~ un'idea** to throw out an idea; **~ una moda** to launch a fashion; **~ un nuovo prodotto** (*market., pubbl.*) to launch (*o* to advertise) a new product; **~ un prestito** (*cred.*) to float a loan.

lancio, *n. m.* **1** throwing, casting; throw, cast. **2** (*fig.*) (*d'un'impresa o società commerciale*) floatation. **3** (*fin., market.*) (*p. es., di titoli sul mercato*) bringing out. **4** (*market., pubbl.*) launching. // **~ della produzione** (*org. az.*) dispatching; **~ pubblicitario** (*market.*) boost.

larghezza, *n. f.* **1** breadth, width. **2** (*abbondanza*) largeness. // **~ di mezzi** largeness of means.

largo, *a.* **1** broad, wide. **2** (*ampio*) ample, large. *n. m.* (*trasp. mar.*) offing. // **al ~** (*trasp. mar.*) in the offing, off shore; **al ~ di** (*trasp. mar.*) out of, off.

lasciapassare, *n. m. inv.* **1** pass, permit. **2** (*dog.*) cart note. **3** (*dog., trasp. mar.*) clearance papers (*pl.*); clearance inwards.

lasciare, *v. t.* **1** to leave★, to depart (from); to quit; to relinquish (*raro*). **2** (*per sempre*) to abandon, to desert. **3** (*permettere*) to let★, to allow. **4** (*leg.*) (*in eredità*) to leave★. // **~ andare in protesto una cambiale** (*cred., leg.*) to dishonour a bill; **~ il banco dei testimoni** (*leg.*) to stand down; **~ la carriera** (*pers.*) to break off one's career; **~ correre** (*fig.*) to let things go their own way; **~ detto a q.** to leave word with sb.; **~ entrare q.** to let sb. in; **~ estinguere** (*un procedimento giudiziario*) (*leg.*) to discontinue; **~ il proprio impiego** (*pers.*) to leave one's job; **~ in eredità** (*leg.*) to bequeath, to leave; (*beni immobili*) to devise; (*con vincolo d'inalienabilità*) to entail; **~ insoluta una cambiale** to dishonour a bill; **~ libera la rotta a una nave** (*trasp. mar.*) to give way to a ship; **~ libera una stanza** (*in albergo*) (*tur.*) to check out; **~ libero** to set free; (*un posto e sim.*) to vacate; **~ un posto** (*pers.*) to resign a position; **~ la presidenza** (*amm.*) to leave the chair, to pass the chair, to resign the chairmanship; **~ q. senza lavoro** (*pers.*) to throw sb. out of employment; **~ transitare** (*trasp.*) to transit; **~ uscire q.** to let sb. out; **~ vuoto** to vacate; **lasciarsi scappare un affare** to miss a bargain; **lasciarsi sfuggire qc.** (*trascurare, non vedere*) to overlook st.

lascito, *n. m.* **1** (*leg.*) legacy, bequest. **2** (*leg.*) (*in proprietà fiduciaria*) trust. // **~ soggetto a vincoli d'inalienabilità** (*leg.*) entailment; **~ testamentario** (*leg.*) bequest, legacy.

«lasta», *n. f.* **1** (*misura di capacità per granaglie pari a 80 «bushels»*) last. **2** (*misura di peso pari a circa 4.000 libbre*) last.

laterale, *a.* lateral; side (*attr.*). *n. f.* (*trasp. aut.*) side road.

latitante, *a.* (*leg.*) absconding, at large. *n. m.* e *f.* (*leg.*) absconder.

latitanza, *n. f.* (*leg.*) absence to avoid arrest.

lato, *n. m.* side. // **~ dell'indirizzo** (*in una busta*) address side; **~ sopravvento** (*trasp. mar.*) windward side, weather side, weather board; **~ sottovento** (*trasp. mar.*) lee side, lee, leeward; **a ~ di** by the side of, beside, alongside.

latore, *n. m.* conveyer, conveyor; bearer. //

il ~ di una lettera the bearer of a letter.

laurea, *n. f.* degree.

laureare, *v. t.* to confer a degree on (sb.); to graduate (*soprattutto USA*).

laurearsi, *v. rifl.* to get★ (*o* to take★) one's degree; to graduate (*specialm. USA*).

laureato, *n. m.* (*pers.*) college graduate, graduate.

lavaggio, *n. m.* **1** washing. **2** (*trasp. aut.*) (*d'automobili, ecc.*) wash. // **~ del cervello** (*per mezzo della propaganda, ecc.*) (*market., pubbl.*) brainwashing.

lavare, *v. t.* to wash. // **«lava e indossa»** (*che non necessita di stiratura*) (*market.*) (*di tessuto*) wash and wear.

lavarsi, *v. rifl.* to wash. // **~ le mani di qc.** to wash one's hands of st.

lavata, *n. f.* wash.

lavatrice, *n. f.* washing machine, washer.

lavatura, *n. f.* **1** washing. **2** (*lavata*) wash.

lavorante, *n. m.* e *f.* (*pers.*) labourer, worker, operative. *n. m.* (*pers.*) man★. *n. f.* (*pers.*) woman★.

lavorare, *v. t.* e *i.* **1** to work, to labour. **2** (*market.*) (*d'un'azienda*) to do★ business. **3** (*org. az.*) (*materie prime, ecc.*) to process, to manufacture. // **~ a contratto** (*pers.*) to work on contract; **~ a cottimo** (*pers.*) to job; **~ a mezzo tempo** to work half-time, to work part-time; **~ a orario ridotto** to work half-time; **~ a tempo pieno** to work full-time; **~ a turno** (*pers.*) to work in shifts; to spell; **~ al carico** (*o* **allo scarico**) **di** (*una nave*) (*trasp. mar.*) to stevedore; **~ in una zona** (*pers.*) (*di commesso viaggiatore*) to work a district, to work an area; **~ su** (*una piazza*) (*pers.*) to travel; **che lavora** working; **chi lavora in ufficio** (*pers.*) white-collar worker; **lavorato a mano** (*market.*) handmade; **non lavorato** (*market.*) (*di prodotto*) unmanufactured.

lavorarsi, *v. rifl.* (*bene, male, ecc.*) (*di sostanza, ecc.*) to work.

lavorativo, *a.* **1** working; work (*attr.*). **2** (*di terreno*) arable.

lavoratore, *n. m.* **1** labourer; laborer (*USA*); worker, workman★. **2 lavoratori,** *pl.* (*econ., pers.*) labour (*collett.*). **3 lavoratori,** *pl.* (*pers., anche*) work-people. // **~ a cottimo** (*pers.*) jobber; **~ a giornata** (*pers.*) day labourer, day man; **~ avventizio** (*pers.*) casual worker; **i lavoratori dell'industria** (*pers.*) industrial workers; **lavoratori «d'assalto»** (*sind.*) shockworkers; **lavoratori indipendenti** (*econ.*) self-employed workers; **lavoratori manuali** (*pers.*) manual workers; **lavoratori migranti** (*econ.*) migrant workers, migratory workers; **i lavoratori portuali** (*trasp. mar.*) the port workers, the dock workers; **un ~ saltuario** (*pers.*) an irregular worker; an on-and-offer (*slang USA*).

lavorazione, *n. f.* **1** working. **2** (*esecuzione, fattura*) workmanship. **3** (*org. az.*) (*della lana, dei metalli, ecc.*) manufacture, processing. // **~ a catena** (*org. az.*) continuous process, line production; **~ a cottimo** (*org. az.*) jobbing; **~ a macchina** (*org. az.*) machining; **~ a mano** handwork; **~ su commessa** (*org. az.*) jobbing; **in ~** in work.

lavoro, *n. m.* **1** work, labour; labor (*USA*). **2** (*singolo lavoro*) piece of work; (*compito*) task. **3** (*occupazione*) business, trade. **4** (*econ.*) labour. **5** (*pers.*) job, occupation. // **~ a contratto** contract work; **~ a cottimo** (*org. az.*) piecework, job work, task-work; **~ a domicilio** (*org. az.*) homework, outwork, home manufacturing; (*nelle campagne*) cottage industry; **~ a giornata** (*org. az.*) work by the day, day labour, chore; **~** (*eseguito*) **a mano** (*market.*) handwork; (*pers.*) handwork, hand labour; **~ a orario ridotto** (*org. az.*) part-time work; (*pers.*) (*l'occupazione*) part-time job; **~** (*retribuito*) **a ore** (*org. az.*) time-work; **~** (*fatto*) **a tavolino** desk work; **~ autonomo** (*econ.*) self-employment; **~ d'agente di cambio** (*Borsa*) stock-broking, stockbroking; **~ d'appalto** (*amm.*) contract work; **~ d'equipe** (*org. az.*) team-work, teamwork; **~ di fattore** (*econ.*) land agency; **~ d'una giornata** (*pers.*) daywork; **~ di gruppo** (*org. az.*) team-work, teamwork, group work; **~ d'impiegato** clerkdom; **~ di manutenzione** (*org. az.*) maintenance; **~ di mediatore** broking; **~ di tavolino** (*pers.*) desk work; **~ d'ufficio** (*org. az.*) office work, clerical work, desk work; **un ~ difficile** (*pers.*) an exacting job; **un ~ duro** (*pers.*) a hard job; **il ~ e il capitale** (*econ.*) Labour and Capital; **~ editoriale** (*giorn.*) editorial work; **~ fatto quando capita** chore; **un ~ fisso** (*pers.*) a regular job, a steady job; **~ full-time** (*pers.*) full-time job, whole-time job; **~ giornaliero** (*pers.*) day's work; **un ~ gravoso** (*pers.*) heavy work; a hard job; **~ in corso** (*org. az.*) work in hand, work in process, work in progress; **«lavori in corso»** (*segnale stradale*) (*trasp. aut.*) «works ahead», «men at work»; **~ in economia** (*org. az.*) work by the day, time-work; **~ in proprio** (*econ.*) self-employment; **~ indipendente** (*econ.*) self-employment; **~ manuale** (*econ.*) manual labour; (*pers.*) hand labour, handwork; **~ notturno** (*pers.*) night work; **lavori occasionali** (*pers.*) odd jobs; **~ pe-**

sante (*pers.*) heavy work; ~ **produttivo** (*econ.*) productive labour; **lavori pubblici** (*amm., leg.*) public works; **un ~ retribuito** (*pers.*) a gainful job; **lavori rimunerativi** (*pers.*) remunerative jobs; **lavori saltuari** (*pers.*) odd jobs; ~ **specializzato** (*pers.*) skilled work; **un ~ stabile** (*pers.*) a regular job; ~ **stagionale** (*pers.*) season work; **lavori stagionali** (*pers.*) seasonal occupations; ~ **straordinario** (*pers.*) extra work; overtime work, overtime; ~ **subordinato** (*econ.*) employment; ~ **temporaneo** (*pers.*) casual labour; ~ **utile** (*econ.*) output; **essere al ~** to be at work; **che fa risparmiare ~** (*org. az.*) labour-saving; **condizioni di ~** (*pers.*) working conditions; **eccesso di ~** overwork; **senza ~** workless (*a.*).

leader, *n. m.* leader. // ~ **d'opinione** (*pubbl.*) opinion former.

leadership, *n. f.* leadership.

«leasing», *n. m.* (*fin.*) leasing. // ~ **finanziario** financial leasing.

lecito, *a.* (*leg.*) lawful, legitimate.

ledere, *v. t.* **1** to hurt★; to prejudice. **2** (*leg.*) to injure. **3** (*leg.*) (*il diritto di proprietà altrui*) to encroach. // ~ **la reputazione di q.** (*leg.*) to injure sb.'s reputation.

lega, *n. f.* **1** (*politica*) league. **2** combination, combine, union. // ~ **operaia** (*sind.*) combination of workers.

legale, *a.* **1** (*leg.*) legal. **2** (*leg.*) (*legittimo*) lawful. **3** (*leg.*) (*giuridico*) juridical, juristic. **4** (*leg.*) (*statutario*) statutory. *n. m.* (*leg.*) lawyer.

legalità, *n. f.* **1** (*leg.*) legality. **2** (*leg.*) (*legittimità*) lawfulness.

legalizzare, *v. t.* **1** (*leg.*) to legalize, to authenticate, to certify, to countersign. **2** (*leg.*) (*di notaio*) to notarize. // ~ **un atto** (*leg.*) to certify a deed; ~ **la copia d'un atto** (*leg.*) to certify a copy of a deed; ~ **una firma** to authenticate a signature.

legalizzazione, *n. f.* (*leg.*) legalization, authentication, certification, countersign. // **la ~ d'un documento** (*leg.*) the legalization of a document; ~ **notarile** (*leg.*) notarization.

legame, *n. m.* **1** (*anche fig.*) bond, tie. **2** (*sentimentale*) attachment. **3** (*connessione*) connection, connexion, link.

legare, *v. t.* **1** (*anche fig.*) to bind★, to tie. **2** (*leg.*) to bequeath. // ~ **un pacco** (*market.*) to tie up a parcel; ~ **per testamento** (*leg.*) to leave by will, to bequeath.

legatario, *n. m.* **1** (*leg.*) legatee. **2** (*leg.*) (*di beni immobili*) devisee. // ~ **universale** (*leg.*) sole legatee.

legato, *a.* bound, tied. *n. m.* (*leg.*) bequest, legacy. // ~ **generale** (*leg.*) general legacy; ~ **particolare** (*leg.*) specific legacy; ~ **universale** (*leg.*) universal legacy.

legge, *n. f.* **1** (*leg.*) law. **2** (*leg.*) (*regolamento*) rule. **3** (*leg.*) (*del Parlamento*) act, statute. // **leggi antimonopolistiche** (*econ., leg.*) anti-trust laws; ~ **contro i monopoli** (*econ., leg.*) anti-trust act; ~ **del Paese di bandiera** (*leg., trasp. mar.*) law of the flag; **la ~ della domanda decrescente** (*econ.*) the law of downsloping demand; **la ~ della domanda e dell'offerta** (*econ.*) the law of supply and demand; ~ **della produttività decrescente** (*econ.*) law of diminishing returns; **leggi economiche** (*econ.*) economic laws; **leggi eque** (*leg.*) equal laws; ~ **finanziaria** (*leg.*) money bill; ~ **fiscale** (*leg.*) revenue act; ~ **moratoria** (*leg.*) stay law; **la ~ non scritta** (*leg.*) the unwritten laws; common law (*in G.B.*); **una ~ normativa** (*leg.*) a normative law; ~ **parlamentare** (*leg.*) parliamentary law; statute law, act of Parliament; «**~-ponte**» (*econ.*) «bridge law»; ~ **quadro** (*leg.*) outline law; ~ **scritta** (*leg.*) written law; ~ **severa** (*leg.*) blue law; **leggi severe** (*leg.*) stringent laws; ~ **speciale** (*leg.*) special act; ~ **sul fallimento** (*leg.*) bankruptcy law; ~ **sulla prescrizione** (*leg.*) statute of limitations; ~ **sulle società** (*leg.*) company law; ~ **sulle società per azioni** (*leg.*) companies act; ~ **valutaria** (*fin.*) currency act; **per ~** (*leg.*) by law; by Act of Parliament.

leggere, *v. t.* to read★. // ~ **da capo a fondo** to read through; **nell'attesa di leggervi** (*comm.*) awaiting to hear from you.

leggero, *a.* **1** light. **2** (*lieve*) slight; soft (*fam.*).

leggina, *n. f.* (*leg.*) by-law, bye-law.

legiferare, *v. i.* (*leg.*) to legislate, to make★ laws.

legislativo, *a.* (*leg.*) legislative.

legislatore, *n. m.* (*leg.*) legislator, lawmaker.

legislazione, *n. f.* (*leg.*) legislation. // ~ **antimonopolistica** (*econ., leg.*) anti-trust legislation, anti-trust laws; ~ **doganale** (*leg.*) customs legislation; ~ **in materia di lavoro** (*leg.*) labour legislation; ~ **internazionale** (*leg.*) international legislation; **legislazioni nazionali** (*leg.*) national laws; ~ **sociale** (*leg.*) social legislation; ~ **sui prodotti alimentari** (*leg.*) food legislation; ~ **sulle società** (*leg.*) company law.

legittima, *n. f.* (*leg.*) legitim (*in Italia, in Scozia*); «jus relictae» (*in Scozia*); reasonable part (*un tempo, in G.B.*).

legittimare, *v. t.* (*leg.*) to legitimate, to legitimize, to legalize.

legittimario, *n. m.* (*leg.*) forced heir.

legittimazione, *n. f.* (*leg.*) legitimation,

legitimization, legalization.

legittimità, *n. f.* (*leg.*) legitimacy, legality.

legittimo, *a.* 1 (*leg.*) legitimate, lawful, legal, rightful. 2 (*leg.*) (*d'un interesse, anche*) vested. // **difesa legittima** (*leg.*) self-defence.

lentezza, *n. f.* slowness; (*anche fig.*) slackness. // ~ **nell'attività commerciale** (*econ.*) slackness in business.

lento, *a.* 1 slow, tardy; (*anche fig.*) sluggish, slack. 2 (*non stretto*) loose.

lesione, *n. f.* 1 lesion; wound. 2 (*leg.*) injury. 3 (*leg.*) (*del diritto di proprietà altrui*) encroachment. // ~ **personale** (*leg.*) personal injury.

leso, *a.* (*leg.*) injured, offended.

lettera, *n. f.* 1 (*comun.*) letter. 2 (*pubbl.*) letter. 3 **lettere,** *pl.* (*corrispondenza*) mail (*collett.*). // ~ **circolare** (*comun.*) circular letter, circular, form letter, form; ~ **circolare di credito** (*simile al travellers' cheque*) (*banca*) circular note; ~ **contabile** accountable document; **la ~ della legge** (*leg.*) the letter of the law; ~ **d'accompagnamento** (*trasp.*) covering letter; ~ **d'affari** business letter; ~ **d'avviso** letter of advice; (*trasp. ferr.*) advice note; ~ **di cambio** (*comm.*) note of hand; ~ **di credito** (*banca, cred.*) letter of credit; ~ **di credito circolare** (*banca, cred.*) circular letter of credit, traveller's letter of credit; ~ **di credito confermata** (*banca, cred.*) confirmed letter of credit; ~ **di credito irrevocabile** (*banca, cred.*) irrevocable letter of credit; ~ **di credito non confermata** (*banca, cred.*) unconfirmed letter of credit; ~ **di credito rotativo** (*banca, cred.*) letter of revolving credit, revolving letter of credit; ~ **di delega** (*leg.*) letter of delegation; ~ **di domanda d'assunzione** (*pers.*) letter of application; ~ **di domanda di pagamento di decimi** (*fin.*) call letter; ~ **d'esenzione doganale** (*dog.*) bill of sufferance; ~ **di garanzia di commissione** commission note; ~ **di garanzia d'indennizzo** (*per eventuali danni alla merce*) (*comm. est.*) letter of indemnity; ~ **d'identificazione** (*banca, cred.*) letter of indication; ~ **d'intenti** (*per un prestito del FMI*) (*fin.*) letter of intention; ~ **d'istruzione dello speditore** (*trasp. aer.*) shipper's letter of instructions; ~ **di notifica dell'emissione d'una tratta** (*cred., USA*) letter of advice; ~ **di presentazione** (*pers.*) letter of introduction, letter of recommendation; testimonial; ~ **di procura** (*leg.*) letter of attorney; ~ **di raccomandazione** (*pers.*) letter of recommendation, letter of introduction; ~ **di reclamo** complaint letter; ~ **di sollecitazione** (*comun.*) dunning letter, follow-up, reminder; ~ **di vendita** (*comun., market.*) sales letter; ~ **di vettura** (*trasp. ferr.*) consignment note, way-bill; ~ **espresso** (*comun.*) express letter; ~ **giacente** (*non ritirata o non consegnata, per irreperibilità del destinatario*) (*comun.*) dead letter; **una ~ inevasa** (*comun.*) an unanswered letter; **lettere iniziali** (*d'un nome e d'un cognome*) initials; ~ **microfilmata, spedita per aereo** (*comun.*) airgraph; **una ~ non datata** (*comun.*) an undated letter; **lettere non raccomandate** (*comun.*) unregistered letters; ~ **per posta aerea** (*comun.*) airmail letter; ~ **raccomandata** (*comun.*) registered letter; ~ **senza data** dateless letter; **alla ~** literally, word for word; literal (*a.*); (*di una somma*) **in lettere** in words.

letto, *n. m.* 1 bed. 2 (*trasp. ferr.*) sleeping-berth. 3 (*trasp. ferr.: vagone letto*) sleeper.

lettore, *n. m.* 1 reader. 2 (*giorn.*) reader.

lettura, *n. f.* reading.

leva, *n. f.* (*anche fig.*) lever. // **le leve del potere economico** the levers of economic power; ~ **d'interlinea** (*o* **di spaziatura**) (*d'attr. uff.*) carriage lever; ~ **finanziaria** (*Borsa, fin.*) (*forte effetto speculativo delle fluttuazioni finanziarie sui titoli ordinari d'una società*) leverage.

levare, *v. t.* 1 (*togliere*) to take* away (*o* off); to remove. 2 (*sollevare*) to lift (up), to raise. // ~ **l'àncora** (*trasp. mar.*) to weight anchor, to weigh, to unanchor, to cast off; ~ **una seduta** to close a sitting.

levata, *n. f.* 1 (*l'alzarsi*) rising. 2 (*delle lettere dalle cassette*) collection. 3 (*market.*) (*acquisto di generi di monopolio*) purchase. // **la ~ d'un sequestro** (*leg.*) the discharge of an attachment.

libbra, *n. f.* (*unità di peso pari a 453 grammi circa*) pound. // ~ **«troy»** (*unità di peso pari a grammi 373,24*) troy pound; **a libbre** (*market.*) by the pound.

liberale, *a.* liberal.

liberalizzare, *v. t.* 1 (*comm. est., econ., fin.*) to liberalize, to free. 2 (*econ., fin.*) to decontrol, to deregulate, to derestrict. 3 (*econ., market.*) (*prezzi*) to unfreeze*. // ~ **gli affitti** (*econ.*) to decontrol (*o* to deregulate) rents; ~ **il commercio estero** to liberalize foreign trade; ~ **i movimenti di capitale nell'ambito della Comunità** to free movements of capital within the Community.

liberalizzato, *a.* 1 (*comm. est., econ.*) liberalized. 2 (*comm. est., econ.*) (*senza tariffe*) tariffless.

liberalizzazione, *n. f.* 1 (*comm. est., econ., fin.*) liberalization. 2 (*econ.*) decontrol, deregulation. 3 (*econ., fin., market.*) (*dei prezzi*) unfreezing. // **la ~ degli scambi** (*comm. est.*) the liberalization of trade; **la ~ dei prezzi interni dei**

prodotti petroliferi (*econ.*) the decontrol of domestic oil prices; ~ **dei traffici** (*econ.*) trade liberalization.

liberamente, *avv.* 1 freely. 2 (*a proprio piacimento*) at discretion.

liberare, *v. t.* 1 to free, to set* free, to release. 2 (*sgombrare*) to clear. 3 (*fin., leg.*) to redeem. 4 (*leg.*) to acquit, to absolve. 5 (*leg.*) (*da un obbligo*) to release, to discharge. // ~ (*i prezzi*) **dai regolamenti (dai controlli,** ecc.) (*econ.*) to unfreeze; ~ **un posto** (*di lavoro*) (*pers.*) to vacate a position.

liberarsi, *v. rifl.* 1 to free oneself, to absolve oneself; to discharge. 2 (*sbarazzarsi*) to get* rid (of). 3 (*pers.*) (*di posto*) to become* vacant. // ~ **dai debiti** (*cred.*) to get out of debt; ~ **di** (*un'obbligazione, un debito, ecc.*) (*leg.*) to discharge; ~ **d'un debito** (*pagandolo*) (*cred.*) to clear a debt, to clear oneself from a debt.

liberazione, *n. f.* 1 liberation, freeing, release. 2 (*fin., leg.*) (*da un impegno finanziario*) redemption. 3 (*leg.*) (*da un obbligo*) release, discharge. // **la ~ d'un'ipoteca** (*fin., leg.*) the redemption (*o* the satisfaction) of a mortgage.

liberismo, *n. m.* (*econ.*) free trade, free market, free enterprise system, laissez-faire, laissez-faire economics.

liberista, *n. m.* e *f.* (*econ.*) free trader.

liberistico, *a.* (*econ.*) laissez-faire (*attr.*).

libero, *a.* 1 free. 2 (*sgombro*) clear, open. 3 (*indipendente*) independent; free-lance (*attr.*). 4 (*pers.*) (*di posto*) vacant, unfilled. 5 (*trasp.*) (*di posto a sedere*) free; available. // **la libera circolazione della manodopera** (*pers., sind.*) the free movement of workers; **la libera circolazione delle merci** (*market.*) the free movement of goods; **libera concorrenza** (*econ.*) free competition; ~ **da dazio (*o* da dogana)** (*dog.*) duty-free; ~ **da imposte (*o* da tasse)** (*fin.*) tax-free; ~ **da ipoteche** (*leg.*) free of mortgage; ~ **dai ghiacci** (*trasp. mar.*) clear of ice; **libera iniziativa** (*econ.*) free enterprise; (*il sistema*) profit system; **libera pratica** (*trasp. mar.*) clearance, pratique; **libera professione** (*d'un medico, ecc.*) private practice; **le libere professioni** the professions; ~ **professionista** professional man; ~ **scambio** (*econ.*) free trade, free market; ~ **-scambista** (*econ.*) free trader; **un giorno** ~ (*pers.*) one day off, an off day.

liberoscambismo, *n. m.* (*econ.*) free market, free trade.

liberoscambista, *n. m.* e *f.* (*econ.*) free marketeer, free trader. *a.* (*favorevole al liberoscambismo*) free-trade minded.

libertà, *n. f.* freedom, liberty. // ~ **contrattuale** (*leg.*) freedom of contract, liberty of contract; ~ **dei traffici** (*econ.*) free trade; ~ **di fare scalo in qualsiasi porto** (*trasp. mar.*) liberty of calling at any port; ~ **di navigazione** (*leg.*) freedom of navigation; ~ **di scelta** freedom of choice; option; ~ **di scelta del consumatore** (*market.*) freedom of choice of the consumer; ~ **di stampa** (*giorn.*) liberty of the press; ~ **economica** (*econ.*) free enterprise; (*il sistema*) profit system; economic freedom (*termine usato soltanto da A. Marshall e dalla sua scuola*); ~ **provvisoria** (*leg.*) conditional discharge; ~ **vigilata** (*leg.*) probation; **accordare a q. la ~ provvisoria** (*leg.*) to let sb. out on bail; **giorno di ~** (*pers.*) off day, day off; **in ~ provvisoria** (*dopo aver pagato la cauzione*) (*leg.*) out on bail.

libreria, *n. f.* 1 (*attr. uff.*) bookcase. 2 (*market.*) bookshop. // ~ **self-service** (*market.*) booketeria (*fam. USA*).

libretto, *n. m.* 1 booklet. 2 (*banca, ecc.*) book. 3 (*pers.*) (*di lavoro*) employment card. 4 (*pers.*) (*di marchette assicurative*) card. // ~ **del depositante** (*banca*) depositor's book; ~ **d'assegni** (*banca*) cheque-book; check-book (*USA*); ~ **di banca** bank book; ~ **di biglietti** (*trasp.*) book ticket; ~ **di biglietti per un viaggio circolare** (*trasp.*) circular tour ticket; ~ **di conto vincolato** (*banca*) deposit account pass-book; ~ **di deposito** (*banca*) pass-book, deposit book; ~ **di deposito vincolato** bank pass-book; ~ **di lavoro** (*pers.*) employment card; ~ **di risparmio** (*banca*) savings-bank depositor's book, bank pass-book; ~ **nominativo** (*banca*) depositor's book; ~ **per i versamenti** (*banca*) paying-in book.

libro, *n. m.* 1 book, volume. 2 (*registro*) register. 3 (*rag.*) book. // ~ **a madre e figlia** (*rag.*) counterfoil book; ~ (*degli*) **acquisti** (*rag.*) bought book, purchase book, invoice book; ~ **bianco** (*amm.*) white paper; ~ (*di*) **cassa** (*rag.*) cash book, cash journal; ~ **catastale** (*amm.*) real estate register; ~ **commissioni** (*org. az.*) order book; ~ **contabile** (*rag.*) account book, register; ~ **contabile dei profitti e delle perdite** (*rag.*) cost-book; **libri contabili** (*rag.*) account books, books of account, books; ~ **copialettere** (*attr. uff.*) copy letter book; ~ **dei bilanci di verifica** (*rag.*) balance book; ~ **dei compensi a terzi** (*fin.*) record of payments to third parties; ~ **dei contratti** (*Borsa*) bargain-book; ~ **dei fidi** (*banca, cred.*) register of credits; ~ **dei saldi** (*rag.*) balance book; ~ **dei soci** (*fin., rag.*) transfer book; stock ledger (*USA*); ~ **dei verbali** (*leg.*) minute book; ~ **delle firme** (*dei clienti*) (*banca*) autograph book, signature book; ~

delle obbligazioni (*fin.*, *rag.*) register of stocks and shares; ~ (*per l'annotazione giornaliera*) **delle operazioni a termine e di riporto** (*fin.*, *rag.*) journal of forward transactions and transactions for the account; ~ **delle ordinazioni** (*org. az.*) order book; ~ **dell'inventario** (*rag.*) balance-sheet book; **libri di bordo** (*trasp. mar.*) ship's books; ~ **di (carico e scarico del) magazzino** (*org. az.*) warehouse book; ~ **(di) piccola cassa** (*rag.*) petty-cash book; ~ **fatture** (*rag.*) invoice book; ~ **giornale** (*rag.*) book of original entry, book of entries, journal; ~ **in brossura** (*pubbl.*) paperback book, paperback, paperbook; ~ **interessi** (*rag.*) interest book; ~ **inventari** (*rag.*) stock-book; ~ **magazzino** (*rag.*) stock-book; ~ **mastro** (*rag.*) ledger; ~ **mastro degli acquisti** (*rag.*) credit ledger; ~ **mastro dei clienti** (*rag.*) clients' ledger; ~ **mastro delle vendite** (*rag.*) debit ledger; ~ **mastro generale** (*rag.*) general ledger; **libri** (*contabili*) **obbligatori** (*leg.*, *rag.*) statutory books; required books; **libri paga** (*rag.*) pay-rolls; **i libri sociali** (*fin.*, *rag.*) the company's books; the corporate books (*USA*); ~ **tascabile** (*pubbl.*) pocket book; ~ (*delle*) **vendite** (*rag.*) sales book, sales day book, sales journal.

licenza, *n. f.* **1** leave, permission, permit. **2** (*comm. est.*) licence, permit. **3** (*leg.*) licence; license (*USA*). **4** (*pers.*) leave of absence, leave; furlough (*USA*). // ~ **d'esportazione** (*comm. est.*) export licence; ~ **di fabbricazione** (*leg.*) manufacturing licence; ~ **d'importazione** (*comm. est.*) import licence; ~ **di vendita** (*leg.*) selling licence; **essere in** ~ (*pers.*) to be on leave.

licenziamento, *n. m.* **1** (*pers.*) dismissal, discharge; boot, sack, sacking, kick, turnout, kickout (*fam.*); mittimus (*fam.*, *ingl.*); ax (*slang USA*). **2** (*pers.*) (*per mancanza d'attività dell'azienda*) layoff. // **il** ~ **d'un impiegato** (*pers.*) the dismissal (*o* discharge) of a clerk; ~ **discriminatorio** (*pers.*) discriminatory discharge; ~ **immotivato** (*leg.*, *pers.*) *V.* ~ **non per giusta causa;** ~ **in tronco** (*pers.*) dismissal without notice; ~ **non per giusta causa** (*leg.*, *pers.*) wrongful dismissal (*o* discharge); ~ **per giusta causa** (*leg.*, *pers.*) dismissal (*o* discharge) for cause; ~ **senza preavviso** (*pers.*) dismissal without notice.

licenziare, *v. t.* **1** (*pers.*) to dismiss, to discharge, to separate, to give★ notice to (sb.), to send★ away; to turn off, to turn out, to fire, to sack, to kick out, to boot, to bounce, to brush off, to shelve, to give★ (sb.) the sack, to give★ (sb.) the boot (*fam.*); to give (sb.) the gate, to can (*slang USA*). **2** (*pers.*) (*per mancanza d'attività dell'azienda*) to lay★ off, to throw★ (sb.) out of employment. // **essere licenziato** (*pers.*) to be dismissed (*o* discharged); to get the boot, to get the kick, to get the sack (*fam.*); to get the gate, to get the air, to get the ax (*slang USA*).

licenziarsi, *v. rifl.* **1** (*accomiatarsi*) to take★ one's leave (from sb.). **2** (*pers.*) (*dimettersi*) to give★ notice (to one's employer); to hand in one's notice, to resign.

licenziatario, *n. m.* (*leg.*) licensee.

licenziato, *a.* dismissed, discharged; broke (*slang*) (*V.* **licenziare**).

licitare, *v. i.* (*leg.*) to bid★ (at an auction).

licitazione, *n. f.* **1** (*leg.*) (*offerta a un'asta*) bid. **2** (*leg.*) (*offerta a una gara d'appalto*) tender. **3** (*market.*) (*vendita all'asta*) auction sale, auction.

lieve, *a* light; (*tenue*) slight. // ~ **diminuzione dell'attività commerciale** (*dopo un periodo inflazionistico, ecc.*) (*market.*) shake-out; **una** ~ **recessione** (*econ.*) a business dip.

lievitare, *v. t.* to leaven. *v. i.* **1** to rise★. **2** (*di prezzi, ecc.*) to rise★; to increase; to go★ up; to swell★.

lievitazione, *n. f.* **1** leavening; rise. **2** (*dei prezzi, ecc.*) rise; increase. // ~ **dei prezzi e dei costi** (*market.*) increase in prices and costs.

lievito, *n. m.* (*anche fig.*) leaven, yeast.

limitare, *v. t.* **1** to limit, to confine, to abridge. **2** (*ridurre: spese e sim.*) to cut★, to curtail, to keep★ (st.) down, to retrench. **3** (*restringere*) to restrict, to restrain. **4** (*leg.*) to qualify. // ~ **i diritti di q.** (*leg.*) to abridge sb.'s rights.

limitarsi, *v. rifl.* to limit oneself, to confine oneself. // ~ **alle istruzioni ricevute da q.** to confine oneself to sb.'s instructions.

limitativo, *a.* restrictive, terminate.

limitato, *a.* **1** limited. **2** (*ristretto*) confined, narrow.

limitazione, *n. f.* **1** limitation, confinement. **2** (*limite*) limit. **3** (*restrizione*) restriction, restraint. **4** (*riduzione*) cut, cutting, curtailing. **5** (*ass.*) (*di copertura*) limitation. **6** (*leg.*) qualification. // ~ **al libero commercio** (*econ.*) restraint of trade; ~ **contrattuale di responsabilità** (*leg.*) contract limitation of liability; ~ **degli scambi** restrictions on trade.

limite, *n. m.* **1** limit, limitation. **2** (*estensione*) extent. **3** (*confine*) boundary, border, mete; (*pietra di confine*) land-mark. **4** (*ass.*) (*di copertura*) limitation. **5** (*mat.*) limit. // ~ **di guardia** (*org. az.*) safety level, safety allowance; ~ **di marea** (*trasp. mar.*) tide-mark; ~ **di tempo** (*per far valere un diritto*) (*leg.*) limitation; ~ (*massimo*) **di velocità** (*trasp. aut.*) speed limit; ~ **massimo** (*ass.*) line; **senza limiti** without limit; limitless.

linea, *n. f.* **1** line. **2** (*rango*) rank. **3** (*comun.*) line; (*del codice Morse*) dash. **4** (*market.*) (*di prodotti*) line. **5** (*org. az.*) (*di produzione*) line. **6** (*trasp.*) line, route. // ~ **aerea** (*trasp. aer.*) airline, airway; ~ **collaterale** (*leg.*) collateral relation; ~ **costiera** (*trasp. mar.*) coast line; ~ **dei rialzi e dei ribassi** (*Borsa*) advance-decline line; ~ **di bandiera** (*trasp. aer., trasp. mar.*) flag carrier; ~ **di carico** (*trasp. mar.*) load line; ~ **di condotta** (*econ.*) policy; ~ **di confine** borderline; ~ **di galleggiamento** (*trasp. mar.*) line of flotation; ~ **d'immersione** (*trasp. mar.*) line of flotation; ~ **di navigazione** (*trasp. mar.*) shipping line, line; ~ **di navigazione a vapore** (*trasp. mar.*) steamship line; ~ **di prodotti** (*d'un'azienda*) (*org. az.*) product line; ~ **di prodotti secondaria** (*rispetto a quella che costituisce oggetto principale di vendita*) (*market.*) side-line; ~ **di volo** (*trasp. aer.*) line of flight; ~ (*telefonica*) **diretta** (*comun.*) direct exchange line; ~ **direttrice** guideline; ~ **ferroviaria** (*trasp. ferr.*) railway line; ~ (*telefonica*) **interurbana** (*comun.*) trunk-line, toll-line; ~ **principale** (*trasp. ferr.*) main line, main stem, trunk-line; ~ **retta** straight line; ~ **telefonica** (*comun.*) telephone line, route; ~ **telegrafica** (*comun.*) telegraph line; **essere in** ~ (*al telefono*) to be through; **in** ~ **retta** in a straight line, straight; (*leg.*) (*di discendente*) lineal (*a.*); (*mat.*) straight-line (*attr.*).

lineare, *a.* linear, lineal.

lineetta, *n. f.* **1** (*comun.*) (*dell'alfabeto Morse*) dash. **2** (*giorn.*) (*lunga*) dash; (*trattino d'unione*) hyphen.

lingotto, *n. m.* ingot, bar. // **un** ~ **d'oro** a gold bar; **oro in lingotti** gold in bullion.

lingua, *n. f.* **1** language. **2** (*parte del corpo*) tongue. // ~ **inglese commerciale** business English.

linguaggio, *n. m.* language. // ~ **della burocrazia** officialese; ~ **misto formato da parole comuni e/o cifrate** (*per telegrammi*) (*comun.*) combination in plain language, code and/or cipher; ~ **tecnico** technical language.

linguetta, *n. f.* (*di scarpa*) tongue. // ~ **sporgente** (*di scheda di casellario, ecc.*) (*attr. uff.*) tab.

liquidabile, *a.* **1** (*ass., cred., fin., leg.*) that can be liquidated. **2** (*ass. mar.*) adjustable.

liquidare, *v. t.* **1** (*ass., leg.*) to liquidate. **2** (*ass. mar.*) to adjust. **3** (*cred.*) (*un debito, ecc.*) to liquidate, to wipe off; (*un creditore, ecc.*) to pay★ off. **4** (*cred., fin.*) (*una società, i conti, ecc.*) to liquidate; (*una società*) to wind★ up, to break★ up. **5** (*fin., market.*) to sell★ off, to sell★ out. **6** (*market.*) (*merce invenduta*) to remainder. // ~ **i propri affari** (*fin.*) to wind up one's business affairs; ~ **un conto** (*rag.*) to discharge an account; ~ **il debito nazionale** (*fin.*) to liquidate the national debt; ~ **un'operazione** (*Borsa*) to close a transaction; ~ **una partita di merci** to clear a parcel of goods; ~ **le rimanenze** (*market.*) to remainder; ~ **una società commerciale** (*fin.*) to wind up a business company; ~ **una società per azioni** (*fin.*) to liquidate a corporation (*USA*).

liquidatore, *n. m.* **1** (*ass., fin., leg.*) liquidator. **2** (*ass. mar.*) adjuster, insurance adjuster. **3** (*leg.*) (*di fallimento*) receiver, official receiver; liquidator (*USA*). // ~ **d'avaria** (*ass. mar.*) average adjuster, average adjustor, average stater, average taker.

liquidazione, *n. f.* **1** (*ass., leg.*) (*di danni, ecc.*) liquidation. **2** (*ass. mar.*) adjustment. **3** (*Borsa*) account, settlement, closing. **4** (*cred., fin.*) liquidation, settling, settling-up, clearing. **5** (*fin., rag.*) (*d'una società, dei conti, ecc.*) wind-up, winding-up, liquidation. **6** (*market.*) (*lo svendere*) selling-off. **7** (*market.*) (*la svendita*) clearance sale, clearing-up sale, sale. **8** (*pers.*) (*indennità di licenziamento senza colpa del dipendente*) severance pay; dismissal wage (*USA*). **9** (*pers.*) (*indennità di fine lavoro all'andata in pensione*) retirement bonus (*non esiste in G.B.*). **10** (*pers.*) (*indennità di buonuscita a militari o impiegati dello Stato*) gratuity. // ~ (*d'avaria*) **all'estero** (*ass. mar.*) foreign adjustment; ~ **coattiva** (*leg.*) compulsory settlement; ~ **corrente** (*Borsa*) current settlement; **la** ~ **dei conti** (*Borsa*) the settlement of accounts; ~ **delle rimanenze** (*market.*) clearing-up sale; ~ **d'avaria** (*ass. mar.*) adjustment of average, average adjustment, average statement; ~ **disposta dall'autorità giudiziaria** (*leg.*) compulsory winding up; ~ **forzata** (*di merce*) compulsory sale; (*d'una società*) compulsory winding-up; ~ **periodica** (*Borsa*) term settlement, settlement; ~ **prossima** (*Borsa*) next account, next settlement; ~ **speciale** (*Borsa*) special settlement; **la** ~ **successiva** (*Borsa*) the ensuing account, the ensuing (*o* following) settlement; ~ **volontaria** (*d'una società*) voluntary winding-up.

liquidità, *n. f. inv.* (*econ., fin., rag.*) liquidity; liquid assets, cash holdings (*pl.*). // ~ **finanziaria** (*fin.*) monetary liquidity; ~ **interna** (*fin.*) domestic liquidity; ~ **internazionale** (*fin.*) international liquidity.

liquido, *a.* (*anche fin.*) liquid. *n. m.* liquid. // ~ **in banca** (*fin., rag.*) cash at the bank; ~ **in**

cassa (*fin., rag.*) cash in hand; **attività liquide** (*fin.*) liquid assets; **denaro** ~ ready cash; **fondi liquidi** (*fin.*) available funds.

lira, *n. f.* (*unità monetaria italiana*) lira. // ~ **commerciale** (*econ., fin.*) commercial lira; ~ **finanziaria** (*econ., fin.*) financial lira; ~ **sterlina** pound sterling, pound.

lista, *n. f.* **1** (*elenco*) list, panel, schedule. **2** (*ruolo*) roll. **3** (*org. az.*) calendar. // ~ **dei disastri marittimi** (*trasp. mar.*) black list; ~ **dei fallimenti** (*cred., fin.*) black list; ~ **dei giurati** (*leg.*) panel; ~ **dei passeggeri** (*trasp.*) way-bill; ~ **delle cause da discutere** (*leg.*) docket; ~ **delle merci ammesse in esenzione doganale** (*dog.*) free list; ~ **delle persone o ditte insolvibili** (*o comunque non raccomandabili per rapporti commerciali*) (*cred., fin.*) black list; ~ **delle spese** (*sostenute per una causa legale*) (*leg.*) fee bill; ~ **d'articoli d'importazione libera** (*dog.*) free list; ~ **d'attesa** waiting list, wait list; ~ **di controllo** (*org. az.*) check list; ~ **di spedizione** (*comun.*) mailing list; ~ **giornaliera degli affari conclusi** (*alla Borsa Valori di Londra; pubblicata dal «Times»*) (*Borsa*) bargains market; ~ **nera** black list.

listino, *n. m.* **1** (*Borsa, fin.*) list. **2** (*market.*) list. // ~ **dei prezzi correnti** (*market.*) current price list, prices current; ~ **dei prezzi di mercato** (*market.*) *V.* ~ **dei prezzi correnti;** ~ **di Borsa** (*fin.*) stock-list; ~ **di chiusura** (*Borsa*) official list; ~ (*dei*) **prezzi** (*d'una ditta*) (*market.*) price-list; ~ **ufficiale** (*Borsa*) official list; ~ **«valori»** (*Borsa*) share-list, stock-list.

lite, *n. f.* **1** dispute, quarrel. **2** (*leg.*) litigation. **3** (*leg.*) (*causa*) lawsuit, suit. // **intentare** (*o* **muovere**) ~ **a q.** (*leg.*) to bring an action against sb.; to sue sb.

litigante, *a.* contending. *n. m.* e *f.* (*leg.*) litigant.

litigare, *v. i.* **1** to contend, to quarrel. **2** (*specialm. tirando sul prezzo*) to haggle. **3** (*leg.*) to litigate.

litigio, *n. m.* **1** dispute, quarrel. **2** (*specialm. mercanteggiando*) haggle.

litigiosità, *n. f.* **1** (*anche leg.*) litigiousness. **2** (*leg.*) barratry.

litigioso, *a.* **1** quarrelsome. **2** (*leg.*) litigious.

litorale, *n. m.* coast, shore, littoral.

litro, *n. m.* litre; liter (*USA*).

livellamento, *n. m.* **1** levelling; leveling (*USA*); equalization, equation. **2** (*trasp. mar.*) (*del carico*) trimming. // **il** ~ **della domanda e dell'offerta** (*econ.*) the equation of demand and supply; **il** ~ **delle differenze sociali** the levelling of social differences.

livellare, *v. t.* **1** to level (down, up), to equalize. **2** (*fin.*) to blanket. **3** (*trasp. mar.*) (*il carico*) to trim. // ~ **i prezzi** (*econ., market.*) to level prices; (*fin., market.*) to bring the rates to the same level; ~ **i redditi** (*fin.*) to equalize incomes.

livellarsi, *v. rifl.* to level; to find★ a common level.

livello, *n. m.* level; (*grado*) standard. // **il** ~ **degli investimenti privati di capitale** (*econ., fin.*) the level of private capital investments; ~ **dei prezzi** (*econ.*) price level; ~ **del mare** (*trasp. mar.*) sea level, water level; ~ **di disoccupazione** (*sind.*) unemployment level; **un** ~ **d'indebitamento assai elevato** (*fin.*) a high debit level; **livelli d'occupazione** (*econ.*) occupational levels; ~ **di sicurezza** (*org. az.*) safety level, safety allowance; ~ **massimo** (*di prezzi, salari, ecc.*) (*fin.*) ceiling; ~ **minimo** (*di prezzi, quotazioni, ecc.*) (*fin., market.*) floor; **il** ~ **minimo di sussistenza** the bare minimum of subsistence; ~ **salariale** (*econ.*) wage level; **oltre il** ~ **massimo** (*previsto, consentito, ecc.*) overceiling (*attr.*); **sopra il** ~ **dell'acqua** above water.

locale, *a.* **1** local. **2** (*settoriale*) sectional. *n. m.* **1** room. **2** (*trasp. ferr.*) local train; way train (*USA*). **3** **locali,** *pl.* premises. **4** **locali,** *pl.* (*comm.*) business premises.

località, *n. f. inv.* **1** place, locality. **2** (*tur.*) resort.

localizzare, *v. t.* **1** to localize. **2** (*econ.*) to locate.

localizzatore, *n. m.* **1** (*econ.*) locator. **2** (*trasp. aer.*) localizer.

localizzazione, *n. f.* **1** localization. **2** (*econ.*) location. // ~ **degli impianti** (*org. az.*) plant location.

locare, *v. t.* (*leg.*) (*dare in affitto*) to rent; to let★.

locatario, *n. m.* (*leg.*) lessee, leaseholder, occupant, occupier, renter, tenant.

locativo, *a.* (*leg.*) rental.

locatore, *n. m.* (*leg.*) lessor, landlord.

locazione, *n. f.* **1** (*leg.*) lease, leasehold, location, tenancy. **2** (*leg., org. az.*) (*di macchinari, ecc.*) leasing. // ~ **di macchinari ed attrezzature** leasing of industrial machinery and equipment; ~ **rinnovata tacitamente** (*leg.*) tenancy at sufferance.

locomotiva, *n. f.* (*trasp. ferr.*) locomotive, railway engine, engine. // ~ **a vapore** (*trasp. ferr.*) steam-engine; ~ **da** (*o* **di**) **manovra** (*trasp. ferr.*) shunting locomotive, yard-locomotive.

lodo, *n. m.* (*leg.*) arbitration award, award. // ~ **arbitrale** *V.* ~.

logoramento, *n. m.* wear, wear and tear.

logorare, *v. t.* to wear★, to wear★ down, to wear★ out. // ~ **la resistenza di q.** to wear down sb.'s resistance.

logorarsi, *v. rifl.* **1** to wear★, to wear★ out. **2** (*di persona*) to wear★ oneself out.

logorio, *n. m.* **1** wear and tear. **2** (*fig.*) strain. **3** (*econ.*) (*di macchine, ecc.*) wear. // **il ~ della vita moderna** the strain of modern life.

Londra, *n. f.* London; the Metropolis (*ingl.*).

lontano, *a.* **1** far-away, far-off, distant, remote. **2** (*trasp.*) long-distance. *avv.* far (*anche fig.*); far away, far off. // **essere ~ dal vero** to be far from the truth.

lord, *n. m.* **1** lord. **2 i Lord,** *pl.* (*amm.*) the Lords (*la Camera Alta inglese*). // ~ **del Sigillo Privato** (*ingl.*) Lord Privy Seal; **lord a vita** (*leg., ingl.*) law-lords.

lordo, *a.* (*comm.*) gross. // «~ **per netto**» (*non si computa la tara*) (*market.*) «gross for net».

losco, *a.* crooked. // **un ~ affare di terreni** a crooked land deal.

lotta, *n. f.* struggle, war (*anche fig.*). // ~ **di classe** (*sind.*) class struggle, class war; ~ **oligopolistica** (*econ.*) competition among the majors.

lottare, *v. i.* to struggle, to fight★, to contend. // ~ **contro l'inflazione** (*econ.*) to combat inflation.

lottizzare, *v. t.* to lot, to lot out, to parcel, to apportion.

lottizzazione, *n. f.* lotting, parcellation, apportionment. // **la ~ di terreni** the apportionment of landed property.

lotto, *n. m.* **1** batch, block. **2** (*di terreno*) plot. **3** (*comm.*) (*di merce: a un'asta*) lot. **4** (*leg.*) (*di terreno*) parcel, lot. // **un ~ fabbricabile** a building lot.

luce, *n. f.* light. // **luci da città** (*trasp. aut.*) town-lights; **luci di posizione** (*trasp. aut.*) town-lights.

lucrare, *v. t.* to gain.

lucrativo, *a.* **1** lucrative, gainful, remunerative, profit-making. **2** (*econ., fin., rag.*) profitable, paying. // **l'esser ~** lucrativeness; **tutt'altro che ~** unremunerative.

lucro, *n. m.* **1** lucre, gain. **2** (*econ., fin., rag.*) profit. // **che non ha fini di ~** non-profit.

lucroso, *a.* **1** lucrative. **2** (*econ., fin.*) profitable.

lunghezza, *n. f.* length. // ~ **d'onda** (*comun.*) wave-length; ~ **in iarde** yardage; ~ **in «piedi»** footage.

lungo, *a.* **1** long. **2** (*a lunga portata*) long-range. *prep.* **1** (*luogo*) along. **2** (*tempo*) (*durante*) during. // **a ~** for a long time; long (*avv.*); long-term (*a. attr.*); **a ~ andare** in the long run; **a lunga scadenza** long-term (*a. attr.*); **a ~ termine** (*econ., fin.*) in the long run; long-term, long-range, long-run (*a. attr.*); **alla lunga** in the long run; **di ~ cabotaggio** (*trasp. mar.*) sea-going; **di ~ corso** (*trasp. mar.*) (*di nave, ecc.*) ocean-going; **nel ~ periodo** in the long term.

luogo[1], *n. m.* place, spot. // ~ **d'approdo o d'ancoraggio** (*di una nave*) (*trasp. mar.*) berth; ~ **di caricamento** (*trasp.*) loading place; ~ **di consegna** (*market.*) place of delivery; ~ **di destinazione** (*trasp. mar.*) place of destination; ~ **di dimora** abiding place; **luoghi d'interesse turistico** (*tur.*) sights; ~ **di lavoro** work-place; ~ **di nascita** place of birth, birthplace; ~ **di residenza** dwelling place; (*leg.*) place of residence; **in ~ di** in place of; «**non ~ a procedere**» (*leg.*) nonsuit.

luogo[2], *pref.* locum-. // **luogotenente** (*chi fa le veci di q.*) locum-tenens.

lusso, *n. m.* luxury.

lussuoso, *a.* luxurious.

M

macchina, *n. f.* 1 machine. 2 (*trasp. aut.*) car, motor car. 3 (*trasp. ferr.*) (*locomotiva*) engine. 4 (*trasp. mar.*) (*di nave*) engine. 5 **macchine,** *pl.* (*org. az.*) machinery. // ~ **a vapore** steam-engine; ~ **affrancatrice** (*macch. uff.*) franking machine, postage meter, postal meter, meter; ~ **calcolatrice** (*macch. uff.*) calculating machine, calculator, comptometer; ~ **contabile** (*macch. uff.*) accounting machine, bookkeeping machine; ~ **contabile automatica** (*macch. uff.*) automatic bookkeeping machine; ~ **da scrivere** (*macch. uff.*) typewriter; ~ **da scrivere elettrica** (*macch. uff.*) electric typewriter; **macchine e impianti** (*org. az.*) machinery and equipment; ~ **fatturatrice** (*macch. uff.*) invoicing machine; ~ **fotografica** camera; **macchine inattive** (*org. az.*) idle machines; ~ **lavatrice** washing machine; ~ **per effettuare la girata d'assegni bancari** (*mediante matrici speciali, per prevenire le contraffazioni*) (*macch. uff.*) cheque endorsing machine; ~ **per fatturazione** (*macch. uff.*) billing machine; ~ **per firmare assegni bancari** (*mediante matrici speciali, per prevenire contraffazioni*) (*macch. uff.*) cheque signer; ~ **per firmare assegni bancari e apporvi la firma di girata** (*mediante matrici speciali, per prevenire contraffazioni*) (*macch. uff.*) cheque signing and endorsing machine; ~ **per impaccare** (*org. az.*) packer; ~ **per stampare le cifre d'un assegno bancario** (*macch. uff.*) check protector, checkwriter; ~ **per stenografare** (*macch. uff.*) stenograph; **macchine per ufficio** (*macch. uff.*) office machines; ~ **utensile** (*org. az.*) tool, machine-tool.

macchinario, *n. m.* (*org. az.*) machinery. // ~ **inoperoso** (*org. az.*) inactive machinery.

macchinista, *n. m.* (*trasp. ferr.*) engine driver; engineer (*USA*).

macroeconomia, *n. f.* (*econ.*) macroeconomics.

macroeconomico, *a.* (*econ.*) macroeconomic.

madre, *n. f.* 1 mother. 2 (*di registro, libretto d'assegni, ecc.*) counterfoil; stub (*USA*). *a. attr.* (*fin.*) parent.

maestranze, *n. pl.* 1 (*org. az.*) (*la «base»*) (the) rank and file. 2 (*pers.*) hands, workers. 3 (*pers.*) (*in genere*) employees. // ~ **d'un cantiere navale** (*pers.*) dockyard hands; **le** ~ **portuali** (*trasp. mar.*) the port workers.

magazzinaggio, *n. m.* 1 (*dog., org. az.*) warehousing. 2 (*dog., trasp.*) (*spese di magazzinaggio*) warehouse dues. 3 (*org. az.*) storage. 4 (*org. az.*) (*spese di magazzinaggio*) storage (charges).

magazziniere, *n. m.* 1 (*dog., org. az., pers.*) warehouse-keeper, warehouseman★, warehouser. 2 (*org. az., pers.*) storekeeper, storeman★, stock clerk.

magazzino, *n. m.* 1 (*dog., org. az.*) warehouse. 2 (*org. az.*) store, store room, stock room. 3 (*org. az.*) (*di deposito*) depot. // ~ **a prezzo ridotto** (*market.*) discount house; ~ **doganale** (*dog.*) customs warehouse, customs store; (*in regime di punto franco*) bonded warehouse, bonded store, entrepôt; ~ **frigorifero** (*market.*) refrigerator warehouse, cold store; ~ **generale** (*dog.*) general warehouse; **magazzini navali** (*trasp. mar.*) marine stores; ~ **nazionale** (*dog.*) national warehouse; **un** ~ **per la stagionatura dei formaggi** (*org. az.*) a store for cheese seasoning; ~ **pezzi finiti** (*org. az.*) finished goods storehouse; ~ **viveri** (*trasp. mar.*) victualling yard; **dal** ~ (*market.*) (*di merce*) ex warehouse; **in** ~ (*org. az.*) on hand, in stock; **in** ~ **doganale** (*dog.*) in bond.

maggioranza, *n. f.* majority. // ~ **assoluta** (*leg.*) absolute majority; ~ **relativa** (*leg.*) plurality; ~ **semplice** (*leg.*) simple majority.

maggiorare, *v. t.* to increase, to raise. // ~ **il prezzo di** (*qc.*) (*market.*) to surcharge; ~ **il prezzo d'acquisto per coprire le spese** to add st. to the purchase price to cover one's expenses.

maggiorazione, *n. f.* 1 increase, raise. 2 (*market.*) (*di prezzo*) surcharge. // ~ **del valore in Borsa dei capitali investiti** (*econ., fin.*) capital gains.

maggiorenne, *a.* (*leg.*) of age, of full age, full-aged. *n. m.* e *f.* (*leg.*) major.

magistrato, *n. m.* 1 (*leg.*) magistrate, judge.

2 (*leg.*) recorder (*in certe città inglesi*).

magistratura, *n. f.* (*leg.*) magistrature, magistrateship, judicature, judiciary; Court, (the) Bench.

magnate, *n. m.* (*fin.*) magnate, grandee; tycoon, baron (*USA*). // **un ~ dell'acciaio** a steel magnate.

magnetico, *a.* magnetic.

magnetofono, *n. m.* (*macch. uff.*) tape recorder, recorder. // **~ a filo** (*macch. uff.*) wire recorder.

magro, *a.* thin; (*scarso*) scanty, scarce, meagre, lean. // **un ~ raccolto** (*econ.*) a scanty crop, a lean harvest.

malato, *a.* sick (*attr.*); ill (*generalm. pred.*). *n. m.* patient, sick person.

malattia, *n. f.* sickness, illness, disease. // **malattie del lavoro** (*pers.*) occupational diseases; **~ mentale** (*leg.*) mental disease; **~ professionale** (*pers.*) industrial disease, occupational disease.

malfattore, *n. m.* (*leg.*) malefactor, evil-doer, wrong-doer.

malo, *a.* bad, ill, evil. // **mala copia** foul copy, rough copy; **in mala fede** (*leg.*) mala fide.

manager, *n. m.* (*amm.*) manager.

manageriale, *a.* (*amm.*) managerial.

mancante, *a.* 1 (*sprovvisto*) lacking (in), in need (of); (*a corto di*) short (of). 2 (*che non si trova più*) missing; (*assente*) absent. // **~ d'elasticità** (*anche econ.*) (*della domanda, ecc.*) inelastic; **~ di qualche requisito essenziale** (*leg.*) imperfect.

mancanza, *n. f.* 1 (*scarsità*) lack, want. 2 (*deficienza*) deficiency, shortage. 3 (*assenza*) absence. 4 (*omissione*) failure. // **~ dei requisiti necessari** (*leg.*) disqualification; **~ d'accettazione** (*cred.*) unacceptance; **~ di competenza** want of competence; **~ di copertura** (*banca, cred.*) absence of consideration; «**~ di copertura**» (*banca, cred.*) «no funds» (*N.F.*); **~ di diversificazione** (*econ.*) lack of diversification; **~ d'elasticità** (*anche econ.*) (*della domanda, ecc.*) inelasticity; **~ d'equilibrio** lack of balance, unbalance; **~ d'eredi** (*leg.*) failure of issue; **~ di fondi** (*fin.*) lack of funds; **~ di fondi per una cambiale** (*banca, cred.*) absence of consideration for a bill; **~ di giurisdizione** (*leg.*) lack of jurisdiction, want of jurisdiction; **~ di notizie d'una nave** (*trasp. mar.*) absence of news of a ship; **~ di prove** (*leg.*) failure of evidence, want of evidence, lack of evidence; **~ di quotazione** (*Borsa*) non-quotation; **~ di titolo** (*leg.*) lack of title; **in ~ di** failing, in default of; **in ~ di accordo** in default of agreement; **in ~ d'istruzioni specifiche** failing specific instructions; **in ~ di prova contraria** (*leg.*) in the absence of contrary evidence; **in ~ d'ulteriori istruzioni** in the absence of further instructions; **per ~ di fondi** for want of funds.

mancare, *v. i.* 1 (*non avere a sufficienza*) to lack, to be lacking. 2 (*essere sprovvisto*) to be short (of), to need. 3 (*non esserci*) to be absent; (*non essere reperibile*) to be missing. 4 (*omettere, tralasciare*) to fail. *v. t.* (*fam.*) (*perdere*) to miss. // **~ a un appuntamento** to miss an appointment; **~ alla parola data** to break one's word; **~ di mezzi** (*fin.*) to be hard up.

mancato, *a.* 1 (*fallito*) unsuccessful. 2 (*che la pretende a*) would-be (*attr.*). // **mancata accettazione** (*d'una cambiale*) (*cred.*) non-acceptance; **~ arrivo** (*trasp.*) non-arrival; **mancata comparizione** (*d'imputato o di teste*) (*leg.*) non-appearance, non-attendance; **mancata comparizione in giudizio** (*leg.*) non-appearance, absence to appear, failure to appear; **mancata consegna** (*market.*) non-delivery; **mancata esecuzione** (*leg.*) failure to perform; **~ imbarco** (*trasp.*) non-shipment; **mancata partenza** (*trasp.*) non-departure; **mancata quotazione** (*Borsa*) non-quotation.

mancia, *n. f.* tip, gratuity, box.

mandante, *n. m.* e *f.* (*leg.*) mandant, mandator, assignor, principal.

mandare, *v. t.* 1 to send★. 2 (*spedire*) to forward, to dispatch; to ship (*USA*). 3 (*spedire per via mare*) to ship. 4 (*trasmettere*) to transmit, to remit. // **~ a chiamare q.** to send for sb.; **~ a prendere** (*ordinare*) (*market.*) to send for; **~ q. «a spasso»** (*licenziarlo*) (*pers., fam.*) to give sb. the sack, to sack sb.; **~ avanti un'azienda** to carry on a business, to keep a business going; **~ avanti la baracca** (*fam.*) to keep one's business going; **~ circolari a q.** to circularize sb.; **~ q. in pensione** (*pers.*) to pension sb. off, to retire sb.; **~ in rovina** to shipwreck, to wreck (*fig.*); **~ per posta** (*comun.*) to mail; **~ un telegramma** (*comun.*) to cable; **~ un telegramma a q.** (*comun.*) to telegraph sb.; **~ via** (*licenziare*) (*pers.*) to send away.

mandatario, *n. m.* 1 (*leg.*) mandatary, mandatory, mandatee. 2 (*leg.*) (*agente*) agent. 3 (*leg.*) (*procuratore*) proxy, assignee, attorney. // **~ commerciale** (*al quale vengono affidate le merci di cui ha la piena disponibilità*) (*leg.*) factor.

mandato, *n. m.* 1 (*incarico*) commission. 2 (*leg.*) order, writ, warrant. 3 (*leg.*) (*citazione*) summons, mandate, mandamus. // **~ commerciale** agency; **~ d'arresto (o di cattura)** (*leg.*)

warrant of arrest, mittimus; ~ **di comparizione** (*leg.*) summons, writ of subpoena, subpoena, process; ~ **di pagamento** (*banca, cred., rag.*) order for payment, order to pay, warrant for payment, card money order, money order; ~ **di rappresentanza** (*leg.*) agency; ~ **di riscossione** cash warrant; ~ **di riscossione sbarrato** (*delle Poste britanniche*) crossed warrant; ~ **di scarico** (*trasp. mar.*) freight release; ~ **generale** (*leg.*) general agency.

maneggiamento, *n. m.* **1** handling. **2** (*manipolazione, falsificazione*) manipulation. **3** (*market.*) (*di prezzi, ecc.*) rig. // ~ **dei materiali** (*org. az.*) materials handling.

maneggiare, *v. t.* **1** to handle. **2** (*manipolare, falsificare*) to manipulate. **3** (*market.*) (*prezzi, ecc.*) to rig. // ~ **(bene) una lingua** to master a language.

manifattura, *n. f.* **1** (*org. az.*) manufacture. **2** (*org. az.*) (*fabbrica*) factory, manufactory, industry. **3** (*org. az.*) (*manufatto*) manufactured article. // ~ **dei tabacchi** tobacco manufacture.

manifatturiere, *n. m.* **1** (*proprietario d'una manifattura*) factory-owner. **2** (*dirigente d'una manifattura*) factory manager. **3** (*operaio*) factory operative (*o* worker).

manifatturiero, *a.* (*org. az.*) manufacturing; factory (*attr.*).

manifestare, *v. t.* **1** to manifest. **2** (*mostrare*) to show★. **3** (*esprimere*) to express. *v. i.* (*fare una dimostrazione*) to demonstrate. // ~ **una tendenza** (*a poco a poco*) to develop a tendency.

manifestazione, *n. f.* **1** manifestation. **2** show. **3** (*dimostrazione*) demonstration. // **una ~ pubblica** a public demonstration; **manifestazioni sindacali** (*sind.*) unions' actions.

manifestino, *n. m.* **1** (*pubbl.*) leaflet. **2** (*pubbl.*) (*distribuito a mano*) handbill; throw-away (*USA*).

manifesto[1], *a.* manifest, evident, express, tangible.

manifesto[2], *n. m.* **1** (*avviso*) notice. **2** (*pubbl.*) (*murale*) poster, placard, bill. **3** (*trasp. aer., trasp. mar.*) manifest. // ~ **di bordo** (*trasp. mar.*) ship's manifest, cargo summary; ~ **di cabotaggio** (*trasp. mar.*) coasting manifest; ~ **di dogana** (*dog.*) customs manifest; ~ **di fabbrica** (*affisso, a cura d'un sindacato, in uno stabilimento, per mostrare che in questo il lavoro è svolto secondo le norme previste dal contratto*) (*sind.*) shop card; ~ **di transito** (*dog.*) transit manifest; ~ **d'uscita** (*trasp. mar.*) outward manifest; ~ **per tram (autobus, metropolitana, ecc.)** (*pubbl.*) car card (*USA*).

manipolare, *v. t.* **1** to manipulate, to handle, to work (out). **2** (*leg.*) to manipulate. **3** (*leg.*) (*adulterare*) to adulterate.

manipolazione, *n. f.* **1** manipulation, handling, working (out). **2** (*leg.*) manipulation. **3** (*leg.*) (*adulterazione*) adulteration. // **manipolazioni chimiche** (*market.*) chemical manipulations; **la ~ delle merci** (*market.*) the manipulation of goods.

mano, *n. f.* **1** hand. **2** (*potere, balia*) hand, power. **3** (*di vernice, ecc.*) coat, coating. // ~ **d'opera** (*econ., pers.*) *V.* **manodopera; a ~** by hand; **contro ~** (*trasp.*) (*di veicoli, ecc.*) on the wrong side of the road; **per le mani** in hand.

manodopera, *n. f.* (*econ., pers.*) labour, manpower, work-people. // ~ **a giornata** (*pers.*) day labour; ~ **contrattuale** (*sind.*) contract labour; ~ **del settore cantieristico** (*trasp. mar.*) shipbuilding labour; ~ **diretta** (*pers.*) direct labour, productive labour; ~ **femminile** (*pers.*) female labour; ~ **indiretta** (*pers.*) indirect labour; ~ **non qualificata** (*pers.*) unskilled labour; ~ **portuale** (*pers.*) dock labour; ~ **qualificata** (*pers.*) skilled labour; ~ **specializzata** (*pers.*) skilled labour; ~ **straniera** (*pers.*) foreign manpower; ~ **temporanea** (*pers.*) contract labour; **ad alto impiego di ~** (*econ.*) labour-intensive (*attr.*); **a corto di ~** (*org. az.*) (*di datore di lavoro*) short-handed; **con ~ insufficiente** (*org. az.*) (*di fabbrica*) underhanded, undermanned.

manomettere, *v. t.* **1** (*aprire indebitamente*) to open unduly. **2** (*leg.*) to tamper (with). // ~ **documenti** (*leg.*) to tamper with documents.

manomissione, *n. f.* **1** unduly opening. **2** (*leg.*) tampering (with).

manoscritto[1], *n. m.* **1** manuscript, handwriting. **2** (*giorn., pubbl.*) (*da stampare*) copy.

manoscritto[2], *a.* handwritten.

manovalanza, *n. f.* unskilled labour; hodmen (*pl.*).

manovale, *n. m.* (*pers.*) unskilled worker, labourer, hodman★; laborer (*USA*).

manovra, *n. f.* **1** manoeuvre, maneuver. **2** (*fig.*) (*manipolazione, raggiro*) manipulation, move. **3** (*market.*) (*per far salire i prezzi*) rig. **4** (*trasp. ferr.*) shunting. **5** (*trasp. mar.*) handling. // ~ **al ribasso** (*Borsa*) bear raid; ~ **del credito** (*fin.*) credit maneuver; **la ~ del tasso di sconto** (*fin.*) the manipulation of the bank rate; **manovre speculative** (*fin.*) speculative manoeuvres; **manovre sulle valute** (*fin.*) currency transactions.

manovrare, *v. t.* **1** to manoeuvre, to maneuver. **2** (*fig.*) (*manipolare, raggirare*) to manipulate. **3** (*market.*) (*prezzi, ecc.*) to rig. **4**

(*trasp. ferr.*) to shunt. **5** (*trasp. mar.*) to handle. // ~ **una locomotiva** (*trasp. ferr.*) to work an engine; ~ **il mercato dei titoli** (*fin.*) to rig the stock market; ~ **una nave** (*trasp. mar.*) to handle a ship, to work a ship; ~ **i prezzi** (*market.*) to rig prices, to manipulate prices; ~ **il tasso di sconto** (*fin.*) to manipulate the Bank rate.

manovratore, *n. m.* **1** (*chi escogita espedienti*) manoeuverer. **2** (*trasp. ferr.*) signalman★, yard-man★, switchman★. // ~ **di scambi** (*trasp. ferr.*) shunter.

mansione, *n. f.* **1** (*incarico*) office; (*dovere*) duty; (*compito*) task. **2** (*pers.*) function, job. // **una** ~ **«chiave»** (*pers.*) a key job; **mansioni d'impiegato** (*pers.*) clerical duties; **le mansioni d'un ragioniere** (*pers.*) the duties of a bookkeeper; **mansioni dirigenziali** (*amm.*) management functions.

mantenere, *v. t.* **1** to maintain, to keep★. **2** (*continuare*) to keep★ up. **3** (*sostenere*) to sustain, to support. // ~ **alto il prezzo di talune merci** (*market.*) to keep up the price of certain goods; ~ **un appuntamento** to keep an appointment; ~ **un certo tenore di vita** (*econ.*) to maintain a certain standard of living; ~ **q. in carica** to continue sb. in office; ~ **un livello di tassi basso** (*fin.*) to hold rates down; ~ **la parola** to stand by one's word; ~ **la parola data** to stick to one's word; ~ **una promessa** to keep a promise; ~ **la rotta** (*trasp. mar.*) to stand on; ~ **stabili i prezzi** (*econ., market.*) to keep prices steady; **non** ~ **un appuntamento** to break an appointment; **non** ~ **la parola** to go back on (*o* upon) one's word.

mantenersi, *v. rifl.* **1** (*alimentarsi, sostentarsi*) to keep★ oneself, to maintain oneself. **2** (*market.*) (*di prezzi: rimanere a un certo livello*) to rule. // ~ **col proprio lavoro** to earn one's keeping (*o* one's living).

mantenimento, *n. m.* **1** maintenance, keeping. **2** (*sostentamento*) support. **3** (*manutenzione*) upkeep. // ~ (*da parte del rivenditore*) **del prezzo di vendita fissato dal produttore** (*market.*) price maintenance; **il** ~ **d'una promessa** the keeping (*o* fulfilment) of a promise.

manuale[1], *a.* manual.

manuale[2], *n. m.* **1** manual, handbook, treatise. **2** (*d'istruzioni, ecc.*) workbook. // ~ **d'accoglimento** (*pers.*) employees' manual; ~ **di manutenzione** (*org. az.*) maintenance handbook; ~ **d'organizzazione** (*org. az.*) organization manual; ~ **di vendita** (*org. az.*) sales manual; ~ **per la conversione di misure, pesi e valute** (*di differenti Paesi*) (*fin., trasp.*) cambist.

manufatto, *n. m.* **1** (*market.*) manufactured article, manufacture, handwork. **2 manufatti,** *pl.* (*market., anche*) manufactured goods.

manutenzione, *n. f.* **1** (*market.*) service. **2** (*org. az.*) maintenance, upkeep. // ~ **correttiva** (*org. az.*) corrective maintenance; **manutenzioni e riparazioni** (*org. az., rag.*) repairs and upkeep; ~ **ordinaria** (*org. az.*) routine maintenance.

marca, *n. f.* (*market.*) brand, brand name, mark, make. // ~ **assicurativa** (*della mutua*) (*leg.*) insurance stamp, stamp; ~ **da bollo** (*leg.*) revenue stamp, stamp; ~ **da bollo per documenti** (*leg.*) documentary stamp; ~ **di fabbrica** (*market.*) trade-mark; ~ **registrata** (*market.*) registered trade-mark; **di (ottima)** ~ first-class, first-rate (*attr.*).

marcare, *v. t.* **1** to mark, to check. **2** (*market.*) to brand, to hallmark. // « ~ **l'ora**» (*all'arrivo sul posto di lavoro*) (*pers.*) to ring in.

marcato, *a.* (*sensibile, pronunciato*) sharp, considerable, remarkable.

«marchetta», *n. f.* (*leg.*) (*della mutua*) insurance stamp, stamp.

marchiare, *v. t. V.* **marcare.**

marchio, *n. m.* **1** (*market.*) brand, brand-name, mark, make. **2** (*market., pubbl.*) (*di garanzia, d'origine, ecc. su un prodotto*) hallmark. // ~ **commerciale** commercial mark; ~ **di fabbrica** (*leg., market.*) trade-mark, trademark, stamp; ~ **(di fabbrica) non registrato** (*leg.*) unregistered trade-mark; ~ **di garanzia** (*su oro e argento*) (*market., pubbl.*) hallmark; ~ **d'origine** (*market.*) certification mark; ~ **d'una società** (*pubbl., USA*) corporate symbol; ~ **registrato** (*leg.*) registered trade-mark; **chi usa illegalmente l'altrui** ~ **di fabbrica** (*leg.*) infringer.

marco, *n. m.* (*unità monetaria tedesca*) mark.

mare, *n. m.* sea. // ~ **aperto** (*trasp. mar.*) high seas, offing; **un** ~ **di debiti** (*fig.*) a sea of debt; ~ **territoriale** (*leg., trasp. mar.*) territorial sea; **che tiene bene il** ~ (*trasp. mar.*) (*di nave*) seakeeping; **in** ~ at sea, afloat; **in** ~ **aperto** (*trasp. mar.*) off shore; **via** ~ (*trasp. mar.*) by sea; by water.

marea, *n. f.* (*trasp. mar.*) tide, water.

margine, *n. m.* **1** margin, edge. **2** (*Borsa, fin.*) cover. **3** (*econ., rag.*) margin, fringe. **4** (*fin.*) margin, range, spread. // **margini degli utili** (*econ.*) profit margins; ~ **del giorno** (*Borsa, fin.*) day's spread; ~ **del «remisier»** (*Borsa, fin.*) bid-and-ask spread; jobber's turn (*ingl.*); dealer spread (*USA*); **margini di fluttuazione delle monete** (*fin.*) fluctuation bands of currencies; **il** ~ **d'una pagina** the margin of a page; ~ **di profitto** (*aggiunto al costo per ottenere il prezzo di vendita*) (*market.*) mark-on, markup; ~ **di sicurezza** (*anche fig.*) leeway; **un ~ di tempo** a margin of time; ~ **lordo** gross margin, contribution margin, margin; **margini lordi d'utile commerciale** (*fin., rag.*) gross trading profits; ~ **rispetto al tasso base d'interesse** (*fin.*) spread.

marina, *n. f.* (*trasp. mar.*) marine, navy. // ~ **mercantile** (*trasp. mar.*) mercantile marine, merchant marine, merchant navy, merchant service, commercial marine, shipping.

marino, *a.* (*trasp. mar.*) marine, nautical; sea (*attr.*).

marittimo[1], *a.* (*trasp. mar.*) maritime, marine, naval; sea (*attr.*).

marittimo[2], *n. m.* (*trasp. mar.*) seaman★.

marketing, *n. m.* (*market.*) marketing. // ~ **di prova** (*market., pubbl.*) test marketing.

massa, *n. f.* **1** mass. **2** (*volume*) bulk, volume. **3** (*grande quantità*) large number, lot(s). // ~ **attiva** (*d'avaria generale*) (*ass. mar.*) values to be made good; ~ **creditizia** (*d'avaria generale*) (*ass. mar.*) values to be made good; ~ **debitrice** (*ass. mar.*) contributory mass, contributing values, contributing interests and values; ~ **dei creditori** (*leg.*) body of creditors; ~ **ereditaria** (*leg.*) legal assets, hereditament; **la ~ fallimentare** (*leg.*) the bankrupt's estate; ~ **passiva** (*ass. mar.*) contributory mass, contributing values, contributing interests and values; **in ~** in bulk, in the lump; (*market.*) wholesale; (*org. az.*) mass (*attr.*).

massima, *n. f.* **1** maxim, precept. **2** (*norma*) rule. // **in linea di ~** as a general rule.

massimale, *a.* maximal, maximum, highest. *n. m.* **1** limit, ceiling. **2** (*ass.*) maximum rate, line. // **un ~ d'aiuti più basso** (*econ.*) a lower ceiling on aids.

massimizzare, *v. t.* **1** (*econ.*) to maximize. **2** (*mat.*) (*una funzione, ecc.*) to maximize.

massimizzazione, *n. f.* **1** (*econ.*) maximization. **2** (*mat.*) maximization, maximation. // ~ **dei profitti** (*econ.*) profit maximation.

massimo, *a.* **1** maximum, greatest, largest, utmost. **2** (*il più alto*) highest; top, peak (*attr.*). *n. m.* **1** maximum★; peak (*fig.*). **2** (*Borsa, fin.*) high. // **massima capacità produttiva** (*di uno stabilimento, ecc.*) (*org. az.*) capacity; **il ~ comun divisore** (*mat.*) the greatest common factor; **il ~ della produttività** (*econ.*) peak productivity; **massimi e minimi** (*Borsa, fin.*) highs and lows; ~ **scoperto** (*banca, cred.*) maximum overdraft.

mastro, *n. m.* (*rag.*) ledger. // ~ **a fogli staccati** (*attr. uff.*) loose-leaf ledger; ~ **acquisti** (*rag.*) bought ledger; ~ **(dei) clienti** (*rag.*) customers' ledger; ~ **(delle) vendite** (*rag.*) debit ledger; ~ **generale** (*rag.*) general ledger; ~ **sussidiario** (*rag.*) subsidiary ledger.

matematica, *n. f.* (*mat.*) mathematics; maths (*fam.*); math (*fam., USA*). // ~ **applicata** (*mat.*) applied mathematics; ~ **superiore** (*mat.*) higher mathematics.

matematico, *a.* (*mat.*) mathematical, mathematic. *n. m.* (*mat.*) mathematician.

materia, *n. f.* **1** matter. **2** (*materiale*) material. **3** (*argomento*) subject, topic, object. **4** (*motivo*) ground, cause. // ~ **di diritto** (*leg.*) matter of law; ~ **di fatto** (*leg.*) matter of fact, matter in deed; **materie grasse** oils and fats; ~ **prima** (*econ.*) raw material, source material, commodity, staple; (*org. az.*) stock; **in ~ di legge** (*leg.*) in point of law.

materiale[1], *a.* material; (*fisico*) physical; (*manuale*) manual.

materiale[2], *n. m.* material, stuff. // ~ **da esposizione** (*market.*) exhibits (*pl.*); ~ **da imballaggio** (*o* **da imballo**) (*market.*) wrapping; ~ **d'archivio** (*attr. uff.*) file material; ~ **d'armamento** (*trasp. mar.*) equipment; **materiali di ricupero** (*ass., org. az.*) salvaged materials, salvage; ~ **diretto** (*org. az.*) direct material; ~ **grezzo** (*econ.*) raw material, staple; (*org. az.*) stock; ~ **illustrativo** (*market., pubbl.*) illustrative material, literature; ~ **per imballaggio** (*market.*) pack; ~ **postale** (*comun.*) mailing; ~ **pubblicitario** (*per pubblicità diretta*) (*pubbl.*) envelope stuffer; ~ **ricuperato** (*da un naufragio, ecc.*) (*trasp. mar.*) salvage; ~ **rotabile** (*trasp. ferr.*) rolling-stock, equipment.

matita, *n. f.* pencil. // ~ **blu** (*attr. uff.*) blue pencil; ~ **copiativa** (*attr. uff.*) copying pencil; ~ **grassa** (*attr. uff.*) greasy crayon.

matrice, *n. f.* **1** matrix★. **2** (*attr. uff.*) (*per ciclostile*) stencil. **3** (*mat.*) matrix★. **4** (*rag.*) (*di registro, libretto, ecc.*) counterfoil, stump, butt; stub (*USA*). // **la ~ d'un libretto d'assegni** (*banca*) the counterfoil of a cheque book; ~ **di ricevuta** counterfoil of receipt.

maturare, *v. i.* **1** to mature. **2** (*cred.*) to fall★ due, to be due. **3** (*fin.*) (*d'interessi*) to accrue.

maturazione, *n. f.* (*anche cred.*) maturity.

meccanico, *a.* mechanical, mechanic. *n. m.* (*pers.*) mechanic, mechanician; (*macchinista*) machinist.

meccanismo, *n. m.* (*anche fig.*) mechanism. // **meccanismi contenziosi** (*leg.*) contentious proceedings; **il ~ dei prezzi** (*econ.*) the price mechanism; **meccanismi d'intervento** (*governativo,* *ecc.*) (*econ.*) support arrangements; **meccanismi di mercato** (*econ., market.*) market mechanisms.

meccanizzare, *v. t.* to mechanize.

meccanizzazione, *n. f.* mechanization. // ~ **del lavoro d'ufficio** (*org. az.*) office mechanization.

media, *n. f.* 1 average. 2 (*mat., stat.*) mean, average. // **al disotto della** ~ below the average; **in** ~ on an average; **pari alla** ~ up to the average; **sopra la** ~ above the average; **sotto la** ~ below the average.

mediante, *prep.* by means of, through, per, via. // ~ **il pagamento d'una piccola somma** (*leg.*) in consideration of the payment of a small sum.

mediatore, *n. m.* 1 (*di liti, ecc.*) mediator. 2 (*market.*) middleman*, intermediary, broker. // ~ **di case** house-agent; ~ **di case e terreni** (*fin.*) estate agent, real agent; realtor (*USA*); ~ **di noleggi marittimi** (*trasp. mar.*) (*che cerca carichi per le navi*) ship-broker; (*che cerca navi per il carico*) chartering agent; ~ **di prodotti** produce-broker; ~ **di terreni** land agent; ~ **giurato** (*fin., leg.*) sworn broker.

mediazione, *n. f.* 1 mediation, mediatorship. 2 (*market.*) brokerage. 3 (*sind.*) mediation. // ~ **di vendita** (*market.*) selling brokerage; ~ **nella compravendita di titoli** (*Borsa*) stock-broking, stock-brokerage; ~ **pagata per aver ottenuto un prestito** (*cred.*) procuration fee, procuration money; ~ **per acquisti** (*market.*) buying brokerage.

medicina, *n. f.* medicine. // ~ **del lavoro** (*org. az., pers.*) industrial medicine; ~ **legale** (*leg.*) legal medicine, forensic medicine, medical jurisprudence; ~ **preventiva** preventive medicine.

medico, *a.* medical. *n. m.* doctor (of medicine), physician. // **un** ~ **«convenzionato»** (*ingl.*) a panel doctor; ~ **generico** general practitioner; ~ **legale** (*ass., pers.*) medical examiner.

medio, *a.* 1 middle, medium, mid. 2 (*di grandezza media*) middle-sized, medium-sized. 3 (*calcolato fra un massimo e un minimo*) mean, average. // **le medie imprese** (*fin.*) the medium-sized companies, the medium-sized enterprises; **medie industrie** (*econ.*) middle-sized industries; ~ **termine prolungato** (*cred.*) extended medium term; **a** ~ (*cred., fin.*) medium-term (*a. attr.*); **a media scadenza** (*cred., fin.*) in the medium term; medium-term (*a. attr.*); (*cred., fin.*) (*di profitti, perdite, operazioni, ecc.*) medium-term; **di media qualità** (*market.*) middling; **nel** ~ **periodo** (*cred., fin.*) in the medium term; medium-term (*a. attr.*).

mediocre, *a.* 1 ordinary, poor, second-class. 2 (*market.*) middling.

mediocredito, *n. m.* (*cred.*) medium-term credit.

membro, *n. m.* member. // ~ **aggiunto d'un comitato** assistant member of a committee; ~ **del consiglio d'amministrazione** (*d'un ente pubblico, d'una scuola, di un ospedale, ecc.*) (*amm.*) trustee; ~ **del personale** (*pers.*) staffer; ~ **della commissione interna** (*pers., sind.*) shop-steward; **i membri dell'equipaggio** (*trasp. mar.*) the members of the crew; ~ **dello staff** (*pers.*) staffer; ~ **d'una commissione** (*leg.*) commissioner; ~ **di giuria** (*leg.*) juryman, juror; **i membri d'una professione** (*collett.*) the profession (*sing.*); **essere** ~ **dell'associazione della Borsa Valori di Londra** (*Borsa, ingl.*) to be on the Stock Exchange; **essere** ~ **di qc.** to be a member of st.; **essere** ~ **di un'assemblea** (*leg.*) to sit on an assembly.

memorandum, *n. m.* 1 memorandum*. 2 (*attr. uff.*) memorandum*, memorandum book, memory book, memo book; memo (*fam.*).

memoria, *n. f.* 1 memory. 2 (*elab. elettr.*) memory, store; storage (*USA*).

meno, *avv.* 1 (*comparativo*) less; (*mat.*) minus, less. 2 (*superlativo relat.*) (*fra due*) (the) less; (*fra più di due*) (the) least. *a.* 1 (*comparativo*) (*con nome sing.*) less; (*con nome pl.*) fewer. 2 (*superlativo relat.*) (*con nome sing.*) the least; (*con nome pl.*) the fewest. *n. m. inv.* 1 (*con valore comparativo*) less; fewer (*pl.*). 2 (*con valore superlativo*) (the) least; (the) fewest (*pl.*). 3 (*mat.*) (*segno di meno*) minus, minus sign, subtraction sign. // ~ **lo sconto** (*market.*) less discount, minus discount.

mensa aziendale, *n. f.* (*org. az.*) cafeteria, canteen.

mensile, *a.* monthly. *n. m.* 1 (*giorn.*) monthly magazine, monthly. 2 (*pers.*) (*retribuzione*) monthly pay; (*salario*) monthly wages; (*stipendio*) monthly salary.

mensilità, *n. f. inv.* 1 (*market.*) (*rata, importo mensile*) monthly instalment. 2 (*pers.*) (*retribuzione mensile*) monthly pay; (*stipendio mensile*) monthly salary.

mensilmente, *avv.* monthly, every month, once a month.

mensualizzazione, *n. f.* (*pers., sind.*) (*dei salari*) mensualisation.

menzionare, *v. t.* to mention.

menzione, *n. f.* mention.

mercante, *n. m.* merchant, trader, dealer.

mercanteggiamento, *n. m.* 1 (*raro*) merchantry, commercial dealings (*pl.*). 2 (*market.*)

(*il tirare sul prezzo*) haggle, haggling, bargaining, higgling, chaffer. // ~ **sulle singole «voci»** (*sui singoli prodotti*) (*econ.*) item-by-item haggling.

mercanteggiare, *v. i.* **1** (*raro*) to deal★ (in). **2** (*market.*) to haggle, to higgle, to bargain, to chaffer, to negotiate.

mercantile, *a.* mercantile, commercial; merchant, trading (*attr.*). *n. m.* (*trasp. mar.*) merchant ship, trading vessel, merchantman★.

mercantilismo, *n. m.* (*econ.*) mercantilism, mercantile system, commercialism.

mercantilista, *a.* (*econ.*) mercantilistic. *n. m.* e *f.* (*econ.*) mercantilist.

mercantilistico, *a.* (*econ.*) mercantilistic.

mercanzia, *n. f.* (*market.*) merchandise.

mercatino, *n. m.* (*Borsa, fam.*) (*Borsa non ufficiale*) street market (*a Londra*); coulisse (*a Parigi*); curb market, curb (*a New York*).

mercato, *n. m.* market; (*il luogo, anche*) market-place. // ~ **a contanti** (*fin.*) cash market; (*market.*) spot market; ~ **a lunga** (*Borsa*) funded debt; ~ **a pronti** (*fin.*) spot market; ~ **a termine** (*Borsa, fin.*) time bargain, settlement bargain, forward market, futures market, option market; ~ **a termine delle valute** (*fin.*) forward exchange market; ~ **al rialzo** (*econ.*) sellers' market, rising market; ~ **al ribasso** (*econ.*) buyers' market; ~ **all'ingrosso** (*market.*) wholesale market; ~ **aperto** (*fin.*) open market; **un** ~ **attivo** (*econ.*) an active market; ~ **azionario** (*fin.*) stock market, share market; **il** ~ **azionario non ufficiale** (*Borsa, fin.*) the off-board market for securities; **il** ~ **Comune allargato** the enlarged Common Market; **il** ~ **Comune Europeo** the European Common Market; **il** ~ **cotoniero** (*market.*) the cotton market; ~ **creditizio interno** (*fin.*) domestic credit market; ~ **degli sconti** (*fin.*) discount market; ~ **dei capitali** (*fin.*) capital market; ~ **dei cereali** (*market.*) corn market; ~ **dei noli** (*trasp. mar.*) freight market, charter market, chartering market; **il** ~ **dei prodotti** (*specialm. agricoli*) (*econ.*) the produce market; ~ **dei prodotti di base** commodity market; ~ **dei titoli finanziari** (*fin.*) stock market; **il** ~ **dei trasporti** (*econ.*) the transport market; ~ **del bestiame** cattle market; ~ **del lavoro** (*econ., sind.*) labour market, job market; ~ **del reddito fisso** (*fin.*) fixed-interest market; **il** ~ **dell'emissione di nuovo capitale** (*fin.*) the new issue market; ~ **della lira interbancaria** (*fin.*) interbank lira market; ~ **delle emissioni** (*fin.*) issue market; ~ **delle euro-obbligazioni** (*fin.*) Euro-bond market; ~ **delle materie prime** commodity market; ~ **delle valute** (*fin.*) foreign-exchange market; ~ **dell'acquirente** (*econ.*) buyers' market; **il** ~ **dell'eurodollaro** (*fin.*) the eurodollar market; ~ **di libera concorrenza** (*econ.*) free market; **i mercati d'oltremare** (*comm. est.*) the overseas markets; ~ **di prova** (*market., stat.*) test market; ~ **disponibile** (*fin.*) spot market; **i mercati esteri** (*comm. est.*) the foreign markets, the overseas markets; ~ **euromonetario** (*fin.*) Eurocurrency market, new money market; **il** ~ **europeo dei capitali** (*fin.*) the European capital market; ~ **favorevole agli acquisti** (*econ.*) buyers' market; ~ **favorevole alle vendite** (*market.*) sellers' market; **un** ~ **fiacco** (*market.*) a dull market, a narrow market; ~ **finanziario** (*fin.*) financial market, capital market; ~ **«grigio»** (*econ.*) (*situazione simile a quella del mercato nero, ma non altrettanto apertamente illegale*) grey market; **il** ~ **immobiliare** (*fin.*) the real-estate market; **un** ~ **inerte** (*econ.*) a sluggish market; ~ **interno** (*econ.*) home market; ~ **ipotecario** (*fin.*) mortgage market; ~ **libero** (*fin.*) open market; ~ **libero e aperto** (*fin.*) free and open market; ~ **marittimo** (*trasp. mar.*) shipping market; **il** ~ **mobiliare** (*fin.*) the securities market; ~ **monetario** (*Borsa, fin.*) money market; ~ **nazionale** (*econ.*) home market; ~ **nero** (*econ.*) black market; **il** ~ **petrolifero** (*fin.*) the oil market; **il** ~ **potenziale** (*market.*) the potential market; ~ **ristretto** (*fin., market.*) thin market, over-the-counter market; **un** ~ **soggetto a forti oscillazioni** (*dei prezzi*) (*econ.*) a volatile market; **un** ~ **sostenuto** (*fin.*) a firm market, a steady market; **un** ~ **stagnante** (*econ.*) a stagnant market; ~ **unico** (*econ.*) single market; **un** ~ **unico per i prodotti agricoli** a single market for agricultural products; **chi compra al** ~ (*market.*) marketer; **chi vende al** ~ (*market.*) marketer, marketeer; **sui mercati stranieri** (*comm. est.*) abroad; **sul** ~ **interno** (*market.*) at home.

merce, *n. f.* goods (*pl.*); commodity, merchandise; ware (*collett., specialm. nei composti; o USA*). // ~ **a cubatura** (*trasp. mar.*) measurement goods, measurement cargo; measurement freight (*USA*); ~ **a domanda costante** (*indipendentemente dalle fluttuazioni economiche*) (*market.*) staple; **merci avariate** damaged goods; ~ **che sembra in ordine e in buone condizioni** (*market.*) goods in apparent good order and condition; ~ **da carico** (*trasp. mar.*) shipper (*USA*); ~ **data in pegno** (*comm.*) goods lying in pledge; **merci deperibili** (*market.*) perishable goods, perishable products, perishables; ~ **di**

(buona) qualità (*market.*) name merchandise; ~ **di cabotaggio** (*trasp. mar.*) coasting cargo; ~ **di contrabbando** contraband goods, smuggled goods; ~ **d'esportazione** (*comm. est.*) export goods, export, exportation; ~ **d'importazione** (*comm. est.*) import goods, import, importation; ~ **d'occasione** (*market.*) bargain lot; **merci di prima necessità** (*econ.*) staple commodities; ~ **di prima scelta** (*market.*) choice goods; ~ **di prim'ordine** (*market.*) high-class goods; ~ **di qualità inferiore** (*market.*) low-class goods; **merci di qualità inferiore a quella normale** (*generalm. vendute senza marca e con forti sconti*) (*market.*) irregulars; ~ **di scarto** (*market.*) rubbish; **merci di seconda qualità** (*market.*) middling goods, seconds; ~ **di transito** (*comm. est.*) transit goods, in-transit goods; **merci d'uso durevole** (*market.*) hard goods; **merci difettose** (*market.*) defective goods, irregulars; ~ **durevole** (*market.*) hard merchandise; **merci esenti da dogana** (*dog.*) free commodities; **merci esportate temporaneamente** (*comm. est.*) temporary exports; **merci flottanti** (*trasp.*) goods afloat; ~ **franca di dazio** (*dog., fin.*) duty-free goods, free goods; ~ **immagazzinata a terra** (*trasp. mar.*) goods stored ashore; ~ **in deposito** (*market.*) goods in consignment; ~ **in deposito nei magazzini doganali** (*dog.*) bonded goods; **merci in dogana** (*dog.*) goods lying in customs; ~ **in magazzino** (*org. az.*) goods in stock, goods on hand, stock-in-trade, stock, inventory; ~ **in transito** (*comm. est.*) goods for temporary admission; ~ **invendibile** (*market.*) unmerchantable goods; ~ **(inviata) in conto deposito** (*market.*) consignment; **merci liquide** wet goods; **merci non deperibili** (*market.*) non-perishable goods; **merci per consumo** (*o* **per uso**) **interno** (*dog.*) goods for home use; **merci pericolose** (*trasp.*) dangerous goods; **merci pesanti** (*market.*) heavy goods, weight goods; (*trasp. aer., trasp. mar.*) weight cargo; **merci pregiate** (*market.*) *V.* **merci preziose; merci preziose** (*market.*) valuable goods, valued goods, value goods, valuable articles, valuables; ~ **pronta per consegna immediata** (*market.*) spot goods, prompt goods; ~ **reimportata** (*comm. est.*) reimportation, reimport; ~ **riesportata** (*comm. est.*) re-exportation, re-export; ~ **sbarcata** (*trasp. mar.*) unload; ~ **scaricata** (*trasp. mar.*) unload; ~ **scelta** (*market.*) choice goods; ~ **schiava di dazio** (*dog.*) goods in bond; ~ **soggetta a dazio** (*dog., fin.*) dutiable goods; **merci solide** dry goods; ~ **spedita** (*market.*) consignment, shipment; (*trasp. mar.*) shipper; **merci trasportate** (*trasp. ferr.*) train-load; **merci trasportate via mare** (*trasp. mar.*) sea-borne goods; ~ **(venduta) a contanti** (*market.*) spots; ~ **(venduta) sottocosto** (*market.*) distress goods; **chi invia** ~ **in conto deposito** (*market.*) consigner.

«merchant banking», *locuz. n.* (*fin., ingl.*) merchant banking.

mercificazione, *n. f.* commoditization.

mercuriale, *n. m.* (*econ.*) market-report, market-list, prices account.

mesata, *n. f.* **1** (*mese*) month. **2** (*pers.*) (*paga d'un mese*) monthly allowance, monthly pay; (*salario*) monthly wages; (*stipendio*) monthly salary.

mescolare, *v. t.* **1** to mix, to merge, to shake★ up. **2** (*market.*) to blend.

mescolatura, *n. f.* **1** mixing, merging. **2** (*market.*) blending.

mese, *n. m.* **1** month. **2** (*pers.*) (*mesata*) monthly allowance, monthly pay. // **il** ~ **corrente** the current month, the present month; **un** ~ **«morto»** (*in cui non si fanno affari*) (*market.*) a slow month; **il** ~ **passato** (*o* **scorso**) last month; **il** ~ **prossimo** (*o* **venturo**) next month; (*fin.*) next; ~ **solare** calendar month; **a un** ~ (*cred.*) (*di pagamento, ecc.*) within a month; **agli ultimi del** ~ late in the month; **ai primi del** ~ early in the month; **al** ~ (*mensilmente*) monthly; **del** ~ **scorso** (*comm.*) ultimo (*abbr.* ult.); **del** ~ **venturo** (*comm.*) proximo (*abbr.* prox.); **di** ~ **in** ~ month after month, month by month; **ogni** ~ monthly; **ogni due mesi** bimonthly.

messa, *n. f.* (*azione del mettere*) putting, laying. // ~ **a bordo** (*trasp. mar.*) loading aboard; ~ **in cantiere** (*d'una nave*) (*trasp. mar.*) laying-down; ~ **in disarmo** (*d'una nave*) (*trasp. mar.*) lay-up; ~ **in liquidazione** (*cred., fin.*) liquidation; ~ **in opera** (*d'un impianto*) (*org. az.*) installation; ~ **in stato d'accusa** (*leg.*) indictment, impeachment.

messaggeria, *n. f.* **1** (*trasp.*) parcel post. **2** **messaggerie,** *pl.* (*trasp.*) transport company.

messaggero, *n. m.* **1** messenger. **2** (*trasp.*) (*addetto al servizio di messaggeria*) carrier.

messaggio, *n. m.* (*comun.*) message, dispatch. // ~ **trasmesso a mezzo telex** (*comun.*) telex; **messaggi urgenti** (*comun.*) urgent messages.

mestiere, *n. m.* **1** trade, handicraft, craft, vocation. **2** (*professione*) profession. **3** (*impiego*) job. **4** (*lavoro*) work. // « ~ **o professione: falegname**» (*su un modulo*) «vocation: joiner»; **mestieri pericolosi** (*pers.*) dangerous trades, dangerous occupations; **di** ~ (*professionale*) professional, vocational.

meta, *n. f.* 1 (*destinazione*) destination. 2 (*traguardo*) goal, target (*anche fig.*).

metà, *n. f. inv.* 1 half★. 2 (*punto medio*) middle; mid (*attr.*). // **a ~ prezzo** (*market.*) half(-)price; **fare a ~ di qc. con q.** to go halves (*o* fifty-fifty) with sb. in st., to split the difference with sb.

metallico, *a.* metallic.

metallo, *n. m.* metal. // **metalli preziosi** precious metals; **metalli vili** base metals.

metallurgia, *n. f.* (*econ.*) metallurgy, metalworking.

metallurgico, *a.* (*econ.*) metallurgic, metallurgical. *n. m.* (*pers.*) metalworker.

metodo, *n. m.* 1 method; (*sistema*) system; (*tecnica*) technique. 2 (*fin.*) (*specialm. di reperire fondi*) ways and means. 3 (*org. az.*) (*di lavorazione*) process. // **~ amburghese** (*per il calcolo degli interessi dei conti correnti fruttiferi*) (*rag.*) balance method; **~ del calcolo della convenienza economica** (*econ.*) comparative cost method; **~ del sopralluogo** (*market.*) observational method; **~ della partita doppia** (*rag.*) double-entry system; **~ della valutazione, in termini d'interessi, del reddito futuro scontato al valore attuale** (*per determinare la convenienza di un investimento*) (*fin., rag.*) discounted-cash-flow method; **~ dell'esperimento** (*market.*) experimental method; **~ (d'ammortamento) a quote costanti** (*rag.*) straight-line method; **~ di classificazione del lavoro** (*org. az.*) job-classification method; **metodi di duplicazione e riproduzione** (*attr. uff.*) duplicating and copying methods; **~ d'imballaggio** (*market.*) method of packing, pack; **~ d'indagine telefonica per il calcolo degli indici di gradimento** (*dei programmi radiotelevisivi*) (*pubbl.*) coincidental telephone method; **metodi di lavorazione** (*org. az.*) processing techniques; **un ~ di produzione antieconomico** (*econ.*) an uneconomic method of production; **~ di valutazione dei danni** (*ass., leg.*) measure of damage; **~ indiretto** (*usato per il calcolo degli interessi dei conti correnti fruttiferi*) (*rag.*) backward method; **~ retrogrado** (*usato per il calcolo degli interessi dei conti correnti fruttiferi*) (*rag.*) backward method.

metodologia, *n. f.* 1 methodology. 2 (*metodo*) method.

metodologico, *a.* methodological.

metrico, *a.* metric, metrical.

metro, *n. m.* metre; meter (*USA*). // **~ cubo** cubic metre; **~ di valutazione** unit of value, yardstick (*fig.*); **~ lineare** running metre; **~ quadrato** square metre.

metropoli, *n. f. inv.* metropolis★.

metropolitana, *n. f.* (*trasp. ferr.*) underground railway, underground; subway (*USA*). // **chi si serve della ~** (*trasp. ferr.*) undergrounder.

metropolitano, *a.* metropolitan. *n. m.* (*guardia urbana*) policeman★.

mettere, *v. t.* 1 to put★; (*porre*) to set★; (*in posizione orizzontale*) to lay★; (*in posizione verticale*) to stand★; (*collocare*) to place. 2 (*impiegare*) to take★. // **~ qc. a disposizione di q.** to make st. available to sb.; **~ a libro** (*rag.*) to book; **~ a riposo** (*amm., pers.*) to retire; **~ a verbale** (*leg.*) to record; **~ q. al corrente di qc.** to acquaint sb. with st.; **~ al lavoro** (*pers.*) to set on; **~ al passivo** (*rag.*) to charge; **~ all'asta qc.** to put st. up for auction; **~ q. alla porta** to show sb. the door; (*pers.*) (*licenziarlo*) to turn sb. out; **~ alla prova** to test; **~ qc. all'incanto** to put st. up for auction; **~** (*un argomento, ecc.*) **all'ordine del giorno** (*org. az.*) to table; **~ annunci su un giornale** (*pubbl.*) to put advertisements in a paper; **~ un annuncio nella rubrica degli oggetti smarriti** to advertise in the lost-and-found column; **~ capitali a riporto** (*Borsa*) to lend money on contango; **~ il cartellino** (*del prezzo*) **a un articolo** (*market.*) to mark an article; **~ da parte** (*risparmiare*) to put aside, to put away; (*porre in disparte*) to lay aside, to lay by, to set aside, to hold over; (*per un particolare scopo*) to earmark; (*trascurare, rimandare*) to put by, to shelve; **~ da parte denaro** to lay aside money, to put by money; to salt down money, to salt away money (*fam.*); **~ l'embargo su** (*navi, merci*) (*leg., trasp. mar.*) to embargo; **~ l'embargo su una nave** (*leg., trasp. mar.*) to lay the embargo on a ship, to put an embargo on a ship; **~ un'etichetta a** (*market.*) to label; **~ il fermo su** (*beni, ecc.*) (*leg.*) to garnishee; **~ il fermo su un assegno** (*banca*) to stop a cheque; **~ in bacino una nave** (*trasp. mar.*) to dock a ship; **~ in banca** (*depositare*) to bank; **~ in bilancio** (*fin., rag.*) to budget; **~ in cantiere** (*una nave*) (*trasp. mar.*) to lay down; **~** (*denaro*) **in cassa** (*market.*) to till; **~ in casse** (*market.*) to pack; **~ in catalogo** (*market.*) to catalogue; **~ in cifra** (*un messaggio*) (*comun.*) to code; **~ in circolazione** (*giorn.*) to issue; **~ in colonna** (*giorn.*) to make up; **~ in comune** (*fondi, risorse, ecc.*) (*fin.*) to pool; **~ in comune i proventi doganali** (*comm. est.*) to pool the revenue from custom duties; **~ in comunicazione** (*al telefono*) (*comun.*) to connect, to put through; **~ q. in congedo** (*pers.*) to grant a leave (of absence) to sb.; **~ in contatto gli interessati** to bring the interested parties together; **~ in conto**

(*far pagare*) to charge; (*rag.*) to carry to account, to bring into account; ~ **q. in difficoltà economiche** to squeeze sb. (*fig.*); ~ **in disarmo una nave** (*trasp. mar.*) to lay up a ship; ~ **in discussione** to dispute; ~ **in esecuzione un disegno** to execute a plan; ~ **in esecuzione una legge** (*leg.*) to execute a law; ~ **in evidenza** to point out, to underline; (*giorn.*) (*una notizia, ecc.*) to feature, to highlight; ~ **in guardia** to warn; ~ **in linea** (*comun.*) to connect; ~ **in liquidazione** (*cred., fin.*) to liquidate; ~ **in liquidazione i beni di q.** (*che è fallito*) (*leg.*) to sell sb. up; ~ **in liquidazione una società** (*fin.*) to put a company into liquidation; ~ (*articoli, ecc.*) **in listino** (*market.*) to list; ~ **in macchina** (*giorn.*) to impose; ~ **in magazzino** (*org. az.*) to store; ~ (*merci*) **in magazzino doganale** (*dog.*) to warehouse; ~ **in mare una nave** (*trasp. mar.*) to launch a ship; ~ **in mostra** (*merce e sim.*) to show, to set out; ~ **in ordine** to order; ~ **in ordine i propri affari** to set one's affairs in order; ~ **q. in pensione** (*pers.*) to retire sb., to cause sb. to retire, to superannuate sb.; ~ **in pericolo** to endanger, to jeopardize; ~ (*una notizia, ecc.*) **in prima pagina** (*giorn.*) to front-page; ~ **in programma** to programme; to program (*USA*); to schedule; ~ **in sacchi** (*market.*) to sack; ~ **in scatola** (*market.*) to box, to pack; ~ (*generi alimentari*) **in scatola** (*di latta*) (*market.*) to tin; to can (*USA*); ~ **in stato d'accusa** (*leg.*) to indict, to impeach; ~ **in vendita** (*market.*) to put up for sale, to market; ~ **in vendita merce** (*o* **merci**) (*market.*) to offer goods on sale; ~ **in vigore** (*leg.*) to bring into force; ~ **una nuova etichetta a qc.** (*market.*) to relabel st.; ~ **ordine nei propri affari** to put one's affairs in order; ~ **per iscritto** to commit to writing; ~ **sotto sequestro** (*leg.*) to sequestrate, to sequester, to seize; ~ **su un negozio** (*market.*) to set up a shop; ~ **il visto su** (*un passaporto e sim.*) (*tur.*) to visa; **esser messo in cassa integrazione** (*sind., ingl.*) (*di dipendente*) to be made redundant; **esser messo in liquidazione** (*fin.*) (*di società, di ente*) to wind up; **esser messo in stato d'arresto** (*leg.*) to be put (*o* placed) under arrest.

mettersi, *v. rifl.* **1** to put★ oneself, to set★ oneself, to place oneself. **2** (*cominciare*) to start, to begin★; to set★ to (st.); to set★ about (doing st.). // ~ **al coperto tramite ricompera** (*Borsa*) to cover oneself by buying back; ~ **al riparo da** (*rischi di perdite finanziarie*) (*fin.*) to hedge; ~ **d'accordo** to come to an agreement, to come to terms, to close with an arrangement, to agree; ~ **in affari** to go into business, to engage in business; ~ **in commercio** to go into business; ~ **in contatto con q.** to get in touch with sb., to contact sb., to liaise with sb.; ~ **in contatto con q. per telefono** (*comun.*) to reach sb. by phone; ~ **in liquidazione** (*fin.*) to go into liquidation; ~ **in relazione con q.** to enter into relation with sb.; ~ **in sciopero** (*sind.*) to go on strike, to go out (on strike); ~ **in società con q.** to go into partnership with sb.; ~ **in tasca** (*anche fig.*) to pocket; ~ **insieme** (*fin.*) (*d'imprese, ecc.*) to pool.

mezzadria, *n. f.* (*econ.*) métayage, métayer system; sharecropping (*USA*).

mezzadro, *n. m.* (*econ.*) métayer; sharecropper (*USA*).

mezzo[1], *a.* **1** (*metà dell'intero*) half, semi-. **2** (*medio*) middle, mean, mid. // **mezza commissione** (*compenso generalm. spettante al remissore*) (*Borsa*) half-commission; ~ **dollaro** half a dollar; half-dollar, half (*USA*); **mezz'e** ~ half-and-half; **mezza festa** (*pers., sind.*) half-holiday; **mezza libbra** half a pound; ~ **per cento** half per cent; **mezza provvigione** (*Borsa*) *V.* **mezza commissione; a mezza paga** (*pers.*) on half pay.

mezzo[2], *n. m.* **1** (*metà*) half★. **2** (*espediente, strumento a un fine*) means (*sing.* o *pl.*); (*modo*) way; (*strumento*) instrument; lever (*fig.*). **3 mezzi,** *pl.* (*denaro*) means. // **mezzi audiovisivi** (*pubbl.*) audio-visual means; **un** ~ **di comunicazione** (*comun.*) a medium of communication; **mezzi di comunicazione di massa** (*giorn., pubbl.*) mass communication media, mass media; **mezzi d'informazione** (*giorn.*) information methods; ~ **di prova** (*leg.*) piece of evidence, element of proof; **mezzi di salvataggio** (*trasp. mar.*) salvage gear (*sing.*); **un** ~ **di scambio** (*econ.*) a medium of exchange, a medium; ~ **di sostentamento** (*econ.*) dependence; **mezzi di sussistenza** (*econ.*) subsistence, living (*sing.*); bread and butter (*fig.*); ~ **di trasporto** (*trasp.*) means of conveyance, means of transportation; vehicle; **mezzi di trasporto** (*trasp.*) transportation facilities; transportation, conveyance (*sing.*); **mezzi di trasporto per via d'acqua** (*trasp., trasp. mar.*) water carriage; **mezzi finanziari** (*fin.*) financial resources; pocket (*fam.*); **mezzi propri** (*econ., fin.*) capital and reserves; **mezzi pubblicitari** (*pubbl.*) advertising media, media; **mezzi tecnici di informazione** (*pubbl.*) media; **a** ~ **ferrovia** (*trasp. ferr.*) by rail; **a** ~ **posta** by mail; **per** ~ **di** by means of, by, through; **per** ~ **di ciò** (*leg.*) hereby.

mezzogiorno, *n. m.* **1** midday, noon. **2** (*le dodici*) twelve o'clock, twelve o'clock noon. // **dopo** ~ (*nel pomeriggio*) in the afternoon; (*nell'indicazione dell'ora*) post meridiem

(*P.M.*); **prima di** ~ (*nella mattinata*) in the morning; (*nell'indicazione dell'ora*) ante meridiem (*A.M.*).

microeconomia, *n. f.* (*econ.*) microeconomics.

microfilm, *n. m.* (*pubbl.*) microfilm.

miglio, *n. m.* (*trasp.*) mile. // ~ **geografico** geographical mile; ~ **marino** (*o* **marittimo,** *o* **nautico**) (*unità di misura pari a 1.853 metri*) (*trasp. mar.*) nautical mile, sea mile; ~ **terrestre** (*misura di lunghezza pari a 1.609 metri*) mile; ~ **ufficiale** (*pari a 1.609 metri*) statute mile.

miglioramento, *n. m.* improvement, betterment, bettering. // ~ **contabile** (*rag.*) improvement in bookkeeping terms; **un** ~ **del tenore di vita** (*econ.*) an upturn in the standard of living; ~ **fondiario** (*econ.*) land improvement; **essere in via di** ~ (*fin., market.*) to be on the up grade.

migliorare, *v. t.* to improve, to better; (*perfezionare*) to perfect. *v. i.* to improve, to make* improvements, to go* better, to get* better; to look up (*fig.*). // ~ **le condizioni d'un'emissione di titoli** (*per facilitarne il collocamento*) (*fin.*) to sweeten an issue of stock; ~ **i prezzi offerti** (*market.*) to improve on the prices offered; ~ **la qualità di** (*un prodotto*) (*market.*) to upgrade.

migliore, *a.* **1** (*comparativo*) better. **2** (*superlativo relat.*) (the) best. // **al** ~ **offerente** to the highest bidder; **della** ~ **qualità** (*fin.*) (*di titoli, ecc.*) gilt-edged (*o* gilt-edge) (*fig.*).

miglioria, *n. f.* **1** betterment, improvement. **2** (*bonifica*) reclamation.

miliardario, *n. m.* multi-millionaire; billionaire (*USA*).

miliardo, *n. m.* milliard, one thousand millions (*ingl.*); billion (*USA*).

milione, *n. m.* million.

militante, *a.* militant, warring. *n. m.* e *f.* militant. // **un** ~ **d'un sindacato** (*sind.*) a trade-union militant.

militare, *v. i.* (*anche fig.*) to militate. // **il** ~ **in un sindacato** (*sind.*) trade-union militancy, union militancy; **chi milita nelle file d'un sindacato** (*sind.*) union militant.

millantato credito, *n. m.* (*leg.*) false pretences.

mille, *num. card.* thousand. // **per** ~ **(‰)** per thousand (‰).

millesimo, *num. ord.* thousandth. *n. m.* **1** thousandth, millesimal. **2** (*data*) date. // ~ **di dollaro** (*unità monetaria usata nei calcoli*) (*fin., USA*) mill.

milligrammo, *n. m.* milligramme, milligram.

millilitro, *n. m.* millilitre; milliliter (*USA*).

millimetro, *n. m.* millimetre; millimeter (*USA*).

mini(-), *pref.* mini(-). // ~ **-convertibilità** (*fin.*) mini-convertibility.

miniera, *n. f.* (*anche fig.*) mine. // ~ **di carbone** coal-mine, coal-pit, colliery, pit; **una** ~ **di notizie** a mine of information.

minimo, *a. superlativo* **1** (*più piccolo*) least, smallest, slightest. **2** (*più basso*) lowest; minimum (*attr.*); (*di prezzo, anche*) knockdown (*attr.*). **3** (*piccolissimo*) very small, very little. **4** (*bassissimo*) very low. *n. m.* **1** minimum*, (the) least. **2** (*Borsa, fin.*) low. **3** (*fin., market.*) floor. // ~ **comune denominatore** (*mat.*) least common denominator, lowest common denominator; ~ **comune multiplo** (*mat.*) least common multiple, lowest common multiple; **il** ~ **della paga** (*pers.*) the minimum pay; **il** ~ **della pena** (*leg.*) the minimum penalty; **il** ~ **tasso di sconto** (*fin.*) the finest rate of discount; ~ **vitale** (*econ.*) bare subsistence level, subsistence.

ministeriale, *a.* ministerial.

ministero, *n. m.* **1** (*funzione*) function(s). **2** (*complesso di Ministri*) ministry; (*Gabinetto*) Cabinet; (*Governo*) Government. **3** (*una delle amministrazioni centrali dello Stato*) ministry, board, office; department (*USA*). // ~ **degli Affari Esteri** Ministry of Foreign Affairs (*in Italia, ecc.*); Foreign Office (*in G.B.*); Department of State (*in U.S.A.*); ~ **degli Esteri** *V.* ~ **degli Affari Esteri;** ~ **degli Interni** Ministry of the Interior (*in Italia*); Home Office (*in G.B.*); Department of the Interior (*in U.S.A.*); ~ **del Bilancio** Ministry of the Budget (*in Italia*); ~ **del Bilancio e della Programmazione** Ministry of Budget and Programming (*in Italia*); ~ **del Commercio** Ministry of Commerce (*in Italia*); Board of Trade (*in G.B.*); Department of Commerce (*in U.S.A.*); ~ **del Commercio Estero** Ministry of Foreign Trade (*in Italia*); ~ **del Lavoro e della Sicurezza Sociale** Ministry of Labour and Social Security (*in Italia*); ~ **del Tesoro** Ministry of the Treasury (*in Italia*); Treasury (*in G.B.*); Department of the Treasury (*in U.S.A.*); ~ **del Turismo** Ministry of Tourism; ~ **dell'Agricoltura e delle Foreste** Ministry of Agriculture and Forestry; ~ **dell'Industria e del Commercio** Ministry of Industry and Commerce; ~ **della Marina Mercantile** Ministry of Merchant Marine; ~ **delle Finanze** Ministry of Finance (*in Italia*); ~ **delle Partecipazioni Statali** Ministry of State Participations in Industry (*in Italia*); ~ **delle Poste e Telecomunicazioni** Ministry of Post and Telecommunications (*in

Italia); Post Office (*in G.B.*); Post Office Department (*in U.S.A.*); ~ **per la Cassa del Mezzogiorno** Ministry of Special Action in the Mezzogiorno and Central-North Depressed Areas (*in Italia*).

ministro, *n. m.* minister; secretary (of State). // ~ **degli Esteri** Minister for Foreign Affairs (*in Italia, ecc.*); Foreign Secretary (*in G.B.*); Secretary of State (*in U.S.A.*); ~ **del Bilancio** Minister of the Budget (*in Italia*); ~ **del Tesoro** Minister of the Treasury (*in Italia*); Chancellor of the Exchequer (*in G.B.*); Secretary of the Treasury (*in U.S.A.*); ~ **delle Finanze** Minister of Finance (*in Italia*); ~ **dell'Interno** Minister of the Interior (*in Italia*); Home Secretary (*in G.B.*); Secretary of State for the Interior (*in U.S.A.*); **Primo** ~ Prime Minister; (*in G.B., anche*) Premier.

minoranza, *n. f.* minority.

minore, *a.* **1** (*più piccolo*) (*comparativo*) smaller; less, lesser (*attr.*); (*superlativo relat.*) (*fra due*) the smaller; (*fra più di due*) the smallest; (*meno importante*) minor. **2** (*più basso*) (*comparativo*) lower; (*superlativo relat.*) (*tra due*) the lower; (*fra più di due*) the lowest. *n. m.* **1** (*d'età, grado, ecc.*) junior. **2** (*leg.*) minor. // ~ **età** (*leg.*) minority; **al** ~ **prezzo** (*market.*) at the lowest (*o* cheapest) price.

minorenne, *a.* (*leg.*) under (full) age. *n. m.* e *f.* (*leg.*) minor, infant; pupil (*scozz.*). // **essere** ~ (*leg.*) to be under-age.

minorile, *a.* (*leg.*) juvenile.

minorità, *n. f. inv.* (*leg.*) minority, non-age.

minuta, *n. f.* minute, draft; (*brutta copia*) foul copy, rough copy, rough draft. // **la** ~ **d'una lettera** the draft of a letter.

minuto, *a.* **1** minute; (*molto piccolo*) (very) small, (very) little. **2** (*particolareggiato*) minute, detailed. *n. m.* minute. // ~ **primo** minute; ~ **secondo** second; **al** ~ (*market.*) by retail, retail.

miracolo, *n. m.* miracle. // ~ **economico** (*econ.*) economic miracle.

miscela, *n. f.* mixture; (*di caffè, tabacco, ecc.*) blend, blending.

miscelare, *v. t.* to mix; (*caffè, tabacco, ecc.*) to blend.

misto, *a.* **1** mixed, mingled. **2** (*market.*) miscellaneous. *n. m.* mixture, compound.

misura, *n. f.* **1** measure, measurement; (*dimensione, taglia*) size. **2** (*provvedimento*) measure, provision, step. // **misure anticongiunturali** (*econ.*) anti-recession measures; **misure correttive** corrective measures; **misure deflazionistiche** (*econ.*) deflationary measures; ~ **della produttività** (*org. az.*) productivity measurement; **misure di sostegno dei prezzi** (*econ.*) measures taken to support prices; **misure illecite** (*leg.*) unlawful measures; ~ **per cereali** (*market.*) dry measure; ~ **per merci solide** (*market.*) dry measure; **misure protezionistiche** (*econ.*) protectionist measures; **misure punitive** (*leg.*) punitive measures; **misure restrittive** restrictive measures; **misure sanitarie** (*org. az.*) sanitary measures.

misurabile, *a.* measurable, mensurable.

misurare, *v. t.* **1** to measure, to measure out (*o* off); (*un terreno*) to survey. **2** (*valutare*) to evaluate, to estimate; (*calcolare*) to calculate. **3** (*limitare*) to limit, to ration. *v. i.* to measure. // ~ **l'indice d'ascolto** (*radiofonico o televisivo*) **di** (*q. o qc.*) (*pubbl.*) to rate.

misuratore, *n. m.* **1** (*chi misura*) measurer; (*di terreni*) land surveyor. **2** (*strumento*) meter.

misurazione, *n. f.* measurement, measuring; (*di terreni*) surveying.

mite, *a.* mild; (*moderato*) moderate.

mittente, *n. m.* e *f.* **1** (*comun.*) sender. **2** (*trasp.*) (*di merce*) consigner, consignor, forwarder.

mobile, *a.* (*che si può muovere*) movable, moveable; (*che si muove facilmente*) mobile, moving. *n. m.* **1** piece of furniture. **2 mobili,** *pl.* furniture (*sing.*). **3 mobili,** *pl.* (*econ.*) movable goods, movables. // ~ **a scomparti per schedario** (*attr. uff.*) filing cabinet; **mobili e arredi** (*org. az.*) furniture and fittings, furnishings; **mobili per ufficio** (*attr. uff.*) office furniture.

mobilia, *n. f.* **1** furniture. **2** (*market.*) furnishings.

mobiliare, *a.* (*leg., rag.*) movable, personal.

mobilio, *n. m.* *V.* **mobilia.**

mobilità, *n. f. inv.* mobility, movability, movableness. // **la** ~ **del lavoro** (*econ., pers.*) the mobility of labour, the fluidity of labour; **la** ~ **della manodopera** (*econ., pers.*) the mobility of labour, the labour turnover; ~ **geografica** (*econ.*) ability to change domicile; **la** ~ **professionale** (*econ., pers.*) the mobility of workers, the ability to change occupation; ~ **sociale** (*econ.*) social mobility.

mobilitare, *v. t.* to mobilize. // ~ **il capitale** (*econ.*) to mobilize capital.

mobilizzare, *v. t.* (*fin.*) to mobilize.

mobilizzazione, *n. f.* (*fin.*) mobilization. // **la** ~ **della ricchezza** (*fin.*) the mobilization of wealth.

moda, *n. f.* (*market.*) fashion, vogue; thing, go (*fam.*). // **alla** ~ (*market.*) in fashion, in vogue (*avv.*); popular, up-to-date (*a.*); todayish (*fam.*); **all'ultima** ~ (*market.*) in the latest fashion (*o* style); **di** ~ (*market.*) in fashion, in vogue (*avv.*); popular, up-to-date (*a.*); new-day (*attr.*); **essere di ~** (*market.*) to be «in», to be all the rage; **essere fuori ~** (*market.*) to be out of fashion, to be unfashionable, to be «out».

modalità, *n. f. inv.* **1** formality. **2** (*modo, maniera*) way, manner. **3 modalità,** *pl.* means. // **modalità d'applicazione delle norme di un regolamento** (*leg.*) arrangements for implementing regulations.

modellare, *v. t.* **1** to model, to fashion, to pattern. **2** (*pubbl.*) to design; to style (*USA*).

modellista, *n. m.* e *f.* **1** model-maker, pattern-maker. **2** (*pubbl.*) designer; stylist (*USA*).

modello, *n. m.* **1** model, pattern. **2** (*norma*) norm, standard. **3** (*market.*) sample, pattern. **4** (*pubbl.*) design; (*alla moda*) style. // **modelli autunnali** (*d'abiti per l'autunno*) (*market.*) fall fashions; **~ depositato** (*leg.*) registered pattern; **il ~ di comportamento del consumatore** (*market.*) the model of consumer action; **~ di serie** (*market.*) current model, standard model; **il ~ di serie d'un veicolo** (*trasp.*) the standard model of a vehicle; **~ fuori serie** (*market.*) special model.

modernizzare, *v. t.* to modernize, to make★ (*o* to render) modern.

modernizzazione, *n. f.* modernization.

moderno, *a.* **1** modern; (*aggiornato*) up-to-date; (*nuovo*) new. **2** (*market., pubbl.*) up-to-date, up-to-the minute; todayish (*fam.*); new-day (*attr.*). // **moderne tecniche pubblicitarie** (*pubbl.*) up-to-date advertising techniques.

modicità, *n. f. inv.* **1** moderateness. **2** (*market.*) (*basso prezzo*) cheapness.

modico, *a.* moderate, reasonable. // **prezzi modici** (*market.*) moderate prices.

modifica, *n. f.* **1** modification, alteration, variation, change. **2** (*org. az.*) modification. // **una ~ allo statuto** (*di una società commerciale*) (*leg.*) an alteration in the articles of association.

modificare, *v. t.* to modify, to alter, to vary, to change. // **~ le condizioni d'un contratto** (*leg.*) to modify the terms of a contract; **~ una legge** (*leg.*) to amend a law; **~ la produzione secondo le esigenze della domanda** (*econ.*) to gear production to demand; **~ i propri progetti** to alter one's plans; **~ i rapporti di cambio** (*fin.*) to devalue (*o* revalue) a currency; **~ la ripartizione dei contingenti di base** (*comm. est.*) to modify the distribution of basic quotas.

modificazione, *n. f. V.* **modifica.**

modo, *n. m.* **1** (*maniera*) way; (*metodo*) method; (*sistema*) system; (*stile*) style. **2** (*mezzo*) means (*sing.* e *pl.*); way. // **~ d'agire** way of acting, behaviour, dealing, proceeding; **il ~ di condurre gli affari** the conduct (*o* management) of business; **~ di pagamento** method of payment, method of paying; **~ di vivere** way of life, way of living, tenor of life; **in ~ impegnativo** committally; **nello stesso ~** in the same way, alike; (*comm., rag.*) ditto, dicto.

modulare, *a.* (*org. az.*) modular.

modulo, *n. m.* (*attr. uff.*) form. // **~ a stampa** printed form, imprinted form; **un ~ ciclostilato** a mimeographed form; **~ della dichiarazione delle imposte (*o* delle tasse)** (*fin.*) tax return form; **~ d'accredito in giroconto** (*banca*) giro slip; **~ d'assegno** (*banca*) cheque form; **~ d'assunzione** (*pers.*) application form, application blank, labour engagement form; **~ di contratto** (*market.*) contract note; **~ di dichiarazione doganale** (*dog.*) customs entry form; **~ di domanda (d'impiego)** (*pers.*) *V.* **~ d'assunzione; ~ di fattura** (*rag.*) billhead (*USA*); **~ d'ordinazione** (*market.*) order form; **~ di polizza di carico** (*trasp. mar.*) form of a bill of lading, bill of lading form; **~ di ricevuta** receipt form; **~ di sottoscrizione per azioni** (*fin.*) form of application for stocks, application form; **~ di trasferimento** (*di titoli*) (*fin.*) form of transfer; **~ di versamento** (*banca*) paying-in slip; deposit slip (*USA*); **~ in bianco** blank form, blank; **~ per un atto legale** (*leg.*) deed form; **~ per cambiale** (*cred.*) bill form; **~ per censimenti** (*market., stat.*) census paper; **~** (*compilato dal datore di lavoro*) **per le detrazioni delle imposte** (*da stipendi e salari*) (*amm., fin.*) tax-deduction card; **~ per ricorsi** claim form; **~ per telegramma** (*comun.*) telegram form; **~ perforato** punched form; **~ «Preti»** (*fin.*) tax return form (*from 1975 onwards*); **~ stampato** printed form; **~ telegrafico** (*comun.*) telegraph form; **~ «Vanoni»** (*fin.*) tax return form (*up to 1974*).

molo, *n. m.* (*trasp. mar.*) jetty, pier; (*banchina*) quay, dock, wharf★. // **~ per il caricamento (e lo scaricamento) del carbone** (*trasp. mar.*) coal wharf.

moltiplicando, *n. m.* (*mat.*) multiplicand.

moltiplicare, *v. t.* **1** to multiply, to increase, to augment, to redouble. **2** (*mat.*) to multiply. // **~ per tre** to multiply by three; (*triplicare*) to triplicate; **~ le spese** (*amm.*) to multiply expenses.

moltiplicatore, *n. m.* **1** (*econ.*) multiplier. **2** (*mat.*) multiplier, multiplicator.

moltiplicazione, *n. f.* **1** multiplication; (*aumento*) increase, augmentation. **2** (*mat.*) multiplication.

momento, *n. m.* **1** moment. **2** (*tempo*) time. // **al ~ della partenza** (*trasp.*) on departure; **al**

~ **dell'arrivo** (*trasp.*) on arrival; **per il** ~ for the time being, for the present.

moneta, *n. f.* **1** (*metallica*) coin, piece; smash (*USA*). **2** (*collett.*) money; smash (*USA*). **3** (*econ., fin.*) tender; (*econ., fin.*) currency. // ~ **a corso forzoso** (*econ., fin.*) fiat paper money, fiat money; ~ **a corso legale** (*econ., fin.*) legal tender currency, legal tender; ~ **cartacea** (*econ., fin.*) paper money, bank paper, soft money; long green (*slang USA*); ~ **che ha corso fiduciario** (*econ., fin.*) fiduciary currency; ~ **circolante** (*econ., fin.*) currency; **una** ~ **comune** (*econ., fin.*) a unified-currency; ~ **corrente** (*econ., fin.*) current money, currency, real money, circulating medium; ~ **da cinque centesimi** (*di dollaro*) five-cent piece; nickel (*USA*); ~ **da dieci centesimi** (*di dollaro*) ten-cent piece; dime (*USA*); ~ **da mezzo dollaro** half-dollar piece; half dollar, half (*USA*); ~ **da 25 centesimi** (*di dollaro*) 25-cent piece; quarter dollar, quarter (*USA*); ~ **debole** (*fin.*) soft money; ~ **decimale** (*econ., fin.*) decimal currency; **una** ~ **d'argento** a silver coin; ~ **di cambio** (*econ., fin.*) money of exchange; ~ **di conto** (*econ., fin.*) money of account; **una** ~ **di rame** a copper coin, a copper; ~ **divisionale** (*econ., fin.*) fractional currency; **monete divisionarie** (*econ., fin.*) token coins; **una** ~ **falsa** a false coin, a counterfeit coin, a bad coin; a duffer (*fam.*); (*collett.*) flash money; smash (*USA*); ~ **forte** (*econ., fin.*) hard currency; overweight coin; **una** ~ **fuori corso** (*econ., fin.*) a coin no longer in circulation; ~ **legale** (*econ., fin.*) legal tender, currency; (*leg.*) lawful money; ~ **metallica** (*econ., fin.*) specie, metallic currency; chip (*fam.*); ~ **nazionale** (*econ., fin.*) national currency, home currency; ~ **non convertibile** (*in oro*) (*econ., fin.*) soft currency; ~ **oscillante** (*econ., fin.*) floating currency; **una** ~ **priva di valore** (*econ., fin.*) a worthless currency; **una** ~ **sana** (*econ., fin.*) a sound currency; ~ **simbolica** (*econ., fin.*) token money; **una** ~ **solida** (*econ., fin.*) a hard currency; ~ **spicciola** small change, change, small money; **una** ~ **stabile** (*econ., fin.*) a stable money, a sound money; **una** ~ **tosata** (*econ., fin.*) a clipped coin; **una** ~ **vile** (*econ., fin.*) a base coin.

monetario, *a.* monetary, pecuniary. // **fautore dell'adozione di misure monetarie** (*per regolare l'economia di un Paese*) (*econ.*) monetarist.

monometallico, *a.* (*econ.*) monometallic.

monometallismo, *n. m.* (*econ.*) monometallism, single standard. // ~ **argenteo** full silver standard; ~ **aureo** full gold standard.

monopolio, *n. m.* (*econ.*) monopoly. // ~ **bilaterale** (*econ.*) bilateral monopoly; **monopoli di Stato** (*econ.*) Government monopolies; ~ **fiscale** (*fin.*) fiscal monopoly; **monopoli nazionali** (*a carattere commerciale*) (*econ.*) Government monopolies, State-trading monopolies; ~ **parziale** (*econ.*) partial monopoly; ~ **perfetto** (*econ.*) absolute monopoly; ~ **verticale** (*econ.*) vertical trust; **in regime di** ~ (*econ.*) under a monopoly system.

monopolista, *n. m.* e *f.* (*econ.*) monopolist, monopolizer.

monopolistico, *a.* (*econ.*) monopolistic.

monopolizzare, *v. t.* (*econ.*) to monopolize.

monopolizzatore, *n. m.* (*econ.*) monopolizer.

monopolizzazione, *n. f.* (*econ.*) monopolization.

monopsonio, *n. m.* (*econ.*) monopsony, buyer's monopoly.

montaggio, *n. m.* **1** (*org. az.*) assembly, assemblage, fitting up. **2** (*pubbl.*) (*cinematografico*) montage, cutting. // ~ **in officina** (*org. az.*) shop-assembly.

montare, *v. t.* **1** (*org. az.*) to assemble. **2** (*pubbl.*) (*un film, ecc.*) to cut★. // ~ **una macchina** (*org. az.*) to assemble a machine.

montatura, *n. f.* **1** (*fig.*) puff, puffing-up, exaggeration. **2** (*fin.*) bubble. // **una** ~ **pubblicitaria** (*pubbl.*) a publicity stunt.

monte, *n. m.* **1** mountain, mount. **2** (*comm., leg.*) (*banca di prestito su pegno*) pawnshop. // ~ **dei Pegni** (*comm., leg.*) *V.* ~ **di Pegno;** ~ **di Pegno** (*comm., leg.*) pawnshop, pawnbroker's shop, pawnbroker's; ~ **di Pietà** (*comm., leg.*) *V.* ~ **di Pegno.**

mora, *n. f.* **1** (*ass.*) grace period. **2** (*leg.*) mora, delay; (*dilazione*) respite. // **essere in** ~ **(con i pagamenti)** (*market.*) to be in arrear(s) (with one's payments).

moratoria, *n. f.* **1** (*ass.*) grace period. **2** (*comm., leg.*) moratorium★.

moratorio, *a.* (*comm., leg.*) moratory.

morosità, *n. f. inv.* (*leg.*) arrearage, laches.

moroso, *a.* (*cred., leg.*) tardy, delinquent; in arrear(s) (*pred.*). // **essere** ~ (*cred., anche*) to be short in one's payments.

morte, *n. f.* death. // ~ **accidentale** (*leg.*) accidental death, misadventure.

morto, *a.* **1** dead, deceased, departed. **2** (*market.*) (*inattivo, di stasi*) dead, slack; off.

mossa, *n. f.* movement; (*anche fig.*) move.

mostra, *n. f.* **1** show, exhibition, display. **2** (*di merci: nella vetrina di un negozio, ecc.*) display, set-out. **3** (*market.*) exhibition, exhibit, show; (*fiera*) fair. **4** (*market.*) (*la vetrina stessa*) show-window, shop-window. // ~ **campionaria** (*market.*) sample fair, trade fair; ~ **dell'agricoltura** agricultural show; **una ~ di bestiame** (*market.*) a cattle show; ~ **itinerante** (*market., pubbl.*) travelling exhibit; **in ~** (*market.*) in view, on view.

mostrare, *v. t.* **1** to show★; (*indicare*) to point out. **2** (*market.*) (*esporre*) to show★, to exhibit, to display. // ~ **il passaporto** (*tur.*) to show one's passport.

motel, *n. m.* (*trasp. aut.*) motel; tourist court, motor court (*USA*).

motivare, *v. t.* **1** (*giustificare adducendo motivi*) to state reasons for, to justify, to ground. **2** (*essere motivo di*) to motivate, to cause. // ~ **una richiesta** to justify a request; ~ **una sentenza** (*leg.*) to state reasons for a judgment.

motivazionale, *a.* (*market., pubbl.*) motivational.

motivazione, *n. f.* **1** motivation. **2** (*motivo*) motive, reason. **3** (*market., pubbl.*) motivation. // **la ~ d'una sentenza** (*leg.*) the grounds of a judgment.

motivo, *n. m.* **1** motive, reason, ground; (*causa*) cause. **2** (*motivazione*) motivation. **3** (*leg.*) ground, reason. // ~ **d'appello** (*leg.*) ground of appeal; ~ **di diritto** (*leg.*) matter of law; **il ~ d'un'eccezione** (*leg.*) the ground of an objection; ~ **di fatto** (*leg.*) matter of fact, matter in deed; **un ~ di lagnanza** (*o* **di reclamo**) a matter of complaint; **motivi procedurali** (*leg.*) reasons of procedure; **a ~ di** owing to, on account of, because of; **chi ha ~ di ricorrere in appello** (*leg.*) person aggrieved.

motobarca, *n. f.* (*trasp.*) motor-boat, power-boat.

motocarro, *n. m.* (*trasp.*) motor-van.

motofurgone, *n. m.* (*trasp.*) motor-van.

motonave, *n. f.* (*trasp. mar.*) motor-ship.

motopeschereccio, *n. m.* (*trasp. mar.*) motor-trawler.

motore, *n. m.* **1** motor, engine. **2** (*fam.*) (*motocicletta*) motor-bike (*fam.*). // ~ **a benzina** (*trasp.*) petrol engine; gasoline engine, gas engine (*USA*); ~ **a combustione interna** (*trasp.*) internal combustion engine; ~ **a due (a quattro) tempi** (*trasp.*) two-(four-) stroke engine; ~ **a scoppio** (*trasp.*) internal combustion engine.

motorista, *n. m.* (*pers.*) engineer.

motorizzare, *v. t.* (*trasp. aut.*) to motorize.

motorizzarsi, *v. rifl.* (*trasp. aut.*) to motorize.

motorizzazione, *n. f.* (*trasp. aut.*) motorization.

motovedetta, *n. f.* (*trasp.*) motor patrol vessel.

motoveicolo, *n. m.* (*trasp. aut.*) motor vehicle.

motrice, *n. f.* **1** (*trasp. aut.*) motor-truck, motor. **2** (*trasp. ferr.*) engine.

movimento, *n. m.* **1** movement; (*moto*) motion; (*mossa*) move. **2** (*flusso*) flow; (*traffico*) traffic. **3** (*market.*) (*di prezzi, ecc.*) movement. **4** (*org. az., pers.*) (*di funzionari*) shake-up. // **movimenti ciclici** (*econ.*) cyclical movements; ~ **(con tendenza) al rialzo** (*fin., market.*) upward movement; ~ **(con tendenza) al ribasso** (*fin., market.*) downward movement; **il ~ cooperativo** (*econ.*) the co-operative movement; ~ **d'affari** (*fin., rag.*) turnover; **movimenti di capitali** (*fin., rag.*) movements of capital, capital movements, capital flows; ~ **di cassa** (*rag.*) cash flow; **movimenti di conto** (*fin., rag.*) movements of capital; ~ **di prezzo** (*econ.*) price adjustment; ~ **(di) viaggiatori** (*trasp.*) passenger traffic; ~ **ferroviario** (*trasp. ferr.*) railway traffic; ~ (*merci o passeggeri*) **locale** (*trasp. ferr.*) local traffic; way traffic (*USA*); **movimenti materiali di titoli** (*econ., fin.*) physical transfers of securities; ~ **merci** (*trasp.*) goods traffic, merchandise traffic, movement of freight; **movimenti occulti di capitali** (*econ., fin.*) hidden capital movements; ~ **sindacale** (*sind.*) labour movement; ~ **stradale** (*trasp. aut.*) road traffic; **movimenti tariffari** (*comm. est., econ.*) tariff adjustments; **il ~ turistico** (*tur.*) the flow of tourists.

mozione, *n. f.* (*leg.*) motion. // **una ~ d'ordine** (*leg.*) a point of order.

multa, *n. f.* **1** (*leg.*) fine, mulct, penalty, forfeit. **2** (*pers.*) docking. **3** (*trasp. aut.*) fine, ticket; tag (*USA*). // ~ **a carico dei ritardatari** (*leg.*) late penalty; ~ **per ritardo** (*leg.*) late penalty.

multare, *v. t.* **1** (*leg.*) to fine, to mulct. **2** (*pers.*) to dock. **3** (*trasp. aut.*) to fine, to ticket; to tag (*USA*).

multilaterale, *a.* multilateral.

multinazionale, *a.* (*comm. est., org. az.*) multinational. *n. f.* (*comm. est., org. az.*) multinational company, multinational.

munire, *v. t.* (*provvedere*) to provide; (*fornire*) to furnish, to supply. // ~ **d'un buono** (*o* **d'uno scontrino**) (*market.*) to voucher; ~ **q. di denaro** to provide sb. with money; ~ (*una cambiale, un assegno, ecc.*) **d'una dicitura a mano** (*o* **a stampa**) (*cred.*) to enface; ~ **un documento della firma** to sign a document.

munirsi, *v. rifl.* (*provvedersi*) to provide oneself, to furnish oneself, to supply oneself.

munito, *a.* provided, furnished, supplied. // ~ **dell'indirizzo del mittente** (*comun.*) (*di busta*) self-addressed.

muovere, *v. t.* to move. // ~ **un'accusa a q.** (*leg.*) to make a complaint against sb., to bring a charge against sb.; ~ **un'accusa formale contro q.** (*leg.*) to swear a charge against sb.; ~ **causa a q.** (*leg.*) to sue sb.; ~ **querela** (*leg.*) to complain.

muoversi, *v. rifl.* **1** to move. **2** (*market.*) (*di prezzi, ecc.*) to move, to budge. // ~ **a spirale** (*market.*) (*di prezzi, ecc.*) to spiral.

mutamento, *n. m.* change; (*variazione*) variation; (*trasformazione*) transformation; (*alterazione*) alteration. // ~ **della composizione del portafoglio** (*fin.*) (*di fondo d'investimento*) change in gearing, shift in portfolio; **un** ~ **di programma** a change in the programme; **un** ~ **in meglio** a change for the better; **un** ~ **in peggio** a change for the worse.

mutare, *v. t.* to change; (*trasformare*) to transform; (*alterare*) to alter. *v. i.* to change; (*alterarsi*) to alter; (*variare*) to vary.

mutua, *n. f.* **1** (*leg.*) (*società di mutuo soccorso*) mutual aid association. **2** (*pers.*) (*per l'assistenza medica*) health insurance association; blue cross (*USA*). **3 le mutue,** *pl.* (*organizzate dallo Stato*) (*pers.*) the national health service. // **della** ~ *V.* **mutualistico; essere in** ~ (*pers.*) to be on sick-leave; to be treated by one's panel doctor; **mettersi in** ~ (*pers.*) to ask for sick-leave; to ask for treatment by one's panel doctor.

mutualistico, *a.* **1** health insurance, national insurance (*attr.*). **2** (*pers.*) (*di medico, ecc.*) working within the national health service; panel (*attr.*). // **assistenza mutualistica** health insurance assistance; **cure mutualistiche** treatment within the national health service; **un medico** ~ (*pers.*) a panel doctor (*in G.B.*).

mutuante, *n. m.* e *f.* (*fin.*) lender.

mutuare, *v. t.* **1** (*cred.*) (*prendere a mutuo*) to borrow. **2** (*cred.*) (*dare a mutuo*) to lend★; to loan (*USA*).

mutuatario, *n. m.* (*cred.*) borrower.

mutuato, *a.* (*pers.*) (*di paziente*) on a (doctor's) panel. *n. m.* **1** patient on a doctor's list (*o* panel). **2 i mutuati,** *pl.* the panel (*collett.*).

mutuo¹, *a.* mutual; (*reciproco*) reciprocal. // ~ **consenso** (*leg.*) mutual consent, mutual agreement, accord and satisfaction; ~ **soccorso** mutual aid; **cassa mutua malattia** health insurance scheme; **società di** ~ **soccorso** (*leg.*) mutual aid association.

mutuo², *n. m.* (*cred.*) loan. // **mutui a breve scadenza** (*cred.*) short-term loans; **mutui a lunga scadenza** (*cred.*) long-term loans; ~ **garantito** (*banca*) secured loan; ~ **ipotecario** (*cred.*) mortgage loan; mortgage (*fam.*).

N

nastro, *n. m.* 1 ribbon. 2 tape. // ~ **adesivo** adhesive tape; ~ **azzurro** (*attr. uff.*) blue ribbon, blue riband; ~ **copiativo** (*per macchine da scrivere*) (*attr. uff.*) copying ribbon; ~ **dattilografico** (*attr. uff.*) type-writing ribbon, inked ribbon; ~ **inchiostratore** (*attr. uff.*) ink roller; ~ **magnetico** magnetic tape, tape.

natale, *a.* native; birth (*attr.*). *n. m.* Christmas; Xmas (*abbr.*).

natura, *n. f.* 1 nature. 2 (*qualità, tipo, anche*) sort, type, kind. // **la** ~ **del contenuto** (*d'una valigia, d'un pacco, ecc.*) (*dog.*) the nature of contents; **in** ~ (*leg.*) in kind.

naturale, *a.* 1 natural. 2 (*market.*) (*opposto a «finto»*) real. 3 (*come risposta: per «certo», «naturalmente»*) of course, naturally.

naufragare, *v. i.* (*trasp. mar., anche fig.*) to be shipwrecked, to shipwreck, to wreck.

naufragio, *n. m.* (*trasp. mar., anche fig.*) shipwreck, wreck, wreckage.

naufrago, *n. m.* (*trasp. mar.*) shipwrecked person. // **un** ~ **sopravvissuto** (*trasp. mar.*) a survivor from a wreck.

nautica, *n. f.* (*trasp. mar.*) art of navigation, navigation, nautical science.

nautico, *a.* (*trasp. mar.*) nautical, naval, marine.

navale, *a.* (*trasp. mar.*) naval, nautical, maritime, marine.

nave, *n. f.* 1 (*trasp. mar.*) ship, vessel; craft (*pl. inv.*). 2 (*trasp. mar.*) (*specialm. mercantile*) bottom. 3 (*trasp. mar.*) boat (*fam.*). // ~ **a cuscino d'aria** (*trasp. mar.*) hovercraft; ~ **a due ponti** (*trasp. mar.*) double-decker; ~ **a un ponte** (*trasp. mar.*) single-decker; ~ **a vapore** (*trasp. mar.*) steamship, steamer; **una** ~ **abbandonata** (*un relitto*) (*trasp. mar.*) a derelict ship; **una** ~ **abbandonata in mare** (*trasp. mar.*) a ship abandoned at sea; ~ **all'àncora** (*trasp. mar.*) ship riding at anchor; ~ **alla fonda** (*trasp. mar.*) ship riding at anchor; ~ **arenata** (*trasp. mar.*) ship aground; ~ **autostivante** (*trasp. mar.*) self-trimmer; ~ **avviso** (*trasp. mar.*) advice boat; ~ **carboniera** (*trasp. mar.*) coal ship, steam collier; ~ **cisterna** (*trasp. mar.*) tankship, tank-steamer, tanker, water boat; ~ **contrabbandiera** (*trasp. mar.*) smuggler, free trader; ~ **costiera** (*trasp. mar.*) coaster; ~ **da carico** (*trasp. mar.*) cargo-ship, cargo boat, cargo steamer, cargo vessel, ocean tramp, freighter; ~ **da carico non di linea** (*trasp. mar.*) tramp, tramp ship, tramp steamer; ~ **del servizio meteorologico** (*trasp. mar.*) weather-ship; **la** ~ **designata** (*trasp. mar.*) the named ship; ~ **di cabotaggio** (*trasp. mar.*) coasting ship, coasting vessel, coaster; ~ **di linea** (*trasp. mar.*) liner; ~ **di linea per passeggeri** (*trasp. mar.*) passenger liner; ~ **di linea transoceanica** (*trasp. mar.*) ocean liner; **una** ~ **di lungo corso** (*trasp. mar.*) an ocean-going ship; ~ **di salvataggio** (*trasp. mar.*) salvage vessel; ~ **di soccorso** (*trasp. mar.*) wrecker; ~ **faro** (*trasp. mar.*) lightship; **navi gemelle** (*trasp. mar.*) sister ships; ~ **guardacoste** (*trasp. mar.*) coast-defence ship; ~ **in armamento** (*trasp. mar.*) ship in commission; **una** ~ **in buone condizioni** (*trasp. mar.*) a sound ship; ~ **in commessa** (*trasp. mar.*) ship on order; **navi in convoglio** (*trasp. mar.*) ships under convoy; ~ **in discarica** (*trasp. mar.*) vessel discharging; ~ **«in entrata»** (*trasp. mar.*) inward-bound ship; ~ **in partenza** (*trasp. mar.*) outward bounder, outgoing ship; ~ **in pericolo** (*trasp. mar.*) ship in distress, distressed ship; ~ **in raddobbo** (*trasp. mar.*) ship under repair; ~ **in secco** (*trasp. mar.*) vessel aground; ~ **in servizio di linea** (*trasp. mar.*) liner; ~ **in stato d'avaria** (*trasp. mar.*) ship under average; ~ **«in uscita»** (*trasp. mar.*) outward-bound ship; ~ **in viaggio d'andata** (*trasp. mar.*) outward-bound ship, outward bounder; ~ **in zavorra** (*trasp. mar.*) ship in ballast, vessel in ballast; ~ **incagliata** (*trasp. mar.*) ship aground; ~ **indenne** (*trasp. mar.*) clean ship; ~ **investitrice** (*trasp. mar.*) colliding ship; ~ **mercantile** (*trasp. mar.*) merchant ship, trading vessel, cargo liner, merchantman, trader, cargo; ~ **naufragata** (*trasp. mar.*) wreck; ~ **noleggiata** (*trasp. mar.*) chartered vessel; ~ **officina** (*trasp. mar.*) repair ship; ~ **per carichi secchi** (*trasp. mar.*) bulk carrier; ~ **per ricuperi** (*trasp. mar.*) wrecker; **navi per il trasporto di cereali** (*trasp.

mar.) dry cargo ships; ~ **per il trasporto di merci e passeggeri** (*trasp. mar.*) cargo and passenger vessel; ~ **postale** (*trasp. mar.*) mail-steamer, packet-ship, packet-boat, packet; ~ **pronta a prendere il mare** (*trasp. mar.*) ship ready for sea; ~ (*di*) **rifornimento** (*trasp. mar.*) victualling ship, victualler; victualing ship, victualer (*USA*); ~ **rinfusiera** (*trasp. mar.*) ocean tramp, tramp; **navi scortate** (*trasp. mar.*) ships under convoy; ~ **sotto carico** (*trasp. mar.*) ship loading; ~ **sotto tutti i riguardi atta al viaggio** (*trasp. mar.*) ship in every way fitted to the voyage; ~ **-traghetto** (*trasp. ferr.*) train-ferry, transfer; ~ **-traghetto che fa servizio notturno** (*trasp. mar.*) night-boat; ~ **«verso casa»** (*in viaggio di ritorno*) (*trasp. mar.*) homeward-bound ship.

navigabile, *a.* **1** (*trasp.*) (*d'un fiume, ecc.*) navigable. **2** (*trasp. aer.*) (*d'un aereo*) airworthy. **3** (*trasp. aer., trasp. mar.*) (*d'aereo, nave, ecc.*) navigable. **4** (*trasp. mar.*) (*d'un'imbarcazione*) seaworthy.

navigabilità, *n. f. inv.* **1** (*trasp.*) (*d'un fiume, ecc.*) navigability. **2** (*trasp. aer.*) (*d'un aereo*) airworthiness. **3** (*trasp. aer., trasp. mar.*) (*d'aereo, nave, ecc.*) navigability. **4** (*trasp. mar.*) (*d'imbarcazione*) seaworthiness.

navigante, *n. m.* (*trasp. mar.*) sailor, seaman★.

navigare, *v. i.* **1** (*trasp., trasp. aer.*) to sail, to navigate. **2** (*trasp. mar.*) to sail, to navigate, to voyage, to be at sea, to be under way. // ~ **con cautela** (*trasp. mar.*) to navigate with caution; ~ **contro vento** (*trasp. mar.*) to sail against the wind; ~ **i mari** (*trasp. mar.*) to sail the seas; ~ **in carico** (*trasp. mar.*) to sail laden; ~ **in cattive acque** (*fin., fam.*) to be in low water; ~ **in zavorra** (*trasp. mar.*) to sail in ballast.

navigatore, *n. m.* (*trasp. mar.*) sailor, seaman★.

navigazione, *n. f.* **1** (*trasp., trasp. aer.*) navigation, sailing. **2** (*trasp. mar.*) navigation, sailing, shipping. // ~ **a vapore** (*trasp. mar.*) steam navigation; ~ **aerea** (*trasp. aer.*) air navigation, aerial navigation; ~ **costiera** (*trasp. mar.*) coasting navigation, coastwise navigation; ~ **di cabotaggio** (*trasp. mar.*) coastwise navigation; ~ **fluviale** (*trasp.*) inland navigation, internal navigation, inland water transport; ~ **in mare aperto** (*trasp. mar.*) off-shore navigation; ~ **interna** (*trasp.*) inland navigation, internal navigation, inland water transport; ~ **per idrovie** (*trasp.*) inland navigation; **atto alla** ~ (*trasp. aer.*) airworthy; (*trasp. mar.*) sea-worthy.

naviglio, *n. m.* **1** (*trasp.*) (*canale navigabile*) ship-canal, canal. **2** (*trasp. mar.*) (*imbarcazione*) boat, ship, vessel. **3** (*trasp. mar.*) (*collett.*) craft. **4** (*trasp. mar.*) (*flotta*) shipping, fleet. // ~ **d'alto mare** (*trasp. mar.*) sea-going vessel, sea-craft; ~ **mercantile** (*d'una nazione o d'un porto, nel complesso*) (*trasp. mar.*) tonnage.

nazionale, *a.* **1** national. **2** (*interno ad una nazione*) home, domestic (*attr.*). **3** (*di dimensioni nazionali*) nationwide.

nazionalità, *n. f. inv.* nationality.

nazionalizzare, *v. t.* (*econ.*) to nationalize.

nazionalizzazione, *n. f.* (*econ.*) nationalization.

nazione, *n. f.* nation; (*Stato*) state; (*Paese*) country. // ~ **autosufficiente** (*econ.*) self-sufficient nation; **una** ~ **commerciale** (*econ.*) a trading nation; ~ **creditrice** (*econ.*) creditor nation; ~ **debitrice** (*econ.*) debtor nation; **la** ~ **(più) favorita** (*econ.*) the most favoured nation (*M.F.N.*); **la** ~ **preferita** (*econ.*) *V.* **la** ~ **(più) favorita; le Nazioni Unite** the United Nations.

necessario, *a.* necessary; (*che si richiede, che si esige*) requisite, required. *n. m.* necessary, necessity.

necessità, *n. f. inv.* **1** necessity. **2** (*bisogno*) need; (*esigenza*) requirement; (*mancanza*) want. // **necessità finanziarie** (*fin.*) pecuniary needs; **in caso di** ~ in case of need.

necessitare, *v. t.* (*rendere necessario*) to render necessary, to require. *v. i.* **1** (*essere necessario*) to be necessary. **2** (*aver bisogno di*) to need.

negare, *v. t.* **1** to deny. **2** (*non concedere*) to deny, to refuse. **3** (*leg.*) to traverse. // ~ **un'accusa** (*leg.*) to deny a charge, to disclaim a charge; ~ **il proprio consenso** (*leg.*) to withhold one's consent; ~ **il permesso** to withhold permission.

negativamente, *avv.* negatively, in the negative.

negativo, *a.* negative.

negazione, *n. f.* **1** negation. **2** (*leg.*) traverse.

negligenza, *n. f.* **1** negligence. **2** (*leg.*) negligence, neglect. **3** (*leg.*) (*morosità, ritardo*) laches. // ~ **grave** (*leg.*) gross negligence; ~ **lieve** (*leg.*) slight negligence; ~ **nell'esercizio professionale** (*leg.*) malpractice; ~ **nello stivaggio** (*trasp. mar.*) improper stowage.

negoziabile, *a.* (*cred.*) negotiable, dealable, marketable. // **non** ~ (*cred.*) (*di documento, titolo, ecc.*) non-negotiable, non-dealable, non-marketable.

negoziabilità, *n. f. inv.* (*cred.*) negotiability, marketability.

negoziante, *n. m.* e *f.* 1 (*market.*) dealer, seller, tradesman*, trader. 2 (*market.*) (*bottegaio*) shopkeeper; storekeeper, merchant (*USA*). // ~ **di bestiame** (*market.*) cattledealer; ~ **in generi diversi** (*market.*) general dealer.

negoziare, *v. t.* 1 to buy* and sell*. 2 (*cred.*) to negotiate. *v. i.* to deal* (in), to trade (in), to treat. // ~ **a termine** (*Borsa*) to deal for the account, to deal for the settlement; ~ **una cambiale** (*cred.*) to negotiate a bill; ~ **per contanti** (*Borsa*) to deal for cash, to deal for money; ~ **titoli** (*fin.*) to negotiate securities.

negoziato, *n. m.* negotiation; talk (*fam.*). // **negoziati commerciali** (*comm. est.*) trade talks; **negoziati per il Kennedy round** (*comm. est.*) Kennedy round negotiations; **negoziati settoriali** (*econ.*) sector-by-sector negotiations; **negoziati tariffari** (*comm. est.*) tariff negotiations; **negoziati tariffari multilaterali** (*comm. est.*) multilateral tariff negotiations; **negoziati tendenti alla riduzione delle tariffe** (*comm. est.*) tariff-cutting negotiations.

negoziatore, *n. m.* negotiator, transactor.

negoziazione, *n. f.* 1 negotiation, transaction, deal. 2 (*Borsa*) dealing. // ~ **a termine** (*Borsa*) dealing for the settlement, dealing for the account; **negoziazioni di divise estere** (*fin.*) negotiations of foreign currency; ~ **per contanti** (*Borsa*) dealing for cash, dealing for money.

negozio, *n. m.* 1 (*market.*) shop, warehouse; wareroom, store, parlor (*USA*). 2 (*market.*) (*affare, impresa commerciale*) bargain, business; dealings (*pl.*). // ~ **al dettaglio** (*market.*) retail shop, outlet; ~ **appartenente a una «catena»** (*market.*) multiple shop, multiple store; multiple (*fam.*); **un** ~ **caro** (*market.*) an expensive shop, an exclusive shop; ~ **del centro** (*market.*) downtown store; ~ **d'abiti confezionati** (*market.*) ready-made shop; ~ **d'articoli usati** (*market.*) thrift shop; ~ (*per la vendita al dettaglio*) **di articoli vari** (*market.*) variety shop, variety store, variety (*USA*); ~ **di generi vari** (*market.*) general store (*USA*); **un** ~ **di lusso** (*market.*) a luxury shop, a fancy shop; ~ **esente da dazio** (*dog., trasp. aer.*) duty-free shop; ~ **giuridico** (*leg.*) legal transaction; ~ **self-service** (*market.*) self-service store; **negozi specializzati** (*market.*) specialty shops.

nero, *a.* black.

netto, *a.* 1 (*pulito, anche fig.*) clean, clear. 2 (*deciso*) decided, distinct, sharp. 3 (*comm.*) net, nett. // **una netta differenza fra i due totali** (*rag.*) a decided difference between the two totals; **un** ~ **miglioramento** a distinct improvement; **una netta ripresa** (*econ.*) a clear-cut revival; **al** ~ **d'aumento o di distribuzione gratuita d'azioni** (*Borsa*) (*di titolo*) ex capitalization; **al** ~ **di tutte le detrazioni** (*fin.*) above all reprises.

nodo, *n. m.* 1 knot. 2 (*trasp. mar.*) (*misura di velocità pari a un miglio marino, o 1.853 metri, all'ora*) knot. // **nodi congiunturali** (*econ.*) slump symptoms; ~ **ferroviario** (*trasp. ferr.*) railway junction, junction; ~ **stradale** (*trasp. aut.*) road junction, junction.

noleggiante, *n. m.* e *f.* 1 (*leg.*) hirer. 2 (*trasp. aer., trasp. mar.*) charterer. 3 (*trasp. mar.*) affreighter.

noleggiare, *v. t.* 1 (*leg.*) (*prendere a nolo*) to hire, to lease. 2 (*leg.*) (*dare a nolo*) to hire (out), to lease, to let*. 3 (*trasp. aer., trasp. mar.*) (*navi o aerei*) to charter. 4 (*trasp. mar.*) (*una nave intera o parte di essa*) to affreight. // ~ **un taxi** to engage a taxi.

noleggiatore, *n. m.* 1 (*leg.*) hirer. 2 (*trasp. aer., trasp. mar.*) charterer. 3 (*trasp. mar.*) affreighter, freighter.

noleggio, *n. m.* 1 (*leg.*) hire, lease. 2 (*trasp. aer., trasp. mar.*) chartering, charter party. 3 (*trasp. mar.*) affreightment, freight, charter party. // ~ **a tempo** (*trasp. mar.*) time charter; ~ **a viaggio** (*trasp. mar.*) voyage charter; ~ **al lordo** (*trasp. mar.*) dead-weight charter; ~ **dell'intera nave** (*trasp. mar.*) affreightment by charter; ~ **d'andata e ritorno** (*trasp. mar.*) round chartering; ~ **d'automobili** (*trasp. aut.*) car hire, car rental; ~ **di banchina** (*trasp. mar.*) quay rent; ~ **di chiatte** (*trasp. mar.*) barge hire; ~ **di scafo nudo** (*trasp. mar.*) demise charter; ~ **parziale** (*trasp. mar.*) part cargo charter; **a** ~ for hire.

nolo, *n. m.* 1 (*leg.*) hire. 2 (*org. az.*) (*affitto di macchinario, ecc.*) rent. 3 (*trasp. aer., trasp. mar.*) charter, chartering, charterage, freight. // ~ **«a corpo»** (*trasp. mar.*) lump freight; ~ **a cuccetta** (*trasp. mar.*) berth freighting; ~ **a forfait** (*trasp. mar.*) through freight; ~ **«a massa»** (*trasp. mar.*) lump freight; ~ **a peso** (*trasp. mar.*) freight by weight; ~ **a tariffa ridotta** (*trasp. mar.*) contract freight; ~ **a tempo** (*trasp. mar.*) time charter, time freight; ~ **a tonnellate** (*trasp. mar.*) freight by measure; ~ **a viaggio** (*trasp. mar.*) voyage charter, voyage freight; ~ **anticipato** (*trasp. mar.*) freight in advance, advanced freight, advance freight; ~ **contrattuale** (*trasp. mar.*) contract freight; ~ **da pagarsi alla partenza** (*trasp. mar.*) freight payable on sailing; ~ **d'andata** (*trasp. mar.*) outward freight; ~ **d'andata e ritorno** (*trasp. mar.*) freight out and home; ~ **di banchina** (*trasp. mar.*) quay rent;

~ **d'entrata** (*trasp. mar.*) inward freight; ~ (*del viaggio*) **di ritorno** (*trasp. mar.*) return freight; ~ **intero** (*trasp. mar.*) full freight; ~ **lordo** (*trasp. mar.*) gross freight; ~ **netto** (*trasp. mar.*) net freight; ~ **non rimborsabile** (*trasp. mar.*) freight earned; « ~ **non rimborsabile** » (*trasp. mar.*) «freight not repayable»; ~ **pagato a destinazione** (*trasp. mar.*) freight forward; ~ **posticipato** (*trasp. mar.*) freight forward; ~ «**pro rata**» (*cioè, in proporzione al tratto di viaggio percorso*) (*trasp. mar.*) freight pro rata, pro rata freight; ~ **proporzionale alla distanza** (*trasp. mar.*) distance freight; ~ **stabilito per contratto** (*trasp. mar.*) chartered freight; ~ **supplementare** (*trasp. mar.*) extra freight; ~ «**vuoto per pieno**» (*trasp. mar.*) dead freight; **a** ~ for hire, on hire; for rent (*USA*).

nome, *n. m.* 1 name. 2 (*fig.*) reputation, repute. 3 (*leg.*) (*ragione sociale*) style. 4 (*market.*) (*d'una classe di cose*) denomination. // ~ **commerciale** (*d'una ditta*) (*leg.*) trade-name, style; **il** ~ **dell'azienda** (*leg.*) the business name; ~ **depositato** (*d'un prodotto*) (*leg.*) trade-name; ~ **di battesimo** first name, Christian name; given name (*USA*); ~ **e cognome** name and surname, full name; ~ **e indirizzo** name and address; ~ **e indirizzo del venditore** (*comun.*) sender's name and address; ~ **fittizio** (*o* **di comodo**) (*leg.*) fictitious name, dummy name; ~ **sociale** (*leg.*) corporate name (*USA*); **a** ~ **di** (*leg.*) on behalf of; **a** ~ **e per conto di q.** for and on behalf of sb.; **in** ~ **della legge** (*leg.*) in the name of the law; **in** ~ **di** (*leg.*) on behalf of.

nomenclatura, *n. f.* nomenclature. // ~ **doganale** (*dog.*) customs nomenclature.

nomina, *n. f.* 1 (*elezione*) nomination, appointment. 2 (*assegnazione*) assignment, constitution. // **la** ~ **a direttore** the appointment as manager; ~ **del difensore d'ufficio per un imputato** (*leg.*) assignment of counsel to a defendant; ~ **provvisoria** (*pers.*) provisional appointment; ~ **soggetta a un periodo di prova** (*pers.*) probationary appointment.

nominale, *a.* nominal.

nominare, *v. t.* 1 to name, to call. 2 (*menzionare*) to mention. 3 (*eleggere*) to nominate, to appoint; (*designare*) to assign, to constitute; (*insediare*) to institute, to establish. // ~ **un arbitro** (**un liquidatore, ecc.**) (*leg.*) to appoint an arbitrator (a liquidator, etc.); ~ **un candidato** (*con votazione*) (*leg.*) to vote a candidate in; ~ **un comitato** (**il consiglio d'amministrazione d'una società, ecc.**) to appoint a committee (the directors of a company, etc.); ~ **il difensore d'ufficio per un imputato** (*leg.*) to assign counsel to a defendant; ~ **q. erede** (*leg.*) to designate sb. as heir; ~ **q. procuratore** (*leg.*) to appoint sb. as proxy.

nominativo, *a.* 1 nominative, nominal. 2 (*fin.*) (*di titolo*) registered. *n. m.* 1 (*nome*) name. 2 (*trasp. mar.*) call sign. // **non** ~ (*fin.*) (*di titolo*) unregistered.

nominato, *a.* named. // ~ **nel testamento** (*leg.*) (*di bene, ecc.*) testate.

norma, *n. f.* 1 norm, standard. 2 (*leg.*) (*regola*) rule, regulation; (*disposizione*) provision; (*principio*) principle; (*precetto*) precept. 3 (*market.*) (*avvertenza*) instruction. // **norme conformi di qualità** (*market.*) quality standards; **le norme contrattuali** (*leg.*) the provisions of a contract; **norme di lavorazione** (*org. az.*) process rules, process standards; **una** ~ **di legge** (*leg.*) a rule of law; **norme di qualità** (*market.*) standards of quality; **norme di sicurezza** safety rules; **norme disciplinari** (*leg.*) disciplinary rules; **norme per l'uso** (*market.*) instructions for use; **norme retroattive** (*leg.*) retroactive laws, retrospective laws; **le norme statutarie** (*fin.*) the provisions of the articles of association; **a** ~ **dello statuto societario** (*fin.*) in accordance with (*o* under) the articles; **a** ~ **di legge** (*leg.*) according to the law; **di** ~ as a rule.

normale, *a.* 1 normal, ordinary, regular. 2 (*che dà una regola*) standard (*attr.*). // ~ **diligenza** (*leg.*) due care.

normalizzare, *v. t.* 1 to bring* back to normal, to normalize. 2 (*standardizzare*) to standardize. // ~ **la produzione** (*org. az.*) to standardize production.

normalizzazione, *n. f.* 1 normalization. 2 (*standardizzazione*) standardization. // **la** ~ **dei rapporti internazionali** the normalization of international relations.

normativa, *n. f.* 1 (*leg.*) (*insieme di norme*) set of rules. 2 (*leg.*) (*legge normativa*) normative law. // ~ **quadro** (*leg.*) outline regulation, outline provisions (*pl.*).

normativo, *a.* (*leg.*) prescribing rules, establishing a norm, normative.

nostrano, *a.* (*market.*) home-grown, national; (*regionale*) regional; domestic (*USA*); home (*attr.*).

nota, *n. f.* 1 note. 2 (*promemoria*) memorandum*, memorial; memo (*fam.*). 3 (*minuta*) minute, account, record. 4 (*lista*) list. // ~ **a piè di pagina** (*o* **in calce**) footnote; **note caratteristiche** distinguishing marks; ~ **delle spese** (*rag.*) account of expenses; ~ **d'accreditamento** (*rag.*) *V.* ~ **d'accredito;** ~ **d'accredito** (*rag.*) credit note, credit advice, credit memo; ~ **d'addebitamento**

(*rag.*) *V.* ~ **d'addebito;** ~ **d'addebito** (*rag.*) debit note, debit advice, debit memorandum, debit memo; ~ **di carico** (*trasp. aer., trasp. mar.*) manifest; ~ **di consegna** (*trasp. ferr.*) delivery note, consignment note; ~ **di consegna a domicilio** (*trasp. aut.*) carman's delivery sheet; ~ **di contratto** (*Borsa*) contract note; ~ **di copertura** (*banca, cred.*) cover note, covering note; ~ **d'imbarco** (*trasp. mar.*) shipping-advice notice; ~ **di pegno** (*dog.*) warrant; ~ **di spese giudiziarie** (*leg.*) bill of costs; ~ **di trasbordo** (*trasp. mar.*) transshipment note; ~ **interna** (*org. az.*) interoffice memo; ~ **spese** (*rag.*) note of expenses, expense account.

notaio, *n. m.* (*leg.*) notary public, notary, scrivener.

notare, *v. t.* **1** to note, to make★ a note of, to write★ down. **2** (*registrare*) to record. **3** (*osservare*) to notice. // ~ **le spese** (*rag.*) to write down expenses.

notarile, *a.* (*leg.*) notarial.

notifica, *n. f.* **1** notice, announcement. **2** (*leg.*) notification, service, summons. // ~ **d'un decreto** (*leg.*) service of a decree; ~ **di licenziamento** (*pers.*) notice of dismissal; walking ticket, walking papers, walking orders (*fam.*); ~ **d'una sentenza** (*leg.*) service of a judgment; ~ **di sfratto** (*leg.*) notice to quit; **la** ~ **d'una vendita** the announcement of a sale.

notificare, *v. t.* **1** to give★ notice of; (*annunciare*) to announce; (*informare*) to inform. **2** (*leg.*) to notify, to serve. // ~ **un atto** (*leg.*) to serve a paper; ~ **un mandato di comparizione a q.** (*leg.*) to subpoena sb.; ~ **un sequestro** (*leg.*) to serve an attachment; ~ **una vendita all'asta** to announce an auction sale.

notificazione, *n. f. V.* **notifica.**

notizia, *n. f.* **1** piece of news, bit of news; (*informazione*) piece of information, bit of information. **2** (*giorn.*) piece of news, news-item. **3 notizie,** *pl.* news (*sing. collett.*); word (*sing.*); (*informazioni*) information, intelligence (*sing. collett.*). // **notizia** (*strettamente*) **confidenziale** (*leg.*) privileged communication; **la** ~ **del sinistro** (*ass.*) the news of the accident; **notizie dell'ultima ora** (*giorn.*) stop-press news, stop press, spot news; ~ **di cronaca cittadina** (*giorn.*) local news, locals; **notizie d'interesse locale** (*giorn.*) local news, locals; **notizie di** (*o* **da**) **prima pagina** (*giorn.*) front-page news; ~ **-lampo** (*trasmessa per radio o per telegrafo*) (*giorn.*) flash; **notizie recentissime** (*giorn.*) stop-press news; stop news, spot news.

notiziario, *n. m.* **1** (*comm.*) (*d'una ditta, ecc.*) newsletter. **2** (*giorn.*) (*radiofonico*) news bulletin, newscast. // ~ **giornaliero** daily report; ~ **mensile** monthly report; ~ **settimanale** weekly report.

noto, *a.* well-known, known.

notorietà, *n. f. inv.* notoriety, renown.

notorio, *a.* well-known, notorius.

nove, *num. card.* nine. // **i Nove** (*econ., fin.*) (*i Paesi della CEE allargata*) the Nine.

novità, *n. f. inv.* **1** (*l'esser nuovo*) newness, novelty. **2** (*innovazione, mutamento*) innovation, change. **3** (*market.*) novelty. **4 novità,** *pl.* (*notizie*) news (*col verbo al sing.*).

noviziato, *n. m.* (*pers.*) (*tirocinio*) apprenticeship.

nubile, *a.* unmarried. *n. f.* **1** unmarried woman★. **2** (*leg.*) spinster.

nudo, *a.* **1** (*spoglio, scoperto*) bare. **2** (*svestito*) naked. // **nuda proprietà** (*leg.*) residuary right of ownership.

nullaosta, *n. m.* (*leg.*) permit.

nullità, *n. f. inv.* (*leg.*) nullity, voidness.

nullo, *a.* (*leg.*) null, void, null and void.

numerale, *a.* e *n. m.* numeral.

numerare, *v. t.* **1** (*segnare con numeri progressivi*) to number. **2** (*contare*) to count. // ~ **i fogli di** (*un libro, ecc.*) to folio, to foliate; ~ **le pagine di** (*un libro, ecc.*) to page, to paginate.

numerario, *n. m.* (*fin.*) ready cash, cash, specie.

numeratore, *n. m.* (*mat.*) numerator.

numeratrice, *n. f.* (*macch. uff.*) numbering machine.

numerazione, *n. f.* **1** system of numbering, numbering. **2** (*mat.*) numeration, notation. // ~ **binaria** (*mat.*) binary notation; ~ **decimale** (*mat.*) decimal notation.

numerico, *a.* **1** numerical. **2** (*mat.*) numerical, numeric.

numero, *n. m.* **1** number. **2** (*giorn.*) (*d'un giornale*) issue. **3** (*market.*) (*di scarpe, ecc.*) size, number. **4** (*mat.*) number, figure, digit. // **numeri arabi** (*mat.*) Arabic numerals, Arabic figures; ~ **arretrato** (*giorn.*) back number; **numeri creditori** (*banca*) credit numbers; **numeri debitori** (*banca*) debit numbers; ~ **decimale** (*mat.*) decimal number; **il** ~ **degli addetti all'agricoltura** (*econ.*) the active farming population; **il** ~ **dei colli** (*trasp.*) the number of packages; ~ **dei passeggeri trasportati** (*trasp.*) number of passengers, traffic; ~ **del telefono** (*comun.*) telephone number, call number; ~ **delle «unità»** (*d'una conversazione telefonica*) (*comun.*) time; ~ **d'azioni** (*d'una società*) **in circolazione sul mercato** (*fin.*) floating supply; ~ **di codice** (*comun.*) code number; ~ **di codice postale**

(*comun.*) zip number; ~ **di controllo** (*org. az.*) control number, check number; ~ **di copie stampate** (*giorn.*) printing; ~ **d'iscritti** number of members; (*sind.*) membership; ~ **di lettori** (*giorn.*) number of readers, readership; ~ **di pagina** (*pubbl.*) page number, folio; ~ **di riferimento** reference number; ~ **di righe** (*di testo a stampa*) (*giorn., pubbl.*) linage; ~ **di schedario** (*rag.*) call number; ~ **di serie** (*di biglietti di banca, ecc.*) (*fin.*) serial number; ~ **di soci** (*fin.*) membership; ~ **di targa** (*trasp. aut.*) plate number, number; ~ **di voti** number of votes, vote; ~ **dispari** (*mat.*) odd number, uneven number; ~ **fisso** (*mat.*) fixed number; ~ **indice** (*stat.*) index number; ~ **indice delle azioni** (*fin., stat.*) share index; **i numeri indici della produzione industriale** (*econ., stat.*) the index numbers of industrial production; ~ **legale** (*leg.*) quorum; **il legale dei creditori** (*leg.*) the quorum of creditors; **numeri neri** (*banca, rag.*) black products; **numeri pari** (*mat.*) even numbers; ~ **periodico** (*mat.*) periodic number, repeater, circulator; ~ **primo** (*mat.*) prime number, prime; **numeri romani** (*mat.*) Roman numerals, Roman figures; **numeri rossi** (*banca, rag.*) red products; ~ **telefonico** (*comun.*) telephone number, call number; ~ **telefonico interno** (*comun.*) extension; ~ **unico** (*di rivista, ecc.*) (*giorn.*) single number, single issue; ~ **zero** (*giorn.*) dry run.

nuovo, *a.* **1** new. **2** (*altro, ulteriore*) other, further, new. // **nuova determinazione d'imposta** (*fin.*) reassessment; ~ **di zecca** brand-new; **la nuova edizione d'una rivista** (*giorn.*) the new edition of a magazine; **una nuova emissione azionaria** (*fin.*) a new issue of stock, a reissue of stock; **un ~ indirizzo di politica industriale** a new industrial approach; **le «nuove leve»** (*di lavoratori*) (*pers.*) the new entrants; **una nuova «linea»** (*market., pubbl.*) a new look; **nuovi metodi di gestione** (*amm.*) new management methods; **la nuova moda** (*market., pubbl.*) the new fashion, the new look; **una nuova ordinazione** (*market.*) a new order; (*delle stesse merci ordinate precedentemente*) a reorder; (*org. az.*) a fresh supply; **nuova registrazione** (*di scritture, ecc.*) (*rag.*) re-entry; **un ~ rifornimento** (*org. az.*) a fresh supply; **nuova spedizione via mare** (*trasp. mar.*) reshipment; **un ~ «stile»** (*market., pubbl.*) a new look; **nuova valutazione** (*d'un danno, ecc.*) (*ass.*) reassessment; **nuova vendita** (*market.*) resale; **col ~** (*cioè: compresa la nuova emissione*) (*Borsa*) «cum» new, with rights; **fino a ~ avviso** until further advice, till further notice.

O

obbligante, *a.* binding. *n. m.* (*leg.*) obliger, obligator.

obbligare, *v. t.* **1** (*costringere*) to oblige, to compel, to constrain. **2** (*forzare*) to force. **3** (*leg.*) (*imporre un vincolo giuridico*) to bind★, to bind★ over, to obligate. // ~ **q. con giuramento** (*leg.*) to bind sb. by oath.

obbligarsi, *v. rifl.* **1** (*impegnarsi, vincolarsi*) to bind★ oneself, to undertake★, to engage (oneself). **2** (*leg.*) (*farsi mallevadore*) to stand★ surety. // ~ **in solido** (*fin.*) to bind oneself jointly and severally.

obbligatario, *n. m.* (*leg.*) obligee.

obbligato, *n. m.* (*leg.*) obligor, obligator.

obbligatorietà, *n. f. inv.* **1** compulsoriness, obligatoriness. **2** (*obbligo*) compulsion, obligation.

obbligatorio, *a.* **1** compulsory, obligatory, obligative. **2** (*leg.*) binding, mandatory. // **non** ~ unbinding.

obbligazionario, *a.* (*fin.*) debenture, bond (*attr.*).

obbligazione, *n. f.* **1** (*fin.*) debenture, debenture bond, debenture stock, stock, security; bond (*USA*). **2** (*leg.*) obligation, liability. // ~ **a premio** (*fin.*) prize bond, lottery bond; ~ (*appartenente a una serie*) **a scadenza periodica** (*fin.*) serial bond; ~ **a termine** (*fin.*) terminable bond; ~ **al portatore** (*fin.*) bearer bond, bearer debenture, coupon bond, bond to bearer; ~ **chirografaria** (*fin.*) chirographary debenture, simple debenture; ~ **con garanzie prive di valore** (*leg.*) straw bond; ~ **consolidata** (*fin.*) funded bond; **obbligazioni convertibili** (*in azioni*) (*fin.*) convertible loan stock, convertible debentures; **obbligazioni dello Stato** (*fin.*) Government bonds; **obbligazioni di partecipazione** (*Borsa, fin.*) income bonds; ~ **esente da imposta** (*fin.*) tax-exempt bond, tax-exempt; ~ **estratta** (*fin.*) called bond; ~ **garantita** (*fin.*) guaranteed bond; ~ **garantita da ipoteca** (*fin.*) mortgage debenture; ~ **garantita da ipoteca su un immobile specifico** (*fin.*) fixed debenture; ~ **incondizionata** (*leg.*) simple obligation, simple bond; ~ **indicizzata** (*fin.*) floating-rate bond; ~ **ipotecaria** (*fin.*) mortgage debenture, mortgage bond, general mortgage bond; ~ **irredimibile** (*fin.*) irredeemable debenture, debenture stock; ~ **nominativa** (*fin.*) registered bond; **obbligazioni non garantite da ipoteca** (*fin., leg.*) naked debentures; ~ **pagabile al portatore** (*banca, cred.*) debenture payable to bearer; ~ **principale** (*leg.*) primary obligation; ~ **redimibile** (*fin.*) callable bond, redeemable bond; ~ **rimborsata** (*fin.*) called bond; **un'** ~ **riscattabile** (*fin.*) a terminable bond; **un'** ~ **senza causa** (*leg.*) an obligation without consideration; **un'** ~ **senza controprestazione** (*leg.*) an obligation without consideration; **un'** ~ **senza garanzia** (*cred.*) an unsecured bond; ~ **solidale** (*leg.*) joint obligation; ~ **tassabile** (*fin.*) taxable bond; **obbligazioni trattate più di frequente** (*Borsa*) free bonds; ~ **ventennale** (*o* **ultraventennale**) (*fin.*) long bond; **chi non adempie un'** ~ (*leg.*) defaulter.

obbligazionista, *n. m.* e *f.* (*fin.*) debenture holder, bondholder.

obbligo, *n. m.* **1** obligation, engagement, compulsion, bond. **2** (*dovere*) duty. // ~ **contrattuale** (*leg.*) contractual obligation; **gli obblighi del proprio stato** the obligations of one's condition; ~ **della residenza** (*leg.*) residential requirement; ~ **morale** moral obligation.

obiettare, *v. t.* e *i.* **1** to object, to except, to raise objections. **2** (*leg.*) to demur. // ~ **su qc.** to object to (*o* against) st.

obiettivo, *a.* **1** objective. **2** (*imparziale*) impartial, unbiased, unprejudiced, fair. *n. m.* **1** objective. **2** (*fig.*) objective, object, target. **3** (*org. az.*) objective, goal. // ~ **aziendale** (*org. az.*) company goal; corporate goal (*USA*); ~ **di bilancio** (*econ., rag.*) budget target; **obiettivi di produzione** (*econ.*) production targets; **obiettivi di sviluppo** (*econ.*) growth targets; **un** ~ **di sviluppo economico** (*econ.*) a target of economic development; **obiettivi minimi** (*org. az.*) minimum goals; **obiettivi prioritari** priority objectives.

obiezione, *n. f.* **1** objection, exception. **2** (*leg.*) demur.

obsolescente, *a.* obsolescent.

obsolescenza, *n. f.* **1** obsolescence, obsoletion. **2** (*org. az.*) obsolescence, depreciation, superannuation. // l'~ **dei macchinari** (*org. az.*) the obsolescence of machinery; ~ **d'un impianto** (*rag.*) depreciation of a plant; ~ **programmata** (*org. az.*) planned obsolescence.

obsoleto, *a.* **1** obsolete, out of date; out-of-date (*attr.*). **2** (*org. az.*) obsolete, superannuated.

occasione, *n. f.* **1** occasion, opportunity, chance. **2** (*circostanza*) occasion. **3** (*market.*) (*buon affare*) bargain. // **merce d'**~ (*market.*) bargain lot; **prezzi d'**~ (*market.*) bargain prices.

occorrendo, *voce verb.* (*banca, cred.*) in case of need.

occorrente, *a.* necessary, required, requisite. *n. m.* what is necessary, what is required, everything necessary, everything requisite. // **l'**~ **per vivere** the necessities of life.

occorrenza, *n. f.* **1** (*bisogno*) necessity, need. **2** (*circostanza*) circumstance, occasion, event. // **all'**~ in case of need, when required.

occorrere, *v. i.* **1** (*impers.: essere necessario*) must, to need, to have (to). **2** (*pers.: essere necessario*) to be needed, to be necessary, to be required, to be wanted. **3** (*abbisognare*) to need, to want.

occultamento, *n. m.* hiding, concealment. // ~ **di utili** (*leg.*) concealment of profits; ~ **doloso** (*di fatti, ecc.*) (*leg.*) fraudulent concealment.

occultare, *v. t.* to hide★, to conceal; (*celare*) to keep★ secret.

occultatore, *n. m.* hider, concealer.

occulto, *a.* hidden, concealed, secret, undisclosed.

occupante, *n. m.* e *f.* (*leg.*) occupant, occupier.

occupare, *v. t.* **1** to occupy, to hold★, to fill. **2** (*di pers.: impiegare il tempo*) to spend★. **3** (*pers.*) (*dar lavoro a*) to employ, to give★ employment to. // ~ **come inquilino** (*leg.*) to tenant; ~ **un impiego** (*pers.*) to take a job; ~ **un posto vacante** (*pers.*) to fill a vacancy, to supply a vacancy.

occuparsi, *v. rifl.* **1** to occupy oneself, to busy oneself, to be interested in; (*trattare*) to deal in, to deal with, to handle. **2** (*provvedere a*) to see★ (to), to see★ (about), to take★ care (of), to take★ charge (of). **3** (*pers.*) (*trovar lavoro*) to find★ work, to find★ a job. // ~ **dei propri affari** to see to one's business; ~ **della corrispondenza** to attend to the correspondence; ~ **di** (*un certo articolo, un ramo d'affari, ecc.*) (*market.*) to merchandise, to merchant; ~ **di affari** to conduct business; ~ **d'una causa** (*leg.*) to attend to a case.

occupato, *a.* **1** (*affaccendato*) occupied, busy. **2** (*non libero*) engaged, taken. // **non** ~ (*pers.*) (*di posto*) vacant, unfilled; (*di persona*) unemployed; **non** ~ **a tempo pieno** (*pers.*) underemployed.

occupazionale, *a.* (*pers.*) occupational.

occupazione, *n. f.* **1** (*atto d'occupare*) occupation. **2** (*econ.*) employment. **3** (*leg.*) occupancy, tenure. **4** (*pers.*) (*attività, impiego*) occupation, employ, engagement; (*lavoro, mestiere*) work, trade, business, job; lay (*fam.*). // **l'**~ **agricola** (*econ.*) employment in agriculture; **l'**~ **femminile** (*econ.*) the employment of women; **l'**~ **illegale d'una proprietà** (*leg.*) the wrongful occupation of a property; ~ **pericolosa** (*pers.*) dangerous occupation, hazardous occupation; **un'**~ **redditizia** (*pers.*) a lucrative job, a gainful job; a gravy job (*fam.*); a gravy train (*fam., USA*); **un'**~ **stabile** (*pers.*) a steady job.

oceanico, *a.* **1** (*dell'oceano*) oceanic. **2** (*trasp. mar.*) (*di nave, ecc.*) ocean-going.

oceano, *n. m.* ocean.

odierno, *a.* **1** (*del giorno d'oggi*) today's. **2** (*attuale*) present. **3** (*moderno*) modern; todayish (*fam.*).

offerente, *n. m.* e *f.* **1** offerer. **2** (*comm.*) tenderer; (*a un'asta, a una gara d'appalto*) bidder. // **il miglior** ~ the highest bidder.

offerta, *n. f.* **1** offer, offering; (*proposta*) proposal. **2** (*cred.*) (*di pagamento d'un debito, ecc.*) tender. **3** (*econ.*) supply. **4** (*fin.*) (*per appalti*) tender; (*all'asta*) bid, bidding. **5** (*market.*) offer. // ~ **a premio** (*market.*) combination offer; **un'**~ **alternativa** an alternative offer; ~ **competitiva** (*econ.*) competitive supply; ~ **complessiva** (*econ.*) aggregate supply; ~ **concorrenziale** (*econ.*) competitive supply; ~ **consorziata** (*fin.*) syndicated bid; ~ **d'appalto** (*fin.*) tender, bid; **un'**~ **d'appalto sigillata** (*fin.*) a sealed tender, a sealed bid; «**offerte d'impiego**» (*giorn.*) «situations vacant»; ~ **d'iscrizione a una società** (*leg.*) bid; ~ **di lavoro** (*econ.*) call for manpower; **offerte di lavoro** (*econ.*) job offers; «**offerte di lavoro**» (*giorn.*) help-wanted column; ~ **di mercato** (*econ.*) market supply; ~ **gratuita** (*d'un prodotto*) (*market.*) free offer; ~ **in blocco** block offer; **un'**~ (*di appalto, ecc.*) **in busta chiusa** (*comm.*) a sealed bid; **un'**~ **minima** a minimum offer, a minimum tender, a knock-down offer; **un'**~ **non vincolante** an unbinding offer; **offerte per un appalto pubblico** (*fin.*) calls for public tender; ~ **premio** (*market.*) premium offer; ~ **pubblica d'acquisto**

(O.P.A.) (*Borsa, fin.*) public purchase offer, public acquisition offer, take-over bid; tender (*USA*); ~ **pubblica d'acquisto in contanti** (*fin.*) cash bid; cash tender (*USA*); ~ **pubblica di scambio** (*fin.*) exchange bid; exchange offer (*USA*); ~ **reale** (*leg.*) tender; ~ **«salvo venduto»** (*market.*) offer subject to goods being unsold; **« ~ speciale»** (*market.*) bargain; **un' ~ stabile** (*market.*) a firm offer; **un' ~ vincolante** a binding offer.

officina, *n. f.* (*org. az.*) workshop, shop, works. // ~ **di montaggio** (*org. az.*) assembly shop; ~ **meccanica** (*org. az.*) machine shop; **dall' ~** (*market.*) (*di merce*) ex works; **essere in ~** (*pers.*) to be at works.

«offresi», *locuz. verb.* (*giorn., pubbl.*) «situations wanted».

offrire, *v. t.* **1** to offer. **2** (*cred.*) (*il pagamento d'un debito, ecc.*) to tender. **3** (*fin.*) to tender; (*all'asta*) to bid*. **4** (*market.*) to offer; (*mettere in vendita*) to put* up (for sale). // ~ **di più di** (*q.*) (*a un'asta, ecc.*) (*comm.*) to outbid, to overbid; ~ **garanzia** (*leg.*) to tender bail; ~ **meno di** (*un concorrente*) (*market.*) to underbid; ~ **merce a un prezzo inferiore a quello di** (*un concorrente*) (*market.*) to underbid; ~ **un prezzo più alto** (*market.*) to go one better; ~ **un programma radiofonico** (*o* **televisivo**) (*pubbl.*) to sponsor a radio (*o* television) broadcast; **essere offerto** (*fin.*) (*di titoli*) to come on offer.

oggetto, *n. m.* **1** object, thing, article. **2** (*argomento*) subject, subject-matter, matter. **3** (*ass.*) subject-matter. **4 oggetti,** *pl.* (*market.*) articles; ware (*sing. collett.*). // **l' ~ assicurato** (*ass.*) the subject-matter insured; **l' ~ del rischio** (*ass.*) the subject-matter of the risk; **l' ~ della causa** (*leg.*) the subject-matter of the action; **l' ~ della controversia** (*leg.*) the matter of the dispute, the matter in controversy; **l' ~ della lite** (*leg.*) the matter of the dispute, the matter in controversy; ~ **di franchigia** (*breve periodo di tempo, piccolo ammontare di danni, ecc.*) (*ass.*) deductible; ~ **di gran moda** (*market.*) big thing (*fam.*); ~ **d'imposta** (*fin.*) taxable basis; **l' ~ d'una lettera commerciale** (*comun.*) the subject-matter of a business letter; ~ **di scarto** (*market.*) reject; **oggetti di valore** valuable goods, valuables; **oggetti di vario genere** sundries; ~ **in mostra** (*market.*) exhibit; **oggetti personali** (*leg.*) personal belongings; **oggetti scompagnati** oddments; **oggetti smarriti** (*leg.*) waifs and strays; ~ **sociale** (*fin.*) corporate purpose (*USA*).

oggi, *avv.* to-day, today, this day. // ~ **a un mese** this day month; ~ **a otto** today week, this day week; ~ **a quindici** a fortnight to-day; **a tutt' ~** to date; **d' ~** today (*attr.*); todayish (*fam.*); **sino a ~** till today, up to now, to date.

oggigiorno, *avv.* nowadays, today.

oleodotto, *n. m.* oil-pipeline.

oligopolio, *n. m.* (*econ.*) oligopoly.

oligopsonio, *n. m.* (*econ.*) oligopsony.

olografo, *a.* (*leg.*) holograph, holographic, holographical. *n. m.* (*leg.*) holograph. // **un testamento ~** (*leg.*) a holographic testament, a holographic will.

oltremare, *avv.* **1** beyond the sea, oversea(s). **2** (*all'estero*) abroad. // **i Paesi d' ~** the overseas Countries, the foreign Countries.

omaggio, *n. m.* **1** homage. **2** (*market.*) premium, giveaway; (*di poco prezzo, offerto da un piazzista*) door opener. **3 omaggi,** *pl.* compliments. **4 «omaggi»,** *pl.* (*market., anche*) free goods. *a. attr. inv.* (*market.*) dividend (*n.*). // ~ (*di scarso valore*) **in busta** (*pubbl.*) letter gadget; **in ~** as a compliment; complimentary (*a. attr.*); **in ~ alla legge** (*leg.*) in observance of the law.

omettere, *v. t.* **1** to omit, to leave* out; to skip (*fam.*); (*sopprimere*) to suppress. **2** (*giorn.*) (*parte d'un articolo, libro, ecc.*) to retrench. **3** (*pubbl.*) to cancel. // ~ **la pubblicazione di notizie** (*giorn.*) to suppress news from publication.

omissione, *n. f.* **1** omission; skip (*fam.*); (*soppressione*) suppression; (*svista*) oversight. **2** (*giorn.*) (*di parte d'un articolo, libro, ecc.*) retrenchment. **3** (*leg.*) failure, non-feasance. **4** (*pubbl.*) cancellation. // **salvo errori e omissioni (S.E.O.)** errors and omissions excepted (*E. & O.E.*).

omologare, *v. t.* (*leg.*) to homologate, to confirm, to approve; (*ratificare*) to ratify, to validate. // ~ **un trattato** (*leg.*) to validate a treaty.

omologazione, *n. f.* (*leg.*) homologation, confirmation, approval, approbation; (*ratificazione*) ratification, validation. // ~ **del tribunale** (*leg.*) approval of the Court, consent of the Court; ~ **d'un concordato fallimentare** (*leg.*) confirmation of a bankruptcy composition.

oncia, *n. f.* ounce. // ~ **«avoirdupois»** (*unità di peso pari a 28,35 grammi*) ounce avoirdupois; ~ **«troy»** (*unità di peso pari a 31,1 grammi*) ounce troy.

ondata, *n. f.* (*anche fig.*) wave. // **un' ~ di ribasso** (*econ.*) a wave of falling prices; ~ **di scioperi** (*econ.*) upturn of strikes; **un' ~ speculativa** (*econ.*) a wave of speculation; **a ondate** in waves.

onere, *n. m.* **1** (*peso, carico*) burden, load,

charge. **2** (*responsabilità*) responsibility. **3** (*leg.*) onus★ (*solo sing.*); burden. // **~ della prova** (*leg.*) onus of proof, onus probandi, burden of proof, burden of proving; **oneri finanziari** (*rag.*) financial charges; **oneri fiscali** (*fin.*) fiscal charges, tax burdens; **oneri previdenziali** (*econ., sind.*) welfare contributions; **oneri salariali** (*econ., rag.*) labour costs; **oneri sociali** (*pers.*) social charges, social-security taxes; **~ tributario** (*fin.*) fiscal drag, taxes paid.

oneroso, *a.* **1** onerous, burdensome; (*pesante*) heavy, hard. **2** (*leg.*) onerous. // **un contratto ~** (*leg.*) an onerous contract.

onestà, *n. f. inv.* **1** honesty, straightforwardness; (*equità*) fairness. **2** (*leg.*) rightfulness.

onesto, *a.* **1** honest, straightforward, straight; (*equo*) fair. **2** (*leg.*) rightful.

onorare, *v. t.* **1** to honour; to honor (*USA*); (*rispettare*) to respect. **2** (*cred.*) to honour, to meet★. // **~ una cambiale** (*cred.*) to honour a bill of exchange, to meet a bill of exchange, to take up a bill.

onorario[1], *a.* honorary.

onorario[2], *n. m.* fee, honorarium★.

onore, *n. m.* honour; honor (*USA*).

onorifico, *a.* honorific, honorary.

opera, *n. f.* **1** (*attività, lavoro*) work, action, deed. **2** (*prodotto d'un'attività*) work, piece of work. **3** (*istituto, ente*) organization, institution, institute, society. // **opere fluviali** (*trasp.*) river works; **~ pia** (*leg.*) charitable institution, charity; **opere portuali (*o* portuarie)** (*trasp. mar.*) harbour works; **opere pubbliche** (*amm., leg.*) public works.

operaia, *n. f.* (*pers.*) workwoman★, worker.

operaio, *n. m.* **1** (*pers.*) workman★, worker, working-man★, workhand, labourer; laborer (*USA*); blue-collar worker, blue collar (man★); hand, help (*fam.*); stiff (*slang USA*). **2** (*pers.*) (*artigiano*) craftsman★. **3** (*pers.*) (*addetto a una macchina*) operator, operative. **4 operai,** *pl.* (*pers., anche*) work-people; (the) rank and file (*fig.*). *a.* **1** (*che lavora*) working, worker. **2** (*di, per operai*) working, workman's, workmen's. // **~** (*che lavora*) **a orario ridotto** (*pers.*) part-time worker; **~** (*retribuito*) **a ore** (*pers.*) time-worker; **un ~ addetto a una macchina** (*pers.*) a machine tender; **~ che fa turni di notte** (*pers.*) night man; **~ che scopre e localizza i guasti** (*d'un macchinario, ecc.*) (*pers.*) troubleshooter; trouble man (*USA*); **operai del commercio** (*pers.*) office workers; **operai del turno di notte** (*pers.*) night shift; graveyard shift (*fam.*); **operai dell'industria** (*pers.*) industrial workers; **~ dell'industria automobilistica** (*pers.*) car worker; **~ di fabbrica** (*pers.*) factory worker, mill-hand; **~ di grado inferiore** (*pers.*) junior; **~ d'officina** (*pers.*) shopman; **~ di riserva** (*adibito a lavori saltuari o alla sostituzione d'un operaio «regolare»*) (*pers.*) spare hand; **~ giornaliero** (*pers.*) journeyman; **operai in forza** (*pers.*) employees on payroll; **operai invalidi** (*pers.*) invalid workmen; **~ metallurgico** (*pers.*) metalworker; **operai non iscritti ai sindacati** (*sind.*) free labour; **~ non qualificato** (*pers.*) unskilled worker, labourer; **operai qualificati** (*pers.*) skill (*inv.*); **un ~ specializzato** (*pers.*) a skilled worker, a specialized worker.

operante, *a.* **1** operant, operating, working. **2** (*leg.*) operative. // **non ~** (*leg.*) inoperative.

operare, *v. i.* **1** to operate, to work, to act. **2** (*Borsa, fin.*) to operate, to deal★. *v. t.* to work, to do★, to carry out. // **~ al rialzo** (*Borsa*) to deal for a rise, to be on the long side of the market; **~ al ribasso** (*Borsa*) to deal for a fall; **~ su un mercato** (*fin.*) to operate on a market.

operativo, *a.* operative, operating, operational.

operatore, *n. m.* **1** operator, worker, agent. **2** (*Borsa, fin.*) operator, dealer. **3** (*market.*) (*a una fiera o mostra*) business visitor. // **~ di Borsa** (*Borsa*) dealer, stockbroker, dealer in stocks; **~ di telescrivente** (*pers.*) teletypist; **~ economico** (*econ.*) transactor; **~ estraneo alla Borsa Valori** (*fin.*) outside broker; **~ finanziario di Wall Street** (*fin., USA*) Wall Streeter (*fam.*); **~ in arbitraggi** (*Borsa*) arbitrager, arbitrageur, arbitragist; **l'~ pubblico** (*econ.*) the State.

operazione, *n. f.* **1** operation, working. **2** (*fin., market.*) transaction, dealing, deal, operation. **3** (*mat.*) operation. **4 operazioni,** *pl.* (*Borsa, anche*) market. // **un'~ a contanti** (*market.*) a transaction for cash, a cash deal, a spot transaction; **un'~ a credito** (*cred.*) a transaction on credit, a credit transaction; **operazioni a premio** (*Borsa, fin.*) option dealings, options; **~ a riporto** (*Borsa*) contango operation; **operazioni a termine** (*Borsa*) dealings for the account, transactions for the account, transactions for the settlement, futures; **~ al rialzo** (*Borsa*) bull transaction, bullish transaction, dealing for a rise; **~ al ribasso** (*Borsa*) bear transaction, bearish transaction, dealing for a fall; **~ allo scoperto** (*Borsa*) bear transaction; **operazioni attive** (*banca*) lending transactions; **operazioni bancarie** (*banca*) banking operations, banking transactions; **un'~ commerciale** a trading transaction; **le operazioni d'una banca** (*banca*) the transactions of a bank; **un'~ di Borsa** (*Borsa*) a transaction on the Stock Exchange; **operazioni di cambio** (*fin.*) exchange transactions; **operazioni di cambio a termine** (*fin.*) exchange for forward delivery; **operazioni di cambio per contanti** (*fin.*) exchange for spot delivery; **operazioni di capitale** (*fin.*) capital operations, capital transactions; **operazioni di carico** (*trasp. mar.*) loading transactions; shipment (*sing.*); **operazioni di carico e scarico** (*trasp. mar.*) loading and unloading operations; ~ **di compensazione** (*banca*) clearing; ~ **di finanziamento in essere** (*banca, fin.*) loans outstanding; **un'~ di fusione** (*fin.*) a merger deal; **operazioni d'inventario** (*org. az.*) stock-taking; **operazioni di magazzinaggio** (*org. az.*) storage operations; **operazioni di magazzinaggio nel commercio all'ingrosso** (*market.*) wholesale warehousing; **operazioni di prestito** (*banca*) lending transactions; **operazioni di ricupero** (*trasp. mar.*) salvage; ~ **di riporto** (*Borsa*) contango; **operazioni di salvataggio** (*trasp. mar.*) salvage operations, search and rescue; **operazioni di scarico** (*trasp. mar.*) unloading operations; ~ **di vendita a contanti contro riacquisto a termine** (*Borsa, fin.*) budla operation, budlaing; ~ **in azioni ancora da emettere** (*Borsa*) dealing in shares for the coming out; ~ **in bianco** (*banca, cred.*) blank deal, blank transaction; ~ (*d'acquisto e vendita*) **in titoli** (*fin.*) turn; ~ **passiva** (*banca*) borrowing transaction; **operazioni sul mercato aperto** (*fin.*) open market operations.

opificio, *n. m.* (*org. az.*) workshop, works, manufactory, factory, mill.

opinione, *n. f.* opinion; (*parere*) mind; view; (*idea*) idea; (*calcolo*) calculation; (*quel che si ha da dire*) say. // **l'~ pubblica** public opinion.

opporre, *v. t.* **1** (*contrapporre*) to oppose. **2** (*obiettare*) to object. // ~ **un'eccezione** (*leg.*) to raise an objection; ~ **un rifiuto** to give a refusal, to refuse.

opporsi, *v. rifl.* **1** to oppose, to set* oneself (against); (*essere contrario*) to be opposed (to), to resist, to counter. **2** (*far obiezione*) to object.

optimum, *n. m.* optimum. // ~ **produttivo** (*econ.*) production optimum.

opulento, *a.* **1** opulent. **2** (*econ.*) affluent.

opulenza, *n. f.* **1** opulence. **2** (*econ.*) affluence.

opuscolo, *n. m.* (*pubbl.*) booklet, brochure. // **opuscoli a stampa** (*market., pubbl.*) literature; ~ **pieghevole** (*pubbl.*) folder; **opuscoli stampati** (*giorn.*) prints.

opzionale, *a.* optional.

opzione, *n. f.* **1** option. **2** (*Borsa, fin.*) option, stock option, straddle; spread (*USA*). **3** (*comm.*) option, refusal.

ora, *n. f.* **1** (*di 60 minuti*) hour. **2** (*nel computo del tempo*) time. **3** (*tempo*) time; (*momento*) moment; (*minuto*) minute. // ~ **dell'Europa centrale** Central European Time, Mid European Time (*M.E.T.*), Mid Europe Time; ~ **dell'Europa occidentale** West European Time, Western European Time, West Europe Time; ~ **dell'Europa orientale** Eastern European Time, East European Time; ~ **d'apertura** (*market.*) opening time; ~ **di chiusura** (*market.*) closing time; ~ (*solare misurata sul meridiano*) **di Greenwich** Greenwich (mean) time, Greenwich civil time; **ore di lavoro diretto imputabili a ciascuna unità di prodotto** (*org. az.*) direct labor hours allowed per unit; **ore di lavoro fisse** (*org. az.*) set working hours; **le ore di punta** (*market., trasp.*) the rush hours, the peak hours; ~ **di scadenza** deadline; **ore d'ufficio** (*org. az.*) office hours, business hours; ~ (*legale*) **estiva** summer time; daylight saving time; daylight saving, daylight time (*USA*); ~ **in cui si deve lasciar libera una camera** (*in albergo, ecc.*) (*tur.*) check-out time; **ore lavorative** (*org. az.*) working hours; **ore lavorative perdute** (*econ.*) working hours lost; ~ **legale** *V.* ~ **estiva;** ~ **legale doppia** (*in anticipo di due ore su quella solare*) double summer time; double daylight saving time (*USA*); ~ **locale** local time, zone time; **ore** (*di lavoro*) **perdute a causa di scioperi** (*econ.*) hours lost through strikes; **ore perdute per conflitti di lavoro** (*econ.*) man-hours lost due to strikes; ~ **solare** standard time; ~ **ufficiale** standard time; ~ **«zero»** (*anche fig.*) zero hour; **a ore** (*org. az.*) by the hour.

orario, *a.* hourly, per hour. *n. m.* **1** (*org. az.*) time; hours (*pl.*). **2** (*trasp.*) (*tabella oraria*) time-table, timetable, time bill, time; schedule (*USA*). **3** (*trasp.*) (*ora, momento*) time. // ~ **di banca** banking hours; **orari di chiusura dei negozi** (*market.*) shops' closing-hours; ~ **di lavoro** (*org. az.*) working hours, working time, hours; ~ **d'ufficio** (*org. az.*) office hours; ~ **ridotto** (*org. az.*) short-time, part time; **orari settimanali** (*org. az.*) weekly time schedules; **chi lavora a ~ ridotto** (*pers.*) part-timer; **in ~** on time; (*org. az.*) on schedule.

ordinamento, *n. m.* (*leg.*) regulations, rules (*pl.*). // ~ **giudiziario** (*leg.*) judicature, judiciary; ~ **giuridico** (*leg.*) legal system; ~ **giuridico comunitario** (*leg.*) Community law.

ordinanza, *n. f.* (*leg.*) ordinance, order, injunction; (*legge*) law, rule; (*mandato*) warrant, writ; (*del giudice a un pubblico ufficiale*) mandamus. // ~ **di riabilitazione** (*d'un fallito*) (*leg.*)

order of discharge; ~ **di sequestro conservativo** (*leg.*) warrant for attachment; ~ **di trapasso delle attività** (*del debitore al curatore fallimentare*) (*leg., ingl.*) receiving order.

ordinare, *v. t.* **1** (*mettere in ordine*) to put★ (*o* to set★) in order, to tidy up, to straighten out, to straighten up; (*classificare*) to sort; (*secondo certi criteri di priorità*) to marshal. **2** (*leg.*) (*comandare*) to order, to appoint; (*decretare*) to decree; (*regolare*) to regulate, to rule. **3** (*market.*) (*commissionare*) to order, to commission, to send★ for; (*soprattutto all'estero*) to indent. **4** (*org. az.*) to calendar. // ~ **un articolo a q.** (*market.*) to order an article from (*o* of) sb.; ~ **le proprie attività patrimoniali** (*riguardo alla disponibilità per la soddisfazione d'obbligazioni*) (*leg.*) to marshal one's assets; ~ **i creditori** (*leg.*) to marshal creditors; ~ (*merci*) **di nuovo** (*market.*) to reorder; ~ **qc. in esame** (*market.*) to send for st. on approval.

ordinario, *a.* **1** (*consueto*) ordinary, customary, usual; (*comune*) common. **2** (*Borsa*) common. **3** (*fin.*) (*di capitolo d'entrata o spesa di bilancio*) above-the-line. // **ordinaria amministrazione** (*org. az.*) routine.

ordinata, *n. f.* (*mat.*) ordinate, y-coordinate, y-axis, y.

ordinativo, *n. m.* order. // ~ **d'imbarco** (*trasp. mar.*) shipping order.

ordinazione, *n. f.* (*market.*) order; (*di merci straniere*) indent; (*proveniente dall'estero*) indent. // **ordinazioni considerevoli** (*market.*) substantial orders; ~ **di prova** (*market.*) trial order; ~ **di vendita** (*market.*) selling order; ~ (*di merci*) **fatta** (*ed eseguita*) **per corrispondenza** (*market.*) mail order; **una ~ fatta una volta per sempre** (*che s'intende rinnovata tacitamente*) (*market.*) a standing order; ~ **inevasa** (*market.*) back order; **ordinazioni inevase** (*market., anche*) backlog (*sing.*); ~ **rinnovata** (*market.*) repeat order; **un'~ su catalogo** (*market.*) an order from catalogue; **un'~ urgente** (*market.*) a rush order; **che lavora su ~** (*market.*) custom (*attr., USA*); **conforme all'~** (*market.*) (*di merce, ecc.*) up to the order; **fatto su ~** (*market.*) made to order, made on order; custom (*attr., USA*).

ordine, *n. m.* **1** (*disposizione*) order, arrangement. **2** (*disciplina*) order, orderliness. **3** (*comando*) command, order. **4** (*leg.*) order, injunction; (*norma*) rule; (*decreto*) decree; (*mandato*) warrant, writ. **5** (*market.*) (*ordinazione*) order. // ~ **a esecuzione immediata** (*Borsa*) immediate or cancel order; ~ (*d'acquisto*) **al meglio** (*Borsa, fin.*) market order; **l'~ degli Avvocati** (*leg.*) the Bar Association, the Bar; ~ **del giorno** order of the day, order of business, business, agenda; (*org. az.*) docket; ~ **del giorno definitivo** approved agenda; ~ **delle ipoteche** (*leg.*) rank of mortgages; ~ **d'acquisto** (*fin., market.*) buying order, buy order, purchase order; ~ **d'acquisto** (*di titoli*) **a un prezzo massimo** (*Borsa*) limited order; ~ **d'acquisto** (*di titoli*) **frazionato** (*circa il tempo dell'operazione e il prezzo*) (*Borsa*) split order to buy; ~ **di bonifico** (*banca*) payment order; ~ **di comparizione** (*leg.*) summons, citation; ~ **di confisca** (*leg.*) extent; ~ **di consegna** (*dog.*) dandy note; (*trasp.*) delivery order; ~ **di fabbricazione** (*org. az.*) shop-order; ~ **di fermo** (*su un assegno*) (*banca*) stop payment; ~ **di grandezza** (*mat.*) order of magnitude; ~ **d'imbarco** (*trasp. mar.*) shipping note; ~ **d'ispezione** (*dei bagagli*) (*dog.*) inspection order; ~ **di lavorazione** (*org. az.*) job order; ~ **di magazzino** (*org. az.*) store order; **un ~ di pagamento** (*rag.*) an order to pay, an order for payment, a money order, a draft; « ~ **di pagamento revocato** » (*banca*) « payment counter-demanded »; **ordini di partenza** (*trasp. mar.*) sailing orders; ~ **di pignoramento presso terzi** (*leg.*) garnishee order; ~ **di prova** (*market.*) trial order, sampling order; ~ **di ricupero di cose immobili** (*illegalmente possedute*) (*leg.*) writ of detinue; ~ **di saggio** (*market.*) sampling order; ~ **di scarico della bolletta di cauzione** (*dog.*) warehouse-keeper's order; ~ **di sequestro** (*leg.*) writ of attachment; (*dei beni di un debitore*) charging order; ~ **di vendita** (*di titoli*) **a un prezzo minimo** (*Borsa*) limited order; ~ **di vendita frazionato** (*fin.*) split order to sell; ~ **pubblico** public order; ~ « **stop** » (*Borsa*) cutting limit order; ~ **valido a revoca** (*Borsa*) good till cancelled order; ~ **vincolato** (*Borsa*) contingent order; **all'~** (*cred.*) (*di titolo di credito*) to order; **fino a nuovo ~** until further orders; **in ~ alfabetico** in alphabetical order; **in ~ cronologico** in chronological order; **in ~ d'età** in order of age; **per ~ del consiglio d'amministrazione** (*fin.*) by order of the board; **per ~ e conto** (*di un cliente: di bonifico bancario, ecc.*) by standing order.

organico, *a.* organic. *n. m.* **1** roll. **2** (*pers.*) (*complesso del personale*) personnel, staff. // **essere in ~** (*pers.*) to be on the roll.

organigramma, *n. m.* (*org. az.*) organization chart.

organismo, *n. m.* **1** organism. **2** (*fig.*) organized body, body, organization; agency (*USA*). // ~ **che fissa livelli qualitativi per la pubblicità** (*pubbl.*) advertising standard authority; ~ **consultivo** advisory body; **organismi d'intervento sul mercato** (*econ., market.*) market-support agencies.

organizzare, *v. t.* **1** to organize, to arrange, to engineer. **2** (*org. az.*) (*un'azienda*) to set* up. // ~ **razionalmente** (*il lavoro*) (*org. az.*) to rationalize; ~ **uno sciopero** (*sind.*) to organize a strike.

organizzarsi, *v. rifl.* to organize, to get* organized.

organizzativo, *a.* organizatory; organizing (*attr.*).

organizzatore, *n. m.* organizer. // ~ **del lavoro d'officina** (*org. az.*) dispatcher.

organizzazione, *n. f.* **1** organization, arrangement. **2** (*org. az.*) organization, set-up. // ~ **aziendale** (*org. az.*) (*la scienza*) business management; (*complesso di persone e beni*) business structure; corporate structure (*USA*); **un'~ commerciale verticale** (*econ., org. az.*) a vertical business organization; **organizzazioni dei consumatori** (*market.*) consumers' organizations; **le organizzazioni dei trasporti** (*trasp.*) transportational organizations; ~ **del personale** (*org. az.*) personnel administration, personnel management; ~ **della produzione** (*org. az.*) production management; ~ **di fabbrica** (*org. az.*) shop-management; ~ **di vendita** (*market.*) sales organization; ~ **per obiettivi** (*org. az.*) management by objectives; ~ **razionale** (*del lavoro*) (*org. az.*) rationalization; ~ **scientifica** (*org. az.*) scientific management; ~ **sindacale** (*sind.*) labour organization; ~ **specializzata nell'incasso di crediti** (*per conto di terzi*) (*fin., USA*) factor.

organo, *n. m.* (*anche fig.*) organ. // ~ **aziendale** (*giorn.*) house organ.

orientamento, *n. m.* **1** orientation. **2** (*fig.*) (*indirizzo, guida*) guidance, guideline, guide. **3** (*fig.*) (*tendenza*) trend. // ~ **professionale** (*pers.*) vocational guidance.

orientare, *v. t.* **1** to orient. **2** (*fig.*) (*indirizzare, guidare*) to guide, to give* principles (to).

originale, *a.* **1** original. **2** (*che è proprio dell'autore*) original. **3** (*nuovo*) original, first-hand, new, novel. *n. m.* original.

origine, *n. f.* origin, beginning, starting point.

orologio, *n. m.* (*portatile*) watch; (*da muro*) clock; (*in genere*) time-piece. // ~ **a cronometro** stop-watch, timer; ~ **da muro** (*attr. uff.*) wall clock; ~ **da polso** wrist-watch; ~ **«marcatempo»** (*pers.*) time clock.

ortofrutticoltore, *n. m.* (*econ.*) market gardener; truck farmer, truck gardener, trucker (*USA*).

ortofrutticoltura, *n. f.* (*econ.*) market gardening; truck farming, truck gardening (*USA*).

oscillante, *a.* (*anche fig.*) oscillating, floating, fluctuating, fluctuant, swinging.

oscillare, *v. i.* (*anche fig.*) to oscillate, to float, to fluctuate, to swing*, to move.

oscillazione, *n. f.* (*anche fig.*) oscillation, floating, fluctuation, fluctuating, swinging, swing, movement. // ~ **ciclica** (*econ.*) cyclical fluctuation; **oscillazioni cicliche dei prezzi** (*econ.*) cyclical fluctuations of prices; **oscillazioni di cambio** (*comm. est., fin.*) fluctuations in exchange rates, fluctuations of exchange.

ossequio, *n. m.* **1** respect, regard, consideration. **2 ossequi,** *pl.* regards, respects. // **in ~ alla legge** (*leg.*) in obedience to the law, in observance of the law; **i miei migliori ossequi** my best regards.

osservanza, *n. f.* **1** observance, compliance. **2** (*ossequio*) regards, respects (*pl.*). **3** (*leg.*) observance. // **con ~** (*comun.*) respectfully Yours; **in ~ alla legge** (*leg.*) in compliance with the law; **in ~ dei vostri ordini** in compliance with your orders.

osservare, *v. t.* **1** to observe, to watch; (*esaminare*) to examine. **2** (*rilevare*) to observe, to remark; (*notare*) to notice, to note. **3** (*leg.*) to observe, to keep*, to comply with, to stand* by. // ~ **un giuramento** to keep an oath; ~ **le leggi** (*leg.*) to observe the laws, to keep the laws; **che osserva** (*leggi, prescrizioni, ecc.*) (*leg.*) observant (*a.*).

osservatore, *n. m.* observer.

ostacolare, *v. t.* to hinder, to set* back, to handicap; (*ostruire*) to obstruct, to block; (*impedire*) to prevent, to bar; (*scoraggiare*) to discourage. // ~ **il traffico** (*trasp.*) to obstruct the traffic.

ostacolo, *n. m.* obstacle, hindrance, setback, handicap; (*ostruzione*) obstruction; (*impedimento*) impediment, bar, prevention. // ~ **alla stipulazione d'un contratto** (*per incapacità d'una delle parti*) (*leg.*) impediment.

ottenere, *v. t.* **1** to obtain, to get*; (*trarre*) to draw*, to derive. **2** (*fin.*) to chalk up. **3** (*leg.*) (*qc., dal tribunale*) to recover. **4** (*market.*) (*realizzare, guadagnare*) to realize, to earn. // ~ **un accomodamento esercitando la mediazione** to mediate a settlement; ~ **un alto interesse** (*fin.*) to earn a high interest; ~ **un anticipo di denaro** (*cred., market.*) to get an advance of money; ~ **un buon impiego** (*pers.*) to get a good position; to step into a good job (*fam.*); ~ **qc. con la propria mediazione** to mediate st.; ~ **denaro per mezzo d'una cambiale di comodo** to kite (*fam.*); ~ **una dilazione di pagamento** (*cred.*) to obtain an extension of time for payment, to get time;

~ **giustizia** (*leg.*) to get legal redress; ~ **una grande rinomanza sul mercato** (*market.*) to earn a great reputation on the market; ~ **un impiego** (*pers.*) to get a situation, to get a job, to get a position; ~ **un impiego per q.** (*pers.*) to get a situation for sb.; ~ **un premio** to obtain a prize, to win a prize; ~ **un prestito su una polizza d'assicurazione** (*cred.*) to raise a loan on an insurance policy; ~ **la rappresentanza d'una ditta** (*market.*) to obtain the agency of a firm; ~ **il ribasso d'un prezzo** (*market.*) to beat down a price; ~ **il risarcimento dei danni** (*leg.*) to recover damages; ~ **una sentenza contro il convenuto** (*leg.*) to recover judgment against the defendant; ~ **un utile** (*rag.*) to realize a profit.

ottenimento, *n. m.* **1** obtainment. **2** (*leg.*) (*di qc., dal tribunale*) recovery. // **l'** ~ **d'un utile** (*rag.*) the realization of a profit.

ottimale, *a.* optimal; optimum (*attr.*).

ottimo, *a.* (*superlativo*) very good; (*eccellente*) excellent, first-rate; (*ottimale*) optimal. // **d'ottima qualità** (*market.*) first-rate, top-level, superior; prime (*attr.*).

otto, *num. card.* eight. // **(gli) «** ~ **giorni»** (*pers.*) warning.

ovest, *n. m.* west. // **l'Ovest** (*il territorio a ovest del Mississippi*) (*USA*) the West; **a** ~ (*avv.*) west.

P

pacchetto, *n. m.* **1** packet, parcel. **2** (*econ., fin.*) package deal, package. **3** (*fin.*) (*di titoli*) lot. // ~ **azionario** (*fin.*) parcel of shares; block of stock (*USA*); ~ **d'aiuti** (*econ.*) aid package; ~ **di misure anticongiunturali** (*econ., fin.*) package of booster measures; ~ **di misure contro la disoccupazione** (*econ.*) jobs package; ~ **di misure di politica dei redditi** (*fin.*) incomes package; **un** ~ **di sigarette** a packet of cigarettes; a pack of cigarettes (*USA*); ~ **industriale** (*econ.*) industrial package.

pacco, *n. m.* **1** parcel, package; (*involto*) pack. **2** (*elab. elettr.*) (*di schede perforate*) pack; deck (*USA*). **3 pacchi,** *pl.* (*comun., anche*) mail. // ~ **assicurato** (*comun.*) value parcel; ~ **contro assegno** (*comun.*) cash on delivery parcel; ~ **(di) valori** (*comun.*) value parcel; ~ **giacente** (*comun.*) dead postal packet; ~ **postale** (*comun.*) post parcel; ~ **postale non consegnato** (*comun.*) undelivered post parcel; **pacchi raccomandati** (*comun.*) registered parcels; ~ **spedito per via aerea** (*trasp. aer.*) airmail parcel; **per** ~ **postale** (*comun.*) by parcel post.

padrona, *n. f.* (*proprietaria*) owner, proprietress, proprietrix. // ~ **di casa** housewife.

padroncino, *n. m.* (*trasp. aut.*) (*camionista proprietario del camion*) truck owner-operator.

padrone, *n. m.* **1** master; boss (*fam.*). **2** (*leg.*) (*proprietario*) proprietor, owner. **3** (*org. az.*) (*principale, datore di lavoro*) principal, employer; boss, boss man* (*fam.*). **4** (*trasp. mar.*) ship's master. // ~ **di casa** householder, landlord.

paese, *n. m.* **1** (*nazione*) country; (*terra*) land; (*luogo*) place. **2** (*villaggio*) village, (little) town. // **paesi a commercio di Stato** (*econ.*) state-trading countries; **paesi acquirenti** (*econ.*) buyer countries; **paesi altamente industrializzati** (*econ.*) highly industrialized countries; **un** ~ **arretrato** (*econ.*) a backward country; ~ **consumatore** (*econ.*) consumer country, consuming country; **paesi d'oltremare** overseas countries; ~ **d'origine** country of origin, one's native land; **paesi eccedentari** (*econ.*) countries with excess production; ~ **esportatore** (*comm. est.*) exporting country, exporter; ~ **fornitore** (*comm. est.*) supplier; **i paesi fuori dell'area del dollaro** (*econ.*) the non-dollar countries; ~ **importatore** (*comm. est.*) importing country, importer; **paesi in via di sviluppo** (*econ.*) developing countries; **paesi industriali** (*econ.*) industrial countries; **paesi industrializzati** (*econ.*) developed countries; ~ **produttore** (*econ.*) producer country, producer, supplier; ~ **soggetto a forte pressione fiscale** (*fin.*) high-tax country; **paesi sottosviluppati** (*econ.*) underdeveloped countries.

paga, *n. f.* (*pers.*) pay, rate of pay; (*salario*) wage (*generalm. al pl.*); (*stipendio*) salary; packet, paycheck (*USA*). // ~ **base** (*pers.*) base pay, base rate, basic wage, standard rate, wage rate; ~ (*minima*) **garantita** (*indipendentemente dalla quantità prodotta*) (*pers.*) guaranteed rate; ~ **giornaliera** (*pers.*) daily wage, daily rate, day rate, day wages; **una** ~ **giusta** (*pers.*) a fair wage; ~ **individuale** (*pers.*) individual rate; **paghe industriali** (*pers.*) industrial wages; ~ **intera** (*senza detrazioni*) (*pers.*) full pay; ~ **mensile** (*pers.*) monthly pay, month's pay, monthly wage; ~ **netta** (*pers.*) take-home pay, take-home pay-packet, take-home; ~ **oraria** (*pers.*) hourly rate; **una** ~ **settimanale** (*pers.*) a weekly pay.

pagabile, *a.* **1** (*cred.*) payable. **2** (*leg.*) due. // ~ **a rate mensili** (*market.*) payable in monthly instalments; ~ **a richiesta** (*cred.*) payable on demand; on call; ~ **a vista** (*cred.*) payable on demand; ~ **al proprio nome** (*cred.*) drawn to self; ~ **al portatore** (*cred.*) payable to bearer; ~ **alla consegna** (*market.*) payable on delivery; «carriage forward»; ~ **alla scadenza** (*cred.*) payable at maturity; ~ **all'ordine** (*cred.*) payable to order; ~ **contro fattura** (*market.*) payable against invoice; ~ **in anticipo** payable in advance; ~ **il 4 settembre** payable on September 4th; **essere (reso) pagabile** to be made payable.

pagamento, *n. m.* **1** payment, paying; (*remunerazione*) remuneration; (*sborso*) disbursement. **2** (*cred.*) (*saldo*) settlement, discharge. // ~ **a contanti** (*market.*) cash payment, down payment, spot cash, cash and carry; ~ **a rate** (*market.*) payment by instalments; spaced payment, time payment; ~ **a saldo** (*cred.*) payment in full, full payment; ~ **«a tamburo battente»** (*market.*) spot cash, payment on the nail; ~ **a un tanto la riga** (*giorn., pubbl.*) linage; ~ **al domicilio del debitore** (*cred.*) payment at the debtor's domicile; ~ **al luogo convenuto** (*cred.*) payment on the place agreed; ~ **alla consegna** (*market.*) payment on delivery, cash on delivery, collection on delivery; ~ **all'ordinazione** (*market.*) cash with order; ~ (*di una somma di denaro*) **all'incaricato della riscossione** consignation; ~ **anticipato** (*cred.*) payment in advance, payment before due date, prepayment; **il ~ anticipato del nolo** (*trasp. mar.*) the prepayment of freight; ~ **arretrato** (*cred.*) payment overdue; ~ **«col contagocce»** (*cred.*) payment in driblets; ~ **contro assegno** (*cred.*) cash on delivery; ~ **contro documenti** (*cred.*) payment against documents, cash against documents; **pagamenti della cassa integrazione** (*sind.*) redundancy payments; ~ **di dazio** (*fin.*) tollage; **il ~ d'un debito** (*cred.*) the discharge of a debt; ~ **di pedaggio** (*trasp.*) tollage; ~ **dilazionato** (*cred.*) time payment; **pagamenti diversi** (*rag.*) sundry payments; ~ **frazionato** (*market.*) spaced payment; **un ~ immediato** (*cred.*) an outright payment, a prompt payment; ~ **in contanti** (*market.*) cash payment, down payment, spot cash, cash and carry; ~ **in conto corrente** (*banca, cred.*) payment on current account; ~ **in natura** (*cred.*) payment in kind; ~ **in piccole somme** (*cred.*) payment in driblets; ~ **in soluzione unica** (*cred.*) single payment, lump-sum payment; **un ~ integrale** (*cred.*) an outright payment; **pagamenti irregolari** (*cred.*) irregular payments; ~ **mediante assegno bancario** (*banca, cred.*) payment by cheque; ~ **parziale** (*cred.*) part payment; ~ **per intervento** (*banca, cred.*) payment per intervention, payment for honour, payment supra protest, supraprotest; ~ **«per l'onore di firma»** (*banca, cred.*) payment for honour; **pagamenti periodici** (*rag.*) terminal payments; ~ **rateale** (*market.*) payment by instalments, spaced payment, time payment; **pagamenti rateali** (*market., anche*) divided payments; ~ **ritardato** (*market.*) delayed payment; ~ **simbolico** (*cred.*) token payment; ~ **straordinario** (*pers., sind.*) bonus, premium; ~ **totale** (*cred.*) full payment; ~ **trimestrale** (*d'imposta, pensione, salario, ecc.*) (*fin., pers.*) quarterage; **pagamenti trimestrali** quarterly payments; ~ **«una tantum»** single payment; **dietro ~ di** against payment of, for payment of; **fino a ~ totale** until fully paid; **mancato ~** (*cred.*) non-payment; (*cred., leg.*) (*d'una cambiale, ecc.*) dishonour, dishonour by non-payment.

pagare, *v. t.* **1** to pay★ (for), to give★ (for); (*rimunerare*) to remunerate; (*un professionista*) to fee. **2** (*cred.*) (*saldare*) to settle, to pay★, to discharge, to pay★ out, to wipe out, to wipe off, to square, to lift. **3** (*cred., leg.*) (*onorare*) to honour, to meet★. // ~ **a contanti** (*market.*) to pay cash, to pay down; ~ **a rate** (*market.*) to pay by instalments; ~ **a saldo** (*cred.*) to pay in full; ~ **a tamburo battente** (*market.*) to pay on the nail, to pay spot cash; ~ **a vista** (*cred.*) to pay on demand; ~ **al portatore** (*cred.*) to pay to bearer; ~ **alla consegna** (*market.*) to pay cash on delivery; ~ **gli arretrati** (*cred.*) to pay up arrears; ~ **un avvocato** to fee a lawyer; ~ **una cambiale alla scadenza** (*cred.*) to pay a bill at maturity, to meet a bill at maturity, to honour a bill at maturity; ~ **la cauzione per q.** (*leg.*) to stand surety for sb., to go bail for sb.; ~ **«col contagocce»** to pay in driblets; ~ **come caparra** (*leg.*) to deposit; ~ **con un assegno** (*cred.*) to pay by cheque; ~ **il conto** to pay the bill, to foot the bill; ~ **un conto** (*cred.*) to settle an account; ~ **i creditori** (*cred.*) to pay (off) one's creditors; ~ **un debito** (*cred.*) to discharge a debt, to satisfy a debt, to quit a debt; (*col ricavato del proprio lavoro*) to work off a debt; ~ **un debito in anticipo** (*cred.*) to anticipate an obligation; ~ **un dividendo** (*fin.*) to pay a dividend; ~ **una fattura** (*cred.*) to settle a bill; ~ **fino all'ultimo centesimo** (*cred.*) to pay to the last penny; ~ **in anticipo** to pay in advance, to prepay; ~ (*una somma di denaro*) **in anticipo** (*leg.*) to deposit; ~ **in anticipo gli interessi su un prestito** (*cred.*) to prepay the interest on a loan; ~ **in contanti** (*market.*) to pay cash, to pay down; ~ **in natura** (*cred.*) to pay in kind; ~ **in piccole somme** (*cred.*) to pay in driblets; ~ **la merce** (*market.*) to pay for the goods; ~ **un occhio della testa** (*fig.*) to pay through the nose; ~ **il pedaggio** (*trasp.*) to pay toll, to toll; ~ **totalmente** (*cred.*) to pay up; **ancora da ~** owing; **chi è tenuto a ~** (*cred.*) payer, payor; **non ~ una cambiale** (*cred.*) to dishonour a bill; **chi paga** (*cred.*) payer, payor; **non essere pagato dopo la scadenza** (*cred.*) (*di debito*) to lie over.

pagato, *a.* **1** paid. **2** (*cred.*) settled. // ~ **a saldo** (*cred.*) settled in full; ~ **in anticipo** (*cred.*) prepaid, paid in advance; **non ~** unpaid; (*cred.*) unsettled, uncollected, outstanding.

pagatore, *n. m.* payer, payor. *a.* paying; pay (*attr.*). // **un agente ~** a pay-clerk.

pagherò, *n. m.* **1** (*cred.*) I owe you (*abbr.*

IOU). **2** (*cred.*) (*cambiario*) promissory note, note of hand; marker (*USA*); dog, good-for (*slang USA*). // ~ **cambiario recante la sola firma dell'emittente** (*e nessuna girata*) (*cred.*) single-name paper.

pagina, *n. f.* page. // **le pagine della pubblicità** (*giorn.*) the advertising pages; **a ~ intera** (*pubbl.*) full-page (*a.*); **a piede** (*o* **piè**) **di ~** at the foot of the page.

paniere, *n. m.* **1** (*anche econ.*) basket. **2** (*fin.*) (*monetario*) basket. // **il ~ dei consumi privati** (*econ.*) the housewife's shopping basket; **il ~ del carovita** (*econ.*) the basket of goods from which price increases are calculated for indexation purposes (*in Italia*); **il ~ della scala mobile** (*econ.*) the cost-of-living basket of goods (*in Italia*).

paragrafo, *n. m.* **1** paragraph. **2** (*giorn.*) section. **3** (*leg.*) section. // **a paragrafi spaziati** (*ma senza rientri a capolinea*) (*di una lettera commerciale*) in block form.

paralisi, *n. f. inv.* (*anche fig.*) paralysis★.

paralizzare, *v. t.* (*anche fig.*) to paralyse; to paralyze (*USA*). // ~ **il risparmio** (*fin.*) to curb the expansion of savings.

paranco, *n. m.* (*trasp. mar.*) tackle. // **sotto ~** (*trasp. mar.*) under ship's tackle.

parcella, *n. f.* honorarium★, fee. // ~ **condizionata** (*al buon esito della causa patrocinata*) (*leg.*) contingent fee; ~ **d'avvocato** (*leg.*) note of counsel's fees, counsel's fees, bill of costs; ~ **fondiaria** (*leg.*) parcel; ~ **supplementare** (*pagata a un avvocato in una causa lunga*) (*leg.*) refresher.

pareggiare, *v. t.* **1** (*rendere pari*) to equalize, to make★ equal. **2** (*rag.*) to balance, to settle, to square. // ~ **il bilancio** (*rag.*) to balance accounts; ~ **il bilancio pubblico** (*fin., rag.*) to balance the budget; ~ **i conti** (*fin.*) to break even.

pareggio, *n. m.* **1** (*il rendere pari*) equalization. **2** (*fin., rag.*) (*saldo*) balance, settlement. // ~ **dei conti** (*fin.*) break-even; **chiudere in ~** (*fin.*) to break even; **in ~** (*rag.*) in balance.

parentesi, *n. f. inv.* parenthesis★; bracket (*generalm. al pl.*). // ~ **quadra** square bracket; **parentesi tonde** round brackets.

parere[1], *n. m.* **1** opinion, advice, counsel. **2** (*leg.*) opinion. // ~ **consultivo** advisory opinion; **il ~ dell'avvocato** (*leg.*) the advice of the counsel, the counsel's advice, the counsel's opinion; **il ~ d'un competente** an expert opinion; ~ **legale** (*leg.*) counsel's advice, counsel's opinion.

parere[2], *v. i.* **1** (*sembrare*) to seem, to appear, to look. **2** (*pensare*) to think★ (*v. pers.*).

pari, *a. inv.* **1** equal, same, like. **2** (*all'altezza di*) equal (to). **3** (*mat.*) (*divisibile per due*) even. *n. m.* **1** (*chi è dello stesso grado, condizione, ecc.*) equal, peer. **2** (*titolo nobiliare ingl.*) Peer, Lord. *n. f.* (*fin.*) par. // ~ **commerciale** (*fin.*) commercial par; ~ **di cambio politico** (*fin.*) arbitrated par of exchange; ~ **di cambio proporzionale** (*fin.*) arbitrated par of exchange; **essere ~ alla domanda** (*econ.*) to meet the demand; **alla ~** (*fin.*) at par, even; **in ~ data** of even date; **sopra la ~** (*fin.*) above par, at a premium; **sotto la ~** (*fin.*) below par, at a discount.

parificare, *v. t.* to equalize, to make★ equal.

parificazione, *n. f.* equalization, equalizing. // ~ **dei sistemi di finanziamento** (*fin.*) equalization of financing methods.

parità, *n. f. inv.* **1** parity; (*uguaglianza*) equality. **2** (*fin.*) parity, par. **3** (*fin.*) peg. // ~ **aurea** (*fin.*) gold standard; **parità cambiarie** (*fin.*) parities of exchange; **parità centrali** (*fra cambi*) (*fin.*) central (exchange) rates; ~ **concorrenziale** (*market.*) equal competitive footing, equal conditions of competition; ~ **del potere d'acquisto** (*di due monete*) (*econ.*) purchasing power parity; ~ **di cambio** (*fin.*) par of exchange, mint par of exchange, currency exchange rates; ~ **di voti** equality of votes; ~ **fissa** (*fin.*) fixed parity; **la ~ fra due tassi di cambio** (*fin.*) the parity between two rates of exchange; ~ **in dollari** (*fin.*) dollar parity; **parità indirette** (*fin.*) indirect parities, cross rates of exchange; ~ **mobile** (*fin.*) crawling peg, shiftable parity; ~ **monetaria** (*econ.*) currency parity; ~ **relativa** (*fin.*) (*dei cambi*) cross rate; ~ **rigida** (*fin.*) rigid parity; ~ **rispetto al dollaro** (*fin.*) dollar parity; ~ **salariale** (*sind.*) equal pay for equal work; ~ **valutaria** (*fin.*) currency exchange rates; **a ~ di condizioni** other things being equal; **a ~ di voti** at a parity of votes.

paritetico, *a.* joint.

parlare, *v. i.* **1** to speak★, to talk. **2** (*trattare parlando*) to speak★; (*trattare scrivendo*) to write★, to mention. **3** (*discutere di*) to discuss, to talk. **4** (*rivolgersi a*) to address. *v. t.* to speak★. // ~ **al telefono** (*comun.*) to speak on the telephone; ~ **d'affari** to talk business.

parola, *n. f.* **1** word. **2** (*promessa, impegno*) word, promise. // ~ **d'onore** word of honour; ~ **in codice** (*comun.*) code word; ~ **per ~** word for word; **parole usate per reclamizzare un prodotto** (*pubbl.*) message (*sing.*); **in parole** in words; **l'ultima ~** the last word; (*market.*) the final offer.

«parquet», *n. m.* **1** (*pavimento a listelli di*

legno) parquet-flooring. **2** (*Borsa*) floor; pit (*USA*).

parsimonioso, *a.* thrifty.

parte, *n. f.* **1** (*porzione*) part, share, portion; (*pezzo*) piece; (*frazione*) fraction; (*quota*) quota; (*sezione*) section; (*fetta, anche fig.*) slice. **2** (*lato*) part, side, way. **3** (*leg.*) party, side. // **la ~ acquirente** (*leg.*) the purchasing party; **~ civile** (*leg.*) plaintiff, complainant; **le parti contraenti** (*leg.*) the contracting parties, the parties; **la ~ del «dare»** (*rag.*) the liabilities side; **la ~ dell'«avere»** (*rag.*) the assets side; **~ di premio rimborsabile in caso di disdetta anticipata** (*della polizza*) (*ass.*) unearned premium; **~ di ricambio** (*org. az.*) spare part, spare; **~ «entrate»** (*di un bilancio*) (*rag.*) income; **~ fabbisogni** (*d'un bilancio*) (*rag.*) requirements; **~ in causa** (*leg.*) litigant; contracting party, real party in interest, party; **le parti in causa** (*leg.*) the parties to the case; **~ in giudizio** (*leg.*) suitor; **la ~ inadempiente** (*leg.*) the defaulting party; **~ integrante** part and parcel; **le parti interessate** (*leg.*) the interested parties, the parties concerned; **la ~ lesa** (*leg.*) the injured party, the offended party; **parti litiganti** (*in giudizio*) (*leg.*) contending parties; **~ residua** (*di eredità: dopo il pagamento di debiti e legati*) (*leg.*) residue; **la ~ soccombente** (*in giudizio*) (*leg.*) the unsuccessful party; **da ~ di** on the part of; (*per conto di*) on behalf of, from; **essere dalla ~ del torto** to be in the wrong; **in ~** partly, in part.

partecipante, *n. m.* e *f.* participant, partaker, sharer. // **i partecipanti a una riunione** the people attending a meeting; **i partecipanti a una «tavola rotonda»** (*fin., market.*) the round table.

partecipare, *v. i.* **1** (*prendere parte*) to participate, to take★ part (in st.), to share (st., in st.), to partake★ (of st., in st.). **2** (*essere presente*) to attend (st.), to be present (at st.). // **~ a un affare** to take part in a business deal; **~ a un'impresa** to take an interest in an enterprise; **~ agli utili** (*fin.*) to share profits, to share in the profits, to take a share in the profits; **~ alla gestione** (*amm.*) to share in the management.

partecipazione, *n. f.* **1** (*il partecipare*) participation, participating, sharing. **2** (*presenza*) presence, attendance. **3** (*fin.*) (*al capitale azionario*) share of stock, share. **4 partecipazioni,** *pl.* (*fin.*) holdings. // **~ agli utili** (*fin.*) sharing of profits, profit-sharing, participation, lay; **~ agli utili con distribuzione in contanti** (*pers., sind.*) cash distribution plan; **partecipazioni azionarie** (*fin.*) equity participations, equity interests; **~ di maggioranza** (*fin.*) controlling interest; **~ (*azionaria*) incrociata** (*fin.*) cross participation; **partecipazioni incrociate** (*fin.*) interwoven holdings; **Partecipazioni Statali** State Participations (in Industry) (*in Italia*); **a ~ statale** (*econ.*) State-controlled (*a.*); **avere una ~ agli utili** (*fin.*) to have a share in the profits.

partenza, *n. f.* **1** departure, leaving. **2** (*trasp. mar.*) sailing. **3** (*tur.*) (*in un albergo*) check-out. // **in ~** (*trasp. mar.*) about to sail, outward-bound; outgoing.

particella, *n. f.* particle, minute part. // **~ catastale** (*leg.*) parcel.

particolare, *a.* particular, special. *n. m.* particular, detail. // **i particolari d'una domanda giudiziale** (*leg.*) the particulars; **i particolari d'un progetto** the details of a plan; **nei particolari** in detail, into detail.

partire, *v. i.* **1** to leave★, to go★ away, to depart. **2** (*trasp. aer.*) (*decollare*) to take★ off. **3** (*trasp. mar.*) (*salpare*) to sail. // **~ da zero** (*fig.*) to start from scratch; **a ~ da** beginning from, starting from, as from, to count from; **a ~ da oggi** beginning today, reckoning from today.

partita, *n. f.* **1** (*fin.*) (*di titoli*) lot. **2** (*market.*) (*di merci*) lot, consignment, parcel, batch. **3** (*rag.*) entry, item. // **~ a credito** (*rag.*) book credit, credit item; **~ a debito** (*rag.*) book debit, debit item; **partite correnti** (*fin.*) current items, current accounts; **una ~ di calzature** (*market.*) a lot of shoes; **partite di debito** (*rag.*) claims (against a business); **~ di giro** (*rag.*) clearing account, clearing transaction; **una ~ di merci** (*market.*) a parcel of goods; **~ di merci disparate** (*market.*) job lot; **una ~ di titoli** (*fin.*) a lot of shares, a block of shares; **~ doppia** (*rag.*) double entry; **partite invisibili** (*della bilancia dei pagamenti*) (*econ.*) invisible items, invisibles; **~ registrata due volte** (*rag.*) amount entered twice; **~ semplice** (*rag.*) single entry; **partite visibili** (*econ.*) visible items, visibles; **le partite visibili della bilancia dei pagamenti** (*econ.*) the visible items in the balance of payments; **partite visibili e invisibili** (*econ.*) visible and invisible items.

partitario, *n. m.* (*rag.*) ledger. // **~ a schede** (*rag.*) card-ledger; **~ clienti** (*rag.*) debtors ledger; **~ fornitori** (*rag.*) creditors ledger.

parziale, *a.* **1** (*che è o avviene soltanto in parte*) partial. **2** (*che favorisce una delle parti*) partial, prejudiced, biased.

passaggio, *n. m.* **1** passage, passing. **2** (*leg.*) conveyance, transfer. **3** (*trasp.*) transit, passage. **4** (*trasp. aer., trasp. mar.*) passage, voyage. // **~ a livello** (*trasp. ferr.*) level crossing; grade crossing (*USA*); **~ da un'occupazione all'altra**

(*pers.*) job-hopping; ~ **di proprietà** (*leg.*) conveyance of property, transfer of property, transfer of title, transfer; **un ~ di responsabilità** a shift of responsibility; **passaggi interni di materie** (*org. az.*) interplant transfers of materials; ~ **marittimo** (*trasp. mar.*) sea passage, pass; ~ **pedonale** pedestrian crossing; walking-way (*USA*).

passaporto, *n. m.* (*tur.*) passport.

passare, *v. i.* **1** to pass, to pass by, to go★ by. **2** (*trascorrere*) to pass, to go★ by, to elapse. **3** (*cessare*) to pass, to cease. **4** (*andare, venire*) to call on (sb.), to call at (a place), to drop in (on sb.). **5** (*leg.*) (*di progetto di legge, ecc.*) to be passed, to pass. **6** (*leg.*) (*di proprietà*) to pass, to lapse. *v. t.* **1** (*oltrepassare*) to pass, to go★ beyond; (*attraversare*) to go★ through, to cross. **2** (*trascorrere*) to pass, to spend★. **3** (*dare*) to give★; (*trasmettere*) to hand, to hand over. **4** (*leg.*) (*approvare*) to pass. **5** (*market.*) (*un'ordinazione*) to pass, to place. // ~ (*una partita*) **a mastro** (*rag.*) to post, to post up; ~ **agli atti** (*leg.*) to file; ~ **al vaglio** to screen; ~ **all'industria** (*econ.*) to go industrial; ~ (*un assegno, ecc.*) **alla stanza di compensazione** (*fin.*) to clear; ~ **di moda** (*market.*) to go out of fashion, to outmode; ~ **in giudizio** (*leg.*) to become final, to become res judicata; ~ **sotto silenzio** to be silent about (*o* on), to ignore; ~ **le vacanze** to spend one's holidays; to vacation (*USA*); **passarsela bene** (*a quattrini*) to be well off; **passarsela male** (*a quattrini*) to be badly off.

passato, *a.* (*trascorso*) past; (*scorso*) last. *n. m.* past, past time. // ~ **di moda** (*market.*) out-of-date, outdated, out.

passeggero, *a.* passing, transitory, temporary. *n. m.* (*trasp.*) passenger, traveller; traveler (*USA*); fare. // ~ **che viaggia sopra coperta** (*trasp. mar.*) deck passenger; ~ **di cabina** (*trasp. mar.*) cabin passenger; **passeggeri di terza classe** (*trasp. mar.*) steerage passengers; **passeggeri trasportati** (*trasp. ferr.*) train-load (*sing.*).

passibile, *a.* (*leg.*) liable, amenable. // ~ **di pena** (*leg.*) indictable; **essere ~ di multa** (*leg.*) to be liable to a fine.

passività, *n. f. inv.* (*rag.*) liability; (*indebitamento*) indebtedness. // **passività a breve scadenza** (*rag.*) current liabilities; **passività a lungo termine** (*rag.*) long-term liabilities; ~ **consolidate** *V.* ~ **a lungo termine; passività correnti** (*rag.*) current liabilities; **passività inesigibili** (*rag.*) non-current liabilities.

passivo, *a.* **1** (*inerte*) passive, inactive, inert. **2** (*rag.*) (*che non dà profitto*) passive, unprofitable. *n. m.* (*rag.*) deficit, indebtedness; liabilities (*pl.*). // ~ **fallimentare** (*leg.*) bankruptcy liabilities; **essere in ~** (*banca, cred.*) to be in the red (*fig.*); **in ~** (*econ.*) lossmaking.

patentato, *a.* **1** licensed, certificated. **2** (*leg.*) (*brevettato*) proprietary.

patente, *n. f.* **1** (*leg.*) (*licenza*) licence, license, permit. **2** (*leg.*) (*brevetto d'invenzione*) patent. **3** (*trasp. mar.*) bill. // ~ **di guida** (*trasp. aut.*) driving licence, driver's licence; ~ **di sanità** (*trasp. mar.*) bill of health; ~ **mercantile** (*trasp. mar.*) demand pass; ~ **provvisoria** (*trasp. aut.*) provisional licence.

paternità, *n. f. inv.* **1** paternity, fatherhood. **2** (*leg.*) (*nome del padre*) father's name.

patrimoniale, *a.* (*leg.*) patrimonial, hereditary. // **asse ~** estate and property; **stato ~** (*rag.*) statement of assets and liabilities.

patrimonio, *n. m.* **1** (*leg.*) (*beni avuti in eredità*) patrimony, heritage, inheritance, estate. **2** (*leg.*) (*beni personali*) estate, property, worth. // ~ **fisico** (*rag.*) tangible net worth; ~ **immobiliare** (*rag.*) real estate, real property; ~ **mobiliare** (*rag.*) personal estate, personal property; ~ **netto** (*rag.*) net assets, net worth; ~ **personale** (*leg.*) personal estate, personal property; ~ **proveniente da eredità** (*leg.*) estate in inheritance.

patrocinante, *a.* patronizing, sponsoring, supporting. *n. m.* (*leg.*) pleader. // **l'avvocato ~** (*leg.*) the counsel.

patrocinare, *v. t.* **1** to patronize, to sponsor; (*sostenere*) to support, to back. **2** (*leg.*) (*una causa*) to plead. // ~ **q.** (*leg.*) to hold a brief for sb.; ~ **una causa** (*leg.*) to plead.

patrocinatore, *n. m.* **1** patronizer, sponsor; (*sostenitore*) supporter. **2** (*leg.*) pleader, counsel.

patrocinio, *n. m.* **1** support. **2** (*leg.*) legal representation, patronage.

patto, *n. m.* **1** (*convenzione, accordo*) agreement, understanding; (*fra nazioni*) treaty. **2** (*ciascuno dei punti convenuti*) term. **3** (*leg.*) pact, compact, covenant, contract. // ~ **arbitrale** (*leg.*) arbitration agreement, arbitration bond; ~ **di riservato dominio** (*leg.*) conditional sale agreement; **a ~ che** on condition that, on the understanding that, provided that.

pattuire, *v. t.* (*anche leg.*) to stipulate, to negotiate, to covenant, to condition; (*fissare*) to fix, to settle. // ~ **una garanzia** (*leg.*) to stipulate a guarantee.

pattuito, *a.* (*anche leg.*) stipulated, agreed upon, negotiated; (*fissato*) fixed, settled. *n. m.* agreement; terms (*pl.*).

pecuniario, *a.* pecuniary, monetary; money (*attr.*). // **non ~** (*leg.*) non-pecuniary; **una pena**

pecuniaria (*leg.*) a pecuniary penalty, a fine.

pedaggio, *n. m.* (*trasp.*) toll, tollage.

pegno, *n. m.* (*leg.*) pawn, pledge, lien, gage, security. // ~ **di merci** (*e/o denaro o altri valori*) (*leg.*) bailment; ~ **marittimo** (*leg.*) maritime lien; **chi costituisce un** ~ (*leg.*) pawnee; **chi ha dato qc. in** ~ (*leg.*) pledger; **chi ha ricevuto qc. in** ~ (*leg.*) pawnee, pledgee.

pena, *n. f.* **1** (*leg.*) (*punizione*) punishment, penalty; (*sanzione*) sanction. **2** (*leg.*) (*sentenza*) sentence, term of imprisonment. // ~ **commutabile** (*leg.*) commutable punishment; ~ **pecuniaria** (*leg.*) pecuniary punishment, fine; **a mala** ~ barely, hardly, scarcely; **sotto** ~ **di** under penalty of.

penale, *a.* (*leg.*) penal, criminal. *n. f.* **1** (*leg.*) penalty, punishment, forfeiture. **2** (*leg.*) (*in un contratto, ecc.*) penalty clause.

penalista, *n. m.* e *f.* **1** (*leg.*) (*esperto del diritto penale*) penologist, criminologist. **2** (*leg.*) (*avvocato in cause penali*) criminal lawyer.

penalità, *n. f. inv.* (*leg.*) penalty, forfeiture, forfeit. // ~ **per ritardo** (*leg.*) penalty for delay.

pendente, *a.* (*leg.*) (*di causa, ecc.*) pendent, pending.

pendenza, *n. f.* **1** (*cred.*) outstanding account, outstanding matter. **2** (*leg.*) pending suit. // **in** ~ (*cred.*) outstanding.

pendolare, *n. m.* e *f.* (*trasp. ferr.*) commuter. // **servizi per i pendolari** (*trasp. ferr.*) commuter services.

penna, *n. f.* (*per scrivere*) pen. // ~ **a sfera** ball-point pen, ball-pen; ~ **stilografica** fountain-pen.

penny, *n. m.* (*ingl.*) (*moneta pari a 1 centesimo di sterlina*) penny★.

pensilina, *n. f.* (*trasp. ferr.*) station-roof, platform-roofing. // ~ **delle partenze** (*trasp. ferr.*) departure platform.

pensionabile, *a.* (*pers., rag.*) pensionable.

pensionamento, *n. m.* (*pers.*) retirement. // ~ **anticipato** (*pers.*) early retirement, beforehand retirement; ~ **posticipato** (*pers.*) delayed retirement.

pensionare, *v. t.* (*pers.*) (*collocare in pensione*) to pension, to retire, to superannuate.

pensionato, *n. m.* **1** (*pers.*) pensioner, pensionary, superannuitant. **2 i pensionati,** *pl.* (*pers.*) the retired personnel (*sing.*). // **un** ~ **statale** (*amm., pers.*) a retired civil servant.

pensione[1], *n. f.* (*pers.*) pension, annuity, allowance, superannuation, retired pension, retired pay. // ~ **agganciata al salario** (*o* **allo stipendio**) **già percepito** (*dal lavoratore*) (*pers.*) earnings-related pension; ~ **alimentare** (*pers.*) allowance for necessaries; ~ **di guerra** war pension; ~ **d'invalidità** (*pers.*) disability pension, invalidity pension; ~ **di reversibilità** (*pers.*) survivorship annuity, reversionary annuity; ~ **di vecchiaia** (*pers.*) old-age pension; ~ **ordinaria** (*per raggiunti limiti d'età*) retirement pension; **che dà diritto a** ~ (*pers., rag.*) pensionable (*a.*); **che ha diritto a** ~ (*pers., rag.*) pensionable (*a.*); **che va in** ~ (*pers.*) retiring; **in** ~ (*pensionato*) (*pers.*) retired (*a.*).

pensione[2], *n. f.* **1** (*tur.*) (*il fornire o ricevere vitto e alloggio*) board and lodging, boarding. **2** (*tur.*) (*luogo in cui si fa pensione*) boarding-house, pension.

percentuale, *a.* per cent, percent; (*proporzionale*) proportional. *n. f.* percentage, centage; (*proporzione*) proportion; (*tasso*) rate. // **la** ~ **degli utili sociali** (*fin., rag.*) the rate of corporate profits; ~ **del valore attuale d'un mutuo** (*spesso aggiunta come compenso di collocazione*) (*cred.*) point; **una** ~ **sugli utili** (*fin.*) a percentage of the proceeds.

percepire, *v. t.* **1** (*riscuotere*) to collect, to cash, to receive. **2** (*pers.*) (*uno stipendio*) to draw★. // ~ **il sussidio di disoccupazione** (*sind.*) to be on relief.

percettore, *n. m.* one who collects (*o* cashes, *o* receives; *V.* **percepire**). // ~ **di un prestito** (*cred.*) borrower; ~ **di reddito** (*fin.*) income earner.

percorrenza, *n. f.* (*trasp. mar.*) endurance.

percorrere, *v. t.* **1** (*attraversare*) to run★ through, to run★ across. **2** (*trasp.*) to travel, to cover. **3** (*trasp., trasp. aer., trasp. mar.*) (*laghi, oceani, ecc.*) to voyage. **4** (*trasp. mar.*) to sail.

percorso, *n. m.* **1** (*tratto che si percorre*) route; (*cammino*) way. **2** (*distanza percorsa*) distance covered. **3** (*trasp.*) (*viaggio*) journey, trip. **4** (*trasp. mar.*) (*d'una corrente*) drift. // ~ **a (vagone) carico** (*trasp. ferr.*) loaded journey, journey loaded; ~ **a (vagone) vuoto** (*trasp. ferr.*) empty journey, journey empty.

perdere, *v. t.* **1** to lose★. **2** (*mancare*) to miss. **3** (*sprecare*) to waste; (*tempo, anche*) to lose★. **4** (*fin.*) (*denaro: in investimenti azzardati, anche*) to sink★. *v. i.* **1** to lose★. **2** (*far acqua*) to leak. // ~ **un appuntamento** to miss an appointment; ~ **una causa** (*leg.*) to lose a lawsuit; ~ **contatto con q.** to lose touch with sb.; ~ **di vista q.** to lose sight of sb.; ~ **un diritto** (*leg.*) to lose a right; ~ **la faccia** (*fig.*) to lose face; ~ **l'impiego** (*pers.*) to lose one's berth, to lose one's job; ~ **un'occasione** to miss an opportunity; to miss the bus (*fig.*); ~ (*un diritto*) **per confisca** (*leg.*) to forfeit; ~ (*un di-*

ritto) **per inadempimento** (*leg.*) to forfeit; ~ (*un diritto*) **per violazione d'una norma** (*leg.*) to forfeit; ~ **tempo** to waste one's time; ~ **il treno** to miss the train; to miss the bus (*fig.*); «**a** ~» (*market.*) not returnable, non-returnable (*a.*).

perdita, *n. f.* **1** loss; (*danno*) damage. **2** (*di tempo*) waste. **3** (*di liquido, ecc.*) leak, leakage. **4** (*ass., fin., rag.*) loss. // ~ **accidentale** (*ass. mar., trasp. mar.*) accidental loss; (*econ.*) windfall loss; ~ **al netto del valore della merce ricuperata** (*ass.*) salvage loss; ~ **con ricupero** (*ass.*) salvage loss; **la** ~ **della nave** (*ass. mar.*) the loss of the ship; ~ (*per oscillazioni*) **di cambio** (*fin.*) loss on exchange; ~ **di denaro** (*da ricuperare*) leeway (*fig.*); **la** ~ **d'un diritto** (*leg.*) the loss of a right; ~ **d'esercizio** (*rag.*) trading loss; ~ **di lavorazione** (*org. az.*) loss in process; ~ **di tempo** (*da ricuperare*) leeway (*fig.*); ~ **effettivamente subita** (*ass.*) actual loss; ~ **inutilizzata** (*di un esercizio passato*) **detraibile dall'imponibile** (*fin.*) carry-back (*USA*); **perdite irreparabili** irrecoverable losses; ~ **netta** (*rag.*) net loss, dead loss; **perdite non deducibili** (*agli effetti fiscali*) (*fin.*) non-deductible losses; ~ **parziale** (*ass.*) partial loss; ~ **per avaria generale** (*ass. mar.*) general average loss; ~ **per colaggio** (*ass. mar.*) loss by leakage; ~ (*d'un diritto*) **per confisca** (*leg.*) forfeiture; ~ (*d'un diritto*) **per inadempimento** (*leg.*) forfeiture; ~ (*d'un diritto*) **per violazione d'una norma** (*leg.*) forfeiture; ~ **secca** (*rag.*) dead loss; **perdite su crediti** (*rag.*) credit losses; ~ **totale** (*ass. mar.*) total loss; ~ **totale con abbandono** (*della nave*) (*ass. mar.*) total loss with abandonment; ~ **totale effettiva** (*ass. mar.*) actual total loss; ~ **totale presunta** (*ass. mar.*) constructive total loss; ~ **totale relativa** (*ass. mar.*) constructive total loss; **in** ~ (*comm.*) at a loss, at a sacrifice; (*econ.*) (*d'azienda, ecc.*) lossmaking.

perequare, *v. t.* to equalize, to make★ equal. // ~ **i redditi** (*econ.*) to equalize incomes.

perequazione, *n. f.* equalization, equal distribution. // **la** ~ **delle imposte** (*fin.*) the equalization of taxes.

perfetto, *a.* perfect.

perfezionamento, *n. m.* **1** (*il perfezionare*) perfecting; (*miglioramento*) betterment, improvement; (*completamento*) completion. **2** (*specializzazione*) specialization, specializing. **3** (*leg.*) (*d'un contratto*) implementation, execution.

perfezionare, *v. t.* **1** to perfect, to make★ perfect; (*migliorare*) to better, to improve; (*completare*) to complete. **2** (*leg.*) (*un contratto*) to implement, to execute. // ~ **un contratto** (*leg.*) to execute a contract.

perfezionarsi, *v. rifl.* **1** (*diventare perfetto*) to become★ perfect; (*migliorare*) to improve. **2** (*fare studi di perfezionamento*) to perfect oneself (in st.), to improve one's knowledge (of st.).

perforare, *v. t.* (*elab. elettr.*) to punch.

perforatrice di schede, *locuz. n.* (*elab. elettr.*) card punch.

perforazione, *n. f.* (*elab. elettr.*) punching.

pericolo, *n. m.* **1** danger, peril, hazard, risk, distress. **2** (*trasp. mar.*) distress, peril, danger. // **i pericoli del mare** (*ass. mar.*) the perils of the sea; **i pericoli della strada** (*trasp. aut.*) the dangers of the road; ~ **imminente** (*trasp. mar.*) imminent peril.

pericoloso, *a.* dangerous, perilous, hazardous; (*malsicuro*) risky, unsafe.

periodico, *a.* **1** periodical, periodic, recurrent, recurring. **2** (*giorn.*) (*di pubblicazione, opuscolo, ecc.*) serial. **3** (*mat.*) recurring. *n. m.* (*giorn.*) periodical, journal, magazine, newspaper. // **un** ~ **mensile** (*giorn.*) a monthly; **un** ~ **popolare** (*giorn.*) a popular magazine; **un** ~ **settimanale** (*giorn.*) a weekly; **un** ~ **sportivo** (*giorn.*) a sports magazine.

periodo, *n. m.* **1** (*intervallo di tempo*) period, lapse; (*stadio*) stage. **2** (*leg.*) (*di tempo*) term. **3** (*mat.*) period, repetend. // ~ (*passato*) **alle dipendenze** (*di q.*) (*pers.*) stretch of work, stretch; ~ **base** (*econ.*) base period; ~ **breve** (*econ.*) short period, short range, short run; ~ **contabile** (*rag.*) accounting period; ~ **d'addestramento** (*pers.*) follow-up; ~ **d'approvvigionamenti** (*org. az.*) purchasing period; ~ **di copertura** (*ass.*) policy period; ~ **di crisi** (*delle vendite, ecc.*) (*market.*) down; ~ **di disoccupazione** (*econ.*) spell of unemployment; ~ **d'imposta** (*fin.*) fiscal year; ~ **d'inattività** (*market.*) slack; (*org. az.*) (*di una macchina, d'una fabbrica o d'un reparto*) downtime, layoff; ~ **di permanenza in carica** (*leg.*) term of office; ~ **di prescrizione** (*leg.*) statutory period; **un** ~ **di prezzi crescenti** (*market.*) a period of rising prices; ~ **di prova** (*pers.*) probationary period, probation; **un** ~ **di restrizioni finanziarie** (*fin.*) a period of financial squeeze; ~ **di ristagno** (*market.*) slack; ~ **di scarsa attività del mercato** (*market.*) narrow market.

perito, *a.* expert, skilled, well-experienced. *n. m.* **1** expert. **2** (*ass.*) insurance adjuster, investigator, surveyor, valuer, valuator. **3** (*leg.*) expert, assessor. **4** (*pers.*) technician. // ~ **commerciale** qualified accountant; ~ **d'avaria** (*ass. mar.*) average surveyor; ~ **industriale** (*pers.*) engineer; ~ **nominato dal tribunale** (*leg.*) expert appointed by the Court; ~ **ragioniere** chartered accountant.

perizia, *n. f.* 1 (*l'essere esperto*) expertness, expertise, skill. 2 (*stima di perito*) appraisement, appraisal, estimate, survey, valuation. 3 (*relazione d'un perito*) expert's report, appraiser's report. 4 (*trasp. mar.*) survey report. // ~ **dei danni** (*ass.*) damage survey; ~ **d'avaria** (*ass. mar.*) damage survey; ~ **di controllo** (*org. az.*) check survey; ~ **in contraddittorio** (*leg.*) control survey; **una** ~ **ufficiale** (*leg.*) an official appraisal.

periziare, *v. t.* to appraise, to estimate, to survey, to value. // ~ **i danni** (*ass.*) to estimate damages.

permesso, *n. m.* 1 permission, leave. 2 (*leg.*) (*licenza, autorizzazione*) licence, permit. 3 (*pers.*) (*d'assentarsi*) leave of absence, leave; furlough (*USA*). // ~ **amministrativo** (*ottenuto mediante il pagamento d'una tassa*) (*leg.*) excise licence; ~ **d'esportazione** (*comm. est.*) export permit; ~ **d'imbarco** (*trasp. mar.*) backed-note; ~ **d'importazione** (*comm. est.*) import permit; ~ **di lavoro** (*pers.*) work permit; ~ **di navigazione** (*trasp. mar.*) navigation permit; (*rilasciato da un'autorità consolare, ecc. a navi non soggette a perquisizione da parte della Guardia di Finanza*) (*trasp. mar., ingl.*) navicert (*abbr. di* navigation certificate); ~ **di passaggio** (*leg.*) way-leave; ~ (*doganale*) **di provvigione a bordo** (*elenco delle provviste in esenzione doganale*) (*trasp. mar.*) victualling bill; ~ **di pubblicazione** (*d'una notizia*) (*giorn.*) release; ~ **di sbarco** (*trasp. mar.*) landing order, landing ticket; ~ **di soggiorno** (*tur.*) residence permit; ~ **di trasbordo** (*trasp. mar.*) transshipment permit; ~ **di visita** (*a un appartamento e sim.*) order to view; ~ **doganale** (*dog.*) customs permit; ~ **retribuito** (*pers.*) leave with pay; ~ **temporaneo d'importazione** (*d'un automezzo: in esenzione di dazio*) (*dog.*) carnet; **essere in** ~ (*pers.*) to be on leave.

permettere, *v. t.* 1 to allow, to permit, to let★. 2 (*leg.*) to license. // ~ **la fluttuazione dello yen** (*econ.*) to float the yen.

permettersi, *v. rifl.* 1 to allow oneself. 2 (*prendersi la libertà*) to take★ the liberty. // ~ **il lusso di** to afford.

permuta, *n. f.* 1 exchange; (*baratto*) barter, truck. 2 (*leg.*) permutation, barter.

permutabile, *a.* permutable, exchangeable; (*intercambiabile*) interchangeable.

pernottamento, *n. m.* 1 overnight stay. 2 **pernottamenti,** *pl.* (*tur.*) nights spent.

perorare, *v. t.* 1 to plead, to advocate. 2 (*leg.*) to plead. // ~ **una causa** (*leg.*) to plead a case; ~ **la causa delle riforme** to plead the cause of (*o* to advocate) reforms.

perpetuo, *a.* 1 (*che non avrà fine*) perpetual, never-ending. 2 (*che dura tutta la vita*) perpetual, permanent, for life. // **una rendita** ~ (*fin.*) a perpetual annuity, a life annuity.

perquisire, *v. t.* 1 to search, to rummage. 2 (*leg.*) to search. // ~ **una nave** (*leg.*) to search a ship, to rummage a ship.

perquisizione, *n. f.* 1 search, searching, rummage. 2 (*leg.*) search, searching, rummaging. // ~ **doganale** (*trasp. mar.*) rummaging.

perseguibile, *a.* (*leg.*) prosecutable, actionable, indictable. // ~ **per legge** (*leg.*) legal.

perseguire, *v. t.* 1 (*cercare di conseguire*) to pursue, to follow up. 2 (*leg.*) (*a termini di legge*) to prosecute. // ~ **il proprio interesse** to consult one's own interests; ~ **un reato** (*leg.*) to prosecute a crime.

persona, *n. f.* 1 person. 2 (*leg.*) person, body. // ~ **a carico** (*sind.*) dependant, dependent, dependent person, encumbrance; ~ **accreditata** (*cred.*) accreditee; ~ **alla quale è affidata la rappresentanza d'una ditta** (*nei contatti ad alto livello*) (*pers.*) contact man; ~ **che «apre» il credito** (*cred.*) opener; ~ **della quale q. altro risponde** (*leg.*) vouchee; ~ **designata** (*a un ufficio*) nominee; ~ **disonesta** (*leg.*) deceitful person, malfeasant; ~ **esente** (*specialm. da imposte*) (*fin.*) exempt; ~ **fallita** (*leg.*) bankrupt; brokee (*slang USA*); ~ **fisica** (*leg.*) individual, individual person, private individual, natural person; ~ **giuridica** (*leg.*) legal person, juridical person, juristic person, corporate body; body corporate; (*società di capitali*) company; corporation, corporation aggregate (*USA*); ~ **nominata** (*a occupare un ufficio*) nominee; ~ **proposta** (*ad assumere un ufficio*) nominee; ~ **sospetta** (*leg.*) suspect; ~ **sottoposta ad addestramento** (*pers.*) trainee; **in** (*o* **di**) ~ in person, personally; **per** ~ (*econ.*) per capita, per head; per-capita (*a. attr.*); **per interposta** ~ through a third party.

personale, *a.* personal; (*privato*) private. *n. m.* (*pers.*) personnel, staff; (*impiegatizio*) clerical staff; (*operaio*) hands (*pl.*); (*di un negozio, ecc.*) attendants (*pl.*). // ~ **ad alto livello** (*pers.*) high-level staff; ~ **che lavora all'edizione del mattino** (*d'un quotidiano*) (*giorn.*) nightside; ~ **di guardia** (*trasp. mar.*) watch; ~ **di ruolo** (*pers.*) permanent staff; ~ **di segreteria** (*pers.*) secretariat; ~ **d'ufficio** (*pers.*) office personnel, office staff; ~ **di vendita** (*pers.*) salespeople (*con v. al plurale*); **il** ~ **direttivo** (*pers.*) the management, the supervisory personnel, the line;

the executives (*pl.*); ~ (*che è*) **nei libri paga** (*org. az.*) pay-roll (*attr.*); ~ **pomeridiano** (*giorn., pers.*) dayside; ~ **ridotto al minimo** (*org. az.*) skeleton staff; ~ **stabile** (*org. az.*) stable personnel; **a corto di** ~ (*org. az.*) (*d'azienda, ecc.*) short-staffed, under-staffed.

personalità, *n. f. inv.* **1** personality. **2** (*leg.*) legal status.

persuadere, *v. t.* to persuade, to convince, to induce. // ~ **un cliente ad acquistare un articolo di prezzo più alto** (*market.*) to trade up a customer.

persuasione, *n. f.* persuasion, inducement.

persuasore, *n. m.* persuader. // **i persuasori occulti** (*pubbl.*) the hidden persuaders.

pertinente, *a.* pertinent, pertaining, proper, relevant. // ~ **a bilancio** (*fin., rag.*) budgetary; ~ **a usufrutto** (*leg.*) usufructuary; ~ **al budget** (*fin., rag.*) budgetary.

pésca, *n. f.* fishing, fishery. // ~ **d'alto mare** deep-sea fishing.

pescaggio, *n. m.* (*trasp. mar.*) draft, draught; sea-gauge. // ~ **a carico** (*trasp. mar.*) load draught; ~ **a poppa** (*trasp. mar.*) aft draught; ~ **a prora** (*trasp. mar.*) forward draught.

peschereccio, *a.* (*trasp. mar.*) fishing. *n. m.* (*trasp. mar.*) fishing-boat, fishing-vessel, fisherman*.

peso, *n. m.* **1** (*anche fig.*) weight. **2** (*importanza*) weight, importance, significance. **3** (*onere, aggravio*) weight, burden, burthen, load. // ~ **a pieno carico** (*di un aereo*) (*trasp. aer.*) all-up weight; ~ **a vuoto** (*d'un veicolo, d'un contenitore, ecc.*) (*market., trasp.*) tare weight; ~ «**abbondante**» (*market.*) overweight, full weight; ~ (*del carico*) **all'imbarco** (*trasp. mar.*) shipping weight; ~ (*accettato*) **allo sbarco** (*trasp. mar.*) landing weight, landed weight, weight delivered; ~ **dei passeggeri** (*trasp.*) live load; ~ **del carico** (*trasp.*) live load; ~ **della merce caricata a bordo** (*trasp. mar.*) intake measurement; **il** ~ **delle tasse** (*fin.*) the burden of taxation; **pesi e misure** weights and measures; **pesi e misure tipo** standards of weight and measure; ~ **giusto** (*market.*) honest weight, exact weight; ~ **imbarcato** (*trasp. mar.*) shipped weight; ~ **in franchigia** (*trasp.*) weight allowed free; ~ **in libbre** poundage; ~ **lordo** gross weight; ~ **massimo** (*trasp.*) maximum load; ~ **massimo per assale** (*trasp.*) maximum axle load; ~ **netto** (*della merce, compreso il peso dell'involucro interno della medesima*) (*market.*) net weight, legal weight, net; ~ **netto effettivo** (*della sola merce*) (*market.*) net net weight; ~ **netto reale** (*della sola merce*) (*market.*) net net weight; ~ **o volume** (*trasp. mar.*) weight or measurement; ~ **onesto** (*market.*) honest weight; ~ **sbarcato** (*trasp. mar.*) landing weight, landed weight; ~ **scarso** (*market.*) short weight; **a** ~ (*market.*) (*di sistema di vendita, valutazione, ecc.*) by weight; **che eccede il** ~ **consentito** (*trasp.*) (*di bagaglio*) over-weight (*a.*).

petrodollaro, *n.* (*econ., fin.*) petrodollar.

petroliera, *n. f.* (*trasp. mar.*) oil-tanker, oil-vessel, tanker.

petroliere, *n. m.* **1** (*addetto alla lavorazione del petrolio*) oil worker. **2** (*industriale petrolifero*) oil magnate, oil baron.

petrolifero, *a.* petroliferous; oil (*attr.*). // **giacimento** ~ oil-field; **pozzo** ~ oil-well.

petrolio, *n. m.* petroleum; oil (*più comune*). // ~ **greggio** (*o* **grezzo**) raw petroleum, crude oil.

petrosterlina, *n. f.* (*fin.*) petrosterling.

pezza, *n. f.* (*market.*) (*di stoffa*) piece. // «**pezze di appoggio**» (*leg.*) supporting documents, documents in support, vouchers; ~ **giustificativa contabile** (*rag.*) bookkeeping voucher; ~ **giustificativa di perdita** (*subita*) (*ass.*) proof of loss; **a pezze** (*market.*) by the piece.

pezzo, *n. m.* **1** piece, bit. **2** (*giorn.*) newspaper article, article. **3** (*org. az.*) (*da lavorare, ecc.*) workpiece, work, piece, part; (*staccato: di macchina, ecc.*) component part. // ~ **di cronaca** (*giorn.*) report; **pezzi di ricambio** (*org. az.*) spare parts, spares; **un** ~ **di terra** a piece of land; **pezzi finiti** (*org. az.*) finished goods; **un** ~ **grosso** (*fig., fam.*) a big shot, a big cheese, a VIP; **pezzi spaiati** (*market.*) oddments; **al** ~ (*market.*) by the piece.

pianificare, *v. t.* (*anche econ.*) to plan, to scheme; (*progettare*) to project; (*programmare*) to programme.

pianificatore, *n. m.* (*anche econ.*) planner, programmer.

pianificazione, *n. f.* (*anche econ.*) planning, programming. // ~ **coercitiva** (*econ.*) centralized planning; ~ **d'una campagna pubblicitaria** (*pubbl.*) campaign planning; ~ **produttiva** (*org. az.*) production control; ~ **scorrevole** (*org. az.*) flexible planning; ~ **urbana** town-planning.

piano[1], *a.* **1** flat, level, even. **2** (*mat.*) plane. *avv.* **1** (*sommessamente*) softly, quietly. **2** (*lentamente*) slowly, slow.

piano[2], *n. m.* **1** (*d'un edificio*) floor, storey; story (*USA*). **2** (*progetto, disegno, anche fig.*) plan, project, design, programme, scheme. **3** (*trasp.*) (*di nave, autobus, ecc.*) deck. // **un** ~ **a**

lunga scadenza a long-term project; ~ **caricatore** (*o* **di caricamento**) (*trasp. ferr.*) loading platform; ~ **dei conti** (*rag.*) chart of accounts; code of accounts (*USA*); ~ **d'addestramento interno** (*org. az.*) in-plant training programme; ~ **d'ammortamento** (*rag.*) sinking plan; ~ **d'azione** (*econ.*) policy; **un** ~ **di lavoro** (*org. az.*) a scheme of work; ~ **di pensionamento** (*pers.*) retirement plan, pension plan; **piani di pensionamento che prevedono contributi** (*da parte sia del datore di lavoro sia dei dipendenti*) (*sind.*) contributory pension plans; ~ **di risanamento** (*econ.*) recovery package; ~ **governativo** (*leg.*) scheme; **un** ~ **poliennale** (*econ.*) a medium-term plan; **il** ~ **preventivo per il nostro bilancio** (*rag.*) the ex-ante plan for our budget; ~ **quinquennale** (*econ.*) five-year plan; ~ **regolatore** urban development plan, urban development scheme, city-plan.

piattaforma, *n. f.* **1** platform. **2** (*sind.*) (*rivendicativa, ecc.*) platform. // **una** ~ **comune di richieste** (*econ.*) a draft package of requests; ~ **di carico** (*trasp. ferr.*) loading-platform; (*alla fine d'un binario*) dock.

piazza, *n. f.* **1** square. **2** (*market.*) market. // ~ **di pagamento** (*d'un effetto, ecc.*) (*banca, cred.*) place of payment; **fare la** ~ (*market.*) to canvass, to tout.

piazzale, *n. m.* **1** square. **2** (*trasp. ferr.*) (*di stazione*) railway-yard, yard. // ~ **di carico** (*trasp. mar.*) loading area; ~ **d'immagazzinaggio** (*org. az.*) store-yard; ~ **doganale** (*dog.*) customs square.

piazzamento, *n. m.* **1** placing, positioning, location. **2** (*market.*) (*d'un'ordinazione*) placement.

piazzare, *v. t.* **1** to place, to position, to locate. **2** (*market.*) (*un'ordinazione*) to place.

piazzista, *n. m.* (*pers.*) commercial traveller, canvasser, tout, touter, direct salesman★, salesman★, town-traveller, runner; bell-ringer (*slang USA*). // **fare il** ~ (*pers.*) to be a commercial traveller, to canvas, to tout.

picchettaggio, *n. m.* (*sind.*) picketing.

picchettare, *v. t.* (*sind.*) (*una fabbrica, ecc.*) to picket.

picchettatore, *n. m.* (*sind.*) picket. // **fila di picchettatori** (*sind.*) picket line.

picchetto, *n. m.* (*sind.*) (*di scioperanti*) picket.

piccolo, *a.* **1** small; little (*di solito attr.*); (*minuscolo*) tiny. **2** (*giovane*) young. **3** (*di poco conto*) petty, minor. **4** (*econ.*) (*d'industria e sim.*) small-scale. // ~ **affittuario** (*econ.*) small holder, crofter; **piccola azienda agricola** (*econ.*) small holding; **piccoli bottegai** (*market.*) petty shopkeepers; **piccola cassa** (*rag.*) petty cash; **un** ~ **commerciante** (*market.*) a small tradesman; **piccole entrate** (*rag.*) petty cash; ~ **fallimento** (*leg.*) small bankruptcy; **piccole imprese** (*econ.*) small companies; **piccola industria** (*econ.*) small industry, small-scale industry, small business; **piccoli negozianti** (*market.*) petty shopkeepers; **piccoli produttori** (*econ.*) petty producers; ~ **proprietario** (*econ.*) small holder, small farmer; **piccola pubblicità** (*giorn.*) classified advertisements; **piccole spese** (*rag.*) petty cash; **piccole spese personali** pocket expenses; **a piccola velocità** (*trasp. ferr.*) by goods train, per goods train.

piede, *n. m.* **1** foot★. **2** (*parte inferiore*) foot★. **3** (*misura di lunghezza pari a cm 30,48*) foot★. // **a** ~ **di pagina** at the foot of the page, below.

piegare, *v. t.* to fold (up); (*flettere*) to bend★.

pieghevole[1], *a.* folding, flexible, bendable.

pieghevole[2], *n. m.* (*pubbl.*) folder, brochure, leaflet, broadside; (*distribuito a mano*) handbill; (*che può essere spedito senza bisogno di busta*) self-mailer.

piego, *n. m. V.* **plico.**

pieno[1], *a.* **1** full (of), filled (with). **2** (*incondizionato, senza riserve*) unconditional. // ~ **carico** (*trasp.*) full load; ~ **impiego** (*econ.*) full employment; **piena occupazione** (*econ.*) full employment; **pieni poteri** full powers.

pieno[2], *n. m.* **1** (*mezzo*) middle; (*colmo*) height. **2** (*trasp.*) (*carico completo*) full load, full cargo.

pignorabile, *a.* **1** (*leg.*) distrainable, attachable, seizable. **2** (*leg.*) (*che si può dare in pegno*) pawnable.

pignoramento, *n. m.* **1** (*leg.*) distraint, attachment, seizure, levy. **2** (*leg.*) (*il dare in pegno*) pawning. // ~ **di rendite** (*leg.*) seizure of incomes; ~ **presso terzi** (*leg.*) garnishment.

pignorare, *v. t.* **1** (*leg.*) to distrain (up) on, to attach, to seize. **2** (*leg.*) (*dare in pegno*) to pawn. // ~ **beni mobili** (*leg.*) to distrain personal chattels.

pinta, *n. f.* **1** (*misura per liquidi, pari a litri 0,57*) pint. **2** (*misura USA per liquidi, pari a litri 0,47, e, per aridi, pari a litri 0,55*) pint. // ~ **imperiale** (*o* **britannica**) (*ingl.*) imperial pint.

piombare, *v. t.* (*leg.*) (*apporre un sigillo di piombo*) to plomb, to seal with lead, to seal.

piombato, *a.* (*leg.*) sealed.

piombatura, *n. f.* (*leg.*) sealing.

piroscafo, *n. m.* (*trasp. mar.*) steamship,

steamboat, steamer, ship. // ~ **a classe unica** (*trasp. mar.*) one-class liner; ~ **per il trasporto di merci e passeggeri** (*trasp. mar.*) cargo and passenger steamer.

pista, *n. f.* 1 (*corsia*) lane, track. 2 (*trasp. aer.*) runway, strip. // ~ **d'atterraggio** (*trasp. aer.*) landing strip; ~ **di decollo** (*trasp. aer.*) take-off strip; ~ **d'emergenza** (*trasp. aer.*) emergency runway (*o* strip); ~ **di prova** (*trasp. aut.*) test track.

«plafond», *n. m.* (*banca, cred.*) line of credit, credit line.

plenario, *a.* plenary.

plenụm, *n. m.* (*leg.*) plenum★.

plico, *n. m.* 1 cover, wrapper; (*busta*) envelope; (*invòlto*) parcel. 2 (*banca*) charge. // **in ~ a parte** (*comun.*) under separate cover; **in ~ separato** (*comun.*) under separate cover.

pluriennale, *a.* pluriannual, multiannual.

plusvalenza, *n. f.* (*econ.*) capital gain.

plusvalore, *n. m.* 1 (*econ.*) surplus value, unearned increment, appreciated surplus. 2 (*fin.*) (*azionario*) share premium. // ~ **accumulato** (*econ.*) accumulated surplus value; ~ **dell'attivo** (*econ., rag.*) appreciation of assets.

podere, *n. m.* farm, holding, estate.

poligrafico, *n. m.* 1 (*giorn.*) (*stabilimento*) printing plant. 2 (*tecnico*) printer.

polipolio, *n. m.* (*econ.*) polypoly.

politica, *n. f.* 1 (*arte del governare uno Stato*) politics (*col v. al sing.*). 2 (*modo d'agire di chi governa*) policy, management. 3 (*vita politica*) politics, political life. 4 (*linea di condotta*) policy. // ~ **agraria** (*econ.*) agricultural policy; ~ **alterna** (*di freni e stimoli della produzione, ecc.*) (*econ.*) stop-and-go policy; ~ **antinflazionistica** (*econ.*) anti-inflationary policy; ~ **autarchica** (*econ.*) self-sufficiency policy; «go it alone» (*fam.*); ~ **aziendale** (*org. az.*) company policy; corporate policy (*USA*); **una ~ che provoca una stretta creditizia** (*econ., fin.*) a policy of tight credit (*o* money); ~ **commerciale** (*econ.*) commercial policy, trade policy; **politiche commerciali bilaterali** (*comm. est.*) bilateral trade policies; ~ **congiunturale** (*econ.*) economic policy, short-term economic policy; ~ **creditizia** (*fin.*) credit policy; ~ **deflazionistica** (*econ.*) deflationary policy; ~ **degli acquisti** (*org. az.*) buying policy; ~ **degli aiuti** (*econ.*) aid policy; ~ **degli investimenti** (*econ., fin.*) investment policy; ~ **dei prezzi** (*econ.*) price policy, pricing policy; ~ **dei redditi** (*econ.*) income policy; **la ~ del pieno impiego** (*econ., sind.*) the policy of full employment; ~ **della concorrenza** (*econ.*) competition policy; ~ **dell'infiltrazione economica come mezzo di potere politico** (*econ.*) dollàr diplomacy; ~ **della spesa pubblica** (*fin.*) public expenditure policy; ~ **delle mezze misure** (*amm.*) half-and-half policy; ~ **delle vendite** (*market.*) selling policy; ~ **di bilancio** (*econ., rag.*) budget policy; ~ **di compressione dei salari** (*o* **degli stipendi**) (*econ.*) pay-restraint policy; ~ **d'espansione** (*org. az.*) expansionist policy; ~ **d'investimenti a medio termine** (*econ.*) medium-term investment policy; **una ~ di libertà dei traffici** (*comm. est.*) an open-door trade policy; ~ **di programmazione** (*econ.*) national planning; ~ **di ricerca e di sviluppo** (*econ.*) research and development policy; **politiche di settore** (*econ.*) sectorial policies; ~ **di vendita** (*market.*) sales policy; ~ **economica** (*econ., org. az.*) economic policy; ~ **economica a medio termine** (*econ.*) medium-term economic policy; **una ~ economica di «centralità»** (*econ.*) a middle-of-the-road economic policy; ~ **fiscale** (*fin.*) fiscal policy, taxation policy; **una ~ globale di concorrenza** (*econ.*) a comprehensive competition policy; **una ~ improvvisata** (*amm.*) a make-do policy; ~ **inflazionistica** (*econ.*) inflation policy; **una ~ liberistica** (*econ.*) a laissez-faire policy; ~ **monetaria** (*fin.*) monetary policy, monetary management; ~ **protezionistica** (*econ.*) protective policy; ~ **regionale** (*econ.*) regional policy; ~ **salariale** (*econ.*) wages policy; **una ~ settoriale** (*econ.*) a policy towards individual industries, a structural policy in specific industries; ~ **sindacale** (*sind.*) union policy; ~ **sociale** (*econ.*) social policy; ~ **strutturale** (*econ.*) structural policy.

politico, *a.* political.

polizia, *n. f.* police (*collett.*); police force. // ~ **costiera** coast police; ~ **ferroviaria** railway police; ~ **stradale** traffic police.

polizza, *n. f.* 1 (*ass.*) policy. 2 (*trasp. mar.*) bill. // ~ **a tempo** (*ass. mar.*) time policy; ~ **a viaggio** (*ass. mar.*) voyage policy; ~ **al portatore** (*ass.*) policy to bearer; ~ **all'ordine** (*ass.*) policy to order; ~ **aperta** (*ass. mar.*) floating policy, open policy, declaration policy; ~ **aperta contro l'incendio** (*ass.*) declaration fire policy; ~ **assicurativa** (*su beni di proprietà*) **a tariffa ridotta** (*e per un periodo dai tre ai cinque anni*) (*ass., USA*) term policy; ~ **assicurativa tipo** (*ass.*) standard insurance policy; ~ **comprensiva di tutti i rischi** (*ass.*) all risks policy, unlimited policy; ~ **con limitazioni di copertura** (*ass.*) limited policy; ~ **con valore dichiarato** (*ass.*) valued policy; ~ **d'assicurazione** (*ass.*) insurance policy, assurance policy; cover (*slang USA*); ~ **d'assicurazione con capitalizzazione**

dei premi (*ass.*) endowment policy; ~ **d'assicurazione contro gli incendi** (*ass.*) fire insurance policy, fire policy; ~ **d'assicurazione marittima** (*ass. mar.*) marine insurance policy; ~ **d'assicurazione sulla vita** (*ass.*) life-insurance policy, life policy; ~ **di carico** (*trasp. mar.*) bill of lading, invoice; ~ **di carico al portatore** (*trasp. mar.*) bill of lading to bearer; ~ **di carico all'ordine** (*trasp. mar.*) bill of lading to order, order bill of lading, calling for orders bill of lading; ~ **di carico annessa ai seguenti documenti...** (*trasp. mar.*) bill of lading attached to the following documents...; ~ **di carico** (*controfirmata dal capitano della nave o dal suo incaricato e*) **attestante che le merci sono state effettivamente caricate a bordo** (*trasp. mar.*) on board bill of lading; ~ **di carico collettiva** (*trasp. mar.*) general bill of lading; ~ **di carico «con riserva»** (*trasp. mar.*) unclean bill of lading, dirty bill of lading; ~ **di carico cumulativa** (*trasp. mar.*) through bill of lading; **una** ~ **di carico diretta** (*trasp. mar.*) a straight bill of lading, a through bill of lading; ~ **di carico per merce imbarcata** (*trasp. mar.*) shipped bill of lading; ~ **di carico per il viaggio d'andata** (*trasp. mar.*) outward bill of lading; ~ **di carico per il viaggio di ritorno** (*trasp. mar.*) homeward bill of lading; ~ **di carico più tratta e polizza d'assicurazione** (*trasp. mar.*) bill of lading accompanied by draft and insurance policy; ~ **di carico provvisoria** (*trasp. mar.*) custody bill of lading; ~ **di carico «pulita»** (*esente da eccezioni e/o riserve*) (*trasp. mar.*) clean bill of lading; ~ **di carico recante girate** (*trasp. mar.*) claused bill of lading; ~ **di carico «sporca»** (*emessa, cioè, con riserve o eccezioni alle clausole generali*) (*trasp. mar.*) foul bill of lading; ~ **di noleggio** (*trasp. mar.*) freight note; ~ **di pegno** (*comm., leg.*) pawnticket; ~ **di rimborso del dazio** (*dog.*) customs debenture, debenture; ~ **distinta** (*ass.*) separate policy; ~ **flottante** (*ass. mar.*) floating policy, open policy, declaration policy; ~ **flottante contro l'incendio** (*ass.*) floating fire policy; ~ (*d'assicurazione*) **generale** (*ass.*) blanket insurance policy; ~ **individuale** (*ass.*) individual policy; ~ **marittima sulle merci** (*ass. mar.*) cargo policy; ~ **mista** (*ass.*) mixed policy, comprehensive policy; ~ **nominativa** (*ass.*) policy to a named person; ~ **priva dell'indicazione del valore assicurato** (*ass.*) unvalued policy; ~ **provvisoria** (*ass.*) covering note, cover note, binder; ~ **relativa a una nave designata** (*ass. mar.*) named policy; ~ **«ricevuto per l'imbarco»** (*trasp. mar.*) «received for shipment» bill of lading; ~ **sul carico** (*trasp. mar.*) policy on cargo; ~ **sul nolo** (*trasp. mar.*) policy on freight; ~ **tipo** (*ass.*) common policy; ~ **valida per nave non nominata** (*ma per rotta specificata*) (*ass. mar.*) floating policy; ~ **valutata** (*ass.*) valued policy.

polizzetta, *n. f.* (*trasp. mar.*) slip. // ~ **definitiva** (*ass. mar.*) definite slip, forward slip; ~ **provvisoria** (*ass. mar.*) original slip.

pollice, *n. m.* **1** thumb. **2** (*misura lineare pari a cm 2,54*) inch. // ~ **cubico** solid inch, cubic inch; ~ **quadrato** square inch.

«pollster», *n. m.* (*pubbl., stat.*) (*chi esegue sondaggi d'opinione pubblica*) pollster.

polo, *n. m.* (*anche fig.*) pole. // ~ **di sviluppo** (*econ.*) pole of development; ~ **di sviluppo industriale** (*econ.*) industrial development pole.

«pool», *n. m.* (*fin.*) (*accordo fra imprese che operano nello stesso settore*) pool. // ~ **dell'oro** (*fin.*) gold pool; ~ **«swap»** (*fin.*) pool swap (*q. V.*).

popolazione, *n. f.* population. // ~ **attiva** (*econ., stat.*) working population.

porre, *v. t.* **1** (*deporre, posare*) to lay★ (down), to put★ (down); (*mettere*) to put★; (*collocare*) to set★, to place. **2** (*presentare*) to submit. // ~ **ai voti una questione** to put a question to the vote; ~ (*qc.*) **come obiettivo** (*o* **traguardo**) (*fig.*) to target; ~ **un freno a** to restrain, to check, to curb; ~ **in commercio** (*market.*) to market; ~ (*merci*) **in magazzino doganale** (*trasp.*) to bond; ~ **q. in quiescenza** (*pers.*) to retire sb., to cause sb. to retire, to superannuate sb.; ~ **obiettivi** (*org. az.*) to establish objectives; ~ **un prezzo a** (*un articolo e sim.*) **inferiore a quello corrente** (*market.*) to underprice; ~ **termine a qc.** to terminate st., to put an end to st.

portacontainers, *n. f.* (*trasp. mar.*) containership.

portafoglio, *n. m.* **1** (*portafogli*) pocket book, wallet, notecase. **2** (*cartella*) portfolio. **3** (*carica ministeriale*) portfolio, ministry. **4** (*ass.*) portfolio. **5** (*banca*) (*ufficio portafoglio*) bills department. **6** (*banca, fin.*) (*complesso di cambiali, titoli, ecc.*) portfolio; paper securities, paper holdings, bills in hand, bills of exchange (*pl.*); holding, box. // ~ **effetti** (*banca, rag.*) bill case; bills of exchange (*pl.*); ~ **estero** (*banca*) foreign bills (*pl.*); ~ **interno** (*banca*) inland bills (*pl.*); ~ **titoli** (*banca*) security department; (*fin.*) investment portfolio.

portamonete, *n. m. inv.* **1** purse. **2** (*attr. uff.*) coin holder.

portare, *v. t.* **1** (*verso l'interlocutore*) to bring★. **2** (*lontano dall'interlocutore*) to take★.

3 (*sostenere, portare con sé; avere una portata di*) to carry. 4 (*condurre, guidare*) to lead★. 5 (*indossare*) to wear★. 6 (*cagionare*) to cause, to bring★ about. 7 (*avere, recare*) to bear★. 8 (*addurre*) to adduce, to bring★ forward, to put★ forward. 9 (*mat.*) (*riportare*) to carry. // ~ **a nuovo** (*rag.*) to carry over (*o* forward); ~ **a nuovo il saldo del conto profitti e perdite** (*rag.*) to carry forward the balance of the profit and loss account; ~ **a termine** to complete, to carry out; ~ **a termine un incarico** to bring a task off; ~ (*qc.*) **al massimo** to peak; ~ **con sé una somma di denaro** to carry a sum of money about oneself; ~ **in porto** (*fig.*) to carry out, to accomplish; (*trasp. mar.*) to bring in; ~ **i prezzi a un livello normale** (*market.*) to bring the rates to level time.

portaspiccioli, *n. m. inv.* (*attr. uff.*) coin holder.

portata, *n. f.* 1 (*fig.*) (*importanza, significato*) importance, significance, bearing, scope. 2 (*leg.*) (*d'una legge*) purview. 3 (*trasp.*) (*di fiume*) flow. 4 (*trasp. mar.*) carrying capacity, deadweight; (*stazza*) tonnage. // ~ **lorda** (*trasp. mar.*) dead-weight capacity, dead-weight tonnage, dead weight.

portatile, *a.* portable.

portatore, *n. m.* 1 (*chi porta*) bearer. 2 (*cred.*) bearer; (*detentore*) holder; (*d'un assegno e sim.*) payee. // **il** ~ **d'una cambiale** (*cred.*) the holder of a bill of exchange; **al** ~ (*fin.*) (*di titolo*) unregistered (*a.*); **pagabile al** ~ (*cred.*) payable to bearer.

portavoce, *n. m.* e *f. inv.* spokesman★ (*m.*); spokeswoman★ (*f.*).

porto[1], *n. m.* (*trasp. mar.*) port, harbour; harbor (*USA*); (*rifugio, asilo*) haven. // ~ **accessibile soltanto con l'alta marea** (*trasp. mar.*) tidal harbour; ~ **alla foce d'un fiume** (*trasp. mar.*) outport; ~ **canale** (*trasp. mar.*) canal harbour; ~ **carbonifero** (*trasp. mar.*) coal port; ~ **costiero** (*trasp. mar.*) coast port; ~ **d'armamento** (*trasp. mar.*) home port, port of origin, port of departure; ~ **d'arrivo** (*trasp. mar.*) port of arrival; ~ **di cabotaggio** (*trasp. mar.*) coasting port; ~ **di caricazione** (*o* **caricamento**) (*trasp. mar.*) port of loading, loading port, lading port; ~ **di destinazione** (*o* **di destino**) (*trasp. mar.*) port of destination; ~ **d'entrata** (*trasp. mar.*) port of arrival; (*di merce importata*) port of entry; ~ **d'imbarco** (*trasp. mar.*) port of departure, port of loading, port of exit, loading port, shipping port; ~ **d'immatricolazione** (*trasp. mar.*) port of registry; ~ **d'indoganamento** (*trasp. mar.*) port of arrival; ~ **di mare** (*trasp. mar.*) seaport; ~ **d'origine** (*trasp. mar.*) port of origin, home port; ~ **di partenza** (*trasp. mar.*) port of departure; ~ **di perizia** (*d'una nave*) (*trasp. mar.*) port of survey; ~ **di provenienza** (*trasp. mar.*) port of origin; ~ **di registrazione** (*trasp. mar.*) home port; ~ **di rifugio** (*trasp. mar.*) harbour of refuge; ~ **di rilascio forzato** (*trasp. mar.*) harbour of refuge; ~ **di sbarco** (*trasp. mar.*) port of delivery; ~ **di scalo** (*trasp. mar.*) port of call; ~ **di scarico** (*trasp. mar.*) port of delivery, discharging port; ~ **di trasbordo** (*trasp. mar.*) transshipping port; ~ **fluviale** (*trasp.*) river port, close port; ~ **franco** (*dog., trasp.*) free port, treaty port, open port; ~ **fuori della sede d'armamento** (*trasp. mar.*) outport; ~ **interno** (*trasp.*) inner port, close port; ~ **naturale** (*trasp. mar.*) natural harbour; ~ **per costruzioni navali** (*trasp. mar.*) building port; ~ **secondario** (*trasp. mar.*) outport; **un** ~ **sicuro** (*trasp. mar.*) a safe port; **un** ~ **sulla Manica** a Channel port; ~ **traghetti** (*trasp. mar.*) ferry port; **essere in** ~ (*trasp. mar.*) to be in port; (*di nave: per riparazioni, ecc.*) to lie up.

porto[2], *n. m.* 1 (*comun.*) (*francatura postale*) postage. 2 (*leg.*) (*permesso, licenza*) certificate, licence. 3 (*trasp.*) (*prezzo del trasporto*) carriage; freight (*USA*). 4 (*trasp. mar.*) freight. // ~ **assegnato** (*trasp.*) carriage forward; freight forward (*USA*); ~ **d'armi** (*leg.*) gun licence; ~ **franco** (*trasp.*) carriage paid; ~ **pagato** (*comun.*) port paid; (*trasp.*) carriage paid.

portuale, *a.* (*trasp. mar.*) of the port, of the harbour; port, harbour (*attr.*). *n. m.* (*trasp. mar.*) docker, dock worker, port worker, harbour worker. // ~ **addetto a una banchina** (*trasp. mar.*) wharfman★.

poscritto, *n. m.* (*comun.*) postscript, postscriptum★ (*abbr.* P.S.).

positivo, *a.* 1 positive. 2 (*mat.*) positive; plus (*attr.*). *n. m.* (*pubbl.*) positive, print. // **un segno** ~ (*mat.*) a plus sign.

posizione, *n. f.* 1 (*anche fig.*) position; (*sito*) situation, location. 2 (*fig.*) position; (*atteggiamento*) attitude. 3 (*condizione, stato*) condition, standing, position, situation. 4 (*grado, posto*) position; rank, capacity, place. 5 (*Borsa*) book. 6 **posizioni,** *pl.* (*banca*) positions. // ~ **al rialzo** (*Borsa*) bull account; **la** ~ **concorrenziale dei prodotti dell'azienda** (*market.*) the competitive position of the company products; ~ **contabile** (*rag.*) accounting position; **le posizioni dei conti dei clienti** (*banca*) the positions of the customers' accounts; ~ **di direttore** (*amm.*) managership; ~ **di ribasso** (*Borsa*) bear position, bear account; ~ **finanziaria** (*banca, cred.*) financial standing; **posizioni valutarie** (*fin.*) foreign exchange positions; **essere in ~ di testa su tutti i concorrenti** (*market.*) to have the lead over one's rivals.

posporre, *v. t.* (*posticipare*) to postpone, to defer, to delay; (*rimandare*) to put★ off; (*aggiornare*) to adjourn.

possedere, *v. t.* **1** (*avere in possesso*) to possess, to own, to hold★, to be in possession of; (*avere*) to have. **2** (*conoscere a fondo*) to master, to possess, to have a good knowledge of. // ~ **azioni d'una società commerciale** (*fin.*) to hold shares in a business enterprise; ~ **terreni** to hold land; **chi possiede** possessor, owner, holder.

possesso, *n. m.* **1** possession, ownership, tenure. **2** (*proprietà immobiliare*) property, estate. **3** (*padronanza, conoscenza approfondita*) mastery, possession. **4** (*leg.*) possession, tenure. // ~ **con limitazioni riguardo alla successione** (*leg.*) fee tail; ~ **d'una carica** tenure of office; ~ **effettivo** (*leg.*) actual possession; ~ **relativo** (*leg.*) constructive possession; **relativo al ~** (*leg.*) possessory.

possessore, *n. m.* **1** possessor; (*proprietario*) proprietor, owner; (*detentore*) holder. **2** (*leg.*) possessor. // ~ **di buona fede d'un titolo di credito** (*leg.*) holder in due course; ~ **di buoni del Tesoro** (*fin.*) bondholder; ~ **di titoli del debito pubblico** (*fin.*) fundholder; ~ **di titoli di Stato** (*fin.*) fundholder; **un ~ in mala fede** (*leg.*) a mala fide possessor.

possessorio, *a.* (*leg.*) possessory. // **azione possessoria** (*leg.*) possessory action.

possibile, *a.* possible, feasible. *n. m.* possible; (*possibilità*) possibility.

possibilità, *n. f. inv.* **1** (*l'essere possibile*) possibility. **2** (*opportunità*) opportunity, chance. // ~ **d'assorbimento d'un mercato** (*econ.*) absorption potential of a market; ~ **di carriera** (*pers.*) career opportunity; **possibilità d'impiego** (*pers.*) job opportunities; **possibilità finanziarie** (*fin.*) availability of finance (*sing.*).

posta, *n. f.* **1** post, mail. **2** (*ufficio postale*) post-office. **3** (*in un gioco d'azzardo e fig.*) stake. **4** (*rag.*) item. // ~ **centrale** General Post Office (*abbr.* G.P.O.); **le poste d'un bilancio** (*rag.*) the items of a balance sheet; ~ **espresso** (*comun.*) express mail; ~ **-giro** (*cred., ingl.*) giro; ~ **in arrivo** (*comun.*) in-coming mail; ~ **in partenza** (*comun.*) out-going mail; ~ **normale** (*che viaggia via terra o via mare, ma non per via aerea*) (*comun.*) surface mail; ~ **pneumatica** (*comun.*) (*sistema di tubi ad aria compressa*) pneumatic dispatch; (*trasmissione della corrispondenza con un sistema di tubi ad aria compressa*) pneumatic post; ~ **raccomandata** (*comun.*) registered mail; ~ **ricevuta in seguito alla pubblicazione** (o **trasmissione radiotelevisiva**) **d'un annuncio pubblicitario** (*pubbl.*) returns (*pl.*); **a giro di ~** (*comun.*) by return of mail, by return of post; **a mezzo ~** (*comun.*) *V.* **per ~**; **per ~** (*comun.*) by post, per post, by mail; **per ~ aerea** (*comun.*) by airmail; **per ~ pneumatica** (*comun.*) by air dispatch.

postale, *a.* (*comun.*) postal; post, mail (*attr.*). *n. m.* **1** (*trasp. ferr.*) mail-train. **2** (*trasp. mar.*) packet-boat, packet-ship, post-boat, mail-steamer, packet.

postdatare, *v. t.* to post-date, to date forward. // ~ **un assegno** (*cred.*) to post-date a cheque.

postergare, *v. t.* (*fin., leg.*) to postpone, to defer. // ~ **un'ipoteca** (*leg.*) to postpone a mortgage.

postergato, *a.* (*fin., leg.*) postponed, deferred.

posteriore, *a.* **1** posterior, back, rear. **2** (*che viene dopo*) posterior, later, subsequent. // **a posteriori** ex post.

posticipare, *v. t.* to put★ off, to postpone, to defer, to lay★ over, to delay.

posticipato, *a.* deferred, delayed.

posticipazione, *n. f.* putting off, postponement, deferment, delaying.

postilla, *n. f.* **1** marginal note, foot-note, side-note; (*chiosa*) gloss. **2** (*leg.*) rider.

posto[1], *a.* placed, situated, located.

posto[2], *n. m.* **1** place. **2** (*spazio*) room, space. **3** (*sito, posizione*) spot, place, location. **4** (*pers.*) (*impiego, lavoro*) position, job, post, situation, appointment, place. **5** (*trasp.*) seat. // **un ~ chiave** (*pers.*) a key position; ~ **d'ancoraggio** (*trasp. mar.*) berth; ~ **di blocco stradale** (*trasp. aut.*) road block; ~ **di caricazione** (*trasp. mar.*) loading place; ~ **di confine** (*comm. est.*) frontier crossing; ~ **di dogana** (*dog.*) customs station; ~ **di frontiera** (*comm. est.*) frontier crossing; ~ **di lavoro** (*pers., anche*) place of business; ~ **di lavoro non occupato** (*org. az.*) unfilled vacancy; ~ **d'ormeggio** (*trasp. mar.*) berth; ~ **di polizia** police station; ~ **di quarantena** (*trasp. mar.*) quarantine anchorage; ~ **di ristoro** (*org. az.*) canteen, cafeteria; **un ~ di ruolo** (*pers.*) a permanent position; ~ **di scarico** (*di una nave*) (*trasp. mar.*) discharging berth; **un ~ stabile** (*pers.*) a permanent position; **un ~ stipendiato** (*pers.*) a salaried position; ~ **vacante** (*pers.*) opening; vacancy.

potenza, *n. f.* **1** power, might; (*forza*)

strength. **2** (*Stato*) power. **3** (*mat.*) power, degree.

potenziale, *a.* potential. *n. m.* potential, potentiality. // ~ **d'acquisto** (*market.*) buying power; ~ **di mercato** (*econ.*) market potential; ~ **di vendita** (*market.*) selling power, sales potential; ~ **economico** (*econ.*) economic potential.

potenzialità, *n. f. inv.* potentiality, potency, power, capacity. // **la** ~ **dell'economia statunitense** (*econ.*) the capacity of the U.S. economy.

potenziamento, *n. m.* potentiation, intensification. // **il** ~ **della ricerca** (*econ.*) the intensification of research.

potenziare, *v. t.* to potentiate, to strengthen.

potere, *n. m.* **1** power. **2** (*influsso*) influence. **3** (*capacità*) capacity, power, leverage. **4** (*autorità*) authority. **5 poteri,** *pl.* (*leg.*) powers; commission (*sing.*). // ~ **assoluto** absolute power; ~ **contrattuale** (*sind.*) bargaining power, bargaining leverage; ~ **decisionale** (*org. az.*) decision-making power; ~ **d'acquisto** (*econ.*) purchasing power, buying power; value in exchange; ~ **d'espropriazione per motivi d'interesse generale** (*leg.*) eminent domain; ~ (*dei sindacati*) **d'ottenere grossi aumenti salariali** (*econ., sind.*) wage-boosting power; **poteri discrezionali** (*leg.*) discretionary powers; ~ **esecutivo** (*leg.*) executive power; ~ **giudiziario** (*leg.*) judicial power, judiciary; **poteri impliciti** (*leg.*) implied powers; ~ **investigativo** (*leg.*) investigative power; ~ **legislativo** (*leg.*) legislative power; **i poteri pubblici** (*leg.*) the public authorities; **poteri straordinari** (*leg.*) extraordinary powers.

prassi, *n. f.* **1** praxis*, (accepted) practice, regular procedure, usual procedure, what is (*o* was) done. **2** (*org. az.*) praxis*. // ~ **bancaria** (*banca*) banking customs; **la** ~ **commerciale** the ordinary course of business.

pratica, *n. f.* **1** practice. **2** (*esperienza, conoscenza*) experience, practice. **3** (*addestramento*) training. **4** (*usanza, consuetudine*) practice, custom, usage; (*prassi*) praxis*. **5** (*affare, faccenda*) matter, affair. **6** (*documento*) paper; (*caso*) case; (*incartamento*) file. **7** (*trasp. mar.*) pratique. // **le pratiche brevettuali** (*leg.*) the necessary steps to obtain a patent; **pratiche che limitano la concorrenza** (*market.*) practices in restraint of competition; ~ **di sdoganamento** (*di nave: per entrare in porto o salpare*) (*dog.*) clearance.

praticante, *a.* practicing. *n. m.* e *f.* **1** (*chi esercita un mestiere o una professione*) practiser. **2** (*pers.*) (*chi fa pratica d'un mestiere*) apprentice. // ~ **d'ufficio** (*pers.*) articled clerk; (*chi accetta lavoro per acquisirne esperienza, pur non essendo retribuito*) improver.

praticare, *v. t.* **1** (*mettere in pratica*) to practise, to put* into practice. **2** (*esercitare una professione, ecc.*) to practise, to follow. // ~ **prezzi proibitivi** (*escludendosi, così, dal mercato*) (*market.*) to price oneself out of the market; ~ **un prezzo** (*market.*) to make a price; ~ **la professione dell'avvocato** to practise law, to practise as a lawyer; ~ **ribassi** (*market.*) to rebate; **essere praticato** (*market.*) (*di prezzo*) to rule.

preavvisare, *v. t.* to inform in advance, to give* notice to, to forewarn.

preavviso, *n. m.* **1** notice, warning; forewarning. **2** (*leg.*) (*di disdetta di contratto di locazione, ecc.*) warning. // ~ **di licenziamento** (*pers.*) notice, warning; **un** ~ **di prelevamento** (*di fondi*) (*banca*) a notice of withdrawal, a withdrawal notice; **con breve** ~ at short notice; **dietro** ~ upon notice; **per mancato** ~ for want of notice; **senza** ~ without notice.

preazione, *n. f.* (*elab. elettr.*) feedforward.

precauzionale, *a.* precautionary, precautional.

precauzione, *n. f.* **1** precaution. **2** (*cautela*) caution, care. // **precauzioni sanitarie** sanitary precautions.

precedente, *a.* **1** preceding, previous. **2** (*anteriore*) former. *n. m.* **1** (*anche leg.*) precedent. **2 precedenti,** *pl.* (*condotta anteriore a un certo momento*) record (*sing.*). // **i precedenti in una relazione d'affari** the background in a business report.

precedenza, *n. f.* **1** precedence; (*priorità*) priority. **2** (*trasp. aut.*) right of way. // ~ **assoluta** (*org. az.*) top priority; **in** ~ (*leg.*) hereinabove, hereinbefore.

precedere, *v. t.* e *i.* **1** to precede, to go* (*o* to come*) before. **2** (*prevenire*) to forestall. // ~ **un concorrente** (*market.*) to forestall a competitor.

precettazione, *n. f.* (*econ., leg.*) (*di scioperanti*) strike ban.

precitato, *a.* above-mentioned, quoted above, mentioned above, aforesaid.

predetto, *a.* **1** mentioned above, above-mentioned, aforesaid, said. **2** (*market.*) (*nelle fatture, negli inventari, ecc.*) ditto.

preferenza, *n. f.* **1** preference. **2** (*gusto*) taste, like. **3** (*parzialità*) partiality. // ~ **alla liquidità** (*fin., rag.*) liquidity preference; **preferenze contrattuali** (*comm. est.*) preference margins; **preferenze del consumatore** (*market.*) consumer preference (*sing.*); **preferenze tariffarie genera-**

lizzate (*comm. est.*) generalized tariff preferences, generalized tariff quotas; **di ~** preferably; (*per lo più*) mostly.

preferenziale, *a.* preferential.

preferire, *v. t.* to prefer, to have a preference for, to like better (*o* best).

prefisso, *n. m.* (*comun.*) (*telefonico*) code number.

pregiare, *v. t.* to appreciate, to esteem, to value.

pregiarsi, *v. rifl.* (*onorarsi*) to have the honour, to be honoured, to beg.

pregiato, *a.* **1** esteemed, valued. **2** (*market.*) name (*attr.*).

pregio, *n. m.* **1** (*considerazione, stima*) regard, esteem. **2** (*ciò che rende q. o qc. degno di stima*) quality, merit. **3** (*valore*) value, worth.

preindirizzato, *a.* (*comun.*) (*di busta, ecc.*) self-addressed.

prelazione, *n. f.* (*leg.*) pre-emption. // **di ~** (*leg.*) pre-emptive (*a.*); **diritto di ~** (*leg.*) right of pre-emption.

prelevamento, *n. m.* **1** (*banca*) (*il prelevare*) withdrawal, withdrawing, drawing. **2** (*banca*) (*somma prelevata*) withdrawal, drawing. **3** (*fin.*) charging, inroad, levy. **4** (*fin., rag.*) appropriation. // **~ di campioni** (*market., stat.*) drawing of samples; **~ di cassa** (*rag.*) cash drawing; **il ~ di materiale d'archivio** (*org. az.*) the requisition of file material; **prelevamenti riscossi nei confronti dei Paesi terzi** (*econ., fin.*) levies charged on imports from non-member Countries; **~ su un conto corrente** (*banca*) drawing on a current account.

prelevare, *v. t.* **1** (*banca*) to withdraw★, to draw★. **2** (*fin., rag.*) to appropriate. // **~ un tanto dai propri risparmi** to appropriate so much out of one's savings.

prelievo, *n. m. V.* **prelevamento.**

preliminare, *a.* preliminary, preparatory. *n. m.* preliminary. // **un ~ di vendita** (*market.*) a preliminary agreement to sell, a promise to sell.

premessa, *n. f.* **1** premise. **2** (*cosa detta precedentemente*) introductory (*o* previous) statement; (*preambolo*) preamble. **3 premesse,** *pl.* (*leg.*) premises. // **le premesse e le conclusioni** (*leg.*) premises and conclusions; **senza tante premesse** without wasting words.

premesso, *a.* premised, stated beforehand, already stated; (*precedente*) preceding, previous. // **~ che** considering that, since; (*leg.*) (*forma introduttiva d'un contratto, e sim.*) whereas; **ciò ~** that being stated.

premettere, *v. t.* to premise, to state beforehand.

premiare, *v. t.* **1** to give★ a prize to, to award a prize to. **2** (*ricompensare*) to reward, to repay★.

premio, *n. m.* **1** prize, award. **2** (*ass.*) premium. **3** (*econ., market.*) bounty, rebate. **4** (*pers., sind.*) bonus. // **~ all'esportazione** (*fin.*) bounty on export, export bounty, export rebate, drawback; **~ annuale** (*ass.*) annual premium; **~ corrente** (*ass.*) current premium; **~ costante** (*ass.*) level premium; **~ del deporto** (*Borsa, fin.*) backwardation; **~ d'acceleramento** (*trasp. mar.*) dispatch money; **~ d'accelerazione** (*sind.*) accelerating premium; **~ d'assicurazione** (*ass.*) premium of insurance, insurance premium; **~ di buonuscita** (*pers.*) retiring allowance; **~ d'emissione azionaria** (*fin.*) premium of shares; **~ d'incoraggiamento** (*sind.*) bounty; **~ «d'operosità»** (*pers.*) override; **~ di partecipazione agli utili** (*ass.*) revisionary bonus; **~ di produttività** (*sind.*) acceleration premium; **~ di produzione** (*pers.*) production bonus; **~ di rinnovo** (*ass.*) renewal premium; **~ di riporto** (*Borsa*) carry-over rate, contango; **~ di salvataggio** (*trasp. mar.*) remuneration for salvage; **~ «di tariffario»** (*ass.*) office premium, gross premium; **~ di vitalizio** (*ass.*) annuity premium; **~ lordo** (*ass.*) gross premium, office premium; **~ netto** (*ass.*) net premium, pure premium, risk premium; **~ per il carico di coperta** (*trasp. mar.*) deck-cargo premium; **~ per il compratore** (*Borsa*) buyer's option; **~ per la produzione** (*sind.*) bounty on production; **~ per il venditore** (*Borsa*) seller's option; **~ supplementare** (*ass.*) extra premium; **~ unico** (*ass.*) single premium; **per un ~ da convenirsi** (*ass.*) at a premium to be arranged.

premista, *n. m.* e *f.* (*Borsa*) stag.

premunire, *v. t.* to forearm, to strengthen.

premunirsi, *v. rifl.* to take★ precautions, to protect oneself, to secure oneself, to provide. // **~ contro i danni** to take protective measures against damages; **~ contro fluttuazioni nei tassi di cambio** (*fin.*) to secure oneself against exchange rate fluctuations.

prendere, *v. t.* **1** to take★. **2** (*cogliere sopraggiungendo*) to catch★. **3** (*assumere*) to take★ over. **4** (*guadagnare, ottenere*) to earn, to get★. **5** (*market.*) (*far pagare*) to charge. **6** (*pers.*) (*assumere*) to engage. *v. i.* (*girare, voltare*) to turn. // **~ a nolo** (*leg.*) to hire; **~ a prestito** to borrow; to loan (*USA*); **~ a riporto** (*Borsa*) to borrow; **~ accordi per** (*una compravendita, ecc.*) (*comm.*) to negotiate; **~ un appuntamento con q.** to make an appointment with sb.; **~ un brevetto** (*leg.*) to take out a patent; ~ **q. come socio in affari** to take sb. into partnership; ~ **contatto con q.** to get in touch with sb., to contact sb.; ~ **una decisione** to adopt a resolution; ~ **denaro a prestito con cambiali di comodo** (*cred.*) to fly a kite; ~ **un impegno** (*leg.*) to take an engagement; ~ **in affitto** (*leg.*) to rent, to hire, to lease; ~ **in consegna qc.** (*org. az.*) to take charge of st.; ~ **in considerazione** to take into consideration, to entertain, to view; ~ **in considerazione una proposta** to entertain a proposal; ~ **in custodia** (*leg.*) to take into custody; ~ **in esame una proposta** to examine a proposal; ~ **q. in parola** to take sb. at his word; ~ (*un locale, ecc.*) **in subaffitto** (*leg.*) to sublease; ~ **indietro** to take back; ~ **informazioni** to make inquiries; ~ **merce a credito** (*market.*) to take goods on account; ~ **nota di** to note, to register, to record, to write down, to take down; ~ **parte a qc.** to participate in st.; ~ **piede** to catch on, to become fashionable; ~ **possesso di qc.** (*leg.*) to take possession of st.; ~ **provvedimenti in vista di qc.** to provide against st.; ~ **un** (*nuovo*) **socio nell'azienda** to take a partner into the business; ~ **titoli a riporto** (*Borsa*) to carry stock.

prendersi, *v. rifl.* **1** (*prendere per sé*) to take★. **2** (*assumere*) to assume, to take★ (up). // ~ **la libertà di fare qc.** to take the liberty of doing st.; ~ **la responsabilità di qc.** to assume the responsibility for st.

prenditore, *n. m.* **1** taker, receiver. **2** (*cred.*) payee. // ~ **in solido** (*leg.*) colessee.

prenome, *n. m.* (*nome di battesimo*) Christian name; given name (*USA*).

prenotare, *v. t.* **1** to book, to reserve; to make★ a reservation for (*USA*). **2** (*trasp., tur.*) to book, to reserve. // ~ **un posto in treno** (*trasp. ferr.*) to book a seat on a train; ~ **una stanza all'albergo** (*tur.*) to book a room in a hotel; ~ **una telefonata** (*comun.*) to book a telephone call, to place a telephone call.

prenotarsi, *v. rifl.* **1** to put★ one's name down (for st.). **2** (*giorn.*) to subscribe.

prenotazione, *n. f.* **1** booking, reservation. **2** (*comun.*) (*d'una chiamata telefonica*) placement. **3** (*trasp., tur.*) reservation, booking. // ~ **del nolo** (*trasp. mar.*) freight booking; **la ~ d'un posto su un aereo** (*trasp. aer.*) the reservation of a seat on a plane.

preparare, *v. t.* to prepare; (*apprestare*) to make★ ready; (*predisporre*) to arrange, to engineer. // ~ **un contratto** (*leg.*) to prepare a contract; ~ **i fondi per il pagamento di** (*una tratta, ecc.*) (*cred.*) to protect; ~ **lo schema d'un contratto** (*leg.*) to draft a contract; ~ **un trattato** to arrange a treaty.

prepararsi, *v. rifl.* to prepare, to get★ ready, to fit oneself. // ~ **a un rialzo** (*Borsa*) to provide against a rise; ~ **a un ribasso** (*Borsa*) to provide against a fall.

preparazione, *n. f.* **1** (*il preparare*) preparation, preparing, making ready, fitting. **2** (*complesso di nozioni acquisite*) attainments (*pl.*). // ~ **del bilancio (di previsione)** (*econ., rag.*) budgeting; **in ~** in preparation; in the works (*USA*).

prepensionamento, *n. m.* (*pers.*) early retirement.

presa, *n. f.* **1** (*atto del prendere*) taking (up), catching. **2** (*elab. elettr.*) jack. // ~ **a domicilio** (*trasp.*) collection at residence; ~ **di possesso** (*leg.*) capture; **la ~ di possesso d'una carica** the taking up of an office.

prescrittibile, *a.* (*leg.*) that may be barred by limitation.

prescritto, *a.* **1** (*stabilito*) prescribed; (*fissato*) fixed; (*obbligatorio*) obligatory. **2** (*vieto*) obsolete, out-of-date. **3** (*leg.*) statute-barred. // **essere ~** (*leg.*) to be barred by the statute of limitations, to be barred by limitation.

prescrivere, *v. t.* **1** to prescribe, to impose; (*fissare*) to fix, to establish. **2** (*leg.*) to prescribe, to debar.

prescriversi, *v. rifl.* (*leg.*) to prescribe; to be barred (by the statute of limitations).

prescrizione, *n. f.* **1** (*il prescrivere*) prescription, prescribing. **2** (*leg.*) prescription, bar of the statute of limitations, barring by limitation, debarment, lapse. // ~ **acquisitiva** (*leg.*) prescription; ~ **contrattuale** (*leg.*) (*ha la durata di sei anni per i contratti semplici e di venti per quelli formali*) period of limitation; **in ~** (*leg.*) stale (*a.*).

presentare, *v. t.* **1** (*mostrare*) to present, to show★; (*esibire, esporre*) to produce. **2** (*proporre*) to propose; (*inoltrare*) to put★ in, to send★ in, to hand in, to submit. **3** (*far fare la conoscenza di q.*) to introduce. **4** (*leg.*) (*un mandato*) to serve; (*un'istanza*) to lodge; (*un documento, ecc.*) to file. **5** (*market.*) (*un conto: a un cliente, ecc.*) to render. **6** (*pubbl.*) (*un articolo, ecc.*) to introduce. **7** (*pubbl.*) (*un programma radio-TV*) to announce; to emcee (*USA*); (*di ditta: «offrirlo»*) to sponsor. // ~ **a una mostra** (*market., pubbl.*) to show; ~ (*titoli*) **all'incasso** (*banca, fin.*) to bank; ~ **un assegno** (*per l'incasso*) (*banca*) to present a cheque; ~ **una cambiale all'accettazione** (*cred.*) to present a bill for acceptance; ~ **una causa al tribunale** (*leg.*) to lay a case before the Court; ~ **i conti** (*rag.*) to present the accounts; ~ **un conto salato** (*comm., fam.*) to salt an account; ~ **le dimissioni** (*pers.*) to send in one's resignation, to tender one's resignation, to send in one's papers; ~ **una gestione passiva** (*fin., rag.*) to run at a deficit; ~ **un'istanza a q.** (*leg.*) to petition sb.; ~ **istanza di fallimento** (*leg.*) to file a petition for bankruptcy, bankruptcy petition; ~ (*una cambiale*) **per il pagamento** (*cred.*) to sight; ~ **una petizione a q.** (*leg.*) to petition sb.; ~ **un progetto di legge** (*leg.*) to introduce a bill; ~ **prove** (*leg.*) to produce evidence, to enter evidence; ~ **un reclamo** (*leg.*) to present a complaint, to lodge a complaint, to raise a claim, to file a claim; ~ **un ricorso a q.** (*leg.*) to petition sb.; ~ **un saldo** (*rag.*) to show a balance; ~ **le proprie scuse** to present one's apologies.

presentarsi, *v. rifl.* **1** to present oneself; (*a rapporto*) to report oneself, to report. **2** (*farsi conoscere*) to introduce oneself. **3** (*capitare*) to occur, to arise★. **4** (*sembrare*) to seem, to appear. **5** (*leg.*) to appear. // ~ **candidato a qc.** to run for st.

presentatore, *n. m.* **1** (*cred., fin.*) bearer, presenter. **2** (*pubbl.*) (*radiotelevisivo*) announcer; emcee (*USA*). // **il** ~ **d'una tratta** (*cred.*) the bearer of a draft.

presentazione, *n. f.* **1** presentation, presentment; (*di documenti e sim.*) showing. **2** (*inoltro*) sending in, putting in, submission. **3** (*il far conoscere una persona a un'altra*) introduction. **4** (*leg.*) lodgment. **5** (*pubbl.*) (*d'un articolo, ecc.*) introduction. // ~ **d'un atto** (*o di un documento, ecc.*) **in tribunale** (*leg.*) profert; **la** ~ **d'una cambiale maturata** (*cred.*) the presentment of a matured bill of exchange; **la** ~ **d'una dichiarazione doganale** (*dog.*) the presentation of a customs entry; **la** ~ **di documenti importanti a un tribunale** (*leg.*) the submission of important papers to a Court; ~ **di prove** (*leg.*) showing of evidence; **la** ~ **di reclami** (*leg.*) the lodgment of complaints; ~ (*d'uno stato patrimoniale, ecc.*) **in modo da fare una buona impressione** (*sul pubblico, ecc.*) window-dressing (*fig.*); ~ **per l'accettazione** (*cred.*) presentation for acceptance; **contro** ~ on presentation; **su** ~ on presentation.

presente[1], *a.* **1** present. **2** (*attuale*) present, current. **3** (*questo*) this. **4** (*leg.*) present, this, within (*attr.*). *n. m.* **1** present. **2 (i) presenti,** *pl.* those present. // **la** ~ **incriminazione** (*leg.*) the within indictment; **la** ~ **(lettera)** this letter; **essere** ~ **a qc.** to witness st.; **al** ~ at present, now; **con il** ~ (*atto, documento, ecc.*) (*leg.*) hereby; **con la** ~ (*scrittura, dichiarazione, ecc.*) (*leg.*) hereby; **nel** ~ **atto** (*leg.*) within.

presente[2], *n. m.* (*dono*) present, gift.

presenza, *n. f.* **1** presence. **2** (*il frequentare*) attendance. **3** (*aspetto fisico*) appearance. **4** (*pers.*) (*sul posto di lavoro, ecc.*) attendance. **5 presenze,** (*pl.*) (*in alberghi, ecc.*) (*tur.*) occupations. // **in** ~ **del pubblico** (*leg.*) in open Court.

presenziare, *v. t.* e *i.* to be present (at), to attend, to take★ part (in). // ~ **a una riunione del consiglio d'amministrazione** to attend a board meeting.

presidente, *n. m.* **1** (*capo supremo d'una repubblica*) President. **2** (*banca*) president (*USA*). **3** (*org. az.*) (*d'una società, d'un'assemblea, ecc.*) chairman★; (the) chair (*slang USA*). // ~ **del consiglio di amministrazione** (*org. az.*) chairman of the board, chairman of directors, board-chairman; ~ **della giuria** (*leg.*) jury foreman; ~ **onorario** honorary president; **non essere più** ~ (*amm.*) to have passed the chair (*fam.*).

presidentessa, *n. f.* **1** (*moglie del presidente*) President's wife★. **2** (*org. az.*) (*donna che presiede*) chairwoman★, lady president.

presidenza, *n. f.* **1** (*atto del presiedere*) presidency, chairmanship; (*seggio di presidente*) chair. **2** (*ufficio di presidente*) presidency, presidentship, chairmanship. **3** (*tempo durante il quale viene esercitata la presidenza*) presidency, presidentship. **4** (*ingl.*) (*ufficio di Presidente del Consiglio dei Ministri*) Premiership. **5** (*USA*) (*ufficio di Presidente della Confederazione*) Presidency.

presiedere, *v. i.* e *t.* **1** to preside (over). **2** (*org. az.*) to act as chairman★, to take the chair, to be in the chair. // ~ **una seduta** to preside over a meeting; ~ **una società** (*org. az.*) to be the chairman of a company.

press agent, *n. m.* (*giorn., pubbl.*) press-agent.

pressione, *n. f.* **1** pressure. **2** (*econ.*) pressure. // **la** ~ **fiscale** (*fin.*) the pressure of taxation; ~ **inflazionistica** (*econ.*) inflationary pressure; **pressioni protezionistiche** (*econ.*) protectionist pressures.

prestanome, *n. m.* (*leg.*) figurehead, dummy, man★ of straw, prêt-nom.

prestare, *v. t.* (*cred.*) to lend★; to loan (*USA*). // ~ **garanzia** (*leg.*) to give security; ~ **giuramento** (*leg.*) to take an oath, to swear; ~ **servizio come interino** (*leg.*) to serve in an acting capacity.

prestarsi, *v. rifl.* **1** to lend★ oneself. **2** (*aiutare*) to help, to make★ oneself useful. **3** (*essere idoneo*) to be fit.

prestatore, *n. m.* (*cred.*) lender, moneylender. // ~ **di denaro** (*cred., fin.*) money lender; lombard (*fam.*); five-for-sixer (*slang USA*); ~ **di lavoro** (*pers.*) workhand; ~ **d'opera** (*pers.*) hired person, employee; ~ **su pegno** (*comm., leg.*) pawnbroker; «**prestatrice d'ultimo appello**» (*fin.*) «lender of last resort».

prestazione, *n. f.* **1** (*professionale*) service. **2** (*org. az.*) (*di macchina, ecc.*) performance. **3 prestazioni,** *pl.* services rendered, services.

prestito, *n. m.* **1** (*cred.*) loan, lending, advance. **2** (*leg.*) (*dello Stato a un privato, per permettergli di far fronte ai suoi debiti*) imprest. // ~ **a cambio marittimo** (*trasp. mar.*) bottomry loan, bottomry; (*con garanzia sul carico*) respondentia; ~ **a interesse** (*cred.*) loan at interest; ~ **a saggio d'interesse fluttuante** (*cred.*) floating-rate loan; ~ **a tasso d'interesse variabile** (*fin.*) variable-rate loan; ~ **a termine** (*cred.*) time loan; ~ (*rimborsabile*) **a vista** (*cred.*) demand loan; ~ **allo scoperto** (*cred.*) loan on overdraft; **prestiti bancari** (*fin.*) bank loans; ~ **bancario rimborsabile a vista** (*col preavviso di un giorno*) (*banca*) call-loan, callable bond; ~ **consolidato** (*fin.*) consolidated loan, funding loan, consol; consols (*pl.*); ~ **di conversione** (*cred.*) conversion loan; ~ **di guerra** (*econ., fin.*) war-loan; ~ **fiduciario** (*fin.*) fiduciary loan; ~ **forzoso** (*fin.*) forced loan; ~ **garantito** (*banca, cred.*) collateral loan; ~ **giornaliero** (*cred.*) daily loan, daily money, day-to-day loan, day-to-day money; **prestiti in eurodollari** (*fin.*) Euro-dollar loans; ~ (*rimborsabile*) **in un'unica soluzione** (*fin.*) non-instalment credit; ~ **ipotecario** (*cred.*) loan on mortgage, mortgage loan; **un ~ irredimibile** (*fin.*) a unredeemable loan, a perpetual loan, a perpetual debt; **un ~ nazionale** (*cred.*) a domestic loan; ~ **non garantito** (*cred.*) unsecured loan; ~ **obbligazionario** (*fin.*) debenture loan; ~ **obbligazionario convertibile** (*in azioni*) (*fin.*) convertible stock loan; **prestiti per operazioni ordinarie** (*cred.*) ordinary loans; ~ **pubblico** (*econ.*) Government loan; ~ **rimborsabile a domanda** (*cred.*) call money; ~ **rimborsabile a rate** (*cred.*) instalment loan; ~ **rimborsabile su domanda** (*cred.*) day-to-day loan, day-to-day money, loan at call; ~ **senza garanzia** (*cred.*) signature loan; **prestiti stilati in eurodollari** (*fin.*) loans denominated in Eurodollars; ~ **su polizza** (*ass.*) policy loan; **prestiti su titoli** (*banca*) advances on securities; **in** ~ (*cred.*) on loan.

presumere, *v. t.* e *i.* to presume; to take★ (st.) for granted; (*supporre*) to assume, to expect; (*pensare*) to think★.

presuntivo, *a.* **1** presumptive. **2** (*leg.*) presumptive. *n. m.* (*fin., rag.*) (*spesa presunta*) estimated expenditure. // **erede** ~ (*leg.*) heir presumptive, presumptive heir.

presunto, *a.* **1** presumed, alleged; (*previsto*) anticipated; (*valutato*) estimated. **2** (*leg.*) presumptive. // ~ **erede** (*leg.*) presumptive heir, heir presumptive; **il ~ ladro** (*leg.*) the alleged thief.

presunzione, *n. f.* **1** (*presuntuosità*) presumption, presumptuousness, self-conceit; cockiness (*fam.*). **2** (*congettura*) presumption, assumption. **3** (*leg.*) presumption. // ~ **di colpa** (*leg.*) presumption of guilt; ~ **di fatto** (*leg.*) presumption of fact; ~ **d'innocenza** (*leg.*) presumption of innocence; ~ **di morte** (*leg.*) presumption of death; ~ **legale** (*leg.*) legal presumption, presumption of law; ~ **legittima** (*leg.*) presumption of law; ~ **relativa** (*leg.*) rebuttable presumption.

presupposto, *n. m.* presupposition, premise, supposition.

pretendere, *v. t.* **1** (*presumere, sostenere*) to claim; to pretend. **2** (*esigere, richiedere*) to claim, to demand, to require. // ~ **la restituzione di** (*qc.*) to claim back, to re-claim; ~ **la restituzione d'un documento importante** to claim back an important paper; ~ **il risarcimento dei danni** (*ass.*) to claim damages.

pretesa, *n. f.* **1** (*presunzione*) pretension, pretence, claim. **2** (*richiesta, esigenza*) demand, claim. **3** (*leg.*) claim, right. // **una ~ fondata** (*leg.*) a valid claim; **una ~ ingiustificata** (*leg.*) an unfounded claim; «**indicare le pretese**» (*pers.*) (*nelle offerte d'impiego*) «state salary required».

pretore, *n. m.* (*leg.*) lower Court judge, (police) magistrate.

pretura, *n. f.* (*leg.*) magistrate's Court.

prevaricare, *v. i.* (*leg.*) to abuse one's office, to embezzle, to peculate, to prevaricate, to graft.

prevaricatore, *n. m.* (*leg.*) embezzler, peculator, grafter, prevaricator.

prevaricazione, *n. f.* (*leg.*) embezzlement, peculation, graft, prevarication.

prevedere, *v. t.* **1** to foresee★, to anticipate; (*aspettarsi*) to expect; (*presagire*) to forecast★, to foretell★. **2** (*leg.*) (*di contratto, legge, ecc.*) to provide, to project.

preventivare, *v. t.* (*rag.*) to estimate, to make★ an estimate of. // ~ **il costo di** (*una merce, un articolo, ecc.*) (*market.*) to cost.

preventivato, *a.* (*rag.*) estimated.

preventivo, *a.* **1** preventive; (*preliminare*) preliminary; ex-ante (*attr.*). **2** (*rag.*) estimative. *n. m.* (*rag.*) estimate, estimation, budget. // ~

dei costi (*rag.*) estimate of costs; ~ **delle spese** (*rag.*) cost estimating; ~ **di cassa** (*rag.*) cash budget; **un** ~ **di massima** (*fin.*) an outside estimate; ~ **troppo basso** underestimate.

previo, *a.* previous, preceding, prior. // ~ **accordo** by previous agreement; ~ **avviso** upon notice.

previsione, *n. f.* **1** (*il prevedere*) prevision, foresight. **2** (*cosa prevista*) prevision, expectation, calculation, anticipation, forecast, prospect. // ~ **a breve termine** (*econ.*) short-range forecast; ~ **a lungo termine** (*econ.*) long-range forecast; **previsioni del tempo** weather forecast; ~ **delle vendite** (*market.*) sales forecast, sales budget; ~ **di bilancio** (*fin., rag.*) budget estimate; ~ **di cassa** (*rag.*) cash forecast, cash requirement, cover for the day; **previsioni pluriennali** (*econ.*) pluriannual forecasts, forecasts covering several years; **al di là d'ogni** ~ beyond expectation(s); **in** ~ **di** in expectation of, in anticipation of.

prezioso, *a.* precious, costly, valuable; (*di gran pregio*) of great value (*pred.*). *n. pl.* **preziosi** valuable goods, value goods, valuables.

prezzo, *n. m.* **1** price; tab, lay. **2** (*econ.*) (*costo*) cost; costs; (*valore*) value worth. **3** (*trasp. ferr.*) (*tariffa*) fare, rate. **4** (*tur.*) (*fatto pagare in un albergo, ecc.*) tariff, rate. **5 prezzi,** *pl.* (*market.*) (*condizioni*) terms, charges. // ~ **a forfait** (*market.*) flat rate, price by the job; ~ **agricolo** (*econ.*) farm price, agricultural price; **prezzi al consumo** (*econ.*) prices to the consumer, consumer prices, retail prices; **prezzi al dettaglio** (*market.*) retail prices; **prezzi al minuto** (*market.*) retail prices; ~ **al netto di ogni tassa o dazio incluso nel prezzo di vendita** (*agli effetti contabili*) (*rag.*) factor cost; ~ **al rivenditore** (*market.*) trade price; **prezzi all'importazione** (*comm. est.*) prices on importation; ~ **all'origine** (*market.*) price at origin; **prezzi all'ingrosso** (*market.*) wholesale prices; **prezzi alti** high prices, strong prices, hard prices; handsome prices, smart prices (*fam.*); ~ **amministrato** (*econ.*) administered price; ~ **base** (*market.*) basis price, base price; **prezzi bassi** (*market.*) low prices; ~ **come da listino** (*market.*) per list price; ~ **concorrenziale** (*market.*) competitive price; ~ **corrente** (*Borsa*) quotation; (*market.*) current price, going price; ~ **corretto** (*Borsa*) adjusted price; **prezzi crescenti** (*market.*) rising prices; **prezzi dei prodotti alimentari** (*econ.*) food prices; ~ **del biglietto** (*trasp.*) fare; ~ **del contratto «dont»** (*Borsa*) call price; **il** ~ **del denaro** (*tasso d'interesse per denaro preso a prestito*) (*cred., fin.*) the price of money; ~ **del dopoborsa** (*Borsa*) price after hours, street price; ~ **del giorno** (*market.*) current price; ~ **del magazzinaggio** (*org. az.*) storage; ~ **del passaggio marittimo** (*trasp. mar.*) pass-money; ~ **del riporto** (*Borsa*) continuation rate; ~ **del trasporto** (*trasp. mar.*) haulage, transportation; ~ **del viaggio** (*trasp. aer., trasp. mar.*) passage; ~ **della corsa** (*trasp.*) fare; ~ **della locazione** (*leg.*) rent; ~ **dell'offerta** (*econ.*) supply price; ~ **della traversata** (*trasp. aer., trasp. mar.*) passage money; ~ **della vendita a premio** (*Borsa*) put price; **prezzi delle carni bovine** (*econ.*) cattle prices; **prezzi delle rimanenze** (*market.*) remainder prices; ~ (*d'un bene*) **determinato secondo la stima del valore di mercato** (*econ.*) valuation; ~ **d'acquisto** (*Borsa, fin.*) bid; (*market.*) purchase price, cost price; (*specialm. d'immobili*) purchase money; **un** ~ **d'affezione** (*market.*) a fancy price; ~ **d'affitto d'un deposito** yardage; ~ **d'affitto d'un recinto** yardage; ~ **d'apertura** (*Borsa*) opening price; (*comm.*) (*in una vendita all'asta*) upset price; ~ **di calmiere** (*econ.*) State-controlled price; ~ **di chiusura** (*Borsa*) closing price; ~ **di compensazione** (*Borsa, ingl.*) making-up price, make-up price, settlement price; ~ **di costo** (*rag.*) cost price; ~ **d'emissione** (*di nuove azioni*) (*fin.*) coming-out price, issue price, price of issue; ~ **d'entrata** (*econ.*) threshold price; ~ **d'equilibrio** (*econ.*) equilibrium price, normal price; ~ **di fabbrica** (*rag.*) factory price; ~ **di fattura** (*market.*) invoice price; ~ **di favore** (*market.*) special price; **prezzi d'intervento** (*econ.*) intervention prices; ~ **d'intervento di base** (*econ.*) basic intervention price; ~ **di liquidazione** (*market.*) bargain price; ~ **di listino** (*market.*) list price; ~ **di mercato** (*econ., market.*) market price, equilibrium price, market; ~ **di monopolio** (*econ.*) monopoly price, monopoly-determined price; (*secondo Keynes*) administered price; ~ **d'obiettivo** (*econ.*) norm price; **prezzi d'offerta** (*fin., market.*) offer prices; ~ **d'orientamento** (*market.*) guide price; ~ **di rescissione** (*Borsa*) default price; ~ **di riacquisto** (*market.*) buying-in price; ~ **di riferimento** (*fin., market.*) reference price; (*del petrolio, ecc.*) posted price; ~ **di rivendita** (*market.*) resale price; ~ **d'un trasferimento** (*di titoli*) (*fin.*) consideration money for a transfer; ~ **di vendita** (*Borsa, fin.*) ask; (*market.*) selling price, sale price, consideration for sale; ~ **di vendita rettificato** (*market.*) adjusted selling price; **prezzi differenziali** (*market.*) graduated prices; **prezzi e condizioni di trasporto** (*trasp.*) transport rates and conditions; ~ **eccessivo** (*market.*) overcharge; **un** ~ **equo**

(*market.*) a fair price, an equitable price; **prezzi fissi** (*market.*) fixed prices; (*imposti dal fabbricante*) settled prices; ~ **forfettario** contract price; **prezzi franchi** (*market.*) delivered prices; ~ **«franco al luogo di partenza»** (*market.*) spot price, loco price; **prezzi futuri** (*market.*) forward prices; ~ **globale** (*market.*) inclusive price, all-in price, overhead price, all-round price; **prezzi imbattibili** (*market.*) record prices; ~ **imposto** (*dal produttore al dettagliante*) (*market.*) resale price; **prezzi in rapido aumento** (*market.*) runaway prices; **prezzi in sterline** (*fin., market.*) sterling prices; **i prezzi in vigore nella Comunità** (*econ.*) the prices in force in the Community; ~ **indicativo** (*econ., market.*) target price; ~ **indicativo di mercato** (*econ.*) market target price; ~ **indice** (*econ., stat.*) price index; **prezzi instabili** (*market.*) unsteady prices; ~ **IVA inclusa** (*market.*) VAT-inclusive price; **prezzi limite** (*econ.*) sluice-gate prices; ~ **lordo** (*market.*) gross price; ~ **massimo** (*econ., fin.*) ceiling price, top price, high; **prezzi massimi e minimi** (*Borsa, fin.*) highs and lows; ~ **medio** (*econ.*) average price, middle price, mean price; ~ **minimo** (*econ., fin.*) floor price, bottom price, floor, low; (*a un'asta pubblica*) reserve price; ~ **minimo garantito al produttore** (*comm., econ.*) minimum price guaranteed to producer; **prezzi modici** (*market.*) moderate prices; **prezzi monopolistici** (*econ.*) monopoly-determined prices, monopoly prices; administered prices (*secondo Keynes*); ~ **netto** (*market.*) net price, net; **un ~ nominale** a nominal price; **prezzi non più validi** obsolete prices; **prezzi normali** (*market.*) standard prices; **prezzi oscillanti** (*market.*) fluctuating prices; **il ~ pattuito** the agreed price; ~ **per una chiamata telefonica** (*comun.*) charge for call; ~ **per contanti** (*market.*) cash price, spot price; **il ~ per la corrente liquidazione** (*Borsa*) the price for current account; **prezzi per futura consegna** (*Borsa*) forward prices; ~ **praticato in condizioni di oligopolio** (*econ.*) administered price (*secondo Keynes*); ~ **raccomandato** (*dal produttore al dettagliante*) (*market.*) resale price; **un ~ ragionevole** (*market.*) a reasonable price; **prezzi reali** (*econ.*) actual prices; **prezzi ridottissimi** (*market.*) rock-bottom prices, close-cut prices, close prices; **prezzi scaduti** obsolete prices; ~ **«sopra luogo»** (*market.*) loco price, spot price; **prezzi stabili** (*market.*) firm prices; **il ~ stipulato** (*market.*) the named price; **prezzi tariffari** (*econ.*) scale charges, scale rates; **prezzi tenuti bassi** (*market.*) stay-low prices; **un ~ teorico** (*market.*) a nominal price; ~ **«tutto compreso»** (*market.*) inclusive price, all-in price; ~ **unico** (*market.*) single price; ~ **unitario** (*econ., market.*) unit price; **prezzi vischiosi** (*econ.*) sticky prices; **a ~ bassissimo** dirt cheap (*a.* e *avv., fam.*); **a un ~** (*richiesto normalmente*) **da** (*un*) **dettagliante** (*market.*) at retail; **a ~ di costo** (*market.*) (at) cost price, at cost; **a prezzi popolari** (*market.*) at popular prices; **a prezzi ribassati** (*market.*) at reduced prices; **a un ~ stabilito** (*market.*) at an arranged price; **a ~ unico** (*market.*) one-price; **a basso** (*o* **a poco**) ~ on the cheap; **a metà** ~ (*market.*) at half price; **al ~ corrente di mercato** (*market.*) at value; **al ~ prevalente** (*Borsa*) at the market; **chi fa salire i prezzi** (*a un'asta*) **con offerte fittizie** (*comm.*) by-bidder; **di poco** ~ inexpensive, cheap; **per un ~ forfettario** at an agreed price (*o* sum); **sotto** ~ (*market.*) at a discount.

primo, *num. ord.* first. *a.* **1** (*passato, precedente*) former. **2** (*prossimo*) next. **3** (*più importante*) principal, chief; main; head, top (*attr.*). *n. m.* **1** first; (*fra due*) former. **2** (*il migliore, il più importante*) the best, the first, the top. // **prima adunanza dei creditori** (*leg.*) first meeting of creditors; **prima classe** (*trasp.*) first class; **prima copia di cambiale** (*fin.*) first of exchange; **prima di cambio** (*fin.*) first of exchange; ~ **giorno** (*dei riporti*) (*Borsa*) carry-over day; **prima nota** (*rag.*) daybook, blotter; ~ **richiamo** (*della somma parziale dovuta come versamento iniziale per l'assegnazione delle azioni*) (*fin.*) first call; **prima, seconda e terza di cambio** (*fin.*) set of exchange; ~ **semestre** (*d'anno finanziario*) (*fin.*) first half; ~ **trimestre** (*d'anno finanziario*) (*fin.*) first quarter; **di prima classe** (*market.*) first class (*V. anche* **di prima qualità**); **di ~ ordine** (*market.*) first-rate (*V. anche* **di prima qualità**); **di prima qualità** (*Borsa*) (*di titoli*) gilt-edged (*o* gilt-edge); (*market.*) first-class, high-class, first-line, first-rate, prime, superior, top; exclusive (*USA*); **di prima scelta** (*market.*) top; exclusive (*USA*) (*V. anche* **di prima qualità**); **di primissima qualità** (*market.*) premium.

principale, *a.* **1** principal, chief, leading, major, main; (*primario*) primary; (*primo*) first; top (*attr.*). **2** (*elab. elettr.*) master. *n. m.* (*org. az.*) principal, employer, chief head; boss (*fam.*).

principio, *n. m.* **1** beginning, start, commencement; (*apertura*) opening. **2** (*massima, norma fondamentale*) principle. **3 principi,** *pl.* (*rudimenti*) principles, rudiments. // ~ **bancario** (*econ., fin.*) banking principle; **il ~ dei costi comparati** (*econ.*) the principle of comparative costs; **il ~ della buona fede** (*ass., leg.*) the principle of good faith; **il ~ dell'indennizzo** (*ass.*) the principle of indemnity; **il ~ dell'interesse assicurabile** (*ass.*) the principle of insurable interest; **il ~ d'accelerazione** (*econ.*) the acceleration principle; **principi di direzione** (*amm.*) principles of management, principles of administration; **i principi di valutazione dell'IVA** (*fin.*) the principles of assessment for VAT purposes.

priorità, *n. f. inv.* **1** priority; (*precedenza*) precedence. **2** (*leg.*) (*d'una terza ipoteca quando la seconda non è stata notificata*) tacking. // **una ~ di diritto** (*leg.*) a priority of claim; **la ~ d'un'invenzione** (*leg.*) the priority of an invention.

privativa, *n. f.* **1** (*spaccio di tabacchi*) tobacconist's (shop). **2** (*leg.*) (*privilegio esclusivo*) exclusive privilege. **3** (*leg.*) (*monopolio*) monopoly.

privatizzare, *v. t.* (*econ., fin.*) to denationalize.

privatizzazione, *n. f.* (*econ., fin.*) denationalization.

privato, *a.* **1** private. **2** (*personale, confidenziale*) private, personal, confidential. *n. m.* private citizen.

privilegiare, *v. t.* (*anche leg.*) to privilege, to grant a privilege to, to invest (sb.) with a privilege.

privilegiato, *a.* **1** privileged, preferential. **2** (*fin., leg.*) preferred; preference (*attr.*). **3** (*leg.*) preferential, privileged, secured. *n. m.* privileged person.

privilegio, *n. m.* **1** (*anche leg.*) privilege. **2** (*leg.*) (*su un bene*) charge, lien. **3** (*leg.*) (*conferito da un'autorità*) franchise, charter. **4** (*leg.*) incident. // **~ del venditore** (*di terreni*) (*leg.*) vendor's lien; **~ dell'armatore** (*sul nolo e le altre spese attinenti al carico*) (*trasp. mar.*) shipowner's lien; **~ generale o speciale per gli agenti e i rappresentanti con deposito** (*in forza del quale essi possono far valere i loro crediti, per spese e provvigioni, sulle merci che hanno in deposito*) (*leg.*) agent's lien; **~ marittimo** (*leg.*) maritime lien; **un ~ revocabile** (*leg.*) a revocable privilege; **un ~ speciale** (*leg.*) a particular lien, a specific lien; (*su un bene*) (*leg.*) charge; **senza privilegi o riserve** (*Borsa*) (*di titolo*) ex-all (*attr.*).

privo, *a.* deprived (of), devoid (of), bare (of), destitute (of); (*mancante*) lacking (in), wanting (in); (*senza*) without; less (*suff.*). // **~ di data** dateless; **~ d'eredi** (*leg.*) heirless; **~ di fondi** out of funds, out of pocket; (*banca*) «no effects» (*scritto su un assegno emesso allo scoperto*); **~ d'indirizzo** (*comun.*) unaddressed; **~ di speciali privilegi** (*come concessioni esclusive, ecc.*) (*leg.*) unchartered; **~ di tariffe** (*comm. est., econ.*) tariffless; **~ di valore** worthless; **esser ~ di (qc.)** to lack (st.), to be lacking in (st.).

pro[1], *n. m. inv.* use, good, advantage, profit, benefit.

pro[2], *prep.* for, in favour of, for the benefit of, to the advantage of. *n. m. inv.* pro. // **« ~ capite»** (*econ.*) per capita; **~ e contro** (*prep.* e *avv.*) pro and con; **i pro e i contro d'una certa politica di mercato** (*market.*) the pros and cons of a certain market policy; **« ~ forma»** pro forma; **« ~ rata»** pro rata.

problema, *n. m.* **1** problem; (*faccenda*) matter, (*questione*) question. **2** (*leg.*) issue. **3** (*mat.*) problem, proposition. // **un ~ che ha precedenza assoluta** a matter of priority; **il ~ dei margini d'utilizzazione degli impianti** (*org. az.*) the problem of plant capacity utilization; **problemi della distribuzione** (*econ.*) distribution problems; **problemi della manodopera** (*pers., sind.*) manpower problems; **i problemi dell'occupazione** (*econ.*) the employment problems; **problemi d'adeguamento** (*org. az.*) problems of adjustment; **problemi di bilancio** (*fin., rag.*) budget matters; **problemi di contingentamento** (*econ.*) problems of quotas; **problemi di direzione** (*amm.*) managerial problems; **problemi d'ordine tecnico** (*org. az.*) problems of a technical nature; **problemi economici regionali** (*econ.*) regional economic problems.

procacciamento, *n. m.* **1** (*il procacciare*) procurement, procuring, getting, obtaining. **2** (*il procacciarsi*) getting, obtaining, earning. **3** (*cred.*) (*di prestiti a favore di terzi*) procuration.

procacciare, *v. t.* to procure, to get★, to obtain; (*provvedere*) to provide.

procacciarsi, *v. rifl.* to procure, to get★, to obtain, to earn. // **~ un lavoro** to get a job.

procacciatore, *a.* busy; (*intrigante*) meddlesome. *n. m.* busybody, meddler. // **~ d'affari** (*market., USA*) solicitor.

procedere, *v. i.* **1** to proceed, to go★ on, to move ahead. **2** (*cominciare*) to start, to proceed. **3** (*comportarsi, agire*) to behave, to act. **4** (*leg.*) to proceed, to start proceedings.

procedimento, *n. m.* **1** (*comportamento*) behaviour, conduct; course. **2** (*leg.*) proceedings (*pl.*). **3** (*org. az.*) process; (*procedura*) procedure. // **~ brevettato** (*leg.*) patent; **~ contabile** (*per il calcolo dell'inventario*) **consistente nel considerare la prima merce entrata in magazzino come la prima uscitane** (*rag.*) first in, first out (*FIFO*); **~ contabile** (*per il calcolo dell'inventario*) **consistente nel considerare l'ultima merce entrata in magazzino come la prima uscitane**

(*rag.*) last in, first out (*LIFO*); **procedimenti di chiusura** (*rag.*) closing procedures; ~ **d'ufficio** (*leg.*) ex officio proceedings; **procedimenti di verifica** (*rag.*) adjusting procedures; ~ **giudiziario** (*leg.*) prosecution; ~ **legale** (*leg.*) process.

procedura, *n. f.* **1** procedure, practice. **2** (*leg.*) procedure; proceedings (*pl.*). // ~ **arbitrale** (*leg.*) arbitration proceedings; ~ **delle trattative** (*sind.*) bargaining procedure; ~ **di gestione** (*org. az.*) administration procedure; **procedure di ridimensionamento aziendale** (*econ.*) layoffs; ~ **di votazione** voting arrangements; ~ **fallimentare** (*leg.*) proceedings in bankruptcy, bankruptcy proceedings; ~ **legale** (*leg.*) proceedings at law; ~ **penale** (*leg.*) criminal proceedings; ~ **sommaria** (*leg.*) summary procedure; **la** ~ **usuale** the regular procedure.

procedurale, *a.* (*leg.*) procedural, of procedure, relating to procedure.

processare, *v. t.* (*leg.*) to try. // ~ **q. per furto** (*leg.*) to try sb. for theft.

processo, *n. m.* **1** (*leg.*) trial, lawsuit, suit; (legal) proceedings (*pl.*); cause, case, prosecution. **2** (*org. az.*) (*produttivo*) process. // ~ **contabile** (*rag.*) accounting process; ~ **decisorio** (*org. az.*) decision making; ~ **di concentrazione** (*econ.*) amalgamating; ~ **di fabbricazione** (*org. az.*) manufacturing process; ~ **di produzione a ciclo continuo** (*pers.*) continuous process; ~ **nullo per vizio di procedura** (*leg.*) mistrial; ~ **produttivo** (*org. az.*) manufacturing process; ~ **scalare** (*org. az.*) scalar process; ~ **verbale** (*leg.*) minutes (*pl.*).

processuale, *a.* (*leg.*) of a trial; trial (*attr.*). // **le spese processuali** (*leg.*) law expenses, costs.

procrastinare, *v. t.* to postpone, to delay, to defer, to put* off. *v. i.* to procrastinate, to delay. // ~ **un pagamento** (*cred.*) to put off a payment.

procura, *n. f.* **1** (*leg.*) (*l'autorità conferita*) power of attorney, procuration, proxy. **2** (*leg.*) (*documento di procura*) warrant of attorney, letter of attorney. **3** (*leg.*) (*documento - più formale della lettera di procura - che ne conferisce l'autorità*) procuration, power of attorney. **4** (*leg.*) (*ufficio del procuratore*) attorney's office. // ~ **generale** (*leg.*) general power of attorney, full power of attorney, general power, general proxy; ~ **legale** (*leg.*) legal power of attorney; ~ **speciale** (*leg.*) special power of attorney, special power; **per** ~ (*leg.*) by proxy, per procuration, «per procurationem», by deputy, per pro.

procuratore, *n. m.* **1** (*leg.*) (*chi esercita un mandato di procura*) proxy. **2** (*leg.*) attorney; procurator (*in Italia*). // **il** ~ **del convenuto** (*leg.*) the solicitor of the defendant; **il** ~ **della Repubblica** the Procurator of the Republic (*in Italia*); ~ **distrettuale** (*leg., USA*) district attorney; ~ **generale** (*leg.*) (*chi ha una procura*) general proxy; (*leg.*) (*magistrato*) Procurator General (*in Italia*); Attorney General (*in U.S.A.*) (*anche Ministro della Giustizia*); ~ **legale** (*leg.*) attorney-at-law, public attorney, law-agent, solicitor.

prodotto[1], *a.* **1** produced, made. **2** (*leg.*) (*addotto, allegato*) produced, exhibited. // « ~ **in Cina** » (*market.*) «produce of China», «made in China».

prodotto[2], *n. m.* **1** product; (*resa, rendimento*) yield. **2** (*econ., market.*) product; (*specialm. agricolo o minerario*) produce (*collett., col v. al sing.*). **3** (*mat.*) product. **4 prodotti,** *pl.* (*econ., market.*) goods. // **prodotti agricoli** (*econ.*) agricultural produce, produce (*col v. al sing.*); agricultural products, farm products; **prodotti alimentari** (*econ.*) food products, foodstuffs; **prodotti che richiedono un largo impiego di manodopera** (*org. az.*) labour-intensive products; **prodotti coloniali** (*market.*) colonial produce; **prodotti concorrenziali** (*market.*) competitive products; **prodotti della terra** (*leg.*) emblements; **prodotti dell'artigianato** (*econ.*) handicrafts; **prodotti destinati al consumo interno** (*econ.*) commodities intended for home consumption; **prodotti destinati al consumo privato** (*market.*) goods for private consumption; **prodotti destinati all'alimentazione umana** (*econ.*) food for human consumption; **prodotti di base** (*econ.*) primary products, basic materials, commodities; **prodotti di concorrenza** (*market.*) competing goods; ~ **d'esportazione** (*comm. est.*) exportation, export; **prodotti di grande consumo** (*market.*) common consumer products; ~ **di grande successo** (*market.*) hit; ~ **d'importazione** (*comm. est.*) importation, import; **prodotti di primissima qualità** (*market.*) premium products; **prodotti di qualità inferiore** (*market.*) subquality products; ~ **di qualità superiore** (*market.*) super; **prodotti di scarto** (*market., org. az.*) waste products; **prodotti fabbricati a mano** (*econ.*) handicrafts, handicraft products; ~ **finale** (*org. az.*) final product; ~ **finito** (*org. az.*) finished product, end product, end-item; **prodotti in corso di lavorazione** (*org. az.*) goods in process, partly-finished goods; **prodotti** (*offerti*) **in omaggio** (*market., pubbl.*) free goods; ~ **invendibile** (*market.*) unsalable product; drug in the market, drug on the market (*slang*); **prodotti lavorati** (*market.*) manufactured goods, manufactured products; ~ **lordo**

(*fin., rag.*) gross product, gross output; ~ **manufatto** (*market.*) manufacture; ~ **marginale** (*econ.*) marginal product; **prodotti nazionali** (*comm. est., market.*) home produced goods, national products, domestic products, domestic goods, home products; ~ **nazionale lordo (PNL)** (*econ.*) gross national product (*GNP*); **il ~ nazionale lordo in termini reali** (*econ.*) the real gross national product; ~ **nazionale netto (PNN)** (*econ.*) net national product (*NNP*); ~ **nazionale netto «pro capite»** (*econ.*) per capita net national product; ~ **netto sociale** (*econ.*) social net product; **prodotti non agricoli** (*econ.*) non-agricultural products; **prodotti non alimentari** (*econ.*) non-food products; **prodotti non destinati all'esportazione** (*econ.*) produce not intended for export; ~ **scalare** (*mat.*) scalar product; **prodotti semilavorati** (*org. az.*) semifinished products, unfinished products, semimanufactures, goods in process; ~ **speciale** (*market.*) specialty goods, specialty; **prodotti trasformati** (*org. az.*) processed commodities; ~ **usato per una dimostrazione** (*pubbl.*) demonstrator; **prodotti zootecnici** (*econ.*) livestock products.

produrre, *v. t.* **1** (*causare, originare*) to cause, to produce, to give★ rise to. **2** (*econ.*) to produce, to bear★, to yield; (*coltivare*) to grow★. **3** (*leg.*) (*documenti, prove*) to produce, to bring★ (forward), to show★, to exhibit, to file. **4** (*org. az.*) to produce, to manufacture, to make★, to put★ out, to turn out. // ~ **documenti in tribunale** (*leg.*) to exhibit documents in Court; ~ **in eccesso** (*econ.*) to over-produce; ~ (*merci, articoli*) **in massa** (*org. az.*) to mass-produce; ~ (*merci, articoli*) **in serie** (*org. az.*) to mass-produce; ~ **interesse** (*fin.*) to yield an interest, to earn; ~ **per l'esportazione** (*econ.*) to produce for export; ~ **testimoni** (*leg.*) to produce witnesses.

produttività, *n. f. inv.* **1** productivity. **2** (*econ.*) productivity. // ~ **crescente** (*econ.*) increasing returns (*pl.*); ~ **decrescente** (*econ.*) diminishing returns (*pl.*); ~ **marginale** (*econ.*) marginal productivity; ~ **massima** (*econ.*) peak productivity.

produttivo, *a.* **1** (*econ.*) productive, yielding, bearing. **2** (*org. az.*) operating. // ~ **d'interesse** (*fin.*) interest-bearing; ~ **di reddito** (*fin.*) revenue-bearing.

produttore, *a.* (*econ.*) producing, manufacturing. *n. m.* **1** (*econ.*) producer, manufacturer, maker. **2** (*econ.*) (*coltivatore*) grower. // ~ **d'assicurazioni** (*ass., pers.*) insurance agent, insurance salesman; ~ **di pubblicità** (*pers., pubbl.*) advertisement canvasser; **produttori nazionali** (*comm. est., market.*) home producers; **dal ~ al consumatore** (*market.*) from the producer to the consumer.

produzione, *n. f.* **1** (*econ.*) production; (*specialm. agricola o mineraria*) produce; (*coltivazione*) growing, growth. **2** (*leg.*) (*di documenti, ecc.*) production, exhibition, show. **3** (*org. az.*) production, manufacture, manufacturing, making. **4** (*org. az.*) (*sotto l'aspetto quantitativo e temporale*) production, output, yield; turnout, throughput (*USA*). // ~ **artigianale** (*econ.*) artisan production; ~ **complessiva** (*org. az.*) overall production, global output; **una ~ da record** (*econ.*) a record-breaking production; ~ **di documenti** (*leg.*) exhibition of documents, show of documents, exhibition; ~ **di massa** (*org. az.*) mass production, volume production; **la ~ d'un testimone** (*leg.*) the production of a witness; ~ **in grande quantità** (*org. az.*) quantity production, volume production; ~ **in lotti** (*econ.*) batch production; ~ **in serie** (*org. az.*) serial production, mass production; ~ **industriale** (*econ.*) industrial production; ~ **insufficiente** (*econ., org. az.*) underproduction; ~ **oraria** (*org. az.*) hourly output; ~ **per il magazzino** (*org. az.*) production for stock; **la ~ per ora lavorativa** (*org. az.*) the output per man-hour; ~ (*d'un articolo*) **secondo le particolari richieste del cliente** (*org. az.*) «one off» production; ~ **su commessa** (*econ.*) job production; ~ **su grande scala** (*econ.*) large-scale production; ~ **su ordine** (*econ.*) job production; **chi attua una ~ di massa** (*market.*) mass-producer; **mancata ~ di documenti** (*leg.*) failure to produce documents.

professionale, *a.* **1** professional, vocational. **2** (*pers.*) occupational.

professione, *n. f.* **1** profession, vocation. **2** (*pers.*) occupation. // **professioni ausiliarie** ancillary occupations; **la ~ bancaria** the banking profession; **la ~ d'avvocato** the profession of a lawyer; **la ~ forense** (*leg.*) the Bar; **chi esercita una ~** practitioner; **di ~** by profession.

professionista, *n. m.* e *f.* practitioner, professional, professional man★ (*m.*); professional woman★ (*f.*).

professionistico, *a.* professional.

profilo professionale, *n. m.* (*pers.*) career brief.

profittabilità, *n. f. inv.* profitability. // ~ **delle imprese** (*econ.*) corporate profitability (*USA*).

profittevole, *a.* **1** profitable. **2** (*fin.*) gainful, lucrative.

profitto, *n. m.* 1 profit, advantage. 2 (*lucro*) lucre. 3 (*econ., fin., rag.*) profit, gain, return, take; proceeds (*pl.*). 4 (*econ., fin., rag.*) (*redditività*) profitability. 5 **profitti,** *pl.* (*econ., fin., rag.*) profits, earnings, makings, receipts, takings. // **profitti in via di maturazione** (*rag.*) incoming profits; **profitti ipotetici** (*rag.*) paper profits; **profitti occulti** (*rag.*) secret profits; **profitti rapidi** (*riguardo al realizzo*) (*fin.*) quick profits; **il ~ sul capitale** (*investito*) (*econ., fin.*) the return on capital.

progettare, *v. t.* to project, to plan, to design, to programme, to scheme; (*avere intenzione*) to contemplate.

progettatore d'impianti, *n. m.* (*pers.*) engineer.

progettazione, *n. f.* projection, planning, design. // **~ d'impianti** (*org. az.*) design of manufacturing systems, equipment design, engineering; **~ modulare** (*org. az.*) modular design.

progettista, *n. m.* e *f.* planner, designer; draftsman★ (*m.*).

progetto, *n. m.* 1 project, plan, design, scheme; (*bozza*) draft; (*programma*) programme; (*divisamento*) device; (*impresa*) enterprise. 2 (*org. az.*) design. // **~ di bilancio** (*fin.*) draft budget; **~ di legge** (*leg.*) bill; **~ di legge finanziaria** (*fin., leg.*) financial bill, finance bill; **un ~ di riconversione** a conversion project; **~ di riduzione dell'imposta sul reddito** (*per gli scioperanti*) (*fin., sind.*) negative income tax scheme; **~ di statuto** (*amm.*) draft articles; **il ~ per un nuovo stabilimento** (*org. az.*) the design for a new plant.

programma, *n. m.* 1 programme; program (*USA*); plan, schedule, scheme; (*progetto*) project. 2 (*fin.*) (*d'una nuova società*) prospectus. 3 (*org. az.*) (*di lavoro, delle consegne, ecc.*) schedule. 4 (*pubbl.*) (*radiotelevisivo*) show, programme, broadcast. // **~ d'addestramento** (*org. az.*) training programme; **~ d'assemblaggio** (*org. az.*) assembly program; **un ~ d'assunzione** (*pers.*) a recruitment plan; **~ d'austerità** (*econ.*) austerity programme; **un ~ d'austerità di bilancio** (*amm.*) a programme of budgetary austerity; **~ di ricerca** (*org. az.*) research programme; **~ di riforma agraria** (*econ.*) agrarian-reform programme; **~ giornaliero** (*org. az.*) daily schedule; **un ~ pluriennale** (*econ.*) a multiannual programme.

programmare, *v. t.* 1 to programme; to program (*USA*); to plan, to project. 2 (*econ.*) to plan. 3 (*econ., rag.*) to budget. // **~ la produzione** (*org. az.*) to plan production.

programmatico, *a.* programmatic.

programmatore, *n. m.* programmer.

programmazione, *n. f.* 1 programming, planning. 2 (*econ.*) planning. // **~ a breve termine** (*econ.*) short-run planning; **~ economica** (*econ.*) economic planning; **la ~ produttiva** (*org. az.*) the planning of production.

proibire, *v. t.* to forbid★, to prohibit.

proibizione, *n. f.* prohibition. // **~ di scioperare** (*econ., leg.*) strike ban.

prolungamento, *n. m.* 1 (*allungamento*) prolongation, protraction, extension. 2 (*proroga*) extension, delay. // **il ~ d'una ferrovia** (*trasp. ferr.*) the extension of a railway.

prolungare, *v. t.* 1 (*rendere più lungo*) to prolong, to protract, to extend. 2 (*prorogare*) to extend, to delay, to put★ off. // **~ la scadenza d'un debito** (*cred.*) to extend the time of payment of a debt.

promemoria, *n. m. inv.* 1 memorandum★, note, minute, reminder. 2 (*org. az.*) memorandum★; memo (*fam.*). // **~ di pagamento** (*rilasciato da un venditore al cliente, e contenente l'indicazione dell'ammontare del debito e la scadenza del medesimo*) (*market.*) prompt note; **~ di scadenza** (*cred.*) reminder of due date; **~ interno** (*org. az.*) interoffice memo; **come ~** as a memorandum, as a reminder.

promessa, *n. f.* promise; (*impegno*) undertaking. // **~ di vendita** (*leg.*) agreement to sell; **~ solenne** formal promise; **~ unilaterale** one-sided promise; **chi fa una ~** (*leg.*) promisor; **chi riceve una ~** (*leg.*) promisee.

promettere, *v. t.* to promise. *v. i.* to promise (well), to be promising.

«promotion», *n. f.* (*market., pubbl.*) promotion, sales promotion.

promotore, *n. m.* 1 promoter, organizer, forwarder. 2 (*fin.*) (*d'una società per azioni*) founder, floater.

promozionale, *a.* (*market., pubbl.*) promotional.

promozione, *n. f.* 1 promotion. 2 (*market., pubbl.*) promotion. 3 (*pers.*) promotion, advancement, step. // **~ delle vendite** (*pubbl.*) sales promotion; **~ per anzianità** (*pers.*) promotion in order of age; **di ~** (*pers.*) promotional (*a.*); **relativo alla ~ delle vendite** (*market., pubbl.*) promotional.

promuovere, *v. t.* 1 (*far progredire*) to promote, to further, to forward, to foster. 2 (*fin.*) (*una società, ecc.*) to promote, to float. 3 (*leg.*) (*una legge, ecc.*) to pass. 4 (*pers.*) to promote, to advance, to upgrade, to step up, to up. // ~ **una nuova impresa** (*econ.*) to further a new enterprise; ~ **la vendita d'articoli più cari** (*market.*) to trade up; ~ **la vendita d'un articolo** (*market., pubbl.*) to promote an article, to sell an article, to merchandise an article; ~ **le vendite** (*market., pubbl.*) to promote sales; **essere promosso** (*pers.*) to step up.

pronto, *a.* **1** ready, prepared. **2** (*rapido, lesto*) prompt, ready, quick. **3** (*pers.*) on deck (*fam.*). // ~ **a prendere il mare** (*trasp. mar.*) (*di nave, battello, ecc.*) ready for sea; **pronta cassa** (*market.*) ready cash, prompt cash, cash down; **a pronta cassa** (*market.*) for prompt cash; **a pronti** (*market.*) for cash; **pagamento a pronti** (*market.*) cash payment, cash down.

prontuario, *n. m.* (*manuale*) manual, handbook. // ~ **degli interessi** (*rag.*) interest table; ~ **di calcoli** (*attr. uff.*) ready reckoner, reckoner, calculator.

propaganda, *n. f.* (*pubbl.*) propaganda, advertising, publicity. // ~ (*fatta in modo*) **capillare** (*pubbl.*) canvassing.

propagandabile, *a.* (*pubbl.*) advertisable.

propagandare, *v. t.* (*pubbl.*) to propagandize, to advertise; (*merce, anche*) to push. // ~ **in modo capillare** (*pubbl.*) to canvass.

propagandista, *n. m.* e *f.* (*pers.*) propagandist; salesman★, runner, tout (*m.*); saleswoman★ (*f.*). // ~ «**capillare**» (*pers.*) canvasser.

propensione, *n. f.* propensity, tendency. // ~ **agli investimenti** (*econ.*) propensity to invest; ~ **al consumo** (*econ.*) propensity to consume; ~ **al risparmio** (*econ.*) propensity to save; ~ **marginale al consumo** (*econ.*) marginal propensity to consume; ~ **marginale al risparmio** (*econ.*) marginal propensity to save.

proponente, *a.* proponent. *n. m.* e *f.* **1** proponent, proposer. **2** (*leg.*) (*d'una mozione in un'assemblea*) mover.

proporre, *v. t.* **1** to propose, to propound; (*suggerire*) to suggest; (*offrire*) to offer. **2** (*indicare*) to set★, to put★, to put★ in. // ~ **condizioni favorevoli** (*market.*) to propose favourable terms; ~ **una domanda in giudizio** (*leg.*) to start legal proceedings.

proporzionale, *a.* **1** proportional, ratable. **2** (*mat.*) proportional. // **la distribuzione** ~ **dei profitti** (*fin.*) the ratable distribution of profits.

proporzionalità, *n. f. inv.* proportionality.

proporzionalmente, *avv.* proportionally, ratably.

proporzionare, *v. t.* to proportion, to proportionate. // ~ **le spese ai redditi** (*econ.*) to proportion one's expenditure to one's income.

proporzionato, *a.* proportionate, proportional, commensurate.

proporzione, *n. f.* **1** proportion; (*relazione*) relation. **2** (*mat.*) proportion, ratio. // ~ **composta** (*mat., rag.*) compound ratio; **in** ~ in proportion, pro rata, ratably (*avv.*); proportional, proportionate (*a.*).

proposta, *n. f.* proposal, proposition; (*fatta a una assemblea*) motion; (*offerta*) offer, bid; (*suggerimento*) suggestion. // **una** ~ **degna di considerazione** a considerable proposal; **una** ~ **d'assicurazione** (*ass.*) a proposal of insurance; ~ **di concordato** (*che deve essere vagliata dai creditori*) (*leg.*) proposal of composition; ~ **di regolamento** (*org. az.*) draft regulation; **una** ~ **di transazione** (*leg.*) a proposal for a compromise; ~ **unica di vendita** (*pubbl.*) unique selling proposition; **quanto alla vostra** ~ as regards your proposal; **secondo la vostra** ~ as suggested by you.

proprietà, *n. f. inv.* **1** (*diritto di disporre di qc.*) property, ownership, proprietorship. **2** (*leg.*) (*ciò che si possiede*) property, estate; possessions, means (*pl.*); holding; (*d'immobili*) demesne. // ~ **a titolo oneroso** (*leg.*) onerous property; **una** ~ **abbandonata** (*leg.*) a vacant estate; ~ **affittata** (*leg.*) lease; ~ **assoluta** (*leg.*) fee simple; ~ **assoluta d'un terreno** (*leg.*) freehold; ~ **collettiva** (*econ.*) collective ownership; **una** ~ **comune** (*leg.*) a joint property; ~ **con vincolo della prova** (*leg.*) burdened estate; ~ **data in affitto** (*leg.*) rental, tenancy; ~ **demaniale** (*leg.*) public domain; ~ **d'una corporazione** (*d'un ente, ecc.*) (*fin.*) corporate property; ~ **d'un terreno** (*basata su una copia di antichi documenti di concessione feudale*) (*leg.*) copyhold; ~ **fondiaria** (*econ.*) landed property, landed estate; ~ **immobiliare** (*fin., leg.*) real property, real estate, realty; ~ **individuale** (*di beni non condivisi con altri*) (*leg.*) severalty; ~ **industriale** (*leg.*) patent rights; ~ **mobiliare** (*fin., leg.*) personal property, personal estate; **una** ~ **non soggetta a imposta** (*fin.*) an untaxed property; ~ **presunta** (*leg.*) reputed ownership; ~ **privata** (*leg.*) private property; «~ **privata**» (*scritto su un cartello, ecc.*) «no trespassing!»; ~ **residua** (*dopo il pagamento di debiti e legati*) (*leg.*) residuary estate; ~ **reversibile** (*leg.*) reversion; ~ **soggetta a imposta** (*fin.*) taxable (property); ~ **soggetta a restrizioni** (*leg.*) qualified property; ~ **tenuta in amministrazione fiduciaria** (*leg.*) trust property, trust estate; **chi è investito d'una** ~ **terriera** (*leg.*) feoffee; **chi pos-**

siede terreni in ~ assoluta (*leg.*) freeholder; **di ~ dello Stato** (*econ.*) State-owned (*a.*); **di ~ riservata** (*leg.*) proprietary (*a.*).

proprietaria, *n. f.* (*leg.*) owner, proprietress.

proprietario, *n. m.* (*leg.*) owner, proprietor, proprietary. // **~ confinante** (*leg.*) adjacent owner; **~ d'un'agenzia di traslochi** (*trasp.*) remover; **~ di banchina** (*trasp. mar.*) wharfinger, wharfmaster; **~ di bene gravato da pegno** (*leg.*) lienee; **~ di bene gravato da privilegio** (*leg.*) lienee; **~ di bene ipotecato** (*leg.*) lienee; **~ di casa** landlord; (*abitata dal medesimo*) owner-occupier; **~ di fattoria** homesteader; **~ legittimo** (*leg.*) legal owner, lawful owner; **~ presunto** (*leg.*) reputed owner; **~ terriero** (*econ.*) landowner, landholder, landed proprietor; **senza ~** (*leg.*) (*di terreno, ecc.*) vacant.

proroga, *n. f.* **1** (*cred.*) extension (of time), respite; (*dilazione*) delay; come again (*fam.*). **2** (*leg.*) (*differimento*) deferment, postponement, continuance, continuation. // **~ di pagamento** (*leg.*) deferment of payment.

prorogabile, *a.* **1** (*cred.*) extendible, extensible, delayable. **2** (*leg.*) liable to deferment.

prorogare, *v. t.* **1** (*cred.*) to extend, to respite, to delay. **2** (*leg.*) (*differire*) to defer, to postpone, to continue; (*rinviare*) to put* off. // **~ la scadenza d'una cambiale** (*cred.*) to prolong a bill, to extend the time of payment of a bill.

prorogato, *a.* (*cred.*) (*d'un pagamento*) extended.

prosecuzione, *n. f.* prosecution; (*continuazione*) continuation. // **la ~ d'un'azione giudiziaria** (*leg.*) the prosecution of a suit.

proseguimento, *n. m. V.* **prosecuzione.**

proseguire, *v. t.* to prosecute, to carry on; (*continuare*) to continue, to go* on with. *v. i.* to prosecute; (*continuare*) to continue, to go* on, to keep* up. // «**far ~**» (*comun.*) (*su una lettera*) «please forward», «to be forwarded».

prospettiva, *n. f.* **1** perspective. **2** (*fig.*) outlook, prospect; opening. **3 prospettive,** *pl.* (*fig.*) prospects; outlook (*sing.*). // **prospettive d'avanzamento** (*pers.*) promotional possibilities; **prospettive economiche a medio termine** (*econ.*) medium-term economic outlook; **prospettive finanziarie** (*fin.*) prospects; **prospettive per l'avvenire** future prospects; **in ~** (*pubbl.*) perspective (*a.*).

prospetto, *n. m.* **1** (*tabella, specchietto*) table, list, schedule, statement. **2** (*rag.*) return. // **~ a due colonne** two-column schedule; **~ dei cespiti ammortizzabili** (*fin., rag.*) statement of redeemable income; **~ della situazione finanziaria** (*rag.*) statement of financial position; **un ~ delle spese** (*rag.*) a return of expenses.

proteggere, *v. t.* to protect, to shelter; (*salvaguardare*) to safeguard. // **~ gli scambi** (*dalla concorrenza straniera, ecc.*) (*econ.*) to shelter trade.

proteggersi, *v. rifl.* **1** to protect oneself. **2** (*fin.*) to hedge. // **~ dalle perdite derivanti da oscillazioni nei prezzi** (*fin.*) to hedge against loss due to price fluctuations; **~ finanziariamente** (*fin.*) to hedge.

protesta, *n. f.* protest, complaint, reclamation. // **~ con asserragliamento nel posto di lavoro** (*sind.*) lock-in (*USA*); **~ del capitano** (*della nave*) **per danni subiti dalla nave o dal carico** (*trasp. mar.*) captain's protest.

protestare, *v. t.* **1** to protest, to declare, to assert. **2** (*leg.*) (*una cambiale*) to protest. *v. i.* to protest, to make* a protest, to remonstrate, to reclaim.

protesto, *n. m.* (*leg.*) formal protest, protest. // **~ cambiario** (*leg.*) protest; **~ marittimo** (*trasp. mar.*) (*dichiarazione giurata dal capitano e dall'equipaggio d'una nave danneggiata, riguardante i danni subiti, le loro cause, ecc.*) ship's protest; **~ per mancata accettazione** (*leg.*) protest for non-acceptance; **~ per mancato pagamento** (*leg.*) protest for non-payment; **~ preliminare** (*leg.*) noting; **mancato ~ di cambiale** (*leg.*) failure to protest a bill.

protettivo, *a.* protective, protecting, defensive. // **una tariffa ~** (*comm. est.*) a protective tariff.

protezione, *n. f.* **1** protection, defence; (*custodia*) custody; (*salvaguardia*) safeguard; (*rifugio*) shelter. **2** (*fin.*) hedge. // **la ~ delle piccole imprese** (*fin.*) the safeguard of small industries.

protezionismo, *n. m.* (*econ.*) protectionism, protection.

protezionista, *a.* e *n. m.* e *f.* (*econ.*) protectionist.

protezionistico, *a.* (*econ.*) protectionist, protective.

protocollare[1], *a.* (*leg.*) protocolar, protocolary.

protocollare[2], *v. t.* **1** to record, to file. **2** (*leg.*) to record in protocol.

protocollo, *n. m.* **1** (*attr. uff.*) register of documents, record, file. **2** (*leg.*) protocol. // **carta (formato) ~** (*attr. uff.*) foolscap; **secondo il ~** (*leg.*) according to the protocol.

prova, *n. f.* **1** (*esperimento, esperienza*) trial,

test, experiment, experience. **2** (*dimostrazione*) proof. **3** (*esame*) examination, exam, test. **4** (*leg.*) evidence (*solo sing.*); proof, substantiation, witness, testimony; (*d'un diritto*) vindication. **5** (*mat.*) proof. **6** (*pers.*) (*periodo di prova*) probation. // ~ **a carico** (*leg.*) evidence for the prosecution; ~ **a discarico** (*leg.*) evidence for the accused; ~ **accessoria** (*leg.*) additional proof, secondary evidence; **prove aggiuntive** (*leg.*) collateral evidence; **una ~ certa** (*leg.*) a positive proof; ~ **conclusiva** (*leg.*) conclusive evidence; ~ **contraria** (*leg.*) contrary evidence; ~ **convincente** (*leg.*) convincing evidence; ~ **decisiva** (*leg.*) conclusive evidence; ~ **di mercato** (*eseguita su un'area ristretta ma rappresentativa*) (*market.*) area test; ~ **di preferenza del consumatore** (*su due prodotti diversi ma presentati in confezioni identiche*) (*market.*) blind test; ~ **documentata** (*leg.*) documentary evidence; ~ **esibita** (*leg.*) exhibit; **una ~ essenziale** (*leg.*) a material piece of evidence; **prove esterne** (*leg.*) external evidence; ~ **falsa** (*leg.*) false evidence; **una ~ fondata** (*sui fatti*) (*leg.*) a positive proof; ~ **in contrario** (*leg.*) evidence to the contrary; ~ **inconfutabile** (*leg.*) incontestable evidence, incontrovertible evidence, unquestionable evidence, prima-facie evidence, primary evidence; **prove indiziarie** (*leg.*) circumstantial evidence, presumptive evidence; ~ **negativa** (*leg.*) negative evidence; ~ **orale** (*leg.*) oral evidence, verbal evidence; ~ **perentoria** (*leg.*) conclusive evidence; ~ **preliminare** (*di danno subìto*) (*ass.*) preliminary proof; ~ **prodotta** (*leg.*) exhibit; ~ **psicotecnica** (*pers.*) attitude test; ~ **scritta** (*leg.*) written evidence, documentary evidence; **una ~ sicura** (*leg.*) a tangible proof; ~ **sostanziale** (*leg.*) substantial proof, substantial evidence; **prove sul prodotto** (*org. az.*) product tests; ~ **testimoniale** (*leg.*) testimonial evidence; ~ **testimoniale diretta** (*leg.*) direct evidence; **prove (testimoniali) verbali** (*leg.*) parol evidence; **esser ~ di** (*leg.*) to testify, to witness; **a ~ di furto** (*leg.*) theftproof; **essere assolto per insufficienza di prove** (*in Italia e in Scozia; non in Inghilterra*) (*leg.*) to be found not proven; **in ~** (*market.*) on trial; (*pers.*) on probation; probationary (*a.*).

provare, *v. t.* **1** (*sperimentare, tentare*) to try. **2** (*dimostrare*) to prove, to show★, to demonstrate. **3** (*leg.*) to evidence, to prove, to establish, to substantiate, to witness, to vouch; (*un diritto*) to vindicate. // ~ **un'accusa** (*leg.*) to substantiate a charge; ~ **il proprio diritto** (*leg.*) to show cause; ~ **per mezzo di testi** (*leg.*) to prove by witnesses; ~ **il valore della cosa assicurata** (*ass.*) to prove the value of the thing insured.

provato, *a.* **1** (*dimostrato*) demonstrated, proved. **2** (*messo alla prova*) proved, tried, experienced, tested. **3** (*leg.*) (*di fatto, atto, ecc.*) of record (*pred.*).

provento, *n. m.* (*rag.*) proceeds, receipts (*pl.*); gain, return. // **proventi delle esportazioni** (*fin.*) export receipts; ~ **incerto** (*fin., rag.*) casual profit; **proventi netti** (*rag.*) net proceeds.

provvedere, *v. t.* to provide, to furnish, to supply. *v. i.* **1** to provide (for st.), to make★ provision (for st.); (*prendersi cura di*) to take★ care of; (*badare a*) to look after, to mind. **2** (*prendere provvedimenti*) to take★ steps, to act. **3** (*procurare, disporre*) to see★ (to *o* about st.), to arrange (for st.). // ~ **di documento giustificativo** (*leg., pers.*) to voucher; ~ **di pezza d'appoggio** (*leg., pers.*) to voucher; ~ **le materie prime per l'industria** (*econ.*) to provide the basic materials for industry.

provvedersi, *v. rifl.* to provide oneself, to furnish oneself.

provvedimento, *n. m.* **1** (*rimedio, riparo*) measure, action, step. **2** (*misura di previdenza*) provision, precaution. // ~ **adottato per rappresaglia** (*econ.*) retaliatory measure; ~ **amministrativo** (*leg.*) decree; **provvedimenti anticongiunturali** (*econ.*) measures taken to stem the recession; **provvedimenti antinflazionistici** (*econ.*) anti-inflationary measures; ~ **compensativo** (*econ.*) compensatory measure; **provvedimenti deflazionistici** (*econ.*) deflationary measures; **provvedimenti di rilancio economico** (*econ.*) measures aimed at boosting the economy; ~ **disciplinare** (*pers.*) disciplinary action; **provvedimenti drastici** (*econ.*) crackdown; **provvedimenti efficaci** constructive measures; **provvedimenti efficaci per tenere a freno l'inflazione** (*econ.*) effective measures to curb inflation; ~ **giudiziario** (*leg.*) decree; **provvedimenti preliminari** preparatory measures; **provvedimenti presi per la salvezza della nave** (*trasp. mar.*) measures taken for the safety of the ship.

provvigione, *n. f.* **1** commission, consideration; (*mediazione, senseria*) brokerage. **2** (*di commissionario*) factorage. // ~ **bancaria** (*banca*) bank commission; ~ **calcolata a un tanto la sterlina** (*o* **la libbra**) (*pers.*) poundage; ~ **«del credere»** (*market.*) del credere commission; ~ **d'incasso** (*per effetti fuori piazza*) (*banca*) exchange charge; ~ **di noleggio** (*trasp. mar.*) freight brokerage; ~ **per acquisti**

(*market.*) buying commission; ~ **per l'incasso d'effetti** (*banca*) commission for collection of bills; ~ **sugli acquisti** (*market.*) commission on purchases; ~ **sui riporti** (*Borsa*) commission on contangoes; ~ **sulle vendite** (*market.*) commission on sales.

provvista, *n. f.* **1** (*il provvedere*) provision, supply. **2** (*cose provvedute*) provision, supply; (*scorta*) store, stock. **3** (*org. az.*) stock, supply. **4** (*rag.*) fund. // **provviste di bordo** (*trasp. mar.*) stores; **la ~ di fondi** (*fin.*) funding, the provision of capital; ~ **in valuta estera** (*banca, fin.*) foreign borrowings.

provvisto, *a.* provided, furnished, equipped. // ~ **d'aria condizionata** air-conditioned; ~ **di fondi** (*fin.*) provided with funds; in pocket (*fam.*); **essere ~ di** (*certa merce, ecc.*) (*org. az.*) to stock.

pubblicare, *v. t.* (*giorn., pubbl.*) to publish, to print, to put★ out, to give★ out; (*dell'editore*) to issue. // ~ **annunzi** (*sui giornali*) (*pubbl.*) to advertise; ~ **un catalogo nuovo ogni sei mesi** (*market., pubbl.*) to put a new catalogue out every six months; ~ **un foglio finanziario** (*giorn.*) to issue a financial paper; ~ **sulla gazzetta ufficiale** (*giorn.*) to gazette; **da non pubblicarsi** (*giorn.*) (*di dichiarazione, intervista, e sim.*) off the record; **essere pubblicato** (*giorn.*) (*di giornale*) to issue.

pubblicazione, *n. f.* **1** (*il pubblicare*) publication, publishing, printing, issue, issuing; issuance (*USA*). **2** (*giorn., pubbl.*) (*opera pubblicata*) publication; (*rivista*) review; («*foglio*») sheet. **3 pubblicazioni,** *pl.* (*giorn., pubbl., anche*) prints. // ~ **bimestrale** (*giorn.*) bimonthly; ~ **bisettimanale** (*giorn.*) semi-weekly; ~ **ciclostilata** mimeograph, mimeo; ~ **mensile** (*giorn.*) monthly; ~ **periodica** (*giorn.*) periodical; ~ **quindicinale** (*giorn.*) bi-weekly, fortnightly, semi-monthly; ~ **settimanale** (*giorn.*) weekly; ~ **trimestrale** (*giorn.*) quarterly.

pubblicista, *n. m.* e *f.* **1** (*giorn.*) (*collaboratore di riviste, giornali, e sim.*) publicist; aide-de-press (*slang USA*). **2** (*leg.*) (*chi è esperto di diritto pubblico*) publicist. // ~ **pagato a un tanto la riga** (*giorn.*) space writer, space man.

pubblicità, *n. f. inv.* **1** publicity. **2** (*l'essere pubblico*) publicity. **3** (*pubbl.*) advertising, advertizing; ballyhoo, bally (*slang USA*). // ~ **a mezzo affissione** (*pubbl.*) poster advertising; ~ **a mezzo timbro postale** (*pubbl.*) postmark advertising; ~ **a nome del rivenditore** (*pubbl.*) cooperative advertising, co-op advertising; ~ **concorrenziale** (*pubbl.*) competitive advertising; ~ **di massa** (*pubbl.*) mass advertising; ~ **diretta** (*pubbl.*) direct advertising, direct mail; ~ **esterna** (*pubbl.*) outdoor advertising; ~ **finanziaria** (*pubbl.*) financial advertising; ~ **industriale** (*pubbl.*) industrial advertising; ~ **invisibile** (*pubbl.*) subliminal advertising; ~ **posta sulla confezione della merce venduta** (*pubbl.*) package advertising; ~ **radio-televisiva** (*pubbl.*) radio and television advertising; ~ (*sulla*) **stampa** (*giorn., pubbl.*) magazine advertising, newspaper advertising; ~ **su tutto il territorio nazionale** (*pubbl.*) national advertising.

pubblicitario, *a.* advertising. *n. m.* (*pubbl.*) media man★, ad writer; booster (*slang USA*).

pubblicizzare, *v. t.* (*giorn., pubbl.*) to publicize, to advertise, to press-agent.

pubblico, *a.* public. *n. m.* **1** public. **2** (*uditorio*) audience.

punto, *n. m.* **1** point. **2** (*argomento, questione, dettaglio*) point, detail. **3** (*momento*) moment, point. **4** (*posto, luogo*) point, place, spot; (*fase, stadio*) stage. **5** (*Borsa, fin.*) (*unità di misura per la quotazione dei titoli*) point, mark. **6** (*giorn.*) (*tipografico*) point. // ~ **a favore dei rialzisti** (*Borsa*) bull point; ~ **della scala mobile** (*econ.*) point of the «scala mobile» (*q. V.*) (*in Italia*); **punti dell'oro** (*econ., fin.*) gold points, bullion points, specie points; ~ **d'acquisto** (*market.*) point of purchase; ~ **d'arresto** (*nella diminuzione di valore d'un titolo*) (*Borsa*) base; ~ **d'incontro dei costi e dei ricavi marginali** (*econ.*) best profit equilibrium; ~ **d'indifferenza** (*econ.*) point of indifference; **il ~ d'intersezione** (*di due rette, ecc.*) (*mat.*) the point of intersection; ~ **d'intervento** (*fin.*) peg, intervention point; ~ **d'intervento ufficiale** (*nei tassi di cambio*) (*fin.*) official intervention point, support limit, support point; ~ **di pareggio** (*econ.*) break-even point; ~ **di rottura** (*econ.*) break-even point; ~ **di saturazione** (*anche fig.*) saturation point; ~ **di vendita** (*market.*) point of sale, sales point, sales office, sales outlet, outlet; ~ **di vendita al dettaglio** (*market.*) retail outlet; **punti e linee** (*del telegrafo*) (*comun.*) dots and dashes; ~ **estremo** (*di una fascia d'oscillazione dei tassi di cambio*) (*fin.*) edge; ~ **franco** (*dog.*) bonded warehouse; (*per merci in transito*) entrepôt; foreign-trade zone (*USA*); **il ~ massimo d'una curva** (*mat.*) the peak of a curve; ~ **metallico** (*attr. uff.*) staple; **punti metallici** (*fin.*) gold points, specie points, bullion points; ~ **morto** standstill, deadlock, impasse; ~ **più alto** (*di un ciclo economico*) crest; ~ **più basso** (*di un ciclo economico*) trough; **i punti principali**

d'un accordo salariale (*sind.*) the outlines of a wage settlement; **punti «qualità»** (*market.*) premium stamps; **da un ~ di vista contabile** (*rag.*) from an accounting standpoint; **mezzo ~** half point, half mark; (*fin.*) 0.50%.

punzonare, *v. t.* **1** to punch, to stamp. **2** (*comun.*) (*indirizzi*) to emboss.

punzonatrice, *n. f.* **1** punch, punching-machine, punch-press. **2** (*attr. uff.*) (*per documenti, lettere, ecc.*) perforator.

punzonatura, *n. f.* **1** punching. **2** (*di documenti, lettere, ecc.*) perforation, perforating. **3** (*comun.*) embossing.

punzone, *n. m.* (*attr. uff.*) embossing plate, perforator.

Q

quaderno, *n. m.* **1** exercise-book, copy book; (*per appunti*) note-book. **2** (*attr. uff.*) book. // ~ **di cassa** (*rag.*) cash-book.

quadrare, *v. t.* **1** (*mat.*) (*calcolare l'area d'una figura bidimensionale*) to square. **2** (*mat.*) (*elevare al quadrato*) to square. **3** (*rag.*) (*verificare che si realizzino determinate uguaglianze nei conti*) to balance, to square. *v. i.* (*mat., rag.*) (*detto d'un conto: essere esatto*) to balance, to agree. // ~ **i conti** (*rag.*) to square accounts.

quadrilione, *n. m.* (*un 1 seguito da 15 zeri*) **1** one thousand billions (*ingl.*). **2** quadrillion (*USA*).

quadro, *n. m.* **1** picture, painting. **2** (*tabella*) table, chart. **3** (*fig.*) framework, frame. **4** **quadri,** *pl.* (*pers.*) cadres. // **un ~ concorrenziale** (*market.*) a competitive framework; ~ **delle partenze** (*trasp. mar.*) sailings board; **quadri direttivi** (*o* **dirigenti**) (*pers.*) executive cadres; **i quadri intermedi** (*pers.*) the intermediate cadres; ~ **riassuntivo** summary; **fare il ~ della situazione** to give a summary of the situation.

quadruplicare, *v. t.* (*mat.*) to quadruplicate, to quadruple, to multiply by four.

quadruplo, *a.* (*mat.*) quadruple, quadruplicate. *n. m.* quadruple.

qualifica, *n. f.* (*leg., pers.*) qualification; (*titolo*) title. // **qualifiche personali** (*pers.*) personal qualifications.

qualificare, *v. t.* to qualify. // ~ **con un titolo** to qualify with a title.

qualificato, *a.* **1** (*fornito delle qualità necessarie*) qualified, competent. **2** (*pers.*) (*d'operaio*) skilled, skilful.

qualificazione, *n. f.* qualification.

qualità, *n. f. inv.* **1** quality; (*natura*) nature. **2** (*genere, tipo*) kind, sort. **3** (*carica, grado, ufficio*) capacity. **4** (*market.*) quality; (*categoria, varietà*) grade; (*grado, livello*) standard; (*marca, tipo*) brand. // ~ **buona media** (*market.*) good average quality, fair average quality; ~ **corrente** (*market.*) current quality, standard quality; ~ **«extrafina»** (*market.*) extra fine quality; ~ **genuina** (*market.*) sterling quality; ~ **inferiore** (*market.*) inferior quality, subquality; ~ **media della produzione** (*org. az.*) process average quality; ~ **richiesta** (*market.*) requirement, requisition; ~ **selezionata** (*market.*) selected quality; ~ **superiore** (*market.*) extra fine quality, super; **di ~ buona media** (*market.*) up to grade (*pred.*); **di ~ inferiore** (*market.*) low-class, low-grade, low-end, subquality, sub-standard (*a.*); **di ~ intermedia fra la seconda e la prima** (*market.*) beta plus; **di ~ migliore** better-quality (*attr.*); **di ~ scadente** (*market.*) second-class, third-class (*attr.*); **essere di ~ scadente** (*market., anche*) to be below the mark; **di ~ superiore** (*market.*) high-grade, superior; fancy (*USA*); **di (buona) ~** (*market.*) name (*attr.*); **in ~ di** (*leg.*) in quality of, in the quality of, as.

qualitativo, *a.* qualitative.

quantità, *n. f. inv.* **1** quantity. **2** (*quantitativo*) quantity, amount; (*volume*) volume. **3** (*un gran numero di; molto*) a lot (of), lots (of), many, a great (*o* good) deal (of). // **una ~ d'affari** a rush of business; ~ **di lavoro** (*assegnata a un operaio*) (*pers.*) work load; ~ **di materia prima messa in lavorazione** (*in una certa unità di tempo*) (*org. az.*) throughput; ~ **di merce esposta per la vendita** (*market., ingl.*) pitch; ~ **di merce trasportata** (*trasp.*) haul; ~ **effettiva** (*in barili, botti, ecc.*) (*dog.*) ullage; ~ **incognita** (*mat.*) unknown quantity, x; ~ **mancante** (*in barili, botti, ecc.*) (*market.*) ullage; **una ~ media** a mean quantity; ~ **ottimale** (*org. az.*) best quantity, economic order quantity; ~ **pari a dodici grosse** (*cioè, 1.728 unità*) great gross; ~ **sufficiente** sufficient quantity, sufficiency; **una ~ sufficiente di materie prime** (*org. az.*) a sufficiency of basic materials.

quantitativo, *a.* quantitative. *n. m.* quantity, amount; (*numero*) number. // ~ **di merce caricata a bordo** (*trasp. mar.*) intake; ~ **minimo trattabile** (*di titoli*) (*Borsa, fin.*) round lot.

quarantena, *n. f.* (*trasp. mar.*) quarantine. // **fuori ~** (*trasp. mar.*) out of quarantine; **in ~** (*trasp. mar.*) in quarantine, under quarantine.

quarto, *num. ord.* fourth. *n. m.* **1** quarter; fourth. **2** (*in senso temporale*) quarter. **3** (*giorn., pubbl.*) quarto. // **quarta di copertina** (*giorn.*)

fourth cover; ~ **di dollaro** quarter (*USA*); ~ **di «gallone»** (*misura per liquidi pari a litri 1,14 circa*) quart; ~ **di «hundredweight»** (*misura di peso pari a kg 12,70 e a kg 11,34 in U.S.A.*) quarter; **un** ~ **di punto** (*Borsa, fin.*) 0.25%; **tre quarti di punto** (*Borsa, fin.*) 0.75%.

quasi, *avv.* **1** almost, nearly. **2** (*con certi nomi composti*) quasi. // ~ **contratto** (*leg.*) quasi-contract; ~ **inflazione** (*econ.*) semi-inflation; ~ **rendita** (*econ.*) quasi income; ~ **ristagno** (*econ.*) near-stagnation; ~ **socio** (*fin.*) quasi partner, partner by estoppel; ~ **«stagnazione»** (*econ.*) near-stagnation; ~ **usufrutto** (*leg.*) quasi usufruct.

quattro, *num. card.* four. // **in** ~ **copie** (*di documento*) quadruplicate (*a.*).

querela, *n. f.* (*leg.*) complaint, lawsuit, suit, action (at law). // **una** ~ **per diffamazione** (*leg.*) an action for libel; **sporgere** ~ **contro** (*leg.*) to bring an action against.

querelante, *n. m.* e *f.* (*leg.*) complainant, plaintiff, prosecutor.

querelare, *v. t.* (*leg.*) to sue (at law), to bring* a suit (*o* an action) against, to make* a complaint against, to prosecute.

querelarsi, *v. rifl.* (*leg.*) to take* legal proceedings.

querelato, *n. m.* (*leg.*) accused, defendant.

querelatore, *n. m. V.* **querelante.**

quesito, *n. m.* **1** (*domanda*) question, query. **2** (*problema*) problem.

questionario, *n. m.* (*market.*) questionnaire, list of questions.

questione, *n. f.* **1** (*discussione, controversia*) question, controversy, issue. **2** (*faccenda*) matter, question. **3** (*leg.*) issue, point, question. // ~ **di competenza** (*leg.*) question of competence; ~ **di diritto** (*leg.*) issue of law, question of law; ~ **di fatto** (*leg.*) issue of fact, question of fact; **una** ~ **di procedura** (*leg.*) a point of order; **questioni interessanti i consumatori** (*econ., market.*) matters of concern to consumers; **la** ~ **operaia** (*sind.*) the labour question; **una** ~ (*legale*) **pendente** (*leg.*) a pending suit.

qui, *avv.* **1** here. **2** (*in frasi temporali*) now. **3** (*leg.*) herein, herewith, within. // ~ **accluso** (*o* **unito**) herein enclosed, herewith enclosed; **di** ~ **a un mese** a month from now.

quiescenza, *n. f.* quiescence, quiescency. // **porre q. in** ~ (*pers.*) to retire sb., to cause sb. to retire, to superannuate sb.; **trattamento di** ~ (*pers.*) pension.

quietanza, *n. f.* (*comm.*) receipt, quittance, acquittance, voucher. // ~ **a saldo** (*market.*) receipt in full; ~ **per nolo** (*trasp. mar.*) freight release.

quietanzare, *v. t.* (*comm.*) to receipt. // ~ **una fattura** (*market.*) to receipt an invoice; ~ **una polizza di carico** (*trasp. mar.*) to receipt a bill of lading.

quindici, *num. card.* e *n. m.* fifteen. // ~ **giorni** a fortnight; **oggi a** ~ a fortnight to-day; **ogni** ~ **giorni** fortnightly (*a.* e *avv.*).

quindicina, *n. f.* **1** (*serie di quindici*) (set of) fifteen. **2** (*circa quindici*) about fifteen. **3** (*quindici giorni*) fortnight, two weeks.

quindicinale, *a.* (*che avviene ogni quindici giorni*) fortnightly, semi-monthly, bi-monthly, bi-weekly. *n. m.* (*giorn.*) fortnightly (publication), semi-monthly (publication), bi-monthly (publication), bi-weekly (publication).

quintale, *n. m.* quintal, 100 kilograms.

quinterno, *n. m.* (*attr. uff.*) five sheets of paper.

quintilione, *n. m.* (*un 1 seguito da 18 zeri*) **1** trillion (*secondo il sistema inglese*). **2** quintillion (*USA*).

quintuplicare, *v. t.* to quintuple, to quintuplicate, to multiply by five.

quintuplo, *a.* quintuple, fivefold, five times as much. *n. m.* quintuple.

quorum, *n. m.* (*leg.*) quorum.

quota, *n. f.* **1** (*porzione*) quota, part, proportion, share, amount. **2** (*fin.*) fee; (*apporto*) contribution. **3** (*fin., rag.*) allocation. **4** (*market.*) (*rata*) instalment. **5** (*stat.*) breakdown. // **quote** (*d'ammortamento*) **decrescenti** (*rag.*) decreasing charges; **quote d'abbonamento** (*giorn.*) subscription rates; ~ **di dividendo pagato ai dipendenti** (*pers.*) wage dividend; ~ **d'immigrazione** immigration quota, immigrant quota; **quote di partecipazione** (*fin.*) participating shares; sub-units; ~ **individuale** (*fin.*) head money; ~ **parte** (*fin.*) proportion, contribution; ~ (*di denaro, ecc.*) **versata** (*o* **da versare**) (*fin.*) subscription; **a quote costanti** (*rag.*) (*d'ammortamento*) straight-line (*attr.*).

quotabile, *a.* (*fin.*) quotable. // **essere** ~ **in Borsa** (*Borsa, anche*) to be a candidate for listing on the stock market.

quotare, *v. t.* (*fin., market.*) to quote, to rate, to state; (*valutare*) to evaluate. // ~ **il «certo per l'incerto»** (*fin.*) to quote fixed exchange; ~ **un corso** (*Borsa, fin.*) to mark a price; ~ **l'«incerto per il certo»** (*fin.*) to quote movable exchange; ~ **il nolo** (*trasp. mar.*) to quote the freight; ~ **un prezzo** (*market.*) to mark a price, to quote a price.

quotato, *a.* (*fin., market.*) quoted, rated, stated; (*valutato*) evaluated. // **non** ~ (*nel li-*

stino ufficiale di Borsa) (*fin.*) unquoted; on the curb (*fam., USA*).

quotazione, *n. f.* (*fin., market.*) quotation, rating; (*di titolo*) market. // **quotazioni a contanti** (*Borsa*) quotations for cash; **quotazioni a termine** (*Borsa*) quotations for the account; ~ **basata sul prezzo di acquisto, più una percentuale** (*spesso determinata da regolamentazioni governative*) (*fin., rag.*) cost plus; **la ~ dei prezzi** (*fin., market.*) the quotation of prices; ~ **d'acquisto** (*Borsa, fin.*) bid; ~ **d'apertura** (*Borsa*) opening price; ~ **di chiusura** (*Borsa, fin.*) day's close, closing quotation; ~ **di comodo del dollaro alla Borsa Valori di Londra** (*fin.*) dummy dollar; **quotazioni di nolo** (*trasp. mar.*) quotations for freight; ~ **di vendita** (*Borsa, fin.*) ask; ~ **doppia** (*Borsa, fin.*) double-barrelled quotation; ~ **in Borsa** (*fin.*) quotation in the list; ~ **massima** (*Borsa, fin.*) high; **quotazioni massime e minime** (*Borsa, fin.*) highs and lows; ~ **minima** (*Borsa, fin.*) low, floor.

quotidiano, *a.* daily, everyday (*attr.*). *n. m.* (*giorn.*) daily paper, daily, journal.

quoziente, *n. m.* (*mat.*) quotient.

R

raccogliere, *v. t.* **1** to pick up; (*cogliere*) to pick. **2** (*mietere*) to crop, to harvest. **3** (*mettere insieme, radunare*) to gather, to collect, to rally. **4** (*fin.*) (*fondi, ecc.*) to raise, to collect. // ~ **notizie** to gather news; ~ **sottoscrizioni** to take up contributions.

raccoglitore, *n. m.* (*attr. uff.*) file holder.

raccolta, *n. f.* **1** (*il raccogliere*) (*cereali*) harvesting; (*cotone, frutta, ecc.*) picking. **2** (*raccolto*) harvest, crop. **3** (*epoca del raccolto*) harvest-time. **4** (*attr. uff.*) file. // ~ **di dati** (*market., org. az.*) information gathering; (*tramite interviste e sperimentazioni all'esterno dell'azienda*) fieldwork; ~ **d'informazioni** gathering of intelligence; ~ **d'informazioni sulla concorrenza mediante clienti «spia»** (*market., org. az.*) service shopping; ~ **di leggi** (*leg.*) body of laws, statute-roll, statute-book; ~ **di notizie** (*sull'attività della concorrenza*) **attuata per mezzo di «falsi clienti»** (*market.*) service shopping.

raccolto, *n. m.* crop, harvest, yield. // ~ **fondamentale** (*econ.*) basic crop; ~ **ottenuto per rotazione** (*econ.*) shift; **un** ~ **record** (*abbondantissimo*) (*econ.*) a record crop; **un** ~ **scarso** (*econ.*) a poor harvest; **raccolti sovrabbondanti** (*econ.*) superabundant crops.

raccomandare, *v. t.* **1** (*appoggiare*) to recommend. **2** (*comun.*) (*una lettera*) to register. **3** (*trasp. mar.*) (*una nave*) to address. // ~ **un pacco** (*comun.*) to register a parcel; ~ **il segreto** to enjoin secrecy.

raccomandata, *n. f.* (*comun.*) registered letter.

raccomandatario, *n. m.* (*trasp. mar.*) ship's husband, ship's agent.

raccomandazione, *n. f.* **1** (*il raccomandare*) recommendation. **2** (*esortazione*) recommendation, exhortation, warning. **3** (*comun.*) (*di lettere*) registration. **4** (*pers.*) reference, recommendation; plug (*slang USA*). **5** (*trasp. mar.*) (*in un contratto di noleggio*) address. // **la** ~ **d'una lettera** (*comun.*) the registration of a letter; **lettera di** ~ (*pers.*) letter of recommendation, reference; **tassa di** ~ (*comun.*) registration fee.

raccordo, *n. m.* **1** joint, connection. **2** (*trasp. ferr.*) siding, feeder. // ~ **anulare** (*trasp. aut.*) ring-road; ~ **ferroviario** (*trasp. ferr., anche*) railway siding.

rada, *n. f.* (*trasp. mar.*) road; roads (*pl.*); harbour; harbor (*USA*); haven.

raddoppiare, *v. t.* **1** (*rendere doppio*) to double, to make★ double; (*duplicare*) to duplicate. **2** (*aumentare fortemente*) to double, to redouble, to increase. // ~ **la proprie entrate** to double one's income; ~ **il prezzo** (*market.*) to double the price.

radiare, *v. t.* **1** to strike★ off (*o* out), to cancel. **2** (*trasp. mar.*) to condemn. // ~ **un'ipoteca** (*leg.*) to extinguish a mortgage.

radice, *n. f.* (*anche mat.*) root. // ~ **cubica** (*mat.*) cube root; ~ **quadrata** (*mat.*) square root.

rafforzamento, *n. m.* strengthening, enforcement, consolidation. // ~ **delle quotazioni** (*di titoli, ecc.*) **dopo un crollo** (*Borsa, fin.*) rally.

rafforzare, *v. t.* to strengthen, to enforce, to consolidate. // ~ **le quotazioni** (*di titoli, ecc.*) **dopo un crollo** (*Borsa, fin.*) to rally.

rafforzarsi, *v. rifl.* to strengthen, to gain strength, to consolidate, to harden.

raffreddamento, *n. m.* (*anche fig.*) cooling, dampening.

raffreddare, *v. t.* (*anche fig.*) to cool down, to dampen. // ~ **la domanda interna** to dampen domestic demand.

raffreddarsi, *v. rifl.* (*anche fig.*) (*dell'economia*) to cool down.

raffrontare, *v. t.* to confront, to compare; (*collazionare*) to collate. // ~ **due documenti** to collate two documents.

raffronto, *n. m.* confrontation, comparing, comparison; (*collazione*) collation. // **il** ~ **dei bilanci economici** (*econ.*) the confrontation of economic budgets; ~ **per fattore** (*pers.*) factor comparison.

raggiungere, *v. t.* **1** to reach, to overtake★. **2** (*ottenere, toccare*) to reach, to attain, to get★. **3** (*market.*) (*un prezzo*) to fetch. // ~ **un accomodamento con q.** to make an arrangement with sb.; ~ **un accordo** to come to an agreement; ~ **una decisione** to arrive at a decision; ~ **il (livello) minimo** (*fin.*) (*di prezzi, ecc.*) to touch bottom; ~ **il numero di** to total; ~ **gli obiettivi** to attain objectives.

raggiungimento, *n. m.* **1** (*il raggiungere*) reaching. **2** (*conseguimento*) attainment, achievement. // ~ **dell'età maggiore** (*leg.*) coming of age.

ragguagliare, *v. t.* **1** (*informare*) to inform; to acquaint (sb. with st.). **2** (*rag.*) to balance. // ~ **le partite** (*rag.*) to balance accounts.

ragguaglio, *n. m.* **1** (*informazione*) piece of information; (*particolare*) particular; (*resoconto*) report. **2** (*rag.*) balance. **3 ragguagli,** *pl.* information (*sing.*).

ragione, *n. f.* **1** reason. **2** (*causa, motivo*) reason, motive, ground. **3** (*diritto, giusto motivo*) right, reason. **4** (*argomentazione*) reason, justification. **5** (*mat., rag.*) (*razione, proporzione*) ratio, proportion; (*tasso*) rate. // ~ **di scambio** (*comm. est.*) terms of trade; **la ~ e il torto** (*leg.*) right and wrong; ~ **sociale** (*d'una ditta*) business name, firm name, style; (*d'una società di capitali*) company title; corporate name (*USA*); **chi usa illegalmente l'altrui ~ sociale** (*leg.*) infringer; **per ragioni d'ordine interno** for internal convenience.

ragioneria, *n. f.* **1** (*rag.*) (*la scienza*) accountancy. **2** (*rag.*) (*ufficio di ragioniere*) counting-house; counting-room (*USA*).

ragioniere, *n. m.* (*pers.*) accountant. // ~ **capo** (*pers.*) chief accountant; (*dello Stato*) paymaster general; ~ **Generale dello Stato** (*amm.*) Accountant and Comptroller General; ~ **iscritto all'albo** chartered public accountant, chartered accountant; certified public accountant (*USA*); ~ **professionista** chartered accountant, public accountant.

ramo, *n. m.* (*comm.*) (*d'affari*) branch, line; lay (*fam.*). // **i rami dell'industria** (*econ.*) the branches of industry; ~ **d'affari meno importante** (*market., org. az.*) side-line.

rango, *n. m.* **1** (*ceto, grado*) rank, social class. **2** (*trasp. mar.*) rating.

rapporto, *n. m.* **1** (*relazione orale o scritta*) report. **2** (*correlazione, attinenza*) relation, relationship, connection, dealing, bearing. **3** (*leg.*) return; (*dichiarazione*) statement. **4** (*mat.*) ratio. // ~ **causa-effetto** (*org. az.*) cause-effect relationship; **un ~ circostanziato** a circumstantial report; **rapporti col pubblico** (*pubbl.*) external relations; **rapporti commerciali** trade relations; ~ **composto** (*mat., rag.*) compound ratio; ~ **consolare** (*comm. est.*) consular report; ~ **del capitano** (*trasp. mar.*) captain's report; **rapporti d'affari** business connections, dealings; **rapporti di cambio** (*fin.*) exchange rates; **i rapporti di cambio fra la lira e le altre monete** (*fin.*) the exchange rates between the lira and other currencies; ~ **di cassa** (*rag.*) (*rapporto fra disponibilità di cassa e crediti esigibili e passività correnti*) cash ratio; ~ **di leva finanziaria** (*fin.*) leverage ratio; ~ **di «leverage»** (*fin.*) leverage ratio; ~ **di surrogazione** (*leg.*) subrogation; ~ **finale** (*org. az.*) final report; ~ **finanziario** (*fin.*) financial report; ~ **fra le attività a breve e le passività correnti** (*rag.*) quick assets ratio, quick ratio, acid-test ratio; ~ **fra i diversi tipi di capitale nella stessa società** (*fin.*) capital gearing; ~ **fra le passività totali d'una ditta e il suo valore patrimoniale** (*rag.*) debt to net worth ratio; **il ~ fra il prezzo delle azioni e i dividendi** the ratio between stock prices and dividends; ~ **fra la quantità di merce prodotta e quella dei fattori produttivi impiegati** (*econ.*) returns to scale of plant; ~ **fra le riserve in contanti e le passività** (*banca*) reserve ratio; ~ **fra il totale del fondo ammortamento e il costo originario d'un immobilizzo** (*org. az.*) depreciation reserve ratio; ~ **fra gli utili** (*annuali*) **d'un'azione e la sua quotazione** (*in un dato momento*) (*fin.*) price-earnings ratio; ~ **fra gli utili d'una società e quelli distribuiti** (*fin.*) cover; ~ **governativo** (*amm.*) white paper; ~ **inverso** (*mat.*) reciprocal ratio; **il ~ manager-imprenditore** (*org. az.*) the manager-owner relationship; ~ **mensile** (*amm., rag.*) monthly report; ~ **prezzo-utili** (*econ.*) price-earnings ratio; **rapporti sindacali** (*pers., sind.*) labour relations; ~ **tra attività e passività correnti** (*econ., rag.*) current ratio; ~ **tra il capitale investito negli impianti e il valore lordo della produzione** (*fin.*) capital-output ratio, capital coefficient; ~ **tra capitalizzazione e depositi** (*banca*) capitalization/deposit ratio; **rapporti tra la direzione e le maestranze** (*pers., sind.*) labour relations; ~ **tra indebitamento e mezzi propri** (*fin.*) leverage ratio; ~ **tra il reddito disponibile e quello risparmiato** (*econ., fin.*) savings ratio; ~ **tra il valore delle uscite per il pagamento dei dividendi e il valore dei profitti** (*d'una società*) (*fin.*) pay-out ratio; **a ~** (*org. az., pers.*) on report; **essere in ~ con q.** to be in relation with sb., to be connected with sb.; **essere in rapporti d'amicizia con q.** to be on a friendly footing with sb.; **mettersi a ~** to demand a hearing; **mettersi in ~ con q.** to get in touch with sb., to contact sb.

rappresaglia, *n. f.* (*leg.*) retaliation, reprisal. // **di ~** (*leg.*) retaliatory (*a.*); **per ~** by way of retaliation.

rappresentante, *a.* representative. *n. m.* 1 (*chi rappresenta un altro*) representative, delegate, deputy; (*portavoce*) spokesman★. 2 (*pers.*) agent, representative agent, sales representative, representative; man★ (*fam.*); rep (*abbr. di* representative), bell-ringer (*slang USA*). // **i rappresentanti della stampa** (*giorn.*) the representatives of the press; ~ **di commercio** (*market., pers.*) commercial traveller, business agent; ~ **di zona** (*pers.*) district representative; ~ **esclusivo** (*market.*) exclusive agent, sole agent; ~ **legale** (*leg.*) legal representative; ~ **sindacale** (*sind.*) bargaining agent.

rappresentanza, *n. f.* 1 (*il rappresentare*) representation, delegation, agency. 2 (*gruppo di persone che rappresentano altri*) representative body, delegation, deputation. 3 (*leg.*) representation, agency. // ~ **di commercio** (*leg.*) mercantile agency; ~ **esclusiva** (*market.*) sole agency, exclusive agency; ~ **legale** (*leg.*) legal representation.

rappresentare, *v. t.* 1 to represent. 2 (*leg.*) to represent, to act as an agent for, to be an agent for. // ~ **graficamente** (*una funzione*) **per mezzo d'una curva** (*mat.*) to plot; ~ **q. in giudizio** (*leg.*) to appear for sb.; ~ **le parti contendenti** (*davanti al tribunale*) (*leg.*) to represent the parties; ~ **per mezzo d'un diagramma** (*o* **d'un grafico**) (*mat.*) to graph.

rappresentativo, *a.* representative; (*di rappresentanza*) representational. // **non** ~ non-representative; **non** ~ **della maggioranza** non-representative of the majority.

rappresentato, *n. m.* (*leg.*) principal.

rappresentazione, *n. f.* 1 representation. 2 (*leg.*) (*nel diritto di successione*) representation.

rassegna, *n. f.* review, report, survey. // ~ **di mercato** (*econ., market.*) market report; ~ **industriale** (*econ.*) industrial review.

rassegnare, *v. t.* to hand in, to give★. // ~ **le dimissioni** (*pers.*) to resign; to give (*o* to hand in) one's resignation; ~ **un reclamo** to resign a claim.

rata, *n. f.* instalment; (*pagamento*) payment; (*quota*) quota. // ~ (*di nolo*) **a cubaggio** (*trasp. mar.*) measurement rate; ~ **di nolo** (*trasp. mar.*) freight rate, rate; ~ **mensile** (*market.*) monthly instalment; **pro** ~ pro rata, in proportion.

rateale, *a.* (*market.*) by instalments, on the instalment plan; instalment (*attr.*).

rateare, *v. t.* (*market.*) to divide into instalments.

rateazione, *n. f.* (*market.*) division into instalments.

rateizzare, *v. t. V.* **rateare.**

rateo attivo, *n. m.* (*rag.*) accrued income.

rateo passivo, *n. m.* (*rag.*) accrued expense, accrued liability, anticipated liability.

ratifica, *n. f.* (*leg.*) ratification, approval, sanction, verification; (*conferma*) confirmation, affirmation. // **la** ~ **d'un trattato** (*leg.*) the ratification of a treaty.

ratificare, *v. t.* (*leg.*) to ratify, to approve, to sanction, to sign, to verify; (*confermare*) to confirm, to affirm. // ~ **un contratto** (*leg.*) to ratify a contract, to bind a contract; ~ **un trattato** (*leg.*) to sign a treaty, to ratify a treaty.

ratificazione, *n. f. V.* **ratifica.**

razionale, *a.* 1 rational. 2 (*mat.*) rational.

razionalizzare, *v. t.* 1 to rationalize. 2 (*mat.*) to rationalize. 3 (*org. az.*) (*il lavoro*) to rationalize. // ~ **il processo produttivo** (*org. az.*) to rationalize the industrial process.

razionalizzazione, *n. f.* 1 rationalization. 2 (*mat.*) rationalization. 3 (*org. az.*) rationalization.

razionamento, *n. m.* (*econ.*) rationing. // **il** ~ **della benzina** (*econ.*) the rationing of petrol; the rationing of gasoline (*USA*).

razionare, *v. t.* (*econ.*) to ration.

razione, *n. f.* 1 (*econ.*) ration, fixed allowance. 2 (*pers.*) (*alimentare*) allowance.

reale, *a.* 1 (*effettivo, vero*) real, actual; (*vero*) true; (*sostanziale*) substantial, substantive. 2 (*mat.*) real. // **un numero** ~ (*mat.*) a real number.

realizzabile, *a.* 1 realizable. 2 (*cred.*) (*riscuotibile*) realizable, encashable. 3 (*fin.*) (*convertibile in contanti*) convertible into cash.

realizzare, *v. t.* 1 (*mettere in atto*) to realize, to accomplish, to carry out. 2 (*cred.*) (*riscuotere*) to realize, to encash. 3 (*fin.*) (*convertire in contanti*) to convert into cash. // ~ **un credito** (*cred.*) to realize a credit; ~ **un utile** (*rag.*) to earn a profit; ~ **il valore attuale di** (*un'annualità, una rendita, ecc.*) (*rag.*) to capitalize.

realizzazione, *n. f.* 1 (*messa in atto*) realization, accomplishment, completion. 2 (*Borsa*) closing. 3 (*cred.*) (*riscossione*) realization, encashment. 4 (*fin.*) (*conversione in contanti*) conversion into cash. // ~ **di titoli in contante** conversion of securities into cash.

realizzo, *n. m.* (*cred.*) realization, encashment, conversion into cash; break-up (*fam.*). // **il** ~ **del contante** (*rag.*) the recovery of cash; **il** ~ **della proprietà d'un fallito** (*leg.*) the realization of a bankrupt's estate; **di facile** ~ (*cred., fin.*) easily cashable, easily cashed.

reato, *n. m.* (*leg.*) offence, crime; (*civile*)

tort; (*di minor gravità*) misdemeanour. // ~ **di complicità** (*leg.*) accessorial crime; ~ **di diffamazione** (*leg.*) slander; ~ **di falsificazione di moneta** (*leg.*) coinage offence; ~ **di stampa** (*leg.*) libel; ~ **minore** (*leg.*) petty offence; ~ **passibile di pena pecuniaria** (*leg.*) pecuniary offence; ~ **penale** (*leg.*) criminal offence; **reati perseguibili a termini di legge** (*leg.*) legal offences, penal offences.

reattivo, *n. m.* (*econ.*) reactor.

reazione, *n. f.* reaction, response. // ~ **a catena** (*anche fig.*) chain-reaction; ~ **difensiva** (*a un processo inflazionistico*) (*econ.*) defensive reaction; **una ~ nelle quotazioni** (*dei titoli*) (*Borsa*) a reaction in stock prices; ~ **passiva** (*a un processo inflazionistico*) (*econ.*) passive reaction.

recapitare, *v. t.* (*comun., trasp.*) to deliver. // **non recapitato** (*comun., trasp.*) undelivered.

recapito, *n. m.* 1 (*comun.*) (*indirizzo*) business address, address; (*ufficio*) office. 2 (*comun., trasp.*) (*consegna*) delivery.

recare, *v. t.* 1 to bring★, to bear★. 2 (*cagionare*) to cause, to bring★. // ~ **danno a** (*q. o qc.*) to damage; **recante la firma e il sigillo di chi lo redige** (*leg.*) (*d'atto*) under seal.

recedere, *v. i.* 1 to recede, to withdraw★. 2 (*rinunciare*) to abandon, to give★ up. 3 (*leg.*) to back down. // ~ **da un contratto** (*leg.*) to recede from a contract, to declare off a contract.

recente, *a.* recent; (*fresco*) fresh; (*nuovo*) new; (*aggiornato*) up-to-date; (*ultimo*) late. // **di ~** recently, lately, newly, of late.

recentissime, *n. pl.* (*giorn.*) stop press (*sing.*); spot news (*sing. collett.*).

recessione, *n. f.* (*econ.*) recession, slump. // ~ **improvvisa** (*econ.*) downswing.

recessivo, *a.* (*econ.*) recessionary. // ~ **e inflattivo** (*a un tempo*) (*econ.*) stagflationary.

reciclaggio, *n. m.* (*econ.*) recycling.

reciclare, *v. t.* (*econ.*) to recycle.

recidiva, *n. f.* (*leg.*) recidivism, recidive.

recidivo, *a.* (*leg.*) recidivist, habitual criminal.

recinto, *n. m.* enclosure; (*cortile*) yard. // ~ **alle grida** (*Borsa*) floor; pit (*USA*); (*di Borsa Merci*) ring; ~ **grida inattivo** (*Borsa*) inactive post.

recipiente, *n. m.* container; (*di latta*) tin; can (*USA*). // **recipienti a rendere** (*market.*) returnable containers; ~ **della capacità d'un «peck»** peck; ~ **vuoto** (*market.*) empty.

reciprocità, *n. f. inv.* 1 reciprocity. 2 (*comm. est.*) reciprocity. // ~ **di trattamento commerciale** (*comm. est.*) reciprocity in trade.

reciproco, *a.* 1 reciprocal, mutual. 2 (*mat.*) reciprocal.

reclamante, *n. m.* e *f.* complainant.

reclamare, *v. i.* 1 to claim, to complain, to make★ (*o* to lodge) a complaint; (*protestare*) to protest. 2 (*leg.*) to claim. *v. t.* 1 to claim, to ask for. 2 (*esigere la restituzione di*) to reclaim, to claim back. // ~ **i propri diritti** (*leg.*) to claim one's rights; ~ **presso q.** to make a complaint to sb.; **chi reclama** complainant; **non reclamato** unclaimed.

réclame, *n. f.* 1 (*pubbl.*) (*pubblicità*) advertising, publicity. 2 (*pubbl.*) (*avviso pubblicitario*) advertisement; ad (*abbr.*).

reclamista, *n. m.* e *f.* (*pubbl.*) self-advertiser.

reclamizzare, *v. t.* (*pubbl.*) to advertise, to merchandise.

reclamo, *n. m.* 1 claim, complaint, contention, grievance; (*pretesa di restituzione*) claiming back, reclamation. 2 (*sind.*) grievance. // ~ **per addebito eccessivo** (*trasp. mar.*) overcharge claim; ~ **per danni** (*leg.*) claim for damages; ~ **per perdita o avaria** (*trasp. mar.*) claim for losses or damage.

reclusione, *n. f.* (*leg.*) imprisonment.

reclutamento, *n. m.* recruitment, recruiting. // **il ~ di personale** (*econ., pers.*) the recruiting of personnel.

reclutare, *v. t.* to recruit. // ~ **manodopera qualificata** (*econ., pers.*) to recruit skilled workers.

record, *n. m.* record. *a.* record (*attr.*); record-breaking.

recto, *n. m.* face; (*di foglio*) recto. // **il ~ d'un certificato azionario** (*fin.*) the face of a stock certificate.

recuperare, *v. t. V.* **ricuperare.**

recupero, *n. m. V.* **ricupero.**

redditività, *n. f. inv.* (*econ., fin., rag.*) profitability.

redditizio, *a.* 1 (*econ., fin., rag.*) profitable, remunerative, paying, payable. 2 (*pers.*) (*d'un lavoro, ecc.*) payable. // **non ~** unprofitable.

reddito, *n. m.* 1 (*econ., fin., rag.*) (*provento*) income, revenue. 2 (*econ., fin., rag.*) (*frutto*) yield, profit, return; pocket book (*fam.*). // **redditi agricoli** (*econ.*) farm incomes; ~ **annuale** (*fin.*) yearly income, annual income; **redditi ascrivibili ai fattori della produzione** (*econ.*) incomes accruing to the factors of production; ~ **commerciale (industriale) netto** (*fin.*) net commercial (industrial) income; ~ **complessivo** (*rag.*) gross income; **il ~ di capitale** (*econ., fin.*) the return on capital, the income from capital; ~ **di fabbricati** (*econ.*) rental; **redditi di lavoro** (*fin.*) earned income, income profits; ~ **di lavoro autonomo di persone fisiche** (*fin.*) income derived from the self-employment of private individuals; ~ **di lavoro subordinato** (*fin.*) income from eployment, income of employed persons; ~ **disponibile** (*fin.*) disposable income; ~ **dominicale** (*econ.*) rental; ~ **effettivo** (*fin.*) flat rate; ~ **esente da imposta** (*fin.*) tax-free income; ~ **familiare** (*econ.*) family income, family wage; ~ **fisso** (*rag.*) fixed income; (*fin.*) fixed interest; ~ **globale** (*fin.*) overall income; ~ **imponibile** (*fin.*) taxable income; ~ **in termini reali** (*econ.*) real income; ~ **lordo** (*fin., rag.*) gross income, gross product; ~ **marginale** (*econ.*) marginal profit; ~ **medio** (*econ.*) average income; ~ **minimo** (*econ., sind.*) basic income; ~ **misto** (*econ.*) mixed income; **un** ~ **modesto** (*econ.*) a moderate income; ~ **nazionale** (*econ.*) national income; ~ **nazionale in termini reali** (*econ.*) real national income; ~ **nazionale netto «pro capite»** (*econ.*) per capita net national income; ~ **netto** (*da imposta*) (*fin.*) disposable income; (*d'un'obbligazione*) yield to maturity; (*rag.*) (*d'esercizio*) net income; net earnings (*pl.*); ~ **non di lavoro** (*econ.*) unearned income; ~ **non tassabile** (*fin.*) non-taxable income; ~ **obbligazionario** (*fin.*) debenture yield; bond yield (*USA*); ~ **permanente** (*econ.*) permanent income; ~ **personale** (*econ.*) personal income; ~ **potenziale** (*econ.*) potential profit; ~ **«pro capite»** (*econ.*) per capita income; **redditi professionali** (*fin.*) professional earnings; ~ **tassabile** (*fin.*) income liable to tax, taxable income; ~ **terriero** (*fin.*) income from farms; **un** ~ **variabile** (*fin.*) a variable yield; **a** ~ **variabile** (*fin.*) variable-yield (*attr.*).

redigere, *v. t.* **1** to write* out, to draw* up, to make* up (*o* out), to word; (*compilare*) to compile. **2** (*leg.*) to execute, to engross, to draw*, to prepare. **3** (*pubbl.*) (*testi pubblicitari*) to copy. // ~ **un atto legale** (*leg.*) to draw a deed, to draw up a deed; ~ **un bilancio** (*fin., rag.*) to draw up a balance sheet, to make up a balance sheet; ~ **la copia d'un contratto** (*leg.*) to write off the copy of a contract; ~ **un estratto-conto** (*banca*) to draw up a statement of account; ~ (*un documento*) **in duplice copia** to indent; ~ **l'originale e due copie di** (*un documento*) to triplicate; ~ **una polizza di carico** (*trasp. mar.*) to draw up a bill of lading.

redimere, *v. t.* (*anche fig.: riscattare*) to redeem.

redimibile, *a.* (*fin., leg.*) redeemable. // **un prestito** ~ (*cred.*) a redeemable loan.

redimibilità, *n. f. inv.* (*fin., leg.*) redeemability, redeemableness.

referendum, *n. m.* referendum.

referenza, *n. f.* (*pers.*) reference; (*benservito*) testimonial. // **referenze bancarie** (*banca*) banker's references; **chi è chiamato a dare referenze** (*su q.*) (*pers.*) reference, referee.

referenziare, *v. t.* (*pers.*) to provide (sb.) with references (*o* with testimonials).

reflazionare, *v. t.* (*econ.*) to reflate.

reflazione, *n. f.* (*econ.*) reflation. // **provocare una** ~ (*econ.*) to reflate.

reflazionistico, *a.* (*econ.*) reflationary.

refrigerare, *v. t.* (*market.*) to refrigerate.

refrigeratore, *n. m.* (*market.*) refrigerator.

refrigerazione, *n. f.* (*market.*) refrigeration.

regalare, *v. t.* **1** to present, to give* (st.) as a present. **2** (*market.*) (*vendere a basso prezzo*) to give* for a song, to give* for nothing, to give* away (*fam.*).

regalia, *n. f.* gratuity, box.

regalo, *n. m.* present, gift, presentation.

regime, *n. m.* (*governo*) régime, rule, system of Government. // **il** ~ **degli scambi** (*comm. est.*) the system of trade; **il** ~ **dei prelievi** (*econ., fin.*) the levy system; ~ **dei prezzi** (*econ.*) price system; ~ **d'aiuti** (*econ.*) aid system; ~ **di cambi fissi** (*fin.*) fixed exchange rate system; ~ **d'importazione** (*comm. est.*) arrangement for importing; ~ **fiscale** (*fin.*) tax treatment, taxation; tax regulations (*pl.*); **il** ~ **fiscale in agricoltura** (*fin.*) taxation in agriculture; **un** ~ **monopolistico** (*econ.*) a monopoly system; **il** ~ **per i titoli d'importazione e d'esportazione** (*comm. est.*) the system of import and export certificates; ~ **tributario** (*fin.*) tax regulations (*pl.*); taxation, tax treatment; ~ **vincolistico** (*econ.*) restriction scheme, control scheme.

regionale, *a.* regional; district (*attr.*).

regione, *n. f.* **1** region, area, zone, district. **2** (*suddivisione amministrativa*) region, department; (*provincia*) province. // ~ **agricola** (*econ.*) agricultural district; ~ **periferica** (*econ.*) peripheral region.

registrare, *v. t.* **1** to register, to record. **2** (*annotare*) to write* down, to take* down, to mark down. **3** (*incidere*) to record; (*su nastro magnetico*) to tape, to tape-record. **4** (*comun.*) (*un programma radiotelevisivo*) to transcribe. **5** (*fin.*) (*il nome del detentore di titoli*) to inscribe. **6** (*leg.*) to enrol, to record; (*ditte, ecc.*) to incorporate; (*una sentenza*) to docket. **7** (*org. az.*) to calendar. **8** (*rag.*) (*scritture contabili*) to record, to enter, to book; (*crediti, ecc.*) to tally; (*di conto, ecc.*) to turn in; (*protocollare*) to file. **9**

(*tur.*) to check in. // ~ **a credito** (*rag.*) to enter on the credit side; ~ **a debito** (*rag.*) to enter on the debit side; ~ **a giornale** (*rag.*) to journalize; ~ **a mastro** (*rag.*) to post, to post up; ~ (*titoli*) **a nome del detentore** (*fin.*) to register; ~ **un atto** (*leg.*) to register a deed; ~ **di nuovo** (*scritture, ecc.*) (*rag.*) to re-enter; ~ **una nave alla dogana** (*trasp. mar.*) to enter a ship; ~ **nella colonna del «dare»** (*rag.*) to debit; ~ **nella colonna dell'«avere»** (*rag.*) to credit; ~ **un'operazione** (*rag.*) to book (*o* to enter) a transaction; ~ **un privilegio ipotecario** (*leg.*) to register a mortgage charge; ~ **uno «storno»** (*rag.*) to pass a transfer.

registrarsi, *v. rifl.* (*tur.*) (*all'arrivo, ecc.*) to sign in, to check in; (*alla partenza*) to sign out, to check out.

registrato, *a.* **1** registered, recorded; (*di documento*) on file, on record. **2** (*rag.*) on the books. // **non** ~ unrecorded, unregistered.

registratore, *n. m.* **1** (*chi registra*) recorder. **2** (*market.*) (*a nastro magnetico o a «cassette»*) recorder. // ~ **a nastro** (*macch. uff.*) tape recorder; ~ **a nastro magnetico** (*macch. uff.*) magnetic tape recorder; ~ **di cassa** (*macch. uff.*) cash register, sales register, check-till, add-lister.

registrazione, *n. f.* **1** registration, recording. **2** (*annotazione*) writing down, taking down, marking down. **3** (*su dischi, nastri magnetici, «cassette», ecc.*) recording, tape-recording. **4** (*comun.*) (*di programma radiotelevisivo*) transcription. **5** (*fin.*) (*del nome del detentore d'azioni*) inscription. **6** (*leg.*) enrolment, record, registration, recordation; (*di ditte, ecc.*) incorporation. **7** (*rag.*) (*contabile*) record, entry, booking; (*di crediti, ecc.*) tally. // ~ **a credito** (*rag.*) credit entry; ~ **a debito** (*rag.*) debit entry; ~ **a giornale** (*rag.*) journal entry; ~ **a mastro** (*rag.*) posting; ~ (*di titoli*) **a nome del detentore** (*fin.*) registration; ~ **ai sensi delle leggi sulle società** (*fin., ingl.*) registration under the Companies Acts; ~ **conforme** (*rag.*) conforming entry; **la** ~ **delle ditte** (*fin., leg.*) the registration of business names; **la** ~ **d'una sentenza** (*leg.*) the enrolment of a decree; ~ **di verifica** (*rag.*) correcting entry; ~ (*contabile*) **doppia** (*rag.*) double application; ~ **e pubblicazione giornaliera dei prezzi quotati** (*Borsa*) marking; ~ **magnetica** magnetic recording; ~ **per storno** (*rag.*) contra entry; ~ **su filo** wire recording.

registro, *n. m.* **1** register; (*ruolo*) roll. **2** (*ufficio statale*) Registrar's office, Registry. **3** (*attr. uff.*) calendar. **4** (*rag.*) register, book. // ~ **a «madre» e «figlia»** (*attr. uff.*) counterfoil book; ~ **acquisti** (*rag.*) bought journal; ~ **ausiliario** (*rag.*) subsidiary ledger; ~ **contabile** (*rag.*) account book, book of accounts; **il** ~ **degli amministratori** (*fin., leg.*) the register of directors; **il** ~ **degli azionisti** (*fin.*) the register of shareholders, the share register, the share ledger; ~ **degli effetti attivi** (*alla stanza di compensazione*) (*fin.*) clearing-in book, bills receivable book; ~ **degli effetti passivi** (*alla stanza di compensazione*) (*fin.*) clearing-out book, bills payable book; **il** ~ **degli obbligazionisti** (*fin.*) the register of debenture-holders; **il** ~ **dei brevetti** (*leg.*) the register of patents; ~ **dei carichi** (*org. az.*) cargo book; ~ **dei certificati** certificate book; ~ **dei nuovi documenti** (*org. az.*) creation register; ~ **dei reclami** claims book; **il** ~ **dei soci** (*fin.*) the register of members; ~ **dei verbali** (*leg.*) minute book; ~ **delle cessioni** (*d'azioni, ecc.*) (*fin., leg.*) transfer-book; ~ **delle fatture** (*rag.*) bill book; ~ **delle ordinazioni** (*org. az.*) order-book; ~ **delle ore di lavoro** (*pers.*) time-book; ~ **delle presenze** attendance book; ~ **delle ricevute** receipt book; ~ **delle sentenze** (*leg.*) judgement book; **il** ~ **delle Società** (*fin., leg.*) the Register of Companies; ~ **delle società che hanno cessato l'attività** dead book (*fam.*); ~ **di carico e scarico** (*rag.*) stock record account; ~ **d'entrata degli effetti** (*banca*) bills received register; ~ **di prenotazione dei noli** (*trasp. mar.*) freight-booking note; ~ **di presenza** (*pers.*) time-book; ~ **di sbarco** (*trasp. mar.*) landing book; ~ **giornaliero degli acquisti** (*rag.*) bought day book; **il** ~ **marittimo** (*o* **navale**) (*trasp. mar.*) the register of shipping.

regola, *n. f.* **1** rule; (*modello, tipo*) standard. **2** (*norma, principio*) norm, principle. **3** (*leg.*) regulation. // ~ **catenaria** (*mat., rag.*) chain rule; ~ **congiunta** (*mat., rag.*) chain rule; **le regole della navigazione** (*trasp. mar.*) the rules of navigation; **regole di stazzatura** (*trasp. mar.*) tonnage rules; **regole «manageriali»** (*amm.*) principles of management; **di** ~ as a rule; **essere in** ~ **coi pagamenti** (*cred.*) to be up-to-date with one's payments.

regolamentare[1], *a.* **1** regular, prescribed; regulation (*attr.*). **2** (*leg.*) statutory.

regolamentare[2], *v. t.* (*leg.*) to regulate, to control by regulations. // ~ **le tariffe di nolo** (*trasp. mar.*) to regulate freight rates.

regolamentazione, *n. f.* (*leg.*) regulation. // **la** ~ **degli affari** the regulation of affairs; ~ **dei cambi** (*fin.*) exchange regulations.

regolamento, *n. m.* **1** (*cred.*) (*di conti*) settlement. **2** (*leg.*) rule, by-law; regulations (*pl.*). // ~ **a termine** (*market., rag.*) credit settlement; ~

dei confini (*leg.*) fixing of boundaries; ~ **dei conti** (*fin.*) settling-up; ~ **d'avaria generale** (*ass. mar.*) general average statement; **il** ~ **d'un sinistro** (*ass.*) the assessment of a loss; **regolamenti doganali** (*dog.*) customs regulations; **regolamenti esecutivi** (*leg.*) rules for the enforcement of a law; ~ **in contanti** (*cred.*) cash settlement; ~ **interno d'una società** (*fin.*) articles of association; **regolamenti intesi a prevenire le collisioni** (*delle navi*) (*trasp. mar.*) collision regulations; ~ **locale** (*leg.*) by-law; **regolamenti portuali** (*trasp. mar.*) port regulations; **regolamenti restrittivi** (*leg.*) restrictive regulations.

regolare[1], *a.* 1 regular. 2 (*costante, uniforme*) steady; (*sistematico*) systematic. // **con** ~ **processo** (*leg.*) by due process of law.

regolare[2], *v. t.* 1 to regulate. 2 (*governare, guidare*) to guide, to rule, to lead★. 3 (*controllare*) to control, to condition. 4 (*cred.*) (*liquidare*) to settle, to square; (*pagare*) to pay★ (up). // ~ **i conti** (*comm.*) to rule off one's accounts, to square accounts; ~ **le spese** to control expenses.

regolarità, *n. f. inv.* regularity. // **la** ~ **d'un atto** (*leg.*) the regularity of a deed.

regolarizzare, *v. t.* 1 to regularize, to regulate. 2 (*cred.*) (*regolare*) to settle. // ~ **i conti** (*cred.*) to settle accounts; ~ **i mercati** (*econ.*) to regularize markets.

regolarizzazione, *n. f.* 1 regularization, regulation. 2 (*cred.*) (*regolamento*) settlement.

regolarsi, *v. rifl.* (*agire*) to act; (*fare*) to do★.

regolazione, *n. f.* regulation, regulating.

regolo, *n. m.* (*mat.*) (*riga*) rule. // ~ **calcolatore** (*attr. uff.*) slide rule, sliding rule.

regresso, *n. m.* 1 regress, regression. 2 (*fig.*) decadence, decline, set-back. 3 (*cred.*) (*cambiario*) recourse. 4 (*trasp. ferr.*) switch-back, back-shunt. // **un** ~ **delle esportazioni** (*comm. est.*) a drop in net exports; **azione di** ~ (*cred.*) action for recovery; **essere in** ~ **d'un tanto per cento** (*market.*) to be a certain percent off; **senza** ~ (*cred.*) without recourse.

reiezione, *n. f.* rejection, rejecting. // **la** ~ **d'una proposta** the rejection of a proposal.

reimbarcare, *v. t.* (*trasp. mar.*) to reship, to re-embark.

reimbarco, *n. m.* (*trasp. mar.*) reshipment, reshipping, re-embarkation, re-embarking.

reimpiegare, *v. t.* 1 to re-employ. 2 (*fin.*) (*capitali*) to reinvest.

reimpiego, *n. m.* 1 re-employment. 2 (*fin.*) (*di capitali*) reinvestment. // **il** ~ **e il riadattamento dei lavoratori** (*sind.*) the re-employment and readaptation of workers.

reimportare, *v. t.* (*comm. est.*) to reimport.

reimportazione, *n. f.* (*comm. est.*) reimportation; (*merce reimportata*) reimport.

reindirizzare, *v. t.* (*comun.*) to redirect.

reintegrare, *v. t.* 1 (*rimettere nello stato originario*) to restore, to reinstate. 2 (*leg.*) (*risarcire*) to refund, to repay★, to indemnify. // ~ **q. nei suoi diritti** (*leg.*) to rehabilitate sb., to restore sb. to his rights; ~ **q. nel possesso di qc.** (*leg.*) to repossess sb.

reintegrazione, *n. f.* 1 (*ripristino*) restoration, reinstatement. 2 (*risarcimento*) refund, indemnification. // ~ (*sotto cauzione*) **di beni mobili** (*leg.*) replevin; ~ (*d'una nave*) **nella classe di registro** (*trasp. mar.*) restoration.

reinvestimento, *n. m.* (*fin.*) reinvestment. // ~ **degli utili in nuovi titoli** (*Borsa, fin.*) pyramiding; **un** ~ **di capitali** (*fin.*) a reinvestment of capitals.

reinvestire, *v. t.* (*fin.*) to reinvest; to plough back (*fam.*).

relatore, *n. m.* reporter; (*portavoce*) spokesman★.

relazionare, *v. t.* to report to (sb.); to inform; to acquaint (sb. with st.).

relazione, *n. f.* 1 report, account, return, statement. 2 connection, relation, liaison. 3 (*conoscenza*) acquaintance, connection. 4 (*contatto*) touch, contact. // ~ **annuale del bilancio** (*fin., rag.*) annual report; **relazioni commerciali multilaterali** (*comm. est.*) multilateral commercial relations; ~ **dei revisori contabili** (*leg.*) auditors' report, report of the auditors; ~ **del consiglio d'amministrazione** (*amm.*) directors' report; **relazioni d'affari** business connections; ~ **di bilancio** (*rag.*) company report; ~ **di perizia** (*trasp. mar.*) survey report; **una** ~ **finanziaria «pro forma»** (*fin.*) a pro forma financial statement; **relazioni finanziarie** (*fin.*) financial relations; ~ **generale** (*rag.*) general report; **relazioni industriali** (*market., pers.*) industrial relations; ~ **interinale** (*org. az.*) interim report; **relazioni internazionali** (*econ.*) foreign relations; ~ **mensile** (*amm., rag.*) monthly report; **una** ~ **particolareggiata sulle tendenze di mercato** (*market.*) a detailed report on market trends; **relazioni professionali** (*pers., sind.*) industrial relations; ~ **provvisoria** (*org. az.*) interim report; **relazioni sui movimenti di cassa** (*rag.*) cash flow statement; ~ **sullo stato dell'economia** (*econ.*) economic survey; **relazioni umane** (*pers.*) human relations; **in** ~ **a** in reference to; **in** ~ **con** relative to; **pubbliche relazioni** public relations.

«remisier», *n. m.* (*Borsa*) stockjobber,

jobber.

remissione, *n. f.* (*leg.*) remission, remittal, withdrawal; (*d'un debito*) release. // **la ~ d'un'ammenda** (*leg.*) the relaxation of a fine; **~ di causa** (*leg.*) desistance from a suit; **la ~ d'un debito** (*cred.*) the remission of a debt; **la ~ d'un delitto** (*leg.*) the remission of an offence; **~ di parte lesa** (*leg.*) desistance of injured party; **~ di querela** (*leg.*) «nolle prosequi», withdrawal of an action.

remissore, *n. m.* (*Borsa*) (*procacciatore d'ordini a un agente di cambio*) half-commission man★.

remunerare, *v. t.* e *derivati V.* **rimunerare** e *derivati.*

rendere, *v. t.* **1** to give★ back, to return, to surrender, to repay★. **2** (*dare, fare*) to give★, to pay★, to render. **3** (*econ., fin.*) (*produrre, fruttare*) to yield, to earn, to bring★ in, to pay★. **4** (*pers.*) (*d'occupazione*) to pay★. // **~ commerciale** (*market.*) to commercialize; **~ conto delle proprie azioni** to render an account of one's actions; **~ conto di qc.** to give an account of st.; **~ q. edotto di qc.** to acquaint sb. with st.; **~ esecutivo** (*leg.*) to enforce; **~ esente** (*leg.*) to frank; **~ illegale** (*leg.*) to outlaw; **~ inattivo** to stagnate, to idle; **~ irreperibile** (*leg.*) to abscond; **~ nullo** (*leg.*) to render void, to void; **~ obsoleto** (*market.*) to outmode, to superannuate; **~ un parere** to give an opinion; **~ pubblica** (*una notizia*) (*giorn.*) to release; **~ qc. retributivo** (*econ., fin.*) to make st. worthwhile; **~ un servizio** to render a service; **~ stabile** to stabilize; **~ stabile una moneta** (*econ.*) to stabilize a currency; **~ testimonianza** (*leg.*) to give evidence, to bear witness; «**a ~**» (*market.*) «to be rendered», «to be returned»; **non «a ~»** disposable.

rendiconto, *n. m.* (*comm., leg.*) statement, statement of account, accounts, return. // **~ della situazione d'una banca** bank statement, bank return; **un ~ delle spese** (*rag.*) a statement of expenses; **~ trimestrale** (*rag.*) terminal accounts.

rendimento, *n. m.* **1** rendering. **2** (*econ.*) (*produzione*) yield,output. **3** (*org. az.*) (*degli impianti*) capacity, performance; (*specialm. della manodopera*) effectiveness. // **~ giornaliero** (*econ.*) daily output; **~ massimo** (*org. az.*) peak efficiency; **~ totale** (*org. az.*) overall efficiency.

rendita, *n. f.* **1** (*econ.*) unearned income, unearned revenue, income, revenue. **2** (*fin.*) yield, rent. **3** (*fin.*) (*annualità*) annuity. **4** (*rag.*) competence. **5 rendite,** *pl.* (*fin.*) stock. // **rendite ammortizzabili** (*fin.*) redeemable stock; **~ annua** (*d'un terreno, d'un'impresa, ecc.*) (*econ., fin.*) year's purchase; **~ annua a termine fisso** (*leg.*) terminable contracts (*pl.*); **una ~ annuale** (*fin.*) a yearly rent; **~ del consumatore** (*econ.*) consumer's surplus; **la ~ del monopolista** (*econ.*) the monopolist's profit; **~ del produttore** (*econ.*) producer's surplus; **la ~ derivante da titoli azionari** (*fin.*) the yield on shares; **~ differita** (*fin.*) deferred annuity; **~ fissa** (*econ.*) sleeping rent; **~ immediata** (*fin.*) immediate annuity; **~ patologica** (*econ.*) pathological income; **~ perpetua** (*fin.*) perpetual annuity; **~ temporanea** (*fin.*) temporary annuity; **~ vitalizia** (*fin.*) life annuity, income for life; **~ vitalizia differita** (*fin.*) deferred annuity.

reparto, *n. m.* **1** department, division. **2** (*market.*) (*di negozio, ecc.*) section, department. **3** (*org. az.*) department, workshop, shop. // **~ al piano interrato** (*di grande magazzino, ecc.*) **per le «offerte speciali»** (*market.*) bargain basement; **~ (articoli) casalinghi** (*market.*) household department; domestics department (*USA*); **~ (articoli di) cancelleria** (*market.*) stationery department; **~ collaudi** (*org. az.*) testing department; **~ contabilità** (*org. az.*) accounts department; **~ corrispondenza** (*org. az.*) correspondence department; **~ di vendita** (*org. az.*) selling department; **~ fatturazione** (*org. az.*) billing department, invoice department; **~ imballaggio e spedizioni** (*org. az.*) packing and despatch department; **~ mezzi pubblicitari** (*pubbl.*) media department; **~ montaggio** (*org. az.*) fitting department; **~ non addetto alla vendita** (*org. az.*) non-selling department; **~ per le ordinazioni per posta** (*org. az.*) mail-order department; **~ statistico** (*org. az.*) statistical department; **~ vendite al minuto** (*market.*) retail department.

reperimento, *n. m.* **1** finding. **2** procurement.

reperire, *v. t.* **1** (*trovare*) to find★. **2** (*procurare*) to procure. // **~ capitali** (*cred., fin.*) to find money.

requisire, *v. t.* **1** (*leg.*) to requisition, to confiscate; (*merci, per uso pubblico*) to impress. **2** (*leg., trasp. mar.*) (*navi, merci*) to embargo.

requisito, *n. m.* **1** requisite, requisition, requirement. **2** (*leg., pers.*) qualification. // **i requisiti d'ammissione** (*pers.*) the requisitions for admission; **~ indispensabile** (*anche leg.*) prerequisite.

requisizione, *n. f.* **1** (*leg.*) requisition, confiscation; (*di merci, per uso pubblico*) impressment. **2** (*leg., trasp. mar.*) (*di navi, merci*) embargo. // **~ ufficiale** (*leg., ingl.*) indent.

resa, *n. f.* **1** surrender. **2** (*cred.*) (*restituzione*) return, repayment. **3** (*econ.*) (*reddito, rendimento*) output, yield, take, profit. **4** (*giorn.*) (*all'editore: di libri, periodici, ecc., invenduti*) returns. // **rese al fornitore** (*rag.*) returns outwards; **la ~ degli investimenti** (*fin.*) the yield on investments; **rese dei clienti** (*rag.*) returns inwards.

rescindere, *v. t.* (*leg.*) to rescind, to cancel, to annul, to avoid, to terminate. // **~ un contratto** (*leg.*) to rescind a contract, to avoid a contract; **~ il contratto d'impiego con q.** (*pers.*) to terminate sb.'s employment.

rescindibile, *a.* (*leg.*) rescindable, cancellable, annullable, avoidable.

rescissione, *n. f.* **1** (*leg.*) rescission, annulment, avoidance, termination. **2** (*pers.*) (*d'un contratto d'impiego, ecc., anche*) severance. // **la ~ d'un contratto** (*leg.*) the termination of a contract, the annulment of a contract; **in caso di ~** (*leg.*) in case of rescission.

rescissorio, *a.* (*leg.*) rescissory.

resi e abbuoni sugli acquisti, *locuz. n.* (*rag.*) purchases returns and allowances.

resi su vendite, *locuz. n.* (*rag.*) sales returns.

residuale, *a. V.* **residuo.**

residuo, *a.* residual, residuary, remaining. *n. m.* **1** remainder, residue, rest, carry over. **2** (*mat.*) remainder. // **~ attivo** (*econ.*) surplus; **~ attivo delle partite correnti** (*fin.*) above-the-line surplus.

resoconto, *n. m.* **1** account, record; (*rapporto*) report; (*relazione*) relation. **2** (*rag.*) account of proceedings. // **~ annuale** (*fin., rag.*) annual report; **un ~ dei fatti** a statement of facts.

respingere, *v. t.* **1** (*spingere indietro*) to repel, to rebut, to resist; (*un attacco, ecc., anche fig.*) to counter. **2** (*non accettare*) to repel, to reject, to refuse, to disallow, to negative. **3** (*comun.*) (*rimandare al mittente*) to return, to send★ back. **4** (*leg.*) to dismiss; (*un addebito, ecc.*) to rebut; (*una proposta di legge, ecc.*) to defeat, to throw★ out. // **~ un'accusa** (*leg.*) to rebut a charge; **~ una domanda** to reject a request; **~ una lettera** (*comun.*) to return a letter; **~ merci di qualità scadente** (*market.*) to return goods of poor quality; **~ una mozione** (*votando contro*) (*leg.*) to vote down a motion; **~ un'offerta** to reject an offer; **~ le proposte di q.** to rebut sb.'s proposals; **~ un reclamo** to reject a claim.

respiro, *n. m.* (*cred., market.*) (*differimento nel pagamento, nella consegna, ecc.*) respite, delay.

responsabile, *a.* **1** responsible, answerable. **2** (*leg.*) accountable, liable. *n. m.* e *f.* **1** person in charge. **2** (*capo*) head. **3** (*direttore*) manager. // **~ civilmente** (*leg.*) civilly liable; **~ degli acquisti** (*pers.*) purchasing agent, purchasing manager; **il ~ della pianificazione** (*pers.*) the head of planning; **i responsabili della politica finanziaria** (*fin.*) the financial policymakers; **il ~ della ricerca** (*pers.*) the head of research; **~ di negligenza grave** (*leg.*) liable for gross negligence; **~ di settore** (*pers.*) superintendent; **~ in solido** (*leg.*) jointly liable; **~ per danni** (*leg.*) liable for damages; **essere ~ di qc. verso q.** to be answerable to sb. for st.; **non ~** (*leg.*) unanswerable.

responsabilità, *n. f. inv.* **1** responsibility. **2** (*fiducia*) trust. **3** (*colpa*) blame. **4** (*leg.*) liability. // **responsabilità chiare e definite** (*org. az.*) definite and clear-cut responsibilities; **~ civile auto (R.C.A.)** (*ass., trasp. aut.*) third-party auto insurance; **~ civile del datore di lavoro** (*ass.*) employer's liability; **~ civile «diversi» (R.C. diversi)** (*ass.*) casualty; **~ collegiale** (*fin., leg.*) corporate responsibility, joint responsibility; **~ collettiva** (*leg.*) joint responsibility; **~ congiunta e solidale** (*leg.*) joint and several liability; **la ~ del datore di lavoro** (*leg., pers.*) the liability for the employer; **la ~ del vettore** (*leg., trasp.*) the liability of the carrier; **~ illimitata** (*fin.*) unlimited liability; **~ incondizionata** (*leg.*) absolute liability; **~ individuale** (*leg.*) several liability, several responsibility; **~ indivisa** (*leg.*) undivided responsibility; **~ limitata** (*leg.*) limited liability; **responsabilità pertinenti a un ufficio** (*pers.*) official responsibilities; **~ solidale** (*leg.*) joint liability; **non ~** (*leg.*) non-liability; **sotto la propria ~** (*leg.*) on one's own responsibility.

restante, *a.* remaining, left over. *n. m.* rest, remainder.

restare, *v. i.* **1** to remain, to stay. **2** (*durare, resistere*) to stay, to last. // **~ disoccupato** (*pers.*) to be thrown out of work; **~ in attesa** (*di qc.*) to wait (for st.); **~ in linea** (*comun.*) to hold the line; **~ in vigore** (*leg.*) (*di contratto, patto, ecc.*) to remain in force.

restituibile, *a.* **1** returnable. **2** (*cred.*) (*rimborsabile*) repayable, reimbursable, refundable.

restituire, *v. t.* **1** (*rendere*) to return, to give★ back, to render. **2** (*comun., trasp.*) (*rispedire*) to send★ back. **3** (*cred.*) (*rimborsare*) to repay★, to return, to refund, to pay★ back. **4** (*leg.*) (*un'offesa, ecc.*) to retaliate. // **~ tasse all'esportazione** (*comm. est.*) to refund taxes on exports; **da ~** (*market.*) (*d'articoli, merce, ecc.*)

returnable; **da non ~** (*cred.*) not repayable; (*market.*) non-returnable, not returnable; **non ~** (*cred., market.*) to detain; **non ~ l'ammontare d'un prestito** (*leg.*) to default a loan.

restituzione, *n. f.* 1 (*il restituire*) restitution, return. 2 (*cred.*) (*rimborso*) repayment, return, refund, paying back. 3 (*leg.*) (*d'un'offesa, ecc.*) retaliation; (*d'una proprietà al possessore precedente*) reconveyance. // **restituzioni all'esportazione** (*fin.*) export refunds, refunds on exports; **restituzioni comunitarie** (*comm. est.*) Community refunds; **la ~ del premio** (*ass.*) the return of premium; **~ dell'IVA all'esportazione** (*fin.*) repayment of VAT on exportation; **~ di dazio** (*dog.*) drawback.

resto, *n. m.* 1 rest, remainder, residue, remnant. 2 (*differenza fra il denaro sborsato e quello dovuto*) change; odd change, odd money (*fam.*). 3 (*cred.*) (*differenza a saldo*) balance. 4 (*mat.*) remainder, residual.

restrittivo, *a.* restrictive.

restrizione, *n. f.* 1 restriction, restraint; (*riserva*) reservation; (*limitazione*) limitation, confinement. 2 (*fig.*) squeeze. 3 (*leg.*) abridg(e)ment, qualification. // **restrizioni alle esportazioni** (*comm. est.*) restrictions on exportation; **restrizioni alle esportazioni di capitale** (*fin.*) capital export restrictions; **~ del credito** (*fin.*) credit rationing, credit squeeze; **restrizioni di cambio** (*fin.*) exchange restrictions; **~ di diritti** (*leg.*) abridgement of rights; **restrizioni quantitative all'importazione** (*comm. est.*) quantitative import restrictions; **restrizioni valutarie** (*fin.*) exchange restrictions; **con restrizioni** (*leg.*) qualified (*a.*).

rete, *n. f.* 1 net. 2 (*anche fig.*) (*complesso di linee incrociate*) network, grid, system. // **~ delle vendite** (*market.*) dealer network; **una ~ di canali** (*artificiali*) (*trasp.*) a network of canals; **~ ferroviaria** (*trasp. ferr.*) railway network, railway system; **una ~ stradale** (*trasp. aut.*) a network of roads, a road network; **una ~ telefonica** (*comun.*) a telephone system (*o* network).

retribuire, *v. t.* to remunerate, to pay★, to repay★, to compensate. // **~ inadeguatamente** (*pers.*) to underpay.

retribuito, *a.* remunerated, paid, repaid, compensated. // **~ a ore** (*pers.*) (*di lavoro*) hourly-rated; **non ~** (*pers.*) unpaid.

retributivo, *a.* (*pers.*) remunerative, compensational.

retribuzione, *n. f.* 1 remuneration, pay, compensation, consideration; (*salario*) wage, wages; (*stipendio*) salary. 2 (*sind.*) emolument. 3 **retribuzioni,** *pl.* (*pers.*) wages and salaries. // **~ a cottimo** (*org. az., sind.*) piecework rates, piece rates; **~ a premio** (*pers.*) premium pay; **~ annuale garantita** (*pers.*) guaranteed annual wage; **~ per il periodo di congedo per malattia** (*pers.*) sick pay.

retro, *n. m. inv.* 1 back. 2 (*di moneta, medaglia, ecc.*) verso, back, reverse. // **sul ~** on the back; (*di una pagina*) overleaf.

retroattività, *n. f. inv.* (*leg.*) retroactivity.

retroattivo, *a.* (*leg.*) retroactive, retrospective. // **effetto ~** (*leg.*) retroactive effect.

retroazione, *n. f.* (*elab. elettr.*) feedback.

retrodatare, *v. t.* to antedate, to date back, to backdate.

retrodatazione, *n. f.* antedating, dating back, backdating.

retrovendita, *n. f.* (*market.*) sale and return, sale or return.

rettangolo, *a.* (*mat.*) right-angled. *n. m.* (*mat.*) rectangle. // **rettangoli disponibili per la pubblicità** (*accanto alla testata d'un quotidiano*) (*pubbl.*) ears.

rettifica, *n. f.* (*correzione*) rectification, correction, amendment, adjustment. // **~ dei corsi** (*Borsa*) correction of prices; **~ dei valori iscritti a bilancio** (*rag.*) adjustment of balance statements; **~ del reddito accertato** (*fin.*) correction of assessed income; **~ d'un conto** (*rag.*) correction of an account; **~ di dichiarazione errata per difetto** (*dog.*) post entry; **~ di dichiarazione errata per eccesso** (*dog.*) over-entry certificate; **rettifiche di fine esercizio** (*rag.*) year-end adjustments; **rettifiche di scritture contabili** (*rag.*) amendmentes to entries; « **~ di valuta** » (*banca*) « adjustment value date ».

rettificare, *v. t.* (*correggere*) to rectify, to right, to correct, to amend, to adjust, to straighten out. // **~ una cifra** (*rag.*) to rectify a figure; **~ conti alla fine dell'esercizio** (*rag.*) to adjust accounts at the end of the accounting period; **~ un conto** (*rag.*) to amend an account; **~ una data** to correct a date; **~ un errore** to rectify a mistake.

rettificativo, *a.* correcting (*attr.*). // **scritture rettificative** (*rag.*) correcting entries.

rettificazione, *n. f. V.* **rettifica.**

reversale, *n. f.* (*rag.*) collection voucher, collection order.

reversibile, *a.* (*leg.*) reversible, reversionary, reversional.

reversibilità, *n. f. inv.* (*leg.*) reversibility. // **~ contingente** contingent reversibility.

reversione, *n. f.* (*leg.*) reversion, reverter.

revisionare, *v. t.* 1 (*rivedere*) to revise, to revision. 2 (*controllare*) to check up, to audit. 3

(*org. az.*) (*macchinari, ecc.*) to overhaul.

revisione, *n. f.* **1** (*il rivedere*) revision, review, revisal. **2** (*controllo*) check-up; (*specialm. contabile*) auditing, audit. **3** (*leg.*) review, rehearing. **4** (*org. az.*) (*dei macchinari, ecc.*) overhaul. // ~ **contabile** (*amm., org. az., rag.*) audit; (*dei conti di un ente pubblico, di un ministero, ecc.*) auditing; (*dei conti di un'azienda: eseguita da professionisti specializzati che svolgono le funzioni attribuite in Italia al collegio dei sindaci*) auditing; ~ **contabile «esterna»** (*eseguita da professionisti specializzati che svolgono le funzioni attribuite in Italia al collegio dei sindaci*) (*org. az., rag.*) external auditing, independent audit; ~ **contabile «interna»** (*org. az., rag.*) internal auditing.

revisore, *n. m.* **1** reviser, revisor. **2** (*giorn., pubbl.*) (*di bozze*) proof-reader. **3** (*pers.*) check clerk, auditor. // ~ **contabile** (*pers.*) auditor; certified public accountant (*USA*); « ~ **Generale dei Conti**» Auditor-General (*in G.B.*).

revoca, *n. f.* **1** (*leg.*) revocation, repeal, retraction, annulment; (*d'una sentenza*) reversal; (*d'un ordine*) countermand. **2** (*market.*) (*di un'ordinazione, ecc.*) cancellation. // ~ **dell'ordine di pagamento** (*banca, cred.*) countermand of payment; **la ~ d'una disposizione** (*leg.*) the repeal of a provision, the revocation of a provision; **la ~ d'un testamento** (*leg.*) the revocation of a will.

revocabile, *a.* (*leg.*) revocable, revokeable, annullable, repealable, reversible.

revocabilità, *n. f. inv.* (*leg.*) reversibility, revocableness.

revocare, *v. t.* **1** (*leg.*) to revoke, to repeal, to retract, to annul; (*una sentenza*) to reverse; (*un ordine*) to countermand. **2** (*market.*) (*un'ordinazione, ecc.*) to cancel. // ~ **una concessione** (*leg.*) to revoke a grant; ~ **una nomina** to annul an appointment; ~ **un'offerta** to retract an offer; ~ **un pegno** (*leg.*) to satisfy a lien; ~ **uno sciopero** (*sind.*) to call off a strike.

revocazione, *n. f. V.* **revoca.**

riabilitare, *v. t.* (*leg.*) to rehabilitate, to reinstate. // ~ **un fallito** (*leg.*) to discharge a bankrupt.

riabilitazione, *n. f.* (*leg.*) rehabilitation, reinstatement. // **la ~ d'un debitore insolvente** (*leg.*) the rehabilitation of an insolvent debtor; **la ~ d'un fallito** (*leg.*) the discharge of a bankrupt.

rialzista, *n. m.* (*Borsa*) bull, long. *a. attr.* (*Borsa*) bull. // **di** (*o* **da**) ~ (*Borsa*) bullish.

rialzo, *n. m.* **1** (*aumento*) rise, increase, advance. **2** (*Borsa*) (*tendenza al rialzo*) bullishness, bull run. **3** (*fin., market.*) rise, upward movement, markup, improvement, lift. // ~ **dei prezzi** (*market.*) price rise, boom; ~ **improvviso** (*delle quotazioni, dei prezzi, ecc.*) (*Borsa, market.*) upsurge; ~ **massimo** (*di quotazioni, ecc.*) (*Borsa, fin.*) peak level, all-time high; **rialzi tariffari** (*comm. est., econ.*) tariff increases; **essere in ~** (*Borsa, fin.*) (*di titolo, ecc.*) to improve, to be on, to be on the up grade; **orientato** (*o* **tendente**) **al ~** (*Borsa*) bullish.

riapertura, *n. f.* **1** reopening. **2** (*market.*) reopening. // **la ~ dei libri** (*contabili*) (*rag.*) the reopening of the books; ~ **d'un processo** (*per scoperta d'un vizio*) (*leg.*) repleader.

riaprire, *v. t.* to reopen. *v. i.* (*market.*) (*di negozio, ecc.*) to reopen. // ~ **un conto** (*rag.*) to reopen an account.

riassetto, *n. m.* (*econ., fin.*) realignment, re-arrangement.

riassicurare, *v. t.* (*ass.*) to reinsure, to reassure, to insure again.

riassicurato, *a.* e *n. m.* (*ass.*) reinsured.

riassicuratore, *n. m.* (*ass.*) reinsurer.

riassicurazione, *n. f.* (*ass.*) reinsurance, reassurance. // ~ **in abbonamento** (*ass. mar.*) treaty reinsurance.

ribassare, *v. t.* (*market.*) (*prezzi, ecc.*) to lower, to abate, to reduce, to cut★; (*merci*) to write★ down. *v. i.* (*market.*) to lower, to decline, to go★ down. // ~ **all'improvviso** (*econ., fin., market.*) (*di prezzi, ecc.*) to slump; ~ **i prezzi** (*market.*) to reduce prices, to abate prices, to cut in prices.

ribassista, *n. m.* (*Borsa*) bear, short. *a. attr.* (*Borsa*) (*di mercato*) bear. // **di** (*o* **da**) ~ (*Borsa*) bearish.

ribasso, *n. m.* **1** (*Borsa*) (*tendenza al ribasso*) bearishness, bear run. **2** (*fin., market.*) (*di prezzi, ecc.*) reduction, abatement, decrease, decline, fall, downswing, drop; (*che riporta i prezzi al livello precedente*) set-back. **3** (*market.*) (*sconto*) discount, rebate, cutting, cut. // **un ~ dei prezzi** (*market.*) an abatement of prices, a decrease in prices, a fall in prices, a cut in prices, a markdown; **un ~ del 15%** (*market.*) a 15% discount; ~ **improvviso** (*di prezzi, ecc.*) (*econ., fin., market.*) slump; **un ~ nei titoli** (*Borsa*) a decline in stocks; **orientato** (*o* **tendente**) **al ~** (*Borsa*) bearish.

ricambio, *n. m.* **1** (*contraccambio*) return, reciprocation. **2** (*org. az.*) turnover, turn-over, turn. **3** (*org. az.*) (*pezzo di ricambio*) spare part, spare. // ~ **del magazzino** (*org. az.*) inventory turnover, stock turnover; ~ **del personale** (*org. az.*) staff turnover; ~ **della manodopera** (*org.

az.) labour turnover; **di ~** spare (*attr.*): **una ruota di ~** a spare wheel.

ricaricamento, *n. m.* (*trasp.*) reload.

ricaricare, *v. t.* (*trasp.*) to reload.

ricavare, *v. t.* (*fin.*) to obtain, to get★, to gain, to make★, to net; (*derivare*) to derive. // **~ un profitto da qc.** (*fin.*) to cash in on st.; **~ un utile** (*rag.*) to turn a profit.

ricavato, *n. m.* (*rag.*) proceeds (*pl.*).

ricavo, *n. m.* (*rag.*) proceeds (*pl.*); revenue, return, receipt, take, making. // «**~ (dei) vostri effetti all'incasso**» (*banca*) «proceeds of bills collected for your account»; «**~ della nostra rimessa (di) effetti all'incasso**» (*banca*) «proceeds of our remittance for collection»; **~ d'esercizio** (*rag.*) operating revenue; **ricavi imprevisti** (*rag.*) incidental incomes.

ricchezza, *n. f.* 1 (*l'essere ricco*) richness. 2 (*averi, sostanze, spesso al pl.*) riches (*pl.*); wealth, worth; money (*fam.*). // **la ~ del suolo** the richness of the soil; **~ mobile** (*econ., fin.*) personal property; **~ nazionale** (*econ.*) national wealth.

ricco, *a.* 1 rich, wealthy, well-to-do, well-off, affluent; moneyed (*fam.*). 2 (*abbondante*) rich (in), abounding (in, with). *n. m.* 1 rich (*o* wealthy) man★. 2 **i ricchi,** *pl.* the rich, the wealthy.

ricerca, *n. f.* 1 search, searching. 2 (*il perseguire*) pursuit, pursuance. 3 (*scienza*) research. 4 (*investigazione, indagine*) inquiry, investigation. // **~ agronomica** (*econ.*) agricultural research; **~ applicata** applied research; **~ dei mezzi d'informazione** (*org. az., pubbl.*) media research; **~ del comportamento del consumatore** (*market.*) consumer behaviour research; **~ del profitto** (*econ.*) profit seeking, pursuit of profit; **la ~ della verità** (*leg.*) the pursuance of truth; **~ di base** basic research, fundamental research; **~ di marketing** (*econ., market.*) marketing research; (*tendente a stabilire gli effetti di un'azione pubblicitaria sulle vendite*) activation research; **~ di mercato** (*econ., market.*) market research; **la ~ di nuovi mercati** (*econ.*) the searching for new markets; **~ e sviluppo** (*econ.*) research and development; **~ esterna** (*market.*) field research, field investigation; **~ motivazionale** (*market., pubbl.*) motivational research; **ricerche pubblicitarie** (*pubbl.*) advertising research; **~ scientifica** (*econ.*) scientific research; **una ~ settoriale** a study by sector.

ricercare, *v. t.* 1 (*cercare di nuovo*) to look for (sb., st.) again. 2 (*cercare con impegno*) to seek★, to seek★ for, to search for. 3 (*esaminare, investigare*) to investigate, to inquire into (st.). 4 (*perseguire*) to pursue.

ricercato, *a.* 1 (*richiesto*) sought-after. 2 (*leg.*) (*cercato*) wanted.

ricercatore, *n. m.* researcher, research worker.

ricettatore, *n. m.* (*leg.*) receiver of stolen goods.

ricettazione, *n. f.* (*leg.*) receiving stolen goods.

ricettività, *n. f. inv.* 1 receptivity. 2 (*tur.*) accommodation. // **~ stagionale** (*tur.*) in-season accommodation.

ricevente, *a.* receiving, recipient. *n. m.* e *f.* receiver, recipient.

ricevere, *v. t.* 1 to receive. 2 (*comun.*) (*una notizia*) to hear★, to receive. 3 (*pers.*) (*un salario, uno stipendio, ecc.*) to receive, to take★, to get★, to draw★, to have. // **~ una buona impressione** (*da q. o qc.*) to be favourably impressed; **~ denaro in deposito** (*fin.*) to receive money on deposit; **~ una dichiarazione giurata** (*leg.*) to take an affidavit; **~ in custodia** to accept in custody; **~ in eredità** (*leg.*) to inherit; **~ notizie** (*da q.*) (*comun.*) to hear; **~ un premio** to be awarded a prize; **~ una promozione** (*pers.*) to step up; **~ regolarmente** (*una pubblicazione, ecc.*) (*giorn.*) to take in; **~ una telefonata** (*comun.*) to receive a (telephone) call; **avere ricevuto** (*comun.*) to be in receipt of; **chi riceve una retribuzione** (*pers.*) pay-roller.

ricevimento, *n. m.* (*il ricevere*) receiving, receipt, reception. // **al ~ della vostra lettera** (*comun.*) upon receipt of your letter.

ricevitore, *n. m.* 1 (*comun.*) (*chi riceve*) receiver. 2 (*comun.*) (*apparecchio*) receiver. 3 (*pers.*) collector. 4 (*trasp. mar.*) shipper. // **~ del premio** (*Borsa*) taker of the rate; **~ delle dogane** (*dog.*) collector of customs; **~ delle imposte** (*fin.*) tax-collector; **~ telefonico** (*comun.*) telephone receiver, headphone.

ricevuta, *n. f.* 1 receipt; (*di una raccomandata, ecc.*) acknowledgement of delivery; (*quietanza*) quittance; (*di pagamento*) quietus. 2 (*market.*) voucher. // **una ~ a saldo** a receipt in full, a receipt for the balance; **~ attestante l'avvenuta consegna dei documenti** (*banca, cred.*) trust letter, trust receipt; **~ del custode del «dock»** (*trasp. mar.*) dock receipt; **~ del custode dello scalo** (*trasp. mar.*) wharfinger's receipt; **~ del magazziniere** (*dog.*) warehouse-keeper's receipt; **~ d'abbonamento** (*giorn.*) subscription warrant; **~ di consegna** (*dog.*) deposit receipt; **~ di deposito** (*Borsa, fin.*) deposit receipt; **una ~ di pagamento** a receipt for payment; **~ di pagamento dei diritti di faro** (*trasp.*

mar.) light bill; ~ **di ritorno** (*comun.*) return receipt; ~ **d'una sottoscrizione** (*di azioni*) (*fin.*) application receipt, subscription warrant; ~ **di versamento** (*d'un vaglia postale*) (*cred.*) certificate of issue; (*per una richiesta di fondi*) call receipt; **una** ~ **in conto** a receipt on account; ~ **provvisoria di imbarco** (*trasp. mar.*) mate's receipt; ~ **ufficiale** accountable receipt.

ricezione, *n. f.* **1** (*atto, effetto del ricevere*) reception, receiving. **2** (*comun.*) receipt. **3** (*tur.*) reception.

richiamare, *v. t.* **1** (*chiamare di nuovo*) to call again. **2** (*chiamare indietro, fare tornare*) to call back. **3** (*attirare*) to attract, to draw★; (*rivolgere*) to direct. // ~ **l'attenzione di q. su qc.** (*anche*) to call sb.'s attention to st.; ~ **una cambiale** (*banca, cred.*) to retire a bill; ~ **i decimi** (*fin.*) to call for subscribed capital.

richiamo, *n. m.* **1** recall. **2** (*pubbl.*) (*in un libro*) cross reference. **3** (*pubbl.*) (*fascino, attrattiva*) pull, appeal. // ~ **dei decimi** (*sulle azioni sottoscritte*) (*fin.*) call; assessment (*USA*); ~ **dell'ultimo versamento** (*fin.*) calling-up of the final instalment.

richiedente, *a.* applying, petitioning. *n. m.* e *f.* **1** applicant, petitioner. **2** (*leg.*) demandant, plaintiff, petitioner.

richiedere, *v. t.* **1** (*chiedere di nuovo*) to ask for (st.) again; (*chiedere in restituzione*) to ask for (st.) back. **2** (*domandare*) to ask, to demand, to require, to request. **3** (*esigere, volere*) to request, to demand. **4** (*necessitare*) to need, to require, to call for, to demand, to exact. // ~ **un certificato** to apply for a certificate; ~ **il pagamento di** (*denaro, ecc.*) (*cred.*) to call in; ~ **spese enormi** to involve great expenditure; **essere richiesto** (*market.*) to be in demand, to be in request.

richiesta, *n. f.* **1** request, demand; (*generalm. scritta*) requisition. **2** (*esigenza, necessità*) requirement; (*desiderio*) desire. **3** (*econ.*) (*domanda*) demand; call; (*mercato*) market. **4** (*leg.*) (*di riconoscimento d'un diritto*) claim. **5** (*pers.*) (*d'impiego*) application. // ~ **a una banca** (*da parte di un funzionario governativo*) **di consegnare le scritture di bilancio** (*fin., USA*) bank call; **una** ~ **che si può accogliere** an allowable claim; **una** ~ **di accreditamento** (*banca, cred.*) a request for credit; **richieste d'aumenti salariali** (*sind.*) wage claims; ~ **di copertura** (*Borsa, fin.*) margin call; ~ **di fondi** (*fin.*) call for funds; ~ **d'informazioni** inquiry; ~ **di informazioni sulla solvibilità** (*d'un cliente potenziale*) (*banca, cred.*) status inquiry; ~ **di pagamento** (*cred., fin.*) call; ~ **di quotazione** (*di un prezzo di listino oppure in Borsa*) (*fin., market.*) application for a quotation; **richieste inoppugnabili** (*leg.*) indefeasible claims; **una** ~ **legittima** a rightful claim; **una** ~ **ragionevole** a reasonable request; **a** (*o* **su**) ~ at request, by request, on request, upon request, on demand; **come da** ~ as requested.

riciclabile, *a.* (*econ.*) recyclable.

riciclaggio, *n. m.* (*econ.*) recycling.

riciclare, *v. t.* (*econ.*) to recycle.

riciclo, *n. m.* (*econ.*) recycling.

ricompera, *n. f.* (*market.*) repurchase, repurchasing, buying back.

riconduzione, *n. f.* (*leg.*) reconduction, renewal of lease, relocation.

riconferma, *n. f.* reconfirmation.

riconfermare, *v. t.* to reconfirm, to confirm (again). // ~ **una notizia** to confirm a piece of news.

riconoscere, *v. t.* **1** to recognize. **2** (*ammettere ufficialmente*) to acknowledge, to recognize. **3** (*ammettere*) to admit, to acknowledge. **4** (*leg.*) to rule. // ~ **la giustizia di** (*qc.*) to recognize; ~ **la validità di** (*qc.*) (*leg.*) to validate; ~ **la validità d'un reclamo** to acknowledge a claim; ~ **il valore di** (*qc.*) to appreciate; **essere riconosciuto colpevole d'un reato** (*leg.*) to stand convicted of an offence; **non** ~ to deny.

riconoscersi, *v. rifl.* to recognize oneself, to acknowledge oneself. // ~ **colpevole** (*leg.*) to plead guilty; ~ **innocente** (*leg.*) to plead not guilty.

riconoscimento, *n. m.* **1** (*il riconoscere*) recognition. **2** (*ammissione ufficiale*) acknowledgment, acknowledgement, recognition; (*del valore di qc. o q.*) appreciation. // ~ **d'un debito** (*cred., leg.*) acknowledgement of a debt, bill of debt; ~ **scritto d'un debito** (*cred.*) IOU (*abbr. di* I owe you); **per** ~ **generale** admittedly (*avv.*).

riconvenzione, *n. f.* (*leg.*) cross summons, cross-action, counter-claim.

riconversione, *n. f.* (*econ.*) (*d'industrie belliche in industrie di pace*) reconversion. // **la** ~ **dei lavoratori che abbandonano l'agricoltura** (*econ., pers.*) the reabsorption of workers leaving the land; ~ **industriale** (*econ.*) industrial reorganization.

riconvertire, *v. t.* (*econ.*) (*industrie*) to reconvert.

riconvertirsi, *v. rifl.* (*econ.*) (*d'industrie*) to reconvert.

ricorrente, *a.* recurrent, recurring. *n. m.* e *f.* (*leg.*) complainant, claimant, petitioner, plaintiff.

ricorrere, *v. i.* **1** (*rivolgersi a*) to apply, to

resort, to have recourse; (*fare appello*) to appeal. 2 (*leg.*) to appeal. // ~ **al risparmio interno** (*econ.*) to call on domestic savings; ~ **alla forza** to resort to force; ~ **alla giustizia** (*leg.*) to go to Court; ~ **all'inflazione** (*econ.*) to inflate; ~ **alla legge** (*leg.*) to have recourse to the law; ~ **alle vie legali** (*leg.*) to resort to legal proceedings.

ricorso, *n. m.* 1 resort, recourse. 2 (*leg.*) petition; (*appello*) appeal; (*reclamo*) claim. // ~ **al prestito pubblico per finanziare spese statali** (*econ.*) deficit financing; ~ (*della compagnia d'assicurazioni*) **contro il capitano** (*quando il danno è dovuto a negligenza di quest'ultimo*) (*ass. mar.*) restaur, restor; ~ **fra assicuratori** (*ass.*) restaur; ~ **per rimborso di dazio** (*dog.*) claim for repayment of duties; **chi fa un** ~ (*leg.*) petitioner, claimant; **far** ~ **a q.** to have resort to sb.; **senza** ~ (*cred.*) «sans recours».

ricuperabile, *a.* 1 (*riacquistabile*) recoverable, reclaimable. 2 (*cred., fin., leg.*) redeemable, collectable.

ricuperare, *v. t.* e *i.* 1 (*riacquistare*) to recover, to reclaim; (*riguadagnare*) to regain, to make★ up for. 2 (*rimettersi*) to recoup. 3 (*Borsa, fin.*) (*di titoli, ecc.*) to rally, to claw back. 4 (*cred., fin., leg.*) to redeem, to collect, to recoup. 5 (*trasp. mar.*) (*un carico, ecc.*) to salvage, to salve. // ~ **crediti inesigibili** (*cred.*) to collect bad debts; ~ **un credito mediante un'azione giudiziaria** (*leg.*) to recover a debt at law; ~ **il proprio denaro** to get one's money back; ~ (*un oggetto venduto a rate, ma non pagato del tutto*) **senza adire le vie legali** (*market.*) to repossess; ~ (*beni mobili*) **sotto cauzione** (*leg.*) to replevy, to replevin; ~ **le spese** to recover expenses; ~ **le spese d'una causa** (*leg.*) to recover costs.

ricuperatore, *n. m.* (*trasp. mar.*) salvager, salvor.

ricupero, *n. m.* 1 (*riacquisto*) recovery, reclamation. 2 (*il rimettersi in sesto, ecc.*) recoupment. 3 (*Borsa, fin.*) (*di titoli, ecc.*) rally, pick-up, clawing back, claw-back. 4 (*cred., fin., leg.*) redemption, collection. 5 (*trasp. mar.*) salvage. 6 «**ricuperi**», *pl.* (*fin.*) inflows. // ~ **degli scarti** (*org. az.*) scrap recovery; ~ **dei crediti** (*cred.*) debt recovery, debt collecting, debt collection; ~ **di beni mobili** (*leg.*) trover; ~ **di capitale** (*rag.*) capital recovery; ~ **pacifico** (*d'un oggetto venduto a rate, ma non pagato interamente*) (*market.*) repossession.

ridimensionamento, *n. m.* 1 retrenchment. 2 (*econ.*) (*delle spese, ecc.*) rescaling.

ridimensionare, *v. t.* 1 to retrench. 2 (*econ.*) (*le spese, ecc.*) to rescale.

ridistribuire, *v. t.* to redistribute.

ridistribuzione, *n. f.* redistribution. // **la** ~ **del reddito** (*econ.*) the redistribution of income.

ridotto, *a.* 1 reduced. 2 (*econ., market.*) (*di volume d'affari, prezzo, ecc.*) depressed; (*di prezzo*) knockdown (*attr.*). // **ridotte restrizioni all'importazione** (*comm. est.*) relaxed restrictions on imports.

ridurre, *v. t.* 1 to reduce, to cut★, to cut★ down, to curtail; (*restringere*) to narrow; (*attenuare*) to lower, to lessen; (*limitare*) to limit. 2 (*econ., fin.*) (*le spese*) to retrench, to slash, to slice; to dock (*fam.*). 3 (*leg.*) (*restrizioni, ecc.*) to relax. 4 (*market.*) (*il volume d'affari, i prezzi, ecc.*) to depress. 5 (*market.*) (*ordinazioni*) to cut★. 6 (*mat.*) (*una frazione: ai minimi termini*) to reduce. // ~ **al minimo** to minimize; ~ **al minimo le spese** (*amm.*) to minimize expenses; ~ **al sistema decimale** (*mat.*) to decimalize; ~ **il costo del denaro** (*fin.*) to force down the cost of credit; ~ **i dazi** (*dog., fin.*) to lower duties; ~ **un disavanzo** (*fin., rag.*) to reduce a deficit; ~ **il disavanzo di cassa** (*fin., rag.*) to cut back the cash deficit; ~ **i dividendi** (*fin.*) to reduce dividends; ~ **drasticamente** (*fondi, spese, ecc.*) (*econ., fin.*) to slash; ~ (*un debito*) **per compensazione** (*cred.*) to defalcate; ~ **il personale** (*org. az.*) to reduce the staff; ~ **il personale di** (*un'azienda, un'industria, ecc.*) (*econ.*) to de-man; ~ **i privilegi** (*leg.*) to retrench privileges; ~ **la produzione** (*org. az.*) to cut down production; ~ (*qc.*) **progressivamente** to scale down; ~ **i salari** (*sind.*) to curtail wages; ~ **le spese** to cut down expenses, to retrench expenses, to retrench; ~ **sterline in lire** to turn pounds into lire; ~ **lo stipendio d'un impiegato** (*sind.*) to dock an employee's salary; ~ **il tasso di sconto** (*fin.*) to reduce (*o* to cut) the discount rate; ~ **il valore nominale di** (*titoli*) (*fin., rag.*) to write down; ~ **un venditore a più miti pretese** (*market.*) to beat down a seller.

ridursi, *v. rifl.* 1 to reduce oneself. 2 (*diminuire*) to lower, to lessen; (*restringersi*) to shrink★; (*scemare*) to slacken.

riduzione, *n. f.* 1 reduction, cut, cutting, curtailing; (*attenuazione*) lowering, lessening. 2 (*econ., fin.*) (*di fondi, spese, ecc.*) slash; docking (*fam.*). 3 (*fin.*) cut-back, rundown, step-down, shrinkage, slackening. 4 (*market.*) (*del volume d'affari, dei prezzi, ecc.*) depression; (*delle ordinazioni*) cut, cutting. 5 (*market.*) discount, rebate. 6 (*mat.*) (*d'una frazione: ai minimi termini*) reduction. // ~ **al sistema decimale** (*mat.*) decimalization, metrication; ~ **degli**

sprechi (*org. az.*) waste-control, saving; ~ **degli utili** (*econ.*) profit squeeze; ~ **dei costi** (*rag.*) cost reduction, cost cutting; **una** ~ **dei costi di distribuzione** (*econ.*) a drop in distribution costs; **una** ~ **dei prezzi** (*market., anche*) a roll-back of prices; ~ **del personale** (*in un'azienda, ecc.*) (*org. az.*) de-manning; **la** ~ **del tasso di sconto** (*banca, cred.*) the reduction of the discount rate; ~ **dell'imposta sul reddito** (*per gli scioperanti*) (*fin., sind.*) rebate of income tax; ~ **della produttività individuale** (*econ.*) job sharing; ~ **delle giacenze** (*org. az.*) stock reduction; **una** ~ **delle imposte** (*fin.*) an abatement of taxes, a tax reduction; **una** ~ **delle limitazioni agli scambi commerciali** (*comm. est.*) a lowering of trade restrictions; ~ **delle scorte** (*org. az.*) inventory reduction; ~ **delle spese** (*rag.*) cost reduction, cost cutting, retrenchment; ~ **delle tariffe** rate cutting; ~ **dell'orario** (*dovuta a interruzioni*) (*org. az., sind.*) broken time; **una** ~ **di capitale** (*rag.*) a reduction of capital; ~ **di debito per compensazione** (*cred.*) defalcation; ~ **di donazione** (*leg.*) abatement of gift; ~ **di legato** (*leg.*) abatement of gift; **riduzioni di prezzo** (*market.*) price cuttings; ~ **di stipendio** (*pers.*) salary cut; ~ **di valore** (*d'un bene*) (*rag.*) depletion; **riduzioni generali delle tariffe doganali** (*applicate ai dazi su un insieme di molti prodotti*) (*dog.*) across-the-board tariff cuts; ~ **nelle spese** (*rag.*) spending cut-back; ~ (*dei prezzi, ecc.*) **ottenuta mediante interventi statali** (*econ., market.*) rollback; ~ **progressiva** scale-down; ~ **tariffaria** (*comm. est., econ.*) tariff cut, tariff reduction; **riduzioni tariffarie** (*previste negli accordi*) **del «Kennedy round»** (*comm. est.*) Kennedy round tariff cuts; **effettuare una** ~ **di personale** (*org. az.*) to de-man.

rientrare, *v. i.* **1** (*entrare di nuovo*) to enter again, to re-enter; (*ritornare*) to return, to go★ back, to come★ back. **2** (*essere compreso, essere contenuto*) to be included in, to fall★ within, to come★ within. **3** (*cred., fin.*) (*di denaro*) to come★ in. // ~ **in possesso di qc.** to re-enter into possession of st., to resume possession of st., to repossess st.; ~ **nei propri diritti** (*leg.*) to be reinstated in one's rights; ~ **nelle spese** to recover one's expenses; ~ **nell'ambito della giurisdizione di q.** (*leg.*) to come under sb.'s jurisdiction.

riesame, *n. m.* **1** re-examination, review. **2** (*leg.*) (*d'una causa*) rehearing, review.

riesaminare, *v. t.* **1** to re-examine, to review. **2** (*leg.*) (*una causa*) to rehear★, to review.

riesportare, *v. t.* (*comm. est.*) to re-export, to export again.

riesportatore, *n. m.* (*comm. est.*) re-exporter.

riesportazione, *n. f.* (*comm. est.*) re-exportation, re-export.

riferimento, *n. m.* reference. // ~ **al mastro** (*rag.*) posting reference; **con** ~ **a** (*comun.*) with respect to, in reference to, with reference to, referring to, in point of; **con** ~ **alla vostra ultima lettera** (*comun.*) in reference to (referring to, with respect to) your last letter; **in** ~ **alla nostra conversazione telefonica** referring to our telephone conversation.

riferire, *v. t.* to report, to relate, to tell★. // ~ **per esteso** (*un avvenimento, ecc.*) (*giorn.*) to cover.

riferirsi, *v. rifl.* **1** to refer, to make★ reference. **2** (*concernere*) to concern, to refer, to cover, to apply, to be related, to attach.

rifiutare, *v. t.* **1** (*non accettare*) to refuse; (*respingere*) to reject, to rebut; (*declinare*) to decline. **2** (*negare*) to refuse, to deny, to withhold★. // ~ **di pagare** (*un assegno, ecc.*) (*cred., leg.*) to dishonour; ~ **di riconoscere** to repudiate; ~ **di riconoscere un debito** (*cred.*) to repudiate a debt; ~ **un'offerta** to turn down an offer; to shut the door upon an offer (*fig.*).

rifiutarsi, *v. rifl.* to refuse, to decline. // ~ **di giungere a un accordo** to stick out (*fam.*); ~ **di pagare** to whithhold payment.

rifiuto, *n. m.* **1** (*il non accettare*) refusal, rejection, rebuttal, declination, turndown. **2** (*il negare*) refusal, denial. **3** (*market.*) reject. **4 rifiuti,** *pl.* (*market., org. az.*) waste products; waste (*sing.*). // **il** ~ **d'un'offerta** the turndown of an offer; ~ **di pagare** (*cred.*) non-payment; **il** ~ **di riconoscere un debito** (*cred.*) the repudiation of a debt.

rifondere, *v. t.* (*rimborsare*) to refund, to reimburse, to pay★ back.

riforma, *n. f.* **1** (*il correggere, il migliorare*) reform, reformation, improvement, amendment. **2** (*leg.*) (*d'una sentenza*) reversal, amendment. // **la** ~ **del sistema monetario internazionale** (*econ.*) the reform of the international monetary system; **la** ~ **d'una sentenza** (*leg.*) the amendment of a judgment; ~ **fiscale** (*fin.*) tax reform; ~ **fondiaria** (*econ.*) land reform; ~ **monetaria** (*econ.*) currency reform; ~ (*del diritto*) **penale** (*leg.*) penal reform; **una** ~ **sociale** a social reform; ~ **tributaria** (*fin.*) fiscal reform.

riformare, *v. t.* **1** (*correggere, migliorare*) to reform, to improve, to mend. **2** (*leg.*) (*una sentenza*) to amend, to reverse.

rifornimento, *n. m.* **1** furnishment, resupply, supply. **2** (*org. az.*) (*del magazzino*) replenishment, restocking. **3** (*trasp. mar.*) replenishment. **4 rifornimenti**, *pl.* (*cose rifornite*) supplies, provisions. // **rifornimenti di bordo** (*trasp. mar.*) stores; ~ **di carbone** (*trasp. mar.*) coaling; ~ **idrico** (*org. az.*) water supply; **un** ~ **in mare** (*trasp. mar.*) a replenishment at sea; **stazione di** ~ (*trasp. aut.*) petrol station, filling-station; gas station (*USA*).

rifornire, *v. t.* **1** to furnish (again), to resupply, to supply. **2** (*org. az.*) (*il magazzino*) to replenish, to stock, to restock. **3** (*trasp. mar.*) to replenish. // ~ (*una nave e sim.*) **di carbone** (*trasp. mar.*) to recoal, to coal; ~ **q. di fondi** (*fin.*) to supply sb. with funds; ~ **di viveri** (*trasp. mar.*) to victual; ~ **una nave in mare** (*trasp. mar.*) to replenish a ship at sea; ~ **un negozio di merci** (*org. az.*) to stock a shop with goods.

rifornirsi, *v. rifl.* **1** to supply oneself (again). **2** (*org. az.*) to restock. **3** (*trasp. mar.*) to replenish. // ~ **di carbone** (*trasp. mar.*) to coal, to recoal; ~ **di viveri** (*trasp. mar.*) to victual.

rifusione, *n. f.* (*rimborso*) reimbursement, refunding, refund; (*risarcimento*) compensation.

rigettare, *v. t.* **1** (*respingere*) to push★ back, to drive★ back. **2** (*non accogliere*) to reject, to turn★ down. **3** (*leg.*) to dismiss, to rebut. // ~ **un'istanza di fallimento** (*leg.*) to dismiss a bankruptcy petition.

rigetto, *n. m.* **1** rejection,rejecting, turning down. **2** (*leg.*) dismissal, rebuttal. // ~ **d'un'istanza** (*leg.*) rejection of a petition, disallowance; ~ **d'una richiesta** (*leg.*) disallowance.

rigidità, *n. f. inv.* **1** rigidity, hardness, stiffness; (*mancanza d'elasticità*) inelasticity. **2** (*fig.: durezza, severità*) rigidity, strictness. **3** (*econ.*) (*di domanda, prezzo, ecc.*) stickiness, inelasticity. **4** (*market.*) (*di prezzi, mercati, ecc.*) flatness. // ~ **della domanda** (*econ.*) inelasticity of demand; ~ **dell'offerta** (*econ.*) inelasticity of supply.

rigido, *a.* **1** (*duro, inflessibile*) rigid, hard, stiff; (*inelastico*) inelastic. **2** (*fig.: duro, severo*) rigid, severe, strict, stringent, hard-and-fast. **3** (*econ.*) (*di domanda, prezzo, ecc.*) sticky, inelastic. **4** (*market.*) (*di prezzi, mercati*) flat.

rilanciare, *v. t.* e *i.* **1** (*fare un'offerta maggiore in un'asta*) to make★ a higher bid. **2** (*fare tornare attuale*) to reactivate.

rilancio, *n. m.* **1** (*maggiore offerta in un'asta*) higher bid. **2** (*il fare tornare attuale*) reactivation. **3** (*econ.*) booster. // **il** ~ **dell'unione economica e monetaria** (*econ.*) the reactivation of the economic and monetary union; **misure per il** ~ (*econ.*) booster measures.

rilasciare, *v. t.* **1** (*consegnare*) to deliver, to consign. **2** (*concedere*) to allow★, to grant, to issue. **3** (*leg.*) (*un detenuto*) to release, to set★ free. // ~ **un diploma** to graduate (*USA*); ~ **un passaporto** to issue a passport; ~ **(una) ricevuta** to make out a receipt, to give (a) receipt.

rilascio, *n. m.* **1** (*consegna*) delivery, consignment. **2** (*concessione*) grant, issue; issuance (*USA*). **3** (*leg.*) (*d'un detenuto*) release, setting free. // «~ **carico**» (*trasp. mar.*) «freight release»; **il** ~ **delle licenze d'importazione e d'esportazione** (*comm. est.*) the issue of import and export licences; **il** ~ **d'un brevetto** (*leg.*) the grant of a patent; ~ **sotto cauzione** (*leg.*) release on bail.

rilevamento, *n. m.* **1** (*topografico*) survey. **2** (*fin.*) (*d'un'azienda*) take-over. **3** (*trasp. mar.*) bearing. // ~ **dei tempi (di lavoro)** (*org. az.*) timekeeping; ~ **della parte d'un socio** (*fin.*) buying out a partner.

rilevare, *v. t.* **1** (*notare*) to notice; (*far notare*) to point out. **2** (*un terreno*) to survey, to plot. **3** (*fin.*) (*un'azienda*) to take★ over, to buy★ out. **4** (*rag.*) (*i saldi contabili, ecc.*) to abstract. **5** (*trasp. mar.*) to take★ the bearing of. // ~ **la parte d'un socio** (*fin.*) to buy out a partner; ~ **i risultati d'un conto** (*rag.*) to abstract the results of an account.

rilevazione, *n. f.* **1** survey; (*osservazione*) observation; (*registrazione*) recording; (*valutazione*) evaluation. **2** (*rag.*) entry. // **la** ~ **dei prezzi** (*market.*) the observation of price trends; ~ **dello stato organizzativo** (*amm.*) management appraisal, management evaluation; ~ **d'apertura** (*rag.*) opening entry; ~ **e stima delle scorte** (*rag.*) inventory and valuation of stocks; ~ (*contabile*) **originaria** (*rag.*) original entry; **rilevazioni statistiche** (*fin.*) gathering of statistical data, statistical findings.

rimandare, *v. t.* **1** (*restituire, mandare indietro*) to send★ back, to return. **2** (*rinviare*) to put★ off, to leave★ over, to lay★ over, to defer, to delay, to postpone; (*aggiornare*) to adjourn; (*una discussione, ecc.*) to shelve. **3** (*leg.*) (*prorogare*) to continue, to stay. // ~ **il pagamento d'un conto** to delay meeting an account; ~ **una riunione** to put off a meeting; ~ (*una mozione, ecc.*) «**sine die**» (*leg.*) to table; **essere rimandato** to lie over, to be deferred.

rimando, *n. m.* **1** (*il posporre*) putting off, leaving over, deferment, deferring, postponement; (*aggiornamento*) adjournment. **2** (*richiamo per il lettore*) cross reference, reference.

rimanente, *a.* remaining, residuary, residual. *n. m.* remainder, remnant; (*resto*) rest; (*residuo*) residue. // **il ~ della merce** (*market.*) the remainder of the goods.

rimanenza, *n. f.* 1 remainder, remnant, surplus. 2 (*fin., rag.*) balance, surplus, overplus, carry over, excess. 3 (*market.*) remainder, surplus stock; inventory; oddments (*pl.*). // **~ di cassa** (*rag.*) cash balance; **rimanenze di materiali** (*rag.*) supplies on hand; **~ finale** (*rag.*) closing stock, ending inventory; **~ iniziale** (*rag.*) opening stock, beginning inventory.

rimanere, *v. i.* 1 to remain, to stay. 2 (*avanzare*) to remain, to be left. 3 (*durare, persistere*) to last, to remain. // **~ a corto di** to run short of; **~ al verde** (*fig.*) to be left broke, to be left penniless; **~ in carica** to remain in office; **~ in porto** (*per riparazioni, ecc.*) (*trasp. mar.*) to lie up; **~ senza lavoro** (*pers.*) to be thrown out of work; **~ sprovvisti (di merce)** (*market.*) to run out of stock.

rimbarcare, *v. t.* (*trasp. mar.*) to reship, to re-embark.

rimbarco, *n. m.* (*trasp. mar.*) reshipment, reshipping, re-embarkation, re-embarking.

rimborsabile, *a.* reimbursable, repayable, returnable, redeemable. // **~ a richiesta** repayable at call; **non ~** not repayable, not returnable.

rimborsabilità, *n. f. inv.* repayability, redeemability.

rimborsare, *v. t.* 1 to reimburse, to refund, to repay★, to pay★ back. 2 (*cred., fin.*) (*parte degli interessi pagati per una somma prestata e che viene restituita in anticipo*) to rebate. 3 (*fin.*) (*obbligazioni*) to redeem. 4 (*leg.*) to recoup. // **~ anticipatamente** to pay back in advance; **~ i creditori** (*cred.*) to repay creditors; **~ obbligazioni** (*fin.*) to call bonds; **~ le spese** to refund expenses.

rimborso, *n. m.* 1 reimbursement, refund, repayment, rebate. 2 (*cred., fin.*) (*di parte degli interessi pagati per una somma prestata e restituita in anticipo*) rebate. 3 (*fin.*) (*d'obbligazioni*) redemption. 4 (*leg.*) recoupment. // **~ anticipato** (*fin.*) advance refunding; **rimborsi anticipati di debiti pubblici** (*fin.*) advance repayments of public debts; **~ dei dazi** (*dog.*) drawback; **un ~ del nolo** (*trasp. mar.*) a rebate of freight; **~ delle perdite** (*ass.*) payment of losses; **un ~ (delle) spese** a reimbursement of expenses; **~ di diritti doganali** (*pagati per merce che viene riesportata*) (*dog.*) customs drawback; **il ~ d'imposte** (*pagate in più del dovuto*) (*fin.*) the return of taxes; **il ~ e il ricupero dei dazi doganali** (*comm. est.*) the refund and remission of custom duties.

rimessa, *n. f.* 1 (*il rimettere*) replacing, replacement. 2 (*Borsa*) commission. 3 (*comm.*) (*in denaro, ecc.*) remittance, transfer; (*di merci*) consignment. 4 (*rag.*) (*perdita*) loss. 5 (*trasp. aer.*) hangar. 6 (*trasp. aut.*) garage. // **una ~ a saldo** (*cred.*) a remittance in settlement; **rimesse degli emigranti** (*econ.*) immigrant remittances; **~ d'assegni salvo buon fine** (*banca*) remittance of cheques subject to payment; **~ in vigore** (*d'una legge*) (*leg.*) re-enactment; **~ per via aerea** (*cred.*) airmail remittance; **~ telegrafica** (*comun., cred.*) cable transfer, cable; **chi effettua una ~** (*comm.*) remitter; «**nostra ~ d'effetti**» (*banca*) «our remittance of bills».

rimettere, *v. t.* 1 to put★ again, to put★ back. 2 (*mandare*) to remit, to send★; (*consegnare*) to hand; (*presentare*) to submit. 3 (*perdere, scapitare*) to lose★, to be out (a sum of money); to be (a sum of money) to the bad (*fam.*). 4 (*affidare*) to refer, to leave★, to entrust. 5 (*leg.*) (*un debito*) to release, to remit. // **~ a nuovo** to renew; **~ un debito** (*cred.*) to remit a debt; **~ denaro** (*comun.*) to send money; **~ denaro in circolazione** (*fin.*) to set money free; **~ in carica** (*leg.*) to rehabilitate; **~ in funzione** to reactivate; **~ in ordine** to reorder; **~ in piedi una società (finanziariamente)** (*fin.*) to rehabilitate a company (financially); **~ in vigore** (*una legge, ecc.*) (*leg.*) to revive, to re-enact.

rimettersi, *v. rifl.* 1 (*ristabilirsi*) to recover. 2 (*affidarsi*) to submit (to sb.), to entrust oneself (to sb.), to rely (on sb.). // **~ al lodo degli arbitri** to refer to the award of the arbitrators; **~ in piedi** (*dopo una caduta; anche fig.*) to regain one's footing; **~ in sesto** (*anche fig.*) to get on one's feet again.

rimozione, *n. f.* 1 removal, removing, displacement; (*eliminazione*) elimination. 2 (*leg.*) removal. 3 (*pers.*) (*da un grado*) removal, dismissal. // **la ~ dei sigilli** (*leg.*) the removal of seals; **la ~ d'una legge ingiusta** (*leg.*) the displacement of an unjust law.

rimpiegare, *v. t. V.* **reimpiegare.**

rimpiego, *n. m. V.* **reimpiego.**

rimunerare, *v. t.* to remunerate, to recompense; (*un professionista*) to fee. // **un'azienda che non rimunera** a firm that yields no profit.

rimunerativo, *a.* 1 remunerative, lucrative, gainful. 2 (*econ., fin., rag.*) (*d'investimento e sim.*) profitable, remunerative, paying, payable. 3 (*pers.*) (*di lavoro, ecc.*) paying. // **non ~** unremunerative.

rimunerazione, *n. f.* 1 remuneration, consideration money, recompense; (*d'un professionista*) fee. **2** (*fin., rag.*) return.

rimuovere, *v. t.* **1** (*allontanare*) to remove, to displace; (*eliminare*) to eliminate. **2** (*pers.*) (*q., da un grado*) to remove, to dismiss. // **~ q. dalla carica** (*pers.*) to remove sb. from office; **~ le frontiere fiscali** (*fin.*) to eliminate fiscal frontiers; **~ un procuratore legale dall'esercizio della professione** (*leg.*) to disentitle a solicitor.

rincarare, *v. t.* (*market.*) (*aumentare il prezzo di*) to increase the price of, to raise the price of. *v. i.* (*market.*) to get★ dearer, to rise★ in price, to become★ more expensive, to go★ up (in price).

rincaro, *n. m.* (*market.*) rise in prices, increase in prices, advance in prices, markup.

rinfusa, *n. f.* (*nella locuz.*) **alla ~** (*market.*) in job lots; (*trasp. mar.*) in bulk.

ringraziamento, *n. m.* thanks (*pl.*).

ringraziare, *v. t.* to thank. // **~ q. di qc.** to thank sb. for st.; **ringraziandovi anticipatamente** thanking you in advance, thanking you beforehand.

rinnovamento, *n. m.* **1** renewal; (*rimodernamento*) updating, modernization. **2** (*sostituzione*) change, renewal.

rinnovare, *v. t.* **1** to renew; (*rimodernare*) to update, to modernize. **2** (*sostituire*) to change, to renew. **3** (*ripetere*) to repeat. // **~ una cambiale** (*banca, cred.*) to renew a bill; **~ un contratto** (*leg.*) to renew a contract; **~ un'ordinazione** (*market.*) to repeat an order; **~ il personale** (*org. az.*) to renew the staff; **non ~ un abbonamento** (*giorn.*) to discontinue a subscription.

rinnovo, *n. m.* **1** renewal; (*rimodernamento*) updating, modernization. **2** (*sostituzione*) change, renewal. **3** (*market.*) repeat. // **~ del contratto d'affitto** (*leg.*) relocation, reconduction; **il ~ d'una cambiale** (*banca, cred.*) the renewal of a bill; **il ~ d'un contratto** (*leg.*) the renewal of a contract; **il ~ d'un diritto d'autore** (*leg.*) the renewal of a copyright.

rinomanza, *n. f.* renown; (*nome*) name; (*fama*) fame. // **la ~ dei nostri prodotti** the renown of our products.

rinomato, *a.* renowned, well-known, famous.

rintracciare, *v. t.* (*anche fig.*) to trace.

rinuncia, *n. f.* **1** (*il rinunciare*) renunciation, renouncement, resignation, relinquishment; (*abbandono*) abandonment. **2** (*leg.*) (*a un diritto*) waiver, renunciation, remise. **3** (*pers.*) vacation. // **~ a un diritto** (*leg.*) quitclaim, disclaimer, remise of a right; **la ~ a far valere un diritto** (*leg.*) the remission of a claim; **la ~ a un'opzione** the abandonment of an option; **~ formale** (*leg.*) disclaimer; **~ implicita** (*leg.*) implied waiver.

rinunciare, *v. i.* **1** to renounce, to resign, to relinquish; (*abbandonare*) to abandon, to give★ up; to step down (*fig.*). **2** (*leg.*) to waive, to renounce, to remise, to recede, to resign, to abdicate. // **~ a un diritto** (*leg.*) to waive a right, to renounce a right, to release a right, to abdicate a right, to disclaim, to quitclaim, to back down; **~ a garanzie reali** (*cred., fin.*) to waive collateral; **~ a un'opzione** to abandon an option; **~ a un posto** (*pers.*) to step down from a position; **~ al proprio diritto a un'eredità** (*leg.*) to relinquish one's claim to an inheritance; **~ all'esecuzione di talune clausole contrattuali** (*leg.*) to waive fulfilment of certain provisions of a contract; **~ alla propria parte in un affare** to compromise one's share in a transaction; **chi rinuncia** (*a qc.*) resigner; **colui in favore del quale q. rinuncia** (*a qc.*) resignee.

rinunzia, *n. f. V.* **rinuncia.**

rinunziare, *v. i. V.* **rinunciare.**

rinviare, *v. t.* **1** (*inviare di nuovo*) to send★ again. **2** (*inviare indietro*) to return, to send★ back. **3** (*differire*) to put★ off, to postpone, to delay, to defer, to lay★ over, to leave★ over; (*aggiornare*) to adjourn. **4** (*leg.*) (*una decisione e sim.*) to stay, to continue; (*una causa a un tribunale inferiore*) to remand; (*un imputato in carcere*) to remand. // **~** (*una causa*) **a un altro tribunale** (*leg.*) to remit; **~ q. a giudizio** (*leg.*) to commit sb. for trial; **~ una causa** (*leg.*) to adjourn a case; **~** (*un contratto a termine*) **da un mese al mese successivo** (*in una Borsa merci*) (*fin.*) to switch; **~ una faccenda** to leave over a matter; **~ un pagamento** to delay a payment; **~ una seduta** to defer a meeting; **~ l'udienza** (*leg.*) to adjourn the hearing; **essere rinviato** to lie over.

rinvio, *n. m.* **1** (*nuovo invio*) sending again. **2** (*l'inviare indietro*) returning, sending back. **3** (*differimento*) putting off, postponement, delay, deferment; (*aggiornamento*) adjournment. **4** (*leg.*) continuation, continuance. // **il ~ d'una causa** (*leg.*) the adjournment of a suit; (*a un altro tribunale*) the remission of a case, the removal of a cause, the change of venue; **il ~** (*al fornitore*) **di merci avariate** (*market.*) the return of damaged merchandise; **~ d'ufficio** (*leg.*) adjournment by the Court.

riorganizzare, *v. t.* **1** to reorganize, to organize again. **2** (*org. az.*) to reorganize, to reorder; (*un'azienda*) to shake★ up.

riorganizzarsi, *v. rifl.* **1** to reorganize. **2**

(*org. az.*) to reorganize.

riorganizzazione, *n. f.* **1** reorganization, reordering. **2** (*org. az.*) reorganization, reordering; (*d'una azienda*) shake-up. // **la ~ del personale** (*org. az.*) the reorganization of the staff.

riparabile, *a.* reparable.

riparazione e manutenzione attrezzature, *locuz. n.* equipment repairs and maintenance.

ripartibile, *a.* divisible, distributable, apportionable, allottable.

ripartire, *v. t.* **1** to divide, to distribute, to portion (out), to apportion, to partition, to share (out), to allot. **2** (*ass. mar.*) (*perdite*) to assess. **3** (*fin.*) (*azioni o obbligazioni*) to allot. **4** (*mat.*) to allocate. // **~ una perdita in modo proporzionale** (*ass. mar.*) to average a loss; **~ proporzionalmente** (*fin., rag.*) to prorate, to average; **~ una somma di denaro fra varie persone** to allocate a sum of money among several persons; **~ gli utili fra i soci** (*anche*) to distribute profits among the members.

ripartizione, *n. f.* **1** (*il ripartire*) division, distribution, portioning (out), apportionment, partition, sharing (out), allotment. **2** (*ognuna delle parti*) division, portion, share. **3** (*ass. mar.*) (*di perdite*) assessment, apportionment. **4** (*fin.*) (*d'una sottoscrizione azionaria o obbligazionaria*) allotment. **5** (*mat.*) allocation. **6** (*rag.*) appropriation. // **~ degli utili** (*fin., rag.*) allocation of profits, division of profits, distribution of profits; **~ dei proventi doganali** (*dog.*) distribution of customs receipts; **~ del lavoro** (*org. az.*) division of work, division of labour; **la ~ dell'utile netto** (*fin.*) the appropriation of the net profit; **la ~ d'una perdita** (*ass. mar.*) the assessment of a loss; **~ proporzionale** (*rag.*) averaging; **senza ~** (*di nuove azioni*) (*Borsa*) (*di titolo*) ex allotment.

riparto, *n. m.* (*fin., rag.*) allocation. // **senza riparti straordinari d'utili** (*Borsa*) (*di titolo*) ex bonus.

riportabile, *a.* (*Borsa*) (*di titolo*) contangoable, continuable.

riportare, *v. t.* **1** (*verso l'interlocutore: portare di nuovo*) to bring★ again; (*portare indietro*) to bring★ back; (*lontano dall'interlocutore: portare di nuovo*) to take★ again; (*portare indietro*) to take★ back. **2** (*riferire*) to report, to relate. **3** (*ottenere, ricevere*) to get★, to receive; (*subire*) to suffer. **4** (*Borsa*) to contango, to continue, to carry over, to borrow. **5** (*mat.*) (*una cifra*) to carry, to carry over. **6** (*rag.*) (*una cifra ad altra colonna, pagina, libro*) to carry over, to carry forward, to bring★ forward. // **~ a nuovo** (*rag.*) to carry forward, to forward, to extend; **~ una posizione da una liquidazione alla successiva** (*Borsa*) to contango a book from one settlement to the next; **~ un saldo** (*rag.*) to forward a balance; **~ il saldo interessi nella colonna capitali** (*rag.*) to carry out the balance of interest in the principal column; **~ titoli** (*Borsa*) to carry stock, to take in stocks; **~ un totale** (*rag.*) to carry over a total; «**a ~**» (*rag.*) «carried forward»; **riportato a nuovo** (*rag.*) (*di cifra, di totale, ecc.*) extended.

riportatore, *n. m.* (*Borsa*) taker.

riporto, *n. m.* **1** (*Borsa*) contango, contangoing, continuation account, continuation, carry-over of securities, carry-over. **2** (*mat.*) carry, carry-over. **3** (*rag.*) (*il procedimento*) bringing forward, carrying forward, carrying over; (*ammontare riportato*) amount brought forward (*o* down), amount carried forward (*o* down), balance brought forward (*o* down), balance carried forward (*o* down), carry-over. // «**riporto**» (*rag.*) «brought forward»; **~ a nuovo** (*rag.*) extension; **il ~ delle perdite** (*rag.*) the carrying over of losses to subsequent years; **~ in cambi** (*fin.*) swap, swop; **~ staccato** (*Borsa, fin.*) hedging; **~ su divise** (*fin.*) continuation on foreign exchanges, swap; **~ valutario** (*fin.*) swap of currency, swap.

riposo, *n. m.* rest. // **a ~** (*pers.*) retired; on the shelf (*pred.*); **collocare q. a ~** (*pers.*) (*per malattia*) to put sb. on the sick-list; (*per raggiunti limiti d'età*) to superannuate sb.

riprendere, *v. t.* **1** (*prendere di nuovo*) to take★ again, to retake★. **2** (*prendere indietro*) to take★ back, to get★ back; (*ricuperare*) to recover. **3** (*ricominciare*) to begin★ again, to resume; (*una discussione, ecc.*) to reopen. *v. i.* (*econ.*) (*d'attività commerciale, ecc.*) to pick up, to catch★ up. // **~ un articolo** (*restituendo al cliente il prezzo che aveva pagato*) (*market.*) to take back an article; **~ il lavoro** (*org. az.*) to resume work; **~ slancio** (*econ.*) to pick up; **~ vigore** (*econ.*) to pick up; **riprendersi qc.** (*leg.*) to resume possession of st.

riprendersi, *v. rifl.* **1** (*anche fig.*) to recover. **2** (*Borsa, fin.*) (*di titoli, ecc.*) to rally.

ripresa, *n. f.* **1** renewal, resumption, restarting; (*d'una discussione, ecc.*) reopening. **2** (*da una malattia e sim.: anche fig.*) recovery. **3** (*Borsa, fin., market.*) (*di titoli, ecc.*) rally, recovery, upswing, snapback. **4** (*econ.*) recovery, catching-up, catch-up, pick-up, go. // **~ a breve termine** (*econ.*) short-term recovery; **~ dell'attività commerciale** (*econ.*) business recovery; **la ~ di possesso** (*leg.*) the resumption of possession; **~ di possesso di beni sottratti illecitamente**

(*leg.*) recaption; ~ **economica** (*econ.*) economic recovery, economic revival; **una ~ produttiva** (*econ.*) a recovery in production, a production recovery; ~ **strisciante** (*econ.*) creeping recovery; **essere in ~** (*Borsa, fin.*) (*di titoli, ecc.*) to recover; (*econ.*) (*di situazione economica*) to recover; (*di domanda, prezzo, ecc.*) to be up.

riprodurre, *v. t.* 1 (*produrre di nuovo*) to reproduce, to produce again. 2 (*copiare*) to copy, to reproduce; (*documenti, ecc.*) to take* off. // ~ (*lettere, disegni, ecc.*) **con uno stampino** (*giorn., pubbl.*) to stencil; ~ (*un originale*) **due volte** to triplicate; ~ **esattamente** (*qc.*) to facsimile; **essere riprodotto** (*bene, male, ecc.*) to reproduce.

risanamento, *n. m.* (*econ.*) recovery; (*del terreno*) reclamation, reclaiming.

risanare, *v. t.* (*econ.*) to recover; (*terreni*) to reclaim. // ~ **il bilancio** (*fin., rag.*) to re-establish the budget on a sound footing; (*con l'eliminazione di crediti inesigibili, ecc.*) to clean up the balance sheet.

risarcibile, *a.* (*leg.*) recoupable, indemnifiable.

risarcimento, *n. m.* (*leg.*) recoupment, refund, redress, reimbursement, recompense, indemnification, indemnity, compensation. // ~ **dei danni** (*ass.*) compensation for damages, damages; ~ **dei danni di guerra** (*econ.*) war-damage compensation; ~ **legale** (*leg.*) legal redress; ~ **per invalidità** (*ass.*) compensation for disability; **a ~ di** (*leg.*) in satisfaction of.

risarcire, *v. t.* (*leg.*) to recoup, to refund, to redress, to reimburse, to recompense, to indemnify, to compensate, to make* good. // ~ **un danno** (*leg.*) to redress a damage; ~ **q. d'una perdita subita** (*ass.*) to make good sb.'s loss; ~ **q. per danni** (*leg.*) to recoup sb. for damages; ~ **una perdita** (*leg.*) to repair a loss; **chi risarcisce** (*leg.*) indemnitor; **chi è risarcito** (*leg.*) indemnitee; **chi ha diritto a essere risarcito** (*leg.*) indemnitee; **chi è tenuto a ~** (*leg.*) indemnitor.

riscattabile, *a.* (*fin., leg.*) redeemable. // **non ~** (*fin., leg.*) unredeemable.

riscattare, *v. t.* 1 (*riacquistare*) to repurchase. 2 (*ass.*) (*una polizza*) to surrender. 3 (*fin., leg.*) to redeem, to buy* in, to buy* off. // ~ **un pegno** (*leg.*) to redeem a pledge; ~ **una polizza** (*ass.*) to surrender a policy; ~ **terreni ipotecati** (*leg.*) to redeem mortgaged land.

riscatto, *n. m.* 1 (*riacquisto*) repurchase. 2 (*ass.*) (*d'una polizza*) surrender. 3 (*fin., leg.*) redemption. // ~ **di stallia** (*trasp. mar.*) dispatch money; **diritto di ~** (*leg.*) right of redemption.

rischiare, *v. t.* to risk, to venture, to hazard; to stake. *v. i.* to run* the risk. // ~ **la propria fortuna in un'impresa** to risk one's fortune in an enterprise; **chi rischia denaro** (*fig.*) venturer.

rischio, *n. m.* 1 risk, venture, hazard; gamble (*fig.*); (*pericolo*) danger. 2 (*ass.*) risk. // ~ **a carico del vettore** (*trasp.*) company's risk; **rischi attinenti alla navigazione** (*ass. mar.*) perils of the sea; **rischi contro terzi** (*ass.*) third-party risks; ~ **d'abbordaggio** (*trasp. mar.*) collision risk; ~ **d'alleggio** (*ass. mar.*) risk of craft, craft risk; ~ **di baratteria** (*ass. mar.*) barratry risk; ~ **di cambio** (*Borsa, fin.*) exchange risk; ~ **di carico** (*trasp. mar.*) loading risk; ~ **di chiatta** (*ass. mar.*) craft risk; ~ **di danno per esposizione alle intemperie** (*ass.*) risk of damage for exposure to weather; ~ **di deviazione** (*ass. mar.*) deviation risk; ~ **di furto** (*ass.*) theft risk; ~ **d'incendio** (*ass.*) risk of fire, fire risk; **rischi di mare** (*ass. mar., trasp. mar.*) marine risks, marine perils, maritime perils; **rischi di passività future** (*rag.*) contingent liabilities; ~ **di quarantena** (*trasp. mar.*) quarantine risk; ~ **di rottura** (*trasp.*) risk of breakage, breakage risk; ~ **di sbarco** (*trasp. mar.*) unloading risk; ~ **di terra** (*ass.*) non-marine risk; ~ **di trasbordo** (*ass. mar.*) transshipment risk; **rischi e pericoli della navigazione** (*ass. mar., trasp. mar.*) marine risks, marine perils, maritime perils; ~ **marittimo** (*ass. mar., trasp. mar., anche*) adventure; **rischi marittimi** (*ass. mar.*) sea risks, sea perils; **rischi marittimi imprevisti** (*ass. mar.*) marine casualties; ~ **massimo** (*ass.*) maximum risk; ~ **negli scali** (*ass. mar.*) calls risk; ~ **per il carico di coperta** (*ass. mar.*) deck-cargo risk; ~ **terrestre** (*ass.*) non-marine risk; **a ~ dei proprietari della merce** (*market.*) at the risk of the owners of the goods; **a ~ del compratore** (*market.*) at (the) buyer's risk; with all faults; **a ~ del destinatario** (*trasp.*) at the consignee's risk; **a ~ dello spedizioniere** (*market.*) at the risk of the shippers; **a ~ e pericolo del committente** (*market.*) at owner's risk; **a ~ e pericolo del compratore** (*o* **dell'acquirente**) (*leg.*) at the buyer's risk; caveat emptor (*lat.*); **a ~ e pericolo del destinatario** (*trasp.*) at owner's risk; **a proprio ~ e pericolo** at one's peril; **chi corre un ~** (*ass.*) risk bearer.

rischioso, *a.* risky, hazardous; (*pericoloso*) dangerous; (*d'affare*) speculative; (*malsicuro*) unsafe.

riscontare, *v. t.* (*banca, cred.*) (*titoli di credito*) to rediscount, to discount again.

risconto, *n. m.* (*banca, cred.*) rediscount, rediscount account. // **risconti attivi** (*rag.*) deferred charges, prepaid expenses; **risconti attivi su fitti** (*rag.*) prepaid rent; **risconti attivi su inte-**

ressi (*rag.*) prepaid interests; ~ **di portafoglio** (*banca*) rebate on bills not due; **risconti passivi** deferred incomes.

riscontrare, *v. t.* **1** (*verificare*) to verify, to check. **2** (*confrontare*) to compare, to collate. **3** (*trovare*) to find★ (out); (*notare*) to notice.

riscontro, *n. m.* **1** (*verifica*) check, verification. **2** (*confronto*) comparison, collation. **3** (*comun.*) (*risposta*) reply, answer, receipt. // ~ **bancario** bank reconciliation; **in** ~ **alla vostra lettera** (*comun.*) in reply to your letter.

riscossione, *n. f.* collection. // ~ **di dazio** (*fin.*) tollage; ~ **di pedaggio** (*trasp.*) tollage; **alla** ~ (*al momento della riscossione*) upon collection.

riscuotere, *v. t.* **1** to collect, to draw★; (*incassare*) to cash. **2** (*fin.*) (*tasse, tributi, ecc.*) to levy, to impose. // ~ **un credito** (*cred.*) to collect a debt; ~ **un dividendo** (*fin.*) to collect a dividend; ~ **le imposte** (*fin.*) to collect taxes, to gather taxes; ~ **la paga** (*pers.*) to receive one's pay; ~ **un tributo** (*fin.*) to levy a tax; **non riscosso** (*cred.*) uncollected.

riscuotibile, *a.* collectible, collectable, cashable. // **non** ~ (*cred.*) uncollectible, uncashable.

riserva, *n. f.* **1** reserve, store, stock, supply. **2** (*restrizione*) reservation, reserve. **3** (*banca, fin., rag.*) reserve; (*costituita dagli utili indivisi che restano dopo il pagamento dei dividendi*) rest. **4** (*econ.*) (*di capitale*) surplus. **5** (*org. az.*) supply; (*di materie prime, merci, ecc.*) stockpile. **6** (*rag., anche*) fund. **7 riserve,** *pl.* (*fin.*) (*di valuta o di preziosi*) coffers. // ~ **aurea** (*banca, econ., fin.*) gold reserve; ~ **bancaria** bank reserve; **riserve danni, tecniche e riporto premi** (*ass.*) risk, contingency and policy reserves; ~ **di denaro** money reserve; (*rag.*) spare cash; **la** ~ **d'un diritto** (*leg.*) the reservation of a right; ~ **di domanda** (*econ.*) backlog of demand; **una** ~ **di legge** (*leg.*) a saving clause; ~ **di previdenza** (*rag.*) contingency reserve; **riserve disponibili** (*fin., rag.*) free reserves, revenue reserves; **riserve e accantonamenti esenti da imposta** (*fin.*) tax-exempt general and special reserves; **riserve in aumento** (*fin., rag.*) growing reserves; ~ **iniziale** (*ass.*) initial reserve; ~ **legale** (*ass., leg., rag.*) legal reserve; ~ **matematica** (*ass.*) life annuity fund; ~ **metallica** (*banca*) metallic reserve, bullion reserve; **riserve monetarie** (*fin.*) monetary reserves; (*d'una persona o d'un'associazione*) exchequer; ~ **netta finale** (*alla chiusura dell'esercizio*) (*ass.*) terminal reserve; ~ **obbligatoria** (*fin.*) compulsory reserve; ~ **occulta** (*rag.*) secret reserve, hidden reserve, inner reserve; ~ **per obsolescenza** (*d'attività fisse*) (*rag.*) reserve for obsolescence; ~ **per sinistri** (*ass.*) loss reserve; ~ **per sinistri da liquidare** (*ass.*) claims reserve; ~ **primaria** (*banca*) primary reserve; ~ **statutaria** (*rag.*) statutory reserve, capital reserve, general reserve; ~ **straordinaria** (*rag.*) extraordinary reserve, surplus reserve; ~ **straordinaria disponibile** (*econ., rag.*) free capital reserve; ~ **tecnica** (*ass.*) actuarial reserve; **riserve ufficiali nette** (*fin.*) official net reserves; **con riserve** (*leg.*) with prejudice; (*d'accettazione cambiaria, ecc.*) qualified (*attr.*); «**con** ~ **di tutti i diritti**» (*leg.*) «all rights reserved»; **con tutte le (dovute) riserve** with all (due) reserves; **in** ~ in hand; **senza alcuna** ~ without reserve, without reservation; **senza riserve** (*leg.*) without prejudice; unconditional (*a.*).

riservare, *v. t.* **1** to reserve, to keep★. **2** (*prenotare*) to book.

riservarsi, *v. rifl.* to reserve (oneself).

risma, *n. f.* (*giorn., pubbl.*) (*unità di misura di fogli di carta*) ream; (*di 516 fogli*) printer's ream; (*di 500 fogli*) long ream; (*di 480 fogli*) short ream.

risolubile, *a.* **1** solvable, resolvable. **2** (*leg.*) defeasible, imperfect.

risolubilità, *n. f. inv.* (*leg.*) defeasibility.

risolutivo, *a.* (*leg.*) resolutive, resolutory.

risolutorio, *a.* (*leg.*) resolutive, resolutory.

risoluzione, *n. f.* **1** (*decisione*) resolution, decision. **2** (*leg.*) (*di un contratto*) cancellation, dissolution, determination, resolution, defeasance, annulment. **3** (*mat.*) resolution, solution, working-out.

risolvere, *v. t.* **1** to resolve, to solve; (*un problema, anche*) to work out, to figure out. **2** (*decidere*) to decide, to resolve. **3** (*comporre*) to settle, to decide, to define. **4** (*leg.*) (*rescindere*) to cancel, to rescind, to dissolve, to determine, to annul. // ~ (*una questione*) **con un compromesso** to compromise; ~ **un contratto** (*leg.*) to annul a contract, to determine a contract, to rescind a contract; (*riducendone i termini*) to cut back a contract; ~ **un problema** (*anche mat.*) to solve a problem; ~ **un problema finanziario** to work out a financial problem.

risolvibile, *a.* **1** solvable, resolvable. **2** (*leg.*) cancellable, annullable.

risorsa, *n. f.* **1** resource; means (*pl.*). **2** (*espediente*) resource, expedient, resort, device. **3 risorse,** *pl.* (*econ., fin.*) resources; (*forze*) strengths. // **risorse finanziarie** (*fin.*) financial resources, moneyed resources; pocket book, pocket (*fam.*); **risorse monetarie a breve** (*fin.*) short-term funds; **risorse naturali** (*econ.*) natural resources; **risorse potenziali** potential resources, potentials; potentiality, potential (*sing.*).

risparmiare, *v. t.* **1** (*mettere in serbo*) to save, to save up, to lay★ aside, to lay★ by, to put★ away, to put★ by; to slice (*fam.*); (*economizzare*) to economize. **2** (*non infliggere*) to spare. **3** (*non distruggere, salvare*) to spare. // **che fa ~** economical; saving (*nei composti*: labour-saving, *ecc.*); **che fa ~ tempo** time-saving.

risparmiatore, *n. m.* **1** saver. **2** (*banca, fin.*) saver, investor.

risparmio, *n. m.* **1** (*il risparmiare*) saving, retrenchment; (*economia*) thrift, economization. **2** (*denaro risparmiato*) savings, economies (*pl.*); ace in the hole (*slang USA*). // **~ a breve termine** (*econ.*) short-term saving; **risparmi cautelativi** (*econ.*) savings motivated by caution; **~ di tempo** (*org. az.*) time saving; **~ familiare** (*econ.*) household saving; **~ forzato** (*econ.*) forced saving, involuntary saving; private savings; **~ negativo** (*econ., fin.*) dissaving.

rispedire, *v. t.* **1** (*comun., trasp.*) (*spedire di nuovo*) to send★ again, to forward again, to reforward, to ship again, to reship, to reconvey. **2** (*comun., trasp.*) (*spedire indietro*) to send★ back, to return. // **~** (*una lettera*) **a un nuovo indirizzo** (*comun.*) to redirect.

rispedizione, *n. f.* **1** (*comun., trasp.*) (*nuova spedizione*) reforwarding, reshipment, reshipping, reconveyance. **2** (*comun., trasp.*) (*spedizione indietro*) sending back, return.

rispettare, *v. t.* **1** to respect. **2** (*osservare*) to observe, to respect, to comply with. // **~ una clausola** (*leg.*) to observe a clause; **~ le clausole d'un contratto** (*leg.*) to comply with the clauses of an agreement; **~ la legge** (*leg.*) to respect the law, to keep the law; **~ le previsioni** to fulfil expectations; **non ~ un accordo** (*leg.*) to break an agreement.

rispondere, *v. t.* **1** to answer, to reply. **2** (*corrispondere*) to answer; to correspond (to); (*soddisfare*) to satisfy. **3** (*farsi garante*) to answer (for), to vouch (for). // **~ a una chiamata telefonica** (*comun.*) to answer a telephone call; **~ a una lettera** to answer a letter; **~ affermativamente** to answer in the affirmative; **~ ai premi** (*Borsa*) to declare an option; **~ di qc.** to answer for st.; **~ di qc. a q.** to answer to sb. for st., to be answerable to sb. for st.; **~ per iscritto** (*comun.*) to reply in writing.

risposta, *n. f.* **1** answer, reply, response; (*replica*) replication, rejoinder. **2** (*Borsa*) (*ai premi*) declaration. // **la ~ a una domanda d'assunzione** (*comun.*) a reply to a letter of application; **una ~ favorevole** a favourable answer; **una ~ negativa** a negative answer, an unfavourable answer, an answer in the negative; **~ pagata** (*comun.*) prepaid reply; **~ premi** (*Borsa*) declaration of option, options settlement; «**con ~ pagata**» (*comun.*) «answer prepaid»; **in ~ alla vostra lettera del 10 giugno** in answer to your letter of June 10th; **senza ~** unanswered (*a.*).

ristagnare, *v. i.* **1** (*anche fig.*) to stagnate. **2** (*fig.*) to slacken, to lag.

ristagno, *n. m.* **1** (*anche fig.*) stagnation. **2** (*fig.*) standstill, slackness. **3** (*econ.*) recession. // **in ~** (*anche fig.*) stagnant (*a.*); **lieve ~** (*econ.*) mild recession.

ristorno, *n. m.* **1** rebound. **2** (*fin.*) drawback. // **ristorni d'imposta** (*fin.*) tax drawbacks.

risultanza, *n. f.* result.

risultare, *v. i.* **1** to result, to turn out, to come★ out, to ensue; (*apparire*) to appear. **2** (*impers.: essere noto*) to hear★, to know★, to understand★ (*verbi pers.*).

risultato, *n. m.* **1** result; (*prodotto*) product, outcome. **2** (*mat.*) result. // **risultati d'esercizio** (*rag.*) trading results; **~ economico di fine esercizio** (*rag.*) year-end profit and loss picture; **risultati lordi di gestione** (*fin., rag.*) gross operating profits; **senza alcun ~** without result.

ritardare, *v. t.* to delay, to set★ back. *v. i.* **1** (*indugiare ad arrivare*) to be delayed, to retard. **2** (*essere in ritardo*) to be late.

ritardatario, *n. m.* late-comer.

ritardo, *n. m.* **1** delay, retardation. **2** (*comm. est., fin.*) (*di pagamento*) lag. **3** (*leg.*) (*morosità*) laches. **4** (*org. az.*) delay. **5** (*trasp.*) (*di nave, carro merci, ecc.*) demurrage. **6** (*trasp. mar.*) detention. // **~ evitabile** (*org. az.*) avoidable delay; **il ~ nell'esecuzione d'un ordine** (*org. az.*) the delay in the execution of an order; **essere in ~** to be late, to be behind time, to fall behind, to be tardy; (*cred.*) (*con un pagamento*) to get into arrears, to be behindhand; (*org. az.*) (*col lavoro, con le consegne, ecc.*) to be behind schedule; (*trasp.*) (*di treno, nave, ecc.*) to be overdue, to be past-due; **senza ~** (*market., trasp.*) without delay.

ritenuta, *n. f.* (*trattenuta*) deduction, stoppage. // **~ alla fonte** (*fin.*) (*il ritenere*) taxation at source, withholding; pay-as-you-earn (*P.A.Y.E.*) (*in G.B.*) (*l'ammontare ritenuto*) withholding tax; **~ d'acconto** (*fin.*) capital gains tax, withholding tax, deduction; **~ sulla paga** (*sind.*) deferred pay.

ritirare, *v. t.* **1** to withdraw★, to take★ back, to draw★ back; (*anche, ritrattare*) to retract. **2** (*riscuotere*) to draw★; (*farsi consegnare*) to collect. **3** (*banca*) (*denaro*) to withdraw★. **4**

(*fin.*) (*circolante e sim.*) to retire, to withdraw★. 5 (*market.*) (*merce e sim.*) to retire, to collect. // ~ **un'accusa** (*leg.*) to withdraw a charge; ~ **una cambiale** (*banca, cred.*) to take up a bill, to clear a bill; ~ **una denuncia** (*leg.*) to withdraw a complaint; ~ **merci dalla dogana** (*dog.*) to remove goods from the customs; ~ **oggetti dati in pegno** (*leg.*) to redeem pledged goods; ~ **titoli** (*fin.*) to retire stocks, to take delivery of securities.

ritirarsi, *v. rifl.* **1** to retire, to recede, to withdraw★; (*da un impegno, ecc.*) to declare off. **2** (*leg.*) (*di tribunale*) to adjourn. // ~ **da un affare** to back out of a bargain; ~ **dagli affari** to retire from business, to retire; to put up the shutters (*fam.*).

ritiro, *n. m.* withdrawal, withdrawing, retirement, retiring. // ~ **(di) effetti** (*banca*) payment of bills; **il** ~ **d'una licenza** (*leg.*) the revocation of a license; **il** ~ **d'una patente** (*leg.*) the cancellation of a licence; **il** ~ **d'un socio** (*da una società*) (*fin.*) the withdrawal of a partner; ~ **sotto cauzione** (*dog.*) removal under bond.

ritoccare, *v. t.* **1** (*fare correzioni*) to retouch, to touch up. **2** (*fin., market., trasp.*) (*prezzi, tariffe, ecc.*) to readjust, to revise.

ritocco, *n. m.* **1** retouch, retouching, touch-up. **2** (*fin., market., trasp.*) (*di prezzi, tariffe, ecc.*) readjustment, revision. // **ritocchi dell'ultimo minuto** (*giorn.*) stop-press corrections.

ritornare, *v. i.* to return; (*andare indietro*) to go★ back; (*venire indietro*) to come★ back. *v. t.* (*restituire*) to return, to give★ back. // « ~ **al mittente** » (*comun.*) « return to sender »; ~ **di moda** to become fashionable again.

ritorno, *n. m.* return. // ~ **in auge** come-back; ~ **in vigore** (*leg.*) (*di leggi, ecc.*) revival; **di** ~ (*trasp.*) inward (*attr.*); (*trasp. mar.*) homeward (*attr.*).

ritorsione, *n. f.* **1** reprisal, retaliation. **2** (*leg.*) retaliation; (*d'una accusa*) retort. // ~ **doganale** (*dog.*) countervailing duty; **per** ~ by way of retaliation.

riunione, *n. f.* **1** (*adunanza*) assembly, meeting, gathering, rally. **2** (*leg.*) session; (*di azioni giudiziarie*) consolidation. **3** (*org. az.*) conference. // ~ **al vertice** (*amm.*) summit; ~ **costitutiva** (*fin., org. az.*) constituent meeting; ~ **del consiglio d'amministrazione** (*fin., org. az.*) meeting of the board (of directors), directors' meeting; **una** ~ **non ufficiale** (*org. az.*) an informal meeting; ~ **rinviata** adjourned meeting; **riunioni ristrette** (*org. az.*) in-house meetings; **essere in** ~ (*org. az.*) to be in conference.

rivalersi, *v. rifl.* **1** (*rifarsi d'un danno o d'una perdita*) to make★ up for (a damage, a loss); to recoup. **2** (*leg.*) to retaliate. // ~ **su q.** (*spiccando una tratta*) (*cred.*) to value on sb.; ~ **su un trasgressore** (*leg.*) to retaliate against a transgressor.

rivalsa, *n. f.* **1** (*cred., leg.*) redraft. **2** (*leg.*) retaliation. // **senza** ~ (*cred.*) without recourse.

rivalutare, *v. t.* **1** (*fin., rag.*) (*valutare di più*) to revalue, to write★ up; (*una moneta, ecc.*) to revaluate, to revalorize. **2** (*rag.*) to appreciate, to appraise again, to revalorize, to revalue, to re-estimate. // ~ **le attività di bilancio** (*rag.*) to revalorize the assets on a balance sheet; ~ **una moneta** (*fin.*) to revalorize a currency; ~ **gli stabili** (*rag.*) to revalue the premises.

rivalutazione, *n. f.* **1** (*fin., rag.*) (*elevazione di valore*) revaluation, write-up, revalorization. **2** (*rag.*) appreciation, reappraisal, revalorization, re-estimation. // **la** ~ **del macchinario** (*rag.*) the write-up of machinery; **la** ~ **della lira sul dollaro** (*fin.*) the revaluation of the lira in terms of the dollar; **la** ~ **d'una proprietà** (*fin.*) the revaluation of a property; ~ **monetaria** (*econ.*) currency appreciation.

rivendere, *v. t.* **1** (*market.*) (*vendere di nuovo*) to resell★, to sell★ again. **2** (*market.*) (*vendere ciò che s'era acquistato*) to resell★. **3** (*market.*) (*vendere al minuto*) to retail.

rivendicazione, *n. f.* (*leg.*) claim, claiming. // **rivendicazioni inflazionistiche** (*d'aumenti salariali*) (*econ., sind.*) inflationary claims; ~ **salariale** (*sind.*) wage claim; **rivendicazioni sindacali** (*sind.*) demands of the trade unions.

rivendita, *n. f.* **1** (*market.*) (*il rivendere*) resale, reselling. **2** (*market.*) (*negozio in cui si rivende*) retail shop.

rivenditore, *n. m.* **1** (*market.*) (*chi rivende*) reseller. **2** (*market.*) (*venditore al minuto*) retailer. // **rivenditori autorizzati** (*market.*) authorized dealers; ~ **specializzato** (*market.*) specialty dealer.

riversibile, *a. V.* **reversibile.**

riversione, *n. f. V.* **reversione.**

rivolgere, *v. t.* (*indirizzare*) to address. // ~ **la parola a q.** to address sb.

rivolgersi, *v. rifl.* **1** (*volgersi a q. o qc.*) to turn; (*indirizzarsi*) to address (sb.). **2** (*ricorrere*) to apply, to refer. // ~ **a** (*q.*) to address (sb.), to appeal to (sb.), to make an appeal to (sb.), to contact (sb.); « ~ **al traente** » (*banca, cred.*) (*formula con la quale una banca rifiuta il pagamento d'un assegno scoperto*) « refer to drawer » (*R/D*).

rogare, *v. t.* (*leg.*) (*di notaio*) to draw★ up.

rogatoria, *n. f.* (*leg.*) rogatory letter; letters

rogatory (*pl.*).

rogito, *n. m.* (*leg.*) (notarial) deed. // **un ~ notarile** (*leg.*) a deed attested by a notary.

rompere, *v. t.* (*anche fig.*) to break★. // **~ un contratto** (*leg.*) to break an agreement, to break a contract; **~ una promessa** to break a promise.

rosso, *a.* e *n. m.* red. // **essere «in ~»** (*banca, cred., fig.*) to be in the red.

rotazione, *n. f.* **1** rotation, turn. **2** (*pers.*) (*delle cariche*) rotation. // **~ agraria** (*econ.*) rotation; **la ~ dei raccolti** (*econ.*) the shift of crops; **la ~ delle colture** (*econ.*) the succession of crops; **~ delle giacenze** (*org. az.*) turnover; **~ delle mansioni** (*org. az.*) job rotation; **~ delle scorte** (*org. az.*) stock turnover.

rotta, *n. f.* (*trasp. aer., trasp. mar.*) course, route. // **~ aerea** (*trasp. aer.*) skyway; **~ atlantica** (*trasp. mar.*) ocean lane; **~ commerciale** (*trasp. mar.*) trade route; **~ navale** (*trasp. mar.*) sea road; **~ oceanica** (*trasp. mar.*) seaway; **~ ordinaria** (*trasp. mar.*) customary route; **fare ~ per** (*trasp. mar.*) to sail to, to make for, to head for; **in ~ per** (*trasp. mar.*) outbound for, sailing to, heading for.

rottura, *n. f.* **1** breaking, breakage. **2** (*fig.*) break, breaking off, breakdown. **3** (*leg.*) breach. // **~ di contratto** (*leg.*) breach of contract; **~ di promessa** (*leg.*) breach of promise.

routine, *n. f.* routine.

rubrica, *n. f.* **1** (*quaderno*) index-book; (*per indirizzi*) address-book. **2** (*giorn.*) column, section.

rullo, *n. m.* **1** roller, roll. **2** (*di attr. uff.*) (*di macchina da scrivere*) cylinder, platen.

ruolo, *n. m.* **1** roll, list. **2** (*leg.*) (*di cause, ecc.*) roll. **3** (*trasp. mar.*) bill. // **un ~ calmieratore dei prezzi** (*market.*) a price-calming factor; **~ dei censi** (*fin.*) rent-roll; **~ dei contribuenti** (*fin.*) tax roll, tax book, tax list; **~ delle cause da discutere** (*leg.*) trial list; **~ delle imposte** (*fin.*) assessment book, tax roll; **il ~ dell'equipaggio** (*trasp. aer., trasp. mar.*) the muster roll, the list of the crew, the crew list; **~ d'anzianità** (*amm., pers.*) seniority list; **essere di ~** (*pers.*) to be on the permanent staff, to be on the regular staff, to be in the employee roll; **passare in ~** (*pers.*) to be put on the employee roll.

S

sacca, *n. f.* (*econ., fig.*) pocket. // **sacche di sottosviluppo** pockets of underdevelopment.

sacchetto, *n. m.* (*market.*) (small) sack, (small) bag. // ~ **di carta** (*market.*) paper-bag, sack.

sacco, *n. m.* **1** sack, bag. **2** (*fam.: grande quantità*) sackful, lot, lots, heap. **3** (*market.*) (*misura per aridi*) sack. // **un** ~ **di farina** a sack of flour; **un** ~ **di soldi** a lot of money; a pretty penny (*fam.*); **sacchi di tela** (*market.*) cloth bags; ~ **postale** (*comun.*) post-bag, mail-bag, mail.

saggiare, *v. t.* to test, to try; (*metalli preziosi, ecc.*) to assay. // ~ **la qualità di** (*merci, ecc.*) (*market.*) to sample.

saggiatore, *n. m.* tester, trier; (*di metalli preziosi, ecc.*) assayer.

saggiatura, *n. f.* test, testing, trial, trying; (*di metalli preziosi, ecc.*) assay, assaying.

saggio, *n. m.* **1** (*operazione sperimentale*) test, trial, assay. **2** (*fin.*) (*tasso*) rate. **3** (*market.*) (*esemplare, campione*) specimen, sample, assay. // **il** ~ **di crescita del prodotto nazionale lordo** (*econ.*) the rate of increase in the gross national product; **saggi di riporto valutario** (*fin.*) swap rates; **il** ~ **di sconto** (*fin.*) the rate of discount; **il** ~ **di svalutazione** (*econ.*) the rate of depreciation, the devaluation rate; **in** ~ (*market.*) by way of trial; specimen (*a. attr.*).

sala, *n. f.* **1** hall, room. **2** (*tur.*) (*d'albergo, ecc.*) saloon. // ~ **(degli) attrezzi** (*org. az.*) tool-room; ~ (*adibita alla mostra*) **dei campioni** (*market., pubbl.*) sample room; ~ **del consiglio** council hall; ~ **(delle) contrattazioni** (*Borsa*) floor; pit (*USA*); ~ **(delle) vendite** (*org. az.*) sale room; ~ **delle vendite all'asta** auction room; ~ **d'aspetto** (*anche trasp. ferr.*) waiting room; ~ **d'attesa** (*anche trasp. ferr.*) waiting room; ~ **d'esposizione** (*market., pubbl.*) show-room; ~ **di montaggio** (*org. az.*) assembly hall; ~ **di mostra** (*delle merci*) (*market.*) wareroom; ~ **di prima classe** (*trasp. mar.*) saloon; ~ **di riunione** assembly room, conference room; (*d'associazioni corporativistiche*) guild-hall; ~ **macchine** (*trasp. mar.*) engine-room; ~ **partenze** (*trasp. aer.*) departure lounge.

salariale, *a.* (*pers.*) of wages; wage, pay (*attr.*).

salariare, *v. t.* (*pers.*) to pay★ wages to, to put★ upon wages; (*stipendiare*) to pay★ a salary to.

salariato, *n. m.* **1** (*pers.*) wage-earner, wage-worker. **2** (*pers., collett.*) wage-earners.

salario, *n. m.* (*econ., pers.*) wage (*generalm. al pl.*); packet, hire; earnings (*pl.*); (*paga*) pay; paycheck (*USA*). // ~ **a cottimo** (*pers.*) piece wage, task-wage, incentive wage; ~ **da incentivo** (*pers.*) merit pay; **salari alti** (*pers.*) high wages; ~ **annuo** (*pers.*) annual wage, yearly wage; ~ **base** (*pers.*) basic rate; **salari bassi** (*pers.*) low wages; **salari da fame** (*pers.*) starvation wages; **salari d'imposizione sindacale** (*sind.*) trade-union enforced wages; **salari e condizioni di lavoro** (*pers., sind.*) wages and terms of employment; ~ **effettivo** (*considerando il potere d'acquisto della moneta*) (*pers.*) real wages; **salari elevati** (*pers.*) high wages; **salari fissi** (*pers.*) set wages; ~ **in arretrato** (*pers.*) arrears of wages; ~ **massimo** (*pers.*) maximum wage; ~ **minimo** (*pers.*) minimum wage; ~ **netto** (*pers.*) take-home wages, take-home pay; **salari reali** (*pers.*) real wages; **un** ~ **sufficiente per vivere** (*pers.*) a living wage; ~ **teorico** (*pers.*) nominal wage; **basato sul** ~ (*di pensione, ecc.*) earnings-related.

salasso fiscale, *locuz. n.* (*econ., fin.*) (*dovuto alla progressività delle aliquote e all'inflazione*) fiscal drag.

saldare, *v. t.* (*cred.*) (*un debito*) to settle, to balance, to square, to sink★, to pay★, to pay★ up, to lift; (*concordando un pagamento inferiore*) to compound; (*un creditore, ecc.*) to pay★ off. // ~ **i conti con q.** (*anche fig.*) to square the accounts with sb.; to fix sb. (*USA*); ~ **un conto** (*cred.*) to settle an account, to balance an account; ~ **il conto** (*di un albergo*) **e andarsene** (*tur.*) to check out; ~ **un debito** (*cred.*) to settle a debt, to settle; ~ **la rimanenza** (*cred.*) to pay the balance.

saldato, *a.* (*cred.*) settled in full, settled,

paid. // **non** ~ (*cred.*) unsettled, undischarged, unpaid.

saldo, *n. m.* 1 (*cred.*) settlement, balance, payment in full, full payment. 2 (*market.*) (*liquidazione*) sale. // ~ **a conto nuovo** (*cred.*) balance carried forward, balance (carried forward) to next account, «account rendered»; ~ **a credito** (*rag.*) credit balance; ~ **a debito** (*rag.*) debit balance; ~ **a riportarsi** (*rag.*) balance carried forward (*o* down), pick-up; ~ **attivo** (*rag.*) credit balance, surplus balance, surplus; **un ~ attivo della bilancia dei pagamenti correnti** (*econ.*) a surplus on current account; ~ **attivo fluttuante** (*fin.*) floating balance; ~ **«avere»** (*rag.*) credit balance; ~ **creditore** (*rag.*) credit balance; **«~ (da effettuare) in seguito»** «balance can remain»; ~ **«dare»** (*rag.*) debit balance; ~ **debitore** (*rag.*) debit balance, balance due; (*d'un conto corrente*) voucher payable; ~ **degli scambi** (*econ., fin.*) balance of trade; ~ **degli utili riportato a nuovo sull'esercizio seguente** (*rag.*) balance of profits carried forward to next account; ~ **dell'esercizio precedente** (*rag.*) balance (brought forward) from last account; ~ **d'apertura** (*rag.*) beginning balance; ~ **di cassa** (*rag.*) cash balance, balance in (*o* on) hand; ~ **di chiusura** (*rag.*) inventory balance; **il ~ d'un conto** (*rag.*) the balance of an account; **saldi di mastro** (*rag.*) ledger balances; ~ **in banca** bank balance, balance at (*o* in) bank; ~ **in contanti** (*rag.*) balance in cash; ~ **iniziale,** *V.* ~ **d'apertura;** ~ **liquidazione titoli** (*banca*) balance on purchase or sale of securities at settlement date; ~ **parziale** (*rag.*) running balance; ~ **passivo** (*fin., rag.*) debit balance, deficit, shortfall, rest; gap; **il ~ precedente** (*rag.*) the previous balance; ~ **prestiti a medio termine** (*fin.*) balance medium-term loans; ~ **rettificato** (*rag.*) adjusted balance; ~ **riportato** (*rag.*) balance brought forward (*o* down); ~ **riportato dall'esercizio precedente** (*rag.*) balance (brought forward) from last account; ~ **totale** (*rag.*) total balance; **a ~ completo** (*cred.*) in full settlement, in full balance.

salone, *n. m.* 1 saloon, hall. 2 (*market.*) parlour; parlor (*USA*). // ~ **da esposizione** (*market.*) exhibition hall.

salvataggio, *n. m.* 1 rescue. 2 (*trasp. mar.*) (*della nave, del carico, ecc.*) salvage. // **compenso di ~** (*trasp. mar.*) salvage money, salvage.

salvezza, *n. f.* salvation; (*scampo*) escape; (*sicurezza*) safety. // **àncora di ~** (*trasp. mar.*) sheet-anchor (*anche fig.*); **per la ~ della nave e del carico** (*trasp. mar.*) for the necessity of the ship and cargo.

salvo, *a.* safe; (*sicuro*) secure. *prep.* except, excepted, with the exception of, subject to, save, barring. // ~ **buon fine** (*cred.*) subject to collection, upon collection, if duly paid; ~ **controrordini** contrary orders excepted; ~ **errori e omissioni** errors and omissions excepted; ~ **imprevisti** barring accidents; ~ **incasso** (*cred.*) subject to collection, upon collection; **«~ prova»** (*market.*) on approval; ~ **venduto** (*market.*) subject to sale, subject to goods being unsold; ~ **vista e verifica** (*market.*) on sale or return, on sale and return, on approval.

sanatoria, *n. f.* (*leg.*) deed of indemnity.

sancire, *v. t.* (*leg.*) to sanction; (*confermare*) to confirm; (*decretare*) to decree; (*ratificare*) to ratify. // ~ **un contratto** (*leg.*) to ratify a contract; ~ **una legge** (*leg.*) to sanction a law; ~ **una nomina** (*leg.*) to ratify a nomination.

sanità, *n. f. inv.* health. // ~ **di porto** (*trasp. mar.*) port sanitary authority; **ufficio di ~** Health Office.

sanitario, *a.* sanitary, medical; health (*attr.*). *n. m.* doctor. // **misure sanitarie** sanitary precautions.

sano, *a.* 1 (*che gode buona salute*) healthy. 2 (*senza difetti*) sound. 3 (*leg.*) (*di mente*) sane. // **sana costituzione** sound constitution; ~ **e salvo** safe and sound.

sanzionare, *v. t.* (*leg.*) (*sancire*) to sanction, to vindicate, to verify; (*ratificare*) to ratify, to pass; (*firmando*) to sign.

sanzione, *n. f.* (*leg.*) sanction, vindication, verification; (*ratifica*) ratification. // **sanzioni economiche** (*econ.*) economic sanctions; ~ **penale** (*leg.*) penalty.

saturare, *v. t.* (*anche fig.*) to saturate, to glut. // ~ **il mercato** (*market.*) to saturate the market.

saturazione, *n. f.* (*anche fig.*) saturation, glut. // ~ **petrolifera** (*o* **dei prodotti petroliferi**) oil glut.

sbaglio, *n. m.* mistake; (*errore*) error; (*colpa, fallo*) fault; (*svista*) oversight, slip. // ~ **compensativo** (*rag.*) compensating error; **per ~** by mistake.

sballare, *v. t.* (*market., trasp.*) to unpack.

sballatura, *n. f.* (*market., trasp.*) unpacking.

sbarcare, *v. t.* (*trasp. aer., trasp. mar.*) (*passeggeri, merci, ecc.*) to disembark, to land, to set★ ashore; (*merci*) to unship, to unload, to deliver. *v. i.* (*trasp. aer., trasp. mar.*) to disembark, to land, to go★ ashore. // ~ **il carico** (*trasp. aer., trasp. mar.*) to land the cargo; ~ **il**

lunario to make both ends meet; ~ **merci** (*trasp. mar.*) to put goods ashore; ~ **passeggeri e scaricare merce** (*trasp. aer., trasp. mar.*) to land passengers and goods.

sbarco, *n. m.* (*trasp. aer., trasp. mar.*) (*di passeggeri, merci, ecc.*) disembarkation, disembarkment, disembarking, landing; (*di merci*) unloading.

sbarra, *n. f.* **1** bar. **2** (*leg.*) bar. **3** (*trasp. mar.*) (*barra del timone*) tiller. // ~ **a bilico** (*trasp. ferr.*) (*di passaggio a livello*) bascule barrier; ~ **spaziatrice** (*d'attr. uff.*) (*di macchina da scrivere*) space bar; **presentarsi alla** ~ (*leg.*) to appear before the Court.

sbarrare, *v. t.* **1** (*anche fig.*) to bar; (*ostruire*) to obstruct, to block. **2** (*banca*) to cross. // ~ **un assegno bancario** (*banca*) to cross a cheque; ~ (*un assegno*) **con sbarratura semplice** (*banca*) to cross generally.

sbarratura, *n. f.* (*banca*) crossing. // ~ **generale** (*banca, cred.*) general crossing; ~ **particolare** (*banca, cred.*) special crossing.

sbilanciare, *v. t.* to unbalance, to overbalance. // ~ **il (bilancio) preventivo** (*rag.*) to overbalance the cash budget.

sbilanciato, *a.* unbalanced.

sbilancio, *n. m.* **1** unbalance, lack of balance. **2** (*econ.*) imbalance. **3** (*fin., rag.*) (*deficit*) deficit; (*eccesso*) excess; (*perdita*) loss; (*somma iscritta in bilancio per pareggiare il dare e l'avere*) balance.

sbloccare, *v. t.* **1** (*anche fig.*) to release. **2** (*cred., fin.*) (*prezzi, fondi, ecc.*) to unfreeze*.

sblocco, *n. m.* **1** (*anche fig.*) release. **2** (*cred., fin.*) (*di prezzi, fondi, ecc.*) unfreezing.

sbocco, *n. m.* **1** (*via d'uscita*) outlet, way out, exit. **2** (*comm.*) opening, outlet. // ~ **commerciale** (*econ.*) market; **sbocchi di mercato** (*econ., market.*) market outlets; ~ **di vendita** (*market.*) sales outlet.

sborsare, *v. t.* **1** to disburse; (*pagare*) to pay* out; (*spendere*) to spend*. **2** (*econ., rag.*) to outlay*.

sborso, *n. m.* **1** (*lo sborsare*) disbursement, paying out, expenditure. **2** (*somma sborsata*) disbursement, money paid out. **3** (*econ., rag.*) (*lo sborsare e la somma sborsata*) outlay.

sbrigare, *v. t.* **1** (*terminare con sollecitudine*) to dispatch, to expedite, to work off. **2** (*risolvere*) to settle, to transact, to arrange. **3** (*market.*) (*ordinazioni, ecc.*) to rush. // ~ **un affare** to transact a bargain; ~ **affari** to dispatch business; to knock off business (*fam.*); ~ **la corrispondenza** to clear off the correspondence, to do the correspondence; ~ **la corrispondenza d'una ditta** to conduct the correspondence of a firm.

scadente, *a.* **1** poor, of poor quality, second-rate. **2** (*market.*) low-class, low-end, low-grade.

scadenza, *n. f.* **1** (*ultima data utile*) deadline. **2** (*termine del tempo convenuto*) expiration, expiry. **3** (*cred.*) maturity, time of payment, due date; (*tempo concesso per il pagamento di cambiali estere secondo le consuetudini locali*) usance. // ~ **del termine utile per comparire davanti al tribunale** (*leg.*) expiration of the time limit for appearance before the Court; ~ **d'un'opzione** (*Borsa*) expiration of an option; **alla** ~ (*cred.*) at (*o* on) maturity; **il giorno precedente la** ~ (*cred.*) the day prior to maturity; **in** ~ (*cred.*) (*di cambiale, ecc.*) mature (*a.*); **in ordine di** ~ (*cred.*) (*di cambiali*) as they fall due; **prima della** ~ (*banca, cred.*) before the expiry, before maturity; **tempo mancante alla** ~ (*cred.*) unexpired time.

scadenzario, *n. m.* (*attr. uff.*) due register, bill-book, tickler. // ~ **delle fatture** (*rag.*) bill diary.

scadere, *v. i.* **1** (*peggiorare*) to fall* off, to worsen, to get* worse. **2** (*finire: del tempo convenuto*) to expire. **3** (*cred.*) to be due, to fall* due, to become* due, to mature. // **lo** ~ **d'una permanenza in carica** (*amm.*) the expiration of a term of office; ~ **di qualità** (*market.*) to go off; ~ **di valore** to decrease in value.

scaduto, *a.* **1** (*di ufficio, carica, ecc.*) expired. **2** (*cred.*) due, past-due, overdue, mature, owing. **3** (*leg.*) stale. // **non ancora** ~ unexpired; (*cred.*) undue, not yet due.

scaffale, *n. m.* (*attr. uff.*) shelf*. // ~ **a muro** (*attr. uff.*) shelf; ~ **da archivio** (*attr. uff.*) filing cupboard.

scafo, *n. m.* (*trasp. mar.*) hull, body.

scaglionare, *v. t.* to stagger.

scala, *n. f.* **1** (*fissa*) staircase, stairway, stair; stairs (*pl.*). **2** (*attrezzo*) ladder. **3** (*geografica, graduata*) scale. **4** (*mat.*) scale. // **la** ~ **dei prezzi** (*market.*) the range of prices; ~ **di colori** (*pubbl.*) colour scale; ~ **di priorità** (*fig.*) scale of priority; ~ **mobile** (*per trasportare persone*) moving staircase, escalator; (*econ.*) (*dei salari, ecc.*) sliding scale, escalator; (*che stabilisce un aggancio fra salari e costo della vita*) cost-of-living wage escalator, system of automatic inflation-linked pay-rises (*non esiste in G.B.*); ~ **mobile dei salari** (*econ., sind.*) sliding wage-scale, wage indexation, automatic wage adjustment (*non esiste in G.B.*).

scalare[1], *a.* (*mat.*) scalar.

scalare², *v. t.* **1** (*abbassare di grado, ordine, ecc.*) to scale down. **2** (*diffalcare*) to deduct. **3** (*cred.*) to pay★ off. // ~ **un debito** (*cred.*) to pay★ off a debt.

scalo, *n. m.* **1** (*trasp. aer.*) landing. **2** (*trasp. mar.*) port of call, place of call, call; (*banchina*) wharf★. // ~ **aereo** (*trasp. aer.*) landing place, landing; ~ **d'alaggio** (*trasp. mar.*) slipway, slip; ~ **d'approdo** (*trasp. mar., USA*) dock; ~ **di costruzione** (*trasp. mar.*) slipway; ways (*pl.*); ~ (*fatto da una nave durante il viaggio*) **di ritorno** (*trasp. mar.*) backward call; ~ **diretto** (*trasp. mar.*) direct call, forward call; ~ **ferroviario** (*trasp. ferr.*) railway-yard, yard; ~ **intermedio** (*trasp. mar.*) indirect call, intermediate port; ~ **merci** (*trasp. ferr.*) goods station; freight depot, freight-yard (*USA*); ~ **per rifornimento di carbone** (*trasp. mar.*) coaling station; ~ **traghetti** (*trasp. mar.*) ferry port; **senza** ~ (*trasp. aer.*) non-stop (*a.* e *avv.*); «**senza scali intermedi**» (*trasp. mar.*) «no calls».

scambiare, *v. t.* **1** to exchange, to change; (*barattare*) to barter. **2** (*spicciolare*) to change.

scambio, *n. m.* **1** exchange, change; (*baratto*) barter, truck. **2** (*trasp. ferr.*) shunt; points (*pl.*); switch (*USA*). **3 scambi,** *pl.* (*econ.*) trade, trading (*sing.*). // ~ **di corrispondenza** (*comun.*) exchange of correspondence; ~ **di merci** exchange of goods; ~ **d'opinioni** exchange of views; **lo** ~ **di valuta fra nazioni** (*econ.*) the interchange of currency between nations; **uno** ~ **equo** a fair exchange, an even exchange; **scambi esteri** (*comm. est.*) external trade; **libero** ~ (*econ.*) free trade.

scambista, *n. m.* **1** (*Borsa*) stockbroker, stock-broker. **2** (*econ.*) free-trader. **3** (*trasp. ferr.*) pointsman★, shunter; switchman★ (*USA*).

scaricamento, *n. m.* **1** discharge, discharging. **2** (*trasp. mar.*) discharge, unloading, breaking the stowage. // **lo** ~ **d'una nave** (*trasp. mar.*) the discharge of a ship.

scaricare, *v. t.* **1** to discharge. **2** (*trasp. aer., trasp. mar.*) to land. **3** (*trasp. mar.*) to discharge, to unload, to unship; (*merce già stivata*) to unstow. *v. i.* (*trasp. mar.*) to unload. // ~ (*merce*) **a un molo** (*trasp. mar.*) to wharf; ~ **un carico** (*trasp. mar.*) to discharge a cargo; ~ **meno di quanto dichiarato nel manifesto** (*trasp. mar.*) to short-land; ~ **una nave** (*trasp. mar.*) to discharge a ship, to unstow a ship; ~ **l'onere della prova** (*leg.*) to shift the burden of proof; ~ **la responsabilità** to shift the responsibility; ~ **la zavorra** (*trasp. mar.*) to discharge ballast, to unballast; **non scaricato** undischarged.

scaricatore, *n. m.* (*pers.*) unloader. // ~ **di porto** (*pers.*) docker, dockhand, stevedore, lumper.

scarico, *a.* **1** (*non carico*) unloaded. **2** (*trasp. mar.*) unloaded; in ballast (*pred.*). *n. m.* **1** (*lo scaricare*) discharge, discharging, unloading. **2** (*leg.*) discharge. **3** (*rag.*) discharge. // ~ **in mare** (*trasp. mar.*) jettison; ~ **senza interruzione** (*trasp. mar.*) continuous discharge.

scartare, *v. t.* **1** (*una cosa incartata*) to unwrap. **2** (*respingere*) to reject, to discard, to scrap; (*mettere da parte*) to put★ aside, to lay★ aside. **3** (*org. az.*) (*macchine, impianti, ecc.*) to supersede. // ~ **un esemplare difettoso** to reject a defective specimen; ~ (*un macchinario*) **perché antiquato** (*org. az.*) to superannuate.

scarto, *n. m.* **1** (*atto d'escludere in una scelta*) discarding, discard. **2** (*cosa scartata*) discarded thing, refuse, trash. **3** (*econ., fin., rag.*) (*margine, differenza*) margin, deviation, range, spread. **4** (*giorn., pubbl.*) (*carta sciupata nel processo di stampa*) spoilage. **5** (*market.*) (*di merce ricevuta da un fornitore*) reject, rejected material. **6** (*org. az.*) (*d'officina*) scrap, waste. // ~ **del giorno** (*Borsa, fin.*) day's spread; ~ **di garanzia** (*Borsa, fin.*) safety margin; **scarti di garanzia nelle operazioni a riporto** (*Borsa, fin.*) safety margins on contango operations; ~ **medio dei prezzi** (*market.*) mean price difference; **di** ~ waste (*attr.*).

scatola, *n. f.* **1** box. **2** (*di latta*) tin; can (*USA*). // ~ **di cartone** cardboard box, carton; ~ **metallica** (*per tè, caffè, tabacco, ecc.*) canister; **a lettere di** ~ in block letters; **comprare qc. a** ~ **chiusa** to buy a pig in a poke; **in** ~ (*market.*) preserved, tinned (*a.*); canned (*a., USA*); **vendere qc. a** ~ **chiusa** to sell a pig in a poke.

scatolame, *n. m.* **1** (*market.*) tins (*pl.*); cans (*pl., USA*). **2** (*market.*) (*commestibili in scatola*) tinned goods (*o* food); canned goods (*o* food) (*USA*).

scatoletta, *n. f.* (*market.*) tin; can (*USA*). // ~ **per cibi conservati** (*market.*) packers' can.

scatto, *n. m.* **1** (*d'un meccanismo*) trigger. **2** (*pers.*) (*di salario, ecc.*) increase. // ~ **di stipendio** (*pers.*) automatic pay increase; ~ **salariale per anzianità** (*pers.*) increase of wages according to age, length of service increase.

scellino, *n. m.* shilling; bob (*fam., inv.*); deaner (*slang ingl.*).

scelta, *n. f.* **1** choice, selection, pick. **2** (*leg.*) (*opzione*) option. // ~ **alternativa** alternative choice; **scelte macroeconomiche** (*econ.*) macroeconomic decisions; **a ~** by choice; optional (*a.*); **a ~ del capitano** (*della nave*) (*trasp. mar.*) at the master's option.

scelto, *a.* selected, select; (*di prima qualità*) first-rate; choice (*attr.*).

scheda, *n. f.* 1 card; (*modulo*) form; (*per votazioni*) ballot-paper, ballot. 2 (*attr. uff.*) file card, card, form. 3 (*elab. elettr.*) card. 4 (*stat.*) card. // **~ con indirizzo** address card; **~ (del) personale** (*pers.*) staff card, employee rating chart; **~ di ciclo di lavorazione** (*org. az.*) route card; **~ di macchina** (*org. az.*) machine-load card; **~ di magazzino** (*org. az.*) stock-card; **~ di posizione** (*pers.*) allocation card; **~ di votazione** (*leg.*) vote, ballot paper, ballot; **~ perforata** (*elab. elettr.*) punched card; **~ posizione** (*org. az.*) bin card.

schedare, *v. t.* to file, to card-catalogue, to calendar.

schedario, *n. m.* (*attr. uff.*) file, card-file, card-holder, card index cabinet, card index. // **~ Generale dei Titoli Azionari** (*fin., leg.*) General Registry of Stocks and Shares; **~ rotante** (*attr. uff.*) rotary file; **~ verticale** (*attr. uff.*) vertical file.

schedato, *a.* (*di documento, ecc.*) on file (*pred.*).

schedatore, *n. m.* (*pers.*) filing clerk, card-compiler.

schedatura, *n. f.* filing.

schema, *n. m.* 1 scheme, outline; (*diagramma*) diagram; (*abbozzo*) draft. 2 (*org. az.*) chart. // **~ d'accordo** (*amm.*) draft agreement; **~ di contratto** (*leg.*) draft contract; **~ di flusso** (*org. az.*) flow chart; (*che evidenzia i difetti riscontrati nella successione delle operazioni*) flow chart; **~ di fusione** (*fin.*) take-over scheme; **~ logico** (*org. az.*) flow chart.

scienza, *n. f.* science. // **~ dell'informazione** information science.

sciogliere, *v. t.* 1 (*disfare un legame; anche fig.*) to loosen, to loose, to let★ loose, to unbind★. 2 (*porre fine a*) to dissolve, to break★ up. 3 (*adempiere*) to fulfil. 4 (*leg.*) (*da un obbligo, ecc.*) to acquit. // **~ l'àncora** (*trasp. mar.*) to weigh anchor; **~ un'assemblea** (*org. az.*) to dismiss an assembly; **~ un contratto** (*leg.*) to dissolve a contract; **~ q. da un obbligo** to acquit sb. from an obligation; **~ un obbligo** (*leg.*) to fulfil an obligation; **~ una seduta** to close a meeting, to break up a meeting; **~ una società** (*di persone*) (*fin.*) to dissolve a partnership; (*di capitali*) (*fin.*) to wind-up a joint-stock company.

scioglimento, *n. m.* 1 (*il disfare un legame; anche fig.*) loosening. 2 (*fine*) dissolution, dissolving, breaking up. 3 (*adempimento*) fulfilment, fulfilling. 4 (*leg.*) (*da un obbligo, ecc.*) acquittal. // **lo ~ d'una società** (*di persone*) (*fin.*) the dissolution of a partnership; (*fin.*) (*di capitali*) the winding-up of a joint-stock company.

sciolto, *a.* 1 loose; (*slegato*) untied, unbound. 2 (*libero*) free, released. 3 (*market.*) (*di merce*) loose; by measure (*pred.*).

scioperante, *n. m.* e *f.* (*sind.*) striker, turnout. // **chi è assunto per sostituire uno ~** (*org. az.*) strike-breaker.

scioperare, *v. i.* (*sind.*) to strike★, to strike★ work, to stick★ out; to walk out, to throw★ down one's tools (*fam.*).

sciopero, *n. m.* (*sind.*) strike, turnout, stick-out, stoppage; walk-out (*fam.*). // **uno ~ a carattere nazionale** (*sind.*) a nationwide strike; **~ «a gatto selvaggio»** (*sind.*) *V.* **~ «selvaggio»**; **~ a oltranza** (*sind.*) strike to the last; **~ a singhiozzo** (*sind.*) intermittent strike, on-off strike; **~ al momento del rinnovo di un contratto collettivo** (*sind.*) end-of-contract strike; **~ bianco** (*sind.*) (*applicazione rigida dei regolamenti, con conseguente rallentamento della produzione*) working to rule, slow-down, go-slow; ca'canny strike, stick-out (*USA*); **~ con occupazione** (*della fabbrica, ecc.*) (*sind.*) stay-in strike, stay-in, sit-down strike, sit-down, sit-in; **~ dei consumatori** (*in attesa d'una diminuzione dei prezzi*) (*market.*) buyers' strike; **~ di solidarietà** (*sind.*) sympathetic strike, secondary strike; **~ generale** (*sind.*) general strike; **uno ~ illegale** (*sind.*) an outlaw strike, an illegal strike, a quickie strike; **~ non autorizzato** (*sind., fam.*) walk-out; **uno ~ paralizzante** (*sind.*) a crippling strike; **~ «selvaggio»** (*sind.*) wildcat strike, wildcat, unofficial strike, unofficial stoppage, illegal strike, quickie strike; **~ senza preavviso** (*sind.*) lightning strike; **essere in ~** (*sind.*) to be on strike; **fare uno ~ bianco** (*sind.*) to go slow.

scissione, *n. f.* (*anche fig.*) split, splitting.

scompartimento, *n. m.* 1 compartment, division. 2 (*trasp. ferr.*) compartment. // **~ a due letti** (*trasp. ferr.*) two-berths compartment; **uno ~ di prima classe** (*trasp. ferr.*) a first-class compartment.

scomparto, *n. m.* *V.* **scompartimento.**

scompensare, *v. t.* (*alterare un equilibrio*) to unbalance. // **~ un bilancio** (*econ., rag.*) to unbalance a budget.

scompensato, *a.* unbalanced.

scompenso, *n. m.* unbalance.

scomporre, *v. t.* 1 to decompose; (*disfare*)

to undo★; (*dividere*) to divide, to split★ up. 2 (*giorn., pubbl.*) (*caratteri di stampa*) to distribute. // ~ **in fattori** (*mat.*) to factorize; ~ **un treno** (*trasp. ferr.*) to split up a train.

scompositore, *n. m.* (*giorn., pubbl.*) distributor.

scomposizione, *n. f.* 1 decomposition; (*divisione*) division, splitting up. 2 (*giorn., pubbl.*) distribution of type, distribution. // ~ **del prezzo di costo nei suoi principali elementi** (*market.*) analysis of the cost price into its chief components; ~ (*di grandi gruppi*) **in sottoclassi** (*più agevolmente trattabili*) (*org. az.*) breakdown.

sconfinamento, *n. m.* (*leg.*) trespass, trespassing.

sconfinare, *v. i.* (*leg.*) to trespass.

scontabile, *a.* (*banca, fin.*) discountable.

scontare, *v. t.* 1 (*banca, fin.*) to discount. 2 (*leg.*) (*una condanna*) to serve. 3 (*market.*) (*detrarre da un conto*) to deduct, to take★ off. // ~ **una cambiale** (*banca*) to discount a bill (of exchange); ~ **di nuovo** (*titoli di credito*) (*banca, cred.*) to rediscount; ~ **un effetto** (*banca*) to discount a bill; **farsi ~ una cambiale** (*banca*) to have a bill discounted.

scontista, *n. m.* e *f.* (*fin.*) discount broker, discounter.

sconto, *n. m.* 1 (*banca, fin.*) (*l'operazione*) discount, discounting; (*compenso spettante a chi anticipa denaro*) discount. 2 (*market.*) (*detrazione*) discount, deduction; (*ribasso*) rebate, abatement; (*abbuono*) allowance. // ~ **bancario** (*banca*) bank discount, bankers' discount; ~ **commerciale** (*market.*) trade discount; ~ **del capitale** (*rag.*) direct discount; ~ **delle cambiali** (*banca*) discounting bills of exchange; ~ **di cassa** cash discount; ~ **di crediti derivanti da vendite d'immobili** (*cred.*) discounting of credits from the sale of real estate; ~ **di effetti bancari** (*banca*) discounting of notes; ~ **d'effetti sull'estero** (*banca*) discount of foreign bills; **sconti e anticipazioni** (*rag.*) discounts and advances; « ~ **effetti Italia** » (*banca*) «discount of bills on Italy»; ~ **per (pagamento in) contanti** discount for cash, cash discount; ~ **razionale** (*mat.*) arithmetical discount, true discount; ~ **sottobanco** (*market.*) kickback (*fam.*); ~ **sugli acquisti** (*market.*) discount on purchases; **uno ~ sul premio** (*ass.*) a rebate of premium; ~ **sulle vendite** (*market.*) discount on sales, sales discounts; ~ **supplementare per pagamento anticipato** (*market.*) anticipation rate; (*di negozio, ecc.*) **che pratica forti sconti** (*sui prezzi*) (*market.*) cut-price (*attr.*).

scontrino, *n. m.* 1 ticket, check, coupon. 2 (*market.*) voucher. // ~ **di bagaglio** (*trasp.*) luggage ticket; baggage-check (*USA*); ~ **di cassa** (*market.*) cash voucher; ~ **di deposito** (*trasp. ferr.*) cloak-room ticket; ~ **di vendita** (*market.*) sales ticket; ~ **doganale** (*dog.*) docket.

scoperto, *a.* 1 discovered, found (out); (*detto di ciò che era celato*) disclosed. 2 (*ass.*) (*di rischio*) uncovered. 3 (*banca*) (*di conto*) overdrawn. 4 (*cred.*) (*d'assegno*) uncovered. 5 (*pers.*) (*di posto di lavoro*) vacant. *n. m.* 1 (*banca*) overdraft. 2 (*Borsa*) bear account, bears. // «**scoperto**» (*banca*) «not sufficient funds»; « ~ **con fido** » (*banca*) overdraft, bank overdraft, fluctuating overdraft, overdraft on current account; ~ **di conto** (*banca*) overdraft; (*cred., fin.*) loan account; **allo ~** (*cred.*) (*di credito*) unsecured, uncovered (*a.*); without security, without cover (*locuz. avv.*); (*di correntista*) overdrawn (*a.*); **essere allo ~** (*banca*) to be overdrawn, to be in the red; (*Borsa*) to be caught short.

scopo, *n. m.* 1 (*fine*) aim, end, object, scope, goal; target (*fig.*). 2 (*org. az.*) (*obiettivo*) objective, goal. // ~ **della società** (*leg.*) corporate purpose (*USA*); **a ~ di lucro** with a view to profit; **che non ha scopi di lucro** (*econ.*) non-profit (*a.*).

scorrere, *v. i.* 1 to run★; (*fluire*) to flow★. 2 (*trasp. mar.*) (*del carico*) to shift.

scorrimento, *n. m.* 1 running, flowing. 2 (*trasp. mar.*) (*del carico*) shifting.

scorso, *a.* 1 last; (*passato*) past. 2 (*comm.*) (*nelle lettere*) ultimo (*abbr.* ult.).

scorta, *n. f.* 1 (*org. az.*) supply, store, stock on hand, stock, inventory. 2 (*trasp.*) convoy, convoying, escort. // ~ **di contanti** cash supply; **scorte disponibili** (*econ., org. az.*) visible supply (*sing.*); ~ **insufficiente** (*di merci, materie prime, ecc.*) (*market., org. az.*) understock; **scorte morte** (*econ.*) dead stock; **scorte vive** (*econ.*) live stock, stock; **di ~** (*di ricambio*) spare (*a. attr.*); **sotto ~** (*trasp.*) under convoy.

scortare, *v. t.* (*trasp.*) to convoy, to escort.

scostamento, *n. m.* (*mat., rag.*) variance. // ~ **dalle cifre di bilancio** (*fin., rag.*) budget variance; ~ **dalle cifre iscritte nel budget per quanto riguarda la capacità produttiva** (*rag.*) capacity variance; ~ **dovuto a incapacità organizzativa** (*rag.*) activity variance; ~ **in meno riscontrato fra le cifre iscritte nel budget e quelle del consuntivo** (*rag.*) decrease.

scrittura, *n. f.* 1 (*lo scrivere*) writing; (*stesura per iscritto*) writing. 2 (*leg.*) (*contratto*) contract. 3 (*leg.*) (*atto notarile*) deed. 4 (*rag.*)

(*contabile*) record; (*a partita doppia*) entry. // ~ (*pubblica o privata*) **che ha effetto legale** (*leg.*) deed; **scritture contabili** (*rag.*) book entries, accounts; ~ **d'accreditamento** (*rag.*) crediting entry, credit entry; **scritture d'apertura** (*dell'esercizio*) (*rag.*) starting entries, opening entries; **scritture di chiusura** (*rag.*) year-end closing entries, closing entries; **scritture di fine esercizio** (*rag.*) year-end closing entries, closing entries; ~ **d'ordine** (*rag.*) suspense entry; **le scritture** (*contabili*) **d'una società** (*rag.*) the records of a company; ~ **di storno** (*rag.*) transfer entry; **scritture di verifica** (*rag.*) correcting entries, adjusting entries, adjustments; ~ **inversa** (*rag.*) contra entry; ~ **privata** (*leg.*) private act, private contract, deed under private seal; ~ **rettificativa** (*rag.*) post entry; **una** ~ **sbagliata** (*a partita doppia*) (*rag.*) a wrong entry.

scrivente, *a.* writing. *n. m.* e *f.* (*comun.*) writer.

scrivere, *v. t.* **1** to write★. **2** (*rag.*) (*registrare*) to enter. // ~ **a macchina** to typewrite, to type; ~ **a mano** to handwrite, to write by hand; ~ (*qc.*) **dando i particolari** to itemize; ~ **in maiuscolo** (*giorn.*) to capitalize; ~ **in stampatello** to print; ~ (*a macchina*) **lasciando uno spazio doppio** to double-space; ~ **lettera per lettera** to spell; ~ **una lettera sotto dettatura** to take a letter; ~ **maiuscolo** (*giorn.*) to capitalize; ~ **il proprio nome in un modulo** to fill in one's name; ~ **un numero in lettere** to spell a number; ~ **una partita** (*rag.*) to make an entry; ~ **per esteso** to write out; ~ (*qc.*) **su una cambiale** (*un assegno, ecc.*) to enface.

scrupolo, *n. m.* **1** scruple. **2** (*misura di peso pari a 20 grani o 1,296 grammi*) scruple.

sdaziare, *v. t.* (*dog.*) to pay★ the customs duties on, to clear.

sdaziato, *a.* (*dog.*) cleared, duty-paid. // **non** ~ (*dog.*) uncustomed.

sdebitarsi, *v. rifl.* **1** (*fig.*) (*disobbligarsi con q.*) to pay★ (sb.) back. **2** (*cred.*) (*pagare i debiti*) to pay★ one's debts; to get★ out of the red.

sdoganamento, *n. m.* (*dog.*) clearance through the customs, customs clearance, clearance, clearing.

sdoganare, *v.t.* (*dog.*) to clear through the customs, to clear. // ~ **merci** (*dog., anche*) to take goods out of bond; **da** ~ (*dog.*) (*di merce*) in bond (*pred.*).

sdoganato, *a.* (*dog.*) cleared, duty-paid, ex bond. // **non** ~ (*dog.*) uncleared, uncustomed.

seconda, *n. f.* **1** (*cred., fin.*) (*di cambio*) second of exchange. **2** (*trasp. ferr.*) second class. **3** (*trasp. mar.*) cabin class. // ~ **di cambio** (*cred., fin.*) second of exchange; second via; ~ **di copertina** (*giorn.*) second cover, inside-front cover; **a** ~ **di** according to, in conformity with.

secondo[1], *num. ord.* **1** second. **2** (*per grandezza*) second largest; (*per importanza*) second most important; (*per qualità*) second best. // **seconda classe** (*trasp.*) second class, tourist class; (*trasp. mar.*) cabin class; **seconda copia** duplicate; ~ **semestre** (*fin.*) second half-year, second half; **di seconda categoria** second-class; **di seconda classe** (*trasp.*) second-class; **di seconda mano** (*market.*) second-hand; (*d'indumento*) hand-me-down; **di second'ordine** minor; **di seconda qualità** (*market.*) second-rate, second-class, middling.

secondo[2], *prep.* according to, in conformity with, in compliance with. *avv.* **1** (*secondo i casi*) that depends. **2** (*in secondo luogo*) secondly, second. // ~ **gli accordi precedenti** as previously agreed upon; ~ **noi** in our opinion; ~ **l'uso** according to custom.

sede, *n. f.* **1** seat; (*residenza*) residence; (*centro*) centre; center (*USA*). **2** (*org. az.*) office, seat, home. // ~ **centrale** (*org. az.*) head office; headquarters (*pl., ma spesso col v. al sing.*); ~ **degli affari** (*org. az.*) seat; premises (*pl.*); ~ **di lavoro** (*pers.*) work-place; **la** ~ **d'una società** (*fin.*) the seat of a company; ~ **legale** (*d'una società*) (*fin.*) registered office; ~ **principale** (*org. az.*) head office, home office; headquarters (*pl., ma spesso col v. al sing.*); inhabitancy, home.

segnale, *n. m.* **1** signal. **2** (*trasp.*) marker, signal. // ~ **a distanza** (*trasp. ferr.*) distant block signal, distant signal; ~ **acustico di «linea libera»** (*al telefono*) dial tone; ~ **acustico di «linea occupata»** (*al telefono*) engaged tone; ~ **di marea** (*trasp. mar.*) tide signal; ~ **di pericolo** (*trasp.*) danger signal, distress signal, distress call; ~ **di soccorso via radio** (*trasp. mar.*) radio distress signal; ~ **di stop** (*trasp. aut.*) stop sign; ~ **meteorologico** (*trasp. mar.*) weather signal; ~ **orario** (*comun.*) time signal; ~ **stradale** (*trasp. aut.*) road signal.

segnaprezzo, *n. m.* (*market.*) tag.

segnare, *v. t.* **1** to mark. **2** (*firmare*) to sign. **3** (*notare*) to note (down), to write★ down. // ~ **l'ora d'entrata** (*pers.*) to ring in; ~ **l'ora d'uscita** (*pers.*) to ring out; ~ **il passo** (*anche fig.*) to mark time; ~ **il prezzo su** (*articoli, ecc.*) (*market.*) to price-mark, to price; ~ **una somma a credito (a debito) di q.** (*cred.*) to credit (to debit) sb. with an amount; ~ **sul conto di q.** to charge to sb.'s account.

segnatario, *n. m.* (*leg.*) (*firmatario*) signatory.

segnatasse, *n. m.* (*comun.*) postage-due stamp.

segretaria, *n. f.* (*pers.*) secretary; girl (*fam.*). // ~ **di direzione** (*pers.*) executive secretary; ~ **tuttofare** (*pers.*) girl friday (*fam.*).

segretariato, *n. m.* 1 (*carica o mansioni di segretario*) secretaryship. 2 (*luogo di lavoro d'un segretario*) secretariat. 3 (*insieme di persone e uffici facenti capo a un segretario*) secretariat.

segretario, *n. m.* (*pers.*) secretary; (*d'accoglimento dei visitatori: nelle mostre, fiere, ecc.*) receptionist. // ~ **comunale** (*pers.*) city clerk, town clerk; ~ **del consiglio d'amministrazione** (*org. az., USA*) corporate secretary; ~ **d'azienda** (*org. az., USA*) corporate secretary; ~ **di direzione** (*pers.*) executive secretary; ~ **di redazione** (*giorn.*) staff secretary; ~ **d'ufficio** (*pers., USA*) desk secretary; **un** ~ **efficiente** (*pers.*) an efficient secretary; ~ **generale** secretary-general; ~ **incaricato della corrispondenza** (*pers.*) corresponding secretary; ~ **particolare** (*pers.*) private secretary, confidential clerk; ~ **privato** (*pers.*) private secretary, confidential clerk.

segreteria, *n. f.* 1 (*org. az.*) secretary's office, secretariat, secretariate. 2 (*pers.*) (*mansioni di segretario*) secretariat, secretariate. // ~ **d'accoglimento** (*dei visitatori: nelle mostre, fiere, e sim.*) (*market., pers.*) reception; **di** ~ (*pers.*) secretarial (*a.*).

segreto bancario, *locuz. n.* (*leg.*) banking secrecy.

séguito, *n. m.* 1 (*insieme di fautori, sostenitori, ecc.*) followers (*pl.*); (*favore, consenso*) following. 2 (*serie, successione*) series, succession, sequence. 3 (*continuazione*) continuation; (*d'un'azione, ecc.*) follow-up. // **a** ~ **di** further to, following; **a** ~ **dell'accordo del 10 maggio 1984** further to the agreement of May 10th 1984; **fare** ~ **a qc.** to follow (up) st.; **in** ~ later on, next, afterwards; (*leg.*) hereinafter; **in** ~ **a** further to, following, in consequence of, as a result of; (*a causa di*) owing to.

selettivo, *a.* selective.

selezionare, *v. t.* to select; (*vagliare*) to screen.

selezione, *n. f.* 1 selection. 2 (*pers.*) selection. // ~ **del personale** (*pers.*) personnel selection; ~ **preliminare** (*pers.*) screening.

self-service, *n. m.* 1 (*market.*) (*tecnica di vendita*) self-service. 2 (*market.*) (*negozio in cui ci si serve da sé*) self-service store, self-service shop. // ~ **all'ingrosso** (*market.*) cash and carry.

semestrale, *a.* semestral, semi-yearly, semi-annual, half-yearly, bi-yearly, six-monthly.

semestralmente, *avv.* semestrally, semi-yearly, semi-annually, half-yearly, bi-yearly, six-monthly.

semestre, *n. m.* semester, half-year.

semilavorato, *a.* (*org. az.*) semifinished, semimanufactured, unfinished. *n. m.* 1 (*org. az.*) semifinished product, semimanufactured product, unfinished product. 2 **semilavorati,** *pl.* (*org. az.*) partly-finished goods, goods in process, semimanufactures.

semiufficiale, *a.* semi-official, half-official.

semplificare, *v. t.* to simplify, to make* simple. // ~ **un processo di lavorazione** (*org. az.*) to simplify a manufacturing process.

semplificato, *a.* simplified.

semplificazione, *n. f.* simplification, simplifying. // ~ **produttiva** (*org. az.*) product simplification.

sensale, *n. m.* broker, agent. // ~ **autorizzato** certified broker; ~ **d'assicurazioni marittime** (*ass. mar.*) marine insurance broker; ~ **di carichi** (*trasp. mar.*) loading broker; ~ **di noli** (*trasp. mar.*) freight broker, charter broker; ~ **di passeggeri** (*trasp. mar.*) passage broker; ~ **marittimo** (*trasp. mar.*) ship-broker.

senseria, *n. f.* brokerage, agency.

senso, *n. m.* 1 (*facoltà di percepire sensazioni*) sense, sensibility. 2 (*significato*) sense, meaning, significance. 3 (*direzione*) direction, way. 4 (*leg.*) (*interpretazione, spiegazione*) construction. // **il** ~ **letterale** the literal meaning, the literal sense; **ai sensi della legge** (*leg.*) under the law, according to the law; **ai sensi di** according to, in conformity with; (*leg.*) pursuant to; **ai sensi della decisione del 20 maggio** pursuant to the decision of May 20.

sentenza, *n. f.* (*leg.*) sentence, judgement, judgment, decision, finding, decree. // **una** ~ **definitiva** (*leg.*) a final judgment; **una** ~ **del tribunale** (*leg.*) a sentence of the Court; ~ **d'un arbitro** (*leg.*) award; ~ **di condanna** (*leg.*) condemnation; ~ **d'esecuzione specifica** (*leg.*) decree for specific performance; ~ **d'un giudice** (*leg.*) award; ~ **d'interdizione** (*leg.*) interdictory decree; ~ **di «non luogo a procedere»** (*leg.*) nonsuit judgment; ~ **dichiarativa di fallimento** (*leg.*) adjudication of (*o* in) bankruptcy, adjudication order, bankruptcy adjudication; ~ **esecutiva** (*leg.*) enforceable judgment; ~ **in assenza della parte** (*leg.*) decision by default; **una** ~ **iniqua** (*leg.*) an unfair judgment; ~ **interlocutoria** (*leg.*) interlocutory judgment; ~ **irrevocabile** (*leg.*) irrevocable judgment; ~ **normativa** (*leg.*) normative judgment; **una** ~ **sigillata** (*leg.*)

a sealed verdict.

senza, *prep.* e *cong.* 1 without. 2 (*Borsa*) (*di titoli*) ex. // « ~ **spese** » (*cred.*) « sans frais »; (*trasp.*) « free of charge »; « franco »; ~ **supplementi** (*market.*) no extra.

sequestrabile, *a.* (*leg.*) (*confiscabile*) confiscable, attachable, distrainable, seizable.

sequestrante, *n. m.* e *f.* (*leg.*) sequestrator, confiscator, garnisher.

sequestrare, *v. t.* 1 (*leg.*) to sequestrate, to sequester; (*confiscare*) to confiscate, to attach, to distrain, to seize. 2 (*leg.*) (*q. a scopo di ricatto*) to kidnap. 3 (*trasp. mar.*) (*navi merci*) to embargo. // ~ **i beni di q. per il mancato pagamento dell'affitto** (*leg.*) to distrain upon sb.'s goods for rent; ~ **merce di contrabbando** (*leg.*) to seize contraband goods.

sequestratario, *n. m.* (*leg.*) sequestrator.

sequestratore, *n. m. V.* **sequestrante.**

sequestro, *n. m.* 1 (*leg.*) sequestration; (*confisca*) confiscation, attachment, distraint, distress, seizure. 2 (*leg.*) (*di q. a scopo di ricatto*) kidnapping. 3 (*trasp. mar.*) (*di navi, merci*) embargo. // ~ **conservativo** (*leg.*) conservatory seizure, preventive attachment, attachment; ~ **dei beni del fallito** (*leg.*) distress on the bankrupt's estate; **un** ~ **giudiziario** (*leg.*) a seizure by order of the Court, a judicial attachment; ~ **immobiliare** (*leg.*) attachment of real property.

serie, *n. f. inv.* 1 series*; (*gamma*) range; (*successione*) succession. 2 (*fin.*) (*di monete, ecc.*) series*. 3 (*market.*) (*di prodotti*) line. 4 (*mat.*) series*. // **di** ~ (*market.*) (*di modello, ecc.*) current; **fuori** ~ (*market.*) (*di modello, ecc.*) special, custom-built; **in** ~ in series; (*market.*) (*di produzione*) mass (*a. attr.*); **numero di** ~ serial number.

serpente, *n. m.* snake. // **il** « ~ **nel tunnel** » (*econ., neol.*) the « snake in the tunnel ».

serracarte, *n. m. inv.* (*attr. uff.*) paper-clip.

serrata, *n. f.* (*pers., sind.*) lockout.

serratura, *n. f.* lock. // ~ « **a combinazione** » dial lock; ~ **a prova di scasso** theftproof lock.

servitù, *n. f. inv.* (*leg.*) easement, servitude, right of user, common. // ~ **fondiaria** (*leg.*) easement appurtenant; ~ **negativa** (*leg.*) negative easement, negative servitude; ~ **personale** (*leg.*) personal servitude; ~ **positiva** (*leg.*) positive easement, positive servitude.

servizio, *n. m.* 1 (*atto del servire*) service. 2 (*attività lavorativa prestata*) service, duty. 3 (*prezzo del servizio*) service. 4 (*econ.*) (*serie di prestazioni fornite dallo Stato, dagli enti pubblici, ecc.*) service. 5 (*giorn.*) story, report, article. 6 (*org. az.*) (*reparto*) department. 7 **servizi,** *pl.* (*org. az.*) (*attrezzature*) facilities. // ~ **a bordo** (*trasp. mar.*) service at sea; ~ **a domicilio** (*market.*) door-to-door service; ~ **a navetta** (*trasp. ferr.*) shuttle service; ~ **accessorio** (*fornito da un rivenditore ai suoi clienti*) (*market.*) customer assistance; ~ **acquisti** (*org. az.*) purchase department; ~ **aereo** air service; **servizi bancari** banking services; ~ **Borsa** (*banca*) investment management; ~ **celere** (*trasp.*) accelerated service; **servizi con andata a (veicolo) carico e ritorno a (veicolo) vuoto** (*trasp.*) out-loaded return-empty services; **servizi con andata a (veicolo) vuoto e ritorno a (veicolo) carico** (*trasp.*) out-empty return-loaded services; ~ **dei pacchi postali** (*trasp.*) parcel post; ~ **di consegna per espresso** (*comun., USA*) special-delivery service; ~ (*telefonico*) **d'elaborazione elettronica delle informazioni** (*comun.*) time-sharing; **il** ~ **d'igiene** (*le autorità sanitarie*) the health authorities; ~ **d'informazioni** (*giorn.*) reporting; ~ **di pacchi per via aerea** airmail parcel service; ~ **di porto** (*trasp. mar.*) harbour service; **il** ~ **d'un prestito** (*cred.*) the service of a loan; ~ **di ricupero** (*trasp. mar.*) wrecking; ~ **di rimorchio** (*trasp. aut., trasp. mar.*) towage service; ~ **di rispedizione** (*trasp. ferr.*) delivery outside prescribed boundaries; ~ **di salvataggio** (*trasp. mar.*) salvage service, wrecking; ~ **di spedizione** (*della posta ordinaria*) **per via aerea** (*comun.*) all-up service; ~ **di spedizioni per espresso** (*trasp.*) dispatch; express (*USA*); ~ **di trasporto a domicilio** (*trasp.*) cartage service; ~ **doganale** (*dog.*) customs service; ~ **fatto per sé dal cliente stesso** (*market.*) self-service; ~ **in esclusiva** (*giorn.*) exclusive; ~ **informazioni** (*telefoniche*) (*comun.*) directory enquiry; ~ **informazioni commerciali** credit reporting service, credit-status inquiry service; ~ **locale** (*fra due stazioni*) (*trasp. ferr.*) shuttle service; ~ **noleggio** (*trasp.*) charter service; **servizi non collegati con il processo di distribuzione delle merci** (*market.*) direct services; ~ **notturno** (*pers.*) night shift; ~ **portafoglio-effetti** (*banca*) bills department; ~ **portuale** (*trasp. mar.*) harbour service; **il** ~ **postale** (*comun.*) the mail service, the postal service; (*d'uno Stato*) the mails, the mail; ~ **pubblico** (*econ.*) public utility service; utility (*USA*); **servizi radio** (*comun.*) wireless service; **servizi resi** services rendered; **servizi resi in luogo del canone d'affitto** (*leg.*) rent-service; **servizi sociali** (*econ.*) welfare works; ~ **su navi da carico** (*trasp. mar.*) cargo service; ~ **vendite** (*org. az.*) sales department; **essere al** ~ **di** (*q.*) to serve; **essere di** ~ (*pers.*) to be on duty;

«**escluso il** ~» «service not included»; **fare** ~ (*org. az.*) (*rif. a reparto, ufficio, ecc.*) to be open; (*trasp.*) (*rif. a mezzi di trasporto*) to run; **fuori** ~ (*org. az.*) (*di macchinario, ecc.: fuori uso*) out of order; (*pers.*) off duty; **in** ~ (*pers.*) on duty; **non essere di** ~ (*pers.*) to be off duty.

settimana, *n. f.* 1 week. 2 (*pers.*) (*salario corrispondente a una settimana di lavoro*) week's pay; week's wages (*pl.*). // ~ «**corta**» (*pers., sind.*) five-day week; ~ (*lavorativa*) **di cinque giorni** (*pers., sind.*) five-day week; ~ **interrotta da una festa** broken week; ~ **lavorativa** (*pers.*) working week, work-week, workweek; **la** ~ **prossima** next week; **la** ~ **scorsa** last week, past week; **alla** ~ (*pers.*) (*di retribuzione*) by the week, weekly; **due settimane** fortnight; **due volte la** ~ twice a week, semi-weekly; **ogni** ~ every week, weekly; **ogni due settimane** every two weeks, every other week, fortnightly.

settimanale, *a.* weekly; week (*attr.*). *n. m.* 1 (*giorn.*) weekly newspaper, weekly periodical, newsweekly, weekly, newspaper. 2 (*pers.*) (*paga d'una settimana*) week's pay; week's wages (*pl.*).

settimanalmente, *avv.* 1 weekly, every week, once a week. 2 (*pers.*) (*di retribuzione*) by the week.

settore, *n. m.* 1 sector. 2 (*econ.*) sector, segment; (*campo*) field; (*d'affari*) line. // **il** ~ **degli affari immobiliari** (*fin.*) the real-estate sector; **il** ~ **dei trasporti** (*econ.*) the transport industry, the transport sector; **il** ~ **della distribuzione** (*econ.*) the services sector; the distributors (*pl.*); ~ **d'attività** (*econ.*) business field, line of business; **i settori di** «**punta**» (*econ., market.*) the leading sectors; ~ **economico** (*econ.*) product sector; **il** ~ **edilizio** (*econ.*) the building sector; **il** ~ **monetario** (*fin.*) the monetary field; **il** ~ **privato** (*econ.*) the private sector; ~ **produttivo** (*econ.*) productive sector; ~ **pubblico** (*econ.*) public sector; public services (*pl.*); ~ (*d'una Borsa*) **riservato a una determinata merce** (*fin., USA*) pit; **il** ~ «**terziario**» (*econ.*) the services sector; **settori utilizzatori** (*econ.*) client industries.

settoriale, *a.* sectorial, sectional.

sezionare, *v. t.* to section, to sectionize, to divide into sections.

sezione, *n. f.* 1 (*parte di qc.*) section, part, division; (*segmento*) segment. 2 (*mat.*) section. 3 (*org. az.*) (*ripartizione d'uffici, istituti, ecc.*) department, division. 4 (*USA*) (*unità di misura di superficie pari a un miglio quadrato*) section. // ~ **avarie** (*ass. mar.*) indemnity club; ~ **civile** (*leg.*) civil division; ~ **controstallie** (*trasp. mar.*) demurrage club; ~ **doganale** (*dog.*) customs division; ~ **locale di sindacato** (*sind.*) local union, local; ~ **noli** (*per il rimborso dei noli perduti*) (*ass. mar.*) freight club.

sfittare, *v. t.* (*leg.*) (*rendere sfitto*) to vacate.

sfittato, *a. V.* **sfitto.**

sfitto, *a.* (*leg.*) (*d'appartamento e sim.*) vacant.

sfrattare, *v. t.* (*leg.*) to turn out, to evict, to eject, to dispossess.

sfrattato, *a.* (*leg.*) turned out, evicted, ejected, dispossessed. *n. m.* (*leg.*) evict, evictee.

sfratto, *n. m.* (*leg.*) turning out, eviction, ejectment, dispossession. // ~ **d'un inquilino** (*leg.*) eviction of a tenant; **chi dà lo** ~ (*leg.*) evictor, dispossessor; **dare l'ordine di** ~ (*leg.*) to give notice to quit; **ricevere l'ordine di** ~ (*leg.*) to receive notice to quit.

sfruttamento, *n. m.* (*anche fig.*) exploitation. // **lo** ~ **degli impianti** (*org. az.*) the utilization of plant facilities; ~ **delle classi lavoratrici** (*sind.*) exploitation of the working classes.

sfruttare, *v. t.* 1 (*anche fig.*) to exploit; (*esaurire*) to exhaust. 2 (*econ.*) (*una miniera e sim.*) to work. 3 (*pers.*) (*dipendenti*) to exploit, to sweat. // ~ **un brevetto** (*leg.*) to work a patent; ~ **i lavoratori** to sweat workers; ~ **le risorse naturali** (*econ.*) to exploit natural resources; **non** ~ **adeguatamente** (*econ.*) to underuse.

sfruttatore, *n. m.* exploiter, profiteer.

sgravare, *v. t.* 1 (*alleggerire*) to lighten, to unload. 2 (*fin.*) (*diminuire tributi*) to relieve (of), to exonerate. // ~ **qc. dei diritti doganali** (*dog.*) to cancel the customs duty on st.; ~ **d'un'imposta** (*fin.*) to relieve of a tax.

sgravio, *n. m.* 1 (*alleggerimento*) lightening, unloading. 2 (*fin.*) relief, exoneration, allowance. 3 (*leg.*) discharge. // ~ **fiscale** (*fin.*) tax relief, tax allowance, tax alleviation, tax cut; ~ (*fiscale*) **per sfitto** (*fin.*) relief for vacant property.

sicurtà, *n. f. inv.* 1 (*leg.*) (*mallevadoria*) security, guarantee. 2 (*leg.*) (*garanzia*) guaranty.

«**sidecar**», *n. m.* (*trasp.*) side-car.

siderurgia, *n. f.* (*econ.*) iron-metallurgy.

siderurgico, *a.* (*econ.*) iron and steel (*attr.*). *n. m.* (*pers.*) iron-worker.

sigillare, *v. t.* (*anche leg.*) to seal, to seal up. // ~ **con piombini** (*leg.*) to seal with lead; ~ **una lettera** to seal a letter.

sigillato, *a.* (*anche leg.*) sealed, sealed up.

sigillatura, *n. f.* (*anche leg.*) sealing, sealing up.

sigillo, *n. m.* (*anche leg.*) seal. // ~ **sociale** (*leg.*) corporate seal (*USA*).

signora, *n. f.* (*titolo di rispetto*) lady; Mrs (*abbr. di* mistress, *usato coi nomi propri e/o coi nomi e cognomi*); Ms (*usato coi nomi propri quando non si conosca, o non si voglia mettere in evidenza, lo stato civile*); madam (*al vocativo, senza nome proprio*). // **Gentile** ~ (*introduzione a una lettera*) Dear Madam.

signore, *n. m.* (*titolo di rispetto*) gentleman*; Mr (*abbr. di* mister, *usato coi nomi propri e/o coi nomi e cognomi*); sir (*usato al vocativo, senza nome proprio*). // **Signor Presidente!** Mr President!; **Egregio** ~ (*introduzione a una lettera commerciale*) Dear Sir; **Egregi Signori** Dear Sirs, Sirs; Gentlemen (*USA*); **Signore e Signori!** Ladies and Gentlemen!

signorina, *n. f.* young lady; Miss (*usato coi nomi propri e/o coi nomi e cognomi*); Ms (*usato coi nomi propri quando non si conosca, o non si voglia mettere in evidenza, lo stato civile*); madam (*al vocativo, senza nome proprio*).

silo, *n. m.* (*org. az.*) silo, storage bin. // ~ **meccanizzato** (*org. az.*) mechanized silo.

simbolo, *n. m.* **1** symbol. **2** (*mat.*) notation. // ~ **di successo** (*econ., pubbl.*) status symbol.

simulare, *v. t.* (*anche leg.*) to simulate, to pretend, to counterfeit, to sham.

simulato, *a.* (*anche leg.*) simulated, pretended, counterfeit; mock (*attr.*).

simulatore, *n. m.* (*anche leg.*) simulator, shammer.

simulazione, *n. f.* (*leg.*) simulation, pretence, sham. // ~ **di reato** (*leg.*) simulation of offence.

sinceramente, *avv.* sincerely, truly; (*onestamente*) honestly; (*fedelmente*) faithfully.

sincerarsi, *v. rifl.* to make* sure. // ~ **di qc.** to make sure of st.

sindacabile, *a.* **1** (*fig.*) (*censurabile*) censurable, criticizable. **2** (*fin., leg.*) (*verificabile*) liable to audit, liable to inspection, controllable.

sindacale, *a.* **1** (*di sindaco di città*) mayoral; syndical (*in Italia*). **2** (*fin.*) (*di sindaco di società*) auditorial. **3** (*sind.*) syndical; trade-union, union (*attr.*).

sindacalismo, *n. m.* (*sind.*) syndicalism, trade-unionism, trades-unionism, labour unionism, unionism. // ~ **combattivo** (*sind.*) militant trade-unionism.

sindacalista, *n. m.* e *f.* (*sind.*) syndicalist, trade-unionist, union officer, union representative, labour leader, organizer. // ~ **viaggiante** (*che visita operai e stabilimenti per controllare l'applicazione delle norme previste dai contratti collettivi di lavoro*) (*sind.*) walking delegate.

sindacare, *v. t.* **1** (*fig.*) (*censurare*) to censure, to criticize. **2** (*fin., leg.*) (*rivedere i conti*) to audit, to inspect, to check, to control.

sindacato, *n. m.* **1** (*fin.*) (*associazione*) syndicate, combine, trust, pool; (*di banchieri, finanzieri, ecc.*) syndicate. **2** (*sind.*) trade-union, trades-union, trade guild, labour union, union. // ~ **aperto** (*a tutti, senza discriminazioni di razza, sesso, ecc.*) (*sind.*) open union; ~ **azionario** (*fin.*) voting trust; ~ **che deriva dalla fusione di vari sindacati minori** (*sind.*) amalgamated union; ~ **d'arbitraggio** (*fin.*) arbitrage syndicate; ~ **di Borsa** (*Borsa*) market syndicate; ~ **di categoria** (*sind.*) craft union; ~ **di compratori** (*fin.*) buying syndicate; ~ **di controllo** (*econ., fin.*) controlling syndicate; ~ **d'operai appartenenti a un'intera industria** (*sind.*) vertical labour union; ~ **dipendente dall'impresa** (*sind.*) company union; ~ **giallo** (*sind.*) company union; **sindacati liberi** (*sind.*) independent unions; ~ **locale** (*sind.*) local union; ~ **nazionale** (*sind.*) national union; **sindacati non confederali** (*sind.*) independent unions; ~ **padronale** (*sind.*) employers' association.

sindaco, *n. m.* **1** (*di città*) mayor, town mayor; syndic (*in Italia*). **2** (*fin.*) (*di società*) auditor.

sinecura, *n. f.* (*pers.*) sinecure. // **chi gode d'una** ~ (*pers.*) sinecurist.

«sine die», *locuz. avv.* (*leg.*) without date, sine die.

sinistrabilità, *n. f. V.* **sinistrosità,** *def. 1.*

sinistro, *a.* **1** left, left-hand. **2** (*di cattivo auspicio*) sinister, ominous. *n. m.* (*ass.*) (*incidente*) accident, casualty; (*automobilistico e sim.*) wreckage, wreck. // ~ **marittimo** (*trasp. mar.*) sea accident.

sinistrosità, *n. f.* **1** (*ass.*) liability to accidents. **2** (*ass.*) (*numero d'incidenti*) number of accidents.

sistema, *n. m.* **1** system. **2** (*mat.*) system. **3** (*org. az.*) system; (*di lavorazione*) process. // **un** ~ **a parità adeguabili** (*fin.*) an adjustable peg system; ~ **a tassi di cambio fissi** (*fin.*) fixed exchange-rate system; ~ (*agricolo*) **a tre colture** (*alternate*) (*econ.*) three-field system, three-course system; ~ (*monometallico*) **aureo** (*econ., fin.*) gold standard; ~ **bancario** banking system; **il** ~ **bancario privato** (*fin.*) the private banking system; ~ **capitalistico** (*econ.*) capitalistic system; ~ **concorrenziale** (*econ.*) competitive system; ~ **creditizio** (*fin.*) credit system; ~ **decimale** (*mat.*) decimal system; **il** ~ **dei doppi cambi per la lira** (*econ.*) the double-tier system for the lira; ~ **dei prezzi** (*econ.*) price system; ~ **del contingentamento** (*econ.*) quota system;

~ **del corso dei cambi fisso** (*fin.*) fixed exchange-rate system; ~ **del punteggio** (*per la valutazione del lavoro*) (*pers.*) point system; ~ **del razionamento della domanda di mercato** (*econ., USA*) market demand prorationing system; ~ **dell'ora standard** (*org. az.*) standard-hour plan; ~ **della retribuzione a premio** (*pers.*) premium system; **il** ~ **delle partecipazioni statali** (*econ.*) the state participation system; **il** ~ **delle preferenze generalizzate** (*econ.*) the system of generalized preferences; ~ **delle tariffe differenziate** (*fra quelli che hanno un contratto con la «Conferenza» e quelli che non l'hanno*) (*trasp. mar.*) contract and non-contract rate system; ~ **delle valute multiple** (*fin.*) multiple currency system; ~ **delle vendite a rate** (*market.*) hire-purchase system; **sistemi di abbuoni sul salario** (*per rendimento, ecc.*) (*org. az., pers.*) bonus systems; ~ **d'aria condizionata** air-conditioning; ~ **di binari per deposito** (*smistamento, ecc.*) (*trasp. ferr.*) railway yard, yard; ~ **di contabilità** (*rag.*) accounting system; **sistemi di contabilità a fogli mobili** (*rag.*) loose-leaf bookkeeping systems; **un** ~ **di contabilità nazionale** (*rag.*) a system of national accounts; ~ **di distribuzione** (*econ.*) distribution system; **un** ~ **di Governo** a system of Government; **sistemi di gratifiche in aggiunta al salario** (*pers.*) bonus systems; ~ **d'incentivi sul lavoro** (*org. az.*) task-and-bonus system; ~ **di lavorazione** (*org. az.*) processing; ~ **di pagamento in natura** (*pers.*) truck system, truck; ~ **di pagamento per lavori a cottimo** (*sind.*) contract system of wage payment; ~ **di razionamento** (*econ.*) rationing system; ~ **di ritenuta alla fonte** (*fin.*) withholding-tax system; ~ **di tariffe a forcelle** (*fin.*) rate-bracket system; ~ **di tassazione per mezzo di ritenute sul salario** (*fin.*) pay-as-you-earn (*P.A.Y.E.*); ~ **di tassazione sul reddito mediante trattenute al momento in cui esso è conseguito** (*fin., USA*) pay-as-you-go; ~ **distributivo** (*econ.*) distribution system; **un** ~ **distributivo poco efficiente** (*econ.*) a clumsy distribution system; ~ **economico** (*econ.*) economic system, economy; ~ **economico chiuso** (*econ.*) closed system; **un** ~ **economico instabile** (*econ.*) an unsteady economic system; **un** ~ **flessibile d'imposte sul reddito** (*fin.*) a flexible income-tax structure; ~ **industriale basato sul lavoro a domicilio** (*econ.*) domestic system; ~ **liberistico** (*econ.*) free enterprise system; **il** ~ **metrico decimale** the metric system, the centimal system; ~ **monetario** (*fin.*) monetary system; ~ **monetario aureo** (*fin.*) gold standard; ~ **monetario basato su carta moneta non convertibile** (*econ., fin.*) paper standard; ~ **monetario basato sul dollaro** (*fin.*) dollar standard; ~ **monetario basato sulla libera convertibilità delle monete** (*rispetto a una moneta «base» a parità aurea*) (*econ., fin.*) gold-exchange standard; ~ **monetario decimale** (*econ.*) decimal currency, decimal coinage; ~ **monetario in corso** (*in un dato momento e in un certo Paese*) (*fin.*) coinage; ~ **monetario manovrato** (*econ., fin.*) managed standard; ~ **previdenziale** (*pers., sind.*) health and welfare plan, social-security plan, employee benefit plan; **un** ~ **proporzionale di contingenti d'immigrazione** (*econ.*) a proportional system of immigration quotas; ~ **protezionistico** (*econ.*) protective system; **un** ~ (*di Governo*) **rappresentativo** a representative Government; **il** ~ **rotativo agrario** (*econ.*) the rotation of crops; ~ (*telefonico*) **simplex** (*comun.*) simplex system; ~ **valutario** (*la cui unità è basata su uno standard metallico*) (*econ.*) normative currency.

situazione, *n. f.* **1** situation, position; (*condizione*) condition; (*stato*) state, status, standing. **2** (*fin., anche*) showing. // **la** ~ **con cui s'è chiusa l'annata** (*rag.*) the year-end position; **una** ~ **concorrenziale** (*market.*) a competitive position; ~ **congiunturale** (*econ.*) business climate; **la** «~ **contabile» dell'Italia nei confronti del resto del mondo** Italy's «accounts» with the rest of the world; **la** ~ **contabile d'un fallito** (*leg.*) the estate of a bankrupt; ~ **dei pagamenti** (*econ.*) payments situation; ~ **del** (*mercato del*) **lavoro** (*pers.*) labour situation; **la** ~ **del mercato** (*fin., market.*) the position of the market; ~ **della domanda** (*econ.*) demand conditions (*pl.*); ~ **dell'offerta** (*econ.*) supply conditions (*pl.*); ~ **di cassa** (*rag.*) cash statement; ~ **economica** (*econ.*) economic situation; ~ **finanziaria** (*fin.*) financial position, financial status; **una** ~ **speculativa in Borsa** (*fin.*) a speculative situation on the exchange.

sleale, *a.* **1** (*che manca di lealtà*) disloyal, unfaithful; (*falso*) false. **2** (*che è fatto in modo sleale*) unfair, foul. // **concorrenza** ~ (*market.*) unfair competition.

slealtà, *n. f.* disloyalty, unfaithfulness, falseness, unfairness.

slittamento, *n. m.* **1** (*di veicoli*) skidding, skid. **2** (*econ., fig.*) sliding. // ~ **salariale** (*econ.*) (*divario fra i livelli retributivi previsti dai contratti collettivi e quelli effettivi aziendali*) wage drift.

slittare, *v. i.* **1** (*detto di veicolo*) to skid. **2** (*econ., fig.*) to slide.

slogan, *n. m.* (*pubbl.*) slogan, catch-phrase, catchword, tag line, message. // ~ **compreso nel**

timbro postale (*sulla corrispondenza affrancata mediante affrancatrice*) (*comun., pubbl.*) meter slogan; **gli slogan dei caroselli televisivi** (*pubbl.*) the messages of TV commercials; **chi inventa slogan** (*pubbl.*) sloganeer (*USA*).

smarrimento, *n. m.* **1** loss, losing. **2** (*trasp.*) (*di merce, ecc.*) miscarriage.

smarrire, *v. t.* **1** to lose★. **2** (*trasp.*) (*merce, ecc.*) to miscarry.

smarrirsi, *v. rifl.* **1** (*non trovare più la via*) to lose★ one's way, to lose★ oneself, to get★ lost, to be lost. **2** (*trasp.*) (*di corrispondenza, merce, ecc.*) to miscarry.

smentire, *v. t.* (*negare*) to deny; (*ritrattare*) to recant; (*sconfessare*) to disavow.

smentita, *n. f.* (*negazione*) denial; (*ritrattazione*) recantation; (*sconfessione*) disavowal. // **una ~ ufficiale** a formal denial.

smerciabile, *a.* (*market.*) saleable, salable, marketable.

smerciare, *v. t.* (*market.*) to sell★, to sell★ off, to market.

smistamento, *n. m.* **1** (*comun.*) (*postale*) sorting, sortation, separation, distribution. **2** (*market.*) (*di merci*) sorting, sortation. **3** (*trasp. ferr.*) shunting, shunt; switching (*USA*). // **lo ~ della corrispondenza** (*comun.*) the sortation of mail.

smistare, *v. t.* **1** (*comun.*) (*la posta*) to sort, to separate, to distribute. **2** (*market.*) (*merci*) to sort. **3** (*trasp. ferr.*) (*un treno*) to shunt; to switch (*USA*). // **~ la corrispondenza** (*comun.*) to sort the mail, to separate the mail; **essere smistato** (*trasp. ferr.*) (*di treno*) to shunt; to switch (*USA*).

smobilizzare, *v. t.* (*econ.*) (*capitali*) to unfreeze★.

smobilizzazione, *n. f. V.* **smobilizzo.**

smobilizzo, *n. m.* (*econ.*) (*di capitali*) unfreezing. // **~ d'un investimento** (*econ.*) disinvestment; **smobilizzi e realizzi** (*rag.*) sales of assets.

snazionalizzare, *v. t.* (*econ.*) to denationalize.

snazionalizzazione, *n. f.* (*econ.*) denationalization.

sociale, *a.* **1** social. **2** (*fin.*) (*di società di persone*) of a partnership; partnership (*attr.*). **3** (*fin.*) (*di società di capitali*) of a company; company (*attr.*); of a corporation (*USA*); corporation, corporate (*attr., USA*).

società, *n. f. inv.* **1** (*complesso d'individui uniti da vincoli*) society. **2** (*associazione*) association, society; (*circolo*) club. **3** (*fin.*) (*di persone*) partnership; (*di capitali*) company; corporation (*USA*). // **~ a capitale variabile** (*fin.*) joint-stock company; **~ a carattere familiare** (*fin.*) family-run company, closed company; closed corporation (*USA*); **~ a economia controllata** (*dallo Stato*) (*econ.*) regulated company; **~ a responsabilità limitata dalle azioni** (*fin.*) company with liability limited by shares, joint-stock limited company, limited company; **~ aderente alla Borsa Valori di New York** (*Borsa, USA*) member corporation; **~ affiliata** (*fin.*) affiliated company, affiliated firm, affiliate; **~ anonima** (*fin.*) joint-stock company; corporation (*USA*); **~ anonima a responsabilità limitata al capitale azionario** (*fin.*) joint-stock company limited by shares; **~ armatrice** (*trasp. mar.*) shipowners' company; **~ capogruppo** (*che possiede titoli d'un'altra, generalm. sotto forma di partecipazioni di controllo*) (*fin.*) holding company; **~ collegata** (*fin.*) associated company, subsidiary company, subsidiary; **~ commerciale che gode di speciali privilegi** (*conferiti dal sovrano o dal Parlamento*) (*fin., ingl.*) chartered company; **una ~ commerciale fittizia** a dummy company; a dummy corporation (*USA*); **~ concessionaria** (*fin.*) concessionary company; **~ consociata** (*fin.*) fellow subsidiary; **~ controllante** (*fin.*) holding company, immediate holding company; proprietary company (*USA*); **una ~ controllata** (*fin.*) a subsidiary company, a subsidiary; (*da una «holding company», q. V.*) holding; **la ~ convenuta** (*leg.*) the defendant company; **~ cooperativa** (*fin.*) co(-)operative society, co(-)operative association; **una ~ costituita** (*fin., leg.*) a corporate body; **~ costituita per scopi illeciti** (*leg.*) illegal partnership; **~ creditrice** (*cred.*) creditor company; **~ da rilevare** (*fin.*) bid-for company, company bid for; **~ debitrice** (*cred.*) debtor company; **la «~ del benessere»** the affluent society; **~ depositaria** (*fin.*) trustee company; **~ d'armamento** (*trasp. mar.*) shipping firm; **~ d'assicurazione** (*ass.*) insurance company; **~ d'assicurazione contro gli incendi** (*ass.*) fire insurance company; **~ di beneficenza** benevolent society, benefit club; eleemosynary corporation (*USA*); **~ di capitali** (*fin.*) company, joint-stock company; corporation (*USA*); **~ di «factoring»** (*fin.*) factoring firm; **~ di finanziamento** (*fin.*) finance company; **~ di finanziamento per l'acquisto o la costruzione di case** (*fin.*) building society; **~ di gestione** (*fin.*) management company; **~ di gestione del portafoglio** (*fin.*) trust company; **una ~ di grandi dimensioni** (*fin.*) a large company, a «technostructure»; **~ d'investimenti mobiliari** (*fin.*) investment company; ~

di «leasing» (*fin.*) leasing company; ~ **di navigazione** (*trasp. mar.*) shipping company; ~ **di persone** (*leg.*) partnership; ~ **di portafoglio** (*fin.*) holding company; ~ **di ricerca** exploitation company; ~ **di ricuperi marittimi** (*trasp. mar.*) salvage company; ~ **di servizi pubblici** (*fin.*) corporation; utility company (*USA*); ~ **di trasporti** (*trasp.*) transport company, carriage company; ~ **dominante** (*fin.*) controlling company; controlling corporation (*USA*); ~ **estera** (*fin.*) foreign company; foreign corporation (*USA*); ~ **ferroviaria** (*fin.*) railway company; railroad company, railroad (*USA*); ~ **fiduciaria** (*fin.*) trustee company; ~ **finanziaria** (*fin.*) holding company; **società finanziarie a controllo pubblico** (*econ.*) public-controlled financial institutes; ~ **gestrice di fondi (comuni) d'investimento** (*fin.*) underwriter; ~ **holding** (*fin.*) holding company; ~ **in accomandita semplice** (*fin.*) limited partnership, special partnership; ~ **in nome collettivo** (*fin.*) general partnership, unlimited partnership, unlimited company, partnership; ~ **in via di sviluppo** (*fin.*) growth company; ~ **legalmente costituita** (*leg.*) company; corporation (*USA*); ~ **liquidata** (*fin.*) defunct company; ~ **madre** (*fin., org. az.*) parent company; parent corporation (*USA*); ~ **mutualistica con organizzazione centralizzata** (*fin.*) accumulating society; ~ **mutuataria** (*fin.*) borrowing company; **una** ~ **nazionale** (*fin.*) a national company; a domestic corporation (*USA*); ~ **non obbligata alla presentazione annuale del bilancio** (*fin., ingl.*) exempt private company; ~ **offerente** (*fin.*) take-over company, bidding company, take-over bidder; ~ **per azioni** (*fin.*) joint-stock company limited by shares, joint-stock limited company, joint-stock company, stock company, limited-liability company, limited company, company; stock corporation, corporation (*USA*); ~ **per azioni a costituzione simultanea** (*fin.*) private limited company, private company, proprietary company; private corporation, close corporation (*USA*); ~ **per azioni costituita tramite pubblica sottoscrizione** (*fin.*) public limited company; ~ **per investimenti finanziari** (*fin.*) investment company; **società petrolifere** (*fin.*) oil companies; ~ **privata** (*fin.*) private company; private corporation (*USA*); ~ **promotrice** (*fin.*) issuing house; ~ **pubblica** (*che esercita funzioni di interesse pubblico*) (*fin.*) corporation, public corporation; Government corporation (*USA*); ~ **sciolta** (*fin.*) defunct company; **una** ~ **senza capitale azionario** (*fin., USA*) a non-stock corporation; ~ **soprannazionale** (*fin.*) supranational company; ~ **specializzata nel collocamento delle azioni d'un fondo comune d'investimento mobiliare** (*fin.*) sponsor; ~ **specializzata nel «venture-capital»** (*fin.*) venture-capital company; ~ **specializzata nella concessione di piccoli mutui a privati** (*fin.*) finance company; ~ **straniera** (*che opera in un dato Paese*) (*fin.*) foreign company; alien corporation (*USA*); ~ **sussidiaria** (*fin.*) subsidiary company, subsidiary, subcompany.

societario, *a.* **1** (*fin.*) (*di società di persone*) of a partnership; partnership (*attr.*). **2** (*fin.*) (*di società di capitali*) of a company; company (*attr.*); of a corporation (*USA*); corporate, corporation (*attr., USA*).

socio, *n. m.* **1** (*membro d'associazione*) member, affiliated member. **2** (*fin.*) partner, affiliate, member; (*consocio*) copartner, consociate. // ~ **accomandante** (*fin., leg.*) limited partner; ~ **accomandatario** (*fin., leg.*) general partner; ~ **che manda avanti un'azienda** (*dopo che gli altri si sono ritirati*) (*fin.*) continuing partner; ~ **corrispondente** corresponding member; ~ **di capitali** (*fin.*) silent (*o* sleeping) partner; **il** ~ **di data più recente** (*fin.*) the junior partner; **il** ~ **di minore importanza** (*fin.*) the junior partner; ~ **d'opera** (*fin.*) active partner; ~ **effettivo** (*fin.*) real partner, active partner; ~ **fondatore** (*fin.*) company promoter, incorporator; charter member (*USA*); ~ **gerente** (*fin.*) managing partner; ~ **nominale** (*fin.*) nominal partner, quasi partner, partner by estoppel; ~ **occulto** (*fin.*) secret partner, silent (*o* sleeping) partner; ~ **onorario** honorary member; **il** ~ **più anziano** (*fin.*) the senior partner; ~ **promotore** (*fin.*) company promoter; (*d'una società per azioni*) foundation member.

socio-economico, *a.* (*econ.*) socioeconomic.

soddisfacente, *a.* satisfactory, satisfying; (*adeguato*) adequate.

soddisfacimento, *n. m.* satisfaction, gratification.

soddisfare, *v. t.* **1** (*appagare*) to satisfy, to fulfil, to gratify, to meet*. **2** (*accontentare*) to satisfy, to please. **3** (*leg.*) (*un debito, ecc.*) to satisfy, to pay* (off). // ~ **i propri bisogni** (*econ.*) to satisfy one's needs; ~ **i propri impegni** (*leg.*) to meet one's engagements; ~ **una richiesta** to meet a demand, to meet a request.

soddisfatto, *a.* **1** satisfied, gratified, pleased. **2** (*adempiuto*) satisfied, fulfilled. **3** (*leg.*) (*di debito, debitore, ecc.: pagato*) paid-off. // **non** ~ unsatisfied.

soddisfazione, *n. f.* **1** (*il soddisfare*) satisfaction, gratification; (*adempimento*) fulfillment. 2 (*compiacimento di chi è soddisfatto*) satisfaction, pleasure. 3 (*leg.*) (*d'un debito*) paying off; (*d'un'offesa*) satisfaction.

sofferenza, *n. f.* 1 (*il soffrire*) suffering, pain. 2 (*cred.*) (*ritardo nel pagamento d'un debito*) delay in paying a debt. // **in** ~ (*fin.*) (*d'assegno bancario, cambiale, ecc.*) outstanding, overdue; afloat (*pred.*).

sofisticare, *v. t.* (*leg.*) (*adulterare*) to sophisticate, to adulterate. // ~ **i vini** to sophisticate wines.

sofisticato, *a.* 1 (*raffinato, ricercato*) sophisticated. 2 (*leg.*) (*adulterato*) sophisticated, adulterated. // **non** ~ unsophisticated.

sofisticatore, *n. m.* (*leg.*) sophisticator, adulterator.

sofisticazione, *n. f.* 1 (*raffinatezza, ricercatezza*) sophistication. 2 (*leg.*) sophistication, adulteration.

soggettivo, *a.* subjective.

soggetto[1], *a.* 1 (*sottoposto: a un'autorità, una condizione, e sim.*) subject. 2 (*esposto a un'azione esterna*) subject, liable. // ~ **a una clausola condizionale** (*leg.*) provisory; ~ **a condizione** (*leg.*) subject to a condition, contingent; ~ **a dazio** (*dog.*) chargeable with duty, customable, dutiable; ~ **a dazio di consumo** (*fin.*) excisable; ~ **a un eccessivo carico fiscale** (*fin.*) overtaxed; ~ **a imposta** (*fin.*) taxable, listable; ~ **a imposta di fabbricazione** (*fin.*) excisable; ~ **a repentini cambiamenti** (*generalm. in aumento*) (*market.*) (*di prezzo*) runaway; ~ **a tassazione** (*fin.*) taxable; ~ **a vincolo doganale** (*dog.*) in bond; ~ **alla giurisdizione d'un dato tribunale** (*leg.*) cognizable; **l'essere** ~ (*a qc., a fare qc.*) (*leg.*) liability; **l'essere** ~ **al pagamento d'imposte** (*fin.*) the liability to pay taxes; **non** ~ **a tariffe** (*comm. est., econ.*) tariffless.

soggetto[2], *n. m.* (*argomento, tema*) subject, subject-matter, matter, topic. // **un** ~ **tassabile** (*fin.*) a subject for taxation, a taxable person.

sola di cambio, *n. f.* (*cred.*) sola, sola of exchange.

soldi, *n. pl.* (*fam.*) money. // ~ **per le piccole spese** spending money, pocket money.

solidale, *a.* 1 (*concorde*) solid. 2 (*leg.*) jointly responsible, jointly liable; (*di responsabilità*) several.

solidalmente, *avv.* 1 (*con solidarietà*) with solidarity. 2 (*leg.*) jointly and severally, jointly.

solidarietà, *n. f.* 1 solidarity. 2 (*leg.*) joint liability, joint responsibility. // ~ **passiva** (*leg.*) several covenant.

sollecitamente, *avv.* (*prontamente*) promptly, readily, quickly, rapidly, speedily.

sollecitare, *v. t.* 1 (*affrettare*) to hasten, to quicken, to speed★ up, to urge, to expedite. 2 (*chiedere insistentemente*) to solicit, to urge, to press for. 3 (*cred.*) (*il pagamento d'un debito*) to dun. 4 (*market.*) (*ordinazioni commerciali, ecc.*) to canvass. // ~ **offerte cauzionali per un'aggiudicazione** (*fin.*) to invite tenders; ~ **ordinazioni** (*market.*) to solicit orders, to tout; ~ **i pagamenti** (*cred.*) to urge payments.

sollecitatore, *n. m.* (*pers.*) (*d'ordinazioni*) runner, tout.

sollecitatoria, *n. f.* (*cred.*) dunning letter, reminder, follow-up.

sollecitazione, *n. f.* (*insistente richiesta*) solicitation, request, entreaty. // ~ **delle consegne** (*org. az.*) expediting.

sollecito, *a.* (*pronto*) prompt, ready, speedy, quick. *n. m.* 1 (*sollecitazione*) solicitation, request, entreaty. 2 (*cred.*) (*sollecitatoria*) dunning letter, reminder, follow-up.

soluzione, *n. f.* 1 solution. 2 (*d'un problema*) resolution, solution, solving. // ~ **di continuità** solution of continuity, break of continuity; **la** ~ **d'un dubbio legale** (*leg.*) the resolution of a legal doubt; **la** ~ **d'un problema** (*anche mat.*) the solution of a problem; **una** ~ **provvisoria** (*un ripiego*) a stopgap; **in** ~ **unica** in one amount.

solvibile, *a.* 1 (*cred.*) solvent, sound; creditworthy. 2 (*econ., fin.*) (*d'uno Stato*) viable.

solvibilità, *n. f.* 1 (*cred.*) solvency; creditworthiness. 2 (*econ., fin.*) (*d'uno Stato*) viability.

somma, *n. f.* 1 (*addizione*) sum, addition. 2 (*risultato d'un'addizione*) sum. 3 (*complesso*) sum total, sum. 4 (*quantità di denaro*) sum (of money), amount (of money). 5 (*mat.*) sum, cast. // ~ **accantonata** (*fin., rag.*) allocation; ~ **complessiva** (*rag.*) grand total; **la** ~ **convenuta** the agreed sum; ~ **degli utili lordi e degli ammortamenti** (*rag.*) gross cash flow; ~ **degli utili non distribuiti e degli ammortamenti effettuati** (*rag.*) net cash flow; ~ **depositata in garanzia** (*leg.*) cover; ~ **di denaro** (*per un certo scopo*) allowance; ~ **di denaro per corrompere** (*leg.*) bribe; ~ **incassata** (*per un assegno e sim.*) **al netto di sconti** (*o provvigioni, ecc.*) (*banca*) proceeds; ~ **offerta** (*specialm. a un'asta*) (*leg.*) bid; ~ **pagata** payment; ~ **pagata tutta in una volta** lump sum; ~ **parziale** (*rag.*) short; ~ **registrata a credito** (*rag.*) credit; ~ **riportata** (*rag.*) amount carried forward (*o* down), amount brought forward (*o* down), extension; ~ **stanziata** (*fin., rag.*) allocation; **la** ~ **totale** the total, the sum total; ~ **tratta allo scoperto** (*banca*) overdraft; ~ **versata**

in conto (*banca*) amount paid on account.

sommare, *v. t.* **1** (*eseguire un'addizione*) to add. **2** (*computare aggiungendo*) to sum, to sum up, to total. **3** (*mat.*) to sum, to cast★.

sommario, *a.* summary, brief. *n. m.* **1** (*compendio*) summary, synopsis★, abstract. **2** (*indice*) table of contents, index★.

sommatoria, *n. f.* (*mat.*) summation.

sondaggio, *n. m.* **1** (*nautico*) sounding. **2** (*market., pubbl.*) (*indagine*) poll. // ~ **della pubblica opinione** (*market., pubbl.*) public-opinion poll, opinion poll; straw vote, straw ballot (*USA*); ~ **di morale aziendale** (*pers.*) attitude survey.

sondare, *v. t.* **1** (*esaminare con la sonda*) to sound. **2** (*market., pubbl.*) (*l'opinione pubblica, ecc.*) to poll.

soppressione, *n. f.* **1** suppression, suppressing. **2** (*abolizione*) abolition; (*distruzione*) destruction. **3** (*leg.*) (*di prove, ecc.*) concealment; (*d'una legge*) abolition; (*rescissione*) rescission. // **la ~ dei dazi doganali** (*dog.*) the abolition of customs duties; ~ **di corrispondenza** (*leg.*) destruction of correspondence; **la ~ d'una pubblicazione** (*giorn.*) the suppression of a publication.

sopprimere, *v. t.* **1** to suppress. **2** (*abolire*) to abolish, to do★ away with, to take★ off. **3** (*leg.*) (*prove, ecc.*) to conceal; (*una legge*) to abolish; (*rescindere*) to rescind. **4** (*pubbl.*) to cancel. // ~ **un dazio doganale** (*fin.*) to abolish a customs duty; ~ **le distorsioni di concorrenza** (*market.*) to abolish distortions of competition; ~ **tutti gli ostacoli agli scambi** (*comm. est.*) to remove all barriers to trade.

sopra, *prep.* **1** (*con contatto*) on, upon. **2** (*senza contatto*) over. **3** (*al di sopra di*) above. *avv.* **1** (*di sopra*) above. **2** (*al piano superiore*) upstairs. **3** (*leg.*) hereinabove, hereinbefore. // ~ **coperta** (*trasp. mar.*) on deck; ~ **indicato** above-mentioned; ~ **il livello del mare** above sea-level; ~ **la pari** (*fin.*) above par; ~ **zero** above zero; **al di ~** over; **come ~** as above.

sopraccennato, *a.* above-mentioned.

sopraccitato, *a.* above-quoted, above-stated, above-cited, above-mentioned; (*sopraddetto*) above-said.

sopraddetto, *a.* above-said, above-mentioned, aforesaid.

sopraffino, *a.* (*market.*) (*d'articolo, ecc.*) superfine, super, extra fine; (*eccellente*) excellent, first-class, first-grade, first-rate.

sopraindicato, *a.* above-mentioned, above-stated, aforesaid.

sopralluogo, *n. m.* investigation, inspection, view.

soprammenzionato, *a.* above-mentioned, aforesaid.

soprammercato, *n. m.* (*nella locuz. avv.*) **per ~** in addition, on the top of it, into the bargain, to boot.

soprannazionale, *a.* supranational. *n. f.* (*fin.*) supranational company.

soprannolo, *n. m.* (*trasp. mar.*) extra freight, back freight; primage.

soprannumerario, *a.* **1** supernumerary; extra (*attr.*). **2** (*pers.*) (*di personale*) redundant.

soprannumero, *a.* e *n. m.* supernumerary. // **l'essere in ~** (*di personale*) redundancy; **in ~** supernumerary (*a.*); in excess (*pred.*); (*di personale*) redundant.

soprappiù, *n. m.* surplus, overplus, extra.

soprapprezzo, *n. m.* (*market.*) surcharge, overprice, excess charge.

soprapproduzione, *n. f.* (*org. az.*) overproduction.

soprapprofitto, *n. m.* (*fin.*) excess profit; excess profits (*pl.*).

soprattassa, *n. f.* **1** (*comun.*) (*su una lettera*) excess postage. **2** (*fin.*) surtax, surcharge, extra tax, extra charge, additional tax, additional charge. // ~ **di bandiera** (*trasp. mar.*) flag surtax; ~ **per posta aerea** (*comun.*) air fee, airmail fee; ~ **sulle importazioni** (*comm. est., fin.*) import surcharge.

soprattassare, *v. t.* (*fin.*) to surtax.

sopravvalutare, *v. t.* **1** to overestimate, to overstate. **2** (*fin.*) to upvalue.

sopravvalutazione, *n. f.* **1** overestimate. **2** (*fin.*) upvaluation.

sopravvenienza, *n. f.* (*ciò che sopravviene*) supervention, unexpected occurrence. // **sopravvenienze attive** (*rag.*) non-recurrent incomes; **sopravvenienze passive** (*rag.*) non-recurrent charges.

sopravvissuto, *a.* surviving. *n. m.* (*ass.*) survivor.

sopravvivenza, *n. f.* (*ass.*) survival, survivorship.

sopravvivere, *v. i.* (*ass.*) to survive.

soprintendente, *n. m.* e *f.* (*pers.*) superintendent, supervisor; (*d'azienda agricola*) estate agent; (*commissario*) commissioner. // ~ **ai lavori** (*pers.*) clerk of the works; **il ~ ai lavori pubblici** the superintendent of public works; ~ **alla zecca** (*fin.*) mintmaster; ~ **alle dogane** (*dog.*) commissioner of customs.

soprintendenza, *n. f.* superintendence, supervision.

soprintendere, *v. i.* to superintend, to supervise.

sorvegliante, *n. m.* e *f.* (*pers.*) watchman★ (*m.*); watchwoman★ (*f.*); watcher, guard, caretaker, keeper; (*soprintendente*) superintendent, supervisor, overseer. // ~ **di banchina** (*trasp. mar.*) wharfman; ~ **doganale** (*dog.*) custom watcher; ~ **notturno** (*pers.*) night watchman.

sorveglianza, *n. f.* watch, guard, caretaking, keeping; (*soprintendenza*) superintendence, supervision, overseeing, oversight. // **di** ~ supervisory (*attr.*); **un comitato di** ~ a supervisory committee.

sorvegliare, *v. t.* to watch, to guard, to take★ care of; (*soprintendere*) to superintend, to supervise, to oversee★.

sospendere, *v. t.* **1** (*interrompere per un dato periodo di tempo*) to suspend, to interrupt, to stop, to stay, to discontinue; (*rinviare*) to postpone, to adjourn, to defer, to put★ off. **2** (*privare, per un certo tempo, d'una carica e sim.*) to suspend. **3** (*leg.*) (*un'azione giudiziaria*) to bar; (*una condanna*) to respite. **4** (*org. az.*) (*il lavoro*) to lay★ off. **5** (*pers.*) (*dal lavoro*) to lay★ off, to suspend, to remove. // ~ **un assegno** (*banca*) to stop a cheque; ~ **dal lavoro** (*i lavoratori, per ottenerne concessioni*) (*pers., sind.*) to lock out; ~ **q. dallo stipendio** (*pers.*) to stop sb.'s salary; ~ **q. dall'ufficio** (*pers.*) to suspend sb. from office; ~ **l'esecuzione di** (*una sentenza*) (*leg.*) to reprieve; ~ **il giudizio** (*leg.*) to suspend judgement; ~ **i lavori** to adjourn; ~ **il lavoro** (*pers., sind.*) to leave off work, to stop working; ~ **momentaneamente il lavoro** (*pers.*) to lie off; ~ **ogni attività** (*fig.*) to shut up shop; ~ **i pagamenti** to stop payments; ~ **la partenza** to put off one's departure; ~ **il procedimento** (*leg.*) to stay proceedings; ~ **le relazioni** to break off connections; ~ **una sentenza** (*leg.*) to remit a sentence, to stay judgement.

sospensione, *n. f.* **1** (*interruzione per un dato periodo di tempo*) suspension, interruption, stoppage; (*il rinviare*) postponement, adjournment, deferment, putting off. **2** (*il privare, per un certo tempo, d'una carica e sim.*) suspension. **3** (*leg.*) (*d'un'azione giudiziaria*) bar, abatement; (*d'una sentenza*) respite. **4** (*org. az.*) (*del lavoro*) layoff. **5** (*pers.*) (*dal lavoro*) layoff, suspension, removal. // ~ **condizionale** (*della pena*) (*leg.*) probation; **la** ~ **dei pagamenti** the suspension of payments; ~ **del lavoro** (*sind.*) cessation from work; **una** ~ **dell'esecuzione** (*d'una sentenza*) (*leg.*) a reprieve, a stay of execution; ~ **d'una causa** (*che può essere ripresa con un atto di riassunzione*) (*leg.*) abatement and revival; ~ **disciplinare** (*pers.*) disciplinary layoff; **puntini di** ~ dots.

sospensiva, *n. f.* **1** postponement, adjournment, delay. **2** (*leg.*) abeyance. // **in** ~ (*leg.*) in abeyance.

sospensivo, *a.* suspensive. // **condizione sospensiva** (*leg.*) suspensive condition, condition precedent.

sospeso, *a.* **1** (*interrotto*) suspended, interrupted; (*rinviato*) postponed, adjourned, put off. **2** (*pers.*) (*dal lavoro*) suspended. // **in** ~ (*in attesa di una definizione*) in abeyance; (*cred.*) (*insoluto, non pagato*) outstanding, unpaid (*a.*); (*leg.*) (*di causa, ecc.*) pending, pendent; (*org. az.*) (*di lavoro: arretrato*) outstanding.

sostegno, *n. m.* **1** support, stand. **2** (*fig.*) support, dependence, protection, prop. // ~ **dei prezzi** (*econ.*) price support; ~ **dei prezzi agricoli** (*econ.*) farm-price support.

sostenere, *v. t.* **1** (*reggere*) to support, to sustain, to hold★ up, to prop. **2** (*sopportare*) to sustain, to bear★. **3** (*difendere*) to support, to defend, to stand★ up for, to side with, to defend. **4** (*affermare, asserire*) to maintain, to claim, to assert. // ~ **l'accusa contro q.** (*leg.*) to prosecute sb.; ~ **un certo tenore di vita** to keep up a certain standard of life; ~ **la concorrenza** (*market.*) to stand up to competition, to meet competition; ~ **la concorrenza di q.** (*market.*) to compete with sb.; ~ **la difesa di q.** (*leg.*) to defend sb.; ~ **un diritto** (*leg.*) to assert a claim; ~ **un esame** to take an exam, to sit for an exam; ~ **finanziariamente** (*fin.*) to stake, to back; (*un'impresa e sim.*) to underwrite; ~ **la propria innocenza** to assert one's innocence; ~ **insieme** to share; ~ **il mare** (*trasp. mar.*) (*detto di nave*) to ride well; ~ **i prezzi** (*econ.*) to keep up prices, to support prices; ~ **i prezzi al dettaglio** (*econ.*) to support retail prices; ~ **un progetto** to back a plan; ~ **una spesa** to meet an expense, to defray an expense.

sostenersi, *v. rifl.* (*sostentarsi*) to support oneself, to sustain oneself, to subsist.

sostenuto, *a.* (*fin.*) (*di prezzo, ecc.*) stable, steady, strong, stiff; (*di mercato, per mancanza di denaro*) stringent. // **una sostenuta campagna di promozione delle vendite** (*d'un articolo, ecc.*) (*pubbl.*) a push; **sterlina sostenuta** (*fin.*) hard pound.

sostituibile, *a.* replaceable.

sostituire, *v. t.* **1** (*mettere al posto d'un altro*) to replace. **2** (*prendere il posto d'un altro*) to replace, to substitute for, to displace. **3** (*org. az.*) (*macchine, impianti, ecc.*) to supersede, to change, to replace. // ~ **q.** (*anche*) to take sb.'s place; to sub for sb. (*fam.*); ~ (*un prodotto di* *qualità inferiore*) **con un prodotto migliore** (*per ottenere un prezzo più alto*) (*market.*) to upgrade.

sostituto, *n. m.* 1 (*leg., org. az.*) locum tenens. 2 (*pers.*) substitute, deputy; sub (*fam.*); alternate (*USA*). // ~ **Procuratore della Repubblica** (*in Italia*) Assistant Public Prosecutor; **un ~ temporaneo** (*pers.*) a stopgap.

sostituzione, *n. f.* replacement, substitution, displacement; (*cambiamento*) change. // ~ **d'impianti** (*org. az.*) plant replacement; ~ **di persona** (*leg.*) personation; **la ~ di tecniche distributive antiquate** (*market.*) the substitution of out-dated marketing techniques; **in ~ di** as a substitute for, in place of.

sotto, *prep.* 1 under. 2 (*più in basso*) below; (*al di sotto*) beneath, underneath. *avv.* 1 under, below, beneath, underneath. 2 (*al piano inferiore*) downstairs. 3 (*leg.*) hereunder, hereinbelow, hereinafter. // ~ **contratto** (*leg.*) under contract; ~ **costo** (*market.*) below cost; ~ **falso nome** under an assumed name; ~ **giuramento** (*leg.*) under oath; ~ **il livello del mare** below sea-level; ~ **il nome di** under the name of; « ~ **paranco** » (*trasp. mar.*) «under ship's tackle», «under ship's derrick», «at ship's rail», «ex ship», «free overside»; ~ **la pari** (*fin.*) below par; ~ **sigillo privato** (*leg.*) under private seal; **essere** ~ (*banca, cred., rag.*) to be in the red; (*fin.*) (*di titoli in Borsa*) to be off.

sottobanco, *avv.* (*market.*) under the counter, under the table, underhand.

sottoccupato, *a.* (*sind.*) underemployed, subemployed.

sottoccupazione, *n. f.* (*econ., sind.*) underemployment, subemployment.

sottocomitato, *n. m.* (*leg., org. az.*) subcommittee.

sottocommissione, *n. f.* (*leg., org. az.*) subcommission, subcommittee.

sottoconto, *n. m.* (*rag.*) subaccount, subsidiary account.

sottocoperta, *n. f.* (*trasp. mar.*) underdeck, lower deck. *avv.* (*trasp. mar.*) below deck.

sottocosto, *locuz. avv.* (*market.*) under price. *a. attr.* (*market.*) (*detto di merce*) distress.

sottofascia, *locuz. avv.* under wrapper, under cover.

sottoindicato, *a.* undermentioned.

sottoporre, *v. t.* 1 (*far subire*) to subject, to expose. 2 (*presentare*) to submit; (*un documento*) to render. // ~ **ad arbitrato una vertenza sindacale** (*sind.*) to arbitrate a labour dispute; ~ (*qc.*) **a condizioni** to qualify; ~ (*q.*) **a giuramento** (*leg.*) to swear; ~ (*una materia prima, ecc.*) **a un processo** (*org. az.*) to process; ~ (*una causa, ecc.*) **a revisione** (*leg.*) to review; ~ (*merci, servizi, ecc.*) **a tariffa** (*comm. est., econ.*) to tariff; ~ (*una nave*) **a visita doganale** (*trasp. mar.*) to visit; ~ **il proprio caso a una commissione** to lay one's case before a commission; ~ **una questione ad arbitrato** (*leg.*) to submit a matter to arbitration, to arbitrate (upon) a matter; **essere sottoposto a** (*prove e sim.*) to undergo.

sottoposto, *a.* submitted, subjected, subject. *n. m.* (*pers.*) subordinate.

sottoprezzo, *locuz. avv.* (*market.*) below price.

sottoprodotto, *n. m.* (*org. az.*) by-product, residual product.

sottoproduttivo, *a.* (*econ., org. az.*) underproductive.

sottoproduzione, *n. f.* (*econ., org. az.*) underproduction.

sottoscritto, *a.* undersigned. *n. m.* undersigned. // **il** ~ the undersigned; Yours faithfully (*fam.*); **io** ~ I the undersigned; **noi sottoscritti** we the undersigned.

sottoscrittore, *n. m.* 1 subscriber. 2 (*fin.*) (*di titoli*) underwriter, applicant.

sottoscrivere, *v. t.* 1 to subscribe, to undersign. 2 (*dare la propria adesione*) to subscribe, to underwrite★. 3 (*fin.*) (*un'emissione di titoli*) to underwrite★. // ~ **un accordo** (*leg.*) to agree to an arrangement; ~ **azioni** (*fin.*) to subscribe for shares, to apply for shares; ~ **capitale azionario** (*fin.*) to underwrite stock; ~ (*un documento e sim.*) **come testimone** (*leg.*) to witness; ~ **un mutuo** (*cred.*) to take up a loan; ~ **una polizza di assicurazione** (*ass.*) to take out an insurance policy, to effect a policy; ~ **un prestito** (*fin.*) to subscribe a loan.

sottoscrizione, *n. f.* 1 subscription, signing; (*firma*) signature. 2 (*raccolta di aderenti, di firme, ecc.*) subscription. 3 (*fin.*) (*di titoli*) underwriting, application. // ~ **d'un'emissione** (*azionaria, ecc.*) (*fin.*) subscription to an issue; **aprire una** ~ to open a subscription.

sottosegretariato, *n. m.* undersecretaryship.

sottosegretario, *n. m.* under-secretary, undersecretary.

sottosviluppato, *a.* (*econ.*) underdeveloped. // **i Paesi sottosviluppati** (*econ.*) the underdeveloped Countries.

sottosviluppo, *n. m.* (*econ.*) underdevelopment. // **il** ~ **delle risorse industriali** (*econ.*) the underdevelopment of industrial resources.

sottovoce, *n. f.* subheading. // ~ **tariffaria**

(*comm. est., econ.*) (*di bilancia commerciale, ecc.*) tariff subheading.

sottrarre, *v. t.* 1 to make★ away with; (*rubare*) to steal★, to abstract; to pocket (*fam.*). 2 (*detrarre*) to deduct. 3 (*mat.*) to subtract.

sottrarsi, *v. rifl.* to escape, to avoid, to evade. // ~ **al fisco** (*fin.*) to dodge taxes; ~ **all'imposta sui redditi** (*leg.*) to evade one's income tax.

sottrazione, *n. f.* 1 (*il sottrarre, il rubare*) stealing, abstraction. 2 (*deduzione*) deduction, deducting. 3 (*mat.*) subtraction. // ~ **dei libri contabili** (*leg.*) abstraction of books; ~ **di attività** (*in un fallimento*) (*leg.*) concealment of assets; **la ~ di beni pignorati** (*leg.*) the removal of distrained chattels; ~ **di documenti** (*leg.*) abstraction of documents, abstraction of papers; ~ **indebita di beni del datore di lavoro** (*da parte d'un dipendente*) (*leg., pers.*) wrongful abstraction.

sovraccaricare, *v. t.* 1 to overload. 2 (*trasp.*) to surcharge. // ~ **una nave** (*trasp. mar.*) to overload a ship.

sovraccarico, *a.* 1 overloaded. 2 (*trasp.*) surcharged. *n. m.* 1 overload. 2 (*trasp.*) surcharge.

sovraimposta, *n. f.* (*fin.*) additional tax.

sovraoccupazione, *n. f.* (*econ.*) overemployment, overfull employment.

sovrappeso, *n. m.* (*market.*) overweight.

sovrapprezzo, *n. m. V.* **soprapprezzo.**

sovrapproduzione, *n. f.* (*econ.*) overproduction.

sovrapprofitto, *n. m. V.* **soprapprofitto.**

sovrimposta, *n. f.* (*fin.*) additional tax.

sovrintendente, *n. m.* e *f. V.* **soprintendente.**

sovrintendenza, *n. f. V.* **soprintendenza.**

sovventore, *n. m.* (*finanziatore*) financial backer.

sovvenzionare, *v. t.* to subsidize, to endow; (*finanziare*) to finance.

sovvenzione, *n. f.* subsidy, endowment, cash grant, grant. // **sovvenzioni al consumo** (*econ.*) consumer subsidies; **sovvenzioni all'agricoltura** (*econ.*) aid to agriculture; ~ **all'esportazione** (*comm. est.*) export bounty; ~ (*governativa*) **alla marina mercantile** (*trasp. mar.*) navigation bounty; **sovvenzioni alla produzione** (*econ.*) production subsidies.

spacchettare, *v. t.* to unpack, to unwrap.

spaziare, *v. t.* (*giorn., pubbl.*) (*in tipografia*) to space, to letterspace.

spaziatura, *n. f.* (*giorn., pubbl.*) spacing, letterspacing. // **a ~ doppia** (*giorn., pubbl.*) double-leaded (*a.*).

spazio, *n. m.* 1 space; (*posto*) room; (*distanza*) distance. 2 (*di tempo*) space, period. 3 (*giorn., pubbl.*) (*per la pubblicità sulla stampa*) space. // ~ **aereo navigabile** (*trasp. aer.*) navigable airspace; ~ **doppio** (*giorn., pubbl.*) double space; ~ (*compreso*) **fra più registrazioni** (*elab. elettr.*) gap; ~ **in bianco** blank space, blank; (*fra caratteri tipografici*) pigeonhole; **gli spazi in bianco** (*d'un modulo e sim.*) the unfilled spaces.

specchietto, *n. m.* (*compendio, sunto*) synopsis★, summary, compendium★.

specialità, *n. f. inv.* 1 (*ramo di studio, di professione, ecc.*) speciality, specialty. 2 (*market.*) specialty. 3 **specialità,** *pl.* (*market.*) specialty goods. // **la ~ della Casa** (*market., tur.*) the specialty of the house; **specialità farmaceutiche** (*market.*) branded pharmaceuticals, proprietary medicines, proprietaries.

specializzare, *v. t.* to specialize. // ~ **un'industria** (*org. az.*) to specialize an industry.

specializzarsi, *v. rifl.* (*org. az.*) to specialize.

specializzato, *a.* 1 specialized. 2 (*pers.*) (*d'operaio*) skilled. // **essere ~** (*org. az.*) to specialize; **non ~** (*pers.*) unskilled.

specializzazione, *n. f.* (*econ., org. az.*) specialization. // ~ **dei compiti** (*org. az.*) division of work; **la ~ industriale** (*econ.*) the specialization of industry.

specifica, *n. f.* (*fin., leg., market.*) bill, detailed list, list.

specificare, *v. t.* to specify, to specialize, to itemize. // ~ **tutte le spese** (*rag.*) to itemize all expenses.

specificato, *a.* specified, itemized. // **come (è) ~ più avanti** (*leg.*) as hereinafter specified.

specificazione, *n. f.* 1 specification. 2 (*leg.*) specification.

specifico, *a.* specific; (*preciso*) precise; (*particolare*) particular, peculiar. // **peso ~** specific weight, specific gravity.

speculare, *v. i.* (*fin.*) to speculate, to gamble, to operate. // ~ **al rialzo** (*Borsa, fin.*) to operate for a rise, to go a bull, to bull; ~ **al ribasso** (*Borsa, fin.*) to operate for a fall, to go a bear, to bear; ~ **in Borsa** (*Borsa, fin.*) to gamble on the Stock Exchange, to play the market.

speculativo, *a.* (*fin.*) speculative.

speculatore, *n. m.* (*Borsa, fin.*) speculator, speculative trader, gambler, player, operator, venturer. // ~ **al rialzo** (*Borsa, fin.*) bull, long; ~ **al ribasso** (*Borsa, fin.*) bear, short; ~ **che tratta in spezzature** (*Borsa*) odd-lot broker, odd-lotter; ~ **di beni immobili** (*Borsa, fin.*) land jobber; ~ **edile** property speculator; ~ **in grande stile** wheeler-dealer (*slang USA*); **uno ~ insolvente** (*Borsa, fin.*) a lame duck; ~ «**professionista**» (*Borsa, ingl.*) jobber, stockjobber; **uno ~ senza scrupoli** (*fin., leg.*) a wildcatter.

speculazione, *n. f.* (*fin.*) speculation, operation, adventure, venture; (*aggiotaggio*) agiotage. // ~ **azzardata** (*fin.*) hazardous speculation; ~ **edilizia** (*caratterizzata dalla fretta e dall'impiego di materiali scadenti*) (*econ.*) jerry building; **una ~ illegale** (*fin., leg.*) a wildcat speculation; ~ **mista** (*Borsa*) cross book.

spedire, *v. t.* **1** to send★, to send★ away; (*merci, anche*) to consign, to forward; to ship, to invoice (*USA*). **2** (*comun.*) (*per posta*) to mail, to post, to dispatch; (*rimettere*) to remit; (*documenti, ecc.*) to route. **3** (*trasp. mar.*) to ship (*in U.S.A. anche via terra*). // ~ (*bagaglio*) **assicurato** (*trasp.*) to register; ~ **come campione** (*comun.*) to send by sample-post; ~ (*merci*) **con accompagnamento della lettera di vettura** (*trasp. ferr.*) to waybill; ~ **contro assegno** (*comun.*) to send cash on delivery (*C.O.D.*); ~ **in conto deposito** (*trasp.*) to consign; ~ (*una nave*) **in dogana** (*dog., trasp. mar.*) to clear outwards, to clear out; ~ **una lettera in busta aperta** (*comun.*) to send a letter as printed matter, to send a letter by book-post; ~ **una lettera in franchigia** (*comun.*) to frank a letter; ~ **merce a un agente in conto deposito** (*perché ne curi la vendita*) (*trasp.*) to consign goods to an agent; ~ **merce per ferrovia** (*trasp. ferr.*) to send goods by rail; ~ **merci a grande velocità** (*trasp. ferr.*) to forward goods by passenger train, to forward goods by fast train; ~ **merci a piccola velocità** (*trasp. ferr.*) to forward goods by slow train; ~ (*una lettera*) **per espresso** (*comun.*) to express; ~ **per ferrovia** (*trasp. ferr.*) to rail (*ingl.*); ~ **per posta** (*comun.*) to post, to mail; ~ **per posta aerea** (*comun.*) to send by air-mail, to airmail; ~ **sotto fascia** (*comun.*) to send under cover.

speditore, *n. m.* sender, consignor, forwarder.

spedizione, *n. f.* **1** (*l'atto di spedire*) sending; (*merce, anche*) consignation, consignment, forwarding; invoicing, shipping, shipment (*USA*); (*di lettere e sim.*) dispatching. **2** (*la merce spedita*) consignment; (*via mare*) shipment (*in U.S.A. anche via terra*). **3** (*viaggio di più persone a scopo di ricerca, studio, ecc.*) expedition, adventure. **4** (*trasp. mar.*) shipping, shipment (*in U.S.A. anche via terra*). // **spedizioni a caricazione completa** (*di vagone*) (*trasp. ferr.*) truck-load consignments; ~ **assicurata** (*di bagaglio*) (*trasp.*) registration; ~ (*di merci*) **fatta dal produttore direttamente al dettagliante** (*e non dal grossista che ha effettuato la vendita*) (*market.*) drop shipment (*USA*); ~ **in dogana** (*dog.*) customs clearance; ~ **marittima** (*trasp. mar.*) (*viaggio di studio, ecc.*) marine adventure; (*invio di merce via mare*) shipping; ~ **per ferrovia** (*trasp. ferr.*) forwarding by rail; ~ **per via di terra** (*trasp.*) overland forwarding; overland shipment (*USA*); **mancata ~** (*trasp.*) nonshipment.

spedizioniere, *n. m.* **1** (*trasp.*) forwarding agent, forwarding merchant, transport agent, forwarder; (*vettore*) carrier, cartage contractor. **2** (*trasp., trasp. mar.*) (*per spedizioni terrestri e marittime*) forwarding and shipping agent. **3** (*trasp. mar.*) shipping agent, shipper (*in U.S.A. anche via terra*); freighter. // ~ **doganale** (*dog.*) customs agent; ~ **marittimo** (*trasp. mar.*) shipping agent, shipper, freighter.

spendere, *v. t.* to spend★, to lay★ out, to outlay★. *v. i.* (*far spese*) to make★ purchases. // ~ **il proprio denaro** to spend one's money; to part with one's money (*fam.*); ~ **in anticipo** to anticipate; **saper ~** to know how to spend one's money.

sperimentale, *a.* experimental, tentative.

sperimentare, *v. t.* to experiment with, to test, to try. // ~ **una macchina** to test a machine.

spesa, *n. f.* **1** expense, charge. **2** (*lo spendere*) expenditure, spending. **3** (*costo*) cost. **4** (*esborso*) disbursement. **5** (*econ., rag., anche*) outlay, outgoing, outgo. **6** (*market.*) (*compra*) buy (*fam.*). **7** (*market.*) (*compere*) shopping. **8 spese,** *pl.* expenses, charges. **9 spese,** *pl.* (*lo spendere*) expenditure, spending. **10 spese,** *pl.* (*banca*) expenses, charges. // «**spese** (*di trasporto*) **a carico del destinatario**» (*trasp.*) «carriage forward»; «**spese** (*di trasporto*) **a carico del mittente**» (*trasp.*) «carriage paid»; **spese a carico della parte soccombente** (*leg.*) costs charged to the loser; **spese accessorie** (*rag.*) incidental expenses; **una ~ aggiuntiva** an extra charge, an extra; **spese amministrative** (*fin., rag.*) administrative expenses; «**spese assegnate**» «charges forward»; **spese bancarie** (*banca*) bank charges; **spese che prevedono un'immediata uscita di numerario** (*rag.*) out-of-pocket expenses; **spese correnti** (*rag.*) running expenses; current spending (*sing.*); ~ **dei risparmi accumulati** (*econ.*) dissaving; **spese d'amministrazione** (*rag.*) administration expenses, administrative expenses; **spese d'avaria** (*ass. mar.,* *trasp. mar.*) average expenses; **spese di bacino** (*trasp. mar.*) dockage; **spese di bollo** (*fin.*) stamp dues, stamp charges; **spese di capitale** (*rag.*) capital charges; **spese di caricazione** (*trasp. mar.*) shipping expenses, loading charges; **spese di carico e scarico** (*trasp. mar.*) loading and unloading charges; **spese di consegna** (*rag.*) delivery charges; **spese di consumo** (*econ.*) consumer spending; **spese di costituzione** (*rag.*) establishment charges, formation expenses; **spese di «dock»** (*trasp. mar.*) dock dues; dockage (*sing.*); **spese di dogana** (*dog.*) customs expenses, customs charges; **spese d'esercizio** (*rag.*) running expenses, operating expenses, working expenses, working costs; **spese di facchinaggio** (*trasp.*) porterage; **spese di gestione** (*rag.*) operating expenses, management expenses; **spese di giudizio** (*leg.*) legal expenses, legal fees; **spese d'imballaggio** (*market.*) packing charges, packing expenses; **spese di imbarco** (*trasp. mar.*) shipping expenses, shipping charges, loading charges; **spese d'imbarco e di spedizione** (*trasp. mar.*) shipping and forwarding charges; **spese d'immobilizzo** (*rag.*) carrying costs; **spese d'incasso** (*banca, rag.*) collection charges; **spese di magazzinaggio** (*rag.*) warehouse charges, warehousing charges, storing charges, storing expenses; **spese di magazzino** (*rag.*) inventory costs, housing costs; **spese di manutenzione** (*rag.*) maintenance charges, handling charges, upkeep expenses; upkeep; **spese di manutenzione e riparazione** (*rag.*) cost of upkeep and repairs (*sing.*); **spese di nolo** (*trasp. mar.*) charges for freight, freight charges; **spese di nolo anticipate** (*trasp. mar.*) prepaid freight charges; **spese di nolo impreviste** (*trasp. mar.*) back freight; **spese di periodo** (*rag.*) period costs; **spese di porto** (*trasp.*) truckage; **spese di protesto** (*leg.*) protest charges; **spese di pubblicità** (*org. az., rag.*) advertising expenses; **spese di rappresentanza** (*rag.*) entertaining expenses; **spese di ricupero** (*trasp. mar.*) salvage charges; **spese di rimorchio** (*trasp. aut., trasp. mar.*) towage fees; towage, trackage (*sing.*); **spese di riparazione** (*rag.*) repair charges, cost of repairs; **spese di sbarco** (*trasp. mar.*) unloading charges, landing charges; **spese di sconto** (*banca*) discount charges; **spese di spedizione** (*trasp.*) forwarding charges; **spese di stivaggio** (*trasp. mar.*) trimming charges; stowage (*sing.*); **spese di trasbordo** (*trasp. mar.*) transshipment expenses; **spese di trasporto** (*trasp.*) charges for carriage, carriage charges; carriage, cartage (*sing.*); freight (*sing., USA*); **spese di trasporto di pacchi per espresso** (*trasp.*) expressage; **spese di trasporto interno** (*org. az., rag.*) handling costs; **spese di trasporto per via d'acqua** (*trasp.*) waterage; **spese di trasporto su chiatte** (*trasp. mar.*) lighterage; **spese d'ufficio** (*rag.*) office expenses; **spese di vendita** (*rag.*) expenses of selling, selling expenses; **spese di viaggio** travelling expenses; **spese dirette** (*rag.*) direct expenses; **spese e competenze** (*di una causa*) (*leg.*) costs and fees; **spese fisse** (*rag.*) fixed charges; **spese generali** (*rag.*) general expenses, indirect expenses, standing expenses, standing charges, general charges, fixed costs, overhead expenses, overhead charges, overheads; oncost (*sing.*); (*voce di bilancio*) selling and administrative expenses; **spese generali di produzione** (*rag.*) manufacturing overhead cost (*sing.*); manufacturing overheads, factory indirect expenses; **spese giudiziarie** (*leg.*) law expenses, law costs; **una ~ imprevista** an unforeseen expense; **~ in eccesso del reddito** (*econ.*) dissaving; **spese indirette** (*rag.*) indirect expenses; oncost (*sing.*); **spese legali** (*leg.*) legal expenses, legal costs, legal fees; **spese minute** petty expenses; **spese non ricorrenti** (*rag.*) non-recurring expenses; **spese notarili** (*leg.*) notarial charges; **spese ordinarie** (*rag.*) ordinary charges; **spese per l'addestramento dei venditori** (*pers.*) outlay on salesmanship (*sing.*); **spese per comunicazioni telefoniche** (*comun.*) charges for telephone calls; **~ per miglio** (*trasp.*) milage, mileage (*sing.*); **spese per la ricerca** (*org. az., rag.*) research expenses; **spese per il turismo** (*partita «invariabile» della bilancia dei pagamenti*) (*fin.*) tourist expenditures; **spese portuali** (*trasp. mar.*) port charges; **spese postali** (*comun.*) postal charges; **le spese processuali** (*leg.*) the costs of the action, the costs; **spese proporzionali** (*rag.*) direct expenses; **spese pubbliche** (*amm., fin.*) public expenditures; expenditure of the public authorities, Government expenditure (*sing.*); **spese rimborsabili** reimbursable expenses; **spese** (*di causa*) **ripetibili** (*leg.*) repayable costs; **la ~ statale** (*fin.*) the expenditure of the State; **spese statali finanziate dal debito pubblico** (*e non da una nuova imposizione fiscale*) (*econ.*) deficit spending (*sing.*); **spese straordinarie** (*rag.*) extraordinary expenses; **~ supplementare** (*rag.*) extra charge, additional charge; **spese urgenti** (*rag.*) pressing expenses; **spese varie** sundry expenses, miscellaneous expenses; **spese vive** out-of-pocket expenses; bread and butter (*slang USA*); **spese voluttuarie** unnecessary expenses; **a spese altrui** at other people's expense; **a nostre spese** (*rag.*) at our expense; **a proprie spese** at one's expense, at one's own charge; **senza spese** (*banca, cred.*) without charges; (*cred., leg.*) (*su una cambiale*) «no noting», «free of charge».

spesare, *v. t.* to pay★ (sb.'s) expenses.

spettabile, *a.* honourable, respectable. // ~ **Ditta Benassati** (*in un indirizzo*) Messrs Benassati.

spettante, *a.* due.

spettanza, *n. f.* **1** (*appartenenza, competenza*) concern, competence. **2** (*ciò che compete di diritto per l'attività prestata*) what is owing (*o* due); (*remunerazione*) remuneration; (*onorario*) fee. // «**a chi di** ~» «to whom it may concern».

spettare, *v. i.* **1** (*concernere per diritto o per dovere*) to be the concern of, to be the duty of, to be up to. **2** (*leg.*) (*appartenere di diritto*) to be due. // ~ (*a q.*) **per riversione** (*leg.*) (*di beni*) to revert, to result.

spezzati, *n. pl.* (*denari spiccioli*) small money, small change, change (*sing.*).

spezzatura, *n. f.* **1** (*lo spezzare*) breaking. **2** (*Borsa*) (*numero d'azioni in quantità inferiore all'unità di contrattazione*) odd lot.

spiccare, *v. t.* (*cred., leg.*) (*emettere*) to issue; (*un titolo di credito*) to draw★. *v. i.* (*risaltare*) to stand★ out, to be conspicuous. // ~ (*un assegno, ecc.*) **allo scoperto** (*cred.*) to kite (*fam.*); ~ **una cambiale** (*cred.*) to draw a bill of exchange; ~ **su q. un ordine di requisizione** (*leg.*) to indent upon sb. for st. (*ingl.*); ~ **tratta** (*cred.*) to draw.

spicciolame, *n. m.* (*quantità di monete spicciole*) small change, small money, change.

spicciolare, *v. t.* (*cambiare in spiccioli*) to break★, to change. // ~ **un biglietto di banca** to change a bank-note, to convert a bank-note into cash.

spicciolo, *a.* small, loose; in coins (*pred.*). *n. m.* **1** small coin. **2 spiccioli,** *n. pl.* small money, odd money, pocket money, broken money, small change, odd change, loose change, change, loose cash, coppers; chicken-feed (*slang USA*).

spillare, *v. t.* **1** (*far uscire vino dalla botte*) to tap. **2** (*fig.*) (*riuscire a prendere usando furbizia o inganno*) to squeeze; to tap (*fam.*). *v. i.* (*trasp. mar.*) to leak.

spillatura, *n. f.* **1** tapping. **2** (*trasp. mar.*) leakage.

spingere, *v. t.* **1** (*anche fig.*) to push. **2** (*fig.*) (*indurre*) to induce; (*stimolare*) to urge; (*motivare*) to motivate. // ~ **le vendite** (*market.*) to force sales.

spinta, *n. f.* **1** (*anche fig.*) push. **2** (*fig.*) (*sollecitazione, pressione*) stress; (*impulso*) impulse; (*motivazione*) motivation. **3** (*econ.*) (*al rilancio*) boost. **4** (*market.*) (*delle vendite*) forcing. **5** (*pers.*) (*raccomandazione per far ottenere un impiego*) plug (*slang USA*). // **la** ~ **dei costi** (*econ.*) the cost push; **la** ~ **dei prezzi** (*econ.*) the cost push; **la** ~ **dei profitti** (*econ.*) the profit push; **la** ~ **della domanda** (*econ.*) the demand pull; **la** ~ **impressa ai consumi** (*econ.*) the boost given to consumption; **spinte inflazionistiche** (*econ.*) inflationary tendencies; ~ **inflazionistica da salari** (*econ.*) wage-push inflation.

spionaggio, *n. m.* espionage. // ~ **industriale** (*leg.*) industrial espionage.

spirale, *n. f.* (*anche fig.*) spiral. // ~ **(dei) costi (e dei) salari** (*econ.*) wage-cost spiral; **la** ~ **dei prezzi** (*econ.*) the spiral of prices, the price spiral; ~ **(dei) prezzi (e dei) salari** (*econ.*) wage-price spiral; ~ **inflazionistica** (*econ.*) inflationary spiral; **essere preso nella** ~ **inflazionistica** (*econ.*) to run away up the inflationary spiral.

sporgere, *v. t.* e *i.* **1** to stretch out, to protrude. **2** (*leg.*) (*una querela*) to prefer. // ~ **denunce** (*leg.*) to lodge accusations.

sportellista, *n. m.* e *f.* (*banca*) teller. *n. m.* (*pers.*) windowman★.

sportello, *n. m.* **1** (*banca, org. az.*) counter, window. **2** (*trasp.*) (*di biglietteria*) ticket-window. // ~ (*di banca*) **cui si accede in automobile** (*banca*) drive-in window; ~ **di cassa** (*org. az.*) cash desk; **chiudere gli sportelli** (*banca*) to stop payments.

spostamento, *n. m.* **1** shift, shifting, drift; (*rimozione*) removal. **2** (*trasp. mar.*) displacement; (*del carico*) shifting. // **lo** ~ **della popolazione dalla campagna alla città** (*stat.*) the drift of population from country to city; **spostamenti nei movimenti internazionali di capitali** (*fin.*) shifts in international capital movements.

spostare, *v. t.* to shift; to displace; (*rimuovere*) to remove.

spostarsi, *v. rifl.* **1** to shift, to move. **2** (*trasp. mar.*) (*del carico*) to shift.

sprovvedere, *v. t.* to deprive.

sprovveduto, *a.* **1** (*che non ha quanto gli è necessario*) unprovided, not supplied. **2** (*impreparato*) unprepared, unready. // **essere** ~ **di** (*un articolo*) (*market.*) to be out of stock.

sprovvisto, *a.* *V.* **sprovveduto.**

spulciare, *v. t.* (*esaminare minuziosamente*) to scrutinize, to go★ through. // ~ **un conto** (*rag.*) to go through an account.

spunta, *n. f.* **1** (*rag.*) (*operazione di revisione e controllo di cifre, voci, ecc.*) reconciliation, check. **2** (*rag.*) (*segno usato per tale operazione*) tick, check.

spuntare, *v. t.* (*rag.*) (*cifre, voci d'un conto,*

ecc.) to reconcile, to tick, to tick off, to check, to check off. *v. i.* (*cominciare a sorgere*) to rise★; (*apparire*) to appear; (*inaspettatamente*) to crop up (*anche fig.*). // ~ **articoli** (*rag.*) to check off items; ~ **le fatture** (*rag.*) to tick off invoices; ~ **un prezzo** (*fin., market.*) to fetch a price; ~ **le voci d'un catalogo** (*market.*) to tick off the items in a catalogue.

spuntatore, *n. m.* (*trasp. mar.*) tallyman★.

squadra, *n. f.* **1** (*attr. uff.*) square. **2** (*pers.*) (*di operai, ecc.*) team, gang; set; (*di turno*) shift. // **capo** ~ (*pers.*) foreman, ganger.

squilibrio, *n. m.* **1** unbalance, imbalance, inbalance, lack of balance, disequilibrium★; (*divario, lacuna*) gap. **2** (*econ.*) imbalance, lack of balance. // ~ **economico** (*econ.*) economic imbalance; ~ **fra l'offerta e la domanda** (*econ.*) imbalance between supply and demand; ~ **sociali ed economici** (*econ.*) social and economic disequilibria.

stabile, *a.* **1** stable, steady, firm. **2** (*permanente*) permanent, standing. *n. m.* (*edificio*) building; (*casa*) house. // **essere in pianta** ~ (*pers.*) to be on the permanent staff.

stabilimento, *n. m.* **1** (*edificio*) establishment. **2** (*org. az.*) factory, plant, mill, workshop, shop; works (*sing.*). // **uno** ~ **non operante** (*che è, cioè, inutilizzato*) (*org. az.*) an inoperative plant; ~ **per la preparazione di cibi in scatola** (*org. az.*) packing house, packing plant, pack house; cannery (*USA*); ~ **tipografico** (*giorn.*) printing works; (*che avviene*) **nell'ambito di uno** ~ (*org. az.*) in-plant (*attr.*).

stabilire, *v. t.* **1** (*collocare, situare*) to establish, to locate. **2** (*fissare*) to fix, to set★, to set★ down, to lay★ down, to state, to schedule. **3** (*sistemare*) to settle, to arrange. **4** (*convenire*) to agree to (st.). **5** (*leg.*) (*di contratto, legge, ecc.*) to provide, to state. **6** (*market.*) (*un prezzo, ecc.*) to name. // ~ **un calendario rigoroso** (*org. az.*) to lay down an exacting timetable; ~ **un contatto con q.** to contact sb., to liaise with sb.; ~ **il costo di** (*qc.*) (*market.*) to cost; ~ **una data per una riunione** to appoint a day for a meeting; ~ **l'imponibile di** (*un bene*) (*fin., ingl.*) to rate; ~ **imposizioni all'importazione** (*fin.*) to levy taxes on imports; ~ **un limite** to assign a limit; ~ **un nuovo prezzo per** (*articoli, merci, ecc.*) (*market.*) to reprice; ~ **obiettivi** (*org. az.*) to establish objectives, to set objectives; ~ **per legge** (*leg.*) to enact; ~ **quote** (*di vendita*) (*market.*) to set quotas; ~ **la propria residenza** (*leg.*) to establish one's residence; ~ **la residenza di** (*q. in un posto*) (*leg.*) to domicile; ~ **il valore imponibile di** (*beni mobili o immobili*) (*fin.*) to assess; «**resta stabilito e inteso che...**» «it is understood and agreed that...».

stabilirsi, *v. rifl.* to establish oneself, to settle, to locate.

stabilità, *n. f.* stability, steadiness, firmness. // ~ **dei prezzi** (*econ.*) price stability; flation; ~ **dei tassi di cambio** (*fin.*) exchange-rate stability; **la** ~ **del personale** (*nel posto di lavoro*) (*org. az.*) the stability of personnel tenure.

stabilito, *a.* established; (*fissato*) fixed, stated; (*convenuto*) agreed.

stabilizzare, *v. t.* to stabilize, to steady, to make★ stable, to give★ stability to. // ~ **i mercati** (*econ.*) to stabilize markets; ~ **i prezzi** (*econ., market.*) to keep prices steady; ~ **il prezzo di** (*titoli, ecc.*) (*Borsa, fin.*) to peg.

stabilizzarsi, *v. rifl.* to stabilize, to steady, to settle, to level off.

stabilizzatore, *n. m.* **1** stabilizer. **2** (*econ.*) stabilizer. // ~ **automatico** (*econ.*) automatic stabilizer, built-in stabilizer.

stabilizzazione, *n. f.* stabilization. // **la** ~ **dei salari** (*econ.*) the stabilization of wages.

staccare, *v. t.* to take★ off, to detach, to cut★ off. *v. i.* (*pers., fam.*) (*cessare il lavoro*) to knock off, to go★ off duty, to stop work. // ~ **un assegno** (*cred.*) to draw a cheque; ~ **una cedola** (*fin.*) to detach a coupon.

stacco, *n. m.* **1** detachment, separation. **2** (*pubbl.*) (*radiotelevisivo*) commercial, cut, message.

stadera, *n. f.* steelyard.

stadio, *n. m.* **1** (*sportivo*) stadium★. **2** (*fig.*) (*fase, periodo*) stage, period, phase.

staff, *n. m.* (*org. az.*) staff, personnel.

«**stagflazione**», *n. f.* (*econ.*) stagflation.

stagionale, *a.* seasonal; in-season (*attr.*). *n. m.* e *f.* (*pers.*) seasonal worker.

stagione, *n. f.* season. // **la** ~ **entrante** the coming season; **la** ~ **morta** (*giorn.*) (*quando i giornali, per mancanza di notizie, si trovano costretti a pubblicare racconti, servizi di scarso interesse, ecc.*) the silly season; (*market.*) the dead season, the dull season, the slack season, the off-season, the layoff; **a** ~ **inoltrata** (*market.*) late in the season; **di** ~ in season; seasonal (*a.*); **fuori** ~ out of season.

stagnante, *a.* (*anche fig.*) stagnant.

stagnare, *v. i.* (*anche fig.*) to stagnate, to be stagnant, to become★ stagnant.

stagnazione, *n. f.* (*econ.*) stagnation.

staio, *n. m.* (*misura di capacità per aridi pari a litri 36,36*) bushel.

stallia, *n. f.* (*trasp. mar.*) lay day, ship's day.

stampa, *n. f.* **1** (*il procedimento*) printing, impression; (*il risultato*) print, issue. **2** (*giorn.*) (*i giornali e i giornalisti*) (the) press; printer's ink (*fig.*). **3** (*pubbl.*) (*fotografica: il procedimento*) printing; (*il risultato*) print, positive. **4** «**stampe**», *pl.* (*giorn.*) (*nella spedizione postale*) «printed matter». // ~ **a grande tiratura** (*giorn.*) mass-circulation press; **la ~ estera** (*giorn.*) the foreign press; ~ **fotografica** (*giorn., pubbl.*) (*il procedimento*) photoprinting; (*il risultato*) photoprint; **la ~ locale** (*giorn.*) the local press; ~ **offset** (*giorn., pubbl.*) (*il procedimento*) offset process, offset printing; (*il risultato*) offset print; **la ~ scandalistica** (*giorn.*) the yellow press; **la ~ «sensazionale»** (*giorn.*) the yellow press; **a ~** printed (*a.*); **fuori ~** out of print; **in ~** in print.

stampaggio, *n. m.* (*stampa*) printing.

stampante, *a.* printing. *n. f.* (*elab. elettr.*) printer.

stampare, *v. t.* **1** (*lasciare l'impronta*) to stamp, to imprint, to impress. **2** (*giorn.*) to print, to publish, to machine, to run* off; (*tirare*) to pull. **3** (*pubbl.*) (*copie fotografiche*) to print. // ~ **a grandi caratteri** (*pubbl.*) to display; ~ **a mano** to print by hand; ~ **banconote** (*fin.*) to print bank-notes; ~ (*qc.*) **con errori** (*giorn., pubbl.*) to misprint; ~ **copie supplementari di** (*una pubblicazione, un inserto speciale, ecc.*) (*giorn.*) to overrun; ~ **l'edizione d'un quotidiano** (*giorn.*) to print the edition of a newspaper; ~ **in fotolito** (*giorn., pubbl.*) to offset; ~ **in offset** (*giorn., pubbl.*) to offset; ~ (*qc.*) **male** (*giorn., pubbl.*) to misprint; ~ **monete** to strike coins; ~ (*qc.*) **su una cambiale** to enface.

stampato, *a.* **1** (*impresso*) stamped, imprinted, impressed. **2** (*giorn.*) printed; (*di libro e sim.*) in print (*pred.*). *n. m.* **1** (*modulo*) printed form, form. **2** (*giorn.*) (*foglio, opuscolo stampato*) printed publication, print. **3** «**stampati**», *pl.* (*giorn.*) (*nella spedizione postale*) «printed matter».

stampatore, *n. m.* (*giorn.*) printer, pressman*, typographer.

stampatrice, *n. f.* (*macchina per la stampa*) printing-machine, printing-press, printer.

stamperia, *n. f.* (*giorn.*) printing-office, printing works (*sing.*).

stampiglia, *n. f.* (*attr. uff.*) stamp.

stampigliare, *v. t.* to stamp.

stampigliatrice, *n. f.* stamping machine. // ~ **per certificare la copertura d'un assegno bancario** (*che acquista così la validità d'un assegno circolare*) (*banca, macch. uff.*) check certifier (*USA*).

stand, *n. m.* (*market.*) stand.

standard, *n. m.* standard. *a.* standard. // ~ **argenteo** (*econ.*) silver standard; ~ **produttivo** (*org. az.*) production standard; **standard qualitativi** (*market.*) quality standards, standards of quality, grades; **prezzo ~** (*market.*) standard price.

standardizzare, *v. t.* to standardize; (*produrre in serie*) to mass-produce.

standardizzato, *a.* standardized; (*prodotto in serie*) mass-produced.

standardizzazione, *n. f.* standardization; (*produzione in serie*) mass-production.

standista, *n. m.* e *f.* (*market.*) (*chi allestisce e/o lavora a uno «stand», q. V.*) standholder; (*chi allestisce*) stand designer; (*addetto*) stand attendant.

stanza, *n. f.* room. // ~ **di compensazione** (*banca, cred., fin.*) bankers' clearing house, clearing house, clearance house; **la ~ di Compensazione di Londra** (*banca, fin.*) the London Bankers' Clearing House; ~ **di compensazione per euro-obbligazioni** (*fin.*) Euroclear; ~ **di lavoro** workroom.

stanziamento, *n. m.* **1** (*fin., rag.*) (*lo stanziare*) appropriation, allocation. **2** (*fin., rag.*) (*la somma stanziata*) appropriation, allocation, sum allocated; (*fondo*) fund. // ~ **di risorse** (*fin.*) allocation of resources; **gli stanziamenti per le spese amministrative** (*amm.*) the sums allocated for administrative expenditure; ~ **pubblicitario** (*org. az.*) advertising budget, budget.

stanziare, *v. t.* (*fin., rag.*) to appropriate, to allocate, to set* apart. // ~ **una certa somma per un fondo speciale d'ammortamento** (*rag.*) to appropriate a certain amount to a special fund for depreciation; ~ (*una somma*) **in bilancio** (*fin., rag.*) to budget; ~ **somme** (*fin., rag.*) to make appropriations.

stanziato, *a.* (*fin., rag.*) (*di fondo*) appropriated. // **non ~** (*fin., rag.*) (*di fondo*) unappropriated.

stare, *v. i.* **1** (*restare, rimanere*) to stay, to remain. **2** (*essere*) to be. **3** (*di salute*) to be. **4** (*abitare*) to live, to reside. **5** (*spettare*) to be up (to sb.). **6** (*mat.*) to be. // ~ **ai patti** to stand by the terms, to stand to the terms, to stand by an agreement, to keep a bargain; ~ **al gioco** (*fig.*) to take one's chance; ~ **al largo** (*trasp. mar.*) to lie off; ~ **certo** to rest assured; **star del credere** (*comm., leg.*) del credere.

stasi, *n. f. inv.* (*fig.*) (*ristagno*) stagnation, standstill; slump (*fam.*). // ~ **dell'attività economica** (*econ.*) bust.

statale, *a.* of the State; state, government

(*attr.*). *n. m.* e *f.* **1** (*pers.*) civil servant. **2** (*trasp. aut.*) (*strada statale*) highway, main road.

statalizzare, *v. t. V.* **statizzare.**

statalizzazione, *n. f. V.* **statizzazione.**

statistica, *n. f.* **1** (*stat.*) (*la scienza*) statistics (*col v. al sing.*). **2** (*stat.*) (*dato statistico*) statistic.

statistico, *a.* (*stat.*) statistical, statistic. *n. m.* (*stat.*) statistician.

statizzare, *v. t.* (*econ.*) to nationalize.

statizzazione, *n. f.* (*econ.*) nationalization.

stato, *n. m.* **1** state, condition. **2** (*in senso politico*) State; (*Paese*) Country; (*nazione*) nation. **3** (*fin.*) (*degli affari, ecc.*) showing. **4** (*leg.*) status. // **lo ~ assistenziale** (*econ.*) the Welfare State; **~ corporativo** (*econ.*) corporative state; **~ del passivo** (*leg.*) statement of liabilities; **~ d'inattività** (*econ.*) stagnation; doldrums (*pl.*); **~ di previsione** (*rag.*) estimation, estimate; **lo ~ di servizio** (*pers.*) the record of service, the record; **lo ~ di servizio d'un aspirante** (*a un posto*) (*pers.*) the record of an applicant; **~ di stagnazione** (*econ.*) stagnation; doldrums (*pl.*); **~ giuridico** (*leg.*) status; **~ patrimoniale** (*rag.*) balance sheet, trading account; **~ patrimoniale di liquidazione** (*rag.*) realization and liquidation account; **lo ~ sociale** (*econ.*) the Welfare State; **chi è messo in ~ d'accusa** (*leg.*) indictee; **chi mette in ~ d'accusa** (*leg.*) indictor; **di ~** State-controlled; State (*attr.*); **essere in ~ d'arresto** (*leg.*) to be (*o* to be held) under arrest, to be in charge, to be in custody.

statuire, *v. t.* (*leg.*) to enact, to decree.

status, *n. m.* status. // **~ quo** status quo; « **~ symbol** » (*econ., pubbl.*) status symbol.

statutario, *a.* (*leg.*) statutory; statute (*attr.*).

statuto, *n. m.* **1** (*leg.*) statute, charter; (*regolamento, leggina*) by-law. **2** (*leg.*) (*d'una società*) charter; (*d'una società di persone*) articles of partnership; (*d'una società di capitali*) articles of association; articles of incorporation (*USA*). // « **~ delle restrizioni** » (*leg.*) statute of limitations, statute of repose.

stazione, *n. f.* **1** station. **2** (*tur.*) (*luogo di villeggiatura*) resort. // **~ aeroportuale** (*trasp. aer.*) air station; **~ balneare** (*tur.*) seaside resort; **~ della metropolitana** (*trasp. ferr.*) underground station; subway station (*USA*); **~ d'arrivo** (*trasp. ferr.*) station of arrival, arrival station; **~ di destinazione** (*trasp. ferr.*) station of destination, destination station; **~ di partenza** (*trasp. ferr.*) station of departure; (*della merce*) forwarding station; **~ di rifornimento** (*trasp. aut.*) petrol station; gas station (*USA*); (*trasp. mar.*) bunkering station; **~ di rifornimento nafta** (*trasp. mar.*) wharf for fuel-oil bunkering; **~ di servizio** (*trasp. aut.*) service station; **~ di smistamento** (*trasp. ferr.*) shunting station; **~ di testa** (*trasp. ferr.*) terminal station, terminal, terminus; **~ di trasbordo** (*trasp. ferr.*) transfer house; **~ di villeggiatura estiva** (*tur.*) summer resort; **~ emittente** (*comun.*) broadcasting station; **~ ferroviaria** (*trasp. ferr.*) railway station; railroad station, depot (*USA*); **~ intermedia** (*trasp. ferr.*) intermediate station; way station (*USA*); **~ principale** (*trasp. ferr.*) main station; **~ radiotrasmittente** (*comun.*) broadcasting station, station; **~ secondaria** (*trasp. ferr.*) local station; way station, way point (*USA*).

stazza, *n. f.* (*trasp. mar.*) tonnage, burden. // **~ lorda** (*trasp. mar.*) gross tonnage; **~ netta** (*trasp. mar.*) net tonnage; **~ netta registrata** (*trasp. mar.*) net registered tonnage; **~ sotto ponte** (*trasp. mar.*) underdeck tonnage.

stazzare, *v. t.* **1** (*trasp. mar.*) (*misurare la stazza di*) to measure the tonnage of. **2** (*trasp. mar.*) (*di nave: avere capacità*) to have a tonnage of.

stazzatore, *n. m.* (*trasp. mar.*) tonnage-measurer.

stazzatura, *n. f.* **1** (*trasp. mar.*) (*misurazione della stazza*) tonnage admeasurement, measurement. **2** (*trasp. mar.*) (*stazza*)) tonnage, burden.

«stellage», *n. m.* (*Borsa*) double option.

stellaggio, *n. m.* (*Borsa*) double option.

stendere, *v. t.* (*mettere per iscritto*) to draw★ up, to draft. // **~ un'accusa** (*leg.*) to draw up an accusation; **~ un contratto** to draw up a contract, to draw a contract; **~ la minuta di** (*qc.*) to minute; **~ il verbale di** (*una riunione, ecc.*) (*leg.*) to minute.

stenodattilografa, *n. f.* (*pers.*) shorthand-typist, stenotypist.

stenodattilografia, *n. f.* shorthand typewriting.

stenodattilografo, *n. m.* (*pers.*) shorthand-typist, stenotypist.

stenografa, *n. f.* (*pers.*) shorthand-writer, stenographer.

stenografare, *v. t.* to write★ in shorthand, to shorthand, to stenograph. // **~ un discorso** to take down a speech in shorthand.

stenografia, *n. f.* shorthand, stenography.

stenografico, *a.* stenographic, stenographical; shorthand (*attr.*).

stenografo, *n. m.* (*pers.*) shorthand-writer, stenographer.

stenogramma, *n. m.* stenograph.

stenotipia, *n. f.* stenotypy.

sterlina, *n. f.* (*ingl.*) pound sterling, pound. *a.* (*nella locuz.* **lira** ~) sterling. // **una ~ forte** (*fin.*) a firm pound sterling; **una lira sterlina** a pound sterling.

stero, *n. m.* (*misura di volume*) stero★, stere, cubic metre.

stesura, *n. f.* writing out, drawing up, wording. // ~ **d'un atto legale** (*leg.*) engrossment; **la ~ d'un contratto** (*leg.*) the drawing up of a contract.

steward, *n. m.* (*trasp. aer., trasp. mar.*) steward.

stima, *n. f.* **1** (*buona opinione*) esteem; (*rispetto*) respect; (*riputazione*) reputation; (*credito*) credit. **2** (*valutazione*) estimate, valuation, rating, appreciation, assessment, appraisement, appraisal; (*computo, calcolo*) computation. **3** (*rag.*) estimate, estimation, valuation. **4** (*stat.*) estimate. // ~ **catastale** (*leg.*) cadastral estimate, cadastral survey; **una ~ dei danni** (*ass.*) an assessment of damages; ~ **della domanda d'un nuovo prodotto** (*market.*) new-product demand estimate; **la ~ d'una proprietà** (*rag.*) the valuation of a property; **una ~ non ufficiale** an unofficial estimate.

stimabile, *a.* **1** (*degno di stima*) estimable; (*rispettabile*) respectable, reputable. **2** (*che si può stimare*) ratable, rateable, appreciable, assessable, appraisable.

stimare, *v. t.* **1** (*avere buona opinione di*) to esteem; (*rispettare*) to respect; (*riputare*) to repute. **2** (*valutare*) to estimate, to value, to rate, to appreciate, to assess, to appraise; (*computare, calcolare*) to compute. **3** (*rag.*) to estimate, to value. // ~ **i danni** (*ass.*) to assess damages; ~ **una proprietà** (*rag.*) to value a property.

stimatissimo, *a.* (*nell'introduzione a una lettera commerciale*) Dear.

stimato, *a.* **1** esteemed; (*rispettato*) respected; (*riputato*) reputed. **2** (*valutato*) estimated, valued, rated, assessed, appraised. **3** (*rag.*) estimated.

stimatore, *n. m.* **1** estimator, appraiser, assessor, valuer, valuator. **2** (*ass., leg.*) valuator.

stipendiare, *v. t.* (*pers.*) to pay★ a salary to, to salary.

stipendiato, *a.* (*pers.*) salaried. *n. m.* (*pers.*) salaried person.

stipendio, *n. m.* (*pers.*) salary, pay; earnings (*pl.*); packet (*fam.*); paycheck (*fam., USA*). // ~ **base** (*pers.*) base salary; ~ **del periodo di prova** (*pers.*) probationary salary; ~ **iniziale** (*pers.*) commencing salary; ~ **netto** (*pers.*) take-home pay; ~ **pensionabile** (*pers., rag.*) pensionable salary; **uno ~ rimunerativo** (*pers.*) a remunerative salary; **basato sullo ~** (*pers.*) (*di pensione, ecc.*) earnings-related; **chi prepara gli stipendi** (*pers.*) paymaster.

stipo, *n. m.* (*attr. uff.*) cabinet.

stipula, *n. f. V.* **stipulazione.**

stipulante, *a.* (*leg.*) stipulating. *n. m.* (*leg.*) stipulator, obligor.

stipulare, *v. t.* **1** (*leg.*) to stipulate; (*concordare*) to agree upon; (*stendere*) to draw★ up; (*pattuire*) to condition; (*di contratto, legge, ecc.*) to provide. **2** (*market.*) (*un prezzo, ecc.*) to name. // ~ **un contratto** (*leg.*) to stipulate a contract, to draw up an agreement; ~ **contratti d'assicurazione** (*ass., anche*) to sell insurance.

stipulato, *a.* **1** (*leg.*) stipulated; (*concordato*) agreed upon. **2** (*market.*) (*di prezzo, ecc.*) named.

stipulazione, *n. f.* (*leg.*) stipulation; (*stesura*) drawing up; (*contratto*) contract; (*accordo*) agreement; (*condizione*) provision, condition.

stiva, *n. f.* (*trasp. mar.*) hold, bulk. // ~ **di poppa** (*trasp. mar.*) after hold; ~ **per il carbone** (*trasp. mar.*) bunker.

stivaggio, *n. m.* (*trasp. mar.*) stowage. // ~ **alla rinfusa** (*trasp. mar.*) stowage in bulk; ~ **difettoso** (*trasp. mar.*) faulty stowage, bad stowage; ~ **e caricazione in sacchi** (*trasp. mar.*) trimming and bagging.

stivare, *v. t.* (*trasp. mar.*) to stow. *v. i.* to trim holds. // ~ **il carico** (*trasp. mar.*) to rummage; ~ **di nuovo** (*il carico*) (*trasp. mar.*) to restow; ~ **merci alla rinfusa** (*trasp. mar.*) to stow goods in bulk.

stivatore, *n. m.* (*trasp. mar.*) stevedore, stower, trimmer.

stoccaggio, *n. m.* (*org. az.*) storage.

stock, *n. m.* (*org. az.*) stock, inventory. // ~ **computato alla chiusura dell'esercizio** (*rag.*) closing stock; **uno ~ di merci** (*org. az.*) a stock of goods; ~ **di riserva** (*fin.*) buffer; (*org. az.*) cushion; ~ **economico** (*org. az.*) economic stock; ~ **fisico** (*org. az.*) physical stock; ~ **«tampone»** (*econ.*) buffer stock.

«stone», *n. m.* (*misura di peso pari a kg 6,350 circa*) stone.

stop, *n. m.* (*comun.*) (*nei telegrammi, ecc.*) stop.

stornare, *v. t.* (*rag.*) to transfer, to divert, to contra; (*una scrittura a partita doppia*) to reverse. // ~ **un'ordinazione** (*market.*) to cancel (*o* to withdraw) an order; ~ **una registrazione** (*rag.*) to reverse an entry, to contra an entry; ~ **una scrittura** (*rag.*) to reverse an entry, to contra an entry.

storno, *n. m.* (*rag.*) transfer, diversion, clearing, contraing; (*di scritture a partita doppia*) reversal. // **storni dalla riserva speciale** (*fin., rag.*) withdrawls from the special reserve; ~ **di denaro pubblico** (*leg.*) diversion of public funds; **lo** ~ **d'un'ordinazione** the cancellation (*o* withdrawal) of an order; **uno** ~ **di scrittura** (*rag.*) a reversal of entry; **lo** ~ **d'una scrittura** (*rag.*) the transfer of an entry; **a** ~ (*rag.*) per contra, in reversal.

stragiudiziale, *a.* (*leg.*) extrajudicial; out of Court.

stragiudizialmente, *avv.* (*leg.*) extrajudicially.

stralciare, *v. t.* **1** (*levare via*) to take* away, to take* off, to remove. **2** (*fin.*) (*liquidare*) to liquidate, to wind* up. // ~ **un articolo da un catalogo** (*market.*) to remove an article from a catalogue; ~ **un'azienda** (*fin.*) to liquidate a firm.

stralcio, *n. m.* **1** (*il levare via*) taking away, taking off, removal, removing. **2** (*fin.*) (*liquidazione*) winding up, liquidation. // ~ **del budget** (*riferito a un particolare settore o ufficio della pubblica amministrazione, e che contempli previsioni di entrate per la vendita di beni o servizi*) (*fin., rag.*) appropriation-in-aid; **vendere a** ~ to sell at bargain prices.

straordinario, *a.* **1** extraordinary; (*insolito*) unusual; (*fuori del comune*) uncommon; (*speciale*) special; (*eccezionale*) exceptional; (*spettacoloso*) spectacular; (*eccessivo*) exceeding; extra, record, smash (*attr.*). **2** (*econ.*) (*di capitolo d'entrata o spesa di bilancio*) below-the-line. *n. m.* **1** (*pers., sind.*) (*lavoro straordinario*) overtime work, overtime. **2** (*pers., sind.*) (*compenso per il lavoro straordinario*) overtime pay. // **edizione straordinaria** (*giorn.*) special (edition).

strappare, *v. t.* **1** (*togliere con forza*) to pull up, to pull out, to tear* up. **2** (*stracciare*) to tear*. **3** (*fig.*) (*riuscire a ottenere, carpire*) to wring*, to wrench. // ~ **a q. una riduzione del 4%** (*su un prezzo*) to knock sb. down 4% (*fam.*).

stretta, *n. f.* **1** (*atto dello stringere*) grasp, grip, hold. **2** (*cred.*) squeeze; crunch (*fam.*). // **una** ~ **creditizia** (*fin.*) a money squeeze, a credit squeeze; ~ **ribassista** (*Borsa*) bear squeeze.

strozzinaggio, *n. m.* (*cred.*) usury, moneygrubbing.

strozzino, *n. m.* (*cred.*) usurer, moneygrubber, loan shark.

strumentale, *a.* **1** instrumental; (*ausiliario*) auxiliary. **2** (*econ.*) (*di beni, ecc.*) inconsumable.

strumento, *n. m.* **1** (*anche fig.*) instrument, tool. **2** (*fig.*) (*mezzo*) means, medium*; (*tramite, veicolo*) vehicle; (*leva*) lever. **3** (*leg.*) instrument, deed, charter. **4** (*org. az.*) implement, tool. **5** **strumenti**, *pl.* (*org. az.*) tackle (*sing. coll.*). // **lo** ~ **adatto per un lavoro** the proper tool for a job; **uno** ~ **d'accelerazione della spesa pubblica** a means of speeding up public spending; **strumenti di precisione** (*org. az.*) precision instruments; ~ **misuratore** measuring instrument, meter; **strumenti negoziabili** (*cred.*) negotiable instruments, bills and notes.

struttura, *n. f.* (*anche fig.*) structure, framework, frame. // ~ **dei salari** (*econ., sind.*) wage structure; ~ **del capitale** (*tipo e numero delle azioni emesse o da emettere*) (*fin.*) capital structure; **strutture dell'approvvigionamento** (*econ.*) supply structures; ~ **direzionale** (*org. az.*) management structure; **la** ~ **distributiva** (*market.*) the frame of distribution; ~ **finanziaria** (*fin.*) capital structure; ~ **funzionale** (*org. az.*) functional structure, staff structure; ~ **gerarchica** (*org. az.*) hierarchical structure; ~ **organizzativa** (*org. az.*) organization structure; ~ **organizzativa orizzontale** (*org. az.*) horizontal organizational structure, flat organization structure; ~ **organizzativa verticale** (*org. az.*) vertical organizational structure, tall organization; ~ **per obiettivi** (*org. az.*) structure by objectives.

strutturale, *a.* structural.

studio, *n. m.* **1** study. **2** (*esame*) examination, study, investigation; (*scientifico*) research; (*ispezione, valutazione*) survey. **3** (*progetto*) plan. **4** (*stanza di studio*) study; (*di professionista*) office. // ~ **comparativo** comparative study; **uno** ~ **comparativo dei mercati europei** (*market.*) a comparative study of the European markets; **studi comparativi di prodotti concorrenziali** (*market.*) comparative studies of competitive products; ~ **della produzione** (*org. az.*) process analysis; ~ **d'avvocato** chambers of a barrister, chambers; ~ **di pubblicità** (*pubbl.*) advertising office; ~ **e analisi dei mercati** (*market.*) marketing; ~ **legale** solicitor's office, chambers (of a barrister); ~ **preliminare** (*market.*) preliminary investigation; ~ **pubblicitario** (*pubbl.*) personal agency; **essere allo** ~ to be under consideration; to be in the works (*USA*).

subaffittante, *n. m.* e *f.* (*leg.*) sublessor.

subaffittare, *v. t.* (*leg.*) to sublet*, to underlet*, to relet*, to sublease, to underlease.

subaffitto, *n. m.* (*leg.*) sublease, underlease, reletting, subtenancy.

subaffittuario, *n. m.* (*leg.*) sublessee, underlessee, subtenant.

subagente, *n. m.* (*org. az.*) subagent, under-agent.

subagenzia, *n. f.* (*org. az.*) subagency.

subalterno, *a.* subaltern; (*subordinato*) subordinate; (*inferiore*) inferior; (*secondario*) secondary. *n. m.* (*pers.*) subordinate, secondary, inferior, junior.

subappaltare, *v. t.* (*leg.*) to subcontract, to sublet★, to job.

subappaltatore, *n. m.* (*leg.*) subcontractor.

subappalto, *n. m.* (*leg.*) subcontract.

subasta, *n. f. V.* **asta.**

subentrante, *a.* incoming.

subentrare, *v. i.* to take★ the place (of), to take★ over, to succeed, to replace.

subentro, *n. m.* replacement.

subire, *v. t.* to undergo★, to go★ through, to experience; (*sostenere*) to sustain; (*soffrire*) to suffer. // ~ **un calo nei prezzi di vendita** (*fin., market.*) to sell off; ~ **una forte flessione** (*econ., fin., market.*) (*di prezzi, ecc.*) to slump, to sag; ~ **un incidente** to suffer an accident; (*trasp.*) (*d'auto, treni, ecc.*) to wreck; ~ **un interrogatorio** (*leg.*) to undergo an examination; ~ **una perdita** (*rag.*) to suffer a loss, to experience a loss, to make a loss; ~ **un processo** (*leg.*) to be on trial; ~ **un tracollo** (*econ., fin., fig.*) to smash.

sublocare, *v. t.* (*leg.*) to sublease, to sublet★.

sublocatario, *n. m.* (*leg.*) sublessee.

sublocazione, *n. f.* (*leg.*) sublease, sublease.

subordinare, *v. t.* to subordinate, to render subordinate, to render dependent, to condition.

subordinatamente, *avv.* subordinately, dependently, conditionally. // ~ **al fatto che la consegna sia eseguita prima della fine della stagione** conditionally to delivery being made within the end of the season.

subordinato, *a.* subordinate, secondary, dependent. *n. m.* (*pers.*) subordinate, secondary, inferior, under-clerk. // ~ **al deposito preliminare degli effetti** (*cred.*) conditional upon the deposit of the bills in advance.

subordinazione, *n. f.* (*leg.*) subordination.

succedaneo, *a.* acting as a substitute, substitute. *n. m.* (*econ., market.*) substitute.

successibile, *a.* (*leg.*) entitled to succeed. *n. m.* (*leg.*) person entitled to succeed.

successione, *n. f.* **1** succession. **2** (*serie, sequela*) series, sequence. **3** (*leg.*) succession. **4** (*amm., pers.*) replacement. // ~ **ereditaria** (*leg.*) hereditary succession; ~ **testamentaria** (*leg.*) testamentary succession; ~ **universale** (*leg.*) universal succession; ~ **vacante** (*leg.*) estate in abeyance; **tassa di** ~ (*fin.*) death duty.

successivo, *a.* successive, next, later, following, ensuing, consecutive; follow-up (*attr.*).

successo, *n. m.* **1** (*anche market.*) success. **2** (*market.*) hit, run. // **un** ~ **strepitoso** a smash success, a smash hit; **che non ha (avuto)** ~ unsuccessful; **senza** ~ with no success; unsuccessfully (*avv.*); unsuccessful (*a.*).

successore, *n. m.* successor.

succursale, *n. f.* (*org. az.*) branch office, branch house, branch, office. // ~ **d'agenzia** (*org. az.*) agency branch; ~ **d'ufficio postale** (*comun.*) branch post-office.

suddetto, *a.* **1** above-said, aforesaid, above-named, above-stated, said, above. **2** (*rag.*) (*nelle fatture, negli inventari, ecc.*) ditto.

suindicato, *a. V.* **sopraindicato.**

summenzionato, *a.* above-mentioned, aforementioned, above-named, above-said, said (*attr.*); mentioned above (*pred.*).

sunnominato, *a. V.* **summenzionato.**

suolo, *n. m.* (*terra, terreno*) ground, soil, land. // ~ **pubblico** communal land.

supermarket, *n. m.* (*market.*) supermarket.

supermercato, *n. m.* (*market.*) supermarket. // ~ **finanziario** (*fin., USA*) financial department store; ~ **per dettaglianti** (*market.*) cash and carry.

supernazionale, *a.* supranational.

supero, *n. m.* (*fin.*) (*soprappiù*) surplus, extra, excess.

superproduzione, *n. f.* (*econ.*) overproduction.

superstite, *a.* surviving. *n. m.* e *f.* (*ass.*) survivor.

supervalutare, *v. t. V.* **sopravvalutare.**

supervisione, *n. f.* (*org. az.*) supervision, oversight.

supervisore, *n. m.* (*pers.*) supervisor, superintendent.

supplementare, *a.* supplementary, supplemental; (*sussidiario*) subsidiary; (*addizionale*) additional; extra (*attr.*).

supplemento, *n. m.* **1** supplement. **2** (*giorn.*) supplement, insert, inset. **3** (*market.*) (*sovrapprezzo*) extra charge, surcharge, extra. **4** (*mat.*) supplement. **5** (*pers.*) extra pay. **6** (*trasp. ferr.*) extra charge. // ~ **di nolo** (*trasp. mar.*) additional freight; ~ **di premio** (*ass.*) additional premium; ~ **di prezzo** (*market.*) additional charge, extra charge; ~ **di salario per spese di vitto non corrisposto** (*pers.*) board wages; ~ **di tariffa** (*trasp. ferr.*) excess fare; ~ **domenicale** (*giorn.*) Sunday supplement.

supplente, *a.* substitute, temporary; temp (*fam.*). *n. m.* e *f.* **1** (*leg., org. az.*) locum tenens. **2** (*pers.*) substitute; sub (*fam.*).

supplenza, *n. f.* **1** (*leg., org. az.*) locumtenency. **2** (*pers.*) temporary post, temporary substitution.

suppletivo, *a.* **1** supplementary. **2** (*leg.*) suppletory.

suppletorio, *a.* **1** supplementary. **2** (*leg.*) suppletory.

supplire, *v. i.* to supply; (*compensare*) to compensate for, to make* up for. *v. t.* to substitute for; to sub for (*fam.*).

surgelati, *n. pl.* (*market.*) frozen food.

«surplus», *n. m.* (*econ.*) surplus. // **surplus agricoli** (*econ.*) farm surpluses; ~ **di capitale** (*fin., USA*) capital surplus.

surrettiziamente, *avv.* (*leg.*) surreptitiously.

surrettizio, *a.* (*leg.*) surreptitious.

surriferito, *a.* above-mentioned, above-stated; afore-said (*attr.*); referred to above (*pred.*).

surriscaldamento, *n. m.* (*anche fig.*) overheating.

surriscaldare, *v. t.* (*anche fig.*) to overheat.

surriscaldarsi, *v. rifl.* (*anche fig.: dell'economia*) to get* overheated, to overheat.

surroga, *n. f. V.* **surrogazione.**

surrogabile, *a.* (*sostituibile*) replaceable; (*supplementare*) supplementary, supplemental, additional; (*alternativo*) alternative.

surrogare, *v. t.* **1** (*mettere in luogo d'un altro*) to subrogate, to substitute for. **2** (*subentrare ad altri*) to take* the place of, to replace.

surrogato, *n. m.* (*econ., market.*) substitute.

surrogazione, *n. f.* (*leg.*) subrogation, substitution.

suspicione, *n. f.* (*leg.*) suspicion.

sussidiare, *v. t.* to subsidize; (*aiutare*) to help, to aid.

sussidiario, *a.* subsidiary, auxiliary, ancillary; (*supplementare*) supplementary.

sussidio, *n. m.* **1** subsidy; (*aiuto*) help, aid; (*appoggio, sostegno*) support. **2** (*pers., sind.*) benefit, allowance. // ~ **agli scioperanti** (*pagato dai sindacati*) (*sind.*) strike pay, strike benefit; **sussidi all'agricoltura** (*econ.*) agricultural support subsidies, farm subsidies; ~ **di disoccupazione** (*sind.*) unemployment benefit, unemployment compensation, dole; ~ **di malattia** (*o* **d'invalidità**) (*pers.*) sickness benefit; ~ **governativo agli Enti locali** (*econ., ingl.*) general grant; ~ **incrociato** (*o* **indiretto**) (*fin.*) cross-subsidy; ~ **(per) malattia** (*pers.*) sick-pay, sick-benefit.

svalutare, *v. t.* **1** (*econ.*) to devalue, to undervalue, to devaluate, to devalorize. **2** (*fin.*) (*monete, ecc., alterandole*) to depreciate, to debase. **3** (*rag.*) (*attività, titoli, ecc.*) to depreciate, to write* off, to write* down. // ~ **un'attività** (*rag.*) to write down an asset; ~ **ufficialmente una moneta** (*econ.*) to decry a coin.

svalutarsi, *v. rifl.* (*econ.*) (*di monete, ecc.*) to depreciate.

svalutato, *a.* undervalued.

svalutazione, *n. f.* **1** (*econ.*) devaluation, undervaluation. **2** (*fin.*) (*di monete, ecc., alterandole*) depreciation, debasement. **3** (*rag.*) (*d'attività, titoli, ecc.*) depreciation, writing-off, writing-down, write-off, write-down. // **una** ~ **a fini di ammortamento** (*rag.*) a write-off for amortization; ~ **del capitale** (*rag.*) depletion of capital; ~ **della moneta** (*econ.*) debasement of the coinage; ~ **di titoli** (*fin.*) depreciation of securities; ~ **fluttuante** (*econ.*) floating devaluation; ~ **monetaria** (*fin.*) currency devaluation, currency depreciation.

svendere, *v. t.* (*market.*) to undersell*, to sell* off, to sell* out, to work off; (*prodotti, specialm. all'estero*) to dump; (*rimanenze*) to remainder. // ~ **merci** (*avendo previsto un crollo dei prezzi*) (*market.*) to unload; ~ **titoli** (*avendo previsto un crollo dei prezzi*) (*fin.*) to unload.

svendita, *n. f.* (*market.*) underselling, selling-off, selling-out; clearance sale, sale, break-up; (*di prodotti, specialm. all'estero*) dumping. // ~ **per cessazione di esercizio** clean-up (*slang USA*).

sviluppare, *v. t.* **1** (*far crescere*) to develop, to expand. **2** (*mat.*) (*un'equazione, ecc.*) to develop, to expand. **3** (*pubbl.*) (*una pellicola*) to develop. // ~ **la propria azienda** (*org. az.*) to develop one's business; ~ **la capacità concorrenziale delle imprese europee** (*econ.*) to develop the competitive capacity of European firms; ~ **un'equazione** (*mat.*) to develop an equation.

svilupparsi, *v. rifl.* **1** to develop. **2** (*crescere*) to grow*, to expand. // ~ **rapidamente** to mushroom.

sviluppo, *n. m.* **1** development, expansion; (*crescita*) growth; (*evoluzione*) evolution. **2** (*market.*) promotion. **3** (*mat.*) (*d'un'equazione, ecc.*) development, expansion. **4** (*pubbl.*) (*fotografico*) development. // ~ **aziendale** (*org. az.*) company growth; corporate growth (*USA*); ~ **coordinato** (*econ., org. az.*) balanced growth; ~ **del prodotto** (*market.*) product development; **lo** ~ **dell'attività commerciale** the evolution of trade; ~ **(delle) vendite** (*pubbl.*) sales promotion; ~ **e formazione manageriale** (*pers.*) management selection and training; ~ **e stampa**

(*pubbl.*) developing and printing; ~ **economico** (*econ.*) economic development, economic growth; « ~ **economico zero** » (*econ.*) zero economic growth (*ZEG*); ~ **edilizio** (*econ.*) housing boom; **uno ~ equilibrato** (*econ., org. az.*) a balanced development, a balanced growth; **lo ~ industriale** (*econ.*) the development of industry; ~ **ottimale** (*econ.*) optimum growth; **in via di ~** (*di un Paese e sim.*) developing.

svincolare, *v. t.* **1** (*dog.*) to clear. **2** (*leg.*) to release, to redeem. // ~ **una proprietà** (*leg.*) to redeem an estate.

svincolarsi, *v. rifl.* to release oneself, to disengage oneself, to free oneself. // ~ **da un impegno** to contract (oneself) out of engagement.

svincolo, *n. m.* **1** (*dog.*) clearing, clearance. **2** (*leg.*) release, redemption.

«swap», *n. m.* (*fin.*) swap, swapping. // ~ **bilaterale** (*fin.*) bilateral swapping.

T

tabella, *n. f.* table; (*prospetto*) schedule; (*lista*) list; (*carta*) chart. // **una ~ dei noli** (*trasp. mar.*) a schedule of freight rates; **~ dei pesi e delle misure** table of weights and measures; **~ dei prezzi** (*market.*) price-list; **~ (*base*) dei salari** (*sind.*) wage scale; **~ delle partenze** (*trasp. mar.*) sailings board; **~ delle partenze dei treni** (*trasp. ferr.*) station-calendar; **~ di marcia** (*anche fig.*) schedule; **~ di previsione delle consegne** (*org. az.*) delivery schedule.

tabellare, *a.* tabular.

tabellone, *n. m.* **1** notice-board. **2** (*per affissioni*) hoarding; bill-board (*USA*). // **~ pubblicitario** (*sul quale si affiggono manifesti*) (*pubbl.*) poster panel, advertisement hoarding.

«tabloid», *n. m.* (*giorn.*) tabloid.

tabulatore, *n. m.* (*di macchina da scrivere*) tabulator.

taccuino, *n. m.* **1** notebook, pocket book. **2** (*attr. uff.*) memorandum book, memory book, memo book.

tachimetro, *n. m.* (*trasp. aut.*) speedometer, tachymeter.

tacitare, *v. t.* **1** (*mettere a tacere*) to silence, to hush up. **2** (*cred.*) (*un creditore*) to satisfy, to pay★ off.

tacito, *a.* **1** (*che tace*) silent, quiet. **2** (*non espresso ma intuibile*) tacit, unexpressed, implied; (*sottinteso*) understood. // **~ accordo** (*leg.*) tacit agreement; **un ~ avvertimento** a tacit warning; **~ consenso** (*leg.*) tacit consent, sufferance.

taglia, *n. f.* **1** (*leg.*) (*premio promesso a chi cattura malviventi*) reward, price. **2** (*market.*) (*d'indumento*) size.

tagliacarte, *n. m. inv.* (*attr. uff.*) paper-knife★, letter opener.

tagliando, *n. m.* coupon. // **~ che conferma l'avvenuta visita d'un piazzista a un cliente** (*market.*) call-slip; **~ da incollare** (*market.*) sticker; **~ di controllo** (*org. az.*) contents slip; **~ di riscontro** (*«madre» o «figlia»*) (*market.*) tally.

tagliare, *v. t.* **1** to cut★; (*staccare tagliando*) to cut★ off; (*cimare, spuntare; anche fig.*) to trim. **2** (*attraversare*) to cut★ across. **3** (*giorn.*) (*parti d'un articolo, libro, ecc.*) to retrench, to cut★. *v. i.* **1** to cut★; (*essere affilato*) to be sharp. **2** (*seguire la via più breve*) to cut★ across. // **~ a metà** (*la differenza fra il prezzo richiesto e quello offerto*) (*comm.*) to split the difference; **~ fuori q.** (*market.*) to freeze sb. out; **~ le spese** (*rag.*) to cut down expenses; **~ la strada a q.** (*trasp. aut.*) to cut sb. in; **~ la testa al toro** (*fig.*) to decide the issue.

taglio, *n. m.* **1** cut. **2** (*econ., fin.*) (*nelle spese previste in bilancio*) retrenchment, cut. **3** (*fin.*) (*di biglietti di banca, ecc.*) denomination. **4** (*giorn.*) (*in un articolo, libro, ecc.*) retrenchment, cut. **5** (*market.*) (*foggia, linea, d'abiti, ecc.*) cut, make; (*stile*) style. **6** (*market.*) (*lunghezza di stoffa*) length. // **un ~ alle spese** (*rag.*) a cut in expenditure; **un ~ di stoffa** (*market.*) a length of material.

tale, *a.* **1** such. **2** (*certo*) certain, one. *pron. indef.* fellow, man★, chap (*m.*); girl, woman★ (*f.*). // **~ quale** (*fin.*) (*di corso*) tel quel, tale quale; flat (*a. attr.*).

talloncino, *n. m.* **1** (*cedola*) talon. **2** (*banca*) slip. **3** (*trasp. mar.*) (*allegato a una polizza di carico*) attachment.

tampone, *n. m.* tampon. // **~ di carta assorbente** (*attr. uff.*) blotting pad, blotting dabber, blotting case; **~ per timbri** (*attr. uff.*) ink-pad.

tangente, *a.* tangent. *n. f.* **1** (*fin.*) (*quota, rata*) quota, share, portion. **2** (*market.*) kick-back. **3** (*mat.*) tangent line, tangent.

tangenziale, *a.* (*mat.*) tangential. *n. f.* (*trasp. aut.*) by-pass.

tara, *n. f.* (*market.*) tare. // **~ convenuta** (*market.*) computed tare; **~ convenzionale** (*market.*) customary tare; **~ d'uso** (*market.*) customary tare, usual tare; **~ media** (*market.*) average tare; **~ percentuale** (*market.*) percentage tare; **~ reale** (*market.*) actual tare, real tare.

tarare, *v. t.* **1** (*regolare uno strumento, un apparecchio, e sim.*) to set★, to adjust. **2** (*market.*) (*fare, o detrarre, la tara*) to tare.

taratura, *n. f.* (*di strumenti, apparecchi e*

sim.) setting, adjustment.

targa, *n. f.* **1** (*lastra di metallo e sim.*) plate. **2** (*trasp. aut.*) number-plate; licence plate (*USA*).

targhetta, *n. f.* (*attr. uff.*) (*per indirizzi*) embossed (metal) plate.

targhettare, *v. t.* (*indirizzi*) to emboss.

targhettatrice, *n. f.* (*attr. uff.*) (*per stampare indirizzi*) addressing machine, addressograph, addresser.

tariffa, *n. f.* **1** tariff, price. **2** (*comm. est., econ., market.*) tariff, rate. **3** (*pers.*) tariff, scale; (*di professionista*) fee. **4** (*trasp.*) tariff, fare. **5** (*tur.*) (*alberghiera*) tariff, term, rate. // ~ **a rischio del vettore** (*trasp. ferr.*) carrier's risk rate; **tariffe adottate per rappresaglia** (*da un Paese nei confronti d'un altro*) (*comm. est.*) retaliatory tariffs, retaliatory duties; ~ **base** (*market.*) basis rate; ~ **combinata** (*trasp.*) combined rate; ~ **comune nei confronti dei Paesi terzi** (*comm. est.*) common external tariff of the Community; ~ **concordata** agreed rate; **tariffe cumulative** (*su cui si accordano due o più vettori*) (*trasp.*) joint tariffs, through rates; ~ **dei premi** (*ass.*) premium rate; **tariffe dei trasporti** (*trasp.*) transport rates; (*di merci*) carriage rates; freight rate (*USA*); **tariffe d'assicurazione** (*ass.*) insurance rates; ~ **di mediazione** (*comm.*) rate of commission, commission rate; ~ **di nolo** (*trasp. mar.*) freight rate; **tariffe di più difficile riduzione** (*o* **abolizione**) (*dog., econ.*) «hard core» tariffs; **tariffe di riferimento** reference tariffs; **tariffe di sostegno** (*econ.*) support tariffs; **tariffe differenziali** (*comm. est.*) differential tariffs, discriminating tariffs; ~ **dimezzata** (*trasp.*) half fare; ~ (*telefonica*) **diurna** (*comun.*) day charge; ~ **doganale** (*dog.*) customs tariff; ~ **doganale comune** (*dog.*) common customs tariff; **tariffe «dure»** (*dog., econ.*) «hard-core» tariffs; **tariffe ferroviarie** (*trasp. ferr.*) railway rates; railroad rates (*USA*); **tariffe ferroviarie differenziali** (*trasp. ferr.*) differential rates on a railway; ~ **fissa** (*cioè, indipendente dalla distanza percorsa*) (*trasp.*) flat rate, standard charge; ~ **flessibile** (*trasp.*) flexible tariff; ~ **forfettaria** standard charge; ~ **generale** (*trasp. ferr.*) carrier's risk rate; ~ **intera** (*comun.*) (*telegrafica, ecc.*) full rate; (*dog.*) full rate; (*trasp.*) full fare; **tariffe** (*per*) **interurbane notturne** (*comun.*) long-distance night rates; **tariffe invisibili** (*econ.*) invisible tariffs; **tariffe «irriducibili»** (*dog., econ.*) «hard-core» tariffs; ~ **ordinaria** (*comun., trasp.*) ordinary rate; ~ **per** (*la spedizione di*) **colli** (*trasp. ferr.*) parcels rate; ~ **per consegna a domicilio** (*trasp. ferr.*) charge for delivery; ~ **per il deposito dei bagagli** (*trasp. ferr.*) cloak-room fee; ~ (*ridotta*) **per famiglie** (*trasp.*) family fare; ~ **per la fornitura idrica** water rate, water rent; ~ (*postale*) **per giornali e periodici** (*giorn.*) newspaper rate; ~ (*postale*) **per lettere** (*comun.*) letter rate; ~ **per noli di transito** (*trasp.*) in-transit freight rate; ~ **per ritiro a domicilio** (*trasp. ferr.*) charge for collection; ~ (*postale*) **per la spedizione di campioni** (*comun.*) sample rate; **la** ~ **per** (*la spedizione degli*) **stampati** (*comun.*) the rate for printed matter; ~ **per telegrammi** (*comun.*) telegraph rate; ~ **per telegrammi urgenti** (*comun.*) urgent rate; **tariffe per trasporti in servizio cumulativo** (*trasp.*) through rates; **tariffe per il trasporto delle merci** (*trasp.*) goods rates; **la** ~ **per tre minuti di conversazione** (*comun.*) the charge for a three minutes' conversation; **tariffe per vagoni completi** (*trasp. ferr.*) truck load rates; ~ **postale** (*comun.*) postal tariff, postage, post; ~ **preferenziale per merce alla rinfusa** (*comm. est.*) bulk supply tariff; **tariffe preferenziali** (*comm. est.*) preferential tariffs; **tariffe proibitive** (*econ., market.*) prohibitive tariffs; **tariffe protezionistiche** (*econ.*) protective tariffs; ~ **pubblicitaria fissa** (*cioè, indipendente dallo spazio occupato*) (*pubbl.*) flat advertising rate; **tariffe pubblicitarie** (*pubbl.*) advertisement rates; **tariffe restrittive** (*econ.*) restrictive tariffs; ~ **ridotta** (*da applicarsi a una «term policy», q.V.*) (*ass., USA*) term rate; **tariffe ridotte** reduced rates; (*trasp.*) half fares; ~ **speciale** (*trasp. ferr.*) owner's risk rate; **tariffe stagionali** (*tur.*) seasonal rates; ~ **tabellare** (*ass.*) schedule rate, specific rate; **a** ~ **ridotta** (*trasp.*) reduced-rate (*a. attr.*).

tariffare, *v. t.* (*comm. est., econ., trasp.*) to tariff.

tariffario, *a.* tariff, price, rate (*attr.*). *n. m.* tariff; (*listino*) price-list. // ~ **degli onorari** (*degli avvocati, ecc.*) fee bill; **non** ~ (*comm. est.*) non-tariff (*a. attr.*).

tasca, *n. f.* pocket.

tascabile, *a.* pocket, pocket-size (*attr.*).

tassa, *n. f.* (*fin.*) tax, duty, fee; (*come gettito*) levy. // «~ **a carico del destinatario**» (*comun.*) «business reply service»; ~ **d'acquisto** (*fin.*) purchase tax; ~ **di bollo** (*fin.*) stamp-duty, stamp-tax; (*pagata su ogni azione emessa da una società*) capital duty; ~ **di circolazione** (*fin., trasp. aut.*) motor-vehicle tax; ~ **di compensazione** (*fin.*) countervailing charge; ~ **di coniatura** (*fin.*) mint charge, mintage; ~ **di licenza** (*fin., USA*) license fee; ~ **di pesatura** (*di merci*) (*trasp., ingl.*) weighage; ~ **di registra-**

zione (*leg.*) booking fee; ~ **di rispedizione** (*postale*) (*comun.*) charge for redirection; ~ **di sdoganamento** (*dog.*) fee for clearance through customs; ~ **di successione** (*fin.*) estate duty, legacy duty, probate duty; death duty (*fam.*); inheritance tax, estate tax, legacy tax (*USA*); ~ **erariale sulle operazioni garantite** (*fin.*) Government tax on secured loans; ~ **ipotecaria** (*leg.*) mortgage duty; ~ **locale** (*fin.*) rate; ~ **pagata per acquisire il diritto d'occupare suolo pubblico con bancarelle** (*chioschi, edicole, ecc.*) (*fin.*) stallage; ~ **per** (*lettera*) **raccomandata** (*comun.*) fee for registration, registration fee; registry fee (*USA*); ~ **per spedizione contro assegno** (*comun.*) cash on delivery fee; ~ **progressiva** (*fin.*) progressive tax; ~ **proporzionale a favore degli enti locali** (*che colpisce la ricchezza individuale sotto qualsiasi forma*) (*fin.*) general property tax (*USA*); **una** ~ **restrittiva dei consumi** (*fin.*) a sumptuary tax; **una** ~ **sugli articoli di lusso** (*fin.*) a tax on luxury articles; ~ **sugli spettacoli** (*fin.*) entertainments duty; ~ **sui sovrapprofitti** (*fin.*) excess-profits duty (*o* tax); ~ **sul biglietto d'ingresso** (*a uno spettacolo; computata in percentuale del prezzo*) (*fin.*) admission tax; ~ **sulla stazza** (*trasp. mar.*) tonnage tax; ~ **sulle concessioni governative** (*fin.*) Government concession tax; ~ **sulle donazioni** (*fin.*) gift tax; ~ **sull'uso** (*d'un certo articolo*) (*fin.*) use tax.

tassabile, *a.* (*fin.*) taxable, chargeable with duty, chargeable, assessable. // **non** ~ (*fin.*) non-taxable, non-assessable.

tassare, *v. t.* (*fin.*) to tax, to assess, to charge, to excise. // ~ **a un tanto per libbra** (*fin.*) to charge by the pound; ~ **gli articoli di lusso** (*fin.*) to tax luxury articles; ~ **di dazio doganale** (*dog.*) to charge with customs duty.

tassazione, *n. f.* (*fin.*) taxation, assessment, charging. // ~ **doppia** (*econ.*) double taxation; ~ **forfettaria** (*fin.*) standard tax; ~ «**forfettaria**» **delle importazioni** (*fin.*) flat-rate taxation of imports.

tasso, *n. m.* (*fin.*) rate. // ~ **a vista** (*fin.*) demand rate; ~ **attivo** (*fin.*) lending rate; ~ **del deporto** (*fin.*) backwardation rate, backwardation fee; ~ **del riporto** (*Borsa*) continuation rate, contango rate, carry over rate; ~ **d'ammortamento** (*rag.*) rate of depreciation; ~ **di cambio** (*fin.*) rate of exchange, exchange rate; **il** ~ **di conversione d'una valuta** (*econ.*) the rate of conversion of a currency; ~ **di copertura** (*fin.*) cover ratio; ~ **di crescita zero** (*econ.*) zero rate of growth; ~ **di disoccupazione** (*sind.*) unemployment rate, jobless rate; ~ **d'incremento** (*econ., fin.*) growth rate; ~ **d'interesse** (*fin.*) rate of interest, interest rate; **tassi d'interesse** «**creditori**» (*banca*) credit interest rates; **tassi d'interesse** «**debitori**» (*banca*) debit interest rates; ~ **d'interesse d'equilibrio** (*econ.*) (*si ha quando il risparmio naturale è uguagliato dagli investimenti*) equilibrium rate of interest; **un** ~ **d'interesse eccessivo** (*fin.*) a rank rate of interest; **il** ~ **d'interesse naturale** (*fin.*) (*quello per cui si ha uguaglianza fra domanda di fondi e offerta di risparmio*) the natural rate of interest; ~ **d'intervento** (*fin.*) peg; ~ **di liquidità** liquidity ratio, liquid ratio; ~ **d'occupazione** (*econ.*) employment rate; **il** ~ **di remunerazione** (*rag.*) the rate of return; **il** ~ **di remunerazione degli investimenti** (*fin.*) the rate of return on capital investment; ~ **di riporto** (*Borsa*) continuation rate, contango rate, carry over rate; ~ **di risconto** (*banca, cred.*) rediscount rate; ~ **di risconto privilegiato** (*banca, cred.*) preferential rediscount rate; ~ **di rotazione del magazzino** (*org. az.*) turnover rate; ~ **di rotazione delle scorte** (*rag.*) rate of turnover; ~ **di sconto** (*fin.*) rate of discount, discount rate; ~ **di sconto del mercato libero** (*fin.*) discount rate of the open market; ~ **di sopravvivenza** (*ass.*) survival rate; ~ **di sviluppo** (*econ.*) rate of growth, growth rate, pace; **il** ~ **di sviluppo dell'inflazione** (*econ.*) the inflation rate; ~ **di sviluppo nullo** (*econ.*) zero rate of growth; **il** ~ **inflazionistico** (*econ.*) the rate of inflation, the inflation rate; ~ **legale d'interesse** (*fin.*) official rate of interest; **un** ~ **minimo** (*fin.*) a minimum rate, a knockdown rate; **i tassi minimi debitori delle banche** (*fin.*) the minimum rates of interest paid on deposits by banks; **un** ~ **nominale** (*fin.*) a nominal rate; ~ **passivo** (*fin.*) borrowing rate; ~ (*d'interesse*) **praticato** (*dalle banche*) **ai clienti meno favoriti** (*fin.*) top rate; ~ **primario** (*fin., USA*) prime rate; ~ **ufficiale di sconto** (*fin.*) official rate of discount, bank rate of discount, bank rate.

tastierista, *n. m.* e *f.* (*elab. elettr.*) keyboard operator.

tecnica, *n. f.* technique. // ~ **bancaria** (*banca*) banking technique; ~ **commerciale** commerce technique, commercial practice; ~ **della catena di montaggio** (*org. az.*) assembly-line technique; ~ **delle ricerche di mercato** (*market.*) marketing; **tecniche d'assicurazione all'esportazione** (*ass.*) export insurance techniques; **tecniche di direzione aziendale** (*amm.*) management techniques, management tools; ~ **industriale** (*econ., org. az.*) industrial technique; ~ **mercantile** (*econ., market.*) commerce technique.

tecnico, *a.* technical. *n. m.* (*pers.*) technician, technicist, engineer. // ~ **specializzato** (*pers.*) engineer.

tecnocrate, *n. m.* e *f.* (*econ.*) technocrat.

tecnocrazia, *n. f.* (*econ.*) technocracy.

tecnologia, *n. f.* (*org. az.*) technology. // ~ **meccanica** (*org. az.*) mechanical technology.

tecnologico, *a.* (*org. az.*) technological, technologic.

tecnosofo, *n. m.* (*econ., neol.*) (*autorevole esperto in problemi tecnologici*) technosophe.

«tecnostruttura», *n. f.* (*econ., neol.*) technostructure.

teleborsa, *n. f.* (*Borsa*) (*apparecchio elettronico che registra e trasmette istantaneamente a tutto il mondo i prezzi e il volume delle contrattazioni in titoli*) stock ticker, tape machine, ticker.

telefonare, *v. t.* e *i.* (*comun.*) to telephone, to phone; to ring★ up (*fam.*).

telefonata, *n. f.* (*comun.*) telephone call, call; ring (*fam.*). // ~ **interurbana** (*comun.*) long-distance call, trunk-call, toll-call.

telefonista, *n. m.* e *f.* **1** (*comun.*) (*alla centrale*) telephone operator, operator; central (*USA*). **2** (*comun.*) (*negli uffici, ecc.*) telephonist, attendant of call office.

telefono, *n. m.* **1** (*comun.*) telephone; phone (*fam.*). **2** (*comun.*) (*servizio pubblico*) telephone service. // ~ **a cuffia** (*attr. uff.*) earphone; ~ **a pagamento (*o* a gettoni)** pay phone; ~ **in duplex** (*comun.*) party-line, party-wire; ~ **interno** (*attr. uff.*) interoffice telephone, house phone; ~ **pubblico** (*comun.*) public telephone, call office; **essere al** ~ to be on the phone; **per** ~ by telephone.

telegiornale, *n. m.* (*comun.*) television newsreel, news broadcast, newscast.

telegrafare, *v. t.* e *i.* (*comun.*) to telegraph, to wire, to telegram.

telegrafia, *n. f.* (*comun.*) telegraphy. // ~ **senza fili** (*comun.*) wireless telegraphy.

telegrafista, *n. m.* e *f.* (*comun.*) telegraph operator, telegraphist.

telegrafo, *n. m.* **1** (*comun.*) telegraph. **2** (*comun.*) (*l'ufficio*) telegraph office. // **per** ~ (*comun.*) by wire.

telegramma, *n. m.* (*comun.*) telegram, wire; telegraph (*USA*). // ~ **cifrato** (*comun.*) code telegram; ~ **con risposta pagata** (*comun.*) reply-paid telegram; ~ **diurno** (*costa meno e viaggia più lento*) (*comun.*) day letter; ~ **-lettera** (*comun.*) day letter telegram, letter telegram; ~ **notturno** (*a tariffa ridotta*) (*comun.*) night lettergram, night letter; **un** ~ **via radio** (*comun.*) a telegram via wireless; **come da vostro** ~ (*comun.*) as per your telegram.

telematica, *n. f.* (*comun., elab. elettr.*) telematics.

telescrivente, *n. f.* (*macch. uff.*) teletypewriter, teleprinter.

telescriventista, *n. m.* e *f.* (*pers.*) teletypist.

telex, *n. m.* (*comun.*) telex.

tel quel, *locuz. a. V.* **tale quale.**

tempo, *n. m.* **1** time. **2** (*atmosferico*) weather. **3** (*fase*) phase; (*stadio*) stage. **4** (*comun., pubbl.*) (*a disposizione di chi fa pubblicità radiotelevisiva*) space. // ~ **assegnato** (*a un operaio*) **per eseguire un certo lavoro** (*pers.*) work load; ~ **cattivo** bad weather; ~ **complessivo di lavoro in ore** (*sind.*) hourage; ~ **concesso per il pagamento delle cambiali estere** (*secondo la consuetudine locale*) (*cred., leg.*) usance; ~ **definito** (*pers., sind.*) part time; ~ **di consegna** (*market., org. az.*) lead time; ~ **di riapprovvigionamento** (*org. az.*) lead time; ~ **fa** a short time ago; ~ **libero** free time, spare time; (*pers.*) off time, leisure time; ~ **permettendo** weather permitting; ~ **pieno** (*pers., sind.*) full time; **a** ~ (*fin., market.*) (*di prezzi*) forward, forwards; (*org. az.*) (*secondo i piani*) on schedule; **a** ~ **debito** in due time, in due course, duly; **a** ~ **indeterminato** (*leg.*) sine die; (*di contratto d'affitto, d'affittuario, ecc.*) at will; **a** ~ **perso** in one's spare time; **a** ~ **pieno** full-time (*a. e avv.*); **a certo** ~ **vista** (*cred.*) day's sight; **a suo** ~ in due time, in due course, duly; **in** ~ **utile** within the time-limit, in time.

tendenza, *n. f.* **1** (*propensione*) tendency, propensity; (*attitudine*) inclination, bent. **2** (*orientamento*) trend, drift. **3** (*econ.*) determination. // ~ **a lungo termine** (*econ.*) long-run trend; ~ **a ridurre la disuguaglianza dei redditi** (*econ.*) egalitarianism; ~ **a salire** (*fin., market.*) upward trend, buoyancy; ~ **al rialzo** (*Borsa*) bullish tendency, bullishness; (*econ.*) upward trend, rising trend, uptrend, upturn; ~ **al ribasso** (*Borsa*) bearish tendency, bearishness; (*econ.*) downward trend, falling trend, downward sloping trend, downtrend, downturn, ease; **una** ~ **alla centralizzazione del potere** a drift towards centralization of power; ~ **all'espansione** (*econ.*) upswing, upturn; ~ **dei prezzi al rialzo** (*econ.*) strength; ~ **di base** (*d'un mercato e sim.*) (*Borsa, fin.*) undertone; ~ **di mercato** (*econ., market.*) market trend; **tendenze inflazionistiche** (*econ.*) inflationary tendencies, inflationary strains; **tendenze protezionistiche** (*econ.*) protectionist trends; **tendenze recessive** (*econ.*) recessionary trends.

«tender», *n. m.* (*trasp. ferr.*) tender.

tendere, *v. t.* **1** to stretch (out), to hold★ out. **2** (*mettere in tensione*) to tighten, to stretch, to strain. *v. i.* **1** to tend, to be inclined, to trend. **2** (*mirare, intendere*) to aim, to intend. // ~ **ad aumentare** (*econ., fin., market.*) (*di prezzi, costi, ecc.*) to trend upward; ~ **a diminuire** (*econ., fin., market.*) (*di prezzi, costi, ecc.*) to trend downward; **tendente a una diminuzione di prezzo** (*fin., market.*) (*di merce, titolo, ecc.*) weak; **tendente al rialzo** (*fin., market.*) (*di mercato, prezzo, ecc.*) stiff.

tenere, *v. t.* **1** to hold★. **2** to keep★. **3** (*prendere*) to take★. **4** (*org. az.*) (*certa merce, ecc.*) to stock. *v. i.* (*Borsa, fin.*) (*di prezzo, titolo, ecc.: mantenersi sostenuto*) to hold★, to hold★ up. // ~ **a bada un creditore** (*cred.*) to stand off a creditor; ~ **a freno l'inflazione** (*fin.*) to curb inflation; ~ **acceso un conto** (*rag.*) to keep an account alive; ~ **aggiornati i conti** (*rag.*) to keep the books up to date; ~ **q. al corrente di qc.** to keep sb. advised about st.; «~ **al fresco**» (*market.*) (*scritto su scatole, ecc.*) «keep cool»; «~ **all'asciutto**» (*market.*) (*su casse, scatole, ecc.*) «keep dry»; ~ **bassi i prezzi** (*econ., market.*) to keep prices down; ~ **una carica fino al termine** (*amm.*) to serve one's term of office; ~ **la contabilità** (*rag.*) to keep accounts, to keep the books; ~ **la contabilità a partita doppia** (*rag.*) to keep the books by double entry; ~ **la contabilità d'un'azienda** (*rag.*) to keep a firm's accounts, to keep a firm's books; ~ **i conti** (*rag.*) to keep accounts, to keep the books; ~ **un conto aperto presso q.** (*rag.*) to keep an account with sb.; ~ **conto delle oscillazioni di cambio** (*fin., rag.*) to make allowance for fluctuations in exchange; ~ **conto di qc.** to make allowance for st., to allow for st.; ~ **denaro in** (*una certa banca*) to bank with; «~ **diritto**» (*market.*) (*su casse, ecc.*) «this side up»; ~ **un discorso** to give a speech; ~ **duro** to hold on, to hold out, to stick out; ~ **fede a un impegno** to keep an engagement; ~ **fede alla parola data** to be true to one's word; ~ **in affitto** (*leg.*) to tenant; ~ **in circolazione effetti** (*cred.*) to keep bills afloat; ~ **in custodia** (*leg.*) to hold in custody; ~ **in quarantena** (*trasp. mar.*) to quarantine; ~ **l'inflazione sotto controllo** (*econ., fin.*) to bring inflation under control; ~ **i libri contabili** (*rag.*) to keep the books; ~ **un (libro) giornale** (*rag.*) to journalize; ~ **il mare** (*trasp. mar.*) (*di nave*) to keep the sea; ~ **una riunione** to hold a meeting; ~ **una seduta** to hold a sitting; ~ **sotto il proprio dominio** to control; ~ **udienza** (*leg.*) to sit; ~ **il verbale d'un'assemblea** (*amm.*) to take the minutes of a meeting; **non** ~ **fede a un impegno** (*leg.*) to break an engagement; **non** ~ **fede a una promessa** to depart from one's promise; **non** ~ **fede alla parola** to deny one's word.

tenersi, *v. rifl.* **1** to hold★ (oneself). **2** to keep★ (oneself). **3** (*attenersi*) to stick★ (to st.); (*seguire*) to follow (st.). // ~ **a galla** (*anche fig.*) to keep afloat; ~ **in contatto con q.** to keep in touch with sb.; ~ **in corrispondenza con q.** to entertain correspondence with sb.; ~ **pronti a salpare** (*trasp. mar.*) to stand by the anchor.

tenitore, *n. m.* (*leg.*) holder.

tenuta, *n. f.* **1** (*possedimento agricolo*) estate, property, holding; (*fattoria*) farm. **2** (*capacità, quantità che può essere contenuta*) capacity, holding. **3** (*abiti, abbigliamento*) clothes (*pl.*); (*uniforme*) uniform. **4** (*leg.*) (*occupazione, possesso*) tenure. // ~ **dei libri** (*rag.*) bookkeeping; ~ **dei libri a partita doppia** (*rag.*) double-entry bookkeeping; ~ **del mare** (*trasp. mar.*) (*d'imbarcazione*) sea-kindliness.

tenutario, *n. m.* (*leg.*) holder; (*proprietario*) owner, proprietor.

tenuto, *a.* **1** (*obbligato*) obliged, forced, bound. **2** (*econ.*) (*di terreno: coltivato*) planted (with); (*lasciato*) kept. // ~ **a barbabietola da zucchero** (*di terreno*) planted with sugar-beet; ~ **a risarcire i danni** (*leg.*) liable for damages; **essere** ~ **a fare qc.** to be expected to do st.; to be supposed to do st.

teoria, *n. f.* theory. // **la** ~ **dei costi comparati** (*econ.*) the theory of comparative costs; **la** ~ **dei monopoli** (*econ.*) the theory of monopolistic competition; **la** ~ **dei prezzi** (*econ.*) the theory of prices; ~ **dei salari** (*econ.*) wage-fund theory, wages-fund theory (*secondo J.S. Mill*); **le teorie dei salari** (*econ.*) the theories of wages; **le teorie del ciclo economico** (*econ.*) the theories of the trade cycle, the theories of the business cycle; **la** ~ **del plusvalore** (*econ.*) the theory of surplus value; **le teorie del valore** (*econ.*) the theories of value; ~ **della capacità contributiva** (*econ.*) ability theory, faculty theory; **la** ~ **della concorrenza monopolistica** (*econ.*) the theory of monopolistic competition; **la** ~ **dell'organizzazione** (*org. az.*) the organization theory; **la** ~ **della probabilità** (*mat.*) the theory of probability; ~ (*Keynesiana*) **della produttività marginale decrescente del capitale** (*econ.*) declining marginal efficiency-of-capital theory; **la** ~ **delle imposte** (*econ., fin.*) the theory of taxation; ~ **dell'equilibrio (economico)** (*econ.*) equilibrium theory; ~ **mercantilistica** (*econ.*) mercantile theory; ~ **metallica (della valuta)** (*econ.*) currency principle; ~ **quantitativa della moneta** (*econ.*) quantity theory of money; **la ~ utilitaristica del valore** (*econ.*) the utility theory of value; **in ~** in theory, theoretically; on paper (*fig.*).

tergo, *n. m.* back. // **a ~** (*di un foglio*) overleaf, over: «**Vedasi a ~**» «please see overleaf», «please turn over».

terminal, *n. m.* (*trasp. aer.*) (*aerostazione urbana collegata all'aeroporto con mezzi di trasporto*) terminal. // «**~ -container**» (*trasp.*) container terminal.

terminale, *a.* terminal. *n. m.* terminal.

termine, *n. m.* **1** (*fine*) end; (*scadenza*) termination, expiration, expiry. **2** (*limite*) limit; (*data*) date. **3** (*tempo*) time. **4** (*parola*) term, word. **5** (*Borsa*) (*alla Borsa Valori*) account. **6** (*cred.*) (*d'una cambiale*) tenor. **7** (*leg.*) time limit. **8** (*leg., market.*) (*condizione*) term, condition. **9** (*mat.*) term. // **~ del mandato** (*leg.*) completion of mandate; **~ di comparizione** (*in giudizio*) (*leg.*) time limit for appearance; **~ d'una diramazione di linea ferroviaria** (*trasp. ferr.*) dead end; **termini di legge** (*leg.*) law terms; **~ di preavviso** (*leg.*) notice period; **~ di prescrizione** (*leg.*) period of limitation; **il ~ di scadenza** (*cred.*) the time of payment; **~ di tempo per il saldo** (*d'un pagamento*) (*cred.*) prompt; **~ perentorio** (*leg.*) peremptory term; **~ ultimo** (*anche giorn., pubbl.*) deadline; (*leg.*) time limit; **il ~ ultimo per la presentazione di documenti** the deadline for sending in documents; **a ~** on credit, upon credit; credit (*attr.*); (*Borsa*) for the account; (*cred., market.*) on term, forward; (*leg.*) (*di contratto*) terminable; **a termini di legge** (*leg.*) according to the law; **a breve ~** in the short run, in the short term, at short range; **a lungo ~** in the long run, in the long term, at long range; **entro il ~ di due settimane** within two weeks; **in termini reali** (*econ.*) (*di valutazione*) real (*attr.*).

terrazzamento, *n. m.* (*econ.*) (*di terreni*) strip-cropping, strip-farming.

terrazzare, *v. t.* (*econ.*) (*terreni*) to strip-crop.

terremoto, *n. m.* earthquake. // **~ finanziario** (*fin.*) financial upheaval; moneyquake (*slang USA*); **~ monetario** (*fin.*) monetary upheaval; moneyquake (*slang USA*).

terreno[1], *a.* **1** ground (*attr.*). **2** worldly, earthly.

terreno[2], *n. m.* **1** ground. **2** (*terra coltivabile, fabbricabile, ecc.*) land; (*proprietà terriera*) landed estate, property. **3** (*suolo*) soil. **4 terreni,** *pl.* (*rag.*) (*voce di bilancio*) landed property, land. // **~ affittato** (*leg.*) lease, leasehold; **~ arato** ploughed land; plowed land (*USA*); plough (*specialm. ingl.*); **~ da costruzione** building land; **terreni da dare in concessione** concessible lands; **terreni demaniali** State lands; Crown lands (*in G.B.*); **~ di proprietà comune** common; **~ in enfiteusi** (*leg.*) fee farm; **~ non occupato** (*leg.*) vacant land; **~ non utilizzato** (*leg.*) vacant land; **~ produttivo** (*econ.*) productive soil; **terreni tassabili** (*fin.*) chargeable lands; **terreni tenuti in affitto** (*leg.*) leasehold (*sing. collett.*); **~ tenuto in proprietà assoluta** (*leg.*) freehold.

terriero, *a.* (*econ.*) landed. // **proprietà terriera** (*econ.*) landed property; **proprietario ~** (*econ.*) landowner.

territoriale, *a.* territorial. // **acque territoriali** (*leg.*) territorial waters.

territorialità, *n. f.* (*leg.*) territoriality. // **~ dell'imposta** (*fin.*) territory to which the tax applies.

territorio, *n. m.* territory; possessions (*pl.*).

terza, *n. f.* **1** (*cred., fin.*) (*di cambio*) third of exchange. **2** (*trasp. ferr.*) third class; third (*fam.*). // **~ di cambio** (*cred.*) third of exchange; **~ di copertina** (*giorn.*) third cover, inside-back cover; **di ~ (classe)** (*trasp.*) third-class (*attr.*).

terziario, *n. m.* (*econ.*) (*il settore terziario*) (the) services sector.

terzo, *num. ord.* third. *a.* (*di copia*) triplicate. *n. m.* **1** (*terza parte*) third. **2** (*leg.*) third party. **3** (*mat.*) third. **4 i terzi,** *pl.* (*leg.*) the third party (*sing.*). **5 i terzi,** *pl.* (*rag.*) the outsiders. // **~ acquirente** (*leg.*) subsequent buyer; **~ arbitro** (*leg.*) umpire; **terzi azionisti** (*fin.*) outside shareholders; **~ copia** (*di documento*) triplicate; **~ di buona fede** (*leg.*) bona fide holder; **il ~ mondo** the third world; **terza pagina** (*giorn.*) literary page; **una terza persona** (*leg.*) a third party; **~ pignorato** (*leg.*) garnishee.

tesaurizzare, *v. t.* (*econ.*) to hoard, to treasure. *v. i.* to accumulate treasures. // **~ oro** (*econ.*) to hoard gold; **~ oro e argento** (*econ.*) to treasure gold and silver.

tesaurizzazione, *n. f.* (*econ.*) hoarding.

tesoreggiamento, *n. m.* *V.* **tesaurizzazione.**

tesoreggiare, *v. t.* e *i.* *V.* **tesaurizzare.**

tesoreria, *n. f.* (*fin.*) treasury. // **la ~ dello Stato** (*fin.*) the State Treasury.

tesoriere, *n. m.* (*fin.*) treasurer, receiver, bursar.

tesoro, *n. m.* **1** treasure. **2** (*fin., ingl.*) (the) Exchequer, (the) Treasury. // **~ trovato** (*leg.*) treasure trove.

tessera, *n. f.* **1** ticket, card. **2** (*trasp.*) (*ferro-*

viaria, ecc.) season ticket. // ~ **del sindacato** (*sind.*) union card; ~ **di commerciante straniero** (*comm. est.*) foreign trader's identity card; ~ **di giornalista** (*giorn.*) press card; ~ **d'iscrizione** membership card.

tesseramento, *n. m.* (*iscrizione*) registration.

tesserare, *v. t.* (*iscrivere*) to register.

tessile, *a.* textile. *n. m.* **1** (*pers.*) (*operaio tessile*) textile worker. **2 tessili,** *n. pl.* (*econ.*) (*prodotti*) textiles.

test, *n. m.* test. // ~ **attitudinale** (*pers.*) aptitude test, capacity test, ability test; ~ **caratterologico** (*pers.*) personality test; ~ **d'assunzione** (*pers.*) entrance test; ~ **d'attitudine al lavoro d'ufficio** (*pers.*) test of clerical aptitude; ~ **d'attitudine meccanica** (*pers.*) mechanical aptitude test; ~ **di capacità** (*pers.*) ability test; ~ **di destrezza** (*pers.*) test of manual dexterity; ~ **d'intelligenza** (*pers.*) intelligence test; ~ **d'interesse** (*pers.*) vocational-interest test; ~ **di personalità** (*pers.*) personality test; ~ **di profitto** (*pers.*) achievement test; ~ **di rendimento** (*pers.*) performance test, proficiency test; ~ **proiettivo** (*pers.*) projective test; ~ **sociometrico** (*pers.*) sociometric test; ~ **standardizzato** (*pers.*) standardized test; ~ **vocazionale** (*pers.*) vocational-interest test.

testamentario, *a.* (*leg.*) testamentary, testamental.

testamento, *n. m.* (*leg.*) will, testament, will and testament. // ~ **congiuntivo e reciproco** (*leg.*) double will; ~ **fatto in punto di morte** (*leg.*) death-bed will; **un** ~ **nuncupativo** (*leg.*) a nuncupative will; ~ **olografo** (*leg.*) holographic will, holograph; **un** ~ **pubblico** (*leg.*) a solemn will; ~ **segreto** (*leg.*) sealed will, mystic testament; **che ha fatto** ~ (*leg.*) (*di persona deceduta*) testate; **fare** ~ (*leg.*) to make one's will; **per** ~ (*leg.*) by will; **senza aver fatto** ~ (*leg.*) intestate (*pred.*).

testare, *v. i.* (*leg.*) to make★ a will. *v. t.* **1** (*market., pers., neol.*) (*sottoporre a un test*) to test. **2** (*pubbl., neol.*) to test. // **capacità di** ~ (*leg.*) testamentary capacity.

testatore, *n. m.* (*leg.*) testator, testate, devisor, bequeather. // ~ **di beni immobili** (*leg.*) devisor; ~ **di beni mobili** (*leg.*) bequeather.

testatrice, *n. f.* (*leg.*) testatrix★.

teste, *n. m.* e *f.* (*leg.*) witness. // ~ **a carico** (*leg.*) witness for the prosecution; ~ **a difesa** (*leg.*) witness for the defence; ~ **a discarico** (*leg.*) witness for the defence; ~ **d'accusa** (*leg.*) witness for the prosecution.

testimone, *n. m.* e *f.* (*leg.*) witness; (*chi fa una deposizione*) deposer, deponent. // ~ **a carico** (*leg.*) witness for the prosecution; ~ **a difesa** (*leg.*) witness for the defence; ~ **a discarico** (*leg.*) witness for the defence; ~ **d'accusa** (*leg.*) witness for the prosecution; ~ **giurato** (*leg.*) sworn witness; ~ **oculare** (*leg.*) eye-witness.

testimoniale, *a.* (*leg.*) of a witness; witness (*attr.*). *n. m.* (*leg.*) evidence. // ~ **d'avaria** (*trasp. mar.*) captain's protest.

testimonianza, *n. f.* (*leg.*) evidence, testimony, witnessing, witness. // ~ **di perito** (*leg.*) expert evidence; ~ **fondata su dicerie** (*leg.*) hearsay evidence; ~ **orale** (*leg.*) verbal evidence; **una** ~ **per procura** (*leg.*) a mediate testimony; ~ **probatoria** (*leg.*) probatory evidence.

testimoniare, *v. t.* (*leg.*) to witness, to evidence; (*attestare*) to testify. *v. i.* (*leg.*) to bear★ witness, to give★ evidence, to witness; (*deporre*) to depose, to depone. // ~ **a favore di q.** (*leg.*) to witness for sb., to give evidence on behalf of sb.

testimonio, *n. m. V.* **testimone.**

testista, *n. m.* e *f.* (*org. az., pers., neol.*) (*esperto di prove psicologiche per valutare le capacità dei candidati a un posto di lavoro*) test expert.

testo, *n. m.* **1** text. **2** (*giorn.*) editorial matter, copy; (*distinto dalle illustrazioni*) letterpress. **3** (*leg.*) (*d'una legge*) purview. **4** (*pubbl.*) (*radiotelevisivo*) script. // **il** ~ **della legge** (*leg.*) the letter of the law; **il** ~ **d'una polizza d'assicurazione** (*ass.*) the text of an insurance policy, the wording of an insurance policy; ~ **unico** (*leg.*) consolidation act.

timbrare, *v. t.* **1** to stamp. **2** (*comun.*) (*una lettera*) to postmark. // ~ **il cartellino** (*pers.*) (*abbandonando il posto di lavoro*) to sign out, to clock out (*o* off), to punch out; (*arrivando sul posto di lavoro*) to sign in, to clock in (*o* on), to punch in.

timbro, *n. m.* **1** (*bollo*) stamp. **2** (*attr. uff.*) (*strumento per imprimere bolli*) stamp. // ~ **a secco** (*attr. uff.*) embossed stamp; ~ **d'annullamento** (*attr. uff.*) cancelling stamp; canceling stamp (*USA*); ~ **di gomma** (*attr. uff.*) rubber stamp; ~ **di ricevuta** (*attr. uff.*) received stamp; ~ **per data** (*attr. uff.*) date stamp, dater; ~ **postale** (*comun.*) postmark.

tipico, *a.* typical; (*esemplare*) exemplary.

tipificare, *v. t. V.* **tipizzare.**

tipificazione, *n. f. V.* **tipizzazione.**

tipizzare, *v. t.* **1** to typify. **2** (*standardizzare*) to standardize.

tipizzazione, *n. f.* **1** typification. **2** (*standardizzazione*) standardization.

tipo, *n. m.* **1** type. **2** (*genere*) type, kind, sort, quality; (*modello*) model; (*norma*) norm, standard. **3** (*giorn., pubbl.*) (*carattere tipografico*) type. **4** (*market.*) (*d'articolo, ecc.*) make, brand. // ~ **a cambio in verghe auree** (*fin.*) gold bullion standard; ~ **a corso forzoso** (*fin.*) fiat standard; ~ **aureo** (*fin.*) gold standard; ~ **dollaro** (*fin.*) dollar standard.

tiraggio, *n. m.* draught, draft. // ~ **reciproco** (*di tratte*) (*cred.*) cross firing.

tirare, *v. t.* **1** to pull, to draw★. **2** (*giorn., pubbl.*) (*stampare*) to print, to pull, to take★ off, to run★ off, to machine. *v. i.* **1** to pull, to draw★. **2** (*fam.*) (*andare bene, andare «forte»*) to be going strong, to go★ strong. // ~ **fuori** (*la merce*) (*market.*) (*spacchettarla, disimballarla*) to unpack; ~ **in lungo un pagamento** (*cred.*) to delay meeting an account; ~ **la paga** (*pers.*) to draw one's wages, to draw one's salary; ~ **le somme** to total; (*fig.*) (*concludere*) to reach a conclusion; (*rag.*) to strike a balance; ~ **lo stipendio** (*pers.*) to draw one's salary; ~ **sul prezzo** (*market.*) to bargain, to chaffer, to haggle, to higgle.

tiratura, *n. f.* **1** (*giorn.*) (*lo stampare*) printing, impression. **2** (*giorn.*) (*copie stampate*) number of copies, issue, run, circulation. // ~ **delle bozze** (*giorn.*) proof-pulling; **una** ~ **di 15.000 copie** (*giorn., pubbl.*) an impression of 15,000 copies; a circulation of 15,000 copies; **una** ~ **forte** (*giorn.*) a long run; **una** ~ **piccola** (*giorn.*) a short run.

tirocinante, *a.* (*pers.*) training. *n. m.* e *f.* (*pers.*) apprentice, trainee, trainer.

tirocinio, *n. m.* (*pers.*) apprenticeship, training, probation. // ~ **collettivo** (*pers.*) collective training; **fare il (proprio)** ~ (*pers.*) to do one's training.

titolare, *a.* titular, regular. *n. m.* e *f.* **1** holder. **2** (*leg.*) (*proprietario*) owner, proprietor. **3** (*pers.*) (*di posto, impiego, ecc.*) occupant. // **il** ~ **d'un'agenzia d'informazioni commerciali** (*market.*) a mercantile agent; ~ **di agenzia di viaggio** (*tur.*) travel agent; ~ **d'agenzia per la vendita di biglietti** (*tur.*) ticket-agent; ~ **di brevetto** (*leg.*) patentee; ~ **d'un conto** (*rag.*) holder of an account, account holder; **il** ~ **d'una ditta** the principal of a firm, the owner of a firm; ~ **d'una polizza** (*ass.*) policy-holder, policy-owner.

titolo, *n. m.* **1** (*di libro, ecc.*) title; (*intestazione*) heading. **2** (*accademico, onorifico*) title. **3** (*fin.*) certificate, document, security; (*azione*) share, stock; (*obbligazione*) debenture; bond (*USA*). **4** (*fin.*) (*d'oro, d'argento*) percentage of precious metal; (*di monete*) fineness. **5** (*giorn.*) (*d'un giornale, ecc.*) headline. **6** (*leg.*) (*diritto*) right, title. **7** (*leg., pers.*) (*qualifica*) qualification. **8 titoli,** *pl.* (*fin.*) (*azionari*) stock (*sing.*). **9 titoli,** *pl.* (*rag., anche*) holding (*sing.*). // **titoli a deporto** backwardized stock (*o* shares); **titoli a dividendo cumulativo** (*fin.*) cumulative stock; **titoli a largo flottante** (*Borsa*) blue chips; ~ **a mercato internazionale** (*Borsa, fin.*) international stock; **titoli a reddito fisso** (*fin.*) fixed-interest securities, fixed-income securities; **titoli a reddito variabile** (*fin.*) variable-yield securities; **titoli a scarso flottante** (*Borsa*) inactive stocks; ~ **a tutta pagina** (*giorn.*) banner headline; ~ **al portatore** (*fin.*) stock to bearer, bearer stock, bearer bond, bearer certificate, bearer security, bearer scrip, bearer warrant; **titoli al 4%** (*d'interesse*) (*fin.*) fours; ~ **azionario** (*fin.*) share; **titoli (azionari) assicurativi** (*fin.*) insurance shares; « ~ **-barometro** » (*Borsa, fin.*) (*titolo il cui prezzo di mercato indica l'andamento generale del mercato*) barometer stock; **titoli che hanno oscillazioni** (*di valore*) **molto ampie** (*fin.*) volatile stocks; **un** ~ **che invita alla speculazione** (*fin.*) a speculative stock; ~ **che si sottrae alle fluttuazioni del mercato** (*per talune caratteristiche particolari*) (*fin.*) specialty; ~ «**che va forte**» (*Borsa*) highflyer, highflier; **titoli consolidati** (*fin.*) consolidation annuities; consolidated stock (*sing. collett.*); consols; **titoli convertibili** (*fin.*) convertible securities; ~ **il cui prezzo non ha subito variazioni** (*a differenza di quello d'altri titoli dello stesso tipo sul mercato*) (*Borsa, fin.*) laggard; ~ **da cassetto** (*fin.*) lock-away; **titoli del** (*prestito*) **consolidato** (*fin.*) consols; consolidated stock (*sing. collett.*); bank annuities; **titoli del debito pubblico** (*fin.*) consolidated annuities, debentures, bonds, funds; **titoli del debito pubblico, emessi per sostituirne altri già giunti a scadenza** (*fin.*) conversion stock; **il** ~ **dell'oro** (*espresso in carati*) (*fin.*) the title of gold; **titoli dello Stato** (*fin.*) Government securities; ~ **d'arbitraggio** (*fin.*) arbitrage share; ~ **d'azienda in espansione** (*fin.*) growth stock; **titoli d'aziende di servizi pubblici** (*fin., USA*) utilities; **titoli di credito** (*cred.*) instruments of credit, documents of credit; bank money, paper (*sing.*); stiffs (*slang USA*); ~ **di credito a breve termine** (*cred.*) short-term paper; ~ **di credito agrario** (*fin.*) agricultural paper; **titoli di credito con buoni requisiti di bancabilità** (*cred.*) eligible paper; **titoli di cui vi è richiesta** (*fin.*) stocks bid for; **titoli di prestito municipali** (*fin.*) corporation stocks; **titoli di prim'ordine** (*fin.*) gilt-edged (*o* gilt-edge) securities, high-grade securities; gilts (*fam.*); **titoli di priorità** (*d'una società*) (*fin.*) senior securities; (*voce di bilancio*) treasury stock, securities owned; ~ **di proprietà** (*leg.*) title-deed to property, document of title; **un ~ di proprietà viziato** (*leg.*) a defective title, a defect of title, a bad title; **titoli di second'ordine** (*fin.*) second-rate securities; cats and dogs (*slang USA*); **titoli di Stato** (*fin.*) Government securities, stocks, funds; **titoli di studio** educational qualifications; ~ **esecutivo** (*leg.*) writ of execution, deed directly enforceable; ~ (*a interesse*) **esente da imposta** (*fin.*) tax-exempt security; **titoli esteri** (*fin.*) foreign securities, foreign stocks; ~ **estratto** (*fin.*) drawn bond; **titoli ferroviari** (*Borsa*) railway shares; rails, railroads (*USA*); **titoli fiduciari** (*fin.*) paper securities, paper holdings; **un ~ girabile** (*cred.*) an endorsable instrument; ~ **giustificativo di proprietà** (*leg.*) proof of ownership; ~ **in corso di stampa** (*giorn., pubbl.*) in-print; **titoli inattivi** (*fin.*) (*per i quali non c'è richiesta*) idle stocks, inactive stocks; ~ **incontestabile** (*leg.*) clear title; **titoli inconvertibili** (*fin.*) unconvertible securities; **titoli** (*d'imprese*) **industriali** (*fin.*) industrials; **titoli irredimibili da parte del detentore** (*e la cui redimibilità è lasciata alla discrezione dell'organismo emittente*) (*fin.*) one-way callable stock; **un ~ legittimo** (*leg.*) a valid title; **titoli nazionali** (*fin.*) home securities, home stocks; **titoli** (*di credito*) **negoziabili** (*cred.*) negotiable instruments, negotiable documents, negotiable securities, negotiable papers; **titoli nominativi** (*fin.*) registered stock, inscribed stock, registered securities; **titoli non negoziabili** (*fin.*) non-marketable securities; ~ **non quotato** (*in Borsa*) (*fin.*) unlisted security; ~ **obbligazionario** (*fin.*) debenture; bond (*USA*); **titoli offerti in garanzia** (*fin.*) securities in pledge; **titoli ordinari** (*fin.*) common stock; **titoli «pesanti»** (*fin.*) heavy stocks; **titoli primari** (*fin.*) gilt-edged securities, gilt-edge securities; gilts (*fam.*); **titoli privilegiati** (*fin.*) preference shares, preference stock; **titoli pubblici** (*fin.*) Government securities, Government stock; ~ **quotato** (*Borsa*) listed security; **titoli redimibili** (*fin.*) redeemable stocks; **titoli riportabili** (*Borsa*) contangoable stocks, continuable stocks; **titoli riportati** (*Borsa*) stock borrowed; ~ **secco** (*senza cedola*) (*fin.*) ex-coupon stock; **titoli sicurissimi** (*fin.*) gilt-edged securities, gilt-edge securities; gilts (*fam.*); **titoli trasferibili** (*fin.*) marketable securities; (*leg.*) marketable titles; **a ~ di favore** as a favour; **a ~ di premio** as a prize; **a ~ di prova** (*market.*) by way of trial; **a ~ gratuito** (*leg.*) free of charge, without consideration; **a ~ oneroso** (*leg.*) for a valuable consideration, for a money consideration; **a ~ personale** in a personal capacity; **a ~ privato** privately.

togliere, *v. t.* **1** to take★ away, to take★ (from), to take★ off, to take★ out. **2** (*impedire*) to prevent. // ~ **il blocco** (*trasp. mar.*) to raise the blockade; ~ **la comunicazione telefonica a q.** (*comun.*) to cut sb. off; ~ **l'embargo su una nave** (*trasp. mar.*) to take off the embargo on a ship; to lift the embargo on a ship; ~ **una imposta** (*fin.*) to take off a tax; ~ **un'ipoteca** (*cred., leg.*) to lift a mortgage; ~ **gli ormeggi** (*trasp. mar.*) to unmoor; ~ **restrizioni a qc.** (*econ., fin.*) to derestrict st.; ~ **la seduta** to close the meeting, to leave the chair, to adjourn; ~ **il sequestro** (*leg.*) to remove the attachment; ~ **i sigilli a qc.** to unseal st.; ~ **un titolo a q.** (*leg.*) to disentitle sb.; **essere tolto** (*di convegno, incontro, e sim.*) to adjourn.

tolleranza, *n. f.* **1** tolerance. **2** (*anche fig.*) leeway. **3** (*market.*) tolerance, allowance. // ~ **di peso** (*market.*) tolerance of weight; ~ **per diminuzione di peso** (*market.*) tolerance for loss of weight; ~ **percentuale di scarti per lotto** (*org. az.*) lot tolerance per cent defective.

tonnellaggio, *n. m.* (*trasp. mar.*) tonnage, burden. // ~ **a nave scarica** (*trasp. mar.*) light displacement tonnage; ~ **a pieno carico normale** (*trasp. mar.*) full load displacement tonnage; ~ **demolito** (*trasp. mar.*) tonnage broken up; ~ **di registro** (*trasp. mar.*) register tonnage, registered tonnage, register; ~ **di spedizione** (*trasp. mar.*) shipping tonnage; ~ **di stazza** (*trasp. mar.*) register tonnage; ~ **lordo** (*trasp. mar.*) gross tonnage; ~ **netto** (*trasp. mar.*) net tonnage; ~ **sotto il ponte** (*trasp. mar.*) tonnage under deck.

tonnellata, *n. f.* **1** ton. **2** (*metrica*) metric ton. // ~ **americana** (*misura di peso pari a kg 907 circa*) short ton, ton; ~ **di dislocamento** (*trasp. mar.*) displacement ton; ~ **di noleggio** (*trasp. mar.*) freight ton; ~ **di portata** (*unità di misura della portata d'una nave mercantile*) (*trasp. mar.*) ton burden; ~ **di portata lorda** (*trasp. mar.*) shipping ton, ton dead weight; ~ **di registro** (*trasp. mar.*) register ton; ~ **di stazza** (*trasp. mar.*) register ton, ton capacity; ~ **inglese** (*pari a kg 1.016 circa*) long ton; ~ **metrica** metric ton, ton; ~ **netta** net ton.

torpedone, *n. m.* (*trasp. aut.*) motor-coach, coach, bus, char-a-banc, charabanc.

totale, *a.* total; (*intero*) whole, entire; (*complessivo, globale*) overall, aggregate; (*lordo*) gross. *n. m.* total, sum total, sum. // ~ **a riportarsi** (*rag.*) pick-up; ~ **complessivo** (*rag.*) grand total, aggregate amount; ~ **del capitale sociale** (*iscritto al valore nominale*) **più gli utili non distribuiti** (*fin.*) stockholders' equity; ~ **delle attività** (*rag.*) total assets; **il ~ d'un'addizione** the total of an addition, the footing-up, the footing; ~ **generale** (*rag.*) grand total; ~ **libertà dei traffici** (*econ.*) global free trade; «~ **partite correnti**» (*fin., rag.*) total current accounts; ~ **parziale** (*rag.*) short; **in ~** on the whole, in all, in the aggregate.

tradizione, *n. f.* **1** tradition. **2** (*leg.*) (*praticamente con forza di legge*) law-way. **3** (*leg.*) (*consegna*) tradition, transfer, delivery. // **la ~ d'una proprietà** (*leg.*) the transfer of an estate; ~ **manuale** (*leg.*) manual delivery.

traffico, *n. m.* **1** traffic. **2** (*market.*) (*commercio*) trade. **3** (*trasp.*) traffic. **4 traffici,** *pl.* (*market.*) trading; trade (*sing.*). // ~ **aereo** (*trasp. aer.*) air traffic; **traffici d'oltremare** (*comm. est.*) overseas trade; ~ **diretto all'estero** (*trasp. mar.*) outbound traffic; ~ **ferroviario** (*trasp. ferr.*) rail traffic; ~ **fluviale** (*trasp.*) river traffic; **un ~ intenso** a heavy traffic; ~ **locale** (*trasp. ferr.*) local traffic; way traffic (*USA*); ~ **marittimo** (*econ., market.*) sea-borne trade; (*trasp. mar.*) sea traffic, shipping, navigation; ~ **misto** (*trasp.*) mixed traffic; ~ **pesante** heavy traffic; ~ **stradale** (*trasp. aut.*) road traffic; ~ (*diretto*) **verso l'est** eastbound traffic; ~ (*diretto*) **verso il nord** northbound traffic; ~ (*diretto*) **verso l'ovest** westbound traffic; ~ (*diretto*) **verso il sud** southbound traffic.

trafiletto, *n. m.* (*giorn.*) paragraph, short article.

traghettare, *v. t.* (*trasp. mar.*) to ferry.

traghettatore, *n. m.* (*trasp. mar.*) ferryman★.

traghetto, *n. m.* **1** (*trasp. mar.*) ferry, transfer. **2** (*trasp. mar.*) (*nave traghetto*) ferryboat.

tragitto, *n. m.* **1** (*trasp.*) journey, trip, passage. **2** (*trasp. mar.*) crossing.

trainare, *v. t.* **1** to haul, to tow, to pull. **2** (*trasp. aut., trasp. mar.*) to tow.

traino, *n. m.* **1** (*il trainare*) hauling, towing, pulling. **2** (*carico trainato*) load.

tram, *n. m. inv.* (*trasp.*) tram; street-car, trolley (car) (*USA*).

tramite, *n. m.* (*via, mezzo*) way, means, medium. *prep.* through, by, via. // ~ **telegramma** (*comun.*) by wire; **per il ~ di** through the agency of, through; **per il ~ di Mr Roberts** per Mr Roberts; **per ~ gerarchico** (*leg.*) through official channels.

transatlantico, *a.* transatlantic. *n. m.* (*trasp. mar.*) Atlantic liner, ocean liner, liner.

transatto, *a.* (*leg.*) settled, compounded.

transazione, *n. f.* **1** (*leg.*) transaction, settlement, composition, compromise, agreement. **2** (*market.*) transaction, dealing, deal. // **una ~ amichevole** (*leg.*) a friendly composition; ~ **commerciale** business transaction, business deal; **transazioni in borsa** (*Borsa*) buying in, selling out, buying in and selling out; **transazioni intergovernative** (*dog., fin.*) intergovernmental transactions; **una ~ stragiudiziale** (*leg.*) an extrajudicial transaction, a settlement out of Court.

transigere, *v. i.* **1** (*venire a patti*) to come★ to an agreement, to come★ to terms. **2** (*leg.*) to settle. *v. t.* (*leg.*) (*una lite*) to compound.

transitabile, *a.* (*trasp. aut.*) passable, negotiable.

transitabilità, *n. f. inv.* (*trasp. aut.*) possibility of transit, negotiability.

transitare, *v. i.* (*trasp. aut.*) to pass, to transit, to run★.

transito, *n. m.* (*trasp.*) transit. // **di ~** (*trasp.*) (*di merce*) transit (*attr.*); in transit (*pred.*); **in ~** (*trasp.*) (*di merce, ecc.*) on passage, in transit; **merce di ~** (*trasp.*) goods in transit.

transitorietà, *n. f. inv.* transitoriness, temporariness.

transitorio, *a.* transitory, transient, temporary. // ~ **disposizioni transitorie** (*leg.*) temporary laws.

transizione, *n. f.* transition.

tranvai, *n. m. inv. V.* **tram.**

tranvia, *n. f.* (*trasp.*) tramway; street-car line (*USA*).

tranviario, *a.* (*trasp.*) tram (*attr.*).

tranviere, *n. m.* **1** (*trasp.*) tram-driver; street-car operator (*USA*). **2** (*trasp.*) (*bigliettario*) tram-conductor.

trapasso, *n. m.* (*leg.*) transfer, conveyance, conveying. // ~ **d'ipoteca** (*leg.*) transfer of mortgage; **il ~ d'una proprietà** (*leg.*) the conveyance of a property.

trarre, *v. t.* **1** (*tirare*) to pull, to draw★. **2** (*prendere*) to take★ (out). **3** (*ricavare*) to obtain, to get★, to derive, to make★. **4** (*banca*) (*denaro*) to draw★. **5** (*cred.*) (*titoli di credito*) to draw★. // ~ **allo «scoperto»** (*banca*) to overdraw; ~ **una cambiale** (*cred.*) to issue a bill of exchange, to draw a bill of exchange; ~ **una cambiale su q.** (*cred.*) to draw on sb.; ~ **profitto** to draw a profit, to profit, to benefit; ~ **su un conto** (*banca*) to draw on an account; ~ **vantaggio da qc.** to get benefit from st., to capitalize on st.

trasbordare, *v. t.* **1** (*trasp. ferr.*) to transfer.

2 (*trasp. mar.*) to transship, to tranship, to reship. *v. i.* 1 (*trasp. ferr.*) to change (trains). 2 (*trasp. mar.*) to transship, to tranship. // ~ **merce da sdoganare** (*trasp. mar.*) to reship bonded merchandise.

trasbordo, *n. m.* 1 (*trasp. ferr.*) transfer. 2 (*trasp. mar.*) transshipment, transhipment. // ~ (*di merci*) **da una nave all'altra** (*trasp. mar.*) reshipment.

trascrivere, *v. t.* 1 to transcribe, to write★ out, to take★ down; (*copiare*) to copy. 2 (*leg.*) to register, to record. // ~ **una legge** (*leg.*) to register a law.

trascrizione, *n. f.* 1 (*l'azione*) transcription, copy, copying; (*il risultato*) transcript, copy. 2 (*leg.*) registration, recording. // ~ **di titoli** (*fin., ingl.*) inscription.

trasferibile, *a.* (*leg.*) transferable, assignable. // «**non** ~» (*banca*) «account payee only»; (*leg.*) (*di titolo*) untransferable, unassignable.

trasferimento, *n. m.* 1 removal, move, transfer, displacement. 2 (*leg.*) transfer, transferance, assignment, conveyance; (*di diritti*) demise; (*di beni, diritti, proprietà*) grant. 3 (*pers.*) transfer. // ~ **a titolo di garanzia** (*leg.*) blank transfer; ~ **bancario** (*banca*) bank transfer; **un** ~ **d'azioni** (*fin.*) a transfer of shares, an assignment of shares, a share transfer; ~ **di capitali** (*fin.*) transfer of funds, displacement of funds, capital transfer; **trasferimenti d'oro e di valuta all'estero** (*per sanare il deficit della bilancia dei pagamenti*) (*fin.*) accommodating movements; ~ **d'una somma ad altro conto** (*rag.*) cross entry; ~ **doloso** (*di beni, a danno dei creditori*) (*leg.*) fraudulent conveyance; ~ **finanziario** (*fin.*) capital transfer; ~ **manuale** (*leg.*) manual delivery; ~ **telegrafico** (*comun.*) telegraphic transfer.

trasferire, *v. t.* 1 to remove, to move, to transfer, to displace. 2 (*leg.*) to transfer, to assign, to make★ over, to convey; (*diritti*) to demise; (*beni, diritti, proprietà*) to grant. 3 (*pers.*) to transfer. // ~ (*cifre, totali, ecc.*) **da una colonna a un'altra** (*rag.*) to extend; ~ **per mezzo d'un atto legale** (*leg.*) to deed; ~ **un titolo mediante girata** (*cred., fin.*) to assign a bond by endorsement.

trasferirsi, *v. rifl.* to transfer, to move, to remove. // ~ (*per motivi di lavoro*) **all'interno d'uno Stato** (*econ.*) to in-migrate, to out-migrate; **chi si trasferisce** (*per motivi di lavoro*) **all'interno d'uno Stato** (*econ.*) in-migrant, out-migrant.

trasferta, *n. f.* 1 (*pers.*) (*l'andare in servizio fuori della propria residenza*) transfer. 2 (*pers.*) (*indennità di trasferta*) travelling indemnity, cost of living bonus; travelling expenses (*pl.*).

trasformare, *v. t.* 1 to transform, to turn (into); (*cambiare*) to change; (*convertire*) to convert. 2 (*org. az.*) to process. // ~ **una società in nome collettivo in una società anonima** (*fin.*) to turn a partnership into a limited company.

trasformazione, *n. f.* 1 transformation; (*cambiamento*) change; (*conversione*) conversion. 2 (*org. az.*) processing. // **la** ~ **d'un'azienda** (*fin.*) the conversion of a firm.

trasgredire, *v. t.* e *i.* (*leg.*) to transgress, to trespass, to infringe. // ~ **la** (*o* **alla**) **legge** (*leg.*) to transgress the law, to contravene the law, to vary from the law, to violate the law.

trasgressione, *n. f.* (*leg.*) transgression, trespass, infringement, violation, wrongdoing, misdemeanour, offence; offense (*USA*). // **una** ~ **alla legge** (*leg.*) an offence against the law.

trasgressore, *n. m.* (*leg.*) transgressor, trespasser, violator, wrongdoer, offender.

traslazione, *n. f.* 1 translation. 2 (*fin.*) (*d'imposta*) shifting. // ~ (*d'imposta*) **all'indietro** (*fin.*) backward shifting; ~ **dell'imposta a un fornitore** (*o* **a un dipendente**) (*fin.*) backward shifting of tax; ~ **d'imposta** (*fin.*) shifting of tax; ~ **di proprietà** (*leg.*) demise; ~ (*d'imposta*) **in avanti** (*cioè, sul consumatore*) (*fin.*) forward shifting.

trasmettere, *v. t.* 1 to transmit, to pass on, to hand on. 2 (*spedire*) to send★. 3 (*comun.*) (*comunicare*) to convey, to message, to transmit. 4 (*comun.*) (*per radio, per televisione*) to transmit, to broadcast★; (*un programma radiotelevisivo registrato*) to transcribe. 5 (*leg.*) to transfer, to convey, to assign. // ~ **a mezzo telex** (*comun.*) to telex; ~ **una cambiale per mezzo della girata** (*cred.*) to transfer a bill by endorsement; ~ **un messaggio** (*comun.*) to send a message; ~ **un'ordinazione a q.** (*comun., market.*) to pass an order on sb.; ~ **per radio** (*comun.*) to wireless; ~ (*qc.*) **per telefono** (*comun.*) to telephone; ~ (*qc.*) **per telegrafo** (*comun.*) to wire, to telegraph, to cable; ~ **per televisione** (*comun.*) to televise, to telecast.

trasmettitore, *n. m.* transmitter.

trasmissibile, *a.* 1 transmissible. 2 (*leg.*) transferable, assignable. // ~ **in eredità** (*leg.*) devisable.

trasmissione, *n. f.* 1 transmission. 2 (*spedizione*) sending (off). 3 (*comun.*) conveyance, transmission. 4 (*comun.*) (*per radio, per televisione: il programma*) broadcast; (*programma radiotelevisivo registrato*) transcription; (*il tra-*

smettere) broadcasting, transmission. **5** (*leg.*) transfer, transmission, conveyance, assignment, tradition. // ~ **locale** (*comun.*) spot broadcasting; ~ **nazionale** (*comun.*) national broadcast; network broadcast (*USA*); ~ **per successione** (*leg.*) transmission by descent; ~ **radiofonica** (*comun.*) radio broadcast, broadcast; (*il trasmettere*) radio broadcasting, broadcasting; ~ **televisiva** (*comun.*) telecast; (*il trasmettere*) telecasting.

trasmittente, *a.* (*comun.*) transmitting. *n. f.* (*comun.*) transmitting station, broadcasting station.

trasportare, *v. t.* **1** (*trasp.*) to transport, to convey, to carry. **2** (*trasp. mar.*) to ship (*in U.S.A. con qualsiasi mezzo*). // ~ **con un carro** (*trasp.*) to cart, to waggon; ~ **con chiatte** (*trasp. mar.*) to lighter; ~ **con un furgone** (*trasp. aut.*) to van; ~ **indietro** (*trasp.*) to reconvey; ~ **la merce al luogo di destinazione** (*trasp.*) to convey (*o* to carry) the goods to the place of their destination; ~ **merci per ferrovia** (*trasp. ferr.*) to convey goods by rail; to railroad goods (*specialm. USA*); **trasportato per via d'acqua** (*trasp.*) water-borne.

trasportatore, *n. m.* **1** (*org. az.*) (*macchina per il trasporto di materiali*) conveyer, conveyor. **2** (*trasp.*) (*vettore*) transporter, carrier, haulage contractor, haulier; hauler (*USA*). // ~ **marittimo** (*di merci*) (*trasp. mar.*) affreighter; ~ (*di merci*) **su strada** (*trasp. aut.*) road haulier.

trasporto, *n. m.* **1** (*trasp.*) transport, conveyance, carrying, carriage; (*solo di merce*) haulage, transportation; transportal (*USA*). **2** (*trasp.*) (*prezzo del trasporto*) transport charges, carriage; (*per via mare*) freight charges, freightage, freight (*in USA anche per via di terra*). **3** (*trasp. mar.*) freight (*in USA con qualsiasi mezzo*). **4 (i) trasporti,** *pl.* (*trasp.*) transport, transportation (*sing.*); (*in senso lato*) (the) distributive trades. // «~ **a carico del cliente**» (*trasp.*) «carriage forward»; «~ **a carico del destinatario**» (*trasp.*) «carriage forward»; «~ **a carico del mittente**» (*trasp.*) «carriage paid»; ~ **a mezzo di autocarri** (*trasp. aut.*) conveyance by motor lorries; ~ **aereo** (*trasp. aer.*) air transport; (*prezzo del trasporto*) freight; **trasporti aerei** (*trasp. aer.*) transportation by air, air transportation; ~ **automobilistico** (*trasp. aut.*) motor transport, road transport; ~ **cumulativo** (*trasp.*) through conveyance; ~ (*interno*) **dei materiali** (*org. az.*) materials handling; **il ~ di merci** (*trasp.*) goods transport, the haulage trade; ~ **di merce su strada** (*trasp. aut.*) road haulage; ~ **di pacchi per espresso** (*trasp.*) expressage; **trasporti ferroviari** (*trasp. ferr.*) rail transport, transport by rail; **i trasporti internazionali** (*trasp.*) the international haulage trade; **trasporti interni** (*org. az.*) materials handling, handling; ~ **marittimo** (*trasp. mar.*) carriage by sea, conveyance by sea; (*delle merci*) affreightment; (*prezzo del trasporto*) freight; ~ **marittimo con nave noleggiata totalmente** (*o per gran parte di essa*) (*trasp. mar.*) affreightment by charter party; ~ **marittimo con polizza di carico** (*trasp. mar.*) affreightment by bill of lading; **trasporti** (*interni*) **meccanizzati** (*org. az.*) mechanical handling; ~ **mediante carro** (*o* **autocarro**) (*trasp.*) truckage, carting, cartage; ~ **misto** (*trasp., trasp. mar.*) sea and land carriage; ~ **motorizzato** (*trasp.*) mechanical transport; ~ **per ferrovia** (*trasp. ferr.*) carriage by rail; ~ **per via d'acqua** (*trasp.*) water carriage, waterage; **trasporti per via d'acqua** (*trasp.*) water transportation; ~ **per via di terra** (*trasp.*) overland transport, land carriage; ~ (*di*) **persone** (*trasp.*) passenger transport; ~ **stradale** (*trasp. aut.*) road haulage, road transport; ~ **su chiatte** (*trasp. mar.*) lighterage; ~ **su strada** (*trasp. aut.*) road haulage, road transport; ~ **terrestre** (*trasp.*) carriage by land; **trasporti urbani** (*trasp.*) local transit.

trassato, *a.* (*cred.*) drawn upon. *n. m.* (*cred.*) drawee.

tratta, *n. f.* **1** (*cred.*) bill of exchange, bill, draft. **2** (*trasp. ferr.*) section, stretch. // ~ **a termine** (*cred.*) time draft; ~ **a vista** (*cred.*) draft at sight, draft payable at sight, sight draft, demand draft, demand bill; ~ **con annotazione per mancata accettazione** (*cred.*) bill noted for non-acceptance; ~ **documentaria** (*cred.*) documentary bill, documentary draft, document bill; ~ **documentaria contro accettazione** (*cred.*) acceptance bill; ~ **documentata** (*cred.*) *V.* ~ **documentaria;** ~ **domiciliata** (*cred.*) domiciled bill; ~ **libera** (*cred.*) clean bill; ~ **non documentata** (*cred.*) clean bill; ~ **spiccata su un banchiere** (*e da lui accettata*) (*banca, cred.*) bank acceptance.

trattabile, *a.* **1** (*di persona*) tractable, amenable. **2** (*comm.*) (*d'articolo, merce, ecc.*) dealable.

trattamento, *n. m.* **1** treatment; deal (*fam.*). **2** (*maneggio*) handling. **3** (*org. az.*) processing. **4** (*pers.*) (*salario*) wages; (*stipendio*) salary; (*paga*) pay. **5** (*pubbl.*) (*d'una pellicola*) processing. **6** (*tur.*) (*vitto*) food; (*vitto e alloggio*) board and lodging. // ~ **di favore** special consideration, discriminating treatment; ~ **di nazione preferita** (*comm. est.*) most-favoured-nation treatment;

preferential treatment, preference; ~ **di quiescenza** (*pers.*) retired pension, retired pay; ~ **tariffario di favore** (*accordato ai Paesi membri del Commonwealth britannico*) (*ingl.*) imperial preference.

trattare, *v. t.* **1** to treat, to deal* with. **2** (*maneggiare*) to handle. **3** (*discutere*) to discuss, to treat. **4** (*negoziare*) to treat, to transact, to negotiate. **5** (*occuparsi di*) to take* care of, to look after. **6** (*Borsa*) (*titoli, ecc.*) to deal* in. **7** (*market.*) (*un articolo, ecc.*) to deal* in, to handle, to merchandise, to merchant, to carry. **8** (*pubbl.*) (*una pellicola*) to process. *v. i.* **1** to treat (with), to deal* with. **2** (*d'un argomento*) to deal* with, to be (about). // ~ **un affare** to conduct a business; ~ **una causa** (*leg.*) to conduct a case, to plead a case; ~ **con q.** (*anche*) to do with sb.; ~ (*un argomento*) **in un trafiletto** (*giorn.*) to paragraph; ~ **un ramo d'affari** (*market.*) to deal in a line; **non trattato in una Borsa ufficiale** (*fin.*) (*di titolo, ecc.*) over-the-counter (*a. attr.*).

trattario, *n. m.* (*cred.*) drawee.

trattativa, *n. f.* negotiation, dealing, deal; (*colloquio*) talk. // **trattativa a livello aziendale** (*sind.*) plant bargaining; **trattative in corso** pending dealings, pending negotiations; ~ **privata** private treaty; ~ **sindacale** (*sind.*) labour negotiation, bargaining; **trattative sindacali collettive** (*sind.*) collective bargaining; **trattative «sotto banco»** indirect dealings.

trattato, *n. m.* **1** (*esposizione d'una dottrina*) treatise; (*manuale*) manual. **2** (*leg.*) (*accordo*) treaty, agreement; (*contratto*) contract. // ~ **commerciale** (*comm. est.*) trade treaty, trade agreement, commercial treaty.

trattazione, *n. f.* (*il trattare un argomento*) treatment.

trattenere, *v. t.* **1** to hold*, to hold* back, to withhold*, to keep*, to keep* back. **2** (*detrarre*) to deduct, to keep* back, to retain. **3** (*far restare*) to detain, to delay. **4** (*frenare*) to curb; (*controllare*) to check; (*reprimere*) to repress. **5** (*leg.*) (*in stato di fermo*) to detain. **6** (*leg.*) (*parte d'una somma dovuta*) to recoup. **7** (*pers.*) (*parte dello stipendio; anche*) to stop. // ~ **a q. lo stipendio** (*pers.*) to stop sb.'s salary; ~ **una polizza di carico** (*trasp. mar.*) to retain a bill of lading; **essere trattenuto in carcere** (*leg.*) (*d'imputato*) to be on remand; **trattenuto in porto dal maltempo** (*trasp. mar.*) (*di naviglio*) weather-bound; **trattenuto in porto dal vento contrario** (*trasp. mar.*) (*di naviglio*) wind-bound.

trattenuta, *n. f.* **1** (*leg.*) (*di parte d'una somma dovuta*) recoupment. **2** (*pers.*) deduction, deduct, check-off, holdback pay, hold-back, stoppage. // ~ **automatica** (*dei contributi sindacali: sulla paga*) (*pers.*) automatic check-off; ~ **d'acconto** (*fin.*) withholding tax; **una ~ sullo stipendio** (*pers.*) a deduction from the salary; ~ **volontaria** (*pers.*) voluntary check-off.

trattore, *n. m.* tractor. // ~ **agricolo** farm tractor, agrimotor.

«traveller's cheque», *locuz. n.* (*cred.*) traveller's cheque; travelers' check (*USA*).

traversare, *v. t.* to cross.

traversata, *n. f.* (*trasp. aer., trasp. mar.*) crossing, voyage, passage. // ~ **su nave da carico** (*trasp. mar.*) cargo passage.

trazione, *n. f.* **1** (*trasp.*) traction. **2** (*trasp. aut.*) drive. // ~ **anteriore** (*trasp. aut.*) front-wheel drive; ~ **meccanica** (*trasp.*) mechanical traction.

tre, *num. card.* three. // **in ~ copie** (*leg.*) (*di documento*) tripartite; **la regola del ~ composto** (*mat.*) the compound rule of three; **la regola del ~ semplice** (*mat.*) the simple rule of three.

tredicesima, *n. f.* (*pers.*) year-end bonus.

tregua, *n. f.* **1** truce. **2** (*pausa*) pause, respite. // ~ **salariale** (*econ., sind.*) wage pause, pay pause; ~ **sindacale** (*sind.*) industrial peace.

«trend», *n. m.* (*econ.*) trend. // ~ **a lungo termine** (*econ.*) long-run trend.

treno, *n. m.* (*trasp. ferr.*) train. // ~ **accelerato** (*trasp. ferr.*) slow train; accommodation train (*USA*); ~ **azzurro** (*trasp. ferr.*) blue train; **un ~ che dalla città principale porta in provincia** (*trasp. ferr.*) a down train; **un ~ che fa la spola fra due stazioni** (*trasp. ferr.*) a shuttle train; ~ **della (ferrovia) elevata** (*trasp. ferr., USA*) elevated train; **un ~ di gomme** (*trasp. aut.*) a set of tyres; ~ **direttissimo** (*trasp. ferr.*) express train; ~ **diretto** (*trasp. ferr.*) through train, non-stop; ~ **diretto in città** (*specialm. a Londra*) (*fam., ingl.*) up train; ~ **diretto in provincia** (*specialm. in partenza da Londra*) (*fam., ingl.*) down train; ~ **diurno** (*trasp. ferr.*) day train, daylight train; **un ~ espresso** (*trasp. ferr.*) an express train, an express; ~ **festivo** (*trasp. ferr.*) extra holiday train; **il ~ in arrivo** (*trasp. ferr.*) the in train; ~ **in coincidenza con un battello** (*che attraversa la Manica*) (*trasp. ferr., ingl.*) boat train; **il ~ in partenza** (*trasp. ferr.*) the out train; ~ **locale** (*trasp. ferr.*) local train, local; way train, accommodation train (*USA*); ~ **merci** (*trasp. ferr.*) goods train, merchandise train; freight train (*USA*); ~ **merci locale** (*trasp. ferr., USA*) local freight, way freight; ~ **misto** (*per merci e* *passeggeri*) (*trasp. ferr.*) passenger and goods train, composite train, mixed train; ~ **notturno** (*trasp. ferr.*) night train; **un ~ «omnibus»** (*trasp. ferr.*) an omnibus train; ~ **postale** (*trasp. ferr.*) mail-train; ~ **rapido** (*trasp. ferr.*) express train; (*per merci deperibili, bestiame, ecc.*) (*trasp. ferr., USA*) manifest; ~ **straordinario** (*trasp. ferr.*) special train, relief train, special; ~ **supplementare** (*trasp. ferr.*) relief train; ~ **viaggiatori** (*trasp. ferr.*) passenger train.

tribunale, *n. m.* (*leg.*) law-court, court, tribunal; (*talora*) judicature. // ~ **arbitrale** (*leg.*) arbitration court; ~ **civile** (*leg.*) civil court, court of equity; ~ **commerciale** (*leg.*) commercial court; ~ **competente** (*leg.*) competent court; ~ **di giurisdizione** (*leg.*) court of records; ~ **di prima istanza** (*leg.*) trial court; district court (*USA*); ~ **fallimentare** (*leg.*) court of bankruptcy, bankruptcy court; **un ~** (*di grado*) **inferiore** (*leg.*) an inferior court of law; **un ~ internazionale** (*leg.*) an international court; **tribunali locali di contea** (*leg.*) county courts; ~ **per processi comuni** (*leg.*) court of common pleas.

tributario, *a.* **1** tributary. **2** (*fin.*) (*fiscale*) fiscal; taxation, tax (*attr.*). // **il sistema ~** (*fin.*) the taxation system.

tributo, *n. m.* **1** tribute. **2** (*fin.*) tax; (*dazio sulle importazioni*) impost. // ~ **fiscale** (*fin.*) revenue tax; **un ~ inesatto** (*fin.*) an uncollected tax.

trilione, *n. m.* (*un 1 seguito da 12 zeri*) **1** billion (*ingl.*). **2** trillion (*USA*).

trimestrale, *a.* quarterly. *n. m.* (*giorn.*) (*pubblicazione trimestrale*) quarterly.

trimestralmente, *avv.* quarterly.

trimestre, *n. m.* **1** (*periodo di tre mesi*) quarter. **2** (*somma da pagare, o da riscuotere, ogni tre mesi*) three-monthly payment; (*rata trimestrale*) three-monthly instalment.

triplice, *a.* treble, triplicate, triple. // ~ **copia** triplicate; **in ~ copia** (*di documento*) in triplicate.

trittico, *n. m.* (*dog., trasp. aut.*) pass-sheet.

tronco, *n. m.* **1** (*anche fig.*) trunk. **2** (*trasp. ferr.*) section. // ~ **di ferrovia** (*trasp. ferr.*) railway section; ~ **di strada** (*trasp. aut.*) road section.

trovare, *v. t.* **1** to find★. **2** (*scoprire*) to find★ (out), to discover; (*rintracciare*) to trace (back). **3** (*pensare*) to think★. **4** (*visitare*) to see★. // ~ **un editore per** (*un manoscritto, ecc.*) (*giorn., pubbl.*) to place; ~ **lavoro per q.** (*pers.*) to find a job for sb., to place sb.; ~ **smercio** (*market.*) (*di merce*) to sell; ~ **il proprio tornaconto in qc.** to find one's account in st.; ~ **il valore massimo di** (*una funzione, ecc.*) (*mat.*) to maximize; ~ **il valore minimo di** (*una funzione, ecc.*) (*mat.*) to minimize.

trovarsi, *v. rifl.* **1** to find★ oneself. **2** (*essere*) to be; (*essere situato*) to be located, to be situated, to lie★; (*risiedere*) to reside. *v. recipr.* (*incontrarsi*) to meet★. // ~ **con una bilancia dei pagamenti favorevole** (*fin.*) to have a balance-of-payments surplus; ~ **d'accordo** to be agreed, to be in agreement; ~ **in buone condizioni finanziarie** to be well off; ~ **in cattive condizioni finanziarie** to be badly off.

truffa, *n. f.* (*leg.*) fraud, swindle, cheat; (*finanziaria*) bubble; (*inganno*) deceit; bunco, con (*slang USA*). // ~ **all'americana** (*leg.*) confidence game, confidence trick; con (*slang USA*).

truffaldino, *a.* (*leg.*) fraudulent, crooked. *n. m.* (*leg.*) swindler, crook; confidence man★, confidence crook, con artist (*slang USA*).

truffare, *v. t.* (*leg.*) to defraud, to cheat, to swindle; (*ingannare*) to deceive. // ~ **con raggiri** (*leg.*) to cheat with false pretence, to defraud with false pretences.

truffatore, *n. m.* (*leg.*) cheat, fraud, swindler, crook; confidence man★, confidence crook; con artist (*slang USA*).

truppa, *n. f.* **1** troop. **2** (*org. az., fig.*) (*gli operai, la «base»*) (the) rank and file.

trust, *n. m.* (*fin.*) trust, combine. // ~ **dei cervelli** brain trust.

tunnel, *n. m. inv.* **1** tunnel. **2** (*econ., fin.*) (*monetario europeo*) tunnel, tube. // ~ **sotto la Manica** (*trasp.*) Channel tunnel; chunnel (*parola composta di «channel» e «tunnel»*).

turbamento, *n. m.* disturbance, perturbation, upset. // ~ **dell'ordine pubblico** (*leg.*) breach of the peace, violation of the peace.

turbare, *v. t.* to disturb, to unsettle, to upset★, to trouble. // ~ **la quiete pubblica** (*leg.*) to disturb the peace.

turbativa, *n. f.* (*leg.*) disturbance, nuisance. // ~ **di possesso** (*leg.*) disturbance of possession.

turismo, *n. m.* **1** (*tur.*) tourism, touring. **2** (*tur.*) (*l'industria turistica*) (the) tourist industry.

turista, *n. m.* e *f.* (*tur.*) tourist, visitor.

turistico, *a.* (*tur.*) tourist (*attr.*).

turnista, *n. m.* e *f.* (*pers.*) shift worker.

turno, *n. m.* **1** turn. **2** (*pers.*) (*di lavoro*) duty, turn, shift, spell. // ~ **a scacchi** (*pers.*) staggered shift; ~ **alternato** (*pers.*) alternate shift; ~ (*di lavoro*) **dalle ore 16 alle 24** (*pers.*) swing shift; ~ **di giorno** (*pers.*) day shift, first shift; **un ~ di lavoro** (*pers.*) a turn of work, a shift; ~ **di notte** (*pers.*) night shift, third shift;

graveyard shift (*fam.*); (*nella redazione d'un giornale*) lobster shift; lobster trick (*fam., USA*); ~ **fisso** (*pers.*) fixed shift; ~ **pendolare** (*pers.*) swing shift; ~ **pomeridiano** (*pers.*) afternoon shift, second shift; **turni rotatori** (*pers.*) rotating shifts.

tutela, *n. f.* **1** (*protezione*) protection. **2** (*leg.*) guardianship, tutorship, custody; (*di minorenne e sim.*) wardship, ward. // ~ **contro l'erogazione d'ammende** (*leg.*) immunity from fines; ~ **della maternità** (*leg., pers.*) maternal welfare; **essere sotto** ~ (*leg.*) to be under wardship.

tutelare[1], *a.* (*leg.*) guardian (*attr.*).

tutelare[2], *v. t.* (*proteggere*) to protect. // ~ (*un libro, ecc.*) **in base alle leggi sui diritti d'autore** (*leg.*) to copyright; ~ **i propri interessi** to protect one's interest; **tutelato da diritto d'autore** (*leg.*) copyright (*attr.*).

tutore, *n. m.* (*leg.*) guardian, tutor, curator, conservator; (*di minore, ecc.: in una causa*) next friend.

tutorio, *a.* (*leg.*) tutelary.

tutto, *a.* **1** all; (*intero*) whole. **2** (*con valore di avv.*) (*completamente*) quite, completely, entirely. *pron.* all; (*ogni cosa*) everything; (*qualsiasi cosa*) anything. *n. m.* whole; (*ogni cosa*) everything. // ~ **compreso** all-in; (*tur.*) «inclusive terms»; **a tutt'oggi** up to date, up to and including today.

U

udienza, *n. f.* **1** audience, hearing; (*colloquio*) interview. **2** (*leg.*) hearing, session, sitting. // ~ **a porte aperte** (*leg.*) hearing in open Court, open Court; ~ **a porte chiuse** (*leg.*) hearing in Chambers; (*penale*) trial «in camera»; ~ **aggiornata** (*che completa un'udienza non definitiva*) (*leg.*) further hearing, further proceedings; **un'** ~ **del tribunale** (*leg.*) a sitting of the Court; ~ **plenaria** (*leg.*) trial at bar; ~ **pubblica** (*leg.*) public hearing, open audience; **udienze trimestrali** (*leg., ingl.*) quarter sessions; **in pubblica** ~ (*leg.*) in open Court; **rinviare l'** ~ (*leg.*) to adjourn the sitting; **sospendere l'** ~ (*leg.*) to adjourn the sitting; **togliere l'** ~ (*leg.*) to close the sitting.

udire, *v. t.* **1** to hear★. **2** (*ascoltare*) to listen to. // ~ **entrambe le parti** (*in giudizio*) (*leg.*) to hear both sides; ~ **i testimoni** (*leg.*) to hear the witnesses.

uditore, *n. m.* **1** hearer. **2** (*ascoltatore*) listener. **3** (*leg.*) auditor.

uditorio, *n. m.* audience; listeners (*pl.*).

ufficiale[1], *a.* official; (*formale*) formal. // **un atto** ~ an official act; **non** ~ unofficial, inofficial; (*non formale*) informal; (*Borsa, fin.*) (*di Borsa Valori*) off-board; (*giorn.*) (*di dichiarazione, intervista, e sim.*) off the record (*pred.*); off-the-record (*attr.*); **una visita** ~ a formal call.

ufficiale[2], *n. m.* **1** (*pers.*) (*funzionario*) official. **2** (*trasp. mar., ecc.*) officer. // ~ **di Stato Civile** (*amm.*) registrar; ~ **doganale** (*dog.*) landing officer, landing waiter, landwaiter, waiter; ~ **giudiziario** (*leg.*) bailiff, sheriff; marshal (*USA*); (*cui compete la notifica di citazione al «convenuto»*) process-server; ~ **pagatore** (*delle Forze Armate*) paymaster general, paymaster; ~ **postale** (*comun.*) postmaster (*m.*); postmistress (*f.*); ~ **sanitario** (*leg.*) officer of health, health-officer, medical officer; **pubblico** ~ public official.

ufficialità, *n. f. inv.* official character. // **l'** ~ **d'una dichiarazione** the official character of a statement.

ufficialmente, *avv.* officially. // **non** ~ unofficially, inofficially, off the record; (*non formalmente*) informally.

ufficio, *n. m.* **1** (*il luogo di lavoro*) office. **2** (*carica*) office, appointment. **3** (*dovere*) duty; (*funzione*) function; (*veste*) capacity. **4** (*amm., org. az.*) (*organo*) board. **5** (*leg.*) (*di un giudice*) camera. **6** (*org. az.*) (*reparto*) department; (*agenzia, sezione*) bureau. **7** (*pers.*) (*impiego, lavoro*) job, place, office. // ~ **acquisti** (*org. az.*) purchasing office, purchasing department, purchasing bureau; ~ **amministrativo** (*org. az.*) counting house; ~ **assistenza** (*org. az.*) service department; ~ **assunzioni** (*pers.*) recruiting office; **un** ~ **ben attrezzato** a well appointed office; ~ **brevetti** (*leg.*) patent office; ~ **cassa** (*org. az.*) cash department, cashier's office, cashier's desk; **uffici contabili** (*org. az.*) accounting offices; ~ **crediti** (*org. az.*) credit department; ~ **del bollo** (*fin.*) stamp office; ~ **del catasto** (*fin.*) land office; ~ **del contenzioso** (*leg.*) disputed claims office; ~ **del dazio** (*trasp.*) tollbooth; ~ **(del) personale** (*org. az.*) personnel department, personnel bureau; ~ **del registro per le società per azioni** (*fin.*) companies' register office; ~ **del telegrafo** (*comun.*) telegraph office; ~ **della dogana** (*dog.*) custom house; ~ **delle compensazioni** (*della Banca d'Inghilterra*) (*banca, fin.*) clearing department; ~ **delle fermo (in) posta** (*comun.*) poste restante; **l'** ~ **(delle) imposte** (*fin.*) the tax office, the Excise; ~ **delle imposte dirette** (*fin.*) direct taxation office; ~ **dello Stato Civile** (*amm.*) register office, registry office; **uffici d'acquisto** (*comm. est.*) buying offices; ~ **di cambio** (*fin.*) exchange office; ~ **di cancelliere** (*di tribunale*) (*leg.*) (*la carica*) clerkship; ~ **di cassiere** (*fin.*) (*la carica*) treasureship; ~ **di collocamento** (*pers., sind.*) labour exchange, employment bureau; public employment office, employment agency (*USA*); (*che inoltre offre assistenza per l'orientamento professionale*) vocational office, vocational bureau; ~ **di contabilità** (*rag.*) counting house; counting room (*USA*); ~ **d'esattore delle imposte** (*fin.*) (*la carica*) collectorate, collectorship; ~ **di facente funzioni** (*leg., org. az.*) (*la carica*) locum-tenency; ~ **di giudice** (*leg.*) (*la carica*) justiceship, judgeship, judicature; (*sede: presso il tribunale*) chamber; ~ **d'un giudice conciliatore** (*leg.*) Court of conciliation; ~ **di notaio** (*leg.*) (*la carica*) notaryship; ~ **di revisore dei conti** (*amm., org. az., rag.*) (*la carica*) auditorship; ~ **di società d'assicurazione contro gli incendi** (*ass.*) fire office; ~ **di sostituto** (*leg., org. az.*) (*la carica*) locum-tenency; ~ **di supplente** (*leg., org. az.*) (*la carica*) locum-tenency; ~ **di tesoriere** (*fin.*) (*la carica*) treasureship; ~ **(distribuzione) pacchi** (*trasp.*) parcels office; ~ **doganale** (*dog.*) customs; ~ **esazioni** (*fin., rag.*) accounts receivable department; ~ **fidi** (*banca*) credit department; ~ **incassi** (*banca*) collecting department, collection department, accounts receivable department; ~ **incendi** (*in una compagnia d'assicurazioni*) (*ass.*) fire department; ~ **informazioni** (*org. az.*) inquiry office, information bureau; (*il banco*) information desk; ~ **informazioni commerciali** (*cred., fin.*) status inquiry agency; credit bureau (*USA*); ~ **Internazionale dei Pesi e delle Misure** International Bureau of Weights and Measures; ~ **legale** (*leg.*) law office; ~ **meteorologico** weather bureau; ~ **paga** (*org. az.*) pay-office; ~ **pagamenti** (*org. az.*) paying office; ~ **per la Riforma della Pubblica Amministrazione** Ministry of the Civil Service; ~ **per la tutela dei diritti d'autore** (*leg.*) copyright office; ~ **portafoglio** (*banca*) bills department; ~ **postale** (*comun.*) post office, post; ~ **prenotazioni** (*trasp.*) booking office; ~ **prestiti** (*cred.*) loan office; ~ **principale** (*org. az.*) head office; ~ **privato** (*org. az.*) private office, back office; ~ **privato del giudice** (*leg.*) chambers; ~ **redazionale** (*giorn., USA*) desk; ~ **spedizione pacchi** (*trasp.*) parcels office; ~ **spedizioni** (*org. az.*) forwarding department, shipping department; ~ **spedizioni postali** (*comun.*) dispatching office, mail room; ~ **statistico** (*org. az.*) statistical department; ~ **titoli** (*banca*) security department, stock department; ~ **turistico** (*tur.*) tourist office; ~ **vendite** (*org. az.*) sales department; **chi tiene un** ~ (*pers.*) office-bearer, office-holder; **d'** ~ (*amm., leg.*) (*senza una previa istanza*) as a matter of course, on one's own initiative, ex officio; **in un** ~ **privato** (*Borsa, fin.*) over the counter; **lavoro d'** ~ (*org. az.*) office work; **nell'** ~ **d'un giudice** (*leg.*) in camera; **orario d'** ~ (*org. az.*) office hours.

ufficiosamente, *avv.* unofficially, officiously, informally, off the record.

ufficiosità, *n. f. inv.* unofficial character, semi-official character, officiousness, informality.

ufficioso, *a.* unofficial, inofficial, semi-official, officious, informal.

uguaglianza, *n. f.* equality; (*parità*) parity. // ~ **dei punti di partenza** (*econ.*) equality of starting points; ~ **di trattamento** equality of treatment.

uguagliare, *v. t.* to equalize, to make★ (st.) equal, to equal; (*livellare*) to level. // ~ **le imposte** (*fin.*) to equalize taxes.

uguale, *a.* **1** equal, like, the same; alike (*pred.*); (*identico*) identical. **2** (*mat.*) equal. // ~ **al campione** (*market.*) up to sample (*pred.*).

ugualmente, *avv.* **1** equally, in the same way. **2** (*lo stesso*) nevertheless, all the same.

ulteriore, *a.* further. // **ulteriori informazioni** additional information, further information.

ulteriormente, *avv.* further, further on.

ultimamente, *avv.* lately, recently, of late.

ultimare, *v. t.* to complete, to finish. // ~ **un lavoro** to complete a work; ~ **la stampa** (*giorn., pubbl.*) to finish the printing.

ultimatum, *n. m.* ultimatum★.

ultimazione, *n. f.* completion.

ultimissime, *n. pl.* (*giorn.*) spot news, latest news.

ultimo, *a.* **1** (*d'una serie*) last. **2** (*il più recente*) latest. **3** (*passato, scorso, trascorso*) past, last. **4** (*finale*) final. // **ultime bozze di stampa** (*prima di andare in macchina*) (*giorn.*) press proofs; ~ **compratore** (*econ.*) ultimate purchaser, ultimate buyer; ~ **consumatore** (*econ.*) ultimate consumer; **l'ultima edizione** (*giorn.*) the latest edition, the final; **l'** ~ **«grido»** (*market., pubbl.*) the last thing, the last word, the latest, the «in» thing; **le** ~ **notizie** (*giorn.*) the latest news; **l'ultima novità** (*market., pubbl.*) the last thing, the last word, the latest, the «in» thing; **l'ultima offerta** the definitive offer; **l'** ~ **prezzo** (*market.*) the lowest price, the closest price; **le ultime quotazioni** (*fin.*) the latest quotations; ~ **scorso** (*comun.*) ultimo (*abbr.* ult.); **ultime volontà** (*leg.*) last will and testament, last will, will and testament, will; **fino all'** ~ **centesimo** down to the last cent, down to the last penny; **ultimissima edizione** (*d'un giornale della sera*) (*giorn.*) extra-special; **ultimissime notizie** (*giorn.*) latest news, spot news; **le ultimissime novità** (*market.*) the very last thing (*sing.*); **all'ultimissima moda** (*market.*) up to the minute.

«underwriting», *n. m.* (*ass., fin.*) underwriting.

unico, *a.* **1** only. **2** (*esclusivo, solo*) exclusive, sole. **3** (*senza pari*) unique. // ~ **agente** (*org. az.*) sole agent; ~ **erede** (*leg.*) sole heir; ~ **proprietario** (*leg.*) sole proprietor; **in un'unica**

somma in one amount; **numero** ~ (*giorn.*) special number.

unificare, *v. t.* **1** to unify. **2** (*standardizzare*) to standardize. **3** (*econ., fin.*) (*fondere, combinare*) to consolidate. // ~ **un debito pubblico** (*fin.*) to consolidate a debt.

unificato, *a.* **1** unified. **2** (*standardizzato*) standardized. **3** (*econ., fin.*) (*combinato, fuso*) consolidated. // **codici unificati** (*leg.*) standardized legal systems.

unificazione, *n. f.* **1** unification. **2** (*standardizzazione*) standardization. **3** (*econ., fin.*) (*fusione*) consolidation. // **l'**~ **della base imponibile dell'IVA** (*Imposta sul Valore Aggiunto*) (*fin.*) the standardization of the basis for assessment of VAT (*Value Added Tax*).

unilaterale, *a.* (*leg.*) unilateral, one-sided.

unilateralità, *n. f. inv.* (*leg.*) unilaterality, one-sidedness.

uninominale, *a.* uninominal. // **collegio** ~ (*leg.*) single-member constituency.

unione, *n. f.* **1** union. **2** (*associazione*) union, association, combine; (*lega*) league. // ~ **dei consumatori** (*market.*) consumers' union; **l'**~ **dell'Europa Occidentale (UEO)** the Western European Union (*WEU*); ~ **doganale** (*comm. est.*) customs union; ~ **economica** (*econ.*) economic union; ~ **Europea dei Pagamenti (UEP)** European Payments Union (*EPU*); ~ **industriale** (*sind.*) employers' association; ~ **monetaria** (*fin.*) monetary union; ~ **postale** (*fra Stati*) (*comun.*) postal union; ~ **tariffaria** (*comm. est.*) tariff union.

unità, *n. f. inv.* **1** unity. **2** (*misura, valore*) unit. **3** (*econ.*) (*dose: d'un bene*) dose. **4** (*mat.*) unity, unit. // ~ **di comando** (*org. az.*) unity of command; ~ **di conto (U.C.)** (*econ., fin.*) unit of account (*u.a.*); ~ **di contrattazione** (*generalm. 100 azioni*) (*Borsa, fin.*) round lot; ~ **di controllo** (*org. az.*) unity of supervision; ~ **di costo** (*rag.*) cost unit; ~ **di direzione** (*org. az.*) unity of direction; ~ **di lavoro** (*econ.*) labour-unit; ~ **di lunghezza** unit of length; ~ **di misura** unit of measurement, denomination; (*fig.*) yardstick; ~ **di misura per liquidi** liquid measure; ~ **di misura usata ai fini della determinazione dell'imponibile** (*fin., leg.*) unit of assessment, unit of value; ~ **di movimento** (*di merci o passeggeri*) (*trasp.*) traffic unit; ~ **di peso** unit of weight; ~ **di salario** (*econ.*) wage-unit; ~ **di valore** unit of value; ~ **marginale** (*econ.*) marginal unity; ~ **monetaria** (*fin.*) monetary unit, pecuniary unit; ~ **normale di contrattazione** (*di titoli*) (*Borsa, fin.*) regular lot; ~ **operativa** (*org. az.*) operating unit; ~ **produttiva** (*org. az.*) production unit, unit, establishment.

unitario, *a.* unitary. // **il prezzo** ~ (*econ., market.*) the average price.

unito, *a.* **1** united; (*congiunto*) joint. **2** (*aggiunto*) added. **3** (*accluso*) enclosed, inclosed.

uomo, *n. m.* **1** man★. **2** (*fam.*) (*operaio*) worker, man★. // **un** ~ «**arrivato**» (*fig.*) a made man; **un** ~ **che s'è fatto da sé** (*fig.*) a self-made man; **un** ~ **della destra (politica)** a right-winger; **l'**~ **della strada** (*fig.*) the man in the street, the man on the street; ~ **d'affari** business man, businessman; ~ **d'affari della City** (*del centro bancario e commerciale di Londra*) (*fin.*) City man; **l'**~ **di casa** the man of the house; ~ **di fatica** man employed for heavy work, blue collar; ~ **di fiducia** confidential man, confidential secretary, personal secretary; man Friday (*fam.*); **un** ~ **di medie capacità** a man of average ability; ~ **di paglia** (*leg.*) man of straw, straw man, figurehead, dummy; **un** ~ **di parola** a man of honour; «**uomo-idea**» (*pers., fig.*) (*persona dotata d'una eccezionale capacità d'immaginare e formulare nuove tecniche, nuovi prodotti o soluzioni a problemi*) idea man; **l'**~ **medio** the common man, the mass man; **l'**~ **qualunque** the man in the street, the man on the street; **un** ~ **reputato solido** (*cred., leg.*) a solvent man, a good man; ~ **sandwich** (*stretto fra due cartelloni pubblicitari che porta in giro*) (*pubbl.*) sandwich man; **un** ~ **solvibile** (*cred., leg.*) a solvent man, a good man.

usanza, *n. f.* **1** (*costume*) custom. **2** (*uso*) usage. **3** (*abitudine*) habit. **4** (*leg.*) usance, custom.

usare, *v. t.* to use, to make★ use of; (*impiegare*) to employ. *v. i.* **1** (*essere comune*) to be customary, to be the custom. **2** (*market., pubbl.*) to be fashionable, to be in fashion, to be the fashion. // ~ **abusivamente** (*denaro altrui*) (*leg.*) to misapply; ~ **attenzione** to be careful; ~ **la forza** to use force; ~ **parsimonia** to be thrifty; ~ **sotterfugi** to dodge.

usato, *a.* **1** used. **2** (*di seconda mano*) second-hand, used. // **non** ~ unused; **non ancora** ~ not yet used, unused.

uscente, *a.* **1** (*di tempo*) expiring. **2** (*amm., pers.*) (*di dipendente, d'organo, ecc.*) retiring. // **il personale** ~ (*pers.*) the retiring personnel.

usciere, *n. m.* **1** (*pers.*) usher. **2** (*pers.*) (*ufficiale giudiziario*) bailiff, distrainor.

uscire, *v. i.* **1** (*andare fuori*) to go★ out, to get★ out. **2** (*venire fuori*) to come★ out, to get★ out. **3** (*giorn.*) (*di giornale*) to issue. // ~ **da** (*abbandonare, lasciare*) to leave; ~ **dal bacino**

(*trasp. mar.*) to undock; ~ **dal bacino di carenaggio** (*trasp. mar.*) to go out of dry dock; ~ **dal porto** (*trasp. mar.*) to leave port; ~ **dalle rotaie** (*trasp. ferr.*) to run off the rails; ~ **di minorità** (*leg.*) to come of age; ~ **di strada** (*trasp. aut.*) to run off the road, to leave the road; ~ **indenne da un'indagine** (*leg.*) to bear enquiry.

uscita, *n. f.* 1 exit; (*anche fig.*) way out. 2 (*econ., rag.*) expenditure, expense, outlay, outgoing, outgo. 3 (*elab. elettr.*) output. 4 (*trasp. aer.*) (*d'aeroporto*) gate. // **uscite invisibili** (*econ.*) invisible imports.

uso, *n. m.* 1 use. 2 usage. 3 (*costume*) custom. 4 (*pratica*) practice. 5 (*abitudine*) habit. 6 (*leg.*) use; (*consuetudine*) custom. // ~ **abusivo** (*di denaro altrui*) (*leg.*) misapplication; **un** ~ **abusivo di marchio di fabbrica** (*leg.*) a misappropriation of trade marks; ~ **commerciale** custom of trade, commercial usage; ~ **della suggestione** (*o* **della persuasione**) **nelle tecniche di vendita** (*market., pubbl.*) soft sell; ~ **d'un molo** (*per caricare e/o scaricare merce*) (*trasp. mar.*) wharfage; ~ **di piazza** (*banca*) local usance; ~ **d'un recinto** (*come deposito, ecc.*) yardage; ~ **e abuso** usage and abusage; ~ **e consumo** wear and tear; **usi e costumi** usages and customs; ~ **illecito dell'altrui marchio di fabbrica** (*leg.*) trade-mark infringement; ~ **illecito dell'altrui ragione sociale** (*leg.*) infringement; ~ **illecito d'un marchio di fabbrica** (*leg.*) trade-mark infringement; **usi in materia commerciale** trade practice; **usi locali** (*leg.*) local customs; **a proprio** ~ **e consumo** at one's own disposal; **d'** ~ **corrente** current; **per** ~ **proprio personale** for one's own personal use; **secondo gli usi del porto di New York** (*trasp. mar.*) as customary at the port of New York.

usucapione, *n. f.* (*leg.*) usucaption, usucapion, prescription.

usucapire, *v. t.* (*leg.*) to prescribe, to acquire (st.) by prescription.

usufruire, *v. i.* 1 (*valersi di qc.*) to take* advantage (of st.). 2 (*leg.*) to enjoy (st.) in usufruct.

usufrutto, *n. m.* (*leg.*) usufruct. // ~ **a vita** (*leg.*) life tenancy; ~ **imperfetto** (*leg.*) quasi-usufruct; ~ **legale** (*leg.*) legal usufruct; ~ **perfetto** (*leg.*) perfect usufruct; ~ **perpetuo** (*leg.*) tenancy for life; **quasi** ~ (*leg.*) quasi-usufruct.

usufruttuario, *a.* e *n. m.* (*leg.*) usufructuary. // ~ **a termine** (*leg.*) termor; ~ **a vita** (*leg.*) life tenant, termor; ~ **vita natural durante** (*leg.*) life tenant.

utente, *n. m.* e *f.* user; (*consumatore*) consumer. // ~ **della pubblicità** (*pubbl.*) advertiser; ~ **diretto** (*econ.*) direct user.

utenza, *n. f.* use; (*consumo*) consumption.

utile[1], *a.* 1 useful, helpful. 2 (*che può servire*) usable; (*proficuo*) profitable; (*pratico*) serviceable.

utile[2], *n. m.* 1 (*vantaggio, utilità*) advantage, benefit. 2 (*econ., fin., rag.*) profit, income, gain; earnings, makings (*pl.*); (*interesse*) interest. 3 (*market.*) (*differenza tra il costo d'acquisto e il prezzo di vendita*) markup. // ~ **aleatorio** (*rag.*) contingent profit; ~ **aziendale addizionale** (*rag.*) excess corporate profit; **utili contabili** (*rag.*) book profits; ~ **da distribuire** (*rag.*) income available for distribution; ~ **derivante dalla vendita d'attività che non erano state acquistate per essere rivendute** (*fin.*) capital profit; **utili di capitale** (*rag.*) capital gains; ~ **d'esercizio** (*rag.*) income for the year, trading profit; ~ **d'impresa** (*fin.*) company profit; corporate profit (*USA*); **utili di impresa soggetti a imposta** (*fin.*) taxable company profits; **utili d'intermediazione** (*fin.*) jobbing profits; **utili diretti** (*derivanti, cioè, dall'attività volta a perseguire il fine principale dell'azienda*) (*rag.*) operating profit; **utili distribuiti** (*rag.*) distributed income; **utili figurativi** (*rag.*) paper profits; **utili indivisi** (*fin.*) undivided profits; ~ **inutilizzato** (*di un esercizio passato*) **detraibile dall'imponibile** (*fin., USA*) carryback; ~ **lordo** (*rag.*) gross profit; gross profits (*pl.*); ~ **lordo d'esercizio** (*rag.*) gross profit; ~ **lordo sulle vendite** (*rag.*) operating profit; ~ **marginale** (*econ.*) marginal profit; ~ **netto di esercizio** (*rag.*) net profit, net income, clear profit; net earnings (*pl.*); **utili non distribuiti** (*fin.*) undistributed profits, retained earnings; ~ **presunto** (*fin., rag.*) anticipated profit; ~ **realizzato** (*rag.*) realized profit; ~ **reinvestito** (*fin.*) accumulated profit; **utili ripartibili** (*rag.*) divisible profits; **l'** ~ **sulle vendite** (*rag.*) the profit on sales.

utilità, *n. f. inv.* 1 usefulness, utility; (*convenienza*) convenience; (*vantaggio*) advantage, benefit. 2 (*econ.*) utility. // ~ **marginale** (*econ.*) marginal utility; final utility (*termine usato da Marshall e Jevons*); ~ **marginale comparata** (*econ.*) equal marginal utility; ~ **marginale decrescente** (*econ.*) diminishing marginal utility; ~ **soggettiva** (*d'un bene*) (*econ.*) subjective utility; ~ **totale** (*econ.*) total utility.

V

vacante, *a.* **1** vacant. **2** (*leg.*) (*di proprietà, di terreno*) vacant. **3** (*org. az., pers.*) (*di posto*) vacant, unfilled, open. // **eredità ~** (*leg.*) vacant succession.

vacanza, *n. f.* **1** holiday, vacation. **2** (*leg.*) (*d'eredità*) vacancy, abeyance. **3** (*org. az., pers.*) (*di carica, posto di lavoro, ecc.*) vacancy. // **~ accidentale** (*pers.*) casual vacancy; **vacanze retribuite** (*pers.*) holidays with pay; **in ~** on holiday, on vacation.

vademecum, *n. m.* vade-mecum.

vaglia, *n. m. inv.* (*cred., fin.*) money order. // **~ cambiario** (*cred., fin.*) promissory note, note of hand; **~ internazionale** (*cred.*) international money order; **~ per l'estero** (*cred.*) foreign money order; **~ postale** (*cred.*) money order; (*fino a un certo ammontare*) postal money order, post-office order; (*con un diverso limite della somma*) postal order, postal note; **~ telegrafico** (*comun., cred.*) telegraphic money order.

vago, *a.* vague; (*indefinito*) indefinite.

vagone, *n. m.* (*trasp. ferr.*) waggon; wagon; car (*USA*); railway carriage, van, truck; (*per passeggeri*) coach. // **~ bestiame** (*trasp.*) cattle wagon, cattle truck; **~ chiuso** (*trasp. ferr.*) covered wagon, covered van, covered truck; **~ completo** (*il contenuto*) (*trasp. ferr.*) truck load; **~ coperto** (*trasp. ferr.*) covered wagon, covered van, covered truck; **~ ferroviario** (*trasp. ferr.*) waggon; car (*USA*); **~ frigorifero** (*trasp. ferr.*) refrigerator car; **~ letto** (*trasp. ferr.*) sleeping-car, sleeping-carriage, sleeper; **~ merci** (*trasp. ferr.*) goods wagon, goods truck; freighter (*USA*); (*chiuso*) box wagon; box car (*USA*); **~ per il trasporto del carbone** (*trasp. ferr.*) coal wagon, coal truck, coaler; **~ postale** (*trasp. ferr.*) postal car, post-office car, mail carriage, mail car; **~ ristorante** (*trasp. ferr.*) lunch wagon; **~ salotto** (*trasp. ferr.*) saloon-carriage, saloon-car.

valere, *v. i.* e *t.* **1** to be worth. **2** (*avere molto merito*) to be worth a great deal. **3** (*essere valido*) to be valid; (*essere in vigore*) to be in force.

valersi, *v. rifl.* to take★ advantage (of), to avail oneself (of), to make★ use (of). // **~ d'un diritto** (*leg.*) to avail oneself of a right.

valevole, *a.* **1** (*utile*) good. **2** (*valido*) valid; (*disponibile*) available. **3** (*fin.*) (*di moneta, ecc.*) current.

validità, *n. f. inv.* **1** validity, availability. **2** (*fin.*) (*di moneta, ecc.*) currency. **3** (*leg.*) (*d'un titolo; anche*) soundness. // **la ~ d'un'assicurazione** (*ass.*) the currency of an insurance; **la ~ d'un atto** (*leg.*) the validity of a deed; **la ~ d'un biglietto ferroviario** (*trasp. ferr.*) the validity of a railway ticket.

valido, *a.* **1** (*anche leg.*) valid, available. **2** (*fin.*) (*di moneta, ecc.*) current. **3** (*leg.*) sound. // **non ~** (*leg.*) invalid, void; (*nullo*) null.

valore, *n. m.* **1** value, worth. **2** (*di persona*) value, worth; (*merito*) merit; weight (*fig.*). **3** (*validità*) validity, value. **4** (*econ.*) value. **5** (*fin.*) (*d'una moneta*) denomination. **6** (*mat.*) value. **7 valori,** *pl.* (*oggetti preziosi*) valuable goods, value goods, valuables. **8 valori,** *pl.* (*banca*) (*assegni, cambiali, ecc.*) papers. **9 valori,** *pl.* (*Borsa, fin.*) (*titoli*) stocks and shares, securities; stock (*sing.*). // **~ aggiunto** (*econ.*) value added, added value; **~ approssimativo** (*rag.*) estimated value, approximate value; **~ assicurabile** (*ass.*) insurable value; **~ assicurato** (*ass.*) insured value; **~ assoluto** absolute value; **valori attivi** (*rag.*) amounts to be made good, assets; **~ attuale** (*mat.*) present value, actual value, present worth, present discounted value; **~ capitalizzato** (*rag.*) capitalized value; **~ complessivo** total value; **~ contabile** (*rag.*) book value; **~ corrente** (*market.*) going value; **valori creditizi** (*rag.*) amounts to be made good; **valori del listino** (*Borsa*) listed shares; **~ derivato** (*econ.*) derived value; **~ d'acquisto** (*rag.*) cost price; **~ d'affezione** sentimental value; **~ di bilancio** (*fin., rag.*) balance-sheet value, book value; **valori di cambio** (*fin.*) exchange values; **~ di carico** (*fin., rag.*) book value; **~** (*massimo*) **di credito** (*che un assicurato sulla vita può ottenere, su garanzia del valore effettivo della polizza*) (*ass.*) loan value; **~ d'inventario** (*fin., rag.*) book value; **~ di mercato** (*econ., market.*)

market value; **valori di portafoglio** (*fin.*) paper holdings, paper securities; ~ **d'una proprietà al netto d'ipoteche** (*leg.*) equity; ~ **di realizzo** (*market.*) break-up value; ~ **di ricupero** (*d'un'immobilizzazione*) (*rag.*) salvage value; ~ **di riduzione** (*del capitale assicurato*) (*ass.*) paid-up policy value; ~ **di rimpiazzo** (*org. az., rag.*) replacement value; ~ **di riscatto** (*rag.*) convertible value; **il ~ di riscatto di una polizza** (*ass.*) the surrender value of a policy; ~ **di sostituzione** (*org. az., rag.*) replacement value; ~ **dichiarato** (*ass., dog.*) declared value, value declared; **valori estremi** (*market.*) extreme values, outliers, extremes; **il ~ estrinseco d'una moneta** (*fin.*) the extrinsic value of a coin; ~ **facciale** (*d'una moneta, banconota, ecc.*) (*fin.*) face value; ~ **imponibile** (*fin.*) taxable value, assessed value; **il ~ imponibile d'una proprietà** (*fin.*) the ratable value of a property; ~ **in capitale** (*rag.*) capital value; ~ **in dogana** (*dog.*) customs value; ~ (*di danni*) **in franchigia** (*ass.*) franchise; **valori** (*d'imprese*) **industriali** (*fin.*) industrials; ~ **intrinseco** (*econ.*) intrinsic value; ~ **locativo** (*leg.*) rental value, letting value, rental; (*per il fisco*) rateable value; ~ **massimo** maximum value; (*mat.*) (*d'una funzione, ecc.*) maximum, peak; ~ **minimo** minimum value; (*mat.*) (*d'una funzione, ecc.*) minimum, trough; **valori mobiliari** (*fin.*) stocks and shares, securities; ~ **monetario** (*fin.*) money value; ~ **nominale** (*econ.*) (*di una moneta, banconota, titolo, ecc.*) denominational value, face value; (*fin.*) nominal value, par value; **il ~ nominale d'un'azione** (*fin.*) the face value of a share; **valori passivi** (*rag.*) liabilities; ~ **patrimoniale** (*rag.*) tangible net worth; ~ **presunto** (*rag.*) constructive value; ~ **reale** true value; ~ **redimibile** (*ass.*) loan value; **valori tabellari** tabular values; ~ **venale** (*fin., rag.*) realizable value, selling price; **senza ~** worthless (*a.*); **senza ~ nominale** (*fin.*) no-par value, no-par (*a. attr.*).

valorizzare, *v. t.* **1** to turn (st.) to account, to use (st.) to advantage; (*sfruttare*) to exploit. **2** (*econ.*) (*un prodotto*) to valorize; (*un terreno, ecc.*) to improve.

valorizzazione, *n. f.* **1** exploitation. **2** (*econ.*) (*d'un prodotto*) valorization; (*d'un terreno, ecc.*) improvement.

valuta, *n. f.* **1** (*fin.*) currency, money, coinage. **2** (*rag.*) (*decorrenza degli interessi*) value date, value. // «~ **al...**» (*banca*) «value date...», «as at...»; ~ **argentea** (*fin.*) silver currency; ~ **aurea** (*fin.*) gold currency, gold standard, gold money; ~ **cartacea** (*fin.*) paper currency, paper money; **una ~ controllata** (*nel suo potere d'acquisto: dalle autorità monetarie*) (*fin.*) a managed currency, managed money; ~ **debole** (*fin.*) soft currency, weak currency; ~ **di conto** (*rag.*) money of account; **valute di riferimento** (*fin.*) reference currencies; ~ **12 aprile** (*banca, anche*) interest to run from April 12th; ~ **estera** (*fin.*) foreign currency; ~ **forte** (*fin.*) hard currency, strong currency, firm currency; «~ **in contanti**» (*banca*) «cash value»; «~ **in conto**» (*banca*) «value in account», «value on account»; ~ **in natura** (*fin.*) commodity-currency; ~ **legale** (*fin.*) legal tender, standard money; ~ **metallica** (*fin.*) metallic currency; ~ **nazionale** (*fin.*) home currency; ~ **non convertibile** (*fin.*) inconvertible currency; **valute ospiti** (*fin.*) guest currencies; ~ **pregiata** (*fin.*) hard currency; ~ **ufficiale** (*fin.*) standard money, legal tender; **in ~ aurea** (*fin.*) in gold; «**per ~ ricevuta**» (*banca*) «(for) value received».

valutabile, *a.* **1** valuable, appraisable, appreciable. **2** (*determinabile*) assessable, ratable; (*misurabile*) measurable; (*calcolabile*) computable, reckonable.

valutare, *v. t.* **1** to value, to evaluate, to estimate, to appraise, to appreciate. **2** (*determinare*) to assess, to rate; (*misurare*) to measure; (*calcolare*) to calculate, to compute, to reckon. **3** (*soppesare*) to weigh (*fig.*). **4** (*rag.*) (*costi*) to cost★. // ~ **al costo** (*rag.*) to value at cost; ~ **al prezzo di mercato** (*rag.*) to value at market price; ~ **il capitale complessivo** (*d'una società*) (*rag.*) to capitalize; ~ **di nuovo** (*un danno, ecc.*) (*ass.*) to reassess; (*fin., rag.*) (*rivalutare*) to revalue, to revaluate, to revalorize; ~ **poco** to underestimate, to underrate; ~ **i risultati** (*org. az.*) to evaluate results; ~ **troppo** to overestimate, to overrate.

valutario, *a.* (*fin.*) monetary; money, currency (*attr.*). // **norme valutarie** (*fin.*) monetary regulations, currency regulations.

valutatore, *n. m.* (*pers.*) evaluator, appraiser, assessor.

valutazione, *n. f.* **1** valuation, evaluation, estimation, appraisal, appraisement, appreciation. **2** (*determinazione*) assessment, rating; (*misurazione*) measurement; (*calcolo*) calculation, computation, reckoning. **3** (*rag.*) (*dei costi*) costing. // ~ **a costi standard** (*rag.*) standard costing; ~ (*d'un bene*) **ai fini della determinazione dell'imponibile** (*fin.*) tax assessment; ~ **dei costi** (*rag.*) costing; ~ **dei creditori** (*fin.*) credit investigation; ~ **del credito** (*di cui gode un individuo o una ditta*) (*cred., fin.*) rating; ~ **del fido concedibile** (*banca*) composite credit appraisal; ~ **del lavoro** (*org. az.*) job evaluation, job rating; ~ **del merito** (*pers.*) merit rating, performance appraisal; ~ **del personale** (*pers.*) *V.* ~ **del merito;** ~ **del reddito** (*econ.*) income estimation; ~ **delle mansioni** (*org. az.*) *V.* ~ **del lavoro;** ~ **delle scorte** (*rag.*) inventory pricing; ~ **dell'attivo e del passivo** (*fin., rag.*) allocation of assets and liabilities; **la** ~ **d'un rischio** (*ass.*) the valuation of a risk; ~ **doganale** (*dog.*) customs valuation; ~ **in termini di risultati** (*org. az.*) merit rating in terms of activities; ~ **mediante punteggio** (*org. az.*) numerical rating; ~ **potenziale** (*org. az.*) potential analysis.

vantaggio, *n. m.* 1 advantage, account; (*interesse*) interest; (*beneficio*) benefit. 2 (*in una gara; anche fig.*) lead. 3 (*pubbl.*) (*tipografico*) galley. // ~ **assoluto** absolute advantage; **vantaggi comparati** (*econ.*) comparative advantages.

vantaggioso, *a.* advantageous, profitable, beneficial; (*favorevole*) favourable.

vapore, *n. m.* 1 vapour, fume. 2 (*acqueo*) steam. 3 (*trasp. mar.*) (*nave a vapore*) steamship, steamboat, steamer. // ~ **da carico** (*trasp. mar.*) cargo steamer; ~ **postale** (*trasp. mar.*) mail-steamer.

vaporetto, *n. m.* 1 (*trasp.*) steamship, steamer. 2 (*trasp.*) (*in servizio di linea su un lago, ecc.*) waterbus.

varare, *v. t.* (*trasp. mar.* e *fig.*) to launch, to set★ afloat. // ~ **un'impresa** (*fin.*) to launch an enterprise; ~ **una legge** (*leg.*) to pass a law; ~ **una nave** (*trasp. mar.*) to launch a ship.

variabile, *a.* variable, varying; (*instabile*) unsteady; (*fluttuante, oscillante*) floating. *n. f.* (*mat.*) variable. // ~ **autonoma** (*mat.*) autonomous variable; ~ **dipendente** (*mat.*) dependent variable; ~ **indipendente** (*mat.*) independent variable; ~ **macroeconomica** (*econ.*) macroeconomic variable.

variazione, *n. f.* 1 variation, change. 2 (*rag.*) (*contabile, ecc.*) change. // ~ **attiva** (*rag.*) active change; **variazioni congiunturali** (*econ.*) short-term changes; ~ **degli stock** (*rag.*) inventory variations; **variazioni dei cambi** (*comm. est., fin.*) fluctuations in exchange rates; ~ **della riserva obbligatoria** (*banca., fin.*) variation of compulsory reserve; ~ **nella domanda e nell'offerta** (*econ.*) change in demand and supply; ~ **passiva** (*rag.*) passive change; **variazioni percentuali dei prezzi al consumo** (*market.*) percent variations in retail prices; **variazioni percentuali del costo della vita** (*econ.*) percent variations in cost of living.

varietà, *n. f. inv.* 1 variety. 2 (*genere, tipo*) variety, kind, type. 3 (*market.*) variety, type, grade. // **una** ~ **di mele** (*market.*) a variety of apples.

vario, *a.* 1 varied. 2 (*diverso*) different, various. 3 **vari,** *pl.* various; (*molti*) many; (*diversi, parecchi*) several. 4 **varie,** *f. pl.* (*giorn.*) (*nei grafici*) miscellaneous. // «**varie ed eventuali**» (*ultima voce d'un ordine del giorno*) (*org. az.*) «general business»; «any other business» (*abbr.* AOB).

varo, *n. m.* (*trasp. mar.*) launch, launching.

vascello, *n. m.* (*trasp. mar.*) vessel; (*nave*) ship.

vedova, *n. f.* (*leg.*) widow.

vedovanza, *n. f.* (*leg.*) widowhood.

vedovile, *a.* (*leg.*) widowed.

vedovo, *n. m.* (*leg.*) widower.

veicolo, *n. m.* 1 (*anche fig.*) vehicle. 2 (*trasp.*) vehicle, conveyance. // ~ **a cuscino d'aria** (*trasp., trasp. mar.*) hovercraft; ~ **a motore** (*trasp.*) motor-vehicle.

veliero, *n. m.* (*trasp. mar.*) sailing ship, sailing vessel, sailer.

velina, *n. f.* 1 (*attr. uff.*) (*carta velina*) tissue-paper, flimsy. 2 (*attr. uff.*) (*copia di lettera*) carbon copy.

velivolo, *n. m.* (*trasp. aer.*) aircraft.

veloce, *a.* fast, quick, speedy.

velocità, *n. f. inv.* speed, velocity. // **la** ~ **di circolazione della moneta** (*econ.*) the velocity of money, the velocity of circulation; ~ **di manipolazione del carico** (*trasp. mar.*) port speed; ~ **economica** (*trasp. mar.*) economical speed; ~ **effettiva** (*trasp. aer.*) true airspeed.

vendere, *v. t.* 1 to sell★. 2 (*leg.*) (*alienare*) to dispose of, to vend. 3 (*market.*) to sell★. 4 (*market.*) (*trattare: una merce, un articolo, ecc.*) to carry, to market. 5 (*smerciare*) to work off; (*liquidare, svendere*) to sell★ out. 6 **vendersi** (*market.*) (*d'articolo: essere venduto*) to sell★, to go★ off, to vend. 7 **vendersi** (*market.*) (*d'articolo: costare*) to cost★. // ~ **a buon mercato** (*market.*) to sell cheaply; to sell for a song (*slang USA*); ~ **a contanti** (*market.*) to sell for cash; ~ **a credito** (*market.*) to sell on credit, to deal on credit, to trust (sb. for st.); ~ **a domicilio** (*market.*) to sell door-to-door, to sell house-to-house; ~ **a lotti** (*market.*) to sell by lots; ~ **a mercato nero** (*market.*) to sell on the black market; ~ **a peso** (*market.*) to sell by weight; ~ **a premio** (*Borsa, fin.*) to take for the call, to give for the put; ~ **a premio con facoltà d'opzione** (*per il compratore*) (*Borsa, fin.*) to sell for the call; ~ **a prezzi più bassi di** (*altri prodotti similari*) (*market.*) to undersell; ~ **a un prezzo inferiore a quello di** (*un concorrente*) (*market.*) to undersell, to undercut; ~ **a rate** (*market.*) to sell on hire-purchase, to sell by instalments; ~ **a termine** (*Borsa*) to sell for the account, to sell for the settlement; ~ **al dettaglio** (*market.*) to sell by retail, to sell retail, to retail, to sell over the counter; **vendersi al dettaglio** (*market.*) (*di merce*) to retail; ~ **al meglio** (*fin., market.*) to sell at best; ~ **al metro** (*market.*) to sell by the metre; ~ **al miglior offerente** (*market.*) to sell to the highest bidder; ~ **al minuto** (*market.*) to sell by retail, to sell retail, to retail, to sell over the counter; **vendersi al minuto** (*market.*) (*di merce*) to retail; ~ **all'asta** to sell by auction, to auction (off); to roup (*scozz.*); ~ **all'incanto** *V.* ~ **all'asta;** ~ **all'ingrosso** (*market.*) to sell wholesale, to sell in bulk, to wholesale; **vendersi all'ingrosso** (*market.*) (*d'articolo*) to wholesale; ~ **allo sbarco** (*trasp. mar.*) to sell ex-ship; ~ **allo scoperto** (*Borsa*) to bear the market, to sell short; ~ **all'ultimo offerente** (*in un'asta*) to sell by inch of candle; ~ **con facoltà di doppia consegna** (*Borsa, fin.*) to give for a put of more; ~ **con facoltà d'opzione** (*Borsa, fin.*) to give for the put; ~ **con patto di riscatto** (*leg.*) to sell with right of redemption, to sell with option to repurchase; ~ **contro assegno** (*market.*) to sell cash on delivery; ~ (*merce*) **di casa in casa** (*market.*) to sell house-to-house, to hawk; ~ **di seconda mano** (*market.*) to sell second-hand, to resell; ~ **in perdita** (*market.*) to sell at a loss, to sell at a sacrifice, to sacrifice; (*titoli, azioni, ecc.*) to slaughter; ~ **merce salvo prova** (*market.*) to sell goods on approval; ~ **merce salvo vista e verifica** (*market.*) to sell goods on approval; ~ **per conto terzi** (*market.*) to sell on commission; ~ **per futura consegna** (*fin.*) to sell for forward delivery; ~ **per** ~ (*market.*) to sell at any price; ~ **più di** (*un collega, un concorrente, ecc.*) (*market.*) to outsell; **vendersi più di** (*un altro articolo*) (*market.*) to outsell; ~ **più** (*merce, ecc.*) **di quanta se ne abbia in magazzino** (*market.*) to oversell; ~ **praticando facilitazioni** (*di pagamento*) (*market.*) to sell on easy terms; ~ **sotto banco** (*market.*) to sell under the counter; ~ (*merce*) **sotto costo** (*market.*) to sell below cost price, to undersell, to discount, to sacrifice; (*specialm. all'estero*) to dump; ~ **titoli senza averne la disponibilità** (*Borsa*) (*di ribassista*) to sell short; **da** ~ **o rimandare** (*market.*) on sale or return; **fare** ~ (*market.*) to sell; «**vendersi**» (*market.*) «for sale», «on sale»; **essere venduto a basso prezzo** (*market.*) (*di un articolo*) to go cheap.

vendibile, *a.* **1** saleable, salable. **2** (*leg.*) (*alienabile*) disposable. **3** (*market.*) saleable, salable, marketable.

vendita, *n. f.* **1** (*il vendere*) selling. **2** (*leg.*) disposal. **3** (*market.*) sale. **4 vendite,** *pl.* (*rag.*) sales. // **una** ~ **a buon mercato** (*market.*) a cheap sale; ~ **a contanti** (*market.*) cash sale, cash-down sale; ~ **a credito** (*market.*) credit sale; ~ **a domicilio** (*market.*) door-to-door sale, house-to-house selling; ~ **a lotti** (*market.*) sale by lots; ~ **a premio** (*Borsa, fin.*) put, put option; (*market.*) premium sale; ~ **a rate** (*market.*) sale by instalments; (*il sistema*) hire purchase; (*il programma*) instalment plan; ~ **a rate con piccoli versamenti mensili** (*da parte di persone considerate quasi come soci di un circolo*) (*market.*) club trading; ~ (*con pagamento*) «**a respiro**» (*market.*) time sale; ~ **a termine** (*Borsa*) sale for the account, sale for the settlement, forward sale; ~ (*d'un articolo, effettuata soltanto se*) **abbinata** (*alla vendita d'un altro prodotto*) (*market.*) tie-in sale; ~ **al dettaglio** (*market.*) sale by retail, retail sale, over-the-counter sale; ~ **al meglio** (*fin., market.*) sale at best; ~ **al miglior offerente** (*market.*) sale to the highest bidder; ~ **al minuto** (*market.*) sale by retail, retail sale; over-the-counter sale; ~ **all'asta** sale by auction, auction-sale; roup (*scozz.*); ~ **all'incanto** *V.* ~ **all'asta;** ~ **all'ingrosso** (*market.*) wholesale, bulk selling, direct sale; ~ **allo sbarco** (*trasp. mar.*) sale delivered ex-ship, sale on ex-ship terms, sale on landed terms; ~ **allo scoperto** (*Borsa*) time bargain, settlement bargain, bear sale, short selling, short sale; ~ **allo scoperto di titoli in possesso di chi opera** (*e che tuttavia non desidera impegnarli*) (*Borsa, fin.*) short sale against the box; **una** ~ **all'ultimo offerente** (*in un'asta*) a sale by inch of candle; ~ **coatta** (*leg.*) forced sale; **una** ~ **con patto di riscatto** (*leg.*) a sale with right of redemption, a sale with option to repurchase; ~ **concordata di titoli a fine anno** (*per la determinazione di perdite e profitti ai fini della dichiarazione dell'imposta sul reddito*) (*fin.*) tax selling; ~ **condizionata** (*market.*) conditional sale; ~ **contro assegno** (*market.*) cash on delivery sale; ~ **d'articoli di poco prezzo** (*market.*) jumble sale; ~ **d'un investimento** (*econ.*) disinvestment; ~ **di liquidazione** (*market.*) clearance sale, sale; ~ **di liquidazione per cessazione di esercizio** (*market.*) close-out sale; ~ **di magazzino** (*market.*) rummage sale; rummage (*USA*); ~ **di merce flottante** (*trasp. mar.*) sale of goods afloat; ~ **di propaganda** (*market., pubbl.*) promotion sale; ~ **di realizzo** (*market.*) clearance sale; **una** ~ **di rimanenze** (*market.*) a bargain sale, an oddments sale; **una** ~ **di scampoli** (*market.*) a remnant sale; ~ **di seconda mano** (*market.*) second-hand sale, resale; ~ **diretta** (*market.*) direct selling, direct sale; ~ **forzosa** (*leg.*) compulsory sale; (*di beni d'un debitore insolvente*) selling-up; **vendite giornaliere** (*market.*) daily sales; ~ **giudiziale** (*leg.*) *V.* ~ **giudiziaria;** ~ **giudiziaria** (*leg.*) judicial sale, sale by order of the Court, foreclosure; **una** ~ **immobiliare** (*fin.*) a sale of real property; ~ **in commissione** (*market.*) consignment sale; ~ **in contanti** (*market.*) cash-down sale, cash sale; ~ **in esclusiva** (*market.*) exclusive agency selling; **vendite nette** (*market.*) net sales; ~ **per contanti** (*market.*) cash sale, cash-down sale; ~ **per futura consegna** (*fin.*) sale for future delivery, forward sale; ~ **privata** (*leg.*) sale by private treaty; ~ **rateale** (*market.*) sale by instalments, instalment selling; ~ **salvo arrivo (della merce)** (*market.*) sale to arrive; ~ **salvo prova** (*market.*) sale on approval; ~ **sotto condizione** (*market.*) conditional sale; ~ **sotto costo** (*market.*) underselling, distress sale; (*specialm. all'estero*) dumping; **una** ~ **speciale** (*market., pubbl.*) a bargain sale; **una** ~ **straordinaria** (*market., pubbl.*) a bumper sale; ~ **su campione** (*market.*) sale by sample; ~ **totale** (*delle rimanenze*) (*market.*) selling-off; ~ **volontaria** (*leg.*) voluntary sale; **essere in** ~ (*market.*) (*d'articolo*) to be on sale, to be on offer, to be in the market, to be on the market; (*specialm.: essere messo all'asta*) to be on the block; «**in** ~» (*market.*) «on sale», «for sale»; **in cima alle vendite** (*market.: di un articolo*) top-selling; **non adibito alla** ~ (*org. az.*) (*di reparto, ecc.*) non-selling; **non in** ~ (*market.*) (*di articolo, ecc.*) out of sale; (*non disponibile*) unavailable; **tecnica di** ~ **basata sull'insistenza nell'offerta della merce** (*market.*) hard sell.

venditore, *n. m.* **1** seller. **2** (*fin., market.*) giver, seller. **3** (*market.*) seller, vendor, vender. **4** (*pers.*) (*rappresentante*) representative agent, representative, agent, salesman★. **5 venditori,** *pl.* (*pers.*) salespeople. // ~ **a domicilio** (*market.*) door-to-door salesman; ~ **allo scoperto** (*Borsa, fin.*) short seller, bear seller; ~ **ambulante** hawker, pedlar, peddler, chapman; **il** ~ **d'un (contratto) «dont»** (*Borsa*) the seller of a call option, the taker for a call.

venire, *v. i.* **1** to come★. **2** (*ammontare a*) to come★ to, to come★ out at (*o* to). **3** (*d'un conto, d'una somma, ecc.*) to work out, to come★ out. **4** (*costare*) to cost★, to come★. **5** (*far visita, «passare»*) to call. // ~ **a un accordo** to come to an arrangement, to come to terms; ~ **a capo di qc.** to finish st., to conclude st., to complete st.; ~ **a un compromesso** to compromise, to compound; ~ **a una conclusione** to come to a conclusion; ~ **a conoscenza** to come to one's knowledge, to get to know, to learn; ~ **a costare** to come, to cost; ~ **a patti** to come to terms; ~ **a sapere** to come to learn, to learn, to understand, to get to know; ~ **a una transazione** (*leg.*) to compound, to compromise; ~ **di moda** to come into fashion, to become fashionable; ~ **fuori** to come out; (*giorn., pubbl.*) (*essere pubblicato*) to be published, to come out; ~ **in aiuto di q.** to come to sb.'s assistance; ~ **in collisione** (*trasp. mar.*) to collide; ~ **meno a un impegno** to break an engagement, to default; ~ **meno a una promessa** to break one's promise; ~ **meno alla parola data** to fail to keep one's word.

venturo, *a.* coming; (*prossimo*) next; (*futuro*) future. // **il mese** ~ next month; **la settimana ventura** next week; **la stagione ventura** the coming season.

verbale, *a.* **1** verbal. **2** (*leg.*) parol. *n. m.* **1** record, roll; minutes (*pl.*); (*d'un'assemblea, ecc.*) proceedings (*pl.*). **2** (*leg.*) (*nei procedimenti giudiziari*) docket. **3** (*leg.*) (*resoconto fatto per la polizia*) statement. // **i verbali del tribunale** (*leg.*) the records of the Court of law; **il** ~ **dell'assemblea degli azionisti** (*fin.*) the minutes of the shareholders' meeting; ~ **d'adunanza** (*org. az.*) board minutes (*pl.*); ~ **d'un processo** (*leg.*) Court record; brief (*USA*); **mettere a** ~ (*leg.*) to take minutes, to record, to minute.

verbalizzare, *v. t.* (*leg.*) (*mettere a verbale*) to record, to minute. *v. i.* (*leg.*) (*redigere il verbale*) to take★ minutes. // ~ **gli atti d'un congresso** (*leg.*) to record the proceedings of a congress; ~ **gli atti d'una seduta** (*leg.*) to minute the proceedings of a meeting.

verbalmente, *avv.* verbally, orally, by word of mouth.

verdetto, *n. m.* (*leg.*) verdict, finding. // **un** ~ **d'assoluzione** (*leg.*) a verdict of not guilty; **un** ~ **di colpevolezza** (*leg.*) a verdict of guilty, a verdict for the plaintiff; **un** ~ **di condanna** (*leg.*) a verdict of guilty, a verdict for the plaintiff; **un** ~ **d'innocenza** (*leg.*) a verdict of not guilty; **un** ~ **emesso a maggioranza** (*dei giurati*) (*leg.*) a majority verdict; **un** ~ **errato** (*leg.*) a false verdict; ~ **parziale** (*leg.*) partial verdict.

verga, *n. f.* bar, rod; (*lingotto*) ingot. // ~ **d'una iarda** (*strumento per misurare*) yardstick.

verifica, *n. f.* verification; (*controllo*) check, checking; (*ispezione, perizia*) survey, inspection; (*esame*) examination; (*prova*) proof. // ~ **dei conti** (*rag.*) examination of business accounts, audit, check-up; ~ **dei crediti** (*nella procedura* *fallimentare*) (*leg.*) proof of debts; ~ **dei fatti** (*leg.*) verification of facts; ~ **di cassa** (*rag.*) cash inspection; **di** ~ (*rag.*) correcting (*a. attr.*); **essere in via di** ~ to be being verified; **scrittura di** ~ (*rag.*) correcting entry.

verificabile, *a.* verifiable.

verificare, *v. t.* **1** to verify; (*controllare*) to check; (*ispezionare*) to survey, to go★ through, to inspect; (*esaminare*) to examine; (*fare la prova di*) to prove. **2** (*rag.*) (*i conti*) to audit. // ~ **la condizione della merce** to verify the condition of the goods, to condition the goods; ~ **il contenuto d'un pacco** (*dog.*) to verify the contents of a packet; ~ **i conti** (*rag.*) to examine the accounts; to audit (the accounts); ~ **un conto e certificarne l'esattezza** (*fin., leg.*) to audit an account.

verificatore, *n. m.* **1** (*pers.*) verifier; (*controllore*) checker; (*ispettore*) surveyor, inspector; (*esaminatore*) examiner. **2** (*rag.*) (*dei conti*) auditor. // ~ **del peso** (*delle merci*) (*pers.*) weigh-master, check-weigher.

versamento, *n. m.* **1** (*pagamento*) payment, paying; (*deposito*) deposit. **2** (*banca*) deposit, paying-in, in-payment. **3** (*fin.*) lodgment. **4** (*market.*) (*della prima rata*) down-payment. // ~ (*di decimi*) **a liberazione** (*fin.*) final instalment, final payment; ~ **alla massa sociale** (*fin.*) capital contribution; ~ **all'atto della sottoscrizione** (*fin.*) application money; ~ **di ripartizione** (*di azioni o obbligazioni*) (*fin.*) allotment money; **un** ~ **in banca** (*banca*) a payment into the bank.

versare, *v. t.* **1** (*pagare*) to pay★, to pay★ out; (*devolvere*) to subscribe; (*depositare*) to deposit. **2** (*banca*) to deposit, to pay★ in, to pay★ into. **3** (*fin.*) to lodge. **4** (*market.*) (*la prima rata*) to pay★ down. *v. i.* (*essere, trovarsi*) to be, to live. // ~ **denaro** (*a un cliente*) (*fin.*) (*di banca*) to pay money out; ~ **denaro in acconto** (*cred., rag.*) to pay money on account; ~ **il proprio denaro in banca** (*banca*) to pay one's money into a bank, to bank one's money.

versato, *a.* **1** (*esperto*) expert, versed, proficient; (*abile*) skilled. **2** (*pagato*) paid; (*depositato*) deposited. // **capitale** ~ (*fin.*) paid-up capital.

vertenza, *n. f.* (*leg.*) controversy, dispute, litigation, difference. // ~ **diplomatica** diplomatic controversy; ~ **giudiziaria** (*leg.*) judicial controversy; ~ **sindacale** (*sind.*) labour dispute, trade dispute, industrial dispute.

verticale, *a.* (*anche fig.*) vertical.

vertice, *n. m.* **1** top. **2** (*amm.*) (*incontro al vertice*) summit meeting, summit, high-level conference.

vessatorio, *a.* (*leg.*) vexatious, oppressive.

vessazione, *n. f.* (*leg.*) vexation, oppression.

veste, *n. f.* **1** (*fig.*) (*capacità*) capacity; (*qualità*) quality. **2** (*fig.*) (*autorità*) authority. // **in** ~ **di** (*leg.*) in the quality of, in quality of, in the capacity of; **in** ~ **ufficiale** (*leg.*) in an official capacity.

veto, *n. m.* (*leg.*) veto. // **diritto di** ~ (*leg.*) right of veto; **porre il** ~ **a una proposta** (*leg.*) to put the veto on a proposal, to veto a proposal.

vetrina, *n. f.* (*market.*) shop-window, show-window, window. // ~ **per esposizione** (*della merce*) (*market.*) display window.

vetrinista, *n. m.* e *f.* (*pers.*) window-dresser, display artist; displayman★ (*m.*).

vettore, *n. m.* **1** (*mat.*) vector. **2** (*trasp.*) common carrier, carrier. **3** (*trasp. aut.*) road haulier. // ~ **aereo** (*trasp. aer.*) air carrier; ~ **ferroviario** (*trasp. ferr.*) rail carrier; ~ **fluviale** (*trasp.*) water carrier; ~ **intermedio** (*trasp.*) intermediate carrier; ~ **marittimo** (*trasp. mar.*) water carrier; ~ **privato** (*trasp.*) private carrier, special carrier.

vettura, *n. f.* **1** (*trasp.*) carriage, coach; (*veicolo*) vehicle. **2** (*trasp. aut.*) (*automobile*) motor car, car. **3** (*trasp. ferr.*) railway carriage, coach; car (*USA*). // ~ **di piazza** taxi; cab (*USA*); ~ **di prima classe** (*trasp. ferr.*) first-class carriage; ~ **di seconda classe** (*trasp. ferr.*) second-class carriage; **una** ~ **diretta** (*trasp. ferr.*) a through carriage; ~ **ristorante** (*trasp. ferr.*) dining-car, diner; ~ **salone** (*trasp. ferr.*) saloon-carriage, saloon-car.

via[1], *n. f.* **1** (*strada*) road, street; (*negli indirizzi italiani*) via. **2** (*passaggio, percorso*) way. **3** (*modo, maniera*) way. **4** (*leg.*) measure, step. // ~ **aerea** (*trasp. aer.*) airway, air route; ~ **d'acqua** (*trasp.*) (*canale navigabile*) waterway; (*trasp. mar.*) (*falla*) leak; **vie di fatto** (*leg.*) violence; assault and battery; ~ **di mezzo** middle course; (*compromesso*) compromise; ~ **di navigazione** (*trasp.*) waterway; ~ **di terra** (*trasp.*) land route; **vie di trasporto** (*trasp.*) transportational routes; **vie legali** (*leg.*) legal steps, legal proceedings, judicial proceedings; **vie navigabili** (*trasp.*) inland waterways; **in** ~ **amichevole** in a friendly way, as a friend; (*leg.*) out of Court; **in** ~ **di diritto** (*leg.*) by right; **in** ~ **eccezionale** by way of exception; **in** ~ **provvisoria** provisionally; **per** ~ **aerea** (*comun.*) by air mail, by air-mail; (*trasp. aer.*) by air; **per** ~ **d'acqua** (*trasp., trasp. mar.*) by water; **per** ~ **d'aria** (*trasp. aer.*) by air; **per** ~ **di terra** (*trasp.*) by land, overland; **per** ~ **fluviale** (*trasp.*) by water; **per** ~ **gerar-**

chica (*leg.*) through official channels.

via², *prep.* (*trasp.*) (*passando per*) via, by way of.

via³, *avv.* **1** away. **2** off.

viabilità, *n. f. inv.* **1** (*trasp. aut.*) (*condizioni della strada*) road conditions (*pl.*). **2** (*trasp. aut.*) (*possibilità di transitare*) use of the road. **3** (*trasp. aut.*) (*rete stradale*) network of roads; roads (*pl.*). // **la ~ ordinaria** (*trasp. aut.*) roads and highways (*excluding motorways*).

viaggiare, *v. i.* **1** (*pers.*) (*fare il rappresentante*) to travel. **2** (*trasp.*) to travel, to journey. **3** (*trasp.*) (*di merci: essere trasportate*) to travel. **4** (*trasp. aer., trasp. mar.*) (*per via d'acqua o via aerea*) to voyage. *v. t.* **1** (*trasp.*) to travel. **2** (*tur.*) to tour. // **~ con un abbonamento ferroviario** (*trasp. ferr.*) to commute; **~ in** (*una zona*) (*pers.*) to travel; **~ in** (*un prodotto*) (*pers.*) to travel in.

viaggiatore, *n. m.* **1** (*pers.*) (*di commercio*) traveller; traveler (*USA*); travelling clerk. **2** (*trasp.*) traveller; (*di nave e sim.*) voyager; (*passeggero*) passenger. // **~ -chilometro** (*stat., trasp.*) passenger-kilometre; **~ di commercio** (*pers.*) commercial traveller, travelling salesman, travelling man, itinerant salesman, salesman, traveller; traveler, drummer (*USA*); **~ di prima classe** (*trasp. ferr.*) first-class passenger; (*trasp. mar.*) saloon-passenger; **viaggiatori di seconda classe** (*trasp.*) second-class passengers; **un ~ di (treno) diretto** (*trasp. ferr.*) a through passenger; « **~-miglio** » (*stat., trasp.*) passenger-mile.

viaggiatrice, *n. f.* (*trasp.*) traveller; traveler (*USA*). // **~ di commercio** (*pers.*) saleswoman.

viaggio, *n. m.* **1** (*specialm. per via di terra*) journey; (*per mare*) voyage. **2** (*gita, viaggetto*) trip. **3** (*trasp. aer., trasp. mar.*) (*traversata*) passage. **4** (*tur.*) tour. // **~ aereo** (*trasp. aer.*) air journey, journey by plane; (*volo*) flight; **~ circolare** (*trasp.*) circular tour; **~ d'affari** business trip; **~ d'andata** (*trasp. mar.*) outward voyage, outward journey, outward passage, outward-bound voyage, passage out; **~ d'andata e ritorno** (*trasp.*) return trip; round trip (*USA*); **~ di mare** (*trasp. mar.*) journey by sea, voyage; (*nella terminologia assicurativa*) marine adventure; **~ di prova** (*trasp. mar.*) trial trip; **~ di ritorno** (*trasp. mar.*) homeward journey, homeward voyage, homeward passage, inward-bound voyage, passage home; **~ di terra** (*trasp.*) journey by land; **~ in automobile** (*trasp. aut.*) drive; **~ in zavorra** (*trasp. mar.*) ballast passage; **il ~ inaugurale** (*d'una nave*) (*trasp. mar.*) the maiden voyage; **~ «tutto compreso»** (*tur.*) package tour; **durante il ~** (*trasp.*) in transit; **in ~** (*trasp.*) (*di persona*) en route; (*di merce*) in transit, on passage; (*trasp. mar.*) (*di merce*) upon the water, on the water; **nel ~ d'andata** (*trasp. mar.*) on the voyage out; **nel ~ di ritorno** (*trasp. mar.*) on the voyage home.

vice-¹, *pref.* (*elemento che, in parole composte, significa «che fa le veci di», ecc.*) vice-, deputy, assistant, under-, sub-. // **~ caposquadra** (*pers.*) straw boss; **~ capostazione** (*pers., trasp. ferr.*) assistant station master; **~ -commissario** (*leg., org. az.*) subcommissioner; **~ redattore capo** (*giorn., pers.*) assistant executive editor; **~ segretario** under-secretary, undersecretary.

vice², *n. m. inv.* (*abbr. di* **vicedirettore** *e sim.*) vice, representative.

vicedirettore, *n. m.* **1** (*amm.*) assistant manager, deputy manager. **2** (*giorn.*) subeditor, assistant editor; deputy editor (*USA*). // **il ~ delle vendite** (*amm.*) the vice-president in charge of sales; **essere il ~ di** (*un giornale*) (*giorn.*) to subedit.

vicedirettrice, *n. f.* (*amm.*) assistant manageress.

vicepresidente, *n. m.* (*amm.*) vice-chairman, deputy chairman. // **~ anziano** (*amm.*) senior vice-president.

vicesegretaria, *n. f.* (*pers.*) assistant secretary.

vicesegretario, *n. m.* (*pers.*) assistant secretary.

vicetesoriere, *n. m.* (*pers.*) vice-treasurer.

videomaster, *n. m.* (*Borsa*) «videomaster».

vidimare, *v. t.* **1** to voucher; (*firmare*) to sign. **2** (*leg.*) (*certificare, attestare*) to certify, to attest; (*autenticare*) to authenticate. **3** (*tur.*) (*detto d'un'autorità consolare, ecc.*) to visa.

vidimazione, *n. f.* **1** (*firma*) signature. **2** (*leg.*) (*certificazione*) certification; (*autenticazione*) authentication. **3** (*tur.*) (*visto*) visa.

vietare, *v. t.* **1** to forbid★, to prohibit. **2** (*leg.*) to forbid★, to prohibit, to interdict, to bar.

vigente, *a.* (*leg.*) in force (*pred.*).

vigile, *a.* vigilant, watchful, alert. *n. m.* **1** (*di polizia urbana*) policeman★; bobby (*fam., ingl.*); cop (*slang USA*). **2** (*del fuoco*) fireman★.

vigilia, *n. f.* eve; (*giorno prima*) day before. // **~ della liquidazione** (*Borsa*) day before the settlement, ticket-day.

vignetta, *n. f.* (*pubbl.*) cartoon, sketch.

vigore, *n. m.* **1** vigour; vigor (*USA*); (*forza*) force, strength; (*energia*) energy. **2** (*leg.*) force, effect. // **il ~ della domanda** (*econ.*) the strength of demand; **essere in ~** (*leg., anche*) to run; **in ~** (*leg.*) in force, in operation, in effect.

vincere, *v. t.* e *i.* **1** to win★. **2** (*sopraffare, superare*) to overcome★. **3** (*battere*) to beat★; (*sconfiggere*) to defeat. // **~ una causa** (*leg.*) to gain a suit at law, to win a case; **~ la concorrenza** (*market.*) to beat the competition, to win competition.

vincolante, *a.* (*anche leg.*) binding, mandatory, mandatary. // **non ~** unbinding.

vincolare, *v. t.* **1** (*anche leg.*) to bind★. **2** (*fin.*) (*capitali, ecc.*) to tie up, to lock up. // **~ q. col versamento d'una cauzione** (*leg.*) to hold sb. to bail; **~ con contratto d'apprendistato** (*pers.*) to bind out; **~ proprietà** (*leg.*) to tie up properties.

vincolato, *a.* **1** (*anche leg.*) bound. **2** (*fin.*) (*di capitali, ecc.*) tied-up, locked-up. // **in conto ~** (*banca*) on deposit.

vincolo, *n. m.* (*anche fig.*) bond, tie. // **libero da ogni ~** (*leg.*) free from any encumbrance; **essere sotto il ~ del giuramento** (*leg.*) to be bound under oath.

violare, *v. t.* (*leg.*) to violate, to break★, to infringe, to invade, to transgress, to contravene. // **~ i diritti di q.** (*leg., anche*) to trespass upon sb.'s rights; **~ il giuramento** (*leg.*) to break one's oath; **~ la legge** (*leg.*) to violate the law, to offend against the law, to strain the law; **~ la legge sul diritto d'autore** (*leg.*) to infringe a copyright; **~ un patto** (*leg.*) to break an agreement; **~ un trattato** (*leg.*) to transgress a treaty.

violatore, *n. m.* (*leg.*) violator, breaker, infringer, transgressor. // **~ della legge** (*leg.*) lawbreaker; **~ di confini** (*leg.*) trespasser.

violazione, *n. f.* (*leg.*) violation, breach, infringement, invasion, transgression, contravention, trespass. // **~ del segreto professionale** (*leg.*) break of professional secrecy; **~ della legge** (*leg.*) infringement of the law, lawbreaking; **~ d'un diritto** (*leg.*) infringement of a right; **~ di domicilio** (*leg.*) housebreaking, burglary; **~ di garanzia** (*leg.*) breach of warranty; **~ di giuramento** (*leg.*) oath breaking; **~ di marchio di fabbrica** (*leg.*) trade-mark infringement; **la ~ d'una promessa** the violation of a promise; **~ di proprietà** (*leg.*) trespass; **~ di sigilli** (*leg.*) breaking of seals.

virgola, *n. f.* **1** comma. **2** (*mat.*) point.

vischiosità, *n. f. inv.* **1** viscosity. **2** (*fig.*) (*l'essere appiccicoso*) stickiness. **3** (*econ.*) downward stickiness, stickiness. // **la ~ dei prezzi** (*econ.*) the downward price stickiness, the price stickiness; **la ~ dei salari** (*econ.*) the downward stickiness of wages.

vischioso, *a.* **1** viscous. **2** (*fig.*) (*appiccicaticcio*) sticky.

visibile, *a.* visible. // **partite visibili** (*econ.*) visible items.

visione, *n. f.* **1** vision. **2** (*il vedere*) sight. // **in ~** (*market.*) (*di merce*) on approval; **prendere ~ d'un documento** to take note of a document.

visita, *n. f.* **1** visit. **2** (*di professionista, rappresentante, ecc.*) visit, call. **3** (*dog.*) examination, inspection, visit. **4** (*trasp. mar.*) (*effettuata dagli istituti di classificazione, per l'assegnazione, conservazione o cambiamento di classe delle navi mercantili*) survey. // **~ alle curiosità d'un luogo** (*tur.*) sightseeing; **~ di controllo** (*trasp. mar.*) search; **~ fiscale** (*leg., pers.*) official medical examination; **~ sanitaria** sanitary inspection.

visitare, *v. t.* **1** (*far visita*) to visit, to call on (sb.), to see★. **2** (*di rappresentante, ecc.*) to visit, to call on (sb.). **3** (*di medico*) to examine. **4** (*leg.*) (*ispezionare*) to inspect, to examine, to search. // **~ i bagagli** (*dog.*) to inspect the luggage.

visitatore, *n. m.* visitor, visiter, caller.

vista, *n. f.* **1** (*facoltà visiva e atto di vedere*) sight. **2** (*panorama*) view. **3** (*cred.*) sight. // **a ~** (*cred.*) at sight, on demand; sight (*attr.*); **a prima ~** at first sight; **a sessanta giorni ~** (*cred.*) sixty days after sight; **essere in ~** (*di persona*) to be in the public eye; (*di cosa*) to stand out; **in ~** in view, in sight; **in ~ del porto** (*trasp. mar.*) within sight of the port; **in ~ di** in view of, in consideration of; **pagabile a ~** (*cred.*) payable at sight.

vistare, *v. t.* **1** to visa, to endorse. **2** (*banca*) (*titoli di credito, ecc.*) to mark. **3** (*tur.*) (*detto d'un'autorità consolare, ecc.*) to visa.

visto, *a.* seen. *n. m.* **1** visa, endorsement. **2** (*banca*) mark. **3** (*tur.*) (*di passaporto e sim.*) visa. // **~ d'ingresso** (*comm. est., tur.*) entry visa; **~ d'uscita** (*comm. est., tur.*) exit visa.

vita, *n. f.* **1** life★. **2** (*durata di tutta una vita*) lifetime. **3** (*durata della vita*) life span, span of life. **4** (*il necessario per vivere*) living; (*esistenza*) subsistence. **5** (*costo della vita*) cost of living. // **la ~ media** (*ass.*) the average life, the mean life; **~ presunta** (*mat. attuariale*) expectation of life.

vitalizio, *a.* life (*attr.*). *n. m.* **1** (*ass.*) straight life annuity, life annuity. **2** (*fin.*) income for life. // **~ corrisposto al beneficiario** (*in caso di morte dell'assicurato*) (*ass.*) survivorship annuity; **chi gode d'un ~** (*ass.*) life annuitant.

vivace, *a.* **1** lively, brisk, spirited; (*attivo*) active. **2** (*di colore*) bright. **3** (*Borsa, market.*) (*dell'attività commerciale, ecc.*) bright.

vivacità, *n. f. inv.* **1** liveliness, briskness. **2**

(*di colore*) brightness. **3** (*Borsa, market.*) (*degli scambi*) brightness.

vivente, *a.* living; alive (*pred.*); live (*attr.*).

vivere, *v. i.* **1** (*essere in vita*) to live. **2** (*abitare*) to live; (*risiedere*) to reside. **3** (*trovare i mezzi di sussistenza*) to live. // **~ di rendita** to live on one's private income.

vizio, *n. m.* (*leg.*) vice, defect, flaw. // **~ intrinseco** (*leg.*) inherent vice; **~ nella cosa venduta** (*leg.*) defect in property sold; **vizi occulti** (*leg.*) latent defects, hidden defects, latent faults.

voce, *n. f.* **1** voice. **2** (*diceria*) rumour, talk, hearsay. **3** (*intestatura*) heading. **4** (*d'elenco, bilancio, e sim.*) item. **5** (*rag.*) (*contabile*) entry. // **le voci d'un catalogo** (*market.*) the items of a catalogue; **una ~ infondata** an unfounded rumour; **voci non confermate** unconfirmed rumours; **voci tariffarie** (*comm. est., econ.*) (*di bilancia commerciale, ecc.*) tariff headings.

voga, *n. f.* fashion, vogue, run. // **essere in (gran) ~** (*market.*) to be in fashion, to be in vogue, to be in, to be popular, to be all the go, to be all the rage.

volantino, *n. m.* (*pubbl.*) handbill, leaflet, fly sheet; throwaway (*USA*).

volare, *v. i.* (*trasp. aer.*) to fly★. // **~ a bassa quota** (*trasp. aer.*) to fly low; **~ a velocità di crociera** (*trasp. aer.*) to cruise.

volere[1], *v. t.* **1** to want. **2** (*desiderare*) to wish, to desire. **3** will, would (*v. modali*). **4** (*esigere, richiedere*) to require. **5** (*quando si offre di fare qc.*) shall I...? shall we...? **6** (*esigere in pagamento*) to want. **7** (*avere intenzione*) to intend, to be going (to). **8 volerci, volercene** to take★, to require, to be required.

volere[2], *n. m.* (*volontà*) will.

volo, *n. m.* **1** flight. **2** (*trasp. aer.*) flight, flying. // **~ charter** (*trasp. aer.*) charter flight; **~ di collaudo** (*trasp. aer.*) test flight; **~ di linea** (*trasp. aer.*) scheduled flight; **un ~ diretto** (*trasp. aer.*) (*senza deviazioni di rotta*) a straightaway flight; (*senza scalo*) a non-stop flight; **voli senza scalo** (*trasp. aer.*) non-stop flights.

voltura, *n. f.* **1** (*leg.*) registration of a transfer deed. **2** (*rag.*) (*scrittura di storno*) reverse entry.

volume, *n. m.* **1** volume. **2** (*quantità*) amount, volume, size. **3** (*libro*) volume. // **il ~ delle contrattazioni** (*Borsa*) the trading volume; **~ delle giacenze** (*org. az.*) stock volume; **il ~ delle importazioni** (*comm. est.*) the volume of imports; **~ delle merci trasportate** (*trasp.*) traffic; **~ delle vendite** (*market.*) turnover; **~ d'affari** (*fin.*) turnover; **~ produttivo** (*org. az.*) production volume.

vuoto, *a.* **1** empty. **2** (*vacante*) empty, vacant, unoccupied. *n. m.* **1** (*spazio vuoto*) empty space; (*spazio in bianco*) blank. **2** (*market.*) (*recipiente vuoto*) empty. // **~ inflazionistico** (*econ., fin.*) (*tipico dell'economia di guerra*) inflationary gap; **~ per pieno** (*trasp.*) dead freight.

W

«warrant», *n. m.* (*dog.*) (*nota di pegno*) warrant.

«wash-and-wear», *locuz. a.* (*market., pubbl.*) (*di tessuto*) wash-and-wear, wash'n'-wear.

«waterproof», *locuz. a.* (*market., pubbl.*) (*di tessuto: impermeabile*) waterproof.

watt, *n. m.* (*unità di misura della potenza elettrica*) watt.

wattora, *n. f.* watt-hour.

wattorametro, *n. m.* watt-hour meter.

week-end, *n. m.* week-end.

X

x, *n. m.* o *f.* **1** x. **2** (*mat.*) (*variabile indipendente*) x.

xerografia, *n. f.* (*giorn.*) xerography.

xerografico, *a.* (*giorn.*) xerographic.

Y

y, *n. m.* o *f.* **1** y. **2** (*mat.*) (*variabile dipendente*) y.

yard, *n. f.* (*misura di lunghezza pari a metri 0,914*) yard.

yen, *n. m.* (*unità monetaria giapponese*) yen.

Z

z, *n. m.* o *f.* **1** z. **2** (*mat.*) z.

zattera, *n. f.* (*trasp. mar.*) lighter, raft.

zatteraggio, *n. m.* (*trasp. mar.*) lighterage.

zavorra, *n. f.* (*trasp. mar.*) ballast. // **~ d'acqua** (*trasp. mar.*) water ballast; **gettare la ~** (*trasp. mar.*) to jettison ballast; **imbarcare ~** (*trasp. mar.*) to take in ballast.

zavorramento, *n. m.* (*trasp. mar.*) ballasting.

zavorrare, *v. t.* (*trasp. mar.*) to ballast. *v. i.* (*trasp. mar.*) to take★ in ballast.

zecca, *n. f.* (*fin.*) mint. // **nuovo di ~** brand-new.

zegista, *n. m.* e *f.* (*econ., neol.*) (*fautore dello «sviluppo economico zero»; dalle iniziali di* Zero Economic Growth) zeggist.

zeppa, *n. f.* (*giorn., pubbl.*) slug.

zero, *n. m.* **1** (*nelle scale graduate, ecc.*) zero. **2** (*al telefono*) o (*con la pronuncia alfabetica della lettera* o). **3** (*fig.*) (*nulla, niente*) zero, nil, null. **4** (*mat.*) nought, cipher, cypher, zero. // **sopra ~** (*di temperatura, ecc.*) above zero; **sotto ~** (*di temperatura, ecc.*) below zero.

zincotipia, *n. f.* **1** (*giorn., pubbl.*) zincotype. **2** (*giorn., pubbl.*) (*cliché*) block.

zincotipista, *n. m.* e *f.* (*giorn., pubbl.*) zincotypist.

zoccolo, *n. m.* **1** clog, sabot. **2** (*architettonico*) base; (*piedistallo*) socle; (*di colonna*) plinth. **3** (*di parete*) wainscot. **4** (*giorn., pubbl.*) (*del cliché*) block.

zona, *n. f.* **1** zone. **2** (*area*) area; (*distretto*) district; (*regione*) region. **3** (*econ.*) area; (*fascia*) belt. **4** (*market.*) territory, area. // **~ commerciale** (*market.*) trade area, trading area; **~** (*di divieto di sosta*) **dalla quale le automobili vengono rimosse** (*con autogru, ecc.*) (*trasp. aut.*) towaway zone; **~ dei negozi** (*market.*) shopping centre; **la ~ del cotone** (*econ.*) the Cotton Belt (*negli USA*); **zone depresse** (*econ.*) depressed areas; **~ di carico** (*trasp. mar.*) loading area; **~ di distribuzione** (*della posta, ecc.*) (*comun.*) delivery area; **zone di sviluppo** (*econ.*) development areas; **~ di vendita** (*market.*) (*d'un viaggiatore, ecc.*) sales territory; **~ di vendita al dettaglio** (*market.*) retail trading zone; **~ franca** (*dog.*) free zone; **~ frontaliera** (*comm. est.*) frontier area; **~ industriale** (*econ.*) industrial area, industrial site, trading estate; **~ portuale** (*trasp. mar.*) port area.

zonale, *a.* regional; area, district (*attr.*).

zumare, *v. t.* e *i.* (*giorn., pubbl.*) (*variare il campo di immagine cinematografica con un obiettivo a lunghezza focale variabile*) to zoom.

zumata, *n. f.* (*giorn., pubbl.*) zoom.